P9-CIU-460

Dictionary of
American Family
Names

Dictionary of American Family Names

PATRICK HANKS

Editor

VOLUME ONE

A–F

OXFORD
UNIVERSITY PRESS
2003

Oxford University Press

Oxford   New York
Auckland   Bangkok   Buenos Aires   Cape Town   Chennai
Dar es Salaam   Delhi   Hong Kong   Istanbul   Karachi   Kolkata
Kuala Lumpur   Madrid   Melbourne   Mexico City   Mumbai
Nairobi   São Paulo   Shanghai   Taipei   Tokyo   Toronto

Published by Oxford University Press, Inc.
198 Madison Avenue, New York, New York, 10016
http://www.oup-usa.org

Oxford is a registered trademark of Oxford University Press

Library of Congress Cataloging-in-Publication Data

Dictionary of American family names / Patrick Hanks, editor.
   p. cm.
Includes bibliographical references.
   ISBN 0-19-508137-4 (set : acid-free paper) — ISBN 0-19-516557-8 (v. 1
: acid free paper) — ISBN 0-19-516558-6 (v. 2 : acid free paper) —
ISBN 0-19-516559-4 (v. 3 : acid free paper)
   1. Names, Personal—United States—Dictionaries.   I. Hanks, Patrick.
   CS2485.D53 2003
   929.4′0973—dc21

                                                              2003003844

Printing number: 9 8 7 6 5 4 3 2 1

Printed in the United States of America
on acid-free paper

EDITORIAL STAFF

CONTRIBUTORS AND CONSULTANTS

For Names from the British Isles

English	David Mills, Patrick Hanks, Kate Hardcastle
Welsh	Hywel Wyn Owen
Scottish	William Nicolaisen, Patrick Hanks
Irish	Kay Muhr
Scottish Gaelic	Kay Muhr

For Names from Western Europe

French	Susan Whitebook
German	Edda Gentry, Jürgen Eichhoff
Dutch	Charles Gehring

For Scandinavian and Finnish Names

Norwegian and Danish	Olav Veka
Swedish	Lena Peterson
Finnish	Hannele Jönsson-Korhola, Kate Moore

For Names from Southern Europe

Spanish and other Iberian Languages	Dieter Kremer Roser Saurí Colomer
Italian	Enzo Caffarelli
Greek	Nick Nicholas, Johanna Kolleca

For Jewish Names

Jewish	Alexander Beider

For Slavic and East European Names

Polish	Aleksandra Cieślikowa
Czech	Dobrana Moldanová
Slovak	Peter Ďurčo
Russian and Ukrainian	Alexander Beider
Armenian	Bert Vaux
Slovenian	Simon Lenarčič
Croatian	Dunja Brozović
Serbian	Svetozar Stijović, Tvrtko Prćić
Hungarian	Gábor Bátonyi
Latvian and Lithuanian	Laimute Balode

For Names from the Middle East and Indian Subcontinent

Indian	Rocky Miranda
Muslim names	Salahuddin Ahmed
Arabic names	Paul Roochnik

For Names from East Asia

Chinese	Mark Lewellen
Japanese	Fred Brady
Korean	Gary Mackelprang

Genealogical Notes
Project team; Additional notes: Marion Harris, M. Tracey Ober

CONTENTS

GENERAL INTRODUCTION

Patrick Hanks

What's in a Name?

DAFN, The *Dictionary of American Family Names*, is the first attempt to explain the history and origin of the 70,000 most frequent family names in the United States, together with some rarer names that are of historical or etymological importance. Each of us has a family name, generally inherited via our parents from our forebears (traditionally through the male line); however, most of us know remarkably little about how, when, and where our family name came into existence, and what it originally meant.

The main purpose of this book is to fill this gap in a systematic way: to provide outline information about where, when, and how our family names originated. Popular interest in family names and their origins has never been greater. Over 85% of Americans will find an entry for their surname in DAFN. Details of how this extremely high coverage was achieved are explained in the article by Ken Tucker which follows this general introduction. Until a few years ago, such an undertaking would have been impossible. Now, thanks to online resources, worldwide scholarship, and computer technology, the task can be attempted. Many American family names, even quite frequent ones, have never been studied at all. In such cases, DAFN has, wherever possible, carried out at least enough research to explain the language of origin of the name, and where possible its etymology. Until very recently, names scholarship has been scarce, and sometimes well-intentioned efforts by untrained amateurs, especially in the 19th and early 20th centuries, have resulted in the perpetuation of false or misleading conclusions. In DAFN, folk beliefs about name origins, which are pervasive, have been discounted or identified as such, though no doubt some may have slipped through. Where the origin of a name remains unidentified or the etymology unexplained, despite the compilers' best efforts, DAFN says so. If an explanation can only be given tentatively, DAFN uses hedges such as "probably," "perhaps," and "possibly." In surnames research there are very few certainties, however, so explanations that are highly probable are not hedged. Uncertainty is expressed only where an explanation is genuinely doubtful.

The Structure of DAFN Entries

The entries in DAFN are structured as follows:

Headword: the surname as found in present-day American name lists, with normalized spacing and capital letters, and no accents or other diacritics.

Comparative Frequency: in parentheses immediately after the headword, giving the frequency of the headword in DAFN's 88.7 million name sample (one-third of the 1997 U.S. population). See the following article by Ken Tucker for details of DAFN's sampling, frequency, and selection policies.

Explanation: the source language and origin of the surname. Within each explanation are included at least some of the following:

Language of Origin: the language or culture in which the surname originated.

Original Spelling: if the surname is written with accents or diacritics in the source language, the accented form is shown as part of the explanation.

Region: if the surname is known to be strongly associated with a particular region of the mother country, DAFN gives this information too.

Typology: a classification of the surname's origin, indicating for example whether it is derived from a place name, from a nickname, from the personal name of a forebear, or from a word denoting the occupation or social status of a forebear.

Etymology: the linguistic history of the surname, generally including the form and meaning of the word from which it is derived.

Cross-references: references, printed in small capitals, to other entries, where more details may be found. There are many, many variant spellings of surnames in America. DAFN treats each major variant as a main entry in its own right. This means that the dictionary is "self-indexing"; the explanations contain an intricate network of cross-references to so-called anchor names, where a fuller explanation of the linguistic, cultural, or historical background is generally given.

Given Names: a limited selection of the most significant "diagnostic" given names (if any) that are associated with the surname in DAFN's sample of 88.7 million American names, together with a statement of the language or languages for which these given names are diagnostic:

Diagnosis and Confidence Measure: a statement of the probable language of origin (if not English) on the basis of the given-name evidence, together with a measure of confidence in the diagnosis, expressed as a percentage. "French 6%" means that, on the basis of given-name evidence, we can have 6% confidence that the surname is French. It does *not* mean that 6% of all bearers are of French origin. See the following article by Ken Tucker for a fuller explanation of diagnostic given names and confidence measures.

Forebears: for a few selected entries, a paragraph on some particularly important aspect of family history or ancestry. Typically, the earliest known bearer in North America of a particular surname may be mentioned. In other cases, forebears are mentioned because they shed light on changes in the linguistic form of the surname. In a very few cases, comments are added on the ancestry of important figures in American history: generally, only the ancestry of presidents and a few other figures of similar historical significance.

In a general work of reference such as DAFN, it is of course impossible to do more than mention a tiny number of selected forebears of particular linguistic or general historical significance for certain names. Systematic research into immigrant forebears is not one of DAFN's objectives. Research into immigrant ancestors starts with ships' passenger lists and immigration records at relevant ports of entry. The Immigrant Ships Transcribers Guild (http://istg.rootsweb.com/) is a good starting point. People sometimes speak as if all immigrants came through Ellis Island, which was the immigration processing center for the port of New York. But of course Ellis Island was only one of dozens of ports of entry and its records cover only a 32-year period (1892–1924). Nevertheless, more than 22 million people, most of them immigrants, came through Ellis Island. Millions of others came through Philadelphia, Boston, Baltimore, New Orleans, and many other ports from the 17th century onward, not to mention the West Coast ports of San Francisco and elsewhere and the border crossings from Canada and Mexico.

Spellings of Family Names

For family historians and genealogists, DAFN does not provide all the answers: far from it. Rather, it provides a starting point, a framework within which family history can be conducted. It provokes questions which can only be answered by dint of detailed research on individual names, research that would be impractical in a work of general scope such as DAFN. Even with this constraint, a very large number of the names in this book have never been researched before, so the editors and contributors were forced to do far more primary research than was originally envisioned.

DAFN gives the basic facts about family names insofar as they are known, summarizing where the name came from, what it meant at the time when it first came into existence, and, where relevant, its history. This turned out to be a massive task. Many names have more than one origin, so research could not stop when one satisfactory explanation had been achieved. All reasonable possibilities had to be considered and explored. Furthermore, the form of some American family names has been altered almost beyond recognition in the course of transmission from generation to generation and from place to place, including adaptation to the English-speaking world. In such cases, the work of individual family historians and names researchers, too numerous to mention individually, has sometimes been of great value. By painstaking primary historical research, family historians have sometimes succeeded in linking a modern American surname to an 18th-century German, Dutch, or French original that may have been very different in spelling and pronunciation from the present-day name. In such cases, DAFN reports the link, and either cross-refers to an existing entry where an etymological explanation is given, or, if no cross-reference is possible, an explanation of the etymology (if known) is given at the new American form.

DAFN has surveyed current surname scholarship, including indigenous scholarship in languages other than English, and summarized the results in a readable form. As far as possible, the present-day form of each name in the book is traced back to its original meaning in the country or region that it came from. In addition, information is give about the comparative frequency of names and, in selected cases, the earliest known bearers of the name in North America.

Sometimes the trail tracking a name to its linguistic origin is long and tortuous: for example, to explain the origins of Sicilian American names requires expertise not only in Italian, but also in Greek, Catalan, and Arabic, which are important source languages for surnames in Sicily alongside Italian. To explain names that come from the British Isles, expertise is needed, not only in Middle English, but also in Old Norman French, Old Norse, Welsh, Cornish, Irish and Scottish Gaelic, and Manx. For this reason, DAFN is very much a team effort. No one individual could possibly explain the origins of all the surnames of America, deriving as they do from all the world's languages. DAFN is very much a cooperative effort among leading names scholars from many different parts of the world.

Further examples of the complex trails of name origins can be given. The Dutch name **Fonda** is of Spanish or Catalan origin, having been brought to the Netherlands in the 16th century via the Italian port of Genoa. Names from the Iberian peninsula are not only of Spanish and Portuguese linguistic origin, but also Catalan and Galician, while a surprisingly large number of Hispanic surnames, including some very frequent and historically important ones such as **Mendoza**, **Ortiz**, and

Aguirre, are ultimately from Basque, the language of the western Pyrenees and adjacent regions, which is unrelated to any other language. Many of the oldest English surnames are not merely of English origin, but come from Old French, Old Norse, medieval Welsh, or Cornish. Scottish names are not only English, French, and Old Norse, but also Gaelic. Many names that are Scottish in form came to North America via northern Ireland. Gaelic names were invariably Anglicized before being brought to North America, often in ways that involved radical alterations in form.

People sometimes claim that one spelling of a name is "more correct" than another. There is no historical or linguistic argument to support such claims. The correct spelling of a name is whatever the family members say it is. If a family prefers to spell its name in a way that reflects a linguistic origin or etymology, or the spelling as found in the country of origin, that is their choice. An equally valid choice is to spell the family name in a way that reflects the development and/or pronunciation of the name in English-speaking America. DAFN explains origins, but origins must not be confused with correctness.

Changing Society: Feminism and Family Names

In Europe, North America, and elsewhere, from the 12th century up to the 1960s, marriage almost invariably involved the adoption of the husband's family name by the wife, while a child's family name was inherited from the father not the mother. In recent years this has begun to change, and family historians must take cognizance of the fact that the traditional notion of the family, which (at least as an ideal) has been comparatively stable for almost a thousand years, is now changing substantially. It is by no means clear how many of the changes to social institutions such as marriage that have occurred in the past forty years and are going on even now will become permanent, how many will be abandoned, and how many will be carried further forward. Certainly, current conventions of childbearing expose the ludicrous irrelevance to the modern world of the literal meaning of the old word *bastard*. In the past, birth out of wedlock was regarded as a sufficient reason for ostracization of both mother and child (though, curiously enough, not the father), but now it is no longer stigmatized, and the term survives only as a meaningless term of abuse or, in Australia, as a cheerful term of reference meaning "regular guy."

Childbirth is no longer an unavoidable concomitant of sexual pleasure; marriage is no longer a commitment entered into early in life, "for better for worse," a sort of desperate lottery in the face of the ever-present possibility of an early death. Instead, marriage is now often entered into by adults who may already have had children, as a signal that they have established what they hope may be a stable relationship. These changes are particularly noticeable among people whose priorities include development of a career—for among conservative families, especially rich ones, marriage as a form of social and political alliance continues to thrive much as it did in the past.

Due in part to the fact that many women now aspire to a career as well as a family, and in part to birth control, enabling families to be planned rather than accidents of nature, the role of childbearing in the marriage contract has diminished. The grinding cycle of annually renewed pregnancies, interspersed with household management, infant mortality, puerperal fever, and concluded by an early death, is no longer a married woman's normal lot, as it all too often was in the past.

Marriage is no longer an essential preliminary to childbearing, and even when people do marry, among many people it is now considered distinctly old-fashioned or unchic for a woman to take the husband's surname. This results in a dilemma for the naming of children. No longer does a child automatically inherit the father's surname. Deciding on a surname has become a matter of choice, not fate. Many children still do receive their father's surname, but others are named with the mother's surname or receive both, joined by a hyphen. Whatever the social implications of these changes, they will certainly add a research dimension for future family historians. Fortunately, however, modern vital records are generally more detailed, more reliable, and more publicly available, than those of past centuries, so the problem may not be as acute as it may seem at first sight.

When Did Family Names Originate?

The obvious answer to the question "When did family names originate?" is that they originated at many different times and in many different places. Nevertheless, some broad trends may be distinguished. The phenomenon of the modern family name is, broadly, of medieval European origin and is associated with the rise of bureaucracies. Tax collectors, beadles and bailiffs, sheriffs and reeves (officers of law enforcement and the courts) had, like their modern counterparts, a particular need for the precise identification of individuals. In a period when the eldest son inherited property and titles, it became normal to inherit the father's surname along with other property.

In Europe family names were unknown before the 11th century (although some clan names existed, which later became family names, for example in Ireland). Within about 250 years, i.e. by the beginning of the 14th century, surnames were established in most of the countries of central and western Europe. By 1300, hereditary surnames were the norm and patronymics were the exception. However, they were less stable than they are today. A person might adopt or acquire a new and different surname at any time.

Older naming traditions, in particular the patronymic tradition, have either been assimilated, in Europe, America, and elsewhere, into the system created by medieval European feudal bureaucracies, or else have been replaced by it.

The Ancient Names of East Asia

Undoubtedly, the oldest surnames in this book are those of Chinese origin. The majority of Chinese surnames are around three thousand years old, while some are believed to date back to the "model emperor" period that began almost fifty centuries ago. Although modern Chinese Americans bear modern American surnames that are derived, linguistically, from these extraordinarily ancient Chinese names, we should not assume that a surname in China had the same function and social status as a modern American surname. For further information about Chinese names and naming, see the article by Mark Lewellen in this volume.

Japanese and Korean surnames are much less ancient than Chinese names, but still older than European names. They originated in the 5th century AD and the 1st century BC respectively. Details are explained by Fred Brady and Gary Mackelprang in their articles below.

At the time when surnames were being formed in East Asia, Europeans surnames as we know them had not yet been formed.

Names and Naming in Ancient Rome

It is hard to know whether to be more impressed by the similarities or the differences between Classical Latin names and modern personal names. Ancient Roman names typically had three parts: a *praenomen* (equivalent to a modern forename), a *nomen* (a clan name, somewhat similar to a modern family name), and thirdly a *cognomen*, a nickname or distinguishing name that was attached to a particular individual, but which could be inherited. When a cognomen was first coined, it was known as an *agnomen*; the term *cognomen* often implies some sort of hereditary use within a family. Thus, the term *crassus* means 'thick-set', and was used as a cognomen by descendants and family members (who may themselves have been tall and slim) of a thick-set individual who acquired the name as an agnomen with reference to the shape of his person.

In Republican Rome, only a few dozen praenomina were in regular use: *Marcus, Lucius, Gaius, Publius,* etc. The number of family names or clan names was not very much larger: *Julius, Antonius,* etc. This made the adoption of a distinguishing cognomen all more important as the size of the population of ancient Rome grew. Thus, contrary to popular belief, the forename of the founder of the Roman empire was not *Julius*: that was his clan name. His praenomen or forename was *Gaius*. And the name by which he is universally known, *Caesar* (which has given rise, indirectly, to numerous European family names and vocabulary words meaning 'ruler' or 'emperor' e.g. Russian *tsar*, German *Kaiser*), was in origin a cognomen or inherited family nickname meaning 'fine head of hair'. The famous Roman military commander Publius Cornelius Scipio (236–184 BC) was a member of the Cornelii clan, with the hereditary cognomen *Scipio* meaning 'rod or staff'. Later, he acquired the agnomen *Africanus*, with reference to his victories over the Carthaginians in North Africa, in a way not dissimilar to the way in which, over two thousand years later, the British generals Montgomery and Alexander were granted the titles "Viscount Montgomery of Alamein" and "Earl Alexander of Tunis," in recognition of *their* victories in North Africa.

Other well-known Roman cognomina were nicknames such as *Ahenobarbus* 'red beard', *Flaccus* 'big ears', and *Posthumus* 'born after the death of his father'. There have been attempts to relate modern Italian surnames to Classical Roman names, but in reality, the naming system of ancient Rome was swept away by the new naming system introduced by the early Christian Church. Ancient Roman names survived only if, as in the case of *Marcus* and *Antonius,* they were also borne by early Christian saints.

Patronymic and Genealogical Naming Systems

Before hereditary surnames became established, a patronymic or genealogical system was the norm throughout central, northern, and western Europe. People were known by their parentage, sometimes supplemented by a nickname. These names were not hereditary. Patronymic naming survives to this day in Iceland, where an individual called Hermann Pálsson is the son of someone called Pál. Alternation between generations is common, so this Pál may well be Pál Hermannsson. Elsewhere in Scandinavia, the patronymic system survived into the 19th century, and there are records of the conservative mirth that greeted the notion that a woman might be known as Anna Andersson (as opposed to Anna Andersdottir—'Anna, daughter of Andrew').

In the Old Icelandic sagas, a rich mixture of patronymics and nicknames is found. Thus, Burnt Njal's Saga begins with a man whose name is *Mord Fiddle, the son of Sighvat the Red*. Before long, the saga mentions a man called Hoskuld, who is given a much fuller genealogical name:

> Hoskuld Dala-Kollsson, son of Thorgerd, daughter of Thorstein the Red, son of Olaf the White, son of Ingjald, son of Helgi and of Thora, daughter of Sigurd Snake-in-the-Eye, son of Ragnar Hairy-Breeches; Thorstein the Red's mother was Aud the Deep-Minded, daughter of Ketil Flat-Nose, son of Bjorn Buna.

In this fine genealogical name, no fewer than seven generations are remembered, with two matrilineal branches and six memorable nicknames.

As in Scandinavia, so also in Wales the patronymic system was in regular use up to the 19th century, long after hereditary surnames had been adopted elsewhere in Britain and Europe. John and Sheila Rowlands mention the example of a certain 16th century gentleman who was *David ap William ap David Lloyd ap Tomas ap Dafydd ap Gwilym ap Dafydd Ieuan ap Howel, ap Cynfrig ap Iorwerth Fychan ap Iorwerth ap Grono ap Tegerin*—12 generations of forebears in a single name! Knowing one's ancestry was important for establishing one's right to the inheritance of land and for other legal purposes.

Examples such as those just given may be colorful, but they are also cumbersome, and it is easy to see why they came to be replaced in most places by the streamlined efficiency of a single hereditary surname, passed down from one generation to the next.

The Rise of Hereditary Surnames

The most ancient hereditary surnames in Europe are probably those that developed from ancient patronymics or clan names. In Ireland surnames such as **Ó Conaill** and **Ó Néill** date back at least to the 10th century and probably beyond. It is only a short step from a name that means 'descendant of Niall' to a hereditary surname.

Elsewhere in Europe during the 11th century, rich and powerful families began to take surnames based on their lands and estates. More humble folk, too, could be known by the name of the place from which they came, if (as was the exception rather than the rule) they ever moved away from that place.

Other hereditary surnames were derived from nicknames, from occupations, and from features of the landscape, as explained in the section on Typology below. It is interesting (and perhaps a little surprising) that, with few exceptions, all the main types of surname are represented in all the languages of Europe. An example of an exception is that there are no Irish Gaelic names of habitational origin; this is probably due to the fact that hereditary Irish Gaelic names are always patronymic in form. The absurdity of a name appearing to state that someone is the son of a place name would be patent.

There are, of course, local differences in proportion among the different types of surname in different countries. Thus, ornamental names (names made up arbitrarily from vocabulary words with more or less pleasant associations) are characteristic of Swedish and Jewish surnames. In Norway habitational names, often deriving from a single farm, are very common. In Italian and Czech, derivatives of pet forms of personal names are especially common.

From an American perspective, it is important to note that most European surnames were well established two or three hundred years before the first European settlements in North America, and had ample opportunity to undergo changes long before they came to this country. The serious student of the origin of a surname must not only know the language of the country of its origin, but must be acquainted with the medieval forms of that language, the medieval meanings of its words, the nature of medieval professions (for many surnames denote occupations that have long since vanished), and the structure of medieval society, for some surnames can only be understood in the context of the medieval feudal system.

Hereditary surnames did not become fixed overnight. In fact, in many records from the 11th to the 14th century it is impossible to be certain whether a surname is hereditary, or merely a distinguishing epithet. Did a medieval Richard Skinner inherit the name **Skinner** from his father, or does it merely indicate that his occupation was skinning animals and making leather goods? If we find that Richard Skinner had a son called John Richardson, it is clear that in this particular case the appellation was not established as a hereditary surname. On the other hand, if we find the surname used alongside an appellation denoting an occupation, e.g. 'Richard Skinner the Baker' or even 'Richard Skinner the Skinner', it is clear that it has become a hereditary surname.

Often, there is variation, and the same individual may be known by more than one name. To take an actual example, Reaney notes in Cornwall in 1297 a certain *Johannes Gyffard dictus le Boeuf* ('John Gifford, called the Bull'). His descendants, if any, could equally well have come to be known by the surname **Gifford** or **Bull**. Unfortunately, records that would enable us to establish hereditary status of these early names in individual cases are few and far between. The process is clear, but the details are lacking. The surname historian must therefore rely to a large extent on probabilities and inferencing from early records.

By the 14th century, hereditary surnames were well established in most parts of continental Europe and the British Isles. And in the 17th century they began to be brought to North America, ready for a new chapter in their development.

Adoptions from Other Naming Systems

In 21st-century America, a hereditary surname is more or less obligatory, for administrative reasons. Immigrants from places where there is no indigenous tradition of hereditary surnames, such as Islamic countries or parts of the Indian subcontinent, have very often adapted their personal names to the American system. Thus, **Muhammad** and **Abdullah** are found as American surnames, in addition to being Arabic personal names found throughout the Muslim world.

By a similar process, among people from southern India personal names such as **Ganesh, Hari**, and **Murthy** have been pressed into service as surnames in an American context, although they are found only as personal names in southern India.

For a few cultures, it was possible to find neither reliable reference works nor a scholar able or willing to explain the history and meaning of the names. All attempts to find a means of explaining Vietnamese, Laotian, Cambodian, and Thai names and naming practices were unsuccessful. Where the evidence points unmistakably to a Vietnamese or other unresearched East Asian origin for an American surname, this fact is noted in DAFN, even though an etymological explanation cannot be given. The total number of names affected is small: under 300 entries altogether.

In other cases, the reader will look in vain for surnames from a particular country or culture. For example, very few American family names of Turkish origin are recorded in DAFN. This is no doubt partly because Turkish family names as such did not exist until 1934, when they were introduced by decree of Mustafa Kemal Atatürk. Being of comparatively recent origin, they are very diverse, so that each one has few bearers, and fewer still have come to America. Fewer than fifty Turkish American family names have reached the selection criterion of 100 bearers in a population sample of 88.7 million. Traditional naming practices in Turkey involved the use of a personal name with an honorific such as *bey,* rather than a surname, and these traditions survive in everyday use in Turkey today. Thus a man whose name (with surname) is officially *Önder Renkliyıldırım* is normally known in everyday use as *Önder Bey.*

African American Family Names

In addition, it must be noted that DAFN contains almost no entries of African linguistic origin. With few exceptions (Ethiopian names being prominent examples), names from the languages of Africa have not reached the U.S. in sufficient numbers to have become established as American family names.

There is no established tradition of names from African languages being used as American surnames. Of course, the vast majority of African Americans bear names that are of English, Scottish, or Irish linguistic origin, these mostly coming from the names of the owners of plantations on which their forebears worked. In other cases, African Americans forebears have adopted the surnames of illustrious historical figures such as **Washington** and **Lincoln.** In a few cases, it has been possible to say that a particular surname, or a particular spelling of a surname, is borne mainly by African Americans, but for the most part African American surnames are inextricably mixed with surnames of British origin. This fact serves to emphasize that the history of surnames, a branch of philology or historical linguistics, is independent of genealogy, the history of families.

The difficulties of disentangling African American surnames from Scottish American and English American ones in no way inhibits African American genealogical research. In recent years, several African American genealogical societies and some excellent web sites have been established, for example Afrigeneas (www.afrigeneas.com) and the African-American Genealogy Ring (http://afamgenealogy.ourfamily.com).

American Indian Names and Naming Systems

It is a matter for regret that it has not been possible to record many details of American Indian names in DAFN, names from native American cultures. This is partly due to the enormous diversity of these cultures, partly to the decimation of the American Indian population from the 17th and early 20th centuries, so that numbers are now small, and partly to the fact that many if not most American Indians have adopted English or Spanish surnames.

DAFN contains a few entries for Navajo names, but very little else. For the most part, names of American Indian linguistic origin are rare. Almost none of them reach the selection criterion of 100 bearers in a population sample of 88.7 million that qualifies a name for entry in DAFN. Here, too, the interested researcher must be directed to native American genealogical societies and relevant websites.

Typology of Family Names

Family names may be classified into a small number of types according to their origin. DAFN uses the classification established in Hanks and Hodges (1988), which is explained below.

Patronymic Names

The oldest and most pervasive type of family name, with many of the highest frequencies, consists of those derived from the personal name of an ancestor. Two main strands in the origins of personal names can be identified: vernacular naming traditions and religious naming traditions. Vernacular names were originally composed, thousands of years ago, of vocabulary elements in a prehistoric form of a language. No doubt, while their meaning was still clear, they were bestowed for their auspicious connotations (e.g. *Raymond* is derived from ancient Germanic elements meaning 'counsel' and 'protection'). In religious naming traditions, on the other hand, names were bestowed in honor of a cult figure. Aside from Jewish names, the most powerful religious influence on naming in Europe has been the Christian Church. There is not a country in Europe that does not have surnames derived from forms of John, Matthew, Mark, Luke, Peter, Paul, and other saints, apostles, and missionaries of the Christian Church. It comes as something of a surprise, therefore, to note that in many countries, especially in northern Europe, baptismal names honoring Christian saints and biblical figures were a fairly recent introduction, at around the time when the bulk of family names were taking shape. These Christian names were in competition with the older and better-established vernacular naming traditions.

Surnames derived from ancient Germanic personal names are found not only in German, but also in Dutch, English, French, and many other languages. The court of Charlemagne (742–814) played an important role: it was Christian and Latin-speaking, but the vernacular language at that time was the Frankish dialect of Old High German, and the personal names in use were Germanic rather than Latinate. These personal names were adopted in many parts of northwest Europe, especially among the ruling classes. They were in use among the Normans; hence, many common English and French names such as *Richard, Robert,* and *William (Guillaume)* are of Germanic origin and have cognates in other European languages.

Some Germanic personal names such as *Siegfried* also have Slavic derivatives, but on the whole the Slavs had their own inventory of personal names. In western Slavic-speaking areas (in particular, in Poland, the Czech lands, and Slovakia), these native Slavic names have also given rise to family names. In Russia, on the other hand, vernacular Slavic names were proscribed as baptismal names by the Orthodox Church in favor of names honoring Christian saints. For this reason, Russian patronymic surnames are mostly derived from saints' names rather than from vernacular Slavic names.

The most basic type of surname derived from a patronymic—that is, from a person's father's given name—simply presents the father's name as a distinguishing epithet alongside the bearer's own given name. Surnames of this type are found in almost all European languages, but in most of them they are considerably less common than names formed with explicitly patronymic endings.

The range of affixes which have been utilized with a patronymic function is very wide. Some are prefixes (Gaelic *mac*, Welsh *ap, ab*, Norman French *fitz*, Italian *fi-*); others (the majority) are suffixes. These were for the most part originally adjectival or possessive in function (English *-s*, North German *-ing* and *-er*, Romanian *-esco*, Russian and Bulgarian *-ov*), or else result from a more or less reduced form of a term meaning 'son of' (English *-son*, Danish/Norwegian *-sen*, Swedish *-son*).

In such cases the surname was almost always originally patronymic in function, although the reference seems occasionally to have been to a grandfather or more distant relative, and in some early examples women are known to have acquired the given name of their husbands as a distinguishing epithet. It is likely that some hereditary surnames are derived from this use.

In this category also belong surnames that are derived from shortened or familiar forms of given names, pet forms, and forms with diminutive suffixes. In the Middle Ages such forms were in common use, often almost to the exclusion of the official baptismal form, hence the frequency of such common English surnames as *Hobson* and *Dobson*, based on vernacular forms of the baptismal name *Robert*, or the equally common northern and central European derivatives of *Johann* or *Hans*, German forms of Latin *Johannes (John)*, or the great profusion of Italian and Czech surnames derived from diminutive forms of given names.

Metronymic Surnames

Much less common than patronymics, with no more than a handful of surviving examples in the majority of European languages, are metronymics, derived from the name of the first bearer's mother. Since European society has been patriarchal throughout the historical period, it was the given name of the male head of the household that was normally handed on as a distinguishing name to successive generations. The few exceptions (e.g. **Catling, Marguerite, Dyott**) seem to be derived from the names of women who were either widows for the greater part of their adult lives, or else heiresses in their own right.

In this respect Jewish naming practice differs from that of the rest of Europe, since metronymics are common among Ashkenazim (see, for example, **Chaikin, Dworkin, Sorkin,** and **Rifkind**). There are several probable reasons for this: (a) both before and after surnames came into use, Ashkenazic Jews often used nicknames, many of them consisting of a parent's given name plus Yiddish possessive *-s*; many of the nicknames containing the mother's given name presumably gave rise to metronymic family names; (b) in other cases, these nicknames consist of the spouse's given name plus Yiddish possessive *-s*, hence men could have taken these nicknames as family names and passed them to their descendants; (c) it is probable that children of deserted mothers (or widows) took family names based on the mother's given name. In connection with (b), there is a class of surnames which seems to exist only among Ashkenazic Jews, indicating explicitly the husband of the woman named, for example **Esterman** 'Esther's husband'. In other cases, we cannot tell whether Ashkenazic family names belong in this category or not: **Roseman,** for instance, might be one of these names (cf. the Yiddish female given name *Royze, Rose*) or it might be merely an ornamental name. **Perlman** is even more complicated: it could be one of these names (cf. the Yiddish female given name *Perl, Pearl*); it might be an ornamental name; or it might indicate someone who dealt in pearls (though this last possibility is the least likely because the relative high frequency of the name is at odds with the small number of Ashkenazic Jews who dealt in pearls).

A fuller account of the origin and meaning of conventional given names may be found in Hanks and Hodges (1990, 2001) and in Pickering (1999).

Kinship and Other Connections

A few surnames derive from some other relationship between the bearer of the surname and the bearer of a given name that forms part of it: for example employment (e.g. **Bateman** 'servant of Bartholomew'), connection by marriage (e.g. **Hickmott** 'Richard's in-law'), or residence in the same dwelling (e.g. **Anttila** 'person from Antti's farm').

A small group of surnames, with representatives in most European languages, identifies the bearer simply by a word denoting a family relationship (e.g. **Neve, Neave, Neff** 'nephew' or 'cousin', **Eames** 'uncle', **Ayer** 'heir'), presumably to some well-known local figure.

Surnames from Lack of Kin

A small but interesting group of surnames are those borne by foundlings, children abandoned by their mothers due to the social stigma of bastardy or simply inability to cope with another mouth to feed. Some surnames based on Christian saints' names are undoubtedly of this origin, being taken from the name of the patron saint of the local church where the baby was abandoned or which ran the local orphanage; however, these are indistinguishable from patronymics.

Other names that have this origin include Dutch **Weese,** Polish **Serota,** French **Jetté** (literally, 'thrown out'), Italian **Innocenti, Comunale** (like English **Parrish,** a name for a child reared at the expense of the community), **D'Amore** (literally, 'of love'), **Di Dio** (literally, 'of god'), and **Esposito** (literally, 'exposed').

Local Names

Surnames derived from words denoting places may be divided into two broad categories: topographic names and habitational names, explained in the next two sections.

Other kinds of local surnames may refer to counties, regions, the names of islands, and indeed whole countries. As a general rule, the further someone had traveled from his place of origin, the broader the designation. Someone who stayed at home might be known by the name of the farm or house where he lived; someone who moved to another town might be known by the name of village that he came from; while someone who moved to a distant city or another county could acquire a surname denoting the region or country from which he originated.

Habitational Names

Habitational names are taken from the names of towns, villages, farmsteads, or other habitations, most of which existed long before surnames came into being. Habitational names include names derived from the names of individual houses with signs on them (where the surname is also the word for the sign, e.g. **Swan, Bell**).

It is sometimes difficult, especially in the case of multiple-element names (in England usually a defining adjective plus a generic noun), to be precise about whether a surname is derived from an identifying topographic phrase such as '(at) the broad ford' or '(by) the red hill' or from an established place name such as **Bradford** or **Redhill**. It is also possible that in some cases what has been thought of as a topographic name is in fact a habitational name from some unidentified place now lost. In Europe, the geographical distribution and linguistic form of surnames is sometimes a source of evidence for local historians of lost places.

Topographic Names

Topographic names are derived from general descriptive references to a feature of the landscape such as a stream, a ford, a tree, or a hill. Topographic surnames can also refer to a river by its name, or to a man-made feature such as a castle, a city wall, an abbey, or a church.

Some surnames that are ostensibly topographic, such as **Hall** and **Monkhouse**, are in fact occupational, for they originally denoted someone who was employed at such a place, for example at a great house or monastery.

Regional and Ethnic Names

Another category of local surnames comprises those denoting origin in a particular region or country. These tended to be acquired when someone migrated a considerable distance from his original home, so that a specific habitational name would have been meaningless to his new neighbors; he would be known simply as coming 'from the East', or 'from Devon', or 'from France'. Many of these names derive from adjectival forms (e.g. **French, Dench, Walsh**); others are in the form of nouns denoting a person's nationality (e.g. **Fleming, Langlois, Moravec**).

In some cases these may have been originally nicknames bestowed with reference to the imagined character traits associated with the inhabitants of the region or country concerned, rather than denoting actual nationality. So, for example, someone in England called **French** may actually have been French, or he may have adopted sophisticated or affected mannerisms and tastes popularly associated with French people and culture. In other cases, such names could denote a trading connection with the place named, especially in the case of a major trading port such as **Danzig.**

House Names

Another type of local appellative is the house name, referring to a distinctive sign of a kind commonly attached to houses before the days of numbered street addresses and general literacy. A number of surnames are documented as having this origin. Several Jewish surnames are derived from the names of houses in the Jewish quarter of Frankfurt-am-Main, for example **Rothschild,** (the house of the) 'red shield'. However, the importance of this category of surname has sometimes been exaggerated; some names that have been so explained are in fact more likely to be nicknames of uncertain significance, or, in the case of Jewish surnames, ornamental names.

Occupational Names

There are many types of surname that are explicitly occupational, in that they refer directly to the particular trade or occupation followed by the first bearer. Buried within this dictionary lies an inventory of the common trades of medieval Europe. These occupations can be divided into classes such as agricultural (e.g. **Sheppard, Bouvier**), manufacturing (e.g. **Smith, Wright, Glover**), retail (e.g. **Monger, Chandler, Draper**), and so on.

They can also be classified according to linguistic criteria. The most basic type of occupational name is represented by words straightforwardly denoting the activity involved, whether as a primary derivative of a verbal roots (e.g. **Webb, Hunt**) or formed by means of an agent suffix attached to a verb (e.g. **Weaver, Baker, Tissier**) or to a noun (e.g. **Webber, Weber, Weaver, Webster, Potter, Stolarz**). Some occupational names are derived from a noun plus an agent noun from a verb (e.g. **Ledbetter, Schuster, Stellmacher**).

Another very common type of surname refers to a calling by metonymy, naming the principal object associated with that activity, whether tool (e.g. **Axe, Pick, Nadel, Swingle, Szydlo**) or product (e.g. **Ballestra, Brott, Maslow**). In other cases, the connection is more indirect (e.g. **Daino** 'fallow deer', denoting a deer hunter).

Particularly in the case of Ashkenazic Jewish surnames, occupational names may have attached to them the explicit suffix *-man(n)* (e.g. **Federman, Hirshman**). This is also occasionally the sense of German *-mann* and English *-man* occupational names (e.g. **Habermann, Zimmermann, Millman**), but this is a semantically complex suffix, with a variety of different meanings.

Another group is similar in form to one type of surname derived from nicknames (see below), but semantically it clearly belongs in the category of occupational names. Members of this group consist of a verb-stem plus a noun, describing the typical action and object involved in the trade of the person concerned, sometimes in a humorous way (e.g. **Catchpole** for a bailiff).

A class of names whose importance has been understated in the past are those that denoted a servant or member of the household of some person of higher social status, ranging from a master craftsman or a humble tenant farmer, to a member of a religious order, a prince of the church, an aristocrat, or royalty. This is the source, for example, of the English surnames **Maidment** and **Parsons**; also, usually, of **Prior, Monk, King,** and **Earl.** Many surnames derived from a term denoting a person of high rank probably have this origin. Occasionally, the servant relationship is made explicit, for example by use of the genitive case or by the German and English suffix *-man(n)* in another of its senses. More often, however, the servant relationship is implied, not stated in the form of a surname.

Status Names

One group of surnames, classified by some as occupational names and by others as nicknames, are names that originated with reference to social status. These for the most part denote a particular role in medieval society (e.g. **Bachelor, Franklin, Knight, Squire**). It must be remembered, however, that many names that are ostensibly status names (e.g. **King, Prince, Duke, Earl, Bishop**) are most unlikely to have denoted a holder of the rank in question. In such cases the name was probably originally borne by a servant of the dignitary mentioned; in other cases it may have been given as an "incident name" to someone who had acted such a role in a pageant or other festivities, or else mockingly to someone who behaved in a lordly manner. Jewish names of this type (e.g. **Kaiser, Graf, Herzog**) are probably all ornamental only.

Other status names (e.g. **Alderman, Beadle, Sherriff, Reeve**) denoted social status with a particular administrative function. For such names, it is not possible to make a clear-cut distinction between status and occupation.

A particular group of status names cannot be understood without reference to the feudal system of land tenure. See, for example, the entries for **Ackerman** and **Huber.** In Czech **Svoboda** literally means 'free' but in particular denoted a free peasant farmer in contradistinction to a serf. **Dvořák** denoted a superior class of farmer, a 'lord of the manor'. A **Sedlák** was a slightly lower class of farmer, but with more land than a **Zahradník,** a smallholder, or a **Chalupník,** a cottager. Similar traces of an older social hierarchy are preserved in the surnames of several other European languages.

Surnames from Nicknames

Surnames derived from nicknames form the broadest and most miscellaneous class of surnames. To some extent this is a catch-all category, encompassing a number of different types of origin. The most typical classes refer adjectivally to the general physical appearance of the person concerned (e.g. **Black, Blake, Schwarz, Russell**), or personality trait (e.g. **Cortes, Hendy, Karg, Kluge**). Others point, with an adjective and noun, to some particular physical feature (e.g. **Whitehead**). Many nicknames refer unambiguously to some physical deficiency (e.g. **Mank, Balfe, Bobo**), while others may be presumed to allude to it (e.g. **Hand, Daum**). Others probably make reference to a favored article or style of clothing (e.g. **Boot, Cape**).

People in past ages were less squeamish and certainly more forthright than we are today, and it will come as a surprise to many Americans that the origin of their surname may draw attention to a physical deformity or indeed may be obscene. It seems at least probable that the surname of England's greatest poet, like **Wagstaff,** is of bawdy origin.

Many surnames derived from the names of animals and birds were originally nicknames, referring to appearance or character, from the attributes traditionally assigned to animals. In the Middle Ages anthropomorphic ideas were held about the characters of other living creatures, based more or less closely on their observed habits, and these associations were reflected and reinforced by large bodies of folk tales featuring animals behaving as humans. The nickname **Fox** (**Foss, Fuchs, Goupil, Lis**) would thus be given to a cunning person, **Lamb** to a gentle and inoffensive one. In other cases, however, **Lamb** might be a metonymic occupational name for a shepherd. In other cases, surnames derived from words denoting animals may be of anecdotal origin (see next paragraph). DAFN normally attempts to explain the likely application of a word as a name, but inevitably there must always be some uncertainty as to the precise application, nowhere more so than in names derived from words denoting animals.

Anecdotal Surnames

Another group of surnames consists of nicknames that arose as the result of some now irrecoverable incident or exploit that involved the bearer. Probable examples include **Followell, Tipper, Mezzanotte, Musil.** In modern nicknames borne by individuals within a community, this type of name is common, but it is also apparent that the reason for the nickname, which may only ever have been known to a few people, is quickly forgotten, whereas the surname may continue to have enduring currency. It is fruitless to try to guess now at the events that lay behind the acquisition of nicknames such as **Death** and **Leggatt** in past centuries.

An unusual class of anecdotal surnames occurs in Czech, with names derived from the past participle of a verb. These are often difficult to gloss in English. Examples include **Doležal,** a nickname for a lazy man meaning something like 'laid back', **Doskočil,** an agile man, literally 'leapt about', **Kratochvíl** 'had a good time', **Kasal** 'bullied', and **Kvapil** 'rushed'.

Seasonal Surnames

Related to such "incident" names are names that refer to a season (e.g. **Winter, Lenz**), month (e.g. **May, Davout**), or day of the week (e.g. **Freitag**). It has been suggested that these names refer to the time of birth, baptism, or conversion. In the cases of more recently acquired surnames, in particular Jewish names, reference is sometimes to the time of official registration of the name. Certainly surnames derived from the names of various Christian festivals (e.g. **Christmas, Toussaint, Ognisanti**) seem to have been acquired in this way. But the seasonal names may also have referred to a 'frosty' or 'sunny' character, while the medieval day names may have referred to feudal service owed on a particular day of the week. No explanation offered for either Christian or Jewish names in this group has been proven conclusively.

Humanistic Names

A small group of names, mostly of Dutch and German origin, are here dubbed "humanistic names." These are Latin forms of vernacular originals, coined during the heyday of Renaissance humanism in the 15th and 16th centuries. In some cases, the alteration consisted of nothing more than adding the Latin -*(i)us* noun ending to an existing name, as in **Bogardus,** based on Dutch *Bogard* 'orchard', or **Goetschius,** from German *Goetsch,* a pet form of *Gottfried.* In other cases, the whole surname was translated into Latin: **Agricola** is a translation of Dutch *Boer* and German *Bauer* 'farmer'; **Faber** is a translation of German *Schmidt* and Dutch *Smit* 'smith'; **Silvius** 'of the woods' represents vernacular names such as Dutch **Van den Bosch** and German **Forster.**

The pattern of forming surnames from Latinate humanistic elements was copied in Sweden in the 18th and 19th centuries, when surnames became generally established there.

Ornamental and Arbitrary Coinages

A category of surname not found in most European language and apparently confined to communities where the adoption of surnames was late and enforced rather than organic, is the ornamental or arbitrary coinage. For further remarks on this class, see the sections on Swedish, Finnish, and Jewish surnames in the area-by-area survey below.

Variants, Diminutives, Augmentatives, and Pejoratives

Certain classes of surnames are derived from base forms of personal names and nicknames, and occasionally from vocabulary words too.

Diminutives include surnames formed from vocabulary words with an affectionate suffix (e.g. Czech **Bajorek** 'little marsh dweller', Italian **Abello** 'little bee', **Castello** 'little castle'), as well as the much more widespread types derived from pet forms of personal names and nicknames (e.g. Polish **Bolek,** a diminutive of *Bolesław*, English **Jess** and **Jessel** from *Joseph*, **Russell** from Old French *rouse* 'red-head'). In practice, it is not always possible to differentiate between a diminutive and a simple variant. More often than not, however, diminutives are distinguished by specifically diminutive suffixes, of which Italian has a particularly rich and productive set. Polish and Czech are not far behind, while diminutives of one kind and another are also found in most other European languages. They are rarer in Spanish, however, which does not boast the wide variety of derivative forms in its surnames that are found in other European languages.

Diminutives and variants are common in all languages. Augmentatives and pejoratives are much rarer. Whereas diminutives mean 'little' and are often affectionate, augmentatives mean 'big'. A typical augmentative ending is Italian -*one*, as in Italian **Iacovone,** 'big Jim', or **Colone,** 'big Nick'. Finally, mention must be made of pejoratives, where an ending that originally had an insulting or derogatory force has been added. A typical pejorative ending is French -*ard*, as in **Bechard**, a nickname for a gossip, from a pejorative derivative of *bec* 'beak'.

Surnames, Genealogy, and Genetics

It has been emphasized that DAFN is a book about the history of names, not the history of families. To some extent, of course, the two go hand in hand: the origins of the surname **Aaberg** are, unsurprisingly, associated with the origins of the Aaberg family. In some cases, it is possible to identify the first person (or one of the first) who bore a particular surname in North America. For example, modern bearers of the surname **Zollicoffer** are descended from Jacob Christoph Zollicoffer, who came to the U.S. from Switzerland in the early 18th century and helped to found the settlement of New Bern, North Carolina.

In some cases, the form of a European surname has been altered to a uniquely American form. Thus, bearers of the American surname **Styron** are almost certainly all descended from a certain George Styring, who came from Yorkshire, England, to North Carolina in about 1720. Americanization is a process particularly characteristic of French, Dutch, and

German surnames during the 18th century, but the process continues to this day. Names of late 19th- and early 20th-century immigrants tend to keep the form that they had in the language of origin, but even so there are exceptions. The comparatively rare Polish name *Bładaśewicz*, for example, was simplified to **Bladey** as an American name in the mid 20th century. On the other hand, at least 199 telephone subscribers have opted not to simplify the distinctively Polish name **Krzywicki**, even though that spelling can be baffling to English speakers unfamiliar with the Polish language. In an American context, the name is often given an American pronunciation (*"Krizwikky"*) rather than a Polish one (*"Krzheeveetsky"*). This special relationship between pronunciation and spelling is characteristic of Polish American names.

The Italian name **Abate** is now sometimes heard in America as two syllables (rhyming with "fate"), rather than as three, as in the original Italian. The surname of Madonna Louise Veronica **Ciccone** similarly varies between two syllables with an initial *S-* (the American way) and three syllables with an initial *Tsh-* (the Italian way), depending on what sort of folk hero the speaker wants her to be.

The words of the English language do not normally carry accents, and this has posed particular problems for immigrants whose family name contained an accent in the language of origin. The Czech surname *Kučera*, for example, is found in two spellings in America. In the one case, **Kucera**, the accent has simply been dropped; in this case the pronunciation is found both as "Kootchera," resembling the Czech original, and as "Koosera," under the influence of the accent-less American spelling. In the other case, **Kuchera,** the spelling has been Americanized to reflect the pronunciation.

In DAFN, surnames as headwords are not accented. Instead, the accented form in the language of origin is given as part of the explanation.

Names with a comparatively low frequency are typically derived from a single ancestor, though it is a matter of chance whether sufficient records still exist to enable lineage back to that ancestor to be traced. On the other hand, very common names such as **Brown, Johnson, Jones, Miller, Smith,** and **Williams** are not only extremely frequent in Britain, the country of their linguistic origin, but also have typically absorbed cognates and translation equivalents from many other languages and indeed have been adopted by people with no previous connection at all with the name, for example on grounds of euphony or simplicity.

If your name is one of these very common names, then tracing your ancestry is virtually impossible, unless reliable family records have been kept by family members in previous centuries (for example in the front or back pages of a family Bible).

Obviously, it would not be practical for a work of general reference such as DAFN to identify and trace the history and descendants of each immigrant. Ideally, every single name in this dictionary merits a whole book to itself. In DAFN, therefore, only the most salient points are mentioned. In particular,

the early immigrants singled out for mention in DAFN are cited as evidence for the linguistic and cultural origins of a name or for changes in its form. The fact that a particular 17th- or 18th-century immigrant is mentioned in DAFN does not necessarily imply that all modern American bearers of a given surname are descended from him.

The tremendous advances in the study of genetics in recent years is beginning to have an impact on family history. The work of the geneticist Bryan Sykes, for example, has shown how DNA can be used to establish whether all (or most) bearers of a particular surname are in fact related. In years to come, no doubt DNA evidence will help to establish systematically, on a basis of probabilities, whether two differently spelled names are variants of the same original name, or whether they are in fact separate and independent. In the next section, some examples are given, drawing on surnames of English origin. There can be little doubt that the history, geographical distribution, and genetics of surnames in most other parts of Europe follow similar patterns. The potential of this work is therefore of relevance to a large proportion of American family names.

Monogenetic and Polygenetic

A distinction is made between monogenetic surnames and polygenetic surnames. Monogenetic surnames are those which are derived from just one original bearer at one particular place and time, whereas polygenetic surnames were coined independently in many different places. **Smith, Brown, Milton**, and **Newton** are good examples of English polygenetic surnames, and one would expect this to be confirmed by DNA studies. On the other hand, **Sykes, Hanks,** and **Hardcastle** are examples of names that are most probably monogenetic: they originated at one place and at one time, i.e. they come from one single ancestor.

It is not normally possible to identify the actual original bearer of a monogenetic surname, for all records of him—rarely her—may have vanished (if they ever existed). However, it is often possible to establish that a name is most probably monogenetic on the basis of its distribution. As long ago as 1890, H. P. Guppy noticed, on the basis a study of Kelly's directories, that many family names are significantly associated with a particular place. On the basis of computational study of the current geographical location of 15,000 British family names, Hanks (1992) concluded that many surnames in Britain are monogenetic, while very many others have "become monogenetic"—i.e. the name may have been coined in more than one place and in more than one time in the Middle Ages, but subsequently the family lines descended from all except one of the original medieval bearers have died out. Meanwhile, the descendants of just one medieval bearer have prospered and multiplied, resulting in the modern distribution of the name.

This was empirical confirmation of a prediction made by statisticians (e.g. Sturges and Hackett 1987; see also Feller 1957), which (broadly) says that frequent names tend to become more frequent, while infrequent names tend to become less frequent and, eventually, die out. Thus **Asquith** and **Auty**, the one a habitational name and the other from a Norse personal name, are both so strongly identified with West Yorkshire that the chances of their being monogenetic must be very high. Possibly, DNA research will establish whether present-day bearers of the surname **Asquith** are all descended from a single individual, or whether there are several lines stretching back to different individuals all from the village of Askwith. The former is more likely than the latter, as is the case with the surname **Sykes.** Even though this name is now widely dispersed in the modern world, and even though there are several places in northern England called Sykes, any one of which might be the source of the surname, the survey of contemporary British surnames described in Hanks 1992 shows a statistically significant association with West Yorkshire. Sykes and Irven (2000) argue that, since male children have consistently inherited both their surname and the Y-chromosome from their father, DNA evidence can be used to confirm or disconfirm the monogenetic hypothesis for any given surname. Combining DNA evidence with geographical distribution and evidence from local history, they show that the majority of present-day bearers of the name are not only related but also can trace their origins back with confidence to a family living in Slaithwaite near Huddersfield in Yorkshire, England, in the 15th century. The name can probably be traced further back, to the 13th century, when William del Sykes held land in Flockton, nine miles to the east of Huddersfield (Redmonds, 1992).

The bringing together in this way of historical and linguistic evidence, statistical studies of geographical and demographic distribution (both modern and historical), and genetic research is in its infancy, but it promises exciting developments in years to come. The examples cited are from England, but there is every reason to hope that these principles can be applied successfully to American family names and indeed on a worldwide basis, not only for monogenetic surnames, but also for different strains of polygenetic surnames.

Genealogical Resources

In 1999–2000, the world of family names research was transformed in a different way, by developments on the Internet. Probably the most important of these was the release of the International Genealogical Index (IGI) as a freely available on-line resource via www.familysearch.org. At the same time, genealogical web sites and in particular discussion forums began to flourish and 19th-century censuses were published in electronic form. With resources like these, research that had previously taken days or was literally impossible can now be accomplished in hours.

The IGI is a vast record of births and marriages (not deaths) from civil and church registrations, and other sources from past centuries, transcribed and compiled by volunteer members of the Church of Jesus Christ of Latter-day Saints (Mormons). Of course, no conclusions can be drawn from frequency (or lack of it) in IGI, for IGI is not a systematic survey such as a census. Also, IGI has a bias in favor of English, German, and Scandinavian records, and in particular it has a policy of avoiding Jewish records, following an agreement between Jewish and Mormon religious leaders.

The entries in IGI have never been subjected systematically to the scrutiny of modern scholarship (indeed, to do this on such a vast scale is almost unimaginable), and there are undeniable blemishes (it has often been pointed out that some entries are clearly errors; a few are merely fanciful; there are variations in details, so that a single individual may occur several times with slight differences in date of birth or spelling of a place name; other entries betray an ignorance by the transcriber of such matters as the geography of language and political boundaries in 18th- and 19th-century Europe). Researchers using IGI should particularly bear in mind the "failure to find" fallacy. For example, failure to find IGI records for a particular surname in Spain or Turkey does not mean that the name is not Spanish or Turkish; it may only mean that the relevant records have not yet been transcribed.

But such blemishes are unimportant to a researcher seeking a broad overview as a starting point for more detailed research. The greatest benefit of IGI to family-name researchers is that, in its electronic form, it gives an immediate overview, showing immediately when and where a particular surname was most frequent in years gone by. It contains hundreds of millions of entries (it is growing all the time), the vast majority of them accurate and reliable.

Other genealogical resources must be treated with equal caution. Studies of particular surnames from the 19th and 20th centuries, often printed privately, are of very variable quality. Some contain priceless information, meticulously researched, with detailed citation of sources and evidence, informed by an understanding of the linguistic and historical processes that conditioned the development of family names. Others are little more than a garbled mishmash of half truths and folk beliefs.

The same wide variability can be observed in contributions to on-line forums and discussion groups. Some contributions are well-informed and reliable; others are of very doubtful reliability. One particularly common characteristic, both of older studies of individual surnames and of modern contributions to genealogical forums, is that researchers of American family names often seem to have a very hazy grasp of the facts of life and language in feudal medieval Europe and the processes of surname formation. It is hoped that DAFN will go at least some way toward remedying this defect.

Despite the undeniable benefits of on-line resources, sooner or later the serious genealogist or family historian will feel a need to visit the local library and historical record offices, both in the places where the surname first became established in North America, and in the locations in Europe or Asia from which it was first brought to America. For the serious one-name researcher, there simply is no substitute for getting to grips with original documents.

Rarer Surnames

If you are among the 15% of Americans for whose name there is no entry in DAFN, you can be sure that your surname is a rare one—specifically, you can be sure that there are fewer than 100 listed telephone subscribers. This is because every surname with a frequency greater than 100 in 88.7 million (the size of Dr. Tucker's database, based on telephone directory sampling) gets an entry. Even if your name is not an entry, there are good chances that it may be a spelling variant of another name that is, for of course the spelling of surnames is notoriously unstable. Therefore, it is worth searching DAFN for names similarly spelled. Vowels, in particular, are unstable. In a few cases (for example, **Wege, Waggy,** and **Wagy**—see the entry for **Wege**), it has been possible to pinpoint precisely when and where certain variants originated; more often, however, precise details about the origin of variants are unknown. In DAFN only the more common variants are recorded: rarer variants, with a frequency below 100 in 88.7 million, do not receive an entry unless they are of particular historic or etymological importance.

So, for example, if your name is **Goodykoontz**, a surname with a frequency of only 56 in 88.7 million (0.63 per million), you will not find your name in DAFN. But with perseverance and a little imagination, you may find your way to the DAFN entry for **Gutekunst** and discover that the latter is a name of German origin, denoting a particularly skilled workman. You will then want to consider the possibility that *Goodykoontz* may be an American variant of *Gutekunst*. If the two names are both found in a similar location at an early date (i.e. in 17th or 18th century America), the likelihood that the former is a variant of the latter is greatly increased. Now, you may decide to consult other sources, starting perhaps with the 1880 U.S. census, which is now available in electronic form, or the International Genealogical Index (IGI) at Familysearch.org (see the section on "Genealogical Resources" above). How frequent was your name in 1880? Well, **Goodykoontz** has 81 occurrences in the 1880 census, when the U.S. population was approximately 50 million (1.62 per million). So the name today seems to be less half as frequent as it was 120 years ago.

If by this time you have got the bit between your teeth, you may also be inspired to check out genealogical discussion forums and websites ("Cyndi's list" of genealogical sites on the Internet is a good guide: http://www.cyndislist.com/), to see whether any research on the history of your family has already been done. You may also decide to ransack second-hand bookstores, or consult the Library of Congress in Washington or the Family History Library in Salt Lake City, in search of a family history. (As it happens, a 16-page booklet on the Goodykoontz family was published in 1914.) You will notice that, although your surname was already widespread in many different states in the 1881 census and is even more diffuse today, 18th-century records of it are centered on Floyd, Virginia, and Frederick, Virginia.

In other cases, a rare family name may be unrelated to any existing DAFN entry. For family historians and genealogists, rare family names are generally easier to research than frequent ones. If your name is **Smith** or **Jones**, it is going to be hard, if not impossible, to distinguish your particular ancestors from literally millions of other Smiths and Joneses who have lived in the past. But if your name is **Aspiras, Babigian, Caraccia,** or **Gopinath** (some of the other surnames with a frequency of only 56 in 88.7 million), it may well be that you are related to all other bearers of that name, and you may decide to start your family history research on this basis.

If your name is not a variant of an existing entry in DAFN, your first step will probably be to establish the country of origin. Here again, comparative frequency is important. A surname that is rare in the U.S. may be very common in the country of origin. A case in point is **Gopinath**, which is not found in the IGI but, it turns out, is frequent in Kerala, India. So in this case, the hypothesis that you are related to all recorded bearers of the name begins to look much less plausible.

Because people are so mobile (a bearer of an Irish Gaelic name may have reached America via Australia; a Chinese via Singapore or Malaysia; a Scot via Canada or New Zealand, and so on and so forth), serious research into American family names must inevitably be conducted on a worldwide basis. Thanks to the Internet, this is now possible.

Acknowledgments

Many individuals and organizations have supported DAFN in various ways during its long gestation period. In 1991 Donnelley Marketing kindly gave permission for use of data on surnames from their files to get the project started, and Kenneth W. Church, of AT&T Bell Laboratories, provided this data in the form of a headword list. James Howes, head of Reference Computing at Oxford University Press in Oxford in the early 1990s, established the text structure, created routines for data conversion, and gave valuable computing support. Kathleen Much helped with the start-up of the editing process. Marion Harris pioneered work on the genealogical notes and helped to recruit and organize the team of consultants and contributors. Flavia Hodges gave support and encouragement, including permission to make use of data from the *Dictionary of Surnames* (1988), coauthored with Patrick Hanks.

In addition to the official project contributors, scholars and genealogists too numerous to mention individually have kindly answered questions about particular names and generously volunteered valuable information. Pirjo Mikkonen vetted the contribution for Finnish names; Xulio Viejo Fernández was consulted with reference to all Asturian names. Małgorzata Calhoun contributed to the editing of Slavic names. Marie Lukášová proofread all the Czech entries, and Vladimir Benko gave valuable computational support in processing Czech and Slovak entries. Anthony Wood provided a systematic identification of Muslim names. Michael Morrell helped to edit the introductory essays.

Thanks are also due to the publishing team at Oxford University Press, both in New York and England, over a twelve-year period. Linda Halvorson helped shape the original project design. Claude Conyers oversaw the long, slow, and (no doubt) frustrating period of project development from 1991 until his retirement in 1998; his support, in keeping the project on course and encouraging the maintenance of editorial standards of coverage and accuracy, overcame many obstacles. Without the support of Edward W. Barry, President of Oxford Univesity Press USA until 1998, the project would never have been possible at all. Tim Benbow, Director of the Dictionaries Department in Oxford until 1997, gave valuable advice and moral support. Frank Abate, formerly head of U.S. dictionaries at Oxford University Press USA, gave valuable advice and encouragement, as did his successors Elizabeth Jewell and Christine Lindberg.

Finally, special mention must be made of Timothy J. DeWerff, who, following his appointment as Director of Editorial Development at Oxford University Press in New York in mid-2002, galvanized the finalization process. His exceptional energy, tact, wisdom, and enthusiasm made it possible to complete the final stages of this huge, complex project in the incredibly short time of six months.

Bibliography

Feller, W. (1957): *Introduction to Probability Theory.* New York: Wiley.

Guppy, H. B. (1890): *Homes of Family Names in Great Britain.* London: Harrison and Sons.

Hanks, Patrick, and Flavia Hodges (1988): *A Dictionary of Surnames.* Oxford University Press.

Hanks, Patrick, and Flavia Hodges (1990, 1996): *Oxford Dictionary of First Names.* Oxford University Press.

Hanks, Patrick, and Flavia Hodges (2001): *A Concise Dictionary of First Names.* 3d ed. Oxford University Press.

Hanks, Patrick (1992): 'The Present-day Distribution of Surnames in the British Isles' in *Nomina,* vol. 16.

Pickering, David (1999): *The Penguin Dictionary of First Names.* Harmondsworth, Eng.: Penguin Books.

Redmonds, George (1992): Yorkshire Surname Series, vol. 2. Huddersfield, Eng.: G. R. Books.

Sturges, Christopher H., and Brian C. Haggett (1987): *Inheritance of English Surnames.* London: Hawgood Computing.

Sykes, Bryan, and Catherine Irven (2000): 'Surnames and the Y-chromosome' in *American Journal of Human Genetics,* vol. 66.

Sykes, Bryan (2001): *The Seven Daughters of Eve.* New York: Norton.

SURNAMES, FORENAMES, AND CORRELATIONS
Some Facts and Figures

D. Kenneth Tucker

Surname Frequencies and Selection of Entries

DAFN is the first surname dictionary for which the selection of entries is based on a study of frequencies of actual surnames as they exist. In the past, content of surname dictionaries has been selected by the author with no systematic account of present-day frequencies or indication of the percentage of the population represented by the content. In his preface to the first edition of *A Dictionary of English Surnames*, for example, P. H. Reaney wrote, that, for space reasons, he had to delete 4,000 surnames from his first draft: "The great majority of those eliminated are local surnames such as Manchester, Wakefield, Essex, etc." We thus see that Reaney selected, or rather deselected, not by coverage but by class. Similarly, in the preface to the second edition of *The Penguin Dictionary of Surnames*, also a dictionary of English surnames, Basil Cottle wrote about the increase in surnames from 12,000 in the first edition to 16,000 in the second edition: "This new word-hoard was largely built up by my mother . . . who . . . went on listing, from the local and national newspaper, all names not in my first volume." Selection of at least these 4,000 was therefore clearly arbitrary. We know that both Reaney (and later Wilson) and Cottle worked with what they had, with the tools then available. The authors of these important dictionaries were unable to discuss the coverage of their works in relation to the population, because the information to do this was unavailable to them.

DAFN makes use of the technology now available to do this. After each surname headword in DAFN there is a statement of the comparative frequency of each surname. Furthermore, entries were selected in large measure on the basis of computational analysis of comparative frequencies.

The challenge in generating a dictionary of surnames has always been source material. Ideally, information from the U.S. Census Bureau information might have been used, but this was not available, so other sources had to be used. A preliminary study was carried out in 1990–91, using data extracted from a list of 7 million names provided by Donnelley Marketing. Name frequencies in this list were studied by research scientists at AT&T Bell Laboratories in the 1980s, mainly for purposes of machine speech recognition and synthesis. Ken Church of Bell Labs went on to process the data for lexicographic purposes, providing a list of 60,000 different surname forms, representing the surnames borne by approximately 224 million Americans, or 80% of the population.

For the main headword list of DAFN, the Bell-Donnelley list was replaced in 1998 by data excerpted from a machine-readable phone directory. This was done partly in order to obtain independent confirmation of the names on the Bell-Donnelley list, and partly in order to obtain a more up-to-date and complete list.

The source data used was the 1997 edition of InfoUSA's ProCD Select Phone product, which lists almost 100 million telephone subscribers. Using the standard export function supplied with the product and the "greater than 50,000 records" export facility authorized by an unlock key from ProCD, the subscriber name(s) for all residential listings were extracted. The extracted data was filtered to remove nonresidential listings such as municipalities, universities, business services, religious organizations, utilities, etc. Listings for "summer residences" and other multiple listings were also removed, as were listings for children's lines, except where separate forenames for these were given.

In about 10% of the listings more than one person's forename was given within an entry. These were expanded into two (or more) entries. For example, a listing for "Jones, Bill & Mary" gives two entries: "Bill Jones" and "Mary Jones." Similarly, "Jones, Mr. & Mrs. Richard" gives two entries: "Richard Jones" and "Unknown Jones." Listings such as "Jones, Fred & May Smith" were rendered as "Fred Jones" and "May Smith."

After filtering, 88.7 million forename-surname records remained. These comprise 1.75 million different surnames (types), stored in the AmSur (American Surnames) database. About 73 million (82%) of these records include an associated forename. The balance of 15.7 million records has "Unknown" for the forename.

At the time when the data used for AmSur was compiled, the U.S. Census Bureau gave the residential population of the United States as 266 million. So AmSur is a sample representing almost exactly 33% of the total population in 1997. (By the beginning of 2003, the U.S. population had climbed to over 290 million.) The sample is geographically proportionately distributed, and there is no reason to suspect that nonlisted individuals bear any particularly characteristic set of surnames.

Not only is AmSur a very large sample; it is also probably as representative a sample of the population of the U.S. as it is possible to obtain. By contrast, it is more than twelve times larger than the 1990 U.S. Census Bureau sample used to create its first name and last name distribution tables (www.census.gov/genealogy/names).

Figure 1: *Surname Distribution in the United States*

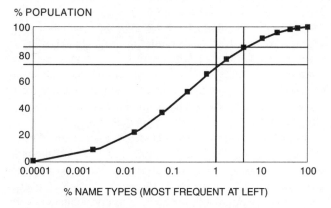

% POPULATION

% NAME TYPES (MOST FREQUENT AT LEFT)

One of the aims of DAFN is to enable the largest number of people to find an entry for their surname in the dictionary, within limits of what is manageable and publishable. We thus want to know the maximum population represented by given number of surnames. Each surname that is different from any other surname is called a *type*. Every example of that surname is called a *token*. We know for each surname type how much of the population it covers—the number of tokens.

Our sample population is 88.7 million, which we arrange by surname in descending frequency order. *Smith* is the most frequent surname with a count of 831,783 tokens and represents almost 1% of the population: in fact 0.937749%. However, it is only one name type in 1.75 million types, or 0.000057% of the surname types. This point (0.937749; 0.000057) is the origin of our graph shown in Figure 1. We can now add the next most frequent name, *Johnson,* with a count of 610,104 tokens to the list where the cumulative effect of adding *Johnson* to *Smith* is to generate a point at 1.625577; 0.000114. We can continue to do this until we have added all the name types in descending

frequency order and arrived at the final point 100; 100. This point says that 100% of the surname types represent 100% of the name tokens, or population, for all the surnames in AmSur. Note that: the "Percentage of Surnames" scale is logarithmic in order to show the shape of the distribution; the graph is cumulative in order to gives a direct read of maximum coverage for a given set of surnames. Note also that the scales have been normalized, so that similar graphs may be compared.

The curve becomes very flat as it approaches the point 100; 100 (top right). This is because there are many surnames with few bearers. There are 706,771 surnames with a count of one in the sample. They include *Ficalowych, Hataisutitum, Kapoakun, Larbaig, Mdududi, Onwubu, Papalz, Quinores, Tuvamontolrat, Xerokostas, Yaddanapudi,* and *Znorkowski.* Some of the singleton entries may be transcription errors, but most of them really are surnames, borne by real people. Of course, since AmSur is a sample of the population, not the whole population, we cannot conclude that all these surnames are unique. For one thing, a single phone listing could represent a family of two or more people. Furthermore, no doubt there are other rare and unique surnames for which no telephone subscriber listings exist. Rare and unique surnames deserve further study, beyond the scope of the present work.

The criteria for selection of entries in DAFN were threefold: frequency, historical importance, and etymological importance. All surnames with a frequency in AmSur greater than 99 were automatically given an entry and researched as far as possible. Names with a frequency less than 100 do not receive an entry in DAFN unless they are of particular historical or etymological importance. In practice, it turned out that very few names with an AmSur frequency lower than 100 are historically or etymologically important. Examples of names entered because of their historical importance are **Faniel** (AmSur frequency 91), an altered form of *Faneuil,* the name of a historically significant Boston family, and **Stuyvesant** (AmSur frequency 74), which was the surname of the director general of New Netherland in 1647–64. Examples of names entered for etymological reasons are **Apostolos** (AmSur frequency 89) and **Brabazon** (AmSur frequency 84), both of which serve as anchor names for cross-references from other entries. Several Chinese names of low frequency carry the main explanation even though they are rare, because of the editorial decision to put the main explanation for Chinese names at the Pinyin romanization, rather than at any of the many folk romanizations. A few Polish and other names with AmSur frequencies lower than 100 survive from earlier phases of the editing: these had been researched, with useful information, and there did not seem to be any good reason to delete them. There is nothing particularly significant about the figure 100; it is nothing more than a convenient cutoff point for editorial purposes. All surnames with a count of 100 or more have been included, with the result that there are 70,315 entries in DAFN. This represents little more than 4% of surname types, but it represents the surnames of over 85% of the population of the U.S.

Normalization of Multiple-Format Surnames

Some surnames—in particular those formed with an initial preposition or definite article, for example names that begin with *La, Le, Li, De, Di, Mac, Mc, Van, Van der,* and so on—exist in a number of different formats as regards spacing and capitalization. For example **De Vito** is also found in the formats *de Vito, Devito, DeVito,* and *deVito.* It would be misleading as well as wasteful to list each of these forms as a different name. The approach adopted was to combine the counts for all forms, rendered in the most appropriate format as determined by the editors from linguistic norms. (There are occasional instances where the same concatenated string represents names of two different roots. In such cases the names are, of course, treated as two separate, independent surnames: e.g., **Vanek,** a name of Czech origin, must be distinguished from Dutch **Van Ek.**)

Forenames and Diagnostic Forenames

How many forenames (given names) are there in the United States, and what is the nature of the association between forename and surname? Recall that 73 million records in AmSur have an associated forename. These comprise 1.25 million discrete forenames (types). The number of forename types is therefore quite similar to the number of surname types, but the distribution, although of the same overall form, is very different. There are fewer forenames than surnames, but the most frequent forenames are very much more frequent than the most frequent surnames, and there are many more singletons. Thus, the most frequent surname is *Smith,* with a count of 831,783, whereas the most popular forename, *John,* has a count of 2,229,952. Furthermore, whereas there are over 70,000 surnames with a frequency greater than 100 in AmSur, there are under 14,000 forenames with a frequency greater than 100. This suggests that fore-naming has been more constrained than sur-naming. If this was true in the past, there is now an observable thrust to invent new forenames in the United States. The distribution curve for U.S. forenames is shown in Figure 2.

Figure 2: *Forename Distribution in the United States*

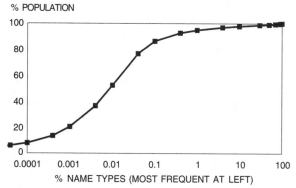

In comparing this curve with the Figure 1—the surname curve—we see that its origin is higher and it rises more steeply and has a long, flat run from about 0.1% of forename types. Furthermore, 95% of the population share 1% of the forenames, or seen from the other end of the telescope, 5% of the population share 99% of the forenames. A forename dictionary the same size as DAFN, i.e. one with over 70,000 entries, would have to include all forenames down to a count of 11, but that would be still less than 6% of the total number of forenames.

By 1996, research for DAFN had already been carried out by the editorial team on over 50,000 surnames, but for more than 20% of those entries it was impossible even to state the language of origin with any confidence, which of course made it impossible to research the etymology. It seemed probable that there was a chance of getting a bearing on the etymology of some of these more obscure surnames if the language of some of the forenames that are associated with them were known. Clearly, many forenames are strongly indicative of cultural, ethnic, or linguistic group (CELG). Even when a surname has been Americanized beyond recognition, the choice of forenames for children is often traditional and reflects the languages of the mother country. A list of all the forenames in the database was therefore sent to the editors, who (with specialist advice where necessary) made the following judgments about each forename:

Is it male or female, both, or unknown?
Is it associated with one or more particular CELG?
Is it diagnostic or nondiagnostic, for one or more
  languages?

These judgments were recorded in a database and used for cluster analysis of forenames. Some forenames are strongly diagnostic in that they are rarely if ever used outside a particular CELG. In other cases, a forename may be weakly diagnostic because it is favored by a particular CELG, even though it may actually be from another language. So, for example, the English forename *Stanley* is favored by Polish Americans, presumably because it is reminiscent of the common Polish forename *Stanisław.* In our terminology, *Stanley* is associated with the Polish CELG and is therefore weakly diagnostic. In the course of cluster analysis, weakly diagnostic names were scored at half the values of strongly diagnostic ones.

Examples of diagnostic and nondiagnostic forenames may be given. *Declan* and *Niamh* are diagnostic for Irish. *Patrick* and *Bernadette* have a statistically significant association with Irish American people, but they cannot be classed as diagnostic, because they are also borne by very large numbers of non-Irish people. *Giuseppe* is diagnostic for Italian. By contrast, it is undeniable that *Antonio* and *Maria* are associated with Italian, but they are associated also with Spanish, Portuguese, and other languages, so these two names are not strongly diagnostic for Italian.

For determining the likely CELG of a surname, all forenames associated with that surname are reviewed and each forename is scored as to whether it is diagnostic, male or female, by CELG, and by count. At the end of the process the total score is normalized to 100, so that we may see results like:

English 72%, Polish 17%, Spanish 4%, Jewish 3%,

with a long tail of very rare other CELG possibilities. English is the default (the object of the exercise being to detect non-English surnames), so the English results are discarded, as are the very low-scoring CELGs. The results in this example point to a likely Polish origin, not an English one, for the surname under consideration.

One problem is that many of the results have quite prominent scores for Spanish where the surname is known not to be Spanish. We believe that this is because of the growing pervasiveness of Spanish naming culture; in some parts of the U.S., Spanish, not English, is the default CELG. Our process was adjusted to accommodate this, by treating Spanish names as diagnostic but weighting the results against Spanish and in favor of rarer CELGs such as Latvian or Dutch.

Finally, the results of the forenames cluster analysis were further processed for separation of CELGs sharing several names in common, of which the most striking two are Italian and Portuguese. Some filtering of results was done, for example to delete low-scoring results for Spanish in the context of high-scoring results for Italian, and vice versa.

The results range from 99% for a few names with CELGs such as Ethiopian, Japanese, Muslim, and East Indian to as low as 4% for some Scandinavian surnames. The high scores show low absorption by the CELG of the mainstream fore-naming patterns, i.e. great cultural and linguistic distinctiveness, whereas the low scores occur either with surnames of English linguistic origin or, more commonly, show almost total absorption into English-American patterns of forename choices, with only an occasional flicker of the heritage. The latter case is typical of surnames that have been in English-speaking North America for some considerable time.

Some normalizing of the results by CELG need to be done. For example it is intuitively easy to understand that a 94% Japanese prediction is very positive, but it is less obvious that a 15% Norwegian result is equally positive. However, despite the fact that much work remains to be done in order to refine this process, it has already yielded very useful results. CELG analysis of forenames enabled the editors to reduce the percentage of "unidentified" names, where the language of origin is unknown, from over 20% to fewer than 3%, where a CELG result could be confirmed from genealogical or linguistic sources in the language or culture indicated.

In DAFN, confidence measures based on forename cluster analysis are declared in the Given Names sections by certain entries. Absence of a Given Names section for a particular surname indicates that not enough diagnostic forenames were found to associate the name with any particular CELG.

A word of caution is necessary concerning the interpretation of the percentages printed in the Given Names section for some entries. The percentages are a measure of confidence in the evidence, not of ethnic origin. For example, "Norwegian 15%" does *not* mean that 15% of all bearers of this surname are of Norwegian extraction. It means that, solely on the basis of forename evidence, we can have confidence that the surname is Norwegian; 15% for Norwegian, as stated above, gives great confidence that the surname is Norwegian. The confidence threshold percentage is different for different CELGs; readers may assume that where the level is published in the dictionary, that level, for that CELG, represents a high level of confidence. When put together with linguistic, historical, and genealogical evidence, this confidence may strengthen or weaken. The choice of forenames is only one of many pieces in the puzzle of identifying the CELG of a particular surname.

Female forenames are, unfortunately, severely underrepresented in the Given Names sections. The main reason for this is that they are severely underrepresented in the source material. Noticeably fewer women than men are listed as telephone subscribers; women are often represented as in "Mr. & Mrs. Richard Jones" or "J. Jones," which tells us nothing about the female forename. Of course, women listing themselves individually as telephone subscribers also sometimes suppress their forenames for security reasons. It should also be noted that female names do not cluster quite so neatly into CELGs as male names; no doubt this is partly because a diagnostic female forename of a woman who has married a man outside her CELG and has taken her husband's surname (neither of which are unusual events) creates a red herring. Such events contribute to the low-scoring "tail" of CELG identification, not printed here.

Data Creation and Data Security

Compiling a book of over 70,000 names over a ten-year period, with many contributors and numerous editorial stages, research, and checking procedures, is a large undertaking needing controlled editing. The data was compiled as a structured text file, using HTML-compatible tags to show information types, fonts, accented characters and special symbols, etc.

Each of these had its own "on" and "off" code: for example the surname at the head of the entry, the headword, began with "<N>" and ended "</N>." A validation routine was developed so that at the end of any editing session unbalanced tagging could be rectified immediately, and this was expanded to include correct sequencing of senses, balancing of brackets, nesting of data, and identification of cross-references. If an entry was deleted in the course of editing, or if the spelling of the name was altered, the editor-in-chief was asked to confirm that the alteration was deliberate. The text-file method used by the compilers had the advantage that any part of the text could be changed quickly and easily without constraint, for example using macros for rapid execution of repetitive or conditional operations. However, the other side of the coin is that free text tends to be insecure and prone to damage caused by human error. Frequent backup into a secure database meant that the DAFN team was able to get the best of both worlds: fast and flexible compilation at the same time as secure backup and structural validation.

Text would be zipped and sent from Oxford, England (later from Boston, Massachusetts), to Ottawa, Ontario, where it was converted into an MS Visual FoxPro database and processed. The text would then be automatically regenerated and sent back for continued editing. Especially toward the end of the process, a major part of the task was ensuring the integrity of the text during final editing. There was an agreed master list of headwords (the 70,315 surnames) and structural elements; deviations were only permitted following explicit confirmation from the editor-in-chief. This proved to be an invaluable aid, especially as the text for the whole book could be validated and turned around in less than 30 minutes.

Bibliography

Hanks, Patrick, and D. Kenneth Tucker (2000): 'A Diagnostic Database of American Personal Names'. *Names, the Journal of the American Name Society,* volume 48, no.1.

Introductions to Surnames of Particular Languages and Cultures

ENGLISH AND SCOTTISH FAMILY NAMES

Patrick Hanks and David Mills

Surname Origins and the Languages of Britain

The present-day family names of the British Isles are of very diverse origins, though not quite as diverse as those of the United States. Britain has its share of immigrants bearing distinctive family names from the Jewish world (see the essay by Alexander Beider in this volume), the Indian subcontinent (see the essay by Rocky Miranda), the Muslim world (see the essay by Salahuddin Ahmed and Paul Roochnik), China (see the essay by Mark Lewellen), Greece (see the essay by Nick Nicholas), and elsewhere. However, in this introductory essay we shall be concerned with the traditional languages from which English family names are derived, i.e. the development of English family names up to the 17th century. Moreover, we shall say nothing about Welsh or Irish and Scottish Gaelic family names, as these are the subject of separate essays by Hywel Wyn Owen and Kay Muhr, respectively. All this leads to a focus on English and French. A brief mention must also be made of the Cornish language. During the Middle Ages (from 1066 to about 1450), three main languages were spoken in England: Latin, the language of the Church and its administration; Norman French, the language of royalty, the aristocracy, and the law courts; and Middle English, the language of the bulk of the populace. Latin was not a source of surnames; thus, almost all traditional English surnames are of Norman French or Middle English origin.

Norman French

The earliest hereditary surnames in England are found within a few decades of the Norman Conquest (1066), and are of Norman French origin rather than native English. The incoming Normans identified themselves by reference to the estates from which they came in northern France. Thus, the aristocratic surname **Mandeville** is from at least three estates in northern France: the Mandevilles who later became earls of Essex came from Manneville in Seine Inférieure; the Devon Mandevilles came from Magneville in La Manche; while a third family derives from Manneville-sur-Risle in Eure. A fourth possible source is Manneville in Calvados. The surname occurs in Domesday Book (1086), both in the Latin form *Goisfridus de Magna Villa* and the French form *de Manneville*; this was the name of a Norman baron who was given estates in both Essex and Kent, superseding the Anglo-Saxon tenant. The surnames **Craker** and **Croaker** are from Crèvecoeur in Calvados, the earliest known English references being in taxation records, to

Helias de Crevequor in Suffolk in 1158 and *Robert de Crevequoer* in Kent in 1195.

It has been commented that the Normans treated warfare like a joint-stock enterprise; they took over lands and power by force in a way analogous to the takeovers of business enterprises by modern industrial tycoons. They also had a rather surprising habit of adopting the local language of the nation on which they imposed themselves. They had done this in France two hundred years earlier, abandoning their native Scandinavian tongue in favor of the local language, which was Old French. It took longer for them to abandon Old French in England in favor of the local language, English, but by the 15th century the transfer was more or less complete. When they reached Ireland, they adopted the local Gaelic language and in many cases Gaelicized their surnames, so that **Bonfield**, for example, came to be Gaelicized as **de Buinnbhíol**.

Within twenty years of William's seizure of the English crown in 1066, his administration had compiled Domesday Book, an inventory of the towns, villages, and estates of England, together with an estimate of the value of each one and the name of the tenant and, where relevant, the former Anglo-Saxon tenant—an invaluable resource for English historians!

In 1124 Norman methods and administration were introduced to Scotland by the new king, David I. David was the sixth son of King Malcolm III of Scotland; following a time-honored practice (described in the entry for **Giesel** in this dictionary), he had been sent to be brought up the English court of Henry I as a pledge of good relations between the two countries. Being the sixth son, he could hardly be expected to succeed to the throne; he made an advantageous marriage to the wealthy countess of Huntingdon and settled down to the comfortable life of an Anglo-Norman baron. However, by the time he was forty, all five of his brothers were dead and he became king. His reign of almost thirty years is notable for its administrative reforms and, from the point of view of the historian of surnames, for the number of English and Norman French names that were taken north by his retainers, many of whom established powerful and aristocratic Scottish families which were to play major roles in subsequent Scottish history. Many of these retainers bore surnames derived from estates in eastern, midland, and southern England; this process explains why names such as **Ramsey**, **Lindsay**, **Hastings**, and **Hamilton** are of such importance in Scottish history.

Equally fascinating is the story of the surname **Sinclair**, originally a habitational name from **Saint-Clair-sur-Elle** in La Manche or **Saint-Clair-l'Évêque** in Calvados. It was the name of a powerful baronial family, recorded in Domesday Book as far afield Somerset and Norfolk, and subsequently in Essex and Sussex. A member of this family accompanied King David in

1124, and was made Earl of Caithness; by the following century, the Sinclairs had established a Scottish clan in Caithness and the Orkneys. As was traditional among Scottish clan members (and many other great families, too, not only in Scotland), the surname came to be borne not only by descendants of the original Sinclair family, but also by their feudal retainers and tenants. This, rather than a proliferation of male children, explains why names such as Sinclair are so common among people from Scotland (including Scottish Americans).

In 1170–72 the Normans reached Ireland. The story here is rather different. By the mid 12th century, the Normans had established themselves throughout England and into Wales. In Wales in particular they built substantial castles to maintain political control; one such castle was at the port of Pembroke, which was of great strategic importance as it controlled seaborne traffic and commerce both in the Bristol Channel and the southern part of the Irish Sea. In 1170 Richard de Clare, Earl of Pembroke, better known as 'Strongbow' (whose surname came from his estate at Clare in Suffolk, eastern England) was invited to intervene in a dispute between two local Irish kings. The Irish got more than they bargained for. **Strongbow** intervened, and many of his retainers stayed on. Not only did **Clare** became established as an Irish surname, but also **Fitzgerald** (borne by descendants of Gerald, constable of Pembroke Castle), **Fitzmaurice**, and **Bermingham** (borne by descendants and associates of Piers de Bermingham, a retainer of **Strongbow**, whose surname came from his estate at Birmingham, which was then nothing but a tiny village in Warwickshire).

Middle English

Middle English is a convenient term for the English language as it was spoken and written from the time of the Norman Conquest in 1066 down to about 1450. It is important for the student of family names to recognize that, whereas English place names were coined in Old English, English surnames were not coined until the Middle English period. Middle English is a direct development of Old English with a rich admixture of vocabulary from Latin, French, and Scandinavian, and with loss of most of the grammatical inflections of Old English. By the end of the Middle English period, English spelling was more or less fixed in its modern form, but the spoken language underwent a further change, known as "the Great Vowel Shift": the qualities of the long vowels shifted dramatically, resulting in the mismatch between spelling and pronunciation which so confuses foreign learners of English. The Great Vowel Shift is explained in more detail in all standard histories of the English language.

English originated as a group of dialects (called Anglo-Saxon or Old English) of the West Germanic language that was spoken in what is now northwestern Germany and Denmark. It was brought across the North Sea to Britain from the 5th century AD onward by three main groups: Angles, who settled in the north of Britain; Saxons, who settled in the south and south-

west; and Jutes, who settled in Kent and the Isle of Wight. The Germanic settlers rapidly displaced the Welsh speakers who were the indigenous inhabitants, putting them to slaughter and driving the survivors into the mountainous areas of western Britain. In the words of the Anglo-Saxon Chronicle entry for the year 473, "The Welsh fled the English as one flees fire," and there are records of several battles in the ensuing two hundred years, in which the Welsh were generally defeated. Thus, there appears to have been comparatively little peaceful coexistence between the Anglo-Saxons and the Welsh.

In the early centuries there were seven Anglo-Saxon kingdoms, which were eventually united into one English kingdom. The majority of names of present-day English towns and villages were coined during the Anglo-Saxon period (c. 450–1066), and, as we shall see, many of these English place names gave rise to present-day English surnames, a large number of which were in turn transported across the Atlantic from the 17th century onward and are now established as American family names.

From the 7th century, Old English was also spoken in eastern Scotland, especially around Edinburgh and Stirling, and here too place names were coined that subsequently gave rise to English and American surnames. (For an account of language history and names in Gaelic-speaking western Scotland, see the essay by Kay Muhr in this volume.)

With a few famous exceptions such as *Edward* and *Alfred*, most Old English personal names died out after the Norman Conquest, being replaced by Norman French names. The Old English names *Æðelstān*, *Ælfstān*, *Beorhtsige*, *Cynebeald*, *Gōdcild*, *Lēofdæg*, *Sigeweard* and *Sæweard*, etc., did not give rise to any modern forenames. However, they survived just long enough after the Norman Conquest of 1066 to give rise to surnames in Middle English, many of which are now also preserved as modern American family names (**Alston**, **Brixey**, **Kimball**, **Goodchild**, **Loveday**, **Seward**).

Toward the end of the Anglo-Saxon period, in the 9th and 10th centuries, a new group of settlers came from across the North Sea: Scandinavians (Vikings) from Denmark and Norway. Contrary to popular belief, the Viking incursions were not all a matter of slaughter, raping, and pillaging; indeed, there seems to have been considerable amount of peaceful coexistence, resulting in the development of a mutually comprehensible spoken language, sometimes referred to as Anglo-Scandinavian. No written records of this language are known; its existence is inferred from the forms of place names and from the forms of many vocabulary words which entered English in the north and east of England. In many cases the new Scandinavian immigrants settled on land that was not previously occupied. Danish settlements took place principally in East Anglia, the East Midlands, and a large part of Yorkshire, while the Norwegians were concentrated in the northwest, especially Lancashire and Cumbria. Viking settlements were also established all around the coastal areas of Scotland, in the Hebrides and west Highlands alongside the Gaelic-speaking peoples who had come from Ireland a couple of centuries earlier. There were also Viking settlements in the Isle of Man and Ireland: Dublin itself was a Viking settlement.

The North Germanic dialects spoken by these Viking settlers were similar in many ways to Old English, although there were striking differences in the sound system, vocabulary, and personal names. So, for example, English place names ending in *-by* 'farm' (e.g. **Darby**, **Kirby**, **Boothby**, **Catesby**) and *-thwaite* 'clearing' (e.g. **Micklethwaite**, **Crosthwaite**) are of Scandinavian origin. The English place names *Skipton* and *Shipton* both mean 'sheep farm', but the former is from the Scandinavian form while the latter is Old English. *Skirt* and *shirt* are, etymologically speaking, the same word, but the former shows Scandinavian influence on its pronunciation, while the latter reflects the palatalization that took place in Old English. Large numbers of Scandinavian words were incorporated into the English language from the 9th century.

Like Old English personal names, Anglo-Scandinavian personal names died out after the Norman Conquest, but not before they had given rise to a further group of English surnames including **Axtell** (from the personal name *Ásketill*), **Gamble** (from the personal name *Gamall*), **Orme** (from the personal name *Ormr*), and **Thurgood** (from the personal name *Þorgautr*).

Cornish

Cornish, a Celtic language closely related to Welsh, died out in the 18th century. During the medieval period, however, it was still spoken throughout Cornwall and gave rise to a number of surnames, some of which crossed the Atlantic and became established as American family names. These include occupational names such as **Angove** 'the smith', nicknames such as **Couch** 'red' or **Keast** 'fat', and many habitational names, typically beginning with *Tre-* 'homestead', *Pol-* 'pool', *Pen-* 'head', 'promontory', or *Bos-* 'dwelling'.

Types of Traditional English Family Names

Habitational Names

A very large number of English surnames are habitational names, derived from place names. In a very few cases, families bearing these names are descended from Norman feudal tenants or subsequent lords of the manor, but the vast majority of English habitational surnames arose simply as distinguishing elements: John 'from Drayton' being distinguished from John 'the Baker' or John who lived 'at the Ford'. Thus, surnames such as **Drayton**, **Preston**, **Henley**, **Langham**, **Houghton**, **Stanley**, **Wootton**, **Gillingham**, **Stratford**, and **Hatfield** abound—all originally denoting the place where someone lived or from whence they had moved to some other place.

Where a place name is unique, as in the case of **Dinsdale**, **Diss**, and **Ramsbottom**, there can be little doubt that a surname spelled the same way is derived from the place name. Sometimes, as in the case of the surname **Brumage**, which is from Bromwich in the West Midlands, the spelling of the surname reflects the normal modern pronunciation of the place name. In the case of **Keighley**, a number of spelling variants are found, including **Keathley**, **Keatley**, **Keightley**, **Keithley**, and **Keithly**.

On the other hand, if a place name denotes more than one place in England, it is often difficult to say with certainty from which particular place called Preston or Gillingham the surname derives. If the surname is very diffuse, the problem may be intractable. However, sometimes statistical studies of geographical distribution can shed light on the problem. The surname **Gillingham**, for example, is very much more common in Dorset than elsewhere. The association is strong enough to be statistically significant, and the name is also found in the adjacent counties of Hampshire and Devon. This makes it very likely that most if not all bearers come from the Gillingham in Dorset, not the Gillingham in Kent or the one in Norfolk. If, furthermore, DNA studies were to demonstrate that most or all bearers of this name are descended from a common ancestor, that would virtually rule out the Kent and Norfolk places of this name as sources of the modern surname. At present, genetic studies of this kind, interacting with historical and statistical evidence of geographic distribution, have hardly begun. In future, however, we may expect interactive studies of this kind to grow considerably.

Topographic Names

Typical English topographic names, with obvious etymologies, include **Hill**, **Dale**, **Marsh**, **Moor**, and **Ford**. However, even in such cases, caution is required: *Ford* is also found as an English place name. Thus, the surname **Ford** may mean 'person from a place called Ford' as well as 'person who lived at or by a ford.' River crossings were important places in medieval times. Topographic names do not only refer to features of the natural world, but also to man-made features, for example **Abbey** and **Castle**.

In other cases, such as **Hurne** 'corner', **Hurst** 'wooded hill', **Toft** 'homestead', the meaning of the name is obscure because the word has simply dropped out of the vocabulary of English since the Middle English period. An additional obscuring factor is misdivision: for example, the surnames **Nash** and **Rash** are variants of **Ash**, from misdivision of Middle English *atten asschen* 'at the ash trees' or *atter ashe* 'at the ash tree'. Similarly, **Noakes** is from *atten okes* 'at the oaks' and is therefore a synonym of **Oakes**.

Norman French Nicknames

In addition to taking names from their estates, the Normans also used nicknames extensively, and many of these have become enshrined as English surnames. The main subcategories are much the same as those of Middle English nick-names and other categories. They include:

> References to physical appearance: **Belcher** 'beautiful face'; **Cave** 'bald'; **Cortney** 'snub-nosed'; **Greeley** 'pock-marked'; **Russell** 'redhead'.
>
> References to personality traits, both flattering and unflattering: **Bone** 'good'; **Curtis** 'courteous'; **Mallory** 'unlucky'; **Barrett** 'trouble', 'strife', or 'fraud'; **Dormer** 'sleeper' or 'sluggard'; **Menter** 'liar'; **Poyner** 'aggressive' (literally, 'fisty'); **Saffer** 'greedy'.
>
> References to animals: **Corbett** 'crow' or 'raven'; **Lever** 'hare'; **Purcell** 'little pig'.
>
> In other cases, the application of the nickname is not clear: for example **Pettiford** is from Norman French *pied de fer* 'iron foot', but was this a reference to the bearer's stern personality or to an artificial limb?

Middle English Nicknames

Nicknames coined during the Middle English period from English or Anglo-Scandinavian words are very numerous. Being coined in the everyday language of the common people, they often reveal aspects of the medieval human condition or medieval attitudes to physical, moral, and mental attributes of individuals. Taken collectively, they reflect and preserve something of the zest and color of life in medieval England. They are often colloquial, sometimes humorous, whimsical, or uncomplimentary. Some are straightforwardly descriptive of physical stature or appearance, for example **Long**, **Short**, **Rudd** 'red', **Blake** 'black', **Nott** 'bald', **Snow** 'white-haired'.

Many names from nicknames are quite flattering (unless, of course, they were applied ironically): **Lovely, Lovejoy, Smart, Sweet, Root** 'happy', **Tait** 'cheerful', **Gentle** 'noble' or 'courteous', **Snell** 'quick', **Goodenough, Scattergood**.

Others allude to some physical characteristic or deformity in a way that might be regarded as politically incorrect today: **Legg, Chinn, Knopp** 'knob' or 'carbuncle', **Niblett** 'beaky nose'. People in medieval times were more forthright and less mealy-mouthed than they are today. Quite a number of English surnames make reference to obesity (**Broad, Body, Cobb, Clapp, Keech** 'fat lump') or its opposite (**Small, Thin**).

Unflattering nicknames include those that comment on some aberration or less than admirable trait of character or behavior (**Sly, Nice** 'foolish', **Boast**, etc.). Some names probably have obscene connotations (**Shakespeare, Wagstaff**), while others describe some philandering anecdote (**Tiplady, Shacklady**).

Large numbers of nicknames are taken from words denoting animals, birds, and fish, presumably because of some fancied resemblance in appearance or behavior: **Catt, Rook, Stork, Swan, Swallow, Bodfish, Herring**. The last of these, however, may be denote someone who caught or sold herrings. When the creature named is domesticate or has a commercial value, the possibility that it may be a metonymic occupational name must always be considered.

Norman French Influence on Given Names and Patronymic Surnames

Another profound effect of the Norman Conquest was that the traditional stock of Old English names such as *Ecgbeorht* (*Egbert*) was gradually replaced by Norman French forms such as *William, Robert, Richard, Hugh*, which eventually more or less entirely replaced the traditional more varied repertoire of Old English personal names, at least among the upper and middle classes. These Norman French names have a particularly interesting history: originating as pagan names in the depths of pre-Christian Europe among Germanic-speaking tribes, with meanings like 'helmet (or protection) of the will' and 'bright renown', they became fashionable and Christianized in the courts of early medieval central Europe, in particular the Frankish court of Charlemagne. Their popularity continued in medieval France, where they were adopted by the Normans, who brought them to England. Here, as elsewhere, they formed the basis for a wide variety of surnames. Thus, for example, forms ending in - *son* (e.g. **Wilson**) are characteristic of northern England, while forms in *-s* (e.g. **Wills**) are more asociated with southern England. The ending *-ks*, as in **Wilks, Jenks, Hanks**, is found especially in the southwest Midlands (Oxfordshire, Gloucestershire, Worcestershire, Warwickshire), corresponding to more northerly forms in *-kinson* (**Wilkinson, Jenkinson, Hankinson**).

The variety of vernacular surname forms derived from some Norman personal names (e.g. **Robson, Hobson, Dobson, Hobbs, Dobbs**, all from *Robert*) bears witness to the difficulty that English speakers had in pronouncing or indeed even recognizing certain Norman French speech sounds, such as initial *R-*.

At the same time, the influence of the Church ensured the rapid spread of New Testament names such as *John, Matthew, Mark, Luke, Paul*, and *Mary*, which were also supplemented by various saints' names such as *Bernard* and *Dominic*.

Surnames of Office and Occupation

Many surnames reflect the different social classes of medieval England and Scotland and the influence of the feudal system on eveyday life. Names such as **Reeve, Bailey, Sargent, Constable, Hayward**, and **Steward** generally denoted manorial officials or administrators, while names such as **Bond, Husband, Cottrell, Cotman**, and **Thrall** refer to various lower ranks in the social hierarchy of agrarian medieval England. The terms of lowly status are mostly from Old English, while many (but by no means all) of the terms denoting administrators are from Norman French.

Names with a more superior significance, such as **Abbott, Bishop, Earl, King** generally denoted someone in the service of such an august personage rather than the man himself. On the other hand, they were probably also bestowed as ironic nicknames on lowly peasants who had inflated ideas of their own importance.

A sharp distinction between status name and occupational name is not always possible. For example, **Butler** literally denotes a servant in charge of the bottles in a household, and this may be the original meaning of the surname in some cases. However, it would be a mistake to take this meaning too literally. Butlers could be immensely powerful and influential officials in a great household—a far cry from mere bottle washers. In 1177, King Henry II's butler, Theobald Fitzwalter, was appointed Chief Butler of Ireland, an office somewhat equivalent to viceroy or colonial governor.

The original meaning of the surname **Marshall** was 'man who looks after horses', but in royal households the marshall was a high official of state, typically one with military responsibilities.

The same is true of the Scottish surname **Stewart**, which originally denoted nothing more than a mere steward. However, the steward of an aristocratic household was an important person in his own right, and this name was borne by a family that rose to royal status in Scotland.

Names from terms denoting medieval occupational surnames are abundant in English. They testify to the diversity and specialization of trades and occupations in medieval England. Many English occupational names (**Smith**, **Baker**, **Cook**, **Mason**, **Shepherd**, etc.) are familiar enough and need no explanation.

In other cases, the occupation in question is no longer practised, or the form of the name has changed and needs some explanation. A **Wright** was a craftsman who made machinery: builders of windmills and watermills were known as wrights. A **Skinner** was a dealer in leather goods; a **Fletcher** made arrows.

For some occupations, different terms were used in different parts of the country: **Baxter** is a Scottish and northern English form of **Baker**; **Webster** is a northern English form of **Weaver**. A **Fuller** (the southeastern English term) was someone who beat cloth or trampled up and down on it in a bath of water and lye, in order to thicken it. In southwestern England, someone engaged in the same occupation was known as a **Tucker**, while in Scotland and northern England he was a **Walker**.

Other occupational names are of the metonymic type, in which the name of an article or product was used to denote a user of the article or a maker or seller of the product. So, for example, **Lock** can be a metonymic occupational name for a locksmith; **Wool** denoted someone who made woolen articles or who sold wool; **Bagge** denoted a maker or seller of bags. **Whitbread** referred to a baker of white bread; **Goodall** 'good ale' and **Godber** 'good beer' no doubt referred to an innkeeper.

Huguenot Surnames

During the 17th century a characteristic group of surnames was brought to Britain, North America, and southern Africa by French Huguenot exiles. The Huguenots were French

Protestants. In 1572 large numbers of them were massacred in Paris on the orders of the queen, Catherine de' Medici, and many of the survivors sought refuge in England and elsewhere. Although the Edict of Nantes (1598) officially guaranteed religious toleration, persecution continued, and when the Edict of Nantes was revoked by Louis XIV in 1685, intolerance became institutionalized: the trickle of emigration became a flood. Many migrated to England, while others joined groups of Dutch Protestants settling around the Cape of Good Hope. Others sailed across the Atlantic to establish themselves in North America. The French surnames which these migrants brought with them were more or less Anglicized, and remain to this day distinctive types of British, American, and South African surnames. **Bosanquet** and **Garrick** are examples of English Huguenot names, **Gasque** and **Bayard** are American examples, and **Du Plessis** is a South African one.

Migration from England and Scotland to North America

The colonial experiences and the background of early migrants from England to North America has been amply documented by many scholars, of whom Boorstin (1958) and Fischer (1989) are perhaps the most outstanding examples. Only the briefest summary can be given here.

Ever since the Pilgrim Fathers made their momentous voyage in the *Mayflower* from Plymouth in southwest England in 1620, there has been a steady flow of immigrants from every part of Britain to North America. In the later 17th and early 18th centuries very different kinds of immigrants, with different agendas for their lives, came from elsewhere in Britain and settled in other parts of eastern North America. Fischer (1985) identifies four American sociocultural threads, which he calls "Folkways" and traces back to different regions of England.

New England. Characteristically, the early 17th-century settlers in Massachusetts, Rhode Island, and Connecticut were Puritans and others with a religious agenda. Their objective was to set up a new society in which they could practice their own forms of worship without interference, a society often based on a written agreement to cooperate (beginning with the famous "Mayflower Compact"). The Puritans came mostly from eastern England. The history of their families in England (and sometimes the origins of their surnames) is typically to be sought in East Anglia and the East Midlands of England.

Virginia. English settlement in Virginia began at Jamestown in 1606, fourteen years before the *Mayflower* pilgrims landed at Plymouth Rock. However, the early years of the Jamestown settlement were troubled with internal strife, conflicts with the local Indians, disease, starvation, and death. Virginia settlements did not really begin to prosper until the 1640s. Unlike the New Englanders, their objectives were commercial rather than religious. They came to make fortunes in growing tobacco and other activities, and they were backed by "merchant adventurers" (venture capitalists, in modern parlance). The great majority of them came from the cities of London and Bristol and their surrounding areas; some of them bore English West Country names such as Berkeley and Throckmorton. Another important group came from Northamptonshire in central England, including the ancestors of George Washington. Many settlers in Virginia were members of aristocratic English families, generally Royalists ("cavaliers"), in some cases fleeing from the victories of the Parliamentarians ("roundheads") in the English Civil War of 1642–51. On the other hand, a penal colony for the transportation of convicts was established in 1618, and many of these transportees eventually founded families in Virginia. In addition, at about the same time, slave labor began to be imported from Africa—among them, no doubt, the earliest ancestors of some modern African American families.

Philadelphia and the Delaware Valley. The earliest settlements in the Delaware Valley, dating from 1640, were Swedish rather than English. In 1682, the city of Philadelphia was founded by William Penn as one of a series of Quaker settlements. Here, as in Massachusetts, a major component of the motive of these settlers was religious freedom. Many of these Quakers came from the North Midlands of England. They settled not only in Philadelphia but all along the Delaware.

Scottish and Scotch-Irish Plantations in the South. In the late 17th century and early 18th century, successive waves of Scottish, northern Irish, and northern English settlers came to Georgia and the southern states of America, often in quite large groups. They went to what Fischer calls "the Backcountry"—in Georgia, the Carolinas, Virginia and West Virginia, spreading into Tennessee and Kentucky—or established large landholdings and began to establish plantations. A lot of the longest-established surnames of the traditional South are linguistically of Scottish or northern English origin, but in many cases they actually came from northern Ireland. This,

incidentally, is why comparatively large numbers of African Americans bear Scottish surnames such as Abernathy, inherited in many cases from North British and northern Irish immigrants who became plantation owners.

Bibliography

Black, George F. (1946): *The Surnames of Scotland*. New York Public Library.

Hanks, Patrick, and Flavia Hodges (1988): *A Dictionary of Surnames*. Oxford University Press.

Hanks, Patrick, and Flavia Hodges (1990): *Oxford Dictionary of First Names*. Oxford University Press.

Hanks, Patrick, and Flavia Hodges (2001): *Concise Dictionary of First Names*. 3d ed. Oxford University Press.

Hey, David (1998): *The Oxford Guide to Family History*. Oxford University Press.

Hey, David (2000): *Family Names and Family History*. London: Hambledon and London.

Mills, David (1998): *Oxford Dictionary of English Place-Names*. Oxford University Press.

Padel, Oliver J. (1985): *Cornish Place-Name Elements*. English Place Name Society.

Reaney, P. H., and R. W. Wilson (1991): *A Dictionary of English Surnames*. 3d ed. Routledge.

Rogers, Colin D. (1997): *The Family Tree Detective: Tracing Your Ancestors in England and Wales*. Manchester University Press.

On Migration from Britain to Colonial North America

Boorstin, Daniel J. (1958): *The Americans: The Colonial Experience*. Random House.

Fischer, David Hackett (1989): *Albion's Seed: Four British Folkways in America*. Oxford University Press.

IRISH AND SCOTTISH GAELIC FAMILY NAMES

Kay Muhr

Language and History

The Gaelic language was spoken throughout Ireland from at least the first century AD. Written literature from the 5th century onward shows little evidence of earlier Celtic and pre-Celtic languages, although early place names confirm that these existed. British Celtic, the language branch from which modern Welsh developed, was closely related.

From northeastern Ireland Gaelic spread to Scotland, and probably also to the Isle of Man, in the 5th century AD. In

Scotland, Gaelic joined two British Celtic languages: Pictish in the northeast, and Cumbric in the southwest. Soon thereafter, Gaelic was followed by the arrival in southeastern Scotland of Anglo-Saxon, the parent language of both Scots and English. A further influence was that of the Vikings, who arrived from Scandinavia in the 8th to 10th centuries and settled in the Isle of Man and the Scottish islands. In Man especially, Gaelic was heavily overlaid by the Norse language, before coming to the fore again in the 12th century.

Most Scottish surnames today are either Gaelic or Anglo-Saxon in origin, with some input from the Vikings and from the

Normans, who arrived from France via England in the 12th century. Normans also settled in Ireland, some via Scotland and Wales. The Norman lords in France had already begun the practice of using as a family surname the name of the lands they held, and this practice continued in Scotland with the adoption of the names of baronies as surnames.

In Ireland, inheritable Gaelic surnames were developing from patronymics as early as the 10th century. This makes them among the first surnames in Europe (Woulfe 1923; Ó Murchadha 1999). The 17th-century Irish historian Geoffrey Keating believed that Irish surnames began by decree of the high king in the reign of Brian Boru (1002–14). The earliest known surname seems to have been **Ó Cléirigh** 'grandson of Cléireach', used in the year 980 and referring to an eponymic ancestor who must have died about 858.

Surnames beginning with *Ó* 'grandson' are typical of Ireland. They were shortly followed by the development of surnames beginning in *mac* 'son' in both Ireland and Scotland.

Patrick Woulfe, author of a foundational work on Irish surnames, writes: "Mac- surnames are in general of later date than Ó- surnames, still I think it must be admitted that by the end of the 12th century surnames were universal among Irish families. . . . It is also true that many Mac- surnames of purely Irish origin are of later date than the Anglo-Norman invasion, but this was due to the break-up of the old surnames into septs."

Certain *Mac* surnames are found in both Scotland and Ulster; it is often difficult to know on which side of the Irish Sea they originated, since there have been comings and goings ever since the Gaelic language was taken to Scotland from Ireland. In some cases the same surnames arose independently in several different localities (e.g., Murphy, Kelly); many other names, now widely dispersed, seem likely to go back to a common ancestor in Ireland or Scotland.

According to a 16th-century Scottish account, surnames there began when King Malcolm Canmore (1057–93) "directed his chief subjects, after the custom of other nations, to adopt surnames from their territorial possessions." This text then gives a list of surnames, none of which is Gaelic. G. F. Black, author of the standard work on Scottish surnames, found surnames in Scottish documents from the second quarter of the 12th century: "From this time onward we find surnames mainly territorial from the possession of land becoming common, though a few are descriptive and some are patronymic."

As happens in any area that has more than one language, Gaelic names were influenced by the naming traditions of coexisting languages, in both Ireland and Scotland. By the time Norman knights arrived in Ireland in the 12th century, they had become English- rather than French-speaking, but they established a number of surnames beginning in *de*, and their patronymics in *fitz* (from *fils* 'son') were easily translated by Gaelic *mac*.

In 1465, the Irish parliament passed an act requiring every Irishman living in the Anglo-Norman counties of Dublin, Meath, Louth, and Kildare to "take to him an English surname of one towne, as Sutton, Chester, Trym, Skryne, Corke, Kinsale; or colour, as white, blacke, browne; or art or science, as smith or carpenter; or office, as cooke, butler." However, the poet Edmund Spenser noted a hundred years later that this ordinance had had little effect.

Despite all these influences, patronymic names remained the norm in Ireland. Although place names of Gaelic origin were used as toponymic surnames in Scotland, this type of surname does not seem to have been significant within the Gaelic-speaking tradition.

Through migration in the period of the English and Scottish Plantations of Ulster in the 16th and 17th centuries, many more English-language surnames arrived in Ireland. Over time, some of these names, such as **Staunton** and **Stapleton**, became much commoner in Ireland than in England, while in other cases some incoming surnames became recognized "English" equivalents of Gaelic types.

Before Gaelic surnames reached their present form, three processes seem to have intervened—the first for speakers of Gaelic, the other two for speakers of English. The first is differentiation in spelling between the Gaelic languages of Ireland and Scotland, which took hold after 1400. The second process, respelling the names according to the sound system of English, was already used by the Normans in the 12th century but increased in Scotland as Gaelic was abandoned by the court, and in Ireland after the 16th-century Tudor occupation. By the third process, based in some cases on attempts at translation or rough phonetic similarity, names of English origin became established as equivalents for some Gaelic names. This seems to have been particularly prevalent in Ireland.

The pronunciation of any language changes over time, and Gaelic pronunciations have changed and often become simplified since the period when surnames arose. In the 1950s, the spelling system of Irish Gaelic was reformed, dropping many consonants that were no longer pronounced in Ireland. Scottish Gaelic remains more conservative. This dictionary, which traces the origins of surnames, uses the historical rather than the reformed spellings. Thus, the reader can see the letters that may be represented in an Anglicized version, so that, for example, a name containing *bh* or *mh* (pronounced as *w*) may preserve a *v* in the modern spelling, as in **McCarvill** (alongside **McCarroll**) from **Mac Cearrbhaill**, whose modern Irish spelling is **Mac Cearúill**. If you want to use the modern Irish spelling of your surname, you will need to use a guide such as *ÓDroighneáin* and *ÓMurchú* 1991, listed in the bibliography.

Reading Gaelic Names

Two rules of Gaelic spelling cause difficulties for those more used to English. First, extra vowels are used to indicate two different types of consonant: *e* and *i* (called "slender vowels") are placed adjacent to those consonants that are pronounced with a slight *y*-sound, while the "broad vowels" *a, o,* and *u* flank those that are not. The "slender" pronunciation is most noticeable with the consonants *d, t, s*; this explains why the personal names *Bríghid*, *Seán*, and *Síle* may be pronounced *Breedge, Shawn,* and *Sheila*. A surname example is **MacFadgean** from *Mac Phaidín*. Second, the (originally Latin) system of adding *h* to certain letters to spell a new sound (*ph, th, ch*) has been extended to include *fh, bh, dh, gh, mh*, which are not found in English. The pronunciations of these are as follows:

ph = English *f*.
th = originally as in English *thin*, later as *h*.
ch = ch in Scottish *loch* or German *Bach*.
bh = usually *v* in Scotland; in Ireland the slender version is *w*.
dh = originally as in English this, later as *gh* below.
gh = *y* when slender, a dry gargle like Parisian French *r* when broad.
mh= as *bh*, but with a nasal timbre.
fh = silent, not pronounced.
sh = *h*.

When two words are put together in the Gaelic languages to form a compound or phrase, the initial consonant of the second may be influenced by the first element, often resulting in one of the sounds written with -*h*. This process of 'lenition' is described below. A somewhat rarer change (not found in Scottish Gaelic) is nasalization. However, word elements are normally quoted in the basic form, insofar as it can still be determined what that is (and with personal names, even more than with other compounds, this may be hard to determine).

Origins of Gaelic Surnames

Patronymics

Knowing one's lineage was very important in Gaelic society. The characteristic question to newcomers in the early literature is not "Who are you?" but "Whose are you?". In texts from the first millennium AD, characters are usually identified by their own and their father's names, and possibly also a grandfather's name: for example, *Aedhan mac Gabrain mic Domangairt* (from the Annals of Ulster, the year 581), or *Dáre macc Findchada maicc Éogain maicc Níalláin* (900). Where Gaelic languages are still spoken, people still are often identified by their own name plus the name of a parent or other relative. There may also be family nicknames or "epithets," based on some distinguishing trait or occupation. In other societies these epithets have become surnames.

The Gaelic interest in genealogy continued. In the 1830s, Roman Catholics by the Lower Bann recited their genealogies at wakes, Maguires in Enniskillen knew theirs, and the O'Hara family of Crebilly, County Antrim, were able to write down their genealogy from an old female retainer. Parallels could certainly be found in Scotland.

Almost all Gaelic surnames are based on the line of descent from the father (*mac* 'son of') or grandfather (*Ó* 'grandson/descendant of'). At first, only actual sons or grandsons were so called, but over time the reference to particular ancestors became fixed, and the patronymic became a genuine surname in the modern sense. Some of the ancestors of the more famous families have been traced in the Irish annals dating to between 858 and 1250. The *Ó* form, now Anglicized to *O'*, belongs particularly to Ireland, beginning in the 10th century, but from a century or so later, many *mac* surnames arose in Gaelic Ireland as well as in Gaelic Scotland.

It is difficult to be sure that a particular historical character was the origin of a patronymic surname, because family pride encouraged the same personal name to be repeated in subsequent generations. Instances are the name *Niall* 'Neil' among the **O'Neills**, or *Rughraidhe* 'Rory' among the **McRory** branch of the **Magennises.**

There have been a very large number of Gaelic personal names, and each often gave rise to further variants and diminutive forms. Many works on surnames also try to explain the meaning of the personal names, but the researcher should remember that the original meanings may not have been understood by their later bearers. Although there was great interest in Gaelic society in the reasons why names were given, the primary reference of a name is always the person or place rather than the linguistic etymology. Despite the prevailing interest in the linguistic meaning of names, even the early texts on the subject do not always explain them correctly.

In a society in which individuals continued to be identified by their own pedigrees, why should one ancestor rather than another be commemorated in a general surname? In most cases, the etymology of his name is an unlikely reason, and a more plausible suggestion is the ancestor's achievements in life. Ó Murchadha's research indicates that, rather than the most famous, the most distinctive eponym (original bearer of a name) was selected for a surname, so that the family would not be confused with others. In a few cases, the name of the surname-ancestor harks back to an even earlier, legendary bearer—for example, **O'Neill** to *Niall Glúndubh* ('Niall of the black knees'), who claimed descent from Niall of the Nine Hostages. However, some personal names were simply more popular than others, and there are many instances where identical surnames arose separately in different parts of Ireland from ancestors who happened to bear the same name.

The important people and events of Irish history before the 17th century are well documented in the Irish annals. The eponyms and bearers of significant surnames are quite likely to have been recorded, but it is clear that many less important surnames and ancestors also existed. Over time, unfamiliar ancestor names might be altered or reinterpreted as language and society changed. The aftermath of the Reformation and Plantation in Ireland meant that many families lost traditional lands or positions and had to migrate to new areas where their names and accents were unfamiliar. Later attempts at translation of surnames into English show that people continued to be interested in the meaning of names, but also that they frequently misinterpreted them.

Gaelic Personal Names

The number of Gaelic personal (given) names is estimated at about twelve thousand in Ó Corráin and Maguire's book on the subject. Many of these, however, were never common. The chief sources from which we know them are medieval Irish genealogies. The origin of septs (divisions of clans) and surnames is often mentioned in later Irish genealogical works. The genealogies mainly give the pedigrees of men, with only occasional reference to wives or mothers, and so far less is known about the personal names of women; surnames, however, are almost all based on names of men.

Some of the oldest personal names are "one-idea" names like *Aodh* 'fire', *Conn* 'sense', *Lugh* (probably 'light'), or *Niall* (possibly 'cloud'). Color names were popular: *Donn* 'brown', *Fionn* 'fair', *Flann* 'blood-red'. Colors also occur as compounds with other elements, and a fuller list includes *breac* 'freckled', *ciar* 'dark', *corcra* 'purple', *crón* 'yellow', *dubh* 'black', *glas* 'green/blue/gray', *gorm* 'dark blue', *lachtna* 'gray', *odhar* 'dun', and *ruadh* 'red'. Many of these refer to hair color, while *flann* and *gorm* have connotations of nobility (like 'blue blood' in English). Animal imagery is seen in many names, including *Art* 'bear', *Bran* 'raven', *Cú* 'hound', *Each* 'horse', *Faol* 'wolf', *Fiach* 'raven', *Madadh* 'dog', and *Mathghamhain* 'bear' (literally, 'good calf').

Most Gaelic personal names are compounds of two ideas: *Cormac* 'raven son' (yet another 'raven' word, etymologically related to Scots *corbie*), *Echu* probably 'horseman'. At the beginning of a name, some of the common elements are *cath-* 'battle', *each-* 'horse', *muir-* 'sea'; at the end, *-gal* 'valor', *-gein* 'birth', *-gus* 'choice' (sometimes interpreted as 'strength'). Examples of such compounds are *Cathal, Cathbharr, Cathmhaol*, 'battle-strong', 'battle-top' (i.e. helmet), 'battle-devotee' or *Ardghal, Conghal, Fearghal, Gormghal, Tnúthghal* 'high valor', 'hound valor', 'man valor', 'noble valor', 'ambition valor'.

As well as compounds, there are two-word names, where the first element is followed either by an adjective or by a noun in the genitive (possessive) form. 'Hound' names are particularly distinctive, made up of *cú, con-* 'hound' plus a further epithet: *Cú Dhubh* 'black hound', *Cú Choigríche* 'hound of the borderland', *Cú Choille* 'hound of the wood', *Cú Mhara*, 'hound of the sea'. Sometimes *Cú* is combined with the names of actual territories: with Irish provinces in names like *Cú Chonnacht, Cú Laighean, Cú Mhidhe, Cú Mhumhan, Cú Uladh*, 'hound of Connaught, Leinster, Meath, Munster, Ulster', or with smaller areas like the Burren in County Clare in *Cú Bhoirne*.

Maol 'tonsured one', 'devotee' often forms names showing Christian influence. It appears in secular names like *Maolchatha, Maolfhoghmhair, Maolmhocheirghe* 'devotee of battle', 'devotee of autumn', 'devotee of early rising', but also, of course, frequently with the genitive of a saint's name, as in *Maoilbhréanainn, Maoilbhrighde, Maoldomhnaigh, Maoilmhichil, Maoilsheachlainn, Maoltuile*, 'devotee of St.

Brendan, St. Brigid, the Lord, St. Michael, St. Secundinus, of the will (of God)'.

Giolla 'lad, servant', spelled *gille* in Scotland, forms personal names with a descriptive adjective, often a color: as in *Giolla Bán* 'fair lad'. It also combines with the genitive of a saint's name or religious attribute.

Popular saints' names differed between Ireland and Scotland, and they might be used in a family to express devotion to a particular saint. Common to both were *Giolla Bhríde, Giolla Chríst, Giolla Íosa, Giolla Mhíchil, Giolla Mhoire* 'servant of Brigid, of Christ, of Jesus, of Michael, of Mary'. In Ireland we also find *Giolla Choinnigh, Giolla Dé, Giolla Eoin, Giolla Seanáin* 'servant of Canice, God, John, Seanán', whereas in Scotland we see Scottish forms such as *Gille Aindreis, Gille Brátha, Gille Eathain* 'servant of Andrew, of Doom, of St. John'.

In contrast to this piety are what one might call "macho" names for men: *Forannán* 'aggressive', *Eigceartach* 'unjust', *Eigneach* 'forceful', *Indreactach, Annrachtach* 'violent', *Cosnamhach* 'contentious'. Uncomplimentary names include *Cennétig* 'ugly head', *Baothgheallach* 'foolish pledger', and women's names such as *Gráinne* 'ugliness', *Brón* 'sorrow'. *Coigleach, Mongach*, and *Mothlach* derive from nicknames referring to hairstyle: 'like a distaff', 'with a mane', 'bushy'.

Many personal names include the diminutive ending *-án*. Established names also have diminutive forms, such as *Dimma, Demmán* from the ancient name *Diarmait*, or *Eachán* from names based on the word *each* 'horse'. With this type it is no longer clear what is the full form of the name being abbreviated. The ending can vary between *-án* and *-ín*, sometimes with the same first element, as with *Casán, Caisín* 'little curly one', *Odhrán, Uidhrín* 'little sallow one'. Another diminutive ending, *-óc*, later *-og*, is more common with female names but forms part of double diminutives in the forms *agán, igín, anán*: *Maolagáin* 'little bald one', *Flannagán* 'little red one', *Branagán* 'little raven'. A large number sound like baby attributes, pet names for 'little old men': for example, *Baothán* 'little foolish one', *Caochán* 'little blind one', *Críonán* 'little withered one', *Lapán* 'little fist', *Maolán* 'little bald one', *Rónán* 'little seal' or 'little hairy one', *Senán* 'little old one', *Tiomán* 'little soft one'. Names like these also occur in patronymic surnames.

Gaelic speakers also borrowed personal names from the Bible and from peoples with whom they came into contact. From Latin and British come *Rumann* 'Roman', *Bréanainn* 'king' (from Welsh), and *Conaing* 'king' (from Old English). Examples of Viking names are *Ivar, Goraidh, Laghmann, Somerled*, and *Ljotr* 'ugly' (which gave the surname **Macleod**). There are names in which Gaelic and Scandinavian names have coalesced, including *Amhalghaidh* or *Amhlaoibh = Amlafr, Annraic = Heimrekr, Bran = Bjorn, Eachdhonn = Haakon, Ruaidhrí = Hrothrekr*, and *Suibhne = Svein*. Personal names of Norman French origin include *Riocard, Gearoid, Gilbert, Seathrún, Roibeard, Seancin, Uidhilin*, and *Uaitear*.

Surnames from Occupations

Some Gaelic surnames derive from the bearer's father's occupation. Scotland and Ireland have different lists in Gaelic: in Scotland we find **MacNider** (*Mac an Fhigheadair* 'son of the weaver'), **Macintosh** (*Mac an Tòisich* 'son of the chief'), **MacNucator** (*Mac an Fhucadoir* 'son of the fuller'), **McWhirter** (*Mac an Chruitire* 'son of the harper'), and **McVittie** (*Mac an Bhiadhtaigh* 'son of the food provider').

Surnames in Ireland with an occupational origin include **Driscoll** (*Ó hEidirsceÓil* 'grandson of the interpreter'), **O'Gowan** (*Ó Gobhann* 'grandson of the smith'), **Hickey** (*Ó hÍcidh* 'grandson of the doctor'), **Gallogly** (*Mac an Galloghlaigh* 'son of the mercenary soldier'), **McAtamney** and **Timoney** (*Mac an Tiompánaigh* 'son of the lute-player'), **McSporran** (*Mac an Sparáin* 'son of the purse-keeper'), and **MacAtee, MacEntee** (*Mac an tSaoi* 'son of the sage').

In both countries, surnames commemorate sons of smiths (*Mac an Ghobhann*: Irish **Magowan**, Scottish **McGowan**), wrights or craftsmen (*Mac an tSaoir:* Irish **McAteer**, Scottish **MacIntyre**), judges (*Mac an Bhreitheamhan:* Irish **Breheny**, Scottish **Brain, Browne, Broome**), doctors (*Mac an Leagha*: **McClay, Macinleich**), and stewards (*Mac an Mhaoir*: **Weir**, Scottish **McNair**). In Scotland, the surnames **Caird** and **Gow**, from Gaelic *ceard* 'craftsman, tinker, tinsmith' and *gabha* 'smith', appear respectively in the 13th and late 16th century. It seems that in some cases these were coined directly from the Gaelic vocabulary words, rather than being shortened from the patronymic forms *Mac an Cheaird* or *Mac an Ghabhann*. In both areas, occupational surnames were quite often translated into their equivalents in English.

Ecclesiastical occupational surnames show some interesting differences between Ireland and Scotland. In Ireland we find *Mac an Airchinnigh* (**McInerney**, 'son of the erenagh, or church overseer') and *Mac an Deagánaigh* (**Digney, Deane**, 'son of the dean'); in Scotland, *Mac an Deoraidh* (**Dewar**, 'son of the pilgrim or guardian of a holy relic'), *Mac an Chlèirich* (**McCleary**, 'son of the cleric'), *Mac an Abadh* (**McNab**, 'son of the abbot'), *Mac an Phearsain* (**McPherson**, 'son of the parson'), *Mac an Phríora* (**McPrior**, 'son of the prior'), and *Mac an Bhiocair* (**McVicar**, 'son of the vicar'); and in both places, *Mac an tSagairt* (**McTaggart**, 'son of the priest').

Surnames apparently derived from aristocratic occupational titles or status names were may also have been complimentary personal names: *Ó Ríoghbhardáin* (**O'Riordan**, 'descendant of the royal poet'), *Ó Flaithbheartaigh* (**O'Flaherty**, 'prince-like', 'generous'), *Ó Flaithfhile* (**Flatley**, 'descendant of the princely poet'), *Ó Tighearnaigh* (**Tierney**, 'descendant of the chieftain'). The *O'Riordans* are recorded as a learned family in an ancient text on Irish writers; *Clann an Bhaird* (**McWard**, 'children of the bard'), *Uí an Cháinte* (**Canty**, 'descendants of the satirist'), and *Mec Con-fhileadh* (**McNeilly** [correctly, *Mic an Fhileadh*]) 'sons of the poet' are named as poets.

Surnames from Nicknames and Epithets

The numbers of descriptive, geographical, or occupational surnames in Gaelic are very small. Scotland has the well-known *Caimbeul* (**Campbell**, 'crooked mouth'), and *Camshrón* (**Cameron**, 'crooked-nosed'), originally nicknames for personage called *Ó Duibhne* in the 13th century and *Mac Domhnaill Duibh* in the 15th century.

Ireland has the adjectival surnames *Breatnach*, now translated as **Walsh** 'Welsh', **Kavanagh** (*Caomhanach*, from an ancestor who was fostered by a successor of St. Caomhán), and **Kinsella** (*Cinnsealach*, an epithet, possibly meaning 'chief warrior', borne by a forebear called Enna Cinnsealach). In Irish and Scottish Gaelic many other appelations are recorded with adjectival variants (usually ending in *-ach*), but these have not become established as surnames.

Colors, though common as epithets, rarely became established as surnames. Those that did include **Bane** from *bán* 'white', **Duff** from *dubh* 'black', and **Roe** or **Roy** from *rua(dh)* 'red'—usually referring to hair color. **Begg** (from *beag* 'small') and **Ogg** (from *Óg* 'young') were used in Scotland in the 13th century.

There are few regional or ethnic names, but we find at least the patronymic forms **McNulty** (*Mac an Ultaigh* 'son of the Ulsterman') and **McAtasney** (*Mac an tSasanaigh* 'son of the Englishman').

Anglicization of Surnames

Gaelic surnames have been adapted in three ways to result in the spellings we have today. These are transliteration, or respelling according to the spelling rules of English; translation, in which an English name of similar meaning was substituted; and the replacement of Gaelic names by unrelated English names.

Transliteration

The most common method of Anglicization has been an attempt to spell the sound of the Gaelic name using the spelling system of English. In the 17th century, initial *Ó* 'grandson, descendant' was retained, but it was frequently dropped later, being considered too much a sign of Irishness and thus of low status. Consonant clusters might also be simplified and the name shortened by dropping unstressed syllables, especially final vowels. *Mac* 'son' was usually retained in both Ireland and Scotland, with the spelling varying between *Mac* and *Mc* according to individual preference. However, it could also be dropped, or reduced to *C-*, a process typical of the Isle of Man but also widespread elsewhere. An example is *Mac Lochlainn* 'son of the Scandinavian', which is variously Anglicized as **McLaughlin, Loughlin**, and **Claflin**, with numerous spelling variants of each.

In 17th-century English, the sound spelled *gh* (originally

pronounced like *ch* in Scottish *loch*, or German *Bach*) was beginning to take on the sound *f,* which it now has in English words like *rough* and *laugh.* Thus, both **O'Haughey** and **O'Haffy** could arise from *Ó hEachaidh.*

That example also shows the 'epenthetic' *h* which was normally inserted after Irish *Ó* if the ancestor name began with a vowel. This is the path by which **O'Hara** developed from *Ó hEadhra,* **Hennessy** from *Ó hAonghusa,* **Hogan** from *Ó hÓgáin.* Similarly, the final *c* of *mac* was often interpreted as beginning the ancestor name, so that **McCartan** derives from *Mac Artáin,* with a reduced Anglicized form **Curtin.** *Mac* followed by an ancestor name beginning with *N* was sometimes Anglicized as *Mac R . . .,* as in **McGreal** from *Mac Néill,* and *l* was sometimes replaced by *r,* as in **Flannery** from *Ó Flannghaile. Mac* often became pronounced *mag* before vowels, resulting in **Maguire** from *Mac Uidhir,* or **Magennis** from *Mac Aonghusa.*

In the older language, an ancestor name beginning with a consonant and following *Ó* or *Mac* normally had its initial unchanged. In the 17th century, however, a new process called "lenition" developed, by which the initial consonant of a proper name in the genitive or possessive case changed to a slightly different sound. Lenition, indicated in Gaelic spelling by adding the letter *h* after the affected consonant, could result in different transliterations of the same surname; thus, **Mac Domhnaill** was Anglicized as **MacDonnell** in Ireland (**MacDonald** in Scotland), while a lenited form of the same name, **Mac Dhomhnaill,** was Anglicized as **MacConnell.** Similar variation can be seen in **MacDonagh** and **MacConaghy** from *Mac D(h)onchadha,* and **MacDowell** and **MacCool** from *Mac D(h)ubhghaill.* These variations caused differences when spelling the name in English, but *Ó* followed by an ancestor name beginning in *F* also caused confusion when spelling the name in Irish, too. Lenited *f* is silent, so that it was possible for a surname like *Ó F(h)loinn* to be understood as *Ó Loinn.* **Flynn** and **Lynn,** and **Flaherty** and **Laverty** (from *Ó F(h)laithbheartaigh*) were thus related surnames originally, but they arose in different places: the forms **Flynn** and **Flaherty** are associated with Munster and Connaught, and **Lynn** and **Laverty** in Ulster.

Some typically Scottish spelling features include *qu* for the sound originally pronounced *ch* or *h,* as in **Farquhar** from *Fearchar,* and *z* for a sound originally pronounced as *y,* as in **Mackenzie** from *Mac Coinnich.*

Translation

Looking at translated names often reveals changes in pronunciation that led people to assume that a surname contained words which in fact it did not. Different attempts at translation of a name might become current in different regions, reflecting the local pronunciation of the name in Irish.

The translations, in the words of Ó Corráin and Maguire, can be "unusual not to say bizarre." They are often naive and rustic, unlike the warrior imagery of many original personal names. The Irish surname *Mac Conaonaigh,* a name that originally

meant 'son of *Cú Aonaigh,* the Hound of the Assembly', was heard as similar to *coinín* 'rabbit' in Connaught, and to *éan* 'bird' in Ulster, and **Rabbit** and **Bird** were used as English forms of that surname in those areas. The translation **Bird** might, furthermore, be used for any name containing a similar syllable: *Ó hÉanna* or *Ó hÉi(gh)nigh,* otherwise **Heaney,** or *Ó hÉidhneáin,* otherwise **Heenan.** *Mac Conchoille* 'son of *Cú Choille,* the Hound of the Wood', was translated as **Woods.** *Ó Maolmoicheirghe* 'son of the devotee of early rising' was translated as **Early.** *Ó Maoltuile* and *Mac Maoltuile,* related surnames from *Maoltuile* 'devotee of the will (of God)', became **Flood** in English, as if based on *tuil* 'flood'. *Ó Fuarghuis* or *Ó hUarghusa* 'descendant of *(F)uarghus,* Cold Choice', was reinterpreted as coming from *fuaruisce* 'cold water' and translated as **Waters** or **Caldwell.** Another variant, *Ó hUaruisce,* was understood as containing *t(h)uaruisc* 'news' and translated as **Tydings.**

English Surnames Adopted as Equivalent

These equivalents tend to be English or Scots surnames current in the locality and perceived as somewhat similar in sound to Gaelic names. If you know that your family used two surnames, one English and one of more Gaelic type, this pair may help you identify their place of origin in Ireland. Families in Ireland may still be aware of, and alternate between, two possibilities. Three Ulster examples may be given: **MacRory** and **Rodgers** from *Mac Ruairí; Mac Cathmhaoil* giving **McCawell,** but also **Campbell** in North Armagh and **Caulfield** in South Tyrone; **Armstrong** alternated with **Trin-Lavery** in North Down, because the epithet *tréan* 'strong' was used for one branch of the family, while the syllable *Lav-* of *Ó Labhradha* (**Lavery**) was interpreted as *lámh* 'hand, arm'.

In Scotland, the use of English patronymic surnames ending in *-son* led to some of these forms being used as equivalents for certain Gaelic surnames, for example **MacFergus, Ferguson; MacIan, Johnson; MacKendrick, Henderson; MacNicol, Nicolson.**

Patterns of Irish Immigration to North America

There was a certain amount of emigration from Ireland from the very start of initial English colonization in North America, but in comparison to the numbers leaving 17th-century England and the scale of later Irish migration across the Atlantic, it was relatively insignificant. In the 18th century, emigration from Ireland to Colonial America became much more significant. Precise estimates are problematic, but it is likely that at least 115,000 Irish entered the American colonies before the Revolutionary War. Approximately 60% of these immigrants were drawn from the northern province of Ulster and the majority of them would have been Presbyterians of

Scottish stock. These immigrants went predominantly to the middle colonies and settled in the Appalachian backcountry. By the early 19th century many of their children and grandchildren peopled the trans-Appalachian migration west.

Small but noticeable numbers of Irish surnames are also found in pre-Revolutionary times in French-speaking areas of North America (sometimes in Frenchified forms such as **DeGuire** from **McGuire**). These are in some cases the names of Irish Jacobite refugees who fled from English rule in Ireland to France in the 17th and 18th centuries; in other cases, they come from Irish soldiers in the British Army who had deserted to the French.

The proportion of Roman Catholics leaving Ireland grew steadily from the 1780s on. By the 1820s Ulster Presbyterians were a declining minority among emigrants. The volume of Irish immigration into the U.S. increased fairly steadily up to the outbreak of the Great Famine in 1845. Over the next five years 1.2 million Irish people came to North America. The mass exodus which the Famine produced was slow to subside. In the following two decades it is estimated that some 2.5 million Irish crossed the Atlantic. Significant Irish immigration continued in the decades down to World War I, but it was declining in absolute terms and particularly in relation to flows of new immigrants from southern and eastern Europe. By the 1920s Britain was overtaking the United States as the primary destination for migrants from Ireland. Whilst more of those post-Famine immigrants ended up "going west" than was once appreciated, there is little doubt that for the majority, immigration meant an experience which was essentially urban or suburban, industrial rather than agricultural, and heavily concentrated in the northeastern quarter of the United States.

Bibliography

Black, George F. (1946): *The Surnames of Scotland; Their Origin, Meaning, and History*. New York: The New York Public Library.

Carney, James (1946): 'De scriptoribus Hibernicis' in *Celtica* vol. 1.

Day, Angélique, and Patrick McWilliams, eds. (1990–98): *Ordnance Survey Memoirs of Ireland*. Belfast: Institute of Irish Studies in association with the Royal Irish Academy, Dublin.

Mac Airt, Seán, and Gearóid Mac Niocaill, eds. (1983): *The Annals of Ulster* (to AD 1131). Dublin: Dublin Institute for Advanced Studies.

MacLysaght, Edward (1957, 1991): *The Surnames of Ireland*. Dublin: Irish Academic Press.

Matheson, Robert Edwin (1909): *Special Report on Surnames in Ireland, with Notes as to Numerical Strength, Derivation, Ethnology, and Distribution*. Dublin: Printed for H. M. Stationery office, by A. Thom and Co. (limited).

O'Brien, M. A. (1962): *Corpus Genealogiarum Hiberniae. Vol. 1*. Dublin: The Dublin Institute for Advanced Studies.

Ó Corráin, Donnchadh, and Fidelma Maguire (1990): *Irish Names*. 2d ed. Dublin: The Lilliput Press.

Ó Droighneáin, M., and M. A. Ó Murchú (1991): *An Sloinnteoir Gaeilge; an tAinmneoir*. Baile Atha Cliath.

Ó Murchadha, Diarmuid (1999): 'The Formation of Gaelic Surnames in Ireland: Choosing the Eponyms' in *Nomina* 22.

Woulfe, Patrick. *Irish Names and Surnames; Collected and Edited with Explanatory and Historical Notes*. Baltimore: Genealogical Pub. Co., 1967.

WELSH FAMILY NAMES

Hywel Wyn Owen

The Welsh Language and Traditional Names

The Celtic languages in Britain are divided broadly into two branches, the Goedelic (Irish, Scottish Gaelic, and Manx) and the Brythonic or Brittonic (Breton, Cornish, and Welsh). Philologists customarily distinguish between the two branches by denoting them as Q-Celtic and P-Celtic, respectively, based on one of the phonological divergences between the two families whereby *qu-* in one family is *p-* in the other. For example, the Scottish Gaelic place names *Kintyre* and *Kinross* correspond to the Welsh place names *Pentir* and *Penrhos*. The word for 'son' in Irish is *mac;* in Old Welsh it was *map* (modern *mab).* In patronymic surnames this distinction has led to Irish and Scottish names in *Mac-* (or *Mc-*) and in Welsh to the patronymic prefix *Ap* (a development of *Map*).

The Brythonic language was the vernacular language of what is now Wales and England until the departure of the Romans in the 5th century. Although Latin and Greek were used in the recorded documents of the Roman empire, place names (such as *Avon* and *Dover*) provide evidence that Brythonic was the vernacular language. After the advent of the Anglo-Saxons from the 5th century onward, the political domination of the Anglo-Saxon kingdoms diminished the Brythonic identity in England itself, and 'Welsh' became the term for the Brythonic language spoken in today's Wales. A related dialect, Cumbric, survived in northwest England and southwest Scotland well into the Middle Ages. Indeed, the earliest literature in the Welsh language refers to "the kingdom of the north," located in the north of England. Some the names associated with those poems, such as Urien, Heledd, and Cynddylan, are still in use today.

The traditional Welsh naming system was patronymic, based on kinship, probably a reflex of a Celtic social structure. Books of pedigrees were vital to show lineage and to provide legal verification of succession. The link between father and son was expressed by *map* 'son (of)', which became *ap* in name sequences (*ab* before names beginning with a vowel), a sequence which was maintained over several generations. Authorities on the patronymic system are fond of citing Lewis Morris of Anglesey (1701–65), who proclaimed his great-great-great-grandfather to have been *David ap William ap David Lloyd ap Thomas ap Dafydd ap Gwilym ap Dafydd Ieuan ap Howel ap Cynfrig ap Iorwerth Fychan ap Iorwerth ap Grono ap Tegerin.*

An additional epithet such as *coch* 'red' or *bychan* 'small' was often used for clarification, usually as *Goch* or *Fychan,* the lenited forms appropriate to adjectives. The word for 'daughter', *merch,* does appear in the genealogies, lenited as *Ferch* and abbreviated as *Ach* or *Uch,* although *Ap* was also occasionally used for the daughter, certainly in documents drafted outside Wales, probably because of a perceived similarity of *Ap* and *Ach.* Latin documents represent *Ap* and *Ach* as *filius* and *filia.* In essence, then, the Welsh system was almost exclusively based on first names. No real need was felt for naming after location, habitation, or occupation.

Until the 16th century, Wales had its own royal courts and its own legal system. The popular belief has long been held that the two Acts of Union of 1536 and 1543 made that model redundant and that Wales was obliged to accept the English legal and administrative system, which found Welsh names largely unintelligible and the patronymic system cumbersome and lengthy, and plainly not conducive to cementing a kingdom united under one legal system. That is a simplistic and narrow interpretation. Certainly, some easing or streamlining of the patronymic system was probably inevitable. For example, even before the 15th century, the patronymic *Ap* was frequently omitted in name sequences. However, the patronymic system continued in use, even in official documents, for over two centuries after 1543.

On the other hand, even in the Middle Ages, imitation of the English system of surnames was not unknown among the gentry, especially the more widely traveled ones. In the 15th and 16th centuries, the rise in power (and eventually to the English throne) of the Tudors, a dynasty whose origins had links with Wales, further stimulated members of the Welsh aristocracy to adopt the English naming system. Indeed, it became clear that social and political preferment depended on adopting the English style in social comportment, language, and naming. Within a very short space of time, the aristocracy, especially those who had moved to London either permanently or temporarily, adopted single family names on the English model.

Formation of Family Names in Wales

The selection of one family name, first by the gentry and then, at a much slower rate, by the middle and lower classes, was frequently quite arbitrary. Most people selected one of the most recent given names, usually the father's. Consequently, Welsh single family names were inevitably based on the personal names which had been the exclusive characteristic of the Welsh patronymic system. That single fact explains the comparatively narrow range of the stock of Welsh family names.

The transformation of Welsh given names into "English" surnames had side effects. It led to an Anglicization of some of the Welsh names both phonologically and orthographically, so that the given name *Hywel* became the surname **Howell(s)** and *Madog* became **Maddock(s).** Some English and Norman-French names which had long been naturalized into "Welsh" forms reverted back to Anglicized forms. For example, *Richard* had become *Rhisiart,* but under the new regime this was readily Anglicized back into **Richards.** *William,* or its Norman French form *Guillaume,* became *Gwilym,* then reverted to **Gwilliam** and **Williams.** *Hugo/Hugh* became *Huw,* then **Hughes.** Some names were adopted as approximations of the Welsh forms, despite there being no actual linguistic link between the two forms, such as *Lewis* for *Llywelyn,* *Hugh* for *Hywel* and *Edward* for *Iorwerth.* Evidently, therefore, the predominant modification was to a recognizable, comparable English form, together with the usual addition of the English possessive or patronymic -*s,* so that *Sion, Dafydd,* and *Ifan* became **Jones, Davies,** and **Evans.**

Welsh names which had been nicknames such as *Goch* and *Fychan* became surnames such as **Gough** and **Vaughan.** Other examples are **Brace** (from *bras* 'ample-girthed'), **Dew** and **Tew** (*tew* 'fat, stout'), **Lloyd** and **Floyd** (*llwyd* 'grey'), **Moyle** (*moel* 'bald'), and **Gwyn/Wynne** (*gwyn* 'white, blessed'). Hypocoristic (or pet) names were also open to adaptation, so that *Siencyn* (a pet form of *Sion*) became *Jenkins, Gutyn* (from *Gruffydd*) became **Gittins,** and *Bedo* (from *Maredydd*) became **Beddowes.**

The all-pervading *Ap* of earlier Welsh patronymics did survive. Occasionally, it was attached to the following name, so that *Ap John* became *Upjohn.* Far more common was the process of assimilation: *Ap Harri* was assimilated to **Parry,** *Ap Huw* to **Puw** and **Pugh,** *Ap Hywel* to **Powell,** *Ap Rhisiart* to **Prichard,** *Ap Rhys* to **Pryce** and **Price,** *Ab Ifan* to **Bevan,** *Ab Owen* to **Bowen.**

The arbitrariness of the choice of the given name taken as a surname can be illustrated by a fictitious example: a son of someone called *Rhisiart ap Huw ap Owain Fychan* could have adopted, as his new family name, any of the following: **Richards, Prichard, Pugh, Hughes, Owen, Owens, Bowen,** or **Vaughan.**

Occupational names may have survived as family names, but it is not always easy to tell, as assimilation to English forms can cause problems. **Saer** and **Sayer,** for example, could be from *saer* 'carpenter' but may also be English **Sawyer**. **Crowther** could be *crythor,* one who played the *crwth* '(Welsh) fiddle', but the same word appeared in Middle English (as *croude,* for the Welsh fiddle) and the family name may have derived from that. **Gooder** may be from Welsh *coedwr* 'woodsman', although it is also from an English personal name.

There are comparatively few Welsh habitational family names. The gentry sometimes adopted surnames from their family seat, such as **Pennant, Blainey,** and **Glynne.** Other names that show people, of whatever class, being associated with their geographic origins are **Powys/Powis, Gwynedd/ Winnet, Clwyd/Cluett, Cogan, Conway, Eyton, Gower, Hanmer, Kyffin, Laugharne, Mostyn, Narberth, Picton, Scourfield, Sully, Trevor,** and **Yale**. But these are the exception, not the rule.

The process of adopting and adapting a single permanent family name was a gradual process, which was swifter in the border counties and among the more English-oriented families. The decline of the patronymic system was far slower in the rural areas.

Two features of the later periods are the religious and the industrial. Seventeenth-century Puritanism and periodic Nonconformist revivals from the 18th to the early 20th century, of varying intensity and permanence, probably account for biblical family names such as **Emanuel, Samuel(s), Elias, Ephraim,** and **Moses**. In parallel, chapel-based culture inspired such given names as *Handel* and *Elgar,* but these do not appear to have transferred into family names. The comparatively narrow range of family names has, almost of necessity, prompted the need to distinguish one *John Jones* from another. This search for what is at the same time an identity and a distinction has certainly prompted people to adopt a second or middle name, and to be regularly known by all three names, such as *Huw Aled Thomas* or *John Davies Jones.* Not surprisingly, the same motivation has given rise to double-barreled names such as **Morris-Jones** and **Parry-Williams.**

The industrial expansion of Wales saw an influx of surnames from England, so that certain areas were and still are notable for characteristic surnames (such as **Hooson** in Flintshire, the name of a family of lead or pottery workers from Derbyshire). At an earlier period, it is interesting to note the appearance of names which designate the bearer as being a *Sais,* 'Englishman', e.g. the surname **Sayce**. This appellation may well have had pejorative connotations, but more probably meant no more than 'able to speak English', having an English parent, or having lived for some time in England. It has a parallel in **Walsh,** an Irish pronunciation of 'Welsh'.

Migration to North America

The migration of Welsh family names to North America was to a large extent the result of industrial and social privation. The decline of the coal and slate industries of north Wales and the coal, iron, and steel industries of south Wales sent thousands to seek a better life elsewhere. North America in particular attracted waves of immigrants from Wales, who took with them their language and their place names (as evidenced by American places with names such as *Wales, Bethesda, Bangor,* and *Bryn Mawr*). Pennsylvania was a particularly favored state for Welsh immigrants.

From 1865, South America saw a migration whose origins were slightly different, in that it was prompted more by a response to religious and social intolerence in the largely agricultural areas of rural mid Wales. The Welsh settlements in Patagonia, too, boast Welsh place names (such as *Trelew, Camwy, Dolafon,* and *Puerto Madryn*) but can also demonstrate Welsh family names being modified by marriage within the Welsh-Spanish communities, such as **de Jones** and **Jones de Ferreira**.

Naming in Present-Day Wales

One of the features of 20th- and 21st-century Wales is a growing sense of national identity in terms of politics, culture, education, and language. Individuals, particularly within what can loosely be described as the professional class, feel the need to express that identity by consciously divesting themselves of the outward signs of Anglicization and reverting to Welsh forms. **Vaughan** can once again be found as **Fychan, Lloyd** as **Llwyd**, and **Griffiths** as **Gruffydd**. English or Norman names may be given the same treatment, so that **Hughes** can be commonly found as **Huws**. Given names redolent of an earlier age have been resurrected, including names from early Welsh literature and history such as *Heledd, Pryderi,* and *Rhodri***.** The natural development of that renaissance is a revival of the patronymic system with *Ap.* The sons of *Hywel Wyn Owen* are *Pryderi Ap Hywel* and *Rhodri Ap Hywel,* where **Ap Hywel** is taken to be the sons' new family name. On the other hand, the daughter's name is *Heledd Wyn Owen,* retaining the existing family name. Several daughters, perhaps jealous of their brothers' ready-made badge of Welsh identity, have taken the opportunity to adopt an alternative by calling themselves, say, *Heledd Wyn* or *Heledd Hywel* where **Wyn** or **Hywel** is taken as the new family name, or simply to adopt **Ap Hywel** regardless of the fact that, strictly, *Ap* has a male significance. Sons are also known to adopt the Welsh versions (or approximations) of their fathers' names, so that an Edward Jones's son or daughter can be **Jones, Ap Sion,** or **Ap Iorwerth** or **Sion** or **Iorwerth**. To what extent these will become established family names only time and usage will tell. Welsh family names, however, appear to have come full circle.

Bibliography

Morgan, T. J., and Prys Morgan (1985): *Welsh Surnames*. Cardiff University Press.

Rowlands, John and Sheila (1996): *The Surnames of Wales*. Federation of Family History Societies.

Owen, Hywel Wyn (1998, 2000): *The Place-names of Wales*. University of Wales Press and The Western Mail, Pocket Guide series.

FRENCH FAMILY NAMES

Susan Whitebook

History

The majority of French family names come from three linguistic sources: Roman Latin, Germanic (mainly Frankish), and the Latinized Hebrew Bible. The Celtic names of the Gauls who inhabited the territory when the Romans arrived have largely been lost, except in the form of place names associated with properties; in the latter case, they were generally Latinized with the ending -*acum* 'property of'.

The Roman style of personal names, with the forename (Latin *praenomen*), the tribal name (*gens*), and the nickname or family name (*cognomen*), came to be abandoned in the north of France as the Germanic tribes overcame the remnants of the empire in the 5th century AD. Thereafter, the Frankish (and general Germanic) style prevailed: a single name, typically composed of two vocabulary elements, one of which was often shared with a parent. *Ro-bert* 'renown-bright' is an example of a name that might bear translation, but as the centuries passed and the Franks themselves became Romanized, names became less full of meaning, and the linguistic pool from which these names drew life stagnated.

With the formal conversion of the Franks to Christianity under Clovis (traditionally 496 AD), a new Oriental fount of names offered such possibilities as *Joseph* and *Mary*, from the New Testament. To this were added the numerous Eastern (Greek and other) names found in the Christian martyrology. Royal names retained their Germanic roots (e.g., *Louis* and *Robert*) and occasionally acquired an epithet ('Charles Martel', 'Louis the Fat'), but these epithets were never inherited.

French is a Romance language, derived mainly from Latin, but its name actually refers to a Germanic people, the Franks, who lived in what is now northern France and western parts of Germany in the early Middle Ages. A late form of Latin (later to become French) was spoken at the courts of their rulers, the most famous of whom was Charlemagne, but their vernacular Germanic (Frankish) language had a considerable influence on French words, and particularly on names.

While the Frankish tribes politically dominated the north of France, a different group of Germanic peoples, the Burgundians, dominated the region of Burgundy, and a further Germanic group consisted of the Visigoths in the southwest. That a family name has its origins in a Germanic language is not, however, an indication of ethnic origin; Germanic names were the fashion even in the south of France in the 10th century, a time when Germanic languages were not spoken there.

When the Northmen or Vikings began to settle in the region that came to be be named for them as Normandy, in the 9th century, they brought a fresh Germanic wave, but they soon abandoned their Norse tongue and adopted the northern Romance language, known as the *langue d'oil* (so named because the word for 'yes' was *oil*, as opposed to the *langue d'oc* [Occitan] in the south, where it was *oc*). When they conquered England in 1066, they brought their Norman dialect with them, and the ruling classes of the islands communicated in Anglo-Norman French for centuries. As they took over Wales, Scotland, and Ireland as well, northern French names such as **Lambert**, **Sinclair**, and **Fitzgerald** became deeply rooted in English, Scottish, and Irish culture. A habitational name such as **Disney** represents a fusion of many traditions: Gaulish *Isina*, a personal name, Romanized with the suffix -*acum,* gave French *Isigny*, the name of a town in Calvados in Normandy. The preposition *de* 'from', 'of' became fused with the locality name, and the whole was contracted to give **Disney** as a surname in England and Ireland. See the essay by Patrick Hanks and David Mills for more details about the Normans in Britain.

It is worth noting here that Norman influence was also felt elsewhere in Europe, for example in Sicily, where a Norman kingdom was established in the 11th century, and where Norman French influence on Italian can be seen in surnames such as **Altieri** and **Guastella**.

In the 12th century, the French language had not yet been "standardized"; in fact, the dialect of Paris would not become the national language until the 19th century, long after the period when family names became fixed. Local dialects, therefore, furnish many of the surnames that are here conveniently grouped under the label "French."

In addition, different regions had different styles of naming. In the Basque region of the Pyrenees, there are many more names deriving from the domaine, the estate or house, than in the northeast, where baptismal surnames prevail. Names deriving from professions were more prevalent in cities than in rural areas.

In the 12th and 13th centuries, with a rapidly growing population and a dramatic decrease in the number of first names currently popular (such as *Guillaume* and *Jean* for men, *Jeanne* and *Marie* for women), surnames became increasingly necessary to distinguish people. By the 14th century, they stabilized and became more and more commonly hereditary.

In 1539, the Ordonnance de Villers-Cotterets ordered that, among various other civil and judicial reforms, village priests must keep registers, duplicated for the civil administration, of all baptisms, marriages, and burials. These would serve as proof in all legal cases involving property, showing, for example, whether the property owner really had died, whether the legatee had really attained the age of majority, and whether he really was the offspring of the couple in question. Therefore, it became urgent to establish good records and to provide conclusive evidence of identity. This gave impetus to even wider use of surnames, now inherited from the father, which became the standard practice.

The French in North America

In the United States, French surnames are concentrated in New England and northern New York state, in Louisiana, and, to a lesser degree, around the Great Lakes. A few of the country's several thousand French place names will help to give an idea of the extent of French involvement in North America: Eau Claire, Wisconsin; Terre Haute, Indiana; Detroit, Michigan; St. Louis, Missouri; Baton Rouge, Louisiana; and Mobile, Alabama.

The first known "French" presence was most likely Breton: by 1500 Bretons were fishing the Grand Banks off Nova Scotia. The many French exploring expeditions in the centuries that followed are remembered in the names of their leaders— **Cartier**, **Champlain**, **Joliet**, **Marquette**, **La Salle**, **Cadillac**, and **Radisson**, which are often preserved in place names. The beaver pelts highly prized in the 17th century brought adventurers (*coureurs des bois,* literally 'woods runners') to seek their fortune on all the lakes and rivers. The common surname **Pelletier** or **Pelkey** means 'fur trapper' or 'fur dealer'. In the struggle for political and economic dominance with Great Britain waged in the late 17th century and the first half of the 18th, an important military presence was established, with forts in Alabama (Fort Toulouse) and Vermont (Fort Saint-Frederic), among many others.

The earliest French outposts in North America, on major waterways like the Great Lakes, the Mississippi, and the Saint Lawrence, were military first and commercial second, so the French men there were drawn from town and country alike, principally from the provinces on the Atlantic: Gascony, Aunis, Saintonge, Poitou, Brittany, Normandy, and Picardy, as well as the Ile-de-France (Paris). Rouen, Bordeaux, and La Rochelle were also important cities of origin.

The French first settled in the Canadian province of Quebec (then called New France) in the early 17th century. The first child born to them was an **Hebert**, in 1619. By far the most significant French immigration to the United States has been from Quebec, where the French-speaking population felt oppressed by British rule, and where economic hardship drove many south of the border in search of jobs and farms. By 1841, the population drain was so severe that a royal commission was appointed to study its causes. Major flows of emigration from French-speaking Canada to the United States occurred in the 1860s, 1880s, and 1930s.

Louisiana (and in the present context we should think of this, not as the modern state, but as the huge Louisiana Territory, sold to the United States in 1803) was first visited by Marquette and Joliet, who in 1673 sailed down the Mississippi River as far as Arkansas and claimed the territory west of the Mississippi for France; in 1685 La Salle reached the mouth of the river. Bienville laid the foundations for New Orleans in 1718. The colony prospered in spite of many difficulties and was left a French possession even after the Seven Years' War ended in British victory in 1763, when France was forced to cede all her other holdings in North America to Britain. Later in the same year, however, the colony was reacquired by Spain, not without resistance. In 1803, ceded back to France, it was promptly sold by France to the newly emergent United States. It had many important French settlements besides New Orleans, perhaps the most distinctively French city in the United States, with its famous French Quarter (Vieux Carré) and the Mardi Gras.

The French-speaking population expanded with the arrival of another group in the late 1750s, the Acadians (the source of the word *Cajuns*), who had been forcibly expelled by the British from their lands in eastern Canada; many found their way to Louisiana, where, given the heavy presence of French-language institutions and the closely bound community, they have retained many of their customs and traditional songs and tales, and, of course, their French names.

The Huguenots in North America

America has long been the goal of refugees, and French refugees included the Huguenots, a group of French Protestants. Some fled the wars of religion of the 16th century, but it was the revocation of the Edict of Nantes in 1685 by Louis XIV that spurred thousands to leave France. The edict had granted Protestants certain limited rights of worship. When these were withdrawn, refugees fled to neighboring countries, in particular Britain, the Netherlands, and the Protestant states of northern Germany. Eventually about two thousand of them came to the colonies, settling at first mainly in Boston, New York (city and colony), and South Carolina. They were readily assimilated among their Protestant English- and Dutch-speaking neighbors. Names such as **Greenleaf** (a translation of *Vertefeuille*) and **Delano** (*DelaNoie*) testify to the presence of Huguenots.

Political refugees would include representatives of factions out of favor at a given historical moment, such as the French Revolution of 1789. The numbers of such refugees in America are impossible to know, but there has been a steady stream, varying with economic and political conditions.

A Typology of French Family Names

There are four main types of French surnames. No scheme, however finely adjusted, could account for all existing names, but let us examine four of the major types of surnames, beginning with the one that seems most closely to spring from an idiosyncrasy or from a feature peculiar enough to leave its mark even today.

Nicknames

The most problematic type of surname to explain is the sobriquet or nickname, which principally reflects a physical characteristic: **LeBlond** 'blond', **LeGros** 'big', 'fat', **LeNain** 'dwarf', **LeBorgne** 'one-eyed'. It may be derived from a habitual phrase, such as **Cadieux** 'by God'; from a particular devotional or occupational phrase, such as *pater noster* 'our father' intoned by a cantor, which produced the surname **Paternoster**, perhaps more familiar to Americans as **Patenaude**. A characteristic phrase is surely the origin of the lovely Canadian name **Vadeboncoeur** 'go with a light (or stout) heart'. The American name **Potvin** (or **Potwine**) may come from the regional name Poitevin 'from the region of Poitou', but it may also be from the nickname Pot-de-Vin, denoting someone willing to take a bribe. Someone might be nicknamed after a hilarious (to everyone else) misadventure: for example, another classic is **Cocu** 'cuckold'—a name that has sometimes been legally changed, for obvious reasons.

Related to these are nicknames derived from animals, such as **Loup** 'wolf', probably the nickname of a particularly bad-tempered man (also a baptismal name from 5th-century Saint Loup, who was formidable enough to stop Attila the Hun; but he in turn may have been named for the animal). **Chouan**, from an Angevin dialectal word for 'screech-owl', evokes a voice happily now silenced. Other evocative animal surnames are **Cochon** 'pig', **Poule** 'chicken', and **LeBoeuf** 'ox'. In this same category could perhaps be placed names derived from body parts associated with moral qualities, such as **Coeur** 'heart', or the Québécois **Jolicoeur** 'lovely (or merry) heart'.

In America, French sobriquet names are especially frequent because of the large 19th-century immigration of French Canadians, whose soldier or sailor ancestors in the 17th century often adopted a nickname as a 'secondary surname' (called 'dit names' by genealogists). These are sometimes derived from words denoting flowers (**Larose**, **LaViolette**), although the name **Lafleur** itself, considered a soldier's or servant's surname in France, is associated with the meaning of *fleur* less as 'flower' than as 'flour'; thus it has sometimes been translated 'Miller'. Secondary surnames often give a vital link between an American branch of a family and its French ancestors. For example, the surname **Baptist** may have been formalized because it was the last audible part of a name such as Olivier dit St-Jean-Baptiste.

Other types of secondary surnames would include personal moral characteristics, such as **Sanssouci** 'carefree', **LaDouceur** 'gentleness', **La Terreur** 'the terror', or **SansPitié** 'merciless'. There are also compound forms, such as **Frappé-d'abord** 'strike first' and **Prêt-à-boire** 'ready to drink'. Of course, not all sobriquets are so easily explained. An example in French of a name difficult to interpret is **Boileau** 'drink-water': is this one who drinks water or, sarcastically, one who never touches it?

Habitational and Topographic Names

For the mobile population of late medieval and early modern France, the town or city of origin formed an important category of surnames; **Rivoire** (a town in Gironde), the family name of Boston immigrants in the 18th century who became known as **Revere**, is such a name. Regional and national origins also contributed to the pool: **Langlais** 'English' or **Langevin** 'from Anjou'.

On a more limited scale, topographical features played an important part. These might be natural features, as in **Duval** 'of the valley', **Dutertre** 'of the hillock', **Delorme** 'of the elm', or **Lafond** 'of the spring'; or they might be man-made, as in **Dupont** 'of the bridge', **Lacroix** 'the cross', **Dupuis** 'of the well', or **Ruelle** 'alley'.

In Canada, the old regional and topographical names gained new life. **Langevin,** especially if it was given as *dit Langevin* 'also called Langevin', at first would have meant that the bearer was actually a native of that region. The regional name **Saintonge** (a region in southwestern France on the Atlantic) is not reported in France itself today, but it is common in Canada and the United States: many of the earliest Canadian settlers came from that seafaring coast. It is routinely split to form **Saint-Onge** or **St. Onge**; **St. Ange** 'holy angel' also appears, by folk etymology.

Secondary surnames derived from topographical features also have practical value in distinguishing two families, or two branches of a family. For example, the **Paquet** *dit LaRivière* would have their holdings on the riverbank, while the **Paquet** *dit LaVallée* would live upland from them.

Occupational Surnames

Occupational surnames tended to be found more in towns and cities than in the countryside. One of the problems in America has been what form of a family name to use. In the 20th century, newcomers have tended to keep their original names, but earlier, especially in the 18th century, a strong assimilationist pull encouraged people to find a corresponding English name by Anglicization or translation, or in some cases by mistranslation. Because occupational surnames are also frequent in English, in most cases the translation worked smoothly. For example, it is easy to get from **Meunier** to **Miller**, from **Chartier** to **Carter**, or from **Boulanger** to **Baker**, and so on.

Sometimes, however, an occupational name fossilizes terminology that has lost currency in everyday speech. **LeFevre** is a good example; it is the most common name in France, just as its equivalent, **Smith,** is in English. But the Old French word *fèvre* was replaced in early modern French with the word *forgeron,* so when translating, people would assimilate the older name to *le fève* 'the bean' and arrive at the surname **Bean**. Secondary surnames, also of the occupational type, are found: *LeFevre dit LeBoulanger,* literally 'the Smith called the Baker'.

Patronymic Names

The most populous category of surnames is derived from the father's baptismal names and nicknames for them. Because a great many of these are also found in English, they presented no problem of transition: **Martin, Robert, Lambert.** Others have ready English equivalents: **Guillaume = William, Jean = John.** The nicknames may be formed by an additional syllable or a substitution of the final syllable: *Nicolas* gives **Nicolet** and **Nicolin,** and those become **Colin (Collins), Colet,** and so on.

Most French patronymics bear no marker of filiation such as the English suffix *-son.* An old-style prefix *fils-* 'son' was brought to Britain by the Normans and is fossilized in such names as **Fitzgerald** and **Fitzwilliam,** but this is the exception rather than the rule.

Canadian French to Northeastern English

For the early migrants coming south from Canada, the names were recorded as they sounded to clerks and were written in conformance with English spelling usage. Thus, *Hébert* became **Abare**; *Ouellette,* **Wallet**; *Houle,* **Wool**; *D'Avignon,* **Devino**; *Beauregard,* **Burgor**. The last of example reflects the Canadian speech habit of rounding *-ar* to *-or*: hence, *Picard* becomes **Pecor,** the *-e-* of the first syllable being the English pronunciation of the sound represented in French by *-i-.*

In names ending in a vowel plus *-t,* where in Continental French the *t* is silent, the modern spelling reflects the Canadian custom of sounding the consonant. Hence, *Chaillot* in France becomes **Chaillotte** or **Shiott**; *Paquet* becomes **Paquette.** This is a very common feature of North American French family names. Also, whereas in modern French a diphthong spelled *oi* is pronounced 'wa', in the 17th century outside Paris, the normal pronunciation was 'way', and this is preserved for example in the spelling and sound of **Benway** (from *Benoit*).

Characteristic Americanizations also involve alteration of sounds difficult for the English ear. Thus, the ending *-tier* is represented by *-key* in **Sharkey** (from *Chartier*) and **Gokey**

(from *Gauthier*). Difficult vowels (for English speakers) were variously accommodated: *L'Heureux* became **Larrow**; *Chaput* became **Shappy.** As the last example shows, French initial *Ch* often appears as American *Sh.* Similarly, an initial soft *G* may often appear as *J;* **Johndrow** (from *Gendron*) illustrates this change. Initial *H* may disappear, and sometimes contractions occur, as in **Dragon** (from *D'Aragon*). The nasal vowels occasionally lose the nasal quality, as in **Demag** (from *Domingue*) but sometimes retain it, as in **Yandow** (from *Guindon*).

The final *o* sound is often represented with a single letter (e.g. **Tebo,** from *Thibault*), though equally often the French spelling is preserved. We have **Breaux** in Louisiana, yet **Brault** and **Brow** in New England from the same name.

People sometimes used translations (e.g. **King** for *Roi*), though some efforts failed. Some names are approximate translations, for example *Terrien* translated as **Landers,** and others are adapted to common similar-sounding English names (e.g. **Kirby** from *Corbeil*; **Bosley** from *Beausoleil*). Finally, there is a category of names whose connections may reflect family associations no longer clear to us, for example *Rouillard* with **Ross,** or *Baillargeon* with **Roe, Rowe.**

Bibliography

Dauzat, Albert (1989): *Dictionnaire étymologique des noms de famille et prénoms de France.* Paris: Larousse.

Deiler, J. Hanno (1909): *The Settlement of the German Coast of Louisiana and the Creoles of German Descent.* Philadelphia: Americana Germanica. Reprinted Saratoga and San Francisco: R. and E. Research Associates, 1968.

Gassette, Véronique (1978): *Mariages de St Joseph de Burlington,* Vermont, 1834–1930. Montreal: Edition Bergeron.

Jetté, René (1983): *Dictionnaire généalogique des familles du Québec.* Montreal: Presse de l'Université de Montréal.

Morlet, Marie-Thérèse (1997): *Dictionnaire étymologique des noms de famille.* 2d ed. Paris.

Tanguay, Cyprien (1871–90): *Dictionnaire généalogique des familles canadiennes depuis la fondation de la colonie jusqu'à nos jours.* 7 vols. Montreal: E. Senécal.

West, Robert Cooper (1986): *Atlas of Louisiana Surnames of French and Spanish Origin.* Baton Rouge: Geoscience Publications, Louisiana State University.

GERMAN FAMILY NAMES

Edda Gentry

German Immigration: A Survey

Statistics

Family names of German origin constitute a very substantial share of American surnames. In addition to the major group comprising the names of immigrants from Germany, German names were also brought to North America and specifically to the United States by immigrants from Switzerland, Austria, Alsace (in present-day France), and from German-language enclaves like Transylvania (in present-day Romania), as well as from the Ukraine and from the area of the so-called Volga Germans, to name just a few. In addition, mention must be made of English names, which, already changed, derive from those of originally German emigrants to England.

German emigration to America took place in several waves from the 17th century onward. Although individual Germans were in the New World almost from the beginning, the first organized emigration occurred in 1683 with the arrival in Pennsylvania of thirteen German Mennonite families from Krefeld in the Rhineland. During the 18th century several small German-speaking religious groups, for instance Swiss Mennonites, Baptist Dunkers, Schwenkfelders, Moravian Brethren, Amish, and Waldensians settled in the British colonies, with the central colonies, especially Pennsylvania, receiving the greatest share of this immigration. Subsequently, Salzburg (Austria) Protestants settled in Georgia. By the end of the 18th century it is estimated that about 100,000 Germans may have immigrated to America, and they and their descendants made up an estimated 8.6 percent of the population of the United States at that time. In Pennsylvania they accounted for 33 percent of the population; in Maryland 12 percent.

By the middle of the 19th century, the range of emigration had expanded considerably: in 1844, for example, Prince Carl of Solms-Braunfels sailed to America with 150 families, settled in Texas, and, in the following year, founded New Braunfels, which was followed by several other Texas German settlements. After the failure of the 1848 Revolution, which had as its aim the establishment of a participatory democracy in Germany, thousands viewed America as an ideal destination and a land where their political dreams might be fulfilled. The largest wave of immigrants was in the 1850s—215,000 arrived in 1854 alone—and an estimated 1.3 million German-born immigrants resided in the United States by 1860. The number swelled to an estimated 2.8 million by 1890, with the majority of the immigrants located in the so-called German triangle: Cincinnati, Milwaukee, and St. Louis. All in all, by the end of the 19th century more than 5 million Germans had arrived.

The years after Hitler came to power in 1933 also witnessed a significant immigration of German and Austrian nationals, especially, but not limited to scientists, writers, musicians, scholars, and other artists and intellectuals, who left Europe in order to escape persecution. By the end of World War II, there were some 130,000 of these refugees living in America. Between 1950 and 1980 approximately 855,000 Germans immigrated to the United States. The dramatic result of these centuries of immigration can be seen in the 1990 U.S. census, in which 58 million Americans claimed to be solely or partially of German descent. In addition, there were about one million Russian Germans living in America in 1990, with their greatest numbers in the Dakotas, Nebraska, Colorado, and Kansas. Thus, while not as impressive as in the 19th century, the number of German immigrants arriving in the United States during the 20th century nonetheless amounted to approximately 2 million.

Corresponding numbers for the immigration of Swiss nationals suggest that more than 400,000 Swiss have settled in North America in the last four centuries. Some 25,000 arrived in the early colonies before 1776, with an approximately equal number following between 1776 and 1820. Swiss immigration continued and the 1990 U.S. census showed more than 1 million U.S. residents claiming Swiss ancestry. In reality the number is probably much higher.

There are no comparable figures on Austrian immigration to America. One reason for this state of affairs is the fact that a variety of ethnic groups—not all of them German-speaking or having German names—populated the Habsburg empire. Further, U.S. census forms in the 19th century provided listing only of national origin and not ethnicity. As a result people from Bohemia, Moravia, Galicia, etc., in addition to those from the western, German-speaking part were counted as Austrians. Moreover, German-speaking Austrians frequently identified themselves or were referred to as Germans. It is known that after the American Civil War immigration from the Austro-Hungarian Empire increased and continued to be reasonably steady later also from what is now the Republic of Austria.

Causes and Origins

German immigration to the American colonies did not gain momentum until the beginning of the 18th century, five decades after the end of the Thirty Years' War (Treaty of Westphalia, 1648). This dreadful conflict was waged over the greater part of Europe and left devastation and great loss of life (6 million—one out of three) in its wake. A further consequence of the war, and one that was significant for emigration, was the rise of a multitude of German principalities (a "patchwork" of more than 300 independent states) and minor territories, each of which made claims on its subjects' loyalties. The rulers of these absolutistic states could and did determine their subjects' religion, according to the maxim "cuius regio, eius religio": the religion of the prince (Protestant or Catholic) became the only religion tolerated in his land.

In addition, since the states' economies were still rooted in the feudal system, tax and tribute burdens as well as service obligations were raised by the prince at whim, in many cases merely to pay for court extravaganzas such as festivals, the acquisition of art works, and military ventures. Agricultural failures, bad crops, and resulting famines contributed to a desperate situation for many farmers and laborers (cotters) along with a scarcity of land in some parts, especially the southwest, where, through repeated divisions according to the then-existing inheritance laws, the resulting land was often no longer sufficient to support a family.

Thus, when in 1708 the British government began to encourage Protestants from Germany to settle in America, a wave of emigration was set in motion, which lasted throughout the century. The Palatinate in southwest Germany was an area where many originated during this phase of emigration. Some of them later bought land on the Mohawk River in New York State and founded towns with names such as Mannheim, Oppenheim, and Herkimer. More than 13,000 Germans reached England during this initial phase, and some 10,000 were shipped onward to her American colonies. About 2,000 Catholics were turned back before the restrictions against Catholic immigration were lifted some time later.

Most of the above-mentioned immigrants, as well as those who arrived up to the middle of the 19th century were craftsmen, farmers, laborers, or merchants, and they had, as a result, strong representation in manufacturing, agriculture, and industry as well as in the mechanical trades and mining. The next group of immigrants stands out for very different reasons, namely the aims and ideals they hoped to realize in the New World.

The notable and celebrated group of political activists known as the Forty-Eighters brought a different element to the United States with their immigration in the thousands around the middle of the 19th century. After the Napoleonic wars there had been a steady and decisive trend in the larger states in Germany toward unity. The major countries in Europe, notably France and England, had been centralized nation-states for centuries, whereas in the majority of German states resources and energy were still being spent or wasted on territorial claims, as well as on those by now old-fashioned and cumbersome traditions in all areas of public life, including the courts. Most of the power and privileges (e.g., education and training for public offices) continued to be concentrated in the hands of the rich and the aristocracy.

The duties and responsibilities of the nobility toward their subjects, however, had been sorely neglected. Since the late 1790s new ideas and ideals had emerged, especially in the classrooms of the universities, concerning the rights, the worth,

and the liberty of an individual. It was on the basis of this realization that scholars, students, and liberals of various backgrounds joined forces in the years leading up to the Revolution of 1848 to bring about political unification, to reduce the power of the aristocracy, and to strive for a type of government that would guarantee basic rights for everyone. A parliament was set up but, mainly due to disagreement and division on fundamental issues, the effort collapsed.

Thousands of reformers left Germany for America, disappointed but hopeful—scholars and students from every branch of scholarly endeavor, writers, artists, ministers, lawyers, and teachers. They brought knowledge and idealism, were devoted to humanitarian issues and education; they founded all sorts of newspapers and periodicals, societies, and clubs (the Turners, for instance) and brought a new and lively spirit into the cultural life in America.

Most arrivals in America up to this time had come from rural backgrounds and tended to settle in agricultural areas. The 19th century, however, especially its last decades, saw more and more immigrants settling in the cities. The Industrial Revolution that brought prosperity to so many also, due to the absence of effective social laws, caused thousands to turn their back on grinding poverty. It is indeed ironic that a very prosperous period in German history, the so-called Gründerzeit, a result of the Industrial Revolution, and one that also saw, for the first time, a modern, unified, centralized Germany (1871), also witnessed a period of the heaviest emigration. Nearly 1.5 million Germans immigrated to the United States during the 1880s: 250,000 in 1882 alone.

The 20th century started out with a slower influx of Germans to the United States. But great economic catastrophe in the 1920s and the uprooting of millions of people due to the devastations of two world wars and political persecution during the Nazi period in Germany had again an enormous impact on the number of German-speaking immigrants.

In 1983 the United States and Germany commemorated the 300th anniversary of German immigration to Pennsylvania. The celebration marked not only an awareness of the German contribution to the United States, but also, as the family names demonstrate, the readiness of the German-speaking immigrants to adapt completely to their new country.

German Family Names: Their Origin and Development

The names that have come down to us in historical and other records, together with the German family names used today in their original form and, in many instances, as will be seen later, in numerous variants and in altered form, constitute the corpus of German surnames or family names.

The practice of name giving in German was not essentially different from that found in most other European countries. In Germanic pre-Christian times, a large body of linguistic elements existed, which in various combinations fashioned personal names. The semantic content of the names coined from these elements was probably rather in conformity with general ideals of the early warrior/tribal society than a designation of the personal valor or other qualities of the name bearer. Some examples (in their Old High German form) of these basic Germanic name elements are: *adal* 'noble, noble origin or clan'; *bald* 'brave, bold'; *ber(a)ht* 'bright'; *burg* 'citadel, protection'; *degan* 'warrior'; *diot* 'people'; *fridu* 'peace'; *ger* 'spear'; *got* 'god'; *hart* 'strong, fast'; *heri* 'army'; *hiltja* 'battle'; *kuoni* 'bold'; *man* 'man, follower'; *mari* 'famous, outstanding'; *ram (raban)* 'raven'; *richi* 'power(ful), rich'; *sig* 'victory, strong'; *waltan* 'to reign, rule'; *wini* 'friend'.

Combinations of these elements allowed several hundred personal names to evolve. The following are examples of the many name-forming combinations of the above elements: *Adelmann, Adelbert, Baldomar, Bertram, Degenhard(t), Gerhard(t), Gottfried, Herbert, Reichard(t), Reichmann, Siegfried, Dietrich, Walther, Winfried;* as well as female names such as *Hildburg* and *Borghild*. All of these ancient Germanic formations have had their influence on modern German surnames.

From the 14th century on, the sources show a considerable loss of the old Germanic names, due to the influx of Christian baptismal names. Hans Bahlow (2002, pp. x–xi) provides a succinct overview of important stages in the development of German family names:

> Some became family names after the canonization of their bearers, some were the reflection of a submerged . . . folk culture: especially names from heroic tales and folk literature (such as **Dietrich, Hildebrand, Siegfried, Ruedeger,** as well as numerous variations). In addition to personal names which were derived from the fathers' names (patronymics) or mothers' names (metronymics) and eventually became inherited family names . . . , there was a number of attributive names or surnames (originally personal in nature) that reflected the everyday realities of the Middle Ages in all social walks of life, farmer and burgher, knight and cleric. The names represent a highly detailed reflection not only of the medieval agrarian economy (with its . . . system of fiefdoms, tributes, and indentured servitude) but to an even greater extent that of the emerging urban culture (with its trade guilds and the widespread separation of labor between production and distribution). The inventory of family names was further enriched by the large group of the ever-popular personal surnames that were given to a "dear" neighbor because of conspicuous physical or mental traits (so-called characterizing or attributive names). Through these sorts of names the bluntness of folk humor often becomes apparent.

Among the oldest surnames are those designating places of residence or habitation, especially in rural areas where scattered farm settlements predominated: for instance, in the mountainous regions of Switzerland, Tyrol, and Bavaria as well as in the Westphalian and Lower Rhine regions. In the cities, some people adopted house names as family names, especially in the Alemannic southwest Alsace, Baden, Württemberg, and Switzerland as well as in Frankfurt and Cologne.

Inland migration also played a role in name formation: the constant movement from the country to the city can be read from family names; the new settlers tended to bear names that referred to their home villages. Family names provide valuable evidence for the large west-east German migration in Europe, which resulted in the settlement and opening up of new territories through enterprising merchants and efficient homesteaders, sometimes resulting in territorial competition with Slavic peoples coming from the east and south.

Upon closer inspection of individual family names, a marked difference can be seen between variants of the same name as it was used in different dialect areas of the German-speaking countries. A dialect map of Germany, Switzerland, and Austria (before 1945) shows approximately the following divisions:

> Low German: Low Saxon, Westphalian, Eastphalian, Brandenburgish, Pomeranian, East Prussian;
> Frisian: East Frisian, North Frisian;
> Central or Middle German: Franconian, Hessian, Thuringian, Saxon, Silesian;
> Upper German: Alemannic (including Swiss German and Alsatian), East Franconian, Bavarian (including Austrian German).

The dialects of some of these divisions, for example East Prussian and Silesian, have been largely lost due to the upheavals of the Second World War, but traces are preserved in the forms of surnames.

The linguistic division into Low German (in the north), Central or Middle German, and Upper German (in the south) provides a rough guideline for identifying variants like (starting in the north) **Pape—Paff—Pfaff; Pieper—Piefer—Pfeiffer; Brüggemann—Brückmann—Bruckmann.**

Dialect-related variability, and hence a great variety of names (or rather, name variants) was a result of the prevalence of the spoken language during the name-giving period. The written forms of German family names became generally fixed around 1600, but in some areas not until the early 1800s, for instance among the Frisians. Different general spelling practices in different periods account for some additional variations, for instance -*dt* in **Gerhardt,** *-ff-* **Kauffmann,** *-pp-* in **Seippel,** and -*ck* in **Merck,** just to name a few.

Typology of German Family Names

The corpus of German family names can be broadly divided into four main groups: personal names and patronymics; nicknames or bynames; occupational names; and habitational, ethnic, and topographic names.

Personal Names and Patronymics

The group of personal names and patronymics comprises names derived from the old Germanic personal names. They were adopted in the Middle Ages as baptismal names, together with a new inventory of biblical and saints' names. Examples include **Hildebrand**, **Dietrich**, **Gerhard**, **Friedrich**, **Konrad**, **Michael**, **Peter**, **Johann**, **Jakob**, **Mark**, and **Matthäus**.

The corresponding patronymic forms, sometimes derived from one element of the name, are widespread and occur in many variants: e.g. (**Hildebrand**) **Hilbrans**; (**Dietrich**, etc.) **Derks**, **Deterding**, **Tjarkes**; (**Gerhard**) **Gerards**, **Gerdes**, **Geertsema**; (**Friedrich**) **Fritz**, **Frerichs(en)**, **Feddersen**; (**Konrad**) **Conrady**, **Kunz**; (**Michael**) **Michels**; (**Peter**) **Peters(en)**; (**Johann(es)**) **Johannsen**, **Jansen**, **Jens**; (**Jakob**) **Jacobi** (Latin genitive of the humanist form **Jacobus**), **Kops**; (**Mark**) **Marx**; (**Matthäus**) **Theissen**, **Tewes**.

Patronymic forms such as **Deterding** or **Geertsema** stand out alongside names bearing the usual *-s* or *-(s)sen* patronymic suffixes and the clan suffix *-ing*. **Deterding** shows a specifically Westphalian patronymic variant, *-ding*, and **Geertsema** exemplifies the Frisian genitive plural form. Such forms attest to the early Germanic social structure in that they express affiliation to a family or clan.

In addition to these easily recognizable patronymics, innumerable dialectal variants of the Germanic family names have also come into use as fixed and inherited family names. Some originated as short forms or pet forms (frequently diminutives) like **Dietz**, **Gerd**, **Fick**, **Kunz**, **Michel**, **Jahn**. Others simply developed according to regional differences in the vowel or consonant system. Examples are: **Hilber**, **Hieber**, **Hickisch** (with a Slavic suffix *-sch*); **Dippert**, **Diebel(s)**, **Daumann**; **Germar**, **Gördt**, **Gierke**; **Fritz**, **Friedmeyer**; **Kuhnert**, **Künzel**, **Keune**; **Peterman**, **Peschel** (Slavic origin), **Patzelt**, **Petzold**; **Janning**, **Jehn**, **Janak** (Slavic origin); **Jäckel**, **Jäggi** (Swiss), **Häckle**; **Debus**, **Mattusch** (Slavic origin), **Mattheck**.

Nicknames or Bynames

Names referring to personal attributes were given from very early on, when the need arose to distinguish different bearers of the same personal name. They were added to the personal names as bynames or nicknames. From the ranks of royalty we know, for example, Charles the Bold, Charles the Fat, Louis the Pious, Louis the German, Otto the Great (**Karl der Kühne**, **Karl der Dicke**, **Ludwig der Fromme**, **Ludwig der Deutsche**, **Otto der Grosse**). The use of nicknames became very popular in the increasingly more populated urban centers from the 13th century on. Names that readily come to mind and which have become established as hereditary family names include **Gross** 'big', **Klein** 'small', **Klug(e)** 'smart, bright', **Weiss** 'white (fair-haired)', **Schwar(t)z** 'black (dark-haired)', **Schlicht** 'smooth', **Schier** 'pure', **Jung** 'young'. But there are

also names like **Beschoren** 'shorn' i.e. tonsured, **Scheel** and **Schiller** 'cross-eyed', **Schieck** 'bent', **Armann** 'poor man', **Frisch** 'fresh, lively', as well as humorous nicknames like **Scheuenpflug** ('avoid the plow') for a run-away farmer's son; **Sparnranft** 'save the crust' and **Schimmelpfennig** 'moldy penny' for a miser; **Rahmschüssel** 'clear the bowl', **Schlick** 'gulp', **Casembrot** 'cheese and bread', and **Brotess** 'bread eater' for voracious eaters; likewise, **Rumsfeld** 'clear the field' and **Morneweg** or **Morgenweg** 'gone tomorrow', and **Schneidewind** 'cut the wind' for unreliable and no doubt unwanted individuals in a community.

In addition, animal names, including bird names, were frequently conferred upon people who were thought to evidence a trait of or some other similarity with the creature or who dealt with them in their profession, for example, **Wolf** 'wolf', **Behr** 'bear', **Reh** 'doe', **Ross** 'horse', **Hahn** 'rooster', **Rindfleisch** 'cow's meat', **Kalbfuss** 'calf's foot', **Ganter** 'gander', **Tax** (= **Dachs**) 'badger', **Hase**, 'hare', **Maus** 'mouse', **Meise** 'titmouse', **Fink** 'fink', **Gimp(e)l** (Austrian) 'bullfinch', **Adler** 'eagle', **Vogel** 'bird'.

Names reflecting urban fashions are, e.g. **Rothkugel** 'red cowl or cap', **Rothärmel** 'red sleeve', **Gelhose** 'yellow trousers'. Tax and service obligations (from the feudal age) are evident in **Freitag**, **Sonntag**, and names of other days of the week as well as in **Sommer** 'summer', **Winter** 'winter', **Dreiheller** 'three coins', **Helbling** 'half coin', and others. They clearly express the day or season when the obligation had to be fulfilled or the amount that was owed.

Occupational Names

The great number of occupational names reflects the diversity of trades and crafts as well as administrative offices, which were necessary in medieval, pre-industrial society. By far the most frequent names (including their variants) in this group in present-day Germany are **Müller** 'miller', **Meyer** 'tenant farmer', 'dairy farmer', **Schmidt** 'blacksmith', **Bauer** 'farmer', **Becker** 'baker', followed by **Weber** 'weaver', **Schneider** 'tailor', **Jäger** 'huntsman', **Schulze** 'village headman', **Schäfer** 'shepherd', and **Wagner** 'cartwright'. If these do not figure at the same frequency in the United States today, it is because in many cases upon immigration they joined the equivalent English names in the form of **Miller** (for **Müller**), **Baker** (for **Becker**), **Smith** (for **Schmidt**), **Weaver** (for **Weber**). Similarly, **Schneider** frequently converted to **Taylor**, **Schumacher** to **Shoemaker**, and **Zimmermann** to **Carpenter**. The majority of occupational names, however, was either adopted with the original German spelling, including numerous dialectal (or spelling) variants, or underwent various spelling transformations in order to adapt to sound combinations with which English speakers were familiar.

Some well-known examples are **Herder** 'shepherd', **Maurer** 'mason', **Schieferdecker** 'slate roofer', **Gerber** 'tanner', **Schreiner**, **Tischler** 'joiner, furniture maker', **Drechsler** 'turner', woodworker', **Metzger** 'butcher', **Töpfer** 'potter',

Kessler 'kettle maker', **Fuhrmann** 'carter', **Seiler** 'rope maker', **Springer** 'jumper, entertainer', **Sangmeister** 'choirmaster'. Family names like **Abt**, **Bischoff**, **Prinz**, **(Mark)Graf**, **Herzog**, **Kaiser**, **König**, **Pabst** obviously do not denote the office contained in the name but presumably were given to men in the employ of an abbot, bishop, prince, margrave, duke. In the case of **König** 'king', **Kaiser** 'emperor', and **Pabst** 'pope', another possible explanation is that the original name bearers may have taken part in a local play and received the names of their roles.

Names like **Richter** 'judge', **Schreiber** 'scribe', **Kanzler** 'chancellor', **Zehntgraf** 'tithe official', 'tax collector', **Burmeister** 'mayor' indicate not only the privileged status but also the administrative duties of the original name bearers. But on the other end of the scale, we find, for instance **Eigenmann** 'bondsman', **Kötter** 'cottager, with no land to farm'.

Occupational nicknames like **Bückeisen** 'bend the iron', **Zerreisen** 'pull the iron' for a blacksmith, **Windschuh** 'turn the shoe' for a shoemaker, were probably applied for good reason to certain members of a trade but then became fixed and in the meantime have been borne by many generations. Since in many cases these longer names have not been understood for some time, many of them have come down to us, on both sides of the Atlantic, in various distorted forms.

Habitational, Ethnic, and Topographic Names

This group of family names shows the geographical or topographic origin of the original name bearers. In the Middle Ages it was mainly the large group of people who moved from the country into the cities who adopted or received names derived from their place of origin, so-called habitational names. But also farmstead names and locative names, names indicating the topographic location of residences and settlements, are included in this group.

Representative samples of family names reflecting the place or town of origin include **Bamberg**, **Dief(f)enbach** (from any of several small towns so named), **Fulda** (from the river or town situated on it), **Lassahn** (a town in Pomerania), **Delbrück** (near Paderborn), **Brabeck** (from a farmstead near Recklinghausen), **Eschenbach** (a village in Franconia). From eastern Germany reflecting the original, large substratum of Slavic population came habitational names, mostly from still existing towns, with the suffix *-ow* as in **Bülow**, **Bahlow**, **Grassow**, **Schadow**; but also **Wendland(t)**, **Wünschmann** (= **Windischmann**), naming the tribe of the Wends (or Sorbs), the Slavic people who in the Middle Ages inhabited territory across what is now northeastern Germany as far west as Lüneburg. Likewise of Slavic origin are names ending in *-i(t)z*, for instance **Leibniz** (from Leubnitz near Dresden), and **Tirpitz** (from a town near Frankfurt/Oder), as well as those ending in *-in* (which is the stress-bearing syllable of the name) like **Ballin**, **Leppin** (both near Neubrandenburg), **Ramien** (near Potsdam and Stettin, respectively).

Related to habitational names are frequently occurring ethnic or regional names such as **Schwab, Bayer, Sachs, Fries(e), Hess(e), Franke, Preuss**—denoting people originally from *Schwaben* (Swabia), *Bayern* (Bavaria), *Sachsen* (Saxony), *Friesland* (Frisia), *Hessen* (Hesse), *Franken* (Franconia), and *Preussen* (Prussia).

Much more frequent are habitational names using the productive suffix *-er* (compare the occupational names discussion above), identifying a man as a former resident from a certain town or region, e.g. **Adenauer** (from Adenau in the Eifel mountains), **Rockefeller** (from Rockenfeld near Neuwied), **Forchhammer** (from Forchheim in Bavaria), **Wertheimer** (from Wertheim on the Main river), **Dändliker** (from Dändlikon in Switzerland), **Schlesinger** (from Schlesien = Silesia), **Meissner** (from Meissen, both a town and a region in eastern Germany), **Dieringer** (= **Thüringer**, from Thuringia), **Würtenberger** (from Württemberg), **Schweitzer** (from Switzerland), **Östreicher** (from Austria), **Unger** (from Hungary), **Brabanter** (in many cases for someone who had business connections with Brabant, a region in Belgium and the Netherlands), **Kumsteller** (for someone who had taken the pilgrim route to Santiago de Compostela in Spain). These are only a few examples from the large variety of habitational family names. They are almost as numerous as the place and regional names themselves in Germany, Switzerland, and Austria. The above examples are all contained in the lexicon.

Various other names derive from the diverse topography of north, central, and south Germany or are typically reflective of the Austrian and Swiss alpine topography. Here we find the following name-forming elements among numerous others: *-beck* 'stream, brook' (**Beckmann, Biederbeck**); *-brink* 'edge, rim' (**Brinkmann, Steinbrink**); *-kamp* 'enclosed field' (**Kampmann, Voskamp**); *-loh* 'wood' (**Lohmeyer, Osterloh**); *-rode, -roth, -reuth(er)* 'clearing in the woods' (**Rohde, Reuter, Herchenröder**); *-feld* 'open field, heath' (**Feldmann, Kleinfelder**); *-leite* 'slope' (**Leitner, Oberleiter**); *-moos* 'reed, swamp' (**Moser, Hintermoser**); *-wang* 'grassy slope' (**Wängler, Binswanger**); *-klamm* 'gorge' (**Klammer, Aufderklamm**).

German Family Names in America[1]

Originally all names, whether given names or family names, were formed and bestowed on the basis of their semantic content; they meant or, in the case of given names, conformed to an ideal of what their linguistic elements said. Over time, changes in the language have frequently obscured the original meanings. This is particularly true of given names. In a surname the original meaning may remain obvious as long as the name stays within the language of its origin, e.g. names such as **Carpenter** and **Weaver** in English or **Zimmermann** and **Weber** in Ger-

[1] This section draws material from an unpublished essay by Jürgen Eichhoff, 'Types of German Surname Changes in America'.

man. Even with less transparent names, a lingering knowledge about a surname's meaning is handed down from generation to generation in most families. But when a person—and his or her name—moves to a different linguistic environment, as is the case upon emigration, what was left of a name's semantic transparency is lost. Also lost is the link to the standard orthography in the originating language, and as a consequence the written manifestation of the name is destabilized. The move to the new linguistic environment brings with it adaptations and, in some cases, drastic changes.

As a nation of immigrants, the United States has become home to millions of families whose surnames were not in harmony with the language and orthographic rules prevailing here. This is certainly the reason for the laissez-faire attitude toward name changes. They have never been prohibited, in some periods they were even encouraged, and given the prevalence of illiteracy, especially in colonial times, and a continual pressure on foreign names to make them "more American," numerous alterations have ensued. When did the name changes of immigrating persons or families occur? Is it true that the British captains or clerks of many immigration vessels were not able to render the passengers' names correctly, as they were mostly pronounced in the latter's German dialect? And it is also obvious that in the absence of a unified, formal immigration process (before the 1890s), the spelling of a name was left to chance. Indeed, from the point of view of the immigrant, the form of the name does not appear to have been of great importance, as long as the principle of *idem sonans* was followed, i.e. that it sounded the same. Thus in most cases where the Americanized spelling produced a semblance of the sound of the German original, a name alteration took place, often with the indifference, tacit consent, or even active participation of the "owner."

Americanization of Pronunciation and Spelling

Retention of German pronunciation is hardly a problem in one-syllable names like **Beck**, **Fick**, **Lind**, **Lipp** or in **Fischer**, **Lippert**, **Keller**, **Becker**. However names like **Lich**, **Zach**, and **Reich** pose a slight difficulty in their final sound, a voiceless (palatal or velar) fricative, represented in German by **-ch-** and generally unfamiliar to English speakers. They mostly resort to a *k*-sound, which often causes the above names to change to **Lick**, **Zack**, and **Rike**, but sometimes a different English sound, as in *rich*, is heard, for example in **Koch**. Initial *z-* as in **Zimmermann**, **Zuck**, but also medial *-z-* as in **Schmelzer** (*-ts-* in German pronunciation) becomes a voiced *-s-* as in *zero*.

Silent *-h-* after *t-* in German is an outdated orthographic leftover and abolished through a spelling reform (1901), except in foreign words such as *Theater, Thron*. In names, however, it is still often found, and in German-American names this spelling results in a different phonetic quality, the *th-* sound as in *thin* instead of a *t-*. Examples are: **Thiel**, **Thode**, **Bethke**, **Roth**, **Wirth**, **Jungbluth**. Also sound clusters such as *schl-, schm-, schn-, schw-* in German names like **Schlegel**, **Schmiel**,

Schnack, **Schwar(t)z** yield to English pronunciation as *sl-, sm-, sn-, sw-* and frequently result in a change in spelling. In the cluster *pf-* in initial position as in **Pfersching**, **Pfeiffer**, **Pfaff**, either the *p-* or the *-f-* is disregarded, mostly the latter.

Another interesting problem is that of the so-called umlauts. How does—or did—an English-speaking environment deal with names like **Töpfer**, **Köhnemann**, **Kühn**, **Wünschmann**, **Käsler**? The symbols *ä, ö,* and *ü* represent sounds that are phonetically quite different from their base vowels (without the umlauts). Upon immigration there have been several ways to handle the problem. Many families converted an umlaut in their name into *ae, oe,* or *ue.* Even in Germany names such as those listed above are also found with this type of humanistic ersatz spelling. In other cases a customary pronunciation took hold: for instance, the long *ü* in the name **Kühn/Kuehn** in some German dialects is the same as in English *keen.* and therefore **Keen** was an acceptable alternative on this continent; *ö* in some German dialects is pronounced as long *e*, similar to the vowel in *cane* (**Köhnemann/Koehnemann**) or short *e* as in yet (**Töpfer/Toepfer**). Another common alternative was simply to drop the umlaut, which in some names resulted in a very different pronunciation of the name. In other cases, especially among more recent immigrants, the umlaut is retained, often to the confusion of the English speaker (or reader), who may nevertheless adapt the pronunciation of a name despite its un-English spelling, e.g. in pronouncing **Löwenbräu** as "Lowenbraw"!

Respelling of a name in order to preserve at least a vestige of the original pronunciation produced probably the largest number of German-American variants. Many German names lend themselves to this process, losing more or less of their original form. In this way **Bruckner** was changed to **Brookner**, **Zug** to **Zook**, **Klein** to **Kline** or **Cline**, **Euler** to **Oiler**, **Kaiser** to **Kizer**, but also **Gerhard** to **Gayheart**. The following changes reflect the central German dialect pronunciation of immigrants' names: **Neuhäuser** to **Nihizer**, **Böhm** to **Bame**, **Göbel** to **Gabel** or **Gable**, **Kühn** to **Keehn**, **Jüngling** to **Yingling**, **Güngerich** to **Ging(e)rich**. In Pennsylvania frequently **Meyer** became **Moyer**. In many names ending in *-el* the ending has been routinely changed to *-le,* as in **Engle** (from **Engel**), **Gable** (from **Göbel**), **Nagle** (from **Nagel**); in others ending in *-heim(er)* the suffix was reduced to *-hime(r),* as in **Inglehimer**; *-bacher* was changed to *-backer*, as in **Rickenbacker** for **Reichenbacher**. Besides these adaptations, the inventory of German-American family names shows several other regular vowel and consonant changes, which contribute to the linguistic integration of the foreign names.

A large number of German surnames are compound names, which often pose a double problem in adapting them to daily use in a different language environment. There is, to be sure, a fairly large number of longer names that have been kept intact, as the Midwestern telephone directories show; e.g. **Bauernfeind**, **Eisenhauer**, **Harnischfeger**, **Schwerdtfeger**, **Seidensticker**, many of which would have been reduced or otherwise altered had it not been for the relatively late arrival of their bearers (from the mid 19th century on), when general literacy had established a predominance of the written word over the spoken medium. In earlier arrivals mostly only one element of the compound name underwent a change, as can be seen (but not heard) in **Eisenhower, Brownstein, Goodweiler, Newmeyer, Messersmith, Steinway** (from **Eisenhauer, Braunstein, Neumeyer, Messerschmidt,** and **Steinweg**).

Substitution and Translation

In many situations and at various times in the history of immigration to the United States, German immigrants and their descendants found it desirable to hide the connections to their German homeland by having their names officially changed. The resulting names look completely English and since nothing in the spelling of their names suggests their German origin, their bearers nowadays very often are not aware of their German origins. In many instances the result of the respelling is a cognate of the original name, as in **Shield** from **Schild(t)**, **Miller** from **Müller**, **Finch** from **Fink**, **Frederick** from **Friedrich**; but also **Grove** from **Graf**, **Idle** from **Eitel**, and **Beam** from **Böhm(e)**. The last three examples show an interesting trend in this process, which sometimes takes place in several stages. **Beam** is a case in point. Gravestone inscriptions in Pennsylvania show for the same family the development from **Böhm** (**Boehme**) to **Bame** to **Beam**; other forms are **Bahme** and **Beahm**. Besides the attempt to achieve a suitable English spelling there is also a subconscious leaning toward meaning, be it ever so far from that of the original name. The regional name **Böhm(e)** meant 'Bohemian'.

Translation of a name requires a conscious effort and interrupts a family tradition. It was therefore done in relatively few cases. It may be assumed that in some instances **Eagle** stands in for **Adler**, **Bird** for **Vogel**, **Woodman** for **Waldmann**, **Taylor** for **Schneider**, **Carpenter** for **Zimmermann**, **Goodbread** for **Gutbrot**. **Turnipseed** for **Rüb(e)sam** is an original translation, resulting in a name which is not of British-English origin. **Rübsam**, however, has tried its luck also in various forms, some of them dialect-related, like **Rubsam**, **Reapsam**, and **Reapsome** with whatever meaning the speakers were able to imply with those variants. The Pennsylvania family name **Pennypacker** joined the group not as a translation but as a folk etymological transformation from **Pfannebecker** 'roof tile maker', along with **Cashdollar**, a successful attempt at transforming the Palatine (Franconian) dialect pronunciation of the topographic name **Kirchthaler** 'person from a village called Kirchthal'.

Numerous Swiss-American surnames, predominantly topographic names, have resulted in a plethora of variants. For instance **Birckenbühl/Birckenbuehl** ('hill of birch trees') sprouted the forms **Perkapeal**, **Pirkeypile** before arriving at **Porcupine**; **Puppikofer**, 'person from the village Puppikon', appears in North America as **Bubickhoffer**, **Bubickopfer**, and finally as **Publicover**.

An interesting subset of German immigration is comprised of originally French-speaking Protestants, the Huguenots. They fled from France to several German states after the Edict of Nantes (1598), which granted them limited religious and civil liberties, was revoked in 1685 by Louis XIV. Names like **Jourdan, Passet, Gorenflo, Transou,** and many others in this dictionary thus became part of the German-American name inventory. (See the essay by Susan Whitebook for further discussion of Huguenot names.)

The above-mentioned changes intend to provide only a rough outline of the much greater variety of name alterations and will perhaps encourage the user of this dictionary to discover other interesting alterations and techniques of adaptation.

Bibliography

Bahlow, Hans (1967, 1980): *Deutsches Namenlexikon*. Hamburg.

Bahlow, Hans (2002): *Dictionary of German Names*. 2d ed. Translated by E. Gentry. Madison, Wisconsin.

Barker, Howard F. (1935): 'How the American Changes His Name' in *The American Mercury* 36, 101–03.

Brechenmacher, Josef (1957): *Etymologisches Wörterbuch der deutschen Familiennamen*. 2 vols. Limburg/Lahn.

Eichhoff, Jürgen. 'Types of German Surname Changes in America'. Unpublished article.

Finsterwalder, Karl (1978): *Tiroler Namenkunde*. Innsbruck. (Very good introduction to the history of Austrian, and in particular Tyrolean names.)

Fulbrook, Mary (2000). *A Concise History of Germany*. Cambridge.

Gottschald, Max (5th and improved ed. by R. Schützeichel, 1982): *Deutsche Namenkunde*. Berlin, New York. (Excellent introduction to the history of German family names.)

Hornung, Maria (1989): *Lexikon österreichischer Familiennamen*. Vienna.

Kunze, Konrad (1998): *DTV-Atlas Namenkunde: Vor- und Familiennamen im deutschen Sprachgebiet*. Munich.

Lehmann, Hartmut, Hermann Wellenreuther, and Renate Wilson, eds. (2000): *In Search of Peace and Prosperity: New German Settlements in Eighteenth-Century Europe and America*. University Park, Pennsylvania.

Meier, Emil, ed. (1989): *Familiennamenbuch der Schweiz*. 3d ed. Zurich.

Naumann, Horst (1987): *Familiennamenbuch*. Leipzig.

Totten, Christine M. (1988): *Roots in the Rhineland*. 2d rev. ed. German Information Center, New York.

Zamora, Juan (1992): *Hugenottische Familiennamen im Deutschen*. Heidelberg.

Zoder, Rudolf (1968): *Familiennamen in Ostfalen*. 2 vols. Hildesheim.

DUTCH FAMILY NAMES

Charles Gehring

The Dutch Language

Dutch and Frisian are members of the Germanic family of languages, which itself is a member of a larger family called Indo-European. The Germanic languages are divided into three groups according to linguistic characteristics: North Germanic includes Icelandic, Faeroese, Norwegian, Danish, and Swedish; East Germanic included the extinct languages of Gothic, Vandalic, and Burgundian; and West Germanic now includes English, German, Dutch, Frisian, and Afrikaans. Most people in the region we call the Low Countries speak one or another dialect of Dutch, except for those speakers in the Dutch province of Friesland who speak Frisian, a distinct language that extends across the border into Germany.

Dutch developed from Franconian and Saxon dialects, diverging from High German dialects that were developing below the so-called Benrath Line (running just south of Düsseldorf, Kassel, Magdeburg, and Frankfurt an der Oder) into a distinct language through a series of vowel and consonant shifts. Compare Dutch *tijd* and English *tide* with German *Zeit* 'time', or English *plow* and Dutch *ploeg* with German *Pflug*, among other regular patterns. This restructuring of consonants through the effects of the the High German sound shift phonetically separated English, Frisian, and Dutch from German. These sound shifts are reflected in linguistically related names, such as Dutch **Timmerman** and German **Zimmermann** 'carpenter'. Dutch is closely related to Low German, and names in the two languages are often closely related or even indistinguishable. (For a discussion of the relationship between Low German and High German, see the essay on German surnames by Edda Gentry.) The English word *Dutch* is cognate with German *Deutsch*, and until the 17th century the word meant both 'Dutch' and 'German'. This is why a variety of German spoken in the eastern United States is generally called 'Pennsylvania Dutch'.

Several closely related Germanic languages are mentioned in the entries in DAFN:

Old Low German, spoken in a region extending from the Elbe River to the North Sea from Roman times until around 1200; the language from which both Dutch and modern Low German are derived.

Middle Low German, the language of Saxony and other parts of northern Germany from about 1200 to 1500, closely related to Middle Dutch.

Modern Low German, the vernacular language still spoken in various dialects throughout northern Germany, especially in rural areas.

Middle Dutch: the Dutch language spoken from about 1200 to 1500, in the earlier part of the period, virtually indistinguishable from Middle Low German. During this period it began to diverge from other dialects of Low German.

Early Modern Dutch, the Dutch language from about 1500 to 1800. It emerged as a national language in 1579, when the United Provinces of Holland, Overijssel, Utrecht, Zeeland, Gelderland, Friesland, and Groningen formed a union under the Treaty of Utrecht, having won independence from Catholic Spain.

Modern Dutch: essentially the same as Early Modern Dutch, minus a few archaisms, but spelled somewhat differently. Older spellings are preserved in many family names.

Dutch and Flemish are the same language, differentiated only for political reasons. Flemish is the dialect of Dutch spoken by the Flemings, who live in Flanders and Brabant, the northern part of present-day Belgium. Frisian is a different language, spoken in the northwestern Netherlands, on offshore islands, and on adjacent parts of the North Sea coast of Germany. It is more closely related to English than other West Germanic languages. Quite a few American family names are of Frisian origin. Characteristic markers of Frisian names are the suffixes *-ma* and *-stra*.

Dutch Names in North America

A traveler to New York encounters many exotic place names. Unusual forms such as *Poughkeepsie, Coxsackie,* and *Schenectady* are inherited from the Native Americans who inhabited the region long before the arrival of Henry Hudson, but what about *Peekskill, Fishkill, Saugerties, Catskill, Kill van Kull, Claverack,* and *Kinderhook*? These are names bestowed during the 17th-century settlement by Europeans from the Low Countries.

From 1614 to 1664, the region between New England and Virginia, including much of what is now New Jersey and New York state, was administered by the Dutch—a vast territory that extended from the Connecticut River to Delaware Bay and was called New Netherland.

Dutch colonization was sponsored by several trading companies, such as the Dutch East India Company. The "patroonship" plan of colonization allowed an investor (the "patroon") to negotiate with the natives for a tract of land upon which he was obligated to settle fifty colonists within four years, at his own expense. Of all the patroonships registered, only Rensselaerswijck on the upper Hudson experienced any degree of long-term success. Dutch colonies were harassed both by

Native Americans and by English colonists from the north, but by the mid-17th century there were thriving settlements on Long Island, New York, at Heemstede (Hempstead), Gravesande (Gravesend), Breuckelen (Brooklyn), and Vlissingen (Flushing). New Amsterdam, the settlement at the tip of Manhattan, officially became a city, and the settlement of Haerlem (Harlem) at the northern end of the island was granted a local court. Other Dutch towns included Bergen, now in New Jersey; Staten Island; and Esopus (now Kingston), a halfway point between Manhattan and Fort Orange. The founding of Schenectady to the north completed the settlement pattern within New Netherland.

In 1664 the Dutch settlements fell to the English, beginning a long process of accommodation, adaptation, assimilation, and development into English-speaking American communities. In 1673, the Dutch regained control of the colony in the third Anglo-Dutch war. During the peace negotiations an English official advised that all the Dutch should be removed from the province, or at least isolated in Albany. Although this drastic measure was not carried out when New Netherland again became New York in 1674, it indicates the concern with which the English viewed the Dutch majority in this province. Fifty years of Dutch commercial exploitation and colonization from the upper Hudson to Delaware Bay had given rise to a distinct non-English entity sandwiched in between New England and Virginia. Although approximately half the colonists sent over by the company were not native-born Netherlanders, they were quickly assimilated into the Dutch colonial society. Norwegians brought over as loggers, German refugees from the Thirty Years' War, Walloons fleeing religious persecution in the Spanish Netherlands, Croatians, Poles, and Bohemians were all required to adhere to the colony's laws. As with most immigrants in a new land, the first requirement was to learn the dominant language.

After the final settlement with England in 1674, assimilation of the colonists of New Netherland was slow and uneven. It has been reported that in New York City by the mid-1700s, only the elderly continued to speak Dutch. However, parts of New Jersey and, especially, the upper Hudson region of New York, with its center at Albany, became strongholds of Dutch.

Dutch social tradition and the Dutch language in which it was articulated did not die out overnight. As late as 1794, a traveler to Albany noted that "the people are of a mixed race, but chiefly Dutch, which language, as they call it, they generally speak, but it is so corrupted, and replete with new words, which a new country, new subjects, and new circumstances would unavoidably require." After almost 130 years of separation, the Dutch language in North America, called *Laeg-duits* or *de taal* by its speakers, had diverged considerably from the language in the fatherland. This was accelerated by the lack of reinforcement from standardizing developments in the Netherlands. The absence of a socially prestigious standard to emulate, especially among the younger generation, caused dialect variants to flourish.

Unless there are still speakers of *de taal* living in some iso-lated region of the Catskills, the only survivals of the language are now represented by a handful of words adopted by American English, and a few traditional nursery rhymes. What does survive linguistically are the numerous placenames of Dutch origin and the thousands of family names deriving from the original settlers of New Netherland. Names beginning in *Van* are quickly recognized as of Dutch origin, but many Dutch family names are now disguised owing to the spelling conventions applied by English-speaking clerks. Names such as *Brouwer, Cuyper, Smidt, Voller, Visscher, Jansz,* and *Pietersz* easily merged with **Brewer, Cooper, Smith, Fuller, Fisher, Johnson,** and **Peters** or **Peterson**; and some names such as *Timmerman* and *Vos* were simply translated as **Carpenter** and **Fox**. Without genealogical research, we cannot hope to recover the Dutch origin of these thoroughly English-sounding family names.

In most cases Dutch names were only slightly modified to conform to the English sound system. Modern family names such as **Prine, Secor**, and **Niver** represent accommodations of sound and spelling from original Dutch *Pruyn, Seger*, and *Knijver*.

Since the 17th and 18th centuries, many thousands more families and individuals have immigrated to the United States from the Netherlands, mostly for political and economic reasons. In the 19th century, a large number of Dutch religious dissidents settled in Michigan, while others continued farther west to Pella, Iowa. The hardships of both world wars drove many more Dutch immigrants to America.

The Dutch Naming System

The Dutch migration to the New World was accompanied by all the cultural baggage associated with the United Provinces in the 17th century. Together with the systems of justice, education, and religion, this included the Dutch naming system, and names shaped by the parameters of Germanic linguistic structure.

Up to the 17th century, the most common way to distinguish one person with the given name *Cornelis* from another in the same locality was by associating each with his father through the use of patronymics. Thus, Cornelis son of Pieter would be known as Cornelis Pietersen, where *-sen* or its variant *-se* represents Dutch *-zoon,* or *-son.* This unaccented syllable is often represented by the medieval abbreviation marker *-z,* most frequently used with names ending in *-s.* Thus, Pieter the son of Cornelis might have a name written *Pieter Cornelisz.*

The feminine equivalent of *-zoon* is *-dochter,* the source of the patronymic marker *-dr.* Thus Pieter's daughter Geertruyt would be identified as *Geertruyt Pietersdr.,* or simply as *Geertruyt Pieters.* The picture is complicated by the fact that there are examples of women in New Netherland who are identified by their husband's given name; thus, Geertruyt Pieters could be the wife of Pieter rather than a daughter of Pieter. This marital association was sometimes applied even to nicknames and occupational names, such as Geertruyt Haps, the wife of Jacob Jansen Hap, and Dirkie Wevers, the wife of Jan Martense de Wever.

In a small community, this system worked fine until duplicates began to cause confusion. The solution was to resort to nicknames, as with Jacob Jansen Hap, who found himself one of six Jacob Jansens in Beverwijck. Another way to avoid confusion was association with place of origin. Most Americans can quickly identify a Dutch origin if *van*, meaning 'of' or 'from', appears in the family name. In the 17th century this was one of several possibilities; sometimes more than one place of origin was associated with an individual, such as Cornelis Segersz van Voorhout, who also appears as Cornelis Segersz van Egmont. Another option was to state your occupation, such **de Timmerman** 'carpenter' or **de Cuyper** 'cooper, barrel-maker'. Often individuals would use one or the other identifier depending on the situation. For example, a certain Jan Hendricksen appears in the records of Beverwijck at various times as Jan Roodthaer, Jan de Timmerman, and Jan van Salsbergen, yielding the biographical information that Jan was the son of Hendrick, had red hair, and was a carpenter from Salzburg.

Bibliography

Debrabandere, Frans (1993): *Verklarend Woordenboek van de Familienamen in Belgie en Noord-Frankrijk.* Brussels.

Ebeling, R. A. (1993): *Voor- en familienamen in Nederland: Geschiedenis, verspreiding, vorm en gebruik.* 's-Gravenhage.

Epperson, Gwenn F. (1994): *New Netherland Roots.* Baltimore.

A Gazetteer of the Netherlands, containing a Full Account of All the Cities, Towns, and Villages in the Seventeen Provinces and the Bishoprick of Liege. London, 1794.

Goodfriend, Joyce D. (1992): *Before the Melting Pot: Society and Culture in Colonial New York City, 1664–1730.* Princeton.

Jacobs, Jaap (1999): *Een zegenrijk gewest: Nieuw-Nederland in de zeventiende eeuw.* Leiden.

Rink, Oliver A. (1986): *Holland on the Hudson: An Economic and Social History of Dutch New York.* New York.

Van der Aa, A. J. (1839): *Aardrijkskundig Woordenboek der Nederlanden.* Gorinchem.

Winkler, Johan (1885): *De Nederlandsche Geslachtsnamen in Oorsprong, Geschiedenis en Beteekenis.* Haarlem.

SCANDINAVIAN FAMILY NAMES

Olav Veka

The European region of Scandinavia comprises three countries: Denmark, Norway, and Sweden, each with its own national language: Danish, Norwegian, and Swedish. These belong to the northern branch of the Germanic languages. There are two other closely related languages in this group, Faeroese and Icelandic, but they have so few speakers (about 270,000 speakers of Icelandic and about 50,000 of Faeroese) and such a small history of immigration in North America that their family names do not occur in this dictionary.

Population figures for the three Scandinavian countries in 2002 were as follows: Denmark, 5.3 million; Norway, 4.4 million; and Sweden, nearly 9 million. Their relative population figures do not, however, correspond to the proportion of immigrants who have come to the United States from each: Sweden, about 1.1 million; Norway, about 800,000; and Denmark, fewer than 300,000. Thus, Norway has had the largest emigration relative to its population, about 18 percent, while Sweden has had an emigration of about 12 percent, and Denmark a little more than 5 percent. The figures for Norway and Sweden are among the highest in Europe; only Ireland has sent a larger percentage of its population as emigrants to the United States than Norway.

Linguistically, Danish, Norwegian, and Swedish are so closely related that they could be termed varieties of the same language. Virtually all Scandinavians can understand one another's native languages, but for historical and political reasons, they are considered separate languages. Since the languages are so similar, one would expect that the inventory of names used by Scandinavian immigrants to the United States would be quite similar, and that it would be difficult to distinguish the groups from one another, but this is not so. In all three countries, the use of hereditary family names began at about the same time, but for various reasons, different types of surnames came to be characteristic of Danes, Norwegians, and Swedes, and these are reflected in the corresponding immigrant groups.

Scandinavian Settlement in the United States

Most Scandinavian immigrants settled in the Midwest. The U.S. census of 1900, from which the figures in Table 1 are drawn, shows that Minnesota was the state with the largest Scandinavian immigrant population, with 115,000 Swedes,

105,000 Norwegians, and 16,300 Danes, while 17,000 Danes lived in Iowa. This table shows the strong concentration of Scandinavians in the Midwest, from Illinois to the Dakotas, with a secondary Swedish center on the Atlantic seaboard.

Table 1.
Scandinavian Immigrant Populations in the United States, U.S. Census of 1900

Denmark	Norway	Sweden
Iowa 17,000	Minnesota 105,000	Minnesota 115,000
Minnesota 16,300	Wisconsin 61,500	Illinois 99,100
Wisconsin 16,200	North Dakota 30,200	New York 42,700
Illinois 15,700	Illinois 30,000	Massachusetts 32,200

Denmark

Danish emigration never reached great numbers, largely because economic conditions were better in Denmark than in Norway and Sweden. As in the other countries, lack of work and land led to the emigration of tenant farmers, or cotters, and farm workers. Almost half the emigrants came from Jutland. When they arrived in the United States, quite a few Danes settled in the cities.

The custom of using hereditary family names spread north from Germany to the Scandinavian countries, first to the gentry and then to the urban bourgeoisie. The fact that Denmark shares its southern border with Germany has resulted in the presence in Denmark of a fairly large number of surnames of German origin, particularly from Low German or Frisian, and many others have been created based on German models. Toward the end of the Middle Ages, about one-third of the Danish aristocracy had taken hereditary family names, and in 1526 the king encouraged all members of the nobility to adopt surnames. Many families took names related to their family crests or coats of arms, such as **Bielke** or **Løvenkrone**. The custom of using hereditary surnames spread through Danish society, and by the end of the 18th century, half of the urban population had taken hereditary surnames of various types—for example, ethnic names (**Friis** 'Frisian', **Holst** 'person from Holstein') and occupational names (**Dreyer** 'turner', **Møller** 'miller').

In the countryside, however, people preserved the old tradition of using a given name and a patronymic (e.g. *Jensen, Nielsen; Jensdatter, Nielsdatter*). Directives in 1828 and 1856 required people to adopt hereditary surnames, with the result that, by the end of the century, patronymics had become hereditary rather than changing from generation to generation. The first actual Danish law on the use of names, passed in 1904, made it permissible for people to change their surnames, among other reasons to avoid the most frequent patronymics, which made it difficult to distinguish between individuals; however, the process was little used.

In Denmark today, almost 70 percent of the native Danish population have patronymics as surnames. As a result, two-thirds of the population share just fifty surnames, and one-fifth of all Danes are named **Jensen, Nielsen,** or **Hansen.** The most common Danish surname, **Jensen,** with 370,000 bearers, can be compared with the most common patronymic in Sweden, **Andersson** (380,000), and with **Hansen** in Norway (60,000). No other country in Europe has so few surnames used by so many citizens as Denmark.

The typology of Danish surnames can be seen in a list of the 100 most frequent surnames in Denmark. The list includes no fewer than seventy-nine patronymics, from **Jensen** down to **Justesen**, which has 2,680 bearers. Among the remaining twenty-one surnames, we find topographical names such as **Lund** 'grove', **Holm** 'small island', and **Skov** 'forest', but few habitational names (an example is **Søndergaard** 'farm to the south'). Other types are occupational names, such as **Møller** 'miller' and **Koch** 'cook', and nicknames or bynames like **Bruun** 'brown' and **Sommer** 'summer'. German forms or spellings are common, such as **Schultz** and **Fischer.** Among the Scandinavian countries, Denmark has the highest number of occupational names, but they are not nearly as widespread as in Germany and England.

As mentioned above, the number of Danish immigrants to the United States was relatively small, and on arrival they dispersed throughout a number of states. Danish surnames have tended to be absorbed by the American body of English-derived surnames. Most Danish emigrants had patronymic surnames, which in many cases were adapted when they arrived in America by changing the ending *-sen* to its common English cognate, *-son.* Names where *-sen* has been preserved are not necessarily typically Danish, since this ending is common in Norway as well as in parts of northern Germany and Frisia. For names with a patronymic ending in *-sen,* only if the root personal name is rarely used in Norway can one be reasonably sure that the name is of Danish and not Norwegian origin. **Thygesen**, which has more than 3,000 bearers in Denmark and fewer than 300 in Norway, is one such example.

Topographical and habitational names are another group that may be easily identified as Danish, particularly farmstead names like **Søndergaard** and **Østergaard** (note that the Danish character *ø* often becomes a plain *o* in the United States). Common final elements in Danish place names are *-borg, -by, -gaard, -rup,* and *-sted.*

Norway

The first organized emigration from Norway took place in 1825, when the sloop *Restauration* sailed across the Atlantic under the leadership of Cleng Peerson, who is considered the "father of Norwegian emigration." The greatest numbers of Norwegians emigrated in the 1860s, in the 1880s, and between 1902 and 1907. A good many of the 800,000 Norwegian migrants went back home, particularly in the period between the world wars.

Most of the migrants were tenant farmers, which explains why of all the immigrant groups, the Norwegians were most likely to settle in rural areas. Concentrations of Norwegians in comparatively small rural communities gave the Norwegian language and culture favorable conditions for maintenance in the new country, and there were numerous associations for immigrants from different regions in Norway, Norwegian newspapers, churches, and other institutions. This partly explains why Norwegian surnames have been preserved quite well in the United States.

The Norwegian gentry class was quite small (it was formally abolished in 1821), and its members followed European naming customs, particularly those of Denmark, by adopting hereditary surnames toward the end of the Middle Ages. In the 17th and 18th centuries, the bourgeoisie started using surnames on European patterns, not least because many of them were immigrant merchants, craftsmen, or laborers from other European countries. Names such as **Schmidt, Møller,** and **Schultz** became common in Norwegian towns. It is generally not possible to determine whether the bearers of such names were actually Norwegian, since their names are identical with corresponding Danish and German names. During the 19th century, the custom of taking hereditary surnames spread to the rural areas, using two basic patterns.

People in rural communities are usually mentioned in official documents with a given name, a patronymic, and the name of the farm where they lived. The given name was an individual's own name, the patronymic indicated the name of his or her father ('son of' or 'daughter of'), and the farm name told where the person lived. Thus, *Lars Halvorsen Haug* was the son of Halvor and lived on Haug Farm, as did his sister *Kari Halvorsdatter Haug*. Most Norwegians followed the Danish custom of writing the oral form *-son* or *-sønn* as *-sen*.

Most laborers and craftsmen in rural communities adopted a patronymic as a hereditary surname. Many of those who moved from rural areas to towns during the Industrial Revolution in the latter half of the 19th century also followed this practice. Farmers and tenant farmers usually took the name of the farm as a surname, and it followed the bearer even when he moved away from the farm or bought another farm with another name.

Only after the passage of legislation in 1923 did hereditary surnames come into common use in Norway. If a patronymic was used, it no longer varied from generation to generation. As an example, the most important politician in Norway after World War II was *Einar Gerhardsen*, born in 1897. As the son of Gerhard, he had a genuine patronymic, *Gerhardsen*, but his sons, who were born after 1923, were given the frozen patronymic *Gerhardsen* as their surname, rather than *Einarsen*.

In Norway today, the most common surname type is the habitational name from a farmstead, names that reflect the varied natural landscape with a finely tuned descriptive vocabulary. Of the 100 most common Norwegian surnames, forty-two are of the farmstead type and fifty-eight are patronymics. Patronymics top the population statistics, however, as the thirteen most widely used names. A good quarter of the Norwegian people have a patronymic surname, while most of the others, slightly fewer than three-quarters, have a farmstead name.

Patronymics number slightly more than 2,000 names, while the number of different farmstead names is well over 40,000. No foreign name types, such as *Møller* or *Schultz*, rank among the 250 most common. The structure of Norwegian surname types, with its large proportion of farmstead names, is almost unique among international surnaming practices.

Sweden

Swedish immigration to the United States began as early as 1638, when a group settled in the Delaware Valley to start a colony with adherence to the Swedish king. The settlers had to give up the idea of a New Sweden in 1655, when the colony was lost to the Dutch. However, Swedish language and culture persisted for a long time in this area.

A new and much larger immigration took place from 1840 on. Up to 1930, 1 million Swedes left for the United States, and Sweden is in seventh place among all countries sending U.S. immigrants from Europe. Unlike the Norwegians, a larger proportion of Swedish immigrants—more than 60 percent—settled in cities.

Sweden was influenced by German naming traditions probably to an even greater degree than Denmark was. In Sweden, the gentry were the first to adopt hereditary surnames, either after the family coat of arms (*Silver-, Gyllen-* 'gold') or based on a habitational name patterned on German.

In the 17th and 18th centuries, the typical two-element surnames came into use among the bourgeoisie, also inspired by German models, at first with the widespread use of the element *-man* (e.g. **Bergman, Björkman, Nyman**). Gradually, topographic elements came into general use, such as *berg* 'mountain', *sjö* 'sea', and *ström* 'river'. In such names, the first element may originate from a place name, such as **Lindberg**, which at least in some cases is from a place name beginning with *Lind-*. Generally, however, the parts of the name were arbitrary and ornamental, and put together without any semantic relation to each other. This name type, consisting of two elements arbitrarily combined, is not found in the other Scandinavian countries and is peculiar to Sweden. Thus, an American with the surname **Lindstrom** (*Lindström*) is almost certainly of Swedish extraction. Other common geographical elements are *holm* 'island', *lund* 'grove', *stedt* 'homestead'.

Many elements forming Swedish ornamental names originate in the realm of plants: *ek* 'oak', *ceder* 'cedar', *lund* 'grove', *blad* 'leaf', *blom* 'flower', *gren* 'branch', *kvist* 'twig', *löv* 'foliage'. The most widely used are *-gren* and *-kvist*. The most common two-element names are *Lindberg* (ranked 19), *Lindström* (20), *Lindgren* (22), and *Lundberg* (24). Names ending in the suffix *-ing* are normally derived from place names (**Nordling, Witting**).

Another easily recognizable Swedish trait is the use of suffixes of Latin origin such as *-el/-ell* (as in **Forsell**), *-en* (as in **Liden**), *-er* (as in **Moder**), or *-(l)in* (as in **Mellin**). In the 1950s there were 3,500 different surnames ending in the suffix *-ell* and *-in,* and about 2,500 surnames had the Latin suffixes *-ius,*

-*aeus*. The suffix -*é* (as in **Linné**) is a shortened form of -*ius*, -*aeus*. The suffix -*ander* (**Bolander, Helander**), originally of Greek origin, is used in more than 1,000 names.

A distinctively Swedish name group consists of the so-called soldiers' names, which originally were nicknames used for men enrolled in the military. Many of these soldiers' names were later taken as family names. They often describe some personal characteristic, such as **Stark** 'strong', **Tapper** 'brave', **Flink** 'agile', **Blixt** 'lightning', **Bång** 'noise', **From** 'pious'. Some denote pieces of military equipment, for example **Granat** 'grenade', **Bagge** 'ram'. Others may reflect an anecdotal association, for example **Appell** 'muster', **Karm** 'covered wagon'.

In addition to these typically Swedish name groups, there are Swedish names of German origin, or names modeled on German ones. In the United States these are difficult to distinguish from German names, for example occupational names, most of which are of German origin, such as **Koch, Müller,** and **Schulz**.

The most frequent surnames are those that are of patronymic origin. As in the other Scandinavian countries, many Swedes took a patronymic as their surname during the latter part of the19th century, and in 1901 hereditary surnames were required by law. In the 1970s, the eighteen most frequent Swedish surnames were patronymics, with **Johansson** and **Andersson** topping the list, and these were used by two-fifths of all Swedes.

All three of the Scandinavian countries chose to pass laws forbidding the use of genuine patronymics, despite the fact that they were in general use during the 19th century in all the countries. According to these laws, a patronymic could be used only as a hereditary surname or as a middle name. Iceland chose to go in the opposite direction, however, and passed a law in 1925 to maintain the old practice of using genuine patronymics.

Scandinavian Names in the United States

Many of the immigrants from Scandinavia did not have hereditary family names with which they identified as individuals. Members of the same family might be registered under several different surnames, but toward the end of the 19th century, this practice was altered in the direction of conformity because the bureaucracy required greater uniformity in family names.

Immigrants had to make a number of choices when they were registered. Should they take a surname in a Scandinavian language form, should they adjust it to American naming practices, or should they take an entirely new name?

The dominant name type was the patronymic, which could easily be adapted to English name forms. Swedes had brought with them the final element -*sson* (**Pettersson**), which would seem even more English if one *s* were removed, and perhaps one *t* as well, producing **Petterson** or **Peterson**. Danish or Norwegian -*sen* was either kept (**Halvorsen**) or replaced with English -*son* (**Halvorson**), which seemed quite suitable at least for Norwegians, since *son* is also a Norwegian word (Old Norse *sonr*). It is often difficult to determine whether a patronymic is Norwegian or Danish, but in this case most of the U.S. bearers would most likely be Norwegians, since **Halvorsen** is much more common in Norway (12,600) than in Denmark (400).

In addition, Norwegians in particular would have to choose whether they wanted to be registered under a patronymic or a farmstead name. Up to the 1870s, patronymics were more common among Norwegian immigrants because they were less deviant in the new language environment. But as the century waned, influential persons agitated for the use of farmstead names as family names, both for ethnic reasons, since they more clearly indicated a Norwegian background, and for practical ones, since they could more easily distinguish individuals from one another as the rate of immigration accelerated. Farmstead names were old, reminiscent of home, and "suitable for this kind of people," as one writer stated. We can get some impression of the difficulties created by the widespread use of patronymics from the case of a village in the Midwest where 54 men of the male population of 312 were named **Olsen**!

As a result of the rising prestige accorded to the use of farmstead names, the large group of immigrants in the 1880s were likely to keep their farmstead names as surnames, because they settled in an environment that was just as Norwegian as it was American. The more immigrants there were in a given district, the easier it was to keep a Norwegian flavor in the family names. Research has shown that farmstead names clearly dominated many immigrant environments; in some rural districts, they comprised as many as two-thirds of the surnames, which is not far from the distribution in the old country.

The Norwegian identity is more obvious in the case of most farmstead names than it is for patronymics, since farmstead names are less usual in the other Scandinavian countries. Frequent elements in Norwegian farmstead names are -*em* (mostly developed from *heim* 'home'), -*land* 'land', -*stad* 'farmstead', -*rud* 'clearing', -*mo* 'sandy heath', -*li* 'slope', -*bakke* 'hill', and -*haug* 'mound'; the latter is also extant in the inflected forms *Haug, Haugen, Hauger, Haugan, Hauge*.

Spelling adaptations were necessary because the Scandinavian letters *æ, ä, ø, ö,* and *å* are not used in English. Norwegian *Sæther* became **Sather**, Swedish *Bäckström* became **Beckstrom**, Danish *Østergaard* became **Ostergaard**, Swedish *Söderström* became **Soderstrom**, Norwegian *Ødegård* became **Odegard**, and Swedish *Åman* became **Ohman**.

At times the name would be written in an English form corresponding to its pronunciation: **Sime** for *Seim*, **Setter** for *Sæther*, or **Lee** for *Lie*. Less often, the name would be translated into English: *Haug* became **Hill**, *Østerhus* became **Easthouse**, and *Askeland* became **Ashland**. It might be replaced by a similar-sounding English name—for example, **Gilbertson** instead of *Gulbrandsen*. A name could be given a slightly more English flavor by respelling it, replacing *k* with *c*, *kv* with *qu*, or *v* with *w* (e.g. **Quammen** instead of *Kvammen*).

Because English and Scandinavian languages are closely related, many changes were easy and seemed natural. Names like *Kleiveland* could easily be changed to **Cleveland**. One of the most typical Scandinavian patronymics in the United States is **Nelson,** which has been used for other forms like *Nilsen, Nilssen, Nielsen,* and *Nilsson,* while the name **Thompson** might encompass, among others, unrelated forms such as *Thorsen, Thorsson, Thorkelsen,* as well as the cognates *Thomassen, Thomsen.* **Johnson** has assimilated many variants, such as *Jansson, Jönsson, Johansson, Johnsen,* and *Jansen.*

When two-element Swedish names were adjusted at all, only one of the elements was normally changed: *Stenberg,* for example, was changed to **Stoneberg,** *Östlund* to **Eastlund,** and *Nyquist* to **Newquist.** The common surname element *Ljung-* 'heather' usually takes the form *Young-*; thus, **Ljungdahl** has become **Youngdahl.** No name in this dictionary has kept the original element **Ljung-.** The Swedish final elements *-quist, -qvist,* and *-kvist* all have the form *-quist* in the United States. Based on the French pattern, accents are common in some suffixes (*Lidén, Norén*), but these have disappeared in the process of making adjustments to American spelling (**Liden, Noren**).

—Translated by Nancy L. Coleman

Bibliography

Jørgensen, Bent (1994): *Stednavneordbog.* Copenhagen: Gyldendal.

Kruken, Kristoffer, and Ola Stemshaug (1995): *Norsk personnamnleksikon.* Oslo: Det Norske Samlaget.

Modéer, Ivar (1989): 'Svenska personnamn' in *Anthroponymica Suecana* 5. Reprinted in *Svenska personnamn: Handbok för universitetsbruk og självstudier.* Lund: Studentlitteratur.

Søndergaard, Georg (2000): *Danske for- og efternavne.* Rødovre: Askholms Forlag.

Swanson, Roy W. (1928): 'The Swedish Surname in America' in *American Speech* 3.

Tegner, Esaias (1882): *Om svenska familjenamn.* Nordisk Tidskrift, reprinted in *Ur sprakens värid: Fem uppsatser av Esaias Tegnér.* Stockholm: Albert Bonniers, 1930.

Veka, Olav (2000): *Norsk etternamnleksikon.* Oslo: Det Norske Samlaget.

FINNISH FAMILY NAMES

Hannele Jönsson-Korhola

History

As family names in most countries of the world reflect the history of the nation, so also the history of Finland and its people is reflected in the Finnish as well as in Finnish American surnames. Present-day Finland was the eastern part of Sweden until 1809. Swedish continued to be the only official language also during the period of Russian rule (1809–1917), until the language edict of 1863, according to which Finnish was to have equal status with Swedish in administrative documents and courts of justice. Behind the edict was a true bearer of Finnish national ideology, Senator Johan Vilhelm Snellman. Already then, Finnish was the language of the majority of the Finnish people. Nowadays close to 94% of the population of Finland is Finnish-speaking, while about 6% are Swedish-speaking Finns. The total population of Finland is now slightly over 5 million. After Finland became independent in 1917, the language law of 1922 stated that Finnish and Swedish are the official national languages.

Finnish belongs to the Finno-Ugric language family, together with Hungarian, Estonian, Saame or Lappish, and Karelian. It is, therefore, unlike Swedish and Russian, a non-Indo-European language. Swedish influence has always been greater both culturally and linguistically in western Finland, whereas Russian and Karelian influence is greater in the eastern parts of the country. Overall, the system of surnames in the western parts of Finland followed common European trails; the naming traditions in the eastern parts deviated more from international paths.

Origins and Types of Finnish Surnames

The oldest Finnish surnames are found in eastern Finland, where they were perhaps already used in pagan times, i.e. before the 12th century AD. The first written sources of bynames that gradually developed into surnames are from 1500 AD in eastern Finland.

The most common Finnish surname ending is *-nen.* The history of *-nen* names is twofold. Originally the ending *-nen* was a diminutive suffix with possessive meaning, expressing (among other concepts) association with a place, the idea of belonging somewhere. For instance, if the father of a family was called *Kauppi* and the son *Heikki,* a kind of patronymic *Kauppinen Heikki* or a compound name *Kauppis-Heikki* was formed, meaning 'Heikki who belongs to the house and family of Kauppi'. As such the name may well have been in everyday use among common people already in the 15th century. Especially in the Savo region in the east, the adding of *-nen* to bynames became very popular. Names such as this could sometimes be written down in documents as if they were Scandinavian patronymics, e.g. *Heikki Kaupinpoika* (poika = 'son'). Gradually the attributive byname, placed before the personal name, turned into a surname placed after it. The name type *Heikki Kauppinen* became so common that it became a set pattern of identification. When the need for surnames grew in the late 19th century, adopted names were also formed according to the same pattern. Usually, though, it is possible to say from the content of the first part of the name whether a particular *-nen* name belongs to the older or more recent layer.

In 1998 there were over 4,000 different Finnish *-nen* surnames, that is 8.6% of all Finnish language names. Altogether there were close to 2 million bearers of names ending in *-nen,* that is, almost 47% of all bearers of Finnish-language names in Finland. In total, there are about 128,000 different surnames borne by the 5.1 million citizens of Finland. Of the total number of surnames about 50,000 (39%) are Finnish or Finnish-sounding and borne by as many as almost 4 million citizens (77% of the population). The 10 most common surnames in Finland in 1998 were: 1. **Virtanen**, 2. **Korhonen**, 3. **Nieminen**, 4. **Mäkinen**, 5. **Mäkelä**, 6. **Hämäläinen**, 7. **Laine**, 8. **Koskinen**, 9. **Heikkinen**, 10. **Järvinen**.

In western Finland, the usage of surnames seems to be more recent. The first few written sources of bynames that later became surnames are from the 15th and 16th century. It is possible, though, that bynames were used commonly among people but the documentation followed more the Swedish pattern of forename followed by a patronymic in Swedish of the type *Jacob Johansson* or *Hilda Johansdotter* ('John's daughter'). The surname could also be derived from a farm or village name, very commonly ending in *-la* or (due to vowel harmony in Finnish) *-lä*, a suffix indicating locality. Examples of farm names that through bynames became surnames are **Mikkola** and **Hirvelä**. Sometimes, for instance in the western central Finnish province of Ostobothnia, a farm could be documented in the parish register as *Martikkala* but the person living there as *Martikainen*. Farm names were derived from first names as *Anttila,* or the location of the farm near a hill, as *Mäki* ('hill'; also *Mäkelä*), or occasionally in relation to another habitation as *Alatalo* ('lower house') contrasted with *Ylätalo* ('upper house'). The original byname indicating locality changed often when the person moved, for example to a farm with another name that then became the new byname.

In past centuries, surnames came also from other sources. Words denoting trades or crafts were used as bynames or nicknames supplementing the forename, giving rise to a few occu-

pational names like **Suutari** ('shoemaker') and **Seppänen** (*seppä* 'smith' + *-nen*). More often, crofters living in towns received Swedish surnames such as **Lundberg** ('grove' + 'mountain') or **Rosendahl** ('rose' + 'valley'), especially in the 17th and 18th centuries. This type of surname had become a surname type or a pattern of its own, in which the two parts together did not necessarily refer to a locality, but included other elements as, for instance, **Lindqvist** ('linden' + 'twig') or the ending *-man* ('-man') as in **Elgman** ('elk' + 'man'). At the end of the Middle Ages the nobility, civil servants, clergymen, soldiers, and university students often adopted Latin or other foreign language surnames. It is only a development of the late 19th century that Finnish-language surnames have more commonly been taken.

Finnish National Romanticism started during the first part of the 19th century, when Finland had become an autonomous Grand Duchy of Finland in the Russian Empire under the tsar. The position of the Finnish language was to be improved and people started to change ("Finnify") also their names into Finnish by adoption or translation in the middle of the 1800s. One important group of the forerunners were Finnish writers such as Alexis Stenvall ('stone wall'; 1834–72), who became the national author of Finland, under the name Aleksis Kivi. The movement culminated in 1906, on the 100th anniversary of the birth of Senator J. V. Snellman, during which celebrations about 100,000 Finns took a Finnish-language surname.

During the name conversion movement of the late 19th and the first decades of the 20th century the newly adopted surnames were often of the earlier surname type with a *-nen* suffix. Many of them are arbitrarily adopted topographic names as **Virtanen** ('stream' + *-nen), ***Mäkinen** ('hill' + *-nen)* or **Koskinen** ('rapids' + *-nen*). The new names could also be just basic words without a suffix. Often, words referring to nature were chosen, resulting in names as **Aalto** 'wave', **Koski** 'rapids', **Lahti** 'bay', **Lehti** 'leaf', or **Nurmi** 'grass'. Surnames could also be translated from an earlier Swedish name, as **Virta,** from Swedish *Ström* 'stream', or **Vapaavuori,** from Swedish *Friberg* 'free mountain'. Also, compound names referring to nature were taken, for example **Koivuniemi** (from *koivu* 'birch' + *niemi* 'cape, point') or **Kalliokoski** (from *kallio* 'rock, mountain' + *koski* 'rapids'). The age of this kind of surnames is sometimes difficult to tell without historical documents because they may have originally referred to a particular place in the natural world, then developed into a farm name and later to a surname. Some names were adopted as such, others formed after the same pattern. During the period around the turn of the 19th century into the 20th, names were adopted as family names to emphasize the family connection or the ideology of Finnishness, or just given or taken for the sake of identification. The most important reason seems, however, to be fashion: the fashion of taking a surname and the fashion of surnames. The first surname law was passed only in 1920 and it stated that everybody had to have a surname.

Finnish Surnames in North America

The emigration of Finns to the United States started as early as in the 1630s, with Delaware on the East Coast as the destination. These early immigrants were mostly so-called forest Finns, who had earlier emigrated from the eastern Savo province into the large forests of central Sweden, on the borders with Norway, to cultivate land with the slash-and-burn technique. They came to Delaware in Swedish immigrant groups and some of them had already taken Swedish names or they had been registered with patronymics. Names in the Delaware region that have been traced back to Finnish names are, for instance, Erik Mattson Hammalin (from **Hämäläinen**) and Olof Thorsson, Tossawa, or (later) Tussey (from **Tossavainen)**. The best-known descendant of this group is probably John Morton (from **Marttinen)**, one of the signers of the Declaration of Independence in 1776.

The greatest flow of Finnish immigration to the United States took place in the years 1880–1930. In this period about 350,000 Finns arrived in America. Of these immigrants, more than 75% came from western Finland, especially the central western province of Ostrobothnia. Therefore, many Finnish surnames in North America bear traces of the western Finnish naming tradition. It is also worth bearing in mind that in those days there were still many people in Finland who had no family name at all. Also, many of those that had a surname when leaving Finland, had had the name only a short time and in some cases represented the first generation bearing a particular name. Although it is believed that most of the Finnish immigrants kept their name as it was written in their documents, some completely new names were taken. In the United States Finnish names were often considered difficult to write and pronounce by Americans, so some changes have taken place in the surnames. Among the typical changes are the following:

Dropping of diacritic marks: *Mäki* to **Maki** or **Maeki**, *Hämäläinen* to **Hamalainen** or **Haemaelaeinen.**

Direct translation: *Järvinen* to **Lake**; *Seppä, Seppälä, Seppänen* to **Smith.**

Shortening, especially of *-(i)nen* and *-la/-lä* names and compound names: *Ahonen* to **Aho**; *Manninen* to **Mann** or **Manning**; *Korpela* to **Korpi**; *Hietaranta* to **Ranta**; *Kalliokoski* to **Koski**; *Järviluoma* to **Jarvi.**

Reversion to a patronymic: *Suutari* to **Antonson** (the father was *Anton*).

Spelling changes: *Hakkarainen* to **Hackray**; *Hämäläinen* to **Hamlin**; *Järvelä* to **Jarvella**; *Nykänen* and *Nykanen* to **Kane**.

Total change to an unrelated term: *Kannisto* to **Hill**; *Kivelä* to **Lake**; *Sulonen* to **Manner.**

The fact that surnames in Finland started to be more commonly taken only after the 1850s and the fairly late law stating that everybody has to have a surname (1920) partly explains the changes in the family names of the Finnish immigrants. The types of changes mentioned above can be of help when tracing family members on both sides of the Atlantic Ocean.

Our indispensable source and authority for Finnish family names has been, in particular, the work of Pirjo Mikkonen and Sirkka Paikkala (1992, 2000). We are very grateful for their help in explaining Finnish surnames in the United States.

Bibliography

Andersson, Paula, and Raija Kangassalo (2003): 'Suomi ja meänkieli Ruotsissa' in *Monena suomi maailmalla: suomalaisia kielivähemmistöjä*, ed. by Hannele Jönsson-Korhola and Anna-Riitta Lindgren. Tietolipas 190. Suomalaisen Kirjallisuuden Seura. Helsinki.

Lindgren, Anna-Riitta. *Tietolipas. Suomalaisen Kirjallisuuden Seura.* Helsinki.

Kolehmainen John (1949): 'Finnish Surnames in America' in *American Speech*, vol. 2. 1949

Mikkonen, Pirjo, and Sirkka Paikkala (1992, 2000): *Sukunimet*. Otava, Keuruu.

Pöyhönen, Juhani (1998): *Suomalainen sukunimikartasto. Atlas of Finnish Surnames*. Suomalaisen Kirjallisuuden Seura. Jyväskylä, Finland.

Virtaranta, Pertti (1991): 'Finskan i America'. Språk i Norden.

Virtaranta, Pertti (1992): *Amerikansuomen sanakirja. A Dictionary of American Finnish*. Siirtolaisuusinstituutti (Institute of Migration). Turku, Finland.

Virtaranta, Pertti, Hannele Jönsson-Korhola, Maisa Martin, and Maija Kainulainen (1993): *Amerikansuomi*. Tietolipas 125. Suomalaisen Kirjallisuuden Seura. Helsinki, Finland.

Wallius, Anna-Liisa (1995). *Amerikansuomalaisten suku- ja etunimistä*. Meddelanden från *Institutionen f ör finska* vid Umeå universitet nr 10. Umeå, Sweden.

SPANISH AND PORTUGUESE FAMILY NAMES

Also Catalan, Basque, Galician, and the Languages of Latin America and the Philippines

Dieter Kremer
with additional comments by Roser Saurí Colomer

One of the most difficult tasks of family name research is the explanation of the names themselves. Their linguistic aspects—etymology (including the original meaning), form, and spelling—are often complex, and even names with straightforward meanings may present problems in understanding their social and cultural background and the legal and administrative aspects of name origins and inheritance. It is not enough to determine the origin of a name; the name's individual history is just as important. Unlike generic nouns, a name individualizes a particular person: a *ferreiro* 'smith' is not the same as a person with the family name **Ferreiro**, a word that has a social function rather than a semantic one, denotation of a class of items. Yet this name goes back to a vocabulary word in Spanish, an occupational term. General dictionaries usually ignore personal names, even those with unambiguous origins. Moreover, someone interested in finding out about the origin of his or her name may not be able to find an explanation of it anywhere. Even if an explanation is found, it may not be reliable. Much research into names in the past has been carried out by enthusiastic amateurs, many of whom lack the necessary grounding in history and historical linguistics.

The *Dictionary of American Family Names,* DAFN, is the first systematic attempt to redress the balance. Many people in the United States bear family names of Iberian origin. Readers of Iberian ancestry will find much of interest in these pages, and, it is hoped, the impetus to look more deeply into their family history. Until the publication of Faure et al. (2001), no comprehensive reference work existed devoted to the surnames of the Iberian Peninsula. There are some books devoted to particular languages (Spanish, Catalan, Basque, and Portuguese), although even some of these provide information that is not always reliable and convincing. For DAFN's research on Iberian names, extensive use was made of specialist sources on the Internet. Of course, a work on such a large scale as DAFN can do no more than provide a general overview; it cannot go into very much detail. Nonetheless, every effort has been made to provide reliable information on a systematic basis, often where none existed before.

Typically, family names go back to other names—first names, place names, nicknames and other epithets, or occupational terms. The family name **López** goes back to the Spanish personal name *Lope* (or Portuguese *Lopo)*; **Romero** goes back to the epithet *romero* 'pilgrim'; **Blanco** to the adjective *blanco* 'white'; **Coelho** to *coelho* 'rabbit'; **Castro** to a place called *Castro.* Even in such cases, however, we have to be careful not to misinterpret coincidence as history. Names have a life of their own, independent of their bearers. A personal name such as *Alfonso* is etymologically of Visigothic origin, but the name bearers were not Goths any more than people named *Johannes* are necessarily Jewish. The place name *Almeida* (like many Iberian place names) is of Arabic origin, but we have to understand it as a place name associated with León or Portugal. It is easy to succumb to the romance of ancient names. So, for example, the family name **Fernández** ultimately derives, linguistically, from the Gothic personal name *Fredenand,* formed from the reconstructed elements *frith* 'peace' and *nanth* 'boldness', but it would be absurd to postulate a Gothic origin for any family of this name. The family name can be traced back no further than the personal name *Fernando* plus the patronymic suffix *-ez.*

Iberian Languages and Names

Any explanation of the history of Hispanic family names must take account of the linguistic context of the Iberian Peninsula, where Spanish and Portuguese are spoken alongside other languages. The languages spoken in present-day Spain are the following:

Galician, spoken in Galicia, in the northwestern part of the peninsula; closely related to Portuguese;

Asturian and **Leonese**, spoken in the northwestern regions of Asturias, León, a part of Zamora province, and also in northern Portugal;

Basque, spoken in the Basque Country, which occupies both the north and south slopes of the western Pyrenees, currently divided between present-day France and Spain;

Aragonese, spoken in northern Aragon, in the central Pyrenees;

Catalan, spoken in Catalonia and Valencia (northeast and east of present-day Spain), North Catalonia (the southeastern corner of present-day France), the Balearic Islands, the state of Andorra, and a small area in the Italian island of Sardinia;

Spanish (sometimes referred to as **Castilian**), historically the language of Castile, and nowadays the official language throughout the country, alongside Galician, Basque and Catalan, which have "co-official" status with Spanish in their respective regions.

In addition to the six above-mentioned languages, Occitan, the vernacular language of southern France (Langue d'Oc), is also spoken in a valley in the Spanish Pyrenees, called Val d'Aran.

In Portugal, the language is almost uniformly **Portuguese**.

Except for Basque, which is of pre-Indo-European origin, all the languages of the Iberian Peninsula are members of the Romance language group, evolved from Latin; nevertheless, they are distinctly different among themselves, and some of their systematic differences are reflected in names. For instance, Castilian **Martín** and its patronymic **Martínez** correspond to Portuguese **Martim** or **Martinho** (patronymic **Martins),** Galician **Martiño** (patronymic **Martís,** among others), and Catalan **Martí.** Often, however, the name forms of some of these languages coincide, and it is not always possible to determine a name's precise origin without added historical background. In this connection it is useful to note the regional distribution of family names, based on modern name inventories or gazetteers.

Beyond Iberia's Romance heritage, there are influences from ancient substrata of indigenous pre-Roman languages (Celtic and Basque, especially in the form of place names), and from post-Roman superstrata, including mainly Germanic languages and Arabic. Later importations came with the ongoing cultural and population exchanges among European countries since the Middle Ages. Unlike place names, which are tied to a spot and are thus important evidence for the history of language settlement, personal names are mobile and subject to changes in fashion. Germanic influence in Iberia, where a Visigothic kingdom existed until 711, is very sparse in terms of vocabulary and place names, but it left an impressive legacy of personal names adopted by the Romance-speaking population. Common Iberian personal names of Visigothic etymology include *Álvaro* (family name **Álvarez, Alves),** *Fernando* (**Fernández, Hernández, Ferrandis, Fernandes),** *Gonzalo* (**González, Gonçalves),** *Rodrigo* or *Rui* (**Rodríguez, Rodrigues, Ruiz),** and *Elvira.* Many place names formed from these personal names (e.g., *villa Roderici* became *Rourís)* are also encountered as family names.

Despite the differences among Iberian languages, it is difficult sometimes to recover the true origin of a family name. This is particularly the case with family names from languages spoken within Spain other than Spanish. With the growth of the Castilian realm during the medieval period, a progressive process of Castilianization began in the areas where Galician, Asturian, Leonese, Basque, Aragonese, and Catalan were spoken. At the peak of emigration to the Americas, Castilian was Spain's only official written language, in all regions. The forms of Galician, Asturian, Leonese, Basque, Aragonese, and Catalan names were generally Castilianized in official records, and generally they were exported in that form. Some family names of those Iberian languages are nowadays only found in their Castilianized form. Nevertheless, the influence of all of these languages is observable, to a greater or lesser extent, on the family names of the Americas, and recorded where relevant in this dictionary.

On the American continent the presence of Spanish has been pervasive among almost all the countries of Latin America since the 16th century. Nowadays, Spanish is the official language of Mexico, most of Central America, Cuba, Puerto Rico, the Dominican Republic, and most of the countries of South America except Brazil, which is Portuguese-speaking. The Philippines, too, were ruled by Spain, and Spanish has been an important language of influence in these islands from the 16th century on. As a consequence, some of the family names of people from that area come originally from Spanish, though others are from indigenous languages. As far as possible, DAFN records these differences too.

Portuguese, which likewise became a major world language during the age of European colonialism, is the official of Brazil (which was Portugal's major American colony); it is also present in other, more recent Portuguese settlements, as for example in Venezuela and Canada.

History

Family names are part of a naming system that developed fairly uniformly in the European context. Family names in the legal sense—that is, administratively fixed, hereditary names for the members of a family—are of comparatively recent origin. An important date for the family historian is the decree by the Council of Trent (1545–63) that pastors of the Roman Catholic Church should keep records of their parishioners' baptisms, marriages, and deaths. As formalized in the Civil Code (Código Civil; in Spain in 1870, Portugal in 1911), the bearing of a uniform family name became a legal requirement, and new individual surnames could not be coined. Until that time, people could and did adopt entirely new family names, although the great majority of surnames had already become fixed, having been used traditionally over many generations. Nowadays, however, the surname—in contrast to the given name or nickname—is no longer a dynamic, productive element of language.

The formation of the Hispanic name system took place over a long period historically, marked throughout with regional variations. Originally, a single name sufficed to individualize a person in his or her social environment, and the supply of available names was large enough to serve a relatively small population. Two phenomena caused the medieval "name revolution," which started at the end of the 10th century, leading to a totally new two-name system, which was firmly established by the 12th century. First, fashions in naming resulted in a situation where just a few names (from a larger stock) became especially popular, so that many persons had the same name, leading to confusion. The second factor was a population explosion and the concentration of similarly named people in medieval cities.

To help resolve the difficulties and confusion that arose, a family name came to be added to the given name (typically a christening name, but not always of Christian origin), distinguishing a particular person from others of the same given name. These surnames fell into three main categories:

patronymics, based on the first name of the father (or rarely, that of the mother); origin names, based on a person's place of residence; and lexically derived names, formed somewhat like nicknames in the vernacular. The third group includes occupational names; it is often hard to tell, when looking at a medieval record, whether the occupation was actually that of the named person, or whether the name was simply inherited.

The Form of Iberian Names

This name system from the Middle Ages is, in principle, still in use today. In contrast to most European countries, official family names in the Iberian Peninsula (Spanish *apellido*, Portuguese and Galician *apelido*, Catalan *cognom*) consist of two parts: the family name of both the father and that of the mother. In extreme cases, the family name may indeed consist of not two, but four different names, in which the names of the grandparents are also present. There is a significant difference in usage between Spanish (or any other of the languages spoken in Spain) and Portuguese. In Spain, the name of the father (by which the family name is alphabetized) comes first; in the Portuguese system, the final name is the one inherited from the father. Thus, a Spaniard named *José Ramón López (Castro) García (Villar)* could be the son of *Manuel López Castro* and *Consuelo García Villar;* whereas a Portuguese named *João Pedro Mendes Martins* would be the son of, say, *Armando Braga Martins* and *Filomena Gaivota Mendes*.

Formally, a family name that is identical to a first name is generally introduced with the particle *de* (*Ramón de Lorenzo Martínez*). In modern Catalan, the paternal and maternal family names are usually separated by the particle *i* 'and' (*Pau Badia i Ferrer*). Both particles, *de* and *i,* have an exclusively connective function; they do not imply membership in the nobility (as similar words do in Italian), and they are not considered in alphabetization.

The two-part family name system is not used, however, in every Spanish-speaking country. Thus, whereas the system used in Mexico is similar to the one employed in Spain, in Argentina, Colombia, and elsewhere only one family name is used. In Brazil, too, only one family name is used.

Names in the Americas

The explanation of Hispanic family names in the United States is especially complex. We must distinguish between names imported via direct immigration from Europe and those that came as a result of migration within the Americas. For immigrants from Europe, the same explanations apply for Spaniards and for Portuguese. For immigrants from Latin America, an intermediate stage is introduced, and direct etymology is not normally possible. Since the sixteenth century, not only have large numbers of Spanish or Portuguese speakers migrated to the Americas, but the European naming system was also applied as the colonists Christianized and acculturated the indigenous populations. Latin American family names include only a very small proportion of names from indigenous languages (although some are recorded in the corpus of the present work), but the name carriers are of richly mixed European and indigenous origin. We cannot normally distinguish the two population groups by their names, for the names are nearly all of Iberian origin, including the names of people with no Iberian ancestry.

Assignment of the label *Spanish* or *Hispanic* is occasionally problematic. On the one hand, it covers some family names that may derive in fact from Amerindian languages such as Nahuatl, Maya, Quechua, or Aymara. On the other hand, there are family names that came originally from Europe but that have died out there. Thus, in Latin America we find numerous family names that are no longer present in Spain, or names that are common in the Americas but rare in Europe. This often reflects the social history of migration. If a group emigrates from a certain place or region for primarily economic reasons, their names may vanish from their abandoned home yet become frequent in the new country, as the families prosper and multiply. This helps to explain the unusually large number of Basque topographical names found in the United States, for example.

The correct interpretation of an American family name ideally requires a scholarly investigation of the family's history, but that is of course far beyond the scope of the present book. In general, only the etymology can be given here. Individual development should, ideally, be determined in detail from linguistic origin down through the various name carriers to the current American family name. We must consider genealogical and nonlinguistic correspondences and the possibility that a name has been adapted to American pronunciation and spelling, or altered more radically, although sound and spelling changes are less frequent in Iberian names than in those of some other ethnic groups.

Names in the Philippines

Names from the Philippines are problematic in a similar way to names from Latin America. On the one hand, the majority of them are of Spanish linguistic origin, introduced into those islands during the period of Spanish rule. Spanish family names among Filipinos is one of the marks left from that period, due to both the Christianization of the Filipino population, and the systematic distribution of family names ordered by the Spanish Governor in 1849—*so* systematic that in some cases names were assigned in alphabetic order, causing some small towns to end up with all family names starting by the same letter.

On the other hand, the label *Hispanic* (especially when found with the comment "unexplained") may be also applied to names original from any of the Filipino languages, such as Tagalog or Ilocano. In spite of the Spanish administration, these family names were preserved, especially among the population of remote areas.

Types of Names

The three main etymological categories of family names, as already noted, are patronymics, habitational names, and lexically derived names. Based on their absolute frequency, patronymic types such as **García, Fernández, González,** or **López** are by far the most widespread Spanish and Portuguese family names. In distant second place are lexically derived names or nicknames like **Romero, Blanco, Rubio.** Finally, we have names like **Ortega, Molina,** and **Castro,** which derive from place names, along with a group of names based on geographical regions (**Navarro, Serrano**). In the case of names of Basque origin, habitational names are the most frequent ones, whereas for Catalan, occupational names are more common.

The most varied development can be seen in the origin and lexically derived names. A formal marker of the Spanish and Portuguese patronymic is the unstressed suffix *-ez, -es* (**López, Lopes**), cognate with Aragonese and Catalan *-is* (**Lopis, Llopis**). It is combined exclusively with first names and means 'son of' (**López** 'son of Lope'), similar to Gaelic *mac-* or Germanic *-son.* In Basque, the element *-(r)ena* (the genitive ending plus an article) often serves this function, but it denotes 'the house of', referring to a family or to its residence; it can be attached to a given name (**Loperina**) or to a lexically derived name (**Amigorena** from Castilian *amigo* 'friend').

In addition to these marked patronymic forms, there are patronymics formed through simple substitution, such as **García.** Others originated in genitive (possessive) forms in the ancestral languages; for instance, **Díaz, Díez** come from the genitive case *Dídaci* '(son) of Didacus', whereas **Diego** comes from the nominative form *Didacus.* In some cases there is no suffix because of sound rules (**Alfonso**) or because a name had been recently imported (**Gil**). There are also "doublets" or parallel forms (**Martín, Martínez**).

Several categories of medieval second names are established family names today. Especially widespread are names associated with Christian cults, particularly that of the Virgin Mary: **Candelaria, Carmen, Concepción, Encarnação, Ramos, Santos, Espírito Santo,** and so on. Given at baptism, these referred to the patronage of the baptismal church or might be related to a woman's name.

There are three clear categories of local names: concrete, identifiable places, the sources of so-called habitational names; generic or topographic place names such as **Prado** 'meadow', **Puente** 'bridge', **Oliveira** 'olive tree', or **Silva** 'thorny brush'; and inhabitant names (so-called *ethnica*), adjectival forms that indicate place origin (e.g. **Toledano** 'from Toledo'), regional origin (**Montañés** 'from the mountains'), ethnicity (**Cigano** 'Gypsy'), or country or region of origin (**Gallego** 'from Galicia'). Some of these inhabitant names have secondary meanings (e.g. **Gallego** can also mean 'northwest wind', 'simple-minded', 'deaf-mute', and a variety of bird). A family name can lead back to an inhabitant name or to

a medieval name formed from it (**Alemán** either means 'from Germany' or is from the personal name *Alemannus*).

The colorful group of lexically derived or descriptive family names claims the greatest linguistic interest, and here "meaning" is easiest for the curious to discover. As a rule, however, this meaning applies to only the first bearer of the name; as soon as the name becomes hereditary, the meaning is lost and it becomes a mere label. As primary categories, we can distinguish affectionate names, nicknames, and occupational and status designations; added to these are function words such as 'the elder' and 'the younger' (e.g., **Mayor, Padre, Viejo, Menor, Hijo, Mozo**). Affectionate names can be abbreviated first names (**Mingo** from *Domingo*), those that are reconstituted hypocoristically (as "baby talk": **Paco** from *Francisco*, or **Pepe** from *José*), and those that are formed with diminutive suffixes (*Juan* can become **Juanico, Juanillo, Juanino, Juanito,** or **Juancho**; *Domingo* yields **Mingote, Minguet, Minguell, Minguall,** or **Mingarro**).

Nicknames are based mostly on physical, intellectual, moral, or professional characteristics. They can take the form of a description (adjectives or phrases like **Curto** 'short' or **Magro** 'skinny'), metaphors (nouns like **Caballo** 'horse'), or metonyms (nouns, with the part representing the whole, as in **Narizes** 'nostrils'). There are numerous nicknames that have to do with food (**Pan** 'bread', **Carnes** 'meat', **Harina** or **Farinha** 'flour') or everyday objects (**Carro** 'cart', **Bote** 'bottle', **Cuchillo** 'knife'). Abstract concepts can supply characterization, too: **Paciencia** 'patience', **Alegría** 'happiness', **Maravilla** 'wonder', or **Verdades** 'truths'.

An especially popular means of caricaturing physical or mental characteristics is the transmitted comparison. Most common are parallels or metaphors drawn from the animal kingdom (**Lobo** 'wolf', **Burro** 'donkey', **Buey** 'ox', **Zorro** 'fox', **Porcel** 'pig', **Gallina** 'chicken', **Halcón** 'falcon', **Caracol** 'snail', **Lagarto** 'lizard', **Sardiña** 'sardine'). More expressive are phrases like **Cabeza de Vaca** 'cow's head', **Seisdedos** 'six fingers', **Pancaliente** 'hot bread', **Matatoros** 'kills bulls', **Manjavacas** 'cow eater', **Cura Vacas** 'tends cattle'.

Family names often allude to a typical activity or occupation. Such names are especially interesting from a social-historical point of view, because many are derived from occupations that have now all but vanished. In all European cultures 'smith' (Spanish **Herrero, Ferrero;** Catalan **Ferrer, Ferré, Farré;** Galician and Portuguese **Ferreiro**) is the most frequent occupational term, followed by 'miller' (Spanish **Molinero,** Catalan **Moliner** or **Moliné,** Portuguese **Moleiro**). Other common Iberian names of occupational origin come from terms meaning 'shoemaker' (Spanish **Zapatero,** Catalan **Sabater** or **Sabaté,** Portuguese **Sapateiro**), 'tailor' (Catalan and Spanish **Sastre,** Portuguese **Alfaiate**), and 'weaver' (Spanish **Tejedor,** Catalan **Teixidor** or **Teixidó,** Portuguese **Tecelão**).

Status names form a special group. In most cases, names such as **Abad** 'abbot', **Cura** 'priest', **Obispo** 'bishop', **Rey** 'king', **Duque** 'duke', **Conde** 'count', and **Hidalgo** 'nobleman' are to be understood as denoting a member of the household of such a person, a servant or retainer, rather than the family itself. In other cases, however, the same name may have arisen as a nickname.

Bibliography

Coromines, Joan, ed. (1989–97): *Onomasticon Cataloniae: Els noms delloc i noms de persona de totes les terres de llengua catalana.* Barcelona: Curial, Caixa d'Estalvis i Pensions de Barcelona, La Caixa.

Faure, Roberto, María Asunción Ribes, and Antonio García (2001): *Diccionario de apellidos españoles.* Madrid: Espasa Calpe.

Machado, José Pedro (1984): *Dicionário onomástico etmológico da língua portuguesa.* Lisboa: Editorial Confluência.

Michelena, Luis (1973): *Apellidos vascos.* San Sebastián.

Moll, Francesc de B. (1982): *Els llinatges catalans (Catalunya, País Vaelencià, Illes Balears).* Mallorca: Editorial Moll.

Tibón, Gutierre (1988, 1995): *Diccionario etimológico comparado de los apellidos españoles, hispanoamericanos y filipinos.* Mexico: Fondo de Cultura Económica

ITALIAN FAMILY NAMES

Enzo Caffarelli

History

The Romans used three-element names. The individual's *praenomen* 'first name' was used by intimates. The middle element, the *nomen* 'name' was for centuries the most important one, identifying the individual's family. Many common Italian personal names derive from the names of families (*gentes*) rather than from praenomina (Roman personal names)—for example, *Giulio* (Julius) and *Claudio* (Claudius) come from the names of the Roman families *Iulia* and *Claudia*. The third element, the *cognomen,* usually originated as an individual's nickname but was used to refer to him by non-intimates and (eventually) became hereditary; examples are the statesman *Cicero* 'chickpea', whose praenomen was *Marcus* and whose family name (*gens*) was *Tullius*, and the playwright *Plautus* 'flat-footed', whose other names were *Titus Macius*.

As the Roman era passed into the Christian era, a one-name system came into use, and this became the usual everyday system of identification throughout the Middle Ages, when any element that could be defined as a family name disappeared. Toward the end of the Middle Ages and during the Renaissance and modern eras, family names that gave rise to modern ones came into general use in Italy. To be considered true surnames, these must have three characteristics: they must show stable or semi-stable transmission from generation to generation; they must be unchangeable; and they must be nonsemantic, i.e. there is no correlation, unless entirely coincidental, between the name and the personal characteristics of the bearer.

In the Middle Ages, the prevailing method used to distinguish one person from another was to add the father's (or occasionally the mother's) name after a person's given name. In small communities, it was logical to distinguish one *Johannes* from another by calling one *Johannes Petri* 'of Peter', another *Johannes Martini* 'of Martin', and so forth. In larger communities, further distinctions developed: two persons with the same given name could also be distinguished by different geographic origin, by the work they did, by their physical appearance, or by some characteristic behavior that was noted in a nickname (which often substituted for a given name). Particularly in small or isolated communities, even today a nickname is often used in place of any other personal name in everyday discourse.

In later medieval documents, we find first names accompanied by a patronymic or a place of origin, expressed using a preposition or the corresponding ethnic adjective—for example **de Napoli** or **Napolitano**—or a word indicating a trade or a nickname. The process used to establish family names did not occur simultaneously in all Italian regions. This was due to their diverse historical, linguistic, and onomastic traditions and their different patterns of social class development (also commerce, craftsmanship, migration patterns, and so forth). Another factor was the widely varying practices of notaries, priests, and other officials charged with issuing documents such as land sales and purchases, marriage certificates, census records, loyalty oaths, and proscription lists. For example, in Venice, some second names were used in a way similar to modern family names even before the year 1000, and in Tuscany, in the very rich documentation we have for the 12th and 13th centuries, single names are rarer as compared to double names or more complex name sets. Conversely, in other regions or in more isolated, less socioculturally developed areas, designation by a hereditary modern family name is a much more recent development. It cannot really be said that all Italians had a true family name until about 150 years ago, after the establishment of civil registry offices in post-unification Italy.

The socioeconomic motivations that caused a family to pass on its surname from one generation to the next were complex, involving, among other factors, inheritance, business transactions, and social status. Whether these causes tended to be more social than economic is uncertain; probably it is not possible to separate the two factors completely. In different places at different times, bearing a family name became a social guarantee, a mark of excellence—nobility, political or economic power, etc.—and so family names came to be used to maintain the power of one's forebears, or to define legal inheritance.

Certainly, family names, or sets of names formed from several elements, initially tended to be used by the highest social classes. Only in later times were they adopted by the middle classes, and still later by the poorest and least educated. This change may have been driven by simple imitation, or by the necessity of differentiation, or in response to edicts from authorities. The last applied (in Italy, as elsewhere) to those members of Jewish communities who did not have family names but were required by the authorities to assume a family name.

Languages of Origin

From the linguistic point of view, each Italian family name can be traced to its etymological root and can be identified by its source language. The successive languages that formed the basis of Italian and contributed to its development, as well as the various dialects that were spoken over the course of the language's history, are reflected in its family names.

With some exceptions—the most important of which is the presence of borrowings from Hebrew for patronymics directly derived from Jewish names (and, more rarely, from appellations)—modern Italian given names refer both to Biblical personages and to aspects of Christian history and liturgy. Etymons (source words) include not only Latin words but also forms from other languages spoken in different parts of Italy at different times: Classical and Byzantine Greek, Germanic (mostly Longobardic and Frankish), Arabic, Catalan, Castilian Spanish, Norman French, early modern French, Albanian, and Slavic languages. Surviving colonies of other speech communities (Greek, Albanian, etc.) still exist in southern Italy, while in the north the border areas have in many places maintained their French, Provençal, German, or Slovene languages, or (even if now Italian-speaking) show the influence of these languages in their family names. Note, however, that the linguistic origin of a present-day family name is quite independent of the ethnic origin of the family's founders.

Categories of Names

Italian family names can be classified into five major categories:

patronymics, derived from the personal names of ancestors (mostly male);

names derived from nicknames, which may refer to someone's physical characteristics or behavior, or to particular events in the life of an individual;

local names, derived from geographic place names, landscape features, and ethnic or place-name adjectives;

occupational names, derived from names of trades or professions, administrative offices, and honorific titles;

invented or innovative names, used particularly for foundlings.

A significant number of Italian family names end in -i. In most cases these are reflexes of Latin genitive patronymics ('of X') that survived into the vernacular, as when *Johannes filius Martini* 'John son of Martin' became *Giovanni Martini*. In other cases, the -i originally indicated a family name in the plural, as in *Giovanni (dei) Martini* 'John of the Martins'. Related to this are names derived from the Latin ablative form ending in -is, such as **De Martinis**. In northern and central Italy, the plural forms are clearly prevalent (with the partial exception of the Piedmont and the Veneto), while in southern Italy, the singular is more prevalent. Where Tuscan, Lombard, and Emilian families are called **Rossi** (Piedmontese **Rosso**), Campania and Sicily have **Russo**. Corresponding to the forms **Ferrari, Bianchi, Bruni, Conti, Galli, Mancini, Lombardi,** and **Leoni,** typical of north and central Italy, the south has **Ferraro, Bianco, Bruno, Conte, Gallo, Mancino, Lombardo,** and **Leone.** Many other Italian family names end in -a, a typical female singular marker; in -n, resulting from dropping of the final vowel from -ino and other suffixes (principally in the Veneto); or in -s, which represents the plural in Sardinian and in "Latinized" notarial acts in other areas of Italy (particularly in Abruzzo and Lazio).

Moreover, markers typical of certain dialects characterize the suffixation of Italian family names. Name suffixes that indicate kinship or descent from a certain family can be specifically identified. An example of a regional name suffix is the typical Venetian ending -ato, which has been added not only to first names (**Bonato, Chinato, Francescato, Lorenzato, Marcato, Zanato**), but also to names that are metaphorical or metonymic in origin (**Cappellato, Lovato, Rossato**), occupational and status names (**Chieregato** 'cleric', **Facchinato** 'porter' or 'scribe'), ethnic names (**Ongarato** 'Hungarian'), and topographical names (**Roncato** 'terraced hillside').

Some suffixes are predominantly or exclusively ethnic markers: -ati, derived from the Italianization of the dialect suffix -at (standard Italian -ate), is used in topographic name suffixes typical of Lombardy and the Piedmont, such as **Casati, Galbiati, Gallarati, Malnati,** and **Vimercati;** -ese (variant -esi) is a pan-Italian suffix (**Abruzzese, Albanese, Calabrese, Genovese, Milanesi, Pugliese, Veronesi**), with the variants -ésio in Piedmont and Liguria (**Genovesio, Novaresio, Pavesio**), -ise in the south (**Campisi, Ferlisi, Puglisi, Scalise, Senise**), -igiàno (itself with variants -esano or -isano, -esàn or -isan) in the north, -iciàno or -isciàno in central Italy, -isano in the south (**Astigiano, Marchigiano, Marchesani, Muiesan, Parmigiani; Angrisano, Formisano, Palmisano, Taurisano**); -itàno (from Greek -ites + Latin -anus), in the south (**Amalfitano, Gancitano, Locritano, Melfitano,**

Napolitano, Riitano, Salernitano, Sciacchitano). The suffixes *-òto* and *-òta,* derived from Greek and neo-Greek *-òtes,* are typically found in the deep south of Italy (**Aliota, Candioto, Castriota, Liparota** and **Liparoti, Milioti**). Also of Greek origin are *-èo* or*-èi* (**Cotroneo, Cataneo, Raguseo, Romeo**) and *-ito* or *-iti* (**Messiniti, Palermiti, Catanzariti**).

Other suffixes indicate origin from a particular place, such as *-aco* and *-ago* in the north, particularly in Lombardy (from the Gallic-Latin toponymic suffix *-acum*). These are often pluralized with final *-i* (**Cambiaghi, Inzaghi, Luraghi**). The suffix *-ano,* which is pan-Italian, often marks personal or ethnic names (**Romano, Cassano, Marano, Napolitano, Pisano**). In historically Greek and neo-Greek areas, the equivalent term is *-anò* (**Germanò, Maranò, Romanò**). In addition, *-asco* continues the Ligurian-Latin suffix *-ascus* and is found mostly in the Piedmont, Liguria, and Lombardy. In the historically Lombard area, *-énga* and*-éngo* (**Mazzenga, Stramenga**) are of Germanic origin, while *-éto* is a suffix used mostly for family names derived from words denoting plants and trees (**Albareti, Carpaneti, Cerretti, Loreto, Roseto**).

Italian has numerous suffixes that can modify names (and generic nouns, too), to create nicknames, which may be either derogatory or complimentary. Their meanings in the Middle Ages, when these names arose, may have differed from their present-day meanings. That is, "nickname" surnames may simply be derived from the name of the head of a family to express both descent/kinship and individuality. A few of these suffixes are *-àcchio, -àcchia,* used principally in Calabria and Sicily (**Agostinacchio, Musacchia**); *-àccio, -àccio/a,* which is pan-Italian; *-acco,* found principally in Friuli; and *-acca* in south central Italy. Of Greek and neo-Greek origin are *-ace, -aci,* and *-achi,* which are typically found in Calabria (**Giannace, Ierace, Morace, Squillace**), Sicily (**Bombaci, Iraci, Nicolaci**), and in the Salento area (**Petrachi, Stefanachi**). Found throughout Italy is *-èllo/-èlla,* with regional variants *-èl, -èi* in the north, *-iéllo* in Campania and Basilicata, *-éddu* in southern Calabria, Sicily, and Sardinia, *-illo* and *-illa* in the south up to Lazio; *-étto* and *-etta,* pan-Italian, with variants *-ét* in the north and *-itto* in the south; *-icchio/a,* especially in the south; *-ino, -ina* and *-ini,* pan-Italian (with the variant *-in* in Veneto); also used with an ethnic adjectival meaning (**Piacentini, Tarantino, Trentin, Visentini**) and in names derived from trades and social conditions; *-òllo/-òlla* in northeastern Italy, in Apulia, and elsewhere in the south, with *-òddu/-òdda* in Sardinia. Although *-òlo/-òla* is pan-Italian, it sometimes also has an ethnic meaning (**Romagnoli, Spagnolo**); its northern variations are *-òl, -úl* (the latter is Friulian), and Tuscan *-uòlo,* southern *-uólo* and *-úlo; -òn, -ún* is pan-Italian.

The northern suffix *-aglia* (**Boscaglia, Chinaglia, Roncaglia**) is a collective suffix having both geographical and ethnic meanings. The suffix *-esco,* plural *-eschi* (corresponding to Latin *-iscus,* Germanic *-isch,* Greek *-iskos*) generally indicates membership of a particular family (**Brunelleschi, Marcheschi, Milaneschi, Simoneschi**). Of Venetian origin, based on a patronymic and having a generically derivative meaning, is *-esso* (**Carlesso, Giorgesso, Grandesso**).

Suffixes that are typical of occupational names are generally derived from Latin words ending in *-arius*. These terminate in *-ai(o)* in Tuscany (**Bagnai, Bottai, Massai**), in *-ario* (**Cravario, Molinario, Vaccario**) and *-ero* (**Cravero, Ferrero, Panero**) in Piedmont, in *-erio* in Lombardy, and in *-aro, -ari* in the rest of Italy (**Cavallari, Ferrari, Massaro, Molinari, Vaccari**). The suffix *-iere* (**Barbieri, Cavalieri, Palmieri**) is French in origin. Another agent suffix comes from Latin *-tor,* which creates nouns from verbs (**Cacciatori, Imperatore, Pescatore**).

Some frequent components of Germanic names over time were reduced to the role of simple suffixes, without any specific semantic value. These were applied to first names that later became family names. This was the case with *-ald* 'nobility' (**Ansaldo, Fuscaldo, Mengaldo**). In Lombardy this became *-oldo, -oldi* (**Gariboldi, Riboldi, Rimoldi**); in Piedmont and Sicily, the form was *-audo, -audi* (**Arnaudo, Baudo, Einaudi**). A similar process occurred with *-ardo, -ardi,* found principally in northern Italy (**Boccardo, Rizzardi, Zanardi**).

The articles and prepositions used in combination with other name elements often have a clear distribution. *Dal* is typically found in the Veneto-Friuli area; *Da* is from Trento and North Veneto. Names formed using *De* and *Di* are pan-Italian. Family names preceded by an article are decidedly southern, found especially in Campania, Puglia, and Sicily. Exclusive to Sicily is *li* (**Licalzi, Li Muli, Li Noce**). Family names that have *lo* or *la* preceding a patronymic (**Lo Mauro**), a trade name or office (**Lo Mastro, Lo Console**), or an ethnic or geographic name (**Lo Greco, Lo Tito**) are generally from Sicily or from Puglia.

Distribution and Frequency of Names

Finally, is there an answer to the question of why some family names are frequent, while others are rare? What made one Italian family name so much more popular than others? From our modern perspective, an obvious guess would be that the proliferation of the family—the number of their descendants—is a primary causal factor. In fact, this is only one of several factors in the patterns created by the interweaving of statistics, demographics, genealogy, medicine and life expectancy, social customs, economics, and the law. There are no quick answers. Generally speaking, however, there are a few factors that help to explain the reasons for the success of a family name. These, of course, often were interrelated.

Some family names originally had more than one motivation. *Rosso* 'red', from which the family name Rossi is derived, was undoubtedly a nickname bestowed on someone for the color of his hair or beard, of his skin, or of his clothing, but it may also have been the name of a political faction. In addition, *Rosso* was frequently used as a first name, independent of its lexical meaning.

Uncommon physical attributes certainly attracted attention in an age when political correctness was unknown, and inspired the creation of nicknames to differentiate as well as denigrate or satirize their owners. For example, a redhead (*rosso*) was rarer than a brunet or a blond, which explains its frequency as a nickname (there is no point in a nickname that fails to differentiate it bearer from the rest of the population). Similarly, the lame (*zoppi*), the deaf (*sordi*), or the mute (*muti*) were rarer than those who could walk, hear, or speak perfectly, so these were common nicknames. The left-handed (*mancini*) were less numerous than the right-handed. All of these nicknames gave rise to more or less common surnames.

Occupational names directly reflected the status and popularity of an occupation or trade. Thus, smiths (*fabbri, ferrai*) had a much higher place on the social scale than goatherds (*caprari*), shepherds (*pecorari*), or cowherds (*vaccari*). Thus, smiths were more inclined to assume and pass on their professional designations. Smiths were also much more numerous than those above them in the social hierarchy, such as notaries (*notari*) or clerics and clerks (*chierici*).

Family names that could be derived from multiple sources were more likely to become established. *Colombo* 'dove', for example, is a Christian first name, but it also has symbolic meaning: it may have been bestowed as a nickname on a peaceable person. *Gallo* 'rooster' also echoes the ethnic name for the Gauls (later, the French). *Leone* 'lion' is a Christian first name but also a nickname recalling the animal.

Family names are also derived from nicknames that were created in a specific place during a specific event (the details of which may no longer be known), then later expanded throughout the region and sometimes even farther. Of course, these are not as numerous as names that arose in several different places and at different times.

Family names derived from a word that was commonly used throughout Italy are, of course, much more common than dialectal forms restricted to a particular region. The vocabulary word *ferraro* 'smith', which was found in almost all Italian dialects, was more "national" than the synonym *fabbro*, or dialect forms *favaro* or *favero* in northeastern Italy, *frau* in Sardinia, and so on, and this is reflected in the comparative frequency of the derived surnames in Italy (though frequencies in America are affected by the different frequencies of the regions from which immigrants came). The nearly equivalent term *magnano* had a more limited distribution, almost exclusively Tuscan-Emilian. Another near-equivalent, *forgione*, was characteristic of an even smaller area, in Campania.

Although *Giovanni* 'John' was the most common male first name in Italy from the early Middle Ages until the end of the 18th century, family names derived from it are not among the top 150 names in frequency, partly because they have been fragmented into derivatives of dialect variants such as *Gianni, Zanni, Nanni, Ianni,* and *Vanni.*

A final, significant factor in determining the frequency of a family name, both in the past and today, relates to diverse demographic patterns and the populations of urban centers.

Over the past few decades, birth rates in the south of Italy have been significantly higher than those in central Italy, and higher still when compared with those in northern Italy. This is reflected both in the statistics for the many family names that are characterized as distinctly southern or northern Italian and in immigration patterns to the United States.

Italian Family Names in North America

Many of the very earliest European explorers of the Atlantic coasts of both North and South America were Italians. Christopher Columbus (Cristobal Colón in Spanish, Cristoforo Colombo in Italian), the most famous of the early European explorers, was a Genoese sailor employed by the court of Spain; his famous first voyage was made in 1492. The continent itself is probably named for Amerigo Vespucci (1451–1512), an Italian born in Florence, who made at least two major voyages of exploration (1499, 1502) along the coast of South America, from the mouths of the Amazon as far south as the coast of Patagonia, also working for the Spanish court. In 1524 Giovanni da Verrazzano, another Florentine, explored northward from the Carolina coast to Nova Scotia, entering what is now New York Harbor. John Cabot (Giovanni Caboto) was a Genoese sailor, commissioned by King Henry VII of England, who landed in present-day Newfoundland and Cape Breton Island. (The American surname **Cabot**, however, is derived from a Channel Islands family of southern French origin; the connection between the Genoese sailor and the Channel Islands surname has not been fully investigated.)

Italians were among the earliest settlers in North America: Italians are recorded in New Amsterdam (present-day New York City) as early as 1639. Groups of Italian Waldensians (Protestant refugees) came to New Amsterdam and the Delaware Valley in the 1650s. Henri de Tonti (Enrico di Tonti, 1649?–1704), an Italian from Gaeta, Italy, was an associate of the French explorer LaSalle; he set up a trading post at the mouth of the Arkansas River in 1686 and is sometimes referred to as the "Father of Arkansas."

Nevertheless, up to about 1890, Italian immigrants were rare compared with other European nationalities. There were, for example, no large and distinctive Italian communities with their own political administration. Such Italian immigrants as there were came mostly from central and northern Italy. All this changed in the 1890s. Driven by poverty, cheap transatlantic fares, and the hope of a better life in the United States, tens of thousands of Italian immigrants poured into the country, settling mostly in the cities rather than in the countryside. About 85% of Italian mass immigration to the United States after 1890 was from the southern regions of Italy and from Sicily. These new immigrants established their own culture and their own customs in tight-knit communities where the Italian language was the norm. As a result, the Italian linguistic form and pronunciation of surnames was preserved in the American context: for example, the final -e of surnames such as **Barone** was almost always given its full value. However, recently, Americanized pronunciations of such names have begun to be heard. Americanizing (English-language) influences, both in spelling and form, can be observed in names such as **Christiano** (Italian **Cristiano**), **De Francis** (Italian **De Francisci**), **De Frank** (Italian **De Franco**), and **De John** (Italian **Di Giovanni**). The Italian surname **Di Napoli** has been "translated" into English as **Naples**. Such variants are evidence for Italian American expressing, simultaneously, their Italian heritage and their (English-speaking) American identity. In other cases, all trace of the Italian original is lost: it is impossible to say how many people called **di Giovanni** now bear the American surname **John** or **Johnson**.

Bibliography

Caffarelli, Enzo (1999, 2000, 2001): *Cognomi italiani. Storia curiosità, significati, e classifiche: 1. I più diffusi a livello nazionale; 2. I più frequenti e tipici regione per regione; 3. I più diffusi e caratteristici in 400 comuni.* Turin: SEAT, Pagine Gialle.

Caracausi, Girolamo (1993): *Dizionario onomastico della Sicilia.* Palermo: Centro di Studi filologici e linguistici siciliani.

De Felice, Emidio (1978): *Dizionario dei cognomi italiani.* Milan: A. Mondadori.

De Felice, Emidio (1980): *I cognomi italiani. Rilevamenti quantitativi dagli elenchi telefonici: informazioni socioeconomiche e culturali, onomastiche e linguistiche.* Rome and Bologna: SEAT, Il Mulino.

Fucilla, Joseph C. (1949): *Our Italian Surnames.* Evanston, Ill.: Chandler.

Lurati, Ottavio (2000): *Perché ci chiamiamo così? Cognomi tra Lombardia, Piemonte e Svizzera italiana.* Lugano; Varese: Fondazione Ticino Nostro; Macchione.

Pittau, Massimo (1990): *I cognomi della Sardegna.* Sassari: Carlo Delfino Editore.

Rohlfs, Gerhard (1974): *Dizionario toponomastico e onomastico della Calabria: Prontuario filologico-geografico della Calabria.* Ravenna: Longo.

Rohlfs, Gerhard (1982): *Dizionario storico dei cognomi salentini.* Galatina: Congedo.

Rohlfs, Gerhard (1985): *Dizionario storico dei cognomi in Lucania: Repertorio onomastico e filologico.* Ravenna: Longo.

GREEK FAMILY NAMES

Nick Nicholas

History

In antiquity, free male Greeks were identified by a proper name, a patronymic, and sometimes by their tribe or native region. A free married woman was identified by the name of her husband rather than that of her father. For example, an Athenian man might be identified as Sokratés the son of Sophroniskos of the deme (district) of Alopéké, or an Athenian woman as Alkimaché wife of Kallimakhos of Anagyrous. The Roman practice of taking cognomens and surnames (*nomina*) did not catch on among Greek speakers during Classical times.

Hereditary surnames as we understand them today became common in Byzantium in the 10th century AD, slightly earlier than in most other parts of Europe. Initially, surnames were predominantly derived from places of habitation, nicknames, or occupations. Thus, the imperial family of the Komnenoi took its name from the city of Komné in Asia Minor, and that of the Laskares from a Persian word for 'warrior', ultimately of Arabic origin. The surname of the Palaiologoi is derived from the words *palaios* 'old' and *-logos* 'collector', and it probably meant not 'antiquarian' but 'garbage collector', although the first Palaiologos we know of was already governor of Thessalonika. This Palaiologos (the father of Emperor Michael VIII, 1259–82), had a triple surname typical of nobles of his time, eager to establish their aristocratic credentials: Andronikos Dukas Komnénos Palaiologos. Commoners made do with single surnames. Among Byzantine intellectuals, Michael Psellos' surname means 'stutterer', while Demetrios Kydonés's surname means 'quince'.

Christianity and Naming

In the first millennium AD, the Greek language was intimately connected with the rise of Christianity. Greek is the original language of the New Testament, and the Greek forms of names such as *Peter, Paul, Mark, Matthew, Luke, John,* and *Mary* have had far-reaching influence on naming practices throughout Europe and elsewhere: thousands of European surnames are derived from the Greek forms of the seven personal names just mentioned.

In many Christian cultures, it was obligatory to select the name of a newborn child from a fairly small inventory of saints' names approved by the church; these later became the foundation for a vast array of European patronymic surnames. Although some saints' names demonstrate continuity with the pagan past (e.g., *Isidore* 'gift of Isis', or *Theresa* 'hunting', originally associated with the goddess Artemis), most of them break with the past, being Semitic in origin, allusions to Christian history and legend (*Christopher*), or novel coinages (*Spyridon*). Differences among saints' cults account for the greater frequency in the Orthodox domain—Greece, Serbia, Bulgaria, Romania, and Russia—of surnames based on Greek *Demetrios, Theodoros, Konstantinos, Athanasios, Vasilios* (Basil), and so on, as well as Orthodox-specific cultic names such as *Stavros* from the Holy Cross, or *Panagiotis* from the Virgin Mary. In Greece itself, accordingly, these religious names are the foundation for a large number of surnames.

The Rise of Patronyms

The major change in Greek family names since Byzantine times has been a massive infusion of patronymic surnames. Many of these originated as late as the 19th century. In fact, patronymic suffixes were widely added to surnames of other origins, especially in the case of suffixes that were strongly associated with a particular region. It is often possible to tell from the patronymic suffix on a surname which region of Greece someone's male lineage is most likely to be from. There are two reasons for this. The first is that patronymic suffixes are usually diminutives, and these vary from dialect to dialect. The second is that patronymic suffixes were always subject to fashion and peer pressure, particularly after this was reinforced by the standardizing influence of universal education. For example, the archaic patronymic suffix *-idis* was adopted by Black Sea Greeks on resettling in Greece, ostensibly to replace the Turkish-sounding surnames some of them had; however, it was adopted even by Black Sea Greeks whose surnames did not end in Turkish *-oğlou,* and often by those whose surnames had no Turkish component at all. Perhaps the most extreme example is that of Crete, where the patronymic suffix *-akis* is found in the surnames of up to 95 percent of the population in some districts. Before the 19th century, this suffix was unknown in Crete, where typical surnames were either Italian, nickname-based, or occupational, or used other patronymic suffixes. The ending *-akis* swept through Crete uniformly, forming **Linardakis** from *Linardos* 'Leonard', **Lykakis** from *Lykos* 'wolf', **Mastorakis** from *Mastoras* 'craftsman', and **Hatzidakis** of *Hatzi-Harkias* 'smith the pilgrim'.

This pervasive change in surnaming practices was accelerated by the fact that education in the Greek language became widely available in the early 19th century. Surname changes were often the prerogative of the child's schoolmaster, rather than of the parents. Similar distinctive regional suffixes are *-idis/-adis* (Asia Minor), *-antis* (Black Sea), *-atos* (Cephallonia, Ithaca), *-eas, -akos* (Mani), *-elis* (Lesbos), *-oudis* (Macedonia, Thrace, Aegean islands), *-ousis* (Chios), *-oglou* (Asia Minor), *-opoulos* (Peloponnese), and genitive or possessive forms (typically *-ou,* as in Cyprus).

Greek Names from Other Languages

The various ethnicities that have contributed to the present-day population of Greece have had a considerable effect on the development of modern Greek surnames. An extensive presence of Italian surnames resulted from the long rule of parts of the Greek-speaking world by Venetians, from the 13th century to the 17th or 18th. The Venetian domain included Crete, much of the Aegean (the remainder being held by other Italian states), the Ionian Islands, and coastal cities in the Peloponnese. Not only did contact with the Venetians result in the borrowing of Italian words into local vocabularies; in addition, many Greek communities—particularly in Crete and the Cyclades became the homes of Italian families that were assimilated into the indigenous population, although they retained their Italian surnames. Common Greek surnames of Italian origin include **Typaldos, Zevgolis, Vitalis, Dandolos,** and **Negrepontis.**

The French-speaking Crusaders held dominion over the Greek-speaking Peloponnese and Cyprus for a shorter period in the 13th to 15th centuries and had a relatively minor influence on Greek surnames. Examples are **Loizos** and **Stinis.**

The Turkish contribution to Greek surnames is extensive, especially in providing vocabulary words on which surnames were based. Ottoman Turkish, with its significant Arabic and Persian components, had a serious impact on the vocabulary of Greek in general, once Greek-speaking lands passed from the Byzantine Empire or the Italian maritime states to the Ottoman Empire; this transfer took place from the 14th century to the 17th and remained in effect until the 19th to early 20th century. In effect, the Ottoman Empire became the successor state to Byzantium, governing not only the bulk of the Greek-speaking world (including the western and northern coasts of Asia Minor), but also the rest of the Balkans. The barrier of religion and political power inhibited assimilation of the Turkish population among Greeks, although the reverse—Greek clans adopting Islam and thenceforth being considered Turks—was not uncommon, especially in Crete. This means that Muslim proper names are not a significant source of Greek surnames, but Turkish vocabulary words are, whether as occupational terms (e.g. **Kavafis** 'cobbler', **Kazandzis/Kazantzakis** 'cauldronmaker') or nicknames (particularly the productive prefixes *Kara-* 'black, dark, moody', *Hatzi-* 'pilgrim', and *Deli-* 'crazy'). In Asia Minor, the much greater proportion of Turks meant that many formerly Greek-speaking Christians ended up speaking Turkish, particularly in hinterlands like Cappadocia; even if they did not, their surnames were often unmistakably Turkish in form, particularly in using the Turkish patronymic suffix *-oğlou (-oğlu)*.

Other non-Greek contributions to Greek surnames come from three populations who have a long history of cohabitation with ethnic Greeks. There is a slight presence of Slavic surnames among Greeks, particularly in Greek Macedonia. The main contributions from ethnic minorities come from the Arvanites and the Vlachs. The Arvanites are the descendants of Albanians who settled in central Greece from the 14th century onward (see the entry for **Arvanitis**). The Vlachs or Aromanians are a traditionally nomadic people living throughout the southern Balkans and speaking a language related to Romanian (see the entry for **Vlachos**). Both populations have been assimilated in language and ethnic consciousness to Greece, but in many cases they retain their non-Hellenic surnames.

The Formation of Modern Greek Surnames

There has long been extensive pressure in Greece for people to Hellenize their names in order to conform to the Greek ideal of nation-building; this pressure was strongly felt in particular by the refugees from Asia Minor, who Hellenized their surnames even when they were not conspiciously Turkish-sounding, as mentioned above. Hellenization as a conscious strategy also means that the morphology of Greek surnames—the components and the way they are combined—is almost always archaic, since that is the form recorded by Greek state institutions, which were long opposed to the use of the vernacular, advocating instead the use of Katharevousa, an artificial language modeled on Classical Greek. For example, surnames based on *George* usually have forms such as **Georgiou**, although that is the archaic genitive, and the modern proper name has the genitive form **Giorgou**. The same holds for **Ioannou** versus *Gianni* (pronounced *Yanni),* and **Dimitriou** versus *Dimitri.*

Another distinctive feature of Greek surnames, which contributes to their legendary length, is the fact that compounding is a highly productive process in this language. This can take several forms. In colloquial use, a man's surname frequently was prefixed to his proper name in order to distinguish him from other bearers of the same name; for example, **Raptomanolis** '*Emmanuel* (Manolis) son of *Raptis* (tailor)'. This compound name could in turn give rise to a patronymic (**Raptomanolakis**).

Alternatively, people might be distinguished by adding descriptive prefixes to their surnames. The most frequent of these are the status indicators *papa-,* indicating a priest (priests being allowed to marry and have offspring in the Greek Orthodox Church), and *hatzi-,* indicating one who had made a pilgrimage to the Holy Land. A third common prefix is the Turkish pejorative *kara-* 'black', hence 'moody' or 'dark'. (See the entries for **Papas, Hatzis,** and **Karas.)** Thus, although a ten-syllable surname like **Papahatzidimitrakopoulos** is a humorous exaggeration, it is not all that far from what actually occurs, and it is easily analyzed: 'son of Father *Little Dimitris,* a pilgrim from the Peloponnese'.

Greek Names Abroad

Such prodigiously long surnames—even when they may have seemed quite straightforward to Greek-speakers—proved undesirable when Greeks began migrating to the United States in the early 20th century. As a result, these Greek migrants tended to abbreviate and/or Anglicize (or rather, Americanize) their surnames on arrival. Anglicization has been less common in Canada and Australia, where Greek immigration took place mostly after World War II.

It is sometimes assumed that American migrants' surnames were mangled by immigration authorities at Ellis Island; it seems, however, that the initiative to make their surnames more manageable in an English-speaking culture was that of the migrants themselves. One result of this is the frequency of the Greek-American surnames **Papas, Hatzis,** and **Karas.** These are, in fact, almost unknown in Greece, since they are properly prefixes rather than independent surnames: identifying someone's father as a priest, pilgrim, or moody would not have narrowed things down sufficiently. These names, therefore, mark the bearer immediately as a Greek-American rather than an indigenous Greek. Other modifications involve the reduction of inflectional endings (e.g., *Karahalios* to **Karahal),** the severance of patronymic suffixes (*Athanasopoulos* to **Athanas** and even **Athan),** and the adoption of similar-sounding English surnames (*Anagnostopoulos* to **Agnew,** *Iliopoulos* to **Lewison,** or *Anastasiou* to **Stanley**).

Outside the Greek-speaking world and recent migrant populations, there are two other major domains in which Greek surnames are found. The first reflects humanistic revivals of classical names as surnames, which were particularly popular in the Netherlands, northern Germany, and Scandinavia (e.g., **Achilles, Alpha,** and the many Scandinavian surnames ending in *-ander*). The other is southern Italy and Sicily, a region colonized by Greeks in antiquity to the extent that it came to be known in Latin as Magna Graecia 'Greater Greece'. When it came under Byzantine dominion in the sixth century, the Greek presence in the region was reinforced, and Greek remained in common use after the 11th century, when Byzantine dominion was extinguished. Today, Greek is spoken only in two rapidly shrinking enclaves in Salento and Calabria, but it made a major contribution to the Romance dialects of the region and is entrenched in the region's surnames. Some Italian vocabulary words—for example, *scarpa* 'shoe'—appear as surnames with Greek diminutive endings (**Scarpace**), and some habitational names display Greek rather than Italian derivational morphology (e.g., **Messineo** from *Messina*). Greek thus joins Norman French, Arabic (including Maltese), and Albanian as a source language for Sicilian and other southern Italian surnames, alongside Italian.

Bibliography
Caracausi, G. (1990): *Lessico Greco della Sicilia e dell'Italia Meridionale. (Lessici Siciliani 6.)* Palermo, Sicily: Centro di Studi Filologici e Linguistici Siciliani.
Karanastasis, A. (1984–92): *Historikon Lexikon tōn Hellēnikōn Idiomatōn tēs Katō Italias.* 5 vols. Athens: Academy of Athens.
Triandafyllidis, Manolis (1981): *Ta Oikogeneiaka-mas Onomata.* Thessalonika: Aristotle University, Institute of Modern Greek Studies.

JEWISH FAMILY NAMES

Alexander Beider

From the Middle Ages up until modern times, there have been three main Jewish diaspora groups: Ashkenazic Jews (whose ancestors are mainly believed to have lived in the German-speaking provinces of Europe), Sephardic Jews (those from the Iberian Peninsula and their descendants), and Oriental Jews (living in the Middle East, Byzantium, Persia, and the Caucasus). The North American Jewish community is largely Ashkenazic. Sephardic names have appeared in the United States only since the 1970s, with the arrival of Israeli Jews. Oriental Jewish names are marginal in North America.

Ashkenazic Names

Before the end of the eighteenth century, most Ashkenazic Jews did not have hereditary family names. In Hebrew documents, individuals were generally called after their proper given name and that of their father: *X ben Y* 'X, son of Y' or *X bat Y* 'X, daughter of Y'. This pattern was not specific to this group: for more than two thousand years, it was traditional for Jews of various origins. In German documents, the principal pattern was *X Y*, meaning 'X, son of Y'; examples are **Simon Abraham** 'Simon, the son of Abraham', **Marcus Nathan**, and **Moses Israel**. In Christian sources, Jews living in Poland were generally referred to either by their given name or by their given name plus a patronymic formed by adding the suffix *-owicz* to the given name of their father.

In Hebrew sources of that period from all European countries, we often find additional names that indicated either descent from the Jewish priestly caste (Kohanim) or Levite origin. Among the expressions that label the Kohanim (that is, the descendants of the biblical Aaron, the brother of Moses), most common are *ha-Kohen* and the acronym *KTz*, which is the abbreviation of Kohen Tzedek, priest of righteousness. Levite origin (corresponding to the descendants of the biblical Levi, one of Jacob's sons) is conveyed by such Hebrew expressions as *ha-Levi* (Levite) as well as the acronym *SGL*, the abbreviation of *SeGan Leviya*, associate of the Levitic order. When in the beginning of the nineteenth century most Ashkenazic Jews were forced to take surnames, these origins were bases for the very common surnames **Kohen, Kohn, Cohn, Kahn, Kon, Kogan,** and **Kagan** (the two last forms are typically Russian, since that language has no equivalent for /h/ and regularly replaces it with the letter *g*). The Levite origin is often expressed by the names **Levi, Levy, Loewy, Lev,** and **Levin**; the latter two are typical for the Russian Empire. The abbreviations *KTz* and *SGL* gave rise to the common surnames **Katz and Segal**, respectively.

There were exceptions with regard to surnames, however; in some places in Europe, Jews regularly adopted them in the 16th through the 18th centuries, several hundred years before Ashkenazic Jews generally were forced to adopt them. Perhaps the most representative of these areas was the Jewish community of Prague, the capital of Bohemia. Almost one-half of the names used there were habitational, derived from various place names, mainly in central Europe. Examples are **Brandeis, Goitein, Eibenschütz, Kisch, Politzer, Taussig,** and **Töplitz.** Patronymics (**Karpeles, Muneles, Schmelkes**) and metronymics (**Bassewi, Jeitelis, Porges**) were also used. Frankfurt was another exception. In that city, two categories encompassed almost the totality of local appellations. As in Prague, the habitational names were quite common. Among the examples are **Bing, Deutz, Emmerich, Flörsheim, Oppenheim(er), Poppart** or **Boppard,** and **Wertheim(er).** The second popular category was specific to Frankfurt. It consisted of names derived from house signs: **Adler** 'eagle', **Birnbaum** 'pear tree', **Grünhut** 'green hat', **Haas** 'hare', **Papagei** 'parrot', **Rindskopf** 'cow's head', **Rothschild** 'red sign', **Schiff** 'ship', and **Strauss** 'ostrich'. However, because there was no legal requirement for Jewish surnames, they were not necessarily inherited by children.

In eastern Europe, in the Polish-Lithuanian Commonwealth, surnames were lacking almost totally. The only exceptions represented some rabbinical families. Among the most famous are **Auerbach, Bachrach, Cheifetz, Eiger, Epstein, Ettingen** or **Ettinger, Frenkel, Ginzburg, Halpern, Heller, Horowitz, Jaffe** or **Joffe, Katzenellenbogen, Landau, Lifschitz, Luria, Margolies, Rappaport, Schorr,** and **Spira** or **Shapiro**. All of them originated in western or central Europe.

The great majority of European Ashkenazic Jews took their surnames during the period that lasted from the end of the 18th century to the middle of the 19th century. In all countries, special laws required the adoption of hereditary names. The first legislation of this kind was promulgated in 1787 by the Austrian emperor Joseph II. At that time, the Hapsburg Empire encompassed not only Austria proper, Hungary, and Bohemia-Moravia, but also—as a result of the first partition of Poland (1772)—the area of southeastern Poland called Galicia. In that province (in which the largest part of the Jewish population of the empire was concentrated) commissions were created for the assignment of surnames for local Jews.

Special instructions regulated the work of these commissions. First, they were to prevent adoption by Jews of common German surnames; thus, the priority was for selection of unusual names. Second, each family within the same locality was to receive a different surname. Jews were free to choose their own names, subject to approval of Austrian officials. If a Jew had not chosen a name himself, one was assigned to him. This was often the case, since many were fearful that the main aim of this process was a census of the Jewish population, which would then be used to determine taxes, enforce military service, and so on. In these cases, the choice of name was subject only to the assigning official's imagination. The fact that the newly adopted surnames had to be approved by the government commissions, in addition to the commissions' power to assign names, gave commission members the opportunity to extort money from local Jews. Bribes could facilitate favorable decisions, and bribery undoubtedly played a role in the adoption of surnames in Galicia.

Several popular legends arose about this practice. According to one, commissioners divided the surnames into categories, requiring larger bribes for those derived from the names of flowers or precious stones (**Rosenthal, Goldstein**) and smaller bribes for surnames drawn from ordinary metals: **Eisen** 'iron' and **Stahl** 'steel'. Free of charge were surnames derived from the names of animals; derogatory surnames were assigned simply to spite their bearers. A detailed study of names adopted in Galicia clearly shows that this story is not based on fact: such categories of names could not have existed in reality.

The number of derogatory names assigned in the province was relatively small. Almost all names were based on German vocabulary. One can distinguish several types. Numerous were names derived from adjectives or common nouns corresponding to personal characteristics: **Bart** 'beard', **Braun** 'brown', **Schwarz** 'black', **Weiss** 'white', **Roth** 'red', **Hellmann** 'light man', **Gross** 'big', **Klein** 'small', **Lang** 'long', **Reich** 'rich', **Jung** 'young', **Ehrlich** 'honest', **Ernst** 'serious'. A large number of names were occupational: **Arzt** 'medical doctor', **Bäcker** 'baker', **Brenner** 'distiller', **Färber** 'dyer', **Fleischer** and **Metzger** 'butcher', **Schneider** 'tailor', **Schnitzer** 'wood carver', **Schreiber** 'scribe'.

The most populous category of names, however, were words taken from the German lexicon that were seemingly unrelated to the personal characteristics of their first bearers. Among them are words designating flora and fauna, metals and stones, natural phenomena, food and household utensils, words associated with the calendar (days of the week, months), and coins. Various terms have been used in onomastic studies to designate these names: arbitrary, ornamental, and artificial. The first is a poor designation, since even if no relationship exists between a name and the characteristics of its bearer, the name is unlikely to have been the result of a completely random decision; some motivation prompted its adoption. The second term, ornamental, is better. Indeed, in many names of that group one can distinguish an unmistakable flourish: the names are drawn from words that have positive associations. However, this is not always the case. In some names, the meaning is neutral, and the fact that derogatory names exist as well makes ornamental a questionable designation. The term artificial thus appears to be the most appropriate.

A large number of artificial names are compound, composed of two roots. The first of these roots generally comes from one of the following series:

precious metals and gems, yielding names such as **Gold** 'gold', **Perl** 'pearl', and **Silber** 'silver';

adjectives designating beauty, giving **Fein** 'fine,' 'excellent' and **Schön** 'beautiful';

adjectives designating colors: **Braun** and **Bron** 'brown', **Gelb** and **Gel** 'yellow', 'light', **Grün** or **Grin** 'green', **Licht** 'light', **Rot** or **Roth** 'red', **Schwarz** or **Schwartz** 'black', **Weiss** 'white';

flora of some type: **Birn** 'pear', **Apfel** 'apple', **Mandel** 'almond', **Rose** 'rose', **Blum** 'flower', **Wein** 'vine';

food: **Korn** 'seed', **Zucker** 'sugar', **Wein** 'wine', **Weiz** 'wheat', **Salz** 'salt';

words related to the heavens: **Himmel** 'heaven', 'sky', **Licht** 'light', **Stern** 'star';

minerals: **Eisen** 'iron', **Kupfer** 'copper';

words designating size: **Klein** 'small', **Gross** 'big'.

Principal second parts in compound surnames come from one of the following two groups:

topographic terms such as *berg* 'mountain,' 'hill', *feld* 'field', *stein* 'stone';

words related to plants: *baum* 'tree'; *blatt* 'leaf'; *blum* 'flower'; *garten* 'garden'; *holz* 'wood'; *zweig* 'branch'.

Name analysis shows that compound surnames existed but were not numerous in the areas where surnames were assigned immediately after the law of 1787. It is reasonable to assume that the Christian officials or the Jewish authorities realized the advantage of creating compound surnames. That pattern allowed numerous names to be constructed from only a few roots. The method was applied on a larger scale in the areas that were annexed by Austria after the third partition of Poland (1795). These new territories included the cities of Kraków, Lublin, Radom, and Kielce. The surnaming took place there during 1805–09.

In the Polish provinces annexed by Prussia in 1795 (covering the Warsaw area), many names were assigned by Prussian clerks after the special law promulgated in 1797. Here, almost all names were also drawn from German vocabulary. However, during the Napoleonic wars, the areas incorporated by both Austria and Prussia after the third partition of Poland became parts of the independent Polish state, and the surnaming process was stopped. After the defeat of Napoleon, these regions were mainly integrated within the Kingdom of Poland, which became a part of the Russian Empire. In 1821 a special law obliged Jews of the kingdom to take hereditary family names. For many people, the appellations assigned previously by Austrian and Prussian officials were restituted. For others, Polish clerks assigned new names that were mainly drawn from Polish vocabulary. Numerous names were artificially constructed from Polish names of birds, fish, animals, and plants. Others designated personal characteristics or occupations. In northeastern Poland, numerous habitational names ending in the standard Polish adjective suffix -ski were chosen. In western and central parts of the country, numerous patronymic names appeared. Examples are **Abramowicz, Jakubowicz, Herszlikowicz,** and **Lewkowicz.** Thus, due to the specific historical circumstances, the names of Jews from the Kingdom of Poland were based either on German or on Polish vocabulary.

In the areas that were annexed by the Russian Empire from Poland in 1772–95—roughly corresponding to modern Belarus, Ukraine (except for the southwestern region that was part of Austrian Galicia), and Lithuania—the situation was different. In that region, also called the Pale of Settlement, the law requiring Jews to acquire family names was promulgated in 1804. During the four following decades, all Jews received surnames. The authorities of the Jewish community (Kahal) were responsible for implementing the surnaming process in Russia, so Russian Jews assumed family names within their own communities. Since there were no regulations concerning the selection of surnames, it seems quite possible that many surnames were chosen by those who bore them. There are many examples, however, in which this appears not to be the case. Instead there was an obvious methodology for constructing a series of surnames. For instance, in several districts of eastern Belarus, about one-third of the surnames were metronymics ending in the suffix -*in*. In northern Ukraine, about one-half of all Jewish inhabitants had surnames that ended in -*man*. Most likely, these names were invented by the Kahal authorities, who used the same patterns in order to create many names during a short period.

The adoption of surnames within the Jewish community reflected linguistic differences. Numerous appellations were created in Yiddish, which was the language spoken by Jews within the Pale of Settlement. There were important regional peculiarities, but there was no single region in which standard Yiddish, the Yiddish of dictionaries and vocabularies, was spoken. The two principal dialects of Yiddish used by Jews in the Russian Empire are designated Southeastern Yiddish (SEY, also called Ukrainian Yiddish) and Northeastern Yiddish (NEY, also called Lithuanian Yiddish). Pronunciation represented the difference between the dialects. To /u/, /o/, and /ey/ of NEY corresponded /i/, /u/, and /oy/ in SEY, respectively. Thus, the surnames **Kuperman, Nodel,** and **Reytman** could be found in NEY territory, while **Kiperman, Nudel,** and **Roytman** were from the SEY region; these can be compared with the German **Kupfermann, Nadel,** and **Rotmann.** The territories in which these differences are found are difficult to specify precisely, but in reference to these vowel alternations, use of the NEY vowels corresponds roughly to Lithuania and Belarus, while the SEY vowels were found in Ukraine and Bessarabia (now Moldova).

Hebrew was also used to create many surnames. Among the Hebrew appellations one can distinguish occupational names (**Sandler** 'shoemaker'; **Chait** or **Khayet** 'tailor'), various artificial forms that correspond to direct quotes from the biblical text (including personal and place names), and numerous acronyms. The latter were mainly created after two patterns: (1) names drawn from the abbreviation of the expressions *Ben Rabbi X* 'son of rabbi *X*,' where *X* can be a single given name, double given name, or single given name to which a nickname

is added); and (2) *Chatan Rabbi X* 'son-in-law of rabbi *X*'. The most numerous names from that category were created in Volhynia (western Ukraine). Examples are **Barak, Barash, Barats, Baraz, Barmak, Charab, Charal, Chari,** and **Charpash**. A large number of names are drawn from Ukrainian and Belorussian words. Often these names were immediately Russified, since Russian was the official language of the empire. In Bessarabia, annexed by Russia in 1812, some names were constructed from Romanian words. Within the Pale of Settlement, German was mainly used to construct artificial compound names such as **Blumenthal, Goldberg, Perelstein, Rosenbaum, Rosenblatt,** and **Silberstein.** However, in Courland (now within Latvia) numerous patronymic and occupational names were based on German, the official language of that province until the end of the nineteenth century.

The surnames adopted in the Russian Empire were of several types. Most were habitational names created from the place names of the Pale of Settlement. They were quite numerous in the Kiev (Ukraine) and Grodno (western Belarus) areas, where they ended mainly in the Slavic suffix -*ski*. In the Mogilev area (eastern Belarus) and in Volhynia and Podolia (both in the Ukraine), many names ended in the Yiddish suffix -*er*. In western Lithuania, numerous names were created after the local place names without any suffix. Patronymics were common in central Belarus. They were generally constructed by using the eastern Slavic suffixes -*ovich* or -*evich* and -*ov* or -*ev*. Metronymics were extremely common in eastern Belarus. Here they terminated in the eastern Slavic possessive suffix -*in*: **Chanin, Dvorkin, Malkin, Shifrin, Zeitlin.** Occupational names and appellations derived from personal characteristics were often created in Ukraine. They were based on Yiddish and Ukrainian words. Artificial surnames were especially common in Volhynia and Podolia.

The ukase of 1804 in Russia preceded corresponding laws in many other regions of Europe: Frankfurt-am-Main (1807), France (July 20, 1808), Baden (1809), Westphalia (1812), Prussia (March 11, 1812), Bavaria (1813), Württemberg (1828), Poznan (1833), and Saxony (1834). In all these German-speaking provinces, as well as in French Alsace and Lorraine, the Jewish population used either German or Yiddish in the vernacular. Almost all new names were German. Among the most popular categories were family names directly drawn from masculine given names (**Abraham, Hirsch, Isaac, Jacob, Joseph, Nathan, Simon, Wolf**) and habitational names (**Bamberger, Feuchtwanger, Hamburg, Hildesheimer, Horkheimer, Landauer**).

Jews from Hungary first adopted surnames at the end of the 18th century following the general law that concerned all Jews who lived in the Hapsburg Empire. Similarly to all the other provinces, these names were mainly based on German vocabulary. However, beginning in the middle of the 19th century, as a result of the Hungarian nationalist movement, some local Jews changed their names using appellations based on the Hungarian vocabulary. Among these "Magyarized" names we find **Kovacs** 'smith', **Meszaros** 'butcher', **Polgar** 'craftsman',

Szabo 'tailor', **Varga** 'shoemaker', **Nemes** 'noble', **Fekete** 'black', **Nagy** 'big', **Kelete** 'oriental', **Farkas** 'wolf'). Other names are habitational and include **Hevesi, Munkacsy, Papai,** and **Szigeti.**

Sephardic Surnames

The names used by Sephardic Jews can be divided into several groups. The first were adopted in the Iberian Peninsula, before the expulsions that occurred during the 1490s. Many names of this category are habitational, mainly derived from Spanish or Portuguese place names. Among them are **Aguilar, Almeida, Belmonte, Castro, Carvallo, Cordova, Dacosta, Franco, Herrera,** and **Spinoza. Segre** comes from the river name in Spain. Certain names from the above list belonged to the Marranos, that is, Jews who were forced to convert to Catholicism but continued to practice Judaism in secret. Representatives of these families regularly emigrated from Spain or Portugal beginning in the 15th century. Their main destinations were the Ottoman Empire and the city of Amsterdam. This group of Sephardic Jews bore typical Spanish or Portuguese surnames; for example **Azevedo, Calderon, Cardoso, Fernandes, Fonseca, Gomes, Hernandez, Lopes, Mendes, Nunes, Pereira,** and **Peres.** Another group of Sephardic surnames was adopted in Arab countries; names in this group are based on Arabic. Among them are **Abbas, Abulafio, Alfandari, Attar, Camhi, Habib, Haddad, Hassan,** and **Hasson.** A series of Sephardic names of Turkic origin were assigned in the Ottoman Empire: **Aslan** 'lion', also a Jewish given name, **Hanci** 'innkeeper', **Karakas** 'black-eyebrowed', **Kucuk** 'small'.

Jews from Italy are of heterogeneous origins. Those from the northern part of the country mainly descended from Ashkenazic Jews who migrated to that area beginning in the thirteenth century. Several common names such as **Luzzato** (most likely, 'from Lausitz'), **Morpurgo** 'from Marburg', and **Ottolenghi** 'from Ettlingen' designate this, as well as the name **Tedesco** 'German'. Many Sephardic Jews appeared in Italy during the 15th and 16th centuries. Finally, a group of local Jews had their roots in the Apennine Peninsula. Numerous names of Italian Jews are habitational, derived from local place names: **Ascoli, Castelnuovo, Cremona, Dancona, Fano, Lucca, Meldola, Modiano, Modigliani, Montefiore, Pontecorvo, Ravenna, Redgio,** and **Volterra.**

Jewish Immigrants in North America

In North America, Jewish immigration became significant between 1850 and 1870. At that time, Jewish immigrants were mainly from Prussia, with a large percentage coming from the province of Poznan, which had been annexed from Poland.

However, it was during the 1880s that the number of immigrants grew dramatically. This new influx was due to the pogroms in Russia that followed the murder of Tsar Alexander II by Russian revolutionaries. From that time until the 1920s, of the total number of Jewish newcomers to the United States, the percentage of Russian Jews was large: from 50 to 70 percent between the end of the 1880s and 1903; and from 70 to 80 percent after 1904. The increase after 1904 was due to a second series of pogroms that corresponded to three years of political instability in Russia from 1905 to 1907.

Emigration from the various provinces of the Russian Empire was not uniform. Numerous Jews emigrated from Ukraine and Bessarabia, the main area affected by the pogroms. Those from the Lithuanian and Belorussian provinces, significantly less affected by the pogroms, were motivated primarily by economic difficulties. The migration of Jews from the Polish provinces annexed by Russia (the Kingdom of Poland) was relatively small. Only the northeastern and eastern parts of that area (Suwałki, Łomża, and Siedlce provinces) provided a considerable number of immigrants. Since the last decade of the 19th century, the second important source of Jewish migration was the Austro-Hungarian Empire. Many immigrants were Jews from Galicia. Taken together, immigrants from Russia and Austria-Hungary made up more than 90 percent of the total number of Jewish immigrants to the United States during the most important period of Jewish immigration, from the 1880s to the 1920s. As a result, the majority of American Jews are Ashkenazic and, more precisely, have their roots in eastern Europe.

Before around 1930, there was a tendency to Americanize names; indeed, numerous names of Jewish European immigrants were changed in the United States. It is popularly believed that names were changed at Ellis Island by U.S. immigration officials—this is a myth. No names were changed by immigration officials. Immigrant name changes were self-imposed, as part of the gradual assimilation process into American society. Several common patterns can be discerned.

anglicizing (phonetic adaptation to English): *Czapnik* to **Chapman**; *Gershovich* to **Gershvin**; *Herszkowicz* and *Herschensohn* to **Harris**; *Kaplan* to **Kopland**; *Rabinowitz* to **Robbins**; *Segal* to **Seagull**; *Trotzky* to **Trevor**; *Wein* to **Wyne**.

truncation (sometimes with concomitant anglicization): *Blatyta* to **Blatt**; *Blumenfeld* to **Fields**; *Davidovich* to **Davidsohn** and *Davimes* to **Davis**; *Goldstein* to **Gold**; *Kabachnik* to **Cabot**; *Koenigfest* to **Koenig**; *Rotkovich* to **Rothko**; *Skidelski* to **Skydell**.

translation to English: *Gruenfeld* to **Greenfield**; *Kleinstein* to **Littlestone**; *Kuznets* to **Smith**; *Silberman(n)* to **Silverman**.

A general tendency was to reject endings that represented typical Slavic suffixes, such as *-owski* or *-ovsky, -owicz* or *-ovich, -ov* or *-ev, -nik* or *-ets.* Numerous names were not Anglicized but Germanized. For example, instead of the original suffix *-owicz* or *-ovich,* the German element *-owitz* was used (**Rabinowitz, Berkowitz, Abramowitz**). Various names of Yiddish origin were replaced by their German counterparts: *Epelboim* became **Apfelbaum;** *Royzenbarg* became **Rosenberg;** *Roitman* became **Rothman;** *Kuperman* became **Kupferman**.

In other cases, Jews chose new names that had nothing in common with their older names. Curiously, among them one finds many names that do not sound English at all, but rather are common Jewish names of German or Hebrew origin. Examples are **Cohen, Friedman, Goldman, Grinberg, Rosenthal, Schwarz,** and **Silberstein.** The reason for such a choice is unknown: the name might have been the surname of a cousin or neighbor, or perhaps it simply appealed to the person adopting it.

In the 1930s name changes became significantly less common. During that period, most Jewish immigrants came from Nazi Germany. The influx of Jews stabilized during the following decades. It was at the beginning of the 1970s that Jewish immigration again increased significantly, due to the arrival of numerous Jews from the Soviet Union. In 1979 Soviet authorities put a halt to immigration. Owing to political changes in the Soviet Union beginning in about 1988, immigration was reestablished. After the collapse of the Soviet Union, several hundred thousand Jews came to the United States from Russia, Ukraine, and Belarus. With respect to family names, it is often not difficult to tell these newcomers from those who had been established in America for several generations, though both groups mainly originated in the same eastern European areas. Those who came in the late 20th century typically arrived with passports using Latin characters; names of the émigrés had already been transliterated from Russian to English by Russian clerks. This was not the case in 1881–1920, when immigration documents used only Cyrillic spelling. The change to the Roman alphabet was done either in the United States or in the European ports (Hamburg, Antwerp) from which passage was begun to North America. Thus, if one encounters the name **Rothstein,** with Russian roots, one is likely to be dealing with a descendant of someone who came to the United States in 1881–1920, while the names **Rotshteyn** or **Rotshtein** typically belong to immigrants who came later. A similar relationship characterizes the pairs **Silberman** and **Zilberman, Weinberg** and **Vaynberg** (or **Vainberg**), **Wiener** and **Viner, Schwarz** and **Shvarts, Cohen** and **Kogan, Rosenzweig** and **Rozentsveig, Feldblum** and **Feldblyum,** and **Herschkowitz** and **Gershkovich.**

Beginning in the late 20th century, the second important source of Jewish immigration to the United States was Israeli Jews. Though in many cases, this immigration has not been definitive (Israelis often move to the United States to work while retaining Israeli citizenship), the number of Jews from Israel who are regularly living in the United States numbers in the hundreds of thousands. The Israeli Jews brought not only standard Ashkenazic and Sephardic names, but also new names created in their country of origin during the 20th century. All these

names are Hebrew. Several categories of new names are patronymic. The first coincides with given names: **Baruch, David, Hayyim, Meir, Moshe, Ovadya, Peretz, Yaakov, Yosef**. The second is constructed after the pattern *Ben (son of) X*. Examples are **Ben Abraham, Ben David, Ben Mordecai, Ben Zvi**. The third pattern used to obtain new patronymic names involves adding the Hebrew possessive suffix *-i* to a masculine given name: **Aharoni, Shimoni, Yitzchaki**. Numerous other names are artificial, often obtained by taking words (common nouns, adjectives, place names, personal names) from the Bible. **Oz, Shamir,** and **Sharon** are among the examples. These new names replaced previous names assigned in the diaspora. In some cases, the old names were Hebraized, replaced either with a Hebrew name that sounded like the old name, or with the direct Hebrew translations of the old name. In other cases, the new name had nothing to do with the old one.

Bibliography

The most comprehensive studies of Jewish names used in the Russian Empire were written by Alexander Beider: *A Dictionary of Jewish Surnames from the Russian Empire* (Teaneck, N.J., 1993) deals with the Pale of Settlement (that is, modern Ukraine, Belarus, Lithuania, Moldova), and Latvia; *A Dictionary of Jewish Surnames from the Kingdom of Poland* (Teaneck, N.J., 1996) treats the area of Congress Poland, popularly called Russian Poland. The present article is mainly based on direct quotations from these books. Both include a dictionary portion, with 50,000 and 32,000 thousand entries, respectively, in which for every name the author describes its geography and suggests an etymology. Both studies also include an introductory section, in which Beider describes the naming practices in the corresponding areas and presents the history of name adoption, the typology of adopted names, and statistics by type, language, and suffix. Also by Beider, *Jewish Surnames in Prague (15th–18th centuries)* (Teaneck, N.J., 1995) is a monograph that suggests the etymology for some seven hundred names that are among the oldest Ashkenazic surnames.

Numerous Jewish entries (mostly Ashkenazic) are present in Patrick Hanks and Flavia Hodges, *A Dictionary of Surnames* (Oxford, 1988). They are mainly compiled by David L. Gold. The suggested etymologies are generally reliable and the information presented is of good quality. The lack of any geographic affiliation is the main drawback of these entries.

Ashkenazic metronymics from various countries are discussed in Erika Timm, *Matronymika im aschkenasischen Kulturbereich* (Tübingen, 1999).

No comprehensive study exists on German Jewish names. The most general work is Gerhard Kessler, *Die Familiennamen der Juden in Deutschland* (Leipzig, 1935). Erwin Manuel Dreifuss, *Die Familiennamen der Juden* (Frankfurt, 1927), is of good quality, but its geographic scope is narrow: the book is mainly focused on the names adopted in the province of Baden. The names used by Frankfurt Jews are studied in A. Schiff, *Die Namen der Frankfurter Juden zu Anfang des 19. Jahrhunderts*

(Freiburg, 1917), and Alexander Dietz, *Stammbuch der Frankfurter Juden* (Frankfurt, 1907).

Important materials concerning German Jewish names can be found in the periodic review *Jüdische Familien Forschung,* which was published in Berlin between 1924 and 1938. The only available study of French Jewish names, *Les noms des Israélites en France, histoire et dictionnaire,* by Paul Lévy (Paris, 1960), is lacking in depth and has numerous errors.

For Sephardic names, the most informative book is Abraham Laredo, *Les noms des juifs du Maroc* (Madrid, 1978); it deals only with names from Morocco.

The most common Jewish surnames in the United States are discussed in Ira Rosenwalke, 'Leading Surnames among American Jews', in *Names* 38, nos. 1–2 (March–June 1990): 32–38.

The most comprehensive bibliographical study on Jewish given names and family names in various countries at different periods is Robert Singerman, *Jewish Given Names and Family Names: A New Bibliography* (Leiden, Boston, and Cologne, 2001).

POLISH FAMILY NAMES

Aleksandra Cieślikowa

Language

The heyday of Polish surname formation was the 14th century, though some surnames are recorded before that, especially among the urban upper classes, while others—especially among the peasantry—did not come into existence until much later. Unsurprisingly, the great majority of Polish surnames derive from Polish vocabulary words and personal names (vernacular as well as Biblical), in many cases exhibiting variations in spelling and pronunciation due to dialect differences. In addition, names originating in other languages—in particular, German and Ukrainian—have been adopted and adapted to Polish forms. For example, the surname **Zajdel,** a respelling of German *Seidel,* was borne in Poland by 2,904 people at the turn of the millennium. The suffix *-uk* is Ukrainian, forming patronymics from forenames, occupational terms, nicknames, and epithets, but today *-uk* is also the sixth most common suffix found in Polish surnames (after *-ski/-cki, -ak, -icz/-ycz, -ik/-yk,* and *-ek*). Surnames ending in *-uk* are now borne by more than 300,000 people in Poland.

Types of Names

Names Based on Place Names and Landscape Features

The most characteristic type of native Polish surnames has the ending *-ski, -cki,* or *-dzki*. Early bearers of this type of surname are often mentioned in historical records and lists of those bearing coats of arms. These surnames are generally habitational names, derived from place names, but some are also topographic, from words denoting features of the landscape. The locations of place names ancestral to habitational surnames are identified in this dictionary by reference to Polish administra-

tive units (voivodeships, or provinces). In this edition, reference is to the forty-nine voivodeships that were valid until the end of 1999, corresponding to the divisions used by Kazimierz Rymut, which are relevant points of reference for historical research. The administrative reorganization of Poland in 1999 resulted in reduction to sixteen voivodeships. Occasionally we use the term province, especially when the relevant locality is outside the present-day borders of Poland.

It is not always possible to link a *-ski* surname with certainty to a particular place. Different places bearing the same name may be found in different regions of Poland and may be very numerous; for example, the surname **Wolski** indicates origin from a village called *Wola* 'free village' (i.e. a village that did have to pay feudal taxes), but there are dozens of villages of this name in various parts of Poland and in the formerly Slavic-speaking regions of eastern Germany. Only detailed family records would enable us to link a family with one particular village of this name, and all too often such records simply do not exist. Moreover, the same surname may come from different place names; thus, **Roguski** can be derived from places called *Rogucko, Roguszyn,* or *Roguzno.* Someone called **Rucki** could come from the locality *Ruta,* but the same name may also derive from *Ruda* via the intermediate form *Rudzki.*

The suffix *-ski* is commonly used in forming habitational names, but *-ski* is also often added to a reduced form of a place name; for example, the surname **Regulski** is from the place name *Regulice,* where the the element *-ice* has been dropped. A more regular formation would be **Regulicki**. In other cases, compound suffixes such as *-owski, -ewski, -iński,* or *-yński* have been added to the basic place-name element. Similar word-forming modifications appear frequently.

Surnames in *-ski* are normally formed in accordance with this model, but in a few cases, the base may be a word that is not a place name at all: some names with this ending are formed from a personal name (e.g. **Adamski** from *Adam*), while others come from some nickname-like appellative (e.g. **Jagodzki** from *jagoda* 'berry').

Patronymics

Patronymics may be said to be the earliest type of surname because they possess the main characteristic of a true surname: attachment to a particular family. They point to the relationship between sons or daughters and their father. Patronymics may come from given names, from surnames that originated from common nouns, or from adapted foreign surnames. The most characteristic suffixes of Polish patronymics are the related forms *-owicz* (**Piotrowicz**), *-ewicz* (**Wojtkiewicz**) and *-icz* or *-ycz* (**Pawlicz, Wronicz**), the Polish form of a patronymic suffix present throughout the Slavic language group.

Surnames from Nicknames and Common Nouns

Very frequent among Polish surnames are those derived from nicknames based on common nouns. A sizable number of common nouns cannot be found in dictionaries of the national colloquial or literary Polish language, but are used in dialects and also appear in surnames. Nicknames generally originated in small social groups. Terms denoting animals were popular sources of nicknames. So, someone who was thought to resemble a herring, a goldfinch, or a wolf might be nicknamed **Śledź, Szczygieł,** or **Wilk.** When such nicknames began to be used to refer to the original owner's whole family—in other words, when they became hereditary and stable—they officially entered the category of surnames.

Surnames derived from nicknames are no less old than those ending in *-ski, -cki.* They were borne not only by peasants but also by the nobility since the Middle Ages, so that we see very old names like **Kiełbasa, Trzaska,** and **Żuk.**

Occupational Names

Just as a person might be given a nickname, he or she might also come to be addressed or referred to by an occupational label, although the latter type lacks the emotional force of a nickname. Examples of occupational names are **Piekarz** 'baker', **Piwowar** 'beer-brewer', **Rybak** 'fisherman', and **Solarz** 'salter'.

Occupational names often originated on the principle of metonymy, i.e. using the part to refer to the whole. Thus, **Płachta** 'canvas' is a metonymic occupational name for a sailmaker. **Plewa** 'husk', 'chaff' is an occupational name for a winnower, but it may also represent a nickname for a worthless man. The diminutive form **Chlebek**, literally 'little bread', is a metonymic occupational name for a baker.

Status Names

Names expressing social status or position in a hierarchy, such as **Wojewoda** 'provincial governor' or **Wolny** 'freedman', are rare in Polish.

Often, both occupational surnames and those denoting social status were used as nicknames. The surname **Krawiec** means 'tailor', but in some cases an individual might be called Krawiec not because he worked as a tailor, but rather because he always wore well-cut clothing. Another might be called **Wojewoda** not because he was a provincial governor, but because he was proud and haughty; while a third might be called **Wolny** because he always behaved *zgodnie z swoją wolą* 'in accordance with his own free will'.

Surnames Based on Given Names

Polish surnames may also be derived from personal names of Christian or Slavic origin, such as **Feliks, Paweł, Piotr,** and **Wojciech**. Alternatively, they may be derived from these by means of various suffixes, as in **Pawełczyk, Pawełek, Pawlaczyk,** and **Pawlik,** all from *Paweł.*

Suffixes with Several Functions

Many suffixes contributing to the formation of Polish surnames are multifunctional. For example, the suffix *-ak* can derive patronymics (e.g. **Pawlak,** patronymic from the personal name *Paweł*), occupational names (**Pielak,** an occupational name for a gardener, from *pielić* 'to weed'), and habitational names (**Podlasiak,** 'from the district of Podlasie' or **Podolak,** 'native or inhabitant of Podolia'). Other multifunctional suffixes include *-czyk, -ek,* and *-ik.*

The fact that suffixes are multifunctional and the impossibility of determining the original motives for naming, along with the presence of foreign elements in surnames, different processes of adaptation, and the partial nature of surviving records, contribute to the difficulties of explaining the etymology of surnames. As mentioned above, similarly spelled surnames may be derived from different bases and may have different historical backgrounds. The information found in records of the coat of arms of a noble family may be of great value for a historian or a genealogist working on that particular family, but it should not be assumed that it is relevant to the genealogy of all the people who have that surname. Discovering the roots of one's own family requires researching not only the name but also other aspects of family history.

Polish Surnames in the United States

The United States and its ideals of independence, free speech, and democracy exerted a strong attraction for Polish people living under repressive foreign rule. Military leaders such as Casimir Pulaski (1748–79) and Tadeusz Kościuszko (1746–1817) had contributed to the birth of the United States during the Revolutionary War. (The latter was actually of Belarussian origin, but he is regarded as a Polish republican patriot. He was educated at the Polish military academy in Warsaw and, after his leading role in the achievement of American independence in 1776–80, returned to Poland, where he led an unsuccessful uprising against the Russians in 1794.)

Surnames of Polish origin in the United States owe their existence there to successive waves of immigration from the late 18th century on. In the 1830s and 1860s many Poles, some of them members of the nobility, who had rebelled against the occupying regimes during the long years when Poland was partitioned among its neighbors (Russia, Prussia, and Austria, 1795–1918), emigrated to the United States. In the second half of the 19th century, Polish emigrants were mainly people from poorer regions of Poland who sought a better livelihood overseas—first peasants, and then also industrial workers. Approximately 4 million Poles (out of a population of 22 million) emigrated to the United States in the two decades leading up to World War I.

At first, the Polish migrants came from the territories occupied at that time by Prussians. Later migrants tended to come from the so-called Kingdom of Poland, which was in fact a Russian puppet state. The last to emigrate were those who lived in Galicia, the Austrian sector of partitioned Poland. A considerable number of the migrants were Jewish.

Polish emigration to the United States increased after World War I, in the 1920s, and again after World War II. The most intense emigration for political and ideological reasons took place in the 1980s, when conditions approaching civil war existed in Poland.

The degree to which Polish names have become Americanized depends to some extent on the length of residence in the United States, as well as on the national consciousness of Poles residing there.

Bibliography

Boniecki, Adam (1899–1913): *Herbarz polski*. 16 vols. Warsaw.

Rodzina. Herbarz szlachty polskiej (1904–1938). 16 vols. Warsaw.

Rymut, K. (1990–94): *Słownik nazwisk współcześnie w Polsce używanych*. 10 vols. Krakow.

Rymut, K. (1999, 2002): *Nazwiska Polaków: Słownik historyczno-etymologiczny*. Vol. 1 (A–K), vol. 2 (L–Z). Krakow.

Skowronek, K. (2001): *Współczesne nazwisko polskie*. Krakow.

CZECH FAMILY NAMES

Dobrava Moldanová

The Czech Language

Czech is the westernmost of the Slavic languages, spoken mainly in Bohemia and Moravia. Even though there are only about 8 million Czech speakers, there are numerous dialect variations, which may affect the form of a surname. Czech forms part of the Western Slavic dialect continuum, stretching from eastern Poland to the German borders. It is closely related to Slovak, less closely related to Polish, and even more distantly related to the Eastern Slavic languages (Ukrainian, Belorussian, and Russian) and South Slavic (Slovenian, Croatian, Serbian, Bulgarian, etc.). The Czech language is very highly inflected, so that in its native environment the form of a surname changes according to the context in which it is used. Moreover, hypocoristics (pet forms) are very widely used, with the result that there are far more derivatives of a basic given name (e.g. Latin *Johannes*) than in English, German, or French. For many years, the Czech lands formed part of the Austro-Hungarian Empire, whose administrative language was German. Inevitably, quite a few German words were borrowed into Czech, but on the whole Czech speakers guarded the independence of their language and culture fiercely.

The Wars of Religion; Czech Migration to North America

In the 15th century the Czech lands were associated with the rise of Protestantism (followers of Jan Hus), but following the defeat of the Protestants at the Battle of the White Mountain in 1620, Bohemia became part of the Austro-Hungarian Empire, whose official religion was Roman Catholicism. Since the 17th century, therefore, most Czechs have been Roman Catholics. Nevertheless, Protestantism survived secretly in some areas, and in 1722 a group of Protestants who came to be known as the Moravian Brethren fled to Herrnhut in Saxony, where they were joined by groups of like-minded Germans. From here they came to North America in successive waves, being noted in particular for their missionary and educational work. Thus, Czechs in North America are of both Roman Catholic and Protestant heritage. Inevitably, however, the bulk of Czech immigrants have been Roman Catholics, bringing with them Roman Catholic customs and naming traditions.

The first important Czech settlements in the United States were founded in Wisconsin in 1848. During the next nine decades a steady flow of Czech immigrants followed, establishing settlements in many different parts of the country. Equally important were the numerous Jewish migrants from the Czech lands to North America (see the essay by Alexander Beider).

The Origins and Typology of Czech Surnames

Czech surnames, like those elsewhere in Europe, are traditionally inherited in the male line, with feminine inflected forms for wives and daughters (e.g., the wife or daughter of Mr. *Navrátil* is Mrs. or Miss *Navrátilová*). In the 21st century, there is an increasing tendency for married women to decide to keep their maiden name or, alternatively, the wife's name may be used by the husband.

Czech personal names, like personal names elsewhere in Europe, comprise a first name and a surname. Typically, the first name is given to a child by its parents soon after the child's birth and reflects the parents' wish that the child succeed in life. This given name was the only, or at least the main, means of identification for a person up to the 18th century. If in a longer text a reference was made to a person several times, the surname appeared only at the first instance, while the first name was used invariably after that.

In the Czech-speaking lands, surnames developed gradually from cognomens (nicknames or epithets), which were not inherited and were used to distinguish the bearer from other persons bearing the same personal name within his of her immediate environment. These cognomens became relevant in cases in which the first name failed to perform its distinguishing function. Thus individuals were recognized by diminutive modifications of their first names. Already in the 15th century the name *Jan* (John) had numerous variations and derivatives, including *Janoušek, Janák, Jeníšek, Janota, Jantásek, Janek, Jech, Ješ,* and *Jíša,* most of which are found as regular surnames in modern Czech. Other given names had an equally rich variety of derived forms, giving rise to surnames.

Typically, individuals were also distinguished by the name of their father, or occasionally by that of their mother or wife, as well as the cognomen. Thus every generation had its own designation. For example, in 1456, we find a record of a certain *Jan Turek,* son of *Václav,* called *Chalupa* (which means 'of the hut'). Sometimes a person had more than one nickname in addition to the patronymic.

Reference to the father (e.g., in 1676, *Jan Martinův,* 'Martin's John's') was the principal motivation for the transformation of cognomens into modern surnames. Sometimes hereditary names were maintained within a family for several generations, although there might be variations in the form by which an individual bearer was known (e.g.: 1416 *Wanyek Piknosy* ('flat-nosed'); 1434 *Wankonis Piknosek*; 1436 *Wenceslai Pikus*; 1436 *Wanconis Piknae*). In 1653 a certain *Jakub Plocek* came to be known as *Jakub Skuhráček* 'Jakub the

Whimperer' after marrying a daughter of a certain *Václav Skuhráček.* The whimpering personality trait belonged, not to this Jakub, but to one of his wife's forebears. In many cases (and actually until quite recently) surnames were associated with a property or a particular house, rather than with a family.

In larger settlements or towns with a higher concentration of population, the need for name differentiation was stronger. People were distinguished by their trade (1546, *Mikuláš Platnýř* 'Nikolas the linen dealer'), by the place of their origin (1581, *Šebastián Záblatský* (Sebastian from Záblatí, 'behind the marshes') son of *Jiřík Kovář* from Záblatí), by their house sign (1525, *Jan od Žab, Jan Žába;* John 'from Frogs', or 'John Frog', who took his name from a house distinguished by the sign of a frog), or by a topographic feature (1585, *Šimek pod Skalkou,* 'Simon under the rock').

An individual's appearance or personality motivated other nicknames and surnames, either directly—**Černý** 'black', **Veselý** 'merry', **Kučera** 'curly', **Pokorný** 'modest', **Skoupý** 'stingy'—or indirectly (metaphorically)—**Růžička** 'little rose', **Jedlička** 'little fir tree', **Bejček** 'young bull', **Volek** (young ox), all diminutives in Czech. In other cases, nicknames were motivated by a habitual phrase, or references to events or incidents in which the bearer played a role (either positive or negative). These nicknames or surnames are distinguished by their expressive nature, which could be either flattering or abusive and mocking.

Czech surnames developed from the 14th through the 18th centuries, adopted first by the aristocracy, later by townspeople and free farmers. The development of society and the increasing complexity of public administration led to a more rigorous maintenance of population records and a consequent stabilization of surnames. Hereditary surnames became compulsory in Bohemia in 1780, with a law that applied to all inhabitants, including landless people and domestics. Since then, the set of Czech surnames has been relatively stable: no new surnames have been introduced, though some rare ones have died out. Czech spelling was standardized in the 1850s, when modern orthography was introduced.

Modern Czech surnames reflect not only centuries of language development but the social changes that Czech society underwent. Surnames also reflect the geographical and dialectal diversity of the region, as well as social stratification in the use of slang. Surnames replaced many first names that are otherwise out of use (and often unknown to us) as well as their derivations. Some names derive from words whose meaning is now obscure, referring to functions and objects that fell out of use.

The Most Common Czech Surnames

The most common Czech surname is **Novák** (*Newman*), borne by almost one hundred thousand Czechs, or 1 percent of the population. It belongs to a category of surnames that established a person's status in a community, in this case marking a newcomer. A related name is **Novotný**, which occupies the second or third place on lists of the most common Czech names, with its related names **Nový** (adjective meaning 'new') and **Nováček** (diminutive of *Novák*).

Surnames could also convey an individual's official status. Those who were free men (royal subjects, with land-holding rights) were called **Svoboda** (freedom), a name sharing second and third places with **Novotný**. In the same way, a man from a manor (in Czech *ze dvora*), might accordingly be called **Dvořák** (fourth or fifth places in terms of frequency). In Moravia, the names **Svoboda** and **Dvořák** were in practice synonymous: someone who occupied a manor house was by definition a free man.

The name **Černý** 'black' is equally popular. Among the Czechs, who were predominantly fair, a black-haired, swarthy man was quite noticeable. This surname has a German counterpart, *Schwarz*, domesticated (adapted) as **Švarc**.

The number of Czech surnames formed from first names is immense, as the number of suffixes used—about 150—suggests. Czech is particularly rich in hypocoristic forms, which yielded a great variety of forms. As is common in all Christian (and especially Roman Catholic) cultures, the largest group comprises names derived from the names of New Testament apostles.

The most popular and therefore the most frequent given names are *Jakub (Jacobus, Jacob, James), Jan (Johannes, John), Martin, Marek (Marcus, Mark), Matouš, Matěj (Matthaeus, Mathias, Mathew), Petr (Petrus, Peter), and Šimon (Simon)*; beside these are various saint's names such as *Mikuláš (Nicholas)* and, of course, *Václav,* from the name of the country's patron saint, *Saint Wenceslas.* To take the first example, the surname **Jakub** and its derivatives are used by about 1.5 percent of the population.

Quite a few first names which form the source of Czech surnames are rarities or no longer found. One of them is *Vavřinec (Laurentius, Lawrence)*, from which derives the surname **Vávra** and its alternates, and *Benedikt (Benedict)*, from which come the common surnames **Beneš, Bendl, Benda,** and so on (occupying the thirteenth through sixteenth places in frequency statistics). This name was brought to Bohemia in the early Middle Ages by the Benedictines, who contributed significantly to Czech society's education, church organization, and management, but it is no longer in regular use.

Some Czech surnames were imports: from the Bible (**Jonáš**, from *Jonas*), from Irish Gaelic via Latin (**Havel**, from *Gallus*), from German and other Western Europe languages (**Jiljí**, from *Egidius*). Some are from pre-Christian Slavic personal names, both compounds such as **Jaromír** ('spring peace'), **Ctibor** ('virtue fight'), and their corresponding abbreviated forms (**Jaroš; Stich**). Quite a few Czech surnames preserve old Germanic names, reflecting German settlements among the Czechs, the German presence at the Bohemian rulers' court (for example, German-speaking wives and their retinues), and a German-speaking adminstration. The first Czech dynasty used Germanic names such as *Konrád, Ota, Bedřich* (cognate with *Friedrich*), and *Oldřich* (cognate with *Ulrich*). These names were adapted to the Czech language.

Surnames can be explained in various ways depending on the place and time of their origin. Not all interpretations are equally conclusive; often one has to rely on conjecture, informed by an overall knowledge of language development, phonological changes, and historical and cultural facts. An important component of such an investigation is etiology, the study of the causes and reasons leading to the choice of name. The etiological investigation presupposes knowledge of the chronological and 'human' context of the period out of which the nickname or surname issued. The researcher must also consider the possibility of interferences in the name as it was recorded over time, involving distortions caused by misinterpretation (mishearing and misreading), artificial "beautification," and inconsistencies stemming from the lack of orthographic stability in Older Czech. Even when spellings had stabilized, illiterate individuals did not know how to spell their names, and different scribes used different spelling standards. Here the investigator of surnames faces a serious problem. Some surnames can be verified using parish registers and property records. But the origin of some names found in old records may never emerge from obscurity.

There are over 40,000 Czech surnames. If distributed equally, each of them would be apportioned to about 250 bearers. Of course, this is not the case: some surnames are common, appearing in many families; others (and they are numerous) are rare, belonging to the descendants of one or just a few families.

Types of Czech Surnames
Patronymics

As mentioned above, patronymics were a main source of surnames. However, unlike such names in other Slavic languages (such as the South Slavic **Petrović**) and those found elsewhere in Europe (*Wilson, MacDonald, O'Brien, Jakobsen, Petropoulos*), Czech patronymics are not typically formed using affixes. Surnames like **Martinů(v), Jakubů(v), Martinic,** and **Petrovic** are exceptional in that they have an explicit patronymic suffix. Historically the normal tendency was to remove the suffix, resulting in simple forms like *Martin* and *Jakub*. Instead of affixes, hypocoristic forms were often used in forming patronymic surnames, although it is generally impossible to tell whether the function of the hypocoristic form is to signal patronymic derivation from a simple form of a given name, or whether the derivation was directly from a hypocoristic form of the father's given name.

While a first name could have become a surname without any change, as in the case of *Ambrož*, most of them underwent some modification, for example leaving only a portion of the name intact, either the first part (1591, *Zachariáš* to *Zach*), the last part (1589, *Ambrožovi* to *Brožovi*), or, rarely, the middle part (*Antonín* to *Ton*).

There are a few instances of female given names giving rise

to surnames, either without any change (1390, *Zdenco dictus Lidmilla*), or from pet forms (e.g. **Důra** from *Dorota*) or diminutives (1531, *od Mikuláše Ančičky kováře* 'from Nicolas Annie, the smith'). Occasionally these feminine forms underwent grammatical masculinization, as in the case of the female name *Zuzana* resulting in the male forms **Zuzan, Zuzánek, Zuzaník,** and **Zuzaňák.**

Czech Habitational Names

Another large and diversified group of Czech surnames is derived from toponyms (place names). From the Middle Ages it was common practice to refer to persons of the aristocracy or upper classes according to their place of origin or their property. These names are of varying derivation. The largest is the group using the suffix *-ský* (e.g. **Komenský**, Latin *Comenius*). Similar are derivatives using terms denoting inhabitants (**Pražák** 'citizen of Prague'), nationality (**Čech** 'Czech'; **Němec** 'German'; **Polák** 'Pole'; **Baloun** 'Walloon'), or ethnic group (**Bavor** 'Bavarian', **Moravec** 'Moravian'). Surnames were also derived from house signs, a symbol, displayed on the house, perhaps taken from a coat of arms, being the medieval equivalent of house numbers. Examples are **Anděl** (owner or inhabitant of a house 'at the sign of the Angel'), **Kotva** (from a house marked by the sign of an anchor), **Závojský** (from the house at a Veil), **Vocloň** (from *vod Slona* 'at the sign of the elephant').

Descriptive Epithets and Nicknames

Another group consists of appellatives (i.e. common nouns, adjectives, verbs, particles, and interjections). It is quite diverse, encompassing the world of old Bohemia and its inhabitants—personal and social life, the natural environment, work, and domestic relations.

Quite a few of these surnames categorize their bearers according to the position they occupy among their contemporaries, according to their employment, according to some physical or mental feature, or according to some event in which they made a (positive or negative) mark. The name might be an explicit statement of an event, but often the surnames are based on an expressive nickname. Thus, for example, the surname **Kovář** (smith) is simply factual and hardly expressive at all, while its derivatives such as the negative **Nekovář** (poor Smith), or the diminutive **Kováříček** (little, young, or insignificant smith) are much more expressive as they include an assessment of the bearer. Some surnames are based on a metaphor that is today no longer evident. This is because the original meaning has vanished over time. It does not seem odd if Mr. **Vrabec** ('sparrow') is a big and strong man of calm disposition, Mr. **Pospíšil** ('he who hurried up') doesn't appear to have ever been in a rush, or that Miss **Hrubá** ('rough'; 'large' in old Czech) is a refined, gentle young lady.

Surnames deriving from words relating to sex and excretion, by contrast, were perceived to be indecent and generally did not become neutral in their meanings over time. Their bearers therefore sought to change them, assisted, perhaps, by the priests controlling the parish records. Nowadays only those surnames that have lost their offensive connotations survive— as, for example, names derived from verbs and nouns that fell out of use or whose meaning became obscure. In the Vienna directory of 1930, one can find quite a few such surnames of Czech origin, with obscene or offensive meanings in Czech. In the German-speaking environment, however, the original appellative meaning has been lost, so the need to change them was felt less strongly, if at all.

Surnames might reflect some prominent mark of the bearer, whether it be a physical characteristic, age, height, or position within the family. A large group of surnames is formed by words referring to social groups and employment, posts and offices, and military rank, either of the bearer or his superior. Another well-represented category is the designation of craftsmen and their products (foodstuffs, for instance: **Smetana** 'cream'; **Vomáčka** 'sauce'; **Polívka** 'soup'). Such names could also be used derogatively. Thus a sluggard might be called **Buchta** 'bun', since all he did was sit like a 'bun on a baking sheet'. The tools that craftspeople worked with were another source of nicknames, which in due course became cognomens and eventually surnames.

Names from Nature

The natural world was also a source of inspiration. Surnames or nicknames taken from nouns denoting animals, recorded since the 11th century, were frequently applied to refer to some feature that an individual had in common with the beast named. Symbolism associated with certain animals also played a role. There were also surnames derived from names of plants and other products of nature.

Anecdotal Surnames

Besides standard nouns, their derivatives (augmentative and diminutive) were applied to depict the bearer's expressive characteristics. In Czech surnames, verbal forms are often represented by past and present tenses, imperatives, and past participles (e.g., **Navrátil** 'returner'). A distinctively Czech group of surnames are the anecdotal cognomens and surnames reflecting full sentences, such as **Drahokoupil** '[He] bought [it] dearly', **Stojespal** '[He] slept standing', **Ontověděl** 'He himself knew it', **Vítámvás** ('[I] welcome you'), and **Skočdopole** 'Jump [imperative] into the field'. Such names represent an encapsulated anecdote, the details of which are lost forever. Surnames originating from certain other parts of speech originated as nicknames, apparently based on sayings or idioms. They come from adverbs (**Tentokrát** 'That time'; **Šak** 'Yet'), particles and conjunctions (**Prej** 'They say'; **Zouplna** 'Quite so'; **Tedáček** 'one who frequently said "you know"', Czech *teda*') and from interjections (*Cvak* [snip], *Řach* [crack], *Tydlidát* [fiddler]). Surnames of this type are comparatively rare.

Czech Names of Foreign Origin

An interesting group of surnames derives from names of foreign origin. They typically appeared in regions influenced by different languages. Because of the location of Bohemia and Moravia in the center of Europe, Czech names can be termed central European In addition to the Slavic roots we find here elements of German and Yiddish as well as influences from the south and west of the continent. French surnames form a comparatively small component. They were brought to Bohemia by cooks, dancing masters, teachers of French, and others who were invited by the nobility. Italian names are used by the descendants of merchants, builders (the common name **Vlach,** which originally meant 'Italian', became virtually synonymous with the word 'bricklayer' during the 16th century), chimney sweepers, and other specialized craftsmen.

The most common surnames from foreign words are of German origin. They are common not because there are many such names but because a few names were adopted in great numbers. The most frequent is **Müller** (and its domesticated Czech forms **Miller** and **Miler**), borne by about 0.15 percent of the Czech population. Ancestors bearing this name came from the neighboring German-speaking lands (Austria, Bavaria, Saxony) or from the adjacent multilingual territories in the north (the Czech-German county of Klodzko in Polish-German Upper Silesia). These were the colonists who came to Bohemia in the 13th and 14th centuries. Many of them became Bohemianized, particularly during the Hussite wars in the 15th century, or settled with the new (usually foreign) owners of the properties vacated due to the Thirty Years' War (1618–1648). Many of them married Czechs and gradually merged linguistically with the local population. In such an environment these surnames lost their German character and many of them presented as dialectal and archaic. On the other hand, some of them were adapted to Czech by means of phonology, inflection, and spelling, frequently undergoing significant changes so that today both original and adjusted forms coexist (as **Müller, Miller,** and **Miler**). The process of adaptation continued by adding Czech affixes to the German roots (thus besides **Kurz** 'short' and its Czech spelling **Kurc** are also recorded **Kurcík** and **Kurcina**). Many German names were acquired by Bohemians in the German environment, referring, for example, to their bearer's origin (**Bém,** from *Böhme* 'Bohemian'; **Prager** 'dweller in Prague'). Some of these may actually be translations of a Czech name, such as **Bauer** (from *Sedlák* 'farmer'), **Schuster** (from *Švec* 'cobbler'), **Bäcker** (from *Pekař* 'baker'), and so on. The process of Germanization under pressure from the German-speaking authorities, especially in the 18th century, stabilized the German alternative name, sometimes with a Czech spelling (e.g. **Šmíd** from *Schmidt* 'smith's).

German etymology of a surname does not necessarily imply German origin; such a name might be based on a Czech common noun the etymology of which is German. This is particularly the case with international words and craftsmen's terminology. The common nouns, in many instances, vanished as a result of social and technological changes, but are preserved in the corresponding surnames. Some words of this kind, particularly at the beginning of the 19th century during the period called the Czech Revival, were replaced with their domestic counterparts, formed in an ad hoc way from Czech or Slavic bases. For example, **Forman** 'Carter', a common surname today, was replaced as a common noun by the word *povozník*.

Bibliography

For Czech Surnames
Beneš, Josef (1998): *Německá príjmení Čechů*. Ustí nad Labem.
Beneš, Josef (1962): *O českých příimeních*. Prague.
Moldanová, Dobrava (1983): *Naše príjmení*. Prague.

For Czech First Names
Knapová, Miroslava (1978): *Jak se bude jmenovat*. Prague.
Kopečný, František (1991): *Průvodce našimi jmény*. Prague.

For Czech Place Names
Hosák, Ladislav, and Rudolf Šrámek (1970–80): *Místní jména na Moravě a ve Slezsku*. 2 vols. Prague.
Profous, Antonín (1947–60): *Místní jména v Čechách*. 5 vols. Prague.

RUSSIAN, UKRAINIAN, AND BELARUSSIAN FAMILY NAMES

Alexander Beider

According to Eastern Slavic tradition, people were generally called by two names. The first was acquired during christening and was from a list composed mainly of Christian saint names authorized by the Orthodox Church. Most of these were of Greek, Latin, and Hebrew origin. The second name was optional and had no religious associations. Sometimes it was a Slavic given name from the period before the adoption of Christianity at the end of the 10th century. In other cases the second, vernacular, name was a sobriquet. In official documents, people were generally referred to by their given name (the first or the second) and the patronymic, constructed by adding special suffixes to the father's given name. The suffix depended on the morphology of the father's name. If the latter ended in a hard consonant or -*o*, then -*ov* was used. If it terminated in a soft consonant or -*e*, then -*ev* was added. If the name had a final -*a* or -*ya*, then the suffix was -*in*. In all these cases, the patronymics took the form of possessive adjectives. The names were not hereditary and changed with every generation. For example, if Ivan Petrov had a son called Boris, the latter's legal name would be Boris Ivanov.

Hereditary family names appeared in Russia in the second part of the 16th century exclusively with respect to the nobility. The merchant class gradually acquired hereditary names as well. Peasants generally did not adopt the practice of hereditary names until the 19th century.

Morphologically, Russian surnames are homogeneous. Almost all take the form of adjectives. Most numerous are those ending in -*ov, -ev,* and -*in*. In these cases, traditional patronymic appellations became fixed as hereditary. Their roots are varied. Most common are those based on masculine given names. Examples are **Andreev, Dmitriev, Fedorov, Ivanov, Nikolaev, Pavlov, Petrov, Stepanov,** and **Yakovlev;** these names are drawn from full forms of given names and are among the most frequent names found in Russia. Numerous names were constructed after the pet forms of masculine names; these include **Demin, Kuzin, Mikhalkov, Savinkov,** and **Yashin.** A large number correspond to occupations: **Bondarev** 'cooper', **Kuznetsov** 'smith', **Pisarev** 'scribe', **Rybakov** 'fisherman'.

The group of appellations derived from place names is also large, and can be discussed in terms of two subgroups. The first consists of names ending in the adjective suffix -*skij* or -*skoj*. For Russians, these names mainly correspond to the nobility; examples are **Obolenskij, Odoevskij, Shujskij, Trubetskoj,** and **Vyazemskij.** They are constructed after the names of towns, villages, and estates owned by noble families. The second are appellations mainly constructed as patronymic forms of the names of inhabitants of various places: **Astrakhantsev** (from *astrakhanets* 'one from Astrakhan') and **Ryazantsev** (from *ryazanets* 'one from Ryazan').

From nicknames based on personal characteristics are drawn **Chernov** 'black', **Gorbachev** 'humpback', **Kosygin** 'squint-eyed', and **Ryzhkov** 'red-haired'. Among the rare examples of Russian names that are not patronymic (but still adjectives) are **Tolstoj** or **Tolstoy** 'fat'.

A specific group encompasses artificial names that belong to the descendants of Russian Orthodox priests. During the 18th and 19th centuries, young men who studied in the theological seminaries often graduated from these institutions with new surnames. Several patterns of name creation were elaborated in the seminaries. A large group of appellations was constructed from the names of religious holidays and churches named after these holidays. All of them include the suffix -*skij*: **Pokrovskij, Preobrazhenskij, Rozhdestvenskij, Troitskij, Voskresenskij, Voznesenskij, Vvedenskij.** Other names were derived from terms issuing from Christianity; these include **Arkhangel'skij** 'archangel', **Bogoslovskij** 'divine', **Petro-**

pavlovskij 'Peter and Paul', **Sinajskij** 'Sinai', **Spasskij** 'salvation'.

Numerous names of an ornamental nature were artificially constructed after Latin roots (**Gilyarovskij, Melioranskij, Sollertinskij, Speranskij, Superanskij).** Other such appellations were created after Russian words: **Lebedev** 'swan', **Rozov** 'rose', **Solntsev** 'sun', **Tsvetkov** 'flower', **Vinogradov** 'grapes'.

Owing to the presence in Russia of people of various ethnic origins, many names borne by Russians are derived from foreign words. There are numerous instances of Turkic names such as **Aksakov, Baskakov, Beklemishev, Berdyaev, Chaadaev, Karamzin, Kurakin, Kutuzov, Nabokov, Timiryazev,** and **Yusupov.** Among names of other origins are **Deribasov** (Italian), **Fonvizin** (German), **Lermontov** (Scottish), **Sheremet'ev** (Persian), and **Turgenev** (Mongolian).

Ukrainian and Belarussian Family Names

In the fourteenth century the southwestern part of modern Ukraine, the area around Lvov, known in historical sources as Red Russia (or Ruthenia), was annexed by Poland. During the same century, the areas that correspond to modern Belarus and greater Ukraine were incorporated into the Grand Duchy of Lithuania. In 1569 the Lublin Union separated Belarussian and Ukrainian lands, with the latter incorporated into Poland and the former continuing as part of Lithuania. However, both countries were joined in a larger configuration, the Polish-Lithuanian Commonwealth.

Because of these historical ties, there are many similarities between Ukrainian and Belarussian Orthodox Christian names. Unlike Russian family names, Ukrainian and Belarussian names were often constructed semantically, without the addition of a suffix. Among these names we find those derived from (1) common nouns (occupational terms, nicknames); (2) adjectives (mainly nicknames having typical endings -*ovy[j]* or -*avy, -aty[j], -ny[j]*); (3) given names (either full forms or, much more frequently, pet or familiar names using the suffixes -*ka* or -*ko, -ejka* or -*ejko, -khno, -ik,* and -*ak*). Several patronymic suffixes are also shared by Ukrainians and Belarussians. Examples are -*enko* (common in eastern Ukraine and eastern Belarus), -*uk,* and -*chuk* (both mainly used in western Ukraine and western and central Belarus). Originally, before becoming patronymic, all of these were diminutive, used to create pet forms of given names. On the other hand, the suffix -*ovich* or -*evich*, more popular among Belarussians than among Ukrainians, is purely patronymic. Names based on habitation are common enough in both ethnic groups. Often these names are constructed by adding the adjective suffix -*skij* (Belarussian) or -*s'kyj* (Ukrainian) to the toponym. The surnames ending in -*ets* were created after the names of inhabitants of various place names.

Differences between the two ethnic groups exist as well. For example, names ending in the patronymic suffix *-ak* constitute about 10 percent of Ukrainian names, while they are rather unusual among Belarussians. On the other hand, the patronymic suffix (genetically diminutive) *-enok* is peculiar to eastern Belarus. In this area we find a large number of patronymic surnames ending in the suffix *-ov* or *-ev* (according to modern Belarussian orthography, the unstressed *-ov* is spelled as *-av*). These names were mainly adopted during the 19th century by peasants who had no hereditary names before that period (as with Russian nobility, the Belarussian nobility acquired their names, mainly ending in *-ovich* or *-evich* and *-skij*, beginning in the 16th century). Ukrainian names ending in *-iv,* the equivalent of *-ov* or *-ev,* are rather unusual. Names ending in *-in* are not rare in eastern Belarus. They are mainly patronymic, created (as their Russian counterparts) from nouns ending in *-a* or *-ya;* metronymic names are rare. On the contrary, Ukrainian names ending in *-in* are almost exclusively metronymic. They are common only in western Ukraine, in the Lvov area. These names are derived from female names that in turn are constructed after the names or occupations of the husband: **Romanishin** from *Romanikha* 'wife of *Roman*', **Yurchishin** from *Yurchikha* 'wife of *Yurko*', **Kovalishin** from *Kovalikha* 'smith's wife'. A large group of Ukrainian family names represent nicknames composed of two roots: **Bilo-did** 'white old man', **Krivo-ruchko** 'crooked arm', **Tverdokhlib** 'hard bread'. Among them, one can distinguish a specific series of names in which the first part is a verb in the imperative mood and the second part is a noun: **Nepijvoda** 'do not drink' + 'water', **Ubijvovk** 'kill' + 'wolf', **Goliboroda** 'shave' + 'beard'.

Eastern Slavic Immigrants in North America

The number of Russian and Belarussian immigrants in North America is not large. Before the 1917 Bolshevik Revolution, Eastern Slavic emigration from the Russian Empire was minimal. The several millions of individuals who emigrated from Russia during the civil war of 1917–23 were not destined for the United States. The main centers for this "first" emigration from Russia were France (Paris), Germany (Berlin), Italy, Czechoslovakia (Prague), and Baltic and Balkan countries. Some of these émigrés later moved to North America. In the "second" emigration, that of people who were displaced by Germans during World War II to western and central Europe and decided not to return to the Soviet Union after the defeat of the Nazis, the United States was a common destination. The "third" emigration (beginning in the 1970s) has mainly involved Jewish émigrés.

In North America, Ukrainian immigrants are much more numerous than Russian and Belarussian immigrants. However, their descendants mainly live in Canada and not in the United States. Many of them came from western Ukraine (former Galicia), when it was part of the Austro-Hungarian Empire.

In many cases, Slavic immigrants changed their names as part of the general process of assimilation. Sometimes they chose new English names that were unrelated to their former surnames. In other cases, the new name was derived from the older one. The main pattern was to truncate the ending: *Bondarenko* to **Bond,** *Buketov* to **Buke,** *Chernoshtan* to **Chern,** *Kormilitsyn* to **Korm,** *Patrikeev* to **Patrick,** *Petropavlovskij* to **Petrop,** *Pobedonostsev* to **Pobie,** and *Znamenskij* to **Znamens.** In several cases, the truncation was accompanied by anglicization: *Grushko* to **Grey,** *Prishchipenko* to **Price,** *Telyat'ev* to **Tolley,** *Trezubov* to **Trey.** Among the most curious cases are those in which the phonetic value of the initial name was kept, while the spelling was altered: *Dubov* to **Du Bow,** *Mikula* to **McCulla,** *Romanishin* to **Romanition.**

Bibliography

The most comprehensive study of Russian family names is Boris O. Unbegaun, *Russian Surnames* (Oxford and New York, 1972). This text relates the history of naming practices in Russia and analyzes the morphologic and semantic features of modern Russian surnames of both local and foreign origins. It also includes brief discussions of names of various ethnic groups living in Russia. The main drawback of the book is the absence of any geographical context; the numerous suffixes discussed are regional.

The geographical context is addressed in V. A. Nikonov, *Geografiya familii* (Moscow, 1988). Nikonov has written several other important studies on Russian surnames, among which should be mentioned *Imya i obshchestvo* (Moscow, 1974) and *Slovar' russkikh familii* (Moscow, 1993).

Sovremennye russkie familii by A. V. Superanskaya and A. V. Suslova (Moscow, 1981) is a good popular treatment of the material discussed in more depth by Unbegaun.

The personal names and nicknames traditionally used by Russians are listed in M. N. Tupikov, *Slovar' drevnerusskikh lichnykh sobstvennykh imen* (St. Petersburg, 1903), and S. B. Veselovskij, *Onomastikon* (Moscow, 1974). Although these books do not deal explicitly with family names, the materials collected in them can be used to explain numerous modern Russian family names.

Yu. K. Red'ko, *Suchasni ukraÿns'ki prizvishcha* (Kiev, 1966), is the most valuable study of Ukrainian family names. The author discusses in detail the typology of names, classified in terms of semantics and morphology, and the origins of various suffixes, and presents numerous examples. All names are also discussed in terms of geography.

F. Bogdan, *Dictionary of Ukrainian Surnames in Canada* (Winnipeg, 1974), includes more than 30,000 names with transliteration and stress, as well as a discussion of name changes.

The most important studies on Belarussian surnames were written by M. V. Biryla. The most detailed information is included in Biryla's thesis 'Belaruskaya antrapanimiya', written in two parts: 'Ulasnuya imeny, imeny-myanushki, imeny pa bats'ku, prozvishchy' (Minsk, 1966) and 'Suchasnyya belaruskiya prozvishchy' (Minsk, 1969). The first includes an analysis of given names and nicknames used by Belarussian Christians from the 15th to the 18th centuries. It was published as a book under the same title (Minsk, 1966). The second deals

with family names. In the introductory material, Biryla presents the geographical distribution of all suffixes found in Belarussian surnames. In the dictionary discussion, he suggests the etymology for a large number of surnames. The book version, *Belaruskaya antrapanimiya,* part 2, *Prozvishchy, utvoranyya ad apelyaywnaj leksiki* (Minsk, 1969), includes only the dictionary, not the analytical discussion.

SLOVENIAN FAMILY NAMES

Simon Lenarčič

Diversity of the Slovenian Language

The Slovenian language, which is spoken by 2.2 million people in the region between the Adriatic Sea, the Alps, and Pannonia, is one of the South Slavic languages. It features more than forty individual dialects—more than any other Slavic language. The dialects include many words that represent significant departures from the modern Slovenian written language. Some of these were borrowed from the neighboring German, Croatian, Hungarian, Italian, and Friulian languages; many others are archaic.

Surnames of Foreign Origin

In terms of its inhabitants Slovenia is relatively homogeneous. Slovenians make up 88 percent of the population; others are mainly of Croatian, Serbian, Bosnian, Albanian (from Kosovo), Macedonian, Hungarian, and Italian origin. But Slovenian surnames are of heterogeneous origin, because the Slovenian territory has been exposed to the influence of various neighboring languages: Latin, Italian, and Friulian from the west, German from the north, West Slavic from the northeast, Hungarian from the east, and South Slavic from the south.

German Influence

The territory of present-day Slovenia and of the early medieval Slovenian state Carantania (now the Austrian provinces Carinthia and Styria) was part of Charlemagne's and the Habsburg Empires for more than a thousand years. German feudal vassals brought many German (especially Bavarian) settlers to the Slovenian territory in the Middle Ages, and many Slovenian surnames were Germanized under the Habsburgs' provincial administration. The German language gradually replaced the

Slovenian one in present-day Carinthia and Styria as a result of this centuries-long Germanization, while the less numerous German settlers in Carniola (the central part of modern Slovenia) and southern Styria (the eastern part of modern Slovenia) adopted the Slovenian language. Their surnames remained in the original form (e.g., **Gartner, Gasser, Schmidt)** or were partly Slovenized (e.g., **Gartnar** and **Gortnar, Gaser, Šmid).** In the Austrian provinces of Carinthia and Styria there is still an autochthonous Slovenian minority. Slovenian surnames in these provinces are often written in German.

Some examples of Slovenian surnames derived from German words: Slovenian equivalents of the English surname **Smith** are **Kovač,** from Slovenian *kovač* 'smith', and **Šmid** or **Šmit,** from German *Schmied* 'smith'. Slovenian equivalents of the English surname **Hunter** are **Lovec,** from Slovenian *lovec* 'hunter' and **Jager,** from German *Jäger* 'hunter'.

Hungarian Influence

Prekmurje, the easternmost part of Slovenia, was under Hungarian rule for many centuries. The influence of the neighboring Hungarian language is therefore quite noticeable in the easternmost Slovenian dialects, and some of the eastern Slovenian surnames are derivatives of Hungarian or Hungarized words (e.g., the surname **Orban** replaced *Urban, Vrban,* or *Verban*). On the other hand, some Hungarian surnames are derived from Slovenian loanwords.

A small minority of autochthonous Slovenians lives in the Raba river region of the western part of Hungary; somewhat more numerous is the autochthonous Hungarian minority living in the easternmost part of Slovenia.

Italian Influence

Many Italians, mostly merchants of Friulian origin, settled in Slovenia during the time of the Habsburg Empire. Their surnames either remained in the original or were partly Slovenized (e.g., **Brunet, Leoni, Simoniti, Tomaduz).**

The Slovenian language is spoken in the adjacent parts of Italy. Slovenian surnames in the easternmost part of Italy are usually written in Italian as the result of long Italianization. Surnames of the numerous autochthonous Slovenian minority in Italy were Italianized mainly by the fascist regime in the first half of the twentieth century (e.g., Slovenian *Ambrožič* to Italian **Ambrosi**, *Bohinc* to **Boccini**, *Franko* to **Franco**, *Ivanc* and *Ivančič* to **Giovannini** and **Giannini**). A small autochthonous Italian national minority lives in the Primorska region in the southwestern part of Slovenia.

Slavic Influence

The first groups of Bosnians, Croatians, and Serbs came to Slovenia in the fifteenth and sixteenth centuries, Christians who fled from the Turks. The memory of these refugees, who were called Uskoki, survive in the Slovenian surnames derived from their nicknames—**Horvat, Hrovat, Turk, Vlah** 'Wallachian'—or family names (e.g., **Markovič**).

Other Croats, Bosnians, Macedonians, Serbs, and Albanians immigrated to Slovenia mainly after 1918, when Slovenia became part of the Kingdom of Serbs, Croats, and Slovenes, and especially after 1945 when Communists took power in Yugoslavia and encouraged immigration from the less-developed parts of Yugoslavia to Slovenia. Surnames of these immigrants remained in the original (e.g., *Andrić, Bašić, Ilić, Milić, Milošević*), or in a Slovenized version (e.g., **Andrič, Bašič, Ilič, Milič, Miloševič**).

Czechs, Slovaks, Poles, and Russians immigrated to Slovenia mainly during the time of the Habsburg Empire. Their surnames (e.g., **Doležal, Sazonov, Smirnov**) are indicators of their origin.

Types of Slovenian Surnames
Habitational and Topographic Names

Some Slovenian surnames derive from the names of villages or countries of people who eventually settled somewhere else. The Slovenian surnames **Bohinc** and **Bohinec** are derived from the name of the Slovenian Alpine region Bohinj; the hundreds of Slovenians with this surname trace their ancestry to that area.

The most common suffixes belonging to Slovenian habitational and topographic names are *-nik, -ec* or *-c, -šek, -an,* and *-ar.* Examples of Slovenian habitational names derived from the topographic name *bukovje* 'beech forest' and the place names Bukovje and Bukovo are **Bukovec, Bukovšek,** and **Bukovnik.**

Patronymics and Metronymics

Slovenian surnames derived from personal names are for the most part patronymics. Metronymics are relatively rare. They are derived mostly from the feminine forenames **Barbara** (e.g., **Barbarič, Barborič, Barbič, Barič**), **Marija** (e.g., **Marinič, Marušič**), and **Magdalena** (e.g. **Magdič, Majdič, Magdalenc, Magdalenič**).

Slovenian patronymics and metronymics are mostly derived from the names of Catholic saints. Some older names and surnames have evolved over the centuries to the point that their derivation is almost unrecognizable. Slovenian surnames derived from the male name **Erazem** (Latin *Erasmus*) are, for example, **Erazem, Oražem, Oraže, Orožen, Orožim, Orož, Ražem, Ražman, Rožman, Rozman, Rožen, Rože,** the patronymic **Rožič,** and **Ažman.** Common suffixes of Slovenian patronymics are *-čič, -ič, -ec, and -c,* but some other suffixes (e.g. *-in, -ka*) may also function as patronymics. Examples of patronymics derived from the Slovenian personal name **Gregor** (Latin *Gregorius*) are **Gregorčič, Gregorič, Gregorc, Gregorec, Gregorin,** and **Gregorka.**

Slovenian patronymics with the suffix *-ovič* originate mainly from the border regions, where the interaction between the Slovenian and Croatian or Serbian language is evident, or are borne by the descendants of Uskoki or other newcomers of Croatian or Serbian origin.

Artificial and Occupational Surnames

Many Slovenian surnames are nicknames derived from animal names: **Bergles, Berglez,** and **Brglez** 'nuthatch', **Gams** 'chamois', **Jazbec** 'badger'. Many also come from plant names: **Grah, Grahek,** and **Grašek** 'pea', **Slak** 'bindweed'; human characteristics: **Gerbec** and **Grbec** 'hunchback', **Okoren** and **Okorn** 'clumsy'; and natural phenomena: **Megla** 'fog', **Mesec** 'moon'.

Surnames derived from occupational names are also very common, and mainly employ the noun suffixes *-ar* and *-ec*; for example, **Tekavec** and **Kavec** 'weaver'.

Slovenian Pronunciation

The Letters *č, š,* and *ž* are written and pronounced like their equivalents in the Czech alphabet (*č* is pronounced like *ch* in English, *š* like *sh* in English, and *ž* like *j* in French). Other Slovenian letters do not have diacritics. Other letters, which are pronounced quite different in Slovenian than in English, are *c,* which is pronounced like *ts* in the English word *tsar* or like *z* in the German word *Zimmer; j,* which is pronounced like *y* in the English word *yes*); and *g,* which is pronounced like *g* in the English word *go.*

Replacement and Omission of Letters

Replacement of the initial letters *p* with *b, b* with *p, v* with *b,* and *b* with *v* can be found in the spellings of Slovenian surnames. The surnames **Burgar, Burger, Purgar,** and **Purger** have the same meaning—they are all derived from the German word *Burger.* Replacement of the final *l* (or *l* before the suffix) with the letter *v* is quite common. The surnames **Debevec** and

Debelec are both derived from *debelec* 'fat person'; the surnames **Bolha** and **Bovha** are both derived from *bolha* 'flea'. Omission of the reduced vowel *e* is also common. The surnames **Debevc** and **Mrhar** are variant forms of the surnames **Debevec** and **Merhar**. Replacement of certain vowels also occurs. The surnames **Avsec** and **Ovsec** are both derived from the word *oves* 'oats'.

Slovenian Surnames Abroad

Hundreds of thousands of Slovenians left their homeland in the second half of the 19th and first half of the 20th centuries. They moved to the United States (the first settlers of Slovenian origin were expelled Protestants, who settled with their German colleagues in Georgia in the 17th century), Germany, France, Argentina, Canada, Australia, and Serbia. Many surnames of Slovenian origin can thus be found in these countries.

Modification of Slovenian Surnames in North America

Many Slovenian surnames, which are not easy to pronounce in English, have been drastically changed or simplified in the American melting pot. Typical Slovenian endings such as -*čič* have often been dropped. Many surnames were respelled. For example, the Slovenian surname **Kolenc** (a nickname derived from the term *kol* 'pale,' 'stake' or *koleno* 'knee', or from the dialectical plant name *kolenc* [*Galium verum* or *Lapsana communis*]) has been in some cases changed to the similarly pronounced English surname **Collins.**

Bibliography

Merku, Pavle (1993): *Svetniki v slovenskem imenoslovju* (Saints in the Slovenian Onomastics). Trieste. (Covers Slovenian surnames and toponyms derived from saints' names.)

Merku, Pavle (1982): *Slovenski priimki na zahodni meji* (Slovenian Surnames on the Western Frontier [i.e., in northeastern Italy]). Trieste. (Covers Slovenian surnames that are characteristic of the Slovenian minority in northeastern Italy.)

See also *Etimološki slovar slovenskega jezika I–III* (Etymological Dictionary of the Slovenian Language). Ljubljana, Slovenia, 1976–95.

HUNGARIAN FAMILY NAMES

Gábor Bátonyi

The Hungarian People and Their Language

Unlike most of the other languages of Europe, Hungarian is not a member of the Indo-European family of languages. The Hungarian people (Magyars) originated in the borderlands of Europe and Asia, in the Ural Mountains. Although the extent of the so-called Uralian homeland is debated, it is thought to include western Siberia and the northern range of the Ural Mountains. The Uralian people spoke a common language there until the fourth millennium BC, when they started to split up into smaller ethnocultural and linguistic units. Around 3000 BC the Uralian languages split into two main branches, the Finno-Ugrians and the Samoyeds. Following a further split in the next millennium the proto-Magyars moved south, where they came into constant contact with Iranian and Turkic peoples. The cultural influence of these peoples can be demonstrated by about 300 words of ancient Turkish origin that have made their way into the Hungarian language. The Magyars settled in their present homeland, in and around the Carpathian Basin, in the ninth century.

Hypotheses aside, the Hungarian language is distantly related to Finnish, Estonian, and some lesser known languages of northern Russia that are now close to extinction, but not to any of the languages in central Europe. There has, however, been considerable intermixture with neighboring peoples, in particular with the Romanians in the east and the Slovaks in the north. In Habsburg times, as a result of the depopulation of various areas by the Ottoman Turkish army, the settlement of Germans (Swabians) and compact groups of South Slavs in the Kingdom of Hungary further complicated the ethnic mix of the Carpathian basin. Consequently, there are many loanwords in the Hungarian language resulting from the period of cohabitation with Germans, Slavs, and Romanians. These linguistic influences between the central European peoples were reciprocal and they are clearly reflected in name-giving. Thus, the Slovak name **Novak** is common in Hungary in the Magyarized form **Novák,** and the German name Bernhard in the form **Bernát.** Characteristically, ethnic names such as **Tót** (Slovak), **Német** (German), **Oláh** (Romanian), **Horvát** (Croatian), **Rác** (Serbian) are very frequent in Hungary, while family names such as **Ungar** and other ethnic names for Hungarians can be found in all neighboring states.

For centuries Hungary has played a major role in central European history. The native rulers of the Árpád dynasty (895–1301) broke with nomadic traditions and built a feudal system resembling that of the west European states. István I (Saint Stephen), crowned as the first king of Hungary on New Year's day in 1001, converted the Magyars to Christianity. The earliest record of the Hungarian language, the charter of Tihany Abbey on the northern shore of Lake Balaton, dates back to 1055. The early medieval period was also important from the point of view of name-giving. King István's nephew, Sámuel Aba, was the first Hungarian monarch to be given a name with more than one element, although this is unrelated to the development of patronymic family names, which occurred only some two centuries later.

Hungary survived Tartar incursions in the 13th century, but the very existence of an independent Magyar state was brought into question by the Turkish occupation of a large section of the country, including the capital Buda, from 1526 to 1686. At the same time, a northern strip of Hungary came under Habsburg rule and provided a basis for the legal fiction of a kingdom that had existed continuously from the start of the second millennium. The historic city of Bratislava (Pressburg) on the Danube, the present-day capital of Slovakia, was at the time the capital of Hungary under the Magyar name **Pozsony.** It remained the seat of the Hungarian diet as late as the early to mid 19th century. The language of Hungarian administration throughout this period was Latin.

The geographical boundaries of Hungary have undergone many changes over the centuries. Croatia was part of medieval Hungary until it was occupied by the Turks; it was reincorporated into the Hungarian state after the retreat of the Ottoman army from Central Europe. Transylvania preserved its independence as a separate principality during the years of Turkish occupation, but under Habsburg rule it was unified with Hungary. After the First World War, the Treaty of Trianon awarded Transylvania to Romania, but a significant part of the population is still Hungarian-speaking.

The Habsburg Empire, from 1867 known as the Austro-Hungarian Monarchy, was a multiethnic state, with more than eleven major linguistic groups. Due to the emancipation of the Jews and the liberal emigration policies in the 19th century, the Jewish population grew rapidly in Hungary, especially in urban centers such as Budapest. The majority of Hungarian Jews perished in the Holocaust, although Admiral Horthy saved the lives of 200,000 Budapest Jews by halting the deportations from the capital in July 1944. (On Jewish names, see the essay by Alexander Beider.)

Origins of Surnames in Hungary

Hungarian social conventions, including naming conventions, are similar in many respects to those of Hungary's nearest neighbors. However, it should be noted that in Hungarian the forename is conventionally placed after the surname. Thus, the composer known in English-speaking contexts as Béla Bartók is Bartók Béla in a Hungarian context. As elsewhere in Europe, the beginning of the use of surnames in Hungary was gradual, and was associated with the development of bureaucracy.

Hungarian surnames, however, are relatively new. It was not until the 14th century or later that the use of surnames was established among the population as a whole. In any case, many Hungarian names can be traced back to the 14th to 17th centuries; their relatively recent origin makes it easier to explain their etymology.

Typology of Hungarian surnames

Pretty well all the surname types found elsewhere in Europe are also represented in Hungary. These types include:

ancient tribal names (e.g. **Kállay, Kér**);

patronymics from ancient, secular, pre-Christian Hungarian personal names (e.g. **Bán, Bátor, Lándor, Macsó, Ormán, Szépe**);

patronymics from secular Slavic personal names (e.g. **László**, from Slavic *Vladislav*; **Radó**, from a Slavic element meaning 'glad');

patronymics from (Latin) biblical names and names of Christian saints (e.g. **Ágoston** from Augustinus; **Balázs** from Blasius; **Ferenc** from Franciscus);

habitational names, often from quite small places (**Almásy, Bányai**); certain place names are found in many different places throughout Hungary, and in many cases it is impossible to say with certainty which one is the source of the surname;

occupational and status names (e.g. **Biró** 'judge'; **Bognár** 'cartwright'; **Deák** 'scribe'; **Fazekas** 'potter'; **Juhász** 'shepherd'; **Kádár** 'cooper'; **Liszt** 'miller'—literally, 'flour');

names from words denoting animals (e.g. **Farkas** 'wolf'—either a nickname or a personal name; **Bárány** 'lamb'—also an occupational name for a shepherd);

nicknames (e.g. **Balog** 'left-handed'; **Barát** 'friend'; **Fehér** 'pale' or 'blond'; **Fekete** 'dark' or 'swarthy'; **Fodor** 'curly'; **Víg** 'cheerful'; **Vörös** 'red');

ethnic names, as previously mentioned (e.g. **Török** 'Turk'—although this may also be a nickname; **Tót** 'Slovak', **Német** 'German', **Oláh** 'Romanian', **Horvát** 'Croatian', **Rác** 'Serb'.

Hungarian Immigration to the United States

Hungarian mass migration to the United States started in the 1880s and intensified in the first decade of the 20th century. The number of Hungarians who left the Habsburg Empire for America was surpassed only by that of the Poles, Slovaks, and Slovenes. By the time of the First World War more than 1,200,000 Magyars lived in the United States. The Second World War and the 1956 revolution triggered further large waves of emigration from Hungary.

For an account of Hungarian migration to North America, readers of Hungarian should consult Julianna Puskás, *Kivándorló Magyarok az Egyesült Államokban* (Budapest, 1982).

Bibliography

Kálmán, Béla (1978): *The World of Names*, Budapest.
Kázmér, Miklós (1993): *Régi Magyar Családnevek Szótára*. Budapest.

LATVIAN AND LITHUANIAN FAMILY NAMES

Laimute Balode

History

Baltic tribes were living on the eastern shore of the Baltic Sea by 2500 BC. Latvian and Lithuanian are the only Baltic languages spoken today, representing one branch of Indo-European language family; a third Baltic language, Old Prussian, died out around the end of the 17th century.

Latvian History

In the 12th century, German traders began entering the Baltic lands. Riga, the present capital of Latvia, was founded in 1201. The Teutonic military order of the Brothers of the Sword crushed Latvian and Livonian tribes and converted them to Christianity. Over 200 years, rivalry and warfare raged among the Roman Catholic Church, the Teutonic Order, and the merchants of Riga in a contest for trade and territory. In 1522, German preachers brought the Protestant Reformation to Latvia. In the Polish-Swedish War (1600–29), Sweden won northern Latvia, while the provinces of Kurzeme and Zemgale were united into a duchy loyal to the Polish-Lithuanian Empire. During the following period, known as the Swedish Occupation, schools were opened, the oppression of peasants lessened, and the Bible was translated into Latvian.

From 1700 until 1721, Sweden and Russia fought for control of Livonia, an ethnically distinct region now divided between Latvia and Estonia. The Russians occupied Latgale, the eastern part of Latvia, in 1795, and controlled the entire country until World War I. Serfdom was abolished in Latvia in 1817–19.

The mixture of nationalist feelings and the demands of the new industrial proletariat made Latvia a hot spot in the abortive 1905 revolution, after which the tsar executed almost 2,000 Latvians. In 1915, the Germans occupied half of Latvia. Latvian independence was declared on November 18, 1918.

President Karlis Ulmanis staged a bloodless coup in May 1934 and ruled as a dictator for six years. Nonetheless, the country grew rapidly, and Latvia had one of the highest living standards in Europe. On the eve of World War II, under the secret protocols of the Molotov-Ribbentrop Pact, Germany and the Soviet Union divided eastern Europe. Latvia and Lithuania fell to the Soviets, whose troops invaded Latvia and Lithuania in 1940.

The German Army took Riga in early July 1941, and the Red Army retook most of Latvia in July–September 1944. In 1941, occupying forces deported tens of thousands of Latvians to Siberia; in 1949, another 42,000 Latvians were deported there. At last, on May 4, 1990, independence was restored to Latvia with the collapse of the Soviet Union.

Lithuanian History

Lithuania was the last state in Europe to be converted to Christianity, in the 14th century. From the 13th to 15th centuries, Lithuania was ruled by grand dukes. It became a powerful grand duchy, which by the mid-16th century extended from the Baltic Sea to the Black Sea. By the terms of Kreva Act (1385), there was a common Polish-Lithuanian kingdom. The Polish-Lithuanian armies decisively defeated the Teutonic knights at the Battle of Tannenberg (Grünwald, 1410).

The Renaissance brought marked cultural advances: the first Lithuanian book was printed in 1547, and the University of Vilnius was founded in 1579. After the Union of Lublin (1568), the Polish-Lithuanian kingdom was merged into a Commonwealth (Rzeczpospolita). Polish became the state language.

The Livonian wars with Russia and Sweden drained the Commonwealth's resources. Weakened by internal dissension, it was ultimately partitioned among Russia, Austria, and Prussia (1795), and Russia absorbed Lithuania. Tsarist rule brought strict censorship and Russification, including a ban on publishing in the Latin script. Patriotic unrest led to a national uprising in 1863. The rising intelligentsia nurtured a national ideal based on the rebirth of the Lithuanian language and the revival of Lithuanian culture. In 1883, the first Lithuanian newspaper was published.

World War I kindled hopes for Lithuanian autonomy. Under German tutelage (1915–18), a Lithuanian Council proclaimed the Republic of Lithuania on February 16, 1918, the Lithuanian Independence Day. In 1920, Poland annexed the capital, Vilnius, and its surrounding region, and the capital was transferred to Kaunas. During the interwar period, independent

Lithuania prospered. Lithuanian independence ended with the Molotov-Ribbentrop Pact (1939), and from 1941 to 1944 Lithuania was occupied by German forces.

The return of Red Army forced the incorporation of Lithuania into the Soviet Union in 1944. Mass deportations to Siberia followed. Many Lithuanians and Latvians, especially the more educated, were forced to emigrate, mainly to the United States, Canada, Australia, Germany, and Sweden. Despite the politics of Sovietization, however, this nation never lost its identity.

After the Soviet period of perestroika, the pro-independence movements in Lithuania and Latvia led to true independence. On March 11, 1990, the Supreme Council declared Lithuanian's independence restored.

Latvian Names

The first surnames in Latvia were adopted after the abolition of serfdom at the beginning of the 19th century. Until that time, Latvians were called by a first or given name and the name of the homestead where they lived. Because many of the officials assigning the surnames were German, many German surnames were adopted in the western part of the country, but in the eastern part there were more family names of Slavic origin. During the period of Latvian independence between 1920 and 1940, surnames underwent a transformation in which many Germanic family names were translated or "calqued" into Latvian equivalents—for example, *Frīdbergs* became **Mierlauks,** and *Grīnbergs* became **Zaļkalns.** Nevertheless, there remain many surnames of Germanic or Slavic origin, as well as borrowings from neighbors; from Lithuanian come **Andrušaitis, Dingaitis, Balčūns,** and **Labutis,** and from Finno-Ugric languages come **Sarja** and **Sika.**

In terms of semantics, the most frequent sources of surnames of Latvian origin are individual characteristics (**Garais, Sirmais, Garkaklis**), place of residence (**Kalniņš, Pakalns, Mežs, Upenieks**), animals (**Ērglis, Lapsa, Vilks**), and plants (**Bērziņš, Ozoliņš, Puķītis**).

In regard to lexical derivation, there are many "primary" surnames with no affixes (**Celms, Kalns),** but there are also names formed with suffixes. The most widely occurring suffixes are -*iņš, -nieks, -āns, -ēns, -ītis, -elis, -ulis, -ēns*. In addition, there are composite names; the most popular first elements are *Mež, Kaln-, Sil-, Lauk-* and *Jaun-, Vec-, Meln-, Liel-*.

Latvian male surnames differ from Latvian female surnames only in the endings. If a Latvian surname has the masculine gender ending -*s* or -*š*, its feminine form ends in -*a* (**Kalns, Kalna**; **Vējš, Vēja**); if the masculine surname ends in -*is*, then the feminine form ends in -*e* (**Balodis, Balode; Valdmanis, Valdmane**).

Lithuanian Names

Surnames were already in use in Lithuania by the 15th century. The most important cause of this was Christianization (1387 in the eastern part, 1413 in the western part). The most intensive period for giving surnames, however, was the 17th and 18th centuries.

Lithuanian surnames originated in several ways: (1) from ancient pre-Christian names (**Ašmantas, Butrimas)** with Lithuanian or Slavic patronymic suffixes; (2) from Christian names (Hebraic, Classical Greek, or Latin) and their Belarussian or Slavic variants (**Abromas, Jackus, Klimas**); (3) from ethnic names (**Latvėnas, Mozūras**); (4) from place names (**Kauniškis, Veliuoniškis**); and (5) from nicknames and other labels. Some old Lithuanian surnames were Slavonized. Many surnames are derived with the Lithuanian patronymic suffixes -*aitis, -ėnas, -onis,* and -*ūnas*. One can also find hybrid surnames in which the root is of Lithuanian origin but the suffix is Slavic (**Alminauskas, Butrimavičius**).

Lithuanian women's surnames originally differed only in their endings (as in Latvian), but in contemporary society Lithuanian unmarried women's names have special endings: -*aitė* (e.g., **Jasaitė**) if the father's surname ends with -*as* (**Jasas**); -*ytė* (**Liesytė**) if the father's surname ends with -*is* or -*ys* (**Liesys**); and -*utė* (**Butkutė**) if the father's surname ends with -*us* and has only two syllables (**Butkus**). A married woman takes the surname of her husband with the ending -*ienė*: **Jasienė, Liesienė, Balkevičienė, Butkuvienė**.

Bibliography

Blese, E. (1929): *Latviešu personvārdu un uzvārdu studijas.* Riga.

Butkus, A. (1996): *Lietuvių pravardės.* Kaunas.

Kuzavinis, K., and B. Savukynas (1987): *Lietuvių vardų kilmės žodynas.* Vilnius.

Lietuvių pavardžių žodynas. Vol. 1, Vilnius, 1985; vol. 2, Vilnius, 1989.

Maciejauskienė, V. (1991): *Lietuvių pavardžių susidarymas 13–18 a.* Vilnius.

Plāķis, J. (1936–39): *Latvijas vietu vārdi un latviešu pavārdi.* Latvijas Universitātes Raksti, Filoloģijas un filozofijas fakultātes sērija. 2 vols. Riga.

Siliņš, K. (1990): *Latviešu personvārdu vārdnīca.* Riga.

Staltmane, V. E. (1981): *Latyshskaya antroponimika. Familii.* Moscow.

Zinkevičius, Z. (1977): Lietuvių antroponimika. Vilnius.

INDIAN FAMILY NAMES

Rocky Miranda

The Indian surnames included in this work come from various states of India, many of which are separate linguistic regions as well. India can be broadly divided into two linguistic areas: the north, or northern states, where the dominant languages belong to the Indo-Aryan language group, and the south, or southern states, where the dominant languages belong to the Dravidian group.

The northern states can be further subdivided into the north-central region, where the principal states are Bihar, Madhya Pradesh, Rajasthan, and Uttar Pradesh; the northeast, with the principal states of Assam, Bengal, and Orissa; the west, which includes Goa, Gujarat, and Maharashtra; and two states outside these groups—the single state known as Jammu and Kashmir, and the Panjab. The official language of north-central states is Hindi. The official languages of the other states mentioned here are Assamese (Assam), Bengali (Bengal), Oriya (Orissa), Konkani (Goa), Gujarati (Gujarat), Marathi (Maharashtra), Kashmiri (Jammu and Kashmir), and Panjabi (Panjab). Among the Indo-Aryan languages, Nepali and Sindhi are also mentioned in this work. Nepali is the language of a separate country, Nepal, and Sindhi is the language of Sind, now part of Pakistan. However, these are recognized among the official languages of India because significant numbers of people speaking Nepali and Sindhi live in India.

The southern states are Andhra Pradesh, Karnataka, Kerala, and Tamil Nadu. The official languages in these states are Telugu (Andhra Pradesh), Kannada (Karnataka), Malayalam (Kerala), and Tamil (Tamil Nadu). Other Indian states have been omitted here because no surnames included in this work are exclusively associated with them. Some names are confined to a single linguistic region, but others are found in more than one.

Hindu Castes and Names

In discussing Hindu surnames, we need to refer to social groups or communities called castes or *jati*s. These are usually endogamous groups (in which people marry only other members of their own group) that are associated with specific occupations. There are numerous such communities in modern India that are supposed to be affiliated with one of four broad social divisions called *varna*s, which have come down from ancient times: the Brahman or priestly class, the Kshatriya or warriors, the Vaishya or merchants, and the Shudra or cultivators and craftspersons. In the case of Brahman names, the jati is usually not identified in this work. In the case of non-Brahman names, however, only the jati is mentioned, because the varna affiliation of several of these jatis is disputed.

Many important non-Brahman communities mentioned in this work include the Ahirs, Banias (see the entry **Banik** for the meaning of *Bania*), Kayasths, and Rajputs of northern India; the Aroras (see **Arora**), Jats, Khatris (see **Khatri**), and Soods (see **Sood**) of the Panjab; the Bhatias of the Panjab and Gujarat (see **Bhatia**); the Vanias (see **Banik**) of Gujarat; the Baidyas (see **Vaidya**) and the Baishyas of Bengal; the Bunts of Karnataka; the Nayars (see **Nair**) of Kerala; and the Reddis (see **Reddy**) of Andhra Pradesh. The Rajputs are a prominent community of the Kshatriya varna. Several other communities (such as the Aroras, the Bhatias, the Khatris, the Soods, and several groups of Banias) also claim Kshatriya origin.

The Banias of northern India, the Vanias of Gujarat, the Aroras, Khatris, and Soods of the Panjab, and the Bhatias of Gujarat and the Panjab are mercantile communities. The Kayasths rose to prominence in medieval India as clerks and accountants and so they are often referred to as the writers' caste. The traditional occupations of the other communities are agriculture or miscellaneous trades. The Banias of northern India are really a cluster of several communities, of which the Agarwal Banias, Oswal Banias, and Porwal Banias are mentioned separately in connection with certain surnames.

Not every Hindu surname can be linked with a special community. Some of them are common to several jatis or varnas (for example, Naik and Prabhu), and some names have no special association with any community (for example, Kumar). In a number of cases, information on the community associated with the name was not available.

Imported Surnames

Many Indian surnames are found among both Hindus and other religious groups: Christian, Jain, Muslim, Parsi, and Sikh. The Jain, Parsi, and Sikh surnames are usually the same as the Hindu surnames in a given area. Many Christians, however, have European surnames. Thus, the Christians whose ancestors were converted by the Portuguese have Portuguese surnames, which are believed to have come from the godfathers of the initial converts. Anglo-Indian Christians usually have British surnames. Christians of southern India, like other people in the south, often use no surnames but place their father's personal names before their own personal names. However, those who move to the United States usually use the father's name as their last name, and it eventually becomes a family name. These new family names are also European because they have evolved from European personal names.

Origins of Names

Full names from ancient India, as found in Sanskrit literature from the first millennium BC to the first millennium AC), typically consist of a single word, either a simple word or a compound word in which the final element often indicates the varna. Some common final elements in such names are *-dāsa* 'servant', *-datta* 'gift', *-deva* 'god', *-gupta* 'secret', *-šarmā* 'joy', *-sena* 'army,' 'armament', *-siṃha* 'lion,' 'eminent person', and *-varmā* 'protection'. Sanskrit dictionaries indicate that *-deva* or *-šarmā* is the final element in the names of Brahmans, as *-varmā* is for Kshatriyas, *-gupta* or *-datta* is for Vaishyas, and *-dāsa* is for Shudras. However, many ancient as well as modern Indian names can be found that contradict this classification. For instance, there are people whose name ends in *-datta* who are not Vaishyas, and there are those whose name ends in *-dāsa* who are not Shudras. These bound elements also have regularly evolved as separate surnames that are among the most common in modern India (see **Das, Datta, Deo, Gupta, Sharma, Sen, Singh** or its variant **Sinha,** and **Varma**).

Later on, many other names evolved similarly—for example, **Chand** from Sanskrit *čandra* 'pleasant,' 'moon'; **Kumar** from Sanskrit *kumāra* 'son'; **Lal** from Hindi *lāl* 'darling', from Sanskrit *lāla* 'cajoling'; **Nath** from Sanskrit *nātha* 'lord'; **Prasad** from Sanskrit *prasāda* 'gift'; and **Raj** from Sanskrit *rājā* 'king'. Some of them occur as independent given names as well, but they all occur as the final elements of compound given names and sometimes as separate surnames. Having had no surnames previously, or having shed the previous surnames for some reason, the bearers of these compound given names split those names to supply new surnames. Most of the split surnames of this second category are not associated with a specific caste or community.

The name of a clan or some similar subgroup of the community to which one belongs is used as a surname quite frequently. Here are some examples.

Arora clan names: **Ahuja, Batra, Chana, Chawla, Dua, Gulati, Kalra, Khurana, Madan, Narang, Sachdev,** and **Taneja.**

Agarwal Bania clan names: **Bansal, Goel, Mittal,** and **Singhal.**

Jat tribal names: **Brar, Dhaliwal, Dhillon, Gill, Grewal, Johal, Khera, Sandhu,** and **Siddhu.**

Kayasth subgroup names: **Bhatnagar, Mathur, Saksena,** and **Srivastava.**

Panjabi Khatri clan names: **Anand, Bahl, Bahri, Bedi, Bhalla, Bhasin, Chadha, Chopra, Dhawan, Kapoor, Khanna, Kohli, Malhotra, Sahni, Sehgal, Sethi, Sodhi, Suri, Talwar, Tandon,** and **Vohra.**

Konkanasth Brahman clan names: **Dev (variant of Deo), Kale.**

Maratha clan names: **Lad, More,** and **Savant.**

Rajput clan names: **Bhatti, Chauhan, Parmar, Rathod,** and **Solanki.**

Reddi clan name: **Bandi.**

Clan names in a subgroup of Saraswat Brahmans of the Panjab: **Bali, Dutt,** and **Mohan.**

The name of the community itself is adopted by some as a surname. Examples are **Agarwal, Arora, Bhatia, Iyengar, Iyer, Khatri, Nair, Reddy,** and **Sood.**

Some Indian surnames come from names or nicknames of ancestors: **Bhargav** 'descendant of **Bhrigu**'; **Bhatti,** ancestor of a Rajput clan; **Lakhani** 'descendant of *Lakh(man)*' In a few cases, the ancestors are mythical. Some of the surnames have overt patronymic suffixes, such as *-jā* and *-ānī*. Some of these surnames are from clan names, but the clan names in turn go back to the name or nickname of the founder of the clan. Examples are **Anand** and **Bedi,** ancestors of Khatri clans.

Other Indian surnames have evolved from ancestral place names, especially in certain parts of India such as Maharashtra and Goa. Since their frequency is not particularly high, only a few names of this type are included in this work—for instance, **Agarwal** 'from Agar or Agroha', **Ahluwalia** 'from Ahlu', **Bhatnagar** 'from Bhatnagar', **Irani** 'from Iran', **Lad** 'from southern Gujarat', and **Mathur** 'from Mathura'.

Many names can be traced back to occupations or offices held by the ancestors of the name bearers—for example, **Bajaj** 'clothier', **Banik** 'merchant', **Bhandari** 'treasurer, keeper of a storehouse', **Chokshi** 'assayer', **Chowdhury** 'chief', **Dalal** 'broker', **Desai** 'district chief', **Deshmukh** 'district chief', **Deshpande** 'district clerk', **Dixit** 'priest performing certain religious rites', **Doshi** 'hawker carrying his wares (clothing) on his shoulder', **Gandhi** 'vendor of perfumes', **Ghosh** 'herdsman', **Jha** 'teacher', **Jhaveri** 'jeweler', **Joshi** 'astrologer', **Kamath** 'cultivator', **Kapadia** 'clothier', **Kothari** 'storekeeper', **Kulkarni** 'village clerk', **Majumdar** 'record-keeper', **Modi** 'grocer', **Nadkarni** 'district clerk', **Pal** 'herdsman', **Parikh** 'assayer', **Patel** 'village headman', **Pathak** 'teacher', **Purohit** 'family priest', **Reddy** 'village headman', **Saha** 'merchant', **Shah** 'merchant', **Shroff** 'money-changer', **Soni** 'goldsmith', **Upadhyaya** 'teacher', and **Vaidya** 'physician'. Among Parsis, one even finds occupational surnames from English, such as **Contractor, Doctor, Merchant,** and **Tailor.**

Some people were awarded titles by native or foreign rulers, by the community, or by themselves. Some titles are simply honorific terms of address that have come down as surnames. Names meaning 'king', 'chief', 'headman', 'lord', 'leader', 'eminent person', 'great one', honorable one', and so on are particularly common: for instance, **Bhatt** 'lord', **Chakraborty** 'emperor', **Chowdhury** 'chief', **Deo** 'god, lord', **Goswami** 'lord of cows, earth, etc.', **Hegde** 'chief', **Mahajan** 'great person', **Maharaj** 'great king, master', **Malik** 'king', **Mehta** 'great one', **Menon** 'exalted one', **Mishra** 'honorable one', **Naidu** 'chief', **Naik** 'leader', **Nair** 'leader', **Nath** 'lord', **Pai** 'lord', **Prabhu** 'lord', **Rai** 'king', **Raja** 'king', **Rana** 'king', **Rao** 'king', **Sarkar** 'lord', **Seth** 'chief', **Setty** 'chief', **Singh** 'lion, eminent one', **Shah** 'king', and **Thakur** 'lord'. It should also be noted that although some names such as **Patel** and **Reddy** 'village headman' go back to an actual office, they are commonly used as respectful terms of address even if the addressee is neither a village headman nor the descendant of one. Names meaning 'scholar', 'expert', 'teacher', and so on are also quite common: **Acharya** 'preceptor', **Bhattacharya** 'learned preceptor', **Jani** 'learned one', and **Upadhyaya** 'teacher'.

In many parts of India, men are respectfully addressed as 'father' or 'brother' and women as 'mother' or 'sister'. These terms are then regularly attached to personal names, as in the case of Gujarati *bhai* 'brother', *ben* 'sister', Kannada *appa* 'father', *aṇṇa* 'older brother', *amma* 'mother', *akka* 'older sister', Marathi *dada* 'older brother', *bai* 'older sister', and *bābū* 'father' in several Indic languages. Occasionally, such attachments have evolved as separate surnames. Thus, Gujarati women who use no surname sometimes give **Ben** as their last name. This cannot be considered a true surname because it is not passed on from one generation to another. However, **Babu** and **Dada** have become inherited surnames. Although the Tamil surnames **Iyer** and **Iyengar** evolved from names of communities, those names go back to a term of address, Dravidian *ayya* 'father, lord'.

Some Hindu surnames are epithets of Hindu gods: **Kumar,** an epithet of Kartikeya, son of the god Shiva; **Lal,** an epithet of the god Krishna; **Mohan,** of Krishna; **Narayan,** of the god Vishnu; **Ram,** an incarnation of Vishnu; and **Basu,** an epithet of Shiva and also of several other gods. These usually go back to ancestral personal names, since epithets of deities are commonly used for personal names. Because many personal names from southern India have been taken as family names in the United States, family names that are epithets of deities are very common among U.S. immigrants from that region.

Some names denoting animals or plants seem to have totemic significance. Examples include **Apte** from *apṭa* 'the plant Bauhinia tomentosa' and **More** from *mor* 'peacock'.

Southern Indian Names

In southern India, the last of a person's names is usually not the family name but the personal name of the individual. The first name may be an ancestral personal name, an ancestral place name, or the father's personal name. In some cases, the father's personal name appears as the middle name. Many people have no middle name and use only the father's personal name as the first name. They have no true surname.

People from southern India who live in the United States usually reorder their names, writing the personal name first and the Indian first name (which might be an ancestral personal name, ancestral place name, or father's personal name) last. Those who have come to use the father's personal name as the last name use it as their children's last name as well, thus converting it into a true surname. As a result, many personal names of southern India—such as **Krishna, Krishnan, Narayanan, Raghavan, Raja, Rajan, Srinivas, Srinivasan, Joseph, Mathew,** and **Philip**—have become surnames in the United States.

Some people with the southern Indian pattern of surname placement have come to use an additional surname that is placed in the final position. In such cases, the surname placed initially is usually an ancestral personal name or ancestral place name whereas the surname placed finally is a title or a name that indicates community or clan. For example, people from Andhra Pradesh with surnames like **Naidu** and **Reddy,** or Konkani-speaking people from Karnataka with surnames like **Kamath, Pai,** and **Shenoy** often have another surname, placed initially, that refers to their ancestral place.

Linguistic Background

The greatest number of Indian surnames are derived from Sanskrit, the ancient language that occupies a position in India similar to that of Latin in Europe. Even in southern India where Dravidian languages are spoken, Sanskrit surnames are quite common. They are adopted with minimal alteration to suit the phonological (sound) patterns of the language of the region. Extensive alteration is found only in a few cases, as in **Khatri.** There are also numerous surnames in the north taken from the modern Indo-Aryan languages of the area. Many of the names in the Dravidian language area are of Indo-Aryan origin, and only their inflectional endings are likely to be Dravidian. Names of Dravidian origin (such as **Bandi, Hegde, Menon, Pillai,** and **Reddy**) are quite few.

Perso-Arabic surnames are the norm among Indian Muslims, but even among Hindus and other non-Muslim Indians, a good number are found: Arabic **Bajaj, Dalal, Jhaveri, Majumdar, Malik,** and **Shroff;** and Persian **Doshi, Sarkar,** and **Sood.** A few occupational surnames, noted above, have come from English. One Indian surname has evolved from Portuguese: **Mistry** from *mestre*.

Variants

Many Indian names have variant forms. For the most part, they are spelling variants: **Bahl** or **Behl** (pronounced 'behl'); **Bava/Bawa** (pronounced 'bawa'), **Bhat/Bhatt, Bora/Borah, Chakrabarti/Chakraborty, Das/Dass/Dash** (pronounced 'dash'), and so on. Some have phonetic variants as well: **Sankar/Shankar, Seth/Sheth.** Some names have Anglicized variants, such as **Bose** for **Basu** and **Ghose** for **Ghosh.** In some cases, Anglicization affects only the spelling, as in **Mullick** for **Mallick** or **Sircar** for **Sarkar.** Some names have Sanskritized variants, analogous to the earlier European practice of Latinizing names (e.g., **Carolus Linnaeus** from Swedish **Carl Linné**): **Bandopadhyay** for **Banerjee, Chattopadhyay** for **Chatterjee, Dwivedi** for **Dube, Mukhopadhyay** for **Mukherjee,** or **Tripathi** for **Tiwari. Bajaj** and **Shroff,** names of Arabic origin, have variants **Bazaz** and **Saraf** that are closer to their Arabic pronunciation.

In this work, the full information on a surname is given under the most frequent variant, although this may not always be closest to the original form of the name. Cognate names with different spelling and pronunciation occurring in entirely different communities are generally not treated as variants. For example, the names **Seth, Setty,** and **Shetty,** which go back to the same Sanskrit source, are listed separately because they differ with respect to spelling, pronunciation, and the social groups in which they occur.

Bibliography
Koul, O. N. (1994): 'Surnames and Nicknames in Kashmiri' in *Mehrotra.*
Krishnamurti, Bh. (1995): 'Dravidian surnames' in *Namenforschung/Name Studies, Les noms propres,* vol. 1: 665–71.

Marykutty, A. M. (1997): *Personal Names of Kerala Christians.* Edamattom, Kerala: Indian Institute of Christian Studies, 1997.
Mehrotra, R. R., ed. (1994):*The Book of Indian Names.* New Delhi: Rupa and Co.
Singh, K. S., ed. (1996): *Communities, Segments, Synonyms, Surnames, and Titles.* (People of India, National Series, vol. 8, of the Anthropological Survey of India). Delhi: Oxford University Press.

ARABIC AND MUSLIM FAMILY NAMES

Paul Roochnik and Salahuddin Ahmed

Language, Names, and Religion

There could be no more dramatic illustration of the complexity of the relationships among language, religion, culture, and naming than those that hold between the Arabic language and Islam. Classical Arabic is the language of the Qur'an, the sacred book of Islam, and many millions of Arabic speakers are Muslims by religion. But in addition, sizeable minorities of people can be found in most Arabic-speaking countries who are not Muslims. Precise figures are impossible to obtain, but it is estimated that at least 35% of the population of Lebanon, 10% of Syrians, 8% of Jordanians, 10% of Egyptians, 8% of Palestinians, and 3% of Iraqis are members of one or other of the Christian sects of the region. Altogether, approximately 5% of Arabic speakers (about 14 million people) are Christians, while a further 2% represent an indigenous Jewish population. Among people from the Middle East, there are many Druze and Christian Arabs, particularly from the Levant (Syria and Lebanon, Jordan and Palestine) among those Arabic speakers who have emigrated to the United States. Christians have also come in large numbers from Iraq and Egypt. Jews from the Arab world have also settled in the United States, but to a lesser extent than that of their Christian counterparts.

The other side of the coin is that Islam is a world religion. Therefore, in addition to being the faith of Arabic speakers, it is also the faith of millions of people whose native language is not Arabic.

All of this affects the choice and usage of names. Clearly, it would be an error to assume that everyone bearing an Arabic name must be a Muslim. Arabic names are borne also by Christians, Druze, and Jews, and people of other faiths too. Conversely, it would be equally erroneous to assume that a person whose name has clear Muslim connotations is necessarily an Arabic speaker. Muslims, even those who do not speak Arabic, regard it as a religious duty to learn classical Arabic so that they can understand the meaning of their daily prayers and

read the Qur'an in the original. Furthermore, they generally choose names that have positive connotations in Islam, typically Arabic names based on attributes of Allah or on the names borne by the Prophet Muhammad, his family, his associates, and his successors. For this reason, a Muslim personal name is not always a good indicator of the national origins of its bearers. For example, the name of a person called Abdul Aziz ('Abd al-'Azīz 'servant of the Mighty') tells us that he is almost certainly of Muslim faith, but his name gives no clue as to whether he or his forebears come from an Arabic-speaking country, from the Indian subcontinent, or elsewhere. Pronunciation differences that may be heard in the spoken form of a name, and which may serve for regional or national identification, are not often reflected in its written forms.

The policy of this dictionary is that, if a name is used by Christian and other non-Muslim Arabic speakers, the label *Arabic* is used. On the other hand, if a name is used by non-Arabic speakers as well as Arabic speakers, the label *Muslim* is used. It must be admitted, however, that there are many cases where the evidence is inconclusive; in such cases, we have made a judgment based on the balance of probability. Given names (*isms*) such as *Fādī* 'redeemer', *'Isa* 'Jesus', *Hanna* 'John', and *Boutros* 'Peter' are preferred by Christian Arabs, although even here there may be no clear-cut distinctions. For example, one might assume that *Mūsā* 'Moses' and *Ibrāhīm* 'Abraham' are Jewish names, but this would be wrong, for in fact these names are also popular among Muslims, Christians, and Druze. *'Isa* is clearly a Christian name, but it is also used by Muslims, for Jesus is regarded as a prophet in Islam. The complexity of these issues, which require much more detailed exposition, lie outside the scope of the present work; they can only be touched on here.

The Arabic Language

Arabic is the sixth most common native language in the world; it is the principal language of eighteen countries, with a combined population of almost 200 million. Arabic became an "official" language of the United Nations in the latter part of the 20th century. Historically speaking, it is a Semitic language, related to Hebrew, Amharic, Berber, and certain other languages of North Africa and the Middle East. Arabic words are composed of two parts: the root and the pattern. The root typically consists of three consonants, giving the underlying basic meaning of the word; the pattern consists of vowels inserted between and around the consonants, giving a specific meaning to the word in particular contexts. Thus *s-l-m* has the underlying meaning 'peace'. With patterns, *salām* means 'peace and security' or 'safety'; *sālim* means 'secure'; *salīm* means 'faultless'; *aslam* means 'most perfect'; *islām* is 'submission (to the will of God)'; *muslim* denotes an adherent of Islam. These different patterns are often reflected in the variety of Arabic names that may be based on the same root.

The Arabic Naming System

Naming conventions in the Arabic-speaking Muslim world are not as cut and dried as they are in the West. All Arab children receive a given name. Their second name comes from the first name of their father. The complexity begins with the third element of the name, which may span five or more elements, as described below. For many Arabs, the given name of the paternal grandfather is taken as an individual's third name, and it often serves as the surname. As an example, if your parents name you *Jamīla*, and your father's first name is *'Alī*, and your paternal grandfather's first name is *Husayn*, then the name which might appear on your official documents is "Jamīla 'Alī Husayn." Other Arabs, however, embrace the concept of an inherited family surname. In this system, you might be named "Jamīla 'Alī Baghdadi," where "Baghdadi" plays the same role as "Milton" or "Bradford" would in the West.

The entries for Muslim and Arabic names in this dictionary generally represent adaptations of different parts of standard Arabic names, as described below, to the American world, insofar as a family name or surname is a conventional and bureaucratic requirement. Any one or more of the five standard elements of a traditional Arabic name may be pressed into service as a modern American "surname" among immigrants from the Arab world. Among second- and third-generation Arab Americans, these names tend to acquire hereditary status on the American model.

Standard Arabic personal names consist of up to five elements. A person might be known by any one of these elements or by combinations of them. The five elements (in the order in which they are used if combined) are as follows:

Kunya: the *kunya* is a kind of nickname, formed with *abū* 'father of' or *umm* 'mother of'. So, for example, the Prophet Muhammad was known by the kunya *Abū-l Qāsem* 'father of Qāsem', and Qāsem was indeed the name of his son. But a kunya could be and often was conventionalized: a childless person or a newborn child could be given a kunya. The Prophet's wife Ayesha was known by the kunya

Umm Abdullah 'mother of Abdullah', although she was in fact childless. In Iran, a kunya is often metaphorical rather than literal, as in the kunya *Abu-l Fazl* 'father of bounty' (i.e. endowed with bounty). In the Indian subcontinent, the kunya is used only informally and literally within the family circle with reference to an actually extant child.

Ism: the *ism* is the individual's personal name or given name. Asmaa' (the plural form) are taken freely from vocabulary words in Arabic, and may be nouns, verbs, or adjectives (including both base forms such as *Ḥamīd* 'praised', 'praiseworthy' and elative forms such as *Aḥmad* 'the most praised'). An ism may be used with or without the definite article *al-*. Abstract nouns are common (e.g. *Nasr* 'victory', *Taufīq* 'success', 'prosperity', *Iqbāl* 'good fortune'), while words denoting features of the natural world (*Suha* 'star', *Ṭalāl* 'gentle rain') are also popular. Asmaa' based on verbs include *Yazīd* 'he increases' and *Ya'ish* 'he lives'. Among Muslims, an ism may be chosen with reference to a noted figure in Muslim history: *Muḥammad*, the name of the messenger of Allah to whom the Qur'an was revealed, remains the most popular choice among Muslim parents for a baby boy, while *Fāṭima*, name of Muhammad's favorite daughter, is a popular choice for girls. Important sources of Muslim asmaa' are the ninety-nine attributes of Allah mentioned in the Qur'an and the Hadith, the holy books of Islam. According to Islamic belief, the relationship between humans and their creator is that of servants to their master. Many Muslims bear a name denoting a servant of one of the attributes of Allah, such as *Abd al-Qadīr* 'servant of the capable' or *Abd al-Karīm* 'servant of the generous'. The Hadith says: "The best names in the sight of God are *'Abdullah* 'servant of God' and *'Abd al-Raḥmān* 'servant of the merciful'."

Nasab: the *nasab* is the lineage name (e.g. *ibn-Saud, ibn al-Khaṭṭāb*), expressing the relationship of a son (*ibn*) or daughter (*bint*) to his or her father, or sometimes to a more distant forebear. Thus, occasionally a nasab could be hereditary for some generations, especially in the case of descendants of a famous forebear. In some cases, a person's nasab expresses relationship with the mother, especially if the mother was remarkable in some way. Generally, the reference of the nasab is to the father's ism, but sometimes it may be to his kunya (e.g. *'Alī ibn Abi Ṭalib*, literally ''Alī the son of the father of Ṭalib'), or to his laqab (e.g. *Muḥammad ibn aṣ-Ṣiddīq* 'Muḥammad, son of the Righteous one', *Dīma bint az-Zayyāt* 'Dima, daughter of the oil man'). The nasab could also be iterated (e.g. *Salamah ibn 'Amr ibn al-Akwā* 'Salamah son of 'Amr, son of al-Akwā').

Nisba: the *nisba* expresses a relation between a person and a locality, generally the person's birthplace, residence, or place where the family originated (e.g. *al-Hāshimī, al-Qurayshī, al-Kuwaitī*).

Laqab: the *laqab* is a distinguishing nickname, which may refer to a physical characteristic (e.g. *al-Aswad* 'the black', *al-Aṣamm* 'the deaf'). Names of animals and birds of prey are common (e.g. *al-Asad* and *al-Ḥaidar*, both meaning 'the lion', *al-Fahd* 'the cheetah', *al-'Uqāb* 'the eagle'); such words can also be used as an ism. A laqab may be an anecdotal nickname; according to Schimmel, a Moroccan politician who habitually interrupted people with the phrase *jūj kelmat* 'just a couple of words' received this expression as his laqab. The laqab could also be an honorific (e.g. *al-Hajji* 'the person who has performed the hajj (pilgrimage to Mecca)'; *al-Nāṣif* 'the just'; *al-Ṣiddīq* 'the truthful'). Another kind of laqab denotes an occupation (e.g. *al-Khayyāṭ* 'the tailor', *al-Ḥaddād* 'the smith', *al-Khayyām* 'the tent-maker').

The elements of this naming system are used, with variations, throughout the Arabic-speaking world and in other Muslim countries. The different elements are used in different social contexts, and conventions vary from country to country. For example, in Arab countries, the kunya may be used among a wide circle of friends, whereas in the Indian subcontinent it may be used informally in family circles, but does not count as part of a family name. The ism is used only among family and intimates, and it is generally a breach of etiquette for an outsider to address a person by his or her ism alone. Famous people are known to history by more or less arbitrary combinations of the ism with the kunya, nasab, nisba, and/or laqab. Name elements including the phrases *ud-Din* 'of the faith', *al-Dawla* 'of the state', *al-Islām* 'of Islam', and *al-Mulk* 'of the kingdom' were a specific type of honorific, used almost exclusively by sultans, qazis, and others of high rank.

In some Muslim countries, legislation was passed in the 20th century to make family names a legal requirement. The best-known example is Turkey, where family names were required by a law passed in 1934. In Egypt, a similar law was enacted as recently as 1970. These developments are too recent to have had much effect on family names among immigrant populations in America.

Other Languages of the Muslim World

As mentioned above, Arabic is not the only language of the Muslim world, though it has had a profound influence on the naming practices of other Muslim communities. From its origin in the Arabian Peninsula in the 7th century CE, Islam proselytized and spread rapidly. To the west, it spread rapidly along the southern shores of the Mediterranean. In the countries of northwest Africa, Arabic found itself competing with Berber and French. Arabic names are found in combination with French forenames among people from Algeria and Morocco, as well as Lebanon and Syria.

Islam crossed the Sahara desert and became the established religion of the Hausa people in northern Nigeria and of certain other peoples of West Africa. It also spread down the coast of East Africa, being most influential there linguistically on Swahili, and culturally in coastal cities such as Zanzibar.

In Europe, Albania and Bosnia contain substantial indigenous Muslim communities, a legacy of the days when the Ottoman Empire extended westward over Greece and much of the Balkans. The surname of the first president of independent Bosnia, Alija Izetbegovich, is a good example of the effects on naming: it contains the Arabic personal name *Izzat* 'honor', the traditional Turkish honorific *beg* 'bey', and the Serbo-Croatian patronymic suffix *-vich* 'son of'.

From the 8th to the 13th century, much of Spain was a Muslim country, under the rule of Moors, who originally came from North Africa. This was a period noted for its cultural and scientific achievements and for its religious tolerance. Although the Moors were driven from Spain in the 13th century, Arabic left indelible traces on Spanish place names, vocabulary, and personal names.

To the east, Islam spread to Persia (Iran) in 642 CE (only ten years after the Prophet's death). From there it continued to spread rapidly northward through the Caucasus and across central Asia, and eastward to the Indian subcontinent.

In the 16th century, the Mughal Empire was established in India, with Islam as its main religion. Some of the princely states of India had already adopted Islam as their main religion, while others remained Hindu. In 1947, India was partitioned and the new Islamic state of Pakistan was created. The main language of Pakistan is Urdu, an Indic language with a strong admixture of both Arabic and Persian vocabulary. Other languages of Pakistan include Pashto (also spoken in Afghanistan), Punjabi, Baluchi, and Sindhi. In 1972, the new state of Bangladesh was formed (formerly East Pakistan). Here the language is Bengali. However, in both Pakistan and Bangladesh, and indeed elsewhere in the Indian subcontinent, Muslim personal names are characteristically Arabic in style, but with many Persian elements.

Further east still, Islam is the main religion in Malaysia and Indonesia, and there are even Muslim communities in western China.

Of all the many languages spoken in the Islamic world, two may be singled out for special mention in addition to Arabic.

Persian (Iranian)

Undoubtedly the most influential language in the Muslim world after Arabic is Persian, the language of Iran (in its modern form generally known as Farsi or, sometimes, Iranian). The Persian language is unrelated to Arabic—it is an Indo-European language, related to Sanskrit and the modern languages of northern India—but it is written using Arabic script and has absorbed many Arabic words.

When Islam swept into Persia within ten years of Muḥammad's death, it brought with it the Arabic naming system and many names themselves derived from Arabic. Under Islam, the Arabic naming system was introduced, and many Arabic words were adopted. In some cases, specifically Persian forms of Arabic names adopted at this time have subsequently spread elsewhere in the Muslim world, for example, *Afzal* (Arabic form *Afḍal*) 'best' or 'learned'; *Fazel* (Arabic form *faḍl*) 'favor' or 'grace'.

Just as, in the traditional Arabic naming system, any vocabulary word (in theory) could be adopted as a personal name (ism), so now Muslims throughout the world (but especially in the subcontinent) found themselves able to choose not only from Arabic but also from Persian words for their names. Names of Persian etymology, for example *Javed* 'eternal',

Firdaws 'paradise', *Jahangir* 'world holder', *Shireen* 'sweet', were added to the standard inventory of Muslim names. These are particularly widely used in Pakistan and the rest of the Indian subcontinent, as well as in Iran itself of course.

In addition to Muslim names, traditional Persian names also survive in use among some groups of Iranians. The Iranian sources for these are the names of the great kings and other legendary people who lived in the time of the ancient Persian Empire, in particular Darius, Cyrus, and Xerxes.

Turkish

The Turkish language is related historically neither to Persian nor Arabic. However, as far as its personal names are concerned, it was powerfully influenced by both. Arabic words in particular are common as elements in Turkish names, while traditional Turkish personal names owed much to the Arabic system.

Under the Ottoman Empire, an individual was known by his personal name, often used in combination with an honorific such as *Bey* or *Uzun* (e.g. *Önder Bey*; *Uzun Ḥasan* 'Ḥasan the tall'), a birth name (e.g. *Ahmed Riza*), an adjective denoting his

place of birth (e.g. *Mekkeli Sabri*), or a genealogical patronymic (e.g. *Akcuraoğlu Yusuf*). All this changed in 1934, when Turks were required by law to take a family name. The set of family names is large and diverse: a great deal of imagination was used in creating new family names, so there are few Turkish family names of any great frequency. This means that very few Turkish family names are recorded in sufficient numbers among Turkish immigrants to America to qualify for entry in this dictionary.

Bibliography

Ahmed, Salahuddin (1999): *A Dictionary of Muslim Names*. New York University Press.

Baker, Mona (1990): 'Common Names in the Arab World' in Patrick Hanks and Flavia Hodges (eds.): *Oxford Dictionary of First Names*. Oxford University Press.

Roochnik, Paul (1993): 'Computer-based Solutions to Certain Linguistic Problems Arising from the Romanization of Arabic Names'. Ph.D. diss., Georgetown University.

Schimmel, Annemarie (1989): *Islamic Names*. Edinburgh University Press.

CHINESE FAMILY NAMES

Mark Lewellen

The exact number of Chinese surnames is unknown, but estimates range from four to eight thousand, and more than six thousand is a widely accepted figure. Perhaps only two thousand of those surnames are in use today, however, and most of those occur rarely, so that a majority of the Chinese people share a remarkably small set of surnames. It is sometimes claimed that Chinese has only a hundred (or five hundred) surnames, but this is a misconception that stems in part from a well-known list whose title is usually translated as "The Hundred Surnames," and more accurately rendered as "The Many Surnames," since the list contains roughly five hundred names.

Almost all Chinese surnames are monosyllabic (of one syllable), but there are a small number of polysyllabic Chinese surnames, such as **Auyeung**. Although a Chinese surname precedes the given name, Chinese people in America have adopted the Western convention of placing the surname last.

The Spelling of Chinese Names

This is a dictionary of American names, so the headwords (entries) reflect the spellings found among Chinese Americans. However, for spelling Chinese words the romanization or

transliteration method used is the *pinyin* standard for the Mandarin dialect, the official language of China and Taiwan. For consistency, *pinyin* is used here even when the American spelling of the name is different; in such a case, the *pinyin* spelling is always identified as such. (However, reference to a headword uses the headword's spelling, not the *pinyin*.) Here are some hints on the pronunciation of *pinyin* consonants:

zh	pronounced like English *j*
j	pronounced like *j* (newscasters often pronounce it like a French *j*, as in *Jacques*)
x	pronounced like *sh*
q	pronounced like *ch*
c	pronounced like *ts*

Other consonants are pronounced much the same as in English.

The pronunciation of vowels is slightly more complex because written vowels often represent more than one possible pronunciation, and some of the Chinese vowel sounds do not occur in English. Additionally, Mandarin Chinese is known for complex diphthongs and triphthongs (combinations of two and three vowels, respectively). Two of the Chinese "medial vowels" are *i* and *u*. When these occur as the first member of a vowel group, *i* is pronounced like *ee* in *see*, and *u* like *oo* in *too*.

To pronounce a diphthong or triphthong, first pronounce *i* or *u* as shown, and then "glide" without interruption to the rest of the vowel cluster. For example, say "chee-yen" for *Qian*, or "jee-yang" for *Jiang*. Remember to make the transition smoothly without a break, though, because each name is actually one syllable, not two. To an English speaker, an initial *i* in a cluster sounds something like the *y* in *you*, and an initial *u* like the *w* in *we*.

History

Chinese surnames have their roots deep in ancient times, and a brief summary of the nation's early history helps us understand how they developed. From the 29th century BC through the 23d, China was ruled by a series of revered emperors, notably Huang Di, Zhuan Xu, Ku, Yao, Shun, and Yu. Because later people desired to trace their lineage to an early ruler, these six appear in many accounts of the origins of Chinese surnames. Huang Di, often considered the father of the Chinese people, supposedly ruled at the time the Egyptians were building their first pyramids; all rulers of the later Zhou dynasty claimed descent from him. His son and successor, Zhuan Xu, was often claimed as an ancestor, as was his son and successor Ku, who was also claimed as an ancestor by rulers of the Shang and Zhou dynasties. Yao, Shun, and Yu were "model emperors" whose virtues were later extolled by Confucius.

Following these emperors, the first dynasty, the Xia, was established in 2205 BC. A recurring motif in Chinese history is apparent in the Xia dynasty: it began with wise and virtuous rulers but decayed over time into cruel and corrupt dictatorship, causing the dynasty to lose the "mandate of heaven" and to be overthrown by another dynasty, initially more virtuous. The Shang dynasty replaced the Xia in either 1766 or 1523 BC, and from that period date the earliest records of Chinese writing, on oracle shells and bones. The last ruler of the Shang dynasty, Zhou Xin, persecuted the prince of the vassal state of Zhou, Wen Wang. Wen Wang has become famous for virtue and loyalty, for, despite imprisonment and mistreatment, he refused to rise up against his sovereign. His son, Wu Wang, did not feel thus restricted, and following his father's death he defeated the Shang dynasty in 1122 BC, establishing the Zhou dynasty.

It is in the Zhou period that many surnames originated. Wen Wang and Wu Wang are involved in many accounts of Chinese surnames, often as ancestors but also as grantors of fiefs that served as sources of surnames. China until the end of the Zhou dynasty in 221 BC is often called a "feudal" society because the European feudal social structure is the closest Western analogue to the elaborate system of titles, relationships, bureaucracies, and land ownership in this period. The king enfeoffed (granted as a fief) states or lands to valued subjects, usually members of his family or direct descendants of an emperor; and the grantee usually was also granted, as one of his names, the place name of the fief. Dukes of individual states could in turn enfeoff lands and titles to others.

Over the course of the Zhou dynasty, central control gradually weakened while the power of the states grew. During the Spring and Autumn period (722–481 BC) of the Zhou dynasty, China became the first culture to enter the Iron Age, and agriculture, water control, warfare, and population consequently developed rapidly. The Warring States period (403–221 BC) saw almost continuous warfare among the states, but nevertheless great societal advancement, with the philosophies of Confucianism, Taoism, and Legalism developing during this period. The triumph of the state of Qin in 221 BC established, in the Qin dynasty, the first true Chinese empire and the end of Chinese feudalism. The ruthless rise to power of the Qin so alienated the populace, however, that their rule lasted only fifteen years, though it made profound changes in Chinese society. By this time, Chinese surnames had developed to essentially the state they exist in today.

The Chinese language does not have one all-encompassing word for 'name'; the words *mingzi* or *ming* perhaps come closest to the larger sense of English *name*, but they refer more to the given name of a person; *xingshi* denotes a surname. Historically, there were additional types of names, and a person might accumulate names throughout his or her life; the higher the social status of the person, the more names he or she might acquire. This is an important clue to the sources of individual surnames, which developed from various other kinds of names. In the earliest recorded times, there was no *xingshi*, but there were types called *xing* and *shi*; there was no *mingzi*, but there were *ming* and *zi*, as well as other types of names.

When the *xing* and *shi* originated, as early as five thousand years ago, the *xing* designated a tribe, while the *shi* designated a subdivision of the tribe. Only people of noble birth bore *xing* and *shi*. The use of *xing* and *shi* developed over time. One's *xing* was generally obtained by inheritance. (Many scholars, noting the high frequency of the component for 'woman' in characters for various *xing*, as well as in the character for the word *xing* itself, argue that the *xing* was originally transmitted through the mother.) Eventually a particular *xing* became associated with the ruling family of a state or a group of states; for instance, the princes of the states of Lu, Jing, Shan, Wei, Yu, and others had the *xing* **Ji**, while princes of the state of Qi had the *xing* **Jiang**, and princes of Qin had the *xing* **Yin**. The *xing* was used to ensure that lines of descent remained sufficiently separate, since people with the same *xing* were prohibited from marrying each other.

Women came to be referred to by their *xing*, while men would be referred to by their *shi*. The *shi* was often granted by a king or higher noble to honor merit. Often the granted name was the same as that of a city, county, or state enfeoffed to a worthy recipient. The majority of modern surnames have their origins in such *shi* and in place names; unfortunately, the historical records rarely indicate how a place name was originally created. Sometimes a *shi* came not from a place name but from one of the names of an honored ancestor.

The term *ming* can be translated as 'given name'. *Zi*, often translated as 'style name', was bestowed when a person reached the age of majority—twenty years for men, fifteen years for women. A person might also be given a posthumous name called *shi* (but written with a character for *shi* different from the one used in *xingshi*) or *shihao*. Sometimes the historical record indicates that a person was simply 'called' (*cheng*) by a certain appellation; such a general appellation might be termed *hao*. Another type of name is *hui*, a 'taboo name' of an important person; a few current surnames have undergone modification in the past in order to distinguish them from *hui*. A descendant might have adopted a character from any of these names (except the taboo *hui*) to serve as a *shi*.

Eventually, by the Warring States period (403–221 BC), the *xing* and *shi* were merging, and people increasingly desired to claim surnames from noble ancestors such as ancient emperors. From the Han dynasty (206 BC–220 AD) on, only *xing*, or *xingshi*, were used by both commoners and nobles. The vast majority of surnames in use today thus existed in fully developed form 2,000 years ago, and most had originated 1,000 to 2,500 years before that.

In this book's discussion of the origins of each name, reference to the rich variety of Chinese name types has been simplified: *xing* and *shi* are referred to as surnames. Mention is also made of 'style names,' posthumously given names, and appellations by which persons were simply "called."

Chinese and Their Surnames in the United States

Through the year 1850, United States immigration records show a total of only 46 Chinese immigrants; however, in the decade of the 1850s the number jumped to 61,000, and it reached a peak of 123,000 in the 1870s before declining rapidly. These numbers represent a small percentage of total immigration to the United States, and half of the Chinese who came to America returned home, so that even at its peak, Chinese immigration was not as large as is often imagined. Nevertheless, in 1882, when people of Chinese ancestry comprised less than 0.2 percent of the U.S. population, Congress passed the first Exclusion Act, which prohibited Chinese workers from entering the country. In 1924, the second Exclusion Act further narrowed the types of people, such as students or those born in the United States, who could enter. It was not until 1943 that the first Exclusion Act was rescinded, and by that time people of Chinese ancestry had declined to roughly 0.05 percent of the U.S. population.

The early immigration came largely from southeastern China in the Cantonese and Min dialect areas. Amazingly, an estimated 60 percent of pre–World War II immigration came from the Taishan (Plateau Mountain) area, just one of the ninety-eight counties of Guangdong, itself just one of more than twenty Chinese provinces. Since World War II, however, immigration from China has become less disproportionately southern, and the Mandarin dialect has become increasingly common in America's Chinatowns. Most American names with Chinese origins, therefore, result from romanizations of names in the Mandarin and Cantonese dialects, with some from the Min dialects of Fujian province and Taiwan. As the following discussion on Chinese dialects and romanization shows, however, the accuracy of such attributions is difficult to gauge because they can rarely be pinpointed by analyzing a romanized name alone. (One interesting aspect of Chinese names in America is that a Chinese name that closely resembles a more familiar English name, or that has sounds familiar in the American English sound system, often is not written according to a standard Chinese romanization, but instead with an American English spelling, as in **Lee** for *Li*, **Yee** for *Yi*, or **Young** for *Yang*.)

The Ambiguity of Chinese Surnames in Romanized Form

One caveat should be kept in mind as you use this book: it is impossible to look at a romanized Chinese name (that is, one written in the roman alphabet rather than in Chinese characters) and to know with absolute certainty which Chinese name is being represented. In fact, the only accurate way to determine the name's origin is to find the Chinese characters with which the name was originally written. For example, even though it is very likely that **Chen, Lee,** or **Chang** refer to three of the most common surnames, it is still possible that these spellings might represent other surnames.

The reasons for this difficulty are several. First, there is a great amount of homophony (words that are pronounced similarly) among the short words of Chinese, particularly when English speakers and writers ignore the tones (pitch features) that are important elements in the meanings of Chinese words. Second, there is great variety of Chinese dialects, so that related names are pronounced quite differently depending on what part of the country they come from. Finally, many substantially different romanization methods have been employed at different times and places. This combination of factors causes great ambiguity when people attempt to represent Chinese names in an alphabetic writing system that does not provide for marking tones. In contrast, these problems are handled well by the "logographic" Chinese writing system, which is not inherently related to pronunciation and allows readers to differentiate among many homophones, while also permitting speakers of different dialects to understand a written text, even though they may pronounce the same words completely differently. Thus, this book's entries for Chinese names often present several of the most common alternatives, though space limitations may prevent our including all possibilities.

Bibliography

Chao, Sheau-yueh J. (2000): *In Search of Your Asian Roots: Genealogical Research on Chinese Surnames*. Baltimore:

Clearfield Company and Genealogical Publishing. (Accounts of the origins of 622 surnames, spelled according to the Wade-Giles system formerly used in Taiwan; traditional characters are employed rather than the simplified characters used in the present work.)

Lewellen, Mark (1998): *Neural Network Recognition of Spelling Variation in Chinese Name Searching.* Ph.D. dissertation, Georgetown University, Washington, D.C. (A description of the types and causes of spelling variation in Chinese names is presented in sections 1.3 and 1.4.)

Louie, Emma Woo (1998): *Chinese American Names: Tradition and Transition.* Jefferson, N.C.: McFarland and Company. (Describes Chinese name traditions and Chinese-American name customs.)

JAPANESE FAMILY NAMES

Frederick Brady

There are approximately 100,000 surnames in Japan. A few—such as Mononobe, Inbe, and Nakatomi—date from at least fifteen centuries ago; their bearers claim to be descended from the Sun Goddess's grandson Ninigi or from his companions. These ancient names, however, have mostly disappeared as descendants took other surnames.

A few more names were created centuries later when, in a process known as "dynastic shedding," descendants of certain emperors were cast out of the imperial clan and ordered to live as commoners. This is the origin of the great **Taira** and **Minamoto** (**Heike** and **Genji**) clans. There were also some ancient noble clans of Korean or Chinese origin whose names were Japanized (e.g., **Hata, Aya, Soga, Sakanoue**). When the great clans became so large that some families within them wanted to be distinguished by new surnames, they sometimes based their new names on their original surnames, or used the name of their residence. It was not uncommon for each son of a lord to take a new surname of his own. Thus, the Fujiwara clan produced the surnames **Satō, Itō, Etō, Gotō,** and others; *-tō* is the Sino-Japanese reading (see below) of the word *fuji.* Only the imperial clan itself has endured to the present without a surname of its own.

All the clans mentioned above were the ancestors of less than 10 percent of the present Japanese population. With few exceptions, the rest of the people were denied the use of surnames until 1870. Surnames became mandatory for all in 1875, when a new civil registration system was instituted. At that time, millions of commoners pulled new surnames out of the air, naming themselves after their former feudal lords, their places of residence, their occupations, or local topographic features. Some were given their surnames by the registrars. Many imaginative surnames, such as **Inu** 'dog', thus arose to bemuse record-keepers and confuse genealogists.

The Writing System and Names

The use in Japan of Chinese characters, called *kanji* in Japanese, causes unique difficulties, especially for descendants of emigrant Japanese. There are thousands of kanji, and each one ordinarily has one or two original Sino-Japanese pronunciations, plus any number (usually two or three) of native Japanese readings. Therefore, the only sure way to know which kanji to use when writing a person's name, when one hears it, is to ask him. For example, there are at least seven ways to write the name **Itō** in kanji. Conversely, a written name may be pronounced several different ways. The two characters 'gold' and 'plain' can be read together as **Kanahara, Kanawara, Kinpara,** or **Kinbara**. More difficulty is caused by variant standards in Roman-alphabet spellings of Japanese names, or the absence of any standard at all.

Japanese Migration

After a period of strict seclusion from about 1640 to 1866, Japanese were allowed to leave their country legally. By the beginning of World War II, nearly 2 million Japanese had emigrated, with some 220,000 settling in North America and Hawaii. The majority of these people came from economically depressed areas in western and southern Japan, including the island of Okinawa, which has many interesting surnames of its own, such as **Arakaki** and **Chinen**.

Probably all these migrants were literate to some degree, but Japanese emigration records were kept by clerks who sometimes wrote a person's name with the wrong kanji. Immigration and employment records abroad were kept by clerks who were not usually familiar with Japanese names, and who at first had no standard romanization scheme to use. Standard romanized systems were developed early in this period, but they took time to be adopted and learned. In addition, the system preferred in the United States differs in several important points from that preferred in Japan. Thus, a Mr. **Miyagishima** may have had his name romanized in one way by a clerk in Hawaii, and in another by a clerk in Oregon, or even shortened to **Miya.** He might have decided to adopt the name as spelled on one record, or he may have preferred his own version.

Searching for Japanese Name Records

As a result, many unrelated people of Japanese origin now have the same surname, or similar-sounding surnames written with different kanji. Some names appear to be the same as the kanji are written, but their pronunciations differ completely—though some of these people may be related anyway. The romanized spelling of any surname may appear in several variants. Even people who know the kanji for their surname may not be able to locate the name in Japanese emigration records if a clerk used the wrong characters (though this is rare). Finally, people who do not know the kanji for their surname may have trouble guessing what they might have been.

It should be emphasized that many kanji have been simplified since 1945, and a kanji dictionary such as Andrew Nelson's *Japanese-English Character Dictionary* should be consulted for the older versions. The name dictionaries by O'Neill and Sakamaki, noted in the bibliography, are very helpful because they give both romanizations and kanji for names, and *Japan: An Illustrated Encyclopedia* provides valuable his-

torical background on noble families. Name research is very popular in Japan, and there are many more books available on the subject than can be listed here.

Bibliography

Japan: An Illustrated Encyclopedia. 2 vols. 1993. Tokyo: Kodansha.

Niwa, Motoji (1985): *Nihon seishi daijiten* (Great dictionary of Japanese surnames). 3 vols. Tokyo: Kadokawa Shoten.

Niwa, Motoji (1981): *Seishi no gogen* (Etymologies of surnames). Tokyo: Kadokawa Shoten.

O'Neill, P. G. (1972): *Japanese Names: A Comprehensive Index by Characters and Readings.* New York: J. Weatherhill.

Ota, Akira (1963): *Seishi Kakei Daijiten* (Great dictionary of surnames and pedigrees). Tokyo: Seishi kakei Daijiten Kankokai.

Sakamaki, Shunzo, ed. (1964): *Ryukyuan Names: Monographs on and Lists of Personal and Place Names in the Ryukyus.* Honolulu and Tokyo.

Sakuma, Ei (1972): *Nihonjin no sei* (Surnames of the Japanese). Tokyo: Rikugei Shobō.

KOREAN FAMILY NAMES

Gary Mackelprang

History

The history of Korean surnames spans fifteen centuries. Most scholars agree that Koreans adopted the use of surnames from the Chinese during the Three Kingdoms Period (*c.* 50 BC–667 AD). Early usage of surnames was restricted to kings, nobles, and scholars who had been exposed to the advanced culture of their Chinese neighbors. The earliest examples of surnames used in Korea appear on stone boundary monuments erected by kings several hundred years after the birth of Christ. Most Korean surnames were imported from China during the Unified Shilla period and the Koryŏ period (668–1392), although additional surnames sporadically entered Korea with refugees fleeing catastrophes in China.

The origins of Korea's oldest surnames are shrouded in mythology. The Pak family, for example, is purported to have originated in 69 BC, when a youth emerged from a gourd-shaped egg and founded the Shilla Kingdom (57 BC–935 AD). The name **Pak** is a Chinese adaptation of a Korean word meaning either 'gourd', referring to the shape of the egg from which the boy is supposed to have emerged, or

'light', referring to the light that is said to have emanated from his person. Several other major surnames have similar mythological origins.

Unlike commoners in old Japan, most free Korean peasants seem to have had surnames by the end of the Koryŏ period. In 1055, Koryŏ's King Munjong decreed that only those with surnames were eligible to take the state civil service examinations. Because successful completion of these examinations later became the key to social and economic success in Korea, this proclamation essentially guaranteed that every free Korean would adopt a surname. The only class without surnames in post-Koryŏ Korea was the slave class. As the institution of slavery was abolished by successive proclamations in 1801 and 1894, newly freed slaves quickly adopted surnames to avoid the stigma of being identified as ex-slaves.

Surnames in Korea Today

There are only about 260 surnames in Korea today. Just under one-half of South Korea's entire population uses only four surnames: **Kim**, **Yi**, **Pak**, and **Ch'oe**. At the other end of the scale, almost 100 surnames were recorded in fewer than 500 house-holds each in a recent census, and seventy of these names were recorded in fewer than 200 households each. Although accurate statistics are not currently available for North Korea, it is reasonable to expect a similar distribution.

With a combined population of around 65 million people and only about 260 surnames, one would imagine that the citizens of North and South Korea would get rather confused about who's who. Surprisingly, however, Koreans seem to have a better sense of their origins and identity than do most people who live in countries with many surnames.

Each Korean surname group is divided into clans. Small surnames may have only one clan; larger ones, like the **Kim** family, may have scores. Clans are designated by their locality of origin, or *pon'gwan*. A clan's pon'gwan distinguishes it from all other clans of the same surname. Hence, it can be seen that individuals with identical surnames may or may not be related, depending on what clan they belong to. This is an important aspect of Korean life, because members of the same clan do not intermarry. Clans are further subdivided into branches, or *p'a*. Each p'a retains a unique identity within the clan and functions as a semiautonomous unit at clan events.

Forming and Writing Names in Korean

Like the Chinese naming system after which it is patterned, the Korean naming system places the surname before the given name. Most surnames consist of a single character (one Chinese character represents a single syllable in Korean), although there are rare two-character surnames. The given name usually consists of two characters, but occasionally it consists of a single character. Traditionally, one of the characters of the given name, the *tollim* character, is determined by the clan elders and indicates the generation in which the individual was born. The other character is usually assigned by a fortune-teller, or, for the less superstitious, by the child's parents or grandparents. A woman retains her birth surname after marriage, and children assume their father's surname. Although strict adherence to traditional naming practices is somewhat diminished in modern society, it nevertheless is still observed by many families, and it will always play a significant role in genealogical research.

Names can be and often are written in the native Korean *han'gŭl* script. Unlike Western names, however, each segment of a traditional Korean name has a unique meaning and is derived from a Chinese character. Because there are many thousands of Chinese characters, and many hundreds of them are pronounced identically in Korean, positive identification of an individual's written name is only possible if it is written in Chinese characters.

Korean Migration to North America

Koreans began migrating to the United States in 1902 as contract laborers. The majority of the first wave of Korean immigrants left their homeland at this time to escape the horrors that were being inflicted on their homeland by the Japanese. Even for the wealthy, life as a laborer in America held more promise than life in a Korea dominated by imperial Japan. Between 1902 and 1905, approximately 8,000 Koreans left their homeland to work in the plantations of Hawaii. Unlike their Japanese and Chinese counterparts, Korean immigrants came from all social classes and from all regions of their homeland.

As the Japanese grip tightened on Korea, fewer Koreans were able to leave. Most of those who did were either political refugees or "picture brides" for Korean men who had already migrated. From 1905 to 1940, Korean immigration to North America ceased almost entirely.

At the conclusion of World War II, many Koreans gained firsthand exposure to Americans when the United States established its occupational administration in South Korea. A few years later, thousands of North American troops poured into the Korean Peninsula as part of the United Nations forces that fought in the Korean War (1950–53). Much of post–Korean War immigration was probably a result of this extended exposure to North Americans. Many Korean women married American or Canadian soldiers and followed them back to North America at the conclusion of the war. Upon arriving in North America, Korean brides would often invite their families to join them.

Students comprise another important segment of post–Korean War immigrants. Many young people who were exposed to Western democracy and technology during the war came to North America as students. Only a minority of the thousands who came to North America immediately after the war ever returned to Korea.

Although there is no one single paradigm to describe modern Korean immigration patterns, most present-day immigrants seem to favor urban settings over rural ones. Many large population centers in the United States and Canada have "Korea towns" with Korean grocery stores, banks, and churches. In some places, recent immigrants have not even found it necessary to learn English.

Within a generation or two of having immigrated to North America, most Korean families adopt Western given names. The rather complicated concepts of tollim, pon'gwan, and clan are not typically taught to second- or third-generation Korean Americans, so the difference between the Kim family of the Kyŏngju district and the Kim family of the Kimhae district becomes blurred or forgotten.

Romanization of Names

Upon arriving in North America, all Koreans are required to romanize their names into the alphabet used to write English. The McCune-Reischauer system of transcription is the official system for romanization used by the Korean government and by scholars, but few Koreans actually use it to convert their names. It is not at all unusual to see a common surname romanized three or four different ways because there is no one-to-one phonemic correspondence between Korean and English. Variant romanizations can complicate positive identification of a surname considerably.

Because many Korean surnames are derived from Chinese surnames, it is not always possible to differentiate between the two nationalities simply be examining the names. The Korean surname **Yi**, for example, is often romanized as **Lee** by Koreans. **Lee** is also a common romanization for more than one major Chinese surname, **Li**, resulting in potential confusion. Even if Koreans were to adhere to the McCune-Reischauer system, some surnames, such as **Ma**, will be romanized identically from Chinese and Korean. Since Koreans use the same Chinese characters for surnames as do the Chinese, the problem of identification is not restricted to romanization. Thus, without additional information it is often impossible to differentiate between Chinese names and Korean names, whether romanized or written in Chinese characters.

Bibliography

Virtually every surname in Korea is represented by a clan organization that publishes official genealogies. These genealogies are usually thorough and accurate, and constitute an excellent secondary source for researchers.

General References (Korean Language)

Han'guk Sŏngssi Taegwan (Compendium of Korean Surnames). Ch'angjosa, Seoul, Korea.

Han'gukin ŭi Sŏngbo: Ch'oidae Sŏngssi wa pon'gwan (Korean Genealogies: updated surnames and clan seats). Samsŏng Munhwasa, Seoul, Korea.

Mansŏngdaedongbo (Compendium of Korean Genealogies). Myŏngmundang, Seoul, Korea.

KEY TO THE DICTIONARY

*Consult the General Introduction and the essay
by D. Kenneth Tucker for further explanation.*

Main entry (one of the more than 70,000 surnames listed in DAFN)

Frequency of this surname in the sample of 88.7 million listings in the DAFN database

Explanation and etymology

Surname type (e.g., occupational, habitational, patronymic, nickname)

Register (3259) English: perhaps from Middle English, Old French *registre* 'register', 'book for recording enactments', hence perhaps a <u>metonymic occupational name</u> for a scribe or clerk.

Language or culture of origin

Region where this surname probably originated

Regner (420) German: **1.** (Bavarian): habitational name for someone from Regen (a place on the Regen river, for which it is named). **2.** from a Germanic personal name composed of the elements *ragin* 'counsel' + *hari, heri* 'army'.

Etymon (a word or element from which the surname is derived; in italics)

Gloss <u>on the etymon (in single quotation</u> marks)

GIVEN NAMES German 4%. *Alois* (2), *Kurt* (2), *Erwin, Franz, Otto*.

Regnier (926) French (**Régnier**): from the personal name *Régnier*, of Germanic origin (see RAYNER 1).

Cross-reference to a related main entry (in capital and small capital letters)

Forebear note for an early bearer of this surname in North America

FOREBEARS A Regnier from La Rochelle, France, is documented in Pointe-aux-Trembles, Quebec, in 1708, with the secondary surname BRION or Brillon.

GIVEN NAMES French 6%. *Lucien* (2), *Micheline* (2), *Pierre* (2), *Andre, Celestine, Felicie, Guilene, Marcel, Marcelle, Patrice, Romain.*

Selection of diagnostic given names from U.S. telephone directories

Number of occurrences of this diagnostic given name with this particular surname in the DAFN database

Rego (1493) **1.** Portuguese and Galician: habitational name from any of the numerous places in Portugal and Galicia called Rego, named with *rego* 'ditch', 'channel', 'furrow'. **2.** Dutch: from a Germanic personal name with the first element *ragin* 'counsel' + *guda* 'god', or *gōda* 'good', or *gauta* 'Goth'. **3.** Dutch: variant of REGA 2. **4.** Hungarian (**Regő**): occupational name for a musician or poet, from *rege* 'song', 'tale'.

Multiple origins

Alternate form in the language of origin (usually with diacritics)

GIVEN NAMES Spanish 15%; Portuguese 9%. *Manuel* (32), *Jose* (25), *Armando* (5), *Eduardo* (5), *Carlos* (4), *Fernando* (4), *Francisco* (4), *Ramon* (4), *Humberto* (3), *Juan* (3), *Luis* (3), *Mario* (3); *Joao* (5), *Duarte* (2), *Adauto, Albano, Goncalo, Guilherme, Serafim.*

Statistical confidence measure that this surname is in fact Spanish, based on analysis of the associated given names

Diagnostic given names grouped by language or cultural group (separated by semicolons)

A

Aaberg (233) **1.** Scandinavian (**Åberg**): ornamental name from *aa, å* 'river' + *berg* 'hill', 'mountain'. **2.** Norwegian: habitational name from a place so named, '(on) the hill by the river'.

Aaby (101) Norwegian and Danish: habitational name from a place called Aaby or Åby, from *å* 'river' + Old Norse *býr* 'farm'.

Aadland (147) Norwegian: habitational name from a place called Ådland, from Old Norse *Árland* 'land by the river'.
GIVEN NAMES Scandinavian 16%; German 5%. *Anders, Lars, Oyvind; Hannes, Otto, Ute.*

Aagaard (134) Norwegian and Danish: variant of **Ågård** (see AGARD).
GIVEN NAMES Scandinavian 13%; German 6%. *Aase, Erik, Knut, Morten; Otto* (2), *Klaus.*

Aagard (115) Norwegian and Danish: variant of **Ågård** (see AGARD).

Aaker (190) Norwegian and Swedish (**Åker**): variant of AKER.
GIVEN NAMES Scandinavian 5%. *Erik, Ove, Sig.*

Aakre (158) Norwegian (**Åkre**): habitational name from any of several places so named, from an inflected form of Old Norse *akr* 'plowed field'.
GIVEN NAMES Scandinavian 14%. *Hjalmer, Knute, Nels, Obert, Selmer, Steinar.*

Aalbers (100) Dutch and Danish: variant of ALBERS.
GIVEN NAMES Dutch 5%. *Geert, Gradus, Marinus.*

Aalto (119) Finnish: ornamental name from *aalto* 'wave'.
GIVEN NAMES Finnish 23%; Scandinavian 4%. *Tauno* (5), *Ensio, Pentti, Reino, Sulo, Tarmo, Wilho; Hilma, Johan.*

Aamodt (331) Norwegian and Swedish (**Åmot**): topographic name for someone who lived by the confluence of two streams, from *aa, å* 'stream' + *mot* 'meeting'. This is also a common habitational name in Norway, from any of the 40 or more farms so named.
GIVEN NAMES Scandinavian 7%. *Lars, Nels.*

Aamot (129) Norwegian and Swedish: variant of AAMODT.
GIVEN NAME Scandinavian 10%. *Aagot.*

Aanenson (119) Norwegian: patronymic from the personal name *Ånund*, from Old Norse *Onundr* ('ancestor' + 'victor').
GIVEN NAMES Scandinavian 6%. *Obert, Ordell.*

Aardema (155) Frisian: patronymic from the personal name *Aart*, a local variant of AREND, + *-ma*, Frisian suffix of origin.
GIVEN NAMES Dutch 4%. *Frans* (2), *Klaas.*

Aarhus (101) Norwegian (**Århus**): habitational name from any of 15 or so farms so named, from Old Norse *á* 'river' + *hús* 'house', 'farmstead'.
GIVEN NAMES Scandinavian 10%; German 5%. *Karsten* (2); *Kurt.*

Aaron (4760) Mainly Jewish: from the Biblical Hebrew personal name *Aharon*, which was borne by the first high priest of the Israelites, the brother of Moses (Exodus 4:14). Like *Moses*, it is probably of Egyptian origin, with a meaning no longer recoverable. In some countries Aaron was also a gentile personal name; not all occurrences of the surname are Jewish.

Aarons (357) Jewish: patronymic from AARON.

Aaronson (650) Jewish (Ashkenazic): patronymic from the personal name AARON.

Aas (135) Norwegian and Swedish (**Ås**): topographic name from *ås* 'ridge', or, in Norway, a common habitational name from any of the numerous farmsteads named with this word.
GIVEN NAMES Scandinavian 10%. *Alf, Erik, Sven.*

Aase (224) Norwegian and Swedish (**Åse**): topographic name from an inflected form of *ås* 'ridge'. This is also a common habitational name in Norway, from any of about 30 places named with this word.
GIVEN NAMES Scandinavian 9%. *Sig* (2), *Anders, Lars.*

Aasen (449) Norwegian and Swedish (**Åsen**): topographic name from *åsen* 'the ridge'. In Norway, this is also a habitational name from any of the numerous farms so named all over the country.
GIVEN NAMES Scandinavian 6%. *Erik* (2), *Gorm, Oddvar, Per.*

Abad (684) **1.** Spanish: nickname from *abad* 'priest' (from Late Latin *abbas* 'priest', genitive *abbatis*, from the Aramaic word meaning 'father'). The application is uncertain: it could be a nickname, an occupational name for the servant of a priest, or denote an (illegitimate) son of a priest. **2.** Muslim: from a personal name based on Arabic *'Abbād* 'devoted worshiper' or 'servant'. The *banu* (tribe) *'Abbād* claims descent from the ancient Lakhmid kings of al-Ḥirah. The founder of the 'Abbadids of

Seville was Muhammad bin 'Abbād (1023–42), whose son 'Abbād succeeded his father as chamberlain to the pretended khalif, but was soon ruling in his own right under the honorific title *al-Muta'id* 'petitioner for justice (from Allah)'.
GIVEN NAMES Spanish 39%. *Jose* (13), *Manuel* (12), *Luis* (9), *Miguel* (6), *Ramon* (6), *Ricardo* (6), *Ernesto* (5), *Jorge* (5), *Armando* (4), *Augusto* (4), *Carlos* (4), *Juan* (4); *Antonio* (8), *Filiberto* (2), *Gino* (2), *Lucio* (2), *Carlo, Cecilio, Eliseo, Enrico, Heriberto, Lirio, Marco, Romeo.*

Abadi (147) **1.** Arabic (**'Abbādī**): denoting someone whose ancestors belonged to the 'Abbād tribe (see ABAD). **2.** Jewish (Sephardic): adoption of the Arabic surname.
GIVEN NAMES Arabic 27%; Jewish 11%. *Hassan* (3), *Abdallah* (2), *Nasrin* (2), *Behruz, Bijan, Ghazanfar, Haisam, Jamal, Mahmoud, Mohammad, Mohammed, Nessim; Chaia, Chaim, Isaak, Meyer, Miriam, Nissim, Pnina, Yehuda, Yitzchak.*

Abadie (453) **1.** Southern French: topographic name for someone living near an *abadie*, which means both 'abbey' and 'family chapel' (from Late Latin *abbatia* 'priest's house'). **2.** Americanized spelling of Hungarian *Abádi*, a habitational name for someone from a place called Abád in Heves county, Abádszalók in Pest county, or other places named after the ancient Aba clan.
GIVEN NAMES French 12%. *Emile* (3), *Jacques* (3), *Andre* (2), *Pierre* (2), *Alain, Amedee, Clothilde, Julien, Leonie, Mathieu, Pascal, Thierry.*

Abair (225) In New England, an Americanized form of French **Hébert** (see HEBERT).
GIVEN NAME French 4%. *Alphonse.*

Abajian (136) Armenian: patronymic from Turkish *abacı* 'maker or seller of coarse woolen cloth or garments', from *aba* 'coarse woolen cloth'.
GIVEN NAMES Armenian 22%; French 4%. *Hagop* (2), *Krikor* (2), *Akop, Arakel, Armen, Dikran, Haig, Herach, Kevork, Viken, Zaven; Antoine, Dominique.*

Abalos (289) Spanish (**Ábalos**): variant of AVALOS.
GIVEN NAMES Spanish 38%; Italian 5%. *Jose* (6), *Jesus* (3), *Alfonso* (2), *Alfredo* (2), *Arsenio* (2), *Arturo* (2), *Gilberto* (2), *Juan* (2), *Roberto* (2), *Adolfo, Alberto, Alejandro, Godofredo; Aldo, Antonio, Lorenzo, Mauro, Quirino.*

Abar (105) Spanish: probably a topographic name, from Basque *abar* 'foliage'.

Abarca (479) Basque, Spanish, and Aragonese: **1.** formerly most common in the Basque country and in Aragon, this name is generally assumed to be from *abarca* 'sandal' (Basque *abarka*), which refers to the traditional Basque peasant sandal or moccasin made of uncured leather. In the past this word was also applied to footwear made from wooden materials, and is probably derived from Basque *abar* 'branch', 'twig'. Some scholars, however, think that *abarka* is an old topographic term referring to a grove of holm oaks or kermes oaks. **2.** habitational name from the village of Abarca in the province of Palencia.
GIVEN NAMES Spanish 53%. *Jose* (11), *Luis* (11), *Miguel* (11), *Francisco* (8), *Jesus* (8), *Juan* (7), *Manuel* (6), *Carlos* (4), *Javier* (4), *Raul* (4), *Ruben* (4), *Alfredo* (3).

Abare (309) In New England, an Americanized form of French **Hébert** (see HEBERT).

Abascal (111) Spanish: habitational name, probably from Abascal de Lemos, a village in Santander province.
GIVEN NAMES Spanish 53%. *Amado* (4), *Jose* (4), *Manuel* (4), *Mario* (3), *Ana* (2), *Arturo* (2), *Bernabe* (2), *Francisco* (2), *Pedro* (2), *Rafael* (2), *Ricardo* (2), *Tomas* (2).

Abate (1289) **1.** Italian: from *abate* 'priest' (from Late Latin *abbas* 'priest', genitive *abbatis*). The application is uncertain: it could be a nickname, an occupational name for the servant of a priest, or denote an (illegitimate) son of a priest. **2.** Jewish (from Italy): either a name indicating descent from a high priest, a calque on Hebrew COHEN, or an occupational name for a rabbi.
GIVEN NAMES Italian 14%. *Salvatore* (10), *Antonio* (6), *Carmelo* (3), *Carmine* (3), *Gaetano* (3), *Vito* (3), *Angelo* (2), *Canio* (2), *Rocco* (2), *Sal* (2), *Aldo*, *Carlo*.

Abato (104) Italian: variant of ABATE.
GIVEN NAMES Italian 10%. *Carmine*, *Nicola*; *Alphonse*.

Abbas (714) **1.** Muslim (widespread throughout the Muslim world): from the Arabic personal name 'Abbās, literally 'stern', 'austere'. 'Abbās was the name of an uncle (died 652) of the Prophet Muhammad, the ancestor of the Abbasid dynasty (see ABBASI). **2.** German: Latinized form of ABT 'abbot'.
GIVEN NAMES Muslim 54%. *Syed* (26), *Ghulam* (12), *Ali* (8), *Mohammad* (7), *Mohammed* (7), *Mohamed* (6), *Farhat* (5), *Abbas* (4), *Asad* (4), *Azhar* (4), *Ahmad* (3), *Amir* (3).

Abbasi (265) Muslim: from the Arabic family name 'Abbāsī, a derivative of the personal name 'Abbās (see ABBAS), denoting someone descended from or associated with someone called 'Abbās, in particular a descendant of the Abbasid dynasty of khalifs, who ruled the Islamic world from 750, when they founded a new capital in Baghdad, to 1258, when they were destroyed by the Mongols.
GIVEN NAMES Muslim 85%. *Mohammad* (7), *Ali* (5), *Abdul* (4), *Adnan* (4), *Tariq* (4), *Arshad* (3), *Mahmood* (3), *Mohammed* (3), *Mousa* (3), *Muhammad* (3), *Nadeem* (3), *Sami* (3).

Abbate (919) Southern Italian: variant of ABATE.
GIVEN NAMES Italian 22%. *Sal* (7), *Angelo* (6), *Salvatore* (6), *Antonio* (4), *Rocco* (3), *Alfonso* (2), *Giuseppe* (2), *Santo* (2), *Silvio* (2), *Alfredo*, *Agostino*, *Carmel*, *Dante*, *Francesca*, *Mario*, *Orlando*.

Abbatiello (249) Southern Italian (Campania): from a diminutive of ABBATE.
GIVEN NAMES Italian 30%. *Antonio* (4), *Carmine* (4), *Agostino* (3), *Biagio* (2), *Domenic* (2), *Giacomo* (2), *Vincenzo* (2), *Alessandro*, *Bartolomeo*, *Domenico*, *Girolamo*, *Giuseppe*.

Abbe (543) **1.** English: variant of ABBEY. **2.** German: from a pet form of the personal name *Albrecht* (see ALBERT). **3.** French (**Abbé**): see LABBE.
FOREBEARS John Abbe (born 1613) emigrated from England to Salem, MA, in 1635.

Abbett (262) English: variant spelling of ABBOTT.

Abbey (1870) English: from Middle English *abbeye*, *abbaye* (Old French *abeie*, Late Latin *abbatia* 'priest's house'), applied as a topographic name for someone living in or near an abbey, or an occupational name for someone working in one.

Abbitt (235) English: variant spelling of ABBOTT.

Abbot (266) English: variant spelling of ABBOTT.

Abbott (20015) English and Scottish: from Middle English *abbott* 'abbot' (Old English *abbod*) or Old French *abet* 'priest'. Both the Old English and the Old French term are derived from Late Latin *abbas* 'priest' (genitive *abbatis*), from Greek *abbas*, from Aramaic *aba* 'father'. This was an occupational name for someone employed in the household of or on the lands of an abbot, and perhaps also a nickname for a sanctimonious person thought to resemble an abbot. In the U.S. this name is also sometimes a translation of a cognate or equivalent European name, e.g. Italian ABATE, Spanish ABAD, or German ABT.
FOREBEARS George Abbot from Yorkshire, England, settled in Andover, MA, in 1640; he had numerous prominent descendants. A certain George Abbott (probably not the same man) died in Rowley, MA, in 1647. James Abbott migrated from Somerset, England, to Long Island, NY, in the 17th century.

Abboud (316) Arabic: from the Arabic personal name 'Abbūd, meaning 'devoted worshiper'. This name is found among Christian Arabs as well as Muslims.
GIVEN NAMES Arabic 26%; French 7%. *Namir* (4), *Bechara* (2), *Fady* (2), *Fayez* (2), *Hoda* (2), *Ibrahim* (2), *Nabil* (2), *Najib* (2), *Abdallah*, *Abdo*, *Adli*, *Amin*; *Antoine* (2), *Raymonde* (2), *Camille*, *Francois*, *Marcelle*, *Pierre*.

Abbruzzese (285) Italian: variant spelling of ABRUZZESE.
GIVEN NAMES Italian 16%. *Carmine* (2), *Antonio*, *Biaggio*, *Carlo*, *Cono*, *Edmondo*, *Geno*, *Lorenzo*, *Sal*, *Vito*, *Vittoria*.

Abbs (186) English (Norfolk): derivative of ABEL, meaning 'son or servant of someone called Abel'.

Abbuhl (109) South German and Swiss German (**Abbühl**): topographic name for someone living 'at the hill', from Middle High German *bühel* 'hill'.

Abby (101) English: variant spelling of ABBEY.

Abdalla (387) Muslim: variant of ABDUL-LAH.
GIVEN NAMES Muslim 53%. *Mohamed* (7), *Abdalla* (5), *Nabil* (5), *Mahmoud* (4), *Mohammed* (4), *Hesham* (3), *Naser* (3), *Tarek* (3), *Ahmad* (2), *Ahmed* (2), *Ali* (2), *Awad* (2).

Abdallah (494) Muslim: variant of ABDUL-LAH.
GIVEN NAMES Muslim 58%. *Ali* (7), *Hassan* (7), *Hussein* (7), *Ahmad* (6), *Ghassan* (6), *Mohammad* (5), *Omar* (4), *Ahmed* (3), *Faisal* (3), *Hasan* (3), *Mahmoud* (3), *Ayman* (2).

Abdella (237) Muslim: variant of ABDUL-LAH.
GIVEN NAMES Muslim 8%. *Mohamed* (2), *Abdul*, *Ahmed*, *Akil*, *Ali*, *Awad*, *Aziza*, *Faiza*, *Hassan*, *Mohammed*, *Munir*, *Redwan*.

Abdelnour (125) Muslim (found throughout the Muslim world): from the Arabic personal name 'Abdul-Nūr, meaning 'servant of the Light'. Al-Nūr 'the Light' is an attribute of Allah.
GIVEN NAMES Muslim 16%; French 8%. *Anees*, *Bassam*, *Fakhry*, *Farid*, *Fayez*, *Ghassan*, *Ibrahim*, *Moheb*, *Nassif*, *Ossama*, *Salem*, *Sameer*; *Camille* (2), *Antoine*, *Jean-Yves*.

Abdelrahman (105) Muslim: from the Arabic personal name 'Abd al-Raḥmān 'servant of the Merciful'. Al-Raḥmān 'the Merciful' is an attribute of Allah.
GIVEN NAMES Muslim 83%. *Mohamed* (8), *Ahmed* (3), *Mahmoud* (3), *Abdel* (2), *Karim* (2), *Omar* (2), *Osama* (2), *Yousry* (2), *Ahmad*, *Ali*, *Ashraf*, *Atef*.

Abdi (211) Muslim: variant of ABDO.
GIVEN NAMES Muslim 77%; Ethiopian 6%. *Mohamed* (9), *Ahmed* (5), *Ali* (5), *Abdullahi* (4), *Abdi* (3), *Hussein* (3), *Omar* (3), *Abdirahman* (2), *Abdul* (2), *Abdulkadir* (2), *Forough* (2), *Halima* (2); *Wondwosen* (4), *Getachew*, *Hirut*, *Jama*, *Yared*, *Yilma*.

Abdo (502) Muslim: from Arabic 'abduh 'his servant', i.e. 'his (Allah's) servant'.

'Abduh is one of the epithets of the Prophet Muhammad.

GIVEN NAMES Muslim 24%. *Ali* (3), *Ayman* (3), *Hatem* (3), *Samir* (3), *Wael* (3), *Farid* (2), *Fouad* (2), *Kamal* (2), *Mohamad* (2), *Mohamed* (2), *Mohammed* (2), *Nasir* (2).

Abdon (147) English: habitational name, probably from the village of Abdon in Shropshire, named from the Old English personal name *Abba* + Old English *tūn* 'settlement'.

Abdoo (118) Muslim: variant of ABDO.

Abdou (160) Muslim: variant of ABDO.

GIVEN NAMES Muslim 57%. *Fathy* (6), *Mohamed* (4), *Nabil* (3), *Saad* (3), *Awny* (2), *Nabih* (2), *Tarek* (2), *Abdou, Ates, Elsayed, Emad, Fadi.*

Abdul (297) Muslim: from Arabic *'abdul, 'abd al* 'servant of the . . .'. *'Abdul* is normally a component of a compound name referring to one of the attributes of Allah mentioned in the Qur'an or the Hadith, for example *'Abdul 'Azīz* 'servant of the Powerful', *'Abdul-Hakīm* 'servant of the Wise', *'Abdul-Qādir* 'servant of the Capable'.

GIVEN NAMES Muslim 64%. *Rashid* (5), *Mohamed* (4), *Mohammed* (3), *Abdul* (2), *Ali* (2), *Amir* (2), *Kadir* (2), *Karim* (2), *Rahman* (2), *Sadiq* (2), *Samad* (2), *Wahid* (2).

Abdulla (213) Muslim: see ABDULLAH.

GIVEN NAMES Muslim 79%. *Ali* (8), *Mohamed* (6), *Ahmed* (3), *Hani* (3), *Khaled* (3), *Mohammed* (3), *Abdul* (2), *Fadel* (2), *Farooq* (2), *Fouad* (2), *Nabeel* (2), *Nadir* (2).

Abdullah (919) Muslim: from the Arabic personal name *'Abdullāh* 'servant of Allah'. This was the name of the father of the Prophet Muhammad, who died before Muhammad was born. In the Qur'an (19:30), Jesus calls himself *'Abdullāh*: 'He (Jesus) said: I am the servant of Allah'. The name is also borne by Christian Arabs.

GIVEN NAMES Muslim 72%. *Muhammad* (21), *Ali* (11), *Ahmed* (10), *Hassan* (7), *Mohamed* (7), *Ibrahim* (6), *Mohammed* (6), *Adnan* (5), *Khalil* (5), *Tariq* (5), *Amin* (4), *Ismail* (4).

Abe (941) Japanese: variously written, with Chinese characters used phonetically. Listed in the Shinsen shōjiroku, the Abe claim descent from Ōhiko, first son of the mythical Emperor Kōgen. There are several places in Japan named Abe, which means 'sun festival' in the Ainu language. Some Ainu connections may be assumed, but the name could also be purely habitational. It is found mostly in northeastern Japan, the island of Kyūshū, and the Ryūkyū Islands.

GIVEN NAMES Japanese 55%. *Hiroshi* (8), *Ayako* (4), *Kaoru* (4), *Masahiro* (4), *Masumi* (4), *Toshio* (4), *Akira* (3), *Haruo* (3), *Hideo* (3), *Kiyoshi* (3), *Koichi* (3), *Kunio* (3).

Abebe (201) Ethiopian: probably from Amharic *abeba* 'flower', 'blossom'.

GIVEN NAMES Ethiopian 79%. *Amare* (3), *Haile* (3), *Mekonnen* (3), *Meskerem* (3), *Tesfaye* (3), *Genet* (2), *Getachew* (2), *Mesfin* (2), *Tadele* (2), *Abiy, Addisu, Admasu; Almaz* (2).

Abed (211) Muslim: variant of ABID.

GIVEN NAMES Muslim 62%. *Mohammad* (4), *Abed* (3), *Bassam* (3), *Khalid* (3), *Mahmoud* (3), *Ali* (2), *Fawzi* (2), *Jamal* (2), *Omar* (2), *Samir* (2), *Zaher* (2), *Abbas.*

Abee (270) **1.** reduced form of Irish MCABEE. **2.** Americanized spelling of Swiss German **Äbi** (see EBY). **3.** possibly an Americanized spelling of French **Abbé** (see ABBE).

Abegg (116) South German and Swiss German: topographic name for someone who lived near the corner of a mountain, from German *ab-* 'off' + *Egg*, dialect form of *Eck(e)* 'promontory', 'corner'.

Abegglen (141) German (Swabian): diminutive of ABEGG.

GIVEN NAMES German 6%. *Hermann* (2), *Gottlieb.*

Abeita (124) Spanish: variant of **Abieta** (see ABEYTA).

GIVEN NAMES Spanish 15%. *Cruz* (2), *Ambrosio, Audelia, Elva, Felipe, Fernando, Juanita, Pablo, Seferino.*

Abel (7185) **1.** Common European surname: from the personal name *Abel*, which is of Biblical origin and was used as a Christian name in many countries of Europe. In the Book of Genesis Abel is a son of Adam, murdered by his brother Cain (Genesis 4:1–8). In Christian tradition he is regarded as representative of suffering innocence. The Hebrew form of the name is *Hevel*, from a vocabulary word meaning 'breath'. **2.** German: from the personal name *Abel*, a pet form of *Albrecht* (see ALBERT).

Abela (136) **1.** Italian: variant of ABELLA or possibly from a feminine form of the Biblical name *Abele* (see ABEL). **2.** Catalan, Galician, Portuguese, and Spanish: variant of ABELLA. **3.** Dutch: variant of ABELE.

GIVEN NAMES Italian 11%; Spanish 11%. *Carmel, Fulvio, Guido, Oreste, Vito; Augusto* (2), *Manuel* (2), *Adan, Alfredo, Eduardo, Graciela, Jorge, Mario.*

Abele (687) **1.** Dutch: habitational name from Abeele in Zeeland. **2.** South German and Swiss German: from a pet form of the personal name *Albrecht* (see ALBERT). **3.** Latvian: from Latvian *ābele* 'apple tree', a topographic name or occupational name for someone who lived by or owned an orchard. **4.** Variant of the Ashkenazic Jewish name ABELES.

GIVEN NAMES German 4%. *Klaus* (2), *Hans, Reinhold, Ulrich, Wolfgang.*

Abeles (268) **1.** Jewish (Ashkenazic): from *Abele* (a pet form of the Yiddish personal name *Abe* (from Hebrew *ab* 'father') or of ABRAHAM) + Yiddish possessive *-s*. **2.** Dutch: variant of ABELE.

GIVEN NAMES Jewish 4%. *Aryeh, Mort, Sol.*

Abell (2711) Variant spelling of ABEL.

FOREBEARS Robert Abell settled in Rehoboth, MA, in about 1630.

Abella (356) **1.** Catalan, Galician, and Spanish: habitational name from any of several places called Abella, in Catalonia, Galicia and Santander. **2.** Catalan and Galician: from *abella* 'bee', hence a nickname for a small, active person or an occupational name for a beekeeper. **3.** Italian: mainly Sicilian variant of AVELLA.

GIVEN NAMES Spanish 35%. *Jose* (4), *Manuel* (4), *Jorge* (3), *Juan* (3), *Luis* (3), *Armando* (2), *Eduardo* (2), *Francisco* (2), *Julio* (2), *Orlando* (2), *Rolando* (2), *Adolfo.*

Abello (119) Catalan (**Abelló**): nickname from a derivative of *abella* 'bee' (see ABELLA).

GIVEN NAMES Spanish 40%. *Manuel* (4), *Carlos* (3), *Jose* (3), *Francisco* (2), *Gustavo* (2), *Alberto, Bernardo, Carols, Edgardo, Eduardo, Fortunato, Guillermo.*

Abelman (133) **1.** Jewish (Ashkenazic): from the personal name *Abele* (see ABELES) + German *Mann* 'man'. **2.** Americanized spelling of German **Abelmann**, which is from the personal name *Abel* (a pet form of *Albrecht*) + *-mann* as a diminutive suffix.

FOREBEARS This surname was brought to PA from Germany by one Heinrich Abelmann in the 18th century.

GIVEN NAME French 5%. *Marie Christine.*

Abeln (244) German: patronymic from the personal name ABEL.

Abels (626) North German: patronymic from the personal name ABEL.

Abelson (489) **1.** Jewish (Ashkenazic): patronymic from *Abele* (see ABELES). **2.** Americanized spelling of Danish **Abelsen** or Swedish **Abelsson**, patronymics from the personal name ABEL.

Abend (298) **1.** German: from Middle High German *ābent* 'evening', hence probably a topographic name for someone living to the west of a settlement. **2.** Jewish (Ashkenazic): ornamental name from German *Abend* 'evening'.

GIVEN NAMES French 4%. *Andre* (2), *Serge.*

Abendroth (389) **1.** German: apparently from the vocabulary word *Abendrot(h)* 'sunset', but in many if not all cases actually a folk-etymological alteration of the habitational name **Appenrodt** or **Appenroth**, from any of several places in northern Germany which are so named from the personal name *Aben* + Middle German *rot* 'cleared land'. **2.** Jewish (Ashkenazic): ornamental name from German *Abendroth* 'sunset', literally 'evening red'. Compare MORGENSTERN.

GIVEN NAMES German 8%. *Fritz* (2), *Hans* (2), *Heinz* (2), *Klaus* (2), *Kurt* (2), *Alfons, Rainer.*

Aber (577) German: from the personal name *Aber*, a North German variant of ALBERT.

Abercrombie (2211) Scottish: habitational name from a place in Fife named Abercrombie (earlier *Abarcrumbach*), which is of Pictish origin, meaning either 'confluence of rivers at a bend' or 'mouth of the bendy river'.

Aberg (165) Americanized spelling of Scandinavian ABERG.
GIVEN NAMES Scandinavian 14%. *Astrid* (2), *Erik* (2), *Fredrik, Helmer, Lennart*.

Aberle (661) South German and Swiss German: from a pet form of the personal name *Albrecht* (see ALBERT).

Aberman (102) Jewish: variant of HABERMANN.
GIVEN NAMES Jewish 8%; Russian 4%. *Ilya, Revekka, Zave; Arkadiy*.

Abernathey (102) Variant spelling of Scottish ABERNATHY.

Abernathy (5834) Scottish: habitational name from Abernethy in southeastern Perthshire. The place name is of Pictish origin, meaning 'mouth of the river Nethy'.
FOREBEARS This was one of the surnames of the Scots who settled in northern Ireland during the 'plantation' in the 17th century, and it was brought to the U.S. as the name of a Southern plantation owner (in a different sense of the word 'plantation').

Abernethy (1354) Scottish: variant of ABERNATHY.

Abert (164) South German and Swiss German: from a southern form of the personal name *Albrecht* (see ALBERT).
FOREBEARS The name was brought to PA by Peter Abert in the 18th century.
GIVEN NAME French 4%. *Vernice*.

Abeyta (1125) Spanish (of Basque origin): variant of **Abieta**, a habitational name from a place named with *a(ha)bi* 'bilberry' + *-eta*, a suffix indicating 'place' or 'group of'.
GIVEN NAMES Spanish 16%. *Jose* (9), *Carlos* (8), *Manuel* (6), *Miguel* (5), *Juan* (4), *Ruben* (4), *Ramon* (3), *Angelina* (2), *Emilio* (2), *Pablo* (2), *Roberto* (2), *Agapito*.

Abid (102) Muslim: from a personal name based on Arabic *'ābid* 'worshiper'. *'Ābid* is also found as a component of compound names referring to one of the attributes of Allah, for example *'Ābidur-Raḥman* 'worshiper of the Most Gracious'.
GIVEN NAMES Muslim 73%. *Syed* (6), *Mohamed* (3), *Mohammad* (3), *Abdul* (2), *Arshad* (2), *Farid* (2), *Khan* (2), *Muhammad* (2), *Ahmed, Bader, Faisal, Hakim*.

Abila (138) Spanish (**Ábila**): habitational name from Ávila (see AVILA), the spelling reflecting confusion in the pronunciation of Spanish between *v* and *b*.
GIVEN NAMES Spanish 34%. *Jose* (3), *Cruz* (2), *Javier* (2), *Ruben* (2), *Agapito, Aida, Alfredo, Amparo, Angel, Efrain, Elena, Eleodoro*.

Abitz (209) German (chiefly eastern): **1.** from a variant of the personal name *A(da)lbert* (see ALBERT). **2.** habitational name from a place name in eastern Germany, of Slavic origin.

Abke (101) German: unexplained.

Able (724) English: variant spelling of ABEL. Probably also an Americanized spelling of the same surname in other languages.

Ableman (152) Variant spelling of ABELMAN.

Abler (283) Variant of German and Jewish **Habler**.
GIVEN NAMES German 6%. *Wolf* (2), *Johann, Othmar, Reinhold*.

Ables (1685) **1.** Scottish: derivative of ABEL, meaning 'son or servant of someone called Abel'. **2.** Possibly a respelling of German ABELS.

Abner (1399) English: from a Biblical personal name, meaning in Hebrew 'God is (my) light', which was popular among the Puritans, especially among early settlers in New England, but also in the southern states. In the First and Second Books of Samuel, Abner is Saul's uncle and the commander of his army, who is eventually cut down by Joab (II Samuel 3:12–39).

Abney (2890) English: habitational name from a place in Derbyshire named Abney, from the Old English personal name *Abba* (+ genitive *-n*) + Old English *ēg* 'island'. The surname is now much more common in the U.S. than in England.

Abood (320) Muslim: variant of ABBOUD. This name is found among Christian Arabs and Jews as well as Muslims in Lebanon and elsewhere.

Aborn (129) English: topographic name for someone who lived near a stream, Middle English *atte borne* 'at the bourn'. The preposition may alternatively be Anglo-Norman French *a*, likewise meaning 'at'.
FOREBEARS Samuel Aborn came to MA from England in 1636; his name is also spelled **Eborne**.

Aboud (187) Muslim: variant spelling of ABBOUD.

Abplanalp (340) South German and Swiss German: topographic name for someone living high on a mountainside, from German *ab-* 'below', 'off' + *Planalp* 'high, flat mountain-meadow'.

Abraha (125) Ethiopian: from the personal name ABRAHAM.
GIVEN NAMES Ethiopian 74%; African 5%. *Girmay* (3), *Abeba* (2), *Belay* (2), *Berhane* (2), *Fetlework* (2), *Haile* (2), *Mebrat* (2), *Mehari* (2), *Mulu* (2), *Nigisti* (2), *Tekeste* (2), *Bruk; Almaz* (2).

Abraham (7637) **1.** From the Hebrew personal name *Avraham*, borne by a Biblical patriarch revered by Jews as the founding father of the Jewish people (Genesis 11–25), and by Muslims as founder of all the Semitic peoples, both Hebrew and Arab (compare IBRAHIM). The name is explained in Genesis 17:5 as being derived from Hebrew *av hamon goyim* 'father of a multi-tude of nations'. It was widely used as a personal name among Christians as well as Jews in the Middle Ages in diverse cultures from northern Europe to southern India. It is also found as a given name among Christians in India, and in the U.S. has come to be used as a family name among families from Kerala. **2.** Irish: English name adopted as an equivalent of Gaelic **Mac an Bhreitheamhan** 'son of the judge'. See McBROOM.
FOREBEARS A bearer of the surname Abraham, from Poitiers, is recorded in Quebec city in 1671.
GIVEN NAMES Indian 6%. *Mathai* (8), *Mohan* (5), *Raju* (5), *Saji* (5), *Prasad* (4), *Anil* (3), *Babu* (3), *Biju* (3), *Leela* (3), *Sajan* (3), *Shibu* (3), *Suma* (3).

Abrahamian (170) Armenian: patronymic from the Biblical personal name ABRAHAM.
GIVEN NAMES Armenian 44%. *Armen* (6), *Sarkis* (4), *Harmik* (2), *Seta* (2), *Zaven* (2), *Adrine, Ara, Avadis, Bedros, Garnik, Hrach, Hrand*.

Abrahams (1061) English, Dutch, and Jewish (Ashkenazic): patronymic from the personal name ABRAHAM.

Abrahamsen (427) Dutch, North German, Danish, and Norwegian: patronymic from the personal name ABRAHAM.
GIVEN NAMES Scandinavian 24%. *Erik* (4), *Alf* (2), *Oddvar* (2), *Sven* (2), *Thor* (2), *Lars, Lief, Per*.

Abrahamson (2091) **1.** Jewish (Ashkenazic): patronymic from the personal name ABRAHAM. **2.** Americanized spelling of Swedish **Abrahamsson**, or Norwegian and Danish ABRAHAMSEN, likewise patronymics from ABRAHAM.
GIVEN NAMES Scandinavian 4%. *Erik* (4), *Aagot, Algot, Anders, Eskil, Lars, Thora*.

Abram (1462) **1.** English, German, Dutch, Polish, Slovenian, and Jewish; Hungarian (**Ábrám**): from a reduced form of ABRAHAM. **2.** English: habitational name from a place near Manchester, formerly *Adburgham*, named in Old English as 'the homestead (Old English *hām*) of a woman called Ēadburg'.

Abramczyk (190) Polish and Jewish (from Poland): from a Polish pet or patronymic form of ABRAM (see ABRAHAM).
GIVEN NAMES Polish 6%; Jewish 5%. *Alicja, Jaroslaw, Jerzy; Mordechai, Shalom*.

Abramo (245) Italian and Jewish (from Italy): from the personal name *Abramo* (see ABRAHAM).
GIVEN NAMES Italian 21%. *Salvatore* (6), *Angelo* (2), *Carmelo, Giuseppe, Guido, Luigi, Nunzio, Sal, Salvator, Saverio, Silvio*.

Abramov (191) Jewish (eastern Ashkenazic) and Russian: patronymic from ABRAM, an Eastern Slavic form of the personal name ABRAHAM.
GIVEN NAMES Russian 37%; Jewish 26%. *Boris* (9), *Oleg* (6), *Mikhail* (4), *Vyacheslav*

(4), *Leonid* (3), *Dmitriy* (2), *Grigoriy* (2), *Iosif* (2), *Vladimir* (2), *Yury* (2), *Aleksey*, *Anatoliy*; *Ilya* (5), *Asaf*, *Avshalom*, *Khaim*, *Malkiel*, *Meir*, *Mier*, *Moisey*, *Naum*, *Pinkhas*, *Ronit*, *Shaul*.

Abramovich (207) Jewish (eastern Ashkenazic): patronymic from ABRAM, a reduced form of the personal name ABRAHAM. In some cases it may be an Americanized spelling of Croatian **Abramović**.
GIVEN NAMES Jewish 23%; Russian 19%. *Ilya* (3), *Aron* (2), *Khaim*, *Lazer*, *Leib*, *Liba*, *Meir*, *Meyer*, *Moysey*, *Shaul*, *Shoshana*, *Sura*; *Lev* (5), *Igor* (4), *Boris* (3), *Mikhail* (3), *Anatoly* (2), *Raisa* (2), *Svetlana* (2), *Aleksandr*, *Anatoliy*, *Arkadiy*, *Garri*, *Grigoriy*.

Abramovitz (268) Jewish (eastern Ashkenazic): variant of ABRAMOWITZ.
GIVEN NAMES Jewish 13%. *Avi* (3), *Asher*, *Iser*, *Malca*, *Meyer*, *Noach*, *Rina*, *Yosef*, *Yoshua*, *Zvi*.

Abramowicz (187) Polish and Jewish (from Poland): patronymic from ABRAM, a reduced form of the personal name ABRAHAM.
GIVEN NAMES Polish 11%; Jewish 4%. *Irena*, *Janusz*, *Ryszard*, *Waclaw*, *Wieslaw*, *Wlodzimierz*, *Yolanta*, *Zbigniew*; *Chaim* (2), *Pola*.

Abramowitz (892) Jewish (eastern Ashkenazic): patronymic from ABRAM, a reduced form of the personal name ABRAHAM.
GIVEN NAMES Jewish 12%. *Sol* (4), *Hyman* (3), *Elkan* (2), *Mayer* (2), *Moshe* (2), *Shloma* (2), *Ari*, *Aron*, *Chain*, *Chana*, *Frima*, *Isador*.

Abramowski (124) Jewish (from Poland): patronymic from ABRAM, a reduced form of the personal name ABRAHAM.
GIVEN NAMES German 4%. *Hedwig*, *Horst*.

Abrams (10057) Jewish (Ashkenazic), Dutch, English, and German: patronymic from a reduced form of the personal name ABRAHAM.

Abramson (2646) Jewish, Dutch, and English: patronymic from ABRAM, a reduced form of the personal name ABRAHAM.
GIVEN NAMES Jewish 5%. *Hyman* (4), *Sol* (3), *Arie* (2), *Emanuel* (2), *Hanoch* (2), *Isadore* (2), *Alter*, *Fira*, *Hymie*, *Moshe*, *Myer*, *Rivka*.

Abrantes (101) Spanish and Portuguese: habitational name from Abrantes, an ancient city in Santarém.
GIVEN NAMES Spanish 31%; Portuguese 14%. *Antonio* (5), *Julio* (3), *Manuel* (2), *Agapito*, *Alejandro*, *Carlos*, *Dulce*, *Felino*, *Francisco*, *Hermes*, *Juan*, *Luis*, *Maria Luisa*; *Paulo*.

Abrego (623) Spanish (also **Ábrego**): from *ábrego*, which originally meant 'African', from Latin *africus*. The vocabulary word in modern Spanish has lost this general sense and now means only 'south wind', literally, 'African (wind)'.

GIVEN NAMES Spanish 49%. *Jose* (19), *Juan* (12), *Luis* (7), *Manuel* (7), *Salvador* (7), *Guadalupe* (5), *Jesus* (5), *Gerardo* (4), *Javier* (4), *Cristobal* (3), *Francisco* (3), *Isidro* (3).

Abrell (156) South German: from Middle High German *aberëlle* 'April'; hence a nickname for a moody or temperamental man, with reference to the changeable weather in that month. In some cases it may have been applied to someone with a particular connection with April, for example as the month in which his annual tax or rent payments were due.

Abresch (121) North German, Dutch, and Jewish (Ashkenazic): from a pet form of the Biblical name ABRAHAM.

Abreu (1969) Portuguese and Galician: habitational name from a place called Abreu in Minho province.
GIVEN NAMES Spanish 44%; Portuguese 12%. *Jose* (62), *Luis* (23), *Rafael* (23), *Carlos* (20), *Manuel* (18), *Juan* (16), *Ana* (15), *Julio* (13), *Jorge* (12), *Pedro* (12), *Ramon* (12), *Francisco* (10); *Joao* (4), *Joaquim* (2), *Paulo* (2), *Amadeu*, *Vasco*.

Abrigo (101) Spanish: variant of ABREGO.
GIVEN NAMES Spanish 32%. *Fernando* (2), *Jose* (2), *Pedro* (2), *Elena*, *Elia*, *Ernesto*, *Felipe*, *Florentino*, *Gonzalo*, *Hipolito*, *Ignacio*, *Imelda*.

Abril (300) Spanish and Portuguese: from an old personal name, *Abril*, based on the name of the month (from Latin *Aprilis*, 'April'). Compare APRIL.
GIVEN NAMES Spanish 40%. *Manuel* (7), *Eduardo* (4), *Juan* (4), *Jesus* (3), *Julio* (3), *Alberto* (2), *Alfonso* (2), *Alvaro* (2), *Dionicio* (2), *Jose* (2), *Luis* (2), *Rodolfo* (2).

Abron (165) Anglicized representation of the French pronunciation of ABRAHAM.
GIVEN NAME French 4%. *Carmelle*.

Abruzzese (191) Italian: regional name for someone from the Abruzzi, from an adjectival form of the place name (see ABRUZZO).
GIVEN NAMES Italian 19%. *Gaetano* (2), *Salvatore* (2), *Angelo*, *Attilio*, *Libero*, *Luigi*, *Pasquale*, *Philomena*, *Rocco*.

Abruzzo (339) Italian: regional name for someone from the Abruzzi, a mountainous region of Italy east of Rome. Compare ABRUZZESE.
GIVEN NAMES Italian 8%. *Salvatore* (3), *Carmine*, *Santo*, *Vita*.

Abshear (110) See ABSHIRE.

Absher (1205) See ABSHIRE.

Abshier (296) See ABSHIRE.

Abshire (1549) Of uncertain origin: **1.** most probably a variant of English **Upshire** (see UPSHUR). **2.** alternatively, perhaps an Americanized form of German **Habicher** 'hawker', i.e. someone who trained hawks for hunting (see HABIG). See also APGAR.
FOREBEARS This is a well-established American family name. Lewis Abshire bought land in VA in 1637, but it is not known

where he came from. In a taxation list for Franklin County, VA, for 1786, there are mentioned William, Abraham, Christian, Jacob, and Lodowick Abshire.

Abston (662) Of uncertain origin; perhaps from an English place name, but not now recorded in England as a surname. One possibility is Abson near Bristol, earlier *Abston*; another is Adstone in Northamptonshire, which is named from an Old English personal name *Ættīn* + Old English *tūn* 'settlement'.

Abt (504) **1.** German and Dutch: from Old Low German or Middle Dutch *abt* 'abbot', hence an occupational name for a servant of an abbot or a nickname for someone thought to resemble an abbot in some way. In some instances it may have been from a house name. **2.** Jewish (central Ashkenazic): from *Abt*, the German name of Opatów in Poland, or from *Apt*, the Yiddish name of this city.
GIVEN NAMES German 5%. *Helmut* (3), *Horst*, *Johann*, *Kurt*.

Abts (270) German and Dutch: variant of ABT.

Abu (123) Muslim and Jewish (Sephardic): from Arabic *abū* 'father', in Muslim names used to form the 'kunya' (name meaning 'father of') in combination with the name of a man's child, usually his firstborn son. Thus, a man might be addressed as *Abū Ḥasan* 'father of Hasan' rather than by his personal name, say 'Alī. In traditional Muslim society, a man is generally known and addressed by his kunya, rather than by his *ism* (his personal name), the use of which can seem unduly familiar. *Abū-Bakr*, literally 'father of the Young Camel' is the name by which Muhammad's son-in-law, the first of the 'rightly guided' khalifs (ruled 632–634) is known. *Abū-Ṭālib* 'father of the Seeker' was an uncle of the Prophet Muhammad. *Abū-Fāḍl*, 'father of the Virtuous one' was the kunya of 'Abbās, another uncle of the Prophet Muhammad. A kunya may also be used to form a nickname, as in the case of *Abū-Turāb* 'Alī 'Alī, father of dust', a kunya of the Khalif Ali, the fourth of the 'rightly guided' khalifs, conferred on him by the Prophet Muhammad.
GIVEN NAMES Muslim 38%; Jewish 6%. *Abu*, *Ahmad*, *Hassan*, *Mohamed*, *Mohammed*, *Muhamad*, *Safi*, *Salah*, *Saleh*, *Talib*, *Usman*, *Walid*; *Hayim*, *Shimon*.

Abundis (114) Hispanic (Mexico): patronymic from the Old Spanish personal name *Abundio*, ultimately from Latin *abundus* 'abundant', 'plentiful'.
GIVEN NAMES Spanish 48%. *Manuel* (3), *Armando* (2), *Carlos* (2), *Ernesto* (2), *Francisco* (2), *Jesus* (2), *Jose* (2), *Juan* (2), *Alejandro*, *Amada*, *Angelina*, *Beatriz*, *Primo*.

Aburto (131) Basque: topographic name from Basque *aburto* 'place of kermes oaks', from *abur* 'kermes oak' + the locative suffix *-lo*.

GIVEN NAMES Spanish 58%. *Jose* (4), *Carlos* (3), *Juan* (3), *Manuel* (3), *Alejandro* (2), *Isidoro* (2), *Pablo* (2), *Pedro* (2), *Adolfo*, *Alfredo*, *Amado*, *Amalia*.

Acampora (290) Southern Italian: variant of **Acanfora**, from the medieval personal name *Canfora*, from *canfora* 'camphor' (from Arabic *kāfūr*).

GIVEN NAMES Italian 11%; French 5%. *Salvatore* (2), *Alfonse*, *Angelo*, *Carmel*, *Gennaro*, *Pasquale*; *Alphonse* (3), *Raoul*.

Accardi (569) Italian: patronymic or plural form of ACCARDO.

GIVEN NAMES Italian 25%. *Salvatore* (6), *Vito* (4), *Mario* (3), *Rosario* (3), *Sal* (3), *Carlo* (2), *Carmelo* (2), *Gasper* (2), *Salvator* (2), *Umberto* (2), *Agostino*, *Angelo*, *Antonino*, *Antonio*.

Accardo (398) Italian (mainly Sicily): of Norman French origin, a derivative of a Germanic personal name composed of the elements *agio* 'edge (of a sword)' + *hard* 'bold', 'hardy'. Compare ACKERT.

GIVEN NAMES Italian 15%. *Angelo* (5), *Salvatore* (4), *Sal* (3), *Paolo* (2), *Antonino*, *Ciro*, *Donato*, *Giacomo*, *Giovanni*, *Giuseppe*.

Accetta (235) Italian: from the female form of southern Italian **Accetto**, a medieval personal name from the Latin name *Acceptus* (from *acceptus* 'welcome', 'well-liked').

GIVEN NAMES Italian 26%. *Matteo* (4), *Salvatore* (2), *Vito* (2), *Angelo*, *Antonella*, *Caesar*, *Carmela*, *Carmelo*, *Caterina*, *Dante*, *Domenic*, *Goffredo*.

Accola (168) Swiss (Romansh): from Latin *accola* 'neighbor', 'inhabitant' (from *accolere* 'to live near'). In medieval Latin *accola* also meant 'tenant (farmer)', which is probably the principal sense of the name.

Accomando (157) Italian (Sicily): from medieval Latin *arcumannus* 'German shepherd dog', presumably a metonymic occupational name for a shepherd or possibly a nickname for someone thought to resemble the dog in some way.

GIVEN NAMES Italian 11%. *Angelo* (2), *Giacomo*, *Gilda*, *Grazia*, *Italo*.

Accordino (127) Italian (Sicily): from a pet form of the personal name *Accordo* (or, more commonly, the compound name *Bonaccordo*), from *accordo* 'agreement'.

GIVEN NAMES Italian 14%. *Carmine* (2), *Salvatore* (2), *Sal*.

Accurso (246) Southern Italian (mainly Sicily): variant of Italian **Accorso**, from a medieval personal name meaning 'help', 'assistance', often also found in the compound form BONACCORSO 'good help'.

GIVEN NAMES Italian 20%. *Angelo*, *Domenica*, *Domenico*, *Gasper*, *Sal*, *Salvatore*, *Santo*.

Ace (401) **1.** English: from a Norman and Old French personal name, *Ace*, *Asse*, from

Germanic (Frankish) *Azzo*, *Atso*, a pet form of personal names containing *adal* 'noble' as a first element. **2.** Possibly an Americanized form of German ATZ, which has the same origin as 1.

Acebo (143) Spanish: habitational name from a place named Acebo, for example in Cáceres province; the place name is from *acebo* 'holly' (Latin *aquifolium*, literally 'sharp-leafed').

GIVEN NAMES Spanish 32%. *Jose* (4), *Alberto* (3), *Francisco* (3), *Angel* (2), *Benito* (2), *Juan* (2), *Nilo* (2), *Pedro* (2), *Alfonso*, *Alicia*, *Amador*, *Aurelio*; *Angelo*, *Antonio*, *Lorenzo*.

Acedo (117) **1.** Basque: habitational name from Acedo, a town in Navarre, Basque Country. **2.** Spanish: nickname for someone of a sour or vinegary disposition, from *acedo* 'sour', 'gone sour' (from Latin *acetum* 'vinegar').

GIVEN NAMES Spanish 52%. *Armando* (2), *Carlos* (2), *Jesus* (2), *Mercedes* (2), *Abelardo*, *Adriana*, *Alberto*, *Alicia*, *Arturo*, *Caridad*, *Ernesto*, *Eugenio*.

Acero (142) Spanish: from *acero* 'steel', 'steelworker' (from Late Latin *aciarium*), an occupational name for a metal worker or an armorer.

GIVEN NAMES Spanish 60%. *Jose* (6), *Pedro* (4), *Guillermo* (3), *Armando* (2), *Carlos* (2), *Jorge* (2), *Juan* (2), *Manuel* (2), *Raul* (2), *Alejandro*, *Alicia*, *Ana*.

Acerra (167) Southern Italian: habitational name from Acerra, in Naples province.

GIVEN NAMES Italian 19%. *Salvatore* (4), *Gaetano* (3), *Caesar*, *Carmela*, *Domenic*, *Giuseppe*, *Sal*.

Aceto (457) Italian: metonymic occupational name for a maker or seller of vinegar, *aceto*, or a nickname from the same word in the sense 'sour'.

GIVEN NAMES Italian 13%. *Rocco* (4), *Domenico* (2), *Camillo*, *Carmine*, *Enzo*, *Francesco*, *Igino*, *Lorenzo*, *Luigi*, *Oreste*, *Pasquale*, *Salvatore*.

Acevedo (4461) Spanish (Castilian and Galician): topographic name from Old Spanish *acebedo*, *azevedo* 'holly grove' (from *azevo* 'holly' + *-edo* 'plantation'). This name is common in Tenerife.

GIVEN NAMES Spanish 50%; Portuguese 10%. *Jose* (117), *Juan* (61), *Luis* (49), *Carlos* (42), *Manuel* (39), *Miguel* (39), *Jesus* (36), *Francisco* (35), *Jorge* (35), *Angel* (30), *Raul* (27), *Rafael* (23); *Wenceslao* (2).

Aceves (777) Spanish: of uncertain origin; perhaps a habitational name from a minor place, named from *acebo* 'holly'.

GIVEN NAMES Spanish 55%. *Jose* (36), *Miguel* (12), *Salvador* (12), *Carlos* (11), *Manuel* (11), *Jesus* (8), *Juan* (8), *Luis* (8), *Alicia* (7), *Francisco* (7), *Rafael* (7), *Guadalupe* (6).

Acey (190) English (East Yorkshire): perhaps from a pet form ACE.

Ach (105) German: topographic name for someone who lived by a spring or stream, from Old High German *aha* 'running water'.

GIVEN NAMES German 8%. *Manfred* (2), *Ilse*.

Acharya (186) Indian: Hindu (Brahman) name, from Sanskrit *ācārya* 'one who knows or teaches (right) conduct', i.e. a spiritual guide or teacher. The term was also applied as an honorific title for a man of learning. It has also been adopted as a surname by some non-Brahman communities.

GIVEN NAMES Indian 96%. *Arvind* (4), *Mukund* (3), *Raj* (3), *Ajay* (2), *Ajit* (2), *Anurag* (2), *Arun* (2), *Bharat* (2), *Harsha* (2), *Harshad* (2), *Jayant* (2), *Madhu* (2).

Achatz (157) German and Dutch: from the personal name *Achatz*, a vernacular form of the Biblical name *Ahaz* (2 Kings 16:1), which means 'he (i.e. God) has made fast'. The Latinate form *Achatius* is attested as a surname in Pforzheim in 1556, and may have a different origin: *Achatius* was a Byzantine saint, a Roman soldier believed to have been crucified, supposedly with 10,000 companions, on Mount Ararat during the reign of Hadrian; his name is probably a derivative of *Achates*, the name of Aeneas's faithful Trojan companion in Virgil's *Aeneid*.

GIVEN NAME German 5%. *Aloysius* (2).

Achee (238) In New England, an Americanized form of French ETHIER. Compare ACHEY.

GIVEN NAMES French 6%. *Achille*, *Charlet*, *Emile*, *Henri*.

Achen (119) **1.** German: habitational name from the city of Aachen in western Germany, near the Dutch and Belgian border. **2.** Dutch: habitational name from Achêne in Namur province, in present-day Belgium.

Achenbach (618) German: habitational name from places in Hesse and Westphalia named Achenbach, from the obsolete word *Ach* or *Ache* (from Middle High German *ahe* 'water', 'stream') + *Bach* 'brook'.

GIVEN NAMES German 5%. *Kurt* (2), *Otto* (2), *Hartmut*, *Horst*, *Orlo*, *Wolfgang*.

Acheson (813) Variant of Scottish ATCHISON. This spelling is of Scottish origin, but since the 17th century has been especially common in northern Ireland.

FOREBEARS Among the individuals who brought this name from northern Ireland to North America was John Acheson (d. 1791). He took up residence in Washington, DC, where he was joined by his brother Thomas *c.* 1786. John founded a business furnishing government troops with supplies in the Indian wars. Their ancestor Archibald Acheson had moved from Gosford, Haddington, Scotland, to Ulster in 1604, where he received lands from King James VI as part of the 'plantation' of Ulster by Protestant Scots.

A certain David Acheson emigrated

from Ulster to North America in 1788 and had numerous prominent descendants.

Achey (311) In New England, an Americanized form of French ETHIER. Various other origins have been proposed, but this seems the most likely.

Achille (183) **1.** Italian and French: from the personal name *Achille*, based on the classical Greek name *Akhilleus* (see ACHILLES). **2.** Variant of ACHILLES.
GIVEN NAMES French 11%; Italian 8%. *Chantale, Ketty, Luckner, Mireille, Pascale, Yolaine*; *Antonio, Carmine, Nichola, Rocco, Salvatore*.

Achilles (270) **1.** German humanistic name or soldier's name, with reference to the prowess and near invulnerability of the classical Greek hero, the leading warrior of the Greek army at the siege of Troy (Greek *Akhilleus*). **2.** In other cases, possibly an Americanized form of names in other languages based on Greek *Akhilleus*, such as Italian *Achille* (three syllables), French *Achille* (two syllables).
FOREBEARS Heinrich Ludwig Achilles was born in *c.* 1746, probably in either Gremscheim or Ammenden, Germany. He emigrated from Brunswick (Braunschweig), and settled in Weare, NH, in 1776. He served in the Hessian army under General Burgoyne at the Battle of Saratoga in 1777.

Achor (163) Variant of French ACORD.

Achord (287) Variant of French ACORD.

Achorn (185) German: topographic name from Middle High German *ahorn* 'maple tree'.

Achter (112) **1.** Dutch: from *achter* 'behind', 'to the rear of', a topographic name for someone living at the back of a main settlement. **2.** Dutch: perhaps a shortened form of ACHTERBERG. **3.** German and Jewish (Ashkenazic): of uncertain origin. Various explanations have been proposed; it may be an agent noun from the verb *achten* 'to reckon or estimate', hence an occupational name for an appraiser or record keeper, or alternatively an altered form of AUCHTER 'watcher' (i.e. someone who watched over a flock or herd).
GIVEN NAMES German 7%; Jewish 5%. *Bernhard, Erna, Guenter, Hans*; *Meyer*.

Achterberg (251) Dutch and North German: topographic name for someone who lived 'behind the hill', from Dutch and Low German *achter* 'behind', 'in back of' + *berg* 'hill', 'mountain'. In some cases the Dutch surname is a habitational name from any of various places so named in the Netherlands and Belgium.
GIVEN NAMES German 5%. *Ernst, Hans, Kurt, Lorenz*.

Achterhof (120) German: topographic name for someone who lived 'behind the manor farm', from Middle Low German *achter* 'behind' + *hof* 'manor farm'.

Achuff (108) Probably a variant of ACUFF.

Achziger (138) German: **1.** (**Achtziger**) from *achtzig* 'eighty' + the agent suffix *-er*, in various possible applications, as for example a member of a council of eighty men, or a man obliged to pay regularly eighty units of currency in taxes. **2.** (in southern Baden) modification of **Achpiger**, a habitational name for someone from Echbeck (Middle High German *Ahbinge*), a village in southern Württemberg situated on a bend (*Bieg*) of the river Aach.

Acierno (233) Italian: habitational name from Acerno in Salerno province, which is named from Latin *acernus* 'of steel'.
GIVEN NAMES Italian 15%. *Alfonse, Aniello, Antonio, Domenico, Ettore, Gelsomina, Gennaro, Luigi, Pasquale, Stefano*; *Gerardo* (2), *Alfonso, Armando*.

Acker (4079) **1.** Dutch and German: topographic name from Middle High German and Middle Dutch *acker* '(cultivated) field', hence a byname for a peasant. **2.** English: topographic name for someone living by a piece of cultivated land, from Middle English *aker* 'acre', 'field' (Old English *æcer*). Compare AKERS. **3.** Jewish (Ashkenazic): ornamental name from German *Acker* 'field' (see 1).

Ackeret (108) Perhaps an altered form of German ECKERT.
GIVEN NAME German 4%. *Gottlieb*.

Ackerley (164) **1.** English (Cheshire): probably a habitational name from a lost or minor place. **2.** Americanized spelling of German **Äckerle** or **Ackerlein**, or Swiss **Aecherli**, all diminutives of ACKER.

Ackerly (266) English: variant spelling of ACKERLEY.

Ackerman (10229) **1.** Dutch: occupational name from *akkerman* 'plowman'; a frequent name in New Netherland in the 17th century. Later, it probably absorbed some cases of the cognate German and Swedish names, ACKERMANN and **Åkerman** respectively. **2.** English: from a medieval term denoting feudal status, Middle English *akerman* (Old English *æcerman*, from *æcer* 'field', acre' + *man* 'man'). Typically, an ackerman was a bond tenant of a manor holding half a virgate of arable land, for which he paid by serving as a plowman. The term was also used generically to denote a plowman or husbandman. **3.** Variant of German and Jewish ACKERMANN.

Ackermann (934) **1.** German: from Middle High German *ackerman* 'plowman', 'peasant'. The German term did not have the same denotation of status in the feudal system as its English counterpart ACKERMAN. **2.** Jewish (Ashkenazic): variant of ACKER.
GIVEN NAMES German 11%. *Kurt* (8), *Otto* (4), *Ernst* (2), *Erwin* (2), *Franz* (2), *Hans* (2), *Rainer* (2), *Armin, Bernd, Dieter, Fritz, Gerhard*.

Ackers (148) **1.** English: variant of AKERS. **2.** Altered form of ACKER.

Ackerson (1123) Americanized form of Dutch ECKERSON.

Ackert (254) **1.** English (of Norman origin): from a personal name, *Aquart*, Old French *Achart*, a derivative of a Germanic personal name composed of the elements *agi(n)* 'edge (of a sword)' + *hard* 'bold', 'hardy'. Compare German ECKHARDT and Italian ACCARDO, which are from the same source. **2.** German: from a Germanic personal name (as in 1). **3.** German: Americanized spelling of ECKERT.

Ackland (193) English: **1.** habitational name from Acland Barton in Landkey, Devon, named with the Old English personal name *Acca* + Old English *lanu* 'lane'. **2.** habitational name from a minor place named from Old English *āc* 'oak' + *land* 'land'. One such was in Oxfordshire.

Ackles (202) Americanized spelling of ACHILLES.

Ackley (2619) **1.** English: from any of various places named in Old English as *āc lēah* 'oak clearing'. Possible sources include Acle in Norfolk, Aykley in Durham, and Ackley Farm in Powys. Compare OAKLEY, which has the same origin. **2.** Americanized spelling of Swiss German EGLI.

Acklin (606) **1.** Americanized spelling of Swiss German EGLIN. **2.** English: perhaps a variant of ACKLAND or a habitational name from places in North Yorkshire and Middlesborough called Acklam, from Old English *æt þēm āc lēaum* (dative plural) 'at the oak clearings'.

Ackman (511) Probably an Americanized spelling of the German occupational name **Achmann** 'water bailiff', or of ECKMANN.

Ackmann (130) German: see ACKMAN.
GIVEN NAMES German 11%. *Wolfgang* (2), *Erwin, Kurt*.

Ackroyd (252) English (Yorkshire): topographic name from northern Middle English *ake* 'oak' + *royd* 'clearing'.

Acoba (112) Filipino: unexplained.
GIVEN NAMES Spanish 37%; Italian 7%. *Andres* (2), *Roberto* (2), *Adriano, Apolinario, Belen, Bonifacio, Brigido, Cerilo, Claudio, Dionicio, Eduardo, Elena*; *Antonio* (3), *Federico, Primo, Romeo*.

Acocella (204) Southern Italian: unexplained.
GIVEN NAMES Italian 30%. *Angelo* (13), *Pasquale* (2), *Agostino, Antonio, Francesco, Giuseppe, Nicola, Rocco*.

Acock (100) English: probably from a Middle English pet name formed from the initial *A-* of a personal name (e.g. ADAM) + the hypocoristic suffix *-cok* (see, e.g., ADCOCK).

Acoff (125) Of uncertain origin. See ACUFF.

Acomb (134) English: **1.** topographic name for a dweller in a valley, Middle English *atte combe* 'at the valley'. **2.** habitational name from one of the places (in Northumberland and Yorkshire) named Acomb, from Old English *æt ācum* 'at the oaks'.

Acord (1149) **1.** German: Americanized spelling of ECKHARDT. **2.** French: variant of **Achard**, which is from an Old French personal name, *Achart*, a derivative of an ancient Germanic personal name composed of the elements *agi(n)* 'edge (of a sword)' + *hard* 'bold', 'hardy'. Compare English ACKERT and Italian ACCARDI, which are from the same Germanic source.
FOREBEARS The name Andreas Lowrence Acord appears on an 18th-century ship's master's list, corresponding to Andreas Arkhard among the signatures of those taking an oath of allegiance in Pennsylvania in October 1753. A will written in Staunton Co., VA, in 1806 begins "In the Name of God, Amen, I, Francis Acord ... " but is signed in German script Frantz Eckhardt.

Acorn (110) Origin uncertain; most probably an Americanized form of German EICHHORN.

Acors (102) English (Kent): variant of AKERS.

Acosta (9603) Portuguese and Spanish: altered form (by misdivision) of DA COSTA.
GIVEN NAMES Spanish 46%; Portuguese 11%. *Jose* (225), *Juan* (107), *Carlos* (91), *Luis* (88), *Jesus* (86), *Manuel* (80), *Jorge* (52), *Miguel* (49), *Julio* (48), *Francisco* (47), *Rafael* (47), *Pedro* (46); *Paulo* (3), *Catarina, Ligia, Nelio*.

Acquaviva (302) Italian: literally 'living water', i.e. 'running water', 'spring'; a habitational name from any of various minor places in central and southern Italy so named on account of their springs of fresh water, as for example Acquaviva Platani in Sicily (until 1862, known simply as Acquaviva).
GIVEN NAMES Italian 10%. *Mauro* (2), *Antonio, Carmine, Martino, Salvatore, Savino, Vito*.

Acquisto (104) Italian: either from the personal name *Acquisto*, from *acquisto* 'acquisition', 'purchase' or from a short form of the personal name *Bonacquisto*, literally 'good buy', 'good acquisition', both names that would have been bestowed on a much wanted child.
GIVEN NAMES Italian 18%. *Carlo* (3), *Salvatore* (3).

Acre (258) **1.** English: probably a variant of ACKER or perhaps **Ackary** (see ACREE). **2.** Possibly also an Americanized spelling of Norwegian AAKRE, or German or Dutch ACKER, or South German EGGER.

Acree (1580) **1.** Americanized spelling of Swedish and Norwegian AKRE. **2.** Possibly an altered form of the English surname *Ackary*, which is derived from the personal name ZACHARIAS, through misdivision in Middle English of Latin *filius Zachariae* 'son of Zachary'.

Acreman (109) **1.** English (Somerset): variant of ACKERMAN. **2.** Americanized spelling of Dutch ACKERMAN or German ACKERMANN.

Acres (289) English and Irish: variant spelling of AKERS.

Acrey (156) See ACREE.

Acri (222) Italian: habitational name from a place in Cosenza province named Acri.
GIVEN NAMES Italian 10%; French 5%. *Rinaldo* (2), *Enrico, Salvatore; Armand* (2).

Acton (1932) English: habitational name from any of several places, especially in Shropshire and adjacent counties, named Acton. Generally, these are from Old English *āc* 'oak' + *tūn* 'settlement'.

Acuff (959) **1.** English: of uncertain origin, perhaps a variant of northern English **Aculf**, from an Old Norse personal name *Agúlfr* 'terror wolf'. **2.** Probably also of German origin: an Americanized form of ECKHOFF or EICKHOFF.
FOREBEARS The name first appears in North America in VA and PA in the early 1700s and later became concentrated in the Appalachian regions of NC and TN. The earliest records of Acuff occur with the personal names Timothy and David, indicating (in PA at least) Episcopal Church membership, thereby implying English origin, although no records of the name have been found in England.

Acuna (1576) Galician (**Acuña**): from *(a)cuña* 'wedge' (Latin *cuneus*).
GIVEN NAMES Spanish 45%; Portuguese 10%; Italian 9%. *Manuel* (22), *Jose* (20), *Carlos* (17), *Antonio* (15), *Juan* (14), *Miguel* (13), *Roberto* (13), *Francisco* (12), *Alfredo* (10), *Jesus* (9), *Arturo* (8), *Fernando* (8), *Luis* (8); *Albano, Wenceslao; Marco* (2), *Sal* (2), *Angelo, Aureliano, Carmela, Fausto, Federico, Leonardo, Marco Antonio, Nino, Sinforosa*.

Acy (120) **1.** French: habitational name for someone from any of various places called Acy, Romano-Gallic *Aciacum* 'estate of Acius'. **2.** English: variant of ACEY.
GIVEN NAME French 5%. *Dominique*.

Adachi (303) Japanese: variously written, usually with characters meaning 'foot' and 'stand', a habitational name, found mainly in northern Japan, from Adachi-ga-hara in Fukushima prefecture. The Adachi of Dewa (now Akita prefecture) descend from Fujiwara no Yamakage (824–888).
GIVEN NAMES Japanese 68%. *Kenji* (5), *Atsushi* (3), *Fumio* (3), *Hiroshi* (3), *Jiro* (3), *Minoru* (3), *Takashi* (3), *Taro* (3), *Yoshiyuki* (3), *Hideyo* (2), *Ichiro* (2), *Masashi* (2).

Adair (6714) Scottish (Galloway) and northern Irish: from the Scottish personal name *Adair*, also spelled *EdÊ'ear*, a form of EDGAR.
FOREBEARS James Adair (*c.*1709–*c.*1783) was an Indian trader in SC from 1735; he was born in Co. Antrim, northern Ireland. A certain Baron William Adair, from Scotland, also settled in SC at around the same period.

Adam (3969) From the Biblical personal name *Adam*, which was borne, according to Genesis, by the first man. It is the generic Hebrew term for 'man', probably from Hebrew *adama* 'earth'. Compare the classical Greek legend that Zeus fashioned the first human beings from earth. It was very popular as a personal name among non-Jews throughout Europe in the Middle Ages, and the surname is found in one form or another in most of the countries of Europe. Jews, however, have never used this personal name, except in recent times under Polish and English influence. Among Scottish and Irish bearers it is sometimes a reduced form of MCADAM.
GIVEN NAMES German 4%. *Erwin* (4), *Hans* (4), *Klaus* (4), *Helmut* (3), *Kurt* (3), *Gerhard* (2), *Gunter* (2), *Heinz* (2), *Reinhold* (2), *Claus, Detlef, Dietmar*.

Adamcik (199) Czech and Slovak (**Adamčík**): from a pet form of the personal name ADAM.

Adamczak (228) Polish and Ukrainian: pet form or patronymic from the personal name ADAM.
GIVEN NAMES Polish 4%. *Zdzislaw* (2), *Janusz*.

Adamczyk (913) Polish: from a pet form or patronymic from the personal name ADAM.
GIVEN NAMES Polish 15%. *Janusz* (5), *Leszek* (4), *Andrzej* (3), *Jerzy* (3), *Jozef* (3), *Agnieszka* (2), *Casimir* (2), *Ryszard* (2), *Stanislaw* (2), *Wladyslaw* (2), *Bogdan, Boleslaw*.

Adame (1273) Basque and Spanish: from the Basque personal name *Adame*, Basque form of ADAM.
GIVEN NAMES Spanish 49%. *Jose* (28), *Juan* (18), *Jesus* (14), *Manuel* (11), *Rafael* (10), *Carlos* (9), *Javier* (9), *Arturo* (8), *Francisco* (8), *Miguel* (8), *Ramon* (8), *Raul* (8).

Adamec (239) Czech and Slovak: from a pet form of the personal name ADAM.

Adamek (525) Czech and Slovak (**Adámek**); Polish: from a pet form of the personal name ADAM.

Adames (397) Spanish (of Basque origin): patronymic from the personal name ADAME.
GIVEN NAMES Spanish 48%. *Jose* (10), *Rafael* (7), *Angel* (6), *Ana* (4), *Aurelio* (3), *Jorge* (3), *Manuel* (3), *Miguel* (3), *Santos* (3), *Alberto* (2), *Andres* (2), *Benigno* (2); *Antonio* (3), *Leonardo* (2), *Cecilio, Clemente, Eligio, Giraldo, Philomena, Rafaelina*.

Adami (353) **1.** German: humanistic patronymic from ADAM, using the Latin genitive. It is attested as a surname of German origin in 18th-century America. **2.** Hungarian: habitational name for someone from a place called Ádám in Bihar county. **3.** Hungarian: patronymic from the personal name *Ádám*, Hungarian form of ADAM. **4.** Italian: patronymic or plural form of ADAMO.

GIVEN NAMES Italian 4%. *Umberto* (2), *Aldo, Giulio, Paolo, Primo, Silvio.*

Adamiak (131) Polish: patronymic from or pet form of the personal name ADAM.
GIVEN NAMES Polish 15%. *Andrzej, Dariusz, Gejza, Jacek, Jozef, Ryszard, Zbigniew.*

Adamian (101) Armenian: patronymic from the personal name ADAM.
GIVEN NAMES Armenian 40%; French 4%. *Haig* (3), *Nerses* (2), *Vahe* (2), *Aram, Aramais, Edik, Gaiane, Gevork, Hagop, Hovsep, Mesrob, Norayr; Germine, Serge.*

Adamic (132) Slovenian (**Adamič**); Serbian and North Croatian (**Adamić**): patronymic from the personal name ADAM.

Adamick (115) Americanized spelling of ADAMIK.

Adamik (151) Polish, Czech, and Slovak (**Adamík**): from a pet form of the personal name ADAM.

Adamo (1223) Italian: from the personal name *Adamo*, Italian equivalent of ADAM.
GIVEN NAMES Italian 16%. *Vito* (9), *Angelo* (6), *Antonio* (6), *Salvatore* (5), *Giuseppe* (3), *Santo* (3), *Giovanna* (2), *Nicola* (2), *Aldo, Baldassare, Carmelo, Carmino.*

Adamovich (133) Russian, Ukrainian, and Belorussian; Serbian and Croatian (Slavonia) (**Adamović**): patronymic from the personal name ADAM.

Adamowicz (207) Polish: patronymic from the personal name ADAM.
GIVEN NAMES Polish 5%. *Aleksander, Jacek, Wieslaw.*

Adams (144377) English (very common in England, especially in the south Midlands, and in Wales) and German (especially northwestern Germany): patronymic from the personal name ADAM. In the U.S. this form has absorbed many patronymics and other derivatives of ADAM in languages other than English. (For forms, see Hanks and Hodges 1988.)
FOREBEARS This American family name was borne by two early presidents of the United States, father and son. They were descended from Henry Adams, who settled in Braintree, MA, in 1635/6, from Barton St. David, Somerset, England. The younger of the two presidents, John Quincy Adams (1767–1848) derived his middle name from his maternal grandmother's family name (see QUINCY).
Another important New England family, established mainly in NH, is descended from William Adams, who emigrated from Shropshire, England, to Dedham, MA, in 1628. James Hopkins Adams (1812–61), governor of SC, was unconnected with either of these families, his ancestry being Welsh; his forebears entered North America through PA.

Adamski (1359) **1.** Polish: from the personal name ADAM + the surname suffix -*ski*. **2.** Polish and Jewish (eastern Ashkenazic): habitational name for someone from Adamy or Adamowo, villages in Poland, or from Adamki in Poland and Belarus.
GIVEN NAMES Polish 5%. *Andrzej* (3), *Jaroslaw* (3), *Jerzy* (2), *Krzysztof* (2), *Andrej, Beata, Casimir, Ignacy, Lech, Mariusz, Piotr, Tadeusz.*

Adamsky (116) Jewish (eastern Ashkenazic): variant spelling of ADAMSKI.
GIVEN NAMES Jewish 7%; Russian 4%. *Aron, Sol; Emanuil, Gennadiy.*

Adamson (6043) Common patronymic form of ADAM, especially in Scotland, where the name is borne by a sept of clan McIntosh. In the U.S., this form may also have absorbed some patronymic forms of ADAM in various other languages. Compare ADAMS.

Adamy (136) German: variant of ADAMI.

Adan (239) **1.** Spanish (**Adán**): from the personal name *Adán*, Spanish form of ADAM. **2.** Scottish: probably a variant of ADAM. **3.** Hungarian (**Ádán**): variant of **Ádám**, from the personal name *Ádám*, Hungarian form of ADAM.
GIVEN NAMES Spanish 41%. *Juan* (5), *Alberto* (4), *Jose* (4), *Adelberto* (3), *Armando* (3), *Alicia* (2), *Angel* (2), *Augusto* (2), *Carlos* (2), *Emilio* (2), *Francisco* (2), *Jesus* (2); *Aldo* (2), *Carlo, Cira, Dante, Heriberto, Marco Antonio.*

Adank (100) Swiss German: possibly a variant of **Hadank**, a variant of the personal name ADAM, probably of Slavic origin.

Aday (460) **1.** Galician and Spanish: habitational name from any of several places called Aday, in particular in Lugo province, Galicia. **2.** Scottish: from the personal name *Aday* or *Adie*, two of the many pet forms of ADAM.

Adcock (4999) English: from one of the many Middle English pet forms of ADAM, formed with the hypocoristic suffix -*cok*.

Adcox (716) English: derivative of ADCOCK. Compare COX.

Addair (185) Scottish and northern Irish: variant spelling of ADAIR.

Addams (138) English: variant spelling of ADAMS.

Addeo (217) Southern Italian (Naples and Sicily): from a short form of the personal name *Donadeo*, meaning 'dedicated to God', or perhaps a nickname for someone who habitually used this as a valedictory expression.
GIVEN NAMES Italian 13%. *Salvatore* (3), *Carmine, Nicola, Rocco, Sal, Santo.*

Adderley (212) English: habitational name from either of two places called Adderley, in Staffordshire and Shropshire; the former is named with the Old English personal name *Ealdrēd* + Old English *lēah* 'woodland clearing', while the latter has as the first element the Old English female personal name *Ealdþrȳð*.

Adderly (120) English: variant spelling of ADDERLEY.

GIVEN NAMES French 7%. *Celestine, Monique, Vernice.*

Addicks (124) Dutch, Frisian, and North German: patronymic from *Addicke*, a pet form of any of several Germanic personal names formed with the element *ad(al)* 'noble' (see ADE).

Addicott (105) English: unexplained; probably a habitational name from a minor or lost place, possibly in Somerset or Devon, where the modern surname is most frequent.

Addie (180) Scottish: from the personal name *Addie*, a pet form of ADAM.

Addington (1897) English: habitational name from any of various places named in Old English as *Eaddingtūn* 'settlement associated with Eadda' or *Æddingtūn* 'settlement associated with Æddi'. Places so named are found in Northamptonshire, Buckinghamshire, Kent, and Greater London.

Addis (1250) Southern English: patronymic from the Middle English personal name *Addy*, a pet form of ADAM.

Addison (4886) Scottish and English: patronymic from the Older Scots or northern Middle English personal name *Addie*, a pet form of ADAM.
FOREBEARS John Addison (died 1706) came from Westmoreland, England, to MD in 1667.

Addleman (274) German and Jewish: Americanized form of ADELMANN or ADELMAN. See also EDELMANN and its Americanized form, EDDLEMAN.

Addonizio (141) Italian: from the personal name DIONISIO, reinforced by the prefix *a*-.
GIVEN NAMES Italian 18%; French 6%. *Angelo* (2), *Carmine, Olympia, Ornella, Salvatore; Armand* (3).

Adduci (186) Italian: probably from a short form of one of the numerous omen names formed from *ducere* 'to bring', as for example *Benaducce* 'bring good'.
GIVEN NAMES Italian 12%. *Angelo* (2), *Fedele, Renzo, Rocco, Sal, Salvatore.*

Addy (907) English (West Yorkshire): from the Middle English personal name *Addy*, a pet form of ADAM.

Ade (445) **1.** Frisian and North German: from the personal name *Ade*, which is a pet form of ADAM or various names beginning with *Ad(al)*-, for example ADOLF, *Adalbrecht* (see ALBRECHT). **2.** English: from the personal name *Ade*, one of the many pet forms of ADAM.

Adee (218) **1.** Scottish or northern English: variant spelling of ADIE. **2.** Altered form of Frisian ADE, written thus to indicate pronunciation in two syllables.

Adel (162) **1.** German: from a short form of any of a number of personal names beginning with Old High German *adal* 'noble'. Compare EDEL. **2.** Jewish (Ashkenazic): ornamental name from *Adel* 'nobility'. **3.** Muslim: from a personal name based on

Arabic *ādil* 'just', 'legally competent (as a witness)'.

GIVEN NAMES Muslim 11%. *Ali, Aman, Ebrahim, Farid, Fawad, Ibrahim, Kaveh, Mohamed, Mohammad, Shahed, Shoeb, Yousef.*

Adelberg (144) **1.** German: habitational name from a place in southwestern Germany called Adelberg, named with Middle High German *adel* 'noble' + *berg* 'mountain'. **2.** Jewish (Ashkenazic): ornamental name composed of German *adel* 'noble' + *Berg* 'mountain'.

GIVEN NAMES German 5%. *Merwin* (2), *Erwin.*

Adell (192) **1.** Jewish: variant of ADEL. **2.** Swedish: from an unexplained first element, *Ad-* (which may represent a personal name or place name beginning with *Ad-*), + *-ell*, a common ending of Swedish surnames derived from the Latin adjectival ending *-elius.*

GIVEN NAMES Jewish 4%. *Gerson, Hirsch, Meyer.*

Adelman (1948) **1.** Jewish (Ashkenazic): ornamental name composed of German *Adel* 'nobility' + *Mann* or Yiddish *man* 'man'. Compare EDEL. **2.** Variant of German ADELMANN.

GIVEN NAMES Jewish 5%. *Emanuel* (3), *Hyman* (3), *Meyer* (3), *Aron* (2), *Chaim* (2), *Gershon* (2), *Isadore* (2), *Faivel, Mechel, Menachem, Miriam, Moshe.*

Adelmann (310) **1.** German (frequent in Württemberg): from *Adalman*, an Old High German personal name meaning literally 'noble man'. **2.** Jewish (Ashkenazic): see ADELMAN.

FOREBEARS Hans Michael Adelmann came to PA from Löwenstein-Wertheim in 1752.

Adelsberger (157) German: habitational name for someone from Adelsberg, a place on the river Main in northern Bavaria.

Adelson (626) Jewish (Ashkenazic): metronymic from the Yiddish female name *Adl* (from a Germanic root meaning 'noble') + German *Sohn* 'son'.

Adelsperger (105) German: variant of ADELSBERGER.

Adelstein (291) **1.** Jewish (Ashkenazic): ornamental name, or ornamental-occupational name for a jeweler, from German *Edelstein* in the sense 'precious stone'. **2.** German: habitational name from a place named with Middle High German *adel* 'nobility' + *stein* 'rock', 'castle'.

GIVEN NAMES Jewish 4%. *Hyman* (2), *Tali, Yaffa.*

Adema (163) Frisian: patronymic from the personal name ADE.

GIVEN NAMES Dutch 6%. *Gerrit* (2), *Pieter.*

Aden (910) **1.** Frisian, Dutch, and North German: patronymic from the personal name ADE. **2.** Scottish: habitational name from the old lands and barony of Auden or Aden in Aberdeenshire.

Ader (578) **1.** North German and Dutch: from a derivative of a Germanic personal name (see ADE). **2.** German and Jewish (Ashkenazic): from Middle High German *ader* 'vein', applied as a metonymic occupational name for a barber-surgeon, one of whose functions was to let blood.

Aderhold (382) North German: topographic name for someone living in a snake-infested wood, from Middle Low German *ader* 'adder' + *holt* 'wood'.

Aderholt (252) Americanized spelling of North German ADERHOLD.

Aderman (191) **1.** German (**Adermann**): variant of the personal name ADER. **2.** Jewish (Ashkenazic): occupational name for a barber-surgeon (see ADER).

Aders (128) German: patronymic from the personal name ADER.

Ades (384) **1.** English: patronymic from the personal name *Ade*, a medieval pet form of ADAM. **2.** Jewish (Ashkenazic): it is unclear whether this name is derived from *Ades*, the Yiddish name for Odessa, or is an English-based Romanization of the Ashkenazic family name **Eydes**, which consists of the Yiddish female personal name *Eyde* (a back-formation from *Eydl*, from Yiddish *eydl* 'noble') + genitive *-s*. The Ashkenazic family name **Adesman** presents the same difficulty.

GIVEN NAMES French 4%. *Yves* (2), *Alain, Edouard, Henri.*

Adey (162) English: from the personal name *Adey*, a medieval pet form of ADAM.

Adgate (109) English: perhaps a variant of AGATE.

Adger (176) Scottish and northern Irish: variant of EDGAR.

GIVEN NAMES Jewish 6%. *Isadore* (2), *Miriam.*

Adickes (125) Frisian: patronymic from a short form of the personal name *Ad(d)ike.*

Adie (130) Scottish: from the personal name *Adie*, a popular medieval pet form of ADAM.

Adinolfi (311) Italian: patronymic or plural form of the personal name *Adinolfo*, which is of Germanic origin, composed of the elements *ad(al)* 'noble' + *wolf* 'wolf'. Compare German ADOLF.

GIVEN NAMES Italian 18%. *Salvatore* (7), *Carlo, Carmela, Francesco, Italia, Luciano, Palma, Rocco, Sal, Vincenzo.*

Adkerson (140) Altered form of English ADKINSON.

Adkins (22808) English: from the Middle English personal name *Adkin*, a pet form of ADAM that was in use particularly in the English Midlands, + patronymic *-s*. Compare ATKINS.

Adkinson (805) Northern English: patronymic from the Middle English personal name *Adkin* (see ADKINS). Compare ATKINSON.

Adkison (1045) Reduced form of English ADKINSON.

Adkisson (1114) Reduced form of English ADKINSON.

Adleman (121) Americanized spelling of German and Jewish (Ashkenazic) ADELMANN or EDELMANN.

Adler (7991) **1.** German: from *Adler* 'eagle', denoting someone living in a house identified by the sign of an eagle. The German noun is from Middle High German *adelar*, itself a compound of *adel* 'noble' + *ar* 'eagle'. This name is widespread throughout central and eastern Europe, being found for example in Czech, Polish, Slovenian, and Hungarian (**Ádler**). **2.** Jewish (Ashkenazic): ornamental name meaning 'eagle'.

GIVEN NAMES German 4%; Jewish 4%. *Kurt* (13), *Hans* (11), *Erwin* (7), *Manfred* (4), *Fritz* (2), *Gunther* (2), *Helmut* (2), *Klaus* (2), *Merwin* (2), *Otto* (2), *Bernhard, Egon; Moshe* (10), *Miriam* (5), *Sol* (4), *Ari* (3), *Arie* (3), *Aron* (3), *Emanuel* (3), *Hillel* (3), *Aryeh* (2), *Avi* (2), *Avram* (2), *Chaim* (2).

Adley (213) English: probably a habitational name, perhaps from a place named Hadley or Hadleigh (see HADLEY).

Admire (419) Americanized form of French **Adémar**, from *Adelmar*, a medieval personal name of Germanic origin, composed of the elements *adal* 'noble' + *mar* 'fame'.

FOREBEARS An Adhémar from Albi was in Quebec by 1667; another, from Menton, is recorded in Quebec in 1720.

Adney (279) English: **1.** habitational name from Adeney in Shropshire, named in Old English as *Ēadwynna ey* 'island of a woman called Ēadwynn'. **2.** English: from a Middle English pet form of ADAM. Forms such as *Adenet, Adinot, Addy,* and *Adey* are all well attested. **3.** Possibly an Americanized spelling of Norwegian **Aadnøy**, a habitational name from a farmstead so named, from Old Norse *ǫrn* 'eagle' + *øy* 'island'.

Adolf (316) German, Dutch, and Scandinavian: from the Germanic personal name *Atha-ulf*, which was widely adopted in other languages throughout central Europe; it is composed of the Old High German elements *ad-* (as in *adal* 'noble') + *(w)ulf* 'wolf'.

GIVEN NAMES German 6%. *Gerhard, Gottlieb, Horst, Reinhold, Rinehart, Waltraud.*

Adolfson (117) Swedish: patronymic from the personal name ADOLF.

GIVEN NAMES Scandinavian 10%; German 5%. *Lennart; Ewald, Ralf.*

Adolph (695) Classicized spelling of ADOLF.

GIVEN NAMES German 5%. *Kurt* (5), *Erwin* (2), *Heinz, Horst, Wolfgang.*

Adolphson (334) Swedish: patronymic from the personal name ADOLPH.

GIVEN NAMES Scandinavian 4%. *Erik, Gudrun, Nils.*

Adomaitis (115) Lithuanian: patronymic from the personal name *Adomas*, the Lithuanian form of ADAM.

GIVEN NAMES Lithuanian 8%; French 5%. *Antanas, Domas, Vytautas*; *Alphonse* (2).

Adornetto (104) Italian: from a pet form of the personal name ADORNO.
GIVEN NAMES Italian 14%. *Filippo, Gaetano, Pasquale.*

Adorno (406) **1.** Southern Italian: from the personal name *Adorno*, meaning 'adorned'. **2.** Italian: from Italian *adorno* denoting a type of hawk, presumably applied as a nickname for someone with hawklike features or a metonymic occupational name for someone who trained hawks.
FOREBEARS The Italian surname Adorno is also established in southern Germany through descendants of an Italian merchant who settled in Swabia in 1680, and in Brazil, where it was taken from Genoa in the 16th century.
GIVEN NAMES Spanish 37%; Italian 8%. *Jose* (10), *Juan* (7), *Luis* (4), *Carlos* (3), *Enrique* (3), *Miguel* (3), *Pedro* (3), *Blanca* (2), *Ernesto* (2), *Jesus* (2), *Ramon* (2), *Raul* (2); *Angelo* (2), *Antonio* (2), *Carmelo* (2), *Sal* (2), *Eliseo, Giovanni, Giuseppe, Heriberto, Leonardo, Luigi, Sebastiano.*

Adragna (232) Italian (Sicily): habitational name from any of various minor places in Sicily named Adragna, of which only one now remains, near Agrigenta.
GIVEN NAMES Italian 27%. *Vito* (8), *Antonio* (2), *Giuseppe* (2), *Salvatore* (2), *Angelo, Domenico, Gaetano, Gaspare, Giacomo, Giovanna, Lucrezia, Maurizio.*

Adrian (1804) English, southern French, and German: from a vernacular form of the Latin personal name *(H)adrianus*, originally an ethnic name denoting someone from the coast of the Adriatic (Latin *Adria*). It was adopted as a cognomen by the emperor who ruled AD 117–138. It was also borne by several minor saints, in particular an early martyr at Nicomedia (died *c.*304), the patron saint of soldiers and butchers. There was an English St. Adrian (died 710), born in North Africa; he was abbot of St. Augustine's, Canterbury, and his cult enjoyed a brief vogue after the discovery of his supposed remains in 1091. Later, the name was adopted by several popes, including the only pope of English birth, Nicholas Breakspear, who reigned as Adrian IV (1154–59).

Adriance (222) Dutch: patronymic from the personal name *Adriaen*, Dutch form of ADRIAN. This was a frequent name in New Netherland in the 17th century.

Adriano (178) Spanish and Italian: from the personal name *Adriano*, from Latin *(H)adrianus* (see ADRIAN).
GIVEN NAMES Spanish 40%; Italian 5%. *Jose* (5), *Felipe* (3), *Carlos* (2), *Fernando* (2), *Manuel* (2), *Adriana, Alejandro, Almario, Apolonia, Araceli, Celso, Edgardo*; *Antonio* (2), *Eliseo, Filippo, Mino, Romeo.*

Adrien (104) French: from the personal name *Adrien*, French form of Latin *(H)adrianus* (see ADRIAN).
GIVEN NAMES French 29%. *Emile, Flore, Francois, Gaspard, Henri, Jacques, Jean-Claude, Magalie, Yolette.*

Adsit (452) Altered spelling of **Adsett**, an English habitational name from Adsett, in Gloucestershire, named in Old English as *Ædda gesetu* 'Addi's fold' or *Eaddas gesetu* 'Eadda's fold'.

Aduddell (135) English: unexplained. In PA in the 18th century this surname alternated with DIDDLE, likewise unexplained. The Shropshire connection suggests a possible Welsh origin, but no relevant Welsh name has been identified.
FOREBEARS William Aduddel (also known as William Adiddle or Diddle) born in 1702/03 in Astly Abbott, Shropshire, England, migrated in the 1740s to PA from England. He and a relative, Thomas Aduddell, both bought land from descendants of William Penn.

Advani (166) Hindu name found among people from Sind, Pakistan, meaning '(descendant) of Adu'. Adu is presumably the personal name of an ancestor.
GIVEN NAMES Indian 82%. *Suresh* (5), *Nihal* (4), *Deepak* (3), *Gopi* (3), *Rajesh* (3), *Ram* (3), *Ramesh* (3), *Arun* (2), *Ashok* (2), *Gautam* (2), *Gope* (2), *Haresh* (2).

Adwell (190) English: **1.** habitational name from a place in Oxfordshire called Adwell, named with the Old English personal name *Eadda* + *wiella* 'stream'. **2.** variant of ATWELL.

Ady (213) English: from the personal name *Ady*, a medieval pet form of ADAM.

Aebersold (129) South German and Swiss German (**Äbersold**): variant spelling of EBERSOLD.
GIVEN NAMES German 7%. *Hanspeter, Kurt.*

Aebi (123) Swiss German (**Äbi**): from a pet form of the personal name *Adalbert* (see ALBERT).
GIVEN NAMES German 15%. *Ernst* (2), *Kurt* (2), *Christoph, Heinz.*

Aegerter (161) South German and Swiss German (**Ägerter**): variant of the Bavarian and Austrian topographic name **Ehgart-(n)er**, from Middle High German *egerte* 'fallow land'.
GIVEN NAMES French 4%. *Marcel, Nicolle.*

Aerni (125) Swiss German (also **Ärni**): from a much altered pet form of the personal name ARNOLD.

Aerts (194) Frisian and Dutch: patronymic from *Aert*, a reduced form of the personal name *Arnout* (see ARNOLD).
GIVEN NAMES French 7%. *Marcel* (2), *Elzear.*

Aeschliman (415) South German and Swiss German (also **Äschlimann**): topographic name for someone who lived near a (small) ash tree or ash wood, from *Esche* 'ash' + the diminutive suffix *-li* + *Mann* 'man'.

Affeldt (315) North German: topographic name for a person living in a distant area of open country, from Middle Low German *af* 'away', 'off' + *velt* 'open country'.
GIVEN NAMES German 5%. *Otto* (2), *Arno, Franz.*

Affinito (154) Italian: from the personal name *Affinito*, an omen name meaning 'perfected', 'completed', 'well done'.
GIVEN NAMES Italian 15%. *Angelo, Carlo, Salvatore, Tullio.*

Affleck (300) Scottish: habitational name, from either Affleck in Angus or Auchinleck (which was formerly pronounced Affleck) in Ayrshire.

Afflerbach (151) German: topographic name for someone living by a stream running by an apple tree, from Middle High German *affal* 'apple' + *bach* 'brook', or a habitational name from a place name with the same meaning.

Affolter (324) German: habitational name or a topographic name, from Middle High German *affolter*, *affalter* 'apple tree', a common South German toponym.
GIVEN NAMES German 4%. *Heinz* (2), *Kurt.*

Afonso (253) Portuguese: variant of ALFONSO.
GIVEN NAMES Spanish 38%; Portuguese 28%. *Antonio* (23), *Jose* (18), *Manuel* (11), *Carlos* (7), *Domingos* (5), *Ana* (3), *Mario* (3), *Abilio* (2), *Alfredo* (2), *Americo* (2), *Arlindo* (2), *Francisco* (2), *Sergio* (2); *Joao* (8), *Joaquim* (2), *Caetano, Lidio.*

Africa (130) Spanish (**África**): ethnic name for a person of African descent or nickname for someone with some other connection with the continent of Africa.
GIVEN NAMES Spanish 14%. *Consuelo* (2), *Gregorio* (2), *Angel, Candido, Carmencita, Faustino, Leandro, Luz, Manuel, Raul, Rogelio.*

Afshar (206) Iranian: ethnic name from the name of a Turkic tribe scattered throughout Iran. *Afshar*, from Persian *feshar*, means 'extraction'.
GIVEN NAMES Muslim 76%. *Nader* (12), *Amir* (5), *Ali* (3), *Ahad* (2), *Ahmad* (2), *Alireza* (2), *Firooz* (2), *Katayoun* (2), *Khalil* (2), *Mahmoud* (2), *Majid* (2), *Maryam* (2).

Afton (113) English: habitational name from a place called Afton, examples of which are found in Devon and on the Isle of Wight.

Afzal (155) Muslim: from Persian *afzal* (Arabic *afḍal*), literally 'better' or 'best', used as an epithet for a learned man.
GIVEN NAMES Muslim 87%. *Mohammad* (28), *Muhammad* (12), *Mohammed* (4), *Syed* (3), *Ali* (2), *Khadija* (2), *Khalid* (2), *Mahammad* (2), *Naeem* (2), *Tariq* (2), *Abida, Adnan.*

Aga (127) **1.** Norwegian: habitational name from either of two farms so named in Hordaland; of uncertain derivation. **2.** Turkish: see AGHA.

GIVEN NAMES Scandinavian 10%. *Lars* (2), *Obert*; *Isak*, *Shaan*.

Agan (806) **1.** Irish: probably a variant of EGAN. **2.** Americanized form of Swiss German EGGEN.

Agans (156) Variant of Irish AGAN, with English patronymic *-s*.

Agar (404) **1.** English: from a Middle English personal name, either *Egar* (see EDGAR) or *Algar* (see ALGER). **2.** Jewish (Sephardic): variant of HAGAR.

Agard (337) **1.** Danish and Norwegian: habitational name from Ågård 'farm by the stream'. **2.** French: from a Germanic personal name composed of the elements *agi(n)* 'edge (of a sword)' + *hard* 'hardy', 'bold'. **3.** Respelling of Hungarian **Agárdi**, a habitational name for someone from any of various places called Agárd, from the vocabulary word *agár* 'hound'. **4.** English: possibly a variant of AGAR.

Agarwal (675) Indian (northern states): Hindu (Bania) and Jain habitational name, from Agroha or Agar + the Hindi or Panjabi adjectival suffix *-wāl* (equivalent to *-er* in English). Agroha in the Hissar district (formerly in the Panjab, now in Haryana) is said to have been the capital city of Agar Sen, a legendary Vaishya king whom the Agarwals claim as their ancestor. Alternatively, the place name in question may be Agar, a city forty miles northeast of Ujjain in Madhya Pradesh. The Agarwals are one of the most prominent mercantile communities of northern India.
GIVEN NAMES Indian 94%. *Anil* (19), *Arun* (10), *Satish* (10), *Sudhir* (10), *Ashok* (8), *Rajesh* (8), *Ramesh* (8), *Sanjay* (8), *Amit* (7), *Mahesh* (7), *Rakesh* (7), *Vivek* (7).

Agate (159) **1.** English: topographic name for someone who lived 'at the gate', i.e. one of the gates of a medieval city. However, in northern counties, Middle English *gate* (from Old Norse *gata*) also meant 'street', and in some instances the surname may derive from this sense. **2.** Southern Italian: from the Greek personal name *Agathē* meaning 'virtuous', 'honest'. **3.** Indian (Maharashtra); pronounced as *ag-tay*: Hindu (Brahman) name, from Marathi *agṭe* 'live coal' (from Sanskrit *agni* 'fire').
FOREBEARS Thomas Agate, a native of Shipley in Yorkshire, settled in Sparta, NY, in the 1790s.
GIVEN NAMES Italian 9%; Indian 5%. *Giuseppe* (2), *Gasper*, *Renzo*, *Salvatore*; *Avinash* (2), *Ameeta*, *Usha*.

Agbayani (121) Ilocano (Philippines): nickname from Ilocano *agbayani* 'to be heroic'.
GIVEN NAMES Spanish 46%. *Orlino* (6), *Jose* (3), *Adoracion*, *Alfonso*, *Amante*, *Artemio*, *Aurelio*, *Bienvenida*, *Celso*, *Dionicia*, *Elena*, *Ernesto*.

Agcaoili (115) Ilocano (Philippines): nickname from Ilocano *agcaoili* 'to hold on'.
GIVEN NAMES Spanish 36%. *Constante* (2), *Florencio* (2), *Rogelio* (2), *Angelito*, *Arturo*, *Ernesto*, *Eulalio*, *Fernando*, *Florentino*, *Francisco*, *Irineo*, *Jesus*.

Age (134) English: perhaps a variant of **Agg**, which is from the Old Scandinavian personal name *Aggi*.

Agee (3651) French (Huguenot): of uncertain origin. Perhaps a variant of **Ajean**, i.e. *(enfant) à Jean* '(child) of John' (see AGENT), or of AGER.

Agen (140) French: habitational name from places in Lot-et-Garonne and Aveyron called Agen.

Agena (159) North German (East Friesland and Schleswig): from an Old Frisian name *Aggo*, cognate with Old High German *ecka* (modern German *Ecke* 'corner') in the sense 'sharp blade (of a sword)'.

Agent (225) French: **1.** status or occupational name from *agent* 'agent', 'representative'. **2.** Americanized spelling (in New Orleans) of French **Ajean**, *(enfant) à Jean* '(child) of John'.

Ager (531) **1.** English (mainly Essex): variant of ALGER. **2.** French: from an Old French personal name of Germanic origin, *Adigari*, equivalent to English EDGAR. **3.** Danish: habitational name from any of several places called Ager, meaning 'plowed land'.

Agers (139) **1.** English: patronymic from AGER. **2.** Possibly also German: variant of EGGERS.

Agerton (161) Possibly a respelling of English EDGERTON.

Aggarwal (362) Indian: variant spelling of AGARWAL.
GIVEN NAMES Indian 93%. *Sanjay* (8), *Anil* (7), *Ashok* (7), *Rajesh* (7), *Vinod* (7), *Ajay* (6), *Arun* (6), *Rakesh* (5), *Vinay* (5), *Raj* (4), *Sanjeev* (4), *Saroj* (4).

Aggen (102) Frisian and North German: from an Old Frisian personal name, *Ag(g)o* (see AGENA).

Agha (130) Muslim: from Turkish *agha* 'leader', 'ruler'. *Aga Khan* is the title of the leader of the Ismaili sect of Shiite Muslims.
GIVEN NAMES Muslim 73%. *Ahmad* (2), *Bilal* (2), *Khaled* (2), *Mahmoud* (2), *Mohamad* (2), *Nader* (2), *Abdul*, *Abul*, *Amer*, *Amir*, *Arif*, *Asghar*.

Agin (412) **1.** Bosnian and Serbian: from *aga*, status name for a Turkish dignitary belonging to the lowest rank of Turkish nobility. **2.** Russian: nickname for an illegitimate child, meaning 'son of Elágin' (a female name), a variant of *Elága*, a pet form of a baptismal name beginning with *El-*.

Agins (124) Origin uncertain. **1.** In some cases it is probably a variant of AKINS. **2.** In the case of at least one family it is a shortened form of Jewish **Aginsky**.

Agius (169) Maltese: possibly a Latinization of Greek *agios* (classical Greek *hagios*) 'saintly', 'holy', applied as a nickname to someone conspicuously virtuous.
GIVEN NAMES Italian 8%. *Angelo*, *Carmel*, *Reno*, *Sal*.

Agle (150) **1.** Norwegian: habitational name from either of two farmsteads in Trøndelag named Agle, the etymology of which is uncertain. **2.** Possibly an Americanized form of South German **Egle**, from a short form of any of various Germanic personal names composed with *egin*, *agin* 'edge (of a sword)'.

Agler (345) German: from the Germanic personal name *Agelhar*, composed of the elements *agi(l)* 'point (of a sword)' (see ECK) + *hari* 'army'.

Agne (228) Greek: variant of AGNES 2 and 3.

Agnello (617) Italian: **1.** from *agnello* 'lamb', applied either as a nickname for a meek and mild person or as a personal name, which was popular because the lamb led to the slaughter was a symbol of the suffering innocence of Christ. **2.** in Sicily, a habitational name from a place named Agnello.
GIVEN NAMES Italian 16%. *Salvatore* (7), *Angelo* (4), *Agostino*, *Antonio*, *Calogero*, *Carlo*, *Carmela*, *Concetta*, *Ercole*, *Gaetano*, *Gerlando*, *Giuseppe*.

Agner (400) **1.** Danish: from the Nordic personal name *Aginharu*, composed of the elements *agior* 'sword' + *haru* 'warrior'. **2.** South German: variant of EGNER.

Agnes (219) **1.** Greek: metronymic from the female personal name *Hagnē*, from *hagnē* 'pure'. **2.** Greek: shortened form of the patronymics **Agnidis** or **Agniadis**, from the male personal name *Agnas*. **3.** Hungarian (**Ágnes**): from the female personal name *Ágnes* (see 2).

Agnew (3475) **1.** Scottish (of Norman origin): habitational name from Agneaux in Manche, France. **2.** Irish and Scottish: Anglicized form of Gaelic **Ó Gnímh** 'descendant of *Gnímh*', a byname meaning 'action' or 'activity'. The Ó Gnímhs were hereditary poets to a branch of the O'Neills; in this family the traditional pronunciation is with the stress on the second syllable.

Agnor (161) Norwegian: habitational name from a place in Akershus, which is apparently named from Old Norse *agnǫr* 'fishhook', 'harpoon barb', presumably with reference to some topographic feature such as the shape of a neighboring mountain or a crook in a stream.

Agopian (112) Armenian: patronymic from the personal name *Yako(v)b*, Armenian form of JACOB. Compare HAGOPIAN.
GIVEN NAMES Armenian 43%. *Agop* (3), *Raffi* (3), *Aram* (2), *Arshag*, *Bedros*, *Dikran*, *Harut*, *Kaloust*, *Kevork*, *Melkon*, *Noubar*, *Nubar*.

Agosta (476) Italian: habitational name from a place named Agosta or Augusta, as for example Augusta in Syracuse province, Sicily.
GIVEN NAMES Italian 19%. *Angelo* (4), *Giovanni* (3), *Giuseppe* (3), *Salvatore* (3),

Santo (3), *Vito* (3), *Antonino* (2), *Carmelo* (2), *Marco, Matteo, Nevio, Nunzio; Mario* (3), *Alberto, Orlando, Roberto, Rosario, Teofilo.*

Agosti (131) **1.** Italian: patronymic or plural form of AGOSTO. **2.** Catalan (**Agostí**): variant spelling of the Catalan personal name *Agustí,* a vernacular form of Latin *Augustinus* (see AUSTIN).

GIVEN NAMES Spanish 8%. *Ricardo* (2), *Eriberto, Ermano, Fernando, Lino, Marta, Orlando, Roberto, Rosario.*

Agostinelli (357) Italian: from a pet form of the personal name *Agosto* (see AUGUSTUS).

GIVEN NAMES Italian 22%. *Antonio* (3), *Nereo* (3), *Concezio* (2), *Adamo, Agostino, Aldo, Alfonso, Angelo, Dino, Domenico, Donato, Fausto, Fernando, Fortunato, Gianni, Gino.*

Agostini (439) Italian: patronymic or plural form of AGOSTINO.

GIVEN NAMES Italian 21%; Spanish 7%. *Dino* (3), *Antonio* (2), *Guido* (2), *Luciano* (2), *Luigi* (2), *Agostino, Angelo, Domenic, Elio, Ennio, Enrico, Geno; Efrain* (3), *Jose* (3), *Domingo, Estelita, Lourdes, Luis.*

Agostino (461) Italian: from a pet form of the personal name AGOSTO.

GIVEN NAMES Italian 26%. *Rocco* (10), *Salvatore* (3), *Antonio* (2), *Nicola* (2), *Vincenzo* (2), *Carlo, Carmelo, Cono, Cosmo, Domenico, Elio, Enzo; Lino* (2), *Armando, Arturo, Atilio, Octavio, Silvana.*

Agosto (575) **1.** Italian and Spanish: from a byname denoting someone born in the month of August, *Agosto.* **2.** Italian: also from the personal name *Agosto,* Latin *Augustus,* from *augere* 'to increase' (see AUGUSTUS).

GIVEN NAMES Spanish 40%. *Jose* (13), *Juan* (10), *Manuel* (8), *Raul* (8), *Luis* (5), *Pedro* (5), *Armando* (4), *Carlos* (4), *Maribel* (4), *Blanca* (3), *Pablo* (3), *Rafael* (3).

Agoston (71) Hungarian (**Ágoston**): from the personal name *Ágoston,* a vernacular form of Latin *Augustinus* (see AUSTIN).

GIVEN NAMES Hungarian 24%. *Tibor* (3), *Attila, Csaba, Gabor, Geza, Istvan, Jeno, Laszlo.*

Agramonte (106) Galician: habitational name from Agramonte in A Coruña and Lugo (Galicia).

GIVEN NAMES Spanish 61%. *Jose* (5), *Altagracia* (3), *Ignacio* (2), *Luis* (2), *Mercedes* (2), *Rafael* (2), *Ramon* (2), *Ramona* (2), *Walfredo* (2), *Adolfo, Ana, Beatriz.*

Agrawal (450) Indian: variant of AGARWAL.

GIVEN NAMES Indian 96%. *Ajay* (8), *Deepak* (8), *Ashok* (6), *Bharat* (6), *Sanjay* (6), *Arun* (5), *Om* (5), *Rakesh* (5), *Sunil* (5), *Amit* (4), *Anil* (4), *Jagdish* (4).

Agre (164) **1.** Americanized spelling of South German EGGER. **2.** Portuguese: probably a nickname from *agre* 'bitter'.

Agrella (108) Italian: from the female personal name *Agrella.*

Agresta (302) Italian: variant of AGRESTI, or from *agresta* 'sour grapes'.

GIVEN NAMES Italian 12%. *Carlo, Cesare, Ezio, Marco, Natale, Rocco, Saverio, Silvio, Valentino.*

Agresti (212) Italian: from a nickname for a peasant or countryman, from *agreste* 'rustic', 'rural'.

GIVEN NAMES Italian 12%. *Pasquale* (2), *Angelo, Antonio, Cosmo, Domenico, Gino, Plinio.*

Agricola (121) German and Dutch: humanistic surname, a translation into Latin of German BAUER or Dutch BOER 'farmer'.

GIVEN NAMES Dutch 6%; German 4%. *Algert* (2), *Cornelis; Aloys, Otto.*

Agro (189) Italian (Sicily): **1.** nickname for a tough individual, from *agro* 'hard', 'bitter' (Sicilian *agru*), from Latin *acer.* **2.** habitational name from Agrò in Sicily, named from Greek *agros* 'field'.

GIVEN NAMES Italian 22%. *Angelo* (6), *Sal* (3), *Carmelo* (2), *Dino* (2), *Antonio, Augustino, Calogero, Concetta, Salvatore.*

Agron (128) **1.** Galician and Spanish: habitational name from either of two places called Agrón, in A Coruña and Granada. **2.** Jewish (eastern Ashkenazic): English transliteration of the eastern Slavic male personal name *Ahron,* a variant of AARON.

GIVEN NAMES Spanish 19%; Jewish 6%. *Juan* (2), *Aida, Alfredo, Ana, Andres, Angel, Elena, Erlinda, Francisco, Gonzalo, Isidoro, Jose; Meyer* (2), *Samoil.*

Agrusa (126) Italian (Sicily): nickname from Sicilian *agruso* 'bitter'.

GIVEN NAMES Italian 30%. *Carlo* (3), *Rosolino* (2), *Vito* (2), *Angelo, Giacomo, Lorenzo, Matteo, Onorato, Salvatore, Santo.*

Aguado (231) **1.** Spanish: apparently a nickname from *aguado* 'watered down', 'diluted'. **2.** Jewish (Sephardic): borrowing of the Spanish surname.

GIVEN NAMES Spanish 45%. *Fernando* (4), *Jose* (4), *Manuel* (4), *Miguel* (4), *Alfredo* (3), *Guillermo* (3), *Juan* (3), *Mario* (3), *Enrique* (2), *Francisco* (2), *Jaime* (2), *Jorge* (2).

Aguas (133) Spanish: topographic name from *aguas* 'waters'.

GIVEN NAMES Spanish 52%. *Carlos* (7), *Luis* (5), *Mario* (3), *Jose* (2), *Vicente* (2), *Alberto, Alicia, Ana Rosa, Angelito, Armando, Arnulfo, Augusto.*

Aguayo (1013) Spanish: habitational name from Aguayo in Córdoba, or from Santa Olalla de Aguayo, in Santander.

GIVEN NAMES Spanish 55%. *Jose* (29), *Jesus* (19), *Manuel* (17), *Juan* (15), *Rafael* (12), *Carlos* (9), *Ruben* (9), *Francisco* (8), *Javier* (8), *Luis* (8), *Miguel* (8), *Pedro* (8).

Agudelo (261) Galician: habitational name from a place in Galicia named Agudelo, from a derivative of *agudo* 'peak'.

GIVEN NAMES Spanish 56%. *Carlos* (11), *Jose* (10), *Alvaro* (5), *Luis* (4), *Beatriz* (3),

Fernando (3), *Guillermo* (3), *Javier* (3), *Juan* (3), *Luz* (3), *Cesar* (2), *Enrique* (2).

Aguero (588) Spanish and Aragonese (**Agüero**): habitational name from places in the provinces of Uesca (Aragon) and Santander named Agüero or from Puente Agüero in Santander province. They are probably named from Late Latin *(vicus) aquarius* 'well-watered (settlement)'.

GIVEN NAMES Spanish 48%. *Jose* (14), *Carlos* (10), *Pedro* (10), *Juan* (7), *Manuel* (7), *Francisco* (6), *Jorge* (5), *Jesus* (4), *Luis* (4), *Mario* (4), *Ricardo* (4), *Roberto* (4).

Aguiar (1485) Galician and Portuguese: habitational name from a common place name, derived from Latin *aquilare* 'haunt of eagles'. Compare Spanish AGUILAR.

GIVEN NAMES Spanish 33%; Portuguese 15%. *Manuel* (49), *Jose* (36), *Carlos* (14), *Luis* (13), *Francisco* (7), *Miguel* (7), *Alvaro* (5), *Juan* (5), *Pedro* (5), *Ramon* (5), *Fernando* (4), *Mario* (4); *Joao* (6), *Paulo* (4), *Serafim* (2), *Goncalo, Henrique, Manoel, Marcio.*

Aguila (497) Spanish (**Águila**): from *águila* 'eagle' (Latin *aquila*). This is either a nickname for a haughty man or one with an aquiline nose, or a habitational name from a place in Salamanca province called Águila.

GIVEN NAMES Spanish 52%. *Jose* (22), *Pedro* (9), *Luis* (8), *Juan* (7), *Fernando* (5), *Sergio* (5), *Francisco* (4), *Jesus* (4), *Mario* (4), *Rafael* (4), *Ramon* (4), *Gerardo* (3); *Antonio* (3), *Aldo, Elio, Federico, Guido, Marco Antonio, Romeo, Salustiano.*

Aguilar (12824) Spanish, Catalan, and Jewish (Sephardic): habitational name from any of numerous places called Aguilar, from Latin *aquilare* 'haunt of eagles' (a derivative of *aquila* 'eagle'), for example Aguilar de Campo in Palencia, Aguilar de la Frontera in Córdoba, and Aguilar de Segarra in Catalonia.

GIVEN NAMES Spanish 50%. *Jose* (354), *Luis* (177), *Juan* (168), *Manuel* (153), *Carlos* (134), *Jesus* (96), *Miguel* (89), *Mario* (82), *Jorge* (73), *Francisco* (69), *Pedro* (69), *Raul* (69).

Aguilera (2381) Spanish: habitational name from a place in Soria province, named Aguilera from *aguilera* 'eagle's nest' (from Latin *aquilaria* 'place of eagles').

GIVEN NAMES Spanish 52%. *Jose* (56), *Juan* (44), *Jesus* (30), *Manuel* (26), *Carlos* (23), *Luis* (22), *Mario* (20), *Miguel* (19), *Jorge* (16), *Ramon* (15), *Enrique* (14), *Rafael* (14).

Aguillard (333) **1.** English: metonymic occupational name for a needle maker from Old French *aguillard,* a variant (with a change of suffix) of *aguillier,* from *a(i)guille* 'needle'. **2.** French: from Old French *aguille* 'needle' + the pejorative suffix *-ard,* hence a derogatory nickname for an irritating person.

GIVEN NAMES French 6%. *Emile, Nicolle, Patrice, Pierre.*

Aguillon (250) French and Southern French (Occitan): perhaps a nickname for an irritating person, from Old French *aguillon* or Occitan *aguilhon* 'sharp point', 'thorn', 'goad' (modern French *aiguillon*).

GIVEN NAMES Spanish 51%. *Jose* (6), *Francisco* (4), *Jesus* (4), *Pablo* (4), *Juan* (3), *Agustin* (2), *Carlos* (2), *Ernesto* (2), *Manuel* (2), *Roberto* (2), *Ruben* (2), *Santiago* (2).

Aguinaga (332) Spanish form of Basque **Aginaga**, a habitational name from a place named with *(h)agin* 'yew tree' + the collective suffix *-aga*.

GIVEN NAMES Spanish 51%. *Jose* (13), *Juan* (7), *Jorge* (6), *Luis* (6), *Salvador* (5), *Jesus* (4), *Blanca* (3), *Carlos* (3), *Francisco* (3), *Isidro* (3), *Julio* (3), *Manuel* (3).

Aguinaldo (180) Hispanic (Philippines, Mexico, etc.): comparatively recent formation from the personal name *Aguinaldo*.

GIVEN NAMES Spanish 37%. *Jorge* (3), *Jose* (3), *Pedro* (3), *Adriano* (2), *Cesar* (2), *Marciano* (2), *Alfredo*, *Amalia*, *Andres*, *Arsenia*, *Caridad*, *Carolina*.

Aguiniga (123) Spanish (**Aguiñiga**): Castilianized form of Basque **Aginaga**, a habitational name from Aginaga, a town in Araba province, Basque Country. The Castilianized form of other Basque towns named Aginaga (as for example in Navarre or Gipuzkoa provinces) is AGUINAGA.

GIVEN NAMES Spanish 48%. *Francisco* (4), *Jose* (4), *Carlos* (3), *Jorge* (3), *Ignacio* (2), *Miguel* (2), *Salvador* (2), *Adan*, *Alfonso*, *Bulmaro*, *Efren*, *Genoveva*.

Aguirre (6908) Spanish form of Basque **Agirre**, a topographic name from Basque *ager*, *agir* 'open space', 'pasture'. This is found as the first element of several place names, reflected in surnames such as **Aguirrezabal(a)** 'broad open space'; the modern surname may be a shortening of any of these.

GIVEN NAMES Spanish 49%. *Jose* (158), *Juan* (83), *Manuel* (81), *Luis* (70), *Jesus* (65), *Carlos* (64), *Raul* (45), *Miguel* (38), *Pedro* (38), *Mario* (34), *Francisco* (33), *Jorge* (33).

Aguon (140) From Guam: unexplained.

GIVEN NAMES Spanish 22%. *Juan* (4), *Francisco* (2), *Jose* (2), *Juanita* (2), *Vicente* (2), *Adelina*, *Ana*, *Ignacio*, *Jesus*, *Joaquin*, *Rafael*.

Agustin (443) Spanish (**Agustín**): from the Spanish personal name *Agustín*, a vernacular form of Latin *Augustinus* (see AUSTIN).

GIVEN NAMES Spanish 49%. *Jose* (5), *Conrado* (4), *Ernesto* (4), *Renato* (4), *Rodolfo* (4), *Salvador* (4), *Antonio* (3), *Carlos* (3), *Francisco* (3), *Manuel* (3), *Adela* (2), *Alfredo* (2), *Alicia* (2).

Ahalt (163) Variant of German **Ehalt**, an occupational name from Middle High German *ēhalt* 'servant'.

Ahart (472) Variant of German **Ehard(t)**, from the personal name *Ehard*, composed of the Old High German elements *ē* 'law', 'order' + *hart(i)* 'hard', 'firm'.

Ahearn (1955) Irish: variant spelling of AHERN.

GIVEN NAME Irish 5%. *Brendan* (2).

Ahern (3419) Irish: Anglicized form of Gaelic **Ó hEachthighearna** 'descendant of *Eachthighearna*', a personal name meaning 'lord of horses', from *each* 'horse' + *tighearna* 'master, lord'. In Ireland, the name is most common in the southwest. Compare HEARN.

GIVEN NAMES Irish 6%. *John Patrick* (2), *Liam* (2), *Aileen*, *Brendan*, *Brigid*.

Aherne (121) Irish: variant spelling of AHERN.

Ahl (641) **1.** German: from a pet form of the personal name *Albrecht* (see ALBERT). **2.** German: from *Aal* 'eel', Middle High German *āl*; generally the application would have been to an eel fisher, but in some cases it may also be a nickname for a 'slippery' person. **3.** German and Jewish (Ashkenazic): metonymic occupational name for a cobbler, from Middle High German *āle* 'awl', German *Ahle*. **4.** Swedish: from *al* 'alder', applied either as a topographic or an ornamental name. The *-h-* in the surname is purely ornamental and does not occur in the vocabulary word.

Ahlberg (489) Swedish: ornamental name composed of the elements *al* 'alder' + *berg* 'mountain', 'hill'.

GIVEN NAMES Scandinavian 9%. *Erik* (2), *Lennart* (2), *Karsten*, *Nils*, *Thor*.

Ahlborn (252) **1.** Swedish: ornamental name composed of the elements *al* 'alder' + *-born*, a Swedish surname suffix derived from German *geboren* 'born'. **2.** North German: from the old personal name *Albern*, from Germanic *adal* 'noble' + *boran* 'born'.

Ahlbrecht (113) German: variant spelling of ALBRECHT.

GIVEN NAMES German 5%. *Erwin*, *Otto*, *Wulf*.

Ahler (143) North German, Dutch, and Danish: from a Germanic personal name composed of the elements *adal* 'noble' + *hari*, *heri* 'army'.

Ahlers (1135) North German and Dutch: patronymic from the personal name *Ahler* (see AHLER).

GIVEN NAMES German 5%. *Heinz* (4), *Kurt* (2), *Beate*, *Erwin*, *Frieda*, *Gerhard*, *Guenter*, *Hans Peter*, *Hartwig*, *Hermann*, *Horst*, *Jurgen*.

Ahlert (130) North German: from the medieval personal name *Alard*, composed of Old High German *adal* 'noble' + *hard* 'hardy'.

Ahles (334) German: patronymic from a short form of any of the many medieval personal names composed with Old High German *adal* 'noble'.

Ahlf (191) German: from a reduced form of the personal name ADOLF.

GIVEN NAME German 4%. *Guenther*.

Ahlgren (507) Swedish: ornamental name composed of the elements *al* 'alder' + *gren* 'branch'.

GIVEN NAMES Scandinavian 5%. *Erik* (2), *Britt*, *Lennart*, *Nils*.

Ahlgrim (205) German: from the Germanic personal name *Ahlgrim*, composed of the elements *adal* 'noble' + *grim* 'warrior's mask', 'helmet'.

Ahlin (223) Swedish: from *al* 'alder' + *-in*, a common ending of Swedish surnames derived from Latin *-inus*, *-inius* 'descendant of'. The surname could be ornamental, but more probably has a topographic sense, having been adopted on account of a prominent alder tree at the home farm.

Ahlman (249) **1.** Altered spelling of German **Ahl(e)mann**, a topographic name, literally meaning 'swamp man'. Ahle(n) is the name of several places in northern Germany named from their situation by a fen or swamp. **2.** Swedish: ornamental name composed of the elements *al* 'alder' + *man* 'man'.

Ahlquist (547) Swedish: ornamental name composed of the elements *al* 'alder' + *quist*, an old or ornamental spelling of *kvist* 'twig'.

GIVEN NAMES Scandinavian 7%. *Bertel*, *Erik*.

Ahlstedt (106) Swedish: ornamental name composed of the elements *al* 'alder' + the German element *-stedt* 'place', a common element of Swedish compound names.

Ahlstrand (183) Swedish: ornamental name composed of the elements *al* 'alder' + *strand* 'shore'.

Ahlstrom (710) Swedish: ornamental name composed of the elements *al* 'alder' + *ström* 'river'.

GIVEN NAMES Scandinavian 6%. *Lars* (2), *Anders*, *Joakim*, *Johan*, *Per*, *Sibel*, *Sven*.

Ahluwalia (234) Indian (Panjab): Sikh name derived from a place name *Ahlu* + *-wāliā*, a Panjabi adjectival suffix. According to Ibbetson (1916), Ahlu is the name of a village near Lahore which was founded by Sada Singh Kalal, a man of the Kalal community. The hereditary occupation of the Kalals was the manufacture of liquors (Sanskrit *kalyapāla* 'distiller of spirituous liquors'), but when that trade was subjected to government regulation in the 19th century, they mostly took to commerce. The title *Ahluwalia* 'one from Ahlu' was first taken by Sada Singh's descendant, Jassa Singh, who is said to have been the most powerful and influential chief that the Sikhs ever had till the rise of Ranjit Singh. The Ahluwalias ruled in Kapurthala, a district in the Panjab which was once a small princely state. The family name Ahluwalia is now found not only among the descendants of Jassa Singh but also among many others who adopted it later.

GIVEN NAMES Indian 90%. *Brij* (3), *Anant* (2), *Anup* (2), *Hardip* (2), *Jagdip* (2), *Sanjay* (2), *Ajay*, *Amrit*, *Amrita*, *Anil*, *Anju*, *Arvind*.

Ahmad (2257) Muslim (widespread throughout the Muslim world): from the Arabic personal name *Aḥmad* 'the most praised', elative adjective from *ḥamid* (see HAMID). This is an epithet of the Prophet Muhammad. In the Qur'an (6:16) Jesus foretells the arrival of Aḥmad (the Prophet Muhammad) in the words: 'I have brought good news about a messenger who will come after me, whose name will be Aḥmad'.
GIVEN NAMES Muslim 87%. *Syed* (52), *Mohammad* (30), *Iftikhar* (22), *Imtiaz* (22), *Bashir* (20), *Ali* (19), *Nasir* (18), *Nazir* (17), *Riaz* (15), *Mushtaq* (14), *Aftab* (13), *Ahmad* (13).

Ahmadi (301) Muslim: Arabic family name meaning 'descended from or associated with Aḥmad' (see AHMAD).
GIVEN NAMES Muslim 76%. *Ahmad* (7), *Mohammad* (7), *Ali* (5), *Hamid* (5), *Mahmoud* (4), *Abdul* (3), *Massoud* (3), *Sultan* (3), *Abbas* (2), *Abdel* (2), *Abdullah* (2), *Amir* (2).

Ahmann (349) German: topographic name for someone living near running water, from Middle High German *ahe* 'water', 'stream' + *man* 'man'.

Ahmed (4409) Muslim: variant spelling of AHMAD.
GIVEN NAMES Muslim 87%. *Syed* (154), *Mohammed* (81), *Mohamed* (64), *Ahmed* (42), *Mohammad* (34), *Ali* (33), *Imtiaz* (24), *Iqbal* (23), *Nasir* (23), *Shakil* (21), *Iftikhar* (20), *Saeed* (20).

Ahn (1963) **1.** Korean: variant of AN. **2.** North German: topographic name from Germanic *an* 'stream' or 'fen'. In Germany the family names **von Ahn** and **von Ahnen** are well established in the Hamburg area. **3.** German: alternatively, perhaps, a status name or nickname from *Ahn* 'grandfather', 'forefather' (Middle High German *ane*, *an*).
GIVEN NAMES Korean 60%. *Young* (28), *Byung* (22), *Chang* (20), *Sung* (18), *Sang* (15), *Yong* (14), *Jung* (12), *Seung* (12), *Jae* (10), *Kwang* (10), *Chong* (9), *Dong* (8), *Jong* (8), *Kyung* (8), *Joon* (7), *Chul* (6), *Myong* (5), *Byung Ho* (4), *Chung* (4), *Hae* (4), *Dong Hyun* (3), *Seong* (3), *Sungsoo* (3), *Byung Chul* (2).

Ahner (316) North German: topographic name from Germanic *an* 'stream' or 'fen' (see AHN 2) + the suffix *-er* denoting an inhabitant.

Ahnert (114) North German: variant of AHNER.
GIVEN NAMES German 13%. *Heinz*, *Horst*, *Kurt*, *Rainer*, *Reinhold*.

Aho (1439) Finnish: from *aho* 'glade', 'forest clearing'. Areas of woodland adjacent to farmhouses were cleared by slash-and-burn techniques to produce glades which

eventually became pastureland. The name is recorded in the Karelian Isthmus in eastern Finland from the 16th century. In northern Finland it was a popular ornamental name, adopted especially among people converting from Swedish surnames to Finnish in the 19th and early 20th centuries. It is now a so-called 'protected' name in Finland, meaning that it may not be adopted except through birthright or marriage. In the U.S. it may also be an abbreviation of AHONEN.
GIVEN NAMES Finnish 9%; Scandinavian 4%. *Reino* (10), *Eino* (7), *Toivo* (6), *Wilho* (4), *Armas* (3), *Aarne* (2), *Aarre* (2), *Aatos* (2), *Arvi* (2), *Kaarin* (2), *Raili* (2), *Sulo* (2); *Alvar* (2), *Swen* (2), *Iver*, *Nels*, *Viljo*.

Ahola (262) Finnish: variant of AHO, with the addition of the local suffix *-la*.
GIVEN NAMES Finnish 9%; German 4%; Scandinavian 4%. *Veikko* (2), *Kimmo*, *Kori*, *Martti*, *Reino*, *Tauno*, *Teuvo*, *Urho*, *Vesa*, *Vilho*; *Fritz*, *Kurt*; *Alvar*, *Gunhild*, *Jalmer*.

Ahonen (210) Finnish: from AHO + the common surname suffix *-nen*.
GIVEN NAMES Finnish 11%; Scandinavian 5%. *Ahti*, *Arvo*, *Erkki*, *Niilo*, *Olavi*, *Petri*, *Reino*, *Tauno*, *Vesa*, *Vieno*; *Erik* (2).

Ahr (222) German: **1.** habitational name from a northern place name derived from old Germanic *ar* 'water', 'stream'. **2.** from a short form of a Middle High German personal name formed with Old High German *aro* 'eagle'. Compare ARNDT.

Ahrendt (458) North German: variant of ARNDT.

Ahrens (4330) **1.** North German and Dutch: patronymic from the personal name *Arend* (see ARNDT). **2.** Jewish (Ashkenazic): assimilation of the Jewish patronymic AARONS to the German name, which has a similar pronunciation.

Ahsan (123) Muslim: unexplained.

Ahuja (322) Indian (chiefly Panjab): Hindu (Arora, Jat) and Sikh name meaning 'descendant of *Ahu*', based on the name of a clan in these communities (see ARORA). *Ahu* is presumably the name of an ancestor; the suffix *-jā* is patronymic.
GIVEN NAMES Indian 90%. *Sunil* (6), *Chander* (5), *Ravi* (5), *Anil* (4), *Madhu* (4), *Rajesh* (4), *Krishan* (3), *Raj* (3), *Sanjay* (3), *Sanjeev* (3), *Sanjiv* (3), *Satya* (3).

Ahumada (425) Spanish: topographic or habitational name from a place named with *ahumar* 'to smoke', possibly denoting a place where ham and other meats were smoked or alternatively a place that had been cleared for settlement by burning. Places named with this word are found in Jaén and Cádiz.
GIVEN NAMES Spanish 48%. *Jose* (15), *Carlos* (7), *Juan* (5), *Angel* (4), *Francisco* (4), *Miguel* (4), *Ruben* (4), *Adriana* (3), *Alfonso* (3), *Enrique* (3), *Felipe* (3), *Jorge* (3).

Aichele (304) South German: variant spelling of EICHEL. Compare EICHE.

GIVEN NAMES German 5%. *Erwin* (2), *Klaus*, *Siegfried*.

Aicher (247) South German: variant spelling of EICHER.

Aide (134) French: either from the masculine noun *aide* meaning 'helper', 'assistant', or the feminine one, *aide*, meaning 'help', 'assistance'.
FOREBEARS There is a large family of French Canadians known as Aide dit Créquy, the progenitor of whom came from La Rochelle, France and married in Neuville in 1689; his four sons had produced 13 children before 1730.

Aiello (3222) Southern Italian: habitational name from any of several places in southern Italy named Aiello, from Latin *agellus*, a diminutive of Latin *ager* 'field'.
GIVEN NAMES Italian 15%. *Salvatore* (21), *Angelo* (15), *Sal* (14), *Carlo* (6), *Vito* (6), *Antonio* (5), *Giuseppe* (5), *Santo* (5), *Neno* (4), *Pasquale* (4), *Rocco* (4), *Carmine* (3).

Aigner (323) South German: variant spelling of EIGNER.
GIVEN NAMES German 5%. *Friedrich*, *Hans*, *Otmar*, *Otto*, *Walburga*.

Aiken (4383) Variant, associated chiefly with northern Ireland, of the Scottish surname AITKEN.
FOREBEARS Aiken is the name of a NH family that was prominent in the 18th century; also of a Charleston family descended from a certain William Aiken, who emigrated from Antrim in Ireland to Charleston in about 1800.

Aikens (1181) Scottish and northern Irish: patronymic form of AIKEN.

Aikey (215) Variant of AKEY.

Aikin (407) Scottish and northern Irish: variant spelling of AIKEN.

Aikins (399) Scottish and northern Irish: variant spelling of AIKENS.

Aikman (456) **1.** Scottish: apparently a nickname meaning 'oak man', from Scots *aik* 'oak' + *man* 'man'. **2.** Scottish: alternatively, perhaps a derivative of an Old English personal name *Agemund*. **3.** Americanized spelling of Dutch **Eyckman** or **Yckman** (more commonly **Eyckmeester**), a 17th-century occupational name for someone whose job was to maintain standards, especially of the contents of wine casks, from Dutch *ijken* 'calibrate', 'measure', 'gauge'.

Ailes (376) English: variant spelling of AYLES.

Ailey (211) English: habitational name, perhaps from a minor place in Herefordshire called Ailey, or alternatively from a place called Hailey (see HALEY).

Ailor (164) Variant spelling of English or German AYLOR.

Ailstock (142) Probably English: this has the form of an English habitational name, but the surname is not now found in England. It could perhaps be from Halstock in Dorset, named in Old English with *hālig* 'religious foundation' + *stoc* '(outlying) farmstead'.

Aime (157) French (**Aimé**): from the personal name *Aimé* 'beloved' (Latin *Amatus*). GIVEN NAMES French 20%. *Jean Claude* (2), *Altagrace, Emile, Guerline, Jean-Claude, Jean-Michel, Magalie, Serge.*

Aimone (215) Northwestern Italian: **1.** from a Germanic personal name, *Haimo, Haimone,* formed with *haimi* 'home', 'world'. This was a popular name in Italy up to and during the Renaissance. **2.** occasionally, it may be from a short form of compound name, for example *Aimeric,* which was much favored in southern France and northwestern Italy in the Middle Ages. GIVEN NAMES Italian 5%. *Angelo* (2), *Caesar, Carlo, Neno.*

Ainley (178) English: habitational name, probably from Ainley Top, near Huddersfield West Yorkshire.

Ainsley (249) English and Scottish: variant spelling of AINSLIE.

Ainslie (437) English and Scottish: habitational name from Ansley in Warwickshire or Annesley in Nottinghamshire (see ANSLEY). The modern surname is found chiefly in the border regions of Scotland and northern England, having been taken north from England to Scotland in the Middle Ages, probably by a Norman baron. FOREBEARS The poet Hew Ainslie (1792–1878) emigrated from Ayrshire, Scotland, to the U.S. in 1822 and became a prominent citizen of Louisville, KY.

Ainsworth (3612) English (Lancashire): habitational name from a place near Manchester named Ainsworth, from the Old English personal name *Ægen* + Old English *worþ* 'enclosure'.

Aird (343) Scottish: habitational name from a place named with Gaelic *àird(e)* 'height', 'promontory', or 'headland', from the adjective *àrd* 'high', 'lofty', cognate with Latin *arduus* 'steep', 'difficult'. There is one such place near Hurlford in Ayrshire, and another in Inch, Wigtownshire. See also ARD.

Airey (294) **1.** German: see AREY. **2.** Possibly also Northern English: habitational name from a minor place named with Old Norse *Eyrará* 'gravel-bank stream', such as Aira Beck in Cumbria. FOREBEARS Cutlip Airey, recorded in 1782 in Augusta Co., VA, is also found as *Gatlive Airy* and *Gottlieb Arey.*

Airgood (100) Americanized spelling of German EHRGOTT.

Airhart (327) Americanized spelling of German EHRHARDT.

Airheart (119) Americanized spelling of German EHRHARDT.

Airington (120) English: variant of ERRINGTON.

Airoldi (115) French (Corsican; also **Airaudi**): from a Germanic personal name

composed of the elements *heri* 'army' + *hard* 'strong', 'hardy'. Compare HERARD. GIVEN NAMES French 13%. *Andre, Chantal, Germaine, Herve, Marcel, Rosaire.*

Aita (127) Southern Italian: habitational name from Aieta in Cosenza, named with Greek *aetos* 'eagle'. GIVEN NAMES Italian 6%. *Fedele, Gilda.*

Aitchison (424) Scottish form of ATCHISON.

Aitken (1799) Scottish: from the Older Scots personal name *Aitken,* a pet form of ADAM. See also AIKEN.

Aitkens (120) Scottish: patronymic from the personal name AITKEN.

Aiton (124) **1.** Scottish: habitational name from Ayton in Berwickshire, 'the settlement on the Eye river'. **2.** English: habitational name from a group of places in North Yorkshire called Ayton, from Old English *ēa* 'river' + *tūn* 'farmstead', 'estate', or from Eyton in Shropshire, named with Old English *ēg* 'island' + *tūn* 'settlement'.

Aja (154) **1.** Spanish: perhaps a metonymic occupational name from *aja* 'chisel', 'adze'. **2.** from an African language, of unknown origin. GIVEN NAMES Spanish 30%. *Manuel* (6), *Joaquin* (3), *Jose* (3), *Basilio* (2), *Diego* (2), *Jesus* (2), *Agustin, Angel, Blanca, Celestino, Domingo, Elena.*

Ajello (108) Italian: variant of AIELLO. GIVEN NAMES Italian 12%. *Antonino, Libero, Mafalda; Alfonso, Margarita, Mario, Marisa.*

Ajemian (111) Armenian: patronymic from Turkish *acem* 'Persian', 'foreigner', from Arabic *a'jam* 'one who speaks Arabic incorrectly'. GIVEN NAMES Armenian 22%. *Mihran* (2), *Anahid, Aram, Bedros, Hagop, Harutun, Hrach, Hratch, Ohannes, Sevag, Vartkes.*

Akagi (117) Japanese: variously written, usually with characters meaning 'red tree'. It may derive from Akagiyama ('Mount Red Castle'), a famous peak in east-central Japan, but the surname is more common in western Japan. GIVEN NAMES Japanese 51%. *Koji* (2), *Shig* (2), *Shigeru* (2), *Aki, Chieko, Fumio, Haruo, Hidetsugu, Hiroshi, Junji, Kanji, Kei.*

Akamine (180) Japanese: 'red peak'; mostly found in western Japan and the Ryūkyū Islands. GIVEN NAMES Japanese 32%. *Masaru* (2), *Shigeru* (2), *Akira, Chika, Haruno, Hatsuko, Hiroshi, Kasumi, Kiyo, Kiyoshi, Masae, Mitsuo.*

Akana (274) Hawaiian: unexplained.

Akard (186) Americanized spelling of German ECKHARDT.

Akau (126) Hawaiian: unexplained.

Akbar (315) Muslim (mainly Pakistan, India, and Bangladesh; also Iran): from a personal name based on Arabic *akbar* 'greater', 'greatest', an elative adjective

from *kabīr* 'great'. *Allāhu Akbar* ('Allah is the Greatest') is a slogan of Muslims throughout the world. The Mughal emperor known in English as Akbar the Great (Jalāl ud-Dīn Akbar; 1542–1605) extended his rule from a base in Panjab to cover most of the Indian subcontinent by the time of his death. His rule was notable for the integration of Hindus and Muslims in positions of power. GIVEN NAMES Muslim 81%. *Ali* (15), *Mohammad* (14), *Syed* (9), *Mohammed* (8), *Muhammad* (4), *Raja* (4), *Aesha* (2), *Alim* (2), *Fatimah* (2), *Ghouse* (2), *Imran* (2), *Jalaluddin* (2).

Akbari (119) Muslim: from an adjective meaning 'associated with or descended from AKBAR'. GIVEN NAMES Muslim 73%. *Ali* (10), *Ahmad* (4), *Mohammad* (3), *Ayub* (2), *Darush* (2), *Majid* (2), *Mohammed* (2), *Shireen* (2), *Syed* (2), *Abdul, Afsar, Alia.*

Ake (586) English: topographic name for someone living by a prominent oak tree, from Middle English *ake* 'oak', or a habitational name from the village of Aike, near Lockington, East Yorkshire, which is named with Old English *āc* 'oak', dative *āce* '(place at) the oak tree'.

Akehurst (121) English (Sussex): habitational name from any of several places named from Old English *ac* 'oak' + *hyrst* 'wooded hill'. The modern spelling of the place name is Oakhurst.

Akel (172) Muslim: from a personal name based on Arabic *'āqil* 'sensible', 'intelligent', 'wise'. GIVEN NAMES Muslim 31%. *Kerim* (2), *Sami* (2), *Hani, Hisham, Karim, Maher, Mohamed, Musa, Najib, Naser, Nuha.*

Akeley (129) **1.** North German form of **Ageley**, from Old High German *agaleia* 'columbine', a plant which was used medicinally in the Middle Ages, or from a female personal name of the same derivation. **2.** Possibly English: habitational name from Akely in Buckinghamshire, named from Old English *ac* 'oak' + *lēah* 'woodland clearing'. GIVEN NAME German 4%. *Kurt.*

Aken (138) **1.** North German and Dutch (**van A(a)ken**): habitational name from the city of Aachen in Germany, near the border with the Netherlands and Belgium. **2.** Variant spelling of Scottish AIKIN. GIVEN NAME German 4%. *Kurt.*

Akens (172) Northern Irish: variant spelling of AIKENS.

Aker (1172) **1.** Norwegian and Swedish (**Åker**): from *åker* 'plowed field', applied either as an ornamental or a topographic name. **2.** Possibly a variant of English, German, and Dutch ACKER or of German EICHER.

Akerley (193) English: variant spelling of ACKERLEY.

Akerman (386) **1.** Dutch: variant spelling of ACKERMAN. **2.** Jewish (Ashkenazic): variant of ACKERMANN. **3.** Swedish: (**Åkerman**): ornamental name composed of the elements *åker* 'field' + *man* 'man'.
GIVEN NAMES Jewish 6%. *Mendy* (2), *Ari, Chaim, Josif, Meir, Moisey, Ruchie*.

Akers (8531) English, Dutch, and Jewish (Ashkenazic): topographic name for someone living by a piece of arable land, from the plural or genitive singular of Middle English *aker* 'acre', i.e. arable land.

Akerson (225) Swedish (**Åkerson**): this is one of a small group of Swedish names ending in *-son* that are not patronymics. It is an ornamental name composed of the elements *åker* 'field' + *son* 'son'.

Akes (118) **1.** North German (Frisian): patronymic of the Old Frisian personal name *Ake*, a variant of *Ag(g)o* (see AGENA). **2.** English: variant of AKERS.

Akey (533) **1.** English: unexplained. **2.** Possibly an Americanized form of German **Eiche** 'oak' (see EICH).

Akhavan (117) Iranian and Jewish (from Iran): from the Persian form of Arabic *'ikhwān* 'brethren', 'friends', 'companions'.
GIVEN NAMES Iranian 73%; Jewish 4%. *Hamid* (4), *Farideh* (2), *Afshin, Ali Akbar, Assad, Bahram, Cyrous, Fatemeh, Habib, Hafez, Haleh, Hashem; Meyer, Shalom*.

Akhtar (418) Muslim: from the Persian personal name *Akhtar* 'star', 'good luck'. *Akhtar* is used in combination with other words, for example *Akhtar-ud-Dīn* 'star of religion (i.e. Islam)'. The name is found in India, Pakistan, and Bangladesh as well as Iran.
GIVEN NAMES Muslim 89%. *Syed* (21), *Mohammad* (15), *Muhammad* (13), *Saeed* (11), *Mahmood* (8), *Malik* (6), *Masood* (6), *Naeem* (6), *Naseem* (6), *Saleem* (6), *Mohammed* (5), *Nasim* (5).

Akhter (129) Muslim: variant of AKHTAR.
GIVEN NAMES Muslim 92%. *Syed* (10), *Mohammad* (4), *Javed* (3), *Mohammed* (3), *Golam* (2), *Iqbal* (2), *Muhammed* (2), *Naheed* (2), *Saeed* (2), *Sayeeda* (2), *Abdul, Asif*.

Aki (205) Japanese: found mostly in western Japan, where it is written with the characters for the former province of Aki (now part of Hiroshima prefecture). The name is written with the character for 'autumn' in the Ryūkyū Islands. Some instances in America could be the result of shortening other Japanese names beginning with *aki*, for example AKIYAMA.
GIVEN NAMES Japanese 7%. *Kiyoshi* (2), *Shota, Toshiya, Yoko*.

Akin (3503) Scottish, northern Irish, and English: variant spelling of AIKEN.

Akina (123) Hawaiian: unexplained.

Akins (5245) Scottish and northern Irish: variant spelling of AIKENS.

Akiona (104) Hawaiian: unexplained.

Akiyama (334) Japanese: meaning 'autumn mountain', it is found mostly in eastern Japan and the Ryūkyū Islands.
GIVEN NAMES Japanese 63%. *Akira* (3), *Kazuo* (3), *Kenji* (3), *Toshio* (3), *Yoshio* (3), *Haruhiko* (2), *Hideo* (2), *Hiroshi* (2), *Masayuki* (2), *Nobuo* (2), *Satoshi* (2), *Shoko* (2).

Akkerman (214) **1.** Dutch: occupational name for a plowman (see ACKERMAN). **2.** Jewish (Ashkenazic): variant spelling of ACKERMAN.
GIVEN NAMES Russian 8%; Jewish 7%. *Vladimir* (2), *Gennady, Glafira, Grigory, Igor, Mikhail, Semyon, Yevsey, Zinoviy; Gershon, Moisey, Muril, Rakhmil, Ruvin*.

Akopyan (154) Armenian: variant of HAGOPIAN.
GIVEN NAMES Armenian 66%; Russian 12%. *Aykanush* (3), *Grigor* (3), *Oganes* (3), *Akop* (2), *Andranik* (2), *Araksya* (2), *Aram* (2), *Ararat* (2), *Knarik* (2), *Mais* (2), *Sarkis* (2), *Tadevos* (2); *Asya, Georgy, Grigory, Grisha, Mikhail, Sergey, Valeriy, Vladimir, Yury*.

Akram (163) Muslim: from a personal name based on Arabic *akram* 'most generous', an elative form of KARIM.
GIVEN NAMES Muslim 90%. *Mohammad* (29), *Mohammed* (10), *Muhammad* (9), *Javed* (3), *Nadeem* (3), *Ahmad* (2), *Aziz* (2), *Mohmmad* (2), *Raja* (2), *Zahid* (2), *Abdul, Abdullah*.

Akre (248) Norwegian and Swedish (**Åkre**): topographic name for someone living by a piece of plowed land, from an inflected form of *aker, åker* 'plowed field'. This is also found as a place name, and so the origin in some cases may be habitational. See AKER.
GIVEN NAMES Scandinavian 6%. *Elert, Ordell, Thor*.

Akridge (676) Possibly English, a habitational name from a place with a name meaning 'oak ridge', as for example Aikrigg in Cumbria (from Old Norse *eik* 'oak' + *hryggr* 'ridge'), or any of the many places called Oakridge (from Old English *āc* + *hrycg*). However, neither Akridge nor Oakridge are found as surnames in current English records.

Akright (130) Variant spelling of English **Ackwright**, itself a variant of ARKWRIGHT.

Aksamit (183) Jewish (from Poland), Polish, Ukrainian, Belorussian, or Czech: from Polish *aksamit* 'velvet' or a cognate word in Czech, Ukrainian, Russian, or Belorussian. The etymology is clear, but not the application or ethnic origin.

Al (70) **1.** Dutch: from a short form of the personal name *Adelhard*, which is of Germanic origin, composed of the elements *adal* 'noble' + *hard* 'bold', 'hardy'. **2.** Swedish: variant of AHL.

Ala (147) Probably a respelling of German **Ahle**, a variant of AHL 2.
GIVEN NAMES German 4%. *Erwin, Kurt*.

Alagna (181) Italian: habitational name from Alagna Lomellina in Pavia province and Alagna Valsesia in Vercelli province, both named for their connection with the ancient Alani.
GIVEN NAMES Italian 20%. *Vito* (3), *Rocco* (2), *Agostino, Alessio, Antonio, Gaetano, Marco, Nicolo, Nino, Salvatore, Tommaso, Vincenza*.

Alaimo (678) Italian (Sicily): from a medieval personal name, *Alaimo*, which is of uncertain origin.
GIVEN NAMES Italian 19%. *Salvatore* (16), *Angelo* (11), *Sal* (6), *Carmelo* (4), *Giovanni* (3), *Calogero* (2), *Antonio, Carmine, Gaspare, Gino, Gioacchino*.

Alam (835) Muslim: **1.** from a personal name based on Arabic *'alam* 'emblem', 'banner', hence an epithet for a distinguished man. 'Alam-al-Huda ('banner of guidance') is an honorific title of the Prophet Muhammad. *'Alam* is generally found in names in combination with other words. **2.** from a personal name based on Arabic *'ālam*, literally 'world'. *'Ālamgir* (in combination with the Persian word *gir* 'conqueror') was a title of the Mughal emperor Aurangzeb (1618–1707), who ruled the Indian subcontinent from 1658 to 1707. This name is found in a variety of compounds, which are popular in the subcontinent, for example *Badrul-'Ālam* 'full moon of the world'.
GIVEN NAMES Muslim 82%. *Mohammed* (58), *Mohammad* (35), *Syed* (23), *Shamsul* (14), *Nurul* (10), *Mohamed* (9), *Muhammad* (6), *Mahbub* (5), *Mahbubul* (5), *Mahmood* (5), *Arif* (4), *Masud* (4).

Alameda (284) Spanish: topographic name from *alameda* 'poplar grove', a collective form of *álamo* 'poplar', or habitational name from any of the many places named with this word.
GIVEN NAMES Spanish 16%. *Manuel* (3), *Juan* (2), *Luis* (2), *Miguel* (2), *Alejandro, Belen, Carlos, Dominga, Efrain, Eladio, Joaquin, Jose*.

Alamillo (193) Spanish: topographic name from *alamillo*, a diminutive of *álamo* 'poplar', or habitational name from any of the many places named with this word, in particular one in Ciudad Real.
GIVEN NAMES Spanish 55%. *Jose* (9), *Jesus* (4), *Pedro* (4), *Ramiro* (3), *Guillermo* (2), *Isidro* (2), *Jose Luis* (2), *Juan* (2), *Manuel* (2), *Miguel* (2), *Ramon* (2), *Ricardo* (2).

Alamo (342) Spanish and Portuguese (**Álamo**): from *álamo* 'poplar' (of uncertain origin), applied either as a topographic name or as a habitational name from any of several places in Spain and Portugal named with this word.
GIVEN NAMES Spanish 43%; Portuguese 10%. *Jose* (9), *Luis* (5), *Alfredo* (4), *Arturo* (4), *Angel* (3), *Carlos* (3), *Jorge* (3), *Alberto* (2), *Alejandro* (2), *Eduardo* (2), *Humberto* (2), *Jaime* (2); *Joao*.

Alan (513) English and Scottish: variant spelling of ALLEN. This is the usual spelling of the personal name in England and Scotland, but is infrequent as a surname.

Aland (100) Scandinavian (**Åland**): topographic name from the Åland Islands in the Gulf of Bothnia.

Alanis (692) **1.** Spanish (**Alanís**) and Portuguese: variant of ALANIZ. **2.** Greek: from *alani* 'open space', 'square' (Turkish *alan*), a nickname for an idler, someone whose time was spent loafing around in the square of a town or village.
GIVEN NAMES Spanish 59%. *Jose* (25), *Juan* (19), *Jesus* (14), *Ricardo* (8), *Ramon* (7), *Ruben* (7), *Carlos* (6), *Arturo* (5), *Guadalupe* (5), *Manuel* (5), *Mario* (5), *Alejandro* (4).

Alaniz (1799) Spanish: habitational name from Alanís in Seville province.
GIVEN NAMES Spanish 49%. *Jose* (40), *Jesus* (24), *Juan* (20), *Manuel* (17), *Carlos* (12), *Pedro* (12), *Ricardo* (12), *Ruben* (11), *Mario* (10), *Alicia* (9), *Luis* (9), *Rogelio* (9).

Alarcon (1579) Spanish (**Alarcón**): habitational name, most probably from Alarcón in Cuenca province.
GIVEN NAMES Spanish 48%. *Jose* (39), *Carlos* (18), *Luis* (18), *Manuel* (15), *Francisco* (12), *Jesus* (12), *Juan* (12), *Rafael* (12), *Raul* (12), *Antonio* (11), *Jorge* (11), *Pedro* (11), *Alfredo* (10).

Alarid (224) perhaps from Catalan *alarit* 'outcry' (Castilian *alarido*). This name is not found in Catalonia, but is very common in Mexico.
GIVEN NAMES Spanish 12%. *Manuel* (4), *Alfonso* (3), *Miguel* (2), *Adolfo*, *Agapito*, *Arturo*, *Carlos*, *Juanita*, *Loyola*, *Maria Guadalupe*, *Octaviano*, *Ramon*.

Alarie (243) French: reflex of the Visigothic personal name *Alaric*, which is composed of Germanic elements meaning 'all power'. This form was established in Quebec from 1681.
FOREBEARS An Alaria, also known as Grandalarie, from Poitiers, France, was recorded in Neuville in 1681.
GIVEN NAMES French 13%. *Andre*, *Camille*, *Dominique*, *Francois*, *Germaine*, *Jean Marc*, *Lucien*, *Michel*, *Pierette*, *Yves*.

Alario (139) Italian: from the personal name *Ilario*, from Latin *Hilarius* (see HILLARY).
GIVEN NAMES Italian 11%. *Orazio* (2), *Carlo*, *Rocco*, *Salvatore*, *Vita*, *Vitina*.

Alas (265) Catalan (**Alàs**): habitational name from a place in Catalonia named Alàs.
GIVEN NAMES Spanish 57%. *Jose* (15), *Ana* (5), *Salvador* (5), *Carlos* (4), *Juan* (4), *Julio* (4), *Ernesto* (3), *Jesus* (3), *Orlando* (3), *Santos* (3), *Delmy* (2), *Francisco* (2).

Alatorre (312) Spanish: topographic name meaning 'at the tower' (see TORRE).
GIVEN NAMES Spanish 54%. *Jose* (12), *Francisco* (8), *Carlos* (6), *Juan* (5), *Jesus* (4), *Ramon* (4), *Leopoldo* (3), *Francisca* (2), *Graciela* (2), *Jose Luis* (2), *Manuel* (2), *Marcos* (2).

Alavi (156) Iranian: from the Persian form of Arabic 'Alawi 'descendant of Ali', name of the son-in-law of the Prophet Muhammad and the first imam of the Shiite Muslims.
GIVEN NAMES Iranian 74%. *Hossein* (5), *Ali* (4), *Farid* (3), *Seyed* (3), *Syed* (3), *Abass* (2), *Hamid* (2), *Hossain* (2), *Saied* (2), *Shahab* (2), *Shirin* (2), *Zafar* (2).

Alba (1453) Spanish, Italian, and Romanian: habitational name from any of the places named in any of these languages with this element. Its meaning is various and disputed; the coincidence in form with Latin *alba* (feminine) 'white' is suggestive, but in many cases the name is pre-Roman and denotes a site on a hill or mountain.
GIVEN NAMES Spanish 37%. *Jose* (28), *Juan* (18), *Luis* (12), *Mario* (12), *Francisco* (10), *Carlos* (9), *Ramon* (9), *Andres* (7), *Jesus* (7), *Jorge* (7), *Manuel* (7), *Pedro* (7); *Antonio* (9), *Angelo* (3), *Lorenzo* (2), *Salvatore* (2), *Alfonse*, *Bartolo*, *Biagio*, *Carlo*, *Carmelo*, *Eligio*, *Elio*, *Eliseo*.

Albach (128) German: habitational name taken from the name of a stream (Middle High German *bach*), of which there are several examples. The surname is Americanized as ALPAUGH and AL(L)BAUGH.
GIVEN NAMES German 9%. *Kurt* (2), *Eberhard*, *Manfred*.

Alban (604) English, German, Spanish (**Albán**), Italian, and French: from the personal name *Alban* (Latin *Albanus*, originally a habitational name for someone from any of the many places in Italy and elsewhere called Alba). This surname has probably also absorbed some cases of Italian or Spanish ALBANO.
GIVEN NAMES Spanish 7%. *Carlos* (4), *Jorge* (3), *Juan* (3), *Manuel* (3), *Alfonso* (2), *Alvaro* (2), *Jaime* (2), *Luis* (2), *Prudencio* (2), *Alberto*, *Andres*, *Guillermo*.

Albanese (2248) Southern Italian: ethnic name from *albanese* '(an) Albanian', applied to someone from Albania or from one of the Albanian settlements in Abruzzo, Apulia, Campania, and Sicily.
GIVEN NAMES Italian 19%. *Salvatore* (16), *Angelo* (11), *Rocco* (10), *Vito* (6), *Antonio* (5), *Sal* (5), *Pasquale* (4), *Domenic* (3), *Raffaele* (3), *Aldo* (2), *Carlo* (2), *Carmine* (2).

Albani (164) Italian: patronymic or plural form of ALBANO.
GIVEN NAMES Italian 31%. *Orlando* (4), *Salvatore* (3), *Aldo* (2), *Cosmo* (2), *Angelo*, *Aniello*, *Dino*, *Gaetano*, *Giovanni*, *Giuseppe*, *Sebastiano*.

Albano (1823) Italian: from the personal name *Albano* (see ALBAN). It could also be a habitational name from any of the places called Albano, for example near Rome, Potenza, and Bergamo, or for someone from a place named Alba (from an adjecti-

val form of the place name), of which there are various examples.
GIVEN NAMES Italian 19%; Spanish 6%. *Rocco* (14), *Salvatore* (10), *Antonio* (8), *Mario* (7), *Alfonso* (6), *Jose* (6), *Angelo* (4), *Sal* (4), *Carmine* (3), *Emilio* (3), *Vito* (3), *Adriana* (2), *Americo* (2), *Canio* (2), *Cosmo* (2), *Crescenzo* (2), *Gennaro* (2), *Pasquale* (2); *Carlos* (2), *Elvira* (2), *Imelda* (2), *Amado*.

Albany (156) Scottish and English: from the title of the Dukes of Albany (House of Stuart), hence a name borne by their retainers. It is an infrequent surname in England and Scotland. The city of Albany, NY (formerly the Dutch settlement of Beverwijck or Fort Orange) was named for James Stuart, Duke of York and Albany; he was the brother of King Charles II and later king in his own right as James II. In 1664 he financed a fleet to take over the Dutch colony of New Netherland (now New York state). The American family name was apparently adopted at this period. The word *Albany* is from Latin *Albania*, Gaelic *Albainn*, genitive of *Alba* 'Scotland'. It is the same word as English *Albion*, an old name for the whole of Britain.

Albarado (364) Spanish: variant of ALVARADO.
GIVEN NAMES Spanish 19%. *Jose* (4), *Juan* (4), *Francisco* (2), *Gilberto* (2), *Guadalupe* (2), *Abiel*, *Agustin*, *Agustina*, *Alberto*, *Alejandro*, *Alphonso*, *Ambrosia*.

Albarran (376) Spanish (**Albarrán**): nickname or occupational name from medieval Spanish *albarrán* 'foreigner', 'alien', also 'chief herdsman or shepherd' (from Arabic *al-* 'the' + *barrāni* 'outside', from *barra* 'out' or *barr* 'land', 'open country').
GIVEN NAMES Spanish 52%. *Jose* (9), *Francisco* (6), *Roberto* (6), *Miguel* (5), *Jesus* (4), *Luis* (4), *Alejandro* (3), *Carlos* (3), *Javier* (3), *Jose Luis* (3), *Juan* (3), *Pedro* (3).

Albaugh (1049) Americanized spelling of German ALBACH.

Albea (139) Variant spelling of English **Alb(e)y** (see ALBEE).

Albee (1019) Variant spelling of English **Alb(e)y**, a habitational name from Alby in Norfolk or Ailby in Lincolnshire, both named with the Old Norse personal name *Áli* + Old Norse *býr* 'farmstead'.
FOREBEARS This is the name of a prominent NH family. Benjamin Albee (1614–53) came to Boston, MA, from Norfolk, England.

Alber (770) South German: **1.** from the personal name *Alber*, a reduced form of either *Adalbert* (see ALBERT) or *Adalbero* (from elements meaning 'noble bear'). **2.** topographic name from Middle High German *alber(boum)* 'white poplar', from Old High German *albari* (ultimately from Latin *albus* 'white', 'pale').
GIVEN NAMES German 5%. *Kurt* (3), *Otto* (3), *Franz*, *Hans*, *Inge*, *Manfred*.

Alberda (107) Dutch: variant of ALBERT.

Alberding (155) German (especially Westphalian): patronymic from ALBERT.

Alberg (281) **1.** Swedish: variant spelling of AHLBERG. **2.** German: reduced form of ADELBERG.

Albergo (180) Italian: **1.** habitational name from some place named in old Italian with *alberga* 'lodging', 'shelter', a word of Germanic origin (modern Italian *albergo* 'inn'). **2.** from a short form of the omen name *Bonalbergo*.

GIVEN NAMES Italian 23%. *Vito* (3), *Angelo*, *Franco, Guiseppe, Marco, Marino, Nicola, Onofrio, Rosario.*

Alberici (120) Italian: patronymic or plural form of ALBERICO.

GIVEN NAMES Italian 14%. *Angelo* (2), *Aldo*, *Attilio, Emedio, Gino.*

Alberico (338) Northern Italian: from the Germanic personal name *Alberic* meaning 'elf king', which was popular in northwestern Italy and southern France in the Middle Ages.

GIVEN NAMES Italian 15%. *Cosmo* (3), *Gino* (2), *Aldo, Amedeo, Angelo, Antonio, Berardino, Fiorino, Geno, Luigi, Marco, Modestino.*

Albers (3976) Dutch, North German, and Danish: patronymic from the personal name ALBERT.

Alberson (366) See ALBERTSON.

Albert (11894) English, French, North German, Danish, Catalan, Hungarian, Czech, Slovak, Slovenian, etc.: from the personal name *Albert*, composed of the Germanic elements *adal* 'noble' + *berht* 'bright', 'famous'. The standard German form is ALBRECHT. This, in its various forms, was one of the most popular of all European male personal names in the Middle Ages. It was borne by various churchmen, notably St. Albert of Prague, a Bohemian prince who died a martyr in 997 attempting to convert the Prussians to Christianity; also St. Albert the Great (?1193–1280), an Aristotelian theologian and tutor of Thomas Aquinas. It was also the name of princes and military leaders, such as Albert the Bear (1100–70), Margrave of Brandenburg. In more recent times it has been adopted as a Jewish family name. FOREBEARS A bearer of the surname Albert, from Saintonge, France, was documented in Quebec city in 1664.

GIVEN NAMES French 4%. *Camille* (5), *Fernand* (5), *Lucien* (5), *Marcel* (5), *Normand* (5), *Cecile* (4), *Adrien* (3), *Armand* (3), *Henri* (3), *Jacques* (3), *Alban* (2), *Andre* (2).

Alberta (158) Italian: from a feminine form of the personal name ALBERTO. This is a rare name in Italy, now confined largely to Foggia province.

GIVEN NAMES Italian 4%. *Angelo, Salvatore.*

Albertelli (106) Italian: from a pet form of the personal name *Alberto*.

GIVEN NAMES Italian 19%. *Guido* (2), *Angelo, Evo, Mino, Pasquale, Quinto, Rocco.*

Alberti (931) **1.** Italian: patronymic or plural form of ALBERTO. **2.** Hungarian: habitational name from a village in Pest county called Alberti. **3.** Hungarian: patronymic from the personal name ALBERT.

GIVEN NAMES Italian 9%. *Angelo* (5), *Antonio* (2), *Carmello* (2), *Salvatore* (2), *Stefano* (2), *Attilio, Carina, Cira, Cosimo, Dino, Domenic, Eustasio; Mario* (5), *Roberto* (3), *Rafael* (2), *Ana, Armando, Elvira, Ernesto, Fernando, Graciela.*

Albertini (365) Italian: from the personal name *Albertino*, a pet form of ALBERTO.

GIVEN NAMES Italian 6%; French 4%. *Carlo* (2), *Angelo, Cristoforo, Dante, Heriberto, Oreste, Remo; Armand* (2), *Damien, Hermite.*

Alberto (510) Spanish, Portuguese, and Italian: from the personal name *Alberto*, Spanish and Italian equivalent of ALBERT.

GIVEN NAMES Spanish 42%; Portuguese 10%; Italian 9%. *Jose* (12), *Juan* (7), *Luis* (7), *Alberto* (4), *Carlos* (4), *Francisco* (4), *Angel* (3), *Gerardo* (3), *Jorge* (3), *Julio* (3), *Andres* (2), *Gregorio* (2); *Heitor; Antonio* (6), *Angelo, Carlo, Domenic, Eliseo, Enrico, Gilda, Gino, Guido, Lorenzo, Mirella, Pasquale.*

Alberts (2491) English, Dutch, and North German: patronymic from the personal name ALBERT.

Albertsen (224) North German, Danish, and Norwegian: patronymic from the personal name ALBERT.

GIVEN NAMES German 7%; Scandinavian 7%. *Ewald* (2), *Hans* (2), *Kurt; Erik, Jeppe.*

Albertson (3650) Patronymic from ALBERT, English in form, but only rarely found as a surname in England or Scotland. In many cases it is probably a respelling of Danish and Norwegian ALBERTSEN, Swedish **Albert(s)son**, or a cognate in some other language.

Alberty (323) Americanized spelling of Italian ALBERTI.

FOREBEARS Frederick Alberti or Alberty was born in Italy in about 1740 and died in 1831 in Surry County, NC.

Albin (1734) English, southern French, German (mainly Austrian), and Hungarian: from the personal name *Albin* (Latin *Albinus*, a derivative of *albus* 'white'). The usual spelling of the French name is AUBIN. The personal name was especially popular in Austria, Lombardy, and Savoy, where it absorbed the Germanic personal name *Albuin* (which is composed of the elements *alb* 'elf' + *win* 'friend'). This was the name of the Lombard leader (died 572) who made himself king of northern Italy, and also of various saints, including a bishop of Brixen (Bressanone) in South Tyrol, whose name was confused with that of St. Aubin of Angers (see AUBIN).

Albini (136) Italian: patronymic or plural form of ALBINO 1.

GIVEN NAMES Italian 34%. *Salvatore* (3), *Antonio* (2), *Pasquale* (2), *Aldo, Amalio, Americo, Armando, Carlo, Caterina, Claudio, Gino, Mario, Maurizio, Nichola, Nicola, Severino, Vittorio.*

Albino (416) **1.** Italian and Spanish: from the personal name *Albino* (see ALBIN). **2.** Italian: habitational name from a place in Bergamo named Albino.

GIVEN NAMES Spanish 20%; Italian 8%. *Jose* (9), *Ramon* (5), *Manuel* (3), *Ana* (2), *Carlos* (2), *Julio* (2), *Luis* (2), *Raul* (2), *Ruben* (2), *Alfonso, Andres, Angel; Pasquale* (2), *Angelo, Antonio, Carmine, Giovanni, Luigi, Sal, Santo, Saverio, Ubalda.*

Albitz (106) German: unexplained.

Albo (179) **1.** Spanish, Italian, and Jewish (Sephardic): from a reduced form of ALBERTO, ALBERICO, or ALBINO. **2.** Hungarian (**Albó**): from a pet form of the personal name ALBERT. **3.** Catalan (**Albó**): from a derivative of ALBA.

GIVEN NAMES Spanish 21%; Italian 6%; Jewish 4%. *Alejandro* (3), *Alberto* (2), *Mario* (2), *Alicia, Arturo, Catalina, Cesar, Edelberto, Guadalupe, Jacobo, Javier, Joaquin; Cecilio, Marco, Romeo; Per* (4); *Irit, Tali, Yitzhak.*

Alborn (106) English: habitational name from Albourne in West Sussex, named from Old English *alor* 'alder' + *burna* 'stream', or possibly from Aldbourne in Wiltshire, which is named with Old English *Ealding* '(people) associated with *Ealda*' + *burna* 'stream'.

Albracht (158) German: variant of ALBRECHT.

Albrecht (7283) German: from the personal name, composed of Germanic *adal* 'noble' + *berht* 'bright', 'famous'. Compare ALBERT. This surname is also found in Slovenia, also in the Slovenized form **Albreht**.

GIVEN NAMES German 5%. *Kurt* (18), *Erwin* (12), *Hans* (7), *Manfred* (6), *Otto* (5), *Horst* (4), *Klaus* (4), *Arno* (3), *Heinz* (3), *Milbert* (3), *Fritz* (2), *Gerhard* (2).

Albright (9610) **1.** Americanized form of German ALBRECHT. **2.** English: from a medieval variant of the personal name ALBERT.

FOREBEARS Jacob Albright (1759–1808), a prominent Methodist preacher, was born in Pottstown, PA, the son of a German immigrant called Johann Albrecht.

Albritton (2371) Variant of English **Al(l)-brighton**, a habitational name from either of two places in Shropshire called Albrighton. The place near Shifnal (*Albricstone* in Domesday Book) was named with the Old English personal name *Æðelbeorh* + *tūn* 'settlement'. The one near Shrewsbury appears in Domesday Book as *Etbritone* and was named in Old English as

'Ēadbeorht's settlement'. Albright Hussey in Shropshire is in the parish of Albrighton (having been part of the same manor) and was also formerly known as Albrighton; this too may be a source of the surname.

Albro (627) English: habitational name from places called Aldborough (in Norfolk and North Yorkshire) or Aldbrough (in East and North Yorkshire), or possibly a variant of ALBURY. All of these places were named with Old English *eald* 'old' + *burh* 'stronghold'.

FOREBEARS A John Albro came to New England from England in 1634 and settled in Rhode Island in 1638.

Albu (140) Romanian: descriptive nickname meaning 'white'.

GIVEN NAMES Romanian 18%. *Nicolae* (3), *Gheorghe* (2), *Valeriu* (2), *Ionel, Mihai, Petre*.

Albuquerque (174) Spanish and Portuguese: habitational name from a place in Badajoz province named Albuquerque. The surname has also been established in Portugal since the 15th century, and it is also found in western India, where it was taken by Portuguese colonists.

GIVEN NAMES Spanish 30%; Portuguese 27%; Indian 6%; Italian 4%. *Jose* (9), *Manuel* (6), *Carlos* (5), *Alberto* (2), *Alvaro* (2), *Fernando* (2), *Pedro* (2), *Armando, Berta, Celestino, Emilia, Felipe; Joao* (3), *Joaquim* (3), *Paulo* (3), *Manoel* (2); *Dinesh* (2), *Anil, Mahesh, Naina, Vijay; Antonio* (7), *Leonardo* (2).

Albury (486) English: habitational name from a place in Hertfordshire or Oxfordshire called Albury, from Old English *eald* 'old' + *byrig*, dative of *burh* 'stronghold'.

Albus (300) German: humanistic name meaning 'white', a translation into Latin of WEISS.

Alcala (1463) Spanish (**Alcalá**): habitational name from any of the numerous fortified villages named during the Moorish occupation of Spain with Arabic *al* 'the' + *qal'ah* 'fortress'.

GIVEN NAMES Spanish 50%. *Jose* (34), *Juan* (18), *Jesus* (17), *Manuel* (17), *Raul* (12), *Ramon* (11), *Alfredo* (10), *Francisco* (10), *Luis* (10), *Rafael* (10), *Ruben* (10), *Carlos* (9).

Alcalde (121) Spanish and Catalan: from *alcalde* 'mayor', from Arabic *al-qāḍī* 'the judge', a title dating from the days of Moorish rule in Spain.

GIVEN NAMES Spanish 50%. *Jorge* (3), *Luis* (3), *Raul* (3), *Carlos* (2), *Emilio* (2), *Juana* (2), *Mario* (2), *Alberto, Ana, Arturo, Bernardino, Celso*.

Alcantar (774) Spanish (**Alcántar**): variant of **Alcántara** (see ALCANTARA).

GIVEN NAMES Spanish 57%. *Jose* (22), *Juan* (14), *Manuel* (12), *Miguel* (10), *Andres* (8), *Ruben* (8), *Jesus* (7), *Rafael* (6), *Salvador* (6), *Carlos* (5), *Javier* (5), *Pedro* (5).

Alcantara (877) Spanish (**Alcántara**): habitational name from any of various places, for example in the provinces of Cáceres, Cádiz, or Castilianized form of Catalan ALCÀNTERA, habitational name from a town in Valencia, all of them named from Arabic *al* 'the' + *qanṭara* 'bridge'.

GIVEN NAMES Spanish 48%. *Jose* (14), *Luis* (9), *Juan* (8), *Carlos* (7), *Francisco* (7), *Jesus* (7), *Pedro* (7), *Eduardo* (5), *Enrique* (5), *Jorge* (5), *Rafael* (5), *Armando* (4).

Alcaraz (730) Spanish: habitational name from a place called Alcaraz, in Albacete province, derived perhaps from the ancient *Alcaratium Orcia*, or possibly from Arabic *al* 'the' + *karaz* 'cherry'.

GIVEN NAMES Spanish 52%. *Jose* (18), *Jesus* (9), *Jorge* (9), *Juan* (9), *Manuel* (8), *Alicia* (6), *Francisco* (6), *Miguel* (6), *Ruben* (6), *Alfredo* (5), *Javier* (5), *Jose Luis* (5); *Antonio* (5), *Angelo, Eliseo, Federico, Gabriella, Heriberto, Leonardo, Marco, Romeo, Sal*.

Alcazar (322) Spanish (**Alcázar**): habitational name from any of various places, for example in the provinces of Ciudad Real, Cuenca, and Granada, named with the word *alcázar* 'citadel' or 'palace' (from Arabic *al* 'the' + *qaṣr* 'fortress', a borrowing of Latin *castrum*; compare CASTRO).

GIVEN NAMES Spanish 55%. *Carlos* (7), *Jose* (6), *Francisco* (4), *Luis* (4), *Manuel* (4), *Juan* (3), *Julio* (3), *Rafael* (3), *Raul* (3), *Ruben* (3), *Alicia* (2), *Gustavo* (2).

Alcocer (289) Spanish and Catalan: habitational name from any of various places called Alcocer, for example in the provinces of Guadalajara and Alacant, from Arabic *al* 'the' + *quṣayr* 'small palace', a diminutive of *qaṣr* 'citadel' (see ALCAZAR).

GIVEN NAMES Spanish 48%. *Jose* (8), *Juan* (6), *Carlos* (4), *Francisco* (4), *Jorge* (3), *Miguel* (3), *Pedro* (3), *Ricardo* (3), *Armando* (2), *Cesar* (2), *Eduardo* (2), *Guadalupe* (2).

Alcock (517) English: from a pet form of any of various personal names beginning with *Al-*, especially *Alan* and *Alexander*. The Middle English hypocoristic suffix *-cok* (see COCKE) was very commonly added to personal names in Middle English; compare for example HANCOCK and WILCOCK.

Alcon (200) Spanish (**Alcón**): from *halcón* 'falcon', 'hawk', applied as a nickname for someone with hawklike features, or a metonymic occupational name for a hawker.

GIVEN NAMES Spanish 20%. *Domingo* (2), *Emilia* (2), *Juan* (2), *Altagracia, Arsenio, Bernabe, Casimiro, Desiderio, Emilio, Erlinda, Fernando, Gaspar*.

Alcorn (2725) Scottish and northern Irish: predominantly Scottish form of the English habitational name ALLCORN. It was established in Scotland by the mid 15th century, and was sometimes altered by folk etymology to **Auldcorn**.

FOREBEARS This surname was brought to Philadelphia from northern Ireland in 1721.

Alcorta (199) Basque: topographic name from Basque *(h)ar(ri)* 'stone', 'rock' + *korta* 'stable', 'corral', with the first *r* changed to *l* by dissimilation.

GIVEN NAMES Spanish 45%. *Jesus* (4), *Jose* (3), *Maximiliano* (3), *Arturo* (2), *Francisco* (2), *Humberto* (2), *Lupe* (2), *Manuel* (2), *Mario* (2), *Ramiro* (2), *Roberto* (2), *Adela*.

Alcoser (111) Spanish: variant of ALCOCER.

GIVEN NAMES Spanish 47%. *Joaquin* (3), *Alfredo* (2), *Jose* (2), *Manuel* (2), *Rafael* (2), *Andres, Carlota, Eloy, Erasmo, Esmeralda, Francisco, Guillermo*.

Alcott (541) English: ostensibly a topographic name containing Middle English *cott, cote* 'cottage' (see COATES). In fact, however, it is generally if not always an alteration of ALCOCK, in part at least for euphemistic reasons.

FOREBEARS Louisa May Alcott (1832–88), author of *Little Women* (1869), was the daughter of Amos Bronson Alcott (1799–1888), who had changed the family name from *Alcox*. The family trace their descent from an Alcocke family who emigrated from England to MA with John Winthrop in 1629.

Aldaco (167) Basque: topographic name from Basque *alde* 'side', 'slope' + the locative suffix *-co*.

GIVEN NAMES Spanish 55%. *Jose* (10), *Juan* (5), *Alfredo* (2), *Carlos* (2), *Jesus* (2), *Manuel* (2), *Natividad* (2), *Pedro* (2), *Rafael* (2), *Raynaldo* (2), *Agripino, Alejandro*.

Aldag (124) German: from one of the typical old North German personal names (actually North Sea Germanic) ending in *-dag* 'day', here prefixed by *al-* 'totally', 'entirely' and meaning 'bright day'.

GIVEN NAMES German 6%. *Kurt, Uwe*.

Aldama (216) Hispanic (Mexico): there is a place in Mexico called Aldama, but it is not known whether the family name is from the place name or vice versa. Probably both go back to a lost original in Spain.

GIVEN NAMES Spanish 47%. *Jose* (4), *Ruben* (4), *Javier* (3), *Jesus* (3), *Juan* (3), *Alejandro* (2), *Cesar* (2), *Eduardo* (2), *Enrique* (2), *Manuel* (2), *Rafael* (2), *Raul* (2).

Aldana (713) Basque: habitational name from a town called Aldana in Biscay province, Basque Country, or topographic name from Basque *alde* 'side', 'slope'. The ending *-ana* is common in Basque place names; its meaning is vague: apparently no more than 'place'.

GIVEN NAMES Spanish 50%. *Jose* (13), *Manuel* (7), *Juan* (6), *Luis* (6), *Cesar* (5), *Jorge* (5), *Miguel* (5), *Ricardo* (5), *Carlos* (4), *Guadalupe* (4), *Guillermo* (4), *Gustavo* (4).

Aldape (223) Spanish form of the Basque surname **Aldabe**, from *alde* 'side', 'slope' + *be(h)e* 'lower part'.

GIVEN NAMES Spanish 47%. *Jose* (6), *Carlos* (5), *Juan* (5), *Jesus* (3), *Ramiro* (3), *Adolfo* (2), *Emilio* (2), *Juanita* (2), *Julio* (2), *Manuel* (2), *Miguel* (2), *Ninfa* (2).

Alday (418) **1.** Spanish form of Basque **Aldai**, a habitational name from any of several places in the Basque country called Alday or Aldai, from Basque *alde* 'side', 'slope'. **2.** Americanized form of German ALDAG. **3.** English: variant spelling of ALLDAY.

GIVEN NAMES Spanish 16%. *Gonzalo* (2), *Manuel* (2), *Ricardo* (2), *Salvador* (2), *Alejandro, Alma Delia, Alonzo, Armando, Arturo, Aurelio, Bonifacio, Catalina.*

Aldaz (157) Castilianized form of Basque **Aldatz**, a habitational name from either of the two towns named with Aldatz in the Basque Country (Larraun-Aldatz and Itza-Aldatz), or possibly also from a variant of ALDAY, with genitive -*z*.

GIVEN NAMES Spanish 47%. *Jose* (3), *Luis* (3), *Arturo* (2), *Claudio* (2), *Ines* (2), *Jesus* (2), *Jose Mario* (2), *Manuel* (2), *Miguel* (2), *Sergio* (2), *Alfonso, Alicia; Lorenzo* (2), *Antonio, Leonardo.*

Aldaz (157) **1.** Castilianized form of Basque **Aldatz**, a habitational name from either of two towns called Aldatz in the Basque Country. **2.** possibly a variant of ALDAY, with genitive -*z*.

GIVEN NAMES Spanish 47%. *Jose* (3), *Luis* (3), *Arturo* (2), *Claudio* (2), *Ines* (2), *Jesus* (2), *Jose Mario* (2), *Manuel* (2), *Miguel* (2), *Sergio* (2), *Alfonso, Alicia; Lorenzo* (2), *Antonio, Leonardo.*

Alden (2322) **1.** English: from a Middle English personal name. This is either *Aldan*, a variant of *Healfdane* (see *Haldane*), or *Aldine*, Old English *Ealdwine*, literally 'old friend', but probably to be interpreted as 'friend of the past'. **2.** Norwegian: habitational name from a farmstead in western Norway, so named because of its situation below a high mountain. FOREBEARS John Alden (*c*.1599–1687) was one of the Pilgrim Fathers who sailed on the *Mayflower* in 1620. He moved from Plymouth to Duxbury, MA, about 1627. Many of his descendants were merchant seamen, among them James Alden (1810–77), who twice circumnavigated the globe.

Alder (1266) **1.** English: topographic name for someone living by an alder tree (Middle English *al(d)re*), or by a group of alders (the surname is often found in the plural form in Middle English). **2.** English: from a Middle English personal name, representing a falling together of two Old English names, *Ealdhere* 'ancient army' and *Æðelhere* 'noble army'. **3.** German: variant of ALTER. **4.** Translation of Swedish AHL. **5.** Translation of Finnish LEPPANEN.

Alderdice (120) Scottish: habitational name from Allardice in Kincardineshire, now part of Aberdeenshire. The first element of

the place name is Old English *alor* 'alder'; the second element is obscure.

Alderete (541) Spanish: habitational name from any various places in Spain and Portugal called Alderete, Aldarete, or Aldrete, probably from a Gothic personal name.

GIVEN NAMES Spanish 27%. *Jose* (7), *Manuel* (7), *Angel* (4), *Carlos* (4), *Luis* (4), *Adolfo* (3), *Armando* (3), *Lupe* (3), *Raul* (3), *Alfonso* (2), *Alfredo* (2), *Juanita* (2).

Alderfer (522) Americanized form of German **Altdörfer**, a habitational name for someone from one of the many places in Switzerland, Austria, and southern Germany called *Altdorf* 'old village'. FOREBEARS Frederick Alderfer (Friedrich Altdörfer) came to PA in 1733 from Steinsfurt in Kraichgau, Germany; his ancestors were from Fehr-Altdorf, Zürich canton, Switzerland.

Alderink (130) Dutch: meaning 'descendant of *Aldert*', a personal name from an ancient Germanic personal name *Aldheri* 'ancient army'. Compare English ALDER 2.

Alderman (3669) Southern English: status name from Middle English *alderman*, Old English *ealdorman*, literally 'elder'. In medieval England an alderman was a member of the governing body of a city or borough; also the head of a guild.

Alders (136) **1.** English: patronymic from the personal name mentioned at ALDER 2 or a variant of the topographic name ALDER. **2.** Dutch: patronymic from the personal name *Aldert* (see ALDERINK).

Alderson (2382) Northern English: patronymic from the personal name mentioned at ALDER 2.

Alderton (306) English: habitational name from any of a number of places called Alderton. Those in Suffolk and Shropshire (*Alretuna* in Domesday Book) are named in Old English as 'the settlement (Old English *tūn*) by the alders (Old English *alor*)'. Those in Gloucestershire, Northamptonshire, and Wiltshire are named as 'settlement associated with Ealdhere'. The one in Essex contains a different personal name, probably the woman's name Æðelwaru. In England, the surname is most common in East Anglia, making the places in Suffolk and Essex the most likely sources.

Aldi (122) Italian: patronymic from the personal name *Aldo*, a short form of various compound names of Germanic origin, formed with *alda* 'old', 'wise', for example *Aldobrando, Arnaldo, Rinaldo.*

GIVEN NAMES Italian 14%. *Angelo, Giovanni.*

Aldinger (560) German: habitational name for someone from Aldingen in Württemberg.

GIVEN NAMES German 6%. *Kurt* (3), *Erwin, Guenter, Helmut, Hermann, Milbert, Otto.*

Aldis (102) **1.** English (East Anglia): variant of ALDOUS. **2.** Possibly also Latvian: from the personal name *Aldonis.*

Aldous (390) English (chiefly East Anglia): from the Middle English female personal name *Aldus*, a pet form of any of the numerous Old English personal names formed with a first element *(e)ald* 'old'. FOREBEARS Nathan Aldis (originally Aldus) came from eastern England to Dedham, MA, in 1638.

Aldred (451) English: from the Middle English personal name *Aldred*, which represents a coalescence of two Old English personal names: *Ealdrǣd* 'ancient counsel' and *Æðelrǣd* (Ethelred) 'noble counsel'.

Aldredge (342) English: variant spelling of ALDRIDGE.

Aldrete (228) Spanish: variant of ALDERETE. GIVEN NAMES Spanish 43%. *Jose* (7), *Carlos* (2), *Enrique* (2), *Guadalupe* (2), *Juan* (2), *Manuel* (2), *Miguel* (2), *Rafael* (2), *Abiel, Agustin, Alberto, Alfonso.*

Aldrich (6915) English: from a Middle English personal name, *Ailric, Alrich, Aldrich*, etc. (Many different forms are recorded.) It represents the coalescence of at least two Old English personal names, *Ælfrīc* 'elf ruler' and *Æðelrīc* 'noble ruler'. FOREBEARS The earliest recorded bearer of this surname in North America is George Alrich, who came from Derbyshire to MA in 1631.

Aldridge (7759) English: **1.** variant of ALDRICH. **2.** habitational name from a place in the West Midlands called Aldridge; it is recorded in Domesday Book as *Alrewic*, from Old English *alor* 'alder' + *wīc* 'dwelling', 'farmstead'.

Ale (112) **1.** English: from the Middle English personal name *Ale*, a short form of any of the various personal names beginning with *Al-*. **2.** Dutch: unexplained. **3.** Estonian: unexplained. **4.** Italian (**Alé**): unexplained.

GIVEN NAMES Spanish 5%. *Carlos Enrique, Cesar, Jose, Maria De Jesus.*

Aleck (103) English: from a short form of the personal name ALEXANDER.

Alegre (248) Spanish and Portuguese: nickname from *alegre* 'bright', 'merry' (Latin *alacer*).

GIVEN NAMES Spanish 40%. *Jose* (4), *Angel* (2), *Jorge* (2), *Luis* (2), *Manuel* (2), *Marcos* (2), *Raul* (2), *Adriano, Alberto, Alejo, Alfonso, Ana; Leonardo, Lucio.*

Alegria (527) **1.** Spanish (**Alegría**) and Portuguese: nickname from Spanish *alegría* or Portuguese *alegria* 'joy', 'happiness'. **2.** Castilianized form of Basque **Alegia**, a habitational name from any of the towns named Alegia in the Basque Country.

GIVEN NAMES Spanish 45%. *Juan* (9), *Alfredo* (5), *Andres* (5), *Fernando* (5), *Carlos* (4), *Jose* (4), *Alfonso* (3), *Enrique* (3), *Felipe* (3), *Francisco* (3), *Guadalupe* (3), *Guillermo* (3).

Alejandre (228) Spanish: variant of ALEJANDRO.

GIVEN NAMES Spanish 60%. *Jose* (5), *Francisco* (4), *Jesus* (4), *Alfonso* (3), *Jorge* (3), *Juan* (3), *Luis* (3), *Miguel* (3), *Pedro* (3), *Salvador* (3), *Santiago* (3), *Alejandra* (2).

Alejandro (676) Spanish: from the personal name *Alejandro*, Spanish form of ALEXANDER.

GIVEN NAMES Spanish 47%. *Juan* (17), *Jose* (16), *Luis* (10), *Alfredo* (5), *Manuel* (5), *Miguel* (5), *Pablo* (5), *Angel* (4), *Armando* (4), *Felipe* (4), *Gerardo* (4), *Jesus* (4).

Alejo (376) Spanish: from the personal name *Alejo*, Spanish form of ALEXIS.

GIVEN NAMES Spanish 57%. *Jose* (11), *Juan* (9), *Enrique* (6), *Luis* (5), *Manuel* (4), *Mario* (4), *Alfonso* (3), *Alfredo* (3), *Francisco* (3), *Jesus* (3), *Jorge* (3), *Julio* (3); *Antonio* (2), *Lorenzo* (2), *Aureliano, Eliseo, Flavio, Marino, Primo, Romeo*.

Alejos (171) Spanish: variant of ALEJO.

GIVEN NAMES Spanish 49%. *Jose* (7), *Juan* (5), *Luis* (4), *Carlos* (3), *Guadalupe* (2), *Roberto* (2), *Abelardo, Agustin, Agustina, Alfonso, Alfredo, Ana*.

Aleman (2086) Spanish (**Alemán**): 1. ethnic name for a German, *alemán*. 2. from the old personal name *Alemannus*, with the same meaning.

GIVEN NAMES Spanish 47%. *Jose* (64), *Juan* (23), *Carlos* (21), *Francisco* (20), *Luis* (17), *Pedro* (16), *Jesus* (14), *Jorge* (14), *Miguel* (13), *Guillermo* (12), *Manuel* (12), *Julio* (11).

Alemany (108) Catalan: 1. ethnic name for a German, *alemany*. 2. from the old personal name *Alemannus*, with the same meaning.

GIVEN NAMES Spanish 42%. *Jose* (3), *Enrique* (2), *Joaquin* (2), *Juan* (2), *Luis* (2), *Modesto* (2), *Alberto, Alicia, Ampara, Ana, Armando, Domingo*.

Aleo (136) Italian (Sicily): habitational name from Alì (also known as *Aleo*) in Messina province, recorded in medieval Latin as *Aleum* (the place name being derived from Arabic *'ālī* 'high').

GIVEN NAMES Italian 16%. *Angelo* (3), *Salvatore* (3), *Antonio* (2), *Vito*.

Alers (111) 1. Of Hispanic origin: apparently a topographic name from Catalan *alers* 'larch'. However, this surname is not found in Spain. 2. Dutch: reduced form of ALDERS.

GIVEN NAMES Spanish 40%. *Juan* (3), *Carlos* (2), *Cesar* (2), *Luis* (2), *Alberto, Alejandro, Alfonso, Alfredo, Ana, Esteban, Fernando, Jaime*.

Ales (276) 1. Italian (Sicily): regional variant of ALESSI. 2. Czech (**Aleš**): from a short form of the personal names *Alexis, Albert, Albrecht*, or *Alexandr*. 3. Slovenian (**Aleš**): from the personal name *Aleš*, a derivative of Latin *Alexius* (see ALEXIS).

GIVEN NAMES Italian 7%. *Salvatore* (4), *Vito* (2), *Angelo, Calogero, Guiseppe, Pasquale, Sal*.

Aleshire (590) Probably an Americanized form of German **Alscher** or **Alischer**, derivatives of the female personal name *Adalheid*, from Old High German *adal* 'noble' + *heit* 'nature', 'quality'.

Alesi (266) Italian: variant of ALESSI.

GIVEN NAMES Italian 10%. *Bruna, Cosmo, Guido, Sal, Salvatore, Santina, Sarina*.

Alessandrini (194) Italian: from the personal name *Alessandrino*, a pet form of ALESSANDRO.

GIVEN NAMES Italian 18%. *Antonio* (2), *Enrico* (2), *Guido* (2), *Rocco* (2), *Aldo, Amedeo, Francesco, Ilio, Luciano, Mario, Ubaldo*.

Alessandro (297) Italian: from the personal name *Alessandro*, from classical Greek *Alexandros* (see ALEXANDER).

GIVEN NAMES Italian 26%. *Nicola* (3), *Biagio* (2), *Domenic* (2), *Natale* (2), *Rocco* (2), *Salvatore* (2), *Angelo, Antonio, Carlo, Carmello, Carmin, Enzo*.

Alessi (1216) Italian: patronymic or plural form of ALESSIO.

GIVEN NAMES Italian 14%. *Salvatore* (14), *Angelo* (8), *Mario* (5), *Sal* (4), *Antonio* (2), *Carmelo* (2), *Gasper* (2), *Santo* (2), *Aldo, Carlo, Carmel, Carmela*; *Liborio, Lino, Margarita, Mariana, Rosalia*.

Alessio (313) Italian: from the personal name *Alessio* (see ALEXIS).

GIVEN NAMES Italian 30%. *Reno* (4), *Lino* (3), *Mario* (3), *Pasquale* (2), *Romeo* (2), *Silvio* (2), *Angelo, Carmine, Concetta, Cono, Dino, Filomena, Francesco, Luigina, Ricardo, Rosalinda, Sergio*.

Alewine (543) English: variant of ALWINE.

Alex (1185) From a short form of ALEXIS or ALEXANDER in any of several languages.

Alexa (138) Czech and Slovak: from a short form of the personal name ALEXIS or ALEXANDER.

Alexander (63462) Scottish, English, German, Dutch; also found in many other cultures: from the personal name *Alexander*, classical Greek *Alexandros*, which probably originally meant 'repulser of men (i.e. of the enemy)', from *alexein* 'to repel' + *andros*, genitive of *anēr* 'man'. Its popularity in the Middle Ages was due mainly to the Macedonian conqueror, Alexander the Great (356–323 BC)—or rather to the hero of the mythical versions of his exploits that gained currency in the so-called Alexander Romances. The name was also borne by various early Christian saints, including a patriarch of Alexandria (AD *c*.250–326), whose main achievement was condemning the Arian heresy. The Gaelic form of the personal name is *Alasdair*, which has given rise to a number of Scottish and Irish patronymic surnames, for example MCALLISTER. *Alexander* is a common forename in Scotland, often representing an Anglicized form of the Gaelic name. In North America the form **Alexander** has absorbed many cases of cognate names from other languages, for example Spanish ALEJANDRO,

Italian ALESSANDRO, Greek **Alexandropoulos**, Russian **Aleksandr**, etc. (For forms, see Hanks and Hodges 1988.) It has also been adopted as a Jewish name.

FOREBEARS A number of Scotch-Irish families of this name landed at New York in the early 18th century. By 1746, six of them were established in NC. Others came in through Philadelphia, for example Archibald Alexander, who came from Londonderry in northern Ireland in 1736 and established himself in VA.

The Revolutionary general William Alexander (1726–83) was always known as 'Lord Sterling' to his compatriots, although his claim to the title was denied by the College of Arms in London. His father, James Alexander, was a Jacobite who had fled to New York after the failure of the Jacobite rising in 1715. The claim to the title arose in connection with their ancestor Sir William Alexander, a courtier and poet at the court of King James VI of Scotland (James I of England), who created him Earl of Stirling in 1633.

Alexandre (491) French and Portuguese: from the personal name *Alexandre* (see ALEXANDER).

GIVEN NAMES French 29%; Spanish 6%; Portuguese 5%. *Pierre* (6), *Michel* (4), *Jacques* (2), *Julien* (2), *Rodolphe* (2), *Andre, Cecile, Colette, Dominique, Eunide, Francoise, Georges*; *Jose* (3), *Fernando* (2), *Adela, Amandio, Amarante, Ana, Beatriz, Carlos, Claudio, Consuelo, Isidro, Joaquina*; *Joaquim* (2), *Aderito, Serafim*.

Alexanian (128) Armenian: patronymic from the personal name ALEXIS.

GIVEN NAMES Armenian 54%. *Nubar* (3), *Andranik* (2), *Berj* (2), *Hrach* (2), *Antranik, Aram, Armen, Aykanush, Bedros, Diran, Garnik, Goharik*.

Alexis (879) French: from the personal name *Alexis*, ultimately from Greek *alexios* 'helping', 'defending'. The personal name owed its popularity in the Middle Ages to St. Alexi(u)s, about whom many legends grew up. The historical St. Alexis is said to have lived in the 4th–5th centuries in Edessa (an early center of Christianity in Syria). His cult was also popular in the Eastern Church, which accounts for the frequency of the Russian personal name *Aleks(e)i*. In North America this surname has probably absorbed Russian and other cognates, mentioned in Hanks and Hodges (1988).

GIVEN NAMES French 15%. *Antoine* (2), *Cecile* (2), *Jacques* (2), *Pierre* (2), *Serge* (2), *Yves* (2), *Andre, Carolle, Ermite, Francois, Gabrielle, Geralde*.

Alexopoulos (152) Greek: from the personal name *Alexios* (see ALEXIS) + the patronymic ending *-poulos*. This ending occurs chiefly in the Peloponnese. It is derived from Latin *pullus* 'nestling', 'chick'.

GIVEN NAMES Greek 31%. *Spyros* (3), *Dimitrios* (2), *Athanasia, Christos, Constan-*

tinos, Costas, Eleni, Evangelos, Georgios, Panagiotis, Soterios, Spiros.

Alexson (113) Origin unidentified; most probably an Americanized form of a patronymic from a short form of the personal name ALEXANDER.

Alexy (158) German (of Slavic origin): from the vernacular Slavic name, variously spelled *Aleksy, Oleksy, Aleksi, Alexej,* etc., of the Latin personal name *Alexius* (see ALEXIS).

GIVEN NAMES German 5%. *Franz, Kurt.*

Aley (254) English (Essex): probably a variant of ALLEY.

Alf (223) **1.** North German: from a reduced form of ADOLF. **2.** Scandinavian: from the personal name *Alf,* a short form of any of several personal names formed with *alf* 'elf' as the first element.

Alfano (1644) Italian: habitational name from Alfano in Salerno province, Campania, a name of disputed etymology.

GIVEN NAMES Italian 16%. *Salvatore* (16), *Angelo* (7), *Vito* (6), *Pasquale* (5), *Carmine* (4), *Domenic* (4), *Luigi* (4), *Sal* (3), *Antonio* (2), *Franco* (2), *Rocco* (2), *Vincenzo* (2).

Alfaro (2472) Spanish: habitational name from a place in Logroño province named Alfaro, apparently from Arabic *al* 'the' + Old Spanish *faro* 'beacon', 'lighthouse'.

GIVEN NAMES Spanish 52%. *Jose* (96), *Carlos* (34), *Juan* (30), *Mario* (26), *Miguel* (26), *Manuel* (24), *Francisco* (21), *Luis* (17), *Pedro* (16), *Rafael* (16), *Jorge* (15), *Ricardo* (14).

Alff (104) Variant spelling of North German **Alf,** a reduced form of the personal name ADOLF.

Alfieri (824) Italian (Sicily): status name for a standard bearer, Sicilian *alfiere,* from Spanish *alférez.*

GIVEN NAMES Italian 21%. *Angelo* (5), *Antonio* (5), *Mario* (4), *Pietro* (3), *Salvatore* (3), *Carmine* (2), *Mauro* (2), *Paolo* (2), *Sal* (2), *Alessandra, Aniello, Bruna, Carlo, Serafina, Theodoro, Tino.*

Alfonsi (151) Southern Italian: patronymic or plural form of ALFONSO.

GIVEN NAMES Italian 16%. *Ferdinando* (2), *Antonio, Benigno, Cesare, Elisabetta, Giuseppe, Italo, Marco, Mario, Mirella, Silvio, Tiberio.*

Alfonso (2067) Spanish and southern Italian: from the personal name *Alfonso,* the name of a number of Spanish and Portuguese kings. It derives from the Visigothic personal name *Adelfonsus,* composed of the elements *hathu* 'war' + *funs* 'ready'.

GIVEN NAMES Spanish 43%; Italian 4%. *Jose* (54), *Juan* (24), *Manuel* (23), *Mario* (21), *Carlos* (18), *Jorge* (16), *Pedro* (15), *Ramon* (15), *Luis* (14), *Rafael* (13), *Jesus* (12), *Gustavo* (11); *Antonio* (12), *Salvatore* (4), *Elio* (3), *Heriberto* (2), *Leonardo* (2), *Lorenzo* (2), *Aldo, Angelo, Annamaria, Antonino, Carmelo, Carmine.*

Alford (10195) English and Scottish: habitational name from any of various places called Alford, for example in Somerset and Aberdeenshire. The first is named with the Old English female personal name *Ealdgyð* + *ford* 'ford'. See also ALVORD.

Alfred (1387) English: from the Middle English personal name *Alvred,* Old English *Ælfrǣd* 'elf counsel'. This owed its popularity as a personal name in England chiefly to the fame of the West Saxon king Alfred the Great (849–899), who defeated the Danes, keeping them out of Wessex, and whose court was a great center of learning and culture.

GIVEN NAMES French 5%. *Andre, Arianne, Armand, Camille, Curley, Germine, Jacques, Jean-Claude, Magalie, Marcel, Michel, Patrice.*

Alfredson (159) Americanized spelling of Swedish **Alfredsson** or Danish and Norwegian **Alfredsen,** patronymics from the personal name ALFRED.

GIVEN NAMES Scandinavian 13%; German 7%. *Nels* (2), *Agnar, Iver, Knute; Kurt.*

Alfrey (424) English: from any of a group of Middle English personal names, *Alfrey, Aufrey,* and *Alfreth,* the origins of which are confused. They almost certainly include some cases of ALFRED, but other Old English names may have contributed too, in particular *Æðelfrið* 'noble peace' and *Ælfric* (see AUBREY).

Alfson (160) Scandinavian: patronymic from the personal name ALF.

Algarin (175) Spanish (**Algarín**): probably a habitational name, from a lost or unidentified place.

GIVEN NAMES Spanish 41%. *Carlos* (4), *Juan* (4), *Nilsa* (2), *Rafael* (2), *Ana Maria, Angel, Aracely, Cruz, Efrain, Emilio, Erasmo, Esmeralda.*

Algee (96) Scottish and northern Irish: variant of ALGEO.

Algeo (210) Scottish: of obscure origin. This name was established at Inchinnan, near Renfrew, from the 16th century onward. A history of Renfrew cited by Black affirms that the family was "of Italian origin, the first of them having come from Rome in the suite of one of the abbots of Paisley." This appears to be no more than speculation based on the fact that the name ends in *-o.* No Italian source has been identified, and *-o* is regularly found as a ending of pet forms in Scottish. It is more likely to be a pet form of the Middle English personal names *Algernon* or *Algar* (see ALGER).

Alger (2261) **1.** English: from one or more Middle English personal names variously written *Alger, Algar, Alcher, Aucher,* etc. These represent a falling together of at least three different Continental Germanic and Old English names: *Adalgar* 'noble spear' (Old English *Æðelgār*), *Albgar* 'elf spear' (Old English *Ælfgār*), and *Aldgar* 'old spear' (Old English *(E)aldgār*). The

Continental Germanic forms were brought to England from France by the Normans. Compare the French cognate AUGER. In Norfolk and northern England, the source is probably the Old Norse name *Álfgeirr* 'elf spear'. The modern English surname is found mainly in East Anglia. **2.** German: from a reduced form of the Germanic personal name *Adalgar* (see 1 above).

FOREBEARS Abiezer Alger was a merchant in Easton, MA, in the 18th century, who had many prominent descendants.

Algiere (108) Italian (mainly Sicily): from a Germanic personal name, *Adalgari,* composed of elements meaning 'noble' and 'spear'.

GIVEN NAMES Italian 13%. *Angelo* (2), *Carmela, Domenica, Natale, Santo.*

Algood (112) English: variant spelling of ALLGOOD.

Alguire (194) Probably an Americanized spelling of German ALLGEIER.

Alhadeff (135) Jewish (Sephardic): from Arabic *al-ḥaddāf* 'the weaver's shuttle'.

GIVEN NAMES Jewish 7%; Italian 4%. *Ari, Nissim; Salvatore* (3).

Ali (5756) Muslim (widespread throughout the Muslim world): from the Arabic personal name *'Ālī* 'high', 'lofty', 'sublime'. *Al-'Ālī* 'the All-High' is an attribute of Allah. *'Abdul-'Ālī* means 'servant of the All-High'. *'Ālī ibn Abī Ṭālib* (*c.* 600–661), the cousin and son-in-law of the Prophet Muhammad, was the fourth and last of the 'rightly guided' khalifs (ruled 656–61) and the first imam of the Shiite Muslims. His assassination led to the appearance of the Shiite sect.

GIVEN NAMES Muslim 78%. *Syed* (227), *Mohammed* (110), *Mohammad* (70), *Ahmed* (53), *Mohamed* (51), *Abdul* (36), *Hassan* (32), *Shaukat* (32), *Ali* (29), *Muhammad* (28), *Ahmad* (23), *Akbar* (22).

Alia (104) Southern Italian (Sicily and Calabria): variant of ELIA.

GIVEN NAMES Italian 22%. *Salvatore* (2), *Carmine, Giacomo, Rocco.*

Aliaga (126) Basque: topographic name, probably formed with Basque *ali* 'food' + the locative suffix *-aga.*

GIVEN NAMES Spanish 45%. *Juan* (4), *Humberto* (2), *Jorge* (2), *Luis* (2), *Manuel* (2), *Raul* (2), *Aida, Alfredo, Arturo, Bernarda, Carlos, Cesar.*

Aliano (176) Southern Italian: habitational name from a place named Aliano, in Matera province, Basilicata.

GIVEN NAMES Italian 12%. *Angelo, Carmelo, Carmine, Paolo, Pasquale, Santo.*

Aliberti (230) Italian: patronymic from the Germanic personal name *Aliberto* (see ALBERT).

GIVEN NAMES Italian 34%. *Rocco* (9), *Angelo* (2), *Giovanni* (2), *Luigi* (2), *Salvatore* (2), *Vito* (2), *Aniello, Antonio, Carmelo, Concetta, Corrado, Dino.*

Alice (114) **1.** French Canadian: altered form of ALIX. **2.** Hispanic: variant of ALICEA. For the etymology, compare English ALLIS.

GIVEN NAMES German 6%. *Gerhart, Theodor*.

Alicea (1190) Hispanic: metronymic from the female personal name *Alicia*. Compare English ALLIS.

GIVEN NAMES Spanish 41%. *Jose* (44), *Angel* (28), *Juan* (17), *Luis* (13), *Pedro* (11), *Julio* (10), *Rafael* (8), *Francisco* (6), *Ana* (5), *Jesus* (5), *Luz* (5), *Margarita* (5); *Antonio* (6), *Carmelo* (3), *Angelo* (2), *Cecilio* (2), *Heriberto* (2), *Leonardo* (2), *Carlo, Carmela, Gasper, Nino*.

Aliff (458) English: variant of **Ayliff(e)**, which is from a Middle English personal name. In most cases, this is Old Norse *Eilífr* 'eternal life', but it could also have absorbed the female name *Ayleve* (Old English *Æðelgifu* 'noble gift'). It could also have absorbed a truncated form of Irish McAULIFFE.

Alig (267) German: from a pet form of any of the many Germanic personal names formed with *adal* 'noble'.

Alioto (389) Italian (Sicily): habitational name for someone from Alì in Messina province. See also ALEO.

GIVEN NAMES Italian 30%. *Angelo* (6), *Mario* (5), *Salvatore* (5), *Gaetano* (3), *Nunzio* (3), *Santo* (3), *Angelina* (2), *Carlo* (2), *Sal* (2), *Antonio, Cosimo, Domenico, Giovanna, Guiseppe*.

Aliotta (99) Southern Italian: from a pet form of the personal name *Alìa*, a variant of ELIA.

GIVEN NAMES Italian 26%. *Salvatore* (3), *Antonino, Francesco, Gaetano, Giuseppe, Paolino*.

Alire (171) Spanish (mainly Mexico): variant of Spanish **Aliri**, a topographic name from Basque *al(h)a* 'pasture' + *iri* 'near'.

GIVEN NAMES Spanish 18%. *Juanita* (3), *Edmundo* (2), *Altagracia, Andres, Elva, Hipolito, Jorge, Manuel, Orlando, Preciliano, Ramon, Vicente*.

Alison (246) English and Scottish: variant spelling of ALLISON.

Alix (382) **1.** French: from the Old French female personal name *Alix* or *Alis*, short form of the Germanic personal name *Adalhaidis* (see ALLIS). **2.** from a short form of ALEXANDER.

GIVEN NAMES French 10%. *Pierre* (4), *Normand* (2), *Emile, Francoise, Gilles, Jean-Guy, Laurier, Marcel*.

Alkema (152) Dutch: habitational name from the city of Alkemade (Alkmaar) in South Holland.

Alker (116) South German: variant of ALGER.

GIVEN NAMES German 7%. *Frieda, Gerhart*.

Alkins (101) English: probably a patronymic from a personal name, *Alkin*, a pet form

of the personal names *Alan* (see ALLEN) or ALEXANDER.

Alkire (1011) Americanized form of German ALLGEIER.

All (312) **1.** English and Scottish: of uncertain origin; in part it may be a shortened form of McCALL. **2.** Probably also an Americanized spelling of AHL or AL.

Allain (754) French form of ALLEN. This is a common spelling of the surname, although the normal spelling of the French personal name is *Alain*.

GIVEN NAMES French 10%. *Andre* (3), *Jean-Paul* (2), *Adelard, Alban, Albenie, Alphonse, Andree, Cyrille, Donat, Emile, Euclide, Francois*.

Allaire (740) French: from an Old French personal name, a variant of *Hilaire* (see HILLARY).

FOREBEARS An Allaire from Poitou, France, is recorded in Quebec city in 1662. Alexandre Allaire, a Huguenot refugee, brought the name to New Rochelle, NY, in 1680.

GIVEN NAMES French 10%. *Normand* (4), *Andre* (3), *Lucien* (2), *Alphonse, Antoine, Armand, Emile, Michel, Pierre, Raoul, Raymonde, Rolande*.

Allam (140) **1.** English: variant spelling of ALLUM. **2.** Muslim: variant spelling of ALAM.

GIVEN NAMES Muslim 23%. *Mohamed* (3), *Abdo, Ahmed, Ali, Amani, Ashraf, Azmy, Elsayed, Faysal, Hamdy, Mahmoud, Mamdouh*.

Allaman (111) Swiss German (**Allamann**): see ALLEMAN 2.

Allan (4198) Scottish and northern English: variant spelling of ALLEN. This is the more common spelling of the name in Scotland and northern England; in Scotland it is often found as an English form of the Gaelic name **McAllan** (see McALLEN).

FOREBEARS One early bearer of this name in North America was William Allan, a British soldier who took his family to the newly founded city of Halifax, Nova Scotia, in 1749. His son John (1746–1805) was a Revolutionary soldier who eventually (1783) founded the settlement of Allan's Island, Passamaquoddy Bay, ME.

Allanson (131) English: variant spelling of ALLINSON.

Allar (181) Americanized spelling of French ALLARD, reflecting the French pronunciation.

Allard (3841) French and English: from the Old French, Norman, and Middle English personal name *A(i)llard*. This is of Germanic origin, being found in the continental form *Adelard* and in Old English as *Æðelheard*, both meaning 'noble hardy'.

FOREBEARS An Allard from Rouen, France, is documented in Quebec city in 1671.

GIVEN NAMES French 8%. *Gilles* (7), *Andre* (5), *Emile* (5), *Normand* (5), *Marcel* (4),

Alain (3), *Armand* (3), *Gaston* (3), *Pierre* (3), *Antoine* (2), *Benoit* (2), *Fernand* (2).

Allaway (142) Variant spelling of English ALLOWAY or Americanized form of any of the French names mentioned there.

Allbaugh (202) Americanized form of German ALBACH.

Allbee (422) See ALBEE.

Allbright (536) Variant spelling of ALBRIGHT.

Allbritten (140) Variant of English **Al(l)-brighton** (see ALBRITTON).

Allbritton (725) Variant of English **Al(l)-brighton** (see ALBRITTON).

Allcock (144) English: variant spelling of ALCOCK.

Allcorn (256) English: habitational name from a lost place in East Sussex, Alchehorne in the parish of Buxted, which was last recorded in 1592.

Allday (204) **1.** English: from a Middle English personal name, *Alday*, which is either a survival of an unrecorded Old English personal name *Æðeldæg* or from a cognate continental form, *Aildag*, imported to England from France by the Normans. The ultimate etymology in both cases is Germanic *adal* 'noble' + *dag* 'day'. **2.** Americanized form of German ALDAG.

Alldredge (830) Variant spelling of English ALDRIDGE.

Allebach (192) Variant of German ALBACH.

Allee (867) **1.** English: variant spelling of ALLEY. **2.** Muslim: variant spelling of ALI.

Allegra (196) Italian: from the feminine form of ALLEGRO.

GIVEN NAMES Italian 20%. *Manlio* (2), *Salvatore* (2), *Alfio, Carmelo, Marcello, Mario, Marisa, Sal, Santo*.

Allegretti (279) Italian: patronymic or plural form of ALLEGRETTO.

GIVEN NAMES Italian 10%. *Cosmo* (2), *Rocco* (2), *Vito* (2), *Carmello, Enzo, Francesca, Geno, Silvio*.

Allegretto (147) Italian: from a diminutive of the nickname or personal name ALLEGRO.

GIVEN NAMES Italian 9%. *Angelo* (3), *Vito*.

Allegro (169) Italian: nickname from *allegro* 'quick', 'lively', 'cheerful', which was also used as a personal name in the Middle Ages.

GIVEN NAMES Italian 12%. *Carlo* (2), *Carmine, Cataldo*.

Alleman (1593) **1.** French: from Old French *Aleman* 'German' (Late Latin *Alemannus*, from a Germanic tribal name, probably meaning 'all the men'), hence a regional or ethnic name for a German-speaker in a predominantly French-speaking area. Compare ALLMAN. **2.** German (**Allemann**): from a Germanic personal name composed of the elements *adal* 'noble' + *man* 'man'.

GIVEN NAMES French 4%. *Alcide* (2), *Emile* (2), *Ulysse* (2), *Andre, Armande, Clovis, Colette, Desire, Easton, Monique, Oneil, Ovide*.

Allemand (359) French: variant of ALLE-MAN, conforming to the usual modern spelling of the vocabulary word meaning 'German', with its non-etymological *-d*.
FOREBEARS An Allemand from La Rochelle, France is recorded in Quebec city in 1685.
GIVEN NAMES French 7%. *Adrien, Alcee, Alphonse, Andre, Curley, Raoul, Vernice.*

Allemang (122) Variant of French ALLE-MAN.

Allen (158845) English and Scottish: from a Celtic personal name of great antiquity and obscurity. In England the personal name is now usually spelled *Alan*, the surname *Allen*; in Scotland the surname is more often *Allan*. Various suggestions have been put forward regarding its origin; the most plausible is that it originally meant 'little rock'. Compare Gaelic *ailín*, diminutive of *ail* 'rock'. The present-day frequency of the surname Allen in England and Ireland is partly accounted for by the popularity of the personal name among Breton followers of William the Conqueror, by whom it was imported first to Britain and then to Ireland. St. Alan(us) was a 5th-century bishop of Quimper, who was a cult figure in medieval Brittany. Another St. Al(l)an was a Cornish or Breton saint of the 6th century, to whom a church in Cornwall is dedicated.
FOREBEARS This name was brought to North America from different parts of the British Isles independently by many bearers in the 17th and 18th centuries. Prominent early bearers include Samuel Allen, who settled in Braintree, MA, about 1629 (died 1648 in Windsor, CT) and whose descendants included Ethan Allen (1737–89), leader of the Green Mountain Boys in VT during the Revolution; and William Allen (died 1725), from Dungannon, Ireland, an early Presbyterian settler in Philadelphia, whose descendants include William Allen (1803–79), governor of OH.

Allenbach (106) German and Swiss German: habitational name from any of several places called Allenbach.

Allenbaugh (259) Americanized form of ALLENBACH.

Allende (213) Spanish: from *allende* 'on the other side', hence a topographic name for someone living on the far side of some natural landmark, such as a mountain.
GIVEN NAMES Spanish 48%. *Juan* (4), *Manuel* (4), *Rafael* (4), *Alberto* (3), *Jorge* (3), *Luis* (3), *Pedro* (3), *Vicente* (3), *Angel* (2), *Gabriela* (2), *Jesus* (2), *Jose* (2).

Allender (745) **1.** English, Scottish, and northern French: unexplained. **2.** Swedish: variant of ALLINDER.

Allendorf (164) German: habitational name from any of ten or more places called Allendorf.

Allenson (100) English: variant spelling of ALLINSON.
GIVEN NAME German 6%. *Otto* (2).

Allensworth (446) Probably English or Scottish, but of unexplained origin. This has the form of an English habitational name, but no such place is known in England or Scotland, and the surname is not found in present-day British records.
FOREBEARS Philip Allensworth is recorded in VA in the 1770s.

Aller (572) German: variant of AHLER.

Allers (303) German: variant of AHLERS.

Allert (174) German: variant of AHLERT.
GIVEN NAMES German 12%. *Fritz* (2), *Beate, Johann, Johannes, Kurt, Lothar.*

Allerton (231) English: habitational name from any of several places so called. Allerton on Merseyside, Chapel Allerton in West Yorkshire, and others in West Yorkshire were named in Old English as *alra tūn* 'settlement by the alders'. One in Somerset (*Alwarditone* in Domesday Book) is 'Ælfweard's settlement'; one in West Yorkshire (Allerton Mauleverer, *Alvertone* in Domesday Book) is 'Ælfhere's settlement'.
FOREBEARS Isaac Allerton (?1586–1658) was among the Pilgrim Fathers who sailed on the *Mayflower* in 1620. His descendants included Samuel Allerton (1828–1914), one of the founders of modern Chicago.

Alles (498) **1.** Dutch and North German: patronymic from the Low German personal name *Aldert* (see ALDERINK) or Frisian *Allo*, a variant of *Adalo*, from Germanic *adal* 'noble'. **2.** English: variant spelling of ALLIS.

Alleva (258) Italian (Lombardy): from a personal name, a short form of the omen name *Diotalleva*, from the phrase *Dio t'alleva* '(may) God help you'.
GIVEN NAMES Italian 13%. *Carmine* (2), *Aldo, Annamarie, Ercole, Gino, Guido, Remo, Rocco, Salvatore.*

Alley (5302) **1.** English: from a Middle English personal name, *Alli, Alleye*, as forms such as *Johannes filius Alli* (Norfolk, 1205) make clear. This is of Scandinavian origin, cognate with Old Danish *Alli*, Old Swedish *Alle*. **2.** Americanized form of French **Hallé** (see HALLEY).

Alleyne (740) English: old spelling of ALLEN, already well established as a surname in England in Tudor times.
GIVEN NAMES French 5%. *Andre* (2), *Camille, Chantal, Julien, Marcell.*

Allford (103) English: variant spelling of ALFORD.

Allgaier (288) German: variant of **Allgäuer** (see ALLGEIER).
GIVEN NAMES German 4%. *Gertraud, Kurt, Leonhard.*

Allgeier (421) German: variant of **Allgäuer**, a regional name for someone from the Allgäu, a district of southern Bavaria, named with Old High German *alb* 'mountain pasture' + *gouw* 'area', 'region'.

Allgeyer (140) German: variant spelling of ALLGEIER.

Allgire (123) Americanized form of German ALLGEIER.

Allgood (1861) English: from the Middle English personal name *Algod, Alegod, Halgod*, of Scandinavian origin. Compare Old Danish *Algot*, from an unattested *Alf-gautr* 'elf Goth' or *Aðal-gautr* 'noble Goth'.

Alli (252) Muslim: variant spelling of ALI.
GIVEN NAMES Muslim 47%. *Mohamed* (11), *Bibi* (10), *Ashraf* (3), *Imran* (3), *Mohamad* (3), *Hassan* (2), *Mohammad* (2), *Rahman* (2), *Abas, Abid, Ahmad, Alim.*

Allie (543) English and French: variant spelling of ALLEY.
GIVEN NAMES French 4%. *Felicien, Fernand, Henri, Yvan.*

Alligood (695) English: variant of ALL-GOOD.

Allin (390) **1.** English (Devon): either a variant spelling of ALLEN or from a derivative of the Norman female name *Adelina*, based on Germanic *adal* 'noble'. **2.** Swedish: variant spelling of AHLIN.

Allinder (209) Swedish: from *al* 'alder' + the common surname suffix *-inder* (probably taken from Greek *andros*, genitive of *anēr* 'man').

Alling (444) **1.** English: variant of ALLEN. **2.** German: habitational name from either of two places called Alling, one in Bavaria and one in Austria. **3.** Danish: habitational name from any of several places called Alling. The etymology of the place name is uncertain; it may be a derivative of *al* 'alder'.
FOREBEARS Roger Alling signed the New Haven, CT, Compact in 1639.

Allinger (175) German: habitational name for someone from a place called Alling (see ALLING).

Allingham (138) English: habitational name from Alvingham in Lincolnshire, named in Old English as *Aluingeham* 'homestead (Old English *hām*) of the family or followers of Ælf(a)'. Reaney also mentions a lost place called Allingham in Kent as a possible source; this is perhaps the same as one of the two places in Kent called ALLINGTON.

Allington (303) Southern English: habitational name from any of at least nine different places called Allington, two in Kent, three in Wiltshire, and one each in Dorset, Devon, Hampshire, and Lincolnshire. These have different origins: those in Devon, Wiltshire near Chippenham, and Kent near Maidstone are from the Old English personal name *Ælla* + *-ing-*, implying association, + *tūn* 'settlement'; those in Dorset, Wiltshire near Devizes, and Lincolnshire are named with Old English *ætheling* 'atheling (prince)' + *tūn*; those in Hampshire and Wiltshire near Amesbury are from the Old English personal name *Ealda* + *tūn*; and the one in Kent near

Lenham is from the Old English personal name *Æþelnōþ* + -*ing-* + *tūn*.

Allinson (257) English (chiefly Yorkshire): patronymic from the personal name ALLEN.

Allio (136) Southern Italian: from the Old Tuscan personal name *Allius*, from Latin *allium* 'garlic'.

GIVEN NAMES French 6%; Italian 4%. *Camille* (2); *Remo* (2), *Angelo*.

Allis (536) English: from the Middle English and Old French female personal name *Alis* (*Alice*), which, together with its diminutive *Alison*, was extremely popular in England in the Middle Ages. The personal name is of Germanic origin, brought to England from France by the Normans; it is a contracted form of Germanic *Adalhaid(is)*, which is composed of the elements *adal* 'noble' + *haid* 'brilliance', 'beauty'.

Allison (19032) English and Scottish: patronymic from a Middle English male personal name: in most cases probably ALLEN, but other possibilities include a variant of ELLIS or a short form of ALEXANDER. In some instances, it may be from a female personal name, *Alise* or *Alice* (see ALLIS).

Alliston (162) English: unexplained; it appears to be a variant of **Allerston**, a habitational name from a place so named in North Yorkshire, but the concentration of the name in Essex and adjoining counties suggests a different source may be involved.

Allman (2978) **1.** English (frequent in eastern England): ethnic name from Norman French *aleman* 'German' or *alemayne* 'Germany' (Late Latin *Alemannus* and *Alemannia*, from a Germanic tribal name that probably originally meant 'all the men'). In some cases the surname may be from the region of Normandy known as Allemagne (south of Caen), probably named as a Germanic-speaking enclave in a Celtic area in Roman times. In North America, the form **Allman** has probably absorbed some cases of cognates from other languages, in particular Spanish ALEMAN and French ALLEMAN. **2.** German (**Allmann**): variant of **Allemann** (see ALLEMAN) or in some cases probably an Americanized form of the same name.

Allmand (106) English: variant of ALLMAN.

Allmaras (118) Variant of French **Almeras**, a topographic name for someone who lived by a prominent elm tree, *olmeras*. The surname is recorded in French-speaking Switzerland and was probably brought to the U.S. from there.

GIVEN NAMES German 7%; French 6%. *Alfons* (2); *Clemence*, *Susette*.

Allmendinger (196) Southwestern German and Swiss German: habitational name for someone from either of two places called Allmending, in Württemberg and Switzerland. The place name is derived from *Allmende* 'common land', 'common pasture', Middle High German *al(ge)meinde* '(that which is) common to all'.

GIVEN NAMES German 9%. *Otto* (2), *Klaus*, *Kurt*.

Allmon (968) Variant spelling of English ALLMAN.

Allmond (442) **1.** English: variant of ALLMAN. **2.** Perhaps also a variant of German **Allmann** (see ALLMAN).

Allnutt (224) English: from the Middle English personal name *Alnoth*, Old English *Æðelnōð* 'noble daring'.

Allocca (190) Italian: from the feminine form of ALLOCCO.

GIVEN NAMES Italian 14%. *Antonio* (2), *Angelo*, *Antimo*, *Carmine*, *Giacomo*, *Luigi*, *Saverio*.

Allocco (217) Southern Italian: nickname from *allocco* 'dunce', 'fool' (feminine *allocca*). This word is of obscure origin; it may be from Arabic *alwaq* (feminine *lawqa*, dialectally *lōqa*), which supposedly means 'foolish', 'crazy'. Compare Spanish *loco* 'crazy'. In Egyptian Arabic the word means 'having a speech defect in pronouncing the letter *r*'.

GIVEN NAMES Italian 15%. *Sal* (3), *Salvatore* (2), *Carmela*, *Ciro*, *Saverio*.

Allor (210) Common Canadian spelling of the French surname ALLARD, reflecting the French pronunciation.

Allore (112) Canadian French: variant of ALLOR.

Alloway (659) **1.** English: from the Middle English personal name *Ailwi*, which represents a falling together of several Old English names: *Æðelwīg* 'noble battle', *Ealdwīg* 'ancient battle', and *Ælfwīg* 'elf battle'. Compare ALVEY. Alloway is a Scottish place name, but the surname is of English rather than Scottish origin. **2.** Americanized form of any of several French surnames, including **Allouis** (from a place in Meung-sur-Yèvre), **Halloy** (from any of various places in Oise, Pas-de-Calais, and Somme), or **Allouet** (a diminutive of **Allou** or **Alleu**, which was a status name for a free tenant, one not bound by feudal dues).

Alloy (128) Probably an Americanized spelling of any of the French names mentioned at ALLOWAY.

Allphin (272) See ALPHIN.

Allport (211) English: habitational name from places in Derbyshire and Shropshire named Alport, from Old English *ealda* 'old' + *port* 'town'.

Allread (119) English: variant of ALLRED.

Allred (5934) English: **1.** from the Middle English personal name *Alured*, a form of ALFRED, which was sometimes written *Alvred*, especially in Old French texts. The *v* was misread as a vowel, since *v* and *u* were written identically and not regarded as distinct letters. **2.** from the Middle English personal name *Alrit*, a variant of ALDRED.

Alls (314) English or Irish: unexplained; perhaps a variant of ALL or a reduced form of ALLIS.

Allsbrook (196) English: variant of ALSOBROOK.

Allshouse (572) Americanized form of German **Alteshaus** (see ALTHAUS).

Allsop (336) English: variant spelling of ALSOP.

Allsopp (191) English: variant spelling of ALSOP.

Allston (139) English: variant spelling of ALSTON.

GIVEN NAME French 5%. *Pierre*.

Allsup (552) English: variant spelling of ALSOP.

Allton (166) English: variant spelling of ALTON.

Alltop (155) **1.** English: variant of **Althorp**, a habitational name from Althorpe in Lincolnshire or Althorp in Northamptonshire. **2.** Possibly also an Americanized form of German ALTHOFF 'old farm'.

FOREBEARS Thomas Altop was transported from London to VA aboard the *Thornton* in 1772. This surname is recorded in the tax records of Harrison County, VA, in 1802.

Allum (170) **1.** English: habitational name from any of various places: Alham in Somerset, which is named for the Alham river on which it stands (a Celtic river name of uncertain meaning), or Alnham in Northumberland, named for the Aln river on which it stands (also of Celtic origin but uncertain meaning), or a regional name from Hallamshire, the district around Sheffield in South Yorkshire, which is named with Old Norse *hallr* or Old English *hall* in a dative plural form, *hallum* '(place at) the rocks'. **2.** Scottish: shortened form of MCCALLUM, an Anglicized form of Gaelic **Mac Coluim** 'son of *Colum*'. **3.** Norwegian: habitational name from any of various farmsteads in southeastern Norway, probably named from Old Norse *Aldheimar*, a compound of *ald* 'high' + *heimar* 'farm'.

Allums (384) English: variant of ALLUM.

Allwardt (117) Variant spelling of German ALWARDT.

Allwein (159) South German: from the personal name *Alwin*, *Adelwin*, from Germanic *adal* 'noble' + *win* 'friend'.

Allwine (114) Americanized form of German ALLWEIN.

Allwood (156) English: variant of ELLWOOD.

Ally (229) **1.** Muslim: variant spelling of ALI. **2.** English and French: variant spelling of ALLEY.

GIVEN NAMES Muslim 53%. *Mohamed* (5), *Syed* (3), *Abdul* (2), *Akbar* (2), *Asgar* (2), *Bibi* (2), *Hussain* (2), *Mohamad* (2), *Mohammed* (2), *Subhan* (2), *Abul*, *Ahamad*.

Allyn (781) English: variant of ALLEN, established in New England in the 17th century.

FOREBEARS Matthew Allyn was one of the founders of Hartford, CT, (coming from

Cambridge, MA, with Thomas Hooker) in 1635.

Alm (890) **1.** Swedish and Danish: ornamental or topographic name from *alm* 'elm'. **2.** Norwegian: habitational name from any of various farmsteads in southeastern Norway named with *alm* 'elm'. **3.** North German: from a medieval personal name, a reduced form of the Germanic name *Adalhelm* 'noble helmet'.
GIVEN NAMES Scandinavian 5%. *Arlys, Erik, Kerstin, Lars, Mauritz, Nels.*

Alma (103) **1.** Italian (Sicily): from the female personal name *Alma*, from Latin *almus* 'nourishing'. **2.** Spanish: from *alma* 'soul' (Latin *anima*). See also ALMAS.
GIVEN NAMES Spanish 14%; Dutch 5%; Italian 5%. *Armando, Efrain, Faustino, Hipolito, Javier, Jorge, Jose, Lopez, Nilda; Willem* (2); *Salvatore* (2).

Almada (191) Portuguese: habitational name from a place near Lisbon named Almada, from *almádena* 'ore mine' (from Arabic *al-ma'āden*).
GIVEN NAMES Spanish 39%. *Carlos* (6), *Manuel* (6), *Jorge* (3), *Jose* (3), *Raul* (3), *Jesus* (2), *Ricardo* (2), *Armindo, Eduardo, Emilio, Enrique, Ernesto.*

Almaguer (548) Catalan: habitational name from a place in Valencia named Almaguer.
GIVEN NAMES Spanish 49%. *Jose* (15), *Juan* (11), *Francisco* (7), *Jesus* (7), *Manuel* (6), *Javier* (5), *Miguel* (5), *Carlos* (4), *Eduardo* (4), *Raul* (4), *Alejandro* (3), *Armando* (3).

Alman (336) **1.** English: variant spelling of ALLMAN. **2.** Swedish: variant spelling of AHLMAN. **3.** German: variant spelling of Ahl(e)mann (see AHLMAN). **4.** Jewish (Ashkenazic): variant spelling of ALMEN 'widower'.
GIVEN NAMES Jewish 6%. *Sol* (3), *Ber, Ilya, Nurith.*

Almand (479) Variant of English ALLMAN, also of French ALLEMAND, both meaning 'German'.

Almanza (1079) Spanish: habitational name from a place in León province named Almanza.
GIVEN NAMES Spanish 47%. *Jose* (30), *Juan* (19), *Manuel* (14), *Miguel* (12), *Jesus* (10), *Alfredo* (7), *Francisco* (7), *Guadalupe* (7), *Jose Luis* (7), *Ruben* (7), *Salvador* (7), *Sergio* (7).

Almanzar (268) Spanish: habitational name from some minor place named with Arabic *al-manẓar* 'the lookout point' or 'the watchtower'.
GIVEN NAMES Spanish 53%. *Jose* (13), *Ana* (6), *Juan* (5), *Rafael* (5), *Ramon* (4), *Altagracia* (3), *Amado* (3), *Dionicio* (3), *Enrique* (3), *Miguel* (3), *Milagros* (3), *Juana* (2).

Almaraz (588) Spanish: habitational name from places in Zamora, Cáceres, and Vallodolid provinces. According to Asín Palacios, these names are derived from Arabic *al-maḥrath* 'the cultivated or arable

land'; another possible origin would be *al-maḥras* 'the guarded or fortified place', 'the sanctuary'.
GIVEN NAMES Spanish 49%. *Jose* (15), *Juan* (11), *Carlos* (8), *Francisco* (6), *Manuel* (5), *Alfredo* (4), *Jesus* (4), *Lupe* (4), *Pedro* (4), *Alberto* (3), *Armando* (3), *Jaime* (3); *Antonio* (5), *Marco* (2), *Sal* (2), *Cecilio, Cesario, Julieta, Leonardo, Mauro.*

Almas (172) **1.** Spanish and Portuguese: from the plural of *alma* 'soul'. **2.** Hungarian (**Almás**): from *alma* 'apple', hence an occupational name for a producer or seller of apples. Probably also a topographic name for someone who lived by an apple orchard.

Almasi (100) **1.** Arabic: from the adjective *almāsi* 'diamond-like'. **2.** Hungarian (**Almási**): see ALMASY.
GIVEN NAMES Muslim 9%; Hungarian 7%; French 5%. *Ali, Hussein, Mehdi, Mehran, Mohammad, Nader, Nahid; Ferenc* (2), *Zoltan; Amie, Pierre.*

Almasy (161) Hungarian (**Almásy**): habitational name for someone from any of 43 places called Almás in 22 counties of the former Hungarian kingdom. All of these places were named for their apple orchards (from *alma* 'apple'). In some cases the family name may derive from a compound place name such as Tóalmás, Bácsalmás, Rácalmás, Hídalmás etc. See also ALMAS.

Almazan (442) Spanish (**Almazán**): habitational name from Almazán in the province of Soria, named in Arabic as *al-makhzan* 'the stronghold', 'the fortified place'.
GIVEN NAMES Spanish 55%. *Jose* (13), *Jose Luis* (6), *Armando* (4), *Juan* (4), *Miguel* (4), *Rafael* (4), *Alicia* (3), *Elena* (3), *Gerardo* (3), *Guadalupe* (3), *Javier* (3), *Jesus* (3).

Alme (121) Norwegian: habitational name from any of the seven farms, most in western Norway, so named, from an inflected form of Old Norse *almr* 'elm'.

Almeda (183) Portuguese and Spanish: variant of ALMEIDA or ALAMEDA.
GIVEN NAMES Spanish 35%. *Jose* (6), *Juan* (3), *Romulo* (3), *Alfredo* (2), *Angel* (2), *Francisco* (2), *Isidro* (2), *Adolfo, Aida, Alfonso, Arturo, Carlos; Antonio* (2).

Almeida (3212) Portuguese and Spanish: habitational name from any of a number of places so named in Portugal or from Almeida in Zamora province, Spain, all named from Arabic as *al-medina* 'the city'. This name is also found in western India, where it was taken by Portuguese colonists.
GIVEN NAMES Spanish 28%; Portuguese 12%. *Jose* (71), *Manuel* (69), *Carlos* (42), *Jorge* (18), *Luis* (14), *Mario* (14), *Fernando* (13), *Juan* (12), *Pedro* (12), *Raul* (8), *Ana* (7), *Armando* (7); *Joao* (10), *Joaquim* (5), *Marcio* (5), *Paulo* (3), *Agostinho* (2), *Amadeu* (2), *Anabela* (2), *Henrique* (2), *Ilidio* (2), *Zulmira* (2), *Afonso, Batista; Antonio* (59), *Angelo* (5), *Marco* (4), *Aldo*

(2), *Emidio* (2), *Carmela, Clementina, Enio, Filomena, Flavio, Florindo, Gasper.*

Almen (103) **1.** Swedish (**Almén**): topographic or ornamental name from *alm* 'elm' + the common surname suffix *-én*, a derivative of Latin *-enius* 'descendant of'. **2.** Norwegian: habitational name from any of various farmsteads named Almen ('the elm'). **3.** Jewish (Ashkenazic): status name from Yiddish *almen* 'widower'.
GIVEN NAMES Scandinavian 6%. *Erik, Lennart.*

Almendarez (357) Spanish (**Almendárez**): variant of ARMENDARIZ.
GIVEN NAMES Spanish 46%. *Jose* (8), *Carlos* (6), *Juan* (4), *Luis* (4), *Ruben* (4), *Jesus* (3), *Pedro* (3), *Angel* (2), *Eugenio* (2), *Felipe* (2), *Jaime* (2), *Javier* (2).

Almendinger (120) German and Swiss German: habitational name for someone from a place called Allmendingen, of which there are two examples in Switzerland, in Bern canton, and one in Baden-Württemberg in Germany.

Almer (154) **1.** German: from the personal name *Adelmar*, composed of the Germanic elements *adal* 'noble' + *mar* 'famous'. **2.** Swedish (**Almér**): topographic or ornamental name from *alm* 'elm' + the common surname element *-ér*, a shortened form of Latin *-erus* 'descendant of'.
GIVEN NAMES French 5%; German 4%. *Andree; Wolf.*

Almeter (173) Variant of Austrian German **Almeder**, a habitational name from a farm in Upper Austria called Almed (recorded in 1451 as *Alm-öd*).

Almgren (205) Swedish: ornamental name composed of the elements *alm* 'elm' + *gren* 'branch'.
GIVEN NAME Scandinavian 8%. *Nils.*

Almodovar (401) Spanish (**Almodóvar**) and Portuguese (**Almodôvar**): habitational name from places called Almodóvar, in the provinces of Ciudad Real and Córdoba and near Cuenca, Spain, or from Almodôvar, Portugal. These are named with Arabic *al-mudawwar* 'the round', 'the circular', referring to a hill, fort, or other topographic feature.
GIVEN NAMES Spanish 45%. *Jose* (9), *Luis* (7), *Carlos* (6), *Angel* (4), *Juan* (4), *Miguel* (4), *Ramon* (4), *Ricardo* (4), *Ana* (2), *Arnaldo* (2), *Ernesto* (2), *Fernando* (2).

Almon (587) **1.** Jewish (Ashkenazic): status name from Ashkenazic Hebrew *almon* 'widower'. Compare ALMEN. **2.** Variant spelling of ALMAN or ALMAND.

Almond (2437) Northeastern English: **1.** from the Middle English personal name *Almund*, from Old English *Æðelmund*, 'noble protection'. **2.** variant of ALLMAN 'German', assimilated by folk etymology to the vocabulary word denoting the tree.

Almonte (910) Spanish: habitational name from a place between Huelva and Sevilla, which was named with a combination of the Arabic article *al-* 'the' with the Spanish noun *monte* 'mountain'.

GIVEN NAMES Spanish 51%. *Jose* (28), *Luis* (14), *Ana* (12), *Juan* (12), *Juana* (8), *Pedro* (8), *Ramon* (8), *Francisco* (7), *Rafael* (7), *Carlos* (6), *Manuel* (6), *Josefina* (5).

Almquist (923) Swedish: ornamental name composed of the elements *alm* 'elm' + *quist*, an old or ornamental spelling of *kvist* 'twig'.

GIVEN NAMES Scandinavian 5%. *Erik* (2), *Erland, Nils, Sig, Sigvard, Walfrid.*

Alms (304) **1.** North German: patronymic from the personal name ALM. **2.** Swedish: variant of ALM.

Almy (501) English: unexplained.

FOREBEARS William Almy came to MA from England in 1631; he settled in RI in 1642.

Alo (123) **1.** Italian (**Alò**): perhaps from an Italian adaption of the Catalan personal name *Eloi*, equivalent of Italian *Eligio*, from French *Eloy*. The cult of St Eligio, patron of horses and blacksmiths, was very popular in the Middle Ages. Alternatively, the family name could be from Greek *alós* 'prisoners', 'captives'. **2.** Spanish: unexplained. **3.** Samoan and Hawaiian: unexplained.

GIVEN NAMES Italian 15%; Spanish 6%. *Olindo* (2), *Angelo, Attilio, Cesare, Silvio; Carlito, Lourdes, Noemi.*

Aloe (101) Southern Italian: variant of ALOI.

GIVEN NAMES Italian 23%. *Orlando* (3), *Aldo, Annunziato, Antonio, Carissima, Carmela, Giovanni, Mario, Matteo.*

Aloi (366) **1.** Southern Italian: from a southern variant of the personal name *Eligio*, Italian form of Latin *Eligius* 'chosen' (see 2). **2.** Americanized form of a French name, probably *Éloi*, which is from a personal name (Latin *Eligius* 'chosen'), borne by a 7th-century saint, bishop of Noyon.

GIVEN NAMES Italian 14%. *Salvatore* (4), *Pasquale* (2), *Carmello, Carmelo, Cosmo, Lorenzo, Santo.*

Aloia (273) Southern Italian: from a feminine form of the personal name ALOI.

GIVEN NAMES Italian 7%; Spanish 6%. *Carmine, Dino, Renaldo; Beatriz, Mercedes, Salvador.*

Aloise (123) Italian: variant of ALOISIO.

GIVEN NAMES Italian 17%. *Aldo, Angelo, Caesar, Domenic, Enrico, Giovanna, Maurizio, Salavatore.*

Aloisi (172) Italian: patronymic or plural form of ALOISIO.

GIVEN NAMES Italian 14%. *Mario* (4), *Gino* (3), *Antonio, Ciro, Dino, Santo, Serafino; Fernando, Orlando.*

Aloisio (267) Italian: from the personal name *Aloisio* (Late Latin *Aloysius*), a derivative of the Germanic personal name *Hlodwig* 'fame (in) battle'. See also LEWIS.

GIVEN NAMES Italian 28%. *Salvatore* (5), *Vito* (4), *Angelo* (3), *Carmine* (2), *Nicola* (2), *Sal* (2), *Amato, Amerigo, Antonio, Dino, Domenico, Franco; Rosario* (2), *Teresita* (2), *Adolfo, Elena, Marisa.*

Alon (103) Jewish (Israeli): ornamental name from Hebrew *alon* 'oak tree'.

GIVEN NAMES Jewish 52%; Spanish 5%. *Ido* (3), *Dov* (2), *Moshe* (2), *Shmuel* (2), *Zvi* (2), *Arie, Binyamin, Doron, Ehud, Eran, Gershon, Hagit; Arturo, Guillermo, Ivette, Virgilio.*

Alonge (216) Italian: probably from a Sicilian dialect variant of the personal name ALONSO (see ALFONSO).

GIVEN NAMES Italian 10%. *Carmelo, Domenic, Gaetano, Sal, Salvatore.*

Alongi (493) Italian (Sicily): variant of ALONGE.

GIVEN NAMES Italian 18%. *Vito* (8), *Angelo* (3), *Salvatore* (3), *Francesco* (2), *Carmel, Carmela, Carmelo, Carmine, Damiano, Giacomo, Gino, Ippolito.*

Alonso (2977) Spanish: from the personal name *Alonso*, a cognate of ALFONSO.

GIVEN NAMES Spanish 52%. *Jose* (117), *Manuel* (44), *Carlos* (42), *Juan* (42), *Jorge* (34), *Francisco* (29), *Pedro* (27), *Luis* (24), *Roberto* (21), *Angel* (19), *Enrique* (19), *Jesus* (19); *Antonio* (28), *Leonardo* (6), *Cecilio* (3), *Dario* (3), *Marco* (3), *Angelo* (2), *Clemente* (2), *Elio* (2), *Heriberto* (2), *Ciriaco, Delio.*

Alonzo (2389) Spanish: variant of ALONSO.

GIVEN NAMES Spanish 37%. *Jose* (40), *Juan* (27), *Manuel* (27), *Mario* (13), *Jesus* (12), *Luis* (12), *Roberto* (12), *Jorge* (11), *Ruben* (11), *Carlos* (10), *Pedro* (10), *Armando* (9); *Antonio* (8), *Leonardo* (3), *Lorenzo* (3), *Alfonse* (2), *Cecilio* (2), *Angelo, Bruna, Camillo, Carina, Clemente, Dario, Domenic.*

Alpaugh (343) Americanized spelling of German ALBACH.

Alper (808) **1.** Jewish (Ashkenazic): variant of HALPERN. **2.** Dutch: from a short form of the personal name ALPERT.

GIVEN NAMES Jewish 6%. *Zalman* (2), *Hyman, Izrail, Jakob, Meyer, Miriam, Mort, Naum, Rimma, Sima, Sol, Yetta.*

Alperin (326) Jewish (Ashkenazic): one of the many variants of HALPERN, that is, the city of Heilbronn in Württemberg.

GIVEN NAMES Jewish 11%. *Myer* (3), *Anat, Aron, Meyer, Mikhael, Sender, Zelman.*

Alpern (338) Jewish (Ashkenazic): one of the many variants of HALPERN, from the city of Heilbronn in Württemberg.

GIVEN NAMES Jewish 7%. *Asher* (2), *Eytan, Mendel, Meyer, Zvi.*

Alpers (386) North German and Dutch: patronymic from ALPERT, a variant of ALBERT.

GIVEN NAMES German 4%. *Kurt* (3), *Helmut.*

Alperstein (115) Jewish (Ashkenazic): one of the many variants of HALPERN, from the city of Heilbronn in Württemberg, with the

addition of the ornamental name element *Stein* 'rock'.

GIVEN NAMES Jewish 7%. *Hyman, Sol.*

Alpert (1776) **1.** Jewish (Ashkenazic): one of the many variants of HALPERN, from the city of Heilbronn in Württemberg. **2.** German and Dutch: variant of ALBERT.

GIVEN NAMES Jewish 6%. *Hyman* (4), *Isadore* (3), *Meyer* (3), *Ari* (2), *Sol* (2), *Avi, Dov, Eliyahu, Emanuel, Hershel, Hymen, Irina.*

Alpha (106) German: Hellenization of the surname **A(a)** (which is probably derived from a river name), adopted with reference to the first letter of the Greek alphabet. *Helene Alpha* is documented in Nuremberg in 1167.

Alphin (442) Origin uncertain. Possibilities include: **1.** English: habitational name from a place of this name near Manchester. **2.** Scottish: reduced and altered form of MCALPINE. **3.** variant of German **Alpfen**, a habitational name from Ober or Unter Alpfen in Baden-Württemberg.

Alphonse (213) French: from the personal name, a borrowing of Spanish ALFONSO, in a Classicized spelling.

GIVEN NAMES French 20%. *Marcel* (2), *Raymonde* (2), *Antoine, Benoit, Clovis, Hermite, Jacques, Michel, Pierre, Ricot, Yves.*

Alphonso (161) Variant of Spanish ALFONSO, in a Classicized spelling.

GIVEN NAMES Spanish 6%; French 5%. *Andres, Belmiro, Eulalia, Gaspar, Manuel; Celestine, Marcel, Pierre.*

Alpizar (121) Spanish (**Alpízar**): habitational name from Alpízar, a place in Huelva province.

GIVEN NAMES Spanish 54%. *Jorge* (3), *Jose* (3), *Luis* (3), *Rafael* (3), *Bernardo* (2), *Elena* (2), *Mario* (2), *Agustin, Ana, Ana Lilia, Angel, Antero.*

Alquist (164) Swedish: variant spelling of AHLQUIST.

Alred (405) English: variant spelling of ALLRED.

Alridge (125) English: variant of ALDRIDGE.

Alsbrook (121) English: variant of ALSOBROOK.

Alsbrooks (158) Variant of English ALSOBROOK.

Alsbury (143) English: evidently a habitational name, perhaps from Aylesbury in Buckinghamshire, which is named from an unattested Old English personal name *Ægel* + Old English *byrig*, dative case of *burh* 'fort'.

Alsdorf (156) German: habitational name from any of several places called Alsdorf.

Alsip (498) English: variant of ALSOP.

Alsman (143) German (**Alsmann**): probably from a Germanic personal name composed with a shortened form of *adal* 'noble' + *man* 'man'.

Alsobrook (427) English: unexplained. The name *Alsebrook* is found in 17th-century

Nottinghamshire parish records; the earliest is Christopher Alsebrook, married in 1657 in Mansfield.

Alsobrooks (151) Variant of English ALSOBROOK.

Alsop (574) English: habitational name from Alsop in Derbyshire, named with the genitive of the Old English personal name *Ælle* + Old English *hop* 'enclosed valley'.

Alspach (420) German: variant of **Alsbach**, a habitational name from any of several places called Alsbach.

Alspaugh (642) Respelling of German ALSPACH.

Alstad (113) Norwegian: habitational name from any of ten or so farms, most in Trondelag, named Alstad, from a personal name + Old Norse *staðr* 'farmstead', 'dwelling'.
GIVEN NAMES Scandinavian 16%. *Erik, Knute, Monrad.*

Alsteen (137) 1. Variant spelling of Swedish **Alsten**, an ornamental name composed of the elements *al* 'alder' + *sten* 'stone'. 2. Dutch: from a Germanic personal name meaning 'noble stone'. The variants **van Alsteen** and **van Alstein** are also found, suggesting that this may be a habitational name from an unidentified place.

Alston (6776) English: 1. from the Middle English personal name *Alstan*, which is a coalescence of several different Old English personal names: *Æðelstān* 'noble stone', *Ælfstān* 'elf stone', *Ealdstān* 'old stone', or *Ealhstān* 'altar stone'. 2. habitational name from any of various places called Alston (in Cumbria, Lancashire, Devon, and Somerset) or Alstone (in Gloucestershire and Staffordshire). With the exception of Alston in Cumbria, which is formed with the Old Scandinavian personal name *Halfdan*, these place names all consist of an Old English personal name + Old English *tūn* 'settlement', for example *Ælfsige* in the case of Alstone in Gloucestershire.
FOREBEARS In 1682 John Alston of Hammersmith, Middlesex, England, began a seven-year apprenticeship to James Jones, merchant, of Charleston, SC. He had many prominent descendants, among whom the name is often spelled **Allston**.

Alstott (105) Americanized form of German **Alstedt**, a habitational name from either of two places called Alstätte or Alstedde, both in Westphalia.

Alstrom (111) Swedish: variant spelling of AHLSTROM.
GIVEN NAME Scandinavian 10%. *Lars.*

Alsup (1275) English: variant of ALSOP.

Alt (2232) German and Jewish (Ashkenazic): from *alt* 'old', typically applied as a distinguishing epithet to the older of two bearers of the same personal name.

Altadonna (122) Italian (Sicily): from a medieval female personal name *Altadonna*, literally 'high lady', also sometimes applied as an ironical nickname.
GIVEN NAMES Italian 15%. *Salvatore* (2), *Carmelo, Giuseppe, Sal, Salvator, Santo.*

Altamirano (781) Spanish: habitational name for someone from any of several place called Altamira, for example the one in the province of Ávila which is famous for its spectacular cave paintings.
GIVEN NAMES Spanish 48%. *Jose* (22), *Juan* (11), *Luis* (9), *Miguel* (9), *Francisco* (8), *Jorge* (8), *Manuel* (7), *Armando* (6), *Arturo* (6), *Roberto* (6), *Ruben* (6), *Angel* (5); *Antonio* (4), *Aldo* (2), *Bartolo, Cecilio, Delio, Fausto, Filiberto, Gabriella, Italo, Leonardo, Marco, Marco Antonio.*

Altamura (125) Italian: habitational name from a place named Altamura, near Bari.
GIVEN NAMES Italian 26%. *Antonio* (2), *Angelo, Ezio, Giuseppe, Ilario, Leonardo, Mauro, Michelina, Pasquale, Romano, Vincenza, Vincenzo.*

Altavilla (123) Italian (Sicily): Italianized form of the Norman family name **Hauteville** (see HAVILL).
GIVEN NAMES Italian 24%. *Carmela, Carmine, Cosimo, Cosmo, Leonardo, Renato, Rocco, Salvatore.*

Altemose (202) German: see ALTEMUS.

Altemus (358) Altered spelling of German **Altemoos**, a topographic name meaning 'old swamp' or 'old fen', from Middle High German *alt* 'old' + *mōs* 'swamp', 'fen'.

Alten (151) 1. German habitational name from a place called Alten, for example the one near Dessau in eastern Germany. 2. Perhaps a shortened form of Dutch **van A(a)lten**, a habitational name for someone from Aalten in Gelderland.

Altenbach (127) German: habitational name from any of numerous places called Altenbach.

Altenburg (397) German: habitational name from any of various places called Altenburg, literally 'old fort', generally denoting the site of a Roman fort or prehistoric earthwork.
GIVEN NAMES German 6%. *Otto* (3), *Kurt* (2), *Florian, Lorenz.*

Altenburger (106) German: habitational name for someone from ALTENBURG.
GIVEN NAMES German 8%. *Kurt, Otto, Rudie.*

Altendorf (133) German: habitational name from any of numerous places in Germany, Austria, and Switzerland, named Altendorf (literally 'old village').

Altenhofen (194) German: topographic name for a person from a place near an old farmstead, from an inflected form of Middle High German *alt* 'old' + *hof* 'farm', 'manor farm'.

Altepeter (112) German: distinguishing epithet denoting 'Peter the elder'.

Alter (1719) 1. German and Jewish (Ashkenazic): distinguishing epithet for the older

of two bearers of the same personal name. 2. Jewish (Ashkenazic): from the Yiddish personal name *Alter*, an inflected form of *alt* 'old'. This was in part an omen name, expressing the parents' hope that the child would live a long life; in part an apotropaic name, given to a child born after the death of a sibling, but also said to have sometimes been assumed by someone who was seriously ill. The purpose is supposed to have been to confuse the Angel of Death into thinking that the person was old and so not worth claiming as a victim.
GIVEN NAMES Jewish 4%. *Sol* (3), *Aron* (2), *Avrohom* (2), *Meyer* (2), *Rivkah* (2), *Alter, Chiam, Haim, Hyman, Uri, Yisroel, Yol.*

Altergott (164) German: from an Old Prussian family name of uncertain origin.
GIVEN NAMES German 6%. *Gottlieb, Otto.*

Alteri (110) Southern Italian: variant of ALTIERI.
GIVEN NAMES Italian 13%. *Domenic, Paolo, Primo, Querino, Rocco.*

Alterio (132) Southern Italian: variant of ALTIERI.
GIVEN NAMES Italian 8%. *Aldo, Angelo, Sebastino.*

Alterman (433) 1. Jewish (Ashkenazic): elaborated form of ALTER or ALT (from the inflected form). 2. Respelling of German **Altermann**, a status name for the head of a craft guild. Compare English ALDERMAN, which was also used in this sense. 3. Belgian: habitational name for someone from Aalter in East Flanders.
GIVEN NAMES Jewish 4%. *Hyman, Irina, Merav.*

Altermatt (126) Swiss German: unexplained.

Alters (119) Variant of German ALTER.

Altes (122) 1. Reduced form of Dutch or German **Althaus** (see ALTIZER). 2. Jewish (Ashkenazic): metronymic from the Yiddish female personal name *Alte* + the genitive ending *-s*.

Althaus (463) German and Jewish (Ashkenazic): from German *altes Haus* 'old house', a habitational name for someone who lived in a building known as 'the old house' or from a place so named, for example in Hessen.

Altheide (139) German: apparently a topographic name denoting someone living on the 'old heath', German *alte Heide*.

Althen (106) German: variant of **Althenn(e)**, a nickname composed of Middle High German *alt* 'old' + *Henne*, a pet form of the personal name JOHANN.
GIVEN NAME German 4%. *Friedrich.*

Altherr (142) Swiss and South German: 1. literally 'old master', hence an older person of high status, as distinguished from a younger member of his family; also a name for a servant in the retinue of such a person. 2. habitational name from a place so called near Leipzig.

GIVEN NAMES German 8%. *Heinz* (2), *Helmut*.

Althoff (962) German (chiefly Westphalia): habitational name for someone who lived at the 'old farmstead', from Middle Low German *olt*, *alt* 'old' + *hof* 'farmstead', 'manor farm'.

Althouse (822) Americanized form of German and Jewish ALTHAUS.

Altic (160) **1.** Croatian or Serbian (**Altić**): patronymic, probably from the German adjective *alt* 'old'. **2.** Perhaps a variant of German ALTIG.

Altice (269) Americanized form of Dutch ALTIS.

Altier (309) French: variant of AUTHIER.

Altieri (1153) Italian (mainly southern): from a medieval personal name, which was probably brought to Sicily from northern France by the Normans. It corresponds to French *Altier*, *Autier*, composed of Germanic *ald* 'old', 'wise' + *hari* 'army'.
GIVEN NAMES Italian 12%. *Angelo* (7), *Carmine* (4), *Antonio* (2), *Domenic* (2), *Sal* (2), *Vito* (2), *Aldo*, *Amato*, *Carlo*, *Carmin*, *Cosmo*, *Dante*.

Altig (141) German: probably from a short form (*Aldico*) of a Germanic personal name composed with *alt* 'old', 'experienced'.

Altimari (100) Italian: southern variant of ALTOMARE.
GIVEN NAMES Italian 19%. *Santo* (3), *Angelo*, *Antonio*, *Carmine*.

Altimus (118) Variant of German **Altemoos** (see ALTEMUS).

Altis (124) **1.** Reduced form of Dutch **Althuyzer** (see ALTIZER). **2.** Jewish (Ashkenazic): variant of ALTES.
GIVEN NAMES German 4%. *Kurt*, *Monika*.

Altizer (911) Americanized form of Dutch **Althuyzer** or German **Althäuser**, topographic name for someone who lived in 'the old house' or a habitational name from Althausen in Germany, named as 'the old houses'. Compare German ALTHAUS.

Altland (319) Jewish (Ashkenazic): ornamental name composed of German *alt* 'old' + *Land* 'land', perhaps adopted with reference to the Jewish homeland before the diaspora.

Altman (7067) **1.** Jewish (Ashkenazic): variant of ALTMANN. **2.** Respelling of German ALTMANN.
FOREBEARS Philip Altman, a Jew from Bavaria, arrived in New York in about 1835. He had numerous prominent descendants.

Altmann (540) German and Jewish (Ashkenazic): from Middle High German *altman*, German *Altmann*, literally 'old man', applied either as a personal name or as a nickname for an older man as distinguished from a younger one.
GIVEN NAMES German 13%. *Markus* (3), *Armin* (2), *Dieter* (2), *Eldred* (2), *Hans* (2), *Kurt* (2), *Claus*, *Erna*, *Ernst*, *Erwin*, *Gertraud*, *Heinz*.

Altmeyer (251) German: status name for an older steward, headman, or tenant farmer, as distinguished from a younger one, from Middle High German *alt* 'old' + *meier* 'steward', 'headman', 'tenant farmer' (see MEYER).

Alto (296) **1.** Respelling of Finnish AALTO. **2.** Portuguese: nickname for a big man, from *alto* 'tall', 'big'.
GIVEN NAMES Finnish 5%. *Arvo* (2), *Reino* (2), *Eino*, *Sulo*, *Waino*.

Altobelli (296) Italian: patronymic or plural form of ALTOBELLO.
GIVEN NAMES Italian 16%. *Aldo* (2), *Dino* (2), *Gino* (2), *Angelo*, *Carlo*, *Domenico*, *Donato*, *Egidio*, *Ettore*, *Giovanni*, *Italo*, *Ivano*.

Altobello (129) Italian: from a medieval personal name, *Altobello*, composed of *alto* 'tall' + *bello* 'handsome'.
GIVEN NAMES Italian 10%. *Giovanni* (2), *Angelo*, *Clemente*, *Dino*.

Altom (317) Probably one of several variants of English HALTON or ALTON, but it could also be an altered form of English **Altham**, which is a habitational name from Altham in Whalley, Lancashire, named in Old English as 'river meadow (*hamm*) of the swans (*elfitu*)'.

Altomare (408) Italian: from a southern variant of *Aldemaro*, a personal name of Germanic origin, composed of the elements *ald* 'old', 'wise' + *mar* 'fame'.
GIVEN NAMES Italian 13%. *Mario* (3), *Sal* (3), *Corrado* (2), *Gasper* (2), *Adolfo*, *Biagio*, *Caesar*, *Carlo*, *Carmin*, *Ennio*, *Enrico*, *Eugenio*, *Mariano*, *Mauro*, *Sergio*, *Tullio*.

Altomari (116) Southern Italian: patronymic or plural form of ALTOMARE.
GIVEN NAMES Italian 12%. *Salvatore* (2), *Angelo*, *Pasquale*.

Alton (1475) English: habitational name from any of the many places called Alton, in Derbyshire, Dorset, Hampshire, Leicestershire, Staffordshire, Wiltshire, Worcestershire, and elsewhere. The origin is various: Alton in Derbyshire and Alton Grange in Leicestershire probably have as their first element Old English *(e)ald* 'old'. Those in Hampshire, Dorset, and Wiltshire are at the sources of rivers, and are named in Old English as 'settlement (*tūn*) at the source (*ǣwiell*)'. Others derive from various Old English personal names; for example, the one in Staffordshire is formed with an unattested personal name, *Ælfa*, and one in Worcestershire, *Eanulfintun* in 1023, is 'settlement associated with (*-ing*) Ēanwulf'.

Altringer (115) German: habitational name for someone from a place called Altringen or Aldingen, of which there are two in Württemberg.

Altschul (206) Jewish (Ashkenazic): from the name of a synagogue in Prague, literally 'old synagogue'.

GIVEN NAMES German 5%. *Ernst*, *Gunther*, *Kurt*.

Altschuler (386) Jewish (Ashkenazic): variant of ALTSCHUL, with the addition of the agent suffix *-er*.
GIVEN NAMES Jewish 5%; German 4%. *Ayelet*, *Iren*, *Yoram*, *Zalman*; *Helmut*, *Otto*.

Altshuler (374) Jewish (Ashkenazic): variant spelling of ALTSCHULER.
GIVEN NAMES Jewish 9%; Russian 7%. *Aron*, *Avram*, *Basya*, *Dafna*, *Khaim*, *Miriam*, *Moisey*, *Yakov*, *Zalman*; *Yury* (4), *Anatoly*, *Dmitry*, *Igor*, *Lev*, *Mikhail*, *Pasha*, *Semyon*, *Vladimir*, *Yefim*.

Altstadt (122) German or Jewish (Ashkenazic): topographic name for someone living in the old quarter of a city, literally 'old city', or a habitational name from a place called Altstadt, as for example in Brandenburg.

Altum (121) See ALTOM.

Altvater (211) German: literally 'old father', used as a distinguishing epithet for a grandfather or father-in-law; probably a surname borne by the servant of a person in the service of the grandfather or father-in-law of a local personage.
GIVEN NAMES German 7%. *Kurt*, *Ulrich*.

Alu (132) Italian (Sicily; **Alú**): from a Sicilian variant of *Alòi*, a variant of ELIA.
GIVEN NAMES Italian 23%. *Salvatore* (5), *Cataldo* (2), *Donato* (2), *Carlo*, *Carmelo*, *Sal*.

Alumbaugh (471) Respelling of German **Allenbach** (see ALLENBAUGH).

Alva (680) Portuguese: habitational name from a place so named (see ALBA).
GIVEN NAMES Spanish 45%. *Juan* (15), *Jose* (11), *Carlos* (8), *Javier* (6), *Enrique* (5), *Ricardo* (5), *Ruben* (5), *Esteban* (4), *Gonzalo* (4), *Guadalupe* (4), *Juana* (4), *Mario* (4).

Alvarado (10074) Spanish: habitational name from a place in Badajoz province called Alvarado.
FOREBEARS This name was taken to Latin America by Pedro de Alvarado (c.1485–1541), Spanish conquistador and companion of Hernán Cortés. He became governor of Tenochtitlán after the conquest of the Aztecs in Mexico.
GIVEN NAMES Spanish 50%. *Jose* (300), *Juan* (140), *Luis* (98), *Manuel* (98), *Carlos* (94), *Jesus* (88), *Francisco* (80), *Raul* (64), *Jorge* (63), *Pedro* (59), *Guadalupe* (53), *Mario* (48).

Alvardo (229) Hispanic (Mexican): variant of ALVARADO.
GIVEN NAMES Spanish 53%. *Jose* (9), *Jesus* (4), *Miguel* (4), *Jorge* (3), *Juan* (3), *Manuel* (3), *Mario* (3), *Ricardo* (3), *Gilberto* (2), *Isauro* (2), *Luisa* (2), *Pedro* (2).

Alvarenga (392) Portuguese: habitational name from a place so named in Alveiro, which probably takes its name from the personal name *Álvaro* (see ALVARO).

Alvares (221) Portuguese: from a patronymic form of the personal name *Álvaro* (see ALVARO).

GIVEN NAMES Spanish 49%; Portuguese 11%. *Jose* (8), *Jorge* (4), *Jesus* (3), *Alfredo* (2), *Andres* (2), *Armando* (2), *Salvador* (2), *Sergio* (2), *Agustin*, *Alberto*, *Alvino*, *Beatriz*; *Joao*, *Omero*.

Alvarez (21200) Spanish (**Álvarez**): from a patronymic form of the personal name *Álvaro* (see ALVARO).

GIVEN NAMES Spanish 49%; Portuguese 11%. *Jose* (688), *Manuel* (266), *Juan* (264), *Luis* (264), *Carlos* (246), *Jesus* (178), *Francisco* (137), *Jorge* (132), *Ramon* (126), *Pedro* (121), *Miguel* (119), *Roberto* (116); *Catarina* (3), *Lidio* (2), *Ligia* (2), *Joaquim*, *Wenceslao*.

Alvaro (246) Spanish (**Álvaro**) and Portuguese: from the personal name *Álvaro*, which is of Germanic (Visigothic) origin, although the exact etymology is not clear.

GIVEN NAMES Spanish 23%; Italian 11%; Portuguese 4%. *Jose* (4), *Francisco* (2), *Raul* (2), *Adelaida*, *Alba*, *Alberto*, *Alejandro*, *Anaya*, *Benito*, *Celestino*, *Chavez*, *Emilia*; *Antonio* (3), *Alfonse* (2), *Angelo* (2), *Cesare*, *Giuseppe*, *Rocco*, *Sal*.

Alvear (211) Spanish: frequent but unexplained, also found as ALVIAR.

GIVEN NAMES Spanish 56%; Portuguese 10%. *Luis* (5), *Carlos* (4), *Jose* (4), *Juan* (4), *Ricardo* (4), *Jaime* (3), *Jesus* (3), *Rafael* (3), *Armando* (2), *Basilio* (2), *Brigido* (2), *Catalina* (2).

Alverez (275) Spanish (**Álverez**): variant spelling of ALVAREZ.

GIVEN NAMES Spanish 42%; Portuguese 12%. *Jose* (7), *Alberto* (3), *Alfredo* (3), *Francisco* (3), *Mario* (3), *Miguel* (3), *Ramon* (3), *Carlos* (2), *Javier* (2), *Luis* (2), *Manuel* (2), *Marcelino* (2); *Antonio* (3), *Angelo* (2), *Annamarie*, *Federico*.

Alvernaz (124) Portuguese: ethnic name, *alvernaz*, for someone from the Auvergne region of France (Portuguese *Alverna*).

GIVEN NAMES Spanish 15%; Portuguese 11%. *Manuel* (5), *Jose* (3), *Ana*, *Carlos*, *Serafin*, *Silverio*; *Joao*, *Ligia*.

Alverson (1243) Respelling of Swedish HALVERSON or of **Alvarsson**, a patronymic from the personal name *Alvar* (composed of Old Norse *alf* 'elf' + *-arr*, an element with various origins).

Alves (3065) Portuguese: the usual Portuguese form of ALVARES.

GIVEN NAMES Spanish 21%; Portuguese 13%. *Manuel* (83), *Jose* (72), *Carlos* (30), *Fernando* (15), *Francisco* (14), *Luis* (11), *Mario* (9), *Domingos* (7), *Sergio* (7), *Alfredo* (6), *Armando* (6), *Ricardo* (6); *Joao* (14), *Joaquim* (5), *Paulo* (3), *Albano* (2), *Ilidio* (2), *Terezinha* (2), *Afonso*, *Aloisio*, *Duarte*, *Guilherme*, *Heitor*, *Henrique*.

Alvey (1744) English: from the Middle English personal name *Alfwy*, Old English *Ælfwīg* 'elf battle'.

Alviar (144) Spanish: unexplained. Compare ALVEAR.

GIVEN NAMES Spanish 41%; Portuguese 9%. *Jose* (5), *Juan* (3), *Jaime* (2), *Ruben* (2), *Sotero* (2), *Alejandro*, *Alfredo*, *Armando*, *Bartolome*, *Basilio*, *Carolina*, *Cesar*.

Alvidrez (294) Spanish (**Alvídrez**): of uncertain origin; perhaps a variant of **Alvírez** (also spelled **Alvires**), a habitational name from a village in León.

GIVEN NAMES Spanish 46%; Portuguese 9%. *Jose* (8), *Juan* (8), *Luis* (5), *Manuel* (5), *Carlos* (4), *Jesus* (4), *Ruben* (4), *Gilberto* (3), *Alberto* (2), *Alfredo* (2), *Arnulfo* (2), *Francisca* (2).

Alvillar (105) Spanish (mainly Mexico; also **Albillar**): possibly related to ALVIAR; unexplained.

GIVEN NAMES Spanish 36%; Portuguese 8%. *Cesar* (2), *Jose* (2), *Manuel* (2), *Alvaro*, *Amparo*, *Armando*, *Efren*, *Eufracio*, *Guadalupe*, *Ignacio*, *Jesus*, *Lilia*.

Alvin (306) **1.** English: from the Middle English personal name *Alvin* or *Alfwin*, Old English *Ælfwine* 'elf friend'. Compare ALWIN. **2.** Swedish: ornamental name from *alv* 'elf' + the common surname suffix *-in*.

Alvino (268) Southern Italian (Campania): from the personal name *Albino* (of uncertain origin; probably from Late Latin *Albinus*, a derivative of *albus* 'white' (see ALBIN)).

GIVEN NAMES Italian 11%; Spanish 11%. *Carmine* (2), *Pietro* (2), *Antonio*, *Ciro*, *Salvatore*, *Savino*; *Sabino* (4), *Aurelio* (2), *Mario* (2), *Elvira*, *Genoveva*, *Gerardo*, *Gilberto*, *Guillermo*, *Lazaro*, *Luz Maria*, *Margarito*, *Maria Carmen*.

Alvis (1253) English: patronymic from ALVIN.

Alviso (110) Spanish (mainly Mexico and Philippines): Castilianized form of Basque **Albiasu**, a habitational name from a town in Navarre province, Basque Country.

GIVEN NAMES Spanish 28%; Portuguese 6%. *Alfredo*, *Amalia*, *Aracely*, *Armando*, *Artemisa*, *Carlos*, *Felicitas*, *Felipe*, *Francisco*, *Gerardo*, *Gregorio*, *Jose*; *Antonio*, *Leonardo*.

Alvizo (105) Spanish: variant of ALVISO.

GIVEN NAMES Spanish 57%; Portuguese 12%. *Alfredo* (3), *Jose* (3), *Alejo* (2), *Jesus* (2), *Juan* (2), *Manuel* (2), *Rafael* (2), *Ana Maria*, *Angel*, *Aristeo*, *Carlos*, *Cesar*; *Mauro* (2), *Antonio*, *Lucio*.

Alvord (814) Southwestern English: variant of ALFORD, from Alford in Somerset; the spelling reflects the southwestern English dialect pronunciation.

FOREBEARS This surname was brought to North America by Alexander Alvord, who came from Devon or Somerset to Windsor, CT, in about 1645. He had many prominent descendants.

Alward (556) **1.** English: variant of AYLWARD. **2.** North German: variant of ALWARDT.

Alwardt (132) North German: from the personal name *Adelward*, composed of the Germanic elements *adal* 'noble' + *ward* 'keeper', 'protector'.

GIVEN NAMES German 8%. *Jutta*, *Kurt*, *Reinhold*.

Alway (143) English: reduced form of ALLOWAY.

Alwin (215) English: from the Middle English personal name *Alwin* or *Elwin*, a falling together of various Old English personal names: *Ælfwine* 'elf friend', *Æðelwine* 'noble friend', *Ealdwine* 'old friend', and others.

Alwine (402) In part, probably a variant of English ALWIN; otherwise an Americanized form of German ALLWEIN.

Alwood (160) English and Irish: variant of ELLWOOD.

GIVEN NAME Irish 4%. *Padraic*.

Alworth (139) English: variant of **Elworth** (see ELLSWORTH).

Aly (266) Muslim: variant spelling of ALI.

GIVEN NAMES Muslim 63%. *Mohamed* (13), *Ahmed* (7), *Aly* (5), *Essam* (3), *Sayed* (3), *Tarek* (3), *Ashraf* (2), *Ayman* (2), *Fawzy* (2), *Hany* (2), *Hassan* (2), *Khalid* (2).

Alyea (235) Americanized form of a French Canadian name, probably **Allier** (of Germanic origin, from *adalhari* 'noble army') or **Elier**, **Hélier**, variants of **Hilaire** (see HILLARY).

Alzate (175) Castilianized form of Basque **Altzate**, a habitational name from a town in Navarre province, or topographic name from Basque *altz* 'alder' + *ate* 'port', 'harbor'.

GIVEN NAMES Spanish 56%; Portuguese 13%. *Jose* (7), *Luis* (6), *Mario* (4), *Angel* (3), *Fabio* (3), *Ruben* (3), *Carlos* (2), *Diego* (2), *Fernando* (2), *Gustavo* (2), *Jaime* (2), *Jorge* (2); *Marino* (2), *Antonio*, *Caesar*, *Marco*, *Silvio*.

Amabile (309) Italian (mainly Naples): from a medieval personal name meaning 'lovable' or (as a Christian name) 'worthy of God's love'.

GIVEN NAMES Italian 18%. *Carmine* (4), *Antonio* (2), *Carmela* (2), *Luigi* (2), *Santo* (2), *Angelo*, *Concetta*, *Orazio*, *Pasquale*.

Amacher (379) **1.** German: topographic name for one who lived *am Ach* 'on the Ach' (a river name), the suffix *-er* denoting an inhabitant. **2.** Swiss German: variant of AMACKER.

FOREBEARS Hans am Acher emigrated from Oberhasle, Switzerland, to the Carolinas in 1742.

Amacker (292) Swiss German: topographic name from *am Acker* 'by the field'.

Amadeo (187) Italian: from the personal name *Amadeo*, *Amodeo*, coined in the early Middle Ages with the meaning 'lover of God' or 'loved by God'.

GIVEN NAMES Italian 15%; Spanish 13%; Portuguese 7%. *Antonio* (3), *Salvatore* (2), *Angelo*, *Mafalda*, *Marco*, *Primo*, *Vincenzo*;

Mario (4), *Jose* (3), *Miguel* (2), *Frederico, Joaquin, Leonila, Luis, Marisol, Rolando.*

Amadio (290) Italian: variant of AMADEO.
GIVEN NAMES Italian 11%. *Massimo* (2), *Antonio, Dante, Marco, Nunzio, Ricco, Rocco, Sante.*

Amado (444) **1.** Spanish and Portuguese: from a medieval personal name, *Amado,* Latin *Amatus* 'beloved (i.e. by God)'. Compare Italian AMATO. **2.** Jewish (Sephardic): adoption of the Spanish family name.
GIVEN NAMES Spanish 27%; Portuguese 11%. *Carlos* (6), *Jose* (4), *Juan* (4), *Francisco* (3), *Manuel* (3), *Miguel* (3), *Alberto* (2), *Ana* (2), *Fernando* (2), *Gerardo* (2), *Jesus* (2), *Jorge* (2); *Joao* (2), *Joaquim* (2), *Manoel, Paulo.*

Amadon (183) See AMIDON.

Amador (2060) Spanish, Portuguese, and Catalan: from a medieval personal name, Latin *Amator* 'lover (i.e. of God)', from *amare* 'to love'. As a personal name it was particularly popular in the 16th century, having been borne by various saints.
GIVEN NAMES Spanish 45%; Portuguese 10%. *Jose* (50), *Juan* (31), *Manuel* (27), *Pedro* (19), *Carlos* (16), *Jorge* (16), *Luis* (14), *Jesus* (13), *Armando* (8), *Eduardo* (8), *Miguel* (8), *Raul* (8); *Henrique, Joaquim, Paulo, Wenceslao.*

Amaker (184) German and Swiss German: variant of AMACKER or AMACHER.

Amalfitano (214) Italian: habitational name for someone from Amalfi, a small city on the Gulf of Salerno, which was once an independent republic and important sea power.
GIVEN NAMES Italian 20%. *Vito* (4), *Carmine* (2), *Aniello, Antonio, Carlo, Guiseppe, Luigi, Rachele, Sal, Saverio.*

Aman (1257) **1.** Americanized spelling of German AMMANN. **2.** Muslim (widespread throughout the Muslim world): from the Arabic personal name *Aman* 'trust', 'safety', 'protection', 'tranquility'. *Aman* is often used in combination with other names, for example *Amān Allāh* (*Amanullah*) 'trust of Allah'.

Amann (1029) German: variant spelling of AMMANN.
GIVEN NAMES German 4%. *Helmut* (2), *Kurt* (2), *Armin, Erhard, Erwin, Franz, Frieda, Otto.*

Amano (175) Japanese: found mostly along the southeastern seaboard of Japan and in the Ryūkyū Islands; in the former case it is probably a habitational name from Amano ('heavenly plain') in Izu (now part of Shizuoka prefecture).
GIVEN NAMES Japanese 62%. *Hiroshi* (5), *Osamu* (2), *Satoru* (2), *Toshio* (2), *Akio, Ayako, Eiji, Etsuko, Hideaki, Hidemi, Hiroaki, Hirohito.*

Amante (191) Italian, Spanish, and Portuguese: from *amante* 'lover', used in the Middle Ages as a Christian baptismal name, in the sense 'he who loves God'.

GIVEN NAMES Spanish 14%; Italian 7%. *Candelario* (2), *Reynaldo* (2), *Aida, Carolina, Erlinda, Fortunato, Jose, Josue, Rosauro, Sofio, Wilfredo, Xavier; Carmine* (2), *Carlo, Carmelo, Salvatore.*

Amantea (101) Italian: variant of AMANTE.
GIVEN NAMES Italian 11%. *Angelo, Salvatore, Saverio.*

Amar (342) **1.** French: Americanized spelling of **Hemard**. **2.** Hindu name found among people from Sind, Pakistan, derived from a personal name based on Sanskrit *amar* 'immortal'. **3.** Jewish (Sephardic): ornamental name from *'amr*, Levantine or Egyptian form of Arabic *qamar* 'moon', or from an Arabic personal name based on *'amr* 'long-lived'.
GIVEN NAMES French 11%; Indian 10%; Jewish 10%. *Jacques* (4), *Aime, Alain, Constant, Edouard, Francois, Germaine, Laurent, Prosper, Solange, Stephane, Thierry; Rajiv* (2), *Ajay, Alka, Amar, Arun, Harish, Lata, Meera, Moti, Narain, Praveen, Ramana; Yossi* (2), *Avi, Avraham, Avram, Chaya, Iian, Itzhak, Mazal, Meryem, Pnina, Shlomo, Shmuel.*

Amara (192) **1.** Italian: variant of AMARO. **2.** Muslim (mainly Pakistan, India, and Bangladesh): probably a variant of OMAR.
GIVEN NAMES Italian 11%; Muslim 4%; Indian 4%. *Angelo* (3), *Salvatore* (2), *Domenic, Enza, Franco; Ahmed* (2), *Fadel, Hasan, Hussein, Iman, Mostafa, Nabil, Nawal; Rao* (2), *Rajeev.*

Amaral (2478) Portuguese: habitational name from any of the numerous minor places called Amaral. The place name is of uncertain etymology, probably from the term *amaral*, denoting a kind of black grape (from Latin *amarus* 'bitter'). Alternatively, the origin may be a collective noun derived from Spanish *maro, amaro* 'cat-thyme' (Latin *marum,* influenced by Spanish *amargo* 'bitter').
GIVEN NAMES Spanish 21%; Portuguese 11%. *Manuel* (84), *Jose* (50), *Carlos* (19), *Mario* (8), *Armando* (7), *Fernando* (7), *Luis* (7), *Jorge* (6), *Eduardo* (5), *Francisco* (5), *Ernesto* (4), *Joaquin* (4); *Joao* (7), *Joaquim* (6), *Paulo* (3), *Guilherme, Serafim, Vasco.*

Amarante (192) Italian (Campania): from an early Christian female personal name, Greek *Amaranthē* 'unfading', bestowed with reference to the adjective *amarantos* as used in I Peter 5:4: 'And when the chief shepherd shall appear, ye shall receive a crown of glory that fadeth not away'. The personal name was sometimes wrongly taken as a derivative of *anthos* 'flower'.
GIVEN NAMES Spanish 21%; Italian 9%; Portuguese 6%. *Celestino* (2), *Jose* (2), *Luis* (2), *Alberto, Ana, Armando, Evelio, Fernando, Gregorio, Jorge, Josefina, Lino; Antonio* (2), *Gaetano, Pasquale, Sal, Sebastiano.*

Amari (213) **1.** Italian (Sicily): see AMARO. **2.** Arabic: variant of AMAR. **3.** Japanese:

'surplus', usually written with characters used phonetically. It appears to be a shortening of *amaribe* 'surplus doors', a reference to the practice among census takers from ancient times up to the era of the Tokugawa shogunate (1603–1867) of listing households in groups of fifty; any households exceeding this number or a multiple of it were referred to as 'surplus'. The surname is found chiefly in northeastern Japan.
GIVEN NAMES Italian 16%. *Angelo* (2), *Marcello* (2), *Vito* (2), *Carmel, Franco, Giulio, Nicolo, Salvatore, Vita.*

Amaro (1101) Italian, Spanish, and Portuguese: of uncertain and multiple origin. In part at least, it is from the Germanic personal name *Amalric,* introduced to northern Italy by the Lombards and to the Iberian peninsula by the Visigoths. In Sicily, it is from a nickname meaning 'bitter', 'unlucky', or 'disappointed' or from an Arabic personal name *'Ammār*. In Portugal, it is from a personal name *Amaro,* of disputed origin.
GIVEN NAMES Spanish 41%; Portuguese 10%. *Carlos* (17), *Jose* (17), *Manuel* (15), *Francisco* (10), *Luis* (10), *Pedro* (10), *Jesus* (7), *Juan* (7), *Mario* (6), *Rafael* (6), *Miguel* (5), *Ana* (4); *Paulo* (2), *Guilherme, Joaquim.*

Amason (428) English: variant spelling of AMISON.

Amato (4220) Italian: from a medieval personal name, *Amato,* Latin *Amatus* 'beloved', i.e. by God.
GIVEN NAMES Italian 16%. *Salvatore* (43), *Angelo* (16), *Sal* (12), *Antonio* (10), *Giuseppe* (10), *Rocco* (9), *Carmine* (8), *Natale* (8), *Vito* (7), *Pasquale* (6), *Gaetano* (5), *Pietro* (5).

Amatucci (115) Italian: from a pet form of AMATO.
GIVEN NAMES Italian 10%; Spanish 5%. *Carmine* (2), *Angelo, Nicola; Amilio, Assunta, Mario, Ramona, Renato.*

Amaya (2212) **1.** Spanish: habitational name, from the name of a mountain and an ancient city in the province of Burgos, probably derived from Basque *amai* 'end' + the article suffix *-a.* **2.** Japanese: usually written with characters meaning 'heavenly valley'. It is pronounced *Amaya* or *Amagai* in eastern Japan and *Amatani* in western Japan.
GIVEN NAMES Spanish 53%; Portuguese 12%. *Jose* (104), *Carlos* (34), *Juan* (26), *Manuel* (25), *Francisco* (22), *Luis* (20), *Miguel* (17), *Pedro* (16), *Jorge* (15), *Raul* (15), *Julio* (14), *Jaime* (13).

Amber (234) **1.** English: unexplained. **2.** Possibly an Americanized spelling of French IMBERT or a translation of German and Jewish BERNSTEIN, which means 'amber'. **3.** Muslim (widespread throughout the Muslim world): from the Arabic personal name *'Anbar,* literally 'perfume', 'ambergris', figuratively 'good', 'pleasant', 'agreeable'.

Amberg (531) **1.** German: habitational name from any of several settlements called Amberg (literally 'by the mountain'), including a city in Bavaria. It could also be a topographic name of identical etymology. **2.** Jewish (Ashkenazic): possibly from 1; alternatively, it may be a habitational name from the city of Hamburg (see HAMBURGER). Many varieties of Yiddish lack *h* and *-burg* is sometimes replaced by *-berg* in Jewish family names.

Amberger (166) German: habitational name for someone from AMBERG.
GIVEN NAME German 4%. *Gerhard.*

Ambers (207) Probably a variant of English AMBROSE or a cognate of it in French or some other European language. The language of origin is uncertain.
GIVEN NAME French 4%. *Camille.*

Amberson (235) **1.** Northern Irish (of Scottish or English origin): most probably a patronymic from AMBROSE, or possibly a variant of EMERSON. **2.** Americanized form of Norwegian and Danish **Ambrossen** and Swedish **Ambrosson**, patronymics from AMBROSE.
FOREBEARS Abraham Amberson is listed in MD court records in 1665–80. Subsequently the name is found among Irish Presbyterians in Amberson Valley, PA, in 1763. Scandinavian bearers of this name came to America in the mid 19th century.

Amble (198) **1.** Norwegian: possibly a habitational name from a farm in Sogn, named from *and* 'against' + *blad* 'leaf', with reference to the shape of an inlet or bay. **2.** Indian (Maharashtra): Hindu (Maratha) name of unknown meaning.
GIVEN NAMES Scandinavian 8%; Indian 5%. *Bjorn, Obert, Peer; Harish, Ravi, Srinivas, Suresh.*

Ambler (814) English (Yorkshire): from Middle English *ambler* 'walker', 'steady-paced horse or mule' (ultimately from Latin *ambulare* 'to walk'), probably applied to someone with a steady, easy-going temperament. Reaney suggests that it may have been a facetious nickname for a fuller.
FOREBEARS Richard Ambler is recorded in MA in 1639, in the New Haven Colony by 1647, and still living in CT in 1700. Many bearers are descended from William Ambler, who was mayor of Doncaster in 1717, at least one of whose sons settled in VA.

Amborn (169) German: topographic name for someone who lived *am Born* 'by the spring or well'.

Ambriz (544) probably Spanish (**Ámbriz**): perhaps a Castilianized form of Asturian-Leonese **Ambres**, a habitational name from Ambres, a village in Asturies.
GIVEN NAMES Spanish 55%; Portuguese 10%. *Jose* (13), *Jesus* (9), *Juan* (9), *Guadalupe* (7), *Carlos* (6), *Francisco* (6), *Manuel* (5),

Miguel (5), *Jaime* (4), *Javier* (4), *Jorge* (4), *Gilberto* (3).

Ambrogi (137) Italian: see AMBROGIO.
GIVEN NAMES Italian 9%; Spanish 8%. *Enrico* (2), *Angelo, Antonio, Franco, Lorenzo, Luigi; Aladino, Claudio, Merino, Octavio, Rosita.*

Ambrogio (180) Italian: from the personal name *Ambrogio* (see AMBROSE).
GIVEN NAMES Italian 20%; Spanish 10%. *Carmelo* (2), *Pasquale* (2), *Sal* (2), *Aldo, Nicola, Rocco, Salvatore, Sebastiano; Fortunato* (2), *Carlos, Gaspar, Valeria.*

Ambroise (106) French: from the personal name *Ambroise*, French equivalent of AMBROSE.
GIVEN NAMES French 52%. *Pierre* (3), *Emile* (2), *Jean Robert* (2), *Serge* (2), *Dominique, Fernande, Herve, Jacques, Jean Baptiste, Lucien, Mathurin, Yva.*

Ambrose (6153) English: from the English form of the medieval personal name, Latin *Ambrosius*, from Greek *ambrosios* 'immortal', which was popular throughout Christendom in medieval Europe. Its popularity was due in part to the fame of St. Ambrose (*c.*340–397), one of the four Latin Fathers of the Church, the teacher of St. Augustine. In North America this surname has absorbed Dutch **Ambroos** and probably other cognates from other European languages. (For forms, see Hanks and Hodges 1988.)

Ambrosi (137) Italian: see AMBROSIO.
GIVEN NAMES Italian 18%; Spanish 10%; French 4%. *Italo* (2), *Marco* (2), *Ambrogio, Antonio, Dino, Filippo, Giampiero, Marino, Reno, Vincenzo; Carlos, Casimira, Consuelo, Emilio, Hernan, Luisa, Mario; Serge.*

Ambrosia (190) **1.** Italian: see AMBROSIO. **2.** Greek: shortened form of the patronymic **Ambrosiadis**, from the personal name *Ambrosios* or *Ambrosiatos*.
GIVEN NAMES Italian 10%. *Angelo* (4), *Antonio, Rocco.*

Ambrosini (347) Italian: see AMBROSINO.
GIVEN NAMES Italian 11%. *Carlo* (3), *Aldo, Angelo, Biagio, Dante, Dario, Elio, Flavio, Fosco, Marco, Renzo, Salvatore.*

Ambrosino (416) Italian: from a pet form of the personal name AMBROSIO.
GIVEN NAMES Italian 17%. *Salvatore* (8), *Antonio* (2), *Cosimo* (2), *Enrico* (2), *Carlo, Ciro, Gaetano, Gennaro, Giro, Giuseppe, Nunzio, Onofrio.*

Ambrosio (689) Italian: from the personal name *Ambrosio* (see AMBROSE).
GIVEN NAMES Spanish 17%; Italian 16%; Portuguese 4%. *Pedro* (5), *Mario* (4), *Andres* (2), *Cristina* (2), *Edmundo* (2), *Emilia* (2), *Erlinda* (2), *Jesus* (2), *Luis* (2), *Albino, Alejandro, Alfonso; Salvatore* (4), *Antonio* (3), *Angelo* (2), *Francesco* (2), *Marco* (2), *Romeo* (2), *Saverio* (2), *Alessio, Aniello, Biagio, Carmela, Carmelo.*

Ambrosius (211) German and Dutch: humanistic surname, from the Latin form of AMBROSE.

Ambroz (103) Czech, Slovak, and Slovenian (**Ambrož**): from the personal name Ambrož, equivalent to AMBROSE. It may also be a shortened form of the Slovenian surname **Ambrožič**, of the same origin.

Ambs (197) German: of uncertain origin. Probably from a Germanic personal name, which also appears in topographic names, whose root is related to German *emsig* with the early sense of 'toil', 'trouble', 'endurance'.

Ambuehl (192) German (chiefly Swiss; **Ambühl**): topographic name from south German dialect *am Bühl* 'at the hill' (see BUEHL).
GIVEN NAME German 5%. *Eldred* (2).

Amburgey (895) Variant of German and Jewish HAMBURGER, under French influence.

Amburgy (131) Variant of German and Jewish HAMBURGER, under French influence.

Amburn (492) Probably an Americanized form of German AMBORN.

Ambush (110) Probably an altered form of **Ambroos**, Dutch form of the personal name AMBROSE.

Amdahl (245) Norwegian and Swedish: habitational name from any of several places named Amdal. The second element of the place name is clearly *da(h)l* 'valley'; the first may be from *alm* 'elm'.

Amdur (192) Jewish (northeastern Ashkenazic): habitational name from *amdur*, the Yiddish name of Indura in Belarus.
GIVEN NAMES Jewish 10%. *Gerson* (2), *Nurit* (2), *Shimon* (2), *Miriam, Sira, Sol.*

Amedee (192) French (**Amédée**): from a personal name meaning 'lover (of God)', which became current in France in the 15th century, having been borne by a succession of counts and dukes of Savoy, especially Amadeus (Amédée) VIII (1383–1451).
GIVEN NAMES French 12%. *Andre* (2), *Emile, Ives, Laurent, Lydie, Oneil, Remy.*

Amedeo (135) Italian: variant of AMADEO.
GIVEN NAMES Italian 19%. *Salvatore* (3), *Carmelo, Elvira, Mario, Onofrio, Santo, Vito.*

Ameen (236) **1.** Muslim: variant spelling of AMIN. **2.** Swedish: from an unexplained first element (it may be the first part of a place name) + a common surname suffix *-én* (Latin *-enius*).
GIVEN NAMES Muslim 25%. *Syed* (4), *Ahmad* (3), *Mohammad* (2), *Mohammed* (2), *Abdul, Abdullahi, Abraham, Anisa, Arshad, Ayesha, Farooq, Hussein.*

Ameling (127) Dutch and German: variant of AMELUNG.

Amelio (159) Italian: from a medieval vernacular form of the Latin personal name *Amelius.*

GIVEN NAMES Italian 18%; Spanish 7%. *Saverio* (2), *Alfonse, Angelo, Antonio, Carmine, Clemente, Domenico, Salvatore, Silvio*; *Sergio* (2), *Alejandro, Rafael, Rosario*.

Amell (355) Americanized spelling of French Canadian HAMEL.

Amelung (116) German: from the Middle High German personal name *Amelung*, which was popular in the 12th and 13th centuries. It was adopted in honor of the *Amelungen* of medieval literature, warriors (in particular followers of Dietrich von Bern and successors of the Gothic royal house) who bore dithematic names of which the first element was *amal* 'strength', 'energy'.

Amen (625) **1.** Respelling of German AMMANN. **2.** Muslim: variant of AMIN.

Amend (748) German: topographic name for someone living at the end of a settlement or street, from Middle High German *am ende* 'at the end'.

Amendola (745) Southern Italian: habitational name from any of several places in southern Italy named Amendola or Mendola, named with the dialect word *amendola* 'almond', 'almond tree' (from Greek *amygdalea*), or a topographic name for someone who lived by an almond tree or trees.

GIVEN NAMES Italian 13%. *Salvatore* (6), *Antonio* (5), *Angelo* (3), *Carmine* (2), *Cosmo, Elio, Giuseppe, Guido, Pietro, Sal, Serafino, Vincenzo*.

Amendt (107) German: variant spelling of AMEND.

Ament (966) **1.** English: from an Old French personal name *Amand, Amant* (from Latin *Amandus* meaning 'loveable'). **2.** German: variant spelling of AMEND.

Amenta (283) Southern Italian (Sicily): habitational name from any of various minor places in Sicily named Amenta, from *menta* 'mint'.

GIVEN NAMES Italian 19%. *Salvatore* (7), *Gaetano* (2), *Guiseppe* (2), *Angelo, Carmelo, Cira, Corrado, Cosmo, Luciano, Massimo, Pasquale, Sal*.

Amer (291) **1.** Muslim: variant of AMIR. **2.** Variant of English AMAR.

GIVEN NAMES Muslim 52%. *Mohamed* (7), *Ahmad* (5), *Mohammed* (5), *Ahmed* (4), *Samir* (3), *Alaa* (2), *Ali* (2), *Amer* (2), *Ashraf* (2), *Jamal* (2), *Maher* (2), *Raed* (2).

Amerine (302) French respelling of German AMREIN.

Amerman (388) **1.** Dutch: occupational name for a charcoal burner. **2.** Americanized spelling of German **Ammermann** (see AMMERMAN).

Amero (244) Altered form of French AMIRAULT.

Amerson (1414) English: variant of EMERSON.

Ames (8951) **1.** English: from the Old French and Middle English personal name

Amys, Amice, which is either directly from Latin *amicus* 'friend', used as a personal name, or via a Late Latin derivative of this, *Amicius*. **2.** German: of uncertain origin. Perhaps a nickname for an active person, from a Germanic word related to Old High German *amazzig* 'busy'. Compare modern German *Ameise* 'ant'.

FOREBEARS William Ames, the son of Richard Ames of Bruton, Somerset, came to Braintree, MA, from England in about 1640. He had numerous prominent descendants.

Amesbury (125) English: habitational name from a place in Wiltshire, recorded in Domesday Book as *Ambresberie*, from an unattested Old English personal name *Ambre* + Old English *byrig*, dative case of *burh* 'fortified place'.

GIVEN NAME German 5%. *Kurt* (2).

Amescua (100) Spanish: variant of AMEZCUA.

GIVEN NAMES Spanish 40%; Portuguese 7%; French 4%. *Jose* (3), *Elba* (2), *Guadalupe* (2), *Jesus* (2), *Luis* (2), *Amparo, Arnulfo, Eliceo, Esperanza, Felipe, Fernando, Genaro*; *Raoul*.

Amesquita (86) Variant spelling of Spanish AMEZQUITA.

GIVEN NAMES Spanish 52%; Portuguese 8%. *Jose* (4), *Carlos* (2), *Guadalupe* (2), *Juan* (2), *Adan, Alfonso, Amparo, Arturo, Basilio, Beatriz, Cosme, Dimas*.

Amey (673) English: **1.** from the Old French personal name *Amé*, Latin *Amatus* 'beloved', a personal name favored by the early Christians, who used it in the sense 'beloved by God'. **2.** possibly a derivative of Old French *ami* 'friend'.

Amezcua (406) Castilianized form of Basque **Amezkoa**, a habitational name from a place in Navarre called Amezkoa, from Basque *ametz* 'Pyrenean oak' + *-ko* (genitive suffix) + *-a* (definite article suffix).

GIVEN NAMES Spanish 58%; Portuguese 12%. *Jose* (21), *Jesus* (8), *Carlos* (7), *Francisco* (6), *Luis* (6), *Jaime* (5), *Miguel* (5), *Javier* (4), *Juan* (4), *Rafael* (4), *Roberto* (4), *Salvador* (4).

Amezquita (266) Spanish (**Amézquita**): Castilianized form (alongside **Amézqueta**) of Basque **Amezketa**, a habitational name from a place in Gipuzkoa province named Amezketa, from Basque *ametz* 'Pyrenean oak' + *-(k)eta* 'group of', 'place of'.

GIVEN NAMES Spanish 51%; Portuguese 10%. *Jose* (10), *Juan* (6), *Manuel* (5), *Jesus* (4), *Alberto* (3), *Carlos* (3), *Rafael* (3), *Roberto* (3), *Salvador* (3), *Alfredo* (2), *Angel* (2), *Ernesto* (2); *Antonio* (3), *Eliseo, Federico*.

Amici (136) Italian: see AMICO.

GIVEN NAMES Italian 16%; French 5%. *Dei, Elio, Enio, Ezio, Ilio, Marino, Nino, Rocco*; *Camille*.

Amick (1951) Probably an Americanized form of German EMIG, a derivative of the

Germanic personal name *Emmerich* (see EMMERICH).

Amico (764) Italian: from a medieval personal name or nickname, *Amicus* (from Latin *amicus* 'friend'), having religious connotations, or from a short form of an omen name such as *Bonamico* (meaning 'good friend').

GIVEN NAMES Italian 16%. *Angelo* (12), *Salvatore* (9), *Sal* (5), *Lorenzo* (3), *Cataldo* (2), *Giovanna* (2), *Antonio, Arcangelo, Carmine, Cosmo, Dante*.

Amicone (157) Italian: from an augmentative of AMICO, probably in the sense 'protégé'.

GIVEN NAMES Italian 8%. *Angelo, Franco*.

Amidei (123) Italian: variant of **Amadei** (see AMADEO).

GIVEN NAMES Italian 10%; French 4%. *Aldo, Amelio, Emidio, Emo, Marco*; *Armand* (2).

Amidon (867) Said to be a French Huguenot name. Family genealogists assert that it is recorded in western France, at La Rochelle and Bordeaux, in the departments of Gironde and Charente, in the spellings *Amidon* and *Amadon*. If this is the source, the etymology is not known.

FOREBEARS Roger Amidon (alias Ammidown, Amadowne) was in MA in 1637; he died there in 1673. According to family tradition, he was a Huguenot who went to England, where he remained for some years before emigrating to America.

Amie (106) Variant spelling of French AMY or English AMEY.

Amiel (113) Jewish and French: from a Biblical personal name.

GIVEN NAMES Jewish 16%; French 13%. *Amnon* (2), *Chaim, Mayer, Ofer, Shai*; *Andre, Jacques, Jean-Claude, Michel*.

Amin (1478) Muslim and Indian (northern states): from an Arabic personal name based on *amīn* 'trustworthy', 'faithful', 'honest'. *Al-Amīn* 'the trustworthy' is an honorific title of the Prophet Muhammad. The term is used in combination with other words to form compound names: for example, *Ruh-ul-Amīn* 'faithful spirit' is an epithet of the Angel Gabriel mentioned in the Qur'an (26:193). Al-Amīn (787–813) was the name of the sixth Abbasid khalif of Baghdad. In India, the name came to be used as a term denoting a government official concerned with investigation of land claims and revenue claims, collection of revenue, and land surveying.

GIVEN NAMES Indian 61%; Muslim 26%. *Ashok* (14), *Mahesh* (12), *Ramesh* (12), *Dilip* (11), *Kirit* (10), *Pravin* (8), *Suresh* (8), *Jagdish* (7), *Mahendra* (7), *Sanjay* (7), *Shailesh* (7), *Yogesh* (7); *Mohammed* (33), *Mohammad* (20), *Muhammad* (12), *Ali* (11), *Mohamed* (10), *Nurul* (8), *Ruhul* (8), *Ahmed* (6), *Khalid* (5), *Abbas* (4), *Hussein* (4), *Tariq* (4).

Amini (248) Muslim: Arabic family name meaning 'descended from or associated with **Amīn**' (see AMIN).

GIVEN NAMES Muslim 72%. *Mohammad* (7), *Ali* (6), *Bijan* (5), *Hossein* (4), *Massoud* (4), *Behzad* (3), *Hassan* (3), *Mohammed* (3), *Ramin* (3), *Ata* (2), *Azita* (2), *Elham* (2).

Amiot (223) French: from a pet form of AMY.

FOREBEARS A bearer of the surname Amiot, from Soissons, Picardy, was documented in Quebec city in 1635.

GIVEN NAMES French 7%. *Armand, Francois, Jean-Paul, Napoleon.*

Amir (258) **1.** Muslim: from a personal name based on Arabic *'amīr* 'prince', 'commander', 'master'. *'Amīr-al-Mu'minīn* 'commander of the faithful' was a title of Muslim khalifs. **2.** Muslim: from a personal name based on Arabic *'āmir* 'prosperous'. **3.** Jewish (Sephardic): adoption of the Arabic name.

GIVEN NAMES Muslim 42%; Jewish 19%. *Mohammad* (6), *Ali* (4), *Syed* (3), *Amir* (2), *Fatemeh* (2), *Javed* (2), *Karim* (2), *Mohamed* (2), *Nader* (2), *Ramy* (2), *Abdul, Achmad, Brahim; Dorit* (2), *Doron* (2), *Emanuel* (2), *Amnon, Arnon, Avner, Ehud, Galit, Haim, Irit, Meir.*

Amirault (247) French: from *amiral* 'admiral' (from Arabic *amīr* 'commander'), most likely applied as an ironic nickname.

GIVEN NAMES French 8%. *Emile, Pierre.*

Amiri (208) Muslim: Arabic family name meaning 'descended from or associated with AMIR'.

GIVEN NAMES Muslim 73%. *Ali* (6), *Amir* (4), *Abdullah* (3), *Ahmad* (3), *Mohammad* (3), *Alireza* (2), *Bahram* (2), *Firouzeh* (2), *Majid* (2), *Mostafa* (2), *Zakia* (2), *Abbas.*

Amis (497) English: variant of AMES.

Amison (142) English: patronymic from AMIS or AMES.

Amitrano (136) Southern Italian: according to Caracausi, possibly a habitational name, from the name of an estate or domain.

GIVEN NAMES Italian 16%; Spanish 6%. *Vito* (2), *Luigi, Pasquale; Assunta, Mariano, Roberto, Sergio, Silverio.*

Amlin (142) Variant of German AMELUNG, HAMLIN, or HAMELIN.

Amling (158) Variant of German AMELUNG.

GIVEN NAMES German 5%. *Jurgen, Kurt.*

Amman (185) Variant of German AMMANN.

Ammann (683) South German and Swiss German: occupational or status name from *Amtmann* 'official', dialect *Ammann* (Middle High German *ambet man*, literally 'retinue man', 'retainer'). This came to denote various kinds of administrator, including a tax farmer.

FOREBEARS Jakob Ammann (c. 1644–1730), for whom the Amish people are named, was a 17th-century, strict Alsatian-Swiss religious reformer of the Anabaptist Mennonite Church. His followers began emigrating to North America in the 1720s, settling chiefly in PA, where they are still present in large numbers, having also spread to OH, Ontario, and elsewhere.

They are noted for their conservative life style (generally including avoidance of modern inventions such as automobiles and telephones), distinctive dress, and close-knit community.

GIVEN NAMES German 8%. *Alois* (2), *Christoph* (2), *Dieter* (2), *Sigi* (2), *Armin, Erwin, Franz, Gerda, Hans, Johannes, Kurt, Rudi.*

Ammar (153) Muslim: from a personal name based on Arabic *ammar* 'virtuous', 'pious'.

GIVEN NAMES Muslim 46%. *Mohammad* (3), *Mustafa* (3), *Ahmed* (2), *Essam* (2), *Hussein* (2), *Abrahim, Adnan, Ahmad, Amal, Atif, Ehab, Emad.*

Ammer (133) German: **1.** from Middle High German *amer* 'bunting' (the bird), hence a nickname for someone with a fine voice, or a flamboyant dresser. **2.** in southern Germany, possibly a topographic name for someone living by the Ammer river.

Ammerman (1181) Americanized spelling of German **Ammermann**, a regional name for someone from Ammerland, an area in Oldenburg.

Ammirati (166) Italian: from the medieval personal name *Am(m)iratus*, derived from the Arabic word *amīr* 'commander' (which also gave rise to AMIRAULT). It is possible that the name was taken to Italy from Spain.

GIVEN NAMES Italian 20%; Spanish 6%. *Carlo* (2), *Pasquale* (2), *Carmela, Carmine, Franco, Graziella, Matteo, Sal; Mario* (2), *Estrellita.*

Ammon (1033) **1.** German: dialect variant of AMMANN. **2.** English: from a Middle English personal name, *Agmund*, of Scandinavian origin, from *agi* 'awe' (or possibly *agi-* 'point of a sword') + *mund* 'protection'. Compare HAMMOND. **3.** Respelling of French HAMON.

Ammons (3014) Variant of English HAMMONDS.

Amo (271) Spanish: occupational name or nickname from *amo* 'tutor', 'guardian', or 'master' (a masculine form of *ama* 'nurse', Late Latin *amma*).

Amodei (157) Italian: see AMODEO.

GIVEN NAMES Italian 21%; Spanish 5%. *Alfonse* (2), *Angelo* (2), *Antonio* (2), *Cosmo* (2), *Aldo, Carmine, Emidio, Giuliano, Riccardo, Sal; Mario* (2), *Erenio.*

Amodeo (573) Italian: variant of AMADEO.

GIVEN NAMES Italian 14%. *Antonio* (2), *Sal* (2), *Salvatore* (2), *Santo* (2), *Biagio, Carlo, Carmine, Ciro, Dante, Filippo, Fulvio, Gaspare.*

Amodio (369) Italian: variant of AMADEO.

GIVEN NAMES Italian 21%. *Angelo* (6), *Antonio* (3), *Francesco* (3), *Pasquale* (3), *Carlo* (2), *Amedeo, Italo, Nicola, Nicoletta, Philomena, Salvatore.*

Amon (730) **1.** Variant spelling of German, English, or French AMMON. **2.** Slovenian: medieval occupational or status name from

a respelling of Bavarian *Amtmann* 'official' (see AMMANN and compare OMAN).

Amond (100) English: variant of AMMON.

Amonett (128) Respelling of French **Amonet**, which is itself a variant of **Hamonet**, a pet form of HAMON.

Amonette (129) Respelling of French **Amonet**, which is itself a variant of **Hamonet**, a pet form of HAMON.

Amor (307) **1.** Spanish and Portuguese: from Spanish and Portuguese *amor* 'love', used to denote an illegitimate child, also as a nickname for a philanderer. **2.** Spanish, Portuguese, and English: from the medieval personal name *Amor* (Latin *amor* 'love'), which was popular in Spain, Italy, and France, and introduced into England by the Normans. There was a St. Amor, of obscure history and unknown date, whose relics were preserved and venerated at the village of St. Amour in Burgundy.

GIVEN NAMES Spanish 27%; Portuguese 7%. *Jose* (12), *Arturo* (3), *Manuel* (3), *Emilia* (2), *Enrique* (2), *Fidel* (2), *Ramon* (2), *Raul* (2), *Alberto, Alejandro, Amador, Angelina.*

Amore (527) Italian: **1.** from a medieval personal name (see AMOR 2), or from a short form of a compound name formed with this element, as for example *Bonamore, Finamore.* **2.** nickname for a philanderer, from *amore* 'love'.

GIVEN NAMES Italian 12%. *Salvatore* (3), *Alfonse, Angelo, Carmelo, Carmine, Domenic, Francesca, Francesco, Giuseppe, Nicola, Olindo, Paolo.*

Amores (114) Spanish and Portuguese: nickname for a philanderer, from *amores* (plural) 'loves' (see AMOR).

GIVEN NAMES Spanish 47%; Portuguese 8%. *Alberto* (2), *Caridad* (2), *Jorge* (2), *Julio* (2), *Alejandro, Amado, Ana Maria, Ariston, Armando, Arsenio, Blanca, Carolina.*

Amorim (133) Portuguese: habitational name from any of the various places named Amorim, originally *(villa) Amorini*, from the name of the estate owner.

GIVEN NAMES Spanish 38%; Portuguese 26%. *Jose* (11), *Manuel* (7), *Maurilio* (3), *Adriano, Americo, Ana, Armando, Candido, Casimiro, Cristina, Fabricio, Isaura; Joaquim* (2), *Vasco* (2), *Almir, Guilherme, Ilidio, Marcio; Antonio* (3), *Giovanni, Silvio.*

Amorin (115) Galician: habitational name from Amorin (see AMORIM).

GIVEN NAMES Spanish 34%; Portuguese 13%. *Jose* (6), *Carlos* (3), *Luis* (3), *Manuel* (3), *Justino* (2), *Raul* (2), *Armondo, Avelino, Enrique, Evaristo, Jose Antonio, Josefa; Antonio* (4), *Dino.*

Amorose (106) Probably a variant of Italian AMOROSO.

GIVEN NAMES German 6%; Italian 6%. *Kurt; Guido, Salvatore.*

Amorosi (128) Italian: see AMOROSO.

GIVEN NAMES Italian 9%. *Angelo, Gaetano.*

Amoroso (1150) Italian (mainly southern): **1.** nickname for a much-loved person, a love-smitten individual, an affectionate person, or a philanderer, from *amoroso* 'amorous' (Latin *amorosus*). **2.** from the personal name *Amorosus*.

GIVEN NAMES Italian 15%; Spanish 5%. *Salvatore* (7), *Carmelo* (4), *Gaetano* (4), *Vito* (4), *Antonio* (3), *Domenic* (3), *Angelo* (2), *Carmine* (2), *Mauro* (2), *Rocco* (2), *Sal* (2), *Silvio* (2); *Ricardo* (3), *Gerardo* (2), *Roberto* (2), *Vicente* (2), *Carlos*, *Consuelo*, *Elena*, *Fabio*, *Jaime*, *Jose*, *Juan*, *Luis*.

Amoruso (181) Southern Italian: variant of AMOROSO.

GIVEN NAMES Italian 13%. *Vito* (2), *Angelo*, *Donato*, *Gasper*, *Gilda*, *Giuseppe*, *Marino*.

Amory (202) English: from a Germanic personal name, *Aimeri*, composed of the elements *haim* 'home' + *rīc* 'power'. (The same elements constitute the etymology of HENRY.) The name was introduced into England from France by the Normans. There has been some confusion with EMERY.

Amos (7218) **1.** Jewish: from the Hebrew personal name *Amos*, of uncertain origin, in some traditions connected with the Hebrew verb *amos* 'to carry', and assigned the meaning 'borne by God'. This was the name of a Biblical prophet of the 8th century BC, whose oracles are recorded in the Book of Amos. This was one of the Biblical names taken up by Puritans and Nonconformists in the 16th–17th centuries, too late to have had much influence on surname formation, except in Wales. **2.** English: variant of AMIS, assimilated in spelling to the Biblical name. It occurs chiefly in southeastern England.

Amoss (148) Variant spelling of AMOS.

Amparan (173) Spanish: probably from a personal name, an omen name from Spanish *amparan* 'may they (i.e. the angels) protect'.

GIVEN NAMES Spanish 33%; Portuguese 9%. *Alfonso* (4), *Jesus* (3), *Juan* (3), *Angel* (2), *Emilio* (2), *Francisco* (2), *Julio* (2), *Manuel* (2), *Raul* (2), *Alfredo*, *Alicia*, *Ana*.

Amparo (108) Spanish and Portuguese: from the Marian epithet meaning 'defenseless'.

GIVEN NAMES Spanish 57%; Portuguese 9%. *Julio* (3), *Jesus* (2), *Jose* (2), *Mercedes* (2), *Alonzo*, *Angel*, *Angelina*, *Carolina*, *Celso*, *Diaz*, *Dionicio*, *Dominga*.

Amrein (257) **1.** South German, chiefly Swiss: topographic name from *am* 'at' + *Rain* 'edge of plowed land'. **2.** Respelling of AMRHEIN.

GIVEN NAMES German 6%. *Benno*, *Hans Peter*, *Kurt*.

Amrhein (624) German and French (Alsace): topographic name for someone living by the Rhine river (German *Rhein*).

GIVEN NAMES French 5%. *Marcel* (3), *Laurette*, *Marielle*.

Amrine (257) Respelling of German AMRHEIN or AMREIN.

Amsbaugh (140) Americanized form of German **Ansbach**, a habitational name from a place of uncertain identity, probably Ansbach near Nürnberg.

FOREBEARS In 1777 two regiments of mercenaries from Ansbach were sent to fight for the British in the Revolutionary War. After the war was over many of them settled in North America, and some became known by this surname.

Amsberry (118) Probably a respelling of English AMESBURY.

Amsden (568) English: probably a habitational name, from a reduced form of the Oxfordshire place name Ambrosden, which is composed of an Old English personal name *Ambre* + Old English *dūn* 'hill'.

FOREBEARS Isaac Amsden was in Plymouth Colony in 1647; he died in Cambridge, MA, in 1659.

Amsel (137) **1.** Jewish (Ashkenazic): patronymic from the Yiddish personal name *Amsl*, from German *Anselm* (see ANSELMO). **2.** German: from *Amsel* '(European) blackbird' (a bird related to the American robin), hence either a nickname for someone fond of singing or an occupational name for a bird catcher.

GIVEN NAMES Jewish 17%; German 5%. *Chaim*, *Cheskel*, *Dovid*, *Hyman*, *Mayer*, *Naftali*, *Rivka*; *Horst*.

Amsler (497) **1.** Swiss German: habitational name from Amslen in Switzerland. **2.** German: occupational name for a fowler (bird-catcher), from an agent derivative of AMSEL. **3.** Jewish (Ashkenazic): habitational name from *Amsle*, Yiddish name of Namsław in Silesia.

Amspacher (166) Southern German: habitational name for someone from a place called Amsbach (see AMSBAUGH).

Amster (418) **1.** Dutch: from a derivative of Amstel, the name of the river that flows through Amsterdam; hence a habitational name for someone from Amsterdam, equivalent of **van Amstel**. **2.** Jewish (Ashkenazic): nickname from German *Hamster* 'hoarder'.

GIVEN NAMES Jewish 7%. *Mayer*, *Pinkus*.

Amsterdam (217) Jewish (Ashkenazic): habitational name from the city of Amsterdam in the Netherlands.

Amstutz (945) Swiss German and Austrian: topographic name for someone living near or at the foot of a steep mountainside, German *am Stutz* 'at the escarpment'.

Amthor (123) German: topographic name, from *am* 'at' + *tor* 'gate' (*Thor* in the early modern spelling). The reference was generally to one of the gates of a city.

GIVEN NAMES Scandinavian 4%; German 4%. *Kerstin*; *Helmut*.

Amundsen (814) Danish and Norwegian: patronymic from a Nordic personal name *Ǫgmundr*, composed of the elements *agi* 'awe' (or possibly *ag* 'point of a sword') + *mund* 'protection'. Compare HAMMOND.

GIVEN NAMES Scandinavian 9%. *Alf* (3), *Erik* (2), *Thor* (2), *Egil*, *Hjordis*, *Iver*, *Per*, *Svein*.

Amundson (3017) Americanized spelling of AMUNDSEN or of the Swedish cognate **Amundsson**.

GIVEN NAMES Scandinavian 4%. *Erik* (4), *Helmer* (3), *Thor* (2), *Alf*, *Anders*, *Arlys*, *Nils*, *Nordahl*, *Obert*, *Per*, *Sig*, *Tor*.

Amuso (116) Southern Italian: of uncertain origin, perhaps a topographic name for someone who lived in a sandy place, from medieval Greek *ammos* 'sand'.

GIVEN NAMES Italian 11%. *Salvatore* (2), *Rocco*.

Amy (629) **1.** French: from Old French *ami* 'friend', which was used both as a nickname and a personal name. **2.** Variant spelling of English AMEY.

Amyot (133) French: variant spelling of AMIOT.

GIVEN NAMES French 19%. *Andre* (3), *Adelard*, *Armand*, *Girard*, *Henri*.

Amyx (344) Southern French: patronymic from Occitan *amic* 'friend'. Compare AMY.

An (1069) **1.** Chinese 安: from the name of the ancient country known in China as AnXi, located in present-day Uzbekistan. Traditional accounts record that the legendary emperor Huang Di (2697–2595 BC) had a grandson named An (the character for 'peace') who moved to the far west to establish AnXi, losing contact with the Middle Kingdom. When the people of AnXi decided to return to China during the Han dynasty (206 BC–220 AD), they adopted their tribal name, An, as their surname. **2.** Korean: there is only one Chinese character for the *An* surname; it means 'peace'. Some sources indicate that there are 109 An clans, but only six can be documented. All had one common founding ancestor, named *Yi Wŏn*, who migrated from China to Shilla Korea in AD 807. Yi's three sons played a major role in resisting Japanese aggression during the reign of the Shilla King Kyŏngmun (861–875) and received the surname as a reward from the king. It is now quite a common Korean surname and can be found throughout the peninsula.

GIVEN NAMES Chinese/Korean 65%; Vietnamese 7%. *Sang* (16), *Sung* (8), *Jae* (7), *Kyung* (7), *Young* (7), *Dong* (5), *Kwang* (5), *Soo* (5), *Hyung* (4), *Kyeong* (4), *Ping* (4), *Sok* (4); *Chong* (8), *Pyong* (8), *Chang* (6), *Min* (5), *Byung* (4), *Byung Yong* (2), *Chang Soon* (2), *Chul* (2), *Dae* (2), *Haekyung* (2), *Jeong* (2), *Seong* (2); *Dung* (2), *Son* (2), *Thi* (2), *Bich*, *Chau Van*, *Cuc Kim*, *Diep*, *Dinh*, *Dinh Thi*, *Ha*, *Hanh*, *Hung*.

Anable (135) English: variant spelling of ANNABLE.

Anacker (215) German: nickname for a day laborer, as opposed to someone who owned

fields, from Middle High German *āne* 'without' + *acker* 'field'.
GIVEN NAMES German 4%. *Lotti* (2), *Wilhelm*.

Anagnos (192) Greek: shortened form of **Anagnostopoulos** 'son of the *Anagnōstēs*', a person appointed to read the Psalms and the Apostles in church, equivalent in responsibility to a Jewish cantor. The office dates from Byzantine times, and was regarded as a high honor.
GIVEN NAMES Greek 7%. *Spiro* (2), *Aristotle*, *Christos*, *Nichlos*.

Anagnost (102) Shortened form of Greek **Anagnostopoulos** (see ANAGNOS).
GIVEN NAMES Greek 9%. *Christos*, *Zissis*.

Anand (409) Indian (Panjab, southern states): Hindu name derived from a male personal name derived from Sanskrit *ananda* 'joy'. In the southern states it is only a given name, but has come to be used as a family name among South Indians in the U.S. It is also a Hindu (Khatri) and Sikh name based on the name of a clan in the Khatri community, probably derived from the name of the founder of the clan.
GIVEN NAMES Indian 87%. *Vijay* (8), *Ajay* (6), *Anil* (4), *Dev* (4), *Raj* (4), *Rakesh* (4), *Suresh* (4), *Vivek* (4), *Atul* (3), *Chandra* (3), *Mohan* (3), *Prem* (3).

Anania (308) Southern Italian and Greek (**Ananias**): from the personal name *Anania*, Greek *Ananias*, from Hebrew *Hananyah*, 'answered by the Lord'. This was the name of a character mentioned in the New Testament (Acts 5), who was struck dead for lying. Despite this, it was a popular name among early Christians and was borne by several saints venerated in the Greek Orthodox Church. As a Greek name it may be a shortened form of the patronymic **Ananiadis**.
GIVEN NAMES Italian 15%. *Salvatore* (5), *Angelo* (3), *Agostino* (2), *Antonio* (2), *Claudio*, *Domenic*, *Ettore*, *Eugenio*, *Gasper*, *Geno*.

Anas (104) Origin unidentified.
GIVEN NAMES Spanish 5%; French 4%. *Manuel* (2), *Cresencio*, *Evangelina*, *Zenaida*; *Jacques*.

Anast (129) Perhaps a shortened form of Greek ANASTAS.

Anastas (181) **1.** Greek: shortened form of patronymic surnames such as **Anastassiadis**, **Anastassopoulos**, **Anastassakopoulos**, and **Anastassakos**, derived from the personal name *Anastasios* 'resurrection'. **2.** Ukrainian: from the personal name *Anastas*, from Greek *Anastassios* (see 1).

Anastasi (576) Italian: see ANASTASIO.
GIVEN NAMES Italian 11%. *Antonino* (2), *Domenic* (2), *Salvatore* (2), *Alesio*, *Amerigo*, *Angelo*, *Cosmo*, *Filomena*, *Gaeton*, *Gasper*, *Marcello*, *Nichola*.

Anastasia (304) Italian: **1.** from the personal name *Anastasia*, feminine form of ANASTASIO. *Anastasia* was a popular per-

sonal name in medieval southern Europe because of the cult of a 4th-century saint who was martyred at Sirmium in Dalmatia. She was widely venerated, especially in the Eastern Church. **2.** in some instances, perhaps a habitational name from the place name Santa Anastasìa, in Naples province.
GIVEN NAMES Italian 8%. *Angelo* (3), *Vito* (3), *Dino*, *Larraine*.

Anastasio (601) Italian: from the personal name *Anastasio* (Latin *Anastasius*, from Greek *anastasis* 'resurrection'). This was widely chosen as a personal name among the early Christians on account of its religious symbolism. See also ANASTASIA.
GIVEN NAMES Italian 15%. *Angelo* (6), *Salvatore* (5), *Carmine* (2), *Pasquale* (2), *Rocco* (2), *Antonio*, *Biagio*, *Dario*, *Gaetano*, *Giacinto*, *Oreste*, *Pietro*.

Anastos (228) Greek: like ANASTAS, a shortened form of patronymic surnames derived from the personal name *Anastasios* 'resurrection', the *-os* representing a masculine inflection.

Anaya (2262) **1.** Basque: from Basque **Anaia**, from *anai* 'brother' + the definite article (suffixed) *-a*. In Basque this was used both as a byname and as a personal name. **2.** Spanish: habitational name from either of two places called Anaya, in Salamanca and Segovia provinces. The place name is probably of Arabic origin.
GIVEN NAMES Spanish 46%; Portuguese 9%. *Jose* (54), *Carlos* (31), *Jesus* (28), *Juan* (28), *Manuel* (26), *Luis* (22), *Francisco* (14), *Miguel* (14), *Raul* (13), *Pedro* (12), *Jorge* (10), *Arturo* (9); *Ligia*.

Ancar (117) French: shortened form of **Ancart**, probably a variant of **Hanecard**, from a derivative of the personal name *(Je)han*, old form of JEAN.
GIVEN NAMES French 17%. *Francois* (2), *Alphonse*, *Etienne*, *Fabien*, *Mireille*.

Ancel (165) **1.** French: status name from Old French *ancel* 'servant'. Compare Latin *ancilla* 'serving maid'. **2.** French: variant spelling of ANSEL. **3.** Jewish (eastern Ashkenazic): patronymic from the eastern Yiddish personal name *Antshl*.

Ancelet (130) French: from a diminutive of *Ancel*.
GIVEN NAMES French 10%. *Clovis*, *Ravis*.

Ancell (279) **1.** English: variant spelling of ANSELL. **2.** Probably a respelling of French or Jewish ANCEL.

Ancheta (465) Spanish (of Basque origin): topographic name from Basque *aintzi* 'swamp' + the collective suffix *-eta*.
GIVEN NAMES Spanish 40%; Portuguese 6%. *Jose* (5), *Andres* (4), *Enrique* (3), *Evelio* (3), *Jaime* (3), *Reynaldo* (3), *Romulo* (3), *Alberto* (2), *Cesar* (2), *Cornelio* (2), *Ernesto* (2), *Filemon* (2); *Wenceslao*; *Antonio* (2), *Angelo*, *Cecilio*, *Eligio*, *Federico*, *Gilda*, *Leonardo*, *Prisco*.

Anchondo (278) Spanish (of Basque origin): topographic name from Basque *aintzi* 'swamp' + *-ondo* 'beside'.
GIVEN NAMES Spanish 51%; Portuguese 11%. *Francisco* (6), *Jose* (6), *Ramon* (6), *Armando* (5), *Jesus* (5), *Manuel* (5), *Raul* (4), *Arturo* (3), *Carlos* (3), *Catalina* (2), *Cristina* (2), *Edmundo* (2).

Anchors (126) English: variant spelling of **Ankers**, itself a variant of ANKER.

Ancira (110) Mexican (also **Ansira**): unexplained.
GIVEN NAMES Spanish 44%; Portuguese 9%. *Jose* (4), *Roberto* (3), *Carlos* (2), *Ernesto* (2), *Lupe* (2), *Alonso*, *Alonzo*, *Amparo*, *Basilio*, *Bernardo*, *Blanca*, *Enrique*.

Ancona (537) Italian and Jewish (from Italy): habitational name from the Adriatic port of Ancona, which was founded by Greek refugees from Syracuse in about 390 BC. Its name is derived from Greek *ankōn* 'elbow', with reference to the shape of the cape on which it is situated.
GIVEN NAMES Italian 14%; Spanish 6%. *Vito* (9), *Antonio* (2), *Angelo*, *Carmine*, *Francesca*, *Gasper*, *Gennaro*, *Gioacchino*, *Girolamo*, *Giuseppi*, *Leonardo*, *Luca*; *Francisco* (2), *Mario* (2), *Alberto*, *Andres*, *Carlos*, *Eduardo*, *Garcia*, *Javier*, *Joaquin*, *Jorge*, *Jose*, *Mauricio*.

Ancrum (216) Scottish: habitational name from a place in Roxburghshire (Borders) called Ancrum, earlier *Alncromb* 'bend in the river Ale', from a word related to Welsh *crwm* 'bent', 'curved'.

Anctil (333) French and English (of Norman origin): from a personal name, *Anquetil* (Old Norse *Ásketill*), composed of the elements *áss* 'god' (earlier *ans*) + *ketill* 'kettle', 'helmet'. Compare HASKELL.
GIVEN NAMES French 17%. *Normand* (3), *Cecile* (2), *Marcel* (2), *Andre*, *Armand*, *Dany*, *Germaine*, *Gilles*, *Henri*, *Hilaire*, *Laurier*, *Valmore*.

Anda (128) **1.** Basque: habitational name from a town named Anda in Araba province, Basque Country. **2.** Norwegian: habitational name from a southwestern farm name, of uncertain origin; it may be from *and* 'duck'. **3.** Hungarian: from a pet form of the personal name *András*, Hungarian form of ANDREAS.
GIVEN NAMES Spanish 18%; Portuguese 5%. *Jose* (4), *Juan* (2), *Alejandro*, *Alma Rosa*, *Carlos*, *Herlinda*, *Jorge*, *Luis*, *Miguel*, *Rodolfo*, *Romulo*.

Andal (101) **1.** Galician: unexplained; it occurs chiefly in Ordes, in Galicia, and is also established in the Philippines. **2.** Norwegian: habitational name from any of four farms so named, most likely from *ahn* 'elm' + *dal* 'valley'.
GIVEN NAMES Spanish 19%; Portuguese 4%. *Jose* (2), *Vicente* (2), *Cesar*, *Domingo*, *Joselito*, *Luzviminda*, *Rafael*, *Virgilio*; *Godofredo*.

Andaloro (102) Southern Italian (Sicily): altered form of **Annaloro**, a status name from Sicilian *annaloru* 'farm worker employed year by year'.
GIVEN NAMES Italian 19%. *Angelo* (2), *Carlo*, *Filippo*, *Gaetana*, *Marco*, *Salvatore*.

Andary (122) Americanized spelling of French **André**, French form of ANDREAS. FOREBEARS Leah and Rachel Andary are recorded in MD in the 1720s and 1730s.
GIVEN NAME French 4%. *Antoine*.

Andaya (141) Basque: topographic name of Basque origin.
GIVEN NAMES Spanish 50%; Portuguese 5%. *Alfredo* (3), *Benedicto* (2), *Eulogio* (2), *Jesus* (2), *Teresita* (2), *Alejandro*, *Alfonso*, *Araceli*, *Bartolome*, *Bernardo*, *Carlos*, *Concepcion*.

Andazola (113) Mexican (also **Andasola**): unexplained; possibly a topographic name of Basque origin.
GIVEN NAMES Spanish 39%; Portuguese 6%. *Adolfo* (2), *Gustavo* (2), *Ruben* (2), *Armando*, *Arnulfo*, *Arturo*, *Camerina*, *Cesar*, *Diego*, *Efren*, *Epigmenio*, *Felipe*.

Andel (276) Czech (**Anděl**) and Slovak: from the personal name *Anděl*, from Greek *angelos* 'angel' (literally 'messenger'). Alternatively, it may be a habitational name for someone who lived in a house bearing the sign of an angel. Compare ANGEL.

Andelman (117) **1.** Jewish (Ashkenazic): variant of HANDELMAN. **2.** German (**Andelmann**): from the Slavic personal name *Anděl* (see ANDEL) + *Mann* 'man', either as a pet form or with the meaning 'servant of Andel'.
GIVEN NAMES Jewish 8%; Russian 6%. *Hyman*, *Polina*; *Aleksandr*, *Mikhail*, *Yasha*.

Ander (153) **1.** German: from the Germanic personal name, *Andahari*, composed of Old Norse *andi* (Old High German *ando* 'breath') or *anti* 'end', 'point' + *hari* 'army'. **2.** Scandinavian: perhaps an American short form of the Swedish surname ANDERSSON or Danish ANDERSEN. **3.** Slovak: derivative of the personal name ANDREAS.

Andera (124) Czech (**Anděra**): derivative of the personal name ANDREAS.

Anderberg (309) Swedish: ornamental name composed of the elements *ander* (an element of uncertain origin, perhaps a derivative of Greek *anēr*, *andros* 'man', as in ALEXANDER) + *berg* 'mountain'.
GIVEN NAMES Scandinavian 8%. *Erik*, *Lars*, *Sven*.

Anderegg (495) South German and Swiss German: topographic name for someone who lived *an der Egge*, dialect for *an der Ecke* 'on the edge (of a village, etc.)'.
GIVEN NAMES German 4%. *Erwin* (3), *Christoph*, *Elfriede*, *Hans*, *Otto*.

Anderer (131) German: probably from a Germanic personal name *Andahari*, composed of *anti* 'end', 'point', 'peak' + *hari* 'army'.

Anderle (225) **1.** German, Slovak, and Slovenian: from a South German pet form

of the personal name ANDREAS. **2.** Czech: from a pet form of German ANDREAS.
GIVEN NAMES German 5%. *Alois*, *Otto*, *Reinhold*, *Wolfgang*.

Anderman (210) German (**Andermann**): from the German personal name ANDER + *Mann* 'man', 'servant'.
GIVEN NAME German 4%. *Kurt*.

Anders (5352) German and Scottish: from the personal name *Anders*, vernacular form of ANDREAS. The German name is also found in Poland and has yielded a family name in Czech (**Anderš**).

Andersen (14853) Danish and Norwegian: patronymic from the personal name *Anders*, a vernacular form of ANDREAS.
GIVEN NAMES Scandinavian 9%. *Erik* (54), *Niels* (19), *Lars* (17), *Nels* (16), *Per* (7), *Anders* (6), *Holger* (6), *Jorgen* (6), *Thor* (6), *Bjorn* (5), *Helmer* (5), *Alf* (4).

Anderson (285232) Scottish and northern English: very common patronymic from the personal name *Ander(s)*, a northern Middle English form of ANDREW. See also ANDREAS. The frequency of the surname in Scotland is attributable, at least in part, to the fact that St. Andrew is the patron saint of Scotland, so the personal name has long enjoyed great popularity there. Legend has it that the saint's relics were taken to Scotland in the 4th century by a certain St. Regulus. The surname was brought independently to North America by many different bearers and was particularly common among 18th-century Scotch-Irish settlers in PA and VA. In the United States, it has absorbed many cognate or like-sounding names in other European languages, notably Swedish ANDERSSON, Norwegian and Danish ANDERSEN, but also Ukrainian *Andreychyn*, Hungarian *Andrásfi*, etc.

Andersson (492) Swedish: patronymic from the personal name *Anders*, a vernacular form of ANDREAS.
GIVEN NAMES Scandinavian 46%; German 7%. *Erik* (7), *Bjorn* (6), *Lars* (6), *Mats* (5), *Lennart* (4), *Nils* (4), *Per* (4), *Anders* (3), *Berndt* (2), *Hokan* (2), *Olle* (2), *Sten* (2); *Hans* (4), *Kurt* (4), *Alfons*, *Ernst*, *Gerd*, *Monika*.

Andert (201) North German: from the Germanic personal name *Anthart*, composed of the elements *Anda* (see ANDER) + *hard* 'strong', 'hard'.
GIVEN NAMES German 5%. *Otto* (2), *Guenter*, *Kurt*.

Anderton (1084) English: habitational name from either of two places, in Cheshire and Lancashire, named with the personal name *Ēanrēd* (Old English) or *Eindriði* (Old Norse) + Old English *tūn* 'settlement'.

Andes (900) **1.** German: variant of ANTHES. **2.** Latvian: variant of ANDIS.

Anding (404) **1.** German: from a pet form of a Germanic personal name composed with *And-* (see ANDER). **2.** Americanized

or Germanized spelling of Latvian **Andiņš**, a derivative of the personal name ANDIS.

Andino (537) Spanish: habitational name from a place in Castile named Andino.
GIVEN NAMES Spanish 44%; Portuguese 11%. *Jose* (18), *Angel* (9), *Luis* (7), *Pedro* (6), *Alberto* (4), *Alicia* (4), *Carlos* (4), *Juan* (4), *Luz* (4), *Rafael* (4), *Ana* (3), *Eduardo* (3); *Paulo*.

Andis (252) **1.** Variant of German ANTHES. **2.** Latvian: from the personal name *Andis*, a variant of *Andrejs* (see ANDREAS).

Andler (234) German and French (Alsace): **1.** habitational name for someone from Andlau in Alsace. **2.** variant of ENDLER.
GIVEN NAMES German 4%; French 4%. *Otto*, *Patrice* (2).

Ando (405) **1.** Japanese (**Andō**): variously written, originally with characters meaning 'peaceful east' or 'pacify the east'; the majority now use characters meaning 'peaceful wisteria'. A branch of the Abe family bears the name in eastern Japan. **2.** Hungarian (**Andó**): from a pet form of the personal name *András*, Hungarian form of ANDREAS.
GIVEN NAMES Japanese 58%. *Akira* (3), *Hiroshi* (3), *Masahiro* (3), *Osamu* (3), *Takashi* (3), *Hideki* (2), *Hiromi* (2), *Kenji* (2), *Makoto* (2), *Minako* (2), *Rie* (2), *Seiji* (2).

Andolina (219) Italian (Sicily): from a diminutive of a personal name, probably one of Germanic origin formed with the stem *And-*.
GIVEN NAMES Italian 8%. *Salvatore* (3), *Antonio*, *Carmelo*.

Andon (111) Galician: variant of ANTON.
GIVEN NAMES Spanish 18%. *Arnando*, *Bartolome*, *Blanca*, *Carlota*, *Cristobal*, *Gaudencio*, *Jorge*, *Marisol*, *Remedios*, *Ruben*, *Socorro*.

Andonian (149) Armenian: patronymic from the personal name *Anton* (see ANTHONY).
GIVEN NAMES Armenian 23%. *Aram*, *Aris*, *Garbis*, *Hagop*, *Haig*, *Hratch*, *Kevork*, *Kourken*, *Krikor*, *Mihran*, *Sarkes*, *Shahen*.

Andra (107) **1.** German (**Andrä**): see ANDRAE. **2.** Indian (Andhra Pradesh): Hindu (Brahman) name of unknown meaning.
GIVEN NAMES Indian 5%. *Ramana*, *Ramesh*, *Sateesh*.

Andrada (260) Spanish and Portuguese: variant of ANDRADE.
GIVEN NAMES Spanish 30%; Portuguese 7%. *Manuel* (4), *Pedro* (3), *Roberto* (3), *Juan* (2), *Ruben* (2), *Abelardo*, *Adelaida*, *Alicia*, *Amada*, *Anacleto*, *Angelito*, *Armando*; *Antonio* (2), *Angelo*, *Lorenzo*, *Lucio*, *Romeo*.

Andrade (6194) Galician and Portuguese: habitational name from any of numerous places in Galicia and Portugal named Andrade, perhaps originally *villa Andr(e)ati* 'estate of a man named ANDREAS'.

GIVEN NAMES Spanish 41%; Portuguese 11%. *Jose* (168), *Manuel* (123), *Juan* (54), *Carlos* (53), *Luis* (49), *Miguel* (35), *Francisco* (34), *Jesus* (32), *Jorge* (25), *Guadalupe* (23), *Pedro* (23), *Ramon* (21); *Joao* (6), *Joaquim* (4), *Paulo* (4), *Serafim* (3), *Afonso* (2), *Ligia* (2), *Marcio* (2), *Anatolio, Conceicao, Duarte, Guilherme, Henrique.*

Andrae (188) German (also written **Andrä**): variant of ANDREAE.
GIVEN NAMES German 8%. *Wilhelm* (3), *Hans* (2), *Kurt.*

Andras (286) Hungarian (**András**): from the personal name *András*, Hungarian form of ANDREAS.
GIVEN NAME French 5%. *Oneil* (4).

Andrasko (113) **1.** Czech (**Andráško**): from a pet form of *Andrasek*, a variant of *Ondrášek*, a derivative of the personal name *Ondřej*, Czech form of ANDREAS. **2.** Slovak (**Andraško**): from a pet form of *Andráš*, a derivative of the personal name *Ondrej*, Slovak form of ANDREAS. **3.** In some cases perhaps from a pet form of the Hungarian personal name *András* (see ANDRAS). **4.** Perhaps a respelling of Bulgarian **Andreasko**, from the personal name, Bulgarian form of ANDREAS.

Andre (2642) **1.** French (**André**): from the personal name *André*, French vernacular form of ANDREAS, also found as a Huguenot name in England in the 17th and 18th centuries. **2.** German: shortened form of ANDREAE. **3.** Swedish: shortened form of ANDREE.
FOREBEARS A bearer of the surname André is recorded in Quebec city in 1653; another, from Charente, is documented there in 1659. Other branches, from Normandy and Burgundy, were recorded in Montreal from 1663.
GIVEN NAMES French 8%. *Pierre* (10), *Jacques* (4), *Jean-Claude* (3), *Emile* (2), *Marcel* (2), *Mirlene* (2), *Pascal* (2), *Alain, Alphonse, Andre, Armand, Arsene.*

Andrea (474) **1.** Filipino: from a local form of the personal name *Andreas*. **2.** Italian: from the personal name *Andrea* (see ANDREAS). It is not found in this form as a surname in Italy. However, compare DE ANDREA.

Andreadis (111) Greek: patronymic from the personal name ANDREAS. The *-ides* patronymic is classical. It was revived in the late 19th and early 20th century, in particular by Greeks from the Black Sea region.
GIVEN NAMES Greek 23%. *Stelios* (3), *Andreas* (2), *Dimitrios, Eleftherios, Georgios, Nikos, Stephanos.*

Andreae (192) German (also written **Andreä**) and Swedish: patronymic from the personal name ANDREAS (from the Latin genitive case).
GIVEN NAME German 4%. *Otto.*

Andreano (172) **1.** Italian: from a derivative of the personal name *Andrea* (see ANDREAS). **2.** Southern Italian: from a variant (*Andreano* or *Andreanò*) of **Andriano, Andrianò**, a habitational name for someone from places called Àndria, in Bari and Apulia.
GIVEN NAMES Italian 17%. *Gino* (2), *Carmela, Fiore, Guido, Marco, Natale, Remo.*

Andreas (931) Greek; also German and Dutch: from the New Testament Greek name *Andreas*, which gave rise to ANDREW in English and vernacular derivatives in almost every other European language. Etymologically, it is from Greek *andreios* 'manly', from *anēr* 'man', 'male' (genitive *andros*). It was the name of the first of Christ's disciples, and is a Greek translation of an Aramaic original. The disciple is the patron saint of both Scotland and Russia, but the Scottish ANDERSON is far more common than its Russian equivalent, **Andreev**. The personal name was popular throughout Europe in various vernacular forms (for example, Italian *Andrea*, French *André*, Scottish, North German, and Scandinavian *Anders*, Dutch *Andries*, Hungarian *András*, Czech *Ondřej*, Slovak *Ondrej*, Polish *Andrzej* and *Jędrzej*, and Russian *Andrei*).
GIVEN NAMES German 5%. *Fritz* (2), *Heinz* (2), *Otto* (2), *Beate, Bernd, Ernst, Ilse, Kurt.*

Andreasen (989) Respelling of Danish, Norwegian, and North German **Andreassen**, a patronymic from the personal name ANDREAS.
GIVEN NAMES Scandinavian 9%; German 4%. *Erik* (3), *Bendt* (2), *Astrid, Ejner, Holger, Kjeld, Knud, Niels, Nils, Ottar, Per*; *Hans* (4), *Egon, Kurt, Otto, Wilhelm.*

Andreason (255) Respelling of Swedish **Andreasson** or of Danish, Norwegian, and North German **Andreas(s)en**, all patronymics from the personal name ANDREAS.
GIVEN NAMES German 6%; Scandinavian 4%. *Kurt* (2), *Klaus.*

Andreassen (165) Danish, Norwegian, and North German: patronymic from the personal name ANDREAS.
GIVEN NAMES Scandinavian 27%; German 6%. *Bjorn* (2), *Knut* (2), *Alf, Dagny, Johan, Lars, Nils, Ove, Svein, Tor*; *Hans, Kurt, Otto.*

Andreatta (191) Northeastern Italian: from a diminutive of the personal name *Andrea* (see ANDREAS).
GIVEN NAMES Italian 14%. *Mario* (4), *Elio* (3), *Antonio* (2), *Aldo, Angelo, Erminio, Fiore, Guido, Leno, Lino, Livio, Nevio, Primo.*

Andree (498) **1.** Americanized spelling of French *André* (see ANDRE). **2.** Variant spelling of German and Swedish ANDREAE.

Andreen (164) Variant spelling of Swedish ANDREN.

Andreini (178) Italian (Sicily): from a pet form of the personal name *Andrea* (see ANDREAS).

GIVEN NAMES Italian 6%. *Dante* (2), *Angelo, Geno.*

Andren (218) Swedish (**Andrén**, earlier **Andrenius**): Latinized patronymic from the personal name ANDREAS.
GIVEN NAMES Scandinavian 12%. *Anders* (2), *Bjorn, Erik, Per.*

Andreola (100) Italian: variant of ANDREOLI.
GIVEN NAMES Italian 9%. *Angelo, Attilio, Emilio, Ildo.*

Andreoli (394) Italian (Naples and Sicily): from a pet form of the personal name *Andrea* (see ANDREAS).
GIVEN NAMES Italian 12%; French 4%. *Aldo* (2), *Domenic* (2), *Angelo, Antonio, Cosmo, Egidio, Flavio, Geno, Lelio, Luigi, Marino, Nazzareno*; *Andre* (3).

Andreoni (169) Southern Italian (Naples and Sicily): from a pet form of the personal name *Andrea* (see ANDREAS).
GIVEN NAMES Italian 12%; Spanish 9%; French 5%. *Aldo* (2), *Carlo, Fulvio, Gino, Giulio, Lido, Marino, Reno*; *Orlando* (5), *Mario* (3), *Aurelio* (2), *Alfonso*; *Armand* (3), *Solange.*

Andreotti (185) Italian (Naples and Sicily): from a pet form of the personal name *Andrea* (see ANDREAS).
GIVEN NAMES Italian 18%. *Aldo* (2), *Dino* (2), *Alessandro, Deno, Elio, Fiorella, Geno, Giuseppe, Levio, Margherita, Reno, Renzo.*

Andreozzi (293) Italian (Naples and Sicily): from a pet form of the personal name *Andrea* (see ANDREAS).
GIVEN NAMES Italian 19%; French 4%. *Rocco* (4), *Angelo* (2), *Gino* (2), *Orazio* (2), *Concetta, Domenic, Egidio, Enrico, Fausto, Gennaro, Luigi, Natale*; *Armand* (3), *Patrice.*

Andrepont (214) French: apparently a habitational name from an unidentified place named as '(Saint) Andrew's Bridge'. This is a frequent Louisiana surname.
GIVEN NAMES French 4%. *Berchman, Yves.*

Andres (2816) From the personal name *Andres*, a vernacular form of ANDREAS in various European languages, including Spanish *Andrés*, French (Breton) *Andrès*, German *Andres*, Czech *Andrejs*, etc.
GIVEN NAMES Spanish 8%. *Francisco* (7), *Jose* (7), *Pedro* (5), *Carlos* (4), *Ernesto* (4), *Juan* (4), *Manuel* (4), *Emilio* (3), *Ramon* (3), *Alberto* (2), *Alejandro* (2), *Andres* (2).

Andresen (1571) Variant of the Danish, Norwegian, and North German patronymic ANDREASSEN.
GIVEN NAMES Scandinavian 8%. *Erik* (6), *Per* (3), *Nord* (2), *Vidar* (2), *Bjorn, Carsten, Erland, Gudrun, Jorgen, Karsten, Odvar, Svein.*

Andreski (145) Reduced form of Polish ANDRZEJEWSKI.

Andreson (118) Respelling of a Scandinavian patronymic from the personal name ANDRES.

Andress (1195) Variant of German ANDRES and English ANDREWS.

Andretta (115) Southern Italian (Naples and Sicily): **1.** from a pet form of the personal name *Andrea* (see ANDREAS). **2.** habitational name from either of two places called Andretta, in Avellino and Campania.
GIVEN NAMES Italian 17%; French 5%. *Donato* (2), *Agostino*, *Cosmo*, *Elio*, *Gaeton*, *Gino*, *Luigi*; *Camille*.

Andreu (225) Catalan and southern French: from the personal name *Andreu*, Catalan and Occitan form of ANDREAS.
GIVEN NAMES Spanish 37%; Portuguese 10%. *Jose* (10), *Angel* (3), *Armando* (3), *Juan* (3), *Luis* (3), *Carlos* (2), *Cristina* (2), *Francisco* (2), *Jesus* (2), *Lazara* (2), *Manuel* (2), *Nieves* (2).

Andrew (4452) English and Scottish: from the usual vernacular English form (recorded from the 13th century onward) of the New Testament Greek personal name ANDREAS.
FOREBEARS The surname Andrew was first brought to North America from England by Robert Andrew (died 1668), who settled in Boxford, MA.

Andrews (46952) English: patronymic from the personal name ANDREW. This is the usual southern English patronymic form, also found in Wales; the Scottish and northern English form is ANDERSON. In North America this name has absorbed numerous cases of the various European cognates and their derivatives. (For forms, see Hanks and Hodges 1988.)
FOREBEARS This was a common name among the early settlers in New England. Robert Andrews emigrated in 1635 from Norwich, England, to Ipswich, MA. Even before 1635, one Thomas Andrews is recorded as being established in Hingham. A certain William Andrews was a member of John Davenport's company, which sailed from Boston in 1638 to found the New Haven colony.

Andriano (137) Italian: variant of ANDRE-ANO.
GIVEN NAMES Italian 15%. *Vito* (2), *Carmela*, *Gaetano*, *Geronimo*, *Rocco*.

Andrich (149) **1.** Serbian and Croatian (**Andrić**): patronymic from the personal name *Andro*, pet form of *Andrija* (see ANDREAS). The Croatian name is found mainly in Slavonia. **2.** Eastern German: from a Sorbian patronymic form of ANDREAS. **3.** Ukrainian: from the personal name *Andrij*, Ukrainian form of ANDREAS.
GIVEN NAMES South Slavic 6%. *Petar* (2), *Miomir*, *Nevenka*.

Andrick (282) **1.** Probably Ukrainian: from a pet form of the personal name *Andrij*, Ukrainian form of *Andreas*. **2.** This spelling is also found as a Sorbian name in eastern Germany. Compare ANDRICH.

Andrie (120) Mainly German: derivative of the personal name ANDREAS. Compare ANDRIES.
GIVEN NAME German 5%. *Kurt*.

Andries (308) Dutch: from the personal name *Andries*, a vernacular form of ANDREAS.
GIVEN NAMES French 4%. *Auguste*, *Gabrielle*, *Leonce*.

Andring (129) Dutch: patronymic from the personal name ANDRIES.

Andringa (189) Frisian: from the personal name ANDRIES + the patronymic suffix -*ing* and genitive plural ending -*a*, i.e. 'descendants of Andries'.
GIVEN NAMES Dutch 5%. *Dirk* (2), *Gerrit*.

Andriola (141) Italian: from a pet form of the personal name *Andrea* (see ANDREAS).
GIVEN NAMES Italian 17%. *Rocco* (2), *Salvatore* (2).

Andris (167) **1.** Greek: shortened form of any of various patronymic surnames derived from ANDREAS. **2.** Lithuanian: patronymic from a variant of the personal name *Andrys* (see ANDREAS). **3.** German and Dutch: variant of ANDRIES.
GIVEN NAMES Greek 5%. *Stavros* (2), *Stathis*.

Andrist (265) Swiss German: variant of ANDRIS, with excrescent -*t*.
GIVEN NAMES German 5%. *Otto* (2), *Fritz*, *Kurt*, *Orlo*.

Andrle (100) German: variant of ANDERLE.
GIVEN NAMES French 6%. *Armand*, *Laure*.

Andros (328) **1.** English: variant of ANDREWS. **2.** Swiss German and Hungarian: derivative of the personal name ANDREAS. **3.** Perhaps a reduced form of Greek **Andronikos**, **Andronidis**, or some other similar surname, all patronymics from ANDREAS.
FOREBEARS William Andros came to VA in 1617 and died there about 1655. Sir Edmund Andros (1637–1714) was the British colonial governor of several provinces in America between 1674 and 1698, most notably NY (1674–81).

Andrus (3470) English: variant of ANDREWS.
FOREBEARS William Andrus came to Boston in 1635 and moved to New Haven in 1639, where he died in 1676.

Andruss (125) Variant of English ANDREWS.

Andry (402) **1.** English: variant of ANDREW, influenced by or borrowed from French *André*. **2.** French: from an Old French personal name of Germanic origin, composed of the elements *agi* 'point of a sword' + *rīc* 'power'. **3.** Northern French variant of **André** (see ANDRE).
FOREBEARS Ellinor Andry is recorded in VA in 1652.
GIVEN NAMES French 10%. *Allain* (7), *Armand* (2), *Emile* (2), *Alcide*, *Christophe*, *Marcel*, *Thierry*.

Andrysiak (101) Polish: patronymic from the personal name *Andrys* (see ANDREAS).

Andrzejewski (570) Polish: habitational name for someone from a place called Andrzejewo, a derivative of the personal name *Andrzej*, Polish form of ANDREAS.
GIVEN NAMES Polish 7%. *Casimir* (2), *Jozef* (2), *Tadeusz* (2), *Halina*, *Jerzy*, *Stanislaw*, *Stas*, *Thadeus*, *Witold*, *Zbigniew*.

Andujar (338) Spanish (**Andújar**): habitational name from Andújar, a city to the east of Córdoba.
GIVEN NAMES Spanish 46%; Portuguese 10%. *Jose* (14), *Miguel* (5), *Carlos* (4), *Rafael* (4), *Bienvenido* (3), *Juan* (3), *Luis* (3), *Luz* (3), *Manuel* (3), *Ramona* (3), *Aida* (2), *Ana* (2).

Andy (175) From a pet form in English (and possibly other languages as well) of the personal names ANDREW or ANDERS (see ANDREAS).

Anello (555) Italian (mainly southern): from the personal name *Anello*.
GIVEN NAMES Italian 19%. *Salvatore* (8), *Angelo* (6), *Vito* (4), *Matteo* (2), *Santo* (2), *Carmela*, *Corrado*, *Gaspere*, *Pietro*, *Rocco*, *Santina*, *Vincenzo*.

Anema (122) Frisian: patronymic from an unidentified personal name.

Anes (117) Portuguese: from a patronymic form of the personal name *João*, a vernacular form of *Johannes* (see JOHN).
GIVEN NAMES Spanish 16%; Portuguese 8%. *Jose* (3), *Angel*, *Dionisio*, *Esperanza*, *Gilberto*, *Ines*, *Juanita*, *Luis*, *Luisa*, *Manuel*, *Manuela*, *Pedro*; *Joao*.

Aney (121) **1.** English: unexplained. **2.** Possibly a respelling of French **Ané**, from a personal name derived from Latin *Asinarius*.
GIVEN NAME French 4%. *Regine*.

Anfinson (295) Swedish and Norwegian: patronymic from *Anfinn*, Old Norse *Arnfinnr*, a personal name composed of the elements *arn* 'eagle' + *Finnr* 'Finn', 'Saami'.

Ang (523) **1.** Chinese 吴: variant of WU 1. **2.** Chinese 伍: variant of WU 4. **3.** Filipino: unexplained.
GIVEN NAMES Spanish 12%. *Jose* (3), *Corazon* (2), *Eduardo* (2), *Jaime* (2), *Pablo* (2), *Ricardo* (2), *Alfonso*, *Alfredo*, *Armida*, *Bernardita*, *Conchita*, *Domingo*.

Ange (456) French: **1.** from the medieval personal name, from *ange* 'angel' (see ANGEL). **2.** (**Angé**): southern variant of the personal name ANGIER.

Angel (4756) **1.** English: from Middle English *angel* 'angel' (from Latin *angelus*), probably applied as a nickname for someone of angelic temperament or appearance or for someone who played the part of an angel in a pageant. As a North American surname it may also be an Americanized form of a cognate European surname, as for example Italian ANGELO, Rumanian **Anghel**, Czech **Anděl**, or Hungarian **Angyal**. **2.** German: ethnic name for a member of a Germanic people on the

Jutland peninsula; members of this tribe invaded eastern and northern Britain in the 5th–6th centuries and gave their name to England. See ENGEL. **3.** Slovenian (eastern Slovenia): from the Latin personal name *Angelus*.

GIVEN NAMES Spanish 11%. *Jose* (32), *Miguel* (13), *Carlos* (12), *Juan* (12), *Manuel* (12), *Jorge* (10), *Luis* (9), *Arturo* (7), *Roberto* (7), *Jesus* (6), *Raul* (6), *Salvador* (6).

Angeles (900) Spanish: **1.** from a short form of the Marian personal name *María de los Ángeles* ('Mary of the angels'). **2.** habitational name from a place named Ángeles (in A Coruña province) or Los Ángeles (for example, in the provinces of Córdoba and Cádiz).

Angeletti (172) Italian: from a pet form of ANGELO.

Angeli (462) Italian: see ANGELO.

GIVEN NAMES Italian 11%. *Geno* (2), *Luigi* (2), *Primo* (2), *Silvio* (2), *Angelo*, *Egidio*, *Franco*, *Marino*, *Pasco*, *Pasquale*, *Raimondo*, *Renzo*.

Angelica (103) Southern Italian: from the personal name *Angelica*, feminine form of ANGELICO.

GIVEN NAMES Italian 13%; French 5%. *Filippo*, *Fiore*, *Gilda*, *Pasco*, *Sal*; *Fabienne*.

Angelico (156) Italian: from the adjective *angelico* 'angelic' (from medieval Latin *angelicus*), which was used as a personal name (a masculine equivalent of the much-favored female personal name *Angelica*), but in some cases may have been applied, possibly ironically, as a nickname.

GIVEN NAMES Italian 10%; French 4%. *Angelo* (2), *Emanuele*.

Angelillo (194) Italian: from a pet form of the personal name ANGELO.

GIVEN NAMES Italian 22%. *Vito* (4), *Amedeo* (3), *Donato* (3), *Carlo*, *Fedele*, *Maurizio*, *Rocco*, *Salvatore*.

Angeline (177) **1.** Dutch: from a pet form of the Latin Christian name *Angelus* (see ANGELO). **2.** Possibly in some cases an altered form of Italian ANGELINI.

GIVEN NAMES Italian 7%. *Dino*, *Gino*, *Salvatore*.

Angelini (616) Italian: see ANGELINO.

GIVEN NAMES Italian 15%. *Domenic* (4), *Rinaldo* (3), *Mario* (2), *Pietro* (2), *Alberto*, *Alfredo*, *Americo*, *Artemio*, *Amelio*, *Caesar*, *Carlo*, *Ciro*, *Concetta*, *Duilio*, *Emidio*, *Erminio*, *Ettore*, *Germano*, *Orlando*, *Sergio*, *Tito*.

Angelino (190) Italian: from a pet form of the personal name ANGELO.

GIVEN NAMES Italian 9%; Spanish 7%; French 5%. *Aldo*, *Angelo*, *Lorenzo*, *Salvatore*; *Mario* (2), *Carlos*, *Juan*, *Pedro*; *Alphonse*, *Jacques*.

Angelis (137) **1.** Greek: variant of ANGELOS. **2.** Italian: see DE ANGELIS.

GIVEN NAMES Greek 21%; Italian 5%. *Konstantinos* (2), *Antonios*, *Athina*, *Christos*,

Dimitrios, *Efthimios*, *Eleftherios*, *Georgios*, *Konstantino*, *Sevasti*, *Stratis*; *Angelo* (3), *Lia*.

Angell (2992) English variant spelling of ANGEL, or an Americanized form of any of the various European cognates mentioned there.

FOREBEARS Thomas Angell came to New England with Roger Williams in 1631. He was one of the earliest settlers of Providence, RI.

Angelle (416) French: from an old personal name, *Angelle*, Latin *Angelus*, from Greek *angelos* 'messenger', 'angel' (considered as a messenger sent from God).

GIVEN NAMES French 7%. *Antoine* (2), *Alphonse*, *Andre*, *Clovis*, *Ferrel*, *Honore*.

Angello (208) Italian: variant spelling of ANGELO.

GIVEN NAMES Italian 11%. *Angelo* (2), *Salvatore* (2), *Aldo*, *Domenic*, *Sal*.

Angelo (2656) Italian: from a popular medieval personal name, *Angelo*, Latin *Angelus*, from Greek *angelos* 'messenger', 'angel' (considered as a messenger sent from God).

GIVEN NAMES Italian 5%. *Sal* (4), *Salvatore* (4), *Santino* (3), *Carlo* (2), *Pasquale* (2), *Rocco* (2), *Aldo*, *Amadeo*, *Anello*, *Angelo*, *Antonio*, *Carmel*.

Angeloff (128) Russian and Bulgarian: alternative spelling of **Angelov**, from *angel* 'angel' + the surname suffix *-ov*. This name and others like it were frequently assigned as religious names to intending Orthodox priests in seminaries.

Angelone (360) Italian: from an augmentative form of the personal name ANGELO.

GIVEN NAMES Italian 15%; Spanish 5%. *Antonio* (2), *Alessandro*, *Angelo*, *Biagio*, *Domenic*, *Dominico*, *Elio*, *Ennio*, *Gaetano*, *Gino*, *Guerino*; *Leandro* (3), *Emilio* (2), *Mario* (2), *Roberto* (2), *Alfonso*, *Amilio*, *Luis*, *Renato*.

Angeloni (190) Italian: see ANGELONE.

GIVEN NAMES Italian 15%; Spanish 6%; French 4%. *Aldo* (2), *Angelo*, *Carmine*, *Dante*, *Dino*, *Elio*, *Lelio*, *Marino*, *Reno*, *Rocco*; *Mario* (2), *Jorge*, *Melio*, *Ramon*, *Sergio*, *Silvia*, *Tavo*; *Almira*, *Armand*, *Patrice*.

Angelopoulos (131) Greek: from the personal name *Angelos* (from *angelos* 'messenger', 'angel') or a shortened form of the personal name *Evangelos* 'bringer of good news' (see EVANGELISTA), + the patronymic ending *-poulos*. This ending occurs chiefly in the Peloponnese. It is derived from Latin *pullus* 'nestling', 'chick'.

GIVEN NAMES Greek 23%. *Andreas* (2), *Dimitrios* (2), *Angelos*, *Athanasia*, *Kostas*, *Nikolaos*, *Pericles*, *Spyridon*, *Spyros*, *Thanos*, *Vassilis*.

Angelos (372) Reduced form of any of various Greek surnames derived from the forename *Angelos* (from *angelos* 'messenger', 'angel'), as for example ANGELOPOULOS.

GIVEN NAMES Greek 6%. *Spiro* (3), *Alexandros*, *Constantine*, *Manos*, *Nikolaos*, *Stavros*, *Vasilios*.

Angelotti (143) Italian: from a pet form of the personal name ANGELO.

GIVEN NAMES Italian 11%. *Carmine* (2), *Antonio*, *Donato*, *Mauro*, *Pasquale*, *Silvio*.

Angelucci (326) Italian: from a pet form of the personal name ANGELO.

GIVEN NAMES Italian 15%. *Dante* (2), *Luigi* (2), *Angelo*, *Domenico*, *Franco*, *Geno*, *Giacinto*, *Marco*, *Massimo*, *Settimio*, *Vincenzo*.

Angelus (107) Most probably a German and Dutch humanistic surname from the Latin word *angelus* 'angel'.

GIVEN NAMES German 7%; Greek 4%. *Theos* (2), *Theodor*; *Constantine*, *Loukas*.

Anger (755) **1.** South German: topographic name from Middle High German *anger* 'meadow', 'village green'. **2.** French and English (of Norman origin): variant of the personal name ANGIER. **3.** French: variant of the habitational name ANGERS.

Angerer (222) South German: topographic name for a dweller by a meadow or village green (see ANGER) or a habitational name for someone from any of numerous places in Bavaria named with this word.

GIVEN NAMES German 4%. *Oskar*, *Otto*.

Angerhofer (101) German: habitational name for someone from Angerhof in Bavaria.

Angerman (197) **1.** Swedish (also **Angermann**): shortened form of the Latinized regional name *Angermannius* 'man from the county of Ångermanland'. **2.** German (**Angermann**): topographic name for a dweller by a meadow or by a village green, from Middle High German *anger* 'meadow', 'village green' + *man* 'man'.

Angermeier (196) German: distinguishing name from Middle High German *anger* 'meadow' + *meier* 'tenant farmer' (see MEYER), i.e. 'tenant farmer of the farm by the meadow'.

GIVEN NAMES German 6%. *Ingo*, *Kurt*, *Willi*.

Angers (342) French and English: habitational name from Angers, the capital of Anjou, France; it was called in Latin *Andrecavis*, being the home of the Gaulish tribe known as the *Andrecavi* in Roman times.

GIVEN NAMES French 18%. *Aime* (2), *Marcel* (2), *Pierre* (2), *Adelard*, *Aristide*, *Eudore*, *Fernand*, *Florent*, *Gilles*, *Henri*, *Jean-Paul*, *Jean-Yves*.

Angert (162) **1.** Jewish (from Ukraine and Belarus): unexplained. **2.** German: variant of ANGER.

GIVEN NAMES Russian 8%; Jewish 7%. *Betya*, *Lev*, *Lyubov*, *Matvey*, *Yefim*, *Yekaterina*, *Yelena*; *Beila*, *Moisey*, *Sol*, *Zelman*.

Angevine (364) French and English: metronymic from a feminine form of the regional name from Old French *angevin* 'man from Anjou'. Anjou is a province of western France that was ruled by a count as an independent territory from the 10th century. It became a property of the English Crown for fifty years at the end of the 12th century.

Angier (244) French and English (both Norman and Huguenot): from the Old French personal name *Angier*, which is of Germanic origin, composed of the elements *ans* 'god' + *gēr* 'spear' (Old Norse *geirr*).
GIVEN NAME French 5%. *Andre*.

Angiolillo (113) Italian: variant of ANGE-LILLO.
GIVEN NAMES Italian 19%. *Domenic* (2), *Lucio*, *Rocco*.

Anglada (117) Catalan: habitational name from any of various minor places in Catalonia, so named from Latin *anglata* 'corner'.
GIVEN NAMES Spanish 23%. *Jose* (4), *Angel* (2), *Luis* (2), *Rafael* (2), *Ana*, *Aniseto*, *Bonifacio*, *Catalina*, *Isaura*, *Juan*, *Liliana*, *Mario*; *Angelo*, *Antonio*.

Angle (1999) **1.** English and Irish (of Norman origin): topographic name from Middle English and Old French *angle* 'angle', 'corner' (Latin *angulus*). As an Irish surname, it can also be habitational, from a place in Pembrokeshire, South Wales, named with this word. **2.** Americanized spelling of German ANGEL or ENGEL.

Anglemyer (227) Americanized spelling of ENGELMEYER, a South German variant of ANGERMEIER.

Anglen (140) Variant spelling of the Irish surname ANGLIN.

Angles (223) **1.** Catalan and southern French (**Anglès**): ethnic name from Catalan and Occitan *anglès* 'English'. **2.** French: from any of at least eight places in France named (Les) Angles '(the place of) the English'.
GIVEN NAMES Spanish 10%. *Joaquin* (2), *Luis* (2), *Aguedo*, *Alberto*, *Cristina*, *Eloisa*, *Gustavo*, *Ignacio*, *Jaime*, *Jesus*, *Juanita*, *Luisita*.

Angleton (160) English: habitational name from a place in Staffordshire named Engleton, from Old English *Engla* (genitive plural of *Engle* 'Angle') + *tūn* 'settlement'.

Angley (140) English: Americanized form of French **Anglais** 'English(man)'.

Anglim (167) Irish: variant spelling of ANGLIN.

Anglin (3243) Irish (Co. Cork): Anglicized form of Gaelic **Ó hAngluinn** 'descendant of *Anglonn*', a personal name from *anglonn* 'champion'.

Angotti (329) Italian: from the Sicilian personal name *Angotto*, possibly brought by the Normans from France (French *Angaut*, *Angot*, from Germanic (Scandinavian) *Ansgaut*).

GIVEN NAMES Italian 11%. *Carmine* (4), *Antonio*, *Dante*, *Italo*, *Salvatore*, *Sando*, *Ugo*.

Angove (154) Cornish: occupational name for a blacksmith, from *an* 'the' + *gof* 'smith'.

Angrisani (119) Southern Italian: from **Angrisano**, a habitational name for someone from Angri in Salerno province.
GIVEN NAMES Italian 24%. *Mario* (4), *Aldo* (2), *Carmine* (2), *Gaetano*, *Roberto*.

Angst (320) South German and Swiss German: topographic name from Middle High German *angest* 'narrowness', i.e. 'narrow place' (whence the modern vocabulary word *Angst* 'anxiety', 'fear'). Bahlow cites an early example, 'Bertschi an der angist' (1382), which is clearly topographical, but in other cases Angst may equally well be a nickname for a timid person.
GIVEN NAMES German 4%. *Kurt* (2), *Ernst*.

Angstadt (493) German in form, but not known as a German surname. Possibly a habitational name of Scandinavian origin.

Anguiano (1134) Spanish: habitational name from Anguiano in the province of Logroño.
GIVEN NAMES Spanish 54%. *Jose* (37), *Juan* (19), *Jesus* (17), *Francisco* (14), *Manuel* (14), *Rafael* (13), *Javier* (10), *Miguel* (10), *Roberto* (9), *Luis* (8), *Ruben* (8), *Carlos* (7).

Anguish (124) English: Reaney suggests this is a variant of ANGUS, citing two late examples from Bardsley: Margaret Anguisshe (1530), Erl of Anguyshe (1563). However, the surname is not found in Scotland (in the 1881 British census it occurs predominantly in East Anglia). It is likely that it is a nickname from Anglo-Norman French *anguisse*, from Old French *angoisse* 'anger', 'violence', cognate with French **Anguise**.

Angulo (1079) Spanish: habitational name from Encima-Angulo in Burgos province.
GIVEN NAMES Spanish 48%. *Jose* (35), *Manuel* (19), *Carlos* (14), *Rafael* (13), *Jesus* (12), *Juan* (12), *Luis* (11), *Jorge* (9), *Pedro* (9), *Miguel* (7), *Ruben* (7), *Armando* (6).

Angus (1479) Scottish and (less frequently) Irish: from the Gaelic personal name *Aonghus*, said to be composed of Celtic *aon* 'one' + *gus* 'choice'. This was borne by an Irish god and a famous 8th-century Pictish king. It is also the name of a county on Tayside (named after him); in some cases the surname may be a regional name from this county.

Angwin (121) **1.** Cornish: nickname for someone with white hair or a pale complexion, from Cornish *gwnn* 'white' + the definite article *an*. **2.** English: regional name for someone from Anjou, France (see ANGEVINE).

Anhalt (361) German: habitational name from a place called Anholt in Westphalia,

which is named from Middle Low German *an* 'at' + *holt* 'wood', or from the old county and castle of Anhalt, named from late Middle High German *anhalt* 'stopping point'.

Anhorn (149) German: habitational name from a place in the Allgäu, Bavaria, named Anhorn, from Middle High German *an* 'at' + *horn* 'horned peak (of a mountain)'.

Anich (120) South German and Austrian: habitational name from a farmstead so named in the Tyrol.

Aniello (103) Italian (Campania, Sicily): variant of AGNELLO 'angel', from an old form (*ainiello*) or Neapolitan dialect form (*aniello*) of the vocabulary word.
GIVEN NAMES Italian 22%. *Ignazio* (2), *Alfio*, *Gaetano*, *Mauro*, *Oreste*, *Pietro*, *Vito*.

Ankenbauer (119) South German and Swiss German: from Middle High German *anken* 'butter' + *būr* 'farmer', hence an occupational name for a dairy farmer. Alternatively, the first element may be a topographic term, *Anke*, meaning 'slight rise in the ground', or an old term *ank* 'watery', hence 'farmer with fields in a wet area'.

Ankeney (158) Swiss German: see ANKNEY.

Ankeny (388) Swiss German: see ANKNEY.

Anker (543) **1.** German: from Middle High German *anker* 'anchor', applied either as an occupational name for a smith who made ships' anchors or as a habitational name from a house identified by an anchor. **2.** English: from the Old French personal name *Anchier* (see ANGIER). **3.** Norwegian and Swedish: probably originally a Swedish soldier's name meaning 'anchor'. This is the name of a powerful and influential Norwegian family, who came to Christiana (Oslo) from Sweden in 1668. **4.** Danish: from a personal name, of which the first element means 'eagle' and the second (probably) 'violent'. **5.** Americanized form of northern French **Anquier**, from a personal name of Germanic origin (see ANGIER).

Anklam (239) German: habitational name from a place in western Pomerania, named in Slavic as *Taglim* 'place of Tagl'.
GIVEN NAMES German 4%. *Hans*, *Kurt*.

Ankney (596) Swiss German: altered form of **Ankner**, an occupational name for a dairyman who made and sold butter, from Swiss German *anke* 'butter', *ankenen* 'to make butter'.
FOREBEARS Dewalt Ankeny (1728–81) came to Philadelphia on the ship *Neptune* in 1746.

Ankrom (589) Variant spelling of Scottish ANCRUM.

Ankrum (288) Variant spelling of Scottish ANCRUM.

Anliker (160) Swiss German: topographic name for someone whose homestead was next to a mountain slope or on the edge of a village, from Middle High German *anligen*, *-licken* 'to lie next to' + *-er* suffix denoting an inhabitant.

Ann (275) English: habitational name from Abbots Ann in Hampshire, named for the stream that runs through it, which is most probably named with an ancient Welsh word meaning 'water'.

Anna (273) Of uncertain origin. It occurs occasionally as a surname in England and Ireland, Italy, and Hungary, most probably being derived from the female personal name *Anna*, which comes through Latin and Greek from the Biblical Hebrew name HANNA.
GIVEN NAME French 4%. *Ketty*.

Annable (219) English (chiefly Nottinghamshire): of uncertain derivation; perhaps from the Middle English female personal name *Amabilia*, from Latin *amabilis* 'lovable'.

Annala (134) Finnish: from the female personal name *Anna* + the local suffix *-la*. Found chiefly in Ostrobothnia.
GIVEN NAMES Finnish 15%. *Arvo, Helvi, Petri, Reino, Toivo, Urho, Waino*.

Annan (254) Scottish: habitational name from a place in Dumfriesshire on the banks of the river Annan, from which its name derives. See also ANNAND.

Annand (146) **1.** Scottish: variant of ANNAN. In the Middle Ages, the place name and surname were most often recorded as *Anand* or *Anant*. The final *d* or *t* is a common feature of early Scottish spelling. Compare *Donald*, from *Donall*. **2.** English: from *Anand*, an East Anglian personal name, from Scandinavian *Anund*, recorded in Domesday Book and elsewhere.

Annas (378) English: variant spelling of ANNIS.

Anne (143) **1.** Indian (Andhra Pradesh); pronounced as two syllables; Hindu name of unknown meaning. **2.** English: variant spelling of ANN.
GIVEN NAMES Indian 29%; African 4%. *Suresh* (2), *Alioune, Anand, Aruna, Bose, Joshi, Madhavi, Pramod, Ramesh, Rao, Ravindra, Seshu; Mamadou, Mame.*

Annear (126) English (Cornish): unexplained.

Annen (283) **1.** German: habitational name from a place named Annen, in the Ruhr valley. **2.** North German: from the medieval German personal name *Anno*. **3.** Swiss German: metronymic from the female personal name *Anne*. **4.** Possibly an altered spelling of Scottish ANNAN.
GIVEN NAMES German 6%. *Kurt* (3), *Math, Otto*.

Annese (316) Italian: **1.** from a variant of *Agnese*, Italian form of the female personal name *Agnes* (see ANNIS). **2.** habitational name from a place in Treviso named Annese.
GIVEN NAMES Italian 19%. *Pasquale* (3), *Rocco* (3), *Salvatore* (3), *Cosmo,*

Domenico, Fedele, Marco, Nino, Pietro, Romeo, Sandro, Vito.

Anness (103) English: variant spelling of ANNIS.

Annett (325) Northern Irish: from a pet form of the English female personal name *Annes* (see ANNIS). This later came to be taken as a pet form of ANN.

Annin (104) Variant spelling of ANNAN or ANNEN.

Annino (166) Southern Italian: of uncertain derivation; possibly a nickname from a diminutive of Greek *amnos* 'lamb', or from a personal name of the same origin.
GIVEN NAMES Italian 17%. *Angelo* (2), *Salvatore* (2), *Alfio, Carmelo, Corrado, Paolo, Romano, Sal, Santi*.

Annis (1755) English: from the Middle English female personal name *Annes*, Old French *Anes*, vernacular form of Late Latin *Agnes*, which is in turn an adaptation of the Greek name *Hagnē* 'pure', 'holy'. St. Agnes was a virgin martyr, one of those who suffered under the persecutions of Diocletian in 303 AD. Her name was associated by folk etymology with Latin *agnus* 'lamb', and in medieval art she is often depicted with a lamb (the lamb of God).

Anno (149) Japanese: meaning 'peaceful plain'. It is rare in Japan proper, and probably originated in the Ryūkyū Islands.
GIVEN NAMES Japanese 5%. *Masayuki, Tadashi, Yoshito*.

Annunziata (518) Italian: from a female personal name, a Marian name (*Maria l'Annunziata*) referring to the Annunciation by the archangel Gabriel to the Virgin Mary of her impending motherhood (Luke 1:20–38). The festival of the Annunciation has been celebrated since the 5th century. It was at first kept on Ember Wednesday during Lent, but was later moved to 25 March, exactly nine months before Christmas Day, replacing pagan festivals celebrating the vernal equinox.
GIVEN NAMES Italian 19%. *Antonio* (4), *Carmine* (4), *Angelo* (3), *Ettore* (2), *Luigi* (2), *Marco* (2), *Salvatore* (2), *Amedeo, Amerigo, Ciro, Domenic, Gaetano*.

Annunziato (223) Italian: from *Annunziato*, masculine form of the female personal name ANNUNZIATA.
GIVEN NAMES Italian 17%. *Angelo* (5), *Carlo* (2), *Antonio, Carmine, Domenic, Gaetano, Sal*.

Ansari (634) Muslim: from the Arabic name *Anṣārī* 'one who traces his lineage to one of the Anṣār'. *Anṣar* is the plural of *Nāṣir* 'friend', 'supporter', a term traditionally used to denote the people of Medina who helped the Prophet Muhammad after the Hegira in 622 AD. Thābit ibn Qais al-Anṣārī was one of the Companions of the Prophet Muhammad, to whom he gave the good news of entry into paradise.
GIVEN NAMES Muslim 79%. *Mohammad* (24), *Mohammed* (10), *Shahid* (7), *Abdul*

(6), *Ali* (6), *Khalid* (6), *Mohsin* (5), *Amir* (4), *Hamid* (4), *Nadeem* (4), *Sajid* (4), *Aftab* (3).

Ansbro (119) Irish: adopted as an English equivalent of Gaelic **Ó hAinmhire** 'descendant of *Ainmhire*', a personal name meaning 'very wild'. This form is found in Co. Galway; a more widespread Anglicization is HANBURY.
GIVEN NAMES Irish 7%. *Kieran, Padraic*.

Anschuetz (112) German: variant spelling of **Anschütz** (see ANSCHUTZ).
GIVEN NAMES German 10%. *Arno, Dieter, Otto*.

Anschutz (351) North German (**Anschütz**): occupational name for someone whose job was to keep a dam or pool filled with water (German *anschützen* 'to fill up'), especially a dam above a water channel serving a mill or mine. The surname is common in northern and eastern Germany.

Ansel (486) **1.** French: from a short form of the Germanic personal name *Anselme* (see ANSELM). **2.** English: variant spelling of ANSELL.

Ansell (789) **1.** English and German: from a vernacular form of the personal name *Anselmus* (see ANSELM). **2.** Swedish: compound name composed of an unexplained first element (perhaps part of a place name) + the common surname ending *-ell*, which is from the Latin adjectival ending *-elius*.

Anselm (167) English and German: from the Germanic personal name *Anselm*, composed of the elements *ans-* 'god' + *helma* 'protection', 'helmet'. The personal name was taken to France and England by St Anselm (*c*.1033–1109), known as the Father of Scholasticism. He was born in Aosta, Italy, joined the Benedictine order at Bec in Normandy, France, and in 1093 became archbishop of Canterbury, England.
GIVEN NAMES German 8%. *Klaus* (3), *Heinz*.

Anselmi (291) **1.** Italian: patronymic or plural form of ANSELMO. **2.** German and Dutch: humanistic surname from the genitive of *Anselmus*, Latin form of ANSELM.
GIVEN NAMES Italian 8%; German 4%. *Angelo* (2), *Ettore* (2), *Antonino, Gino, Guido, Leno, Lorenzo, Primo, Renzo, Sebastiano; Kurt* (4).

Anselmo (893) Italian and Spanish: from the personal name *Anselmo*, which is of Germanic origin (see ANSELM). This was a distinctively Langobardic name, and was especially common in Lombardy in the Middle Ages.
GIVEN NAMES Italian 16%; Spanish 9%. *Sal* (5), *Angelo* (3), *Antonio* (2), *Carlo* (2), *Dario* (2), *Enrico* (2), *Ernesto* (2), *Gaetano* (2), *Rocco* (2), *Romeo* (2), *Battista, Carmela, Carmelo; Salvador* (3), *Julio* (2), *Manuel* (2), *Carlos, Cesar*.

Anshutz (106) Americanized spelling of North German **Anschütz** (see ANSCHUTZ).

Ansley (1301) English: habitational name from such places as Ansley in Warwickshire or Annesley in Nottinghamshire. The former is named with Old English *ānsetl* 'hermitage' + *lēah* 'woodland clearing'; the latter with an Old English personal name *An* ('the solitary one') + *lēah*. In some cases the American surname may be a respelling of Scottish ANSLIE.

Anslinger (104) German (**Änslinger**): habitational name from Langenenslingen in Baden-Württemberg.
GIVEN NAME German 4%. *Kurt.*

Anslow (127) English: habitational name from Anslow in Staffordshire, which is named with the Old English female personal name *Eanswīth* + *lēah* 'woodland clearing'.

Anson (1393) English (found mainly in Yorkshire): patronymic from one of several Middle English personal names. Reaney and Wilson have it as 'son of HANN' or 'son of HAND'. Bardsley explains it as 'son of Anne', but *Anne* was not common as a Middle English personal name, although this is very probably the sense of the Scottish surname **Anisoun**. More plausible in a medieval context, perhaps, is 'son of Agnes' (see ANNIS), or even 'son of ANSELM'.

Ansorge (126) German: nickname for a carefree person, someone 'without sorrow', Middle High German *ane sorge*.
GIVEN NAMES German 9%. *Gerhard, Guenter, Kurt.*

Anspach (685) German: habitational name from a place named Anspach, of which there is one in Hesse and another near Frankfurt on the Oder.
GIVEN NAMES German 4%. *Ernst* (2), *Helmut* (2), *Gerhard, Kurt.*

Anspaugh (202) Americanized form of German ANSPACH.

Anstead (232) **1.** Americanized form of German ANSTETT. **2.** English: of uncertain derivation; perhaps a variant of **Hampstead**, a habitational name for someone from Hampstead in Greater London, Hampstead Norreys or Hampstead Marshall in Berkshire, or either of two places called Hamstead, in the West Midlands and the Isle of Wight. All are named as 'the homestead', from Old English *hām-stede*.

Ansted (117) **1.** German: variant of AN-STETT. **2.** English: variant of ANSTEAD.

Anstett (357) South German: **1.** from the medieval German personal name *Anstett.* This is a vernacular derivative of Greek *Anastasios* (see ANASTASIO). **2.** habitational name for someone from Anstedt in Lower Saxony.

Anstey (288) English: habitational name from any of the dozen places in England called Anstey or Ansty, from Old English *ānstiga*, a compound of *ān* 'one' + *stīg* 'path', denoting a short stretch of road forking at both ends. The surname is found principally in Somerset and the West Country.

Anstine (358) Americanized spelling of the German topographic name **Anstein** 'at the rock', from Middle High German *an* 'at' + *stein* 'rock'.

Antal (436) Hungarian: from the personal name *Antal*, a Hungarian form of *Antonius* (see ANTHONY).

Antalek (115) Hungarian: from the personal name ANTAL + the Slavic diminutive suffix *-ek.*

Antar (110) Arabic: from the personal name *'Antar*, a hero of Arabian romantic mythology, originating in Mecca. **'Antar** is also the name of a tribal subdivision in Iraq.
GIVEN NAMES Muslim 23%; French 5%. *Jamal* (2), *Mohamed* (2), *Hassan, Huda, Ibrahim, Marwan, Mohammad, Musa, Ramy, Randa, Salah, Walid; Antoine, Marcelle.*

Antaya (193) French: secondary surname for PELLETIER, of American Indian origin and unexplained etymology.
FOREBEARS This surname is said to have originated when François Pelletier married an Indian woman in 1661.
GIVEN NAMES French 12%. *Armand* (2), *Andre, Clovis, Donat, Germaine, Gilles.*

Antcliff (137) English: habitational name from somewhere in northern England. Ancliffe Hall in Lancashire is a possibility, but Reaney and Wilson derive it from Arncliffe, Arnecliff, or Ingleby Arncliffe, in Yorkshire, all of which are named from Old English *earn* 'eagle' (genitive plural *earna*) + *clif* 'cliff'.

Antczak (330) Polish: patronymic from a pet form of the personal name *Antoni* (see ANTHONY).
GIVEN NAMES Polish 8%. *Jerzy* (2), *Tadeusz* (2), *Agnieszka, Ewa, Halina, Jadwiga, Mietek, Mikolaj.*

Ante (109) **1.** North German and Dutch: from *ante* 'duck', probably applied as an occupational name for a fowler, or as a nickname for someone thought to resemble a duck. **2.** Spanish: unexplained; possibly from Spanish *ante* 'elk', 'suede'.
GIVEN NAMES Spanish 16%. *Alejandro, Amparo, Enrique, Fernando, Jose, Juan, Luis, Luisa, Mercedita, Ramon, Raul.*

Antee (126) Origin uncertain; presumably a variant of ANTE.

Antell (195) **1.** English: variant spelling of ANTILL. **2.** Swedish: perhaps a compound of an unexplained first element + the common surname ending *-ell*, which is taken from the Latin adjectival ending *-elius*. Compare ANSELL.

Antenucci (226) Variant of Italian ANTO-NUCCI.
GIVEN NAMES Italian 16%. *Edmondo* (2), *Luigi* (2), *Albo, Amedeo, Damiano, Dario, Gaetano, Giovanna, Giulio.*

Antes (402) German: **1.** variant spelling of ANTHES. **2.** Humanistic Hellenization of **Blume**, literally 'flower', with reference to the Greek vocabulary word *anthos* 'flower'.

FOREBEARS Henry Antes (1701–55), German-American religious leader in PA, was a descendant of a certain Baron von Blume of Mainz, said to have altered his name to Antes to escape religious persecution during the Thirty Years' War.

Anthes (215) **1.** German: from a vernacular form, common in the Rhineland, of the personal name *Antonius* (see ANTHONY). **2.** German: variant of ANDER. **3.** Greek: metronymic from *Anthē* (genitive *Anthēs*), a female personal name derived from *anthos* 'flower', or a reduced form of any of various other names ending in *-anthē* such as *Rhodanthē* 'rose flower'.

Anthis (164) Greek: metronymic from *Anthēa, Anthē*, a female personal name derived from *anthos* 'flower', or a reduced form of patronymics or metronymics derived from this and similar names, such as **Anthidis**.

Anthon (163) German: from an older spelling of the personal name ANTON (see ANTHONY).
FOREBEARS George Christian Anthon was a surgeon in the British Army, stationed at Detroit, MI, from 1767 to 1786, after which he moved with his family to New York City. He was of German origin, from Salzungen in Saxe-Meiningen.

Anthony (16822) **1.** English: from the personal name *Anthony*, Latin *Antonius*. See also ANTON. This, with its variants, cognates, and derivatives, is one of the commonest European personal names. Many of the European forms have been absorbed into this spelling as American family names; for the forms, see Hanks and Hodges 1988. Spellings with *-h-*, which first appear in English in the 16th century and in French (as *Anthoine*) at about the same time, are due to the erroneous belief that the name derives from Greek *anthos* 'flower'. The popularity of the personal name in Christendom is largely due to the cult of the Egyptian hermit St. Anthony (AD 251–356), who in his old age gathered a community of hermits around him, and for that reason is regarded by some as the founder of monasticism. It was further increased by the fame of St. Anthony of Padua (1195–1231), who long enjoyed a great popular cult and who is believed to help people find lost things. **2.** South Indian: this is only a given name in India, but has come to be used as a family name among Christians from South India in the U.S.
FOREBEARS John Anthony of Hampstead, Middlesex, England (now part of north London) migrated to Boston, MA, in 1634. By 1640 he had moved to Providence, RI, where his descendants are still established.

Antico (197) Italian: nickname from the adjective *antico* 'ancient'.
GIVEN NAMES Italian 27%. *Dino* (2), *Gaetano* (2), *Francesco, Franco, Paolo, Renato, Rocco, Rolando, Salvatore, Vito.*

Antil (107) English: variant spelling of ANTILL.

Antill (348) **1.** English and French: variant of ANCTIL. **2.** English: possibly a habitational name from Ampthill in Bedfordshire, named from Old English *ǣmette* 'ants' + *hyll* 'hill', or from an Ampthill, now lost, in Cumbria.

Antilla (176) Altered spelling of Finnish ANTTILA.

Antillon (129) Aragonese: habitational name from Antillón in Uesca province, Aragon.
GIVEN NAMES Spanish 45%. *Jose* (5), *Sergio* (3), *Carlos* (2), *Manuel* (2), *Pedro* (2), *Rafael* (2), *Rafaela* (2), *Alejandro*, *Alfredo*, *Alicia*, *Cosme*, *Edmundo*.

Antin (131) French: see DANTIN.
GIVEN NAME French 11%. *Jacques* (2).

Antinori (118) Southern Italian: from the Greek personal name *Antēnor*.
GIVEN NAMES Italian 12%. *Antonio* (2), *Santino* (2), *Santo* (2), *Angelo*.

Antis (154) Variant of German ANTHES.

Antisdel (145) Origin uncertain; possibly English, but unexplained.
FOREBEARS Lawrence Antisell (1688–1759) married Mary Armstrong in Norwich, New London, CT, in 1730.

Antkowiak (188) Polish: patronymic from a pet form of the personal name *Antoni* (see ANTHONY).
GIVEN NAMES Polish 9%. *Danuta* (2), *Casimir*, *Tadeusz*, *Wieslawa*.

Antle (577) **1.** English (Dorset and Somerset): possibly a variant spelling of ANTILL. **2.** Variant of South German **Antli** 'little duck' (see ANTLEY 2).

Antley (466) **1.** English: habitational name from Antley in Lancashire, which is named from Old English *ǣmette* 'ant' + *lēah* 'woodland clearing'. **2.** English: possibly a variant of ANTILL, assimilated to the common English surname ending *-ley*. **3.** Americanized spelling of Swiss **Antli**, from a nickname meaning 'little duck'.

Antman (118) Jewish: unexplained.
GIVEN NAMES Jewish 6%. *Zev*, *Zipora*.

Antoine (1555) French: from the personal name *Antoine*, French equivalent of ANTHONY.
GIVEN NAMES French 13%. *Jacques* (5), *Michel* (4), *Pierre* (3), *Francoise* (2), *Jean Claude* (2), *Marcel* (2), *Pascal* (2), *Patrice* (2), *Alouis*, *Ancil*, *Andre*, *Camille*.

Antol (157) Polish (also **Antoł**): from a derivative of the personal name *Antoni*, Latin *Antonius* (see ANTHONY).

Antolick (107) Respelling of Slovak **Antolík** (see ANTOLIK).

Antolik (219) Slovak (**Antolík**): from a pet form of ANTOL.

Antolin (122) **1.** Spanish (**Antolín**): from the personal name, a vernacular form of *Antoninus*, a name borne by thirteen saints. **2.** Slovenian (eastern Slovenia): patronym-

ic from the personal name *Antol*, an old derivative of *Anton*, Latin *Antonius* (see ANTHONY).
GIVEN NAMES Spanish 40%. *Esperanza* (2), *Julito* (2), *Orlino* (2), *Ruben* (2), *Alvaro*, *Asuncion*, *Bernardo*, *Carlos*, *Eduardo*, *Fidel*, *Froilan*, *Inocencio*.

Antolini (143) Italian: from the personal name *Antolino*, a pet form of ANTONIO.
GIVEN NAMES Italian 18%. *Antonio*, *Dario*, *Domenic*, *Domenico*, *Enrico*, *Enzo*, *Ezio*, *Guerino*, *Pasquale*.

Anton (2248) From *Anton*, a vernacular form of Latin *Antonius* (see ANTHONY) in Spanish (**Antón**), German, Swedish, Czech (**Antoň** or *Anton*, short forms of *Antonín*), and several other languages.

Antonacci (507) Southern Italian: from a derivative of the personal name *Antonio* (see ANTHONY).
GIVEN NAMES Italian 15%. *Gino* (3), *Angelo* (2), *Gaetano* (2), *Natale* (2), *Pasquale* (2), *Sal* (2), *Beniamino*, *Domenic*, *Filomena*, *Giuseppe*, *Guiseppe*, *Leonardo*.

Antone (534) Dutch: variant of ANTOON.

Antonelli (1669) Italian: from *Antonello*, a pet form of the personal name *Antonio* (see ANTHONY).
GIVEN NAMES Italian 17%. *Rocco* (9), *Antonio* (6), *Carmine* (6), *Domenic* (4), *Donato* (4), *Enrico* (4), *Gino* (4), *Aldo* (3), *Dino* (3), *Giuseppe* (3), *Luigi* (3), *Silvio* (3).

Antonellis (264) Italian: shortened form of **De Antonellis**, meaning 'from the Antonello family'.
GIVEN NAMES Italian 24%. *Domenic* (4), *Nunziato* (4), *Angelo* (2), *Nino* (2), *Amato*, *Antonio*, *Biagio*, *Carmela*, *Cesidio*, *Domenico*, *Donato*.

Antonetti (220) Italian: from a pet form of the personal name *Antonio* (see ANTHONY).
GIVEN NAMES Spanish 11%; Italian 7%. *Margarita* (3), *Jose* (2), *Mario* (2), *Alberto*, *Alfredo*, *Alina*, *Amalia*, *Ana*, *Eduardo*, *Elba*, *Francisca*, *Jere*; *Amelio*, *Angelo*, *Carlo*, *Franco*, *Marco*, *Paolo*.

Antoni (168) **1.** German: humanistic patronymic from the genitive case of the Latin personal name *Antonius* (see ANTHONY). **2.** Italian: from the personal name *Antonio* (see ANTHONY). **3.** Greek (**Antonis**): from the personal name *Antonios* (see ANTHONY), or a shortened form of **Antoniadis** or **Antonidakis**, patronymics from this name.
GIVEN NAMES German 17%. *Erwin* (2), *Willi* (2), *Dieter*, *Hans*, *Konrad*, *Kurt*, *Ralf*, *Reinhold*, *Volker*, *Wolf*.

Antoniak (114) Polish: from a pet form or patronymic from the personal name *Antoni* (see ANTHONY).
GIVEN NAMES Polish 12%. *Janusz*, *Kazimierz*, *Pawel*, *Stanislaw*.

Antonich (125) **1.** Serbian and Croatian (**Antonić**) or Slovenian **Antonič**: patronymic from the personal name *Anton*, from Latin *Antonius* (see ANTHONY). **2.** Ukrain-

ian: patronymic from the personal name ANTON.
GIVEN NAME French 4%. *Chantal*.

Antoniewicz (118) Polish: patronymic from the personal name *Antoni* (see ANTHONY).

Antonik (112) Polish: from a pet form of the personal name *Antoni* (see ANTHONY).
GIVEN NAMES Polish 5%; German 4%. *Czeslaw*, *Mariusz*; *Berthold*.

Antonini (356) Italian: patronymic or plural form of ANTONINO.
GIVEN NAMES Italian 24%; French 4%. *Carlo* (3), *Angelo* (2), *Dante* (2), *Orlando* (2), *Alberto*, *Alfredo*, *Antonino*, *Antonio*, *Attilio*, *Celestino*, *Claudio*, *Dario*, *Francesco*, *Franco*, *Gildo*, *Guillermo*, *Italo*; *Marcel*, *Pierre*.

Antonino (137) Italian: from the personal name *Antonino* (Latin *Antoninus*), a pet form of ANTONIO.
GIVEN NAMES Spanish 7%; Italian 6%. *Jose* (2), *Filomeno*, *Manuel*, *Pedro*, *Ramon*, *Ricardo*, *Sergio*; *Carlo*, *Luciano*, *Nino*.

Antonio (1292) Spanish and Portuguese: from the personal name *Antonio* (see ANTHONY).
GIVEN NAMES Spanish 31%; Portuguese 7%. *Jose* (16), *Manuel* (14), *Luis* (8), *Ernesto* (5), *Francisco* (5), *Eduardo* (4), *Juan* (4), *Mario* (4), *Orlando* (4), *Reynaldo* (4), *Wilfredo* (4), *Alberto* (3), *Catarina* (2), *Afonso*, *Henrique*, *Joao*, *Joaquim*.

Antonioli (124) Italian: from the personal name *Antoniolo*, a pet form of the personal name ANTONIO.
GIVEN NAMES Italian 7%. *Angelo*, *Marino*, *Reno*.

Antoniou (159) Greek: patronymic from the genitive case of the personal name *Antonios* (see ANTHONY). Genitive patronymics are particularly associated with Cyprus.
GIVEN NAMES Greek 37%. *Antonios* (6), *Andreas* (3), *Konstantinos* (3), *Costas* (2), *Panayiotis* (2), *Constantinos*, *Dimitris*, *Eleni*, *Georgios*, *Konstantinos*, *Pantelis*, *Prodromos*.

Antonoff (114) Russian and Bulgarian: alternative spelling of **Antonov**, a patronymic from the personal name *Anton* (see ANTHONY).
GIVEN NAMES Russian 5%. *Alexei*, *Kiril*.

Antonopoulos (176) Greek: patronymic from the personal name *Antonios* (see ANTHONY) + the patronymic ending *-poulos*. This ending occurs chiefly in the Peloponnese. It is derived from Latin *pullus* 'nestling', 'chick'.
GIVEN NAMES Greek 23%. *Anastasios* (2), *Athanasios*, *Christos*, *Constantinos*, *Costas*, *Evangelos*, *Fotini*, *Georgios*, *Spiros*, *Spyridon*, *Spyros*, *Vaios*.

Antonsen (197) Danish and Norwegian: patronymic from *Anton* (see ANTHONY).
GIVEN NAMES Scandinavian 15%; German 5%. *Alf*, *Arnt*, *Knud*, *Kristoffer*, *Lasse*,

Morten, Nils, Per; Hans (2), *Erwin, Kurt, Markus.*

Antonson (279) Americanized spelling of Swedish **Antonsson**, a patronymic from the personal name *Anton* (see ANTHONY) or the Danish and Norwegian patronymic ANTONSEN.

Antonucci (1045) Italian: from a pet form of the personal name ANTONIO.
GIVEN NAMES Italian 16%. *Angelo* (10), *Salvatore* (6), *Carmine* (4), *Antonio* (3), *Amadeo* (2), *Carlo* (2), *Ciro* (2), *Dante* (2), *Gino* (2), *Agostino, Bartolo, Biagio.*

Antony (328) Variant spelling of English ANTHONY. Etymologically, this is the 'correct' spelling, but it is now much less common. It is also found as a given name among Christians in India, and in the U.S. is used as a family name among people from southern India.
GIVEN NAMES Indian 4%; French 4%. *Anila, Anuja, Suresh, Veena; Armand* (2), *Patrice* (2), *Andree.*

Antoon (145) **1.** From the Arabic form of *Antonius* (see ANTHONY), used by Christians in the Levant. **2.** Dutch: from the personal name *Antoon*, one of the Dutch forms of ANTHONY.
GIVEN NAMES Arabic 5%. *Alia, Duraid, Farid, Faris, Ismail, Maroun, Sameer.*

Antos (343) **1.** Hungarian: from a pet form of *Antal*, Hungarian form of ANTHONY. **2.** Jewish (from Hungary): adoption of the Hungarian surname. **3.** Polish (**Antosz**); Czech and Slovak (**Antoš**): from a short form of the personal name *Anton* (see ANTHONY).
GIVEN NAMES Polish 5%. *Janina* (2), *Casimir, Stanislaus, Witold.*

Antosh (191) Americanized spelling of Hungarian **Antos**, Polish **Antosz**, or Czech and Slovak **Antoš** (see ANTOS).

Antoun (106) Arabic: variant of ANTOON.
GIVEN NAMES Arabic 28%; French 14%. *Zoher* (3), *Gamil* (2), *Afif, Antoun, Basim, Maged, Manal, Munir, Nabil, Nazir, Saad, Salwa; Georges* (2), *Antoine, Emile, Jacques, Michel.*

Antrim (662) Evidently from the name of the county in northern Ireland. Irish surnames are not normally derived from place names, and this surname is not found in Ireland. It may be a U.S. coinage, perhaps adopted for sentimental reasons by people of northern Irish descent. For the process involved, compare CLYDE.

Antrobus (205) English: habitational name from a place in Cheshire, recorded in Domesday Book as *Entrebus*, apparently from an Old Norse personal name *Eindriði, Andriði* + Old Norse *buski* 'bush', 'thicket'.

Anttila (229) Finnish: habitational name for someone who lived or worked at a farm named Anttila, from the personal name *Antti* (a vernacular form of ANDREAS) + the local suffix *-la*. This is one of the most common farm names in Finland; consequently, the surname is also very frequent.
GIVEN NAMES Finnish 14%. *Eino* (3), *Seija* (2), *Timo* (2), *Aino, Raimo, Tapio, Toivo, Veikko, Vesa.*

Antuna (162) Asturian-Leonese (**Antuña**): habitational name from a place in Asturies named Antuña, apparently from a lost place called Villa Antonia.
GIVEN NAMES Spanish 40%. *Ignacio* (3), *Juan* (3), *Enrique* (2), *Jesus* (2), *Juana* (2), *Pedro* (2), *Aurelio, Carlos, Eduardo, Elvira, Emilia, Eneida.*

Antunes (367) Portuguese: patronymic from the personal name *António*, a vernacular form of *Antonius* (see ANTHONY).
GIVEN NAMES Spanish 35%; Portuguese 21%. *Jose* (25), *Manuel* (16), *Antonio* (13), *Alfredo* (2), *Americo* (2), *Ana* (2), *Dionisio* (2), *Jose Luis* (2), *Luis* (2), *Pedro* (2), *Silvino* (2), *Sueli* (2), *Abilio; Joaquim* (5), *Joao* (2), *Serafim* (2), *Ademir, Agostinho, Aloisio, Zulmira.*

Antunez (302) Spanish (**Antúnez**): patronymic from a dialect form of the personal name ANTONIO.
GIVEN NAMES Spanish 63%. *Jose* (9), *Juan* (9), *Francisco* (5), *Arturo* (3), *Carlos* (3), *Eduardo* (3), *Jesus* (3), *Jorge* (3), *Ofelia* (3), *Alejo* (2), *Andres* (2), *Angel* (2).

Antwine (286) Americanized spelling of French ANTOINE.

Anwar (346) Muslim (widespread throughout the Muslim world): from a personal name based on Arabic *anwar* 'brighter', an elative adjective derived from *nur* 'light'. *Anwār* (with a long *a*) is the plural of *nūr* (see NOOR) and means 'rays (of light)'.
GIVEN NAMES Muslim 88%. *Mohammad* (35), *Muhammad* (16), *Mohammed* (10), *Syed* (7), *Mohamed* (6), *Aftab* (5), *Hamid* (5), *Imran* (5), *Khalid* (4), *Muhammed* (4), *Asif* (3), *Javed* (3).

Anway (154) Altered form of Welsh NANNEY.
FOREBEARS George Nanney, also called Anway, was baptized 1746 in Long Island, NY, a descendant of Captain John Nanny, who was born 1596 in Merionethshire, Wales.

Anzai (101) Japanese: literally 'pacify the west'; this pronunciation is more common in eastern Japan and the island of Okinawa. In western Japan, the same characters are usually pronounced *Yasunishi.*
GIVEN NAMES Japanese 57%. *Yoji* (2), *Akira, Hidehiro, Hisao, Keiji, Kenichi, Kenji, Koichiro, Makoto, Masaaki, Masamitsu, Masao.*

Anzaldua (308) Basque: topographic name from Basque *aintzi* 'swamp' + *aldu* 'high' + *-a* (article suffix).
GIVEN NAMES Spanish 39%. *Jose* (8), *Manuel* (5), *Adolfo* (3), *Amalio* (3), *Juan* (3), *Rodolfo* (3), *Alonzo* (2), *Amador* (2), *Arturo* (2), *Carlos* (2), *Guadalupe* (2), *Leticia* (2).

Anzalone (1216) Southern Italian (Sicily and Naples): probably a variant of **Ansalone**, an augmentative of the personal name *Ansaldo*, which is of Germanic origin, composed of the elements *ans* 'god' + *walda* 'power'. Alternatively, it may be a variant of the Biblical personal name *Absalone* 'Absalom'.
GIVEN NAMES Italian 16%. *Salvatore* (17), *Angelo* (11), *Sal* (5), *Antonio* (4), *Carmine* (4), *Concetta* (3), *Giuseppe* (3), *Vito* (3), *Aniello* (2), *Gaetano* (2), *Luigi* (2), *Attilio.*

Anzelmo (142) Southern Italian (Sicily and Naples): variant of ANSELMO.
GIVEN NAMES Italian 9%. *Natale* (2), *Attilio, Giuseppe.*

Anzivino (128) Italian (Naples): from the personal name *Ansuino, Ansovino*, composed of the Germanic elements *ans* 'god', 'divinity' + *wīn* 'friend'.
GIVEN NAMES Italian 13%. *Rocco* (2), *Angelo, Florio.*

Anzures (105) Spanish or Portuguese: variant of **Ansures**, probably a patronymic form of the medieval personal name *Ansur*, which is of uncertain etymology.
GIVEN NAMES Spanish 38%. *Adan* (2), *Alfonso* (2), *Blanco, Edgardo, Enriqueta, Ismaela, Jaime, Juana, Juanita, Luis, Manuel, Miguel.*

Ao (51) Chinese 敖: from the name of Da Ao, a teacher of the legendary emperor Zhuan Xu (26th century BC).

Aoki (619) Japanese: literally 'green tree'. This surname is mostly found in central Japan and the Ryūkyū Islands. One family, descended from the TAKEDA branch of the MINAMOTO clan, takes its name from *Aokimura* in Kai (now Yamanashi prefecture). Others have FUJIWARA connections.
GIVEN NAMES Japanese 61%. *Kenji* (6), *Yoshio* (5), *Minoru* (4), *Mitsuo* (4), *Shigeru* (4), *Toshio* (4), *Hiroshi* (3), *Isamu* (3), *Kazuo* (3), *Makoto* (3), *Miho* (3), *Nobuo* (3).

Aoyama (132) Japanese: 'green mountain'. This surname is found throughout Japan, a country filled with green mountains, and the Ryūkyū Islands. One family, lords of Mikawa (now part of Aichi prefecture), was descended from the FUJIWARA clan.
GIVEN NAMES Japanese 65%. *Shigeru* (4), *Wataru* (2), *Yasutaka* (2), *Yoshihiro* (2), *Hiroaki, Hiroshi, Hisao, Kazumasa, Kazuo, Keiko, Keisuke, Manabu.*

Apa (121) **1.** Southern Italian: from Sicilian and southern Italian *apa, lapa* 'bee', applied as a nickname for someone thought to resemble a bee in some way or as a metonymic occupational name for a beekeeper. **2.** Hungarian: from *apa* 'father', one of various surnames derived from relationship terms which were presumably originally applied with reference to someone of importance; other examples include **Bátya** 'brother', **Fi** 'son' **Fia** 'his son', **Gyermek** 'child', **Unoka** 'grandchild'. **3.** Hungarian:

from an old secular personal name *Appa*. The Transylvanian royal name *Apafi* is a patronymic from this name.
GIVEN NAMES Italian 8%; French 4%. *Enzo*; *Armand* (2).

Aparicio (964) Portuguese and Spanish: from a personal name, bestowed especially on children born on or around the Feast of the Epiphany (6 January), Spanish *Aparición*, which celebrates the appearance of Christ to the Magi. The Spanish vocabulary word *aparición* means 'appearance' or 'manifestation'. In Portugal and Spain, however, this is found as a forenames only, not a surname.
GIVEN NAMES Spanish 49%; Portuguese 11%. *Jose* (28), *Manuel* (14), *Carlos* (13), *Juan* (11), *Luis* (9), *Alejandro* (7), *Mario* (7), *Alberto* (6), *Ana* (6), *Julio* (6), *Ricardo* (6), *Roberto* (6); *Figueroa*, *Wenceslao*.

Aparo (110) Southern Italian (Sicily): occupational name from Sicilian dialect *aparu* 'beekeeper'.
GIVEN NAMES Italian 30%. *Salvatore* (4), *Sal* (3), *Angelo* (2), *Santo* (2), *Carmelo*, *Giuseppe*, *Paolo*.

Apel (723) **1.** Dutch and North German: variant of APPEL 'apple'. **2.** North German and Dutch: from a pet form of ALBRECHT. **3.** Dutch (**van Apel**): habitational name from a place called Ap(p)el, near Groningen. **4.** Jewish (Ashkenazic): Yiddish-German variant of APFEL. See also APPEL. **5.** Czech: from the German personal name (see 2).
GIVEN NAMES German 7%. *Armin* (2), *Dietrich* (2), *Hans* (2), *Arno*, *Fritz*, *Gerhard*, *Horst*, *Klaus*, *Kurt*, *Lothar*, *Mathias*, *Rudie*.

Aper (113) Hungarian: unexplained.

Apfel (383) **1.** German: from Middle High German *apfel* 'apple', hence a metonymic occupational name for a grower or seller of the fruit. **2.** Jewish (Ashkenazic): ornamental or metonymic occupational name from German *Apfel* 'apple'.
GIVEN NAMES German 4%. *Gunther*, *Irmgard*.

Apfelbaum (142) German and Jewish (Ashkenazic): from German *Apfelbaum* 'apple tree'; either a metonymic occupational name for a grower of the fruit or, as a Jewish surname, an ornamental name.
GIVEN NAMES Jewish 17%. *Mayer* (3), *Este*, *Heshy*, *Mendel*.

Apgar (896) Origin uncertain; probably Dutch or North German. It could be a habitational name from a village in the Rhineland called Epgert. Early American spellings include **Apgard**, **Ebcher**, **Aepjer**, and **Apker**. See also ABSHER.
FOREBEARS Sergeant Peter Apgar served in the Hunterdon Co., NJ, militia in the American Revolutionary War.

Apicella (387) Southern Italian: from a diminutive of *apa* 'bee', probably applied as a nickname for an industrious person, or

possibly as a metonymic occupational name for a beekeeper.
GIVEN NAMES Italian 11%; French 4%. *Aldo*, *Alfonse*, *Angelo*, *Antonio*, *Carlo*, *Carmine*, *Franco*, *Guido*, *Salvatore*, *Taddeo*; *Alphonse* (3), *Achille* (2), *Oneil*.

Apitz (118) **1.** Eastern German: variant of ABITZ. **2.** Eastern German: from the short form of a Germanic personal name (*Ab(b)o*), based on *addal* 'clan', 'nobility'.
GIVEN NAMES German 9%. *Hans*, *Horst*, *Ingeborg*, *Otto*.

Apkarian (113) Armenian: patronymic from the Syriac personal name *Abgar*, which was borne for example by a king of Edessa.
GIVEN NAMES Armenian 31%. *Arsen* (3), *Ara* (2), *Artine* (2), *Avedis* (2), *Vartan* (2), *Arpi*, *Berj*, *Gagik*, *Garabet*, *Hovsep*, *Varoujan*, *Vatche*.

Apland (102) English: variant of APPLING.

Apley (128) English: habitational name from any of several minor places in Lincolnshire and Shropshire (Apley) or the Isle of Wight and Somerset (Appley), named with Old English *æppel* 'apple' + *lēah* 'woodland clearing'.

Aplin (437) English (Dorset and Somerset): variant of APPLING.

Apling (103) English (Devon): variant spelling of APPLING.

Apodaca (1957) Castilianized form of Basque **Apodaka**, a habitational name from a place in Araba province, Basque Country. The place name is of disputed etymology; it may be based on the word *abi* or *ahabi* 'bilberry'.
GIVEN NAMES Spanish 5%. *Jose* (20), *Manuel* (20), *Juan* (10), *Jesus* (9), *Lupe* (8), *Ramon* (7), *Armando* (6), *Miguel* (6), *Alfonso* (5), *Carlos* (5), *Ricardo* (5), *Francisco* (4).

Apolinar (148) Spanish and Portuguese: from a medieval personal name, a variant of *Apolinario*, via Latin from Greek *Apollinaris*, which means 'belonging to the god Apollo'. This rather inappropriate Christian name was borne by various saints, including the first bishop of Ravenna, who was martyred in about 260.
GIVEN NAMES Spanish 41%. *Andres* (3), *Gaspar* (2), *Guadalupe* (2), *Jesus* (2), *Jose* (2), *Juan* (2), *Alberto*, *Alicia*, *Ana*, *Arturo*, *Beatriz*, *Camilo*.

Apollo (136) Italian and Spanish: from the Greek personal name *Apollo*. There are several saints Apollo in the Christian Church, including an Egyptian hermit and monastic leader who died in 395 AD. The personal name derives from the name in classical mythology of the sun god, *Apollo*, an ancient Indo-European name, found for example in Hittite as *Apulana* 'god of the gate' (from *pula* 'gate', cognate with Greek *pylē*), therefore 'protector', 'patron'.
GIVEN NAMES Italian 7%; Spanish 6%. *Carmin*, *Sal*, *Salvatore*; *Benito*, *Carlos*, *Juanita*.

Aponte (1709) Galician and Portuguese: from a misdivision of **Daponte**, a topographic name from *da ponte* 'from the bridge'.
GIVEN NAMES Spanish 44%. *Jose* (52), *Carlos* (34), *Luis* (24), *Juan* (22), *Angel* (21), *Miguel* (16), *Francisco* (11), *Rafael* (10), *Jorge* (9), *Julio* (8), *Ramon* (8), *Luz* (7); *Antonio* (10), *Marco* (3), *Angelo* (2), *Carmelo* (2), *Graciliano* (2), *Annamaria*, *Carmelina*, *Ceasar*, *Federico*, *Giovanni*, *Heriberto*, *Leonardo*.

Apostle (115) **1.** Americanized form of Greek APOSTOLOS. **2.** Americanized form of Spanish and French APOSTOL or German *Apostel*. These were generally derived from nicknames for a man of serious, pious demeanor, though Bahlow suggests that the German name may have denoted one who played the part of an apostle in the passion play.

Apostol (273) **1.** Shortened form of Greek APOSTOLOS. **2.** Spanish (**Apóstol**) and French: nickname for a pious or serious man, from Greek *apostolos* 'apostle' (Old French *apostol*, French *apôtre*; the Old French word was also used to denote the Pope). See also APOSTLE. **3.** Hungarian: from the old ecclesiastical personal name *Apostol*, a vernacular form of APOSTOLOS.
GIVEN NAMES Spanish 18%. *Augusto* (2), *Emilio* (2), *Wilfredo* (2), *Angelito*, *Aurea*, *Cesar*, *Eduardo*, *Ernesto*, *Felipa*, *Filipina*, *Imelda*, *Javier*.

Apostolos (89) Greek: from *apostolos* 'apostle', which was used as a personal name, or a reduced form of patronymics from this name, such as **Apostolakis**, **Apostolidis**, **Apostoliadis**, and **Apostolatos**. The term *apostolos* was adopted by early Christians in honor of Christ's twelve apostles and as a symbol of their own commitment to spreading the Christian message. The original meaning of the Greek word *apostolos* is 'messenger', 'one sent with a message', from *apostellein* 'to send'. The word was used in the Septuagint as a translation of Hebrew *saleh* 'messenger', 'apostle'.
GIVEN NAMES Greek 4%. *Aphrodite*, *Despina*.

Apostolou (134) Greek: from the genitive case of the personal name APOSTOLOS. Genitive patronymics are particularly associated with Cyprus.
GIVEN NAMES Greek 15%. *Demos*, *Dimitrios*, *Konstantions*, *Panagiotis*, *Panagis*, *Spyridon*, *Stefanos*.

App (232) German: from a short form of the personal name *Apprecht*, a variant of ALBRECHT. See also ALBERT.

Appel (3453) **1.** German: from the personal name *Appel*, a pet form of *Apprecht* (common especially in Thuringia and Franconia), itself a variant of ALBRECHT. **2.** German, Dutch, and Jewish (Ashkenazic): from Low German *Ap(p)el*, Middle Dutch *appel*, or Yiddish *epl* 'apple', hence an occupational name for a grower or seller of the fruit. As a Jewish ornamental name, it is generally ornamental rather than occupational. **3.** Jewish (Ashkenazic): variant spelling of APEL.

Appelbaum (718) Jewish (Ashkenazic) and North German: variant of APFELBAUM. See also APPEL.

GIVEN NAMES Jewish 5%. *Benzion, Boruch, Emanuel, Miriam, Morty, Sol, Yetta, Yosef.*

Appelhans (180) German: **1.** from a compound of the personal name *Appel*, a pet form of *Albrecht* (see APPEL 1) + the personal name *Hans* (see JOHANN), i.e. 'Appel's (son) Hans'. **2.** from the North German dialect word *Appel* 'apple' + the personal name *Hans*, hence a distinguishing name for a fruit grower or seller named Hans.

GIVEN NAMES German 5%. *Fritz, Gerd, Reinhold.*

Appell (542) **1.** Swedish: probably a soldier's name from *appell* '(military) call', 'muster'. **2.** Perhaps a respelling of APPEL.

Appelman (188) **1.** North German (**Appelmann**) and Jewish (Ashkenazic): from Middle Low German *appel* 'apple' + *man* 'man', an occupational name for a grower or seller of the fruit. **2.** Dutch: occupational name from Middle Dutch *apelmanger* 'apple seller'.

Appelt (311) German: from the personal name *Appel*, with the addition of a non-etymological *-t*. See APPEL 1.

GIVEN NAMES German 6%. *Otto* (2), *Bernd, Helmut, Herta, Siegfried.*

Appenzeller (231) German: habitational name for someone from Appenzell (city or canton) in northeastern Switzerland. The place name derives ultimately from Latin *abbatis cella* 'abbot's cell', in reference to the summer residence of the abbots of St. Gallen.

Apperson (801) Dutch: variant of EPPERSON.

Appiah (140) Ghanaian: unexplained.

GIVEN NAMES African 14%. *Kwame* (3), *Osei* (2), *Akwasi, Kwabena, Kwaku.*

Apple (2739) **1.** English: from Middle English *appel* 'apple' (Old English *æppel*), acquired as a surname in any of various senses: a topographic name for someone living by an apple orchard; an occupational name for a grower or seller of apples; or a nickname for someone supposed to resemble an apple in some way, e.g. in having bright red cheeks. The economic importance in medieval northern Europe of apples, as a fruit that could be grown in a cold climate and would keep for use throughout the winter, is hard to appreciate in these days of rapid transportation and year-round availability of fruits of all kind. **2.** Americanized form of APPEL or APFEL.

Applebaum (972) Part Americanized form of German and Jewish APPELBAUM or APFELBAUM.

GIVEN NAMES Jewish 4%. *Emanuel, Hyman, Hymen, Isadore, Mayer, Miriam, Sol.*

Applebee (493) English: variant spelling of APPLEBY.

Appleberry (176) **1.** Americanized spelling of Swedish **Ap(p)elberg**, an ornamental name composed of the elements *apel* 'apple tree' + *berg* 'mountain'. **2.** English: the surname **Applebury** is recorded in England in the 19th century, perhaps a habitational name from a lost place.

Appleby (2200) Northern English: habitational name from any of various places, for example in Leicestershire, Lincolnshire, and Cumbria, named from Old English *æppel* 'apple' or Old Norse *epli* + Old Norse *býr* 'farm'.

Applegarth (330) Northern English and Scottish: topographic name from northern Middle English *applegarth* 'apple orchard' (Old Norse *apaldr* 'apple tree' + *garðr* 'enclosure'), or a habitational name from a place so named, of which there are examples in Cumbria and North and East Yorkshire, as well as in the county of Dumfries.

Applegate (4403) Northern English: extremely common variant of APPLEGARTH, in which the less familiar final element has been assimilated to the northern Middle English word *gate* 'road' or to modern English *gate*.

Appleget (111) Variant of northern English APPLEGATE.

Appleman (593) **1.** Respelling of German **Appelmann** (see APPELMAN). **2.** Jewish (Ashkenazic): Americanized form of the German Jewish surname **Apfelmann** 'apple man', an ornamental name or a metonymic occupational name for a seller of the fruit.

Applequist (149) Americanized form of Swedish **Apelkvist**, an ornamental name composed of the elements *apel* 'apple tree' + *kvist* 'twig'.

GIVEN NAME Scandinavian 4%. *Alvar.*

Appler (156) Dutch or German: variant of EPPLER.

Appleton (2195) English: habitational name from any of the many places in all parts of England, for example in Cheshire, Oxfordshire, and North Yorkshire, named in Old English as *æppeltūn* 'orchard' (literally 'apple enclosure').

FOREBEARS This surname was brought to North America in 1635 by Samuel Appleton, who migrated from Ipswich, England, to Ipswich, MA.

Applewhite (833) English: habitational name from a place named Applethwaite, from Old Norse *apaldr* 'apple tree' + *þveit* 'meadow'. There are two or three such places in Cumbria; Applethwaite is also recorded as a surname from the 13th century in Suffolk, England, pointing to a possible lost place name there. The form Applewhite, now found predominantly in

Lincolnshire, goes back to the 16th century in Suffolk.

Appley (100) English: variant of APLEY.

Appleyard (295) Northern English: topographic name for someone who lived by an apple orchard, Middle English *appleyard* (an Americanized form of APPLEGARTH, which in Scandinavian-speaking areas replaced the native APPLETON). There are several places named with this term, of which the most significant as a source of surnames is in West Yorkshire.

Applin (292) English: variant of APPLING.

Appling (909) English: patronymic from ABEL, which was a popular Middle English personal name. Compare APLIN.

Appold (108) German: habitational name from Apolda in Thuringia, or alternatively from the Germanic personal name *Adabald*, composed of *adal* 'clan', 'nobility' + *bald* 'brave', 'courageous'.

GIVEN NAME German 4%. *Erhardt.*

Apps (179) **1.** English (Kent): from Middle English *apse* 'aspen tree' (Old English *æpse*). See also ASP. Generally, this was a topographic name for someone who lived by an aspen or a habitational name from a place named with this word, as for example Apps in Surrey, Apse on the Isle of Wight, or Asps in Warwickshire. Occasionally it may have been applied as a nickname for a timorous person, with reference to the trembling leaves. **2.** Dutch: variant of EPPS.

Aprahamian (113) Armenian: variant of ABRAHAMIAN.

GIVEN NAMES Armenian 27%. *Souren* (2), *Ara, Araxie, Arpenik, Bedros, Harout, Hrair, Kapriel, Misak, Neshan, Norair, Vahe.*

Aprea (184) Italian: habitational name for someone from Prea in Campania (*da Prea*, reinterpreted as *d'Aprea*).

GIVEN NAMES Italian 24%. *Aniello* (4), *Carmine* (2), *Luigi* (2), *Antonio, Bernardo, Carlo, Ciro, Filippo, Gennaro, Giovanni, Giuseppe, Graziano, Luca, Mario, Nadina, Silverio.*

April (479) **1.** Translation of a European surname meaning 'April' (Latin *aprilis*), for example Italian APRILE, German **April(l)**, **Abrell**, Polish **Kwiecień**. There were various possible connections between the month and the surname; for example, it may have been applied to someone who rendered homage or paid rent to an overlord in April, or as a personal name bestowed on a child born in April. **2.** Jewish (Ashkenazic): ornamental name from German *April* 'April'. **3.** April is found in England as a surname from the 13th and 14th centuries onwards, which Reaney and Wilson explain as "a nickname, perhaps with reference to the changeable weather of the month, 'changeable', 'vacillating', or with reference to spring or youth."

GIVEN NAMES French 7%. *Armand* (2), *Lucien* (2), *Alcide, Andre, Simonne, Yvon.*

Aprile (221) Southern Italian: from *aprile* 'April' (see APRIL).
GIVEN NAMES Italian 29%. *Salvatore* (3), *Angelo* (2), *Armando, Carmela, Carmelo, Gino, Gioacchino, Mario, Sal, Salvator, Santo, Vito.*

Aprill (106) German: variant of ABRELL.

Apsey (187) English: of uncertain derivation; perhaps a variant of **Apsley**, a habitational name from a place named Apsley or Aspley (in Bedfordshire), from Old English *æspe, æpse* 'aspen' + *lēah* 'woodland clearing'.

Apt (254) **1.** German: variant of ABT. **2.** Jewish (eastern Ashkenazic): habitational name from Apt, the Yiddish name of Opatów in Kielce voivodeship, Poland. The place name (in German, Yiddish, and Polish) is from a root meaning 'abbot', the place having been named for the local abbey.

Apte (104) Indian (Maharashtra); pronounced as *ap-tay*: Hindu (Brahman) name found among the Konkanasth Brahmans, probably from Marathi *apṭa*, denoting the tree *Bauhinia tomentosa*.
GIVEN NAMES Indian 72%. *Anjali* (4), *Atul* (2), *Avinash* (2), *Dilip* (2), *Meena* (2), *Uday* (2), *Ajit, Aruna, Ashok, Balkrishna, Girish, Hemant.*

Apter (211) Jewish (Ashkenazic): habitational name for someone from APT.
GIVEN NAMES Jewish 7%. *Miriam* (2), *Avrohom, Bronya, Eliezer, Naftali.*

Apuzzo (237) Southern Italian (Campania): from a derivative of Italian *ape* 'bee', Sicilian *apa*, hence an occupational name for a bee keeper or a nickname for an industrious person.
GIVEN NAMES Italian 16%; French 4%. *Salvatore* (5), *Franco* (2), *Cosmo, Dino, Ferdinando, Pasquale, Remo*; *Alphonse, Luc.*

Aquila (220) Italian: **1.** nickname from *aquila* 'eagle', denoting a lordly or a sharp-eyed man. **2.** habitational name from L'Aquila in Abruzzo or from any of various smaller places called Aquila.
GIVEN NAMES Italian 18%. *Lucio* (2), *Salvatore* (2), *Dante, Giuseppe, Italia, Palma, Rocco.*

Aquilar (86) Variant spelling of Spanish AGUILAR.
GIVEN NAMES Spanish 50%. *Jose* (4), *Juan* (3), *Pedro* (2), *Alfredo, Emilio, Enrique, Fidelina, Gildardo, Jesus, Jose Antonio, Josefina, Laureano*; *Antonio* (2), *Marco, Paolo.*

Aquilina (289) Italian: from a diminutive of AQUILA or from the female personal name *Aquilina.*
GIVEN NAMES French 5%; Italian 5%. *Chantal*; *Sal* (2), *Carmel, Riccardo.*

Aquilino (385) Italian: **1.** from the personal name *Aquilino*, from Latin *Aquilinus*, from the family name *Aquilius*, which appears to be from *aquila* 'eagle' but is probably actu-

ally of Etruscan origin. **2.** nickname from *aquilino* 'eagle-like', presumably with reference to keen eyesight or arrogant bearing.
GIVEN NAMES Italian 16%; French 4%. *Angelo* (3), *Carmine* (2), *Donato* (2), *Rocco* (2), *Amato, Antonio, Matteo, Romeo, Salvatore*; *Armand* (2), *Clemence.*

Aquino (2709) **1.** Spanish, Portuguese, and Italian: from a personal name bestowed in honor of the great theologian St. Thomas Aquinas (*Tommaso d'Aquino* in Italian). **2.** Italian: habitational name from a place called Aquino (see D'AQUINO).
GIVEN NAMES Spanish 37%; Portuguese 7%; Italian 7%. *Jose* (33), *Carlos* (16), *Antonio* (15), *Pedro* (15), *Juan* (13), *Manuel* (13), *Mario* (10), *Ana* (8), *Jesus* (8), *Jorge* (7), *Josefina* (7), *Julio* (7), *Luis* (7), *Paulo* (2), *Catarina, Joao*; *Romeo* (6), *Luigi* (4), *Salvatore* (4), *Clemente* (3), *Leonardo* (3).

Arabia (139) **1.** Italian (**Aràbia**) and Spanish: ethnic name for someone from Arabia or some other Arabic-speaking country or a nickname for someone who had visited or traded with one of these countries. **2.** Americanized form of French ARABIE.
GIVEN NAMES Spanish 8%; Italian 4%. *Andres, Evelia, Natividad, Rigoberto, Rosalinda*; *Domenic.*

Arabian (140) Armenian: patronymic from the ethnic term *arab* 'Arab'.
GIVEN NAMES Armenian 28%. *Aram* (2), *Ano, Ara, Artin, Bedros, Gitti, Grigor, Haig, Harout, Hovsep, Kevork, Khachig, Nerses, Youses.*

Arabie (264) French: ethnic name denoting someone from Arabia or an Arabic-speaking person.
GIVEN NAMES French 4%. *Alceste, Andrus.*

Arace (103) Italian: unexplained. This is a name from Campania, the ending *-ace*, suggesting that it could be of Greek origin.
GIVEN NAMES Italian 21%. *Vito* (3), *Carmine, Gaetano, Pasquale, Raffaele.*

Arafat (43) Muslim (**'Arafāt**): ornamental religious name adopted with reference to a plain lying twelve miles southwest of Mecca, where pilgrims spend a day praying during the hajj.

Aragon (3378) Spanish (**Aragón**) and French: regional name from Aragon, an independent kingdom from 1035 to 1479, which took its name from the river Aragón that arises in its northwestern corner. The river name is of obscure origin; it may be related to Basque *(h)ara(n)* 'valley'. In Basque, Aragon is called *Aragoa* or *Aragoi*, which may mean 'high valley'. See also DRAGON, DERAGON.
GIVEN NAMES Spanish 30%. *Jose* (51), *Manuel* (34), *Carlos* (30), *Juan* (20), *Ruben* (13), *Fernando* (12), *Jesus* (12), *Julio* (12), *Luis* (12), *Raul* (10), *Mario* (9), *Alfonso* (8).

Aragona (243) Italian (mainly southern) and Spanish: regional name for someone

from the Spanish kingdom of Aragon, which conquered and dominated southern Italy from 1282. See also ARAGON.
GIVEN NAMES Italian 18%; Spanish 6%. *Angelo* (2), *Carmine, Ciro, Domenic, Domenico, Gaspare*; *Carolina, Ninfa, Rosario.*

Arai (309) Japanese: variously written, usually with characters meaning 'new well'; the original meaning is 'new residence'. It is also written with characters pronounced as IMAI, and is found in eastern Japan, especially in Saitama prefecture.
GIVEN NAMES Japanese 77%. *Kaz* (4), *Takashi* (4), *Hiroshi* (3), *Kenichi* (3), *Kenji* (3), *Kiyoshi* (3), *Shinji* (3), *Akira* (2), *Hideki* (2), *Hideo* (2), *Hirokazu* (2), *Mamoru* (2).

Araiza (621) Basque: topographic name from *ara, haran* 'valley' + *-itz*, a common topographic suffix, + the article suffix *-a*, that is, 'the place in the valley'. In some cases it may be a variant of **Areyza**, from *areitz* 'oak' (variant of *(h)aritz*) + the article suffix *-a*. Because it is somewhat unusual in terms of Spanish orthography, the latter surname may have been assimilated to the former, which is more common and more regular in form.
GIVEN NAMES Spanish 48%. *Jose* (19), *Juan* (14), *Jesus* (10), *Alicia* (5), *Luis* (5), *Miguel* (5), *Rafael* (5), *Raul* (5), *Rodolfo* (5), *Carlos* (4), *Cesar* (4), *Francisco* (4).

Arakaki (480) Japanese: habitational name from the Ryūkyū Islands, written with characters meaning 'wild enclosure', but actually denoting the enclosure around a Shintō shrine.
GIVEN NAMES Japanese 33%. *Kiyoshi* (3), *Minoru* (3), *Takeo* (3), *Yoshio* (3), *Hiroshi* (2), *Isamu* (2), *Jiro* (2), *Masao* (2), *Shinya* (2), *Tsuru* (2), *Genji, Haruko.*

Arakawa (352) Japanese: topographic name meaning literally 'wild river', probably referring to the Arakawa River, which drains the Kantō Plain into Tōkyō Bay. There are other rivers of the same name. This surname is mostly found in eastern Japan.
GIVEN NAMES Japanese 47%. *Hiroshi* (3), *Masahiro* (3), *Michiyo* (3), *Takeshi* (3), *Kasumi* (2), *Osamu* (2), *Teruko* (2), *Toyoko* (2), *Yasushi* (2), *Yoichi* (2), *Yoshiko* (2), *Akio.*

Arakelian (384) Armenian: patronymic from the personal name *Arak'eal*, literally 'sent', i.e. 'apostle', a calque on Greek APOSTOLOS.
GIVEN NAMES Armenian 38%. *Agop* (4), *Haig* (3), *Kevork* (3), *Sarkes* (3), *Vartan* (3), *Arakel* (2), *Aram* (2), *Ararat* (2), *Armen* (2), *Artin* (2), *Garabed* (2), *Kerop* (2).

Araki (280) **1.** Japanese (found in western Japan): meaning 'wild tree' or 'new tree'; mostly written with characters for the former. It is listed in the Shinsen shōjiroku. **2.** Hungarian: habitational name for someone from a place called Arak in Moson county.

GIVEN NAMES Japanese 60%. *Akira* (3), *Mika* (3), *Takashi* (3), *Haruo* (2), *Hisashi* (2), *Kenji* (2), *Makoto* (2), *Shinichi* (2), *Tetsuo* (2), *Yoshi* (2), *Yoshio* (2), *Akio*.

Arambula (455) Basque: probably a variant of **Aramburu**, from Basque **Aranburu**. This is a topographic name for someone who lived at the upper end of a valley, from Basque *aran* 'valley' (see ARANA) + *buru* 'head', 'top'.

GIVEN NAMES Spanish 50%. *Jose* (13), *Jesus* (11), *Juan* (9), *Guadalupe* (7), *Manuel* (6), *Raul* (6), *Carlos* (5), *Ramon* (4), *Mario* (3), *Miguel* (3), *Ricardo* (3), *Salvador* (3); *Antonio* (6), *Angelo* (2), *Caterina*, *Cecilio*, *Donato*, *Lorenzo*.

Arana (777) Basque: topographic name from *aran* 'valley' + the Basque definite article -*a*. The name in the U.S. may have absorbed some instances of **Araña**, from Spanish *araña* 'spider', a nickname for a weaver or for an industrious or opportunistic person.

GIVEN NAMES Spanish 51%. *Jose* (22), *Carlos* (11), *Jesus* (9), *Juan* (7), *Manuel* (7), *Ramon* (7), *Beatriz* (6), *Enrique* (6), *Francisco* (6), *Jaime* (6), *Mario* (6), *Cesar* (5).

Arand (107) Variant spelling of English **Arrand**, an unexplained Lincolnshire name.

Aranda (1717) Spanish: habitational name from any of various places, for example Aranda de Duero in Burgos province, which bears a name of pre-Roman, probably Celtic, origin.

GIVEN NAMES Spanish 51%. *Jose* (41), *Juan* (36), *Jesus* (18), *Manuel* (18), *Luis* (16), *Ruben* (15), *Pablo* (12), *Pedro* (12), *Jaime* (11), *Sergio* (11), *Carlos* (10), *Jorge* (10).

Arango (804) Castilianized form of Asturian-Leonese **Arangu**, a habitational name from a place named Arangu in Asturies.

GIVEN NAMES Spanish 52%. *Luis* (23), *Juan* (14), *Jose* (13), *Jorge* (12), *Carlos* (10), *Alberto* (6), *Fernando* (6), *Luz* (6), *Alfonso* (5), *Ana* (5), *Jaime* (5), *Julio* (5).

Arant (618) German: variant of ARNDT.

FOREBEARS Herman Arant and his wife Anna Margretha came to Philadelphia on the ship *Hope* in 1733 with their sons Peter, Conrad, and Jacob, from whom all present-day bearers seem to be descended.

Arata (589) **1.** Italian (northern): topographic name for someone who lived near an area of cultivated land, from (*terra*) *arata* 'cultivated (land)', or a habitational name from a place named with this word, as for example Arata in Piedmont. **2.** Japanese: rare name, meaning 'wild rice paddy' or 'new rice paddy', listed in the Shinsen Shōjiroku. Characters for the latter meaning tend to be pronounced NITTA or *Shinden* in Japan proper; the reading Arata

is from the Ryūkyū Islands. All three versions are found in western Japan.

Araujo (1921) Portuguese (and Galician): habitational name from any of various places called Araújo: in Portugal, in Coimbra, Elvas, Estremoz, Lisbon, Moncorvo, Monsão, Serpa, Setúbal, and Villa Verde; also in Ourense, Galicia.

GIVEN NAMES Spanish 39%; Portuguese 13%. *Jose* (52), *Manuel* (35), *Antonio* (29), *Carlos* (27), *Juan* (17), *Fernando* (16), *Luis* (16), *Miguel* (11), *Jorge* (10), *Mario* (9), *Pedro* (9), *Francisco* (8), *Armando* (7), *Marco* (7); *Joao* (9), *Paulo* (3), *Joaquim* (2), *Afonso*, *Albano*, *Almir*, *Aloisio*, *Duarte*, *Guilherme*, *Terezinha*.

Arauz (235) Castilianized form (alongside **Araoz**) of Basque **Araotz**, a habitational name from a town called Araotz in Gipuzkoa province, Basque Country; or possibly also a topographic name from Basque *ara(n)* 'valley' + an unidentified suffix, or alternatively a reduced form of **Aranotz**, from *aran* 'valley' + *otz* 'cold'.

GIVEN NAMES Spanis 9%. *Juan* (7), *Jose* (6), *Carlos* (4), *Cesar* (3), *Alberto* (2), *Edgardo* (2), *Eduardo* (2), *Enrique* (2), *Jose Orlando* (2), *Julio* (2), *Luis* (2), *Miguel* (2).

Arave (146) Probably of French origin: unexplained.

Araya (356) **1.** Castilianized form of Basque and Catalan **Araia**, a habitational name from any of various places called Araia, for example in Araba, Basque Country, and Catelló de la Plana, Valencia. **2.** Spanish: habitational name from any of the places called Araya, as for example the one in Canary Islands. **3.** Japanese: meaning 'wild valley' or 'new valley'; found in eastern Japan and pronounced *Aratani* in western Japan. Neither version is particularly common.

GIVEN NAMES Spanish 35%; Ethiopian 16%. *Juan* (8), *Luis* (7), *Carlos* (5), *Jorge* (5), *Jose* (4), *Manuel* (4), *Alejandro* (3), *Eduardo* (3), *Mario* (3), *Rodrigo* (3), *Ana* (2), *Enrique* (2); *Mesfin* (4), *Genet* (3), *Abiy*, *Abraha*, *Alemu*, *Araya*, *Asfaw*, *Aynalem*, *Biniam*, *Binyam*, *Derege*, *Desta*.

Arb (127) German: variant of ERB.

Arballo (117) Catalan (**Arballó**): possibly a topographic name for someone who lived by a ditch or channel, from a variant of Catalan *arbelló* 'channel', 'groove'.

GIVEN NAMES Spanish 31%. *Ruben* (3), *Carlos* (2), *Felipe* (2), *Jesus* (2), *Adriana*, *Alberto*, *Angel*, *Jesus Antonio*, *Jorge*, *Juan*, *Lupe*, *Marta*; *Alfio*, *Lorenzo*, *Nicoletta*.

Arbanas (104) Croatian and Serbian: ethnic name for an Albanian. Some bearers are from the village of Arbanasi near Zadar in Dalmatia, inhabited by Catholic Albanians who arrived in the 18th century, fleeing from the Turks.

GIVEN NAMES South Slavic 4%. *Branko*, *Goran*.

Arbaugh (635) Americanized form of German **Arbach**, a habitational name from any of several places called Arbach, as for example a village in the Rhineland, west of Koblenz, which is named from Middle High German *ar(n)* 'eagle' + *bach* 'brook'. Compare ERBAUGH.

Arbeiter (155) German (southeast): occupational name from Middle High German *arbeiter* 'laborer'.

Arbelaez (145) Spanish (**Arbélaez**): topographic name from Basque *albel* 'slate' + (*h*)*aitz* 'rock'.

GIVEN NAMES Spanish 53%. *Jose* (6), *Carlos* (5), *Luis* (4), *Jorge* (3), *Adriana* (2), *Beatriz* (2), *Bernardo* (2), *Guillermo* (2), *Ignacio* (2), *Juan* (2), *Raul* (2), *Alberto*.

Arber (127) **1.** English: variant of HARBER. **2.** South German: either from Middle High German *arber* 'tree' (related to Latin *arbor*), an occupational name for a forester or perhaps a habitational name from some place named with this word, or from *Arbihari*, a Germanic personal name composed of Old High German *arbi* 'inheritance' + *hari* 'army'.

Arbo (180) Respelling of French **Harbaud**, a personal name of Germanic origin.

Arbogast (2009) Southwest German and French (Alsace): from a Germanic name composed of *arbi* 'inheritance' + *gast* 'stranger'. St. Arbogast was a 7th-century bishop of Strasbourg and is the patron saint of Alsace.

Arboleda (252) Spanish: topographic name from *arboleda* 'grove of trees', from *árbol* 'tree' (Latin *arbor*), or a habitational name from a place named with this word, as for example Caserío de Arboleda in Logroño province.

GIVEN NAMES Spanish 48%. *Carlos* (7), *Luis* (4), *Fernando* (3), *Gustavo* (3), *Rodrigo* (3), *Alberto* (2), *Alicia* (2), *Angel* (2), *Arnulfo* (2), *Jorge* (2), *Manuel* (2), *Mario* (2).

Arbon (109) English (East Anglia): from a personal name, Old Norse *Arnbjǫrn*, Old Danish and Old Swedish *Arnbiorn*.

Arbour (467) **1.** Variant of English HARBOUR. **2.** It is also found as a French name in Quebec, from Rouen, from 1691 onwards. A French origin is therefore also likely: perhaps it is one of the many variants of HERBERT or **Harbaud**.

GIVEN NAMES French 9%. *Adrien* (2), *Amelie* (2), *Normand* (2), *Armand*, *Emile*, *Francois*, *Herve*, *Jean Marie*, *Jean-Marie*, *Pierrette*, *Yvon*.

Arbuckle (1679) Scottish: habitational name from Arbuckle (earlier *Arnbuckle*) in the parish of Airdrie, Lanarkshire, named in Gaelic as *earrann buachaille* 'herdsman's portion (of land)'.

FOREBEARS Captain Matthew Arbuckle (1741–81) was a prominent VA frontiersman. The name was brought to Pittsburgh in the early 19th century by a certain Thomas Arbuckle.

Arbuthnot (288) Scottish and northern Irish: habitational name from a place called Arbuthnott, south of Aberdeen, earlier *Aberbuthnot*, a Pictish place name from *aber* 'confluence' + the stream name *Buadhnat* (the Gaelic form) meaning 'virtuous' or 'healing', i.e. the stream was regarded as holy, with healing properties.

Arcand (459) French: of uncertain origin, perhaps from a personal name containing the Old High German element *ercan* 'precious', 'excellent' (borrowed, via Latin, from Greek *archi-* 'the first', 'the highest'). Compare ARCHAMBAULT.

FOREBEARS Simon Arcand 'dit Bourdelais' (i.e. 'from Bordeaux') married Marie-Anne Inard in 1687 in Batiscan; their five sons had some thirty children before 1730.

GIVEN NAMES French 6%. *Normand* (2), *Adelard, Andre, Armand, Gabrielle, Lucien.*

Arcara (134) Italian: habitational name from Alcara in Messina province, Sicily, named from Arabic *al-hārah*.

GIVEN NAMES Italian 11%. *Angelo* (2), *Salvatore.*

Arcari (148) Italian: patronymic or plural form of ARCARO.

GIVEN NAMES Italian 21%. *Carmine* (2), *Donato, Enrico, Ercole, Gino, Giuseppe, Libero, Pasquale, Rino.*

Arcaro (280) Italian: **1.** occupational name for a maker or seller of bows, *arcaro.* **2.** from *arcaro*, from Latin *arcarius* 'treasurer', an agent noun from *arca* 'chest', 'coffer'; hence a status name for the treasurer of a city, guild, or other institution.

GIVEN NAMES Italian 19%. *Angelo* (5), *Antonio* (3), *Cosmo* (2), *Riccardo* (2), *Rocco* (2), *Attilio, Carmela, Ermanno, Vincenzo.*

Arce (1844) Spanish: habitational name from places in the provinces of Santander and Navarra called Arce. Their name is a Castilianized spelling of Basque *artze* 'stony place' (from *arri* 'stone' + the suffix of abundance *-tz(e)*).

GIVEN NAMES Spanish 48%. *Jose* (33), *Juan* (28), *Carlos* (27), *Luis* (22), *Francisco* (13), *Jesus* (12), *Manuel* (12), *Angel* (10), *Efrain* (9), *Jorge* (9), *Miguel* (9), *Ricardo* (9).

Arcement (231) French: of uncertain origin. If this comes through the French Canadian tradition, it could be an alteration of a German name ending in *-mann*, for example **Hartzmann**. The process is seen in the Alsatian name **Impelmann**, which changed to **Amplement**.

GIVEN NAMES French 9%. *Remy* (2), *Sylviane.*

Arceneaux (1728) Variant spelling of French ARSENAULT.

GIVEN NAMES French 8%. *Andre* (8), *Antoine* (3), *Leonce* (3), *Alcide* (2), *Curley* (2),

Elodie (2), *Emile* (2), *Andrus, Camille, Celina, Easton, Elzina.*

Arceo (334) Galician: habitational name from a place named Arceo, in A Coruña province, Galicia.

GIVEN NAMES Spanish 53%. *Jose* (7), *Francisco* (5), *Rafael* (5), *Jesus* (4), *Juan* (4), *Luis* (4), *Armando* (3), *Ignacio* (3), *Salvador* (3), *Alvaro* (2), *Blanca* (2), *Enrique* (2); *Constantino* (4), *Antonio* (2), *Fausto, Filiberto, Francesca, Gilda, Julieta, Romeo.*

Arch (493) **1.** English: topographic name for someone living by a bridge, from Middle English, Old French *arche* 'arch'. **2.** Possibly Jewish: a translation into English of BOGEN.

Archacki (123) Polish and Ukrainian: unexplained. Possibly a derivative of Greek *archos* 'ruler', 'lord'.

GIVEN NAME Polish 4%. *Jozef.*

Archambault (1625) French: from an Old French personal name of Germanic origin, composed of Old High German *ercan* 'precious', 'excellent' (see ARCAND) + *bald* 'bold', 'daring'.

FOREBEARS Bearers of the name Archambault were recorded in Quebec in 1651 (from Poitou) and Montreal in 1660.

GIVEN NAMES French 11%. *Armand* (6), *Jacques* (6), *Lucien* (6), *Normand* (5), *Marcel* (3), *Amie* (2), *Alcide, Andre, Berard, Damien, Emile, Fernand.*

Archambeau (399) French: variant of ARCHAMBAULT.

Archambeault (295) French: variant spelling of ARCHAMBAULT.

GIVEN NAMES French 6%. *Armand, Laurier, Serge.*

Archambo (121) Respelling of French ARCHAMBAULT.

Archbold (434) Northern English: variant of Scottish ARCHIBALD. This form of the name is especially common in Northumberland.

Archdeacon (103) English: occupational name from Middle English *archedekene* 'archdeacon' (Old English *arcedīacon*, Old French *arc(h)ediacne*), probably denoting someone in the service of an archdeacon.

Archer (12164) English: from Old French *arch(i)er*, Middle English *archere*, hence an occupational name for an archer. This Norman French word partially replaced the native English word *bowman* in the 14th century. In North America this surname may have absorbed some cases of European cognates such as French **Archier**.

Archey (355) English: probably from a variant of ARCHER, but in some cases it could be of Scottish origin, from a pet form of ARCHIBALD.

Archibald (2927) Scottish: from a Scottish personal name, *Archibald*, of Anglo-Norman French and (ultimately) Continental Germanic origin (see ARCHAMBAULT). In the Highlands of Scotland it was

taken as an Anglicized equivalent of the Gaelic personal name *Gille Easbaig* 'servant of the bishop' (see GILLESPIE), probably because of the approximate phonetic similarity between *Arch(i)bald* and *easbaig.* Both *Archibald* and *Gillespie* are personal names much favored among Clan Campbell.

FOREBEARS This is the name of a leading Nova Scotia family, taken there by four brothers who emigrated from Londonderry, northern Ireland, in 1750–62.

Archibeque (317) Spanish and French: from a variant of Old French *archevesque* 'archbishop', either denoting a member of an archbishop's household or used as an ironic nickname.

GIVEN NAMES Spanish 11%; French 4%. *Jose* (4), *Gilberto* (2), *Alfonso, Cristina, Emiliano, Emilio, Ernesto, Fidel, Francisco, Hilario, Ignacio, Isidro; Andre, Marcell.*

Archie (1480) Scottish: from a short form of the personal name ARCHIBALD.

Archila (117) Possibly a variant spelling of Spanish ARCILA.

GIVEN NAMES Spanish 49%. *Jose* (5), *Miguel* (3), *Carlos* (2), *Jaime* (2), *Juan* (2), *Julio* (2), *Mario* (2), *Ana, Benigno, Cristina, Esperanza, Genaro; Marco Antonio.*

Archuleta (2584) Castilianized form of Basque **Aretxuloeta**, a topographic name meaning 'oak hollow', from *aretx*, Biscayan variant of *(h)artiz* 'oak' + *zulo* 'hole', 'hollow' + *-eta* 'place or group of'.

GIVEN NAMES Spanish 17%. *Jose* (39), *Manuel* (22), *Juan* (12), *Alfonso* (5), *Jacobo* (5), *Orlando* (5), *Ruben* (5), *Alonzo* (4), *Carlos* (4), *Ramon* (4), *Salomon* (4), *Ana* (3).

Archuletta (177) Respelling of ARCHULETA.

GIVEN NAMES Spanish 5%. *Amador, Angelina, Juan, Marcos, Mondo, Ricardo.*

Arcia (119) Spanish: probably variant of **García** (see GARCIA).

GIVEN NAMES Spanish 50%. *Alberto* (5), *Francisco* (3), *Arturo* (2), *Dagoberto* (2), *Enrique* (2), *Jose* (2), *Ramiro* (2), *Adalberto, Aleida, Alejandro, Alfredo, Amalia.*

Arcidiacono (155) Southern Italian: from *arcidiàcono* 'archdeacon', probably a nickname for someone who behaved in a pompous way or was in the service of an archdeacon, rather than an occupational name for an archdeacon.

GIVEN NAMES Italian 23%. *Salvatore* (3), *Alfio* (2), *Nunzio* (2), *Angelo, Carmelo, Orazio, Salvator, Vito.*

Arcieri (140) Southern Italian: occupational name from *arciere* 'archer'.

GIVEN NAMES Italian 23%; Spanish 8%. *Alberto* (2), *Mario* (2), *Amore, Anello, Carmela, Rocco; Natividad* (2), *Osvaldo* (2), *Carlos.*

Arciero (118) Southern Italian: occupational name from Old French *archier* 'archer', 'bowman'.
GIVEN NAMES Spanish 8%; Italian 7%. *Elena, Ernesto, Esequiel, Mario, Ovidio, Ramon, Vila; Rocco* (2), *Domenic, Silvio.*

Arcila (106) Spanish: in most cases probably a variant of a topographic name from *arcilla* 'clay' (Latin *argilla*).
GIVEN NAMES Spanish 59%. *Carlos* (4), *Jose* (3), *Alfredo* (2), *Amparo* (2), *Beatriz* (2), *Fabio* (2), *Fernando* (2), *Juan* (2), *Ramon* (2), *Alberto, Arturo, Candelaria.*

Arciniega (272) Castilianized form of Basque **Artziniega**, a habitational name from a place in Araba province named Artziniega, from Basque *artzain* 'shepherd' + *(h)egi* 'ridge' + the article suffix -*a*.
GIVEN NAMES Spanish 45%. *Jose* (10), *Pedro* (4), *Juan* (3), *Luis* (3), *Manuel* (3), *Ramon* (3), *Armando* (2), *Enrique* (2), *Florencio* (2), *Jesus* (2), *Jorge* (2), *Mario* (2).

Arco (122) **1.** Spanish: habitational name from any of the places called Arco in the provinces of Cáceres, Pontevedra, Santander, and Salamanca, or a topographic name from *arco* 'archway'. **2.** Italian: metonymic occupational name for a bow maker or bowman, from *arco* 'bow', or a habitational name from a place named with this word, as for example Arco Felice in Naples province.
GIVEN NAMES Spanish 9%; Italian 8%. *Emilio* (3), *Alberto, Carlos, Celestino, Juanita, Manuel, Miguel; Angelo, Nino.*

Arcos (266) Spanish: habitational name from any of several places called Arcos or Los Arcos, with reference to their arches or arcades.
GIVEN NAMES Spanish 54%. *Carlos* (8), *Jose* (5), *Luis* (5), *Armando* (4), *Raul* (4), *Guadalupe* (3), *Jesus* (3), *Juan* (3), *Pedro* (3), *Ana* (2), *Francisco* (2), *Humberto* (2).

Arcuri (774) Southern Italian: variant of **Arcudi**, which is from the Greek personal name *Arcadio* (Latin *Arcadius*), conflated by folk etymology with modern Greek *arkouda* 'bear' (classical Greek *arktos*). There were several Saints Arcadius, including a fourth-century Mauretanian martyr, a fifth-century Spanish martyr, and a sixth-century French bishop. The name Arcadius (*Arkadios*) originally denoted someone from the region of Arcadia in the Peloponnese.
GIVEN NAMES Italian 24%. *Salvatore* (7), *Angelo* (5), *Santo* (5), *Antonio* (2), *Carmine* (2), *Domenico* (2), *Giuseppe* (2), *Ignazio* (2), *Rosario* (2), *Dino, Domenica, Fabio, Gino, Renato.*

Ard (2144) Scottish: habitational name from any of several places called Aird, including one near Hurlford in Ayrshire, another near Stranraer in Galloway, and the Aird, the higher part of the Vale of Beauly, near Inverness. These place names are derived from Gaelic *àird(e)* 'height', 'promontory', from *àrd* 'high'.

Ardelean (130) Romanian: habitational name for someone from Transylvania, Hungarian name *Erdély* (see ERDELYI).
GIVEN NAMES Romanian 18%; French 4%. *Constantin* (2), *Vasa* (2), *Cornel, Doru, Gheorghe, Petre, Petru, Simion, Tiberiu, Todor; Aurel* (2).

Ardell (133) Swedish: from an unexplained first element + the common suffix of surnames -*ell* (from Latin -*elius*).

Arden (825) English: habitational name for someone from the district of Arden in Warwickshire or from Arden in North Yorkshire. Both place names are derived from a Celtic word meaning 'high', and are cognate with *Ardennes*, name of a forested region on the borders between northeastern France and eastern Belgium.

Ardinger (126) German: habitational name for someone from a place in Bavaria called Erding (earlier *Ardingen*).

Ardis (499) **1.** Scottish: reduced form of **Allardice** (see ALDERDICE). **2.** Possibly a variant of ARTIS.

Ardito (412) Italian: nickname from *ardito* 'bold', 'daring', from *ardire* 'to venture', a word of Germanic origin.
GIVEN NAMES Italian 16%. *Vito* (6), *Francesco* (2), *Aldo, Angelo, Annamaria, Carlo, Carmel, Dante, Domenico, Gaetano, Gino, Giuseppe.*

Ardizzone (224) Italian (common in Sicily): from a medieval personal name of Germanic origin, from *Ardizon*, the oblique case of *Ardizo*, a pet form of any of various Italian names beginning with the element *ard-* 'hard'. Compare English HARDY.
GIVEN NAMES Italian 26%. *Mario* (4), *Salvatore* (2), *Aurelio, Giovanni, Giuseppe, Leonardo, Nunziata, Pietro, Rocco, Santo, Vito.*

Ardoin (1245) French: variant of **Hardouin**, from a personal name of Germanic origin (see HARDING).
FOREBEARS This is a very common Louisiana name. There was an Ardouin or Hardouin from Saintonge recorded in Quebec city in 1665. Other early settlers bearing this surname came from Clermont, Saintes, Bordeaux, Bayonne, and Languedoc. Etienne Ardouin of Montreal settled in Detroit around 1770; sometime later the family moved down the Mississippi, and are now concentrated around Ville Platte, LA.
GIVEN NAMES French 5%. *Silton* (2), *Sylvian* (2), *Anatole, Camille, Curley, Delphin, Desire, Easton, Eugenie, Leandre, Lucien.*

Ardolino (213) Italian: probably from a variant of the personal name *Arduino* (see ARDUINI).
GIVEN NAMES Italian 6%. *Antonio, Carmela, Carmino, Pasquale.*

Ardon (166) **1.** Hispanic (mainly El Salvador): habitational name from Ardón in León province, Spain. **2.** Dutch: probably from a variant of the personal name

Hardewijn, French *Ardouin*, composed of the Germanic elements *hard* 'hardy', 'brave' + *win* 'friend'.
GIVEN NAMES Spanish 53%. *Jose* (7), *Luis* (6), *Ana* (2), *Carlos* (2), *Marina* (2), *Roberto* (2), *Salvador* (2), *Adan, Alfredo, Alirio, Amalia, Andres.*

Ardrey (354) Scottish and northern Irish: habitational name from Airdrie, the name of several farms and minor places in Nairn, Fife, and Kirkcudbrightshire, as well as Airdrie near Glasgow. The origins of the place names are uncertain; in some cases it is said to represent Gaelic *árd ruigh* 'high reach' or 'high slope'.

Arduini (207) Italian: patronymic or plural form of ARDUINO.
GIVEN NAMES Italian 18%. *Angelo* (4), *Antonio* (2), *Biagio, Giacomo, Gino, Giuseppe, Nicola, Romano, Tommaso.*

Arduino (127) Southern Italian: from the personal name *Arduino*, which is of Germanic origin, akin to HARDING 2.
GIVEN NAMES Spanish 34%. *Francisco* (2), *Jose* (2), *Luis* (2), *Marina* (2), *Alberto, Alfonso, Alturo, Angel, Arturo, Azucena, Basilio, Carlos; Antonio* (2), *Gabino.*

Arebalo (154) Spanish (**Arébalo**): variant spelling of AREVALO.
GIVEN NAMES Spanish 44%. *Antonio* (2), *Francisco* (2), *Jose* (2), *Luis* (2), *Marina* (2), *Alberto, Alfonso, Alturo, Angel, Arturo, Azucena, Basilio, Carlos.*

Arechiga (278) Castilianized variant (**Aréchiga**) of Basque **Aretxaga**, a habitational name from a town called Aretxaga in Araba province, Basque Country, or a Basque topographic name meaning 'oak grove', from *aretx* 'oak' + -*aga* 'place or group'.
GIVEN NAMES Spanish 53%. *Jose* (10), *Juan* (8), *Francisco* (4), *Jaime* (4), *Manuel* (4), *Raul* (3), *Carlos* (2), *Jorge* (2), *Lupe* (2), *Ramon* (2), *Ricardo* (2), *Rogelio* (2).

Arehart (534) Americanized spelling of German EHRHARDT.

Arel (371) Probably a variant of Scottish **Arrol**, a habitational name from a place called Arrol, later Errol, in Tayside, Scotland. The variant **Arrell** is found in Scotland.
GIVEN NAMES French 12%. *Armand* (3), *Cecile* (2), *Lucien* (2), *Normand* (2), *Alphonse, Andre, Fernand, Jacques, Marcel, Phillippe, Rosaire, Serge.*

Arellanes (245) Spanish: probably a patronymic from ARELLANO, used as a personal name or later interpreted as such. On the other hand, it may be an alternative plural alongside the standard *Arellanos*, based on an unrecorded but possible variant of the singular, *Arellán*.
GIVEN NAMES Spanish 35%. *Juan* (3), *Arturo* (2), *Cesar* (2), *Guadalupe* (2), *Jorge* (2), *Manuel* (2), *Mario* (2), *Roberto* (2), *Agustina, Armida, Cirilo, Concepcion.*

Arellano (3743) Spanish: habitational name from Arellano in Navarre, named in Late Latin as *fundus Aurelianus* 'the farm or estate of Aurelius'.
GIVEN NAMES Spanish 48%. *Jose* (92), *Juan* (43), *Jesus* (41), *Manuel* (36), *Francisco* (29), *Luis* (25), *Carlos* (21), *Mario* (21), *Miguel* (20), *Ramon* (19), *Jorge* (18), *Rafael* (18).

Arena (2181) Italian (southern) and Spanish: habitational name from any of numerous places named with *arena* 'sand', 'sandy place', also 'arena', '(bull) ring'.
GIVEN NAMES Italian 18%; Spanish 7%. *Salvatore* (22), *Angelo* (11), *Rosario* (6), *Sal* (6), *Mario* (5), *Antonio* (4), *Vito* (4), *Natale* (3), *Rocco* (3), *Aldo* (2), *Claudio* (2), *Domenic* (2), *Maurizio* (2), *Nunzio* (2), *Pietro* (2); *Jose Fernando* (3), *Juanita* (2), *Salvador* (2), *Alfonso, Alvaro, Angelina, Armando, Berta*.

Arenas (951) Spanish: habitational name from any of numerous places called Arenas, from the plural of *arena* 'sand' (Latin *(h)arena*).
GIVEN NAMES Spanish 49%. *Jose* (22), *Juan* (15), *Carlos* (11), *Jorge* (11), *Luis* (11), *Mario* (10), *Francisco* (8), *Pedro* (8), *Jesus* (7), *Fernando* (6), *Miguel* (6), *Roberto* (6).

Arenberg (104) Jewish (Ashkenazic): ornamental name composed of the personal name *A(a)ron* + German *Berg* 'mountain'.
GIVEN NAMES Jewish 6%; German 4%. *Miriam*; *Egon*.

Arencibia (224) Spanish (of Basque origin): habitational name from some minor place named with Basque *arantz(e)* or *arantz(a)* '(haw)thorn' + *ibi* 'ford' + *-a* (article suffix).
GIVEN NAMES Spanish 60%. *Jose* (12), *Juan* (6), *Alberto* (4), *Alfredo* (4), *Carlos* (4), *Orlando* (4), *Pedro* (4), *Andres* (3), *Julio* (3), *Lazaro* (3), *Luis* (3), *Miguel* (3).

Arend (695) Dutch and North German: from a personal name of Germanic origin, derived from the elements *arn* 'eagle' + *wald* 'rule'. Compare German ARNDT.

Arendale (102) **1.** English: variant of ARUNDEL. **2.** Perhaps an altered spelling of Swedish ARENDALL.

Arendall (128) **1.** English: variant of ARUNDEL. **2.** Respelling of a western Swedish habitational name, **Arendal**, composed of an unexplained first element + *dal* 'valley'.

Arender (142) Jewish (eastern Ashkenazic): Germanized or Yiddishized form of Polish *arendarz* 'leaseholder' or 'publican'.
GIVEN NAME Jewish 5%. *Hershel* (3).

Arends (1192) Dutch and North German: patronymic from AREND.

Arendt (1089) **1.** German: variant of ARNDT. **2.** Jewish (Ashkenazic): adoption of the German personal name as a surname, in part probably on account of its resemblance to the Jewish name AARON. Compare AHRENS.

GIVEN NAMES German 4%. *Kurt* (3), *Erwin* (2), *Armin, Dieter, Gunter, Hans, Hedwig, Monika, Wolfram*.

Arens (1200) Dutch and North German: variant of ARENDS.

Arensberg (148) North German: habitational name from a place named as 'eagle's mountain' (see AREND and BERG), probably Ahrensberg in Mecklenburg.

Arensdorf (146) German: habitational name from a place called Arensdorf or Ahrensdorf, 'village of A(h)rens' (see AREND and DORF). There is one Arensdorf near Frankfurt an der Oder and there are several places called Ahrensdorf north and south of Berlin.
GIVEN NAMES French 5%. *Amie* (2), *Patrice*.

Arenson (289) Jewish (Ashkenazic): variant spelling of AARONSON.

Arent (397) **1.** Dutch: variant of AREND. **2.** Altered form of German ARNDT.

Arentz (223) German and Dutch: variant of ARENDS.

Arenz (317) German and Dutch: variant of ARENDS.

Ares (278) Galician: probably a habitational name from places called Ares, in the provinces of A Coruña and Lugo in Galicia, either from the plural of *ar* 'wind', 'air' (compare Buenos Aires, Galician *Bos Ares*), or from the medieval personal name *Arias* (*Aires*), which is probably of Germanic origin.
GIVEN NAMES Spanish 28%; French 5%. *Jose* (6), *Manuel* (5), *Angel* (3), *Carlos* (3), *Luis* (3), *Ruben* (3), *Ana* (2), *Francisco* (2), *Ignacio* (2), *Juan* (2), *Mercedes* (2), *Orlando* (2); *Adrien, Jean-Claude, Jean-marie, Micheline*.

Aresco (122) Southern Italian: nickname from Greek *areskos* 'lovable'.
GIVEN NAMES Italian 34%. *Mario* (4), *Salvatore* (4), *Angelo* (3), *Benito, Carmelo, Emanuele, Filomena, Rosario, Sal, Santo*.

Aretz (128) German: from a variant of ARNDT.

Arevalo (1631) Spanish (**Arévalo**): habitational name from places called Arévalo, in the provinces of Ávila and Soria, or from various places named with this word.
GIVEN NAMES Spanish 52%. *Jose* (59), *Luis* (29), *Juan* (21), *Carlos* (18), *Manuel* (18), *Francisco* (12), *Jesus* (11), *Jorge* (11), *Roberto* (10), *Armando* (9), *Jaime* (9), *Julio* (9).

Arey (700) **1.** English: variant spelling of AIREY. **2.** variant of AVERY. **3.** Respelling of German ERICH or, in some cases, IHRIG.
FOREBEARS Richard Arey was in Salisbury, MA, in 1646. By 1652 he was in Martha's Vineyard, where he drowned in 1669. William Arey, who died in Boston in 1687, was in Dedham, MA, in 1650. In this case at least, the name is probably a variant of AVERY.
In the Shenandoah Valley of VA the name Arey is probably from German

ERICH. Compare *Cutlip Airey*, mentioned in the note at AIREY. The Arey family of Rowan Co., NC, are descended from Peter Ihrig, who arrived at Philadelphia in 1749. His place of origin was probably near Mosbach on the Neckar river in Baden, Germany. At some time before 1757 he arrived in NC, where his and his children's surname was spelled Eary, and by the next generation, Arey.

Arford (112) English: habitational name from Arford in Hampshire.

Arfsten (104) Possibly of Scandinavian origin: unexplained.
GIVEN NAME German 7%. *Lorenz* (2).

Arft (113) North German and Frisian: from Germanic *arbi-*, Dutch *erf* 'heritage'.

Argabright (311) Americanized form of German **Erkenbrecht** (see ARGENBRIGHT).

Argabrite (108) Americanized form of German **Erkenbrecht** (see ARGENBRIGHT).

Argall (187) Northern Irish: variant of Scottish ARGYLE.
FOREBEARS Philip Argall (1854–1922), from Newtownards, northern Ireland, was a prominent mining engineer in CO. He had ten children.

Arganbright (175) Americanized form of German **Erkenbrecht** (see ARGENBRIGHT).

Argenbright (178) Americanized form of German **Erkenbrecht**, from a Germanic personal name composed of Old High German *erkan* 'pure', 'perfect' + *berht* 'bright'.

Argenio (112) Italian: unexplained.
GIVEN NAMES Italian 10%; Jewish 5%. *Carmine* (2), *Franca*; *Miriam* (2).

Argent (176) English: from Old French *argent* 'silver', hence probably a nickname for someone with silver-gray hair, or possibly an occupational nickname for a silversmith or moneyer.

Argenta (102) Italian: **1.** variant of ARGENTO. **2.** habitational name from Argenta in Emilia-Romagna.
GIVEN NAMES French 6%; Italian 6%. *Numa*; *Pio*.

Argenti (104) Italian: patronymic or plural form of ARGENTO.
GIVEN NAMES Italian 16%. *Angelo* (2), *Caesar* (2), *Aldo, Domenic*.

Argentieri (151) Italian: occupational name for a silversmith, *argentiere*.
GIVEN NAMES Italian 19%. *Angelo* (7), *Carlo* (2), *Aldo*.

Argento (357) Italian: from *argento* 'silver', perhaps sometimes applied as a nickname for someone with silvery gray hair, but more often a metonymic occupational name for a silversmith.
GIVEN NAMES Italian 33%. *Salvatore* (9), *Angelo* (4), *Sal* (4), *Antonio* (3), *Calogero* (2), *Giuseppe* (2), *Carmella, Claudio, Dino, Filippo, Mario, Natale, Paolo, Pasquale, Renato, Rocco*.

Argenziano (107) Italian: unexplained; perhaps from a derivative of the personal name *Argenzio*, from Latin *argenteus* 'silver'.

GIVEN NAMES Italian 11%. *Mario* (3), *Gaetano*, *Sal*.

Argetsinger (134) Americanized spelling of German **Ergetzinger** or **Erge(n)zinger**, a habitational name for a person from Ergenzingen in Württemberg.

Argiro (144) Italian (Sicily): from a Greek personal name derived from *argyros* 'silver'. See ARGYROS.

GIVEN NAMES Italian 23%. *Rocco* (4), *Angelo* (2), *Anello*, *Antonio*, *Cosmo*.

Argo (1460) **1.** Scottish (Aberdeen): unexplained. Perhaps of the same Gaelic origin as ARGUE 2, or a variant of ARGYLE. **2.** Italian (**Argò**): either a variant of **Agró**, from Greek *agros* 'field', or a nickname from Greek *argos* 'lazy', 'slothful'. Compare AGRO.

Argue (281) **1.** Americanized form of French **Argoud** or **Argaud** (from the Germanic personal name *Argwald* 'fierce governor') or **Argoux** (from the Germanic personal name *Argwulf* 'raging wolf'). **2.** Irish: probably from Gaelic *Mac Giolla Fhearga* 'son of the servant of (Saint) Fearga'. In Ireland this name is found mainly in Co. Cavan and may also appear as **McIlhargy** (see McHARGUE).

Arguelles (529) Asturian-Leonese and Spanish (**Argüelles**): habitational name from any of various places called Argüelles, mainly the one in Asturies.

GIVEN NAMES Spanish 47%. *Jose* (16), *Carlos* (11), *Fernando* (10), *Ramon* (7), *Juan* (5), *Alfredo* (4), *Joaquin* (4), *Jorge* (4), *Orlando* (4), *Angel* (3), *Armando* (3), *Eduardo* (3); *Antonio* (2), *Donato* (2), *Cecilio*, *Enrico*, *Federico*, *Lorenzo*, *Romeo*, *Silvano*.

Arguello (996) Spanish (**Argüello**): habitational name from any of various minor places called Arguello, from Old Spanish *arboleo* 'well-wooded'.

GIVEN NAMES Spanish 39%. *Jose* (20), *Carlos* (12), *Eduardo* (8), *Mario* (8), *Juan* (7), *Manuel* (7), *Francisco* (6), *Ramon* (6), *Roberto* (6), *Ana* (5), *Jorge* (5), *Luis* (5).

Argueta (909) Basque: topographic name from Basque *argi* 'light' + *-eta* 'place or abundance of', and so probably denoting a clearing.

GIVEN NAMES Spanish 58%. *Jose* (73), *Carlos* (15), *Mario* (14), *Julio* (11), *Luis* (10), *Francisco* (9), *Juan* (9), *Santos* (9), *Ana* (7), *Manuel* (6), *Jorge* (5), *Ramon* (5).

Arguijo (171) Spanish: habitational name from a place called Arguijo, in Zamora province.

GIVEN NAMES Spanish 38%. *Jose* (5), *Arturo* (3), *Armando* (2), *Gilberto* (2), *Jesus* (2), *Santiago* (2), *Santos* (2), *Serapio* (2), *Adriana*, *Armondo*, *Carlos*, *Efrain*.

Argus (160) Cornish: unexplained. The name is recorded in Cornwall and South Wales in the 19th century.

GIVEN NAMES French 6%. *Camille*, *Musette*.

Argyle (377) Scottish: from the regional name Argyll, a county of southwestern

Scotland, named in Gaelic as *Earre Ghàidheal* 'coast of the Gaels'. Argyll was the earliest part of Scotland to be settled by Gaelic speakers from Ireland from the 6th century onwards. The origin of Argyle as a surname owes more to its use to denote retainers of the powerful and influential earls and dukes of Argyll, heads of Clan Campbell, than to use as a habitational name.

Argyros (114) Greek: from the personal name *Argyrios*, or patronymics formed from it, such as **Argyroglou** or **Argyropoulos**, all ultimately derived from the adjective *argyros* 'silvery'.

GIVEN NAMES Greek 43%. *Anastasios* (2), *Christos* (2), *Costas* (2), *Dimitrios* (2), *Evangelos* (2), *Apostolos*, *Demos*, *Eleni*, *Fotios*, *Georgios*, *Ioannis*, *Konstantinos*.

Ariail (146) French: unexplained.

Arian (103) **1.** Arabic: unexplained. **2.** Jewish (Sephardic): adoption of the Arabic name.

GIVEN NAMES Arabic 18%; Jewish 6%. *Akram* (2), *Muhammad* (2), *Afshin*, *Amir*, *Jawed*, *Mehdi*, *Nabil*, *Rahim*, *Ramin*, *Zia*; *Asher*, *Avram*, *Einat*, *Eyal*.

Arias (4599) **1.** Spanish: from the popular medieval personal name *Arias* which is probably of Germanic origin. **2.** Jewish (Sephardic): adoption of the Spanish family name.

GIVEN NAMES Spanish 52%. *Jose* (151), *Carlos* (68), *Luis* (65), *Juan* (62), *Manuel* (42), *Jorge* (36), *Jesus* (34), *Arturo* (33), *Ramon* (33), *Pedro* (29), *Francisco* (28), *Miguel* (26).

Arick (124) Perhaps a respelling of German ERICH or, alternatively, of Dutch **Arik**, a nickname from Middle Dutch *haderic*, the name of a spice or herb, or from a Germanic personal name composed of the elements *hathu* 'battle', 'combat' + *rik* 'powerful'.

Arico (278) Southern Italian (**Aricò**): nickname for a countryman, from medieval Greek dialect *a(g)riko* 'rural', 'rustic' (classical Greek *agroikos*).

GIVEN NAMES Italian 17%. *Carmine* (2), *Salvatore* (2), *Santo* (2), *Franco*, *Grazia*, *Nicolina*, *Pietro*, *Sal*.

Ariel (131) Jewish: from the Biblical place name Ariel, said to mean 'lion of God' in Hebrew. It is mentioned in the prophecies of Ezra (8:16) and Isaiah (29:1–2).

GIVEN NAMES Jewish 29%. *Yoram* (2), *Yosef* (2), *Amram*, *Ari*, *Avi*, *Gitty*, *Haim*, *Ilan*, *Miriam*, *Moshe*, *Yaacov*, *Yaakov*.

Aries (138) **1.** Scottish: habitational name from either of two places in Kirkcudbrightshire named Airies (earlier written *Aries*, *Aryes*). **2.** French (**Ariès**): from the medieval personal name *Yrieix*, Latin *Aredius*, which was borne by a 6th-century saint, an abbot of Limoges.

GIVEN NAMES Spanish 7%. *Luis* (3), *Jose*, *Jose Luis*, *Ramon*, *Salvador*.

Arif (117) Muslim (**'Ārif**): from the Arabic adjective *'ārif* 'learned', 'expert'.

GIVEN NAMES Muslim 88%. *Mohammad* (18), *Mohammed* (12), *Muhammad* (8), *Syed* (4), *Ahmed* (3), *Abdul* (2), *Riaz* (2), *Abdurahman*, *Ahmad*, *Alaa*, *Anjum*, *Ehab*.

Arima (105) Japanese: 'owns a horse'; the name is found mostly in western Japan and the Ryūkyū Islands. It is habitational, taken from the Arima hot spring near the city of Kōbe. The original bearers were lords in the district, descended from the MINAMOTO clan.

GIVEN NAMES Japanese 58%. *Kenji* (2), *Akinori*, *Fumi*, *Goro*, *Haruo*, *Haruto*, *Hideki*, *Hiroko*, *Hiroyuki*, *Jiro*, *Junichi*, *Kazuo*.

Aring (125) Americanized spelling of German **Ehring**.

Arington (185) English: variant spelling of ARRINGTON.

Ariola (226) Variant spelling of ARRIOLA.

GIVEN NAMES Spanish 12%. *Gerardo* (2), *Edgardo*, *Erlinda*, *Gregoria*, *Hilaria*, *Jose*, *Leopoldo*, *Leticia*, *Manuela*, *Marcelo*.

Aris (166) **1.** French: unexplained. **2.** Galician: probably a habitational name from a place called Aris in Galicia. **3.** Latvian: from the personal name *Ārijs*.

GIVEN NAMES French 4%. *Andre*, *Matilde*.

Arispe (291) Spanish variant of ARIZPE.

GIVEN NAMES Spanish 44%. *Juan* (8), *Manuel* (8), *Jose* (4), *Ernesto* (3), *Raul* (3), *Agustin* (2), *Armando* (2), *Aurelio* (2), *Carlos* (2), *Guadalupe* (2), *Humberto* (2), *Juanita* (2).

Aristizabal (102) Spanish (**Aristizábal**; of Basque origin): topographic name for someone who lived by a large oak wood, from Basque *areitz* 'oak' + *zabal* 'broad', 'wide'.

GIVEN NAMES Spanish 57%; Italian 7%. *Eduardo* (4), *Gustavo* (3), *Jose* (3), *Carlos* (2), *Fabio* (2), *Juan* (2), *Liliana* (2), *Luis* (2), *Orlando* (2), *Alfredo*, *Alvaro*, *Amparo*; *Silvio* (3), *Marco* (2).

Arita (182) Japanese: written with characters meaning 'has' or 'owns' and 'rice paddy', the actual meaning could be 'rice paddy of ants'. It is a habitational name most common west-central Japan.

GIVEN NAMES Japanese 35%; Spanish 11%. *Akira* (2), *Satoru* (2), *Taiji* (2), *Yukie* (2), *Akiko*, *Atsuko*, *Fumio*, *Hidehito*, *Hideyuki*, *Hiroko*, *Hiroyuki*, *Katsuki*; *Aida*, *Alejandro*, *Alfredo*, *Alicia*, *Arnoldo*, *Carlos*, *Ernestina*, *Felicita*, *Jorge*, *Juan Carlos*, *Luis*, *Miguel*.

Ariza (276) **1.** Castilianized form of Basque **Aritza**, a topographic name from Basque *(h)aritz* 'oak' + the article suffix *-a*. **2.** Spanish: habitational name from a place so named in Zaragoza province in Aragón.

GIVEN NAMES Spanish 47%. *Jose* (7), *Jorge* (4), *Jaime* (3), *Juan* (3), *Luis* (3), *Miguel* (3), *Ramon* (3), *Asdrubal* (2), *Jairo* (2), *Jesus* (2), *Luz* (2), *Manuel* (2).

Arizmendi (228) Castilianized form of Basque **Aritzmendi**, a topographic name from Basque *(h)aritz* 'oak' + *mendi* 'mountain'.

GIVEN NAMES Spanish 54%. *Jose* (5), *Fernando* (3), *Javier* (3), *Jorge* (3), *Juan* (3), *Alfredo* (2), *Armando* (2), *Efrain* (2), *Guadalupe* (2), *Hernan* (2), *Jaime* (2), *Jesus* (2).

Arizpe (146) Castilianized form of Basque **Aritzpe**, a topographic name from Basque *(h)aritz* 'oak' + *-be* 'below', 'under'.

GIVEN NAMES Spanish 49%. *Jose* (5), *Juan* (4), *Raul* (3), *Alfonso* (2), *Carlos* (2), *Emilio* (2), *Fermin* (2), *Homero* (2), *Juanita* (2), *Ramiro* (2), *Ricardo* (2), *Antonieta*.

Arjona (139) Spanish: habitational name from Arjona in Jaén province.

GIVEN NAMES Spanish 61%. *Juan* (5), *Enrique* (4), *Jose* (3), *Manuel* (3), *Carlos* (2), *Francisco* (2), *Leticia* (2), *Mauricio* (2), *Orlando* (2), *Rafael* (2), *Ruben* (2), *Alicia*.

Ark (122) Dutch (**van Ark**): habitational name from a place called Ark in Gelderland.

Arkell (142) English: from a Scandinavian personal name: Old Norse *Arnkell*, Old Danish *Arnketil*, Old Swedish *Arkil*.

Arkin (501) Jewish (eastern Ashkenazic): patronymic from *Arke*, an eastern Yiddish pet form of the personal name AARON.

Arko (225) Jewish (eastern Ashkenazic): from a pet form of the personal name *Aron*, Slavic form of the Biblical name AARON.

Arkwright (130) English: occupational name for a chest maker, from Middle English, Old French *arc* 'chest', 'bin' + Middle English *wright* 'maker', 'craftsman' (see WRIGHT).

Arledge (954) English: variant of ALDRICH or ALDRIDGE. A few bearers of the name are recorded in southern England in the 17th–19th centuries, but the name appears to have died out in Britain.

FOREBEARS Isaac Arledge died in Fairfield co., SC, in 1790. He was a slave owner; many present-day bearers are African Americans.

Arlen (207) In at least a few cases, this is a respelling of German **Erlen**. However, the original surname of the composer Harold Arlen was **Arluck** (a name of obscure origin), while the playwright Michael Arlen was **Kouyoumdjian**, an Armenian name.

Arline (308) Americanized spelling of German **Ehrlein**.

Arling (101) **1.** English: variant of HARLIN. **2.** German: possibly from a Germanic personal name derived from Old High German *aro* 'eagle'.

GIVEN NAME German 4%. *Matthias*.

Arlinghaus (129) German: perhaps a habitational name from Oerlinghausen in North Rhine-Westphalia.

GIVEN NAMES German 4%. *Heinrich*, *Ilse*.

Arlington (216) English: habitational name from any of three places called Arlington: in Devon, Gloucestershire, and East Sussex. Earlier forms of the place names show that each contains a different Old English personal name (respectively, *Ælffrith*, *Ælfrēd*, and *Eorl(a)*) + *-ing-*, denoting association with, + *tūn* 'settlement'.

Arlotta (153) Italian (Sicily): from the French personal name *Arlot*, recorded in the Latinized form *Arolottus* from the 13th century.

GIVEN NAMES Italian 18%. *Angelo* (3), *Carmine* (2), *Domenico*, *Vincenza*.

Arlt (359) German: from the personal name, a reduced form of ARNOLD. It is frequent in Silesia and Upper Lausitz, where the change in form is amply documented from the 16th century.

Armacost (268) Hispanic: variant of ARMAGOST.

Armagost (271) Hispanic: from the Germanic personal name *Aringast*, composed of the elements *arn* 'eagle' + *gast* 'stranger', 'host'.

Arman (281) **1.** Variant of French ARMAND. **2.** German (**Armann**): nickname for a impoverished person, Middle High German *ar(m)mann* 'poor man'. There has been some confusion with the more common medieval Germanic personal name *Heriman* 'army man' (see HERMANN).

GIVEN NAMES French 4%. *Armand* (3), *Michel*.

Armand (668) French: from the personal name *Arman(d)* or *Harman(d)*, which is of Germanic origin, composed of the elements *hardi* 'bold', 'hardy' + *man* 'man', with excrescent *-d*. This surname is also found in Germany as a Huguenot name.

FOREBEARS An Armand from Rouen is documented in Quebec city in 1663.

GIVEN NAMES French 14%. *Pierre* (4), *Lucien* (2), *Philippe* (2), *Serge* (2), *Alain*, *Andre*, *Andree*, *Camille*, *Etienne*, *Francoise*, *Gabrielle*, *Gardy*.

Armando (119) Spanish, Portuguese, and Italian: from *Armando*, a personal name of Germanic origin, cognate with ARMAND.

GIVEN NAMES Spanish 26%; Italian 4%. *Navarro* (2), *Alvarado*, *Andrade*, *Armando*, *Diaz*, *Emiliano*, *Garcia*, *Jimenez*, *Jorge*, *Martinez*, *Ramon*, *Sanchez*; *Angelo*, *Vito*.

Armani (100) Italian: from the medieval personal name *Armanno* (Latinized as *(H)ariman(n)us*), a Lombardic name, from Germanic *hariman* 'freeman'.

GIVEN NAMES Italian 6%; Armenian 5%. *Giorgio* (2), *Angelo*, *Carlo*; *Artin* (2), *Nerses*.

Armanini (100) Italian: from the personal name *Armanino*, a pet form of *Armanno* (see ARMANI).

GIVEN NAMES Italian 22%. *Dario* (2), *Dino* (2), *Geno* (2), *Angelo*, *Carlo*, *Renzo*.

Armantrout (180) See ARMENTROUT.

Armao (124) Portuguese (**Armão**) and Southern Italian: from the Germanic personal name *Armando*. Compare German ARMAND.

Armas (608) Spanish: from *armas* 'arms', hence a metonymic occupational name for a maker of arms or a soldier.

GIVEN NAMES Spanish 47%. *Jose* (23), *Juan* (9), *Armando* (6), *Alberto* (5), *Alfredo* (5), *Carlos* (5), *Francisco* (5), *Manuel* (5), *Miguel* (4), *Pedro* (4), *Raul* (4), *Angel* (3); *Antonio* (4), *Carina*, *Lorenzo*, *Luciano*, *Olivero*, *Oreste*.

Armata (125) Southern Italian (Sicily): variant (feminine form) of ARMATO.

GIVEN NAMES Italian 11%. *Antonio*, *Giacomo*, *Nicola*, *Salvatore*.

Armato (249) Italian (Sicily): from *armato* 'armed', hence an occupational or status name for a soldier or guard.

GIVEN NAMES Italian 9%. *Carlo* (2), *Sal* (2), *Aldo*, *Marco*, *Salvatore*, *Vito*.

Armbrecht (156) German: from a personal name composed of Old High German *arn* 'eagle' or *irmin* 'world', 'great' + *berht* 'bright', 'famous'.

Armbrister (228) Altered form of German ARMBRUSTER.

Armbrust (701) German: from Middle High German *armbrust*, earlier *arbrust* 'crossbow', hence a metonymic occupational name for a maker of crossbows or for a soldier who used one. This term is adapted from Old French *arbalestre*, Late Latin *arcuballista*, a compound of *arcus* 'bow' + *ballista* 'catapult'. In Middle High German it was altered by folk etymology as if composed of the elements *arm* 'arm' + *berust* 'weaponry'. When the latter term became obsolete it was replaced by *brust* 'chest'.

GIVEN NAMES German 6%. *Kurt* (6), *Hans* (2), *Florian*, *Heinz*, *Horst*, *Manfred*, *Reinhold*.

Armbruster (2078) German (also **Armbrüster**): occupational name for a soldier armed with a crossbow or for a maker of crossbows, from an agent derivative of *armbrust* 'crossbow' (see ARMBRUST).

GIVEN NAMES German 4%. *Kurt* (3), *Manfred* (3), *Otto* (3), *Ueli* (2), *Wolfgang* (2), *Aloysius*, *Bernhard*, *Dieter*, *Erwin*, *Gerhard*, *Gernot*, *Guenter*.

Armel (237) French: from a Celtic personal name, *Arthmael* 'bear prince', Latin *Armagilus*. This was the name of a saint who was the subject of a local cult in Brittany.

GIVEN NAMES Jewish 4%. *Inna* (2), *Miriam*.

Armellino (108) Italian: of uncertain origin; possibly from a masculinized form of *Armellina*, a old female personal name derived from Latin *animula*, a diminutive of *anima* 'spirit', 'soul'.

GIVEN NAMES Italian 16%. *Domenic*, *Gianna*, *Guilio*, *Luciano*, *Michelangelo*, *Pasquale*.

Armendarez (147) Spanish: variant of **Armendáriz** (see ARMENDARIZ).

GIVEN NAMES Spanish 38%. *Jose* (4), *Domingo* (2), *Emilio* (2), *Jesus* (2), *Juan* (2), *Roberto* (2), *Ruben* (2), *Adalberto*, *Adan*, *Alberto*, *Alfredo*, *Alonzo*.

Armendariz (1258) **1.** Spanish (**Armendáriz**; of Basque origin): patronymic from the Basque personal name *Armendari* or *Armentari*, from Latin *armentarius* 'herdsman'. **2.** Spanish and French variant of **Armendaritze**, a habitational name from a village in Low Navarre named Armendaritze. The place name is commonly said to be composed of the elements *ar(ri)* 'rock' + *mend(i)* 'mountain' + *aritz* 'oak'. However, this is probably a folk etymology; the place name is more likely the same as the patronymic surname, except that *-itz* here is to be interpreted as a locative suffix: 'Armendari's place' or perhaps 'herdsman's place'.
GIVEN NAMES Spanish 46%. *Jose* (21), *Manuel* (18), *Carlos* (17), *Juan* (17), *Ruben* (12), *Alfredo* (11), *Arturo* (11), *Jesus* (8), *Raul* (8), *Armando* (7), *Enrique* (7), *Fernando* (7).

Armenia (104) Italian: from the feminine form of **Armenio**, from Greek *Armenios* 'Armenian'.
GIVEN NAMES Italian 6%. *Carmelo* (2), *Giuseppe*.

Arment (319) Catalan and French: **1.** from the vocabuarly word *arment* 'herd'. See ARMENTA. **2.** Perhaps a variant of ARMAND.

Armenta (1040) Spanish: from Latin *armenta* 'herd(s)', applied to cattle and horses and, by extension, to places and persons involved with them, hence either an occupational name for a herdsman or a topographic name for someone who lived at a place where cattle or horses were raised.
GIVEN NAMES Spanish 40%. *Jose* (26), *Juan* (13), *Manuel* (13), *Miguel* (9), *Carlos* (6), *Armando* (5), *Francisco* (5), *Javier* (5), *Jesus* (5), *Ramon* (5), *Salvador* (5), *Felipe* (4).

Armenteros (111) Spanish: habitational name from either of two places called Armenteros, in the provinces of Ávila and Salamanca, from the plural of *armenatero* 'cowherd', from Latin *armenta* 'herd(s)'.
GIVEN NAMES Spanish 57%. *Luis* (7), *Jose* (5), *Jorge* (4), *Guillermo* (2), *Gustavo* (2), *Juan* (2), *Margarita* (2), *Orlando* (2), *Pedro* (2), *Agustina*, *Alfredo*, *Alina*; *Angelo* (3), *Guido*.

Armenti (155) Italian: patronymic or plural form of ARMENTO.
GIVEN NAMES Italian 16%. *Amedio*, *Biagio*, *Giovanni*, *Nicola*, *Vito*.

Armento (133) Italian (chiefly Molise): from *armento* 'herd' (from Latin *armentum*), hence probably a metonymic occupational name for a herdsman.
GIVEN NAMES Italian 9%. *Rocco* (2), *Antonietta*, *Marco Antonio*.

Armentor (159) Respelling of French **Armentaire**, an occupational name for a

herdsman, from a derivative of Old French *arment* 'cattle'.
GIVEN NAMES French 6%. *Amie*, *Minos*.

Armentrout (1456) Altered form of the German surname **Ermentraut**, a metronymic from a female Germanic personal name, of which the English cognate is *Ermintrude*. It is composed of the elements *ermin-* 'world', 'great' + *drūd* 'strength' or *trūt* 'beloved'.

Armer (616) English: occupational name for a maker of arms and armor, from Anglo-Norman French *armer* 'armsmaker' (Old French *armier*). Originally this was a separate name from ARMOUR, but in due course the two became inextricably confused.

Armes (974) **1.** English: variant of HARMS. **2.** German: from a short form of a Germanic personal name containing the element *ermin-* 'world', 'great'. See for example, ARMENTROUT.

Armetta (153) Italian (Sicily): from a diminutive of Sicilian *arma* 'soul' (Italian *anima*).
GIVEN NAMES Italian 14%. *Vito* (2), *Antonio*, *Pietro*, *Sal*, *Salvatore*, *Vincenzo*.

Armfield (448) English: probably a variant of **Arnfield**, a habitational name from Arnfield in Cheshire, named with the Old English personal name *Earnwīg* + Old English *feld* 'open land used for pasture or cultivation'.

Armiger (254) English: status name for a squire, from Latin *armiger* 'bearer of arms or armor' (from *armas gerere* 'to bear arms'), which acquired the specialist sense 'squire'.

Armijo (1488) Southern Spanish: unexplained.
GIVEN NAMES Spanish 22%. *Jose* (11), *Manuel* (9), *Orlando* (5), *Roberto* (5), *Francisco* (4), *Ramona* (4), *Carlos* (3), *Diego* (3), *Ernesto* (3), *Jesus* (3), *Luis* (3), *Lupe* (3).

Armington (198) Evidently an English habitational name, probably from Ermington in Devon, which is of uncertain etymology but probably from an Old English personal name *Earma* + the connective particle *-ing-* + *tūn* 'settlement', 'estate'.

Arminio (118) Southern Italian: from a personal name, Latin *Arminius*, which is of Germanic origin (see HERMANN).
GIVEN NAMES Italian 21%. *Angelo* (2), *Antonio* (2), *Vito* (2), *Alfonse*, *Carmine*, *Romeo*, *Silvio*.

Armintrout (118) See ARMENTROUT.

Armistead (1100) English: topographic name for someone who lived by a hermit's cell, from Middle English *(h)ermite* 'hermit' + *stede* 'place'.
FOREBEARS William Armistead (born 1610, died before 1660) brought the name from Yorkshire, England, to VA in 1635.

Armitage (1598) English: topographic name from Middle English, Old French

(h)ermitage 'hermitage' (a derivative of Old French *(h)ermite* 'hermit'), or a habitational name from a place named with this word. The name is very common in Yorkshire, where it has been traced to Hermitage Bridge, a locality in Almondbury, near Huddersfield.
FOREBEARS The name was first brought to North America by Enoch Armitage (born 1677) of Wooldale, Yorkshire, England.

Armold (188) German: from the Germanic personal name *Irminold*, composed of *irmin* 'total', 'all-embracing' + *-old* from *waltan* 'to rule'.

Armon (230) Respelling of French ARMAND. This is also found as an English surname, probably of the same origin.

Armond (198) Respelling of French ARMAND. This is also found as an English surname, probably of the same origin.
GIVEN NAMES French 8%. *Berard*, *Celina*, *Easton*, *Pierre*.

Armor (325) Variant spelling of Scottish and northern Irish ARMOUR, now found predominantly in England.

Armour (2682) Scottish and northern Irish: from Middle English, Old French *armure*, blended with the agent noun *armer* (see ARMER), hence an occupational name for a maker of arms and armor. The collective noun *armure* denoted offensive weapons as well as the more recently specialized sense of protective gear.

Arms (1339) **1.** English: variant of HARMS. **2.** German: variant of ARMES 2.

Armstead (1632) English: reduced form of ARMISTEAD.

Armstong (169) Altered form of English ARMSTRONG.

Armstrong (46612) **1.** English (common in Northumberland and the Scottish Borders): Middle English nickname for someone who was strong in the arm. **2.** Irish: adopted as an English equivalent of Gaelic **Ó Labhradha Tréan** 'strong O'Lavery' or **Mac Thréinfhir**, literally 'son of the strong man', both from Ulster.
FOREBEARS This is a very common surname in North America. It was brought to PA, NJ, and NH in the early 18th century by several different families of northern Irish and northern English Protestants. One such was James Armstrong, who emigrated from Fermanagh to Cumberland Co., PA, in 1745; another was John Armstrong (1720–95), who settled in Carlisle, PA, in about 1748. The Cumberland Valley of PA early became the most concentrated area of Scotch-Irish immigration in America.

Armwood (147) Perhaps an English habitational name from Arnwood in Hampshire or Earnwood in Shropshire, both named from Old English *earn* 'eagle' + *wudu* 'wood'. The surname, however, does not appear in present-day English records.

Army (115) Probably an Americanized form of French **Armée**, literally 'armed', hence a byname for a soldier or guard.

Arn (315) **1.** Swedish: from a short form of any of the many Norse names of which *arn* 'eagle' is the first element, for example *Arnbjorn*, *Arnfinn*, and *Arnsten*. **2.** Swiss German: habitational name from Arn near Zürich, or from a house name, Middle High German *arn* 'eagle'. **3.** Variant spelling of English ARNE.

Arnall (249) English: **1.** habitational name from either of two places called Arnold, in Nottinghamshire and East Yorkshire, from Old English *earn* 'eagle' + *halh* 'nook'. **2.** variant of ARNOLD.

Arnao (119) Castilianized variant of Catalan **Arnau**, a patronymic name from *Arnal(d)*, a personal name of Germanic origin, equivalent to ARNOLD. The surname, corresponding to the Italian form **Arnaldi**, is also found in Italy.
GIVEN NAMES Spanish 21%; Italian 11%. *Manuel* (2), *Rudolfo* (2), *Aurelio, Carlos, Cesar, Enrique, Genaro, Herminia, Jose, Orestes, Pedro, Roberto*; *Luciano, Nunzio, Santo*.

Arnason (100) Americanized form of Norwegian and Danish ARNESEN or Swedish ARNESON.
GIVEN NAMES Scandinavian 19%; German 12%. *Arni* (2), *Gudrun* (2), *Sig*; *Fritz* (2), *Hannes, Matthias*.

Arnaud (473) French: from the medieval personal name *Arnaldus* (see ARNOLD).
FOREBEARS The birth of an Arnaud or Renaud is recorded in Quebec city in 1637, and an Arnaud from Poitou is documented there in 1668.
GIVEN NAMES French 12%. *Michel* (5), *Antoine* (2), *Jacques* (2), *Altagrace, Anatole, Andre, Angelle, Christophe, Lucien, Philippe*.

Arndorfer (151) Southern German: habitational name for someone from a place called Arndorf, of which there are three examples in Bavaria, Germany and one in Styria, Austria.

Arndt (5791) German, Danish, and Swedish: from a personal name of Germanic origin, composed of the elements *arn* 'eagle' + *wald* 'rule'. Compare English ARNOLD.
GIVEN NAMES German 5%. *Otto* (13), *Kurt* (6), *Helmut* (5), *Erwin* (4), *Heinz* (4), *Hans* (3), *Klaus* (3), *Willi* (3), *Armin* (2), *Arno* (2), *Eberhard* (2), *Ernst* (2).

Arne (211) **1.** Northern English and Swedish: from the medieval personal name *Arne*, a short form of ARNOLD or, in Scandinavia, any of the many other Norse names of which *arn* 'eagle' is the first element, for example *Arnbjörn*, *Arnfinn*, and *Arnsten*. **2.** Norwegian: habitational name from a farmstead in western Norway, so named from a fjord name meaning 'the streaming', 'the fjord with the waves'.

3. English: habitational name from Arne, a place in Dorset, which is most probably named with Old English *ærn* 'building', 'house'.
GIVEN NAME Scandinavian 4%. *Juel* (2).

Arnell (291) **1.** English: variant spelling of ARNALL. **2.** Swedish: from the personal name *Arne* (see ARNE) + *-ell* (from Latin *-elius*), a common suffix of Swedish surnames.

Arner (550) **1.** German: from Middle High German *arnaere* 'reaper', 'day laborer' (from *arn* 'harvest'). **2.** Swiss German: habitational name for someone from a place called Arn, near Zürich.

Arnesen (343) Norwegian and Danish: patronymic from the common Scandinavian personal name *Arne*, a short form of any of various Norse names of which *arn* 'eagle' is the first element. See ARNE.
GIVEN NAMES Scandinavian 23%. *Erik* (3), *Aksel, Alf, Arndt, Egil, Niels, Ottar*.

Arneson (1964) Respelling of Swedish **Arnesson** or Norwegian and Danish ARNESEN, patronymics from ARNE. **Arnison** is a frequent surname in northern England, and in some cases Arneson could be a respelling of this.
GIVEN NAMES Scandinavian 4%. *Erik* (3), *Helmer* (2), *Alf, Arnt*.

Arness (105) English: variant of HARNESS.

Arnet (103) **1.** Swiss and South German: variant of ARNOLD. **2.** English: variant spelling of ARNETT.
GIVEN NAMES French 4%; German 4%. *Marie-Noelle*; *Urs*.

Arnett (5528) **1.** English: from a Middle English personal name, probably a pet form of ARNOLD, although Reaney has it as a survival of the Old English personal names *Earngēat* (male) 'eagle Geat' (a tribal name) or *Earngȳð* (female) 'eagle battle'. **2.** Variant of French ARNETTE.

Arnette (864) French: from a pet form of ARNOLD.

Arney (1239) **1.** Americanized form of the Scandinavian and North German surname ARNE or of some other name with *arn* 'eagle' as a first element. **2.** Perhaps an altered form of Norwegian **Arnøy**, a habitational name from any of a number of farmsteads named for the islands on which they stand; the original derivation of such names being either from the Old Norse personal name *Arni*, or from *ǫrn* 'eagle' + *øy* 'island'.

Arnhart (114) German: from a Germanic personal name, composed of the elements *arn* 'eagle' + *hard* 'hardy', 'strong'.

Arnhold (167) German: variant of ARNOLD.
GIVEN NAMES German 14%. *Kurt* (2), *Winfried* (2), *Dietmar, Rainer, Ute, Wolfgang*.

Arnholt (202) German: variant of ARNOLD.

Arning (123) **1.** German: patronymic from the personal name ARNE. **2.** Swedish: probably of the same origin as the German

name, but in Swedish the suffix *-ing* is commonly used in forming ornamental names from many different vocabulary words and from place names, as well as from personal names; the underlying etymon could be *arn* 'eagle'.
GIVEN NAMES Scandinavian 8%; German 4%. *Erland* (2), *Holger*; *Juergen, Klaus*.

Arnn (199) Variant of German ARN.

Arno (511) **1.** Italian (**Arnò**): from the medieval Greek personal name *Arnos* meaning 'lamb'. **2.** From a reduced form of the Italian personal name *Arnao* (see ARNOLD). **3.** Dutch and German: from a short form of the personal name *Arnout* or ARNOLD. **4.** Respelling of French ARNAUD.

Arnold (50733) **1.** English and German: from a very widely used personal name of Germanic origin, composed of the elements *arn* 'eagle' + *wald* 'rule'. In addition, it has probably absorbed various European cognates and their derivatives (for the forms, see Hanks and Hodges 1988). **2.** English: habitational name from either of the two places called Arnold (see ARNALL). **3.** Jewish (Ashkenazic): adoption of the German personal name, at least in part on account of its resemblance to the Jewish name AARON.
FOREBEARS Arnold is a widespread and important family name in North America. In particular, it is borne by a prominent RI family, descended from a certain Thomas Arnold, who emigrated to New England before 1635.

Arnoldi (192) **1.** Italian: patronymic from the personal name *Arnoldo*, of Germanic origin (see ARNOLD). **2.** German: humanistic patronymic (using a Latin genitive) from ARNOLD.
GIVEN NAMES Italian 4%. *Antonio, Carlo, Donato, Gianfranco, Luigi*.

Arnoldy (175) German: variant spelling of ARNOLDI.

Arnone (1044) Southern Italian: from a personal name *Arnone*, of Germanic origin.
GIVEN NAMES Italian 13%. *Salvatore* (9), *Angelo* (6), *Aldo* (3), *Giuseppe* (3), *Sal* (3), *Domenico* (2), *Francesco* (2), *Luigi* (2), *Rocco* (2), *Antonio, Calogero, Carmine*.

Arnot (263) **1.** Scottish and English: variant spelling of ARNOTT. **2.** German: variant of ARNOLD.

Arnott (929) **1.** Scottish and English: habitational name from a place called Arnot, near Kinross. **2.** Scottish and English: variant of ARNOLD. **3.** Respelling of German ARNOT, **Arnoth** or **Arnodt**, variants of ARNOLD.

Arnoult (112) French: variant of ARNAUD.
GIVEN NAMES French 11%. *Jacques* (2), *Patrice, Pierre*.

Arnow (183) **1.** Jewish (Ashkenazic): Americanized form of ARONOV. **2.** Perhaps also an Americanized spelling of the French surname ARNAUD.

Arns (234) Variant of German ARNTZ.

Arnsdorff (117) Variant spelling of German **Arnsdorf**.

Arnson (148) Variant of Scandinavian and German ARNTSON, or Norwegian and Danish ARNESEN or the Swedish cognate **Arnesson**.

GIVEN NAMES Scandinavian 6%. *Erik, Iver*.

Arnst (191) Probably a variant of German ERNST.

GIVEN NAMES German 5%. *Achim, Kurt, Otto*.

Arnstein (199) German: habitational name from either of two places in northern Bavaria named Arnstein 'eagle's crag'.

GIVEN NAME German 5%. *Ignatz* (2).

Arnt (123) Variant spelling of the German and Scandinavian surname ARNDT.

GIVEN NAMES German 5%. *Mathias, Matthias*.

Arntsen (118) North German and Scandinavian: variant of ARNTSON.

GIVEN NAMES Scandinavian 12%. *Arnt, Erik*.

Arntson (251) North German and Scandinavian: patronymic from the personal name *Arn(d)t* (see ARNDT).

GIVEN NAMES Scandinavian 4%. *Algot, Jarl*.

Arntz (337) North German and Danish: patronymic from the personal name *Arn(d)t* (see ARNDT).

Arntzen (192) Danish, Norwegian, and North German: patronymic from the personal name *Arn(d)t* (see ARNDT).

GIVEN NAMES Scandinavian 13%; German 5%. *Sven* (3), *Bjorn, Ketil, Morten, Unni; Kurt* (2), *Guenther, Hans*.

Arnwine (292) Possibly a respelling of German **Ernwein**, from the personal name *Ernwin*, probably from Middle High German *ēre* 'honor' + *win* 'friend'.

Arnzen (206) Variant of Danish, Norwegian, and North German ARNTZEN.

Aro (223) **1.** Finnish: topographic and ornamental name from *aro* 'hard, relatively infertile ground' or 'wet meadow', 'swamp', found both as a place name and as a surname throughout Finland. In many cases the surname was adopted during the name conversion movement in the 19th and early 20th centuries, especially in southern Finland. In the U.S. this is also a shortened form of names such as **Kiviaro**, of which the first element is *kivi* 'stone', 'rock'. **2.** Spanish: habitational name, in some cases from Aro in Galicia, in others probably from Haro in Rioja.

GIVEN NAMES Finnish 7%; Spanish 6%. *Eero, Hannu, Pentti, Waino; Angelina, Cayetano, Eufronio, Gerardo, Hernando, Luis, Maria Teresa, Raul, Tomas, Victorina*.

Arocha (225) Spanish (and Portuguese): possibly from the Basque occupational name **Arotxa, Arotza**, from *arotz* (*arotx*) 'smith', 'carpenter' + the article suffix *-a*, or alternatively a topographic from *a rocha* 'the rock' (with the Portuguese or Galician article). This name is chiefly associated with the Canary Islands.

GIVEN NAMES Spanish 43%. *Ernesto* (4), *Francisco* (4), *Jose* (4), *Eduardo* (3), *Juan* (3), *Adelina* (2), *Alejandro* (2), *Angel* (2), *Carlos* (2), *Jesus* (2), *Jorge* (2), *Luisa* (2); *Antonio, Cira, Guido, Marco*.

Arocho (271) Hispanic (Puerto Rico): unexplained.

GIVEN NAMES Spanish 44%. *Luis* (7), *Jose* (6), *Angel* (3), *Manuel* (3), *Candido* (2), *Carlos* (2), *Florencio* (2), *Jesus* (2), *Juan* (2), *Julio* (2), *Pedro* (2), *Rafael* (2); *Antonio* (2), *Angelo, Carmelo, Heriberto*.

Arola (140) **1.** Finnish: variant of ARO, with the local suffix *-la*. **2.** Italian: habitational name from any of several places named Arola, in Piedmont, Emilia-Romagna, Marche, and Campania.

GIVEN NAMES Finnish 6%; German 4%. *Antti, Arvo, Sulo, Wiljo; Markus*.

Aron (877) Jewish: variant of AARON.

GIVEN NAMES Jewish 5%. *Jakob* (2), *Mordche* (2), *Oded* (2), *Sol* (2), *Eliyahu, Girsh, Hersh, Ilya, Miriam, Shoshana, Tauba*.

Arone (170) Italian: from the Biblical personal name *Aron(n)e* (see AARON).

GIVEN NAME Italian 8%. *Domenic* (2).

Aronhalt (158) **1.** Respelling of German **Ehrenhold(t)**, an occupational or status name from Middle High German *erhalt, heralt* 'herald'. **2.** Alternatively perhaps, a respelling of German ARNHOLT.

Aronica (124) Ialian (Sicilian): unexplained.

GIVEN NAMES Italian 22%. *Angelo* (3), *Salvatore* (3), *Sal* (2), *Armando, Carmela, Enza, Gasper*.

Aronin (117) Jewish (eastern Ashkenazic): patronymic from the personal name *Aron*, a variant of AARON.

GIVEN NAMES Jewish 13%; Russian 7%. *Aron, Hyman, Ilya, Isaak, Khaim; Boris, Gennadiy, Grigoriy, Oleg*.

Aronoff (493) Jewish (eastern Ashkenazic): alternative spelling of ARONOV.

GIVEN NAMES Jewish 6%. *Isadore* (2), *Miriam* (2), *Avram, Emanuel, Shifra, Yael*.

Aronov (169) Jewish (eastern Ashkenazic): patronymic from the personal name AARON.

GIVEN NAMES Russian 32%; Jewish 28%. *Boris* (7), *Mikhail* (5), *Igor* (3), *Vladimir* (3), *Yuriy* (3), *Aleksandr* (2), *Anatoliy* (2), *Arkady* (2), *Iosif* (2), *Yefim* (2), *Anatoly, Auram; Aron* (3), *Ilya* (3), *Yakov* (3), *Uziel* (2), *Ari, Gavriel, Isaak, Khaim, Mikhel, Moshe, Naum, Rimma*.

Aronow (227) Jewish (eastern Ashkenazic): variant of ARONOV.

GIVEN NAMES Jewish 4%. *Sol* (2), *Eliezer, Kerith*.

Aronowitz (326) Jewish (eastern Ashkenazic): patronymic from AARON; a Germanized spelling of either Polish **Aronowicz** or Russian **Aronovich**.

GIVEN NAME Jewish 6%. *Yaffa*.

Arons (319) **1.** Jewish (Ashkenazic): variant spelling of AARONS. **2.** Latvian: from the personal name *Ārons*.

Aronson (2861) **1.** Jewish: variant spelling of AARONSON. **2.** Variant of Swedish **Aronsson** or Americanized form of Norwegian **Aronsen**, patronymics from the personal name *Aron* (see AARON).

Aronstein (114) Jewish (Ashkenazic): ornamental name composed of the personal name *A(a)ron* + German *Stein* 'stone'.

GIVEN NAMES Jewish 7%. *Moshe, Naum*.

Arora (618) Indian (Panjab): Hindu and Sikh name based on the name of a mercantile community of the Panjab. It is derived from a place name, Aror (now known as Rohri, in Sind, Pakistan). According to legend the Aroras are of Kshatriya stock, but denied their Kshatriya origin in order to escape persecution by Paras Ram (*paraśu-rāma* in Sanskrit means 'Rama with the axe'), calling themselves *Aur*, which means 'someone else' in Hindi and Panjabi. Some believe the Aroras to be related to another prominent mercantile community of the Panjab, the Khatris.

GIVEN NAMES Indian 93%. *Sanjay* (11), *Vijay* (9), *Arun* (8), *Sanjeev* (8), *Ajay* (7), *Anil* (7), *Om* (7), *Raj* (7), *Satish* (7), *Vivek* (7), *Ashok* (6), *Ashish* (5).

Aros (142) **1.** Hungarian (**Áros**): occupational name for a merchant, or a shopkeeper, from *árus* 'seller'. **2.** Norwegian (**Åros**): habitational name from any of several farmsteads named Åros, from *å* 'stream' + *os* 'estuary'. **3.** Spanish: apparently of Galician origin (Tui) and probably a topographic name related to *aro* 'hoop'.

GIVEN NAMES Spanish 16%. *Jose* (5), *Alvaro, Arnulfo, Carlos Francisco, Jaime, Jeremias, Manuel, Mario, Otila, Socorro*.

Arp (1341) **1.** German: variant of ERB. **2.** North German, Dutch, and Danish: from the personal name *Arp*, derived from Middle Low German *erp* 'dark brown'.

Arpin (360) **1.** French: variant of the occupational name HARPIN 'harper'. **2.** French: Savoy dialect form of the topographic name **Alpin** 'dweller in the Alps'.

FOREBEARS An Arpin or Herpin from Poitiers was in St. Ours by 1689.

GIVEN NAMES French 10%. *Alcid* (2), *Andre* (2), *Armand* (2), *Rodolphe* (2), *Alphonse, Gisele, Laurent, Ovila, Pierre*.

Arpino (149) Italian: habitational name from Arpino in Frosinone province, Latium, Latin *Arpinum*.

GIVEN NAMES Italian 26%. *Pasquale* (3), *Angelo, Aniello, Antonio, Carlo, Constantino, Dino, Donato, Gennaro, Nicolo, Rosaria*.

Arps (261) **1.** North German: patronymic from ARP. **2.** Americanized form of ERBES.

Arquette (328) French: from *arquet* 'little bow' or 'little arch' (diminutive of *arche*, from Latin *arcus*). It was originally an occupational name for an archer, but the French word *arquet(te)* is also found in the sense 'market trader' (originally, perhaps, one with a stall underneath an arch). The surname looks feminine, but French Canadian surnames from nouns ending in -*et* are regularly spelled -*ette*, indicating that the *t* is pronounced, not because they have any feminine sense.

Arquilla (127) Spanish: probably from a diminutive of the vocabulary word *arca* 'chest', 'coffer', hence an occupational name for a chest maker. The name also occurs in Italy, possibly of Spanish origin.
GIVEN NAMES Italian 12%. *Velio* (2), *Dario*, *Guido*, *Marco*, *Primo*.

Arra (142) Galician: habitational name from a place in Galicia called Arra.
GIVEN NAMES Spanish 5%. *Elena*, *Juan*, *Mariano*, *Susana*.

Arrambide (136) Basque: topographic or habitational name from Basque *arran(o)* 'eagle' + *bide* 'road', 'way'.
GIVEN NAMES Spanish 34%. *Jaime* (3), *Armando* (2), *Francisco* (2), *Isidro* (2), *Jose* (2), *Juan* (2), *Lilia* (2), *Alejandro*, *Carlos*, *Dominga*, *Emilia*, *Enrique*.

Arrant (315) Variant of German ARANT, which is itself a variant of ARNDT.

Arrants (237) Variant of German and Dutch ARENDS.

Arras (273) **1.** English and French: habitational name from the city of Arras in Artois, northern France, or one of the other places in France so named. **2.** Scottish: habitational name from Airhouse, a locality in Channelkirk, Berwickshire. **3.** English: habitational name from a place called Arras in East Yorkshire, earlier spelled *Erghes*, from the plural of Old Norse *erg* 'hut', 'shelter'. **4.** German: metonymic occupational name for a cloth merchant, from a type of woolen cloth for which the city of Arras in Flanders was famous in the Middle Ages. This name is also established in Mexico.
GIVEN NAMES Spanish 8%; German 4%. *Armando* (2), *Jose* (2), *Manuel* (2), *Angelina*, *Araceli*, *Benigno*, *Cruz*, *Estela*, *Homero*, *Jesus*, *Juan*, *Lucila*; *Erwin* (2), *Heino*, *Kurt*, *Manfred*.

Arrasmith (302) English: variant spelling ARROWSMITH.

Arredondo (2408) Spanish: habitational name from a place in Santander province named Arredondo, from *redondo* 'round', because of the roundish shape of the hill on which it stands.
GIVEN NAMES Spanish 49%. *Jose* (64), *Juan* (36), *Manuel* (34), *Jesus* (29), *Guadalupe* (18), *Carlos* (16), *Francisco* (16), *Mario* (16), *Jorge* (14), *Miguel* (13), *Ricardo* (13), *Raul* (12).

Arreguin (438) Spanish (**Arreguín**; of Basque origin): variant of **Arreguí**, Spanish spelling of Basque **Arregi**, which clearly contains the Basque word *arri* 'stone'. This is either an occupational name for a stonecutter (with the agent suffix -*gin*), or a topographic name for someone who lived

on stony ground (with the locative suffix -*egi*) or on a stony slope (with *egi* 'slope').
GIVEN NAMES Spanish 49%. *Jose* (25), *Juan* (10), *Alfredo* (5), *Francisco* (5), *Javier* (5), *Jorge* (5), *Alberto* (3), *Manuel* (3), *Salvador* (3), *Agustin* (2), *Angel* (2), *Angelina* (2).

Arrellano (150) Variant spelling of Spanish ARELLANO.
GIVEN NAMES Spanish 62%. *Jose* (5), *Juan* (3), *Arnulfo* (2), *Catalina* (2), *Enrique* (2), *Humberto* (2), *Jesus* (2), *Miguel* (2), *Alfonso*, *Alvaro*, *Ana Luisa*, *Aquileo*.

Arrendale (117) English: variant of ARUNDEL.

Arrendondo (146) Spanish: variant of ARREDONDO.
GIVEN NAMES Spanish 49%. *Fernando* (3), *Eduardo* (2), *Jose* (2), *Lupe* (2), *Mario* (2), *Ramon* (2), *Rogelio* (2), *Socorro* (2), *Adan*, *Aldolfo*, *Alfonso*, *Amalia*; *Antonio* (2), *Lucio* (2), *Flavio*.

Arreola (1382) Variant of ARRIOLA.
GIVEN NAMES Spanish 58%. *Jose* (44), *Juan* (29), *Jesus* (23), *Manuel* (18), *Roberto* (14), *Francisco* (13), *Fernando* (11), *Luis* (11), *Rafael* (11), *Carlos* (10), *Javier* (10), *Salvador* (10).

Arriaga (1284) Basque: habitational name from a town named Arriaga in Araba province, Basque Country, or topographic name from Basque *arri* 'stone' + -*aga* 'place or group of'.
GIVEN NAMES Spanish 53%. *Jose* (40), *Juan* (26), *Jesus* (18), *Carlos* (14), *Francisco* (14), *Luis* (13), *Miguel* (12), *Manuel* (11), *Raul* (10), *Jorge* (8), *Pedro* (7), *Salvador* (7).

Arriaza (130) Basque: topographic name for someone who lived on a stony area of land, from Basque *arri* 'crag', 'rock', 'stone' + the locative suffix -*a(t)z* 'abundance of'.
GIVEN NAMES Spanish 56%. *Jose* (3), *Luis* (3), *Raul* (3), *Carlos* (2), *Esperanza* (2), *Francisco* (2), *Julio* (2), *Sergio* (2), *Ana*, *Augusto*, *Bernardo*, *Blanca*.

Arrick (167) See ARICK.

Arrieta (509) Basque: habitational name from any of the places called Arrieta, for example in the provinces of Araba, Biscay, Gipuzkoa and Navarre, from Basque *arri* 'stone' + the suffix -*eta* 'place or group of'.
GIVEN NAMES Spanish 50%. *Jose* (13), *Jesus* (8), *Carlos* (6), *Roberto* (6), *Alfredo* (5), *Jorge* (5), *Juan* (5), *Julio* (5), *Luis* (5), *Manuel* (5), *Rafael* (5), *Enrique* (4).

Arrighi (184) Italian: from the personal name ARRIGO.
GIVEN NAMES Italian 9%; French 5%. *Aldo* (2), *Enrico*, *Giovanni*, *Giuseppe*, *Lorenzo*, *Pietro*, *Ugo*; *Gaile*, *Jean Michel*.

Arrigo (578) Italian: from the medieval personal name *Arrigo*, a variant of *Enrico* (see HENRY).
GIVEN NAMES Italian 16%. *Angelo* (3), *Antonio* (3), *Pasquale* (3), *Salvatore* (3),

Sal (2), *Santo* (2), *Vincenzo* (2), *Antonino*, *Franco*, *Mario*, *Natale*, *Vito*.

Arrigoni (205) Italian: from an augmentative form of the personal name ARRIGO.

Arrington (6383) English: **1.** habitational name from Arrington, a place in Cambridgeshire, named from an Old English byname, *Earn(a)*, meaning 'eagle' + -*inga*- 'people or followers of' + *tūn* 'settlement'. **2.** variant of HARRINGTON.

Arriola (944) Basque: habitational name from any of the places named Arriola, from Basque *arri* 'stone(s)' + -*ola* 'place of', for example in the provinces of Gipuzkoa and Araba.
GIVEN NAMES Spanish 40%. *Jose* (17), *Francisco* (9), *Juan* (9), *Luis* (8), *Manuel* (7), *Felipe* (6), *Arturo* (5), *Ernesto* (5), *Jesus* (5), *Miguel* (5), *Alberto* (4), *Fernando* (4).

Arrison (159) Variant of English HARRISON.

Arritt (109) Origin unidentified.

Arrow (172) **1.** English: habitational name from Arrow in Warwickshire or Arrowe in Cheshire. The first takes its name from the Arrow river, a Celtic or pre-Celtic term meaning 'stream'; the second, recorded *c.* 1245 as *Arwe*, is from Old Norse *erg* 'shieling'. **2.** Perhaps in some cases a translation of French **La Flèche** ('the arrow').

Arrowood (1479) **1.** Probably a variant of English HARWOOD. **2.** There is also a Cherokee connection, but it is not known whether this name is derived from a Cherokee original.

Arrowsmith (464) English: occupational name for a maker of iron arrowheads, from Old English *arwe* 'arrow' + *smið* 'smith'.

Arroyave (113) Castilianized variant of Basque **Arroiabe**, a habitational name in Araba province, probably from Basque *arro* 'gorge', 'ravine' + *be(h)e* 'below'.
GIVEN NAMES Spanish 57%. *Carlos* (4), *Efrain* (4), *Guillermo* (4), *Jose* (4), *Raul* (3), *Adriana* (2), *Fabio* (2), *Mario* (2), *Rocio* (2), *Alejandro*, *Augusto*, *Bernardo*.

Arroyo (4108) Spanish: habitational name from any of numerous places named with *arroyo* 'watercourse', 'irrigation channel' (a word of pre-Roman origin).
GIVEN NAMES Spanish 49%. *Jose* (111), *Juan* (51), *Luis* (46), *Jesus* (34), *Manuel* (33), *Carlos* (29), *Miguel* (29), *Rafael* (26), *Francisco* (25), *Javier* (25), *Angel* (24), *Jorge* (24).

Arruda (1241) Portuguese: habitational name, probably in most cases from Arruda dos Vinhos, a place north of Lisbon, which takes its name from the plant *arruda* 'rue' (from Latin *rūta*).
GIVEN NAMES Spanish 14%; Portuguese 12%. *Manuel* (42), *Jose* (13), *Carlos* (5), *Luis* (4), *Hermano* (3), *Mario* (3), *Altino* (2), *Eduardo* (2), *Elvira* (2), *Jaime* (2), *Manual* (2), *Alexandrina*; *Duarte* (4), *Joao* (4), *Guilherme* (2), *Joaquim* (2), *Armanda*, *Catarina*, *Paulo*, *Serafim*.

Arscott (137) English (mainly Devon): habitational name, perhaps from Arscott in Shropshire, which is named from an unexplained first element + Old English *cot* 'hut', 'cottage'.

Arsenault (3435) French: occupational name for a gunmaker, a seller of guns, or the keeper of an arsenal. The French word *arsenal* (Italian *arsenale*) is from Arabic *dār aṣ-ṣinā'a* 'house of fabrication', 'workshop'. This spelling of the surname, which is much more common in North America than in France, has been assimilated to that of other French surnames ending in -*ault*, for example THIBAULT.

FOREBEARS An Arsenault, also written Arsonneau, of unknown origin, was documented in Cap-de-la-Madeleine in 1665. A Pierre Arsenault went to Acadia from France in 1671.

GIVEN NAMES French 8%. *Armand* (7), *Aime* (4), *Yvon* (4), *Adelard* (3), *Adrien* (3), *Alphonse* (3), *Andre* (3), *Lucien* (3), *Normand* (3), *Urbain* (3), *Alphee* (2), *Henri* (2).

Arseneau (477) French: variant spelling of ARSENAULT.

GIVEN NAMES French 8%. *Alcide* (2), *Ancil, Armand, Camille, Georges, Laurier, Marcel, Raymonde, Rejean.*

Arseneault (219) French: variant spelling of ARSENAULT.

GIVEN NAMES French 15%. *Marcel* (2), *Andre, Clovis, Emile, Fleurette, Gaston, Normand, Ovila, Rejean, Sylvie, Treffle.*

Arshad (139) Muslim: from a personal name based on Arabic *arshad* 'more reasonable', 'more rightly guided', an elative adjective derived from RASHID.

GIVEN NAMES Muslim 91%. *Mohammad* (33), *Mohammed* (6), *Muhammad* (6), *Syed* (5), *Ali* (3), *Mian* (3), *Amer* (2), *Jameela* (2), *Kaleem* (2), *Sheikh* (2), *Abdul, Abrar.*

Arslanian (187) Armenian: patronymic from a personal name based on *arslan* 'lion', a word of Turkish origin. Compare ASLAN. *Arslan* was a title of the shahs of Iran.

GIVEN NAMES Armenian 32%. *Armen* (4), *Ara* (3), *Hagop* (2), *Haig* (2), *Krikor* (2), *Sark* (2), *Agop, Antranig, Arda, Diran, Garabet, Garbis.*

Art (258) **1.** Dutch and German: from a reduced form of the personal names ARNOLD and Dutch *Alaert* or German AHLERT. The Dutch name could also be derived from *Adriaan*, a Dutch form of ADRIAN. **2.** Irish: from the Gaelic personal name *Art* meaning 'bear' (see MCCART).

Artale (170) Italian (Sicily and Naples): **1.** from the personal name *Artale*, from Aragon (*Artal*). **2.** habitational name from a village in Sicily named Artale.

GIVEN NAMES Italian 27%. *Ignazio* (2), *Angelo, Antonino, Benito, Carmela, Giovanni, Matteo, Salvatore, Santo, Stefano.*

Arteaga (1391) Basque: habitational name from any of several places in the province of Biscay named with *arte* 'holm oak' + the locative suffix -*aga* 'place or group of'.

GIVEN NAMES Spanish 55%. *Jose* (52), *Juan* (24), *Manuel* (15), *Carlos* (13), *Luis* (13), *Francisco* (11), *Jorge* (11), *Mario* (11), *Jesus* (10), *Miguel* (8), *Ramon* (8), *Salvador* (8).

Arter (593) Scottish and English: variant of ARTHUR, the form being influenced perhaps by the Gaelic form of the personal name, *Artair*.

Arterberry (231) Variant of English ATTERBERRY.

Arterburn (445) Of uncertain origin. It invites the interpretation 'Arthur's burn,' but no place with such a name is known in the British Isles, and the surname is not found in current records. It may well be a variant of ATTEBERRY.

Arters (139) Northern Irish: variant of ARTHURS.

Arth (316) German: **1.** Variant of ART. **2.** Alternatively perhaps a habitational name. There is a place in Schwyz canton, Switzerland, with this name and also a village in Bavaria south of Regensburg.

FOREBEARS Family historians report an Art/Arth family arriving in Ohio from Mittelbollenbach, Germany in 1848.

Arther (111) Scottish and Irish: shortened variant of MCARTHUR.

Arthur (9964) Scottish, Irish, Welsh, English, and French: from the ancient Celtic personal name *Arthur*. In many cases it is a shortened form of Scottish or Irish MCARTHUR, the patronymic *Mac*- often being dropped in the 17th, 18th, and 19th centuries under English influence. The personal name is most probably from an old Celtic word meaning 'bear'. Compare Gaelic *art*, Welsh *arth*, both of which mean 'bear'. It has been in regular use as a personal name in Britain since the early Middle Ages, owing its popularity in large part to the legendary exploits of King Arthur and the Knights of the Round Table, which gave rise to a prolific literature in Welsh, French, English, German, and other European languages.

FOREBEARS President Chester Alan Arthur (1830–86) was the son of a VT Baptist preacher, William Arthur (1797–1875), who emigrated from Ballymena in northern Ireland in about 1815.

Arthurs (732) Northern Irish: patronymic from ARTHUR, or a variant of MCARTHUR.

Artiaga (168) Variant of Basque ARTEAGA.

GIVEN NAMES Spanish 47%. *Jesus* (5), *Salvador* (3), *Francisco* (2), *Guadalupe* (2), *Jorge* (2), *Jose* (2), *Manuel* (2), *Manuela* (2), *Otilia* (2), *Adela, Agustin, Alejandra.*

Artiga (107) Spanish and Catalan: topographic name from *artiga* 'clearing'.

GIVEN NAMES Spanish 56%. *Jesus* (3), *Raul* (3), *Ana* (2), *Eladio* (2), *Francisco* (2), *Juana* (2), *Miguel* (2), *Adalberto, Adela, Alicia, Ana Luz, Carlos.*

Artigue (107) French: topographic name from *artica*, a term meaning 'fallow land', or a habitational name from a minor place named with this word.

GIVEN NAME French 4%. *Antoine.*

Artiles (134) Spanish (especially Canary Islands): unexplained.

GIVEN NAMES Spanish 62%. *Juan* (6), *Jose* (5), *Carlos* (3), *Jorge* (3), *Rafael* (3), *Ramon* (3), *Ruben* (3), *Digna* (2), *Jesus* (2), *Manuel* (2), *Adriana, Alberto; Antonio* (3), *Leonardo* (2), *Cecilio, Fausto, Julieta, Vita.*

Artim (127) Czech and Slovak: unexplained.

Artinian (123) Armenian: patronymic from the personal name *Artin*, western Armenian form of *Arutyun* (see ARUTYUNYAN).

GIVEN NAMES Armenian 55%. *Artin* (4), *Avo* (4), *Ara* (3), *Garo* (3), *Sarkis* (2), *Agop, Anoush, Antranig, Aram, Artine, Garabed, Garen.*

Artino (131) **1.** Italian (Sicily): origin unknown. **2.** Greek (**Artinos**): habitational name for someone from the city of Arta in Epirus.

GIVEN NAMES Italian 19%. *Orlando* (2), *Benedetto, Gino; Ignatius.*

Artis (1808) **1.** English: regional name for someone from the French province of Artois, from Anglo-Norman French *Arteis* (from Latin *Atrebates*, the name of the local Gaulish tribe). **2.** French: from Old French *artis* 'woodworm', Old Occitan *arta* 'moth', possibly applied as a nickname for someone suffering from a wasting disease, perhaps leprosy.

Artist (118) Variant of English or French ARTIS.

Artley (238) English: variant of HARTLEY.

Artman (780) **1.** Dutch and German: variant of HARTMAN. **2.** Americanized spelling of South German **Artmann** 'plowman' or 'peasant', from Middle High German *art* 'farming', 'agriculture' + *man* 'man'.

Artrip (350) Probably Danish or southern Swedish in origin, a respelling of a habitational name formed with -*rup* 'village', 'hamlet' (Old Norse *þorp*) as the second element.

Arts (239) North German and Dutch: variant of ARTZ.

GIVEN NAMES French 4%. *Alphonse, Desire, Henri.*

Artus (169) French and German: from a medieval variant of ARTHUR.

GIVEN NAME German 4%. *Klaus.*

Artuso (127) Italian: from the personal name *Artuso*, a form of ARTHUR, influenced by medieval French ARTUS.

GIVEN NAMES Italian 17%. *Angelo* (2), *Meo, Saverio.*

Artz (1182) **1.** North German and Dutch: patronymic from the personal name *A(a)rt*, a reduced form of *Arnt* (see ARNDT, ARNOLD), or sometimes from a reduced form of the personal name *Alaert* or *Adriaan*. **2.** German and Jewish (Ashkenazic): variant of ARZT 'physician'.

Artzer (122) German: derivative of ARTZ 2, with the agent suffix -*er*.

Arundel (129) English: **1.** habitational name from a place in West Sussex, seat of the Dukes of Norfolk, named Arundel, from Old English *hārhūne* 'horehound' (a plant) + *dell* 'valley'. **2.** (of Norman origin): nickname for someone supposedly resembling a swallow, from Old French *arondel*, diminutive of *arond* 'swallow' (Latin *hirundo*, confused with *(h)arundo* 'reed').
GIVEN NAME French 4%; Welsh 4%. *Patrice* (2).

Arutyunyan (120) Armenian: patronymic from the personal name *Arutyun*, from classical Armenian *yarut'iwn* 'resurrection', a calque on Greek *Anastasios*.
GIVEN NAMES Armenian 57%; Russian 12%. *Anait* (2), *Asmik* (2), *Garnik* (2), *Grayr* (2), *Vazgen* (2), *Akop*, *Alvard*, *Andranik*, *Arsen*, *Artush*, *Gagik*, *Garen*; *Georgy*, *Grigoriy*, *Maksim*, *Natela*, *Shelya*, *Vladmir*, *Yevgeniya*, *Yuriy*.

Arvanitis (174) Greek: ethnic name from *Arvanitis*, the medieval Greek term for an Albanian, still used to refer to the descendants of the Albanians who settled in central Greece from the 13th to 16th centuries. It may also be from a nickname meaning 'headstrong' or 'boorish', from an informal meaning of the same word that developed following the prevalent ethnic stereotype.
GIVEN NAMES Greek 19%. *Costas* (2), *Stratis* (2), *Andreas*, *Argyrios*, *Athanasios*, *Demetrios*, *Nikolaos*, *Panos*, *Pantelis*, *Toula*, *Voula*, *Yannis*.

Arvay (151) Hungarian and Slovak (**Árvay**): habitational name for someone from Árva county in the former Hungarian kingdom, now in Slovakia.

Arvelo (152) Portuguese and Spanish (frequent in Canary Islands): probably a nickname from Portuguese and Galician *arvela*, a variant of *alvéloa* a species of bird (*Motacilla alba*).
GIVEN NAMES Spanish 46%. *Jose* (6), *Juan* (5), *Alberto* (2), *Alfonso* (2), *Ana* (2), *Carlos* (2), *Justina* (2), *Luz* (2), *Miguel* (2), *Americo*, *Bienvenida*, *Demetrio*.

Arvey (100) English: variant of HARVEY.

Arvidson (661) Americanized form of Swedish **Arvidsson** or Norwegian and Danish **Arvidsen**, patronymics from the personal name *Arvid*, composed of Old Norse *arn* 'eagle' + *víðr* 'wood'.
GIVEN NAMES Scandinavian 7%; German 4%. *Anders*, *Britt*, *Erik*, *Lars*, *Nordahl*, *Ove*; *Kurt* (2), *Erwin*, *Fritz*.

Arvie (115) Origin unidentified. Perhaps an altered spelling of French **Hervé** (see HARVEY).
GIVEN NAMES French 6%. *Monique*, *Patrice*.

Arvin (857) Probably a variant of Irish IRVIN.
FOREBEARS Thomas Arvin is recorded in MD in 1735.

Arviso (126) Hispanic (Mexico): variant of ARVIZU.
GIVEN NAMES Spanish 7%. *Alfonso*, *Armando*, *Celso*, *Epifanio*, *Juan*, *Manuel*.

Arvizo (116) Hispanic (Mexico): variant of ARVIZU.
GIVEN NAMES Spanish 37%. *Alvaro* (2), *Eraclio* (2), *Guadalupe* (2), *Jorge* (2), *Jose* (2), *Juan* (2), *Manuel* (2), *Ramon* (2), *Alfonso*, *Cristina*, *Felipe*, *Francisco*.

Arvizu (483) Basque: variant of **Arbizu**, a habitational name from a place in Navarre named Arbizu, from Basque *arbizu* 'turnip field', from *(h)arbi* 'turnip' + the suffix -*zu* 'abundance of'.
GIVEN NAMES Spanish 42%. *Jesus* (11), *Jose* (10), *Francisco* (7), *Manuel* (6), *Miguel* (6), *Luis* (5), *Armando* (4), *Enrique* (4), *Ernesto* (4), *Juan* (4), *Carlos* (3), *Jorge* (3).

Arwine (116) Variant of English IRWIN 2.

Arwood (735) English: variant of HARWOOD.

Ary (518) **1.** Americanized spelling of French HARY. **2.** English: variant spelling of AIREY.

Arya (153) Indian (northern states): Hindu name found in several communities, from Sanskrit *ārya* 'honorable man' or 'man of the Aryan race'. In the Panjab it is a Jat name based on the name of a Jat clan.
GIVEN NAMES Indian 86%. *Ram* (4), *Satya* (4), *Arun* (2), *Brahm* (2), *Ravi* (2), *Sarla* (2), *Sudhir* (2), *Sumit* (2), *Suresh* (2), *Veena* (2), *Yashpal* (2), *Ajay*.

Arzate (281) Basque: topographic name for someone living in a mountain pass named for its abundance of stones, from *artza* 'stony place' (from *(h)ar(ri)* 'stone' + -*tza* 'abundance of') + *ate* 'pass'.
GIVEN NAMES Spanish 59%. *Manuel* (10), *Jose* (5), *Arturo* (4), *Jesus* (4), *Raul* (4), *Armando* (3), *Fernando* (3), *Juan* (3), *Miguel* (3), *Ramon* (3), *Andres* (2), *Ernesto* (2).

Arzola (352) Basque: topographic or habitational name, from *artza* 'abundance of stones' (from *(h)arri* 'stone') + -*ola* 'place', 'hut', 'cabin'.
GIVEN NAMES Spanish 47%. *Jose* (7), *Jesus* (5), *Pedro* (5), *Francisco* (4), *Ricardo* (4), *Juan* (3), *Luis* (3), *Roberto* (3), *Alberto* (2), *Alfredo* (2), *Angel* (2), *Arturo* (2).

Arzt (193) **1.** North German: variant of the patronymic ARTZ. **2.** German and Jewish (Ashkenazic): occupational name for a physician, German *Arzt*.
GIVEN NAMES Jewish 8%; German 6%. *Aron*, *Isidor*, *Itzchak*, *Noam*, *Sholom*; *Elke* (2), *Franz* (2), *Alois*, *Hans*.

Arzu (100) Basque: topographic name, probably from Basque *arri* 'stone' + the suffix -*zu* 'abundance of'.

GIVEN NAMES Spanish 35%. *Ricardo* (3), *Adriana*, *Alba*, *Alberto*, *Alfredo*, *Ana*, *Augusto*, *Benito*, *Eloina*, *Eufracio*, *Guillermo*, *Gustavo*.

Asa (151) **1.** Japanese: variously written, sometimes with characters used phonetically. It can mean 'morning', but the most likely meaning is 'hemp', making it a topographic or occupational name. Both forms are found mostly in Amami, one of the Ryūkyū Islands. **2.** Hungarian: from *Assa*, a pet form of the ecclesiastical personal name *Asbót* (see OSWALD).
GIVEN NAMES Spanish 5%. *Juan* (2), *Eugenio*, *Jaime*, *Ludivina*, *Rolando*.

Asad (117) Muslim: variant of ASSAD.
GIVEN NAMES Muslim 72%. *Syed* (4), *Mazen* (3), *Mohammed* (2), *Ramadan* (2), *Abdelrahim*, *Abdul*, *Abu*, *Ahmad*, *Ameen*, *Amer*, *Azmi*, *Bashir*.

Asai (139) Japanese: 'shallow well'. This name is found mostly along the southeastern seaboard of Japan.
GIVEN NAMES Japanese 70%. *Akira* (2), *Hiroshi* (2), *Hiroyuki* (2), *Kiyoshi* (2), *Osamu* (2), *Yasuhiro* (2), *Akinori*, *Haruo*, *Hidehiko*, *Hidenori*, *Hideo*, *Hiroki*.

Asano (166) Japanese: meaning 'shallow plain'; probably derived from two places of that name, one in Mino (now southern Gifu prefecture), the other in Owari (now Nagoya prefecture). Both families descend from the MINAMOTO clan through the Toki family.
GIVEN NAMES Japanese 78%. *Hiroko* (4), *Takashi* (4), *Hiroshi* (3), *Akira* (2), *Koichi* (2), *Koji* (2), *Toshio* (2), *Toshiyasu* (2), *Tsuyoshi* (2), *Yumiko* (2), *Aki*, *Akihiko*.

Asante (119) Ghanaian: name for a member of the Ashante people of Ghana, West Africa.
GIVEN NAMES African 18%. *Kwame* (3), *Akua*, *Kofi*, *Kwaku*, *Kwasi*, *Kwesi*.

Asare (102) Ghanaian: unexplained.
GIVEN NAMES African 12%. *Kwabena* (2), *Kwame* (2), *Kofi*, *Kwaku*.

Asaro (550) Italian: from the unexplained medieval personal name *Ássoro*.
GIVEN NAMES Italian 22%. *Vito* (9), *Mario* (6), *Salvatore* (5), *Sal* (3), *Santo* (3), *Angelo* (2), *Francesco* (2), *Gaspare* (2), *Vincenzo* (2), *Alessandra*, *Antonella*, *Antonio*, *Bartolo*, *Bernardino*, *Carmella*, *Mateo*, *Pasqual*, *Rosario*.

Asato (332) Japanese: variously written; the version listed in the Shinsen shōjiroku is written with characters meaning 'morning' and 'door'. Another version, written with characters meaning 'safe' and 'village', is found in the Ryūkyū Islands, where it is sometimes pronounced *Yasuzato*. One family of this name originated in Asatsu village in Satsuma province (present-day Kogoshima prefecture), and any of four places called Asato in the Ryūkyū Islands could also have given rise to the surname.

GIVEN NAMES Japanese 35%. *Hideo* (2), *Masaki* (2), *Masaru* (2), *Minoru* (2), *Noboru* (2), *Shigeo* (2), *Yoshito* (2), *Akio*, *Eisuke*, *Fumie*, *Goro*, *Hajime*.

Asay (701) English: probably a variant of ACEY.

FOREBEARS A certain Joseph Asay is recorded in Salem County, NJ in 1755.

Asbell (686) Probably an altered form of English **Aspell**, a habitational name from Aspall in Suffolk or Aspull in Greater Manchester. The first is named from Old English *æspe* 'aspen' + *halh* 'nook', 'corner'; the second from Old English *æspe* + *hyll* 'hill'.

Asberry (620) English: variant spelling of ASBURY.

Asbill (384) See ASBELL.

Asbridge (178) English: probably a variant of ASHBRIDGE.

Asbury (2848) English (West Midlands): **1.** habitational name from Astbury in Cheshire, named from Old English *ēast* 'east' + *byrig*, dative of *burh* 'manor', 'fortified place'. **2.** from either of two places, in Oxfordshire and Devon, named Ashbury, from Old English *æsc* 'ash tree' + *byrig*.

Asby (160) English: habitational name from Asby or Great or Little Asby in Cumbria, named from Old Norse *askr* 'ash tree' + *býr* 'farmstead'.

Ascencio (438) Spanish and Italian: from the personal name (Latin *Ascensius*), favored by the early Christians, by whom it was bestowed with reference to the ascension of Christ (Late Latin *ascensio*).

GIVEN NAMES Spanish 57%. *Jose* (22), *Salvador* (8), *Miguel* (7), *Jesus* (6), *Manuel* (6), *Raul* (5), *Javier* (4), *Juan* (4), *Pedro* (4), *Ramon* (4), *Carlos* (3), *Eduardo* (3).

Asch (525) **1.** North German: from a Middle Low German personal name, *Asc*, originally meaning 'spearman' (see ASH). **2.** German: habitational name from any of various minor places named with *asch* 'ash (tree)'. Compare ASCHER. **3.** Jewish (Ashkenazic): variant of ASH. **4.** English: variant spelling of ASH. See also ASCHE.

Aschbrenner (104) Reduced form of German ASCHENBRENNER.

Asche (446) **1.** North German: variant of ASCH. **2.** English: variant spelling of ASH (*asche* was the regular Middle English spelling of this word).

Ascheman (135) Respelling of German **Aschmann**, habitational name from a place named Asch, Ascha, or Aschau.

Aschenbach (167) German: variant of ESCHENBACH.

GIVEN NAME German 5%. *Hans* (2).

Aschenbrener (109) Variant of German ASCHENBRENNER.

GIVEN NAMES German 7%. *Aloys*, *Eldred*, *Leonhard*.

Aschenbrenner (655) German: occupational name for someone who prepared ash from wood fires for use in glassworks and soapworks, from Middle High German *asche*, *esche* 'ashes' + *brenner* 'burner'.

GIVEN NAMES German 4%. *Johann* (2), *Aloys*, *Franz*, *Frieda*, *Kurt*, *Urs*.

Ascher (597) **1.** German (often **Äscher**): occupational name for an ashmaker (see ASCHENBRENNER), from Middle High German *escher* 'ashes'. **2.** German: topographic name for someone who lived by an ash tree or ash grove, from Middle High German *asch* 'ash' + *-er*, suffix denoting an inhabitant. **3.** German: habitational name from any of the numerous minor places named with the element *asch*, including Ascha, Aschach, Aschau. **4.** Jewish (Ashkenazic): see ASHER.

GIVEN NAMES German 4%. *Ernst* (2), *Erwin*, *Heinz*, *Helmut*, *Kurt*, *Monika*, *Wolf*.

Aschoff (205) German (especially Westphalia): habitational name from a farmstead named from Middle Low German *esch*, *asch* 'ash tree' + *hof* 'manor farm', 'yard'. In German the usual form of the name is **Aschhoff**.

Ascione (138) Southern Italian (Campania): perhaps from an augmentative form of *ascia* 'axe', 'hatchet', or from the Ascione mountain in the Sila range (Calabria).

GIVEN NAMES Italian 14%; French 5%. *Angelo*, *Aniello*, *Enrico*, *Guido*, *Raffaele*, *Salvatore*; *Armand*, *Philippe*.

Ascolese (103) Southern Italian: habitational name for someone from Ascoli Satriano in Foggia, or less likely, from Ascoli Piceno in the Marches, from an adjectival form of the place name element.

GIVEN NAMES Italian 14%. *Americo*, *Renato*, *Salvatore*.

Asel (134) Variant of German **Esel** (see EZELL).

Aseltine (153) Variant of English HASELTINE.

Asencio (309) Spanish: from a personal name, from Latin *Ascensius* 'ascension' (see ASCENCIO).

GIVEN NAMES Spanish 48%. *Diego* (5), *Jose* (5), *Alfredo* (4), *Angel* (4), *Carlos* (4), *Juan* (4), *Francisco* (3), *Luis* (3), *Pedro* (3), *Rafael* (3), *Roberto* (3), *Santos* (3); *Antonio* (3), *Angelo*, *Ceasar*.

Asfaw (100) Ethiopian: unexplained.

GIVEN NAMES Ethiopian 69%. *Alemayehu* (3), *Amha* (2), *Girma* (2), *Mengistu* (2), *Negussie* (2), *Teferi* (2), *Yared* (2), *Abate*, *Abeba*, *Abebe*, *Araya*, *Ayele*.

Asfour (114) Arabic: **1.** probably from the adjective *'asfūr* 'yellow', 'saffron-colored'. **2.** alternatively, a nickname from Arabic *'usfūr* 'sparrow', 'small bird'.

GIVEN NAMES Arabic 55%. *Walid* (3), *Amin* (2), *Emad* (2), *Ghassan* (2), *Hani* (2), *Khalil* (2), *Maher* (2), *Shihab* (2), *Adib*, *Ahmad*, *Antoun*, *Ayman*.

Asghar (114) Arabic: from a distinguishing epithet from Arabic *aşghar* 'younger', 'smaller', comparative of *şaghīr* 'young'.

GIVEN NAMES Arabic 85%. *Ali* (10), *Mohammad* (9), *Muhammad* (7), *Syed* (7), *Masood* (3), *Mohammed* (3), *Ghulam* (2), *Khan* (2), *Nafees* (2), *Abdul*, *Afshan*, *Arshad*.

Ash (7347) **1.** English: from Middle English *asche* 'ash tree' (Old English *æsc*), hence a topographic name for someone living by an ash tree or a habitational name from any of the many places in southern and central England named with this word (Derbyshire, Dorset, Hampshire, Herefordshire, Kent, Surrey, Shropshire, Somerset, and elsewhere). **2.** In New England, Ash is commonly found for French DUFRESNE, with the same meaning. **3.** Jewish (Ashkenazic): from an acronym for Yiddish *AltSHul* (see ALTSCHUL) or *AyznSHtot* (see EISENSTADT).

Ashabranner (125) Respelling of German ASCHENBRENNER.

Ashbaugh (1124) Respelling of German ESCHBACH.

Ashbeck (139) Possibly an English habitational name from Ashbeck Gill in Cumbria, but more likely an Americanized form of German ESCHBACH.

Ashbridge (112) English: habitational name from any of numerous minor places named 'the bridge (Old English *brycg*) by the ash tree (Old English *æsc*)', as for example the one in Shropshire.

Ashbrook (719) **1.** English: habitational name from a place in Gloucestershire, recorded in Domesday Book as *Estbroce*, from Old English *ēast* + *brōc* 'nook'. **2.** In some instances, the surname may be a literal translation of German ESCHBACH.

Ashburn (1494) English: habitational name from Ashburnham in Sussex (*Esseborne* in Domesday Book), Ashbourne in Derbyshire, or Ashburton in Devon (*Æscburnan land* in a document of 1008), all named from Old English *æsc* 'ash tree' + *burna* 'stream'.

Ashby (6045) English: habitational name from any of the numerous places in northern and eastern England called Ashby, from Old Norse *askr* 'ash' or the Old Norse personal name *Aski* + *býr* 'farm'.

Ashcraft (3625) Altered form of English ASHCROFT.

Ashcroft (614) English (chiefly Lancashire): topographic name from Middle English *asche* 'ash tree' + *croft* 'enclosure', or a habitational name from a minor place named with these elements.

Ashdown (305) English: habitational name from Ashdon in Essex, Ashdown Forest in East Sussex, or Ashdown in Berkshire (now lost). The first two are named from Old English *æscen* 'growing with ash trees' + *dūn* 'hill'. The last may be from an Old English personal name *Æsc* or Old English *æsc* 'ash tree' + *dūn* 'hill'.

Ashe (2624) Irish and English: variant spelling of ASH, found mainly in Ireland.

FOREBEARS This is the name of a prominent NC family; John Baptist Ashe settled in NC before 1720. It is not known where he came from: his personal name suggests that he may have been of French extraction, perhaps originally named Jean-Baptiste Dufresne.

Ashenbrenner (114) Respelling of German ASCHENBRENNER.
GIVEN NAME German 5%. *Erwin* (2).

Ashenfelter (331) Respelling of German **Eschenfelder**, a topographic name for someone living by an ash tree or ash wood in open country, from Middle High German *esche* 'ash' + *feld* 'open country'.

Asher (4462) **1.** English (mainly Sussex and Hampshire): topographic name denoting someone dwelling by an ash tree, from Middle English *asche* 'ash tree' + the habitational suffix -*er*. **2.** Jewish: from the Hebrew personal name *Asher* 'blessed'. **3.** Americanized spelling of German ASCHER.

Ashey (109) Probably an altered spelling of French **Hachet** or **Hachée** (see HACHEY).
GIVEN NAME French 5%. *Placide*.

Ashfield (110) English: habitational name from any of numerous places called Ashfield, as for example in Nottinghamshire and Suffolk; these are named from Old English *æsc* ash + *feld* 'open country'.

Ashford (2506) English: habitational name from any of several places called Ashford. Those in Essex, Devon, Derbyshire, and Shropshire are named from Old English *æsc* 'ash' + *ford* 'ford'. One in Surrey is first recorded in 969 as *Ecelesford*, probably from a personal name *Eccel*, a diminutive of *Ecca* 'edge (of a sword)' + *ford*. The one in Kent is from *æscet* 'clump of ash trees' + *ford*.

Ashikaga (9) Japanese: meaning 'place of reeds' (usually written phonetically with characters meaning 'foot' and 'advantage'), a habitational name from a place in Shimotsuke (now Tochigi prefecture). Although not a common surname now, it is one of the great names in Japanese history. Founded by Minamoto Yoshiyasu (1126?–57), the family gained prominence when Ashikaga Takauji (1305–58) established the Ashikaga (or Muromachi) Shogunate in 1338; the institution endured until 1573. The family produced many warriors and artists of renown, and several other important families are descended from them. The famous Ashikaga Gakkō, a school of military and Confucian studies which operated until 1872, was reputedly founded by Yoshiyasu's son, Yoshikane (1147?–99). Another Ashikaga family, unrelated to the above, is descended from the FUJIWARA clan.

Ashkenazi (103) Jewish: nickname applied by Jews in Slavic countries for a Jew from Germany; it was also used to denote a Yiddish-speaking Jew who had settled in an area where non-Ashkenazic Jews were in the majority. *Ashkenaz* is a Biblical place name (Genesis 10:3, Jeremiah 51: 27), etymologically related to Greek *Skythia* 'Scythia'. However, since the 9th century AD, if not earlier, it has been applied to Germany.
GIVEN NAMES Jewish 46%; Russian 5%. *Chaim* (2), *Zalman* (2), *Anshel*, *Avi*, *Avraham*, *Batia*, *Gilad*, *Hershel*, *Inna*, *Liat*, *Polina*, *Shaul*; *Aleksandr*, *Anatoliy*.

Ashland (227) **1.** English and Scottish: topographic or habitational name for residence on or near land covered with ash trees. There are minor places called Ashland(s) in Hampshire and Leicestershire, Staffordshire, and Galloway. Asland, a river name in Lancashire, refers to the lower reaches of what is more generally known as the Douglas river. It is named from Old Norse *askr* 'ash' + Old English *lanu* 'lane'. **2.** Americanized form of Norwegian **Ask(e)land** (see ASKELAND). **3.** Probably an Americanized form of the common French Canadian name ASSELIN. Compare ASHLINE.
FOREBEARS In the U.S., Ashland is the name of two counties and at least thirteen cities, towns, and villages. Most, perhaps all, were named after Ashland in Lexington, KY, home of Henry Clay (1777–1852), who is said to have named his estate from a characteristic feature of the site, not from anyone's surname.

Ashley (12499) English: habitational name from any of the numerous places in southern and central England named Ashley, from Old English *æsc* 'ash' + *lēah* 'woodland clearing'.
FOREBEARS The name of Capt. John Ashley appears in the VA Charter of 1609. For more than two centuries his descendants were prominent in Norfolk, VA. A branch of the family settled in Pittsburgh in the early 19th century.

Ashlin (110) English and Swedish: variant of ASLIN.

Ashline (405) English form of the French name ASSELIN. This is found in medieval England, from the Anglo-Norman French personal name *Asceline*. In 19th-century VT, the process took place all over again, with conversion of French Canadian Asselin into Ashline.

Ashlock (854) English: from a medieval personal name, *Aslak*, found in Norfolk; it is from the Old Norse personal name *Áslákr*, composed of the elements *áss* 'god' + *leikr* 'game', 'fight'.

Ashman (994) **1.** English: from the Middle English personal name *Asheman* (Old English *Æscmann*, probably originally a byname from *æscman* 'seaman' or 'pirate', i.e. one who sailed in an ash-wood boat). **2.** Americanized spelling of German **Aschmann**, an occupational name from Middle High German *aschman* 'kitchen servant' or 'boatman'. **3.** Variant of German and Swiss ESCHMANN.

Ashmead (163) English: habitational name from Ashmead Green or Ashmead House in Gloucestershire, named from Old English *æsc* 'ash' + *mēd* 'meadow', or a topographic name with the same meaning.

Ashmore (2293) English: habitational name from any of several minor places, generally named from Old English *æsc* 'ash' + *mōr* 'moor', 'marsh', 'fen'. In the case of Ashmore in Dorset, however, the early forms show that the second element is Old English *mere* 'lake'.

Ashmun (108) Variant of German **Aschmann** or English **Ashman** (see ASHMAN).
GIVEN NAMES German 6%. *Fritz*, *Heinz*.

Ashraf (293) Muslim: from an Arabic personal name, *Ashraf*, meaning 'most honorable' or 'most distinguished', an elative adjective based on SHARIF.
GIVEN NAMES Muslim 88%. *Mohammad* (41), *Mohammed* (14), *Muhammad* (14), *Syed* (14), *Ali* (4), *Bibi* (3), *Ovais* (3), *Ahmad* (2), *Aziz* (2), *Fareed* (2), *Iqbal* (2), *Javaid* (2).

Ashton (4289) English: habitational name from any of the numerous places so called, especially Ashton-under-Lyne near Manchester. Most are named from Old English *æsc* 'ash tree' + *tūn* 'settlement'; the one in Northamptonshire is *(æt þæm) æscum* '(at the) ash trees'. Others have been assimilated to this from different sources. The one in Devon is 'the settlement *(tūn)* of Æschere', while the one in Hertfordshire is 'the settlement of Ælli'.

Ashurst (310) English: habitational name from any of various places called Ashurst, from Old English *æsc* 'ash tree' + *hyrst* 'wooded hill'. The most significant of these places are in Kent and West Sussex, but in England the surname is now found chiefly in south Lancashire, where it probably derives from Ashurst Beacon near Wigan.

Ashwell (293) English: habitational name from any of various places, in Essex, Hertfordshire, Rutland, and elsewhere, named Ashwell, from Old English *æsc* 'ash tree' + *well(a)* 'spring', 'stream'.

Ashwill (101) English: variant of ASHWELL.

Ashwood (267) English: habitational name from a place in Staffordshire named Ashwood, from Old English *æsc* 'ash' + *wudu* 'wood'.

Ashworth (3771) English (chiefly Lancashire): habitational name from any of various places called Ashworth, in Lancashire and elsewhere, from Old English *æsc* 'ash tree' + *worð* 'enclosed settlement'.

Ask (249) **1.** Swedish and Norwegian: from *ask* 'ash tree', applied either as a habitational name from a place named with this word or as an ornamental name. **2.** English: habitational name from a place in North Yorkshire named Aske, from Old

English as *æsc* 'ash tree', later replaced by the Old Norse cognate *askr*.

GIVEN NAME Scandinavian 7%. *Oddvar*.

Askeland (154) Norwegian: habitational name from any of five places in western Norway named with Old Norse *ask* 'ash tree' + *land* 'land', 'piece of land'.

GIVEN NAMES Scandinavian 15%. *Erik, Selmer, Thorval*.

Askelson (138) Scandinavian: patronymic from a reduced form of the Old Norse personal name *Ásketill* (see HASKELL).

Asker (127) **1.** Turkish: occupational name from *asker* 'soldier', from Arabic *'askarī*. This name is also found in Iran and the Indian subcontinent. **2.** Arabic: variant of ASGHAR. **3.** Greek: shortened form of **Askeris**, from Turkish *asker* 'soldier', or from **Askeridis** or **Askeropoulos**, patronymics from this word. Compare LASKARIS. **4.** Norwegian and Swedish: habitational name from any of several farmsteads named Asker, in particular those near Oslo, from an inflected form of *ask* 'ash tree'. **5.** English (Norfolk): topographic name for someone who lived by an ash tree, Middle English *ask* (from Old Norse *asker*) + the habitational suffix *-er*. **6.** English: from Middle English *asker(e)* 'collector of tolls or revenues' or (in a legal context) 'plaintiff' or 'prosecutor' (an agent derivative of Middle English *aske(n)* 'to ask', 'to demand').

GIVEN NAMES Muslim 13%; Scandinavian 5%. *Adil, Ahmed, Amr, Isam, Kamal, Latif, Mohamed, Nazeeh, Ribhi, Talal, Widad, Yehya*.

Askew (4107) Northern English: habitational name from a place in North Yorkshire named Aiskew, from Old Norse *eik* 'oak' + *skógr* 'wood'.

Askey (456) Northern English: **1.** from an early Middle English personal name of Scandinavian origin, related to Old Danish *Aski*, a derivative of *askr* 'ash tree'. **2.** variant of ASKEW.

Askin (478) English (of Norman origin): from a Middle English and Anglo-Norman French personal name, *Askin* or *Asketin*, a pet form of *Asketill*, *Askell*, which is of Old Norse origin and related to HASKIN and HASKELL.

Askins (1231) English: variant of HASKINS.

Askren (315) Northern English: unexplained.

Aslakson (141) Americanized spelling of Norwegian **Aslaksen** and Swedish **Aslaksson**, patronymics from the personal name *Aslak*, Old Norse *Áslákr*, from elements meaning 'god' + 'giant' or 'battle'.

Aslam (221) Muslim: from a personal name based on Arabic *Aslam* 'most perfect', 'faultless', an elative form of the adjective *salīm* (see SALIM).

GIVEN NAMES Muslim 89%. *Mohammad* (44), *Mohammed* (19), *Muhammad* (9), *Syed* (5), *Mohamed* (4), *Ahmed* (2),

Ambreen (2), *Javed* (2), *Tanveer* (2), *Tariq* (2), *Zahid* (2), *Aamer*.

Aslan (107) Turkish, Iranian, and Jewish (from Turkey and Iran): from the personal name *Aslan*, a variant of Turkish *arsaelan* 'lion'.

GIVEN NAMES Muslim 13%; Jewish 8%; Spanish 6%. *Ali, Aslan, Azzam, Dursun, Muhammed, Mustafa, Suat; Shlomo* (3), *Iren; Ana, Andres, Eduardo, Francisco, Ines, Jose, Pablo, Silvia*.

Aslanian (207) Armenian: patronymic from the personal name *Aslan*, from Turkish *aslan* 'lion'.

GIVEN NAMES Armenian 37%. *Vahik* (2), *Varoujan* (2), *Antranig, Antranik, Aram, Armen, Arsen, Ashot, Asmik, Babken, Berge, Garabed*.

Asleson (249) Norwegian: patronymic from *Asle*, ultimately from Old Norse *Atli*, literally 'little father'. The personal name *Attila* is of the same origin.

GIVEN NAME Scandinavian 4%. *Ordell* (2).

Aslin (232) **1.** English: from the Old French personal name *Asceline*, a pet form of the personal name *Asse* (see ASSELIN). **2.** Swedish (**Åslin**): topographic or ornamental name from *ås* 'ridge', with the addition of *-lin*, a suffix of Swedish family names.

Aslinger (124) Altered form of German ESSLINGER or of **Asslinger**, a habitational name for someone from Assling in Bavaria.

Asman (273) Americanized form of German **As(s)mann**, a much altered derivative (pet form) of the personal name *Erasmus*, which was popular among humanists in the Netherlands, Denmark, and northern Germany during the 16th century (see RASMUSSEN).

GIVEN NAME German 4%. *Ernst*.

Asmar (161) Muslim: from a personal name derived from Arabic *asmar* 'brown', 'dark-skinned'. This is also the name of a region of Afghanistan.

GIVEN NAMES Muslim 32%; French 11%. *Amal* (2), *Faiz* (2), *Hoda* (2), *Abdel, Ali, Amir, Bashar, Basim, Dhia, Ghanim, Ghazi, Hasib; Pierre* (2), *Antoine, Edouard, Michel*.

Asmus (845) Danish, Dutch, and North German: from a short form of *Erasmus* (Latinized form of Greek *Erasmos*, a derivative of *erān* 'to love'). Compare RASMUSSEN.

GIVEN NAMES German 4%. *Hans* (2), *Wolfgang* (2), *Frieda, Hellmuth, Helmut, Kurt*.

Asmussen (476) Danish (also found in northern Germany): shortened form of RASMUSSEN.

GIVEN NAMES German 5%. *Hans* (5), *Arno, Detlef, Kurt, Manfred*.

Asp (335) **1.** Swedish: ornamental name from *asp* 'aspen tree'. **2.** Norwegian: habitational name from a farmstead named with *asp* 'aspen tree'. **3.** German and English: topographic name from Middle High Ger-

man *aspe*, Middle English *aspe* 'aspen tree'. **4.** English: habitational name from a minor place named with Old English *æspe*, *æpse* 'aspen tree' (see APPS).

GIVEN NAMES Scandinavian 6%. *Anders, Erik*.

Aspden (100) English: habitational name from a lost or unidentified place, probably in Lancashire, where the surname is most frequent.

Aspell (118) English: habitational name from Aspull in Greater Manchester, named from Old English *æspe* 'aspen' + *hyll* 'hill', or from Aspall in Suffolk.

Aspen (128) **1.** Norwegian: habitational name from a place named Aspen, from an inflected form of *asp* 'aspen tree'. **2.** English: topographic name for someone living by an aspen tree.

GIVEN NAMES Scandinavian 9%. *Alf, Erik, Ludvig, Sven*.

Aspenson (132) Possibly an Americanized form of a Scandinavian patronymic from a variant of the Old Norse personal name *Ásbjǫrn* ('god' + 'bear').

Asper (366) South German, Austrian, Swiss, and Norwegian: topographic name for someone living by aspen trees, from Middle High German *aspe*, or a habitational name from a place named with this word. Compare ASP.

Aspinall (325) English: reduced form of ASPINWALL.

Aspinwall (513) **1.** English: habitational name from a place in the parish of Ormskirk, Lancashire called Aspinwall (also Asmall), from an Old English word *æspen* 'growing with aspen trees' + *wæll(a)* 'stream'. There has probably also been some confusion with another Lancashire habitational surname, **Aspinhalgh**, the second element of which is Old English *halh* 'nook'. **2.** According to Einar Haugen, the Norwegian family name **Asbjørnsen** has been assimilated to Aspinwall in America. FOREBEARS Peter Aspinwall was one of the four thousand Puritans who followed the Pilgrim Fathers to New England in 1630. He settled in Brookline, MA.

Asplin (106) English (Midlands): from a reduced form of the Biblical name *Absalom* (probably meaning 'father of peace' in Hebrew).

Asplund (502) **1.** Swedish: ornamental name composed of the elements *asp* 'aspen' + *lund* 'grove'. **2.** Norwegian: habitational name from any of several farms named Asplund, of the same derivation as 1.

GIVEN NAMES Scandinavian 6%. *Nils* (2), *Britt, Elof, Lennart*.

Asquith (240) English: habitational name from a village in North Yorkshire named Askwith, from Old Norse *askr* 'ash tree' + *viðr* 'wood'.

Assad (317) Muslim: **1.** from an Arabic personal name, *As'ad* 'happiest', 'luckiest', a superlative adjective derived from *saʿīda* 'to be lucky or happy'. Compare SAID. **2.** nickname or ornamental name from Arabic *asad* 'lion'. This was adopted as a surname by Ḥafeẓ al-Assad (1928–2000), president of Syria from 1971 until his death.

GIVEN NAMES Muslim 23%. *Assad* (2), *Mohamed* (2), *Mohammed* (2), *Sader* (2), *Saleh* (2), *Sheikh* (2), *Abed*, *Abeer*, *Abrahim*, *Adnan*, *Akram*, *Amer*.

Assaf (232) **1.** Muslim and Christian Arabic: from an Arabic personal name *āsaf*, of unknown etymology. This was the name of Suleiman's grand wazir, whence it came to be used proverbially as a name for any wise counselor. **2.** Jewish (Sephardic): either an adoption of the Arabic name or from the Biblical name *Asaph*, name of a counselor of King David and King Solomon, to whom authorship of twelve of the Psalms is attributed (1 Chronicles 16:4–5; Psalms 50, 73–83).

GIVEN NAMES Muslim 30%; French 5%; Jewish 4%. *Fadi* (3), *Sami* (3), *Ali* (2), *Hussein* (2), *Marwan* (2), *Samir* (2), *Abdulaziz*, *Abdullah*, *Aboud*, *Ahmad*, *Amal*, *Assaf*, *Emile* (2), *Antoine*, *Jacques*; *Mendel*, *Moshe*, *Yehuda*.

Assante (147) Italian (mainly Naples): unexplained.

GIVEN NAMES Italian 14%; French 5%. *Angelo*, *Antonio*, *Carmela*, *Ciro*, *Marco*, *Paolo*, *Salvatore*; *Amelie*, *Andre*, *Armand*.

Assefa (133) Ethiopian: unexplained.

GIVEN NAMES Ethiopian 72%. *Almaz* (3), *Mulugeta* (3), *Alemayehu* (2), *Girma* (2), *Yeshi* (2), *Zewdu* (2), *Alem*, *Amanuel*, *Araya*, *Bekele*, *Belay*, *Dereje*, *Genet*.

Asselin (686) **1.** French: from a frequent Old French personal name, a pet form of *Ace* or *Asse*, Germanic *A(t)zo*, a pet form of any of the many Germanic compound names that had *adal* 'noble' as their first element. **2.** Dutch: from the Dutch cognate of this personal name, *Asselijn*.

FOREBEARS An Asselin from Rouen was in Chateau Richer by 1662.

GIVEN NAMES French 21%. *Andre* (6), *Armand* (5), *Lucien* (4), *Germain* (3), *Jacques* (3), *Normand* (3), *Amedee* (2), *Fernand* (2), *Gilles* (2), *Laurent* (2), *Alphee*, *Benoit*.

Asselta (143) Probably Italian; the surname is found in two small communities in Apulia, suggesting that it may be a habitational name from a lost place. However, there is no documentary evidence to support this.

GIVEN NAMES Italian 10%. *Rocco* (3), *Carmine*.

Assink (122) Dutch: unexplained.

GIVEN NAMES French 4%. *Andre*, *Colette*.

Assmann (108) German: from a much altered pet form of the personal name ASMUS.

GIVEN NAMES German 7%. *Gerhard*, *Ingeborg*, *Willi*.

Ast (415) **1.** German and Jewish (Ashkenazic): from Middle High German *ast* 'knot (in wood)', 'branch', hence a nickname for a tough or awkward individual or a metonymic occupational name for a lumberjack. **2.** North German: occupational name, from Middle Low German *arste* 'physician', a variant of ARZT. **3.** Southern French: from Occitan *ast* 'pike or lance', probably an occupational name for a maker of these weapons.

GIVEN NAMES German 6%. *Erwin* (2), *Dieter*, *Gunter*, *Hans*, *Jurgen*, *Manfred*, *Trud*.

Asta (204) Southern Italian: **1.** habitational name from a place in Sicily called Asta. **2.** perhaps also from a medieval byname, either a short form of *Astancollo* (from *asta in collo* 'lance in neck'), or directly from *asta* 'lance'.

GIVEN NAMES Italian 9%; French 7%. *Giacomo* (2), *Pasquale*, *Vito*; *Henri* (2), *Marcel*.

Astacio (114) Spanish: probably from a variant of the personal name *Estacio* (*Eustachius*; see EUSTACE). In Spain, the name is concentrated in Alcalá de Guadaira, in Seville province.

GIVEN NAMES Spanish 43%. *Jose* (4), *Miguel* (3), *Jorge* (2), *Julio* (2), *Justo* (2), *Luis* (2), *Aida*, *Alberto*, *Andres*, *Angel*, *Carlos*, *Domingo*.

Astarita (150) Southern Italian: of uncertain derivation; possibly a nickname from Greek *astrítēs* 'asp' (a type of snake), from *astēr* 'star'.

GIVEN NAMES Italian 6%. *Salvatore* (2), *Gianni*, *Tommaso*.

Astbury (116) English: habitational name from Astbury in Cheshire, named from Old English *ēast* 'east' + *burh* 'manor', 'stronghold' (dative *byrig*).

Aster (143) **1.** German: nickname from Middle High German *agelster* 'magpie', which was known especially in the Middle Ages for mischievous tricks. **2.** English: perhaps a variant of EASTER.

Asti (117) Italian: nickname from the plural of *asta* 'staff', 'pole', 'shaft'.

GIVEN NAMES French 6%; Italian 5%. *Pierre*; *Guido*, *Veto*, *Vito*.

Astin (388) English: from a reduced form of the Anglo-Norman French personal name *Asketin*, a diminutive of Old Norse *Ásketill*, composed of the elements *áss* 'god' + *ketill* 'kettle', 'helmet' (see HASKELL, ASKIN).

Astle (465) **1.** English: habitational name from a place in Cheshire called Astle, from Old English *ēast* 'east' + *hyll* 'hill'. There may also have been some confusion with *Asthall* and ASTLEY. **2.** German: variant of **Ast(e)l**, probably a nickname for a crude person, from Middle High German *ast* 'branch', 'bough', 'knot'.

Astleford (114) Origin unidentified. This has the form of an English habitational name, but no place of this name is known in Britain, and the surname is found mainly in Ireland.

Astley (147) English: habitational name from a place in Warwickshire named Astley, from Old English *ēast* 'east' + *lēah* 'woodland clearing'. There are several other places in western and northwestern England so named, but the modern surname seems to be particularly associated with the one in Warwickshire. See also ASTLE.

Aston (1399) English: **1.** habitational name from any of several places in England called Aston. Most were named from Old English *ēast* 'east' + *tūn* 'settlement'. In a few cases the first element is *æsc* 'ash tree'. **2.** from a Middle English personal name, *Astan(us)*, which is probably a survival of Old English *Æðelstān* or one of the other names mentioned at ALSTON.

Astor (331) **1.** Southern French and German: from Occitan *astor* 'goshawk' (from Latin *acceptor*, variant of *accipiter* 'hawk'), used as a nickname characterizing a predacious or otherwise hawklike man. The name was taken to southwestern Germany by 17th-century Waldensian refugees from their Alpine valleys above Italian Piedmont. **2.** English: variant spelling of ASTER.

FOREBEARS Astor is the name of a famous American family of industrialists and newspaper owners. John Jacob Astor I (1763–1848) was born at Walldorf near Heidelberg, Germany, the son of a butcher. He followed his brother Henry to New York and made a fortune in the fur trade, which was greatly increased by his descendants in industry, hotels, and newspapers. They built the Waldorf-Astoria Hotel in New York. The great-grandson of John Jacob I, William Waldorf Astor (1848–1919), moved to England in 1890, becoming an influential newspaper proprietor and taking British citizenship in 1899. In 1917 he was created Viscount Astor of Hever. His son, the 2nd Viscount (1879–1952), married Nancy Shaw (née Langhorne) (1879–1964), daughter of a VA planter. She became the first woman to sit in the British House of Commons as a member of Parliament.

Astorga (323) Asturian-Leonese and Spanish: habitational name from the ancient city of Astorga in León province, named in Latin *Asturica*.

GIVEN NAMES Spanish 51%. *Jose* (8), *Luis* (7), *Juan* (6), *Francisco* (4), *Mario* (4), *Arturo* (3), *Jesus* (3), *Ruben* (3), *Adolfo* (2), *Ana* (2), *Benito* (2), *Cruz* (2).

Astorino (216) Southern Italian: from a diminutive of the nickname *astore*, literally 'goshawk'. Italian *astore* is an adaptation of Occitan *astor*, which displaced its Old Italian cognate *accettore* in the era of the troubadours. Both forms are derived from Latin *acceptor* 'hawk'

GIVEN NAMES Italian 13%. *Salvatore* (3), *Angelo* (2), *Luigi* (2), *Carmine*, *Giuseppe*, *Pasquale*, *Sal*.

Astudillo (193) Spanish: habitational name from a place in Palencia province called Astudillo.

GIVEN NAMES Spanish 55%. *Luis* (5), *Carlos* (4), *Jose* (3), *Juan* (3), *Manuel* (3), *Roberto* (3), *Rogelio* (3), *Beatriz* (2), *Francisco* (2), *Guillermo* (2), *Juan Carlos* (2), *Pablo* (2).

Asuncion (477) Spanish (**Asunción**): metronymic from the female personal name *Asunción*, bestowed with reference to the Marian title *Nuestra Señora de la Asunción* 'Our Lady of the Assumption'.

GIVEN NAMES Spanish 38%. *Jose* (4), *Juan* (3), *Alberto* (2), *Andres* (2), *Demetrio* (2), *Erlinda* (2), *Filemon* (2), *Lito* (2), *Luz* (2), *Nestor* (2), *Otilia* (2), *Reynaldo* (2); *Carmelo* (3), *Antonio* (2), *Romeo* (2), *Donato*, *Filiberto*, *Ireneo*, *Lorenzo*, *Marcello*, *Mauro*, *Valentino*.

Aswad (105) Arabic: **1.** from a distinguishing epithet, *aswad* 'black'. **2.** from a personal name based on Arabic *as'ad* 'happier', 'luckier', comparative of the adjective *sa'īd* 'happy' (see SAEED).

GIVEN NAMES Arabic 17%. *Adnan* (2), *Amin*, *Bassam*, *Kaleel*, *Maha*, *Mostafa*, *Nageeb*, *Saleem*, *Samir*, *Taha*.

Aswegan (116) Dutch (**Van Aswegan**): unexplained. This name is common in South Africa.

GIVEN NAMES German 4%. *Erwin*, *Gerhart*.

Aswell (101) English: variant of HASWELL.

Atallah (201) Muslim: from an Arabic personal name, *'Aṭāllāh*, literally 'gift of God'.

GIVEN NAMES Muslim 42%; French 11%. *Akram* (2), *Ali* (2), *Maroun* (2), *Nabil* (2), *Omar* (2), *Sami* (2), *Wajdi* (2), *Adnan*, *Ahmad*, *Ahmed*, *Atallah*, *Bakr*; *Antoine* (2), *Michel* (2), *Andre*, *Camil*, *Dany*, *Francois*, *Pierre*.

Atamian (164) Armenian: variant of ADAMIAN.

GIVEN NAMES Armenian 23%. *Raffi* (2), *Agavni*, *Aram*, *Araxi*, *Garabet*, *Garo*, *Haig*, *Hripsime*, *Kohar*, *Manouk*, *Nazaret*, *Nerses*.

Atcher (119) English: variant of HATCHER.

Atcheson (315) Scottish and northern Irish: variant spelling of ATCHISON.

Atchinson (195) Scottish and northern Irish: variant of ATCHISON.

Atchison (2924) Scottish and northern Irish: palatalized form of ATKINSON or ADDISON, each a patronymic from one of the many medieval pet forms of ADAM, for example *Atty*, *Addie*, and (with the diminutive suffix *-kin*) *Atkin*, *Aitkin*, and *Adkin*.

Atchley (2365) English: habitational name from Atchley in Shropshire.

Aten (721) Frisian, Dutch, and North German: variant of ADEN.

Atencio (853) Spanish: unexplained.

GIVEN NAMES Spanish 17%. *Alfonso* (5), *Carlos* (4), *Jose* (4), *Manuel* (4), *Jesus* (3), *Ramona* (3), *Abelino* (2), *Armando* (2), *Isidoro* (2), *Marita* (2), *Pedro* (2), *Reynaldo* (2).

Ater (401) **1.** English: unexplained. **2.** German: unexplained; possibly a variant of EDER or **Ader**, from a Germanic personal name *Adheri*, composed of *adal* 'clan', 'nobility' + *heri* 'army'.

FOREBEARS Johann Georg Ater was born in about 1745–50 in Clarksburg, OH.

Ates (355) **1.** Dutch: unexplained. **2.** Filipino: unexplained.

Atha (593) Variant of Irish ATHY or English ATHEY.

Athan (114) Greek: from a short form of the personal name *Athanasios* (see ATHANAS).

GIVEN NAMES Greek 6%. *Athina*, *Vasiliki*.

Athanas (196) Greek and Albanian: from the Greek personal name *Athanasios* 'immortal'. St. Athanasius (*c.*297–373), bishop of Alexandria, was one of the most influential of the fathers of the Christian Church. He is venerated especially in the Eastern Church.

GIVEN NAMES Greek 5%. *Dinos*, *Nikolaos*, *Spiro*.

Athanasiou (104) Greek: from the genitive case of the personal name *Athanasios* (see ATHANAS). Genitive patronymics are particularly associated with Cyprus.

GIVEN NAMES Greek 35%. *Andreas* (3), *Christos* (2), *Athanasia*, *Constantine*, *Constantinos*, *Costas*, *Evangelos*, *Ioannis*, *Kostantinos*, *Kostas*, *Nikolaos*, *Panagiotis*.

Athans (175) Greek: reduced form of ATHANAS or any of the various other names derived from the personal name *Athanasios* 'immortal', for example the patronymic **Athanassopoulos**.

GIVEN NAMES Greek 7%. *Demetrios* (3), *Athanasios*, *Constantine*, *Despina*.

Athas (176) Greek: from a reduced form of the personal name *Athanasios* (see ATHANAS).

GIVEN NAMES Greek 5%. *Aristotle* (2), *Constantine*.

Athearn (172) English: unexplained. Various proposals about the origin of the name have been put forward, the most plausible being that it is a topographic name from early Middle English *atte hærn* 'at the stones' (see HERN 5).

FOREBEARS Simon Athearn (*c.*1643–1714) was one of the earliest settlers on Martha's Vineyard, MA. His family is believed to have originated in Kent, England.

Athens (183) **1.** Americanized form of Greek **Atheneos** 'Athenian' or **Athenakis**, habitational name for someone from the city of Athens. These terms were also used as nicknames for people who had spent time in Athens and liked to show off their worldliness. **2.** Americanized form of surnamed based on the Greek personal name *Athanasios* (see ATHANAS).

Atherholt (117) Americanized form of North German ADERHOLD.

Atherley (124) English (Midlands and Lancashire): topographic name for someone living 'at the clearing or meadow', Middle English *ater lee* (from Old English *lēah* 'woodland clearing'). Compare ATLEE. This name is also well established in Barbados.

GIVEN NAMES Spanish 6%. *Agustin*, *Berta*, *Raul*, *Reinaldo*, *Xiomara*.

Atherton (2575) English: habitational name from a place near Manchester named Atherton, from the Old English personal name *Æðelhere* + Old English *tūn* 'settlement'.

FOREBEARS Major-General Humphrey Atherton arrived from England in 1636, settling at Dorchester, MA, and becoming governor of the colony. Joshua Atherton (1737–1809), probably a descendant of the major-general, was an early antislavery campaigner in MA.

Athey (1185) **1.** English (mainly Yorkshire): topographic name for someone dwelling 'at the enclosure', Middle English *atte hey* (from Old English *(ge)hæg* 'enclosure'). **2.** Irish: variant of ATHY.

Athmann (115) German: elaborated form of ATER, shortened in the first part, + *man* 'man'.

Athy (108) **1.** Irish: one of the very few Irish surnames derived from a place name, namely Athy in county Kildare, Gaelic *Áth í* 'ford of the yew tree'. This was adopted by Norman settlers in Ireland in the form *de Athy*, which was re-Gaelicized as *Ataoi* and borne by one of the 'tribes of Galway', who first settled in Co. Kildare about 1300. **2.** English: variant spelling of ATHEY.

GIVEN NAME Irish 8%. *Brendan*.

Atienza (214) Spanish: habitational name from a place in Guadalajara province named Atienza.

GIVEN NAMES Spanish 46%. *Elpidio* (3), *Pedro* (3), *Roberto* (3), *Ariston* (2), *Armando* (2), *Ernesto* (2), *Ranulfo* (2), *Renato* (2), *Ricardo* (2), *Agripino*, *Agustina*, *Aissa*; *Romeo* (4), *Antonio* (2), *Albertina*, *Lorenzo*.

Atilano (210) Spanish and Portuguese: from the personal name *Atilano*, a Latinized form of the Visigothic personal name *Attila*.

GIVEN NAMES Spanish 47%. *Jose* (9), *Jesus* (3), *Luis* (3), *Enrique* (2), *Guillermo* (2), *Hilario* (2), *Juan* (2), *Manuel* (2), *Ruben* (2), *Rufino* (2), *Agustin*, *Alejandro*.

Atiyeh (128) Arabic: from a personal name based on Arabic *'aṭiyyah* 'gift', 'present'.

GIVEN NAMES Arabic 25%. *Anis* (2), *Fadi* (2), *Aboud*, *Arif*, *Aziz*, *Bassam*, *Habib*, *Hasan*, *Houda*, *Ibrahim*, *Jamil*, *Omar*.

Atkerson (170) Variant of English ATKINSON.

GIVEN NAMES German 5%. *Kurt*, *Willi*.

Atkeson (143) English: variant of ATKIN-SON.

Atkin (893) English: from the Middle English personal name *Atkin*, one of the many pet forms of ADAM. Compare Scottish AITKEN.

Atkins (16924) English: patronymic from the personal name ATKIN.

Atkinson (19001) Northern English: patronymic from the personal name ATKIN.

Atkison (278) Reduced form of English ATKINSON.

Atkisson (380) Reduced form of English ATKINSON.

Atlas (811) Jewish (Ashkenazic): ornamental name from German *Atlas* or Polish *atłas*, both meaning 'satin' (ultimately from an Arabic word meaning 'smooth'). It was probably also used as a metonymic occupational name for a merchant dealing in satin goods.
GIVEN NAMES Jewish 5%. *Aron, Hersz, Hyman, Igal, Ilan, Jakob, Meyer, Zeev.*

Atlee (156) English: topographic name for someone whose dwelling was 'by the clearing or meadow', Middle English *atte lee*. The word *lea* or *lee* (Old English *lēah*) originally meant 'wood', thence 'clearing in a wood', and, by the Middle English period, 'grassy meadow'.
FOREBEARS This is the name of a family that was prominent in Lancaster, PA, in the 18th century.

Atmore (113) English (Norfolk): topographic name from Middle English *atte more* 'at the marsh'.

Atnip (417) English: of uncertain origin; perhaps from Middle English *atte knappe* (from Old English *cnæpp* 'hill' or 'summit'), a topographic name for someone who lived at the top of a hill.

Aton (208) English: variant of EATON.

Ator (196) **1.** Dutch or German: variant of ATER. **2.** Filipino: unexplained.

Attanasio (420) Italian: from a medieval personal name, Latin *Athanasius*, Greek *Athanasios* 'immortal'. St. Athanasius (*c.* 297–373), bishop of Alexandria, was one of the most influential of the fathers of the Christian Church. He is venerated especially in the Eastern Church.
GIVEN NAMES Italian 14%. *Salvatore* (4), *Angelo* (2), *Carmine* (2), *Pasquale* (2), *Sal* (2), *Cosimo, Enrico, Filomena, Franco, Guido, Luigi.*

Attar (162) Muslim (**Aṭṭār**): occupational name from Arabic *aṭṭār* 'perfumer'.
GIVEN NAMES Muslim 44%. *Adnan* (4), *Mohamad* (3), *Monzer* (3), *Ahmad* (2), *Ghassan* (2), *Sana* (2), *Wahib* (2), *Abdullah, Ammar, Essa, Farouk, Faten.*

Attard (239) **1.** Maltese: variant of Italian ATTARDO. **2.** English: of uncertain origin, perhaps a topographic name for someone living 'at the hard'. The noun *hard*, in Essex and elsewhere, denotes a short causeway leading from the shore into the

sea, used by fishermen. Alternatively, the reference may have been to an area of firm ground in a marshy area.
GIVEN NAMES French 6%. *Renald* (2), *Emanuelle, Pascal; Carmel* (2), *Sal.*

Attardo (164) Italian: from the medieval personal name *Attardo*, of Germanic origin.
GIVEN NAMES Italian 20%. *Angelo* (3), *Salvatore* (3), *Ciro* (2), *Antonio, Corrado, Dino, Giuseppi, Luigi, Pasquale.*

Attaway (1165) English: topographic name from Middle English *atte weye* 'by the road', or a habitational name for someone from Atway or Way, both in Devon. The word *way* (Old English *weg*) was the usual term for a road in Old and Middle English, as opposed to a *stræt* 'paved road' (usually a Roman road). The term *rād* or *road*, originally meaning 'act of riding', 'outing on horseback', did not come to mean 'highway' until Shakespeare's time.

Atteberry (831) English: topographic name from Middle English *atte bery*. This generally denoted a servant 'at the manor house', but the Middle English word *bery* also meant 'castle' or 'stronghold'. In form it is from Old English *byrig*, dative singular of *burh* 'fortress' or 'fortified town'. (The nominative case gave rise to the Middle English word *burgh* 'borough', 'town'; compare BURROUGHS and BURY.)

Attebery (366) Variant of English ATTE-BERRY.

Attebury (157) English: variant of ATTE-BERRY.

Atterberry (467) English: from Middle English *at ther bery* 'at the manor house', a slightly older form of ATTEBERRY. The *-ter-* spelling represents a survival into early Middle English of *þære*, Old English feminine dative of *se* 'the'.

Atterbury (312) English: variant of ATTER-BERRY.

Attia (190) **1.** Arabic: variant of ATIYEH. **2.** Jewish (Sephardic): from Arabic *'aṭiyyah* 'gift', 'present'; most likely a calque of a Jewish personal name with a similar meaning in Hebrew (for example, NATHAN, JONATHAN, or NATHANIEL).
GIVEN NAMES Arabic 55%; French 8%; Jewish 5%. *Mohamed* (4), *Safwat* (4), *Ednan* (3), *Fouad* (3), *Emad* (2), *Khaled* (2), *Mahmoud* (2), *Mohsen* (2), *Ramsis* (2), *Tarek* (2), *Ahamed, Ahmed; Michel* (3), *Andre, Gilles, Jacques, Monique, Sylvie; Anat* (2), *Arie, Meir, Shlomo, Yossi, Zvi.*

Attias (125) Jewish (Middle Eastern): probably a ornamental name from Arabic *'aṭiyyah* 'gift', 'present'. Compare Arabic ATIYEH.
GIVEN NAMES Jewish 16%; French 7%; Spanish 7%. *Amram, Avraham, Haim, Moises, Moshe, Nissim; Chantal, Prosper, Thierry; Rafael* (2), *Reina* (2).

Attig (207) German: from a short form of a Germanic personal name formed with Old

High German *adal* 'noble'. Compare ADDICKS.

Attkisson (168) Altered form of English ATKINSON.

Attridge (239) English: ostensibly a topographic name for someone dwelling 'at the ridge', but in most if not all cases actually a derivative of the Middle English personal name *Atteriche*, Old English *Æðelrīc* (see ETHERIDGE).

Attwood (360) English: variant spelling of ATWOOD.

Atwal (102) Indian (Panjab): Sikh name of unknown meaning, based on the name of a Jat tribe.
GIVEN NAMES Indian 88%. *Ajit* (2), *Harnek* (2), *Nasib* (2), *Sukhbir* (2), *Amar, Arjun, Dilawar, Govind, Gurbax, Kewal, Lachhman, Raghbir.*

Atwater (1465) English: topographic name for someone whose dwelling was by a river or lake, Middle English *atte water* 'at the water'.
FOREBEARS This surname was established from an early date in New England. David Atwater was one of the group of settlers who founded the New Haven colony in 1638.

Atwell (3036) English: topographic name from Middle English *atte welle* 'by the spring or stream'.

Atwill (145) English: variant of ATWELL.

Atwood (6442) English: topographic name from Middle English *atte wode* 'by the wood'.

Atz (133) South German: from the Germanic personal name *Azzo* (see ACE).

Au (1585) **1.** South German, Swiss, and Austrian: topographic name from dialect *Au* 'water meadow', 'stream' (see AUE). **2.** Chinese 歐: variant of OU 1. **3.** Vietnamese: unexplained.
GIVEN NAMES Vietnamese 15%; Chinese 14%. *Hung* (7), *Long* (5), *Minh* (4), *Muoi* (3), *Phan* (3), *Phat* (3), *Vinh* (3), *Cuong* (2), *Hien* (2), *Hoa* (2), *Lam* (2), *Lan* (2); *Wing* (6), *Chi* (4), *Kin* (4), *Cheuk* (3), *Chi Wai* (3), *Chuen* (3), *Hon* (3), *Keung* (3), *Wah* (3), *Wai* (3), *Chiu* (2), *Ho* (2).

Aube (570) **1.** French (**Aubé**): from the Old French personal name *Aube*, a variant of ALBERT. This is a common surname in VT. **2.** English (of Norman origin): nickname from Old French *aube, albe* 'white' (i.e. blond), from Latin *albus*. Compare ALBIN.
GIVEN NAMES French 14%. *Lucien* (3), *Marcel* (2), *Adrien* (2), *Armand* (2), *Evariste* (2), *Alderic, Andre, Emile, Fernand, Germain, Gilles, Jeremie.*

Aubel (170) **1.** German: variant of ABEL 2. **2.** German: from a Germanic personal name composed of the elements *ōd* 'possession', 'property' + *bald* 'bold', 'strong'. **3.** French: patronymic from the nickname *Lebel* 'the handsome (one)': *(fils) à Lebel* '(son) of Lebel'. **4.** Altered spelling of Slovenian **Avbelj** or **Aubelj**, both probably of German origin, from an old personal name (see 2).

Auberry (143) English: variant spelling of AUBREY.

Aubert (561) **1.** French and English (of Norman origin): from the Old French personal name *Aubert*, a variant of ALBERT. **2.** German (Swabian): variant of ALBERT.
FOREBEARS An Aubert from Normandy, France, is recorded in New France in 1643.
GIVEN NAMES French 9%. *Armand* (2), *Marcel* (2), *Michel* (2), *Andre*, *Antoine*, *Celestine*, *Celina*, *Laurent*, *Leontine*, *Maryse*, *Phillippe*, *Remy*.

Aubertin (111) French: from a pet form of the personal name AUBERT.
GIVEN NAMES French 15%. *Andre*, *Jacques*, *Lucien*, *Rufine*, *Simonne*.

Aubin (1144) French: from the personal name *Aubin* (Latin *Albinus*, a derivative of *albus* 'white'). This was the name of several minor early Christian saints, including a famous bishop of Angers (died *c.* 554). At an early date, this name became confused with the Germanic personal name *Albuin* (see ALBIN).
FOREBEARS A bearer of the surname Aubin, from Perche, was in Ste. Famille by 1670.
GIVEN NAMES French 10%. *Lucien* (4), *Andre* (3), *Normand* (3), *Armand* (2), *Cecile* (2), *Emile* (2), *Henri* (2), *Monique* (2), *Adelard*, *Aime*, *Alcid*, *Aldege*.

Auble (281) Americanized spelling of AUBEL.

Aubrecht (103) German: variant of ALBRECHT.

Aubrey (1465) **1.** English: from the Norman and Old French personal name *Aubri*, from the Germanic personal name *Alberic*, composed of elements meaning 'elf power'. **2.** Respelling of French AUBRY.

Aubry (564) French form of AUBREY, also a variant spelling of this found in English. In French-speaking Canada, Aubry is found as a Frenchification of **O'Brennan** among the Irish who fought alongside the French against the English in the mid 18th century; they found it expedient to adopt a French identity after the defeat at the Plains of Abraham.
FOREBEARS An Aubry, also called La Brière, from Normandy, France, was recorded in Canada in 1666; another, also called Thecle, from Dublin, was married in New France in 1670.
GIVEN NAMES French 10%. *Marcel* (3), *Michel* (2), *Pierre* (2), *Emile*, *Gaston*, *Germaine*, *Jacques*, *Jean Claude*, *Jean Michel*, *Jean-Michel*, *Luce*, *Stephane*.

Aubuchon (946) French: of uncertain origin, probably from the patronymic prefix *au* (see AUCLAIR) + *buchon*, a dialect term for a woodcutter (standard French *bûcheron*).
GIVEN NAMES French 4%. *Andre* (4), *Adrien*, *Donat*, *Marcel*, *Pierre*, *Remi*.

Aubut (127) Northern French: nickname from *(l'homme) au but* '(the man) with the (long) torso', from Old French *buc*, *bu(t)* 'trunk', 'body'.
GIVEN NAMES French 24%. *Armand* (4), *Napoleon* (2), *Adelard*, *Adrien*, *Andre*, *Elphege*, *Fernand*, *Lucien*.

Auch (343) **1.** South German (common in Stuttgart): metonymic occupational name for someone who minded cattle at night, from Middle High German *uhte* 'night watch', 'night pasture', or 'time just before dawn'. **2.** Possibly also French: habitational name from the southern town of Auch.
GIVEN NAMES German 4%. *Egon*, *Hermann*, *Otto*.

Auchincloss (104) Scotland: habitational name from the lands so named in Kilmarnock parish.

Auchter (175) **1.** South German: occupational name for someone who minded cattle at night, from Middle High German *uhte* 'night watch', 'night pasture', or 'time just before dawn'. **2.** Scottish: topographic name from Gaelic *uachdar* 'upland', 'summit', or a habitational name from a place in Perthshire named with this word.

Auciello (112) Italian: nickname from *uccello* 'bird', 'cock', 'fowl', from Latin *aucellus* (see UCCELLO).
GIVEN NAMES Italian 29%. *Antonio* (3), *Alfonso* (2), *Rocco* (2), *Carmine*, *Dante*, *Domenico*, *Francesca*, *Gaetano*, *Pasqualina*, *Saverio*, *Vito*.

Auck (151) Respelling of German AUCH.

Aucker (102) Americanized form of Dutch ACKER.

Auclair (533) French: patronymic from the personal name *Clair* (see CLAIR) or the nickname LECLAIR ('the cheerful one'): *(fils) à Leclair* '(son) of Leclair'. It has also absorbed cases of *Auclerc* (from LECLERC).
FOREBEARS A bearer of the surname Auclair, from La Rochelle, is recorded in Charlesbourg in 1679.
GIVEN NAMES French 19%. *Armand* (8), *Marcel* (3), *Raoul* (3), *Andre* (2), *Fernand* (2), *Ovila* (2), *Alphonse*, *Cecile*, *Gaston*, *Germaine*, *Jacques*, *Jean-Paul*.

Aucoin (1885) French (northern and southwestern): **1.** from an Old French personal name, *Alcuin*, of Germanic origin, composed of the elements *alh* 'temple' and *win* 'friend'. This name was borne by a famous English scholar and theologian (*c.* 735–804), an influential figure at the court of Charlemagne. The surname has been assimilated by folk etymology to the French phrase *au coin* 'at the corner'. **2.** topographic name for someone who lived *au coin* 'on the corner (of a street)' or 'in a corner (of land)'.
GIVEN NAMES French 7%. *Normand* (4), *Camille* (3), *Emile* (3), *Andre* (2), *Herve* (2), *Monique* (2), *Albon*, *Angelle*, *Armand*, *Benoit*, *Chantel*, *Constant*.

Aucutt (100) English: variant of ALCOTT.

Aud (275) Variant of Scottish AULD.

Audas (153) English: variant of ALDOUS.
GIVEN NAME French 4%. *Jean-Paul*.

Aude (124) **1.** North German: from a Low German variant of *Ohde* (from *Oderik*), which in turn is a variant of the personal name ULRICH. **2.** French: from a female personal name based on the Germanic word *alda* 'old', 'elder'. *Aude la belle* was the name of the beloved of Roland in the Charlemagne romances. **3.** French: regional name from Aude department or a topographic name for someone who lived by the Aude river. **4.** Variant of AULD.

Audet (875) Southern French: nickname from Gascon dialect *audet* 'bird', variant of standard Occitan *ausèl* (modern French *oiseau*).
FOREBEARS An Audet from Poitiers is recorded in Île d'Orleans in 1670.
GIVEN NAMES French 17%. *Armand* (5), *Pierre* (4), *Alain* (2), *Alphonse* (2), *Emile* (2), *Marcel* (2), *Michel* (2), *Normand* (2), *Benoit*, *Camil*, *Donat*, *Edouard*.

Audette (1004) Respelling of French AUDET, written thus to make it clear to French speakers that the *t* is sounded.
GIVEN NAMES French 10%. *Armand* (8), *Andre* (4), *Laurent* (2), *Marcel* (2), *Normand* (2), *Pierre* (2), *Adrien*, *Alcide*, *Aurore*, *Emile*, *Fernand*, *Flore*.

Audi (150) Italian: variant of ALDI.
GIVEN NAMES Italian 5%. *Antonio*, *Guiseppe*, *Massimo*; *Essa* (2), *Aiman*, *Farid*, *Hiam*, *Issam*, *Nabila*, *Naziha*.

Audia (202) Italian: from the personal name *Alda*, feminine form of *Aldo* (see ALDI). The surname now occurs chiefly in two areas of Italy: Turin and San Giovanni in Fiore, Calabria.
GIVEN NAMES Italian 16%. *Salvatore* (5), *Domenic*, *Francesco*, *Luigi*, *Santo*.

Audibert (123) French: from the Germanic personal name *Adalberht* (see ALBERT).
GIVEN NAMES French 6%; German 4%. *Lorette*, *Philippe*.

Audino (191) Italian: from a pet form of the personal name *Audo*, a variant of *Aldo* (see ALDI).
GIVEN NAMES Italian 18%. *Rosario* (2), *Nicola*, *Salvatore*.

Audiss (107) English: variant of ALDOUS.

Audley (143) English: habitational name from Audley in Staffordshire, named from the Old English female personal name *Aldgȳth* + Old English *lēah* 'woodland clearing'.

Audrey (55) English: **1.** from the Anglo-Norman French personal name female *Audrey*, via Old French from Germanic *Aldric* 'ancient power'. Compare French AUTRY. **2.** metronymic from the Middle English personal name *Aldreda*, representing a coalescence of various Old English female personal names: *Æðelðrȳð* 'noble strength', *Ælfðrȳð* 'elf strength', and *Ealhðrȳð* 'temple strength'.

Aue (151) German: topographic name from Middle High German *ouwe* 'water meadow', 'stream' (modern German *Au(e)*), or a habitational name from any of numerous places in southern Germany and Switzerland named with this word.

GIVEN NAMES German 5%. *Maximilian, Otto.*

Auen (178) German: plural or inflected variant of AUE.

Auer (1515) German (chiefly Bavaria): topographic name for someone living by a water meadow, German *Au*, or a habitational name for someone from a place named AU or AUE.

GIVEN NAMES German 4%. *Alois* (4), *Hans* (3), *Erwin* (2), *Matthias* (2), *Siegfried* (2), *Bernd, Bernhard, Erna, Franz, Fritz, Hermann, Horst.*

Auerbach (1595) German and Jewish (Ashkenazic): habitational name from any of several places in southern Germany called Auerbach 'the stream at the water meadow'. Compare AU and BACH.

GIVEN NAMES Jewish 5%. *Hyman* (4), *Miriam* (3), *Moshe* (3), *Emanuel* (2), *Isidor* (2), *Bronia, Chaim, Faigy, Menachem, Meyer, Sol, Yechezkel.*

Aufderheide (180) German (chiefly Westphalia): topographic name for someone who lived *auf der Heide* 'on the heath'.

Aufiero (259) Italian: Neapolitan and southern variant of ALFIERI.

GIVEN NAMES Italian 16%; Spanish 7%; French 4%. *Angelo* (3), *Antonio* (2), *Carmine, Concetta, Lorenzo*; *Xavier* (3), *Alejandro*; *Alphonse, Armand.*

Aug (121) German: variant of AUGE 2.

Auge (296) **1.** French (**Augé**): southern variant of AUGER. **2.** German: nickname for someone with a defect or peculiarity of the eyes, from Middle High German *ouge* 'eye' (modern German *Auge*). **3.** German: variant of AU.

GIVEN NAMES French 6%. *Elodie* (2), *Philippe, Thierry.*

Augello (317) Italian (Campania): dialect variant of UCCELLO 'bird', hence either a nickname for a diminutive, birdlike person or an occupational name for a fowler. Compare AUCIELLO.

GIVEN NAMES Italian 21%. *Salvatore* (3), *Vito* (3), *Angelo* (2), *Carmelo* (2), *Mario* (2), *Alfonso, Carmine, Cosmo, Dominico, Filomena, Gaspare, Giuseppe, Guido, Lorenzo, Mariano, Sabino.*

Augenstein (428) German: from an altered form of the personal name *Augustin* (see AUSTIN).

GIVEN NAMES German 6%. *Helmut* (5), *Manfred* (2).

Auger (1561) **1.** French and English (of Norman origin): from the Old French personal name *Auger* or *Alger* (see ALGER). **2.** German: variant of AUER, the *g* reflect-

ing Frisian *-oog* contained in place names like Wangeroog.

FOREBEARS An Auger from Maine was in Montreal by 1653; another, from Poitou, by 1685.

GIVEN NAMES French 15%. *Armand* (8), *Andre* (5), *Gaston* (4), *Lucien* (4), *Marcel* (4), *Mederic* (3), *Normand* (3), *Raoul* (3), *Cecile* (2), *Emile* (2), *Fernand* (2), *Gaetan* (2).

Augeri (167) Italian: southern form of a personal name of Germanic origin, found in the north in the forms **Uggeri** and **Oggeri**. These names were evidently adaptations of Old French *Og(i)er*, from the Germanic personal name *Adalgari*, composed of the elements *audha-* 'wealth', 'power' + *gaira*, from *gaiza* 'lance'.

GIVEN NAMES Italian 17%. *Salvatore* (6), *Sal* (2), *Attilio, Gino, Sebastiano.*

Aughenbaugh (281) Americanized form of German ACHENBACH.

Aughinbaugh (107) Americanized form of German ACHENBACH.

Augsburger (398) German: habitational name for someone from the city of Augsburg in Bavaria, named as the city (*burg*) of the Roman Emperor *Augustus*, in whose reign it was founded.

GIVEN NAMES German 4%. *Kurt* (3), *Lorenz.*

Augspurger (248) German: variant of AUGSBURGER.

Augur (139) English: variant spelling of AUGER.

August (2190) **1.** From the German, Dutch, and Scandinavian personal name *August* (vernacular form of the classical and medieval Latin personal name AUGUSTUS) or Americanized form of French **Auguste** or some other European cognate. **2.** Translation of a European surname acquired with reference to the month of August, which was named after the Roman Emperor Augustus (63 BC–AD 14). There were various connections between the month and the surname: for example, derivation from a baptismal name given to a child or a convert who was baptized in August. August is not found as a personal name or a native surname in Britain.

Augusta (352) Italian: habitational name from Augusta in Syracuse province, Sicily.

GIVEN NAMES Italian 5%. *Vito* (3), *Gaetano*; *Americo, Aurelio, Mario, Rosita, Ruben.*

Auguste (348) French: from the personal name *Auguste*, the French vernacular form of AUGUSTUS.

GIVEN NAMES French 30%. *Andre* (2), *Jean Claude* (2), *Luce* (2), *Philippe* (2), *Yves* (2), *Altagrace, Dieuseul, Francklin, Gaston, Jacques, Jean-Claude, Jean-Marie.*

Augustin (1124) French and German: from the personal name *Augustin*, from Latin *Augustinus* (see AUSTIN).

GIVEN NAMES French 16%; German 7%. *Pierre* (6), *Andre* (2), *Fernand* (2), *Jacques* (2), *Jean Claude* (2), *Monique* (2), *Renold*

(2), *Andree, Antoine, Arsene, Celine, Dany*; *Kurt* (4), *Fritz* (3), *Gunter* (2), *Hans* (2), *Erwin, Georg, Gerda, Inge, Juergen, Klaus, Matthias, Otto.*

Augustine (4370) Americanized form of any of various European surnames from personal names derived from Latin *Augustinus* (see AUSTIN).

Augustino (102) Italian: from a derivative of Latin *Augustus* (compare AGOSTINO).

GIVEN NAMES Italian 10%. *Angelo* (2), *Mario.*

Augusto (211) Spanish and Portuguese: from a vernacular form of the Latin personal name AUGUSTUS.

GIVEN NAMES Spanish 23%. *Manuel* (5), *Fernando* (3), *Ana* (2), *Cesar* (2), *Jose* (2), *Abilio, Acacio, Arlindo, Augusto, Bernardino, Jaime, Jorge*; *Aderito, Henrique, Vasco.*

Augustson (168) Respelling of Swedish **Augustsson**, a patronymic from the personal name AUGUST.

GIVEN NAMES Scandinavian 6%. *Anders, Erik.*

Augustus (704) Humanistic re-creation of the Latin personal name *Augustus* on the basis of its medieval vernacular derivatives, principally AUGUST. The Latin name is from an adjective meaning 'venerable', from *augere* 'to increase'. Examples include German, Dutch, and Scandinavian AUGUST (though the family name does not exist in Scandinavia), French AUGUSTE, Italian AGOSTO, and Portuguese AUGUSTO. The month of August was named in honor of the Emperor Augustus (63 BC–AD 14), after whom it became conventional for Roman emperors to adopt *Augustus* as a title on their accession. The personal name became popular among early Christians, who read into it the implication that the bearer had become greater by being baptized.

Augustyn (529) Polish: from the personal name *Augustyn*, Polish form of Latin *Augustinus* (see AUGUSTINE, AUSTIN).

GIVEN NAMES Polish 7%. *Andrzej, Boguslaw, Elzbieta, Ewa, Irena, Kazimierz, Krystyna, Maciej, Mariusz, Piotr, Wieslaw, Wladyslawa.*

Augustyniak (273) Polish: patronymic or pet form from the personal name AUGUSTYN.

GIVEN NAMES Polish 11%. *Jerzy* (2), *Tadeusz* (2), *Arkadiusz, Elzbieta, Jozef, Karol, Lech, Leszek, Piotr, Wojtek.*

Aukamp (120) German (Westphalia): topographic name for someone living by an area of land by a river, from Middle High German *ouwe* 'water meadow', 'stream' + *kamp* 'field', 'domain'.

Auker (409) **1.** Americanized spelling of Dutch ACKER. **2.** English: variant of **Alker**, which has two possible origins: either from a Middle English survival of the Old English personal name *Ealhhere* meaning 'altar army'; or a habitational name from Altcar in Lancashire, named from the Celtic river name *Alt* (meaning 'muddy river') + Old Norse *kiarr* 'marsh'.

Aukerman (312) Americanized form of Dutch ACKERMAN. This was a frequent name in New Netherland in the 17th century.

Aukes (118) Dutch: unexplained.

Aul (247) German: **1.** variant of the North German personal name *Ohl*, a short form of *Aul(e)rich*, modern *Ulrich*. **2.** altered spelling of the northwestern German byname *Ahl*, which may be from a word meaning 'eel' (modern German *Ahl*) or from one denoting the shoemaker's awl (see AHL). **3.** variant spelling of **Auel**, a metonymic occupational name for a potter, from Middle High German *ûle* 'pot' (related to Latin *olla*).
GIVEN NAMES German 4%. *Aloysius, Frieda, Kurt.*

Aulbach (140) German: topographic name from a creek of this name. See also ALBACH, AULENBACH.

Auld (1148) Scottish spelling of OLD, a distinguishing epithet for the older of two bearers of the same personal name.

Auldridge (112) Probably a respelling of ALDRICH or ALDRIDGE.

Aulds (197) Scottish: patronymic or possessive from AULD.

Aulenbach (117) German: **1.** habitational name from a creek or place so named in Württemberg, where there is also a place called Aulendorf. **2.** variant of German **Allenbach** (see ALLENBAUGH).

Auletta (198) Southern Italian (Campania): habitational name from a place in Salerno province named Auletta, from a diminutive of *aula* 'sheepfold'.
GIVEN NAMES Italian 23%. *Carmine* (6), *Angelo* (2), *Egidio, Gino, Giocondo, Giovanni, Margherita, Pasquale, Salvatore.*

Aulicino (108) Southern Italian: probably from a dialect word, *aulecene* (Neapolitan) or *aulicina* (Calabrian) denoting a type of plum.
GIVEN NAMES Italian 8%. *Franco, Pasquale.*

Aulick (103) Americanized form of German **Auligk**, a habitational name from a place in Saxony so named.

Aull (426) German: habitational name from a place near Limburg in Hesse called Aull.

Ault (2992) German: variant of ALT.

Aultman (982) Americanized spelling of German ALTMANN.

Aumack (128) Probably of Dutch or German origin: see AUMICK.
GIVEN NAME German 5%. *Otto* (2).

Auman (1103) Americanized spelling of German AUMANN.

Aumann (322) German: topographic name from Middle High German *ouwe* 'water meadow', 'stream' + *man* 'man'.
GIVEN NAMES German 10%. *Kurt* (6), *Alois, Dieter, Ekkehard, Erwin, Siegfried.*

Aument (163) Americanized form of German AMEND.

Aumick (119) Probably a much altered form of the German and Dutch name EMMERICH. Compare AMICK, EMIG.

Aumiller (376) Americanized form of German **Aumüller**, from Middle High German *ouwe* 'water meadow', 'stream' + *Müller* 'miller'; as a surname it is both topographic and occupational. Aumühle is a frequent place name in various parts of Germany.

Aune (811) Norwegian: habitational name from a farm name found in several places in Norway, derived from Old Norse *auðn* 'wasteland', 'desolate place'. This became common as a habitational name in the 15th and 16th centuries when places that had been deserted as a result of the Black Death were resettled.
GIVEN NAMES Scandinavian 7%. *Bjorn* (2), *Arnt, Eilif, Erik, Juel, Knut, Knute, Selmer.*

Aung (103) Southeast Asian: unexplained.
GIVEN NAMES Southeast Asian 43%; Vietnamese 10%. *Tun* (4), *Thein* (3); *Kyaw* (8), *Soe* (5), *Khin* (2), *Chan, Maung, Sein; Than* (4), *Tin* (2); *Myo* (3).

Aungst (452) Respelling of German ANGST.

Aupperle (178) German: Swabian variant of **Auberle**, from a pet form of ABEL. See also ABERLE and ALBERT.

Aurand (705) French (Huguenot): variant of French **Auran**, which is probably of Germanic origin.
FOREBEARS According to family tradition, the Huguenot family of this name which eventually settled in the U.S. fled from France to Holland to escape religious persecution, and then moved to Germany in the 17th century before coming to North America.

Aurelio (244) Italian and Spanish: from a personal name derived from the Roman family name *Aurelius*, earlier *Auselios*, said to be of Sabine origin.
GIVEN NAMES Italian 19%; Spanish 9%; French 4%. *Salvatore* (3), *Marco* (2), *Ciriaco, Domenic, Emidio, Ernesto, Gino, Romeo, Santo; Jose* (2), *Aida, Alicia, Carmelito, Cirilo, Froilan, Hilario, Julio, Luis, Mamerto; Pierre, Reynald.*

Auricchio (128) Italian (mainly Naples): nickname from a dialect variant of *orecchio* 'ear' (Latin *auricula*).
GIVEN NAMES Italian 18%. *Carmine* (2), *Angelo, Ciro, Ferdinando, Francesca, Salvatore, Veto.*

Aurich (147) German: habitational name from a place in East Friesland named Aurich.
GIVEN NAMES German 5%. *Hans, Heinz, Sieg.*

Auriemma (279) Italian (Naples): from an old female personal name composed of the elements *aur(o)* 'gold' + *gemma* 'gem' (*iemma* in southern dialects).

GIVEN NAMES Italian 17%. *Angelo* (4), *Antonio* (2), *Carmine* (2), *Salvatore* (2), *Donato, Geno, Luigi, Sal, Vincenzo.*

Aurigemma (124) Southern Italian: variant of AURIEMMA.
GIVEN NAME Italian 9%. *Pasquale.*

Aurilio (103) Italian: variant of AURELIO.
GIVEN NAMES Italian 17%. *Carmel, Erminio, Marco, Paolo, Sal, Valentino.*

Auringer (115) German: **1.** habitational name for someone from Auringen in Hesse. **2.** Germanized form of a Slavic topographic name, from Sorbian or Czech *jawor* 'maple tree', found as such among the Salzburg emigrants in East Prussia.

Aurora (172) Indian: see ARORA.
GIVEN NAMES Indian 34%. *Narain* (2), *Amrit, Ashok, Deepak, Dinesh, Gopi, Manish, Meena, Navneet, Om, Pankaj, Rajeev.*

Aus (156) Variant spelling of Scandinavian AAS.
GIVEN NAMES Scandinavian 9%. *Alf, Dagny, Erik.*

Ausborn (163) North German (especially Hamburg): from the medieval personal name *Osbern*, from Germanic *ans* '(heathen) god' + *bero* 'bear'.

Ausbrooks (161) Variant of English ALSOBROOK.

Ausburn (223) Altered form of German AUSBORN or English OSBORNE.

Ausherman (175) Altered form of German **Aschermann**, an occupational name for someone who prepared ash for use in making glass or soap. Compare ASCHENBRENNER.

Auslander (244) German (especially Baden) and Jewish (Ashkenazic): literally 'foreigner' (Middle High German *ûzlender*), a byname bestowed on a newcomer to a district or on a farmer who cultivated land outside a community's bounds.
GIVEN NAMES Jewish 7%; German 4%. *Hyman, Meyer, Orli, Shalom.*

Ausley (235) English: probably a variant of OWSLEY or HORSLEY.

Ausman (257) **1.** German (**Ausmann**): from Middle High German *ûzman* 'outsider', 'stranger', hence a byname for a newcomer to a district. **2.** Americanized form of German **As(s)mann** (see ASMAN).

Ausmus (480) Variant of Dutch, North German, and Danish ASMUS.

Aust (665) German: from a reduced form of AUGUST or AUGUSTIN.
GIVEN NAMES German 4%. *Dietmar, Erwin, Gerhard, Gunter, Jurgen, Kurt, Rudi, Willi.*

Austad (293) Norwegian: habitational name from any of several places in Norway named Austad. The second element is *stad* (from Old Norse *staðr* 'farmstead', 'dwelling'); the first can be, among other things, from the Old Norse personal names *Auði* or *Ǫlvir*.
GIVEN NAMES Scandinavian 7%. *Knut, Steinar.*

Austell (161) **1.** Respelling of German **Austel**, from a pet form of AUGUST. **2.** English: possibly a variant of ASTLE. There is a place in Cornwall called St. Austell (from the dedication of its church to a certain St. Austol), but this is unlikely to be the source of the surname.

Austen (325) **1.** English: variant spelling of AUSTIN, associated chiefly with southeastern England, especially Kent. **2.** German: from a reduced form of the personal name AUGUSTIN.

Auster (161) German: variant of OSTER, a topographic name for someone living to the east of a settlement.

Austerman (125) German (**Austermann**): Westphalian variant of OSTERMANN.

Austgen (106) German (Saarland) and French (Alsace–Lorraine): unexplained.

Austill (163) See AUSTELL.

Austin (38911) **1.** English, French, and German: from the personal name *Austin*, a vernacular form of Latin *Augustinus*, a derivative of AUGUSTUS. This was an extremely common personal name in every part of Western Europe during the Middle Ages, owing its popularity chiefly to St. Augustine of Hippo (354–430), whose influence on Christianity is generally considered to be second only to that of St. Paul. Various religious orders came to be formed following rules named in his honor, including the 'Austin canons', established in the 11th century, and the 'Austin friars', a mendicant order dating from the 13th century. The popularity of the personal name in England was further increased by the fact that it was borne by St. Augustine of Canterbury (died *c.* 605), an Italian Benedictine monk known as 'the Apostle of the English', who brought Christianity to England in 597 and founded the see of Canterbury. **2.** German: from a reduced form of the personal name AUGUSTIN.
FOREBEARS This was the name of a merchant family that became well established in eastern MA in the 17th century, notably in Charlestown. Richard Austin came from England and landed at Boston in 1638, and his son Anthony was clerk of Suffield, CT, in 1674. The surname is very common in England as well as America; this Richard Austin was only one of a number of bearers who brought it to North America.
In 1821 Stephen F. Austin (1793–1836), born in Austinville VA, founded the first Anglo colony in TX.

Auston (158) English: variant spelling of AUSTIN.

Austria (227) **1.** Spanish: ethnic name for someone from Austria. **2.** Americanized or Latinized form of German **Österreich(er)** 'Austria(n)'.
GIVEN NAMES Spanish 38%. *Virgilio* (4), *Ramon* (3), *Roberto* (3), *Alfredo* (2), *Eduardo* (2), *Jaime* (2), *Jesus* (2), *Almario*,

Amado, Anastacio, Angelito, Arsenio; Antonio, Federico, Rizalino.

Auten (1082) Americanized form of Dutch or German ADEN.

Autenrieth (112) South German: topographic name from Middle High German *ūhte* 'night pasture' + *riet* 'wet land', or a habitational name from any of several places called Autenried, notably in Bavaria.

Autery (121) Variant spelling of English or French AUTRY.

Auth (409) German: from a short form of any of the numerous Germanic personal names formed with *od-* 'possession' (Old High German *ōt*), as for example *Othmar* and OTTO.

Authement (441) French: of uncertain origin. It may be an Alsatian name derived from a Frenchified form of German HAUPTMANN 'captain'. This is a common Louisiana surname, dating from around 1800, when the first settlers arrived from Provence.
GIVEN NAMES French 7%. *Gervais* (2), *Armand, Fernand, Raoul.*

Authier (177) French: from an old name of Germanic origin, formed with either *aud(a)* 'property', 'riches' or *ald(a)* 'old', 'wise' + *hari* 'army'. See also ALTIERI.
GIVEN NAMES French 11%. *Camille, Fernand, Gabrielle.*

Autin (338) French: from the personal name *Autin*, a vernacular form of Latin *Augustinus* (see AUSTIN). In French this name is a homophone of *Hautin* 'haughty' and *Hottin* 'maker or bearer of baskets'.
GIVEN NAMES French 7%. *Alphonse, Andre, Armand, Camille, Celina, Etienne, Eves, Kearney, Maxime, Octa.*

Autio (215) Finnish: topographic name from *autio* 'uninhabited', 'abandoned', denoting a farm or field that had fallen into disuse. In northern Finland the word means 'spacious', 'wide' and is a frequent place name; there are also farms so named in eastern areas, which gave rise to the surname. It spread to the south with the name conversion movement in the 19th and early 20th centuries.
GIVEN NAMES Finnish 9%; Scandinavian 5%. *Eino* (2), *Ahti, Antti, Sulo, Waino; Erik.*

Auton (265) **1.** English: variant spelling of the habitational name **Aughton**, from any of three places, in Lancashire, East and South Yorkshire, named Aughton, from Old English as *āc* 'oak' + *tūn* 'settlement'. **2.** Possibly French: there are several places in France named Authon and it could be a habitational name from any of these.

Autrey (1345) Variant spelling of English and French AUTRY 1.

Autry (2884) **1.** French and English: habitational name from any of the places in France named Autrey or Autry. **2.** French: from the Old French personal name *Audry*, from Germanic *Aldric* 'ancient power'. There are also places in Allier, Ardennes,

and Loiret (at least) bearing this name; it could be a habitational name from any of them.

Auvenshine (106) Americanized form of German OBENCHAIN.

Auvil (342) Probably an Americanized form of German AUBEL or **Auwel**, a habitational name from a place in the Rhineland called Auwel.
FOREBEARS This name was common in WV in the 18th century.

Auxier (540) French: regional name for someone from Auxerre.

Au Yeung (233) Chinese 欧阳: variant spelling of OU YANG.
GIVEN NAMES Chinese 31%; Vietnamese 7%. *Ho* (5), *Ching* (2), *Keung* (2), *Kwan* (2), *Tat* (2), *Wing* (2), *Yau* (2), *Cheung, Chi Hung, Chi Sing, Chiu, Fung Yee; Nghi* (2), *Anh Kim, Hung.*

Auzenne (266) French: together with the variants **Ozenne** and **Ozanne**, this is a Louisiana name. The progenitor seems to have spelled it *Ozanne*, and to have come from St. Lo, Normandy, France, in 1726. This form would suggest a derivation from the medieval female personal name *Hosanna*.
GIVEN NAMES French 7%. *Adrien, Anatole, Antoine, Leonce.*

Avakian (423) Armenian: patronymic from classical Armenian *awag*, literally 'first', 'greatest'. This was used as a personal name, usually for a firstborn son. Compare German *Max*, from Latin *maximus* 'greatest'. It was also an occupational name for a priest.
GIVEN NAMES Armenian 33%. *Sarkis* (5), *Armen* (4), *Avak* (3), *Anahid* (2), *Arra* (2), *Avadis* (2), *Hagop* (2), *Haig* (2), *Hovsep* (2), *Vahe* (2), *Vartan* (2), *Anoush.*

Avallone (480) Southern Italian: topographic name for someone who lived in a deep valley, from *vallone* 'deep valley', 'gorge' (augmentative of *valle* 'valley'), with initial *a* probably acquired by reinterpretation of *da vallone* 'from or at (the) gorge' as *d'avallone.*
GIVEN NAMES Italian 15%. *Cesare* (2), *Ennio* (2), *Pasquale* (2), *Angelo, Antonino, Gennaro, Matteo, Nicola, Oreste, Rocco, Salvatore, Valentino.*

Avalos (2463) Spanish (**Ávalos**): habitational name from Ábalos, a place near Haro in Soria province, on the edge of the Basque country. A Basque origin of the place name has been suggested, involving the stem *abar-* 'kermes oak', but this is highly conjectural.
GIVEN NAMES Spanish 52%. *Jose* (90), *Juan* (41), *Jesus* (34), *Luis* (26), *Francisco* (21), *Carlos* (18), *Javier* (17), *Roberto* (15), *Manuel* (14), *Ricardo* (13), *Fernando* (12), *Pedro* (12).

Avans (136) **1.** Probably a variant of Welsh EVANS. **2.** Possibly Latvian, from a dialect form of *auns* 'ram', 'wether'.

Avant (1612) English (Devon): variant spelling of AVENT.

Avants (308) Perhaps a variant of English AVENT.
FOREBEARS Johannes Avants is recorded in MD in 1745.

Avara (130) **1.** Origin unidentified; perhaps a variant of English AVERY. **2.** Italian: feminine form of **Avaro**.

Avary (100) English: variant spelling of AVERY.

Ave (103) **1.** French (also **Avé**): from Old French *havet* 'hook', 'pick', hence a metonymic occupational name for someone who made picks or worked with a pick. **2.** probably also Galician: either from a river name or from *ave* 'bird'.
GIVEN NAMES Spanish 7%; German 5%; Dutch 4%. *Erlinda, Melanio, Purita, Ruperto; Kurt* (2); *Willem*.

Avedisian (217) Armenian: patronymic from the personal name *Awetik'*, 'good news', a calque on Greek *Evangelos* (see EVANGELISTA).
GIVEN NAMES Armenian 17%. *Avedis* (2), *Haig* (2), *Vahan* (2), *Ara, Aram, Aris, Armen, Armik, Gayane, Harutiun, Herand, Mihran*.

Avelar (512) Portuguese: topographic name from *avelar* 'hazel grove', or a habitational name from any of various places named with this word.
GIVEN NAMES Spanish 53%; Portuguese 12%. *Jose* (25), *Luis* (8), *Juan* (7), *Manuel* (7), *Jesus* (6), *Francisco* (5), *Ruben* (5), *Alfredo* (4), *Carlos* (4), *Arturo* (3), *Efrain* (3), *Guillermo* (3); *Joaquim*.

Avelino (106) Spanish and Portuguese: from the personal name *Avelino*, which was borne by Saint Andrea Avellino and is taken from the city of Avellino in Campania, Italy.
GIVEN NAMES Spanish 51%. *Demetrio* (2), *Jose* (2), *Juana* (2), *Ricardo* (2), *Consuelo, Francisco, Gaspar, Guadalupe, Hilario, Horacio, Jaime, Josefina*.

Avella (245) **1.** Italian: habitational name from a place named Avella, in Avellino province, Campania; it is an ancient settlement which was named *Abella* in Latin. **2.** Catalan, Galician and Spanish: variant of ABELLA.
GIVEN NAMES Italian 18%; Spanish 9%. *Nicola* (3), *Angelo* (2), *Gino* (2), *Francesco, Pietro, Rocco; Francisco* (2), *Adriana, Alberto, Amparo, Gerardo, Jaime, Javier, Josue*.

Avellaneda (138) Spanish: habitational name from any of three places called Avellaneda (in Ávila, Toledo, and Biscay), from *avellana* 'hazel' + *-eda* 'agglomeration', 'mass'.
GIVEN NAMES Spanish 61%. *Jose* (4), *Catalina* (2), *Eduardo* (2), *Francisco* (2), *Ignacio* (2), *Manuel* (2), *Miguel* (2), *Rafael* (2), *Ramon* (2), *Alberto, Alvaro, Ambrocio; Marco* (3), *Fausto, Rino*.

Avellino (247) Italian: habitational name from Avellino in Campania, from Latin *Abellinum*.
GIVEN NAMES Italian 23%. *Aldo, Carlo, Dino, Luigi, Rocco, Salvatore, Severino, Silverio, Victorio, Vincenzo*.

Aven (240) **1.** Scandinavian: unexplained. **2.** English: variant spelling of AVON. **3.** German: patronymic from the Frisian personal name *Ave*. The surname is frequent in the areas of Oldenburg and Jeverland. **4.** Dutch: metonymic occupational name from Middle Dutch *haven* 'pot'. **5.** Americanized form of French **Avenne** or **Avoine**, literally 'oats', hence a metonymic occupational name for a grain grower or merchant.
GIVEN NAMES Scandinavian 4%. *Jarl* (2), *Lennart*.

Avena (224) **1.** Spanish and Italian: metonymic occupational name for a grain grower or merchant, from *avena* 'oats', 'oatmeal' (Latin *avena*). **2.** Italian: habitational name from a place in Calabria called Avena.
GIVEN NAMES Spanish 22%; Italian 19%. *Jose* (3), *Alberto, Ana, Arturo, Blanca, Domingo, Felipe, Francisco, Gerado, Gerardo, Gilberto, Guillermo; Angelo* (3), *Rocco* (3), *Antonio* (2), *Carmine* (2), *Giuseppe* (2), *Leonardo* (2), *Vito* (2), *Carmela, Ettore, Salvatore, Vincenzo*.

Avendano (331) Spanish (**Avendaño**): habitational name from Abendaño in Araba province, Basque Country. The place name is of obscure, probably Basque, origin.
GIVEN NAMES Spanish 54%. *Luis* (6), *Jorge* (5), *Jose* (5), *Juan* (5), *Carlos* (4), *Jesus* (4), *Enrique* (3), *Fernando* (3), *Gerardo* (3), *Mario* (3), *Ricardo* (3), *Alberto* (2); *Antonio* (2), *Donato* (2), *Eliseo* (2), *Clementina, Fausto, Geronimo, Heriberto*.

Aveni (230) Italian: either a metonymic occupational name for a seller of oats (see AVENA) or from the Latin personal name *Avenius*.
GIVEN NAMES Italian 18%. *Antonio* (2), *Domenic, Enza, Gino, Pasquale, Philomena, Vincenzo; Elva, Nestor, Ricardo, Rosario*.

Avent (692) English (of Norman origin): probably from a reduced form of the Anglo-Norman French personal name or nickname *Avenant* 'suitable' or 'handsome'.
FOREBEARS Family historians record an Isham Avent in the Carolinas in the 1760s. His father was Colonel Thomas Avent from England.

Avera (544) Origin unidentified. Probably a variant of AVERY.
FOREBEARS A Jacob Avera is recorded in Johnson Co., NC, in 1764.

Averbach (111) **1.** Jewish (eastern Ashkenazic): variant of AUERBACH. **2.** German: variant of AVERBECK, with the second ele-

ment changed into the standard German form.
GIVEN NAMES Jewish 10%. *Charna, Emanuel, Faina, Ofer*.

Averbeck (168) German (chiefly Westphalia): topographic name for someone living 'on the other side of the stream', from Middle Low German *over, aver* 'over', 'across' + *beke* 'stream'.
GIVEN NAMES German 7%. *Ernst* (2), *Heinz, Jurgen*.

Averett (965) English: variant of EVERETT.

Averette (437) Variant of English EVERETT.

Averhart (108) Probably an Americanized spelling of German EBERHARDT.
GIVEN NAME French 5%. *Celestine* (2).

Averill (1520) English: of uncertain origin. **1.** Reaney and Wilson cite 13th- and 14th-century examples such as *Richard Averil*, which they associate with the name of the month (see APRIL; the Old French word *Avrill* was taken into Middle English as *Averil* before being altered under Latin influence to *April*). **2.** As a North American surname, it may be a habitational name from Haverhill in Suffolk, which is probably named from Old English *hafri* 'oats' + *hyll* 'hill'. The traditional English pronunciation of this place name was *Have-rill*. Compare AVERY.
FOREBEARS William Averill (*c.*1590–1635) brought his family from Worcestershire, England, to VA in 1635. A different William Averill (alias Avery) came from England to Ipswich, MA, in or about 1637.

Averitt (537) Variant of English EVERETT.

Averitte (100) Variant of English EVERETT, under French influence.

Avers (250) Probably an altered form of German EVERS.

Aversa (418) Southern Italian: habitational name from Aversa in Campania.
GIVEN NAMES Italian 26%. *Angelo* (4), *Antonio* (4), *Rocco* (4), *Armando* (2), *Domenic* (2), *Giovanni* (2), *Luigi* (2), *Salvatore* (2), *Carlo, Chiara, Ciro, Cosmo, Domenico; Alfonso, Claudio, Fabio, Mario, Marisa, Olimpia, Rafael, Ruben, Tino*.

Aversano (216) Southern Italian: habitational name for a native or inhabitant of a place called AVERSA.
GIVEN NAMES Italian 27%. *Salvatore* (3), *Armando* (2), *Sal* (2), *Santi* (2), *Aniello, Edoardo, Francesco, Gaetano, Ignazio, Loredana, Nunzio, Pasquale, Raffaela*.

Avery (12920) English: from the Anglo-Norman French personal name *Auvery*, a Norman form of ALFRED. It could also be from a variant of the Anglo-Norman French personal name *Aubri* (see AUBREY). At least in the case of the original Puritan settlers in New England, there has been some confusion with AVERILL.
FOREBEARS Christopher Avery emigrated from England to Salem, MA, in or before 1630. William Avery (alias Averill) was one

of the Puritan settlers who emigrated from England to Ipswich, MA, in or about 1637.

Aves (112) English: variant of EAVES or possibly AVIS.

GIVEN NAME German 5%. *Otto* (2).

Avey (641) **1.** English (mainly East Anglia and southern counties): unexplained. **2.** Possibly a shortened form of **Mac Avey**, a variant of MCEVOY and MCVEY. **3.** Possibly an altered form of French **Hévé**. **4.** Alternatively, perhaps, an Americanized form of German EWIG.

Avila (7951) **1.** Spanish (**Ávila**): habitational name from Ávila in old Castile. Its name, first recorded in the Latin forms *Avela* and *Abulia*, is of unknown derivation and meaning. **2.** Portuguese and Galician: from **Davila**, a topographic name for someone from a town or village, *da vila*, reinterpreted as *d'Avila*.

GIVEN NAMES Spanish 47%; Portuguese 11%. *Jose* (211), *Manuel* (123), *Juan* (71), *Francisco* (69), *Luis* (67), *Jesus* (65), *Carlos* (59), *Pedro* (49), *Jorge* (48), *Miguel* (43), *Armando* (39), *Javier* (37); *Ligia* (3), *Joaquim* (2), *Guilherme*, *Henrique*, *Joao*, *Paulo*, *Vasco*.

Aviles (2109) **1.** Asturian-Leonese (**Avilés**): habitational name from Avilés, a place in Asturies on the coast west of Xixón (Gijón in Spanish). The place name is derived either from a pre-Roman cognomen, *Abilus*, or from the Latin name *Abilius*, from the place name formed with (Villa) *Abilius* + the suffix *-ensis*. **2.** Spanish: possibly also habitational name for someone from Ávila (see AVILA).

GIVEN NAMES Spanish 48%. *Jose* (58), *Juan* (40), *Carlos* (26), *Luis* (22), *Ramon* (20), *Angel* (19), *Francisco* (18), *Ana* (13), *Manuel* (13), *Jorge* (12), *Pedro* (12), *Margarita* (11); *Antonio* (16), *Carmelo* (3), *Angelo* (2), *Constantino* (2), *Lucio* (2), *Marco* (2), *Albertina*, *Annamarie*, *Carmel*, *Cira*, *Ciro*, *Clemente*.

Avilez (234) Spanish variant of Asturian-Leonese **Avilés** (see AVILES), with the ending interpreted as the patronymic suffix *-ez*.

GIVEN NAMES Spanish 47%. *Roberto* (4), *Carlos* (3), *Julio* (3), *Manuel* (3), *Raul* (3), *Alfonso* (2), *Armando* (2), *Francisco* (2), *Jose* (2), *Alba*, *Alejandro*, *Araceli*.

Avilla (281) Portuguese and Galician: variant of AVILA 1.

GIVEN NAMES Spanish 9%; Portuguese 5%. *Jose* (2), *Alberto*, *Alfredo*, *Ana*, *Avelino*, *Enrique*, *Javier*, *Luis*, *Pedro*, *Ramiro*, *Ricardo*, *Rocio*; *Fernandes*.

Avina (556) Galician (**Aviña**): probably from a topographic name for someone who lived by a vineyard, *da viña* 'from the vineyard', reinterpreted as *d'Aviña*.

GIVEN NAMES Spanish 51%. *Jose* (19), *Luis* (8), *Miguel* (8), *Jesus* (7), *Carlos* (6), *Juan* (6), *Jorge* (5), *Manuel* (5), *Pedro* (5), *Roberto* (5), *Gustavo* (4), *Rafael* (4).

Avinger (180) **1.** Americanized form of German **Ewinger**, a habitational name for someone from a place called Eubigheim in Württemberg (earlier *Ewbickein*). **2.** The surname is also said to be of Frisian origin. During the Reformation, a Frisian family named **Aebinga** moved to Switzerland, where the name changed to **Aebinger**.

Avino (128) **1.** Spanish (**Aviñó**): probably a Castilianized form of Catalan **Avinyó**, a habitational name from Avinyó in the district of El Bages in Catalonia. **2.** Spanish: habitational name from Avignon in southern France (Occitan name *Avinhon*). **3.** Southern Italian: unexplained.

GIVEN NAMES Italian 15%. *Aniello*, *Attilio*, *Carlo*; *Adolfo*, *Alfredo*, *Jorge*, *Leopoldo*, *Noemi*.

Avis (636) **1.** English: from the Norman female personal name *Avice* (Old French *Avice*, Latin *Avitia*, also found in a masculine form, *Avitius*). This is of uncertain origin, perhaps from a Celtic (Gaulish) name. **2.** French: Tanguay and Jetté have people named **Avice**, **Avisse** in Quebec from 1666. Nègre has an **Avèze** (Puy-de-Dome) also deriving from *Avitius*.

Avitabile (184) Southern Italian: apparently from *abitabile* 'habitable'; it is not clear how came to be applied as a surname.

GIVEN NAMES Italian 17%. *Pasquale* (3), *Angelo* (2), *Camillo* (2), *Alberico* (2), *Gaetano*, *Grazia*, *Guido*, *Romeo*.

Avitia (258) Spanish: from the Latin female personal name *Avitia* (see AVIS).

GIVEN NAMES Spanish 66%. *Antonio* (5), *Jose* (5), *Juan* (3), *Roberto* (3), *Salvador* (3), *Sergio* (3), *Alonso* (2), *Carlos* (2), *Cristina* (2), *Cruz* (2), *Felipe* (2), *Francisco* (2), *Javier* (2).

Avner (120) Jewish: from the biblical male given name *Avner* (see ABNER).

GIVEN NAMES Jewish 12%. *Sol* (2), *Hirsh*, *Isidor*, *Yeshaya*.

Avolio (173) Italian (mainly Naples): either a habitational name from Avolio, a minor place in Sicily, or, more likely, from Sicilian *avoliu* 'ivory', Italian *avorio*, applied as a metonymic occupational name for an ivory worker or dealer, or possibly as a nickname for someone with pale skin.

GIVEN NAMES Italian 17%. *Armando* (3), *Antonio*, *Carmine*, *Egidio*, *Gennaro*, *Guerino*, *Guido*, *Salvatore*.

Avon (174) English: possibly a habitational name from a settlement on one of the rivers or small streams called Avon or Aven. These river names derive from the Celtic word for 'river', as reflected in Welsh *afon* and Gaelic *abhainn*. The modern surname is concentrated in Somerset and Wiltshire, England, suggesting it is associated chiefly with the Avon river that rises on the Gloucester-Wiltshire border and flows through Wiltshire and Somerset into the Severn.

Avram (130) Jewish (of Slavic or Romanian origin): variant of ABRAHAM.

GIVEN NAMES Romanian 15%. *Florin* (2), *Cornel*, *Gheorghe*, *Mihai*, *Radu*, *Vasile*.

Avrett (105) Variant of English EVERETT.

Avril (115) French: from *avril* 'April' (Latin *aprilis*) (see APRIL).

GIVEN NAMES French 8%. *Franck*, *Joffre*.

Awad (743) Arabic: **1.** from a personal name based on '*awad* 'reverence', 'kindness'. **2.** occupational name from *awwad* 'lute maker' or 'lute player'. **3.** possibly also from '*awwā* 'one who compensates or indemnifies'.

GIVEN NAMES Arabic 58%. *Mohamed* (9), *Mohammed* (7), *Nabil* (6), *Ghassan* (5), *Youssef* (5), *Abdel* (4), *Ahmed* (4), *Ibrahim* (4), *Mahmoud* (4), *Samir* (4), *Ahmad* (3), *Ali* (3).

Awalt (333) Probably a respelling of German EWALD.

Awan (167) Muslim: from an Arabic personal name, probably based on *Āwān* 'times', 'seasons'.

GIVEN NAMES Muslim 89%. *Malik* (8), *Mohammad* (8), *Azhar* (6), *Muhammad* (6), *Khalid* (4), *Akhtar* (3), *Ghulam* (3), *Javed* (3), *Mushtaq* (3), *Abdul* (2), *Aftab* (2), *Amir* (2).

Awbrey (305) English: variant spelling of AUBREY.

Awe (334) German: **1.** variant of AUE. **2.** from a variant of the Frisian personal name *Ave*.

Awtrey (178) Respelling of English or French AUTRY.

Awtry (111) Respelling of English or French AUTRY.

Ax (157) German: variant of AXT.

GIVEN NAMES German 7%. *Kurt* (2), *Eberhard*.

Axe (456) **1.** English: evidently a metonymic occupational name for a woodman. A further possible origin is from the French place name element *Ax* (etymologically identical to *Aix*), from Latin *aquis* (dative or ablative plural) 'near the waters', denoting a spa. **2.** In some cases perhaps an altered form of German AXT.

FOREBEARS A George Axe is recorded in VA in 1679.

Axel (287) **1.** Scandinavian, Dutch, and North German: from the personal name *Apsel*, Danish and North German vernacular form of the Biblical name *Absolom*. As a Scandinavian surname it is a shortened form of the patronymic forms **Axelsson** or **Axelsen**. **2.** Belgian and Dutch: habitational name for someone from either of two places, Aksel in East Flanders or Axel in Zeeland.

Axelrad (157) Jewish: variant of AXELROD.

GIVEN NAMES French 6%. *Mireille*, *Mirelle*, *Mirielle*.

Axelrod (1358) Jewish (Ashkenazic): from the Yiddish personal name *Akslrod*, which is of uncertain derivation, perhaps from ALEXANDER.

GIVEN NAMES Jewish 5%. *Hyman* (2), *Rivka* (2), *Sol* (2), *Avi, Benzion, Emanuel, Myer, Yetta.*

Axelsen (184) Danish and Norwegian: patronymic form of AXEL.

GIVEN NAMES Scandinavian 17%; German 5%. *Bjorn* (2), *Nils* (2), *Knud, Knut, Niels, Per; Claus, Hans.*

Axelson (698) Swedish: patronymic form of AXEL.

GIVEN NAMES Scandinavian 7%. *Bjorn* (2), *Nils* (2), *Erik, Hilma, Lennart, Nels, Olle.*

Axford (275) English: habitational name from places in Wiltshire and Hampshire called Axford. The first is named from Old English *æsc* 'ash tree' + *ford*; the second from Old English *æsc* + *ōra* 'slope'.

Axler (113) Jewish (Ashkenazic): variant spelling of **Achsler**, an ornamental name from German *Achsel* 'shoulder'.

GIVEN NAMES French 5%; Jewish 4%. *Marcel, Patrice; Isadore.*

Axley (257) **1.** English: probably a variant of EXLEY or OXLEY. **2.** Americanized spelling of German **Echsle** or **Öchsle**, from a diminutive of Middle High German *ohse* 'ox', applied as a nickname for someone dealing with oxen (especially a plowman), or a habitational name for someone who lived at a house distinguished by the sign of an ox.

Axline (212) Americanized spelling of German **Echsl(e)in** or **Öchsl(e)in**, from a diminutive of *Ochse* 'ox', used as a nickname or house name (see AXLEY).

Axness (105) Norwegian: habitational name from any of eight farmstead named Aksnes, usually from *ask* 'ash tree' + *nes* 'promontary', 'headland'.

GIVEN NAME Scandinavian 4%. *Gudrun.*

Axon (186) English: most probably the Middle English surname *Ackeson*, a patronymic from the Middle English personal name *Acke* (Old English *Acca*). It may also be from *Anketin* or *Asketin*, Norman forms of the Old Norse personal name *Asketill* (see HASKELL), or even a variant of ASHTON.

Axsom (252) English: variant of AXSON.

Axson (120) English (Lancashire and Cheshire): variant spelling of AXON.

Axt (301) German: metonymic occupational name for a woodcutter, carpenter, or maker of axes, from Middle High German *ackes*, *axt-* 'axe'.

Axtell (1241) English and Scottish: from the Old Norse personal name *Ásketill*, composed of the elements *áss* 'god' + *ketill* 'kettle', 'helmet' (see HASKELL). This name was in use both among Scandinavian settlers in northern England and among the Normans.

Axtman (260) Respelling of German **Axtmann**, occupational name for a woodcutter, carpenter, or maker of axes, from

Middle High German *ackes*, *axt-* 'axe' + *man* 'man'.

Axton (307) English: habitational name from Axton in Kent, named from the Old English personal name *Acca* + Old English *stān* 'stone'.

Ayala (7126) Basque: habitational name or topographic name from Basque *ai* 'slope', 'hillside' + *al(h)a* 'pasture'.

GIVEN NAMES Spanish 51%. *Jose* (238), *Juan* (102), *Luis* (68), *Carlos* (67), *Manuel* (65), *Jesus* (60), *Miguel* (49), *Pedro* (46), *Francisco* (45), *Raul* (42), *Jorge* (41), *Rafael* (40).

Ayars (348) English: variant spelling of AYERS.

Aybar (194) Spanish (of Basque origin): habitational name, in most cases probably from Aibar in Navarre, but in some cases perhaps a variant of Eibar, the name of a place in Gipuzkoa. The place names are from Basque *ai* 'side', 'slope' + *ibar* 'flood plain', 'valley'.

GIVEN NAMES Spanish 51%. *Jose* (9), *Juan* (7), *Ana* (6), *Francisco* (4), *Rafael* (4), *Ramon* (3), *Alejandro* (2), *Armando* (2), *Guadalupe* (2), *Manuel* (2), *Miguel* (2), *Alfonso; Antonio, Fausto, Romeo.*

Aycock (2306) English: from a pet form of any of various personal names beginning with A-. It is generally a pet form of a pet form, i.e. from a pet form of ADAM such as *Ade* or *Aitkin* + the Middle English hypocoristic suffix *-cok* (see COCKE), which was very commonly added to personal names in Middle English; compare, for example, ADCOCK, ALCOCK, HANCOCK, WILCOCK.

Aycox (119) English: patronymic from AYCOCK.

Aydelott (245) Variant spelling of French AYDELOTTE.

Aydelotte (282) French: from the personal name *Edelot*, a pet form of any of various Old French names of Germanic origin containing the element *edel* 'noble'. American families bearing this name, as well as French families named **Aydalot**, are traceable to Gascony and Guyenne.

Aydin (125) Muslim: variant of UDDIN.

GIVEN NAMES Muslim 78%. *Ali* (4), *Metin* (3), *Ahmet* (2), *Dursun* (2), *Fatima* (2), *Hasan* (2), *Levent* (2), *Mahmut* (2), *Selahattin* (2), *Suleyman* (2), *Zeki* (2), *Abdurrahman.*

Aydt (199) German: variant spelling of EIDT.

Aye (208) **1.** German and Dutch: patronymic from a short form of a Germanic (Frisian) personal name with *agi* 'sword' as its first element. **2.** Scottish: from a shortened form of the Gaelic personal name *Adhamh* 'Adam'.

Ayer (1450) English: from Middle English *eir*, *eyer* 'heir' (Old French *(h)eir*, from Latin *heres* 'heir'). Forms such as *Richard le Heyer* were frequent in Middle English,

denoting a man who was well known to be the heir to the main property in a particular locality, either one who had already inherited or one with great expectations.

Ayers (13852) English: derivative of AYER. The *-s* most probably represents a trace of the Latin nominative singular in *heres* 'heir', but it may also signify the son or servant of someone known as 'the heir', i.e. someone who was heir to some great estate.

Ayler (143) English: variant spelling of AYLOR.

Ayles (176) English (Hampshire and Dorset): of uncertain origin, perhaps representing a patronymic from a personal name such as those that appeared in Old English as *Ægel* and *Ædel* (see AYLESWORTH and AYLING).

Aylesworth (385) English: habitational name from a place in Cambridgeshire named Ailsworth, from an Old English personal name *Ægel* + Old English *worþ* 'enclosure'.

Ayling (238) English: from Old English *æðeling* 'prince', a derivative of *æðel* 'noble'. This word was commonly used as a byname among Anglo-Saxons before and after the Norman Conquest, and was in use for a time as a personal name. The surname derives from this use rather than from a nickname; still less does it denote descent from noble Anglo-Saxon blood.

Aylor (650) **1.** English: occupational name from Old French *aillier* 'garlic seller', from *ail* 'garlic' (from Latin *allium*). **2.** Americanized spelling of German EHLER or **Öhler** (see OHLER).

Aylsworth (268) Variant spelling of English AYLESWORTH.

Aylward (906) English: from a Middle English personal name, *Ailward*, representing a coalescence of at least two Old English names: *Æðelweard* 'noble guardian' and *Ælfweard* 'elf guardian'.

Aymond (322) French or English (of Norman origin): from the Old French personal name *Aimon* (see HAMMOND).

GIVEN NAMES French 5%. *Cecile, Emile, Octave, Silton, Theophile.*

Aynes (161) Probably from the Welsh personal name *Einws*, a pet form of *Einion* (see HAYNES).

Ayo (218) Spanish: occupational or status name, from *ayo* 'tutor', 'guardian', probably from a Visigothic word *hagja* 'attendant', 'steward'.

GIVEN NAMES Spanish 6%. *Luis* (3), *Eulalia, Fernando, Jesus, Jose, Juan, Rolando, Teresita, Valeriano.*

Ayon (313) French and Spanish: topographic name from *hayon*, a diminutive of *haie* 'hedge'. See also HAY.

GIVEN NAMES Spanish 48%. *Jose* (9), *Carlos* (5), *Francisco* (4), *Efren* (3), *Guadalupe* (3), *Juan* (3), *Miguel* (3), *Consuelo* (2), *Manuel* (2), *Ramon* (2), *Rosario* (2),

Salvador (2); *Antonio* (4), *Lorenzo* (3), *Clemente, Erminio, Santo.*

Ayoob (107) Muslim: variant spelling of AYOUB.

GIVEN NAMES Muslim 9%. *Ameen, Kalil, Maqsood, Mohammad, Mohammed, Naseem, Nemer.*

Ayotte (1238) Altered spelling (common in Quebec) of the French occupational name **Aillot** or **Hayot** 'garlic seller', from *ail* 'garlic'.

GIVEN NAMES French 8%. *Lucien* (3), *Normand* (2), *Pierre* (2), *Adelard, Alcide, Alphonse, Alyre, Andre, Camille, Carmelle, Cecile, Fernand.*

Ayoub (644) Muslim: from Arabic Ayyūb, the Arabic form of the Hebrew (Biblical) name *Iyōb* 'Job'. In the suras he is regarded as a messenger of Allah. This name is borne by Christians (in Lebanon and elsewhere) as well as by Muslims. The spread of the name among Muslims is partly due to the fame of Ṭalāḥ ad-Dīn Yūsuf ibn Ayyūb (Saladin), founder of the Ayyubid dynasty.

GIVEN NAMES Muslim 40%. *Mohamed* (6), *Samir* (6), *Nabil* (5), *Kamal* (4), *Ahmed* (3), *Fadi* (3), *Fouad* (3), *Issa* (3), *Nader* (3), *Selim* (3), *Akram* (2), *Ali* (2).

Ayre (325) English: variant spelling of AYER.

Ayres (4554) English: variant spelling of AYERS.

Ayscue (432) Variant of English ASKEW.

Ayson (108) Filipino: unexplained.

GIVEN NAMES Spanish 27%; Italian 7%. *Reginaldo* (2), *Alejandro, Erlinda, Faustino, Herminio, Jose, Juanita, Milagros, Monico, Pedro, Raul, Rodolfo; Dante* (2), *Fausto, Severiano.*

Aytes (140) English (county Durham): unexplained.

Ayub (112) Muslim: variant spelling of AYOUB.

GIVEN NAMES Muslim 63%; Spanish 8%. *Mohammad* (7), *Mohammed* (4), *Muhammad* (4), *Abdul* (3), *Salim* (3), *Muhammed* (2), *Nasim* (2), *Afshan, Ali, Ayaz, Choudhry, Faisal; Carlos* (2), *Alonso, Eduardo, Felipe, Jorge, Juan, Otilia, Pablo, Ricardo.*

Ayvazian (111) Armenian: patronymic from Turkish *ayvaz* 'footman', 'manservant'. This was also used as a given name; it is the name of the beautiful youth in the Köroğlu epic.

GIVEN NAMES Armenian 37%; Dutch 4%. *Haig* (2), *Anait, Antranik, Arax, Armen, Arpine, Arsen, Babken, Berge, Hagop, Harout, Nerses; Henrik, Laurens.*

Azad (180) Muslim (mainly Iranian): from a status name or personal name based on Persian *āzād* 'free man' (as opposed to a slave).

GIVEN NAMES Muslim 80%. *Abul* (21), *Mohammed* (6), *Mohamed* (4), *Abdul* (3), *Ali* (3), *Ghulam* (2), *Hamid* (2),

Mohammad (2), *Nasser* (2), *Abbas, Abdolreza, Abdullah.*

Azam (154) Muslim: variant spelling of AZZAM.

GIVEN NAMES Muslim 88%. *Mohammad* (22), *Mohammed* (13), *Syed* (6), *Muhammad* (5), *Khalid* (3), *Abdool* (2), *Ahmad* (2), *Ahmed* (2), *Ali* (2), *Farooq* (2), *Kazi* (2), *Mohamed* (2).

Azar (989) **1.** Iranian: from a personal name based on Persian *azer* 'fire', also denoting the ninth month of Persian solar year. **2.** Ethnic name for an Azeri. The Azeri people (so named from Persian *azer* 'fire', because they were originally fire worshipers) are Shiite Muslims who mostly live in Azerbaijan, on the Caspian Sea to the north of Iran.

GIVEN NAMES Muslim 21%. *Khalil* (5), *Nabil* (4), *Sami* (4), *Basem* (3), *Fouad* (3), *Ibrahim* (3), *Marwan* (3), *Mohammad* (3), *Ahmad* (2), *Amin* (2), *Aziz* (2), *Hamid* (2).

Azarian (155) Armenian: patronymic, apparently from Turkish *Azar* 'March', but more probably from a first name *Azaria*, from Hebrew *'Azariāh* 'God's help'.

GIVEN NAMES Armenian 24%. *Aghavni, Anahid, Antranig, Arshag, Avadis, Avanes, Bedros, Garo, Hagop, Medik, Mihran, Ohannes.*

Azbell (241) See ASBELL.

Azbill (224) See ASBELL.

Azcona (106) Castilianized form of Basque **Azkona**, a habitational name from Azkona in Navarre province, Basque Country, so named from Basque *azko(i)n* 'badger'.

GIVEN NAMES Spanish 48%. *Jose* (3), *Manuel* (3), *Ana* (2), *Carlos* (2), *Ramon* (2), *Alejandro, Alfredo, Andres, Arturo, Asela, Cruz, Ernesto.*

Azer (119) Muslim: ethnic name for an Azeri, a member of a Shiite Muslim people living mostly in Azerbaijan, on the Caspian Sea to the north of Iran.

GIVEN NAMES Muslim 45%. *Samir* (4), *Ashraf* (2), *Medhat* (2), *Morcos* (2), *Youssef* (2), *Anwar, Atef, Emad, Girgis, Kamilia, Mervat, Mounir.*

Azevedo (1641) Portuguese: topographic name for someone whose dwelling was by a clump of holly bushes. Compare ACEVEDO.

GIVEN NAMES Spanish 15%; Portuguese 14%. *Manuel* (42), *Jose* (20), *Mario* (6), *Fernando* (5), *Carlos* (4), *Alberto* (3), *Luis* (3), *Adelino* (2), *Alvarino* (2), *Alvaro* (2), *Anselmo* (2), *Claudio* (2); *Joao* (3), *Paulo* (3), *Agostinho* (2), *Joaquim* (2), *Aderito* (2), *Albano, Damiao, Duarte, Guilherme, Henrique, Ligia, Marcio.*

Azimi (131) Muslim: from the Arabic adjectival form of *'aẓīm* 'mighty', 'magnificent', 'glorious'.

GIVEN NAMES Muslim 75%; Indian 4%. *Abdul* (4), *Said* (4), *Amir* (3), *Mohammad* (3), *Ahmad* (2), *Azam* (2), *Kaveh* (2),

Mojgan (2), *Abdullah, Alireza, Amin, Assad; Mani* (2), *Asis.*

Aziz (871) Muslim (widespread throughout the Muslim world): from the Arabic personal name *'Abd al-'Azīz* 'servant of the mighty' or 'servant of the beloved'. *Al-'Azīz* 'the Invincible' or 'the Beloved' is an attribute of Allah. *Al-'Azīz* (955–996) was the fifth Fatimid khalif of Egypt (975–996), noted among other things for his religious tolerance.

GIVEN NAMES Muslim 71%. *Abdul* (30), *Mohammad* (11), *Mohammed* (11), *Ahmed* (10), *Khalid* (6), *Tariq* (6), *Abdel* (5), *Abdullah* (5), *Amir* (4), *Aziz* (4), *Rahmat* (4), *Salim* (4).

Azizi (184) **1.** Muslim: Arabic family name (*'Azīzī*), a derivative of *'Azīz* (see AZIZ), denoting a descendant or associate of *'Azīz*. **2.** Jewish (Sephardic): adoption of the Arabic name.

GIVEN NAMES Muslim 78%; Jewish 4%. *Abdul* (10), *Mohammad* (5), *Mehrdad* (4), *Said* (3), *Abdullah* (2), *Fawzia* (2), *Ghulam* (2), *Mohammed* (2), *Pedram* (2), *Sultan* (2), *Abbas, Abdul Hakim; Mayer* (3), *Hadassa, Sima.*

Azlin (106) Variant spelling of English or Swedish ASLIN.

Azua (109) Basque: variant of **Asua**, a habitational name from Asua, in Biscay province, or possibly a topographic name from Basque *(h)artsu* 'stony'.

GIVEN NAMES Spanish 53%. *Agustin* (2), *Alfonso* (2), *Fernando* (2), *Jose* (2), *Rodolfo* (2), *Alejandro, Alicia, Amado, Armando, Arturo, Bibiano, Carlos.*

Azuma (104) Japanese: an archaic word used to mean 'east', originally applied to the fifteen northern and eastern provinces of Japan. According to legend, the hero Prince Yamatotakeru, on his mission to conquer the eastern barbarians, was badly homesick and cried 'Azuma wa ya!' ('Oh, my wife!') when he viewed the Kantō Plain from a high pass, and this incident gave the name to the region. The family name is most commonly written with the character for 'east' (*higashi*), but some families write it using different characters phonetically. The name *Azuma* is found mostly in western Japan and the Ryūkyū Islands, while the name HIGASHI is more common along the southeastern seaboard.

GIVEN NAMES Japanese 63%. *Akira* (2), *Hiroko* (2), *Shoji* (2), *Yoichi* (2), *Chieko, Chika, Eiko, Fumiko, Hideaki, Kenji, Koichi, Kyoichi.*

Azure (293) Origin unidentified. Evidently from French *azure* 'blue', but the details of the origin as a family name are unclear. There are several Azure families living on the Turtle Mountain Chippewa Reservation.

Azzam (126) Muslim: from an Arabic personal name, *'Azzām*, meaning 'very determined', 'resolute'.

GIVEN NAMES Muslim 67%. *Samir* (4), *Marwan* (3), *Ayoub* (2), *Fouad* (2), *Hani* (2), *Imad* (2), *Issam* (2), *Jamil* (2), *Nabil* (2), *Said* (2), *Walid* (2), *Ali*.

Azzara (237) Southern Italian: **1.** from a personal name based on Arabic *az-zahrah* 'the flower'. **2. (Azzarà)**: occupational name from medieval Greek *opsaras* 'fisherman'.

GIVEN NAMES Italian 13%. *Cosmo* (2), *Salvatore* (2), *Carmine, Nicola, Saverio*.

Azzarello (225) Italian: from a diminutive of AZZARO.

GIVEN NAMES Italian 14%. *Sal* (2), *Salvatore* (2), *Agostino, Angelo, Francesco, Guido, Lorenzo, Pietro, Santo*.

Azzaro (165) Italian (chiefly northern): of problematic and probably multiple origin. The most likely sources are *az(z)aro*, an occupational name for a producer or supplier of hatchets or battleaxes, from *az(z)a* 'hatchet', 'battleaxe', or a metonymic occupational name for maker or supplier of steel or swords, from Italian *acciaio* 'steel' (from Latin *ac(c)iar(i)um*).

GIVEN NAMES Italian 20%. *Antonino, Carmine, Claudio, Salvatore, Silvio*.

Azzi (126) Muslim: **1.** Perhaps a variant of AZIZ. **2.** possibly a personal name based on Persian *izzi* 'power', 'honor', 'glory', or 'to be dear to', from Arabic *'izz*.

GIVEN NAMES Muslim 21%; French 13%. *Salah* (2), *Tanios* (2), *Amal, Anis, Bechara, Fadi, Ghassan, Kamal, Maroun, Nasr, Nazem, Nazira*; *Pierre* (2), *Andre, Antoine, Georges*.

Azzopardi (151) Italian (Sicily) and Maltese: ethnic name for a person of African descent or occupational name for a mercenary soldier, from medieval Greek *atsoupas*, plural *atsoupades* 'black', 'person from Mauritania', or 'mercenary soldier'. The word probably derives ultimately from Old Persian *takhma spada* 'army', modern Persian *sipah* 'army'.

GIVEN NAMES Italian 8%. *Carmel* (2), *Aldo, Guido, Sal*.

B

Ba (115) **1.** African: unexplained. Compare BAH. **2.** Arabic: from a shortened form of *Abā*, accusative case of *Abu* 'father'. **3.** Vietnamese: unexplained. **4.** Chinese 巴: from the name of the kingdom of Ba, which existed in Sichuan during the Zhou dynasty (1122–221 BC). Descendants of some of the ruling class adopted the name of the kingdom as their surname. This character still has as one of its meanings an ancient name for Sichuan province. Researchers believe that another branch of the Ba clan came from Shanxi province during the Han dynasty (206 BC–220 AD). Additionally, when Manchus and Mongolians came from the north to China several hundred years ago, many adopted the surname Ba.
GIVEN NAMES African 44%; Muslim 20%; Vietnamese 10%. *Amadou* (9), *Ousmane* (4), *Demba* (3), *Mamadou* (3), *Thierno* (2), *Aissatou, Fatou, Mame, Oumar*; *Daouda* (2), *Ibrahima* (2), *Mohamed* (2), *Abdoul, Abdoulaye, Abou, Fatime, Moussa, Yassin*; *Dung* (2), *Thai Van, Tho, Thuy, Toan, Tong Van, Tran.*

Baab (188) German: from a variant of *Babo*, a name derived from baby talk (like English *Papa*), or a short form of the Germanic personal name *Badubrecht*, related to Old Saxon *beada* 'battle' + *berht* 'bright'.

Baack (330) North German (Frisian) and Dutch: either from a reduced form of the Germanic personal name *Baldeke* (a short form of any of the compound names with the first element *bald* 'bold', for example *Baldewin*) or from Middle Low German *baec, bake* 'pork', 'bacon', hence a metonymic occupational name for a butcher or pig farmer.
GIVEN NAMES German 5%. *Frieda, Fritz, Orlo, Otto, Reinhard, Rudie.*

Baade (401) North German: variant of BADE.

Baal (103) German: variant of BAHL.
GIVEN NAME German 4%. *Mathias.*

Baalman (156) North German (**Baalmann**): from the personal name *Bole*, a popular medieval short form of Middle Low German *Bol(d)ewin*, from Germanic *bald* 'bold', 'brave' + *win* 'friend'. Compare BAHLMAN.

Baar (371) **1.** German: habitational name from either of two places called Baar, one in the Eifel region and the other in Bavaria. **2.** North German and Dutch: variant of BEER. **3.** Czech: from a short form of the personal name *Bartoloměj* (see BARTHOLOMEW).
GIVEN NAMES German 4%. *Erwin* (2), *Volkert.*

Baars (224) **1.** Dutch: from *baars* 'bass', 'perch', applied as a derogatory nickname or possibly from a house name for someone who lived at a house distinguished by the sign of a perch. **2.** Dutch: variant of the habitational name BEERS. **3.** German (North Sea area): variant of BARSCH.
GIVEN NAMES German 9%. *Kurt* (2), *Arno, Reinhard.*

Baas (658) **1.** North German and Dutch: nickname or occupational name from Dutch and Low German *baas* 'master', 'overseer', 'boss', also 'well-respected person'. **2.** Dutch: patronymic from the Germanic personal name *Baso*.

Baasch (155) **1.** North German: variant of BAAS. **2.** South German: from a dialect short form of SEBASTIAN.

Baase (102) Dutch: variant of BAAS.

Baatz (212) Dutch: patronymic from a short form of a Germanic personal name beginning with the element *badu-* 'strife', 'battle'.

Baba (380) **1.** Japanese: from a word meaning 'horse-riding ground', 'race track'; a common place name. The surname is found mostly in west central Japan. One Baba family in Kai (now Yamanashi prefecture) were samurai, vassals of the TAKEDA family. **2.** Czech, Slovak, Polish, and Hungarian: from the Slavic word *baba* 'old woman', 'grandmother', 'witch', hence an unflattering nickname for a man thought to resemble an old woman. In Czech *baba* can also mean 'coward'. **3.** Hungarian (**Bába**): habitational name from one of many places called Bába, in Abaúj, Borsod, Somogy, and Vas counties of Hungary, and Közép-Szolnok county, now in Romania. **4.** Arabic (**Bābā**): from a diminutive of *Abū* 'father'.
GIVEN NAMES Japanese 29%; Arabic 9%. *Takashi* (5), *Tetsuo* (3), *Seiji* (2), *Tsutomu* (2), *Akifumi, Arata, Ayako, Haruo, Haruyo, Hideo, Hikari, Hiroaki*; *Abbas, Akram, Ali, Bader, Daouda, Essam, Fadi, Fawaz, Faysal, Fuad, Hajji, Idrees.*

Babayan (155) Armenian: patronymic from Turkish *Baba* 'father'.
GIVEN NAMES Armenian 41%; Russian 16%. *Ara* (4), *Armen* (2), *Garo* (2), *Vartan* (2), *Vazgen* (2), *Andranik, Anoush, Antranik, Araxy, Arpenik, Avetik, Azniv*; *Svetlana* (3), *Volodya* (2), *Zhanna* (2), *Aleksandr, Anzhelika, Artem, Boris, Galina, Lyudmila, Misha, Ninel, Sergei.*

Babb (4702) **1.** English (chiefly Devon): probably from a Middle English nickname, *bab(e)* 'baby', but possibly from the female personal name *Babb(e)*, a pet form of *Barbara* (see BARBARY), or the Old English personal name *Babba*, found in several place names, including Babbacombe in Devon and Babington in Somerset. **2.** Variant of German **Bobb** (see BOB).

Babbit (139) English: variant spelling of BABBITT.

Babbitt (2065) English: **1.** from the personal name *Babot*, a medieval pet form of *Barbara*, or *Bobet*, a pet form of ROBERT. **2.** Alternatively, perhaps, a nickname from Middle English dialect *babbit* 'baby'.
FOREBEARS The founder of the American Babbitt family was Edward Bobet, who came to Plymouth Colony in 1643.

Babbs (317) English: patronymic or metronymic from BABB.

Babcock (8705) English: from a pet form of the Middle English personal name BABB.
FOREBEARS James Babcock settled in Portsmouth, RI, in 1642.

Babe (170) **1.** Jewish (Ashkenazic): from the personal name Baba (babe or bobe in Yiddish), from Slavic baba 'grandmother', 'old woman'. This name was sometimes given to a tenderly guarded or seriously sick child. **2.** German: recorded in Eastphalia as a surname since the 15th century but of uncertain origin. In eastern areas of Germany the Sorbian (Slavic) word *baba* 'old woman' (see 1) may be involved; in the south perhaps a development from baby talk like Babo. Compare BAAB **3.** Perhaps also an Americanized form of BAAB, BABA, or some similar name.

Babel (442) **1.** Jewish (Ashkenazic): ornamental name from German or Polish *Babel* 'Babylon' (which was named with the Assyrian elements *bāb* 'gate' + *ilu* 'god'). The Jewish people were held in captivity in Babylon from 597 to about 538 BC, and the name was sometimes adopted with reference to being an oppressed minority in a foreign culture. **2.** French: from a medieval personal name bestowed in honor of St. Babylas, a 3rd-century Christian patriarch of Antioch, whose name is of uncertain origin. **3.** German: variant of the personal name *Babo*, a name developed from baby talk, also a pet form of PAUL.

GIVEN NAMES German 4%. *Eberhard* (2), *Gerda, Klaus, Otto*.

Baber (1874) **1.** English (Gloucester, Somerset, and Wiltshire): unexplained. **2.** German: habitational name from either of two places called Baben, in Silesia and Brandenburg.

Babers (155) Origin unidentified. Perhaps a variant of English BABER.

Babey (103) Americanized form of Jewish or German BABE.

Babiak (237) Polish and Ukrainian: patronymic from BABA.

GIVEN NAMES Polish 6%. *Wasyl* (2), *Chrystyna, Irena, Jerzy*.

Babiarz (302) Polish: nickname from *baba* 'woman' (see BABA), sometimes applied to a womanizer.

GIVEN NAMES Polish 13%. *Andrzej* (2), *Boleslaw* (2), *Bronislaw* (2), *Casimir, Franciszek, Janina, Jerzy, Leslaw, Piotr, Stanislaw*.

Babic (249) **1.** Serbian and Croatian (**Babić**); Slovenian, Czech, and Slovak (all **Babič**): metronymic or a nickname from *baba* '(old) woman', 'grandmother', denoting a descendant of an older woman, or a child raised by a grandmother. **2.** With a long rising accent, this is a Bosnian name from Turkish *babo* 'grandfather'. Compare BABICH.

GIVEN NAMES South Slavic 20%. *Marko* (2), *Borka, Darko, Davorin, Djordje, Drago, Gojko, Goran, Ivica, Jovanka, Lazar, Marijan*.

Babich (769) **1.** Americanized spelling of **Babič** or **Babić** (see BABIC). **2.** Ukrainian: metronymic from *babich* 'old woman', 'grandmother' (see BABIN).

Babicz (126) **1.** Polish: patronymic from *baba* 'old woman', 'midwife', 'witch'. See BABA. **2.** Jewish (eastern Ashkenazic): metronymic from BABE. **3.** Jewish (eastern Ashkenazic): habitational name from any of the villages named Babichi in Ukraine and Belarus.

GIVEN NAMES Polish 12%. *Aniela, Jacek, Krzysztof, Stanislaw, Waclaw*.

Babik (150) Czech and Slovak (**Babík**); Polish: from a pet form of BABA or *babas* 'son', 'husband'.

Babin (2273) **1.** French: from a pet name derived from the personal name *Babylas*; it was the name of patriarch of Antioch who was beatified in the 3rd century. **2.** Jewish (from Belarus): metronymic from the personal name BABE. **3.** Jewish (from Belarus): habitational name from Babino, a village in Belarus. **4.** Russian, Ukrainian, and Polish (**Babyn**): metronymic or patronymic from *baba* 'grandmother', 'old woman', either meaning son of an old woman or a nickname denoting a fussy man. **5.** Serbian: nickname from *baba* 'grandmother' or *babo* 'father'.

FOREBEARS A bearer of the name Babin from the Poitou region of France was documented in Montreal in 1691, with the secondary surname Lacroix. A secondary surname of Lasource is documented with a family from the Maine region.

Most Louisiana families bearing this name descend from Acadian refugees who first settled in MD after the expulsion of 1755.

GIVEN NAMES French 6%. *Emile* (5), *Alcide* (2), *Andre* (2), *Colette* (2), *Lucien* (2), *Alcee, Amede, Amedee, Ancil, Angelle, Aurele, Benoit*.

Babine (153) Variant of French BABIN.

Babineau (609) French: variant of BABINEAUX.

GIVEN NAMES French 10%. *Emile* (3), *Andre* (2), *Marcel* (2), *Alcide, Alphee, Amedee, Antoine, Camille, Edmour, Herve, Leandre, Lucien*.

Babineaux (834) French: from a pet form of BABIN. This name is characteristic of Louisiana.

FOREBEARS Louisiana bearers of this name are descended from Louis-Charles Babineau, an Acadian who, after the expulsion of 1755, emigrated to the West Indies and then resettled in Louisiana around 1765.

GIVEN NAMES French 6%. *Antoine* (3), *Alcide, Alphonse, Chantal, Curley, Desire, Elzina, Marcel, Remy, Ulysse, Vernice*.

Babinec (123) Czech and Slovak: nickname from Old Czech *babinec* 'coward'.

Babington (256) English: habitational name for someone from Babington in Somerset or Great or Little Bavington in Northumberland, named with the Old English personal name *Babba* (see BABB) + the connective particle *-ing-* 'associated with', 'named after' + *tūn* 'settlement'.

Babino (175) **1.** Italian: probably from a diminutive of the personal name, *Babbo*, of Germanic origin. **2.** Northwestern Italian: nickname from *baba* 'gossip', 'talkative person', 'babbler', or alternatively, possibly from a diminutive of the personal name *Barnaba*. The name is particularly common in Ravenna. **3.** Altered spelling of French BABINEAU.

GIVEN NAMES Italian 14%. *Cono* (4), *Marco* (2), *Angelo, Carmine, Giuseppe, Salvatore, Vito*.

Babinski (305) **1.** Polish (**Babiński**) and Jewish (from Poland): habitational name for someone from a place called Babin or Babino. **2.** Russian, Belorussian, and Jewish (eastern Ashkenazic): habitational name for someone from a place called Babino or Babinka (now in Belarus), or Babin (now in Ukraine).

GIVEN NAMES Polish 5%. *Andrzej, Casimir, Krystyna, Piotr, Zbigniew*.

Babish (115) **1.** Altered form of English (Devon) **Babbage**, of unexplained origin. **2.** Possibly also an altered form of Slovak

Babiš, Czech or Slovenian **Babičš**, or Serbian **Babić** (see BABIC, BABICH).

Babka (151) Polish, Czech, and Slovak: from a diminutive of BABA.

Bable (102) Jewish (Ashkenazic) or French: variant spelling of BABEL.

Babler (334) German: from a pet form of the personal name *Babo* (see BAAB).

GIVEN NAMES German 4%. *Alois* (2), *Egon, Horst, Manfred*.

Babson (391) Presumably a patronymic from English BABB. It is now extremely rare in the British Isles.

Babst (119) German: variant of PABST.

Babu (203) Indian (Gujarat, Maharashtra, southern states): Hindu name meaning 'father', derived from Prakrit *bappa*, used as a respectful term of address for a man, also as a term of endearment for a male child. In Gujarat and Maharashtra the family name comes from the respectful term of address, while in the southern states the term of endearment evolved into a male given name, which is used as a family name among South Indians in the U.S.

GIVEN NAMES Indian 76%. *Suresh* (10), *Ramesh* (7), *Nikhil* (3), *Arun* (2), *Arunachalam* (2), *Bhupesh* (2), *Geetha* (2), *Mohan* (2), *Ratna* (2), *Ravi* (2), *Satesh* (2), *Sharath* (2).

Babula (198) Polish: from a derivative of BABA.

GIVEN NAMES Polish 7%. *Casimir* (2), *Henryk, Irena*.

Babyak (292) Ukrainian: variant of BABIAK.

Baca (4918) **1.** Spanish: variant of VACA. **2.** Croatian, Czech and Slovak (**Bača**); Polish; Hungarian (**Bacsa**); Romanian: occupational name from Romanian *baciu* 'shepherd'. Many Romanians were shepherds. In the mountains of Croatia *bača* denotes a senior shepherd. **3.** Croatian (**Baća**): from *baća*, a pet name meaning 'brother'. **4.** Hungarian: nickname from *baca* 'simple-minded' or 'obstinate'.

GIVEN NAMES Spanish 21%. *Jose* (38), *Manuel* (34), *Juan* (26), *Carlos* (25), *Jesus* (15), *Ruben* (14), *Ernesto* (10), *Luis* (9), *Francisco* (8), *Ramon* (8), *Trinidad* (8), *Benito* (7).

Bacak (115) Slovak (**Bačák**) and Croatian (Bačak): occupational name for a senior shepherd, from an augmentative form of *bača* 'shepherd' (see BACA).

Bacallao (121) Spanish: from *bacalao* 'codfish', hence either a nickname for someone who resembled the fish in some way or a metonymic occupational name for a fisherman.

GIVEN NAMES Spanish 57%. *Jorge* (4), *Jose* (4), *Juan* (4), *Mario* (4), *Armando* (3), *Carlos* (3), *Lazaro* (3), *Raul* (3), *Alfredo* (2), *Damaso* (2), *Enrique* (2), *Juana* (2); *Aldo* (2).

Bacani (103) Filipino: unexplained.

GIVEN NAMES Spanish 44%. *Alberto* (2), *Bienvenido* (2), *Diosdado* (2), *Adelino*,

Adoracion, Alfredo, Alicia, Asuncion, Bernardo, Delfin, Dionisio, Dominador.

Bacca (98) Southern Italian: **1.** variant of VACCA (from *vacca* 'cow'), a metonymic occupational name denoting a cowherd or a nickname for a rough-mannered or unsophisticated person. **2.** from *bacca* 'berry', perhaps applied as a metonymic occupational name for a gatherer or seller of berries.

Baccam (132) **1.** Chamorro (from Guam): unexplained. **2.** East Asian: unexplained.
GIVEN NAMES Southeast Asian 47%. *Chan, Deng, Dong, Eun, Seng*; *Phong, Souk, Then, Tinh*; *Manivanh, Noi, Nouane*; *Dac, Ha, Houng, Hung, Khong, Khue, Khuyen, Long, Ly, Rang, Thanh, Thiem.*

Baccari (195) Southern Italian: patronymic or plural form of BACCARO.
GIVEN NAMES Italian 28%. *Mario* (4), *Gerardo* (3), *Carmine* (2), *Angelo, Antonio, Carlo, Corrado, Domenic, Donato, Franco, Lucio, Sal.*

Baccaro (107) Italian: variant of VACCARO, an occupational name for a cowherd.
GIVEN NAMES Italian 17%. *Angelo* (2), *Pasquale* (2), *Antonio.*

Bacchi (175) Central Italian (Emilia-Romagna and Tuscany): variant of BACCI.
GIVEN NAMES Italian 8%. *Santo* (2), *Remo.*

Bacchus (539) **1.** English: variant of BACKUS. The form of the name appears to have been assimilated by folk etymology to the name of *Bacchus*, the Greek god of wine. **2.** Variant of German BACKHAUS. **3.** Muslim: probably a variant of BACHO.
GIVEN NAMES Muslim 20%. *Mohamed* (6), *Bibi* (4), *Abdool* (2), *Fazal* (2), *Mahmood* (2), *Abdel, Afzal, Alim, Ayube, Azam, Azeez, Azim.*

Bacci (207) Italian: from the personal name *Baccio*, a reduced form of various pet names, as for example *Iacobaccio, Bartolaccio,* and *Brunaccio.*
GIVEN NAMES Italian 14%. *Dante* (2), *Amedeo, Amelio, Carlo, Enea, Ettore, Giancarlo, Leonardo, Romano, Romeo, Spartaco, Vincenzo.*

Bacco (119) Italian: from the personal name *Bacco*, from Greek *Bacchus.*
GIVEN NAMES Italian 7%. *Franco, Vincenzo.*

Baccus (534) **1.** English: variant of BACKUS. **2.** Variant of German BACKHAUS. **3.** Muslim: variant of BACCHUS.

Bach (4578) **1.** German: topographic name for someone who lived by a stream, Middle High German *bach* 'stream'. This surname is established throughout central Europe and in Scandinavia, not just in Germany. **2.** Jewish (Ashkenazic): ornamental name from German *Bach* 'stream', 'creek'. **3.** English: topographic name for someone who lived by a stream, Middle English *bache.* **4.** Welsh: distinguishing epithet from Welsh *bach* 'little', 'small'. **5.** Norwegian: Americanized spelling of the topographic name **Bakk(e)** 'hillside' (see BAKKE). **6.** Polish, Czech, and Slovak:

from the personal name *Bach*, a pet form of *Bartomolaeus* (Polish *Bartłomiej*, Czech *Bartoloměj*, Slovak *Bartolomej* (see BARTHOLOMEW) or possibly in some cases of BALTAZAR or SEBASTIAN).
GIVEN NAMES German 4%. *Otto* (6), *Hans* (5), *Kurt* (4), *Fritz* (3), *Klaus* (3), *Horst* (2), *Johann* (2), *Alfons, Bernhard, Eldred, Erna, Ernst.*

Bacha (229) **1.** French (Alsace), German, Czech, and Polish: from a vernacular pet form of the Latin personal name *Bartolomaeus* (see BARTHOLOMEW). **2.** Americanized spelling of Norwegian **Bakka**, a variant of BAKKE.
GIVEN NAMES French 4%. *Andre, Henri.*

Bachand (727) French: unexplained. This name is associated with the secondary surname Vertefeuille; it is found in an Americanized form as **Bashaw** or **Bushaw**.
FOREBEARS A bearer of the name Bachand from Paris is documented in Boucherville, Quebec, in 1692.
GIVEN NAMES French 8%. *Armand* (3), *Normand* (3), *Gaston* (2), *Emile, Fernand, Jacques, Laurent, Onezime.*

Bachar (188) **1.** Jewish (Sephardic) and Turkish: occupational name for a spicer, from Turkish *bahar* 'spices', 'aroma'. **2.** Polish: derivative of BACH 6, a pet form of the personal name *Bartłomiej* (see BARTHOLOMEW). **3.** Polish: nickname from the dialect terms *bach* 'child' or *bachorz* 'belly'. **4.** Americanized spelling of Slovenian **Bačar**, a topographic name for someone living by the ravine of the river Bača, or a habitational name from Bača in western Slovenia, probably named with a reduced form of *globača* 'ravine', 'gorge'.
GIVEN NAMES Jewish 10%. *Yitzchak* (2), *Avi, Haim, Idit, Itzhak, Morty, Shlomit.*

Bacharach (202) Jewish (Ashkenazic): habitational name from a place on the Rhine near Koblenz, recorded in the earliest Latin documents as *Bacaraca*. The place name seems to be the same as that of Baccarat in the Vosges; both are of Celtic origin but unknown meaning.
GIVEN NAMES German 9%. *Fritz* (2), *Ernst, Gerhart, Kurt, Siegfried.*

Bache (389) **1.** German and English: variant of BACH 1, 3. **2.** German, French (Alsace), and central European: from a vernacular pet form of the personal name *Bartholomaeus* (see BACH 6, BARTHOLOMEW). **3.** Americanized spelling of Norwegian and Danish BAKKE.
FOREBEARS New York merchant and U.S. Postmaster General Richard Bache (1737–1811) was born in Settle in North Yorkshire. He came to New York in 1756, his brother Theophylact (a merchant) having arrived there in 1751. In 1767 he married Benjamin Franklin's daughter Sarah.

Bachelder (661) English: variant of BATCHELOR, altered by false association with *elder.*

Bacheller (156) Variant of English BATCHELOR, under French influence.
GIVEN NAME French 7%. *Pierre* (3).

Bachelor (410) English: variant spelling of BATCHELOR.

Bacher (753) **1.** German: topographic name from Middle High German *bach* 'stream' + the suffix *-er* denoting an inhabitant, or a habitational name from any of various places named with this word, for example Bach or Bachern. **2.** Jewish (Ashkenazic): variant of BACHAR. **3.** Danish: probably of German origin (see 1). **4.** Respelling of Norwegian **Bakker**, a habitational name from any of the farmsteads so named (see BACK). **5.** English: variant of BAKER.
GIVEN NAMES German 6%. *Lothar* (2), *Lutz* (2), *Ulrich* (2), *Armin, Claus, Hans, Hasso, Klaus, Kurt, Otto.*

Bachert (314) German: variant of BECKERT.
GIVEN NAMES German 8%. *Kurt* (3), *Erwin, Gerd, Gerhard, Manfred, Volkert.*

Bachhuber (126) German: status name for a peasant who owned a measure of farmland known as a *hube* (see HUBER) beside a stream (see BACH).

Bachicha (110) Hispanic (Mexico, Philippines): unidentified; compare the Brazilian Portuguese nickname *bachichá* 'stranger'.
GIVEN NAMES Spanish 8%. *Claudio* (2), *Aurelio, Fernando, Juan, Manuel.*

Bachler (164) South German (**Bächler**): variant spelling of BECHLER.

Bachman (5392) **1.** Jewish (Ashkenazic): ornamental name from German *Bach* 'stream', 'creek' + *Mann* 'man'. **2.** Respelling of German BACHMANN.
FOREBEARS According to family tradition, a Bachman family from Berne canton, Switzerland, came to PA with William Penn in 1677.

Bachmann (1575) **1.** German: topographic name for someone who lived by a stream, from Middle High German *bach* 'stream' + *man* 'man'. **2.** Jewish (Ashkenazic): variant spelling of BACHMAN.
GIVEN NAMES German 7%. *Hans* (4), *Heinz* (4), *Kurt* (4), *Johannes* (2), *Otto* (2), *Beate, Benno, Dieter, Dietmar, Elke, Ewald, Franz.*

Bachmeier (543) German: from Middle High German *bach* 'stream' + *meier* 'steward', 'tenant farmer' (see MAYER), denoting a farmer whose farm lay beside a stream.
GIVEN NAMES German 4%. *Florian, Hans, Heinrich, Kurt, Mathias, Otto.*

Bachner (282) South German: variant of BACHER.
GIVEN NAMES German 7%. *Gerhard, Heinrich, Helmut, Johann, Matthias, Otto.*

Bacho (110) Muslim: probably from Persian *bachcha* 'child', which is used as an affectionate nickname in the Indian subcontinent.
GIVEN NAMES Muslim 5%. *Huda, Kareem, Mahmoud, Wassim.*

Bachrach (371) Jewish (Ashkenazic): variant of BACHARACH.

GIVEN NAMES German 5%; Jewish 5%. *Erwin* (2), *Berthold, Fritzi, Kurt; Hillel* (4), *Shlomo, Sima, Yaakov, Yetta.*

Bachtel (322) German (**Bächtel**): variant of BECHTEL.

Bachtell (226) Variant spelling of German **Bächtel** (see BECHTEL).

Bachus (322) **1.** English: variant of BACKUS. **2.** Variant of German BACKHAUS.

Bacigalupi (202) Italian: patronymic or plural form of BACIGALUPO.

GIVEN NAMES Italian 8%. *Dante* (2), *Aldo, Giovanna, Giovanni, Guido, Paolo.*

Bacigalupo (248) Southern Italian: of uncertain origin; perhaps from *bacigare* (an unattested verb related to *baciare* 'to kiss') + *lupo* 'wolf'.

Bacik (146) Polish: nickname from *bacik*, a diminutive of *bat* 'whip'.

Bacino (139) Italian: from a diminutive of **Baccio** (see BACCI).

Back (2741) **1.** English: from Middle English *bakke* 'back' (Old English *bæc*), hence a nickname for someone with a hunched back or some other noticeable peculiarity of the back or spine, or a topographic name for someone who lived on a hill or ridge, or at the rear of a settlement. **2.** English: from the Old English personal name *Bacca*, which was still in use in the 12th century. It is of uncertain origin, but may have been a byname in the same sense as 1. **3.** English: nickname from Middle English *bakke* 'bat' (apparently of Scandinavian origin), from some fancied resemblance to the animal. **4.** Altered spelling of BACH 1, 2, or 6. **5.** North German: from Middle Low German *back* 'kneading trough', hence a metonymic occupational name for someone who made or used such vessels. **6.** Americanized spelling of Norwegian **Bakk(e)** (see BAKKE).

Backe (237) **1.** Scandinavian (especially Norwegian): variant spelling of BAKKE. **2.** Frisian: from a pet form of the Germanic personal name *Baldo*, a short form of the various compound names with the first element *bald* 'bold'. See BALD. **3.** German: nickname from Middle High German *backe* 'cheek', 'buttock'.

Backen (128) **1.** Americanized spelling of Norwegian BAKKEN. **2.** Frisian: patronymic from BACKE 1.

Backer (1334) **1.** North German (**Bäcker**) and Dutch: variant of BECKER. **2.** Northern English: topographic name for someone who lived on a hill or at the rear of a settlement, from Middle English *bakke* 'back', 'spine' + the suffix *-er* denoting an inhabitant. **3.** Danish and Norwegian: probably of German origin (see 1), but in Norway this is also a spelling variant of the habitational name BAKKER.

Backes (932) **1.** German: variant of BACKHAUS. **2.** Possibly a variant of English BACKUS.

Backhaus (540) German: from Middle High German *backhūs* 'bakehouse', hence a topographic name for someone who lived at a communal bake oven.

GIVEN NAMES German 9%. *Dieter* (2), *Math* (2), *Otto* (2), *Reinhold* (2), *Wilhelm* (2), *Erwin, Gunter, Hans, Juergen, Kurt, Lorenz, Siegfried.*

Backhus (151) **1.** North German form of BACKHAUS. **2.** English: variant of BACKUS.

GIVEN NAMES German 6%. *Heinz* (2), *Erwin.*

Backlund (542) Swedish: **1.** ornamental name composed of the elements *back(e)* 'hill' + *lund* 'grove'. **2.** (**Bäcklund**): ornamental name composed of the elements *bäck* 'stream' + *lund* 'grove'.

GIVEN NAMES Scandinavian 8%. *Nels* (2), *Sven* (2), *Anders, Evald, Jan Erik, Nils.*

Backman (1320) **1.** English (mainly northern): topographic name for someone who lived on a hill or at the rear of a settlement, from Middle English *bakke* 'back', 'spine' + *man* 'man'. Compare BACKER. **2.** Swedish: ornamental name composed of the elements *back(e)* 'hill' + *man* 'man'. **3.** Swedish (**Bäck(man)**): ornamental name composed of the elements *bäck* 'stream' + *man* 'man'. **4.** German: variant of BACHMANN. **5.** German: occupational name for a baker or employee of a master baker, from *backen* 'to bake' + *man(n)* 'man'. Compare BECKMANN.

GIVEN NAMES Scandinavian 6%. *Bjorn, Egil, Erik, Hilma, Lasse, Nels, Sven.*

Backs (218) **1.** German: variant of BACKHUS. **2.** Latvian (**Baks**): derivative of the German surname. **3.** English: patronymic from BACK 2.

GIVEN NAMES German 4%. *Guenther, Jochen.*

Backstrom (802) Americanized spelling of Swedish **Backström**, an ornamental name composed of the elements *back(e)* 'hill' + *ström* 'stream' or **Bäckström**, an ornamental name composed of the elements *bäck* 'brook', 'stream' + *ström* 'stream'.

GIVEN NAMES Scandinavian 5%. *Joakim, Lars, Lennart, Nels, Niklas.*

Backus (2596) **1.** English: from Middle English *bakehous* 'bakehouse' (Old English *bæchūs*), hence a topographic name for someone who lived or worked in a bakery. See also German BACKHAUS. **2.** Lithuanian (**Bačkus**): from Lithuanian *bačka* 'barrel', 'cask', hence either a nickname for a short, fat man or an occupational name for a cooper.

FOREBEARS Among the original settlers of Norwich (later Franklin), CT, in 1660 was a certain Stephen Backus.

Bacon (11205) **1.** English and French: metonymic occupational name for a preparer and seller of cured pork, from Middle English, Old French *bacun, bacon* 'bacon' (a word of Germanic origin, akin to BACK 1).

2. English and French: from the Germanic personal name *Bac(c)o, Bahho*, from the root *bag-* 'to fight'. The name was relatively common among the Normans in the form *Bacus*, of which the oblique case was *Bacon*.

FOREBEARS An immigrant from Normandy, France, called Bacon or Bascon was documented in Quebec city in 1647.

A Michael Bacon from England arrived in Dedham, MA, in 1640. Nathaniel Bacon (1647–76) from Friston Hall, Suffolk, emigrated to VA and settled at Curl's Neck on the James river. Another Nathanial Bacon, from Stratton, Cornwall, arrived at Barnstaple, MA, in 1639.

Bacorn (147) Dutch or German: unexplained. The surname **Beckhorn** is also found, which may be a variant of this.

FOREBEARS The baptismal records of the Dutch Church in Sleepy Hollow, Westchester Co., NY, have an entry for November 20, 1736, for Job, son of Job Becoren and his wife Jannetie.

Bacot (194) French: from a derivative of the unexplained root *Bac-*.

FOREBEARS A family of Huguenots called Bacot, from the Touraine region of France, settled in SC.

GIVEN NAME French 4%. *Arnaud.*

Bacote (235) Probably an altered spelling of BACOT preserving the final *-t*, which is not normally pronounced in French.

Bacus (205) Respelling of English BACKUS or German BACKHUS.

Baczewski (145) Polish: **1.** habitational name for someone from Bacze in Ciechanów voivodeship. **2.** alternatively, perhaps a derivative of the personal name *Bacz*, a pet form of *Bartłomej* (see BARTHOLOMEW).

GIVEN NAMES Polish 14%. *Zygmunt* (2), *Bogdan, Bronislaw, Danuta, Jerzy, Zbigniew, Zigmund, Zygfryd.*

Baczkowski (109) Polish: habitational name for someone from either of two places called Baczków, in Siedlce and Tarnów voivodeships.

GIVEN NAMES Polish 15%. *Andrzej, Arkadiusz, Jaroslaw, Wojciech, Zbigniew.*

Badal (206) Indian (Panjab): Sikh name found in the Jat community; in Hindi and Panjabi it means 'cloud', from Sanskrit *vārdala* 'water'.

GIVEN NAMES Indian 5%. *Anjanie, Dushan, Mohi, Ramdeo, Sangeeta.*

Badalamenti (303) Southern Italian (Sicily): from an Arabic personal name or nickname '*Abd al-Amān* 'servant of peace'.

GIVEN NAMES Italian 38%. *Salvatore* (7), *Vito* (7), *Sal* (6), *Vincenzo* (3), *Angelo* (2), *Antonio* (2), *Giuseppe* (2), *Caesar, Giacomo, Gino, Italia, Nunzio.*

Badami (156) **1.** Iranian and Indian (Gujarat): Muslim name, from an adjectival form of Persian *bādām* 'almond'. **2.** Indian (Karnataka): Hindu name, which goes back

to a place name. The town of Badami is situated in the northern part of Karnataka. It was formerly known as *Vatapi* and was the capital of the Chalukya kingdom from the 6th to the 8th century AD. **3.** Italian (Sicily): patronymic or plural form of BADAMO.
GIVEN NAMES Indian 17%; Italian 9%. *Sujal* (2), *Ajit, Asha, Binay, Chandana, Dinesh, Mohan, Umesh, Vinay, Vinod, Vivek; Angelo, Caterina, Ciro, Santo.*

Badamo (104) Italian (Sicily): from a personal name of uncertain etymology, probably of Arabic origin.
GIVEN NAMES Italian 19%. *Carlo* (2), *Matteo, Paolo, Salvatore, Vita.*

Badaracco (105) Italian: unexplained.
GIVEN NAMES Italian 6%; Spanish 5%. *Andrea, Giovanni, Giuseppe; Alicia, Rogelio, Ruben.*

Baddeley (104) English: variant of BADLEY.

Badder (126) English, of Welsh origin: Anglicized form of Welsh *ap Adda* 'son of *Adda*', a byform of ADAM.

Badders (276) English, of Welsh origin: variant of BADDER, with English patronymic -*s* added.

Baddour (112) Muslim: probably an altered form of the Persian personal name *Bahadur*, from an adjective meaning 'brave' or 'magnanimous'.
GIVEN NAMES Muslim 12%. *Abla, Awad, Faouzi, Mazen, Nabil, Ramez.*

Bade (944) **1.** English: probably from a Middle English survival of the Old English personal name *Bad(d)a*, which is of uncertain origin, perhaps a short form of the various compound names with the first element *beadu* 'battle'. **2.** North German: from a short form of a Germanic personal name composed with *badu* 'strife', 'battle'. **3.** North German: occupational name from Middle Low German *bade* 'messenger'.

Badeau (182) French: variant of BADEAUX.
GIVEN NAMES French 10%. *Marcel* (2), *Francois, Laurent, Normand.*

Badeaux (492) French: from Occitan *badau* 'stupid', 'gullible', a derivative of *badar* 'to be open-mouthed', 'to gape'. The name is frequent both in New England and in Louisiana.
FOREBEARS A bearer of the name from La Rochelle is documented in Quebec city in 1651.
This is also the name of a French Huguenot family in Tarrytown, NY, one of whose members, Adam Badeau (1831–95) was a writer and officer on General Grant's staff in the Civil War.
GIVEN NAMES French 5%. *Alphonse* (2), *Andre, Angelle, Antoine, Camille, Eulice.*

Baden (815) North German and Danish: patronymic from BADE.

Badenhop (109) North German: from a field name composed of the Germanic personal name *Bade* + Middle Low German *hōp* 'heap', 'settlement', the connecting -*n*- indicating ownership, i.e. 'Bade's plot of land for cultivation'.

Bader (3865) **1.** German and Jewish (Ashkenazic): occupational name for an attendant in or owner of a public bath house, from an agent derivative of Middle High German *bat* 'bath' (Old High German *bad*), German *Bad*. In former times, such attendants undertook a variety of functions, including blood-letting, tooth-pulling, and hair-cutting. **2.** Southern French: variant of **Badié** (see BADIE).

Badertscher (307) German: variant of **Bartscher**, an occupational name for a barber (a compound of Middle High German *bart* 'beard' + *scher* from *scheren* 'to cut or clip').
GIVEN NAMES German 5%. *Fritz* (2), *Kurt* (2), *Hans.*

Badger (2851) English (West Midlands): **1.** habitational name from a place in Shropshire named Badger, probably from an unattested Old English personal name *Bæcg* + Old English *ofer* 'ridge'. **2.** occupational name for a maker of bags (see BAGGE 1) or for a peddler who carried his wares about with him in a bag. It is unlikely that the surname has anything to do with the animal (see BROCK 2), which was not known by this name until the 16th century.
FOREBEARS A Giles Badger from England was in Newbury, MA, by about 1635.

Badgerow (101) Origin uncertaiin: possibly English, but unexplained.

Badgett (1034) **1.** Variant of English BAGGOTT. **2.** Jewish (American): adoption of the English surname in place of some like-sounding Jewish name.

Badgley (865) English: perhaps a variant of BADLEY.

Badham (112) English, of Welsh origin: reduced form of the patronymic *ap Adam* 'son of ADAM', the spelling having been altered by folk etymology as if from an English place name.

Badia (180) Spanish, Catalan, and Italian: habitational name from any of numerous places called Badia or Abbadia, or a topographic name for someone living near an abbey, Spanish *abadía*, Catalan *abadia*, and Italian *badia* (from Latin *abbatia*). In some cases the surname may have arisen as a metonymic occupational name for someone who worked in an abbey or who looked after one.
GIVEN NAMES Spanish 30%; Italian 12%. *Jose* (3), *Ramon* (3), *Carlos* (2), *Joaquin* (2), *Rafael* (2), *Sergio* (2), *Alejandro, Alfonso, Americo, Armando, Arturo, Blanca; Antonio, Carmela, Dante, Domenico, Giulio, Ignazio, Leonardo, Luigi, Pietro.*

Badie (123) **1.** Muslim: respelling of a personal name based on Arabic *badī* 'original', 'wonderful', 'unique'. *Al-Badī* 'the Sole Creator' is an attribute of Allah.

2. French: shortened form of ABADIE.
3. French (**Badié**): southern (Occitan) occupational name from medieval Latin *baderius* 'janitor'.
GIVEN NAMES Muslim 13%. *Ahmad, Alireza, Amin, Badie, Fuad, Saeid, Shirin.*

Badilla (158) Spanish: variant of BADILLO.
GIVEN NAMES Spanish 39%. *Luis* (3), *Jesus* (2), *Jose* (2), *Juan* (2), *Maria Elena* (2), *Porferio* (2), *Alfredo, Carlos, Efren, Elpidio, Emilio, Enrique.*

Badillo (765) Spanish: topographic name from a diminutive of *vado* 'ford' (Latin *vadum*) or a habitational name from either of two places named with this word: Valillo de la Guarena in Zamora province or Vadillo de al Sierra in Ávila.
GIVEN NAMES Spanish 49%. *Jose* (17), *Mario* (10), *Jesus* (9), *Juan* (9), *Manuel* (8), *Carlos* (6), *Francisco* (6), *Pedro* (5), *Alejandro* (4), *Angel* (4), *Guadalupe* (4), *Jorge* (4).

Badley (220) English: habitational name from Badley in Suffolk or Baddeley Green in Staffordshire, both named with the Old English personal name *Bad(d)a* + *lēah* 'woodland clearing'.

Badman (198) English: probably an occupational name for the servant of someone called *Badd* or BATT, but possibly in some cases a nickname for a reprobate, from Middle English *badde* 'bad', 'worthless', 'evil'.

Bado (113) Altered spelling, under Spanish influence, of French BADEAUX.
GIVEN NAMES Spanish 8%. *Carlos* (2), *Jose, Ricardo, Silvestre.*

Badolato (299) Italian: habitational name from a place named Badolato, in Catanzaro province, Calabria; the place name is derived ultimately from Latin *vadum latum* 'broad path'.
GIVEN NAMES Italian 22%. *Angelo* (4), *Domenic* (3), *Mario* (2), *Antonio, Domenico, Gino, Gregorio, Vincenzo.*

Badon (278) French: from a short form of a personal name of West Frankish origin beginning with the element *Bad-*. It could alternatively be from a nickname meaning 'fat belly' or a habitational name from a place so named. This family name is frequent in Louisiana.
GIVEN NAMES French 4%. *Monique* (2), *Remy.*

Badour (170) **1.** French: probably a variant of **Badou(x)**, from a short form of a personal name of West Frankish origin formed with *Bad-* as the first element. **2.** alternatively, a nickname from Occitan *badou* 'stupid'. Compare BADON, BADEAU. This is a frequent name in MI. **3.** Muslim: variant of BADDOUR.

Badowski (126) Polish: habitational name for someone from a place called Badowo in Skierniewice voivodeship.
GIVEN NAME Polish 4%. *Stanislaw.*

Badura (244) Polish: nickname for a dawdler or time-waster, from the dialect verb *badurać (się)* 'to dawdle or waste time'.

GIVEN NAMES German 5%. *Guenter, Heinz, Juergen.*

Bady (161) French: variant of BODY.

Bae (865) Korean: variant of PAE.

GIVEN NAMES Korean 70%. *Jung* (15), *Young* (14), *Sang* (13), *Jong* (8), *Sung* (8), *Jin* (6), *Kyung* (6), *Yong* (6), *Jae* (5), *Soon* (5), *Hyun* (4), *Keum* (4); *Chang* (4), *Jung Sook* (3), *Byung* (2), *Jinsoo* (2), *Jung Hwan* (2), *Nam* (2), *Sang Joon* (2), *Seong* (2), *Sook* (2), *Young Hwan* (2), *Ae, Bok Soon.*

Baechle (185) South German (**Bächle**): Swabian variant of BACH, from a diminutive of Middle High German *bach* 'stream'.

Baecker (178) German: alternative spelling of **Bäcker**, a variant of BECKER.

GIVEN NAMES German 14%. *Siegfried* (2), *Bodo, Gerhardt, Heinz, Horst, Kurt, Waltraud.*

Baeder (149) German and Jewish (Ashkenazic): alternative spelling of **Bäder**, a variant of BADER.

GIVEN NAME German 4%. *Fritz.*

Baehler (141) German: **1.** habitational name for someone from a place called Bahlen, of which there are several examples in northern Germany. **2.** variant spelling of BEHLER or **Böhler** (see BOEHLER).

GIVEN NAMES German 4%; French 4%. *Juerg; Constant, Odette.*

Baehr (710) German and Jewish (Ashkenazic): variant spelling of BAER.

GIVEN NAMES German 4%. *Kurt* (2), *Lutz* (2), *Bernhard, Fritz, Wolfgang.*

Baek (397) Korean: variant of PAEK.

GIVEN NAMES Korean 73%. *Sung* (7), *Young* (6), *Kwang* (5), *Seung Ho* (5), *Seung* (4), *Yong* (4), *Ho* (3), *Myung* (3), *Won* (3), *Dong* (2), *Duk* (2), *Eunsook* (2); *Chong* (4), *Nam* (3), *Woon* (3), *Choon* (2), *Chung* (2), *Eun Ju* (2), *Kyu Hyun* (2), *Seung Chul* (2), *Wonkyu* (2), *Byung, Chong Son, Chul.*

Baena (120) Spanish: habitational name from Baena in Córdoba province.

GIVEN NAMES Spanish 49%. *Jose* (4), *Alvaro* (3), *Julio* (3), *Miguel* (3), *Fernando* (2), *Pablo* (2), *Adriana, Alfredo, Armando, Aurelio, Beatriz, Carlos.*

Baenen (147) Dutch: metronymic from the old Germanic female personal name *Bana.*

Baer (7155) **1.** German (**Bär**): from Middle High German *ber* 'bear', a nickname for someone thought to resemble the animal in some way, a metonymic occupational name for someone who kept a performing bear, or a habitational name for someone who lived at a house distinguished by the sign of a bear. In some cases, it may derive from a personal name containing this element. **2.** Jewish (Ashkenazic): **3.** Jewish (Ashkenazic): from the Yiddish male personal name *Ber*, from Yiddish *ber* 'bear'. **4.** Dutch: from Middle Dutch *baer* 'naked', 'bare'. Debrabandere suggests it may have

been a nickname for someone who wore ragged clothes.

FOREBEARS The family name Baer was established in Northampton Co., PA, in 1743.

Baerg (165) German (**Bärg**): variant of BERG.

GIVEN NAMES German 5%. *Gerhard, Kurt.*

Baert (117) Dutch: **1.** patronymic from a pet form of the personal name *Bartolomaeus* (see BARTHOLOMEW). **2.** nickname from Middle Dutch *baert* 'beard'. See also BEARD. **3.** from a short form of any of the various Germanic personal names with the final element *baert* (*berht*), for example *Isebaert, Notebaert.*

GIVEN NAME French 5%. *Aime.*

Baerwald (158) German (also **Bärwald**): variant spelling of BERWALD.

GIVEN NAMES German 7%. *Hans, Kurt.*

Baese (108) German: variant of **Bese** (see BEESE).

GIVEN NAME German 4%. *Kurt.*

Baessler (118) German: **1.** habitational name for someone from Basel in Switzerland (see BESLER), or from any of various places called Basse or Bassen in northern Germany. **2.** Alternatively, perhaps from a derivative of Middle Low German *baseln* 'to act in a confused manner', hence a nickname for someone who was absent-minded or forgetful.

GIVEN NAMES German 12%. *Gottfried, Kurt, Urs, Volker.*

Baeten (248) Dutch: metronymic from a short form of the female personal name *Beatrix* (see BEATRICE).

Baetz (216) German: variant spelling of BETZ.

Baez (2546) Spanish (**Báez**): of uncertain derivation, but possibly a variant of PAEZ.

GIVEN NAMES Spanish 51%. *Jose* (65), *Luis* (45), *Juan* (36), *Carlos* (32), *Rafael* (24), *Manuel* (23), *Angel* (22), *Ramon* (19), *Pedro* (16), *Julio* (15), *Ana* (14), *Francisco* (14).

Baeza (834) Spanish: habitational name from a place of this name in the province of Jaén.

GIVEN NAMES Spanish 51%. *Jose* (21), *Manuel* (16), *Jesus* (12), *Juan* (12), *Ramon* (10), *Ruben* (9), *Miguel* (8), *Carlos* (7), *Cruz* (7), *Armando* (6), *Luis* (6), *Raul* (6).

Baffa (134) Italian: **1.** perhaps from *baffo* 'moustache', with the feminine (*-a*) ending, probably due to the influence of the Italian word *famiglia* 'family'. **2.** perhaps of Albanian origin, but unexplained etymology.

GIVEN NAMES Italian 8%. *Antonietta, Raffaele, Ruggero.*

Bafford (115) English: variant of PAFFORD.

Bafus (112) Altered form of German **Beifuss** 'mugwort' (see BEILFUSS).

Bagan (179) Ukrainian and Polish: of uncertain origin. **1.** possibly from a place named with *bagno* 'marsh'. **2.** alternatively a nickname for a destructive person, from *baganić* 'to destroy'. **3.** Jewish (east-

ern Ashkenazic): habitational name from a place called Bagny or Bagno, now in Poland.

GIVEN NAMES Polish 5%. *Jerzy, Krystyna, Krzysztof, Zofia.*

Bagby (2073) **1.** English: habitational name from Bagby in North Yorkshire, recorded in Domesday Book as *Baghebi*, from the Old Norse personal name *Baggi* + Old Norse *býr* 'farmstead', 'village'. **2.** Scottish: possibly from Begbie in East Lothian.

FOREBEARS James Bagby, a Scot, arrived in Jamestown, VA, in about 1628. One of his descendants, Arthur Pendleton Bagby (1794–1858), was governor of Alabama (1837–1841) and a U.S. senator (1841–48).

Bagdasarian (194) Armenian: patronymic from the western Armenian personal name *Bagdasar*, variant of classical Armenian *Baltasar* (see BALTAZAR).

GIVEN NAMES Armenian 29%. *Ara* (3), *Aram* (2), *Armen* (2), *Sarkis* (2), *Vahan* (2), *Andranik, Antranig, Antranik, Araik, Armine, Bagdasar, Diran.*

Bagdon (154) Origin unidentified; probably of German or English origin.

Bagdonas (139) Lithuanian: patronymic from the personal name *Bagdon*, Lithuanian form of Polish BOGDAN.

GIVEN NAMES Lithuanian 10%; Polish 5%. *Adolfas, Kazys, Vincas, Vitas; Casimir, Halina.*

Bagent (145) Origin unidentified. It is found in southern England, where it may be of French (possibly Huguenot) origin.

FOREBEARS A William Bageant went to America in 1755 with General Edward Braddock's army; his descendants are found mainly in Virginia and Maryland.

Bagg (299) English: variant spelling of BAGGE.

Baggarly (109) English: variant of BAGLEY.

Bagge (189) **1.** English: from Middle English *bagge* 'bag', hence a metonymic occupational name for a maker of bags and sacks of various kinds, including wallets and purses. **2.** English: from the Germanic personal name *Bac(c)o, Bahho* (see BACON 1). **3.** Swedish: nickname or soldier's name from Swedish *bagge* 'ram'. **4.** Danish: from a personal name of uncertain derivation.

GIVEN NAME Scandinavian 7%. *Asger* (2).

Baggerly (232) English: variant of BAGLEY.

Baggett (4753) English: from a pet form of BAGGE 2.

Baggott (354) English: from a pet form of BAGGE 2.

GIVEN NAME Irish 5%. *Malachy.*

Baggs (685) English: patronymic from BAGGE 2.

Bagheri (117) Muslim: unexplained. There may be a link with the name of Bughra Khan, a king of Khwarazm.

GIVEN NAMES Muslim 79%. *Ali* (6), *Hamid* (3), *Mohammad* (3), *Mohsen* (3), *Abbas*

(2), *Abbass* (2), *Hossein* (2), *Kayvon* (2), *Nader* (2), *Ahmad*, *Amir*, *Arash*.

Baginski (504) Polish (**Bagiński**): habitational name for someone from a place called Bagno or Bagna, named with *bagno* 'marsh'.

GIVEN NAMES Polish 15%. *Tadeusz* (4), *Wieslaw* (4), *Danuta* (2), *Jerzy* (2), *Jolanta* (2), *Jozef* (2), *Slawomir* (2), *Arkadiusz*, *Beata*, *Bogdan*, *Bronislawa*, *Casimir*.

Bagley (6105) English: habitational name from any of the places so called, mainly in Berkshire, Shropshire, Somerset, and West Yorkshire. These get their names either from the Old English personal name *Bacga* + Old English *lēah* 'woodland clearing' or from an unattested Old English word, *bagga*, for a 'bag-shaped' animal (probably the badger) + *lēah*.

Baglien (107) Norwegian: unexplained.

Baglio (202) **1.** Italian: from *baglio* 'bailiff', 'steward', 'official' (Late Latin *baiulivus*), an occupational name for an administrative, judicial, or political functionary of some kind (the precise meaning of the term varied from region to region and time to time), or sometimes perhaps a nickname for an officious person. **2.** Sicilian: topographic name from *bbàgliu*, *bbàgghiu* 'farmyard', from Old French *bail*.

GIVEN NAMES Italian 14%. *Salvatore* (3), *Angelo*, *Cataldo*, *Cosimo*, *Filippa*, *Filippo*, *Rocco*.

Bagnall (554) English: habitational name for someone from Bagnall in Staffordshire, named with the Old English personal name *Badeca*, *Baduca* (from a short form of the various compound names with the first element *beadu* 'battle') + Old English *halh* 'nook', 'recess' (see HALE) or *holt* 'wood' (see HOLT).

Bagnasco (112) Southern Italian: habitational name from Bagnasco in Cuneo province, which is probably named from the Latin personal name *Banius*.

GIVEN NAMES Italian 11%. *Carlo* (2), *Carmela*, *Dante*, *Gino*.

Bagnato (178) Southern Italian: **1.** nickname from *Bagnato* 'bathed', from the past participle of *bagnare* 'to bathe'. **2.** habitational name from any of various minor places named with a derivative of *bagno* 'bath' (Latin *balneum*).

GIVEN NAMES Italian 15%; German 4%. *Rocco* (2), *Carmelo*, *Concetto*, *Natale*, *Vincenzo*; *Reiner*, *Uwe*.

Bagnell (232) English: variant spelling of BAGNALL.

Bagnoli (136) Italian: habitational name from any of numerous places named or named with Bagnoli (meaning 'little baths'), as for example a place near Messina, a quarter of Naples, and Bagnoli Irpino near Avellino.

GIVEN NAMES Italian 16%. *Constantino* (2), *Angelo*, *Enzo*, *Luca*, *Martino*, *Nicola*, *Olindo*, *Sisto*.

Bagot (169) English: from a pet form of BAGGE 2.

Bagsby (134) Probably a variant of English BAGBY (or possibly BIGSBY). This name is not found in the British Isles.

Bagshaw (347) English: habitational name from a place so named in Derbyshire. The first element of the place name is either the Old English personal name *Bacga* or an unattested Old English word, *bagga*, for a 'bag-shaped' animal (probably the badger); the second is Old English *sceaga* 'copse'.

Bagwell (3927) English: of uncertain origin. It may be a variant of **Backwell**, a habitational name from Backwell in Somerset, named with Old English *bæc* 'ridge' + *wella* 'spring', 'stream', or possibly from Bakewell in Derbyshire (see BAKEWELL). Alternatively, it may be from a minor place named with an unattested Old English word, *bagga* ' badger' + *wella* 'spring', 'stream'.

Bah (198) **1.** African: unexplained. Compare BA. **2.** Slovenian: unexplained.

GIVEN NAMES African 38%; Muslim 33%. *Mamadou* (11), *Thierno* (5), *Amadou* (4), *Boubacar* (2), *Fatmata* (2), *Fatoumata* (2), *Mariama* (2), *Oumou* (2), *Umaru* (2), *Aboubacar*, *Aissatou*, *Alieu*; *Mohamed* (6), *Abdulai* (5), *Ibrahima* (5), *Abdul* (4), *Abdoul* (2), *Ibrahim* (2), *Abou*, *Abu*, *Abubakar*, *Ali*, *Hassane*, *Mahmoud*.

Baham (526) English: habitational name from Bayham in Kent (near Tunbridge Wells), named in Old English with *bēag* 'river bend' + *hamm* 'water meadow'.

Bahamonde (59) Galician: habitational name from one of the Galician places called Baadmonde (earlier written Bahamonde) in the province of Lugo, most probably Santiago de Baamonde (Begonte). This is a characteristic example of the numerous (over a thousand) medieval places which were named after their owners, in this case *Badamundus*.

GIVEN NAMES Spanish 52%. *Jose* (5), *Rodrigo* (3), *Roberto* (2), *Javier*, *Jesus*, *Juan*, *Juana*, *Manuel*, *Pepe*, *Rafael*, *Reinaldo*.

Bahan (172) Ukrainian: see BAGAN.

Bahar (109) Arabic, Turkish, and Jewish (Sephardic): **1.** from Arabic *bahār* 'spice', an occupational name for a spicer or perhaps a personal name. **2.** perhaps a variant of **Bāhir**, an Arabic personal name meaning 'brilliant', 'superb'.

GIVEN NAMES Arabic 44%; Jewish 8%. *Aisha* (3), *Ali* (3), *Hassan* (3), *Habib* (2), *Mohammad* (2), *Salam* (2), *Abbass*, *Adnan*, *Bijan*, *Fereidoon*, *Imad*, *Jamilah*; *Ephraim*, *Erez*, *Igal*, *Izak*, *Rina*.

Bahe (222) German: variant of BADE.

Bahena (446) Spanish: habitational name from Baena in the province of Córdoba.

GIVEN NAMES Spanish 65%. *Juan* (14), *Jose* (9), *Mario* (7), *Francisco* (6), *Pedro* (6), *Alejandro* (5), *Alfredo* (5), *Bernardo* (5),

Carlos (5), *Leticia* (5), *Armando* (4), *Jesus* (4).

Bahl (687) **1.** Indian (Panjab): Hindu (Khatri) and Sikh name, probably from Sanskrit *bahala* 'strong', based on the name of a clan in the Khatri community. **2.** North German: from the Germanic personal name *Baldo*, a short form of the various compound names with the first element *bald* 'bold'. **3.** Eastern German: from *Bahl*, a Sorbian form of the personal name *Valentinus* (see VALENTINE).

GIVEN NAMES Indian 22%. *Satish* (4), *Arun* (3), *Ramesh* (3), *Krishna* (2), *Lalit* (2), *Neeraj* (2), *Om* (2), *Sandeep* (2), *Sanjeev* (2), *Vijay* (2), *Akash*, *Anand*.

Bahler (274) German: **1.** habitational name from any of several places so named, for example near Bremen and in Mecklenburg. **2.** possibly an altered spelling of BEHLER.

GIVEN NAMES German 4%. *Armin*, *Kurt*.

Bahlman (121) Respelling of German BAHLMANN.

Bahlmann (101) German: from BAHL 2 or 3 + *mann* 'man'.

Bahls (190) North German: **1.** patronymic from BAHL. **2.** shortened form of **Bahlsen**, a habitational name for someone from a place called Balehusen.

Bahm (386) South German: variant of BAUM.

Bahn (496) German: **1.** from a topographic name from Middle High German or Middle Low German *bān* 'open space', 'public area', or in eastern Germany from Sorbian *bahno* 'swamp'. **2.** from a Germanic personal name of uncertain origin.

Bahner (263) German: variant of BAHN 1, the *-er* suffix denoting an inhabitant.

GIVEN NAMES German 5%. *Gerhard*, *Kurt*, *Wilfried*.

Bahnsen (344) North German: **1.** patronymic from BAHN. **2.** habitational name from a place named Bahnsen, near Ülzen, Lower Saxony.

GIVEN NAMES German 5%. *Bernhard*, *Erwin*, *Hans*, *Harro*, *Kurt*, *Lorenz*.

Bahnson (104) Variant of North German BAHNSEN.

Bahr (3064) North German: from Middle Low German *bar(e)* 'bear', hence a nickname for someone thought to resemble the animal, a metonymic occupational name for someone who kept a performing bear, or a habitational name for someone who lived at a house distinguished by the sign of a bear. In some cases, it may derive from a personal name containing this element.

GIVEN NAMES German 4%. *Claas* (3), *Erwin* (3), *Gunter* (3), *Otto* (3), *Hans* (2), *Eberhard*, *Ewald*, *Florian*, *Frieda*, *Fritz*, *Gerhard*, *Heinz*.

Bahrami (113) Iranian: from an adjective based on *Bahrām*, 'the planet Mars', also '20th day of every solar month', borne as a personal name by several kings of Persia.

GIVEN NAMES Iranian 70%. *Ali* (5), *Hamid* (3), *Ahmad* (2), *Abdollah, Arsalan, Bahram, Jalil, Maryam, Massoud, Mohamad, Mohammad, Mostafa.*

Bahre (101) German: variant of BAHR.
GIVEN NAME German 4%. *Kurt.*

Bahrenburg (114) German: habitational name for someone from Barenburg, west of Hannover.

Bahri (83) **1.** Muslim: probably from Arabic *baḥrī* 'maritime', a derivative of *baḥr* 'sea'. This could also be an ethnic name for someone from Bahrain. **2.** Indian (Panjab): Hindu (Khatri) and Sikh name, said to be from Panjabi *bā'rā* 'twelve'. The Bahris are one of the major subdivisions of the Khatri community and comprise twelve clans: CHOPRA, DHAWAN, KAPUR, KHANNA, MEHROTRA, SEHGAL, SETH, TALWAR, and VOHRA, and (not included in this dictionary) **Tannan, Maindharu**, and **Wadhaun**.
GIVEN NAMES Muslim 59%; Indian 16%; French 4%. *Kamal* (4), *Adnan* (3), *Salim* (2), *Sami* (2), *Youssef* (2), *Abbas, Abdulaziz, Ahmed, Amer, Amira, Azadeh, Fady*; *Jyotika, Minoo, Raj, Rajeev, Ramesh, Sujata, Sunil; Camille, Georges.*

Bahrke (100) German: pet form of BAHR.

Bai (335) **1.** Chinese 柏: according to legend, this name comes from Bai Huang, the name of a prehistoric Chinese leader. At a later date, the kingdom of Bai in the area of present-day Henan province gave its name to descendants of its ruling clan. The Chinese character for this name may also mean 'cypress'. **2.** Chinese 白: from the name of the Victorious Duke Bai of the kingdom of Chu, who lived during the Zhou dynasty (1122–221 BC). This Chinese character may also mean 'white' or 'clear'. **3.** Korean: variant of PAE.
GIVEN NAMES Chinese/Korean 45%. *Li* (3), *Yong* (3), *Bin* (2), *Hong* (2), *Joon* (2), *Niu* (2), *Yun* (2), *Baolin, Chu, Dawei, Dong*; *Chang, Hyun Ho, In Soo, Sooil, Young Hwa, Young Joon, Young Sik*; *Lan* (2), *Byoung, Hao, Quan.*

Baiamonte (126) Italian: possibly a derivative of the Germanic personal name *Boiamund, Baiamund.*
GIVEN NAMES Italian 14%. *Giuseppe* (2), *Santo* (2), *Vita.*

Baich (102) Slovenian: unexplained.

Baier (2139) German: variant spelling of BAYER.
GIVEN NAMES German 4%. *Kurt* (5), *Armin* (2), *Dieter* (2), *Hans* (2), *Hilde* (2), *Otto* (2), *Claus, Eldred, Erhart, Ernst, Florian, Frieda.*

Baierl (136) South German: from a pet form of BAIER.

Baig (390) Muslim (common in Pakistan): from the Turkish word *beg* 'bey', originally a title denoting a local administrator in the Ottoman Empire, but subsequently widely used as a title of respect. Compare BEG.

GIVEN NAMES Muslim 88%. *Imran* (6), *Muhammad* (5), *Abdul* (4), *Azam* (4), *Mohammad* (4), *Mohammed* (4), *Saleem* (4), *Amir* (3), *Arif* (3), *Babar* (3), *Tariq* (3), *Zahid* (3).

Baik (299) Korean: variant of PAEK.
GIVEN NAMES Korean 72%. *Young* (9), *Seung* (8), *Hyung* (5), *Sung* (5), *Ok* (3), *Soo* (3), *Chan* (2), *In Sang* (2), *Chang Ho, Choong, Chul Kyu, Chun*; *Chang* (3), *Nam* (3), *Chul* (2), *Eun Hee* (2), *Sang Hoon* (2), *Seoung* (2), *Byung, Eun Young, Hae Jung, Hee Sook, Hyong, In Soo.*

Bail (302) **1.** English: topographic name for someone who lived by the outer wall of a castle, Middle English *baile*, from Old French *bail(le)* 'enclosure' (see BAILEY 2). **2.** Spanish: variant of BAILE. **3.** Indian (Karnataka): Hindu (Brahman) name, probably a topographic name from Tulu *bail* 'low-lying land' (Dravidian *vayal* 'plain', 'field').
GIVEN NAMES Indian 4%. *Ashok, Mahesh, Rama, Ravi, Sumanth.*

Baile (147) **1.** English: variant of BAIL. **2.** Spanish: status name for a steward or official, from Old Spanish *baile*, Late Latin *baiulivus*; cognate with English BAILEY.

Bailen (105) **1.** Spanish (**Bailén**): habitational name from Bailén in Jaén province. **2.** German: unexplained.

Bailer (265) **1.** South German: probably an occupational name for a gauger or sealer of barrels, from an agent derivative of Middle High German *beil* 'barrel inspection'. See also BEILER. **2.** Altered spelling of **Böhler** (see BOEHLER). **3.** English: variant spelling of BAILOR.

Bailes (1004) English: **1.** variant of BAYLISS. **2.** from the genitive case of Middle English *bail(e)* 'bailey', 'outer wall of a castle', hence a topographic name for someone who lived beside a castle. Compare BAIL and BAILEY.

Bailey (93393) English: **1.** status name for a steward or official, Middle English *bail(l)i* (Old French *baillis*, from Late Latin *baiulivus*, an adjectival derivative of *baiulus* 'attendant', 'carrier' 'porter'). **2.** topographic name for someone who lived by the outer wall of a castle, Middle English *bail(l)y, baile* 'outer courtyard of a castle', from Old French *bail(le)* 'enclosure', a derivative of *bailer* 'to enclose', a word of unknown origin. This term became a place name in its own right, denoting a district beside a fortification or wall, as in the case of the Old Bailey in London, which formed part of the early medieval outer wall of the city. **3.** habitational name from Bailey in Lancashire, named with Old English *beg* 'berry' + *lēah* 'woodland clearing'. **4.** Anglicized form of French BAILLY.
FOREBEARS The surname Bailey was established early on in North America by several different bearers; one of them, James Bailey, was one of the founders of Rowley, MA.

A family of Huguenots of this name settled in CT, also using a variant spelling **Besly**.

Bailie (500) Scottish: status name for one of the senior members of a city council, or (earlier) the chief magistrate in a barony, Older Scots *baili*. Etymologically, this is the same word as BAILEY, but the functions as well as the spelling of the two officials were different in England and Scotland.

Bailiff (315) English: occupational name for an officer of a court of justice, from the English vocabulary word *bailiff*, which is from the objective case of Old French *bailis* (see BAYLISS).

Bailin (203) Variant spelling of the Ashkenazic Jewish name **Beylin**, a metronymic from the Yiddish female personal name *Beyle* meaning 'beautiful' (related to French *belle*).
GIVEN NAMES Jewish 5%. *Gershon, Miriam.*

Baillargeon (828) French: diminutive of **Baillarger**, a metonymic occupational name for a cereal farmer, from *baillarge*, a type of barley. Some branches of the family in North America have adopted the names ROE or ROWE as an English equivalent.
FOREBEARS A bearer of the name from the Angoumois region of France was documented in Trois Rivières, Quebec, in 1650.
GIVEN NAMES French 14%. *Andre* (6), *Normand* (5), *Armand* (4), *Jacques* (4), *Marcel* (2), *Alain, Alcide, Amede, Calix, Colette, Cyrille, Emile.*

Baillie (660) Scottish: variant spelling of BAILIE.

Bailly (270) French: occupational name for a steward or official, from Old French *baillis*. Compare BAILEY, BAYLISS.
FOREBEARS A Bailly, dit Lafleur, is documented in Montreal in 1661.
GIVEN NAMES French 7%. *Andre, Armand, Emile, Marcel, Philippe.*

Bailon (232) Spanish (**Bailón**): **1.** probably a nickname from *bailón* 'dancer', an agent derivative of *bailar* 'to dance'. **2.** Aragonese and southern Spanish (**Bailón**): probably from a diminutive of Aragonese *baile* 'judge'. **3.** Aragonese (**Bailón**): perhaps also from a derivative of Aragonese **Bailo**, a habitational name from Bailo, a town in Uesca, Aragon.
GIVEN NAMES Spanish 44%. *Francisco* (4), *Jose* (4), *Ana* (2), *Angel* (2), *Jesus* (2), *Juan* (2), *Luis* (2), *Pedro* (2), *Roberto* (2), *Tano* (2), *Abelino, Adela.*

Bailor (310) English: unexplained; possibly from the legal term *bailor* 'one who delivers goods'.

Bails (211) English: variant spelling of BAILES.

Baily (547) English: variant spelling of BAILEY.

Baim (184) Alternative spelling of Jewish (eastern Ashkenazic) BEIM.
GIVEN NAME Jewish 4%. *Hyman.*

Baima (130) Origin uncertain. Perhaps a variant of Frisian BAJEMA.

Bain (6499) **1.** Scottish: nickname for a fair-haired person, from Gaelic *bàn* 'white', 'fair'. This is a common name in the Highlands, first recorded in Perth in 1324. It is also found as a reduced form of MCBAIN. **2.** Northern English: nickname meaning 'bone', probably bestowed on an exceptionally tall, lean man, from Old English *bān* 'bone'. In northern Middle English *-ā-* was preserved, whereas in southern dialects (which later became standard), it was changed to *-ō-*. **3.** Northern English: nickname for a hospitable person, from northern Middle English *beyn*, *bayn* 'welcoming', 'friendly' (Old Norse *beinn* 'straight', 'direct'). **4.** English and French: metonymic occupational name for an attendant at a public bath house, from Middle English, Old French *baine* 'bath'. **5.** French: topographic name for someone who lived by a Roman bath, from Old French *baine* 'bath' or a habitational name from a place in Ille-et-Vilaine, named with this word. **6.** Possibly an altered spelling of North German BEHN.
FOREBEARS George Luke Scobie Bain (1836–91) was born in Stirling, Scotland. He ran away to sea and successively lived and worked in Portland, ME, Chicago, and St. Louis, where he was a miller and flour merchant and a very prominent citizen.

Bainbridge (1291) English: habitational name from Bainbridge in North Yorkshire, named for the Bain river on which it stands (which is named with Old Norse *beinn* 'straight') + Old English *brycg* 'bridge'.
FOREBEARS A family of this name was very prominent in Princeton, NJ, from the mid 17th century.

Baine (499) English and French: variant spelling of BAIN.

Bainer (120) Origin unidentified. Probably of English or German origin.

Baines (1742) **1.** Scottish and northern English: nickname meaning 'bones'. Compare BAIN 2. **2.** Scottish: reduced form of MCBANE, with English patronymic *-s*. **3.** English, of Welsh origin: Anglicized form of Welsh *ab Einws* 'son of *Einws*', a pet form of the personal name *Einon* (see EYNON). **4.** English: from a derivative of BAIN.

Bains (498) **1.** Indian (Panjab): Sikh name based on that of a Jat tribe. It is believed that *Bains* was the name of the ancestor of this clan. **2.** Scottish and English: variant of BAINES.
GIVEN NAMES Indian 56%. *Avtar* (2), *Dharam* (2), *Harcharn* (2), *Jagdish* (2), *Joga* (2), *Mohan* (2), *Raj* (2), *Shangara* (2), *Sohan* (2), *Ajit*, *Ajmer*, *Amar*.

Bainter (503) German: topographic name with numerous variants, from Middle High German *biunte* (modern *Bünd-*) 'enclosed

plot of land (for cultivation or a farmstead)'. See POINTER.

Bainum (126) English, of Welsh origin: variant of BEYNON.

Baio (222) Italian: nickname for someone with light brown or reddish brown hair or beard, from *baio* 'bay (horse)' (from Late Latin *badius* 'red-brown').
GIVEN NAMES Italian 23%. *Angelo* (6), *Sal* (4), *Salvatore* (4), *Carmelo* (3), *Antonio*, *Carmine*, *Dino*, *Filomena*, *Fiore*, *Pietro*.

Baiocchi (104) Italian: variant of **Baiocco**, which is probably a derivative of BAIO.
GIVEN NAMES Italian 21%. *Gino* (2), *Aldo*, *Angelo*, *Enrico*, *Enzo*, *Gianpaolo*, *Italo*, *Livio*, *Lucrezia*, *Reno*.

Bair (4219) Altered spelling of German BAER.

Baird (14003) Scottish: occupational name from Gaelic *bàrd* 'bard', 'poet', 'minstrel', or of Gaelic **Mac an Baird** 'son of the bard'.
FOREBEARS This is the name of a PA (Pittsburgh) family which reached America from Scotland, via northern Ireland.

Baires (109) Hispanic: unexplained.
GIVEN NAMES Spanish 58%. *Jose* (4), *Luis* (4), *Carlos* (3), *Alberto* (2), *Felipe* (2), *Juan* (2), *Julio* (2), *Roberto* (2), *Adalberto*, *Adelina*, *Alfredo*, *Alicia*; *Amadeo* (2).

Bairos (116) Variant of Portuguese **Bairros**, a habitational name from any of various places called Bairros, as for example in Aveiro, Braga, and Porto provinces.
GIVEN NAMES Spanish 29%; Portuguese 24%. *Jose* (9), *Manuel* (6), *Altino*, *Augusto*, *Dinis*, *Eduardo*, *Ernesto*, *Francisco*, *Helio*, *Isidro*; *Joao* (2), *Agostinho*, *Henrique*, *Serafim*; *Antonio* (6), *Agnelo*, *Angelo*.

Baisch (333) South German: from a dialect short form of SEBASTIAN.

Baisden (867) English: unexplained. It may be a variant of BASTIN, or perhaps a habitational name from a lost or unidentified place. In Britain the surname now occurs mainly in Essex.

Baise (158) **1.** Variant of English BASS. **2.** French: variant of BAIZE.

Baisley (380) English and Scottish: variant of English BAZLEY or Scottish PAISLEY.

Baitinger (113) German: habitational name from Beutingen in Baden-Württemberg.
GIVEN NAMES German 5%. *Kurt*, *Otto*.

Baity (628) Variant of Scottish and northern Irish BEATTY.

Baiz (115) **1.** Variant of Spanish **Báez** (see BAEZ). **2.** Variant of German BEITZ.
GIVEN NAMES Spanish 19%. *Luis* (3), *Carlos*, *Estefana*, *Ignacio*, *Jose*, *Leandro*, *Luiz*, *Manuel*, *Pascual*, *Salvador*, *Sotero*.

Baiza (121) Variant spelling of Spanish **Baeza**, a habitational name from a place so named in the province of Jaén.
GIVEN NAMES Spanish 37%. *Jose Antonio* (2), *Lupe* (2), *Ramiro* (2), *Alberto*, *Angel*, *Armando*, *Carlos*, *Elida*, *Elpidio*, *Jesus*, *Jose Mario*, *Juan*.

Baize (572) **1.** French: possibly an Americanized spelling of **Bèze**, a habitational name from a place in Burgundy taking its name from the river of the same name. As an American surname it is most frequent in the Old South, especially TX. **2.** Perhaps an altered spelling of German *Böse*, see BOESE.

Bajaj (185) Indian (Panjab and Rajasthan): Hindu (Arora, Bania, Khatri), Jain, and Sikh name, from Panjabi *bəjāj* or *bəzāz* 'clothier', from Arabic *bazzāz*. The Aroras, Khatris, and also the Banias have clans called Bajaj. See also ARORA, KHATRI.
GIVEN NAMES Indian 91%. *Anil* (4), *Ashok* (4), *Prem* (4), *Ajay* (3), *Avinash* (3), *Ravi* (3), *Vijay* (3), *Vinod* (3), *Amit* (2), *Balwinder* (2), *Dinesh* (2), *Harish* (2).

Bajek (126) Polish: nickname for a story teller, from *bajać* 'to tell stories'.
GIVEN NAMES Polish 12%. *Janusz*, *Mariusz*, *Mieczyslaw*, *Tadeusz*.

Bajema (150) Frisian: patronymic from an unidentified personal name.
GIVEN NAME German 5%. *Otto* (3).

Bajor (119) Polish: topographic name from *bajor* 'marsh', 'pond'.
GIVEN NAMES Polish 19%. *Jerzy* (2), *Andrzej*, *Dariusz*, *Franciszek*, *Jozef*, *Jurek*, *Krystyna*, *Zbigniew*.

Bajorek (193) Polish: topographic name for someone who lived by a marsh, from a diminutive of *bajor* 'marsh', 'pond'.
GIVEN NAMES Polish 10%. *Bronislawa*, *Grzegorz*, *Henryk*, *Ignacy*, *Ireneusz*, *Jozefa*, *Krzysztof*, *Pawel*.

Bajwa (207) Indian (Panjab): Sikh name based on that of a Jat tribe.
GIVEN NAMES Indian 54%; Muslim 35%. *Ajay* (2), *Jagdish* (2), *Amolak*, *Amrit*, *Anupa*, *Balwinder*, *Deep*, *Dilip*, *Gursharan*, *Harjeet*, *Jag*, *Jagdev*; *Naseer* (4), *Tanvir* (4), *Iqbal* (2), *Mohammad* (2), *Mohsin* (2), *Abid*, *Ali*, *Amna*, *Asif*, *Atiq*, *Ayesha*, *Chaudhry*.

Bak (968) **1.** Polish, Czech, Slovak, and Hungarian: from the medieval personal name *Bak*. This personal name probably existed in Polish and Ukrainian too, but Rymut derives the surname from *bakać* 'to scold or yell'. **2.** Slovenian: unexplained. The Slovenian name comes from the southern part of the Kras region of southwestern Slovenia. **3.** Dutch: variant of BAKKE. **4.** Korean: variant of PAK.
GIVEN NAMES Polish 11%. *Bogdan* (3), *Jerzy* (3), *Jozef* (3), *Stanislaw* (3), *Andrzej* (2), *Dariusz* (2), *Dorota* (2), *Jacek* (2), *Ryszard* (2), *Tadeusz* (2), *Benedykt*, *Boguslaw*.

Baka (196) **1.** Czech, Slovak, and Hungarian: patronymic from the personal name BAK. **2.** Hungarian: possibly also from *baka* 'foot soldier', hence a status name for an ordinary soldier. **3.** Polish: from a derivative of BAK.

Bakal (104) **1.** Jewish (from Moldavia): occupational name from Turkish *bakkal* 'grocer'. **2.** Jewish (from Belarus): nickname from Belorussian *bakalo* 'gaper'.

GIVEN NAMES Jewish 8%; Russian 7%. *Uri, Yitzhak; Konstantin, Lyudmila, Vasily.*

Bakalar (167) Czech (**Bakalář**), Slovak (**Bakalár**), and Polish (**Bakalarz**): from medieval Latin *baccalarius* 'school teacher'. Compare BACHELOR.

Bakas (132) Greek: **1.** nickname for a small, rotund man, from Albanian *baq, baqth* 'lower belly'. It may also be a reduced form of surnames beginning with *Bak-* as a prefix, such as **Bakogiannis** 'Belly John'. **2.** offensive nickname from a dialect word meaning 'fool'.

GIVEN NAMES Greek 13%; Spanish 5%. *Constantine* (4), *Angelos, Athanasios, Dimitrios, Eleftheria, Kalliopi, Pericles; Sergio* (2), *Ana Maria, Jaime, Susana.*

Bake (221) **1.** English: probably an occupational name for a baker. **2.** German (northern Frisian): from a short form of the personal name *Balke*, itself a reduced form of *Baldeke*, a pet form of *Baldewin* (see BALDWIN). **3.** Dutch: variant of BAEK.

Bakehouse (27) English: variant of BACKUS.

Bakeman (224) Americanized spelling of Dutch **Baekman** or one of its variants (see BAEK).

Baker (148669) **1.** English: occupational name, from Middle English *bakere*, Old English *bæcere*, a derivative of *bacan* 'to bake'. It may have been used for someone whose special task in the kitchen of a great house or castle was the baking of bread, but since most humbler households did their own baking in the Middle Ages, it may also have referred to the owner of a communal oven used by the whole village. The right to be in charge of this and exact money or loaves in return for its use was in many parts of the country a hereditary feudal privilege. Compare MILLER. Less often the surname may have been acquired by someone noted for baking particularly fine bread or by a baker of pottery or bricks. **2.** Americanized form of cognates or equivalents in many other languages, for example German **Bäcker**, **Becker**; Dutch **Bakker**, **Bakmann**; French **Boulanger**. For other forms see Hanks and Hodges (1988).

FOREBEARS Baker was well established as an early immigrant family name in Puritan New England. Among others, two men called Remember Baker (father and son) lived at Woodbury, CT, in the early 17th century, and an Alexander Baker arrived in Boston, MA, in 1635.

Bakes (162) Of multiple origin, including **1.** Czech and Slovak (**Bakeš**): from a derivative of the personal name BAK. **2.** English (Yorkshire): unexplained.

Bakewell (315) English: habitational name from Bakewell in Derbyshire, named with the Old English personal name *Badeca, Baduca* (from a short form of the various

compound personal names with the first element *beadu* 'battle') + *well(a)* 'spring', 'stream'.

Bakey (126) Americanized form of Dutch BAKKE.

Bakke (1571) **1.** Dutch: from Middle Dutch *bac* 'bucket', 'bin', 'beaker', hence a metonymic occupational name for a maker of such vessels. **2.** Dutch: nickname for someone with a peculiarity of the mouth, jaw, or cheek, from Dutch *bakke* 'cheek', 'side'. **3.** Norwegian: habitational name from any of numerous farmsteads named with Old Norse *bakki* 'hillside', 'bank'.

GIVEN NAMES Scandinavian 5%. *Erik* (3), *Jalmer* (2), *Anders, Astrid, Bergit, Bjorn, Dagny, Gudrun, Helmer, Knute, Ordell, Tollef.*

Bakken (1786) Scandinavian (especially Norway): variant of BAKKE, with the addition of the definite article *-n*. Like BAKKE, this is one of the most frequent surnames in Norway.

GIVEN NAMES Scandinavian 6%. *Erik* (3), *Lars* (3), *Helmer* (2), *Nels* (2), *Johan, Maren, Per, Sig, Tor.*

Bakker (1250) **1.** Dutch: occupational name for a baker, Dutch and Low German *bakker*. Compare English BAKER. **2.** Norwegian: variant of BAKKE, using a plural formation.

GIVEN NAMES Dutch 9%; German 4%. *Gerrit* (7), *Dirk* (6), *Klaas* (3), *Cornelis* (2), *Cornie* (2), *Durk* (2), *Frans* (2), *Kees* (2), *Michiel* (2), *Pieter* (2), *Aaltje, Adrianus; Konrad* (5), *Claus, Erwin, Frieda, Gerhard, Hans, Hertha, Johannes.*

Bakko (100) Variant spelling of Hungarian BAKO.

Bakkum (109) Dutch: unexplained.

Bakley (173) Origin uncertain. **1.** Perhaps an altered spelling of Dutch or Belgian *Backele*, from a diminutive of **Bachelier**, French form of BATCHELOR. **2.** Alternatively, perhaps, an Americanized form of German BAECHLE.

Bako (139) **1.** Hungarian (**Bakó**): patronymic from BAK. **2.** Hungarian: from *bakó*, an occupational name for an executioner. **3.** Croatian: nickname from the archaic word *bako* 'bull'. The name is frequent in Istria and Dalmatia.

GIVEN NAMES Hungarian 12%. *Zoltan* (3), *Balazs, Gabor, Lajos, Sandor.*

Bakos (523) **1.** Hungarian: derivative of the medieval personal name BAK. **2.** Croatian (**Bakoš**): from the personal name *Bakoš*, a pet form of BALTAZAR or of a Slavic name such as *Bratoljub*.

GIVEN NAMES Hungarian 4%. *Geza* (2), *Csaba, Ferenc, Janos, Sandor, Tamas, Zsolt.*

Bakowski (150) Polish (**Bąkowski**): habitational name from any of a number of places called Bąkow, Bąkowa, or Bąkowo.

GIVEN NAMES Polish 12%; French 6%. *Elzbieta, Janusz, Jerzy, Lech, Pawel, Zygmunt; Andre, Camille, Aloysius.*

Baksa (106) **1.** Hungarian: from a derivative of the personal name *Bak* (see BAK). **2.** Hungarian: habitational name from a place called Baksa. **3.** Czech (**Bakša**); Slovak (**Baksa** or **Baxa**); Croatian (**Baksa** or **Bakša**): nickname from a derivative of *bak* 'bull'. **4.** Croatian (**Bakša**): from a pet form of the personal name *Bratoljub*. The Croatian family name is found mostly in Istria.

GIVEN NAMES Hungarian 4%. *Sandor, Tibor.*

Baksh (264) Muslim (Iranian, also found in Pakistan, India, and Bangladesh): from a Persian personal name, *Bakhsh*, based on the Persian word *bakhsh* meaning 'fate', 'destiny', 'portion', 'share'.

GIVEN NAMES Muslim 70%; Indian 4%. *Mohamed* (11), *Bibi* (7), *Mustapha* (5), *Abdul* (3), *Karim* (3), *Mohammed* (3), *Nadir* (3), *Amin* (2), *Anwar* (2), *Fareed* (2), *Hanif* (2), *Mohammad* (2); *Jasodra, Leela, Nandi, Radica, Sharmila.*

Bakshi (180) Indian (Panjab): Hindu and Sikh name, from Persian *bakhshī* 'paymaster', originally the title of an official who distributed wages in the Muslim armies.

GIVEN NAMES Indian 79%. *Amar* (2), *Daya* (2), *Deepak* (2), *Krishan* (2), *Mahesh* (2), *Pradeep* (2), *Ranvir* (2), *Sanjay* (2), *Saroj* (2), *Vikram* (2), *Ajay, Anil.*

Bakst (177) Jewish (from Belarus): habitational name from Bakshty in Belarus.

GIVEN NAMES Jewish 10%. *Yehudah* (2), *Jakob, Leib, Meir, Meyer, Nosson.*

Bakula (166) **1.** Polish (**Bakuła**): from a derivative of the personal name BAK. **2.** Polish: nickname for a habitual liar, from *bakulić* 'to lie in one's throat'. (The Polish idiom translates literally as 'to lie in one's eyes'.) **3.** Serbian or Croatian (Dalmatia): derivative of BAKO 'bull'.

GIVEN NAMES Polish 6%. *Wieslaw* (2), *Casimir, Wieslawa.*

Bal (297) **1.** Indian (Panjab): Sikh name based on the name of a Jat tribe, from Sanskrit *bala* 'strength'. **2.** Polish: from a reduced form of the personal name BALTAZAR. **3.** French: from a short form of a personal name of Germanic origin formed with *bald* 'bold' as the first element.

GIVEN NAMES Indian 27%; Polish 4%. *Krishan* (2), *Avtar, Balwinder, Ganesh, Gursharan, Hardev, Karnail, Mahendra, Raj, Ravi, Subhash, Sudarshan; Kazimierz* (2), *Janusz, Malgorzata, Piotr, Wojciech.*

Bala (354) **1.** Indian (Gujarat and Bombay city): Parsi name, probably from Persian *bālā* 'high', 'exalted'. **2.** Indian (southern states): variant of BALAN, particularly among speakers of Tamil and Malayalam who have migrated away from their home state. In India it is only a given name, but it has come to be used as a family name among South Indians in the U.S. **3.** Polish: from a reduced form of the personal name

BALTAZAR. **4.** Hungarian: from a pet form of the personal name *Balázs*, a vernacular form of BLASIUS.

GIVEN NAMES Indian 23%. *Deepa* (2), *Manju* (2), *Nisha* (2), *Pranab* (2), *Ravi* (2), *Adarsh, Arul, Chandran, Ganesan, Indu, Karthik, Kavita.*

Balaban (534) **1.** Ukrainian, Belorussian, Romanian, and Jewish (eastern Ashkenazic): from a Russian word meaning 'hawk', probably usually applied as a descriptive nickname, although it could also be an occupational name for a falconer. In Ukrainian and Belorussian *balaban* also means 'chatterer'. In patronymic form (**Balabanov**) it is also found as a Russian and Bulgarian surname. **2.** Greek: nickname for a big man, from Turkish *balaban* 'tame bear', or a shortened form of some other family name derived from this word, such as **Balabanis, Balabanidis, Balabanos,** or **Balabanopoulos.**

GIVEN NAMES Jewish 6%. *Emanuel* (3), *Yakov* (2), *Zev* (2), *Chaja, Chaya, Moisey.*

Balaguer (123) Catalan: habitational name from Balaguer in Lleida province.

GIVEN NAMES Spanish 36%. *Jorge* (3), *Jose* (3), *Luis* (3), *Enrique* (2), *Jaime* (2), *Joaquin* (2), *Alberto, Arnulfo, Carlos, Domingo, Emiliano, Francisco.*

Balakrishnan (135) Indian (Kerala, Tamil Nadu): Hindu name from Sanskrit *bālakṛṣṇa* 'child Krishna' (from *bāla* 'child' + *kṛṣṇa*, name of an incarnation of the god Vishnu, meaning 'black'), + the Tamil-Malayalam third-person masculine singular suffix *-n*. This is only a personal name in India, but has come to be used as a family name in the U.S.

GIVEN NAMES Indian 95%. *Arun* (3), *Ramesh* (3), *Sivakumar* (3), *Ashok* (2), *Govind* (2), *Karthik* (2), *Prasad* (2), *Sankaran* (2), *Sekar* (2), *Suresh* (2), *Usha* (2), *Anant.*

Balan (243) **1.** Spanish (Mexico): unexplained. **2.** Variant of French **Baland, Balland,** possibly a nickname from *balland* 'dancer'. **3.** Czech (**Balán**): from a reduced and altered form of the personal name BALTAZAR. **4.** Romanian: descriptive nickname from Romanian *bălan* 'blond'. **5.** Indian (Kerala, Tamil Nadu): Indian (Kerala, Tamil Nadu): Hindu name from Sanskrit *bāla* 'child' + the Tamil-Malayalam third-person masculine singular suffix *-n*. This is only a given name in India, but has come to be used as a family name in the U.S.

FOREBEARS A Balan with the secondary surname Lacombe is documented in Beaumont, Quebec, in 1699.

GIVEN NAMES Spanish 17%; Indian 12%; Russian 5%; French 4%; Romanian 4%. *Cesar* (2), *Leopoldo* (2), *Pablo* (2), *Reynaldo* (2), *Traian* (2), *Alicia, Amalia, Arnaldo, Carlos, Domingo, Edgardo, Emeterio*; *Ajay, Ajit, Chandra, Dinesh, Mahesh, Prakash, Rajasekhar, Ramesh, Sanjay, Shankar, Siva, Subra*; *Aleksandr,*

Boris, Gennady, Lyudmila, Mikhail, Nikolay, Svetlana, Vladimir; *Micheline, Mireille*; *Corneliu, Cosmin, Danut, Ilie, Toader.*

Balas (517) **1.** Hungarian (**Balás**): from a form of the personal name *Balázs* (see BALAZS). **2.** Polish; Czech and Slovak (**Baláš**); and Croatian (northern and eastern Croatia; **Balaš** and **Balas**): either from a reduced form of the personal name BALTAZAR or from Slavic forms of the Hungarian personal name *Balázs* (see BALAZS).

Balasco (104) Spanish (of Basque origin): see VELASCO.

Balash (255) **1.** Americanized spelling of Czech and Slovak **Balaš** or Hungarian **Balász** (see BALAZS), from vernacular forms of the Latin personal name BLASIUS. **2.** Albanian: from *balash*, denoting an animal with a white facial marking.

Balasubramanian (116) Indian (Kerala, Tamil Nadu): Hindu name from Sanskrit *bālasubrahmaṇya* 'child Subrahmanya' (from *bāla* 'child' + *subrahmaṇya* 'dear to Brahmans', an epithet of the god Kartikeya, son of the god Shiva) + the Tamil-Malayalam third-person masculine singular suffix *-n*. This is only a given name in India, but has come to be used as a family name in the U.S.

GIVEN NAMES Indian 96%. *Bala* (3), *Ganesh* (3), *Usha* (3), *Gopi* (2), *Kumar* (2), *Shankar* (2), *Sundar* (2), *Vijay* (2), *Amita, Anitha, Bhavani, Janaki.*

Balay (100) **1.** French: habitational name from any of various minor places and localities so named. **2.** Indian (Gujarat): Hindu (Bhatia) name based on the name of a Bhatia subgroup.

GIVEN NAMES Indian 5%. *Rajesh, Satish.*

Balazs (421) Hungarian (**Balázs**): from the Hungarian personal name *Balázs*, vernacular form of BLASIUS.

GIVEN NAMES Hungarian 16%. *Tibor* (5), *Laszlo* (4), *Antal* (2), *Attila* (2), *Gabor* (2), *Ildiko* (2), *Imre* (2), *Sandor* (2), *Zoltan* (2), *Csaba, Denes, Dezso.*

Balbach (207) German (Franconia): habitational name from Balbach on the Tauber river, near Karlsruhe.

GIVEN NAMES German 4%. *Kurt, Otto.*

Balbi (111) Italian: patronymic or plural form of BALBO.

GIVEN NAMES Italian 18%; Spanish 11%. *Salvatore* (3), *Carmelo* (2), *Adolfo, Angelo, Cornelio*; *Alejandrina, Dominga, Isidra, Jose, Mariano, Pablo.*

Balbo (140) Italian: nickname for someone with a speech impediment, from Latin *balbus* 'stammering', 'stuttering'.

GIVEN NAMES Italian 14%. *Salvatore* (2), *Angelo, Giuseppe, Gregorio, Italo, Mario, Sal.*

Balboa (263) Galician: habitational name from the city of Balboa, named with Latin *vallis bona* 'pleasant valley'.

GIVEN NAMES Spanish 40%. *Jose* (13), *Ramon* (3), *Emilio* (2), *Genaro* (2), *Guadalupe* (2), *Jesus* (2), *Juan* (2), *Luisa* (2), *Marcos Antonio* (2), *Mario* (2), *Raul* (2), *Ruben* (2).

Balboni (414) Italian: from *Balbone*, an inflected form of the personal name BALBO.

GIVEN NAMES Italian 18%. *Angelo* (2), *Dante* (2), *Giorgio* (2), *Mauro* (2), *Antonio, Federico, Marco, Nino, Renzo, Salvatore.*

Balbuena (257) Asturian-Leonese: habitational name from either of two places called Valbuena ('pleasant valley') in the provinces of Asturies and Lléon. Compare BALBOA.

GIVEN NAMES Spanish 52%. *Juan* (6), *Luis* (6), *Miguel* (5), *Amparo* (3), *Angel* (3), *Arturo* (3), *Jorge* (3), *Jose* (3), *Manuel* (3), *Alberto* (2), *Carolina* (2), *Felipe* (2).

Balcazar (129) Spanish: variant of BALTAZAR.

GIVEN NAMES Spanish 56%. *Miguel* (4), *Mario* (3), *Raul* (3), *Arturo* (2), *Carlos* (2), *Jose* (2), *Pablo* (2), *Alba, Alberto, Angel, Ascencion, Beatriz.*

Balcer (340) Polish (**Balcerz**) and Czech: from a vernacular form of the personal name BALTAZAR.

GIVEN NAME French 4%. *Georges.*

Balcerak (117) Polish: variant of BALCERZAK.

Balcerzak (221) Polish: pet form or patronymic from BALCER.

GIVEN NAMES Polish 6%. *Casimir, Henryk, Zigmunt.*

Balch (1819) **1.** English: from Middle English *balch, belch* 'balk', 'beam' (Old English *bælc, balca*), possibly denoting someone who lived in a house with a roof beam rather than in a simple hut; alternatively it may have been a nickname for a man built like a tree trunk, i.e. one of stocky, heavy build. **2.** English: nickname from Middle English *balche, belche* 'swelling' (Old English *bælc(e)*). This was probably chiefly given in the sense 'swelling pride', 'overweening arrogance', but it can also mean 'eructation', 'belch' and may therefore in some cases have been acquired by a man given to belching. **3.** Welsh: from the adjective *balch*, which has a range of meanings—'fine', 'splendid', 'proud', 'arrogant', 'glad'—but the predominant meaning is 'proud' and from this the family name probably derives.

FOREBEARS The surname Balch was established in MD *c.*1650.

Balchunas (169) Lithuanian (**Balčiūnas**): patronymic from the personal name *Balčius*, from Lithuanian *baltas* 'white'.

Balcom (988) Altered spelling of English **Balcombe**, a habitational name from Balcombe in West Sussex, which is named with Old English *bealu* 'evil', 'calamity' (or the Old English personal name *Bealda*) + *cumb* 'valley'.

Balcomb (100) Variant of English **Balcombe** (see BALCOM).

Bald (353) **1.** Dutch and German: from the Germanic personal name *Baldo*, or a short form of the various compound names such as BALDWIN, formed with the first element *bald* 'bold', 'strong'. **2.** Scottish: nickname for a bald man, from Middle English *balled* 'rounded like a ball', from *bal(le)* 'ball' (Old English *ball* or Old Norse *bǫllr*).
GIVEN NAMES German 5%. *Hans* (2), *Inge* (2), *Karl-Heinz, Konrad, Kurt, Otto.*

Balda (117) **1.** Catalan: from Arabic *dabla* 'stick', 'pole'. **2.** Basque: variant of **Alda**. **3.** from the Germanic personal name *Baldo* (see BALDO).
GIVEN NAMES Spanish 8%; French 5%. *Alfredo, Carlos, Jose, Juan, Marcelo*; *Emile, Marcel.*

Baldacci (130) Italian: from **Baldacco**, a derivative of the personal name BALDO.
GIVEN NAMES Italian 4%. *Angelo, Caesar, Vasco.*

Baldasare (105) Variant spelling of Italian BALDASSARRE.
GIVEN NAME Italian 8%. *Rocco* (2).

Baldassano (110) Italian (Sicilian): unexplained; perhaps from a derivative of the personal name BALDO.
GIVEN NAMES Italian 16%. *Salvatore* (2), *Sal.*

Baldassare (136) Italian: variant of BALDASSARRE.
GIVEN NAMES Italian 23%. *Mario* (2), *Aldo, Camillo, Elvira, Geremia, Remo, Sarina.*

Baldassari (160) Italian: variant of BALDASSARRE.
GIVEN NAMES Italian 14%. *Angelo, Carlo, Dino, Emelio, Giovanni, Mafalda, Riccardo, Ugo.*

Baldassarre (160) Italian: from the Biblical personal name *Baldassarre*, Italian form of BALTAZAR.
GIVEN NAMES Italian 24%. *Italo* (2), *Angelo, Antonio, Ennio, Ezio, Guido, Luigi, Mauro, Rocco.*

Baldauf (506) South German: from the Germanic personal name *Baldolf* ('bold wolf'), altered by folk etymology as if it were a combination of Middle High German *bald* 'soon' + *auf* 'up' (earlier *uf*), and hence taken as a nickname for a rash or intolerant person, quick to judge, or for an early riser.
GIVEN NAMES German 4%. *Gunther, Hans, Herwig, Kurt.*

Baldelli (148) Italian: from a diminutive of the personal name BALDO.
GIVEN NAMES Italian 6%. *Dario* (2), *Angelo, Nino, Reno.*

Balder (173) German: **1.** from the Germanic personal name *Balderam* (from the adjective *bald* 'hardy', 'bold', 'strong'). **2.** see BALTER.

Balderas (1165) Spanish: habitational name from Valderas in León province, so named as *valle de eras* 'valley of *eras*'; *era*, from Latin *area*, denoted variously, an area of firm flat land used as a threshing floor, a clearing, or a fertile patch.

GIVEN NAMES Spanish 52%. *Jose* (37), *Juan* (20), *Jesus* (14), *Manuel* (14), *Carlos* (11), *Ricardo* (9), *Alberto* (7), *Alfredo* (7), *Alfonso* (6), *Alicia* (6), *Angel* (6), *Arturo* (6).

Balderrama (407) Variant of Spanish VALDERRAMA.
GIVEN NAMES Spanish 45%. *Juan* (7), *Jose* (6), *Armando* (4), *Raul* (4), *Ruben* (4), *Francisco* (3), *Gustavo* (3), *Manuel* (3), *Tomas* (3), *Carlos* (2), *Enrique* (2), *Javier* (2).

Balderson (544) English: assimilated form of BALDERSTON, rather than a patronymic from *Balder*, appearances to the contrary notwithstanding.

Balderston (294) **1.** English: habitational name from either of two places in Lancashire called Balderston(e), deriving their names from the genitive case of the Old English personal name *Baldhere* (composed of the elements *bald* 'bold', 'brave' + *here* 'army') + Old English *tūn* 'enclosure', 'settlement'. **2.** Scottish: habitational name from Balderston in West Lothian, which has the same etymology as 1.

Baldes (109) Asturian-Leonese: variant of **Valdé** (see VALDES).
GIVEN NAMES Spanish 5%. *Jose* (2), *Juanita, Luis, Miguel.*

Baldi (520) **1.** Italian: patronymic or plural form of BALDO. **2.** Hungarian (**Báldi**): habitational name for someone from a place called Báld in Kolozs county in Transylvania, now in Romania.
GIVEN NAMES Italian 15%. *Angelo* (3), *Carmine* (3), *Salvatore* (3), *Aldo* (2), *Enzo* (2), *Marco* (2), *Alessandro, Dante, Dino, Enrico, Francesca, Gaetano.*

Balding (410) English: from the unattested Old English personal name *Bealding*, a derivative of *Beald*, or in some cases a variant of BALDWIN.

Baldinger (268) German and Jewish (Ashkenazic): habitational name for someone from a place called Baldingen, either in Württemberg, Germany, or Aargau, Switzerland.
GIVEN NAMES Jewish 4%. *Bronia* (2), *Ilan, Levi.*

Baldini (472) Italian: patronymic or plural form of BALDINO.
GIVEN NAMES Italian 16%. *Angelo* (2), *Carlo* (2), *Dino* (2), *Domenic* (2), *Elio* (2), *Luigi* (2), *Vito* (2), *Aldo, Alessandra, Amerigo, Camillo, Elisabetta.*

Baldino (549) Italian: from a pet form of the Germanic personal name BALDO.
GIVEN NAMES Italian 16%. *Rocco* (4), *Angelo* (3), *Carlo* (2), *Ciro* (2), *Cosmo* (2), *Domenic* (2), *Salvatore* (2), *Carmello, Carmelo, Gino, Giovanna, Paride.*

Baldner (159) German: probably a variant of **Balt(e)ner**, an occupational name from Middle High German *balteniere* (medieval Latin *paltonarius*) 'pilgrim', 'vagrant in a pilgrim's cloak'.

Baldo (255) Italian: from a short form of a personal name of Germanic origin formed with *bald* 'bold' as the second element, for example *Ubaldo, Teobaldo, Garibaldo, Rambaldo.*
GIVEN NAMES Italian 17%; Spanish 8%. *Antonio* (4), *Elio, Federico, Leonardo, Marcello, Reno, Salvatore, Valentino*; *Luis* (2), *Jose, Juan, Juanita, Julio, Rosario.*

Baldocchi (106) Italian: variant of **Baldocci**, from a derivative of the personal name BALDO.
GIVEN NAMES Italian 17%. *Gino* (2), *Angelo, Evo, Giovanni, Guido, Marco, Umberto.*

Baldock (373) English: habitational name from a place in Hertfordshire, first named in the 12th century by the Knights Templar, who held the manor there. It was named in commemoration of the city of Baghdad, known in Middle English and Old French as *Baldac*; its Arabic etymology is said to be 'city of *Dat*', the personal name of a dervish.

Baldon (90) English: possibly a habitational name from one of the group of places in Oxfordshire named Baldon, from the Old English personal name *Bealda* + *dūn* 'hill', or a variant of BALDWIN.

Baldonado (332) Spanish: variant of **Maldonado**, a nickname from Latin *male dolatus* 'ill fashioned' or *male donatus* 'ill favored'. This was the name of a well-known medieval family from Galicia, which had numerous branches in Portugal and Spain.
GIVEN NAMES Spanish 30%. *Jose* (6), *Manuel* (3), *Ramon* (3), *Avelino* (2), *Eloy* (2), *Francisco* (2), *Rudolfo* (2), *Adela, Alfonso, Alfredo, Alicia, Arsenio.*

Baldoni (168) Italian: from an augmentative of BALDO (see BALDELLI).
GIVEN NAMES Italian 9%; Spanish 6%. *Armando, Carlo, Dino, Enrico, Libero, Nazareno*; *Carlos, Luis, Marcos, Mercedes.*

Baldree (364) Variant of English BALDRY.

Baldridge (2143) **1.** English: from a Middle English personal name, *Baldrik* (see BALDREE). In the British Isles, the name now occurs chiefly in northeastern England. **2.** Possibly an altered spelling of the cognate German name **Baldrich**.

Baldry (142) English: from a Germanic personal name composed of the elements *bald* 'bold', 'brave' + *rīc* 'power'. This may have been present in Old English in a form *Bealdrīc*, but it was reintroduced by the Normans as *Baldri, Baudri*, and it is from these forms that the surname is derived.

Balducci (430) Italian: from a diminutive of BALDO.
GIVEN NAMES Italian 17%. *Angelo* (3), *Carlo* (2), *Giulio* (2), *Leno* (2), *Rino* (2), *Vito* (2), *Aldo, Amelio, Antonio, Domenic, Enrico, Geno.*

Balduf (117) South German: variant of BALDAUF.
GIVEN NAME German 4%. *Otto.*

Baldus (339) Frisian, Dutch, and North German: from a reduced and altered form of the personal name *Balthasar* (see BALTAZAR).

Baldwin (28430) **1.** English: from a Germanic personal name composed of the elements *bald* 'bold', 'brave' + *wine* 'friend', which was extremely popular among the Normans and in Flanders in the early Middle Ages. It was the personal name of the Crusader who in 1100 became the first Christian king of Jerusalem, and of four more Crusader kings of Jerusalem. It was also borne by Baldwin, Count of Flanders (1172–1205), leader of the Fourth Crusade, who became first Latin Emperor of Constantinople (1204). As an American surname it has absorbed Dutch spellings such as **Boudewijn**. **2.** Irish: surname adopted in Donegal by bearers of the Gaelic name **Ó Maolagáin** (see MILLIGAN), due to association of Gaelic *maol* 'bald', 'hairless' with English *bald*.

FOREBEARS A John Baldwin from Buckinghamshire, England, arrived in the U.S. in 1638 and settled in Milford, CT.

Baldy (142) **1.** Scottish and northern Irish: from the personal name *Baldy* or *Baldie*, a pet form of ARCHIBALD. **2.** English: possibly from an Old English female personal name, *Bealdgȳð*, meaning 'bold combat', first recorded *c.*1170 as *Baldith*, and in others from the Old Norse personal name *Baldi*.

Baldyga (259) Polish (**Bałdyga**): unflattering nickname from dialect *bałdyga* 'oaf', 'large and clumsy or lazy man'.
GIVEN NAMES Polish 11%. *Bogumil, Casimir, Eugeniusz, Faustyn, Jaroslaw, Jozef, Mieczyslaw, Tadeusz, Wieslaw.*

Bale (962) **1.** English: variant of BAILE. **2.** Americanized spelling of German BOEHL(E) or BOELL.

Balek (131) Czech and Slovak (**Bálek**): from a pet form of *Bal*, shortened form of the personal name BALTAZAR.
GIVEN NAME French 6%. *Michel.*

Balent (138) **1.** Catalan: variant of **Valent**, a nickname from Catalan *valent* 'courageous'. **2.** Croatian: from a Croatian form of the Hungarian personal name BALINT.
GIVEN NAME French 4%. *Mechelle.*

Balentine (977) Variant of Scottish BALLENTINE.

Bales (4825) **1.** English: variant spelling of BAILES. **2.** Czech (**Baleš**) and Slovak (**Báleš**): from a pet form of *Bal*, a shortened form of the personal name BALTAZAR.

Balestra (158) Italian and southern French: from Italian, Occitan *balestra* 'crossbow' (Latin *ballista* '(military) catapult'), hence a metonymic occupational name for a maker of crossbows or a soldier armed with a crossbow.
GIVEN NAMES Italian 21%. *Antonio* (3), *Attilio, Carmel, Fulvio, Geno, Luigi, Nicola, Sante, Santo, Silvio, Sylvana, Valentino.*

Balestreri (106) Italian: variant of BALESTRIERI.
GIVEN NAMES Italian 23%. *Mario* (3), *Antonio, Ignazio, Pietro.*

Balestrieri (301) Italian: occupational name from *balestriere* 'crossbowman', 'crossbow maker', from Latin *ballistarius* 'catapult maker' (see BALESTRA). De Felice notes that the *-ieri* suffix shows the influence of Old French *balestrier* 'crossbowman', owing to the importance of these troops in the Angevin militias in southern Italy in the 13th and 14th centuries.
GIVEN NAMES Italian 17%. *Mario* (6), *Salvatore* (4), *Sal* (3), *Angelo* (2), *Nino* (2), *Domenic, Gaeton, Natale, Sebastiano.*

Baley (312) Variant of English BAILEY.

Balfanz (165) German (Pomerania): unexplained.

Balfe (220) Irish: Anglicized form of Gaelic **Balbh** meaning 'stammering', 'dumb', itself probably a translation of a Norman family name of similar meaning, for example **Baube** 'stammering', from Latin *balbus*, itself used as a Roman family name.
GIVEN NAMES Irish 6%. *Liam, Onora.*

Balfour (831) Scottish: habitational name from any of several places in eastern Scotland named with Gaelic *bail(e)* 'village', 'farm', 'house' + *pùir*, genitive case of *pór* 'pasture', 'grass' (lenited to *phùir* in certain contexts). The second element is akin to Welsh *pawr* 'pasture'. The principal British family bearing this name derives it from lands in the parish of Markinch, Fife. According to the traditional pronunciation, the accent falls on the second syllable, but these days it is found more commonly on the first.

Bali (129) **1.** Indian (Panjab): Hindu (Brahman) name based on the name of a clan in the Mohyal subgroup of Saraswat Brahmans. It is probably derived from an ancestral personal name. **2.** Hungarian: from a pet form of the personal names BALINT or BALAZS.
GIVEN NAMES Indian 56%; Hungarian 7%. *Arun* (2), *Lokesh* (2), *Savita* (2), *Shiv* (2), *Vijay* (2), *Ajay, Anil, Arvind, Ashish, Brij, Dhirendra, Harish; Janos* (2), *Sandor* (2), *Laszlo.*

Balian (274) Armenian: patronymic of uncertain origin, perhaps from Turkish *bal* 'lord', 'master', a word of Arabic origin.
GIVEN NAMES Armenian 42%. *Armen* (4), *Aram* (3), *Garabed* (3), *Zareh* (3), *Dikran* (2), *Garbis* (2), *Haroutun* (2), *Hrair* (2), *Sarkis* (2), *Vartan* (2), *Anahid, Antranik.*

Balich (98) **1.** Croatian (**Balić**): patronymic from the personal name *Bali*, a pet form of the personal names *Baltazar* or *Balint*. **2.** Bosnian (**Balić**): patronymic from *balija*, a status term for the lowest rank in a Muslim village.

Balicki (232) Polish: habitational name for someone from a place called Balice.

GIVEN NAMES Polish 6%. *Henryk, Jaroslaw, Jozef, Wieslaw, Zdzislaw.*

Balik (159) **1.** Polish and Slovak (**Balík**): from a pet form of *Bal*, a short form of the personal name BALTAZAR or of Hungarian **Balázs** (see BALAZS). **2.** Hungarian: perhaps from Turkish *balyq* 'fish'.

Balin (177) **1.** Jewish (Ashkenazic): habitational name for someone from Balin, a village in Ukraine. **2.** Possibly French, from a pet form of BAL.
GIVEN NAMES Jewish 5%. *Meyer, Rina.*

Balinski (150) Polish (**Baliński**): habitational name for someone from a place called Balin.
GIVEN NAMES Polish 8%. *Mieczyslaw, Tomasz, Urszula.*

Balint (661) **1.** Hungarian (**Bálint**): from the personal name *Bálint*, Hungarian form of VALENTINE. **2.** Slovak, Romanian, Croatian, and Serbian: from the Hungarian personal name.

Balis (288) **1.** English: variant of BAYLISS. **2.** Hungarian and Croatian (**Bališ**): from the personal name *Bali*, a pet form of *Baltazar* or *Balint*. **3.** Perhaps also Greek: occupational status name from Turkish *balija* 'workman', 'low-ranking man'.

Balistreri (511) Southern Italian (Sicily): occupational name from Sicilian *balistreri* 'crossbowman', 'crossbow maker'. Compare BALESTRIERI.
GIVEN NAMES Italian 13%. *Salvatore* (3), *Angelo* (2), *Antonio* (2), *Franco* (2), *Gaetano* (2), *Pietro* (2), *Antonino, Carlo, Ceasar, Marcello, Natale, Vincenzo.*

Balius (139) Origin unidentified. Possibly a respelling of Greek **Balias**, a nickname from Albanian *balë* 'white-headed' (used of sheep).

Balk (768) **1.** German: from a short form of a Slavic equivalent of the personal name *Valentinus*. **2.** Dutch: from *balk* 'timber', 'beam', hence a metonymic occupational name for a carpenter or a nickname for a big man.

Balkan (110) **1.** Regional name for someone who lived in the Balkans, originally a Turkish word denoting a range of mountains in this area. **2.** Possibly a variant of English **Balcombe** (see BALCOM).

Balkcom (242) Variant of English **Balcombe** (see BALCOM).

Balke (570) **1.** German: from *Balke* 'timber', 'beam'; hence a metonymic occupational name for a carpenter. **2.** German: variant of BALK. **3.** Norwegian: habitational name from a farmstead named Balke, from Old Norse *balkr* 'beam', used in the sense 'ridge'.
GIVEN NAMES German 5%. *Fritz* (2), *Hans* (2), *Bodo, Hartwig, Horst, Manfred, Otto.*

Balkema (132) Frisian: from the personal name *Baleke*, a pet form of *Baldewin* (see BALDWIN).

Balkin (164) Jewish (Ashkenazic): from the Yiddish female personal name *Beyle* meaning 'beautiful' (related to French *belle*).
GIVEN NAMES Jewish 5%. *Emanuel* (3), *Herschel, Miriam, Sol.*

Balko (387) Hungarian (**Balkó**) and Slovak: from a pet form of **Balázs** (see BALAZS) or **Bálint** (see BALINT).

Balkus (118) Lithuanian: nickname for a person with white hair or a pale complexion, from a derivative of Polish *biały* 'white'.

Ball (28646) **1.** English: nickname for a short, fat person, from Middle English *bal(le)* 'ball' (Old English *ball*, Old Norse *bǫllr*). **2.** English: topographic name for someone who lived on or by a knoll or rounded hill, from the same Middle English word, *bal(le)*, used in this sense. **3.** English: from the Old Norse personal name *Balle*, derived either from *ballr* 'dangerous' or *bǫllr* 'ball'. **4.** South German: from Middle High German *bal* 'ball', possibly applied as a metonymic occupational name for a juggler, or a habitational name from a place so named in the Rhine area. **5.** Dutch and German: short form of any of various Germanic personal names formed with the element *bald* (see BALD).
FOREBEARS William Ball (1616–80) emigrated from Suffolk, England, to VA about 1650 and was one of the founders of Millenbeck on the Rappahannock.

Balla (458) **1.** Hungarian: from a short form of *Ballabás*, variant of the personal name *Barnabás* (see BARNABY). **2.** Italian: from *balla*, which in its earliest sense meant 'dance' but from the 14th century was used to denote 'goods packed for transport', 'bale', 'bundle (of merchandise)' and was hence probably a metonymic occupational name for a carrier.
GIVEN NAMES Hungarian 6%. *Arpad, Atilla, Endre, Eszter, Gabor, Istvan, Janos, Jozsef, Laszlo, Tamas, Zsolt.*

Ballagh (124) Irish: from Gaelic *ballach* 'speckled', 'marked'.

Ballam (102) English: variant of **Balham**, a habitational name from a place in Surrey (now part of south London), named with Old English *bealg* 'smooth' or 'round' + *hamm* 'water meadow', 'land hemmed in by water'.

Ballance (814) English: metonymic occupational name for someone who used a balance (scales), Anglo-French and Middle English *balaunce*, from Old French *balance*.

Ballantine (594) Scottish: variant spelling of BALLENTINE.

Ballantyne (1011) Scottish: variant spelling of BALLENTINE.

Ballard (20800) English and Scottish: derogatory nickname from a derivative of *bald* 'bald-headed' (see BALD 2).

Ballas (596) **1.** Greek: nickname for someone who was short and fat, from *bal(l)a*

'ball', from Italian *balla* 'ball', 'bullet', 'cannonball'. **2.** Syrian and Jewish (from Syria): unexplained. **3.** German: variant of **Baldas**, from a reduced form of the personal name BALTAZAR.

Ballay (100) Americanized spelling of Dutch BALLE.
GIVEN NAMES French 6%; German 5%. *Jean-Pierre; Wolfgang.*

Balle (135) **1.** Dutch: from a reduced form of any of various Germanic personal names formed with the element *bald* (see BALD). **2.** English: variant spelling of BALL 1. **3.** Danish: habitational name from a farmstead named Balle, meaning 'slope', 'hill'. **4.** Catalan: respelling of **Batlle**, status name for a steward or official, from Catalan *batlle*.
GIVEN NAMES Spanish 6%. *Corina, Elidoro, Fernando, Geraldo, Humberto, Joaquin, Ruben.*

Ballek (111) Origin uncertain. Probably Slovenian, perhaps from a shortened form of the personal name BALTAZAR.

Ballen (140) Dutch: variant of BALLE.

Ballengee (288) Probably an Americanized form of Dutch **(van) Baelinghem** or **(van) Belenghien**, habitational names from places in the Netherlands so called.

Ballenger (1785) English: variant spelling of BALLINGER (see BERINGER).

Ballentine (1401) Scottish: habitational name from either of two places (in Roxburgh and Selkirk) called Bellenden, of unknown origin.

Baller (262) **1.** English: variant of BALL 2, the suffix *-er* denoting an inhabitant. **2.** German: variant of the Germanic personal name *Balther* (from *bald* 'bold', 'strong').

Ballerini (135) Italian (mostly Lombardy and Tuscany): occupational name or nickname for a dancer, Italian *ballerino*, an agent derivative of *ballare* 'to dance'.
GIVEN NAMES Italian 26%. *Albano* (3), *Mario* (2), *Sal* (2), *Antonio, Dante, Giuliano, Lino, Nicola, Orlando, Rocco, Romolo, Umberto, Valdo.*

Balles (163) **1.** Catalan: habitational name from El Vallès, a Catalan district in Barcelona province, Catalonia. **2.** Spanish: habitational name from one of the places named Valles, from the plural of *valle* 'valley'. **3.** German: from a variant of *Baldes*, a short form of the personal name *Balthasar* (see BALTAZAR). **4.** Variant spelling of English BALLS.
GIVEN NAMES Spanish 8%. *Alfredo, Cipriano, Eduardo, Graciela, Jose, Jose De Jesus, Juan, Lupe, Manuel, Mariano, Miguel, Ricardo.*

Ballester (151) **1.** Catalan: occupational name for a maker of crossbows or a soldier armed with a crossbow, from Catalan *ballester* 'crossbowman' or 'crossbow maker', an agent derivative of *ballesta* 'crossbow' (Latin *ballista* '(military) cata-

pult'). **2.** English and German: occupational name, cognate with 1, from an agent derivative of Middle English, Old French *baleste* 'crossbow'.
GIVEN NAMES Spanish 43%. *Ricardo* (6), *Jose* (4), *Luis* (3), *Domingo* (2), *Jorge* (2), *Juan* (2), *Magda* (2), *Pilar* (2), *Roberto* (2), *Ana, Andres, Aura; Aldo, Antonio, Franco, Gilda.*

Ballesteros (870) Spanish: habitational name from any of various places in Spain, for example Ballesteros de Calatrava in the province of Ciudad Real, Los Ballesteros (Huelva), Ballesteros (Cuenca), and others no longer identifiable, which were probably so named because of their association with *ballesteros* 'crossbowmen', plural of *ballestero*, an agent derivative of *ballesta* 'crossbow' (see BALLESTER).
GIVEN NAMES Spanish 46%. *Jose* (17), *Francisco* (13), *Juan* (11), *Alfredo* (9), *Fernando* (9), *Manuel* (9), *Jaime* (8), *Jesus* (6), *Luis* (6), *Carlos* (5), *Jorge* (5), *Lupe* (5).

Ballew (2846) Altered spelling of BALLOU or BELLEW.

Balli (320) **1.** Spanish: adaptation of French **Vailly**. **2.** Italian: variant of BALLO. **3.** Eastern French and Swiss French: variant of BAILLY. **4.** Greek: variant of BALLIS.
GIVEN NAMES Spanish 30%. *Jose* (7), *Juan* (5), *Manuel* (4), *Jesus* (3), *Alberto* (2), *Eloy* (2), *Mercedes* (2), *Roberto* (2), *Rolando* (2), *Ruben* (2), *Abelardo, Adolfo; Giorgio* (3), *Angelo, Clemente, Eliseo, Fabrizio.*

Balliet (668) Perhaps an altered spelling of French **Baillet**, a nickname for someone with light-brown or reddish-brown hair, from a derivative of *bai* 'bay (horse)', from Latin *badius*. Compare BAIG, BAIO.

Balliett (165) See BALLIET.

Ballin (318) **1.** German and Danish: habitational name for someone from a place so named near Neubrandenburg; the *-in* ending suggests Slavic origin. **2.** French: metonymic occupational name for a maker of straw mattresses, Old French *ballin*. **3.** Jewish (Ashkenazic): variant of BALIN. **4.** Asturian-Leonese: habitational name from any of the places in Asturies named Vallín, from a diminutive of *valle* 'valley'.
GIVEN NAMES Spanish 7%. *Lupe* (2), *Ana Isabel, Armando, Gonzalo, Guadalupe, Hilaria, Jose, Juan, Juan Carlos, Juana Maria, Macario, Mario.*

Balling (265) **1.** German (**Bälling**): patronymic from the Germanic personal name *Baldo* (see BALD), or a nickname from Middle High German, Middle Low German *ballinc* 'outlaw'. **2.** Danish: habitational name from a farm so named, from a derivative of BALLE.
GIVEN NAMES German 5%. *Claus, Kurt, Willi.*

Ballinger (2718) English, French, and German: variant of BERINGER.

Ballis (128) **1.** German: Alemannic variant of BALLAS or BALLES. **2.** Greek: variant of

BALIS. **3.** Greek: nickname from Turkish *balli* 'honeyed', from *bal* 'honey'.

Ballman (429) **1.** variant of German BALL-MANN. **2.** Ballman is also found in Britain, where it may be a respelling of the German surname (see 1) or alternatively a variant of the English surname **Balman**, which is from an Old English personal name *Bealdmann*.

Ballmann (104) German (**Ballmann**): **1.** from a compound of the Germanic personal name *Baldo* (see BALD) + *man* 'man'. **2.** variant of BAHLMANN.
GIVEN NAME German 4%. *Dieter.*

Ballmer (157) Variant of German BALMER.

Ballo (185) **1.** Italian: nickname from *ballo* 'dance', from *ballare* 'to dance'. **2.** Hungarian (**Balló**): from a pet form of the personal name *Barnabás* (see BARNABY). **3.** Lapp: unexplained. **4.** African: unexplained.
GIVEN NAMES Hungarian 5%; African 5%. *Bela* (3), *Istvan*; *Aboubacar* (2), *Mamadou, Mohamadou.*

Ballon (154) **1.** Spanish: of uncertain origin. Theoretically it could be a variant of *vallón*, from *valle* 'valley', but neither form is attested as a vocabulary word or as a place name element. Alternatively, it could be a Castilian spelling of Catalan **Batlló**, **Balló**, nicknames from diminutives of *batlle* 'dancing'. **2.** English: variant spelling of BALON.
GIVEN NAMES Spanish 15%; Jewish 4%. *Jose* (2), *Sergio* (2), *Alfonso, Cesar, Conchita, Emigdio, Enrique, Felipe, Francisco, Jose Luis, Julio, Ruben; Hyman, Isadore.*

Ballor (101) Possibly an altered form of French BALLARD, reflecting the Canadian pronunciation. It is found chiefly in MI.

Ballou (2271) **1.** French: of uncertain origin; possibly related to BAL. **2.** Possibly a variant spelling of BELLEW.
FOREBEARS A certain Maturin Ballou settled in Providence, RI, in the mid 17th century.

Ballow (333) Of uncertain origin; perhaps a respelling of BALLOU or BELLEW. As an American surname, **Ballow(e)** seems to have become inextricably mixed up with several similar names. For example, a census compilation from Albemarle County, VA, in 1785 lists Peter and Solomon Ballow; another, from 1787, lists them as Peter and Sollomon Belew. A will book from Halifax County, VA includes, dated June 26, 1809, 'Inventory of Thomas Ballow (Ballou)'.

Ballowe (186) Variant of BALLOW.

Balls (214) English: patronymic form of the Old Norse personal name *Balle* (see BALL 3).

Balluff (125) South German: variant of BALDAUF.
GIVEN NAMES German 4%. *Gerhard, Wilhelmina.*

Ballweber (114) German: unexplained.

Ballweg (495) German: sometimes said to be a reduced form of *Baldhinweg*, a nick-

name composed of the elements *bald* 'soon' + *hinweg* 'away', i.e. 'soon to be gone', but more likely to be a variant of the Germanic personal name *Baldwig*, a compound of *bald* 'bold' + *wīg* 'battle'.
GIVEN NAMES German 4%. *Alphons, Crescentia, Ewald, Florian, Gerhard, Kurt, Math.*

Bally (209) Swiss French: variant spelling of BAILLY.
GIVEN NAMES French 8%; German 4%. *Marcel* (2), *Andre, Emile, Francois; Fritz, Kurt.*

Balma (104) **1.** Italian: perhaps a topographic name from the dialect word *balma* 'grotto', 'cave', 'jutting rock'. **2.** Dutch: unexplained.
GIVEN NAMES Italian 6%. *Giorgio, Martino.*

Balmer (1087) **1.** English and Scottish: occupational name for a seller of spices and perfumes, from an agent derivative of Middle English, Old French *basme, balme, ba(u)me* 'balm', 'ointment' (Latin *balsamum* 'aromatic resin'). **2.** South German and Swiss German: habitational name from any of the places in Switzerland and Baden called Balm, which almost certainly get their names from a Celtic word meaning 'cave'. **3.** German: from the Germanic personal name *Baldemar*, composed of the elements *bald* 'bold' + *mar* 'famous'.

Balmes (158) Catalan: topographic name from *balma* 'cave', 'hollow' (of pre-Roman origin), a common element of place names.
GIVEN NAMES Spanish 5%. *Maxima* (2), *Anastacio, Arturo, Esteban, Manuel, Rosita.*

Balog (990) Hungarian: variant of BALOGH. This name is also found in Slovakia, Croatia, and Ukraine.

Baloga (143) Slovak: see BALOG.

Balogh (1279) Hungarian: from *balog* 'left-handed', from *bal* 'left', hence a nickname for a left-handed or clumsy person.
GIVEN NAMES Hungarian 10%. *Laszlo* (7), *Tibor* (5), *Zoltan* (5), *Bela* (4), *Karoly* (4), *Attila* (3), *Sandor* (3), *Andras* (2), *Arpad* (2), *Geza* (2), *Lajos* (2), *Balint.*

Balok (105) Variant spelling of Hungarian BALOGH.

Balon (309) **1.** English: from Old French *balon* 'bundle', 'roll', 'pack', hence a nickname for a small, rotund man or possibly a metonymic occupational name for a carrier of goods and merchandise. **2.** French (**Bâlon**): generally regarded as a habitational name from Baalons in the Ardennes, it may however simply be from *balon* 'ball', 'roll' (see 1) or a derivative of BAL.

Balough (118) Altered spelling of Hungarian BALOGH or of BALLOW.

Baloun (142) Czech: variant of *Valon*, ethnic name for a Walloon, also used as an offensive nickname meaning 'boor', 'stupid peasant'.

Balow (171) **1.** German: habitational name from Balow, a place in Mecklenburg. The

name is of Slavic origin. **2.** In some cases possibly an altered spelling of BALLOW.

Balsam (343) **1.** Jewish (Ashkenazic): ornamental name from German *Balsam* or Yiddish *balzam* 'balm', 'balsam'. **2.** German: occupational name for a seller of spices and perfumes, from Latin *balsamum* 'balsam', 'aromatic resin'. **3.** German: variant of **Balsel** (see BALTZELL). **4.** English: habitational name from Balsham in Cambridgeshire, named with an Old English personal name, *Bæll(i)*, + *hām* 'homestead', 'village', or Balstone in Devon.

Balsamo (737) Southern Italian (Naples): from the medieval personal name *Balsamo*, meaning 'balsam', 'balm', 'comfort', bestowed upon a child who is (or is expected to be) a comfort to his parents, typically one born following the death of an older child.
GIVEN NAMES Italian 24%. *Salvatore* (14), *Gaetano* (3), *Mario* (3), *Angelo* (2), *Gaspare* (2), *Gasper* (2), *Giuseppe* (2), *Liborio* (2), *Rocco* (2), *Rolando* (2), *Saverio* (2), *Aniello, Antonietta, Antonio, Biagio; Angelina, Cristina, Gaspar, Nilda, Salvador, Serafina.*

Balsano (126) Probably a variant spelling of BALZANO.
GIVEN NAMES Italian 17%. *Angelo* (2), *Giuseppe* (2), *Giovanni, Silvio, Vito.*

Balsbaugh (132) Americanized spelling of German **Pfaltzbach**, a habitational name from a place so named in the Palatinate. The variants **Balschbach**, **Baltsbach** are also found.
FOREBEARS This name was brought to the U.S. in 1751 by a family from Fahrenbach, Germany, who settled in PA.

Balser (770) **1.** German: reduced form of the personal name *Balthasar* (see BALTAZAR). **2.** shortened form of Lithuanian **Balseris**, a patronymic from a reduced form of the personal name *Baltazaras* (see BALTAZAR). **3.** Jewish: habitational name for someone from Bolsi, a place in Ukraine.

Balsiger (209) German and Swiss German (mainly Bern canton): habitational name for someone from Palzing in Bavaria or some other place similarly named.
GIVEN NAMES German 6%. *Eugen, Fritz, Joerg.*

Balsinger (105) German: variant of BALSIGER.

Balsley (559) Probably of German origin: an Americanized spelling of Swabian **Bälzle** or Swiss **Balzli**, both of which are from pet forms of the personal name *Balthasar* (see BALTAZAR).

Balson (129) English: **1.** variant of BALSAM. **2.** alternatively, it may be a patronymic from an unidentified personal name. Compare BOLSON.

Balstad (104) **1.** Swedish: habitational name from any of various places called Bålstad, Bålsta, or Balsta. **2.** Norwegian:

habitational name from any of various farmsteads so named, from an uncertain first element, most likely a personal name, + Old Norse *staðir*, plural of *staðr* 'farmstead', 'dwelling'.
GIVEN NAME Scandinavian 12%. *Ottar*.

Balster (271) **1.** English: reduced form of BALLESTER. **2.** North German: from a reduced form of the personal name BALTAZAR. **3.** German: variant of BALLESTER. **4.** German: in some cases, possibly a habitational name from a place so named in Brandenburg.

Baltazar (879) Spanish, Portuguese, German, Dutch, Polish, Czech, Slovak, Hungarian (**Baltazár**), etc. It is derived from the Biblical personal names *Balthazar* and *Belshazzar*, which were originally distinct but by medieval times had come to be regarded as variants of a single name. The first is from Aramaic *Balshatzar*, Babylonian *Baal tas-assar* 'may Baal preserve his life', the second from Babylonian *Baal shar-uzzur* 'may Baal protect the king'. The latter was borne by the Chaldean king for whom Daniel interpreted the writing on the wall (Daniel 5); the main reason for the popularity of the first in medieval Italy and Germany was that, according to legend, it was the name of one of the three Magi from the East who attended Christ's birth. His supposed relics were venerated at first in Milan, but after 1164 in Cologne, where they had been taken by Rainald of Dassel.
GIVEN NAMES Spanish 47%; Portuguese 9%. *Jose* (14), *Juan* (11), *Pedro* (8), *Guadalupe* (7), *Jesus* (6), *Luis* (6), *Gustavo* (5), *Jorge* (5), *Manuel* (5), *Miguel* (5), *Roberto* (5), *Francisco* (4); *Godofredo, Joao, Joaquim, Wenceslao; Antonio* (10), *Romeo* (4), *Lorenzo* (3), *Ciro* (2), *Carmela, Cecilio, Clemente, Clementina, Fausto, Flavio, Leonardo, Marco*.

Balter (362) **1.** Jewish (eastern Ashkenazic): habitational name for someone from the town of Balta in southern Ukraine. **2.** German: from a reduced form of the personal name BALTAZAR. **3.** German: in Tyrol, Austria, a variant of WALTER. **4.** German: possibly also a reduced form of Swabian *Balt(e)ner*, from Middle High German *balteniere* 'pilgrim', 'beggar', 'vagrant'. Compare BALDNER.
GIVEN NAMES Jewish 5%. *Miriam* (2), *Yoel* (2), *Naum, Rakhil, Shlomo, Sima*.

Baltes (487) Dutch and German (Rhineland): from a shortened form of the personal name *Balthasar* (see BALTAZAR).

Balthaser (207) Variant of BALTAZAR.

Balthazar (225) Predominantly French variant of BALTAZAR.
GIVEN NAMES French 11%. *Pierre* (2), *Alphonse, Celine, Constant, Monique, Murielle*.

Balthazor (297) German: variant of BALTAZAR.
GIVEN NAME German 4%. *Kurt* (3).

Balthis (124) **1.** Swiss German: from a pet form of BALTAZAR. **2.** Lithuanian: variant of **Baltis**, a descriptive nickname from *baltas* 'white'.

Balthrop (302) English: habitational name from a lost place, probably in Cambridgeshire, where the surname is recorded in the 17th century. The second element of the place name is a metathesized form of Old English *þorp* 'settlement'; the first element is of uncertain origin. The surname is now extinct in the British Isles.
FOREBEARS William Baltrop, Baldrop, or Boltrop came to VA from England in about 1664.

Baltierra (151) Variant of VALTIERRA.
GIVEN NAMES Spanish 38%. *Enrique* (3), *Juan* (3), *Jose* (2), *Rafael* (2), *Raul* (2), *Ascension, Carolina, Cipriano, Claudio, Domingo, Francisco, Gerardo*.

Baltimore (554) American: apparently from the city in MD or from the title of the English Barons Baltimore, borne by members of the Calvert family, who were Lords Proprietors of the colony of MD in the 17th century and for whom the state capital was named. As a family name, Baltimore seems to have originated in America (appearing in VA in the 1660s). There is no record of any Calvert descendants having assumed the title as a surname.

Baltodano (106) Spanish: unexplained, probably from Granada province.
GIVEN NAMES Spanish 45%. *Carlos* (3), *Francisco* (2), *Luis* (2), *Manuel* (2), *Amparo, Ana, Arnoldo, Auxiliadora, Carlos Mario, Cesar, Eduardo, Elena*.

Baltus (138) Dutch, German, and Latvian: from a short form of the personal name *Balthasar* (see BALTAZAR).

Baltz (768) German: from a shortened form of the personal name *Balthasar* (see BALTAZAR).

Baltzell (354) Altered spelling of German **Balsel**, from a pet form of the personal name *Balthasar* (see BALTAZAR).

Baltzer (429) German: from a reduced form of the personal name *Balthasar* (see BALTAZAR).

Baluch (109) **1.** Polish: from the personal name *Baluch*, a reduced form of BALTAZAR. **2.** Muslim: ethnic name for someone from Baluchistan.
GIVEN NAMES Muslim 19%. *Abdul, Aftab, Akram, Fatima, Hashem, Hassan, Mohammed, Muhammad, Munawar, Murad, Nasim, Nasir*.

Balusek (123) Czech (**Bálušek**) and Slovak (**Balušík**): from a pet form of the personal name *Balus*, a reduced form of BALTAZAR.

Balvin (141) Perhaps a reduced form of Irish **O'Ballevan**, an Americanized form of **Ó Balbhán** 'descendant of the little dumb one' (see BALFE).

Balyeat (147) Probably a variant of French BALLIET.

Balz (180) German: from a reduced form of the personal name *Balthasar* (see BALTAZAR).
GIVEN NAMES German 7%. *Fritz, Gunther, Kurt, Merwin, Rainer*.

Balzano (464) Italian: possibly a nickname from *balzano* 'strange', 'odd'.
GIVEN NAMES Italian 20%. *Carmine* (4), *Antonio* (3), *Gennaro* (3), *Vito* (2), *Amerigo, Angelo, Cristoforo, Dante, Eliseo, Giovanni, Giuseppe, Guido*.

Balzarini (191) Italian: from a reduced diminutive of the personal name *Baldassare*, Italian form of BALTAZAR.
GIVEN NAMES Italian 14%. *Gino* (3), *Angelo* (2), *Aldo, Attilio, Eligio, Elio, Pasco, Piero, Remo, Romeo, Silvio*.

Balzer (1248) German: from a reduced form of the personal name *Balthasar* (see BALTAZAR).

Bambach (193) Probably a variant of German BAUMBACH, or a habitational name from a lost place in northern Germany.
GIVEN NAMES German 5%. *Fritz, Hans, Kurt, Viktor*.

Bambenek (108) Czech: unexplained.

Bamber (266) **1.** English: habitational name from Bamber Bridge in Lancashire, probably named with Old English *bēam* 'tree trunk', 'beam' + *brycg* 'bridge'. **2.** German: nickname for a short fat person.

Bamberg (393) German and Jewish (western Ashkenazic): habitational name from the city of Bamberg in Bavaria (formerly in Upper Franconia). Between 1007 and 1702 it was the capital of a powerful ecclesiastical state, and in the 15th century the bishops of Bamberg were raised to princely rank.

Bamberger (633) German and Jewish (Ashkenazic): habitational name for someone from BAMBERG.
GIVEN NAMES German 5%; French 4%. *Ernst, Helmut, Helmuth, Juergen, Otto; Gabrielle* (3), *Julien, Manon*.

Bambino (116) Italian: from *Bambino*, a byname meaning 'child' (see CHILD), or a personal name given with reference to *Gesù Bambino*, 'the Christ child', the use of *Gesù* as a personal name being considered taboo in Italy.
GIVEN NAMES Italian 12%. *Carmine* (2), *Angelo*.

Bambrick (218) Origin uncertain: this is a well-established surname in Britain and Ireland. It may have come to the UK from Germany, in which case it is most probably a variant of BAMBERG.
GIVEN NAMES Irish 5%. *Brendan, Liam*.

Bamburg (285) Variant of German BAMBERG.

Bame (379) Americanized spelling of German BOEHM or BEHM.

Bamford (802) English: habitational name from any of various places (the two main ones being in Derbyshire and Lancashire) named with Old English *bēam* 'tree', 'beam' + *ford* 'ford', i.e. a ford beside a plank bridge for those who wished to keep their feet dry.

Bamonte (115) Italian: in Campania, probably a reduced form of **Baiamonte**, **Buiamonte**, a nickname for a very large or strong man, from *buia*, an aphetic form of *abbuia* 'obscures' + *monte* 'mountain'.

GIVEN NAMES Italian 17%. *Angelo* (2), *Carmine* (2), *Biagio*, *Marco*, *Salvatore*.

Bamrick (111) Variant spelling of BAMBRICK.

Ban (461) **1.** Hungarian (**Bán**): from the old Hungarian personal name *Bán*. **2.** Hungarian, Serbian, and Croatian: from Slavic *ban* or Hungarian *bán* 'governor' (from Avar *bajan* 'rich', 'rich man'), historically a status name for a regional military or administrative leader (for example the governor of Croatia in the Habsburg Empire). **3.** Slovenian: probably from a reduced form of the personal name *Urban*. **4.** German: variant spelling of BANN. **5.** Japanese: 'comrade'. This name is found mostly in eastern Japan. Some families pronounce the same character as *Tomo*. **6.** Chinese 班: according to legend, during the Spring and Autumn period (722–481 BC), a noble of the state of Chu was raised and suckled by a tiger. This tiger's skin bore markings that resembled the character for *Ban*, and his descendants adopted this character, which may also mean 'team', 'class', 'group' as their surname. **7.** Korean: variant of PAN.

GIVEN NAMES Japanese 9%; Chinese/Korean 6%; Hungarian 4%. *Yoshimi* (2), *Akihiko*, *Hiroki*, *Junji*, *Keiko*, *Keisuke*, *Koji*, *Masanori*, *Masataka*, *Misa*, *Misao*, *Naoki*; *Yong* (2), *Young* (2), *Chea*, *Chun Hung*, *Chunsheng*, *Dong*, *Eun*, *Hee*, *Hyun*, *Hyung*; *Zoltan* (3), *Bela* (2), *Imre*, *Laszlo*, *Tibor*.

Banach (697) Polish: from a pet form of the personal name *Benedykt*, from Latin *Benedictus* (see BENEDICT).

GIVEN NAMES Polish 8%. *Bogdan*, *Elzbieta*, *Ewa*, *Grazyna*, *Grzegorz*, *Jerzy*, *Jozef*, *Krzysztof*, *Leszek*, *Pawel*, *Piotr*, *Stanislaus*.

Banahan (130) Variant spelling of Irish **O'Ban(n)aghan**, Anglicized form of Gaelic **Ó Beannacháin** 'descendant of *Beannachán*', a byname from a diminutive of *beannach* 'peaked'.

Banales (146) Spanish (**Bañales**): from *bañ(o)* 'bath' (Latin *balnea* 'baths') + *-al* 'place' + the plural suffix *-es*, hence a topographic name for someone who lived near public baths, or a habitational name from a place of this name in the province of Zaragoza.

GIVEN NAMES Spanish 46%; Italian 7%. *Jose* (3), *Evangelina* (2), *Francisco* (2), *Manuel* (2), *Margarito* (2), *Mario* (2), *Rafael* (2), *Raul* (2), *Roberto* (2), *Sergio* (2), *Amador*, *Buena*; *Antonio* (3), *Clemente*, *Federico*, *Marco*, *Sal*.

Banas (968) Polish (**Banaś** or **Banasz**): from a pet form of the personal name *Benedykt*, a vernacular form of *Benedictus* (see BENEDICT).

GIVEN NAMES Polish 6%. *Boleslaw* (2), *Franciszek* (2), *Janusz* (2), *Danuta*, *Eugeniusz*, *Grzegorz*, *Iwona*, *Izabela*, *Jacek*, *Kazimerz*, *Kazimierz*, *Miroslaw*.

Banasiak (186) Polish: from a pet form of the personal name *Benedykt*, a vernacular form of *Benedictus* (see BENEDICT).

GIVEN NAMES Polish 12%. *Jerzy* (2), *Alicja*, *Andrzej*, *Krystyna*, *Slawomir*, *Zygmund*, *Zygmunt*.

Banasik (139) Polish and Belorussian: from a pet form of the personal name *Benedykt*, a vernacular form of Latin *Benedictus* (see BENEDICT).

GIVEN NAMES Polish 16%. *Andrzej* (2), *Casimir*, *Czeslaw*, *Janusz*, *Piotr*, *Stanislaw*, *Wieslaw*, *Witold*.

Banaszak (445) Polish: from the personal name *Banasz*, a pet form of *Benedykt*, vernacular form of Latin *Benedictus* (see BENEDICT).

Banaszek (85) Polish: from a pet form of *Banadyk*, variant spelling of the personal name *Benedykt*, a vernacular form of *Benedictus* (see BENEDICT).

GIVEN NAME Polish 7%. *Wlodzimierz*.

Banaszewski (102) Polish: habitational name for someone from a place named with the personal name **Banaszyk**, a pet form of *Benedykt* (see BENEDICT).

GIVEN NAME Polish 6%. *Zdzislaw*.

Banaszynski (100) Polish (**Banaszyński**): habitational name for someone from a place named with the personal name *Banasz*, a pet form of *Benedykt* (see BENEDICT), + *-yński*, common ending of surnames.

GIVEN NAME German 5%. *Kurt*.

Banbury (210) English: habitational name from Banbury, a place in Oxfordshire, named with the unattested Old English personal name *Ban(n)a* (possibly a byname meaning 'felon', 'murderer') + Old English *burh* 'fort', dative *byrig*.

Banchero (110) Italian (Genoa): occupational name from *banchero* 'banker' or from Genoese *bancà* 'carpenter'. This surname is also established in Spain.

GIVEN NAMES Spanish 9%. *Natalio* (3), *Carlos*.

Bancroft (2156) English: habitational name from any of various minor places called Bancroft, from Old English *bēan* 'beans' (a collective singular) + *croft* 'paddock', 'smallholding'.

FOREBEARS John Bancroft came to MA on board the 'James' in 1632.

Band (315) **1.** English, German, and Jewish (Ashkenazic): metonymic occupational name for a maker of hoops and bands, etc., from Middle English *band*, *bond*, Middle High German, Middle Low German *bant*, German *Band* denoting something used for tying or binding: 'hoop', 'metal band', 'fetter', 'shackle'. **2.** Old spelling of the Dutch cognates **Bant**, **Bande**, from Middle Dutch *bant* 'band'.

GIVEN NAMES Jewish 4%. *Hyman*, *Isidor*, *Myer*.

Banda (1269) **1.** Spanish: habitational name from various places named with *banda*, probably in the sense 'side', 'edge', 'part'. **2.** Hungarian: of uncertain origin; probably from the old secular personal name *Bán*. **3.** Jewish (from Poland): metonymic occupational name from Polish *banda* 'ribbon'. **4.** In some instances, perhaps an altered spelling of German and Dutch **Bande** (see BAND). **5.** Croatian or Serbian: nickname for a bandit, from *banda* 'band', 'gang'. This name originates from the Kordun and Krajina region on the former border between Croatia and Bosnia.

GIVEN NAMES Spanish 47%. *Juan* (29), *Francisco* (15), *Jose* (15), *Jesus* (14), *Manuel* (14), *Pedro* (9), *Carlos* (8), *Guadalupe* (8), *Raul* (7), *Javier* (6), *Mario* (6), *Alejandro* (5).

Bandel (281) **1.** South German and Jewish (Ashkenazic): from a diminutive of BAND. **2.** South German: occupational name for a ribbon-maker. Compare BENDEL. **3.** German: possibly a variant of **Pandel**, from a pet form of the personal name *Pantaleon* (see PANTALEO). **4.** Slovenian: possibly a medieval respelling of the Latin personal name *Pantaleon*, originating in western Slovenia. It may also be an Americanized form of the surname *Bandelj*, which is of the same origin.

GIVEN NAMES Jewish 5%. *Zvi* (3), *Emanuel*, *Hyman*, *Meir*.

Bandemer (112) **1.** French: unexplained. **2.** German: from a Germanic personal name composed of the elements *bandu* 'banner' + *mari* 'famous' or from the Slavic personal name *Bandomir*, composed of an unknown first element + *mir* 'fame'.

GIVEN NAMES French 6%. *Marat* (2), *Armand*, *Martial*, *Mechelle*.

Bander (137) German (**Bänder**) and Jewish (Ashkenazic): occupational name for a cooper (see BENDER).

GIVEN NAMES Jewish 5%. *Meyer*, *Yigal*.

Bandera (152) **1.** Spanish: from *bandera* 'banner', 'flag', hence presumably a status name for a standard bearer. **2.** Ukrainian: unexplained.

GIVEN NAMES Spanish 26%; Italian 7%. *Jose* (3), *Alberto* (2), *Alfonso*, *Andres*, *Angelina*, *Aurelio*, *Blanca*, *Cesar*, *Cesareo*, *Cristina*, *Fernando*, *Guadalupe*; *Angelo*, *Antonio*, *Fausto*, *Marino*, *Nicolo*.

Bandi (136) **1.** Italian: from the personal name *Bando*, which may be a short form of any of the various Germanic compound names with the unattested element *band-wo-* meaning 'banner', 'flag', 'insignia', or, more likely from a short form of a personal name formed with *-brand-* 'sword (blade)',

for example *Ildebrando*. **2.** Swiss German (from Oberwil near Büren, Bern canton): probably from a Germanic personal name of the same origin as the Italian. **3.** Hungarian (**Bándi**): habitational name for someone from a place called Bánd in Veszprém county and Marosszék in Transylvania. **4.** Indian (Andhra Pradesh): Hindu name, from Telugu *baṇḍi* 'carriage', 'cart', based on the name of a REDDY clan.
GIVEN NAMES Italian 13%; Indian 12%. *Salvatore* (2), *Antonio*, *Filippo*, *Giovanni*; *Ram* (3), *Upendra* (2), *Pratima*, *Rajendra*, *Rajesh*.

Bandler (110) German: occupational name for a maker of band of ribbon or lace, from an agent derivative of Middle High German, Middle Low German *bandel*, a diminutive of *bant* 'band' (see BAND).

Bando (120) Japanese (**Bandō**): meaning 'east of the slope', referring to provinces east of Ōsaka ('great slope'). Two characters meaning 'slope' and a third character, meaning 'wooden board' but similar in appearance to the two meaning 'slope', are used to write it. The name is found mostly in western Japan.
GIVEN NAMES Japanese 18%. *Akiko* (2), *Keizo* (2), *Atsushi, Katsuhiro, Katsuyo, Seiko, Takeshi, Toshiaki*.

Bandow (118) German: habitational name from Bandow in Mecklenburg-West Pomerania.

Bandstra (152) Frisian: **1.** habitational name for someone from a place named Band. **2.** possibly a topographic name for someone who lived by a road, a topographic derivative of Dutch *baan* 'road'
GIVEN NAMES Dutch 4%. *Gerrit, Wouter.*

Bandt (154) German: variant spelling of BAND.

Banducci (194) Italian: from a derivative of BANDI.
GIVEN NAMES Italian 15%. *Amato* (2), *Carlo* (2), *Gino* (2), *Luigi* (2), *Elio, Ilio, Pasquale.*

Bandura (136) **1.** Polish: unflattering nickname from *bańdura* 'chatterer'. **2.** Ukrainian: from *bandura* 'bandore', hence a metonymic occupational name for a musician.

Bandy (3019) **1.** English: unexplained. **2.** Probably a variant of Swiss German BANDI, or German BENDER or **Bänder** (see BANDER). **3.** Hungarian (**Bándy**): variant of BANDI.

Bane (1989) **1.** English: variant spelling of BAIN. **2.** Irish: variant of BAIN 1. **3.** Perhaps French, an occupational name from Old French *ban(n)e* 'hamper', 'large basket'.

Banegas (244) Spanish: from a characteristic (but rare) hybridization, in this case of Semitic *(i)ben* 'son' + *Egas*, a personal name of Visigothic origin. More widespread is the Portuguese equivalent, **Viegas**.
GIVEN NAMES Spanish 39%. *Jose* (7), *Miguel* (4), *Juan* (3), *Juana* (3), *Pedro* (3), *Estevan*

(2), *Fernando* (2), *Jaime* (2), *Javier* (2), *Julio Cesar* (2), *Manuel* (2), *Santos* (2).

Banerjee (485) Indian (Bengal) and Bangladeshi: Hindu (Brahman) name, the first element of which, *Ban-*, is a shortened form of the village name Bandoghat. The final element *-jee* is derived from *jhā* (greatly reduced form of Sanskrit *upādhyāya* 'teacher'); thus, *Banerjee* 'teacher from the village of Bandoghat'. In Bengali names formed with *-jee*, the initial element is believed to indicate a village granted by Ballal Sen, a legendary ancient king of Bengal, to the ancestor of the person bearing the surname. A Sanskrit version of this name, **Vandyopadhyaya**, was coined later, from the elements *vandya* 'venerable' + *upādhyāya* 'teacher'.
GIVEN NAMES Indian 85%. *Partha* (9), *Amit* (6), *Soumya* (6), *Aniruddha* (4), *Dilip* (4), *Bharati* (3), *Bhaskar* (3), *Ranjan* (3), *Shampa* (3), *Swapan* (3), *Tapan* (3), *Utpal* (3).

Banes (604) **1.** Variant of Scottish and English BAINES. **2.** Spanish (**Bañes**): habitational name from a place in Palencia named Bañes. **3.** German: perhaps a variant or a patronymic from the Frisian personal name **Bane**, from *ban* 'decree', 'ban'.

Banet (201) **1.** French: from a diminutive of BANE. **2.** Jewish (from Poland): unexplained.

Baney (806) **1.** English: nickname from Middle English *bani* 'bony', from Old English *bān* 'bone'. Compare BAIN 2. **2.** Americanized spelling of south German and Swiss **Bä(h)ni**, from a pet form of the personal name BERNHARD.

Banez (103) Spanish (**Báñez**): shortened form of *Ibáñez* (see IBANEZ).
GIVEN NAMES Spanish 44%. *Jose* (3), *Juanito* (2), *Aida, Arturo, Beatriz, Catalino, Conrado, Domingo, Erlinda, Eugenio, Gaspar, Julio.*

Banfield (921) **1.** English: habitational name from any of various places named in Old English from *bēan* 'beans' (collective singular) + *feld* 'field', 'open land', as for example Benville in Dorset. **2.** Irish: variant of the Norman family name BANVILLE (see BONFIELD), associated primarily with county Wexford.

Banfill (143) Irish: variant of the Norman family name **Banville** (see BONFIELD).
GIVEN NAME French 6%. *Dominique.*

Banford (149) English: variant of the English habitational name BAMFORD or Norman BANVILLE. See also BONFIELD.

Bang (1085) **1.** Korean: variant of PANG. **2.** Norwegian: habitational name for someone who lived at a farm named Bang, from *bank* 'flat hill-top', 'terrace'. **3.** Danish: from Old Danish *bang* 'noise', hence a nickname for a loud or brash person. **4.** German: nickname for a timid person, from Middle High German, Middle Low German *bang* 'fearful', 'nervous'.

GIVEN NAMES Korean 24%; Scandinavian 4%. *Sung* (5), *Hyun* (4), *Soo* (4), *Yong* (4), *Young* (4), *Dong* (3), *Hong Shik* (3), *Jung* (3), *Seung* (3), *Chan* (2), *Jong* (2), *Joon* (2); *Chong* (3), *Byung* (2), *Chang* (2), *Dae* (2), *Inho* (2), *Moon* (2), *Nam* (2), *Young Ok* (2), *Byung Sun, Chul, Hyeyoung, Hyong*; *Anders* (2), *Lasse* (2), *Bjorn, Helmer, Jorgen, Lars, Nils, Thorvald.*

Bange (304) German: variant of BANG 4.

Bangert (859) German: **1.** southern reduced form of BAUMGARTEN. **2.** in southern Germany, also in Alsace, from the occupational name *Banwart* 'field and forest ranger'. **3.** variant of BANKERT.

Bangerter (294) South German and Swiss German: **1.** variant of BAUMGARTNER. **2.** variant of BANGERT.

Banghart (357) German: from a Germanic personal name, perhaps composed of Germanic *banga* 'to beat' + *hard* 'hard', 'strong'.

Bangle (191) Altered spelling of German **Bangel**, which probably is a variant of BANG or of BENGEL, or derives from a field name in the district of Lüneburg.
GIVEN NAME French 5%. *Marcel.*

Bango (191) **1.** Asturian-Leonese: habitational name from Bango in the district of Conceyu de Corvera, Asturies. **2.** Hungarian: from *bangó* 'awkward', hence a nickname for a mentally or physically, or socially handicapped person.
GIVEN NAMES Spanish 15%. *Francisco* (3), *Luis* (3), *Reinaldo* (3), *Abelino, Adalberto, Angel, Enrique, Eugenio, Jesus, Jose, Lourdes.*

Bangs (1001) English: variant of BANKS 1.
FOREBEARS Edward Bangs of Chichester, England, came to Plymouth Colony on board the 'Anne' in 1623; he is believed to have been born in about 1592.

Bangura (122) Muslim: unexplained.
GIVEN NAMES Muslim 42%; African 14%. *Abdul* (3), *Abu* (3), *Mohamed* (3), *Abass* (2), *Ahmed* (2), *Abdul Rahman, Abdullah, Alhaji, Dauda, Hassan, Ibrahim, Ismail*; *Fatmata* (4), *Aminata* (2), *Isatu* (2), *Kadiatu, Mariama.*

Banh (278) Vietnamese: unexplained.
GIVEN NAMES Vietnamese 46%; Chinese 27%. *Minh* (5), *Sanh* (5), *Anh* (3), *Cuong* (3), *Hao* (3), *Hoa* (3), *Khanh* (3), *Thanh* (3), *Tran* (3), *Chau* (2), *Diep* (2), *Duc* (2); *Chi* (3), *Xia* (3), *Han, Ping, Sen, Tong*; *Phong* (2), *Tinh* (2), *Chong, Nam, Sinh, Tam, Thai.*

Banholzer (105) South German: topographic name for someone who live in a *Banholz* 'protection wood', i.e. a forest grown for protection against avalanches.
GIVEN NAMES French 4%; German 4%. *Mechelle* (2); *Kurt.*

Bania (186) Polish: from *bania* 'gourd', 'globe', 'round, bulging object', probably applied as a nickname for a small fat man.
GIVEN NAMES Polish 8%. *Andrzej, Casimir, Eugeniusz, Henryk, Wladyslaw.*

Banick (189) Germanized or Americanized spelling of Polish or Slovak BANIK.

Banicki (116) Polish: from the personal name *Banasz*, a pet form of *Benedykt* (see BENEDICT).

Banik (208) **1.** Polish and Slovak (**Baník**): occupational name for a miner. **2.** Polish: from a reduced form of *Benedikt* or *Benedykt*, vernacular forms of *Benedictus* (see BENEDICT). **3.** Indian (Bengal, Assam, and Orissa) and Bangladeshi: Hindu (Baishya) name, from Sanskrit *vaṇik* 'merchant'.
GIVEN NAMES Indian 12%. *Asit, Gautam, Gour, Niranjan, Pranav, Somnath, Utpal, Uttam.*

Banis (147) **1.** Greek: of uncertain origin; possibly a nickname meaning 'hut-dweller', from Albanian *banë* 'hut'. **2.** Lithuanian (also **Banys**): from a vernacular form of the personal name *Benediktas*, Latin *Benedictus* (see BENEDICT). **3.** Dutch: from a vernacular form of Latin *Benedictus* (see BENEDICT).

Banish (170) Americanized form of Polish BANACH or **Banaś** (see BANAS).

Banister (1160) English: variant of BANNISTER.
FOREBEARS The naturalist John Banister (1650–92) was born in Gloucestershire, England, and came to VA in 1678.

Bank (980) **1.** German, Dutch, and Jewish (Ashkenazic): from Middle High German or Middle Low German *banc*, or Yiddish *bank* 'bench', 'table', 'counter', in any of various senses, e.g. a metonymic occupational name for anyone whose work required a bench or counter, for example a butcher, baker, court official, or money changer. **2.** Danish and Swedish: topographic name from *bank* '(sand)bank' or a habitational name from a farm named with this word. **3.** Danish and Swedish: from *bank* 'noise', hence a nickname for a loud or noisy person. Compare BANG. **4.** Danish: habitational name from the German place name Bänkau. **5.** English: probably a variant of BANKS. **6.** Americanized spelling of Polish **Bąk**, literally 'horsefly'; perhaps a nickname for an irritating person. **7.** Hungarian (**Bánk**): from a pet form of the old secular personal name *Bán*.
GIVEN NAMES Jewish 4%. *Mort* (2), *Sol* (2), *Ari, Avraham, Galit, Hyman, Isadore, Mirra, Zvia.*

Banka (158) **1.** Polish (**Bańka**) and Slovak (also **Baňka**): nickname for a short fat man, from *bańka* 'bulb'. **2.** Hungarian (**Bánka**): see BANK.
GIVEN NAMES Polish 13%. *Casimir* (2), *Stanislaw* (2), *Henryk, Jerzy, Zbigniew.*

Bankard (129) Possibly an Americanized spelling of French **Ban(c)quart**, metonymic occupational name for a carter, from Old French *bancart* 'bench of a wagon or cart', later a particular type of cart.

Banke (190) German: variant of BANK.

GIVEN NAME German 4%. *Egon.*

Banken (120) Dutch: variant of BANK.

Banker (1484) **1.** English: topographic name from northern Middle English *bank(e)* 'hillside slope', 'riverbank' + the suffix *-er* denoting an inhabitant (see BANKS). **2.** Scottish: habitational name from Bankier in Stirlingshire. **3.** Jewish (Ashkenazic): occupational name from Polish *bankier* 'banker'. **4.** German (**Bänker**): occupational name from an agent derivative of Middle Low German *banc* 'bench', 'counter' (see BANK).

Bankert (499) German and Dutch: nickname for an illegitimate child, from Middle High German, Middle Low German *banc-hart*, Dutch *bankaard* 'fathered on a bench'.

Bankes (355) English and Scottish: variant spelling of BANKS 1.

Bankey (148) Americanized form of North German BEHNKE.

Bankhead (1008) Scottish and northern Irish: topographic name for someone who lived at the top or end of a bank or hill (see BANKS 1) or habitational name from a place with this origin. There are several minor places in Scotland so called, but the most likely source of the surname is one on the border between the parishes of Kilmarnock and Dreghorn in Ayrshire.

Banko (406) **1.** Hungarian: from a pet form of the old secular personal name *Bán*. **2.** Slovak, Croatian (Istria), and Slovenian: derivative of *ban* 'governor' (see BAN).

Bankowski (195) Polish (**Bańkowski**): habitational name for someone from a place named Bańki, from *bańka* 'bulging vessel', 'bubble'.
GIVEN NAMES Polish 8%. *Ewa, Irena, Jacek, Zbigniew, Zigmond.*

Banks (27242) **1.** English and Scottish: topographic name for someone who lived on the slope of a hillside or by a riverbank, from northern Middle English *banke* (from Old Danish *banke*). The final *-s* may occasionally represent a plural form, but it is most commonly an arbitrary addition made after the main period of surname formation, perhaps under the influence of patronymic forms with a possessive *-s*. **2.** Irish: Anglicized form of Gaelic **Ó Bruacháin** 'descendant of *Bruachán*', a byname for a large-bellied person. The English form was chosen because of a mistaken association of the Gaelic name with *bruach* 'bank'.

Bankson (375) Swedish: variant of BANKSTON.

Bankston (2270) Americanized form of Swedish **Bengtsson** (see BENGTSON).
FOREBEARS Andrew Bankston, alias Anders Bengtsson, came to New Sweden on the Delaware river in 1656; he died in Philadelphia in 1706.

Bann (200) **1.** German: from Middle High German *ban* 'area (of fields or woods) banned from agricultural or other use',

hence probably a topographic name for someone who lived by such a reserve. See also BANWART. **2.** English: of uncertain origin. Reaney suggests that it may be from an unrecorded Old English personal name *Banna*, or a metonymic occupational name for a basket maker, from Old French *bane*, *banne* 'hamper', 'pannier'. Compare French BANE.

Bannan (356) Irish: variant spelling of BANNON.

Banner (1766) **1.** English (Midlands): metonymic occupational name for a standard bearer, from Anglo-Norman French *banere* 'flag', 'ensign' (see BANNERMAN). **2.** German: occupational name for a standard bearer, Middle High German *banier*, Middle Low German *banner*, from French *bannière* 'flag', 'standard'.

Bannerman (490) Scottish: occupational name for a standard bearer, from Anglo-Norman French *banere* 'flag', 'ensign' (Old French *baniere*, Late Latin *bandaria*) + Middle English *man* 'man'.

Bannick (156) Americanized spelling of Polish or Slovak BANIK.

Banning (1263) **1.** English: unexplained. **2.** German: patronymic from a personal name formed with *Ban-* 'decree', 'command' or *Band-* 'band', 'tie'.

Bannister (2737) English: metonymic occupational name for a basket weaver, from Anglo-Norman French *banastre* 'basket' (the result of a Late Latin cross between Gaulish *benna* and Greek *kanistron*). The term denoting a stair rail is unconnected with this name; it was not used before the 17th century.

Bannon (1962) Irish: Anglicized form of Gaelic **Ó Banáin**, 'descendant of *Banán*', a personal name representing a diminutive of *ban* 'white'.

Banos (237) **1.** Spanish (**Baños**): habitational name from any of numerous places named for their public baths, *bañnos* (from Latin *balnea*). In some instances the name may have arisen as a metonymic occupational name for an attendant at a public bath house. **2.** Hungarian (**Bános**): from a pet form of the old secular personal name *Bán*.
GIVEN NAMES Spanish 46%. *Luis* (7), *Alfredo* (4), *Blanca* (3), *Carlos* (3), *Orlando* (3), *Abilio* (2), *Alberto* (2), *Ernesto* (2), *Francisco* (2), *Javier* (2), *Jose* (2), *Juan* (2).

Bansal (241) Indian (northern states): Hindu (Bania), Jain, and Sikh name, which appears to be related to Sanskrit *vamśa* 'lineage', also meaning 'bamboo'. The Agarwal Banias have a clan called Bansal (see AGARWAL), as have the Ramgarhia Sikhs.
GIVEN NAMES Indian 93%. *Rajesh* (7), *Anil* (6), *Arun* (6), *Anju* (5), *Krishan* (4), *Raj* (4), *Satish* (4), *Ashok* (3), *Ravi* (3), *Sudhir* (3), *Suresh* (3), *Vinay* (3).

Banse (152) **1.** German: from Middle Low German *banse* 'granary', '(wood or coal) shed next to a barn' hence a topographic name for someone who owned or lived by such a building. In some instances a nickname for a fat person, from dialect *Pansen* 'belly', or in Bavaria a metonymic occupational name for a barrel maker from *Banz*, *Banse* 'barrel'. **2.** French: from a Germanic personal name, short form of any of various names beginning with the element *bant* 'bond', 'tie'.
GIVEN NAMES German 6%. *Ingo* (2), *Helmut*.

Banta (2104) Frisian: probably a habitational name for someone from Bant, in the 17th century an island in Friesland, now the village north of Emmeloord in the Noordoostpolder.
FOREBEARS The name Banta was first attested as a family name in New Netherland in 1696, the founder, Epke Jacobs Banta, having arrived in New Netherland in 1659. A family of this name, prominent in NJ in the 1780s, went with the Low Dutch Company to settle in KY.

Banter (104) English and Scottish: unexplained.

Bantle (165) German: **1.** altered spelling of **Bantel(e)**, from an Alemannic-Swabian short form of the personal name *Pantaleon* (see PANTALEO). **2.** habitational name from Banteln near Hildesheim.
GIVEN NAMES German 6%. *Alfons, Helmut, Lorenz*.

Banton (580) English: habitational name of uncertain origin. There is a place so called in Strathclyde region and a Banton House in Lancashire; the present-day concentration of the surname in the Derbyshire area suggests the latter may be the more likely source. In some instances the name may have arisen from a place called Bampton, in particular, one in Cumbria, named with Old English *bēam* 'trunk', 'beam' + *tūn* 'farmstead', 'settlement'.

Bantz (415) German: variant spelling of BANZ.

Banuelos (1490) Spanish (**Bañuelos**): habitational name from any of various places, primarily Bañuelos de Bureba in Burgos, named for their public baths, from a diminutive of *baños* 'baths' (see BANOS).
GIVEN NAMES Spanish 55%. *Jose* (44), *Manuel* (24), *Juan* (19), *Jesus* (16), *Pedro* (15), *Francisco* (13), *Jorge* (11), *Raul* (11), *Carlos* (10), *Luis* (10), *Javier* (9), *Ruben* (9).

Banville (269) French, English, and Irish (of Norman origin): habitational name from Banville in Calvados, France, recorded in the 13th century as *Badanvilla* 'estate of a woman called Bada'. Compare BONFIELD.
GIVEN NAMES French 10%. *Normand* (2), *Alban, Andre, Armand, Benoit*.

Banwart (184) German: occupational name for a field or forest ranger, Middle High German *banwart*, from *ban* 'restricted area' (see BANN) + *wart* 'warden'.

Banwell (115) **1.** English (Somerset): habitational name from Banwell in Somerset, named from Old English *bana* 'killer' + *wella* 'stream', 'spring'. **2.** Irish (of Norman origin): variant of BANVILLE or BONFIELD.

Banyai (153) Hungarian (**Bányai**): habitational name for someone from any of over forty places named with *bánya* 'mine', especially the Transylvanian city of Nagybánya ('great mine').
GIVEN NAMES Hungarian 6%. *Laszlo* (2), *Istvan, Vilmos*.

Banyas (167) **1.** Hungarian (**Bányás**): from *bánya* 'mine', hence a metonymic occupational name for a miner or a topographic name for someone who lived near a mine. **2.** Americanized spelling of Hungarian **Bányász**, occupational name for a miner.

Banz (124) South German: **1.** habitational name from a place in Franconia so named, or a topographic name from Old High German *banz*, which denotes the administrative area of a tribe and is probably the origin of the place name. **2.** In Bavaria, from Middle High German *banz*, denoting a barrel or drinking vessel which was used by reapers in the fields, hence probably a metonymic occupational name for a farm laborer or a maker of such vessels.

Banzhaf (176) German (South): metonymic occupational name for a maker of vats and drinking vessels, from *banz* (see BANZ) + *hafen* 'pot'.
GIVEN NAMES German 10%. *Winfried* (2), *Elfriede, Kurt*.

Bao (311) **1.** Chinese: there are three different surnames that are Romanized in pinyin as **Bao**. Other Romanizations include **Bau**, **Pao**, and **Pau**. **2.** Chinese 鲍: this character also means 'abalone', but the name comes from an old place name. The area of Bao was granted to a chief counselor of the state of Qi during the Spring and Autumn period (722–481 BC). His son took the place name as his surname and was called Bao Shuya. Bao Shuya was famous for his lofty moral character and was skilled at delegating authority, eventually becoming the first 'Chief King' of the Spring and Autumn period. **3.** Chinese 包: this Chinese character means 'to wrap' or 'package'. The name is derived from the name of Shen Baoxu. Shen Baoxu was a senior official who lived 2500 years ago in the state of Chu. When the state of Chu was attacked by the state of Wu, Shen Baoxu went to the State of Qin to beg for aid. There, he reportedly cried for seven days and nights until the duke of Qin was moved to help rescue the state of Chu. **4.** Chinese 暴: this character means '(violently) sudden'. It comes from the name of Bao Xingong, a duke during the Yin dynasty (1401–1122 BC).
GIVEN NAMES Chinese 42%; Vietnamese 18%. *Jian* (3), *Cheng* (2), *Gang* (2), *Han* (2), *Ling* (2), *Ming* (2), *Yung* (2), *Bin*, *Chuang, Fei, Feng, Hong; Huan* (3), *Hoa* (2), *Yen* (2), *Be Thi, Dang, Duc, Hai, Hanh, Hien, Hoai, Hoan, Khoi; Thai* (2), *Shen, Yiming, Yiping*.

Bapst (112) German: variant of PABST.

Baptist (497) **1.** English: variant of BAPTISTE. **2.** Americanized form of cognate names in other languages; for example, BAPTISTA, BAPTISTE, BATISTA, and BAUTISTA.

Baptista (759) From Latin *Baptista* 'Baptist' (see BAPTISTE), a form found in Portugal, Spain (Castile), Germany, and some other countries.
GIVEN NAMES Spanish 18%; Portuguese 11%. *Manuel* (15), *Jose* (14), *Luis* (5), *Jorge* (4), *Alvaro* (3), *Augusto* (3), *Alfredo* (2), *Carlos* (2), *Eduardo* (2), *Fernando* (2), *Helio* (2), *Mauricio* (2); *Joao* (6), *Joaquim*.

Baptiste (1630) French and English: from a medieval personal name, derived from the distinguishing epithet of St. John the Baptist, who baptized people, including Jesus Christ, in the river Jordan (Mark 1:9), and was later beheaded by Herod. The name is from Latin *Baptista* (Greek *baptistēs*, a derivative of the verb *baptizein* 'to dip in liquid', 'to baptize').
FOREBEARS A Baptiste from the Île-de-France is documented in Quebec city in 1668 with the secondary surname St. Amour.
GIVEN NAMES French 12%. *Andre* (3), *Pierre* (3), *Yves* (3), *Germaine* (2), *Jacques* (2), *Jean Claude* (2), *Ricot* (2), *Agathe, Anite, Antoine, Cecile, Charlemagne*.

Baquero (136) Spanish: variant of **Vaquero** (see VAQUERA).
GIVEN NAMES Spanish 44%; Italian 9%. *Carlos* (3), *Ines* (3), *Armando* (2), *Fermin* (2), *Gilberto* (2), *Javier* (2), *Jose* (2), *Julio* (2), *Mario* (2), *Albaro, Alberto, Angel; Marco* (3), *Fausto, Lorenzo, Marcello, Salustiano*.

Bar (218) **1.** Jewish (Ashkenazic): from the Yiddish male personal name *Ber* (see BAER). **2.** Variant spelling of German BAHR or BAER. **3.** Polish and Czech: from a short form of the personal name *Bartolomaeus* (Polish *Bartłomiej*, Czech *Bartoloměj*; see BARTHOLOMEW). **4.** Hungarian (**Bár**): from the old secular personal name *Bár*.
GIVEN NAMES Jewish 25%; French 4%; German 4%. *Moshe* (4), *Giora* (3), *Ilan* (2), *Arie, Eliahu, Hadassa, Haim, Menashe, Mordechai, Nadav, Nir, Noam; Dany, Francois, Henri; Hans* (2), *Gerhard, Willi*.

Bara (363) **1.** Scottish: habitational name from Bara, the name of an old manor and parish in East Lothian. **2.** Polish, Czech, and Slovak (**Bára**): from a reduced vernacular form of the Latin personal name *Bartolomaeus*, Polish *Bartłomiej*, Czech

Bartoloměj (see BARTHOLOMEW), or possibly from a pet form of the personal name *Barbara*. **3.** Hungarian: from a short form of the personal name *Barabás* (see BARABAS). **4.** French: nickname for a quarrelsome or deceitful person, from Old French *barat* 'commerce', 'dealings', a derivative of *barater* 'to barter'. Compare BARRATT. **5.** Aragonese: habitational name from Bara in Uesca province, Aragon. **6.** Catalan (**Barà**): respelling of Catalan **Berà** in Tarragona, Catalonia (see BERA).

Barabas (201) Hungarian (**Barabás**), Polish (**Barabasz** or **Barabaś**), Czech and Slovak (**Barabáš**), and Spanish (**Bar(r)abás**): from the New Testament personal name *Barabas* (Greek *Barabbas*) 'son of Aba'. This was the name borne by the thief whose life was demanded by the crowd in Jerusalem in preference to that of Jesus (Matthew 27:15–21). In central Europe it was sometimes adopted as a personal name by a repentant sinner.
GIVEN NAMES Hungarian 13%. *Attila* (2), *Zoltan* (2), *Akos, Bela, Gabor, Istvan, Miklos, Sandor*.

Barach (165) Jewish (eastern Ashkenazic): acronymic surname from a Hebrew patronymic phrase *Ben Rabi Hayyim* 'son of rabbi Hayyim'.

Barackman (104) Of German origin: see BARICKMAN.

Barad (106) **1.** Indian (Gujarat): Hindu (Brahman) name of unknown meaning. **2.** Indian (Panjab): variant of BRAR. **3.** Jewish (eastern Ashkenazic): acronymic surname from the Hebrew patronymic phrase *Ben Rabi David* 'son of Rabbi David'.
GIVEN NAMES Indian 16%; Jewish 5%. *Dipti* (2), *Vijay* (2), *Arun, Manish, Rama; Shimshon*.

Barahona (497) Spanish: habitational name from a place in Soria province.
GIVEN NAMES Spanish 51%. *Jose* (23), *Luis* (10), *Carlos* (8), *Juan* (8), *Mario* (7), *Roberto* (7), *Ana* (6), *Rafael* (6), *Francisco* (5), *Blanca* (4), *Jorge* (4), *Ricardo* (4).

Barajas (2914) Spanish: habitational name from places in the provinces of Cuenca and Madrid; the latter is now the site of an international airport.
GIVEN NAMES Spanish 56%. *Jose* (114), *Juan* (55), *Jesus* (50), *Miguel* (32), *Francisco* (30), *Luis* (28), *Salvador* (24), *Javier* (23), *Manuel* (21), *Ramon* (21), *Jorge* (20), *Rafael* (19).

Barak (257) **1.** Jewish (Ashkenazic): from a Hebrew Biblical name meaning 'lightning'. **2.** Jewish (eastern Ashkenazic): acronymic surname from a Hebrew patronymic phrase *Ben Rabi Kalonymos* 'son of rabbi Kalonymos'. **3.** Czech (**Barák**): status name for the owner of a cottage without land, from *barák* 'cottage', 'shanty', 'cabin'. **4.** Hungarian: habitational name

from a place called Barak, or from a pet form of one of two personal names, *Bertalan* (see BARTHOLOMEW) or *Barabás* (see BARABAS). **5.** Turkish, Bosnian, and Croatian (Kordun): nickname from *barak* 'shaggy-haired'. **6.** Croatian (Dalmatian coast): derivative of the personal name *Bare*, a pet form of *Bartol* (see BARTHOLOMEW) or *Branimir*.
GIVEN NAMES Jewish 17%. *Pinhas* (3), *Yoram* (2), *Avital, Doron, Dov, Erez, Haim, Hanoch, Moshe, Ronit, Shai, Shimon*.

Barakat (359) Muslim (widespread, especially in Egypt, Iran, Pakistan, India, and Bangladesh): from a personal name based on Arabic *barakāt* 'blessings', 'good fortune', 'prosperity', often found in combinations such as *Barakāt-ullah* 'blessings of Allah'.
GIVEN NAMES Muslim 62%. *Ahmad* (5), *Bassam* (4), *Ibrahim* (4), *Amin* (3), *Emad* (3), *Farouk* (3), *Hamid* (3), *Hassan* (3), *Hisham* (3), *Mohamed* (3), *Abdul* (2), *Abed* (2).

Baral (110) Indian (Bengal) and Bangladeshi: Hindu (Swarnabonik) name of unknown meaning. It is found in a community of gold merchants; the community name *Swarnabonik* means 'gold trader'.
GIVEN NAMES Indian 30%. *Asok* (2), *Arun, Chitta, Himanshu, Panna, Ram, Subhash, Suresh, Swapan, Uday*.

Baran (2161) **1.** Polish, Ukrainian, Russian, Czech, Slovak, and Hungarian (**Bárány**): nickname from *baran* 'ram', borne by either a forceful, lusty man or else by a shepherd. **2.** Jewish (eastern Ashkenazic): ornamental name from the same word, *baran* 'ram'.
GIVEN NAMES Polish 8%. *Andrzej* (5), *Stanislaw* (4), *Jacek* (3), *Jozef* (3), *Zbigniew* (3), *Bogdan* (2), *Czeslawa* (2), *Ewa* (2), *Grzegorz* (2), *Jaroslaw* (2), *Mieczyslaw* (2), *Piotr* (2).

Baranek (217) Polish, Czech, Slovak, Ukrainian, and Jewish (eastern Ashkenazic): from a diminutive of BARAN.
GIVEN NAMES Czech and Slovak 4%; German 4%. *Milan* (2), *Jaroslav, Stanislav; Kurt*.

Baranello (113) Italian (Molise): habitational name from Baranello, a mountain community in Campobasso province.
GIVEN NAMES Italian 13%. *Angelo* (2), *Nunzio, Pasquale*.

Baranoski (141) Polish and Jewish (eastern Ashkenazic): variant of BARANOWSKI.

Baranowski (1198) Polish and Jewish (eastern Ashkenazic): habitational name for someone from the village of Baranów, or from any of many other places (Baran, Barany, Baranowice, Baranovo, Baranovka, etc.) named with Polish *baran* 'ram'.
GIVEN NAMES Polish 5%. *Andrzej* (2), *Bronislaw* (2), *Janina* (2), *Stanislaw* (2), *Zygmunt* (2), *Aniela, Casimir, Jacek, Krystyna, Lech, Miroslaw, Wieslaw*.

Baranski (463) Polish (**Barański**), Ukrainian, and Jewish (eastern Ashkenazic): habitational name for someone from a place called Baran or Barany, Polish *baran* 'ram'.
GIVEN NAMES Polish 8%. *Andrzej* (3), *Janusz* (2), *Bogdan, Bronislaw, Jacek, Jozef, Thadeus, Wieslaw, Wlodzimierz, Zigmunt*.

Barany (167) Hungarian (**Bárány**): from *bárány* 'lamb', hence a metonymic occupational name for a shepherd or a nickname for someone thought to resemble a lamb in some way.
GIVEN NAMES Hungarian 14%. *Istvan* (2), *Laszlo* (2), *Attila, Bela, Endre, Sandor, Zoltan*.

Barasch (241) Jewish (Ashkenazic): variant of BARASH.
GIVEN NAMES Jewish 6%. *Morry* (2), *Elihu, Sol*.

Barash (370) Jewish (Ashkenazic): acronymic surname from the Hebrew patronymic phrase *Ben Rabi Shelomo, Shemuel, Shimon, Shimshon*, etc., i.e. 'son of (rabbi) SOLOMON, SAMUEL, SIMON, SAMSON', or some other male personal name beginning with Sh-.
GIVEN NAMES Jewish 11%; Russian 6%. *Shlomo* (3), *Naum* (2), *Devorah, Isaak, Mariya, Meyer, Musya, Rozalia, Srul, Yerachmiel; Mikhail* (2), *Semyon* (2), *Zoya* (2), *Arkady, Galina, Liliya, Yefim, Yelena, Yuriy*.

Barath (163) Hungarian (**Baráth**): from the vocabulary word *barát* 'friend', hence a nickname for a companionable person. Alternatively, in some cases it may be an occupational name for a monk, from another meaning of the same word.
GIVEN NAMES Hungarian 15%. *Laszlo* (3), *Gaza* (2), *Antal, Barna, Endre, Miklos, Tibor*.

Baratta (653) Italian: occupational name for a market trader, especially in northern Italy, from *baratta* 'exchange', 'sale', 'buying and selling', a derivative of *barattare* 'to barter'. See also BARRETT.
GIVEN NAMES Italian 9%. *Angelo* (3), *Carmine* (2), *Pasquale* (2), *Alfonse, Antonio, Carmela, Guido, Salvatore, Vincenzo*.

Baratz (152) Jewish (Ashkenazic): acronymic surname from a Hebrew patronymic phrase *Ben Rabi Tsvi* 'son of rabbi Tsvi'.
GIVEN NAME Jewish 6%. *Sol*.

Barb (575) Possibly an altered spelling of French BARBE.

Barba (1566) **1.** Spanish, Catalan, Italian, Portuguese, and southern French: nickname for a man noted for his beard, from *barba* 'beard' (Latin *barba*). **2.** Italian: from a byname from a southern dialect word meaning 'uncle' (from Latin *barba* 'beard' via Lombardic *barba, barbane*), as characterizing a man of wisdom and authority. **3.** Greek: see BARBAS. **4.** Slovenian: unexplained. This name comes from the Brkini region in southwestern Slovenia.

GIVEN NAMES Spanish 34%; Italian 5%. *Jose* (26), *Jesus* (13), *Manuel* (13), *Carlos* (12), *Juan* (12), *Luis* (11), *Salvador* (8), *Francisco* (7), *Roberto* (7), *Ramon* (6), *Alfonso* (5), *Guadalupe* (5); *Antonio* (7), *Lorenzo* (5), *Salvatore* (5), *Silvano* (3), *Angelo* (2), *Piero* (2), *Agostino*, *Aldo*, *Carmela*, *Clemente*, *Eliseo*, *Federico*.

Barbagallo (360) Italian (especially eastern Sicily): nickname from *barba (di) gallo*, literally 'cock's beard', i.e. wattle, probably a nickname for someone with a dewlap.
GIVEN NAMES Italian 29%. *Sal* (4), *Carmelo* (3), *Salvatore* (3), *Antonino* (2), *Cirino* (2), *Stefano* (2), *Angelo*, *Antonio*, *Carlo*, *Cesario*, *Enzo*, *Gaeton*.

Barbano (159) Italian: variant of BARBA 2.
GIVEN NAMES Italian 7%. *Attilio*, *Carlo*, *Constantino*, *Ugo*.

Barbara (615) **1.** Italian, Spanish and Portuguese (**Bárbara**), and English: from the female personal name *Barbara*, which was borne by a popular saint, who according to legend was imprisoned in a tower and later put to death by her own father for refusing to recant her Christian beliefs. The name comes from a feminine form of Latin *barbarus*, Greek *barbaros* 'foreign(er)' (originally an onomatopoeic word formed in imitation of the unintelligible babbling of non-Greeks). **2.** Catalan (**Barbarà**): variant of BARBERA.
GIVEN NAMES Italian 20%; Spanish 12%. *Salvatore* (4), *Mario* (3), *Carlo* (2), *Francesco* (2), *Caesar*, *Domenic*, *Giuseppe*, *Rosaria*, *Sal*, *Santo*, *Vito*; *Jose* (2), *Ana*, *Andres*, *Eloy*, *Jorge*, *Leticia*, *Lourdes*, *Luis*, *Manuel*.

Barbare (97) Variant of English or French BARBARY.

Barbaree (170) Variant spelling of English or French BARBARY.

Barbaria (105) Italian: variant of BARBARO.
GIVEN NAMES Italian 20%. *Angelo* (2), *Antonio*, *Nunzio*, *Reno*.

Barbarino (144) Italian: from a diminutive of BARBARO.
GIVEN NAMES Italian 20%. *Alfio* (2), *Orazio* (2), *Salvatore* (2), *Angelo*.

Barbaro (501) Italian: **1.** from the imperial Roman personal name *Barbarus* (for the etymology see BARBARA 1). **2.** from *Barbaro*, a byname or nickname also originally denoting a person of non-Greek or Roman origin, which in the Middle Ages came to mean a non-Christian, specifically an Arab or Saracen. Compare BARBARY. **3.** from *barbarus*, from Castilian *bravo* 'fierce', 'brave'.
GIVEN NAMES Italian 21%. *Antonio* (5), *Salvatore* (5), *Carmine* (4), *Rocco* (4), *Vito* (3), *Cosmo* (2), *Alessandro*, *Alfonse*, *Amelio*, *Domenic*, *Fiore*, *Gaspare*.

Barbary (125) **1.** English: from a pet form of the female personal name *Barbara* (see BARBARA). **2.** Southern French: from a diminutive of Occitan *barbari* 'barbarous', 'barbarian'. In particular, this word came to

denote a Moor or Berber from the Barbary Coast in North Africa, and hence was then applied to a man of swarthy appearance or uncouth habits.
FOREBEARS An immigrant from the Périgord region of France was variously documented in Montreal in 1668 as Barbary and Barbarin, with the secondary surname Grandmaison.

Barbas (126) **1.** Greek: from a term of address, *barbas*, indicating either respect for an older man or friendly familiarity, from Italian *barba* 'uncle', 'man with a beard' (see BARBA). It may also be a reduced form of surnames beginning with *Barba*, for example *Barbagiannis* 'Uncle John'. **2.** Portuguese and Spanish: from the plural of *barba* 'bearded' (Latin *barba* 'beard'), a nickname for a bearded man. **3.** Hungarian (**Barbás**): see BARABAS.
GIVEN NAMES Greek 4%. *Konstantinos*, *Panos*.

Barbash (123) Americanized spelling of Hungarian **Barbás** (see BARABAS).

Barbati (131) Italian: patronymic or plural form of BARBATO.
GIVEN NAMES Italian 22%. *Gino* (3), *Angelo* (2), *Emidio* (2), *Nicola* (2), *Carmine*, *Pellegrino*, *Sal*, *Salvatore*.

Barbato (906) Italian: descriptive nickname from *barbato* 'bearded', from *barba* 'beard' (Latin *barba*).
GIVEN NAMES Italian 15%. *Pasquale* (6), *Angelo* (4), *Gaetano* (3), *Salvatore* (3), *Carmela* (2), *Luca* (2), *Luigi* (2), *Marco* (2), *Anella*, *Biagio*, *Camillo*, *Carmel*.

Barbay (139) **1.** Belgian variant of French BARBEAU. **2.** Respelling of French **Barbé**, meaning 'bearded', from an adjectival derivative of *barbe* 'beard' (see BARBE).

Barbe (401) **1.** French: nickname for someone with a beard, Old French *barbe* (Latin *barba*). **2.** French: from the female personal name, French form of BARBARA. **3.** German: from Middle High German *barbe*, the name of a species of fish resembling the carp; hence by metonymy an occupational name for a fisherman or fish dealer, or possibly a nickname for someone thought to resemble the fish in some way.
FOREBEARS A man called Barbe, born in London, England, under the name BEARD, is documented in Pointe-aux-Trembles, Quebec, in 1699. He was also known as Abel, Bear, and Buard.
GIVEN NAMES French 9%. *Emile* (2), *Laurent* (2), *Andre*, *Gillis*, *Jean Pierre*, *Serge*, *Sylvie*, *Thierry*, *Yves*.

Barbeau (685) French: **1.** from *barbeau* 'barbel', a type of fish, hence a metonymic occupational name for a fisherman, or a nickname for a man with a sparse beard, the fish being distinguished by beardlike growths on either side of its mouth. **2.** nickname from a derivative of Old French, Occitan *barbel* 'point', 'tooth'.
FOREBEARS A Barbeau from the Poitou re-

gion of France is documented in Quebec city, in 1669 with the secondary surname Laforest. Another, from the Saintonge region, is recorded in Boucherville, Quebec, in 1686 with the secondary surname Boisdoré. A third, from the Poitou region, is documented in Lachenaie, Quebec, in 1690 with the secondary surname Poitevin.
GIVEN NAMES French 9%. *Andre* (4), *Pierre* (3), *Monique* (2), *Alcide*, *Alphonse*, *Amiee*, *Armand*, *Gisele*, *Jean Francois*, *Lucien*, *Lucienne*, *Michel*.

Barbee (3856) Dutch: variant of BARBE or French **Barbé** (see BARBAY).

Barbella (118) Italian: from a diminutive of BARBA.
GIVEN NAMES Italian 20%. *Angelo*, *Rogelio*, *Salvatore*, *Saverio*.

Barben (121) Dutch: derivative of French BARBE 'beard'.
GIVEN NAME French 5%. *Micheline*.

Barber (26826) **1.** English: occupational name for a barber, Anglo-Norman French *barber*, Old French *barbier*, from Late Latin *barbarius*, a derivative of *barba* 'beard'. In the Middle Ages barbers not only cut hair and shaved beards, but also practised surgery and pulled teeth. **2.** Jewish (Ashkenazic): occupational name from German *Barbier* 'barber'. **3.** Catalan: occupational name for a barber, *barber* (see 1). **4.** Americanized form of any of numerous cognates of 1 in different languages, for example Spanish BARBERO, Portuguese **Barbeiro**, French BARBIER, Italian BARBIERI.

Barbera (1171) **1.** Southern Italian: derogatory nickname from *barbera* 'barber's wife', a term also used to denote a prostitute or dishonest woman. **2.** Catalan (**Barberà**): habitational name from a place in Tarragona province, named with Late Latin *Barbarianum* 'place of *Barbarius*', a derivative of *Barbarus* (see BARBARO).
GIVEN NAMES Italian 13%. *Salvatore* (12), *Angelo* (4), *Sal* (4), *Francesco* (2), *Nunzio* (2), *Pietro* (2), *Vittorio* (2), *Antonino*, *Biagio*, *Carlo*, *Gasper*, *Gino*.

Barberi (197) Italian: patronymic or plural form of BARBERIO.
GIVEN NAMES Italian 19%; Spanish 8%. *Pasquale* (3), *Francisco* (2), *Ubaldo* (2), *Carlo*, *Ignazio*, *Nicolo*, *Salvatore*; *Alfonso*, *Berenice*, *Bibiana*, *Carlos*, *Elfego*.

Barberio (272) Italian: from a variant of *barbiere* 'surgeon', 'barber'.
GIVEN NAMES Italian 14%. *Antonio* (4), *Luigi* (2), *Pasquale* (2), *Pierino* (2), *Angelo*, *Arduino*, *Petrina*, *Rocco*.

Barberis (114) **1.** Northern Italian (Piedmont): variant of BARBERI. This is one of a class of surnames typified by the genitive plural suffix *-is* imparting the sense 'belonging to', 'of', in this case 'the barber's (or surgeon's) family'. **2.** Greek: occupational name from *barberis* 'barber', from Italian *barbiere* (see 1), or a shortened form of a patronymic derived from this, such as **Barberopoulos**.

GIVEN NAMES Spanish 13%. *Carlos* (2), *Juan* (2), *Jaime, Jose, Tito.*

Barbero (347) Spanish: occupational name for a barber-surgeon (see BARBER), Spanish *barbero*, from Late Latin *barbarius*, a derivative of *barba* 'beard' (Latin *barba*).

GIVEN NAMES Spanish 7%; Italian 6%; French 4%. *Ricardo* (2), *Alvino, Ana, Angel, Arsenio, Fernando, Gustavo, Jaime, Jose, Maribel, Mario, Nenita; Aldo* (2), *Angelo* (2), *Domenic, Ernani, Giulio, Italo; Emile, Yves.*

Barbery (116) English (Cornwall): variant spelling of BARBARY.

GIVEN NAMES Spanish 8%. *Carlos* (2), *Jorge* (2), *Emilio, Luis, Normando, Soledad.*

Barbetta (133) Italian: nickname from a diminutive of *barba* 'beard' (Latin *barba*) or from *barbetta* in the sense 'short beard'.

GIVEN NAMES Italian 12%. *Angelo* (2), *Agostino, Santo.*

Barbey (115) Respelling of French **Barbé**, a nickname from *barbet* 'bearded', an adjectival derivative of *barbe* 'beard' (see BARBE).

GIVEN NAMES French 12%. *Adrien, Henri, Jacques, Marcel.*

Barbian (251) Of German origin: unexplained.

Barbier (574) French: occupational name for a barber-surgeon (see BARBER), Old French *barbier* (from Late Latin *barbarius*, a derivative of *barba* 'beard').

FOREBEARS A Barbier from the Nivernais region of France is documented in Montreal in 1650 with the secondary surname Le Minime.

GIVEN NAMES French 10%. *Dominique* (3), *Emile* (2), *Pierre* (2), *Alexandre, Gilles, Jacques, Laurent, Laurette, Manon, Marcel, Marcellin, Michel.*

Barbieri (1634) Italian: occupational name from *barbiere* 'barber-surgeon' (see BARBER), from Late Latin *barbarius*, a derivative of *barba* 'beard'.

GIVEN NAMES Italian 15%. *Antonio* (9), *Salvatore* (9), *Angelo* (6), *Vito* (5), *Rocco* (4), *Aldo* (2), *Cosmo* (2), *Dino* (2), *Domenic* (2), *Geno* (2), *Giovanna* (2), *Guido* (2).

Barbin (268) French: diminutive of BARBE 1.

GIVEN NAMES French 4%. *Angelle, Marcel.*

Barbo (214) **1.** Italian, Spanish, and Portuguese: from *barbo* 'barbel' (the fish), hence a metonymic occupational name for a fisherman or possibly a nickname for a man with a sparse beard, the fish being distinguished by beardlike growths on either side of its mouth. **2.** Slovenian (from south central Slovenia): unexplained.

GIVEN NAMES Italian 4%. *Carmine, Gino, Giordano, Quirino, Sal, Salvator.*

Barbone (168) Italian: descriptive nickname from *barbone* 'full, thick beard', an augmentative of *barba* 'beard' (Latin *barba*), or alternatively, from the same word used on the Adriatic coast to denote the red mullet.

GIVEN NAMES Italian 28%. *Salvatore* (3), *Luigi* (2), *Arminda, Generoso, Guido, Luca, Luciano, Soccorso, Virginio.*

Barbosa (1845) Portuguese: topographic name from *barba*, a type of plant, + *-oso* 'place rich in this plant'.

GIVEN NAMES Spanish 41%; Portuguese 15%. *Jose* (55), *Manuel* (40), *Juan* (20), *Francisco* (15), *Miguel* (13), *Luis* (12), *Pedro* (12), *Alfredo* (11), *Carlos* (11), *Ricardo* (10), *Angel* (8), *Armando* (8); *Joao* (12), *Joaquim* (6), *Paulo* (4), *Agostinho, Manoel, Serafim, Vanderlei; Antonio* (27), *Marco* (6), *Angelo* (2), *Carmelo* (2), *Eliseo* (2), *Leonardo* (2), *Sal* (2), *Albertina, Cesario, Constantino, Fausto, Flavio.*

Barbour (5424) Scottish and northern Irish: occupational name from Old French *barbeor* 'barber'. Compare the English form BARBER.

FOREBEARS George Barbour sailed from England on the *Transport* in 1635. He became a freeman of Dedham, MA, in 1647 and settled eventually at Medfield.

A Scottish merchant named Barbour settled in eastern VA in the latter half of the 17th century.

Barboza (1032) Portuguese: variant spelling of BARBOSA.

GIVEN NAMES Spanish 35%; Portuguese 7%. *Manuel* (16), *Jose* (10), *Carlos* (9), *Juan* (7), *Ricardo* (6), *Javier* (5), *Jesus* (5), *Jorge* (5), *Luis* (5), *Alejandro* (4), *Jose Luis* (4), *Mario* (4); *Armanda, Joao, Marcio, Paulo.*

Barbre (330) Variant of English or French BARBARY.

Barbush (101) Origin unidentified.

Barbuto (349) Italian: descriptive nickname from *barbuto* 'bearded', from *barba* 'beard' (Latin *barba*).

GIVEN NAMES Italian 24%. *Vito* (5), *Rocco* (4), *Salvatore* (4), *Carmine* (2), *Ambrogio, Angelo, Bartolomeo, Concetta, Filomena, Giuseppe, Onofrio, Sal.*

Barby (105) Dutch: respelling of French **Barbé** (see BARBEY). This spelling is found in areas of German settlement in North America.

GIVEN NAMES German 8%; French 4%. *Merwin, Otto, Wolfgang; Celestine, Pierre.*

Barca (276) **1.** Spanish and Italian: from *barca* 'boat', 'small boat' (Latin *barca*), hence a metonymic occupational name for a sailor, a shipbuilder, or the owner of a boat. **2.** Spanish and Portuguese: habitational name from any of various places named with this word, which is probably of pre-Roman origin. **3.** Hungarian: habitational name from a place called Barca in Borsod county. In some cases the family name could be a derivative of the personal name

Bertalan, Hungarian form of BARTHOLOMEW. **4.** Romanian: from *barca* 'curly fleeced sheep', hence probably a metonymic occupational name for a shepherd, or a nickname for someone with curly hair.

GIVEN NAMES Italian 11%. *Antonio* (2), *Salvatore* (2), *Angelo, Antonino, Libero, Sal, Santo, Sebastiano.*

Barcellona (112) Italian (Sicily): habitational name which may have denoted someone from a place so named (now united with Pozzo di Gotto) in Sicily, or possibly from the city of Barcelona in Catalonia.

Barcellos (178) Portuguese: habitational name for someone from the northern town of Barcelos (formerly spelled *Barcellos*).

GIVEN NAMES Spanish 10%; Portuguese 6%. *Manuel* (5), *Avelino* (3); *Guilherme; Antonio.*

Barcelo (315) Catalan (**Barceló**): apparently from a personal name *Barcelonus* (feminine *Barcelona*), originally denoting someone from the city of Barcelona (see BARCELONA).

GIVEN NAMES Spanish 41%. *Jose* (6), *Luis* (6), *Carlos* (5), *Mario* (4), *Francisco* (3), *Juan* (3), *Ruben* (3), *Arturo* (2), *Eduardo* (2), *Humberto* (2), *Ignacio* (2), *Jaime* (2); *Antonio* (5), *Federico, Lorenzo, Marco Antonio, Nino.*

Barcelona (252) Catalan and Spanish: habitational name from Barcelona, the principal city of Catalonia. The place name is of uncertain, certainly pre-Roman, origin. The settlement was established by the Carthaginians, and according to tradition it was named for the Carthaginian ruling house of *Barca*; the Latin form was *Barcino* or *Barcilo*.

GIVEN NAMES Spanish 8%; Italian 7%. *Alfredo, Amelita, Elvira, Jaime, Luis, Manuel, Mariano, Orlando, Ramon, Romelia; Angelo* (3), *Sal* (3), *Antonio.*

Barcena (119) Spanish: variant of BARCENAS.

GIVEN NAMES Spanish 46%. *Juan* (4), *Jose* (3), *Blasa* (2), *Carlos* (2), *Fernando* (2), *Luis* (2), *Raul* (2), *Alicia, Apolonio, Armando, Arturo, Esequiel.*

Barcenas (337) Spanish (**Bárcena(s)**): habitational name from any of various places throughout Spain named Barcenas, from an unattested pre-Roman topographical element *bargina*, denoting an area of cultivated land.

GIVEN NAMES Spanish 56%. *Jose* (11), *Manuel* (7), *Juan* (6), *Alfredo* (4), *Arturo* (4), *Jorge* (4), *Luis* (4), *Francisco* (3), *Jesus* (3), *Mario* (3), *Pedro* (3), *Alicia* (2).

Barch (325) **1.** North German: topographic name from a Low German dialect form of *Berg* 'mountain', 'hill' (see BARG). **2.** Americanized spelling of Hungarian **Barcs**, from the personal name *Barcs*.

Barcia (261) **1.** Galician: habitational name from any of numerous places so named in Galicia and in Galician-speaking western

Asturias. **2.** Southern Italian: probably a habitational name of Albanian origin, for it is found, along with **Barshi**, in Piana degli Albanesi in Palermo province, and the place names *Barci* and *Bartsi* are common in Albania.

GIVEN NAMES Spanish 15%; Italian 12%. *Jose* (3), *Manuel* (3), *Carlos* (2), *Amparo*, *Caridad*, *Cristina*, *Francisco*, *Joaquin*, *Jorge*, *Julio*, *Luis*, *Mariano*; *Salvatore* (5), *Gasper* (3), *Antonio* (2), *Angelo*, *Ciro*, *Dario*, *Gaspare*, *Sal*.

Barck (108) German: variant of BARK.

Barclay (4470) Scottish: habitational name of English origin, from Berkeley in Gloucestershire, named in Old English with *be(o)rc* 'birch' + *lēah* 'woodland clearing'.

FOREBEARS The surname was brought to Scotland from southwest England in the 12th century; Walter de Berchelai or Berkelai was Chamberlain of Scotland in 1165.

Barclift (179) Origin uncertain; perhaps an altered form of Scottish BARCLAY.

Barco (362) **1.** Spanish: variant of BARCA 1, from an earlier form. **2.** Spanish and Galician: habitational name from any of various places called (El or O) Barco, in particular Barco de Ávila (Ávila, Castile) and O Barco (Ourense, Galicia). These are of uncertain origin, possibly from the Celtic element *bar-* 'height', 'eminence'. **3.** Spanish and Portuguese: metonymic occupational name for a boatman, from Spanish, Portuguese *barco* 'boat'. **4.** Italian (especially Piemonte, Lombardy, and Veneto): from *barco*, which meant 'boat' (possibly derived from Spanish) and also 'garden', 'park', 'farmyard', 'cowshed', hence a metonymic occupational name for either a boatman or a boatbuilder, or for a park keeper or farmer.

GIVEN NAMES Spanish 18%. *Jose* (5), *Alejandro* (3), *Felipe* (2), *Jorge* (2), *Abelardo*, *Andres*, *Cesar*, *Claudio*, *Colon*, *Eduardo*, *Eleazar*, *Emilio*.

Barcomb (412) **1.** Americanized form of French BERTHIAUME. **2.** Perhaps an English habitational name from any of various places in Devon, Somerset, and East Sussex called Barcombe, or possibly from Barkham in Berkshire.

GIVEN NAMES French 4%. *Armand*, *Jacques*, *Marcel*, *Marcelle*.

Barcroft (204) English (also established in Ireland): habitational name from for example Barcroft in Haworth, West Yorkshire, so named with Old English *bere* 'barley' + *croft* 'paddock', 'smallholding'.

FOREBEARS This is the name of a family established in Ireland by William Barcroft (1612–96). They can be traced to the parish of Barcroft, Lancashire, in the reign of Henry III (1216–72).

Barcus (957) Lithuanian: variant spelling of BARTKUS.

Barczak (387) Polish: **1.** patronymic from a reduced pet form of the personal name *Bartłomiej* (see BARTHOLOMEW). **2.** patronymic from a pet form of the personal name *Bartołt*, Polish form of German BERTHOLD.

Bard (2355) **1.** Scottish: occupational name from Gaelic *bàrd* 'poet', 'minstrel', 'singer'. See also BAIRD. **2.** Scottish: perhaps also a habitational name (early forms such as Henry de Barde and Richard de Baard are recorded, and 'de' usually signifies 'from'), but no suitable place has been identified. **3.** French: habitational name from any of the several minor places called Bar(d), from the Gaulish element *barro* 'height', 'hill'. Compare BARRE. **4.** French: metonymic occupational name for someone who used a handcart or barrow in his work, from Old French *bard* 'barrow'. **5.** French: from Old French *bart* 'mud', 'clay' (Late Latin *barrum*, apparently of Celtic origin), in which case it is either a topographic name for someone living in a muddy area or an occupational name for a builder or bricklayer. **6.** Hungarian (**Bárd**): metonymic occupational name for a butcher, woodcutter or carpenter, from *bárd* 'hatchet', 'cleaver'. Derivation from *bárd* 'poet' is unlikely because the word was borrowed from Gaelic only in the late 18th century. **7.** Jewish (Ashkenazic): nickname for someone with a luxurious beard, from a blend of German *Bart* and Yiddish *bord*, both meaning 'beard'. **8.** Probably also an altered spelling of German BART.

FOREBEARS Peter Bard, a French Huguenot, came via London to DE and from there to Burlington, NJ, in the late 17th century.

GIVEN NAMES French 4%. *Michel* (2), *Aime*, *Alphonse*, *Alphy*, *Armand*, *Cecile*, *Celestine*, *Emile*, *Fernand*, *Germaine*, *Gilles*, *Jacques*.

Bardales (141) Spanish: topographic name, from the plural of bardal 'covered with thorns'.

GIVEN NAMES Spanish 49%. *Jose* (5), *Javier* (3), *Luis* (3), *Mario* (3), *Ana* (2), *Gilberto* (2), *Guillermo* (2), *Juan* (2), *Raul* (2), *Sergio* (2), *Alfredo*, *Arnoldo*; *Antonio*, *Lucio*, *Romeo*.

Bardeen (103) Irish: Anglicized form of Gaelic **Ó Bairdín** 'descendant of the bard'.

Bardell (266) English: variant of BARDWELL.

Barden (2168) English: habitational name from places in North and West Yorkshire named Barden, from Old English *bere* 'barley' (or the derived adjective *beren*) + *denu* 'valley'.

Bardes (122) French (**Bardès**): habitational name for someone from a place called Barès, examples of which are found in Côte-d'Or, Loire, and Haute Saône. The place name is derived from a Gallic word, *barr* 'height', 'eminence'.

Bardi (113) Italian: patronymic or plural form of BARDO.

GIVEN NAMES Italian 15%; Spanish 5%. *Gino* (2), *Angelo*, *Pio*, *Salvatore*; *Adolfo* (2), *Augusto*, *Jorge*, *Luis*, *Mario*.

Bardin (618) **1.** English: variant spelling of BARDEN. **2.** French: from a pet form of the Germanic personal name *Bardo*, from Old High German *barta* 'battle axe'. **3.** Russian: from *barda* 'distillery refuse'; the reasons for the adoption of this name are not clear.

Bardo (364) Italian: **1.** from the medieval personal name *Bardo*, a short form of *Isembardo*, *Lombardo*, or *Bernardo*, for example. **2.** (Sicily) possibly from Arabic *balad* 'plot', 'village'.

Bardon (302) **1.** English: variant spelling of BARDEN. **2.** Possibly also a variant of German PARDON. **3.** French: from a pet form of the Germanic personal name *Bardo* (see BARDIN). **4.** Czech: from a pet form of the personal name *Bartoloměj* (see BARTHOLOMEW).

Bardsley (683) English: habitational name from Bardsley in Lancashire, so named from the genitive case of the Old English personal name *Beornrēd* (composed of the elements *beorn* 'young warrior' + *rēd* 'counsel', 'advice') + Old English *lēah* 'woodland clearing'.

Bardwell (1089) English: habitational name from Bardwell in Suffolk, so named with an unattested Old English byname *Bearda*, a derivative of *beard* (see BEARD) + Old English *well(a)* 'spring', 'stream'. Alternatively, the first element may be from a dissimilated form of Old English *bre(o)rd* 'brim', 'bank'.

Bardy (126) **1.** English (Yorkshire): unexplained. **2.** French: from a diminutive of BARD 5. **3.** Hungarian (**Bárdy**): habitational name for someone from a place called Bárd in Somogy county or in Máramaros, (now Maramures in Romania).

Bare (2410) **1.** English: nickname from Old English *bær* 'bare', which in medieval times in addition to the sense 'naked', 'uncovered', also meant 'unarmed', 'defenseless', 'unconcealed', 'destitute'. **2.** Altered spelling of German **Bär** (see BAER).

Barefield (691) English: variant of BARFIELD.

Barefoot (1614) **1.** English: nickname for someone who was in the habit of going about his business unshod, from Old English *bær* 'bare', 'naked' + *fōt* 'foot'. It may have referred to a peasant unable to afford even the simplest type of footwear, or to someone who went barefoot as a religious penance. **2.** In some instances, probably a translation of German BARFUSS, the northern form **Barfoth**, or the Danish cognate **Barfo(e)d**.

Bareford (118) English (Cambridgeshire): possibly a variant of **Barford**, a habitational name from any of various places so named, from Old English *bere* 'barley' + *ford*. In this case the most likely source is the place in Norfolk, although there are other examples in Bedfordshire, Oxfordshire, Warwickshire, Wiltshire.

Bareis (139) German: habitational name for someone from Paris, France, or perhaps more likely a nickname for someone who had trading or other links with the city.

Barela (1334) **1.** Galician: variant of Galician VARELA. **2.** Polish (**Bareła**): from Polish *baryła* 'barrel', hence a metonymic occupational name for a cooper.
GIVEN NAMES Spanish 20%. *Jose* (14), *Manuel* (9), *Luis* (7), *Carlos* (6), *Juan* (4), *Mario* (4), *Ramon* (4), *Adolfo* (3), *Emilio* (3), *Juanita* (3), *Pedro* (3), *Ruben* (3).

Barella (125) Italian: from a derivative of BARONE.
GIVEN NAMES Italian 16%. *Abelino, Emilio, Guillermo, Humberto, Luca, Mario, Ramona.*

Barentine (194) Altered form of Scottish BALLENTINE.

Bares (412) **1.** Czech and Slovak (**Bareš**): from a pet form of the personal name *Bartoloměj* (see BARTHOLOMEW). **2.** German: probably from a Germanic personal name based on *bero* 'bear' (the animal). **3.** English: unexplained; perhaps a variant of BARRS or BARRAS. **4.** Galician: habitational name from Bares in A Coruña province.

Barfield (4026) English: **1.** habitational name, probably from Bardfield in Essex, which is named with an unattested Old English *byrde* '(river) bank', 'border' + *feld* 'open land'. The name is still most common in northern Essex. **2.** topographic name for someone who lived in an area where barley was cultivated, from Middle English *berefeld*.

Barfknecht (195) German: **1.** most probably a nickname from Middle Low German *berve* (*bederve*, modern *bieder*) 'honest', 'trustworthy' + *knecht* 'vassal', 'man', 'servant'. **2.** alternatively perhaps a variant of **Barbknecht**, an occupational name or nickname for a barber's assistant, from *Barb(ier)* 'barber' + *knecht* 'servant'.

Barfoot (297) **1.** Scottish: probably a variant of the English nickname BAREFOOT, although Black says that it is 'doubtless of local origin'. **2.** Americanized form of German BARFUSS.

Barfuss (195) German: nickname for someone who was in the habit of going unshod, from Middle High German *bar* 'bare', 'naked' + *vuoz* 'foot', or for a member of the monastic order of the Barefoot Monks.
GIVEN NAME German 5%. *Manfred.*

Barg (442) North German: topographic name for someone who lived on a hill, Low German *barg*. Compare High German BERG.
GIVEN NAMES German 4%. *Bernhard, Erwin, Hans, Mathias, Wilfried.*

Barga (293) North German: variant of BERGER.

Barganier (185) Origin unidentified. This name occurs mainly in AL, GA, and TX.

Bargar (227) Variant of Dutch and North German BARGER.

Bargas (378) Spanish: variant of the habitational name VARGAS, from Bargas in Toledo in particular.
GIVEN NAMES Spanish 23%. *Jose* (3), *Luis* (3), *Mario* (3), *Ruben* (3), *Francisco* (2), *Juan* (2), *Manuel* (2), *Adelaida, Alberto, Albino, Anastacio, Andrade.*

Barge (732) **1.** English and French: metonymic occupational name for a boatman, from Middle English, Old French *barge* 'boat', 'barge'. **2.** Dutch: variant of BERG.

Bargen (104) Dutch and North German: topographic name from *bargen* 'hills', dative plural of BARG.
GIVEN NAMES German 9%. *Ewald, Johann, Otto.*

Barger (5301) **1.** Dutch and North German: variant of standard German BERGER. **2.** Variant of French BERGER.

Bargeron (247) French: from a diminutive of **Barger** (see BERGER).

Bargerstock (111) Origin unidentified.

Bargiel (116) Polish (**Bargieł**): from Polish *bargieł* 'nuthatch', presumably applied as a nickname for someone thought to resemble the bird in some way.
GIVEN NAMES Polish 6%; German 4%. *Ewa, Zdzislaw; Alois, Kurt.*

Bargman (155) Respelling of North German BARGMANN.
GIVEN NAMES German 5%; Russian 4%. *Fritz, Otto; Valeriy, Yefim, Yekaterina.*

Bargmann (209) North German: variant of BARG 'hill', with the addition of *-man* 'man'. Compare BERGMANN.
GIVEN NAMES German 7%. *Franz* (2), *Egon, Kurt, Ute.*

Bargo (315) Variant of Dutch BARGER.

Barham (2276) English: habitational name from any of the various places so called. Most, for example those in Cambridgeshire and Suffolk, are named with Old English *beorg* 'hill' + *hām* 'homestead'. The one in Kent, however, is from an unattested Old English byname *Biora, Beora* (a derivative of *bera* 'bear') + *hām*.

Barhorst (316) North German: probably a habitational name from a place called Barkhorst.

Bari (265) **1.** Muslim: from an Arabic personal name based on *bāri* 'originator'. *Al-Bāri'* 'the Creator' is an attribute of Allah. The personal name *Abd-al-Bāri'* means 'servant of the Creator'. **2.** Italian: habitational name from the Adriatic port of Bari, chief city of Apulia.
GIVEN NAMES Muslim 31%. *Mohammad* (6), *Mohammed* (6), *Abdul* (4), *Akm* (4), *Syed* (2), *Abbas, Ashraf, Asif, Aziz, Azizul, Bashar, Farhat.*

Baria (142) **1.** Indian (Panjab): Hindu (Rajput) name based on the name of a Rajput clan. **2.** Spanish or Galician: unexplained.

Baribault (112) Of French origin; possibly related to BARIBEAU or perhaps a variant, **Barigault**, itself a variant of **Baricault**, from a derivative of Gascon *bar(r)iko* 'barrel', 'cask'.

Baribeau (240) French: unexplained; perhaps a variant of BARBEAU.
FOREBEARS A Baribeau of unknown origin is documented in Quebec city in 1670.
GIVEN NAMES French 9%. *Adelard, Armand, Lucien, Marcel, Rejean.*

Barich (246) Croatian (**Barić**) and Slovenian (**Barič**): patronymic from the male personal name *Bare*, a pet form of *Bartul* or *Bartolomej* (see BARTHOLOMEW), or a metronymic from the female personal name *Bara*, a pet form of BARBARA.

Barickman (155) Americanized form of German **Barichmann**, a Rhenish variant, reflecting the local pronunciation, of BARGMANN.
FOREBEARS The original bearer of this name in the U.S., a native of Hesse, fought with the Hessian troops against the rebellious Americans in the Revolution in 1776.

Barie (129) German: unexplained. The name occurs mainly around Stuttgart and Karlsruhe.
GIVEN NAME German 4%. *Lorenz* (2).

Baril (686) French: from Old French *baril* 'barrel', applied as a metonymic occupational name for a cooper, or a nickname for a rotund man.
FOREBEARS A bearer of this name from the Saintonge region of France was documented in Batiscan, Quebec, in 1674. The secondary surnames Baricourt, Ducheny, and Saintonge are also recorded.
GIVEN NAMES French 10%. *Marcel* (3), *Andre* (2), *Normand* (2), *Alain, Armand, Ghislaine, Jacques, Jean-Marc, Jean-Pierre, Lucien, Monique, Phillippe.*

Barile (605) Italian: from *barile* 'barrel', hence a metonymic occupational name for a cooper, or a nickname for a fat man.
GIVEN NAMES Italian 13%. *Angelo* (3), *Rocco* (3), *Domenico* (2), *Pasquale* (2), *Aldo, Alessandro, Antonio, Bruna, Carlo, Carmela, Gennaro, Gino.*

Barilla (263) Italian: occupational name from medieval Greek *barellas* 'cooper', from *barella* 'barrel' (a loanword from Italian), with the occupational suffix *-(e)as*. See also BARILE.
GIVEN NAMES Italian 19%. *Salvatore* (3), *Santo* (3), *Rocco* (2), *Angelo, Antonio, Fortunato, Francesco, Gino, Orlando, Rigoberto.*

Barillaro (104) Italian: occupational name for a cooper, from a derivative of *barile* 'barrel' (see BARILE).
GIVEN NAMES Italian 25%. *Alfredo, Angelo, Atilio, Emilio, Fortunato, Nicola, Rocco, Salvatore.*

Barillas (223) **1.** Spanish: variant of BARILLA. **2.** Basque: habitational name from a place so named in Navarre, Basque Country.

GIVEN NAMES Spanish 54%. *Carlos* (10), *Jose* (6), *Mario* (6), *Cesar* (3), *Ana* (2), *Armando* (2), *Estela* (2), *Francisco* (2), *Guadalupe* (2), *Gustavo* (2), *Jorge* (2), *Nefi* (2); *Eliseo, Fabrizio, Marco, Marco Antonio.*

Barineau (108) French: variant spelling of BARRINEAU.

Baringer (251) German (**Bähringer**): **1.** variant of BEHRINGER 2. **2.** possibly an altered spelling of the habitational surname **Böhringer** (see BOEHRINGER).

Baris (185) **1.** Dutch: unexplained. Perhaps a habitational name for someone from Paris, France, or perhaps more likely a nickname for someone who had trading links with the city. **2.** Albanian, Italian (of Albanian origin), and Greek: occupational name from Albanian *bari* 'goatherd', 'shepherd'. **3.** Perhaps also Jewish, a variant of BARISH. **4.** Possibly an altered spelling of English BARRAS.

GIVEN NAMES Greek 4%. *Marinos* (2), *Constantine, Despina.*

Barish (399) Jewish (Ashkenazic): acronymic surname from a Hebrew patronymic phrase starting with *Ben Rabi* 'son of rabbi' and ending in a compound male personal name whose parts begin with I- and Sh-, e.g. *Isaac Shimon.*

Bark (463) **1.** English: from Middle English *bark* 'bark' (Old Norse *bǫrkr*), hence a metonymic occupation name for a tanner. See also BARKER. **2.** North German: topographic name for someone who lived by a birch tree or in a birch wood, from *berke* 'birch', or alternatively for someone who lived on a mountain (see BARG). **3.** Jewish (eastern Ashkenazic): of uncertain origin, perhaps a variant of BARAK.

Barkalow (208) Probably an altered form of Scottish **Buccleugh** (see BUCKLEW).

Barkan (357) Jewish (from Belarus): from a Hebrew-Aramaic patronymic phrase *bar Kohen* 'son of a descendant of the high priest' (see COHEN).

GIVEN NAMES Jewish 10%. *Aron* (2), *Nir* (2), *Ari, Bluma, Moisey, Mordecai, Moshe, Nissin, Semen.*

Barkdoll (230) Americanized spelling of Swedish BERGDAHL.

Barkdull (241) Americanized spelling of Swedish BERGDAHL.

Barke (204) English: variant spelling of BARK.

GIVEN NAMES German 7%. *Manfred* (2), *Gerhard, Otto, Siegfried.*

Barkell (107) English (Devon): unexplained. Possibly an irregular variant of BIRCHALL.

Barkema (132) Frisian: unexplained. It looks like a Frisian patronymic, but may in fact be a variant of the Dutch topographic name BARKMAN.

Barker (32221) **1.** English: occupational name for a tanner of leather, from Middle English *bark(en)* 'to tan', tree bark having been used as the tanning agent. **2.** English: occupational name for a shepherd, Anglo-Norman French *bercher* (Late Latin *berbicarius*, from *berbex* 'ram', genitive *berbicis*). With the change of *-ar-* to *-er-* in Middle English, this became indistinguishable from the preceding name. **3.** Altered spelling of German BARGER or BERGER.

Barkes (141) English: variant of BARK or BARKUS.

Barkett (225) English: variant of BIRKETT.

Barkey (328) **1.** Variant spelling of BERKEY. **2.** German: presumably from a habitational name in northern Germany. See also PARKEY.

GIVEN NAMES French 4%. *Henri* (2), *Colette.*

Barkhurst (230) Origin uncertain: perhaps an altered form of English PARKHURST.

Barkin (275) Jewish (from Belarus): variant of BARKAN.

Barkley (4388) Northern Irish variant of BARCLAY.

Barklow (160) Probably of Dutch origin: unexplained.

Barkman (677) **1.** Swedish: ornamental compound, probably influenced by German formations, of *bark* 'bark' + *man* 'man'. **2.** Dutch: topographic name for someone who lived by a birch or birch grove, Dutch *berk*. **3.** Probably a respelling of German **Barkmann**, a northern form of the topographic name BERGMANN.

Barko (148) Hungarian (**Barkó**): **1.** from a pet form of the personal name *Barnabás* (see BARNABY). **2.** variant of **Berkó**, from a derivative of the personal name *Bertalan* (see BARTHOLOMEW).

GIVEN NAMES Hungarian 5%. *Attila* (2), *Geza.*

Barkow (216) Eastern German: habitational name from any of several places so named in Mecklenburg and Pomerania.

Barks (583) English: variant of BARKUS or BARK.

Barksdale (2878) Origin uncertain. It looks like an English place name, but no such place is known in the British Isles. It may be an Americanized form of an original in some other language.

FOREBEARS The Barksdale family became established first in VA, in the early 18th century, and later in TN.

Barkus (223) **1.** English: probably a reduced form of **Barkhouse**, a topographic name for someone who lived by a tannery, Middle English *barkhous*, or an occupational name for someone who worked in one. **2.** Lithuanian: variant of BARTKUS. **3.** Czech and Slovak: unexplained.

GIVEN NAMES Lithuanian 5%. *Vytautas* (3), *Arunas.*

Barlage (244) German: habitational name from a place near Oldenburg, so named

from Middle Low German *bār* 'bear' or 'bare' + *lage* 'open fields between woods'.

Barland (112) Scottish: unexplained.

Barlas (111) **1.** Scottish: habitational name for someone from the French city of Bordeaux, from a reduced form of the Old French adjective *bordelais*. **2.** Iranian: from the Persian personal name or epithet *barlas* 'brave man of noble stock', from Mongolian *barlas* 'brave', the name of the Mongolian tribe of which Tamerlane's father was a member. **3.** Greek: perhaps a nickname from Aroumin (a language related to Romanian, spoken in Greece) *bărliv* 'tormented', 'long-suffering', from Bulgarian *bŭlivŭ* 'ill'.

GIVEN NAMES Muslim 7%; Greek 6%. *Sajid* (2), *Ali, Humaira, Mohammed, Rehan; Dimitrios, Spiro, Spiros.*

Barlet (130) English: variant of BARLETT.

Barlett (439) English: from the Middle English personal name *Berelot*, a double diminutive of the personal name *Berard*.

Barletta (577) Italian: **1.** habitational name from Barletta, in Bari province, Apulia. **2.** possibly from a diminutive of BARILE.

GIVEN NAMES Italian 25%; Spanish 8%. *Rocco* (5), *Angelo* (4), *Antonio* (4), *Franco* (2), *Mario* (2), *Rosaria* (2), *Salvatore* (2), *Arcangelo, Carlo, Carmine, Ciriaco, Constantino, Dominico; Jose* (3), *Eraldo* (2), *Carmelita, Carmella, Florencia, Jose Luis, Juanita, Julio.*

Barley (1406) **1.** English: habitational name from any of various places called Barley. Those in Lancashire and West Yorkshire are named with Old English *bār* 'wild boar' or *bere* 'barley' + *lēah* 'woodland clearing'. A place of the same name in Hertfordshire has as its first element an unattested Old English byname *Be(o)ra* (from *bera* 'bear'). **2.** English: metonymic occupational name for a grower or seller of barley, from Old English *bærlic*, originally an adjective derivative of *bær* 'barley' (a byform of *bere*). **3.** Altered spelling of South German **Behrle** or **Beerli**, from a Germanic personal name formed with Old High German *bero* 'bear' (the animal).

Barling (130) English: habitational name from Barling in Essex.

Barlow (10759) English: habitational name from any of several places called Barlow, especially those in Lancashire and West Yorkshire. The former is named with Old English *bere* 'barley' + *hlāw* 'hill'; the latter probably has as its first element the derived adjective *beren* or the compound *bere-ærn* 'barn'. There is also a place of this name in Derbyshire, named with Old English *bār* 'boar' or *bere* 'barley' + *lēah* 'woodland clearing', and one in Shropshire, which is from *bere* 'barley' + *lēah*.

Barlowe (195) English: variant of BARLOW.

Barman (319) **1.** Variant spelling of German BARMANN. **2.** Indian (Bengal) and

Bangladeshi: Hindu (Rajbanshi) name from Sanskrit *varman* 'armor', 'protection'. This is a cognate of north central Indian VARMA.

GIVEN NAMES Indian 10%. *Dilip* (2), *Rajesh* (2), *Ajit, Anoop, Dinesh, Narayan, Nil, Nishi, Pooran, Prashant, Raju, Shikha.*

Barmann (125) **1.** North German: see BAER. **2.** German (mostly **Bahrmann**): status name from Middle High German *barman* 'person with some (feudal) tax or rent obligation'.

Barmore (523) English and Scottish: habitational name from a place named Barmore or Barmoor, numerous examples of which are found in Derbyshire, North Yorkshire, and Northumberland, as well as the Scottish regions of Angus, Galloway, and Strathclyde. In Britain the surname is now rare and is found only in Manchester.

Barna (1112) **1.** Italian: from the ancient Germanic personal name *Barna*. **2.** Italian: possibly from a short form of the personal name BARNABA (see BARNABY 1). **3.** Hungarian: from a short form of the personal name *Barnabás* (see BARNABY 1). **4.** Polish (also Slovak and Ukrainian): from a derivative of the personal name *Biernat*, Polish form of German BERNHARD. **5.** Possibly from Polish dialect *barna*, *brona* 'harrow', hence a metonymic occupational name for a peasant who used a harrow.

Barnaba (134) Italian and southern French: from the personal name *Barnaba*, Italian and Occitan form of *Barnabas* (see BARNABY 1).

GIVEN NAMES Italian 11%; French 5%. *Angelo* (2), *Franco, Paolo, Vito; Numa, Pierre.*

Barnaby (711) English: **1.** from the Middle English vernacular form of the personal name *Barnabas*, which was borne by the companion of St Paul (Acts 4:36). This is of Aramaic origin, from *Barnabia* 'son of Nabia', a personal name perhaps meaning 'confession'. **2.** habitational name from Barnaby in North Yorkshire, named with the Old English personal name *Beornwald* (composed of the elements *beorn* 'young warrior' + *wald* 'rule') + Old Norse *býr* 'settlement'.

Barnard (7929) English and French: variant of BERNARD.

FOREBEARS This name was brought independently to New England by many bearers from the 17th century onward.

John Barnard was one of the founders of Hartford, CT, (coming from Cambridge, MA, with Thomas Hooker) in 1635.

Another John Barnard, born in Boston in 1681, was a Congregational clergyman who served as minister of Marblehead, MA, from 1716 to 1770.

Barnas (257) Polish (**Barnaś**): from a derivative of the personal name *Biernat*, Polish form of BERNHARD.

GIVEN NAMES Polish 10%. *Bronislawa, Jerzy, Leszek, Pawel, Stanislaw, Tadeusz, Zbigniew.*

Barndt (421) German: variant of BERNDT.

Barnell (175) English: reduced form of BARNHILL.

Barner (1499) **1.** Southern English: habitational name for someone who lived by a barn. **2.** North German: derivative of the old Germanic personal name *Barnher* or *Bernher* (see BERNER 6).

Barnes (70136) **1.** English: topographic name or metonymic occupational name for someone who lived by or worked at a barn or barns, from Middle English *barn* 'barn', 'granary'. In some cases, it may be a habitational name from Barnes (on the Surrey bank of the Thames in London), which was named in Old English with this word. **2.** English: name borne by the son or servant of a *barne*, a term used in the early Middle Ages for a member of the upper classes, although its precise meaning is not clear (it derives from Old English *beorn*, Old Norse *barn* 'young warrior'). *Barne* was also occasionally used as a personal name (from an Old English, Old Norse byname), and some examples of the surname may derive from this use. **3.** Irish: possibly an Anglicized form of Gaelic **Ó Bearáin** 'descendant of *Bearán*', a byname meaning 'spear'. **4.** French: variant of BERN. **5.** Jewish: variant of PARNES.

Barnet (370) **1.** English: variant spelling of BARNETT. **2.** French: variant of BERNET.

Barnett (33020) English: **1.** habitational name from various places, for example Chipping (High) Barnet, East Barnet, and Friern Barnet in Greater London, named with Old English *bærnet* 'place cleared by burning' (a derivative of *bærnan* 'to burn', 'to set light to'). **2.** from a medieval personal name, a variant of BERNARD.

Barnette (3031) **1.** French: variant of BERNET. **2.** perhaps also a variant of English BARNETT, under French influence.

Barney (5302) English: **1.** habitational name from Barney in Norfolk, which is probably named with an Old English personal name *Bera* (with genitive *-n*) + Old English *ēg* 'island', 'dry ground in a marsh'. **2.** from the personal name *Barney*, a pet form of BERNARD.

FOREBEARS A William Barney from England came to Baltimore county, MD, in about 1695. Joshua Barney, born in that county in 1759, was an outstanding naval officer during the War of 1812.

Barnfield (149) English: habitational name from any of various minor places called Barnfield (near Egerton in Kent) or Barnfields (in Herefordshire and Staffordshire), probably from Middle English *barn* 'barn' + *feld* 'area of open country'.

Barngrover (133) Americanized form of German **Berngruber**, a topographic name for someone who lived by or kept a bear pit,

from Middle High German *ber* 'bear' + *gruobe* 'pit' + the suffix *-er* denoting an inhabitant.

Barnhard (202) Dutch: variant spelling of BARNHART.

Barnhardt (970) Dutch: variant spelling of BARNHART.

Barnhart (7432) Dutch: from the personal name *Barnhart*, Dutch form of BERNHARD.

Barnhill (3269) English: topographic name for someone who lived by a hill with a barn on it, from Middle English *barn* 'barn' + *hille* 'hill', or a habitational name from a place named Barnhill, possibly the one near Broxton in Cheshire named with Old English *bere-ærn* 'barn' + *hyll* 'hill'.

Barnhouse (642) English: topographic name for someone who lived in a house by a barn, from Middle English *barn* 'barn', 'granary' + *hous* 'house', or a habitational name from Barn House in Brightling, Sussex, or from Barnhouse Farm in Shipley, Sussex.

Barnick (318) **1.** German (of Sorbian origin): nickname from a Slavic word meaning 'ram'. **2.** German: variant of BERNICK. **3.** Ukrainian (**Barnyk**): nickname from *barnyk*, denoting a species of bird.

GIVEN NAMES German 4%. *Otto* (2), *Kurt.*

Barnicle (211) **1.** English: from Middle English *bernacle, barnakyll*, a diminutive of *bernak*, from Old French *bernac*, a type of severe bit, which was also used as an instrument of torture; the term may have been applied as a nickname for a tamer of restive horses, for a man with an unruly temperament, or for a torturer. Alternatively, the surname may have originated as a nickname for someone thought to resemble a barnacle goose (Middle English *barnakyll*) in some way. **2.** Americanized spelling of German **Barnickel, Barnikel**, from a byname of uncertain origin for someone who was cross-eyed or suffering from an eye disease; or presumably from a personal name, a compound of *Bern(o)* + *Nickel* (pet form of *Nicolaus*).

Barnier (159) French: variant of BERNIER.

GIVEN NAMES French 4%. *Laurent, Pierre.*

Barnish (163) English: nickname from Old French *barnage*, a contraction of *baronage*, a term denoting the attributes of a baron, namely courage, fortitude, etc.

Barno (221) **1.** Perhaps a variant of French BARRINEAU. **2.** Ukrainian: nickname from Ukrainian *barna* 'dark ox' (dark red or dark gray in color).

Barnoski (105) Variant of Polish and Jewish (eastern Ashkenazic) BARANOWSKI.

Barnosky (118) Variant of Polish and Jewish (eastern Ashkenazic) BARANOWSKI.

Barns (429) English: variant spelling of BARNES 1 and 2.

Barnthouse (107) Origin unidentified. Apparently an English habitational name, but no place of this name has been identified in Britain.

Barnum (2121) English: habitational name from any of various places called Barnham, for example in Norfolk, Suffolk, and West Sussex. They are probably all named with the Old English byname *Beorn(a)* (see BARNES 2) or Old English *beorn* 'warrior' + *hām* 'homestead'.

Barnwell (1551) English: habitational name from a place so called; there is one in Cambridgeshire and another in Northamptonshire, both named with Old English *beorn* 'warrior' (genitive plural *beorna*) or the Old English personal name *Beorna* + *well(a)* 'stream'.
FOREBEARS A John Barnwell (*c.*1671–1724) emigrated to SC from Ireland at the end of the 17th century.

Baro (187) **1.** Spanish: from a medieval personal name, *Baro(ne)*, from the status name *baró* 'free man', 'baron'. **2.** Catalan (**Baró**): from Germanic *bero* 'bear' or the status name *baró* 'free man', 'baron' (see BARON 1). **3.** Hungarian (**Báró**): status name from *báró* 'baron'. In the form **Baró**, it could be from a pet form of the personal names *Barabás* (see BARABAS) or *Bertalan*.
GIVEN NAMES Spanish 30%. *Mario* (5), *Manuel* (4), *Ana* (2), *Angel* (2), *Carlos* (2), *Cesar* (2), *Fernando* (2), *Jesus* (2), *Jose* (2), *Orlando* (2), *Ramon* (2), *Rosalia* (2); *Guido* (2), *Angelo*, *Carmelo*, *Federico*, *Lucio*.

Barocas (131) Jewish (Sephardic, from Portugal): unexplained.

Baron (6435) **1.** English and French: from the title of nobility, Middle English, Old French *baron*, *barun* (of Germanic origin; compare BARNES 2). As a surname it is unlikely to be a status name denoting a person of rank. The great baronial families of Europe had distinctive surnames of their own. Generally, the surname referred to service in a baronial household or was acquired as a nickname by a peasant who had ideas above his station. The title was also awarded to certain freemen of the cities of London and York and of the Cinque Ports. Compare the Scottish form BARRON. **2.** English and French: from an Old French personal name *Baro* (oblique case *Baron*), or else referred to service in a baronial household or was acquired as a nickname by a peasant who had ideas above his station. **3.** German: status name for a freeman or baron, *barūn* 'imperial or church official', a loan word in Middle High German from Old French (see 1). **4.** Spanish (**Barón**): from the title *barón* 'baron' (see 1). **5.** Irish: Anglicized form of Gaelic **Ó Bearáin** (see BARNES). **6.** Jewish (eastern Ashkenazic): ornamental name meaning 'baron', from German, Polish, or Russian. In Israel the surname is often interpreted, by folk etymology, as being from *Bar-On* 'son of strength'.
FOREBEARS A bearer of the name Baron from the Champagne region of France was documented in Montreal in 1676 with the secondary surname Lupien. Another, from the Angoumois region, is recorded in Boucherville, Quebec, in 1679, and a third bearer, from Normandy, France, was documented in Île d'Orléans in 1698 with the secondary name Le Baron. Secondary surnames Bélair and Lafrenière are also recorded.

Barone (4393) Italian: from the Germanic personal name *Baro*, or to a lesser extent the title *barone* 'baron', both derivatives of an unattested word *bara-* 'free man' (see BARON 1).
GIVEN NAMES Italian 15%. *Salvatore* (30), *Angelo* (19), *Antonio* (9), *Carmine* (9), *Sal* (9), *Rocco* (7), *Vito* (7), *Carmela* (6), *Enrico* (6), *Giovanni* (6), *Pasquale* (6), *Domenic* (4).

Baroni (468) Italian: variant of BARONE.
GIVEN NAMES Italian 10%. *Angelo* (3), *Gino* (3), *Giorgio* (2), *Aldo*, *Carlo*, *Domenica*, *Ettore*, *Fabiano*, *Matteo*, *Remo*, *Ricco*, *Ugo*.

Baronian (101) Armenian: patronymic meaning 'son of the baron'. Middle Armenian *baron* 'baron', 'nobleman' (from French) was also used as a respectful term of address.
GIVEN NAMES Armenian 19%. *Souren* (2), *Ara*, *Avedis*, *Haig*, *Hrair*, *Karo*, *Ohannes*, *Satenig*.

Baroody (233) Origin unidentified.
GIVEN NAMES *Anas*, *Bahij*, *Bahjat*, *Joumana*, *Malek*, *Najla*, *Raja*, *Rami*, *Shakib*.

Baros (274) **1.** Portuguese or Spanish: habitational name from any of several places called Barros, named with *barro* 'loam', 'clay'. **2.** Hungarian: from a pet form of the personal names *Barnabás* (see BARNABY) or *Bertalan* (see BARTHOLOMEW). **3.** Czech and Slovak (**Baroš**): from a pet form of the personal name *Bartoloměj* (see BARTHOLOMEW). **4.** Polish: from a pet form of a personal name beginning with *Bar-* (*Bartłomiej*, *Bartołt*, or *Barnaba*). **5.** Greek: nickname from Albanian *mbarë* 'happy', 'lucky'.
GIVEN NAMES Spanish 6%. *Eloy* (3), *Guillermo*, *Jose*, *Manuel*, *Maurilio*, *Onofre*, *Orlando*, *Soledad*.

Barousse (151) French: regional name from an area so named to the north of Luchon. The surname is found chiefly in Louisiana.
GIVEN NAMES French 7%. *Andrus*, *Laurent*.

Barquero (102) Spanish: occupational name for a boatman, *barquero*.
GIVEN NAMES Spanish 47%; Italian 7%. *Jose* (4), *Guillermo* (3), *Manuel* (3), *Juan* (2), *Mario* (2), *Alberto*, *Alvaro*, *Ana*, *Armando*, *Arturo*, *Berta*, *Dimas*; *Antonio*, *Federico*, *Ferdinando*, *Gilda*, *Marco*.

Barr (17204) **1.** Scottish and northern Irish: habitational name from any of various places in southwestern Scotland, in particular Ayrshire and Renfrewshire, named with Gaelic *barr* 'height', 'hill' or a British cognate of this. **2.** English: topographic name for someone who lived by a gateway or barrier, from Middle English, Old French *barre* 'bar', 'obstruction'. **3.** English (of Norman origin): habitational name from any of various places in northern France called Barre. See BARRE. **4.** English: habitational name from any of various places in England called *Barr*, for example Great Barr in the West Midlands, named with the Celtic element *barro* 'height', 'hill'. **5.** English: from the vocabulary word *barr* 'bar', 'pole', either a metonymic occupational name for a maker of bars, or perhaps a nickname for a tall, thin man. **6.** Irish: from **Ó Bairr**, Donegal form of **Ó Báire** (see BARRY 2).

Barra (578) **1.** Southern Italian: probably a topographic name from Sicilian *bharra* 'bar', 'barrier' or a habitational name from a place named with this word. **2.** Galician: habitational name from places named Barra, in the provinces of Lugo and Ourense. **3.** Southern French: dialect variant of BARRE. **4.** Hungarian: from the personal name *Barna*, short form of *Barnabás*, Hungarian equivalent of BARNABY.
GIVEN NAMES Italian 17%; Spanish 7%. *Angelo* (2), *Marina* (2), *Antonio*, *Augusto*, *Biagio*, *Carlo*, *Domenic*, *Flavio*, *Gennaro*, *Lorenzo*, *Luciano*, *Rocco*, *Salvatore*; *Jorge* (2), *Carlos*, *Diego*, *Enrique*, *Jaime*, *Juan*, *Manuel*.

Barrack (306) Scottish: habitational name from the lands of Barroch or Barrauch in the parish of Bourtie, Aberdeenshire.

Barraclough (347) English (mainly Yorkshire): habitational name from Barrowclough near Halifax in West Yorkshire, named with Old English *bearu* 'grove' + *clōh* 'ravine'.

Barraco (213) Italian (Sicily): nickname from Arabic *barrāq* 'shining', 'brilliant'.
GIVEN NAMES Italian 14%; French 4%. *Adriana*, *Salvatore*, *Vincenza*; *Pierre* (2), *Christophe*.

Barragan (1556) Spanish (**Barragán**): **1.** nickname for a strong or brave man, from Spanish *barragán* 'young man', 'warrior'. **2.** metonymic occupational name for a maker or seller of fustian, a kind of material, Spanish *barragán* (from Arabic *barrakân*).
GIVEN NAMES Spanish 55%. *Jose* (47), *Jesus* (29), *Luis* (21), *Jorge* (19), *Francisco* (18), *Manuel* (18), *Salvador* (17), *Juan* (15), *Carlos* (14), *Alfonso* (13), *Rafael* (13), *Roberto* (13).

Barrall (120) Possibly a variant spelling of BARRELL.

Barranco (434) Spanish: habitational name from any of various minor places named with the topographical term *barranco* 'ravine', 'gorge' (of pre-Roman origin).
GIVEN NAMES Spanish 23%; Italian 8%. *Juan* (4), *Angel* (3), *Jose* (3), *Luis* (3), *Adalberto*

(2), *Enrique* (2), *Guillermo* (2), *Jorge* (2), *Roberto* (2), *Adriana*, *Aida*, *Alberto*; *Salvatore* (5), *Angelo* (2), *Marco Antonio*, *Marino*, *Sal*.

Barrand (108) **1.** English (Lincolnshire): unexplained. **2.** French: from the present participle of *barrer* 'to bar', 'to close or shut off'.

Barrantes (126) Spanish: habitational name from Barrantes in Cáceres province.
GIVEN NAMES Spanish 46%. *Juan* (3), *Luis* (3), *Ricardo* (3), *Adolfo* (2), *Carlos* (2), *Fernando* (2), *Gerardo* (2), *Jorge* (2), *Manuel* (2), *Adelaida*, *Alejandro*, *Amancio*.

Barras (693) **1.** English: of uncertain origin; perhaps a topographic name for someone who lived by the outworks of a fortress, Old French *barrace*, or a variant of BARRS. **2.** French (Midi): from an augmentative of BARRE.
GIVEN NAMES French 7%. *Antoine* (3), *Emile* (2), *Alberie*, *Alcee*, *Alexandre*, *Angelle*, *Aurelien*, *Cyprien*, *Julien*, *Maudry*, *Oneil*, *Remy*.

Barrasso (172) Southern Italian (common in Abruzzo, Molise, and Campania): from a personal name of disputed derivation, recorded in the 14th century as *Barrasius*.
GIVEN NAMES Italian 16%. *Pasquale* (3), *Antonio*, *Domenic*, *Franca*, *Gennaro*, *Lorenzo*, *Orazio*, *Stefano*.

Barratt (516) English: variant spelling of BARRETT.

Barraza (1468) Spanish: of uncertain origin; perhaps from an augmentative of *barra* 'pole', 'post'.
GIVEN NAMES Spanish 53%. *Jose* (41), *Jesus* (22), *Manuel* (17), *Juan* (15), *Carlos* (12), *Francisco* (12), *Raul* (11), *Armando* (9), *Javier* (9), *Ricardo* (8), *Angel* (7), *Fernando* (7).

Barre (603) French: **1.** habitational name from any of various places called Barre. Barre-en-Ouche in Eure or Barre-de-Semilly in Manche are named with Old French *barre* 'bar', 'obstruction', 'gateway'. Others, for example Barre in Lozère, derive their name from the Celtic element *barr* 'height'. **2.** (**Barré**) from *barré*, the past participle of Old French *barrer*, a derivative of *barre* 'bar' (see 1). The meaning of the surname derived from this word is uncertain. It may sometimes have been a topographic name for a person who lived in a place that was naturally cut off or particularly well fortified, but in many cases it was probably a nickname meaning 'striped', referring to a habitual wearer of striped clothing or possibly to someone with a noticeable birthmark. In the Middle Ages the term was also applied to the Carmelite Friars, who wore habits striped in black, yellow, and white, and it may have been used as a nickname for someone thought to resemble a Carmelite in some way. The name is also found in Germany, attested as

a Huguenot name, for example in Magdeburg in 1703.
FOREBEARS A bearer of the name from Normandy, France, is documented as Barré in Montreal in 1667; another, from Picardy, is recorded in Chambly, Quebec, in 1722.
GIVEN NAMES French 8%. *Anatole* (2), *Emile* (2), *Pierre* (2), *Alphonse*, *Andre*, *Cecile*, *Henri*, *Herve*, *Jacques*, *Marcel*, *Regean*, *Yves*.

Barreau (102) French: possibly a variant of **Barreur**, an agent derivative of *barrer* 'to bar', 'to close or block off', hence possibly an occupational name for a jailer or doorkeeper.
GIVEN NAMES French 20%. *Fresnel*, *Gabrielle*, *Jean-Louis*, *Jean-Marie*, *Jeanty*, *Michel*, *Michelene*, *Pierre*.

Barreca (207) **1.** Southern Italian (chiefly Calabria): nickname from Sicilian *bbarreca* 'person with a paunch'. **2.** Possibly Portuguese, a topographic name from a derivative of *barra* 'pole', 'rod', 'post'.
GIVEN NAMES Italian 14%. *Salvatore* (2), *Antonio*, *Giuseppe*, *Lorenzo*, *Santo*.

Barreda (167) Spanish: habitational name from any of numerous places called Barreda, named with *barro* 'clay', 'loam', especially the one in Cantabria.
GIVEN NAMES Spanish 45%. *Jose* (6), *Miguel* (3), *Pedro* (3), *Ramon* (3), *Alfredo* (2), *Jesus* (2), *Jorge* (2), *Pablo* (2), *Ricardo* (2), *Ubaldo* (2), *Amalia*, *Amilia*; *Antonio* (3), *Clemente* (2).

Barreira (108) Galician (and Portuguese): habitational name from any of numerous places in Galicia and Portugal named Barreira, from barreira 'clay or loam hollow'.
GIVEN NAMES Spanish 31%; Portuguese 21%. *Manuel* (7), *Alvaro* (2), *Ana* (2), *Carlos* (2), *Fernando* (2), *Mario* (2), *Adelino*, *Adelmo*, *Arsenio*, *Emilio*, *Jorge*, *Jose*; *Agostinho*, *Joao*, *Joaquim*; *Antonio*.

Barreiro (364) Galician and Portuguese: habitational name from any of the numerous places in Galicia and Portugal named with *barro* 'clay', 'loam'.
GIVEN NAMES Spanish 44%; Portuguese 13%. *Jose* (10), *Manuel* (6), *Jorge* (4), *Agustin* (3), *Andres* (3), *Carlos* (3), *Jesus* (3), *Lazaro* (3), *Ramon* (3), *Roberto* (3), *Alejandro* (2), *Fernando* (2); *Agostinho* (2), *Joao*.

Barrell (305) English: **1.** from Old French *baril* 'barrel', hence a metonymic occupational name for a cooper or a nickname for a fat man or an immoderate drinker. **2.** habitational name from Barwell in Leicestershire, named with Old English *bār* 'wild boar' + *well(a)* 'spring', 'stream'.
FOREBEARS A cooper named George Barrell came to Boston, MA, in 1637 from Suffolk, England.

Barrella (106) Italian: variant spelling of BARELLA.

GIVEN NAMES Italian 20%. *Gaetano*, *Rocco*, *Rosaria*, *Salvatore*.

Barren (192) English: probably a variant spelling of BARON.

Barrentine (526) Probably a variant of Scottish BALLENTINE.

Barrera (5233) **1.** Spanish and Catalan: topographic name for someone who lived near a gate or fence, from Spanish and Catalan *barrera* 'barrier'. **2.** topographic name for someone who lived by a clay pit, Spanish *barrera*, *barrero* (a derivative of *barro* 'mud', 'clay').
GIVEN NAMES Spanish 49%; Portuguese 9%. *Jose* (129), *Juan* (81), *Carlos* (63), *Manuel* (53), *Jorge* (37), *Jesus* (33), *Mario* (33), *Luis* (29), *Roberto* (29), *Pedro* (27), *Alfredo* (26), *Miguel* (26); *Anatolio* (2), *Catarina*.

Barreras (468) Spanish: topographic or habitational name from any of numerous watercourses, mountains, and other place named Barrera or Barreras, from *barrera* 'barrier', 'obstacle'; 'clay pit'.
GIVEN NAMES Spanish 29%. *Jose* (6), *Juan* (3), *Luis* (3), *Ruben* (3), *Candelario* (2), *Enrique* (2), *Felipe* (2), *Fidel* (2), *Francisco* (2), *Jesus* (2), *Joaquin* (2), *Manuel* (2).

Barrere (110) French (**Barrère**): occupational name for a gatekeeper or for someone who lived by a gate or barrier, from a derivative of Old French *barre* 'bar', 'obstruction' (see BARRE). See also BARRIERE.

Barrero (104) Spanish: topographic name from *barro* 'clay', 'loam'. Compare BARREIRO.
GIVEN NAMES Spanish 46%. *Benigno* (2), *Francisco* (2), *Jesus* (2), *Jose* (2), *Julio* (2), *Sergio* (2), *Agustin*, *Alfonso*, *Alida*, *Amalia*, *Ana*, *Anselmo*; *Marco*.

Barrese (113) Italian (Sicily): habitational name for someone from a place named Barra, from *barra* 'barrier', 'bar', 'obstacle'; there is a large district of Naples so named, as well as many minor places in southern Italy.
GIVEN NAMES Italian 21%. *Rocco* (2), *Salvatore* (2), *Gaetano*.

Barresi (373) Italian: variant of BARRESE.
GIVEN NAMES Italian 19%. *Angelo* (4), *Salvatore* (3), *Vito* (3), *Orazio* (2), *Aldo*, *Alfio*, *Antonino*, *Antonio*, *Carlo*, *Gaetana*, *Gasper*, *Giacoma*.

Barret (215) **1.** English: variant spelling of BARRETT. **2.** French: from a diminutive of BARRE.
GIVEN NAMES French 7%. *Matthieu*, *Mirlande*, *Philippe*.

Barreto (1048) **1.** Portuguese: probably a metonymic occupational name for a cap maker, from a variant of *barrette* 'cap'. Compare BERRETTA. This name is also found in western India, where it was taken by Portuguese colonists. **2.** Spanish: possibly a derivative of *barreta*, *barreto*, from *bara* '(crow)bar', presumably a metonymic occupational name or a topographic name.

GIVEN NAMES Spanish 46%; Portuguese 14%. *Jose* (35), *Luis* (25), *Angel* (9), *Carlos* (9), *Juan* (9), *Manuel* (9), *Jorge* (8), *Raul* (8), *Roberto* (8), *Francisco* (7), *Miguel* (7), *Rafael* (7); *Joaquim* (2), *Paulo* (2), *Henrique*, *Joao*; *Antonio* (6), *Angelo* (2), *Leonardo* (2), *Marco* (2), *Bartolo*, *Clementina*, *Ernani*, *Federico*, *Gabino*, *Mauro*, *Plinio*.

Barrett (35914) English: of much discussed but uncertain origin. **1.** It may be from a medieval personal name, but if so the form is unclear. **2.** Alternatively, it may be a nickname for a quarrelsome or deceitful person, from Middle English *bar(r)et(t)e*, *bar(r)at* 'trouble', 'strife', 'deception', 'cheating' (Old French *barat* 'commerce', 'dealings', a derivative of *barater* 'to haggle'). It is possible that the original sense of *barat* survived unrecorded into Middle English as a word for a market trader; the Italian cognate BARATTA has this sense. It could also be a nickname or metonymic occupational name from Old French *barette* 'cap', 'bonnet'.

Barretta (265) Italian: probably from a diminutive of *barra* 'barrier', 'bar' or from Calabrian dialect *barretta* 'cap'.
GIVEN NAMES Italian 28%. *Santo* (4), *Carmine* (2), *Giuseppe* (2), *Carmela*, *Cataldo*, *Gaetano*, *Giacomo*, *Giovanna*, *Leonardo*, *Luigi*, *Nunzia*, *Salvatore*.

Barrette (781) North American spelling of French **Baret**, from a diminutive of *Bar*.
GIVEN NAMES French 11%. *Lucien* (4), *Jacques* (3), *Antoine* (2), *Armand* (2), *Pierre* (2), *Aldor*, *Andre*, *Elmire*, *Eudore*, *Luc*, *Marcel*, *Marcellin*.

Barretto (224) **1.** Spanish: variant of BARRETO. **2.** Italian: variant of BARRETTA or of Spanish BARETO.
GIVEN NAMES Spanish 26%; Italian 7%. *Alberto* (7), *Jose* (4), *Fernando* (2), *Rafael* (2), *Ramon* (2), *Bonifacia*, *Candido*, *Carlos*, *Cesar*, *Gonzalo*, *Josefina*; *Antonio* (2), *Roberto* (2), *Marco*, *Severiano*.

Barrick (1925) English: variant spelling of BARWICK.

Barricklow (182) Origin uncertain: possibly a respelling of English BARRACLOUGH.

Barrickman (152) Americanized spelling of German **Barichmann** (see BARICKMAN).

Barrie (959) Scottish: habitational name from any of various places, especially one in Angus, generally named with Gaelic *barr* 'height', 'hill', or from a British cognate of this word.

Barrientes (273) Hispanic: variant of BARRIENTOS.
GIVEN NAMES Spanish 40%. *Jose* (6), *Juan* (4), *Ruben* (4), *Juanita* (3), *Santiago* (3), *Alfredo* (2), *Arturo* (2), *Ernesto* (2), *Esteban* (2), *Javier* (2), *Justo* (2), *Manuel* (2).

Barrientez (120) Hispanic: variant of BARRIENTOS.

GIVEN NAMES Spanish 41%. *Juan* (5), *Jesus* (3), *Alejandro* (2), *Alfonso* (2), *Manuel* (2), *Mario* (2), *Blanca*, *Cervando*, *Dionisia*, *Fernanda*, *Francisco*, *Guadalupe*.

Barrientos (1317) Spanish: habitational name from a place in León province named Barrientos, from *barrio* 'outlying region'.
GIVEN NAMES Spanish 51%. *Jose* (40), *Juan* (21), *Mario* (17), *Manuel* (16), *Carlos* (15), *Jesus* (13), *Jorge* (10), *Luis* (10), *Miguel* (10), *Guadalupe* (9), *Enrique* (8), *Francisco* (8).

Barrier (961) French: see BARRIERE.

Barriere (155) French (**Barrière**): occupational name for a gatekeeper, from Old French *barier*, an agent derivative of *barre* 'bar' (see BARRE). In the U.S. **Barrière** is also documented in the translated form GATES. Compare English PORTER.
GIVEN NAMES French 12%. *Emile*, *Gaston*, *Monique*, *Philippe*.

Barriga (380) Spanish: nickname for someone with a large belly, from Spanish *barriga* 'belly', 'paunch'.
GIVEN NAMES Spanish 51%. *Jose* (8), *Jesus* (6), *Francisco* (5), *Raul* (5), *Carlos* (4), *Juan* (4), *Ramon* (4), *Alfredo* (3), *Celso* (3), *Enrique* (3), *Fernando* (3), *Guillermo* (3); *Antonio* (3), *Eliseo* (2), *Annamaria*, *Gabino*, *Marco*, *Riccardo*, *Severiano*.

Barriger (161) Probably a variant of BARRINGER.

Barrile (92) Italian: variant spelling of BARILE.
GIVEN NAMES Italian 18%. *Gelsomina*, *Luigi*, *Salvatore*.

Barrilleaux (372) Respelling of French **Barilleau**, from a diminutive of BARIL. It is concentrated in LA.
GIVEN NAMES French 6%. *Alcide* (2), *Chantel*, *Gaston*, *Julien*, *Odette*.

Barrineau (404) French: unexplained. Possibly a Huguenot name. It occurs principally in SC.

Barringer (2332) Americanized spelling of German BEHRINGER.
FOREBEARS Rufus Barringer (1821–95) was the grandson of Paulus Behringer of Württemberg, who went first to Philadelphia in 1743 and later settled in NC.

Barrington (1634) **1.** English: habitational name from any of several places called Barrington. The one in Gloucestershire is named with the Old English personal name *Beorn* + *-ing-* denoting association + *tūn* 'settlement'. In the Somerset place name the first element is an unattested Old English personal name *Bāra*, which also occurs, in the genitive form, as the first element of the Cambridgeshire place name. **2.** Irish: adopted as an English form of Gaelic **Ó Beáráin** (see BARNES 3).

Barrio (176) Spanish: variant of BARRIOS.
GIVEN NAMES Spanish 41%. *Jose* (4), *Juan* (4), *Jorge* (3), *Luis* (3), *Enrique* (2), *Lourdes* (2), *Manuel* (2), *Miguel* (2), *Rafael* (2), *Roberto* (2), *Rodolfo* (2), *Sergio* (2).

Barrios (3000) Spanish: habitational name from any of the numerous places named with Spanish *barrio* 'outlying suburb' (especially an impoverished one), 'slum', from Arabic *barr* 'suburb', 'dependent village'. It may also be a topographic name for someone originating from a barrio.
GIVEN NAMES Spanish 45%. *Jose* (67), *Juan* (33), *Carlos* (29), *Luis* (28), *Manuel* (23), *Jorge* (21), *Jesus* (17), *Francisco* (16), *Mario* (16), *Angel* (14), *Pedro* (14), *Guadalupe* (13).

Barris (416) English: probably a variant of BARRAS.

Barrish (175) **1.** Jewish (Ashkenazic): variant spelling of BARISH. **2.** Possibly also an Americanized spelling of German **Behrisch** (see BERISH).
GIVEN NAMES Jewish 5%. *Chaim*, *Rebekah*.

Barritt (363) English: variant spelling of BARRETT.

Barro (106) Spanish and Galician: widespread habitational name, especially in Galicia, from any of numerous places named with *barro* 'clay', 'loam', in particular Barro in Pontevedra.
GIVEN NAMES Spanish 30%; Italian 8%. *Jose* (5), *Jesus* (2), *Lino* (2), *Manuel* (2), *Roberto* (2), *Alberto*, *Aurelio*, *Isidro*, *Jose Luis*, *Juan*, *Leandro*, *Otilio*; *Angelo*, *Antonio*, *Geno*, *Leonardo*.

Barron (12632) Scottish, northern English, and Irish: **1.** status name from Middle English *barron* (see BARON). A baron in Scotland was a member of a class of minor landowners who had a certain degree of jurisdiction over the local populace living in his barony. **2.** of Norman origin: from an Old French personal name *Baro* (oblique case *Baron*) (see BARON).
GIVEN NAMES Spanish 7%. *Jose* (60), *Juan* (25), *Jesus* (22), *Manuel* (18), *Francisco* (17), *Carlos* (15), *Miguel* (15), *Raul* (12), *Pedro* (10), *Ruben* (10), *Alfredo* (9), *Luis* (9).

Barrons (113) English: probably a variant of BARON.

Barros (1165) Spanish, Galician, and Portuguese: widespread habitational name from any of numerous places named with *barro* 'clay', 'loam'.
GIVEN NAMES Spanish 28%; Portuguese 14%. *Manuel* (35), *Jose* (20), *Luis* (10), *Carlos* (7), *Mario* (6), *Ana* (6), *Julio* (5), *Domingo* (4), *Francisco* (4), *Alberto* (3), *Casimiro* (3), *Ernesto* (3); *Joao* (8), *Joaquim* (4), *Paulo* (2), *Ligia*, *Manoel*, *Mateus*, *Nelio*; *Antonio* (12), *Angelo* (2), *Fausto* (2), *Annamarie*, *Ceasar*, *Clemente*, *Filomena*, *Gabriella*, *Leonardo*, *Ludovina*, *Marco*.

Barroso (546) Galician and Portuguese: topographic name for someone who lived in an area of clay or loamy soil, from *barroso* 'clayey', 'loamy' (from *barro* 'loam').
GIVEN NAMES Spanish 50%; Portuguese 14%. *Jose* (19), *Juan* (15), *Luis* (14), *Jorge* (9), *Manuel* (9), *Jesus* (8), *Mario* (8), *Fernando*

(5), *Francisco* (5), *Angel* (4), *Carlos* (4), *Jose Luis* (3); *Joao* (2), *Joaquim*, *Margarida*, *Paulo*; *Antonio* (4), *Caio*, *Cecilio*, *Cesario*, *Elvio*, *Filiberto*, *Giraldo*, *Heriberto*, *Paolo*, *Romeo*, *Rosangela*, *Sal*.

Barrow (5682) English: **1.** habitational name from any of the numerous places named with Old English *bearo*, *bearu* 'grove' (dative *bear(o)we*, *bearuwe*), for example in Cheshire, Derbyshire, Gloucestershire, Lancashire, Leicestershire, Lincolnshire, Shropshire, Suffolk, and Somerset, or a topographic name with the same meaning. **2.** topographic name for someone who lived by an ancient burial mound, Middle English *berwe*, *barwe*, or a habitational name from a place named with this word (Old English *beorg*, dative *beorge*), of which there is one near Leicester and another in Somerset. **3.** habitational name from Barrow in Furness, Cumbria, which is named with an unattested Celtic word, *barr*, here meaning 'promontory', + Old Norse *ey* 'island'.

Barrowman (152) English: variant of BORROWMAN.

Barrows (3036) English: topographic name for someone who lived by a grove (see BARROW 1) or an ancient burial mound (see BARROW 2).

Barrs (476) English (Midlands and northwest): **1.** topographic name for someone who lived by one or more barriers or obstructions, from a plural or possessive form of BARR 2. **2.** metonymic occupational name for a maker of bars, or perhaps a nickname for a tall, thin man. See BARR 4.

Barrus (491) English: probably a variant of BARROWS.

Barry (18355) **1.** Irish: Anglicized form of Gaelic **Ó Beargha** 'descendant of *Beargh*', a byname meaning 'plunderer'. **2.** Irish: Anglicized form of Gaelic **Ó Báire** 'descendant of *Báire*', a short form of either of two Gaelic personal names, *Bairrfhionn* or *Fionnbharr*. **3.** English, of Welsh origin: patronymic from HARRY, the medieval English vernacular form of HENRY, preceded by Welsh *ap* 'son of'. Compare PARRY. **4.** Variant spelling of BARRIE 1.
GIVEN NAMES Irish 6%. *Brendan* (8), *Donal* (4), *Aidan* (2), *Ciaran* (2), *Eoin* (2), *John Patrick* (2), *Kaitlin* (2), *Kieran* (2), *Murphy* (2), *Aileen*, *Brigid*, *Caitlin*.

Barsalou (111) French: unexplained.
FOREBEARS This name was brought to Montreal some time before 1702 from Agen in Lot-et-Garonne, France, by Gerard Barsalou (1673–1721).
GIVEN NAMES French 7%. *Aime*, *Normand*.

Barsamian (215) Armenian: patronymic from the personal name *parsam*, from Syriac *Barṣauma*, a derivative of *ṣauma* 'fast'.
GIVEN NAMES Armenian 26%. *Raffi* (3), *Ara* (2), *Arsen* (2), *Dikran* (2), *Haig* (2), *Vahan*

(2), *Vartan* (2), *Agop*, *Aram*, *Armen*, *Goarik*, *Hagop*.

Barsanti (228) Central Italian: unexplained.
GIVEN NAMES Italian 5%. *Umberto* (2), *Angelo*, *Gino*, *Ilio*.

Barsch (212) German: **1.** from Middle High German *bars* 'perch', hence a nickname, probably uncomplimentary, for someone thought to resemble a fish in some way, or a metonymic occupational name for a fish dealer or fisherman. **2.** nickname from Low German *barsch* 'harsh', 'rude'.
GIVEN NAMES German 8%. *Ekkehard*, *Gerda*, *Gerhard*, *Hans*, *Heinrich*, *Otto*, *Udo*.

Barse (181) French: from the Germanic personal name *Berizo*, a pet derivative of *bero* 'bear'.

Barsh (192) Americanized spelling of German BARSCH.

Barshinger (128) Probably an Americanized form of Swiss German **Baertschiger**.

Barsi (108) **1.** Central Italian: unexplained. **2.** Hungarian: habitational name for someone from a village called Bars (with the common -i suffix -i of Hungarian local names), from the Turkic personal name *Bars*, *Bors*. Borsod county in the north of Hungary was named with the same Turkic (Khabar, Uze, Pecheneg, or Cumanian) personal name.
GIVEN NAMES Italian 10%. *Dante* (2), *Enzo*, *Reno*.

Barski (125) Polish form and variant spelling of Jewish and Ukrainian BARSKY.
GIVEN NAMES Polish 12%; Jewish 4%. *Stanislaw* (2), *Mieczyslaw*, *Wieslaw*, *Zbigniew*; *Moshe*, *Naama*.

Barsky (490) Jewish (from Ukraine) and Ukrainian: habitational name for someone from the city of Bar, now in Ukraine. In the 16th century this was an important frontier fortress of the Polish Empire against the Turks and the Tartars, which in the 18th century became the center of a confederation. Its original name was Rów; it was given its present name in honor of the Italian city of Bari by Bona Sforza, Duchess of Bari, wife of King Zygmunt Stary (Sigismund the Old).
GIVEN NAMES Russian 7%; Jewish 7%. *Lev* (4), *Arkady* (2), *Boris* (2), *Anatoly*, *Gleb*, *Grigory*, *Igor*, *Masha*, *Matvey*, *Oleg*, *Raisa*, *Semyon*; *Hyman* (2), *Emanuel*, *Ilya*, *Nachman*, *Rimma*, *Zev*.

Barsness (408) Norwegian: habitational name from a farmstead so named in the county of Sogn og Fjordane, possibly from a compound of the Old Norse personal name *Baldrekr* + *nes* 'point', 'headland'.
GIVEN NAME Scandinavian 5%. *Nels*.

Barson (206) English: patronymic from a short form of BARTHOLOMEW.

Barsotti (307) Italian (Tuscany): unexplained.
FOREBEARS Charles (Carlo) Barsotti (1850–1927) came to the U.S. in 1872 from Pisa,

Italy, and founded *Il Progresso*, the first Italian daily newspaper in America.
GIVEN NAMES Italian 9%. *Aldo* (2), *Antonio*, *Carlo*, *Cesare*, *Enrico*, *Enzo*, *Ezio*, *Rinaldo*, *Rocci*.

Barsoum (120) Aramaic (a name used among the Christians of Lebanon and Syria and the Chaldeans of Iraq): from *bar* 'son' + *ṣūm* 'fasting', literally 'son of fasting', i.e. one who fasts (for religious reasons).
GIVEN NAMES Arabic 60%. *Emad* (4), *Kamal* (4), *Nabil* (3), *Mourad* (2), *Amal*, *Amani*, *Amir*, *Bassem*, *Fady*, *Hany*, *Ibraham*, *Ibrahim*.

Barss (142) Altered form of English and Welsh BEARSE.

Barstad (326) Norwegian: habitational name from any of various farmsteads named Barstad, from the Old Norse personal name *Bǫrkr* or *Barði* + *stad* (from Old Norse *staðir*, plural of *staðr* 'farmstead', 'dwelling').
GIVEN NAMES Scandinavian 4%. *Lars*, *Obert*.

Barstow (859) English: habitational name from Bairstow in West Yorkshire, probably named with Old English *beger* 'berry' + *stōw* 'place'. The surname is still most common in Yorkshire.

Barszcz (135) Polish: nickname from *barszcz* 'beetroot soup'.
GIVEN NAMES Polish 9%. *Andrzej*, *Henryk*, *Jadwiga*.

Bart (909) **1.** German: variant of BARTH, or from a Germanic personal name, cognate of Old High German *beraht* 'bright', 'shining', as in BERTHOLD. **2.** English, Dutch, German, and Czech: from the personal name *Bart*, a short form of *Bartolomaeus* or its vernacular derivatives (see BARTHOLOMEW).

Barta (1826) Hungarian; Slovak and Czech (**Bárta**): from a pet form of the personal name *Bartolomaeus* (Hungarian *Bertalan*; Czech *Bartoloměj*, from Latin *Bartolomaeus* (see BARTHOLOMEW)).

Bartak (164) Czech and Slovak (**Barták**): from a pet form of BARTA.

Bartch (134) Altered spelling of German BARTSCH.

Bartczak (96) Polish: patronymic from *Bartcz*, a pet form of the personal name *Bartłomiej* (see BARTHOLOMEW).
GIVEN NAMES Polish 8%. *Casimir*, *Halina*, *Ryszard*.

Barteau (136) French: metonymic occupational name for a basket maker, from a derivative of *berte* 'basket'.

Bartee (811) Probably an altered spelling of Scottish **Bartie**, from a pet form of the personal name BARTHOLOMEW.

Bartek (605) Polish, Czech, Slovak, and eastern German: from a pet form of a vernacular form of the personal name *Bartolomaeus* (Czech *Bartoloměj*, Polish *Bartłomiej*, German *Bartolomäus*) (see BARTHOLOMEW).

Bartel (2165) **1.** German: from a pet form of the Germanic personal name BART, a short form of BERTHOLD. **2.** German, Polish, Czech, and Slovak: from a pet form of a vernacular form of the personal name *Bartolomaeus*, German *Bartolomäus*, Polish *Bartłomiej*, Czech *Bartoloměj* (see BARTHOLOMEW). **3.** Possibly also an Americanized form of Slovenian **Bartelj**, from a vernacular form of the personal name *Bartolomej*, Latin *Bartolomaeus* (see BARTHOLOMEW).

Bartell (1657) English: from a medieval pet form of BARTHOLOMEW.

Bartelme (151) German and central European: from the genitive form, *Bartholomaei*, of the Latin personal name *Bartholomaeus* (see BARTHOLOMEW).

Bartels (3636) German: patronymic from BARTEL 1 or 2.
GIVEN NAMES German 4%. *Kurt* (6), *Otto* (5), *Dieter* (2), *Erwin* (2), *Frieda* (2), *Heinz* (2), *Helmuth* (2), *Adelheid, Alois, Arno, Bernhard, Christoph*.

Bartelson (174) Respelling of Danish and Norwegian BERTELSEN or its Swedish cognate **Bertilsson**.

Bartelt (1033) German: variant of BERTHOLD.

Barten (247) English: variant spelling of BARTON.

Barter (827) English: nickname from Old French *barateor, barateur* 'rogue', 'cheat', 'fraud'; alternatively, in some instances it may be from Old Norse *barátta* 'beating', 'fight', 'battle', hence by extension a troublemaker or quarrelsome man.

Bartgis (114) Origin unidentified. Possibly a variant of BARTKUS.

Barth (6009) German: **1.** nickname for a bearded man, from Middle High German *bart* 'beard'. See also BEARD 1. **2.** variant of BART 2. **3.** habitational name from a place so named in Pomerania.
GIVEN NAMES German 4%. *Otto* (11), *Hans* (5), *Kurt* (4), *Franz* (3), *Erwin* (2), *Florian* (2), *Gerhard* (2), *Gunther* (2), *Klaus* (2), *Manfred* (2), *Armin, Arno*.

Bartha (223) Hungarian: variant spelling of BARTA.
GIVEN NAMES Hungarian 9%. *Bela* (2), *Gabor* (2), *Arpad, Dezso, Geza, Tamas, Tibor*.

Barthe (110) **1.** French: topographic name for someone who lived on a piece of land overgrown with bushes or scrub, Old French *barthe* (a word probably of Gaulish origin). **2.** German: metonymic occupational name for someone who made (battle)axes, from Middle High German *barte*, Middle Low German *barde* 'axe'.
FOREBEARS A Barthe or Barte from the Languedoc region of France is recorded in Varennes, Quebec, in 1707, together with the secondary surnames Belleville and Larivière.
GIVEN NAMES French 12%. *Alphonse, Ghyslaine, Raymonde*.

Barthel (1217) German (**Bärthel**): variant spelling of BARTEL.
GIVEN NAMES German 6%. *Kurt* (4), *Fritz* (2), *Hans* (2), *Monika* (2), *Reinhard* (2), *Aloys, Armin, Bernhard, Eldred, Ewald, Franz, Frieda*.

Barthelemy (453) French (**Bart(h)élemy**): from the personal name *Bart(h)élemy*, French form of BARTHOLOMEW. It is found chiefly in New England.
FOREBEARS A Barthelemy from the Languedoc region of France is recorded in Quebec City in 1690.
GIVEN NAMES French 17%. *Pierre* (3), *Philippe* (2), *Alain, Alphonse, Andre, Camille, Clemence, Francois, Frenel, Jacques, Jean Michael, Jesula*.

Barthelmes (116) German: altered form of the personal name *Bartolomaeus* (see BARTHOLOMEW).

Barthelmess (94) German: altered form of German BARTHELMES.
GIVEN NAME German 4%. *Kurt*.

Barthels (110) German: variant spelling of BARTELS.
GIVEN NAMES German 4%. *Egon, Erna*.

Barthlow (154) Americanized spelling of any of various vernacular derivatives of the personal name *Bartholomaeus* (see BARTHOLOMEW).

Barthol (174) German and central European: variant spelling of BARTOL.
GIVEN NAME German 5%. *Gottfried* (2).

Barthold (269) North German: variant of BERTHOLD.
GIVEN NAMES German 6%. *Wolfgang* (2), *Erwin, Fritz*.

Bartholf (133) North German form of **Bertolf**, from a Germanic personal name composed of the elements *berht* 'bright', 'famous' + *wolf* 'wolf'.

Bartholomay (232) German and central European: from the genitive form, *Bart(h)olomaei*, of the personal name *Bart(h)olomaeus* (see BARTHOLOMEW).

Bartholomew (5521) English: from a medieval personal name, Latin *Bart(h)olomaeus*, from the Aramaic patronymic *bar-Talmay* 'son of Talmay', meaning 'having many furrows', i.e. rich in land. This was an extremely popular personal name in Christian Europe, with innumerable vernacular derivatives. It derived its popularity from the apostle St. Bartholomew (Matthew 10:3), the patron saint of tanners, vintners, and butlers. As an Irish name, it has been used as an Americanized form of **Mac Pharthaláin** (see MCFARLANE).

Bartholow (315) Americanized spelling of any of various vernacular derivatives of the personal name *Bartholomaeus* (see BARTHOLOMEW).

Bartik (111) Czech (**Bártík**) and Slovak (also **Bartík**): from a pet form of the personal name *Bartoloměj*, a vernacular form of *Bartolomaeus* (see BARTHOLOMEW).

Bartimus (107) German: variant of **Bartemes**, from a reduced form of the personal name *Bartolomaeus* (see BARTHOLOMEW).

Bartkiewicz (105) Polish: patronymic from BARTEK.
GIVEN NAMES Polish 16%. *Andrzej, Bogdan, Dariusz, Janusz, Krystyna, Rafal, Zofia*.

Bartko (326) Polish and Slovak: from a vernacular pet form of the personal name *Bartolomaeus* (see BARTHOLOMEW).

Bartkowiak (345) Polish: patronymic from BARTEK.

Bartkowicz (65) Polish: patronymic from BARTEK.
GIVEN NAMES Polish 9%. *Janusz, Kazimierz*.

Bartkowski (268) Polish: **1.** habitational name for someone from any of various places called Bartkowa, Bartkowo, or Bartków. **2.** from a derivative of the personal name BARTEK.
GIVEN NAMES Polish 9%. *Witold* (2), *Andrzej, Kazimir, Mieczyslaw, Thadeus, Zigmund, Zofia*.

Bartkus (270) Lithuanian form of Polish BARTKO.

Bartl (197) German: variant of BARTEL.
GIVEN NAMES German 5%. *Elfriede, Franz, Nikolaus*.

Bartle (802) **1.** English: from a pet form of the medieval personal name BARTHOLOMEW. **2.** German (Swabian: **Bärtle**): from a pet form of *Bartolomäus* (see BARTHOLOMEW) or BERTHOLD. It is also found as an altered spelling of BARTEL.

Bartlebaugh (199) Origin uncertain; probably German, possibly an altered form of **Bartenbach**, a habitational name from a place named Bartenbach, in Württemberg, where there is a large family of that name.

Bartles (319) Americanized spelling of German BARTELS.

Bartleson (400) Americanized spelling of any of the various Scandinavian surnames beginning *Bertel-, Bartel-, Barthel-* + the patronymic ending *-(s)son* or *-sen*.

Bartlett (17309) English: from the Middle English personal name *Bartlet*, a pet form of BARTHOLOMEW.
FOREBEARS This is the name of a well-established New England family. Its members include Josiah Bartlett (1729–95), who was born in Amesbury, MA, and became governor of NH (1790–94). A Richard Bartlet(t) settled in Newbury, MA, in 1635.

Bartlette (109) English: variant spelling of BARTLETT.

Bartley (5646) **1.** English: habitational name from Bartley in Hampshire, or from Bartley Green in the West Midlands, both of which are named with Old English *be(o)rc* 'birch' + *lēah* 'woodland clearing'; compare BARCLAY. **2.** Americanized spelling of German (Swabian) BARTLE and the Swiss cognate **Bartli**.
FOREBEARS The surname Bartley was brought to VA from Northumberland in 1724.

Bartling (679) German (Westphalia): patronymic from a pet form of BERTHOLD.
GIVEN NAMES German 4%. *Kurt* (3), *Gerhard, Helmuth, Hermann*.

Bartlow (415) Americanized spelling of any of various vernacular derivatives of the personal name *Bartholomaeus* (see BARTHOLOMEW).

Bartman (572) Respelling of German **Bartmann**, a nickname from Middle High German, Middle Low German *bart* 'beard' + *man* 'man'.

Bartmess (201) German: reduced form of BARTHELMESS.

Bartness (109) Altered form of German BARTMESS.

Bartnick (227) Eastern German: occupational name from Slavic *bartnik* 'bee keeper'.
GIVEN NAMES German 4%. *Heinz, Hermann*.

Bartnicki (150) Polish: habitational name from a place called Bartniki.
GIVEN NAMES Polish 7%. *Henryk, Jadwiga, Mieczyslaw, Witold*.

Bartnik (195) Polish: occupational name from Polish *bartnik* 'bee keeper'.
GIVEN NAMES Polish 13%. *Janina* (2), *Zdzislaw* (2), *Casimir, Janusz, Jolanta, Leszek, Wojciech, Zbigniew*.

Barto (1463) **1.** Italian: from a variant of the personal name BERTO or a short form of BARTOLO. **2.** Hungarian (**Bartó**): from a pet form of *Bertalan*, Hungarian form of BARTHOLOMEW. **3.** Albanian: unexplained.

Bartoe (128) Variant spelling of BARTOW.
GIVEN NAME French 4%. *Renald*.

Bartok (270) Hungarian (**Bartók**): from a pet form of *Bartalan*, a variant of *Bertalan*, Hungarian form of the personal name BARTHOLOMEW.

Bartol (437) Polish, Eastern German, and Slovenian: from a short form of the Latin personal name *Bartolomaeus* (see BARTHOLOMEW).

Bartoletti (204) Italian: from the personal name *Bartoletto*, a pet form of the personal name *Bartolomeo*, Italian form of BARTHOLOMEW.
GIVEN NAMES Italian 10%. *Dante* (2), *Angelo, Geno, Guido, Luca, Primo, Sereno*.

Bartoli (369) **1.** Italian: patronymic or plural form of BARTOLO. **2.** Catalan (**Bartolí**): variant of the Catalan name **Bertolí** (see BERTOLI).
GIVEN NAMES Italian 23%; Spanish 7%. *Mario* (3), *Claudio* (2), *Corrado* (2), *Cosmo* (2), *Marco* (2), *Renato* (2), *Americo, Bartolomeo, Carlo, Dino, Edoardo, Elio, Evo, Gino, Lino, Martino, Mauro; Miguel* (2), *Jose* (2), *Pablo*.

Bartolini (291) Italian: from the personal name *Bartolino*, a diminutive of the personal name BARTOLO.
GIVEN NAMES Italian 16%. *Angelo, Arduino, Bruna, Carlo, Emidio, Fabrizio, Gino, Giulio, Guido, Julieta, Leonardo*.

Bartolo (385) Italian: from a short form of the personal name *Bartolomeo*, Italian form of BARTHOLOMEW.
GIVEN NAMES Spanish 16%; Italian 6%. *Manuel* (3), *Jose* (2), *Marcial* (2), *Pedro* (2), *Alberto, Alredo, Anastacio, Argemiro, Arnulfo, Artemio, Domingo, Eduardo; Domenico* (2), *Sal* (2), *Aureliano, Carmela, Federico, Guido, Raffaele, Romeo, Silvio*.

Bartolome (245) Spanish (**Bartolomé**): from the personal name *Bartolomé*, Spanish form of BARTHOLOMEW.
GIVEN NAMES Spanish 40%; Italian 8%. *Jose* (4), *Alfredo* (3), *Francisco* (3), *Juan* (3), *Manuel* (3), *Pedro* (3), *Carlos* (2), *Marcelino* (2), *Rufino* (2), *Adolfo, Adriano, Alberto; Antonio* (2), *Cecilio* (2), *Dante, Filomena, Gabriele, Luciano, Romeo, Severino*.

Bartolomei (295) Italian: patronymic or plural form of BARTOLOMEO.
GIVEN NAMES Italian 20%; Spanish 8%. *Aldo* (3), *Mario* (3), *Ceasar* (2), *Emidio* (2), *Aida, Alberto, Angelo, Bartolo, Emo, Fernando, Gino, Giulio, Imelda, Paolo; Juan* (2), *Luis* (2), *Jose, Lourdes, Norberto*.

Bartolomeo (391) Italian: from the personal name *Bartolomeo*, Italian form of BARTHOLOMEW.
GIVEN NAMES Italian 17%. *Angelo* (5), *Dante* (2), *Gino* (2), *Aldo, Antonio, Attilio, Benedetta, Franco, Gaetano, Giosue, Marco*.

Bartolomucci (158) Italian: from a diminutive of the personal name *Bartolomeo*, Italian form of BARTHOLOMEW.
GIVEN NAMES Italian 10%. *Angelo, Biagio, Carlo, Dario, Dino, Guido*.

Bartolone (187) Italian: from an augmentative form of the personal name BARTOLO.
GIVEN NAMES Italian 24%. *Salvatore* (2), *Mariano* (2), *Aldo, Ciro, Domenic, Giovanni, Ignazio, Pasquale, Rosaria, Sal*.

Bartolotta (503) Italian: from a diminutive of the personal name BARTOLO.
GIVEN NAMES Italian 22%. *Angelo* (9), *Salvatore* (7), *Sal* (4), *Calogero* (3), *Antonio* (2), *Matteo* (2), *Vito* (2), *Antoninette, Carmela, Carmelo, Francesco, Giuseppe*.

Bartolotti (112) Italian: patronymic from a pet form of the personal name BARTOLO.
GIVEN NAMES Italian 16%. *Salvatore* (2), *Guido, Libero, Riccardo*.

Bartolucci (185) Italian: patronymic from a pet form of the personal name BARTOLO.
GIVEN NAMES Italian 8%. *Guido* (3), *Dino, Enzo, Reno, Santo*.

Barton (24981) **1.** English: habitational name from any of the numerous places named with Old English *bere* or *bær* 'barley' + *tūn* 'enclosure', 'settlement', i.e. an outlying grange. Compare BARWICK. **2.** German and central European (e.g. Czech and Slovak **Bartoň**): from a pet form of the personal name *Bartolomaeus* (see BARTHOLOMEW).

Bartone (284) Southern Italian: **1.** from a derivative of the personal name *Bartolomeo*, Italian form of BARTHOLOMEW. **2.** variant of BERTONE.
GIVEN NAMES Italian 11%. *Pasquale* (3), *Biagio, Carmela, Pasqualina, Rocco, Sal, Vito*.

Bartoo (158) Most probably an Americanized spelling of French **Bartou** (or the variants **Barthou, Bartoux,** or **Barthoux**), from a Germanic personal name composed of the elements *berht* 'bright', 'famous' + *wolf* 'wolf'.

Bartos (1042) **1.** Hungarian, Czech and Slovak (**Bartoš**), and eastern German: from a vernacular pet form of the personal name *Bartolomaeus* (Hungarian *Bertalan*, Czech *Bartoloměj*, Slovak *Bartolomej*) (see BARTHOLOMEW). **2.** Polish: variant of BARTOSZ.

Bartosch (160) German: variant of Slavic *Bartoš* (see BARTOS).
GIVEN NAMES German 6%. *Kurt* (2), *Elfriede, Erwin*.

Bartosh (468) **1.** Americanized spelling of German BARTOSCH, Hungarian BARTOS, or Polish BARTOSZ. **2.** Ukrainian: from a pet form of the personal name *Bartolomij*, Ukrainian form of BARTHOLOMEW.

Bartosiewicz (154) Polish: patronymic from the personal name BARTOSZ.
GIVEN NAMES Polish 11%. *Andrzej, Ewa, Ryszard, Stanislaw, Tadeusz, Zofia*.

Bartosik (181) Polish: from a pet form of the personal name *Bartłomiej* (see BARTHOLOMEW).
GIVEN NAMES Polish 15%. *Bogdan* (2), *Alicja, Beata, Czeslawa, Grazyna, Karol, Kazimierz, Lucyna, Ludwik, Tadeusz, Wieslawa, Zbigniew*.

Bartosz (140) Polish: from a pet form of the personal name *Bartłomiej* (see BARTHOLOMEW).
GIVEN NAMES Polish 10%. *Benedykt, Boguslaw, Karol, Krystyna, Stanislaw, Zdzislaw*.

Bartoszek (193) Polish: from a pet form of the personal name *Bartłomiej* (see BARTHOLOMEW).
GIVEN NAMES Polish 6%. *Alicja, Teofil*.

Bartow (800) Eastern German: **1.** habitational name for someone from the place so named north of Neubrandenburg, which is of Slavic origin. **2.** variant of BARTHOL or BARTHOLD.

Bartram (914) English and North German: variant of BERTRAM.
FOREBEARS William Bartram, a Quaker, had a large farm near Darby, PA, when his eldest son, John, the first American botanist, was born in 1699. John conducted botanical experiments at his own farm in Kingsessing, PA, near Philadelphia.

Bartron (131) English: perhaps a variant of BARTRAM.

Bartruff (131) Origin unidentified. Probably of German origin.

Barts (218) Dutch: patronymic from a short form of the personal name *Bartolomeus* (see BARTHOLOMEW).
GIVEN NAME French 4%. *Vernice*.

Bartsch (1068) German (also **Bärtsch**): from a Slavic short form of the personal name *Bartholomaeus* (see BARTHOLOMEW).
GIVEN NAMES German 7%. *Detlef* (2), *Horst* (2), *Otto* (2), *Siegfried* (2), *Uwe* (2), *Alfons*, *Arno*, *Benno*, *Dieter*, *Ewald*, *Guenter*, *Gunther*.

Bartunek (295) Czech (**Bartůněk**): from a pet form of **Bartoň** (see BARTON).

Bartus (248) **1.** Czech and Slovak (**Bartuš**): from a short form of the personal name *Bartoloměj*, Czech form of BARTHOLOMEW. **2.** Hungarian: variant of BARTOS.

Bartusek (110) Czech (**Bartušek, Bartůšek**): from a pet form of the personal name *Bartuš* (see BARTUS).

Bartz (2311) **1.** German: from a pet form of the personal name *Bartolomäus* (see BARTHOLOMEW). **2.** South German: from Middle High German *barz*, *borz* 'tree stump', hence a nickname for a short, stocky man. **3.** Eastern German: nickname from Slavic *barzy* 'quick'.

Baruch (459) Jewish: from the Hebrew male personal name *Baruch* meaning 'blessed', 'fortunate'. This was borne by a disciple of Jeremiah, the supposed author of one of the books of the Apocrypha.
FOREBEARS Simon Baruch (1840–1921), physician, came from Schwersen, Germany. He received medical training in SC, served as a surgeon in the Civil War, and settled in New York City in 1881.
GIVEN NAMES Jewish 13%. *Amnon* (4), *Aharon* (2), *Avi* (2), *Arie*, *Chaim*, *Cohen*, *Devorah*, *Dror*, *Isak*, *Meyer*, *Miriam*, *Moshe*.

Baruth (140) German: habitational name for someone from a place so named in the provinces of Brandenburg and Saxony.

Barwick (1424) **1.** English: habitational name from any of various places called Barwick, for example in Norfolk, Somerset, and West Yorkshire, from Old English *bere* 'barley' + *wīc* 'outlying farm', i.e. a granary lying some distance away from the main village. **2.** North German: habitational name from a place called Berwick, near Soest, in Westphalia.

Bary (114) Probably a variant of BARRY.
FOREBEARS The name in this spelling is found in Belgium. It also seems to have reached Argentina via New Orleans.

Barylski (108) Polish: metonymic occupational name for a cooper, from *baryła* 'barrel' + the common surname ending -*ski*.

Barz (231) German: variant spelling of BARTZ.
GIVEN NAMES German 12%. *Otto* (4), *Guenter* (2), *Kurt* (2), *Deiter*, *Erwin*, *Hans*, *Wolfgang*.

Barzee (117) **1.** Dutch: unexplained. Perhaps a shortened form of **Barzeele**: **2.** from Middle Dutch *bariseel*, Old French *barisel* 'vat', 'barrel', hence a metonymic occupational name for a cooper or wine merchant. **3.** alternatively, perhaps, a habitational name from Bazel in East Flanders, Belgium.

Bas (111) **1.** Basque: topographic name for someone who lived by a wood, from Basque *baso* 'wood'. **2.** Catalan: habitational name from a place so named in the Catalan district of La Garrotxa, Catalonia. **3.** Slovenian (**Baš**): from a medieval short form of the personal name *Sebastjan* (see SEBASTIAN).
GIVEN NAMES Spanish 17%; Slavic 11%. *Jose* (3), *Mauricio* (3), *Abelardo*, *Florencio*, *Francisco*, *Jorge*, *Luis*, *Manuel*, *Pedro*, *Soledad*, *Vicente*; *Dmytro*, *Esfira*, *Liya*, *Pyotr*, *Sergey*, *Semen*.

Basa (184) **1.** Spanish (of Basque origin): topographic name from Basque *baso* 'wood', 'forest'. **2.** Catalan: variant spelling of **Bassa**, a topographic name from Catalan *bassa* 'pool', 'pond'. **3.** Hungarian: from the old secular personal name *Basa*, or from *Bazsa*, a pet form of the ecclesiastical name *Bazsil*, from Greek *Basileios* (see BASIL). In some cases the Hungarian family name could be a derivative of the Turkish *başa* (see BASHA), probably as a nickname for a self-important person or someone who had dealings with the Turkish authorities or occupying forces. **4.** Polish: metonymic occupational name for a musician, from *basa*, dialect form of *basy* 'musical instrument'. **5.** Balkan (Muslim): variant of Turkish PASHA.
GIVEN NAMES Spanish 34%. *Jose* (3), *Rogelio* (3), *Amelita* (2), *Arturo* (2), *Elena* (2), *Elpidio* (2), *Juanito* (2), *Nenita* (2), *Adoracion*, *Angelina*, *Basilio*, *Bernabe*; *Romeo* (3), *Antonio*, *Mauro*, *Severiano*.

Basak (103) Indian (Bengal) and Bangladeshi: Hindu (Baishya) name of unknown meaning.
GIVEN NAMES Indian 32%. *Arup* (2), *Amitabha*, *Anima*, *Apurba*, *Aroon*, *Indrani*, *Jayati*, *Madhuri*, *Mamta*, *Raj*, *Sanjay*, *Saroj*.

Basaldua (146) Basque: habitational name from Basaldua in Urduña, in Biscay province, or a topographic name from *baso* 'wood', 'forest' + *aldu* 'high' + the definite article -*a*.
GIVEN NAMES Spanish 42%. *Jose* (3), *Armando* (2), *Arturo* (2), *Dionicio* (2), *Jesus* (2), *Jose Luis* (2), *Manuel* (2), *Miguel* (2), *Roel* (2), *Tomas* (2), *Alberto*, *Celestino*.

Basara (157) **1.** Polish: of uncertain origin; possibly a nickname from the dialect word *basior* 'male wolf', *basiora* 'inflorescence', or *basiora* 'sheep or ram'. **2.** Ukrainian: variant of **Basarab**, a regional name for someone from Bessarabia, now Moldova. **3.** Serbian: from Turkish *basar*

'physical beauty'. **4.** Arabic: variant of BISHARA.
GIVEN NAMES Polish 7%. *Jacek*, *Wieslaw*, *Wladyslawa*, *Zofia*.

Basch (619) **1.** German (also **Bäsch**): from a southern short form of SEBASTIAN. **2.** Jewish: acronymic surname from the Hebrew patronymic phrases *Ben Shelomo*, *Shemuel*, *Shimon*, or *Shimshon*. See also BROCK.
GIVEN NAMES German 4%; Jewish 4%. *Mathias* (2), *Erwin*, *Theodor*; *Aron*, *Heshy*, *Meir*, *Miriam*, *Naftali*, *Shlomo*, *Yakov*, *Yehoshua*.

Basche (101) German: variant of BASCH.

Basciano (132) Southern Italian (Naples): from a palatalized derivative of the Latin personal name *Bass(i)anus*.
GIVEN NAMES Italian 12%. *Dino*, *Peppino*.

Basco (400) Spanish: ethnic name for a Basque, Spanish *vasco*, or a regional name for someone who lived in Basque country. See VASCO.
GIVEN NAMES Spanish 8%. *Jose* (3), *Jaime* (2), *Rodolfo* (2), *Alfonso*, *Buenaventura*, *Carlos*, *Carmelita*, *Catalina*, *Digna*, *Elvira*, *Emilia*, *Juan*.

Bascom (786) English: habitational name from either of two places called Boscombe (in Dorset and Wiltshire), both named with Old English *bors* 'spiky plant' + *cumb* 'valley'.
FOREBEARS Alpheus Bascom, said to be of Huguenot stock, was in Hancock, NY, by 1796.

Bascomb (106) English: variant spelling BASCOM.

Bascue (103) Respelling of French **Bascou**, an ethnic name for a Basque. See VASCO.

Basden (454) English: unexplained. It may be a variant of BASTIN, or a habitational name from a lost or unidentified place. Compare BAISDEN.

Base (271) **1.** Variant spelling of BASS. **2.** German (**Bäse**): variant of **Bese** (see BEESE).

Basehore (138) See BASHORE.

Basel (339) **1.** German: habitational name from the Swiss city of Basel. **2.** from a short form of Germanic personal names formed with Old High German *ber* 'bear' (the animal) or Old Norse *bodh* 'battle'. **3.** from a pet form, *Božel*, from Slavic *Božidar* 'gift of God'.

Baselice (115) Altered form of Italian **Basilace**, from the Greek personal name *Basilakes*, a pet form of *Basileios* (see BASIL).
GIVEN NAMES Italian 12%. *Angelo*, *Carmine*, *Donato*, *Marco*, *Marino*.

Baseman (141) **1.** Altered spelling of German **Besemann**, a habitational name for someone from a place named Beesem (near Dannenberg) or Beesen (Westphalia and Schleswig-Holstein). **2.** Possibly an altered spelling of German **Bösemann** (see BOSEMAN).

Basey (287) **1.** Of German origin: probably an altered spelling of German **Böse**, a variant of BAZE 2. **2.** Also English: unexplained.

Basford (395) English (chiefly north Midlands): variant of BASSFORD.

Basgall (202) German: probably a variant of the personal name *Pascall* (see PASQUALE).

Bash (1139) **1.** English: variant of BACH 3. **2.** Americanized spelling of German or Jewish BASCH. **3.** Americanized spelling of Slovenian **Baš** (see BAS 3).

Basha (153) Muslim: variant of Turkish PASHA.

GIVEN NAMES Muslim 25%. *Fozia* (2), *Imad* (2), *Nabil* (2), *Alaa, Anwer, Ashraf, Bassem, Farhana, Fati, Fatima, Hassan, Karima.*

Basham (3027) English: habitational name of uncertain origin. It may be from places in Norfolk and Suffolk called Barsham, from the genitive case of the Old English byname *Bār* 'wild boar' + Old English *hām* 'homestead'.

Bashara (147) Muslim: variant of BISHARA.

Bashaw (892) **1.** Americanized spelling of French **Bachard** (see BACHAR). **2.** Probably an altered spelling of German *Beschore* (see BASHORE).

Basher (177) Muslim: variant of BASHIR.

GIVEN NAMES Muslim 9%. *Abul* (3), *Mohammed* (2), *Ali, Anwar, Isam, Nisim, Nurul, Sayed.*

Bashford (273) English: variant of BASSFORD.

Bashir (252) Muslim: from a personal name based on Arabic *bashīr* 'bringer of good news'. This is an attribute of the Prophet Muhammad.

GIVEN NAMES Muslim 82%. *Mohammad* (18), *Khalid* (6), *Muhammad* (6), *Shahid* (5), *Abid* (3), *Amir* (3), *Rifaat* (3), *Salah* (3), *Tariq* (3), *Abdul* (2), *Ahmad* (2), *Atif* (2).

Bashor (323) See BASHORE.

Bashore (714) Americanized form of Dutch or North German **Boesshaar**, of uncertain origin, probably a Low German form of the personal name BOSSHART. This name is found in a rich variety of Americanized forms, including **Basehore, Beshore, Bosher, Paysore**, etc. There has also been some confusion with derivatives of French BOUCHARD and BRASSEUR. FOREBEARS This name was already well established in PA in the 18th century. Johannes Boesshaar, for example, also known as Basehor, was born in 1760 in Lancaster Co., PA, and died there in 1837.

Basic (122) Bosnian (**Bašić**): patronymic from *baša* 'senior', 'headman', from Turkish *baş* 'head'. *Baša* was used as a title for a distinguished Muslim in the Ottoman Empire who was not an aga or a bey.

GIVEN NAMES Muslim 12%; South Slavic 10%. *Suad* (2), *Damir, Fuad, Halil, Haris, Mohamed, Muharem, Nihad, Rasim, Safet; Dunja, Frane, Marijan, Natasa, Stjepan, Zlatan.*

Basich (175) Bosnian: see BASIC.

GIVEN NAME South Slavic 6%. *Bosiljka.*

Basil (648) English and French: from a medieval personal name, ultimately from Greek *Basileios* 'royal'. The name was borne by a 4th-century bishop of Caesarea in Cappadocia, regarded as one of the four Fathers of the Eastern Church; he wrote important theological works and established a rule for religious orders of monks. Various other saints are also known under these and cognate names. The popularity of *Vasili* as a Russian personal name is largely due to the fact that this was the ecclesiastical name of St. Vladimir (956–1015), Prince of Kiev, who was chiefly responsible for the introduction of Christianity to Russia. As an American surname, this has also absorbed some Greek, Russian, and other derivatives of Greek *Vasili*.

Basile (2691) **1.** Southern Italian: from a personal name derived from medieval Greek *Basilis*, a reduced form of *Basileios* (see BASIL). **2.** French: variant of BASIL.

GIVEN NAMES Italian 16%. *Angelo* (17), *Salvatore* (16), *Vito* (9), *Antonio* (8), *Carlo* (8), *Sal* (5), *Carmelo* (4), *Carmine* (4), *Rocco* (4), *Domenic* (3), *Giuseppe* (3).

Basilio (255) Italian and Portuguese (**Basílio**): from the personal name *Basilio* (from Latin *Basilius*) (see BASIL).

GIVEN NAMES Spanish 44%; Portuguese 8%; Italian 7%. *Jose* (4), *Pedro* (4), *Domingo* (3), *Roberto* (3), *Carlos* (2), *Ricardo* (2), *Albertino, Alejandro, Almario, Altagracia, Andres, Armando; Ilidio; Antonio* (3), *Gennaro* (2), *Anastasio, Federico, Marco, Quirino.*

Basilone (111) Italian: from an augmentative form of the personal name BASILE.

GIVEN NAMES Italian 8%; French 4%. *Dario; Alphonse, Armand.*

Basinger (1450) Altered form of the Swiss and German family name **Bäsiger**, Alemannic form of **Bösinger**, a habitational name for someone from either of two places in Württemberg named Bösingen (near Freudenstadt and Rottweil), or a patronymic from a Germanic personal name beginning with the element *Bos-*. Compare also BAYSINGER.

Basinski (157) Polish (**Basiński**): **1.** habitational name for someone from a place called Basin. **2.** from the personal name *Basia*, a pet form of BARBARA.

GIVEN NAMES Polish 4%; German 4%. *Jerzy, Tadeusz; Erwin, Kurt.*

Basista (183) Polish, Czech and Slovak: occupational name for a double-bass player.

Baska (110) Slovak (**Baška**) and Croatian: unexplained.

Baskerville (913) English (of Norman origin): habitational name from Boscherville in Eure, France, named with Old Anglo-Norman French *boschet* 'copse', 'thicket' (a diminutive of BOIS) + *ville* 'settlement', 'town'.

Baskett (673) English: **1.** from Middle English *basket* 'basket', hence a metonymic occupational name for a basket maker, or perhaps, as Reaney suggests, for someone who carried baskets of stone to a lime kiln. In some cases, it appears to have been a topographic name for someone who lived at a house distinguished by the sign of a basket (who was therefore probably a basket maker). **2.** habitational name for someone from Bascote in Warwickshire, probably so named with an unattested Old English personal name *Basuca* + *cot* 'cottage'.

Baskette (209) Altered spelling, under French influence, of English BASKETT.

Baskin (2404) Jewish (from Belarus and Ukraine): metronymic from the Yiddish female personal name *Baske*, a pet form of the Biblical name *Bath Seba* under the influence of Polish *Basia*, a pet form of *Barbara*.

Baskind (106) Jewish (from Belarus and Ukraine): variant of BASKIN.

GIVEN NAME Jewish 4%. *Ofer.*

Baskins (310) Origin unidentified.

Basler (1086) German: **1.** habitational name for someone from the city of Basel in Switzerland. **2.** from an agent derivative of Middle Low German *baseln* 'to behave in a confused manner', hence a nickname for a scatterbrained person.

Basmajian (131) Armenian: patronymic from Turkish *basmaci*, an occupational name for a maker or seller of textiles, from *basma* 'printed textile'.

GIVEN NAMES Armenian 25%; French 4%. *Haig* (3), *Ara* (2), *Vahan* (2), *Aram, Armen, Arusyak, Diran, Noubar, Onnik, Varant, Vasken; Armand* (3).

Basner (141) **1.** German: nickname from an agent derivative of Middle Low German *basen* 'to talk or behave in a nonsensical manner'. **2.** Altered spelling of German **Bösner**, a habitational name for someone from Bösen, a place northeast of Hannover.

GIVEN NAME Jewish 4%. *Yakob.*

Basnett (240) Irish: from *basynet*, French *bassinet*, a type of hood or helmet. The name was prominent in Dublin throughout the 16th century, but is now found mainly in Liverpool, England.

Basnight (348) **1.** Probably an Americanized form of German FASNACHT. **2.** Perhaps an altered spelling of Irish BASNETT.

Basom (155) Origin uncertain; possibly an altered spelling of English BASON.

Bason (279) **1.** German: unexplained. It may be an altered form of a French Huguenot name, possibly BASSIN. **2.** English and Scottish: patronymic from BATE.

Basore (267) Of Dutch or North German origin: see BASHORE.

Basque (137) French: ethnic name for a Basque. See VASCO.

GIVEN NAMES French 7%. *Cecile, Marcel.*

Basquez (201) Galician: patronymic (**Básquez**) probably from a Galician personal name, *Basco*, from Basque *Belasco*, formed with *bele* 'raven' + the diminutive suffix -*sk*.

GIVEN NAMES Spanish 21%. *Jose* (3), *Juan* (3), *Jesus* (2), *Raul* (2), *Adelina, Angel, Benito, Cristina, Cruz, Domingo, Fernando, Gavino.*

Bass (19484) **1.** English: from Old French *bas(se)* 'low', 'short' (Latin *bassus* 'thickset'; see BASSO), either a descriptive nickname for a short person or a status name meaning 'of humble origin', not necessarily with derogatory connotations. **2.** English: in some instances, from Middle English *bace* 'bass' (the fish), hence a nickname for a person supposedly resembling this fish, or a metonymic occupational name for a fish seller or fisherman. **3.** Scottish: habitational name from a place in Aberdeenshire, of uncertain origin. **4.** Jewish (Ashkenazic): metonymic occupational name for a maker or player of bass viols, from Polish, Ukrainian, and Yiddish *bas* 'bass viol'. **5.** German: see BASSE.

Bassani (114) Italian: patronymic or plural form of BASSANO.

GIVEN NAMES Italian 22%. *Albeno, Angelo, Candido, Cristiano, Domenico, Giuseppe, Nino, Salvatore.*

Bassano (119) Italian (Lombardy and Venetia): **1.** also Jewish (from Italy): habitational name from any of numerous places in northeastern and central Italy named with this word, including Bassano del Grappa (Vicenza), Bassano Bresciano (Brescia), San Bassano (Cremona), and Bassano Romano (Viterbo), which had a large Jewish community. **2.** from the personal name *Bassano*, a derivative of *basso* 'low', 'short in stature', Latin *bassus* 'thickset' (see BASSO). The name was popularized by the cult of St. Bassano, a contemporary of St. Ambrose of Milan.

GIVEN NAMES Italian 11%. *Carmine, Enrico, Sylvio.*

Basse (256) **1.** German: habitational name from any of the places called Basse, for example near Wunstorf and Rostock. **2.** Danish: from Old Danish *basse* 'wild boar'. **3.** French: from Old French *basse* 'low-born' or 'short' (see BASS).

GIVEN NAMES German 8%; French 6%. *Arno* (2), *Hans* (2), *Gernot, Heinz, Inge, Kurt, Udo; Francois, Laurent.*

Bassett (7869) English: from Old French *basset*, a diminutive of *basse* 'low', 'short', either a nickname for a short person or a status name for someone of humble origins.

FOREBEARS William Bassett (*c.* 1598–1667) came to Plymouth, MA, from Kent,

England, in the 1620s; in about 1650 he moved to Duxbury and subsequently to Bridgewater. He had many prominent descendants, among them one of the earliest families on Martha's Vineyard.

Bassette (142) Altered spelling reflecting the Canadian pronunciation of French **Basset**, from a diminutive of Old French *bas* 'low', either in the sense 'low-born' or 'short'.

FOREBEARS A bearer of the name Basset from Paris, also known as Deslauriers, is documented in Montreal in 1659.

GIVEN NAMES French 5%. *Andre, Pierre.*

Bassetti (178) Italian: from a diminutive of BASSO.

GIVEN NAMES Italian 6%. *Camillo, Emidio, Giorgio, Silvio.*

Bassford (299) English: habitational name from any of several places called Basford, especially the one in Staffordshire. There are others in Nottinghamshire and Cheshire. All are named with a personal name (variously Old English *Beorcol* and *Basa*, and Old Norse *Barkr*) + Old English *ford* 'ford'.

Bassham (524) English: variant spelling of BASHAM.

Bassi (389) **1.** Italian: patronymic or plural form of BASSO. **2.** Indian (Panjab): Sikh name based on the name of a Jat clan.

GIVEN NAMES Indian 16%; Italian 8%. *Ajit, Amrit, Ashwani, Atma, Bhim, Dinesh, Jasvir, Manju, Nisha, Pawan, Rani, Sewa; Antonio* (2), *Vito* (2), *Aldo, Alessio, Antonella, Donato, Enzio, Giorgio, Maurizio, Mauro, Sandro.*

Bassin (286) **1.** Jewish (eastern Ashkenazic): metronymic from the Yiddish female personal name *Basye*, a pet form of the biblical name *Bath Sheba* under the influence of Polish *Basia*, a pet form of *Barbara*. **2.** French: from *bassin* 'small basin', 'ladle', hence a metonymic occupational name for a maker or seller of such vessels.

GIVEN NAMES Jewish 5%. *Abbe, Myer, Sol.*

Bassinger (173) Variant spelling of German **Bäsiger** (see BASINGER).

Bassler (639) German (also **Bässler**): variant of BASLER.

Bassman (161) **1.** German (**Bassmann**): variant of the habitational name BASSE, with the addition of Middle High German *man* 'man'. **2.** Jewish (Ashkenazic): variant of BASS 4, with the addition of Yiddish *man* 'man'.

GIVEN NAMES Jewish 13%. *Gershon* (2), *Faigy, Hyman, Meyer, Naftoli, Yaakov.*

Basso (1367) **1.** Italian: in some cases from *Bassus*, a family name of the Republican period, from Latin *bassus* 'thickset', i.e. wide as opposed to tall; in others from a medieval nickname *Basso* meaning 'short', 'low', a derivative of *bassus*. **2.** Catalan: variant of BESSO.

GIVEN NAMES Italian 10%. *Salvatore* (5), *Angelo* (4), *Carmine* (4), *Rocco* (3), *Vito*

(3), *Aldo* (2), *Guido* (2), *Silvio* (2), *Amadeo, Antonella, Antonio, Attilio.*

Bast (996) **1.** German: from a short form of the personal name SEBASTIAN. **2.** French: from *bast* 'saddle pad for a beast of burden', hence perhaps a metonymic occupational name for a maker of such saddles or more probably a derogatory nickname.

Basta (434) Albanian: perhaps a derivative of the Arabic name *Bāsiṭ* 'enlarger' (an attribute of Allah). This name is also found in Italy, among the Albanian speakers of Calabria and Sicily.

GIVEN NAMES Muslim 5%. *Nabil* (5), *Adly, Attia, Hakeem, Hassan, Karim, Makram, Medhat, Mervat, Mohamed, Onsy, Sameh.*

Bastarache (166) French (of Basque origin): from Basque **Basterreche**, a topographic name for someone who lived in a house by a boundary, or on the edge of a settlement or the corner of a street, from *bazter* 'border', 'edge', 'corner' + *eche* 'house'.

GIVEN NAMES French 14%. *Raoul* (2), *Donat, Gisele, Michel, Ovila.*

Bastedo (186) Origin uncertain. Probably Dutch, of Southern French or Catalan origin, a topographic name for someone who lived by a fortification, French *bastide*, Occitan *bastido*. It may be a Huguenot name.

FOREBEARS This name was established in the early 18th century in NY and NJ.

Basten (199) German and French: variant of BASTIAN.

Bastian (2365) German and French: from a short form of the personal name SEBASTIAN.

FOREBEARS A Bastien or Basquin from Paris is documented in Montreal in 1690.

Bastianelli (158) Italian: from the personal name *Bastianello*, a pet form of *Sebastiano* (see SEBASTIAN).

GIVEN NAMES Italian 8%. *Alfredo* (2), *Amando* (2), *Guido* (2), *Antonella, Antonio, Enrico, Luciano, Rafael, Renaldo, Roberto, Umberto.*

Bastidas (148) Spanish: habitational name from Bastidas in Murcia, so named with Occitan *bastide* 'building' (Late Latin *bastita*, feminine singular or neuter plural past participle of *bastire* 'to build', of Germanic origin).

GIVEN NAMES Spanish 55%. *Carlos* (5), *Ruben* (4), *Cesar* (2), *Jose* (2), *Luis* (2), *Manuel* (2), *Miguel* (2), *Rafael* (2), *Alberto, Alfredo, Alvaro, Ana.*

Bastien (789) French: from *Bastien*, a short form of the personal name *Sébastien* (see SEBASTIAN).

GIVEN NAMES French 15%. *Andre* (3), *Armand* (3), *Emile* (2), *Gregoire* (2), *Jean Pierre* (2), *Lucienne* (2), *Marcel* (2), *Pierre* (2), *Yves* (2), *Alphonse, Camille, Edline.*

Bastin (705) **1.** English: from a reduced form of the personal name SEBASTIAN. **2.** French: from a diminutive of BAST.

Basting (118) English: unexplained; possibly a hypercorrected spelling of BASTIN.

Bastion (149) Southern French: from a diminutive of **Bastide**, a topographic name from Occitan *bastide* 'building' (Late Latin *bastita*, feminine singular or neuter plural past participle of *bastire* 'to build', of Germanic origin). The term was used in particular for a number of small fortified villages that were established in the 13th and 14th centuries in Gascony and Perigord and inhabited by free citizens.

Basto (113) Portuguese (and Spanish): habitational name from one of the places named Basto in Portugal, from *basto* 'dense (wood)'.
GIVEN NAMES Spanish 30%; Portuguese 7%. *Carlos* (4), *Jose* (2), *Reynaldo* (2), *Alejandro, Andres, Carlito, Humberto, Jaime, Javier, Lilia, Luiz, Luz*; *Guilherme*.

Baston (351) **1.** French and English: from Old French *bastun* 'stick', hence a nickname for a person of authority, an officious person, or perhaps for a beadle or verger. **2.** English: habitational name from Baston in Lincolnshire, named with the Old Norse personal name *Bak* + Old English *tūn* 'farmstead'.
GIVEN NAMES French 5%. *Andree* (2), *Almira, Pierre*.

Bastone (175) Italian: metonymic occupational name for a maker of seller of staffs and sticks, or from a nickname for a thin or rigid-looking person, from *bastone* 'stick'.
GIVEN NAMES Italian 22%. *Ettore* (2), *Cesare, Pasquale, Pietro, Santo, Vincenzo*.

Bastos (144) Portuguese and Galician: habitational name from any of various places in Portugal and Galicia (notably in Valgas, Pontevedra) called Bastos.
GIVEN NAMES Spanish 32%; Portuguese 18%; French 5%. *Fernando* (4), *Manuel* (4), *Ricardo* (2), *Abilio, Alberto, Ana Maria, Armindo, Augusto, Carlos, Carolina, Claudio, Gerado; Joao, Serafim; Antonio* (6), *Francesco; Andre, Dominique, Gisele*.

Bastow (178) English: variant of BARSTOW.

Bastyr (169) Czech (**Baštýř**): occupational name from *baštýř* 'fish master', 'pond keeper'.

Basu (364) Indian (Bengal) and Bangladeshi: Hindu (Kayasth) name, from Bengali *bošu* (from Sanskrit *vasu*, which has many meanings including 'wealth', 'gem', 'radiance'). It is an epithet of Shiva and of several other gods.
GIVEN NAMES Indian 82%. *Sankar* (5), *Amit* (4), *Amrita* (3), *Anindya* (3), *Asish* (3), *Gautam* (3), *Kalyan* (3), *Partha* (3), *Prabir* (3), *Shankar* (3), *Sharmila* (3), *Somnath* (3).

Basulto (140) Spanish (of Basque origin): variant of BASURTO.
GIVEN NAMES Spanish 49%. *Jose* (18), *Alfonso* (2), *Francisco* (2), *Javier* (2), *Manuel* (2), *Rafael* (2), *Trinidad* (2), *Amalia, Ana, Angel, Armando, Aurelio; Elio*.

Basurto (206) Castilianized form of Basque **Basurtu**, a habitational name from a town so named in Biscay, Basque Country, or topographic name from *basu* 'wood', 'forest' + an unattested *aurte* 'middle'.
GIVEN NAMES Spanish 48%. *Guadalupe* (4), *Jose* (4), *Juan* (4), *Roberto* (4), *Francisco* (3), *Ricardo* (3), *Alfonso* (2), *Alfredo* (2), *Guillermo* (2), *Gustavo* (2), *Raul* (2), *Adolfo; Antonio, Franco, Leonardo, Lucio*.

Baswell (259) Origin unidentified. It may be a variant of Scottish BOSWELL.

Basye (344) Variant of BASEY.

Bata (159) **1.** Turkish and Arabic: perhaps from Arabic *baṭṭa* 'duck'. **2.** Hungarian: from the old secular personal name *Bata*. **3.** Czech and Slovak (**Baťa** or **Bát'a**): from *bat'a* 'brother', 'mate', also used as a colloquial nickname for a blockhead.
GIVEN NAMES Muslim 6%. *Ahmed, Amer, Amin, Asif, Mazin, Munir, Sanaa, Shabir, Shiraz*.

Bataille (122) French: nickname for a bellicose man, from *bataille* 'battle', from Latin *battualia*.
GIVEN NAMES French 13%. *Brunel, Celine, Jacques*.

Batch (246) English and Welsh: variant of BACH 3 and 4.

Batchelder (1896) English: altered form of BATCHELOR, showing the folk-etymology influence of the word *elder*, with which it is not in fact connected.

Batcheller (242) English: variant of BATCHELOR.

Batchelor (3480) English: status name for a young knight or novice at arms, Middle English and Old French *bacheler* (medieval Latin *baccalarius*), a word of unknown ultimate origin. The word had already been extended to mean '(young) unmarried man' by the 14th century, but it is unlikely that many bearers of the surname derive from the word in that sense.
FOREBEARS The Reverend Stephen Bachiler (*c*.1561–1656) was a Puritan nonconformist, born in Hampshire, England, who came to New England in 1632, at the age of 71. In 1638/9 he was the leader of the founders of Hampton, NH.

Batcher (123) German (**Bätcher**): dialect variant of **Böttcher** (see BOETTCHER), or the Frisian cognates **Bätjer, Bötjer**.

Batchler (112) English: reduced form of BATCHELOR.

Batcho (104) Origin unidentified.

Batdorf (419) German: habitational name from an unidentified place, perhaps one called **Betdorf**.

Bate (705) English and Scottish: from the Middle English personal name *Bat(t)e*, a pet form of BARTHOLOMEW.

Bateman (6886) English and Scottish: occupational name meaning 'servant of Bate' (see BATE).

Baten (142) Muslim: from an Arabic personal name *Bāṭin*, literally 'inward', 'within'. *Al-Bāṭin* 'the Inner One' is one of the names of Allah.
GIVEN NAMES Muslim 17%. *Abdul* (8), *Mohammed Abdul* (2), *Mohammad, Mohammed, Samir, Shahriyar*.

Batenhorst (124) German: habitational name from a place near Gütersloh, Westphalia, named Batenhorst.
GIVEN NAME German 4%. *Kurt*.

Bater (106) English (Devon): occupational name from Old French *bateor* 'one who beats', possibly denoting a textile or metal worker.

Bates (32709) **1.** English: patronymic from BATE (see BARTHOLOMEW). **2.** Americanized form of German BETZ. See also BETTS.

Bateson (483) Northern English and Scottish: patronymic from BATE (see BARTHOLOMEW).

Batey (1062) English (mainly Northumberland): from a pet form of BARTHOLOMEW.

Bath (1052) **1.** English: habitational name from the city of Bath in western England, which is the site of sumptuous, but in the Middle Ages ruined, Roman baths. The place is named with the dative plural of Old English *bæð* 'bath'. In some cases the surname may have originated as a metonymic occupational name for an attendant at a public bath house. **2.** Scottish: reduced and altered form of McBETH. **3.** German: variant of BATHE. **4.** Indian (Panjab): Sikh name based on the name of a Jat clan.
GIVEN NAMES Indian 4%. *Dalbir, Renu, Sandeep, Suneet, Tarlok, Vikram*.

Bathe (163) **1.** English: habitational name from the city of Bath (see BATH 1) or from Bathe Barton in Devon, which is named with the same word. **2.** German: from a Germanic personal name formed with the element *badu* 'battle'.

Bathgate (184) Scottish: habitational name from a place in West Lothian, recorded *c*.1160 as *Batchet*, and probably derived from Brittonic *baeddgoed* 'boar wood'.

Bathke (268) German (**Bäthke**): variant spelling of German BETHKE.

Bathon (116) Origin unidentified; possibly a variant of French BATON (see BASTON).
GIVEN NAME French 4%. *Michel*.

Bathrick (172) Origin uncertain. Probably a variant of English **Battrick**, a Dorset name derived from the Old English personal name *Beadurīc* ('battle powerful').

Bathurst (331) English: habitational name from Bathurst in the parish of Warbleton, Sussex, named with the Old English personal name *Bada* (a short form of the various compound names formed with *beadu* 'battle') + Old English *hyrst* 'wooded hill'.

Batie (301) Scottish: pet form of BARTHOLOMEW.

Batista (1754) Spanish, Catalan, and Portuguese: from a medieval personal name (see BAPTISTE).

GIVEN NAMES Spanish 46%; Portuguese 14%. *Jose* (59), *Carlos* (22), *Juan* (20), *Rafael* (17), *Luis* (16), *Manuel* (16), *Julio* (15), *Pedro* (11), *Fernando* (10), *Francisco* (10), *Raul* (9), *Alberto* (8); *Joao* (9), *Joaquim* (3), *Afonso, Agostinho, Almir, Duarte, Paulo, Valentim, Vasco, Wenceslao; Antonio* (31), *Marino* (5), *Carmelo* (4), *Fausto* (3), *Sal* (2), *Amadeo, Annamarie, Filomena, Giorgio, Giovanna, Guido, Heriberto.*

Batiste (1201) French: variant of BAPTISTE.

GIVEN NAMES French 7%. *Antoine* (4), *Monique* (2), *Nolton* (2), *Alphonse, Anatole, Camille, Celina, Nelma, Pierre.*

Batko (117) Polish, Ukrainian, and Jewish (eastern Ashkenazic): from Ukrainian *batko* 'daddy'.

GIVEN NAMES Polish 14%. *Marcin* (2), *Halina, Janusz, Lukasz, Stanislaw.*

Batley (233) English: habitational name from Batley in West Yorkshire, named with the Old English personal name *Bata* (see BATT 2) + Old English *lēah* 'woodland clearing'.

Batliner (111) Swiss German (Liechtenstein): unexplained.

FOREBEARS Josef Batliner came to America from Liechenstein in the early 1830s.

GIVEN NAME German 4%. *Mathias.*

Batman (308) English: status name meaning 'servant of Batte' (see BATT).

Baton (116) French (**Bâton**): see BASTON.

Bator (459) Hungarian (**Bátor**) and Polish: nickname from Hungarian *bátor* 'bold' 'brave'. In some cases the Hungarian name may be from the old secular personal name *Bátor* (which is from the vocabulary word). The Transylvanian Báthori dynasty of the 16th–17th centuries was named for one of the family's estates, the village of Bátor. One of its rulers, István Báthori (Stefan Batory in Polish), became king of Poland, hence the spread of the name into Poland.

GIVEN NAMES Polish 7%. *Danuta* (2), *Zbigniew* (2), *Aleksander, Andrzej, Boguslaw, Casimir, Irena, Krzysztof, Miroslaw, Zofia.*

Batra (278) Indian (Panjab): Hindu (Arora) and Sikh name of unknown meaning, based on the name of a clan in the Arora community.

GIVEN NAMES Indian 90%. *Anil* (8), *Sanjay* (6), *Ashok* (4), *Harish* (4), *Raj* (4), *Rajeev* (4), *Subhash* (4), *Devender* (3), *Dinesh* (3), *Manju* (3), *Rajiv* (3), *Rakesh* (3).

Batres (329) Spanish: habitational name from Batres in Madrid province. There are many bearers of this name in Guatamala and Mexico.

GIVEN NAMES Spanish 52%. *Jose* (21), *Carlos* (6), *Francisco* (5), *Juan* (5), *Ana* (3), *Arturo* (3), *Javier* (3), *Jorge* (3), *Julio* (3), *Luis* (3), *Pedro* (3), *Ricardo* (3).

Batson (3215) English: patronymic from BATT 1 and 2.

Batt (1333) **1.** English: like BATE, a derivative of the Middle English personal name *Batte*, a pet form of BARTHOLOMEW. **2.** English: possibly from a Middle English survival of an Old English personal name or byname *Bata*, of uncertain origin and meaning, but perhaps akin to *batt* 'cudgel' and so, as a byname, given to a thickset man or a belligerent one. **3.** English: topographic name, of uncertain meaning. That it is a topographic name seems clear from examples such as Walter atte Batte (Somerset 1327), but the meaning of the term is in doubt although it is found in medieval field names. **4.** German: from a medieval personal name (Latin *Beatus* 'Blessed'), bestowed in honor of the apostle who was reputed to have brought Christianity to Switzerland and southern Germany.

Batta (142) Indian (Panjab): Hindu name of unknown meaning, based on the name of a subgroup among the Tank goldsmiths of Panjab.

GIVEN NAMES Indian 16%. *Anil, Raghu, Rajiv, Ram, Ramesh, Ravi, Satish.*

Battaglia (2901) Italian: from *battaglia* 'battle', 'fight' (a feminine noun from the Late Latin neuter plural *battualia* 'military exercises'), applied as a nickname for a combative person, or a topographic name for someone who lived at a place remembered as the site of a battle.

GIVEN NAMES Italian 13%. *Salvatore* (11), *Angelo* (8), *Sal* (7), *Santo* (6), *Rocco* (5), *Cosmo* (4), *Domenic* (4), *Vito* (4), *Antonino* (3), *Antonio* (3), *Biagio* (3), *Concetta* (3).

Battaglini (184) Italian: patronymic or plural form of BATTAGLINO.

GIVEN NAMES Italian 14%. *Dante* (2), *Antonio, Dino, Dominico, Giuseppe, Guido, Mauro, Pasquale, Tullio.*

Battaglino (124) Italian: from a diminutive of BATTAGLIA.

GIVEN NAMES Italian 18%. *Luigi* (2), *Alfonso, Antonio, Emilio, Mario.*

Batte (281) English: variant spelling of BATT.

Batten (2746) English: from a pet form of BATT (1 or 2).

Battenfield (199) Americanized form of German **Battenfeld**, a habitational name from a place so named in Hesse (near Frankenberg). *Batten* may be the genitive of a Germanic personal name meaning 'battle'.

Batterman (296) German (**Battermann**): of uncertain origin. It could be an occupational name for a merchant or peddler, from *Bartermann*, or possibly from a short form of BERTRAM + Middle High German *man* 'man'.

GIVEN NAMES German 4%. *Erwin, Frieda, Helmuth, Kurt.*

Battersby (396) English: habitational name from Battersby in North Yorkshire, named with the genitive case of the Old Norse personal name *Bǫðvarr* (composed of the elements *baðwa* 'battle' + *harjaz* 'warrior') + Old Norse *býr* 'settlement'.

Battershell (206) English: probably a habitational name from a lost or unidentified place; the forms **Battershall** and **Battershill** are also found.

Batterson (431) English: patronymic from *Batten* or *Batty*, pet forms of BATT 1 and 2.

Batterton (364) English: probably a habitational name from a lost or unidentified place.

Battey (389) **1.** English: variant spelling of BATTY. **2.** Americanized spelling of German **Bethe**, from a short form of the personal names *Elisabeth, Bertold*, or *Bertram*.

Battiato (122) Southern Italian (Sicily): nickname from the Sicilian dialect word *battiatu* 'baptized', by extension 'Christian'. The name was probably added routinely to the personal name or names of a new Christian convert.

GIVEN NAMES Italian 9%. *Angelo, Matteo.*

Battin (497) English: from a pet form of BATT 1 or 2.

Battis (160) Reduced form of French BAPTISTE.

Battista (1480) Italian: from the personal name *Battista*, derived from the distinguishing epithet of St. John the Baptist, *San Giovanni Battista.*

GIVEN NAMES Italian 14%. *Angelo* (8), *Carmine* (5), *Donato* (4), *Gino* (4), *Guido* (4), *Vito* (4), *Antonio* (3), *Luigi* (3), *Cosmo* (2), *Dante* (2), *Domenic* (2), *Elio* (2).

Battiste (342) French Canadian variant of BAPTISTE.

GIVEN NAMES French 4%. *Alphonse, Fontane, Francois, Jacques.*

Battistelli (134) Italian: patronymic from *Battistello*, a pet form of the personal name BATTISTA.

GIVEN NAMES Italian 9%. *Angelo, Paolo.*

Battisti (313) Italian: patronymic or plural form of BATTISTA.

GIVEN NAMES Italian 15%; French 4%. *Angelo* (2), *Egidio* (2), *Amadeo, Carlo, Fiorino, Gino, Giuseppe, Ignazio, Italo, Manlio, Rocco, Romeo; Armand* (3).

Battistoni (191) Italian: from a derivative of the personal name BATTISTA.

GIVEN NAMES Italian 6%. *Angelo, Domenic, Fabrizio, Gino, Nicola.*

Battle (5730) English and Scottish (of Norman origin): habitational name from a place named as having been the site of a battle, from Old French *bataille* 'battle'. In some cases, this may be Battle in Sussex, site of the Battle of Hastings, but this name was taken to Scotland by a family from Umfreville, France, in the early 13th century.

FOREBEARS A John Battle from Yorkshire, England, settled in 1654 on the Nansemond, a stream in VA. His descendants became prominent in NC and GA.

Battles (2190) English: variant of BATTLE.

Batton (835) **1.** English: from a pet form of BATT 1 or 2. **2.** French: variant of BASTON. FOREBEARS Huguenot families named Bat(t)on from Picardy settled in SC in the early 18th century.

Batts (2364) English: patronymic from BATT 1 or 2.

Batty (750) English (chiefly Yorkshire): from a pet form of BATT 1 or 2.

Baty (1204) English (chiefly Northumberland): variant spelling of BATTY.

Batz (431) Swiss German: **1.** from Alemannic, Swabian *Batz* 'pile', 'large quantity', possibly applied as a nickname either for a man of large physical proportions or for a man of wealth. The term also denoted a coin and may have been used metonymically for a coiner. The name of the coin is believed to have been derived from its imprint of a bear, known in folklore as *Betz* or *Petz*. **2.** (Bätz): see BETZ.

Batzel (226) South German: from a diminutive of BATZ (the coin).

Batzer (152) German (**Bätzer**): Swabian nickname for a braggart, from an agent derivative of *bätzen* 'to boast or show off'.

GIVEN NAME German 4%. *Siegfried.*

Bau (164) **1.** German: of uncertain origin; probably from Old High German *būan* 'to live at a place', or an occupational name from Middle High German *bū, bou* 'cultivation' or perhaps from a short form of compounds with this element, such as *Bauhofer*, BAUMANN. **2.** French: of uncertain origin. Perhaps a variant of BEAU meaning 'handsome', though it has also been suggested that it may derive from an obsolete personal name of Germanic origin. **3.** Chinese 鮑: variant of BAO 1. **4.** Chinese 包: variant of BAO 2. **5.** Chinese 暴: variant of BAO 3.

FOREBEARS A Bau from the Angoumois region in France is recorded in Montreal in 1667; another, also known as Lebeau and Lalouette, from the Poitou region, is documented in Boucherville, Quebec, in 1672.

Baublitz (266) Variant spelling of German **Boblitz**, a habitational name from a place near Bautzen.

Bauch (577) German: nickname for a fat man, from Middle High German *būch* 'belly', 'paunch' or from a homonym meaning 'stick', 'cudgel'.

GIVEN NAMES German 8%. *Kurt* (3), *Gerhard* (2), *Siegfried* (2), *Eldred, Ewald, Helmut, Lotti, Manfred.*

Bauchman (100) German (**Bauchmann**): nickname for a man with a protruding stomach, from Middle High German *būch* 'belly', 'paunch' + *man* 'man'.

Bauck (107) Probably a respelling of German BAUCH.

GIVEN NAMES German 5%. *Juergen, Theodor.*

Baucom (1657) Altered spelling of English **Balcombe** (see BALCOM).

Baucum (450) Altered spelling of English **Balcombe** (see BALCOM).

Baudendistel (194) German: nickname for a poor peasant farmer, meaning 'grow the thistle', recorded in late Middle High German as *Buwendistel*, from *būwen* 'to grow' + *distil* 'thistle'.

GIVEN NAMES German 5%. *Kurt, Mathias.*

Bauder (919) German (Swabian): nickname for a pugnacious person, from an agent derivative of Middle High German *buden* 'to hit'.

Baudhuin (118) French: variant spelling of BAUDOIN.

Baudin (102) French: from a pet form of a Germanic personal name from *bald* 'bold', 'brave'.

GIVEN NAMES French 14%. *Antoine, Clothilde, Jacques, Jean-Paul, Pierre.*

Baudo (122) Italian: Piedmontese variant (also found in Sicily) of Italian BALDO.

GIVEN NAMES Italian 16%. *Salvatore* (3), *Carmello.*

Baudoin (544) French: from a Germanic personal name composed of the elements *bald* 'bold', 'brave' + *win* 'friend' (see BALDWIN).

GIVEN NAMES French 10%. *Raywood* (3), *Camille* (2), *Etienne* (2), *Adrien, Alcide, Andre, Firmin, Francoise, Jean-Yves, Laurent, Minos, Sylvain.*

Bauer (27069) German and Jewish (Ashkenazic): status name for a peasant or nickname meaning 'neighbor', 'fellow citizen', from Middle High German *(ge)būr*, Middle Low German *bur*, denoting an occupant of a *būr*, a small dwelling or building. Compare Old English *būr*, modern English *bower*. This word later fell together with Middle High German *būwære*, an agent noun from Old High German *būan* 'to cultivate', later also (at first in Low German dialects) 'to build'. The German surname thus has two possible senses: 'peasant' and 'neighbor', 'fellow citizen'. The precise meaning of the Jewish surname, which is of later formation, is unclear. This surname is also found elsewhere in central and eastern Europe, for example in Slovenia, where it may also be a translation of KMET.

GIVEN NAMES German 4%. *Kurt* (44), *Hans* (22), *Otto* (21), *Erwin* (15), *Fritz* (8), *Helmut* (8), *Heinz* (7), *Manfred* (7), *Franz* (6), *Gerhard* (6), *Johannes* (5), *Wolfgang* (5).

Bauerle (550) South German (**Bäuerle**): from a Swabian diminutive of BAUER.

GIVEN NAMES German 5%. *Bernhard* (2), *Albrecht, Helmut, Horst, Lothar, Merwin, Otto.*

Bauerlein (131) German (**Bäuerlein**): standardized diminutive of BAUER, originally occurring in southern dialects as **Bäuerle**, **Beuerle**, **Beyerle**.

GIVEN NAMES German 5%. *Gerhard, Gunther.*

Bauermeister (223) German: modernized spelling of BURMEISTER.

GIVEN NAMES German 9%. *Kurt* (2), *Hans, Kuno, Otto.*

Bauernfeind (199) South German: literally 'enemy of the peasants' (from Middle High German *gebūr(e)* 'farmer', 'peasant' + *vīant* 'enemy'), used as a nickname for a robber knight or mercenary soldier.

Bauers (348) German: patronymic from BAUER.

Bauersfeld (100) German: topographic name, a variant of **Bauerfeld**, perhaps a standardized form of Middle Low German *būr-esch* 'open, unfenced field for cultivation' + *feld* 'open country'.

Baugh (4284) **1.** Anglicized form of Welsh BACH. **2.** Americanized form of German BACH.

Baughan (357) Welsh: from *bychan*, a diminutive of *bach* 'little' (see BACH 4).

FOREBEARS A Welsh family of this name was established from an early date in Great Rollright, Oxfordshire, England. The name was probably brought to North America from Oxfordshire rather than Wales.

Baugher (1253) Americanized spelling of German **Bager** or **Bäger** (see BEGER), or BACHER.

FOREBEARS This is the name of a Pennsylvania family descended from Johann Georg Bager, a Lutheran clergyman who migrated to Lebanon country, PA, in 1752.

Baughman (5379) Probably an Americanized form of German and Jewish BACHMANN.

Baughn (802) Welsh: variant spelling of BAUGHAN.

Bauguess (282) See BAUGUS.

Baugus (359) Probably an altered form of English **Boggess** (see BOGGS).

Bauknecht (191) German (Württemberg): occupational name for a farm worker, from Middle High German *būknecht* 'plowboy', 'farmhand'.

GIVEN NAMES German 7%. *Ewald, Gottlob, Heinz, Kurt.*

Bauknight (168) Partly Americanized form of German BAUKNECHT.

Baulch (121) English: variant of BALCH.

Bauler (145) German: **1.** probably a variant of BAUER. **2.** from a derivative of PAUL, a nickname for a lay person who worked at a Paulinian monastery or who was connected with one in some other way.

Bault (132) French: **1.** from the Germanic personal name *Baldo*, a short form of the various compound names with the first element *bald* 'bold'. **2.** nickname for a lively person, from Old French *baud* 'joyful', 'abandoned' (a word of Germanic origin—see above—but with an altered sense).

Baum (7096) **1.** German: topographic name for someone who lived by a tree that was particularly noticeable in some way, from Middle High German, Old High

German *boum* 'tree', or else a nickname for a particularly tall person. **2.** Jewish (Ashkenazic): ornamental name from German *Baum* 'tree', or a short form of any of the many ornamental surnames containing this word as the final element, for example **Feigenbaum** 'fig tree' (see FEIGE) and *Mandelbaum* 'almond tree' (see MANDEL). **3.** English: probably a variant spelling of **Balm**, a metonymic occupational name for a seller of spices and perfumes, Middle English, Old French *basme*, *balme*, *ba(u)me* 'balm', 'ointment' (see BALMER).

Bauman (7194) Respelling of German BAUMANN or Jewish (Ashkenazic) or Scandinavian spelling of the same name.

Baumann (6177) German, Dutch, Jewish (Ashkenazic): status name for a peasant or a nickname meaning 'neighbor', 'fellow citizen' (see BAUER).

GIVEN NAMES German 6%. *Kurt* (15), *Hans* (12), *Erwin* (8), *Otto* (7), *Gerhard* (5), *Ernst* (4), *Heinz* (4), *Guenter* (3), *Armin* (2), *Dieter* (2), *Erna* (2), *Friedrich* (2).

Baumbach (674) German: habitational name from a place named Baumbach, for example in Hesse, Baden, Westphalia.

GIVEN NAMES German 4%. *Erwin* (2), *Klaus* (2), *Frieda*, *Kurt*, *Otto*, *Wolf*.

Baumberger (352) German: **1.** habitational name for someone from any of several places called Bamberg, for example in Rhineland and Bavaria, from Old High German *boum* 'tree' + *berg* 'mountain', 'hill'. **2.** possibly a variant of the habitational name BAMBERGER, from an earlier form of the place name, *Bomberg*.

GIVEN NAMES German 4%. *Kurt* (2), *Horst*.

Baumeister (683) German: occupational name for a builder, from Middle High German *būwen* 'to build' + *meister* 'master'.

GIVEN NAMES German 4%. *Alfons*, *Ernst*, *Gerhard*, *Hans*, *Hans-Peter*, *Konrad*, *Kurt*, *Mechthild*, *Wolfgang*.

Baumel (179) **1.** South German and Austrian: (**Bäumel**): either from a diminutive of BAUM, or from a contracted form of **Baumhöwel**, an occupational name for a tree feller. **2.** Jewish (eastern Ashkenazic): ornamental name from German *Baumöl* 'olive oil', literally 'tree oil'.

GIVEN NAMES French 5%; Jewish 4%. *Monique*, *Raoul*; *Faina*.

Baumer (781) German: **1.** (also **Bäumer**) from an agent derivative of BAUM 1. **2.** in Westphalia *Bäumer* denotes an occupational name for a border or customs official, from Middle Low German *bōm* 'barrier' + *-er* suffix of agent nouns.

GIVEN NAMES German 4%. *Erwin* (5), *Christoph*, *Gerhard*, *Kurt*, *Manfred*, *Otto*.

Baumert (365) German: variant of BAUMER, an occupational name for a tree farmer or a woodman.

GIVEN NAMES German 4%. *Alfons*, *Egon*, *Hans*, *Kurt*, *Wilfried*.

Baumgard (154) German and Jewish (Ashkenazic): variant of BAUMGARTEN.

Baumgardner (2321) Partial Americanized form of BAUMGARTNER.

Baumgardt (163) German: variant of BAUMGARTEN.

GIVEN NAMES German 5%. *Fritz*, *Horst*.

Baumgarner (151) German and Jewish (Ashkenazic): variant of BAUMGARTNER.

Baumgart (1040) German and Jewish: variant of BAUMGARTEN.

GIVEN NAMES German 6%. *Otto* (4), *Helmut* (3), *Kurt* (3), *Hans* (2), *Alfons*, *Dietrich*, *Eldor*, *Erwin*, *Fritz*, *Gerhard*, *Guenther*, *Hanns*.

Baumgartel (109) South German (**Baumgärt(e)l**): from a pet form of BAUMGARTEN.

GIVEN NAMES German 8%. *Armin* (2), *Kurt*.

Baumgarten (1107) German and Jewish (Ashkenazic): topographic or metonymic occupational name for someone who owned or lived by an orchard or was employed in one, from Middle High German *boumgarte* 'orchard' (a compound of *boum* 'tree' + *garte* 'enclosure'), German *Baumgarten*. There are also several villages named with this word, and so in some cases the surname may have originated as a habitational name from one of these. As a Jewish name, it is mainly ornamental.

GIVEN NAMES German 6%. *Kurt* (5), *Erwin* (2), *Hans* (2), *Horst* (2), *Klaus* (2), *Otto* (2), *Ewald*, *Lothar*, *Wilhelm*.

Baumgartner (4728) German and Swiss German (also **Baumgärtner**): occupational name for someone who owned or worked in an orchard, from an agent derivative of BAUMGARTEN, or habitational name for someone from any of various minor places called Baumgarten.

GIVEN NAMES German 4%. *Kurt* (12), *Fritz* (4), *Hans* (4), *Helmut* (4), *Alois* (3), *Otto* (3), *Erwin* (2), *Johann* (2), *Meggan* (2), *Dietmar*, *Ernst*, *Franz*.

Baumhardt (179) German: nickname for a man 'as strong as a tree', from Middle High German *boum* 'tree' + *herte* 'hardy', 'strong'. Compare BAUMSTARK.

Baumhover (147) German: habitational name for someone from Baumhof in Bavaria, or a topographic name from a field name meaning 'orchard', 'enclosed stand of trees'.

Baumiller (126) Partly Americanized form of German **Baumüller**, from a status or occupational name for a miller who owned a farm or who was under a feudal obligation to run one.

Baumler (304) German (mostly **Bäumler**): from an agent derivative of BAUM 1, as a topographic name for someone who lived by a large or otherwise remarkable tree, or an occupational name for a tree warden, a specialist employed by a community to look after the trees, in particular fruit trees,

from Middle High German *boumen* 'to make tree plantings'.

GIVEN NAMES German 6%. *Fritz*, *Gunther*, *Hans*, *Johann*, *Kurt*, *Otto*.

Baumstark (168) German: nickname for a strong man, from Middle High German *boum* 'tree' + *starc* 'strong'.

GIVEN NAMES German 7%. *Alfons*, *Kurt*, *Viktor*.

Baumunk (104) German: unexplained.

GIVEN NAME German 5%. *Siegmund* (2).

Baun (339) Probably a reduced form of Welsh BAUGHAN.

Baunach (107) German: habitational name from a place near Bamberg called Baunach, which lies near the confluence of the Baunach river with the Main.

GIVEN NAME German 5%. *Albrecht*.

Baune (173) French: **1.** habitational name from a place named Beaune, examples of which are found in Allier, Côte-d'or, and Loire. The place name is derived from Gallic *Belena*, feminine form of *Belenos*, the name of a Gallic deity. **2.** (**Bauné**): habitational name from Bauné in Maine-et-Loire.

Baur (1178) South German: variant of BAUER.

GIVEN NAMES German 5%. *Hans* (4), *Kurt* (3), *Uli* (2), *Ulrich* (2), *Alfons*, *Arno*, *Erwin*, *Friedrich*, *Fritz*, *Urs*, *Wilhelm*, *Wolfgang*.

Baures (104) German: probably an altered form of **Baureis**, of uncertain origin, or an altered spelling of BARES.

Baus (438) German: **1.** of Slavic origin but uncertain meaning. **2.** perhaps from a Swabian dialect word meaning 'armful', 'great many', 'feast', and hence a nickname for a gourmand. Compare FAUS.

Bausch (721) South German: **1.** from Middle High German *būsch* 'fluffy ball', a nickname for a puffed-up person or someone with a touchy personality. **2.** variant of BAUS.

GIVEN NAMES German 5%. *Dieter* (2), *Kurt* (2), *Erwin*, *Friedrich*, *Gebhard*, *Otto*, *Sigfried*.

Bauser (111) South German: nickname for a heavy drinker and eater or spendthrift, from an agent derivative of Middle High German *būzen* 'to feast'.

Bauserman (309) South German: variant of BAUSER.

Bausman (232) South German (**Bausmann**): variant of BAUSER.

Baust (107) German: **1.** in southern Germany, a variant of BAUSCH, with the addition of an inorganic *-t*, but more often from a reduced form of the personal name SEBASTIAN. **2.** in eastern Germany, a variant of **Paust**, which is possibly a topographic name from Sorbian *pūst* (Polish *pusty*) 'bleak', 'desolate', 'uncultivated', or a nickname from Middle Low German *pūsten* 'to blow', 'to breathe with difficulty'.

GIVEN NAME French 4%; German 4%. *Otto*.

Baustian (120) German: variant of BAS-TIAN.

Bautch (218) Altered spelling of German BAUCH.

Baute (135) **1.** French: variant of BAULT. **2.** German: unexplained.
GIVEN NAMES Spanish 4%. *Alfonso, Caridad, Estrella, Noemi, Raimundo.*

Bautista (3732) Spanish: from the personal name *Bautista*, Spanish form of BAPTIST.
GIVEN NAMES Spanish 51%; Italian 9%. *Jose* (91), *Juan* (59), *Jesus* (31), *Francisco* (30), *Manuel* (28), *Luis* (22), *Mario* (22), *Carlos* (21), *Miguel* (18), *Roberto* (18), *Guadalupe* (17), *Jorge* (16); *Antonio* (29), *Romeo* (7), *Lorenzo* (6), *Constantino* (3), *Leonardo* (3), *Carlo* (2), *Carmelina* (2), *Ciro* (2), *Dario* (2), *Erminio* (2), *Federico* (2), *Lucio* (2).

Bautz (186) South German: nickname from Middle High German *butz* 'apple core', 'little fellow'.

Bauwens (182) Dutch and German (Lower Rhine): patronymic from *Bauwen, Boude-wijn*, a Germanic personal name composed of the elements *bald* 'bold', 'brave' + *wine* 'friend' (see BALDWIN), or according to one authority from *Bau, Bauwe*, an unexplained element.
GIVEN NAME French 4%. *Andre.*

Bauza (153) Catalan (**Bauzà**): unflattering nickname from *bausà* 'foolish', 'silly'.
GIVEN NAMES Spanish 31%. *Juan* (3), *Jose* (2), *Miguel* (2), *Pedro* (2), *Ramon* (2), *Adelaida, Alejandro, Amalia, Ana, Arminda, Arturo, Carlos*; *Antonio* (2), *Angelo, Giraldo.*

Bava (156) **1.** Italian: derogatory nickname from *bava* 'dribble', 'slime'. **2.** Indian: variant of BAWA.
GIVEN NAMES Italian 11%; Indian 4%. *Antonio* (3), *Aldo* (2), *Gino* (2); *Sharmila.*

Bavaro (321) Italian: ethnic name from *bavaro* 'Bavarian', i.e. someone from Bavaria, now part of Germany, but former-ly an independent kingdom.
GIVEN NAMES Italian 23%. *Vito* (5), *Angelo* (3), *Antonio* (2), *Gaetano* (2), *Onofrio* (2), *Antoninette, Benedetto, Carmela, Damiano, Dino, Domenico, Gino.*

Baver (172) **1.** English (York): perhaps a variant of BEAVER. **2.** Dutch: unexplained. Perhaps a variant of BAUER.

Bavis (110) English: probably a variant spelling of BEVIS.

Bawa (120) Indian (Panjab): Sikh name based on the name of a Jat clan. It is also a title given to the male descendants of the first three Sikh gurus.
GIVEN NAMES Indian 73%; Muslim 9%. *Raj* (2), *Ajay, Alpana, Anju, Arvind, Balraj, Darshan, Deepak, Devendra, Gurmukh, Harish*; *Abdul, Altaf, Kamal, Nazir, Salah, Shaheda.*

Bawcum (100) Respelling of English **Balcombe** (see BALCOM).

Bawden (421) English: from a late variant of the Norman personal name BALDWIN.

Bax (533) **1.** English: patronymic from BACK 2. **2.** German: from a short form of a Germanic personal name, related to Old High German *bāgan* 'to fight'. **3.** North German form of BACKHAUS.

Baxa (269) French and Spanish: unex-plained.
GIVEN NAMES Spanish 6%. *Alfonso* (2), *Alicia, Artemio, Benedicto, Efren, Francisca, Jose, Joselito, Marciano, Pacifico, Rudolfo, Teresita.*

Baxendale (207) English (Lancashire): habitational name, probably an altered form of **Baxenden**, a place near Accring-ton, which is named with an unattested Old English word *bæcstān* 'bakestone' (a flat stone on which bread was baked) + *denu* 'valley'. Middle English *dale* was some-times substituted for Old English *denu* in northern place names.

Baxley (2505) English: probably a variant of BEXLEY.

Baxter (17839) Northern English and Scottish: occupational name from Old Eng-lish *bæcestre* 'baker', variant (originally a feminine form) of *bæcere* (see BAKER).

Bay (2198) **1.** English, French, and Dutch: nickname for someone with chestnut or auburn hair, from Middle English, Old French *bay, bai*, Middle Dutch *bay* 'red-dish brown' (Latin *badius*, used originally of horses). **2.** English: from the Middle English personal name *Baye*, Old English *Bēaga* (masculine) or *Bēage* (feminine). **3.** Scottish: reduced form of MCBETH. **4.** German: from the Germanic personal name *Baio*. **5.** The name is also found in Denmark and Norway, where it may be a short form of German BAYER or from *baygh*, originally a loan word from French denoting a type of fabric.

Bayard (479) English and French: **1.** nick-name for a reckless person, from Middle English, Old French *baiard, baiart* 'fool-hardy' (the name—a derivative of *baie* 'reddish brown'—of the magnificent but reckless horse given to Renaud by Charle-magne, according to medieval romances). **2.** metonymic occupational name for a car-rier, from Middle English, Old French *ba-iard, baiart* 'hand barrow', 'open cart'.
FOREBEARS A Huguenot family of this name migrated from France to Antwerp in the 16th century. In 1647 Anna Bayard, widow of Samuel Bayard, and her three young children accompanied her brother Peter Stuyvesant to New Amsterdam aboard the *Princess*. Her sons Petrus and Nicolas Bayard, both born in Alphen, Netherlands, had many prominent descendants in North America. Peter Stuyvesant's wife Judith was a Bayard.
GIVEN NAMES French 6%. *Pierre* (2), *Vilaire* (2), *Alcee, Antoine, Franck, Ghislaine, Marcel.*

Baye (231) English and Dutch: variant spelling of BAY.

Bayer (4250) German, Scandinavian, and Jewish (Ashkenazic): regional name for someone from Bavaria (German *Bayern*). This region of southern Germany derives its name from that of the Celtic tribe of the *Boii* who once inhabited this area. They were displaced in the 6th century AD by a Germanic people, the *Boioarii* or *Baiuarii*, whose name is derived from that of their Celtic predecessors.
GIVEN NAMES German 4%. *Helmut* (5), *Kurt* (4), *Otto* (4), *Klaus* (3), *Manfred* (3), *Bernd* (2), *Bernhard* (2), *Erwin* (2), *Franz* (2), *Hans* (2), *Johann* (2), *Juergen* (2).

Bayerl (140) German: from a pet form of BAYER.

Bayers (149) German: variant of BAYER.
GIVEN NAMES German 4%. *Elfriede, Kurt.*

Bayes (701) English: patronymic from the Middle English personal name *Baye* (see BAY).

Bayha (124) German: variant of **Böhm** (see BOHM).
GIVEN NAMES German 8%. *Hedwig, Otto.*

Bayle (185) French and English: topograph-ic name for someone who lived by the outer wall of a castle (see BAILEY 2).
GIVEN NAMES French 11%. *Emile* (2), *Aime, Henri, Jean Claude, Pierre.*

Bayles (1130) English: variant spelling of BAILES.

Bayless (2404) English: variant spelling of BAYLISS.

Bayley (773) English: variant spelling of BAILEY.

Bayliff (183) English: variant of BAILIFF. See also BAYLISS.

Baylin (102) Jewish: variant spelling of BAILIN.
GIVEN NAMES Jewish 10%. *Kahn, Meyer.*

Baylis (662) English: variant of BAYLISS.

Bayliss (865) English: occupational name for an officer of a court of justice, whose duties included serving writs, distraining goods, and (formerly) arresting people. In England formerly it was also a status name for the chief officer of a hundred (adminis-trative subdivision of a county). The deriva-tion is from Middle English, Old French *bailis*, from Late Latin *baiulivus* (adjec-tive), 'pertaining to an attendant or porter' (see BAILEY).
FOREBEARS Thomas Baylies, a prominent Quaker, came to Boston from London in 1737.

Baylon (130) Spanish: variant of **Bailón** (see BAILON).
GIVEN NAMES Spanish 36%. *Jose* (4), *Francisco* (2), *Mario* (2), *Raul* (2), *Renato* (2), *Armando, Baudelio, Cristina, Edmundo, Felipe, Florencio, Guillerma*; *Angelo, Antonio, Leonardo, Romeo.*

Baylor (1868) **1.** English: variant spelling of BAILOR. **2.** Respelling of German BAILER or **Bayler** (see BEILER).

Bayly (340) English: variant spelling of BAILEY.

Bayman (178) **1.** English (mainly Lancashire): unexplained; perhaps 'servant of BAY'. **2.** Altered spelling of German **Beumann** or **Bäumann**, variants of BAUMANN.

Baynard (466) English: from a Germanic personal name introduced to Britain from France by the Normans, composed of an unexplained first element (possibly akin to Old Norse *beinn* 'straight') + *hard* 'brave', 'hardy', 'strong'.

Bayne (2087) Scottish, English, and French: variant spelling of BAIN.

Baynes (871) English: variant spelling of BAINES.

Baynham (174) English (West Midlands and Wales): variant of Welsh BENNION.

Bayona (101) **1.** Galician: habitational name from Bayona in Pontevedra province, Galicia. **2.** Castilianized form of Basque **Baiona**, a habitational name from a town in the Basque province of Lapurdi.
GIVEN NAMES Spanish 52%. *Luis* (3), *Raul* (3), *Delfina* (2), *Eduardo* (2), *Jose* (2), *Manuel* (2), *Roberto* (2), *Arturo*, *Belkys*, *Blanca*, *Carlos*, *Cesar*.

Bays (2191) English: patronymic from BAY.

Baysden (136) English: unexplained; compare BAISDEN.

Bayse (130) English (East Midlands): variant of BAYES.

Baysinger (714) Americanized spelling of German **Bösinger** (see BASINGER).

Bayuk (183) Ukrainian: nickname from a noun derivative of *bayaty* 'to entertain or amuse people'.

Bayus (160) **1.** Probably a variant spelling of English BAYES. **2.** Lithuanian (**Bajus**): nickname for a rich man, from a derivative of Belorussian or Russian *bai* 'rich'.

Baz (110) Arabic: from a personal name meaning 'falcon', borne by, among others, Lebanese Christians. It is also found as a Spanish name, of the same origin.
GIVEN NAMES Spanish 23%; Arabic 8%; French 7%. *Luis* (4), *Javier* (3), *Jose* (2), *Raul* (2), *Alberto*, *Carlos*, *Donaldo*, *Librada*, *Rogelio*, *Xavier*; *Afif*, *Amr*, *Ghassan*, *Imad*, *Inaam*, *Maan*, *Maher*; *Chantal* (2), *Jacques*.

Bazaldua (133) Variant of Basque BASALDUA, a habitational name from Basaldua in Biscay province.
GIVEN NAMES Spanish 60%. *Juan* (5), *Efrain* (3), *Jose* (3), *Mario* (3), *Pablo* (3), *Guadalupe* (2), *Jorge* (2), *Pedro* (2), *Salvador* (2), *Adela*, *Alberto*, *Alfredo*.

Bazan (992) **1.** Spanish (**Bazán**; of Basque origin): Castilianized form of Basque **Baztan**, a habitational name from Baztan in Navarre province, named from Basque *aza*, *azta* 'bramble' + the locative suffix *-an*, with the addition of initial *B-*. **2.** Polish and Ukrainian: from Polish *bażant* 'pheasant' (from Middle High German *fasan(t)*), hence a nickname for some-

one thought to resemble the bird in some way.
GIVEN NAMES Spanish 34%. *Jose* (16), *Juan* (15), *Carlos* (12), *Jorge* (7), *Mario* (6), *Pedro* (6), *Miguel* (5), *Francisco* (4), *Guadalupe* (4), *Manuel* (4), *Ricardo* (4), *Rodolfo* (4).

Bazar (281) Polish, Ukrainian, and Jewish (eastern Ashkenazic): **1.** from *bazar* 'market', 'marketplace', hence a metonymic occupational name for a market trader. **2.** Jewish (from Ukraine): habitational name from a place in Ukraine called Bazar.

Baze (447) **1.** German and French: from the Germanic personal name *Boso* (see BOOS). **2.** German: Americanized form of BOESE, nickname for a bad or worthless person, from Middle High German *bœse* 'evil', 'mean'.

Bazemore (1103) Respelling of German **Bessemer**, an occupational name for a broom maker, from an agent derivative of Middle High German *besem* 'broom'.

Bazen (151) Variant of French BAZIN.

Bazer (139) Jewish (Ashkenazic): variant spelling of BEISER.
GIVEN NAMES Russian 4%. *Arkadiy*, *Modest*.

Bazil (167) French: variant spelling of BASIL.
GIVEN NAMES French 6%. *Andre*, *Anite*, *Maryse*, *Raoul*.

Bazile (368) French: variant spelling of BASIL.
GIVEN NAMES French 23%. *Antoine* (2), *Ghislaine* (2), *Gisele* (2), *Jacques* (2), *Marie Anne* (2), *Pierre* (2), *Yanick* (2), *Clemile*, *Dominique*, *Emile*, *Eugenie*, *Eunide*.

Bazin (149) French: **1.** from a Germanic personal name, based on *badu-* 'battle'. **2.** metonymic occupational name for a maker or seller of *(bom)basin*, a kind of cheap cotton cloth (Italian *bombagine*).
FOREBEARS A bearer of this name from Normandy, France, is documented in Quebec City in 1654.
GIVEN NAMES French 15%; German 6%. *Andre*, *Armand*, *Arnaud*, *Martial*, *Pierre*, *Wesner*, *Fritz* (2).

Bazinet (349) French: from a diminutive of BAZIN.
FOREBEARS A Bazinet from the Périgord region of France is recorded in Montreal in 1669 with the secondary surname Tourblanche.
GIVEN NAMES French 12%. *Normand* (2), *Adrien*, *Alain*, *Andre*, *Armand*, *Benoit*, *Fernande*, *Jean Guy*, *Lucien*, *Marcel*, *Philippe*, *Sylvain*.

Bazley (124) English: variant of BASIL, from the feminine form of the personal name, Middle English and Old French *Basil(l)(i)e*. St. Basilla (died AD 304) was a Roman maiden who, according to legend, chose death rather than marry a pagan.

Bazzano (176) Italian: habitational name from any of various places called Bazzano,

in Bologna, L'Aquila (Abruzzo), Perugia (Umbria), and Parma (Emilia-Romagna). The place name is derived from the Latin personal name *Badius* + the suffix *-anu* (later *-ano*), indicating ownership.
GIVEN NAMES Italian 24%. *Carmelo* (6), *Salvatore* (4), *Gaetano* (2), *Pasquale* (2), *Rocco* (2), *Santo* (2), *Lorenzo*, *Sabastian*.

Bazzell (414) Altered spelling of BASIL.

Bazzi (148) Iranian and Arabic: probably from Arabic *baezii* 'foster brother(s)', unrelated children breast-fed by the same wet nurse.
GIVEN NAMES Muslim 82%. *Hassan* (8), *Ali* (6), *Hussein* (5), *Ahmad* (4), *Kayed* (4), *Mohamed* (4), *Kamel* (3), *Mahmoud* (3), *Mohamad* (3), *Amer* (2), *Rafic* (2), *Samir* (2).

Bazzle (200) Altered spelling of BASIL.

Bea (238) Spanish: habitational name from a place of this name in Teruel.

Beaber (176) Americanized spelling of German **Bieber** or **Biber**, from Middle High German *biber* 'beaver', hence a nickname for someone thought to resemble the animal in some way, a topographic name for someone who lived in a place frequented by beavers or by a field named with this word, or a habitational name from any of various place names in Hesse containing this element.

Beabout (193) Probably an Americanized form of French **Bibeau**.

Beach (11382) **1.** English: topographic name for someone who lived by a stream, Middle English *beche*, Old English *bece*, a byform of *bæce*. Compare BACH 3. **2.** English: topographic name for someone who lived by a beech tree or beech wood, from Middle English *beche* 'beech tree' (Old English *bēce*). **3.** Perhaps also an Americanized form of German BISCH.
FOREBEARS John Beach came from England to New Haven, CT, in about 1635. Thomas Beach came from England to Milford, CT, in 1638. It is not clear whether they are related.

Beacham (1182) English: variant spelling of BEAUCHAMP.

Beachem (166) English: variant spelling of BEAUCHAMP.

Beacher (109) English: variant spelling of BECHER.

Beachler (363) Americanized spelling of German **Büchler** (see BUECHLER).

Beachley (139) **1.** English: habitational name from Beachley in Gloucestershire, recorded in the 12th century as *Beteslega* 'woodland clearing of a man called Betti'. **2.** Americanized form of German BUECHLER or **Büchle** or of the Swiss form **Büchli** (see BUECHEL).

Beachum (294) Altered spelling of English BEAUCHAMP.

Beachy (976) **1.** Swiss German: probably an Americanized spelling of **Büchi** (see BUECHE), a pet form of BURKHARDT; this is a common PA German name (see PEACHEY). **2.** Probably also an altered spelling of the English topographic surname **Beechey**, from Old English *bēce* 'beech tree' + *(ge)hæg* 'enclosure'.

Beacom (379) Northern Irish: variant of BEAUCHAMP.

Beadle (1562) English: occupational name for a medieval court official, from Middle English *bedele* (Old English *bydel*, reinforced by Old French *bedel*). The word is of Germanic origin, and akin to Old English *bēodan* 'to command' and Old High German *bodo* 'messenger'. In the Middle Ages a beadle in England and France was a junior official of a court of justice, responsible for acting as an usher in a court, carrying the mace in processions in front of a justice, delivering official notices, making proclamations (as a sort of town crier), and so on. By Shakespeare's day a beadle was a sort of village constable, appointed by the parish to keep order.

Beadles (544) English: patronymic meaning 'son of the beadle' (see BEADLE).

Beadling (162) English (Northumberland and Durham): unexplained. Compare BUDLONG.

Beadnell (158) English: habitational name from Beadnell in Northumberland or Bednall in Staffordshire, both named with the genitive case of the Old English personal name *Bēda* + Old English *halh* 'nook'.

Beagan (166) Altered spelling of the Irish surnames **Beaghan** (see BEHAN), or, more likely, **Ó Beagáin** (see BEGIN).

Beagle (1073) **1.** English: unexplained; possibly a variant of BEADLE, or a nickname from the breed of small hound called a *beagle*. **2.** Alternatively, it may be from French *bégueule* 'gaper', Old French *begueulle* 'noisy shouting person', a word which has been proposed as the etymology of the English term for the dog. **3.** Possibly an Americanized spelling of German BIEGEL.

Beagles (153) English (Cambridgeshire): unexplained. See BEAGLE.

Beagley (259) **1.** Probably a variant of BEGLEY. **2.** Possibly an Americanized form of German **Büchle** or Swiss German **Büchli** (see BUECHEL).

Beahan (178) Respelling of Irish BEHAN.

Beahm (536) Respelling of German **Böhm** (see BOEHM).

Beaird (942) Altered spelling of Scottish BAIRD.

Beakley (160) Possibly a respelling of BEGLEY.

Beal (7328) **1.** English (of Norman origin): from Old French *bel(e)* 'fair', 'lovely' (see BEAU), either a nickname for a handsome man or a metronymic from this word used as a female personal name. **2.** English: habitational name from places so named in Northumberland and West Yorkshire. The former of these (*Behil* in early records)

comes from Old English *bēo* 'bee' + *hyll* 'hill'; the latter (*Begale* in Domesday Book) is from Old English *bēag* 'ring', here probably used in the sense 'river bend', or an unattested personal name *Bēaga* derived from this word + *halh* 'nook', 'recess'. **3.** French (**Béal**): topographic name for someone who lived by a mill race, from the Lyonnaise dialect term *béal, bezale, bedale* (of Gaulish origin). **4.** Americanized spelling of German **Biehl** or **Bühl** (see BUEHL).

FOREBEARS Lt. Col. Thomas Beal(e) (*c.*1621–*c.*1676) of London settled in York Co., VA, about 1650.

Beale (2704) English: variant spelling of BEAL.

FOREBEARS Thomas Beale came from England to York Co., VA, in 1645.

Bealer (503) Americanized spelling of German BIEHLER or BUEHLER.

Beales (172) English: patronymic from BEAL.

Beall (3897) English and Scottish: variant spelling of BEAL.

FOREBEARS Ninian Beall, a Scottish Royalist, emigrated to Calvert co., MD, in about 1650, after King Charles I was beheaded.

Bealmear (136) Possibly an altered spelling of French topographic name **Balmier**, from an agent derivative of the pre-Latin term *balma* 'cave', 'grotto' (in the east 'hillock', 'bank').

Beals (2587) English: patronymic from BEAL.

Beam (5411) **1.** English: from Old English *bēam* 'beam', 'post', a term with various applications. It denoted the beam of a loom and was therefore in some cases a metonymic occupational name for a weaver. In others it was a topographic name for someone who lived by a post or tree, or by a footbridge made from a tree trunk. **2.** Americanized form of German BOEHM, or sometimes of BAUM.

Beaman (2165) English: variant spelling of BEEMAN.

FOREBEARS Gamaliel Beaman came from Bridgenorth, Shropshire, England to MA in 1635 as a 12-year-old boy.

Beamer (1395) **1.** English: occupational name for a trumpeter, Middle English *bemere* (Old English *bēmere, bīemere*). **2.** Americanized spelling of German BOEHMER or **Bäumer** (see BAUMER).

Beames (125) English: variant of BEAMISH

Beamesderfer (115) Of German origin; probably a habitational name for someone from an unidentified place, perhaps Biensdorf in Saxony.

GIVEN NAME German 4%. *Kurt.*

Beamish (352) **1.** English and Irish (of Norman origin): habitational name from various places in northern France: Beaumais-sur-Dire in Calvados, Beaumetz in Somme, or any of three places called Beaumetz in Pas-de-Calais. They are

named in Old French as *beu* 'fair', 'lovely' + *més* 'dwelling'. Compare MAS. A place called Beamish in County Durham is an Anglo-Norman French place name of the same origin, first mentioned in the 13th century; it is possible that in some cases the surname is from this place. **2.** Americanized spelling of German **Behmisch** or **Böhmisch**, ethnic names for someone from Bohemia (see BOHM).

Beamon (1035) Probably a variant spelling of BEEMAN.

Beams (555) Irish and English: variant of BEAMISH.

Bean (13641) **1.** English: metonymic occupational name for a grower or seller of beans, from Old English *bēan* 'beans' (a collective singular). Occasionally it may have been applied as a nickname for a someone considered of little importance. **2.** English: nickname for a pleasant person, from Middle English *bēne* 'friendly', 'amiable' (of unknown origin; there is apparently no connection with BAIN or BON). **3.** Scottish: Anglicized form of the Gaelic personal name *Beathán*, a diminutive of *beatha* 'life'. **4.** Translation of German BOHNE, or an altered spelling of BIEHN. See also BIHN. **5.** Mistranslation of French LEFEVRE. As the vocabulary word *fèvre* 'smith' was replaced by *forgeron*, the meaning of the old word became opaque, and the surname was reinterpreted as if it were *La fève*, from *fève* '(fava) bean'. Lefevre is the most common name in French Canada; great numbers of them migrated to the US, where many adopted the name Bean, in the belief that it was a translation of **Lefèvre**. See also LAFAVE.

Beanblossom (160) Translation of the Swiss German ornamental name **Bohnenblust**, a compound of *Bohne* 'bean' + Alemannic *Blust* 'blossom'.

Beane (2133) Variant spelling of BEAN.

Beaner (125) English: probably an occupational name for a grower or seller of beans, from an agent derivative of Old English *bēan* 'beans' (see BEAN).

Beanland (108) English (Yorkshire): topographic name for someone who lived by land on which beans were grown, from Old English *bēan* + *land*.

GIVEN NAME French 4%. *Jean Marie.*

Beans (381) **1.** English: variant of BEAN. **2.** Probably a translation of German BOHNE, which while singular in standard German is also a dialect plural (the singular form being *Bohn*), or an Americanized spelling of BINZ.

Bear (2826) **1.** English: from the Middle English nickname *Bere* meaning 'bear' (Old English *bera*, which is also found as a byname), or possibly from a personal name derived from a short form of the various Germanic compound names with this first element. Compare for example BERNHARD. The bear has generally been regarded with a mixture of fear and amusement because of its strength and unpredictable temper on the one hand and its clumsy gait on the other, and in the medieval period it was also thought to typify the sins of sloth and gluttony. All these characteristics are no doubt reflected in the nickname. Throughout the Middle Ages the bear was a familiar figure in popular entertainments such as bear baiting and dancing bears. **2.** English: variant spelling of the habitational name BEER. **3.** Probably a translation of cognates of 1 in other languages, for example German BAER, and also an Americanized spelling of German BAHR.

Bearb (107) Possibly a respelling of French **Béard**, a nickname for a gormless person, from a derivative of *béer* 'to gape'.
GIVEN NAMES French 9%. *Aurelien, Camille, Micheline, Pierre*.

Bearce (417) Probably a variant of English and Welsh PIERCE.

Beard (17071) English: **1.** nickname for a bearded man (Middle English, Old English *beard*). To be clean-shaven was the norm in non-Jewish communities in northwestern Europe from the 12th to the 16th century, the crucial period for surname formation. There is a place name and other evidence to show that this word was used as a byname in the Old English period, when beards were the norm; in this period the byname would have referred to a large or noticeable beard. As an American surname, this name has absorbed cognates and equivalents in other languages, in particular German BART. **2.** habitational name from a place in Derbyshire, which derives its name by dissimilation from Old English *brerd* 'rim', 'bank'.

Beardall (180) **1.** English (Nottinghamshire): possibly a habitational name from Beard Hall Farm in Derbyshire, named with Old English *brerd* 'edge', 'hillside' + *hall* 'hall', 'manor house'. **2.** Possibly an Americanized spelling of German **Bärt(h)el** (see BARTEL).

Bearden (4674) Possibly an English habitational name, a variant of BARDEN, or from places in Devon and Cornwall called Beardon, from Old English *burh* 'manor' + *dūn* 'hill'. In the British Isles the surname is now rare occurring chiefly in Kent.

Beardmore (245) English: probably a habitational name from some lost place (probably in Staffordshire, where the surname is particularly common).

Beardslee (651) Variant of English BEARDSLEY.

Beardsley (2753) English: possibly a variant of BARDSLEY, or alternatively a habitational name from an unidentified place (possibly in Nottinghamshire, where the surname is particularly common).
FOREBEARS William Beardsley, mason, came to New England in 1635 from London aboard the *Planter*.

Beare (295) English: variant spelling of BEER.

Bearer (182) English: unexplained.

Bearfield (126) English: habitational name for someone from Great or Little Bardfield or Bardfield Saling in Essex, all named with Old English *byrde* 'bank', 'border' + *feld* 'open country'.

Bearman (328) English: **1.** occupational name for a keeper of a dancing bear or one who kept bears for baiting (see BEAR). **2.** variant of BERMAN 3.

Bears (205) **1.** Possibly a variant of Welsh and English PIERCE or (less probably) of BEERS. **2.** Possibly a respelling of German BEERS or the cognate **Behrs**.

Bearse (299) Variant of Welsh and English PIERCE. Compare BEARCE.
FOREBEARS Augustine Bearse (born 1618) arrived at Plymouth, MA, from Southampton, England on April 24, 1638 aboard the *Confidence*. A year later he was one of the founders of Barnstable, on Cape Cod.

Bearss (229) Probably a variant of English and Welsh PIERCE.

Bearup (153) **1.** Northern English and Scottish: unexplained. **2.** Possibly also Scandinavian, an Americanized form of a name ending in *-rup*, a common element of Danish and southern Swedish habitational names, from Old Scandinavian *þorp* 'outlying farmstead', 'hamlet'.

Beary (322) Irish: Anglicized form of Gaelic **Ó Béara** (see O'BERRY).

Beas (165) **1.** Spanish (common in Mexico): habitational name from any of the places in Andalusia named Beas. **2.** Variant spelling of English BEES. **3.** Possibly also a variant spelling of German BIES.
GIVEN NAMES Spanish 47%. *Jose* (8), *Arturo* (3), *Carlos* (3), *Enrique* (2), *Jesus* (2), *Juan* (2), *Pedro* (2), *Roberto* (2), *Ruben* (2), *Abdias, Andres, Angel*.

Beasley (15515) English: habitational name from a place in Lancashire named Beesley, perhaps from Old English *bēos* 'bent grass' + *lēah* 'woodland clearing'.

Beason (1618) Probably a variant spelling of the English surname BEESON, itself a variant of **Beeston** (see BEASTON).

Beaston (256) English: habitational name from any of the various places called Beeston (the more common form of the family name in England). Most of them, for example those in Bedfordshire, Norfolk, Nottinghamshire, and West Yorkshire, are named with Old English *bēos* 'rough grass' + *tūn* 'enclosure', 'settlement'. The one in Cheshire is probably named with Old English *byge* 'trade', 'commerce' + *stān* 'stone', meaning 'rock where a market was held'. A few other Beestons have different derivations.

Beat (148) **1.** Scottish: variant of BATE or BEATH. **2.** English and Scottish: from a short form of the female personal name *Beton* (see BEATON 2).

Beath (142) Scottish: either a habitational name from Beath in Fife or a reduced form of McBEATH, a variant of McBETH.

Beatie (131) Scottish: variant spelling of BEATTY.

Beatley (106) English (Norfolk): unexplained.

Beato (219) Spanish, Portuguese, and southern Italian: from the personal name *Beato*, an omen name from Latin *beatus* 'blessed', 'happy', 'prosperous', bestowed on a child in the hope of bringing him good fortune.
GIVEN NAMES Spanish 33%; Portuguese 9%; Italian 8%. *Jose* (8), *Ana* (2), *Carlos* (2), *Ernesto* (2), *Juan* (2), *Juana* (2), *Pedro* (2), *Alejandro, Amarilis, Bienvenido, Cruz Maria, Damaso*; *Zulmira* (3); *Vito* (3), *Amedeo, Giuseppe, Luca, Nino*.

Beaton (1569) Scottish **1.** (of Norman origin) habitational name from Béthune in Pas-de-Calais, France (see BETHUNE). **2.** from the medieval personal name *Be(a)ton*, a pet name from a short form of BARTHOLOMEW or BEATRICE. **3.** Anglicization of Gaelic **Mac Beath** (see McBETH).

Beatrice (386) Italian and French (**Béatrice**): from a medieval female personal name borne in honor of a 4th-century saint, martyred together with her brothers Simplicius and Faustinus. Her name was originally *Viātrix* meaning 'traveler' (a feminine form of *viātor*, from *via* 'way'), a name adopted by early Christians in reference to the journey through life, and Christ's description of himself as 'the way, the life, and the truth'; it was later altered as a result of folk etymological association with Latin *beatus* 'blessed'.
GIVEN NAMES Italian 10%. *Carmine* (4), *Angelo* (2), *Attilio, Dante, Luigi, Pellegrino, Pietro, Rocco, Salvatore, Vincenzo*.

Beatson (165) Scottish and English: patronymic from the personal name *Beat* (see BEAT).

Beattie (3849) Scottish: variant of BEATTY.

Beatty (9446) Scottish and northern Irish: **1.** from the personal name *Beatie*, a pet form of BARTHOLOMEW. **2.** reduced Anglicized form of Gaelic **Mac Bhiadhtaigh** 'son of the victualer', from *biadhtach* 'victualer'.

Beaty (4665) Scottish and northern Irish: variant spelling of BEATTY.

Beau (112) French: nickname for a handsome man (perhaps also ironically for an ugly one), from Old French *beu, bel* 'fair', 'lovely' (Late Latin *bellus*). See also BEL.
FOREBEARS A Beau, also called Desjardins, from Brittany is documented in Canada in 1726.
GIVEN NAMES French 12%. *Andre, Laurent, Pascal, Remi*.

Beaubien (488) French: evidently a complimentary nickname formed from a combination of *beau* 'fine', 'handsome' + *bien* 'well'.

FOREBEARS In New France this was a secondary surname for Trotier or Trottier. A bearer from the Perche region of France is documented in Quebec city in 1646. Beaubien was apparently used as a primary name for the first time in 1742 in Detroit. GIVEN NAMES French 6%. *Armand* (4), *Lucien* (2), *Alphonse, Celine, Luc, Marcel*.

Beaucage (146) French: variant spelling of **Bocage**, a topographic name from *boscage* 'copse'. A document of 1696 records it as a secondary surname of Baillargeon.
GIVEN NAMES French 21%. *Lucien* (2), *Cecile, Fernand, Jacques, Normand, Pierre, Raynald, Solange*.

Beauchaine (207) Variant of French BEAUCHESNE.
GIVEN NAME French 5%. *Donat*.

Beauchamp (4355) English (or Norman origin) and French: habitational name from any of several places in France, for example in Manche and Somme, that are named with Old French *beu, bel* 'fair', 'lovely' + *champ(s)* 'field', 'plain'. In English the surname is generally pronounced *Beecham*.
FOREBEARS Two families of this name which were prominent in the 13th and 14th centuries in England. One was established in Somerset, the other in Warwickshire, and there is no apparent connection between them.
Beauchamp is also found as a Frenchification of the Scottish family name CAMPBELL, due to an erroneous Latinization of the latter as *Campo Bello*.
Beauchamp lines in Canada descend from two brothers from La Rochelle, whose father was called Deschamps as well as Beauchamp. They were in Montreal by 1661. One was also known as *Le Grand Beauchamp* and the other as *Le Petit Beauchamp*.
GIVEN NAMES French 4%. *Antoine* (3), *Jacques* (3), *Yves* (3), *Andre* (2), *Armand* (2), *Emile* (2), *Fernand* (2), *Marcel* (2), *Marthe* (2), *Remi* (2), *Alcide, Camille*.

Beauchemin (637) French: Canadian secondary surname (meaning 'fair way') to the primary names Petit-Hus, Millet, Pinard, Rèche, and Fleurant.
GIVEN NAMES French 13%. *Armand* (5), *Marcel* (4), *Herve* (2), *Aldor, Andre, Chantal, Denys, Emile, Francoise, Henri, Jean Louis, Jean-Marc*.

Beauchene (198) French: variant of BEAUCHESNE.
GIVEN NAMES French 8%. *Armand* (3), *Adelard* (2), *Philippe*.

Beauchesne (387) French (**Beauchêne**): topographic name composed of Old French *beu*, which in medieval times could also mean 'high', 'tall' as well as 'lovely', + *chesne* 'oak'.
GIVEN NAMES French 12%. *Armand* (3), *Normand* (3), *Auguste, Emile, Fernand, Laurier, Marcel, Mederic, Oliva, Sylvie*.

Beaudet (572) French: variant spelling of **Baudet**, a diminutive of *Baud* meaning 'joyful'.

FOREBEARS As Beaudet and Baudet, this name is recorded in Canada in 1666, borne by an immigrant from La Rochelle. Another, from the Poitou region, arrived in Canada in 1664. Documented in association with Beaudet is the secondary surname Ducap.
GIVEN NAMES French 19%. *Pierre* (5), *Emile* (3), *Marcel* (3), *Normand* (3), *Armand* (2), *Lucien* (2), *Adelard, Adrien, Aime, Andre, Benoit, Donat*.

Beaudette (635) Variant spelling of French *Baudet* (see BEAUDET). The *-ette* ending is not feminine, but reflects the Canadian pronunciation, in which the final *-t* is sounded.
GIVEN NAMES French 7%. *Armand* (2), *Lucien* (2), *Philippe* (2), *Adrien, Andre, Emilien, Herve, Monique, Nicolle, Solange*.

Beaudin (599) French: variant spelling of **Baudin**, a diminutive of *Baud* meaning 'joyful'.
FOREBEARS As Beaudin and Bodin, this name is recorded in Quebec city in 1669, borne by an immigrant from the Poitou region of France.
GIVEN NAMES French 8%. *Armand* (3), *Urbain* (2), *Alcid, Andre, Briand, Donat, Fernand, Gilles, Marcel, Renald, Stephane*.

Beaudoin (2620) French: variant spelling of BAUDOIN.
GIVEN NAMES French 13%. *Armand* (9), *Marcel* (8), *Andre* (7), *Serge* (6), *Jacques* (5), *Gilles* (4), *Laurent* (4), *Normand* (4), *Pierre* (4), *Alcide* (3), *Lucien* (3), *Raoul* (3).

Beaudreau (250) French: unexplained.
FOREBEARS A Baudreau, also called Graveline, from the Maine region of France, is documented in Montreal in 1664.
GIVEN NAMES French 9%. *Armand, Cecile, Henri, Marcel, Monique, Valere, Viateur*.

Beaudrie (102) French: variant spelling of BEAUDRY.
GIVEN NAMES French 6%. *Amie, Romain*.

Beaudry (1668) French: from a Germanic personal name composed of the elements *bald* 'bold' + *rīc* 'power'.
FOREBEARS A Beaudry or Baudry, also known as Lamarche, from the Anjou region of France, is recorded in Trois Rivières, Quebec, in 1647; another, also called L'Épinette, from the Maine region of France, is documented in Montreal in 1665; and a Beaudry from La Rochelle was documented in Montreal in 1670. The secondary surname Desbuttes was recorded in Quebec city in 1682.
GIVEN NAMES French 10%. *Normand* (6), *Andre* (5), *Armand* (4), *Pierre* (4), *Amedee* (3), *Gilles* (2), *Laurent* (2), *Rosaire* (2), *Aime, Celine, Charlemagne, Elphege*.

Beauford (406) English: variant of BEAUFORT.

Beaufort (142) English (of Norman origin) and French: habitational name from various places in France named Beaufort, for example in Nord, Somme, and Pas-de-

Calais, from Old French *beu, bel* 'fair', 'lovely' + *fort* 'fortress', 'stronghold'.
FOREBEARS A powerful English family of this name originated with the bastard children of John of Gaunt and Catherine Swinford, who were legitimized by Act of Parliament. Their name was derived from their father's castle, Beaufort, in Champagne.
The English admiral Sir Francis Beaufort (1774–1857), who devised the Beaufort scale, used for measuring wind velocity, was the grandson of a French Huguenot refugee, Daniel de Beaufort, who became pastor of a church in Spitalfields, London.
GIVEN NAME French 5%. *Normand*.

Beaulac (205) French: topographic name meaning 'beautiful lake', from French *beau* 'fair', 'lovely' + *lac* 'lake'.
FOREBEARS In Canada Beaulac is recorded as a secondary surname to Desmarais, Lefebvre, and Marest.
GIVEN NAMES French 13%. *Armand* (3), *Gaetan, Gillis, Jean Marie, Marcelle, Raoul, Rosaire, Urgel*.

Beaulieu (4140) French: habitational name from any of the extremely numerous places in France named with Old French *beu, bel* 'fair', 'lovely' + *lieu* 'place', 'location'. The name is occasionally also found in England; it is then either a Norman name from one of the French places just mentioned or derives from an English place name of the same origin, Beaulieu (pronounced *byoo-lee*) in Hampshire, seat of the Montagu family.
FOREBEARS In Canada Beaulieu has been used as a secondary name to Diers, Dufresne, Hudon, Lebel, Martin, Montpelier, Palmier, Philippe, and Thomas. It is documented independently in Montreal in 1726 as the name of an immigrant from Gascony, France.
GIVEN NAMES French 15%. *Marcel* (12), *Armand* (11), *Normand* (10), *Andre* (9), *Lucien* (9), *Emile* (6), *Jacques* (6), *Pierre* (6), *Camille* (5), *Gilles* (5), *Laurier* (5), *Raoul* (5).

Beauman (109) Variant of English and French BEAUMONT.

Beaumier (189) French: variant of Occitan **Baumier**, a topographic name meaning 'person who lives in a cave', from *baume*, Occitan form of *balme* 'cave'.
FOREBEARS A Beaumier from the Poitou region of France arrived in Quebec city in 1665, where the name is common today. In the mid 19th century it was Americanized as Beauman in southern IL by Doric François Beaumier (Doric Frank Beauman), who was born in Trois Rivières, Quebec.
GIVEN NAMES French 14%. *Armand* (2), *Lucien* (2), *Cecile, Gaston, Jacques, Valmont, Yves*.

Beaumont (1784) English (of Norman origin) and French: habitational name from any of the five places in Normandy or several others elsewhere in France so named.

The place name comes from Old French *beu*, *bel* 'fair', 'lovely' + *mont* 'hill'. There are also places in England so named under Norman influence (in Cumberland, Lancashire, and Essex, the last of which changed its name in the 12th century from *Fulepet* 'foul pit' to *Bealmont* 'beautiful hill'); these may also have given rise to cases of the surname. The surname is now widespread throughout England, but most common in Yorkshire.

FOREBEARS Many American bearers of this surname are descendants of John Beaumont (1612–1647), who came to North America from England in 1630.

William Beaumont came from England to Cambridge, MA, in 1635 and subsequently moved to CT.

A Beaumont from the Anjou region of France, with the secondary surnames Piquefeu and Boutefeu, is recorded as having arrived in Quebec city in 1665; another, from the Poitou region is recorded in 1674 in Quebec city.

GIVEN NAMES French 4%. *Andre* (4), *Gilles* (3), *Gaetan*, *Honore*, *Jacques*, *Jean-Guy*, *Marcel*.

Beauparlant (103) French: nickname for someone with a gift for oratory, literally 'fine speaking'.

GIVEN NAMES French 8%. *Andre*, *Michel*.

Beaupre (1033) French (**Beaupré**): topographic name from Old French *beu* 'lovely' + *pred* 'meadow'. The nautical term *beaupré* 'bowsprit' may have given rise to its use as a secondary surname for a sailor.

FOREBEARS Beaupré is recorded as a secondary surname for Brisset. A Bonhomme, also called Beaupré, was in Detroit in 1724.

GIVEN NAMES French 10%. *Armand* (5), *Andre* (3), *Colette* (2), *Laurier* (2), *Treffle* (2), *Adelard*, *Alphonse*, *Dany*, *Fernand*, *Germaine*, *Gilles*, *Henri*.

Beauregard (1952) French: habitational name from any of various places in France named Beauregard for their fine view or fine aspect, for example in Ain, Dordogne, Drôme, Lot, and Puy-de-Dôme, from *beau* 'fair', 'lovely' + *regard* 'aspect', 'outlook'.

GIVEN NAMES French 11%. *Marcel* (7), *Andre* (6), *Pierre* (6), *Normand* (5), *Laurent* (4), *Adrien* (3), *Armand* (3), *Adelard* (2), *Donat* (2), *Gilles* (2), *Lucien* (2), *Simonne* (2).

Beausoleil (437) French: habitational name from any of various minor places named with French *beau* 'lovely', 'fair' + *soleil* 'sun', probably denoting a place that was exposed to the sun. This name has been translated as **Prettyson**, which in turn gave rise to the frequent version *Peterson*. It has also been rendered into English as BOSLEY.

FOREBEARS Beausoleil is recorded as a secondary name for Audirac, Besnard (1744), Derumé, Hengard (1736), Lepage, Maigré, Malbeuf, Moreau, Normandin, Quatrefage, Rousseau, Saunier, and Villat. It was first used independently around 1700.

GIVEN NAMES French 17%. *Andre* (4), *Briand* (2), *Marcel* (2), *Aime*, *Alcide*, *Armand*, *Bibiane*, *Camille*, *Cecile*, *Jean Claude*, *Laurent*, *Lucien*.

Beauvais (844) French: habitational name from a place so named in Oise, or alternatively from any of numerous minor places throughout France named Beauvoir or Beauvir 'lovely view'.

FOREBEARS A bearer from the Perche region of France is recorded in Montreal in 1654 with the secondary surnames Saint-Gemme and Saint-Jemme. The secondary surnames Bouvret, Crenet, and Emery are also documented.

GIVEN NAMES French 9%. *Armand* (2), *Chantelle*, *Clelie*, *Denys*, *Edouard*, *Germain*, *Guilene*, *Laurette*, *Ludger*, *Marcel*, *Michel*, *Olivier*.

Beavan (122) Mostly a variant spelling of Welsh BEVAN; possibly in some cases of English BEAVIN.

Beaven (341) Mostly a variant spelling of Welsh BEVAN, but possibly in some cases of English BEAVIN.

Beaver (7774) **1.** English (of Norman origin): habitational name from any of several places in France called Beauvoir, for example in Manche, Somme, and Seine-Maritime, or from Belvoir in Leicestershire. All of these are named with Old French *beu*, *bel* 'fair', 'lovely' + *veïr*, *voir* 'to see', i.e. a place with a fine view. **2.** English: nickname from Middle English *bevere*, Old English *beofor* 'beaver', possibly referring to a hard worker, or from some other fancied resemblance to the animal. The existence of patronymic forms such as BEAVERSON suggest that this may also have been a personal name. **3.** Probably a translation of cognates of 2 in other languages, in particular Dutch BEVER and German BIEBER. **4.** Possibly a variant of Welsh BEVAN.

FOREBEARS George Beaver, a Huguenot from Alsace, came to Philadelphia, PA, in 1744.

Beavers (5284) English: origin uncertain. Possibly it is a variant of Welsh BEVANS.

FOREBEARS William Walter Beavers, from whom many bearers of this American family name are descended, was born in Wales on July 25, 1755 and married Elizabeth Ragsdale in Lunenburg Co. VA. He died in about 1807 in Elbert Co., GA.

Beaverson (212) Evidently a patronymic from BEAVER.

Beavin (184) **1.** Welsh: variant spelling of BEVAN. **2.** English (of Norman origin): nickname for a wine drinker, from Old French *bei(vre)*, *boi(vre)* 'to drink' + *vin* 'wine'.

Beazer (159) English (Gloucestershire): unexplained.

Beazley (611) English: variant spelling of BEASLEY.

Bebb (180) English: perhaps a variant of BABB. In the British Isles it is now most common in mid-Wales and in the border county of Shropshire, where it is recorded from the 16th century.

FOREBEARS William Bebb (1802–73), Governor of OH 1846–48, was a descendant of an immigrant from Montgomeryshire, Wales.

Bebber (191) German: habitational name from a place so named near the Deister hills, west of Hannover.

GIVEN NAME German 4%. *Otto* (2).

Bebeau (182) French: variant spelling of BIBEAU.

GIVEN NAME French 5%. *Alcide*.

Bebee (335) Variant spelling of English BEEBY.

Beber (176) Central German: nickname from the dialect word *Beber* 'beaver'. See also BEVER, BIEBER.

Bebo (145) Americanized spelling of French BIBEAU.

Bebout (674) Most probably an Americanized form of French BIBEAU, or an altered form of a Middle English and Old French nickname for a heavy drinker, *beivrebout*, from Old French *beivre* 'to drink' + *bo(u)t* 'wine cask'. Compare BEAVIN.

FOREBEARS This name is recorded in NY and NJ in the early 18th century, so it is probably of English, French Huguenot, or Dutch origin.

Becerra (2484) Galician and Spanish: nickname, probably for a high-spirited person, from *becerra* 'young cow', 'heifer'. It may also have been a metonymic occupational name for a cowherd.

GIVEN NAMES Spanish 53%. *Jose* (86), *Juan* (46), *Jesus* (32), *Manuel* (29), *Carlos* (28), *Miguel* (24), *Luis* (21), *Rafael* (21), *Pedro* (18), *Ramon* (18), *Francisco* (17), *Jorge* (16).

Becerril (223) Spanish: habitational name from any of several places so named, for example Becerril in Segovia, Becerril de Campos in Palencia, and Becerril de la Sierra in Madrid. The place name means 'cowshed'.

GIVEN NAMES Spanish 58%. *Jose* (11), *Carlos* (5), *Jorge* (5), *Ramon* (4), *Adolfo* (3), *Arturo* (3), *Fernando* (3), *Luis* (3), *Mario* (3), *Enrique* (2), *Maria Elena* (2), *Miguel* (2); *Antonio* (2), *Gabino*, *Marco Antonio*.

Bech (114) **1.** Danish and Norwegian: unexplained. **2.** German: metonymic occupational name for a pitch gatherer and/or tar maker, from Middle High German *pech* 'pitch', 'tar' (see PECH).

GIVEN NAMES Scandinavian 10%; German 9%. *Knud*, *Vidar*; *Claus*, *Fritz*, *Inge*, *Klaus*.

Bechard (772) Probably a variant spelling of French **Becard** or **Béchart**, nicknames for a gossip, from *bec* 'beak' + the pejorative suffix *-ard*, *-art*.

FOREBEARS An immigrant from the Limousin region of France was variously documented in Quebec in 1691 as Béchard, Béchet, Bechéque, and Beriade.

GIVEN NAMES French 7%. *Armand* (3), *Adrien, Alain, Andre, Antoine, Emile, Laurent, Leandre, Lucien, Marcel, Octave.*

Bechdel (113) Variant of German BECHTEL.

Bechel (155) South German: topographic name for someone who lived by a stream, from a diminutive of BACH 1.

Bechen (121) German: habitational name from Bechen in North Rhine-Westphalia or near Kempten in the Allgäu area.

Becher (901) **1.** German: occupational name for a maker of wooden vessels, a shortened form of BECHERER, the loss of the final syllable having occurred in the 15th century. **2.** German: occupational name for someone who distilled or worked with pitch, for example in making vessels watertight, from an agent derivative of Middle High German *bech, pech* 'pitch'. **3.** Scandinavian: either the German name (see 1 and 2 above) or a variant spelling of BECKER. **4.** Jewish (Ashkenazic): metonymic occupational name from Yiddish *bekher* 'cup'. **5.** English: topographic name, a variant of BEECH with the habitational suffix *-er*.

GIVEN NAMES German 4%. *Ilse* (2), *Inge* (2), *Armin, Arno, Erwin, Heinz, Jutta, Otto.*

Becherer (267) German: occupational name for a turner of wooden vessels, Middle High German *becherer*, an agent derivative of *becher* 'cup', 'mug'.

Bechler (271) German: **1.** topographic name for someone who lived by a stream, from a southern diminutive of Middle High German *bach* 'stream' + the suffix *-(l)er* denoting an inhabitant. **2.** dissimilated form of BECHERER. **3.** variant of BECHER 2.

GIVEN NAMES German 4%. *Gerhard, Klaus, Kurt.*

Becht (536) Southwestern German: from a short form of a personal name beginning with *becht* (for instance **Bechtold**), a dialect variant of Germanic *berht* 'bright', 'famous'.

Bechtel (2712) Southwestern German: from a pet form of BECHT or a short form of BECHTOLD.

Bechthold (183) Variant spelling of German BECHTOLD.

GIVEN NAME German 6%. *Kurt* (4).

Bechtle (175) Variant of German BECHTEL.

GIVEN NAME German 5%. *Helmut* (2).

Bechtol (460) German: variant of BECHTOLD.

Bechtold (1554) Southwestern German: from the personal name *Bechtold*, a dialect variant of BERTHOLD.

Beck (37463) **1.** English: topographic name for someone who lived beside a stream, from northern Middle English *bekke* 'stream' (Old Norse *bekkr*). **2.** English (of Norman origin): habitational name from any of various places in northern France, for example Bec Hellouin in Eure, named with Old Norman French *bec*

'stream', from the same Old Norse root as in 1. **3.** English: probably a nickname for someone with a prominent nose, from Middle English *beke* 'beak (of a bird)' (Old French *bec*). **4.** English: metonymic occupational name for a maker, seller, or user of mattocks or pickaxes, from Old English *becca*. In some cases the name may represent a survival of an Old English byname derived from this word. **5.** German and Jewish (Ashkenazic): occupational name for a baker, a cognate of BAKER, from (older) South German *beck*, West Yiddish *bek*. Some Jewish bearers of the name claim that it is an acronym of Hebrew *ben-kedoshim* 'son of martyrs', i.e. a name taken by one whose parents had been martyred for being Jews. **6.** North German: topographic name for someone who lived by a stream, from Low German *Beke* 'stream'. Compare the High German form BACH 1. **7.** Scandinavian: habitational name for someone from a farmstead named Bekk, Bæk, or Bäck, or a topographic name for someone who lived by a stream.

Becka (160) German: eastern variant of BECK 'baker'.

Beckel (352) Altered spelling of German BECHEL or of **Böckel**, a nickname from a diminutive of Middle High German *boc* 'buck', 'ram'.

Beckemeyer (136) North German: distinguishing name for a tenant farmer living by a stream (see BECK + MEYER).

GIVEN NAME French 4%. *Marcel.*

Becken (124) **1.** North German: variant of BECK 6. **2.** Norwegian: habitational name for someone living at a farmstead named *Bekken*, from *bekk* 'stream'.

GIVEN NAME German 4%; Scandinavian 4%. *Thor.*

Beckendorf (127) German: habitational name from either of two places in Mecklenburg-West Pomerania called Beckendorf.

Becker (37882) **1.** Dutch, German, Danish, and Jewish (Ashkenazic): occupational name for a baker of bread, or brick and tiles, from *backen* 'to bake'. **2.** English: occupational name for a maker or user of mattocks or pickaxes, from an agent derivative of Old English *becca* 'mattock'.

FOREBEARS This name is recorded in Beverwijck in New Netherland in the mid 17th century, but it was also brought independently to North America by many other bearers.

Beckerdite (107) Probably a variant of English (Yorkshire) **Bickerdike**, a topographic name for someone who lived by a disputed boundary ditch, from Middle English *bicker* 'quarrel', 'dispute' + *dike* 'ditch'.

Beckerle (129) South German: from a diminutive of BECKER.

Beckerman (668) German (**Beckermann**) and Jewish (Ashkenazic): variant of BECKER.

GIVEN NAMES Jewish 4%. *Miriam* (3), *Avi, Liba, Sol.*

Beckers (280) Dutch: patronymic from BECKER.

GIVEN NAMES German 6%; French 4%. *Ewald, Gerda, Hans, Klaus, Kurt, Wendelin, Wilhelmina; Jacques, Thierry.*

Beckert (399) German: from *Begehart* 'Beghard', a member of a lay brotherhood founded in Flanders in the 13th century, the male counterpart of the Beguines (see BEGUE), or simply an enlarged form of BECKER.

GIVEN NAMES German 4%. *Dietmar, Heino, Wilhelm.*

Beckes (103) Variant of English, German, or Dutch BECKS.

Becket (102) English and Irish: variant spelling of BECKETT.

Beckett (4111) **1.** English: from a diminutive of BECK 3 or, more rarely, of BECK 1. **2.** English: habitational name from places called Beckett in Berkshire and Devon. The former is named with Old English *bēo* 'bee' + *cot* 'cottage', 'shelter'; the latter has as its first element the Old English personal name *Bicca*. This surname is also found in Ireland. **3.** Possibly an Americanized spelling of French **Béquet** (see BEQUETTE).

Beckey (128) **1.** English (Somerset): unexplained. **2.** Probably an altered spelling of German **Becke**, a variant of BECK.

Beckford (649) English: habitational name from a place now in Worcestershire (formerly in Gloucestershire) named Beckford, from the Old English byname *Becca* (see BECK 4) + Old English *ford* 'ford'.

GIVEN NAMES French 4%. *Clovis, Eulalie, Leonie, Marcelle, Oneil.*

Beckham (3268) English: habitational name from a place in Norfolk named Beckham, from the Old English byname *Becca* (see BECK 4) + Old English *hām* 'homestead'.

Becking (110) Dutch and English: unexplained.

Beckius (184) Swedish: ornamental name composed of the elements *bäck* 'stream' + the common suffix of family names *-ius*.

Beckler (638) **1.** Probably an Americanized spelling of German BECHLER. **2.** Americanized spelling of German **Böckler**, occupational or status name for a shield-bearer, from Middle Low German *bokeler*.

Beckles (292) English: habitational name from a place in Norfolk named Beccles, from Old English *bec(e), bæce* 'stream' + *lǣs* 'meadow'.

GIVEN NAMES Spanish 5%. *Alphonso* (2), *Conrado* (2), *Mario* (2), *Berta, Carmelita, Rodolfo, Wilfredo, Yajaira.*

Beckley (1959) **1.** English: habitational name from any of the various places, in Kent, Oxfordshire, and Sussex, named Beckley, from the Old English byname *Becca* (see BECK 4) + Old English *lēah* 'woodland clearing'. **2.** Altered spelling of the South German and Swiss topographic names **Bächle**, **Bächli** (see BACH 1).

FOREBEARS Richard Beckley was one of the free planters who assented to the 'Fundamental Agreement' of the New Haven Colony on June 4, 1639.

Becklund (189) Altered spelling of Swedish **Bäcklund** (see BACKLUND).

Beckman (6176) **1.** English: topographic name for someone who lived beside a stream, from northern Middle English *bekke* 'stream' (Old Norse *bekkr*) + *man* 'man'. **2.** Swedish (**Bäckman**): ornamental name composed of the elements *bäck* 'stream' + *man* 'man'. **3.** Respelling of German BECKMANN. **4.** Jewish (Ashkenazic): variant of BECK.

Beckmann (1357) North German: variant of BECK 6.

GIVEN NAMES German 7%. *Klaus* (3), *Otto* (2), *Alois*, *Dieter*, *Dietrich*, *Gerd*, *Gerda*, *Gerhard*, *Gunter*, *Gunther*, *Hans*, *Heino*.

Beckmeyer (162) German: variant of BECKEMEYER.

GIVEN NAME French 4%. *Armand*.

Becknell (447) English: variant of BICKNELL.

Beckner (1883) Americanized spelling of German **Bechner**, a variant of BECHER 2, or of BECKER.

Beckom (167) **1.** Variant spelling of English BECKHAM. **2.** Possibly an Americanized spelling of Norwegian **Bekkum** (see BECKUM).

Becks (276) **1.** variant of German or English BECK. The origin and significance of the final *-s* is unclear. **2.** variant of Dutch BEEK.

Beckstead (643) **1.** North German: partly Americanized form of the topographic name **Beckstedde** from Low German *Beck* 'stream' + *-stedde* 'stead', 'place', or a habitational name from Beckstedt near Wildeshausen, Oldenburg. **2.** Possibly an Americanized spelling of Swedish **Beckstedt**, an ornamental name composed of the elements *bäck* 'stream' + *stedt* (of German origin) 'place'.

Beckstrand (197) Swedish: ornamental name composed of the elements *bäck* 'stream' + *strand* 'shore'.

Beckstrom (647) Americanized spelling of Swedish **Bäckström** (see BACKSTROM).

Beckum (248) **1.** Americanized spelling of Norwegian **Bekkum**, from the dative plural case of *bekk* 'stream', hence a topographic name for someone who lived 'by the streams'. **2.** Possibly a variant spelling of English BECKHAM.

Beckwith (4653) English: habitational name from a place in West Yorkshire named Beckwith, from Old English *bēce* 'beech' + Old Norse *viðr* 'wood' (replacing the cognate Old English *wudu*).

FOREBEARS Most if not all present-day bearers of the surname are probably descended from a certain William Beckwith who held the manor of Beckwith in 1364. In the U.S. the name also occurs in the elaborated form **de la Beckwith**.

Beckworth (294) English: variant of BECKWITH, now found chiefly in Nottinghamshire.

Becnel (626) Possibly a respelling of Dutch **Becknel**, which Debrabandere suggests could either be from Middle Dutch *beckenell* 'helmet', 'skull' or from French **Becquerel** 'prattler', 'babbler', the name of several watermills.

GIVEN NAMES French 10%. *Michel* (3), *Oneil* (3), *Fernand* (2), *Amelie*, *Antoine*, *Emile*, *Fabien*, *Francois*, *Gaston*, *Onezime*, *Pierre*, *Raoul*.

Becotte (101) French: unexplained.

GIVEN NAMES French 10%. *Armand*, *Emile*, *Lucien*.

Becraft (574) English: variant of BEECROFT.

Becton (734) Altered spelling of **Beckton**, a Scottish habitational name from Beckton, near Lockerbie in Dumfriesshire.

Becvar (191) Czech (**Bečvář**): occupational name for a maker of casks, from *bečka* 'cask'.

Bedard (2408) French: nickname for someone with a fat belly, from a derivative of *bedaine*, a regional variant of *boudaine* 'fat'. Alternatively, it may be a variant of **Bedat**, a habitational name from a place so named.

FOREBEARS A Calvinist family called Bedard from La Rochelle is documented in Charlesbourg, Quebec, in 1666.

GIVEN NAMES French 15%. *Armand* (13), *Marcel* (9), *Normand* (8), *Andre* (7), *Emile* (7), *Lucien* (7), *Adelard* (4), *Pierre* (3), *Raoul* (3), *Yvon* (3), *Antoine* (2), *Camille* (2).

Beddingfield (621) English: habitational name for someone from Bedingfield in Suffolk. The place name is recorded in Domesday Book as *Bedingefelda*, from the Old English personal name *Bēda* + the connective particle *-ing-* 'associated with', 'named after' + *feld* 'open country'.

Beddoe (151) Welsh: variant of BEDDOW.

Beddow (427) Welsh: from the personal name *Bedo*, a pet form of *Meredydd* (see MEREDITH).

Bedel (219) French and German: occupational name from Old French *bedel*, a word with many senses in medieval Europe, among them 'beadle' 'bailiff', 'janitor', and 'soldier' (from Late Latin *pedellus*, *bedellus* 'messenger', 'servant'). It is cognate with English BEADLE.

FOREBEARS A Bedel from Toulouse, with the secondary surname St. George, was recorded in Canada in 1759.

Bedell (2232) **1.** English: variant spelling of BEADLE. **2.** Possibly a variant of French and German BEDEL.

Bedenbaugh (422) Americanized spelling of German **Biedenbach**, a habitational name from Biedenbach in northern Hesse.

Beder (162) German and Jewish (Ashkenazic): variant of BADER.

Bedford (2945) English: habitational name from the county seat of Bedfordshire, or a smaller place of the same name in Lancashire. Both are named with the Old English personal name *Bēda* + Old English *ford* 'ford'. The name is now very common in Yorkshire as well as Bedfordshire.

Bedgood (401) English: unexplained. Possibly a habitational name from an Anglicized form of the Welsh place name *Betws-y-coed* 'prayer house in the wood'.

Bedi (214) Indian (Panjab): Hindu (Khatri) and Sikh name, based on the name of a clan in the Khatri community. The name is derived from Sanskrit *vedī* 'one who knows the Vedas'. Guru Nanak (1469–1539), the founder of the Sikh religion, was from the Bedi clan. It is said that the founder of the clan studied the Vedas in Banaras and came to be known as Vedi or Bedi.

GIVEN NAMES Indian 69%. *Ashok* (3), *Deepak* (2), *Sanjay* (2), *Sonu* (2), *Subhash* (2), *Ajit*, *Amar*, *Anil*, *Anoop*, *Arjun*, *Arvind*, *Dalip*.

Bedient (228) Possibly of English origin: unexplained.

Bedillion (125) Origin unidentified.

Bedinger (160) Americanized form of German **Büdinger**, a habitational name for someone from Büdingen in Hesse, so named with the personal name *Bodo* or *Budo* + the suffix *-inge(n)* which denotes belonging, i.e. 'the people or followers of a man called Bodo'. Today the surname is common around Darmstadt.

FOREBEARS Adam Büdinger was a German-speaking emigrant to PA from Alsace. George Michael Bedinger was born in York Co., PA, in 1756, and was an early settler in KY.

Bedingfield (468) English: variant spelling of BEDDINGFIELD.

Bedinghaus (118) Probably an altered spelling of the German habitational name **Böddinghaus**, from a place called Böddinghausen near Altena, Westphalia.

Bednar (1703) **1.** Czech (**Bednář**), Slovak (**Bednár**), and Slovene: occupational name meaning 'cooper'. Compare BODNAR. **2.** Americanized spelling of Polish BEDNARZ 'cooper'.

Bednarczyk (368) Polish: from a diminutive of *bednarz* 'cooper' (see BEDNARZ).

GIVEN NAMES Polish 16%. *Zbigniew* (3), *Grzegorz* (2), *Slawomir* (2), *Andrze*, *Casimir*, *Dorota*, *Jerzy*, *Jurek*, *Karol*, *Kazimierz*, *Leszek*, *Ludwik*.

Bednarek (516) Polish: from a diminutive of *bednarz* 'cooper' (see BEDNARZ).

GIVEN NAMES Polish 6%. *Andrzej* (3), *Stanislaw* (2), *Bogdan*, *Casimir*, *Janina*, *Karol*, *Wieslaw*, *Zofia*.

Bednarik (204) Czech (**Bednařík**), Slovak (**Bednárik**), and Slovenian: from a diminutive of *bednář*, *bednar* 'cooper' (see BEDNAR).

Bednarski (600) **1.** Polish and Jewish (from Poland): habitational name for someone from a place called Bednary, Bednarze, or Bednarskie. **2.** Jewish (from Poland): patronymic from Polish *bednarz*, an occupational name for a cooper (see BEDNARZ).
GIVEN NAMES Polish 9%. *Andrzej* (2), *Piotr* (2), *Tomasz* (2), *Zbigniew* (2), *Bronislawa*, *Danuta*, *Dorota*, *Janusz*, *Krzysztof*, *Pawel*, *Wieslaw*, *Wladyslaw*.

Bednarz (924) Polish and Jewish (from Poland): occupational name for a cooper, Polish *bednarz*.
GIVEN NAMES Polish 8%. *Jozef* (3), *Zbigniew* (3), *Janina* (2), *Leszek* (2), *Tadeusz* (2), *Aloisius*, *Andrej*, *Benedykt*, *Boguslaw*, *Czeslaw*, *Danuta*, *Ewa*.

Bedner (175) German: variant of **Bittner** (see BUETTNER).

Bednorz (111) Polish: Silesian variant of BEDNARZ.

Bedolla (372) Spanish: variant of BEDOYA. This name is common in Mexico.
GIVEN NAMES Spanish 55%. *Jose* (15), *Jorge* (6), *Jesus* (5), *Carlos* (4), *Juan* (4), *Manuel* (4), *Marcos* (4), *Armando* (3), *Eduardo* (3), *Jaime* (3), *Javier* (3), *Jose Luis* (3).

Bedor (151) See BEDORE.

Bedore (378) New England spelling of French BEDARD, reflecting the North American pronunciation.

Bedoya (332) Spanish (of Basque origin): habitational name from a minor place in Santander province named Bedoya. The place name is from Basque *bedi* 'pasture', 'grazing' + the locative suffix *-ona*.
GIVEN NAMES Spanish 51%. *Jose* (12), *Carlos* (7), *Luis* (7), *Manuel* (5), *Juan* (4), *Luz* (4), *Pedro* (4), *Ricardo* (4), *Ruben* (4), *Alvaro* (3), *Eduardo* (3), *Gustavo* (3).

Bedrick (157) Americanized spelling of **Bedřich**, Czech form of FRIEDRICH.

Bedrosian (444) Armenian: patronymic from the western Armenian personal name *Bedros*, classical Armenian *Pedros* (see PETER).
GIVEN NAMES Armenian 18%. *Aram* (5), *Bedros* (4), *Hagop* (2), *Haig* (2), *Karnig* (2), *Taniel* (2), *Vartan* (2), *Yeprem* (2), *Agop*, *Andranik*, *Araxy*, *Armenak*.

Bedrossian (141) Armenian: variant of BEDROSIAN.
GIVEN NAMES Armenian 49%. *Bedros* (3), *Aram* (2), *Herand* (2), *Anahid*, *Anahit*, *Andranik*, *Antranig*, *Arshalous*, *Avedis*, *Berge*, *Boghos*, *Garabed*.

Bedsaul (206) See BEDSOLE.

Bedsole (542) Americanized form of German PETZOLD.

Bedsworth (127) English: perhaps a variant of **Bedworth**, a habitational name from a place in Warwickshire, so named with an Old English personal name *Bē(a)da* + *worð* 'enclosure'.

Bedwell (1607) English: variant of BIDWELL.

Bee (1279) **1.** Scottish: reduced form of MCBEE, a variant of MCBETH. **2.** English: from Middle English *be* 'bee', Old English *bēo*, hence a nickname for an energetic or active person or a metonymic occupational name for a beekeeper. Compare BEEMAN 2.

Beebe (5962) English (Midlands): probably a variant of BEEBY.

Beebee (117) English (Staffordshire): variant spelling of BEEBY.

Beeber (111) Respelling of German **Bieber** or **Biber** (see BEABER). Beeber and Biber are both recorded in England (Staffordshire) in the 19th century, but may well be of German origin.

Beebout (114) Variant of BEBOUT.

Beeby (148) English: habitational name from a place in Leicestershire named Beeby, from Old English *bēo* 'bee' + Old Norse *býr* 'settlement', 'village'.

Beech (1420) English: variant spelling of BEACH.

Beecham (542) English: variant spelling of BEAUCHAMP, reflecting the normal English pronunciation.

Beecher (2027) **1.** Southern English: variant of **Beech** (see BEACH), the *-er* suffix having a locative sense. **2.** Americanized form of German **Bücher** (cognate with 1) (see BUCHER).

Beeching (110) English (Kent and Sussex): topographic name, from either Old English *bece*, *bæce* 'stream' or Old English *bēce* 'beech', hence denoting a dweller by a stream or a beech tree.

Beechler (210) Americanized form of German **Büchler** (see BUECHLER).

Beeck (166) Dutch: variant spelling of BEEK.

Beecroft (336) English: topographic name for someone who lived at a place where bees were kept, from Middle English *bee* 'bee' + *croft* 'paddock', 'smallholding', or a habitational name from some minor place named with these elements.

Beed (113) English: from the Old English personal name *Bēda*, of which the most famous bearer was the Venerable Bede, the 8th century theologian and historian. Use of the personal name, though rare, continued long enough into the medieval period to give rise to the surname.

Beede (481) Variant spelling of English BEED.

Beedle (574) English: variant spelling of BEADLE.

Beedy (250) Irish spelling of Scottish **Beedie**, itself a variant of BEATTY.

Beeghly (181) Origin unidentified. **1.** It may be a variant of Irish BEGLEY. **2.** Alternatively, perhaps, an Americanized spelling of German BIEGEL or **Büchle** (see BUECHLER).

Beegle (647) Americanized spelling of German BIEGEL.

Beehler (529) Americanized spelling of German **Biehler** or **Bühler** (see BUEHLER).

Beek (223) Dutch: **1.** habitational name from any of various places called Beek, in Limburg, Gelderland, and North Brabant. **2.** topographic name for someone who lived by a stream or creek, *beek*.
GIVEN NAMES German 6%. *Ernst*, *Johannes*, *Kurt*, *Otto*.

Beeker (296) North German and Dutch: habitational name for someone who lived by a stream, from Middle Low German *beke* 'stream', 'brook' + the suffix *-er*, denoting an inhabitant.

Beekman (929) Dutch: topographic name for someone who lived by a stream or creek, from *beek* 'stream' + *-man* 'man'. FOREBEARS This name is recorded in Beverwijck in New Netherland in the mid 17th century.

Beeks (387) **1.** Dutch: variant of BEEK. **2.** English: unexplained.

Beel (210) **1.** English: variant spelling of BEAL. **2.** Americanized spelling of German BIEHL or **Bühl** (see BUEHL).

Beeler (3097) **1.** Americanized spelling of German **Biehler** (see BUEHLER). **2.** Possibly a habitational name for someone from places called Bielen, Bielau, or Biehla, all in eastern Germany, or from Biel in Switzerland. Compare BIELER 3.

Beeley (114) English: habitational name from Beeley in Derbyshire, which is named with the Old English personal names *Bēage* (female) or *Bēga* (male) + *lēah* 'woodland clearing'.

Beem (723) Dutch and North German: ethnic name for a native or inhabitant of Bohemia. Compare BOEHM.

Beeman (2422) **1.** English: variant of BEAUMONT. **2.** English: occupational name for a beekeeper, from Middle English *be* 'bee' + *man* 'man'. **3.** Americanized spelling of German **Biemann**, which is probably a reduced form of **Bineman** or **Bileman**, habitational names from Bien near Lingen and Biela or Bielau.

Beemer (717) **1.** English: variant spelling of BEAMER. **2.** German and Jewish (Ashkenazic): variant of BEHMER.

Been (444) **1.** Dutch: nickname from *been* 'leg', probably a nickname for a cripple. **2.** Dutch: occupational name for a butcher. **3.** Dutch: from a short form of any of the various Germanic personal names beginning with the element *Ber(n)-* 'bear', as for example BERNHARD. **4.** English: variant spelling of BEAN.

Beene (1307) Variant of English BEAN, Dutch BEEN, or German BIEN.

Beeney (141) English (Sussex and Kent): probably a variant of BINNEY.

Beenken (174) North German: variant spelling of BEHNKEN.
GIVEN NAMES German 4%. *Erwin*, *Gerhard*.

Beer (2430) **1.** English (West Country): habitational name from any of the forty or so places in southwestern England called Beer(e) or Bear(e). Most of these derive their names from the West Saxon dative case, *beara*, of Old English *bearu* 'grove', 'wood' (the standard Old English dative *bearwe* being preserved in BARROW). Some may be from Old English *bǣr* 'swine pasture'. **2.** North German and Dutch: from Middle Low German *bāre*, Middle Dutch *bēre* 'bear', applied as a nickname for someone thought to resemble the animal in some way, or as a metonymic occupational name for someone who kept a performing bear. Alternatively, it could have been a habitational name for someone who lived at a house distinguished by the sign of a bear, or from a Germanic personal name with this as the first element. See also BAER, BAHR. **3.** Respelling of Swiss German BIER.

GIVEN NAMES German 4%. *Kurt* (4), *Otto* (3), *Erhard* (2), *Hans* (2), *Heinz* (2), *Aloys, Bodo, Erna, Ernst, Frieda, Friedhelm, Hanni.*

Beerbower (239) Americanized spelling of German **Beerbauer** or **Bierbauer**, probably an occupational name for a farmer who kept a boar and raised hogs, from Low German *beer* 'boar' + *bauer* 'farmer'.

Beere (137) English and German: variant of BEER.

Beerman (502) **1.** Respelling of German BEERMANN or BIERMANN. **2.** Dutch: occupational name from Middle Dutch *berman* 'laborer'.

Beermann (167) North German form of BIERMANN.

GIVEN NAMES German 11%. *Dieter, Egon, Ingo, Kurt, Otto, Ulrich.*

Beers (4280) **1.** Irish or English (mainly northern Ireland): unexplained. **2.** Dutch: shortened form of **van Beers**, a habitational name from any of the places called Beers in Friesland, Overijssel, North Brabant, and near Antwerp. **3.** German: variant of BAER.

Beery (1183) **1.** Possibly a reduced variant of the Irish surname O'BERRY. **2.** Americanized spelling of Swiss German BIERI. **3.** Americanized spelling of Hungarian **Béry**, a habitational name for someone from any of various places called Bér, in Baranya, Komárom, Nógrád, Pest, Vas, or Zala counties.

Bees (166) English or Welsh (Bristol and Cardiff): perhaps a variant of BISS.

Beese (259) **1.** English or Welsh (Bristol and Gwent): perhaps a variant of BISS. **2.** German: from Middle Low German *bēse* 'reed', 'bulrush', hence a metonymic occupational name for someone who used reeds in his work, for example a brush maker. **3.** Americanized spelling of **Biese**, a North German variant of 2.

Beesley (956) English: variant spelling of BEASLEY.

Beeson (2764) English: variant of the habitational name **Beeston** (see BEASTON). The spelling reflects the local pronunciation of the Nottinghamshire place name, although this form is now quite widespread in England.

Beetham (136) English: habitational name from Beetham in Cumbria, probably named from a dative plural form, *bjothum*, of an Old Norse *beth* 'embankment', i.e. '(place near) the embankments'.

Beeton (102) English (eastern England): variant of BEATON.

Beets (569) **1.** Dutch: patronymic from a short form of a Germanic personal name beginning with the element *berht* 'bright', 'famous'. **2.** Dutch: habitational name from a village in Friesland called Beets. **3.** English: outside East Anglia, possibly a respelling of Scottish **Beats**, a variant of BEAT. In East Anglia, however, where the name is concentrated, it is of Dutch origin (see 1, 2), as evidenced by the census of 1881. **4.** Probably a respelling of German BEETZ.

Beetz (118) **1.** German: habitational name from a place so named on the Havel river, northwest of Berlin. **2.** Dutch: variant spelling of BEETS.

GIVEN NAMES German 7%. *Erwin, Hans, Juergen.*

Beever (310) **1.** English (Yorkshire): variant spelling of BEAVER. **2.** Variant of Dutch and North German BEVER.

Beevers (209) **1.** English (Yorkshire): variant of BEAVER. **2.** Variant of Dutch and North German BEVER.

Beezley (314) English: variant spelling of BEASLEY.

Beffa (163) Italian: nickname for a practical joker, from Italian *beffa* 'trick', 'prank'.

Befort (239) French: assimilated form of **Belfort**, a habitational name from any of various places so named, from Old French *bel* 'beautiful' + *fort* 'fort', 'fortified castle'.

Beg (111) **1.** Turkish and Bosnian: from Turkish *beg* 'bey', a title of respect. Compare BAIG. **2.** Slovenian: nickname from *beg* 'escape', 'getaway', probably denoting a refugee.

GIVEN NAMES Muslim 75%. *Khalid* (3), *Faisal* (2), *Gulam* (2), *Humayun* (2), *Islam* (2), *Anjum, Anwar, Anwer, Azam, Azeez, Azim, Babar.*

Bega (104) Spanish: variant of VEGA.

GIVEN NAMES Spanish 27%. *Jose* (3), *Rafael* (3), *Justo* (2), *Manuel* (2), *Cesar, Dalia, Juan, Ruben, Trinidad, Reis* (2).

Began (123) Variant spelling of Irish BEGIN or **Beaghan** (see BEHAN).

Begay (517) Navajo: unexplained.

Begeman (216) German (**Begemann**): habitational name for someone from a settlement on the Bega river, in the Lippe area.

GIVEN NAMES German 5%. *Fritz, Kurt.*

Beger (134) **1.** South German: from an agent derivative of Middle High German *bāgen* 'to quarrel', 'to pride oneself', hence a nickname for a quarrelsome or boastful person. In some cases, it may be a derivative of **Beyer**, through the intermediate form **Beiger**, a regional name for someone from Bavaria (see BAYER). **2.** French: adoption of 1, or possibly in some cases a variant of **Béguer**, **Béguier**, an occupational name for a medieval official, a type of magistrate.

GIVEN NAMES German 5%. *Kurt, Manfred.*

Begg (413) Scottish and northern Irish: nickname or byname for a small man, from Gaelic *beag* 'small'.

Beggs (1919) Chiefly northern Irish: variant of BEGG.

Begin (1060) **1.** Jewish (from Belarus): variant of BEGUN. **2.** Variant of the Irish surname **Beggin**, Anglicized form of Gaelic **Ó Beagáin** 'descendant of *Beagán*', a personal name from the diminutive of *beag* 'small'.

GIVEN NAMES French 14%. *Andre* (4), *Armand* (3), *Benoit* (3), *Rolande* (3), *Alcide* (2), *Antoine* (2), *Camille* (2), *Jacques* (2), *Luc* (2), *Normand* (2), *Renaud* (2), *Aime.*

Begle (108) Possibly a reduced form of German **Begele**, a nickname from a derivative of Middle High German *bāgen* 'to scold'.

GIVEN NAMES German 10%. *Otto* (2), *Kurt, Othmar.*

Begley (2910) **1.** Irish (Donegal): Anglicized form of Gaelic **Ó Beaglaoich** 'descendant of *Beaglaoch*', a personal name composed of the elements *beag* 'small' + *laoch* 'hero'. **2.** Possibly an altered spelling of German **Böckle** or Swiss **Böckli**, variants of BOCK or of **Böckler**, an occupational name for a buckle maker or carrier, Middle Low German *bokeler*.

Begnaud (404) French: unexplained. This name occurs chiefly in LA.

GIVEN NAMES French 8%. *Alcide, Andre, Andrus, Camille, Celestine, Chantel, Clemence, Clovis, Fernand, Irby.*

Begnoche (174) French: unexplained. There are bearers of the name in VT and KS, which is consistent with a French origin, many Vermonters having moved to Kansas in 1830–50.

GIVEN NAMES French 13%. *Napoleon* (2), *Antoine, Armand, Gaston, Lucien, Normand.*

Begue (173) French (**Bègue**): nickname for someone afflicted with a stammer, from a derivative of Old French *beguer* 'to stammer' (from Middle Low German *beggen* 'to chatter'). In the 12th century in Liège a priest called Lambert le Begue ('Lambert the Stammerer') founded a Christian sisterhood whose members followed an austere rule of life; they came to be known as the *Béguines*. A century later an order of lay brothers modeled on this sisterhood was founded in Flanders, the Beghards (see BECKERT). The name is frequent in LA.

GIVEN NAMES French 4%. *Christophe, Jean Louis.*

Begum (194) Muslim (chiefly Pakistan and India): honorific title for a respectable lady. Not really a surname at all, but in America sometimes taken as such.

GIVEN NAMES Muslim 83%; Indian 5%. *Sakina* (5), *Mumtaz* (4), *Nargis* (3), *Nazma* (3), *Razia* (3), *Anees* (2), *Dilara* (2), *Rehana* (2), *Shamim* (2), *Syeda* (2), *Akhtar, Akhter; Nawab.*

Begun (182) Jewish (from Belarus): nickname from Belorussian *begun* 'runner', 'one who walks quickly'.

GIVEN NAMES Jewish 9%. *Aron, Yakov, Yerachmiel.*

Beh (127) German: possibly one of many variants of BOEHM.

Beha (100) German: one of many variants of BOEHM.

GIVEN NAME German 7%. *Wilhelm* (2).

Behan (989) Irish: **1.** Anglicized form of Gaelic **Ó Beachain** 'descendant of *Beachán*', a personal name from a diminutive of *beach* 'bee'. **2.** Anglicized form of the Gaelic personal name *Beathán*, a derivative of *beatha* 'life' (see BEAN 3).

GIVEN NAMES Irish 6%. *Conan* (3), *Aileen.*

Behanna (134) Variant of Cornish **Behenna**, which is of unknown etymology.

Behar (646) Spanish (**Béhar**) and Jewish (Sephardic): variant spelling of BEJAR.

GIVEN NAMES Jewish 11%; Spanish 10%; French 4%. *Jose* (7), *Alberto* (6), *Roberto* (6), *Hortensia* (3), *Isidoro* (3), *Ruben* (3), *Ana* (2), *Jaime* (2), *Marcos* (2), *Mauricio* (2), *Rafael* (2), *Salomon* (2); *Moises* (3), *Sol* (3), *Gady* (2), *Arie, Isadore, Isak, Menahem, Miriam, Moshe, Nissin, Ori, Yoshua*; *Jacques* (2), *Andre, Armand, Henri, Lucien, Marcel, Raymonde, Yves.*

Beharry (142) Name found among people of Indian origin in Guyana and Trinidad: from Hindi **bihārī**, a common final element in Hindu personal names in India, from Sanskrit *vihārī* 'one who roams about for pleasure', or 'beautiful'.

GIVEN NAMES Indian 24%. *Basdeo, Devanand, Dhanraj, Indra, Jagan, Lilowtie, Mahadeo, Oudit, Parmanand, Rajendra, Savitri, Seeta.*

Behe (141) German: one of many variants of BOEHM.

Behel (161) Altered form of German BEHL or **Böhl** (see BOEHLE).

Beheler (244) Altered form of German **Böhler** (see BOEHLER).

Behen (131) Variant spelling of Irish BEHAN.

Behl (404) **1.** German: habitational name from a place in Holstein named Behl. **2.** Altered spelling of German **Böhl** (see BOEHLE). **3.** Indian: variant of BAHL.

GIVEN NAMES Indian 11%. *Ajay* (2), *Swadesh* (2), *Aditya, Anil, Ashok, Dev, Nikhil, Pradeep, Rajesh, Ramesh, Sanjay, Santosh.*

Behle (148) German: **1.** habitational name from a place so named in Silesia. **2.** variant of BEHLEN, recorded in early documentation as *Bele(n)*.

Behlen (126) German: metronymic from *Abele* or *Hebele*, pet forms of the female personal name *Elisabeth* (see ELIZABETH), the suffix -*n* being the (weak) genitive ending; thus '(husband or son) of *Bele*'.

GIVEN NAMES German 5%. *Fritz, Kurt.*

Behler (416) German: **1.** habitational name for someone from either of two places named Behla, near Donau-Eschingen or on the Netze river in eastern Germany. **2.** variant of **Böhling** (see BOHLING).

Behling (1152) German: **1.** habitational name for someone from Behling in the Ruhr district (near Hagen), or possibly from Behlingen, Württemberg. **2.** variant of **Böhling** (see BOHLING).

GIVEN NAMES German 4%. *Otto* (3), *Hans* (2), *Kurt* (2), *Erwin, Ewald, Heinz, Monika, Reinhold.*

Behlke (198) German: **1.** variant of **Böhlke** (see BOEHLKE). **2.** in rare cases, from a pet form of **Bele** (see BEHLE 2).

GIVEN NAME German 4%. *Bernhardt* (2).

Behm (1865) German: variant of BOEHM. Until the late 17th century this was the usual form of the name, the -*o*- spelling becoming the more frequent after that time.

Behme (103) German: one of the many variants of BOEHM.

GIVEN NAMES German 16%. *Kurt* (2), *Erwin, Heinz, Hermann, Manfred.*

Behmer (171) German: variant of BOEHMER.

GIVEN NAME German 4%. *Kurt* (2).

Behn (492) North German: **1.** from a short form of the personal name BERNHARD. **2.** in some cases, perhaps a variant of BEIN, from Middle Low German *bēn* 'bone', 'leg'.

Behne (289) North German: variant of BEHN 1.

Behnen (118) Probably a variant of German BEHN 1.

Behner (160) German: probably a variant of BEHN 1.

Behney (236) Altered spelling of German BEHNER, BOEHNE, or possibly BOEHNING.

Behning (134) North German: patronymic from BEHN.

GIVEN NAME German 4%. *Kurt.*

Behnke (2539) North German: from a pet form of the personal name BERNHARD.

GIVEN NAMES German 4%. *Kurt* (4), *Erna* (2), *Erwin* (2), *Heinz* (2), *Otto* (2), *Alfons, Arno, Eldor, Hans, Hermann, Inge, Manfred.*

Behnken (291) North German: patronymic from the personal name BEHN.

GIVEN NAMES German 8%. *Claus, Gunther, Heinz, Holger, Johann, Matthias, Otto.*

Behr (1686) German and Dutch: variant of the personal name **Bähr** (see BAER).

GIVEN NAMES German 5%. *Arno* (4), *Claus* (3), *Hans* (3), *Erwin* (2), *Horst* (2), *Armin, Bernd, Ernst, Fritz, Gerda, Gerhard, Heinz.*

Behre (117) German and French (Alsace-Lorraine): variant of BAER.

GIVEN NAME French 4%; German 4%. *Guenther.*

Behrend (636) Dutch and North German: from a variant of the personal name *Bernd*, a short form of BERNHARD.

GIVEN NAMES German 6%. *Bernhard* (3), *Erwin* (3), *Arno, Eldred, Hans, Helmut, Inge, Kurt, Lisl, Siegbert.*

Behrends (817) Dutch and North German: patronymic from BEHREND.

Behrendt (1020) Dutch and North German: variant of BEHREND.

GIVEN NAMES German 7%. *Kurt* (5), *Gerda* (2), *Horst* (2), *Bernhard, Dietmar, Erna, Ernst, Gerhard, Guenter, Gunter, Heinz, Hertha.*

Behrens (4347) Dutch and North German: patronymic from BEHREND, variant of BERNHARD. According to documentary evidence, the earlier form **Be(h)rendes** was generally replaced by **Behrens** during the 17th century.

GIVEN NAMES German 5%. *Kurt* (15), *Otto* (6), *Erwin* (4), *Hans* (4), *Eldred* (2), *Erna* (2), *Ernst* (2), *Frieda* (2), *Guenther* (2), *Bernhard, Claus, Elke.*

Behring (208) German: patronymic from the personal name BEHR.

GIVEN NAMES German 5%. *Fritz, Heinrich, Kurt.*

Behringer (561) **1.** German: habitational name for someone from either of two places called Behringen, near Soltau and in Thuringia, or from Böhringen in Württemberg. **2.** German: patronymic from *Bering, Berning*, or some other personal name with the Germanic element *bero* 'bear'.

GIVEN NAMES German 5%. *Hans* (3), *Berthold, Dieter, Friedrich, Guenther, Leonhard, Reinhard.*

Behrle (231) **1.** German (Württemberg): from a pet form of BEHR. **2.** Altered spelling of Norwegian **Berle**, a habitational name from a farmstead in the county of Sogn og Fjordane, so named with Old Norse *barð* 'rim', 'edge'.

Behrman (653) **1.** Jewish (Ashkenazic): variant spelling of BERMAN. **2.** Respelling of German BEHRMANN, also found in Sweden.

Behrmann (361) **1.** German: variant of BERMANN 2. **2.** North German: spelling variant, dating from the 17th century, of BIERMANN. **3.** Jewish (Ashkenazic): variant spelling of BERMAN.

GIVEN NAMES German 7%. *Hans* (2), *Heinz* (2), *Otto* (2), *Aloys, Eckhard, Ernst, Frieda.*

Behrns (178) Reduced form of German BEHRENS.

Behun (116) Variant spelling of Irish BEHAN.

Behunin (162) Probably a variant spelling of Irish BOHANNON.

Behymer (325) German: from an old form of BOEHMER (see BOEHM).

Beich (100) Possibly a variant of German BAUCH or a respelling of German **Beiche**, a habitational name from Beicha or Beucha, both on the Saale river, or from Beichau in Silesia.
GIVEN NAMES German 6%. *Fritz, Uwe.*

Beichler (121) **1.** German: of uncertain origin; perhaps a variant of **Beuchler**, from a short form of a Germanic personal name related to Middle High German *bouc* 'arm band', 'necklace'. **2.** Altered spelling of German **Büchler** (see BUECHLER).

Beichner (139) Altered spelling of German **Büchner** (see BUCHNER).

Beidelman (104) Probably an altered spelling of German **Beutelmann**, a variant of BEUTLER, or a variant of BEIDLER 2.

Beideman (108) Probably an altered spelling of German BIEDERMANN.

Beidleman (180) Probably a variant (**Beidlmann**) of BEIDLER 2, or possibly a respelling of German **Beutelmann**, a variant of BEUTLER.

Beidler (391) **1.** Probably an altered spelling of German BEUTLER. **2.** habitational name for someone from Beidl, Oberpfalz (Bavaria).

Beier (1101) German, Danish, and Jewish (Ashkenazic): variant spelling of BAYER.
GIVEN NAMES German 6%. *Kurt* (4), *Hans* (3), *Klaus* (3), *Ernst* (2), *Dieter, Erwin, Hartmut, Heinz, Matthias, Theodor.*

Beierle (299) German: from a diminutive of BEIER (see BAYER).
GIVEN NAMES German 5%. *Fritz, Gottlieb, Otto, Udo.*

Beiermann (113) German: regional name for someone from Bavaria (German *Bayern*).
GIVEN NAMES German 4%. *Aloys, Math.*

Beigel (225) Jewish (Ashkenazic): metonymic occupational name for a baker of bagels, from Yiddish *beygl* 'bagel'.
GIVEN NAMES Jewish 8%; German 5%. *Chaim, Fishel, Hersh, Hirsch, Zalman; Juergen, Kurt, Othmar.*

Beighle (110) See BEIGHLEY.

Beighley (330) Origin uncertain. **1.** It may be an Americanized form of German BUECHLER or *Büchle* or of the Swiss form **Büchli** (see BUECHEL). Compare BEACHLEY 2. **2.** Alternatively, it could be an altered spelling of Irish BEGLEY.

Beightol (229) Americanized spelling of German BECHTOL, a dialect variant of BERTHOLD.

Beil (771) **1.** South German: from Middle High German, Middle Low German *bīl* 'axe', hence a metonymic occupational name for someone who made or used axes and similar implements, in particular a carpenter. **2.** Dutch: cognate of 1, from Dutch *bijl* 'axe'.

Beilby (110) English: variant spelling of BIELBY.

Beiler (457) German (Alemannic): from Middle High German *beigel, beile* 'measuring stick' (Late Latin *pagella*), hence an occupational name for an inspector of measures or a maker of measuring sticks.

Beilfuss (299) German: probably from the name of the aromatic plant *Beifuss* 'mugwort' (*Artemisia vulgaris*), Middle High German *bībōz*, but by the 13th century reinterpreted as *bīvōt* 'for the foot', with reference to the common belief that strapped to the legs the plant would ward off fatigue on a journey. The excrescent -*l*- is evidence of a further reinterpretation, as *Beilfuss* 'axe foot', suggestive of a deformity of the foot such as club foot.
GIVEN NAMES German 4%. *Erwin, Lorenz, Waltraut.*

Beilke (444) **1.** Probably an altered spelling of the German habitational name **Beilcke**, from a place called Belicke near Magdeburg. **2.** German: from a pet form of *Beile*, itself a pet form of *Elisabeth* (see ELIZABETH). Compare BEHLEN.
GIVEN NAMES German 5%. *Erwin* (4), *Kurt* (2), *Gerhard, Helmuth, Otto.*

Beilman (203) Probably an altered spelling of German **Bielmann**, a habitational name for someone from any of the places in eastern Germany named Biela, Bielau, or Biele.

Beilstein (169) German: habitational name from any of several places called Beilstein, in Hesse, Mosel, and Württemberg, named with an old Germanic field name, from *bīl* 'steep rock', 'cone-shaped mountain' + *stein* 'rock'.

Beim (101) Jewish (eastern Ashkenazic): ornamental name from northeastern Yiddish dialect *beym* 'tree'.
GIVEN NAMES Jewish 5%. *Schmuel, Yakov.*

Bein (345) **1.** German: from *Bein* 'bone', 'leg', as a nickname for a cripple or for someone who was exceptionally long-legged. In some cases it may be a short form of a compound name containing this element such as **Langbein** ('long leg'), **Stelzbein** ('peg leg'). **2.** North German: from a short form of the personal name BERNHARD. In Low German the older short form *Behn* (see BEHN) was diphthongized to *Bein*.
GIVEN NAMES German 4%. *Kurt, Wolf, Wolfgang.*

Beine (220) North German: variant of BEHNE (see BEHN).

Beiner (115) German: possibly a variant of the nickname BEIN 'leg' + -*er*, suffix of animate nouns, but more probably from a Germanic personal name composed with *win* 'friend' as the first element.
GIVEN NAME German 4%. *Ernst.*

Beining (167) North German: patronymic from BEIN 2 (short form of BERNHARD).

Beinke (112) North German: variant of BEHNKE.

Beinlich (103) German: from Middle High German *beinlinc* 'trouser leg', perhaps applied as a nickname for a tailor.
GIVEN NAMES German 6%. *Friedrich, Kurt.*

Beins (100) Dutch and North German: patronymic from the personal name *Bein*, a reduced form of BERNHARD.
GIVEN NAMES German 9%. *Guenter, Gunter, Otto.*

Beiriger (100) French (Alsace): probably an altered form of German BEHRINGER or French **Béringer** (see BERINGER).
GIVEN NAME French 4%. *Jeanmarie.*

Beirne (674) Irish: variant spelling of BYRNE. (In Ireland *O'Beirne* is found in Connacht, *O'Byrne* in Leinster.)
GIVEN NAMES Irish 6%. *Fintan, Padraic.*

Beise (119) German: topographic name for someone who lived by the Beise river, a tributary of the Fulda.

Beisel (469) German: **1.** variant spelling of BEISSEL. **2.** (Württemberg): from a pet form of the Germanic personal name *Biso*.

Beiser (345) **1.** German: occupational name for a falconer, Middle High German *beizaere* 'one who hunts with falcons'. **2.** Jewish (eastern Ashkenazic): nickname for a wicked or aggressive person, from Yiddish *beyzer* 'wicked', 'severe', 'bad', 'angry', 'fierce'.

Beishline (105) Probably an Americanized form of a German name: unexplained.

Beisler (117) South German: of uncertain origin. Possibly a variant of BESLER, or from *Beisel* 'small inn', an Austrian word from Yiddish and thieves' cant *bajis* 'house', hence an occupational name for an innkeeper.

Beisner (346) South German: **1.** occupational name for a falconer or hunter, from an agent derivative of Middle High German *beizen* 'to hunt with falcons', early modern German *beissen*. Compare BEISER. **2.** from a short form of a Germanic personal name, related to Old High German *bittan* 'to ask for' or *bītan* 'to endure or withstand'.

Beissel (183) German (Swabian): from the Swabian word for a breeding boar, hence a nickname for someone who kept such an animal or was thought to resemble one in some way.

Beisser (103) South German: nickname from Middle High German *beysser* 'biter', 'one who bites'.
GIVEN NAMES German 11%. *Franz* (2), *Alfons.*

Beiswanger (104) German: variant of BEISWENGER.

Beiswenger (192) German: habitational name from a place in Württemberg named Beiswang.
GIVEN NAME German 4%. *Kurt* (2).

Beitel (285) South German: **1.** variant of BEUTEL. **2.** see BEITLER 2.

Beiter (407) German: occupational name for a beekeeper, from a derivative of Middle High German *biute* 'beehive'.
GIVEN NAMES German 5%. *Otto* (3), *Gerhard, Kurt.*

Beith (127) Scottish: probably a reduced and altered form of MCBETH.

Beiting (103) German: probably a patronymic from a Germanic personal name (short form *Bito*) formed with *bītan* 'to endure'.
GIVEN NAME German 5%. *Otto* (2).

Beitler (420) South German: **1.** variant of BEUTLER. **2.** from a Germanic personal name related to Old High German *wīt* 'far'.

Beito (105) Norwegian: habitational name from a farm in Valdres, so named from a river name formed with an element meaning 'pasture' or 'freezing cold'.

Beitz (417) **1.** German: possibly a habitational name from places in eastern Germany named Baitz or Beitzsch. **2.** South German: from Middle High German *beiz* 'tanning liquid', 'lye', or 'falcon hunt', hence an metonymic occupational name for a tanner or someone who hunted with falcons, or in some cases perhaps a derogatory nickname. **3.** variant of BEITLER 2.

Beitzel (451) South German: variant of BEITZ 3.

Bejar (179) Spanish (**Béjar**) and Jewish (Sephardic): habitational name for someone from a place called Béjar in Salamanca province. The place name is of pre-Roman origin and unknown meaning; the original form seems to have been *Bigerra.*
GIVEN NAMES Spanish 52%. *Jose* (6), *Juan* (4), *Manuel* (4), *Alfredo* (2), *Francisco* (2), *Ignacio* (2), *Jacobo* (2), *Jorge* (2), *Miguel* (2), *Pedro* (2), *Rogelio* (2), *Alberto.*

Bejarano (679) Spanish and Jewish (Sephardic): habitational name, an adjectival derivative of **Béjar** (see BEJAR).
GIVEN NAMES Spanish 47%. *Jose* (19), *Manuel* (12), *Luis* (9), *Carlos* (8), *Jorge* (8), *Juan* (7), *Armando* (6), *Javier* (6), *Mario* (5), *Rafael* (5), *Raul* (5), *Ruben* (5).

Bek (105) **1.** Jewish (Ashkenazic): variant of BECK 5 'baker'. **2.** Slovenian: unexplained. Perhaps a variant of BEG.
GIVEN NAME Jewish 4%. *Izrail.*

Bekele (204) Ethiopian: unexplained.
GIVEN NAMES Ethiopian 64%; African 10%. *Girma* (5), *Berhanu* (3), *Dereje* (3), *Mekdes* (3), *Azeb* (3), *Dawit* (2), *Eyob* (2), *Frehiwot* (2), *Mesfin* (2), *Tamrat* (2), *Abenet, Admasu; Almaz* (2), *Fassil, Konjit.*

Bekker (277) **1.** Variant spelling of German and Jewish (Ashkenazic) BECKER. **2.** Danish: as 1, or an occupational name for a baker, from Dutch BAKKER.
GIVEN NAMES Russian 23%; Jewish 17%. *Leonid* (6), *Boris* (4), *Vladimir* (4), *Aleksandr* (3), *Lev* (3), *Mikhail* (3), *Galina* (2), *Grigoriy* (2), *Igor* (2), *Semyon* (2),

Yefim (2), *Yuriy* (2); *Semen* (3), *Aron* (2), *Yakov* (2), *Inna, Isaak, Moisey, Moysey, Naum, Polina, Ronya, Srul, Zalman.*

Bel (145) **1.** English and French: nickname for a handsome man (perhaps also ironically for an ugly one), from Old French *beu, bel* 'fair', 'lovely' (Late Latin *bellus*). **2.** Hungarian (**Bél**): from the old secular Hungarian name *Bél*, or alternatively from *bél* 'internal part', probably an occupational name for a servant who worked in the household. **3.** Czech (**Běl**) from Czech *bílý* 'white'.
GIVEN NAME German 4%. *Liselotte.*

Belair (569) French: see BELAIRE.
GIVEN NAMES French 11%. *Andre* (3), *Armand* (2), *Emile* (2), *Fernand* (2), *Lucien* (2), *Aime, Auguste, Aurele, Carmelle, Normand, Raoul, Rolande.*

Belaire (190) French: respelling of French **Belleaire**, a nickname for someone with a pleasant demeanor, from *belle* 'lovely' + *aire* 'demeanor', 'manner'.
FOREBEARS In Canada this is documented as a secondary surname for Dusault, Gaudreau, Hémério, Hérault, Moreau, Plessis, Ragaut, Vetu. There is also a Belair-Beaupré recorded in 1715.
GIVEN NAMES French 6%. *Amede, Placide.*

Belak (137) Croatian and Slovenian: nickname meaning 'fair-haired' or 'pale-skinned'. Compare BELAN, BELICH.

Belan (133) **1.** Croatian and Serbian: nickname for someone with white or very fair hair or a pale complexion, from *bijel, beo* 'white'. **2.** Czech (**Bělán**) and Slovak (**Belán**): nickname from Czech *bílý,* Slovak *biely* 'white', or derivative of the female personal name *Běla* (see BELIN). **3.** French (**Bélan**): unexplained.
FOREBEARS A bearer of the name Bélan was buried in Quebec city in 1688; his origins are unknown.

Beland (664) French: probably an altered form of BRELAND.
GIVEN NAMES French 9%. *Normand* (3), *Armand* (2), *Andre, Aurore, Cecile, Donat, Emilien, Gaetan, Laurent, Lucienne, Marcel, Stephane.*

Belanger (5221) French: variant of **Béringer** (see BERINGER).
FOREBEARS A Belanger from Normandy, France, is documented in Quebec city in 1637; the secondary surname Catherine is associated with it.
GIVEN NAMES French 13%. *Andre* (16), *Armand* (14), *Normand* (13), *Emile* (11), *Marcel* (10), *Jacques* (8), *Lucien* (7), *Fernand* (6), *Adrien* (5), *Germain* (5), *Adelard* (4), *Camille* (4).

Belardo (129) Italian: from a dissimilated form of the personal name BERARDO.
GIVEN NAMES Spanish 22%; Italian 15%; French 5%. *Rafael* (2), *Roberto* (2), *Ana, Angel, Angelito, Arsenio, Encarnacion, Jesus, Jorge, Jose, Juana, Julio; Aldo* (2),

Salvatore (2), *Aniello, Antonio, Carmelo, Matteo; Camille, Raynald.*

Belasco (268) Spanish (of Basque origin): from the Basque personal name *Belasco* (from *bela* 'raven' + the diminutive suffix *-sk*).
GIVEN NAMES Spanish 6%. *Manuel* (2), *Marcos* (2), *Aureo, Carlos, Genaro, Jorge, Juan, Medardo, Oswaldo, Salvador.*

Belay (139) Ethiopian: unexplained.
GIVEN NAMES Ethiopian 64%. *Dawit* (2), *Ermias* (2), *Fana* (2), *Haile* (2), *Yared* (2), *Abeba, Amare, Amha, Anteneh, Ayele, Eyassu, Fetlework.*

Belcastro (380) Southern Italian: habitational name from a place called Belcastro ('beautiful castle') in Catanzaro, Calabria.
GIVEN NAMES Italian 17%. *Angelo* (2), *Luigi* (2), *Amedeo, Antonio, Camillo, Carlo, Deno, Domenic, Domenico, Giuseppe, Nicolo, Piero.*

Belch (323) **1.** English: variant of BALCH. **2.** German: nickname, from Middle High German *belche* 'coot' (bird), for someone who was thought to resemble the bird in some way.

Belcher (9595) English: **1.** (of Norman origin): nickname from Old French *beu, bel* 'fair', 'lovely' + *chere* 'face', 'countenance'. Although it originally meant 'face', the word *chere* later came to mean also 'demeanor', 'disposition' (hence English *cheer*), and the nickname may thus also have denoted a person of pleasant, cheerful disposition. There has been some confusion with BOWSER. **2.** nickname for someone given to belching. See BALCH.
FOREBEARS Andrew Belcher came before 1654 from London, England, to Cambridge, MA, where he kept a tavern. His family was originally from Wiltshire. His descendant Jonathan Belcher (1682–1757), a weathy merchant, was governor of MA and NH. Subsequently, as governor of NJ, he was one of the founders of the College of New Jersey (now Princeton).

Belcourt (170) French and English (of Norman origin): habitational name from a place named Bellecour(t) 'lovely farm'.
FOREBEARS In the form Belcour this is recorded as a secondary surname for Desruisseaux, De la Fontaine de Belcourt, and Trotier; as Bellecourt, it is a secondary surname for Lefebvre.
GIVEN NAMES French 8%. *Henri* (2), *Adrien, Gilles, Jean Noel.*

Beld (129) Origin unidentified. Possibly of Dutch or German origin, from a pet form of the personal name *Baldo* (see BALD).

Belden (1831) English: **1.** variant of the English habitational name **Bayldon**. **2.** possibly also a variant of BALDING.
FOREBEARS Many if not all bearers of this surname are descended from Richard Bayldon, who came from England to CT in 1645.

Beldin (146) English: variant of BELDING.

Belding (698) English: variant of BALDING.

Beldon (146) English: variant spelling of BELDEN.

Belen (222) **1.** Spanish (**Belén**): from the personal name derived from the Biblical place name *Bethlehem*, birthplace of Jesus Christ. **2.** Jewish (Sephardic): adoption of the Spanish name.

GIVEN NAMES Spanish 27%; Jewish 4%. *Jose* (4), *Luis* (3), *Ernesto* (2), *Jesus* (2), *Luz* (2), *Alfredo, Alicia, Ana, Andres, Augusto, Carlos, Conrado; Maier* (2), *Ari.*

Belew (1167) English and Irish: variant spelling of BELLEW.

Beley (111) English: most probably a variant of BEELEY.

Belfer (183) Jewish (Ashkenazic): occupational name from Yiddish *be(he)lfer, ba(he)lfer* 'teacher's assistant' (someone who conducts children to school).

GIVEN NAMES Jewish 10%; Russian 7%. *Esfir, Inna, Naum, Shira; Anatoly* (2), *Boris* (2), *Aleksandra, Galina, Sofiya, Yury.*

Belfi (121) Italian (Belluno): probably from an old personal name *Belfiglio* meaning 'beautiful son'.

Belfield (336) **1.** English (chiefly West Midlands): habitational name from a place in Greater Manchester called Belfield, from the name of the Beal river + Old English *feld* 'open country'. The river name is possibly from Old English *bēogol* 'winding'. **2.** Possibly an Americanized spelling of French BELLEVILLE.

Belfiore (428) Italian: **1.** from the personal name *Belfiore*, meaning 'beautiful (as a) flower'. **2.** habitational name from any of numerous minor places called Belfiore, as for example in Verona province.

GIVEN NAMES Italian 24%. *Salvatore* (4), *Sal* (3), *Mario* (2), *Angelo, Aniello, Biagio, Domenico, Ernesto, Ezio, Gerardo, Gregorio, Nino, Rocco, Silvestro, Vito.*

Belflower (230) Probably a partly Americanized form of BELFIORE or BELLEFLEUR.

Belford (842) English: habitational name from a place in Northumberland named Belford, from Old English *belle* 'bell-shaped hill' + *ford* 'ford'.

Belgard (256) French: variant of BELGARDE.

Belgarde (241) French: variant of **Belle-garde**, a widespread topographic name for someone living in a secure, protected location, from French *beau* (feminine *belle*) 'beautiful', 'lovely' + *gard* 'shelter', 'refuge'. The name is frequent in New England.

Belger (224) **1.** Dutch and North German: from a Germanic personal name composed of *bald* 'bold' + *gēr, gār* 'spear'. **2.** German: habitational name from any of several places called Belgern, near Torgau and in Saxony. **3.** English: variant of BOLGER.

Belgrave (255) English: habitational name from a place in Leicestershire, recorded in Domesday Book as *Merdegrave*. The original name derived from Old English *mearð* 'marten' + *grāf* 'grove', but after the Norman Conquest the first element was taken to be Old French *merde* 'dung', 'filth', and changed to Old French *beu, bel* 'fair', 'lovely', to remove the unpleasant association. A mid 12th-century writer refers to the place as '*Merthegrave, nunc* (now) *Belegrava*'.

Belgum (118) Norwegian: habitational name from a farm name derived from Old Norse *belgr* 'animal skin'.

GIVEN NAMES Scandinavian 8%; German 8%. *Gerhard, Kurt.*

Belhumeur (158) French: nickname for a well-tempered or genial person, from Old French *bel* 'lovely' + *humeur* 'humor', 'disposition'.

FOREBEARS As a secondary surname this is associated with the surnames Ardouin, Badeau, Blanche, Blosse, Bloze, Dupont, Janot, Montauban, Naudet, and Philippe.

GIVEN NAMES French 14%. *Armand* (2), *Emile, Herve, Jeanpaul, Normand, Pierre.*

Belich (149) **1.** Serbian and Croatian (**Belić**) or Slovenian **Belič**: nickname for a fair-skinned or fair-haired person, from Serbian *beo*, Croatian *bijel*, Slovenian *bel* 'white', 'light', 'fair', feminine *bela*. **2.** Jewish (eastern Ashkenazic): habitational name (Yiddish **Belic** or **Belich**) from a place called Belitsa in western Belarus.

Beliles (111) Probably an Americanized form of French BELLE-ISLE.

Belin (495) **1.** Czech (**Bělín**): either a nickname from Czech *bílý* 'white' or a derivative of the female personal name *Běla* (which also means 'white'), denoting the son or husband of a woman so named. **2.** Serbian: variant of BELAN. **3.** Jewish (eastern Ashkenazic): metronymic from the Yiddish female personal name *Beyle* meaning 'beautiful' (related to French *belle*).

Belinski (122) Polish: variant spelling of **Bieliński** (see BIELINSKI).

Belinsky (183) **1.** Russian and Jewish (Ashkenazic): habitational name from Belin in Ukraine. **2.** Czech (**Bělinský**) and Slovak (**Belinský**): habitational name from a place called Bělín. **3.** In some cases perhaps an altered spelling of Polish **Bieliński** (see BIELINSKI).

GIVEN NAMES Jewish 8%; Russian 4%. *Avi, Hyman, Slava, Srul; Leonid* (2), *Alexei, Vladimir.*

Belisle (1454) French: variant of BELLE-ISLE.

FOREBEARS A Belisle from the Anjou region of France is recorded in Quebec city in 1690. Belisle is also associated as a secondary name with Chévrefils, Germain, Goguet, Goyer, Lamarre, Rotureau.

GIVEN NAMES French 11%. *Lucien* (5), *Andre* (4), *Armand* (4), *Normand* (3), *Pierre* (3), *Adelard* (2), *Emile* (2), *Valmore* (2), *Camille, Cecile, Clovis, Edmour.*

Belitz (171) Jewish (from Belarus and Ukraine): habitational name for someone from Belitsa in Belarus.

GIVEN NAMES German 6%. *Dietrich, Gunter, Hans, Kurt.*

Beliveau (767) French: from a derivative of Old French *beli, beslif* 'diagonal', which Morlet suggests may have been a nickname for a drunkard, with reference to his staggering walk.

FOREBEARS The name is recorded in Quebec in the mid 18th century.

GIVEN NAMES French 17%. *Armand* (6), *Andre* (4), *Chantel* (2), *Marcel* (2), *Michel* (2), *Normand* (2), *Pierre* (2), *Adelard, Adrien, Alain, Alphonse, Cecile.*

Belizaire (157) French: unexplained.

GIVEN NAMES French 43%; German 6%. *Altagrace* (2), *Antoine* (2), *Pierre* (2), *Chantal, Colette, Flore, Jeanty, Josseline, Ketty, Louise Marie, Micheline, Philomene; Gerda, Ralf.*

Belk (1941) English: variant of BALCH.

Belka (189) **1.** Polish: nickname for a tall, upright man, from *belka* 'beam', 'timber'. **2.** Czech (**Bělka**) and Slovak (also **Bielka**): from a pet form of the female personal name *Běla* meaning 'white', or, in some cases, possibly a nickname from *bělka* 'squirrel'. **3.** Jewish (Ashkenazic): from a pet form of the Yiddish female personal name *Beyle* meaning 'beautiful' (related to French *belle*).

Belke (191) **1.** German: possibly a habitational name for someone from Belkau in eastern Germany (near Stendal). **2.** North German: from Middle Low German *belke* 'beam', 'rafter', hence a nickname for an exceptionally tall person. **3.** Altered spelling of German BOEHLKE, **Bölke**.

GIVEN NAMES German 7%. *Erna, Hans, Helmut, Kurt.*

Belken (110) Origin unidentified. Possibly a variant of BELKIN.

Belkin (453) **1.** Jewish (eastern Ashkenazic): metronymic from *Beylke*, a pet form of the Yiddish female personal name *Beyle* (see BELIN), with the Slavic suffix *-in*. **2.** Russian: patronymic from the nickname *Belka* meaning 'squirrel' (a derivative of *bely* 'white', referring to the animal's white stomach).

GIVEN NAMES Jewish 11%; Russian 8%. *Sol* (2), *Aron, Avram, Emanuel, Esfir, Hershel, Hyman, Ilya, Irina, Miriam, Rifka, Shimshon; Mikhail* (4), *Arkadiy* (3), *Aleksandr, Alexey, Arkady, Boris, Galina, Iliya, Lev, Semyon, Yafim, Yurity.*

Belknap (1375) English: probably a habitational name from a lost or unidentified place, the second element of which is most likely Middle English *knappe* 'hilltop'.

FOREBEARS Abraham Belknap (*c.*1588–*c.*1643) emigrated from Latton, Essex, England, to Lynn, MA, in the 1630s.

Belko (187) Hungarian: unexplained.

Bell (89728) **1.** Scottish and northern English: from Middle English *belle* 'bell', in various applications; most probably a metonymic occupational name for a bell ringer or bell maker, or a topographic name for someone living 'at the bell' (as attested by 14th-century forms such as *John atte Belle*). This indicates either residence by an actual bell (e.g. a town's bell in a bell tower, centrally placed to summon meetings, sound the alarm, etc.) or 'at the sign of the bell', i.e. a house or inn sign (although surnames derived from house and inn signs are rare in Scots and English). **2.** Scottish and northern English: from the medieval personal name *Bel*. As a man's name this is from Old French *beu*, *bel* 'handsome', which was also used as a nickname. As a female name it represents a short form of *Isobel*, a form of *Elizabeth*. **3.** Scottish: Americanized form of Gaelic **Mac Giolla Mhaoil** 'son of the servant of the devotee' (see MULLEN 1). **4.** Jewish (Ashkenazic): Americanized form of one or more like-sounding Jewish surnames. **5.** Norwegian: habitational name from a farmstead in western Norway named Bell, the origin of which is unexplained. **6.** Scandinavian: of English or German origin; in German as a habitational name for someone from Bell in Rhineland, Germany, or possibly from Belle in Westphalia. **7.** Americanized spelling of German **Böhl** or **Böll** (see BOEHLE, BOLL).

Bella (639) **1.** Italian: from the medieval female personal name *Bella*, meaning 'beautiful', 'lovely'. **2.** Italian: possibly a habitational name from Basilicata Bella, in Potenza, probably so named with Latin *labellum* 'little basin'. **3.** Greek: reduced form of BELLAS.
GIVEN NAMES Italian 16%; Spanish 8%. *Romeo* (3), *Salvatore* (3), *Aldo*, *Alfonso*, *Alfredo*, *Antonio*, *Berto*, *Carlo*, *Dario*, *Italia*, *Napoli*, *Sebastiano*, *Vita*; *Miguel* (2), *Carmelita*, *Eleuterio*, *Elida*, *Graciela*, *Juan*, *Lazaro*, *Maria De La Luz*.

Bellack (112) **1.** Germanized or Americanized spelling of Slovenian *Belak*, a nickname denoting a fair-haired or pale-skinned person, from *bel* 'white', 'light', 'fair'. **2.** Respelling of German **Bellach**, a nickname from a derivative of Sorbian *bely* 'white'.
GIVEN NAMES German 6%. *Arno*, *Florian*, *Kurt*.

Bellafiore (119) Italian: variant of BELFIORE originating in an area where the noun *fiore* 'flower' is treated as feminine, as for example in Sicily.
GIVEN NAMES Italian 21%. *Vito* (3), *Salvatore* (2), *Filippo*, *Francesco*, *Rosaria*, *Sal*.

Bellah (407) Variant of Irish BALLAGH.
FOREBEARS Bearers of this surname are descended from John Bellah, Bellagh, or Ballagh, born in about 1645 in county Antrim, Ireland, died 8 November 1717 in Charleston, SC. His son William is generally regarded as the immigrant.

Bellaire (141) French: see BELAIRE.
Bellairs (115) Anglicized variant of French BELAIRE.
Bellamy (4562) English and Irish (of Norman origin), French: literal or ironic nickname meaning 'fine friend', from French *beau* 'fair', 'handsome' (*bel* before a vowel) + *ami* 'friend'.
Bellan (156) Probably an altered spelling of BELAN, BELAND, or BELLAND.
Bellanca (242) Italian (Sicily): nickname meaning 'beautiful (*bella*) hip (*anca*)'.
GIVEN NAMES Italian 11%. *Cataldo*, *Cosimo*, *Guido*, *Nicolo*, *Sal*, *Salvatore*, *Vito*.

Belland (376) **1.** French: probably a variant of BRELAND. **2.** Norwegian: habitational name from any of the farmsteads in Agder so named, from an unexplained first element + *land* 'land'.
GIVEN NAMES French 5%. *Antoine* (2), *Michel* (2), *Andre*.

Bellanger (270) English and French: variant of BERINGER.
GIVEN NAMES French 11%. *Serge* (3), *Alain*, *Armand*, *Francoise*, *Gaetan*, *Georges*, *Wilbrod*.

Bellante (153) Italian: **1.** from a derivative of the nickname BELLO. **2.** habitational name from Bellante in Teramo province.
GIVEN NAMES Italian 16%. *Sal* (2), *Carmelo*, *Santo*.

Bellanti (113) Italian: patronymic or plural form of BELLANTE.
GIVEN NAMES Italian 15%. *Salvatore* (2), *Domenico*, *Guiseppe*, *Sal*.

Bellantoni (261) Italian: from a nickname composed of the elements *bello* 'handsome' + the personal name *Antonio*.
GIVEN NAMES Italian 22%. *Rocco* (8), *Antonino*, *Antonio*, *Concetta*, *Cosimo*, *Filomena*, *Nino*, *Salvatore*.

Bellar (370) English: **1.** from French *bélier* 'ram', hence a nickname for someone thought to resemble a ram in some way or possibly a metonymic occupational name for a shepherd. **2.** variant spelling of BELLER.

Bellard (654) **1.** English: unexplained. In the British Isles the name is now found chiefly in Lancashire. **2.** French: dissimilated form of **Bérard** (see BERARD).
GIVEN NAMES French 7%. *Andre* (2), *Leonce* (2), *Albon*, *Laurent*, *Nolton*, *Orelia*, *Vernice*.

Bellas (341) **1.** English: topographic name for someone who lived by a belltower, from a compound of Middle English *belle* 'bell' + *hous* 'house'. The surname is now found chiefly in Yorkshire. **2.** Greek form of the Italian surname BELLA, or alternatively a nickname derived from Slavic *bel* 'white'.

Bellavance (331) French: compound of *belle* 'beautiful' (feminine of *beau*) + *avance* 'advance', 'overture', presumably applied as a nickname. It is frequent in New England.
FOREBEARS In Canada Bellavance is associated as a secondary surname with **Gagné**.

GIVEN NAMES French 11%. *Henri* (2), *Napoleon* (2), *Alcide*, *Alphonse*, *Andre*, *Fernand*, *Gabrielle*, *Germaine*, *Germine*, *Josee*, *Normand*.

Bellavia (274) Italian (Sicily): probably from French *bellevue* 'good view' or *bellevie* 'good life' rather than Italian *bella via* 'good road'.
GIVEN NAMES Italian 23%; French 4%. *Mario* (4), *Salvatore* (4), *Angelo* (3), *Sal* (3), *Carmelo* (2), *Antonino*, *Antonio*, *Nino*, *Vito*; *Alphonse* (3).

Belle (970) **1.** Italian (**Bellé**): from a reduced derivative of BELLO, for example *Belletto*. **2.** French: from *Belle* meaning 'beautiful'. In medieval times this epithet was often combined with a baptismal name, e.g. *Bellemarie*. **3.** German: habitational name from a place so named in the Lippe district. **4.** German spelling of Slovenian *Bele*, nickname denoting a fair-haired or pale-skinned person, a derivative of *bel* 'white', 'light', 'fair', formed with the suffix *-e*, typically denoting a young person.

Belleau (269) French: **1.** nickname from *beau*, *bel* 'handsome', 'beautiful' + the diminutive suffix *-eau* (from Latin *ellu*). **2.** habitational name from places so named in Aisne and Meurthe-et-Moselle; the latter is recorded as early as 1047 as *Bella Aqua* 'lovely water' (French *beau*, *bel* 'lovely' + *eau* 'water').
FOREBEARS A Belleau from the Périgord region of France is documented in Quebec city in 1673, with the secondary surname Larose.
GIVEN NAMES French 4%. *Lucien*, *Marcel*.

Bellefeuille (372) French: from Old French *beu*, *bel* 'lovely' + *fueille*, *foille* 'leaf', perhaps as a nickname for a woodsman. It is particularly common in New England.
FOREBEARS In Canada it is associated as a secondary surname with Houde, Lefebvre, Pelletier, Poiriau, and Poiriot.
GIVEN NAMES French 8%. *Marcel* (2), *Adrien*, *Armand*, *Gillis*, *Jean Louis*, *Laurent*, *Ovide*.

Bellefleur (157) French: from Old French *beu*, *bel* 'lovely' + *flor*, *flour* 'flower', possibly applied ironically as a soldier's nickname. The name is found chiefly in New England.
GIVEN NAMES French 16%. *Fernande* (2), *Camille*, *Carmelle*, *Collette*, *Marcel*, *Monique*, *Normand*.

Belle-Isle (104) French: topographic name from Belle Isle (literally 'beautiful island'), an island in the Gulf of Morbihan, or from some other place so named.
GIVEN NAMES French 7%. *Cecile*, *Jacques*, *Patrice*.

Bellemare (228) Altered spelling of French **Bellemère**, a metronymic meaning 'mother-in-law' or 'step-mother'. As a surname, this may originally have been applied as a nickname.

GIVEN NAMES French 21%. *Marcel* (4), *Jacques* (2), *Pierre* (2), *Alcide*, *Dominique*, *Francois*, *Germain*, *Gilles*, *Laurent*, *Michel*, *Normand*, *Valmore*.

Bellemore (110) **1.** Variant spelling of English BELMORE. **2.** Possibly a respelling of French **Bellemère** (see BELLEMARE).

GIVEN NAMES French 8%. *Aime*, *Marcel*.

Bellenger (112) German and French: variant of BERINGER 1.

Beller (1413) **1.** English: occupational or topographic name, from a derivative of BELL 1. **2.** German: habitational name from any of several places so named in Westphalia. **3.** German: nickname from Middle High German *bellen* 'to pinch'. **4.** German: from the Germanic personal name *Baldher* (see BELTER). **5.** Hungarian (**Bellér**): variant of **Böllér** (see BOLLER).

Bellerive (130) French: topographic name from Old French *beu*, *bel* 'lovely'; also 'grand', 'high' + *rive* 'bank', 'shore'.

GIVEN NAMES French 16%. *Alain*, *Andre*, *Armand*, *Emile*, *Florent*, *Origene*, *Philibert*.

Bellerose (274) French: from Old French *beu*, *bel* 'lovely' + *rose* 'rose'; perhaps a metronymic or a soldier's nickname.

GIVEN NAMES French 14%. *Normand* (2), *Andre*, *Aurele*, *Camille*, *Emile*, *Emilien*, *Gilberte*, *Jacques*, *Jean Louis*, *Michel*.

Belles (607) Spanish, Galician, and Catalan: either from a place of this name (in A Coruña province, Galicia), or from a Catalan descriptive nickname meaning 'beauties'.

Bellet (109) French: from a derivative of *bel* 'handsome'.

GIVEN NAME French 4%. *Alain*.

Belleville (393) French: habitational name from several places called Belleville (for example in Rhône and Meuse) or named with this word (for example Belleville sur Vie in Vendée), from Old French *beu*, *bel* 'lovely' + *ville* 'settlement', 'domain'.

FOREBEARS A bearer of the name from Paris is documented in Quebec city in 1666.

GIVEN NAMES French 8%. *Marcel* (2), *Andre*, *Carmelle*, *Gaston*, *Henri*, *Normand*, *Pierre*.

Bellew (901) English and Irish (of Norman origin): habitational name from any of the various places in northern France, such as Belleu (Aisne), named in Old French with *bel* 'beautiful' + *l(i)eu* 'place', or from Belleau (Meurthe-et-Moselle), which is named with Old French *bel* 'lovely' + *ewe* 'water' (Latin *aqua*), or from Bellou (Calvados), which is probably named with a Gaulish word meaning 'watercress'. Compare French BEAULIEU.

FOREBEARS In 1651 a Major William Bellew was granted 406 acres of land in Henrico Co., VA. In 1652 Lieut. Col. Bellew (possibly the same man), with another, was granted 1050 acres in James City Co. An Irish family of this name trace their descent from

an early settler, Adam de Bella Aqua, who was living in 1210. They have given their name to Bellewstown in County Louth and Mountbellew in County Galway.

Bellezza (132) Italian: from *Bellezza*, a nickname or personal name meaning 'beauty', 'loveliness'.

GIVEN NAMES Italian 15%. *Vito* (2), *Antonietta*.

Bellflower (140) See BELFLOWER.

Belli (621) Italian: patronymic or plural form of BELLO.

GIVEN NAMES Italian 14%. *Angelo* (7), *Aldo* (3), *Remo* (3), *Caesar* (2), *Dino* (2), *Guido* (2), *Antonio*, *Edo*, *Elio*, *Enrico*, *Ferdinando*, *Guilio*.

Bellia (111) Italian (Sicily) and Maltese: variant of BELLA 'beautiful'.

GIVEN NAMES Italian 32%. *Angelo* (2), *Antonio* (2), *Augustino* (2), *Carmela* (2), *Sal* (2), *Salvatore* (2), *Agatino*, *Attilio*, *Carmelo*, *Francesco*, *Gaetano*.

Bellile (101) Variant spelling of French BELLE-ISLE.

Bellin (495) **1.** German: habitational name from any of several places in northeastern Germany named Bellin. **2.** French: variant spelling of BELIN. **3.** Welsh: Americanized form of **Belyn**, from the personal name of a shadowy Welsh hero who died in 627.

Bellina (208) **1.** Italian: from a diminutive of the female personal name BELLA. **2.** Italian or German spelling of Slovenian **Belina**, nickname denoting a fair-haired or pale-skinned person, from *bel* 'white', 'light', 'fair', with the augmentative suffix *-ina*.

GIVEN NAMES Italian 10%. *Carmine*, *Emanuele*, *Pio*, *Salvatore*.

Belling (329) **1.** German: habitational name from any of several places called Belling, in Pomerania, Baden, Hesse, Thuringia, and elsewhere. **2.** Welsh: see BELLIN.

Bellinger (1757) **1.** English (of Norman origin) and French: variant of BERINGER. **2.** German: habitational name for someone from a place called Belling (see BELLING).

Bellingham (201) English: habitational name from places called Bellingham, in Greater London (formerly in Kent) and Northumberland. The former is named with Old English *Beringahām* 'homestead (Old English *hām*) of the followers of *Be(o)ra*', a byname meaning 'bear'; the latter seems to have been originally named as the 'homestead of the dwellers at the bell', from Old English *belle* used in a transferred sense of a bell-shaped hill.

FOREBEARS Richard Bellingham (c.1592–1672) came from Boston, Lincolnshire, England, to Boston, MA, in 1634. He was a controversial political figure in the new colony, an opponent of John Winthrop. He was elected governor of MA in 1641 and again in 1654 and 1665–72.

An Irish family of this name trace their

descent from William de Bellingham, who was sheriff of Tynedale, Northumbria, in 1279. They were established in Ireland by Robert Bellingham, who settled in County Longford in 1611. They gave their name to Castlebellingham in County Louth, Ireland.

Bellinghausen (161) German: habitational name from a place so named in northern Germany.

Bellini (393) Italian: patronymic or plural form of BELLINO.

GIVEN NAMES Italian 16%. *Angelo* (5), *Dante* (3), *Gino* (3), *Carmine* (2), *Luigi* (2), *Antonio*, *Carlo*, *Dino*, *Giovanna*, *Ivano*, *Neno*, *Philomena*.

Bellino (619) Italian: from a diminutive of BELLO.

GIVEN NAMES Italian 16%. *Angelo* (5), *Vito* (4), *Salvatore* (3), *Carmine* (2), *Aldo*, *Antonio*, *Constantino*, *Dino*, *Domenic*, *Donato*, *Gaetano*, *Geno*.

Bellis (963) Welsh: **1.** Anglicized form of Welsh *ap Elisedd* 'son of *Elisedd*' (see ELLIS). **2.** English: variant of BELLOWS, from an old form of the word, which persisted generally until the 16th century and much later in various dialects.

Bellisario (140) Italian: from the (now rare) personal name *Belisario*, *Bellisario*, derived via Latin from Greek *Belisarios*, a name that is probably of Illyric origin. The diffusion of the name was promoted by the fame of the general Belisarius, who served the emperor Justinian.

GIVEN NAMES Italian 23%. *Egidio* (2), *Pasquale* (2), *Attilio*, *Ciro*, *Domenic*, *Domenico*, *Enrico*, *Ermanno*, *Filomena*, *Nunzio*, *Sebastiano*, *Vincenzo*.

Bellissimo (197) Italian: from a nickname meaning 'most handsome' or the personal name *Bellissimo*.

GIVEN NAMES Italian 19%; French 4%. *Vito* (3), *Angelo* (2), *Sal* (2), *Domenic*, *Pasquale*, *Soccorso*; *Emile* (2).

Belliston (125) Scottish: habitational name from Belliston in Fife.

Belliveau (852) French: variant spelling of BELIVEAU.

GIVEN NAMES French 9%. *Emile* (3), *Alcide* (2), *Adrien*, *Allain*, *Alyre*, *Amedee*, *Andre*, *Andree*, *Armand*, *Collette*, *Evariste*, *Joffre*.

Bellizzi (212) Southern Italian (Campania): habitational name from either of two villages, Bellizzi in Salerno, or Bellizzi Irpino in Avellino, so named with a variant of *bellezza* 'beauty'.

GIVEN NAMES Italian 22%. *Angelo* (4), *Elena* (2), *Giovanni* (2), *Biagio*, *Carlo*, *Gennaro*, *Gino*, *Mario*, *Osvaldo*, *Paolo*, *Ricardo*.

Bellm (160) German: habitational name from Bellheim (Palatinate), which is pronounced *Bellem* locally, or from Belm, near Osnabrück, formerly Bellheim.

GIVEN NAME German 4%. *Kurt* (2).

Bellman (724) **1.** English: occupational name for a bell ringer, in particular one whose duty was to make public announcements, after ringing a bell to attract attention. Compare BELL. **2.** Americanized or Swedish spelling of German **Bellmann**, a North German habitational name from Belle in Westphalia, Bell in the Rhineland, or Bellen near Bremen.

Bellmer (145) German: habitational name for someone from Belm near Osnabrück or from Bellheim near Mainz (see BELLM).
GIVEN NAME German 5%. *Kurt* (2).

Bellmore (309) **1.** Variant spelling of English BELMORE. **2.** Possibly a respelling of French **Bellemère** (see BELLEMARE).

Bello (2243) **1.** Spanish and Italian: from *bello* 'handsome' (Late Latin *bellus*), hence a nickname for a handsome man or perhaps in some instances ironically for an ugly one. In medieval Italy the word was also applied as a personal name, which also gave rise to the surname. **2.** Catalan (**Belló**): variant of **Abelló** (see ABELLO). **3.** Galician: variant of **Vello**, from a personal name which is either a variant of VELA or a derivative of Latin *vetulus*, a diminutive of *vetus* 'old'.
GIVEN NAMES Spanish 27%; Portuguese 8%; Italian 8%. *Jose* (36), *Luis* (24), *Manuel* (14), *Juan* (13), *Jorge* (9), *Mario* (9), *Roberto* (9), *Eduardo* (8), *Sergio* (8), *Alberto* (7), *Ernesto* (7), *Julio* (7); *Joaquim, Paulo*; *Antonio* (13), *Angelo* (6), *Salvatore* (5), *Carmine* (3), *Natale* (3), *Vito* (3), *Eliseo* (2), *Luciano* (2), *Sal* (2), *Aldo, Amato*.

Bellock (100) English (of Norman origin): from a Norman French dialect form of the common French place name *Beaulieu*.
GIVEN NAME German 4%. *Kurt*.

Bellofatto (140) Southern Italian: from the personal name *Bellofatto* meaning 'happy event', 'well done'.
GIVEN NAMES Italian 22%. *Angelo, Carmine, Mario, Rocco, Sal, Silvio*.

Belloli (116) Italian: pet form of BELLO.
GIVEN NAMES Italian 11%. *Primo* (2), *Angelo, Marcello, Stefano*.

Bellomo (430) Italian: nickname from *bello* 'handsome', 'lovely' + *uomo* 'man' (Latin *homo*).
GIVEN NAMES Italian 29%. *Angelo* (6), *Salvatore* (5), *Antonio* (3), *Gaspare* (2), *Gasper* (2), *Mario* (2), *Santo* (2), *Alessandro, Carlo, Donato, Eliseo, Giacomo, Giuseppe*.

Bellomy (506) Probably an altered spelling of BELLAMY.

Bellon (424) **1.** French: from a medieval diminutive of BEAU. **2.** Spanish (**Bellón**): unexplained.
GIVEN NAMES Spanish 8%. *Jose* (4), *Alvaro* (2), *Amando, Claudio, Consuelo, Diego, Jorge, Leopoldo, Ondina, Oneida, Pablo, Ramon*.

Bellone (212) Italian: from an augmentative of BELLO.
GIVEN NAMES Italian 8%; French 4%. *Carlo, Gaetano, Giuseppe, Salvatore, Stefano, Vincenza*; *Baptiste, Camille*.

Belloni (110) Italian: patronymic or plural form of BELLONE.
GIVEN NAMES Italian 24%. *Ricardo* (2), *Alessandra, Alessio, Alfonso, Carlo, Franco, Gabriella, Giovanni, Mario, Mauricio, Narcisso, Ruggero*.

Bellot (104) Catalan: probably a derivative of **Abelló** (see ABELLO).
GIVEN NAMES Spanish 12%. *Benito* (2), *Manuel* (2), *Alejandra, Felipe, Jovita, Juan, Maricela, Pedro*.

Bellotti (300) Italian: patronymic from a pet form of BELLO.
GIVEN NAMES Italian 16%. *Sergio* (3), *Aldo* (2), *Carlo, Carmine, Cesare, Enrico, Ireneo, Renzo, Alberto, Alfredo, Fabio, Mario, Renato, Rosalia*.

Bellow (327) **1.** English: variant of BELLEW. **2.** English: metonymic occupational name for a bellows maker or someone who pumped the bellows, for example for a blacksmith or for a church organ, from Middle English *beli*. Until the early 15th century the term was normally used in the singular. **3.** Variant spelling of Jewish (eastern Ashkenazic) and Russian BELOFF.

Bellows (1448) English: metonymic occupational name for a maker or user of bellows. See BELLOW.
FOREBEARS John Bellows emigrated from England to MA on the *Hopewell* in 1635. Benjamin Bellows was one of the founders of Walpole, VT, in the mid 18th century.

Bellucci (475) Italian: from a diminutive of BELLO.
GIVEN NAMES Italian 17%. *Antonio* (3), *Sante* (2), *Amerigo, Angelo, Antonietta, Bartolomeo, Concetta, Cosmo, Enrico, Ettore, Guido, Italo*.

Belluomini (179) Italian: variant (plural) of **Belluomo** (see BELLOMO).
GIVEN NAMES Italian 17%. *Angelo* (3), *Antonio* (2), *Dante, Dino, Enrico, Gino, Guido, Marino, Matteo, Paolo*.

Bellus (134) English: variant of BELLOWS.

Bellville (308) Variant spelling of French BELLEVILLE.
GIVEN NAMES French 4%. *Armand, Colette, Francois*.

Belman (217) **1.** Hispanic (Mexico): unexplained. **2.** Altered spelling of German **Bellmann** (see BELLMAN). **3.** Jewish (eastern Ashkenazic): metronymic from the Yiddish female personal name *Beyle* meaning 'beautiful' (related to French *belle*) + Yiddish *man* 'husband'.
GIVEN NAMES Spanish 20%; Jewish 4%; Russian 4%. *Jose* (3), *Guadalupe* (2), *Roberto* (2), *Esteban, Filemon, Gustavo, Heraclio, Hipolito, Humberto, Inocencio, Jose Carmen, Lito*; *Orli, Shira*; *Grigoriy, Grigory, Khasya, Leonid, Mikhail, Yefim*.

Belmares (80) Hispanic (Mexico): unexplained.
GIVEN NAMES Spanish 47%. *Jose* (2), *Luis* (2), *Pedro* (2), *Ramiro* (2), *Amado, Ascencion,*

Fabiola, Felipa, Felipe, Fernando, Francisco, Hermelinda; *Antonio, Cesario, Ciro*.

Belmont (1034) **1.** English: variant of BEAUMONT. **2.** Catalan: from the place name Bellmont, a variant of *Bellmunt* 'beautiful mountain'. Compare Spanish BELMONTE.

Belmonte (841) Spanish, Portuguese, Jewish (Sephardic), and Italian: habitational name from any of numerous places called Belmonte ('beautiful mountain'), especially one in Portugal and another in Cuenca province, Spain.
FOREBEARS Belmonte is the name of a Sephardic Jewish family in Germany, who originated in the city of Belmonte in Portugal, spread to Italy, and reached Germany via the Spanish Netherlands before being brought to North America.
GIVEN NAMES Spanish 15%; Italian 12%. *Jose* (4), *Rafael* (3), *Salvador* (3), *Arturo* (2), *Beatriz* (2), *Carlos* (2), *Guadalupe* (2), *Guillermo* (2), *Jesus* (2), *Juan* (2), *Miguel* (2), *Reynaldo* (2); *Salvatore* (5), *Angelo* (4), *Antonio* (4), *Carmine* (3), *Aldo* (2), *Caesar* (2), *Gino* (2), *Ireneo* (2), *Pietro* (2), *Antonietta, Biagio, Domenica*.

Belmontes (103) Spanish: habitational name from any of the places called Belmonte (see BELMONTE).
GIVEN NAMES Spanish 54%. *Jose* (5), *Francisco* (3), *Jesus* (3), *Armando* (2), *Rogelio* (2), *Salvador* (2), *Adriana, Agustin, Anastacio, Angelina, Brigido, Camilo*; *Antonio* (5), *Federico*.

Belmore (336) English: possibly a habitational name from Belmore Farm in Shropshire, Belmore House in Hampshire, or Bellmoor Farm in Somerset.

Belnap (386) Variant of English BELKNAP.

Belo (151) Portuguese: nickname for a handsome man (perhaps in some instances ironically for an ugly one), from *belo* 'handsome'. Compare Spanish BELLO.
GIVEN NAMES Spanish 16%; Portuguese 8%. *Carlos* (2), *Jose* (2), *Manuel* (2), *Alfredo, Amalia, Armando, Emilia, Florencio, Francisca, Luiz, Nilo, Panfilo*; *Joao*.

Beloff (139) Jewish (from Belarus and Ukraine): alternative spelling of **Belov**, a patronymic from a nickname or personal name based on the adjective *belyj* 'white', 'pale'.

Beloin (110) French: from a Germanic personal name composed of the elements *bili* 'gentle', 'soft', 'kind' + *win* 'friend'.
GIVEN NAMES French 14%. *Alcide, Emile, Fernand*.

Belongia (253) Americanized spelling of French BELANGER.

Belot (114) French: from a derivative of BEL.
GIVEN NAMES French 7%. *Emile, Raymonde*.

Belote (630) Of uncertain origin: perhaps German, a nickname from Swabian dialect *bellode* 'idiot', 'silly person'.

Belotti (117) Italian: from a reduced pet form of the Biblical personal name *Abele* (see ABEL).
GIVEN NAMES Italian 15%. *Carmine* (2), *Angelo, Giovanni, Reno.*

Below (422) **1.** English: variant spelling of BELLOW. **2.** German: habitational name from any of three places in Mecklenburg named Below. **3.** Jewish (eastern Ashkenazic) and Russian: variant of BELOFF.

Belrose (156) French: variant spelling of BELLEROSE.

Belschner (134) South German: variant of **Bel(t)zner**, an occupational name for a furrier, from an agent derivative of Middle High German *bel(lī)z* 'fur', 'pelt' (see BELTZ).

Belser (454) German: habitational name for someone from Belsen in Württemberg.

Belshaw (175) English: variant of BELCHER.

Belshe (196) Respelling of eastern German (Silesian) **Bölsche**, probably of Slavic origin, from *Bolcze*, a short form of the personal name *Boleslaw*.

Belsito (224) Italian: habitational name from any of numerous places called Belsito ('fine place'), as for example in Catania and Cosenza.
GIVEN NAMES Italian 8%. *Angelo, Domenic, Natale, Rocco.*

Belsky (528) Russian and Jewish (eastern Ashkenazic): habitational name for someone from the city of Bielsk.
GIVEN NAMES Jewish 9%. *Hillel* (2), *Miriam* (2), *Zvi* (2), *Aron, Aryeh, Boruch, Chanie, Mendel, Pinchus, Yehuda, Yisroel, Yochanan.*

Belson (359) **1.** English: patronymic from the personal name *Bel(e)* (see BEAL 1) or a metronymic from a short form of the female personal name *Isabel* (see ISBELL). **2.** Jewish (Ashkenazic): metronymic from the Yiddish female personal name *Beyle* (see BELIN) + German *Sohn* 'son'.

Belt (3007) **1.** English and North German: metonymic occupational name for a leather belt or strap maker, from Middle English *belt(e)*, Middle Low German *balt*. **2.** German: from a short form of the Germanic personal name *Baldher* (see BELTER). **3.** North German: habitational name from a place called Beelte (see BELTER 2).

Belter (471) German: **1.** possibly from the Germanic personal name *Baldher*, a compound of *bald* 'bold' + *her(i)* 'army'. **2.** North German: habitational name for someone from a place named Beelte. **3.** occupational name for a belt and (leather) strap maker, Middle Low German *baltære*.

Belton (2061) **1.** English: habitational name from any of various places called Belton, for example in Leicestershire, Lincolnshire, and Suffolk. The first element, *bel*, is of uncertain origin; the second is Old English *tūn* 'enclosure', 'settle-

ment'. **2.** Irish: the name WELDON, relatively common in Ireland, has sometimes been Gaelicized as *de Bhéalatún* and re-Anglicized as **Veldon** and Belton.

Beltram (135) Spanish and southern French: from a Germanic personal name composed of the elements *berht* 'bright', 'famous' + *hrabn* 'raven'. See also BERTRAM.
GIVEN NAMES Spanish 14%; Italian 6%. *Amalia, Francisca, Gilberto, Graciela, Guillermo, Jesus, Jose, Juan, Manuel, Pedro, Rafael, Rolando; Carmelo, Dario, Giorgio, Raffaele, Romeo.*

Beltrami (162) Italian: from the personal name *Beltrame*, from a Germanic personal name composed of the elements *berht* 'bright', 'famous' + *hrabn* 'raven'. See also BERTRAM.
GIVEN NAMES Italian 9%. *Dante, Dino, Marco, Pio, Sal, Tullio.*

Beltramo (150) Italian: from the medieval personal name *Beltramo* (Latinized as *Beltramus* and *Bertramus*), of Germanic origin (see BERTRAM).
GIVEN NAME Italian 5%. *Angelo* (2).

Beltran (3612) Spanish (**Beltrán**), Catalan, and southern French: from a Germanic personal name composed of the elements *berht* 'bright', 'famous' + *hrabn* 'raven'. See also BERTRAM.
GIVEN NAMES Spanish 49%. *Jose* (94), *Juan* (58), *Manuel* (42), *Carlos* (36), *Jesus* (33), *Luis* (33), *Pedro* (24), *Jorge* (23), *Mario* (19), *Ricardo* (19), *Francisco* (17), *Rafael* (16).

Beltre (106) Spanish: unexplained; possibly Catalan in origin.
GIVEN NAMES Spanish 56%. *Ana* (2), *Balbino* (2), *Ernesto* (2), *Jose* (2), *Juan* (2), *Luz* (2), *Rafael* (2), *Silvia* (2), *Alba, Alfredo, Altagracia, Angel; Leonardo.*

Beltz (1533) South German: probably a metonymic occupational name for a furrier, from Middle High German *bel(lī)z* 'fur', 'skin', (from Late Latin *pellicia*).

Belue (452) Variant of English BELLEW or its French cognate BELLEAU, or of French BALLOU.

Belval (112) French: habitational name from any of various places called Belval ('beautiful valley'), as for example in Ardennes, Manche, and Vosges.
GIVEN NAMES French 18%. *Octave* (2), *Fernand, Lorette, Marcel.*

Belveal (174) Americanized spelling of French BELLEVILLE.

Belvedere (154) **1.** English: see BEAVER 1. **2.** Italian: habitational name from any of numerous places called Belvedere, from *bello* 'beautiful' + *vedere* 'to see', 'to look at', for example Belvedere Marittimo in Cosenza and Belvedere di Spinello in Catanzaro. In some instances the surname may have arisen from a nickname with the same meaning.
GIVEN NAMES Italian 9%. *Angelo, Fiore, Marco, Ottavio.*

Belville (328) French: variant spelling of BELLEVILLE.

Belvin (647) English (of Welsh origin): Anglicized form of Welsh *ab Elfyn* 'son of Elfyn'.

Belyea (387) Americanized spelling of French **Bélier**, a nickname from Old French *belier* 'ram'. The nickname no doubt refers in many cases to sexual prowess, but since *belier* also means 'battering ram', it may sometimes have been applied to a man of powerful build. This name is now frequent in New England.

Belyeu (249) French: **1.** most probably an altered form of BILLEAUD (compare BILYEU, BELLEW). **2.** Alternatively, perhaps, a variant of the habitational name BEAULIEU. In the U.S. this is a southern name, concentrated in AL.

Belz (756) **1.** South German: see BELTZ. **2.** Eastern German: nickname of Slavic origin, from Slavic *belu* 'white', probably referring to the color of the named person's hair.

Belzer (515) **1.** German: occupational name for a furrier, from an agent derivative of Middle High German *bel(lī)z* 'fur', 'pelt' (see BELTZ). **2.** Jewish (eastern Ashkenazic): habitational name for someone from Belz in Ukraine.

Bem (114) Polish: from German *Böhm* (see BOHM), an ethnic name for someone from Bohemia.
GIVEN NAME Polish 4%. *Marcin.*

Beman (240) **1.** English: variant spelling of BEEMAN. **2.** Americanized spelling of German **Biemann**, a habitational name for someone from Biene, Bien, or Bienen, all places in the Rhine-Ems area.

Bembenek (206) Polish (**Bębenek**): from *bębenek* 'side drum', 'tambour' hence presumably a metonymic occupational name for someone who played such an instrument.

Bembry (327) Origin unidentified. Perhaps an American variant of English BANBURY.

Bement (564) English: variant of BEAUMONT.

Bemiller (126) Americanized form of German **Biemüller**, a compound of a northern German place name, Bien or Biele, + Middle High German *müller* 'miller' (see MUELLER).

Bemis (1955) English: variant of BEAMISH.

Bemiss (167) Variant of Irish and English BEAMISH.
GIVEN NAME Irish 5%. *Fitzgerald* (2).

Bemus (122) Variant of Irish and English BEAMISH.

Ben (585) **1.** Muslim: abstracted as a surname from Arabic *ben* 'son of', as in *Bensoussan*. This is quite commonly used as a surname among Muslims living in France. **2.** Italian (also **Del Ben**): from a dialect form of *bene* 'well'. This form, without the preposition, is found only in Belluno province, in particular in Taibon Agordino. **3.** Indian (Gujarat): from Gujarati *ben* 'sister', from Sanskrit *bhaginī*, a title often attached to their given name by Gujarati women. It is not a true family name, but is sometimes used as a last name by women who do not have a surname.

Bena (174) **1.** Northern Italian (Piedmont): from a reduced form of the medieval personal name *Benenato* (see BENENATI). **2.** Czech (**Béňa**) and Slovak (**Beňa**): from a pet form of the personal name *Benedikt* (see BENEDICT). **3.** Hungarian (**Béna**): nickname from *béna* 'lame', or from a pet form of *Benedek*, Hungarian form of BENEDICT.

Benac (129) French: habitational name from places in Ariège and Hautes Pyrénées named Bénac, from the Romano-Gallic personal name *Benos* + the locative suffix *-acum*.

Benak (220) Czech and Slovak (**Beňák** or **Benák**): from a pet form of the personal name *Benedikt* (see BENEDICT).

Benally (188) Navajo: unexplained.

Benanti (155) Italian: from a derivative of *Bene*, a short form of the various omen names formed with this element (from Latin *bene* 'well'), such as BENEDETTO, BENVENUTO, etc.
GIVEN NAMES Italian 10%. *Sal* (3), *Antonio*, *Carmelo*, *Salvatore*.

Benard (578) French (also **Bénard**): variant of BERNARD.
FOREBEARS A Bénard or Besnard from the Anjou region of France, also called Bourjoli, is documented in Three-Rivers, Quebec, in 1666. Another, with the secondary surname Lajeunesse is recorded in Quebec city in 1672. The secondary surname Carignan is documented in 1689. Another Benard, from Paris, with the secondary surname Laterreur is documented in Montreal in 1723. The secondary surname Bonenfant is recorded in Montreal in 1724. Other secondary surnames include Beausoleil, La Tourmente, and Lavignon.
GIVEN NAMES French 8%. *Andre* (3), *Alain* (2), *Armand* (2), *Emile*, *Francois*, *Henri*, *Jacques*, *Patrice*, *Pierre*, *Serge*.

Benassi (158) Italian: probably a variant of **Benazzi**, a derivative of BENE.
GIVEN NAMES Italian 16%. *Geno* (2), *Carlo*, *Carmello*, *Dante*, *Marco*, *Paolo*, *Primo*.

Benavente (200) Spanish: habitational name from any of several places, in the provinces of Badajoz, Uesca, and Zamora, named in Latin as *Beneventum*. The Latin place name seems to mean 'welcome' (from *bene* 'well' + *ventum*, past participle of *venire* 'to come'), but this may be no more than a folk etymological distortion of an earlier name.
GIVEN NAMES Spanish 43%. *Carlos* (4), *Jesus* (3), *Jorge* (3), *Miguel* (3), *Andres* (2), *Jose*

(2), *Juan* (2), *Manuel* (2), *Ramon* (2), *Ruben* (2), *Angel*, *Blanca Estela*.

Benavides (2820) Spanish: patronymic from the common medieval personal name *Ben Avid*, of Arabic origin, from *ibn 'Abd* 'son of the servant (of God); see BENAVIDEZ.
GIVEN NAMES Spanish 48%. *Jose* (54), *Carlos* (38), *Juan* (30), *Manuel* (29), *Jesus* (23), *Raul* (22), *Armando* (19), *Jaime* (17), *Ricardo* (16), *Ruben* (16), *Luis* (15), *Roberto* (15).

Benavidez (1630) Spanish (**Benavídez**): variant of BENAVIDES.
GIVEN NAMES Spanish 35%. *Juan* (19), *Jose* (18), *Manuel* (15), *Ruben* (9), *Jesus* (8), *Roberto* (8), *Armando* (7), *Ricardo* (7), *Fernando* (6), *Andres* (5), *Carlos* (5), *Guadalupe* (5).

Benbow (732) English (Shropshire): from Middle English *bend(en)* 'to bend' + *bowe* 'bow', hence a metonymic occupational name for an archer.

Benbrook (195) English (Essex): probably a habitational name from either of two places called Binbrook. The one in Cambridge is named with Old English *binnan* 'within' + *brōc* 'brook'; the other, in Lincolnshire, is named with the Old English personal name *Bynna* + Old English *brōc*.

Bence (558) **1.** English: from a medieval personal name, *Bence*, *Benz*, derived from Old German *Benzo*. **2.** Possibly also an Americanized spelling of German BENTZ or BENZ. **3.** French: from *Benzi*, an Italian form of the Germanic personal name *Bandizo*. **4.** Hungarian (also found in Slovenia): from a short form of the old ecclesiastical name *Bencenc*, from Latin *Vincentius*. See also VINCE. From the 16th century onward, *Bence* was confused with *Bencse*, a pet form of *Benedek* (see BENEDICT), and various derivatives of the personal name *Benjámin* (see BENJAMIN).

Bench (979) **1.** English (West Midlands): of uncertain origin; perhaps a topographic name for someone who lived by a bank or raised piece of ground, Middle English *benche* (from Old English *benc* 'bench'). This transferred sense of the word is not well attested, however, and some other sense of the word may be in question; perhaps one who sat on a bench in a hall, i.e. a retainer. **2.** Possibly an altered spelling of German BENSCH.

Benchoff (124) Bulgarian: alternative spelling of **Benchov**, a patronymic from the personal name *Bencho*, a pet form of *Benefacij*, Bulgarian form of BONIFACE.

Bencivenga (232) Italian (mainly Naples): from a personal name, an omen name composed of the elements *bene* 'well' + *ci* 'to us' + *venga* 'come', i.e. 'God bless us'.
GIVEN NAMES Italian 24%. *Angelo* (4), *Rocco* (3), *Nicola* (2), *Cono*, *Dante*, *Dino*,

Edoardo, *Enrico*, *Ermanno*, *Pasquale*, *Pietro*.

Bencivengo (133) Italian: variant of BENCIVENGA.
GIVEN NAMES Italian 13%. *Dante*, *Pasquale*, *Rocco*, *Vito*.

Benck (142) North German: from a reduced form of BENECKE.

Bencomo (287) Spanish (Canary Islands): unexplained.
GIVEN NAMES Spanish 45%. *Jose* (6), *Manuel* (5), *Ramon* (5), *Armando* (4), *Raul* (4), *Eloy* (3), *Esteban* (3), *Pedro* (3), *Alicia* (2), *Felipe* (2), *Fernando* (2), *Jesus* (2).

Benda (910) **1.** Eastern German, Czech, Slovak, Slovenian, Hungarian, and Jewish (Ashkenazic): from a short form of a personal name derived from Latin *Benedictus* (see BENEDICT). **2.** Southern French: occupational name for a merchant or tradesman.

Bendall (303) English: variant of BENTHALL.
GIVEN NAME French 4%. *Denys*.

Ben-David (161) Jewish: patronymic meaning 'son of David'.
GIVEN NAMES Jewish 35%. *Shula* (3), *Ilan* (2), *Meir* (2), *Meyer* (2), *Ari*, *Avi*, *Ayal*, *Haim*, *Limor*, *Menashe*, *Mordechai*, *Moshe*.

Bendel (454) **1.** South German: metonymic occupational name for a maker or seller of ribbons and cords, from a diminutive of Middle High German *band* 'band', 'cord'. **2.** English: variant spelling of BENDELL.

Bendele (274) German: probably from a pet form of the personal name *Pantaleon* (see PANTALEO).
GIVEN NAMES German 6%. *Armin* (2), *Fritz* (2), *Erwin*, *Goetz*.

Bendell (153) **1.** English: variant of BENTHALL. **2.** In some cases, probably a respelling of German BENDEL.

Bender (15221) **1.** German: occupational name for a cooper, a short form of FASSBENDER. **2.** English: from an agent derivative of Old English *bendan* 'to bend (the bow)', hence probably a metonymic occupational name for an archer. Compare BENBOW. **3.** Hungarian: from *bender* 'curl', hence a nickname for someone with curly hair.

Bendick (166) **1.** Scottish: variant of BENEDICT. **2.** North German: variant of the personal name *Benedikt* (see BENEDICT).

Bendickson (299) Americanized spelling of several Scandinavian patronymics from the personal name *Benedictus* (see BENEDICT).
GIVEN NAMES Scandinavian 4%. *Anders*, *Thor*.

Bendig (147) German: variant of *Benedikt* (see BENEDICT).

Bendik (141) Czech and Slovak (also **Bendík**): from a pet form of BENDA.

Bendix (263) North German, Danish, and Jewish (Ashkenazic): from a reduced form of Latin *Benedictus* (see BENEDICT).

GIVEN NAMES German 6%. *Armin, Gerhard, Gerhart, Gunter.*

Bendixen (277) North German, Danish, and Norwegian: patronymic from the medieval personal name *Bendix, Bendikt* (see BENEDICT).

GIVEN NAMES Scandinavian 12%; German 9%. *Alf, Jorgen, Knut; Hans* (3), *Kurt* (2), *Adelheid, Claus, Erwin, Rainer.*

Bendle (123) **1.** English (mainly Wales): variant of BENTHALL. **2.** In some cases, probably an altered spelling of German BENDEL.

Bendler (135) German: occupational name for a maker or seller of ribbons and cords, from an agent derivative of Middle High German *bendel* 'ribbon', 'cord' (see BENDEL).

Bendon (101) English: probably a variant of **Benden**, which may be a habitational name from Benenden in Kent, named from the Old English personal name *Bionna* + *-ing-* denoting association with + *denn* 'woodland pasture'.

Bendorf (212) German: habitational name from Bendorf, a place near Koblenz.

Bendt (217) **1.** Danish: from the medieval personal name *Bendt*, Danish form of BENEDICT, or from the Germanic personal name BERNHARD. **2.** German: habitational name from a place so named near Hannover.

GIVEN NAMES German 4%. *Fritz, Johannes, Katharina.*

Bendure (178) Origin unidentified.

Bendy (99) **1.** English and German: from a pet form of the personal name BENEDICT. **2.** In some cases it may be of Welsh origin, a variant of **Bendry**, patronymic from the personal name HENDRY (from Welsh *ap Hendry*). Compare PARRY.

Bene (287) **1.** Hungarian: from a short form of the personal name *Benedek*, Hungarian form of BENEDICT. **2.** Italian: from the personal name *Bene*, an omen name meaning 'well', 'good', or a short form of the various compound omen names beginning with this element, such as *Benvenuto* (meaning 'welcome') and *Benenato* ('well born'). **3.** German: from a short form of BENEKE.

GIVEN NAMES Hungarian 5%. *Imre* (2), *Istvan, Janos, Sandor, Tibor.*

Benecke (235) North German: variant spelling of BENEKE.

GIVEN NAMES German 6%. *Heinrich, Horst.*

Benedek (158) Hungarian: from the personal name *Benedek*, Hungarian equivalent of BENEDICT.

GIVEN NAMES Hungarian 17%. *Dezso* (2), *Zoltan* (2), *Balazs, Gabor, Kalman, Laszlo, Miklos, Sandor, Szabolcs.*

Benedetti (1095) Italian: variant of BENEDETTO.

GIVEN NAMES Italian 21%. *Mario* (9), *Angelo* (6), *Gino* (4), *Dante* (3), *Sergio* (3), *Adelfo* (2), *Carlo* (2), *Eduardo* (2), *Enrico* (2),

Nino (2), *Primo* (2), *Rafael* (2), *Reno* (2), *Aldo, Amerigo, Antonio, Caesar, Camerino, Colombo, Guillermo, Gustavo.*

Benedetto (1190) Italian: from the medieval personal name *Benedetto* meaning 'blessed', Latin *Benedictus* (see BENEDICT).

GIVEN NAMES Italian 14%. *Rocco* (11), *Angelo* (7), *Vito* (5), *Domenic* (4), *Pasquale* (3), *Sal* (3), *Vittorio* (3), *Carmelo* (2), *Corrado* (2), *Filomena* (2), *Salvatore* (2), *Amato.*

Benedick (221) **1.** English: variant of BENEDICT. **2.** Americanized spelling of Slovenian **Benedik**, from an old form of the personal name *Benedikt* (see BENEDICT).

Benedict (6788) English and Dutch: from the medieval personal name *Benedict* (Latin *Benedictus* meaning 'blessed'). This owed its popularity in the Middle Ages chiefly to St. Benedict of Norcia (*c*.480–550), who founded the Benedictine order of monks at Monte Cassino and wrote a monastic rule that formed a model for all subsequent rules. No doubt the meaning of the Latin word also contributed to its popularity as a personal name, especially in Romance countries.

Benedix (159) Dutch: patronymic from the personal name BENEDICT.

Benedum (151) German (Palatinate): unexplained.

Benefiel (660) Probably English, a variant of the Norman family name BANVILLE.

Benefield (2028) English: **1.** variant of BANFIELD or BONFIELD. **2.** topographic name from Middle English *bent* 'bent-grass' + *feld* 'open country' or 'land converted to arable use', or a habitational name from a place named with these elements (Old English *beonet* + *feld*), such as Binfield in Berkshire.

Beneke (433) North German: from a short form of BERNHARD.

Benenati (207) Southern Italian (especially Sicily): from the medieval personal name *Benenato*, an omen name meaning 'well born'.

GIVEN NAMES Italian 12%. *Aldo, Antonio, Girolamo, Lorenzo, Luciano, Rocco, Vita, Vito.*

Benenson (145) Jewish (from Russia): patronymic from the Yiddish male personal name *Benye* (a pet form of *Beniamin*; see BIEN, BENJAMIN) + German *Sohn* 'son'.

GIVEN NAMES Jewish 6%; Russian 5%. *Vladimir* (2), *Boris, Igor, Iosif.*

Benes (809) Czech and Slovak (**Beneš**): from a reduced form of the personal name *Benedikt*, Czech form of BENEDICT. This is one of the most common Czech family names, also well established elsewhere in central Europe.

Benesch (311) Germanized spelling of Czech **Beneš** (see BENES) occurring chiefly in Austria and eastern Germany.

GIVEN NAMES German 4%. *Erhard, Horst, Otto.*

Benesh (449) Americanized spelling of Czech and Slovak **Beneš** (see BENES) or German BENESCH.

Benet (145) **1.** Catalan: from the Catalan form of the Latin personal name *Benedictus* (see BENEDICT). **2.** English: variant of BENNETT.

GIVEN NAMES Spanish 7%. *Alfonso, Eduardo, Jere, Jorge, Jose, Luis, Migdalia.*

Benetti (145) Italian: **1.** from a derivative of *Bene*, a short form of the various personal names formed with this element (from Latin *bene* 'well'), such as BENEDETTO, BENVENUTO. **2.** reduced form of BENEDETTI.

GIVEN NAMES Italian 10%. *Santo* (2), *Dante, Gino, Giuseppe.*

Benevento (378) Italian: **1.** habitational or regional name from the city or province of Benevento in southwestern Italy. **2.** from the personal name *Benevento*, an omen name meaning 'welcome'.

GIVEN NAMES Italian 17%. *Angelo* (3), *Rocco* (3), *Nunzio* (2), *Antonio, Concetta, Donato, Enrico, Fiore, Luigi, Marcello, Orazio, Pasquale.*

Benevides (370) Altered spelling of Spanish BENAVIDES.

GIVEN NAMES Spanish 19%; Portuguese 9%. *Manuel* (10), *Carlos* (4), *Luis* (4), *Jose* (3), *Bento* (2), *Alipio, Ana, Armando, Arnoldo, Domingos, Edgardo, Elena; Joao* (2), *Serafim.*

Ben-Ezra (174) Jewish: patronymic from the Hebrew male personal name *Ezra* meaning 'help'. Ezra was a Biblical prophet, author of the Old Testament book that bears his name.

GIVEN NAMES Jewish 12%. *Hanon* (2), *Isak, Meir, Meyer, Miriam, Shlomo, Yossi.*

Benfer (361) German: habitational name from a place called Benfe or Banfe, near Laasphe in Hesse.

Benfield (1742) English: variant of BENEFIELD.

Benford (952) English: habitational name from a lost or unidentified place, possibly somewhere in the East Midlands, where the name is most frequent today.

Benge (1613) **1.** German: habitational name from a place named Bengen in Rhineland. **2.** Hungarian: from a place in Baranya county called Benge, one of only a few Hungarian habitational names without the *-i* suffix.

Bengel (291) German and Jewish (Ashkenazic): **1.** habitational name from a place so named, for example in Bavaria and the Mosel area. **2.** from Middle High German *bengel* 'club', 'cudgel' or in a transferred sense 'hooligan', 'lout', hence a nickname for a boorish man.

Bengston (520) Metathesized spelling of Swedish BENGTSSON.

GIVEN NAMES Scandinavian 6%. *Erik, Helmer, Nels, Nils.*

Bengtson (1289) Americanized spelling of Swedish BENGTSSON, a patronymic from the personal name *Bengt*, Swedish form of BENEDICT.
GIVEN NAMES Scandinavian 6%; German 4%. *Anders* (2), *Nils* (2), *Algot, Britt, Kjersten, Lars, Nels; Kurt* (4), *Alphild, Ernst, Erwin, Gerhard, Manfred, Otto.*

Bengtsson (110) Scandinavian (mostly Swedish): patronymic from the personal name *Bengt*, Swedish form of BENEDICT.
GIVEN NAMES Scandinavian 39%; German 5%. *Nils* (3), *Erik, Gunnel, Kerstin, Lars, Per, Sven; Hans, Ulrika.*

Benham (1954) English: habitational name from a place in Berkshire named with the Old English personal name *Benna* + Old English *hamm* 'river meadow'.
FOREBEARS John Benham was one of the free planters who assented to the 'Fundamental Agreement' of the New Haven Colony on June 4, 1639.

Benhart (122) Probably a variant of German BERNHARD.

Benhoff (106) Variant of North German BENNINGHOFF.

Beni (104) French: from *beni* 'blessed', the past participle of *bénir* 'to bless' (from Latin *benedicere*), presumably applied as a nickname, possibly with Christian overtones.
GIVEN NAME French 7%. *Henri* (2).

Benigni (115) Italian: patronymic or plural form of BENIGNO.
GIVEN NAMES Italian 18%. *Livio* (2), *Alessandro, Ezio, Lucrezia, Reno, Stefano.*

Benigno (303) Italian: from the personal name *Benigno* meaning 'kindly', 'good', 'benign', from the Roman Imperial name *Benignus.*
GIVEN NAMES Italian 21%; Spanish 7%. *Salvatore* (5), *Angelo* (3), *Sal* (3), *Caesar, Ceasar, Enrico, Fiore, Lorenzo, Luigi, Mario, Pedro, Rico, Rocco, Romeo, Vito; Felipe* (2), *Efren, Lourdes, Salvador, Vargas.*

Benik (119) Czech and Slovak (**Beník**); Polish: from a pet form of the Latin personal name *Benedictus* 'blessed' (see BENEDICT).

Benike (102) Origin unidentified. Perhaps a variant spelling of Dutch or North German **Benicke**, from a pet form of BEHN.

Beninati (201) Italian: variant of BENENATI.
GIVEN NAMES Italian 21%. *Angelo* (5), *Sal* (2), *Salvatore* (2), *Carlo, Carmela, Enrico, Vincenza.*

Beninato (101) Italian: from the personal name *Benenato* (see BENENATI).
GIVEN NAMES Italian 14%. *Concetto* (2), *Salvatore, Vito.*

Benincasa (273) Southern Italian: from the personal name *Benincasa*, an omen name meaning 'welcome in the home', bestowed on a much wanted child.

GIVEN NAMES Italian 15%. *Salvatore* (2), *Ugo* (2), *Angelo, Caesar, Luigi, Luigia, Pina, Vittoria.*

Bening (114) German: patronymic from BEHN.

Benis (108) **1.** Jewish (eastern Ashkenazic): patronymic from the Yiddish male personal name *Benye* (a pet form of *Beniamin*; see BIEN, BENJAMIN) + the Yiddish possessive and patronymic suffix *-s*. **2.** Latvian: from a shortened form of the personal name *Benedikts* (see BENEDICT).
GIVEN NAMES Russian 5%; Jewish 4%. *Leonid, Mikhail, Vladimir.*

Benisch (138) Eastern German: Germanized spelling of Czech and Slovak **Beniš**, a derivative of the personal name *Benedikt* (see BENEDICT).

Benish (526) Americanized spelling of BENISCH.

Benison (136) **1.** English: variant spelling of BENNISON. **2.** Jewish (Ashkenazic): variant of BENENSON.
GIVEN NAMES Jewish 5%; French 4%. *Isadore, Tikva; Sylvie* (2).

Benites (280) Variant of Spanish BENITEZ.
GIVEN NAMES Spanish 49%. *Jose* (7), *Manuel* (5), *Juan* (4), *Luis* (3), *Julio* (3), *Miguel* (3), *Alejandro* (2), *Alfredo* (2), *Carlos* (2), *Pablo* (2), *Pedro* (2), *Pilar* (2).

Benitez (3687) Spanish (**Benítez**): patronymic from BENITO.
GIVEN NAMES Spanish 53%. *Jose* (126), *Juan* (57), *Manuel* (51), *Carlos* (36), *Jesus* (34), *Miguel* (32), *Luis* (31), *Jorge* (30), *Pedro* (26), *Mario* (25), *Francisco* (24), *Rafael* (24).

Benito (242) Spanish: from the medieval personal name *Benito*, from Latin *Benedictus* (see BENEDICT).
GIVEN NAMES Spanish 46%. *Carlos* (6), *Mario* (5), *Jose* (4), *Eduardo* (3), *Fernando* (3), *Jaime* (3), *Jorge* (3), *Juan* (3), *Urbano* (3), *Javier* (2), *Luis* (2), *Mariano* (2).

Benitz (138) German: habitational name from any of two places so named near Gifhorn and Güstrow in northern Germany.
GIVEN NAMES Spanish 12%. *Angel* (2), *Ana, Artemio, Candido, Ernesto, Fermin, Guadalupe, Jorge, Jose, Juan, Mario, Orlando.*

Benjamin (11201) Jewish, English, French, and Hungarian (**Benjámin**): from the Hebrew male personal name *Binyamin* 'Son of the South'. In the Book of Genesis, it is treated as meaning 'Son of the Right Hand'. The two senses are connected, since in Hebrew the south is thought of as the right-hand side of a person who is facing east. Benjamin was the youngest and favorite son of Jacob and supposed progenitor of one of the twelve tribes of Israel (Genesis 35:16–18; 42:4). It is rare as an English and French surname; the personal name was not common among Gentiles in the Middle Ages, but its use was sanctioned by virtue of having been borne by a saint martyred in Persia

in about AD 424. In some cases in medieval Europe it was also applied as a byname or nickname to the youngest (and beloved) son of a large family; this is the sense of modern French *benjamin.*
FOREBEARS John Benjamin (1598–1645) came from England to Watertown, MA, in 1632.
A man called Benjamin, of unknown origin, was recorded in Repentigny, Quebec, in 1704, with the secondary surname Saint-Aubin.

Benke (478) Hungarian: from a pet form of the personal name *Benedek* (see BENEDICT).

Benker (177) German: variant of BENKERT.
GIVEN NAMES German 12%. *Wilhelm* (3), *Ewald, Fritz, Hans, Kurt, Lotti.*

Benkert (369) South German: habitational name for someone from a place named Benk, of which there are several examples in Bavaria, or from either of two places in Switzerland named Benken, in Basel and Zurich cantons. In some instances it may be an occupational name for a carpenter, from an agent derivative of Middle High German *benken* 'to make benches'.
GIVEN NAMES German 5%. *Ernst, Erwin, Gunther, Kurt, Markus, Otto.*

Benko (686) Hungarian (**Benkó** or **Benkő**), Slovak, Slovenian, and Ukrainian: from a pet form of a personal name derived from Latin *Benedictus*, e.g. Hungarian *Benedek*, Slovak *Beňadik*, Slovenian *Benedikt*, Ukrainian *Benedykt* (see BENEDICT).

Benkowski (125) Polish: variant of BIENKOWSKI.
GIVEN NAME Polish 4%. *Tadeusz.*

Benn (1501) **1.** English: from the Middle English personal name *Benne*, which is in part a short form of *Benedict* and in part a form of the Old Norse personal name *Bjorn* meaning 'bear cub', 'warrior'. **2.** North German: from a short form of the personal name BERNHARD.

Bennardo (102) Italian: variant of BERNARDO.
GIVEN NAMES Italian 13%. *Carmela, Gilda, Giovanni, Sal, Salvatore.*

Benne (293) **1.** North German: variant of BENN. **2.** French: metonymic occupational name for the maker or driver of a cart, *benne.*

Bennefield (267) Respelling of the English surname BENEFIELD.

Benner (4647) **1.** South German: occupational name for a basket and bassinet maker, from an agent derivative of Middle High German *benne* 'work basket', 'bassinet', 'cradle'. **2.** In some cases probably an altered spelling of German BENDER. **3.** English (East Midlands): possibly a variant of BENDER.

Bennet (544) English: variant spelling of BENNETT.

Bennett (86539) English: from the medieval personal name *Benedict* (Latin

Benedictus meaning 'blessed'). In the 12th century the Latin form of the name is found in England alongside versions derived from the Old French form *Beneit*, *Benoit*, which was common among the Normans. See also BENEDICT.

Bennette (232) Respelling of the French surname **Bennet**, a diminutive of BENNE.

Bennetts (312) English (chiefly Devon and Cornwall): patronymic from BENNETT.

Benney (164) English (Devon and Cornwall): from a pet form of the personal name *Benne* (see BENN).

Bennick (225) **1.** North German: probably a variant of BENECKE. **2.** Swedish: probably an adoption of the German name (see 1 above).

Bennie (299) Scottish: **1.** from a pet form of the personal name *Benne* (see BENN). **2.** habitational name from a place so named near Perth.

Bennight (117) Fanciful spelling of English BENNETT.

Bennin (107) East German: habitational name from a place so named near Ludwigslust in Mecklenburg.

Benning (1168) North German: patronymic from a short form of the personal name BERNHARD or its variant *Benno*.

Benninger (417) **1.** South German: habitational name for someone from either of two places called Benningen in Württemberg. **2.** English: variant of BERINGER.

Benningfield (509) English: probably an altered form of BENEFIELD 2.

Benninghoff (208) German: habitational name from a north German farmstead, so named after the original owner or tenant (see BENNING) + Middle Low German *hof* 'farmstead', 'manor farm'.
GIVEN NAMES German 4%. *Gunter*, *Hans*, *Kurt*.

Bennington (1113) English: habitational name from either of two places called Benington, in Hertfordshire and Lincolnshire, or from Long Bennington in Lincolnshire. The first is recorded in Domesday Book as *Benintone* 'farmstead or settlement (Old English *tūn*) by the Beane river'; both Lincolnshire names are derived from the Old English personal name *Beonna* + *-ing-*, a connective particle denoting association, + *tūn*.

Bennink (163) Dutch: patronymic from a short form of BERNHARD.
GIVEN NAMES German 4%. *Berthel*, *Otto*.

Bennion (555) Welsh: Anglicized form of Welsh *ap Einion*, 'son of *Einion*' (see EYNON).

Bennis (384) **1.** Dutch: patronymic from a reduced form of the personal name BERNHARD. **2.** English: patronymic from the personal name *Benne* (see BENN).

Bennison (237) English: variant of BENSON.

Bennitt (141) English: variant spelling of BENNETT.

Benns (101) English: patronymic from the personal name BENN.

Benny (232) English: variant spelling of BENNEY.

Beno (444) **1.** Hungarian (**Benő**): from a dialect variant of **Benyő** (see BENYO). **2.** Slovak (**Beňo**): from a pet form of the personal name *Beňadik*, Slovak form of BENEDICT.

Benoist (250) Variant of French BENOIT.
GIVEN NAMES French 9%. *Alain* (2), *Jacques* (2), *Andre*, *Jean Jacques*, *Pierre*.

Benoit (6835) French (**Benoît**): from the personal name *Benoit*, French form of BENEDICT.
FOREBEARS A Benoît, also called La Ruine, is recorded in Quebec city in 1666; another from the Nivernais is recorded in Montreal in 1658, with the secondary surnames Nivernois and Livernois, and one from Paris is recorded in Champlain, Quebec, in 1665, with the secondary surname Laforest. A bearer of the name from the Poitou region of France is recorded in Château-Richter in 1665; another, from Saintonge, is documented in Montreal in 1670 with the secondary surname Lajeunesse; and a third, from the Angoumois region, was recorded in Montreal in 1729 with the secondary surname Laguerre. The secondary surname Abel, from a father's forename, is recorded in 1694 in Île-d'Orléans. The LA lines seem to have descended from various Acadian refugees of the 18th century.
GIVEN NAMES French 8%. *Andre* (12), *Normand* (12), *Marcel* (10), *Armand* (8), *Pierre* (8), *Raoul* (8), *Michel* (6), *Emile* (5), *Jacques* (5), *Alphonse* (4), *Laurent* (4), *Arsene* (3).

Benowitz (150) Jewish (eastern Ashkenazic): patronymic from a pet form of the personal name *Beniamin* (see BIEN, BENJAMIN).
GIVEN NAMES Jewish 5%. *Morty*, *Sol*.

Benoy (162) Altered spelling of French BENOIT.

Bens (109) Dutch and North German: patronymic from a short form of BERNHARD.
GIVEN NAMES German 7%; French 5%. *Dieter*, *Heinz*; *Andre*, *Myrtha*.

Bensch (233) German: from a reduced form of BENESCH.
GIVEN NAMES German 8%. *Klaus* (2), *Kurt* (2), *Otto*, *Rudi*.

Benschoter (119) Dutch: perhaps a topographic for someone who lived by an enclosure for cattle, Middle Dutch *sco(o)t(t)e*, or by a corner of woodland or heathland in a marshy area, Middle Dutch *scoet*. Compare VAN BENSCHOTEN.

Benscoter (270) Variant of Dutch BENSCHOTER.

Bense (147) **1.** French: see BENCE. **2.** German: variant of BENSEN.

Bensel (145) German: nickname from Middle High German *bensel*, *pensel* '(paint)brush'; it also meant 'opinionated fool' and it is no doubt from this sense that the name arose.
GIVEN NAMES German 7%. *Heinz* (2), *Oskar*.

Bensen (531) **1.** German: habitational name from any of several places in northern Germany named Bensen. **2.** Altered form of **Bengtsson**, **Bendtsen** and the like, patronymics from *Bengt*, *Bendt*, Scandinavian forms of BENEDICT.
GIVEN NAME Scandinavian 4%. *Britt* (2).

Benshoff (119) German: habitational name from a farmstead so named after its original owner or tenant, *Basino* (or a later form of this name), + Middle Low German *hof* 'farmstead', 'manor farm'.

Benshoof (235) Variant spelling of German BENSHOFF.

Bensing (198) German: patronymic from the personal name *Bens(o)*.

Bensinger (488) Variant of German BENZINGER.

Benskin (194) English: from a pet form of the personal name *Benne* (see BENN).

Bensley (312) English: habitational name from a lost or unidentified place, possibly, in view of the present-day concentration of the name in Norwich, in East Anglia.

Bensman (270) North German (**Bensmann**): variant of **Bensemann**, a compound of BENSE + *-man* 'man'.

Benson (32425) **1.** English: patronymic from the medieval personal name *Benne*, a pet form of *Benedict* (see BENN). **2.** English: habitational name from a place in Oxfordshire named Benson, from Old English *Benesingtūn* 'settlement (Old English *tūn*) associated with *Benesa*', a personal name of obscure origin, perhaps a derivative of *Bana* meaning 'slayer'. **3.** Jewish (Ashkenazic): patronymic composed of a pet form of the personal name *Beniamin* (see BIEN, BENJAMIN) + German *Sohn* 'son'. **4.** Scandinavian: altered form of such names as **Bengtsson**, **Bendtsen**, patronymics from *Bengt*, *Bendt*, etc., Scandinavian forms of BENEDICT.

Benston (100) Origin uncertain. This has the form of an English habitational name, and there are places in Shetland and Strathclyde named Benston which could have given rise to the surname; however, the surname is rare in the British Isles. It could perhaps be a variant of BENSON 2; alternatively, it may be an Americanized form of an original in some other language.

Bent (1348) English: topographic name for someone who lived on a patch of land on which grew bent grass, rushes, or reeds (Middle English *bent*).

Bente (154) North German: habitational name from a place called Benthe, near Hannover (see BENDT).

Benter (233) German: **1.** habitational name for someone from Benthe near Hannover.

2. topographic name for someone living by an enclosed portion of an area of common land (see BUNDE 2).

Benthall (183) English: habitational name from a place in Shropshire named Benthall, from Old English *beonet* 'bent grass' + *halh* 'nook', 'recess'.

Bentham (118) English: habitational name from any of various places, for example in North Yorkshire and Gloucestershire, named Bentham, from Old English *beonet* 'bent grass' + *hām* 'homestead' or *hamm* 'enclosure hemmed in by water'.

Benthin (164) German: habitational name from a place called Bentin in Mecklenburg.

Bentivegna (259) Italian (Sicily): from a personal name, an omen name composed of the elements *bene* 'well' + *ti* 'to you' + *venga* 'come', i.e. 'God bless you'.
GIVEN NAMES Italian 22%. *Salvatore* (4), *Carlo* (2), *Santo* (2), *Saverio* (2), *Angelo*, *Domenic*, *Francesco*, *Giacomo*, *Ignazio*, *Orazio*, *Pasquale*, *Sal*.

Bentle (133) In some cases probably an Americanized spelling of South German **Bentl** or **Bentele**, from short forms of the personal name *Pantaleon* (see PANTALEO); in others perhaps an altered spelling of English BENDLE.

Bentler (230) German: **1.** perhaps a patronymic from *Bentele* (see BENTLE). **2.** variant of BENDLER.

Bentley (13759) **1.** English: habitational name from any of various places, the chief of which are in Derbyshire, Essex, Hampshire, Shropshire, Staffordshire, Suffolk, Warwickshire, Worcestershire, and East and South Yorkshire. The place name is from Old English *beonet* 'bent grass' + *lēah* 'woodland clearing'. **2.** Probably an Americanized spelling of Swiss *Bandle* or *Bandli* or German *Bentele*, all short forms of the medieval personal name *Pantaleon* (see PANTALEO).

Bento (433) Portuguese: from the personal name, Portuguese form of BENEDICT.
GIVEN NAMES Spanish 18%; Portuguese 10%. *Jose* (8), *Manuel* (6), *Carlos* (4), *Luis* (3), *Sergio* (3), *Augusto* (2), *Lino* (2), *Mario* (2), *Adelino*, *Alberto*, *Alvaro*, *Eduardo*; *Joaquim* (2), *Vasco*; *Antonio* (12), *Marco* (3), *Carlo*.

Benton (12923) English: habitational name from a pair of villages in Northumbria named with Old English *bēan* 'beans' (a collective singular) or *beonet* 'bent grass' + *tūn* 'enclosure', 'settlement'. The name is now most frequent in the West Midlands, however, so it may be that a place of the same name in that area should be sought as its origin.

Bentrup (129) German: habitational name from a place named Bentrup, in the Lippe district.
GIVEN NAME German 6%. *Eldor* (2).

Bents (182) Variant of German BENZ.

GIVEN NAMES German 7%. *Reinhold* (2), *Gerd*, *Kurt*, *Theodor*.

Bentsen (284) North German, Danish, and Norwegian: patronymic from *Bengt*, *Ben(d)t*, short forms of *Benignus*, *Benedikt* (see BENEDICT).
GIVEN NAMES Scandinavian 13%; German 6%. *Bent* (2), *Per* (2); *Kurt* (4), *Otto*.

Bentson (335) Norwegian and Danish: variant of BENTSEN.
GIVEN NAMES Scandinavian 4%. *Nels* (2), *Monrad*.

Bentz (2347) South German: variant spelling of BENZ.

Bentzel (174) German: from a pet form of BENTZ.

Bentzen (181) Norwegian, Danish, and North German: variant spelling of BENTSEN.
GIVEN NAMES Scandinavian 19%; German 6%. *Erik* (5), *Thorwald*; *Inge* (2), *Erwin*, *Kurt*, *Otto*.

Bentzinger (113) Variant spelling of German BENZINGER.

Benveniste (156) Italian and Jewish (Sephardic): from a personal name based on the Italian expression *benveniste* 'welcome', Latin *bene venistis* 'you have arrived well'. Compare BENVENUTI.
GIVEN NAMES Jewish 8%; French 5%. *Etty*, *Mayer*; *Jacques*, *Raoul*.

Benvenuti (230) Italian: patronymic or plural form of BENVENUTO.
GIVEN NAMES Italian 22%. *Dante* (2), *Menotti* (2), *Remo* (2), *Carlo*, *Dario*, *Dino*, *Emo*, *Enzo*, *Gianni*, *Guido*, *Ilio*, *Italo*.

Benvenuto (459) Italian: from the medieval personal name *Benvenuto*, meaning 'welcome' (from Old Italian *bene* 'well' + *venuto* 'arrived'). Generally it was an omen name given to a long-awaited and much-desired child.
GIVEN NAMES Italian 19%. *Antonio* (3), *Gino* (3), *Mario* (3), *Angelo* (2), *Donato* (2), *Riccardo* (2), *Vito* (2), *Belisario*, *Carlo*, *Elia*, *Elvira*, *Natale*, *Pina*, *Ricardo*, *Rocco*, *Sal*, *Santo*, *Sergio*.

Benware (310) Americanized spelling of French BENOIT, with a slightly different resolution of the Americanization from that of the more frequent BENWAY.

Benway (550) Americanized spelling of French BENOIT, reflecting the Canadian pronunciation, which retains the diphthong *wé* that in metropolitan France was replaced in the 17th century by the current *wa*.

Benya (104) Altered form of BENYO.

Benyo (231) Hungarian (**Benyó** or **Benyő**): from a pet form of the personal name *Benedek*, Hungarian form of BENEDICT.

Benz (2356) South German: (in Alemannic areas) from a short form of the Germanic personal name BERTHOLD, or to a lesser extent of BERNHARD.
GIVEN NAMES German 5%. *Erwin* (4), *Gerhard* (3), *Kurt* (3), *Otto* (3), *Ernst* (2),

Fritz (2), *Gunther* (2), *Heinz* (2), *Erhard*, *Georg*, *Gerhardt*, *Heiner*.

Benza (111) Italian: from a feminine form of the personal name *Benso*, *Benzo*, pet forms of a Germanic name such as BERNARDO, or from a medieval name such as *Bene*, *Beno* with the addition of the Germanic suffix *-izo*.
GIVEN NAMES Italian 8%. *Gaetano* (2), *Carlo*, *Sal*.

Benzel (445) German: from a pet form of BENZ.

Benzie (148) Scottish: perhaps from a pet form of the Middle English personal name *Benne*, which is in part a short form of *Benedict* and in part a form of the Old Norse personal name *Bjorn* meaning 'bear cub', 'warrior'.

Benziger (125) Swiss German: variant of BENZINGER.

Benzing (408) South German: see BENZINGER.

Benzinger (330) South German: habitational name for someone from Benzingen in Württemberg, near Sigmaringen.
GIVEN NAMES German 4%. *Erwin* (2), *Frieda*, *Rudi*.

Benzschawel (107) German: probably an altered form of **Binsschaubel** or **-schäubel**, a nickname for a tall, skinny man, from Middle High German *biese* (modern German *Binse*) 'reed' + *schoup* 'bundle', or from a house name with a sign depicting this.

Beougher (254) Origin unidentified. Possibly an Americanized spelling of Dutch BOER or German BAUER. This name is particularly associated with Hocking, OH.

Bequette (451) Variant spelling of French **Béquet**, a diminutive of **Bec**, a nickname for a gossipmonger, from *bec* 'beak'. See also BECHARD.
FOREBEARS A Becquet from Normandy, France, is recorded in Quebec city in 1666; another, a Calvinist from La Rochelle, France, is recorded in Charlesbourg, Quebec, in 1666.

Ber (102) Jewish (Eastern Ashkenazic): from the Yiddish male personal name *Ber* (see BAER).
GIVEN NAMES Russian 8%; Jewish 8%; Polish 4%. *Leonid* (2), *Evgeny*, *Fanya*, *Mikhail*; *Herschel*; *Andrzej*.

Bera (223) **1.** Indian (Bengal) and Bangladeshi: Hindu (Kayasth) name of unknown meaning. **2.** Hungarian: from a pet form of the personal name *Bertalan* (Hungarian form of BARTHOLOMEW) or *Bernát* (see BERNHARD). **3.** Basque: habitational name from Bera, a town in Navarre, Basque Country. **4.** Catalan (**Berà**): habitational name from Berà, a place in Tarragona, Catalonia.
GIVEN NAMES Indian 12%; Spanish 6%. *Madan* (2), *Dilip*, *Girish*, *Kanta*, *Mansukh*, *Raj*, *Rajesh*, *Rajiv*, *Ranjan*, *Sonali*, *Tapan*;

Ruben (4), *Ana*, *Balentina*, *Gilberto*, *Gonzalo*, *Juana*.

Beran (819) Czech and Jewish (Ashkenazic): from *beran* 'ram', hence a nickname for someone thought to resemble a ram in some way, for example, someone with curly hair. It is also found as a nickname for a pig-headed or arrogant person and as a derogatory nickname for a Protestant.

Beranek (700) Czech (**Beránek**): from *beránek* 'lamb', a nickname for someone with curly hair or a mild temperament, or a habitational name for someone who lived at a house distinguished by the sign of a lamb.

Berard (1391) French (**Bérard**): from a personal name of Germanic origin, formed with *ber* 'bear'.
FOREBEARS The name is recorded in Neuville, Quebec, in 1673 with the secondary surname Lépine.
GIVEN NAMES French 12%. *Marcel* (5), *Emile* (3), *Leandre* (3), *Normand* (3), *Antoine* (2), *Armand* (2), *Laurent* (2), *Pierre* (2), *Adrien, Alcide, Amiee, Andre*.

Berardi (1113) Italian: patronymic or plural form of BERARDO.
GIVEN NAMES Italian 20%. *Luigi* (6), *Vito* (6), *Rocco* (5), *Amato* (4), *Angelo* (4), *Carmine* (4), *Antonio* (3), *Pasquale* (3), *Domenic* (2), *Domenico* (2), *Enrico* (2), *Gaetano* (2).

Berardinelli (223) Italian: from a diminutive of the Germanic personal name BERARDO; the double suffix is a typical feature of Italian family names.
GIVEN NAMES Italian 23%. *Domenic* (3), *Antonio* (2), *Carlo* (2), *Giacomo* (2), *Amerigo, Caesar, Camillo, Elio, Ettore, Gildo, Gino*.

Berardino (167) Italian: from a diminutive of the Germanic personal name BERARDO.
GIVEN NAMES Italian 18%. *Sabino* (2), *Antonio, Carmine, Emilio, Luigi, Nicola, Rocco, Silvio*.

Berardo (172) Italian: from the Germanic personal name *Berardo*, formed with *ber* 'bear'.
GIVEN NAMES Italian 16%. *Carmine, Donato, Florindo, Guido, Luigi, Vittorio*.

Berarducci (146) Italian: from a diminutive of the Germanic personal name BERARDO.
GIVEN NAMES Italian 15%. *Gino, Pasquale, Sante, Silvio*.

Berber (118) **1.** Catalan: probably a variant of BARBER. **2.** German: possibly a habitational name from a place called Berber near Kevelaer.
GIVEN NAMES Spanish 48%. *Jose* (4), *Salvador* (4), *Guillermo* (3), *Juan* (3), *Manuel* (3), *Francisco* (2), *Luis* (2), *Adriana, Alfredo, Angelina, Armando, Carlos*.

Berberian (351) Armenian: patronymic from the Turkish loanword *berber* 'barber', from Arabic.
GIVEN NAMES Armenian 34%. *Karnig* (4), *Ara* (3), *Haig* (3), *Kevork* (3), *Aram* (2),

Artin (2), *Diran* (2), *Misak* (2), *Nubar* (2), *Roupen* (2), *Sarkis* (2), *Vahe* (2).

Berberich (646) Bosnian (**Berberić**): occupational name for a barber, from *berber(in)* 'barber', from Turkish.
GIVEN NAMES German 5%. *Kurt* (4), *Otto* (2), *Alois, Aloysius*.

Berberick (141) Americanized form of Bosnian BERBERICH.

Bercaw (240) Americanized spelling of German **Berkau**, a habitational name from either of two places in central Germany named Berkau (near Stendal and Wittenberg), or possibly of BERKA.

Bercegeay (115) French: from Old French *berser* 'to shoot (with a bow and arrow)' + *gay* 'magpie' (Latin *gajus*). It may have been an occupational name for someone whose job was quite literally to control magpies.
GIVEN NAMES French 12%. *Andre* (2), *Leonce, Odile, Valmond*.

Berch (243) **1.** Shortened form of Dutch **van den Berch**, a variant of VANDENBERG. **2.** Variant of German **Bercht**, from a short form of the personal names BERTHOLD or *Albrecht* (see ALBERT).

Berchem (136) Dutch: habitational name from any of several places in the Netherlands so called.
GIVEN NAMES German 4%. *Gunther, Mathias*.

Berchtold (302) German: variant of BERTHOLD.
GIVEN NAMES German 5%. *Hans* (3), *Raimund* (2).

Bercier (167) French: occupational name for an archer, from an agent derivative of *berser* 'to shoot (with a bow and arrows)'.
GIVEN NAMES French 10%. *Camille, Laurier, Octave, Pierre, Remi*.

Bercik (101) Czech and Slovak (**Berčík**); Polish: pet form of BERK.

Berck (118) Variant spelling of German or Dutch BERK.

Berdahl (198) Norwegian: variant of the habitational name **Berdal(en)**, a compound of Old Norse *bera* 'female bear' or *ber* 'berry' + *dal* 'valley'.
GIVEN NAMES Scandinavian 5%. *Juel, Nels*.

Berdan (297) Variant of French BARDIN.

Berdine (232) Variant of French **Berdin**, itself a variant of BARDIN.

Berding (134) German: patronymic from a Germanic personal name (short form *Bardo*) composed with *bart* 'beard' or *barta* 'battle ax'.

Beren (139) Dutch: from a derivative of BERNHARD.

Berenato (112) Italian: variant of BERNARDO.
GIVEN NAMES Italian 18%. *Domenic* (2), *Angelo, Antonio, Palma, Salvatore*.

Berenbaum (110) Jewish (Ashkenazic): variant of BIRNBAUM.
GIVEN NAMES Jewish 18%. *Asher, Elchonon, Hyman, Khaim, Mandel, Shlomo, Shmuel*.

Berend (249) German: variant spelling of BEHREND.

Berendes (109) German: patronymic from BEREND.
GIVEN NAMES German 5%. *Christoph, Heinz*.

Berends (401) North German and Dutch: variant of BEHRENS.

Berendsen (132) North German and Dutch: patronymic from the personal name BEHREND, a variant of BERNHARD.
GIVEN NAME French 4%; German 4%. *Fritz*.

Berendt (237) North German: variant spelling of BEHREND. This is also found as a Danish and Swedish name.
GIVEN NAMES German 6%. *Horst, Kurt, Otto, Wolfgang*.

Berendzen (103) Dutch: patronymic from the personal name BEREND (see BERNHARD).

Berens (1245) North German: variant spelling of BEHRENS.

Berenson (503) **1.** Jewish (Ashkenazic): patronymic composed of the Yiddish personal name *Ber* meaning 'bear' + German *Sohn* 'son'. **2.** Variant spelling of German BERENDSEN.
GIVEN NAMES Jewish 6%. *Hyman* (2), *Ari, Meyer, Miriam, Sima*.

Berent (193) Polish form of German BEHREND (see BERNARD).

Beres (939) Hungarian (**Béres**): occupational name for a farm laborer or casual harvest hand, *béres*, a derivative of *bér* 'wage', 'payment'.

Beresford (573) English: habitational name from a place in the parish of Alstonfield, Staffordshire named Beresford, from Old English *beofor* 'beaver' (or possibly from a byname from this word) + Old English *ford* 'ford'. This name also became established in Ireland.

Beretta (178) Northern Italian: variant spelling of BERRETTA.
GIVEN NAMES Italian 13%; French 5%. *Aldo* (4), *Dante* (3), *Alessandra, Enrico, Gianluigi; Lisanne* (2), *Armand, Marcel*.

Bereza (104) Ukrainian and Polish: topographic name from Ukrainian *bereza* 'birch tree'. Compare BRZOZA.
GIVEN NAMES Russian 6%; Polish 5%. *Lyudmila, Mikhail, Raisa; Andrzej, Wencel*.

Berezin (135) **1.** Jewish (eastern Ashkenazic): habitational name for someone from any of various villages called Berez(i)no, Berez(i)na, and Bereza, in Belarus and Ukraine, all derived from an Eastern Slavic noun meaning 'birch tree'. **2.** Russian: topographic name for someone who lived by a birch tree, from Russian *bereza* 'birch' + the Russian possessive suffix *-in*.
GIVEN NAMES Russian 21%; Jewish 10%. *Boris* (3), *Gennadiy* (2), *Yuriy* (2), *Aleksandr, Aleksey, Arkadiy, Iosif, Nikolay, Pesya, Vitaliy, Vladimir, Yori; Mordechai* (2), *Gershon, Moshe*.

Berfield (107) English: possibly a habitational name from Burghfield in Berkshire, named from Old English *beorg* 'hill' + *feld* 'open country'.

Berg (21581) **1.** German or Dutch: topographic name for someone who lived on or by a hill or mountain, from Middle High German *berc*. This name is widespread throughout central and eastern Europe. **2.** Scandinavian: habitational name for someone who lived at a farmstead named with Old Norse *bjarg* 'mountain', 'hill'. In Sweden this is commonly found as an element of ornamental names. **3.** Jewish (Ashkenazic): ornamental name from German *Berg* 'mountain', 'hill', or a short form of any of the many ornamental surnames containing this word as the final element, for example **Schönberg** (see SCHOENBERG) and GOLDBERG.
GIVEN NAMES Scandinavian 4%. *Erik* (24), *Lennart* (6), *Bjorn* (5), *Lars* (5), *Nils* (5), *Alf* (4), *Nels* (4), *Thor* (4), *Tor* (4), *Knute* (3), *Selmer* (3), *Anders* (2).

Bergamini (171) Italian: occupational name from *bergamino* 'cowherd', 'dairy farmer', a derivative of the place name Bergamo, the cowherds of the Po valley having originally come from Bergamo and the Bergamese Alps.
GIVEN NAMES Italian 11%. *Angelo* (2), *Carlo* (2), *Antonio, Giuseppe, Romeo*.

Bergamo (213) Italian: habitational name from Bergamo in Lombardy, northern Italy.
GIVEN NAMES Italian 10%. *Pietro* (2), *Agostino, Dante, Francesco, Lorenzo, Luigi*.

Bergan (836) **1.** Norwegian: habitational name for someone from any of various farms in southeastern Norway named with Norwegian *berg* 'mountain' (Old Norse *bjarg*). **2.** In some cases, perhaps a variant spelling of the Irish surname BERGIN.

Bergdahl (151) Swedish: ornamental name composed of the elements *berg* 'mountain', 'hill' + an ornamental spelling of *dal* 'valley'.
GIVEN NAMES Scandinavian 7%. *Johan, Lars*.

Bergdoll (214) Americanized spelling of Swedish BERGDAHL.

Bergdorf (107) Origin unidentified. Possibly a German habitational name from places in Hamburg and Lower Saxony called Bergedorf, Bargdorf in Lower Saxony, or Bergsdorf in Brandenburg.

Berge (1498) **1.** Norwegian and Swedish: variant of BERG, from the dative form. **2.** German: variant (from the oblique case) of BERG or a habitational name from any of several places so named, notably in Westphalia. **3.** French: topographic name for someone who lived on a steep bank, from Old French *berge* 'bank' (apparently of Gaulish origin). **4.** French: hypercorrected spelling of BARGE.

GIVEN NAMES Scandinavian 9%. *Maren* (3), *Johan* (2), *Karsten* (2), *Alf, Bent, Erik, Gudmund, Knud, Peer, Per, Sten, Thor*.

Bergeman (182) Respelling of German BERGEMANN.

Bergemann (334) North German: variant of BERGE, with the addition of *-mann* 'man'.
GIVEN NAMES German 6%. *Eldor, Ewald, Georg, Kurt*.

Bergen (2414) **1.** Dutch: topographic name for someone who lived on or by a hill, or a habitational name from any of various places named with this word. **2.** German: inflected variant of BERG (originally after a preposition, as in *an* or *zu Bergen*). **3.** Swedish: variant of BERG. **4.** Jewish (Ashkenazic): habitational name from any of the various German places called Bergen.

Bergendahl (140) Swedish: ornamental name composed of the elements *berg* 'mountain', 'hill' + an older spelling of *dal* 'valley'.

Bergener (109) German: habitational name for someone from any of the many places called Bergen, especially in Bavaria.

Berger (19688) **1.** German, Dutch, Swedish, and Jewish (Ashkenazic): topographic name for someone who lived in the mountains or hills (see BERG). As a Jewish name it is mainly ornamental. It is found as a surname throughout central and eastern Europe, either as a surname of German origin or as a German translation of a topographic name with similar meaning, for example Slovenian **Gričar**, HRIBAR, **Gorjan** or **Gorjanc**. **2.** Norwegian: habitational name from any of various farms so named with the plural of BERG 'mountain'. **3.** French: occupational name for a shepherd, from Old French *bergier* (Late Latin *berbicarius*, from *berbex* 'ram').

Bergeron (7724) French (of Norman origin): from a diminutive of BERGER. The name is common in both New England and LA.
FOREBEARS A bearer of the name is documented in Lauzon, Quebec, in 1673. Another, from the Poitou region of France, is recorded in Trois Rivières, Quebec, in 1676; and a third, from Gascony, was documented in Quebec city in 1698. The LA families are descendants of a Jean-Baptiste Bergeron from IL, who was in New Orleans by 1725. A French soldier, Guillaume Bergeron (also called St. Onge), was in LA by 1740. Several Acadian families of this name settled in LA after the dispersal of 1755.
GIVEN NAMES French 11%. *Normand* (21), *Andre* (17), *Armand* (16), *Marcel* (16), *Lucien* (15), *Emile* (11), *Gaston* (8), *Michel* (8), *Pierre* (8), *Camille* (6), *Alphonse* (5), *Fernand* (5).

Bergerson (553) Swedish (**Bergersson**): patronymic from a personal name, *Berger*, variant of BIRGER.
GIVEN NAMES Scandinavian 6%. *Berger, Bjorn, Ove, Selmer, Sven*.

Berges (245) **1.** German: topographic name from a reduced form of *Berghaus*, a compound of *Berg* 'mountain', 'hill' + *Haus* 'house'. The name is found in the Lower Rhine. Compare BACKES. **2.** French (**Bergès**): Gascon variant of **Vergès** (see VERGES).
GIVEN NAMES Spanish 6%. *Alvaro* (2), *Jose* (2), *Carlos, Cesar, Florina, Gustavo, Luis, Margarita, Mariana, Mercedes, Ramon, Xavier*.

Bergesen (123) Danish and Norwegian: variant of BERGERSON.
GIVEN NAMES Scandinavian 19%. *Berent, Berger, Britt, Monrad, Sig*.

Bergeson (896) Swedish: variant of BERGERSON.

Berget (188) Norwegian: variant of BERG, from the definite singular form of *berg* 'mountain', 'hill'.
GIVEN NAME Scandinavian 12%. *Knut*.

Bergevin (303) French: variant spelling of **Burgevin**, a nickname for a roisterer, from Old French *burger* 'to strike', 'to steal or carry off', 'to make a noise' + *vin* 'wine'. In Canada, it was first recorded in the forms **Bréchevin** and **Brugevin**, also called *Langevin* (meaning '(the) one from Anjou'), in 1668 in Quebec city. The North American forms appear in no modern dictionary of French names.
GIVEN NAMES French 6%. *Lucien* (2), *Andre, Gaston, Jean-Rene*.

Bergey (535) In part, an altered spelling of Swiss German **Bürki**, from a pet form of the personal name *Burkhard* (see BURKHARDT).

Bergfeld (275) German: habitational name from any of various places called Bergfeld in northern Germany, for example near Brunswick.

Berggren (1060) Swedish: ornamental name composed of the elements *berg* 'mountain', 'hill' + *gren* 'branch'
GIVEN NAMES Scandinavian 7%. *Erik* (3), *Nels* (3), *Alvar, Holger, Lars, Lennart, Sven, Thor*.

Bergh (836) **1.** Scandinavian: ornamental spelling of BERG. **2.** Dutch: in some cases, possibly a shortening of **van den Bergh**, a topographic name denoting someone living on a hill (see VANDENBERGH). **3.** Dutch: possibly also from Middle Dutch *barg*, *berg* 'castrated pig', either as an occupational name for a pig farmer or possibly as a nickname.
GIVEN NAMES Scandinavian 7%. *Johan* (2), *Anders, Arndt, Owe, Per, Sigvard, Sven, Syvert*.

Berghoff (254) North German: Westphalian habitational name from a farmstead named Berghoff ('mountain farm').

Bergholz (119) German: folk-etymological variant of the personal name *Berchtold* (see BERTHOLD), probably via **Bercholz**, another variant; or from a respelling of the Low German topographic name **Berkholt** 'birchwood', from Middle Low German *berk(e)* 'birch' + *holt* (High German *Holz*) 'wood'.

Berghorn (142) North German: topographic name for someone who lived by the corner of a mountain, from *Berg* 'mountain', 'hill' + *Horn* 'corner'.

Berghorst (120) German: topographic name for someone who lived by a wilderness area on a mountain, from *Berg* 'mountain', 'hill' + *Horst* 'wilderness' (see HORST).

Berghuis (228) Dutch: habitational name for someone from any of several places called Berghuizen, in the provinces of Gelderland and Drente.

Bergin (1683) **1.** Irish: Anglicized form of Gaelic **Ó Beirgin** or **Ó Meirgin**, an altered form of **Ó hAimheirgin** 'descendant of *Aimheirgin*', a personal name of early Irish mythology and historical tales, perhaps composed of the elements *amhra* 'wonderful' + *gin* 'birth'. **2.** Swedish: variant of BERG, with the addition of *-in*, a common suffix of Swedish family names.
GIVEN NAMES Irish 5%. *Aileen, Brendan, Colm, Donal, Eoin, Kiernan, Padraic, Siobhan.*

Bergkamp (121) North German: probably originally **Berkkamp**, a topographic name for someone who lived by a field with birches, from Middle Low German *berk(e)* 'birch' + *Kamp* 'field'.
GIVEN NAME French 4%. *Michel.*

Bergland (363) Norwegian: habitational name from any of several farmsteads named Bergland, from *Berg* 'mountain', 'hill' (Old Norse *bjarg*) + *land* 'land', 'farm'.
GIVEN NAMES Scandinavian 4%. *Helmer, Jarl.*

Berglin (161) Swedish: variant of BERG, with the addition of *-lin*, a suffix of Swedish family names.

Berglund (2397) Swedish: ornamental name composed of the elements *berg* 'mountain', 'hill' + *lund* 'grove'.
GIVEN NAMES Scandinavian 6%. *Erik* (4), *Sven* (4), *Nils* (3), *Anders* (2), *Helmer* (2), *Bjorn, Elof, Erland, Hasse, Hilma, Lars, Nelle.*

Bergman (7618) **1.** Swedish and Dutch: from BERG, with the addition of *man* 'man'. **2.** Variant spelling of German BERGMANN.

Bergmann (2140) German (also found in Sweden): variant of BERG, reinforced by the addition of the suffix *-man(n)* 'man', a topographic name in most cases, but in some an occupational name for a miner.
GIVEN NAMES German 7%. *Otto* (8), *Klaus* (4), *Ernst* (3), *Guenter* (3), *Elfriede* (2),

Elke (2), *Gerd* (2), *Hans* (2), *Kurt* (2), *Siegfried* (2), *Bernhardt, Eugen.*

Bergmark (110) Swedish: ornamental name composed of the elements *berg* 'mountain', 'hill' + *mark* 'ground', 'field', 'land'.
GIVEN NAME Scandinavian 5%. *Nels.*

Bergmeier (115) German: distinguishing name for a tenant farmer living on a mountainside, composed of Middle High German *berc* 'mountain' + *meier* 'tenant farmer' (see MEYER).

Bergner (603) **1.** German and Jewish (Ashkenazic): habitational name for someone from any of various places called Bergen (notably in Bavaria). **2.** Swedish: variant of BERG, with the addition of the suffix *-ner*.
GIVEN NAMES German 4%. *Erwin* (3), *Hans* (2), *Eldred, Otto, Wolfgang.*

Bergo (143) **1.** Norwegian: habitational name from any of various farmsteads named Bergo, from the dative plural form of *berg* 'mountain', 'hill'. **2.** In some instances, perhaps a respelling of French **Bergaud**, from a Germanic personal name composed of the elements *berg-* (from Middle High German *bergan* 'to conceal') + *wald* 'rule'.

Bergold (104) German: variant of BERTHOLD.

Bergquist (1819) Swedish: ornamental name composed of the elements *berg* 'mountain', 'hill' + *quist*, an old or ornamental spelling of *kvist* 'twig'.
GIVEN NAMES Scandinavian 7%. *Thor* (3), *Erik* (2), *Lars* (2), *Lennart* (2), *Algot, Alrik, Anders, Johan, Nels, Nils, Per, Sigfrid.*

Bergren (679) Variant of Swedish BERGGREN.

Bergs (143) Latvian form of Swedish or German BERG.
GIVEN NAMES Latvian 12%. *Ansis* (2), *Arturs, Arvids, Harijs, Ivars, Juris.*

Bergschneider (154) German: topographic name for someone living by a mountain trail (cut into the hillside), from *Berg* 'mountain', 'hill' + *Schneit* 'trail', 'path running on a border' (Old High German *sneita*).

Bergsma (271) Frisian: probably a topographic name for someone who lived on or by a hill, a derivative of Middle Low German *berg* 'hill'.

Bergson (102) Jewish (from Poland): variant spelling of BERKSON.
GIVEN NAME Jewish 5%. *Hyman.*

Bergstedt (283) Swedish: ornamental name composed of the elements *berg* 'mountain', 'hill' + *stedt* 'place' (of German origin).

Bergstein (246) Jewish (Ashkenazic): ornamental compound of German *Berg* 'mountain', 'hill' + *Stein* 'stone'.
GIVEN NAMES Jewish 7%. *Sol* (2), *Chaim, Hyman, Shalom, Yitzchok.*

Bergsten (196) Swedish: ornamental name composed of the elements *berg* 'mountain', 'hill' + *sten* 'stone'.
GIVEN NAMES Scandinavian 6%. *Erland, Nils.*

Bergstrand (145) Swedish: ornamental name composed of the elements *berg* 'mountain', 'hill' + *strand* 'shore'.

Bergstresser (234) Americanized spelling of German **Bergsträsser**, a regional name denoting someone from the Bergstrasse, an area north of Heidelberg, or a topographic name for someone who lived by a mountain road, from *Berg* 'mountain', 'hill' + *Strasse* 'street', 'road'.

Bergstrom (3790) Swedish (**Bergström**): ornamental name composed of the elements *berg* 'mountain', 'hill' + *ström* 'river'.
GIVEN NAMES Scandinavian 6%. *Erik* (4), *Lars* (4), *Nels* (4), *Nils* (4), *Alf* (2), *Iver* (2), *Lennart* (2), *Thor* (2), *Anders, Bernt, Bjorn, Elof.*

Bergt (111) German: from a pet form (*Perhto*) of the personal name BERCHTOLD.
GIVEN NAMES German 9%. *Dieter, Erwin, Gerhard.*

Bergthold (163) Variant spelling of German BERCHTOLD.
GIVEN NAMES German 4%. *Frederich, Kurt.*

Bergum (384) Norwegian: habitational name from a farmstead named Bergum, from the dative plural of *berg* 'hill', 'mountain'.
GIVEN NAMES Scandinavian 4%. *Dagny, Erik.*

Bergwall (113) Origin unidentified.

Berhane (125) Ethiopian: unexplained.
GIVEN NAMES Ethiopian 63%; African 5%. *Amanuel* (2), *Asmeret* (2), *Freweini* (2), *Hagos* (2), *Saba* (2), *Yared* (2), *Abebe, Ayele, Azeb, Beyene, Dawit, Ermias; Almaz.*

Berhe (124) Ethiopian: unexplained.
GIVEN NAMES Ethiopian 72%. *Berhane* (3), *Almaz* (2), *Dawit* (2), *Mehari* (2), *Mulugeta* (2), *Selamawit* (2), *Tesfai* (2), *Abera, Abrehet, Alazar, Alemnesh, Amanuel, Asfaw; Aron, Yosef.*

Berhorst (123) German: variant of BERGHORST.

Berhow (208) Origin unidentified. Possibly an Americanized form of German **Berkau** (see BERCAW).

Bering (176) North German: patronymic from the Germanic personal name *Ber* (meaning 'bear') or from a short form of any of the various compound names formed with this element (for example BERNHARD).
GIVEN NAMES German 8%. *Wilhelm* (2), *Kurt.*

Beringer (630) **1.** German and Dutch: from the Germanic personal name *Beringer*, composed of the elements *berin* + *gēr* '(warrior) fighting with a spear'. **2.** German: variant spelling of BEHRINGER 1. **3.** French (**Béringer**) and English (of Norman origin): from the Old French personal name *Berenger*, derived from the same Germanic personal name as 1. It owed its popularity in medieval England in part to the fact that it was the name of one of the characters in the Charlemagne romances.

Berisford (107) English: variant spelling of BERESFORD.

Berish (265) Americanized spelling of German **Behrisch**, from a pet form of the Slavic personal name *Beruslaw* or *Boruslaw*.

Berk (1762) **1.** Dutch, Czech, and Polish: from a reduced form of a Germanic personal name formed with *ber* 'bear' (see BERNHARD). **2.** Dutch and North German (**van Berk**): topographic name for someone who lived by a birch tree or in a birch wood, from Middle Dutch, Middle Low German *berke* 'birch'. **3.** German: of Slavic (Sorbian) origin, an occupational name for a collector of taxes. **4.** Slovenian: unexplained. **5.** Jewish (Ashkenazic): variant of BERG.

Berka (226) **1.** Czech, Slovak, and Polish: from a pet form of the Germanic personal name BERNHARD. **2.** Hungarian: from a pet form of the personal names *Bernát* (see BERNHARD) or *Bertalan* (see BARTHOLOMEW). **3.** German: habitational name from any of several places named with Germanic *birka* 'birch tree', notably in Hesse and Thuringia.

Berke (1022) **1.** German: topographic name for someone who lived by a birch tree or birch grove, Middle Low German *berke*. In Westphalia *Berke*, *Birke* also means 'brook', 'stream', and in some cases it may have been a topographic name for someone who lived by a stream. **2.** German: possibly a variant of BERKA. **3.** Altered spelling of Swiss German **Bürki**, from a pet form of the personal name *Burkhard* (see BURKHART). **4.** Dutch: variant of BERK. **5.** Slovenian: unexplained. **6.** Jewish (Ashkenazic): from the Yiddish personal name *Berke*, a pet form of *Ber*.

Berkebile (446) Possibly an altered spelling of German **Berkebiel**, a topographic name from Low German *Berke* 'birch' + *Biel*, a field name meaning 'swampy land'.

Berkel (190) German: habitational name for someone from Berkel (Berklo) near Hamelin.

Berkeley (563) **1.** English: habitational name from Berkeley in Gloucestershire, named in Old English with *be(o)rc* 'birch' + *lēah* 'woodland clearing'. Compare Scottish BARCLAY. **2.** Jewish (American): assimilated form of BERKOWITZ.

Berkemeier (162) German (Westphalia): distinguishing name for a tenant farmer whose farm was by a birch wood, from Middle Low German *berke* 'birch' + *meier* 'tenant farmer' (see MEYER).

Berkemeyer (100) German: variant spelling of BERKEMEIER.

GIVEN NAME German 5%. *Otto*.

Berken (187) Dutch: patronymic from the personal name BERK.

GIVEN NAMES German 5%. *Guenther, Kurt, Reinhard*.

Berkery (177) Irish: Anglicized form of Gaelic **Mac Bearthagra** or **Mac Biorthagra**, literally 'son of sharp pleading', the name of an Ulster family who were Gaelic lawyers to the O'Neills.

GIVEN NAME Irish 5%. *Niall*.

Berkes (190) **1.** North German: topographic name for someone who lived among birch trees, from a derivative of Middle Low German *berke* 'birch'. **2.** Hungarian: from a pet form of the ecclesiastical names *Bernát*, Hungarian form of BERNHARD, or *Bertalan*, Hungarian form of BARTHOLOMEW. **3.** English: variant spelling of BIRKS (see BIRCH).

GIVEN NAMES German 4%. *Kurt, Otto*.

Berkey (1302) **1.** Americanized spelling of Swiss German *Bürki*, or an altered spelling of BERKE (see BERKE 2). **2.** Possibly an Americanized spelling of Hungarian **Berki**, a habitational name from a village called Berki, in Pest county, or a topographic name from *berek* 'marsh with groves'. **3.** English: unexplained.

Berkheimer (442) South German: habitational name for someone from either of two places called Berkheim, near Biberach and near Esslingen in Württemberg. The place name is a compound of Old High German *berg* 'hill', 'mountain' + the common suffix of place names *-heim* (related to English *home*). In some cases it may possibly be a habitational name from any of various places in Hesse and Alsace named Bergheim.

Berkheiser (146) **1.** Altered spelling of German **Birkhäuser**, a habitational name for someone from any of several places (in Westphalia, Bavaria, and Thuringia) named Birkhausen, a compound of Old High German *birka* 'birch' + *hūs* 'house'. **2.** Altered spelling of German **Berghäuser**, a habitational name for someone from any of numerous places called Berghausen, for example in Württemberg.

Berkland (221) Probably an altered spelling of Norwegian BERGLAND.

Berkley (1635) **1.** English: variant of BERKELEY. **2.** Jewish (Ashkenazic): assimilated form of BERKOWITZ.

Berkman (805) **1.** Dutch: topographic name for someone who lived by a birch tree or in a birch wood, from Middle Dutch *berke* 'birch' + *man* 'man'. **2.** Jewish (Ashkenazic): variant of BERKE 4. **3.** Variant of BERGMAN or BERGMANN.

GIVEN NAMES Jewish 5%. *Aron* (3), *Aaron David, Eliezer, Meyer, Miriam, Yaacov, Yakov*.

Berkner (172) German: variant of BERGNER.

GIVEN NAMES German 6%. *Heinz, Horst, Klaus, Lutz*.

Berko (168) **1.** Jewish (Ashkenazic): variant of BERKE. **2.** Hungarian (**Berkó**): from a pet form of the personal name *Bertalan*, Hungarian form of BARTHOLOMEW. **3.** Slovenian: from the personal name *Berko*, a pet form of BERNHARD.

Berkovich (185) **1.** Jewish (eastern Ashkenazic): see BERKOWITZ. **2.** Slovenian (**Berkovič**): patronymic from the personal name *Berko*, a pet form of BERNHARD.

GIVEN NAMES Russian 29%; Jewish 22%. *Vladimir* (5), *Leonid* (4), *Yefim* (4), *Igor* (3), *Arkadiy* (2), *Mikhail* (2), *Aleksandr, Anatoliy, Anatoly, Arkady, Dmitriy, Efim*; *Naum* (5), *Semen* (2), *Aron, Feyga, Ilya, Marat, Mazal, Mendel, Moisey, Moysey, Ronit*.

Berkovitz (177) Jewish (eastern Ashkenazic): variant of BERKOWITZ.

GIVEN NAMES Jewish 13%; German 5%. *Moshe* (2), *Aharon, Isadore, Mandel, Varda, Zvi*; *Markus* (2).

Berkow (114) Jewish (Ashkenazic): patronymic from the Yiddish male personal name BERKE.

Berkowitz (3556) Jewish (Ashkenazic): patronymic from the Yiddish male personal name BERKE, Germanized form of either the Polish spelling *Berkowicz* or eastern Slavic *Berkovich*.

GIVEN NAMES Jewish 9%. *Meyer* (9), *Chaim* (6), *Moshe* (5), *Sol* (5), *Miriam* (4), *Isadore* (3), *Hyman* (2), *Levi* (2), *Mort* (2), *Rebekah* (2), *Shira* (2), *Zvi* (2).

Berks (107) **1.** English: variant spelling of BIRKS (see BIRCH). **2.** North German: variant of BERKES.

Berkshire (445) English: regional name denoting someone from the county of Berkshire in central southern England. The place name is derived from a Celtic name meaning 'hilly place' + Old English *scīr* 'shire'.

Berkson (262) Jewish (eastern Ashkenazic): patronymic composed of the personal name BERKE + German *Sohn* 'son'.

Berkstresser (169) Americanized spelling of German **Bergsträsser** (see BERGSTRESSER).

Berl (137) **1.** German: variant of BEHRLE. **2.** German: habitational name from a place in Westphalia named Berl. **3.** Jewish (Ashkenazic): pet form of the Yiddish male name BER.

GIVEN NAMES Jewish 5%. *Aron, Chaim, Eliezer*.

Berland (376) **1.** Jewish (eastern Ashkenazic): variant of **Brillant**, an ornamental name from Yiddish *barlyant* 'diamond', 'jewel'; compare BRILLIANT. **2.** French: from a Germanic personal name composed of the elements *ber* 'bear' + *land* 'country'. **3.** Norwegian: habitational name from any of numerous farms in southwestern Norway named Berland, from Old Norse *bjarg* 'hill', 'mountain' or *ber* 'berry' + *land* 'land'.

Berlanga (241) Spanish: habitational name from a place so named in Badajoz province, or from Berlanga de Duero in Soria, or Berlanga del Bierzo in León.
GIVEN NAMES Spanish 42%. *Jose* (11), *Pedro* (4), *Alfredo* (3), *Domingo* (3), *Armando* (2), *Benito* (2), *Jesus* (2), *Juan* (2), *Luis* (2), *Lupe* (2), *Manuel* (2), *Roberto* (2).

Berley (159) **1.** English: variant spelling of BURLEY. **2.** Probably an altered spelling of Swiss German **Beerli**, from a short form of the Germanic personal name *Berilo*, from Old High German *bero* 'bear'. **3.** Possibly an Anglicized spelling of French **Berlet**, from a diminutive of **Berle**, a topographic name from Old French *berle* 'water parsnip' (of Celtic origin, compare Welsh *berur*, Gaelic *biorar* 'watercress'), or perhaps an occupational name for a grower of the plant.

Berlin (3360) Jewish (Ashkenazic) and German: habitational name from the city of Berlin, capital of Germany. This city takes its name from a West Slavic word meaning 'river rake', a scaffold of beams built over a river to prevent logs from jamming; the river in question is the Spree. Folk etymology, however, has put a bear into the arms of the city, as if the name were derived from *Bärlin*, a diminutive of *Bär* 'bear'. The German name is also found in the Hamburg area, where it may be derived from the village of the same name, but uncertain origin, in Holstein. In some cases the Jewish name may be a patronymic from a pet form of the Yiddish personal name *Ber* (see BERENSON).

Berliner (756) Jewish (Ashkenazic) and German: habitational name for someone from the city of Berlin (see BERLIN).
GIVEN NAMES Jewish 4%; German 4%. *Asher*, *Blyuma*, *Este*, *Itzhak*, *Leibel*, *Miriam*, *Sol*; *Bernhard* (2), *Ernst* (2), *Erwin* (2), *Hans* (2), *Kurt*, *Otto*.

Berling (306) German and Scandinavian: perhaps, as Søndergaard suggests, from German *Berlingk*, a patronymic from *Berit*, a dialect form of the personal name BERTHOLD.

Berlinger (258) Swiss and German: habitational name from Beroldingen, Switzerland, and any of several places called Berlingen in the Eifel and Mosel districts of Germany.

Berlinski (132) Polish (**Berliński**) and Jewish (eastern Ashkenazic): habitational name for someone from Berlin (see BERLIN).
GIVEN NAMES German 6%; Polish 5%. *Erik* (2), *Frieda*; *Casimir*, *Dariusz*.

Berlinsky (100) Jewish (eastern Ashkenazic): variant of BERLINSKI.
GIVEN NAMES French 4%; Jewish 4%. *Dany*; *Hyman*.

Berman (9090) **1.** Jewish (Ashkenazic): from the Yiddish male personal name *Berman*, meaning 'bear man'. **2.** Respell-

ing of German BERMANN 1–3. **3.** English: occupational name for a porter, Middle English *berman* (Old English *bærmann*, from *beran* 'to carry' + *mann* 'man'). **4.** English: possibly from a Middle English personal name, *Ber(e)man*, which may be derived from Old English *Beornmund*, composed of the elements *beorn* 'young man', 'warrior' + *mund* 'protection'.
GIVEN NAMES Jewish 7%. *Sol* (22), *Hyman* (12), *Isadore* (11), *Miriam* (11), *Meyer* (10), *Ari* (4), *Emanuel* (4), *Zev* (4), *Elihu* (3), *Irina* (3), *Naum* (3), *Aba* (2).

Bermann (92) **1.** German: occupational name for a swineherd, from Middle High German *bēr* 'boar' + *man* 'man'. **2.** German: occupational name for someone who exhibited a bear (see BEARMAN). **3.** North German: from a short form of any of the various medieval personal names derived from Germanic compound names with the first element *ber(n)* 'bear'. **4.** Jewish (Ashkenazic): variant spelling of BERMAN.
GIVEN NAMES German 12%. *Fritz*, *Manfred*.

Bermea (234) Hispanic: unexplained.
GIVEN NAMES Spanish 42%. *Jose* (5), *Jesus* (3), *Juan* (3), *Armando* (2), *Arnoldo* (2), *Eleazar* (2), *Felipe* (2), *Sergio* (2), *Trinidad* (2), *Alicia*, *Amador*, *Ana*.

Bermejo (165) Spanish: nickname for a man with red hair or a ruddy complexion, from Spanish *bermejo* 'red', 'ruddy' (Late Latin *vermiculus*, from *vermis* 'worm', since a red dye was obtained from the bodies of worms).
GIVEN NAMES Spanish 57%. *Carlos* (4), *Juan* (4), *Miguel* (4), *Angelina* (2), *Francisco* (2), *Isidra* (2), *Jesus* (2), *Jose* (2), *Leticia* (2), *Luz* (2), *Pablo* (2), *Pedro* (2).

Bermel (295) German: habitational name from a place in Rhineland named Bermel.

Bermingham (377) Irish (of English origin): variant spelling of BIRMINGHAM. This spelling is found chiefly in Ireland.
FOREBEARS The Bermingham family take their surname from lands held at what is now a great city in the West Midlands of England, but it was brought to Ireland as early as the 12th century. The Norman baron Robert de Bermyngeham was a follower of Strongbow (see CLARE); his name is found on a number of Irish charters between 1175 and 1179. The family was also known as *Mac Fheorais* (**(Mc)Corish**) in Ireland, named for Piers (Gaelic *Feoras*) de Bermyngeham, the father of Robert.
GIVEN NAMES Irish 5%. *Liam*, *Sinead*.

Bermudes (140) Spanish and Portuguese: variant of BERMUDEZ.
GIVEN NAMES Spanish 49%. *Jose* (5), *Carlos* (3), *Jesus* (3), *Miguel* (2), *Pedro* (2), *Alfredo*, *Angel*, *Armando*, *Cesar*, *Eduardo*, *Elivia*, *Emigdio*.

Bermudez (2375) Spanish (**Bermúdez**): patronymic from *Bermudo*, a Germanic (Visigothic) personal name of uncertain etymology.

GIVEN NAMES Spanish 50%. *Jose* (60), *Juan* (35), *Luis* (32), *Carlos* (28), *Manuel* (27), *Jesus* (20), *Francisco* (16), *Pedro* (15), *Eduardo* (14), *Jorge* (14), *Raul* (14), *Miguel* (13).

Bern (374) **1.** German and Scandinavian: from the personal name *Berno*, a pet form of BERNHARD. **2.** South German: habitational name from Bern, Switzerland, notably in the south; in other parts from the personal name *Berno*.

Berna (371) Swiss and Italian: **1.** from the Italian personal name BERNARDO, or from any other Germanic personal name beginning with *Bern-*. **2.** habitational name from the Swiss city of Bern.

Bernabe (361) Spanish, Italian, and French (**Bernabé**): from the personal name *Bernabé* (see BARNABY).
GIVEN NAMES Spanish 48%; Italian 4%. *Jose* (12), *Jaime* (4), *Pedro* (4), *Salvador* (4), *Alberto* (3), *Jose Luis* (3), *Juan* (3), *Luis* (3), *Roberto* (3), *Carlos* (2), *Damaso* (2), *Emilio* (2); *Antonio* (2), *Aldo*, *Angelo*, *Cecilio*, *Filiberto*, *Lucio*, *Marco*.

Bernabei (172) Italian: from the personal name *Bernabeo*, a variant of *Barnaba*, Italian form of *Barnabas* (see BARNABY).
GIVEN NAMES Italian 20%. *Domenic* (3), *Aldo*, *Angelo*, *Camillo*, *Geno*, *Giacomo*, *Guglielmo*, *Leno*, *Primo*.

Bernacchi (113) Italian: from a derivative of a short form of the personal name BERNARDO.

Bernacki (229) Polish: variant of BIERNACKI.
GIVEN NAMES Polish 6%. *Kazimierz* (2), *Jozef*.

Bernal (3921) Catalan: from the personal name *Bernal*, a variant of Spanish *Bernaldo* (see BERNARD).
GIVEN NAMES Spanish 43%. *Jose* (95), *Juan* (48), *Manuel* (43), *Carlos* (25), *Luis* (23), *Miguel* (23), *Francisco* (22), *Jesus* (19), *Jorge* (19), *Pedro* (19), *Raul* (19), *Ramon* (18).

Bernard (12443) **1.** English, French, Dutch, Polish, Czech, and Slovenian: from a Germanic personal name (see BERNHARD). The popularity of the personal name was greatly increased by virtue of its having been borne by St. Bernard of Clairvaux (*c.*1090–1153), founder and abbot of the Cistercian monastery at Clairvaux. **2.** Americanized form of German BERNHARD or any of the other cognates in European languages; for forms see Hanks and Hodges 1988.
FOREBEARS The first bearer of the name in Canada was from the Lorraine region of France. He is documented in Quebec city in 1666 as Jean Bernard. He and some of his descendants bore the secondary surnames Anse and Hanse, because his original forename must have been Hans (the German equivalent of French Jean, English John). Another bearer, from La Rochelle, is docu-

mented in Quebec city in 1676; and a third, from the Poitou region of France, was also documented in Quebec city, in 1713, with the secondary surname Léveillé. Other documented secondary names are Jolicoeur, Larivière, and Lajoie.

The Bernard families of LA have origins in France, Acadia, the West Indies, and Germany; they have been in the U.S. since the earliest days of settlement.

GIVEN NAMES French 6%. *Armand* (8), *Emile* (8), *Jacques* (8), *Marcel* (8), *Pierre* (8), *Andre* (6), *Lucien* (5), *Normand* (5), *Henri* (4), *Michel* (4), *Cecile* (3), *Gabrielle* (3).

Bernardez (101) Spanish (**Bernárdez**): patronymic from the personal name *Bernardo* (see BERNHARD).

GIVEN NAMES Spanish 41%. *Luis* (3), *Jose* (2), *Juan* (2), *Manuel* (2), *Basilio, Berardo, Carlos, Carolina, Celso, Domingo, Eduardo, Felipe*; *Antonio* (2), *Constantino, Gino, Lorenzo*.

Bernardi (1154) Italian: patronymic or plural form of BERNARDO.

GIVEN NAMES Italian 29%. *Mario* (7), *Angelo* (6), *Armando* (5), *Silvio* (4), *Antonio* (3), *Dino* (3), *Gino* (3), *Aldo* (2), *Emilio* (2), *Franco* (2), *Leno* (2), *Marco* (2), *Rocco* (2), *Sandro* (2), *Timoteo* (2), *Alfeo, Amerigo, Artemio, Avelino*.

Bernardin (224) French: from a pet form of the personal name BERNARD.

GIVEN NAMES French 10%. *Chantal, Georges, Jacques, Marthe, Pierre, Wilner*.

Bernardini (464) Italian: patronymic or plural form of BERNARDINO.

GIVEN NAMES Italian 18%; Spanish 9%; French 4%. *Mario* (7), *Dante* (3), *Angelo* (2), *Carlo* (2), *Remo* (2), *Reno* (2), *Alessandro, Antonella, Antonio, Elio, Evo, Fausto, Gino*; *Jorge* (2), *Ana, Carlos, Jaime, Lilia, Mercedes*; *Armand, Dominique, Serge*.

Bernardino (284) Spanish, Portuguese, and Italian: from a pet form of the personal name BERNARDO.

GIVEN NAMES Spanish 39%; Portuguese 10%; Italian 4%. *Jose* (7), *Carlos* (4), *Miguel* (4), *Estela* (3), *Rafael* (3), *Armando* (2), *Jaime* (2), *Juan* (2), *Lourdes* (2), *Manuel* (2), *Adriana, Alejandro*; *Joao, Paulo, Wenceslao*; *Antonio* (2), *Amedio, Angelo, Gilda, Leonardo, Primo*.

Bernardo (1577) Spanish, Portuguese, and Italian: from the personal name *Bernardo* (see BERNHARD).

GIVEN NAMES Spanish 19%; Portuguese 6%; Italian 6%. *Jose* (18), *Manuel* (17), *Carlos* (6), *Eduardo* (5), *Luis* (4), *Ricardo* (4), *Arturo* (3), *Fernando* (3), *Mario* (3), *Alfredo* (2), *Benito* (2), *Conrado* (2); *Joao, Joaquim, Margarida, Mateus, Paulo*; *Antonio* (9), *Angelo* (3), *Aldo* (2), *Antonino, Carlo, Carmela, Carmelo, Carmine, Cesare, Cosmo, Domenico*.

Bernards (224) **1.** Dutch and North German: patronymic from the personal name

Bernard (see BERNHARD). **2.** Latvian form of the personal name BERNHARD.

Bernardy (278) **1.** French: from a pet form of BERNARD. **2.** German: humanistic name representing a respelling of the Latin genitive form, *Bernardi*, of the personal name *Bernardus* (see BERNHARD).

Bernas (242) **1.** Polish (**Bernaś**) and Czech (**Bernáš**): from a derivative of the personal name BERNARD. **2.** French: from a derivative of BERN.

GIVEN NAMES German 4%. *Egon, Kurt, Otto*.

Bernasconi (200) Italian (chiefly Milan): habitational name for someone from Bernasca in Como province.

GIVEN NAMES Italian 8%; Spanish 5%. *Angelo* (2), *Guido* (2), *Dario, Edo, Giorgio, Santo*; *Andres, Armando, Carlos, Francisco, Mario, Ricardo*.

Bernat (601) **1.** Southern French and Catalan: from the personal name *Bernat* (see BERNHARD). **2.** Hungarian (**Bernát**): from the personal name *Bernát*, Hungarian form of BERNHARD. **3.** Slovenian: from a derivative of the personal name BERNARD. Compare BERNOT.

Bernath (446) Hungarian (**Bernáth**): from the personal name *Bernát*, Hungarian form of BERNHARD.

Bernatowicz (107) Polish: patronymic from the personal name *Bernat*, Polish form of German BERNHARD.

GIVEN NAMES Polish 15%. *Beata, Grazyna, Janusz, Krystyna, Ludwik, Remigiusz*.

Bernau (130) German: habitational name from any of several places called Bernau (see BERNAUER).

GIVEN NAMES German 11%. *Dieter* (2), *Hans* (2), *Klaus* (2).

Bernauer (252) German: habitational name for someone from any of the places called Bernau, for example in Baden, Bavaria, or Württemberg.

Bernbaum (105) Jewish (Ashkenazic): variant of BIRNBAUM.

Bernd (265) German: from a reduced form of the personal name BERNHARD (see BERNDT).

GIVEN NAMES German 5%. *Kurt, Matthias, Otto*.

Berndsen (104) Danish and North German: patronymic from the personal name *Bernd*, a local form of BERNHARD.

Berndt (2540) North German form of BERNHARD.

GIVEN NAMES German 5%. *Otto* (6), *Erwin* (4), *Kurt* (3), *Johannes* (2), *Manfred* (2), *Christoph, Erna, Ernst, Eugen, Ewald, Franz, Fritz*.

Berne (255) **1.** Irish: variant spelling of BYRNE. **2.** French: variant spelling of BERN. **3.** Variant spelling of Swiss German BERNI. **4.** Slovenian: from a derivative of the personal name BERNARD.

Bernecker (123) German: habitational name for someone from Berneck (the name of places in Franconia and Württemberg).

GIVEN NAMES German 9%. *Erwin* (2), *Helmut* (2), *Theresia*.

Berner (2001) **1.** English: from the Norman personal name BERNIER. **2.** English: from Old English *beornan* 'to burn', hence an occupational name for a burner of lime (compare German KALKBRENNER) or charcoal. It may also have denoted someone who baked bricks or distilled spirits, or who carried out any other manufacturing process involving burning. **3.** English: occupational name for a keeper of hounds, from Old Norman French *bern(i)er, brenier* (a derivative of *bren, bran* 'bran', on which the dogs were fed). **4.** Southern English: topographic or occupational name for someone who lived by or worked in a barn, from Middle English *bern, barn* 'barn' + the suffix *-er*. Compare BARNES. **5.** German: habitational name, in Silesia denoting someone from a place called Berna (of which there are two examples); in southern Germany and Switzerland denoting someone from the Swiss city of Berne. **6.** German: from the Germanic personal name *Bernher* meaning 'lord of the army'. **7.** North German: occupational name for a lime or charcoal burner (cognate with 2), from an agent derivative of Middle High German *brennen* 'to burn'.

GIVEN NAMES German 4%. *Kurt* (5), *Heinz* (2), *Lothar* (2), *Bernhard, Erwin, Gerhard, Helmut, Reimund, Wolf*.

Bernero (102) Italian: reduced form of BERNARDO.

GIVEN NAMES Italian 6%. *Giulio, Marco*.

Bernert (135) German: variant of BERNER or BERNHARD.

GIVEN NAME German 4%. *Heinz*.

Bernet (277) French: from a pet form of BERNARD.

Bernett (191) Altered spelling of Scottish and English BURNETT or French BERNET.

Berney (486) **1.** English: variant spelling of BURNEY. **2.** French: from a pet form of BERNARD. **3.** Jewish (American): from a derivative of the Yiddish personal name BER.

Bernfeld (140) Jewish (Ashkenazic): ornamental name from the Yiddish personal name *Ber* ('bear') + German *Feld* 'open country'.

GIVEN NAMES Jewish 17%; German 4%. *Chaim* (2), *Avrum, Chanie, Gersh, Hyman, Mordche, Moshe, Shimon, Sol*; *Hans, Siegfried, Siegmund*.

Bernhagen (165) German: habitational name from a place in Pomerania named Bernhagen.

Bernhard (1675) Dutch, German, and Scandinavian: from the Germanic personal name *Bernhard*, composed of the elements *ber(n)* 'bear' + *hard* 'brave', 'hardy', 'strong'. In the 13th and 14th centuries it vied with ARNOLD as the most popular personal name in the Netherlands and northern Germany. It was borne by St. Bernard of

Menthon (923–1008), founder of Alpine hospices and patron saint of mountaineers, whose cult accounts for the frequency of the name in Alpine regions. See also BERNARD.
GIVEN NAMES German 4%. *Alfons, Detlef, Dieter, Erwin, Friedhelm, Fritz, Gerhard, Hertha, Horst, Kurt, Manfred, Otto.*

Bernhardt (3174) German and Scandinavian: variant spelling of BERNHARD.
GIVEN NAMES German 5%. *Kurt* (5), *Armin* (3), *Juergen* (3), *Ernst* (2), *Erwin* (2), *Helmut* (2), *Otto* (2), *Elfriede, Franz, Frieda, Fritz, Gerd.*

Bernhart (265) German and Scandinavian: variant spelling of BERNHARD.

Bernheim (203) Jewish (Ashkenazic): ornamental name from the Yiddish personal name *Ber* ('bear') + German *Heim* 'home'.
GIVEN NAMES French 5%; German 4%. *Armand, Chantal, Jean Francois; Kurt* (2).

Bernheisel (120) Altered form of a German habitational name from any of numerous places named with *ber(n)* 'bear' + a diminutive of *Haus* 'house', probably a minor place or farmstead called *Bernhäusel.*

Berni (153) **1.** Italian: probably from a short form of BERNARDO, but see also BERNA. **2.** German (Alemannic): from a pet form of BERNHARD.
GIVEN NAMES Italian 11%; French 6%; Spanish 5%. *Luigi* (2), *Amedeo, Arrigo, Donato, Egidio, Silvio; Emile, Marcelle; Francisco* (2), *Fabio, Juan, Rafael, Xavier.*

Bernick (222) **1.** German: from a nickname derived from Sorbian *baran* 'ram'. **2.** North German: from a pet form of BERNHARD. **3.** German: nickname for someone with a growth such as a sty on the eyelid. **4.** German or American spelling of Slovenian **Bernik**, from the northern part of central Slovenia, probably an archaic nickname from the noun *bera* 'collecting', from *brati* 'to collect', 'to pick', perhaps denoting a beggar or an impoverished man.

Bernier (3622) **1.** French: from the personal name *Bernier*, from a Germanic personal name composed of the elements *bern* 'bear' + *hari* 'army'. **2.** German (from Slavic): habitational name from a place so named in Mecklenburg.
FOREBEARS A Bernier from Paris, also called Jean de Paris, is recorded in Quebec city in 1656. Another, from the Poitou region of France, was documented in Quebec city in 1670, with the secondary surname La Marzelle.
GIVEN NAMES French 13%. *Marcel* (12), *Normand* (9), *Andre* (8), *Fernand* (8), *Armand* (7), *Adrien* (6), *Michel* (6), *Camille* (5), *Jacques* (5), *Lucien* (5), *Benoit* (3), *Laurent* (3).

Berning (1037) North German: habitational name from Behring, which during the 15th century is recorded as *Berning* and *Bernynge.*

Berninger (265) North German (mainly Eastphalia): habitational name for someone from Behring (see BERNING).

GIVEN NAMES German 5%. *Egon* (2), *Kurt, Raimund.*

Bernitt (100) Variant spelling of Scottish and English BURNETT.
GIVEN NAMES German 5%. *Eldred, Otto.*

Bernius (118) **1.** German: Latinized form of BERNER. **2.** Lithuanian: occupational name from a derivative of *bérnas* 'lad', 'farmhand'.

Bernosky (142) Jewish (from Belarus): habitational name from the village of Bernovo in Belarus.

Bernot (129) **1.** French: from a pet form of BERNARD. **2.** Slovenian: from a derivative of the personal name BERNARD. Compare BERNAT.
GIVEN NAMES French 5%. *Micheline, Remy.*

Bernotas (107) Lithuanian: from a variant of the personal name *Bernardas*, Lithuanian form of BERNARD.
GIVEN NAMES Lithuanian 9%; Polish 4%. *Aleksas, Alfonsas, Bronius, Vytautas; Casimir.*

Berns (1217) **1.** Dutch and North German: patronymic from *Bern*, a variant of BERND. **2.** Latvian: from a short form of the personal name *Bernards* (see BERNHARD).

Bernsen (148) **1.** North German: reduced form of BERENDSEN. **2.** Danish and Norwegian: patronymic from the personal name *Bernt* (see BERNHARD).

Bernson (172) **1.** Swedish: patronymic from the personal name *Bernt* (see BERNHARD). **2.** Americanized spelling of BERNSEN. **3.** Jewish (Ashkenazic): patronymic from the Yiddish personal name *Ber* ('bear').

Bernstein (10279) **1.** Jewish (Ashkenazic): ornamental name from German *Bernstein* 'amber' (from Middle Low German *bernen* 'to burn' + *stēn* 'stone'; it was thought to be created by burning, although it is in fact fossilized pine resin). **2.** German: habitational name from a place named Bernstein, of which there is one example in Bavaria and another in what used to be East Prussia (now Pełczyce in northwestern Poland). Both of these probably get their German names from the notion of a 'burnt stone', for example in brick making, rather than from the usual modern meaning, 'amber'. The name may also be derived from Bärenstein, a common field and place name, especially in Bavaria and Austria. **3.** German and Jewish (Ashkenazic): in some cases perhaps a metonymic occupational name for a craftsman or dealer in amber.
GIVEN NAMES Jewish 5%. *Sol* (18), *Isadore* (14), *Hyman* (12), *Meyer* (7), *Miriam* (6), *Emanuel* (4), *Giora* (4), *Ari* (3), *Aron* (3), *Morty* (3), *Noach* (3), *Avi* (2).

Bernt (194) Scandinavian and North German: from a short form of BERNHARD.
GIVEN NAMES German 6%; Scandinavian 4%. *Helmut* (2), *Benno.*

Bernthal (149) Jewish (Ashkenazic): ornamental name from the Yiddish personal name *Ber* ('bear') + German *Thal* (now spelled *Tal*) 'valley'.
GIVEN NAMES German 5%. *Erwin, Frieda.*

Berntsen (342) Norwegian and Danish: patronymic from the personal name *Bernt* (see BERNHARD).
GIVEN NAMES Scandinavian 13%. *Bernt* (2), *Erik* (2), *Knut.*

Berntson (299) Altered spelling of Norwegian and Danish BERNTSEN or Swedish **Berntsson**, also a patronymic from *Bernt* (see BERNHARD).
GIVEN NAMES Scandinavian 8%. *Alf* (2), *Bernt, Lars, Lennart, Thor.*

Bero (428) **1.** German and French (Alsace): unexplained. **2.** Possibly a respelling of French **Berot**, which Morlet identifies as an altered form of **Berost**, a pet form of a Germanic compound name formed with *ber* 'bear'.

Beron (164) **1.** French (**Béron**): from a pet form of the Germanic personal name *Bero*, from *ber* 'bear'. **2.** Jewish (eastern Ashkenazic): variant of BARON 6.
GIVEN NAMES Spanish 6%; Jewish 4%; German 4%. *Alberto, Alfredo, Carlos, Horacio, Josefa, Maximo, Nestor, Pedro; Leizer, Mechel; Kurt, Wilhelm.*

Berquist (518) Altered form of the Swedish ornamental name BERGQUIST.
GIVEN NAMES Scandinavian 5%. *Arlys, Dagny, Knut, Lisen, Thor.*

Berra (342) Spanish: of uncertain origin; possibly a nickname from a derivative of *berrar* 'to scream or shout'.

Berres (288) German: from a short form of *Liborius*, the patron saint of the city of Paderborn, probably of Celtic origin.
GIVEN NAME French 4%. *Andre.*

Berreth (331) German: variant form of **Berroth**, a family name in Württemberg imported by (French) Waldensians in 1699, recorded subsequently as *Perrot* and *Perrault*. The name is derived from the Germanic personal name *Berwald*, composed of the elements *ber* 'bear' (the animal) + *wald-* 'to wield', 'rule'.
GIVEN NAMES German 6%. *Milbert* (2), *Otto* (2), *Helmuth, Hertha, Reinhold.*

Berrett (400) French: from *berret* 'hooded cloak' (Latin *birrus*), later 'headdress', 'bonnet', hence a metonymic occupational name for a maker of such headgear or a nickname for an habitual wearer. In the modern sense of a flat brimless hat, *béret* was not coined until the 19th century.

Berretta (132) Italian: from *berretta*, originally meaning 'hooded cloak' (Latin *birrus*), later 'headdress', 'bonnet', hence a metonymic occupational name for a maker of such headgear or a nickname for an habitual wearer.
GIVEN NAMES Italian 19%. *Angelo* (3), *Gino, Reno, Salvatore, Vito.*

Berrey (255) Variant of BERRY.

Berrian (234) Variant of French BERRIEN.

Berridge (384) English: variant of BEVERIDGE.

Berrie (181) Scottish: **1.** variant of BARRIE. According to Black, this is the name of an ancient family in Fife. **2.** variant of BERRY.

Berrien (167) French: regional name for someone from Berry (see BERRIER) or from Berrien, in the department of Finistere.

FOREBEARS The name is borne by a French Huguenot family who fled from religious persecution in France in the 17th century, first to the Netherlands and then to North America. Cornelius Jansen Berrien (died 1689) arrived in Flatbush (now a section of Brooklyn, NY) in 1669. In 1685 he moved to Newtown, Long Island.

Berrier (939) French: regional name (from Old French *berruyer*) for someone from Berry (see BERRY 4). However, the distribution of the name in North America is not consistent with a French origin, and it may be that another source should be sought.

Berrigan (332) Irish: Anglicized form of Gaelic **Ó Beirgin** or **Ó Meirgin**, a variant of **Ó hAimheirgin** 'descendant of *Aimheirgin*', a personal name in early Irish mythology and historical tales, perhaps composed of the elements *amhra* 'wonderful' + *gin* 'birth'. (The Gaelic pronunciation would have an extra vowel between the *r* and the *g*, as shown in the Anglicized spelling.)

Berriman (130) English: variant spelling of BERRYMAN.

Berringer (258) **1.** English: variant spelling of BERINGER. **2.** In some instances, possibly an altered form of German BEHRINGER or French **Béringer** (see BERINGER).

Berrio (135) Basque: habitational name from Berrio in Biscay province, Basque Country, or a topographic name, probably from Basque *berri* 'new'.
GIVEN NAMES Spanish 33%. *Carlos* (2), *Cristina* (2), *Francisco* (2), *Jesus* (2), *Juan* (2), *Angel, Bernardo, Consuelo, Ernesto, Jairo, Jorge, Jose*.

Berrios (1285) Variant of Spanish BARRIOS.
GIVEN NAMES Spanish 45%. *Jose* (52), *Luis* (24), *Carlos* (19), *Juan* (17), *Miguel* (15), *Ana* (12), *Angel* (11), *Pedro* (10), *Jorge* (9), *Julio* (8), *Rafael* (8), *Roberto* (8).

Berrones (133) Spanish: unexplained; perhaps a topographic name from the plural of *berrón* denoting a kind of bird.
GIVEN NAMES Spanish 45%. *Jose* (6), *Manuel* (4), *Alberto* (3), *Gerardo* (3), *Alfredo, Alicia, Ana Maria, Arturo, Carlos, Dimas, Eduardo, Elpidio; Carmela, Marco*.

Berrong (249) According to family tradition, this is a variant of French **Béringer** or Dutch BERINGER.

Berry (46082) **1.** Irish (Galway and Mayo): Anglicized form of Gaelic **Ó Béara** or **Ó Beargha** (see BARRY 1). **2.** Scottish and northern Irish: variant spelling of BARRIE. **3.** English: habitational name from any of several places named with Old English

byrig, dative case of *burh* 'fortified manor house', 'stronghold', such as Berry in Devon or Bury in Cambridgeshire, Greater Manchester, Suffolk, and West Sussex. **4.** French: regional name for someone from Berry, a former province of central France, so named with Latin *Boiriacum*, apparently a derivative of a Gaulish personal name, *Boirius* or *Barius*. In North America, this name has alternated with BERRIEN. **5.** Swiss German: pet form of a Germanic personal name formed with Old High German *bero* 'bear' (see BAER).

Berryhill (1910) English or Scottish habitational name from any of numerous places in England and Scotland named Berryhill, for example in Berkshire, Gloucestershire, Nottinghamshire, Staffordshire, Lothian, Tayside, and Orkney.

Berryman (2786) English: topographic or habitational name, ultimately from the dative case, *byrig*, of Old English *burh* 'stronghold', 'fortified place' + *man* 'man'.

Bersani (135) Italian: habitational name from a place so named in Emilia-Romagna.
GIVEN NAMES Italian 10%; German 4%. *Angelo* (2), *Antonio* (2), *Luigi, Silvio; Kurt*.

Bersch (282) German (Alemannic and Swabian): variant spelling of BERTSCH.

Bershad (106) Jewish (from Ukraine): habitational name from the town of Bershad, Ukraine.
GIVEN NAMES Jewish 7%. *Emanuel, Vigdor*.

Berson (541) Jewish (Ashkenazic): patronymic from the Yiddish male personal name *Ber* ('bear').
GIVEN NAMES Jewish 5%. *Isadore* (2), *Aron, Emanuel, Miriam, Myer*.

Berst (167) Variant of German BERTZ or BREST.

Berstein (116) Jewish (Ashkenazic): variant of BERNSTEIN.
GIVEN NAMES Jewish 6%. *Isadore, Ziva*.

Berstler (121) Of German origin. Compare BERST.

Bert (607) English and French: from the Germanic personal name *Berto*, a short form of the various compound personal names formed with *berht* 'bright', 'famous' (see for example BERTHOLD, BERTHOLF, and BERTRAM).
GIVEN NAMES French 4%. *Philibert, Pierre*.

Berta (590) **1.** Italian and Hungarian: from the personal name *Berta*, a short form of the various Germanic compound personal names formed with *berht* 'bright', 'famous'. **2.** Hungarian: from a short form of the personal name *Bertalan*, Hungarian form of BARTHOLOMEW.

Bertagnolli (188) Italian: from a double diminutive of BERTO.
GIVEN NAMES Italian 7%. *Angelo* (2), *Corrado, Ettore, Leno, Libero*.

Bertani (141) Italian: from a derivative of the personal name *Berto*.

GIVEN NAMES Italian 19%. *Dante* (2), *Giorgio* (2), *Reno* (2), *Alberto, Amadeo, Angelo, Ceasar, Eusebio, Javier, Mario*.

Bertch (136) Altered spelling of German BERTSCH.

Berte (290) **1.** French: from a variant of *Berta*, feminine form of BERT. **2.** Hungarian: from a pet form of *Bertalan*, Hungarian form of BARTHOLOMEW.
GIVEN NAMES Italian 6%. *Dino, Domenic, Domenico, Salvatore, Santo, Saverio*.

Berteau (114) French: from the Germanic personal name *Berto* (see BERT).
GIVEN NAMES French 12%. *Lucien* (3), *Leonce*.

Bertel (112) **1.** German, Swedish, and Danish: from a pet form of the personal name BERTHOLD. **2.** French: from a derivative of Old French *berte* 'basket', 'pannier'.
GIVEN NAMES Scandinavian 5%; French 5%; German 4%. *Erik* (2); *Eugenie, Numa; Otto*.

Bertelli (176) Italian: from a diminutive of BERTO.
GIVEN NAMES Italian 10%. *Gianluigi* (2), *Antonio, Caesar, Carlo, Dino*.

Bertels (155) German and Swedish: from the personal name BERTEL. The genitive *-s* is either a patronymic suffix or denotes possession (of a house, for instance).
GIVEN NAMES German 7%. *Claus* (3), *Eldor*.

Bertelsen (626) German, Danish, and Norwegian: patronymic from *Bertel*, a pet form of BERTHOLD.
GIVEN NAMES Scandinavian 8%. *Erik* (4), *Bertel, Iver, Niels, Nils, Sven, Viggo*.

Bertelson (253) Americanized spelling of BERTELSEN or the Swedish cognate **Bertelsson**.
GIVEN NAMES Scandinavian 4%. *Erik, Nils*.

Berth (114) German: probably from the female personal name BERTA.

Bertha (187) German and Hungarian: from the female personal name *Bertha* (see BERTA).

Berthel (110) German and Swedish: variant of BERTEL.

Berthelot (582) French: from a pet form of the personal name *Barthélemy* (see BARTHOLOMEW) or possibly of any of the Germanic personal names mentioned at BERT. It is quite commonly found as a Huguenot name outside France.

FOREBEARS A Bertholet from Normandy is documented in Quebec city in 1659. Another, from the Anjou region of France, is recorded in Quebec city in 1674, with the secondary surname Le Loutre, as well as Du Veau, dit des Cormiers. Others originated in Paris and the Saintonge region; the secondary surname La Giroflée is also documented. The Berthelot families of LA claim descent from Urbain Berthelot, who came to Mobile before 1720.
GIVEN NAMES French 8%. *Alcide* (3), *Antoine* (3), *Aubert, Firmin, Gervais, Jean-Pierre, Reynaud, Yves*.

Berthelsen (159) Danish and Norwegian: variant spelling of BERTELSEN.
GIVEN NAMES Scandinavian 11%. *Holger* (2), *Einer, Maren, Viggo.*

Berthiaume (1051) French: from a Germanic personal name composed of the elements *berht* 'bright', 'famous' + *helm* 'helmet'.
FOREBEARS The immigrant ancestor of the Berthiaume families is recorded as Berthéome in Cap Rouge or in Sillery, Quebec, in 1667.
GIVEN NAMES French 13%. *Armand* (7), *Adlore* (2), *Gaston* (2), *Henri* (2), *Lucien* (2), *Marcel* (2), *Normand* (2), *Aime, Andre, Celine, Collette, Elrick.*

Berthold (555) German and Scandinavian: from the Germanic personal name *Bertwald*, composed of the elements *berht* 'bright', 'famous' + *wald* 'rule'. The second element has been altered by association with German *hold* 'lovely', 'splendid'.
GIVEN NAMES German 8%. *Erwin* (4), *Hans* (2), *Juergen* (2), *Claus, Fritz, Gerhard, Goetz, Guenter, Helmut, Merwin, Otto, Siegried.*

Bertholf (233) German: from the Germanic personal name *Bertolf*, composed of the elements *berht* 'bright', 'famous' + *wolf* 'wolf'.

Berti (385) **1.** Italian: patronymic or plural form of BERTO. **2.** Hungarian: from a pet form of the personal name *Bertalan*, Hungarian form of BARTHOLOMEW.
GIVEN NAMES Italian 26%. *Aldo* (3), *Angelo* (3), *Gino* (3), *Luciano* (3), *Alberto* (2), *Dante* (2), *Orlando* (2), *Silvio* (2), *Agostino, Alfredo, Annibale, Antonio, Berto, Dario, Ferruccio, Geno, Marina, Sergio.*

Bertin (301) French: from a pet form of BERT.
FOREBEARS A Bertin, also called Languedoc, from the Languedoc region of France, is recorded in Quebec city in 1670; another, from the Saintonge region, is recorded with the secondary surname Larouge in Quebec city in 1717.
GIVEN NAMES French 10%. *Armand* (2), *Francois* (2), *Amedee, Andre, Colette, Gabrielle, Marcel, Michel, Patrice, Solange, Stephane.*

Bertini (253) Italian: patronymic or plural form of BERTINO.
GIVEN NAMES Italian 17%. *Graziano* (2), *Vito* (2), *Aldo, Dino, Francesco, Fulvio, Guiseppe, Marino, Nino, Reno, Rino, Rocco.*

Bertino (441) Italian: from the personal name *Bertino*, a diminutive of BERTO.
GIVEN NAMES Italian 14%. *Cosmo* (4), *Santo* (3), *Salvatore* (2), *Alfio, Carmela, Crispino, Ignazio, Natale, Philomena, Remo, Rocco, Sal.*

Bertke (363) North German: probably from a pet form of BERTA.

Bertling (252) North German: **1.** patronymic from BERTHOLD. **2.** habitational name from Bertlingen in Westphalia.

Bertman (126) Respelling of eastern German **Bertmann**, a variant (altered by folk etymology) of BERTRAM.
GIVEN NAMES German 5%. *Frieda, Wilhelm.*

Berto (137) **1.** Italian: from the personal name *Berto*, a short form of any of various Germanic names formed with *bert* (from *berht* 'bright', 'famous'), for example *Alberto, Gilberto, Norberto, Roberto, Umberto.* **2.** Hungarian (**Bertó**): from a pet form of the personal name *Bertalan*, Hungarian form of BARTHOLOMEW.
GIVEN NAMES Spanish 6%; Italian 5%. *Jose* (2), *Mario* (2), *Jose Cruz, Manuel, Virgilio; Dario, Mauro, Vito.*

Bertocchi (101) Italian: from a pet form of the personal name BERTO.

Bertola (123) Italian: variant of BERTOLI.
GIVEN NAMES Italian 7%. *Deno* (2), *Guido* (2), *Primo* (2).

Bertolami (109) Italian: from a derivative of BERTOLI.
GIVEN NAMES Italian 22%. *Salvatore* (5), *Ugo* (3), *Lorenzo.*

Bertoldi (157) Italian: from the Germanic personal name *Bertoldo*, Italian form of BERTHOLD.
GIVEN NAMES Italian 16%. *Guido* (2), *Ciro, Livio, Maurizio, Pasquale, Remo.*

Bertolet (133) French: from a pet form of the personal name *Barthélemy* (see BARTHOLOMEW) or any of the Germanic personal names mentioned at BERT. Compare BERTHELOT.
FOREBEARS There are Huguenots of this name, who came from the Swiss canton of Vaud and settled in PA.
GIVEN NAME French 4%. *Camille.*

Bertoli (184) **1.** Italian: from the personal name *Bertolo*, a variant of BARTOLO. **2.** Catalan (**Bertolí**): from the personal name *Bertolí*, from the Germanic personal name *Berthilin*.
GIVEN NAMES Italian 7%. *Luigi* (2), *Aldo, Antonio, Gildo, Giorgio, Tullio.*

Bertolini (407) Italian: patronymic or plural form of BERTOLINO.
GIVEN NAMES Italian 15%. *Angelo* (4), *Alessandro* (2), *Attilio* (2), *Giovanni* (2), *Silvio* (2), *Aldo, Carmela, Cesare, Dino, Elio, Fausto, Gino.*

Bertolino (534) Italian: from a diminutive of the personal name *Bertolo* (see BERTOLI).
GIVEN NAMES Italian 17%. *Angelo* (7), *Salvatore* (4), *Antonio* (3), *Vita* (3), *Carlo* (2), *Giovanna* (2), *Vito* (2), *Aldo, Attilio, Augustino, Baldassare, Calogero.*

Bertolotti (149) Italian: from a diminutive of the personal name *Bertolo* (see BERTOLI).
GIVEN NAMES Italian 22%; Spanish 10%. *Aldo* (3), *Paolo* (2), *Angelo, Caterina, Dino, Enzo, Ferdinando, Fulvio, Giacomo,*

Guido, Leno, Luigi; Miguel (2), *Angel, Ines, Joaquin, Moreno, Otilia, Palmira, Romana.*

Bertolucci (128) Italian: from a diminutive of BERTOLI.
GIVEN NAMES Italian 8%. *Pietro* (2), *Angelo, Antonio, Geno.*

Berton (354) **1.** French: from a pet form of BERT. **2.** Perhaps also a variant spelling of English BURTON.

Bertone (442) Italian: from an augmentative form of BERTO.
GIVEN NAMES Italian 15%. *Antonio* (3), *Carmine* (3), *Angelo* (2), *Nicola* (2), *Aldo, Attilio, Concetta, Dino, Domenic, Giovanni, Ottavio, Rosaria.*

Bertoni (314) Italian: patronymic or plural form of BERTONE.
GIVEN NAMES Italian 11%. *Aldo* (2), *Alessandro* (2), *Gino* (2), *Angelo, Domenic, Domenico, Fiore, Giancarlo, Guido, Italo, Riccardo.*

Bertorelli (104) Italian: from a pet form of the personal name BERTO.
GIVEN NAMES Italian 24%. *Alfredo* (2), *Giuseppe* (2), *Antonio, Giacomo, Gildo, Giovanni, Guiseppe, Mario, Migdalia.*

Bertozzi (114) Italian: variant of **Bertozzo**, a pet form of the personal name BERTO.
GIVEN NAMES Italian 17%. *Carlo* (2), *Amadeo, Angelo, Enrico, Gino, Guido, Luca, Marco, Stefano.*

Bertram (3186) German, English, Scottish, French, and Danish: from the Germanic personal name *Bertram*, composed of the elements *berht* 'bright', 'famous' + *hrabn* 'raven'. The raven was the bird of Odin, king of the gods, in Germanic mythology. The personal name was common in France throughout the Middle Ages, where its popularity was increased by the fame of the troubadour Bertrand de Born (?1140–?1214). The spelling *Bertrand* is French, coined by folk etymology under the influence of the present participle ending *-and*, *-ant*. The name was taken to England by the Normans in the forms *Bertran(d)*, *Bertram*, and *Bartram.*

Bertran (141) French, Southern French (Occitan), and Catalan: variant of BERTRAM or BERTRAND.
GIVEN NAMES Spanish 32%; French 4%. *Jose* (5), *Jorge* (4), *Eduardo* (2), *Enrique* (2), *Joaquin* (2), *Ricardo* (2), *Aleida, Ana, Ana Maria, Elena, Felipe, Jeronimo; Andre* (2).

Bertrand (4335) English and French: variant of BERTRAM.
FOREBEARS A Bertrand from La Rochelle, France, is documented in Cap Rouge, Quebec, in 1666; another, from the Saintonge region, is documented in Charlesbourg in 1685. A bearer of the name from Normandy was recorded with the secondary surname Saint Arnaud in Batiscan in 1697. Another is documented from the Poitou region in 1697, and one from Guyenne is recorded in

Laprairie, Quebec, in 1699 with the secondary surnames Raymond and Toulouse.

The LA Bertrand families trace ancestry to a number of forebears of the very early 18th century from France, Canada, Acadia, and Switzerland.

GIVEN NAMES French 7%. *Marcel* (6), *Andre* (4), *Armand* (4), *Monique* (4), *Francois* (3), *Gilles* (3), *Raoul* (3), *Emile* (2), *Herve* (2), *Jacques* (2), *Jean-Marie* (2), *Odette* (2).

Bertsch (1641) German (Alemannic and Swabian): from an Alemannic pet form of the personal name BERTHOLD.

GIVEN NAMES German 4%. *Otto* (4), *Ewald* (2), *Reinhard* (2), *Darrold*, *Hans*, *Helmuth*, *Lorenz*, *Mathias*, *Ulrich*, *Wolfgang*.

Bertsche (187) German: variant of BERTSCH.

GIVEN NAMES German 9%. *Otto* (3), *Georg*, *Gerhard*.

Bertschy (137) Swiss German: variant of BERTSCHE.

Bertucci (665) Italian: from a diminutive of BERTO.

GIVEN NAMES Italian 14%; French 4%. *Vito* (4), *Giorgio* (3), *Rocco* (3), *Antonio* (2), *Enrico* (2), *Giacomo* (2), *Salvatore* (2), *Angelo*, *Carlo*, *Gino*, *Guido*, *Marco*; *Emile* (4).

Bertuzzi (105) Italian: variant of BERTUCCI.

GIVEN NAMES Italian 17%. *Gino* (2), *Gaetano*, *Lorenzo*, *Renzo*, *Romeo*, *Santo*.

Bertz (215) German: from a variant of the Germanic personal name *Bero* (see BAER).

Berube (2381) French (**Bérubé**): habitational name from some minor place named with Old French *bel ru* 'beautiful stream', with the subsequent pleonastic addition of *bé*, variant of *bel* 'beautiful'.

FOREBEARS A person called Bérubé from Normandy, France, is recorded in L'Islet, Quebec, in 1679.

GIVEN NAMES French 13%. *Normand* (15), *Armand* (8), *Emile* (8), *Andre* (7), *Lucien* (4), *Pierre* (4), *Adelard* (2), *Amedee* (2), *Berthe* (2), *Fleurette* (2), *Gaetan* (2), *Marcel* (2).

Berumen (510) Hispanic (Mexico): unexplained.

GIVEN NAMES Spanish 46%. *Jose* (19), *Miguel* (10), *Jesus* (9), *Armando* (7), *Manuel* (7), *Juan* (6), *Raul* (5), *Salvador* (5), *Luis* (4), *Eduardo* (3), *Fernando* (3), *Jorge* (3).

Berven (141) Norwegian: habitational name from a farmstead named Berven, from *berg* 'mountain', 'hill' (Old Norse *bjarg*) + *vin* 'meadow'.

GIVEN NAMES Scandinavian 5%. *Ordell*, *Ove*.

Berwald (184) **1.** German, Danish, and Swedish: from the Germanic personal name *Ber(n)wald*, composed of the elements *ber(n)* 'bear' + *wald* 'ruler' but altered by folk etymology as if from German *Bär* 'bear' + *Wald* 'forest'. **2.** German: in some cases, a habitational name from a place called Bärwalde or Beerwalde, of which there are several examples in eastern Germany.

GIVEN NAMES German 7%. *Erhardt*, *Erwin*, *Klaus*, *Winfried*.

Berwanger (163) South German and Austrian: habitational name for someone from a farm or hamlet named Berwangen, originally a field name from Middle High German *bēr* 'bear' + *wange* 'grassy mountain slope'.

Berwick (528) **1.** Scottish: habitational name from Berwick-on-Tweed, on the Northumbrian coast at the mouth of the Tweed river, a border town that regularly changed hands between the Scots and the English. **2.** English: variant of BARWICK.

Berzins (267) Latvian (**Bērziņš**): topographic name for someone living among birch trees, or a diminutive form, from *bērzs* 'birch'.

GIVEN NAMES Latvian 24%; Lithuanian 20%; German 4%. *Arvids* (2), *Elmars* (2), *Gunars* (2), *Ivars* (2), *Ojars* (2), *Aivars*, *Alberts*, *Alfreds*, *Arturs*, *Edvins*, *Rudolfs*; *Juris* (4), *Laimonis* (4), *Inta* (3), *Valdis* (3), *Andris* (2), *Ilze* (2), *Karlis* (2), *Maris* (2), *Talivaldis* (2), *Vilnis* (2), *Aldis*, *Ansis*; *Erna*, *Herta*, *Wilhelmina*.

Besancon (187) French (**Besançon**): habitational name from Besançon in Doubs, which is probably named with a Celtiberian element *ves* 'mountain' + the suffix *-unt*, with a further Latin suffix *-io* (genitive *-ionis*). In folk etymology there has been some association with Old French *bison*, the (European) bison, which appears in the arms of the city.

FOREBEARS A Prélas or Prélat with the secondary surname Besançon was documented in Quebec city in 1759.

GIVEN NAMES French 8%. *Jacques*, *Jean Pierre*, *Renaud*.

Besaw (678) Americanized spelling of French **Bessan(d)**, a habitational name from Bessan in Hérault, recorded in 940 as *Betianum* and in 1150 as *Bessanum*, from the personal name *Bettius* or *Bessius* + the suffix *-anum*.

Besch (526) South German: from a short form of the personal name SEBASTIAN.

Beschta (104) Origin unidentified.

Besco (121) Altered spelling of Breton **Bescou**, from a derivative or plural of **Besq**, a nickname denoting someone who was disfigured or mutilated in some way, or who had lost a limb.

Besecker (308) North German: from the personal name *Bäsecke*, a vernacular form of the saint's name *Basilius* (see BASIL). In some cases it may also be a derivative of BERNHARD.

Beseda (125) Czech and Slovak: nickname for a talkative person, from *beseda* 'talk', 'chat'.

Besel (122) German: variant of BESSEL.

GIVEN NAME German 4%. *Reinhart*.

Besemer (181) German: occupational name for a broom maker, Middle High German *besemer*, from an agent derivative of *besem* 'broom'.

Beshara (210) Muslim: variant of BISHARA.

GIVEN NAMES Muslim 8%; French 4%. *Hany* (3), *Amal* (2), *Ahmed*, *Amin*, *Farid*, *Mazen*, *Nabeeh*, *Raafat*, *Rafaat*, *Zahia*; *Amie*, *Michel*.

Beshear (139) See BESHEARS.

Beshears (668) Americanized variant of French BOUCHARD or BRASSEUR.

Beshore (155) **1.** Americanized form of Dutch or North German **Boesshaar** (see BASHORE). **2.** Americanized form of French BOUCHARD and BRASSEUR. Compare BESHEARS.

Beske (206) **1.** Eastern German: probably from the personal name *Peske* or *Peschke*, vernacular forms of *Petrus* (see PETER). **2.** Danish: from the old word *bieske* 'bitter', 'acrid', a nickname common since the 17th century.

Besler (209) German: **1.** from Middle Low German *beseler*, a kind of long dagger, hence a metonymic occupational name for a maker of such weapons. **2.** German: variant of BASLER.

Besley (112) English: southern variant of BEASLEY.

Besner (112) Possibly a respelling of French **Besnard**, a variant of BERNARD.

GIVEN NAMES French 8%; Jewish 4%. *Andre*, *Henri*, *Rejean*; *Emanuel* (2), *Mort*.

Beson (128) English: probably a variant spelling of BEESON.

Bess (2842) **1.** English: unexplained. Apparently a metronymic from the female personal name *Bess*, pet form of *Elizabeth*. **2.** German: short form of BETZ. **3.** In some cases it is probably an altered spelling of French BESSE.

Besse (635) Southern French: topographic name for someone who lived by a birch tree or in a birch wood, from Late Latin *bettia* 'birch wood', a word of Gaulish origin.

Bessel (115) German: of uncertain derivation; possibly from the name of a place or river.

GIVEN NAMES German 8%. *Kurt* (2), *Otto*.

Besselman (124) German: elaborated form of BESSEL.

GIVEN NAME German 5%. *Kurt*.

Bessent (249) English: from Middle English *besant*, the name of a gold coin (via Old French from Latin *(nummus) byzantius*, so called because it was first minted at Byzantium). The surname arose as a metonymic occupational name for a minter or moneyer or else as a nickname for a man who was considered to be rich or miserly.

Besser (723) German: **1.** occupational name for a collector of fines, from Middle High German *bezzerære*, an agent derivative of *bezzern* 'to collect fines'. **2.** habitational name from any of various places in Germany named Besser, Bessing, or Bessingen.

Bessert (149) South German variant of BESSER.

Bessett (132) French: variant of BESSETTE. GIVEN NAME French 4%. *Andre*.

Bessette (1703) French: variant of **Besset**, from a diminutive of *bès* 'birch', or possibly of French **Basset** (see BASSETTE). The ending is not feminine, but reflects the Canadian custom of pronouncing a final *-t*, which is generally silent in metropolitan French.
FOREBEARS A Besset with the secondary surname Brisetout arrived in Chambly, Quebec, in 1665.
GIVEN NAMES French 11%. *Andre* (7), *Marcel* (6), *Armand* (5), *Adrien* (4), *Normand* (4), *Alphonse* (3), *Lucien* (3), *Cecile* (2), *Herve* (2), *Jacques* (2), *Laurent* (2), *Aime*.

Bessey (639) French: habitational name from places in Côte-d'Or and Loire named Bessey, from the Romano-Gallic estate *Bassiacum*, from the Roman personal name *Bassius* + the locative suffix *-acum*.

Bessinger (306) German: **1.** habitational name for someone from any of several places called Bessingen. **2.** variant of **Bäsiger** (see BASSINGER).

Bessire (187) Origin unidentified. This is predominantly a Texan name.

Bessler (440) German: **1.** variant of BESSLER. **2.** occupational name for someone who does odd jobs or a tinkerer, hobby worker (modern German *Bastler*), of uncertain origin.

Besso (133) Catalan (**Bessó**): nickname for a twin, *bessó*, a derivative of Latin *bis* 'twice'.

Besson (349) Southern French: nickname for a twin, from Occitan *besson* 'twin', a derivative of Latin *bis* 'twice'.
FOREBEARS A Besson from La Rochelle is documented in Quebec city in 1720.
GIVEN NAMES French 6%. *Celine, Dominique, Frederique, Joffre, Marcel, Stephane*.

Best (13095) **1.** English, northern Irish, and French: from Middle English, Old French *beste* 'animal', 'beast' (Latin *bestia*), applied either as a metonymic occupational name for someone who looked after beasts—a herdsman—or as a derogatory nickname for someone thought to resemble an animal, i.e. a violent, uncouth, or stupid man. It is unlikely that the name is derived from *best*, Old English *betst*, superlative of *good*. By far the most frequent spelling of the French surname is *Beste*, but it is likely that in North America this form has largely been assimilated to *Best*. **2.** German: from a short form of SEBASTIAN.

Beste (377) **1.** English and French: variant spelling of BEST. **2.** German: topographic name for someone who lived by the Beste river, a tributary of the Trave, or a habitational name from any of various villages called Besten, said by Bahlow to be named with a Middle Low German word for poor soil.

GIVEN NAMES German 4%. *Alois, Aloys, Juergen, Kurt*.

Bester (359) **1.** English: occupational name for someone who looked after animals, Middle English *bester*, from *beste* 'beast' (see BEST). **2.** German: habitational name for someone from a place called BESTE. **3.** Slovenian (Gorenjska; also **Bešter**): probably a derivative of VESTER 3, a reduced form of the personal name *Silvester*. Replacement of initial *V-* with *B-* is quite common in Slovenian surnames.

Bestgen (101) German: from a reduced form of the personal name SEBASTIAN + the suffix *-gen*, the Rhineland and Central German diminutive and suffix of endearment, parallel to Low German *-jen*, *-ken* and standard German *-chen*.
GIVEN NAME French 5%. *Roch*.

Bestor (147) Variant spelling of English BESTER, possibly also of the German name.

Bestul (178) Origin unidentified.
GIVEN NAMES German 4%. *Gerhard, Kurt*.

Bestwick (153) English: variant of BESWICK.

Beswick (488) English: habitational name from places in Lancashire and East Yorkshire named Beswick. The second element is clearly Old English *wīc* 'outlying (dairy) farm' (see WICK). The first element of the Lancashire name may be an Old English personal name *Bēac*; that of the Yorkshire name is possibly an Old Norse personal name *Bōsi* or *Besi*.

Betances (143) Spanish and Hispanic (Dominican Republic and Mexico): unexplained; probably related to Betanzos, the name of a town near A Coruña in Galicia.
GIVEN NAMES Spanish 55%. *Luis* (9), *Carlos* (4), *Jose* (4), *Miguel* (3), *Alberto* (2), *Ana* (2), *Juanita* (2), *Luz* (2), *Pura* (2), *Rodolfo* (2), *Alba, Alicia*.

Betancourt (2335) Spanish (Canary Islands) and Portuguese: from **Béthencourt** (see BETTENCOURT), the name (with many variants) of the first conqueror of the Canary Islands (1417), a knight of Norman-French origin. This name is also common and widespread in Latin America.
GIVEN NAMES Spanish 48%. *Jose* (61), *Luis* (35), *Carlos* (28), *Jorge* (23), *Manuel* (23), *Raul* (21), *Juan* (20), *Miguel* (18), *Ruben* (16), *Jesus* (15), *Ana* (14), *Angel* (14).

Betancur (136) Spanish (also Mexico): variant spelling of BETANCOURT.
GIVEN NAMES Spanish 54%. *Jose* (5), *Alvaro* (2), *Jaime* (2), *Jorge* (2), *Juan* (2), *Luis* (2), *Roberto* (2), *Rodrigo* (2), *Abelardo, Alberto, Alfonso, Amparo*.

Betcher (393) Americanized spelling of German BOETTCHER.

Betesh (139) Jewish: unexplained.
GIVEN NAMES Jewish 11%. *Sol* (3), *Avi, Shabtay, Shaul, Sima*.

Beth (427) **1.** Scottish: reduced form of MCBETH. **2.** North German: from a short form of the Germanic personal name

BERTHOLD or from a short form, *Bete*, of the female personal name *Elisabeth* (see ELIZABETH). **3.** Jewish: ornamental name from Hebrew *bet* 'house'.
GIVEN NAMES German 5%; Jewish 4%. *Ewald, Manfred, Otto, Uwe; Shalom* (4), *Rochel*.

Bethany (273) English: possibly a topographic name from an Old English plant name, *betonice* 'betony'. The form of the name has been altered by folk association with the New Testament place name.

Bethard (189) Probably English: unexplained.
FOREBEARS Ancestry of bearers of this name has been traced to William Bedder (*c*.1656–1718) of Somerset Co., MD. He was probably of English descent.

Bethards (187) Variant of BETHARD.

Bethea (2454) Origin unidentified. Possibly an Anglicized variant of Welsh BETHEL.
FOREBEARS The name was brought to VA by John Bethea (known as 'English John') (1684– after 1750), who settled in Nansemond, VA.

Bethel (2426) Welsh: Anglicized form of Welsh *ab Ithel* 'son of *Ithael*', a personal name meaning 'bountiful lord'. Compare IDLE.

Bethell (243) Welsh: variant of BETHEL.

Bethke (1059) North German: from a pet form of the Germanic personal names BERTRAM or BERTHOLD. See also BETH.
GIVEN NAMES German 4%. *Kurt* (3), *Eldor, Ewald, Otto, Rudi, Wilhelmina*.

Bethmann (102) North German: **1.** from a pet form of the personal name BERTRAM. **2.** occupational name for a tax collector of the *bede penninc*, a tax requested (*erbeten*) from freemen in the Middle Ages.
GIVEN NAMES German 8%. *Hans* (2), *Helmut*.

Bethune (1056) French (**Béthune**) and Scottish (of Norman origin): habitational name from Béthune in Pas-de-Calais, Picardy, France, recorded in the 8th century in the Latin form *Bitunia*, probably an adjective (with *villa* understood) derived from the oblique form of a Germanic personal name *Betto*, a hypocoristic formation. Compare BETTENCOURT, BEATON.

Betit (120) French: variant of PETIT.
GIVEN NAMES French 13%. *Andre* (2), *Cecile* (2), *Normand*.

Betka (105) Polish form of German BETHKE.
GIVEN NAMES Polish 12%. *Miroslaw, Ryszard, Wojciech, Zofia*.

Betke (156) Dutch and North German: **1.** variant spelling of BETHKE. **2.** variant spelling of **Böttge**, from a pet form of the personal name *Bodo* (see BODE).
GIVEN NAMES Dutch 5%. *Egbert* (2), *Hendrik*.

Betker (227) Dutch and North German: occupational name for a cooper. Compare German BOETTCHER.

GIVEN NAMES German 4%. *Reinhardt* (2), *Kurt*.

Betlach (119) Czech and German: metonymic occupational name for a weaver or seller of bedsheets, from Middle High German *bett(e)* 'bed' + Middle Dutch, Middle Low German *laken* 'piece of woven material', which transferred into Middle High German as *lahhen*, *lachen* (modern German *Laken*).

Betler (119) German: **1.** descriptive name for a beggar, Middle High German *bëtelære*, or a very poor person. **2.** habitational name; in northwestern Germany for someone from Bethel in Westphalia; in Austria from Bettlern in Bohemia (earlier *Bettler*; the Czech name of the place is *Žebrák*, from *žebrák* 'beggar'), which was probably originally a settlement for homeless or dispossessed people.

Betley (224) English: habitational name from either of two places, in Staffordshire and Sussex, named Betley, from an Old English female personal name *Bette* + *lēah* 'woodland clearing'.

GIVEN NAMES German 4%. *Erwin* (2), *Elke*, *Jutta*.

Betsch (214) South German (Alemannic): from a short form of the Germanic personal names BERNHARD or BERTHOLD.

Betschart (157) German: from an altered form of the personal name BERNHARD. A similar alteration is **Betschold** from *Berthold*.

GIVEN NAMES German 8%. *Alois*, *Franz*, *Fritz*, *Johann*, *Reinhard*.

Betsill (207) Americanized spelling of South German **Betzel**, from a pet form of the personal name BETZ.

Betsinger (114) Respelling of German **Betzinger**, a habitational name for someone from Betzingen in Baden-Württemberg.

Betson (116) English: patronymic or metronymic from the medieval personal name *Bett*, a short form of *Bartholomew*, *Beatrice*, or *Elizabeth*.

GIVEN NAME French 5%. *Constant*.

Bett (109) English and Scottish (Fife and Angus): variant of BETTS.

Bettcher (196) Americanized spelling of German BOETTCHER.

GIVEN NAMES German 7%. *Kurt* (2), *Ewald*, *Juergen*.

Betten (197) **1.** Probably German, from a variant of *Bete* (see BETH). **2.** Possibly a shortened form of any of various German habitational names such as BETTENDORF or BETTENHAUSEN.

GIVEN NAMES German 5%. *Claus*, *Dieter*, *Manfred*.

Bettencourt (2280) French: habitational name from any of various places so called, with minor variations in spelling, of which the main one is in Somme. They are named with a Germanic personal name *Betto* (an assimilated form of *Berto* (see BERT) + Old

French *court* 'farm(yard)'). The name is now very frequent in Portugal, where it first occurred in the 15th century (see BETANCOURT).

GIVEN NAMES Spanish 9%; Portuguese 6%. *Manuel* (57), *Jose* (10), *Jorge* (4), *Luis* (4), *Ana* (3), *Carlos* (3), *Joaquin* (3), *Aires* (2), *Arlindo* (2), *Armando* (2), *Francisco* (2), *Mario* (2); *Joao* (6), *Adao*, *Albano*, *Conceicao*, *Duarte*, *Ilidio*, *Paulo*, *Serafim*.

Bettendorf (258) German: habitational name from any of several places called Bettendorf, for example on the Rhine, near Luxembourg, and in Alsace.

Bettenhausen (236) German: habitational name from any of several places named Bettenhausen, for example in Hessen and Württemberg.

Better (199) **1.** Translation of French LEMIEUX. **2.** English: nickname from Old English *bētere* 'fighter', 'beater'. Reaney suggests it may also be a short form of the various occupational names ending with *-better*, for example LEADBETTER. **3.** German (Bavarian): metonymic occupational name for a maker of rosaries, from Bavarian *better* 'rosary' (from *beten* 'to pray').

Betteridge (157) English: from the Old English personal name *Beaduric*, composed of the elements *beadu* 'battle' + *rīc* 'power'.

Betterley (102) English: probably a variant of **Betteley**, from a place called Betley, of which there is one in Staffordshire and another in Sussex, the former being named from an Old English female personal name *Bette* + *lēah* 'woodland clearing'.

Betterly (101) Variant of English BETTERLEY.

Betterman (104) Translation of French LEMIEUX.

Betters (378) Translation of French LEMIEUX.

GIVEN NAMES French 4%. *Monique* (2), *Napoleon*.

Betterton (379) English: habitational name from a place in Berkshire named Betterton, probably from an Old English personal name *Bēthere* + *-ing-* (implying association) + *tūn* 'settlement'.

Bettes (256) English: variant spelling of BETTS.

Bettger (132) German: variant of BOETTCHER.

Betthauser (109) German: probably an altered form or variant of **Bettenhauser**, a habitational name from any of several places in north and central Germany called Bettenhausen.

Betti (224) Italian: **1.** from the personal name *Betto*, a reduced form of *Benedetto*, or a short form of any of various personal names with this ending (*Iacobetto*, for example). **2.** from a diminutive of BERTO.

GIVEN NAMES Italian 13%. *Eliseo* (2), *Enrico* (2), *Gino* (2), *Guido* (2), *Riccardo*, *Rino*, *Salvatore*, *Silvio*, *Tiziano*.

Bettin (313) **1.** German: habitational name of Slavic origin of a deserted settlement in northeastern Germany. **2.** Italian (Venice): variant of BETTINI.

GIVEN NAMES German 4%. *Kurt*, *Lutz*, *Otto*, *Wolfgang*.

Bettinger (757) **1.** French: habitational name for someone from Betting in Moselle department. **2.** German: habitational name for someone from any of several places called Bettingen, for example near Cologne, Trier, and in Baden.

Bettini (173) Italian and Corsican: from *Bettino*, a diminutive of the personal name *Betto* (see BETTI).

GIVEN NAMES Italian 13%; French 4%. *Carmine* (2), *Luca* (2), *Carlo*, *Dino*, *Gino*, *Renzo*, *Santino*; *Eugenie*, *Gisele*.

Bettis (1997) English: variant of BETTS, or possibly a topographic name meaning '(dweller) by the hollows', from Old English *bytt* 'butt', 'cask', used in a transferred sense.

Bettner (125) German: possibly an altered, unrounded form of **Böttner**, a variant of **Büttner** 'cooper', hence an occupational name.

Betton (179) English and Scottish: variant of BEATON or BEETON.

Bettridge (101) English: reduced form of BETTERIDGE.

Betts (6748) **1.** English: patronymic or metronymic from the medieval personal name *Bett*, a short form of *Bartholomew*, *Beatrice*, or *Elizabeth*. **2.** Americanized spelling of German BETZ.

Betty (410) English: from a pet form of the personal name *Bett* (see BETTS).

GIVEN NAMES French 4%. *Francois*, *Jean-Paul*.

Betz (3980) South German: from a pet form of the personal names BERTHOLD or BERNHARD. Compare BETSCH.

Betzen (117) Origin unidentified. Possibly an altered spelling of **Betzin**, a habitational name of a place so named in Brandenburg, Germany.

GIVEN NAMES French 4%; German 4%. *Marcellin*; *Aloys*, *Gerhard*.

Betzer (218) German: variant of BETZ.

Betzler (188) German: **1.** from Middle High German *betzeler* 'young knight' (from Old French *bachelier*, Italian *baccalare*, which gave rise to *baccalaureus*). **2.** possibly a variant of the old German surname **Becceler**, itself a variant of **Böckeler** (see BOECKEL).

GIVEN NAMES German 5%. *Heinz*, *Monika*.

Betzner (134) German: from a topographic name, frequent in Rhineland, meaning 'meadow', or a Germanized form of Czech *pecnář* 'baker'.

Betzold (224) German: **1.** in southern areas, a variant of **Betschold**, itself a variant of BERTHOLD. **2.** in eastern areas, a variant of PETZOLD, from a vernacular form of the New Testament name *Petrus* (see PETER).

Beu (160) North German: **1.** variant of BOYE. **2.** topographic name for someone who lived in a place surrounded by water, Low German *böu*, Middle Low German *buge*, *bü*, *boy*.
GIVEN NAMES German 6%. *Kurt, Otto, Wolfgang.*

Beucler (148) **1.** Perhaps an altered spelling of Dutch **Beukelaer**, a metonymic occupational name from Middle Dutch *bokelare* 'buckler' (a type of small shield with a boss or knob in the center). **2.** Alternatively, perhaps, an Americanized form of French **Bouclier**, an occupational name for a maker of buckles.

Beuerlein (122) South German: variant spelling of BAUERLEIN.

Beukelman (128) North German and Dutch: occupational name for a maker or user of a buckle shield, from Dutch and German dialect *beukel* 'shield'.

Beukema (217) Frisian: topographic name for someone who lived by a beech tree or beech wood, from *beuk* 'beech' + *ma* 'man'.

Beumer (238) Altered spelling of German **Bäumer** (see BAUMER).

Beuning (103) Americanized spelling of German **Böhning** (see BOHNING).

Beury (103) Possibly an Americanized form of German **Böhre**, a variant of BOHR.

Beus (188) Dutch and German: patronymic from the Old Frisian personal name *Boy(e)* (see BEY).

Beutel (444) German: metonymic occupational name for a maker of bags, from Middle High German *biutel* 'bag', 'purse'. Compare BEITEL.
GIVEN NAMES German 6%. *Gerhard* (2), *Kurt* (2), *Erwin, Hans, Heinz, Helmut, Helmuth.*

Beutler (764) German: occupational name for a bag maker, from an agent derivative of Middle High German *biutel* 'bag', 'purse' (see BEUTEL).
GIVEN NAMES German 4%. *Hans* (2), *Otto* (2), *Ernst, Gerhard, Guenter, Helmut, Kaethe, Manfred.*

Bevacqua (399) Italian: variant of BEVILACQUA.
GIVEN NAMES Italian 11%. *Nicola* (3), *Pietro* (2), *Amato, Angelo, Antonio, Carmela, Egidio, Saverio.*

Bevan (1605) Welsh: Anglicized form of Welsh *ap Iefan* 'son of *Iefan*', Welsh equivalent of JOHN.

Bevans (674) English, of Welsh origin: variant of BEVAN, with the addition of the regular English patronymic suffix *-s*.

Bevard (314) French: from *buvard* 'drinker' (from *boire* 'to drink').

Bevel (371) English: variant of BEVILL.

Bevels (104) Origin unidentified; perhaps a variant of English BEVILL.

Bevens (206) English: variant of BIVENS.

Bever (1020) **1.** Dutch and North German: nickname from *bever* 'beaver', possibly referring to a hard worker, or from some other fancied resemblance to the animal. **2.** English: variant spelling of BEAVER.

Beverage (459) Scottish: variant of BEVERIDGE.

Beveridge (1258) Scottish: probably from Middle English *beverage* 'drink' (Old French *bevrage*, from *beivre* 'to drink'). The term was used in particular of a drink bought by a purchaser to seal a bargain, and the surname may have been acquired as a nickname in this context. Reaney adduces evidence that suggests that the nickname may have been bestowed on a man who made a practice of getting free drinks by entering into bargains which he did not keep.

Beverley (377) English: habitational name from the city in East Yorkshire, the name of which contains Old English *beofor* 'beaver', combined with a second element, *licc*, that may mean 'stream'.

Beverlin (181) Origin unidentified.

Beverly (3248) English: variant spelling of BEVERLEY.

Bevers (558) German: patronymic from BEVER.

Beversdorf (101) German: habitational name from a place so called in Pomerania.

Bevier (332) French: from Old French *bevier*, a measure of land; hence probably a nickname for someone who owned or worked such a piece of land.

Bevil (253) English: variant of BEVILL.

Bevilacqua (953) Italian: nickname from the expression *bevi l'acqua* 'drinks water', probably applied ironically to a heavy drinker of alcohol. The surname is also found in France.
GIVEN NAMES Italian 20%. *Mario* (13), *Angelo* (5), *Carmine* (5), *Rocco* (4), *Enrico* (3), *Dario* (2), *Domenic* (2), *Emilio* (2), *Giulio* (2), *Giuseppe* (2), *Guido* (2), *Amerigo, Caesar, Claudio, Eugenio, Fernando, Liborio, Marisa, Modesto.*

Bevill (641) English (of Norman origin) and French: habitational name from Beuville (Calvados) or Bouville (Seine-Inférieure) in France.

Beville (497) French and English: variant of BEVILL.

Bevington (538) English (southwest Midlands): habitational name from either of two places, in Warwickshire and Gloucestershire, named Bevington, from the Old English personal name *Bēofa* + Old English *-ing-* implying association + *tūn* 'settlement'.

Bevins (1421) English: variant of BEVANS.

Bevis (1076) English (of Norman origin): **1.** habitational name from Beauvais in

Oise, France. **2.** from a term of endearment, from Old French *beu*, *bel* 'handsome' (also used in the sense 'dear') + Anglo-Norman French *fiz* 'son'.

Bewick (167) Northern English: habitational name from places in Northumberland and East Yorkshire named Bewick, from Old English *bēo* 'bee' + *wīc* 'outlying farm', hence an outlying station for the production of honey.

Bewley (1134) English: habitational name from Bewley Castle in the former county of Westmorland (now part of Cumbria), from Bewley in Durham, or from Beaulieu in Hampshire (see BEAULIEU), all named with *beu* 'lovely' + *lieu* 'place'.

Bex (146) Southern French: variant of BESSE.
GIVEN NAMES French 5%. *Chantal, Yves.*

Bexley (142) English: habitational name from Bexley (now Bexleyheath in Greater London), which was named from Old English *byxe* 'box tree' + *lēah* 'woodland clearing'.

Bey (1096) **1.** North German and Frisian: from the Old Frisian personal name *Beyo* or *Boy(e)* (see BOYE). **2.** French: habitational name from any of the places so named, in Ain, Meurthe-et-Moselle, or Saône-et-Loire. **3.** French (Burgundy): topographic name for someone who lived by a mill stream. **4.** Muslim: from *beg* 'bey', a Turkish title of respect. Compare BAIG.
GIVEN NAMES Muslim 5%. *Mohammed* (5), *Abdullah* (2), *Dawoud* (2), *Fatima* (2), *Jamaal* (2), *Rasheedah* (2), *Shakoor* (2), *Zaib* (2), *Aisha, Akil, Ameen, Aminah.*

Beyda (170) Jewish: unexplained.
GIVEN NAME Jewish 8%. *Shmuel.*

Beydler (105) German: variant of BEIDLER.

Beydoun (110) Muslim: ethnic name for a Bedouin, a member of a nomadic Arab people, from a variant of standard Arabic **Badawī**.
GIVEN NAMES Muslim 79%. *Ali* (6), *Jamal* (4), *Samir* (4), *Ahmed* (3), *Amin* (3), *Hassan* (3), *Ahmad* (2), *Houssam* (2), *Ikram* (2), *Nassar* (2), *Sanaa* (2), *Youssef* (2).

Beye (127) Dutch and North German: variant of BEY.

Beyea (145) Origin unidentified. Probably of French origin, but unexplained.

Beyene (130) Ethiopian: unexplained.
GIVEN NAMES Ethiopian 68%. *Mulugeta* (4), *Abeba* (2), *Debebe* (2), *Tekle* (2), *Abebe, Abebech, Abera, Abraha, Alem, Berhane, Dawit, Desta, Tarek.*

Beyer (7660) German, Dutch, Scandinavian, and Jewish (Ashkenazic): variant of BAYER.
GIVEN NAMES German 4%. *Kurt* (13), *Hans* (12), *Otto* (7), *Erwin* (4), *Ewald* (3), *Klaus* (3), *Alois* (2), *Arno* (2), *Gerhard* (2), *Gunter* (2), *Heinz* (2), *Theodor* (2).

Beyerle (152) German: from a Swabian diminutive of BAUER.

Beyerlein (151) German: from a diminutive of BAUER.

GIVEN NAME German 9%. *Fritz* (4).

Beyers (708) German: variant of BEYER.

Beyersdorf (200) German: habitational name from any of several places in Saxony, Thuringia, Bavaria, Brandenburg, and Pomerania.

Beyke (101) German (Westphalia): unexplained.

Beyl (188) Variant of German BEIL.

Beyler (135) German: variant spelling of BEILER.

Beymer (258) Variant of German **Bäumer** (see BAUMER).

Beynon (346) Welsh: variant of BENNION.

Bezak (106) Croatian (northern and eastern Croatia): topographic name from a derivative of *beza*, northern dialect form of *bazga* 'elder'.

GIVEN NAMES German 5%; Slavic 5%. *Helmut*; *Bogdan, Cecylia*.

Bezanson (290) Americanized spelling of French **Besançon** (see BESANCON).

Bezdek (207) Czech (**Bezděk**): probably from the adverb *bezděky* 'involuntarily', 'unintentionally', possibly in the sense 'carefree', 'untroubled'. The application as a surname is not clear. There are several place names in the Czech lands formed with this element, and although the surname is not a habitational name in form, it may nevertheless be derived from one of these. Moldanová cites a certain Jan Bezděcký from Bezděčí Hora, recorded in 1576.

Bezek (193) **1.** Czech, Slovak, Slovenian, and Croatian (northern Croatia; also from the Dalmatian island of Korčula): topographic name from Czech *bez*, Slovak *baza* 'elder' or 'lilac', Slovenian and northern Croatian dialect *beza*, dialect form of *bazga* 'elder'. **2.** Slovenian (**Bežek**): perhaps a medieval nickname for a refugee, from an agent noun based on *bežati* 'to flee'.

Bezio (135) Italian: unexplained; quite probably from a personal name.

Bezner (156) German: variant spelling of BETZNER.

GIVEN NAMES French 4%. *Alban, Camille.*

Bezold (170) German: variant spelling of BETZOLD.

Bhagat (254) Indian (northern states): Hindu and Jain name, from modern Indo-Aryan *bhəgət* 'devotee', 'votary', from Sanskrit *bhakta*, a derivative of the verb root *bhaj-* 'to serve or adore'. As a Hindu name it is found in several communities, including the Banias in several states and the Marathas in Maharashtra.

GIVEN NAMES Indian 89%. *Jagdish* (5), *Ravi* (5), *Ramesh* (4), *Naresh* (3), *Pravin* (3), *Ram* (3), *Urvashi* (3), *Alok* (2), *Amit* (2), *Arun* (2), *Bharti* (2), *Chandravadan* (2).

Bhakta (424) Indian (Gujarat, Karnataka): Hindu (Bhatia, Brahman) name, from Sanskrit *bhakta* 'devotee'. It is found in the

Bhatia community in Gujarat and among Saraswat Brahmans of Goa who have migrated to coastal Karnataka.

GIVEN NAMES Indian 95%. *Bharat* (11), *Rajendra* (7), *Dipak* (6), *Hasmukh* (6), *Suresh* (6), *Arvind* (5), *Pravin* (5), *Ramesh* (5), *Sanjay* (5), *Sanmukh* (5), *Bhupendra* (4), *Ishwar* (4).

Bhalla (228) Indian (Panjab): Hindu (Khatri) and Sikh name based on the name of a clan in the Khatri community. It is derived from Sanskrit *bhalla* meaning (among other things) 'auspicious', 'missile', and 'bear'.

GIVEN NAMES Indian 93%. *Anil* (6), *Ravi* (5), *Sanjeev* (4), *Vijay* (4), *Arun* (3), *Niti* (3), *Rajesh* (3), *Subhash* (3), *Suresh* (3), *Sushil* (3), *Vinod* (3), *Amita* (2).

Bhandari (197) Indian: Hindu name, from Sanskrit *bhāṇḍā(gā)rika* 'treasurer', 'keeper of a storehouse', from *bhāṇḍā(gā)ra* 'treasury', 'storehouse'. The name is found in many different communities; there is a Bhandari clan among the Panjabi Khatris.

GIVEN NAMES Indian 94%. *Sanjay* (6), *Anil* (5), *Ramesh* (5), *Arvind* (4), *Ashok* (4), *Deepak* (4), *Raj* (4), *Rajesh* (4), *Vinod* (4), *Amit* (3), *Rahul* (3), *Ravi* (3).

Bhardwaj (160) Indian (northern states): Hindu (Brahman) name, from Sanskrit *bhāradvāja* 'descendant of *bharadvāja*', *bharadvāja* meaning 'one who has strength or vigor' (a compound of *bharat* 'bearing' + *vāja* 'vigor'). According to legend, Bharadvaja (*bharadvāja*) was the name of one of the great sages.

GIVEN NAMES Indian 91%. *Ramesh* (4), *Sushma* (4), *Anil* (3), *Harish* (3), *Prem* (3), *Rakesh* (3), *Sunil* (3), *Usha* (3), *Vijay* (3), *Vinod* (3), *Ajay* (2), *Anish* (2).

Bhargava (241) Indian (chiefly Gujarat): Hindu (Brahman) name, from Sanskrit *bhārgava* '(descendant) of *Bhrigu*'. Bhrigu is the name of one of the great sages of Hindu legend.

GIVEN NAMES Indian 93%. *Ajay* (7), *Bharat* (7), *Ashok* (6), *Anil* (5), *Vivek* (5), *Deepak* (4), *Pankaj* (4), *Rahul* (4), *Vijay* (4), *Alok* (3), *Amit* (3), *Arvind* (3).

Bhasin (149) Indian (Panjab): Hindu (Khatri) and Sikh name based on the name of a clan in the Khatri community, generally believed to be derived from Sanskrit *bhāsin* 'sun'.

GIVEN NAMES Indian 87%. *Sunil* (4), *Vijay* (4), *Ashok* (3), *Ajay* (2), *Anuradha* (2), *Deepak* (2), *Maneesh* (2), *Sandeep* (2), *Sushma* (2), *Aditya, Amar, Anand.*

Bhat (301) Indian: variant of BHATT, common in the southern states.

GIVEN NAMES Indian 93%. *Sanjay* (5), *Gajanan* (4), *Narayan* (4), *Narendra* (4), *Dinesh* (3), *Ganesh* (3), *Hari* (3), *Kiran* (3), *Narayana* (3), *Seema* (3), *Shrikant* (3), *Suresh* (3).

Bhatia (780) Indian (Gujarat, Bhatia): Hindu (Bhatia) and Sikh name, based on

the name of this mercantile community. The Bhatias claim relationship with the Bhatti Rajputs. See also BHATT and BHATTI.

GIVEN NAMES Indian 90%. *Prem* (12), *Anil* (11), *Raj* (9), *Sanjay* (8), *Subhash* (8), *Sunil* (8), *Vijay* (8), *Ashok* (7), *Ram* (7), *Shashi* (7), *Kamlesh* (6), *Rajesh* (6).

Bhatnagar (210) Indian (northern states): Hindu (Kayasth) name from Hindi *bhəṭnāgər*, the name of a subgroup of the Kayasth community, denoting association with Bhatnagar or Bhatner, a city in Rajasthan. The place name Bhatner ('city of Bhats') is a compound of *bhəṭ-* (from Sanskrit *bhaṭṭa* 'learned one') + *ner* (from Sanskrit *nagara* 'town').

GIVEN NAMES Indian 93%. *Ashok* (4), *Deepak* (4), *Mohit* (4), *Amit* (3), *Anil* (3), *Manoj* (3), *Pankaj* (3), *Rajiv* (3), *Rakesh* (3), *Rashmi* (3), *Sunil* (3), *Anish* (2).

Bhatt (747) Indian: Hindu (Brahman) name, from Sanskrit *bhaṭṭa* 'lord', 'learned one', from *bhartr-* 'lord', 'husband', a derivative of *bhar-* 'to bear', 'support'.

GIVEN NAMES Indian 93%. *Bharat* (11), *Kiran* (9), *Harish* (7), *Nikhil* (7), *Praful* (7), *Ashok* (6), *Atul* (6), *Dilip* (6), *Harshad* (6), *Jitendra* (6), *Mahesh* (6), *Rajesh* (6).

Bhattacharya (266) India (Bengal and Assam): Hindu (Brahman) name, from Sanskrit *bhaṭṭācārya*, from *bhaṭṭa* 'learned one' (see BHATT) and *ācārya* 'teacher', 'preceptor' (see ACHARYA). Originally, it was a title given to a learned man or a celebrated teacher.

GIVEN NAMES Indian 86%. *Arun* (4), *Atanu* (3), *Som* (3), *Utpal* (3), *Ajit* (2), *Amar* (2), *Amit* (2), *Amitava* (2), *Arjun* (2), *Arup* (2), *Ashok* (2), *Dilip* (2).

Bhattacharyya (153) Indian: variant spelling of BHATTACHARYA.

GIVEN NAMES Indian 86%. *Amit* (3), *Biswa* (3), *Aniruddha* (2), *Anjali* (2), *Anjan* (2), *Arun* (2), *Ashim* (2), *Asit* (2), *Mita* (2), *Aditi, Ajit, Alok.*

Bhatti (396) Indian (Panjab, Rajasthan): Hindu (Rajput) and Sikh name believed to be from the eponymous ancestor of the Bhatti tribe. Etymologically, the name is related to Sanskrit *bhaṭṭa* 'lord' (see BHAT). This tribe is by far the largest and most widely distributed of the Rajput tribes of the Panjab. There is also an area in the Panjab called Bhattiana, which was once ruled by the Bhattis. Bhatti occurs as a personal name in Sanskrit literature and was the name of a well-known Sanskrit poet of the 6th century.

GIVEN NAMES Muslim 68%; Indian 20%. *Mohammad* (15), *Muhammad* (9), *Mohammed* (8), *Abdul* (7), *Javed* (5), *Rashid* (5), *Zia* (4), *Hamid* (3), *Imtiaz* (3), *Khalid* (3), *Shahid* (3), *Ahsan* (2); *Awtar* (2), *Nanak* (2), *Niranjan* (2), *Ajit, Amrit, Anuradha, Chander, Deepak, Dharam, Dinesh, Harjeet, Jagat.*

Bhavsar (143) Indian (Gujarat and Maharashtra): Hindu (Bhavsar) and Jain name of unexplained origin. The Bhavsars claim to be of Kshatriya descent. Their traditional occupations were dyeing and calico printing.

GIVEN NAMES Indian 92%. *Hemant* (3), *Indra* (3), *Jayesh* (3), *Bharat* (2), *Haresh* (2), *Jagdish* (2), *Kirti* (2), *Prakash* (2), *Rajendra* (2), *Ramesh* (2), *Sudhir* (2), *Anila*.

Bhuiyan (119) Bangladeshi: from Bengali *bhuyyan* 'landlord', 'chieftain'. Bearers of this surname claim descent from one of the twelve chieftains (nine Muslims and three Hindus), who ruled the Sultanate of Bengal (1336–1576). They frequently declared their independence from the imperial rule of the Mughals. The chieftain Isa Khan of Sonargaon defeated the Mughals in a naval blockade in September 1584, but in the end the sultanate was brought under Mughal administration.

GIVEN NAMES Muslim 84%. *Mohammed* (15), *Mohammad* (7), *Abdul* (4), *Abu* (2), *Jasim* (2), *Kabir* (2), *Rifat* (2), *Abdul Karim*, *Abdullah*, *Abul*, *Akhter*.

Bi (102) **1.** Chinese 毕: probably from the name of a people living to the west of China in ancient times, who integrated with the Han Chinese during the Han dynasty (206 BC–220 AD). The character also means 'finish', 'conclude'. **2.** Vietnamese: unexplained. **3.** Scandinavian: unexplained.

GIVEN NAMES Chinese 54%; Vietnamese 20%. *Weihua* (2), *Cheng*, *Hui*, *Keping*, *Kun*, *Lei*, *Li Ping*, *Ming*, *Qi*, *Tao*, *Weizhen*, *Wenyi*; *Chau*, *Hai*, *Hao*, *Hung*, *Mui*, *Nguyen*, *Nhung*, *Tran*, *Tuan*.

Biafore (109) Italian (Calabria): unexplained.

GIVEN NAMES Italian 12%. *Pasquale*, *Vito*.

Biaggi (109) Italian: variant spelling of BIAGI.

GIVEN NAMES Italian 9%. *Ovidio* (2), *Mario*.

Biagi (342) Italian (Tuscany): from the personal name *Biagio*, from Latin BLASIUS.

GIVEN NAMES Italian 8%. *Angelo* (2), *Ettore* (2), *Dante*, *Enrico*, *Giancarlo*, *Gildo*, *Guido*, *Marino*, *Mauro*.

Biagini (300) Italian: from a diminutive of the personal name *Biagio* (see BIAGI).

GIVEN NAMES Italian 8%. *Emo* (2), *Guido* (2), *Aldo*, *Angelo*, *Gino*, *Giulio*, *Pio*, *Reno*, *Salvator*, *Salvatore*.

Biagioni (124) Italian: from an augmentative form of the personal name *Biagio*.

GIVEN NAMES Italian 25%. *Ettore* (2), *Gino* (2), *Aldo*, *Alicia*, *Anselmo*, *Emilio*, *Ferdinando*, *Quinto*, *Juliano*, *Santa*, *Sergio*.

Biagiotti (114) Italian: from a pet form of the personal name **Biagio** (see BIAGI).

GIVEN NAMES Italian 16%. *Eliseo* (2), *Adriano*, *Aldo*, *Domenica*, *Filippo*, *Lino*, *Mario*, *Sandro*.

Bialas (332) Polish (**Białas**): from Polish *białas* 'blond', from *biały* 'white', hence a nickname or byname for a fair-haired person.

GIVEN NAMES Polish 9%; German 5%. *Stanislaw* (2), *Alicja*, *Arkadiusz*, *Bogdan*, *Casimir*, *Franciszek*, *Henryk*, *Lucyna*, *Maciej*, *Mariusz*, *Zofia*; *Florian* (2), *Ernst*, *Fritz*, *Horst*, *Kurt*, *Manfred*.

Bialecki (226) Polish (**Białecki**): habitational name for someone from any of the places called Białka, Białki, or Biała.

GIVEN NAMES Polish 9%. *Wieslaw* (2), *Wojciech* (2), *Bogdan*, *Casimir*, *Jerzy*.

Bialek (479) Polish (**Białek**): nickname for someone with very fair or white hair, from *biały* 'white'.

GIVEN NAMES Polish 12%. *Boguslaw* (2), *Dorota* (2), *Stanislaw* (2), *Bronislawa*, *Casimir*, *Dariusz*, *Genowefa*, *Grazyna*, *Jacek*, *Janusz*, *Jerzy*, *Jolanta*.

Bialik (146) Polish and Jewish (eastern Ashkenazic): nickname for a person with fair hair or a pale complexion, from *biały* 'white'.

Bialk (126) Polish (**Białk**): dialect variant of BIALIK.

Bialkowski (156) Polish (**Białkowski**): habitational name for someone from a place called Białkowo in Płock and Toruń voivodeships, Białków in Konin voivodeship, or Białkowice in Piotrków voivodeship. See also BIALEK.

GIVEN NAMES Polish 10%. *Ewa*, *Krzystof*, *Mieczyslaw*, *Piotr*, *Zygmunt*.

Bialy (208) Polish (**Biały**) and Jewish (eastern Ashkenazic): nickname for a blond or white-haired person or someone with a pale complexion, from Polish *biały* 'white'.

GIVEN NAMES Polish 12%. *Andrzej*, *Dariusz*, *Jerzy*, *Krystyna*, *Leszek*, *Ryszard*, *Tadeusz*, *Wojciech*.

Biamonte (162) Italian: probably a variant of **Baiamonte** or **Baiamonti**, derived from an old Germanic personal name, *Boiamund* or *Baiamund*.

GIVEN NAMES Italian 11%. *Ermanno* (2), *Ignazio*, *Raffaele*.

Bianca (241) Southern Italian: **1.** from the female personal name *Bianca* meaning 'white'. **2.** possibly, especially in Tuscany, a shortened form of **Biancalani**, literally 'white wool', hence an occupational name for a fuller.

GIVEN NAMES Italian 22%. *Angelo* (3), *Carmelo* (2), *Domenica*, *Nunzio*, *Rocco*, *Sal*, *Salvator*, *Salvatore*, *Vittorio*.

Biancalana (124) Italian (Tuscany): occupational or nickname name, from *(im)biancalana*, denoting someone who cleaned and bleached wool.

GIVEN NAMES Italian 8%. *Dante*, *Gino*, *Guido*, *Reno*.

Biancardi (150) Italian: from the medieval personal name *Biancardo*, a derivative, probably via the French *Blanc(h)ard*, of a Germanic personal name composed of the elements *blank* 'white', 'shining' + *hard* 'strong', 'brave'.

GIVEN NAMES Italian 25%; Spanish 8%. *Marco* (2), *Saverio* (2), *Carlo*, *Luigi*, *Mario*, *Pasquale*, *Sal*, *Sebastiano*, *Sergio*, *Stefano*, *Vittorio*; *Elia*, *Narciso*, *Osvaldo*, *Raul*.

Bianchi (3036) Italian: from BIANCO.

GIVEN NAMES Italian 11%. *Angelo* (13), *Rocco* (7), *Aldo* (6), *Carlo* (6), *Guido* (5), *Antonio* (4), *Dante* (4), *Giuseppe* (4), *Marino* (4), *Marco* (3), *Romeo* (3), *Salvatore* (3).

Bianchini (542) Italian: from *Bianchino*, a diminutive of BIANCO.

GIVEN NAMES Italian 13%. *Guido* (3), *Aldo* (2), *Angelo* (2), *Mauro* (2), *Vito* (2), *Alessandro*, *Antonella*, *Antonio*, *Attilio*, *Dino*, *Donato*, *Emanuele*.

Bianco (2769) Italian: from Italian *bianco* 'white' (of Germanic origin; compare Old High German *blanc* 'bright', 'shining', 'white', 'beautiful'), originally applied as a nickname for a man with white or fair hair or a pale complexion, or for someone who habitually wore white, especially in jousting or other competitions, and later used as a personal name.

GIVEN NAMES Italian 16%. *Vito* (16), *Angelo* (14), *Salvatore* (14), *Carmine* (12), *Antonio* (6), *Rocco* (5), *Aniello* (4), *Francesco* (4), *Luca* (4), *Luigi* (3), *Pasquale* (3), *Sal* (3).

Bianconi (150) Italian: from an augmentative form of BIANCO.

GIVEN NAMES Italian 8%. *Carlo*, *Fabrizio*, *Natale*, *Reno*, *Vitaliano*.

Bianculli (159) Southern Italian: from a diminutive of BIANCO.

GIVEN NAMES Italian 14%. *Angelo* (2), *Silvio*.

Bias (1441) **1.** French: habitational name from places in Landes and Lot-et-Garonne named Bias. **2.** English: possibly a variant spelling of BYAS.

Biasi (181) Italian: variant of BIAGI.

GIVEN NAMES Italian 14%. *Reno* (2), *Corrado*, *Franco*, *Gino*, *Pasquale*, *Primo*, *Vito*.

Biba (126) Czech and Slovak: unflattering nickname for a drunkard, from Latin *bibere* 'to drink'.

Bibb (1400) English (chiefly West Midlands): from the medieval female personal name *Bibb*, a pet form of *Isabel* (see ISBELL).

Bibbee (248) Variant spelling of English BIBBY.

Bibbins (275) English: metronymic from a pet form of BIBB.

Bibbo (188) Southern Italian (Campania): unexplained.

GIVEN NAMES Italian 13%. *Fiore* (2), *Amleto*, *Gennaro*, *Nicola*, *Pasquale*, *Raffaele*, *Salvatore*.

Bibbs (754) English: metronymic from BIBB.

Bibby (578) English (Lancashire): from a pet form of BIBB.

Bibeau (590) French (**Bibaud**, **Bibaut**): nickname for a heavy drinker, from a derivative of Latin *bibere* 'to drink'.
GIVEN NAMES French 10%. *Andre* (2), *Aime*, *Armand*, *Edmound*, *Emile*, *Florent*, *Gabrielle*, *Gaston*, *Marcel*, *Monique*, *Ovila*, *Patrice*.

Bibeault (153) French: variant of **Bibeau**.
GIVEN NAMES French 23%. *Lucien* (3), *Normand* (3), *Cecile* (2), *Gaston* (2), *Andre*, *Armand*, *Celine*, *Herve*, *Rosaire*.

Bibee (175) Probably an altered spelling of BIBBY or BEEBY.

Biber (254) German: variant of BIEBER.
GIVEN NAMES German 6%. *Klaus* (3), *Viktor*.

Bible (1281) **1.** English: from the female personal name *Bibel*, a pet form of BIBB. **2.** Perhaps an altered spelling of South German **Biebl**, a variant of BIEBEL.

Bibler (383) Altered spelling of South German **Biebler**, a variant of BIEBEL.

Biby (213) English: variant spelling of BIBBY.

Bice (2401) **1.** Americanized spelling of German **Beiss(e)**, a variant of BEITZ 2. **2.** English: perhaps a variant of BISS. Compare BEESE, BISE, BUYS, BYCE. **3.** Hungarian: nickname for someone with a limp or a peculiar gait, from *bice* 'limp'.

Bichler (279) **1.** South German: topographic name for someone who lived on a hill, from Bavarian dialect *Bichel* 'hill', variant of *Bühel* (see BUEHLER). **2.** Jewish (Ashkenazic): occupational name for a seller or binder of books, from Yiddish *bukh* 'book' + the agent suffix *-ler*.
GIVEN NAMES German 5%. *Kurt* (2), *Francis Fritz*, *Johann*.

Bichsel (224) Swiss German: probably from **Büchsel**, a metonymic occupational name for a maker of small boxes or a woodworker, from a diminutive of Middle High German *bühse* 'box', from Latin *buxus* 'box (tree)'.

Bick (690) **1.** Dutch and German: from Middle Dutch and Middle High German *bicke* 'pickaxe' or 'chisel', hence a metonymic occupational name for a stonemason or someone who made or worked with such tools. **2.** German: from a pet form of the personal name BURKHART. **3.** English: of uncertain origin, perhaps from the Old English personal name *Bicca*. Alternatively, Reaney suggests it may be from Middle English *bike* 'nest of wild bees or wasps' and hence a metonymic occupational name for a beekeeper. Compare BICKER. **4.** Jewish (eastern Ashkenazic): German or English spelling of eastern Yiddish *bik*, Polish *byk*, or Russian *byk*, all meaning 'ox' or 'bull'. This may be a translation of SHOR.

Bickel (2842) **1.** Dutch and German: from *bickel* 'pickaxe' or 'chisel', hence a metonymic occupational name for someone who made pickaxes or worked with a pickaxe or for a stonemason. Compare BICK. **2.** Ger-man: nickname for a dice player, from the same word in the sense 'die'. **3.** South German: from a pet form of BURKHART. **4.** Jewish (eastern Ashkenazic): from a diminutive of BICK. **5.** English: variant spelling of BICKELL.

Bickelhaupt (140) South German: probably from Middle High German *becken-* or *beckelhübe* 'bowl-shaped helmet', applied as a nickname for someone who wore one, but later reinterpreted through folk etymology as *Bickel* 'pickaxe' + *Haupt* 'head', i.e. 'thick head' or 'pointed head'.
GIVEN NAMES German 6%. *Gottlieb*, *Heinz*, *Matthias*.

Bickell (219) **1.** English (Devon): unexplained. **2.** American spelling of Dutch or German BICKEL.

Bicker (169) **1.** Dutch and German: occupational name for a stonemason or someone who used or made pickaxes or chisel, from *bicke* 'pickaxe', 'chisel' + the agent suffix *-er*. Compare BICK. **2.** English: occupational name for a beekeeper, Middle English *biker* (from Old English *bīcere*). Bees were important in medieval England because their honey provided the only means of sweetening food (sugar being a more recent importation); honey was also used in preserving. **3.** English: habitational name from Bicker in Lincolnshire or Byker in Tyne and Wear, both named with the Old English preposition *bī* 'by', 'beside' + Old Norse *kjarr* 'wet ground', 'brushwood'.
FOREBEARS Cars Bicker was a wealthy merchant and one of the commissioners to New Netherland under the West India Company's 1621 charter.

Bickers (529) English: patronymic from BICKER.

Bickerstaff (705) English: variant of BIGGERSTAFF.

Bickert (210) French (Alsace and Lorraine): from a Germanic personal name composed of the elements *bek* (a borrowing of Latin *beccus* 'beak') + *hard* 'hardy', 'strong'.
GIVEN NAME French 5%. *Arnaud*.

Bickerton (251) English: habitational name from any of the various places (for example in Cheshire, Northumberland, and North Yorkshire) named Bickerton, from Old English *bīcere* 'beekeeper' + *tūn* 'enclo-sure', 'settlement'.

Bickett (604) **1.** Scottish (of Norman origin): habitational name from Bequet, Bechet, or Le Becquet in Oise, France. **2.** Possibly an Americanized spelling of BICKHART.

Bickford (3382) English: habitational name from a place named Bickford, from the Old English personal name *Bicca* + Old English *ford* 'ford'. There is one such place in Staffordshire, but the surname is more common in Devon, where it is derived from Bickford Town in Plympton St. Mary parish.

Bickham (953) English: habitational name from places so named in Devon and Somerset, most of which are most probably named with an Old English personal name *Bicca* + Old English *cumb* 'valley'. The first element could alternatively be from *bica* 'pointed ridge'.

Bickhart (171) German: presumably from a personal name derived from Old High German *pichan*, Middle High German *bicken* 'to hack or pound'.

Bicking (210) **1.** German: habitational name from a place so named near Herzberg on the Elster river (tributary of the Elbe). **2.** Altered spelling of German **Bücking**, from Middle Low German *bücking* 'smoked herring', hence a nickname or a metonymic occupational name for a seller of smoked herrings. See also PICKING.

Bickle (517) German: variant of BICKEL 1.

Bickler (241) German and Jewish: variant of PICKLER or BICHLER.
GIVEN NAMES German 4%. *Kurt* (2), *Wendelin*.

Bickley (1076) English: habitational name from any of the places called Bickley, in Worcestershire, Cheshire, and Kent, or Bickleigh in Devon, all of which are possibly named with an Old English personal name *Bicca* + Old English *lēah* 'woodland clearing'. The first element could alternatively be an Old English word, *bic* 'pointed ridge'.

Bickmore (255) English: unexplained; possibly a habitational name from a lost or unidentified place.
FOREBEARS This name was brought to New England by Thomas Bigmore or Bickmore, whose son Samuel Bickmore was born in 1635 in Boston, MA.

Bicknell (1259) English: **1.** habitational name from Bickenhill in Warwickshire or Bickenhall in Somerset. Both are named with the Old English personal name *Bicca* + Old English *hyll* 'hill', but in the Somerset name the final element alternates with Old English *h(e)all* 'hall'. **2.** variant of BIGNELL.

Bicknese (144) North German: nickname for someone with a pointed nose, from *Bicke* 'pickaxe' + Low German *Nese* 'nose'.
GIVEN NAME German 5%. *Gunther*.

Bicksler (146) Altered spelling of German **Büchsler**, an occupational name for a maker of wooden boxes, from Middle High German *bühse* 'box' (from Latin *buxus* 'box tree') + the agent suffix *-ler*.

Biddick (147) English (Cornwall): topographic name from Old English *bī dīc* 'by the ditch'. It could also be a habitational name from a place in County Durham named Biddick.

Biddinger (333) Americanized spelling of the German habitational name **Büdinger** (see BUDINGER).

Biddison (146) English: variant of **Beddison**, but of unexplained etymology.

Biddix (305) English: variant of BIDDICK.

Biddle (3390) **1.** English: variant of BEADLE. **2.** Americanized spelling of German BITTEL or its variant **Büttel**.

Biddulph (154) English (Midlands): habitational name from a place in Staffordshire, recorded as *Bidolf* in Domesday Book, from Old English *bī* 'beside' + *dylf* 'digging' (a putative derivative of *delfan* 'to dig'), i.e. a mine or quarry.

Biddy (411) English: unexplained.

Biderman (148) **1.** Americanized spelling of German BIEDERMANN. **2.** Jewish (Ashkenazic): variant of BIEDERMANN.

GIVEN NAMES Jewish 15%. *Chaim* (2), *Moshe* (2), *Avrohom*, *Miriam*, *Sol*.

Bidgood (183) English: nickname from Middle English *biddan* 'to ask', 'to pray' + *God* 'God'.

Bidinger (193) German: variant of **Büdinger** (see BUDINGER).

GIVEN NAMES German 5%. *Franz*, *Kurt*, *Merwin*.

Bidlack (262) Probably a respelling of the English habitational name **Bidlake**, from a place in the parish of Bridestow, Devon, named Bidlake, probably from Old English *byde(n)* 'tub' + *lacu* 'stream'.

Bidleman (108) Possibly an Americanized spelling of a German **Beidlmann** (see BEIDLER 2; compare BEIDLEMAN).

GIVEN NAME German 4%. *Orlo*.

Bidstrup (120) Danish: habitational name from a place so named in Jutland. The first element is from *bis(ko)p* 'bishop'; the second from Old Norse *þorp* 'outlying farmstead', 'village'.

GIVEN NAME Scandinavian 6%. *Lars*.

Bidwell (1826) English: habitational name from any of various minor places called Bidwell, for example in Hertfordshire, from Old English *byde(n)* 'tub' + *well(a)* 'spring', 'stream'.

Biebel (212) South German: **1.** topographic name from an old word *bibl* denoting water of some kind, or a habitational name from any of various places named with this word, for example Biebelried in Bavaria or Biblis in Hesse. **2.** from a pet form of a Germanic personal name formed with the elements *bītan* 'to endure' or *bittan* 'to ask for', 'to wish'.

Bieber (1849) German and Jewish (Ashkenazic): from Middle High German *biber* 'beaver', German *Biber*, or Yiddish *biber*, hence a nickname, possibly a nickname for a hard worker, or from some other fancied resemblance to the animal. In some cases the surname may be habitational, from a house or some other place named with this word. As a Jewish name it is largely ornamental.

GIVEN NAMES German 4%. *Otto* (4), *Klaus* (3), *Gerhard* (2), *Kurt* (2), *Alois*, *Erwin*,

Florian, *Frieda*, *Hans*, *Helmut*, *Horst*, *Mathias*.

Biechler (100) South German: variant of BICHLER.

Bieda (161) Polish: nickname for a needy person, from *bieda* 'poverty' (Old Polish *biada*, *bida*).

GIVEN NAMES Polish 8%. *Andrzej*, *Ludwik*, *Mieczyslaw*, *Stanislaw*.

Biedenbach (135) German: habitational name from Biedenbach in Schwalm, Hesse.

Biedenharn (130) North German: topographic name meaning 'at the hills', from Low German *bi den Ha(a)ren*, from Middle Low German *hare* 'hill'.

Biederman (775) German or Jewish (Ashkenazic): see BIEDERMANN.

Biedermann (316) **1.** German: nickname for an honest man, from a compound of Middle High German *biderbe* 'honorable' + *man* 'man'. Associated with it is the surname **Biedermeier** (see MAYER), adopted in 1853 by a group of German humorists as the name of a fictitious writer, Gottlob Biedermeier, satirized as an unimaginative bourgeois philistine. The name came to be used to refer to the stolid style of furnishing and decoration that was popular in mid 19th-century Germany. **2.** Jewish (Ashkenazic): surname adopted because of its honorific meaning, from modern German *bieder* 'honest', 'upright' + *-mann* 'man'.

GIVEN NAMES German 12%. *Guenther* (2), *Manfred* (2), *Armin*, *Arno*, *Egon*, *Erna*, *Hans*, *Helmut*, *Konrad*, *Kurt*, *Siegfried*.

Biediger (102) German: probably an altered spelling or variant of German **Büdinger**, a habitational name for someone from Büdingen in Hesse. Compare BEDINGER.

Biedron (136) Polish (**Biedroń**): nickname, either from dialect *biedron* 'spotted bullock', or for someone with conspicuous or deformed hips, from a derivative of dialect *biedro* 'hip'.

GIVEN NAMES Polish 8%. *Andrzej*, *Casimir*, *Janusz*, *Tadeusz*.

Biedrzycki (187) Polish: habitational name for someone from a place called Biedrzyce, for example in Ostrołęka voivodeship.

GIVEN NAMES Polish 6%. *Andrzej*, *Jadwiga*, *Karol*, *Tadeusz*.

Biegel (352) South German: **1.** topographic name for someone living on or by a hill, from Middle High German *bühel* 'hill', 'knoll'. **2.** topographic name for someone who lived by a curve in a street or river or in a nook, from Middle High German *biegel* 'nook', 'curve'.

Bieger (139) German: **1.** nickname for a quarrelsome or pugnacious person, Middle High German *bieger* 'quarreler'. **2.** of Slavic origin, from a personal name (*bēgati* 'to run'). **3.** variant of BIEGEL 2.

Biegert (115) German: variant of BIEGER.

GIVEN NAMES German 5%. *Johannes*, *Lothar*.

Biegler (375) South German: **1.** see BIGLER. **2.** variant of BUEHLER.

GIVEN NAMES German 5%. *Lorenz* (2), *Ernst*, *Hans*, *Klaus*.

Biehl (1094) German: **1.** from Middle Low German *bil* 'hatchet', Middle High German *biel*; hence a metonymic occupational name for someone who made or used hatchets. **2.** in southern Germany, a variant of **Bühl** (see BUEHL). **3.** habitational name from places so named in Baden and Bavaria.

Biehle (218) German: **1.** possibly a topographic name from *Biel* 'sloping rock', or a habitational name from any of several places called Bielau, in Silesia, or Biehla in eastern Germany, or Biele on the Oder river. **2.** (Westphalia) topographic name for someone who lived by a field that had the shape of a hatchet, from Middle Low German *bīl* 'hatchet', 'axe'.

Biehler (299) South German: variant of BUEHLER.

Biehn (286) German: **1.** possibly a habitational name from any of several places named Bienen (Lower Rhine) or from Biene near Lingen. **2.** variant spelling of BIEN.

Bieker (534) German: variant of **Biecker**, from a Germanic personal name related to Old High German *pichan* 'to hack or stab'.

Biel (883) **1.** Polish, Czech, and Slovak: nickname for a white- or fair-haired person, from Polish *biel*, Old Czech *bielý*, Slovak *biely* 'white'. **2.** Czech: habitational name for someone from Biehlau, Biehla, or some other place named with German BIEHL. **3.** German: variant spelling of BIEHL.

Biela (184) **1.** Polish: variant of BIEL. **2.** German: habitational name for someone from any of several places of Slavic origin called Biela, or from Biehla in Saxony or Bielau in Silesia.

GIVEN NAMES Polish 12%. *Casimir* (2), *Aleksander*, *Bernadeta*, *Ewa*, *Grazyna*, *Ludwik*, *Malgorzata*, *Wladyslaw*.

Bielak (216) **1.** Polish: patronymic from **Biały** (see BIALY). **2.** Polish and Jewish (from Poland): nickname for someone who was a fast runner, from *bielak* 'mountain hare' (*Lepus variabilis*).

GIVEN NAMES Polish 9%. *Andrzej*, *Elzbieta*, *Irek*, *Janina*, *Wieslaw*, *Wladyslaw*.

Bielat (171) Polish: nickname from dialect *bielaty* 'whitish'.

Bielawa (112) Polish: nickname for someone with fair hair or a pale complexion, from *biały* 'white'.

Bielawski (409) Polish: habitational name for someone from any of various places called Bielawy or Bielawa.

GIVEN NAMES Polish 14%. *Jerzy* (3), *Tadeusz* (3), *Jacek* (2), *Jaroslaw* (2), *Aleksander*, *Andrzej*, *Bogdan*, *Darek*, *Janusz*, *Karol*, *Kazimierz*, *Ludwika*.

Bielby (171) English: habitational name from a place of this name in East Yorkshire, named with the Old Norse personal name

Beli + Old Norse *býr* 'farmstead', 'settlement'.

GIVEN NAME German 5%. *Erwin* (4).

Biele (110) Italian: variant of VIELE.

GIVEN NAME Italian 6%. *Angelo* (2).

Bielec (110) Polish: nickname for a man with white hair or a blond beard, from *biały* 'white'.

Bielecki (457) Polish: habitational name for someone from a place called Bielcza in Tarnów voivodeship.

GIVEN NAMES Polish 9%. *Boguslaw* (2), *Jerzy* (2), *Andrzej*, *Bogdan*, *Krzysztof*, *Leszek*, *Mieczyslaw*, *Pawel*, *Tomasz*, *Wincenty*, *Zbigniew*.

Bielefeld (260) German and Jewish (western Ashkenazic): habitational name from the city of this name in Westphalia. See also BIEHLE.

GIVEN NAMES German 5%. *Hermann*, *Lothar*, *Otto*.

Bielefeldt (178) Variant spelling of BIELEFELD, also found in Denmark.

GIVEN NAME German 4%. *Otto*.

Bielen (158) Polish (**Bieleń**): nickname for a person with white or fair hair or a pale complexion, from a derivative of *biały* 'white'. Compare BIEL.

GIVEN NAMES Polish 8%. *Halina*, *Stanistaw*, *Wladyslaw*, *Zofia*.

Bielenberg (213) German: habitational name from a place named Bielenberg, near Glückstadt in Schleswig-Holstein.

Bieler (297) **1.** Jewish (Ashkenazic): habitational name from any of the many places in eastern Europe whose name incorporates the Slavic element *byel-* 'white'. **2.** German: occupational name for someone who used or made hatchets; a variant of BIEHL, with the addition of the agent suffix *-er*. **3.** German: habitational name for someone from Bielen in Thuringia. **4.** Altered spelling of BIEHLER (a variant of BUEHLER), or a habitational name from any of places mentioned at BIEHLE 1.

GIVEN NAMES German 5%; Jewish 4%. *Dieter*, *Fritz*, *Rudiger*; *Meyer* (2), *Hirsch*.

Bielicki (157) Polish and Jewish (from Poland): habitational name for someone from a place called Bielice.

GIVEN NAMES Polish 16%. *Beata* (2), *Jacek* (2), *Wieslaw* (2), *Krzysztof*, *Stanislaw*, *Witold*.

Bielinski (274) Polish (**Bieliński**) and Jewish (eastern Ashkenazic): habitational name for someone from a place called Bielin in Volhynia or any of various other places in Poland such as Bielina, Bielino, or Bieliny.

GIVEN NAMES Polish 5%. *Boleslaw*, *Jacek*, *Jaroslaw*, *Jozef*, *Witold*, *Zbigniew*.

Bielke (130) **1.** Scandinavian: variant of **Bjelke**, a noble family name dating back to around 1500, from *bjelke* 'beam', a device which appears in their coat of arms. **2.** German: reduced form of **Bielecke**,

from a pet form of a personal name formed with the Germanic stem *bil* 'axe'.

GIVEN NAMES German 6%. *Arno*, *Wolfgang*.

Biello (136) Italian: from the personal name *Viello* (see VIELE).

GIVEN NAMES Italian 22%. *Carmine* (3), *Angelo* (2), *Domenic* (2), *Dante*, *Rino*.

Bielski (568) Polish and Jewish (eastern Ashkenazic): habitational name for someone from Biała, Białe, Bielsk, Bielsko, or various other places in Poland and in Ukraine with a name that incorporates the Slavic element *biel-* 'white' + the surname suffix *-ski*.

GIVEN NAMES Polish 5%. *Danuta*, *Ewa*, *Janusz*, *Piotr*, *Stanislaw*, *Teofil*, *Wieslaw*, *Zygmunt*.

Bien (692) **1.** Polish (**Bień**): from a short form of the personal names *Benedykt* (see BENEDICT) or *Beniamin* (see BENJAMIN). **2.** Jewish (eastern Ashkenazic): from a pet form of the personal name *Beniamin* (see BENJAMIN). **3.** Jewish (Ashkenazic): ornamental name from Yiddish *bin* 'bee', German *Bien(e)*, or a metonymic occupational name for a beekeeper. **4.** German: from the dialect word *Bien* 'bee', hence a metonymic occupational name for a beekeeper or nickname for an industrious person. **5.** Vietnamese (**Biên**): unexplained.

GIVEN NAMES Vietnamese 4%. *Anh*, *Chanh*, *Cuc*, *Duc Van*, *Hau*, *Hieu*, *Hoang*, *Hung Ngoc*, *Khanh*, *Thanh*, *Thanh Thi*, *Thuy*.

Bien-Aime (184) French: literally 'well-loved', a nickname for a popular person or, more probably, from the same phrase used as a given name.

GIVEN NAMES French 44%. *Antoine* (2), *Michel* (2), *Micheline* (2), *Altagrace*, *Andre*, *Dieuseul*, *Dominique*, *Emile*, *Jean Claude*, *Jean Robert*, *Joanel*, *Julien*.

Bieneman (109) German (**Bienemann**): occupational name for a beekeeper.

Bienenfeld (108) Jewish (Ashkenazic): ornamental name from German *Bienenfeld* 'open country where bees lived'.

GIVEN NAMES Jewish 6%. *Moshe*, *Yaakov*.

Biener (123) **1.** Jewish (Ashkenazic) and German: occupational name for a beekeeper, a variant of BIEN, with the addition of the *-er* agent suffix. **2.** German: possibly a habitational name from a place name of Slavic origin, such as Bienau in eastern Germany.

GIVEN NAMES Jewish 8%; German 4%. *Zalman* (2), *Aron*; *Kurt*.

Bieniek (403) Polish: from a pet form of the personal names *Benedykt* (see BENEDICT) or *Beniamin* (see BENJAMIN).

GIVEN NAMES Polish 10%. *Jerzy* (2), *Stanislaw* (2), *Andrzej*, *Beata*, *Iwona*, *Janusz*, *Teofil*, *Zigmund*, *Zygmunt*.

Bienkowski (227) Polish (**Bieńkowski**): habitational name for someone from any of various places called Bieńkowice, Bieńkowiec, or Bieńkowo.

GIVEN NAMES Polish 12%. *Andrzej* (2), *Dariusz*, *Grzegorz*, *Henryk*, *Iwona*, *Jerzy*, *Mariusz*, *Wieslaw*.

Bienstock (249) Jewish (Ashkenazic): ornamental name or an occupational name for a beekeeper, from Yiddish *binshtok* 'beehive'.

GIVEN NAMES Jewish 8%; German 4%. *Hyman* (3), *Hanka*, *Isadore*, *Sol*; *Wolf*.

Bienvenu (471) French: from the personal name *Bienvenu* (feminine *Bienvenue*) meaning 'welcome', an omen name given to a much wanted child.

FOREBEARS A Bienvenu from La Rochelle, with the secondary surname Delisle, is documented in Detroit in 1701.

GIVEN NAMES French 10%. *Marcel* (2), *Andre*, *Camille*, *Eugenie*, *Henri*, *Ludger*, *Marcelle*, *Monique*, *Ovide*, *Pierre*, *Yvrose*.

Bienvenue (219) French: variant of BIENVENU.

GIVEN NAMES French 17%. *Adrien*, *Andre*, *Armand*, *Emile*, *Eulalie*, *Fernand*, *Germain*, *Marcelle*, *Monique*, *Reynald*, *Yves*.

Bienz (140) South German: **1.** variant of BENZ. **2.** habitational name from a place, now in Poland, called Bienitz, near Bunzlau, Silesia.

Bier (833) **1.** German and Jewish (Ashkenazic): from Middle High German *bier* 'beer', German *Bier*, Yiddish *bir*, a metonymic occupational name for a brewer of beer or a tavern owner, or in some cases perhaps a nickname for a beer drinker. **2.** South German: from the short form of a personal name formed with Old High German *bero* 'bear'. **3.** Northern English and Scottish: variant of BYERS.

GIVEN NAMES German 5%. *Franz* (2), *Lutz* (2), *Erwin*, *Guenter*, *Gunther*, *Horst*, *Kurt*, *Otto*, *Rudi*.

Bierbaum (426) German: topographic name for someone who lived by a pear tree, Middle Low German *bērbōm*. Compare BIRNBAUM.

GIVEN NAMES German 4%. *Ewald*, *Ilse*, *Kurt*.

Bierbower (122) Americanized form of an unidentified German name.

Bierce (177) Variant of Welsh and English PIERCE.

Biere (115) Variant of German BIER.

Bierer (285) South German: occupational name for a fruit dealer or grower, Middle High German *birer*, a derivative of *bir(e)* 'pear'.

Bieri (426) Swiss German: probably from a pet form of *Birr*, *Pirr*, which is a short form of French *Pierre* or of *Pirmin* (the name of an 8th century bishop who founded several monasteries in southern Germany, including Reichenau and Murbach). This is a typical Pennsylvania German name; in Switzerland it is common in Emmental and the canton Bern.

GIVEN NAMES German 5%. *Otto* (2), *Bernhard*, *Heinz*, *Kurt*, *Reinhold*.

Bierig (101) Variant of Swiss German BIERI.
GIVEN NAMES German 5%. *Christoph, Kurt.*

Bierl (104) South German: from a pet form of a Germanic personal name formed with *ber(o)* 'bear' (the animal) as the first element (see BERNARD).
GIVEN NAME German 6%. *Otmar.*

Bierle (123) South German and Swiss: from a diminutive of BAUER, an unrounded form of Alemannic **Bürle**.
GIVEN NAME German 4%. *Otto.*

Bierlein (260) German: hypercorrected or standardized form of BIERLY.
GIVEN NAMES German 7%. *Gerhard* (2), *Ewald, Lorenz, Otto.*

Bierley (177) Variant of BIERLY.

Bierly (491) **1.** English: habitational name from a place in West Yorkshire named Bierley, from Old English *burh* 'fortified place' (genitive *byrh*) + *lēah* 'woodland clearing'. **2.** German: from a short form of a personal name formed with Old High German *bero* 'bear', or a topographic name from a variant of Middle High German *birling* 'hay barn'.

Bierma (164) Frisian: late formation from German *Bier* 'beer' + Frisian *-ma* 'man', probably an occupational name for a beer merchant or brewer.
GIVEN NAMES Dutch 4%. *Hessel, Pieter.*

Bierman (1990) **1.** Dutch and Jewish (Ashkenazic): occupational name for a beer merchant, brewer, or tavern owner or a nickname for a beer drinker. **2.** Respelling of the German cognate BIERMANN.

Biermann (640) German and Jewish (Ashkenazic): occupational name for a brewer or tavern owner or a nickname for a drinker; a variant of BIER.
GIVEN NAMES German 6%. *Kurt* (5), *Achim, Franz, Hans, Manfred, Otto.*

Biernacki (361) Polish: habitational name for someone from a place called Biernaty, for example in Ostrołęka voivodeship, or Biernatki, for example in Poznań voivodeship, places named with the personal name *Biernat*, Polish form of BERNARD.
GIVEN NAMES Polish 12%. *Zigmund* (4), *Casimir* (2), *Czeslaw, Darek, Jacek, Jerzy, Leszek, Wiktor, Zbigniew, Zigmond, Zigmunt.*

Biernat (290) Polish: from the personal name *Biernat*, Polish form of BERNARD.
GIVEN NAMES Polish 14%. *Krzysztof* (2), *Wladyslaw* (2), *Andrzej, Bogdan, Dorota, Henryk, Irek, Jadwiga, Jerzy, Jozef, Kazimierz, Slawomir.*

Biers (168) English: variant spelling of BYERS.

Bierschbach (118) German: habitational name from a lost or unidentified place.

Bierschenk (106) German: perhaps an occupational name for a tavern owner. Literally it means 'beer pourer'.

Bierstedt (112) North German: habitational name from a place so named, near Salzwedel, for instance.
GIVEN NAME German 7%. *Heinz* (2).

Bierwagen (101) German: literally 'beer wagon', an occupational name for a drayman (a man who delivered beer to taverns and inns).
GIVEN NAMES German 8%. *Klaus* (2), *Bernhard, Hans.*

Bierwirth (187) German: occupational name for an innkeeper mainly serving beer, Middle High German *birwirt*.
GIVEN NAME German 5%. *Otto.*

Biery (504) Variant spelling of Swiss German BIERI.

Bies (379) **1.** Dutch and North German: from *bies* 'rush', either a topographic name for some who lived where rushes grew, or metonymic occupational name for a weaver of rush matting. **2.** Polish: unflattering nickname from *bies* 'devil', 'Satan'.

Bieschke (145) Eastern German: of Slavic origin, either from a personal name *Bēg* (from *bēgati* 'to run') or a nickname for someone who always ran.
GIVEN NAMES German 5%. *Florian* (2), *Hertha, Kurt.*

Biese (162) German and Dutch: variant of BIES 'reed'.

Biesecker (316) German: derivative of **Biesecke**, probably a variant of **Besecke** (see BESECKER) or BESKE.

Bieser (180) German: perhaps from an occupational or topographic name from Low German *Biese* 'reed' (in northern Germany reed was used for thatched roofs) or a habitational name from Biesen in the Lippe district or Mark Brandenburg.
GIVEN NAMES German 6%. *Dietrich* (2), *Gerhard.*

Biesiada (122) Polish: nickname from *biesiada* 'feast', 'banquet', probably for someone who liked to feast.

Biesinger (122) German: habitational name for someone from any of several places called Biesingen, Bisingen, or Bissingen, all in southern Germany.

Biesterfeld (122) German: habitational name from either of two places called Biesterfeld, in Lippe and Oldenburg.
GIVEN NAMES German 6%. *Kurt* (3), *Hans.*

Bietz (171) German: variant of BITZ.

Biever (296) **1.** English: variant spelling of BEAVER. **2.** German: variant of BIEBER.

Bifano (158) Southern Italian: from the medieval personal name *Epifanio*, ultimately from Greek *Epiphanios*, a derivative of *epiphainesthai* 'to appear', a name typically given to children born on 6th January, with reference to the Christian festival of the Epiphany, which commemorates the manifestation of Christ to the Magi.
GIVEN NAMES Italian 12%. *Angelo, Cosmo, Salvatore.*

Biffle (326) Americanized spelling of German **Büffel**: **1.** from late Middle High German *büffel* 'buffalo' (in some areas 'bull'); the surname may have arisen from a house name or a nickname for a loutish person.

2. from a pet form of the Old German personal name *Bodefrit*.

Bifulco (205) Southern Italian: nickname from Sicilian *bbifurcu* 'scoundrel', 'rascal', or from Italian *bifolco* 'plowman', 'boor', both from Late Latin *bufulcus, bubulcus*.
GIVEN NAMES Italian 13%. *Antonio* (2), *Gennaro* (2), *Salvatore* (2), *Annamarie, Giuseppe, Luigi.*

Big (110) English: see BIGG.

Biga (138) Polish: possibly from *biga* 'two-wheeled cart' and hence an occupational name for a carter.

Bigalke (125) German: variant of Polish *Biegałka*, a nickname from *biegać* 'to run'.

Bigbee (313) Variant spelling of BIGBY.

Bigbie (166) Variant spelling of BIGBY.

Bigby (301) English: habitational name from a place in Lincolnshire named Bigby, from an Old Norse personal name *Bekki* + Old Norse *býr* 'settlement', 'farmstead'.

Bigelow (4493) English (Merseyside and Cheshire): probably a habitational name from a place in Cheshire named Big Low in the township of Rainbow. This place name is not on early record; it means 'big mound', from early Modern English *big* + *low* 'mound', 'hill' (Old English *hlāw*).

Bigford (161) English: variant of BICKFORD. In Britain this form is found mainly in the Wolverhampton area, suggesting it probably arose from Bickford in Staffordshire.

Bigg (130) **1.** English: presumably a descriptive nickname for a large, strong person, but compare BIGGS. **2.** Scottish: variant of BEGG.

Biggar (402) Scottish: habitational name from a place in east Lanarkshire, probably named with Old Norse *bygg* 'barley' + *geiri* 'triangular plot of land'.

Biggart (168) Scottish: variant of BIGGAR.

Bigge (115) English: variant spelling of BIGG.

Bigger (847) **1.** Scottish: variant spelling of BIGGAR. **2.** English: occupational name for a builder, from Middle English *bigger* '(house) builder', an agent derivative of *bigge(n)* 'to build' (from Old Norse *bygg-ja*).

Biggers (1661) **1.** English: patronymic from BIGGER. **2.** Perhaps German: from a variant of a personal name formed with Germanic *pichan* 'to hack or stab'.

Biggerstaff (1225) English: habitational name from Bickerstaffe in the parish of Ormskirk, Lancashire, so named with Old English *bīcere* 'beekeeper' + *stæð* 'landing place'. In Britain, this spelling of the surname is now found predominantly in northern Ireland.

Biggie (125) Scottish and northern English: presumably a descriptive nickname for a large man.

Biggins (663) English: habitational name from any of the various places in England named with northern Middle English *bigging* 'building' (from Old Norse). This word came to denote especially an outbuilding, and is still used in and around Northumberland and Cumbria.

Biggio (188) Italian: nickname from *bigio* 'dull', 'gray', hence a nickname for someone with mousy gray hair or beard, or for someone who habitually dressed in drab colors.

Biggs (7849) **1.** English: nickname for a large or stout person, Middle English *bigge* + unexplained *-s*. **2.** English: records of names such as *William de Bigges* (Cambridgeshire 1327) and *Laurentia atte Bigge* (Somerset 1327) suggest that it must also have a topographic or habitational origin, but the etymology is obscure. **3.** Scottish and northern Irish: variant of BEGGS.

Bigham (2094) Scottish: habitational name from a place called Bigholm(e); there are lands so called in Dumfriesshire and Ayrshire.

Bigler (1508) South German: topographic name for someone who lived by a curve in a street or river, or in a nook, from Middle High German *biegel* 'nook', 'corner'.

Bigley (898) Irish: see BEGLEY.

Biglin (208) English: habitational name from Biglands in Cumbria or Bigland in Lancashire, which are both named with Old Norse *bygg* 'barley' + *land* 'land'.

Biglow (193) English: variant of BIGELOW.

Bigman (105) Origin uncertain. Perhaps an Americanized form of Dutch BEEKMAN.

Bignell (223) English: **1.** habitational name from Bignell near Bicester, Oxfordshire, so named with an Old English personal name *Bicga* + Old English *hyll* 'hill'. **2.** variant of BICKNELL.

Bigner (105) German (Austria): unexplained.

Bigos (269) Polish and Jewish (from Poland): from *bigos*, formerly denoting anything that was chopped or slashed, now a particular dish composed of hash and sauerkraut; also 'confusion'; hence perhaps a nickname for someone who caused confusion.
GIVEN NAMES Polish 5%. *Jaroslaw, Jozef, Krystyna, Slawomir.*

Bigsby (265) English: habitational name from a lost or unidentified place. See BIXBY.

Bigwood (175) English: from the Germanic personal name *Bigwald*, composed of an unexplained first element + *wald* 'rule'.

Bihl (146) **1.** German: variant spelling of BIEHL or BUEHL. **2.** Danish: from Old Danish *biil* 'axe', 'hatchet'. Compare German BIEHL.

Bihler (116) German: variant of BIEHLER or BUEHLER.
GIVEN NAMES German 9%; French 6%. *Kurt (2), Hans, Siegfried; Armand, Marcel.*

Bihm (164) German: variant of BOEHM, found also in Siebenbürgen, the German settled area of Romania.

Bihn (148) German: variant of BIEHN.

Bila (114) **1.** Czech (**Bílá**) and Slovak (also **Bilá**): nickname for a fair-haired person, from *bílý* 'white'. **2.** Italian: unexplained.
GIVEN NAMES Italian 8%. *Matteo, Salvatore, Vito.*

Bilak (104) Slovak (**Bilák**) and Ukrainian: nickname meaning 'pale' or 'fair', from Slavic *bilak*, noun derivative of *bily* 'white'. See BILY, BILA.
GIVEN NAME French 6%. *Andre (2).*

Bilal (180) Muslim (widespread throughout the Muslim world): from a personal name based on Arabic *bilāl* 'moist'. This was the name of one of the Companions of the Prophet Muhammad, who became the first muezzin (caller to prayer) in Islam.
GIVEN NAMES Muslim 64%. *Mohammad (5), Hassan (4), Abdul (3), Abdullah (2), Muhammad (2), Naimah (2), Wali (2), Aaliyah, Abdel, Abubakr, Aisha, Alaa.*

Bilas (105) Polish: nickname for a person with white or fair hair or a pale complexion, from a derivative of *biały* 'white'. Compare BIEL.
GIVEN NAMES Polish 6%. *Casimir, Jozef.*

Bilbao (214) Spanish (of Basque origin): habitational name from the city of Bilbao, in Biscay province, which was founded in the 13th century on the site of an ancient settlement.
GIVEN NAMES Spanish 35%. *Carlos (5), Jorge (5), Jose (4), Miguel (3), Francisco (2), Mario (2), Ofelia (2), Pedro (2), Aida, Alicia, Amalia, Ana; Antonio (3), Angelo, Cecilio, Geronimo.*

Bilberry (137) English: **1.** Probably a variant of BILBRO. **2.** habitational name from Bilberry in Cornwall.

Bilbo (485) Irish and English: unexplained. Perhaps a habitational name, either from a place called *Bilbo* in Scotland (although the surname is not found in Scotland), or from an altered form of an unidentified English place name.

Bilbrey (1352) Probably an altered form of the English habitational name **Bilborough** (see BILBRO), but see also BILBERRY.

Bilbro (179) Probably an altered spelling of the English habitational names **Bilbrough** or **Bilborough**, from Bilbrough in North Yorkshire or Bilborough in Nottinghamshire. Both places are named with an Old English personal name, *Bila* or *Billa*, + Old English *burh* 'stronghold', 'fortification'.

Bilby (414) English: habitational name from a place in Nottinghamshire, so named with the Old Norse personal name *Billi* + Old Norse *býr* 'settlement', 'farmstead'.

Bilder (140) Jewish (eastern Ashkenazic): occupational name for a teacher, from an agent derivative of Yiddish *bildn* 'to educate', 'to cultivate'.

Bilderback (556) German: habitational name from any of the three places in northern Germany named Billderbeck, formerly *Bilderbeck*.

Bilek (395) Czech (**Bílek**): nickname for a fair-haired person, from *bílek* 'whiteness', a derivative of *bílý* 'white'.
GIVEN NAMES German 4%. *Alois (2), Otto (2), Gerhard.*

Bilello (313) Italian (Sicily): from the Arabic personal name *Bilāl*.
GIVEN NAMES Italian 17%. *Pasquale (3), Aurelio (2), Carlo (2), Salvatore (2), Domenica, Francesco, Gaspare, Gasper, Leonardo, Lorenzo, Mario, Palma.*

Biles (1110) English: topographic name for someone who lived on a promontory or elevation, from Old English *bil(e)*, literally denoting the bill or beak of a bird, but also used in a transferred sense.

Bilger (612) German: nickname for someone who had been on a pilgrimage, from Middle High German *bilgerīm* 'pilgrim'.

Bilicki (177) Polish and Ukrainian: habitational name, a variant of BIELICKI.
GIVEN NAME Polish 5%. *Zigmond (2).*

Bilik (105) **1.** Jewish (eastern Ashkenazic): occupational nickname for someone who worked for a low wage, from Yiddish *bilik* 'cheap'. **2.** Ukrainian and Polish (**Bielik**): nickname from Ukrainian *bilik*, Polish *bielik* 'golden eagle', or else a nickname for someone with fair hair or a pale complexion (see BIELEN).
GIVEN NAMES Russian 18%; Jewish 7%; Polish 6%; German 4%. *Vasily (2), Aleksandr, Boris, Daniil, Leonid, Nadezhda, Sergei, Vladimir, Yefim; Ilya, Yakov; Beata, Jozef.*

Bilinski (334) Polish (**Biliński**) and Ukrainian: habitational name for someone from a place called Bielino; a variant of BIELINSKI.
GIVEN NAMES Polish 11%. *Casimir (2), Kazimir (2), Tadeusz (2), Zbigniew (2), Aleksander, Jaroslaw, Zdzislaw, Zygmund.*

Bilka (153) Czech (**Bílka**): nickname for a fair-haired person, from *bílý* 'white'.

Bill (1646) **1.** English and German: from a Germanic personal name, either a short form of compound names such as BILLARD, or else a byname *Bill(a)*, from Old English *bil* 'sword', 'halberd' (or a Continental cognate). (*Bill* as a short form of *William* was not used until the 17th century.) **2.** English: metonymic occupational name for a maker of pruning hooks and similar implements, from Middle English *bill*, from Old English *bil* 'sword', with the meaning shifted to a more peaceful agricultural application (see BILLER 5).

Billadeau (111) French: variant of BILODEAU.

Billard (199) French: **1.** from a short form of the personal name *Robillard*, a derivative of ROBERT. **2.** from the Germanic personal name *Bilhard*, composed of the elements *bil* 'sword' + *hard* 'brave', 'hardy', 'strong'. The spelling has been influenced by Old French *bille* 'piece of wood', 'stick'. Compare BILLET 2.

GIVEN NAMES French 13%. *Pierre* (4), *Jean-Louis, Jean-Pierre, Sebastien*.

Bille (225) Danish: **1.** altered form of **Bielde**, a Danish noble name. **2.** from the Old Norse personal name *Bille* meaning 'axe', 'hatchet'.

Billeaud (146) French: from a personal name composed of the Germanic elements *bil* 'sword' (or possibly *bili* 'gentle') + *wald* 'ruler'.

FOREBEARS A Billeaud from Brittany, with the secondary surname Montplaisir, is documented in Quebec city in 1717.

GIVEN NAMES French 9%. *Raoul* (2), *Andre, Jacques, Marcelle*.

Billeci (114) Southern Italian: unexplained.

GIVEN NAMES Italian 15%; French 5%. *Sal* (2), *Carlo, Francesco, Ignazio, Nino*; *Andre* (2), *Pierre*.

Billen (123) **1.** Dutch and North German: from a reduced form of the personal name *Boudewijn* (see BALDWIN). **2.** English: variant of BULLEN.

GIVEN NAME German 4%. *Kurt*.

Biller (1046) **1.** German: southern form of BUEHLER. **2.** German: possibly from Middle High German *bil(le)* 'sculpture' (from *billen* 'to cut stone'), hence an occupational name for a stonemason or sculptor. **3.** German: possibly a variant of **Büller**, a nickname from Middle High German *büllen* 'to bark', 'bawl'. **4.** Danish: altered form of German BUEHLER. **5.** English: occupational name for a maker of billhooks or pruning forks (bills), from Middle English *billere*. Compare BILL-MAN.

GIVEN NAMES German 4%. *Helmut* (2), *Kurt* (2), *Otto* (2), *Achim, Almut, Armin, Fritz, Hannelore, Hans, Ingeburg, Johann, Manfred*.

Billerbeck (115) German: habitational name from any of several places called Billerbeck in Eastphalia and Westphalia.

Billet (333) French and English: **1.** from a reduced form of *Robillet*, itself a pet form of ROBERT. **2.** metonymic occupational name for a carpenter, from a diminutive of Old French *bille* 'piece of wood', 'stick' (a word of Gaulish origin). **3.** metonymic occupational name for a secretary, from a diminutive of Old French *bulle* 'letter'. This sense of *billet* did not become established until the 15th century, however, rather late for surname formation. **4.** Jewish (Ashkenazic): metonymic occupational name for a banker or money changer, from German *Billet* 'note', 'banknote'.

GIVEN NAMES Jewish 4%. *Hadassa, Herschel, Mendel, Mertie*.

Billeter (210) Swiss German: **1.** habitational name for someone from Bilten (formerly *Biliton*) in the canton of Glarus. **2.** occupational name for a military quartermaster

from French *billet*, here 'certificate or voucher' (held by soldiers to be given lodgings), a loan word dating back to the Thirty Years War.

GIVEN NAME German 4%. *Kurt* (2).

Billett (292) English: variant spelling of BILLET.

Billey (118) **1.** Southern English: unexplained. **2.** French: habitational name from Billey in the Côte d'Or, of the same derivation as BILLY.

Billheimer (145) German: habitational name for someone from Pillham in Bavaria, (formerly recorded as *Pilhaim*).

Billick (261) German: variant spelling of BILLIG.

Billie (309) **1.** Scottish: habitational name, according to Black, from the lands of Billie in the parish of Bunkle. **2.** Navajo: unexplained.

Billiet (104) French: variant of BILLET.

Billig (480) German: **1.** habitational name from a place named Billig, near Cologne. **2.** nickname from Middle High German *billich* 'proper', 'appropriate'.

Billing (477) **1.** English: either from a Middle English survival of an Old English personal name, *Billing*, or a habitational name from a place in Northamptonshire called Billing, probably '(settlement of) the followers (Old English *-ingas*) of a man called *Bill(a)*'. **2.** German: from a Germanic personal name, formed with a cognate of Old Saxon *bīl* 'sword'. **3.** Danish and Norwegian: from an Old Danish personal name, *Billing*. **4.** Swedish: shortened form of various habitational names such as **Billinge, Billingsfors**, etc.

Billinger (260) German: from the personal name *Billung* or *Billing* (see BILLING 2).

Billingham (202) English: habitational name from a place called Billingham. There is one such place in Stockton on Tees (formerly in County Durham), which probably derives its name from Old English *Billingahām* 'homestead (Old English *hām*) of the people of *Bill(a)*'. However, in the British Isles the surname is found chiefly in the Midlands (Staffordshire), and the distribution, together with evidence from other names, suggests that it may be derived from a lost place in Staffordshire or nearby.

Billings (7935) English: patronymic from BILL.

Billingslea (417) English: variant of BILLINGSLEY.

Billingsley (3969) English: habitational name from a place in Shropshire named Billingsley, from Old English *Billinges-lēah*, probably 'clearing (Old English *lēah*) near a sword-shaped hill' (see BILL).

Billingsly (149) English: variant of BILLINGSLEY.

Billington (1345) English: habitational name from any of three places called Billington, in Lancashire, Staffordshire,

and Bedfordshire. The first of these is first recorded in 1196 as *Billingduna* 'sword-shaped hill' (see BILL); the second is in Domesday Book as *Belintone* 'settlement (Old English *tūn*) of *Billa*'; the one in Bedfordshire is recorded in 1196 as *Billendon*, from an Old English personal name *Billa* + *dūn* 'hill'. The place in Lancashire is the most likely source of the surname.

FOREBEARS John Billington (1580–1630), from Spalding, Lincolnshire, was a passenger on the *Mayflower* in 1620 and an early settler in Plymouth Colony. Governor Bradford called him 'the profanest' of the settlers; eventually he was hanged for murder. His son Francis married and had children.

Billiot (611) Variant of French **Billot**, itself a variant of BILLEAUD.

GIVEN NAMES French 8%. *Antoine* (3), *Emile* (3), *Amelie, Camile, Camille, Cecile, Easton, Jean Marie, Marcelin, Patrice*.

Billips (232) Probably an altered form of English BILLUPS.

Billiter (262) English: occupational name for a bell-founder, Middle English *belleyetere*, from Old English *belle* + *gēotere*. It is unlikely that there would have been enough work to keep anyone employed exclusively in making bells, and there is evidence that bell makers were general founders, engaged for the most part in making smaller domestic items, such as pots and buckles.

Billman (1210) **1.** German (**Billmann**): variant of *Bellmann* see BELLMAN 2, or a name denoting a dweller by the Bille river near Hamburg. **2.** Perhaps a respelling of Swiss German **Bielmann**, a variant of BIEHLER, itself a variant of BUEHLER. **3.** English (East Anglia): possibly an occupational name for someone who made or used billhooks. Compare BILLER.

Billmeyer (200) German: variant of **Billmann** (see BILLMAN 2).

GIVEN NAMES German 6%. *Kurt* (2), *Erwin, Reinhard*.

Billock (126) English: possibly a variant of BULLOCK.

Billotte (133) French: **1.** most probably from French *billot* 'plank', occupational name for someone whose job was to saw wood into planks. **2.** perhaps from a shortened form of the personal name *Robillot*, pet form of ROBERT.

Billow (263) English: probably a variant of BELLOW or BELLEW.

Bills (3289) Origin unidentified. In some cases at least it is a derivative of Dutch *bijl* 'axe'; in other cases it is clearly of English origin.

Billue (104) Probably a variant of English or Irish BELLEW.

Billups (1567) English (South Yorkshire): unexplained.

Billy (568) **1.** French: habitational name from any of various minor places so named, for example in Aisne, Côte d'Or, and Nièvre. The place name is from Romano-Gallic *Billiacum*, from a Gallic personal name *Billios* (Latin *Billius*) + the locative suffix *-acum*. **2.** English: unexplained. Compare BILLEY.

FOREBEARS A man named de Billy, from Paris, is documented in Canada in 1665, and possibly in Quebec city. Documented secondary surnames are Courville, Léveillé, Verrier, Saint Louis.

Bilodeau (1807) French: from a pet form of the personal name BILLEAUD.

FOREBEARS A Bilodeau from the Poitou region of France is recorded in Quebec city in 1654.

GIVEN NAMES French 15%. *Normand* (12), *Armand* (8), *Marcel* (7), *Andre* (4), *Alphonse* (3), *Laurent* (3), *Adrien* (2), *Benoit* (2), *Cecile* (2), *Emile* (2), *Florent* (2), *Gaston* (2).

Bilotta (452) Southern Italian: **1.** from a French personal name, *Bil(l)ot*, which may be a short form of *Robillot*, a pet form of ROBERT. **2.** from Old French *billotte* denoting a ball game using small balls, presumably a nickname for an inveterate player.

GIVEN NAMES Italian 16%. *Amedeo* (2), *Amedio*, *Angelo*, *Carmine*, *Domenic*, *Donato*, *Francesco*, *Giuseppe*, *Luigi*, *Palma*, *Pasquale*, *Santo*.

Bilotti (269) Italian: **1.** variant of BILOTTA. **2.** variant of **Bellotti**, from a diminutive of BELLI or BELLO.

GIVEN NAMES Italian 26%. *Americo* (2), *Carlo* (2), *Mario* (2), *Antonio*, *Armando*, *Dino*, *Gaetano*, *Orlando*, *Roberto*, *Sabino*, *Sal*, *Salvatore*, *Vincenzo*.

Bilow (183) **1.** Jewish (Ashkenazic): patronymic from Ukrainian *bilyj* 'white'. See also BELOFF. **2.** Variant of German *Bülow* (see BUELOW).

GIVEN NAME German 4%. *Kurt*.

Bilski (506) Polish: habitational name for someone from a place called Bilsko, or possibly a variant of BIELSKI.

GIVEN NAMES Polish 5%. *Czeslaw* (2), *Jadwiga*, *Janusz*, *Jerzy*, *Piotr*, *Tadeusz*, *Zygmunt*.

Bilsky (176) Jewish (Ashkenazic): variant of BIELSKI.

Bilson (148) English: variant of BELSON or an altered spelling of **Billson**, a patronymic from BILL 1.

Bilton (251) English: habitational name from places in Northumberland and Yorkshire named Bilton, from an Old English personal name *Billa* + Old English *tūn* 'enclosure', 'settlement'. There is also a Bilton in Warwickshire, of which the first element is probably Old English *beolone* 'henbane', but this place does not seem to have yielded any surviving surnames.

Biltz (230) German: possibly a variant spelling of **Pilz** or **Piltz** (in Saxony, Silesia), from Middle High German *büless* 'mush-

room' (a loanword from Latin *boletus*), hence a nickname or a metonymic occupational name for a gatherer or seller of mushrooms.

Bily (195) Czech (**Bílý**), Slovak (**Biely**), and Ukrainian: nickname for a fair-haired person, from *bílý* 'white'.

Bilyeu (1229) Probably an altered form of French BILLEAUD. Compare BELYEU.

Bilyk (144) Ukrainian: from a derivative of *bilyj* 'white', hence a nickname for someone with white or fair hair or a pale complexion.

GIVEN NAMES Russian 6%; Ukrainian 4%. *Fedor*, *Nikolay*, *Sergey*, *Vasiliy*; *Andrij*, *Taras*.

Bilz (121) German: variant of **Pilz** 'mushroom', (from Latin *boletus*), probably an occupational nickname for a mushroom gatherer.

GIVEN NAME German 4%. *Kurt* (2).

Bina (378) **1.** Muslim: from a derivative of Arabic *bannā'* 'builder'. **2.** Northern Italian: variant of BINI. **3.** Northern Italian: from a short form of *Jacobina* or of any of various other feminine personal names ending in *-bina*. **4.** Czech (**Bína**): from a variant of *Ben*, a short form of the personal name *Benedikt* (see BENEDICT).

GIVEN NAMES Muslim 7%. *Bijan* (2), *Massoud* (2), *Amin*, *Behzad*, *Haroun*, *Hossein*, *Majid*, *Mansour*, *Pari*, *Rashid*, *Saiid*, *Shahab*.

Binda (127) **1.** French: unexplained; possibly of Italian origin (see 2). **2.** Italian: unexplained; possibly a feminized variant of **Bindi**, from the male personal name *Bindo*, a reduced form of *Aldobrandino* which was popular in medieval Tuscany.

GIVEN NAMES French 7%; Italian 5%. *Andre*, *Lucien*; *Aldo*, *Domenic*, *Egidio*, *Guido*, *Reno*.

Bindas (125) Probably a shortened form of Lithuanian **Bindokas** or **Bindokaitis**, derivatives of the personal name *Benediktas* (see BENEDICT).

Bindel (168) German: **1.** possibly from a pet form of the personal name *Bindhart*. **2.** topographic name for someone who lived by a *Beunte*, an area of the land under cultivation in a farming community, typically one that was enclosed and subject to different uses and rules.

Binder (4012) German and Jewish (Ashkenazic): **1.** one of the many occupational names for a cooper or barrel maker, German *(Fass)binder*, an agent derivative of *binden* 'to bind'. Less often the same word was used to denote a bookbinder. The surname is found principally in southern Germany and Switzerland, but also in Denmark and Slovenia. Compare BOETTCHER, BUETT-NER, and SCHAEFFLER. **2.** German: variant of BUNDE 2.

GIVEN NAMES German 4%. *Otto* (6), *Alfons* (3), *Hans* (3), *Kurt* (3), *Alois* (2), *Ernst* (2),

Erwin (2), *Fritz* (2), *Rainer* (2), *Arno*, *Dietrich*, *Florian*.

Bindl (126) South German: variant spelling of BINDEL.

GIVEN NAMES German 4%. *Alois*, *Florian*, *Lorenz*.

Bindner (116) German: variant of BINDER.

Binegar (279) **1.** Possibly an Americanized spelling of German **Beinger**, a habitational name for someone from Biengen, near Staufen in Breisgau, earlier spelled Beingen. **2.** See PINEGAR.

Bines (165) Jewish (Ashkenazic): metronymic from the Yiddish female personal name *Bine* (from Yiddish *bin* 'bee', used as a translation of the Hebrew female personal name *Devora* 'Deborah', the literal meaning of which is 'bee'). *Bine* is often folk-etymologized as being from the Hebrew noun *bina* 'understanding'.

Binette (402) Altered spelling of French **Binet**, a short form of *Robinet*, a pet form of ROBERT. The spelling reflects the French Canadian custom of pronouncing the final *-t*, which would be silent in metropolitan French.

FOREBEARS A bearer of the name Binet from the Poitou region of France appears in the records of Quebec city for 1667; another, from Picardy, was documented in Boucherville, Quebec, in 1670 with the secondary surname Lespérance.

GIVEN NAMES French 20%. *Armand* (5), *Marcel* (4), *Cecile* (3), *Normand* (2), *Raoul* (2), *Alain*, *Alphe*, *Donat*, *Fernand*, *Francois*, *Gedeon*, *Gilles*.

Binetti (159) Italian: **1.** from a diminutive of *Bino* (see BINI). **2.** Italianized form of French **Binet** (see BINETTE). **3.** habitational name from a place called Binetto (named with Latin *vinetum* 'vineyard') in Bari province.

GIVEN NAMES Italian 36%. *Vito* (6), *Pasquale* (3), *Giulio* (2), *Lorenzo* (2), *Marco* (2), *Mario* (2), *Sergio* (2), *Cosmo*, *Damiano*, *Dino*, *Elvio*, *Florindo*, *Mauro*, *Nerina*.

Binford (812) English: habitational name from Binneford in Crediton, Devon, so named with the Old English personal name *Beonna* + Old English *ford* 'ford'.

Bing (1129) **1.** English: of uncertain derivation; probably a topographic name for someone living near a *bing*, a northern dialect word recorded with the senses 'heap', 'bin', 'receptacle' (probably from Old Norse *bingr* 'stall'). **2.** Jewish (western Ashkenazic) and Danish: habitational name from *Bing*, a shortened form of BINGEN. **3.** Danish: metonymic occupational name, from *bing* 'storage bin for grain', for someone who either made or used such containers.

Bingaman (1213) Altered spelling of German **Bingemann**, probably a habitational name for someone from any of the various places called Bingen or Bingum, or a topographic name from *Binge* 'trench', applied also to a kettle-shaped depression or a collapsed shaft in a mine (see BINGEL).

Bingel (158) German: topographic name from a diminutive of Middle High German *binge* 'depression', 'ditch', 'pit', or a Westphalian nickname for a pedantic person, *pingel*.

Bingen (140) **1.** Jewish (western Ashkenazic): habitational name from Bingen in the Rhineland, Germany. **2.** Norwegian: habitational name from a farmstead so named with Old Norse *bingr* 'cow stall', 'field', 'small farm'.

Bingenheimer (175) German: habitational name for someone from Bingenheim on the Eder river.

Binger (608) **1.** German, Danish, and Jewish (Ashkenazic): habitational name for someone from Bingen on the Rhine in Germany. **2.** German: variant of the topographic name BINGEL.

Binggeli (115) Swiss German: unflattering nickname for someone little, a whippersnapper.

GIVEN NAMES German 9%. *Heinz* (2), *Fritz*, *Klaus*.

Bingham (8838) **1.** English: habitational name from a place in Nottinghamshire called Bingham, from an unattested Old English clan name, *Binningas*, or an Old English word *bing* '(a) hollow' + Old English *hām* 'homestead'. The name is also established in Ireland. **2.** Jewish (American): Americanized form of various like-sounding habitational names such as BINGEN-HEIMER.

FOREBEARS The Bingham family of Melcombe Bingham in Dorset can trace their descent back to Robert de Bingham, recorded in 1273, who probably came from Bingham in Nottinghamshire. His descendants included the Earls of Lucan. A branch of the family was established in Ireland, where they gave their name to Binghamstown in County Mayo. Sir Richard Bingham (*c.*1528–99) was Marshal of Ireland. Charles Bingham (1735–99) was created earl of Lucan in 1795.

William Bingham, born in Philadelphia in 1752, was a prominent land speculator and founder of the Bank of North America in 1781. Hiram Bingham, born in Bennington, VT, in 1789, was a missionary to the Sandwich Islands (Hawaii).

Bingle (226) Americanized spelling of BINGEL.

Bingley (157) English: habitational name from Bingley in West Yorkshire, recorded in Domesday Book as *Bingelei*, from the Old English personal name *Bynna* (or alternatively Old English *bing* 'hollow') + *-inga* 'of the people of' + *lēah* 'woodland clearing'.

GIVEN NAME French 4%. *Andre*.

Bingman (502) Probably an Americanized form of German **Bingemann** (see BINGA-MAN).

Bini (118) Italian: from the personal name *Bino*, a short form of any of the various personal names ending in *-bino* (or *-vino*), such as *Iacobino, Albino, Cherubino*.

GIVEN NAMES Italian 19%; French 5%. *Dante* (2), *Mario* (2), *Aldo, Dario, Dino, Elisabetta, Franco, Graziano, Guido, Luciano, Nicolo, Romano*; *Achille, Collette*.

Binion (876) Welsh: variant of BENNION.

Bink (159) **1.** English: topographic name for someone living by a *bink*, a northern dialect term for a flat raised bank of earth or a shelf of flat stone suitable for sitting on. The word is a northern form of modern English *bench*. **2.** Variant of Polish **Binek**, itself a variant of BIENIEK.

Binkerd (117) Origin unidentified.

Binkley (2835) **1.** Altered spelling of the Swiss name **Binckli** or **Bünckli**, probably a pet form of the personal name *Buno*, of unexplained origin. **2.** English: possibly a variant of BINGLEY.

Binkowski (386) **1.** Polish: habitational name for someone from a place called Binkowice, in Tarnobrzeg voivodeship. **2.** variant of BIENKOWSKI.

GIVEN NAMES Polish 5%. *Jerzy* (2), *Casimir, Janusz, Kazimierz*.

Binks (115) English: variant of BINK; this is much the commoner form of the surname in the British Isles.

GIVEN NAME Scottish 5%. *Alastair*.

Binner (242) **1.** English: occupational name for a maker of bins, from a derivative of Old English *binn* 'bin', 'manger'. **2.** Welsh: variant of BONNER. **3.** German: variant of BINDER.

GIVEN NAME German 4%. *Kurt*.

Binney (319) **1.** English (chiefly South Yorkshire): topographic name for someone who lived on land enclosed by a bend in a river, from Old English *binnan ēa* 'within the river', or a habitational name from places in Kent called Binney and Binny, which have this origin. **2.** Scottish: habitational name from Binney or Binniehill near Falkirk, named in Gaelic as *Beinnach*, from *beinn* 'hill' + the locative suffix *-ach*.

Binnie (155) Scottish: variant of BINNEY.

Binning (352) English and Scottish: of uncertain derivation; possibly related to BING.

Binnion (102) Welsh: variant of BENNION.

Binns (1364) **1.** English (Yorkshire): patronymic from the Middle English personal name *Binne*, Old English *Binna* (of uncertain origin). **2.** Altered spelling of German and Swiss BINZ.

Bins (127) Variant spelling of English BINNS.

Binsfeld (151) German: habitational name for someone from any of the various places called Binsfeld, for example near Düren, Karlstadt, and Wittich. The first element of the place name is from Old High German *binuz* 'reed'; the second is *feld* 'open country'.

GIVEN NAMES German 4%. *Benno, Wilhelm*.

Binstock (280) **1.** German: metonymic occupational name for a beekeeper, from Middle High German *bīnstoc* 'beehive'. **2.** Jewish (Ashkenazic): variant of BIENSTOCK.

GIVEN NAMES Jewish 4%. *Hyman, Isadore, Moshe, Rina*.

Bintliff (139) Origin unidentified.

Bintz (210) German: variant of BENZ.

Binz (211) German: variant of BENZ.

GIVEN NAMES German 5%. *Ernst, Klaus, Otto*.

Biondi (866) Italian: patronymic or plural form of BIONDO.

GIVEN NAMES Italian 13%. *Angelo* (6), *Giuseppe* (2), *Riccardo* (2), *Aldo, Amato, Antonio, Attilio, Bruna, Carmelo, Carmine, Dino, Elio*.

Biondo (874) Italian: nickname for someone with fair hair or beard or a light complexion, from *biondo* 'light', 'fair'.

GIVEN NAMES Italian 21%. *Angelo* (10), *Salvatore* (10), *Sal* (7), *Vito* (6), *Carmela* (3), *Gaetano* (2), *Guiseppe* (2), *Mauro* (2), *Santo* (2), *Sebastiano* (2), *Antonino, Arcangelo*.

Biondolillo (193) Southern Italian: **1.** most probably a nickname from Sicilian *biunnuliddu* 'little fair one' (see BIONDO). **2.** possibly also from a personal name composed of the elements BIONDO + LILLO.

GIVEN NAMES Italian 8%. *Sal* (2), *Filippo, Luca, Lucio, Pasquale, Salvatore*.

Bippus (147) Moldavian: unexplained.

GIVEN NAMES German 6%. *Fritz, Hans, Otto*.

Bir (185) Indian (Panjab): Hindu (Khatri) and Sikh name meaning 'brother', 'hero' (from Sanskrit *vīra* 'brave', 'heroic').

GIVEN NAMES Indian 6%. *Ajay, Rajindar*.

Birch (4401) English, German, Danish, and Swedish: topographic name for someone who lived by a birch tree or in a birch wood, from a Germanic word meaning 'birch' (Old English *birce* 'birch', Middle High German *birche*, Old Danish *birk*). In some cases, the German name may be derived from places named with this word, such as Birch in Aargau (see BIRKE). In Swedish, the name is in many instances ornamental.

Birchall (267) English: probably a habitational name from Birchill in Derbyshire or Birchills in Staffordshire, both named in Old English with *birce* 'birch' + *hyll* 'hill'.

Birchard (324) English: from the Old English personal name, *Burgheard* (see BURKETT).

Birchell (106) English: variant of BIR-CHALL.

Birchem (103) Variant of English **Bircham**, habitational name from a place so called in Devon.

Birchenough (110) English: habitational name from a place so called in Greater Manchester.

Bircher (415) **1.** South German, Swiss German: topographic name for someone who

lived by a birch tree or in a birch wood, from Middle High German *birche* 'birch' + the suffix *-er* denoting an inhabitant. **2.** English: habitational name from Birchover in Derbyshire or Bircher in Hereford, both named as from Old English *birce* 'birch' + *ofer* 'ridge'.
GIVEN NAMES German 4%. *Erwin* (2), *Albrecht, Hans, Kurt, Otto, Ulrich.*

Birchett (171) Southern English: variant of BURCHETT.

Birchfield (1220) **1.** English: variant spelling of BURCHFIELD. **2.** Americanized form of German BIRKENFELD, a topographic or habitational name, cognate with 1.

Birchler (236) Swiss German: variant of BIRCHER.
GIVEN NAMES German 4%. *Kurt* (2), *Otmar.*

Birchmeier (203) Swiss German: distinguishing name for a tenant farmer whose farm was by a birch wood, from Middle High German *birche* 'birch' + *meier* '(tenant) farmer' (see MEYER).

Birckhead (207) **1.** English: variant of English BIRKETT. Compare BIRKHEAD, BURKHEAD. **2.** Possibly an altered spelling of German **Birkert**, a variant of BIRKNER.

Bird (12713) **1.** English and Scottish: from Middle English *bird, brid* 'nestling', 'young bird' (Old English *bridd*), applied as a nickname or perhaps occasionally as a metonymic occupational name for a bird catcher. The metathesized form is first found in the Northumbrian dialect of Middle English, but the surname is more common in central and southern England. It may possibly also be derived from Old English *burde* 'maiden', 'girl', applied as a derisory nickname. **2.** Irish: Anglicization of Gaelic **Ó hÉanacháin** or **Ó hÉinigh**, in which the first element (after Ó) has been taken as Gaelic *éan* 'bird' (see HENEGHAN). **3.** Jewish: translation of various Ashkenazic surnames meaning 'bird', as for example VOGEL.

Birden (160) Probably a variant spelling of English BURDEN.

Birdsall (1318) English (Yorkshire): habitational name from Birdsall, near Malton, in North Yorkshire, so named with the genitive case of the Old English byname *Bridd* meaning 'bird' + Old English *halh* 'nook', 'recess'.

Birdsell (507) English: variant of BIRDSALL.

Birdsey (126) English: unexplained; probably a habitational name from a lost or unidentified place. The surname (together with the variant **Birdseye**) was brought to CT from England in the 17th century.

Birdsong (1875) Translation of German VOGELSANG or French **Chandoiseau**, both meaning 'bird song', presumably applied as a nickname.

Birdwell (1665) English: habitational name from a place in South Yorkshire named Birdwell, from Old English *bridd* 'bird' +

wella 'spring', 'stream', or from Bridwell in Devon or Bridewell in Wiltshire, the first element of which may be an Old English word, *brȳd* 'surging'. The surname is now very rare in the British Isles.

Bireley (134) **1.** English: variant spelling of BYERLY. **2.** Americanized spelling of German BEYERLE.

Biren (102) Dutch: probably from the personal name BERNARD.

Birenbaum (241) German and Jewish (Ashkenazic): variant of BIRNBAUM.
GIVEN NAMES Jewish 6%. *Ilya, Isidor, Naum.*

Bires (254) **1.** Northern English and Scottish: probably a variant spelling of BYERS. **2.** Slovak (**Bíreš**): unexplained.

Birge (822) Hungarian: metonymic occupational name for a shepherd, from *birga*, a variant spelling of *birka* 'sheep'.

Birger (119) **1.** Jewish (eastern Ashkenazic): nickname or ornamental name from Yiddish *birger* or German *Bürger* 'citizen'. **2.** Swedish: from a personal name, *Birger* 'one who saves, protects, or helps'.
GIVEN NAMES Jewish 10%; Russian 8%; Scandinavian 5%. *Ari, Irit, Leyb, Revekka, Yakov; Leonid* (3), *Efim, Gennadiy, Igor, Sofya; Anders, Erik, Nils.*

Biringer (100) German, French, or English: variant of BERINGER.

Birk (1214) **1.** Danish, Swedish, and northern English: variant of BIRCH. **2.** German: northern habitational name from any of various places called Birk, Birke, or Birken. **3.** German: southern variant of BUERK. **4.** Slovenian: unexplained.
GIVEN NAMES German 4%. *Udo* (2), *Bernd, Bernhardt, Gerhard, Gerhart, Hans, Hedwig, Karlheinz, Klaus, Kurt, Manfred, Otto.*

Birkbeck (135) **1.** English: habitational name from a minor place in Cumbria named after the river on which it stands. The river name derives from Old Norse *birki* 'birch' + *bekkr* 'stream'. **2.** Americanized form of either Swedish **Björkbäck** or Danish **Birkebæk**, which have the same origin as the English river name.

Birke (145) **1.** North German: variant of BIRK 2. **2.** Perhaps a shortened form of any of various Danish and Norwegian surnames beginning with *Birke-*, for example BIRKELAND and **Birkelund** ('birch grove'). **3.** Swedish: ornamental name from *birk* 'birch'.
GIVEN NAMES Ethiopian 4%. *Lakew, Mesfin, Sisay.*

Birkel (257) **1.** South German: from the personal name *Bürkle*, a pet form of BURKHART. **2.** Probably a variant of the habitational name BERKEL.

Birkeland (385) Norwegian: habitational name from any of some 40 places named Birkeland, from Old Norse *birki* 'birch' + *land* 'land'.

GIVEN NAMES Scandinavian 20%. *Anders* (2), *Toralf* (2), *Bjorn, Erik, Jorgen, Kristoffer, Lars, Nils, Sig, Sigvard.*

Birkenfeld (153) German: habitational name from any of several places in western Germany named Birkenfeld.
GIVEN NAMES German 6%. *Heinz, Wilhelm.*

Birkes (169) English: variant spelling of *Birks*, itself a variant of BIRCH.

Birkett (493) Northern English: topographic name for someone who lived by a grove of birch trees, from Old English *bircet* 'birch copse', a derivative of *birce* 'birch'. There has been some confusion with BURKETT.

Birkey (210) Americanized spelling of Swiss German **Bürki** (see BURKEY).

Birkhead (317) **1.** English: variant of BIRKETT. **2.** Possibly an altered spelling of German **Birkert**, a variant of BIRKNER.

Birkhimer (150) Respelling of German **Birkheimer**, a habitational name for someone from Birkheim in the Hunsrück Mountains.

Birkhofer (108) German: habitational name for someone from any of several places called Birkhof, for instance in Bavaria.
GIVEN NAME German 4%. *Otto.*

Birkholz (670) Altered spelling of German **Berkholz**, a topographic name for someone who lived by a birch wood, from *Birke* 'birch' + *Holz* 'wood', or a habitational name from any of various places named Birkholz.
GIVEN NAMES German 4%. *Armin, Dietrich, Gerhard, Hans, Manfred, Willi.*

Birkland (184) Altered spelling of Norwegian BIRKELAND.
GIVEN NAMES Scandinavian 8%. *Alf, Bergit.*

Birkle (162) German (Württemberg): from the personal name *Bürkle*, a pet form of *Burkhard* (see BURKHART).
GIVEN NAMES German 5%. *Frieda, Fritz, Kurt.*

Birkner (269) German: topographic name, a variant of BIRKE, with the addition of the suffix *-ner* denoting an inhabitant, or a habitational name for someone from any of the various places called Birken or Birk.
GIVEN NAMES German 9%. *Franz* (4), *Armin, Hans, Matthias, Otto.*

Birks (410) Northern English: variant of BIRCH.

Birky (275) **1.** Danish and Norwegian: either a variant of BIRKE or a habitational name from any of numerous places named with forms of Old Norse *bjǫrk* or *birki* 'birch'. **2.** Altered spelling of Swiss German **Bürki** (see BURKEY).

Birman (232) Variant spelling of Dutch and Jewish (Ashkenazic) BIERMAN or an altered spelling of the German cognate BIERMANN.
GIVEN NAMES Jewish 11%; Russian 10%. *Yakov* (2), *Amnon, Anat, Gitla, Irina, Isak, Sol; Igor* (4), *Leonid* (2), *Vladimir* (2), *Betya, Boris, Grigoriy, Lev, Lilya, Oksana, Vyacheslav.*

Birmingham (2258) English: habitational name from Birmingham in the West Midlands. In Domesday Book the name is already found as *Bermingeham*, but it seems likely that it was originally *Beornmundingahām* 'homestead (Old English *hām*) of the people of (*-inga-*) *Beornmund*', a personal name composed of the elements *beorn* 'young man', 'warrior' + *mund* 'protection'. This name is well established in Ireland (see BERMINGHAM).

Birnbach (107) Jewish (Ashkenazic): ornamental name from German *Birn* 'pear' + *Bach* 'stream'.

Birnbaum (1737) **1.** German: topographic name for someone who lived by a pear tree, from Middle High German *bir* 'pear' + *boum* 'tree'. **2.** Jewish (Ashkenazic): from German *Birnbaum* 'pear tree', applied mainly as an ornamental name, possibly occasionally as a topographic name.
GIVEN NAMES Jewish 7%. *Emanuel* (6), *Meyer* (4), *Sol* (4), *Avrohom* (3), *Hyman* (3), *Menashe* (2), *Arie*, *Benzion*, *Chaskel*, *Irina*, *Isadore*, *Mendel*.

Birnberg (123) Jewish (Ashenazic): ornamental name from German *Birn* 'pear' + *Berg* 'mountain'.

Birner (139) German: **1.** habitational name for someone from Pirna in Saxony or Birnau in Württemberg. **2.** occupational name for a coiner or assayer of precious metals, from an agent derivative of Middle High German *birnen* 'to smelt'.
GIVEN NAME German 4%. *Otto*.

Birney (532) **1.** Scottish: habitational name from a place in Morayshire, recorded in the 13th century as *Brennach*, probably from Gaelic *braonach* 'damp place'. **2.** Variant spelling of English or Irish BURNEY.

Birnie (264) Scottish: variant of BIRNEY.

Birns (107) Irish: variant of BURNS.

Biro (569) Hungarian (**Bíró**): occupational name from *bíró* 'judge', 'local administrative leader' (*Szolgabíró*). In some cases the name was given to a relative, assistant, or servant of a judge.
GIVEN NAMES Hungarian 11%. *Bela* (4), *Imre* (3), *Zoltan* (3), *Endre* (2), *Sandor* (2), *Tamas* (2), *Arpad*, *Atila*, *Attila*, *Geza*, *Istvan*, *Janos*.

Biron (695) **1.** French: habitational name from any of the places called Biron, in Charente-Maritime, Dordogne, and Basses Pyrénées. The Latin form of the name is *Biriacum*, from a Gaulish personal name *Birius* + the locative suffix *-acum*. **2.** English: variant spelling of BYRON.
FOREBEARS A Biron is documented at Trois Rivières, Quebec, in 1686.
GIVEN NAMES French 13%. *Normand* (3), *Andre* (2), *Lucien* (2), *Monique* (2), *Amedee*, *Armand*, *Aurelien*, *Benoit*, *Donat*, *Emile*, *Fernard*, *Germaine*.

Biros (211) **1.** Polish: from a dialect form of standard Polish **Bierosz**, a derivative of

brać 'to take'. **2.** Greek: from Albanian *bir* 'son'.

Birr (413) German and French (Alsace): from a short form of the personal name *Pirmin*, the name of an 8th century bishop and founder of several monasteries in southern Germany, or, according to some sources, from the French personal name *Pierre* (see PETER).

Birrell (274) Scottish: variant of BURRELL.

Birrer (104) **1.** French (Alsace): unexplained. Compare BIRR. **2.** Swiss German: unexplained.

Birschbach (181) German: variant of BIERSCHBACH.

Birt (856) **1.** English: variant spelling of BURT. **2.** German: habitational name for someone from any of several places in the Rhineland named Birth or Birten.

Birtcher (103) English: variant spelling of BIRCHER.

Birth (145) German: variant of BIRT 2.
GIVEN NAME German 5%. *Ralf*.

Bisaillon (180) French: possibly a derivative of *bisaille* 'peas and vetch used as hen food', hence presumably an occupational name for a grower or supplier of poultry food.
FOREBEARS A Bisaillon from the Auvergne region of France is recorded in Laprairie, Quebec, in 1685.
GIVEN NAMES French 26%. *Emile* (2), *Alain*, *Antoine*, *Arsene*, *Cecile*, *Celine*, *Fernand*, *Germain*, *Ghislain*, *Gilles*, *Ludger*, *Micheline*.

Bisbee (878) English: variant spelling of BISBY.

Bisbing (150) Variant spelling of German BISPING.

Bisby (121) English (South Yorkshire): habitational name of uncertain origin; probably a variant of BUSBY.

Biscardi (229) Southern Italian: **1.** from a Germanic personal name composed of the elements *wisa* 'wise' + *hard* 'brave', 'hardy'. **2.** (in Calabria and Sicily) from Sicilian *biscardu* 'cunning', 'shrewd', 'astute'.
GIVEN NAMES Italian 20%. *Angelo* (3), *Carmine* (3), *Pasquale* (3), *Salvatore* (2), *Biagio*, *Ciro*, *Franco*, *Giovanni*, *Giuseppe*, *Liberato*.

Bisceglia (325) Italian: habitational name from Bisceglie in Bari (earlier recorded as Bisceglia, Bisceglie).
GIVEN NAMES Italian 14%. *Angelo* (2), *Cosimo* (2), *Domenic* (2), *Matteo* (2), *Vito* (2), *Antonio*, *Chiara*, *Egidio*, *Gaspare*, *Marco*, *Massimo*, *Pasquale*.

Bisch (211) Swiss German: of uncertain origin.

Bischel (198) South German: of uncertain origin.
GIVEN NAMES German 7%. *Helmuth* (2), *Benno*, *Lorenz*.

Bischof (629) German: variant of BISCHOFF.
GIVEN NAMES German 6%. *Ernst* (2), *Gunter* (2), *Aloysius*, *Christoph*, *Guenter*, *Hans*, *Jutta*, *Manfred*, *Markus*, *Mathias*.

Bischoff (2799) German: from Middle High German *bischof*, Middle Low German *bischop* 'bishop', probably applied as a nickname for someone with a pompous manner or as a metonymic occupational name for someone in the service of a bishop. See also BISHOP.
GIVEN NAMES German 5%. *Kurt* (10), *Otto* (5), *Erwin* (4), *Bernhard* (2), *Hans* (2), *Klaus* (2), *Lorenz* (2), *Alois*, *Armin*, *Arno*, *Dieter*, *Fritz*.

Biscoe (250) English: probably a habitational name from Burscough in Lancashire, so named with Old English *burh* 'fortified place' + Old Scandinavian *skógr* 'wood'.

Bise (487) **1.** French and Swiss (French part): metonymic occupational name for a baker, from Old French *bise* 'large round loaf'. **2.** English and Scottish: perhaps a variant of BISS. Compare BEESE, BICE, BUYS, BUYS.

Bisek (219) Polish: possibly from *biesek*, a diminutive of *bies* 'devil', 'Satan'.

Bisel (319) South German: of uncertain origin, possibly a habitational name from a place so named in Alsace.

Biser (338) Swiss German: of uncertain origin.

Bisesi (173) Italian (Sicily): from Arabic, either an occupational name from *bazzāz* 'clothes dealer' or a nickname from *bizāz* 'breasts'.
GIVEN NAMES Italian 11%. *Salvatore* (2), *Carmelo*, *Gabriella*, *Nicolo*.

Bish (1211) **1.** Americanized spelling of German BISCH. **2.** English: variant of BUSH.

Bishara (149) Arabic: from a personal name based on *bishāra* 'good news'. Compare BASHIR.
GIVEN NAMES Arabic 53%. *Hany* (3), *Nabil* (3), *Amin* (2), *Essa* (2), *Fadi* (2), *Fawzy* (2), *Maher* (2), *Abdul*, *Anis*, *Atif*, *Ayad*, *Fouad*.

Bisher (210) Americanized spelling of German **Büscher** (see BUESCHER).

Bishoff (401) Americanized spelling of German BISCHOFF.

Bishop (42290) English: from Middle English *biscop*, Old English *bisc(e)op* 'bishop', which comes via Latin from Greek *episkopos* 'overseer'. The Greek word was adopted early in the Christian era as a title for an overseer of a local community of Christians, and has yielded cognates in every European language: French *évêque*, Italian *vescovo*, Spanish *obispo*, Russian *yepiskop*, German *Bischof*, etc. The English surname has probably absorbed at least some of these continental European cognates. The word came to be applied as a surname for a variety of reasons, among them service in the household of a bishop, supposed resemblance in bearing or appearance to a bishop, and selection as the 'boy bishop' on St. Nicholas's Day.

Bisig (185) Swiss German: possibly a variant of **Biesike**, **Biesecke**, from Sorbian *pesk* 'sand', hence a topographic name or a nickname for a farmer who worked sandy soil.

Bisignano (170) Southern Italian: habitational name from either of two places called Bisignano: one, the more likely source of the surname, in Cosenza province; the other in the province of Ascoli Piceno. The place name is derived from the Latin personal name *Visinius*, with the suffix *-anu*.

GIVEN NAMES Italian 23%. *Alfio, Annamarie, Antonino, Carlo, Carmelo, Concetta, Cosimo, Sal, Salvatore, Santo.*

Bisio (141) Italian: variant of BIGGIO.

GIVEN NAMES Italian 21%. *Mario* (5), *Angelo, Attilio, Cesare, Clemente. Leopoldo, Luigi, Marco, Nino, Palmiro.*

Biskup (276) Polish, Czech, and Slovak: from a word meaning 'bishop', a local form of German *Bischof*, Greek *episkopos* 'overseer' (see BISHOP). This was either an occupational name for someone in the service of a bishop or a nickname for someone thought to resemble a bishop in some way.

GIVEN NAMES Polish 7%. *Bronislawa, Jolanta, Katarzyna, Kazimier, Krystna, Waclaw, Witold.*

Bisnett (146) Probably a variant of Irish BASNETT.

Bisogno (106) Italian: from *bisogno* 'want', 'need', 'lack' (medieval Latin *bisonium*), possibly applied as a nickname for a poor person.

GIVEN NAMES Italian 23%. *Gaetano, Genaro, Marcelo, Mario, Palma, Vito.*

Bisping (152) German: habitational name from Bispingen near Soltau, which is named with a reduced form of *biskoping* 'belonging to the bishop'.

Biss (330) **1.** English and Scottish: from Middle English *bis, biss(e), bice, byse* 'dingy', 'dark', 'gray', 'murky'; 'dark fur used for trimming and lining garments' (Old French *bis(e)*, of Germanic origin), hence a nickname for someone with an unhealthy complexion or someone who habitually dressed in particularly drab garments, or (from the noun) a metonymic occupational name for a furrier or maker of fur-trimmed garments. **2.** South German: nickname for a cutting, sarcastic person, from *Biss* 'bite'.

Bissell (2228) **1.** English: from Middle English *buyscel, busshell, bysshell* 'bushel', 'measure of grain' (Old French *boissel, buissel*, of Gaulish origin), hence a metonymic occupational name for a grain merchant or factor, one who measured grain. The name may also have been applied to a maker of vessels designed to hold or measure out a bushel. **2.** English: from a

diminutive of BISS. **3.** Respelling of German **Biesel**, a habitational name from Bisel in Alsace.

Bissen (199) **1.** German: habitational name from either of the places so named, one near Oldenburg, another in Rhineland. **2.** Danish: altered form of the German surname BISPING.

Bisset (264) **1.** Scottish: variant spelling of BISSETT. **2.** French: from a diminutive of Old French *bisse* 'fine linen', as a metonymic occupational name for weaver of or dealer in fine linen.

Bissett (858) **1.** English and Scottish: from a diminutive of BISS. **2.** French: variant of BISSET.

Bissette (373) Variant of French BISSET. The spelling reflects the French Canadian custom of pronouncing the final *-t*, which is silent in metropolitan French.

Bissey (163) English: nickname from Old English *bysig* 'busy'.

Bissinger (267) Jewish (western Ashkenazic): habitational name for someone from any of five places called Bissingen in Swabia.

Bisso (129) **1.** Italian: metonymic occupational name for a weaver or dealer in linen, from *bisso* 'linen' (from Latin *byssus*). **2.** Possibly an altered spelling of French **Bissot**.

GIVEN NAMES French 4%; Italian 4%. *Angelo, Rocco.*

Bisson (1502) French: **1.** possibly from a diminutive of Old French *bisse* 'fine linen' (see BISSET). **2.** (Normandy) topographic name for someone who lived in an area of scrub land or by a prominent clump of bushes, from Old French *buisson* 'bush', 'scrub' (a diminutive of *bois* 'wood').

FOREBEARS A Bisson from the Maine region of France appears in the records of Quebec city for 1666, with the secondary surname Saint-Côme; another, from Comtat-Venaissin, is documented in Trois Rivières, Quebec, in 1669, with the secondary surname Provençal. Another line, from the Poitou region, is recorded in Quebec city in 1670, with the secondary surname Lépine.

GIVEN NAMES French 13%. *Armand* (9), *Marcel* (4), *Emile* (3), *Gilles* (3), *Jean-Paul* (3), *Rosaire* (3), *Andre* (2), *Laurier* (2), *Normand* (2), *Urbain* (2), *Adelard, Adrien.*

Bissonette (490) French: variant of BISSONNETTE.

GIVEN NAMES French 4%. *Aime, Juliene, Laurier, Normand.*

Bissonnette (926) North American spelling of French **Bissonet**, a topographic name from a diminutive of Old French *buisson* 'bush', 'scrub' (see BISSON).

FOREBEARS A bearer of this name, from the Poitou region of France, was recorded in Quebec city in 1660. La Favry and La Faverie are documented secondary surnames.

GIVEN NAMES French 13%. *Andre* (5), *Marcel* (4), *Armand* (3), *Normand* (3), *Fernand* (2), *Gilles* (2), *Lucien* (2), *Adelard, Adrien, Alain, Camil, Cecile.*

Bistany (123) Origin unidentified.

Bistline (223) Origin unidentified; said to be of German origin, but not satisfactorily explained.

Bistodeau (172) French: unexplained.

Biswas (226) Indian (Bengal) and Bangladeshi: Hindu (Kayasth) name, from Sanskrit *viśvāsa* 'trust'.

GIVEN NAMES Indian 80%. *Dilip* (5), *Kalpana* (3), *Amit* (2), *Amitava* (2), *Arunava* (2), *Arup* (2), *Ashok* (2), *Dipak* (2), *Gopal* (2), *Mrinal* (2), *Rahul* (2), *Sumita* (2).

Biswell (179) English: unexplained. Probably a habitational name from a lost or unidentified place.

Bitar (270) **1.** Arabic (Egypt and Syria): probably from a personal name based on the Arabic root *btr* 'wild' or 'proud'. **2.** Possibly an altered spelling of French **Bitard**, from a noun derivative of Middle French *bite* (from Old Norse *biti* 'tooth'), later 'piece of wood', 'tiller', used as a nickname for a surly man, or possibly an occupational name for a boatman.

GIVEN NAMES Muslim 36%; French 6%. *Kamal* (5), *Ghassan* (4), *Khalil* (4), *Samir* (3), *Ali* (2), *Amer* (2), *Jamal* (2), *Loutfi* (2), *Mohammad* (2), *Samer* (2), *Afif, Badih; Antoine* (2), *Emile* (2), *Camille, Georges, Michel.*

Biter (117) Origin unidentified.

Bithell (115) Welsh: variant of BETHEL.

Bither (214) Probably an altered spelling of German **Beuther**, an occupational name for a beekeeper, from an agent derivative of Middle High German *biute* 'beehive'.

Bitler (389) German: from an agent derivative of Middle High German *bitelen* 'to ask or solicit', hence a nickname or occupational name for a suitor, a bidder, or intermediary; later it became confused with *Bettler* 'beggar' (an agent derivative of *betelen* 'to beg') and the two words were used synonymously.

Bitner (1305) Eastern German and Jewish (Ashkenazic): variant of BUETTNER.

Bitney (165) Americanized form of French **Bétourné**, descriptive epithet for a malformed person.

Bitonti (122) Southern Italian: habitational name for someone from Bitonto, a place near Bari.

GIVEN NAMES Italian 18%. *Biagio* (2), *Antonio, Gino, Luigi, Mario, Rosario, Salvatore, Saverio.*

Bittel (302) German (Württemberg and Swabia): occupational name for a beadle, from Middle High German *bütel* 'bailiff', 'beadle'.

Bittenbender (230) Altered form of German **Bittenbinder**, an occupational name for a cooper, from Middle High German *büte(n)* 'cask', '(wine) barrel' + *binder*

'binder' (agent derivative of *binden* 'to bind'). Compare FASSBENDER.

Bitter (782) **1.** Dutch and German: from Dutch or German *bitter* 'harsh', 'bitter', hence a nickname for a sour, embittered, or severe person. **2.** German: from an agent derivative of Middle High German *bitten* 'to bid', hence a nickname or occupational name for a bidder, broker, the municipal alms collector, or a suitor. Compare BITNER. **3.** Jewish (Ashkenazic): occupational name from 2.

GIVEN NAMES German 4%. *Gerhardt, Hans, Heinrich, Jutta, Volker.*

Bitterman (552) German (**Bittermann**) and Jewish (Ashkenazic): variant of BITTER 2, 3.

GIVEN NAMES German 4%; Jewish 4%. *Erna, Erwin, Eugen, Kuno, Otto; Aron, Mayer, Meyer, Miriam, Shem, Zelman.*

Bitters (225) Dutch: variant of BITTER.

Bittick (297) German: nickname from Slavic *ptak* 'bird'.

Bitting (551) German: possibly a habitational name from any of the places mentioned at PITTINGER.

Bittinger (830) German: **1.** variant of PITTINGER. **2.** possibly an altered form of the habitational name **Büdinger** (see BUDINGER).

Bittle (1103) Respelling of German BITTEL.

Bittman (243) Jewish (Ashkenazic): metonymic occupational name from Yiddish *bit* 'tub', 'vat' + *man* 'man'.

GIVEN NAMES German 5%. *Kurt, Monika, Otto.*

Bittner (3864) German and Jewish (Ashkenazic): variant of BUETTNER.

Bitto (115) **1.** Hungarian: from the old ecclesiastical name *Bitó, Bittó*, altered form of a Slavic derivative of Latin *Vitus*. **2.** Italian: probably from a Germanic personal name formed with *Bid-* or *Wid-*.

GIVEN NAMES Hungarian 9%; Italian 9%. *Attila* (3); *Domenic* (2), *Domenico.*

Bitton (316) **1.** Jewish: unexplained. **2.** English: habitational name from a place in Gloucestershire named Bitton. The place takes its name from the Boyd river, a Celtic river name of uncertain origin + Old English *tūn* 'settlement', 'farmstead'.

GIVEN NAMES Jewish 10%; French 8%. *Meyer* (3), *Yoram* (3), *Aharon, Haim, Ilan, Itsik, Menashe, Miriam, Moshe, Ronen, Tali, Yosef; Michel* (3), *Yvan* (2), *Alain, Armand, Herve, Jacques, Josephe.*

Bitz (496) South German and Swiss German: **1.** probably from a topographic name for someone living near an enclosure, i.e. a fenced plot such as an orchard, from Middle High German *bīzūne* 'enclosure'. **2.** habitational name from a place named with this word, in particular one near Balingen, Württemberg. **3.** Americanized spelling of **Bütz(e)** (see BUTZ 2).

Bitzer (614) German: topographic name for someone living near an enclosure (see

BITZ) or habitational name for someone from a place called Bitz or Bütz(e).

Biven (170) Welsh: variant spelling of BEVAN.

GIVEN NAME Welsh 5%. *Llewellyn* (3).

Bivens (2877) English, of Welsh origin: variant of BIVEN, with English patronymic *-s*.

Biviano (154) Italian (Sicily): from the personal name (now *Viviano*), from Latin *Vivianus* (see VIVIAN).

GIVEN NAMES Italian 17%. *Angelo* (7), *Carmelo, Nunzio, Onofrio, Sal.*

Bivin (185) Welsh: variant of BEVAN.

Bivins (1641) English, of Welsh origin: variant of BIVENS.

Bivona (409) Italian (Sicily): habitational name from either of two places called Bivona, in the provinces of Agrigento and Vibo Valentia.

GIVEN NAMES Italian 9%; French 5%. *Carmela* (2), *Sal* (2), *Salvatore* (2), *Antonio, Baldassare, Gino, Giuseppe, Leonardo, Vincenzo; Michel, Philomene.*

Biwer (152) Possibly an altered form of German **Biewer**, a variant of BIBER.

Bixby (1701) English: habitational name from a lost or unidentified place, probably somewhere in East Anglia, where the name is most frequent.

Bixel (153) Swiss German: variant spelling of BICHSEL.

Bixler (2452) Of German origin: variant spelling of BICKSLER.

Bizier (130) French: unexplained; perhaps an altered form of **Béziers**, a habitational name from Béziers in Hérault.

GIVEN NAMES French 29%. *Marcel* (3), *Gaetan* (2), *Normand* (2), *Alain, Emile, Gaston, Laurier, Leonce, Luc, Michel, Raynald.*

Bizjak (116) **1.** Slovenian (western and central Slovenia): nickname for someone from the western and southwestern edges of the former Slovenian-speaking regions, in particular Monfalcone (Slovenian name *Tržič*) and Gorizia (Slovenian name *Gorica*), two cities in the present-day Italian province of Friuli-Venezia Giulia (annexed to Italy after World War I), or from Istria (now divided between Slovenia and Croatia). **2.** (also Croatian): variant spelling of the nickname *Bezjak*, literally 'man without eggs' (Croatian *bez jaja* 'without eggs'), also found as a nickname for a silly or rude person. In Slovenia this term was used as a nickname for someone from the region between the Sava and Drava rivers; in Croatia it was used for a speaker of the Kajkavian dialect of Croatian, which is close to Slovenian.

Bizon (110) Polish: nickname from *bizon* 'whip', used for a big, ponderous person.

GIVEN NAME Polish 5%. *Thadeus.*

Bizub (135) Polish (mainly southeastern Poland): probably a nickname for a toothless person, from a variant of *bez* 'without' + the dialect word *zub* 'tooth'.

GIVEN NAMES Polish 4%. *Kazimierz, Stanislaw.*

Bizzaro (102) Italian: variant spelling of BIZZARRO.

GIVEN NAMES Italian 8%. *Angelo, Reno, Silvio.*

Bizzarro (120) Italian: nickname from *bizzarro* 'odd', 'eccentric'; earlier, also 'irascible'.

GIVEN NAMES Italian 27%. *Angelo* (4), *Saverio* (2), *Annamarie, Ciro, Francesco, Gennaro, Giovanni, Giuseppe.*

Bizzell (707) English: variant of BISSELL.

Bizzle (130) English: variant of BISSELL.

Bjelland (223) Norwegian: habitational name from any of 24 farms in southwest Norway, named with Old Norse *bær* 'farm', 'farmstead' + *land* 'land'.

GIVEN NAMES Scandinavian 14%. *Erik* (2), *Carsten, Lars, Ove.*

Bjerk (121) Scandinavian: variant of BJERKE.

Bjerke (1012) Scandinavian: ornamental or topographic name from Old Norse *birki* 'birch'.

GIVEN NAMES Scandinavian 6%. *Astrid* (2), *Bjorn* (2), *Helmer* (2), *Egil, Erik, Hakon, Iver, Juel, Ordell, Selmer, Tor.*

Bjorge (231) Norwegian (**Bjørge**): habitational name from *bjarg, berg* 'mountain', 'hill', i.e. 'the farm below the mountain'.

GIVEN NAMES Scandinavian 8%. *Astrid, Monrad, Svein.*

Bjork (1421) Swedish (**Björk**) and Norwegian (**Bjørk**): habitational name from any of the many farms named with a word meaning 'birch' (Old Norse *bjǫrk*). The Swedish name can also be of ornamental origin.

GIVEN NAMES Scandinavian 6%. *Erland* (3), *Erik* (2), *Kerstin* (2), *Lars* (2), *Anders, Fredrik, Jarle, Klas, Lennart, Nils, Olle, Stellan.*

Bjorklund (1154) Swedish (**Björklund**) and Norwegian (**Bjørklund**): habitational name from any of the many farms named with the words *björk* 'birch' + *lund* 'grove'. The Swedish name can also be of ornamental origin.

GIVEN NAMES Scandinavian 8%. *Erik* (4), *Anders* (3), *Ansgar, Bertel, Eskil, Hilmer, Iver, Nils, Per, Swen, Thora, Tor.*

Bjorkman (575) Swedish (**Björkman**): ornamental name from *björk* 'birch' + *man* 'man'.

GIVEN NAMES Scandinavian 9%. *Johan* (2), *Lars* (2), *Astrid, Bjorn, Erik, Knut, Nels, Olle, Per.*

Bjorkquist (109) Swedish (**Björkquist**): ornamental name from *björk* 'birch' + *quist*, an old or ornamental spelling of *kvist* 'twig'.

GIVEN NAMES Scandinavian 11%. *Erik* (3), *Nels.*

Bjorn (188) Danish and Norwegian (**Bjørn**); Swedish (**Björn**): from a personal name and nickname meaning 'bear' (Old Norse bjørn). The Norwegian name is often a shortened form of any of various habitational names from places named with this word, e.g. **Bjørnsplass**. In Swedish it is ornamental in some cases.

GIVEN NAMES Scandinavian 9%. *Erik* (2), *Lars*, *Walfrid*.

Bjornberg (113) Swedish: ornamental name meaning literally 'bear mountain'.

GIVEN NAME German 4%. *Eldred*.

Bjornsen (134) Danish and Norwegian: patronymic from the personal name *Bjørn* (see BJORN).

GIVEN NAMES Scandinavian 14%; German 4%. *Steinar* (2), *Bjorn*, *Knut*; *Fritz*, *Hans*.

Bjornson (580) Respelling of Swedish **Björnsson** or Norwegian **Bjørnsen** 'son of *Björn*' (see BJORN).

GIVEN NAMES Scandinavian 13%. *Bjorn* (4), *Erik* (3), *Sig* (3), *Arni*, *Berger*, *Birgit*, *Lars*, *Ove*, *Selmer*, *Thor*.

Bjornstad (393) Norwegian (**Bjørnstad**): habitational name from a farm named as 'Bjørn's farm' (see BJORN), of which there are many examples, especially in southeastern Norway.

GIVEN NAMES Scandinavian 7%; German 4%. *Bjorn*, *Carsten*, *Erik*, *Fredrik*, *Peer*; *Otto* (3).

Bjur (101) Swedish: from *bjur* 'beaver', probably a shortened form of any of several place names formed with this element.

Bjurstrom (115) Swedish (**Bjurström**): ornamental name or topographic name from *bjur* 'beaver' + *ström* 'river'.

Blaauw (104) Dutch: from the adjective *blauw* 'blue'. Compare German BLAU.

GIVEN NAMES Dutch 8%. *Coen*, *Hannie*, *Hendrik*.

Blach (130) Polish: **1.** possibly a descriptive nickname from the dialect word *blach* 'birthmark'. **2.** alternatively perhaps a metonymic occupational name from Old Polish *blach* 'skeet iron', 'metal fittings'.

GIVEN NAMES Polish 6%; German 5%. *Agnieszka*, *Andrzej*; *Heribert*, *Siegfried*.

Blache (109) French (southeastern): topographic name from French dialect *blache* 'oak plantation' (see BLACHER).

Blacher (132) **1.** Southern French: topographic name for someone who lived by an oak grove, originating in the southeastern French dialect word *blache* 'oak plantation' (said to be of Gaulish origin), originally a plantation of young trees of any kind. **2.** Jewish (eastern Ashkenazic): occupational name for a tinsmith, a Yiddishized form of Polish *blacharz* or Ukrainian *blyakhar*.

Blachly (162) English: variant spelling of BLATCHLEY.

Black (53244) **1.** Scottish and English: from Middle English *blak(e)* 'black' (Old English *blæc*, *blaca*), a nickname given from the earliest times to a swarthy or dark-haired man. **2.** Scottish and English: from Old English *blāc* 'pale', 'fair', i.e. precise-

ly the opposite meaning to 1, and a variant of BLAKE 2. *Blake* and *Black* are found more or less interchangeably in several surnames and place names. **3.** English: variant of BLANC as a Norman name. The pronunciation of the nasalized vowel gave considerable difficulty to English speakers, and its quality was often ignored. **4.** Scottish and Irish: translation of various names from Gaelic *dubh* 'black' (see DUFF). **5.** Danish and Swedish: generally, probably the English and Scottish name, but in some cases perhaps a variant spelling of **Blak**, a nickname from *blak* 'black'. **6.** In some cases, a translation of various names meaning 'black', for example German and Jewish SCHWARZ.

Blackaby (118) English: variant of BLACKERBY.

Blackard (562) **1.** English, Scottish, and northern Irish: of uncertain etymology: perhaps a derivative of the nickname *black heart*, or from *blackguard*, a Tudor term denoting a group of the lowest-class menials in a household. **2.** Perhaps also an altered spelling of German BLACKERT.

Blackbourn (111) English: variant of BLACKBURN.

Blackburn (14213) English: habitational name from any of various places called Blackburn, but especially the one in Lancashire, so named with Old English *blæc* 'dark' + *burna* 'stream'. The surname is mainly found in northern England.

Blacker (630) **1.** English: probably an occupational name for a bleacher of textiles, from Middle English *blāken* 'to bleach or whiten'. Compare BLEACHER. Alternatively, it could be an agent noun from *blæc* 'black', an occupational name for an ink maker. Compare 2. **2.** German (**Bläcker**): probably from Middle Low German *black* 'black ink', hence an occupational name for an ink maker.

Blackerby (436) English: unexplained. Probably a habitational name from a lost or unidentified place.

Blackert (106) German: of uncertain origin. **1.** It may be from an old Germanic personal name. **2.** Alternatively, perhaps, a nickname from a noun derivative of Low German *blackern* 'to laugh foolishly', 'cackle'.

GIVEN NAMES German 5%. *Hartmut*, *Hermann*.

Blacketer (252) Scottish: habitational name from the lands of Blackadder in Berwickshire.

Blackett (263) English: **1.** from a diminutive of BLACK. **2.** nickname for a person with dark hair, or a topographic name for someone who lived by a dark headland, from Middle English *blak(e)* 'black' + *heved* 'head'.

Blackford (1625) English: habitational name from any of various places called Blackford, for example in Somerset, from

Old English *blæc* 'black', 'dark' + *ford* 'ford'.

Blackham (271) English: habitational name from some place so called, presumably deriving its name from Old English *blæc* 'black', 'dark' (or the Old English personal name *Blaca*) + *hām* 'homestead'. Reaney associates the name with Blakenham in Suffolk, but in England the surname is now found mainly in the West Midlands.

Blackhurst (276) English: habitational name from a minor place named Blackhurst, as for example in Cheshire or Lancashire, where the surname is chiefly found. This would be derived from Old English *blæc* 'black', 'dark' + *hyrst* 'wooded hill'.

Blackie (130) Scottish: **1.** from a diminutive of BLACK. **2.** nickname for a person with dark eyes or one who was reputed to have the power of casting the evil eye on someone, from Middle English *blak(e)* 'black', 'dark' + *ie* 'eye'.

Blackiston (132) Scottish or English: variant of BLACKSTONE.

Blackketter (102) Variant of Scottish BLACKETER.

Blackledge (824) English: habitational name from Blacklache near Leyland, Lancashire, named with Old English *blæc* 'black', 'dark' + *læc(e)* 'boggy stream'.

Blackler (127) English (Devon): habitational name from a place in Devon named Blackler, from Old English *blæc* 'black' + *alor* 'alder'.

Blackley (424) Scottish: variant of BLAKELY.

Blacklidge (120) English (Lancashire): variant spelling of BLACKLEDGE.

Blacklock (387) Northern English: nickname for someone with dark hair, Middle English *blakelok*, from Old English *blæc* 'black', 'dark' + *locc* 'lock (of hair)'. Although *blake* might mean either 'dark' or 'fair' (see BLAKE), the meaning 'dark hair' is the most probable since this name contrasts with WHITLOCK.

Blackman (4759) English, Scottish, and Irish: descriptive nickname for someone of swarthy complexion or hair, or else someone with a pale complexion or hair (see BLACK).

Blackmar (145) English: variant of BLACKMER or BLACKMORE.

Blackmer (764) English: topographic name for someone living by a dark lake, from Old English *blæc* 'black', 'dark' + *mere* 'mere', 'lake', or a habitational name for someone from a place named with these words, such as Blakemere in Herefordshire. See also BLACKMORE.

Blackmon (5787) English: variant of BLACKMAN.

Blackmore (1367) English: habitational name from any of various places so named with Old English *blæc* 'black', 'dark' + *mōr* 'moor', 'marsh' or *mere* 'lake'. *Mōr* is the second element of places called Blackmore in Essex, Wiltshire, and Worcestershire, as well as Blackmoor in Dorset; *mere*, on the other hand, is the second element of Blackmore in Hertfordshire and Blackmoor in Hampshire, the early forms of which are *Blachemere, Blakemere*.

Blackmun (103) English: variant of BLACK-MAN.

Blacknall (101) English: probably a habitational name from any of various places called Blakenhall, in particular one in Cheshire, named with Old English *blæc* 'black' (dative *blacan*) + *halh* 'nook', 'hollow'.

Blackner (124) English (Midlands): perhaps a variant of BLACKMER.

Blackney (114) English: variant of BLAKENEY.

Blackshaw (125) English and Scottish: habitational name from any of various minor places in northwest England and Scotland, named with Old English *blæc* 'black' + *sceaga* 'thicket'.

Blackshear (936) Variant of English BLACKSHAW.

Blacksher (198) Variant of English BLACK-SHAW.

Blackshire (272) Variant of English BLACK-SHAW.

Blacksmith (136) English: occupational name for a smith who worked in iron ('black metal'), as opposed to tin ('white metal'). This was never established as a surname in England or Scotland, which suggests that the name may have been adopted in North America as a translation of an occupational name for a blacksmith from some other language (see SMITH).

Blackson (198) English: unexplained.

Blackstock (1078) English and southern Scottish: topographic name from Middle English *blak(e)* 'black', 'dark' + *stok* 'stump', 'stock'.

Blackston (461) English: variant of BLACK-STONE.

Blackstone (1292) English: topographic name for someone who lived by a dark (boundary) stone, from Middle English *blak(e)* 'black', 'dark' (Old English *blæc*) + *stān* 'stone', or a habitational name from a place named with these words, for example Blaxton in South Yorkshire.

Blackwelder (1139) Partly translated form of German **Schwarzwälder**, denoting someone from the Black Forest (German *Schwarzwald*). The first element *Black* is a translation of German *Schwarz* (Old High German *swarz*), while the second element is a respelling of *-wälder* 'forest dweller' (from Old High German *wald* 'forest').

Blackwell (15291) English: habitational name from any of various places, for example in Cumbria, Derbyshire, County Durham, Warwickshire, and Worcestershire, named Blackwell, from Old English *blæc* 'black', 'dark' + *wæll(a), well(a)* 'spring', 'stream'.

Blackwood (2961) Scottish and English: habitational name from any of various places, for example in Dumfries, Strathclyde, and Yorkshire, named Blackwood, from Old English *blæc* 'black', 'dark' + *wudu* 'wood'.

Blad (125) Jewish (eastern Ashkenazic): nickname from Polish *blady* 'pale-faced'.
GIVEN NAME Jewish 4%. *Leiv* (3).

Blade (457) English: metonymic occupational name for a cutler, from Middle English *blade* 'cutting edge', 'sword'.

Bladen (282) English: habitational name from Bladon in Oxfordshire or Blaydon in Tyne and Wear (formerly in County Durham). The first takes its name from a pre-English name (of uncertain origin and meaning) of the Evenlode river; the second is named with Old Norse *blár* 'cold' + Old English *dūn* 'hill'.

Blades (1618) English: **1.** variant of BLADE, from the plural or genitive singular form. **2.** habitational name from a place of uncertain location and origin. Its status as a habitational name is deduced from early forms cited by Reaney, such as Alan de Bladis (Leicestershire 1230), Hugh de Bladis (Staffordshire 1258), and William de Blades (Yorkshire 1301).

Bladow (172) **1.** English: unexplained. **2.** German: possibly a variant of **Platow**.

Blaes (149) Dutch: variant of BLAS.

Blaeser (169) German (**Bläser**): variant of BLASER.
GIVEN NAMES German 4%. *Hans, Kurt*.

Blaesing (156) German (**Bläsing**): patronymic from a derivative of the personal name BLASIUS.

Blagg (830) English and Scottish: variant of BLACK.

Blaha (1323) Czech (**Bláha**) and Slovak: from a short form of the personal names *Blahoslav, Blahomil*, or *Blažej*, all formed with *blaho* 'good'.

Blahnik (383) Czech (**Blahník**): pet form of **Bláha** (see BLAHA).

Blahut (189) Czech and Slovak: see BLAHA.
GIVEN NAME German 4%. *Dieter*.

Blaich (150) German: variant of **Bleich**, a nickname for a person with a pale complexion, from Middle High German *bleich* 'pale', 'whitish'.

Blaikie (140) Scottish: nickname from a pet form of BLAKE.

Blain (1670) **1.** Scottish: Anglicized form of the Gaelic personal name *Bláán*, a diminutive of *blá* 'yellow'. This was the name of an early Celtic saint. **2.** Scottish: shortened form of **MacBlain**. **3.** Scottish and northern English: nickname for a person suffering from boils, from Middle English *blain* 'blister', 'pustule'. **4.** Variant of **Blin**, a reduced form of French BELIN. Possibly also a reduced form of **Abelin**, a pet form of ABEL.
FOREBEARS A Blain or Abelin from the Saintonge region of France is recorded in

Contrecoeur, Quebec, in 1681. Lajeunesse is documented as a secondary surname in 1721.
GIVEN NAMES French 6%. *Donat* (2), *Jacques* (2), *Michel* (2), *Cecile, Elzear, Ermite, Fernand, Gaston, Germain, Gisele, Jean Claude, Jobe*.

Blaine (2356) Scottish: variant of BLAIN.

Blair (27379) Scottish and northern Irish: habitational name from any of the numerous places in Scotland called Blair, named with Scottish Gaelic *blàr* (genitive *blàir*) 'plain', 'field', especially a battlefield (Irish *blár*).

Blais (2332) French: variant of BLAISE.
FOREBEARS Quebec city records for 1666 show a Blais from the Poitou region of France. Another bearer, from the Angoulême region, was documented in Ste. Famille, Quebec, in 1669.
GIVEN NAMES French 17%. *Marcel* (11), *Normand* (11), *Andre* (10), *Emile* (6), *Fernand* (5), *Lucien* (5), *Aime* (4), *Gilles* (4), *Julien* (4), *Michel* (4), *Yvon* (4), *Alphonse* (3).

Blaisdell (1678) English (Cumbria and Lancashire): habitational name from a place in the Lake District named Blaisdell, from the Old Norse byname *Blesi* (from *blesi* 'blaze', 'white spot'), or from the same word used in the sense of a white spot on a hillside, + Old Norse *dalr* 'valley'.

Blaise (483) French and English: from the medieval personal name *Blaise*, a vernacular form of Latin BLASIUS.
FOREBEARS A Blaise from the Orléanais region of France is documented in Montreal in 1685.
GIVEN NAMES French 11%. *Dominique, Edrice, Evens, Guerline, Jean-Claude, Kettly, Marthe, Monique, Murielle, Serge, Yves*.

Blaize (175) Variant spelling of French or English BLAISE.

Blake (24190) **1.** English: variant of BLACK 1, meaning 'swarthy' or 'dark-haired', from a byform of the Old English adjective *blæc, blac* 'black', with change of vowel length. **2.** English: nickname from Old English *blāc* 'wan', 'pale', 'white', 'fair'. In Middle English the two words *blac* and *blāc*, with opposite meanings, fell together as Middle English *blake*. In the absence of independent evidence as to whether the person referred to was dark or fair, it is now impossible to tell which sense was originally meant. **3.** Irish: Anglicized form of Gaelic **Ó Bláthmhaic** 'descendant of *Bláthmhac*', a personal name from *bláth* 'flower', 'blossom', 'fame', 'prosperity' + *mac* 'son'. In some instances, however, the Irish name is derived from Old English *blæc* 'dark', 'swarthy', as in 1 above. Many bearers are descended from Richard Caddell, nicknamed *le blac*, sheriff of Connacht in the early 14th century. The

English name has been Gaelicized **de Bláca**.

Blakeley (1129) English (mainly West Yorkshire and Lancashire): from any of several places so named in Staffordshire, Cheshire, Derbyshire, Cumbria, and elsewhere (see BLAKELY).

Blakely (3809) English, Scottish, and northern Irish: habitational name from any of various places in northern England and the Scottish Borders called Blakeley, named with Old English *blæc* 'black', 'dark' (see BLACK) + *lēah* 'woodland clearing'. The Scottish surname may also have absorbed some cases of **Blakelaw**, from a place in the Borders named with Old English *blæc* 'black' + *hlāw* 'hill'.

Blakeman (1260) English and Scottish: variant of BLACKMAN.

Blakemore (1112) English: variant of BLACKMORE.

Blakeney (1289) English: habitational name from places so named in Gloucestershire and Norfolk or from Blackney Farm in Stoke Abbott, Dorset. The first two are named with Old English *blæc*, dative *blacan* 'black', 'dark' + *ēg* 'island', 'promontory'; the third is from Old English *blæc* + *hæg* 'enclosure'.

Blakenship (109) Variant of English BLANKENSHIP.

Blaker (625) English: variant of BLACKER.

Blakes (192) English: variant of BLAKE.

Blakeslee (1436) English: habitational name from a place in Northamptonshire named Blakesley, from an Old English personal name *Blæcwulf* + *lēah* 'woodland clearing', 'glade'.

Blakesley (457) English: variant of BLAKESLEE.

Blakeway (113) English (West Midlands): habitational name, probably from Blakeway Farm near Much Wenlock, Shropshire. The place name is derived from Old English *blæc* 'black', 'dark' + *weg* 'road', 'path', 'way'.

Blakey (1208) English (Northumberland): variant of BLACKIE.

Blakley (1858) English (northern Ireland): variant of BLAKELY.

Blakney (530) English: variant of BLAKENEY.

Blalack (249) Variant of English BLALOCK.

Blalock (4315) English: variant of BLACKLOCK.

Blamer (113) English: possibly an altered form of northern English **Blamire**, which is of uncertain origin. It may be a habitational name from a place named with the Old Norse elements *blár* 'dark' + *mýrr* 'swamp', 'marsh'. The place Blamires in West Yorkshire takes its name from the surname rather than vice versa.

Blan (193) **1.** English: unexplained. **2.** French: altered form of BLANC.

Blanc (817) **1.** French and Catalan: descriptive nickname for a man with white or fair hair or a pale complexion, from Old French, Catalan *blanc* 'white'. **2.** Jewish (Ashkenazic): ornamental name from German *blank* 'bright', 'shiny'.
GIVEN NAMES French 11%. *Henri* (3), *Andre* (2), *Philippe* (2), *Alain, Berthony, Damien, Elysee, Emile, Fabienne, Fernand, Florent, Francois.*

Blancas (164) Spanish: habitational name from a place in Teruel province named Blancas, from *blanco* 'white'.
GIVEN NAMES Spanish 54%. *Jesus* (5), *Jose* (4), *Armando* (3), *Carlos* (3), *Jaime* (3), *Ruben* (3), *Salvador* (3), *Alfonso* (2), *Arturo* (2), *Guillermo* (2), *Jorge* (2), *Luis* (2).

Blancato (129) Italian: **1.** hypercorrected form of BRANCATO. **2.** variant of **Biancato**, from a Venetian term meaning 'white'.
GIVEN NAMES Italian 18%. *Angelo* (2), *Vincenzo* (2), *Santo, Sebastiano, Vito.*

Blancett (269) Variant of French BLANCHET.
GIVEN NAME French 4%. *Michel* (2).

Blanch (445) English and French: from Old French *blanche* 'fair', 'white', feminine form of *blanc* (see BLANC). The surname may have arisen from a nickname or from a personal name derived from this word.

Blanchard (14319) French and English: from the French medieval personal name **Blancard, Blanchard**, from a Germanic personal name composed of the elements *blank* 'white', 'shining' + *hard* 'strong', 'brave'.
FOREBEARS A bearer of this name from the Saintonge region of France appears in the records of Quebec city in 1665; another, from Brittany, was documented in Quebec city in 1665, with the secondary name Belleville.
Huguenots named Blanchard came to NY from La Rochelle, while the Blanchards of southern LA claim descent from Acadian refugees after the 1755 expulsion. They in turn are reputed to descend from a Guillaume Blanchard, from the Poitou region of France, who is said to have arrived in Acadia before 1640.
GIVEN NAMES French 4%. *Armand* (8), *Pierre* (8), *Andre* (7), *Marcel* (5), *Emile* (4), *Monique* (3), *Camille* (2), *Dominique* (2), *Euclide* (2), *Germaine* (2), *Leonce* (2), *Lucien* (2).

Blanche (354) French: **1.** variant of BLANC, from the feminine form. **2.** from the female personal name *Blanche* meaning 'white'.

Blancher (102) Southern French: occupational name for a tanner, literally 'whitener', from the verb *blancher* 'to make white'.
GIVEN NAME French 4%. *Jean-Marc.*

Blanchet (425) French: from a diminutive of BLANC.

GIVEN NAMES French 19%. *Pierre* (4), *Jacques* (3), *Andre* (2), *Adrien, Alain, Armand, Chantal, Francois, Georges, Laurent, Lucien, Marcel.*

Blanchett (199) Altered spelling of BLANCHET, reflecting the customary French Canadian pronunciation of the final -*t*.
GIVEN NAMES French 6%. *Hilaire, Jacques, Raywood.*

Blanchette (2461) **1.** French: from a diminutive or pet form of BLANCHE. **2.** Canadian respelling of BLANCHET.
GIVEN NAMES French 13%. *Armand* (7), *Normand* (6), *Pierre* (5), *Jacques* (4), *Alcide* (3), *Andre* (3), *Camille* (3), *Girard* (3), *Marcel* (3), *Adrien* (2), *Alphonse* (2), *Cecile* (2).

Blanchfield (339) Irish (of Norman origin): habitational name for someone from Blancheville in Haute Marne, France.

Blanck (519) German: nickname for a man with white or fair hair or a pale complexion, from Middle High German *blanc* 'bright', 'shining', 'white', 'beautiful'.

Blanco (4542) **1.** Spanish: nickname for a man with white or fair hair or a pale complexion, from *blanco* 'white'. **2.** Italian (Sicily): variant of BIANCO, perhaps influenced by French *blanc* and Spanish (see 1 above).
GIVEN NAMES Spanish 47%. *Jose* (141), *Manuel* (61), *Juan* (58), *Carlos* (57), *Jorge* (45), *Luis* (39), *Raul* (33), *Francisco* (30), *Miguel* (30), *Julio* (28), *Pedro* (27), *Jesus* (24).

Bland (8248) **1.** English: habitational name from a place in West Yorkshire called Bland, the origin of which is uncertain. Possibly it is from Old English *(ge)bland* 'storm', 'commotion' (from *blandan* 'to blend or mingle'), with reference to its exposed situation. The modern English adjective *bland* did not come into English (from Latin) until the 15th century, and is therefore unlikely to have given rise to surnames. **2.** French: nickname from Old French *blant* 'flattering' (Latin *blandus*).

Blanda (263) Italian: from a feminine form of BLANDO.
GIVEN NAMES Italian 10%. *Angelo* (2), *Carlo, Carmelo, Filippo, Giorgio, Salvatore.*

Blandford (886) English: habitational name from Blandford Forum and other places called Blandford in Dorset (*Blaneford* in Domesday Book), probably named in Old English with *blǣge* 'gudgeon' (genitive plural *blǣgna*) + *ford* 'ford'.

Blandin (266) French: from a diminutive of BLAND.

Blanding (662) English: variant of BLANTON.

Blandino (231) Italian: from a diminutive of BLANDO.
GIVEN NAMES Spanish 14%; Italian 10%. *Adela* (2), *Enrique* (2), *Jose* (2), *Pedro* (2), *Alejandro, Colomba, Eulalia, Francisco,*

Guillermo, Herberto, Marcos, Mario; Pasquale (2), *Antonio, Carmelo, Giovanni, Giuseppa, Rocco, Sal, Salvatore, Silvio.*

Blando (206) Italian and Spanish: nickname from *blando* 'flattering', 'caressing', 'smooth', 'gentle', 'mild' (Latin *blandus*).
GIVEN NAMES Italian 13%; Spanish 9%; Polish 4%. *Salvatore* (2), *Amadeo, Angelo, Ceasar, Gino, Petrina, Vincenzo, Vito; Domingo, Eduardo, Ernesto, Jesus, Joaquin, Luis, Manuel, Marcela, Margarita, Mercedes; Krzysztof, Lech.*

Blandon (236) Spanish (**Blandón**): Andalusian (Huelva, Sevilla), from *blandón* 'wax torch'.
GIVEN NAMES Spanish 50%. *Jose* (9), *Carlos* (6), *Luis* (4), *Luz* (4), *Juan* (3), *Eduardo* (2), *Jorge* (2), *Mauricio* (2), *Ramon* (2), *Rodolfo* (2), *Sergio* (2), *Adela.*

Blane (269) Variant spelling of Scottish BLAIN.

Blaney (1438) Irish (of Welsh origin): topographic name from Welsh *blaenau*, plural of *blaen* 'point', 'tip', 'end', i.e. uplands, or remote region, or upper reaches of a river.
FOREBEARS The first recorded bearer of this name is a certain Ieuan Blaenau, who appears as Evan Blayney in a list of burgesses of Welshpool in 1406. Edward Blayney went to Ireland with the Earl of Essex in 1598; he was knighted in 1603 and elevated to the peerage of Ireland as Lord Blayney, Baron of Monaghan. The name was brought to North America in the 18th century from Ireland rather than Wales. The Welsh line died out in 1795 with Arthur Blayney of Gregynog, Montgomeryshire.

Blanford (565) English: variant of BLANDFORD.

Blank (5410) **1.** Dutch and German: nickname for a man with white or fair hair or a pale complexion, from Middle Low, Middle High German *blanc* 'bright', 'shining', 'white', 'beautiful', Middle Dutch *blank* 'fair', 'white'. **2.** Variant spelling of the English and Jewish (Ashkenazic) cognate BLANC or the German cognate BLANCK.

Blanke (523) German and Dutch: variant of BLANK.

Blanken (284) Dutch: patronymic from BLANK.

Blankenbaker (320) Americanized spelling of German **Blankenbacher**, a habitational name for someone from either of two places called Blankenbach, in Thuringia or Hesse.

Blankenbeckler (155) German: variant of **Blankenbacher** (see BLANKENBAKER).

Blankenberg (105) Dutch and Belgian (**van Blankenberg**): habitational name from any of various places so called, in particular in Hennef and Gelderland, or from Blankenberge in West Flanders, Belgium.

Blankenbiller (105) Dutch: habitational name from a place called Blankenbijl or similar.

Blankenburg (285) **1.** German: habitational name from any of several places called Blankenburg, in Brandenburg, the Harz Mountains, and Thuringia. **2.** Perhpas also an altered spelling of Dutch BLANKENBERG.
GIVEN NAMES German 8%. *Kurt* (2), *Heinz, Rainer.*

Blankenheim (135) German: habitational name for someone from any of several places named Blankenheim, for example near Fulda, Hesse, and in Thuringia.

Blankenhorn (184) German: habitational name from a place called Blankenhorn, for example a castle near Brackenheim in Württemberg.
GIVEN NAMES German 6%. *Kurt, Otto.*

Blankenship (14884) Northern English: variant of the English surname **Blenkinsop**, a habitational name from a place called Blenkinsopp in Northumberland.
FOREBEARS This name was brought to America in about 1686 by Ralph Blankinship (1662–1714), who probably came from Cumberland, England.

Blankinship (542) English: variant of BLANKENSHIP.

Blankley (188) English: habitational name from a place in Lincolnshire named Blankney, from an Old English personal name *Blanca* + *ēg* 'island'.

Blankman (172) Jewish (Ashkenazic): variant of BLANC.

Blanks (1704) English: patronymic from BLANK.

Blann (280) Southern English: unexplained. Compare BLAN.

Blansett (389) Probably an altered spelling of French BLANCHETTE.

Blanshan (103) Americanized form of French **Blanchon**, a diminutive of BLANC.

Blansit (115) Americanized form of French BLANCHET.

Blanton (8572) English: unexplained; perhaps a habitational name from a lost or unidentified place. It has been suggested that it might be an altered form of Scottish BALLANTINE, but the distribution and variants (including BLANDING) make it more probable that it is an altered form of a French original.

Blas (406) **1.** Spanish and Dutch: from the medieval personal name *Blas*, a derivative of BLASIUS. **2.** Jewish (Ashkenazic): nickname for a pale person, from Yiddish *blas* or modern German *blass* 'pale'.
GIVEN NAMES Spanish 33%. *Manuel* (4), *Rogelio* (4), *Alicia* (3), *Francisco* (3), *Guadalupe* (3), *Jose* (3), *Pedro* (3), *Alejandro* (2), *Angel* (2), *Jesus* (2), *Juan* (2), *Lourdes* (2).

Blasberg (131) Jewish (Ashkenazic): ornamental compound of Yiddish *blas* or German *blass* 'pale' + *berg* 'hill', 'mountain'.
GIVEN NAME French 5%. *Serge.*

Blaschke (430) German (of Slavic origin): from a vernacular pet form of the personal name BLASIUS.
GIVEN NAMES German 4%. *Hans* (3), *Erwin* (2), *Otto.*

Blaschko (108) German (of Slavic origin): from a vernacular pet form of the personal name BLASIUS.

Blasco (350) Spanish: variant of BELASCO.
GIVEN NAMES Spanish 11%. *Eduardo* (2), *Alberto, Alfredo, Armando, Carmelita, Consuelo, Edgardo, Enrique, Estela, Estelita, Francisco, Gonzalo.*

Blasdel (214) English: variant of BLAISDELL.

Blasdell (180) English: variant of BLAISDELL.

Blase (615) North German: derivative of BLASIUS.
GIVEN NAMES German 4%. *Kurt* (2), *Horst, Jutta, Otto.*

Blaser (1167) **1.** German, Swiss German (also **Bläser**), and Jewish (Ashkenazic): from Middle High German *blāsaere* 'blower', German *Bläser*, hence an occupational name for a musician who played a wind instrument. **2.** Jewish (Ashkenazic): variant of BLAS.
GIVEN NAMES German 4%. *Fritz* (2), *Kurt* (2), *Wolf* (2), *Ernst, Franz, Frieda, Gerhard, Hermann, Joerg, Otto, Urs.*

Blash (154) Altered spelling of German **Blasch(e)**, probably a pet form of BLASIUS. Compare BLASCHKE.

Blasi (700) **1.** Italian, Catalan, and southern French: from a medieval personal name, from Latin BLASIUS. **2.** Swiss German (**Bläsi**): from a pet form of BLASIUS.
GIVEN NAMES Italian 11%. *Rocco* (8), *Aldo* (2), *Libero* (2), *Luigi* (2), *Pasquale* (2), *Salvatore* (2), *Vito* (2), *Angelo, Carmel, Enrico, Reno, Saverio.*

Blasier (105) French (Alsace): French form of German BLASER.
GIVEN NAME German 5%. *Kurt* (2).

Blasing (191) German: variant of BLAESING.

Blasingame (808) English: variant of **Bletchingdon**, habitational name from a place so called in Oxfordshire, named with the Old English personal name *Blecci* + *-ing-*, implying association, + *don* 'hill'.

Blasius (295) German, Dutch, and Scandinavian: from the Latin personal name *Blasius*. This was a Roman family name, originating as a byname for someone with some defect, either of speech or gait, from Latin *blaesus* 'stammering' (compare Greek *blaisos* 'bow-legged'). It was borne by a Christian saint martyred in Armenia in 316, whose cult achieved wide popularity, in particular as the patron saint of carders by virtue of the fact that he was 'carded' to death, i.e. his flesh was scraped off in small pieces with metal combs.

Blaske (164) **1.** Sorbian: from a pet form of the Latin personal name BLASIUS.

2. Germanized form of the Slavic name *Blažek* (see BLAZEK).

GIVEN NAMES German 9%. *Frieda* (2), *Fritz* (2), *Bernd*.

Blaski (102) Polish: nickname from the dialect word *blaski* 'gray', 'pale blue'.

GIVEN NAME Polish 5%. *Zigmund*.

Blasko (693) Croatian, Slovenian, and Slovak (all **Blaško**): derivative of the personal name *Blaž*, Slovak *Blažej*, local pet forms of Latin BLASIUS, with the diminutive suffix *-ko*.

Blaskovich (111) Croatian (**Blašković**): patronymic from the personal name *Blaško*, a pet form of *Blaž*, Latin BLASIUS, formed with the diminutive suffix *-ko*.

Blaskowski (143) Germanized or Americanized spelling of Polish **Błaszkowski** or **Błazkowski**, habitational names for someone from a place called Błaszków or Błaszkóv.

GIVEN NAMES French 4%; German 4%. *Florien*; *Kurt*.

Blass (628) **1.** German: nickname for a bald-headed man or alternatively for a weak person, from Middle High German *blas* 'bare', 'pale', 'weak', 'insignificant'. **2.** North German: from the personal name *Blass*, a vernacular form of BLASIUS. **3.** Jewish (Ashkenazic): variant of BLAS.

Blassingame (415) English: variant of BLASINGAME.

Blaszak (223) Polish (**Błaszak**): patronymic from *Błasz*, a short form of the personal name *Błażej*, a vernacular form of BLASIUS.

GIVEN NAMES Polish 5%. *Lech* (2), *Casimir*.

Blaszczak (99) Polish (**Błaszczak**): patronymic from *Błaszek*, a pet form of the personal name *Błażej*, a vernacular form of BLASIUS.

GIVEN NAMES Polish 10%. *Gerzy*, *Jerzy*, *Wojciech*.

Blaszczyk (206) Polish (**Błaszczyk**): from a pet form of the Polish personal name *Błażej*, a vernacular form of BLASIUS.

GIVEN NAMES Polish 16%. *Ireneusz*, *Iwona*, *Jerzy*, *Jozefa*, *Krzysztof*, *Mieczyslaw*, *Miroslaw*, *Wieslaw*, *Wlodzimierz*, *Zofia*, *Zosia*.

Blaszkiewicz (68) Polish (**Błaszkiewicz**): patronymic from *Blaszek*, a pet form of the personal name *Błażej*, a vernacular form of BLASIUS.

GIVEN NAMES Polish 11%; Czech and Slovak 5%. *Casimir*, *Ryszard*.

Blatchford (420) English (chiefly Devon): habitational name from Blatchford in Sourton, Devon, which is probably named with the Old English personal name *Blæcca* + Old English *ford* 'ford'.

Blatchley (211) English: variant of the habitational name **Bletchley**, from places so named in Buckinghamshire and Shropshire. The first is named from the Old English personal name *Blæcca* + *lēah* 'woodland clearing'; the second has the

same second element combined with a personal name *Blæcca* or *Blecci*.

Blatnick (103) Altered form (under German, French, or English influence) of BLATNIK.

GIVEN NAME French 4%. *Ignace*.

Blatnik (219) **1.** Czech (**Blatník**): topographic name from *blata* 'moorland' (from *bláto* 'mud'). **2.** Slovenian: topographic name for a person from a muddy or miry place or a swamp, from *blato* 'mud', 'mire', or from Slovenian dialect *blata* 'swamp'. **3.** Slovenian: habitational name for someone from any of several Slovenian villages called Blato or Blate. **4.** Slovenian: possibly also a nickname or topographic name from *blatnik* 'pond lily' (*Nuphar luteum*).

Blatt (1669) **1.** German and Jewish (Ashkenazic): from German *Blatt*, Yiddish *blat* 'leaf'. As a Jewish name this is normally a shortened form of a compound name with *Blatt* as a second element, adopted as ornamental surnames in the 18th and 19th centuries. **2.** German: topographic name from Middle High German *blate* 'flat surface', 'ledge', 'plateau', hence a topographic name for someone who lived at a farm on a ledge on a mountainside.

GIVEN NAMES Jewish 4%. *Sol* (5), *Aron*, *Benyamin*, *Etan*, *Hanoch*, *Mendel*, *Meyer*, *Mort*, *Pinchos*, *Tova*.

Blattel (113) South German (**Blättel**): probably a topographic name for someone who lived at a farm on a ledge, from Middle High German *plate*, *blate* 'flat surface', 'plateau'.

Blattenberger (103) German: habitational name for someone from a place called Blattenberg.

Blatter (311) South German and Swiss German: **1.** topographic name for someone who lived on a plateau, from Middle High German *plate*, *blate* 'flat surface', 'plateau' + the suffix *-er* denoting an inhabitant. **2.** habitational name for someone from Blatten near St. Gallen, Switzerland. The place name refers to a promontory of the Alps, a wide elevated plateau.

GIVEN NAMES German 6%. *Hans* (2), *Ernst*, *Erwin*, *Ewald*, *Fritz*, *Lothar*.

Blattner (606) South German and Swiss German: occupational name for an armorer, Middle High German *blatenaere*, a derivative of *blate* 'armor', 'plate'.

Blatz (446) South German: **1.** habitational name from any of various farms so named, from Middle High German *plaz*, *blaz* 'place'. Compare PLATZ. **2.** metonymic occupational name for a baker, from *Blatz*, a type of flat loaf.

Blau (1382) **1.** German: from Middle High German *blā* 'blue' (Old High German *blāo*), applied as a nickname with various senses: someone who habitually wore blue clothes, a dyer, someone with blue eyes, a sickly or pale person, someone with a

bluish complexion resulting from poor circulation, etc. **2.** Jewish (Ashkenazic): ornamental name, one of the many such Ashkenazic surnames taken from names of colors. **3.** Catalan: from *blau* 'blue'.

GIVEN NAMES Jewish 5%; German 4%. *Arnon* (2), *Binyamin* (2), *Shulem* (2), *Zalmen* (2), *Akiva*, *Chaim*, *Dov*, *Emanuel*, *Gavriel*, *Hersch*, *Hyman*, *Isador*; *Kurt* (3), *Eugen* (2), *Gerda* (2), *Otto* (2), *Alfons*, *Ernst*, *Inge*, *Siegfried*.

Blauch (163) Swiss German: perhaps a variant of BLECH.

Blauer (176) South German and Jewish (Ashkenazic): variant of BLAUERT 'dyer', or an inflected form of the adjective BLAU.

Blauert (108) German: occupational name for a dyer, from *Blau* 'blue' (see BLAU).

GIVEN NAME German 4%. *Otto*.

Blaufuss (143) German: metonymic occupational name for a falconer, from *Blaufuss* (literally 'blue foot'), a species of falcon.

GIVEN NAMES German 14%. *Armin* (2), *Otto* (2), *Kurt*.

Blaum (173) Possibly an altered spelling of German BLOHM.

Blauser (291) German (Swabia): variant of BLOSSER.

Blausey (104) Americanized form of a German family name, probably **Blauser** (see BLOSSER).

Blaustein (424) Swedish and Jewish (Ashkenazic): ornamental name from German *blau* 'blue' + *Stein* 'stone', i.e. lapis lazuli.

GIVEN NAMES Jewish 7%. *Miriam* (2), *Hyman*, *Zeev*.

Blauvelt (842) Dutch: topographic name for someone living in a place known as 'the blue pastureland'.

Blaxton (133) English: variant spelling of BLACKSTONE.

Blay (304) **1.** English: variant of BLISS 2. **2.** Catalan: variant of BLASI.

Blaydes (213) English: variant spelling of BLADES.

Blaylock (3282) English (Cumbria): perhaps a variant of BLACKLOCK.

Blayney (200) Irish: variant spelling of BLANEY.

Blaze (239) English: variant spelling of BLAISE.

Blazejewski (164) Polish (**Błażejewski**): habitational name for someone from Błażejewo, Błażejewice, Błażejewko, or another place named with *Błażej*, a vernacular form of the personal name BLASIUS.

Blazek (1177) **1.** Polish (**Błażek**): from a pet form of the personal name *Błażej*, a vernacular form of BLASIUS. **2.** Czech and Slovak (**Blažek**): from a pet form of the personal name *Blažej*, Czech and Slovak form of BLASIUS, or a pet form of an Old Czech personal name formed with *Blaži-*, such as *Blažislav* or *Blažibor*. **3.** Croatian (northwestern Croatia) and Slovenian (western and eastern Slovenia) (all

Blažek): from a pet form of the personal name *Blaž*, Latin Blasius.

Blazer (1010) **1.** Dutch: from Middle Dutch *blaser* 'blower', hence an occupational name for a player of the trumpet or other wind instrument, or a nickname for a braggart or boaster. **2.** Americanized spelling of German **Bläser** (see Blaser).

Blazevich (123) Croatian (**Blažević**): patronymic from the personal name *Blaž*, Latin Blasius.

Blazey (109) English (Norfolk): probably from a personal name, a pet form of Blaise (see Blasius).

Blazier (371) English: unexplained. Possibly an altered form of Brazier.

Blazina (188) **1.** Czech (**Blažina**): from a pet form of the personal name *Blažej* (see Blazek). **2.** Slovenian and Croatian (also **Blažina**): from the personal name *Blaž* + the augmentative suffix -*ina*. As a Croatian surname this originates mainly from Labin in Istria.

GIVEN NAME French 4%. *Gabrielle.*

Blazo (103) Probably an Americanized form of a name of Slavic origin such as Blazevich.

Blea (324) **1.** English (Midlands): unexplained; perhaps a variant of Bligh. Compare Blee. **2.** Hispanic (Mexico): unexplained; perhaps a variant of Galician Brea.

GIVEN NAMES Spanish 20%. *Manuel* (8), *Carlos* (3), *Jose* (3), *Julio* (2), *Adolfo, Adolpho, Amado, Armando, Benito, Claudio, Concha, Enrique.*

Bleacher (124) Probably an Americanized form of German Bleicher or Dutch Bleecker, although it could also be a palatalized variant of English Blacker. All three names denote someone whose job was to bleach cloth.

Bleak (131) English: possibly from *bleak* 'pale' (first attested in the 16th century, but probably a much older word, derived from Old Norse *bleikr*, a cognate of Old English *blāc*). The name *John Bleke* is recorded at Haddenham, near Ely, in 1585. However, the Low German or Dutch name **Bleeke** was introduced to England by a waterman recorded at Gravesend, Kent, in 1653, and this may account for some if not all examples of the name.

Bleakley (413) English (northern Ireland): variant of Blakely.

Bleakney (184) English (northern Ireland): probably a variant of Blakeney.

Bleam (175) Americanized spelling of German **Blüm**, a variant of Blum 1.

Blease (131) English (Cheshire and Lancashire): probably a variant of Blaise.

Bleau (431) French: reduced form of Belleau.

FOREBEARS A bearer of this name from Normandy, France, is documented in Montreal in 1672.

GIVEN NAMES French 6%. *Alphonse, Amede, Gilles, Girard, Normand.*

Bleazard (107) **1.** Perhaps a variant of English Blizzard. **2.** Alternatively, perhaps an altered form of Dutch Blazer.

GIVEN NAMES Dutch 4%. *Dirk, Marlous.*

Blech (141) German and Jewish (Ashkenazic): generally a metonymic occupational name from Middle High German *blech* 'sheet metal'; German *Blech* 'tin' or Yiddish *blekh*, denoting a worker in tin or some other metal.

GIVEN NAMES Jewish 11%; German 5%. *Ari, Benzion, Ilan, Morry, Moshe, Nukhim; Erwin, Reinhold.*

Blecha (419) German: nickname for someone small, from Czech *blecha* 'flea', 'little guy'.

Blecher (268) German and Jewish (Ashkenazic): occupational name for a worker in tin (see Blech).

Blechinger (111) German: occupational name for a worker in tin, a derivative of *blech* 'tin' (see Blech).

GIVEN NAME German 6%. *Otto.*

Blechman (241) German and Jewish (Ashkenazic): occupational name for a worker in tin (see Blech).

GIVEN NAMES Jewish 5%. *Izaak, Moshe, Sol.*

Bleck (327) **1.** North German: from a field name or any of various other locations so named. **2.** Jewish (Ashkenazic): North American variant of Bleich.

GIVEN NAMES German 5%. *Rainer* (2), *Helmuth, Otto.*

Blecker (175) **1.** Dutch and North German: variant of Bleecker. **2.** South German: from an agent derivative of Middle High German *blecken* 'to show off', 'to show one's teeth', hence a nickname for a boastful person.

Bleckley (123) English: variant of Blakely.

Bledsoe (6130) English: habitational name from a place in Gloucestershire named Bledisloe, from the Old English personal name *Blīð* (a byname meaning 'cheerful') + Old English *hlāw* 'mound', 'tumulus'.

Blee (141) Northern Irish: variant of Bligh 2.

Bleecker (306) Dutch: occupational name for a bleacher of textiles, a launderer, or the owner of a public bleaching ground.

FOREBEARS Jan Jansen Bleecker and his wife came to New Netherland in 1658 and settled in Beverwijck (subsequently renamed Albany, NY). They had 10 children, two of whom (Johannes and Rutger) went on to become mayors of Albany.

Bleeker (381) Dutch: occupational name for a bleacher of textiles, Middle Dutch *ble(e)kere*.

Blees (108) Dutch: from the personal name *Blass*, a vernacular form of Blasius.

GIVEN NAMES German 9%; Dutch 6%. *Johann* (2), *Fritz; Willem* (2), *Gerrit.*

Blegen (234) Norwegian: habitational name from any of various farms, especially in southeastern Norway, named Bleiken, from *bleik* 'pale', 'light-colored' + -*en* from *vin* 'meadow'.

Blehm (297) German: unexplained.

GIVEN NAMES German 5%. *Erna, Frieda, Otto.*

Bleiberg (114) **1.** Dutch: habitational name from a place so named in Luxembourg province, Belgium. **2.** Jewish (Ashkenazic): ornamental name compound from German *Blei* 'lead' + *Berg* 'hill'.

GIVEN NAMES Jewish 5%; German 5%. *Isadore; Manfred, Oskar.*

Bleich (463) German and Jewish (Ashkenazic): nickname from German *bleich* 'pale'.

GIVEN NAMES German 6%. *Horst* (2), *Otto* (2), *Erwin, Hermann, Kurt.*

Bleicher (208) German and Jewish (Ashkenazic): occupational name for a bleacher of textiles, a launderer, or the owner of public bleaching ground, from Middle High German *blīcher*, German *Bleicher*. Compare Bleecker.

GIVEN NAMES German 6%. *Fritz, Hans, Johann, Markus.*

Bleichner (122) German: variant of Bleicher.

Bleier (467) German and Jewish (Ashkenazic): occupational name for a lead miner or lead worker, from a derivative of Middle High German *blī* 'lead'. Compare Bley.

GIVEN NAMES Jewish 4%. *Chaim, Emanuel, Morty, Shlomie, Sol, Zvi.*

Bleigh (111) Irish: variant spelling of Bligh.

Bleil (173) German: metonymic occupational name for anyone whose work involved the use of an instrument for pounding, crushing, or beating, from German *Bleil(e)* 'pestle', 'beater'.

GIVEN NAMES German 4%. *Klaus, Kurt.*

Bleile (154) German: variant of Bleil.

Bleiler (278) German: occupational name for someone whose work involved the use of an instrument for pounding, crushing, or beating, from Bleil + the agent suffix -*er*.

GIVEN NAME German 4%. *Franz* (2).

Bleiweiss (121) German and Jewish (Ashkenazic): metonymic occupational name for a producer of white lead (used as a pigment), from Middle High German *blīwīss*, German *Bleiweiss* 'white lead'.

GIVEN NAMES Jewish 8%; German 4%. *Sol* (2), *Avi; Erwin.*

Blend (145) **1.** Possibly English, an infrequent surname of uncertain origin; perhaps a variant of Bland. **2.** German: unexplained.

Blender (124) **1.** German: habitational name from a place so named near Verden an der Weser. **2.** South German: from an agent derivative of Middle High German *blenden* 'to darken', hence an occupational name for a dyer of silk, or for a painter, plasterer, or someone who erected shingle siding.

Blenker (100) German (Lower Rhine): topographic name for someone living in a treeless area (very unusual in the Middle Ages), from Middle High German *blank* 'shining', 'treeless' + *-er* denoting an inhabitant.

GIVEN NAMES German 6%. *Florian, Gerhard.*

Bleser (166) Dutch: variant of BLAZER.

Blesi (161) Swiss German: from a pet form of the personal name BLASIUS.

Bless (255) Swiss German: variant of BLASIUS.

Blessing (1981) **1.** German: patronymic from a variant of the personal name BLASIUS. **2.** German: probably a habitational name from a place called Blessing or Bläsing. **3.** English or Irish: unexplained.

Blessinger (229) German: habitational name for someone from a place called Blessing or Bläsing.

GIVEN NAMES German 4%. *Kurt, Othmar.*

Blessington (170) English (now most common in northern Ireland): probably a habitational name from a lost or unidentified place, most likely somewhere in Lancashire or Yorkshire.

Blessman (114) German (**Blessmann**): unexplained.

GIVEN NAME German 5%. *Uwe* (2).

Bleth (105) Origin unidentified.

Blethen (258) Welsh: Anglicized form of Welsh *ap Ble(i)ddyn* 'son of *Ble(i)ddyn*', a byname meaning 'wolf cub', from *blaidd* 'wolf' + the diminutive suffix *-yn*. *Blaidd* was used in medieval Welsh as a term for a hero, and sometimes for a cruel man or for an enemy who feigned friendship.

Blevens (250) English, of Welsh origin: variant of BLEVINS.

Blevins (12296) English, of Welsh origin: Anglicized form of Welsh *ap Ble(i)ddyn* (see BLETHEN), with the addition of the English patronymic suffix *-s*.

Blew (318) Jewish (Ashkenazic): variant of BLUE.

Blewett (558) English: from Middle English *bluet* 'blue woolen cloth' or *bleuet* 'cornflower', perhaps applied as a nickname for a habitual wearer of blue clothes or for someone with blue eyes. Both terms are from Old French *bleuet*, a diminutive of *bleu* 'blue', a word of Germanic origin (see BLAU).

Blewitt (238) English: variant spelling of BLEWETT.

Bley (602) **1.** German: metonymic occupational name for a lead miner or lead worker, from Middle High German *blī* 'lead'. **2.** Jewish (eastern Ashkenazic): variant of German **Blei** (Yiddish *blaj*), due to replacement of the *-ei* or *-aj* with Russian *-ej*.

GIVEN NAMES German 4%. *Hans* (2), *Eckhard, Ernst, Fritz, Joerg, Volker.*

Bleyer (140) German (also found in Sweden): occupational name for a lead miner (see BLEY).

GIVEN NAME Scandinavian 4%. *Knute.*

Blick (527) **1.** English: unexplained; possibly from Middle English *bleik, blek(e)* 'pallid', 'sallow' (from Old Norse *bleikr* 'pale') with alteration of the vowel, although Reaney suggests it may be a nickname derived from Middle English *blikie(n)* 'to shine or gleam' (from Old English *blīcian*). **2.** Jewish (Ashkenazic): origin uncertain; possibly from German *Blick* or Yiddish *blik* 'glance', 'look', and based on some now irrecoverable anecdote. **3.** German: Prussian variant of **Blek**, a nickname from Middle High German *blic* 'shine'. **4.** German: short form of the Low German occupational name **Blickslager** 'tinsmith'. Compare BLECK. **5.** German: from a short form of the Germanic personal name *Bligger, Blickhart*, based on *blic* 'gleam', 'shine', later 'pale'.

Blickensderfer (123) Swiss German **Blickensdorfer**: habitational name from a place called Blickensdorf (see BLICKENSTAFF).

Blickenstaff (365) Americanized form of Swiss German **Blickensdorf**, a habitational name from a place so named.

Blickhan (107) North German: probably a compound nickname for a pale person, from BLICK + a short form of **Johann** (see JOHN).

Blickle (102) South German: pet form of the personal name **Blickhart** (see BLICK 5).

GIVEN NAMES German 10%. *Kurt* (2), *Juergen.*

Bliek (103) Dutch: nickname from *bliek* 'bream', presumably applied to someone thought to resemble the fish, or possibly an occupational name for a fish seller.

Blier (166) **1.** French: reduced form of **Belier**, a nickname for a powerful, forceful person, from *bélier* 'ram', 'battering ram'. **2.** South German: variant of BLEIER.

GIVEN NAMES French 13%. *Aurele* (2), *Adrien, Armand, Emile, Michel, Normand.*

Bliese (133) German: short form of the Slavic personal name *Blisemer*.

GIVEN NAME German 4%. *Wilhelmine.*

Bliesner (125) German: habitational name from a place called Bliesen in the Saarland.

GIVEN NAMES German 4%. *Erwin, Manfred.*

Bligh (298) **1.** English: variant of BLYTHE. **2.** Irish: Americanized form of the Connacht name **Ó Blighe** 'descendant of *Blighe*', a personal name probably derived from the Old Norse byname *Blígr* (from *blígja* 'to gaze'). **3.** Cornish: nickname from Cornish *blyth* 'wolf'. Compare BLETHEN.

Blight (228) Irish or English: variant of BLIGH.

Bliley (135) Probably an Americanized spelling of German **Bleile**, a variant of BLEIL.

Blincoe (230) English: habitational name from Great or Little Blencow in Cumbria, named with a Celtic word *blain* 'summit' and an obscure second element to which Old Norse *haugr* 'hill' has been added.

Blind (280) **1.** English: descriptive epithet for a blind man, from Old English *blind* 'blind'. **2.** German and Jewish (Ashkenazic): cognate of 1, from Middle High German *blint*, German or Yiddish *blind* 'blind'.

Blinder (190) German and Jewish (Ashkenazic): variant of BLIND 2, from a noun derivative meaning '(the) blind man'.

GIVEN NAMES Jewish 12%; Russian 7%. *Hyman, Isak, Mayer, Meyer, Nyusya, Yehuda; Boris* (3), *Aleksandr, Lev, Liudmila, Losif, Semyon.*

Blinderman (123) Jewish (Ashkenazic): descriptive epithet meaning 'blind man'.

GIVEN NAMES Jewish 14%. *Meyer* (2), *Aron, Blyuma, Emanuel, Yuly.*

Bline (111) English: unexplained; perhaps a variant spelling of Scottish BLAIN.

Blink (147) **1.** English: unexplained. **2.** Swedish: unexplained. It may have been a soldier's name.

Blinkhorn (102) English: habitational name from Blencarn in Cumbria, named with the Old Welsh elements *blain* 'summit' + *carn* 'rock', 'cairn'.

Blinn (854) German: variant of **Blinne**, itself a variant of BLIND.

Blish (233) Probably English: unexplained. The surname seems to have died out in Britain.

Bliss (5842) **1.** English: nickname for a cheerful person, from Middle English *blisse* 'joy'. Compare BLYTHE 1. **2.** English (of Norman origin): habitational name from the village of Blay in Calvados, France, recorded in 1077 in the form *Bleis* and of unknown origin. The village of Stoke Bliss in Worcestershire was named after a Norman family de Blez, recorded several times in the county from the 13th century. **3.** German: nickname for a cheerful person, from Middle High German *blīde* 'happy', 'friendly'. Compare 1. **4.** Americanized spelling of French BLOIS.

Blissett (253) English: nickname for a fortunate person, from Middle English *(i)blescede, blissed* 'blessed' (from Old English *blētsian* 'to bless'). The word also appears to have been in use in the Middle Ages as a female personal name, and some cases of the surname may be derived from this.

Blitch (305) Possibly German (**Blitsch**), a variant of BLISS 3.

Blitstein (143) Jewish (Ashkenazic): ornamental compound meaning 'blossom stone' (see BLUTH, STEIN).

Blitz (576) German and Jewish (Ashkenazic): from German *Blitz(er)* 'lightning' (Middle High German *blicze*), presumably a nickname for a fast mover.

GIVEN NAMES Jewish 5%. *Moshe* (2), *Ari, Arie, Herschell, Hyman, Miriam, Sol, Yetta.*

Blitzer (231) German and Jewish (Ashkenazic): variant of BLITZ.

Bliven (563) Welsh: variant of BLEVINS.

Blix (129) Swedish: variant of BLIXT.

Blixt (247) Swedish: a soldier's name or ornamental name, from *blixt* 'lightning'.

GIVEN NAMES Scandinavian 7%; German 5%. *Per; Hans* (3), *Kurt* (2), *Manfred.*

Blizard (234) English: variant spelling of BLIZZARD.

Blizzard (1482) English: variant of BLISSETT, altered by folk etymology under the influence of the vocabulary word *blizzard.*

Bloch (2411) **1.** Jewish (Ashkenazic): regional name for someone in Eastern Europe originating from Italy, from Polish *włoch,* meaning 'Italian' (originally 'foreigner'). See VLACH. **2.** German and Swedish: variant of BLOCK. **3.** Danish: from *blok* 'block (of wood)', hence a nickname for a large lumpish person, or from German BLOCK.

GIVEN NAMES German 6%; Jewish 4%. *Kurt* (7), *Hans* (4), *Heinz* (4), *Otto* (4), *Konrad* (2), *Manfred* (2), *Angelika, Arno, Beate, Bernhard, Ewald, Fritz; Aron* (3), *Miriam* (3), *Baruch* (2), *Ephraim* (2), *Meir* (2), *Moshe* (2), *Chana, Eyal, Igal, Mendy, Meyer, Mort.*

Blocher (627) German: from a derivative of Middle High German *bloch* 'block of wood', 'stocks', hence presumably a metonymic occupational name for a jailer. See also BLOCK.

Block (10236) **1.** German and Dutch: from Middle High German *bloch,* Middle Dutch *blok* 'block of wood', 'stocks'. The surname probably originated as a nickname for a large, lumpish man, or perhaps as a nickname for a persistent lawbreaker who found himself often in the stocks. **2.** English: possibly a metonymic occupational name for someone who blocks, as in shoemaking and bookbinding, from Middle English *blok* 'block'. **3.** Jewish (Ashkenazic): Americanized spelling of BLOCH (see VLACH).

FOREBEARS Adriaen Coertsz Block was a Dutch-born merchant-explorer who traded along the CT coast and Long Island shortly after Hudson's voyage to the region in 1609. Block Island, between the north fork of Long Island and RI, which he used as a base of operations, is named after him.

Blocker (2652) **1.** German (**Blöcker**): occupational name for a jailer (see BLOCK 1). **2.** English: occupational name for a shoemaker or bookbinder (see BLOCK); a person called Henry le Blocker is recorded in York in 1212. However, in some cases the English name is of German origin (see 1 above); the census of 1881 records, amongst others, a Herman Blocker and a John Blocker, both born in Germany.

Blodgett (2883) Origin unidentified. Perhaps an Americanized form of Dutch **Bloetgoet** (see BLOODGOOD).

Bloedel (153) South German: nickname for a weak, timid, or foolish person, from a diminutive of Middle High German *blæde* 'fragile', 'weak', 'ignorant'.

Bloedorn (201) North German (also **Blödorn**): topographic name from Low German *Blödorn* 'blossoming brier'.

Bloedow (111) German: habitational name from Blodau, an unlocated, deserted settlement.

GIVEN NAME German 6%. *Otto.*

Bloem (154) Dutch and North German (in the Lower Rhine area): from Dutch *bloem,* Middle Low German *blōm* 'flower', possibly applied as a nickname, an ornamental name, or a metonymic occupational name for a gardener or florist.

GIVEN NAMES Dutch 4%; German 4%. *Adriaan, Dirk; Wessel, Wilhelm.*

Bloemer (194) Dutch and North German: ornamental or occupational name from an agent derivative of Dutch and Middle Low German *blōm* 'flower' (see BLOEM). In the Lower Rhine area and Westphalia the vowel cluster -*oe*- is not pronounced with an umlaut; instead, the -*e*- indicates a lengthening of the vowel.

Bloemker (176) Possibly a variant of German **Blömke**, a diminutive of BLOEM.

Blohm (956) **1.** North German (also **Blöhm**): nickname or ornamental name, from Middle Low German *blōme* 'flower'. **2.** Swedish: ornamental name, a variant of BLOM.

GIVEN NAMES German 4%. *Hans, Kurt, Manfred, Otto, Uwe.*

Blois (108) French and English (of Norman origin): habitational name from either of two places in France called Blois, in Loire-et-Cher and Jura.

GIVEN NAME French 4%. *Camille.*

Bloise (140) **1.** Italian (Calabria): from the medieval personal name *Bloise,* a vernacular form of Latin BLASIUS. Compare BLASI, BIAGI. **2.** English: variant of BLOIS.

GIVEN NAMES Italian 23%; Spanish 8%. *Rolando* (2), *Salvatore* (2), *Biagio, Carmelo, Giulio; Alejandro, Ines, Jose, Juan Antonio, Luis.*

Blok (228) Dutch and Jewish (Ashkenazic): variant spelling of BLOCK.

GIVEN NAMES Dutch 9%. *Adriaan* (2), *Marten* (2), *Bastian, Gerrit, Willem.*

Blom (1291) **1.** Scandinavian: ornamental name from *blom* 'flower'. **2.** Norwegian: habitational name from two farms so named in western Norway; unexplained. **3.** German and Jewish (Ashkenazic): variant of BLUM. **4.** Dutch: variant of BLOEM.

GIVEN NAMES Scandinavian 5%. *Erik* (3), *Gunner, Helmer, Knud, Knut.*

Blomberg (1029) **1.** Swedish: ornamental name composed of the elements *blom* 'flower' + *berg* 'mountain', 'hill'. **2.** Danish: habitational name from a place so named. **3.** German: habitational name from a place named Blomberg, in Lippe district and Friesland.

GIVEN NAMES Scandinavian 6%. *Sven* (2), *Erik, Jorgen, Pontus.*

Blome (360) **1.** German: variant of BLUM. **2.** Dutch: variant of BLOEM. **3.** Swedish: variant of BLOM.

GIVEN NAMES German 5%. *Fritz, Heinz, Horst, Lothar.*

Blomgren (622) Swedish: ornamental name composed of the elements *blom* 'flower' + *gren* 'branch'.

GIVEN NAME Scandinavian 4%. *Mauritz.*

Blomme (135) Dutch: variant of BLOEM.

GIVEN NAME French 4%. *Marcel.*

Blommel (131) North German and Dutch: from a diminutive of BLOEM 'flower'.

Blommer (110) Dutch and North German: variant of BLOEMER.

GIVEN NAMES French 6%; German 4%. *Camille; Aloys.*

Blomquist (1540) Swedish: ornamental name composed of the elements *blom* 'flower' + *quist,* an old or ornamental spelling of *kvist* 'twig'.

GIVEN NAMES Scandinavian 7%. *Nils* (2), *Sven* (2), *Alrik, Arni, Bertel, Britt, Erik, Erland, Gothard, Iver, Lennart, Ove.*

Blomstrom (167) Swedish (**Blomström**): ornamental name composed of the elements *blom* 'flower' + *ström* 'river'.

GIVEN NAMES Scandinavian 5%. *Kali, Knute.*

Blond (144) **1.** Jewish (Ashkenazic): nickname for a fair-haired person, from German, Yiddish *blond* 'blonde'. **2.** French: nickname for someone with fair hair or a light complexion, from Old French *blund, blond* 'blond', of Germanic origin. This name was taken to Denmark in the 18th century by the Huguenots.

GIVEN NAMES Russian 6%; Jewish 5%. *Aleksandr* (2), *Marik; Ilya, Izak.*

Blondeau (119) French: from a diminutive of BLOND.

GIVEN NAMES French 15%. *Yves* (2), *Gilles, Marcel.*

Blondell (244) **1.** English: perhaps a variant spelling of **Blundell**, a diminutive of BLUNT 1. **2.** Swedish: ornamental name composed of the elements *Blond* + -*ell,* a common suffix of Swedish surnames, taken from the Latin adjectival ending -*elius.*

GIVEN NAMES French 4%. *Antoine, Emile.*

Blonder (159) **1.** Dutch: occupational name for a brewer. **2.** Jewish (Ashkenazic): from an inflected form of BLOND.

GIVEN NAMES Jewish 11%. *Avi, Ayelet, Hyman, Meir, Ofra, Rebekah.*

Blondin (494) **1.** French: from a diminutive of BLOND. **2.** Swedish: ornamental name composed of the elements *blond* 'blond' + the suffix -*in,* from Latin -*in(i)us* 'descendant of'.

FOREBEARS A Sureau, also called Blondin, from the Poitou region of France, is documented in Quebec city in 1691. Secondary surnames include Avon, Bellemer, Bilmer, Bernesse, Catignon, Guillimin, Roquet, Simon.

Charles Blondin (1824–97), born Jean-François Gravelet in St. Omer, France, was a tightrope walker, famous for crossing Niagara Falls in 1859 on a high wire suspended 100 feet above the water.

Blong (130) English (Merseyside): unexplained.

Bloniarz (112) Polish: metonymic occupational name for a maker of windows from animal membranes, from *błona* 'membrane'. GIVEN NAMES Polish 8%. *Wincenty, Wladyslaw*.

Blonigen (119) North German (Rhineland): unexplained.

Blonski (120) Polish (**Błoński**): habitational name for someone from Błonie, a place named with *błonie* 'meadow'. GIVEN NAMES Polish 7%. *Krzysztof, Slawomir, Wladyslaw*.

Blood (2280) **1.** English: evidently from Old English *blōd* 'blood', but with what significance is not clear. In Middle English the word was in use as a metonymic occupational term for a physician, i.e. one who lets blood, and also as an affectionate term of address for a blood relative. **2.** Welsh: Anglicized form of Welsh *ap Llwyd* 'son of *Llwyd*' (see LLOYD).

Bloodgood (373) Americanized form of Dutch **Bloetgoet**, unexplained. FOREBEARS Franz or François Bloetgoet, alias Francis Bloodgood (1635–76) came in 1658 from Amsterdam in the Netherlands to Flushing, Long Island, NY.

Bloodsaw (109) Origin unidentified.

Bloodsworth (247) English: variant of BLOODWORTH.

Bloodworth (1446) English: habitational name from *Blidworth* in Nottinghamshire, named with the Old English personal name *Blīþa* + Old English *worð* 'enclosure'.

Bloom (11144) **1.** Jewish (American): Americanized spelling of BLUM. **2.** Americanized spelling of Dutch BLOEM. **3.** Swedish: variant of BLOM. **4.** English: metonymic occupational name for an iron worker, from Middle English *blome* 'ingot (of iron)'. The modern English word *bloom* 'flower' came into English from Old Norse in the 13th century, but probably did not give rise to any surnames.

Bloomberg (671) **1.** Jewish (American): partly Americanized ornamental name, a compound meaning 'flower hill' (from Yiddish *blum* 'flower' or German *Blume* + German *Berg* 'mountain', 'hill'). **2.** Variant of Scandinavian BLOMBERG.

Bloome (129) **1.** Swedish (**Bloomé**): variant of BLOM, with the addition of the ornamental suffix -*é*. **2.** Probably an Americanized spelling of BLUM.

Bloomer (1610) **1.** English: occupational name for an iron worker, Middle English

blomere (see BLOOM). **2.** Americanized form of Dutch BLOEMER or German **Blümer** (see BLUMER).

Bloomfield (2154) **1.** Jewish (American): Americanized form of **Blumfeld**, an ornamental compound of Yiddish *blum* 'flower' + *feld* 'field'. **2.** English: variant of the Norman habitational name **Blundeville**, from Blonville-sur-Mer in Calvados, France. The first element is probably an Old Norse personal name; the second is Old French *ville* 'settlement'. In the 16th and 17th centuries in England, the endings -*field* and -*ville* were often used interchangeably; one branch of the **Blundeville** family continued using the -*ville* spelling while another chose Blom(e)field or Bloomfield.

Bloomingdale (178) Jewish (American): Americanized form of German BLUMEN-THAL or Dutch *Bloemendaal*, both of which are ornamental names composed of elements meaning 'flower' and 'valley'.

Bloomquist (1187) Respelling of the Swedish ornamental name **Blomqvist** (see BLOMQUIST). GIVEN NAMES Scandinavian 4%. *Bertel, Erik, Erland*.

Bloor (198) English (Midlands): variant of BLORE.

Blore (104) English: habitational name from Blore in Staffordshire, possibly named from Old English *blōr* 'swelling', 'hill'.

Blosch (103) Swiss German: variant of BLOSS or BLASS. Its variant, **Blöschli**, denotes a bald-headed man.

Blose (591) German (**Blöse**): from a vernacular form of the personal name BLASIUS.

Bloss (968) **1.** German: from Middle High German *blōz* 'naked', 'destitute', applied as a nickname for a poor person, or for someone who dressed inappropriately, or for a man without a beard. **2.** German: variant of BLASS. **3.** Swedish: unexplained; possibly an adoption of the German name.

Blosser (1448) Swiss German: variant of BLASER, or in some cases possibly a nickname from a derivative of BLASS 1.

Blossom (657) English: nickname from Old English *blōstm(a)*, *blōsma* 'blossom', according to Reaney 'used in the 15th century of one lovely and full of promise.'

Blouch (206) German: unexplained. Compare BLAUCH.

Blough (1188) Americanized form of German BLAUCH.

Blouin (1012) French: nickname for someone with an unusually pale complexion, from a derivative of Old French *blou* 'blue'. FOREBEARS A Blouin with the secondary surname La Violette, from the Poitou region of France, is recorded in Château Richer, Quebec, in 1669. GIVEN NAMES French 15%. *Jacques* (5), *Andre* (4), *Marcel* (4), *Aime* (2), *Armand*

(2), *Germaine* (2), *Laurent* (2), *Normand* (2), *Raoul* (2), *Bibiane, Calix, Collette*.

Blount (5757) English: variant of BLUNT.

Blouse (105) Americanized spelling of German BLOSS.

Blout (102) Jewish: unexplained. GIVEN NAME Jewish 7%. *Elkan* (3).

Blow (1077) **1.** English: from Middle English *blowe, blaa, bloo* 'pale', hence a nickname for someone with an exceptionally pale complexion. **2.** Americanized spelling of French BLEAU.

Blowe (187) English: variant spelling of BLOW.

Blower (225) **1.** English: from Middle English *blōwere* 'one who blows'. The name was applied chiefly to someone who operated a bellows, either as a blacksmith's assistant or to provide wind for a church organ. In other cases it was applied to someone who blew a horn, i.e. a huntsman or a player of the musical instrument. **2.** Welsh: Anglicized form of Welsh *ab Llywarch* 'son of *Llywarch*'. Compare FLOWER.

Blowers (824) English (East Anglia): patronymic from BLOWER 1.

Bloxham (374) English: habitational name from Bloxham in Oxfordshire and Bloxholm in Lincolnshire, both of which are recorded in Domesday Book as *Blochesham*, from an unrecorded Old English byname *Blocc* (presumably referring to a large, ungainly fellow; compare BLOCK 1) + Old English *hām* 'homestead'.

Bloxom (311) Variant of English BLOX-HAM.

Bloxsom (136) Variant of English BLOX-HAM.

Bloyd (327) Welsh: Anglicized form of Welsh *ap Llwyd* 'son of *Llwyd*' (see LLOYD).

Bloyer (172) French: perhaps, as Morlet proposes, an occupational name for someone who separated the fibres of hemp or flax.

Blubaugh (649) Americanized form of an unidentified German name.

Blucher (187) German (**Blücher**): habitational name from a place of this name, of Slavic origin, near Boizenburg on the Elbe.

Bludau (122) German: habitational name from a place in the former East Prussia. GIVEN NAME German 6%. *Frieda*.

Bludworth (114) English: variant spelling of BLOODWORTH.

Blue (6877) English: generally a fairly recent Americanized form of German BLAU or the French cognate *Bleu*.

Bluemel (200) South German (**Blümel**): from a diminutive of Middle High German *bluome* 'flower', hence a metonymic occupational name for a gardener or florist, or in some cases possibly denoting someone who lived at a house distinguished by the sign of a flower.

GIVEN NAMES German 8%. *Kurt* (3), *Hermann, Ralf.*

Bluestein (463) Jewish (American): partly Americanized form of BLAUSTEIN.

GIVEN NAMES Jewish 7%. *Hyman, Meyer, Miriam, Myer, Sol.*

Bluestone (239) Jewish (American; also found in England): Americanized form of BLAUSTEIN.

GIVEN NAMES Jewish 5%. *Avi, Fishel, Isadore.*

Bluett (149) English: variant spelling of BLEWETT.

Bluford (203) Possibly English, a habitational name from a lost or unidentified place. The name occurs in records of the 19th century but is now very rare if not extinct in the British Isles. In the U.S. it is found chiefly in TX and TN.

Bluhm (1126) German: variant spelling of BLUM.

Bluitt (162) English: variant spelling of BLEWETT.

Blum (8135) **1.** German: from Middle High German *bluom* 'flower', hence an occupational name for a flower gardener or a florist. **2.** Jewish (Ashkenazic): ornamental name from German *Blume*, Yiddish *blum* 'flower'. **3.** Swedish: variant of BLOM 1.

Blumberg (1720) **1.** Jewish (Ashkenazic): ornamental compound of German *Blume* 'flower' + *Berg* 'mountain', 'hill'. **2.** German: habitational name from any of various places called Blumberg.

GIVEN NAMES Jewish 4%. *Emanuel* (5), *Herschel* (2), *Aryeh, Aviva, Avrom, Chaim, Girsh, Leib, Myer, Shmuel, Sol, Zelig.*

Blume (2481) **1.** German and Jewish (Ashkenazic): variant of BLUM. **2.** Swedish: variant of BLOM 1.

Blumenauer (102) German: habitational name for someone from any of several places called Blumenau.

Blumenberg (195) **1.** Jewish (Ashkenazic): ornamental name composed of German *Blume* 'flower' + German *Berg* 'mountain', 'hill'. **2.** German: habitational name from any of several places called Blumenberg, for example in Brandenburg. This is also found as a Swedish name.

GIVEN NAMES German 7%; Jewish 6%. *Heiner* (2), *Horst; Herschel, Pinchas, Shraga.*

Blumenfeld (813) **1.** Jewish (Ashkenazic): ornamental name composed of German *Blume* 'flower' + *Feld* 'field'. **2.** German: habitational name from any of several places called Blumenfeld or Blumenfelde.

GIVEN NAMES Jewish 7%. *Sol* (3), *Gershon* (2), *Yair* (2), *Aron, Avram, Gersh, Herschel, Isadore, Isak, Leizer, Meyer, Morry.*

Blumenschein (139) German: from Middle High German *bluomenschīn* 'flower splendor', probably denoting someone who lived at a house distin-

guished by a sign depicting a bunch of flowers or decorated with flower designs, or noted for its flower garden.

GIVEN NAMES German 8%. *Erwin* (2), *Erna, Ewald.*

Blumenshine (141) Partly Americanized form of German BLUMENSCHEIN.

Blumenstein (279) Jewish (Ashkenazic): ornamental name composed of German *Blume* 'flower' + *Stein* 'stone'.

GIVEN NAMES German 4%. *Hans, Kurt, Otto.*

Blumenstock (218) Jewish (Ashkenazic): ornamental name composed of German *Blume* 'flower' + *Stock* 'stem'.

Blumenthal (2134) Jewish (Ashkenazic) and Swedish: ornamental name composed of German *Blumen* 'flowers' + *Thal* (now spelled *Tal*) 'valley'.

GIVEN NAMES Jewish 4%; German 4%. *Chana* (2), *Isidor* (2), *Sol* (2), *Ari, Hyman, Hymen, Irit, Isadore, Meyer, Myer, Shula, Smadar; Erwin* (3), *Kurt* (3), *Manfred* (3), *Horst* (2), *Benno, Bernhard, Bernhardt, Gerd, Gerda, Gitta, Inge, Lothar.*

Blumer (855) **1.** Jewish (Ashkenazic): ornamental name based on Yiddish *blum* or German *Blume* 'flower'. **2.** English: variant of BLOOMER. **3.** German (mostly **Blümer**): variant of *blume* (see BLUM).

Blumhagen (132) German: older form of **Blumenhagen**, a habitational name from a place near Prenzlau, so named with *Blum(e)* 'flower' + *Hagen* 'hedge'.

GIVEN NAMES German 6%. *Arno, Otto.*

Blumhardt (109) German: from a Germanic personal name composed of *bluomo* 'flower' + *hart* 'strong'.

Blumstein (233) Jewish (Ashkenazic): ornamental name composed of German *Blume* 'flower' + German *Stein* 'stone'.

GIVEN NAMES Jewish 7%. *Heshy, Igal, Isidor, Meyer, Simche.*

Blunck (229) German: variant spelling of BLUNK.

GIVEN NAMES German 4%. *Hans, Kurt.*

Blundell (588) **1.** English (chiefly Lancashire): from a diminutive of BLUNT. **2.** Swedish: ornamental name from *Blund* (of unexplained origin) + the suffix *-ell*, taken from the Latin adjectival ending *-elius*.

Blunden (108) English: probably a nickname from Middle English *blonde(n)* 'blond', 'fair-haired'.

Blunk (615) German: habitational name from a place named Blunk, near Segeberg in northern Germany.

Blunt (2107) English: **1.** nickname for someone with fair hair or a light complexion, from Anglo-Norman French *blunt* 'blond' (Old French *blund, blond*, of Germanic origin). **2.** nickname for a stupid person, from Middle English *blunt, blont* 'dull', 'stupid' (probably from Old English *blinnan* 'to stop', or Old Norse *blundr* 'sleep').

Blurton (230) English (Staffordshire and Derbyshire): habitational name from Blurton in Staffordshire, so named with an Old English word *blōr*, possibly 'hill', + Old English *tūn* 'settlement'.

Blush (101) **1.** English: unexplained. **2.** Alternatively, perhaps, a respelling of German BLOSCH.

Blust (407) German: ornamental name from Middle High German *bluost* 'blossom', 'flower'.

Blustein (117) Jewish (Ashkenazic): variant of BLAUSTEIN, reflecting a southern Yiddish pronunciation of Yiddish *blo* 'blue'.

Bluth (255) **1.** German and Jewish (Ashkenazic): ornamental name from Middle High German *bluot*, German *Blüte* 'bloom', 'flower head'. **2.** German: possibly from Middle High German *bluot* 'blood', an allusion to kinship or family, as in the name **Jungblut**.

GIVEN NAMES Jewish 7%. *Elimelech* (2), *Simcha* (2), *Avraham, Chaya, Mordecai.*

Bly (1750) **1.** English: variant spelling of BLIGH. **2.** German: variant of **Blei, Bley**, a metonymic occupational name for a lead miner or lead worker, from Middle High German *blī* 'lead'. **3.** Dutch: nickname for a cheerful, happy man, Dutch *blij*. **4.** Swedish: possibly German in origin (see 2 above) or a soldier's name. **5.** Americanized form of a Norwegian habitational name from a farmstead in Hardanger named Bleie, from a river name from Old Norse *bleikr* 'gray', 'pale' + *vin* 'meadow'.

Blydenburgh (111) Belgian (also **Van Blydenbergh**): habitational name from Blijenberg (formerly *Bleidenberg*) in Brabant, Belgium.

Blye (228) English: variant spelling of BLIGH.

Blyler (167) Dutch or North German: occupational name for someone whose work involved the use of an instrument for pounding, crushing, or beating (see BLEILER).

Blystone (553) Americanized form of the Jewish (Ashkenazic) surname **Bleistein**, an ornamental name composed of German *Blei* 'lead' + *Stein* 'stone'.

Blyth (440) Scottish and English: variant spelling of BLYTHE.

Blythe (2946) English and Scottish: **1.** nickname for a cheerful person, from Old English *blīðe* 'merry', 'cheerful'. **2.** habitational name from any of several places called Blyth or Blythe, especially Blyth in Northumberland, named for the rivers on which they stand. The river name is from Old English *blīðe* 'gentle', 'pleasant'.

Bo (159) **1.** Danish and Swedish: patronymic from the personal name *Bo* 'farmer' (see BOE). **2.** Chinese 薄: according to legend, some descendants of Shen Nong, a legendary emperor (2734–2697 BC), were granted an area named Bo in modern-day Shandong province, and adopted the place name as their surname. Additionally, an official of the state of Song during the Spring and Autumn period (722–481 BC) was granted a town named Bo in modern-day Henan province, and his descendants also adopted the place name as their surname. The character also means 'thin' or 'slim', and 'weak'. **3.** Chinese 伯: from the name of Bo Yi, a famous adviser to the model emperors Shun and Yao around 2200 BC. This character also means 'oldest brother', and is often used as a personal name with this sense. **4.** Vietnamese: unexplained. **5.** Other Southeast Asian: unexplained.

GIVEN NAMES Vietnamese 17%; Chinese 10%; Other Southeast Asian 9%; Scandinavian 8%. *Dat* (2), *Bay Van, Binh, Chau Minh, Dai, Hiep Van, Hung, Khien, Nguyen, Sau, Sen Thi; Zhang* (2), *Fan, Heang, Heng, Jiang, Li, Peng, Won, Yan; Chea, Quanz, Soeun; Olav, Stig.*

Boag (131) Scottish: variant of BOAK.

Boak (301) Scottish: perhaps a habitational name from Boak in the parish of Kirkcolm, or a topographic name from the dialect word *boak* 'ridge (as a boundary)'.

Boal (416) **1.** English, Welsh, and northern Irish: variant of BOWELL. **2.** Irish: variant of BOYLE.

Boals (406) English: probably a variant spelling of BOWLES.

Boan (486) **1.** Galician: habitational name from a place called Boán, in Lugo province, Galicia. **2.** Perhaps a respelling of German BOHN. **3.** Scottish: unexplained.

Board (1289) English: from Old English *bord* 'board', 'plank', 'table', hence a metonymic occupational name for a carpenter or a topographic name for someone who lived in a plank-built cottage.

Boardley (126) English: variant spelling of BORDLEY.

Boardman (2651) English (chiefly Lancashire): occupational name for a carpenter or a topographic name for someone who lived in a plank-built cottage (see BOARD).

Boardway (121) Origin uncertain. **1.** It may be an altered form of French BEAUDOIN. Compare BOARDWINE. **2.** Alternatively, perhaps, it is a metathesized form of BROADWAY.

Boardwine (142) Probably an altered form of French BEAUDOIN.

Boarman (356) **1.** English: variant spelling of BOORMAN. **2.** Probably a respelling of German BORMANN.

Boarts (113) Probably an Americanized spelling of German BORTZ.

Boas (411) Jewish, English, and Scottish: from the Biblical personal name *Boas* or BOAZ. In 18th-century Britain this surname was found as far apart as St. Ives in Cornwall and Dundee in Scotland.

Boase (123) **1.** Jewish: variant of BOAZ. **2.** Indian: variant of BOSE.

GIVEN NAME Indian 4%. *Subhas* (2).

Boast (154) English (East Anglia): nickname for a boastful person, from Middle English *bost* 'brag', 'vainglory'.

Boat (103) Origin uncertain. The surname is recorded in England in the 1881 English census and may be of English origin, a metonymic occupational name for a boatman or boat builder, from Middle English *bot(e)* 'boat'. However, in part at least, it is an Americanized form of some other name, most probably Dutch and North German BOOT.

GIVEN NAME German 4%. *Otto.*

Boateng (212) Ghanaian: unexplained.

GIVEN NAMES African 22%. *Kofi* (4), *Kwaku* (4), *Kwabena* (3), *Kwasi* (3), *Kwame* (2), *Akwasi, Osei, Owusu.*

Boatman (1852) English: occupational name from Middle English *bot(e)* 'boat' + *man* 'man'.

Boatner (514) Possibly an Americanized spelling of German BODNER.

Boatright (2019) English: variant of BOATWRIGHT.

Boatwright (2206) English: occupational name for a boat builder, from Middle English *bot(e)* 'boat' + *wright* 'maker', 'craftsman'.

Boaz (1196) Jewish (Ashkenazic): from the Hebrew personal name *Boaz* (of uncertain etymology). In the Bible this was borne by Ruth's rich kinsman who later became her husband. This is also found as a gentile surname in Britain and Sweden.

Bob (333) Jewish (eastern Ashkenazic): **1.** variant of BOBE. **2.** from eastern Yiddish *bob* 'broad bean', 'bean(s)', hence a metonymic occupational name for a grower of beans or a nickname for a tall thin man.

Boback (207) **1.** Ukrainian: see BOBAK. **2.** Americanized spelling of Czech, Slovak, or Polish BOBAK. **3.** Americanized spelling of the German habitational name **Bobach**, a habitational name derived from various farmsteads or rivers so named, or from place names such as Bobeck and Bobek. **4.** Possibly a Swedish ornamental name composed of the elements *bo* 'farm' + *back* 'hillside' or an altered spelling of Swedish **Bobäck**, an ornamental compound of *bo* + *bäck* 'stream'.

Bobadilla (300) Spanish: habitational name from any of various places, as for example Bobadilla in Logroño province or Bobadilla del Campo in Valladolid.

GIVEN NAMES Spanish 54%. *Jose* (6), *Juan* (6), *Armando* (5), *Miguel* (4), *Ramon* (4), *Angel* (3), *Jesus* (3), *Lupe* (3), *Manolito* (3), *Pedro* (3), *Raul* (3), *Amado* (2); *Luciano* (2), *Marco* (2), *Antonio, Dante, Gabriella, Heriberto, Lorenzo, Mauro.*

Bobak (284) Polish; Czech and Slovak (**Bobák**): nickname from a derivative of Slavic *bob* 'bean', 'broad bean'.

GIVEN NAMES Polish 10%. *Wladyslaw* (3), *Franciszek* (2), *Tadeusz* (2), *Boguslaw, Janina, Krystyna, Wojciech.*

Bobal (102) **1.** Czech, Slovak (**Bobál'**): nickname from a derivative of Slavic *bob* 'bean', 'broad bean'. **2.** Indian (Panjab): Hindu and Sikh name of unknown meaning.

GIVEN NAMES Indian 4%. *Darshan, Pritam.*

Bobay (132) Origin unidentified.

Bobb (1060) **1.** English: variant of BUBB. **2.** German: variant of BOPP.

Bobbett (198) English: variant spelling of BOBBITT.

Bobbitt (2307) English: from a pet form of *Bobb* (see BUBB).

Bobby (295) English (mainly East Anglia and Kent): probably from a pet form of the personal name ROBERT.

Bobe (151) **1.** Catalan (**Bobé**): respelling of **Bover**, occupational name for a herdsman, from Catalan *bover* 'oxherd', 'cowherd' (Late Latin *bovarius*). **2.** Jewish (eastern Ashkenazic): from the Yiddish personal name *bobe, babe*, from a Slavic word meaning 'old woman' or 'grandmother'. This was bestowed on girls in the hope that they would live a long life and grow old.

GIVEN NAMES Spanish 16%. *Agripina, Alicia, Ana, Angel, Carlos, Crisanta, Efrain, Francisco, Fulgencio, Gumersindo, Herminio, Ines.*

Bobeck (170) **1.** German: habitational name from a place name in Thuringia, which is of Slavic origin. **2.** Jewish (from Poland): variant of BOBEK 1. **3.** Respelling of Czech, Slovenian, or Croatian BOBEK. **4.** Respelling of Swedish **Bobäck**, an ornamental name composed of the elements *bo* 'farm' + *bäck* 'stream'.

Bobek (228) **1.** Polish and Jewish (from Poland): topographic name from *bobek* 'bayberry'. **2.** Czech and Jewish (eastern Ashkenazic): nickname for a small rotund person, from *bobek* 'goat droppings'. **3.** Slovenian and Croatian (northwestern Croatia): nickname from a diminutive of *bob* 'horse bean', formed with the diminutive suffix *-ek*. Compare BOBIK and BOBICH. **4.** German: habitational name from a place in Schleswig-Holstein named Bobek. **5.** Swedish: variant spelling of BOBECK.

GIVEN NAMES Czech and Slovak 5%; Polish 5%. *Miroslav* (2), *Jaroslav, Ludmila, Zdenek; Stanislaw* (2), *Ryszard.*

Bobel (114) Dutch and German (**Böbel**): nickname for a small, insignificant person, from Dutch *bobbel* 'pustule', 'boil', German dialect *Bebel, Böbbele.*

Bober (862) Eastern German and Jewish (from Ukraine and Poland): from Polish *bóbr* 'beaver', Yiddish *bober*, applied as an ornamental name or as a nickname for someone thought to resemble the animal in some way.

GIVEN NAMES Polish 5%. *Gustaw* (2), *Andrzej, Bogdan, Ewa, Jerzy, Jozef, Kazimierz, Ludwik, Stanislaw, Tomasz, Wieslaw.*

Boberg (374) **1.** German: habitational name from a place so named east of Hamburg and in Lippe district. **2.** Swedish: ornamental name composed of the elements *bo* 'dwelling', 'farm' + *berg* 'mountain', 'hill'. **3.** Norwegian: habitational name from any of various farmsteads named Boberg, from *bo* 'dwelling', 'farm' or the Old Norse personal name *Baugi* + *berg* 'mountain', 'hill'.

Bobich (107) **1.** Slovenian (**Bobič**) and Croatian (**Bobić**): probably a nickname from a diminutive of *bob* 'horse bean', formed with the diminutive suffix *-ič*. Compare BOBEK, BOBIK. **2.** Croatian and Serbian (**Bobić**): patronymic from *Bobo* or *Boba*, old pet forms of the personal names *Bogdan*, *Slobodan*.

Bobick (185) Americanized spelling of BOBIK.

Bobier (198) French: variant spelling of **Baubier**, a nickname for a stutterer (ultimately from Latin *balbus* 'stammering').

Bobik (123) Czech (**Bobík**), Slovak, Polish, and Slovenian (from historically Slovenian-speaking Styria): from a diminutive of Slavic *bob* 'bean' (Slovenian: 'horse-bean'), hence a metonymic occupational name for a grower of beans or a nickname for someone tall and thin. Compare BOBEK and BOBICH.

Bobinger (100) German: habitational name for someone from places called Bobingen in Bavaria and Switzerland.
GIVEN NAME German 5%. *Otto*.

Bobinski (157) Polish (**Bobiński**): habitational name for someone from a place called Bobin or Bobino.
GIVEN NAMES Polish 8%. *Andrzej, Maciej, Tadeusz, Waclaw*.

Bobko (117) Russian: unexplained.
GIVEN NAMES Russian 4%. *Mikhail, Vasiliy*.

Boblett (109) See BOBLITT.

Boblitt (146) Origin uncertain. **1.** Perhaps an Americanized form of German **Boblitz** (see BAUBLITZ). **2.** Alternatively, possibly English: from a pet form of the personal name *Bob*, itself a pet form of ROBERT.

Bobo (2884) **1.** Altered form of a French (Huguenot) name, probably **Bobeaux**, which is unexplained. **2.** Spanish: nickname for a sufferer from a speech defect, from Spanish *bobo* 'stammering' (Latin *balbus*). **3.** Hungarian (**Bobó**): from the old secular personal name *Bobó*.
FOREBEARS The first American bearer of this name on record is Elizabeth Bobo, who in 1719 received a land grant in King and Queen Co., VA, from the Proprietors of the VA Company. Sampson Bobo, a Protestant born in France about 1735, married Sarah Simpson of Caroline Co., VA, and became the progenitor of a large and prominent southern family. Except for Revolutionary soldier Joseph Bobo of Prince William Co., VA, the entire Bobo clan seems to have moved to the counties of Spartanburg and Laurens, SC, between 1772 and 1792.

Bobola (106) Polish: from a derivative of *bób* 'bean'.

Bobowski (105) Polish: habitational name for someone from a place called Bobowa, Bobowo.
GIVEN NAME Polish 4%. *Karol*.

Bobrow (263) Jewish (from Belarus): habitational name from a place called Bobr or Bobrovo in Belarus or other villages named with Slavic *bobr* 'beaver'.
GIVEN NAMES Jewish 10%. *Meyer* (3), *Hersh* (2), *Arieh, Mort, Shlomo*.

Bobrowski (273) Polish and Jewish (from Poland): habitational name for someone from a place called Bobrowa, Bobrowo, Bobrowce, or Bobrowiec.
GIVEN NAMES Polish 5%. *Bogumil, Jozef, Mariusz, Zygmund*.

Bobst (262) German: probably a variant of PABST.

Bobzien (180) German: habitational name from either of two places in Mecklenburg called Bobzin.

Bocan (50) Czech and Slovak (**Bočan**) or Serbian (**Bokan**): nickname for a tall, gangling person, from *bočan* 'stork'. Compare BOCIAN.

Bocanegra (536) Spanish: nickname from *boca* 'mouth' + *negra* 'black', denoting a foul-mouthed or abusive person. In the form **Boccanegra**, this surname has also been long established in Italy.
GIVEN NAMES Spanish 51%. *Jose* (17), *Juan* (12), *Jesus* (6), *Eduardo* (5), *Fernando* (5), *Manuel* (5), *Ruben* (5), *Ignacio* (4), *Raul* (4), *Carlos* (3), *Efren* (3), *Francisco* (3).

Bocchino (443) Italian: from a diminutive of **Bocca**, a nickname for a talkative or indiscreet person, an orator, or a person with a large or deformed mouth, from *bocca* 'mouth' (Latin *bucca* 'cheek').
GIVEN NAMES Italian 17%. *Angelo* (6), *Salvatore* (3), *Antonio, Camillo, Carlo, Carmin, Carmine, Francesca, Gino, Matteo, Philomena, Raffaele*.

Bocci (148) Italian: patronymic or plural form of BOCCIO.
GIVEN NAMES Italian 20%. *Angelo, Armando, Carmine, Constantino, Guido, Margarita, Mario, Roberto*.

Boccia (328) Italian: **1.** nickname from *boccia* 'bottle', 'glass pot'. **2.** nickname for a humpback, from French *boche* 'hunch'.
GIVEN NAMES Italian 24%. *Luigi* (3), *Salvatore* (2), *Angelo, Antonio, Carlo, Carmine, Corrado, Enrico, Franco, Gaetano, Giuseppe, Marcello*.

Boccio (238) Italian: probably a variant form of BOCCIA, or alternatively a short form of a personal name formed with the hypocoristic suffix *-boccio*.
GIVEN NAMES Italian 17%. *Salvatore* (4), *Angelo, Ciro, Francesco, Gilda, Sal*.

Boccuzzi (144) Italian: from a diminutive of *bocca* 'mouth' (see BOCCHINO).
GIVEN NAMES Italian 29%. *Angelo* (3), *Vito* (3), *Carmine* (2), *Elio* (2), *Lorenzo* (2), *Giraldo, Giuseppe, Pasquale, Quinto, Rocco, Salvatore, Silvio*.

Bocek (210) Czech (**Boček**): **1.** from a pet form of a personal name beginning with *Bo-*, for example *Bohuslav*, or *Bohumil*. **2.** nickname for an illegitimate child, from *boček*, a diminutive of *bok* 'side'.

Boch (230) **1.** German: Alemannic variant of BOCK 1. **2.** Swedish and Danish spelling of German BOCK. **3.** Polish: from a pet form of a personal name such as *Bogdan*, *Bogusław*, or *Bolesław*.
GIVEN NAME French 4%. *Armand*.

Boche (141) **1.** German: habitational name from any of several places in Rhineland and Westphalia named Bochen. **2.** French (Normandy and Picardy): nickname for a hunchback, from Old French *boce*.
GIVEN NAMES German 6%. *Hermann, Jurgen, Kurt*.

Bochenek (293) Polish: from *bochenek*, a diminutive of *bochen* 'loaf (of bread)'; presumably a metonymic occupational name for a baker.
GIVEN NAMES Polish 14%. *Alicja* (2), *Jerzy* (2), *Zigmund* (2), *Andrzej, Beata, Casimir, Genowefa, Krzysztof, Ryszard, Stanislaw, Wieslaw, Wojciech*.

Bochicchio (176) Southern Italian (Basilicata): variant of **Bocchicchio**, a nickname meaning 'little mouth'.
GIVEN NAMES Italian 24%. *Salvatore* (4), *Vito* (4), *Rocco* (2), *Biagio, Donato, Sal, Silvio*.

Bochner (197) Jewish (from Poland and Ukraine): habitational name for someone from a place called Bochnia.
GIVEN NAMES Jewish 19%; German 5%. *Chaim* (2), *Mandel* (2), *Benzion, Chaskel, Mordechai, Naftali, Schlomo, Shalom, Shimon; Kurt* (2), *Gerhard, Hans*.

Bocian (191) Polish and Jewish (from Poland): nickname for a tall, gangly person from *bocian* 'stork'. In some cases the Jewish name is ornamental.
GIVEN NAMES German 4%. *Kurt, Manfred*.

Bock (5506) **1.** German: nickname for a man with some fancied resemblance to a he-goat, Middle High German *boc*, or a habitational name from a house distinguished by the sign of a goat. **2.** Altered spelling of German **Böck** (see BOECK) or BACH. **3.** Jewish (Ashkenazic): ornamental name from German *Bock* 'he-goat'. **4.** English: variant of BUCK.
GIVEN NAMES German 4%. *Kurt* (7), *Erwin* (5), *Heinz* (3), *Manfred* (3), *Otto* (3), *Eldor* (2), *Ernst* (2), *Ewald* (2), *Reinhold* (2), *Wolf* (2), *Alois, Claus*.

Bockelman (381) North German (**Bockelmann**): habitational name from Bockel, the name of several places between Bremen and Soltau.

Bockenstedt (138) German: habitational name from a place so called.

Bocker (101) Dutch (**Boeker**) and North German (**Böcker**), and Danish: occupational name for a cooper (see BOECKER).
GIVEN NAMES German 5%; Dutch 5%; Scandinavian 4%. *Manfred*; *Harm, Klaas*; *Anders*.

Bockholt (107) Dutch and North German: topographic name for someone who lived near a beech wood, from Middle Low German *bōk* 'beech' + *holt* 'wood'.

Bockhorst (116) German: habitational name from a place in Westphalia, so named with Middle Low German *boke* 'beech tree' + *horst, hurst* 'thicket', 'undergrowth'.
GIVEN NAMES German 7%. *Gerhard, Kurt*.

Bockman (475) **1.** Altered spelling of North German **Böckmann** (see BOECKMANN). **2.** Swedish: probably from German (see 1).

Bockoven (104) German: see BOCKOVER.

Bockover (120) Respelling of German **Backofen**, a topographic name for a person living next to the village baking oven or a metonymic occupational name for a baker, from *back(en)* 'to bake' + *ofen* + the suffix *-er* denoting an occupation. Alternatively, though less likely, it could be from **Bockhof(f)er**, a habitational name for someone from Bockhop near Vechta.

Bockrath (164) North German: probably a topographic name for someone who lived in a clearing in a beech wood, from Middle Low German *boke* 'beech' + *rath* 'clearing'.

Bockus (177) Lithuanian (**Bočkus**): variant of **Bačkus** (see BACKUS).

Bocock (243) English (Yorkshire and Lancashire): from the Middle English personal name *Bawcok* or *Bolcok*, a pet form of BALDWIN + the hypocoristic suffix *-cok* (see COCKE).

Bocook (161) English: variant of BOCOCK.

Boczar (130) Polish and Ukrainian: occupational name for a cooper.
GIVEN NAMES Polish 7%. *Andrzej, Bogdan*.

Boczek (68) Polish: from *boczek* 'bacon' (from *boczek* 'side', hence the meat from the side of the animal), applied as a nickname or possibly a metonymic occupational name for a supplier of bacon.
GIVEN NAMES Polish 8%. *Darek, Mariusz*.

Boda (294) **1.** Spanish: nickname from *boda* 'wedding' (Latin *vota* '(marriage) vows', plural of *votum*, from *vovere* 'to vow'). The reasons for its adoption as a surname are probably anecdotal. **2.** Hungarian: from a derivative of *Bod* a personal name, believed by some to be derived from a Turkic word meaning 'twig', but the etymology is uncertain. In Hungary such one-element personal names of pagan origin were given to servants, usually before the 14th and 15th centuries when Christian names became dominant. **3.** Hungarian: possibly from *Bóda*, a pet form of the personal name *Boldizsár*, Hungarian form of BALTHAZAR. **4.** Bulgarian: from *Bogda*, a short form of the male personal name *Bogdan*, or the female personal name *Bogdana* (see BOGDAN).
GIVEN NAMES Hungarian 4%. *Attila, Bela, Mihaly, Tibor, Tivadar*.

Bodak (102) Polish, Ukrainian, and Slovak (**Bodák**) and Polish:: topographic name from *bodak* 'thistle', or nickname for a prickly person.

Bodamer (154) German: variant of BODMER.

Bodart (140) Belgian and northern French variant of Dutch **Boddaert**, from a Germanic personal name composed of the elements *bodo* 'messenger' + *hard* 'bold', 'hardy'.

Bodden (674) **1.** Dutch: from a pet form of the Germanic personal name *Bod(d)o* (see BODE). **2.** German: variant of BODEN 2.

Boddicker (126) Americanized form of Dutch or North German **Bödeker** (see BODEKER).

Boddie (911) **1.** English: variant spelling of BODY. **2.** Possibly an altered form of the German habitational name **Boddi(e)n**, from either of two places so named, in Mecklenburg and Brandenburg.

Boddy (634) **1.** English: variant spelling of BODY. **2.** Possibly also an altered spelling of Hungarian **Bódi** (see BODI).

Bode (2480) **1.** Dutch and German: occupational name for a messenger or representative, Dutch *bode*, Middle Low German *bode*. A *bode* was a medieval official with a variety of different functions. **2.** German and Danish: from the North German personal name *Bodo*, a derivative of Old Saxon *bodo* 'messenger'. **3.** North German and Dutch: a topographic name from Middle Low German *bōde*, *būde* 'booth', 'small house'. **4.** Danish: habitational name from a place named Bode.
GIVEN NAMES German 4%. *Erwin* (4), *Otto* (3), *Gerd* (2), *Gerhard* (2), *Helmut* (2), *Armin, Dieter, Erna, Ewald, Friedhelm, Fritz, Gunter*.

Bodeen (108) Swedish: topographic name from *bod* 'small hut' + the adjectival suffix *-én*, a derivative of Latin *-enius*. Alternatively, it may be from a place name containing the element *bod*.
GIVEN NAME Scandinavian 4%. *Erik*.

Bodek (125) Jewish: occupational name from Hebrew *bodek* 'ritual slaughtering inspector'.
GIVEN NAMES Jewish 11%. *Hillel* (2), *Arie, Golde, Mayer, Mendel, Zev*.

Bodeker (114) Dutch and North German (**Bödeker**): occupational name for a cooper, from Middle Low German *bodek* 'tub', 'vat' + the agent suffix *-er*. Compare BOECKER.
GIVEN NAME German 4%. *Heinz*.

Bodell (422) **1.** English (Midlands): of uncertain origin; perhaps a variant of BEADLE. **2.** Swedish: from *bod* 'small hut' + *-ell*, a frequent suffix of surnames, from the Latin adjectival ending *-elius*. **3.** Perhaps an altered spelling of German **Bodelle**, an occupational name for a beadle. Compare BITTEL.

Boden (1591) **1.** North German: patronymic from the personal name BODE, or from a short form of any of the many compound names with the element *Boden*. **2.** German: topographic name for someone living in a valley bottom or the low-lying area of a field, Middle High German *boden* 'ground', 'bottom'. Compare English BOTTOM. **3.** Swedish (**Bodén**): ornamental name, possibly from *bod* 'small hut' + the common surname suffix *-én*, a derivative of Latin *-enius* 'descendant of'. **4.** English: according to Reaney, a late variant of BALDWIN. **5.** Irish: Anglicized form of Gaelic **Ó Buadáin**.

Bodenhamer (471) Respelling of German and Jewish BODENHEIMER.

Bodenheimer (403) German and Jewish (western Ashkenazic): habitational name for someone from any of the several places in the Rhineland called Bodenheim.
GIVEN NAMES German 5%. *Ernst, Fritzi, Hans, Kurt, Siegfried*.

Bodenschatz (143) German: metonymic occupational name for someone who collected or had to pay *Bodenschatz*, a levy on produce from his ground (property) or on wine sold in barrels, from Middle High German *boden* 'bottom', 'ground' + *schatz* 'tax', 'rent', 'tithe'.
GIVEN NAMES German 7%. *Eberhard, Kurt*.

Bodenstein (185) **1.** German: habitational name from any of various places called Bodenstein, in Bavaria and northern Germany. **2.** Jewish (eastern Ashkenazic): ornamental name composed of German *Boden* 'ground' + *Stein* 'stone'.
GIVEN NAMES German 8%; Jewish 7%. *Dieter, Dietrich, Klaus, Wolfgang*; *Arie* (2), *Avrohom* (2), *Tzvi*.

Bodensteiner (203) German: habitational name for someone from a place called BODENSTEIN.

Bodette (137) Respelling of French BEAUDET.

Bodey (211) English: variant of BODY.

Bodge (146) English: probably a variant of BUDGE.

Bodi (267) Hungarian (**Bódi**): **1.** from a short form of *Bódizsár*, a variant of the personal name *Boldizsár*, Hungarian form of BALTHAZAR. **2.** nickname from *bódi* 'fat', 'rotund', or from the same word in the sense 'mad', 'crazy'. **3.** written *Bodi*, possibly a habitational name for someone from a place called Bod in Heves county.
GIVEN NAMES Hungarian 5%. *Csilla, Istvan, Lajos, Sandor, Zoltan*.

Bodie (715) English: variant spelling of BODY.

Bodiford (726) Origin uncertain. It is probably a variant of English **Bideford**, habitational name from a seaport in North Devon, named with the Cornish river name *Bȳd*, name of a local stream, + Old English *ea* 'river', + *ford* 'ford'. Alternatively, it may perhaps be from Buddleford in Devon, so named with Old English *boðl* 'dwelling', 'house' + *ford* 'ford'.

Bodily (431) English (Northamptonshire): perhaps a variant of **Baddeley**, a habitational name from Baddeley Green in Staffordshire, so named with the Old English personal name *Badda* + Old English *lēah* 'woodland clearing'.

Bodin (891) **1.** French and English: from an Old French personal name *Bodin*, a pet form of any of the various Germanic personal names beginning with the element *Bod-* 'messenger'. **2.** Altered spelling of French BEAUDOIN. **3.** Swedish: variant of **Bodén** (see BODEN). **4.** German: probably from a Germanic personal name, see 1, or from the habitational name *Boddin*, name of several places in Mecklenburg and Brandenburg.
GIVEN NAMES French 5%. *Raywood* (3), *Emile, Jean Claude, Leonie, Luc, Philippe, Theophile.*

Bodine (1818) French: possibly derived from the Germanic root *bald* 'bold'.
FOREBEARS A Huguenot family of this name, from the Saintonge region of France, settled in Staten Island, NY, at the end of the 17th century.

Bodkin (715) Irish: from *Bowdekyn*, an English pet form of BALDWIN, a Norman name well established in Ireland, described by McLysaght as the name of one of the 'Tribes of Galway'.

Bodkins (206) English: variant of BODKIN.

Bodle (323) English: topographic name for someone who lived or worked at a particular large house, from Old English *boðl, botl* 'dwelling house', 'hall', or a habitational name for someone who came from a place named with this element, probably Bodle Street near Hailsham, Sussex.

Bodley (357) English (West Midlands): habitational name of uncertain origin: probably from a lost settlement called Buddeley in Tabley Superior, Cheshire. Another possibility is Budleigh in Devon (*Bodelie* in Domesday Book), named with Old English *budda* 'beetle' (or the same word used as a byname) + *lēah* 'woodland clearing'.

Bodman (228) **1.** English: from Old English *boda* 'messenger' or *(ge)bod* 'message' + *mann* 'man', 'servant', hence an occupational name denoting a messenger or the servant of a messenger. **2.** German: variant of **Bodemann**, a habitational name from Boden near Uelzen, or from the Bode river in the Harz Mountains. **3.** Jewish (from Belarus): occupational name for the keeper of a bathhouse, from Yiddish *bod* 'bathhouse' + *man* 'man'.

Bodmer (318) Swiss German: **1.** topographic name for someone who dwelt in a valley bottom, from Middle High German *bodem* 'floor', 'bottom', or a habitational name from either of two places in Switzerland: Bodmen near Zurich or Bodman on Lake Constance. **2.** occupational name for someone who put down floors, from the same word as 1.
GIVEN NAMES German 4%. *Kurt* (2), *Erwin, Fritz, Heinz.*

Bodnar (2053) **1.** Ukrainian: occupational name for a cooper, from *bodnja* 'tub'. **2.** Polish and Slovak (**Bodnár**): from Low German, a borrowing of either *Böddener* 'cooper' or *Bodner* 'cottager'. **3.** Hungarian (**Bodnár**): occupational name from the Slavic loanword *bodnár* 'cooper', of German origin.

Bodner (871) **1.** German: topographic name for someone who dwelt in a valley bottom, from an agent derivative of Middle High German *boden* 'floor', 'bottom'. **2.** North German: nickname for someone who lived in a small dwelling, from a derivative of Middle Low German *bōde, būde* 'booth', 'small house', 'cottage'. **3.** Jewish (Ashkenazic): topographic name as in 1 or an occupational name from East Yiddish *bodner* 'cooper' (from Belorussian or older Ukrainian *bodnár*) (see BODNAR).
GIVEN NAMES Jewish 5%. *Moishe* (2), *Yakov* (2), *Beila, Feige, Inna, Leib, Mayer, Meyer, Mordechai, Ronit.*

Bodo (256) **1.** Hungarian (**Bodó**): from the old secular name *Bodó*, a derivative of the personal name *Bod*. **2.** Polish: perhaps from a pet form of the Old Slavic personal name *Ostrobod*, composed of the elements *ostro* 'sharp' + *bod*, from *bodę* 'to stab', 'prick'. **3.** Respelling of French **Baudot**, from a personal name derived from the Germanic root *bald* 'bold', 'brave'.
GIVEN NAMES Hungarian 8%. *Arpad* (2), *Sandor* (2), *Antal, Gabor, Imre, Kalman, Laszlo.*

Bodoh (146) Hungarian: variant of BODO.

Bodor (132) Hungarian: variant of BODO.
GIVEN NAMES Hungarian 12%. *Laszlo* (2), *Andras, Geza, Gyula, Magdolna, Zoltan.*

Boduch (108) Polish: derivative of BODO.
GIVEN NAMES Polish 10%. *Cecylia, Janina, Stanislaw, Wladyslaw.*

Bodwell (290) English: origin uncertain. Perhaps a variant of BIDWELL or possibly BARDWELL.

Body (469) **1.** English: nickname from Middle English *body*, Old English *bodig* 'body', 'trunk', presumably denoting a corpulent person. In Middle English the word was also used in the sense 'individual', 'person'. **2.** English: occupational name for a messenger, Middle English *bode* (Old English *boda*; compare BOTHE), with the spelling altered to preserve a disyllabic

pronunciation. This development can be clearly traced in Sussex. **3.** French: variant of BODIN. **4.** Hungarian (**Bódy**): variant of **Bódi** (see BODI).

Boe (1512) **1.** Swedish (**Boé**): from *bo* 'farm', 'dwelling' + the ornamental suffix *-é*. **2.** Respelling of Norwegian **Bø** or **Bøe**, a topographic name from Old Norse *býr* 'farm'. **3.** Danish: from *Bo*, a derivative of the Nordic personal name *Bui*. **4.** Dutch and North German: reduced form of BODE, originally pronounced as two syllables. **5.** Frisian (**Böe**): from the personal name *Boye*.
GIVEN NAMES Scandinavian 6%. *Erik* (2), *Alf, Bertel, Carsten, Egil, Gunvor, Holger, Iver, Knud, Knute, Nels, Nils.*

Boebel (114) German (**Böbel**): variant of **Böbel** (see BOBEL).
GIVEN NAMES German 5%. *Frieda, Ottmar.*

Boeck (601) **1.** South German (**Böck**): occupational name for a baker, a variant of BECK. **2.** North German: topographic name from Middle Low German *boke*, *böke* 'beech tree' or a habitational name from a place so named in Pomerania.
GIVEN NAMES German 6%. *Otto* (3), *Friedrich* (2), *Hilde* (2), *Dieter, Ernst, Hans, Jochen, Kurt, Liselotte, Manfred, Ute.*

Boeckel (179) North German (**Böckel**): habitational name from any of several places called Böckel, in the Rhineland, Westphalia, and Lower Saxony.
GIVEN NAMES German 7%. *Manfred* (2), *Eberhard, Otto.*

Boecker (343) North German (also **Böcker**) and Dutch: **1.** reduced form of **Bödeker** 'cooper' (see BOEDEKER). **2.** habitational name from any of several places in northern Germany named with Middle Low German *boke, böke* 'beech tree' (see BOECKMANN).
GIVEN NAMES German 7%. *Bernhard, Ewald, Gerd, Heinz, Ilse, Ulrich, Ulrike, Wolfgang.*

Boeckman (477) **1.** Dutch: topographic name for someone who lived by a beech tree, from Middle Dutch *boeke* 'beech' + *man* 'man'. **2.** Respelling of the German cognate **Böckmann** (see BOECKMANN).

Boeckmann (257) North German (**Böckmann**): topographic name for someone who lived by a beech tree or beech wood, from Middle Low German *boke, böke* 'beech tree' + *man* 'man', or a habitational name for someone from any of the places named with this word: *Böck, Böcke,* or *Böcken.*
GIVEN NAMES German 10%. *Heinz* (2), *Johannes* (2), *Claus, Ernst, Hans, Irmgard, Kurt, Othmar, Otto, Wendelin.*

Boedecker (195) Variant spelling of Dutch and German BOEDEKER.

Boedeker (519) North German (**Bödeker**) and Dutch: one of several occupational names for a cooper, from Middle Low German *bodeker, bödeker*, an agent derivative of *bodek*, *budik* 'vat', 'barrel'. Compare BOETTCHER.

GIVEN NAMES German 6%. *Hans* (4), *Fritz* (2), *Dietrich, Heinz, Hermann, Kurt, Otto*.

Boeder (208) German (**Böder**): occupational name from an agent derivative of Middle Low German *bodern* 'to wash'.

GIVEN NAMES German 4%. *Erna, Ernst, Lorenz*.

Boedigheimer (167) German (**Bödigheim**): habitational name for someone from a place called Bödigheim near Heilbronn.

Boeding (221) Probably a German habitational name (**Böding**) denoting someone from a place in Thuringia named Bodungen.

Boege (137) North German (**Böge**): 1. variant of the personal name **Böe** (see BOE 5). 2. from Middle Low German *boge* 'flexible', 'supple' or 'arch', 'curve', 'bow', hence a nickname for a lithe person or a topographic name for someone who lived by the bend in a river, road, or field.

Boegel (120) German: 1. metonymic occupational name for an archer, *bögel* 'bow', or for a maker or seller of harness equipment, from the same word in the sense 'stirrup', 'ring', or 'yoke'. 2. from the short pet form (*Bogo*) of a Germanic personal name formed with *bogo* 'bow' as the first element.

Boeger (246) North German (**Böger**): see BOGER.

GIVEN NAMES German 7%. *Frieda, Guenther, Hans, Helmut, Kurt, Willi*.

Boeglin (122) German: from a diminutive of BOEGEL.

GIVEN NAMES German 7%; French 4%. *Aloysius, Erwin, Kurt, Markus; Alphonse, Marcel*.

Boeh (176) German and Dutch: variant of **Böe** (see BOE 5).

Boehl (153) German: variant of BOEHLE.

GIVEN NAMES German 8%. *Hans, Helmut, Herta*.

Boehle (223) 1. German (**Böhl(e)**): patronymic from a pet form of a personal name composed of the Germanic elements *bald* 'bold', 'hardy', 'strong' + *win* 'friend'. Compare BALDWIN. 2. North German: variant of BOHLE 1. 3. North German: topographic for someone who lived by a boardwalk, from Middle Low German *bōle* (*f.*) 'plank', 'beam'.

GIVEN NAMES German 5%. *Klaus, Kurt, Reinhard*.

Boehler (574) German (**Böhler**): habitational name for someone from any of several places in Saxony named Böhle or Böhlen.

GIVEN NAMES German 4%. *Aloysius, Horst, Juergen, Markus, Oskar*.

Boehlert (106) German: variant of BOEHLER.

Boehlke (376) German (**Böhlke**): from the personal name *Boleke*, a pet form of a personal name composed of the Germanic

elements *bald* 'bold', 'hardy', 'strong' + *win* 'friend'. Compare BALDWIN.

GIVEN NAMES German 4%. *Ulrich* (3), *Armin, Kurt*.

Boehm (4590) German (**Böhm**), Dutch, and Jewish (Ashkenazic): ethnic name for a native or inhabitant of Bohemia (now the western part of the Czech Republic), from *Böhmen*, German name of Bohemia (Middle High German *Böheim, Bēheim*). This derives its name from the tribal name *Baii + heim* 'homeland'; the *Baii* were a tribe, probably Celtic, who inhabited the region in the 1st century AD and were gradually displaced by Slavic settlers in the period up to the 5th century. The same tribe also gave their name to *Bavaria* (see BAYER). Bohemia was an independent Slavic kingdom from the 7th century to 1526, when it fell to the Habsburgs. In 1627 it was formally declared a Habsburg Crown Land, and by the Treaty of Versailles it became a province of the newly formed Czechoslovakia in 1919. This is also found as a Swedish name.

GIVEN NAMES German 6%. *Kurt* (11), *Hans* (9), *Otto* (6), *Fritz* (5), *Gerhard* (5), *Horst* (5), *Bernd* (3), *Dieter* (3), *Helmut* (3), *Wolfgang* (3), *Erwin* (2), *Guenter* (2).

Boehme (963) German and Dutch: variant of BOEHM.

GIVEN NAMES German 6%. *Heinz* (2), *Helmut* (2), *Kurt* (2), *Reinhold* (2), *Detlef, Diethelm, Erwin, Hans, Juergen, Klaus, Otto, Wolf*.

Boehmer (1020) 1. German (**Böhmer**): ethnic name for a native or inhabitant of Bohemia (see BOEHM). 2. North German: topographic name for someone who lived by a barrier (German *Schlagbaum*), or perhaps a metonymic occupational name for a customs collector. Alternatively, in some cases it may have been an occupational name for someone who grew or tended trees or a topographic name for someone who lived by a conspicuous tree. 3. Swedish: probably from German.

Boehmke (171) North German (**Böhmke**): from a diminutive of Middle Low German *bom*, which in addition to meaning 'tree' was also used to denote a beam or joist, so that the name may have been either topographical or a metonymic occupational name for a carpenter.

Boehne (223) North German (**Böhne**) and Dutch: topographic name for someone who lived in a loft, from Middle Low German *böne* 'raised platform', 'hay loft', 'attic'.

Boehner (264) North German (**Böhner**): 1. occupational name from an agent derivative of Middle Low German *bönen* 'to board', 'to lay a floor' 2. topographic name for someone who lived in a loft, a variant of BOEHNE + the suffix *-er* denoting an inhabitant.

Boehning (197) North German (**Böhning**): patronymic from BOHN. See also BOENING.

Boehnke (212) North German (**Böhnke**): occupational name for a grower of beans, from a diminutive of BOHN 1 or a variant of **Bohneke**.

GIVEN NAMES German 10%. *Uwe* (3), *Manfred* (2), *Kurt, Otto*.

Boehnlein (226) German (**Böhnlein**): from a diminutive of BOHN, literally 'little bean'.

Boehringer (267) German (**Böhringer**): habitational name for someone from any of three places in Baden-Württemberg called Böhringen.

GIVEN NAMES German 7%. *Kurt* (3), *Hans, Orlo*.

Boeke (283) Dutch and North German (**Böke**): topographic name for someone who lived near a beech tree or beech grove, from Middle Low German *boke, böke* 'beech tree'.

Boeker (200) Dutch and North German (**Böker**): variant of the topographic name **Böke** 'beech' (see BOEKE), + the suffix *-er* denoting an inhabitant.

GIVEN NAMES German 8%. *Wolfgang* (2), *Arno, Rainer*.

Boelens (134) Dutch and North German: patronymic from **Bolen**, itself a patronymic from the Germanic personal name *Bole* (see BOHL).

Boelke (141) North German (**Bölke**): variant of *Böhlke* (see BOEHLKE).

Boell (134) Variant of German BOEHLE.

Boelman (151) Altered spelling of German **Böhlmann**, a variant of **Bohlmann**, a compound formed with the Germanic personal name *Bole* or the Slavic stem *bol* 'more'.

Boelter (690) German (**Bölter**): occupational name from Middle High German *bolter* 'maker of bolts (for crossbows)'.

GIVEN NAMES German 4%. *Erwin* (2), *Claus, Erna, Franz, Frederich, Hans, Otto*.

Boen (496) 1. Dutch: variant of BOONE. 2. Norwegian (**Bøen**): habitational name from a common farm name **Bøen** 'The Farm', from *bø* 'farm' or 'meadow' (Old Norse *býr*) + the definite article *-en*. 3. Respelling of Swedish **Böen**, cognate with 2.

Boender (122) Dutch: from Middle Dutch *boender*, a measure of land equivalent to about two and a half acres, hence a status name for someone who farmed a landholding of this size.

GIVEN NAMES Dutch 9%. *Cornie* (3), *Michiel* (2).

Boenig (145) German (**Bönig**): presumably from the Slavic personal name *Bon*, a derivative of *boniti* 'to scare'.

GIVEN NAMES German 8%; French 5%. *Arno, Helmuth, Lutz; Pierre, Sylvie*.

Boening (222) North German (**Böning**): 1. patronymic from BOHN 1. 2. habitational name from a place called Boninge, now known as Bönnien, near Hildesheim. 3. variant of BOENIG.

GIVEN NAMES German 8%. *Franz, Gerhard, Hans, Helmut, Willi.*

Boenker (110) German: of uncertain origin. Possibly a habitational name from a place called Bonk in the former West Prussia, or a variant or alteration of **Bönke**, from a Slavic personal name *Bon* (from *boniti* 'to scare'), or an occupational name for a carpenter, a rounded form of **Benker**, from Middle High German **bank** 'bench' + the *-er* agent suffix.

GIVEN NAME German 6%. *Kurt.*

Boepple (169) South German (**Böpple**): from a pet form of BOPP.

Boer (480) Dutch and North German: occupational name for a farmer, from Middle Low German *būr* 'dweller', 'citizen', 'neighbor', 'farmer' (see BAUER).

GIVEN NAMES German 6%; Dutch 5%. *Ralf (5), Hans (2), Kurt; Gerret (2), Marinus (2), Adriaan, Cornelis, Egbert, Gerrit, Gert, Kees.*

Boerboom (125) Dutch: topographic name for someone who lived by a tree under which the inhabitants of a village would meet.

Boerema (146) Variant of Frisian *Boerma* (see BOERSMA).

Boerger (561) North German (**Börger**): **1.** status name for a freeman of a borough, especially one who was a member of its governing council (see BURGER). **2.** in some cases a habitational name from a place named Börger, near the hills of Hümmling.

Boerman (201) Dutch: occupational name for a peasant, from *boer* 'peasant', from BOER + *man* 'man'.

Boerner (1014) North German (**Börner**): topographic name for someone who lived beside a well, from a northern and western term *born* 'well' + the suffix *-er* denoting an inhabitant.

GIVEN NAMES German 6%. *Otto (7), Kurt (5), Ernst (2), Gerhard (2), Arno, Hannelore, Joerg.*

Boers (265) **1.** German (**Börs**): from the personal name *Boers*, a short form of the medieval personal name *Liborius*. **2.** Dutch: patronymic from BOER.

Boersema (101) Frisian: variant of BOERSMA.

Boersma (654) Frisian: occupational name for a farmer or peasant.

Boerst (131) German (**Börst**): nickname for someone with an aggressive temperament, from German *Börst* 'bristle'.

Boes (912) German (**Bös**): **1.** variant of **Böse** (see BOESE). **2.** patronymic from BOE 5.

Boesch (692) **1.** South German (**Bösch**): from a short form of the personal name SEBASTIAN. **2.** North German: variant of BOSCH.

Boeschen (105) North German: topographic name from Middle Low German

bosch 'bush', 'woods', the dative plural indicating a location near a wood.

GIVEN NAMES German 9%. *Erwin, Gerhard, Helmut, Reinhard.*

Boese (1011) German (**Böse**): nickname from Middle High German *bœse* 'bad', 'poor quality', 'sickly', later 'furious', 'angry'.

GIVEN NAMES German 4%. *Klaus (2), Erna, Erwin, Frieda, Inge, Kurt, Otto.*

Boesel (206) German (**Bösel**): habitational name from any of two places so named Bösel, near Oldenburg or Lüneburg.

GIVEN NAME German 6%. *Fritz (2).*

Boesen (303) Swedish and Danish: patronymic from the personal name *Bo* 'farmer' (see BOE).

Boester (114) North German (**Böster**) from a reduced form of the personal name SEBASTIAN.

Boetcher (153) German: variant of BOETTCHER.

GIVEN NAME German 5%. *Kurt (2).*

Boettcher (2850) German (**Böttcher**): occupational name for a cooper, from Middle High German *botecher, bötticher, büttticher*, an agent derivative of *botech(e), bottich, bütte* 'vat', 'barrel'. See also BINDER, BUETTNER, and SCHAEFFLER.

GIVEN NAMES German 6%. *Horst (6), Gerhard (5), Hans (5), Kurt (4), Otto (4), Erwin (3), Fritz (2), Helmuth (2), Juergen (2), Klaus (2), Siegfried (2), Armin.*

Boettger (491) German: variant of BOETTCHER.

GIVEN NAMES German 8%. *Gerhard (2), Kurt (2), Claus, Erhard, Gerd, Heinz, Otto, Ralf.*

Boettner (309) German: variant of BUETTNER.

GIVEN NAMES German 4%. *Fritz, Gunther, Helmut, Klaus.*

Boeve (308) Dutch: derogatory nickname from Middle Dutch *boef, boeve* 'rogue', 'scoundrel'.

Boever (127) Dutch: variant of BOEVE.

Boevers (116) Dutch: variant of BOEVE.

GIVEN NAMES German 4%. *Ewald, Kurt.*

Boff (139) **1.** English: from Old French *boeuf* 'bull', a nickname for a powerfully built man. In some cases it may have been originally a metonymic occupational name for a herdsman. Compare BOUVIER. **2.** German (**Böff**): from the short form of a Germanic personal name with *bod-* (Old Saxon *bodo* 'messenger'), as in *Bodo*.

GIVEN NAMES French 6%. *Gabrielle, Henri.*

Boffa (184) Italian (Piedmont): probably a nickname for a person who suffered from shortness of breath, or was in the habit of breathing rapidly or heavily, from Old Italian *boffare* 'to pant', 'to puff'.

GIVEN NAMES Italian 15%. *Antonio (4), Mario (3), Antonino, Armando, Attillo, Biagio, Emilio, Gino, Martino, Sal.*

Bogaard (116) Dutch: variant of BOGARD.

GIVEN NAMES Dutch 5%. *Dirk, Godfried.*

Bogacki (182) Polish: **1.** habitational name for someone from a place called Bogacko or Bogate, for example. **2.** nickname from *bogaty* 'rich'.

GIVEN NAMES Polish 10%. *Casimir, Jacek, Przemyslaw, Stanislaw, Szczepan, Zbigniew.*

Bogacz (217) Polish: nickname from Polish *bogacz* 'rich man'.

GIVEN NAMES Polish 7%. *Bronislaw, Urszula, Wladyslaw, Zbigniew, Zdzislaw.*

Bogaert (106) Dutch: variant of BOGARD.

GIVEN NAMES French 6%; German 4%. *Armand, Remi; Erwin.*

Bogan (2289) Irish: Anglicized form of Gaelic **Ó Bogáin** 'descendant of *Bogán*', a diminutive of *bog* 'soft', 'tender'.

Bogar (418) **1.** Variant, especially in French-speaking areas, of Dutch BOGARD. **2.** Hungarian (**Bogár**): from *bogár* 'bug', also found as a nickname for someone with dark hair or black eyes. **3.** In some cases, possibly from the old Hungarian secular name *Bogár*.

Bogard (1301) Dutch: shortened form of **van den Bogaard**, a topographic name for someone living by an orchard, Dutch *Boomgaard*, or a habitational name from any of various places named with this word.

Bogardus (671) Humanistic surname in Germany and the Netherlands, a Latinized form of BOGARD.

FOREBEARS The name in this spelling is recorded in Beverwijck in New Netherland in the mid 17th century.

Bogart (2442) Dutch and North German: variant of BOGARD 'orchard', German BAUMGARTEN.

FOREBEARS This name is recorded in Beverwijck in New Netherland in the mid 17th century, but it was also brought independently to North America by other bearers.

Bogda (102) Variant of Polish BOGDAN.

Bogdan (1105) **1.** Polish, Slovak, Slovenian (Prekmurje, i.e. easternmost Slovenia), and Serbian: from the common Slavic personal name *Bogdan, Bohdan*, composed of the elements *Bog* 'God' + *dan* 'gift'. This was not a Christian name sanctioned by the Orthodox Church, but was common as a familiar vernacular name, equivalent to Greek *Theodōros* 'gift of God' (see THEODORE) or *Theodōtos* 'given by God'. As an American surname, it may also be a shortened form of any of numerous other Slavic surnames formed from this personal name. This is also found as a Romanian name. **2.** Hungarian (**Bogdán**): habitational name for someone from any of numerous places called Bogdány, in Abaúj, Pest, Szabolcs, and Veszprém counties, or in Máramaros, now in Romania. **3.** Jewish (eastern Ashkenazic): habitational name from any of numerous places in Belarus and Poland called Bogdany.

GIVEN NAMES Romanian 4%. *Cornel* (4), *Mircea* (4), *Radu* (4), *Alexandru* (2), *Doru* (2), *Nicolae* (2), *Gheorghe*, *Mihaela*, *Vasile*.

Bogdanoff (168) **1.** Alternative spelling of Russian, Bulgarian, and Macedonian **Bogdanov**, a patronymic from the personal name BOGDAN meaning 'gift of God'. Among the Orthodox it was sometimes used to denote an illegitimate child or foundling. **2.** Jewish (from Belarus): habitational name for someone from any of the various places in Belarus called Bogdanovo or Bogdany.

Bogdanovich (140) **1.** Belorussian and Ukrainian; Serbian and Croatian (**Bogdanović**): patronymic from the personal name BOGDAN. **2.** Jewish (eastern Ashkenazic): habitational name for someone from Bogdany in Poland or from the various places in Belarus called Bogdanovo, Bogdanovichi, or Bogdany.

GIVEN NAMES South Slavic 7%; Russian 6%. *Darko*, *Petar*, *Spasoje*, *Zorka*; *Luka*, *Lyubov*, *Valeriy*.

Bogdanowicz (156) Polish: patronymic from BOGDAN.

GIVEN NAMES Polish 18%. *Wojciech* (3), *Benedykt*, *Bogdan*, *Mieczyslaw*, *Miroslaw*, *Zbigniew*, *Zigmunt*, *Zofia*.

Bogdanski (279) **1.** Polish (**Bogdański**) and Jewish (Ashkenazic): habitational name for someone from any of the various villages called Bogdany, in Poland, Belarus, Ukraine, and elsewhere, all named with the personal name BOGDAN. **2.** Bulgarian: patronymic from the personal name BOGDAN.

GIVEN NAMES Polish 7%. *Alojzy*, *Janina*, *Lucjan*, *Tadeusz*, *Zigmund*.

Bogden (224) Variant of Slavic BOGDAN.

Bogdon (188) Variant of Slavic BOGDAN.

Boge (279) **1.** Frisian: variant of **Böe** (see BOE 5). **2.** Norwegian: habitational name from any of various farms in southwestern Norway named Boge, from Old Norse *bugr* 'hook', 'bay', 'bend', with reference to an inlet or a bend in a river.

Bogel (132) North German (**Bögel**): **1.** from a pet form of *Bogo*, itself a short form of the personal name *Bogenhart*. **2.** from Middle Low German *bog(h)el* 'stirrup', 'bow', 'yoke ring', hence possibly a metonymic occupational name for a maker or user of such items.

GIVEN NAME German 4%. *Dieter*.

Bogen (446) **1.** German: metonymic occupational name for an archer, bowman, or bow maker, from Middle High German *boge* 'bow'. **2.** Jewish (Ashkenazic): ornamental name from German *(Regen)bogen* 'rainbow' or from German *Bogen* (Yiddish *boigen*) 'arch', 'bow'. **3.** Norwegian: habitational name from any of various farmsteads, so named with Old Norse *bugr* (see BOGE) + the definite article *-en*. **4.** Perhaps also an altered spelling of Irish BOGAN.

GIVEN NAMES German 4%. *Otto* (2), *Fritz*, *Kurt*.

Bogenrief (120) German: metonymic occupational name for an archer or a bowmaker, from Middle High German *bogen* 'bow' + *reif*, an agent noun from *reifen* 'to bend'.

Bogenschutz (162) German (**Bogenschütz**): occupational name for an archer, from Middle High German *bogen* + *schütze* 'archer'.

Boger (1532) **1.** German: occupational name from Middle High German *bogære* 'bow maker', 'bowman', 'archer'. **2.** German: from a personal name formed with Old High German *bogo* 'bow'. **3.** Norwegian: variant of BOGE.

Bogert (821) shortened and altered form of Dutch **van den Bogaard** (see BOGARD).

Boggan (559) Irish: variant of BOGAN.

Boggess (1755) English: nickname from Middle English *boggish* 'boastful' or 'haughty' (see BOGGS).

Boggiano (121) Northern Italian (mainly Liguria): probably a habitational name from a place in Pistoia province named Buggiano, from the Latin personal name *Abudius* + the adjectival suffix *-anus*.

Boggio (309) Northern Italian (mainly Piedmont): probably a habitational name from either of the common place names Boggio or Boggia.

GIVEN NAMES Italian 6%. *Raul* (2), *Romulo* (2), *Angelo*, *Catalina*, *Cesar*, *Gino*, *Guido*, *Massimo*, *Paulina*, *Riccardo*, *Renato*, *Zulma*.

Boggs (9692) English: nickname from Middle English *boggish* 'boastful', 'haughty' (a word of unknown origin, perhaps akin to Germanic *bag* and *bug*, with the literal meaning 'swollen', 'puffed up'). The name (in the forms *Boge(y)s*, *Boga(y)s*) is found in the 12th century in Yorkshire and East Anglia, and also around Bordeaux, which had trading links with East Anglia.

Boggus (200) **1.** English: variant of BOGGS. **2.** Lithuanian: respelling of Polish BOGUSZ or shortened form of the Lithuanian family names **Bogušas**, **Boguša**, **Bogušauskas**, or **Bogusevičius**, all derivatives of BOGUSZ.

Bogh (105) Norwegian: habitational name from a placed named with Old Norse *bugr* 'hook', 'bay', 'bend' (see also BOGE).

GIVEN NAMES Scandinavian 7%. *Bjorg*, *Nels*, *Niels*.

Boghosian (214) Armenian: variant of BOGOSIAN.

GIVEN NAMES Armenian 27%. *Sarkis* (4), *Ara* (2), *Boghos* (2), *Haig* (2), *Krikor* (2), *Agob*, *Aram*, *Garen*, *Hagop*, *Masis*, *Menas*, *Missak*.

Boghossian (128) Armenian: variant of BOGOSIAN.

GIVEN NAMES Armenian 33%. *Hagop* (3), *Razmik* (2), *Agop*, *Aris*, *Bedros*, *Goorgen*, *Hrair*, *Hrayr*, *Kegham*, *Krikor*, *Noune*, *Ohannes*.

Bogie (291) Scottish: habitational name from a place in Fife, first recorded as *Bolgyne*. The modern Gaelic name is *Srath* '(valley)' *Bhalgaidgh*. The origin of the place name is uncertain. Watson suggests a connection with Gaelic *bolg* 'bag', 'sack', in the sense 'bag-shaped pool'.

Bogin (174) **1.** Jewish (from Belarus): habitational name from a village called Bogin. **2.** Jewish (eastern Ashkenazic): Russianized form of BOGEN.

GIVEN NAMES Jewish 7%. *Asher* (3), *Irina*, *Rimma*, *Sinai*.

Bogle (1848) **1.** Scottish and northern Irish: nickname for a person of frightening appearance, from older Scots *bogill* 'hobgoblin', 'bogy' (of uncertain origin, possibly Gaelic). **2.** South German (**Bögle**): metonymic occupational name for a bowman or bow maker, from a diminutive of Middle High German *boge* 'bow' (see BOGEL), or from the pet form of a Germanic personal name formed with an element akin to Old High German *bogo* 'bow'.

Bognar (333) Hungarian (**Bognár**): occupational name from *bognár* 'cartwright', 'wheelwright'.

GIVEN NAMES Hungarian 7%. *Andras* (3), *Istvan* (2), *Attila*, *Bela*, *Miklos*, *Sandor*, *Tibor*.

Bogner (938) German: metonymic occupational name for a bowman or for a maker or seller of bows, from Middle High German *bogenære*. Compare BOGER.

GIVEN NAMES German 5%. *Kurt* (4), *Hans* (2), *Reinhold* (2), *Franz*, *Lorenz*, *Manfred*, *Matthias*, *Otto*, *Siegmund*, *Theodor*, *Viktor*.

Bogosian (304) Armenian: patronymic from the western Armenian personal name *Bołos*, classical Armenian *Pawłos* (see PAUL).

GIVEN NAMES Armenian 18%. *Armen* (4), *Sarkis* (3), *Aram* (2), *Arshag* (2), *Garabet* (2), *Vasken* (2), *Zaven* (2), *Avak*, *Garegin*, *Hovanes*, *Megerdich*, *Ovsanna*.

Bogren (115) Swedish: ornamental name composed of the elements *bo* 'dwelling', 'farm' + *gren* 'twig'.

GIVEN NAMES Scandinavian 13%. *Erik*, *Lennart*, *Nels*, *Thor*.

Bogucki (356) Polish: habitational name for someone from a place called Boguty, Bogucice, Bogucin, or Bogucino, which are all diminutives of *Boguta*, a derivative of the personal name *Bogusław* (see BOGUSLAWSKI).

GIVEN NAMES Polish 9%. *Bogdan*, *Bronislaw*, *Ewa*, *Henryk*, *Jacek*, *Janina*, *Krzysztof*, *Lukasz*, *Tadeusz*, *Wit*, *Zigmund*.

Bogue (1365) Irish (Cork): Anglicized form of Gaelic **Ó Buadhaigh** 'descendant of *Buadhach*', a personal name meaning 'victorious'. (The British name *Boudicca* or *Boadicea*, borne by the Queen of the Iceni who in AD 62 led a revolt against the Roman occupation of her country, is a cognate.)

Bogues (137) Origin uncertain. Perhaps a variant of English BOGGS or Irish BOGUE.
GIVEN NAMES French 5%. *Andree, Patrice.*

Bogus (377) **1.** German (of Slavic origin): from the short form of a Slavic personal name (*Bogumil* 'dear to God', for example), equivalent to *Gottlieb*, with the same meaning. **2.** Polish and Ukrainian (**Boguś**): variant of BOGUSZ.

Bogush (105) Americanized spelling of Polish and Ukrainian BOGUS.
GIVEN NAME Russian 4%. *Yuriy.*

Boguslawski (128) **1.** Polish (**Bogusław-ski**) and Jewish (from Poland): habitational name for someone from a place called Boguslaw or Boguslawice, from the personal name *Bogusław* (composed of Slavic *Bog* 'God' + *slav* 'glory'). **2.** Jewish (from Ukraine): habitational name for someone from a place called Boguslav in Ukraine.
GIVEN NAMES Polish 8%. *Jaromir, Tadeusz, Zbigniew, Zygmunt.*

Bogusz (172) Polish: from a short form of the personal name *Bogusław* (composed of the Slavic elements *Bog* 'God' + *slav* 'glory').
GIVEN NAMES Polish 14%. *Andrzej, Bogdan, Grazyna, Jozef, Leszek, Malgorzata, Mariusz, Pawel, Piotr, Wieslaw.*

Bohac (325) Czech and Slovak (**Boháč**): nickname for a rich man, from *bohatý* 'rich'.

Bohach (126) Americanized spelling of Czech and Slovak **Boháč** (see BOHAC), or German **Bohatsch**, a Germanized form of this name.

Bohall (204) Origin unidentified.

Bohan (876) Irish: Anglicized form of Gaelic **Ó Buadhacháin**, a diminutive of *buadhach* 'victorious'.
GIVEN NAMES Irish 6%. *Connor* (2), *John Patrick* (2), *Brendan, Liam.*

Bohanan (711) Irish: variant of BOHANNON.

Bohannan (685) Irish: variant of BOHANNON.

Bohannon (3287) Irish: Anglicized form of Gaelic **Ó Buadhachanáin**, a double diminutive of *buadhach* 'victorious'.

Bohanon (490) Irish: variant of BOHANNON.

Bohart (204) Origin unidentified.

Bohaty (117) Czech (**Bohatý**): nickname from *bohatý* 'rich'.

Bohen (166) **1.** French: habitational name from Bohain-en-Vermandois in Aisne, France, or from Bohan in Namur province, now in Belgium. **2.** Variant of the Irish surname BOHAN.

Bohl (1307) **1.** North German: from the Germanic personal name *Baldo*, a short form of the various compound names with the first element *bald* 'bold'. **2.** North German: habitational name from either of two places called Bohl, near Düren and

Cologne. **3.** North German: variant of BOHLE. **4.** Swedish: of German origin.

Bohland (175) German: **1.** habitational name from a place in Baden called Bohland, or from any of the places mentioned at BOLANDER. **2.** possibly in some cases an ethnic name for someone from Poland, commonly known in the Middle Ages as *Boland*.

Bohlander (327) **1.** Swedish and German: variant of BOLANDER. **2.** German: variant of BOHLAND.

Bohle (225) **1.** North German: nickname for a male relative, colleague in a guild or fraternity, or lover, Middle Low German *bōle*. **2.** German: habitational name from any of the various places so named in Rhineland and Schleswig-Holstein. **3.** Norwegian (**Bøhle**): variant of **Bøle** (see BOLE).
GIVEN NAME French 4%. *Henri.*

Bohlen (666) **1.** German: patronymic from BOHL 1. **2.** German: habitational name from a place in Westphalia named Bohlen. **3.** German (**Böhlen**): habitational name from any of several places in Saxony named Böhlen. **4.** Swedish (**Bohlén**): ornamental name from BOHL 1 + the suffix *-én*, a derivative of Latin *-enius* 'descendant of'.

Bohlender (130) Swedish: variant of BOLANDER.
GIVEN NAME German 4%. *Otto.*

Bohler (430) **1.** German: variant of BOLER. **2.** German (**Böhler**): see BOEHLER. **3.** Norwegian (**Bøhler**): variant of *Bøler* (see BOLER).

Bohley (135) **1.** Americanized form of German BOLEY. **2.** Possibly a variant spelling of Irish **O'Bohelly**, an Anglicization of Gaelic **Ó Buachalla** (see BUCKLEY).

Bohlin (246) Swedish: variant spelling of BOLIN.
GIVEN NAMES Scandinavian 7%. *Swen* (2), *Lars.*

Bohling (586) North German (also **Böhling**): patronymic from BOHL 1.

Bohlinger (145) German: habitational name for someone from a place called Bohling in Baden or Bohlingen in Württemberg.

Bohlke (211) Variant of North German BOHLKEN.
GIVEN NAME German 4%. *Manfred.*

Bohlken (185) North German: from a pet form of BOHL.
GIVEN NAMES German 4%. *Gerda, Ingo.*

Bohlman (601) Americanized spelling of North German BOHLMANN.

Bohlmann (388) **1.** North German (also **Böhlemann, Böhlmann**): **2.** variant of BOHL. **3.** from Middle Low German *bōle* (f.) 'plank', 'beam' + *man* 'man', hence an occupational name for a carpenter or a topographic name for someone who lived by a board walk.

GIVEN NAMES German 8%. *Hans* (3), *Kurt* (2), *Otto* (2), *Elfriede, Erwin, Joerg, Lorenz.*

Bohls (151) North German: patronymic from BOHL.

Bohm (1076) **1.** German (**Böhm**) and Jewish (Ashkenazic): ethnic name for a native or inhabitant of Bohemia: see BOEHM. **2.** North German: from Middle Low German *bōm* 'tree', hence a topographic name for someone who lived by a particularly conspicuous tree, a habitational name for someone who lived at a house distinguished by the sign of a tree, or perhaps in some cases a metonymic occupational name for someone who tended trees. This is also found as a Swedish surname.
GIVEN NAMES German 5%. *Friedrich* (3), *Jurgen* (2), *Arno, Claus, Erna, Fritz, Hans, Karl-Heinz, Konrad, Manfred, Monika.*

Bohman (676) **1.** Respelling of German BOHMANN. **2.** Swedish: variant of BOMAN.
GIVEN NAMES German 4%. *Kurt* (2), *Ralf* (2), *Wenzel.*

Bohmann (138) German: reduced form of **Bodemann** (see BODE).

Bohmer (203) **1.** German (**Böhmer**): see BOEHMER. **2.** Jewish (western Ashkenazic): variant of BOHM.
GIVEN NAMES German 6%. *Alois, Christoph, Hilde, Ulrich.*

Bohn (3864) **1.** North German: variant of BODE. **2.** German: metonymic occupational name for a grower of beans, from Middle High German, Middle Low German *bōne* 'bean'. Beans were a staple food in the Middle Ages, especially the broad bean, *Vicia faba*; the green bean, *Phaseolus vulgaris*, was not introduced from South America until the late 16th century.

Bohne (587) North German: variant of BOHN.
GIVEN NAMES German 5%. *Fritz* (3), *Kurt* (2), *Erna.*

Bohnen (165) German: **1.** variant of BOHN. **2.** (mainly in northern Germany) patronymic from BOHN(E). **3.** habitational name from a place named Bohnen, near Zerbst, Saxony-Anhalt.

Bohnenkamp (257) German: from Middle High German, Middle Low German *bōne* 'bean' + late Middle High German, Middle Low German *kamp* 'field', 'domain', hence a topographic name for someone who lived by a field or domain where beans were grown.

Bohner (530) **1.** South German: variant spelling of BONER 2 'bean grower'. **2.** German (**Böhner**): topographic name for someone who lived in a loft (see BOEHNER). **3.** Swedish (**Bohnér**): ornamental name from *bo* 'farm', 'dwelling' + the suffix *-ner*.

Bohnert (632) German: **1.** variant of BOHNER. **2.** habitational name from a place in Schleswig-Holstein named Bohnert.

3. (Böhnert): variant of **Böhner** (see BOEHNER).

Bohnet (234) German: perhaps an altered spelling of BOHNERT. The name is recorded in Switzerland, having been taken there in 1858 and 1912 by immigrants from Germany.
GIVEN NAMES German 4%. *Arno, Kurt.*

Bohnhoff (149) German: habitational name from any of two places near Siegburg (Rhineland) or in Bavaria from any of several other minor localities in the same area. The second element is Middle Low German *hof* 'court', 'farmstead', 'manor farm' (see HOFF); the first is probably from *bōne* 'bean', a staple item of diet in the Middle Ages; alternatively, it may be from a personal name with the common Germanic element *Bon*, cognate with Old English *Buna*. Compare BONHAM 2.
GIVEN NAME German 6%. *Heinz.*

Bohning (149) North German (**Böhning**): **1.** habitational name from a place near Hildesheim called Bönnien, the *-ing* suffix denoting affiliation. **2.** patronymic from *Bone*, a Germanic personal name of unknown origin.

Bohnsack (392) German: occupational name for a bean grower, from a word meaning 'beanbag', a compound of BOHN + Middle High German *sac* 'bag', Middle Low German *sak*.

Bohnstedt (103) German: habitational name from a place of this name.

Bohon (495) Possibly a variant spelling of the Irish surname BOHAN.

Bohorquez (151) Spanish (**Bohórquez**): habitational name from a minor place called Bohorques in Santander province.
GIVEN NAMES Spanish 49%. *Carlos* (5), *Luis* (5), *Eduardo* (4), *Jorge* (4), *Jaime* (3), *Jose* (3), *Mario* (3), *Alberto* (2), *Blanca* (2), *Elena* (2), *Ernesto* (2), *Fernando* (2); *Marco* (2), *Aldo, Antonio, Federico.*

Bohr (649) **1.** German: from a short form of a personal name of Slavic origin (see BORIS), or from a reduced form of the medieval personal name *Liborius*, patron saint of the city of Paderborn. **2.** Danish and Swedish: from German *Baar, Bahr* (see BEER), recorded in Denmark since the 18th century.

Bohren (180) **1.** Swiss German: see BOHR 1. **2.** Swedish (**Bohrén**): variant of BOHR, with the addition of the suffix *-én*, a derivative of Latin *enius* 'descendant of'.
GIVEN NAMES German 4%; French 4%. *Fritz; Andre, Marthe.*

Bohrer (1317) German: **1.** occupational name from Middle High German *born* 'to bore or drill'. **2.** German: topographic name from Slavic *bor* 'pine forest', 'conifer'. Compare BORAK.

Boice (1123) English: variant spelling of BOYCE.

Boicourt (110) French: probably a habitational name from Buicourt in Oise.

Boie (179) **1.** Frisian, North German, and Danish: variant spelling of BOYE. **2.** Probably an Americanized spelling of French BOIS.
GIVEN NAMES French 6%. *Camille, Emile, Fernand.*

Boies (330) Variant spelling of French BOIS.

Boik (155) Variant of North German BOYKE, a diminutive of BOYE.

Boike (310) Variant of North German BOYKE, a diminutive of BOYE.

Boiko (103) **1.** Jewish (eastern Ashkenazic): nickname from Russian *boykiy* 'bold, daring'. **2.** Ukrainian: ethnic name from Ukrainian *boyko*, a designation for inhabitants of an area of western Ukraine.
GIVEN NAMES Jewish 8%; Russian 7%. *Inna, Mayer; Anatoli, Anatoly, Nikolai.*

Boilard (145) Respelling of French **Boillard**, a pejorative nickname for a corpulent individual, from a derivative of Latin *botulus* 'guts', 'belly'. In Burgundy *boille* also denotes a large basket for collecting grapes and it is possible that in this area the name arose as a metonymic occupational name for someone who made or used such baskets.
FOREBEARS The surname Boilard is documented in L'Islet, Quebec, in 1680, having been brought there by an immigrant from the Poitou region of France. The secondary surname Beaurivage is recorded in 1730 in Quebec city.
GIVEN NAMES French 17%. *Armand* (3), *Adelard, Andre, Elphege, Emile, Jacques, Lucien, Marcel, Pierre.*

Boileau (477) French: from the Old French verb *boi(re)* 'to drink' + the definite article *l'* + *eau* 'water', hence a nickname, perhaps for a teetotaler, perhaps for a drinker, or perhaps for someone who was so parsimonious he was prepared to run the risk of drinking water. Compare DRINKWATER.
FOREBEARS An English and Irish family called Boileau is descended from Étienne Boileau, who was governor of Paris under Louis IX in 1255. A number of the family later became Huguenots, and so exiles who brought the name to North America and elsewhere. Charles Boileau (1673–1733) was a senior commander in the forces under the Duke of Marlborough, and his sons settled in Dublin.
The name was brought to Canada from Poitou, France, being documented in Boucherville in 1706.
GIVEN NAMES French 11%. *Armand* (2), *Jacques* (2), *Marcel* (2), *Michel* (2), *Agathe, Alphonse, Andre, Edouard, Emile, Francois, Leonide, Marie Claude.*

Boire (164) French: topographic name for someone who lived by a watering hole, or, in the south, a nickname for an imbecile, from *boire* 'buzzard'.
GIVEN NAMES French 16%. *Andre* (2), *Marcel* (2), *Germain, Lucien, Renaud, Yvan.*

Bois (316) French: topographic name for someone living or working in a wood, from Old French *bois* 'wood' (Late Latin *boscum* 'bush', 'shrub', 'undergrowth', of Germanic origin). Compare the much more frequent form DUBOIS.
GIVEN NAMES French 10%. *Alcide, Antoine, Donat, Marcel, Ovide, Ovila, Raoul, Serge.*

Boisclair (272) French: topographic name from Old French *bois* 'wood' (see BOIS) + *clair* 'clear', 'light', or in some cases possibly a habitational name for someone who lived at a place known as 'Clair's wood', from the same second element as a personal name.
GIVEN NAMES French 18%. *Normand* (4), *Marcel* (2), *Aldege, Alphonse, Arsene, Edmour, Emile, Leopaul, Prudent, Rejean, Remi, Yves.*

Boise (367) English: variant spelling of BOYCE.

Boisen (191) **1.** Variant spelling of BOYSEN. **2.** Danish: patronymic from the German personal name *Boie*, of unexplained etymology.

Boisse (129) French: variant of BOISSEAU.
GIVEN NAMES French 20%. *Armand* (2), *Monique* (2), *Andre, Emile, Fernand, Laurette, Marcell, Normand.*

Boisseau (317) French: metonymic occupational name for a corn merchant or factor, one who measured grain, from Old French *boisse(l), buissel*, 'bushel', 'measure of grain', of Gaulish origin. The name may also have been applied to a maker of vessels designed to hold or measure out a bushel.
FOREBEARS A Boisseau from Brittany in France is recorded in Sillery, Quebec, in 1667, while a man named Boissel from the Perche region is documented in Quebec city in 1666.
GIVEN NAMES French 6%. *Adrien, Armand, Chantel, Jacques.*

Boisselle (155) French: Variant of BOISSEAU.
GIVEN NAMES French 13%. *Armand* (3), *Luc, Normand, Pierre.*

Boissonneault (197) Characteristic New England spelling of French **Boissonneau**, a topographic name for someone who lived near a clump of bushes, *buisson* (a derivative of *bois* 'wood', 'copse'), or in an area characterized by such vegetation.
GIVEN NAMES French 16%. *Adrien, Aurore, Francois, Germain, Luc, Lucien, Marcel, Pierre, Yvon.*

Boisvert (1934) French: topographic name for someone who lived in a dense forest or perhaps a copse of evergreens, from Old French *bois* 'wood' (see BOIS) + *vert, verd* 'green'. This name is sometimes translated as GREENWOOD.
GIVEN NAMES French 17%. *Marcel* (12), *Armand* (11), *Andre* (7), *Donat* (6), *Lucien*

(6), *Jacques* (5), *Gaston* (4), *Normand* (4), *Pierre* (4), *Gilles* (3), *Herve* (3), *Adrien* (2).

Boitano (175) Northern Italian (Liguria): possibly a habitational name for someone from a lost place named Boita.
GIVEN NAMES Italian 5%. *Dino, Ettore.*

Boiter (105) French (also Scottish): descriptive epithet for a man with a limp, from French *boiter* 'to limp'.

Boitnott (251) Origin unidentified.

Boivin (879) French: nickname for a wine drinker, from Old French *bei(vre)*, *boi(vre)* 'to drink' + *vin* 'wine'. This name is sometimes translated as Drinkwine.
FOREBEARS A Boivin from the Normandy region of France is documented in Quebec city in 1646, with the secondary name Bontemps. Another, from the Anjou region, is recorded in Montreal in 1665, with the secondary name Panse.
GIVEN NAMES French 14%. *Andre* (3), *Armand* (3), *Luc* (3), *Emile* (2), *Gaston* (2), *Leonce* (2), *Lucien* (2), *Marcel* (2), *Rejean* (2), *Adrien, Alphonse, Aurele.*

Bojanowski (155) Polish: habitational name for someone from a place called Bojanow or Bojanowo.
GIVEN NAMES Polish 7%. *Casimir, Lucja, Pawel, Tadeusz.*

Bojarski (245) **1.** Polish and Jewish (from Poland and Belarus): habitational name for someone from Bojary in Poland, or (in the case of the Jewish name) from Boyary in Belarus. **2.** Polish: nickname from *bojar* 'boyar' (a member of the old Russian aristocracy). **3.** Jewish (from Ukraine): habitational name for someone from Boyarka, a place in Ukraine.
GIVEN NAMES Polish 6%. *Halina* (2), *Karol, Zbigniew.*

Boje (127) Dutch: variant spelling of BOYE.
GIVEN NAMES German 6%. *Goetz, Johannes.*

Bojko (125) Polish: probably from a pet form of an Old Polish personal name such as *Budziboj*, containing the element *boj* 'fight'.
GIVEN NAMES Polish 11%. *Jadwiga, Jozef, Miroslaw, Myroslaw, Orysia, Tadeusz.*

Bojorquez (434) Spanish (**Bojórquez**): variant of BOHORQUEZ.
GIVEN NAMES Spanish 46%. *Jose* (7), *Manuel* (7), *Carlos* (5), *Francisco* (5), *Jesus* (4), *Alvaro* (3), *Juan* (3), *Miguel* (3), *Armando* (2), *Blanca* (2), *Eduardo* (2), *Enrique* (2).

Bok (284) **1.** Dutch: nickname for a man with some fancied resemblance to a he-goat, *bok*. **2.** Swedish: ornamental name from *bok* 'beech'. **3.** Variant spelling of Jewish BOCK. **4.** Slovenian: unexplained.

Boka (112) Dutch: variant of BOEKE or BOK.

Bokelman (135) German (**Bokelmann**): habitational name for someone from any of several places called Bokel.

Boker (123) **1.** German: topographic name from Middle Low German *boke* 'beech' +

the suffix *-er* denoting an inhabitant. **2.** German: reduced form of **Bödeker** (see BOEDEKER). **3.** Jewish (Israeli): ornamental name from Hebrew *boker* 'morning'.
GIVEN NAMES German 7%; Jewish 4%. *Heinz, Helmut; Aharon, Eldad.*

Bokor (200) Hungarian: topographic name from Hungarian *bokor* 'shrub'.
GIVEN NAMES Hungarian 10%. *Bela* (2), *Zoltan* (2), *Ferenc, Gabor, Gyula, Janos.*

Bol (236) **1.** Dutch: variant of BOLLE. **2.** French: from *Bolo, Bollo*, short forms of the Germanic personal name *Baldo* (see BOLL).
GIVEN NAMES Dutch 11%; German 5%. *Gerrit* (4), *Cornelis* (3), *Kees* (2), *Dirk, Klaas, Pieter; Erwin, Gerhard, Otto.*

Bolam (162) English (Northumberland): habitational name from places called Bolam in Northumberland and County Durham. These place names could derive from the dative plural (*bolum*) of either of two unattested Old English words, *bola* 'tree trunk' (compare Old Norse *bolr*) or *bol* 'rounded hill' (compare Middle Low German *bolle* 'round object').

Bolan (658) Irish: variant of BOLAND.

Boland (4771) **1.** Irish (Sligo and Munster): Anglicized form of Gaelic **Ó Beólláin** 'descendant of *Beóllán*', an old Irish name of uncertain origin. **2.** English: habitational name from any of various places such as Bowland in Lancashire and West Yorkshire, Bowlands in East Yorkshire, and Bolland in Devon. All of these are most probably named with Old English *boga* 'bow' (in the sense of a bend in a river) + *land* 'land'. **3.** German: of uncertain origin; possibly from Slavic *polan* 'rural person', 'peasant', or a variant of BOLANDER, or an altered spelling of **Böhland**, a name of Slavic origin, from Old Slavic *belu* 'white', a descriptive nickname for a fair-haired person.
GIVEN NAMES Irish 6%. *Brendan* (2), *Aidan, Bridie, Caitlin, Donal, Finbar, Maeve.*

Bolander (640) **1.** Swedish: ornamental name composed either of *bo* 'farm' + the suffix *-(land)er* or of *bol* 'farm' + *ander*, probably taken from Greek *anēr* 'man', genitive *andros*. **2.** German: habitational name for someone from Bolanden in the Palatinate, Bolande in Schleswig-Holstein, or Bohland in Baden. The first takes its name from a 13th century castle and neighboring village, which is derived from an older (12th century) field name, *Bonlande(n)*, meaning 'bean field'. **3.** German: probably an altered spelling of Böhlander, regional name for a Pole, Middle High German *Polan, Poland* (from Slavic *poljane* 'plain').

Bolanos (801) Spanish (**Bolaños**): habitational name from either of two places, Bolaños de Calatrava in Ciudad Real province or Bolaños de Campos in Vallado-

lid, so named with the plural of Spanish *bolaño* 'stone ball'.

Bolar (248) Of uncertain origin. **1.** possibly in part Spanish, a topographic name for someone who lived on a patch of soil of a particular type known as *tierra bolar*. **2.** alternatively perhaps Irish, a variant of BOLLARD under French or Spanish influence.

Bolas (125) English: habitational name from Great Bolas in Shropshire, named in Old English with an unidentified first element (possibly an unattested word *bogel* meaning 'bend in a river') + *wæsse* 'land beside a river liable to flood'.

Bolash (103) Variant of English BOLAS.

Bolch (179) German: nickname from *Bolch*, a term denoting a large salted or dried fish, especially cod.

Bold (487) **1.** English: nickname from Middle English *bold* 'courageous', 'daring' (Old English *b(e)ald*, cognate with Old High German *bald*). In some cases it may derive from an Old English personal name (see BALD). **2.** English: topographic name for someone who lived or worked at the main house in a settlement, from Old English *bold*, the usual West Midland and northwestern form of Old English *bōðl*, *bōtl* 'dwelling house', 'hall'. **3.** English: habitational name for someone from Bold in Lancashire, which is named with Old English *bold* 'dwelling', as in 2 above. **4.** German: from the Germanic personal name *Baldo*, a short form of the various compound names with the element *bald* 'bold', notably BALDWIN in the north, and *Reinbold* in the south. **5.** Swedish: probably of German origin.

Bolda (188) **1.** Polish: from the German personal name **Bold** (see BOLD 4). **2.** Hungarian: from a pet form of the personal name *Boldizsár*, Hungarian form of BALTHAZAR.

Bolden (4630) **1.** English: variant of BOLDING. **2.** Swedish (**Boldén**): ornamental name.

Boldin (229) **1.** English: variant of BOLDING. **2.** Swedish: variant of BOLDEN.

Bolding (1272) **1.** English and German: patronymic from BOLD as a personal name. **2.** Danish: habitational name from a place so named in Jutland.

Boldman (235) **1.** German (**Boldmann**): possibly a variant of **Boldemann**, from a compound of the Germanic personal name *Baldo* (see BOLD 4) + *man* 'man'. **2.** Variant of BOLLMANN.

Boldon (198) English: unexplained. Compare BOLDEN.

Boldrey (108) English: variant of BALDREE.

Bolds (350) Perhaps an Americanized spelling of German BOLZ 1 or a variant of English BOLD.

Boldt (1827) German and Danish: from the Germanic personal name *Baldo*, a short form of the various compound names with the first element *bald* 'bold'.

GIVEN NAMES German 4%. *Hermann* (3), *Kurt* (2), *Bernhard, Dieter, Egon, Eldred, Gerd, Gerhard, Gunter, Gunther, Heinz, Hilde.*

Bolduc (2241) French: unexplained. The name is very frequent in New England.

FOREBEARS A Bolduc from Paris is recorded in Quebec city in 1668.

GIVEN NAMES French 14%. *Andre* (14), *Armand* (7), *Marcel* (7), *Normand* (6), *Lucien* (5), *Emile* (4), *Fernand* (4), *Germain* (4), *Michel* (3), *Alain* (2), *Benoit* (2), *Dominique* (2).

Bole (415) **1.** Irish: variant of BOYLE. **2.** Altered spelling of German BOHLE or BOLL. **3.** Norwegian (**Bøle**): habitational name from any of the farmsteads so named, from Old Norse *bøli* 'farm'. **4.** Slovenian: probably from a medieval altered short form of the personal name *Valentin* (see VALENTINE). Replacement of initial *V* with *B* and alternation between the vowels *a* and *o* is quite common in Slovenian surnames.

Bolejack (125) Probably an Americanized form of Czech **Boleček**, from a pet form of the personal names *Boleslav* or *Bolebor*.

Bolek (325) Polish and Czech: from a pet form of a personal name (Polish *Bolesław*, Czech *Boleslav*), composed of the Slavic elements *bole* 'greater' + *slav* 'glory'.

Boleman (134) North German (**Bolemann**): from an elaborated form of *bōle*, used as a term of endearment (see BOHLE 1), or possibly a respelling of German BOHLMANN or BOLLMANN.

Bolen (3219) **1.** Czech: from a pet form of the personal names *Boleslav* or *Bolebor*. **2.** Polish (**Boleń**): from a pet form of the personal name *Bolesław*. **3.** Variant spelling of German BOHLEN. **4.** Swedish (**Bolén**): ornamental name composed of an unexplained first element + the common surname suffix *-én*, a derivative of Latin *-enius* 'descendant of'. **5.** English: variant of BULLEN.

Bolenbaugh (181) Americanized spelling of the German habitational name BOLLENBACH.

Bolender (399) Variant of Swedish BOLANDER.

Boler (591) **1.** English: variant of BOWLER. **2.** German: variant of BOLLER. **3.** Norwegian (**Bøler**): habitational name from various farms in southeastern Norway named Bøler, from Old Norse *bøli* 'farm'. Compare BOHLE.

Bolerjack (130) Americanized spelling of Czech *Boleček* (see BOLEJACK).

Boles (5218) Origin uncertain; possibly an altered spelling of English BOWLES, a variant of BOWELL or BOWLER, or of German BOLZ or BOHLS.

Boleware (171) See BOULWARE.

Boley (1698) **1.** South German: patronymic from a personal name derived from *Pelagius* (from Greek *Pelagios*, a derivative of *pelagos* 'sea'; compare Spanish PELAYO). Saint Pelagius is the patron saint of Constance. **2.** English: variant of BULLEY.

Boleyn (171) English: variant of BULLEN.

Bolf (202) Apparently of Czech origin; possibly a variant of **Volf** (see WOLF).

Bolger (1251) **1.** English: occupational name for a leather worker, from Middle English, Old French *boulgier*, an agent derivative of Old French *boulge* 'leather bag', 'wallet' (Middle English *bulge*). **2.** Irish (South Leinster): Anglicized form of Gaelic **Ó Bolguidhir** 'descendant of *Bolgodhar*', a personal name composed of the elements *bolg* 'belly' + *odhar* 'yellow', 'sallow'. **3.** Perhaps an altered spelling of German BOHLINGER or BOLINGER.

GIVEN NAMES Irish 5%. *Brendan* (3), *Aileen, Ciaran, Maeve.*

Bolhuis (138) Belgian: habitational name from a place called Bolhuis, in the Belgian province of Brabant.

Bolich (222) **1.** Serbian (**Bolić**): from *Bole*, a pet form of the personal name BOGDAN or *Božidar*. **2.** German: from a Slavic personal name formed with *bol* 'more' (as in *Boleslaw*).

Bolick (1266) Americanized spelling of Czech and Slovak **Bolík**, from a pet form of the personal names *Boleslav* or *Bolebor*.

Boliek (101) Variant of Slavic **Bolik** (see BOLICK).

Bolig (109) German spelling of Slavic **Bolik** (see BOLICK).

Bolin (4509) **1.** Swedish: ornamental name composed of the elements *bo* 'farm' + *-lin*, suffix of Swedish family names. **2.** Czech: from a pet form of the personal names *Boleslav* or *Bolebor*.

Bolinder (141) Swedish: probably a variant of BOLANDER.

GIVEN NAME German 5%. *Kurt* (2).

Boline (213) Of uncertain origin; perhaps an altered spelling of Swedish BOLIN or English BULLEN. Compare BOLEYN.

Boling (2794) **1.** altered spelling of German **Böhling** (see BOHLING, BOLLING). **2.** altered spelling of English BOLLING.

Bolinger (1698) **1.** Variant spelling of German BOLLINGER. **2.** Altered spelling of German BOHLINGER.

Bolinsky (109) German spelling of Polish POLINSKI.

Bolio (168) Italian: from the Genoese equivalent of Italian *boglio* 'stew' (from *boglire* 'to cook').

GIVEN NAMES Spanish 5%. *Carlos* (2), *Abimael, Alicia, Ernesto, Gonzalo, Jorge, Rafael.*

Bolitho (150) Cornish: habitational name from either of two places in Cornwall named Bolitho, from Cornish *bos*, *bod*

'dwelling' + a personal name of uncertain form.

Bolivar (363) Spanish (**Bolívar**): Castilianized form of Basque **Bolibar**, a habitational name from any of several places named Bolibar, for example in Biscay province, from Basque *bolu* 'mill' (Latin *molinum*) + *ibar* 'meadow', 'riverbank'.

GIVEN NAMES Spanish 44%. *Jose* (8), *Luis* (8), *Alvaro* (5), *Carlos* (4), *Julio* (4), *Consuelo* (3), *Cruz* (3), *Eduardo* (3), *Jesus* (3), *Juan* (3), *Manuel* (3), *Rafael* (3).

Boliver (142) Welsh and English (Shropshire): Anglicized form of Welsh *ap Oliver* 'son of Oliver' (see OLIVER).

Boll (1153) **1.** German and Danish: topographic name from Middle High German *boll* 'rounded hill', or a habitational name from any of several places called Boll, named with this word. **2.** German (**Böll**): derivative of the Germanic personal name *Baldo* (see BOLD 4). **3.** Swedish: possibly a soldier's name or else an ornamental adoption of 1 or 2.

Bolla (229) **1.** Catalan and Spanish: from *bolla* 'sphere', 'ball'. How it was acquired as a surname is unclear; it may have been a nickname for a fat person. In Spanish *bolla* is also a regional term denoting various types of cakes and pastries and in some cases the surname may have arisen from this sense. **2.** Hungarian: variant of *Balla*, pet form of the personal name *Barabás*, or *Barnabás* (see BARNABY).

Bolland (189) **1.** Variant spelling of Irish BOLAND. **2.** German: habitational name from a place in Mecklenburg named Bolland.

GIVEN NAMES German 4%. *Ernst, Frieda, Jurgen.*

Bollard (168) **1.** English and Irish: according to MacLysaght, this is a surname of Dutch origin which was taken to Ireland early in the 18th century. **2.** French: from a personal name composed of the Germanic elements *boll* 'friend', 'brother' + *hard* 'hardy', 'strong'.

Bolle (279) **1.** German: from the Germanic personal name *Baldo*, a short form of the various compound names with the first element *bald* 'bold'. **2.** German: nickname in the south for a short fat man or a topographic name in the north from Middle Low German *bolle* 'knoll', 'rounded hill'. **3.** Dutch: from Middle Dutch *bolle* 'ball', 'bread bun', hence a metonymic occupational name for a baker or a nickname for a ball player. **4.** Norwegian: habitational name from a farm in northern Norway, so named with *bolle* 'rounded hill'. **5.** Swedish: variant of BOLL.

GIVEN NAMES German 6%; Scandinavian 4%. *Hans* (2), *Ilse* (2), *Kurt, Manfred, Otto; Arlys.*

Bollen (272) English: variant of BULLEN.

Bollenbach (175) German: habitational name from a place in Baden called Bollenbach.

Bollenbacher (288) German: habitational name for someone from BOLLENBACH.

Boller (902) **1.** South German and Swiss German (also **Böller**): habitational name for someone from any of several places called Boll (see BOLL). **2.** South German and Swiss German: nickname for a noisy blustering person, from Middle High German *bollen* 'to bluster'. **3.** Hungarian (**Böllér**): occupational name for a butcher's apprentice, *böllér*.

Bolles (940) German (also **Bölles**): of uncertain origin, perhaps a dialect variant of BOLLE or BOLL 2, or a variant of BALLES.

Bollich (105) Variant of German BOLICH.

Bollier (191) French: variant of BOULIER.

GIVEN NAMES French 5%. *Andre, Marcel.*

Bollig (475) Variant of German BOLICH.

Bolliger (216) Swiss German: variant of BOLLINGER.

GIVEN NAMES German 8%. *Hans* (4), *Ernst, Frieda, Heinz, Markus.*

Bollin (370) Swedish: **1.** ornamental name, the first element an adoption of Middle High German *boll* 'rounded hill' + the suffix *-lin*. **2.** variant of Swedish BOLIN.

Bolling (2067) **1.** English: nickname for someone with close-cropped hair or a large head, Middle English *bolling* 'pollard', or for a heavy drinker, from Middle English *bolling* 'excessive drinking'. **2.** German (**Bölling**): from a pet form of a personal name formed with Germanic *bald* 'bold', 'brave' (see BALDWIN). **3.** Swedish: either an ornamental name composed of BOLL + the suffix *-ing* 'belonging to', or possibly a habitational name from a place named Bolling(e).

Bollinger (4886) Swiss German: habitational name for someone from any of three places called Bollingen, in Schwyz, Württemberg, and Oldenburg, or from Bohlingen near Lake Constance (which is pronounced and was formerly written as *Bollingen*).

Bollman (1107) Variant of German BOLLMANN, found in Scandinavia as well as North America.

Bollmann (205) **1.** German: elaborated derivative of the Germanic personal name *Baldo* (see BOLD 4). **2.** German: topographic name for a man who lived on a rounded hill, from Middle High German *boll* 'rounded hill' + *man* 'man', or a habitational name from any of several places called Boll (see BOLL).

Bollom (106) English: habitational name from Bolham in Nottinghamshire, probably named in Old English with the dative plural (*bolum*) of either of two unattested Old English words, *bola* 'tree trunk' (compare Old Norse *bolr*, modern English *bole*) or *bol* 'rounded hill' (cognate with Middle

Low German *bolle* 'round object'). Compare BOLAM.

Bolls (190) German: patronymic from BOLL 2.

Bolman (126) Dutch and American spelling of German BOLLMANN.

GIVEN NAMES French 4%. *Marcelle* (2); *Pieter; Eldred; Boris, Oleg.*

Bolmer (113) **1.** English: variant of BULMER. **2.** Dutch: probably from the Germanic personal name *Baldemar*, composed of the elements *bald* 'bold' + *mar* 'famous'.

Bolner (112) Probably an Americanized form of German **Böhlner**, a habitational name for someone from a place in Saxony called Böhlen.

Bologna (608) Italian: habitational name from the city of Bologna in northern Italy. In early classical times this was an independent Tuscan city called *Felsina*, but was renamed *Bononia* (a derivative of Celtic *bona* 'foundation', 'settlement') when it became a Roman colony in 190 BC.

GIVEN NAMES Italian 37%. *Angelo* (4), *Vito* (4), *Antonio* (3), *Gino* (3), *Mario* (3), *Carmine* (2), *Ciro* (2), *Domenic* (2), *Enza* (2), *Gasper* (2), *Geno* (2), *Salvatore* (2), *Sante* (2), *Vincenza* (2), *Aurelio, Enzo, Giovanni.*

Bolognese (164) Italian: habitational name for someone from Bologna (see BOLOGNA), from the adjectival form of the place name.

GIVEN NAMES Italian 28%. *Alicia, Attilio, Nunzio, Ottavio, Paolo, Pasquale.*

Bolon (199) Polish (**Boloń**): from a derivative of the personal names *Bolesław* or *Boleczest.*

Bolotin (180) **1.** Jewish (from Belarus): habitational name from a place in Belarus called Boloto. **2.** Russian and Jewish (from Belarus): topographic name for someone who lived near a marsh or swamp, Russian *boloto.*

GIVEN NAMES Jewish 8%; Russian 6%. *Hyman, Meyer, Miriam, Moshe; Lev* (2), *Aleksandr, Arkady, Boris, Michail, Vladimir; Maris; Vulf.*

Bolser (303) **1.** Possibly a variant of German BALSER or POLZER. **2.** Catalan: occupational name for a bag or pouch maker, *bosser, bolser.*

Bolsinger (116) Variant of German **Bösinger** (see BASINGER).

Bolson (136) English: unexplained. It may be a variant of BALSON (see BALSAM) or BULSON.

Bolstad (582) Norwegian: habitational name from any of 14 farmsteads in southern Norway named Bolstad, from Old Norse *bólstaðr* 'farmstead', 'dwelling'.

GIVEN NAMES Scandinavian 7%. *Jens* (2), *Leif* (2), *Arne, Bjorn, Erik, Erling, Jons, Nels, Sverre, Thor; Mi; Irmgard; Ilene.*

Bolster (717) German: variant of POLSTER.

Bolstridge (100) English (Midlands): unexplained.

Bolt (2606) **1.** English (chiefly West Country): from Middle English *bolt* 'bolt', 'bar' (Old English *bolt* 'arrow'). In part this may have originated as a nickname or byname for a short but powerfully built person, in part as a metonymic occupational name for a maker of bolts. **2.** Danish: variant of BOLDT. **3.** Variant of BOLD. **4.** German: from a short form of the personal names *Baldwin* or *Reinbold.*

Bolte (969) **1.** German: variant of BOLDT. **2.** Slovenian: from *Bolte*, an old short form of the personal name *Boltežar* (see BALTHAZAR). It may also be an Americanized form of the Slovenian surname **Boljte**, which has the same origin. **3.** English: variant spelling of BOLT.

GIVEN NAMES German 4%. *Hans* (2), *Juergen* (2), *Siegfried* (2), *Armin, Bernhard, Kurt, Manfred.*

Bolten (195) **1.** German: variant of BOLTE. **2.** German: habitational name from short form of a compound place name such as Boltenhagen, of which there are six examples in Mecklenburg and Pomerania. **3.** Swedish (**Boltén**): from BOLT + the ornamental suffix *-én.*

GIVEN NAMES German 6%. *Ernst, Hermann, Inge, Otto.*

Bolter (215) **1.** English: occupational name for a bolter or sifter of flour, from Middle English *bo(u)lt* 'to sift' (Old French *buleter*, of Germanic origin). **2.** English: occupational name for a maker of bolts or bars, from an agent derivative of Middle English *bolt* (see BOLT). **3.** German: habitational name for someone from a lost place named Bolt. It is the name of a large family from Hechingen, Württemberg. **4.** German (also **Bölter**): occupational name for a maker of wooden bolts for crossbows, Middle High German *bolter.*

GIVEN NAMES German 6%. *Horst* (2), *Ernst, Erwin.*

Bolthouse (154) Probably an Americanized spelling of German *Balthasar* via the German variant *Baldhauser* (see BALTHAZAR), also recorded in the U.S. as **Baltenhouse** and **Boltenhouse**.

Boltin (129) Slovenian: from an old short form of the Slovenian personal name *Boltežar* (see BALTHAZAR).

Bolton (11337) English: habitational name from any of the numerous places in northern England named Bolton, especially the one in Lancashire, from Old English *boðl* 'dwelling', 'house' (see BOLD 2) + *tūn* 'enclosure', 'settlement'.

Boltz (1302) **1.** German: from the personal name *Boltz*, a reduced form of BALDWIN. **2.** South German: metonymic occupational name for a maker of bolts for crossbows or for a bowman, or a nickname for a tall stiff man, from Middle High German *boltz* 'crossbow bolt'.

Bolus (156) **1.** English (West Midlands): perhaps a nickname from the early modern

English word *bolus* 'pill', often used contemptuously. **2.** Belgian: variant of BOLHUIS.

Bolyard (1084) English: unexplained; perhaps a variant of BULLARD.

Bolz (488) German: **1.** variant spelling of BOLTZ. **2.** variant of BOHLS.
GIVEN NAMES German 7%. *Wolfgang* (3), *Otto* (2), *Alois, Dieter, Hans, Jutta, Kurt, Madel, Wolf.*

Boman (944) **1.** Swedish: generally an ornamental name composed of the elements *bo* 'dwelling', 'farm' + *man* 'man', occasionally applied as a topographic name for someone who lived on an outlying homestead. **2.** English: variant spelling of BOWMAN.

Bomar (1204) Variant of Swiss German BOMMER.

Bomba (400) Portuguese, Spanish, Polish, Ukrainian, Czech, and Slovak: from *bomba* 'bomb', (Latin *bombus*), hence probably a nickname for someone with an explosive temperament, or a metonymic occupational name for an artilleryman.
GIVEN NAMES Polish 5%. *Casimir, Irena, Pawel, Waclaw, Wojciech, Zuzanna.*

Bombara (124) Italian: topographic name for someone who lived in a noisy or resonating place, from a derivative of Latin *bombarus* 'rumble', 'resonance'.
GIVEN NAMES Italian 7%. *Salvatore* (2), *Francesca.*

Bombard (625) French: from Old French *bombarde* 'bombard', 'device for throwing large stones', possibly applied as a metonymic occupational name or a nickname.

Bombardier (329) French: occupational name from French *bombardier* 'bombardier', 'artilleryman'.
FOREBEARS Recorded in Montreal in 1706 is a person called Bombardier from Flanders with the secondary surnames Labombarde and Passepartout.
GIVEN NAMES French 11%. *Andre* (2), *Armand* (2), *Yvon* (2), *Gaston, Nicolle, Pierre, Romain.*

Bomberger (479) German and Jewish (western Ashkenazic): habitational name for someone from Bamberg in Germany.

Bomboy (133) Belgian French: habitational name from a place in Luxembourg province, Belgium, called Bombaye.

Bomer (260) Variant of German Böhmer, an ethnic name for an inhabitant of Bohemia (see BOEHM).

Bomgaars (125) Dutch and Jewish (from the Netherlands): occupational name for someone who owned or worked in an orchard, from a reduced form of Dutch BOMGARDNER.
GIVEN NAMES Dutch 5%; Jewish 4%. *Marinus; Arie* (5).

Bomgardner (258) Dutch and North German: occupational name for someone who owned or worked in an orchard, Dutch

boomgaard. Compare German **Baumgärtner** (see BAUMGARTNER).

Bomhoff (111) Dutch and North German: topographic name composed of Middle Low German *bōm* 'tree' + *hof* 'farmstead', 'manor farm'.

Bomkamp (172) Dutch and North German: topographic name composed of Middle Low German *bōm* 'tree' + *kamp* 'field', 'domain'.

Bommarito (609) Italian (Sicily): nickname from *buon marito* 'good husband'.
GIVEN NAMES Italian 20%. *Vito* (8), *Salvatore* (7), *Angelo* (6), *Domenic* (4), *Antonio* (2), *Guido* (2), *Marco* (2), *Ambrogio, Caesar, Carmelo, Ciro, Cosimo.*

Bommer (219) **1.** German: habitational name for someone from Bommen in Switzerland. **2.** Altered spelling of German BAUMER.
GIVEN NAMES German 7%. *Arno* (3), *Aloysius, Otto.*

Bommersbach (110) German: habitational name from a place of this name.

Bon (267) **1.** French: approbatory (or ironic) nickname, from Old French *bon* 'good' (Latin *bonus*). **2.** French: occasionally from the Latin personal name *Bonus* (likewise meaning 'good'), which was borne by a minor 3rd-century Christian saint, martyred at Rome with eleven companions under the Emperor Vespasian. It was adopted as a personal name partly in his honor and partly because of the transparently well-omened meaning. **3.** Hungarian: from a short form of the old ecclesiastical name *Bonifác* (see BONIFACE).
FOREBEARS A Bon, of unrecorded origin, with the secondary name Lacombe is documented in St. Ours, Quebec, in 1671.
GIVEN NAMES Spanish 6%; Italian 5%. *Armando* (2), *Agustin, Alfredo, Anselmo, Blanca, Eneida, Florencio, Jaime, Jose, Luis, Ramon, Xavier; Giovanni* (3), *Aldo, Livio, Lorenzo, Luigi.*

Bona (581) **1.** Italian: from the female personal name *Bona*, feminine form of BONO. **2.** Hungarian (**Bóna**) and Polish: from a pet form of the personal name *Bonifác* (Hungarian), *Bonifacy* (Polish) (see BONIFACE).
GIVEN NAMES Italian 7%. *Dino* (3), *Angelo* (2), *Aldo, Federico, Gasper, Gino, Giovanni, Luigi, Oreste, Quinto.*

Bonacci (716) Italian: from a derivative of the personal name BONO or BONA.
GIVEN NAMES Italian 16%. *Angelo* (6), *Salvatore* (5), *Carmine* (3), *Vito* (3), *Carmino* (2), *Nicola* (2), *Antonio, Carlo, Carmin, Domenic, Domenica, Enrico.*

Bonaccorsi (106) Italian: patronymic or plural form of BONACCORSO.
GIVEN NAMES Italian 24%. *Angelo* (3), *Adelmo, Alfredo, Benito, Marco, Sal.*

Bonaccorso (117) Italian: from a medieval personal name composed of the elements *bono* (*buono*) 'good' + *accorso* 'aid' (Late

Latin *accursus*, from *adcurrere* 'to aid', literally 'to run up'), often bestowed as an expression of gratitude upon a longed-for child.
GIVEN NAMES Italian 20%. *Pasquale* (2), *Salvatore* (2), *Matteo, Orazio, Santino, Santo, Vita.*

Bonadies (131) Italian: variant of BONADIO, from Latin *bona dies* 'good day'.
GIVEN NAMES Italian 11%. *Franco, Luca, Rocco.*

Bonadio (175) Italian: from a personal name composed of the elements *bona* (*buona*) 'good' + Old Italian *die* 'day', often bestowed as an expression of gratitude upon a long-awaited child.
GIVEN NAMES Italian 11%. *Antonio* (3), *Giovanni, Luigi, Reno, Santo.*

Bonadonna (163) Italian: from a nickname composed of the elements *bona* 'good' + *donna* 'woman'. In some instances the first element may be the medieval feminine personal name *Bona* (which is still used in Sardinia); the name was bestowed as an augural or well-wishing name (that the child would grow to be a good woman).
GIVEN NAMES Italian 11%. *Angelo, Gaetano, Salvatore.*

Bonafede (202) Italian: from a personal name composed of Latin *bona* 'good' (feminine form) + *fides* 'faith', given as an omen name meaning '(one who will have) great faith'.
GIVEN NAMES Italian 20%. *Salvatore* (5), *Mario* (4), *Americo, Mariano, Pino, Salvadore, Santo.*

Bonagura (113) Italian: reduced form of **Bonaugura**, from the personal name, an omen name meaning 'good omen'.
GIVEN NAMES Italian 12%. *Sal* (3), *Salvatore.*

Bonanni (291) Italian: patronymic or plural form of BONANNO.
GIVEN NAMES Italian 28%. *Mario* (4), *Emilio* (3), *Fernando* (3), *Renato* (3), *Angelo* (2), *Domenic* (2), *Silvano* (2), *Adalgisa, Aldo, Alessandro, Americo, Antonio, Cataldo, Fabrizio, Filomena, Gaetano, Giacomo, Orlando, Roberto.*

Bonanno (1346) Italian: from the medieval personal name *Bonanno*, an omen name meaning 'good year'.
GIVEN NAMES Italian 18%. *Salvatore* (16), *Antonio* (6), *Santo* (6), *Carmelo* (4), *Domenic* (4), *Giovanni* (3), *Vito* (3), *Amedeo* (2), *Bartolo* (2), *Giovanna* (2), *Rocco* (2), *Alessandro.*

Bonano (121) Italian: variant of BONANNO. The name is also established in Spain (**Bonaño**), taken there in the Age of Discoveries, and Brazil.
GIVEN NAMES Spanish 22%; Italian 4%. *Carlos* (3), *Alba, Angel, Benito, Cristino, Eulogio, Jaime, Luis, Luz, Maribel, Mercedes, Miguel; Fiore.*

Bonaparte (418) Italian: from a personal name composed of the elements *bona* (*buona*) 'good' + *parte* 'solution', 'match', a name bestowed as an expression of satisfaction at the child's arrival. The name has also been adopted as a Jewish surname and by admirers of the Emperor Napoleon in North America and the Caribbean.

FOREBEARS The family of the French Emperor Napoleon Bonaparte (1769–1821) had originally come to the island of Corsica from Tuscany in 1512. They were landowners, proud of their noble Italian background, and they claimed descent from a 10th-century count of Pistoia. Jerome Bonaparte, Napoleon's brother, married Elizabeth Patterson in Baltimore, MD, in 1803, but the emperor refused to recognize the marriage and it was annulled. Many years later her son's legitimacy was recognized by Napoleon III. Her grandson Charles Joseph Bonaparte (1851–1921) was secretary of the navy and U.S. attorney general. Another grandson, Jerome Napoleon Bonaparte II, graduated from West Point in 1852, but resigned from the U.S. Army to serve with the French army.

GIVEN NAMES French 5%. *Collette, Napoleon, Pierre.*

Bonar (957) **1.** Scottish and northern Irish: variant of BONNER. **2.** Irish (Donegal): Scottish name adopted as a translation of Gaelic **Ó Cnáimhsighe** 'descendant of *Cnáimhseach*', a byname meaning 'midwife'. This word seems to be a derivative of *cnámh* 'bone' (with the feminine ending *-seach*), but if so the reason for this is not clear. **3.** Polish: from German **Bo(h)ner** 'bean grower' (see BONER).

Bonardi (129) Italian: from BONO. The combination, as here, of a Latin personal name (*Bonus*) and a Germanic element (*hard*) used as a suffix without semantic function, was not uncommon in the medieval period.

GIVEN NAMES Italian 16%. *Aldo* (2), *Alba, Alberto, Armando, Assunta, Natale, Silvio, Tiziano.*

Bonasera (156) Italian (Sicily): from the expression *bona sera* 'good evening', applied as a nickname either for someone who made frequent use of this salutation (compare BONGIORNO) or as a personal name, bestowed on a child as an expression of gratitude in the sense 'it was a good evening when you were born'.

GIVEN NAMES Italian 13%. *Salvatore* (3), *Angelo, Antonio, Giuseppe.*

Bonato (107) Italian: **1.** Lombardic nickname from *bonat, bonato* 'good natured person', 'kindly person'. **2.** habitational name from Bonate in Bergamo province.

Bonaventura (246) Italian: from the personal name *Bonaventura* meaning 'good fortune', bestowed as an omen or well-wishing name.

GIVEN NAMES Italian 13%. *Alfio* (2), *Salvatore* (2), *Gino, Rocco.*

Bonaventure (165) French: adaptation of the Italian personal name BONAVENTURA.

FOREBEARS In Canadian documents Bonaventure is recorded with the secondary names Frapier, Hilaire and Lejeune.

Bonavita (264) Italian: from a personal name derived from *bona* 'good' + *vita* 'life', bestowed as an omen or well-wishing name.

GIVEN NAMES Italian 22%. *Sal* (5), *Carlo* (2), *Salvatore* (2), *Antonio, Carmine, Livio, Rosario, Sebastiano, Sebastino.*

Bonawitz (215) Altered spelling of Polish **Bonowicz**, a habitational name for someone from Boniowice in Galicia.

Bonczek (187) Polish (**Bọczek**): derivative of **Bạk** (see BANK 6).

GIVEN NAMES Polish 4%. *Janina, Krystyna.*

Bond (18577) **1.** English: status name for a peasant farmer or husbandman, Middle English *bonde* (Old English *bonda, bunda*, reinforced by Old Norse *bóndi*). The Old Norse word was also in use as a personal name, and this has given rise to other English and Scandinavian surnames alongside those originating as status names. The status of the peasant farmer fluctuated considerably during the Middle Ages; moreover, the underlying Germanic word is of disputed origin and meaning. Among Germanic peoples who settled to an agricultural life, the term came to signify a farmer holding lands from, and bound by loyalty to, a lord; from this developed the sense of a free landholder as opposed to a serf. In England after the Norman Conquest the word sank in status and became associated with the notion of bound servitude. **2.** Swedish: variant of BONDE.

Bondar (234) Ukrainian, Polish, and Jewish (from Ukraine and Belarus): occupational name for a cooper, Ukrainian *bondar*.

GIVEN NAMES Russian 22%; Jewish 8%. *Vladimir* (3), *Leonid* (2), *Mikhail* (2), *Vasiliy* (2), *Yelena* (2), *Aleksey, Anatoliy, Efim, Evgeny, Inessa, Konstantin, Leya; Ilya* (2), *Aron, Leyb.*

Bondarenko (135) Ukrainian: occupational name for a cooper, Ukrainian *bondar,* + *-enko*, patronymic suffix.

GIVEN NAMES Russian 31%. *Oleg* (4), *Vladimir* (4), *Yuriy* (2), *Aleksandr, Anatoliy, Anatoly, Gennady, Grigoriy, Igor, Konstantin, Lyubov, Lyudmila.*

Bonde (402) **1.** English: variant spelling of BOND. **2.** Scandinavian: status name for a farmer, from Old Norse *bóndi* 'farmer'. Compare BOND. In Sweden *Bonde* is both a personal name and the name of an old aristocratic family. **3.** Norwegian: habitational name from a farmstead named Bonde, from Old Norse *bóndi* 'farmer' + *vin* 'meadow'.

GIVEN NAMES Scandinavian 5%. *Anders, Erik.*

Bonder (137) Variant of Polish BONDAR.

GIVEN NAMES Polish 4%. *Halina, Zygmund.*

Bondeson (110) Swedish: patronymic from the personal name BONDE.

GIVEN NAME Scandinavian 5%; German 5%. *Wilhelm.*

Bondi (644) **1.** Italian: from a personal name *Bondí*, an omen name from *buon di* 'good day' (see BONADIO). **2.** Italian: from a reduced form of the personal name *Abbondio*, from the Latin personal name *Abundius*, from *abundus* 'abundant'. **3.** Italian (Tuscany): from a short form of any of various personal names beginning with *Bond-*, for example *Bondelmonte*. **4.** Hungarian: patronymic from the old personal name *Bond*.

GIVEN NAMES Italian 10%. *Amedeo* (2), *Angelo* (2), *Pasquale* (2), *Salvatore* (2), *Carmelo, Elio, Manlio, Nunzio, Onofrio, Philomena, Sal, Vincenzo.*

Bondoc (157) Tagalog: topographic name (alongside the variant **Bundoc**) from Tagalog *bondoc* 'mountain'.

GIVEN NAMES Spanish 32%; German 5%. *Jose* (3), *Rolando* (3), *Atilano* (2), *Teresita* (2), *Adelaida, Armando, Arturo, Carlos, Conrado, Domingo, Eduardo, Francisca; Romeo* (2), *Antonio, Carlo, Cesario, Dante; Rommel* (2), *Armin.*

Bonds (3631) English: patronymic from BOND.

Bondurant (1092) French: nickname from *bon* 'good' + the personal name *Durand*, literally 'good Durand'. This is a Huguenot name that was brought to North American in about 1690.

Bondy (701) Jewish: from the Sephardic personal name *Bondia*, related to Latin *bonus dies* 'good day', used as a translation of Hebrew *yom tov* 'Jewish holiday' (literally 'good day'). The surname was borne by a family of Sephardic origin that settled in Prague, hence its occurrence chiefly in Bohemia and neighboring countries.

Bone (3839) **1.** English (of Norman origin): nickname meaning 'good', from Old French *bon* 'good'. **2.** English: nickname for a thin man, from Middle English *bōn* 'bone' (Old English *bān*; compare BAIN 2). **3.** Hungarian (**Bóné**): from *bóné* denoting a particular kind of fishing net, hence a metonymic occupational name for a fisherman or perhaps for a maker of such nets.

Bonebrake (473) Possibly an Americanized form of German **Beinbrech**, literally 'bone break', from Middle High German *bein* 'bone' + *brec* 'break'.

Bonecutter (147) Translation of German **Knochenhauer**, occupational name for a butcher.

GIVEN NAME French 4%. *Serge.*

Bonelli (524) Italian: patronymic or plural form of BONELLO.

GIVEN NAMES Italian 14%. *Rocco* (6), *Angelo* (2), *Marco* (2), *Salvatore* (2), *Antonella, Antonio, Carlo, Carmine, Enrico, Ezio, Giorgio, Guido.*

Bonello (222) **1.** Italian: from a diminutive of BONO. **2.** Scottish: Italianized form of a

habitational name from a place name, Bonaly near Edinburgh or Banaley in Fife.
GIVEN NAMES Italian 20%. *Salvatore* (4), *Cosmo* (2), *Vincenzo* (2), *Antonino, Antonio, Carmela, Giuseppe, Guiseppe, Ignazio, Nicola*.

Bonenberger (186) German: topographic name from Middle High German *bōne* 'bean(s)' + *berc* 'hill'.

Bonenfant (324) French: nickname, probably slightly mocking in tone, from Old French *bon* 'good' + *enfant* 'child'.
FOREBEARS A Bonenfant of unknown origin is recorded in Montreal for 1648.
GIVEN NAMES French 14%. *Leandre* (2), *Andre, Damien, Felicien, Gaetan, Jacques, Jean Pierre, Laureat, Laurent, Laurier, Marcel*.

Boner (596) **1.** Scottish and English: variant spelling of BONNER or BONAR. **2.** German: occupational name for a grower of beans, from Middle High German *bōne* 'bean' + the agent suffix *-er*. **3.** Swedish (**Bonér**): variant of BOHNER.

Bones (466) **1.** English: variant of BONE 2. **2.** Jewish (eastern Ashkenazic): metronymic from the Yiddish female personal name *Bone*, of Latinate origin.

Boness (134) South German: derisive nickname meaning 'bean-eater' (from a compound of Middle High German *bone* 'bean' + *ezzen* 'to eat'), used to denote a bean-grower or a poor person whose diet consisted mainly of beans.

Bonesteel (362) **1.** Americanized spelling of North German **Bohnestiel**, a metonymic occupational name for a bean grower or a nickname for a very tall person, from Low German *Bohne* 'bean' + *Stiel* 'stalk'. **2.** Americanized spelling of French **Bonôtal** 'good hotel'.

Bonet (302) **1.** Catalan: from a medieval personal name, from a diminutive of *bon* 'good'. **2.** French: variant of BONNET (mainly 2).
FOREBEARS A bearer of the name from the Angoumois region of France is documented in Montreal in 1670, with the secondary surname Lafortune. Other secondary surnames on record are Delisle, La Rochelle, Latour, and Tranchemontagne.
GIVEN NAMES Spanish 41%. *Jose* (5), *Jaime* (3), *Lourdes* (3), *Pedro* (3), *Ana* (2), *Angel* (2), *Armando* (2), *Carlos* (2), *Domingo* (2), *Ernesto* (2), *Eudaldo* (2), *Gilberto* (2).

Bonetti (427) Italian: **1.** nickname from a diminutive of BONO. **2.** from the Latin personal name *Bonitus*, a derivative of *bonus* 'good' (see BONO). **3.** metonymic occupational name for a milliner, or a nickname for a wearer of unusual headgear, from medieval Latin *abonnis*.
GIVEN NAMES Italian 20%; Spanish 8%. *Mario* (4), *Guido* (3), *Salvatore* (2), *Claudina, Dante, Enrico, Gino, Giovanni, Marco, Massimo, Pasquale, Ricci, Ricco; Jaime, Jorge, Jose, Luz, Pedro*.

Bonewitz (121) Germanized spelling of Polish **Boniewicz**, a patronymic from the personal name *Bonifacy* (see BONIFACE).

Boney (1261) English: nickname from the adjective *bony*, denoting a scrawny individual with prominent bones.

Bonfanti (161) Italian: from the personal name *Bonfante*, from *bono* 'good' + *infante* 'child', probably bestowed therefore in the hope that the child would be good.
GIVEN NAMES Italian 8%. *Corrado, Premo, Sal, Tullio*.

Bonfield (259) Irish and English (of Norman origin): habitational name, altered by folk etymology, from any of three places in northern France called Bonneville, from Old French *bonne* 'good' + *ville* 'settlement'. In the 16th and 17th centuries in England, the endings *-field* and *-ville* were confused; one branch of a family might continue using the first spelling while another chose the second.
FOREBEARS This was one of the earliest Norman names to be taken in the 12th century to Ireland, where it was Gaelicized as **de Buinnbhíol**.

Bonfiglio (646) Italian: from the personal name *Bonfiglio*, an omen name meaning 'good son'.
GIVEN NAMES Italian 11%. *Salvatore* (6), *Angelo* (2), *Antonio* (2), *Aldo, Alessia, Carmelina, Filomena, Francesco, Gaetano, Lucio, Nino, Santo*.

Bong (353) **1.** Swedish: originally a soldier's name, from *bång* 'noise'. **2.** Belgian: unexplained. **3.** Malaysian or Indonesian: unexplained.

Bongard (328) **1.** German: from Middle Low German *bōm* 'tree' + *gard* 'garden', hence a topographic name for someone who lived by an orchard or a nickname for someone who owned or worked in one. Compare BAUMGARTEN. **2.** Dutch: variant of **Boomgaard** (see BOOMGARDEN). **3.** French: nickname for a trusted servant, from *bon* 'good' + *gars* 'servant', 'lad'.

Bongers (204) Dutch: variant of **Boomgaard** (see BOOMGARDEN).

Bongiorno (687) Italian: from the medieval personal name *Bongiorno* (composed of *bono* 'good' + *giorno* 'day'), bestowed on a child as an expression of the parents' satisfaction at the birth ('it was a good day when you were born').
GIVEN NAMES Italian 20%. *Salvatore* (8), *Sal* (4), *Angelo* (3), *Gaetano* (3), *Domenic* (2), *Filippo* (2), *Giuseppe* (2), *Stefano* (2), *Vito* (2), *Amadeo, Antonio, Benedetto*.

Bongiovanni (612) Italian: from a personal name composed of the elements *bon* 'good' + *Giovanni*, Italian equivalent of JOHN.
GIVEN NAMES Italian 19%. *Mario* (5), *Antonio* (3), *Dante* (2), *Salvatore* (2), *Santo* (2), *Antonino, Domenic, Gaetano, Geno, Giacomo, Gilda, Luciano, Nino*.

Bonham (2579) **1.** English: nickname from Old French *bon homme* (Latin *bonus*

homo). This had two senses relevant to surname formation; partly it had the literal meaning 'good man', and partly it came to mean 'peasant farmer'. **2.** Americanized form of French BONHOMME.

Bonhomme (171) French: nickname from Old French *bon homme* 'good man'.
FOREBEARS Documented in the records of Trois Rivières, Quebec, for 1640 is a bearer of the name Bonhomme from the Normandy region of France. The secondary surnames Beaupré and Dulac are also recorded.
GIVEN NAMES French 25%. *Pierre* (2), *Andre, Arnaud, Dominique, Ghislaine, Gilles, Lucienne, Marie-Christine, Michel, Micheline, Pascal, Regine*.

Boni (468) **1.** Italian: patronymic or plural form of BONO. **2.** Hungarian: from a pet form of the personal name *Bonifác* (see BONIFACE). **3.** Bulgarian: from a pet form of the personal name *Bojan*. **4.** Altered spelling of Swiss German **Bohni**.
GIVEN NAMES Italian 9%. *Rocco* (3), *Angelo* (2), *Dino* (2), *Alfonse, Attilio, Cesare, Leno, Lido, Marino, Salvatore*.

Bonica (148) Italian: probably from a personal name of Germanic origin.
GIVEN NAMES Italian 9%; Romanian 5%. *Angelo, Giovanni; Vasile* (3).

Boniface (345) English and French: from the medieval personal name *Boniface* (see BONIFACIO). Among the noted bearers of the name was an early Christian saint (*c.* 675–754) who was born in Devon and martyred in Friesland after evangelical work among Germanic tribes.

Bonifacio (236) Italian, Portuguese (**Bonifácio**): from the personal name *Bonifacio* (Latin *Bonifatius*, from *bonum* 'good' + *fatum* 'fate', 'destiny'). In Late Latin *-ti-* and *-ci-* came to be pronounced identically; the name was thus often respelled *Bonifacius* and assigned the meaning 'doer of good deeds', derived by folk etymology from Latin *facere* 'to do'. *Bonifatius* was the name of the Roman military governor of North Africa in 422–32, who was a friend of St. Augustine. It was also borne by various early Christian saints and was adopted by nine popes. The personal name was always more popular in Italy (in its various cognate forms) than elsewhere; the original sense 'well fated' remained transparent in Italian, so the name was often bestowed there for the sake of the good omen.
GIVEN NAMES Spanish 32%; Italian 10%. *Andres* (4), *Alfredo* (2), *Jose* (2), *Rodolfo* (2), *Altagracia, Ana, Armando, Bienvenida, Carmelita, Catalina, Dionisio, Edgardo; Antonio, Caesar, Dino, Ennio, Filippo, Lorenzo, Romeo, Sal, Tullio*.

Bonifas (195) English: variant of BONIFACE.

Bonifay (146) French: possibly a variant of BONIFACE.

Bonifield (197) Variant of English BONFIELD or an Americanized form of the French BONNEVILLE, which has the same origin.

Bonilla (3755) Spanish: habitational name from Bonilla in Cuenca province or Bonilla de la Sierra in Ávila province.
GIVEN NAMES Spanish 50%. *Jose* (147), *Carlos* (61), *Luis* (61), *Juan* (55), *Jorge* (39), *Miguel* (31), *Pedro* (31), *Mario* (28), *Manuel* (26), *Francisco* (24), *Angel* (19), *Roberto* (16).

Bonin (1496) French: from a diminutive of BON.
GIVEN NAMES French 10%. *Armand* (4), *Pierre* (4), *Ulysse* (4), *Aymar* (3), *Lucien* (3), *Marcel* (3), *Gilles* (2), *Herve* (2), *Alcide, Desire, Emile, Etienne*.

Bonine (351) Variant of French BONIN.

Bonini (295) Italian: patronymic or plural form of BONINO.
GIVEN NAMES Italian 5%. *Angelo, Carlo, Fortunata, Gilda, Maurizio*.

Bonino (207) Italian: from a diminutive of BONO.
GIVEN NAMES Italian 9%. *Angelo, Antonino, Carlo, Domenic, Fulvio, Geno*.

Bonis (131) **1.** Hungarian (**Bónis**): from a pet form of the old ecclesiastical name *Bonifác* (see BONIFACIO). **2.** Jewish: variant of BONES.

Bonito (231) **1.** Southern Italian: from the personal name *Bonito*, from Latin *Bonitus*. **2.** Italian: habitational name from the village of Bonito in Avellino province, Campania. **3.** Spanish and Portuguese: nickname from *bonito* 'pretty'. **4.** Spanish and Portuguese: possibly from *bonito* 'tuna', probably denoting a fisherman.
GIVEN NAMES Italian 19%; Spanish 6%. *Americo* (2), *Angelo, Carmel, Carmine, Dante, Fedele, Filomena, Gaetano, Mauricio, Mauro, Rocco, Salvatore, Vito; Alicia, Carlos, Francisco*.

Bonitz (144) German: nickname of Slavic origin, from *boniti* 'to scare'.
GIVEN NAME German 4%. *Heinz*.

Bonjour (201) French: nickname from Old French *bon* 'good' + *jorn, jour* 'day', presumably denoting someone who made frequent use of this salutation.
GIVEN NAMES French 5%. *Monique, Pierre*.

Bonk (1084) **1.** Americanized spelling of Polish and Jewish **Bąk** (see BANK 6). **2.** North German and Dutch: variant of BUNK.

Bonkoski (119) Polish: variant of BONKOWSKI.

Bonkowski (308) Polish (**Bąkowski**) and Jewish (from Poland): habitational name for someone from a place called Bąkowa, Bąkowice, Bąkowiec, or Bąkowo.

Bonn (840) **1.** English: variant of BONE 1. **2.** German: variant of BONITZ.

Bonnar (139) Scottish and northern Irish: variant spelling of BONNER.

Bonne (191) **1.** French: from the nickname *Bonne*, feminine form of BON. **2.** Danish: status name for a farmer, from Old Norse *bóndi*. See also BOND. **3.** German: topographic name from Romance *bonna* 'border', or a variant of BONN 2.
GIVEN NAMES French 5%. *Henri* (2), *Emile*.

Bonneau (773) French: from the medieval personal name *Bonellus*.
FOREBEARS A Bonneau from the Poitou region of France is documented in Ste Famille, Quebec, in 1670, with the secondary surname La Bécasse; the secondary surname Lajeunesse is also recorded.
GIVEN NAMES French 12%. *Armand* (4), *Philippe* (3), *Aurore* (2), *Henri* (2), *Marcel* (2), *Normand* (2), *Alphonse, Benoit, Cecile, Emile, Euclide, Gaetan*.

Bonnell (1786) **1.** Altered spelling of French **Bonnel**, a variant of BONNEAU. **2.** English: variant of BUNNELL.

Bonnema (350) Frisian: patronymic from the Old Frisian personal name *Bonne*.

Bonner (10272) **1.** English, Scottish, and Irish: nickname from Middle English *boner(e)*, *bonour* 'gentle', 'courteous', 'handsome' (Old French *bonnaire*, from the phrase *de bon(ne) aire* 'of good bearing or appearance', from which also comes modern English *debonair*). **2.** Welsh: Anglicized form of Welsh *ap Ynyr* 'son of Ynyr', a common medieval personal name derived from Latin *Honorius*. **3.** Swedish: unexplained.

Bonnes (167) North German: variant of BONESS.

Bonness (102) North German: variant of BONESS.

Bonnet (626) **1.** French: from the medieval personal name *Bonettus*, a diminutive of Latin *bonus* 'good'. **2.** French: occasionally, a Gascon variant of BONNEAU. **3.** English and French: metonymic occupational name for a milliner, or a nickname for a wearer of unusual headgear, from Middle English *bonet*, Old French *bon(n)et* 'bonnet', 'hat'. This word is found in medieval Latin as *abonnis*, but is of unknown origin. **4.** In Germany the name was borne by Waldensians, of French origin.
FOREBEARS A Bonnet from the Charente region of France is documented in Montreal in 1670 with the secondary surname Lafortune.
GIVEN NAMES French 8%. *Pierre* (3), *Adrien, Andre, Georges, Guillaume, Henri, Jean-Paul, Marie Carmel, Michel, Philippe, Thierry*.

Bonnett (1430) Variant of French BONNET.

Bonnette (985) Altered spelling of French BONNET, reflecting the Canadian pronunciation of the final *-t*, which is not sounded in metropolitan French.
GIVEN NAMES French 4%. *Andre, Armand, Colette, Elzear, Germaine, Jean-Paul, Marcel, Nicolle, Silton*.

Bonneville (381) French: habitational name from any of the numerous places called Bonneville, from Old French *bonne* 'good' + *ville* 'settlement'.
FOREBEARS The name is recorded in Quebec city in 1743, brought there by a bearer from Franche-Comté in France. Secondary surnames recorded in Canadian documents are Bellefleur, Poupeville, Prouville.
GIVEN NAMES French 6%. *Andre, Francois, Liette, Normand, Pierre*.

Bonney (1709) **1.** English (chiefly Lancashire): nickname for a handsome person, especially a large or well-built one, from northern dialect *bonnie* 'fine', 'beautiful' (still in common use in northern England and Scotland). **2.** French: eastern variant of BONNET 2.

Bonnici (105) Maltese: unexplained.
GIVEN NAME French 5%; Italian 4%. *Salvatore*.

Bonnie (181) Scottish: nickname for a handsome person, from Scots *bonnie* 'fine', 'beautiful'.

Bonnin (234) French: from a diminutive of BON. This name is also found in Mallorca and Italy (Turin).
GIVEN NAMES Spanish 9%; French 5%. *Carlos* (2), *Francisco* (2), *Jose* (2), *Alicia, Ana, Arturo, Elba, Fernando, Juan, Luis, Miguel, Nestor; Dominique, Lucien, Serge*.

Bonniwell (144) **1.** Possibly English: of uncertain origin (see BONWELL). **2.** Perhaps an Americanized form of French BONNEVILLE or *Bonville*.

Bonno (127) Altered spelling of French BONNOT.

Bonnot (120) French: from a diminutive of BON.
GIVEN NAMES French 9%. *Emile, Francoise, Henri, Marcelle*.

Bonny (155) **1.** English and Irish: variant of BONNEY or Scottish BONNIE. **2.** Swiss French: variant of BONNET.
GIVEN NAMES French 6%. *Gardy, Odette, Yanick*.

Bono (1511) **1.** Italian: from the personal name *Bono* meaning 'good', from the Latin personal name *Bonus*, which was borne by a minor 3rd-century Christian saint, martyred at Rome with eleven companions under the Emperor Vespasian. It was adopted as a personal name partly in his honor and partly because of the transparently well-omened meaning. **2.** Italian: nickname from *b(u)ono* 'good' (Latin *bonus*). **3.** Hungarian (**Bonó**): from a pet form of the personal name *Bonifác* (see BONIFACIO).
GIVEN NAMES Italian 10%. *Salvatore* (6), *Vito* (5), *Gaspare* (3), *Antonino* (2), *Carlo* (2), *Gino* (2), *Rocco* (2), *Saverio* (2), *Vincenzo* (2), *Alfonse, Angelo, Antonio*.

Bonomi (149) Italian: patronymic or plural form of BONOMO.
GIVEN NAMES Italian 8%. *Angelo* (2), *Aldo, Dante, Flavio, Marco, Mauro, Pietro*.

Bonomo (720) Italian: **1.** from the personal name *Bonomo*, an omen or well-wishing

name meaning '(we hope that he will be a) good man'. **2.** occupational name for various elected officials, for example in 12th-century Florence, who bore this title.
GIVEN NAMES Italian 13%. *Salvatore* (6), *Angelo* (3), *Carmelo* (2), *Philomena* (2), *Rocco* (2), *Vito* (2), *Carmela*, *Carmine*, *Concetta*, *Cosmo*, *Francesca*.

Bonsack (117) Americanized spelling of German **Bohnsack** 'bean bag'.
GIVEN NAME German 4%. *Konrad*.

Bonsall (562) English: habitational name from a place in Derbyshire recorded in Domesday Book as *Bunteshale* 'nook or corner of land (Old English *halh*) of a man called *Bunt*'.

Bonsell (136) English (Leicestershire): variant spelling of BONSALL.

Bonser (459) English (Nottinghamshire): nickname from Old French *bon sire* 'good sir', given either to a fine gentleman (perhaps ironically), or to someone who made frequent use of this term of address. Compare BOWSER.

Bonsignore (323) Italian: nickname from *bon signore* 'good sir', probably bestowed on someone who was, or aspired to be, a fine gentleman, or to someone who made frequent use of this expression as a term of address.
GIVEN NAMES Italian 11%. *Angelo* (2), *Salvatore* (2), *Matteo*, *Natale*, *Sal*.

Bonson (117) **1.** English: unexplained. **2.** Swiss French (Vaud): unexplained. **3.** German: unexplained.
GIVEN NAME French 5%. *Henri*.

Bonta (256) **1.** Hungarian: from *bonta* 'multicolored', 'mixed with black and white stripes or patches', hence a nickname for someone with patchy gray beard or hair. **2.** Czech: from the personal names *Bonifác* (see BONIFACIO) or BONAVENTURA.

Bonte (146) French: see LABONTE.
GIVEN NAMES French 16%. *Andre* (2), *Serge* (2), *Lucien*, *Marcel*, *Maryse*, *Mireille*.

Bontempo (345) Italian: from the personal name *Bontempo*, meaning literally 'good time', i.e. 'it was a good time, an auspicious moment, when you were born', from Old Italian *bono* 'good' + *tempo* 'time' (Latin *tempus* 'time', 'weather', 'season'). This was a name bestowed as an expression of gratitude for the birth of a much wanted child.
GIVEN NAMES Italian 13%; French 5%. *Angelo* (5), *Domenic* (2), *Alfonse*, *Dante*, *Gasper*, *Ignazio*, *Marco*, *Renzo*, *Salvatore*; *Colette*, *Emile*.

Bontrager (1238) German (**Bonträger**): variant of **Bornträger** (see BORNTRAGER).
FOREBEARS The name was brought to the U.S. in 1767 by Martin Bonträger; his sons John, Christian, and Andrew, all Amish, settled in OH and VA.

Bonura (347) Italian (Sicily): from the personal name *Bonora*, an omen name meaning '(it was a) good time (when you were

born)', bestowed as an expression of gratitude, or perhaps signifying a child that was born in the early morning or one that had been long awaited, from *buonora* in the sense 'finally', 'at last'.
GIVEN NAMES Italian 15%. *Carlo* (4), *Angelo* (2), *Salvatore* (2), *Carmelo*, *Guiseppe*, *Innocenzo*, *Lia*.

Bonus (157) **1.** French, German, and Dutch: humanistic Latinization of vernacular names meaning 'good', for example French LEBON or Dutch *de Goede* (see DE GOOD). **2.** Czech (**Bonuš**): from a pet form of the personal name *Bonifác*, Czech form of BONIFACIO. **3.** Lithuanian: shortened form of **Bonusevičius**.

Bonventre (126) Italian: from the personal name *Bonventre* 'good belly', bestowed on a newborn probably with reference to the mother's womb.
GIVEN NAMES Italian 23%. *Vito* (4), *Antonino*, *Gasper*, *Martino*, *Pietro*, *Sal*, *Santo*, *Veto*, *Vita*.

Bonvillain (244) French: nickname from Old French *bon* 'good' + *vilain* 'farmer'.
GIVEN NAMES French 5%. *Emile* (2), *Amie*, *Cecile*.

Bonville (167) French: variant of BONNEVILLE.

Bonvillian (124) Altered spelling of French BONVILLAIN.
GIVEN NAMES French 7%. *Marcelle* (2), *Dominique*.

Bonwell (168) **1.** English: possibly a habitational name from Bunwell in Norfolk, which is named with Old English *bune* 'reed' + *wella* 'spring', 'stream'. Alternatively it could be a variant of the Norman habitational name BONFIELD. **2.** Possibly an Americanized form of French BONNEVILLE.

Bonzo (156) Northern Italian (Piedmont): probably from a reduced form of the medieval personal name *Bónizo*, of Germanic origin.

Boo (120) **1.** Dutch: reduced form of BODE 1. **2.** Scottish: unexplained. **3.** Malaysian and other East Asian: unexplained. **4.** Korean: variant of PU.
GIVEN NAMES Southeast Asian 13%; Korean 5%. *Chi*, *Chin*, *Ming*, *Sang*, *Soon*, *Sung*; *Jinyoung*, *Kyung Sook*, *Myong*, *Sung Chul*, *Sungtae*, *Youngil*.

Boock (172) **1.** Dutch: topographic name for someone who lived by a beech tree or in a beech wood, from Middle Low German *buche*. **2.** German: habitational name from any of various places so named, in Altmark and Pomerania.
GIVEN NAMES German 4%. *Erwin*, *Otto*.

Boody (226) English: variant of BOOTY.

Booe (334) German (**Buhe**): unexplained.
FOREBEARS The surname was brought to Philadelphia in 1738 by Philip Jacob Buhe (born 1683 in Baden, Germany) aboard the *Snow Fox*.

Boogaard (105) Dutch: reduced form of **Boomgard** (see BOGARD).
GIVEN NAMES Dutch 6%. *Gerrit*, *Pieter*.

Booher (2538) Of German origin: probably an Americanized spelling of BUCHER.

Book (2246) **1.** Probably an Americanized spelling of German and Jewish (Ashkenazic) BUCH or BUCK. **2.** German: from a Germanic personal name *Bogo*, Old High German *bogo* 'bow' (weapon). **3.** The surname Book appears occasionally in English records; it may be a variant spelling of BUCK or from the same source as 1.

Bookbinder (202) **1.** Jewish (Ashkenazic): Americanized form of BUCHBINDER. **2.** English: occupational name for a bookbinder, from Middle English *bokbynder*.
GIVEN NAME Jewish 4%. *Meyer*.

Booke (124) **1.** Americanized spelling of German BUCHE. **2.** English: see BOOK.

Booker (9092) **1.** English: occupational name for someone concerned with books, generally a scribe or binder, from Middle English *boker*, Old English *bōcere*, an agent derivative of *bōc* 'book'. **2.** English: variant of BOWKER. **3.** Americanized form of German BUCHER.

Bookhout (109) Probably an Americanized spelling of Dutch **Bouckhout**, **(van) Boeckhout**, etc., a habitational name from any of numerous minor places in Belgium named or named with Boekhout(e), Bochout(e), Boechout(e), meaning 'birch wood'.

Bookman (662) German (**Bo(o)kmann**): North German cognate of BUCHMANN, of which this may also be an Americanized spelling.

Bookout (864) Americanized spelling of the Dutch habitational name **Bouchout**, from any of numerous places called Boekhout(e), Boechout(e), or Bochoute.

Books (477) North German and Dutch: derivative of BOOCK.

Bookwalter (292) Americanized form of German **Buchwalter**, a habitational name for someone from any of several places called Buchwald(e), the name of which means 'beech forest'.

Boom (390) Dutch and North German: from Middle Dutch *boom*, Middle Low German *bōm* 'tree', hence a nickname for a particularly tall person or a topographic name for someone who lived by a tree that was particularly conspicuous.

Boomer (724) **1.** Dutch: from an agent derivative of *(sluit)boom*, 'sluice gate', hence an occupational name for a man who operated such a gate on a waterway. **2.** North German: variant of **Bäumer** (see BAUMER 2).

Boomershine (182) Americanized form of the German habitational name **Bommersheim**, from a place so named in Hesse.

Boomgaarden (109) Variant of the Dutch topographic name **Boomgaard** 'orchard'. See also BOGARD.

Boomgarden (139) Altered form of the Dutch topographic name **Boomgaard** 'orchard'. See also BOGARD.

Boomhower (249) Altered spelling of Dutch and North German **Bohmhauer**, literally 'wood cutter', an occupational name for a woodsman or lumberjack, Middle Low German *bomhowere*.

Booms (189) Dutch and North German: variant of BOOM.

Boomsma (200) Frisian: habitational name for someone from a place named with Boom 'tree'.

Boon (779) English or Dutch: variant of BOONE.

Boone (16494) **1.** English (of Norman origin): from a nickname meaning 'good', from Old French *bon* 'good'. Compare BONE 1. **2.** English (of Norman origin): habitational name from Bohon in La Manche, France, of obscure etymology. **3.** Dutch: from Middle Dutch *bone*, *boene* 'bean', hence a metonymic occupational name for a bean grower or a nickname for a man of little importance (broad beans having been an extremely common crop in the medieval period), or possibly for a tall thin man (with reference to the runner bean). FOREBEARS The renowned American frontiersman Daniel Boone (1734–1820) was born in Reading, PA, into a Quaker family. His grandfather was a weaver who had emigrated from Exeter in England to Philadelphia in 1717.

Boonstra (321) Frisian: metonymic occupational name for a grower or seller of beans, from an agent noun derived from *boon* 'bean'. It may also have been a derogatory nickname for a man regarded as of little importance.

Boop (224) Altered spelling of German BUB. In this form, also written **Boob**, the name is frequent in PA.

Boor (497) **1.** English: from Old English *bār* 'boar', hence probably a nickname for a keen hunter of wild boar or for someone thought to resemble the animal in some way. **2.** Variant spelling of BOER.

Booras (164) Greek: from Albanian *burrë* 'man', 'husband'. GIVEN NAMES Greek 8%. *Speros* (2), *Stavros* (2), *Vasilios*.

Boord (242) English: variant spelling of BOARD.

Boore (133) **1.** English: variant spelling of BOOR. **2.** Possibly a shortened form of Dutch **van den Boore**, a variant of **van den Borne** (see BORNE). GIVEN NAME French 4%. *Monique*.

Boorman (274) English: variant of BOWERMAN.

Boorse (114) Probably an Americanized spelling of French or German BURSE.

Boortz (143) Possibly an altered spelling of the Dutch surname **Boorts**, which Debrabandere suggests may be a hypercorrected form of **Boots** (see BOOT). Alternatively, it

may be an Americanized spelling of German **Burtz**, a nickname for a little man, from the base form of the word *Bürzel* 'rump', 'stump'. GIVEN NAME German 4%. *Otto* (2).

Boos (1516) Dutch and German: from a Germanic personal name, *Boso*, most probably from an element meaning 'leader', 'nobleman', or 'arrogant person'.

Boosalis (100) Greek: derivation unknown. It may be a derivative of the personal name *Bousias*, a pet form of *Kharalambos* (see HARRIS). GIVEN NAMES Greek 15%. *Costas, Panagiotis, Tasos*.

Boose (662) **1.** Dutch: variant of BOOS. **2.** Altered spelling of North German BUSE.

Boot (243) **1.** English: metonymic occupational name for a maker or seller of boots, from Middle English, Old French *bote* (of unknown origin). **2.** Dutch and North German: metonymic occupational name for a boatman, from Dutch *boot* 'boat'.

Boote (125) English: variant spelling of BOOT.

Booten (135) Dutch: from a pet form of the Germanic personal name *Bodo* (see BODE).

Booth (18561) Northern English and Scottish: topographic name for someone who lived in a small hut or bothy, Middle English *both(e)*, especially a cowman or shepherd. The word is of Scandinavian origin (compare Old Danish *bōth*, Old Norse *būð*) and was used to denote various kinds of temporary shelter, typically a cowshed or a herdsman's hut. In the British Isles the surname is still more common in northern England, where Scandinavian influence was more marked, and in Scotland, where the word was borrowed into Gaelic as *both(an)*. FOREBEARS Robert Booth (1604–72) is mentioned in the colonial records of Exeter, NH, in 1645. He subsequently moved to ME.

Boothby (700) English: habitational name from a place in Lincolnshire (now Boothby Graffoe and Boothby Pagnell), recorded in Domesday Book as *Bodebi*, from Old Danish *bōth* 'hut', 'shed' + *bý* 'farm', 'settlement'.

Boothe (2878) Northern English and Scottish: variant spelling of BOOTH.

Boothman (164) Northern English: variant of BOOTH.

Boothroyd (217) English (Yorkshire): habitational name from a place in West Yorkshire named Boothroyd, from northern Middle English *both(e)* 'hut', 'shed' + *royd* 'clearing'.

Booton (283) English: habitational name, probably from a place in Norfolk named Booton, from an Old English personal name (*Bōta* or *Bō*) + *tūn* 'settlement'. The present-day concentration of the surname is in the West Midlands and Wales.

Boots (1116) Dutch: variant of BOOT.

Booty (240) English (East Anglia and Essex): unexplained.

Bootz (163) Dutch: **1.** variant of BOOT. **2.** nickname for a ridiculous person (see BOOZ 2). GIVEN NAME French 4%. *Antoine*.

Booz (260) **1.** Dutch: variant of BOOS. Debrabandere suggests it may also be habitational name for someone from Booze in Trembleur in the Belgian province of Liège. **2.** South German and Swiss German: regional (Alemannic) nickname from Middle High German *boese* 'ridiculous person', 'low-standing servant' or from a Germanic personal name *Bozo* (See BOSSHART 1).

Booze (623) Variant of Dutch BOOZ.

Boozer (1464) English (Kent): of uncertain derivation: **1.** it could be a topographic name for someone living in an area planted with bushes, French *bussière*, or a habitational name from any of various minor places in Essex, perhaps named with this word. **2.** alternatively it may be a nickname for a heavy drinker, from an agent derivative of Middle English *bouse(n)* 'to drink', 'to booze' (from Middle Dutch *būsen*) or Middle English *bous, boos* 'intoxicating drink' (from Middle Dutch *būse*). **3.** lastly, it could be an occupational name for a stockman, from a derivative of Middle English *bos(e), buse* 'stall for livestock', 'cowstall', 'manger' (from Old English *bōs*).

Bope (100) Probably an Americanized form of German BOPP.

Bopp (1254) German: from a Germanic personal name *Boppo*, of uncertain origin and meaning, perhaps originally a nursery name or a short form of a personal name such as *Bodobert*, a Germanic personal name meaning 'famous leader', composed of the elements *Bodo* 'messenger', 'leader' (see BODE) + *berht* 'bright', 'famous'. See also POPP.

Boquet (154) Variant spelling of French BOUQUET. GIVEN NAMES French 6%. *Alce, Sylvie, Yves*.

Boquist (166) Swedish: ornamental name composed of the elements *bo* 'dwelling', 'home' + *quist*, an old or ornamental spelling of *kvist* 'twig'.

Bor (104) **1.** Jewish (eastern Ashkenazic): habitational name from the village of Bor in Belarus. **2.** Dutch: variant of BOER. GIVEN NAMES Jewish 9%; Russian 7%; Dutch 4%. *Eyal, Haya, Irina; Leonid, Sergey, Yelena, Yury; Cornelis, Imrich*.

Bora (176) **1.** Indian (Gujarat): Muslim name based on the name of a Muslim community in Gujarat. It is believed to be a derivative of Sanskrit *vyavahāra* 'trade'. However, only one subgroup of the Boras is engaged in trade. **2.** Indian (Assam): Hindu name of unknown meaning. **3.** Romanian: from a feminine form of *Boro*, a short form of the personal name

BORIS. **4.** Polish: from a pet form of the personal names *Borzysław* or *Bolebor*. **5.** Hungarian: variant of *Bara*, a short form of the personal name *Barabás*, Hungarian form of BARNABY.

GIVEN NAMES Indian 10%; Muslim 7%; Romanian 6%; Polish 4%. *Girish, Renu, Sudhir, Sunder, Sunil, Varsha; Yusuf* (4), *Ahmet, Ali, Iqbal, Irfan, Nesrin, Salim; Vasile* (3), *Floare, Ilie; Danuta, Janusz, Tadeusz.*

Borah (344) Indian: variant of BORA.

Borak (232) **1.** Polish: from a pet form of *Borzysław, Bolebor*, or any of various other personal names formed with *bor*. **2.** Czech (**Borák**): habitational name for someone from one of many places named with *bor* 'pine forest'; alternatively from a short form of the personal names *Dalibor* or *Bořivoj*, containing the element *-bor* 'battle'.

Boram (151) English (Essex and Kent): possibly a variant of the habitational name BARHAM.

Boran (136) **1.** Irish: Anglicized form of Gaelic **Ó Bodhráin** 'descendant of the deaf one', from *bodhar* 'deaf'. **2.** Czech (also **Bořan**): from a personal name beginning or ending with the element *bor* 'battle' e.g. *Bořivoj* or *Bořislav*, or *Dalibor*.

GIVEN NAME Irish 6%. *Colm.*

Borash (108) Origin unidentified.

Borawski (265) Polish: habitational name for someone from a place called Borawe, Borawskie, or Borawy.

GIVEN NAMES Polish 13%. *Kazimierz* (3), *Dariusz, Iwona, Lech, Slawomir, Stanislaw, Wieslawa, Zbigniew, Zdzislaw.*

Borba (475) Portuguese: habitational name from a place named Borba, for example in Alentejo.

GIVEN NAMES Spanish 14%. *Manuel* (11), *Jose* (9), *Carlos* (5), *Luis* (3), *Ana* (2), *Fernando* (2), *Alicia, Camilo, Climaco, Dimas, Lilia, Marcelo.*

Borbely (138) Hungarian (**Borbély**): occupational name for a barber, Hungarian *borbély*. See also BARBER.

GIVEN NAMES Hungarian 18%. *Zoltan* (3), *Antal* (2), *Ferenc* (2), *Ildiko, Kalman, Laszlo, Miklos.*

Borbon (156) Spanish (**Borbón**): variant of BOURBON.

GIVEN NAMES Spanish 52%. *Jose* (12), *Ana* (2), *Jesus* (2), *Marta* (2), *Miguel Angel* (2), *Tomas* (2), *Ademar, Alfredo, Ana Maria, Bernabe, Berta, Carlos; Antonio* (2), *Bartolo, Fausto, Julieta.*

Borchard (281) North German: variant of BORCHARDT.

Borchardt (1673) Dutch and North German: from the medieval personal name *Burkhard* (see BURKHART).

GIVEN NAMES German 4%. *Hans* (5), *Otto* (3), *Bodo, Dieter, Gerhard, Heinz, Katharina, Klaus, Kurt, Math, Meinhard, Wolfgang.*

Borchelt (153) North German: from a pet form of the personal name *Borko* (itself a short form of BORCHARDT).

Borcher (111) Variant of German BORCHARDT.

Borcherding (461) North German: patronymic from BORCHARDT.

Borchers (1279) Dutch and North German: patronymic from the personal name BORCHARD. See also BURKHART.

GIVEN NAMES German 4%. *Ernst* (2), *Bernhard, Dieter, Erwin, Ewald, Guenter, Heiner, Heinz, Helmuth, Kurt, Otto.*

Borchert (1028) North German: variant of BORCHARDT.

GIVEN NAMES German 6%. *Ernst* (2), *Gerd* (2), *Otto* (2), *Uwe* (2), *Berthold, Erwin, Florian, Fritz, Gunter, Gunther, Klaus, Kurt.*

Borck (274) **1.** Eastern German: variant spelling of BORK. **2.** Eastern German: from the personal name *Borek*, a pet form of *Boruslaw*. **3.** Danish: topographic name from *bork* 'fortress' or a habitational name from a place named with this word.

Bord (138) Jewish (eastern Ashkenazic): nickname from Yiddish *bord* 'beard'.

GIVEN NAMES Russian 7%; Jewish 6%; French 5%. *Aleksandr, Boris, Dmitry, Igor, Leonid, Vladimir; Rivka, Shmuel; Jacques, Monique.*

Borda (292) **1.** Catalan: topographic name for someone who lived in a plank-built cottage, from Catalan *borda* 'board'. **2.** Hungarian: see BORDAS.

GIVEN NAMES Spanish 21%; French 6%. *Carlos* (4), *Juan* (3), *Jaime* (2), *Roberto* (2), *Adriana, Alberto, Alejandro, Alfonso, Augusto, Cesar, Elba, Elena; Andre* (2), *Arnaud, Jean-Paul, Monique.*

Bordas (179) **1.** Catalan: respelling of **Bordes**, the plural of BORDA. **2.** Hungarian (**Bordás**): from *takácsborda*, denoting part of a loom, hence a metonymic occupational name for a maker of looms or a weaver.

GIVEN NAMES Hungarian 5%; Spanish 5%. *Csaba* (2), *Attila, Lajos; Ernesto, Jaime, Juan, Juana, Lino, Pedro, Ricardo, Vicenta.*

Borde (137) **1.** Southern French: topographic name for someone who lived in a plank-built cottage, from Frankish *bord* 'plank'. Later, this word came to designate a farm. **2.** German: see BORDES 3. **3.** Indian (Maharashtra); pronounced as *borday*: Hindu (Maratha) name of unknown meaning.

GIVEN NAMES Indian 7%; French 6%. *Arvind, Madhusudan, Shekhar, Sushama; Armand, Emile, Marcel.*

Bordeau (310) French: **1.** variant of BORDEAUX. **2.** topographic name for someone who lived on a small farm, Old French *bordeau.*

Bordeaux (968) French: habitational name from the city in Gironde, the Latin name of which is *Burdigala*, of ancient and unexplained origin.

GIVEN NAMES French 4%. *Aldea, Andre, Andree, Clovis, Jean Claude, Jean-Luc, Leonce.*

Bordeleau (109) French: from a diminutive of BORDE.

GIVEN NAMES French 24%. *Gilles* (2), *Armande, Berthe, Cecile, Jacques, Lucien, Michel, Venance.*

Bordelon (2502) Southern French: from a diminutive of BORDE.

FOREBEARS The Bordelon families of LA and eastern TX claim descent from Laurent (Nicholas) Bordelon of Le Havre, France, who came to New Orleans around 1728.

GIVEN NAMES French 4%. *Gaston* (4), *Leonce* (3), *Andre* (2), *Armand* (2), *Alphonse, Camile, Celestine, Celina, Colette, Curley, Emile, Germaine.*

Borden (5667) English: habitational name from a place in Kent named Borden, perhaps from Old English *bār* 'boar' or *bor* 'hill' + *denu* 'valley' or *denn* '(swine) pasture'.

Bordenave (145) Southern French: topographic name originally denoting someone who lived at the 'new cottage', from Occitan *borde* 'plank-built cottage' + *nave* 'new'. See BORDE.

GIVEN NAMES French 12%; Spanish 10%. *Pierre* (2), *Altagrace, Cecile, Edouard, Gaston, Ketty; Pedro* (3), *Jaime* (2), *Carlos, Concepcion, Manuel, Martinez, Rafael.*

Bordenkircher (142) Respelling of German **Partenkircher**, a habitational name for someone from the twin cities of Garmisch-Partenkirchen in Bavaria.

Border (810) English: topographic name for someone who lived at the edge of a village or by some other boundary, Middle English *border*, from Old French *bordure* 'edge'.

Borders (2972) English: topographic name for someone who lived at the edge of a village or by some other boundary, Middle English *border*, from Old French *bordure* 'edge'.

Bordes (204) **1.** French: variant of BORDE. **2.** Catalan: variant (plural) of BORDA. **3.** German: from the genitive form of a personal name formed with *Bord* (Gothic *baurd*, Old Norse *bordh* 'shield'), for example *Herbord*.

GIVEN NAMES French 18%. *Francois* (2), *Pierre* (2), *Anselme, Cyrille, Germaine, Guylaine, Lucien, Magalie, Marcel, Marie Yolene, Michel, Rolande.*

Bordley (133) English: habitational name, probably from a place in North Yorkshire named Bordley, from Old English *bord* 'board' + *lēah* 'woodland clearing'.

Bordner (747) German: probably a variant spelling of **Bartner**, an occupational name for a (battle) axe maker, from an agent derivative of Middle Low German *barde*, Middle High German *barte* 'axe'.

Bordon (103) **1.** Spanish (**Bordón**): from *bordón* 'pilgrim's staff', hence a nickname for a pilgrim. **2.** Spanish (**Bordón**): habitational name from a place so named in Teruel province. **3.** French: variant of BOURDON.

GIVEN NAMES Spanish 17%. *Juan* (2), *Alicia, Armando, Carlos, Cristina, Enrique, Ernesto, Francisco, Jose, Julio, Luis, Marcelo*; *Alessandra, Dario, Elio, Umberto.*

Bordonaro (478) Italian (Sicily): **1.** occupational name for a muleteer (strictly speaking, a driver of hinnies, the offspring of a female donkey and a male horse), Italian *bordonaro*, Sicilian *bburdunaru* (from Latin *burdonarius*). The Sicilian word also means 'tuna fishing net', thus the name may have been a metonymic occupational name for a fisherman in some instances. **2.** from a derivative of *bordone* 'pilgrim's staff', probably applied as a nickname for someone who had made a significant pilgrimage.

GIVEN NAMES Italian 23%. *Salvatore* (12), *Santo* (7), *Angelo* (6), *Antonio* (2), *Cosmo* (2), *Leonardo* (2), *Sebastiano* (2), *Biagio, Ciro, Corrado, Luigi, Marco.*

Bordwell (230) English: variant spelling of the Lancashire surname **Boardwell**, which is probably from a lost or unidentified place.

Borecki (80) Polish: habitational name for someone from a place called Borek or Borki, from *bór* 'pine forest'. Compare BORKOWSKI.

GIVEN NAMES Polish 8%. *Henryk, Wojtek.*

Boreen (105) Irish: probably a variant of **Burrane**, an Anglicized form of Gaelic Ó **Bodhráin** 'descendant of the deaf one', from *bodhar* 'deaf'.

Borek (566) **1.** Polish: from a derivative of *Borzysław, Bolebor*, or some other personal name formed with *bor*. **2.** Polish and Jewish (from Poland): habitational name from Borek, so named with Polish *bór* 'pine forest' + the diminutive suffix *-ek*. As a Jewish name, it could sometimes be from a Polonized form of the Yiddish personal name *Borukh*.

GIVEN NAMES Polish 6%. *Bronislaw, Jacek, Janina, Jerzy, Kazimierz, Stanislaw, Zbigniew, Zofia, Zygmunt.*

Borel (624) **1.** French: from a diminutive of **Boure**, probably a nickname for someone who habitually dressed in brown, or a metonymic occupational name for a worker in the wool trade, from Old French *b(o)ure*, a type of coarse reddish brown woolen cloth with long hairs (Late Latin *burra* 'coarse untreated wool'). However, the word had many other senses in Old French, among them 'cushion', 'harness', 'collar', 'crest', and 'headdress'; the surname could equally have arisen as an occupational name for a maker or seller of any of these items, or as a nickname derived from one of these other senses. **2.** French: occupational name for a judicial torturer, from Old French *bourreau*, a derivative of *bourrer*, literally 'to card wool' and by extension 'to maltreat or torture'. It may also be an occupational name for a wool carder, but the corresponding vocabulary word in Old French does not seem to be recorded in this sense. **3.** In some cases the name may be of English origin, a variant of the cognate BURRELL. This name is found chiefly in LA and TX.

FOREBEARS A Borel from the Auvergne in France is documented in Baie St-Paul, Canada, in 1747.

GIVEN NAMES French 9%. *Armand* (2), *Clovis* (2), *Emile* (2), *Minos* (2), *Alain, Chantelle, Dominique, Francoise, Henri, Marcel, Odile, Pascale.*

Borell (181) English: variant of BURRELL.

Borella (172) Possibly a variant of Italian BORELLO.

GIVEN NAMES Italian 8%. *Aldo* (2), *Vito* (2), *Angelo, Dante, Pietro, Primo.*

Borelli (717) Northern Italian: patronymic or plural form of BORRELLO.

GIVEN NAMES Italian 13%. *Angelo* (5), *Carmine* (4), *Primo* (3), *Giuseppe* (2), *Luigi* (2), *Serafino* (2), *Antonio, Carmin, Caterina, Dario, Dino, Donato.*

Borello (210) Northern Italian: variant spelling of BORRELLO.

GIVEN NAME Italian 6%. *Domenic* (2).

Boreman (143) **1.** Dutch: variant of BORNEMAN. **2.** Probably in some cases an altered spelling of German BORMANN; in others of English *Borman* or *Boorman*, variants of BOWERMAN.

Boren (2762) **1.** Czech (**Boreň**): see BORAK. **2.** Possibly also an altered spelling of German BORN. **3.** Swedish: ornamental name composed of an unexplained first element + the common surname suffix *-en*, from Latin *-enius* 'descendant of'.

Borenstein (471) Dutch form or Jewish (from Poland) variant of BERNSTEIN.

GIVEN NAMES Jewish 15%. *Sol* (4), *Isak* (2), *Moshe* (2), *Nachman* (2), *Simcha* (2), *Boruch, Chaim, Chani, Chanie, Chaya, Dov, Dovid.*

Borer (565) **1.** English: occupational name for one whose job was to bore holes in something, Middle English *borer*. **2.** Swiss German: variant of BOHRER.

Bores (260) **1.** Czech (**Boreš**): see BORAK. **2.** Probably an altered spelling of any of the various German names derived from pet forms of the medieval personal name *Liborius*, such as **Börs, Böres, Borries**. See also BERRES.

Borg (1919) **1.** Scandinavian: habitational name from various farms and other minor places so named, from Old Norse *borg* 'fortification', 'stronghold'. In some cases the name is topographical, often referring to a hill that resembles a fortification, rather than an actual fortification. **2.** North German: habitational name from the common place name Borg, a Low German form of BURG. **3.** Jewish (eastern Ashkenazic): metonymic occupational name for a money lender, from Yiddish *borg* 'credit'.

GIVEN NAMES Scandinavian 6%. *Erik* (4), *Lars* (4), *Anders* (2), *Swen* (2), *Bjorn, Evald, Jorgen, Karsten, Knut, Lennart, Nels.*

Borgardt (119) North German: from the medieval personal name *Burkhard* (see BURKHART).

Borgatti (107) French (Corsica): topographic name for someone who lived in a fortified town, from a Corsican cognate of French *bourget* 'fortified town' (see BOURGET).

GIVEN NAMES French 9%; Spanish 6%; Italian 5%. *Raoul* (2), *Armand; Mando* (2), *Mario* (2), *Narcisa; Angelo.*

Borge (334) **1.** Spanish and Portuguese: variant of BORGES, or a habitational name from Borge in Málaga province. **2.** Danish and Norwegian: variant of BORG 'fortification', from the dative case, meaning 'at the fortification'.

GIVEN NAMES Spanish 11%; Scandinavian 4%. *Manuel* (4), *Carlos* (3), *Sergio* (3), *Alejandro* (2), *Alberto, Alvaro, Angel, Avelina, Cesar, Francisco, Guillermo, Humberto.*

Borgelt (162) Possibly a variant of German BORCHELT.

GIVEN NAME German 4%. *Kurt.*

Borgen (794) Danish and Norwegian: variant of BORG.

GIVEN NAMES Scandinavian 5%. *Erik* (5), *Bjorn, Jan Erik.*

Borger (935) **1.** North German and Dutch: variant of BURGER. **2.** Jewish (Ashkenazic): nickname from Yiddish *borger* 'borrower' or 'lender'. **3.** Norwegian and Swedish: habitational name for someone from a place called BORG or topographic name for someone living by a fortification or near a hill resembling a fortification.

Borgerding (306) German: variant of **Borcherding** (see BORCHERS).

Borgerson (114) Scandinavian: patronymic from BORGER.

Borgert (156) North German: variant of BORCHARDT.

Borges (2509) **1.** Catalan: habitational name from any of several places called with Borges in Catalonia, for example Les Borges Blanques, in Lleida, or Les Borges del Camp, in Tarragona. **2.** Portuguese: of disputed etymology; possibly a habitational name for someone from Bourges in France. **3.** German: from a short form of the medieval personal name *Liborius*. **4.** Danish: from the German patronymic BORCHERS.

GIVEN NAMES Spanish 24%; Portuguese 10%. *Jose* (44), *Manuel* (35), *Carlos* (25), *Francisco* (13), *Luis* (12), *Julio* (10), *Mario* (10), *Eduardo* (9), *Jorge* (9), *Ana* (8), *Jesus* (7), *Orlando* (7); *Joao* (4), *Afonso* (2),

Manoel (2), *Duarte, Heitor, Joaquim, Marcio, Neuza, Paulo, Vasco.*

Borgese (135) Italian: variant of BOR-GHESE.

GIVEN NAMES Italian 16%. *Domenic* (2), *Salvatore* (2), *Antonio, Sal.*

Borgeson (463) Scandinavian: patronymic probably from *Børge*, which is from the Old Norse personal name *Byrgir.*

GIVEN NAMES Scandinavian 5%. *Erik* (2), *Anders, Sigfrid.*

Borghese (123) Italian: from the medieval personal name *Borghese*, from the adjective *borghése* 'burgher', an inhabitant and (usually) freeman of a (fortified) town, a burgher, especially one with municipal rights and duties (Late Latin *burgensis*).

GIVEN NAMES Italian 13%. *Guido* (2), *Carmine, Francesca, Giovanna, Livio, Marco.*

Borghi (165) Northern Italian: variant of BORGO.

GIVEN NAMES Italian 17%. *Angelo* (3), *Deno* (2), *Dino* (2), *Gaetano* (2), *Aldo, Egidio.*

Borgia (346) Italian: habitational name from Borgia, a place in Catanzaro province, or from Borja in Spain (see BORJA).

FOREBEARS The powerful and notorious Borgia family in Renaissance Rome was of Spanish origin. Rodrigo BORJA (1431–1503), born in Játiva, Spain, became Pope as Alexander VI. Among his four children by his mistress Vannozza Catanei were Cesare Borgia (1475–1507) and Lucrezia Borgia (1480–1519). Cesare was a brilliant but unscrupulous soldier and politician, who was made a cardinal at the age of 17 and was implicated in the murders of both his elder brother and his sister's husband. Lucrezia was rumored to have been a poisoner and to have had incestuous relations with her father and her brother, but she led a conventional life after her marriage to her third husband, Alfonso d'Este, Duke of Ferrara, in 1501, and became a patron of the arts and sciences.

GIVEN NAMES Italian 15%; French 5%. *Angelo* (6), *Vito* (2), *Elio, Giovanni, Salvatore, Tullio; Andre* (2), *Colette, Gaetan.*

Borgman (796) **1.** Respelling of BORGMANN. **2.** Swedish: variant of BORG, with the addition of *man* 'man'.

Borgmann (388) **1.** North German: from Middle Low German *borgman* or *borchman* 'man of the castle', hence an occupational name for someone who worked at a castle or was a vassal of the feudal lord, or for a citizen of a (fortified) town. **2.** Jewish (Ashkenazic): variant of BORG.

GIVEN NAMES German 6%. *Egon* (2), *Hans* (2), *Reinhold* (2), *Bernhard, Christoph, Claus.*

Borgmeyer (192) German: status name for a free farmer or peasant with feudal obligations to a castle or town, from Middle Low German *borg* 'castle', 'town' + *Meyer* 'tenant farmer'.

GIVEN NAME French 5%. *Roch.*

Borgo (114) **1.** Northern Italian (and Spanish): habitational name from any of a number of towns and villages so named, from Italian *borgo* 'hamlet', 'village', or a topographic name from the same word. **2.** Italian: from a short form, *Burgi*, of a Germanic personal name formed with this element.

GIVEN NAMES Spanish 7%. *Mario* (2), *Anselmo, Jose, Jose Luis, Miguel.*

Borgstrom (304) Swedish (**Borgström**): ornamental name composed of the elements *borg* 'castle', 'fortification', 'stronghold' + *ström* 'river'.

GIVEN NAMES Scandinavian 9%; German 6%. *Arlis, Erik, Lennart, Per, Tor; Kurt* (2), *Wilhelm.*

Borgwardt (228) North German: from a personal name composed of Middle Low German *borg* 'castle' + *wart* 'guard', 'watchman'.

GIVEN NAMES German 5%. *Kurt* (2), *Hans, Irmgard.*

Boria (137) Catalan: unexplained.

GIVEN NAMES Spanish 32%; Italian 9%. *Jose* (3), *Juan* (3), *Jorge* (2), *Justo* (2), *Agustin, Alfredo, Angel, Augustina, Carlos, Catalino, Consuelo, Domingo; Dante* (2), *Angelo, Dario, Luigi, Luigino, Romeo.*

Borich (144) Serbian (**Borić**): from the personal name *Bora*, a pet form of *Borislav.*

GIVEN NAMES South Slavic 7%. *Milorad* (2), *Vuk* (2), *Rade.*

Borie (108) French (central and southern): topographic name for someone who lived in an isolated house in the country, Occitan *borio.*

GIVEN NAMES French 7%. *Alain, Andre.*

Borin (185) **1.** Russian: patronymic from a pet form of BORIS. **2.** Slovenian: probably a topographic name from *bor* 'pine tree'.

Boring (2046) North German: perhaps a patronymic from a personal named formed with Slavic *bor* 'pine (forest)', 'conifer' or 'strife', 'struggle' (see BORIS).

Borino (109) Italian: from a diminutive of **Borio**, which is probably from a pet form of the personal name *Liborio.*

GIVEN NAMES Italian 14%. *Angelo* (2), *Leno, Pasquale.*

Boris (928) **1.** Bulgarian and Slovak: from the personal name *Boris*, which is of disputed etymology. It is sometimes taken as a shortening of an Old Slavic personal name, *Boroslav*, from *bor* 'struggle', 'conflict' + *slav* 'glory', but more probably it is an alteration of the Old Bulgarian personal name *Bogoris*, borne by the king of the Bulgars (sometimes known as Boris) who was converted to Christianity in 864. This is a byname from Turkic *bogori* 'small'. *Boris* is one of the very few names of non-Byzantine origin admitted as a baptismal name in the Orthodox Church, largely because of the popular cult of St. Boris (died 1010), patron saint of Moscow (whose baptismal name was ROMAN). **2.** Hungarian:

from *Boris*, a pet form of the female personal name *Borbála*, or in some cases possibly from the male personal name *Barabás.*

Borish (110) Americanized spelling of German **Bo(h)risch**, a topographic name from Slavic *bor* 'pine (forest)', 'conifer' or in some cases from a Slavic personal name with the element *bor* 'struggle', 'strife'. Compare BORIS.

GIVEN NAME German 4%; Jewish 4%. *Myer.*

Borja (677) **1.** Spanish: habitational name from a place in Zaragoza province, named with Arabic *borj* 'tower', 'farmhouse'. Compare BORGIA. **2.** Norwegian (**Børja**): variant of BORG.

GIVEN NAMES Spanish 41%. *Jose* (15), *Jesus* (9), *Francisco* (6), *Carlos* (5), *Juan* (5), *Alfredo* (4), *Jorge* (4), *Manuel* (4), *Ricardo* (4), *Roberto* (4), *Angel* (3), *Armando* (3).

Borjas (259) Spanish: **1.** Castilianized form of Catalan BORGES. **2.** variant (plural) of BORJA.

GIVEN NAMES Spanish 43%. *Jose* (6), *Carlos* (3), *Ramon* (3), *Adolfo* (2), *Alberto* (2), *Blanca* (2), *Eduardo* (2), *Javier* (2), *Jesus* (2), *Luis* (2), *Manuel* (2), *Mario* (2); *Antonio* (4), *Gabino* (2), *Lucio, Mauro, Saturnina.*

Borjon (101) Spanish (**Borjón**): unexplained.

GIVEN NAMES Spanish 59%. *Jose* (4), *Juan* (4), *Francisco* (2), *Jesus* (2), *Manuel* (2), *Alejos, Alfonso, Cesar, Enrique, Esperanza, Felicitas, Felipe.*

Bork (1319) **1.** Eastern German: habitational name from either of two places so named, in Pomerania and Lausitz, or from Borek in Upper Saxony; all are named with Slavic *bor-* 'pine', 'conifer'. **2.** German: patronymic from a pet form of a Slavic personal name such as *Boroslaw* (see BORIS). **3.** Dutch: shortened form of **Van der Borck**, a variant of VANDENBURG. **4.** Danish: from a German variant of BORCK.

GIVEN NAMES German 4%. *Erwin* (4), *Guenter* (2), *Bernhardt, Frieda, Fritz, Hedwig, Hellmut, Kurt, Otto.*

Borke (113) German (also **Börke**): **1.** from a pet form of a Slavic personal name containing the element *bor* 'to fight'. **2.** topographic name for someone living near a pine forest, from Slavic *bor* 'pine tree', 'fir tree', 'coniferous forest'.

GIVEN NAME German 7%. *Fritz* (2).

Borkenhagen (194) German: habitational name from either of two places called Borkenhagen, in Pomerania and Mecklenburg.

GIVEN NAMES German 4%. *Arno, Erna.*

Borkowski (1638) Polish and Jewish (eastern Ashkenazic): habitational name for someone from a place called Borki, Borkowice, or Borek, all named with Polish *bór* 'pine forest', or from Borków, which derives from the personal name *Borek* + the possessive suffix *-ow.*

GIVEN NAMES Polish 7%. *Wieslaw* (3), *Andrzej* (2), *Jacek* (2), *Janusz* (2), *Piotr* (2), *Ryszard* (2), *Slawomir* (2), *Witold* (2), *Beata, Bogdan, Boguslaw, Casimir.*

Borland (1513) Scottish: habitational name from any of several places called Bor(e)land or Bordland, which are named with Old or Middle English *bord* 'board', 'table' + *land* 'land', i.e. land that supplied the lord's table, in other words 'home farm'.

Borman (1089) **1.** Dutch and North German: variant of BORMANN. **2.** English: variant of BOWERMAN.

Bormann (628) North German: variant of BORNEMANN.

GIVEN NAMES German 6%. *Fritzi* (2), *Manfred* (2), *Arno, Eldor, Erna, Hellmut, Horst, Kurt, Reinhold.*

Born (2571) **1.** English: variant spelling of BOURNE. **2.** North German, Danish, and Dutch: from Middle Low German *born* 'well', 'spring', a topographic name for someone who lived beside a well or spring, or a habitational name from a place named with this word.

GIVEN NAMES German 4%. *Hans* (4), *Kurt* (3), *Otto* (3), *Heinz* (2), *Helmut* (2), *Berthold, Frieda, Friedrich, Fritz, Gerhard, Horst, Jutta.*

Borne (925) **1.** English: variant spelling of BOURNE. **2.** French: nickname for a person with only one eye or with a squint, from Old French *borgne* 'squinting', of unknown origin. **3.** In some cases, possibly a shortening of the Dutch surname **van den Borne**, a habitational name for someone from Born in the province of Limburg (Netherlands) or from a place associated with the watercourse of the Borre river in French Flanders.

GIVEN NAMES French 6%. *Emile* (4), *Leonce* (3), *Octave* (2), *Andre, Anicet, Camille, Chantelle, Etienne, Gaston, Mederic.*

Borneman (476) **1.** Respelling of German BORNEMANN. **2.** Dutch: variant of BORNE, with the addition of *man* 'man'.

Bornemann (357) North German: topographic name denoting someone who lived by a well or spring, from Middle Low German *born* 'spring', 'well' + *man* 'man'.

GIVEN NAMES German 7%. *Hermann* (2), *Dieter, Erwin, Franziska, Gerhard, Klaus.*

Borner (263) **1.** Southern English: topographic name for someone who lived beside a stream, from BOURNE + the suffix *-er*, denoting an inhabitant. **2.** North German (also **Börner**): variant of BORN, + the suffix *-er* denoting an inhabitant. **3.** North German: occupational name for a stockman, from Middle Low German *bornen* 'to water (farm animals)'.

GIVEN NAMES German 4%. *Gerd* (2), *Hans, Irmgard.*

Bornheimer (118) German: habitational name for someone from any of various places called Bornheim, near Frankfurt, for example.

Bornhoft (142) German (**Bornhöft**) and Danish (**Bornhøft**): habitational name from Bornhöved, a place in Holstein.

Bornholdt (185) German: habitational name from any of the places so named, especially in the Hamburg region.

Bornhorst (186) German: habitational name from a place named Bornhorst, near Oldenburg.

Bornman (152) Variant of German BORNEMANN.

Bornmann (108) German: variant of BORNEMANN.

Borns (181) North German: shortened form of **Bornsen** or **Börnsen**, patronymics from a Danish and Norwegian personal name *Björn*, meaning 'bear'.

Bornstein (1282) Dutch form or Jewish (from Poland) variant of BERNSTEIN.

GIVEN NAMES Jewish 8%. *Chaim* (3), *Isadore* (3), *Sol* (3), *Herschel* (2), *Menachem* (2), *Myer* (2), *Aron, Avraham, Avram, Danit, Emanuel, Hinda.*

Bornt (110) German: unexplained.

Borntrager (175) German (**Bornträger**): from Middle High German *burne* 'spring', 'well' (Middle Low German *born*) + an agent derivative of *tragen* 'to carry', hence an occupational name, originally for a water carrier and then for a transporter of liquids (wine, beer, etc.). See also BONTRAGER.

Boro (183) **1.** Hungarian (**Boró**): variant of BALLO. **2.** Perhaps also a respelling of French **Borreau**, an occupational name for a torturer (see BOREL 2).

Boroff (300) **1.** Bulgarian: alternative spelling of **Borov**, a patronymic from the personal name *Boro*, a pet form of BORIS. **2.** Jewish (eastern Ashkenazic): shortened form of BOROWSKI or BOROFSKY.

Borofsky (123) Jewish (eastern Ashkenazic): habitational name for someone from any of the many places in Belarus and Ukraine called Borovka, or from Borovaya, Borovye, or Borovoe in Belarus, or any other place named with Slavic (Russian) *bor* 'pine forest'. Compare BOROWSKI.

GIVEN NAME Jewish 6%. *Meyer* (2).

Borom (117) English: variant of **Boreham**, a habitational name from places so called in Essex, Hertfordshire, and Sussex.

Boron (370) **1.** French: habitational name from a place so called in Franche Comté. **2.** Polish (**Boroń**): from a pet form of the personal names *Borzysław* or *Borzymir*. **3.** Jewish (Ashkenazic): see BARON.

GIVEN NAMES Polish 7%. *Krystyna* (2), *Edyta, Leszek, Mieczyslaw, Mieczyslawa, Wladyslaw.*

Boros (455) **1.** Hungarian: from *boros* 'tipsy', 'drunk' (a derivative of *bor* 'wine'), hence a nickname for a heavy drinker or in some rare cases a metonymic occupational name for a wine merchant or a wine producer. **2.** Hungarian: probably a spelling variant of *Baros*, from a pet form of the

personal name *Barnabás*, Hungarian form of BARNABY. **3.** Czech and Slovak (**Boroš**): nickname from Hungarian *boros* 'drunk' (see 1 above); or alternatively from a Slavic personal name such as *Dalibor*, or *Bořivoj*. **4.** Polish (also **Boroś**, **Borosz**): from a Slavic personal name such as *Borzysław* or *Bolebor*.

GIVEN NAMES Hungarian 9%. *Laszlo* (4), *Imre* (2), *Jeno* (2), *Tibor* (2), *Zoltan* (2), *Aranka, Attila, Gabor, Geza, Zsolt.*

Boroski (150) Polish: variant of BOROWSKI.

Boroughs (307) English: variant spelling of BURROWS.

Borow (104) **1.** Germanized spelling of Bulgarian BOROV. **2.** Jewish (Ashkenazic): variant spelling of BOROFF. **3.** English: variant spelling of **Borrow**.

GIVEN NAMES German 5%; Jewish 4%. *Franz; Yaakov.*

Borowiak (245) Polish: from a derivative or patronymic form of the personal name BOROWY.

GIVEN NAMES Polish 4%. *Casimir, Krysztof, Zigmond.*

Borowicz (329) Polish: patronymic from a pet form of *Borowy*, or from *Borzysław*, *Bolebor*, or some other personal name formed with the element *bor* 'to fight'.

GIVEN NAMES Polish 5%. *Jozef, Leszek, Marcin, Zygmund.*

Borowiec (184) Polish: from a derivative of the personal name *Borowy*.

GIVEN NAMES Polish 15%. *Pawel* (2), *Stanislaw* (2), *Andrzej, Arkadiusz, Dariusz, Krystyna, Mariusz, Zbigniew.*

Borowitz (116) Germanized spelling of Jewish **Borowicz**, a habitational name from Borow in Poland.

Borowski (1395) **1.** Polish: habitational name for someone from a place named with *Bor*, a short form of the personal names *Borzysław* or *Bolebor* (composed of Slavic *borzy, bor* 'to fight' + *sław* 'glory' or *bole* 'greater' + the possessive suffix *-ow*). **2.** Polish and Jewish (eastern Ashkenazic): habitational name for someone from a place named with *bór* 'pine forest'. See also BOROFSKY.

GIVEN NAMES Polish 7%. *Andrzej* (3), *Jerzy* (3), *Bogdan* (2), *Boguslaw* (2), *Casimir* (2), *Krzysztof* (2), *Stanislaw* (2), *Ewa, Henryk, Jaroslaw, Jozef, Lech.*

Borowsky (172) Jewish (eastern Ashkenazic): variant of BOROWSKI or BOROFSKY.

GIVEN NAME German 8%. *Kurt* (4).

Borowy (197) Polish: occupational name from *borowy* 'forester'.

GIVEN NAMES Polish 6%. *Danuta, Stanislaus, Zofia.*

Borquez (148) Spanish (**Bórquez**): probably a variant of Spanish **Bohórquez** (see BOHORQUEZ).

GIVEN NAMES Spanish 33%. *Carlos* (3), *Jose* (3), *Jesus* (2), *Juan* (2), *Julio* (2), *Mario* (2), *Miguel* (2), *Rosario* (2), *Ernestina, Ernesto, Evangelina, Francisco.*

Borr (141) **1.** Dutch and northern French: unexplained; perhaps a respelling of BORRE. **2.** Swedish: soldier's name of unexplained meaning. **3.** Possibly a variant spelling of Scottish or English BURR.

Borra (131) **1.** Dutch: nickname for a swindler or trickster, from Middle Dutch *baraet, beraet*, Old French *barat* 'fraud', 'trick', 'swindle'. **2.** Spanish and Italian: from *borra* 'coarse woolen cloth' (compare French BOREL), or, in Spanish, possibly also from the same word in the sense 'young sheep'. **3.** French: southern dialect form of BORRE. **4.** Indian (Andhra Pradesh): Hindu name of unknown meaning.
GIVEN NAMES Italian 11%; Indian 7%. *Angelo* (2), *Antonio, Gianni, Gildo, Secondo*; *Jyothi, Madhu, Rammohan, Ranjan.*

Borras (136) Catalan (**Borràs**): patronymic from the personal name *Borràs.*
GIVEN NAMES Spanish 31%. *Andres* (2), *Manuel* (2), *Alba, Ana, Ana Milena, Bernardo, Cosme, Elena, Enrique, Esperanza, Eugenio, Gregorio.*

Borrayo (104) Spanish: unexplained; perhaps from *borrajo, borrallo* 'burning ash'.
GIVEN NAMES Spanish 52%. *Carlos* (4), *Jose* (4), *Alfredo* (2), *Francisco* (2), *Ignacio* (2), *Jorge* (2), *Miguel* (2), *Alberto, Arnulso, Belkys, Cristobal, Felicitas.*

Borre (164) **1.** French: of uncertain origin; possibly a nickname from *borre* 'stuffing' or possibly a habitational name from Borre in Nord. **2.** Dutch (also **van den Borre**): unexplained. **3.** Danish: variant of BORG.

Borrego (919) Spanish and Portuguese: from *borrego* 'lamb', probably applied as a nickname in Spanish for a simpleton or in Portuguese for a gentle person.
GIVEN NAMES Spanish 40%; Portuguese 9%. *Jose* (23), *Jesus* (9), *Manuel* (9), *Armando* (7), *Juan* (6), *Raul* (6), *Carlos* (5), *Emilio* (5), *Ernesto* (5), *Fernando* (5), *Luis* (5), *Pedro* (5); *Paulo.*

Borrell (333) **1.** English: variant of BURRELL. **2.** Catalan: nickname from *borrell* 'red-haired'.
GIVEN NAMES Spanish 6%. *Angel* (2), *Osvaldo* (2), *Alejandro, Alvaro, Blanca, Carlos, Enrique, Francisco, Jose Ramon, Julio, Luis, Manuel.*

Borrelli (1091) Southern Italian: patronymic or plural form of BORRELLO.
GIVEN NAMES Italian 15%. *Angelo* (8), *Salvatore* (7), *Carmine* (5), *Antonio* (4), *Luigi* (3), *Carmela* (2), *Gaetano* (2), *Pasquale* (2), *Amedeo, Cesare, Dino, Domenic.*

Borrello (189) Southern Italian: topographic name from *borro* 'gully', 'hole', 'grave', from Late Latin *borra*, or a habitational name from either of two Sicilian places called Borrello.
GIVEN NAMES Italian 13%. *Vito* (2), *Filippo, Luigi, Salvatore.*

Borrero (443) Spanish: occupational name from *borrero* 'executioner', 'hangman'.
GIVEN NAMES Spanish 44%. *Jose* (14), *Juan* (6), *Angel* (5), *Luis* (5), *Miguel* (5), *Andres* (3), *Carlos* (3), *Guillermo* (3), *Manuel* (3), *Mercedes* (3), *Orlando* (3), *Ricardo* (3).

Borresen (107) Danish and Norwegian (also **Børresen**): patronymic from *Børre*, from the Old Norse personal name *Byrgir.*
GIVEN NAMES Scandinavian 28%. *Thor* (5), *Anders, Erik, Jarl, Lars, Lasse, Sven.*

Borreson (169) Swedish: patronymic from *Børre*, from the Old Norse personal name *Byrgir.*
GIVEN NAME Scandinavian 9%. *Berndt.*

Borriello (132) Southern Italian (Naples): variant of BORRELLO.
GIVEN NAMES Italian 17%. *Gennaro* (2), *Salvatore* (2), *Angelo, Antonio, Ciro, Luigi.*

Borries (132) German: variant of BERRES, from a short form of *Liborius*, the patron saint of the city of Paderborn.

Borris (183) **1.** Variant of German **Borries**, from a short form of the personal name *Liborius.* **2.** Ulster variant of the English surname **Burris**, itself a variant of BURROWS.
GIVEN NAMES German 5%; French 4%. *Armin, Gunther, Kurt; Jacques, Marcel.*

Borrmann (108) German and Dutch: variant of BORMANN.
GIVEN NAMES German 11%; Dutch 4%. *Hans* (2), *Dieter, Horst; Dirk.*

Borromeo (136) Spanish: habitational name from the Borromean Islands in Lago Maggiore, Italy, borne by St. Carlo Borromeo (16th century).
GIVEN NAMES Spanish 34%. *Carlos* (4), *Alfredo* (2), *Miguel* (2), *Reynaldo* (2), *Angelita, Carmelita, Eduardo, Felipe, Jorge, Jose, Jose Roberto, Karina.*

Borron (122) English: unexplained.

Borror (464) Americanized spelling of German BOHRER.

Borrowman (151) English: status name from Middle English *burghman, borughman* (Old English *burhman*) 'inhabitant of a (fortified) town' (see BURKE), especially one holding land or buildings by *burgage* (see BURGESS).

Borruso (184) Southern Italian (Sicily): **1.** probably from the Arabic personal name *Abūr-ruwūs.* **2.** perhaps also, in the form **Vurroso**, from Late Latin *burlosus*, related to Italian *burla* 'joke'.
GIVEN NAMES Italian 20%. *Vito* (4), *Sal* (2), *Camillo, Pietro, Placido, Salvatore, Santo, Vincenzo.*

Bors (228) **1.** German (**Börs**): from a short form of the medieval personal name *Liborius.* **2.** Hungarian: from the old secular personal name *Bors.* **3.** Hungarian: from *bors* 'pepper', 'hot spice', hence probably a metonymic occupational name for a spice merchant or a cook.
GIVEN NAMES German 4%. *Konrad, Wolfgang.*

Borsa (111) Italian: probably a metonymic occupational name for a maker of bags, from *borsa* 'bag'.
GIVEN NAMES Italian 15%. *Rocco* (2), *Alessandro, Angelo, Ferdinando, Vito.*

Borsari (128) Italian: from the occupational name *borsaro* 'bag maker', an agent derivative of *borsa* 'bag'
GIVEN NAMES Italian 7%. *Evo* (2), *Attilio, Gino, Luciano.*

Borsch (151) **1.** German (**Börsch**): from a pet form of the medieval personal name *Liborius.* **2.** Possibly an altered spelling of **Borsche**, from a pet form of the Slavic personal name *Borislav.* **3.** Ukrainian and Jewish (from Belarus): nickname from *borshch* 'borscht (beet soup)'.
GIVEN NAMES German 5%. *Bernhard, Johann.*

Borsellino (144) Southern Italian (Sicily): from *borsellino* 'little purse', 'moneybag', hence an occupational name for a purse maker, or perhaps a nickname for someone who was mean.
GIVEN NAMES Italian 27%. *Gaspare* (2), *Angelo, Carmella, Ettore, Giovanna, Giovanni, Leonardo, Mario, Nicolo, Pietro, Santo, Vincenza.*

Borseth (164) Norwegian: habitational name from any of various farms in central Norway named Borseth, Børseth, or Børset, from Old Norse *borg* 'stronghold', 'fortification', Old Norse *birki* 'birch', or the river name *Bera* + *set* 'dwelling', 'farmstead'.

Borsheim (119) Norwegian: habitational name from either of two farmsteads: Borsheim in Rogaland (from an uncertain first element + *heim* 'home', 'farmstead'); and Børsheim in Hordaland (from Old Norse *byrgi* 'enclosure' + *heim*).
GIVEN NAMES Scandinavian 4%. *Oystein, Thor.*

Borski (287) **1.** Jewish (eastern Ashkenazic): habitational name for someone from any of various places called Bor, Bori, or Borki, in Ukraine and Belarus. **2.** Polish: habitational name for someone from a place called Bór or Bory.

Borsos (139) Hungarian: **1.** variant of BORS. **2.** (**Borsós**): from *borsó* 'pea', hence a metonymic occupational name for a grower or seller of peas.
GIVEN NAMES Hungarian 7%. *Tibor* (2), *Geza, Imre, Lajos.*

Borst (1463) **1.** German (also **Börst**): from Middle High German *borst(e)* 'bristle', 'brush', hence a nickname for someone with a prickly temperament. **2.** Dutch: short form of **de Borst**, a nickname for someone with a peculiarity of the chest, from Middle Dutch *borst* 'chest', 'breast'. Alternatively it may be a short form of **van der Borst**, a habitational name for someone from Burst in East Flanders (Belgium), or a topographic name for someone who lived by a fortification, Middle Dutch *burcht*.

Borstad (140) Norwegian: habitational name from various farms named Borstad or Børstad, from the Old Norse personal names *Byrgir* or *Borgar*, or from Old Norse *borg* 'fortification', 'stronghold' + *staðr* 'farmstead', 'dwelling'.
GIVEN NAMES Scandinavian 5%; French 4%. *Jarl, Selmer; Collette, Louise Marie.*

Borstel (27) **1.** North German: habitational name from any of several places, for example in Holstein and Hannover, so named with Old Saxon *bur* 'small house' + *stel* 'place' or 'house frame'. **2.** Dutch: nickname for someone with bristly hair, from Middle Dutch *borstel* 'brush'.
GIVEN NAMES French 11%; German 9%. *Henri; Ernst.*

Borsuk (187) Ukrainian, Polish, and Jewish (from Ukraine and Poland): nickname, sometimes denoting a dirty unkempt individual, from *borsuk* 'badger'. As a Jewish surname it can sometimes be a habitational name from Borsuki, a village in Ukraine.

Bort (244) **1.** Jewish (eastern Ashkenazic): nickname for a man with a remarkable beard, from Yiddish *bord* combined with German *Bart*, both meaning 'beard'. **2.** Polish: from *borta* 'braid', 'galloon', a loanword from German (*Borte*).

Bortel (104) Dutch: see BORTELL.

Bortell (136) **1.** Possibly an altered form of Dutch **van Bortel**, which Debrabandere suggests may be a habitational name from a place named Bortlo in the Belgian province of Limburg. **2.** It may alternatively be a variant of German BARTEL.

Borth (556) German: **1.** perhaps a variant spelling of BARTH. **2.** in northern Germany the name and its variants **Bordt** and **Bordemann** are topographic names from Middle Low German *borde* 'legal and administrative district' (compare modern German *Börde* 'district'), also in the sense of 'limit' or 'border'.

Borthwick (379) Scottish: habitational name from a place near Hawick in southern Scotland, where a family of this name held Borthwick Castle since the 14th century. The place name is from Old English *bord* 'board', 'table' + *wīc* 'outlying village', 'dairy farm'.

Bortle (174) **1.** Probably an Americanized spelling of Dutch BORTELL. **2.** Alternatively, from German **Bartel**, pet forms of the personal name *Bart(h)olomaeus* (see BARTHOLOMEW).
GIVEN NAME German 4%. *Eldred* (2).

Bortnem (106) Norwegian: unexplained.

Bortner (462) German and Jewish (Ashkenazic): occupational name for a maker of braiding, from Middle High German *borte*, German *Borte* 'braiding'.

Bortnick (184) Ukrainian and Jewish (from Ukraine): occupational name for a beekeeper, Ukrainian *bortnik*.
GIVEN NAME Jewish 6%. *Avi.*

Borton (1121) English: variant of BURTON.

Borts (137) Jewish (eastern Ashkenazic): variant spelling of BORTZ.

Bortz (1017) **1.** German: nickname for a little fellow, from Low German dialect word meaning 'buttocks', 'stump'. Compare BOORTZ. **2.** Jewish (eastern Ashkenazic): habitational name from a place in Lithuania, called Bortsi in Russian.

Boruch (169) **1.** Polish: from a derivative of *Borzysław, Bolebor*, or some other personal name formed with *bor* 'to fight'. **2.** Jewish (Ashkenazic): Yiddish variant of BARUCH.
GIVEN NAMES Polish 8%; French 4%. *Bronislaw, Czeslawa, Dariusz, Mieczyslaw, Wasyl; Colette, Constant.*

Borucki (317) Polish: habitational name for someone from places called Boruty, in Ostrołęka and Radom voivodeships, Borucino in Piła voivodeship, Borucin, or Borucinek.

Boruff (313) Origin unidentified.

Borum (677) **1.** Danish: habitational name from any of several places whose name means 'dwelling place on the edge'. **2.** English: probably a variant of **Boreham**, habitational name from a place in Essex, probably named with Old English *bor* (unattested) 'hill' + *ham* 'homestead', or from Boreham Street in Sussex, or Borehamwood in Hertfordshire, which has the same etymology.

Borunda (292) Basque (also **Burunda**): topograhic name formed with Basque *buru* 'peak', 'summit'.
GIVEN NAMES Spanish 39%. *Jose* (4), *Armando* (3), *Ricardo* (3), *Ruben* (3), *Ernesto* (2), *Francisco* (2), *Jaime* (2), *Jesus* (2), *Juan* (2), *Luis* (2), *Lupe* (2), *Manuel* (2).

Borup (192) Danish: habitational name from any of various places called Borup. The place name is derived from a Danish word meaning 'rim', 'edge' or from the personal name *Bowi* + Old Norse *þorp* 'outlying farmstead', 'dwelling'.
GIVEN NAMES Scandinavian 8%. *Erik* (2), *Bjorn, Niels, Oluf.*

Boruta (107) Polish: from a derivative of *Borzysław, Bolebor*, or some other personal name formed with *bor* 'to fight'.
GIVEN NAMES Polish 6%. *Bronislaw, Tadeusz.*

Borys (311) Ukrainian and Polish (also **Boryś**): variant of BORIS.
GIVEN NAMES Polish 8%. *Alicja, Czeslaw, Feliks, Ferdynand, Iwona, Jacek, Jerzy, Karol, Kazimierz, Krystyna.*

Borza (140) **1.** Hungarian: nickname from Hungarian *borzas* 'unkempt', 'tousled', 'disheveled'. **2.** Slovak (also **Borža**): unexplained.

Bos (1379) **1.** Reduced form of Dutch **Van den Bos**, a variant of the topographic name VANDENBOSCH. **2.** South German and French: from the Germanic personal name *Boso* (see BOOS). **3.** French (central France): variant of BOIS. **4.** Hungarian (**Bős**): from a pet form of the old secular personal name *Bő*. **5.** Hungarian: habitational name for someone from a place called Bős, formerly in Pozsony county, Hungary, now part of Slovakia. **6.** Hungarian (**Bós**): from the old Magyar secular name *Bós*. **7.** Polish (**Boś**): from a pet form of the personal names *Bolesław* or *Bogusław*.
GIVEN NAMES Dutch 5%. *Gerrit* (7), *Hendrik* (4), *Willem* (2), *Berend, Cor, Corniel, Derk, Geert, Gysbert, Klaas, Maarten, Piet.*

Bosak (472) **1.** Polish and Jewish (eastern Ashkenazic): nickname for a poor man or beggar, from Polish *bosak* 'barefoot man', or possibly a metonymic occupational name from *bosak* 'boat hook'. **2.** Czech and Slovak (**Bosák**): nickname for a poor person or beggar, from *bosý* 'barefoot'.

Bosanko (103) Cornish: habitational name from a place called *Bosanketh*, named with Cornish *bos, bod* 'dwelling' + an unidentified personal name. In England in the 18th century this surname became confused with French **Bosanquet**, the name of a French family of Huguenot refugees who settled in Cornwall.

Bosarge (502) French: unexplained. Perhaps a respelling of of **Boussagues**, a habitational name from a minor place in Hérault so named from the Romano-Gallic domain name *Bucciacas*.

Boscarino (139) Southern Italian: nickname for a solitary and retiring person, from Sicilian *bbuscarinu* 'reclusive'.
GIVEN NAMES Italian 11%. *Angelo* (2), *Salvatore, Santo, Sebastiano.*

Bosch (2596) **1.** Dutch and North German: topographic name from Middle Dutch *bussch*, meaning 'wood' rather than 'bush', also found in place names, such as 's Hertogenbosch (Bois-le-Duc). **2.** German (**Bösch**): see BOESCH. **3.** Catalan: habitational name from a place named with Bosc(h), from Late Latin *boscus* 'wood'.

Bosche (110) Variant of Dutch BOSCH.
GIVEN NAMES French 7%; German 4%. *Michel, Serge; Hermann.*

Boschee (236) **1.** Altered form, under French influence, of Dutch BOSCH. **2.** Possibly derivative of French **Bauché**, an occupational name for a tiler, from *bauche* 'clay tile'.
FOREBEARS A Bosché, also known as Bauché, from Rennes in Brittany is recorded in L'Ange-Gardien, Quebec, in 1697. He was also known as Beauheur, Boheur, Boisverd, and Morency.
GIVEN NAMES German 5%. *Milbert* (2), *Otto.*

Boschen (175) Variant of Dutch or German BOSCH, perhaps from the oblique case, a shortening of *zen Boschen* 'at the thicket', or from a shortened form of a compound surname such as **Böschenstein**.
GIVEN NAMES German 6%. *Jurgen, Kurt.*

Boschert (468) **1.** Swiss German: variant of BOSSHART. **2.** Probably an altered spelling of Dutch **Boschaert**, a variant of VANDENBOSCH.

Boschetti (106) Italian: from a diminutive of BOSCO.
GIVEN NAMES Italian 10%. *Mario* (2), *Angelina, Antonio, Guido, Rosario.*

Boscia (205) Albanian family name that is widespread in southern Italy, especially in Greci, an ancient Albanian-speaking place in Avellino province, Campania.
GIVEN NAMES Italian 15%. *Salvatore* (2), *Angelo, Biaggio, Carlo, Domenic, Filomena, Nicola, Oreste, Vito.*

Bosco (1446) Italian: topographic name for someone living or working in a wood, from Late Latin *boscus* 'shrub', 'undergrowth' (of Gallic or Germanic origin), or a habitational name from a place named with this word. De Felice suggests that in some cases it may have been an occupational name for a woodsman or forester and, by extension, a nickname for a surly or rough person.
GIVEN NAMES Italian 15%. *Angelo* (10), *Salvatore* (10), *Carmine* (4), *Sal* (4), *Ignazio* (3), *Antonio* (2), *Attilio* (2), *Cosimo* (2), *Francesco* (2), *Gaspare* (2), *Luigi* (2), *Saverio* (2).

Bose (947) **1.** German and English: from a Germanic personal name, *Boso* (see BOOS). **2.** French: probably a variant of BOIS. **3.** Indian (Bengal) and Bangladeshi: Anglicized form of BASU.
GIVEN NAMES Indian 32%. *Gautam* (5), *Salil* (4), *Alok* (3), *Arun* (3), *Chandra* (3), *Kunal* (3), *Partha* (3), *Somesh* (3), *Subhas* (3), *Amit* (2), *Anindya* (2), *Anjan* (2).

Bosecker (101) German: probably a variant of **Boseck**, a nickname meaning 'barefoot', from a Slavic word.

Boseman (324) German (**Bösemann**): nickname for an unpleasant person or a person of low standing, from Middle Low German, Middle High German *böse* 'bad' 'evil', 'common', 'weak'.

Bosen (141) German: probably a shortened form of a compound surname such as **Bosenberg** or a patronymic from BOSE.

Boser (370) German (also **Böser**): nickname for a malicious man, from an agent derivative of Middle High German *bösen* 'to do evil'.
GIVEN NAMES German 4%. *Bernhard, Gerhard, Heinz, Otmar, Wendelin.*

Bosetti (134) Italian: from a diminutive of the personal name BOSO.

Bosh (244) Americanized spelling of BOSCH.

Boshart (305) Americanized spelling of German BOSSHART.

Boshears (275) Americanized variant of French BOUCHARD or BRASSEUR.

Boshell (207) English: variant of BISSELL.

Bosher (227) **1.** Americanized form of Dutch or North German **Boesshaar** (see BASHORE). **2.** Perhaps also of French origin, a variant BOSHEARS.

Boshers (178) **1.** Of Dutch or North German origin: variant of BOSHER. **2.** Possibly also of French Huguenot origin: variant of BOSHEARS.

Bosi (123) **1.** Italian: patronymic or plural form of BOSO. **2.** Hungarian: habitational name for someone from a place called Bós in the former Hunyad and Kolozs counties of Hungary or the Marosszék district of Transylvania.
GIVEN NAMES French 6%; Italian 5%. *Benoit* (2); *Antonio, Luciano, Silvio, Ugo.*

Bosier (116) French (Huguenot): variant of BOSSIER.

Bosio (146) Italian: **1.** variant of BOSO. **2.** from a Latin personal name, *Bosius*.
GIVEN NAMES Italian 19%; Spanish 8%; French 4%. *Angelo* (2), *Tino* (2), *Aida, Alberto, Aldo, Caterina, Mario, Roberto; Julio* (2), *Adelmo, Alicia, Carlos, Jose, Juan, Lilia; Eloi, Remy.*

Bosko (243) **1.** Serbian and Croatian (**Boško**): from the personal name *Boško*, a derivative of *Božko*, pet form of *Božo* or any of various other personal names composed with *bog* 'God' (e.g. *Božidar* 'gift of God'). **2.** Shortened form of **Bošković** (see BOSKOVICH). **3.** Polish: nickname from a derivative of *bosy* 'bare-footed'.

Boskovich (123) **1.** Serbian and Croatian (**Bošković**): patronymic from any of various personal names such as *Božan, Božidar,* and *Božimir,* all composed with *bog* 'god'. **2.** Jewish (western Ashkenazic): habitational name for someone from Blansko in Moravia (German name *Boskowitz*).

Bosler (493) **1.** German: habitational name from a place so named near Jülich. In Switzerland *Bossler* means 'ruffian' (from Middle High German *bôssen* 'to hit'; compare BOSSHART), and in some cases the surname may have arisen from a nickname from this sense. **2.** Swabian (**Bösler**): nickname for a sickly person, from Swabian *Bösele* 'ulcer', 'boil', 'abscess'.

Bosley (2452) **1.** English: habitational name from a place in Cheshire named Bosley, from the Old English personal name *Bōsa* or *Bōt* + *lēah* 'woodland clearing'. **2.** Americanized spelling of French BEAUSOLEIL, especially in New England. **3.** Altered spelling of German BOSLER.

Bosma (578) Frisian: topographic name for someone who lived by a wood, from *bos* 'wood'. Compare BOSCH.
GIVEN NAMES Dutch 4%. *Willem* (2), *Gerrit, Heiko, Klaas, Leendert, Marinus, Marten, Roelof.*

Bosman (496) Dutch: occupational name for a forester (see BOSCH).
GIVEN NAMES German 4%. *Franz, Johann, Orlo, Otto.*

Boso (185) Italian: from the medieval personal name *Boso*, from a Germanic personal name derived from a pejorative nickname meaning 'leader', 'nobleman', or 'arrogant person'. Compare Dutch BOOS.

Bosque (181) Spanish: from *bosque* 'wood' (Late Latin *boscus*), hence a topographic name for someone living or working in a wood.
GIVEN NAMES Spanish 39%. *Ana* (4), *Jose* (4), *Carlos* (3), *Jorge* (3), *Ramon* (3), *Alvaro* (2), *Evelio* (2), *Juan* (2), *Mario* (2), *Alfredo, Alina, Amado; Antonio* (3).

Bosquez (216) Spanish (**Bósquez**): possibly an altered spelling of Spanish **Bosques**, a variant (plural) of BOSQUE.
GIVEN NAMES Spanish 40%. *Juan* (7), *Ana* (3), *Carlos* (3), *Jose* (3), *Manuel* (3), *Ruben* (3), *Abelardo* (2), *Enrique* (2), *Eufemia* (2), *Segundo* (2), *Tomas* (2), *Trinidad* (2).

Boss (2924) **1.** English: nickname for a hunchback, from Old French *bossu* 'hunchbacked' (a derivative of *bosse* 'lump', 'hump'; compare BOSSARD 2). **2.** German: from a short form of the personal name **Borkhardt**, a variant of BURKHART. **3.** Possibly an altered spelling of South German **Bös** (see BOS). **4.** Danish: medieval variant of **Buus**, a surname of uncertain origin, perhaps from German *būsemen* 'devil', 'ghost'.

Bossard (419) **1.** French and English: from a Germanic personal name composed of the elements *bos* 'audacious' + *hard* 'hardy', 'brave'. **2.** French: nickname for a hunchback, from Old French *bosse* 'hump', 'hunched back' (of unknown origin) + the pejorative suffix *-ard*. **3.** Swiss German: variant of BOSSHART.

Bossart (249) **1.** Swiss German: variant of BOSSHART. **2.** French: variant of BOSSARD.

Bosscher (102) Dutch: variant of BUSKER.

Bosse (1521) **1.** French (also **Bossé**): nickname for a hunchback, from Old French *bossu* 'hunchbacked' (a derivative of *bosse* 'lump', 'hump'). **2.** French: metonymic occupational name for a cooper, from *bosse* 'barrel', 'keg'. **3.** South German, Swiss German, and Danish: from a pet form of the personal name *Burkhard* (see BURKHART). **4.** Dutch: variant of BOSCH.
FOREBEARS The records of Cap St. Ignace in Quebec for 1692 document a Bossé from the Poitou region of France.
GIVEN NAMES French 9%. *Marcel* (4), *Normand* (4), *Armand* (2), *Aurele* (2), *Herve* (2), *Laurent* (2), *Laurier* (2), *Lucien* (2), *Yvon* (2), *Alphe, Alphonse, Alphy.*

Bosselman (114) North German (**Bosselmann**): **1.** habitational name from Bossel near Hagen, Westphalia. **2.** Dutch: nickname for someone with bristly hair, from Middle Dutch *borstel* 'brush' (see BORSTEL).
GIVEN NAMES German 7%. *Frieda, Gerhard, Kurt.*

Bossen (150) **1.** North German: possibly a patronymic from BOSSE or a shortened form of **Bossenstein**, a habitational name from Am Bosenstein, Aschern. **2.** Danish: patronymic from the Nordic personal names *Bo, Butse,* or *Borch*.

Bosserman (427) German (**Bosser-mann**): **1.** from Middle High German *bosser* 'bowls player', probably applied as a nickname for a skilled or enthusiastic player. **2.** probably a variant of **Basser-mann**, itself a variant of **Wassermann** (see WASSERMAN).

Bossert (824) Swiss and South German: variant of BOSSHART.

FOREBEARS This is a widespread Amish name, found mainly in Ontario, MI, IN, IA, and NE.

Bosshard (104) German: variant of BOSS-HART.
GIVEN NAMES German 15%. *Fritz, Gerda, Heinz, Kurt, Otto.*

Bosshardt (154) German: variant of BOSSHART.
GIVEN NAMES German 4%. *Hans, Kurt.*

Bosshart (206) **1.** German: from a Germanic personal name composed of the elements *bos* 'audacious' + *hard* 'hardy', 'brave'. **2.** Swiss German: from Middle High German *bōz* 'blow', 'push' + *hart* 'hardy', 'brave', probably a nickname for someone who was pugnacious.
GIVEN NAMES German 5%. *Armin, Hans, Otto, Rudi.*

Bossi (307) Northern Italian: variant of BOSSIO or BOSSO.
GIVEN NAMES Italian 8%. *Domenic* (2), *Attilio, Dino, Enrico, Fiore, Guido, Vittoria.*

Bossie (257) Of French origin: possibly a variant of **Bossu**, a nickname for a hunchback (see BOSSE 1).
GIVEN NAME French 4%. *Camille.*

Bossier (173) French: occupational name for a cooper, from an agent derivative of Old French *bosse* 'barrel'. The name is frequent in the southern States; it was probably brought to North America by Huguenots.
GIVEN NAMES French 7%. *Emile, Marcel.*

Bossio (153) Italian: variant of BOSSO.
GIVEN NAMES Italian 24%. *Carmine* (6), *Angelo* (2), *Salvatore* (2), *Antonio, Genoveffa, Gino, Libardo, Mario, Nino.*

Bossler (234) German: **1.** nickname for an aggressive or pugnacious person, from *Bossler* 'fighter', 'ruffian'. **2.** Swabian (Württemberg): occupational name for an odd-job man, from *bosseln* 'to potter around'.

Bossman (163) Dutch (also **Bossmann**): topographic name for someone living or working in a wood (see BOSCH).

Bosso (186) Italian: **1.** from *bosso* 'box tree', probably applied as a topographic name but possibly also as a metonymic occupational name for a wood carver or turner. **2.** variant of BOSO.
GIVEN NAMES Italian 5%. *Angelo, Massimo, Philomena.*

Bossom (127) English (Sussex): variant of **Bosham**, a habitational name from Bosham in Sussex, named in Old English

with the personal name *Bōsa* + *hām* 'homestead' or *hamm* 'promontory' or 'water meadow'.

Bosson (103) French and Dutch: from *Bosson*, a patronymic from the Germanic personal name *Boso* (see BOOS).
GIVEN NAMES French 4%. *Jean-Jacques, Laurent.*

Bossong (100) Variant of French BOSSON, found mainly in Alsace.

Bossung (100) German variant of French BOSSON.

Bost (2209) **1.** French (central France): variant of BOIS. **2.** German: from a reduced form of the personal name SEBASTIAN. **3.** North German: nickname for a self-important man, from Low German *bost* 'chest', 'breast'.

Bostelman (185) North German (**Bostelmann**) and Dutch: nickname for someone with bristly hair, from Middle Dutch *borstel* 'brush' (see BORSTEL).
GIVEN NAMES German 6%. *Eldor, Otto, Winfried.*

Boster (483) North German (also **Böster**) from a reduced form of the personal name SEBASTIAN.

Bostian (501) German: variant of BASTIAN, a short form of the personal name SEBASTIAN.

Bostic (3070) Slovenian (**Bostič, Boštič**): patronymic from an old short form of the Slovenian personal name *Sebastijan* and its vernacular form *Boštjan* (see SEBASTIAN). It may also be a reduced form of **Boštjančič**, which has the same origin.

Bostick (2408) **1.** English: variant of BOSTOCK. **2.** Possibly an Americanized spelling of BOSTIC.

Bostock (324) English: habitational name from Bostock in Cheshire (*Botestoch* in Domesday Book), so named with an Old English personal name *Bōta* (see BOTT) + Old English *stoc* 'place'.

Boston (4627) **1.** English: habitational name from the place in Lincolnshire, the name of which means 'Bōtwulf's stone'. This has been considered to refer to St. Botulf, and to be the site of the monastery that he built in the 7th century, but it is more likely that the Bōtwulf of the place name was an ordinary landowner, and that the association with the saint was a later development because of the name. **2.** Probably an altered spelling of German *Basten* and perhaps BASTIAN.

Bostrom (867) Swedish (**Boström**): ornamental name composed of the elements *bo* 'dwelling', 'farm' + *ström* 'river'.
GIVEN NAMES Scandinavian 10%; German 4%. *Lars* (3), *Anders* (2), *Knute* (2), *Thor* (2), *Alf, Berger, Erik, Maren, Nels, Niels, Ylva; Kurt* (5), *Mathias, Otto, Reinholdt.*

Bostwick (1791) English (South Yorkshire): **1.** habitational name from a lost or unidentified place, possibly BESWICK. **2.** perhaps a variant of BOSTOCK.

Boswell (7914) Scottish (of Norman origin): habitational name from Beuzeville in Seine Maritime, France, named with Old French *Beuze* (a personal name probably of Germanic origin) + *ville* 'settlement'. The final element has been altered as a result of association with the common place name ending -*well* 'spring', 'stream'.

Bosworth (2182) English: habitational name from Market Bosworth in Leicestershire, so named with an Old English personal name *Bōsa* + Old English *worð* 'enclosure'. Husbands Bosworth in Leicestershire (*Baresworde* in Domesday Book) has a different origin: an Old English personal name, *Bār* (from *bār* 'boar') + *worð*.

Boteler (338) North German (**Böteler**): possibly an occupational name from an agent derivative of Low German *böteln* 'to pound', for someone who either made wooden mallets (*bötel*) or used one; this was an implement commonly used by the North Sea to pound down the turfs on the dikes.

Botelho (1300) Portuguese: from *botelho*, which can denote a measure of grain, a grain sack, or seaweed, and was probably applied as an occupational name for a grain dealer or a gatherer of kelp or seaweed.
GIVEN NAMES Spanish 15%; Portuguese 11%. *Manuel* (50), *Jose* (12), *Luis* (5), *Fernando* (4), *Eduardo* (3), *Jaime* (3), *Mario* (3), *Alberto* (2), *Alda* (2), *Ana* (2), *Edmundo* (2), *Francisco* (2); *Joao* (3), *Guilherme* (2), *Agostinho, Anabela, Armanda, Duarte, Henrique, Joaquim, Marcio, Paulo.*

Botello (920) Galician or Spanish: probably from Galician *botella* 'little bottle'.
GIVEN NAMES Spanish 46%. *Jose* (27), *Juan* (15), *Luis* (9), *Manuel* (9), *Miguel* (8), *Jesus* (7), *Salvador* (6), *Armando* (5), *Pedro* (5), *Raul* (5), *Roberto* (5), *Angel* (4); *Antonio* (10), *Geronimo* (2), *Heriberto* (2), *Marco* (2), *Mauro* (2), *Amadeo, Carlo, Cecilio, Donato, Eliseo, Leonardo, Lorenzo.*

Botero (210) Spanish: from *botero*, an occupational name for a bottler or a boat owner.
GIVEN NAMES Spanish 48%. *Jorge* (8), *Juan* (7), *Carlos* (5), *Mario* (4), *Alfredo* (3), *Diego* (3), *Fernando* (3), *Mauricio* (3), *Alvaro* (2), *Cesar* (2), *Consuelo* (2), *Fabio* (2).

Both (350) North German and Dutch: variant of BOTHE.
GIVEN NAMES German 7%. *Ernst* (3), *Johann, Otto, Ulrich, Wilhelm.*

Botham (106) English: variant of BOTTOM.

Bothe (372) North German and Dutch: from a Low German personal name *Bode*.
GIVEN NAMES German 7%. *Dieter* (3), *Detlef, Manfred, Wolfgang.*

Bothell (133) English: habitational name from any of various places called Bothel(l), of which there are examples in Cumbria and Northumberland, named with Old English *bōðl* 'dwelling house', 'hall', or a topographic name from this word, denoting someone who lived or worked at the main house in a settlement.

Bothum (106) **1.** Variant of Norwegian **Bøthun** (see BOTHUN). **2.** Variant of English BOTHAM.

GIVEN NAME Scandinavian 5%. *Bjorn*.

Bothun (190) Americanization of Norwegian **Bøtun**, a habitational name from any of various farms in southwestern Norway, so named with Old Norse *bær* 'farm' + *tun* 'enclosure', 'farm'.

Bothwell (913) Scottish and northern Irish: habitational name from a place in Lanarkshire named Bothwell, from Middle English *both(e)* 'bothy', 'small hut' + *well(a)* 'spring', 'stream'.

Botkin (1130) Probably an altered spelling of the English surnames **Bodkin** or **Batkin**. The first is from Middle English *bodkin*, *bodekin* 'dagger', 'short pointed weapon', and hence a metonymic occupational name for a maker or seller of such weapons; the second is a pet form of the personal name *Bate*, itself a reduced form of BARTHOLOMEW.

Botkins (164) English: variant of BOTKIN.

Botner (163) **1.** Norwegian: habitational name from a farm named Botner, from Old Norse *botn* 'small valley', 'end of a valley'. **2.** Respelling of the North German occupational name **Bottner** or **Böttner** 'cooper'. Compare BUETTNER.

Botos (127) Hungarian: **1.** occupational name for a herdsman, *botos*, a derivative of *bot* 'stick'. **2.** (**Bótos**) occupational name for a shopkeeper or merchant, from *boltos* 'trader'.

GIVEN NAMES Hungarian 6%. *Istvan, Laszlo, Sandor*.

Botros (129) Arabic: variant of BOUTROS.

GIVEN NAMES Arabic 65%. *Samir* (4), *Emad* (3), *Kamal* (3), *Maher* (2), *Nader* (2), *Ramzi* (2), *Basem, Bassam, Farid, Fayek, Hany, Heba*.

Botsch (105) German: variant of BOSS (short form of **Burkhard**) and BOTZ combined. Compare BUTZ.

GIVEN NAME German 5%. *Erwin*.

Botsford (689) English: habitational name from either of two places, in Lincolnshire and Leicestershire, named Bottesford, from Old English *botl* 'building' + *ford* 'ford'.

Bott (2275) **1.** English: probably from an Old English personal name of uncertain origin; perhaps a cognate of BOTHE or akin to BUTT. However, forms such as Walter le Botte (Oxfordshire 1279) seem to point to a nickname or occupational name, perhaps from Old French *bot* 'butt', 'cask', or *bot* 'toad'. Compare BOTTRELL. **2.** South German: occupational name for a messenger, from Middle High German *bote* 'messenger', 'emissary'. **3.** Danish: according to

Søndergaard, from Dutch *bot, both* 'flounder' (the fish).

Botta (384) Italian: **1.** from *botta* 'blow', 'bump', hence a nickname for someone who was clumsy or violent. **2.** variant of BOTTE. **3.** from Calabrian dialect *botta* 'fig flower'.

GIVEN NAMES Italian 23%; Spanish 5%. *Antonio* (2), *Armando* (2), *Pasquale* (2), *Rocco* (2), *Sergio* (2), *Carlo, Duilio, Eduardo, Enrico, Francesca, Genesio, Nunzio, Roberto, Romano, Salvatore, Sandro, Silvio; Carlos* (3), *Juan* (2), *Vincente* (2), *Horacio, Rafael*.

Bottari (203) Italian: patronymic or plural form of BOTTARO.

GIVEN NAMES Italian 9%. *Antonio* (2), *Enrico, Nicolo, Vincenza*.

Bottaro (123) Italian: occupational name for a maker, seller, or repairer of boots, from an agent derivative of *botte* 'boot'.

GIVEN NAMES Italian 25%. *Angelo* (2), *Mario* (2), *Salvatore* (2), *Alvaro, Gaetano, Sebastiano*.

Bottcher (289) German (**Böttcher**): see BOETTCHER.

GIVEN NAMES German 9%. *Otto* (3), *Gerhard* (2), *Frieda, Hermann, Kurt*.

Botte (129) Italian (two syllables) and French (one syllable): metonymic occupational name for a maker or seller of boots, from Old French *bote*, Italian *botte* 'boot' (of unknown origin). In some cases it may have been a nickname, perhaps for a heavy drinker (who 'drank out of a boot').

GIVEN NAMES Italian 6%. *Carmel, Pasquale*.

Bottemiller (113) Apparently a part translation of a German or Dutch occupational name of which the second element means miller, with an unexplained first element.

Botten (212) **1.** English: metonymic occupational name for a maker or seller of buttons, from Old French *bo(u)ton* 'knob', 'lump'. **2.** English: possibly a topographic name for someone who lived in a valley, from Old Norse *botn* 'valley bottom', or a habitational name from a place named with this word, as for example Botton in Lancashire or Botton Cross in North Yorkshire. **3.** Norwegian: habitational name from any of various farms named Botn, Botten, or Botnen, from Old Norse *botn* 'small valley', 'valley end'. Compare BOTNER.

Bottenfield (177) German: perhaps an altered form of **Bothfeld**, habitational name from either of two places so named near Hannover or Merseburg.

Bottger (236) Americanized spelling of German **Böttger** (see BOETTCHER).

GIVEN NAMES German 4%. *Claus, Erna, Erwin*.

Botti (426) Italian: patronymic or plural form of BOTTO.

GIVEN NAMES Italian 13%. *Carmine* (5), *Aldo* (3), *Italo* (2), *Livio* (2), *Rocco* (2), *Dino, Domenico, Geno, Lido, Paolo*.

Botticelli (171) Italian: from *botticella* 'little boot' (see BOTTA).

GIVEN NAMES Italian 12%. *Antonio, Cosmo, Domenico, Francesca, Gilda, Guido, Pietro, Salvatore*.

Bottiglieri (120) Italian: from **Bottigliere**, an occupational name for a tavern keeper or cellarman, Old Italian *bottigliere*.

GIVEN NAMES Italian 15%. *Carmine* (3), *Sal, Salvatore, Teodoro*.

Botting (215) English: patronymic from BOTT.

Bottini (266) Italian: patronymic or plural form of BOTTINO.

GIVEN NAMES Italian 8%. *Carlo* (2), *Aldo, Amelio, Angelo, Clemente, Giuliano, Secondo*.

Bottino (167) Italian: from a diminutive of BOTTO.

GIVEN NAMES Italian 8%. *Alfonse, Gino, Nunzio, Salvatore*.

Botto (335) Italian: **1.** from a personal name, from an old Germanic name *Boddo* or *Bot(t)o*. **2.** variant of BOTTA.

GIVEN NAMES Italian 12%; Spanish 7%. *Aida, Giorgio* (2), *Dante, Dominico, Enrico, Lorenzo, Mario, Pierino, Piero, Sergio; Luis* (2), *Melida* (2), *Alejandro, Juan, Manuel, Miguel*.

Bottom (559) **1.** Northern English: topographic name for someone who lived in a broad valley, from Old English *botm* 'valley bottom'. **2.** In some cases, a mistranslation of French *Lafond*, in which Old French *la fond* 'fountain' is confused with modern French *le fond* 'the bottom'.

Bottomley (639) English (Yorkshire and Lancashire): habitational name from a place in West Yorkshire named Bottomley, from Old English *botm* 'broad valley' + *lēah* 'woodland clearing'.

Bottoms (1553) English: variant of BOTTOM.

Bottone (264) Italian: **1.** from a derivative of BOTTO. **2.** from an augmentative of BOTTE.

GIVEN NAMES Italian 18%. *Salvatore* (5), *Fiore* (2), *Sal* (2), *Angelo, Antonio, Caesar, Gaetano, Tullio*.

Bottoni (130) Italian: possibly from a derivative of the Germanic personal name *Bodo* (see BODE).

GIVEN NAMES Italian 26%. *Rocco* (3), *Angelo* (2), *Gino* (2), *Amato, Domenico, Ettore, Giuseppe, Guido, Marco, Marino, Massimo, Tonino*.

Bottorf (165) German: variant of BOTTORFF.

Bottorff (826) German: possibly a habitational name from a place named Bottorf near Quakenbrück.

Bottrell (161) English: probably of Norman origin, a habitational name from Les Bottereaux in Eure, France, apparently so named from being infested with toads. The place name is recorded in the late 12th century in the Latin form *Boterelli*, from a diminutive of Old French *bot* 'toad' (of Germanic origin). It has also been suggested that the name originated as a Norman nickname, from Old Norman French *bottereau* 'toad', or as an occupational name for a worker in a buttery, Middle English *butterer*.

GIVEN NAME Jewish 4%. *Herschell.*

Botts (1670) **1.** English: patronymic from BOTT. **2.** Americanized spelling of German BOTZ.

Bottum (123) English: variant of BOTTOM.

Botwin (102) Jewish (Ashkenazic): occupational name for a greengrocer, from Yiddish *botvine* 'leaves of beets'.

Botwinick (155) Jewish (from Belarus): occupational name for a greengrocer, from Yiddish *botvine* 'leaves of beets' or from Belorussian *botva* 'greens'.

GIVEN NAMES Jewish 9%. *Shifra* (2), *Aryeh, Avi, Moshe.*

Botz (297) German: variant of BUTZ or BATZ.

Bou (178) **1.** Catalan and southern French: from Catalan and Occitan *bou* 'ox' (from Latin *bos*, genitive *bovis*), probably a metonymic occupational name for a herdsman. **2.** Cambodian or other Southeast Asian: unexplained.

GIVEN NAMES Spanish 27%; Other Southeast Asian 5%; French 4%. *Jose* (4), *Miguel* (3), *Javier* (2), *Rafael* (2), *Ana, Concepcion, Consuelo, Elena, Enrique, Eusebia, Fernando, Gilberto*; *Phan, Phanh, Samnang, Tha*; *Jean-Charles, Pierre.*

Bouch (255) English: variant of BUDGE.

Bouchard (5244) French: **1.** from a Norman personal name, *Bou(r)chart*, composed of the Germanic elements *bourg* 'fort' + *heard* 'hardy', 'brave', 'strong'. **2.** nickname for someone with a big mouth (possibly in either a literal or figurative sense), from French *bouche* 'mouth' + the pejorative suffix *-ard.*

FOREBEARS A Bouchard from Picardy is recorded in Sillery or Cap Rouge, Quebec, in 1650, with the secondary surname Dorval. Claude Bouchard (1626–99), known as Le Petite Claude, came from Sarthe, Perche, France, to Quebec city before 1654. A further bearer of the name from Paris was in Quebec city by 1657, and another, from La Rochelle, was in Château Richer by 1662. This is a very common surname in Canada and New England.

GIVEN NAMES French 13%. *Armand* (21), *Marcel* (18), *Andre* (17), *Michel* (8), *Normand* (8), *Pierre* (8), *Cecile* (7), *Gilles* (7), *Lucien* (7), *Alphonse* (5), *Jacques* (5), *Alain* (4).

Bouche (254) French (**Bouché**): **1.** metonymic occupational name for a hawker or trader, from *bou(s)che* 'large bundle'. **2.** nickname for someone with a large or otherwise remarkable mouth, from *bouche* 'mouth'. **3.** possibly a variant of BOUCHER.

GIVEN NAMES French 7%. *Georges* (3), *Adrien.*

Boucher (7847) French and English: occupational name for a butcher or slaughterer, Middle English *bo(u)cher*, Old French *bouchier* (also with the transferred sense 'executioner'), a derivative of *bouc* 'ram'. Compare BUCK 1.

FOREBEARS A family of this name which was very prominent in the early history of Quebec traces its ancestry to a Marin Boucher from Mortagne in the Perche region of France. His marriages, first to Julienne Baril and then to Perrine Mallet, are recorded in Quebec city. A relative of his, Gaspard Boucher, arrived in Quebec in 1634 with his wife, Nicole Lemaire. Their son, Pierre Boucher, for whom Boucherville is named, was very influential in the new colony. He was married in Trois Rivières in 1649 to Marie-Madeleine Ouébadinoukoé dit Chrétienne. In 1652 he married a second time, Jeanne Crevier, whose numerous children founded many of today's dynasties.

A Boucher from Normandy is documented in Quebec city by 1664 with the secondary surname Vin d'Espagne. Other secondary surnames include Pitoche (1663), Desroches (1671), Desrosiers (1689), and Belleville (1696).

GIVEN NAMES French 10%. *Armand* (31), *Normand* (13), *Andre* (11), *Marcel* (9), *Emile* (7), *Gilles* (6), *Lucien* (6), *Yvon* (6), *Adrien* (5), *Jacques* (5), *Laurent* (5), *Alcide* (4).

Bouchey (219) French: eastern variant of BOUCHER.

Bouchie (192) French: variant of BOUCHER.

GIVEN NAMES French 4%. *Patrice, Pierre.*

Bouchillon (216) French: occupational name from a variant of Old French *boschillon* 'woodcutter'.

Bouck (555) Dutch: **1.** from *bok* 'he-goat', applied probably as a derogatory nickname. **2.** occupational name for a butcher.

Boudinot (110) French: from a pet form of BOUDIN.

Boudoin (192) French and Dutch: from a Germanic personal name composed of the elements *bald* 'bold', 'brave' + *wine* 'friend', which was extremely popular among the Normans and in Flanders in the Middle Ages. See also BALDWIN.

GIVEN NAME French 4%. *Clemile.*

Boudreau (4083) New England variant of French BEAUDREAU.

GIVEN NAMES French 8%. *Armand* (9), *Pierre* (5), *Girard* (4), *Jacques* (4), *Marcel* (4), *Camille* (3), *Emile* (3), *Gaston* (3), *Gilles* (3), *Lucien* (3), *Yvon* (3), *Alban* (2).

Boudreaux (5546) LA variant of French BEAUDREAU.

FOREBEARS The LA Boudreaux family is of Acadian origin. They trace their ancestry to Michel Boudrot from La Rochelle and his wife, Michelle Aucoin, who were in Acadia by about 1642.

GIVEN NAMES French 6%. *Emile* (5), *Lucien* (4), *Michel* (4), *Ulysse* (4), *Antoine* (3), *Curley* (3), *Leonce* (3), *Alcide* (2), *Aldes* (2), *Anatole* (2), *Andre* (2), *Chantal* (2).

Boudrie (106) Perhaps an Americanized form of French BEAUDREAU.

Boudrot (118) French: variant of BEAUDREAU.

Bouffard (743) French: nickname for a glutton, a pejorative term from Old French *bouffer* 'to stuff oneself', earlier 'to puff out the cheeks' (a word probably of imitative origin).

GIVEN NAMES French 13%. *Armand* (4), *Lucien* (4), *Alphee* (2), *Andre* (2), *Benoit* (2), *Pierre* (2), *Achille, Alphonse, Aurore, Cecile, Emile, Flore.*

Boufford (123) New England spelling of BOUFFARD, reflecting the rounding of the vowel characteristic of North American pronunciation.

Bough (315) **1.** English and Irish (pronounced *Bow*): variant spelling of BOW. **2.** English (pronounced *Boff*): from a Norman form of Old French *boeuf* 'bull', 'ox', hence a nickname for a powerfully built man, or in some cases a metonymic occupational name for a herdsman.

Boughan (177) Irish: variant of BOHAN or BOWEN.

Bougher (261) Americanized spelling of German BUCHER.

Boughey (106) English (West Midlands): unexplained. Perhaps a variant spelling of BOWIE.

Boughman (148) Origin uncertain. In some cases the name may be an Americanized spelling of German BACHMANN or BUCHMANN; in others, it may be an altered spelling of English BOWMAN.

Boughner (457) Americanized spelling of German BUCHNER.

Boughter (151) Origin unidentified.

Boughton (1227) English: habitational name from any of the numerous places so named. Those in Cambridgeshire (formerly Huntingdonshire), Lincolnshire, Norfolk, Northamptonshire, and Nottinghamshire are named from the Old English byname *Bucca* (see BUCK 1) + Old English *tūn* 'enclosure', 'settlement'; those in Cheshire and Kent are named with Old English *bōc* 'beech' + *tūn.*

Bougie (259) Probably French: perhaps a metonymic occupational name for a candlemaker, from *bougie* 'candle'.

GIVEN NAMES French 12%. *Laurent* (3), *Andre* (2), *Fernand* (2), *Normand, Pierre, Yvon.*

Bouie (323) Variant of French **Bouis**, a topographic name for someone who lived by a particular box tree or in an area characterized by box, Old French *bois* (from Latin *buxus*).

GIVEN NAMES French 4%. *Evest, Germaine.*

Bouillion (158) French: variant of BOUILLON.

GIVEN NAMES French 8%. *Antoine, Emile, Eves, Renella.*

Bouillon (160) French: from a diminutive of **Bouille**, a topographic name for someone who lived by a marsh, Old French *bouille* (a derivative of *boue* 'mud', of Celtic origin), or for someone who lived by a birch grove, from the Old French dialect term *bouille* (from Late Latin *betul(l)ia*, a derivative of *bettius* 'birch'). *Bouillion* is the more common spelling in LA; elsewhere the spellings *Bouillon* and *Boullion* predominate.

GIVEN NAMES French 6%. *Fernand, Marcel, Pascal, Pierre.*

Bouknight (498) Americanized form of German BAUKNECHT.

Boulais (175) French: variant of BOULAY.

GIVEN NAMES French 16%. *Normand* (2), *Yves* (2), *Gaetane, Gilles, Jacques, Marcel, Oliva, Pierre.*

Boulanger (1036) French: occupational name for a baker, originally the man responsible for dividing the dough into *boules* 'balls'. The name is comparatively late in origin (12th century) and replaced the older FOURNIER only in northern France.

FOREBEARS A bearer of the name Boulanger from Normandy, France, is documented in Quebec city in 1671.

GIVEN NAMES French 17%. *Camille* (6), *Jacques* (4), *Armand* (3), *Emile* (3), *Marcel* (3), *Normand* (3), *Andre* (2), *Antoine* (2), *Fernand* (2), *Luc* (2), *Lucien* (2), *Patrice* (2).

Boulay (515) French: topographic name for someone who lived by a grove of birch trees, from a collective form of Old French *boul* (Late Latin *bettulus*, a diminutive of *bettius*).

GIVEN NAMES French 11%. *Adrien* (2), *Armand* (2), *Henri* (2), *Lucien* (2), *Marcel* (2), *Alain, Camille, Fernand, Francois, Germaine, Gilles, Raoul.*

Boulden (543) English: **1.** probably a variant of BOULDIN or possibly of BOLDEN or BOLDON. **2.** Alternatively, it may be a habitational name from a place in Shropshire called Bouldon.

Bouldin (1164) English: variant of **Boulding**, a patronymic from the Germanic personal name *Baldo*, a short form of any of the various compound names with the first element *bald* 'bold'.

Boule (250) French: from Old French *boule* 'ball' (Latin *bulla*), probably a metonymic occupational name or a nickname for, amongst other possibilities, a bowls player or a short rotund man.

GIVEN NAMES French 13%. *Normand* (2), *Adelard, Jean-Marie, Lucien, Marcelle, Theophile, Yvon.*

Bouler (179) English: possibly a variant spelling of BOWLER.

Boulet (440) French: from a diminutive of BOULE.

GIVEN NAMES French 18%. *Andre* (3), *Gaetan* (2), *Laurier* (2), *Monique* (2), *Yvan* (2), *Armand, Emile, Emilien, Gabrielle, Gaston, Gilles, Henri.*

Boulette (155) Altered spelling of French **Boulet**, reflecting the Canadian pronunciation of the final *-t*, which is silent in metropolitan French.

Bouley (689) Eastern French: variant of BOULE.

GIVEN NAMES French 8%. *Marcel* (3), *Andre* (2), *Normand* (2), *Albenie, Aurele, Autrey, Laurent, Napoleon, Ovila, Rosaire.*

Boulier (173) French: occupational name for a maker of balls or the organizer of a game of boules, from an agent derivative of *boule* 'ball'.

Boullion (196) Variant spelling of French BOUILLION.

GIVEN NAME French 5%. *Emile* (2).

Boulos (262) Arabic and Greek: from the personal name *Boulos*, Arabic form of PAUL.

GIVEN NAMES Arabic 43%; French 4%. *Samir* (4), *Kamil* (3), *Mounir* (3), *Nabil* (3), *Bahaa* (2), *Nader* (2), *Riad* (2), *Sami* (2), *Sherif* (2), *Shirine* (2), *Ziad* (2), *Akram*; *Emile* (2), *Fernand* (2).

Boulter (452) English: variant of BOLT.

Boultinghouse (222) Americanized form of the German habitational name **Böddinghaus**, from Böddinghausen near Altena, Westphalia.

Boulton (946) English: variant spelling of BOLTON.

Boulware (1217) Probably a variant of English **Bulwer**, a Norfolk surname of unexplained origin, probably a variant of BOWLER.

FOREBEARS The name is associated with Fairfield Co., SC, in the 18th century. The marriage of Nancy Boleware and Fredrick Vaughn is recorded on February 5, 1781.

Bouma (620) Frisian: status name for a peasant or land worker or a nickname meaning 'neighbor' (see Dutch BOUMAN).

Bouman (316) Dutch: status name for a peasant or land worker or a nickname meaning 'neighbor', Middle Dutch *bouman*.

GIVEN NAMES Dutch 4%. *Aldert* (2), *Bastian, Frans, Geert, Rutger.*

Bound (169) English: variant of BOND.

Bounds (2839) English: patronymic from BOND.

Boundy (187) English: variant of BOND.

Bouquet (214) French: from a diminutive of **Bouc**, a nickname for a man with some fancied resemblance to a he-goat, from *bouc* 'billy goat'.

GIVEN NAMES French 10%. *Andre* (2), *Edouard, Jean-Pierre, Marcel, Pierre.*

Bour (246) **1.** Scottish: status name for someone who lived in a small cottage, from Older Scots *būr* 'bower', 'cottage'. See also BOWER. **2.** French (Normandy): nick-

name from Old Norman French *bourc* 'bastard'.

Bouras (130) **1.** Greek: variant of BOORAS. **2.** Southern French and Catalan (**Bourras**): from Occitan *bourras*, Catalan *bourràs* 'frieze', a type of coarse reddish brown woolen cloth with long hairs (Late Latin *burra* 'coarse untreated wool'), applied as a nickname for someone who habitually wore brown or a metonymic occupational name for a worker in the wool trade.

GIVEN NAMES Greek 13%. *Andreas, Antonios, Marinos, Nickolaos, Sotiria, Theodoros.*

Bourassa (1125) Southern French: from a diminutive of French **Bourrasse** (see BOURAS).

FOREBEARS A bearer of the name Bourassa, also known as Bourasseau, from the Poitou region of France, is recorded in Quebec city in 1665.

GIVEN NAMES French 11%. *Andre* (3), *Armand* (3), *Marcel* (3), *Adrien* (2), *Alain* (2), *Emile* (2), *Gisele* (2), *Jacques* (2), *Ludger* (2), *Normand* (2), *Anselme, Aurelie.*

Bourbeau (440) French: topographic name for someone who lived in a muddy place, from Old French *borbe* '(thick) mud'.

GIVEN NAMES French 14%. *Armand* (3), *Andre* (2), *Emile* (2), *Laurent* (2), *Lucien* (2), *Normand* (2), *Alphonse, Gilles, Jacques, Josee, Laurette, Michel.*

Bourbon (218) French: habitational name from a village in Allier, the site of the (now ruined) castle of Bourbon, or from another place so named, for example one in Saône-et-Loire. The place name is of uncertain origin, according to Dauzat derived from a 'Celtic and pre-Celtic' element *borb-* describing a well or hot spring. Many bearers of the surname claim a connection with the former French royal family, but the name is also derived from residence in these villages and from the Bourbonnais, a former province in central France around Bourbon in Allier.

FOREBEARS The house of Bourbon, which provided generations of monarchs of France and Spain and other European royalty, takes its name from the castle of Bourbon in Allier, which was held by Adhémar, a 9th-century noble. His descendant Beatrice, heiress of Bourbon, married Robert of Clermont, 6th son of King Louis IX of France, in 1272, and these two are considered founders of the royal house. Robert's son Louis was created Duke of Bourbon in 1327. By the 16th century they had added much of southern France, the dukedom of Vendôme, and the kingdom of Navarre to their fiefs, and in 1589 a Bourbon succeeded to the throne of France as Henry IV. His grandson, Louis XIV, called 'the Sun King', reigned 1643–1715, presiding over a golden age of French literature and art and attempting to establish

French supremacy in Europe. The Bourbons ruled France until the Revolution in 1793 and again 1815–48. The present claimants to the French throne are descended from Louis XIV's brother, Philippe, Duke of Orléans. The Bourbons acquired the Spanish throne in 1700, when a grandson of Louis XIV succeeded as Philip V; they ruled until 1931 and were restored, in the person of King Juan Carlos, in 1975. The Bourbon kings of the Two Sicilies (i.e. Sicily and Naples), 1759–1861, and Bourbon dukes of Parma, 1748–1860, were descended from the Spanish branch of the family.

Bourbonnais (107) French: habitational name, from an adjectival form of the place name, for someone from either of two places named Bourbon: Bourbon-l'Archambaut in Allier or Bourbon-Lancy in Saône-et-Loire.
GIVEN NAMES French 23%. *Pierre* (3), *Andre* (2), *Gilles* (2), *Jean Guy, Jean-Pierre, Sebastien.*

Bourcier (173) Northern French: occupational name for a maker of purses and leather wallets, from an agent derivative of Old French *bourse* 'purse', Late Latin *bursa*, whence also Old English *purs* (see PURSER).
FOREBEARS A bearer of this surname from the Saintonge region of France is recorded in Montreal in 1673, with the secondary surname Lavigne.
GIVEN NAMES French 11%. *Laurent* (2), *Lucien* (2), *Armand, Emile.*

Bourcy (100) Perhaps a habitational name for someone from Bourcy in Luxembourg, in French-speaking Belgium.
GIVEN NAME French 4%. *Laurent.*

Bourdage (111) French: unexplained; perhaps a variant of Walloon **Bourdange**, from Walloon *bourdouh* 'somersault', 'leap', hence possibly a metonymic occupational name for a tumbler or a nickname for an exhuberant person.
GIVEN NAMES French 7%. *Eudore, Normand.*

Bourdeau (678) Altered spelling of French BORDEAU.
GIVEN NAMES French 11%. *Andre* (2), *Anais, Antoine, Armand, Dominique, Emile, Germain, Lucien, Marcel, Marie Alice, Marie Josette, Normand.*

Bourdo (157) Probably an altered spelling of French **Bourdot**, a nickname for a habitual liar, from Old French *borde* 'tall story', Old Occitan *bourde* 'fib', 'untruth'.

Bourdon (715) French: from Old French *bourdon*, a word with several meanings, from any or each of which the surname could have arisen: 'pilgrim's staff', as a nickname for a pilgrim; 'bumblebee', as a nickname for someone thought to resemble the insect in some way; and 'bagpipes', as a metonymic occupational name for a piper or pipe-maker.

GIVEN NAMES French 8%. *Andre* (4), *Adrien, Armand, Donat, Fabien, Francois, Francoise, Ghislaine, Gilles, Jacques, Luc, Marcel.*

Bourg (979) French: topographic name for someone who lived in a town as opposed to one who lived in a village, from Old French *bourg* 'fortified town'.
GIVEN NAMES French 7%. *Camille* (3), *Antoine* (2), *Cecile* (2), *Emile* (2), *Alcide, Anatole, Clovis, Easton, Ferrel, Leonce, Oneil, Onile.*

Bourgault (334) French: from a Germanic personal name composed of the elements *burg* 'fortification' + *wald* 'rule'.
FOREBEARS A Bourgault from Brittany is documented in Contrecoeur, Quebec, in 1694, with the secondary surname Lacroix.
GIVEN NAMES French 17%. *Urbain* (2), *Alain, Alban, Armand, Dominique, Emile, Francois, Gilles, Gisele, Jacques, Jean Marc, Luc.*

Bourgeois (4866) French: status name from Old French *burgeis* 'inhabitant and (usually) freeman of a (fortified) town', 'burgess' (from *bourg* 'fortification').
FOREBEARS The records of Beaupré, Quebec, for 1667 document a Bourgeois from Picardy, with the secondary surnames Le Picard and Le Grand Picard. Another bearer of the name, from the Périgord region of France, is recorded in La Durentaye in 1697 with the secondary surname Laverdure.
In LA, the name can be traced back to the early 18th century; most present-day bearers of the name are believed to be descended from refugees from Acadia in the mid 1760s.
GIVEN NAMES French 8%. *Andre* (14), *Marcel* (7), *Emile* (6), *Alphonse* (4), *Armand* (4), *Camille* (4), *Gaston* (4), *Monique* (4), *Pierre* (4), *Lucien* (3), *Michel* (3), *Normand* (3).

Bourget (429) French: topographic name for someone who lived in a fortified town from a diminutive of BOURG.
GIVEN NAMES French 15%. *Normand* (3), *Jacques* (2), *Lucien* (2), *Pierre* (2), *Aime, Andre, Fernand, Germaine, Laurent, Ludger, Marcel, Marcell.*

Bourgoin (494) French: regional name denoting someone from Burgundy (Old French *Bourgogne*), a region of eastern France having Dijon as its center. The area was invaded by the *Burgundii*, a Germanic tribe from whom it takes its name, in about AD 480. The duchy of Burgundy, created in 877 by Charles II, King of the Western Franks, was extremely powerful in the later Middle Ages, especially under Philip the Bold (1342–1404; duke from 1363).
FOREBEARS A bearer of the surname from the Poitou region of France is recorded in Quebec city in 1667, with the secondary surname Bourguignon.
GIVEN NAMES French 10%. *Alphee, Alyre, Andre, Armand, Aurore, Celina, Emile,*

Gilberte, Jacques, Laurent, Lucienne, Olivier.

Bourgoyne (142) Variant of French BOURGOIN.
GIVEN NAME French 7%. *Emile* (2).

Bourguignon (128) French: variant of BOURGOIN.
GIVEN NAMES French 10%. *Jacques* (2), *Mathieu.*

Bourke (1011) English: variant spelling of BURKE.
GIVEN NAMES Irish 5%. *Brendan, Dermot, Liam, Murphy.*

Bourland (982) Scottish: variant spelling of BORLAND.

Bourn (677) English: variant of BOURNE.

Bourne (3387) English: topographic name for someone who lived beside a stream, Old English *burna, burne* 'spring', 'stream', or a habitational name from a place named with this word, for example Bourn in Cambridgeshire or Bourne in Lincolnshire. This word was replaced as the general word for a stream in southern dialects by Old English *brōc* (see BROOK) and came to be restricted in meaning to a stream flowing only intermittently, especially in winter.

Bournival (107) French: probably a habitational name from Bornival in the province of Brabant, Belgium.
GIVEN NAMES French 18%. *Andre, Gilles, Laurent, Lucien, Marcelle.*

Bourns (108) English: topographic name for someone who lived by a stream or streams, from the Middle English nominative plural or genitive singular of *burne* (see BOURNE).

Bourque (3331) French: reduced form of **Bourrique**, from a personal name, probably a derivative of *bourre* 'tawny', 'fawn' (from Latin *burrus*), hence denoting a man with tawny hair.
FOREBEARS A Bourque or Bours from Le Puy in France is recorded in Beauport, Quebec, in 1696, with the secondary surname Lachapelle.
GIVEN NAMES French 11%. *Armand* (7), *Lucien* (7), *Pierre* (6), *Andre* (4), *Aurele* (3), *Camille* (3), *Emile* (3), *Fernand* (3), *Henri* (3), *Jacques* (3), *Marcel* (3), *Normand* (3).

Bourquin (444) French: from a diminutive of BOURG.
GIVEN NAMES French 4%. *Marcel* (2), *Pascal, Pierre.*

Bourret (200) French: **1.** occupational name for a manufacturer of or dealer in frieze, a coarse woolen cloth, Old French *b(o)ure* (see BOURAS). **2.** in the Massif Central, a nickname from a word meaning 'young bull'.
GIVEN NAMES French 22%. *Normand* (3), *Andre* (2), *Camille, Emile, Emilien, Francois, Gaetan, Georges, Herve, Joselle, Laurent, Lucien.*

Bouse (486) **1.** Czech (**Bouše**): see BOUSKA. **2.** Possibly a variant of North German BUSE.

Bouska (338) **1.** Czech (**Bouška**): from a short form of the personal names *Bohuslav* or *Bohumil*, both formed with Slavic *Bog* 'God'. **2.** Respelling of French BOUSQUET.

Bouslog (108) Origin unidentified.

Bousman (272) Dutch: **1.** from *Boso*, a Germanic personal name derived from an element meaning 'audacious'. **2.** topographic name for someone who lived or worked in a wood (see BOSCH).

Bousquet (1010) Southern French: topographic name for someone living or working in a wood, from a diminutive of BOIS.
GIVEN NAMES French 9%. *Marcel* (3), *Lucien* (2), *Andre, Colette, Elzina, Emile, Gilles, Gisele, Henri, Jean Pierre, Luc, Mechelle.*

Boustead (113) English: habitational name from a minor place so named.

Boutell (193) French: variant of BOUTELLE.

Boutelle (296) Altered spelling of French **Bouteille**, a metonymic occupational name for a butler or a bottle maker, from Old French *bouteille* 'bottle'.

Boutet (108) French: from pet form of a Germanic personal name, *Boto*, from Old High German *bodo* 'messenger'.
GIVEN NAMES French 21%. *Cecile* (2), *Andre, Gilles, Jacques, Monique, Pierre, Prosper.*

Bouthillette (105) French: occupational name for a wine steward or butler, from a diminutive of *bouteillier*, 'butler'.
GIVEN NAMES French 27%. *Marcel* (3), *Lucien* (2), *Gilles, Lucienne, Michel, Normand, Raoul.*

Bouthillier (168) French: variant of BOUTI-LIER.
GIVEN NAMES French 22%. *Andre* (5), *Armand* (3), *Jacques, Normand, Philippe, Yves.*

Boutiette (119) French: variant of BOUT-HILLETTE.
GIVEN NAME French 4%. *Marcel.*

Boutilier (389) French: occupational name for a wine steward or butler, usually the chief servant of a medieval household, from Old French *bouteillier*, 'butler'. This name is often Americanized as BUTLER.
FOREBEARS A bearer of the name from Brittany is documented in Boucherville, Quebec, in 1686; another, from La Rochelle, is recorded in Montreal in 1695, with the secondary surname Tétu.

Boutin (1366) French: from a diminutive of **Bout**, which in some cases is derived from Old French *bout* 'end', 'extremity', hence a topographic name for someone who lived at the edge of a town or village, and in others from a Germanic personal name formed with *bodo* 'messenger'.
FOREBEARS Documented in Château Richer, Quebec, in 1661 is a Boutin from the Saintonge region of France with the secondary surname Laplante; and a Boutin or Bouterin is recorded in Charlesbourg in 1669. Other secondary surnames documented are Dubord and Langoumois.

GIVEN NAMES French 17%. *Armand* (9), *Normand* (7), *Emile* (6), *Andre* (5), *Lucien* (5), *Francois* (4), *Jacques* (3), *Marcel* (3), *Alcide* (2), *Gaetane* (2), *Gilles* (2), *Monique* (2).

Bouton (908) French: **1.** from the Old French oblique case of the Germanic personal name *Bodo* meaning 'messenger', 'herald' (see BOTHE). **2.** nickname for someone with a prominent wart, carbuncle, or boil, from Old French *bo(u)ton* 'knob', 'lump', 'excrescence' (from *bo(u)ter* 'to thrust or strike'). **3.** metonymic occupational name for a maker or seller of buttons, from Old French *bo(u)ton*, the same word as in 2, specialized to mean 'button'.
FOREBEARS A Bouton from the Lyonnais region of France is documented in Trois Rivières, Quebec, in 1702, while Huguenots of this name are recorded in Staten Island.

Boutot (184) Variant spelling of French **Boutaud** (or the variants **Boutaut**, *-ault, -eau*), from a Germanic personal name composed of the elements *bod-* 'messenger' + *wald* 'rule'. This surname occurs mainly in New England.
FOREBEARS A person called Bouteau, also called Laramée, was briefly in Quebec city in 1665.
GIVEN NAMES French 18%. *Albenie, Alberie, Alcide, Andre, Armand, Camille, Jean Louis, Lucien, Marcel, Monique, Rosaire.*

Boutros (185) Arabic: from a French spelling of the Arabic personal name *Butros* 'Peter' (Greek *Petros*), found among Christians, especially in Egypt.
GIVEN NAMES Arabic 59%; French 6%. *Samir* (4), *Ayman* (3), *Amal* (2), *Ashraf* (2), *Fadi* (2), *Fouad* (2), *Kamel* (2), *Mounir* (2), *Nabil* (2), *Ramzi* (2), *Saad* (2), *Sameh* (2); *Antoine, Camille, Laure, Monique, Odette, Pierre.*

Boutte (850) French: variant of **Bout** (see BOUTIN). This is a common surname in LA.
GIVEN NAMES French 9%. *Andre* (3), *Armand* (3), *Marcel* (2), *Odile* (2), *Achille, Aime, Alcide, Clovis, Esme, Etienne, Kossuth, Laurent.*

Boutwell (1786) Possibly English: unexplained.

Bouvier (740) French: occupational name for a herdsman, Old French *bouvier* (Late Latin *bovarius*, a derivative of *bos*, genitive *bovis*, 'ox').
GIVEN NAMES French 9%. *Laurier* (2), *Pascal* (2), *Adrien, Armand, Christophe, Constant, Dominique, Edouard, Jean Pierre, Jean-Paul, Lucien, Marcel.*

Bouwens (208) Dutch: variant of BAUWENS.
GIVEN NAMES French 5%. *Yves* (2), *Michel.*

Bouwkamp (167) Dutch: topographic name for someone who lived by a field or domain that was under cultivation.
GIVEN NAMES Dutch 5%; German 4%. *Gerrit* (2), *Gert* (2), *Pieter.*

Bouwman (312) Dutch: **1.** derivative of the personal name *Boudewijn* (see BALDWIN). **2.** variant of BOUMAN.
GIVEN NAMES Dutch 4%. *Marinus* (2), *Cornelis, Gerrit, Gradus, Teunis.*

Bouyea (119) Americanized spelling of French BOUYER.
GIVEN NAME French 4%. *Normand.*

Bouyer (147) Southern French: regional variant of BOUVIER.
GIVEN NAMES French 6%. *Frederique, Monique, Napoleon.*

Bouza (161) Galician: habitational name from any of various places in Galicia named Bouza, from *bouza* 'fenced plantation of trees' or 'infertile land'.
GIVEN NAMES Spanish 27%. *Jorge* (5), *Jose* (4), *Cesar* (2), *Juan* (2), *Manuel* (2), *Roberto* (2), *Agustin, Alfredo, Avelino, Blanca, Cesareo, Concepcion; Antonio, Dario.*

Bova (1335) Italian (southern Calabria): habitational name from a place in Calabria called Bova.
GIVEN NAMES Italian 10%. *Salvatore* (10), *Angelo* (7), *Carmine* (4), *Rocco* (4), *Antonio* (2), *Agostino, Carmelo, Cosimo, Cosmo, Dino, Domenico, Enrico.*

Bovaird (132) Irish (Donegal): variant of French **Bouvard** (see BOVARD).

Bovard (384) Variant of French **Bouvard**, from a Germanic personal name composed of the elements *bōv(o)* 'boy' + *hard* 'hardy', 'strong'. This form is found in Switzerland and the Netherlands, as well as in North America; it is probably a Huguenot name.

Bove (1387) **1.** Italian and Catalan (**Bové**): from Italian *bove*, Catalan *bové* 'ox' (from Latin *bos*, genitive *bovis*), applied as a metonymic occupational name for a plowman or herdsman or as a nickname for someone thought to resemble an ox in some way, for example in being fat or patient. **2.** Danish: nickname from *bouæ* 'villain', 'wretch', or from the old personal name *Bovi*.
GIVEN NAMES Italian 11%. *Antonio* (4), *Dante* (3), *Antonietta* (2), *Carlo* (2), *Carmine* (2), *Edo* (2), *Gennaro* (2), *Salvatore* (2), *Aldo, Amato, Biagio, Ciro.*

Bovee (1105) **1.** French (**Bovée**): habitational name from a place named Bovée-sur-Barboure in Meuse. **2.** Possibly an altered spelling of the French habitational name BEAUVAIS.

Bovell (125) English (of Norman origin) and French: habitational name from Bouville (Seine-Inférieure) in France. This surname is now common in Barbados.
GIVEN NAMES Spanish 4%. *Aurelio, Luz, Orlando.*

Boven (211) **1.** Dutch: from a derivative of the Germanic personal name *Bovo*, from *bōv(o)* 'boy'. **2.** Swedish (**Bovén**): probably a topographic name from *bo* 'farm' + the adjectival suffix *-(v)én*, a derivative of Latin *-enius*.

Bovenzi (141) Southern Italian (Campania): from an unattested personal name, *Bovenzo*, of unexplained etymology.

GIVEN NAMES Italian 12%. *Angelo, Egidio, Pino, Rocco, Salvatore*.

Bovey (205) English (Devon): habitational name from either of two places in Devon, Bovey Tracey or North Bovey, which take their names from the Bovey river, on which they stand.

Bovino (156) Italian: probably a habitational name from Bovino in Apulia or, less likely, from a diminutive of BOVE.

GIVEN NAMES Italian 21%. *Angelo* (3), *Vito* (3), *Antonio, Giuseppe, Rocco, Sal, Severino*.

Bow (496) **1.** English: metonymic occupational name for a maker or seller of bows, from Middle English *bow* (Old English *boga*, from *būgan* 'to bend'). Before the invention of gunpowder, the bow was an important long-range weapon for shooting game as well as in warfare. *Boga* is also found as a personal name in Old English, and it is possible that this survived into Middle English and so may lie behind the surname in some instances. In other cases (for example, Richard *atte Bowe*, 1306), the name is topographic, from the same word in the transferred sense 'arched bridge', 'river bend', an allusion to their similarity in shape to a drawn bow. **2.** Irish: Anglicized form of Gaelic **Ó Buadhaigh** (see BOGUE).

Bowar (184) Scottish: variant of BOWER.

GIVEN NAMES French 4%. *Camille, Colette*.

Boward (174) Scottish: variant of **Bowar** (see BOWER).

Bowcutt (149) English: variant of BOCOCK.

Bowden (8645) **1.** English: habitational name from any of several places called Bowden or Bowdon. Bowden in Devon and Derbyshire and Bowdon in Cheshire are named with Old English *boga* 'bow' + *dūn* 'hill', i.e. 'hill shaped like a bow'; one in Leicestershire (*Bugedone* in Domesday Book) comes, according to Ekwall, from the Old English personal name *Būga* (masculine) or *Bucge* (feminine) + *dūn*. There are also Scottish places of this name, but there are comparatively few bearers of the surname Bowden north of the border. In England the surname is found most frequently in Lancashire and in the West Country. In Devon and Cornwall there has been some confusion with the Norman personal name BALDWIN. **2.** English: habitational name from Bovingdon, Hertfordshire, so named with the Old English phrase *būfan dūne* 'on, upon the hill'. The surname may also have arisen as a topographic name from the same phrase used independently, for someone who lived at the top of a hill. **3.** Irish: Anglicized form of Gaelic **Ó Buadáin** 'descendant of *Buadán*', an Old Irish personal name.

Bowdish (296) Probably an altered form of the English surname BOWDITCH. Alternatively, it could be Americanized spelling of the eastern German family name **Baudisch**, from the Old Slavic stem *buditi* 'to wake'.

Bowditch (244) English: probably a habitational name from a place in Devon named Bowditch, from the Old English phrase *būfan dīce* 'above the ditch'.

FOREBEARS The surname Bowditch is well known in New England. Nathaniel Bowditch (1773–1838), author of *The Practical Navigator* (1772), a standard work that went through more than sixty editions, was born in Salem, MA, the son of a shipmaster. The family can be traced back, via a clothier who settled in New England in 1671, to Thorncombe in Devon in the early 16th century.

Bowdle (145) English: altered spelling of **Bowdell**, which is of unexplained origin. This spelling is now rare in England.

Bowdoin (350) Americanized spelling of **Baudouin**, French form of BALDWIN, or of any of the numerous variant forms of this name found in France and Belgium.

Bowdre (107) Americanized spelling of French BEAUDRY.

Bowdry (117) Americanized spelling of French BEAUDRY, or a variant spelling of English **Baudry**, which has the same origin.

Bowe (2280) Variant spelling (chiefly Irish) of BOW.

Bowell (208) **1.** Welsh: variant of POWELL (see HOWELL). **2.** English (of Norman origin): habitational name from Bouelles in Seine Maritime, France, so named with Old Norman French *boelle* 'enclosure', 'dwelling'.

Bowen (28131) **1.** English, of Welsh origin: Anglicized form of Welsh *ap Owain* 'son of *Owain*' (see OWEN). **2.** Irish: Anglicized form of Gaelic **Ó Buadhacháin** 'descendant of *Buadhachán*', a diminutive of *Buadhach* 'victorious' (see BOHAN).

Bowens (1680) **1.** English, of Welsh origin: variant of BOWEN, with the addition of the regular English patronymic suffix *-s*. **2.** Altered spelling of Dutch **Bouwens**, a variant of BAUWENS.

Bower (8497) **1.** Scottish: occupational name for a bow maker, Older Scots *bowar*, equivalent to English BOWYER. **2.** English and Scottish: from Middle English *bur*, *bour* 'bower', 'cottage', 'inner room' (Old English *būr*), hence a topographic name for someone who lived in a small cottage, an occupational name for a house servant who attended his master in his private quarters (see BOWERMAN), or a habitational name from any of various places, for example in Essex, named Bower or Bowers from this word.

Bowerman (1394) **1.** English: occupational name for a house servant who attended his master in his private quarters (see BOWER 2). **2.** Americanized spelling of German **Bauermann**, a variant of BAUER.

Bowermaster (181) Americanized form of German **Bauermeister**, the standardized German form of BURMEISTER.

Bowers (24220) English: variant of BOWER.

Bowersock (407) Probably an Americanized spelling of German **Bauersack**, a derisive nickname for a peasant.

Bowersox (952) Americanized spelling of German **Bauersachs**, a name indicating descent from Hans Bauer, nicknamed *Sachs* 'the Saxon', a forester who lived in Judenbach, Franconia, *c*.1555. An alternative derivation is from **Bauerochs**, literally 'farmer ox', a nickname or byname for the farmer who kept the breeding bull in a community.

Bowery (243) English: unexplained.

Bowes (1907) **1.** Northern English: habitational name from Bowes (formerly in North Yorkshire, now in County Durham), or from some other place so called, the place name being derived from the plural of Old English *boga* 'bow', here referring to bends in a river (see BOW). **2.** Irish: Anglicized form of Gaelic **Ó Buadhaigh** (see BOGUE).

Bowhay (109) English (Devon and Cornwall): unexplained.

Bowick (122) Northern English: variant of BEWICK.

GIVEN NAME French 4%. *Emile*.

Bowie (3387) Scottish and Irish: nickname from Gaelic *buidhe* 'yellow', 'fair-haired', or possibly an Anglicized form of **Ó Buadhaigh** (see BOGUE).

Bowker (1635) English (chiefly Manchester): occupational name for someone whose job was to steep cotton or linen in lye (a strong alkali) to cleanse it, from an agent derivative of Middle English *bouken* 'to wash' (from Middle Dutch *būken*).

Bowlan (129) **1.** English: variant of BOLAND. **2.** Irish: Anglicized form of Gaelic **Ó Beólláin**, 'descendant of *Bjolan*', a Norse personal name.

GIVEN NAME French 6%. *Susette*.

Bowland (402) **1.** Variant spelling of BOLAND 1 and 2. **2.** Altered spelling of Dutch **Bouwland**, a topographic name for someone who lived by land that was under cultivation.

Bowlby (694) English: habitational name from Boulby in North Yorkshire or Bulby in Lincolnshire, both of which are named with the Old Norse byname *Boli* (from *boli* 'bull') + Old Norse *býr* 'farmstead', 'settlement'.

Bowlds (251) English: unexplained. Possibly a variant of BOLD.

Bowlen (217) Perhaps an Americanized spelling of BOHLEN.

Bowler (1702) English (chiefly Nottinghamshire): from Middle English *boller* (from Old English *bolla* 'bowl', 'drinking vessel' + the agent suffix *-er*), an occupational name for a maker or seller of bowls. Medieval bowls were made of wood as well as of earthenware.

Bowles (8549) English and Irish: variant of BOWELL or BOWLER.

Bowley (647) English: habitational name from either of two places called Bowley, near Leominster in Herefordshire and in Devon. The first is named with Old English *bula* 'bull', perhaps a byname (see BULL) + *lēah* 'woodland clearing'. The second is from Old English *boga* 'bow', 'river bend' + *lēah*.

Bowlin (2386) English: probably a variant of BOWLING.

Bowling (8808) **1.** English: variant of BOLLING. **2.** Partly Americanized form of German BOLLING or BOHLING.

Bowlsby (105) English: probably a variant of BOWLBY.

Bowlus (227) Origin unidentified. Perhaps an altered spelling of German **Paulus** (see PAUL).

Bowman (37045) **1.** English and Scottish: occupational name for an archer, Middle English *bow(e)man*, *bouman* (from Old English *boga* 'bow' + *mann* 'man'). This word was distinguished from BOWYER, which denoted a maker or seller of the articles. It is possible that in some cases the surname referred originally to someone who untangled wool with a bow. This process, which originated in Italy, became quite common in England in the 13th century. The vibrating string of a bow was worked into a pile of tangled wool, where its rapid vibrations separated the fibers, while still leaving them sufficiently entwined to produce a fine, soft yarn when spun. **2.** Americanized form of German **Baumann** (see BAUER) or the Dutch cognate BOUMAN.

Bowmaster (135) Americanized spelling of German BAUMEISTER or the Dutch cognate **Bouwmeester**, occupational names for a master builder.

Bowmer (169) **1.** English: variant of BULMER. **2.** Americanized spelling of German BAUMER.

Bown (627) English: variant of BOONE.

Bownds (171) English: probably a variant spelling of BOUNDS.

Bowne (455) English: variant of BOONE. FOREBEARS John Bowne (*c.* 1627–95), a Quaker, came from Matlock, Derbyshire, England, to Boston, MA, in 1651.

Bownes (112) English: variant of BOONE.

Bowns (150) English: variant of BOONE. In England this form of the name is found chiefly in South Yorkshire and the Midlands.

Bowring (152) English: topographic name for someone who dwelt in a small cottage, from an unattested Old English word *būring*, a derivative of *būr* 'bower', 'cottage' (see BOWER).

Bowron (218) English: habitational name for someone from Boldron in County Durham (formerly in North Yorkshire), so named with Old Norse *boli* 'bull' + *rúm* 'clearing'.

Bowser (4764) **1.** English: nickname from the Norman term of address *beu sire* 'fine sir', given either to a fine gentleman (perhaps ironically), or to someone who made frequent use of this term of address. Compare BONSER. **2.** Americanized spelling of German BAUSER.

Bowsher (452) **1.** German: variant of **Bauscher** or **Boesshaar** (see BASEHORE). **2.** English: variant of BELCHER.

Bowyer (1553) English: occupational name for a maker or seller of bows (see BOW), as opposed to an archer. Compare BOWMAN.

Box (3730) English: from Middle English, Old English *box* 'box tree' (Latin *buxus*), in any of a number of possible applications. It may have been a topographic name for someone who lived by a box thicket, a habitational name from one of the places called Box, in Gloucestershire, Hertfordshire, and Wiltshire, or a metonymic occupational name for someone who worked box wood, which is very hard and for this reason was used to make a variety of tools. In some cases it may even have been a nickname for a person with pale or yellow skin, for example as the result of jaundice, a reference to the color of box wood.

Boxberger (197) German and Jewish (western Ashkenazic): habitational name for someone from any of the eight places called Boxberg, in Baden, Hesse, former Silesia (now Poland), and Rhineland. GIVEN NAME German 5%. *Kurt* (3).

Boxell (199) English: habitational name from a lost hamlet near Kirford, Sussex, called Boxholte, from Old English *box* 'box' + *holt* 'wood'. The surname has been found in the area since the 14th century.

Boxer (533) **1.** English: variant of BOX, with the addition of the agent suffix *-er*. **2.** Jewish (from Poland and Ukraine): from an Americanized spelling of Yiddish *bokser* 'St. John's bread', presumably an ornamental name.

Boxler (104) Swiss German: variant spelling of German **Büchsler**, an occupational name for a maker of wooden boxes (see BICKSLER).

Boxley (387) **1.** English: habitational name from a place in Kent named Boxley, from Old English *box* 'box (tree)' + *lēah* 'woodland clearing', or some other place similarly named. **2.** Americanized form of Swiss German BOXLER.

Boxwell (171) English: habitational name from a place in Gloucestershire named Boxwell, from Old English *box* 'box (tree)' + *wella* 'spring', 'stream'.

Boxx (214) Variant spelling of English BOX.

Boy (313) **1.** Dutch, Frisian, and North German: variant of BOYE. **2.** French: southwestern spelling variant of BOIS. GIVEN NAMES German 6%. *Hans Peter* (3), *Heinz, Horst*.

Boyack (194) Scottish: possibly a variant of BOAK. It has been recorded in Scotland since the 16th century.

Boyadjian (170) Armenian: variant of BOYAJIAN. GIVEN NAMES Armenian 61%. *Sarkis* (4), *Hakop* (3), *Minas* (3), *Noubar* (3), *Agop* (2), *Armen* (2), *Boghos* (2), *Hagop* (2), *Haroutioun* (2), *Hayg* (2), *Kevork* (2), *Nerses* (2).

Boyajian (509) Armenian: patronymic from an occupational name for a painter, from Turkish *boyacı* 'painter'. GIVEN NAMES Armenian 17%. *Aram* (4), *Armen* (4), *Karnig* (3), *Krikor* (2), *Sarkis* (2), *Vahan* (2), *Vahe* (2), *Anahid, Antranig, Ara, Arax, Araxie*.

Boyan (184) Americanized spelling of Polish **Bojan**, a nickname for a timorous person, from a derivative of *bać się, bojać się* 'to be afraid'.

Boyar (217) **1.** Jewish (eastern Ashkenazic): habitational name from a place named Boyary, in Belarus, Latvia, or Lithuania. **2.** Americanized spelling of Polish **Bojar**, a status name or nickname from *bojar* 'boyar' (a member of the old Russian aristocracy).

Boyarsky (135) Jewish (from Belarus and Ukraine): habitational name for someone from Boyary in Belarus or Boyarka in Ukraine. GIVEN NAMES Jewish 8%. *Malkah, Meir*.

Boyatt (109) Probably a variant of French BOYETTE.

Boyce (9371) **1.** Scottish, northern Irish, and English: topographic name for someone who lived by a wood, from Old French *bois* 'wood'. **2.** English: patronymic from the Middle English nickname *boy* 'lad', 'servant', or possibly from an Old English personal name *Boia*, of uncertain origin. Examples such as Aluuinus Boi (Domesday Book) and Ivo le Boye (Lincolnshire 1232) support the view that it was a byname or even an occupational name; examples such as Stephanus filius Boie (Northumbria 1202) suggest that it was in use as a personal name in the Middle English period. **3.** Irish: Anglicized form of Gaelic Ó Buadhaigh (see BOGUE). **4.** Anglicized spelling of French BOIS, cognate with 1.

Boyd (49945) Scottish: habitational name from the island of Bute in the Firth of Clyde, the Gaelic name of which is *Bód* (genitive *Bóid*).

Boyda (104) Origin unidentified.

Boyden (914) English: from the Old French personal name *Bodin*, a variant of *Baudin* (see BALDWIN).

Boydston (848) Scottish: habitational name from a place called Boydston near Glasgow. This surname is no longer found in the British Isles.

Boydstun (423) Scottish: variant of BOYDSTON.

Boye (354) **1.** English, North German, Dutch, Frisian, and Danish: from a Germanic personal name, *Boio* or *Bogo*, of uncertain origin. It may represent a variant of BOTHE, with the regular Low German loss of the dental between vowels, but a cognate name appears to have existed in Old English (see BOYCE), where this feature does not occur. *Boje* is still in use as a personal name in Friesland. **2.** Dutch: nickname from Middle Dutch *boy(e)* 'boy', 'lad'.
GIVEN NAMES French 5%; Scandinavian 5%. *Olivier; Erik* (3).

Boyea (371) Americanized spelling of French BOUYER.

Boyens (105) North German: patronymic from the personal name BOYE.
GIVEN NAME German 7%. *Georg* (2).

Boyer (18944) **1.** Altered spelling of German BAYER or BEYER. **2.** German: habitational name for someone from Boye (near Celle-Hannover). **3.** English: variant of BOWYER. **4.** Danish: habitational name from a place so named. The surname is also found in Norway and Sweden, probably from the same source.

Boyers (414) English: possibly a variant of BOWYER.

Boyes (768) **1.** English (chiefly Yorkshire): variant spelling of BOYCE. **2.** Americanized spelling of French BOIS.

Boyet (107) Variant of French BOYETTE.

Boyett (1627) Variant of French BOYETTE. Also found in England.

Boyette (1893) French: of uncertain origin; perhaps a variant of the French surname **Boyau**, **Boyault**, occupational name for a sausage merchant, from *boyaux* 'intestines', 'gut'.

Boyington (488) English: variant of BOYNTON.

Boyke (102) Dutch: from a pet form of the personal name BOYE (see BOYKINS).

Boyken (138) **1.** Dutch and North German: from a pet form of the personal name BOYE (see BOYKINS). **2.** Possibly also a variant spelling of English BOYKIN.

Boykin (4892) English: from a pet form of the Middle English personal name BOYE.
FOREBEARS Jarvis Boykin was one of the free planters who assented to the 'Fundamental Agreement' of the New Haven Colony on June 4, 1639.

Boykins (688) Americanized spelling of Dutch **Boykens**, which is either from a pet form of the personal name *Boy* (see BOYE), or a patronymic from the personal name *Boudewijn*, Dutch equivalent of BALDWIN.

Boyko (692) Ukrainian: regional name from *bojko* 'inhabitant of western Ukraine'.

GIVEN NAMES Russian 6%. *Sergey* (3), *Galina* (2), *Konstantin* (2), *Vladimir* (2), *Aleksandr, Aleksandra, Fedor, Leonid, Nikolay, Oksana, Raisa, Sheyva.*

Boylan (2553) **1.** Irish: Anglicized form of Gaelic **Ó Baoigheálláin**. It was the name of a sept of Dartry, County Monaghan. **2.** English: variant of BOYLAND.
GIVEN NAMES Irish 6%. *Brigid, Finbar.*

Boyland (397) **1.** English: habitational name from places in Devon and Norfolk named Boyland. The Norfolk place name is derived from the Old English personal name *Boia* + *lund* 'grove' (Old Norse *lundr*). **2.** Irish: variant of BOYLAN.

Boyle (16018) Irish (Donegal): Anglicized form of Gaelic **Ó Baoithghill** 'descendant of *Baoithgheall*', a personal name of uncertain meaning, perhaps from *baoth* 'rash' + *geall* 'pledge'.
GIVEN NAMES Irish 5%. *Brendan* (11), *Liam* (3), *Declan* (2), *Fergus* (2), *John Patrick* (2), *Padraic* (2), *Seamus* (2), *Aileen, Brigid, Cathal, Colm, Conn.*

Boylen (225) Variant spelling of Irish BOYLAN.

Boyles (4191) Irish: variant of BOYLE.

Boyll (144) Variant of Irish BOYLE.

Boylston (174) Scottish: habitational name from a place named Boylston in Strathclyde, Scotland.
FOREBEARS Thomas Boylston came to Watertown, MA, in 1635. His grandson Zabdiel Boylston (c. 1679–1766) introduced inoculation against smallpox to North America.

Boyne (371) Irish: MacLysaght suggests this may be a modern form of **Mac Baoithin** 'son of *Baothin*', a byname from *baoth* 'foolish', which was formerly Americanized as **Mac Boyheen**.

Boynton (2946) English: habitational name from a place in East Yorkshire named Boynton, from the Old English personal name *Bōfa* + the connective particle *-ing-* denoting association + *tūn* 'settlement'. Alternatively, the name may have arisen from Boyton in Wiltshire (recorded in Domesday Book as *Boientone*) or from Boyington Court in Kent (recorded in 1207 as *Bointon*), both of which are named with the Old English personal name *Boia* + *tūn* 'settlement'.
FOREBEARS John Boynton emigrated from England to Salem, MA, 1638.

Boys (317) **1.** English (chiefly Yorkshire): variant spelling of BOYCE. **2.** Americanized spelling of French BOIS.

Boyse (112) Variant of English BOYCE or French BOIS.
GIVEN NAME French 4%. *Camille.*

Boysel (118) French: variant spelling of **Boissel**, a variant of BOISSEAU.

Boysen (864) North German and Scandinavian: patronymic from BOYE.

GIVEN NAMES German 4%. *Gerd* (2), *Hans* (2), *Erwin, Hermann, Juergen, Lorenz, Siegfried.*

Boyson (177) **1.** North German and Scandinavian: Americanized spelling of BOYSEN. **2.** English: patronymic from the Middle English nickname *boy* 'lad', 'servant', or possibly from an Old English personal name *Boia*. See BOYCE.

Boyster (110) Probably of Irish origin, but unexplained.

Boyt (285) English: unexplained. Compare BOYETT.

Boyte (352) Possibly a variant spelling of BOYT. However, this surname is frequent in LA and TX and may be French in origin; perhaps an Americanized spelling of **Boîteux**, documented in 1701 in Lachine from Dauphin in France.

Boyter (357) Scottish: from French BOITER.

Boyum (421) Norwegian (**Bøyum**): habitational name from a farm in Sogn, named from Old Norse *bær, býr* 'farm'.
GIVEN NAMES Scandinavian 8%. *Asmund* (2), *Iver, Syvert.*

Boza (199) **1.** Hispanicized spelling of Galician BOUZA. **2.** Hungarian: from the old secular personal name *Boza* or *Bozás*; possibly also a metonymic occupational name from *boza* 'beer'.
GIVEN NAMES Spanish 33%. *Jose* (6), *Luis* (3), *Marcelo* (3), *Reinaldo* (3), *Francisco* (2), *Jorge* (2), *Rafael* (2), *Adalberto, Arnaldo, Arturo, Celestino, Diosdado.*

Bozak (112) Croatian (from northern Croatia; **Božak**): derivative of the personal name **Božo**, a pet form of *Božidar* meaning 'gift from God'.

Bozard (216) **1.** Possibly an altered spelling of French **Bosard**, from the Germanic personal name *Burghard* (see BURKHART). **2.** See BOZARTH.

Bozarth (1335) Probably a reduced form of Swiss German **Bozenhardt**, a habitational name from Botzenhardt in Württemberg.

Boze (362) Origin uncertain. **1.** In part at least it is English, a variant of BOSE. **2.** Probably also a variant of BOAZ in some cases. **3.** French: probably a variant of BOIS.

Bozek (524) **1.** Polish (**Bożek**): from a pet form of the personal names *Boguchwał* 'praise of God', *Bogdan* 'gift of God', or *Chwalibog* 'praise God'. **2.** Polish and Ukrainian: from *bożek* 'idol', 'pagan divinity'.
GIVEN NAMES Polish 6%. *Casimir* (3), *Krystyna* (2), *Tadeusz* (2), *Izabela, Janina.*

Bozell (127) Respelling of South German **Bosl**, from the Germanic personal name *Boso* (see BOOS).

Bozeman (2284) **1.** Dutch: nickname for a wicked man. **2.** Probably an Americanized spelling of the German cognate **Bösemann** (see BOSEMAN).

Bozic (169) **1.** Croatian and Serbian (**Božić**): patronymic from *Božo*, short form

of the personal name *Božidar*, meaning 'gift from God'. **2.** Slovenian (**Božič**) and Croatian (**Božić**): nickname for someone born between Christmas Day and Epiphany, or for someone who had some particular connection with the Christmas season, from *božič* 'Christmas', from a diminutive of *Bog* (in the sense 'son of God').
GIVEN NAMES South Slavic 7%. *Krsto, Nenad, Obren, Zeljko, Zivko.*

Bozich (312) Americanized spelling of BOZIC.

Bozick (118) Americanized or Germanized spelling of Czech **Božík** (see BOZIK).

Bozik (123) Czech (**Božík**): from a short form of the personal names *Bohuslav* or *Bohumil*, both formed with Slavic *Bog* 'God'.

Bozman (394) Possibly a variant of Dutch BOZEMAN or an Americanized form of the German cognate **Bösemann** (see BOSEMAN).

Bozza (207) Italian: **1.** variant of BOZZO. **2.** possibly a nickname from Sicilian *bbhozza, vozza* 'crop (of a chicken)'.
GIVEN NAMES Italian 16%. *Antonio, Armando, Carlo, Cosimo, Fausto, Gino, Guido, Mario, Orlando.*

Bozzelli (119) Italian: from a diminutive of BOZZO.
GIVEN NAMES Italian 15%. *Fedele, Pasquale, Valentino.*

Bozzi (224) Italian: patronymic or plural form of BOZZO.
GIVEN NAMES Italian 18%. *Aldo* (5), *Vito* (3), *Carmine* (2), *Angelo, Camillo, Domenic, Innocenzo, Rocco, Salvatore, Tommaso.*

Bozzo (319) Italian: from a Germanic personal name *Boz(z)o*.
GIVEN NAMES Italian 11%. *Gino* (2), *Luigi* (2), *Aldo, Alessandra, Angelo, Biagio, Fedele, Natale, Paolo, Salvatore, Santino, Vito.*

Bozzuto (174) Italian: possibly a nickname from a derivative of *bozzo* 'cuckold'.
GIVEN NAME Italian 4%. *Salvatore.*

Braaksma (183) Frisian: topographic name for someone who lived by a piece of wasteland or newly cultivated land, from Frisian, Dutch *braak* 'fallow', 'waste' + Frisian *ma* 'man'. Compare BRACH.

Braam (129) Dutch: variant of ABRAHAM.
GIVEN NAMES Dutch 5%. *Cornelis, Pieter.*

Braasch (421) North German and Danish: nickname from *braasch* 'noisy', 'fresh' (Middle Low German *bräsch* 'noise').
GIVEN NAMES German 5%. *Kurt* (2), *Claus, Frederick, Gerhard, Hans, Helmut, Inge, Otto.*

Braaten (1192) **1.** Norwegian: habitational name from Bråten, a common farm name in southeastern Norway, derived from Old Norse *broti* 'land cleared for cultivation by burning'. **2.** Dutch: perhaps a nickname for a trickster, from a derivative of Old

French *barat*, Middle Dutch *baraet, beraet* 'deceit', 'ruse', 'tumult'. Compare BRADT.
GIVEN NAMES Scandinavian 5%. *Karsten* (2), *Arndt, Iver, Lars, Nels, Nordahl, Selmer.*

Braatz (622) North German: nickname for a fat or clumsy person, from Low German *bratsch, bratz* 'plump'.
GIVEN NAMES German 4%. *Erwin* (4), *Eldred, Gerhard, Hildegarde.*

Braband (113) French and English: variant of BRABANT.

Brabant (416) Ethnic name (in France and England as well as Germany and the Low Countries) for a native of Brabant, a medieval duchy (capital Brussels), which extended from what is now central Belgium northwards into the Netherlands. The name of the duchy is of Dutch origin. See also BRABAZON.
FOREBEARS There is a Brabant or Brébant documented in Sillery, Quebec, from the Berry region of France, with the secondary surname Lamothe. Another, with the secondary surname Lecomte, from La Rochelle, is recorded in Montreal in 1696.
GIVEN NAMES French 5%. *Aime, Aristide, Marcel, Normand, Ovila, Yvan.*

Brabazon (84) English and French: from Anglo-Norman French *brabançon*. This was originally an ethnic term for a native of the duchy of Brabant (see BRABANT). By the 13th century it had passed into generic use as an occupational name for a mercenary, specifically a member of one of the more or less independent marauding bands of mercenaries, noted for their lawlessness and cruelty. These originated in Brabant and Flanders, but in the course of time accepted recruits from anywhere.

Brabec (391) Czech: nickname from *brabec* 'sparrow' (literary *vrabec*).

Brabender (184) German and Dutch: ethnic name for a native of Brabant (see BRABANT), or an occupational name for a mercenary (see BRABAZON).

Brabham (713) English: variant of BRABANT, altered by association with English habitational names ending in *-ham*.

Brabson (279) English: variant of BRABANT, altered by association with English patronymics ending in *-son*.

Bracamonte (301) Spanish and Portuguese: habitational name from the French town of Bracquemont, near Dieppe.
GIVEN NAMES Spanish 36%. *Carlos* (6), *Ernesto* (3), *Jose* (3), *Juan* (3), *Manuel* (3), *Alvaro* (2), *Armando* (2), *Jorge* (2), *Luis* (2), *Luis Carlos* (2), *Mateo* (2), *Orlando* (2).

Bracamontes (178) Variant of Spanish and Portuguese BRACAMONTE.
GIVEN NAMES Spanish 52%. *Alberto* (3), *Jesus* (3), *Jose* (3), *Ramon* (3), *Beatriz* (2), *Carlos* (2), *Francisco* (2), *Juan* (2), *Leticia* (2), *Luis* (2), *Miguel* (2), *Raul* (2).

Bracci (167) Italian (mainly central Italy): from the plural of *braccio* 'arm', hence a

nickname for someone with strong, deformed, or otherwise noticeable arms, also used as a personal name in medieval Italy. **Fortebraccio** 'strong arm' was the surname of a noble family of Perugia.
GIVEN NAMES Italian 27%. *Carlo* (3), *Angelo* (2), *Mario* (2), *Aldo, Alfonso, Americo, Armondo, Emelio, Emilio, Luciano, Lucio, Nazzareno, Nino, Nilo, Piera, Reno, Sergio, Silvano.*

Braccia (119) Italian: feminized form of **Braccio**, from a medieval personal name, a short form of *Fortebraccio* ('strong arm'). The feminine form is probably due to association with the Italian word *famiglia* 'family'.
GIVEN NAMES Italian 28%. *Vito* (2), *Amato, Amedeo, Angelo, Carmine, Giuseppe, Luciano, Romeo.*

Bracco (501) Italian: **1.** from *bracco* 'hunting dog', 'bloodhound' (from Old High German *brakko* via French *brac*), probably a nickname for someone thought to resemble a hunting dog. **2.** in southern Italy, most likely a nickname from Calabrian *braccu* 'small and chubby'. **3.** possibly a habitational name from a place named Bracco, for example in Liguria province.
GIVEN NAMES Italian 19%. *Angelo* (8), *Salvatore* (4), *Carmine* (3), *Ignazio* (3), *Sal* (3), *Silvio* (2), *Aldo, Carmela, Donato, Elio, Gino, Pasquale.*

Brace (1766) English: probably from Middle English, Old French *brace* 'arm', also denoting a piece of armor covering the arm. In most cases it is probably a metonymic occupational name for a maker or seller of armor, specifically armor designed to protect the upper arms, but it could also have been a nickname for someone with strong arms (compare ARMSTRONG) or a deformed or otherwise noticeable arm.

Bracero (173) Spanish: from *bracero*, an occupational name, most likely for a day laborer or farm hand, although the term could also mean 'brewer' and 'sure-armed man' (i.e. one with a good aim in throwing or shooting) and these senses cannot be excluded.
GIVEN NAMES Spanish 45%. *Jose* (6), *Julio* (3), *Angel* (2), *Delfin* (2), *Eladio* (2), *Rafael* (2), *Alfonso, Alida, Bernardo, Blanca, Carlos, Catalina.*

Bracewell (627) Northern English: habitational name from a place in Lancashire (formerly in West Yorkshire), named in Anglo-Scandinavian as 'Breith's stream', from the Old Norse byname *Breiðr* meaning 'broad' (which possibly replaced earlier Old English *Brægd*, meaning 'trick') + Old English *well(a)* 'spring', 'stream'.

Bracey (1460) English (of Norman origin): habitational name from either of two places in France called Brécy, in Aisne and Ardennes.

Brach (487) **1.** German and Jewish (Ashkenazic): topographic name from Middle

High German *brache* 'fallow land', 'pastureland', originally 'newly plowed land'. **2.** Jewish (Ashkenazic): variant of BARACH. **3.** English: topographic name from Middle English *breche*, Old English *brēc* 'newly cultivated land' (a derivative of *brecan* 'to break', i.e. 'land broken by the plow'), or a habitational name from any of the places named with this element, as for example Brache in Luton, Bedfordshire, and Breach in Maulden, Bedfordshire.
GIVEN NAMES Jewish 12%. *Cheskel* (5), *Moshe* (3), *Chaim* (2), *Mendel* (2), *Pinchas* (2), *Bernat, Hershel, Meyer, Moche, Mort, Rivka, Rivky.*

Bracher (235) **1.** English: variant of BRACH 2, + the suffix *-er* denoting an inhabitant. **2.** Swiss German: variant of German **Brachman** (see BRACHMAN).

Brachfeld (101) Jewish (Ashkenazic): ornamental name from German *Brachfeld* 'fallow field'.
GIVEN NAMES Jewish 17%. *Emanuel* (3), *Mendel* (2), *Benzion, Chaim, Chanie, Dov, Heshy, Ori.*

Brachman (146) German (**Brachmann**): variant of BRACH, with the addition of Middle High German *man* 'man'.
GIVEN NAMES French 5%. *Armand, Voldemar.*

Bracht (317) German and Dutch: **1.** habitational name from places called Bracht, in Westphalia, Rhineland, and Hesse. **2.** from a short form of any of the various personal names containing the second element *-bracht* (a local variant of *-brecht* in Rhineland, Westphalia, and elsewhere), such as *Albrecht* (see ALBERT).
GIVEN NAMES German 4%. *Gunther, Juergen, Wilhelmina.*

Brack (1172) German and English: metonymic occupational name for a master of hunting dogs or a nickname for someone thought to resemble a hunting dog, Middle High German *bracke*. The cognate Middle English word was derived via Old French *brachez* (plural of *brachet*, a diminutive form). Compare BRAKKE.

Brackbill (187) Americanized spelling of Swiss German **Brechbühl** (see BRECHBILL).

Bracke (112) German: variant of BRACK.
GIVEN NAMES German 12%. *Helmut, Horst, Kurt, Markus.*

Brackeen (375) Irish: variant of BRACKEN.

Bracken (3061) **1.** Irish: Anglicized form of Gaelic **Ó Breacáin** 'descendant of *Breacán*', a personal name from a diminutive of *breac* 'speckled', 'spotted', which was borne by a 6th-century saint who lived at Ballyconnel, County Cavan, and was famous as a healer; St. Bricin's Military Hospital, Dublin is named in his honor. **2.** English: topographic name from Middle English *braken* 'bracken' (from Old English *bræcen* or Old Norse *brakni*), or a habi-

tational name from a place named with this word, such as Bracken in East Yorkshire or Bracon Ash in Norfolk. **3.** German: especially in the north, probably a topographic name from Middle Low German *brake* 'brushwood', 'fallow land', 'copse', an element of many field and place names.

Brackenbury (194) English: habitational name from any of several minor places named with Middle English *braken* 'bracken' (from Old English *bræcen* or Old Norse *brakni*) + Old Norse *berg* 'hill', among them Brackenber in West Yorkshire and Cumbria, Brackenborough in Lincolnshire, and Breckenbrough in North Yorkshire.

Brackenridge (141) Scottish and English: variant of BRECKENRIDGE.

Brackens (181) Variant of Irish BRACKEN.

Bracker (148) **1.** German: occupational name from Middle Low German *brāken* 'to plow fallow land' or from *braken* 'to crush flax'. **2.** Possibly an altered spelling of Swiss German BRACHER. **3.** Swiss German (**Bräcker**): variant of **Brägger** (see BRAGER).
GIVEN NAMES German 5%. *Heinrich, Sigfried.*

Brackett (4013) English: from Middle English, Old French *brachet*, denoting a type of hound. The word was also used as a term of abuse.
FOREBEARS Captain Richard Brackett (1610–c. 1691) came to Boston, MA, in about 1629, and moved to Braintree, MA, in 1641.

Brackin (1044) Irish: variant spelling of BRACKEN.

Brackins (302) Variant spelling of Irish BRACKENS.

Brackley (126) English: habitational name from a place in Northamptonshire named Brackley, from an Old English personal name *Bracc(a)* + Old English *lēah* 'woodland clearing'.

Brackman (511) **1.** North German (**Brackmann**): variant of BROCKMANN or a topographic name from Middle Low German *bra(c)k*. According to Brechenmacher this denotes a breach point in a dike, or an area of stagnant water behind one. **2.** Americanized spelling of German **Brachmann** (see BRACHMAN).

Brackmann (120) German: see BRACKMAN.
GIVEN NAMES German 6%. *Hans, Kurt.*

Bracknell (144) English: habitational name from a place in Berkshire named Bracknell from an Old English personal name *Bracca* (genitive *-n*) + *halh* 'nook or corner of land'.

Brackney (423) Probably an altered spelling of North German **Brackner** or South German **Brachner**, topographic names from Middle Low German *brāk*, Middle High German *brāch* 'fallow', 'uncultivated (land)', the suffix *-ner* denoting an inhabitant.

Bracy (1037) English: variant spelling of BRACEY.

Brad (115) **1.** English: unexplained. **2.** Variant of Dutch BRADT. **3.** Romanian: unexplained.
GIVEN NAMES Romanian 6%. *Anca, Vasile.*

Bradac (113) Czech and Slovak (**Bradáč**), Slovenian (**Bradač**): nickname meaning 'bearded man', from a derivative of *brada* 'beard'.
GIVEN NAME German 5%. *Detlef.*

Bradach (147) Americanized spelling of BRADAC.

Bradberry (1103) English: variant spelling of BRADBURY.

Bradburn (883) English (Lancashire): habitational name from Bradbourne in Derbyshire or Brabourne in Kent, both named with Old English *brād* 'broad' + *burna* 'stream'.

Bradbury (3357) English: habitational name from any of various minor places so called, in several counties, all first recorded fairly late. The etymology is generally Old English *brād* 'broad' + *burh* 'fort' (see BURY), but Bradbury in County Durham is recorded in Old English as *Brydbyrig*, the first element probably being Old English *bred* 'board'. This is probably also the first element in Bradbury, Cheshire.

Bradby (143) English: habitational name from an unidentified or lost place; perhaps a reduced form of BRADBURY.

Braddock (1733) English: topographic name for someone living by a notable broad oak, from Old English *brād* 'broad' + *āc* 'oak', or a habitational name from a minor place so named, such as Broad Oak in Symondsbury, Dorset. Braddock in Cornwall (*Brodehoc* in Domesday Book) may have this origin; the second element may however be Old English *hōc* 'hook of land', 'hill spur'.

Braddy (1009) **1.** English (Essex): variant of the topographic name BROADY 'broad island' or 'broad enclosure'. **2.** variant of Irish BRADY.

Bradeen (209) Irish: from a pet form of BRADY or BRADEN.

Braden (4760) Irish: Anglicized form of Gaelic **Ó Bradáin** 'descendant of *Bradán*', a personal name meaning 'salmon'. The Gaelic name was sometimes translated into English as SALMON or FISHER.

Brader (367) German (**Bräder**): **1.** from an Old German personal name *Brado*. **2.** occupational name for a cook, from an agent derivative of Middle Low German *brāden* 'to fry or cook'.

Bradfield (1601) English: habitational name from any of the places in Berkshire, Devon, Essex, Suffolk, South Yorkshire, and elsewhere named Bradford, from Old English *brād* 'broad' + *feld* 'open country'.

Bradford (17380) English: habitational name from any of the many places, large and small, called Bradford; in particular the city in West Yorkshire, which originally rose to prosperity as a wool town. There are others in Derbyshire, Devon, Dorset, Greater Manchester, Norfolk, Somerset, and elsewhere. They are all named with Old English *brād* 'broad' + *ford* 'ford'.

FOREBEARS This name was brought independently to North American by many different bearers from the 17th century onward. William Bradford (1590–1657), born in Austerfield in South Yorkshire, England, the son of a yeoman farmer, was among the Pilgrim Fathers who emigrated to America on the *Mayflower* in 1620. He was a signer of the Mayflower Compact and in 1621 he was elected governor of Plymouth colony, being re-elected thirty times.

Another William Bradford (1663–1752), printer, came from Barnwell, Leicestershire, England, to Philadelphia, PA, in 1685, subsequently moving to New York, where he set up a printing press and founded a paper mill. His grandson, also called William Bradford (1721–91), was known as 'the patriot printer', famous for his Philadelphia newspaper, which among other things denounced the Stamp Act, "which no American can mention witout abhorrence".

Bradham (465) English: probably a habitational name from places in Buckinghamshire and Norfolk named Bradenham, from Old English *brād* (dative *-an*) 'broad' + *hām* 'homestead' or *hamm* 'river meadow', 'enclosure hemmed in by water'.

Bradigan (102) Irish (Roscommon): reduced Americanized form of **Ó Bradagáin** 'descendant of *Bradagán*', a byname possibly derived from *bród* 'pride'.

Brading (151) English (Hampshire and the Isle of Wight): habitational name from a place on the Isle of Wight named Brading, from Old English *brerd* 'hillside' + *-ingas* 'dwellers at', i.e. '(settlement of) the dwellers on the hillside'.

Bradish (465) Of Irish origin: unexplained; perhaps from Gaelic **ÓBrádaigh** (see BRADY).

Bradle (110) Altered spelling of South German **Bradl**, a metonymic occupational name for a cook, from Middle High German *brāte* 'roast'.

Bradley (45011) 1. English: habitational name from any of the many places throughout England named Bradley, from Old English *brād* 'broad' + *lēah* 'woodland clearing'. 2. Scottish: habitational name from Braidlie in Roxburghshire. 3. Irish (Ulster): adopted as an English equivalent of Gaelic *Ó Brolcháin*.

Bradner (305) 1. English (mainly Somerset): habitational name from Bradnor in Herefordshire, so named with Old English *brād* 'broad' (dative *-an*) + *ōra* 'hill slope'. 2. Possibly an altered spelling of the South German surname **Brettner**, an occupational name for someone who cut shingles or boards, from an agent derivative of Middle

High German *bret* 'board', or in some cases perhaps a habitational name for someone from Bretten in Baden.

Bradney (119) English: habitational name from a place in Somerset named Bradney, from Old English *brād* 'broad' (dative *-an*) + *ēg* 'island'.

Bradow (101) 1. English (Derbyshire): unexplained. 2. German: perhaps a variant of BREDOW.

Bradshaw (14320) English: habitational name from any of the places called Bradshaw, for example in Lancashire and West Yorkshire, from Old English *brād* 'broad' + *sceaga* 'thicket'.

Bradsher (463) Origin uncertain; possibly an old variant spelling of English BRADSHAW or BRATCHER; alternatively, it may be an altered spelling of the German occupational name **Bretscher** (see BRATCHER).

Bradstreet (501) English: topographic name for someone living by a Roman road or other great highway, from Old English *brād* 'broad' + *strēt* 'paved highway', 'Roman road' (see STREET), or habitational name from some minor place named with these elements.

FOREBEARS The poet Anne Bradstreet (1612–72) was born Anne Dudley, probably in Northampton, England. She and her husband Simon Bradstreet came to MA with Winthrop in 1630. Simon (1603–97) came from an old Suffolk family. He served in various public offices and was governor of MA from 1679 to 1686 and again in 1686–92.

Bradt (714) 1. Dutch: nickname for a trickster, from Old French *barat*, Middle Dutch *baraet*, *beraet* 'deceit', 'fraud', 'ruse'. 2. Norwegian: variant of BRAATEN or BRATT.

FOREBEARS Albert Andriessen Bradt (1607–1686), a settler in Rensselaerswijck on the upper Hudson, was of Norwegian origin, from Fredrikstad, Norway. He was also known as **de Norrman** 'the Norwegian'. See NORMAN.

Bradtke (114) 1. Dutch: from a diminutive of BRADT. 2. German: of uncertain origin.

Bradway (552) English: topographic name from Old English *brād* 'broad' + *weg* 'way', 'track', or a habitational name from a place so named, notably Bradway in South Yorkshire. See also BROADWAY.

Bradwell (256) English: habitational name from a place named Bradwell, of which there are examples in Buckinghamshire, Derbyshire, Essex, Somerset, Suffolk, and elsewhere, from Old English *brād* 'broad' + *well(a)* 'spring', 'stream'.

Brady (26787) Irish: Anglicized form of Gaelic **Ó Brádaigh** 'descendant of *Brádach*', a byname the meaning of which is not clear. It is unlikely to be connected with Gaelic *bradach* 'thieving', 'dishonest', which has a short first vowel.

GIVEN NAMES Irish 6%. *Brendan* (9), *Ciaran* (3), *Colm* (3), *John Patrick* (3), *Kieran* (3), *Seamus* (3), *Aidan* (2), *Conal* (2), *Patrick Michael* (2), *Aileen, Assumpta, Brigid.*

Braeger (122) German (also **Bräger**): habitational name for someone from any of several places called Bräg in Germany and Switzerland.

GIVEN NAMES German 5%. *Gerhard, Otto.*

Braff (202) 1. Jewish (from Poland): probably an ornamental name from German *brav* 'good', 'upright'. 2. Swedish: an old spelling of **Brav**, possibly a soldier's name.

GIVEN NAMES Scandinavian 4%; Jewish 4%. *Erik*; *Emanuel, Shimon, Shoshi.*

Brafford (444) English: variant of BRADFORD.

Brafman (112) Jewish: variant of BRAFF.

GIVEN NAMES Jewish 18%; Russian 6%. *Ari, Chaim, Hyman, Leibish, Yaakov, Zev*; *Arkadiy, Reisa, Yevgeniy.*

Braford (122) English: variant of BRADFORD.

Braga (844) Portuguese and Galician: habitational name from Braga, a city in northern Portugal. As *Bracara Augusta*, it was the capital of the Roman province of Gallaecia.

GIVEN NAMES Spanish 16%; Portuguese 10%. *Manuel* (18), *Jose* (14), *Francisco* (4), *Luis* (3), *Mario* (3), *Sergio* (3), *Alvaro* (2), *Carlos* (2), *Luiz* (2), *Reginaldo* (2), *Virginio* (2), *Adriana*; *Paulo* (3), *Duarte* (2), *Joao* (2), *Albano*; *Antonio* (21), *Filomena* (4), *Larraine, Marco, Mauro, Reno.*

Bragan (147) Irish: Anglicized form of Gaelic **Ó Bragáin**, an unexplained name, recorded from the 12th century but now rare in Ireland.

Bragdon (895) English: most probably a variant of BROGDEN.

Brager (379) 1. Norwegian: habitational name from any of various farms so called in eastern Norway, which may have originally derived their name from a river name meaning 'roaring', 'thundering'. 2. South German (**Bräger**): habitational name for someone from Bräg in Bavaria. 3. Altered spelling of Swiss German **Bräg(g)er**, a habitational name for someone from Bräg in Toggenburg district.

Bragg (7536) English: nickname for a cheerful or lively person, from Middle English *bragge* 'lively', 'cheerful', 'active', also 'brave', 'proud', 'arrogant' (of unknown origin).

Braggs (443) English: variant of BRAGG.

GIVEN NAMES French 4%. *Alphonse* (2), *Celestine, Jacques, Patrice.*

Braham (467) 1. English: habitational name from either of two places called Braham, in Cambridgeshire and West Yorkshire, both probably named with Old English *brōm* 'broom' + *hām* 'homestead' or *hamm* 'flood plain', 'water meadow'. 2. Jewish: reduced variant of ABRAHAM.

Brahler (142) German: nickname for a boaster, from an agent derivative of Middle Low German *prālen* 'to swagger'.

Brahm (414) **1.** German and Jewish (Ashkenazic): from a reduced form of ABRAHAM. **2.** North German: topographic name from Middle Low German *brām* 'broom', 'gorse', or a habitational name from a place named with Low German *brām* 'swampy thicket', for example Am Brahm, near Oldenburg (denoting a location by a canal). **3.** German: topographic name for someone who lived by a bramble thicket, from Middle High German *brāme* 'blackberry', 'bramble'.

Brahmbhatt (118) Indian (Gujarat): Hindu (Brahman) name, from Sanskrit *brahma* 'pertaining to Brahman (the ultimate reality in Hinduism) or to the Brahmans' + *bhaṭṭa* 'lord', 'learned one' (see BHATT).
GIVEN NAMES Indian 95%. *Ashok* (7), *Mahesh* (3), *Pankaj* (3), *Rajendra* (3), *Ashish* (2), *Bansi* (2), *Hitesh* (2), *Jagdish* (2), *Jayesh* (2), *Pravin* (2), *Shyam* (2), *Trupti* (2).

Brahms (110) German: patronymic from *Brahm*, a reduced form of ABRAHAM.
GIVEN NAME German 5%. *Gerhard*.

Braid (244) Scottish: **1.** variant of BROAD. **2.** habitational name from a place called Braid, south of Edinburgh.

Brailey (176) English: habitational name from Brayley Barton in Devon, which is named with the Bray river (a back formation from High Bray, which is from Celtic *brez* 'hill') + Old English *lēah* 'woodland clearing'.

Brailsford (298) English (East Midlands): habitational name from a place in Derbyshire named Brailsford, possibly from an Old English word *brægels*, a metathesized form of *bærgels*, itself a byform of *byrgels* 'tumulus', 'barrow', + *ford* 'ford'.

Brain (543) Irish and Scottish: reduced Anglicized form of Scottish Gaelic **Mac an Bhreitheamhan** 'son of the judge', from *breitheamh* 'judge'.

Brainard (1621) English: unexplained.
FOREBEARS Daniel Brainerd came to Hartford, CT, in 1649 at around the age of eight. There is a widespread belief that he came from Braintree, Essex, England, and that his surname may be an altered form of that place name, but there is no documentation to support this. In 1662, at the age of 21, he became one of the founders of Haddam, CT.

Brainerd (665) English: variant of BRAINARD.

Brais (112) French: perhaps a variant of **Brès**, from the Gaulish personal name *Brictius*.
GIVEN NAMES French 17%. *Marcel* (2), *Aldea, Andre, Cecile, Fernande, Stephane*.

Braisted (131) Origin unidentified. Probably English, but unexplained.

Braithwaite (1124) Northern English: habitational name from any of the places in Cumbria and Yorkshire named Braithwaite, from Old Norse *breiðr* 'broad' + *þveit* 'clearing'.

Brake (2029) **1.** English: topographic name for someone who lived by a clump of bushes or by a patch of bracken. *Brake* 'thicket' and *brake* 'bracken' were homonyms in Middle English. The first is from Old English *bracu*; the second is by folk etymology from northern Middle English *braken, -en* being taken as a plural ending. After the words had fallen together, their senses also became confused. **2.** North German: habitational name from any of several places so named, notably the town on the Weser, or a topographic name from Middle Low German *brāk* 'clearing', 'coppice'.
FOREBEARS Wilhelm Joseph Dietrich, Baron von Brake, of Hannover (Germany), is said to have settled in Nansemond, VA, about 1730. His son Johann Jacob (John) Brake was the progenitor of the VA and WV Brakes; another son, also named Jacob Brake, settled in Edgecombe Co., NC, in 1742, where he sired seven sons and two daughters.

Brakebill (303) Americanized spelling of Swiss German **Brechbühl** (see BRECHBILL).

Brakefield (524) English: topographic name from Middle English *brake* 'thicket', 'bracken' (see BRAKE) + *feld* 'open country', 'cleared land'.

Brakel (111) Dutch (**van Brakel**): habitational name from any of several places so called, named with a diminutive of Dutch *braek* 'fallow', 'uncultivated'.
GIVEN NAMES Dutch 7%; German 4%. *Willem* (2), *Maarten; Erwin, Horst*.

Braker (278) **1.** Swiss German (**Bräker**): probably a habitational name for someone from Bräg in the district of Toggenburg. Compare BRAGER. **2.** Jewish (eastern Ashkenazic): nickname or occupational name from Yiddish *braker* 'chooser (of inferior goods)'.
GIVEN NAMES German 5%; Jewish 4%. *Erwin* (3), *Fritz* (2), *Ingo; Moishe, Rakhil, Shoshana*.

Brakke (266) Dutch: from Middle Dutch *bracke, brakke* 'bloodhound', 'hunting dog', hence possibly an occupational name for a hunter or a keeper of hounds. Compare BRACK.
GIVEN NAME Scandinavian 5%. *Nels*.

Braley (1429) **1.** English: probably a variant spelling of BRAILEY. **2.** French: from a diminutive of **Brael**, from Old French *braiel*, a belt knotted at the waist to hold up breeches, presumably an occupational name for a maker of such belts. There may be some connection with **Breilly** (see BRALLIER). This is a New England name.

Bralley (167) Probably a variant spelling of BRAILEY or BRALEY.

Brallier (159) French: occupational name for a belt maker, from Old French *braielier*

(from *braiel* 'belt' + *braie* 'hose', 'breeches').

Braly (387) **1.** Variant spelling of BRALEY or BRAILEY. **2.** Possibly an altered spelling of German **Brelie**, a habitational name from Brelingen near Hannover.

Bram (343) **1.** German: variant of BRAHM 2. **2.** Jewish (Ashkenazic and Sephardic): from a reduced form of the Biblical name *Abraham* (see ABRAHAM). **3.** Danish and Swedish: from the Nordic personal name *Bram*. **4.** French: variant of BRAME.

Braman (959) North German (**Bramann**): topographic name from Middle Low German *brām* 'swampy thicket' + *man* 'man', or a respelling of **Brahmann**, a contracted form of **Brademann**, of uncertain origin.

Bramante (129) Italian: from a derivative of *bramare* 'to desire', 'to long for', presumably applied as a nickname.
GIVEN NAMES Italian 29%. *Salvatore* (3), *Domenic* (2), *Concetta, Giuseppe, Nicola, Nunzio, Pietro, Sal, Vittorio*.

Brambila (217) Altered spelling of Italian **Brambilla**, a habitational name, common in Milan, for someone from Brembilla, a place in Bergamo. In this form, which is not found in Italy, the surname has been brought to the U.S. via Mexico, where it is also well established.
GIVEN NAMES Spanish 58%. *Jose* (5), *Juan* (5), *Francisco* (3), *Jaime* (3), *Manuel* (3), *Miguel* (3), *Alfredo* (2), *Armando* (2), *Asuncion* (2), *Isidro* (2), *Luis* (2), *Rafael* (2).

Bramble (1002) English: **1.** from Old English *brēmel, braemel* 'bramble', 'blackberry bush', hence a topographic name for someone who lived by a blackberry thicket or possibly a nickname for a prickly person. **2.** variant of BRAMHALL.

Bramblett (764) English: variant of BRAMLETT.

Brame (1025) **1.** English: variant of BREAM 1. **2.** French: from Old Occitan *brame* 'cry', 'howl', presumably applied as a nickname.

Bramel (255) **1.** German: habitational name from Bramel near Stade, Lower Saxony. **2.** German: nickname for a person with a sharp tongue, from Middle Low German *breme, brame*, 'thorn bush', later 'horsefly'. **3.** English: altered form of BRAMHALL reflecting the local pronunciation. Compare BRAMMELL.

Bramer (691) **1.** German: topographic name in the south for someone who lived where brambles grew (see BRAHM 3). **2.** German (**Brämer**): variant of BREMER. **3.** Jewish (eastern Ashkenazic): occupational name for a janitor, Yiddishized form of Polish *bramarz*.
GIVEN NAMES German 4%. *Kurt* (6), *Otto* (2), *Dieter*.

Bramhall (497) English: habitational name from either of two places, in Greater Manchester (formerly in Cheshire) and

Sheffield, South Yorkshire, named with Old English *brōm* 'broom' + *halh* 'nook', 'recess'. See also BRAMWELL.

Bramlage (151) North German: habitational name from a place near Oldenburg named Bramlage.
GIVEN NAME French 4%. *Damien.*

Bramlet (182) English: variant of BRAMLETT.

Bramlett (2005) English: unexplained. This American family name was widespread recorded in England in the 17th century, especially in Durham and Yorkshire, but has died out in present-day England.

Bramlette (163) Frenchified spelling of BRAMLETT.

Bramley (347) English (North Midlands): habitational name from any of various places (in Derbyshire, Hampshire, Surrey, Yorkshire, and elsewhere) named Bramley, from Old English *brōm* 'broom', 'gorse' + *lēah* 'woodland clearing'.

Brammeier (143) German: distinguishing name for a tenant farmer (see MEYER) who farmed land on which there was a swampy thicket, Middle Low German *brām*.
GIVEN NAMES German 7%. *Alois, Lorenz, Otto.*

Brammell (133) **1.** English: variant of BRAMHALL or BRAMWELL. **2.** Altered spelling of German **Brammel**, a variant of BRAMEL.

Brammer (1804) **1.** German; Danish and Swedish (of German origin): habitational name from either of two places called Brammer, near Rendsburg and Verden. **2.** English: variant of BRAMHALL, or possibly a habitational name from Breamore in Hampshire (from Old English *brōm* 'broom' + *mōr* 'moor', 'marsh'). **3.** Possibly a variant of BREMMER.

Bramson (232) **1.** English: patronymic from BRAND 1. **2.** Jewish (Ashkenazic): patronymic from *Bram*, a reduced form of ABRAHAM. **3.** Americanized spelling of Danish **Bramsen**, a patronymic from BRAM.
GIVEN NAMES Jewish 5%. *Gadi, Mort, Noam.*

Bramstedt (129) North German: habitational name from any of several places so named in northern Germany.
GIVEN NAMES German 8%. *Fritz* (2), *Kurt* (2).

Bramwell (458) English: habitational name, apparently from a lost or unidentified places called Bramwell (named in Old English *brōm* 'broom', 'gorse' + *well(a)* 'spring', 'stream'). However, it may well be a variant of BRAMHALL.

Bran (160) **1.** Scottish: nickname from Gaelic *bran* 'raven'. **2.** Galician: habitational name from either of two places in Lugo province called Bran. This is a common name in Mexico.
GIVEN NAMES Spanish 35%. *Manuel* (4), *Carlos* (3), *Jose* (3), *Cesar* (2), *Miguel* (2), *Beatriz, Blanca, Candido, Concepcion, Elena, Fernando, Gerardo.*

Branagan (286) Irish: variant of BRANNIGAN.

Branam (757) Variant of English BRANHAM.

Branaman (240) **1.** Americanized spelling of North German **Brannemann**, a habitational name for someone from a place named Brande, near Hamburg. **2.** Americanized spelling of Swiss German **Brennemann** (see BRENNEMAN).

Branan (334) Variant of Irish BRANNAN.

Branca (523) Italian: **1.** from *branca* 'claw', 'hand', hence a nickname for someone with a deformity of the hand or possibly for a grasping person. **2.** from a short form of a compound personal name formed such as *Brancaleone* ('lion's paw').
GIVEN NAMES Italian 11%. *Salvatore* (3), *Guido* (2), *Rocco* (2), *Angelo, Carmine, Constantino, Francesco, Lorenzo, Natale, Nunzi, Pasco, Raffaele.*

Brancaccio (189) Southern Italian: **1.** from a metathesized form of the personal name *Pancrazio*, Latin *Pancratius*, from Greek *Pankratios* (see PANKRATZ). **2.** habitational name from a place named Brancaccio, as for example near Palermo, Sicily.
GIVEN NAMES Italian 14%; French 5%. *Carmine, Ciro, Gino, Giovanna, Lia, Pasquale, Salvatore; Armand* (2), *Alphonse.*

Brancato (694) Italian (Sicily): variant of BRANCACCIO, probably from the Greek form of the personal name.
GIVEN NAMES Italian 15%. *Salvatore* (10), *Vito* (7), *Santo* (3), *Carmela* (2), *Carmelo* (2), *Cosmo, Enza, Gaetano, Giacomo, Gilda, Giorgio, Marco.*

Branch (9994) English: from Middle English, Old French *branche* 'branch' (Late Latin *branca* 'foot', 'paw'), the application of which as a surname is not clear. In America it has been adopted as a translation of any of the numerous Swedish surnames containing the element *gren* 'branch', and likewise of French LABRANCHE, German ZWEIG, and Finnish **Haara, Oksa**, and **Oksana**.

Branchaud (150) Variant of French **Branchereau**, a diminutive of BRANCHE.
FOREBEARS A bearer of the name Branchaud or Branchereau, also called Lacombe, from the Saintonge region of France is recorded in St. Laurent, Quebec, in 1694.
GIVEN NAMES French 18%. *Armand* (3), *Andre* (2), *Jacques* (2), *Jean Claude, Julien.*

Branche (278) French: from Old French *branche* 'branch' (Late Latin *branca* 'foot', 'paw'), the application of which as a surname is not clear. Compare BRANCH.
FOREBEARS A Branche from the Poitou region of France is documented in Quebec city in 1665; another, from Toulouse, is recorded at Champlain in 1699, with the secondary surname Tous les Jours.
GIVEN NAMES French 5%. *Andre, Jacques, Marcel.*

Brancheau (208) Variant of French **Branchereau**, a diminutive of BRANCHE.
GIVEN NAME French 4%. *Andre.*

Branciforte (146) Italian (Sicily): nickname from *branc(h)i* 'claws', 'hands' (plural of *branca*) + *forte* 'strong'.
GIVEN NAMES Italian 32%. *Angelo* (7), *Salvatore* (4), *Sal* (3), *Alfonso, Carmelo, Emilio, Gasper, Giuseppe, Mario, Rosario, Santo, Vito.*

Branco (679) Portuguese: nickname for a man with white or fair hair or a pale complexion, from Portuguese *branco* 'white'.
GIVEN NAMES Spanish 21%; Portuguese 13%. *Manuel* (18), *Jose* (14), *Carlos* (5), *Mario* (4), *Antero* (3), *Domingos* (3), *Fernando* (2), *Helio* (2), *Marcelo* (2), *Nuno* (2), *Adelino, Adilia; Joao* (4), *Joaquim* (3); *Antonio* (23), *Cesario* (2), *Angelo, Flavio.*

Brand (7168) **1.** English, Scottish, Scandinavian, North German, and Dutch: from the Germanic personal name *Brando*, a short form of various compound personal names containing the element *brand* 'sword' (a derivative of *brinnan* 'to flash'), of which the best known is HILDEBRAND. There is place name evidence for *Brant(a)* as an Old English personal name; however, the Middle English personal name *Brand* was probably introduced to England from Old Norse; *Brandr* is a common Old Norse personal name. **2.** English: topographic name for someone who lived by a place where burning had occurred, from Old English *brand*, or a habitational name from a minor place named with this word, as for example The Brand in Northamptonshire and Nottinghamshire. **3.** German: variant of BRANDT 1. **4.** Scandinavian: from the personal name *Brand, Brant*, from Old Norse *Brandr* (see 1). **5.** Swedish: ornamental name from *brand* 'fire'. **6.** Jewish (Ashkenazic): ornamental name or nickname from German *Brant* 'fire', 'conflagration'.

Branda (188) Italian: **1.** from Germanic *branda-* 'sword' (via French *brand, brande*). **2.** possibly a variant of BRANDO, or of **Blanda**, from the female personal name, from the feminine form of the adjective *blando* 'soft', 'mild'.
GIVEN NAME Italian 4%. *Pasquale.*

Brandao (147) Portuguese (**Brandão**): from the medieval Latin form, *Brendanus*, of the old Irish personal name *Brénainn* (English *Brendan*).
GIVEN NAMES Spanish 28%; Portuguese 19%; Italian 9%. *Jose* (5), *Manuel* (4), *Fernando* (2), *Roberto* (2), *Sergio* (2), *Augusto, Carlos, Domingo, Edgardo, Elvira, Evandro, Fabio; Joao* (2); *Antonio* (5), *Caio, Filomena, Vitorino.*

Brandau (481) German: habitational name from any of several places called Brandau, in Hesse, Bavaria, and former East Prussia.

Brande (134) Variant of BRAND.

Brandeberry (210) Probably an Americanized form of German BRANDENBERG or BRANDENBURG.

Brandeis (118) Jewish (Ashkenazic): habitational name from the Czech town of Brandýs, on the Labe (Elbe) river, called Brandeis in German.

Brandel (512) **1.** German: from a pet form of the personal name BRAND 1. **2.** Altered spelling of South German **Brändle** (see BRANDLE). **3.** Swedish: from the Germanic personal name *Brand* (see BRAND 1) + *-ell*, a common suffix of Swedish surnames, taken from the Latin adjectival ending *-elius*. **4.** Swedish: habitational name for someone from a place named with *brand* 'fire'.

Brandell (142) Swedish: variant spelling of BRANDEL.

Branden (129) **1.** Swedish: ornamental name composed of the personal name BRAND 1 (or the place name element *brand*) + the adjectival suffix *-én*, from Latin *-enius*. **2.** Possibly a respelling of English BRANDON, or alternatively a shortened form of any of the various German family names beginning with *Branden-* (see the following entries).

Brandenberg (129) German and Swiss German: habitational name from any of several minor places called Brandenberg, for example in Bavaria and Rhineland, or in some cases probably a variant of BRANDENBURG.

Brandenberger (251) Swiss German: habitational name for someone from a place called BRANDENBERG.

Brandenburg (3594) German: regional and habitational name from Brandenburg, the name of a former province, now a state of eastern Germany, its principal city, and numerous other places.

Brandenburger (246) German: regional and habitational name for someone from BRANDENBURG.

Brandenstein (163) German: habitational name from any of various places in central Germany, particularly castles, named Brandenstein.

Brander (332) **1.** Dutch: occupational name for an inspector of weights and measures. **2.** German and Swiss German: habitational name for someone from any of the many places called Brand or Brandt (see BRANDT). **3.** Jewish (Ashkenazic): perhaps an occupational name for fireman or distiller, from German *Brand*, Yiddish *brand* 'conflagration'. **4.** Dutch: nickname for a fire raiser. **5.** Danish: habitational name for someone from a place called Brande.

Brandes (1274) **1.** German: patronymic from the personal name BRAND. **2.** German and Jewish (Ashkenazic): variant of BRANDEIS
GIVEN NAMES German 5%. *Kurt* (4), *Hans* (2), *Monika* (2), *Eldred, Ewald, Fritz, Guenther, Heinz, Karlheinz, Otto, Ute.*

Brandewie (125) Probably an altered form of German BRANDWEIN.

Brandhorst (206) North German: habitational name from any of several places called Brandhorst, in Westphalia and Saxony-Anhalt, the element *-horst* denoting a thicket or a hillock in a swamp.
GIVEN NAMES German 5%. *Armin, Helmut.*

Brandi (290) Italian: patronymic or plural form of BRANDO.
GIVEN NAMES Italian 19%. *Guido* (3), *Antonio* (2), *Angelo, Attilio, Cinzia, Emilio, Luigi, Onorato, Otilia, Rico.*

Brandin (111) Swedish: unexplained ornamental name.
GIVEN NAMES Scandinavian 19%. *Alf* (2), *Erik* (2), *Lennart, Per.*

Brandis (217) **1.** Swiss and German: habitational name from a former Brandis castle in Emmental near Bern, Switzerland, or from any of the places so named in Saxony, Germany. **2.** Jewish (Ashkenazic): variant of BRANDEIS.

Brandl (638) German (**Brändl**): from a pet form of the personal name BRAND 1.
GIVEN NAMES German 5%. *Alois* (2), *Bernd, Erwin, Franz, Hans, Klaus, Reinhardt, Siegmund, Wenzel.*

Brandle (226) South German (**Brändle**): from a pet form of the personal name BRAND 1.
GIVEN NAMES German 4%. *Hans, Kurt.*

Brandley (164) Americanized spelling of German BRANDLE or BRANDLI.

Brandli (132) Swiss German (**Brändli**): topographic name for someone who lived near a burnt area (in the woods or in a town).
GIVEN NAMES German 4%. *Gottlieb, Monika.*

Brandman (117) Jewish (Ashkenazic): ornamental name, a derivative of BRAND 6.
GIVEN NAMES Jewish 10%. *Ephraim, Faina, Naftula, Yigal, Yossi.*

Brandmeyer (125) German: distinguishing name for a tenant farmer (see MEYER) who farmed land that had been cleared by burning (see BRANDT).
GIVEN NAME German 4%. *Otto.*

Brandner (534) Altered form of German BRANTNER.
GIVEN NAMES German 4%. *Kurt* (2), *Gerhard, Heinz, Math.*

Brando (103) Italian: from the Germanic (Lombardic) personal name *Brando*, a short form of the various compound personal names formed with *brand* 'sword', particularly *Aldobrando* and *Ildebrando*.
GIVEN NAMES Italian 25%; Spanish 8%. *Antonio* (2), *Carmela, Concetta, Cono, Dante, Salvatore, Vito; Carlos* (2), *Juan* (2), *Juan Carlos.*

Brandom (108) English: variant of BRANDON.

Brandon (7897) **1.** English: habitational name from any of various places called Brandon, in County Durham, Northumbria, Norfolk, Suffolk, Warwickshire, and elsewhere. Most are named with Old English *brōm* 'broom', 'gorse' + *dūn* 'hill'. One in Lincolnshire, however, may be named with the Brant river, on which it stands; Ekwall derives the river name from Old English *brant* 'steep', presumably with reference to its steep banks. **2.** Irish (Kerry): Anglicized form of Gaelic **Mac Breandáin** 'son of *Breandán*'. **3.** French: from the Old French oblique case of the personal name *Brand*, of Germanic origin (see BRAND 1).

Brandow (542) Variant of German BRANDAU.

Brands (413) German and Dutch: patronymic from the personal name BRAND 1.
GIVEN NAMES German 5%. *Otto* (3), *Detlef, Ewald.*

Brandsma (135) Frisian: topographic name for someone who lived in an area that had been cleared by fire. Compare German BRANDT.

Brandstetter (304) German: habitational name for someone from any of the many places called Brandstatt, Brandstädt, Brandstätt, Brandstett, and Brandstetten, all from element meaning 'place cleared by burning'.
GIVEN NAMES French 4%; German 4%. *Alois, Franz, Wolf.*

Brandt (15519) German: **1.** topographic name for someone who lived in an area that had been cleared by fire, Middle High German *brant* (from *brennen* 'to burn'). **2.** variant of BRAND 1.

Brandvold (250) Norwegian: habitational name from any of various farms named Brandvoll, from *brand-* 'fire', 'burning' + *voll* (from Old Norse *vǫllr* 'green field').

Brandwein (236) Jewish (Ashkenazic) and German: occupational name for a distiller, from German *Branntwein* 'spirits', 'brandy'.
GIVEN NAMES Jewish 7%. *Avraham, Mechel, Mordecai, Shmuel, Yitzchok.*

Brandy (244) Americanized form of BRANDWEIN or a variant or cognate of this name.

Braner (149) Possibly an altered spelling of German BREINER.

Branford (119) English: habitational name from Bramford in Suffolk or Brampford Speke in Devon. Both places are named with Old English *brōm* 'broom' + *ford* 'ford'.

Brangers (105) Dutch and Belgian: Flemish variant of BRANDER.

Branham (4390) English: habitational name, possibly from Bramham in West Yorkshire or Brantham in Suffolk. The first is named with Old English *brōm* 'broom' + *hām* 'homestead' or *hamm* 'river meadow'; the second is from the Old English personal name *Branta* + *hām* or *hamm*.

Braniff (246) Irish: Anglicized form of Gaelic **Ó Branduibh** 'descendant of *Brandubh*', a personal name composed of the elements *bran* 'raven' + *dubh* 'black'.

Branigan (496) Irish: variant spelling of BRANNIGAN.
GIVEN NAME Irish 5%. *Donal.*

Branin (192) Probably an altered spelling of Irish BRANNAN.

Brank (146) **1.** Altered form of German **Branke**, from a pet form of the Slavic personal name *Branislaw*. **2.** Slovenian form of FRANK.

Brann (1312) **1.** English: nickname from Gaelic and Welsh *bran* 'raven'. **2.** Jewish (Ashkenazic): Hebrew acronym consisting of *ben-rabi* 'son of' + the initials of some personal name (for example *Nachman*, *Nahum*, *Nathan*).

Brannam (171) English: variant of BRANHAM.
GIVEN NAME French 5%. *Collette.*

Brannan (2698) Irish: variant of BRENNAN.

Brannen (1615) Irish: variant of BRENNAN.

Branner (242) **1.** Danish: variant of BRANDER. **2.** German: variant of BRANTNER.

Brannick (159) Irish: Anglicized form of Gaelic *Breathnach* 'Briton' (*Breithneach* in Donegal and Ulster), typically applied to a Welsh speaker.

Brannigan (551) Irish: Anglicized form of Gaelic **Ó Branagáin** 'descendant of *Branagán*', a personal name from a double diminutive of *bran* 'raven'. Compare BRENNAN and BYRNE.
GIVEN NAME Irish 5%. *Brendan.*

Brannin (131) Variant of Irish BRENNAN.

Branning (497) German: derivative of BRAND 1, the suffix *-ing* denoting affiliation, i.e. 'the people of Brand'.

Brannock (594) Irish: habitational name, taken to Ireland by medieval settlers from Brecknock in Wales.

Brannon (5647) Variant of Irish BRENNAN.

Brannum (249) Variant of English BRANHAM.

Branom (125) Variant of English BRANHAM.

Branon (204) Variant of Irish BRENNAN.

Branscom (184) Variant of English BRANSCOMB.

Branscomb (256) English: habitational name from Branscombe in Devon, which is named from the Celtic personal name *Branoc* + Old English *cumb* 'valley'. The usual English spelling is *Branscombe*, as in the place name.

Branscome (345) Variant of English BRANSCOMB.

Branscum (830) Variant of English BRANSCOMB.

Bransfield (218) Scottish and northern Irish: habitational name from a farm so named in the Strathclyde region of Scotland, south of Glasgow.

Bransford (423) English: habitational name from a place in Worcestershire, named Bransford, from Old English *bræġen* 'hill' + *ford* 'hill'.

Bransky (114) Jewish (eastern Ashkenazic): habitational name from a place called Brańsk in eastern Poland.

Bransom (158) English and Irish: variant of BRANSON 2.
GIVEN NAMES Irish 4%. *Deirdre*, *Delma.*

Branson (3999) English: **1.** habitational name from any of several places: Branston in Leicestershire, Lincolnshire, and Staffordshire, Brandeston in Suffolk, Brandiston in Norfolk, or Braunston in Leicestershire and Northamptonshire. All are named with the Old English personal name *Brant* + *tūn* 'settlement'. **2.** (of Norman origin) habitational name from a place called Briençun in northern France. Compare BRINSON. **3.** patronymic from the personal name *Brand* (see BRAND).

Branstad (100) Swedish: habitational name from any of various places called Brandsta, Brandstad, Bransta, Brånsta, or Brånstad.

Branstetter (1010) German: variant of BRANDSTETTER.

Branstrom (118) Swedish (**Brännström** or **Brändström**): ornamental name composed of the elements *bränna* 'to burn' + *ström* 'stream', or habitational name from a place named with these elements.

Brant (3620) English, German, Jewish (Ashkenazic), and Dutch: variant of BRAND.

Branting (102) Swedish: probably a habitational name from a place name formed with *brant* 'steep', 'steep hill' + the suffix *-ing*.
GIVEN NAME Scandinavian 4%. *Morten.*

Brantingham (111) English (Durham): habitational name from Brantingham in East Yorkshire, named in Old English as 'the homestead (*hām*) of the people of *Branta*', or possibly as 'homestead of the people living on a hillside', from Old English *brant* 'hillside', 'steep slope'.

Brantley (6502) Americanized spelling of Swiss German **Brändle** and **Brändli** (also **Brändly**), topographic names for someone who lived near a place where there had been a forest fire or in an area of town that had been burned down.

Brantly (167) Variant of Swiss German **Brändle** or **Brändli** (see BRANTLEY).

Brantner (730) German (also **Bräntner**): topographic name for a settler on land cleared by fire, from Middle High German *brant* 'burnt' + the suffix *-ner* denoting an inhabitant.

Branton (1031) English: habitational name from places called Branton in South Yorkshire (formerly in West Yorkshire) and Northumberland or from Braunton in Devon. The first and last are named with Old English *brōm* 'broom' + *tūn* 'farmstead', 'settlement'. The second is from an Old English word *brēmen* 'overgrown with broom' + *tūn* 'farmstead'.

Branum (1019) Variant of English BRANHAM.

Branyan (145) English: unexplained.

Branyon (213) English: unexplained.

Branz (169) South German: **1.** from a pet form of BRAND 1. **2.** (of Slavic origin) from a pet form of *Franciscus* (see FRANCIS).

Brar (244) Indian (Panjab): Sikh name based on the name of a tribe in the Jat community.
GIVEN NAMES Indian 84%. *Gurdarshan* (3), *Ajit* (2), *Jagroop* (2), *Navdeep* (2), *Pritam* (2), *Raj* (2), *Saroj* (2), *Ajmer*, *Amar*, *Avtar*, *Balwinder*, *Bhola.*

Bras (107) **1.** Dutch and North German: from Old French and Middle Dutch *bras* 'arm'. This was probably a descriptive nickname for someone with some peculiarity of the arm, but the word was also used as a measure of length, and may also have denoted a surveyor. **2.** Spanish: from the personal name, a vernacular form of BLASIUS, popularized through the cult of the 4th century Christian martyr. Compare Portuguese BRAZ
GIVEN NAMES Spanish 12%; French 8%; Portuguese 7%. *Rafael* (3), *Armando*, *Cesar*, *Gilberto*, *Jorge*, *Jose*, *Juaquin*, *Julio*; *Andre*, *Francois*, *Thierry*; *Joao.*

Brasch (478) **1.** North German and Danish: variant of BRAASCH. **2.** German: from a reduced form of the Latin personal name *Ambrosius* (see AMBROSE).

Brase (423) North German: variant of BRASS 2.

Brasel (528) **1.** German (**Bräsel**): from a reduced pet form of the Latin personal name *Ambrosius* (see AMBROSE). **2.** North German: nickname for a forgetful or scatter-brained person, from Low German *braselich*. **3.** Jewish: unexplained.
GIVEN NAMES Jewish 4%. *Menachem*, *Mirra*, *Yakov.*

Braselton (189) English: variant of BRAZELTON.

Brasfield (781) See BRASSFIELD.

Brash (254) **1.** Scottish: probably a nickname for an impetuous person, from northern English dialect *brasche* 'rash', 'impetuous' (associated with *brasche* 'assault', 'attack', a word of imitative origin). **2.** Americanized spelling of German BRAASCH.

Brashear (1757) Of French (Huguenot) origin: Americanized variant of BRASSEUR. The traditional pronunciation is with the stress on the second syllable.
FOREBEARS **Brasseur** is a Huguenot family name that was brought to VA and MD around 1635. The family multiplied greatly, and the name is found in a profusion of different spellings, including **Brashear**, **Boshears**, and **Bashear**. The variant **Beshears** arose in 18th-century TN.

Brashears (826) Americanized form of French (Huguenot) BRASSEUR. Compare BRESHEARS.

Brasher (2297) **1.** English: occupational name for a brewer, from Old French *brasser* 'to brew' (Late Latin *braciare*, a derivative of *braces* 'malt', of Gaulish origin). **2.** English: variant of BRAZIER. **3.** Of French (Huguenot) origin: Americanized form of BRASSEUR, assimilated to the English name.

Brashers (154) Variant of BRASHER.

Brashier (479) Americanized form of French BRASIER or BRASSEUR.

Brasier (372) **1.** French: according to Morlet, an occupational name for a cook, from an agent derivative of *braise* 'embers'. **2.** English: variant spelling of BRAZIER.
GIVEN NAMES French 4%. *Celina, Raoul.*

Brasil (208) Portuguese and Spanish: ethnic name for someone from Brazil.
GIVEN NAMES Spanish 35%; Portuguese 23%. *Jose* (13), *Manuel* (13), *Luis* (3), *Orlando* (3), *Carlos* (2), *Isidro* (2), *Jorge* (2), *Adriano, Alberto, Alvaro, Ana, Armando*; *Duarte* (2), *Joao* (2), *Albano, Conceicao, Guilherme*; *Antonio* (9), *Angelo, Filomena, Sandro.*

Brasington (333) English: variant spelling of BRASSINGTON.

Brass (934) **1.** English (Northumberland): variant of BRACE. **2.** North German (also **Bräss**): nickname from Middle Low German *brās* 'noise', 'pomp', a related form of *brāsch* (see BRAASCH). **3.** German: topographic name from *Brass* 'broom', 'gorse', a common name element in the Lower Rhine and Ruhr.

Brassard (682) French: **1.** from a derivative of Old French *braz* 'arm', possibly applied as a nickname for someone of exceptional strength or a pugilist. **2.** metonymic occupational name for an armorer, from *brassard* 'armor for the arm'. **3.** occupational name for a brewer, from a derivative of *brasser* 'to brew (beer)'.
FOREBEARS A bearer of the name from Normandy is recorded in Quebec city in 1637. The secondary surnames Deschenaux and Bordet are documented in 1711 and 1723, respectively.
GIVEN NAMES French 12%. *Andre* (3), *Jacques* (2), *Lucien* (2), *Amedee, Amie, Antoine, Armand, Emile, Fernand, Florent, Gaston, Germaine.*

Brasseaux (284) Altered spelling (characteristic of LA) of French **Brasseau**, a variant of BRASSELL.
GIVEN NAMES French 6%. *Nelma* (2), *Clemile, Easton, Euclide.*

Brassel (105) **1.** French: from a variant of Old French *bracel* 'bracelet'. **2.** French: from a derivative of Old French *brace*, a measure of length equivalent to two outstretched arms, hence probably a metonymic occupational name for someone whose job involved taking measurements. **3.** German: nickname for a glutton, from Swabian *prasslen* 'to indulge or feast'.

Brassell (375) Altered spelling of BRASSEL.

Brasser (141) Dutch: nickname for a heavy drinker, from an agent noun derivative of *brasser* 'to carouse'.
GIVEN NAME German 5%. *Kurt* (2).

Brasseur (278) French and English (of both Norman and Huguenot origin): occupational name for a brewer, from Old French *brasser* 'to brew'. See also BRASHER.
GIVEN NAMES French 11%. *Michel* (5), *Georges, Jean Claude, Martial, Yves.*

Brassfield (657) English: unexplained. It has the form of a habitational name, possibly of Norman origin, but no source has been identified.

Brassil (149) Irish: variant of BRAZIL.

Brassington (155) English: habitational name from a place in Derbyshire, which is probably named as 'the settlement (Old English *tūn*) associated with a man named *Brandsige*'. *Brandsige*, composed of the elements *brand* 'sword' + *sige* 'victory', is not attested as an Old English personal name, but seems plausible.

Brasuell (152) Perhaps a variant of English BRACEWELL.

Braswell (4655) English: perhaps a variant of BRACEWELL.

Bratcher (2745) **1.** English: variant of BRACH 2, the suffix -*er* denoting an inhabitant. **2.** Probably a partly Americanized form of Swiss German **Bretscher**, an occupational name for a sawyer, from *Brett* 'plank', 'board' + *scher*, a reduced form of *Scherer* 'cutter', a derivative of *scheren* 'to cut', 'sever'.

Bratek (103) Slovak and Slovenian: nickname meaning 'little brother', from a diminutive of *brat* 'brother'.

Brathwaite (628) English: variant of BRAITHWAITE.

Bratland (144) Norwegian: habitational name from a farm so named, from *bratt* 'steep' + *land* 'farm land'.
GIVEN NAME Scandinavian 6%. *Per.*

Bratsch (182) German (also **Brätsch**): from a diminutive of the Slavic word *brat* 'brother'.

Bratt (711) **1.** English (West Midlands): of uncertain origin; possibly a nickname for an unruly child, or somebody who behaved like one, though this sense of *brat* is not recorded by OED before the 16th century. Alternatively, it may be derived from the older word *brat(te)* 'apron', 'pinafore' (of Celtic origin), as a nickname for someone who habitually wore one. **2.** Swedish and Norwegian: from the Old Norse personal name *Brattr* meaning 'majestic', 'proud' (also, of places, 'steep'). See also BRADT.

Brattain (289) Scottish: variant of BRATTEN.

Bratten (444) **1.** Scottish: Anglicized form of the Gaelic surname **Mac an Bhreatnaich** 'son of the Briton', originally denoting a Strathclyde Welsh-speaking Briton. It was applied in Ireland also to people from Brittany. Compare BRETT, MCBRATNEY.

2. Swedish (**Brattén**): ornamental name composed of the personal name *Bratt* + the surname suffix -*én*, from Latin -*enius* 'descendant of'. **3.** variant of Norwegian BRAATEN.

Brattin (197) Scottish: variant of BRATTEN.

Brattle (1) English: habitational name from the village of Brattle, near Ashford in Kent. FOREBEARS Thomas Brattle (*c.*1624–83) was reckoned, at the time of his death, to be the wealthiest man in New England. His son, also called Thomas Brattle (1658–1713), treasurer of Harvard College from 1693 to 1713, was a man noted for his rationality and humanism, which included opposition to the Salem withccraft trials of 1692.

Bratton (3360) **1.** Scottish and northern Irish: variant spelling of BRATTEN. **2.** English: habitational name from any of the places called Bratten (in Shropshire, Somerset, and Wiltshire) or from Bratton Clovelly or Bratton Fleming in Devon. The Shropshire and Somerset places are named with Old English *brōc* 'hook' + *tūn* 'settlement'. The Wiltshire and Devon names are from Old English *brǣc* 'newly cultivated ground' + *tūn*.

Bratvold (104) Norwegian: habitational name from a farm so named, from *bratt* 'steep' + *voll* 'meadow', 'grassy field'.

Bratz (307) German: from a diminutive of the Slavic word *brat* 'brother'.

Brau (210) **1.** South German (**Bräu**): from a primitive form of the agent noun for a brewer, Middle High German *briuwe*. **2.** North German: from Middle Low German *brüw(e)* denoting 'a set quantity brewed at once'. **3.** Catalan and southern French: nickname from *brau* 'wild', from Latin *barbarus* 'barbarian', 'ruffian'.

Brauch (311) South German: from a derivative of Middle High German *brüchen* 'to enjoy', hence a nickname for a gourmet or self-indulgent person.

Braucher (144) German: from an agent derivative of Middle High German *brüchen* 'to enjoy' (see BRAUCH).

Brauchle (119) German: nickname for a gourmet or gourmand, from a pet form of BRAUCH.
GIVEN NAMES German 9%. *Kurt* (2), *Aloysius, Otto.*

Braucht (113) German: probably a variant of BRAUCH, with the addition of an excrescent -*t*.

Braud (776) French: **1.** from a reduced form of the Germanic personal name *Ber(n)wald*, composed of the elements *ber(n)* 'bear' + *wald* 'rule'. Compare BRAULT. **2.** habitational name from a place in Gironde named Braud.
GIVEN NAMES French 4%. *Colette, Dominique, Elphege, Ferrel.*

Braude (178) Jewish (eastern Ashkenazic): Germanized form of Yiddish *Broyd*, the Jewish name for the town in Moravia called

Ungarisch Brod in German and Uhersky Brod in Czech.

GIVEN NAMES Jewish 13%; Russian 12%. *Avi* (2), *Baruch, Irina, Miriam, Mordechai, Ruvim, Yaakov; Elizaveta, Igor, Iosif, Konstantin, Leonid, Lyudmila, Maks, Mikhail, Nikolay, Vladimir, Yuliy.*

Brauer (2122) North German and Ashkenazic Jewish, or Americanized form of German **Bräuer**, an occupational name for a brewer of beer or ale, from Middle Low German *brūwer* or Middle High German *briuwer* 'brewer'.

GIVEN NAMES German 5%. *Otto* (6), *Kurt* (4), *Dieter* (2), *Erwin* (2), *Ewald* (2), *Gerhard* (2), *Benno, Claus, Elke, Gunther, Hans, Harro.*

Braughton (184) English: probably a variant spelling of BROUGHTON.

Brault (791) French: variant of BRAUD. This is the more common spelling in Canada and New England, where it is most frequent. It is sometimes Americanized as BROW or BROWN.

FOREBEARS A Brault from La Rochelle, bearing the secondary surname Pomainville, is documented in Quebec city in 1665. Another, from the Saintonge region, is documented in Montreal in 1697 with the secondary surname Lafleur.

GIVEN NAMES French 13%. *Armand* (4), *Adelard* (3), *Alain* (2), *Andre* (2), *Gilles* (2), *Rosaire* (2), *Solange* (2), *Cecile, Emile, Francoise, Germaine, Girard.*

Braum (111) **1.** Americanized form of German BRAHM. **2.** Jewish (Ashkenazic): perhaps a variant of BRAUN.

Braun (14113) German and Jewish (Ashkenazic): nickname from German *braun* 'brown' (Middle High German *brūn*), referring to the color of the hair, complexion, or clothing, or from the personal name *Bruno*, which was borne by the Dukes of Saxony, among others, from the 10th century or before. It was also the name of several medieval German and Italian saints, including St. Bruno, the founder of the Carthusian order (1030–1101), who was born in Cologne.

GIVEN NAMES German 4%. *Kurt* (24), *Hans* (12), *Ernst* (9), *Otto* (8), *Alois* (6), *Gerhard* (5), *Helmut* (5), *Fritz* (4), *Heinz* (4), *Joerg* (4), *Wolfgang* (4), *Egon* (3).

Braunagel (116) German: metonymic occupational name for a nail smith, from *braun* 'brown' + *nagel* 'nail'.

GIVEN NAMES German 9%. *Wendelin* (2), *Egon.*

Braund (287) English (Devon): variant of BRAND 1.

Braune (181) German: variant of BRAUN.

GIVEN NAMES German 12%. *Kurt* (2), *Dietmar, Erwin, Fritz, Siegfried.*

Brauner (608) **1.** German: from a Germanic personal name, a compound of *Brun(o)* + *her* 'army'. **2.** German: from a term denoting a follower of the Brunones, a

dynasty of medieval (Lower) Saxony. **3.** German: habitational name for someone from Brauna near Kamenz, Saxony, or from Braunau in Austria. **4.** Jewish (Ashkenazic): from German *Brauner* 'the brown one'. **5.** Swedish and Danish: of German origin.

GIVEN NAMES German 7%. *Gunther* (2), *Otto* (2), *Wolf* (2), *Friedrich, Fritz, Hans, Klaus, Kurt, Wenzel.*

Brauning (133) German (**Bräuning**): patronymic from a Germanic personal name *Brun(o)*, becoming **Brüning** in northern Germany and **Bräuning** in the south.

GIVEN NAMES German 8%. *Gernot, Gunther, Helmut.*

Braunlich (105) German (**Bräunlich**): variant of **Bräunling**, from a Germanic personal name (see BRAUNING).

GIVEN NAMES German 8%. *Elke, Fritz, Helmut.*

Brauns (163) Dutch, German, and Latvian: patronymic from the personal name *Bruno* (see BRAUN).

Braunschweig (245) German and Jewish (western Ashkenazic): habitational name from the city of Braunschweig in Lower Saxony, known in English as Brunswick. The place name is from the genitive case of the Germanic personal name *Bruno* (borne by the Duke of Saxony who founded the city in 861) + Old Saxon *wīk* 'dwelling place', 'settlement'.

GIVEN NAMES German 8%. *Heinz, Juergen, Kurt, Otto, Reinhold.*

Braunstein (1111) Jewish (Ashkenazic): ornamental name composed of German *braun* 'brown' + *Stein* 'stone'.

GIVEN NAMES Jewish 6%. *Mozes* (2), *Shlomo* (2), *Blima, Chaim, Elihu, Faigy, Lazer, Lipot, Mendel, Sol, Yehuda, Yetta.*

Brause (155) German: **1.** from a vernacular pet form of the Latin personal name *Ambrosius* (see AMBROSE). **2.** nickname for a stormy, tempestuous person, from Middle High German *brūs* 'noise', 'roar'.

GIVEN NAMES German 13%. *Eckhard* (2), *Gerhard* (2), *Manfred, Otto.*

Brausen (120) German: habitational name from either of two places called Brausen, in former East and West Prussia.

GIVEN NAMES German 8%. *Aloysius, Gunter, Kurt, Reinhard, Reinhardt.*

Brautigam (485) German (**Bräutigam**): from a kinship term, Middle High German *briutegome* 'bridegroom'.

GIVEN NAMES German 4%. *Horst* (2), *Hans, Hermann, Kurt.*

Brautigan (131) Variant of German BRAUTIGAM.

GIVEN NAMES German 6%. *Erwin, Reiner.*

Bravard (118) French: nickname for a cruel or fierce man, from a derivative of *brave*, 'fierce', 'courageous' (from Latin *barbarus* 'barbarian', 'ruffian').

Brave (143) **1.** French: nickname from *brave* 'fierce', 'courageous'. **2.** Jewish

(eastern Ashkenazic): Yiddishized form of Russian *bravyj* 'good', 'honest'.

Braver (201) Jewish (from Poland and Ukraine): **1.** nickname from the inflected form of Yiddish *brav* 'good', 'honest'. **2.** Slavicized form of German BRAUER.

GIVEN NAMES Jewish 14%. *Mendel* (2), *Moshe* (2), *Cheskel, Gitty, Moysey, Shaya.*

Braverman (1104) Jewish (from Poland and Ukraine): variant of BRAVER.

GIVEN NAMES Jewish 7%. *Miriam* (4), *Hyman* (3), *Aron* (2), *Eitan, Froim, Hymen, Ilya, Isaak, Isadore, Izidor, Rakhil, Sol.*

Bravo (3347) Spanish and Portuguese: nickname from *bravo* 'fierce', 'violent', 'courageous' (from Latin *barbarus* 'barbarian', 'ruffian').

GIVEN NAMES Spanish 49%; Portuguese 10%. *Jose* (90), *Carlos* (43), *Juan* (42), *Luis* (34), *Jesus* (30), *Jorge* (29), *Francisco* (25), *Manuel* (24), *Miguel* (22), *Angel* (18), *Rafael* (18), *Guadalupe* (15); *Joao, Joaquim; Antonio* (28), *Lorenzo* (6), *Marco* (6), *Leonardo* (5), *Angelo* (4), *Carmine* (4), *Sal* (4), *Carlo* (3), *Fausto* (3), *Flavio* (3), *Aldo* (2), *Eliseo* (2).

Brawdy (138) English: origin uncertain. It may be a habitational name from a place in Pembrokeshire, Wales, called Brawdy, or a variant spelling of Irish BRADY.

Brawer (112) Jewish (Ashkenazic): Polish or German spelling of BRAVER.

GIVEN NAME Jewish 5%. *Naftali.*

Brawley (1457) Irish (Derry): Anglicized form of Gaelic **Ó Brólaigh** 'descendant of *Brolach*', a personal name possibly derived from *brollach* 'breast'.

Brawn (338) **1.** English: perhaps, as Reaney suggests, a variant of BRAND. **2.** Possibly a respelling of German BRAUN.

Brawner (1470) Respelling of German and Jewish BRAUNER.

Braxton (2725) English: habitational name of uncertain origin, perhaps from Branxton in Northumberland, which is named with the Celtic personal name *Branoc* + Old English *tūn* 'settlement'.

Bray (11827) English: habitational name from places in Berkshire and Devon. The former is probably named with Old French *bray* 'marsh', the latter from the Cornish element *bre* 'hill'.

Brayboy (290) Origin unidentified.

Brayer (198) **1.** Scottish and northern Irish: reduced form of Scottish MCBRAYER. **2.** The surname is also established in England, where it may be an occupational name for a maker of pestles, from Old French *breie, broie* 'pestle'. **3.** Jewish (Ashkenazic): occupational name from Yiddish *brayer* 'brewer'.

GIVEN NAMES Jewish 4%. *Menachem, Mirra, Yakov.*

Brayfield (145) English: habitational name from Cold Brayfield in Buckinghamshire or from Brafield-on-the-Green in Northamptonshire. Both are named with an Old

English *bragen* 'higher ground' + *feld* 'open country'.

Brayman (398) Respelling of German **Breymann**, from Middle High German *brī* 'porridge' + *man* 'man', hence an occupational name for someone who worked in or owned a grist mill or for someone involved in the production of millet, millet having been the main cereal used for cooking in medieval Europe.

Braymer (111) Americanized spelling of BREHMER or BREMER.

Brayshaw (126) English (chiefly West Yorkshire): variant of BRADSHAW.

Brayton (1019) English: habitational name from places in Cumbria and North Yorkshire named Brayton, from Old Scandinavian *breithr* 'broad' or the personal name *Breithi* + Old English *tūn* 'farmstead'.

Braz (217) Portuguese: from an old spelling of the personal name *Brás*, a vernacular form of BLASIUS.
GIVEN NAMES Spanish 19%; Portuguese 11%. *Jose* (5), *Manuel* (5), *Evandro* (2), *Marcos* (2), *Orlando* (2), *Alvaro*, *Americo*, *Armando*, *Augusto*, *Aurelio*, *Eduardo*, *Elisio*; *Joao*; *Antonio* (6), *Dino* (2), *Constantino*, *Ottavio*, *Silvio*.

Brazda (154) Czech and Slovak (**Brázda**): nickname, presumably for a worrier, from *brázda* 'furrow'.

Brazeal (584) Irish: variant of BRAZIL. Compare BRAZIEL.

Brazeau (425) French: unexplained.
FOREBEARS Nicolas Brazeau came to Montreal in 1681 from St-Denis d'Amboise, Touraine. A Brazeau from Paris is documented in Pointe-aux-Trembles, Quebec, in 1683.
GIVEN NAMES French 7%. *Andre*, *Fernand*, *Gaetan*, *Germain*, *Marcel*, *Pierre*, *Viateur*, *Yvon*.

Brazee (360) Possibly an altered spelling of French **Brazey**, a habitational name from a place so named in Côte d'Or. The place name is from Gallo-Roman *Brasiacum*, from the personal name *Brasius* + the locative suffix *-acum*.

Brazel (323) Irish: variant of BRAZIL.

Brazell (1182) Irish: variant of BRAZIL.

Brazelton (639) English: unexplained. Possibly a variant of BRASSINGTON.

Brazie (152) Altered spelling of French **Brazey** (see BRAZEE).

Braziel (475) Irish: variant of BRAZIL 1.

Brazier (941) **1.** English: occupational name for a worker in brass, from Old English *bræsian* 'to cast in brass' (a derivative of *bræs* 'brass'). **2.** French: variant of BRASIER.

Brazil (1642) **1.** Irish: Anglicized form of Gaelic **Ó Breasail** 'descendant of *Breasal*', a byname meaning 'strife'. The accent is on the first syllable. **2.** Spanish and Portuguese: variant of BRASIL.

Brazile (185) See BRAZZELL.

Brazill (239) Irish: variant spelling of BRAZIL.

Brazzel (168) Irish: variant spelling of BRAZIL.

Brazzell (354) **1.** Variant of Irish BRAZIL. **2.** Possibly a respelling of Spanish and Portuguese BRASIL, French BRASSELL, or German *Brassel* (see BRASSELL).

Brazzle (152) Irish: variant spelling of BRAZIL.

Brea (137) Galician: topographic from Galician *brea* 'footpath', or in some cases possibly a nickname from Spanish *brea* 'pitch'.
GIVEN NAMES Spanish 51%; French 5%. *Juan* (5), *Leandro* (4), *Luis* (4), *Manuel* (4), *Cesar* (3), *Jose* (3), *Julio* (3), *Altagracia* (2), *Francisco* (2), *Juana* (2), *Alba*, *Amador*; *Marcel*, *Matilde*, *Serge*.

Breach (146) English and Irish: variant of BRACH 2.
GIVEN NAME Irish 4%. *Donal*.

Bready (162) **1.** English: variant of BROADY. **2.** Irish: variant of BRADY.

Breaker (184) Americanized spelling of Swiss German **Bräker** (see BRAKER).

Breakey (179) English (northwest): unexplained. This name is also fairly frequent in Ireland, notably in Co. Monaghan and adjacent areas, where it has been recorded since the 17th century.

Breakfield (263) English: variant spelling of BRAKEFIELD.

Breakiron (106) Americanized (translated) form of German BRECHEISEN.

Breakstone (139) Perhaps a variant of English BRAXTON.

Bream (309) English: **1.** habitational name from Bream in Worcestershire, which is probably named in Old English as 'the place where broom grows', from *brēme*, an unattested dialect variant of *brōm* 'broom'. **2.** nickname for a fierce or energetic person, from Middle English *brem(e)*, *brim(me)* 'fierce', 'vigorous' (from Old English *brēme* 'famous', 'noble'). **3.** variant of BRAHAM.

Brean (120) Irish: variant of BREEN or BRAIN.
GIVEN NAME French 4%. *Camille*.

Breard (138) French (**Bréard**): metathesized form of *Bérard* (see BERARD).
GIVEN NAMES French 10%. *Armand*, *Camille*, *Reneau*.

Brearley (220) English (Yorkshire): variant spelling of BRIERLEY.
FOREBEARS John Brearly came from Yorkshire, England, to Trenton, NJ, in 1680.

Breau (266) French (**Bréau**): variant of **Bréaux** (see BREAUX).
GIVEN NAMES French 16%. *Ulysse* (3), *Alcide*, *Antoine*, *Aurore*, *Girard*, *Leonide*, *Mederic*, *Ovila*, *Raoul*, *Yves*, *Yvon*.

Breaud (123) French (**Bréaud**): variant of **Bréaux** (see BREAUX).

GIVEN NAMES French 7%. *Urbain* (2), *Nemour*.

Breault (1400) French (**Bréault**): variant of **Bréaux** (see BREAUX).
GIVEN NAMES French 9%. *Armand* (4), *Lucien* (3), *Aime* (2), *Andre* (2), *Emile* (2), *Eugenie* (2), *Gilles* (2), *Marcel* (2), *Adrien*, *Aldor*, *Alphonse*, *Amie*.

Breaux (4179) French (**Bréaux**): metathesized form of *Beraud*, a Germanic personal name composed of the elements *ber(n)* 'bear' + *wald* 'rule'. Compare BRAUD, BRAULT.
FOREBEARS The Breaux families of LA trace their origins to one Vincent Brault from La Chaussé in present-day Vienne département, who arrived in Acadia sometime before 1661. After the expulsion of the Acadians, several of his descendants found their way to LA.
GIVEN NAMES French 6%. *Lucien* (3), *Oneil* (3), *Ulysse* (3), *Andre* (2), *Andree* (2), *Antoine* (2), *Curley* (2), *Gaston* (2), *Gracien* (2), *Kearney* (2), *Pierre* (2), *Raoul* (2).

Breazeale (954) Variant of Irish BRAZIL.

Brech (115) German: variant of BRACH or BRECHT.

Brechbiel (127) Variant of Swiss German **Brechbühl** (see BRECHBILL).

Brechbill (147) Americanized spelling of Swiss German **Brechbühl**, a topographic name for someone who lived by a hill (*bühl*) owned by or associated with a man called BRECHT.

Brecheen (156) Irish: Anglicized form of Gaelic **Mac an Bhreitheamhnaigh** 'son of the judge' (see BREHENY, MCBRATNEY).

Brecheisen (251) German: from Middle High German *brecheysen* 'crowbar', hence a nickname for a manual worker or for large strong man.

Brecher (453) **1.** English: variant of BRACH 2, the *-er* suffix denoting an inhabitant. **2.** German and Jewish (Ashkenazic): from an agent derivative of German *brechen* 'to break', an occupational name for someone who crushed hemp or flax, or possibly a nickname for a lawbreaker.
GIVEN NAMES Jewish 11%; German 5%. *Chaim* (3), *Miriam* (2), *Yosef* (2), *Baila*, *Chana*, *Ephraim*, *Herschel*, *Hershel*, *Meir*, *Meyer*, *Pnina*, *Shimon*; *Armin* (3), *Oskar* (3), *Bernd*, *Erwin*, *Gerhard*.

Brecht (937) South German: from a short form of any of various personal names formed with Germanic *berht* 'bright', 'famous' as the second element, for example ALBRECHT, *Ruprecht*.

Brechtel (225) South German: from a reduced pet form of the personal name ALBRECHT or, in the southwest, from a pet form of *Bechtold* (see BERTHOLD).

Breck (370) **1.** Scottish: nickname from Gaelic *breac* 'speckled'. **2.** English: unexplained. **3.** German: topographic name related to Middle Low German *brāke* 'uncultivated land'.

FOREBEARS Breck was the name of a Massachusetts Bay family prominent in the earliest settlement. Edward Breck settled in Dorchester, MA, in 1636, and died there in 1662.

Brecke (114) German: variant of BRECK.

GIVEN NAMES German 4%. *Erwin, Fritz.*

Breckel (107) South German: nickname from Middle High German *bracke* 'hunting dog', 'tracker dog'. See also BRACK.

GIVEN NAME German 5%. *Gottlieb.*

Breckenridge (1768) Scottish, northern Irish, and English: habitational name from Brackenrig in Lanarkshire, so named with northern Middle English *braken* 'bracken' (Old Norse *brækni*) + *rigg* 'ridge' (Old Norse *hryggr*), or from a similarly named place in northern England.

FOREBEARS Alexander Breckenridge emigrated from northern Ireland to VA in about 1738. He had many prominent descendants, most of whom spelled the name Breckinridge.

Brecker (203) German: variant of **Brägger** (see BRAGER).

Breckinridge (103) Variant of Scottish and English BRECKENRIDGE.

Breckner (110) German: possibly a topographic name for someone who settled on land that was fallow or still uncultivated, from Low German *Breck* (High German *Brache*).

GIVEN NAMES German 8%. *Egon, Ernst, Heinz.*

Breckon (118) Welsh: habitational name from the district in South Wales of this name, named for a Welsh prince of the 5th century called *Brychan*.

Breda (311) 1. Italian: topographic name from medieval Latin *braida* 'grassy meadow', 'flat grassland adjoining a settlement', or a habitational name from any of the places named with this word, such as the districts (now suburbs) of Genoa, Milan, Mantua, and Brescia called Breda or Brera. 2. Dutch: habitational name from the city of this name in North Brabant.

GIVEN NAMES Italian 8%. *Aldo* (2), *Angelo, Dino, Domenic, Donato, Egidio, Geno, Massimo, Quintino, Sante, Ugo.*

Bredahl (167) 1. Norwegian: habitational name from a farmstead named Bredahl, from *bre* 'broad' + *dahl* 'valley'. 2. Danish: habitational name from a place so named (with the same derivation as 1).

Bredbenner (130) North German: status name for a farmer who owned two units (Middle Low German *brēde*, literally 'breadth', 'width'), in this case of peat land (Middle Low German *benne*).

Brede (326) 1. North German: topographic name for someone living in an area of marshy lowland, Middle Low German *brede*. 2. English: variant spelling of BREED.

Bredehoeft (126) North German (**Bredehöft**): Low German form of **Breithaupt**, from Middle Low German *brede* 'broad', 'wide' + *höft* 'head'.

GIVEN NAMES German 7%. *Eldred, Erwin, Otto.*

Bredehoft (132) North German (**Bredehöft**): nickname for someone with a broad head, from Middle Low German *brēd* 'broad' + *hovet* 'head'.

Bredemeier (141) North German: distinguishing name for a tenant farmer (see MEYER) who owned or worked a double unit of land, known as a *brede* (from Middle Low German *brēd* 'broad', 'wide'). Alternatively, the surname could have denoted a farmer whose land was swampy (see BREDE).

GIVEN NAMES German 10%. *Gerhart, Hermann, Lorenz, Reinold, Wolfgang.*

Bredemeyer (131) German: variant spelling of BREDEMEIER.

GIVEN NAMES German 6%. *Hans* (2), *Jurgen.*

Breden (205) 1. North German and Danish: habitational name from any of various places so named. 2. Swedish: ornamental name formed with the suffix *-en*, *-én*, a shortened form of Latin *-enius* 'descendant of'. 3. English: perhaps a variant spelling of BREEDEN.

GIVEN NAMES Scandinavian 5%. *Thor* (2), *Lief, Sven.*

Bredenberg (111) 1. Danish and North German: habitational name from any of several farmsteads named with Middle Low German *brēd* 'wide' + *berg* 'mountain', 'hill'. 2. Swedish: ornamental name composed of the same elements as 1 above.

Bredesen (143) Norwegian: patronymic from the personal name *Brede*.

Bredeson (399) Altered spelling of Norwegian BREDESEN.

Bredeweg (102) North German: topographic name for someone who lived by a broad road, from Middle Low German *brede* 'broad', 'wide' + *weg* 'way', 'path', '(unpaved) road'.

Bredin (115) Irish: Anglicized form of Gaelic **Mac Giolla Bhrídín**, diminutive form of **Mac Giolla Bhrighde** 'son of the servant of (Saint) Brighid' (see McBRIDE). This name was once found in an ecclesiastical family in County Down, but it has not survived in Ireland.

GIVEN NAMES Irish 8%. *Brendan, Siobhan.*

Breding (101) Probably an American variant of Irish BREDIN.

Bredow (141) German: habitational name from either of two places called Bredow, one on the Havel river, the other near Stettin.

GIVEN NAME German 4%. *Udo.*

Bredthauer (128) German: variant spelling of **Bretthauer**, an occupational name for a

carpenter, from Middle High German *bret* 'board' + *houwer* 'cutter'.

Bree (226) 1. Irish (Counties Sligo and Mayo): Anglicized form of Gaelic Ó **Breaghaigh** 'descendant of *Breagha*', a byname meaning 'hill dweller', from *brí* 'hill', 'height', genitive *breagh*. 2. Dutch: nickname for a well-built man, from Middle Dutch *breet* 'broad'. 3. Jewish: unexplained.

GIVEN NAMES Irish 6%; French 5%; Jewish 4%. *Declan, Dermot, Siobhan; Germaine* (2), *Francoise; Chana, Meyer, Yaakov.*

Breece (710) Variant spelling of English or German BREESE or Welsh PREECE.

Breech (174) 1. English: variant of BRACH 2. 2. Possibly an altered spelling of **Breetsch**, a North German habitational name from a place so named in the Altmark area.

Breed (1015) English: habitational name from any of various minor places, for example Brede in Sussex, named with Old English *brǣdu* 'breadth', 'broad place' (a derivative of *brād* 'broad').

FOREBEARS Modern bearers of the American surname **Breed** are in many cases descended from Alan Breed, who came to Salem, MA, from England in 1629, and subsequently settled at Saugus, MA.

Breeden (3793) 1. English: habitational name from Bredon in Worcestershire or from Breedon on the Hill in Leicestershire, both of which are named from an unattested Celtic word *brez* 'hill' + the tautologous addition of Old English *dūn*. 2. Americanized form of German BREDEN.

Breeding (1946) North German: probably a patronymic form of a now-lost Germanic personal name, or a topographic name from Low German *brēde* 'open field'. Compare BREITING.

Breedlove (2992) English: probably a nickname for an amiable or popular person, from Middle English *brede(n)* 'to breed', 'to produce' + *loue* 'love'.

Breeland (227) Norwegian: variant of BRELAND.

Breen (5171) Irish: either a shortened form of McBREEN or an Anglicized form of Gaelic Ó **Braoin** 'descendant of *Braon*', a byname meaning 'moisture', 'drop'.

GIVEN NAMES Irish 7%. *Brendan* (3), *Brennan, Conan, John Patrick, Kiera, Niall.*

Breene (110) Irish: variant of BREEN.

GIVEN NAME Irish 8%. *Brennan* (2).

Breer (186) 1. German: reduced form of BREGER or **Breder**, a variant of BREDE. 2. Variant spelling of English **Brear**, from Old English *brǣr* 'thorn bush', hence a nickname for a sharp or prickly person.

Brees (357) Dutch: habitational name from any of the various places in France named Buré, for example in Orne and Meurthe-et-Moselle, or from a Dutch form of the personal name *Brictius*.

Breese (1164) **1.** English: nickname for an irritating person, from Middle English *breeze* 'gadfly' (Old English *brēosa*). **2.** Americanized spelling of the Welsh patronymic **ap Rhys** 'son of *Rhys*' (see REESE). **3.** German: habitational name from any of numerous places called Breese or Breesen, in Mecklenburg, Wendland (near Hannover), Brandenburg, and Pomerania. In some cases the place name is derived from West Slavic *brjaza* 'birch'.

Breeze (784) **1.** Variant spelling of BREESE. **2.** Anglicized spelling of the Welsh patronymic **ap Rhys** 'son of *Rhys*' (see REESE).

Bregar (122) Slovenian: topographic name for a person who lived on a hillside, from *breg* 'slope' + the suffix *-ar*.

GIVEN NAMES German 4%. *Erna, Kurt.*

Brege (145) German: nickname for someone with a loud, strident voice, from a noun derivative of *bregen* 'to roar'.

Bregenzer (128) German: habitational name for someone from Bregenz in Austria.

Breger (182) German: **1.** topographic name from Slavic *breg* 'slope', 'bank', 'mountainside' + the suffix *-er* denoting an inhabitant. Compare Slovenian BREGAR. **2.** from a German thieves' jargon term meaning 'beggar'. **3.** nickname for someone with a loud, strident voice, from a noun derivative of *bregen* 'to roar'.

Bregman (520) **1.** German and Jewish (Ashkenazic): metathesized form of BERGMAN or BERGMANN. **2.** Jewish (eastern Ashkenazic): topographic name for someone who lived near a river or stream, from eastern Yiddish *breg* 'shore', 'bank', 'coast' (from Polish *brzeg*) + *-man*.

GIVEN NAMES Jewish 5%. *Ilya* (2), *Arie, Basya, Batia, Emanuel, Heshy, Moshe.*

Breheny (147) Irish: Anglicized form of Gaelic **Mac an Bhreitheamhnaigh** 'son of the judge' (see McBRATNEY).

Brehm (2308) **1.** South German: nickname for a restless, cantankerous man, from Middle High German *brem(e)* 'horsefly', a derivative of *bremen* 'to buzz or grumble'. **2.** German: topographic or habitational name from a field named with *Brem* 'swampy bank', simply as Brehm, Brem, or Bräm, or in compounds such as Bremgarten, Bremkamp. In Switzerland the regular spelling of this name is **Bräm**.

Brehmer (678) German: **1.** topographic name, a variant of BREHM 2, or a habitational name from Brehme near Duderstadt or Brehmen near Mergentheim. **2.** variant spelling of BREMER.

Brei (140) German: variant of **Bräu** (see BRAU).

Breidenbach (620) German: variant of BREITENBACH.

Breidenstein (218) German: variant of BREITENSTEIN.

Breiding (154) German: **1.** variant of **Breiting**, a habitational name from either of two places called Breitungen, on the Werra river and in the Harz Mountains. **2.** in southwestern Germany, a metronymic from *Breide*, a short form of the female personal name *Brigida*.

Breidinger (119) German: habitational name from either of two places called Breitungen (see BREIDING 1).

Breier (388) German and Jewish (Ashkenazic): variant of BREUER or **Bräuer** (see BRAUER).

GIVEN NAMES Jewish 6%. *Zvi* (3), *Rina* (2), *Beril, Moshe, Uri, Uzi.*

Breig (132) German: **1.** variant of **Braig**, a habitational name from any of several places so named in Württemberg. **2.** possibly a nickname from an old agent derivative of Swabian *bräugen* 'to cry', 'to roar'.

Breighner (168) Altered spelling of German **Brüchner**, a topographic name from Middle High German *bruoch* 'swamp'.

Breihan (100) German: occupational nickname for a (beer) brewer, one of the many variants (e.g., **Breu-**, **Brey-**, **Broyhan**), from Middle High German *briuw(er)* 'brew(er)' + a short form of the common personal name *Johann(es)* (see JOHN).

GIVEN NAMES German 5%. *Erwin, Kurt.*

Breiner (623) German (also well established in Sweden and Denmark): occupational name for a cereal grower, from a derivative of Middle High German *brīe* 'porridge', 'mush'.

Breinholt (122) German: from a rare Germanic personal name *Brin(no)*, probably composed of element related to Middle High German *brünne* 'armor' + *walt* 'rule'.

Breinig (128) German: variant of BREUNIG.

Breining (198) **1.** German: variant of **Breuni(n)g** (see BREUNIG). **2.** Danish: habitational name from any of several places called Breining 'place with bracken'.

Breininger (147) German: variant of **Breuninger**, a variant of BREUNIG.

Breisch (259) German: unexplained.

Breit (515) German: nickname for a stout or fat person, from Middle High German *breit* 'broad'.

GIVEN NAMES German 4%. *Heinz* (3), *Alphons, Erwin.*

Breitbach (374) German: habitational name from a place in Bavaria named Breitbach, from Middle High German *breit* 'broad' + *bach* 'stream'. Compare BREITENBACH.

Breitbart (119) German, Alsatian, and Jewish (Ashkenazic): variant of BREITBARTH.

GIVEN NAME French 4%. *Jacques.*

Breitbarth (176) German, Alsatian, and Jewish (Ashkenazic): nickname for a man with a full beard, from German *breit* 'broad' + *Bart* 'beard'.

GIVEN NAMES German 4%. *Eldor, Hans.*

Breitenbach (625) German and Jewish (western Ashkenazic): habitational name from any of the numerous places called Breitenbach or Breidenbach, meaning 'broad stream', for example in Westphalia, Rhineland, and Hesse. Compare BREITBACH.

GIVEN NAMES German 4%. *Kurt* (3), *Dieter, Fritz, Juergen, Otto.*

Breitenfeldt (124) German: habitational name from any of several places meaning 'broad, open pasture'.

GIVEN NAMES German 5%. *Irmgard, Lorenz.*

Breitenstein (410) German: topographic name from Middle High German *breit* 'broad' + *stein* 'rock', or a habitational name from a place named Breitenstein or Breidenstein (with the same meaning), for example in Hesse.

GIVEN NAMES German 5%. *Kurt* (3), *Gottfried.*

Breiter (166) South German: from *Breite*, a noun derivative of Middle High German *breit* 'broad', denoting a broad, flat, fertile area of farmland, hence a topographic or status name for someone who lived on and farmed such land.

GIVEN NAME German 8%. *Manfred* (4).

Breithaupt (509) German: nickname for a man with a broad head, from Middle High German *breit* 'broad' + *houpt* 'head'. Compare BREDEHOFT.

Breitinger (105) German: habitational name for someone from either of two places named Breitingen, near Leipzig and in Württemberg.

GIVEN NAME German 4%. *Kurt.*

Breitkreutz (247) German: probably a nickname for a person with a broad butt. *Breitkreutz* replaced an earlier, more transparent form of the surname, *Breitarsch*, the use of *Kreuz* (literally 'cross') as a euphemism for 'buttocks' first occurring in the 17th century.

Breitling (190) German: **1.** from the name of a fish, hence a nickname for someone thought to resemble a fish in some way. **2.** habitational name for someone who lived at the widening of the Warnow river near Rostock which is so named, from *breit* 'broad' + the suffix *-ling* denoting affiliation.

Breitman (176) Jewish (Ashkenazic): nickname for a stout or fat person, from German *breit* 'broad' + *Mann* 'man', or Yiddish *breyt* + *man*.

GIVEN NAMES Jewish 5%. *Jakov, Sol.*

Breitner (109) German: variant of BREITER.

Breitweiser (177) Altered spelling of German BREITWIESER.

Breitwieser (137) German: topographic name for someone living by a broad meadow, from Middle High German *breit* 'broad', 'wide' + *wise* 'meadow' + the suffix *-er* denoting an inhabitant.

GIVEN NAME German 4%. *Helmut.*

Breitzman (173) Altered spelling of **Breitzmann**, an eastern German topographic name for someone who lived by a birch wood, from the Slavic stem *brēs* 'birch'.

Brekhus (114) Norwegian: habitational name from a farm so named in Voss, from *brek* 'slope', 'steep ascent' (see BREKKE) + *hus* 'house', 'farm'.
GIVEN NAME Scandinavian 4%. *Johan.*

Brekke (980) Norwegian: habitational name from any of numerous farms named Brekke, from Old Norse *brekka* 'hill', 'slope', 'steep ascent' (often with reference to a steep track or approach).
GIVEN NAMES Scandinavian 9%. *Bernt* (2), *Knute* (2), *Tor* (2), *Aksel, Alf, Britt, Erik, Hilmer, Lars, Nils, Nord, Selmer.*

Brekken (152) Norwegian: habitational name from any of numerous farms named Brekken ('the slope'), from the definite singular form of BREKKE.

Breland (1823) **1.** French: from Old French *brelenc* 'card table' (or a specific card game), hence a name for a card player or gambler. **2.** Norwegian: habitational name from any of various farms named Breland, from *bre* 'glacier' or *breid* 'wide' + *land* 'land'.

Brelje (110) German: habitational name for someone from a place called Brelingen near Hannover.
GIVEN NAMES German 5%. *Frieda, Gerhard.*

Brelsford (463) English: variant of BRAILSFORD.

Brem (294) German: variant of BREHM.

Bremer (2809) **1.** German (also Swedish and Danish, of German origin): **2.** habitational name for someone from Bremen in northern Germany, or a namesake in Württemberg. **3.** spelling variant of BREHMER.

Bremmer (275) **1.** German: nickname for an obnoxious or grumpy person, from an agent derivative of Middle High German *bremen* 'to buzz or grumble'. **2.** Probably an altered spelling of BREMER.

Bremner (550) Scottish: regional name for someone from Brabant in the Low Countries, from Older Scots *Brebner*, *Brabanare*, 'native or inhabitant of Brabant' (see BRABANT).

Brems (154) North German: variant of BREHM, from Low German *Brems* 'horsefly'.
GIVEN NAMES French 5%. *Ferrel, Georges.*

Bremser (127) German: **1.** nickname for an irascible person, from dialect *bremsen* 'to rage'. **2.** habitational name from Brömse near Frankfurt.

Bremseth (115) Norwegian: habitational name from a farm in Trøndelag, so named from an uncertain first element + *set* 'dwelling', 'farmstead'.

Bren (346) Jewish (Ashkenazic): presumably a nickname for a very active person, from Yiddish *bren* 'heat', 'fervor', 'ardor'.

Brenan (148) Probably an altered spelling of the Irish surname BRENNAN.

Brenchley (155) English: habitational name from a place in Kent named Brenchley, from an Old English personal name *Brænci* (of uncertain origin) + Old English *lēah* 'woodland clearing'.

Brendel (837) South German: from a pet form of the personal name *Brando* (see BRAND 1).
GIVEN NAMES German 4%. *Aloys, Erwin, Georg, Juergen, Jutta, Rainer, Viktor.*

Brendemuehl (101) German (**Brendemühl**): habitational name from a place named Brendemühle near Stettin (Szczecin in Polish).

Brenden (346) Norwegian: habitational name from any of numerous farms in southeastern Norway named Brenden, from *brenna* 'land cleared for cultivation by burning' + the definite singular article *-en*.

Brender (157) **1.** German and Danish: probably of the same derivation as BRENNER. It may also have denoted the wax-light bearer (*ceroferarius*) in Christian ceremony. **2.** Jewish (Ashkenazic): variant of BRANDER.
GIVEN NAMES Jewish 6%. *Aaron David, Hyman, Ofer.*

Brendle (696) South German: variant spelling of BRENDEL.

Brendlinger (177) German (**Brändlinger**): topographic name for someone who lived near a burned area of a forest or town. Since fire was a great threat in the Middle Ages this name may also have been a derisive nickname for a presumed arsonist, in which case the suffix *-linger* is to be understood as an intensifying agent suffix.

Breneman (857) **1.** Swiss German (**Brenemann**): probably a variant of BRENNER. Compare BRENNEMAN. **2.** Jewish: variant of BRENNER.

Brener (208) Jewish: variant spelling of BRENNER.
GIVEN NAMES Jewish 11%; Russian 9%. *Gerson, Hyman, Igal, Mariya, Miriam, Moisey, Tsilya, Yakov, Yehuda; Leonid* (2), *Aleksandr, Anatoliy, Grigory, Iosif, Khava, Lyudmila, Mikhail, Yelizaveta, Zachar.*

Brenes (217) Asturian-Leonese and Galician (**Breñes**): possibly variant of Asturian-Leonese **Brañes**, and Galician **Brañas**, habitational names from any of the places named Brañes (in Asturies), and Brañas (in Galicia).
GIVEN NAMES Spanish 45%. *Carlos* (7), *Jose* (7), *Juan* (6), *Francisco* (3), *Jorge* (3), *Manuel* (3), *Ana* (2), *Mario* (2), *Ricardo* (2), *Roberto* (2), *Adolfo, Alejandro.*

Brengle (170) Altered spelling of German **Brengel**, of uncertain origin.

Brenizer (195) Americanized spelling of German **Brenneiser**, an occupational name for a blacksmith. It is a derivative of **Brenneisen**, literally 'burn (the) iron' (from Middle High German *brennen* 'to

burn' + *īsen* 'iron'), a name given to young journeymen by the craft guild.

Brenke (104) North German: variant of the topographic name BRINK, or habitational name from a place named with this word.

Brenn (184) German: from Middle High German *brennen* 'to burn something', an occupational name either for someone who cleared forest land by burning, or for a distiller of spirits. Compare BRENNER.
GIVEN NAMES German 6%. *Reinhart* (2), *Eldor, Hans.*

Brenna (285) **1.** Italian (Lombardy): habitational name from a place in Lombardy named Brenna. **2.** Norwegian: habitational name from any of numerous farms in southeastern Norway named Brenna, from *brenna* 'land cleared for cultivation by burning'.

Brennan (19969) Irish: **1.** (predominantly southern) Anglicized form of Gaelic Ó Braonáin 'descendant of *Braonán*', a personal name from a diminutive of *braon* 'moisture', 'drop'. Compare BREEN. **2.** (predominantly northern) Anglicized form of Gaelic Ó Branáin 'descendant of *Branán*', a personal name meaning 'little raven' (see BRANNIGAN).
GIVEN NAMES Irish 5%. *Brendan* (6), *Ciaran* (6), *Kieran* (6), *Liam* (4), *Dermot* (3), *Eamon* (3), *Seamus* (3), *Siobhan* (3), *Brigid* (2), *Colm* (2), *Eamonn* (2), *Niall* (2).

Brennecke (288) North German and Dutch: variant of **Brende(c)ke**, from a Low German pet form of the personal name BRAND.
GIVEN NAMES German 7%. *Bernd* (2), *Fritz* (2), *Kurt, Otto.*

Brenneis (128) German: occupational name for a blacksmith, a variant of **Brenneisen** (see BRENIZER).
GIVEN NAME French 4%. *Marcel.*

Brenneke (123) North German and Dutch: see BRENNECKE.
GIVEN NAME German 5%. *Heida.*

Brenneman (1978) German (**Brennemann**): probably a variant of BRENNER.

Brennen (489) Probably a shortened form of a German surname formed with the element *Brennen*, for example **Brennenstuhl**.

Brenner (7146) **1.** German: from an agent derivative of Middle High German *brennen* 'to burn', in various applications. Often it is an occupational name for a distiller of spirits; it may also refer to a charcoal or lime burner or to someone who cleared forests by burning. **2.** Jewish (Ashkenazic): occupational name for a distiller, from German *Brenner*, literally 'burner' (see 1). **3.** English: metathesized variant of BERNER 2 and 3.

Brennick (146) **1.** Origin uncertain: possibly an altered spelling of Irish **Brennock**, a variant of BRANNOCK. **2.** Probably a variant spelling of German **Brennicke** (see BRENNECKE).

Brenning (169) German: patronymic from BRAND.

Brenny (169) Probably an altered spelling of German BRENNING.

Brensinger (177) German (Rhineland): habitational name for someone from a place near Waldbröl called Brenzingen.

Brent (2589) English: **1.** topographic name for someone who lived by a piece of ground that had been cleared by fire, from Middle English *brend*, past participle of *brennen* 'to burn'. **2.** habitational name from any of the places in Devon and Somerset named Brent, probably from Old English *brant* 'steep', or from an old Celtic (British) word meaning 'hill', 'high place'. **3.** byname or nickname for a criminal who had been branded; compare Henry *Brendcheke* ('burned cheek'), recorded in Northumbria in 1279.

FOREBEARS Giles Brent (died 1672) came from Gloucestershire, England, to MD in 1638.

Brentlinger (294) German: variant of BRENDLINGER.

Brenton (702) English (Devon): habitational name primarily from Brenton near Exminster, possibly named in Old English as *Brȳningtūn* 'settlement (Old English *tūn*) associated with *Brȳni*' (a personal name from Old English *bryne* 'fire', 'flame'), or from any of the places mentioned at BRINTON.

Brents (373) Probably an altered spelling of German **Bren(t)z**, a pet form of the personal name *Brando* (see BRAND 1).

Brenzel (100) German: pet form of the personal name **Bren(t)z** (see BRENTS).

Breon (474) French: variant spelling of BRION.

Brereton (487) English: habitational name from places called Brereton, in Cheshire and Staffordshire. The former is named with Old English *brǣr*, *brēr* 'briar' + *tūn* 'enclosure', 'settlement'; the latter originally had as its final element Old English *dūn* 'hill'.

Brescia (611) Italian: habitational name from the city of Brescia in northern Italy.
GIVEN NAMES Italian 12%. *Franco* (3), *Salvatore* (3), *Carlo* (2), *Donato* (2), *Pasquale* (2), *Rocco* (2), *Vito* (2), *Angelo*, *Antonio*, *Duilio*, *Quirino*.

Bresciani (104) Italian: habitational name for someone from the city of Brescia, from the adjectival form of the name.
GIVEN NAMES Italian 12%. *Luigi* (2), *Silvio* (2), *Alessandra*, *Angelo*, *Guerino*, *Marino*.

Bresee (331) Probably of Dutch origin, but the etymology is unexplained.

Bresett (134) French: see BRESSETTE.

Bresette (222) French: see BRESSETTE.

Breshears (899) Americanized form of French (Huguenot) BRASSEUR. Compare BRASHEARS.

Breske (156) German: topographic name from Slavic *bres* 'birch'.

Breslau (125) Jewish (Ashkenazic): habitational name from Breslau, German name of the Polish city of Wrocław, which for a long time was part of Germany.

Breslauer (131) German and Jewish (Ashkenazic): habitational name for someone from Breslau (German name of the Polish city of Wrocław, which for a long time was part of Germany).
GIVEN NAMES Jewish 4%. *Izak*, *Miriam*.

Bresler (429) Jewish (Ashkenazic): habitational name for someone from Bresle, Yiddish name of the Polish city Wrocław. Compare BRESLAUER.
GIVEN NAMES Jewish 8%. *Yakov* (3), *Isaak* (2), *Genya*, *Isadore*, *Miriam*, *Mordechai*, *Sholom*, *Shraga*, *Sol*, *Yehoshua*.

Breslin (1782) Irish (Sligo and Donegal): Anglicized form of Gaelic **Ó Breisláin** 'descendant of *Breisleán*', a diminutive of the personal name *Breasal* (see BRAZIL).

Breslow (372) Jewish (Ashkenazic): variant of BRESLAU.
GIVEN NAMES Jewish 4%. *Aron*, *Meyer*.

Bresnahan (1457) Irish: Anglicized form of Gaelic **Ó Brosnacháin** 'descendant of *Brosnachán*', a personal name derived from Brosna, name of a town and river in County Kerry.
GIVEN NAMES Irish 6%. *Brendan* (4), *Aileen*, *Brian Patrick*.

Bresnan (217) Irish: variant of BRESNAHAN.
GIVEN NAME Irish 4%. *Niall*.

Bresnick (176) Origin unidentified. Perhaps an altered form of German **Bresnitz**, a habitational name from any of several places in Silesia.

Bress (194) Probably a variant of French **Bresse**, ethnic name for someone from the region of France called Bresse, or habitational name from any of various places of this name, derived from the Gallo-Roman personal name *Bricius* (see BRICE).
GIVEN NAMES Jewish 4%. *Meyer* (2), *Sol*.

Bressan (107) **1.** Italian: habitational name for someone from Brescia, from a northern variant, *Bressan(o)*, of *Bresciano*, an adjectival form of the place name. **2.** French: Probably a variant of French **Bresse**, ethnic name for someone from the region of France called Bresse, or habitational name from any of various places of this name, derived from the Gallo-Roman personal name *Bricius* (see BRICE).
GIVEN NAMES Italian 10%; Spanish 10%. *Reno* (3), *Enrico*, *Olindo*; *Germano* (2), *Ines* (2), *Renato* (2), *Americo*, *Mario*, *Pablo*.

Bresser (141) Dutch: variant of BRASSER.
GIVEN NAMES German 6%. *Rudi* (2), *Hans*, *Johannes*, *Kurt*.

Bressette (224) North American form of French **Bresset**, from a pet form of the personal name *Brès*, a variant of BRICE.

Bressi (156) Italian: **1.** variant of **Bresci**, itself a variant of BRESCIA. **2.** habitational name from Bresso in Milan province, showing the same regularization of form, characteristic of northern Italy.

Bressler (1704) German and Jewish (Ashkenazic): variant of BRESLAUER.

Bressman (167) Probably a variant of Jewish PRESSMAN.

Bresson (221) French: from a pet form of the personal name *Brès* (see BRICE).
GIVEN NAMES German 4%. *Elke*, *Franz*.

Brest (205) German: nickname from Middle High German *brast* 'boastfulness'.

Brester (187) German: **1.** habitational name, probably for someone from Brest in Moravia. **2.** nickname for a boastful person, from an agent derivative of Middle High German *brast* 'boastfulness'. Compare BREST.

Breth (195) Shortened form of German BRETHAUER.

Brethauer (246) German: variant spelling of BRETTHAUER.

Bretl (166) German: from a pet form of *Brado*, an unexplained old Germanic personal name.

Breton (1274) French and English: ethnic name for a Breton, from Old French *bret* (oblique case *breton*) (see BRETT).

FOREBEARS A bearer of the surname Breton from the Poitou region of France was recorded in Quebec city in 1668. Another, from Normandy, was documented in Champlain, also in 1668; and a third, also called Lebreton and Lardoise, from Brittany, is recorded in Château Richer in 1687.
GIVEN NAMES French 19%. *Marcel* (7), *Andre* (5), *Normand* (4), *Renald* (4), *Adelard* (3), *Alphonse* (3), *Armand* (3), *Gaetan* (3), *Laurent* (3), *Serge* (3), *Adrien* (2), *Aime* (2).

Bretschneider (181) German: variant spelling of BRETTSCHNEIDER.
GIVEN NAMES German 5%. *Fritz*, *Ilse*, *Oskar*.

Brett (2210) English and French: ethnic name for a Breton, from Old French *bret*. The Bretons were Celtic-speakers driven from southwestern England to northwestern France in the 6th century AD by Anglo-Saxon invaders; some of them reinvaded England in the 11th century as part of the army of William the Conqueror. In France and among Normans, Bretons had a reputation for stupidity, and in some cases this name and its variants and cognate may have originated as derogatory nicknames. The English surname is most common in East Anglia, where many Bretons settled after the Conquest. In Scotland it may also have denoted a member of one of the Celtic-speaking peoples of Strathclyde, who were known as *Bryttas* or *Brettas* well into the 13th century.

Bretthauer (173) German: occupational name for a sawyer, from Middle High

German *bret* 'board' + *houwer* 'cutter', 'chopper'. Compare BRETTSCHNEIDER.

GIVEN NAMES German 7%. *Elfriede, Ewald, Kurt.*

Brettschneider (137) German: occupational name for a sawyer, Middle High German *bretsnīder*. Compare BRETTHAUER.

GIVEN NAMES German 9%. *Heinz, Horst, Konrad, Otto, Reimund.*

Bretz (1291) German: probably habitational name from Breetz near Lüneburg, Lower Saxony.

Breu (111) German: variant of BREUER.

GIVEN NAMES German 5%. *Alois, Bernd.*

Breuer (1368) German and Jewish (Ashkenazic): occupational name for a brewer of beer or ale, from Middle High German *briuwer* 'brewer'.

GIVEN NAMES German 6%; Jewish 4%. *Hans* (4), *Erwin* (2), *Franz* (2), *Helmut* (2), *Horst* (2), *Klaus* (2), *Kurt* (2), *Dietmar, Frieda, Gerd, Gerhard, Guenter; Aron* (2), *Aba, Chaim, Feivel, Gershon, Hershel, Lazer, Mechel, Menachem, Mendel, Naftoli, Shachar.*

Breuker (141) German: topographic name for someone living near a bog or marsh, from Low German *brök* 'bog' + the suffix *-er* denoting an inhabitant.

Breunig (621) German: from the popular medieval personal name *Brüning*, a patronymic from *Bruno* (see BRUNING), which was diphthongized to *Breuni(n)g* in the 17th century.

GIVEN NAMES German 6%. *Kurt* (5), *Florian, Franz, Math, Siegfried, Winfried.*

Breuninger (159) German: variant of BREUNIG.

GIVEN NAMES German 10%. *Kurt* (2), *Fritz, Ulrich.*

Brevard (297) French: nickname from Old French *bref* 'small' + the derogatory suffix *-ard.*

Brevig (172) Norwegian: variant of BREVIK.

GIVEN NAMES Scandinavian 6%. *Per, Thora.*

Brevik (231) Norwegian: habitational name from any of several farms named Brevik, from *bre* 'broad' + *vik* 'bay' (or *vig*, an older (Danish) spelling of this word).

GIVEN NAMES Scandinavian 5%. *Anders, Arndt, Sig.*

Brew (658) **1.** Irish: Anglicized form of Gaelic **Ó Brughadha** 'descendant of *Brughaidh*', a byname meaning 'strong farmer', 'prosperous farmer'. **2.** Manx: Anglicized form of the Gaelic occupational term *breitheamh* 'judge', 'deemster' (see BRAIN). **3.** Probably an Americanized spelling of German and Swiss **Breu**, a variant of BREUER.

Brewbaker (184) Americanized form of Swiss German BRUBACHER.

Brewer (35110) **1.** English: occupational name for a brewer of beer or ale, from an agent derivative of Old English *brēowan* 'to brew'. Compare BREWSTER. **2.** English (of

Norman origin): anglicized form of French **Bruyère** (see BRUYERE), habitational name from a place so called in Calvados, France. **3.** Translation of Dutch BROUWER, German BRAUER or BREUER, etc., all occupational names meaning 'brewer'.

Brewin (108) **1.** English (Leicestershire): of uncertain origin; perhaps variant spelling of BRUIN, or alternatively the Irish name (see 2). **2.** Irish: Anglicized form of Gaelic **Ó Braion** 'descendant of *Braon*', a byname meaning 'moisture', 'drop'.

Brewington (1512) English: habitational name from a lost or unidentified place, probably in East Anglia.

Brewster (6439) Northern English and Scottish: occupational name for a brewer of beer or ale, from Old English *brēowan* 'to brew'. *Brewer* is the usual term in southern England, while *Brewster* is mainly midland, northern, and Scottish.

FOREBEARS The *Mayflower* Pilgrim William Brewster (1567–1644) was the son of the bailiff of the manor of Scrooby, Nottinghamshire, home of one of the earliest Puritan congregations. He was a prominent leader in Plymouth Colony from the 1620s until his death.

Brewton (1008) English: variant spelling of the habitational name **Bruton**, from a place in Somerset, so named with a Celtic river name meaning 'brisk' + Old English *tūn* 'farmstead'.

Brey (847) **1.** Americanized spelling of German **Bräu** (see BRAU). **2.** North German: variant of BREDE 2.

Breyer (585) Americanized spelling of German **Bräuer** (see BRAUER).

GIVEN NAMES German 4%. *Lorenz* (2), *Eberhard, Elke, Gottlieb, Johannes, Rudie, Walther.*

Breyfogle (220) Respelling of German **Breyvogel**, a nickname from Middle High German *brī* 'grain mush', 'porridge' + *vogel* 'bird'. See also BRAYMAN.

Breza (178) Czech (**Březa**) and Slovak: topographic name for someone who lived by a birch tree, Czech *bříza*; a common surname in Bohemia.

Brezina (343) Czech and Slovak (**Březina**): topographic name from *březina* 'birch forest'.

Brezinski (301) **1.** Americanized spelling of Polish **Brzeziński** (see BRZEZINSKI). **2.** Jewish (eastern Ashkenazic): habitational name from a place name formed with a root from either Russian *beryoza* or Polish *brzoza*, both meaning 'birch'.

Bria (226) Italian (Calabria): perhaps a reduced form of BRIGLIA.

GIVEN NAMES Italian 12%. *Amerigo, Angelo, Fiore, Girolamo, Pasquale.*

Brian (1297) **1.** Irish and English: variant spelling of BRYAN. **2.** French and English: from the Celtic personal name *Brian*, which contains the element *bre-* 'hill', with the transferred sense 'eminence'. See also

BRYAN. **3.** French: nickname from Old Occitan *brian* 'maggot'.

Briand (284) French: variant of BRIAN 2.

FOREBEARS A Briand from the Angoumois region of France is documented in Repentigny, Quebec, in 1722, with the secondary surname Sansregret.

GIVEN NAMES French 14%. *Alain* (2), *Jacques* (2), *Alban, Alphonse, Andre, Benoit, Florent, Francois, Olivier.*

Brians (113) Irish: variant of Irish BRYAN, formed with the addition of English patronymic *-s.*

Briant (326) **1.** Irish: variant of BRYAN. The addition of *-t* is due to English speakers' perception of the devoicing of Gaelic final *-n*. **2.** French: variant of BRIAN 2.

GIVEN NAMES French 4%. *Pierre* (2), *Andre, Laure.*

Briar (164) Scottish and northern Irish: reduced form of **McBriar** (see MCBRAYER).

GIVEN NAME French 4%. *Cecile* (2).

Bricco (197) Origin unidentified; possibly an Italian form of a Germanic personal name, *Brico*, but it is unknown in Italy. An alternative possibility is a topographic name from northern Italian dialect *bricco* 'steep place' 'precipice'.

Brice (3180) **1.** French, English, and Scottish: from a personal name of Celtic origin (Latinized as *Bri(c)tius, Bric(c)ius*, or *Brixius*), which was borne by a 5th-century saint who succeeded St. Martin as bishop of Tours. Consequently, it became a popular given name in France and Germany in the early Middle Ages. It was imported to England and Scotland by the Normans. **2.** Welsh: Anglicized form of the patronymic *ap Rhys* 'son of Rhys' (see REESE).

GIVEN NAMES French 4%. *Andre, Antoine, Cecile, Chantal, Chantale, Damien, Donat, Franck, Ghislaine, Jacques, Jean Claude, Jean Francois.*

Briceno (403) Spanish (**Briceño**): **1.** patronymic from the personal name *Bricio*, of Celtic origin (see BRICE). **2.** possibly a habitational name from a place so named in Colombia.

GIVEN NAMES Spanish 46%. *Jose* (12), *Luis* (7), *Carlos* (6), *Antonio* (5), *Jorge* (5), *Mario* (5), *Juan* (4), *Manuel* (4), *Pedro* (4), *Rafael* (4), *Raul* (4), *Eugenio* (3), *Francisco* (3).

Brich (110) English, German, and Danish: unexplained. Possibly a derivative of the personal name *Briccius* (see BRICE).

Brichacek (116) Czech (**Břicháček**): nickname for a fat man, from a derivative of *břichatý* 'pot-bellied', from *břicho* 'abdomen'.

Brick (1379) **1.** Irish: Anglicized form of Gaelic **Ó Bruic** 'descendant of *Broc*', i.e. 'Badger' (sometimes so translated) or **Ó Bric** 'descendant of *Breac*', a personal name meaning 'freckled'. **2.** English: possibly, as Reaney suggests, a nickname from

Old English *brȳce* 'fragile', 'worthless'. **3.** German: topographic name for someone who lived in a swampy wood, *brick, breck* 'swamp', 'wood'. **4.** Jewish (Ashkenazic): from Yiddish *brik* 'bridge', probably a topographic name. **5.** Altered spelling of German **Brück** (see BRUCK). **6.** In some cases it may be an altered spelling of Slovenian **Bric**, regional name for someone from the hilly region of western Slovenia called Brda, a plural form of *brdo* 'rising ground'.

Brickel (173) **1.** Americanized form of South German and Swiss German **Brückel, Brückl**, a topographic name for someone who lived by a small bridge, from a diminutive of Middle High German *brücke* 'bridge'. **2.** South German: nickname perhaps for a stocky, squat person, related to the word *Bröckel*, a diminutive of *Brocken* 'chunk'.

Brickell (396) English or Welsh: habitational name from Little and Great Brickhill in Buckinghamshire or from Brickil in Flintshire, both probably named with Old Welsh *brig* 'hilltop' + Old English *hyll* 'hill'.

Bricken (102) Scottish (Aberdeen): probably a variant of **Brechin**, a habitational name from Brechin in Angus.

Bricker (3024) **1.** Respelling of German **Brücker** or **Brügger**, habitational names for someone from any of numerous places in southern Germany, Austria, and Switzerland named Bruck or Brugg, or a topographic name for someone who lived by a bridge (see BRUCKER). **2.** Altered spelling of German **Brücher**, a topographic name for someone who lived by a swamp, from Middle High German *bruoch* 'swamp' + the suffix *-er*, denoting an inhabitant. **3.** English (Somerset): unexplained; perhaps a variant of BROOKER.

Brickett (144) English: metathesized variant of BIRKETT.

Brickey (1214) Probably a respelling of German BRICKER.

Brickhouse (591) Perhaps an altered form of the English habitational name **Brighouse**, from a place in West Yorkshire, so named from Old English *brycg* 'bridge' + *hūs* 'house', or alternatively a topographic name from Middle English *briggehouse* 'house or tower at or over the entrance to a bridge', or for someone who lived at a house made of bricks or at a place where bricks were made, Middle English *brike* 'brick' + *hous* 'house'.

Brickle (176) German: **1.** Americanized spelling of BRICKEL. **2.** Possibly also an altered spelling of South German **Briechle**, from Swabian *Brüchle* 'gourmet', 'self-indulgent person'. Compare BRAUCH.

Brickler (166) Variant spelling of German **Brückler**, a habitational name for someone who lived by a small bridge, from Middle High German *brücke* 'bridge' + the diminu-

tive suffix *-ler* denoting an inhabitant.
GIVEN NAMES German 5%. *Gunther* (2), *Mathias*.

Brickley (813) **1.** English: habitational name from a lost or unidentified place, or perhaps a variant of BRACKLEY. **2.** Irish (co. Cork): habitational name from the place name BERKELEY.

Brickman (981) **1.** Jewish (Ashkenazic): from Yiddish *brik* 'bridge' (altered by folk etymology in English-speaking countries as if derived from English *brick*) + *man* 'man'; possibly an ornamental name or an occupational name for a bridge keeper. Compare BRUCKMAN. **2.** Altered spelling of German **Brückmann** 'bridge keeper' (see BRUCKMAN). **3.** Altered spelling of Slovenian *Bricman*, derived from an old personal name *Bric* (Latin *Bricius* or *Brictius*; see BRICE) + the suffix *-man*, German *-mann*.
GIVEN NAMES Jewish 4%. *Isadore* (2), *Miriam* (2), *Avrohom, Chaya, Hyman, Meyer*.

Brickner (1010) **1.** Jewish (Ashkenazic): from Yiddish *brik* 'bridge' (altered by folk etymology in English-speaking countries as if derived from English *brick*) + the suffix *-ner*; possibly an ornamental name or an occupational name for a bridge keeper. Compare BRUCKNER. **2.** Altered spelling of German **Brückner** (see BRUCKNER).

Brickson (106) Origin unidentified.

Briddell (150) Probably an altered spelling of English **Bridle**, a metonymic occupational name for a bridle maker, from Old English *brīdel* (compare BRIDEN), or a variant of BRIDEWELL.

Bride (344) **1.** Irish and Scottish: reduced form of MCBRIDE. **2.** Perhaps also a reduced form of Scottish KILBRIDE. **3.** English: metathesized variant of BIRD.

Brideau (191) French: metonymic occupational name for a maker or seller of bridles and harness, from Old French *bride* 'bridle'.
GIVEN NAMES French 12%. *Emile* (2), *Venance* (2), *Alcide, Armand, Benoit, Napoleon*.

Briden (158) Scottish: variant spelling of BRYDEN.

Bridenbaugh (212) Americanized spelling of the German habitational name **Breidenbach**, a variant of BREITENBACH.

Bridenstine (218) Americanized spelling of German BREITENSTEIN.

Bridewell (116) English (Wiltshire): topographic name for someone who lived by a well dedicated to St. Bride or by a stream frequented by birds (Old English *bridd*).

Bridge (2508) English: from Middle English *brigge* 'bridge', Old English *brycg*, applied as a topographic name for someone who lived near a bridge, a metonymic occupational name for a bridge keeper, or a habitational name from any of the places named with this element, as for example

Bridge in Kent or Bridge Sollers in Herefordshire. Building and maintaining bridges was one of the three main feudal obligations, along with bearing arms and maintaining fortifications. The cost of building a bridge was often defrayed by charging a toll, the surname thus being acquired by the toll gatherer.

Bridgeford (304) English: habitational name, probably from Bridgeford in Northumberland, Bridgford in Staffordshire, or East or West Bridgford in Nottinghamshire, which are named with Old English *brycg* 'bridge' + *ford* 'ford'.

Bridgeforth (287) Scottish: probably a variant of the habitational name BRIDGEFORD.

Bridgeman (1443) **1.** English: topographic name for someone who lived by or kept a bridge (see BRIDGE). **2.** Americanized form of German **Bruckmann** (see BRUCKMAN).
FOREBEARS James Bridgeman or Bridgman (1620–76) came to Hartford, CT, from Winchester, Hampshire, England, in 1640.

Bridger (632) **1.** English: variant of BRIDGE. **2.** Americanized form of German **Brücker** (see BRUCKER).

Bridgers (830) English: probably an altered spelling of BRIDGES.

Bridges (17868) English: variant of BRIDGE. The *-s* generally represents the genitive case, but may occasionally be a plural. In some cases this name denoted someone from the Flemish city of Bruges (Brugge), meaning 'bridges', which had extensive trading links with England in the Middle Ages.

Bridgett (221) English and Irish: perhaps, as MacLysaght suggests, a shortened form of the Welsh patronymic *ap Richard,* assimilated to the name of one of the patron saints of Ireland. In England the name is found chiefly in the Midlands. It has been recorded in Ireland (chiefly Ulster) since the 17th century.

Bridgewater (1218) English: habitational name from Bridgwater in Somerset; the water which the bridge at Bridgwater crosses is the Parrett river, but the place name actually derives from *Brigewaltier*, i.e. 'Walter's bridge', after Walter de Dowai, the 12th-century owner.

Bridgford (133) English: variant spelling of BRIDGEFORD.

Bridgforth (113) Variant of English BRIDGEFORD.
GIVEN NAMES German 6%. *Monika* (2), *Otto*.

Bridgham (195) English: habitational name, perhaps from a place in Norfolk named Bridgham, from Old English *brycg* 'bridge' + *hām* 'homestead' or *hamm* 'enclosure hemmed in by water', or from Bridgeham Grange in Surrey, which probably has the same origin.
GIVEN NAME French 4%. *Minot*.

Bridgman (909) English: variant spelling of BRIDGEMAN.

Bridgmon (116) Variant of English BRIDGE-MAN.

Bridgwater (118) English: variant spelling of BRIDGEWATER.

Bridwell (1306) English: habitational name from some minor place called Brid(e)well, as for example Bridwell in Uffculme, Devon, or Bridewell Springs in Westbury, Wiltshire; both are named with Old English *brȳd* 'surging' or *brȳd* 'bride' + *well(a)* 'spring' (perhaps a spring associated with a fertility cult). There may be other places so called with different derivations, for example from Old English *bridd* 'nestling', 'young bird' or from St. Bride (see KIL-BRIDE).

Brief (139) **1.** German and Jewish (Ashkenazic): from Middle High German *brief* 'letter', 'missive', German *Brief*, hence a metonymic occupational name for a letter carrier or scribe. **2.** French: nickname from *bref* 'short'.
GIVEN NAMES German 7%; Jewish 6%; French 5%. *Kurt* (2), *Wolf*; *Chaskel*, *Hyman*, *Mayer*; *Benoit*, *Monique*.

Briegel (147) German: topographic name from Middle High German *bruogel* 'wet, fertile meadow'. Compare BRUEHL.
GIVEN NAMES German 4%. *Erwin*, *Hans*, *Heinz*.

Brieger (146) German and Jewish (Ashkenazic): from a place in Silesia called Brieg in German.
GIVEN NAMES German 8%; Jewish 5%. *Gunther* (2); *Eluzer* (2), *Yosef*.

Briel (201) **1.** German and Swiss German: topographic name for someone who lived by a water meadow, a variant of BRUEHL. **2.** Dutch: topographic name for someone who lived in an area of marshland, from Celtic *brogilo*, or a habitational name from the Dutch city in Zeeland so named (also spelled variously Brielle, Brill) or from various minor places in present-day Belgium and Netherlands named with this word.
GIVEN NAMES German 5%. *Erna*, *Philo*.

Brien (917) **1.** Irish: reduced form of O'BRIEN. **2.** French and English: variant spelling of BRIAN.
FOREBEARS A bearer of this name from Brittany with the secondary surname Desroches is recorded in Montreal in 1681.
GIVEN NAMES French 5%. *Armand* (2), *Marcel* (2), *Emile*, *Esme*, *Fernand*, *Heloise*, *Henri*, *Herve*, *Luc*, *Ovila*, *Telesphore*.

Brienza (307) Southern Italian: habitational name from Brienza in Potenza province.
GIVEN NAMES Italian 13%; French 4%. *Rocco* (2), *Vito* (2), *Angelo*, *Carmela*, *Carmelo*, *Domenico*, *Fiorino*, *Gino*, *Pasquale*, *Sal*, *Salvatore*; *Armand*, *Camille*.

Brier (735) **1.** English (Yorkshire): topographic name for someone who lived by a briar patch, Middle English *brere*. This was also applied as a nickname for a prickly, difficult person. **2.** Scottish and northern Irish: reduced form of **McBriar** (see

MCBRAYER). **3.** Americanized form of German BREUER.

Briere (466) French (**Brière**): topographic name from a regional variant of *bruyère* 'heather'.
FOREBEARS A Brière from Normandy, France, is documented in Quebec city in 1658, also as Labriére and Labruyère.
GIVEN NAMES French 14%. *Armand* (5), *Andre* (2), *Pierre* (2), *Adrien*, *Aurele*, *Benedicte*, *Benoit*, *Colette*, *Fernand*, *Gaston*, *Marcel*, *Micheline*.

Brierley (403) English: habitational name from any of the places called Brierl(e)y, in the West Midlands, West and South Yorkshire, and elsewhere, all of which are named with Old English *brǣr* 'briar' + *lēah* 'woodland clearing'.

Brierly (262) English: variant of BRIERLEY.

Brierton (147) English: habitational name from Brierton in County Durham (formerly in West Yorkshire) or Brearton in North Yorkshire, which are both named with Old English *brēr* 'briar' + *tūn* 'farmstead', or Brereton in Cheshire, which has the same origin (see BRERETON).

Bries (139) Dutch and German: from a vernacular form of the Celtic personal name *Brixius* (see BRICE).
FOREBEARS This name is recorded in Beverwijck in New Netherland (Albany, NY) in the mid 17th century.
GIVEN NAMES German 5%. *Kurt*, *Otto*, *Waltraud*.

Briese (343) German: habitational name from a place so named in Silesia, related to Slavic *brēs-* 'birch'.

Brieske (129) German: habitational name from a place in Lusatia (Lausitz) named Brieske.

Brietzke (126) German: habitational name from a place in Brandenburg named Brietzke.
GIVEN NAME French 4%. *Jean-Marie*.

Brigance (376) Possibly an altered spelling of German **Bregenz**, a habitational name from the place so named in Austria.

Brigandi (223) Italian (also **Brigandí**): probably a variant of BRIGANTE.
GIVEN NAMES Italian 13%. *Natale* (2), *Carlo*, *Francesco*, *Gaetano*, *Onofrio*, *Salvatore*.

Brigante (194) Italian: derogatory nickname from *brigante* 'brigand', 'bandit'.
GIVEN NAMES Italian 21%. *Giro* (2), *Rocco* (2), *Angelo*, *Cosimo*, *Gennaro*, *Lia*, *Matteo*, *Salvatore*.

Briganti (260) Italian: variant of BRIGANTE.
GIVEN NAMES Italian 17%; French 4%. *Aldo*, *Carmelo*, *Cosimo*, *Cosmo*, *Michelangelo*, *Nicola*, *Rocco*, *Sebastiano*; *Armand*, *Camille*.

Briggeman (121) Dutch: topographic name for someone living by a bridge.

Briggs (20440) Northern English form of BRIDGE, from Old Norse *bryggja*.
FOREBEARS The surname Briggs is found chiefly in West Yorkshire. A family of gen-

try have held lands at Keighley in West Yorkshire continuously for 500 years. The mathematician Henry Briggs (1561–1631), who invented logarithms, was born in Halifax, Yorkshire, England.

Brigham (2570) English: habitational name from either of two places in East Yorkshire and Cumbria named Brigham, from Old English *brycg* 'bridge' + *hām* 'homestead' or *hamm* 'enclosure hemmed in by water'.
FOREBEARS Thomas Brigham (c. 1603–53) came from London to Cambridge, MA, in 1635.

Bright (10933) **1.** English: from a Middle English nickname or personal name, meaning 'bright', 'fair', 'pretty', from Old English *beorht* 'bright', 'shining'. **2.** English: from a short form of any of several Old English personal names of which *beorht* was the first element, such as *Beorhthelm* 'bright helmet'. Compare BERT. **3.** Americanized form of German BRECHT. **4.** Americanized spelling of German BREIT.

Brightbill (367) Americanized spelling of Swiss German *Brechbühl* or the variant **Brächtbühl** (see BRECHBILL).

Brightman (729) English: occupational name for a servant of a man called Bright', or a variant of BRIGHT 1.

Brighton (511) English: habitational name from Breighton in East Yorkshire, on the river Derwent. This place is named with Old English *beorht* 'bright' or an unattested personal name *Beohta* + *tūn* 'enclosure', 'settlement'. The surname is unlikely to derive from Brighton in Sussex, which was known as *Brighthelmestone* until the end of the 18th century.

Brightwell (957) English: habitational name from any of various places, for example in Berkshire, Oxfordshire, and Suffolk, named Brightwell, from Old English *beorht* 'bright', 'clear' + *well(a)* 'spring', 'stream'.

Briglia (127) Italian: of uncertain derivation; possibly a habitational name from a minor place named with this word.
GIVEN NAMES Italian 8%. *Assunta*, *Domenic*, *Sal*.

Brigman (1124) **1.** English: variant of BRIDGE. **2.** Americanized form of German **Brüggemann** (see BRUEGGEMAN).

Brignac (463) French: habitational name from either of two places called Brignac, in Corrèze and Hénault. Both are named with Roman personal names (*Brinnius* and a reduced form of *Aprionus* respectively) + the suffix *-acus*, denoting ownership.
FOREBEARS The Brignac families of LA are descended from three brothers from the Mobile area, whose father, Jacques-Simon Brignac, had been a soldier at Fort Toulouse, AL. His birthplace in France is unknown. The surname is rare outside LA.
GIVEN NAMES French 9%. *Ferrel* (2), *Jacques* (2), *Pierre* (2), *Aldes*, *Amedee*, *Antoine*, *Camille*, *Eulalie*, *Leonce*, *Remi*.

Brigner (143) Altered spelling of German **Brückner** (see BRUCKNER) or the variant **Brüggener**.

Briguglio (153) Southern Italian (Sicily): unexplained.

GIVEN NAMES Italian 29%. *Carmine* (2), *Rocco* (2), *Salvatore* (2), *Carmel*, *Pietro*, *Sabastian*, *Sal*, *Vincenzo*.

Briles (518) Americanized form of German **Breil** or **Breyhel**, a variant of BRUEHL. Compare BROYLES.

Briley (1874) English: of uncertain origin; perhaps a variant of BRIERLEY.

Brilhart (108) Swiss German: variant spelling of German BRILLHART.

Brill (3844) **1.** English: habitational name from Brill in Buckinghamshire, named with the Celtic element *bre-* 'hill' + Old English *hyll* also 'hill'. **2.** North German and Dutch: habitational name from any of various places in northwestern Germany and the Netherlands named Brill, from Middle Low German *brūl*, *brōil* 'wet lowland'. Compare German BRUEHL. **3.** German: from Middle Low German *brill* 'eyeglasses', hence a metonymic occupational name for a maker of spectacles or perhaps a nickname for someone who wore them. **4.** Jewish (Ashkenazic): acronymic surname from Hebrew *ben rabi* 'son of . . . ' and the first letter of each part of a Yiddish double male personal name, most likely Yude (Juda) Leyb. Many Ashkenazic family names beginning with *Br-* and *Bar-* are probably of acronymic origin, but without detailed evidence from family histories it is impossible to specify the personal name from which each is derived.

Brilla (120) Origin unidentified.

Brillant (109) French: nickname for a charismatic person, from *brillant* 'shining'. Compare BRILLIANT.

GIVEN NAMES French 32%. *Lucien* (3), *Muguette* (3), *Alcide*, *Benoit*, *Gaetan*, *Marcel*, *Martial*, *Philippe*, *Romain*.

Brillhart (603) German and Dutch: unexplained. Possibly a variant of German **Brillert**, which is itself of unexplained origin, or of Dutch **Brillard**, from a derivative of Old French *bril* 'trap', 'snare for catching birds'.

Brilliant (265) Jewish (Ashkenazic): ornamental name from German *Brillant* 'diamond of the finest cut' (from French *brillant*, present participle of *briller* 'to shine or glitter'), or from the Polish cognate *brylant*, which has the same meaning, or from the Yiddish cognate *brilyant*, which has a more general meaning, 'diamond', 'jewel'. Compare DIAMOND.

GIVEN NAMES Jewish 10%. *Avi* (2), *Mayer* (2), *Meyer* (2), *Shalom*.

Brillon (131) French: from a derivative of Old French *beril* (feminine *berille*) 'trap (for birds)', hence an occupational name for a bird catcher.

GIVEN NAMES French 7%; Spanish 6%. *Marcel*, *Rodolphe*; *Epifanio*, *Jaime*, *Javier*, *Juan*, *Rosauro*.

Brim (1125) **1.** English: variant of BREAM 2. **2.** Jewish (Ashkenazic): acronymic surname from Hebrew *ben rabi* 'son of . . . ', and the first letter of each part of a Yiddish double male personal name. See also BRILL.

Brimage (110) English: probably a variant of **Bromage** (see BRUMAGE).

Brimberry (161) Probably an altered spelling of German **Brimberg**, of uncertain origin or of **Bremberg**, a habitational name from a place so named in Hesse.

Brimer (530) Scottish (Fife): most probably a variant of the ethnic name BREMNER, denoting someone from Brabant in the Low Countries.

Brimeyer (153) Respelling of North German **Breymeyer**, a variant of **Brei(t)- meyer**, which is probably a standardized form of BREDEMEIER.

Brimhall (543) English: variant of BRAM- HALL.

Brimley (159) English: habitational name, perhaps from Brimley in Devon or Brimbley in Stoke Abbott, Dorset, both named with Old English *brōm* 'broom' + *lēah* 'woodland clearing'.

Brimm (336) English: variant spelling of BRIM.

Brimmer (720) German: nickname for a grouse or grumbler, from an agent derivative of Middle High German *brimmen* 'to grumble'.

Brin (358) **1.** Jewish (Ashkenazic): habitational name from Brin, the Yiddish name for Brno, a city in Moravia. **2.** Jewish (Ashkenazic): acronymic surname from Hebrew *ben rabi* 'son of . . . ', and the first letter of each part of a Yiddish double male personal name. See also BRILL. **3.** French: nickname for a loud or quarrelsome man, from Old French *brin* 'noise', 'tumult'.

GIVEN NAMES French 7%; Jewish 4%. *Donat* (2), *Aime*, *Alain*, *Amie*, *Henri*, *Marcel*; *Mariya*, *Yakov*, *Yisroel*.

Brincefield (131) Variant spelling of BRINS- FIELD.

Brinck (161) North German, Dutch, Swedish, and Danish: variant spelling of BRINK.

GIVEN NAMES Scandinavian 9%; German 5%. *Bent*, *Lars*, *Per*, *Vibeke*; *Fritz*, *Wolfgang*.

Brinckerhoff (155) Dutch: variant spelling of BRINKERHOFF.

Brincks (155) Variant spelling of BRINKS.

Brindamour (109) French: unexplained. Possibly a nickname for someone who wore a sprig of heather or some other plant in his hat as a love token, from French *brin* 'sprig' (especially one worn in a hatband) + *d'amour* 'of love'.

Brindisi (232) Italian: habitational name from Brindisi, a port of southern Italy named in Latin as *Brundisium*.

GIVEN NAMES Italian 16%. *Rocco* (2), *Alfio*, *Angelo*, *Gaetano*, *Natale*, *Ricco*, *Salvatore*.

Brindle (871) **1.** English (Lancashire): habitational name from a place in Lancashire named Brindle, from Old English *burna* 'stream' + *hyll* 'hill'. **2.** Altered spelling of South German **Brindl**, **Bründl**, a topographic name for someone who lived by a spring or stream, from a diminutive of Middle High German *brun(ne)* 'spring', 'stream', or of BRENDLE or BRENDEL.

Brindley (886) English (chiefly Cheshire, Staffordshire, and southern Lancashire): habitational name from a place in Cheshire named Brindley, from Old English *berned* 'burnt' + *lēah* 'woodland clearing'.

Brine (263) **1.** Americanized spelling of Dutch BRUIN. **2.** English: of uncertain origin; possibly from Old English *bryne* 'burning', i.e. a topographic name for a clearing made by burning.

Brinegar (776) Americanized spelling of German **Breuniger** (see BREUNIG), or of the habitational name **Briniger**, denoting someone from Brinnig in southern Bavaria.

Briner (764) **1.** Swiss German: habitational name for someone from Brin in Grison canton (Graubünden) or from the Brin valley. **2.** Probably also an Americanized spelling of BREINER.

Brines (214) **1.** Jewish (Ashkenazic): metronymic from the Yiddish female personal name *brayne* (a back formation of the Yiddish female personal name *brayndl*, which is a diminutive of Yiddish *broyn* 'brown') + the genitive ending *-s*. **2.** English: variant of BRINE.

Briney (509) English: unexplained. perhaps a habitational name, from a lost or unidentified place, possibly in Worcestershire, where the surname is frequent.

Bring (185) Variant spelling of BRINK, or a shortened form of a German compound name beginning with *Bring-*.

Bringas (131) Basque: unexplained; mainly in Biscay.

GIVEN NAMES Spanish 44%. *Fernando* (3), *Jesus* (2), *Jose* (2), *Manuel* (2), *Marta* (2), *Pablo* (2), *Ramon* (2), *Raul* (2), *Adriana*, *Ana*, *Andres*, *Augusto*.

Bringer (105) Dutch: variant of BERINGER.

Bringhurst (348) Scottish: habitational name, probably from a place in Leicestershire, England, called Bringhurst. This was named in Old English with *Brȳninga* + *hyrst* 'wooded hill', i.e. 'wooded hill on lands associated with someone called Brȳni'.

Bringle (214) Of German origin: see BRENGLE.

Bringman (275) Variant of German BRINK- MANN.

Brining (186) **1.** English (chiefly Yorkshire): unexplained; perhaps a variant

of BROWNING. Compare BRUNNING.
2. Americanized spelling of German
Breuning (see BREUNIG).

Brininger (103) Americanized spelling of German BREUNINGER.

Brink (4613) North German, Dutch, Danish, and Swedish: topographic name for someone who lived by a pasture or green, from Middle Low German *brinc* 'edge', 'slope', 'grazing land', especially a raised meadow in low-lying marshland. In both Danish and Swedish *brink* is a borrowing of Dutch *brinck* 'waterside slope'; in Danish it means 'where the water runs deep'.

Brinker (2065) Dutch and North German: topographic name from BRINK, the suffix -*er* denoting an inhabitant.

Brinkerhoff (1095) Dutch and German: habitational name from a place so called (there is one in North Rhine-Westphalia), originally named as 'the farmstead (*hof*) in low-lying pastureland (see BRINK)'.
FOREBEARS Joris Brinkerhoff came to New Netherland from the Netherlands in 1638.

Brinkley (4329) English: habitational name from places in Cambridgeshire and Nottinghamshire named Brinkley; the first is most probably named with the Old English personal name *Brynca* (of uncertain origin) + Old English *lēah* 'woodland clearing'.

Brinkman (4141) Dutch and Danish: topographic name for someone who lived by a meadow in low-lying marshland (see BRINK).

Brinkmann (679) North German: topographic name for someone who lived by a meadow in low-lying marshland (see BRINK).
GIVEN NAMES German 12%. *Klaus* (4), *Erwin* (3), *Ulrich* (3), *Elke* (2), *Heinz* (2), *Helmut* (2), *Arno*, *Elfriede*, *Ewald*, *Fritz*, *Gerd*, *Gernot*.

Brinkmeier (183) German: variant of BRINKMEYER.

Brinkmeyer (363) North German: distinguishing name for a tenant farmer (see MEYER) whose farm was on the edge of low-lying grazing land, Middle Low German *brinc* (see BRINK).

Brinks (418) German: variant of BRINK, with the genitive ending -*s*.

Brinkworth (135) English: habitational name from a place in Wiltshire named Brinkworth, from the Old English personal name *Brynca* + *worð* 'enclosed settlement'.

Brinlee (248) Variant spelling of BRINLEY.

Brinley (400) English: probably a variant of BRINDLEY.

Brinn (314) Jewish (Ashkenazic): variant spelling of BRIN.
GIVEN NAME Jewish 4%. *Sol* (2).

Brinser (135) Probably a respelling of German **Brinzer** or **Prinser**, from a (Celtic?) personal name *Brinno*, or related to Old High German *brinnan* 'to burn'.

Brinsfield (213) Probably an Americanized form of Dutch **Bronsveld**, a habitational name from a place called Braunsfeld in Keulen.

Brinson (3414) English (of Norman origin): habitational name from Briençun in northern France. Compare BRANSON.

Brint (114) **1.** English: probably a variant of BRENT. **2.** Apparently also French: unexplained.
GIVEN NAMES French 7%. *Armand*, *Camille*, *Patrice*.

Brintnall (122) Perhaps an altered spelling of German **Brentnagel**, an occupational nickname for a cooper, from Bavarian *Brente* 'tub' + *Nagel* 'nail'. Alternatively, it may be an altered spelling of the English surname **Brentnall**, which is of unknown derivation.

Brinton (922) English: habitational name from Brinton in Norfolk, named in Old English as *Brȳningtūn* 'settlement (Old English *tūn*) associated with (-*ing*-) *Brȳni*' (a personal name based on Old English *bryne* 'fire', 'flame'), or from any of various other places with names of the same origin, such as Brineton in Staffordshire, Brimpton in Berkshire, Brenton in Devon, Brington in Cambridgeshire or (Great and Little) Brington in Northamptonshire.
FOREBEARS William Brinton (1635–99) came from Staffordshire, England, to West Chester, PA, in 1684–85.

Briody (296) Irish: Anglicized form of Gaelic **Ó Bruaideadha** 'descendant of *Bruaided*', an old Irish personal name.

Brion (373) Spanish (**Brión**) and French: habitational name from any of several places called Brion. Most of them derive from the Gaulish element *briga* 'height', 'hill' + the suffix -*one*.

Briones (1358) Spanish: probably a habitational name from a place in Logroño province named Briones.
GIVEN NAMES Spanish 44%. *Jose* (31), *Juan* (23), *Francisco* (11), *Luis* (11), *Jesus* (10), *Jorge* (9), *Manuel* (9), *Pedro* (9), *Carlos* (7), *Mario* (7), *Tomas* (7), *Armando* (6).

Brisbane (326) Scottish: nickname from Old French *bris(er)* 'to break' + Old English *bān* 'bone'. The sense of this hybrid name is not clear; it may have been used for someone crippled by a broken bone or for a violent man who broke other people's bones.

Brisbin (468) Variant spelling of Scottish BRISBANE.

Brisbois (276) French: from Old French *briser* 'to break' + *bois* 'wood', 'forest', hence possibly a nickname for someone who cleared land.
GIVEN NAMES French 5%. *Emile*, *Jacques*.

Brisbon (175) Variant spelling of Scottish BRISBANE.

Brisby (132) English: habitational name from a lost or unidentified place.

Brisco (764) Variant of northern English BRISCOE.

Briscoe (4360) Northern English: habitational name from any of various places so named. Briscoe in Cumberland is named with Old Norse *Bretaskógr* 'wood of the Britons' (see BRETT). Brisco in Cumberland and Briscoe in North Yorkshire are named with Old Norse *birki* 'birch' + *skógr* 'wood'.

Brisendine (357) English: variant of BRISSENDEN.

Briseno (951) Spanish (**Briseño**): variant spelling of **Briceño** (see BRICENO).
GIVEN NAMES Spanish 48%. *Jose* (22), *Juan* (16), *Jesus* (11), *Manuel* (9), *Javier* (8), *Miguel* (8), *Carlos* (7), *Francisco* (6), *Guadalupe* (6), *Guillermo* (5), *Luis* (5), *Raul* (5).

Brisk (191) Jewish (eastern Ashkenazic): habitational name from Brisk, the Yiddish name of two cities: Brest Litovsk in Belarus, and Brześć Kujawski in Poland.
GIVEN NAMES Jewish 9%. *Aharon*, *Avrohom*, *Hershel*, *Naftali*, *Naftaly*, *Yakov*, *Yehuda*.

Briske (143) **1.** East German: topographic name from Slavic *bris* 'birch' (see BRITZ). **2.** Variant of *Brisske*, nickname meaning 'brother' in German thieves' cant.

Brisker (133) **1.** English: variant of BRISCOE. **2.** Jewish (eastern Ashkenazic): habitational name from Yiddish *brisker* 'native or inhabitant of *brisk*' (see BRISK).
GIVEN NAMES Jewish 4%. *Emanuel*, *Ilya*.

Briskey (231) **1.** English: variant of BRISCOE. **2.** Americanized spelling of German BRISKE.

Briski (223) German: variant of BRISKE.
GIVEN NAMES German 4%. *Aloysius*, *Friedrich*, *Kurt*.

Briskin (200) Jewish (Ashkenazic): variant of BRISK.
GIVEN NAMES Russian 6%; Jewish 6%. *Galina* (2), *Boris*, *Igor*, *Leonid*, *Yury*, *Zinovy*; *Isaak* (2), *Isadore*.

Brisky (178) **1.** Variant of English **Briskey** (see BRISCOE). **2.** Americanized form of German BRISKE.

Brisley (113) English: habitational name from a place in Norfolk named in Old English with *brīosa* 'gadfly' + *lēah* 'woodland clearing'.

Brislin (204) **1.** Variant of Irish BRESLIN. **2.** Altered spelling of Swiss and South German **Brüstlin**, from a diminutive of Middle High German *brust* 'chest', 'breast' (see BRUST). **3.** Americanized form of South German **Brüslin**, a nickname for a poor person, from an old dialect word *Brüslin* 'crumb'.

Brison (419) Scottish, northern English, and Irish: variant spelling of BRYSON.

Brissenden (105) English: from either of two places in Kent named Brissenden (one near Frittenden, the other near Tenterden), both named with the Old English personal name *Brēosa* (a byname from *brēsa* 'gadfly') + Old English *denn* 'woodland pasture (for swine)'.

Brissett (135) French: variant of BRISSETTE.

GIVEN NAME French 4%. *Andre*.

Brissette (641) French: from a pet form of **Brès** (see BRICE).

FOREBEARS The name is recorded in Canada in 1668 and in Champlain in 1672 (with the secondary surname Courchesne); it is also associated with the secondary surnames Beaupré and Dupas.

GIVEN NAMES French 7%. *Aime* (2), *Armand* (2), *Normand* (2), *Alcid*, *Arsene*, *Herve*, *Laurier*, *Marcel*.

Brissey (180) **1.** Possibly an Americanized spelling of the French surname **Brisset** (or the variant **Brissez**), a pet form of the personal name *Brès* (see BRICE). **2.** Possibly an altered spelling of the South and Swiss German family name **Brütschi**, a variant of BRITSCH.

Brisson (1092) French: from a pet form of *Brès* (see BRICE).

FOREBEARS A Brisson from the Aunis region of France is recorded in Ange Gardien, Quebec, in 1664, with the secondary surname Laroche.

GIVEN NAMES French 12%. *Andre* (3), *Jacques* (3), *Marcel* (3), *Alberic* (2), *Benoit* (2), *Gilles* (2), *Lucien* (2), *Pierre* (2), *Aime*, *Alcide*, *Armand*, *Donat*.

Brister (1752) English: variant of BRISTOW.

Bristol (2658) English: variant of BRISTOW, respelled to conform to the spelling of the modern place name.

Bristor (100) Variant of English BRISTOW.

Bristow (2667) English: habitational name from the city of Bristol, named in Old English with *brycg* 'bridge' + *stōw* 'assembly place'. The final *-l* of the modern form is due to a regional pronunciation.

Britain (366) English: variant spelling of BRITTAIN.

Britcher (159) **1.** English: variant of BRACHER (see BRACH). **2.** South German: variant of BRITSCH.

Brite (370) Altered spelling of English BRIGHT or German BREIT.

Britnell (166) English: of uncertain origin; perhaps a habitational name from a place named as 'the hall of the Britons'. Compare BRINTNALL.

Brito (1948) Portuguese: habitational name from any of various places called Brito. The place name is probably related to the root *britt-*. Compare BRETON.

GIVEN NAMES Spanish 48%; Portuguese 12%. *Jose* (44), *Manuel* (30), *Juan* (29), *Francisco* (26), *Pedro* (19), *Luis* (17), *Ana* (16), *Carlos* (13), *Miguel* (13), *Javier* (11), *Jorge* (11), *Rafael* (11); *Paulo* (4), *Joao* (3), *Joaquim* (3), *Duarte*, *Martinho*; *Antonio* (25), *Aldo* (3), *Eliseo* (3), *Leonardo* (3), *Luciano* (3), *Ceasar* (2), *Cesario* (2),

Clemente (2), *Eligio* (2), *Guido* (2), *Heriberto* (2), *Lorenzo* (2).

Britsch (182) Swiss German and German: variant of **Brütsch**, a nickname for a sullen or moody person, from the dialect word *Brütsch* 'pouting mouth'.

GIVEN NAMES German 7%. *Hans*, *Heinz*, *Uwe*.

Britt (10607) **1.** English: ethnic name for a Celtic-speaking Briton or a Breton, from Middle English *brit*, *bret*, Old French *bret* (see BRETT). **2.** German: from a vernacular form of the personal name *Brixius* (see BRICE).

Brittain (3323) English: ethnic name for a Celtic-speaking Briton or Breton (see BRETT). In more recent times, this surname was adopted by immigrants to Britain as a token of their new patriotism.

Brittan (231) English: variant of BRITTAIN.

Britten (811) English: variant of BRITTAIN.

Brittenham (178) English: variant of BRITTINGHAM.

Brittian (282) English: altered spelling of BRITTAIN.

Brittin (192) English: variant spelling of BRITTAIN.

Britting (133) **1.** South German: patronymic from BRITT. **2.** In some cases, perhaps a hypercorrected form of BRITTIN.

Brittingham (1327) English: habitational name from either of two places, in Norfolk and Suffolk, named Brettenham, from Old English *Bretta* 'of the Britons' (genitive of *Brettas*) + *tūn* 'farmstead'.

Brittle (203) English (West Midlands): from a diminutive of BRETT.

Britto (303) Spanish: variant of BRITO.

GIVEN NAMES Spanish 6%. *Manuel* (3), *Alvaro*, *Dominga*, *Eufemia*, *Fermino*, *Josue*, *Juana*, *Pedro*, *Romulo*, *Serafin*.

Britton (9684) English: variant spelling of BRITTAIN.

Britts (137) Probably an Americanized spelling of BRITZ, or alternatively a variant of English BRITT (see BRETT).

Britz (541) **1.** German and Jewish (western Ashkenazic): habitational name from a place in Brandenburg named Britz. **2.** German: topographic name from Slavic *bris* 'birch', from which the place name is derived. **3.** German: from a vernacular form of the Celtic personal name *Brixius* (see BRICE). **4.** Jewish (eastern Ashkenazic): acronymic surname from Hebrew *ben rabi* 'son of . . .' and the first letter of each part of a Yiddish double male personal name. See also BRILL.

Brix (329) Danish and North German: from a vernacular form of the personal name *Brixius* (see BRICE).

GIVEN NAMES Scandinavian 5%. *Bent*, *Holger*.

Brixey (399) English: from an Old English personal name composed of the elements *beorht*, *briht* 'bright' + *sige* 'victory'.

Brixius (146) German: Latinized form of the Celtic personal name BRICE, found in Silesia and Lusatia (Lausitz).

GIVEN NAMES German 5%. *Erwin*, *Kurt*.

Brizendine (635) Variant of English BRISSENDEN.

Brizuela (198) Spanish: habitational name from a place named Brizuela in Burgos province.

GIVEN NAMES Spanish 57%. *Jose* (7), *Carlos* (3), *Juan* (3), *Marcos* (3), *Alfredo* (2), *Edgardo* (2), *Enrique* (2), *Hernan* (2), *Manuel* (2), *Rafael* (2), *Roberto* (2), *Ruben* (2).

Brizzi (162) Italian: **1.** from a short form of the personal names *Albrizzo* (a diminutive of *Alberico*) or *Fabrizio*. **2.** from an unattested Germanic personal name, *Berizo*. **3.** ethnic name from Latin *Brittius* 'Breton'.

GIVEN NAMES Italian 11%. *Benvenuto*, *Gianni*, *Saverio*, *Vito*.

Brizzolara (187) Northern Italian (Liguria): habitational name from a place called Brizzolara, near Genoa.

Bro (193) **1.** Scandinavian: habitational name from any of various places named with Swedish or Danish *bro*, Norwegian *bro* or *bru* 'bridge'. **2.** Possibly an altered spelling of Irish **Broe** (see BREW).

Broach (820) Scottish: habitational name from Broats in the Dumfries and Galloway region of Scotland.

Broad (817) English: **1.** nickname for a stout or fat person, from Middle English *brode*. **2.** from the Old English personal name *Brāda* (from *brād* 'broad').

Broadaway (198) English: variant of BROADWAY.

Broadbent (1303) Northern English: habitational name from a minor place in Lancashire, near Oldham, named Broadbent, from Old English *brād* 'broad' (see BROAD) + *beonet* 'bent grass'.

Broaddus (790) English (western England and south Wales): **1.** probably a variant (reflecting a local pronunciation) of the English topographic name **Broadhouse**, from Old English *brād* 'broad', 'extensive' + *hūs* 'house'. **2.** alternatively, perhaps, a habitational name from Broadwas in Worcestershire, which is named with Old English *brād* + an unattested element *wæsse* 'alluvial land'.

Broaden (121) Scottish: unexplained. **1.** Perhaps a topographic name for someone who lived in a broad valley, Old English *brād* 'broad' + *denu* 'valley'. **2.** Alternatively, perhaps, an altered spelling of Irish BRADEN.

Broadfoot (362) Scottish (also **Braidfoot**): from Old English *brād* 'broad' + *fōt* 'foot', probably a descriptive nickname but in some cases possibly a topographic name for someone who lived at the foot of a mountain.

Broadhead (860) **1.** English (Yorkshire): topographic name for someone who lived by a broad headland, i.e. a spur of a mountain, from Middle English *brode* 'broad' + *heved* 'head'. **2.** Americanized form of German BREITHAUPT or any of the cognates in other languages.

FOREBEARS Captain Daniel Brodhead came to North America in 1664 as part of the force whose mission was to seize New York from the Dutch

Broadhurst (708) English: habitational name from a minor place called Broadhurst, for example in Sussex, from Old English *brād* 'broad' + *hyrst* 'wooded hill', or a topographic name with the same meaning.

Broadie (229) **1.** Scottish: variant of BRODIE. **2.** English: variant of BROADY.

Broadley (178) Scottish and English: variant of BRADLEY.

Broadnax (1010) English: unexplained.

FOREBEARS Thomas Broadnax (*c.*1586–*c.*1658) came from Godmersham, Kent, England, to VA in the early 17th century.

Broadrick (162) Variant of Irish BRODERICK.

Broadstone (117) Origin unidentified. **1.** Possibly English, a variant of **Bradstone**, which is probably a topographic name from Old English *brād* 'broad' + *stān* 'stone'. **2.** Alternatively, it may be a translation of a name with similar meaning from some other language, for example the German habitational name **Breitenstein**, from any of various places so named.

Broadstreet (140) English: topographic name from Old English *brād* 'broad' + *strēt* '(Roman) road', or a habitational name from any of numerous minor places so named. This spelling of the surname is no longer found in the British Isles, although an older form, **Bradstreet**, is still found.

Broadus (856) English and Welsh: variant of BROADDUS.

Broadwater (1221) English: habitational name from a place in West Sussex named Broadwater, from Old English *brād* 'broad' + *wæter* 'water', 'river', or a topographic name with the same meaning.

Broadway (1928) English: **1.** habitational name from places called Broadway, in Worcestershire and Somerset, from Old English *brād* 'broad', 'extensive' + *weg* 'way', 'road', or a topographic name with the same meaning. See also BRADWAY. **2.** possibly a habitational name from Broadwey in Dorset, 'the broad manor on the Wey river', named with Old English *brād* 'broad' prefixed to *Wey*, an ancient pre-English river name.

Broadwell (709) English: habitational name from places in Gloucestershire, Oxfordshire, and Warwickshire named Broadwell, from Old English *brād* 'broad' + *wella* 'spring', 'stream', or a topographic name with the same meaning.

Broady (460) English: **1.** habitational name from any of various minor places called Broad(e)y, named with Old English *brād* 'broad' + *(ge)hæg* 'enclosure'. **2.** habitational name from a place named as 'broad island', from Old English *brād* 'broad' + *ēg* 'island'. There is a district of Stafford so named, on the western edge of the medieval town.

Broas (138) **1.** Portuguese: probably from the plural of *broa* 'corn bread'. **2.** Norwegian (**Broås**): habitational name from any of several farms so named, from *bru* 'bridge' + *ås* 'hill'.

Brobeck (183) **1.** German: variant of **Brotbeck**, an occupational name for a baker, from Middle High German *brōt* 'bread' + *beck* 'baker'. **2.** Probably a respelling of Swedish **Brobäck**, an ornamental name composed of the elements *bro* 'bridge' + *bäck* 'stream', or the Norwegian cognates **Brobekk**, **Brubekk**, which may be topographic or habitational names.

GIVEN NAME German 5%. *Kurt.*

Broberg (621) Swedish: ornamental name composed of the elements *bro* 'bridge' + *berg* 'mountain', 'hill'.

Brobst (776) German: variant of PROBST.

Brocato (754) Italian (Sicily): **1.** variant of BRUCATO. **2.** metonymic occupational name for a weaver or cloth merchant, from Sicilian *brucato* 'brocade'.

GIVEN NAMES Italian 10%. *Angelo* (4), *Sal* (3), *Salvatore* (3), *Santo* (3), *Cosimo* (2), *Antonio*, *Carmelo*, *Carmine*, *Michelina*, *Pasquale*, *Santi.*

Brocco (151) Italian: from *brocco* 'bud', 'shoot', 'sprout', also 'nail', 'stud', 'boss' (from Latin *broccus* 'having protruding teeth'), probably applied as a nickname or perhaps a metonymic occupational name.

GIVEN NAMES Italian 10%. *Cosmo*, *Gino*, *Nicola*, *Rocco*, *Stefano.*

Broccoli (152) Italian: from a diminutive of *brocco* (see BROCCO).

GIVEN NAMES Italian 26%. *Angelo* (2), *Biagio* (2), *Carmine* (2), *Dante* (2), *Aldo*, *Antimo*, *Benedetto*, *Carmelo*, *Dino*, *Domenic*, *Luigi*, *Silvio.*

Broce (229) French: variant spelling of **Brosse**.

Brochu (889) French: from *brochu* 'to provide with a lance or spear' or an equivalent of *broché* 'brocade', 'brocading'.

FOREBEARS A Brochu from the Poitou region of France is documented in Ste-Famille, Quebec, in 1669.

GIVEN NAMES French 18%. *Andre* (5), *Armand* (5), *Aime* (4), *Fernand* (4), *Emile* (3), *Laurent* (3), *Marcel* (3), *Cecile* (2), *Donat* (2), *Gaetan* (2), *Gilles* (2), *Jacques* (2).

Brocious (318) Altered spelling of German BROSIUS.

Brock (20854) **1.** English, Scottish, and North German: variant of BROOK. **2.** English, Scottish, and Scandinavian: nickname for a person supposedly resembling a badger, Middle English *broc(k)* (Old English *brocc*) and Danish *brok* (a word of Celtic origin; compare Welsh *broch*, Cornish *brogh*, Irish *broc*). In the Middle Ages badgers were regarded as unpleasant creatures. **3.** English: nickname from Old French *broque*, *brock* 'young stag'. **4.** Dutch: from a personal name, a short form of *Brockaert*. **5.** South German: nickname for a stout and strong man from Middle High German *brocke* 'lump', 'piece'. **6.** Jewish (Ashkenazic): probably an acronymic family name from Jewish Aramaic *bar-* or Hebrew *ben-* 'son of', and the first letter of each part of a Yiddish double male personal name. Compare BRILL. **7.** Jewish (from Poland): habitational name from Brok, a place in Poland.

Brockbank (193) English: variant of **Brocklebank**, a habitational name from Brocklebank in Cumbria or Brockabank in West Yorkshire, both named from Old English *brocc-hol* 'badger's sett' + Old Danish *banke* 'bank', 'slope'.

Brockel (196) German (also **Bröckel**): **1.** habitational name from Bröckel near Celle or from Brökeln on the Weser. **2.** in southern Germany, a variant of BROCK 3.

GIVEN NAMES German 4%. *Gottlieb*, *Kurt.*

Brockelman (125) German: **1.** (**Brockelmann**): habitational name for someone from Brockel in Württemberg. **2.** (**Bröckelmann**): habitational name for someone from Bröckel near Celle or Brökeln on the Weser river.

Brockenbrough (106) English: habitational name from Brackenborough in Lincolnshire or a similarly named place elsewhere (see BRACKENBURY). This name is found in VA from an early date.

Brocker (373) North German (**Bröcker**): topographic name for someone who lived by a swamp, from Middle Low German *brook* 'bog' + the suffix *-er* denoting an inhabitant.

Brockert (181) German: probably a metathesized variant of BURKHART.

Brockett (1059) **1.** Scottish: habitational name from a place called Brocket in Ayrshire. **2.** Scottish and English: from Middle English *bro(c)ket*, a term denoting a stag in its second year with its first horns (diminutive of Old French *brock*), probably applied as a nickname.

FOREBEARS John Brockett (died 1690) was one of the founders of New Haven, CT, in 1637/8.

Brockhaus (269) German: habitational name from a place named Brockhusen or Brockhausen, of which there are numerous instances, for example in Hannover, Oldenburg, and Westphalia.

Brockhoff (218) German: habitational name from any of the numerous farmsteads in northwestern Germany so named, from Middle Low German *brook* 'bog', 'swamp' + *hof* 'farmstead', 'manor farm'.
GIVEN NAME German 4%. *Hans* (2).

Brockhouse (144) **1.** English: variant of BROOKHOUSE. **2.** Americanized form of German BROCKHAUS.

Brockie (117) Scottish: diminutive of BROCK 2.

Brockington (663) English: habitational name, probably from a place in Dorset named Brockington, from Old English *brōchǣme* 'brook dweller' + *tūn* 'settlement'.

Brocklehurst (193) English (Lancashire): habitational name from a place near Accrington named Brocklehurst, from Old English *brocc-hol* 'badger's sett' + *hyrst* 'wooded hill'.

Brockman (4259) **1.** English: topographic name for someone who lived by a brook or stream, an elaborated form of BROCK 1. **2.** Jewish (Ashkenazic): unexplained. **3.** Respelling of German BROCKMANN.

Brockmann (431) **1.** North German: topographic name for someone who lived by a marsh, from Middle Low German *brook* 'bog', 'swamp' + *man* 'man'. **2.** Jewish: variant spelling of BROCKMAN.
GIVEN NAMES German 7%. *Ernst, Heinrich, Juergen, Kurt, Siegfried, Uwe, Wilhelm.*

Brockmeier (277) German: variant of BROCKMEYER.
GIVEN NAMES German 4%. *Eldred, Otto.*

Brockmeyer (451) North German: distinguishing name for the tenant farmer (see MEYER) of a farm on boggy ground, from Middle Low German *brook* 'swamp', 'bog'.

Brockmiller (107) Part-translation of North German **Brockmüller**, **Brockmöller**, a distinguishing name for a miller (Low German *möller*) who lived by a marsh (Middle Low German *brōk, brūk*).
GIVEN NAME French 4%. *Emile.*

Brockner (100) German: unexplained.

Brocks (106) Eastern German: **1.** variant of **Prox**, from a short form of *Procopius* (of which the vernacular form was *Prokop*); this was the name of the patron saint of Bohemia. **2.** from a short form of the personal name *Burkhard* (see BURKHART).

Brockschmidt (134) German: distinguishing name for a smith (see SCHMIDT) who lived by a bog, Middle Low German *brook*.

Brocksmith (138) Americanized form of German BROCKSCHMIDT.

Brockus (142) English: variant of BROOKHOUSE.

Brockway (1901) English: topographic name from Middle English *broke* 'brook' + *weye* 'way', 'road'.

Brockwell (555) English: probably a habitational name from an unidentified minor place named with Old English *brocc* 'badger' + *wiella* 'spring', 'stream' or *hol* 'hole', 'hollow'. Old English *brocchol* is known to have developed into *Brockwell* in at least one instance, in Derbyshire. Both Brockwell Park in London and Brockwell Farm in Buckinghamshire are of comparatively recent origin, probably deriving their names from the surname rather than vice versa.

Brod (550) Jewish (Ashkenazic): variant of BRODSKY or BRAUDE.

Broda (356) **1.** Polish and Jewish (from Poland): nickname from *broda* 'beard'. **2.** German: habitational name from a place named Broda or Brodau.
GIVEN NAMES Polish 6%. *Wieslaw* (2), *Danuta, Jozef, Tadeusz, Wladyslawa, Zbigniew.*

Brodbeck (656) German and Jewish (Ashkenazic): occupational name for a baker, from Middle High German *brōt* 'bread' + *becke* 'baker'.

Brodd (128) Swedish: topographic or ornamental name based on *bro* 'bridge'.
GIVEN NAMES Scandinavian 10%. *Anders, Evald.*

Brode (453) Jewish (from Poland): **1.** Yiddishized form of BRODA. **2.** Variant of BRAUDE.

Brodell (109) English (Lincolnshire): origin uncertain; perhaps a variant of **Braddle**, itself a variant of BRADWELL.

Broden (238) Swedish (**Brodén**): ornamental name or topographic name, probably composed of the elements *bro* 'bridge' + the adjectival suffix *-én*, from Latin *-enius*.

Broder (634) **1.** North German: from a personal name occasionally used for a younger son, i.e. the brother (Middle Low German *broder*) of someone important, or a byname for a guild member. **2.** Jewish (Ashkenazic): Yiddish variant of BRODSKY.
GIVEN NAMES Jewish 5%. *Sol* (5), *Mayer* (2), *Hershel, Isidor, Meyer.*

Broderick (4163) **1.** Irish: Anglicized form adopted as an equivalent of Gaelic **Ó Bruadair** 'descendant of *Bruadar*', a Norse personal name. **2.** Welsh: Anglicized form of Welsh *ap Rhydderch* 'son of *Rhydderch*' (see PROTHERO, RODERICK).
GIVEN NAMES Irish 7%. *Brendan, Connor, Kieran, Kilian, Malachy, Siobhan.*

Broders (157) North German: patronymic from BRODER 1.
GIVEN NAMES German 4%. *Gunther, Kurt.*

Brodersen (549) North German, Danish, and Norwegian: patronymic from BRODER as a personal name.
GIVEN NAMES German 6%; Scandinavian 4%. *Hans* (7), *Ewald, Franz, Fritz, Heinz, Lorenz, Ruediger; Astrid, Bendt, Carsten, Iver.*

Broderson (319) Jewish (from Poland and Belarus): perhaps a nickname from German *Brudersohn* 'son of a brother'.

Brodeur (1683) French: occupational name for an embroiderer, *brodeur*, from *broder* 'to embroider'.
FOREBEARS A Brodeur from the Poitou region of France is recorded in Boucherville, Quebec, in 1679, with the secondary surname Lavigne.
GIVEN NAMES French 13%. *Armand* (12), *Adrien* (6), *Lucien* (5), *Normand* (3), *Andre* (2), *Cecile* (2), *Henri* (2), *Laurent* (2), *Pierre* (2), *Rosaire* (2), *Valmore* (2), *Yvon* (2).

Brodhead (329) English: variant of BROAD-HEAD.

Brodie (2437) Scottish: habitational name from Brodie Castle in Moray. The place name is probably from Gaelic *brothach* 'muddy place' rather than *bruthach* 'steep place'.

Brodigan (119) Irish: variant of BRADIGAN, found chiefly in counties Meath and Louth.

Brodin (213) Swedish (**Brodín**): ornamental name formed with *bro* 'bridge' + the adjectival suffix *-ín*, from Latin *-enius*.
GIVEN NAMES Scandinavian 8%. *Erik* (2), *Per.*

Brodine (112) Variant of Swedish BRODIN.

Brodkin (152) Jewish (from Belarus): habitational name from Brodki, a village in Belarus.
GIVEN NAMES Jewish 5%. *Isadore, Miriam.*

Brodman (173) Jewish (Ashkenazic): variant of BROTMAN.
GIVEN NAME German 4%. *Lothar.*

Brodnax (294) Variant spelling of English BROADNAX.

Brodowski (164) Polish and Jewish (Ashkenazic): habitational name for someone from Brodowo in Łomża voivodeship or Brodów in Wolhynia. See also BRODA.
GIVEN NAMES Polish 4%. *Jozef, Zigmund.*

Brodrick (300) Irish and Welsh: variant of BRODERICK.

Brodsky (1952) **1.** Czech and Slovak (**Brodský**): habitational name for someone from any of numerous places, notably in Bohemia, named Brod, from Slavic *brod* 'ford'. **2.** Americanized spelling of Polish **Brodzki**, a habitational name for someone from the various places in Poland called Brody. **3.** Jewish (eastern Ashkenazic) and Ukrainian: habitational name for someone from Brody, a place in Galicia (now Ukraine), which was an important center of Jewish life up to the time of Hitler
GIVEN NAMES Jewish 7%; Russian 4%. *Isadore* (3), *Yakov* (3), *Hyman* (2), *Ilya* (2), *Elihu, Elik, Emanuel, Jascha, Leib, Meyer, Miriam, Moisey; Leonid* (9), *Boris* (7), *Mikhail* (7), *Iosif* (3), *Arkady* (2), *Gennady* (2), *Igor* (2), *Lev* (2), *Lyudmila* (2), *Yefim* (2), *Alevtina, Grigory.*

Brodt (399) Jewish (Ashkenazic): variant of BROD.
GIVEN NAMES Jewish 4%. *Aron, Chaim, Chaya, Hyman, Jakob, Moshe, Shimshon.*

Brody (3129) **1.** Hungarian (**Bródy**), Slavic, and Jewish (Ashkenazic): habitational name for someone from any of the many towns and cities in central and eastern Europe named with Slavic *brod* 'fort'. **2.** Variant spelling of Scottish BRODIE.
GIVEN NAMES Jewish 4%. *Emanuel* (4), *Miriam* (4), *Sol* (4), *Avrohom* (3), *Moshe* (3), *Gershon* (2), *Hyman* (2), *Isadore* (2), *Mendle* (2), *Chana*, *Eluzer*, *Feivel*.

Brodzik (119) Polish: topographic name for someone living by a ford, from Slavic *brod* 'ford'.

Brodzinski (174) Polish (**Brodziński**): habitational name for someone from a place called for example Brudzyń (formerly Brodzino) in Konin voivodeship, or Brodna in Piła voivodeship. See also BRODA.
GIVEN NAMES Polish 6%. *Janusz*, *Miroslaw*, *Zygmunt*.

Broe (205) **1.** Irish: variant spelling of BREW. **2.** Americanized spelling of French BRAUD. **3.** Altered spelling of Scandinavian BRO.

Broeckel (104) **1.** German and Dutch: from a pet form of the personal name **Broekaert**, a variant of BURGHART. **2.** South German (**Bröckel**): nickname for a thickset individual.

Broecker (242) North German (**Bröcker**) and Dutch: variant of the personal name **Broekaert**, itself a variant of BURGHART.
GIVEN NAMES German 5%. *Guenter*, *Hans*, *Kurt*.

Broeder (120) Dutch: from *broeder* 'brother', generally a status name for a member of a trade association or guild.
GIVEN NAME German 7%. *Otto* (3).

Broekemeier (105) Dutch and North German: distinguishing name for a tenant farmer (see MEYER) whose farm lay in a marsh (see BROEKER).

Broeker (385) Dutch: **1.** variant of the personal name *Broekaert*, itself a variant of BURGHART. **2.** topographic name for someone living in a marsh, an agent derivative of Middle Dutch *broek*.

Broer (159) Dutch: from Middle Dutch *broeder* 'brother', a byname sometimes used for a younger son, i.e. the brother of someone important; alternatively, denoting a member of a guild. *Broer* was also used as a personal name.
GIVEN NAMES Dutch 4%; German 4%. *Dirk*; *Hans*, *Kurt*.

Broeren (107) Dutch: patronymic from the personal name BROER.

Broering (154) Dutch: patronymic from the personal name BROER.

Broerman (214) Dutch: variant of BROER 'brother', with the addition of *man* 'man'.

Broers (197) Dutch and North German: patronymic from the personal name BROER.

Broersma (137) Frisian: patronymic from the personal name BROER.
GIVEN NAMES Dutch 4%. *Berend*, *Joost*.

Brogan (2740) Irish: Anglicized form of Gaelic **Ó Brógáin** 'descendant of *Brógán*', a personal name probably derived from a diminutive of *bróg* 'shoe'.
GIVEN NAMES Irish 6%. *Brendan*, *Michael Patrick*.

Brogden (669) English (Yorkshire): habitational name from Brogden in West Yorkshire, so named with Old English *brōc* 'brook' + *denu* 'valley'.

Brogdon (1489) English: variant spelling of BROGDEN.

Broge (104) German (**Bröge**): nickname for an ostentatious person, from Middle High German *brogen* 'to be resplendent', 'to flaunt'.

Broggi (113) Italian: from a short form of the personal name *Ambrogio*, Italian form of AMBROSE.
GIVEN NAMES Italian 8%. *Aldo* (2), *Domenic*, *Lorenzo*, *Umberto*.

Brogna (234) Sicilian and southern Italian: metonymic occupational name for a swineherd, from Sicilian *bbrogna* 'shell used for calling pigs', from Late Latin *ebornea (bucina)* 'ivory horn', or alternatively a nickname for someone with a large nose, from the same word in the sense 'pig's snout'.
GIVEN NAMES Italian 14%. *Donato* (2), *Sal* (2), *Angelo*, *Antonio*, *Carlo*, *Carmine*, *Federico*, *Fiore*, *Gaetano*, *Salvatore*, *Sebastiano*, *Vincenzo*.

Brogren (108) Swedish: ornamental name composed of the elements *bro* 'bridge' + *gren* 'branch'.
GIVEN NAMES Scandinavian 15%; German 4%. *Erik*, *Nels*; *Hans*.

Brohl (108) German: variant of BRUEHL.

Broich (195) German: Lower Rhine variant of BROOK.

Brokaw (1389) Altered form of the Dutch personal name *Brokaert* (see BROEKER).

Brokenshire (114) English: variant of BURKINSHAW.

Broker (417) Dutch: Americanized form of BROEKER.

Brokke (107) Dutch: topographic name for someone living by a marsh, Middle Dutch *broek*.
GIVEN NAMES Dutch 5%. *Cees*, *Cornelis*.

Brolin (152) Swedish: ornamental name composed of the elements *bro* 'bridge' + the common surname suffix *-lin*.

Broll (154) German: nickname for a fat man, from Swabian *brollig* 'fat'

Brom (292) German: **1.** from *Brohm*, a variant of BRAHM. **2.** altered spelling of BROMM.

Broman (600) **1.** English: from the Middle English personal name *Bruman*, *Bruneman*, Old English *Brūnmann*. **2.** Swedish: ornamental name composed of the elements *bro* 'bridge' + *man* 'man'.

GIVEN NAMES Scandinavian 7%. *Erik* (2), *Bjorn*, *Lennart*, *Niklas*.

Bromberg (945) Jewish (eastern Ashkenazic): habitational name from Bromberg (from *Brom(beere)* 'bramble' + *Berg* 'mountain', 'hill'), the Yiddish or German name of the city of Bydgoszcz in Poland.
GIVEN NAMES Jewish 7%; Russian 4%. *Yechiel* (4), *Aba*, *Aron*, *Avraham*, *Avrohom*, *Chiam*, *Filipp*, *Lipman*, *Mendel*, *Meyer*, *Rakhil*, *Reuven*; *Boris* (5), *Mikhail* (5), *Grigoriy*, *Iosif*, *Leonid*, *Lev*, *Pyotr*, *Sofiya*, *Yevsey*.

Bromell (118) English: perhaps a variant of BROMWELL or BROOMHALL.

Bromfield (272) English: variant spelling of BROOMFIELD.

Bromley (2192) English: habitational name from any of the many places called Bromley, in Essex, Hertfordshire, Kent (now in Greater London), Greater London, Greater Manchester, Staffordshire, and elsewhere. Most are named with Old English *brōm* 'broom' + *lēah* 'woodland clearing', but Bromley (near Bow) in Greater London is from Old English *bræmbel* 'bramble' + *lēah*.

Bromm (183) German: variant of BRUMM 2.
GIVEN NAMES German 7%. *Othmar*, *Otto*.

Brommer (225) German: variant of BRUMMER.

Broms (112) Dutch: see BRONS.

Bromwell (191) English: habitational name from Broomwell in Herefordshire named in Old English with *brōm* 'broom' + *wella* 'spring', 'stream'.

Bronaugh (263) **1.** Irish: variant of **Branagh** (see BRANNICK). **2.** Possibly an altered spelling of German **Bronnach**, **Braunach**, or **Braunagel**, occupational names for a nailsmith.

Bronder (202) Dutch: variant of BRANDER.

Broner (170) **1.** Dutch and Jewish (Ashkenazic): topographic name for someone who lived by a well (see BRUNNER). **2.** Jewish (Ashkenazic): variant of BRAUNER.
GIVEN NAMES Jewish 10%. *Aron* (2), *Miriam*, *Peleg*, *Shaul*, *Shmuel*, *Sol*.

Bronfman (114) Jewish (eastern Ashkenazic): metonymic occupational name for a seller of spirits, from Yiddish *bronfman* 'alcohol', 'vodka', 'spirits' + *man* 'man'.
GIVEN NAMES Russian 19%; Jewish 15%. *Grigoriy* (2), *Yefim* (2), *Aleksandr*, *Dmitriy*, *Mikhail*, *Sofiya*, *Yuriy*, *Yuzef*, *Zoya*; *Bina* (2), *Arie*, *Iakov*, *Marat*, *Ruvin*, *Zinaida*.

Brong (150) Dutch: variant of BRONK.

Bronikowski (137) Polish: habitational name from any of several places called Broniki or Bronikowo, in Konin, Leszczno, Piła, and Sieradz provinces.

Bronk (418) **1.** Dutch: probably a variant of BRINK. **2.** Jewish (eastern Ashkenazic): habitational name from the village of Bronki, in eastern Poland.
FOREBEARS Jonas Bronck (1600–43), for whom the Bronx in NY is named, was a

Dutch sea captain born in Småland, Sweden, probably of Dutch ancestry. In the 1620s he was based in the Netherlands. In 1629 he sailed to New Amsterdam in the ship *Fire of Troy* and staked out a claim of approximately 500 acres just north of the confluence of the Harlem and the East rivers.

Bronkema (170) Frisian: unexplained.

Bronkhorst (104) Dutch: habitational name from a place called Bronkhorst, in Steenderen, Gelderland.

Bronnenberg (121) German (Rhineland): habitational name from a place called Brauneberg in the Rhineland-Palatinate.

Bronner (693) German: variant of BRUNNER.

GIVEN NAMES German 4%. *Annice, Dieter, Eldred, Fritz, Gerhard, Kurt*.

Bronowski (77) Polish and Jewish (from Poland): habitational name for someone from a place called Bronów, Bronowo, or Bronowice, from *brona* 'harrow', or from a short form of various Slavic personal names.

Brons (141) Dutch: from Middle Dutch *broem, brom* 'broom', probably a topographic name, although Debrabandere suggests it may have been a nickname for a poor farmer, one whose land was covered with broom.

Bronson (3884) English: variant of BRUNSON.

Bronstad (124) Probably Norwegian: habitational name from a farm named Brunstad, from the Old Norse personal name *Brúni* + Old Norse *staðir*, plural of *staðr* 'farmstead', 'dwelling'.

Bronstein (910) Jewish: variant of BRAUNSTEIN.

GIVEN NAMES Jewish 9%. *Hyman* (3), *Aron* (2), *Chaim* (2), *Hillel* (2), *Myer* (2), *Sol* (2), *Anshel, Fishel, Ilya, Irina, Isador, Isadore*.

Bronston (127) Jewish (Ashkenazic): Americanized spelling of BRONSTEIN (see BRAUNSTEIN).

Bronte (68) Altered form of Irish PRUNTY. The change in spelling was probably an early 19th-century development, due to romantic admiration for the English admiral Lord Nelson, on whom the title Duke of Bronte was conferred in 1799 by Ferdinand, King of the Two Sicilies. Bronte is the name of a place in Sicily, literally meaning 'thunder'.

Brook (1679) 1. English: topographic name for someone who lived by a brook or stream, from Middle English *brook*, Old English *brōc* 'brook', 'stream'. 2. North German and Dutch: topographic name for someone who lived by a water meadow or marsh, from Low German *brook*, Dutch *broek* (cognate with German BRUCH and Old English *brōc*; see 1). 3. Americanized spelling of German and Jewish BRUCK or German BRUCH.

Brookbank (248) English (Yorkshire): habitational name from a minor place called Brooksbank, named with Middle English *brokes* (genitive of *broke* 'brook') + *bank* 'bank'. There are places of this name in Bradfield and Agbrigg, West Yorkshire.

Brooke (2022) English: variant spelling of BROOK, which preserves a trace of the Old English dative singular case, originally used after a preposition (e.g. 'at the brook'). FOREBEARS In 1650, Robert and Mary Mainwaring Brooke brought ten children and a number of servants with them from England to MD, where Robert became governor. Although the fourteen known contemporary Brooke immigrants in VA included Robert's brothers Richard and Humphrey, the relationships of the others are unknown. Brooke family memorials remain in the Anglican church at Whitchurch, Hampshire, England.

Brookens (247) English: variant spelling of BROOKINS.

Brooker (1695) English: topographic name for someone who lived by a stream, a variant of BROOK.

Brookes (651) English: variant of BROOK, which preserves the Old English genitive case (i.e. 'of the brook').

Brookfield (168) English (Lancashire): habitational name from any of various minor places named with Old English *brōc* 'brook' + *feld* 'open country', in particular Brookfield House in Nether Peover, Cheshire, recorded as *le Brocfeld* in the late 13th century.

Brookhart (437) Americanized form of Dutch *Brockaert* or German **Brockhardt**, metathesized forms of BURKHART.

Brookhouse (127) 1. English: topographic name for a house by a stream, from Middle English *brok(e)* 'brook' + *hous* 'house'. 2. Americanized form of German BROCKHAUS.

Brooking (403) English: variant of BROOKINS. This is the most frequent form of the surname in the British Isles.

Brookings (119) English: variant of BROOKINS.

Brookins (1346) English: topographic name for someone who lived by a stream, from a derivative of Old English *brōc* 'stream' (see BROOK). In Britain the form **Brooking** is much commoner.

Brookman (863) 1. English: variant of BROOK. 2. Americanized form of Dutch BRUGMAN.

Brookover (433) Americanized spelling of German **Brockhöfer**, a variant of BROCKHOFF, or of **Bachofer**, a topographic name for a farmer living by a stream (see BACH + HOFER).

Brooks (78647) 1. English: from the possessive case of BROOK (i.e. 'of the brook'). 2. Jewish (Ashkenazic): Americanized form of one or more like-sounding Jewish

surnames. 3. Americanized spelling of German BRUCKS.

FOREBEARS This name was brought independently to North America from England by numerous different bearers from the 17th century onward. Among them were William Brooks, who brought the name to Scituate, MA, from Kent, England, in 1635, and Henry Brooks, who came to Woburn, MA, in or before 1649.

Brooksher (128) Respelling of English BROOKSHIRE.

Brookshier (229) Respelling of English BROOKSHIRE.

Brookshire (1933) English: unexplained; possibly related to another unexplained English surname, **Brookshaw**.

Broom (1629) English: habitational name from any of various places called Broom(e) or Brome, from Old English *brōm* 'broom', 'gorse'. There are such places in Bedfordshire, County Durham, Norfolk, Shropshire, Suffolk, Worcestershire, and elsewhere.

Broomall (166) Perhaps an altered spelling of English BROOMHALL, reflecting a local pronunciation, but see also BROMWELL.

Broome (3613) English: variant spelling of BROOM.

Broomell (115) English: probably a variant of BROOMHALL.

Broomfield (653) English: habitational name from any of the places named with Old English *brōm* 'broom', 'gorse' + *feld* 'open country', for example Broomfield in Essex, Kent, and Somerset, or Bromfield in Cumberland and Shropshire.

Broomhall (121) English: habitational name from a place called Broomhall, most probably the one in Cheshire, which takes its name from Old English *brōm* 'broom', 'gorse' + *halh* 'nook', 'hollow'.

Broomhead (116) English: habitational name from Broomhead, now a district of Sheffield.

Brooner (129) Probably an Americanized spelling of the German and Jewish name BRUNNER.

Brophy (2627) Irish: Anglicized form of Gaelic **Ó Bróithe** 'descendant of *Bróth*', a personal name or byname of unknown origin. Also Anglicized as **Broy**.

GIVEN NAMES Irish 6%. *Brendan* (2), *Maeve*.

Brosch (266) German: 1. from a vernacular pet form of the Latin personal name *Ambrosius* (see AMBROSE). 2. from a Sorbian pet form of the Slavic personal name *Bronislaw*.

GIVEN NAMES German 6%. *Alois, Friedl, Gerhardt, Hermann, Inge*.

Brose (723) German: from a vernacular short form of the Latin personal name *Ambrosius* (see AMBROSE).

Brosey (109) Americanized form of German BROSE.

Brosh (197) Americanized spelling of German BROSCH.

GIVEN NAMES Jewish 4%. *Amnon* (2), *Dov, Moshe, Shai.*

Broshears (150) Americanized form of French (Huguenot) BRASSEUR. Compare BRASHEARS.

Brosi (105) German: variant of BROSIG or BROSE.

GIVEN NAMES German 7%. *Gunter, Juergen, Kurt.*

Brosig (136) German: from a vernacular pet form of the Latin personal name *Ambrosius* (see AMBROSE).

GIVEN NAMES German 12%. *Kurt* (2), *Erwin, Hans, Heinz, Klaus.*

Brosious (206) Americanized spelling of German BROSIUS.

Brosius (813) German: from a short form of the Latin personal name *Ambrosius* (see AMBROSE).

Broskey (117) Americanized spelling of German BROSKI.

Broski (155) Eastern German: **1.** Slavicized variant of Low German **Broske**, a reduced pet form of the Latin personal name *Ambrosius* (see AMBROSE). **2.** pet form of the personal name BROSS.

Brosky (240) Eastern German: variant spelling of BROSKI.

Brosman (123) Respelling of German **Brossmann**, a variant of BROSS.

Brosmer (102) German (Baden): unexplained.

GIVEN NAME French 4%. *Alphonse.*

Brosnahan (286) Irish: variant of BRESNAHAN.

Brosnan (918) Irish: Anglicized form of Gaelic Ó **Brosnacháin** (see BRESNAHAN).

GIVEN NAMES Irish 7%. *Brendan* (5), *Dermot, Nuala, Pegeen.*

Brosnihan (100) Irish: variant of BRESNAHAN.

Bross (903) **1.** German: from a reduced form of the Latin personal name *Ambrosius* (see AMBROSE). **2.** German: from Middle High German *brossen* 'to sprout or bud', hence an affectionate nickname for a young son. Compare BROTZ. **3.** Eastern German: from the Slavic personal name *Prus*, related to German *Preusse* 'Prussian'.

Brossard (287) French: nickname from *brosse* 'brush' + the pejorative suffix *-ard*.

FOREBEARS A Brossard from the Anjou region of France is recorded in Montreal in 1669.

GIVEN NAMES French 8%. *Andre, Cyrille, Henri, Jean Charles, Pierre, Rosaire.*

Brossart (249) Altered spelling of BROSSARD.

Brosseau (551) French: from a diminutive of BRUSSE (probably in the topographic sense).

FOREBEARS A bearer of the name from Brittany is documented in Quebec city in

1668 as Brossard or Broussard, with the secondary surname Laverdure.

GIVEN NAMES French 11%. *Andre* (4), *Adelard* (2), *Lucien* (2), *Pierre* (2), *Alphonse, Emile, Gaston, Jacques, Laurier, Lucienne, Michel, Rosaire.*

Brossett (143) Altered spelling of French **Brosset**, a diminutive of BRUSSE (probably in the topographic sense).

Brossette (162) French: from a diminutive of BRUSSE.

Brossman (282) German: variant of BROSS.

Brost (732) German: occupational name for an official, from Middle High German *brobest* 'supervisor' (from Latin *praepositus*).

GIVEN NAMES German 4%. *Mathias* (3), *Erwin, Frieda, Kurt, Otto.*

Brostrom (292) Swedish (**Broström**): ornamental compound of *bro* 'bridge' + *ström* 'river'.

GIVEN NAMES Scandinavian 4%. *Evald, Helmer, Nels.*

Brosz (142) Polish: from a pet form of *Ambrozy*, Polish form of the Latin personal name *Ambrosius* (see AMBROSE).

Brotemarkle (117) Altered spelling of German **Brotmerkel**, an occupational nickname for a baker, from *Brot* 'bread' + a pet form of personal name *Mark* (as in *Markward*).

Broten (255) **1.** German: probably a shortened form of any of various compound names containing the element *Braten* 'roast' (from Middle High German *brāte*), as for example **Bradenahl** ('baked eel') or **Bratengeiger**, a nickname for a fiddler (from a derivative of Middle High German *gīge* 'fiddle', 'violin') who was paid in food rather than cash. **2.** Variant spelling of Norwegian **Bråten** (see BRAATEN).

Brother (132) **1.** English: from a byname occasionally used for a younger son, i.e. the brother (Old English *brōðor*) of someone important, or for a guild member (*brother* was used in this sense in Middle English). **2.** English and Irish: from the cognate Old Norse *Bróðir*, which was in use as a personal name, originally for a younger son.

GIVEN NAME French 4%. *Andre.*

Brothers (4142) **1.** Irish: Anglicization of Irish Ó **Bruadair**, an ancient Donegal sept name: it has also been derived, probably wrongly, from Gaelic *bruadar* 'dream', 'reverie'. **2.** In New England, an Americanized form of French BRODEUR.

Brotherson (186) **1.** Americanized form of North German, Norwegian, and Danish BRODERSEN, or Jewish BRODERSON. **2.** English: perhaps a variant of BROTHERTON.

Brotherton (1872) English: habitational name from either of two places called Brotherton, in North Yorkshire and Suffolk; both are named with Old English *brōðor* 'brother' or the Old Scandinavian personal

name *Bróðir* + Old English *tūn* 'farmstead', 'enclosure'.

Brotman (391) **1.** altered spelling of German **Brotmann**, an occupational name for a baker and peddler of breads and pastries, from Middle High German *brōt* 'bread' + *man* 'man'. **2.** Jewish Ashkenazic: cognate of 1, from German *Brot* 'bread' + *Mann* 'man'.

GIVEN NAMES Jewish 5%. *Sol* (4), *Emanuel, Isidor, Meyer.*

Brott (623) **1.** German and Jewish (Ashkenazic): from German *Brot* 'bread' (Middle High German *brōt*), hence a metonymic occupational name for a baker **2.** German: from a Germanic personal name related to Old High German *proz* 'budding growth'.

Brotz (160) German: **1.** variant of PROTZ. **2.** from a dialect variant of BROTT.

Brotzman (310) German (**Brotzmann**): from a dialect variant of **Brotmann** (see BROTMAN).

Broudy (164) Jewish (American): Americanized spelling of BRAUDE. Compare BROWDY.

Brough (1202) **1.** English: habitational name from any of various places called Brough, of which there are several in Yorkshire and Derbyshire as well as elsewhere. The place name is from Old English *burh* 'fortress' and in most cases these are the sites of Roman fortifications. The pronunciation is usually 'bruff'. **2.** Possibly an altered spelling of German BRAUCH.

Brougham (242) English: habitational name from a place in Cumbria named Brougham, from Old English *burh* 'fortress' + *hām* 'homestead'. The pronunciation is 'broo-um'.

FOREBEARS The type of four-wheeled horse-drawn carriage known as a *brougham* was named after Henry, Lord Brougham (1778–1868). He was descended from a certain Henry Brougham, who had bought the manor of Brougham in 1726.

Brougher (281) Americanized spelling of German **Braucher**, a variant of BRAUCH.

Broughman (337) Americanized spelling of German **Brauchmann** or **Brauckmann**, variants of BROCKMANN or of **Brachmann** (see BRACHMAN).

Brought (104) Possibly English: unexplained.

Broughton (3974) English: habitational name from any of the many places in all parts of England called Broughton. The first element is variously Old English *brōc* 'brook', *burh* 'fortress', or *beorg* 'hill', 'mound'; the second is in all cases Old English *tūn* 'enclosure', 'settlement'.

Brouhard (175) French: from Old French and Occitan *brou* 'broth'. Morlet suggests this was a nickname for someone who lived on soup.

FOREBEARS A Brouart is documented in Quebec city in 1641.

Brouillard (627) French: habitational name from any of the places so named, from Old Occitan *brohl*, *brouil* 'copse enclosed by a wall or hedge'. Compare BREAULT.

FOREBEARS A Brouillard from the Poitou region of France is documented in Montreal in 1688. Another, from Angoumois, is documented at La Pérade in 1706, with the secondary surname Lavigueur.

GIVEN NAMES French 13%. *Armand* (6), *Lucien* (3), *Marcel* (3), *Fernand* (2), *Alain*, *Aurele*, *Camille*, *Damien*, *Donat*, *Euclide*, *Herve*, *Ovila*.

Brouillet (212) French: variant of BROUILLARD.

GIVEN NAMES French 10%. *Fabien*, *Fernand*, *Jean-Luc*, *Marcel*, *Michel*, *Pierre*.

Brouillette (1224) Respelling of French BROUILLET.

GIVEN NAMES French 6%. *Armand* (4), *Jacques* (3), *Lucien* (2), *Adlore*, *Amie*, *Anatole*, *Andre*, *Clovis*, *Colette*, *Gaston*, *Herve*, *Jean-Paul*.

Broun (144) Of uncertain origin; possibly a variant spelling of Scottish BROWN.

GIVEN NAMES French 6%; Russian 4%. *Clemence*; *Boris*, *Lyubov*, *Sergey*.

Brous (168) Variant of German BRAUSE 2.

Brouse (582) **1.** French: altered form of **Brosse**, which has at least two possible origins: **2.** a topographic name for someone who lived in a scrubby area of country, from Old French *broce* 'brushwood', 'scrub' (Late Latin *bruscia*), or a habitational name from any of various minor places named with this word. **3.** occupational name for a brush maker, from the same Old French word in the transferred sense 'brush'.

Broussard (8992) Southern French: variant of BROSSARD.

FOREBEARS The Broussard families of LA trace their ancestry to two Acadian brothers, Joseph and Alexandre, also called Beausoleil, who arrived in New Orleans in 1765.

GIVEN NAMES French 6%. *Andre* (11), *Alcide* (6), *Antoine* (6), *Pierre* (5), *Emile* (4), *Evest* (4), *Fernand* (4), *Minos* (4), *Ulysse* (4), *Alphe* (3), *Curley* (3), *Jacques* (3).

Brousseau (999) Southern French: variant of BROSSEAU.

FOREBEARS A bearer of the name from the Poitou region of France is documented in Quebec city in 1683.

GIVEN NAMES French 10%. *Andre* (5), *Armand* (3), *Lucien* (3), *Chantal* (2), *Jacques* (2), *Laurent* (2), *Alcide*, *Alphonse*, *Benoit*, *Camille*, *Celine*, *Emile*.

Brouwer (1017) Dutch: occupational name for a brewer of beer or ale, Middle Dutch *brouwer*.

GIVEN NAMES Dutch 5%; German 4%. *Gerrit* (5), *Frans* (3), *Harm* (3), *Dirk* (2), *Egbert*, *Hendrick*, *Herm*, *Jacobus*, *Mieke*, *Onno*, *Pim*, *Wim*; *Kurt* (3), *Hans* (2), *Eldor*, *Wilfried*, *Wilhelm*, *Wilhelmina*.

Brouwers (107) Dutch: patronymic from BROUWER, i.e. 'son of the brewer'.

GIVEN NAMES French 8%; Dutch 5%; German 4%. *Jacques*, *Olivier*; *Pim*; *Hans* (2).

Brovold (133) Norwegian: habitational name from any of various farms named Brovold, Brovoll, or Bruvoll, from *bru* 'bridge' + *voll* 'green field'.

Brow (577) **1.** English: either a descriptive nickname for someone with bushy or otherwise distinctive eyebrows, from Middle English *browe* 'eyebrow', 'eyelid' (Old English *brū*), but, more likely, a topographic name for someone who lived at the brow of a hill from a transferred use of the same word; surnames of the type *de la Browe* are recorded from the end of the 13th century. **2.** Americanized spelling of French BRAUD. **3.** Americanized spelling of Dutch **Brouw**, an occupational name for a brewer, from a derivative of Middle High Dutch *brouwen* 'to brew'.

Browder (2105) Americanized form of Dutch **Brouder** 'brother' or of German BRODER.

Browdy (111) Jewish (American): Americanized spelling of BRAUDE. Compare BROUDY.

GIVEN NAMES Jewish 5%. *Emanuel*, *Myer*.

Browe (156) Variant spelling of BROW.

Browell (103) English (Northumberland; of Norman origin): habitational name from Breuil in Calvados or from any of numerous places elsewhere in France called La Breuil.

Brower (5621) **1.** English: variant of BREWER. **2.** Respelling of BRAUER or BROUWER.

Browers (101) Americanized spelling of Dutch BROUWERS.

Brown (447208) English, Scottish, and Irish: generally a nickname referring to the color of the hair or complexion, Middle English *br(o)un*, from Old English *brūn* or Old French *brun*. This word is occasionally found in Old English and Old Norse as a personal name or byname. *Brun-* was also a Germanic name-forming element. Some instances of Old English *Brūn* as a personal name may therefore be short forms of compound names such as *Brūngar*, *Brūnwine*, etc. As a Scottish and Irish name, it sometimes represents a translation of Gaelic *Donn*. As an American family name, it has absorbed numerous surnames from other languages with the same meaning.

Brownback (137) Americanized form of the German surname **Braunbach**, a topographic name from Middle High German *braun* 'brown' + *bach* 'stream'.

Browne (8347) Irish and English variant of BROWN.

FOREBEARS In Galway the name Browne is borne by descendants of a 12th-century Norman called *le Brun*. It is Gaelicized as **de Brún**.

A John Browne, who died in 1662 in Wannamoisett, RI, was a magistrate in Plymouth Colony, MA, 1635–54.

Brownell (2967) English: habitational name from any of various places called Brownell, for example in Yorkshire, Cheshire, and Staffordshire, from Old English *brūn* 'brown' + *hyll* 'hill'.

FOREBEARS Thomas Brownell came from England to Little Compton, RI, in about 1650.

Browner (379) Americanized form of BRAUNER.

Brownfield (1519) **1.** Jewish (American): Americanized form of an ornamental compound, **Braunfeld**, from German *braun* 'brown' + *Feld* 'field'. **2.** English: variant of BROOMFIELD.

Browning (16084) English: from the Middle English and Old English personal name *Brūning*, originally a patronymic from the byname *Brūn* (see BROWN).

FOREBEARS This name was brought independently to North America from England by numerous different bearers from the 17th century onward. William Browning was one of the free planters who assented to the 'Fundamental Agreement' of the New Haven Colony on June 4, 1639.

Brownlee (3615) Scottish and English: habitational name from Brownlee in Lanarkshire or Brownley in Warwickshire, both named with Old English *brūn* 'brown' + *lēah* 'woodland clearing'.

Brownley (174) English: variant of BROWNLEE.

Brownlie (216) Scottish: variant of BROWNLEE.

Brownlow (779) English: habitational name from places in Greater Manchester, Cheshire, and Staffordshire named Brownlow, all probably from Old English *brūn* 'brown' + Old English *hlāw* 'hill', 'mound'.

Brownridge (102) English: variant of BROWNRIGG.

Brownrigg (262) English: habitational name from any of several places in Cumbria named Brownrigg, from Old English *brūn* 'brown' + *hrycg* 'ridge'.

Brownsberger (150) Part-translation of German **Braunsberger**, a habitational name from any of numerous places called Braunsberg.

Brownson (518) English: variant of BRUNSON.

FOREBEARS John Brownson or Bronson was one of the original settlers of Hartford, CT, in 1635.

Brownstein (960) Jewish (American): partly Americanized form of BRAUNSTEIN.

GIVEN NAMES Jewish 7%. *Binyamin* (2), *Sol* (2), *Avrohom*, *Ilissa*, *Meier*, *Miriam*, *Mordechai*, *Morty*.

Brox (127) German: variant spelling of BROCKS.

GIVEN NAME German 5%. *Gunter*.

Broxson (338) English: patronymic from BROCK 2.

Broxterman (185) German (**Broxtermann**): topographic name from BROCK, for someone living by a stream, or a habitational name from Broxten near Osnabrück, named with the same word.

Broxton (364) **1.** English: habitational name from Browston in Suffolk, recorded in Domesday Book as *Brockestuna*, from the Old English personal name *Brocc* (from Old English *brocc* 'badger') + Old English *tūn* 'settlement', or from Broxton in Cheshire, an obscure name, possibly from Old English *burgæsn* 'burial place'. **2.** Possibly an altered spelling of German **Broxten**, a variant of *Broxtermann* (see BROXTERMAN).

Broy (145) Irish: see BROPHY.
GIVEN NAMES French 5%. *Gilles, Gillis*.

Broyhill (198) English: variant of **Broughhill**, a habitational name from Broughall in Shropshire, named in Old English with *burh* 'fortified place' + an uncertain second element, probably *hyll* 'hill'.
FOREBEARS James Broughill, born at Sutton Maddock, Shropshire, England, in 1714, emigrated to Caroline County, VA, in or before 1732.

Broyles (3723) Americanized form of German **Breil** or **Breyhel**, a variant of BRUEHL. Compare BRILES.
FOREBEARS Johannes Breyhel and his family, from Oetisheim in Württemberg, were among a group of German colonists sponsored by VA Governor Alexander Spotswood in 1714. They founded a settlement called Germanna in Orange County. Hans Jacob Breyhel (born 1705) was the ancestor of the Broyles family, while his brother Conrad was founder of the Briles family.

Broz (566) Polish (**Broż**), Czech and Slovak (**Brož**), Croatian, and Slovenian: from a short form of the personal names *Ambroży* (Polish), *Ambrož* (Czech and Slovenian), *Ambrozije* (Croatian), all from Latin *Ambrosius* (see AMBROSE).

Brozek (357) Polish (**Brożek**) and Czech and Slovak (**Brožek**): from a pet form of the personal name *Broż* (Polish), *Brož* (Czech) (see BROZ).
GIVEN NAMES Polish 6%. *Janina* (2), *Grazyna, Krystyna, Lucyna, Piotr, Stanislawa, Tomasz, Wladyslaw*.

Brozik (104) Czech and Slovak (**Brožík**): from a pet form of the personal name *Brož* (see BROZ).

Brozovich (233) Croatian (**Brozović**): patronymic from the personal name *Broz*, shortened form of *Ambrozije*, Slovenian form of AMBROSE.

Brozowski (174) Americanized spelling of Polish BRZOZOWSKI.
GIVEN NAMES Polish 5%. *Ignatius, Zigmond, Zigmund*.

Bru (119) **1.** Catalan: from the Catalan personal name *Bru*, equivalent to BRUNO, or nickname from Catalan *bru* 'dark (hair or skin)', for someone with dark hair and skin. **2.** Norwegian: habitational name from a farmstead so named in western Norway, from *bru* 'bridge'.
GIVEN NAMES Spanish 26%; Scandinavian 7%. *Luis* (4), *Guillermo* (3), *Juan* (3), *Carlos* (2), *Francisco* (2), *Jose* (2), *Alberto, Jaime, Lourdes, Miguel, Rafael, Ricardo*.

Brubach (101) German: habitational name for someone from Bruebach, near Mulhouse, Alsace, or from any of various places called Braubach.

Brubacher (169) German and Swiss German: habitational name for someone from a place called BRUBACH.

Brubaker (4585) Americanized spelling of BRUBACHER.

Brubeck (194) Americanized spelling of the German habitational name **Brubach** (see BRUBACHER), or of Norwegian *Brubekk* (see BROBECK).

Brucato (288) Italian (Sicily): probably a habitational name from a place named with Sicilian *bbrica, bbruca* 'tamarisk'.
GIVEN NAMES Italian 11%. *Angelo* (2), *Salvatore* (2), *Cosmo, Ignazio, Mafalda, Nunzio, Orfeo*.

Bruce (19142) Scottish and English (of Norman origin): habitational name from a place in Normandy which has not been certainly identified. Traditionally, it is believed to be derived from Brix near Cherbourg, but Le Brus in Calvados and Briouze in Orne have also been proposed as candidates.

Bruch (810) German: topographic name for someone who lived by a marsh or a stream that frequently flooded, from Middle High German *bruoch* 'water meadow' or 'marsh'. Compare BROOK.
GIVEN NAMES German 4%. *Reinhard* (2), *Bernd, Ernst, Guenter, Hans, Hertha, Kurt*.

Bruck (997) **1.** German (also **Brück**): topographic name for someone who lived near a bridge, or an occupational name for a bridge keeper or toll collector on a bridge, from Middle High German *bruck(e)* 'bridge'. *Bruck* remained the Bavarian and Austrian form, reflected in place names such as Innsbruck, whereas in central and northern Germany *Brück(e)* was the regular and ultimately standard form, as for example in the place name *Osnabrück*. Switzerland has both forms. See also BRUECK. **2.** Jewish (from Poland and Belarus): from Polish, Belorussian, or Yiddish *bruk* 'pavement', possibly a metonymic occupational name for a paver.
GIVEN NAMES Jewish 4%. *Hyman* (2), *Naftali* (2), *Eliahu, Hershel, Meyer, Miriam, Ruvim, Shloime, Sol, Yoav*.

Brucker (1128) **1.** German: topographic name for someone who lived near a bridge, or an occupational name for a bridge

keeper or toll collector on a bridge (see BRUCK). **2.** Jewish (eastern Ashkenazic): occupational name, either from a Yiddishized form of Polish *brukarz* 'paver' or from an agent noun based on Yiddish *bruk* 'pavement'. **3.** English: variant spelling of BROOKER.

Bruckman (283) **1.** German (**Bruckmann**): variant of BRUCK, with the addition of the suffix -*mann* 'man'. **2.** English: variant spelling of BROOKMAN.

Bruckner (1125) **1.** South German: topographic name for someone living by a bridge or an occupational name for a bridge toll collector; a variant of BRUCK with the addition of the suffix -*ner*. **2.** Jewish (Ashkenazic): occupational name for a paver, from Yiddish *bruk* 'pavement' + the agent suffix -*ner*.
GIVEN NAMES German 4%. *Albrecht, Arno, Gunther, Hans, Helmut, Juergen, Kurt, Markus, Oskar, Wolfgang*.

Brucks (227) German (northwest): probably a habitational name from Brucks (also Brux) which derived from Middle Low German *brōk* 'low-lying marsh'. A north German family by this name reportedly (1820) derive their name from Flemish immigrants from a place called *Broex*.

Bruder (1175) **1.** German and Swiss German: from a byname meaning 'brother', occasionally used for a younger son, i.e. the brother of someone important, or for a guild member. **2.** Jewish (Ashkenazic): possibly derived from German *Bruder* 'brother' or Yiddish *bruder*; the reason for its adoption as a surname is not clear.
GIVEN NAMES German 4%. *Kurt* (3), *Beate, Bernhard, Egon, Erhardt, Erwin, Klaus, Otto*.

Brue (353) **1.** Americanized spelling of Norwegian BRU. **2.** Possibly an altered spelling of the French surname **Bru**, in part a topographic name for someone who lived on moorland, from Old Occitan *bruc* 'heather', 'heath', or a habitational name from any of the various minor places named with this word (for example Bru in Lot, or Le Bru in Cantal, Corrèze, and Dordogne); otherwise from *bru* 'daughter-in-law'.
GIVEN NAMES Scandinavian 4%. *Nordahl* (2), *Erik, Nils*.

Brueck (255) German (**Brück**): see BRUCK.
GIVEN NAMES German 4%. *Heinz, Hermann*.

Brueckner (436) German (**Brückner**): from Middle Low German *brugge*, Middle High German *brugge, brücke, brügge* 'bridge' + the agent suffix -*ner*, hence a topographic name for someone living by a bridge, an occupational name for a bridge toll collector, or in the southeast (Silesia for example) a bridge keeper or repairer. *Brücke* also meant 'plank road' or 'paved road', and the Middle Low German forms *brügger* and *brüggeman* especially denoted a street paver (see BRUEGGER, BRUEGGEMAN).

GIVEN NAMES German 7%. *Otto* (2), *Claus, Elke, Erwin, Guenter, Hans, Heinz, Kurt, Monika, Rudi, Siegbert.*

Brueggeman (510) Variant of German BRUEGGEMANN.

GIVEN NAMES German 4%. *Erna* (2), *Fritz* (2), *Erwin, Otto.*

Brueggemann (404) North German (**Brüggemann**): topographic name for someone who lived near a bridge or a metonymic occupational name for a bridge keeper or street paver, Middle Low German *brügge-man* (see BRUCKMAN, BRUECKNER).

GIVEN NAMES German 6%. *Fritz* (2), *Aloys, Erwin, Gerd, Johannes, Juergen, Reiner, Waltraud.*

Brueggen (166) German (**Brüggen**): habitational name from any of several minor places so named.

Bruegger (186) North German (**Brügger**): occupational name for a bridge keeper, paver, or road builder, Middle Low German *brügger*. Compare BRUEGGEMANN.

GIVEN NAMES German 4%. *Armin* (2), *Hans.*

Bruehl (220) **1.** German (**Brühl**): topographic name for someone who lived in a swampy area, Middle High German *brüel*, Middle Low German *brül* 'swampy land with brushwood'. **2.** German and Jewish (western Ashkenazic): habitational name from Brühl in Germany.

GIVEN NAMES German 9%; French 4%. *Hans* (2), *Armin, Dieter, Frieda, Horst, Lothar; Colette, Regine.*

Bruemmer (397) German (**Brümmer**): variant of BRUMMER.

GIVEN NAMES German 5%. *Claus, Gretche, Kurt, Udo, Waldron.*

Bruen (394) **1.** Irish: variant of BREEN. **2.** English: probably a variant of BROWN. **3.** North German (**Brün**): from Middle Low German *brün* 'brown', hence probably a nickname for someone with brown hair or a dark complexion or for someone who habitually wore brown clothes. Compare BRAUN.

GIVEN NAMES Irish 5%. *Dermot, Finbarr.*

Bruening (702) North German (**Brüning**): from the personal name *Brüning*, a derivative of *Bruno* (see BRAUN).

GIVEN NAMES German 4%. *Fritz* (3), *Beate, Ekkehard, Erwin, Joerg, Klaus, Nicolaus.*

Bruer (276) **1.** North German: occupational name for a brewer, a dialect (Low German) form of BRAUER. **2.** Possibly an altered spelling of the cognate BREUER. **3.** Possibly Norwegian: habitational name from a farm named Bruer, from the plural of *bru* 'bridge'.

Bruesch (118) German (**Brüsch**): topographic name from Middle High German *brüsch* 'broom', 'brushwood'.

Bruesewitz (113) German (**Brüsewitz**): habitational name from places in Pomerania and Mecklenburg called Brüsewitz.

Brueske (160) Eastern German (**Brüske**): probably from the Slavic stem *brus* 'whetstone', which is also a personal name, *Brus.*

GIVEN NAMES German 7%. *Erna* (2), *Kurt, Otto.*

Bruestle (123) South German: from a diminutive of BRUST.

GIVEN NAMES German 10%; Scandinavian 4%. *Kurt* (3), *Erna, Erwin.*

Bruett (108) South German (**Brütt**): unexplained.

GIVEN NAME German 4%. *Georg.*

Bruff (212) English: variant spelling of BROUGH.

Bruffett (107) Origin unidentified.

Bruffey (123) Americanized spelling of Irish BROPHY.

Bruffy (107) Probably an Americanized spelling of Irish BROPHY.

GIVEN NAMES French 7%. *Jacques, Lucienne.*

Brugge (104) German: **1.** variant of BRUCK. **2.** nickname from Sorbian *bruk* 'beetle'.

Bruggeman (949) **1.** North German (**Brüggemann** or **Bruggemann**): see BRUEGGEMANN. **2.** Dutch: variant of BRUGMAN, cognate with 1.

Bruggemann (118) North German: variant of **Brüggemann** (see BRUEGGEMANN).

Brugger (954) **1.** South German variant or Americanized spelling of North German *Brügger* (see BRUEGGER). **2.** habitational name for someone from any of various (southern) places called Bruck or Brugg in Bavaria and Austria.

GIVEN NAMES German 5%. *Ulrich* (7), *Ewald, Gerhard, Hans, Hans Peter, Kurt, Manfred, Otto.*

Bruggink (124) Dutch: perhaps from a derivative of Middle Dutch *brugg(h)e* 'bridge'.

Bruggman (104) Dutch: see BRUGMAN.

Brugh (338) English: variant spelling of BROUGH.

Brugman (329) **1.** Dutch: topographic name for someone who lived near a bridge or a metonymic occupational name for a bridge keeper, from Dutch *brugge* 'bridge' (see BRIDGE); in some cases, it is a habitational name for someone from the Flemish city of Bruges (or Brugge), meaning 'bridges'. **2.** Altered spelling of Swiss **Bruggmann** 'bridge keeper'.

GIVEN NAMES German 5%. *Helmut* (2), *Erna, Kurt.*

Bruha (174) From German **Brühan** or **Bruhan**, the name of an old family of beer brewers, composed of early modern German *breu* 'brew' + the personal name *(Jo)han* (John), a common nickname for a helper.

Bruhl (177) German (**Brühl**) and Dutch: see BRUEHL.

GIVEN NAMES German 4%. *Gunther, Heinz.*

Bruhn (1247) North German, Danish, and Swedish: variant of BRUN.

GIVEN NAMES German 5%. *Otto* (4), *Hans* (3), *Bernd* (2), *Bernhard* (2), *Dieter* (2), *Kurt* (2), *Gerhard, Heinz, Johann, Wolfgang.*

Bruhns (121) **1.** German, Danish, and Swedish: variant of BRUHN. **2.** Estonian: unexplained.

GIVEN NAMES German 7%; Scandinavian 6%. *Bodo, Johannes, Merwin; Erik.*

Bruin (225) **1.** Dutch: from a personal name based on Middle Dutch *bruun* 'brown', or a nickname referring to the color of the hair or complexion. See also BRAUN. **2.** English: of uncertain origin. Reaney suggests that the name may simply reflect a pronunciation of French BRUN. **3.** Altered spelling of Swiss *Bruhin.*

Bruington (171) English: see BREWINGTON.

Bruins (254) Frisian and Dutch: patronymic from BRUIN.

GIVEN NAMES Dutch 4%; German 4%. *Albertus, Berend, Dirk, Gerrit; Johanes, Otto.*

Bruinsma (257) Frisian: patronymic from BRUIN.

Bruland (108) Norwegian: habitational name from a farmstead so named in western Norway, from *bru* 'bridge' + *land* 'land', 'farmstead'.

GIVEN NAMES German 7%; Scandinavian 5%. *Caspar, Hans, Kurt; Ove.*

Brule (403) French (**Brûlé**): topographic name for someone living in a place cleared for use by burning, from Old French *brusle* 'burnt', past participle of *brusler* 'to burn'. Some instances of the name may derive from the same word used with reference to disfigurement by burning, either accidentally or as a medieval ordeal or punishment. Compare BRENT 3.

FOREBEARS Étienne Brûlé, from the Marne region of France, was with Samuel de Champlain as an interpreter for the Hurons in 1608–10 expedition to North America; he is credited with the discovery by Europeans of Lake Superior.

GIVEN NAMES French 12%. *Fernand* (2), *Lucien* (2), *Andre, Laurent, Marcel, Monique, Normand, Phillippe, Pierre, Raoul, Yvan, Yves.*

Bruley (280) French and English: variant spelling of **Brûlé** (see BRULE). As an English name, this may be both a Norman and a Huguenot importation. It is recorded in Oxfordshire and Worcestershire in the 13th and 14th centuries, and was also common in East London in the 18th century.

Brull (190) **1.** Jewish (Ashkenazic): variant spelling of BRUEHL. **2.** Possibly from German *Brüll*, a dialect word meaning 'minnow' (the fish).

GIVEN NAMES Jewish 11%. *Boruch* (2), *Eliezer* (2), *Chaim, Chana, Menachem, Mendel, Osher, Yehuda.*

Brulotte (139) Altered spelling, reflecting Canadian pronunciation patterns, of French **Brulot**, a diminutive of *Brûlé* (see BRULE).
FOREBEARS A Brûlot is documented in Beaupré, Quebec, in 1667.
GIVEN NAMES French 10%. *Armand, Normand, Yvon.*

Brum (361) **1.** German: variant of BRUMM. **2.** Jewish (eastern Ashkenazic): nickname from Yiddish *brum* 'hum', 'roar'. **3.** Portuguese name of Flemish origin, taken to Portugal by a 15th-century immigrant from Flanders and now found mainly in Madeira.
GIVEN NAMES Spanish 17%; Portuguese 8%. *Jose* (8), *Manuel* (6), *Luis* (3), *Isauro* (2), *Angelina, Anselmo, Celso, Dimas, Diniz, Domingos, Eduino, Enrique; Paulo* (2), *Marcio.*

Brumage (118) English: variant of **Bromage**, a habitational name from Bromwich in the West Midlands, named in Old English with *brōm* 'broom' (the shrub) + *wīc* 'outlying dairy farm'.

Brumagin (115) English: from the informal England adjective *Brummagem* 'of or relating to Birmingham', hence a habitational name for someone from the city of Birmingham in the West Midlands.

Brumbach (258) German: habitational name from any of various places called Brombach, in Hesse, Baden, and Bavaria.

Brumback (537) Americanized spelling of German BRUMBACH.

Brumbalow (108) Variant of BRUMBELOW.

Brumbaugh (2004) Americanized spelling of German BRUMBACH.

Brumbeloe (111) Variant of BRUMBELOW.

Brumbelow (359) Origin uncertain. **1.** It is probably a variant of English **Rumbelow**, itself of uncertain origin; most likely a habitational name from a place in Aston, Birmingham, called *the Rumbelow*, from a misdivision of the Old English locative phrase *æt þæm þreowān hlāwum* 'at the three hills'. The Old English word *hlāw* meant 'small hill' or 'tumulus'. **2.** Alternatively, it may be an Americanized form of the German habitational name **Brummerloh**, from a place so named near Varel, Lower Saxony.

Brumberg (122) Jewish (eastern Ashkenazic): variant of BROMBERG.
GIVEN NAME Jewish 7%. *Yaacov.*

Brumble (131) English; probably a variant of BRAMHALL.

Brumby (136) English: habitational name from a place in Lincolnshire named Brumby, from the Old Norse personal name *Brúni* or from Old Norse *brunnr* 'well' + *býr* 'farmstead', 'village'.

Brumer (168) German and Jewish (Ashkenazic): variant of BRUMMER 2.
GIVEN NAMES Jewish 6%. *Haim, Semen.*

Brumett (187) Altered spelling of BRUMMITT.

Brumfield (3576) English: variant spelling of BROOMFIELD.

Brumit (287) English: variant of BRUMMITT.

Brumitt (138) English: variant of BRUMMITT.

Brumleve (156) North German: probably a nickname meaning 'roaring lion', or a habitational name from a house bearing the sign of a roaring lion, from an altered form of Middle Low German *brüllen* 'to roar' + *leve* 'lion'.
FOREBEARS Five Brümleve brothers came to North America from Lengerich, near Lingen, Emsland, Germany in 1846–51. Two of them settled in Teutopolis, IL, and three in Louisville, KY. Other members of the family, also from Emsland, settled in St. Louis, and Americanized the name by spelling it as **Bruemleve**.

Brumley (2307) English: variant of BROMLEY.

Brumlow (160) Probably a variant of **Bromlow**, an English topographic name, from Old English *brōm* 'broom' + *hlāw* 'hill', 'mound', or possibly a habitational name from a minor place named with these elements. But see also BRUMBALOW.

Brumm (672) German: **1.** nickname for a noisy or restless person, from a derivative of Middle High German *brummen* 'to buzz'. Compare BRUMMER. **2.** from *Brumo*, a short form of a Germanic personal name formed with Old High German, Old Saxon *brūn* 'brown'.

Brummel (525) English: variant of BRAMHALL.

Brummell (190) English: variant of BRAMHALL.

Brummer (857) **1.** German: nickname for a curmudgeon, from an agent derivative of Middle High German *brummen* 'to buzz or grumble'. **2.** German: variant of BRUMM 2. **3.** Jewish (Ashkenazic): nickname from 1, or alternatively for a person who hummed, Yiddish *brumer.*

Brummet (184) Variant of English BRUMMETT.

Brummett (1866) English: Reaney identifies this surname as a variant of the habitational name **Broomhead**, from a locality in Hallamshire, now part of Sheffield, South Yorkshire, so named with Old English *brōm* 'broom' or *brōmig* 'growing with broom' + Old English *hēafod* 'headland'. In England the name is more commonly spelled **Brummitt**.

Brummitt (441) English: variant of BRUMMETT.

Brummond (282) Variant of German BRUMMUND.

Brummund (108) German: from a medieval personal name, *Brunomund* (see BRUMM).

Brumwell (127) English: variant of BRAMWELL, possibly in some instances of BRAMHALL.

Brun (669) **1.** French: descriptive nickname, *le Brun* 'the brown one', from Old French *brun*, referring to the color of the hair, complexion, or clothing (see BROWN). This name is also Catalan and Swiss (in the French as well as the German speaking parts). **2.** North German and Scandinavian: nickname Germanic *brūna* 'brown', referring to the color of the hair, complexion, or clothing or from a Germanic personal name, *Bruno*, with the same meaning. See also BRAUN.
GIVEN NAMES French 10%. *Normand* (2), *Patrice* (2), *Philippe* (2), *Pierre* (2), *Thierry* (2), *Armand, Georges, Henri, Jean Michael, Jean-Marc, Lorette, Lucien.*

Bruna (174) Italian (Calabria): from the feminine personal name *Bruna.*
GIVEN NAMES Spanish 5%. *Emilio* (3), *Juan* (2), *Gustavo.*

Brundage (1706) English: habitational name from Brundish in Suffolk, so named with Old English *burna* 'stream' + *edisc* 'pasture'.

Brundidge (335) Variant of English BRUNDAGE.

Brundige (416) Variant of English BRUNDAGE.

Brundrett (142) English: variant of **Brandreth**, a habitational name from Brandirth in North Yorkshire.

Brune (1142) **1.** German (**Brüne**): habitational name from Brüne in Lower Saxony or Brünen near Wesel, Lower Rhine. **2.** German: nickname meaning 'brown', from a dialect form (Alemannic and Low German) of BRAUN. **3.** French: from the feminine form of BRUN.
GIVEN NAMES German 4%. *Erwin, Guenter, Hans, Helmut, Ingeborg, Johannes, Jurgen, Wilfried.*

Bruneau (651) French: from a diminutive of BRUN.
FOREBEARS A bearer of the name from the Poitou region of France was documented in Quebec city in 1668. A Bruneau or Drouineau was recorded in Quebec city in 1699, with the secondary surname Jolicoeur.
GIVEN NAMES French 9%. *Pierre* (3), *Patrice* (2), *Alcide, Amie, Andre, Arianne, Armand, Cecile, Emile, Jean-Claude, Lucien, Napoleon.*

Brunell (698) **1.** English: from Old French *brunel*, a diminutive of *brun* 'brown' (see BRUN). **2.** Swedish: ornamental name from *brun* 'brown' + the suffix *-ell*, taken from the Latin adjectival ending *-elius*. **3.** German (also **Brünell**): nickname meaning 'brown' (see BRUN). **4.** Catalan: from *brunell*, a diminutive of *bru* 'brown'.

Brunelle (1750) French: from diminutive of BRUN.
FOREBEARS Documented as Brunel, the name appears in the records of Boucherville, Quebec, for 1677, borne by an immigrant from Normandy, France.

GIVEN NAMES French 10%. *Armand* (8), *Normand* (5), *Alphonse* (4), *Lucien* (4), *Henri* (3), *Jacques* (3), *Laurier* (3), *Marcel* (3), *Pierre* (3), *Alphee* (2), *Andre* (2), *Clovis* (2).

Brunelli (288) Italian: from a diminutive of BRUNO.

GIVEN NAMES Italian 7%. *Angelo* (4), *Caesar*, *Leno*, *Massimo*, *Quinto*.

Bruner (5868) **1.** German: nickname from Old High German, Old Saxon *Brūn* (see BRUN). **2.** German and Jewish: variant spelling of BRUNNER.

Brunet (1084) **1.** English, French, and Catalan: from a diminutive of *brun* 'brown' (see BROWN, BRUN). **2.** German: from a personal name (*Brunhard*) composed with Old High German, Old Saxon *brūm* 'brown'. But this is also a Waldensian name in Germany, in which case it is of French origin, see 1.

FOREBEARS A Brunet from the Charente Maritime region of France is documented in Montreal in 1663, with the secondary surname Belhumeur. Another, from the Perche region, is documented in Quebec city in 1667, with the secondary surname Létang. Other secondary surnames recorded are Bourbonnais, La Sablonnière, and Saint-André. A Calvinist from La Rochelle, with the secondary surname Bonvouloir, is documented in Quebec city in 1698.

GIVEN NAMES French 14%. *Pierre* (7), *Andre* (5), *Emile* (4), *Armand* (3), *Marcel* (3), *Elphege* (2), *Fernand* (2), *Michel* (2), *Antoine*, *Armande*, *Cecile*, *Christophe*.

Brunett (290) French: variant of BRUNET.
GIVEN NAMES French 5%. *Emile*, *Jean Claude*, *Pierre*, *Romain*.

Brunette (1230) French: variant of BRUNET, reflecting the French Canadian pattern of pronouncing the final -*t*, which is not pronounced in metropolitan French.
GIVEN NAMES French 5%. *Jacques* (3), *Armand* (2), *Aime*, *Fernand*, *Gilles*, *Marcel*, *Micheline*, *Normand*, *Pierre*, *Yvon*.

Brunetti (716) Italian: patronymic or plural form of BRUNETTO.
GIVEN NAMES Italian 15%. *Vito* (7), *Angelo* (2), *Dante* (2), *Dino* (2), *Francesco* (2), *Guido* (2), *Leno* (2), *Nicola* (2), *Sal* (2), *Antonio*, *Attilio*, *Battista*.

Brunetto (233) Italian: from *Brunetto*, a diminutive of BRUNO.
GIVEN NAMES Italian 9%. *Angelo*, *Carmelo*, *Concetta*, *Domenic*, *Gaetano*, *Sal*.

Bruney (139) Variant of French BRUNET.

Brungard (218) German: variant of BRUN-GARDT.

Brungardt (598) German: from an early medieval personal name (presumably *Brungard*) formed with Old High German, Old Saxon *brūn* 'brown'.

Brunger (130) **1.** German (**Brünger**): from the Old German personal name *Brunger* meaning 'brown spear'. **2.** English: from the same name as 1 or from *Brūngār*, the

Old English form of the personal name. **3.** Possibly an altered spelling of the Swiss habitational name **Brüngger**, denoting someone from Brünggen in Switzerland.

Bruni (821) Italian: patronymic or plural form of BRUNO.
GIVEN NAMES Italian 16%. *Angelo* (4), *Carlo* (3), *Ugo* (3), *Domenic* (2), *Francesco* (2), *Gino* (2), *Luigi* (2), *Santo* (2), *Vittorio* (2), *Aldo*, *Amadeo*, *Antonio*.

Brunick (178) Altered form of North German **Brunik** or **Brünicke**, variants of **Brüning** (see BRUNING).

Bruning (1198) North German (**Brüning**) and Dutch: patronymic from the Germanic personal name *Brun(o)* or the byname *Brūn* (see BRAUN).
GIVEN NAMES German 4%. *Ilse* (2), *Otto* (2), *Bismark*, *Ernst*, *Fritz*, *Gunter*, *Klaus*, *Kurt*.

Brunjes (182) North German (**Brünjes**): patronymic from *Brüni*; an Eastphalian form of *Brüning* (see BRUNING).

Brunk (1412) Variant of German BRUNKE.

Brunke (331) **1.** South German: from Middle High German *brunke* 'splendor', hence probably a nickname for an ostentatious dresser. **2.** North German (and Frisian): from a pet form of the personal name *Brun(o)* or the byname *Brün* (see BRUN).
GIVEN NAMES German 4%. *Erhardt*, *Ernst*, *Erwin*, *Otto*.

Brunken (236) **1.** North German and Frisian: patronymic from BRUNKE 2. **2.** German: habitational name from places called Brunken, in Brandenburg and Rhineland.
GIVEN NAME German 7%. *Manfred*.

Brunker (239) German: habitational name for someone from Brünken near Stettin or from either of two places called Brunken, in the Rhineland and Brandenburg.

Brunkhorst (246) German: habitational name from a place named Brunkhorst, in Gelderland, Netherlands.

Brunkow (261) Eastern German: habitational name from Brunkau near Stendal.

Brunmeier (145) Altered form of German **Brunnmeier** or **Brunnenmeier**, distinguishing name for a tenant farmer (see MEYER) whose farm lay by a spring, from Middle High German *brun(ne)* 'spring'.
GIVEN NAMES German 6%. *Eldor*, *Kurt*, *Otto*.

Brunn (540) **1.** German: habitational name from any of several places called Brunn 'spring', 'well', or a topographic name with the same meaning. **2.** Swedish: ornamental name from *brunn* 'well', 'spring'.
GIVEN NAMES German 5%. *Erwin*, *Ewald*, *Helmut*, *Karl Heinz*, *Katharina*, *Kurt*, *Willi*.

Brunner (6108) German and Jewish (Ashkenazic): topographic name for someone who lived beside a spring or well, Middle High German *brun(ne)* 'spring', or habitational name for someone from a place named with this word.

Brunning (117) English (Suffolk): variant of BROWNING.

Bruno (9392) **1.** Italian and Portuguese: from a Germanic personal name, *Bruno* (see BRUN). **2.** Italian: nickname from *bruno* 'brown', referring to the color of the hair, complexion, or clothing. **3.** Italian: possibly a habitational name from a place named Bruno, for example in Asti province.
GIVEN NAMES Italian 11%. *Angelo* (34), *Salvatore* (27), *Rocco* (16), *Sal* (15), *Antonio* (14), *Carmine* (12), *Carlo* (11), *Pasquale* (11), *Vito* (9), *Domenic* (8), *Filomena* (7), *Gaetano* (7).

Brunot (104) French: from a diminutive of *brun* 'brown' (see BRUN).

Brunow (127) German: habitational name from one of four places in eastern Germany named Brunow, for example in Pomerania and Mecklenburg, or from Brunau near Saarbrücken.
GIVEN NAMES German 5%. *Eldor* (2), *Erwin*.

Bruns (4756) **1.** North German and Dutch: patronymic from BRUN, BRUIN. **2.** Altered spelling of a patronymic from *Bruhn*, a variant of the personal name *Brun(o)* (see BRUHN).

Brunsell (132) Probably an altered spelling of German **Brunzel**, from a pet form of the Slavic personal name *Bronislaw*, or a pet form of *Brun(o)* (see BRUNO 2).

Brunskill (147) **1.** Northern English: unexplained. **2.** Possibly also Dutch, perhaps a habitational name from an unidentified place named with *kil* 'stream'.
GIVEN NAME French 4%. *Patrice*.

Brunsman (188) Probably an altered spelling of North German **Brunsemann**, a habitational name for someone from Brunsen near Gandersheim.

Brunson (4730) **1.** English: patronymic from BROWN, either as a nickname or as an existing surname. Formation of new surnames ending in -*son* from existing surnames was a relatively common phenomenon in northwestern England. **2.** Variant of Dutch **Brunsen**, a patronymic from BRUN.

Brunsvold (199) Norwegian: habitational name from a farmstead in Hallingdal named Brunsvoll. The first element of the place name is probably a male personal name, Old Norse *Brúnn*, from *brúnn* 'brown'; the second element is *voll* 'meadow', 'grassy field'.
GIVEN NAME German 5%. *Otto*.

Brunswick (513) **1.** English: habitational name from the city in Saxony now known in German as Braunschweig (see 2). **2.** German: habitational name from the original Middle Low German name (a compound of *Bruns* + *wik* 'Bruno's settlement') of Braunschweig (Brunswick); the standard German form was adopted in 1573.

Brunt (597) English: variant of BRENT.

Brunton (867) Scottish and northern English: habitational name from Brunton in Fife, or either of two places in Northumberland so named, from Old English *burna* 'stream' + *tūn* 'enclosure', 'settlement'.

Brunty (183) Irish: Anglicization of Gaelic **Ó Proinntigh** (see PRUNTY). Compare BRONTE.

Bruntz (175) German: possibly a short form of **Brunzel** (see BRUNSELL) or a variant spelling of BRUNZ.

Brunz (103) German: patronymic from a short form of *Bruno* (see BRUN).

Brus (221) **1.** Polish, Slovenian, and Jewish (eastern Ashkenazic): from Slavic *brus* 'whetstone', presumably a metonymic occupational name for someone who honed or sharpened blades; possibly also a nickname for a clumsy or coarse fellow. **2.** Slovenian: from an old dialect short form of the personal name *Ambrož* (see AMBROSE). **3.** French: topographic name for someone living on a heath, from Occitan *brusc* 'heather'.

Brusca (208) Southern Italian (Sicily): **1.** topographic name from southern Italian *brusca*, *bruscia* 'butcher's broom', the name of a plant. **2.** short form of a compound name formed with *brusca*, such as **Bruscalupi**.
GIVEN NAMES Italian 23%. *Salvatore* (3), *Nunzio* (2), *Antonio*, *Benedetto*, *Mario*, *Orlando*, *Pietro*, *Sal*, *Vincenza*.

Bruschi (168) Italian: from BRUSCA or BRUSCO.
GIVEN NAMES Italian 16%. *Aldo* (3), *Amerigo*, *Angelo*, *Caesar*, *Enrico*, *Giorgio*, *Giovanni*, *Pietro*.

Brusco (224) Italian: nickname for an uncouth or prickly person, from *brusco* 'rude', 'coarse', 'abrupt', from Late Latin *bruscus*.
GIVEN NAMES Italian 25%. *Domenic* (5), *Salvatore* (4), *Alfonso* (3), *Francesco* (2), *Mario* (2), *Dino*, *Ernesto*, *Eugenio*, *Fernando*, *Franco*, *Giacomino*, *Osvaldo*.

Bruse (145) **1.** German: from a short form of the medieval personal name *Ambrosius* (see AMBROSE). Perhaps from the Slavic stem *Brus* (as in BRUSKY or the place name Bruschewitz). **2.** Swedish: possibly from a Nordic personal name *Bruse*, from Old Norse *brúsi* 'he-goat'.
GIVEN NAMES German 6%. *Claus*, *Gerhardt*.

Brush (2645) **1.** English: of uncertain origin. It may be a nickname for someone thought to resemble a brush (Middle English *brusche*, from Old French *brosse*), or a metonymic occupational name for a brush maker. It could also be from a related word, *brusche* 'cut wood', 'branches lopped off trees' (Old French *brousse*), applied as a metonymic occupational name for a forester or woodcutter, or a topographic name for someone who lived in a scrubby area of country, from Old French *broce* 'brushwood', 'scrub', 'thicket' (Late Latin *bruscia*). **2.** Respelling of German **Brusch** or **Brüsch**, a topographic name from the field name Brüsch (Middle High German *brüsch* 'heather', 'broom' or 'brush').

Brushaber (159) North German (**Brüsehaber**): associated particularly with the area to the north east of Bremen, this is of uncertain etymology. It may be an occupational name for an oat farmer, from Middle Low German *haber*, *haver*, if *brüs* denoted a particular variety of the plant. However, if the first element derives from *bross*, *bröss* 'brittle', 'crumbly', the name would have been a derisive nickname for an oat farmer. Brechenmacher proposes the gloss 'bruise the oats' as a metonymic occupational name for a miller.
GIVEN NAMES German 6%. *Konrad* (2), *Kurt* (2).

Brushwood (107) English: unexplained.

Bruske (110) German (**Brüske**, of Slavic origin): **1.** variant of **Brüsch** (see BRUSH 2). **2.** from a Sorbian personal name, *Brus*, from a word meaning 'whetstone'.
GIVEN NAME German 4%. *Otto*.

Bruski (204) Polish: habitational name for someone from a place called Brus.

Brusky (187) **1.** German: unexplained. **2.** Variant spelling of Polish BRUSKI.
GIVEN NAMES German 4%. *Aloys* (2), *Erwin*.

Bruso (468) Americanized spelling of French *Brousseau*, frequent in New England. See BRUSSEAU.

Bruss (691) **1.** German (**Brüss**): from a short form of the medieval personal name *Ambrosius* (see AMBROSE). **2.** Perhaps an altered spelling of Slavic BRUS or French **Brousse** (see BROUSE).
GIVEN NAMES German 4%. *Otto* (2), *Eldor*, *Reinhard*, *Rudie*, *Wilhelm*.

Brusse (75) French: **1.** topographic name for someone living in a scrubby area of country, from Old French *broce* 'brushwood', 'scrub' (Late Latin *bruscia*). **2.** metonymic occupational name for a brush maker, from Old French *brusse* 'brush'.

Brusseau (299) Probably an Americanized spelling of French **Brousseau**, a derivative of **Brousse** (see BRUSSE).
FOREBEARS The name is documented in Trois Rivières, Quebec, in 1667.

Brussel (102) French: variant of **Broussel**, a topographic name from a derivative of *brosse* 'brushwood', 'scrub'.
GIVEN NAME French 4%. *Gabrielle* (2).

Brusso (117) Respelling of French **Brousseau**, a derivative of *Brousse*, a variant of BRUSSE. This spelling is found chiefly in MI.
GIVEN NAME German 5%. *Mathias* (2).

Brust (1057) **1.** German: from Middle High German *brust* 'chest', 'breast'; also 'vest', presumably a nickname for someone with a particularly broad chest or alternatively for the wearer of a distinctive upper garment. **2.** Swiss German: topographic name for someone living near a down-fault in a mountain range, probably a crevasse, from *Brust*, a noun derivative of *bresten* 'to burst'. **3.** French: from Old French *brost* 'shoot', 'young growth'. Morlet suggests this is a topographic name for someone who lived by an area of low growth suitable for grazing. **4.** Jewish (Ashkenazic): presumably from German *Brust* 'chest' (see 1) or from the Yiddish equivalent, *brust*.
GIVEN NAMES German 4%. *Aloysius*, *Bernhardt*, *Hermann*, *Kurt*, *Rainer*, *Reinhold*, *Wilfried*.

Brustad (149) Norwegian: habitational name from any of several farmsteads so named, from an uncertain first element, or in some cases *bru* 'bridge', + *stad* (from Old Norse *staðr* 'farmstead', 'dwelling').

Bruster (152) **1.** English: variant of BREWSTER. **2.** English: occupational name for an embroiderer, Middle English *broudestere* (from Old French *brouder* 'to embroider', of Germanic origin). The suffix *-ster(e)* was originally feminine, but by the Middle English period was being used interchangeably for both men and women in words like BREWSTER and BAXTER, and in some regions such as East Anglia was the standard occupational suffix for men as well as women. Nevertheless, there is no evidence that men did very much embroidery. **3.** Swiss German: variant of BRUST 2, the suffix *-er* denoting an inhabitant.

Bruton (2259) English: habitational name from a place in Somerset named Bruton, 'settlement (Old English *tūn*) on the *Brue* river'. The river name is derived from a British element cognate with Welsh *bryw* 'brisk', 'vigorous'.

Brutsche (116) Possibly a variant of German **Brütsch**, a nickname for a grumpy, sullen individual, from *Brütsch*, *Brutsche* 'pout'.
GIVEN NAME French 4%. *Dominique*.

Brutus (172) Black name, adopted with reference to Lucius Junius Brutus (fl. 509 BC), founder of the Roman republic.
GIVEN NAMES French 33%. *Pierre* (4), *Allain*, *Alphonse*, *Antoine*, *Evens*, *Jacques*, *Micheline*, *Odette*, *Prosper*, *Remy*, *Serge*, *Stephane*.

Bruun (247) Danish, Norwegian, and Swedish: variant of BRUN 1.
GIVEN NAMES Scandinavian 17%; German 4%. *Erik* (3), *Anders*, *Helmer*, *Klas*, *Nels*, *Per*; *Hans*, *Kurt*.

Bruxvoort (153) Dutch: habitational name from an unidentified place.
GIVEN NAMES German 6%; Dutch 4%. *Gerrit* (2), *Herm* (2).

Bruyere (177) French (**Bruyère**): from Old French *bruyere* 'heather', hence a topographic name for someone who lived in a place where heather grew, or a habitational name from one of the places in France (for example in Calvados) named with this word.
GIVEN NAMES French 8%. *Andre*, *Fernand*, *Jacques*, *Marcel*.

Bruyn (107) Dutch: variant of BRUIN.
GIVEN NAME Dutch 6%. *Dirk* (2).

Bruzek (113) Czech: unexplained.

Bruzzese (236) Italian: reduced form of ABRUZZESE.

GIVEN NAMES Italian 33%. *Natale* (3), *Domenic* (2), *Domenico* (2), *Gerardo* (2), *Rocco* (2), *Alfredo, Annamarie, Antonio, Eduardo, Filippo, Gaetano, Gino, Giuseppe, Salvatore*.

Bry (135) French and Dutch: habitational name from any of various places in France and Belgium called Bry(e), Brie, or Bré (see DEBREE).

Bryan (21290) **1.** English (of Norman origin): habitational name (*de Brionne*) from either of two places called Brionne in northern France (in Eure and Creuse). **2.** Irish and English: from the Celtic personal name *Brian* (see O'BRIEN). Breton bearers of this name were among the Normans who invaded England in 1066, and they went on to invade and settle in Ireland in the 12th century, where the name mingled with the native Irish name *Brian*. This native Irish name had also been borrowed by Vikings, who introduced it independently into northwestern England before the Norman Conquest.

Bryans (289) Northern Irish: variant of BRYAN, with the addition of the English patronymic *-s*.

Bryant (57723) English (mainly southwestern England): variant of BRYAN.

FOREBEARS The American poet William Cullen Bryant (1794–1878) came of a New England family, being descended from Stephen Bryant, who had settled in Plymouth Colony in 1632.

Bryars (250) Scottish and English: variant of BRIER.

Bryce (1622) Scottish: from the personal name *Brice*, Gaelic *(Gille) Bhris* '(servant of) (Saint) Bricius' (see BRICE).

Bryde (106) Scottish and Irish: reduced form of McBRIDE.

Bryden (520) Scottish, of uncertain derivation: **1.** probably a habitational name from a place now lost. The surname is most common in southwestern Scotland. **2.** Reaney suggests that it is a metonymic occupational name for a bridle maker, from Old French *bridon* 'bridle'.

Brydges (162) English: variant spelling of **Bridges**, a variant of BRIDGE.
GIVEN NAME German 4%. *Bernd* (2).

Brydon (305) Scottish: variant spelling of BRYDEN.

Brye (169) French: variant of BRY. This is also found in England as a Huguenot name.

Bryer (548) English: variant spelling of BRIER.

Bryers (125) **1.** English: variant of BRIER. **2.** German: Americanized form of BREUER.
GIVEN NAMES German 5%. *Hans, Kurt*.

Bryk (269) **1.** Polish: nickname for a gambler, from *brykać* 'to gamble'. **2.** Jewish (from Poland): Polish spelling variant of BRICK.
GIVEN NAMES Polish 7%. *Tadeusz* (2), *Bogdan, Marcin, Miroslaw, Zygmunt*.

Brymer (289) Scottish (Fife): variant spelling of BRIMER, which is probably a variant of the ethnic name BREMNER, denoting someone from Brabant in the Low Countries.

Bryn (123) Welsh: topographic name meaning 'hill'.

Bryne (134) **1.** English: variant spelling of BRINE. **2.** Norwegian: habitational name from a farm called Brynes, for example in Rogaland, from Old Norse *brún* 'brim', 'edge' + *vin* 'meadow'.

Bryner (689) Swiss German: variant of BRINER.

Bryngelson (188) Swedish: patronymic from the personal name *Bryngel*, an Old Swedish dialect form of Old Norse *Bryniólfr*.

Bryon (106) English: probably a variant spelling of BRIAN.

Brys (161) Welsh: see BRICE 2.

Bryson (6275) **1.** Scottish: patronymic from the personal name *Brice*, Gaelic *(Gille) Bhris* '(servant of) (Saint) Bricius' (see BRICE). **2.** Irish (Donegal): Anglicized form of Gaelic **Ó Briosáin**, an altered version of **Ó Muirgheasáin** (see MORRISSEY).

Brzezinski (836) Polish (**Brzeziński**) and Jewish (from Poland): habitational name for someone from a place called Brzezina, Brzeziniec, Brzezinka, Brzezie, or Brzeziny, named with *brzezina* 'birch forest'.

FOREBEARS The oldest of the several Polish noble families by the name Brzeziński can be traced back to the 14th century. The American statesman Zbigniew Brzezinski (born 1928) is of Polish descent.
GIVEN NAMES Polish 8%. *Andrzej* (3), *Zbigniew* (2), *Beata, Bogdan, Casimir, Darek, Halina, Henryk, Janusz, Jaroslaw, Jozef, Lech*.

Brzoska (175) Altered spelling of Polish **Brzózka**, from a diminutive of BRZOZA.
GIVEN NAMES Polish 7%. *Casimir, Slawek, Wladyslaw*.

Brzoza (59) Polish: topographic name from *brzoza* 'birch tree'.
GIVEN NAMES Polish 22%. *Danuta, Miroslaw, Teofil, Wieslaw, Zdzislaw*.

Brzozowski (597) Polish: habitational name for someone from a place named with *brzoza* 'birch tree', for example Brzozowa, Brzozowice, or Brzozowo.
GIVEN NAMES Polish 11%. *Kazimierz* (3), *Boleslaw* (2), *Dariusz* (2), *Jerzy* (2), *Krzysztof* (2), *Miroslaw* (2), *Andrzej, Beata, Dorota, Ireneusz, Janina, Leszek*.

Brzycki (137) Polish: from a personal name *Brzykcy, Brykcy*, of Celtic origin.

Bu (95) **1.** Norwegian: variant of BO. **2.** Chinese 卜: this character means 'to divine' or 'to predict'. In ancient China there existed government officials for fortune-telling. In honor of their forebears, the descendants of several such officials adopted **Bu** as their surname. **3.** Chinese 步: from the town of Bu in the state of Jin (in present-day Shaanxi province) during the Spring

and Autumn period (722–481 BC). Descendants of a man who was enfeoffed with this area subsequently adopted the place name as their surname. This character also means 'a (walking) step'.

Bua (228) Italian (mainly Sicily): metonymic occupational name for a herdsman, or a nickname for a powerfully built man, from *bue* 'ox', an old variant of *bove* (from Latin *bos, bovis* 'bull').
GIVEN NAMES Italian 30%. *Mario* (3), *Angelo* (2), *Salvatore* (2), *Vito* (2), *Albo, Carlo, Ciro, Cosmo, Gasper, Giuseppe, Massimo, Sal*.

Bub (244) South German: nickname meaning 'boy', Middle High German *buobe* (originally a nursery word). The word was also used to denote a menial servant, and took on a derogatory meaning.

Bubak (107) Polish: patronymic from the personal name *Buba* (see BUBEL).
GIVEN NAME Polish 5%. *Tadeusz*.

Buban (147) Slovak: nickname from *bubák* 'ghost', hence for a frightful person (see BUBEL 1).

Bubar (332) Jewish (from Ukraine): nickname for someone who was illegitimate, from Ukrainian *bubar* 'bastard'.

Bubb (620) **1.** English: from an Old English personal name, *Bubba*. **2.** Variant of German BUB.

Bubeck (199) **1.** German: from a field name which gave its name to a farmstead in Württemberg. **2.** Americanized spelling of Slavic **Bubek**, a nickname from a diminutive of *buba* 'fright', 'idiot'.

Bubel (172) **1.** Polish and Czech: nickname from *buba* 'fright'. **2.** Polish: nickname from *bubel* 'unsaleable article'. **3.** German: from a Sorbian nickname denoting someone with chubby cheeks. Compare BUCEK. **4.** German: from a diminutive of BUB.

Bubier (208) Possibly of French origin; there are a small number of bearers in the British Isles, whence the name may have been brought to the U.S.

Bublitz (670) German: habitational name from a place named Bublitz, in Pomerania.
GIVEN NAMES German 4%. *Kurt* (2), *Bernhardt, Ewald, Gerhard, Otto*.

Buboltz (188) German: from a derivative of the personal name *Poppo*, which, like BUB, originated as a nursery name.

Bubolz (175) German: variant of BUBOLTZ.
GIVEN NAMES German 6%. *Armin, Gerhardt*.

Bucalo (123) Southern Italian: variant of BUCOLO.
GIVEN NAMES Italian 11%. *Antonio, Carmelo, Carmine, Cosmo, Gasper, Pasquale*.

Bucaro (145) Southern Italian (Sicily): **1.** probably from an Arabic personal name *Bū'l-hayr* meaning 'father of good'. **2.** possibly, though less likely, a variant of BUCALO (see BUCOLO).
GIVEN NAMES Italian 29%. *Rosario* (5), *Vito* (3), *Carlo* (2), *Salvatore* (2), *Biagio, Innocenzo, Luigi, Roberto*.

Bucca (121) Italian: nickname for a talkative or indiscreet person, an orator, or a person with a large or deformed mouth, from Sicilian *bbucca* 'mouth' (standard Italian *bocca*).

GIVEN NAMES Italian 19%. *Antonio, Carmello, Carmelo, Gaspare, Sal, Salvatore, Santo.*

Buccellato (222) Italian: from *buccellato* 'ring-shaped loaf', 'long-keeping bread' (from Latin *buccellatum* 'biscuit'), applied as metonymic occupational name for a baker or as a nickname for someone who was well preserved or long lived.

GIVEN NAMES Italian 19%. *Salvatore* (3), *Vito* (3), *Gasper, Giuseppa, Giuseppe, Nicolo, Rocco, Veto, Vita.*

Bucceri (106) Italian (Sicilian): from a plural form of **Buccero**, occupational name for a butcher or slaughterman, Sicilian dialect *bbuccero*, from French *boucher*.

GIVEN NAMES Italian 16%. *Salvatore* (2), *Gianni, Sal, Santo.*

Buccheri (171) Southern Italian: habitational name from a place called Buccheri in Sicily.

GIVEN NAMES Italian 28%. *Salvatore* (5), *Sal* (2), *Santo* (2), *Vincenzo* (2), *Vito* (2), *Benedetto, Corrado, Filippo, Nicola, Sebastiano.*

Bucci (1826) Italian: from a short form of any of various personal names ending with *-bucci*, for example **Iacobucci**, from *Iacobo* (see JACOB).

GIVEN NAMES Italian 15%. *Angelo* (6), *Antonio* (4), *Guido* (4), *Pasquale* (4), *Dante* (3), *Rocco* (3), *Vincenzo* (3), *Carlo* (2), *Carmine* (2), *Cosmo* (2), *Domenic* (2), *Donato* (2).

Bucciarelli (247) Italian: from a diminutive of the personal name *Buccio*, a short form of a personal name such as **Iacobucci** (see BUCCI).

GIVEN NAMES Italian 14%. *Carmine* (2), *Antonio, Bruna, Camillo, Carlo, Domenic, Giovanni, Giuseppe, Marco, Natale, Rocco, Romano.*

Buccieri (183) Southern Italian (Calabria and Sicily): patronymic or plural form of BUCCIERO.

GIVEN NAMES Italian 19%. *Biagio* (2), *Salvatore* (2), *Silvio* (2), *Fiore, Guiseppe, Rocco, Sal.*

Bucciero (111) Italian: variant of **Buccero** (see BUCCERI).

GIVEN NAMES Italian 18%. *Angelo, Antonio, Gaetano, Oresto, Pasquale, Salvatore.*

Buccini (133) Italian: patronymic or plural form of BUCCINO.

GIVEN NAMES Italian 13%. *Carmelo, Domenic, Donato, Ercole, Giuliano, Stefano.*

Buccino (185) Italian: **1.** habitational name from a place called Buccino in Salerno, Campania. **2.** from a diminutive of the personal name *Buccio* (see BUCCI).

GIVEN NAMES Italian 11%. *Sal* (2), *Angelo, Antonio, Carlo, Constantino, Rocco, Salvatore, Vito.*

Bucco (165) Italian: **1.** from a southern variant of *bocca* 'mouth', applied as a nickname for someone who had a large, deformed, or otherwise remarkable mouth or for someone who was talkative, indiscreet, or persuasive. **2.** from the Germanic personal name *Buco*.

GIVEN NAMES Italian 19%. *Angelo, Claudio, Donato, Mario, Mauro, Olinto, Vito.*

Buccola (202) Italian: **1.** from a diminutive of BUCCA. **2.** nickname for someone with curly hair, from *buccola* 'curl'. **3.** possibly from Albanian *bukura* 'beautiful', the surname being extremely common in the ancient Albanian-speaking community of Piana degli Albanesi, in Palermo province.

GIVEN NAMES Italian 13%. *Sal* (2), *Domenic, Gaspare, Salvatore.*

Bucek (196) **1.** Czech: from a pet form of the personal name *Budislav*. **2.** Czech and Sorbian: nickname from *bucek* 'chubby'. **3.** Czech and Slovak (**Buček**): topographic name from a diminutive of *buk* 'beech tree'. **4.** Slovenian (**Buček**): nickname from *buček* 'comic or ludicrous fellow'. It may also be derived from an identical dialect word meaning 'small jug-like vessel'.

Bucey (143) English: of uncertain origin; possibly a variant of **Bussey** (see BUSEY).

Buch (883) **1.** German: topographic name for someone who lived by a beech tree or beech wood, from Middle High German *buoche*, or a habitational name from any of the numerous places so named with this word, notably in Bavaria and Württemberg. (The beech tree is the main tree in the forests of central Europe.) **2.** Danish: from German (see 1) or a nickname from *buk* 'he goat'. **3.** Indian (Gujarat and Bombay city): Hindu (Brahman) and Parsi name of unknown meaning. **4.** Indian (Panjab): Sikh name based on the name of a Jat clan.

GIVEN NAMES Indian 6%; Scandinavian 4%; German 4%. *Dhaval* (2), *Nimish* (2), *Abhinav, Akshay, Deep, Deepak, Devyani, Haren, Harish, Hemant, Jawahar, Ketan*; *Morten* (2), *Fredrik*; *Otto* (2), *Erwin, Frieda, Gerda, Hans, Juergen, Jurgen, Wilhelm.*

Buchalski (113) Polish: **1.** habitational name from a place called Buchałowice. **2.** from the personal name *Buch*, a pet form of *Budzisław*.

GIVEN NAMES Polish 6%. *Dymitr, Stanislaw.*

Buchalter (258) **1.** Jewish (Ashkenazic): from German *Buchhalter* 'bookkeeper', probably an occupational name for someone who kept the books of the Jewish community. **2.** Respelling of South German **Buchhalter**, a topographic name for someone who lived on a beech-covered slope, from Middle High German *buoche* 'beech tree' + *halde* 'slope'.

Buchan (1108) Scottish: regional name from a district north of Aberdeen. There was also a barony of *Buchquane* in Strathore, Fife, a settlement called Buchan in Kirkcudbrightshire, and several other places in Scotland so named, but these are less likely to be the source of the surname.

Buchanan (23213) Scottish: habitational name from Buchanan, a place near Loch Lomond, perhaps named with Gaelic *buth chanain* 'house of the canon'.

FOREBEARS The name Buchanan was brought independently to North America from Scotland by several different bearers in the 17th and 18th centuries. George Buchanan came to MD in 1698.

James Buchanan (1791–1868), 15th President of the U.S. (1857–61), was born near Mercersburg, PA, the son of a successful land speculator and store keeper, who had emigrated to PA from Scotland in 1783. The surname originated in the 13th century when the place name Buchanan was taken as a surname by Gilbrid McAuslan, head of a cadet branch of the clan McAuslan.

Buchannan (148) Scottish: variant of BUCHANAN.

Buchannon (100) Scottish: variant of BUCHANAN.

Buchanon (232) Scottish: variant of BUCHANAN.

Buchberger (188) German: habitational name for someone from any of the numerous places called Buchberg.

GIVEN NAMES German 6%. *Franz, Kurt, Wolfgang.*

Buchbinder (260) German and Jewish (Ashkenazic): occupational name for a bookbinder, German *Buchbinder*.

Buche (207) **1.** German: habitational name for someone from any of numerous places called Buchau (Bavaria) or Bucha (eastern Germany). Alternatively, it may be a topographic name from Middle High German *buoche* 'beech tree'. **2.** French: perhaps a metonymic occupational name for a woodsman, from *buche* 'log'.

Buchele (120) South German (**Büchele**): **1.** topographic name for someone who lived on a hill, from Middle High German *bühel* 'hill', 'mound'. **2.** from a field name *Büechelin* 'beech grove'.

Buchen (164) German (**Büchen**): habitational name from Buchen, a place east of Hamburg, in Odenwald district, so named with Middle High German *buoche* 'beech tree', 'beech wood'.

GIVEN NAMES German 6%. *Ernst, Horst, Walther.*

Bucher (3001) **1.** English: variant spelling of BUTCHER. **2.** German: topographic name for someone who lived by a beech tree or beech wood, from Middle High German *buoche* 'beech tree' + the suffix *-er* denoting an inhabitant. **3.** German: habitational name for someone from any of numerous places called Buch. **4.** French (**Bûcher**): occupational name for a logger or woodsman, from a derivative of *buche* 'log'.

FOREBEARS One of the earliest immigrants of the Bucher family came from Würzenhaus, Switzerland, to Philadelphia in 1735.

Buchert (430) German: variant of BUCHER.

Buchheim (130) German: habitational name from any of numerous places called Buchheim or Puchheim, literally 'beech settlement'.

GIVEN NAMES German 10%. *Gerd, Gunther, Kurt, Siegfried.*

Buchheit (639) German: topographic name from *Buchheide*, literally 'beech heath', denoting an open plain with scattered beech trees.

Buchholtz (463) German: variant of BUCH-HOLZ.

GIVEN NAMES German 4%. *Erwin, Franz, Fritz, Siegfried.*

Buchholz (3333) **1.** German: topographic name for someone who lived near a beech wood, from Middle High German *buoch* 'beech' + *holz* 'wood', or a habitational name from a place named Buchholz, of which there are numerous examples, especially in northern Germany. **2.** Jewish (Ashkenazic): ornamental name from German *Buchholz* 'beech wood' (see 1).

GIVEN NAMES German 5%. *Kurt* (9), *Otto* (9), *Hans* (4), *Gerda* (3), *Heinz* (3), *Reinhardt* (3), *Gunter* (2), *Hermann* (2), *Ilse* (2), *Arno, Claus, Dietmar.*

Buchinger (194) German and Jewish (Ashkenazic): habitational name for someone from a place in Bavaria named Buching or either of two places in Lorraine named Buchingen. The place names derive from Old High German *buohha* 'beech'.

GIVEN NAMES Jewish 13%. *Yitzchak* (3), *Yitzchok* (2), *Chaim, Ephraim, Feivel, Mendel, Miriam, Mordche, Pinchas.*

Buchko (217) Ukrainian: nickname for a noisy person, from a diminutive of *bucha* 'noise', 'outcry'.

Buchler (258) German (**Büchler**): see BUECHLER.

Buchli (102) Swiss German (**Büchli**): see BUECHEL.

Buchman (1173) Jewish or Americanized spelling of German BUCHMANN.

Buchmann (427) German and Jewish (Ashkenazic): variant of BUCH, with the addition of Middle High German *man* 'man'. In some instances *Buch* may have been used as a nickname in the sense 'book', as an occupational name for a scholar or scribe.

GIVEN NAMES German 10%. *Hans* (5), *Darrold, Gerhard, Guenter, Gunter, Klaus, Kurt, Otto, Reinhard, Siegfried.*

Buchmeier (120) German: distinguishing name for a tenant farmer (see MEYER) who lived by a beech tree or beech wood (Middle High German *buoche*).

GIVEN NAME German 6%. *Kurt.*

Buchmiller (132) Partly Americanized form of German **Buchmüller**, a distinguishing name denoting a miller (Middle High German *mülner*) who lived by a beech tree (Middle High German *buoche*).

GIVEN NAME German 4%. *Otto.*

Buchner (723) **1.** German: topographic name for someone who lived by a beech tree or beech wood, a variant of BUCH + the suffix -*(n)er* denoting an inhabitant, or a habitational name from any of various places called Buchen, for example in Baden (east of Heidelberg). **2.** Jewish (Ashkenazic): occupational name for a scholar or scribe, from German *Buch* 'book', Yiddish *bukh* + the agent suffix -*ner*.

GIVEN NAMES German 4%. *Wolfgang* (2), *Gerhard, Hans, Jutta, Klaus, Kurt.*

Bucholtz (518) Variant of German BUCH-HOLZ.

Bucholz (483) Variant of German BUCH-HOLZ.

Buchs (152) German: topographic name for someone who lived by a box tree or thicket, Middle High German *buhs*. Compare BOX.

GIVEN NAME French 4%. *Andre.*

Buchsbaum (219) **1.** German: topographic name for someone who lived by a box tree, from Middle High German *buhs* (see BUCHS) + *boum* 'tree'. **2.** Jewish (Ashkenazic): ornamental name from German *Buchsbaum* 'box tree' (see 1).

GIVEN NAMES Jewish 7%. *Yael* (2), *Sol.*

Buchta (428) **1.** German: habitational name from a place near the Czech border named Buchbach, pronounced and also recorded as *Buchba*, from a variant of which the surname arose. **2.** German: habitational name from a place named Buchte in Brandenburg. **3.** In eastern Germany, possibly from the Sorbian personal name *Buchta*, ultimately a derivative of *Boguslav*. **4.** Czech, Slovak, Polish, and eastern German: from *buchta* 'baked yeast dumpling' (see BUCHTEL 2). **5.** Czech: possibly from a derivative of *Budislav* or some other personal name formed with *budi-* 'to awaken or inspire'.

GIVEN NAMES German 4%. *Bernhard, Klaus, Konrad, Kurt, Monika.*

Buchtel (121) Czech: **1.** from a pet form of the personal name *Bohuslav*. **2.** alternatively, it may be from *Buchtel* 'oven-baked yeast dumpling', used as a occupational name for a baker of these, also as a nickname for someone resembling a little boy.

Buchter (184) Probably a variant of German **Buchtler**, an occupational name for a baker of yeast dumplings (see BUCHTEL).

GIVEN NAME German 4%. *Egon.*

Buchwald (464) **1.** German: topographic name for someone who lived by a beech forest, from Middle High German *buoche* 'beech' + *walt* 'forest', or a habitational name from any of numerous minor places so named, mainly in eastern Germany. **2.** Jewish (Ashkenazic): habitational name, as in 1, or an ornamental adoption of it.

GIVEN NAMES German 5%. *Kurt* (2), *Ekkehard, Erwin, Helmut, Manfred, Otto.*

Buchwalter (131) German: variant of **Buchwalder**, a habitational name for someone from any of various places called Buchwald or Buchwalde in Saxony and Pomerania.

Bucio (204) Hispanic (Mexico): unexplained.

GIVEN NAMES Spanish 65%. *Jose* (6), *Miguel* (6), *Carlos* (5), *Salvador* (5), *Enrique* (3), *Jesus* (3), *Juan* (3), *Candido* (2), *Francisco* (2), *Ignacio* (2), *Jose Luis* (2), *Josefina* (2).

Buck (16925) **1.** English: nickname for a man with some fancied resemblance to a he-goat (Old English *bucc(a)*) or a male deer (Old English *bucc*). Old English *Bucc(a)* is found as a personal name, as is Old Norse *Bukkr*. Names such as *Walter le Buk* (Somerset 1243) are clearly nicknames. **2.** English: topographic name for someone who lived near a prominent beech tree, such as *Peter atte Buk* (Suffolk 1327), from Middle English *buk* 'beech' (from Old English *bōc*). **3.** German: from a personal name, a short form of *Burckhard* (see BURKHART). **4.** North German and Danish: nickname for a fat man, from Middle Low German *būk* 'belly'. Compare BAUCH. **5.** German: variant of BOCK. **6.** German: variant of PUCK in the sense 'defiant', 'spiteful', or 'stubborn'. **7.** German: topographic name from a field name, *Buck* 'hill'.

FOREBEARS Emanuel Buck came from England to Plymouth Colony in the 1640s and in 1647 settled in Wethersfield, CT.

Buckalew (708) Altered form, under French influence, of Scottish **Buccleugh**. Compare BUCKLEW.

Buckallew (138) Altered form of Scottish **Buccleugh** (see BUCKLEW).

Buckaloo (100) Altered spelling of Scottish **Buccleugh** (see BUCKLEW).

Buckbee (243) Probably an altered spelling of the English surname **Buckby**, a habitational name from a place in Northamptonshire named Buckby, from the Old Norse personal name *Bukki* + Old Norse *býr* 'farmstead', 'settlement'.

Buckel (296) **1.** German: from a pet form of the personal name BURKHART. **2.** German: descriptive nickname for a person with a hunchback. **3.** Possibly a German metonymic occupational name for a metalworker, from Middle High German *buckel* '(embossed) buckle on a shield'. **4.** English: variant spelling of BUCKLE.

Buckelew (552) Altered spelling of Scottish **Buccleugh** (see BUCKLEW).

Buckels (181) **1.** English: variant of BUCKLE. **2.** German: patronymic from BUCKEL.

Bucker (101) English: variant spelling of BOOKER.

GIVEN NAME French 4%. *Honore.*

Buckert (142) Variant of South German BURKERT.

Buckey (264) English: possibly a variant spelling of Scottish **Buckie**, a habitational name from either of two places so called in northeast Scotland.

Buckhalter (204) Respelling of German and Jewish **Buchhalter** (see BUCHALTER).

Buckheit (113) Altered spelling of German BUCHHEIT.

Buckholtz (194) Altered spelling of German BUCHHOLZ.

Buckholz (280) Altered spelling of German BUCHHOLZ.

Buckhout (137) Altered spelling of the Dutch topographic name **Boekhout** denoting someone who lived by a beech wood or a habitational name from any of the many places named with this word.

Bucki (100) Polish: habitational name from any of numerous places called Budy.
GIVEN NAME Polish 4%. *Miroslaw.*

Buckingham (3023) English: habitational name from the former county seat of the county of Buckinghamshire, Old English *Buccingahamm* 'water meadow (Old English *hamm*) of the people of (*-inga-*) *Bucc(a)*'.

Buckland (1279) English: habitational name from any of the many places in southern England (including nine in Devon) named Buckland, from Old English *bōc* 'book' + *land* 'land', i.e. land held by right of a written charter, as opposed to *folcland*, land held by right of custom.

Buckle (426) **1.** English: metonymic occupational name for a maker of buckles, from Middle English *bokel* 'buckle'. **2.** Americanized spelling of German BUCKEL.

Bucklen (107) Variant of English BUCKLAND.

Buckler (1272) **1.** English: occupational name for a maker of buckles, Middle English *bokeler*, Old French *bouclier* (see BUCKLE). **2.** Americanized spelling of German **Büchler** (see BUECHLER).

Buckles (1749) English: variant of BUCKLE.

Bucklew (424) Altered spelling, reflecting the pronunciation, of Scottish **Buccleugh**, the title of a ducal family associated with the town of Buccleuch in the Scottish Borders. Compare BUCKALEW.

Buckley (15804) **1.** English: habitational name from any of the many places so named, most of which are from Old English *bucc* 'buck', 'male deer' or *bucca* 'he-goat' + *lēah* 'woodland clearing'. Places called Buckley and Buckleigh, in Devon, are named with Old English *boga* 'bow' + *clif* 'cliff'. **2.** English: possibly a variant of BULKLEY, from the local pronunciation. **3.** Irish: Anglicized form of Gaelic **Ó Buachalla** 'descendant of *Buachaill*', a byname meaning 'cowherd', 'servant', 'boy'. **4.** Altered spelling of German **Büchler** (see BUECHLER), or of **Büchle**, a variant of BUECHEL.

Bucklin (700) Variant of either English BUCKLAND or **Butlin**, a nickname from Old French *boute-vilain* 'hustle or beat the churl', presumably denoting a severe or bullying master.

Buckman (2179) English: **1.** occupational name for a goatherd, Middle English *bukkeman* (from Old English *bucca* 'he-goat' + *mann* 'man'). **2.** occupational name for a scholar or scribe, Middle English *bocman* (from Old English *bōc* 'book' + *mann* 'man'). **3.** possibly also a habitational name, a reduced form of BUCKINGHAM or a metathesized form of BUCKNAM.

Buckmaster (947) English: habitational name from Buckminster in Leicestershire, named with the Old English personal name *Bucca* (see BUCK) + Old English *mynster* 'minster', 'large church'.

Buckmiller (105) Americanized form of German **Buchmüller** (see BUCHMILLER).

Bucknam (230) English: **1.** habitational name from a place in Norfolk named Buckenham, from the Old English personal name *Bucca* (with genitive *-n*) + Old English *hām* 'homestead'. **2.** reduced form of BUCKINGHAM.

Bucknell (241) English: habitational name from places called Bucknell, in Oxfordshire and Shropshire, or Bucknall, in Lincolnshire and Somerset. These are all named with the Old English byname *Bucca* (see BUCK) or Old English *bucca* 'he-goat' (with genitive *-n*) + *hyll* 'hill' in the first two examples or *healh* 'nook', 'hollow' in the latter two.

Buckner (8005) Variant of German BUCHNER.

Bucko (305) **1.** Polish (**Buczko**): topographic name from *buk* 'beech' (see BUKOWSKI). **2.** Ukrainian: variant of BUCHKO.
GIVEN NAMES Polish 9%. *Andrzej* (2), *Bronislaw, Ewa, Janusz, Jozef, Ryszard, Stanislaw, Wojciech.*

Buckridge (112) English: habitational name from a place in Worcestershire called Buckridge, from Old English *bōc* 'beech' + *hrycg* 'ridge', 'hill'.

Bucks (180) **1.** Probably an altered spelling of German BUCHS. **2.** Possibly also English or German, a patronymic from BUCK 1 or 3.

Buckson (100) English: unexplained; either a patronymic from BUCK, or possibly an altered form of BUXTON.

Buckwalter (874) Americanized spelling of German **Buchwalder**.

Bucolo (117) Italian: occupational name for a cowherd, from Greek *boukolos*.
GIVEN NAMES Italian 14%. *Carmelo, Domenic, Giovanni, Placido, Salvatore.*

Bucy (688) **1.** There is a French habitational name **Bucy**, from places so called in Aisne and Loiret. The place name is from *Bucciacum*, the name of a Gallo-Roman estate, composed of the personal name *Buccius* + the locative suffix *-acum*. However, the distribution of the surname in the U.S. is not consistent with a French origin. **2.** Possibly a variant spelling of English BUSSEY. **3.** Altered spelling of German BUSSE.

Buczek (492) Polish: **1.** nickname from *buczeć* 'to hum', 'to blubber'. **2.** topographic name from a diminutive of *buk* 'beech' (see BUKOWSKI).
GIVEN NAMES Polish 8%. *Grazyna* (2), *Zigmund* (2), *Boguslaw, Irena, Jadwiga, Jaroslaw, Pawel, Przemyslaw, Stanislaw, Wieslawa, Zofia.*

Buczkowski (374) Polish: habitational name for someone from places called for example Buczkowa, Buczkowo, Buczków, Buczek, or Buczkowice, all named with a diminutive of *buk* 'beech' (see BUCZEK).
GIVEN NAMES Polish 4%. *Tadeusz, Wasyl, Witold.*

Buczynski (305) Polish (**Buczyński**): habitational name for someone from places called Buczyn or Buczyna.
GIVEN NAMES Polish 4%. *Bogdan* (2), *Dariusz, Zosia.*

Buda (639) **1.** Polish, Ukrainian, Czech, and Slovak: topographic name from Polish and Ukrainian *buda*, Czech *bouda* 'hut', 'cabin', 'shack', 'stall'. **2.** Polish and Ukrainian: from a short form of any of various compound personal names beginning with *Budzi-*. **3.** Czech and Slovak: from a short form of the Czech personal name *Budislav*, composed of the elements *budi-* 'to awaken or inspire' + *slav* 'glory', or of any other personal name formed with *budi-* as the first element. **4.** Hungarian: habitational name from the name of the old capital of Hungary (see BUDAI). **5.** Slovenian (western Slovenia): perhaps a derivative from *buditi* 'to awaken'.
GIVEN NAMES Italian 8%. *Salvatore* (4), *Angelo* (3), *Rocco* (3), *Caesar, Enrico, Lorenzo, Sal.*

Budai (147) Hungarian: habitational name for someone from Buda, the old capital of Hungary, today part of Budapest. The etymology of the place name is uncertain, but is probably a derivative of *Bod* or *Bud*, a personal name of Turkic origin (see BODA). There are other places so called in Heves and Zala counties, and in former Kolozs county in Transylvania (now in Romania), which may also have given rise to the surname.
GIVEN NAMES Hungarian 10%. *Attila, Ferenc, Karoly, Laszlo, Sandor.*

Buday (275) **1.** Hungarian: variant spelling of BUDAI. **2.** Slovak and Ukrainian (**Budaj**): from a short form of the personal names *Budimir* or *Budislav*.
GIVEN NAMES Hungarian 4%. *Laszlo* (2), *Gabor, Zoltan.*

Budd (3182) **1.** English: from an Old English byname, *Budde*, which was applied to a thickset or plump person. By the Middle English period it had become a common personal name, with derivatives formed with hypocoristic suffixes, *Budecok* and *Budekin*. Reaney derives it from Old English *budda* 'beetle'. **2.** Shortened form of German BUDDE.

FOREBEARS John Budd was one of the free planters who assented to the 'Fundamental Agreement' of the New Haven Colony on June 4, 1639.

Budde (1079) **1.** North German: metonymic occupational name for a cooper, from Middle Low German *budde* 'tub', 'vat'. Compare BUETTNER. **2.** German and Danish: from a derivative of the Germanic personal name *Bodo*, cognate with English BUDD. **3.** English: variant spelling of BUDD.

Buddemeyer (136) North German (Westphalia): distinguishing name for the tenant farmer (see MEYER) of a bogland farm, from Middle Low German *budde* 'morass', 'bog'.

Budden (314) **1.** English: from a pet form the Old English personal name *Budda*. **2.** German: possibly from a shortened form of a North German farm name such as **Buddenbrock**, **Buddendiek**, or **Buddensiek**, all containing the element *budde(n)* 'morass', 'bog'.

Buddenhagen (201) German (Westphalia): from a farm name composed of Middle Low German *budde(n)* 'morass', 'bog' + *hag(en)* 'hedge'.

GIVEN NAMES German 5%. *Erwin, Kurt.*

Buddin (122) **1.** English: variant spelling of BUDDEN. **2.** Possibly an altered spelling of or German BUDDEN.

Buder (120) **1.** German: variant of BUDNER. **2.** German: in Swabia, a nickname for a bully, from *Buder* or *Bauder* 'stroke', 'blow', from Middle High German *buden* 'to hit'. **3.** Jewish (eastern Ashkenazic): habitational name from villages called Buda or Budy, in Ukraine and Belarus.

GIVEN NAMES German 5%; Jewish 5%. *Manfred; Aron, Dorit.*

Budge (529) **1.** English (mainly Devon and Cornwall): nickname from Norman French *buge* 'mouth' (Late Latin *bucca*), applied either to someone with a large or misshapen mouth or to someone who made excessive use of his mouth, i.e. a garrulous, indiscreet, or gluttonous person. The word is also recorded in Middle English in the sense 'victuals supplied for retainers on a military campaign', and the surname may therefore also have arisen as a metonymic occupational name for a medieval quartermaster. **2.** Scottish (Caithness and Orkney): unexplained.

Budig (106) Eastern German: from a short form of the Slavic personal names *Budimir* or *Budislav*.

GIVEN NAMES German 10%. *Fritz* (2), *Kurt, Otto.*

Budin (216) **1.** Jewish (eastern Ashkenazic): habitational name for someone from

Budy, a village in Ukraine and another in Belarus. **2.** Croatian and Slovenian: from the Old Slavic personal name *Budin*, from *buditi* 'to awaken', or from a shortened form of the personal names *Budimir* or *Budislav*, containing the same element + *mir* 'peace' and *slav* 'glory'. It may also be a nickname from *buden* meaning 'wide awake'.

Budinger (182) **1.** German (**Büdinger**): habitational name for someone from any of several places called Büdingen, in Hesse and the Saarland. **2.** Dutch and Belgian: habitational name for someone from Budingen in the province of Brabant.

GIVEN NAME French 4%. *Jean-Paul.*

Budish (102) Respelling of eastern German BUDIG or **Budich**, a variant.

Budka (139) Polish: from a diminutive form of BUDA.

Budke (308) German: of Slavic origin, a variant of BUDKA.

Budlong (287) English: of uncertain origin; said to be an Anglicized form of a French Huguenot name. It may be a variant of BEADLING. It is also found as a surname in the Philippines.

FOREBEARS The name was brought to Warwick, RI, some time in or before 1668, probably from England, by Francis Budlong (died 1675).

Budman (146) Jewish (southeastern Ashkenazic): occupational name for the keeper of a bathhouse, from Yiddish *bod* 'bathhouse' + German *Mann* 'man'.

GIVEN NAMES Jewish 10%. *Fira, Meyer, Naum, Sima, Yakov.*

Budner (147) **1.** German: status name for a tenant who held a cottage in return for performing certain services, from a derivative Middle High German *buode* 'hut', 'shack'. Compare COTTER. **2.** Jewish (from Poland): habitational name for someone from Budne, a village in Poland.

Budney (247) Americanized spelling of Polish and Ukrainian BUDNY.

GIVEN NAMES Polish 4%. *Thadeus, Zigmond.*

Budnick (613) Americanized spelling of Polish and Ukrainian BUDNIK.

Budnik (439) Polish and Ukrainian: occupational name for a stallholder, *budnik*, a derivative of *buda* 'stall'.

Budny (244) Polish and Ukrainian: see BUDA, BUDNIK.

GIVEN NAMES Polish 8%. *Casimir, Janusz, Lech, Piotr, Tomasz, Zygmund.*

Budreau (290) Altered form of French BEAUDREAU.

Budrow (177) Altered form of French BEAUDREAU.

Budz (197) Polish: from a short form of the compound personal names *Budziwoj* or *Budzimir*.

GIVEN NAMES Polish 16%. *Jozef* (3), *Tadeusz* (2), *Bronislaw, Danuta, Franciszek, Grazyna, Janina, Jerzy, Katarzyna, Kazimierz, Stanislaw, Tomasz.*

Budzik (140) Polish: **1.** from a pet form of BUDZ. **2.** from a derivative of *budzić* 'to waken'.

GIVEN NAMES Polish 10%. *Karol, Ludwik, Marcin, Wieslaw.*

Budzinski (515) Polish: variant of BUDZYNSKI.

GIVEN NAMES Polish 5%. *Casimir* (2), *Jacek, Piotr, Stanislaw, Zygmund.*

Budziszewski (103) Polish: habitational name for someone from places called Budziszewo.

GIVEN NAMES Polish 5%. *Janusz, Pawel.*

Budzynski (224) Polish (**Budzyński**): habitational name for someone from places called Budzyn (also written Budzin), Budzyno, Budzyń.

GIVEN NAMES Polish 5%. *Tadeusz, Wojciech, Zbigniew.*

Bue (292) Norwegian: habitational name from a farm so named, most probably from *bu* 'small house', 'shelter' (compare BUER).

GIVEN NAMES Scandinavian 5%. *Ragnhild, Sig, Svein.*

Bueche (387) South German and Swiss German (**Büche**): **1.** variant of BUCHE. **2.** from a pet form of a Germanic personal name formed with an element akin to Old High German *burg* 'castle', 'protection'. Compare BURKHART.

Buechel (431) South German (**Büchel**): **1.** variant of BUEHL. **2.** from a field name, *Büchelin* 'beech grove', 'beech stand' or a habitational name from any of several places so named.

GIVEN NAMES German 5%. *Alfons, Eldred, Fritz, Monika.*

Buechele (195) South German (**Büchele**): variant of BUECHEL.

GIVEN NAMES German 5%. *Heinz* (2), *Hans, Juergen.*

Buechler (952) German (**Büchler**): **1.** from the common field name *Büchle* 'beech stand', the -*er* suffix denoting an inhabitant. **2.** from *buchel* 'beech nut', hence a metonymic occupation name for someone who owned or worked in an oil mill producing oil from beech nuts. **3.** variant of BUEHLER.

Buechner (491) German (**Büchner**): variant of BUCHNER.

Buecker (118) German (**Bücker**): **1.** habitational name for someone from Bücken, near Hoya. **2.** from a Germanic personal name formed with Old High German *burg* 'castle', 'protection'. **3.** respelling of **Bücher**, a topographic name for someone who lived by a beech tree, a variant of BUCHER 2.

Buege (323) **1.** German (**Büge**): perhaps a habitational name from a place in eastern Germany. **2.** Probably also an altered spelling of Swiss French **Bueche** or **Buège**, unexplained.

Buehl (218) South German (**Bühl**): topographic name for someone who lived on a hillside, from Middle High German *bühel* 'hill', or a habitational name from a place called Bühl, for example in Baden.

Buehler (2704) South German (**Bühler**): from Buehl, with the addition of the suffix *-er* denoting an inhabitant.
GIVEN NAMES German 5%. *Hans* (7), *Kurt* (5), *Fritz* (3), *Otto* (3), *Heinz* (2), *Armin*, *Arno*, *Dieter*, *Eberhard*, *Erwin*, *Frieda*, *Gerhard*.

Buehner (519) German (**Bühner**): **1.** habitational name for someone from any of three places called Bühne (in Westphalia, the Harz Mountains, and Altmark). **2.** in the south, possibly a topographic name from *Bühne* 'scaffold', 'barn loft'.
GIVEN NAMES German 5%. *Fritz* (3), *Kurt* (2), *Frieda*, *Leonhard*.

Buehrer (307) German (**Bührer**): habitational name for someone from any of the places called Bühren, in Westphalia, near Hannover, and near Oldenburg, or from Büren in Westphalia. The last is named with Middle Low German *bur* 'dwelling', 'settlement'.
GIVEN NAMES German 5%. *Kurt* (2), *Gerhart*, *Hans*, *Otto*.

Buehring (171) German (**Bühring**): patronymic from Buhr, or from a personal name *Bur(o)*, perhaps cognate with Old Norse *buor* 'son'.
GIVEN NAMES German 10%. *Klaus* (2), *Eldor*, *Harro*, *Juergen*, *Konrad*, *Kurt*.

Buehrle (211) South German (**Bührle**): variant of Bauer + diminutive ending; this form is congruent with a derivative from Old High German *būr* 'dwelling place', 'house', or a personal name *Bührlen*, from *Bur(o)*, cognate perhaps with Old Norse *buor* 'son'.

Bueker (182) North German (**Büker**): occupational name for a fabric worker who softened linen in beech lye, from Middle Low German *boken*, Low German *büken* + *-er* denoting activity.

Buel (321) Variant of Buell.

Buell (2662) **1.** Welsh: variant of Bowell. **2.** Dutch: occupational name for a hangman.
FOREBEARS William Buell came from Wales to Windsor, CT, in or about 1639.

Buelna (131) Asturian-Leonese and Spanish: habitational name from any of the places called Buelna in Asturies and Cantabria.
GIVEN NAMES Spanish 30%. *Francisco* (3), *Jose* (3), *Enrique* (2), *Adriana*, *Armando*, *Carlos*, *Concepcion*, *Eduardo*, *Feliciano*, *Hermelinda*, *Jesus*, *Luis*.

Buelow (764) German (**Bülow**): habitational name from any of various places in Mecklenburg named Bülow, or from any of the places in Brandenburg called Bühlow, or from Bühlau in Saxony.

Bueltel (117) German: unexplained.

Buenaventura (158) Spanish: from the personal name *Buenaventura* meaning 'good

fortune', bestowed as an omen name or with specific reference to the Italian bishop and theologian St Bonaventura (canonized in the 14th century).
GIVEN NAMES Spanish 48%; Italian 9%. *Raul* (6), *Jose* (3), *Ricardo* (3), *Eduardo* (2), *Josefina* (2), *Luis* (2), *Manuel* (2), *Teresita* (2), *Alfredo*, *Andres*, *Celestina*, *Conrado*; *Romeo* (3), *Angelo*, *Antonio*, *Carmela*, *Clemente*, *Dino*, *Donato*, *Italo*, *Pio*.

Buendia (206) Spanish (**Buendía**): **1.** probably a habitational name from Buendía in Cuenca province, Spain. **2.** occasionally, a nickname from Spanish *bueno* 'good' + *día* 'day', presumably denoting someone who made frequent use of this salutation. *Buendía* was also occasionally used as a personal name in the Middle Ages, bestowed on a child as an expression of the parents' satisfaction at the birth, or for the sake of a good omen.
GIVEN NAMES Spanish 50%. *Juan* (8), *Jorge* (6), *Jose* (5), *Roberto* (4), *Miguel* (3), *Ana* (2), *Beatriz* (2), *Camilo* (2), *Felipe* (2), *Luis* (2), *Adan*, *Adriano*.

Buenger (269) German (**Bünger**): see Bunger.
GIVEN NAMES German 6%. *Bernhard*, *Johann*, *Klaus*, *Otto*.

Buening (241) German (**Büning**): variant of the patronymic **Bünning** (see Bunning).

Bueno (1642) Spanish: generally an approving (or ironic) nickname, from Spanish *bueno* 'good'.
GIVEN NAMES Spanish 47%. *Jose* (29), *Manuel* (23), *Juan* (22), *Carlos* (16), *Luis* (16), *Raul* (12), *Francisco* (10), *Ramon* (10), *Ana* (9), *Miguel* (8), *Javier* (7), *Jorge* (7); *Antonio* (13), *Clemente* (3), *Lorenzo* (3), *Dario* (2), *Gabino* (2), *Leonardo* (2), *Amadeo*, *Antonino*, *Cenovio*, *Fabiano*, *Federico*, *Franco*.

Buenrostro (413) Spanish: nickname for a handsome man, from *bueno* 'good' + *rostro* 'face'.
GIVEN NAMES Spanish 61%. *Jose* (24), *Jesus* (11), *Juan* (10), *Francisco* (6), *Luis* (5), *Raul* (5), *Sergio* (5), *Carlos* (4), *Guillermo* (4), *Jorge* (4), *Salvador* (4), *Efrain* (3).

Buentello (274) Hispanic (Mexican): unexplained.
GIVEN NAMES Spanish 42%. *Jose* (7), *Manuel* (4), *Raul* (4), *Gonzalo* (3), *Gustavo* (3), *Mario* (3), *Sergio* (3), *Arturo* (2), *Enrique* (2), *Gilberto* (2), *Juan* (2), *Pedro* (2).

Buer (185) **1.** North German: probably a habitational name from a place so named near Essen, or a variant of Buhr. **2.** Norwegian: habitational name from the common farm name Buer, from the plural of *bu* 'booth', 'temporary dwelling' (from Old Norse *búð*).
GIVEN NAMES German 6%; Scandinavian 5%. *Eldred*, *Hans*, *Kurt*, *Otto*.

Buerge (105) German (**Bürge**): see Burge.

Buerger (517) German (**Bürger**): variant of Burger.

GIVEN NAMES German 10%. *Fritz* (2), *Kurt* (2), *Otto* (2), *Willi* (2), *Dieter*, *Florian*, *Franz*, *Georg*, *Gernot*, *Hans*, *Heinz*, *Hermann*.

Buerk (160) German (**Bürk**): from a short form of the personal name *Burkhardt*, a variant of Burkhart.

Buerkle (325) German (**Bürkle**): from a pet form of the personal name *Burkhardt* (see Burkhart).
GIVEN NAMES German 7%. *Frieda*, *Fritz*, *Hartmut*, *Hellmut*, *Kurt*, *Manfred*, *Reinhold*.

Buermann (101) German: unexplained.

Buescher (640) German (**Büscher**): topographic name for someone who lived near a copse, from Middle High German *busch* 'copse', or a habitational name from any of various places named with this word or from any of the numerous places called Busch.
GIVEN NAMES German 4%. *Juergen* (2), *Klaus* (2), *Gerhard*, *Kurt*, *Lorenz*.

Buesing (347) North German (**Büsing**): possibly a nickname for a glutton, from Middle Low German *büsen* 'to drink and feast'. Compare Bauser.
GIVEN NAMES German 4%. *Gerhard*, *Kurt*, *Lutz*, *Otto*.

Bueter (142) North German (**Büter**): **1.** from an agent derivative of Middle Low German *bute* 'booty', 'barter', 'exchange', hence an occupational name for a trader or dealer or perhaps a nickname for someone who drove a hard bargain. **2.** from a Germanic personal name, *Botthar*, cognate with Old High German *boto* 'messenger'.

Bueti (128) Italian (Calabria): from a Calabrian word meaning 'little ox', from *bue* 'ox' + the diminutive suffix *-etto*, or, more likely, via French **Bouvet**, **Bouet**, with the same meaning.
GIVEN NAMES Italian 42%; Spanish 11%. *Rocco* (9), *Serafino* (6), *Antonio* (4), *Antonino* (2), *Carmela* (2), *Carmelo* (2), *Pasquale* (2), *Attilio*, *Fortunata*, *Giovanni*, *Nicola*, *Sal*; *Diego* (4), *Elena*, *Ernesto*.

Buetow (287) German (**Bütow**): habitational name from a place in Mecklenburg named Bütow; the place name is of Slavic origin.
GIVEN NAMES German 6%. *Berthold*, *Erna*, *Fritz*, *Klaus*, *Kurt*.

Buettner (1447) German (**Büttner**): occupational name for a cooper or barrel-maker, German *Büttner*, an agent derivative of Middle High German *büte(n)* 'cask', 'wine barrel'. This name occurs chiefly in eastern German-speaking regions. Compare Binder, Bittenbender, Boettcher, Schaeffler.
GIVEN NAMES German 5%. *Erwin* (4), *Helmut* (2), *Otto* (2), *Bernd*, *Erhard*, *Gerhard*, *Hartmut*, *Hubertus*, *Klaus*, *Kurt*, *Manfred*, *Reinhold*.

Bufalini (118) Italian: patronymic or plural form of Bufalino.

GIVEN NAMES Italian 19%. *Angelo, Ezio, Giovanni, Mario, Orlando, Santina, Ubaldo.*

Bufalino (102) Italian: from a diminutive of *buf(f)alo, bufolo, bubalo* 'buffalo' (from Late Latin *bufalus*), presumably applied as a nickname for someone thought to resemble the animal in some way, or as a metonymic occupational name for a herdsman.
GIVEN NAMES Italian 26%. *Angelo* (4), *Giuseppe, Nicolo, Salvatore.*

Bufano (162) Southern Italian (Apulia): **1.** from a reduced and altered form of the personal name *Epifanio.* **2.** habitational name from any of several minor places called Bufano (probably also derived from *Epifanio*), for example in Foggia province.
GIVEN NAMES Italian 16%. *Rocco* (3), *Carlo, Cesare, Saverio, Vito.*

Buff (957) **1.** German: nickname for a violent, aggressive person, from Middle High German *buf* 'push', 'shove'. **2.** German: from the Old German personal name *Bodo* or the compound name *Bodefrit*, containing the Old High German element *buitan* 'to bid or order' or *boto* 'messenger'. **3.** English: of uncertain derivation; possibly a nickname, either variant of BOFF 1, or alternatively from Old French *buf(f)e* 'blow', 'slap in the face'. Compare BUFFIN.

Buffa (457) Italian: **1.** nickname from Sicilian *bbuffa* 'toad', from Latin *bufo.* **2.** possibly also a nickname for a trickster, from old Italian *buffa* 'trick', 'joke'.
GIVEN NAMES Italian 28%. *Antonio* (4), *Salvatore* (4), *Vito* (4), *Angelo* (3), *Carlo* (2), *Gaetano* (2), *Gasper* (2), *Guido* (2), *Mario* (2), *Paolo* (2), *Sal* (2), *Ulisse* (2), *Vincenzo* (2), *Armando, Juanita, Manuel, Rosario.*

Buffalo (253) Origin unidentified; possibly am American nickname from *buffalo* (the animal), perhaps denoting a large, powerfully built man.

Buffaloe (332) Variant spelling of BUFFALO.

Buffenbarger (102) German: probably a habitational name of unexplained origin.
GIVEN NAME German 4%. *Kurt.*

Buffett (135) Probably a respelling of French **Buffet**, from Old French *buffet*, which meant variously 'table', 'cupboard', 'stall', or 'cheap wine'.

Buffin (173) English: **1.** possibly of Flemish origin, from a pet form of the Germanic personal name *Bufo.* **2.** alternatively, perhaps, from a diminutive of Old French *bufe, buffe* 'blow', 'slap in the face', hence probably a nickname for a rough or uncouth man.
GIVEN NAMES French 5%. *Gaile, Yvon.*

Buffington (3334) Possibly a respelling of the English habitational name **Bovington**, from Bovington in Dorset, which is named with the Old English personal name *Bōfa* + *-ing-* implying association with + *tūn* 'settlement'.

Buffkin (369) English: variant of BUFKIN.

Buffo (235) Italian: **1.** nickname for a foolish or clownish man, from *buffo* 'ridiculous', 'amusing'. **2.** possibly a nickname from *buffa* in the sense 'fat', 'corpulent' (see BUFFA).
GIVEN NAMES Italian 5%. *Domenic* (2), *Guido, Sal.*

Buffone (260) Italian: nickname from *buffone* 'buffoon', 'joker'.
GIVEN NAMES Italian 17%. *Angelo* (4), *Luigi* (3), *Aldo, Antonio, Damiano, Domenic, Filomena, Francesco, Giovanni, Nicolino, Rocco, Romeo.*

Bufford (597) English: variant of BUFORD.

Buffum (487) English: variant spelling of **Buffham**, apparently a habitational name from a lost or unidentified place, possibly in Lincolnshire, where the surname is concentrated.

Bufkin (513) English: probably of Flemish origin, from a pet form of the Germanic personal name *Bufo.* Compare BUFFIN.

Buford (2565) **1.** English: most probably a variant of BEAUFORT. **2.** Possibly an Anglicized spelling of French **Buffard**, which is from Old French *bouffard*, a term which meant 'puffing and blowing', hence an unflattering nickname for an irascible or self-important man.
FOREBEARS American bearers of this name are mostly descended from Richard Beauford or Beaufort, who came from England to Lancaster co., VA, in 1635.

Bufton (138) English (Hereford and Wales): topographical name from Middle English *(a)bove* 'above' (Old English *on būfan*) + *toun* 'village', 'hamlet', i.e. denoting someone who lived above the village, or a habitational name from a minor place named with these elements, such as Bufton End in Cambridgeshire.

Bugaj (168) Polish, Ukrainian, and Jewish (eastern Ashkenazic): from Polish *bugaj*, Ukrainian *bugay* 'ox', 'bull', hence a nickname for a big and vigorous man. The Polish word *bugaj* also means 'bend in a river'; in some instances the surname may therefore be topographical.
GIVEN NAMES Polish 12%. *Jerzy, Tadeusz, Wieslaw, Zbigniew, Zdzislaw.*

Bugajski (117) Polish: habitational name from any of numerous places called Bugaj.
GIVEN NAMES Polish 21%. *Tadeusz* (4), *Tomasz* (2), *Andrzej, Ignatius, Janusz, Krzysztof, Mieczyslaw, Zygmunt.*

Bugarin (260) Galician: habitational name from either of two places in Pontevedra province named Bugarin.
GIVEN NAMES Spanish 52%; Portuguese 12%. *Jose* (10), *Jesus* (3), *Juan* (3), *Luis* (3), *Ruben* (3), *Basilio* (2), *Esperanza* (2), *Francisco* (2), *Genaro* (2), *Javier* (2), *Jorge* (2), *Josefina* (2); *Joao.*

Bugay (181) Americanized spelling of Polish BUGAJ.
GIVEN NAMES Polish 4%. *Casimir, Zigmund.*

Bugbee (734) English: variant spelling of **Bugby**, a Northamptonshire variant of **Buckby** (see BUCKBEE).

Bugenhagen (115) German: habitational name from a place in western Pomerania called Buggenhagen.
GIVEN NAMES German 5%. *Erwin, Otto.*

Bugg (1306) English: nickname for an uncouth or weird man, from Middle English *bugge* 'hobgoblin', 'scarecrow' (perhaps from Welsh *bwg* 'ghost'). Compare BOGLE 1.

Bugge (213) **1.** Scandinavian: habitational name from a place so named in Denmark. **2.** Scandinavian: from the old Danish personal names *Buggi* or *Bukki*, short forms of various German compound names. **3.** English: variant spelling of BUGG.
GIVEN NAMES Scandinavian 9%; German 5%. *Erik* (3), *Thor*; *Hans, Kurt.*

Buggs (667) English: variant of BUGG.

Buggy (159) English: of uncertain derivation. Reaney suggests it may be from Middle English *bugee, buggye* 'lambskin', and hence probably a metonymic occupational name for someone who prepared such skins.
GIVEN NAME Irish 5%. *Fintan.*

Bugh (170) Welsh: Anglicized form of Welsh *ap Huw* 'son of *Huw*' (see HUGH).

Bugher (166) Probably an altered spelling of German BUCHER.

Buglione (119) Italian: habitational name from any of various minor places with names related to *bollire* 'to boil'.
GIVEN NAMES Italian 24%. *Antonio* (2), *Petrina* (2), *Sal* (2), *Angelo, Aniello, Nicola, Salvatore, Sergio.*

Bugni (177) Italian: **1.** metonymic occupational name for a beekeeper, from *bugno* 'beehive', from an unattested Celtic word, *būnia.* **2.** from *bugna* 'dressed stone', 'ashlar', hence a metonymic occupational name for a stonemason or possibly a nickname for someone with a protrusion on the forehead.
GIVEN NAMES Italian 8%. *Domenic* (2), *Guido* (2), *Angelo, Dino, Oreste.*

Bugos (101) Hungarian: probably an Anglicized spelling of either *Buga* or *Bagos*, both Magyar secular personal names.

Buhl (993) German: **1.** nickname for a male relative (i.e. a member of an important family who was not the head of it), from Middle High German *buole* 'kinsman' (Old High German *buolo*, also used as a personal name). **2.** nickname for a lover or the (illegitimate) child of a lover, from the same word in the later sense 'paramour', 'lover', 'mistress'. **3.** respelling of BUEHL.

Buhler (1216) German (**Bühler**): see BUEHLER.

Buhman (156) North German (**Buhmann**): Low German form of **Baumann**, a variant of BAUER.
GIVEN NAME French 4%. *Michel.*

Buhr (1016) German: variant of BAUER or BUR.

GIVEN NAMES German 5%. *Gerhard* (2), *Heinz* (2), *Christoph*, *Erwin*, *Frieda*, *Hans*, *Hans Peter*, *Heinrich*, *Hermann*, *Otto*.

Buhrman (388) German (**Buhrmann**): occupational name for a farmer or, in some cases, for the owner of a large farm (see BAUER) or of the German habitational name **Bührmann**, a variant of BUEHRER.

Buhrow (213) Possibly an altered spelling of the German habitational name **Burow**, from any of various places so named in Mecklenburg and Pomerania.

Buhs (108) Altered spelling of North German **Buhse**, a variant of BUSE.

Bui (3042) **1.** Vietnamese (**Bùi**): unexplained. **2.** Belgian French and Dutch: from a northern French dialect variant of BOIS.

GIVEN NAMES Vietnamese 79%. *Thanh* (46), *Hung* (45), *Dung* (35), *Khanh* (27), *Minh* (27), *Hai* (21), *Hien* (20), *Thuy* (20), *Tuan* (20), *Hoa* (19), *Tam* (19), *Chau* (18), *Lan* (18), *Hong* (12), *Nam* (11), *Phong* (10), *Sang* (9), *Man* (8), *Sinh* (8), *Thai* (8), *Chi* (7), *Dong* (6), *Tinh* (6), *Ho* (5), *Thach* (5), *Tuong* (5), *Uyen* (5), *Chien* (4), *Hang* (4), *Tong* (4), *Chung* (2), *Hon* (2), *Lai* (2), *Manh* (2), *Phoung* (2), *Tanh* (2).

Buice (574) Probably a variant of Scottish, northern Irish, and English BOYCE.

Buick (143) **1.** Scottish and northern Irish: variant spelling of BEWICK. **2.** Dutch: variant spelling of BUYCK.

Buie (1762) Scottish: nickname from Gaelic *buidhe* 'yellow', 'fair-haired'. See also BOWIE.

Buikema (228) Frisian: patronymic from the nickname *Buick* (see BUYCK).

Buis (486) **1.** French: from French *buis* 'box (tree)', in any of a number of possible applications. It may have been a topographic name for someone who lived by a box thicket, or a metonymic occupational name for a worker in the wood (see BOX). **2.** Dutch: patronymic from the Germanic personal name *Buso*, *Boso*.

FOREBEARS An immigrant from the Perigord region of France was variously documented in Champlain, Quebec, in 1670, as Buy, Bouy, or Lebuis, with the secondary surname Lavergne.

Buisson (130) French: topographic name for someone who lived near clump of bushes, *buisson* (a derivative of *bois* 'wood', 'copse'), or in an area characterized by such vegetation.

GIVEN NAMES French 18%. *Emile* (3), *Andre*, *Armand*, *Jean-Paul*, *Matilde*.

Buist (303) Scottish (Fife): unexplained.

Buitrago (249) Spanish: habitational name from Buitrago in Soria province or possibly Buitrago del Lozoya in Madrid province, so named with the Late Latin personal name *Vulturius* (a derivative of *vultur* 'vulture') + the locative suffix *-acum*.

GIVEN NAMES Spanish 56%. *Jose* (11), *Jaime* (6), *Carlos* (5), *Jorge* (5), *Fernando* (4), *Juan* (4), *Alvaro* (3), *Gustavo* (3), *Luis* (3), *Luz* (3), *Armando* (2), *Blanca* (2).

Buitron (166) **1.** Spanish (**Buitrón**): habitational name possibly from El Buitrón (in the provinces of Huelva and Andalusia). **2.** also possibly Galician: habitational name from Buiturón (in A Coruña), so named with *buitrón* 'fish trap' or an augmentative of *buitre* 'vulture'.

GIVEN NAMES Spanish 46%. *Carlos* (6), *Juan* (6), *Ignacio* (2), *Jose* (2), *Juanita* (2), *Luis* (2), *Oralia* (2), *Pedro* (2), *Ricardo* (2), *Adelina*, *Alejandra*, *Alicia*.

Bujak (186) Polish: nickname either from Old Polish *bujak* 'impertinent person', or from *bujać* 'to develop or grow quickly'.

GIVEN NAMES Polish 21%. *Stanislaw* (3), *Boguslaw*, *Czeslawa*, *Danuta*, *Dariusz*, *Ewa*, *Halina*, *Henryk*, *Leszek*, *Miroslaw*, *Tadeusz*, *Witold*.

Bujalski (130) Polish: nickname for a storyteller, Polish *bujała*.

GIVEN NAMES Polish 16%; German 5%. *Ewa*, *Juliusz*, *Lucjan*, *Wieslaw*, *Zbigniew*, *Zdzislaw*; *Hildegarde*.

Bujnowski (142) Polish: habitational name for someone from a place called Bujnowo or Bujnow, named with *bujny* 'luxuriant', 'bushy', 'fertile'.

GIVEN NAMES Polish 12%. *Jerzy* (2), *Arkadiusz*, *Krzysztof*, *Tadeusz*.

Bujold (158) Of French origin: unexplained; perhaps an altered form of **Bujard**, **Bujart**, a metonymic occupational name for a launderer, from a derivative of Occitan *bugua* 'washing tub', 'lye vat'.

GIVEN NAMES French 11%. *Emile* (3), *Martial*, *Micheline*.

Buker (571) German: **1.** (**Büker**): see BUEKER. **2.** possibly an altered spelling of BUCHER.

Bukoski (143) **1.** Variant of Polish BUKOWSKI. **2.** Variant of Bulgarian **Bukovski**, a habitational name for someone from a place called Bukovo or Bukovec, or other places named with *buk* 'beech'.

Bukovac (116) Serbian and Croatian: topographic name for someone who lived in a place where beeches grow (from *bukva* 'beech tree') or habitational name for someone from a village called Bukva.

Bukowski (1241) Polish and Jewish (eastern Ashkenazic): habitational name for someone from a place called Buków, Bukowo, or Bukowa, from *buk* 'beech'.

GIVEN NAMES Polish 5%. *Tadeusz* (3), *Zygmunt* (2), *Beata*, *Boguslaw*, *Bronislaw*, *Casimir*, *Ewa*, *Ferdynand*, *Janina*, *Janusz*, *Jarek*, *Jerzy*.

Bula (204) **1.** Czech, Slovak, and Polish: nickname for a fat man, from *bula* (Polish *buła*) 'hard roll', 'large roll of wheaten bread'. As a Polish name it may also be from *bula* 'bruise'. This name is also well established in German-speaking areas. **2.** Ukrainian: nickname from *bulya* 'potato'. **3.** Spanish (Mexico, Argentina): unexplained.

GIVEN NAMES Spanish 7%. *Julio* (3), *Adolfo*, *Angel*, *Carlos*, *Jose*, *Lupe*, *Marta*, *Rafael*, *Torres*.

Bulat (126) Polish (**Bułat**): from *bułat* 'scimitar', presumably a metonymic occupational name for a swordsmith.

GIVEN NAMES Polish 5%. *Janusz*, *Stanislawa*.

Bulen (157) **1.** German: unexplained. **2.** Probably also English: variant spelling of BULLEN.

Buley (267) **1.** English: variant of the Norman habitational name BEAULIEU, or possibly a variant of BULLEY. **2.** Americanized spelling of Czech and Slovak **Bulej** (see BULA). **3.** Perhaps a variant of German **Puley**, from a short form for the medieval saint's name *Pelagius* (see BOLEY).

Bulger (1247) English: variant of BOLGER.

Bulgrin (150) German: habitational name from a place in Pomerania called Bulgrin.

GIVEN NAMES German 5%. *Erwin* (2), *Juergen*.

Bulick (129) **1.** Probably an altered spelling of the English surname **Bullick**, probably a habitational name from Bolwick in Norfolk or Bulwick in Northamptonshire, named with Old English *bula* 'bull' + *wīc* 'outlying settlement'. The surname is now found mainly in northern Ireland. **2.** Perhaps an Americanized form of Serbian and Croatian **Bulić**, which is either a patronymic from a personal name such as *Budimir* or possibly a derivative of the old nickname *bula*, pejorative term for a Muslim woman in areas of former Turkish occupation in the Balkans. **3.** Altered spelling of Polish **Bulik** (see BULA).

Bulin (149) Czech and Slovak (**Bulín**); eastern German (of Slavic origin): nickname for a fat man (see BULA).

Bulinski (102) Polish: see BULA.

Bulkeley (111) English: habitational name from a place in Cheshire named Bulkeley, from Old English *bulluc* 'bullock' + *lēah* 'woodland clearing'.

FOREBEARS Peter Bulkeley (1583–1659), Puritan divine, who came from Bedfordshire, England, was a founder of Concord, MA, in 1636.

Bulkley (456) English: variant of BULKELEY.

Bull (4507) **1.** English: nickname for a strong, aggressive, bull-like man, from Middle English *bul(l)e*, *bol(l)e*. Occasionally, the name may denote a keeper of a bull. Compare BULMAN. **2.** German (mainly northern): from a byname for a cattle breeder, keeper, or dealer. Compare South German OCHS. **3.** South German: nickname for a short fat man, a variant of BOLLE, or a nickname for a man with the physical characteristics of a bull.

Bulla (458) Italian (southern): from *bulla* 'bubble', a regional variant of *bolla*; either a habitational name from any of several minor places with hot springs that have names derived from this word, or a nickname for a person with a skin complaint causing bubble- or blister-like swellings.

Bullard (7997) English: **1.** most probably from *bullward*, an occupational name for someone who looked after a bull. **2.** alternatively, it may be a nickname for a fraudster, from Old French, Middle English *bole* 'fraud', 'deceit' + the pejorative suffix *-(h)ard*, or a nickname for a rotund man, from a pejorative derivative of Old French *boule* 'round'.

Bullen (910) English: habitational name from the French Channel port of Boulogne, recorded in Latin sources both as *Gessoriacum* and as *Bononia*. The latter name is clearly the source of the modern place name. It is ostensibly a derivative of Latin *bonus* 'good' (compare BOLOGNESE), but may in fact come from a Gaulish element *bona* 'foundation'. Boulogne has long been a major trading port between England and France.

Buller (1673) **1.** English: occupational name for a scribe or copyist, from an agent derivative of Middle English, Old French *bulle* 'letter', 'document'. **2.** English (of Norman origin): habitational name from a place in Normandy that has not been identified. If it is Bouillé, and so identical with BULLEY 1, the *-er(s)* may have arisen by analogy with other Norman place names in *-ière(s)* (see for example VILLERS). **3.** German: nickname for a man with a loud voice, from an agent derivative of Middle High German *bullen* 'to roar' (of imitative origin).

Bullerman (141) North German: nickname for a rowdy, boisterous man, from Middle High German *bulderen* 'to bluster' (modern German *poltern*), the *-ld-* having been assimilated as *-ll-*.

Bullers (132) English: variant of BULLER 2.

Bullett (122) Variant spelling of French **Bullet**, from a diminutive of *Bulle*, from Old French *bul(l)e*, a term denoting a lump of lead used to seal documents, and later the documents themselves.

FOREBEARS This is the name of a Huguenot family which settled at Port Tobacco, MD, in 1685.

GIVEN NAMES French 5%. *Alcide, Michel.*

Bulley (141) English: **1.** Norman habitational name from any of several places in northern France called Bouillé or Bully, from a Gaulish personal name of uncertain form and meaning + the locative suffix *-acum*. **2.** habitational name from Bulleigh in Devon or Bulley in Gloucestershire, both named with Old English *bula* 'bull' + *lēah* 'woodland clearing'.

Bullinger (460) **1.** Swiss German: habitational name for someone from Bohlingen in Switzerland which was formerly named Bollingen (see BOLLINGER). **2.** English:

occupational name for a baker, from Old French *bolonger, boulengier*.

GIVEN NAMES German 5%. *Kurt* (2), *Otto* (2), *Wendelin* (2), *Bauer, Rainer.*

Bullington (1510) English: **1.** variant of BILLINGTON, found as such in colonial VA. **2.** There are also two places in England named Bullington, in Leicestershire and Buckinghamshire, and it is possible that either or both of these could have given rise to the surname.

Bullins (474) English: perhaps a variant of BULLEN or an altered form of **Bullions**, a variant of BULLION.

Bullion (429) **1.** English: probably a variant of BULLEN. **2.** Scottish: habitational name from any of various minor places of this name, perhaps from an unrecorded Scottish Gaelic cognate of Irish *bullán*, a term denoting a round spring or a hollow in a rock containing rainwater.

Bullis (1225) **1.** English (Cambridgeshire): probably a metonymic occupational name for someone employed in a cattle shed, or a topographic name for someone who lived by one, from a reduced form of Middle English *bulehus* 'bull house', from *bul(l)e, bol(l)e* 'bull' + *h(o)us* 'house'. **2.** Latvian: nickname or metonymic occupational name from *bullis* 'bull'.

Bullman (303) **1.** English: variant of BULMAN. **2.** Altered spelling of German BOLLMANN or **Bullmann**, a variant of BULL 2.

Bulloch (494) Scottish: habitational name from Balloch, a locality in Bonhill, Dumbartonshire, named with Gaelic *beallach* 'pass'. The change of vowel is probably due to confusion with BULLOCK.

Bullock (14112) English: from Middle English *bullok* 'bullock' (Old English *bulluc*), referring to a young bull rather than a castrated one, probably applied as a nickname for an exuberant young man, or a metonymic occupational name for a keeper of bullocks.

Bullough (122) **1.** English (Lancashire): unexplained. **2.** Possibly an Americanized spelling of French **Bullot**, a metonymic occupational name for a scribe, from a diminutive of Old French *bul(l)e* '(lead) seal'.

GIVEN NAME French 5%. *Pierre* (2).

Bulls (167) **1.** North German: perhaps altered spelling of **Buls**, presumably a variant of BULL 2. **2.** Perhaps a variant of English BULL.

Bulluck (295) Variant spelling of English BULLOCK.

Bulman (597) English: occupational name for the keeper of a bull or bulls, from Middle English *bule* 'bull' + *man* 'man'.

Bulmer (502) English: habitational name from either of two places called Bulmer, in North Yorkshire and Essex, or from Boulmer in Northumberland. The first, recorded in Domesday Book as *Bolemere*, is named in Old English with *bula* 'bull' + *mere*

'lake', as is Boulmer; the second, found in early records as *Bulenemera*, is from *bulena* (genitive plural of *bula*) + *mere* 'lake'.

Bulow (213) German (**Bülow**): habitational name from any of several places in Mecklenburg named Bülow.

Buls (114) Jewish: unexplained.

GIVEN NAMES Jewish 5%. *Hyman, Hymie.*

Bulson (304) English: unexplained; most probably a patronymic from an unidentified medieval personal name, but compare BALSON and BOLSON.

Bult (218) Dutch: nickname from Middle Dutch *bult(e)* 'hump', 'hunchback'.

Bultema (181) Frisian: patronymic from the descriptive nickname BULT.

Bultemeier (118) German (**Bültemeier**): distinguishing name for a tenant farmer (see MEYER) whose farm was on a knoll or hump, an area of upland surrounded by marsh, Middle Low German *bulte*.

Bulter (217) North German (**Bülter**): topographic name for someone who lived on a low hill or an area of raised ground, from Middle Low German *bult(e), bülte* 'hump', 'knoll' + the suffix *-er* denoting an inhabitant.

Bulthuis (205) Dutch: from Middle Dutch *bulte* 'knoll', 'hump' + *huis* 'house', hence either a topographic name from a house on a low hill surrounded by marshland or a house inhabited by a hunchback (especially in the Groningen area).

Bultman (536) German (**Bultmann**): topographic name for someone who lived on a knoll or area of raised ground, from Middle Low German *bulte* 'knoll' + *man* 'man'.

Buma (113) Probably Frisian: unexplained.

GIVEN NAMES German 5%. *Kurt, Madel.*

Buman (165) Respelling of North German BUMANN.

Bumann (187) North German: variant form of **Baumann** (see BAUER).

Bumb (140) **1.** German: variant of **Pump**, metonymic occupational name for a pump maker. **2.** German: possibly also a variant of **Bump** (see BUMP). **3.** Indian (Maharashtra): Hindu (Maratha) name, from Marathi *bəmb* 'stout'. Compare BUMP.

GIVEN NAMES Indian 5%. *Amar, Balu, Raj.*

Bumbalough (245) Genealogical evidence suggests that this is an altered form of BRUMBELOW.

Bumbarger (185) Respelling of German BAMBERGER.

Bumbaugh (199) Respelling of German BAUMBACH.

Bumford (112) English: variant of BAMFORD.

Bumgardner (1634) Respelling of German BAUMGARTNER.

Bumgarner (2470) Respelling of German BAUMGARTNER.

Bump (1044) Possibly an altered spelling of German **Bumpf**, a nickname for a blusterer, from the onomatopoeic word *Bumpf* 'thump'.

Bumpas (262) English: variant spelling of BUMPUS.

Bumpass (268) English: variant spelling of BUMPUS.

Bumpers (346) Probably an altered spelling of BUMPUS or one of its variants.

Bumpus (1003) English: nickname, of Norman origin, for someone who was a swift walker, from Old French *bon* 'good' + *pas* 'pace'. It may also have been a topographic name, with the second element used in the sense 'passageway'. Compare MALPASS.

Bumstead (251) English: habitational name from Bumpstead in Essex, recorded in Domesday Book as *Bumesteda*, from Old English *bune* 'reed' + *stede* 'place', 'site'.

Bun (149) **1.** English: perhaps an occupational name for a baker of buns or a nickname for a short, round individual. **2.** Cambodian: unexplained.
GIVEN NAMES Cambodian 58%. *Leng* (3), *Sun* (3), *Chhay, Chheng, Han, Heng, In, Khin, Khun, Pin, Seng, Yeng* (2), *Phon* (2), *Thy* (2), *Loeung* (2), *Pheng* (2), *Savuth* (2), *Thoeun* (2), *Boeun, Bopha, Chhorn, Hak, Ly, Minh, Saroeun, Than, Thong, Thoung, Phorn, Samoeun, Savoeun, Soeun, Soeung, Sokheng, Yoeum*.

Bunce (1568) **1.** English: unexplained. Perhaps a respelling of BUNTS. **2.** Probably an altered spelling of Swiss German **Bunz** or **Bünz**, from Alemannic *bunz* 'little barrel', hence a nickname for a short fat man, or of German BANZ, or from pet form of an Old High German personal name *Bun(n)o*, of unexplained etymology.

Bunch (7338) English: nickname for a hunchback, from Middle English *bunche* 'hump', 'swelling' (of unknown origin).

Bunda (180) **1.** Hungarian, Polish, Czech, Slovak, and Ukrainian: from Slavic and Hungarian *bunda* 'fur coat', hence a metonymic occupational name for a furrier or a nickname for someone who habitually wore a fur coat. **2.** Hispanic: unexplained.
GIVEN NAMES Spanish 6%. *Jose* (2), *Angelito, Mario, Rodolfo, Rosauro, Ruben, Santiago, Traian*.

Bunde (298) **1.** North German: status name for a farmer Middle Low German *bunde, bunne*, related to Danish, Swedish *bonde* 'free peasant' (see BOND). **2.** German (**Bünde**): topographic name from Old High German *biunda* 'enclosed fertile pasture' (modern German *Bünde, Beunte*), a derivative of *biwenden* 'to bend or weave', with reference to the practice of making fences from woven branches. There are many different local forms and communal implications concerning the use of the land. **3.** North German (**Bünde**): habitational name for someone from a place in Westphalia, so named with the same word as 2.

GIVEN NAMES German 5%. *Ernst, Gerhard, Hans, Kurt*.

Bunderson (135) Scandinavian: probably a variant of Danish **Bundesen** or Swedish **Bondesson**, a patronymic from BONDE.

Bundick (372) English: variant of **Bundock**, a surname of unexplained origin, associated chiefly with Essex and Kent.

Bundrant (116) Americanized form of French BONDURANT.

Bundren (166) Americanized form of French BONDURANT.

Bundrick (358) English: unexplained.

Bundschuh (165) German: from Middle High German *buntschuoch*, a term denoting the type of shoe tied with thongs that was worn by peasants in the Middle Ages. This was the emblem on the banner of the peasants involved in the revolt of 1525, and presumably the surname could have arisen as a nickname for someone involved in the insurrection.
GIVEN NAME German 9%. *Kurt* (3).

Bundy (4102) English: variant of BOND.

Bungard (269) **1.** German: variant spelling of BONGARD. **2.** Possibly an altered spelling of Danish **Bundgaard**, **Bundgård**, a habitational name from any of the numerous farms so named.

Bunge (618) **1.** German: from Middle High German, Middle Low German *bunge* 'drum', hence probably a metonymic occupational name for a drummer or drum maker. **2.** German (**Bünge**): in Hesse, a variant of **Bünde** (see BUNDE 2).
GIVEN NAMES German 6%. *Kurt* (2), *Dietrich, Ewald, Harro, Lothar, Otto, Reinhard, Siegfried*.

Bunger (665) German (**Bünger**): **1.** occupational name for a drummer or drum maker, from a derivative of Middle High German, Middle Low German *bunge* 'drum'. Compare BUNGE. **2.** topographic name, a variant of BINGER, itself a variant of BINGEL.

Bungert (158) Variant spelling of German BANGERT.
GIVEN NAMES German 7%. *Kurt* (2), *Wilhelm*.

Bungo (115) Probably of English or Scottish origin, but unexplained.

Bunin (138) **1.** Jewish (from Belarus): metronymic from the Yiddish female personal name *Bune*, of Romance origin, with the addition of the East Slavic suffix *-in*. **2.** Russian: patronymic from *Buna*, a nickname for a haughty or boring person, from *bunet* 'to drone'.
GIVEN NAMES Jewish 11%; Russian 8%. *Rina* (2), *Sol* (2), *Haim, Shalom*; *Mikhail* (2), *Anatoliy, Andrei, Igor, Leonid*.

Bunk (362) North German: from a contracted form of the Old Saxon-Frisian personal name *Buniko*.
GIVEN NAMES German 5%. *Kurt* (2), *Egon, Klaus*.

Bunke (241) German: variant of BUNK.
GIVEN NAME German 4%. *Kurt*.

Bunker (2773) **1.** English: nickname, of Norman origin, for a reliable or good-hearted person, from Old French *bon* 'good' + *cuer* 'heart' (Latin *cor*). **2.** German: variant of BOENKER.
FOREBEARS Bunker Hill in Charlestown, MA, was named as land assigned in 1634 to George Bunker of Charlestown, who had emigrated from Odell in Bedfordshire, England.

Bunkers (189) **1.** Perhaps an altered spelling of German **Bongartz**, a variant of BAUMGARTEN. **2.** English: variant of BUNKER.

Bunkley (302) Of English origin: probably a habitational name from a lost or unidentified place; possibly a variant of BINGLEY. The surname was established in VA in the 18th century.

Bunn (3931) **1.** English: variant of BONE 1. **2.** German: perhaps from BUNDE 1.

Bunnell (2442) English: in part, a habitational name for someone from Bunwell in Norfolk. The place name is from Old English *bune* 'reed' + *wella* 'spring', 'stream'. Old forms of the surname suggest a second, non-habitational source.

Bunner (693) **1.** German: of uncertain origin. Probably related to BUNDE 1 or 2. **2.** Welsh: variant of BONNER.

Bunney (273) English (Devon): possibly a nickname, as Reaney suggests, for someone having a prominent lump or swelling, from Middle English *boni, buny* 'swelling', 'bunion' (see BUNYAN). It is also possibly a topographic name from the southwestern English dialect word *bunny* 'ravine'.

Bunning (225) German (**Bünning**): patronymic from the Frisian personal name *Bunno*.

Bunt (521) **1.** German: from Middle High German *bunt*, a term which originally described black and white coloration, specifically of a fur. Later, by extension, it came to denote the fur itself. It was probably applied as a nickname, but in which sense is no longer clear, and the matter is further complicated by the fact that in some areas *bunt* meant 'multicolored' (its modern meaning is 'colorful'). **2.** English: probably a metonymic occupational name for a maker of sieves, from Middle English *bonte, bunte*.

Buntain (151) English: variant of BUNTING.

Bunte (251) **1.** German (**Bünte**): most likely a variant of **Bünde** (see BUNDE 2). **2.** English: variant spelling of BUNT.

Bunten (379) **1.** English: variant of BUNTING. **2.** German: from Middle High German *bund*, the noun from *binden* 'to bind', 'to tie'; in what sense it became the basis for a name is unclear.

Buntin (665) English: variant of BUNTING.

Bunting (3221) **1.** English: nickname from some fancied resemblance to the songbird (*Emberiza spp.*). **2.** German: patronymic from an unexplained Frisian-Lower Saxon personal name, or a derivative of *Bunt-* (see BUNTEN).

FOREBEARS Sarah Bunting (1686–1762), born in Matlock, Derbyshire, became a noted Quaker minister in Cross Wicks, NJ. It is believed but not certain that other members of her family, including her father, John Bunting, came with her to NJ sometime before 1704, when her marriage to William Murfin is recorded.

Bunton (1241) English: variant of BUNTING.

Buntrock (243) German: from Middle Low German *bunt* 'striped or piebald fur' (see BUNT) + *rock* 'tunic', 'smock', hence presumably a nickname for an habitual wearer of such an item of clothing or possibly a metonymic occupational name for a furrier. Alternatively, the first element is believed by some to derive from *binden* 'to tie'. Compare BUNDSCHUH.

GIVEN NAMES German 8%. *Arno* (3), *Guenter*, *Ulrich*.

Bunts (105) **1.** Probably an Americanized spelling of the Swiss German surname *Bunz* (see BUNCE). **2.** English: possibly a variant of BUNT.

Buntyn (191) Probably an altered spelling of BUNTING.

Bunyan (255) English (Bedfordshire): nickname for someone disfigured by a lump or hump, from a diminutive of Old French *bugne* 'swelling', 'protuberance'. The term *bugnon* was also applied to a kind of puffed-up fruit tart, and so the surname may also have been a metonymic occupational name for a baker of these.

Bunyard (383) English: from a metathesized form of a Germanic personal name introduced to Britain from France by the Normans in the form BAYNARD.

Buol (175) Swiss German: of uncertain origin, possibly Ladin or Romansh.

Buonaiuto (115) Italian: from the personal name *Bonaiuto*, an omen name meaning 'good help'.

GIVEN NAMES Italian 15%. *Carmine* (2), *Umberto* (2), *Delfino*, *Federico*.

Buonanno (221) Italian: from the personal name *Buonanno*, composed of the elements *b(u)ono* 'good' + *anno* 'year', a name expressing satisfaction at the child's birth ('(it was a) good year (when you were born)'), possibly bestowed on a child born at the beginning of the year.

GIVEN NAMES Italian 22%. *Carmine* (2), *Americo*, *Amerigo*, *Angelo*, *Antonio*, *Armando*, *Bernardino*, *Ferdinando*, *Guido*, *Pasquale*, *Valentino*, *Vito*.

Buono (1074) Southern Italian: nickname from *buono* 'good'.

GIVEN NAMES Italian 16%. *Angelo* (7), *Salvatore* (7), *Carlo* (3), *Natale* (3), *Vito* (3), *Antonio* (2), *Concetta* (2), *Domenic* (2), *Rocco* (2), *Agostino*, *Aniello*, *Carmine*.

Buonocore (390) Southern Italian: nickname for a reliable or good-hearted person,

from *buono* 'good' + *core* 'heart', an old, dialect, or poetic form of *cuore* (Latin *cor*).

GIVEN NAMES Italian 14%. *Angelo* (2), *Ciro* (2), *Salvatore* (2), *Amedeo*, *Antonio*, *Carmine*, *Fiore*, *Francesca*, *Michelina*, *Pasquale*, *Sal*, *Vincenzo*.

Buonomo (282) Italian: nickname from *buono* 'good' + *uomo* 'man'.

GIVEN NAMES Italian 14%. *Angelo* (3), *Sal* (2), *Amedeo*, *Antonio*, *Carlo*, *Cosmo*, *Domenic*, *Ettore*.

Buonopane (158) Italian: from *buono* 'good' + *pane* 'bread', a nickname for a person 'as good as bread', or possibly a metonymic occupational name for a baker.

GIVEN NAMES Italian 13%. *Angelo* (2), *Costantino*, *Dino*, *Domenic*, *Gabriele*, *Prisco*.

Buote (107) French: habitational name from any of various places in France called Le Buot, Le Buat, or (Le) Buet, named with the Frankish word *buka* 'stream', 'watercourse'.

Buoy (166) English (Gloucestershire): unexplained.

Bupp (361) German: from a short form of the late medieval personal name *Buppelin*, associated chiefly with *Burkhard* (see BURKHART).

Buquet (121) Respelling of French BOUQUET.

GIVEN NAMES French 6%. *Andre*, *Celina*, *Marcel*.

Bur (166) **1.** Swiss and North German variant of BAUER. **2.** French: from a short form of a Germanic personal name formed with *bur* 'dwelling', 'settlement'. **3.** Czech: topographic name, from *bur* 'pine wood'. **4.** Czech: descriptive nickname from *burý* 'dark'.

Burack (214) **1.** Americanized spelling of Slavic and Jewish BURAK. **2.** Respelling of the German and Jewish habitational name **Burach**, from a place so named near Ravensburg.

GIVEN NAMES Jewish 5%. *Ari* (2), *Emanuel*, *Hyman*.

Buracker (104) Respelling of German **Buracher**, a habitational name for someone from a place called Burach (see BURACK).

Burak (447) **1.** Ukrainian, Belorussian, Polish, and Jewish (eastern Ashkenazic): from Slavic *burak* 'beet'. **2.** Polish: nickname from *bury* 'dark brownish gray', probably denoting hair or eye color. **3.** Czech: nickname for someone with dark hair, dark eyes, or a swarthy complexion, from Old Czech *burý* 'dark'.

Buran (183) Czech: topographic name from *bur* 'pine wood'.

Burandt (182) Eastern German: of Slavic origin, related to the personal name *Bureslav*.

GIVEN NAMES German 5%. *Horst* (2), *Hans*, *Kurt*.

Burant (121) German (**Burandt**): unexplained.

Buras (462) **1.** Variant of French **Bura(t)**, from Old French *b(o)ure* 'frieze', a type of coarse woolen cloth, and hence a metonymic occupational name for a maker or seller of such cloth. **2.** Norwegian (**Burås**): habitational name from a farm named Burås, from *bu* 'booth', 'temporary dwelling' (from Old Norse *búð*) + *ås* 'hill'. **3.** Polish: nickname from *bury* 'dark, brownish gray', probably denoting hair or eye color.

FOREBEARS The Louisiana Buras family traces its descent from a Jean-Guillaume Burat, a soldier from Saleure, Switzerland, who was married in Mobile, AL, in 1725.

GIVEN NAMES French 5%. *Emile*, *Lucien*, *Olivier*.

Buratti (110) Italian: perhaps an occupational name from Old Italian *buratta*, *burattino* 'sifter' or a metonymic occupational name for a sieve maker or flour sifter, from *buratto* 'sieve'.

GIVEN NAMES Italian 6%. *Aldo*, *Carmel*.

Burau (142) German: habitational name from a place in Silesia called Burau (now in Poland).

Burba (464) Polish: possibly from a dialect form of Polish *burbot* 'rumbling' or *burbułka* 'soap bubble'.

Burbach (669) German: habitational name from Burbach in Baden or Hesse, or from Bauerbach, Baden.

GIVEN NAMES German 4%. *Kurt* (2), *Otto*, *Reinhold*, *Willi*.

Burback (301) Americanized spelling of BURBACH.

Burbage (510) English: habitational name from places in Wiltshire, Derbyshire, and Leicestershire, so named with Old English *burh* 'fort' + *bæc* 'hill', 'ridge' (dative *bece*).

GIVEN NAMES French 4%. *Andre* (2), *Cecile*.

Burbank (1757) English: habitational name, perhaps from Burbank House in Dacre, Cumbria, possibly named with Old English *burh* 'stronghold', 'manor' + Old Danish *banke* 'bank', 'ridge'.

Burbee (101) See BURBY.

Burbey (116) English: see BURBY.

Burbidge (249) English: variant spelling of BURBAGE.

Burbine (105) Probably French, but unexplained; perhaps an altered form of **Burban**, a nickname for a vain or arrogant man, from Old French *burban* 'splendour', or alternatively a much altered form of **Bourbon** (see BOURBONNAIS).

Burbridge (533) English: perhaps a variant of BURBAGE, altered by folk etymology, or possibly a habitational name from a lost place so named.

Burbrink (126) Dutch or North German: topographic name for someone who lived on the edge of low-lying grazing land (see BRINK), with an unexplained first element.

Burby (218) **1.** English: perhaps a habitational name from a lost or unidentified place. **2.** Perhaps a variant of BARBY.

Burcaw (105) Origin unidentified. Perhaps a metathesized variant of Dutch BROKAW.

Burch (12698) **1.** English: variant spelling of BIRCH. **2.** North German: habitational name from any of several places called Burg, in northern Germany originally denoting a fortified town or a fortified residence within a town. The form reflects the north German pronunciation of *Burg*.

Burcham (2036) English: probably a variant spelling of **Bircham**, a habitational name from a group of villages in Norfolk (Great Bircham, Bircham Newton, and Bircham Tofts), named with Old English *brēc* 'newly cultivated ground' + *hām* 'homestead'. There is also a Bircham in Devon, named with Old English *birce* 'birch' + *hām* or *hamm* 'enclosure hemmed in by water', which could have given rise to the surname.

Burchard (773) **1.** English: from the Old English personal name *Burgheard* (see BURKETT). **2.** Dutch and German: variant of BURKHARDT.

FOREBEARS Thomas Burchard came from London, England, to MA in 1635 aboard the *True Love*, and by 1652 he was in Edgartown on Martha's Vineyard.

Burchardt (139) German and Danish: variant of BURKHART.

GIVEN NAMES Scandinavian 6%; German 5%. *Erland, Per; Hans* (2), *Bernd.*

Burchell (907) English: variant spelling of BIRCHALL.

Burcher (199) English: variant spelling of BIRCHER.

Burchett (2638) Southern English: topographic name for someone who lived by a grove of birch trees, from Old English *byrcet* 'birch copse', a derivative of *birce* 'birch'. Compare the northern English equivalent BIRKETT.

Burchette (595) Frenchified spelling of English BURCHETT.

Burchfiel (110) Altered spelling of English BURCHFIELD.

Burchfield (2441) English: habitational name from any of various minor places called Birchfield, from Old English *birce* 'birch' + *feld* 'open country', or a topographic name with the same meaning.

Burchill (379) English: variant spelling of BIRCHALL.

Burciaga (393) Hispanic (Mexico): unexplained, but probably a topographic name of Basque origin.

GIVEN NAMES Spanish 54%. *Jesus* (13), *Jose* (10), *Manuel* (7), *Juan* (6), *Miguel* (6), *Carlos* (5), *Raul* (5), *Jaime* (4), *Armando* (3), *Guadalupe* (3), *Lupe* (3), *Ramiro* (3).

Burck (261) Possibly a shortened form of any of the various German names beginning *Burk-* or *Burch-* or of the Dutch name **de Burck**, which Debrabandere suggests

may be an altered form of **(de) Bok** (see BOK).

Burckhalter (101) Swiss German: variant of BURKHALTER.

Burckhard (218) Dutch and German: variant of BURKHART. This spelling is also found in Alsace and Lorraine.

Burckhardt (208) German: variant of BURKHART.

GIVEN NAMES German 9%. *Dieter* (3), *Ewald, Inge, Jochem, Klaus.*

Burczyk (156) Polish: nickname for a grouse or complainer, from *burczeć* 'to grumble'.

Burd (2057) **1.** English: variant spelling of BIRD. **2.** Jewish (from Poland and Ukraine): nickname for a man with a notable beard, from a southern Yiddish pronunciation of Yiddish *bord* 'beard'.

Burda (712) **1.** Czech, Slovak, and Ukrainian: nickname for a large, loutish fellow, from the vocabulary word *burda*. **2.** Polish and Jewish (eastern Ashkenazic): nickname for a troublemaker, from Old Polish *burda* 'disturbance', 'brawl' (originally meaning 'burden', 'load').

Burdell (177) English: origin uncertain; perhaps a variant of BEARDALL or BARDWELL.

Burden (3925) English (chiefly West Country): **1.** (of Norman origin) from the Old French personal name *Burdo* (oblique case *Burdon*), probably of Germanic origin, but uncertain meaning. **2.** nickname for a pilgrim or one who carried a pilgrim's staff, Middle English, Old French *bourdon*. **3.** habitational name from any of various places called Burdon or Burden. Burden in West Yorkshire and Great Burdon in County Durham are named with Old English *burh* 'stronghold', 'fortified place' + *dūn* 'hill'; Burdon in Tyne and Wear is named with Old English *būre* 'byre' + *denu* 'valley'.

Burdeshaw (154) Perhaps an Americanized spelling of German **Badertscher**, an occupational name for a barber, from Middle High German *bart* 'beard' + *scher* 'cutter', 'shearer', an agent derivative of *scheren* 'to clip'.

Burdett (1450) French and English (of Norman origin): from a pet form of the Old French personal name *Burdo* (see BURDON).

Burdette (4084) French: variant spelling of BURDETT.

Burdge (588) English: southwestern dialect variant of BRIDGE, from a metathesized form of Old English *brycg*. Compare BURGE.

Burdi (134) Italian (Bari province): probably from an old German personal name, *Burdo*.

GIVEN NAMES Italian 22%. *Saverio* (2), *Aldo, Angelo, Antonietta, Carmine, Gianfranco, Pasquale, Rocco, Sal, Vincenzo.*

Burdick (5529) English: unexplained; possibly a variant of BURDETT.

FOREBEARS Robert Burdick was a freeman of Newport, RI, in 1655.

Burdin (227) **1.** French: possibly a derivative of Occitan *burdir* 'to sport or amuse oneself' or a variant of BORDEAU. **2.** Southern French: variant of **Bourdin**, a nickname or metonymic occupational name, from medieval Latin *burdinus* 'mule', 'hinny'. **3.** Russian and Jewish (Ashkenazic): see BURDA. **4.** English: variant spelling of BURDON.

Burdine (1161) Possibly an altered spelling of BURDIN.

Burditt (429) French and English: variant spelling of BURDETT.

Burdo (258) **1.** Jewish (eastern Ashkenazic): variant of BURDA. **2.** In some instances, possibly an altered spelling of the French surname **Burdeau**, a topographic name derived from BORDE, or perhaps of BORDEAU.

Burdock (109) English: unexplained; perhaps from either of two medicinal and edible plants commonly known by this name (*Arctium lappa* and *A. minus*). However, the word is not recorded in OED before 1597, rather too late for surname formation.

Burdon (123) **1.** English: variant spelling of BURDEN. **2.** Polish: nickname for a troublemaker (see BURDA).

Burdorf (109) Variant of German BURGDORF.

GIVEN NAMES German 5%. *Erwin, Reiner.*

Burdsall (213) English: variant spelling of BIRDSALL.

Bureau (370) French: from Old French, Old Occitan *bureau, burel* 'frieze', 'coarse woolen material' (see BOREL).

FOREBEARS A bearer of the name from Brittany is documented in L'Ancienne Lorette, Quebec, in 1685, with the secondary surname Sanssoucy; another, from the Nivernais region, is recorded in Quebec city in 1699.

GIVEN NAMES French 16%. *Marcel* (3), *Gaetan* (2), *Luc* (2), *Aime, Amie, Andre, Armand, Dany, Fernand, Gaston, Gilles, Jean Louis.*

Burek (402) Polish: nickname from a derivative of *bury* 'auburn(-haired)'.

GIVEN NAMES Polish 4%. *Ewa, Irena, Jadwiga, Jozefa, Ryszard, Tadeuz.*

Burel (151) French: variant of BOREL.

GIVEN NAMES French 7%. *Henri, Julienne, Patrice, Serge.*

Burell (196) Altered spelling of French *Burel* (see BOREL), or of the English cognate BURRELL.

FOREBEARS A Burel from Paris, whose family was said to be established in Mobile, LA (AL not yet existing), was married in Cap St. Ignace, Quebec, in 1682.

Buren (263) **1.** Dutch: patronymic from a short form of any of the Germanic personal names beginning with the element *Boro*.

2. Dutch: short form of VAN BUREN.
3. German (**Büren**; also **Buhren**, **Bühren**): from Old High German *bür* 'small house', 'chamber', hence a topographic name for someone who lived 'near the houses' or a habitational name from any of various places throughout Germany and in parts of Switzerland named with this word.

Bures (388) Czech and Slovak (**Bureš**): from a pet form of BURIAN.
GIVEN NAMES Czech and Slovak 4%. *Milan* (4), *Jaroslav* (2).

Buresh (564) **1.** Americanized spelling of Czech *Bureš* (see BURES). **2.** Americanized spelling of German *Buresch*, from the Slavic personal name *Bureslaw*.

Burfeind (169) North German form of BAUERNFEIND.

Burfield (281) English: habitational name from Burghfield in Berkshire or Burfield in Sussex. The first is named with Old English *beorg* 'hill' + *feld* 'open country'. The second is from Old English *burh* 'stronghold', 'fortified manor' + *feld*.

Burford (1958) English: habitational name from places in Oxfordshire and Shropshire, so named with Old English *burh* 'stronghold', 'fortified manor' + *ford* 'ford'.

Burg (2089) **1.** German (also **Bürg**): topographic name, from Middle High German *burc* 'fortification', 'castle', or a habitational name from any of the numerous places called Burg. **2.** German: from a short form of the personal name *Burkhard* (see BURKHART). **3.** Dutch: short form of VANDERBURG. **4.** Dutch: from a short form of the Germanic personal name *Burgo*. **5.** Jewish: variant of BURGER. **6.** Probably in some cases an altered spelling of BURGH.

Burgamy (179) English: unexplained.

Burgan (777) English: variant spelling of BURGIN.

Burgard (603) Altered spelling of BURKHART.

Burgardt (153) Altered spelling of BURKHART.

Burgart (112) Altered spelling of BURKHART.

Burgdorf (409) German: habitational name from any of various places so named in northern Germany, Austria, and Switzerland.
GIVEN NAMES German 6%. *Otto* (4), *Hans* (3), *Juergen*, *Jurgen*, *Nikolaus*.

Burge (3764) **1.** English (chiefly Somerset and Dorset): variant of BRIDGE, Old English *brycg*, with metathesis of *u* and *r*, as exemplified in several place names of this origin in various parts of southern England. **2.** German (**Bürge**): from Middle High German *bürge* 'bailsman', 'guarantor'. **3.** In some cases maybe an altered spelling of Swiss **Bürgi** (see BURGI).

Burgee (114) Variant spelling of BURGY.

Burgen (120) English: variant spelling of BURGIN.

Burgener (389) German: habitational name for someone from Burgheim near Breisach. The form of the surname reflects the local pronunciation of the place name.

Burger (7926) **1.** German, English, and Dutch: status name for a freeman of a borough, especially one who was a member of its governing council, a derivative of Middle High German *burc*, Middle English *burg* '(fortified) town', Middle Dutch *burch*. The English name is found occasionally as a surname from the 13th century onwards but is not recorded as a vocabulary word until the 16th century. The usual English term was the Old French word *burgeis* 'burgess' (see BURGESS). This name is frequent throughout central and eastern Europe. It also occurs as an Ashkenazic Jewish family name, but the reasons for its adoption are uncertain. **2.** German: habitational name for someone from any of the many places called Burg.

Burgers (109) Dutch: variant of BURGER.
GIVEN NAMES French 5%; German 4%; Dutch 4%. *Henri*, *Pierre*; *Hans*, *Wilhelmus*; *Frans* (2), *Gerrit*.

Burgert (217) German and Czech: from the German personal name BURKHART.
GIVEN NAMES German 4%. *Gitta*, *Konrad*.

Burges (167) English: variant spelling of BURGESS.

Burgeson (510) Perhaps an Americanized spelling of a Scandinavian patronymic from the Old Norse personal name *Byrgir*, *Birgir*, for example **Bergesen**, **Børgesen**, **Byrgesen**.

Burgess (25253) English and Scottish: status name from Middle English *burge(i)s*, Old French *burgeis* 'inhabitant and (usually) freeman of a (fortified) town' (see BURKE), especially one with municipal rights and duties. Burgesses generally had tenure of land or buildings from a landlord by *burgage*. In medieval England burgage involved the payment of a fixed money rent (as opposed to payment in kind); in Scotland it involved payment in service, guarding the town. The *-eis* ending is from Latin *-ensis* (modern English *-ese* as in *Portuguese*). Compare BURGER.
FOREBEARS Thomas Burgess came from England to MA in about 1630 and eventually settled in Sandwich, MA.

Burget (289) Czech: from the German personal name BURKHART.

Burgett (1797) English: topographic name for someone who lived by a castle or city gate, Middle English *burgate*, or a habitational name from a place named Burgate, from Old English *burh-geat* with the same meaning, examples of which are found in Hampshire, Suffolk, and Surrey.

Burggraf (243) German: occupational or status name for the highest ranking judge of a castle and its adjacent territory or the governor of a town, from Middle High German *burc* 'castle' + *grāve* 'highest (territorial) judge', such a person being appointed by the king.

Burggraff (143) Respelling of German BURGGRAF.

Burgh (155) English: habitational name from any of the places in Cumbria, West Yorkshire, Lincolnshire, Norfolk, and Suffolk named Burgh, from Old English *burh* 'fortified manor', 'stronghold'.

Burghard (116) German: variant of BURKHART, also frequent among Czech speakers.
GIVEN NAMES German 8%. *Otto*, *Willi*.

Burghardt (686) German: variant of BURKHART.
GIVEN NAMES German 6%. *Kurt* (4), *Detlef*, *Erna*, *Friedrich*, *Horst*, *Klaus*, *Lothar*, *Theresia*.

Burghart (269) German: variant of BURKHART, also frequent among people of Czech origin.

Burgher (372) English and Dutch: variant spelling of BURGER.

Burgi (146) **1.** Italian: from the plural of BURGIO 1. **2.** Swiss German (**Bürgi**): from a pet form of the personal name *Burkhard* (see BURKHART).

Burgin (1869) **1.** English: regional name for someone from Burgundy, Old French *Bourgogne* (see BURGOYNE). **2.** Swiss German (**Bürgin**): from a pet form of the personal name *Burkhard* (see BURKHART).

Burgio (435) Italian (Sicily): **1.** topographic name from Sicilian *bùrgiu* 'tower', 'fortified town'. **2.** habitational name from Burgio in Agrigento province.
GIVEN NAMES Italian 18%. *Salvatore* (7), *Vito* (3), *Angelo* (2), *Antonio* (2), *Pietro* (2), *Sal* (2), *Corrado*, *Enzo*, *Francesca*, *Giovanni*, *Guiseppe*, *Marcello*.

Burgman (209) Americanized spelling of German **Burgmann**, from Middle High German *burc* 'fortified town', 'castle' + *man* 'man', 'vassal', a status name for a vassal of the lord of a castle, or a chatelain, or an occupational or status name for a town justice.

Burgmeier (171) German: occupational name for the tenant farmer of an estate belonging to a castle or fortified town, from Middle High German *burc* '(fortified) town', 'castle' + *meier* 'tenant farmer' (see MEYER).

Burgner (252) German: probably an altered spelling of **Burgmer**, a habitational name for someone from Burgheim near Lahr, Baden, or from a personal name formed with Old High German *burc* 'castle'.

Burgo (193) **1.** Spanish: habitational name from any of the many places in Spain called Burgo, from Spanish *burgo* 'fortified place', 'hamlet'. **2.** Italian: topographic name from *borgo* 'tower', 'fortified town'.
GIVEN NAMES Spanish 14%; Portuguese 8%; Italian 5%. *Manuel* (3), *Porfirio* (2), *Carolina*, *Domingos*, *Eduardo*, *Elvira*, *Jaime*, *Jose*, *Jose Luis*, *Rafael*, *Tiago*; *Joaquim* (2), *Joao*; *Rocco* (2), *Santo*.

Burgon (105) Variant of English BUR-GOYNE.

Burgoon (522) Variant of English BUR-GOYNE.

Burgos (2281) Spanish: habitational name from Burgos, the capital of old Castile.
GIVEN NAMES Spanish 47%. *Jose* (64), *Luis* (36), *Juan* (25), *Angel* (20), *Carlos* (20), *Rafael* (20), *Ana* (18), *Miguel* (17), *Manuel* (14), *Jorge* (13), *Francisco* (12), *Jesus* (11).

Burgoyne (839) English: regional name for someone from Burgundy (Old French *Bourgogne*), a region of eastern France having Dijon as its center. The area was invaded by the *Burgundii*, a Germanic tribe from whom it takes its name, in about AD 480. The duchy of Burgundy, created in 877 by Charles II, King of the West Franks, was extremely powerful in the later Middle Ages, especially under Philip the Bold (1342–1404, duke from 1363).

Burgstahler (116) German: **1.** occupational name for an armorer, from *Burg* 'castle' + *Stahl* 'steel' + *-er* suffix of agent nouns. **2.** Possibly a respelling of German **Burgstaller**, a habitational name for someone from any of numerous places called Burgstall (generally designating a 'place where a castle stands or stood').
GIVEN NAMES German 7%. *Ewald*, *Frieda*.

Burgus (103) German: unexplained.

Burgy (201) **1.** French: habitational name from a place in Sâone-et-Loire named Burgy, from a Gallo-Roman personal name *Burgius* + the locative suffix *-acum*. **2.** Swiss German (**Bürgy**): variant of **Bürgi** (see BURGI).

Burham (91) English: habitational name from a place in Kent named Burham, from Old English *burh* 'stronghold', 'fortified place' + *hām* 'homestead'.

Burhans (410) German: from Middle Low German *būr* 'farmer', 'peasant' + the personal name *Hans*, a short form of *Johannes* (see JOHN), hence 'farmer John'. See also BURIAN.

Burhoe (119) Origin unidentified.

Burhop (121) North German: topographic name from Middle Low German *būr* 'farmer', 'peasant' + *hōp*, 'pile', or, as a suffix in place names, 'gathering', 'assembly'. The term *hōp* is a common element in place names of the northwestern coastal area of Germany, for example Hope, Hoopen, Hoople.

Buri (164) **1.** Swiss German: from an Alemannic pet form of the personal name *Burkhard* (see BURKHART). **2.** Eastern German: variant of **Buresch** (see BURESH).
GIVEN NAMES German 6%. *Markus* (2), *Kurt*.

Burian (416) **1.** Czech, Slovak, and Polish: from *Burian*, an Old Slavic personal name of uncertain origin. **2.** North German: variant of BURHANS, formed with *Jan* (John) in place of *Hans*.

Burianek (122) Czech and Slovak (**Buriánek**): from a diminutive of BURIAN.
GIVEN NAME German 5%. *Otto* (2).

Burich (329) **1.** Czech (**Buřič**) and Slovak (**Burič**): nickname from *buřič* 'rebel'. **2.** Americanized spelling of Serbian and Croatian **Burić**, a patronymic of uncertain origin. In Serbia it is probably from a descriptive nickname based on *bur* 'dark brownish gray'. In the mountains of Croatia, it is more probably a shepherd's nickname from Rumanian *bur* 'good'. On the Dalmatian coast it is thought to be from a nickname given to children 'blown in by the north wind', i.e. born when the north wind called the *bura* was blowing. **3.** German: variant of German **Burisch**, from a derivative of the Slavic personal name *Bureslav*.

Burick (146) **1.** Ukrainian (**Burik**): nickname from *bur* 'dark brown', 'gray'. **2.** See BURICH.

Burk (5881) **1.** Swiss German: from an Alemannic short form of the personal name *Burkhard* (see BURKHART). **2.** German: habitational name from the common place names Burk and Burg. **3.** Northern English: variant of BIRCH.

Burka (152) Jewish (from Ukraine): habitational name for someone from Burki, a village in Ukraine.

Burkard (561) German: variant of the personal name BURKHART.

Burkart (1071) **1.** English: variant of BURKETT. **2.** Dutch and German (also Swiss): from the personal name BURKHART.

Burke (47014) **1.** Irish (of Anglo-Norman origin): habitational name from Burgh in Suffolk, England. This is named with Old English *burh* 'fortification', 'fortified manor'. **2.** Norwegian: Americanized form of **Børke**, a habitational name from any of eight farms in southeastern Norway, named with Old Norse *birki* 'birch wood'. **3.** German: variant of BURK.

FOREBEARS Burke owes its importance as an Irish surname to William FitzAdelm de Burgo, a Norman knight whose family held lands at Burgh in Suffolk, from which they took their name. He took part in Henry II's expedition to Ireland in 1171 and received the earldom of Ulster, along with large tracts of land in Connacht. His descendants quickly associated themselves with the native population, Gaelicizing their name as **de Búrca**. Thomas Burke (1747–1783) was born in Co. Galway, Ireland, settled in VA after immigration, then moved to NC in 1771, where he became a prominent revolutionary statesman.
GIVEN NAMES Irish 8%. *Brendan* (27), *Kieran* (4), *Siobhan* (4), *Aileen* (3), *Brennan* (3), *Brigid* (3), *Donovan* (3), *Liam* (3), *Murphy* (3), *Ulick* (3), *Aidan* (2), *Dermot* (2).

Burkeen (338) **1.** American pet form of Irish BURKE, not found as a surname in Ireland. **2.** Possibly an altered spelling of

the Swiss family name **Bürgin** (see BUR-GIN).

Burkel (236) German (also **Bürkel**): from a pet form of one of the various personal names beginning with the element *Burg-* or *Burk-*, for example *Burkhard* (see BURK-HART).
GIVEN NAMES French 4%. *Raynald*, *Remy*.

Burkemper (187) North German (Westphalia): habitational name from a place called Burgkamp, named with Middle Low German *būr* 'farmer', 'peasant' + *kamp* 'field', 'meadow'.

Burken (111) English: variant of **Birkin** (see BURKINS).

Burker (113) English: variant of BURGER.

Burkert (406) German: variant of BURK-HART.
GIVEN NAMES German 5%. *Helmut* (2), *Erwin*, *Gunther*, *Heinz*, *Willi*.

Burkes (872) English: variant spelling of BIRKS.

Burket (704) Variant of English BURKETT and German BURKHART.

Burkett (6599) **1.** English: from an Old English personal name, *Burgheard*, composed of the elements *burh*, *burg* 'fort' (see BURKE) + *heard* 'hardy', 'brave', 'strong'. The name was reintroduced into Middle English by the Normans in the forms *Bou(r)chart*, *Bocard*. In the form *Burkhard* it was a very popular medieval German name. There has been considerable confusion between this English surname and BIRKETT. **2.** Perhaps also a variant of German BURKHART.

Burkette (111) Frenchified spelling of English BURKETT.

Burkey (1484) Altered spelling of German **Bürki**, from an Alemannic pet form of the personal name *Burkhard* (see BURKHART).

Burkhalter (1921) Swiss German: topographic name composed of the Middle High German elements *burc* 'castle' (originally also 'protection') + *halter* from *halde* 'slope', hence a name for someone living by a castle or fortified town.

FOREBEARS The earliest immigrant of the Burkholder family, Hans Burkhalter, from Bern canton, Switzerland, settled in Lancaster county, PA, in 1717.

Burkham (146) Americanized form of the German habitational name **Burkheim** (see BURKHEIMER).

Burkhammer (152) Americanized form of German BURKHEIMER.

Burkhard (541) German: variant of BURK-HART.

Burkhardt (3212) German: variant of BURKHART.
GIVEN NAMES German 5%. *Hans* (4), *Kurt* (4), *Otto* (4), *Erwin* (3), *Dieter* (2), *Lorenz* (2), *Ueli* (2), *Dietmar*, *Eberhard*, *Eugen*, *Fritz*, *Gerlinde*.

Burkhart (5923) German and Dutch: from the medieval personal name *Burkhard*, composed of the elements *burg* 'fort', 'castle' + *hard* 'hardy', 'brave', 'strong'.

Burkhead (860) **1.** English: variant spelling of BIRKHEAD (see BIRKETT). **2.** Americanized form of German BURKHART.

Burkheimer (109) German: habitational name from either of two places called Burkheim, in Baden and Bavaria. Compare BURKHAMMER.

Burkholder (3463) Americanized form of Swiss German BURKHALTER.

Burki (130) **1.** South German (**Bürki**): from a pet form of the personal name BURKHART. **2.** Muslim (prevalent in Pakistan): unexplained.
GIVEN NAMES Muslim 11%; German 7%; French 7%. *Aamir, Amir, Jamal, Khalid, Mohammed, Sajjad, Shahid, Tariq*; *Kurt, Otto*; *Henri, Marcel, Yves*.

Burkins (198) English: variant of **Birkin**, **Burkin**, a habitational name from the parish of Birkin in West Yorkshire, so named with Old English *bircen* 'birch grove', a derivative of *birce* (see BIRCH).

Burkinshaw (123) English: habitational name from Birkenshaw in West Yorkshire, named from Old English *bircen* 'birches' + *sceaga* 'copse'.

Burkitt (295) English: variant spelling of BURKETT.

Burkland (270) Possibly an Americanized form of one of the common Scandinavian compounds of *bjørk* 'birch' (Old Norse *birki*) + *land* 'land' (see, for example, BIRKELAND).

Burkle (443) Respelling of South German **Bürkle**, **Bürkel**, or **Birkle**, all from a pet form of the personal name *Burkhard* (see BURKHART).
GIVEN NAMES German 4%. *Erwin, Kurt, Rainer*.

Burkley (394) **1.** Altered form of Swiss and South German **Bürkle**, **Bürkli** (see BURKLE). **2.** English: variant of BERKELEY.

Burklow (211) Probably an altered form of Swiss and South German **Bürkle**, **Bürkli** (see BURKLE).

Burklund (255) Probably a respelling of various Scandinavian ornamental or habitational names (from farms) formed with a first element meaning 'birch' + *lund* 'grove', as for example **Birkelund**, **Bjørklund**, **Bjerklund**.

Burkman (428) **1.** English: variant of BURMAN. **2.** Possibly an altered spelling of German **Bergmann** or **Burgmann** (see BERGMAN and BURGMAN).

Burks (7868) English: variant spelling of BIRKS.

Burky (128) South German (**Bürky**): variant of BURKI.

Burl (196) Altered spelling of the English occupational name **Burle**, from Old English *byr(e)le* 'cup bearer', 'butler'.

Burlage (153) German: habitational name from any of several places near Hannover, named Burlage from Middle Low German *būr* 'dwelling place', 'peasant', 'farmer' + *lage* 'open space or field within a forest'.

Burland (141) English: habitational name from places in Cheshire and East Yorkshire named Burland. The first is named with Old English *(ge)būr* 'peasant' + *land* 'land'; the second from Old English *bȳre* 'byre', 'cow shed' + *land*.

Burleigh (1186) English: variant spelling of BURLEY 1.

Burleson (4635) English: perhaps a patronymic (meaning 'son of the butler') from BURL.
FOREBEARS Aaron Burleson emigrated from England to NC in 1726.

Burlew (440) Probably a variant of BURLEY 1 or 2.

Burley (2697) **1.** English: habitational name from any of various places, for example in Hampshire, Rutland, Shropshire, and West Yorkshire, named Burley from Old English *burh* 'fortified manor', 'stronghold' + *lēah* 'woodland clearing'. **2.** Americanized spelling of Swiss German **Bürli**, from a diminutive of *būr* 'peasant', 'farmer' (see BAUER).

Burlin (126) **1.** English: possibly, as Reaney proposes, an ethnic name for someone from Burgundy, France, from a variant Old French *bouguignon* 'Burgundian', but more probably a variant of the more frequent English surname BURLING. **2.** Altered spelling of BERLIN.

Burling (472) English (Essex and Cambridgeshire): probably a habitational name from a place in Kent named Birling, from an Old English personal name *Bērla* + the suffix *-ingas* denoting 'family or followers'. There is also a Birling (of the same derivation) in Northumberland, but this appears not to have contributed significantly to the modern surname.

Burlingame (1587) Variant of English BURLINGHAM.
FOREBEARS Joel Burlingame was a Methodist exhorter and lay preacher at New Berlin, NY, in the 1820s. His son Anson Burlingame, born in New Berlin in 1820, headed the first diplomatic mission to China and negotiated the Burlingame Treaty (1868).

Burlingham (292) English (East Anglia): habitational name from Burlingham in Norfolk 'homestead (Old English *hām*) of Bærla's or Byrla's people', or from Birlingham in Worcestershire 'enclosure (Old English *hamm*) of Byrla's people'.

Burlington (144) English: habitational name from Bridlington in East Yorkshire. The place name, which was formerly pronounced locally as *Burlington*, is recorded in Domesday Book as *Bretlinton* 'estate (Old English *tūn*) associated with a man called *Berhtel*'.

Burlison (663) English: variant spelling of BURLESON.

Burlock (105) English: unexplained.

Burman (1216) **1.** English: status name, from Middle English *burghman*, *boroughman* (Old English *burhmann*) 'inhabitant of a (fortified) town' (see BURKE), especially one holding land or buildings by *burgage* (see BURGESS). **2.** Americanized spelling of German *Buhrmann* (see BUHRMAN).

Burmaster (273) Partly Americanized form of German BURMEISTER.

Burmeister (1859) North German: status name for the mayor or chief magistrate of a town, from Middle Low German *būr* 'inhabitant, dweller', 'neighbor', 'peasant', 'citizen' + *mēster* 'master'.
GIVEN NAMES German 5%. *Kurt* (13), *Erwin* (4), *Klaus* (2), *Otto* (2), *Ewald, Fritz, Gerhardt, Gernot, Hans, Horst, Juergen, Ulrike*.

Burmester (362) North German: see BURMEISTER.
GIVEN NAMES German 4%. *Hans, Kurt*.

Burn (544) English: variant of BOURNE.

Burnam (528) English: variant spelling of the habitational name BURNHAM.

Burnaman (120) Americanized form of German BORNEMANN.

Burnap (140) English: unexplained. The spelling *Burnap* is associated chiefly with Kent, while other forms (**Burnop**, **Burnup**, etc.) occur predominantly in Northumberland and Durham.

Burnard (211) English: variant of BERNARD.

Burne (109) English: variant of BOURNE.

Burnell (1344) English: from a metathesized diminutive of Middle English *brun* 'brown' (see BROWN).

Burner (822) English: topographic name for someone who lived by a stream, from Middle English *burn* 'stream' + the suffix *-er* denoting an inhabitant.

Burnes (764) Scottish: variant of BURNS 2.

Burness (158) Scottish: variant of BURNS 2.

Burnet (241) **1.** Scottish: variant spelling of BURNETT. **2.** French: variant spelling of BURNETTE.

Burnett (20213) Scottish and English: descriptive nickname from Old French *burnete*, a diminutive of *brun* 'brown' (see BROWN).

Burnette (5598) French: **1.** descriptive nickname from Old French *burnete* 'brown' (see BURNETT). **2.** possibly also a reduced form of **Buronet**, from a diminutive of Old French *buron* 'hut', 'shack'.

Burney (2736) **1.** English (of Norman origin) and Irish: habitational name from Bernay in Eure, France, named with a Gaulish personal name *Brenno* + the locative suffix *-acum*. **2.** Irish: Anglicized form of Gaelic **Mac Biorna** 'son of *Biorna*', a Gaelic form of the Old Norse personal name *Bjarni* (from *björn* 'bear cub', 'warrior'). **3.** English: variant of BARNEY 1.

Burnham (6375) English: habitational name from any of several places called Burnham. Those in Buckinghamshire (Burnham Beeches), Norfolk (various villages), and Essex (Burnham-on-Crouch) are named with Old English *burna* 'stream' + *hām* 'homestead'. In the case of Burnham-on-Sea in Somerset, however, the second element is Old English *hamm* 'water meadow', while Burnham in Lincolnshire is named from *brunnum*, dative plural of Old Norse *brunnr* 'spring', originally used after a preposition, i.e. '(at) the springs'.
FOREBEARS In 1635 Robert Burnham and his two brothers came from England to Ipswich, MA, after their ship was wrecked on the coast of Maine. In the mid 18th century John Burnham and his son, also called John, were among the early settlers in what became the state of VT. In 1785, the younger John Burnham established himself at Middletown, CT.

Burningham (297) English: unexplained. Most probably a habitational name from a lost or unidentified place.

Burnison (133) English: probably a patronymic from Old Norse *Bjarni* (see BURNEY 2).

Burnley (580) English (Lancashire and Yorkshire): habitational name from Burnley in Lancashire, so named with the Old English river name *Brun* (from *brūn* 'brown' or *burna* 'stream') + *lēah* 'woodland clearing'.

Burno (117) Of Italian origin: unexplained.
GIVEN NAMES Italian 6%. *Calogero, Pasqualino, Vincenzo.*

Burnor (132) New England spelling of French BERNARD, reflecting the Franco-Canadian pronunciation.

Burns (60369) **1.** Scottish and northern English: topographic name for someone who lived by a stream or streams, from the Middle English nominative plural or genitive singular of *burn* (see BOURNE). **2.** Scottish: variant of **Burnhouse**, habitational name from a place named with *burn* 'stream' + *house* 'house'. **3.** Irish: Anglicized form of Gaelic **Ó Broin** (see BYRNE). **4.** Jewish (American): Americanized and shortened form of BERNSTEIN.

Burnsed (363) Americanized spelling of Scottish and northern Irish BURNSIDE.

Burnside (2785) Scottish and northern Irish: topographic name for someone living beside a burn or stream, or a habitational name from one of the many places so named.

Burnstein (260) Jewish (Ashkenazic): variant of BERNSTEIN or BURSTEIN.
GIVEN NAME Jewish 4%. *Naphtali* (2).

Burnsworth (194) English: see BURNWORTH.

Burnum (113) Probably an altered spelling of BURNHAM.

Burnworth (371) English: probably a habitational name from Burnworthy in Devon, which is named with the Old English personal name *Beorna* + Old English *worð* or *worðig* 'enclosure'; the interchange between *worth* and *worthy* is common in Middle English names in the southwest. The surname has died out in the British Isles.

Buro (117) **1.** Italian (especially Campania and Apulia): possibly from a Germanic personal name, *Buro.* **2.** Possibly an altered spelling of French **Bureau** (see BUREL).
GIVEN NAMES Italian 15%. *Natale* (2), *Carmela, Carmine, Giovanni, Pasquale, Sal.*

Buroker (231) German: probably an occupational name for a wig maker, from an agent noun based on *Perücke* 'wig', a loanword from Italian *parucca*. If this is right, the surname is a late formation, the vocabulary word first being attested in German in the 17th century.

Buron (118) **1.** French: status name from Old French *buron* 'small house', a derivative of Germanic *būr* 'hut'. **2.** Spanish (**Burón**): habitational name from Burón in León province.
GIVEN NAMES French 11%; Spanish 5%. *Raoul* (2), *Benedicte, Gaston, Pierre; Enrique, Felipe, Oliverio.*

Buros (101) Greek: variant of BOORAS.

Burow (332) German: habitational name from places so named in Mecklenburg and Pomerania.
GIVEN NAMES German 6%. *Fritz* (3), *Armin, Dietrich, Otto.*

Burpee (422) Probably French in origin: unexplained. Compare BURPO.

Burpo (226) The form **Burpeau** is also found and the name may be French in origin but the original form and etymology are unknown. Compare BURPEE.

Burr (6036) **1.** English: of uncertain origin. Reaney explains this as a nickname for a person who is difficult to shake off, from Middle English *bur(r)* 'bur' (a seedhead that sticks to clothing). *Burre* occurs as a surname or byname as early as 1185, but the vocabulary word is not recorded in OED until the 14th century. Another possibility is derivation from Old English *būr* 'small dwelling or building' (modern English *bower*), but there are phonological difficulties here too. **2.** German: perhaps a variant spelling of BUR, or a topographic name from *Burr(e)* 'mound', 'hill', or in the south a variant of BURRER.
FOREBEARS The American political leader Aaron Burr (1756–1836) was the son of a clergyman and academic, president of Princeton University. On his mother's side he was descended from the Puritan preacher Jonathan Edwards; on his father's from

Jehu Burr, who emigrated from England with John Winthrop to MA in 1630.

Burrage (515) English: variant spelling of BURRIDGE.
FOREBEARS John Burrage came from Norfolk, England, to Charlestown, MA, in 1637.

Burrell (6913) English, Scottish, and northern Irish: probably a metonymic occupational name for someone who made or sold coarse woolen cloth, Middle English *burel* or *borel* (from Old French *burel*, a diminutive of *b(o)ure*); the same word was used adjectively in the sense 'reddish brown' and may have been applied as a nickname referring to dress or complexion. Compare BOREL.

Burrer (168) German: from an agent derivative of Middle High German *burren* 'to buzz or complain', probably applied as a nickname for a noisy or cantankerous person.

Burres (177) Probably an Americanized spelling of German **Börries** or **Borres**, short forms of the personal name *Liborius*, the name of the patron saint of Paderborn.

Burress (1569) **1.** English: probably a variant of BURROWS. Compare BURRISS. **2.** Probably also an Americanized spelling of German **Börries** (see BURRES).

Burri (213) Swiss German: from a pet form of the personal name *Burkhard* (see BURKHART).
GIVEN NAMES German 5%. *Armin, Erna, Hans.*

Burrichter (102) German (Westphalia): unexplained. Compare BURRIGHT.

Burridge (361) English: **1.** habitational name from any of three places in Devon named Burridge, from Old English *burh* 'fort' (see BURKE) + *hrycg* 'ridge'. **2.** from the Middle English personal name *Burrich*, Old English *Burgrīc*, composed of the elements *burh*, *burg* 'fortress', 'stronghold' + *rīc* 'power'.

Burrier (417) Probably an altered spelling of French **Bourrier**. In eastern France this was an occupational name for a harness maker, from a derivative of Old French *bourrel* 'harness', 'collar'. In western France *burrier* denoted a thin wisp of straw, and was probably applied as a metonymic occupational name for a winnower.

Burright (167) Americanized form of German **Burricht**, of unexplained origin.

Burrill (848) English: variant spelling of BURRELL.
FOREBEARS George Burrill was one of the early settlers at Lynn, MA, in 1638, and the founder of a prominent family in colonial MA. He is believed to have come from Boston in Lincolnshire, England.

Burrington (301) English: habitational name from any of the places called Burrington, for example in Avon, Devon, and Herefordshire. The first and last are named with Old English *burh* 'fortified place' + *tūn* 'farmstead', 'enclosure'; the second is recorded in Domesday Book as *Bernintone* 'estate associated with a man called Beorn'.

FOREBEARS George Burrington (*c*.1680–1759), born in Devon, England, was a colonial governor of NC (1723–25, 1731–34).

Burris (8956) **1.** English: variant of BURROWS. **2.** Possibly an altered form of German **Börries** or **Borr(i)es** (see BURRESS).

Burriss (523) **1.** English: variant of BURROWS. **2.** Possibly an altered form of German **Börries** or **Borr(i)es** (see BURRESS).

Burritt (405) English: **1.** from the Middle English personal name *Burret*, Old English *Burgrǣd*, composed of the elements *burh*, *burg* 'fortress', 'stronghold' + *rǣd* 'counsel'. **2.** possibly a nickname for someone with thick and disheveled hair, from Old French *b(o)ure* 'coarse woolen cloth' + Middle English *heved* 'head'.

Burrola (186) Hispanic (Mexico): unexplained.
GIVEN NAMES Spanish 42%. *Manuel* (3), *Jesus* (2), *Julio* (2), *Raul* (2), *Ruben* (2), *Alfonso*, *Alicia*, *Andres*, *Arturo*, *Avelino*, *Consuelo*, *Dagoberto*.

Burros (130) Probably a variant of English BURROWS. Compare BURRIS, BURRUS.

Burrough (402) English: variant spelling of BURROW.

Burroughs (6077) English: variant spelling of BURROWS.

Burrous (212) Probably a variant of English BURROWS.

Burrow (2768) English: variant of BURROWS.

Burrowes (276) English: variant spelling of BURROWS.

Burrows (6362) English: topographic name for someone who lived by a hill or tumulus, Old English *beorg*, a cognate of Old High German *berg* 'hill', 'mountain' (see BERG). This name has become confused with derivatives of Old English *burh* 'fort' (see BURKE). Reaney suggests a further derivation from Old English *būr* 'bower' + *hūs* 'house'.

Burruel (117) Hispanic (Mexico): unexplained, but most probably Aragonese in origin.
GIVEN NAMES Spanish 30%. *Eduardo* (3), *Manuel* (3), *Armando* (2), *Jesus* (2), *Adolfo*, *Alfonso*, *Alicia*, *Carlos*, *Ernesto*, *Guillermo*, *Heberto*, *Jose*.

Burrus (1351) English: probably a variant of BURROWS. Compare BURRIS.

Burruss (672) English: unexplained; perhaps a variant of BURROWS. Compare BURRIS.

Burry (423) **1.** English: possibly a topographic name meaning 'dweller by the borough (Old English *burg*) enclosure (Old English *(ge)hæg)*', or alternatively a variant spelling of BURY. **2.** Swiss German: variant of BURRI.

Bursch (250) German: from a byname meaning 'young man', from Middle High German *burse*, originally denoting a student fraternity at a medieval university (from Late Latin *bursa* 'purse', i.e. a cash fund from which the students supported themselves), and later also other male societies, such as soldiers' or craftsmen's guilds. Eventually the term *Bursch(e)* came to denote an individual member rather than the institution, and was pluralized as *Burschen*.

Burse (498) **1.** Possibly also an altered spelling of French **Bourse**, a metonymic occupational name for a maker of purses, Old French *bourse* (from Late Latin *bursa*). **2.** German (**Bürse**): variant of BURSCH.
GIVEN NAMES French 4%. *Celestine*, *Jean Marie*, *Marcel*, *Patrice*.

Bursell (132) **1.** English: habitational name from Burshill in East Yorkshire, so named with Old English *bryst* 'landslip', 'rough ground' + *hyll* 'hill'. **2.** Swedish: probably from *Burs-*, a place name with any of several possibly origins, + *-ell*, a common ending of Swedish surnames derived from the Latin adjectival ending *-elius*.
GIVEN NAME Scandinavian 7%. *Sven* (2).

Bursey (399) English: **1.** (of Norman origin) habitational name from Burcy in Calvados, France. **2.** from the Old English personal name *Beorhtsige*.

Burski (49) Polish: habitational name for someone from a place called Bursz, in Ciechanów voivodeship, or Bursy.

Bursley (125) English: probably from a variant of *Burslem* in Staffordshire, which is named from the Old English term *burgweard* 'castle keeper' (or the same word as a personal name) + *Lyme*, the ancient Celtic name of the district in which the town is situated.

Burson (1799) English: unexplained; apparently a patronymic, but from an unidentified medieval personal name. It may be a variant of BARSON. On the other hand, there appears to be a French connection with the villages of Hardanges and La Chapelle au Riboul, whence bearers of this name are recorded as having emigrated to Canada.

Burst (197) German: from Middle High German *burst* 'bristle', hence a nickname either for someone with spiky, unkempt hair or for a brush maker.

Burstein (818) Jewish (Ashkenazic): Germanized spelling of Yiddish *burshtin* 'amber', Polish *bursztyn* (see BERNSTEIN).
GIVEN NAMES Jewish 9%. *Sol* (6), *Miriam* (5), *Ari* (2), *Hyman* (2), *Ilan* (2), *Isaak* (2), *Haim*, *Isadore*, *Meyer*, *Yakov*, *Yisroel*, *Yonah*.

Burston (140) **1.** English: habitational name from any of various places called Burston, in Buckinghamshire, Norfolk, and Staffordshire, which have different origins.

The Buckinghamshire place name is from an Old English personal name *Briddel* + Old English *þorn* 'thorn tree'; the place in Norfolk is named with Old English *byrst* 'rough ground', 'landslip' + *tūn* 'farmstead'; the Staffordshire place name has the same second element, the first being an Old English personal name *Burgwine* or *Burgwulf*. **2.** English: possibly from an unrecorded Old English personal name, *Burgstān*. **3.** Jewish (American): Americanized spelling of BURSTEIN (see BERNSTEIN).

Burt (9874) **1.** English and Scottish: from the Old English personal name *Byrht*, a byform of *Be(o)rht* 'bright'. Compare BERT. **2.** German: Middle High German *burt* 'that which is due or proper', therefore a nickname for someone who has fulfilled his obligations properly. **3.** Jewish (from Poland and Ukraine): variant of BURD.
FOREBEARS Richard Burt came from England to Taunton, MA, in about 1634.

Burtch (495) Variant of German BERTSCH.

Burtis (495) English: unexplained.

Burtner (412) Americanized form of North German **Pörtner** or standard German **Pförtner** 'gatekeeper', 'doorkeeper' (see FORTNER).

Burtness (168) Americanized form of Norwegian **Börtnes**, a habitational name from a farmstead so named, from Old Norse *birki* 'birch' + *nes* 'headland', 'promontory'.

Burtnett (229) Origin unidentified.

Burton (35486) English: habitational name from a place name that is very common in central and northern England. The derivation in most cases is from Old English *burh* 'fort' (see BURKE) + *tūn* 'enclosure', 'settlement'.

Burts (316) Probably an altered spelling of German **Bur(t)z**, from Middle High German *borz*, *barz* 'tree stump', hence a nickname for a short, stocky man.

Burtt (446) English: variant spelling of BURT.

Burtz (117) South German: nickname for a small man, from *burz* 'rump', 'stump'.
GIVEN NAME French 5%. *Yvon*.

Burum (131) Americanized spelling of English BURHAM.

Burwell (2032) English: habitational name from a place named Burwell, of which there are examples in Cambridgeshire and Lincolnshire, named with Old English *burh* 'fort' + *wella* 'spring'.

Burwick (218) Scottish: habitational name from Burwick in Sandwick, Orkney.

Bury (1096) **1.** English: habitational name from Bury in Lancashire (now part of Greater Manchester), or from some other similarly named place. The place name comes from the dative case, *byrig*, of Old English *burh* 'fortified place'. Compare BURKE, originally used after a preposition (e.g. Richard *atte Bery*). **2.** French: habitational name from places so named in Marne and Oise. The place name is from *Buriacum*, the name of a Gallo-Roman estate, composed of the personal name *Burius* + the locative suffix *-acum*. **3.** German: probably a variant spelling of BURI. According to Gottschald, however, it is from French *Purry*. **4.** Czech (**Burý**): topographic name from *bur* 'pine wood'. **5.** Czech (**Burý**): descriptive nickname from *burý* 'dark'.

Burzinski (102) Polish: variant spelling of BURZYNSKI.

Burzynski (541) Polish (**Burzyński**): habitational name from places called Burzyn in the voivodeships of Tarnów or Łomża, apparently named with *burza* 'tempest', 'storm'.

GIVEN NAMES Polish 9%. *Leszek* (3), *Andrzej* (2), *Miroslaw* (2), *Casimir*, *Feliks*, *Halina*, *Janusz*, *Karol*, *Ryszard*, *Stanislaw*, *Wiesia*, *Zigmund*.

Bus (101) **1.** Dutch: variant of BOS. **2.** Danish: variant of BUUS.

GIVEN NAMES Dutch 6%; French 6%. *Jacobus*, *Sievert*, *Willem*; *Andre* (2).

Busa (338) **1.** Italian: probably an occupational name for a collector or seller of stalks of *ampelodesmo*, a graminaceous plant. **2.** Czech and Slovak (**Buša**): probably from a reduced form of the personal name *Bohuslav*. **3.** Hungarian: nickname from *busa* 'stocky', 'big-headed'.

GIVEN NAMES Italian 8%. *Angelo* (5), *Amerigo*, *Antonino*, *Antonio*, *Marco*, *Pasquale*, *Salvator*.

Busacca (105) Italian: unexplained.

GIVEN NAMES Italian 24%. *Sal* (3), *Angelo* (2), *Mario* (2), *Alessandro*, *Luigi*.

Busack (147) Germanized spelling of Czech **Bušák** (see BUSA).

GIVEN NAME French 4%. *Germain*.

Busalacchi (244) Italian (Sicily): from the Arabic personal name *(A)bū Zallāq* 'father of Zallaq'.

GIVEN NAMES Italian 20%. *Mario* (2), *Alicia*, *Cosimo* (2), *Antonio*, *Gasper*, *Ignacio*, *Pietro*, *Rosario*, *Salvatore*.

Busam (168) South German: from Old High German *buosam* 'bosom', probably a nickname for someone with a conspicuous feature on this part of the body. The word was used for both sexes.

GIVEN NAME German 4%. *Kurt*.

Busbee (711) English: variant spelling of BUSBY.

Busbey (134) English: variant spelling of BUSBY.

Busbin (144) Origin unidentified.

Busboom (216) Dutch (**Bosboom**) and North German: topographic name from Middle Low German *busbōm* 'box tree'.

GIVEN NAMES German 6%. *Claus*, *Kurt*, *Lorenz*, *Otto*.

Busby (5466) English: habitational name from a place in North Yorkshire, recorded in Domesday Book as *Buschebi*, from Old

Norse *buskr* 'bush', 'shrub' or an Old Norse personal name *Buski* + *býr* 'homestead', 'village', or from some other place so called.

Buscaglia (217) Southern Italian: from a derivative of *bosco* 'forest', hence a topographic name for someone living in or near a forest, an occupational name for someone who worked in one, for example a woodcutter, or a nickname for a rough or uncouth person.

GIVEN NAMES Italian 22%; Spanish 9%. *Salvatore* (5), *Angelo* (2), *Camillo*, *Carlo*, *Franco*, *Gaspare*, *Gerlando*, *Giuseppi*, *Marco*, *Sal*, *Sergio*, *Tosca*; *Enrique* (2), *Jose* (2), *Edgardo*.

Buscemi (678) Southern Italian: habitational name from Buscemi in Sicily; the place name is of Arabic origin.

GIVEN NAMES Italian 18%. *Salvatore* (8), *Angelo* (6), *Vito* (4), *Francesco* (2), *Gaetano* (2), *Marcello* (2), *Santo* (2), *Carlo*, *Carmelo*, *Carmine*, *Concetta*, *Cosmo*.

Busch (7263) German (also **Büsch**): topographic name for someone who lived by a thicket or wood, from Middle High German *busch* 'bush', or a habitational name from a place named with this word.

GIVEN NAMES German 4%. *Kurt* (8), *Erwin* (6), *Bernd* (4), *Hans* (4), *Wolfgang* (4), *Klaus* (3), *Lorenz* (3), *Dieter* (2), *Erna* (2), *Ernst* (2), *Helmut* (2), *Meinrad* (2).

Busche (419) German: variant of BUSCH.

GIVEN NAMES German 4%. *Eldred*, *Fritz*, *Gerhardt*, *Guenther*, *Liselotte*, *Otto*.

Buscher (652) **1.** German: topographic or habitational name, a variant of BUESCHER. **2.** North German: occupational name for a butcher, from Middle Low German *buscher* 'non-guild butcher or meat retailer'

Busching (128) North German: **1.** patronymic (in the north) or a topographic name from BUSCH. **2.** from French *Bouchain*.

Buschman (375) Respelling of German BUSCHMANN.

Buschmann (385) German: variant of BUSCH, with the addition of Middle High German *man* 'man'.

GIVEN NAMES German 10%. *Dieter* (2), *Claus*, *Erna*, *Erwin*, *Gunther*, *Mathias*, *Oskar*, *Rainer*, *Siegfried*, *Wilhelm*.

Buschur (119) Possibly a respelling of **Buschaert**, a Dutch occupational name for a butcher, but see also BUSHAW.

GIVEN NAME French 4%. *Alphonse*.

Buse (672) North German (also **Büse**): from Middle Low German *buse* 'fishing boat', specifically of the kind used to catch herring, and hence a metonymic occupational name for a maker of such boats or for a herring fisher.

Buseman (192) German (**Busemann**): nickname for a gourmand, from a derivative of Middle Low German *busen* 'to indulge' + *man* 'man'.

GIVEN NAMES German 4%. *Erwin*, *Heinz*.

Busenbark (195) Probably an Americanized spelling of German **Busenberg**, a habitational name from a place so named near Kaiserslautern.

Buser (781) **1.** German (also **Büser**): nickname for a glutton, Middle Low German *buser*, an agent derivative of *busen* 'to indulge'. Compare BUSEMAN. This name is also found in Slovenia. **2.** Swiss German: habitational name for someone from a place called Buus.

Busey (404) English: probably a variant spelling of BUSSEY or of **Boosey**, which is possibly a topographic name from Middle English *bosy* 'cow or ox stall'.

Bush (28430) **1.** English: topographic name for someone who lived by a bushy area or thicket, from Middle English *bush(e)* 'bush' (probably from Old Norse *buskr*, or an unrecorded Old English *busc*); alternatively, it may derive from Old Norse *Buski* used as a personal name. **2.** Americanized spelling of German BUSCH.

Busha (294) Possibly an Americanized spelling of Czech **Buša** (see BUSA).

Bushard (163) Americanized spelling of German **Buschardt** (see BUSHART).

Bushart (215) Americanized spelling of German **Buschardt**, a southwestern variant of BURKHART under the influence of French *Bouchard*, or possibly of BOUCHARD itself.

Bushaw (343) Of uncertain origin. Said to be an Americanized spelling of French BACHAND, but see also BUSCHUR and BRASHEAR.

Bushby (131) Northern English: habitational name from Bushby in Leicestershire.

Bushee (436) Variant of English BUSHEY.

Bushek (114) Americanized spelling of Czech **Bušek**, from a pet form of the personal names *Budimír*, *Budislav*, or *Budivoj*. Compare BUSA.

Bushell (432) English: variant of BISSELL 1.

Busher (266) **1.** Americanized spelling of German BUSCHER. **2.** Americanized variant of French BOUCHARD.

Bushey (2010) **1.** English: habitational name from Bushey in Hertfordshire, so named with an Old English *bysce* or *byxe* 'box' + *hæg* 'enclosure'. **2.** Americanized spelling of French BOUCHER. **3.** Americanized spelling of German **Büsche** (see BUSCHE) or Swiss German **Büschi**, a variant of BUSCH.

Bushman (1756) Americanized form of German BUSCHMANN.

Bushnell (2035) English: unexplained.

FOREBEARS Francis Bushnell came to New Haven, CT, in 1639, and was a founder of Guilford, CT.

Bushner (103) Americanized form of German **Buschner**, a variant of BUESCHER.

Bushong (1026) **1.** Americanized spelling of French **Bouchon**, a habitational name from a place in Somme, so named with the personal name *Buccius* + Gallic *duros* 'fortress', or a topographic name for someone who lived in an area of bushes, from Old French *bousche* 'bush'. **2.** Possibly an altered spelling of German **Buschang**, which is of Slavic origin (see BUSHEK).

Bushor (116) Americanized form of French BOUCHARD.

Bushue (181) Origin uncertain; perhaps a respelling of a French surname. Compare BUSHWAY, BUSHAW, BUSHOR.

Bushway (203) Americanized spelling of French BOURGEOIS, frequent in New England.

Bushy (103) Variant of BUSHEY.

Busic (195) Serbian and Croatian (**Busić**): patronymic from a pet form of the personal names *Budimir*, *Budislav*, or *Budivoj*. Compare BUSHEK.

Busick (748) Americanized or Germanized spelling of an unidentified Slavic name, for example Czech **Bušek** (see BUSHEK).

Busing (127) **1.** North German (**Büsing**): presumably from an old personal name. **2.** habitational name from Büsum in Schleswig-Holstein.

Busk (195) Danish and Swedish: topographic name from *busk(e)* 'bush', or a habitational name from a place in Denmark named Busk. The surname is also established in England.

FOREBEARS The English surname Busk is not of English origin. The family of this name has been traced to Jacob Hans Busck (died 1755), a wool merchant from Gothenburg, who settled in England in 1712.

Buske (497) **1.** German: of Slavic origin. **2.** German: from a pet form of *Busse*, a short form of the personal name *Burkhard* (see BURKHART). **3.** Danish and Swedish: variant of BUSK.

Busker (243) Dutch: occupational name for a lumberman, Middle Dutch *bosscere*.

Buskey (326) English: topographic name from northern Middle English *busk* 'bush' + *hey* 'enclosure'.

Buskirk (1032) Americanized form of Dutch **Boskerck**, a habitational name from an unidentified place named as 'the church in the woods', from Middle Dutch *bos* 'woodland' + *kerk* 'church'.

Busko (124) Polish (**Buśko**): **1.** from a pet form of the personal name *Budzisław*. **2.** habitational name from Busko-Zdrój in Kielce voivodeship.
GIVEN NAME German 4%. *Viktor*.

Busler (277) Probably an altered spelling of German BUSSLER.

Busman (117) Respelling of German BUSSMANN.

Busque (105) Possibly a respelling of the French topographic name **Busquet**, a variant of **Bosquet**, from a derivative of *bosc* 'wood', a southern variant of *bois*.

GIVEN NAMES French 28%. *Marcel* (2), *Andre, Donat, Fernand, Gedeon, Ghislain, Gilles, Herve, Jean-Yves, Oliva*.

Buss (3768) **1.** English: metonymic occupational name for a cooper or else a nickname for a rotund, fat man, from Middle English, Old French *busse* 'cask', 'barrel' (of unknown origin). The word was also used in Middle English for a type of ship, and the surname may perhaps have been given to someone who sailed in one. The byname seems to occur already in Domesday Book, where a Siward Buss, and a John and Richard Buss are recorded at Brasted in Kent. **2.** German and Swiss German: from a pet form of the personal name *Burkhard* (see BURKHART). **3.** Danish: variant of BUUS.

Bussa (223) Italian: probably a topographic name, a variant of **Busso**, from Latin *buxus* 'box tree'.
GIVEN NAMES Italian 4%. *Cosmo* (2), *Angelo, Battista, Tillio*.

Bussan (129) Origin unidentified. **1.** Perhaps a variant of German BUSSEN. **2.** Alternatively, possibly an American variant of French **Baussant**, a nickname for someone with a freckled or mottled complexion, from Old French *baucent, baussant* 'spotted', 'flecked'.

Bussard (1051) **1.** Variant of German **Busshardt** (see BOSSHART). **2.** Possibly an altered spelling of French **Boussard**, a variant of BOSSARD.

Busscher (128) **1.** Dutch: variant of BUSKER. **2.** German (**Büsscher**): variant of BUSCHER 1.

Busse (2240) **1.** German: variant of BUSS. **2.** North German (**Büsse**): metonymic occupational name for a maker of boxes and containers or for a gunsmith, from Middle Low German *büsse, busse* 'box', 'gun', 'rifle'. **3.** English: variant spelling of BUSS.
GIVEN NAMES German 4%. *Ewald* (3), *Ernst* (2), *Fritz* (2), *Konrad* (2), *Claus, Eberhard, Eckhard, Eldred, Frieda, Fritzi, Gerhard, Helmuth*.

Bussell (1493) English: variant of BISSELL 1.

Bussen (166) German: variant (from the genitive form) of BUSSE 1.

Busser (209) **1.** German (**Büsser**): occupational name for a cobbler or tinker, from an agent derivative of Middle High German *büessen* 'to mend or repair'. **2.** Perhaps a shortened form of Dutch **De Busser**, a variant of BUSKER.

Bussert (193) German: **1.** variant of BOSSHART. **2.** from a pet form of the personal name *Burkhard* (see BURKHART).

Bussey (2370) **1.** English (of Norman origin): habitational name from any of several places in Normandy, France: Boucé in Orne, from which came Robert de Buci mentioned in Domesday Book, Bouce (Manche), or Bucy-le-Long (Aisne). All

are named with a Latin personal name *Buccius* (presumably a derivative of *bucca* 'mouth') + the locative suffix *-acum*. **2.** Altered spelling of German BUSSE.

Bussie (139) Scottish spelling of BUSSEY.

Bussiere (512) French (**Bussière**): topographic name for someone who lived by a box thicket, from *buis* 'box (tree)'.
FOREBEARS A Bussière from the Guyenne region of France is documented in Sainte-Famille, Quebec, in 1671, with the secondary surname Laverdure.
GIVEN NAMES French 14%. *Normand* (5), *Emile* (3), *Aurel* (2), *Remi* (2), *Alain, Andre, Armand, Benoit, Fernand, Gaston, Ghislaine, Jacques*.

Bussing (231) North German (**Büssing**): patronymic from BUSS.

Bussinger (128) Swiss German: probably, like Swiss **Busslinger**, a derivative of a pet form of the personal name BURKHART.

Bussler (150) German: from Middle High German *bōzeln* 'to knock or beat' or later 'to tinker', hence a nickname for someone who did minor jobs or puttered around.

Bussman (208) Respelling of German and Swiss BUSSMANN.

Bussmann (132) German and Swiss German: either a northern variant of BUSCH or a variant of BUSS.
GIVEN NAMES German 6%. *Konrad* (2), *Egon, Ingeborg*.

Bussone (114) Italian: from *Boson*, an inflected form of the Germanic personal name BOSO.
GIVEN NAME Italian 4%. *Gilda* (2).

Busta (208) Czech (**Bušta**): see BUSA.

Bustamante (2416) Spanish: habitational name from Bustamante in Santander province, so named with Late Latin *bustum Amantii* 'pasture (see BUSTO) of *Amantius*', a personal name derived from Late Latin *Amans*, genitive *Amantis*, meaning 'loving'.
GIVEN NAMES Spanish 46%. *Jose* (34), *Manuel* (33), *Carlos* (29), *Juan* (26), *Luis* (26), *Jorge* (18), *Jesus* (15), *Ruben* (15), *Jaime* (14), *Javier* (14), *Sergio* (12), *Alberto* (11).

Bustard (144) English: nickname for someone thought to resemble the bird in some way, from Old French *bistarde, bustarde*.

Busteed (111) Irish: unexplained. According to MacLysaght, the surname is found almost exclusively in County Cork, having been recorded there since the first half of the 17th century; it may be of English origin.

Buster (988) Austrian German (Tyrol and Allgäu): nickname from a derivative of *Buste* 'pock mark', 'boil' (from Latin *apostema* 'boil').

Bustillo (235) Spanish: habitational name from any of numerous places called Bustillo, from a diminutive of *busto* (see BUSTOS).

GIVEN NAMES Spanish 46%. *Jose* (5), *Mario* (5), *Juan* (4), *Manuel* (4), *Miguel* (4), *Pedro* (4), *Andres* (3), *Carlos* (3), *Javier* (3), *Jorge* (3), *Ana* (2), *Felipe* (2); *Cecilio* (2), *Deno, Lorenzo, Marco.*

Bustillos (519) Spanish: apparently a habitational name; however, no place of this name is now known in Spain, and the surname may be a Castilian rendering of Galician **Bustelos**, from places so named in Ourense and Pontevedra provinces, Galicia.

GIVEN NAMES Spanish 48%. *Jose* (17), *Manuel* (10), *Luis* (9), *Juan* (6), *Ruben* (6), *Francisco* (4), *Andres* (3), *Carlos* (3), *Enrique* (3), *Jesus* (3), *Miguel* (3), *Ramon* (3).

Bustin (247) **1.** Asturian-Leonese (**Bustín**): from a diminutive of BUSTO. **2.** Castilianized form of Basque *buztin* 'clay', hence probably a topographic name for someone who lived on clay ground or possibly a metonymic occupational name for a potter.

Bustle (234) Possibly an altered spelling of South German **Bastl**, from a pet form of the personal name SEBASTIAN or of English BUSSELL.

Busto (164) Spanish, Asturian-Leonese, and Galician: habitational name from any of the numerous places so named, from *busto* 'meadow', 'willow'. In Asturian-Leonese, this name is a Castilianized form of Asturian-Leonese **Bustu**, of the same origin. Busto (and its equivalent Bustu) is one of the commonest place names of northwestern Iberia.

GIVEN NAMES Spanish 36%. *Jose* (5), *Carlos* (3), *Eugenio* (3), *Manuel* (3), *Ana* (2), *Armando* (2), *Juan* (2), *Mario* (2), *Mercedes* (2), *Raul* (2), *Alejandro, Alvaro; Antonio, Eliseo, Vito.*

Bustos (1560) Spanish, Asturian-Leonese, and Galician: topographic name from the plural of *busto* 'meadow', 'willow', or a habitational name from either of the places so named, in León and Galicia (see BUSTO).

GIVEN NAMES Spanish 44%. *Jose* (28), *Juan* (20), *Manuel* (13), *Carlos* (12), *Jesus* (11), *Alberto* (8), *Luis* (8), *Armando* (7), *Mario* (7), *Miguel* (7), *Andres* (6), *Fernando* (6).

Buswell (745) English (East Midlands): probably a variant spelling of Scottish BOSWELL.

Butala (224) **1.** Indian (Gujarat): Hindu name of unknown meaning. **2.** Slovenian (south central Slovenia): unexplained.

GIVEN NAMES Indian 14%; German 4%. *Alpa, Ameet, Amit, Ashvin, Atul, Dipika, Govind, Kirit, Nilesh, Parul, Rajesh, Rajiv; Aloys, Math, Mathias.*

Butch (389) Altered spelling of German *Butsch*, a variant of BUTZ.

Butchart (212) **1.** Scottish (Angus): variant of BUTCHER. **2.** Respelling of **Buttschard**, **Buschart**, southwestern German variants

of BURKHART, influenced by French BOUCHARD.

GIVEN NAME French 4%. *Gabrielle* (3).

Butcher (7807) English: occupational name for a butcher or slaughterer, Middle English *bo(u)cher* (Old French *bouchier*, a derivative of *bouc* 'ram').

Butchko (316) Americanized spelling of Ukrainian BUCKO.

Bute (233) English: unexplained; possibly a variant of BUTT.

Buteau (291) French: unexplained. **1.** Most probably an altered form of French **Buteux**, a nickname for someone who was in the habit of pushing or hitting, also an occupational name for someone whose job was to unload goods or cargo, from Old French *bouteor*. **2.** alternatively it could be an altered form of **Butaud**, from the personal name *Botwald*, composed of the Germanic elements *bod(o)* 'messenger' + *waldan* 'ruler'. This name is found chiefly in New England.

FOREBEARS A bearer of the name Buteau from La Rochelle, France, was documented in Sillery in 1669.

GIVEN NAMES French 15%. *Andre* (2), *Emile* (2), *Michel* (2), *Armand, Cecile, Edwige, Jacques, Leandre, Lucien, Marcel, Normand, Philibert.*

Butenhoff (195) North German: topographic name for someone who lived on an outlying farm, from Low German *buten* 'outside' + *hof* 'farmstead', 'manor farm'.

GIVEN NAMES German 5%. *Kurt, Otto, Uwe.*

Buter (103) Of uncertain origin; this surname is recorded in England in the 19th century, also spelled **Boot(i)er**, suggesting that it could be of French origin, perhaps a respelling of **Boutier** (or the variants **Buthier** or **Buttier**), from the Germanic personal name *Bothari*.

Butera (1032) Southern Italian (Sicily): habitational name from a place named Butera, in Caltanisetta, Sicily.

GIVEN NAMES Italian 16%; French 4%. *Angelo* (12), *Salvatore* (9), *Antonio* (3), *Sal* (3), *Massimo* (2), *Matteo* (2), *Umberto* (2), *Vincenzo* (2), *Carmela, Carmine, Cataldo, Evo; Camille, Laure.*

Buterbaugh (531) Americanized form of a German habitational name from an unidentified place, perhaps Budenbach near Koblenz or Boudlerbach in Luxembourg, near the German border.

FOREBEARS Johann, Peter, and George (sic) Putterbach landed in Philadelphia on September 15, 1752.

Buth (400) North German: **1.** perhaps from an Old Prussian personal name *Buth* or *Butt*, or a nickname from Low German *but* 'dumb', 'crude'. **2.** variant of BUTT 4.

Butikofer (138) German: unexplained.

GIVEN NAMES German 4%. *Eldred, Hans.*

Butka (173) Czech: from a diminutive of *bota* 'shoe'.

Butkiewicz (292) Variant spelling of Polish **Budkiewicz**, a patronymic from the personal name BUDKA.

GIVEN NAMES Polish 6%. *Danuta* (2), *Andrze, Janusz, Maciek.*

Butkovich (302) Croatian (**Butković**): patronymic from **Butko**, pet form of any of several personal names formed with the prefix Bud- (e.g. *Budimir, Budislav*), derived from *buditi* 'to awaken'.

Butkowski (120) Altered spelling of Polish **Budkowski**, a habitational name for someone from places called Budkowo or Budkow.

Butkus (497) Lithuanian: from a personal name based on Lithuanian *būti* 'to be', 'to exist'.

Butland (125) English (Devon): habitational name from Butland in Devon.

Butler (70457) **1.** English and Irish: from a word that originally denoted a wine steward, usually the chief servant of a medieval household, from Norman French *butuiller* (Old French *bouteillier*, Latin *buticularius*, from *buticula* 'bottle'). In the large households of royalty and the most powerful nobility, the title came to denote an officer of high rank and responsibility, only nominally concerned with the supply of wine, if at all. **2.** Anglicized form of French BOUTILIER. **3.** Jewish (from Poland and Ukraine): occupational name for a bottle maker, from Yiddish *butl* 'bottle' + the agent suffix *-er*.

FOREBEARS This name was brought independently to New England by many bearers from the 17th century onward. William Butler was one of the founders of Hartford, CT, (coming from Cambridge, MA, with Thomas Hooker) in 1635.

A Massachusetts family called Butler is descended from Nicholas Butler, who came to Dorchester, MA, from Ashford, Kent, England, in 1636 and subsequently moved to Martha's Vineyard.

The name is also very common in Ireland. Irish bearers trace their ancestry to Theobald FitzWalter, who accompanied Henry II to Ireland in 1170 and in 1177 was created 'Chief Butler' (i.e. overlord) of Ireland by the king. FitzWalter's descendant James Butler (1665–1745), 2nd Duke of Ormonde, was a staunch Protestant and supporter of William of Orange in 1685. He served as Lord Lieutenant of Ireland and became Commander-in-Chief of the British army. But after the death of Queen Anne he opposed the accession of George I and took part in a Jacobite rising (1715), after which he spent the rest of his life in exile.

Butman (243) **1.** North German (**Butmann**): from Middle Low German *butenman* 'stranger', 'foreigner' (from *buten* 'outside' + *man* 'man'). **2.** North German (**But(t)mann**): perhaps an occupational name for a fish seller (see BUTT 5). **3.** Jewish (eastern Ashkenazic): unexplained.

GIVEN NAMES Jewish 4%. *Shmuel, Velvel, Yosef.*

Butner (703) **1.** English: occupational name for a maker or seller of buttons, Old French *boutonier*, from *bo(u)ton* 'knob', 'lump', specialized to mean 'button'. **2.** Altered spelling of German **Büttner** (see BUETTNER).

Butorac (186) Croatian: of uncertain origin; perhaps a derivative of the personal name *Butko* (see BUTKOVICH), altered by association with the archaic word *butora* 'bundle'.

Butrick (161) Altered spelling of the English habitational name BUTTRICK.

Butrum (131) English: variant spelling of BERTRAM.

Butsch (208) German: **1.** from a pet form of the personal name *Burkhard* (see BURKHART). **2.** variant of BUTZ.

GIVEN NAMES German 6%. *Ernst, Otto, Rainer.*

Butson (245) English: patronymic from BUTT 2.

Butt (1930) **1.** English: topographic name for someone who lived near a place used for archery practice, from Middle English *butte* 'mark for archery', 'target', 'goal'. In the Middle Ages archery practice was a feudal obligation, and every settlement had its practice area. **2.** English: topographic name from Middle English *butte* 'strip of land abutting on a boundary', 'short strip or ridge at right angles to other strips in a common field'. **3.** English: from Middle English *butte, bott* 'butt', 'cask', applied as a metonymic occupational name for a cooper or as a nickname possibly for a heavy drinker or for a large, fat man. **4.** English: from a Middle English personal name, *But(t)*, of unknown origin, perhaps originally a nickname meaning 'short and stumpy', and akin to late Middle English *butt* 'thick end', 'stump', 'buttock' (of Germanic origin). **5.** German and English: in both Middle Low German and Middle English the word *but(te)* denoted various types of marine fish, originally a fish with a blunt head, for example halibut (German *Heilbutt*) or turbot (German *Steinbutt*), and the surname may in some cases be a metonymic occupational name for a seller of fish or salt fish. **6.** Kashmiri: variant of BHATT.

FOREBEARS Robert Butt came from Kent, England, to NC in 1640.

GIVEN NAMES Muslim 18%. *Mohammad* (22), *Tariq* (8), *Muhammad* (6), *Abdul* (5), *Nasir* (5), *Mohammed* (4), *Abid* (3), *Arif* (3), *Khalid* (3), *Nadeem* (3), *Shahid* (3), *Tahir* (3).

Butta (148) **1.** Italian: from a short form of a compound name formed with *butta-* 'throw', as for example BUTTACAVOLI. **2.** Italian: from an old German feminine personal name *Butta*. **3.** Italian: variant of BOTTA.

GIVEN NAMES Italian 14%. *Salvatore* (3), *Enrico, Sal, Vincenzo.*

Buttacavoli (161) Italian (Sicily): nickname composed of the elements *butta* 'throw' + *cavoli* 'cabbages'.

GIVEN NAMES Italian 10%. *Carmine* (2), *Calogero, Ciro, Domenic, Giovanni.*

Buttars (268) Perhaps a Scottish spelling of English BUTTERS.

Butte (202) English: unexplained; possibly a variant spelling of BUTT.

Butter (202) **1.** English: nickname for someone with some fancied resemblance to a bittern, perhaps in the booming quality of the voice, from Middle English, Old French *butor* 'bittern' (a word of obscure etymology). **2.** English and German: metonymic occupational name for a dairyman or seller of butter, from Old English *butere* 'butter', Middle High German *buter*. **3.** German: possibly a short form of any of the various compound names formed with *Butter* 'butter' (see 2).

GIVEN NAMES German 8%. *Arno, Gerhard, Mathias, Reinhart.*

Butterbaugh (345) See BUTERBAUGH.

Butterfield (4405) English: topographic name for someone who lived by a pasture for cattle or at a dairy farm, or a habitational name from a place named Butterfield (for example in West Yorkshire), from Old English *butere* 'butter' + *feld* 'open country'.

FOREBEARS Benjamin Butterfield came to Massachusetts Bay Colony in 1638. John Butterfield (1801–69) was born in Berne, NY, and founded an express company that merged with other companies to form the American Express Company (1850).

Butterly (107) English: habitational name from either of two places called Butterley, in Derbyshire and Herefordshire, or from Butterleigh in Devon. All are named with Old English *butere* 'butter' + *lēah* 'pasture'.

Butterman (105) English and German (**Buttermann**): occupational name for a dairyman or seller of dairy produce (see BUTTER 2).

Buttermore (318) Origin uncertain. It may be an altered spelling of the Irish surname **Buttimer**, which MacLysaght describes as a well-known County Cork name since the 16th century, from an earlier English form *Botymer*. Alternatively, it may be an English habitational name from either of two places, in Cumbria and Wiltshire, named Buttermere, from Old English *butere* 'butter' + *mere* 'lake'. The surname, however, is absent from current English records, and of the six bearers recorded in the 1881 British census, one was born in Ireland and two in the Netherlands.

Butters (919) **1.** English: patronymic from BUTTER 1. **2.** English: occupational name for a servant working in a wine cellar, Norman French *boterie* (see BUTTERY),

with the Middle English genitive *-s*. **3.** German: variant of BUTTER 2.

Butterworth (1873) English (Lancashire and Yorkshire): habitational name from places named Butterworth in Lancashire (near Rochdale) and in West Yorkshire. Both are so named with Old English *butere* 'butter' + *worð* 'enclosure'. The surname is recorded from an early date in each of these two places; it probably arose independently in each.

Buttery (315) English: from Anglo-Norman French *boterie* 'buttery' (Late Latin *botaria*, a derivative of *bota* 'cask'), hence a metonymic occupational name for the keeper of a buttery. The term originally denoted a store for liquor but soon came to mean a store for provisions in general.

Buttitta (137) Italian (Sicily): variant of **Bottitta**, from a diminutive of *botta*, probably in the sense 'boot' (see BOTTA).

GIVEN NAMES Italian 14%. *Cosmo, Giacomo, Leonardo, Pietro.*

Buttke (262) German: probably of Slavic origin, perhaps from the personal name *Budislav*.

Buttler (251) **1.** English: variant spelling of BUTLER. **2.** German: occupational name for a village tavern owner, from French *bouteillier* 'butler'. **3.** Respelling of the German habitational name **Buttlar**, from a place so named in Thuringia.

Buttles (118) English: unexplained; perhaps a variant of **Bottle**, from the medieval personal name *Bottyll*, of Scandinavian origin.

Buttner (407) German (**Büttner**): see BUETTNER.

GIVEN NAMES German 6%. *Gerhard, Hans, Hartmut, Kurt, Manfred, Reiner, Siegfried.*

Butto (104) Italian (Naples): perhaps, as Caracausi proposes, either an Italianized form of French **Boutaud** (see BOUTOT), or a variant of BOTTO 1.

GIVEN NAMES Italian 12%. *Antonio, Rocco, Santo.*

Buttolph (147) English (mainly Norfolk): from the medieval personal name *Botolph* or *Botolf*. St. Botolph (d. 680) is said to have introduced the Benedictine rule into England and brought Christianity to East Anglia. Boston in Lincolnshire was named in Old English as *Botulves stan* 'St. Botolph's stone'.

Button (2798) English: metonymic occupational name for a maker or seller of buttons, from Old French *bo(u)ton* 'knob', 'lump', specialized to mean 'button'. Compare BUTNER.

Buttram (636) English: variant of BERTRAM.

Buttrey (367) English: variant spelling of BUTTERY.

Buttrick (250) English: habitational name from a place named Butterwick, for example in County Durham, Lincolnshire, North Yorkshire, and North Lincolnshire. The place name is from Old English *butere* 'butter' + *wīc* 'farmstead'.

FOREBEARS William Buttrick came from Kingston-upon-Thames, Surrey, England, to Concord, MA, in 1640.

Buttrum (192) English: variant of BERTRAM.

Buttry (272) English: reduced form of BUTTERY.

Butts (7768) English: patronymic from BUTT 3.

Butz (1825) German: **1.** (mainly Switzerland) from a derivative of *Butzo*, a pet form of the personal name *Burkhard* (see BURKHART). **2.** (**Bütz(e)**): topographic name for someone who lived near a well, from Middle High German *bütze* 'well', 'puddle' (from Latin *puteus*). **3.** South German: nickname from Middle High German *butze* denoting something small: an apple core, a small piece of sometning left over, a small person, a poltergeist.

Butzen (139) German: **1.** habitational name for someone from a place so named in Brandenburg or from a shortened form of any of several compound names with *Butzen*. **2.** in Swabia possibly a topographic name from Middle High German *bütze* 'well', 'puddle' (from Latin *puteus*), with *-en* indicating the oblique case (*bī dem butzen*).

Butzer (213) German: **1.** nickname for a small person, from South German *Butz* 'stump', 'stub' or from Middle High German *butze* 'poltergeist'. **2.** nickname for a bully, from an agent derivative of Middle High German *butzen* 'to push'.

Butzin (158) German: from a name of Slavic origin.

GIVEN NAMES German 8%. *Kurt* (3), *Otto*.

Butzke (140) German: from a short form of the Slavic personal name *Budislaw*.

GIVEN NAMES German 10%. *Hans, Heinz, Horst, Lorenz, Otto*.

Butzlaff (122) German: **1.** from a Slavic personal name, *Budislaw* or *Bogislaw*. **2.** habitational name from a place in Pomerania called Butzlaff.

GIVEN NAMES German 5%. *Dieter, Gerhard*.

Buuck (158) North German form of BAUCH.

GIVEN NAMES German 4%. *Gerhard, Winfried*.

Buus (174) Danish: either from a nickname *Bus* (of unexplained etymology), or from German *būseman* 'devil', 'ghost'.

GIVEN NAMES Scandinavian 5%. *Niels* (2), *Carsten, Nils*.

Buwalda (142) Dutch: probably a habitational name from an unidentified place.

GIVEN NAMES Dutch 6%. *Pieter* (2), *Wiebe*.

Buxbaum (471) German and Jewish (Ashkenazic): variant spelling of BUCHSBAUM.

GIVEN NAMES Jewish 5%. *Anshel, Asher, Avrom, Chaim, Devorah, Hadassa, Mayer, Miriam, Sol, Yakov*.

Buxman (112) Americanized spelling of German **Buchsmann**, a topographic name

from Middle High German *buhs(boum)* 'box (tree)' (an early loanword from Latin *buxus* of the same meaning) + *man* 'man'.

Buxton (3017) English: **1.** habitational name from Buxton in Derbyshire, which in Middle English was called *Buchestanes, Bucstones* (i.e. 'bowing stones', from Middle English *b(o)ugen*, Old English *būgan* 'to bow' + *stanes* 'stones'). It is probably named for logan stones in the vicinity. (Logan stones are boulders so poised that they rock at a touch.) **2.** less commonly, a habitational name from Buxton in Norfolk, which is named with the genitive case of the Old English personal name *Bucc* (see BUCK 1) + Old English *tūn* 'settlement', 'enclosure'.

Buyck (130) Dutch: nickname for a fat man, from Middle Dutch *buuc* 'stomach'.

GIVEN NAMES French 5%. *Albertine, Monique*.

Buyer (129) Altered form of German BAYER of Scottish BYER, by folk-etymological association with the English vocabulary word *buyer*.

Buyers (109) Scottish (Aberdeen): variant of BYERS.

Buynak (114) Probably an altered spelling of Czech BENAK or Slovak **Bujnák**.

Buys (441) **1.** Dutch: variant spelling of BUIS. **2.** English: perhaps a variant of BISS. Compare BEESE, BICE, BISE, BYCE.

Buysse (292) French: variant of BUIS.

Buza (283) **1.** Hungarian (**Búza**): from *búza* 'wheat', hence a metonymic occupational name for someone who grew, milled, or sold wheat. **2.** Czech: from a pet form of the personal name *Budislav*. **3.** Polish: nickname for a scold, from *buza* 'reprimand', 'scolding'; in some dialects this word also has the meaning 'porridge', 'soft pulp made from cereals', and in some cases the nickname may have arisen from this sense.

Buzan (197) Of Slavic origin; probably Czech, a derivative of BUZA.

Buzard (400) Altered spelling of English BUZZARD.

Buzas (100) Hungarian (**Búzás**): of Slavic origin; probably from Czech, a derivative of BUZA.

GIVEN NAMES Hungarian 5%. *Imre, Zoltan*.

Buzbee (461) English: variant spelling of BUSBY.

Buzby (291) English: variant spelling of BUSBY.

Buzek (194) Czech: **1.** from a diminutive of the personal name *Budislav*. **2.** (**Bůžek**): from the personal names *Božetěch, Bohuchval*, or *Bohuslav*.

GIVEN NAME French 4%. *Andre*.

Buzick (128) Americanized spelling of BUZEK.

Buzza (128) Italian: variant (feminine form) of **Buzzo** (see BUZZI).

Buzzard (1170) **1.** English: from Middle English *busard, bosard* 'buzzard' (Old

French *busart*), hence a nickname for someone thought to resemble the bird in some way. The buzzard was considered an inferior bird of prey, useless for falconry, and the nickname was therefore probably a derogatory one. **2.** Americanized spelling of Swiss German BOSSHART or any of its variants.

Buzzell (1062) **1.** Altered spelling of English *Bussell* (see BISSELL 1). **2.** Possibly a shortened form of Italian BUZZELLI.

Buzzelli (283) Italian: **1.** from *Buzzello*, a diminutive of **Buzzo**, itself a variant of BOZZO. **2.** from a diminutive of *Buccio* (see BUCCI).

GIVEN NAMES Italian 11%. *Antonio* (3), *Marco* (2), *Amedeo, Angelo, Filomena, Geno, Nicola, Salvatore*.

Buzzeo (109) Italian: perhaps from a short form of a personal name ending with *-buzzeo*, for example *Iacobuzzeo*, from *Iacobo* (see JACOB).

GIVEN NAMES Italian 18%. *Pasquale* (2), *Angelo, Clementina, Domenico, Gianni*.

Buzzi (130) Italian: from a short form of a personal name ending with *-buzzi*, for example *Iacobuzzi*, from *Iacobo* (see JACOB).

GIVEN NAMES Italian 19%. *Julio* (3), *Carlo* (2), *Adriano, Angelina, Dario, Libero, Luigi, Mario, Renato, Riccardo*.

Byam (343) English: probably a habitational name from Bytham in Lincolnshire, so named with Old English *bythme* 'valley bottom' + *hām* 'homestead'.

Byard (684) English: topographic name from Middle English *bi yerd* 'by the enclosure'.

Byars (2366) **1.** Scottish: variant spelling of BYERS. **2.** Possibly also an Americanized spelling of German BAYER.

Byas (307) English: topographic name for someone who lived at a house by a bend, from Middle English *bye* 'bend' + *hous* 'house'.

Byassee (165) Origin unidentified.

Bybee (1653) Origin unidentified; perhaps an altered spelling of English BEEBY.

Byce (136) English: perhaps a variant of BISS. Compare BEESE, BICE, BISE, BUYS.

Byczek (109) Polish: nickname from *byczek* 'bullock'.

GIVEN NAMES Polish 9%; German 4%. *Casimir, Jozef, Krystyna, Stanislaw; Fritz*.

Bye (1449) **1.** English: topographic name for someone who lived near a bend, for example in a river, from Middle English *bye* 'bend' (from Old English *byge*, a derivative of *būgan* 'to bow'). Reaney suggests that occasionally it may be from an Old English personal name of obscure origin. **2.** Norwegian and Swedish: habitational name from any of various farms named By, from Old Norse *býr* 'farm'.

Byer (1242) Scottish: variant of BYERS.

Byerley (592) English: variant spelling of BYERLY. In England this is the more frequent spelling.

Byerly (2125) **1.** English: habitational name from either of two places called Birley, in Derbyshire and Herefordshire, or from Bierley in West Yorkshire (see BIERLEY). **2.** Americanized spelling of German BEIERLE.

Byers (11246) **1.** Scottish and northern English: topographic name for someone who lived by a cattleshed, Middle English *byre*, or a habitational name with the same meaning, from any of several places named with Old English *bȳre*, for example Byers Green in County Durham or Byres near Edinburgh. **2.** Americanized spelling of German BAYERS.

Byfield (282) English: topographic name for someone who lived near a patch of open land, from Middle English *by* 'by', 'beside' + *felde* 'open land, for pasture or cultivation', or a habitational name with the same meaning, from a place named Byfield, from Old English *bī* + *feld*, for example in Northamptonshire.

Byford (423) English: **1.** habitational name from a place named Byford, from Old English *byge* 'bend' + *ford* 'ford'. There is one such on the Wye near Hereford. **2.** topographic name for someone who lived by a ford, from Middle English *by* 'by', 'beside' + *ford*.

Byington (1226) This has the form of an English habitational name, but no source has been identified, and the surname is rare in the British Isles.

Byk (101) Jewish (eastern Ashkenazic): variant of BICK 4.
GIVEN NAMES Russian 12%; Jewish 9%. *Mikhail* (4), *Aleksandr, Leonid, Svetlana, Yefim; Jakov, Khana.*

Byker (109) Dutch: occupational name for a stonemason (see BICKER).
GIVEN NAME Dutch 4%. *Gerrit* (3).

Bykowski (242) Polish: habitational name for someone from a place called Bykowice or Byków.
GIVEN NAMES Polish 4%. *Casimir, Wojciech.*

Byl (154) Dutch: **1.** from the female personal name *Bijl*, a reduced form of a female personal name such as *Amabilia* or *Sibilia*. **2.** metonymic occupational name for a maker of axes or adzes, from Dutch *bijl* 'axe', 'adze'.
GIVEN NAMES Dutch 5%. *Aart, Dirk, Laurens.*

Byland (207) **1.** English: habitational name from Byland in North Yorkshire.
2. Swedish: ornamental name from a compound of Old Norse *býr* 'farm' + *land* 'land'.

Byle (130) Americanized spelling of Dutch *Bijl* (see BYL) or German BEIL.

Byler (1173) Americanized spelling of German BEILER.

Byles (192) English: variant spelling of BILES.
GIVEN NAME French 4%. *Valmore.*

Bylsma (332) Frisian: derivative of the personal name *Bijl* (see BYL).
GIVEN NAMES German 4%. *Otto* (3), *Erwin.*

Bylund (211) Swedish and Norwegian: ornamental name composed of the elements *by* 'farm' (from Old Norse *býr*) + *lund* 'grove'.
GIVEN NAMES Scandinavian 10%. *Sten* (2), *Erik.*

Byman (101) Swedish: ornamental name or occupational name from *by* 'farm' + *man* 'man'.
GIVEN NAMES Scandinavian 8%. *Erik, Iver, Lars.*

Bynes (189) Jewish: variant spelling of BINES.

Bynoe (188) Origin unidentified. It is a well-established name in Barbados, and may be of Irish origin.
GIVEN NAMES Irish 4%. *Fitzgerald, Oneil.*

Bynog (112) Origin unidentified.

Bynum (4751) Probably Welsh, a variant spelling of **Beynon** (see BENNION).

Byous (104) English: variant spelling of BYAS.
GIVEN NAME French 4%. *Dominique.*

Byram (1027) English: variant of BYRON.

Byrd (28163) English: variant spelling of BIRD.

Byrdsong (115) See BIRDSONG.

Byrer (179) Probably an altered spelling of German **Beurer**, a habitational name for someone from any of various places called Beuren, from Old High German *būr* 'small dwelling' (see BAUER).

Byrge (315) Altered spelling of English or German BURGE.

Byrley (126) Variant spelling of BYERLY or BURLEY.

Byrn (276) Altered spelling of Irish BYRNE.

Byrne (12342) Irish: Anglicized form of Gaelic **Ó Broin** 'descendant of *Bran*', a personal name based on *bran* 'raven'. Bran was the name of a son of the King of Leinster, who died at Cologne in 1052, and also of the hero of an 8th century voyage tale.
GIVEN NAMES Irish 6%. *Brendan* (15), *Eamon* (6), *Aidan* (3), *Liam* (3), *Niall* (3), *Declan* (2), *Eamonn* (2), *Fergus* (2), *John Patrick* (2), *Keelin* (2), *Kieran* (2), *Siobhan* (2).

Byrnes (4683) Irish: variant of BYRNE, formed with the addition of English patronymic -*s*.
GIVEN NAMES Irish 5%. *Brendan* (3), *Conley* (2).

Byrns (514) Irish: variant of BYRNES.

Byrnside (100) Variant spelling of Scottish and northern Irish BURNSIDE.

Byrom (665) English: variant of BYRON.

Byron (2519) **1.** English: habitational name from Byram in West Yorkshire or Byrom in Lancashire, both named with Old English *bȳrum* 'at the cattle sheds', dative plural of *bȳre* 'byre'. **2.** This name and the variants **Biron** and **Biram** have occasionally been adopted as Jewish surnames, presumably as Americanized forms of Jewish names that cannot now be identified.

Byrum (2220) Variant of English BYRON.

Bystrom (298) Swedish (**Byström**): ornamental name composed of the elements *by* 'hamlet', 'farm' + *ström* 'stream'.
GIVEN NAMES Scandinavian 10%. *Johan, Sven.*

Byun (406) Korean: variant of **Pyŏn** (see PYON).
GIVEN NAMES Korean 69%. *Sung* (9), *Jong* (5), *Jung* (5), *Young* (5), *Soon* (4), *Jae* (3), *Kyung* (3), *Yong* (3), *Hee* (2), *Jin* (2), *Seung* (2), *Won* (2); *Chang* (6), *Chong* (3), *Dae* (3), *Byung* (2), *Jeong* (2), *Soon Ja* (2), *Yeon* (2), *Chong Sun, Chul Ho, Dae Won, Dong Soo, Eun Sook.*

Byus (173) English: variant spelling of BYAS.

Bywater (343) **1.** English: topographic name for someone living by a lake or river, from Middle English *by* 'by', 'beside' + *water* 'water'. **2.** Irish: pseudo-translation (due to confusion with *sruth* 'stream') of Gaelic **Ó Srutháin** 'descendant of *Sruithán*', a personal name from a diminutive of *sruith* 'sage', 'elder'. Bywater is found as the English form of this Gaelic name in County Cork, while in Mayo the usual Anglicization is RYAN.

Bywaters (155) English and Irish: variant of BYWATER.

C

Caamano (168) Galician (**Caamaño**): habitational name from either of two places called Caamaño, both in A Coruña province.
GIVEN NAMES Spanish 51%. *Jose* (8), *Juan* (8), *Jorge* (4), *Manuel* (3), *Agustin* (2), *Armando* (2), *Gonzalo* (2), *Margarita* (2), *Ramon* (2), *Alejandro, Alonso, Amador*.

Caba (240) Spanish and Catalan: variant of CAVA.
GIVEN NAMES Spanish 34%. *Jose* (8), *Juan* (4), *Ramon* (4), *Angel* (3), *Rafael* (3), *Ana* (2), *Eladio* (2), *Juana* (2), *Miguel* (2), *Alberto, Armenia, Cesar*.

Cabal (121) Southern French and Catalan: nickname for a rich man, from Catalan and Occitan *cabal* 'rich'.
GIVEN NAMES Spanish 31%. *Alvaro, Ana, Armando, Arturo, Camilo, Carlos, Catalina, Emilio, Ernesto, Fermin, Francisco, Jaime*.

Caballero (2801) Spanish: occupational name from *caballero* 'knight', 'soldier', 'horseman' (from Late Latin *caballarius* 'mounted soldier').
GIVEN NAMES Spanish 46%. *Jose* (69), *Luis* (30), *Juan* (23), *Manuel* (21), *Mario* (21), *Francisco* (20), *Carlos* (19), *Jesus* (15), *Raul* (15), *Jorge* (14), *Miguel* (14), *Pedro* (14).

Caban (716) Southern French and Catalan (**Cabañ, Caban**): possibly from Occitan *caban, gaban* 'coat wth large sleeves', applied as an occupational nickname for a Provençal farmer, or perhaps a topographic name, from a masculine form of *cabana, cabanya* 'cabin', 'hut' (Late Latin *capanna*). The form **Cabañ** would be the Castilianized form of **Cabany**.
GIVEN NAMES Spanish 38%. *Jose* (18), *Luis* (10), *Angel* (6), *Rafael* (6), *Carlos* (5), *Juan* (5), *Luz* (5), *Miguel* (5), *Julio* (4), *Juana* (3), *Manuel* (3), *Marisol* (3).

Cabana (442) Spanish (**Cabaña**) and Portuguese: habitational name from a place named with Spanish *cabaña* 'hut', 'cabin' (Late Latin *capanna*, a word of Celtic or Germanic origin).
GIVEN NAMES French 10%; Spanish 8%. *Andre* (2), *Armand* (2), *Adrien, Blanchard, Camille, Herve, Marcel, Normand, Philippe, Valmond; Carlos* (2), *Juan* (2), *Rolando* (2), *Alberto, Alfredo, Aniceta, Armando, Augusto, Blanca, Cornelio, Elena, Elina*.

Cabanas (202) Spanish (**Cabañas**) and Portuguese: habitational name from a place

named with Spanish *cabaña* or Portuguese *cabanha* 'hut', 'cabin' (see CABANA).
GIVEN NAMES Spanish 46%. *Eduardo* (6), *Manuel* (6), *Justo* (4), *Jose* (3), *Luis* (3), *Carlos* (2), *Humberto* (2), *Jorge* (2), *Lazaro* (2), *Rafael* (2), *Ramon* (2), *Adolfo; Antonio* (2), *Dante, Heriberto, Marco*.

Cabanilla (114) Spanish: topographic name from a diminutive of *cabaña*, i.e. 'little hut' (see CABANA).
GIVEN NAMES Spanish 29%. *Eduardo* (2), *Gerardo* (2), *Angelito, Arcadio, Arturo, Beatriz, Emilio, Enrique, Ernesto, Felipe, Florencio, Francisco; Romeo* (2), *Gino, Leonardo, Lorenzo*.

Cabaniss (637) Southern French: variant spelling of **Cabanis**, a habitational name from any of various places in Gard named Cabanis, from Late Latin *capannis* 'at the huts', ablative plural of *capanna* 'hut' (see CABAN). This name was established in North American in the 18th century, probably by Huguenots.

Cabbage (159) **1.** Translation of German KOHL. **2.** English: from Middle English *caboche, cabage* 'cabbage', hence a nickname or perhaps a metonymic occupational name for a cabbage grower. The Middle English word also denoted a kind of freshwater fish, and in some cases the surname may have arisen from this sense.

Cabe (874) Irish: reduced form of MCCABE.

Cabell (555) **1.** Catalan: nickname for a bald man, equivalent to Spanish CABELLO. **2.** English: variant spelling of CABLE. **3.** Possibly a respelling of German **Göbel** (see GOEBEL) or KABEL.
FOREBEARS William Cabell, of Bugley near Warminster, in Wiltshire, England, trained in surgery and migrated to Virginia in the 18th century. The emigrant ancestor of a distinguished VA family, he married in 1726 and by 1741 had carried settlements 50 miles westward. As a pioneer during VA's westward push, the surgeon had a private hospital from which he handed out medicines and wooden legs crafted by his artisans.

Cabello (475) Spanish: from *cabello* 'hair' (Latin *capillus*, a collective noun), applied as a nickname for a man with a particularly luxuriant growth of hair, or perhaps ironically for a bald man.
GIVEN NAMES Spanish 48%. *Jose* (17), *Luis* (11), *Francisco* (9), *Carlos* (8), *Juan* (7), *Manuel* (6), *Ramon* (6), *Ricardo* (5),

Alejandro (3), *Guillermo* (3), *Jesus* (3), *Alberto* (2).

Cabeza (133) Spanish: either a nickname for someone with a big head, from *cabeza* 'head' (Late Latin *capitia*), or a topographic name from any of the numerous minor places named with this word, which was commonly used to denote a small hill.
GIVEN NAMES Spanish 45%. *Manuel* (4), *Guillermo* (3), *Mario* (3), *Luis* (2), *Margarita* (2), *Miguel* (2), *Orlando* (2), *Pedro* (2), *Alberto, Aristedes, Arturo, Carlos; Angelo, Guido*.

Cabezas (314) Spanish: topographic name for someone living on or by a cluster of hillocks, from the plural of *cabeza* 'head', 'hillock' (see CABEZA).
GIVEN NAMES Spanish 49%. *Luis* (8), *Manuel* (8), *Jorge* (7), *Jose* (7), *Miguel* (6), *Carlos* (4), *Fernando* (4), *Jesus* (4), *Juan* (4), *Magda* (3), *Pablo* (3), *Alberto* (2).

Cabiness (193) Variant of CABANISS.

Cable (3658) **1.** English: metonymic occupational name for a maker of rope, especially the type of stout rope used in maritime applications, from Anglo-Norman French *cable* 'cable' (Late Latin *capulum* 'halter', of Arabic origin, but associated by folk etymology with Latin *capere* 'to seize'). **2.** English: possibly from an Old English personal name, *Ceadbeald*. **3.** English: metonymic occupational name for a horseman, from Middle English *cabal* 'horse'. **4.** From German **Göbel** (see GOEBEL), assimilated to the English name.

Cabler (196) Altered form of German GABLER.

Cabot (634) Southern French: from *cabot*, a diminutive of Occitan *cap* 'head', hence a nickname for someone with some peculiarity of the head.
FOREBEARS John Cabot, born in Jersey in the Channel Islands in 1680, settled in Salem, MA, in 1700. Although not among the earliest American immigrants, the Cabots were, by the end of the 18th century, the preeminent family of New England. By 1800 they were extremely rich, largely on account of privateering during the American Revolution, smuggling, and trade in slaves and opium. In the 19th century, they branched out into oil and gas production, railroads, and chemicals. The Cabots sustained their wealth and social position well into the 20th century, largely by carefully arranging their marriages and sending most of their sons to Harvard.

Cabral (4089) Portuguese and Galician: habitational name from any of the many places named with Late Latin *capralis* 'place of goats', from Latin *capra* 'goat'.

GIVEN NAMES Spanish 24%; Portuguese 11%. *Manuel* (104), *Jose* (88), *Francisco* (19), *Fernando* (18), *Luis* (18), *Juan* (16), *Carlos* (13), *Armando* (10), *Ana* (9), *Mario* (9), *Miguel* (7), *Ricardo* (7); *Joao* (8), *Duarte* (6), *Joaquim* (5), *Paulo* (4), *Henrique* (2), *Vasco* (2), *Zulmira* (2), *Conceicao*, *Gonsalo*, *Heitor*, *Margarida*, *Messias*.

Cabrales (272) Asturian-Leonese: habitational name from a place in Asturies called Cabrales, meaning 'place of goats' (see CABRAL).

GIVEN NAMES Spanish 56%. *Jose* (12), *Juan* (7), *Jorge* (5), *Miguel* (4), *Alberto* (3), *Alfredo* (3), *Carlos* (3), *Rafael* (3), *Sergio* (3), *Felipe* (2), *Fernando* (2), *Francisco* (2).

Cabrera (6757) Catalan and Spanish: habitational name from any of various minor places called Cabrera, from Late Latin *capraria* 'place of goats' (a derivative of Latin *capra* 'goat').

GIVEN NAMES Spanish 51%; Portuguese 11%. *Jose* (197), *Juan* (110), *Luis* (83), *Carlos* (74), *Manuel* (60), *Jorge* (57), *Francisco* (54), *Rafael* (54), *Jesus* (51), *Pedro* (46), *Miguel* (43), *Ramon* (41); *Lidio* (2), *Wenceslao* (2), *Anatolio*, *Joao*, *Ligia*, *Marcio*; *Antonio* (59), *Marco* (13), *Leonardo* (6), *Lorenzo* (6), *Carmela* (5), *Romeo* (5), *Donato* (4), *Lucio* (4), *Mauro* (4), *Carmelo* (3), *Federico* (3), *Heriberto* (3).

Cacace (323) Southern Italian (Naples): derogatory nickname from dialect *cacace* 'wicked', from medieval Greek *kakakēs*, a diminutive of *kakos* 'bad', 'wicked'.

GIVEN NAMES Italian 15%. *Salvatore* (3), *Antonio*, *Carmine*, *Ciro*, *Dante*, *Franco*, *Gaspare*, *Luigi*, *Nicola*, *Palma*, *Sal*, *Vita*.

Caccamise (158) Italian (Sicily): derivative of CACCAMO, used to distinguish one branch of the family from others.

Caccamo (264) Italian (Sicily): habitational name from Càccamo, near Palermo, Sicily.

GIVEN NAMES Italian 22%. *Angelo* (2), *Emilio* (2), *Enrico* (2), *Aldo*, *Antonio*, *Carlo*, *Carmine*, *Dario*, *Fortunato*, *Giorgio*, *Liborio*, *Marisa*, *Nunzio*, *Sal*, *Salvatore*, *Santo*.

Caccavale (234) Italian: of uncertain derivation; perhaps from *cacare* 'to shit' + *vale* 'valley'.

GIVEN NAMES Italian 23%. *Salvatore* (5), *Carmine* (2), *Gino* (2), *Sal* (2), *Gaetano*, *Gennaro*, *Guido*, *Luca*, *Marco*, *Onofrio*, *Rocco*.

Caccese (121) Italian (Campania): unexplained.

GIVEN NAMES Italian 10%. *Carlo*, *Dino*.

Cacchione (130) Italian (Molise and Apulia): unexplained.

Caccia (172) Italian: **1.** metonymic occupational name for a huntsman, from *caccia* 'hunting'. **2.** short form of any of numerous compound surnames derived from nicknames formed with *caccia* 'hunting' (from *cacciare* 'to hunt', 'to chase'), for example **Cacciabue** 'chase (the) ox', **Cacciafeda** 'hunt (the) wild animal'.

GIVEN NAMES Italian 11%. *Orazio* (2), *Enrico*, *Salvatore*.

Cacciatore (469) Italian: occupational name from *cacciatore* 'huntsman'.

GIVEN NAMES Italian 24%. *Angelo* (9), *Rocco* (4), *Salvatore* (4), *Alfonso* (2), *Alfonzo* (2), *Domenico* (2), *Enrico* (2), *Antonio*, *Carmela*, *Carmelo*, *Giacomo*, *Giuseppe*, *Sal*.

Cacciola (318) Italian: from a diminutive of CACCIA.

GIVEN NAMES Italian 17%. *Santo* (3), *Angelo* (2), *Antonio* (2), *Carmelo* (2), *Salvatore* (2), *Dante*, *Domenic*, *Domenico*, *Marco*, *Sal*.

Caceres (1084) Spanish (**Cáceres**): habitational name from the city of Cáceres in Estremadura, named with the plural of Arabic *al-qaṣr* 'the citadel'.

GIVEN NAMES Spanish 50%. *Jose* (35), *Carlos* (25), *Jorge* (15), *Juan* (15), *Luis* (15), *Manuel* (9), *Ana* (8), *Julio* (8), *Mario* (8), *Pedro* (8), *Francisco* (7), *Miguel* (7).

Cacho (228) Portuguese and Spanish: nickname from *cacho* 'thick neck'.

GIVEN NAMES Spanish 45%. *Francisco* (4), *Jose* (4), *Gilberto* (3), *Jaime* (3), *Ricardo* (3), *Rogelio* (3), *Alberto* (2), *Ana* (2), *Ana Maria* (2), *Eduardo* (2), *Jorge* (2), *Juan* (2).

Cacioppo (460) Southern Italian (Sicily): from Sicilian dialect *cacioppu* 'dried tree trunk', presumably applied as a nickname for someone with wizened skin, or from *caciopu* 'short-sighted' (from Greek *kakiopēs*, literally 'having bad eyes').

GIVEN NAMES Italian 16%. *Gasper* (3), *Angelo* (2), *Sal* (2), *Vita* (2), *Carmine*, *Dino*, *Gaspare*, *Salvatore*, *Veto*, *Vito*.

Cackowski (122) Polish (**Czaczkowski**): habitational name for someone from a place called Czaczki in Białystok voivodeship, or some other place named with *cacko*, a derivative of Old Polish *czacz* 'toy', 'bauble'.

Cada (203) **1.** Czech (**Čáda**): descriptive nickname from Old Czech *čad-* 'smoke', applied to someone with dark skin. **2.** Filipino: unexplained.

Cadarette (117) Altered spelling of French CADORET.

GIVEN NAME French 4%. *Michel*.

Cadavid (112) Galician (also **Cadavide**): unexplained, probably a topographic name, related to *cádavo*, *cádava* 'stump of a burned tree or bush'.

GIVEN NAMES Spanish 57%. *Luis* (5), *Jose* (4), *Alvaro* (3), *Gonzalo* (3), *Carlos* (2),

GIVEN NAMES Italian 7%; German 4%. *Ottavio*; *Otto*.

Jaime (2), *Luz* (2), *Rosalba* (2), *Ana*, *Aracelly*, *Blanca*, *Cesar*.

Cadd (147) English: variant of CADE.

Caddell (1296) Welsh: from an Old Welsh personal name, *Cadell*, formed with Welsh *cad* 'battle'. It was popular in the Middle Ages as a result of the fame of Cadell ab Urien, a 7th-century saint who founded the chapel of Llangadell ('church of Cadell') in Glamorgan. The surname is also found in Scotland and Ireland; in Scotland it is a variant of CALDER.

Cadden (410) Northern Irish and Scottish: reduced form of McCADDEN.

GIVEN NAMES Irish 5%. *Brendan*, *Seamus*, *Siobhan*.

Caddick (153) Welsh: from an Anglicized form of the Welsh personal name *Cadog*, a pet form of *Cadfael*, a personal name formed with *cad* 'battle' (compare CADDELL).

GIVEN NAME French 4%. *Ancil* (2).

Caddy (334) **1.** English: from a pet form of the Old English personal name or byname *Cada* (see CADE). **2.** Altered spelling of French **Caddé**, a variant of CADE.

Cade (2470) **1.** English: from a Middle English personal name, *Cade*, a survival of the Old English personal name or byname *Cada*, which is probably from a Germanic root meaning 'lump', 'swelling'. **2.** English: metonymic occupational name for a cooper, from Middle English, Old French *cade* 'cask', 'barrel' (of Germanic origin, probably akin to the root mentioned in 1). **3.** English: nickname for a gentle or inoffensive person, from Middle English *cade* 'domestic animal', 'pet' (of unknown origin). **4.** French (**Cadé**): topographic name from *cade* 'juniper' (from Latin *catanus*). FOREBEARS Bearers of the name Caddé, from Amiens, were documented in Quebec city by 1670.

Caden (102) Irish and Scottish: reduced and altered form of McCADDEN.

Cadena (1235) Catalan: metonymic occupational name for a maker of chains or perhaps for a jailer, from Catalan and Spanish *cadena* 'chain' (Latin *catena*). This form (singular) is rare as a surname in Castile, but frequent in Catalonia; the plural (**Cadenas**) occurs in both regions but is more frequent in the former.

GIVEN NAMES Spanish 49%. *Jose* (25), *Juan* (20), *Manuel* (15), *Raul* (11), *Jesus* (10), *Jorge* (10), *Miguel* (10), *Alfredo* (8), *Armando* (8), *Carlos* (7), *Pablo* (7), *Ruben* (7).

Cadenas (141) Spanish, Catalan, and Portuguese: variant (plural) of CADENA. In Catalan, this form is a respelling of **Cadenes**.

GIVEN NAMES Spanish 53%. *Jose* (7), *Carlos* (4), *Julio* (4), *Alejandro* (2), *Aramis* (2), *Jesus* (2), *Juan* (2), *Luis* (2), *Manuel* (2), *Maria Isabel* (2), *Pedro* (2), *Roberto* (2);

Antonio (2), *Federico, Filiberto, Marco Antonio*.

Cadenhead (432) Scottish: topographic or habitational name for someone who lived at the head of Caddon Water in the parish of Stow in the Scottish Borders.

Cadet (419) Southern French: nickname from Old Occitan *cadet*, 'small dog', or perhaps from Gascon *capdet*, a term designating the youngest member of a family (however, this term is not recorded in French until the 15th century).
GIVEN NAMES French 45%. *Pierre* (8), *Antoine* (2), *Francois* (2), *Jacques* (2), *Luc* (2), *Marthe* (2), *Yanick* (2), *Yves* (2), *Andre, Andree, Chantal, Chantel*.

Cadieux (516) French: from the Old French nickname *Capdiou* 'God's head', applied to someone who habitually uttered this oath.
FOREBEARS There are Cadieux documented in Montreal from 1657; it is not known where they came from.
GIVEN NAMES French 13%. *Marcel* (5), *Andre* (2), *Armand* (2), *Pierre* (2), *Alban, Emile, Euclide, Gaston, Gervais, Jacques, Jean-Guy, Normand*.

Cadigan (397) Welsh and Irish: variant of CADOGAN.

Cadiz (295) Spanish (**Cádiz**): habitational name from the great seaport of this name in southwestern Spain (earlier *Gades*), which was founded in the 1st millennium BC by Phoenician colonists from Tyre.
GIVEN NAMES Spanish 37%. *Jose* (4), *Ernesto* (3), *Juan* (3), *Alfredo* (2), *Andres* (2), *Carlos* (2), *Deogracias* (2), *Eugenio* (2), *Julio* (2), *Luis* (2), *Manuel* (2), *Mariano* (2); *Antonio, Dante, Eliseo, Quirino*.

Cadle (809) **1.** English and Welsh: variant spelling of CADDELL. **2.** Probably a variant spelling of German KADEL.

Cadman (494) English: occupational name meaning 'servant (Middle English *man*) of Cade' (see CADE).

Cadmus (262) Origin uncertain; probably a Dutch humanistic name taken from the Latin form of classical Greek *Kadmos*, name of the son of the Phoenician King Agenor, founder of Thebes, the person reputed to have introduced the alphabet to the Greeks, a mythological representation of the acquisition of the alphabet from the Phoenicians.

Cadogan (269) Welsh and Irish (of Welsh origin): from a traditional Welsh personal name, *Cadwgan*, probably from *cad* 'battle' + *gwgan* 'scowler'. See also WOGAN.
GIVEN NAME Irish 5%. *Dermot*.

Cadoret (113) French: from an old Breton personal name *Catuuoret* meaning 'protector in combat'.
FOREBEARS A bearer of the name Cadoret is documented in Quebec city in 1657.
GIVEN NAMES French 13%. *Ghislain, Gisele, Normand, Remi, Rolande*.

Cadorette (312) Respelling of French CADORET.
GIVEN NAMES French 10%. *Lucien* (2), *Andre, Fernand, Jacques, Normand, Pierre*.

Cadotte (194) Canadian spelling, reflecting the local pronunciation, of French **Cadot**, a nickname meaning 'little dog'. Compare CADET.
FOREBEARS A bearer of the name is documented in Montreal in 1688.

Cadwalader (127) Welsh: variant spelling of CADWALLADER.

Cadwallader (828) Welsh: from a personal name composed of the elements *cad* 'battle' + *gwaladr* 'leader'.
FOREBEARS John Cadwallader (died 1734) came from Pembroke, Wales, to PA in the late 17th century. The name Cadwal(l)ader appears in 18th-century Philadelphia, PA, including Thomas Cadwalader (1707–1799), a physician, and his sons, John (1742–1786) and Lambert (1743–1823), both revolutionary war soldiers.

Cadwell (1125) **1.** English, Scottish, and northern Irish: variant of CALDWELL. **2.** Perhaps also an Anglicized variant of Welsh CADWALLADER.

Cady (3711) **1.** English (Suffolk): probably a variant of CADDY. **2.** Possibly an Americanized spelling of French **Cadé** (see CADE) or CADET. **3.** Perhaps an Americanized spelling of German **Gäde** (see GADE), **Göde** (see GOEDE), or **Köthe**, all from the medieval personal name *Godo*.

Caesar (897) From the Latin family name of the first Roman emperor, Gaius Julius Caesar (100–44 BC), which gave rise to vocabulary words meaning 'emperor' or 'ruler' in German (*Kaiser*), Russian (*tsar*), Arabic (*qaysar*), and other languages. As a modern family name it is probably most often a humanistic re-translation into Latin of German KAISER, but it is also found as an Americanized form of Italian CESARE and French **César** and **Césaire**. It is also found as an English surname, derived either from a medieval personal name taken from the Latin or a nickname for someone who had played the part of the emperor Julius Caesar in a pageant.

Caetano (254) Portuguese: from the personal name *Caietano*, bestowed in honor of the Italian Saint Gaetano (1480–1547) (see GAETANO).
GIVEN NAMES Spanish 21%; Portuguese 15%. *Manuel* (7), *Jose* (5), *Carlos* (4), *Ana* (2), *Luis* (2), *Abilio, Ademar, Agusto, Alfredo, Alvaro, Enrique, Fernando; Joaquim* (2), *Duarte, Joao, Paulo, Vasco; Antonio* (4), *Angelo* (2).

Cafarella (170) Italian: variant (feminine form) of CAFARELLI.

Cafarelli (245) Italian: diminutive of CAFARO.
GIVEN NAMES Italian 13%. *Rocco* (3), *Ettore* (2), *Angelo, Antonio, Enzo, Marco, Romeo*.

Cafaro (464) Southern Italian: from southern Italian dialect *càfaro* 'unbeliever', from Arabic *kāfir* 'infidel'.
GIVEN NAMES Italian 21%; Spanish 6%. *Angelo* (4), *Antonio* (3), *Carmine* (2), *Nicola* (2), *Alessandro, Arcangelo, Carlo, Cono, Constantino, Domenic, Elio, Erminio, Rosario; Carlos, Guadalupe, Javier*.

Cafasso (122) Italian: variant of **Cafa**, from medieval Greek *Kaiaphas*, derived in turn from a Hebrew personal name.
GIVEN NAMES Italian 18%. *Amerigo* (4), *Guido* (3), *Carmine*.

Cafe (211) Italian (**Cafè**): unexplained.
GIVEN NAMES Italian 16%; Spanish 10%; French 6%. *Angelo* (2), *Luigi* (2), *Carmel, Carmine, Enrico, Franco, Giuseppe, Graziella, Luciano, Michelangelo, Napoli, Nicola; Alberto, Alonso, Eufemia, Flores, Marcos, Mercado, Navarro, Paulina, Pepe, Rudolfo, Teodoro; Andre, Camille*.

Caffee (497) Irish: reduced form of McAFEE.

Cafferty (368) Irish: reduced form of McCAFFERTY.
GIVEN NAME Irish 8%. *Brendan*.

Caffery (248) Irish and Scottish: reduced form of McCAFFERY.

Caffey (956) Irish: reduced form of McAFEE.

Caffrey (1207) Irish and Scottish: reduced form of McCAFFREY.
GIVEN NAMES Irish 5%. *Liam* (2), *Brendan, Declan*.

Cafiero (291) Southern Italian: probably a derogatory nickname from Arabic *kāfir* 'infidel'. Compare CAFARO.
GIVEN NAMES Italian 17%. *Sal* (4), *Salvatore* (3), *Luca* (2), *Pasquale* (2), *Angelo, Aniello, Antonio, Carlo, Gasper*.

Caflisch (111) Swiss German: possibly a dialect shortened form of *Kalbfleisch*, literally 'calf meat', a nickname for a young, immature, 'half-baked' person. According to the *Schweizer Idiotikon*, veal was of inferior quality.

Cagan (208) Jewish (eastern Ashkenazic): variant of COHEN.
GIVEN NAMES Jewish 5%. *Isadore, Reuven, Shimon, Sholom*.

Cage (1316) **1.** Reduced form of Irish **McCage**, a variant of McCAIG. **2.** English (East Anglia): from Middle English, Old French *cage* 'cage', 'enclosure' (Latin *cavea* 'container', 'cave'), hence a metonymic occupational name for a maker and seller of small cages for animals or birds, or a keeper of the large public cage in which petty criminals were confined for short periods of imprisonment.

Cager (94) English: occupational name for a maker of cages or a jailer, Middle English *cager* (from Old French *cagier*), an agent derivative of CAGE 2.
GIVEN NAME French 6%. *Antoine*.

Caggiano (859) Southern Italian: habitational name from a place in Salerno province named Caggiano, from the Latin personal name *Cavius*.
GIVEN NAMES Italian 16%. *Angelo* (7), *Rocco* (4), *Antonio* (3), *Carmine* (3), *Donato* (2), *Fiore* (2), *Guido* (2), *Pasquale* (2), *Sal* (2), *Antonella, Cosmo, Marco*.

Cagle (6364) Americanized spelling of **Kagel** (see KEGEL), **Kögel** (see KOEGEL), or KOGEL.

Cagley (237) Americanized spelling of German KEGLER or of Swiss German **Kaegly**, a variant of **Kägi** (see KAEGI).

Cagney (239) Irish: Anglicized form of Gaelic **Ó Caingnigh** 'descendant of *Caingneach*', a personal name meaning 'pleader' or a byname for a contentious person.
GIVEN NAME Irish 6%. *Brendan*.

Cagnina (136) Italian (Sicily): from the feminine form of **Cagnino**, a diminutive of the personal name *Cagno*, from Latin *Canius*.
GIVEN NAMES Italian 19%. *Salvatore* (5), *Angelo, Luciano, Luigi*.

Cagwin (115) English: unexplained. Perhaps an altered version of the Cornish personal name *Keigwin*.

Cahalan (397) Irish: Anglicized form of Gaelic **Ó Cathaláin** (see CALLAN 1).
GIVEN NAMES Irish 4%. *Brendan, Kieran*.

Cahalane (153) Irish: Anglicized form of Gaelic **Ó Cathaláin** (see CALLAN 1).

Cahall (383) Irish: variant spelling of CAHILL.

Cahan (207) **1.** Irish: reduced form of McCAHAN or **O'Cahan** (see O'KANE). **2.** Jewish: variant of COHEN.
GIVEN NAME Jewish 5%. *Nissen* (3).

Cahill (8202) Irish: Anglicized form of Gaelic **Ó Cathail** 'descendant of *Cathal*', a personal name meaning 'powerful in battle'.
GIVEN NAMES Irish 5%. *Brendan* (5), *Liam* (4), *Donal* (3), *Conor* (2), *Eamon* (2), *Kieran* (2), *Ronan* (2), *Aidan, Aileen, Brigid, Colm, James Patrick*.

Cahn (836) **1.** Jewish: variant of COHEN. **2.** Americanized spelling of North German KAHN.
GIVEN NAMES German 5%. *Otto* (2), *Arno, Frieda, Horst, Kurt*.

Cahoon (1771) Irish spelling (reflecting the traditional pronunciation) of the Scottish surname COLQUHOUN.

Cahow (111) English: **1.** habitational name of Norman origin from Caien, France (earlier recorded as *Cahou*, 1195), a lost place near Boulogne-sur-Mer in northern France. **2.** habitational name from Kew in Greater London (earlier *Cayho*, 1327), which is probably named with Old English *cǣg* 'key' (used here in the sense 'projecting land') + *hōh* 'hill spur'.

Cahoy (122) Filipino: unexplained.

Cai (768) Chinese 蔡: from the name of the former state of Cai, in present-day Henan province. When the Zhou dynasty displaced the Shang dynasty in 1122 BC, the defeated Shang were allowed to rule in the area of their old capital of Yin, under the stewardship of Zhou appointees. However, these Zhou appointees, among them Cai Shu, the 14th son of Wen Wang and younger brother of the new king, joined forces with the Shang in revolt. After the rebellion was suppressed, Cai Shu was banished, but his son was granted the state of Cai along with the title Earl of Cai. His descendants later adopted the place name Cai as their surname. Other spellings of this name, due to dialect differences and variation in Romanization, include **Tsai, Choi, Choy**, and **Tsoi**.
GIVEN NAMES Chinese 67%; Vietnamese 7%. *Wei* (11), *Li* (7), *Hong* (6), *Xin* (5), *Yang* (5), *Feng* (4), *Jian* (4), *Liming* (4), *Ming* (4), *Rong* (4), *Yi* (4), *Hui* (3); *Quan* (2), *Anh, Chau, Dinh, Huong Thi, Huyen, Khiem, Loan Kim, Long, Nga, Nhi, Oanh*.

Caiazza (131) Italian: variant (feminine form) of CAIAZZO.
GIVEN NAMES Italian 14%; Irish 5%. *Pasquale* (2), *Aniello, Biagio, Modestino, Rocco, Vittorio*.

Caiazzo (295) Italian: **1.** habitational name from a place called Caiazzo, in Caserta. **2.** from a diminutive of the personal name *Caio* (from Latin *Caius*).
GIVEN NAMES Italian 18%. *Salvatore* (3), *Angelo* (2), *Carmine* (2), *Attilio, Carmela, Lia, Pasquale, Raffaela, Vito*.

Caicedo (235) Castilianized form of Basque **Kaizedo**, a habitational name from Kaizedo Behekoa (Caicedo de Yuso in Spanish) or Kaizedo Goikoa (Caicedo Sopeña in Spanish), two towns in the Basque province of Araba.
GIVEN NAMES Spanish 52%. *Luis* (7), *Carlos* (6), *Jorge* (5), *Jose* (5), *Hernando* (4), *Juan* (4), *Julio* (3), *Alvaro* (2), *Eduardo* (2), *Fernando* (2), *Gustavo* (2), *Ines* (2).

Cail (404) French: **1.** in Normandy and Picardy, a topographic name for someone who lived on a patch of stony soil, from Old Norman French *cail(ou)* 'pebble', 'stone' (of Celtic origin). **2.** in southern France, a metonymic occupational name for a dairy worker, from Occitan *cail* 'curds' (Latin *coagulum*, from *coagulāre* to congeal).

Caillier (166) French: probably an occupational name for a catcher of quails, from an agent noun from Old French *caille* 'quail' (Latin *quaccula*).
FOREBEARS The name **Caillé**, from La Rochelle, is documented in La Prairie, Canada, by 1675. A family called **Cailler** or **Cahié** was in Quebec city by 1669.
GIVEN NAMES French 6%. *Andre* (2), *Antoine*.

Caillouet (269) French: topographic name for a person living on pebbly ground, from a diminutive of *caillou* 'stone'.

FOREBEARS The variant **Cahouet** is documented in Cap St. Ignace, Canada, in 1693.
GIVEN NAMES French 5%. *Antoine, Lucien, Marcel*.

Cain (21548) **1.** Scottish: Anglicized form of Gaelic **Mac Iain**, patronymic from *Iain*, one of the Gaelic forms of JOHN. This name is found in many other spellings, including McCAIN, KEAN, and McKEAN. In some cases it may also be a variant of COYNE. **2.** English: variant spelling of CANE. **3.** English (of Norman origin): habitational name from Caen in Calvados, France, named with the Gaulish elements *catu* 'battle' + *magos* 'field', 'plain'. **4.** French (**Caïn**): from the Biblical name *Cain* (Hebrew *Qayin*), probably applied as a derogatory nickname for someone who was considered to be treacherous. **5.** Spanish (**Caín**): habitational name from a place called Caín in León.

Caine (1435) **1.** Scottish, English, and French: variant spelling of CAIN. **2.** French: derogatory nickname for a peevish or bad-tempered person, from *caigne* 'bitch'.

Caines (538) English (of Norman origin): habitational name from Cahaignes in Eure, France, or Cahaynes in Calvados, France, both probably named with a Celtic element meaning 'juniper bush'.

Cains (125) English: variant spelling of CAINES.

Caiola (204) Southern Italian (Sicily): from Sicilian dialect *càiula* 'lace', 'baby's bonnet', a diminutive of medieval Latin *caia* 'cap', 'bonnet'.
GIVEN NAMES Italian 10%; German 5%. *Salvatore* (2), *Enrico, Guiseppe, Marcello*; *Hedwig* (4).

Caira (157) **1.** Southern Italian (Calabria): probably from Arabic *khayr* 'good', 'well'. **2.** Galician: habitational name from Caira Lugo in Galicia.
GIVEN NAMES Italian 27%. *Aldo* (2), *Benedetto* (2), *Gino* (2), *Luigi* (2), *Mario* (2), *Adriana, Armando, Amedeo, Angelo, Antonio, Attilio, Bernardo, Concetta, Giuseppina, Guido, Marcello*.

Caird (130) Scottish: occupational name from Gaelic *ceard* 'tinker'.
GIVEN NAME Scottish 4%. *Iain*.

Caire (170) Southern French and Catalan: topographic from **1.** from *caire* 'edge', 'square rock' (Latin *quadrum*) **2.** French: habitational name from any of three places called Le Caire.
GIVEN NAMES Spanish 9%. *Emilio* (5), *Eloy* (2), *Rafael* (2), *Conception, Manuel*.

Caires (171) Southern French and Catalan: variant (plural) of CAIRE.
GIVEN NAMES Spanish 6%. *Manuel* (3), *Jose* (2), *Armando, Claudio, Mario, Roberto*.

Cairnes (162) Variant spelling of Scottish CAIRNS.

Cairney (100) Irish: Anglicized form of Gaelic **Ó Ceithearnaigh** 'descendant of the foot soldier (Gaelic *ceithearnach*)'.

Cairns (2263) Scottish: from Gaelic *carn* 'cairn', a topographic name for someone who lived by a cairn, i.e. a pile of stones raised as a boundary marker or a memorial.

Cairo (539) Italian (Sicily): habitational name from any of various places in Sicily named Cairo.
GIVEN NAMES Italian 19%; Spanish 8%. *Alberto* (2), *Rigoberto* (2), *Salvatore* (2), *Aldo, Angelo, Attilio, Carlo, Carmela, Carmine, Guido, Oreste, Palma, Remo, Reno*; *Luis* (2), *Mercedes* (2), *Ruben* (2), *Jorge, Juan*.

Caison (297) Variant spelling of French **Caisson**, a metonymic occupational name for a chest maker (see CAISSE).

Caisse (307) French: metonymic occupational name for a chest maker, from Middle French *caisse* 'wooden chest' (derivative of Latin *capsa*). This surname has sometimes been Americanized as CASE.
GIVEN NAMES French 4%. *Armand, Lucien.*

Caissie (181) French: probably a habitational name from a place called Caissie.
GIVEN NAMES French 13%. *Aurel, Desire, Gilles, Maxime, Normand, Sylvain.*

Caito (351) Italian (Sicily): occupational name from *càjitu* 'official', 'leader', Sicilian variant of Italian *gàito*, a derivative of Arabic *qāḍī* 'judge'.
GIVEN NAMES Italian 6%. *Salvatore* (2), *Angelo, Antonio, Gaetano, Ignazio, Sal.*

Cajigas (151) Spanish (also **Cagigas**): topographic name from the plural of Spanish *cajiga, quejigo* 'gall oak'.
GIVEN NAMES Spanish 38%. *Jose* (4), *Juan* (3), *Aida* (2), *Felicidad* (2), *Jaime* (2), *Luis* (2), *Luz* (2), *Pedro* (2), *Rafael* (2), *Alberto, Alejandro, Alfonso*; *Antonio* (3), *Clemente, Gilda, Heriberto.*

Cake (165) English: from the Middle English *cake* denoting a flat loaf made from fine flour (Old Norse *kaka*), hence a metonymic occupational name for a baker who specialized in fancy breads. It was first attested as a surname in the 13th century (Norfolk, Northamptonshire).

Cal (136) **1.** Spanish: topographic name for someone who lived by an area of limestone, from *cal* 'lime(stone)' (from Late Latin *cals*, Latin *calx*). **2.** Spanish: variant of CALLE. **3.** Portuguese: reduced variant of CANAL. **4.** Polish (**Cał**): nickname from an Old Polish variant of *cały* 'whole', 'entire'.
GIVEN NAMES Spanish 15%. *Osvaldo* (2), *Benito, Enrique, Genaro, Jose, Luis, Mario, Ruben, Santiago.*

Cala (271) **1.** Spanish and southern Italian (Sicily): habitational name from any of numerous minor places in eastern and southern Spain, and one in Sicily, called Cala, from a proto-Romance word *cala* 'bay', 'cove'. **2.** Southern Italian: nickname from medieval Greek *kalas* 'good', 'beautiful'

(ancient Greek *kalos*). **3.** Czech (**Čála**): from a reduced form of an unidentified personal name beginning with *Ča-*. **4.** Polish (**Cała**): variant of **Cał** (see CAL).
GIVEN NAMES Spanish 14%; Italian 8%. *Avelino* (3), *Inocencia* (2), *Jose* (2), *Adriana, Carlos, Carmella, Dionisio, Epifanio, Estanislao, Eudaldo, Francisca, Jesus*; *Antonio* (2), *Luigi* (2), *Salvatore* (2), *Angelo, Santo.*

Calabrese (3046) Italian: regional name from the adjective *calabrese* 'Calabrian' (see CALABRIA).
GIVEN NAMES Italian 17%. *Angelo* (21), *Salvatore* (14), *Rocco* (9), *Carlo* (7), *Pasquale* (6), *Sal* (6), *Carmine* (4), *Santo* (4), *Vito* (4), *Aldo* (3), *Antonio* (3), *Domenic* (3).

Calabretta (150) Italian: from a diminutive of CALABRIA; it may have served to distinguish one person who had come from Calabria from another in the same family or community.
GIVEN NAMES Italian 21%. *Antonietta, Carmela, Giuseppe, Mario, Rocco, Salvatore, Rosario, Teodoro.*

Calabria (412) Italian: regional name from Calabria in southern Italy.
GIVEN NAMES Italian 17%. *Sal* (3), *Salvatore* (3), *Angelo* (2), *Antonio* (2), *Marco* (2), *Carlo, Dino, Domenico, Fausto, Gennaro, Gildo, Luigi.*

Calabro (1057) Italian: regional name for a man from Calabria, from Italian *càlabro* 'Calabrian', 'inhabitant of Calabria'; in southern Italy this is *calabró*, from Greek *kalabros*.
GIVEN NAMES Italian 17%. *Santo* (8), *Carmela* (4), *Carmelo* (4), *Sal* (4), *Salvatore* (4), *Antonio* (3), *Italia* (3), *Carmine* (2), *Domenic* (2), *Domenico* (2), *Gaetano* (2), *Nino* (2).

Calafiore (108) Italian (Sicilian **Calafiura**): hypercorrected form of **Calaciura**, from Greek *Kalokyrēs, Kalokyrios* meaning 'good man', or more likely from the variant *Kalokioures*.
GIVEN NAMES Italian 31%. *Salvatore* (4), *Carmela* (2), *Antonio, Carmelo, Concetta, Domenica, Elio, Gaetano, Giovanni, Nunzio, Sal, Santo.*

Calahan (628) Irish: variant spelling of CALLAHAN.

Calais (196) French: habitational name from the French port of Calais or from a minor place of the same name in Sarthe.
GIVEN NAME French 5%. *Onezime.*

Calaman (110) French: respelling of German **Kahl(e)mann**, a nickname for a bald man (from Middle High German *kal(wes)* 'bald' + *man* 'man'), or possibly of German KALLMAN.

Calamari (266) Italian: **1.** occupational name from medieval Latin *calamarius* 'scribe', 'copyist' (from Latin *calamus* 'reed'). **2.** habitational name from Calamaro in Sicily, named with medieval Latin

calamarium 'writing stand', probably denoting a place rich in reeds.

Calame (253) French: from a derivative of Latin *calamus* 'reed', denoting a feather pen, and hence, by metonymy, a scribe or clerk. However, the distribution of the name in North America is not compatible with normal French migration patterns, and it may be that it was brought via another country or that a different source is involved.

Calamia (227) Southern Italian (Sicily): topographic name from medieval Greek *kalamia*, plural of *kalamos* 'reed'. Reeds were used for wattling and thatching.
GIVEN NAMES Italian 13%. *Rocco* (3), *Carmela* (2), *Angelo, Domenic, Santo, Vito.*

Calandra (602) Italian: from *calandra* 'skylark' (Latin *calandra*), probably a nickname for someone with a fine singing voice.
GIVEN NAMES Italian 16%. *Salvatore* (8), *Angelo* (4), *Antonio* (3), *Rocco* (3), *Francesca* (2), *Vito* (2), *Aldo, Carmel, Egidio, Franco, Giacomo, Gino.*

Calandrino (100) Southern Italian (Calabria and Sicily): from a diminutive of CALANDRA.
GIVEN NAMES Italian 27%. *Gaspare* (2), *Angelo, Battista, Gilda, Gino, Sal, Santo, Valentino.*

Calandro (181) Italian: variant of CALANDRA.
GIVEN NAMES Italian 11%. *Carmelo, Pasquale, Rocco, Sal, Santo, Vito.*

Calarco (207) Italian: from Greek *kalos arkhōn* 'good nobleman'. This name is sometimes Americanized as CLARK.
GIVEN NAMES Italian 17%; French 4%. *Rocco* (2), *Angelo, Carmelo, Fausto, Nunziato, Salvatore*; *Jean Pierre, Marcel, Pascal.*

Calaway (540) English: variant spelling of CALLAWAY.

Calbert (234) English: variant of ALBERT, probably due to misdivision of a personal name such as *Rick Albert*.

Calcagni (288) Italian: variant (plural) of CALCAGNO.
GIVEN NAMES Italian 8%. *Antonio* (2), *Aldo, Angelo, Dante, Mirella, Philomena, Stefano, Ugo.*

Calcagno (615) Italian: from *calcagno* 'heel' (medieval Latin *calcaneum*).
GIVEN NAMES Italian 26%; Spanish 6%. *Sal* (7), *Angelo* (6), *Salvatore* (6), *Aldo* (2), *Alfonso* (2), *Giuseppe* (2), *Mario* (2), *Anello, Antonino, Carlo, Domenic, Domenico, Elvio, Filippo*; *Salvador* (2), *Blanca, Enrique, Luis, Miguelina, Salvador.*

Calcaterra (413) Italian: nickname from *calcare* 'to tread', 'to stamp' + *terra* 'land', 'earth', 'ground', probably denoting a short person, someone who walked close to the ground, or an energetic walker.
GIVEN NAMES Italian 7%. *Angelo* (3), *Attilio, Benedetto, Orfeo, Sal.*

Calcote (467) English: habitational name from any of the numerous places (in Bedfordshire, Berkshire, Cambridgeshire, Cheshire, Northamptonshire, Warwickshire, and elsewhere) named Caldecote or Caldecott, from Old English *cald* 'cold' + *cot* 'cottage', 'dwelling'. It has been suggested that in Old English this expression denoted an unattended shelter for wayfarers, although in fact some places with this name were of considerable status by 1086, when they appear in Domesday Book. In some instances this and some of the other contracted forms may have arisen from Calcot in Berkshire, Collacott(s) in Devon, or Calcutt in Wiltshire, in all of which the first element apparently comes from the Old English personal name *Cola* (see COLE 2) or the word *col* '(char)coal', in which case the meaning would be something like 'coalshed'.

Calcutt (218) English: variant of CALCOTE.

Caldarella (115) Italian: metonymic occupational name for a tinker or maker of large cooking pots, from a diminutive of *caldara* 'cauldron', or, in Sicily, for a bricklayer or mason, from the same word in the sense 'bricklayer's bucket'.
GIVEN NAMES Italian 15%. *Angelo, Carlo, Rocco, Salvatore, Santo.*

Caldarelli (122) Italian: patronymic or plural form of CALDARELLA.
GIVEN NAMES Italian 8%. *Angelo, Attilio, Elio, Romeo.*

Caldarera (108) Italian: probably a topographic name for someone who lived in a place where there were copper workings or, less likely, a feminine form of **Caldarero**, an occupational name from medieval Latin *caldararius* 'coppersmith', 'tinker'.
GIVEN NAMES Italian 8%. *Antonio, Mario.*

Caldarone (141) Italian: from an augmentative form of *caldara* 'cauldron'.
GIVEN NAMES Italian 20%. *Salvatore* (3), *Angelo, Caesar, Giorgio, Nicola, Remo, Vittorio.*

Caldas (123) Galician, Catalan, and Portuguese: habitational name from any of the places named Caldas (in Galician and Portuguese) and Caldes (in Catalan) for their hot springs, especially in Galicia and Catalonia. The Catalan form is a respelling of **Caldes**.
GIVEN NAMES Spanish 37%; Portuguese 16%; Italian 8%. *Jose* (5), *Adolfo* (2), *Gustavo* (2), *Manuel* (2), *Pablo* (2), *Alfredo, Arlindo, Carlos, Consuelo, Cristina, Eloisa, Emilio*; *Joao* (2); *Antonio* (3), *Constantino, Rosangela, Silvio.*

Caldeira (221) Portuguese: metonymic occupational name for a tinker or maker of large cooking vessels, from *caldeira* 'kettle' (Latin *caldarium* 'hot bath').
GIVEN NAMES Spanish 12%; Portuguese 7%. *Manuel* (4), *Adelino* (2), *Ernesto* (2), *Luis* (2), *Americo, Anselmo, Arnaldo, Christi-*

ano, Eduarda, Geraldo, Joaquin, Lilia; *Joao, Paulo.*

Calder (1881) **1.** Scottish: habitational name from any of the various places called Calder, Caldor, or Cawdor. Calder in Thurso is recorded in the early 13th century in the form *Kalfadal* and was named with Old Norse *kalfr* 'calf' + *dalr* 'valley'. The others are probably the same as in 2 below. **2.** English: habitational name from Calder in Cumbria, named from the river on which it stands. This is probably a British name, from Welsh *caled* 'hard', 'violent' + *dwfr* 'water', 'stream'.

Caldera (622) Spanish: topographic name from *caldera* 'basin', 'crater', 'hollow' (Latin *caldarium* 'hot bath'), a common element of stream and mountain names.
GIVEN NAMES Spanish 41%; Portuguese 10%. *Jose* (18), *Manuel* (11), *Juan* (9), *Francisco* (7), *Mario* (5), *Miguel* (5), *Gustavo* (4), *Jesus* (4), *Leticia* (4), *Roberto* (4), *Carlos* (3), *Javier* (3); *Joaquim.*

Calderaro (176) Italian: occupational name from Italian *calderaro* 'boilermaker'.
GIVEN NAMES Italian 13%. *Biaggio, Carmine, Giuseppe, Guiseppe, Nunzia.*

Calderin (112) Asturian-Leonese (**Calderín**): Asturian diminutive of CALDERA.
GIVEN NAMES Spanish 49%; Italian 7%. *Jose* (6), *Roberto* (4), *Alberto* (3), *Andres* (2), *Fernando* (2), *Jorge* (2), *Juan* (2), *Manuel* (2), *Mario* (2), *Agustin, Ana, Ania*; *Ciro* (2), *Lorenzo* (2), *Aldo, Antonio.*

Calderon (6248) Spanish (**Calderón**): topographic name from an augmentative of *caldera* 'basin', 'crater', 'hollow', a common element of stream and mountain names, or a habitational name from a place named with this word, as for example Calderón in Valencia province. Alternatively, it may be a metonymic occupational name from the same word in the sense 'kettle', 'cauldron'.
GIVEN NAMES Spanish 49%. *Jose* (167), *Carlos* (90), *Juan* (74), *Manuel* (60), *Luis* (54), *Jorge* (52), *Jesus* (47), *Miguel* (39), *Francisco* (34), *Pedro* (34), *Roberto* (32), *Fernando* (29).

Calderone (1077) Italian: from an augmentative of Spanish *caldera*, Italian *caldara* 'cauldron', hence a topographic name for someone living in a crater or hollow or a metonymic occupational name for a maker of large cooking pots.
GIVEN NAMES Italian 18%; Spanish 12%. *Salvatore* (7), *Angelo* (6), *Domenic* (5), *Santo* (4), *Carmelo* (3), *Vito* (3), *Antonio* (2), *Cosimo* (2), *Gino* (2), *Mario* (2), *Ambrogio, Benito, Carlo*; *Juan* (3), *Carlos* (2), *Jose* (2), *Luis* (2), *Bolivar, Jorge.*

Calderwood (723) Scottish: habitational name from Calderwood in Lanarkshire, named from the river name *Calder* (see CALDER 2) + Middle English *wode* 'wood'.

Caldon (127) Irish: shortened altered form of **McCalden**, which is unexplained, perhaps a variant of McCALLION.

Caldwell (31426) English, Scottish, and northern Irish: habitational name from any of several places in England and Scotland, variously spelled, that are named with Old English *cald* 'cold' + *well(a)* 'spring', 'stream'. Caldwell in North Yorkshire is one major source of the surname; Caldwell in Renfrewshire in Scotland another.
FOREBEARS Several Caldwells emigrated from Scotland to America by way of Ireland in the 18th century. James Caldwell (1734–81), son of settler John Caldwell, was born in Charlotte Co., VA, and was a militant clergyman during the revolutionary war. Andrew Caldwell, a Scottish farmer, emigrated to America in 1718 and started a family in Lancaster Co., PA. His son David was a Presbyterian clergyman and well-known revolutionary war patriot.

Cale (1036) **1.** French (**Calé**) and English: from Old French *calé*, adjectival derivative of *cale* 'close-fitting cap', hence a nickname for someone who wore such a cap. **2.** Southern Italian (**Calè**): variant of CALIA. **3.** Dutch: variant spelling of KALE. **4.** Americanized spelling of German KEHL.

Caleb (175) **1.** Reduced and altered form of Scottish and Irish McKILLIP, a Gaelic patronymic from PHILIP. The form of the name, originally *Killip*, has been assimilated to that of the Biblical personal name *Caleb*. **2.** English and Welsh: from the Biblical Hebrew personal name *Caleb*, the name of one of the only two men who set out with Moses from Egypt to live long enough to enter the promised land (Numbers 26:65). This name, which is derived from a Hebrew word meaning 'dog', was popular among the Puritans in the 17th century and was brought by them as a personal name to America.

Caleca (120) Southern Italian: probably from the medieval Greek personal name *Kalēkes*, a derivative of *kalos* 'good' or 'beautiful'.
GIVEN NAMES Italian 30%. *Vito* (3), *Antonino* (2), *Antonio* (2), *Salvatore* (2), *Angelo, Benedetta, Cosmo, Gaspere, Sal.*

Calef (190) Probably a variant of English **Calf(e)** (see CALIFF).

Calegari (114) Italian: variant of CALLEGARI. This name is found especially in French-speaking areas of North America.
GIVEN NAMES French 8%; Italian 5%. *Jean-Claude, Jean-Paul, Pierre*; *Dario, Gino, Sylvio.*

Calender (136) **1.** Variant of English and Scottish CALLENDER. **2.** Variant of German **Kalander** (see KOLANDER).

Calendine (112) Variant of English **Calla(n)dine**; unexplained.

Caler (261) Americanized spelling of German KAHLER or **Köhler** (see KOHLER).

Calero (312) Spanish: metonymic occupational name for a burner or seller of lime, from *calero* 'lime'. Lime (calcium carbonate) is a product of some historical importance, obtained from limestone by heating or 'burning'. It has various agricultural, domestic, and industrial applications, including fertilizing soil, treating furniture, bleaching, and making mortar.
GIVEN NAMES Spanish 49%. *Jose* (12), *Julio* (6), *Juan* (5), *Ana* (4), *Jorge* (4), *Luis* (4), *Angel* (3), *Francisco* (3), *Gilberto* (3), *Rodolfo* (3), *Armando* (2), *Arturo* (2); *Antonio, Fausto, Manfredo*.

Cales (520) **1.** Galician: habitational name from any of various places in Galicia called Cales, in Lugo, Ourense, and Pontevedra provinces. **2.** French: habitational name, a derivative of pre-Latin *kal* 'rock', from either of two places so called, in Lot and Dordogne.

Caley (633) **1.** English (of Norman origin): habitational name from places in Eure and Seine-Maritime, France, called Cailly, from a Romano-Gallic personal name *Callius* + the locative suffix *-acum*. **2.** English: habitational name from a minor place called Caley in the parish of Winwick, Lancashire, named with Old English *cā* 'jackdaw' + *lēah* 'woodland clearing'. **3.** Irish: reduced and altered form of MCCAULEY. **4.** Manx: variant of CALLOW.

Calfee (611) English or Scottish: unexplained. The name is recorded in VA from the 18th century on. It could be a variant of English **Calf(e)** (see CALIFF), or a reduced and altered form of Scottish MCALPINE.

Calhoon (802) Irish: variant of Scottish COLQUHOUN.

Calhoun (13836) Irish: variant of Scottish COLQUHOUN.
FOREBEARS This prominent early American name was brought across the Atlantic Ocean by Scotch-Irish pioneers who entered Pennsylvania in about 1733. The American statesman John C. Calhoun (1782–1850), born in Abbeville District, SC, served in both houses of Congress, was secretary of war, and vice president of the U.S. (1825–32).

Cali (902) Southern Italian (**Calì**) and Greek (**Kalis**): from the female personal name *Kalē*, from the feminine form of the adjective *kalos* 'good', 'beautiful', or possibly from a shortened form of the male name *Kallistos* 'best'.
GIVEN NAMES Italian 14%. *Salvatore* (16), *Angelo* (4), *Filippo* (3), *Rocco* (3), *Sal* (3), *Pietro* (2), *Vito* (2), *Amedeo, Calogero, Carmela, Concetta, Cosimo*.

Calia (180) Southern Italian: nickname from medieval Greek *kaleas* 'good or beautiful person' (from *kalos* 'good', 'beautiful' + the personalizing suffix *-eas*).
GIVEN NAMES Italian 9%. *Vito* (2), *Sal*.

Calicchio (117) Italian: from a pet form of CALI.

GIVEN NAMES Italian 16%; German 4%. *Dante* (2), *Angelo, Carmine, Giancarlo; Irmgard, Wolfgang.*

Calico (177) Probably an altered form of English CALCOTE. Compare CALLICOAT.

Caliendo (519) Italian: of uncertain derivation, perhaps a variant of **Calenda**, a topographic name from *calendula* '(pot) marigold' (*Calendula officinalis*).
GIVEN NAMES Italian 15%. *Angelo* (7), *Gennaro* (3), *Antonio* (2), *Rocco* (2), *Sal* (2), *Salvatore* (2), *Alfonse, Giacomo, Gino, Giovanni, Luigi, Michelina.*

Califano (317) Italian: from a nickname from Greek *kaliphanēs* 'one who shines beautifully'.
GIVEN NAMES Italian 18%. *Angelo* (3), *Antonio* (2), *Gaetano* (2), *Sal* (2), *Aldo, Alfonse, Carmela, Ciro, Francesco, Giovanni, Giuseppe, Lorenzo.*

Califf (201) English: probably a variant of English **Calf(e)**, a nickname from Middle English *calf* 'calf'.
FOREBEARS The name was brought to Roxbury, MA, by Robert Calfe (1648–1719), from Stanstead, England. He is buried in the Eustis Street Burying Ground in Boston.

Caligiuri (338) Southern Italian (Calabria): variant of CALOGERO.
GIVEN NAMES Italian 13%. *Angelo* (3), *Amedeo* (2), *Antonio* (2), *Matteo* (2), *Natale* (2), *Biagio, Pasquale, Sal, Salvatore.*

Caliguire (104) Altered form of Italian CALIGIURI.
GIVEN NAME Italian 6%. *Angelo.*

Caliri (182) Southern Italian (Sicily and Calabria): from the medieval Greek personal name *Kallirēs*, a derivative of classical Greek *Kallirhoos* 'one who flows beautifully'.
GIVEN NAMES Italian 18%. *Angelo* (2), *Carmelo, Domenic, Fortunata, Francesca, Lorenzo, Mario, Santo.*

Calise (465) Southern Italian (Sicily, Naples): perhaps from Arabic *khalīṣ* 'pure', 'sincere'.
GIVEN NAMES Italian 21%. *Vito* (6), *Salvatore* (4), *Gaetano* (3), *Angelo* (2), *Antonio* (2), *Domenic* (2), *Sal* (2), *Aniello, Attilio, Carlo, Carmela, Concetta.*

Calistro (107) Italian, Spanish, and Portuguese: variant of **Calisto**, from the Latin personal name *Callistus* (see CALIXTO).
GIVEN NAMES Italian 7%. *Antonio, Sal.*

Calitri (142) Italian: unexplained.
GIVEN NAMES Italian 23%. *Angelo* (4), *Carmine* (2), *Domenic* (2), *Santo, Vito.*

Caliva (117) Italian (Sicily; **Calivà**): topographic name of medieval Greek origin, from *kalyba* 'hut', 'shelter'.
GIVEN NAMES Italian 9%. *Mario* (2), *Alfredo, Ernesto, Marcello.*

Calix (146) Catalan and Portuguese (**Càlix**): unexplained; it seems to refer to Portuguese *cálice*, Catalan *càliç* 'communion cup'; or in Catalan it could perhaps be from

calitx denoting a throwing game, with the same etymology.
GIVEN NAMES Spanish 45%. *Luis* (6), *Jose* (5), *Jorge* (4), *Roberto* (4), *Cesar* (3), *Carlos* (2), *Juan* (2), *Miguel* (2), *Alberto, Alonso, Andres, Angel.*

Calixte (135) French: from the personal name *Calixte* (see CALIXTO).
GIVEN NAMES French 58%; German 5%. *Jacques* (3), *Evens* (2), *Pierre* (2), *Solange* (2), *Andre, Dieudonne, Dominique, Euclide, Fernand, Francois, Julien, Luckner; Ernst.*

Calixto (225) Spanish and Portuguese: from the Latin personal name *Calixtus*, borne by several early popes, of whom the first (217–222) was canonized as a saint. The personal name is from Greek *kallistos* 'most beautiful'.
GIVEN NAMES Spanish 57%. *Jose* (7), *Enrique* (5), *Guadalupe* (5), *Juan* (5), *Francisco* (2), *Jorge* (2), *Julio* (2), *Luis* (2), *Luz* (2), *Manuel* (2), *Rafael* (2), *Roberto* (2); *Nicola* (2), *Antonio, Valentino.*

Calk (238) **1.** English: possibly a habitational name from Calke in Derbyshire '(place on) the chalk or limestone', from Old English (Anglian) *calc*. **2.** Americanized spelling of German KALK.

Calkin (254) Irish: variant of CULKIN.

Calkins (3638) Irish: variant of CULKIN, with English patronymic *-s* added.

Call (5434) **1.** Irish: reduced form of MCCALL. **2.** English: from Middle English *calle* 'close-fitting cap for women' (from Old French *cale*), probably applied as a metonymic occupational name. Compare CALE. **3.** Catalan: topographic name from *call* 'narrow track' (Latin *callis*). Compare CALLE. **4.** Possibly an Americanized spelling of German KOLL or GOLL.

Calla (128) **1.** Italian: variant spelling of CALA. **2.** Catalan (**Callà**): respelling of **Catllà** or **Catllar**, two habitational names from any of the towns so named, mainly Catllà, a town in the district of El Conflent, northern Catalonia (called Catllar in French), and El Catllar, a town in the district of El Tarragonès, in Catalonia.
GIVEN NAMES Italian 17%. *Domenic* (2), *Salvatore* (2), *Damiano, Enzo, Guido.*

Callaghan (2530) Irish: reduced form of O'CALLAGHAN (see CALLAHAN).
GIVEN NAMES Irish 6%. *Brendan* (3), *Caitlin* (3), *John Patrick, Kieran, Thomas Patrick.*

Callaham (393) English: most probably a respelling of Irish CALLAHAN, influenced by the common element of English habitational names, *ham.*

Callahan (19766) Irish: reduced Anglicized form of Gaelic **Ó Ceallacháin** 'descendant of *Ceallachán*', a diminutive of the personal name *Ceallach*, possibly meaning 'lover of churches', from *ceall* 'church', or (more likely) 'bright-headed', from *cen* 'head' + *lach* 'light'. This name was borne by a 10th-century king of Munster, from whom many present-day bearers of the surname claim descent.

GIVEN NAMES Irish 6%. *Brendan* (4), *Aidan*, *Brennan*, *Bridie*, *Clancy*, *Connor*, *Conor*, *Delma*, *Eamon*, *Gearold*, *Keane*, *Kieran*.

Callais (330) French: variant spelling of CALAIS.

GIVEN NAMES French 4%. *Octave*, *Orelia*, *Renette*.

Callan (1849) **1.** Irish: reduced Anglicized form of Gaelic **Ó Cathaláin** 'descendant of *Cathalán*', a personal name representing a diminutive of *Cathal* (see CAHILL). **2.** Irish and Scottish: Anglicized form of Gaelic **Mac Ailin**, a patronymic from an old Gaelic personal name derived from *ail* 'rock'. **3.** Irish and Scottish: Anglicized form of Gaelic **Mac Cailin** 'son of *Cailin*' (see COLLIN).

GIVEN NAMES Irish 5%. *Colm* (2), *Dermot* (2), *Aidan*, *Brennan*, *Donovan*, *Eamon*, *Ethna*, *Grainne*.

Callanan (789) Irish (Munster): Anglicized form of Gaelic **Ó Callanáin** 'descendant of *Callanán*', a personal name of uncertain origin.

GIVEN NAMES Irish 7%. *Brendan* (2), *Liam*, *Seamus*.

Calland (153) **1.** English (Lancashire): unexplained; possibly a variant of Scottish and Irish CALLAN. **2.** French: metonymic occupational name for someone who owned or sailed a large cargo vessel, from a Picard or southern French variant of Old French *chaland* 'large cargo vessel'. **3.** Norwegian: habitational name from any of several farmsteads in Agder and Vestlandet named Kalland or Kaland, generally from Old Norse *Kalfaland*, a compound of *kalfr* 'calf' + *land* '(piece of) land'.

Callander (313) **1.** Scottish: habitational name from Callendar near Falkirk or Callander in Perthshire. The original form and meaning of both place names is unclear, but it is certain that they were once distinct; later the former name was transferred to Perthshire under the Livingstones, Earls of Linlithgow. **2.** Swedish: probably a variant of **Carlander**, from *karl* 'man' + *-ander*, ornamental suffix from classical Greek *anēr*, *andros* 'man'. **3.** Variant spelling of German **Kalander** (see KOLANDER). **4.** In some instances, probably a variant spelling of English CALLENDER.

Callard (149) **1.** English (Devon): unexplained. **2.** Respelling of French **Calard**, a derivative of Old French *cale*, denoting a kind of close-fitting cap worn by women (see CALE). **3.** Possibly an Americanized spelling of German **Kallart** or **Kellert**, variants of KELLER.

GIVEN NAMES French 4%. *Pierre*, *Raymonde*.

Callari (213) Southern Italian (**Càllari**): probably a habitational name from Cagliari, the chief city of Sardinia, which is documented in Latin as *Callari* (Latin *Caralis*), before Sardinia was ruled by the

Aragonese. Alternatively, it may be of Greek origin.

GIVEN NAMES Italian 13%. *Antonio* (3), *Angelo* (2), *Aldo*, *Aniello*, *Giulio*, *Rocco*, *Salvatore*.

Callas (459) Greek: **1.** short form of any of several compound surnames composed with the first element *kalos* 'good', 'beautiful', for example **Kalogiannis** 'good John'. **2.** short form of the surname **Kalogeropoulos** (see CALOGERO).

Callaway (5122) English (of Norman origin): habitational name from Caillouet-Orgeville in Eure, France, named with a collective form of Old Northern French *cail(ou)* 'pebble' (see CAIL).

Calle (404) **1.** Spanish: topographic name for someone who lived in an alley, Spanish *calle* (from Latin *callis*). **2.** French: variant of **Calé** (see CALE).

GIVEN NAMES Spanish 51%. *Jose* (16), *Luis* (15), *Juan* (8), *Jorge* (7), *Manuel* (6), *Miguel* (6), *Carlos* (5), *Angel* (4), *Jaime* (4), *Raul* (4), *Fernando* (3), *Guillermo* (3).

Callegari (184) Italian: occupational name for a maker of footwear and leggings, from an agent derivative of Italian *callega* 'shoe' (Latin *caliga* 'military boot').

GIVEN NAMES Spanish 6%; Italian 5%. *Carlos* (2), *Eduardo* (2), *Andres*, *Fernando*, *Francisco*, *Lino*, *Mario*, *Zulma*; *Alessandro*, *Antonio*, *Dante*, *Luciano*, *Sal*, *Salvatore*.

Calleja (277) Spanish: topographic name from a diminutive of CALLE 'street'.

GIVEN NAMES Spanish 21%. *Jose* (8), *Angel* (3), *Emilio* (2), *Francisco* (2), *Jorge* (2), *Luis* (2), *Mario* (2), *Amalia*, *Amando*, *Ambrosio*, *Ana*, *Armando*; *Carmel* (2), *Carmela*.

Callejas (225) Spanish: variant (plural) of CALLEJA.

GIVEN NAMES Spanish 53%. *Jose* (11), *Roberto* (6), *Juan* (4), *Miguel* (4), *Ana* (3), *Luis* (3), *Mario* (3), *Orlando* (3), *Ricardo* (3), *Salvador* (3), *Carlos* (2), *Jorge* (2); *Antonio*, *Heriberto*, *Sal*.

Callejo (101) Spanish: variant of CALLEJA.

GIVEN NAMES Spanish 29%. *Carlos* (2), *Jose* (2), *Adela*, *Adelfa*, *Alfredo*, *Andres*, *Basilio*, *Beatriz*, *Carmelita*, *Catalina*, *Dionisio*, *Filipina*; *Heriberto* (2), *Lucio*.

Callen (1141) Irish and Scottish: variant spelling of CALLAN.

Callender (1744) **1.** English: occupational name for a person who finished freshly woven cloth by passing it between heavy rollers to compress the weave. The English term for such a worker, *calender*, is from Old French *calandrier*, *calandreur*, from the verb *calandrer*. **2.** Scottish: variant spelling of CALLANDER. **3.** Variant spelling of German **Kalander** (see KOLANDER).

Callens (209) Dutch and northern French: metronymic from the female personal name *Calle*, a short form of *Katelijne*, Dutch equivalent of CATHERINE.

GIVEN NAMES French 5%. *Andre*, *Pierre*, *Remi*.

Calleros (111) Spanish (Canary Islands): from the plural of *callero*, an unrecorded word which appears to derive from *calle* 'street' and is probably a topographic name meaning 'living near the street', 'neighbour', or alternatively, it could be a derivative of *callos* 'innards'.

GIVEN NAMES Spanish 52%. *Jose* (4), *Amador* (2), *Salvador* (2), *Adriana*, *Agustin*, *Alejandro*, *Anacleto*, *Anastacia*, *Armando*, *Armida*, *Cristina*, *Efrain*.

Callery (325) Irish: reduced Anglicized form of Gaelic **Mac Giolla Riabhaigh** (see McELRATH).

Calles (241) Spanish: probably a habitational name from Calles in Valencia province.

GIVEN NAMES Spanish 45%. *Jose* (15), *Jorge* (3), *Elva* (2), *Jesus* (2), *Juan* (2), *Julio* (2), *Manuela* (2), *Margarita* (2), *Mauricio* (2), *Ramon* (2), *Adilio*, *Adolfo*.

Calley (302) **1.** Irish and Scottish: reduced and altered form of McCAULEY. **2.** Manx: variant of CALLOW.

Callicoat (207) English: variant of CALLICOTT.

Callicott (210) English: habitational name from any of the numerous places (in Bedfordshire, Berkshire, Cambridgeshire, Cheshire, Northamptonshire, Warwickshire, and elsewhere) named Caldecote or Caldecott, from Old English *cald* 'cold' + *cot* 'cottage', 'dwelling'. See also CALCOTE.

Callicutt (299) English: variant of CALLICOTT.

Callier (315) French: **1.** from an Old French term denoting earthenware and, by extension, a particular type of earthenware vessel from which new wine was drunk, hence probably a metonymic occupational name for a maker of such crocks. **2.** from *caielier*, an occupational name for a chair maker, from an agent derivative of *caiel* 'chair'.

Callies (527) **1.** French (**Calliès**): habitational name from Caille, near Nice. **2.** Variant spelling of the German habitational name KALLIES.

GIVEN NAMES German 5%. *Otto* (2), *Gerhard*, *Helmuth*, *Ilse*, *Reinhold*.

Calligan (149) Irish: variant of CALLAHAN.

Calliham (126) Altered form of Irish CALLAHAN, influenced by the common element found in English habitational names, *-ham*. Compare CALLAHAM.

Callihan (1180) Irish: variant of CALLAHAN.

Callin (102) Manx: variant of CALLAN.

Callinan (256) Irish: variant spelling of CALLANAN.

GIVEN NAME Irish 7%. *Brigid*.

Callins (109) Irish: variant of COLLINS.

Callis (1458) **1.** English and Irish (of Norman or Huguenot origin): habitational name from the French port of Calais. **2.** Greek: variant of KALLIS.

Callison (1337) Scottish or Irish: reduced form of **McAlison**, a Gaelic patronymic based on the personal name *Alison* (see ALLISON).

Callister (296) Scottish: reduced form of McALLISTER.

Callon (120) French: possibly from a derivative of *calle* 'cap'.

Callow (472) **1.** English: habitational name from any of several places called Callow, including one in Herefordshire which is named with Old English *calu* 'bare' in the sense 'bare hill', Callow near Hathersage and Callow near Wirksworth, both in Derbyshire, which are named with Old English *cald* 'cold' + *hlāw* 'hill', and Calow near Chesterfield, also in Derbyshire, which is named with Old English *calu* 'bare' + *halh* 'nook of land'. **2.** English: nickname for a bald man, from Middle English *calue*, *calewe* 'bald' (Old English *calu*). **3.** Manx: Anglicized form of Gaelic **Mac Caoladhe**, a patronymic from the personal name *Caoladhe*, a derivative of *caol* 'slender', 'comely'.

Calloway (4117) English: variant spelling of CALLAWAY.

Callum (169) Scottish: reduced form of MCCALLUM.

GIVEN NAME Scottish 4%. *Moray*.

Calma (137) Spanish (Filipino): most probably from Spanish *calma* 'stillness' (of sea, ocean); 'dull'. The surname, however, is not documented in Spain.

GIVEN NAMES Spanish 41%. *Jose* (2), *Alejandro, Araceli, Armando, Bernadino, Bernardo, Cesar, Conrado, Dionisio, Edilberto, Eduardo, Esteban; Calogero, Clemente.*

Calman (100) **1.** French: respelling of German **Kahl(e)mann**, a nickname for a bald man (from Middle High German *kal(wes)* 'bald' + *man* 'man'), or possibly of German KALLMAN. **2.** altered spelling of Hungarian **Kálmán** (see KALMAN).

GIVEN NAME French 5%. *Michel*.

Calmes (375) Possibly a French topographic name for a person living on a high barren plateau, from the Celtic term *calmis*. However, the name is concentrated in MS and KY, an unlikely distribution for French.

Calnan (391) Irish: reduced form of CALLANAN.

GIVEN NAMES Irish 5%. *Brendan, Padraig*.

Calo (463) **1.** Southern Italian (**Calò**): from the personal name *Calò*, from Greek *kalos* 'beautiful', 'good'. **2.** Southern Italian: habitational name from Calò in Sicily. **3.** Galician: habitational name from a place in A Coruña province, Galicia, called Calo. **4.** possibly also Catalan (**Caló**): habitational name from El Caló, a place in Mallorca.

GIVEN NAMES Italian 18%; Spanish 12%. *Rocco* (5), *Antonio* (2), *Carmelo* (2), *Sal* (2), *Salvatore* (2), *Aida, Alberto, Ambrosio, Edo, Franco, Gaetano, Gerardo, Giovanni, Giuseppe, Ireneo, Lorenzo; Domingo* (2), *Jose* (2), *Juana* (2), *Marcial* (2), *Carlos, Enrique, Fernando*.

Calogero (228) **1.** Southern Italian: from the personal name *Calogero* (from Greek *Kalogeros*, literally 'handsome-old'). In Sicily especially this name was popularized by the cult of St. Calogero, a 5th-century martyr from Constantinople, who had stayed on the island for a time. **2.** Possibly a short form of any of various Greek family names based on the personal name *Kalogeros* (see 1), as for example **Kalogeropoulos** (with the patronymic suffix *-poulos*), **Kalogerogiannis** (with the personal name *Giannis* 'John'), **Kalogeromikhalis** (with the personal name *Mikhalis* 'Michael'). Compare CALLAS.

GIVEN NAMES Italian 10%; Spanish 6%; French 4%. *Agatino, Carmela, Cesare, Dante, Giorgio, Mario, Raffaele, Rosario, Sirio; Pablo* (2); *Pascal* (3).

Calpin (139) Scottish: reduced form of **McAlpin**, a variant of McALPINE.

Caltabiano (189) Italian: habitational name from a place in Sicily named Calatabiano, from Arabic *qal'at* 'fortress' + (possibly) *al-bayān* 'announcement'.

GIVEN NAMES Italian 34%. *Salvatore* (6), *Angelo* (4), *Carmelo* (3), *Carmine* (2), *Agatino, Antonio, Cosimo, Gaeton, Mario, Pietro, Rosario, Sal, Santo*.

Caltagirone (175) Italian: habitational name from a place called Caltagirone in Catania province, Sicily.

GIVEN NAMES Italian 27%. *Paolo* (4), *Salvatore* (2), *Angelo, Calogero, Gaetano, Giuseppina, Leopoldo, Mario, Pasquale, Ricardo*.

Calton (692) English: habitational name from either of two places, in Staffordshire and North Yorkshire, named Calton, from Old English *calf* 'calf' + *tūn* 'farmstead', 'settlement'. There are also numerous minor places so named, notably in Yorkshire and Derbyshire, and they may also have given rise to the surname in some instances.

Caltrider (158) Americanized form of German **Kaltritter** (literally 'cold knight'), altered by folk etymology from **Kaltreuter**, a topographic name from Middle High German *kalt* 'cold' + *riute* 'clearing for settlement or farming'.

Calvanese (116) Italian: habitational name for someone from any of the places called Calvano, probably named with the personal name **Galvano**.

GIVEN NAMES Italian 12%. *Ciro, Guiseppe, Salvatore*.

Calvano (194) Italian: perhaps from a variant of the personal name *Galvano*, from Latin *Galbanus* (see GALVAN) or a habitational name from a place named with this word. Compare CALVANESE.

GIVEN NAMES Italian 22%; Spanish 7%. *Emilio* (2), *Flavio* (2), *Silvia* (2), *Antonio, Donato, Enrico, Salvatore; Salvador* (3), *Veneranda*.

Calver (125) English (mainly East Anglia): **1.** habitational name from Calver in Derbyshire, named in Old English with *calf* 'calf' + *ofer* 'slope', 'ridge'. **2.** variant of CALVERT.

Calverley (228) English: habitational name from Calverley in West Yorkshire, named with Old English *calfra* (genitive plural of *calf* 'calf') + *lēah* 'woodland clearing'.

Calvert (6722) English: occupational name from Middle English *calfhirde*, from Old English (Anglian) *calf* 'calf' + *hierde* 'herdsman'.

Calvery (125) **1.** English: reduced form of CALVERLEY. **2.** Possibly an Americanized spelling of German **Kälberer** (see KALBERER).

Calvetti (132) Italian: diminutive of CALVO.

GIVEN NAMES Italian 12%; Spanish 7%. *Enrico* (2), *Alfredo, Angelo, Arturo, Evo; Ruben* (2), *Jose, Juan Luis, Luis, Milagros*.

Calvey (205) **1.** Irish: shortened Anglicized form of **McCalvey**, which is recorded as a variant Anglicized form of Gaelic **Mac Giolla Bhuidhe** (see McELWEE), although Woulfe treats it as an Anglicized form of Gaelic **Mac an Chalbhaigh**, possibly from *calbhach* 'bald'. **2.** In some cases possibly an Americanized spelling of the southern French surname **Calvé**, a nickname from Old Occitan *calv* 'bald'.

Calvi (249) Italian: **1.** patronymic or plural form of CALVO. **2.** habitational name from Calvi in Benevento province.

GIVEN NAMES Italian 29%. *Dante* (3), *Rocco* (3), *Antonio* (2), *Romolo* (2), *Salvatore* (2), *Aldo, Carlo, Carmela, Ciro, Giuseppe, Lorenzo, Luigi, Mario, Rico*.

Calvillo (778) Spanish: from *calvo* 'bald', either a nickname for a bald man or a topographic name in the sense 'barren tract of land'.

GIVEN NAMES Spanish 47%. *Jose* (23), *Francisco* (13), *Luis* (12), *Jesus* (10), *Manuel* (10), *Juan* (9), *Carlos* (6), *Sergio* (6), *Miguel* (5), *Ramon* (5), *Raul* (5), *Armando* (4).

Calvin (2733) **1.** Southern French: nickname for a bald man, from a diminutive of Old Occitan *calv* 'bald' (from Latin *calvus*). **2.** Spanish (**Calvín**): from a regional variant of a diminutive of *calvo* 'bald'.

Calvo (1063) Spanish, Portuguese, and Italian: nickname for a bald-headed man, from *calvo* 'bald' (Latin *calvus*).

GIVEN NAMES Spanish 40%; Portuguese 9%; Italian 5%. *Jose* (25), *Juan* (21), *Jorge* (16), *Manuel* (11), *Raul* (9), *Luis* (7), *Carlos* (6), *Fernando* (6), *Miguel* (6), *Enrique* (5), *Ramon* (5), *Eduardo* (4); *Wenceslao*;

Antonio (5), *Marco* (5), *Salvatore* (4), *Angelo, Carmela, Dario, Fausto, Federico, Giraldo, Rocco, Sebastiano, Vincenzo.*

Calzada (405) Spanish: habitational name from any of numerous places called Calzada or La Calzada, from *calzada* 'paved road' (Latin *calciata via*, from *calx* 'stone').

GIVEN NAMES Spanish 47%. *Jose* (12), *Juan* (9), *Angel* (4), *Francisco* (4), *Jesus* (4), *Rafael* (4), *Ana* (3), *Ernesto* (3), *Guillermo* (3), *Humberto* (3), *Manuel* (3), *Ramon* (3).

Calzadilla (125) Spanish: habitational name from any of the places called Calzadilla or La Calzadilla, from a diminutive of *calzada* 'paved road', as for example Calzadilla in Cáceres province.

GIVEN NAMES Spanish 52%. *Raul* (4), *Carlos* (3), *Felipe* (3), *Jose* (3), *Luis* (3), *Francisco* (2), *Jorge* (2), *Rafael* (2), *Ramon* (2), *Ana, Angel, Armando; Antonio* (2), *Giovanni, Leonardo, Marco, Mauro.*

Cam (193) **1.** Vietnamese: unexplained. **2.** English (of Norman origin): habitational name from Caen in Calvados, France (see CAIN). **3.** English: habitational name from Cam in Gloucestershire. **4.** Czech (**Čam**): from the personal name *Čamir*.

GIVEN NAMES Vietnamese 22%; Chinese 7%. *Ba, Chau, Coung, Cun, Cuong, Duc, Giao, Hai, Hieu, Hoa, Hoanh, Hung, Kinh Van; Kang, Wing, Ying, Young.*

Camacho (5424) Portuguese: unexplained. This very common Portuguese surname seems to have originated in Andalusia, Spain.

GIVEN NAMES Spanish 47%; Portuguese 10%. *Jose* (136), *Juan* (64), *Luis* (63), *Carlos* (57), *Manuel* (36), *Francisco* (35), *Jorge* (35), *Jesus* (34), *Pedro* (32), *Angel* (29), *Mario* (26), *Miguel* (24); *Agostinho, Anatolio, Vasco.*

Camara (1346) Portuguese (**(da) Câmara**) and Spanish (**Cámara**): from *cámara* '(main) room' (from Latin *camera*), hence an occupational name for a courtier or servant who had access to the private living quarters of a king or noble.

GIVEN NAMES Spanish 18%; Portuguese 9%; African 4%. *Manuel* (32), *Carlos* (13), *Jose* (12), *Jorge* (8), *Ana* (5), *Francisco* (5), *Luis* (5), *Pedro* (4), *Juan* (3), *Alejandro* (2), *Armando* (2), *Augusto* (2); *Joao* (5), *Duarte* (2), *Joaquim* (2), *Afonso, Heitor, Manoel, Marcio, Messias; Mamadou* (4), *Boubacar* (3), *Mamady* (3), *Aboubacar* (2), *Amadou* (2), *Bakary* (2), *Fatou* (2), *Ousmane* (2), *Babacar, Balla, Brahima, Hamidou.*

Camarata (303) Italian: variant of Sicilian CAMMARATA.

GIVEN NAMES Italian 5%. *Angelo, Nunzio, Ricci, Salvatore.*

Camarda (354) Southern Italian (Sicily): habitational name from Camarda in Sicily, named with *camarda* 'shrub', possibly from Greek *kamarda*, denoting a type of tent.

GIVEN NAMES Italian 20%. *Salvatore* (6), *Angelo* (3), *Vito* (2), *Antonio, Carlo, Cosmo, Gaetano, Giacomo, Mattia, Nunzio, Onofrio.*

Camardo (142) Southern Italian: variant of CAMARDA.

GIVEN NAMES Italian 12%. *Camillo, Nicola, Reno.*

Camarena (741) Spanish: habitational name from Camarena in Toledo province or Camarena de la Sierra in Teruel.

GIVEN NAMES Spanish 52%. *Jose* (27), *Juan* (14), *Carlos* (13), *Jesus* (10), *Francisco* (9), *Manuel* (9), *Armando* (6), *Jorge* (6), *Andres* (5), *Pedro* (5), *Ramon* (5), *Alfonso* (4).

Camargo (704) Spanish: habitational name for someone from a place in Andalusia called Camargo.

GIVEN NAMES Spanish 50%. *Jose* (17), *Carlos* (13), *Jaime* (9), *Mario* (8), *Miguel* (7), *Salvador* (7), *Francisco* (6), *Juan* (6), *Pedro* (6), *Manuel* (5), *Sergio* (5), *Luis* (4); *Marco* (5), *Antonio* (4), *Ciro* (3), *Bartolo, Dante, Filiberto, Lorenzo, Lucio.*

Camarillo (937) Spanish: unexplained, but most probably from a derivative of *cámara* 'chamber', 'room'.

GIVEN NAMES Spanish 47%. *Jose* (17), *Jesus* (15), *Juan* (10), *Manuel* (10), *Miguel* (7), *Raul* (7), *Armando* (6), *Ramon* (6), *Carlos* (5), *Enrique* (5), *Fernando* (5), *Francisco* (5).

Camba (104) **1.** Southern French: nickname for someone with long legs, from Occitan *cambe, camba* 'leg', a cognate of French *jambe*. **2.** Galician: habitational name from any of the places called Camba in Galicia.

GIVEN NAMES Spanish 41%. *Arsenia* (2), *Gregorio* (2), *Guadalupe* (2), *Jorge* (2), *Aurelio, Domingo, Eriberto, Fernando, Guillermo, Imelda, Jaime, Javier.*

Cambareri (126) Italian: variant of **Cammareri**, an occupational name from Sicilian *cammareri* 'servant'. Compare CHAMBERS.

GIVEN NAMES Italian 48%. *Rocco* (10), *Antonio* (4), *Carmelo* (3), *Giuseppe* (3), *Antonino* (2), *Fortunato* (2), *Francesca* (2), *Francesco* (2), *Giovanni* (2), *Salvatore* (2), *Carmela, Cosmo, Rosario.*

Cambell (229) variant spelling of Scottish CAMPBELL.

Camber (107) English: variant of COMER.

Cambio (133) Italian (Sicily): from a short form of the personal name *Buoncambio*, a compound of *buono* 'good' + *cambio* 'change' (from Latin *cambiare*); this was an omen name often bestowed on a child born soon after the death of a sibling.

GIVEN NAMES Italian 25%. *Orlando* (2), *Angelo, Antonio, Carmine, Cosmo, Domenic, Pasco, Vito.*

Camblin (132) Scottish and Irish: perhaps a variant of CAMPLIN.

Cambra (427) **1.** Catalan, Galician, and Portuguese: from Catalan *cambra*, a variant

of Galician and Spanish **Cámara** or a variant of Portuguese **Câmara** (see CAMARA). **2.** Galician and Portuguese: habitational name from any of several places called Cambra, for example in Viseu, Portugal.

GIVEN NAME French 4%. *Celestine.*

Cambre (392) French: Norman or Picard occupational name denoting someone who worked in the private quarters of his master, rather than the public halls of the manor, from *c(h)ambre* 'room'.

GIVEN NAMES French 5%. *Andre, Caliste, Francois, Lucien.*

Cambria (324) Italian (Sicily): habitational name from a place in Sicily called Cambria, probably of Arabic origin.

GIVEN NAMES Italian 18%. *Salvatore* (4), *Carmine* (2), *Angelo, Carmel, Cosimo, Gaetano, Gasper, Nino, Pietro, Sal, Santino.*

Cambridge (400) **1.** Irish: reduced form of MCCAMBRIDGE. **2.** English: habitational name for someone from either of two places called Cambridge: one in Gloucestershire, the other in Cambridgeshire (the university city). Until the late 14th century the latter was known as *Cantebrigie* 'bridge on the (river) Granta', from a Celtic river name meaning 'marshy river'. Under Norman influence *Granta-* became *Cam-*. It seems likely, therefore, that the surname derives mainly from the much smaller place in Gloucestershire, recorded as *Cambrigga* (1200–10), and named for the Cam, a Celtic river name meaning 'crooked', 'winding'.

Cambron (732) **1.** Spanish (**Cambrón**): habitational name from places in the provinces of Cácares and Murcia called Cambrón. **2.** French: from a diminutive of *c(h)ambre* 'room' (see CAMBRE). **3.** French: habitational name from places in Somme and Aisne called Cambron.

Camburn (203) English: probably a habitational name from Camborne in Cornwall, named with Cornish *camm* 'crooked' + *bronn* 'hill'.

Camby (100) English: unexplained; perhaps of French origin, a variant of **Cambe**, a nickname for someone with a limp or other peculiarity of the leg, from a southern French form of *jambe* 'leg'.

Camden (1082) English: possibly a habitational name from Broad Campden or Chipping Campden in Gloucestershire, both named with Old English *camp* 'enclosure' + *denu* 'valley'.

Camejo (194) Spanish (Canary Islands) and Portuguese: unexplained.

GIVEN NAMES Spanish 57%. *Armando* (8), *Pedro* (6), *Raul* (6), *Carlos* (5), *Jose* (5), *Jorge* (3), *Justo* (3), *Orlando* (3), *Ramon* (3), *Agustin* (2), *Eduardo* (2), *Francisco* (2).

Camel (187) **1.** English and French: from the word denoting the animal, Norman French *came(i)l*, Latin *camelus*, classical

Greek *kamēlos*. The surname may have arisen from a nickname denoting a clumsy or ill-tempered person. It may also be a habitational name for someone who lived at a house with a sign depicting a camel. **2.** English: from an assimilated pronunciation of CAMPBELL. **3.** English: possibly a habitational name from Queen Camel and West Camel in Somerset, *Camel(le)* in Domesday Book (1086), possibly a Celtic name from *canto-* 'border', 'district' and *mēl* 'bare hill'. **4.** Probably an Americanized spelling of KAMEL.
GIVEN NAMES French 5%. *Andre, Napoleon, Patrice.*

Camelio (112) Italian: from late Greek *khamaileos*, denoting a plant belonging to the genus *Pseudolentiscus*.
GIVEN NAMES Italian 16%. *Cosmo* (2), *Attilio, Carmine, Romeo.*

Camenzind (101) Swiss German: perhaps an occupational name for a builder of fireplaces and chimneys or a derogatory nickname for someone who allowed his chimney to catch fire (for which the owner was fined), from Middle High German *kamen* 'chimney', 'fireplace' + the base of the agent noun from the verb *zünden* 'to set on fire', 'burn'.
GIVEN NAMES German 13%. *Franz* (3), *Hans, Kurt.*

Camerer (215) Americanized form of the German occupational name KAMMERER.

Camerino (102) **1.** Italian: habitational name from a place in Macerata province called Camerino (Latin *Camerinum*). **2.** Spanish: unexplained, but possibly from a derivative of *cámara* 'chamber', 'room'.
GIVEN NAMES Spanish 12%; Italian 4%. *Nestor* (3), *Alberto, Carlos, Evaristo, Fernando, Rolando, Teresita.*

Camero (189) Spanish: habitational name from Camero (Camero Viejo, Camero Nuevo), a mountainous area in the Rioja region.
GIVEN NAMES Spanish 38%. *Luis* (4), *Alfredo* (3), *Francisco* (3), *Roberto* (3), *Alberto* (2), *Cresencio* (2), *Eduardo* (2), *Jose* (2), *Mario* (2), *Bernabe, Celestina, Cesar; Federico, Leonardo, Lorenzo, Sylvana.*

Cameron (19196) Scottish: **1.** as a Highland clan name it is from a nickname from Gaelic *cam* 'crooked', 'bent' + *sròn* 'nose'. **2.** in the Lowlands it is also a habitational name from any of various places called Cameron, especially in Fife.

Camerota (116) Southern Italian: from Greek *Kamerōtēs*, habitational name from Camerota in Salerno province.
GIVEN NAMES Italian 24%. *Ciro* (3), *Salvatore* (2), *Angelo, Carmel, Emilio, Pasquale.*

Camfield (261) English: probably a variant of CANFIELD.

Camhi (189) Jewish (Sephardic): metonymic occupational or nickname from Hebrew *kamkhi* 'of wheat'.

GIVEN NAMES Jewish 13%. *Hyman* (2), *Yael* (2), *Emanuel, Sol.*

Camille (174) French: from the personal name *Camille*, derived from the Latin name *Camillus*, which denoted a youth of noble birth who helped the priest with sacrifices.
GIVEN NAMES French 18%. *Calixte, Chantal, Georges, Jacques, Jean Francois, Jean-Claude, Marie Josette, Pascal, Rodrigue, Serge, Yves.*

Camilleri (500) Southern Italian (Sicilian): occupational name for a camel driver, from medieval Latin *camelarius*, medieval Greek *kamēlarios*.
GIVEN NAMES Italian 12%. *Angelo* (3), *Salvatore* (3), *Carmel* (2), *Alessio, Carmelo, Cesare, Domenico, Francesca, Giuseppe, Luigi, Nunzio, Stefano.*

Camilli (231) Italian: patronymic or plural form of CAMILLO.
GIVEN NAMES Italian 16%; Spanish 6%. *Emilio* (2), *Guido* (2), *Carmelo, Dante, Elio, Fabio, Pasquale, Reno; Ramon* (2), *Helio, Jorge, Navarro.*

Camillo (285) Italian: from the personal name *Camillo*, a derivative of Latin *Camillus*, from a term which originally denoted a youth of noble birth who assisted at sacrifices.
GIVEN NAMES Italian 11%; French 5%. *Carmine* (2), *Pasquale* (2), *Angelo, Antonio, Lorenzo, Nuncio, Rocco; Michel* (2), *Armand, Henri.*

Camilo (152) Spanish and Portuguese: from the personal name *Camilo*, a derivative of Latin *Camillus* (see Italian CAMILLO).
GIVEN NAMES Spanish 50%; Portuguese 12%. *Jose* (10), *Luis* (3), *Juan* (2), *Manuel* (2), *Marta* (2), *Noemi* (2), *Rafael* (2), *Alina, Angel, Bienvenida, Caonabo, Cayetano; Joaquim; Clemente, Clementina, Federico, Severino.*

Caminiti (351) Italian: habitational name for someone from Camini in Calabria.
GIVEN NAMES Italian 18%. *Carmelo* (4), *Natale* (3), *Angelo* (2), *Antonio* (2), *Cosmo* (2), *Domenic* (2), *Rocco* (2), *Salvatore* (2), *Carmela, Carmine, Grazia.*

Camino (229) **1.** Spanish: topographic name for someone who lived by a thoroughfare, from *camin* 'path', 'way' (from Late Latin *caminus*), or a habitational name from any of numerous places named with this word. **2.** Italian: topographic name from *camino* 'root', 'hearth', 'furnace', or 'olive press'.
GIVEN NAMES Spanish 25%; Italian 9%. *Jose* (7), *Angel* (2), *Bernardo* (2), *Francisco* (2), *Manuel* (2), *Miguel* (2), *Adolfo, Alfonso, Alfredo, Ana, Asuncion, Carlos; Carmine* (2), *Domenic* (2), *Ciriaco, Egidio, Gino, Saverio.*

Camire (394) Americanized spelling of German KAMMEYER or the variant **Kammeier**.
GIVEN NAMES French 16%. *Lucien* (4), *Marcel* (2), *Adrien, Alcide, Andre, Armand,*

Elphege, Emile, Henri, Honore, Laurette, Normand.

Camisa (126) Southern Italian, Spanish, and Portuguese: from Italian *camicia*, Spanish and Portuguese *camisa* 'shirt' (from Latin *camisia*), probably applied as an occupational name for a shirt-maker.
GIVEN NAMES Italian 11%. *Aldo, Matteo, Umberto.*

Camlin (121) Scottish and Irish: perhaps a variant of CAMPLIN. Compare CAMBLIN.

Camm (213) **1.** English (of Norman origin): habitational name for someone from Caen in Normandy, France. **2.** English: habitational name from Cam in Gloucestershire, named for the Cam river, a Celtic river name meaning 'crooked', 'winding'. **3.** Scottish and Welsh: possibly a nickname from Gaelic and Welsh *cam* 'bent', 'crooked', 'cross-eyed'. **4.** Americanized spelling of German KAMM.

Cammack (981) **1.** Irish: reduced form of McCAMMACK. **2.** English: habitational name from Cammock in Settle, North Yorkshire, possibly a Celtic name meaning 'crooked one', referring to a lofty hill in a bend of the Ribble river. **3.** English: perhaps a nickname for a prickly person, from Old English *cammoc* 'thorny shrub'.

Cammarano (227) Italian: habitational name from a place named Cammarano or Cammarana.
GIVEN NAMES Italian 16%. *Angelo, Arcangelo, Carmelo, Gaetano, Giovanni, Mauro, Pompeo, Salvator.*

Cammarata (782) Southern Italian (Sicily): habitational name from any of various places in Sicily named Cammarata, from Latin *cameratus* 'vaulted', as for example in Agrigento province.
GIVEN NAMES Italian 18%. *Angelo* (12), *Sal* (7), *Rocco* (5), *Salvatore* (4), *Antonino* (2), *Nunzio* (2), *Santo* (2), *Bartolo, Biagio, Carmelo, Domenic, Domenica.*

Cammarota (173) Southern Italian: habitational name for someone from any of various places called Camara, from an adjectival form of the place name.
GIVEN NAMES Italian 19%. *Aldo* (2), *Angelo* (2), *Salvatore* (2), *Carmine, Concetta, Giuseppe, Guerino, Peppino, Rocco, Savino.*

Cammer (152) **1.** English: variant of COMER. **2.** Respelling of German KAMMER.

Cammisa (132) Southern Italian: from Sicilian dialect *cammisa* 'shirt', 'jacket', presumably applied as a metonymic occupational name for a maker of such garments.
GIVEN NAMES Italian 13%. *Romeo* (2), *Agostino, Guido, Marco, Pasquale.*

Cammon (223) Scottish and Irish: reduced form of McCAMMON.
GIVEN NAMES French 6%. *Andre, Marcel, Oneil.*

Camozzi (119) Italian: of uncertain derivation, perhaps from the personal name *Comozzi*, a dialect diminutive of *Giacomo*, Italian equivalent of JAMES.
GIVEN NAMES Italian 5%. *Angelo* (2), *Umberto*.

Camp (11717) **1.** Dutch (also **van den Camp**) and North German: from *de camp* 'the field' (from Latin *campus* 'plain'), hence a topographic name or a status name denoting a small farmer or peasant (see KAMP). **2.** French: Norman, Picard, or southern form of CHAMP.

Campa (585) **1.** Spanish, Galician, and Asturian-Leonese: habitational name from any of various places named with *campa* 'ditch', for example Campa in Lugo and Biscay provinces, or La Campa in Asturies. **2.** Slovenian (**Čampa**): see CHAMPA.
GIVEN NAMES Spanish 41%. *Jose* (18), *Carlos* (7), *Jesus* (5), *Jorge* (5), *Juan* (5), *Manuel* (4), *Marcelino* (4), *Adriana* (3), *Andres* (3), *Blanca* (3), *Fernando* (3), *Francisco* (3).

Campagna (1603) Italian: habitational name from any of numerous places called Campagna.
GIVEN NAMES Italian 13%. *Salvatore* (12), *Angelo* (5), *Rocco* (4), *Antonio* (2), *Gaetano* (2), *Guido* (2), *Nicola* (2), *Sal* (2), *Saverio* (2), *Silvio* (2), *Vincenzo* (2), *Adamo*.

Campana (1059) Italian and Spanish: metonymic occupational name for a bell-ringer or bell-maker, from Italian and Spanish *campana* 'bell' (abbreviated from the Latin phrase *vasa campana* 'Campanian vessels', since bells were first produced in Campania).
GIVEN NAMES Italian 21%; Spanish 14%. *Mario* (6), *Angelo* (5), *Gino* (3), *Alfonso* (2), *Antonio* (2), *Biagio* (2), *Caesar* (2), *Dino* (2), *Falco* (2), *Sisto* (2), *Alessandra*, *Amerigo*, *Carlo*, *Cosmo*; *Manuel* (4), *Jose* (3), *Jorge* (2), *Luis* (2), *Roberto* (2), *Agustin*, *Amado*.

Campanale (147) Italian (Apulia): unexplained; perhaps a variant of CAMPANILE.
GIVEN NAMES Italian 19%. *Rocco* (4), *Vito* (2), *Cosimo*, *Luigi*, *Marco*, *Salvatore*.

Campanaro (342) Southern Italian: **1.** occupational name for a bell ringer, sexton, or sacristan, from an agent derivative of *campana* 'bell'. **2.** habitational name from a place named Campanaro, for example in Sicily and Campania.
GIVEN NAMES Italian 20%; Spanish 6%. *Mario* (4), *Alfonso* (3), *Alberico* (2), *Caesar*, *Domenica*, *Domenico*, *Filomena*, *Rocco*; *Luis*, *Luz*, *Raul*.

Campanella (1022) Italian: from a diminutive of *campana* 'bell', applied as a metonymic occupational name for a maker of small bells or handbells, or as a means of distinguishing one branch or member of a family called CAMPANA from another.
GIVEN NAMES Italian 14%. *Angelo* (9), *Salvatore* (8), *Santo* (5), *Sal* (4), *Rocco* (3), *Calogero* (2), *Cosmo* (2), *Domenic* (2), *Vito* (2), *Aldo*, *Annamarie*, *Antonio*.

Campanelli (591) Italian: patronymic or plural form of CAMPANELLA.
GIVEN NAMES Italian 17%. *Rocco* (7), *Salvatore* (3), *Vito* (3), *Angelo* (2), *Grazio* (2), *Marco* (2), *Sal* (2), *Anello*, *Canio*, *Carmela*, *Domenico*, *Donato*.

Campanile (329) Italian (Bari): topographic name for someone who lived by a bell tower, *campanile*, or a habitational name from a place named for its bell tower.
GIVEN NAMES Italian 22%. *Angelo* (4), *Rocco* (4), *Vito* (3), *Giovanni* (2), *Luigi* (2), *Sante* (2), *Caesar*, *Dario*, *Gaetano*, *Giacomo*, *Guido*, *Leonardo*.

Campano (163) **1.** Southern Italian: regional name from medieval Greek *kampanos* 'from Campania'. **2.** Spanish: either a habitational name from Campano in Cádiz province or from *campano* 'cow bell', hence by metonymy an occupational name for a cowherd.
GIVEN NAMES Italian 16%; Spanish 12%; French 7%. *Angelo* (2), *Pasco* (2), *Domenic*, *Giacomo*, *Pasquale*, *Saverio*; *Sixto* (3), *Manuel* (2), *Nicanor* (2), *Catalina*, *Emilio*, *Luis*, *Marcelo*, *Mario*, *Noemi*, *Ricardo*; *Gaston* (2), *Marcell*.

Campany (132) English (of Norman origin): variant of **Champney**, a regional name for someone from Champagne, France, from Old French *Champeneis*.

Campau (259) Variant of French CAMPEAU, itself a variant of CHAMPEAU.

Campbell (132126) **1.** Scottish: nickname from Gaelic *cam* 'crooked', 'bent' + *beul* 'mouth'. The surname was often represented in Latin documents as *de bello campo* 'of the fair field', which led to the name sometimes being 'translated' into Anglo-Norman French as BEAUCHAMP. **2.** In New England documents, Campbell sometimes occurs as a representation of the French name HAMEL.
FOREBEARS The founder of the clan Campbell (and the bearer of the nickname) was Gillespie Ó Duibhne, who lived at the beginning of the 13th century. He married Eva Ó Duibhne, heiress of Lochow, and from them descended a long line of Lairds of Lochow and immensely powerful Scottish aristocrats, including the dukes of Argyll. For centuries they wielded enormous power in Scotland. As with many Highland Scottish clan names, the surname was adopted not merely by descendants but also retainers of the original clan founders. John Campbell (1653–1727/8), born in Scotland, was postmaster general of Boston and published the *Boston News-Letter* (1704–22), the first continuously published newspaper in America.

Campe (136) German: variant spelling of KAMPE.

Campeau (492) French: Norman or Picard variant of CHAMPEAU.

FOREBEARS Etienne Campeau and Catherine Paulo were married in Montreal in 1663, where they raised fourteen children. Two of their sons, Michel and Jacques, with their families, joined the Sieur de Cadillac in the extension of New France to the Detroit area in 1707–08. Descendants of another son, François, followed later to what is now MI and WI. It is believed that all U.S. bearers of the name Campeau are descended from these three brothers.
GIVEN NAMES French 13%. *Normand* (3), *Gilles* (2), *Jacques* (2), *Marcel* (2), *Yves* (2), *Alain*, *Benoit*, *Fernand*, *Georges*, *Germain*, *Gillis*, *Lucien*.

Campen (239) **1.** Dutch and North German: variant of KAMPEN. **2.** English (Essex; of Norman origin): habitational name from any of several places in Pas-de-Calais and elsewhere in France named Campagne, or from a Norman form of a regional name from Champagne in northeastern France.

Camper (1061) Respelling of German KAMPER or **Kämpfer** (see KAMPFER). The surname **Camper** is recorded in England, in the London and Essex area, in the 19th century; its origin is uncertain, but it may have been taken there from continental Europe.

Campfield (396) English: possibly a variant of CANFIELD.

Campi (216) Italian: **1.** habitational name from any of various places called Campi or named with this word, the plural of *campo* 'field' (see CAMPO). **2.** (**Campì**): southern habitational name from any of various places named or named with Campì, ultimately also from Latin *campus*.
GIVEN NAMES Italian 8%. *Florio* (2), *Domenic*, *Enrico*, *Silvio*.

Campillo (118) Spanish: habitational name from any of various places called Campillo, from a diminutive of *campo* 'field', 'country(side)' (see CAMPO).
GIVEN NAMES Spanish 39%; French 4%. *Jose* (3), *Pedro* (3), *Carlos* (2), *Luis* (2), *Abelardo*, *Acencion*, *Adriana*, *Beatriz*, *Benito*, *Celedonio*, *Graciela*, *Horacio*; *Georges*, *Lucien*.

Campion (1488) English (of Norman origin) and French: status name for a professional champion (see CHAMPION, KEMP), from the Norman French form *campion*.
GIVEN NAMES Irish 4%. *Ronan* (2), *Conley*.

Campione (381) Italian: **1.** occupational name for a professional champion, from Late Latin *campio*, genitive *campiōnis* (see CHAMPION, and compare KEMP). **2.** habitational name from a place called Campione, of which there is one in Lombardy.
GIVEN NAMES Italian 19%. *Angelo* (3), *Salvatore* (3), *Alfio*, *Antonino*, *Carlo*, *Carmela*, *Carmelo*, *Carmine*, *Cataldo*, *Gino*, *Girolamo*, *Giuseppe*.

Campisano (148) Southern Italian (Sicily and Calabria): nickname for a country dweller, from a derivative of CAMPO.
GIVEN NAMES Italian 10%. *Antonio, Caterina, Vito.*

Campise (231) Italian: nickname for a country dweller, from a derivative of CAMPO.
GIVEN NAMES Italian 11%. *Gasper* (2), *Rocco* (2), *Gino, Sal, Salvatore.*

Campisi (657) Southern Italian: **1.** patronymic or plural form of CAMPISE. **2.** occupational name from Sicilian *campisi* 'bowman'.
GIVEN NAMES Italian 24%. *Angelo* (8), *Salvatore* (5), *Vito* (5), *Luciano* (3), *Rosario* (3), *Baldassare* (2), *Carlo* (2), *Gaetano* (2), *Orlando* (2), *Sal* (2), *Antonio, Carmine, Corrado, Cosmo, Isidoro, Norberto, Placido.*

Campitelli (128) Italian: probably a habitational name from any of various places called Campitelli or Campitello; otherwise possibly from a diminutive of **Campiti**, an adjectival form of CAMPO.
GIVEN NAMES Italian 25%. *Enrico* (2), *Antonio, Carlo, Florentino, Guido, Oswaldo, Reinaldo.*

Camplin (155) English: from Anglo-Norman French, Middle English *camelin* 'camel' (Latin *camelinus*, a derivative of *camelus*), hence a metonymic occupational name for a maker or seller of camel-hair cloth. Compare CAMEL.

Campman (115) Respelling of North German **Kampmann**, a topographic name for someone who lived by a field or enclosure, Low German *Kamp*.
GIVEN NAMES German 6%. *Ingeborg, Kurt.*

Campo (1811) **1.** Italian and Spanish: habitational name from any of numerous places named with *campo* 'field', 'country(side)', a derivative of Latin *campus* 'plain'. **2.** Possibly a respelling of French CAMPEAU.
GIVEN NAMES Italian 14%; Spanish 10%. *Salvatore* (14), *Antonio* (7), *Gaspare* (7), *Sal* (7), *Angelo* (4), *Carmine* (4), *Vito* (4), *Alfredo* (3), *Giuseppe* (2), *Marco* (2), *Rocco* (2), *Santino* (2), *Attilio; Manuel* (8), *Carlos* (7), *Jose* (6), *Juan* (6), *Fernando* (5), *Ana* (3), *Enrique* (3), *Luis* (3), *Eduardo* (2), *Francisco* (2).

Campobasso (127) Italian: habitational name from Campobasso in Molise, named with *campo* 'field' + *basso* 'low'.
GIVEN NAMES Italian 19%. *Vito* (3), *Enrico* (2), *Agostino, Carina, Costantino, Domenico, Gaetano, Geno.*

Campodonico (107) Italian (Genoa): habitational name from a place in the Apennines called Campodonico.
GIVEN NAMES Spanish 9%; Italian 8%. *Luis* (3), *Julio, Liliana, Ricardo; Aldo, Lia, Marco, Sal, Salvatore.*

Campoli (229) Italian: habitational name from any of various places in central and southern Italy named with Campoli or Campolo, from Latin *campulus* 'little field', as for example Campoli Appennino in Frosinone province or Campoli del Monte Taburno in Benevento.
GIVEN NAMES Italian 17%. *Salvatore* (3), *Luigi* (2), *Rocco* (2), *Duilio, Gabriele, Lorenzo, Pasquale, Remo.*

Campolo (134) Italian (Calabria): from medieval Latin *campulus* 'little field', a diminutive of CAMPO.
GIVEN NAMES Italian 8%. *Fortunato, Silvio.*

Campopiano (149) Italian: topographic name from *campo* 'field' + *piano* 'flat' (from Latin *planus*) or a habitational name from Campo Piano in Laviano, near Salerno.
GIVEN NAMES Italian 19%. *Remo* (4), *Angelo* (2), *Domenic, Franca, Onorato, Siena.*

Camporeale (109) Italian: habitational name from a place called Camporeale in Sicily.
GIVEN NAMES Italian 26%. *Antonio* (2), *Ignazio* (2), *Angelo, Antonietta, Corrado, Fortunato, Nilda, Sal.*

Campos (8129) Portuguese: topographic name from *campos* 'fields', denoting someone who lived in the countryside as opposed to a town.
GIVEN NAMES Spanish 49%; Portuguese 10%. *Jose* (243), *Juan* (101), *Carlos* (81), *Manuel* (75), *Luis* (65), *Jesus* (56), *Francisco* (53), *Pedro* (50), *Miguel* (42), *Jorge* (41), *Ramon* (41), *Mario* (39); *Joao* (4), *Joaquim* (3), *Agostinho* (2), *Paulo* (2), *Goncalo, Gonsalo, Ligia, Marcio, Omero, Vasco.*

Campoverde (117) Spanish and Galician: habitational name from any of various places named Campoverde ('green field'), especially in Galicia. This is a common surname in Ecuador and Mexico.
GIVEN NAMES Spanish 57%; Italian 7%. *Angel* (7), *Humberto* (3), *Jose* (3), *Luis* (3), *Vicente* (3), *Agueda* (2), *Blanca* (2), *Carlos* (2), *Francisco* (2), *Jesus* (2), *Manuel* (2), *Adolpho; Ceasar, Cesario, Flavio.*

Campoy (104) Spanish: unexplained, but most probably from a derivative of *campo* 'field'. This is a frequent surname in southeastern Spain (Murcia, Almería).
GIVEN NAMES Spanish 43%. *Joaquin* (3), *Carlos* (2), *Jesus* (2), *Rafael* (2), *Alberto, Arnoldo, Cesar, Enrique, Facundo, Jorge, Jorge Luis, Juana.*

Camps (281) **1.** Catalan and southern French: topographic name from *camps* 'fields', or a habitational name from a place named with this word. **2.** French: Norman and Picard variant of the plural of CHAMP, etymologically identical with 1 above.
GIVEN NAMES Spanish 24%. *Jose* (4), *Candido* (3), *Jorge* (3), *Juan* (3), *Manuel* (3), *Mario* (3), *Ricardo* (3), *Carolina* (2), *Enrique* (2), *Fidel* (2), *Juan Carlos* (2), *Luis* (2).

Campton (221) English: habitational name from Campton in Bedfordshire, named in Old English as 'settlement (Old English *tūn*) by the Camel river' (a lost river-name of Celtic origin).

Campus (103) Italian: Sardinian variant of CAMPO.
GIVEN NAMES Italian 11%. *Flavio, Innocenzo, Leonardo, Roberto, Salvatore.*

Campuzano (284) Spanish: habitational name from the village of Campuzano in Santander province.
GIVEN NAMES Spanish 48%. *Carlos* (6), *Mario* (5), *Jose* (4), *Juan* (4), *Eduardo* (3), *Francisco* (3), *Jesus* (3), *Roberto* (3), *Alfredo* (2), *Armando* (2), *Blanca* (2), *Gustavo* (2); *Antonio* (2), *Fausto* (2), *Adalgisa, Bartolo, Carlo, Cira, Ciro, Filiberto, Leonardo, Lorenzo.*

Camus (210) French: nickname for someone with a snub nose, Old French *camus*.
FOREBEARS A bearer of the name Camus, also called Tonnerre ('thunder'), from Évreux is documented in Quebec city by 1756.
GIVEN NAMES French 9%; Spanish 6%. *Andre, Armand, Emile, Jacques, Michel, Philippe, Raoul; Jose* (2), *Luis* (2), *Alonso, Augusto, Concepcion, Emilio, Erlinda, Gregorio, Milagros, Rafael, Ricardo, Susana.*

Camuso (227) Southern Italian: nickname from *camuso* 'snub-nosed'.
GIVEN NAMES Italian 7%. *Pasquale* (2), *Marco, Pasco, Sal, Vito.*

Can (123) **1.** Spanish: nickname from Spanish *can*, a synonym of *perro* 'hound'. **2.** French: descriptive nickname for a gray-haired man, Latin *canutus*. Compare CANUEL, CANO. **3.** Muslim: variant of KHAN. **4.** Vietnamese: unexplained.
GIVEN NAMES Muslim 33%; Vietnamese 14%; Spanish 7%. *Yakup* (3), *Adil* (2), *Ali* (2), *Abdullah, Ahmet, Arif, Bayram, Ebru, Eyup, Faris, Halil, Hasan; Bang, Doan, Duong, Ha Van, Hien, Khang, Quan, Tho, Thu, Tong Thanh, Tu, Tung; Cesar, Jorge, Jose, Miguel, Pascual, Raul, Reyna.*

Canaan (227) **1.** Jewish (American and Israeli): modern Hebrew name from *Canaan*, name of the promised land in the Bible. See also KANAAN. **2.** Irish: variant of CANNAN.

Canada (2584) **1.** Spanish (**Cañada**): topographic name from *cañada* 'glen', 'valley'. **2.** Possibly also French, from a derivative of Old French *chanée*, a term denoting a type of elongated pitcher, from Latin *canna* 'reed'.

Canaday (1274) Americanized form of Irish–Scottish KENNEDY.

Canady (2522) Americanized form of Irish–Scottish KENNEDY.

Canal (259) **1.** Spanish, Catalan, and Portuguese: habitational name from any of numerous places named with *canal* 'channel', 'conduit', from Latin *canalis*.

2. Spanish (**Cañal**) and Portuguese: habitational name from a place named with Spanish *cañal*, Portuguese *canal* 'reedbed', a derivative of Latin *canna* 'reed'. **3.** Italian: variant of CANALE.
GIVEN NAMES Spanish 27%; Italian 5%. *Jose* (9), *Emilio* (4), *Luis* (4), *Roberto* (3), *Avelino* (2), *Carlos* (2), *Manuel* (2), *Mercedes* (2), *Raul* (2), *Adolfo, Alberto, Ana; Carlo* (2), *Carmela, Ciro, Clemente, Dario, Eliseo, Lucio, Oreste, Reno*.

Canale (829) Italian: habitational name from any of numerous places called Canale, from Latin *canalis* 'channel', 'conduit'.
GIVEN NAMES Italian 13%. *Salvatore* (10), *Angelo* (2), *Antonio* (2), *Cinzia* (2), *Gildo* (2), *Caterina, Dino, Ferdinando, Filippa, Francesco, Gaetano, Gino*.

Canales (2484) Spanish: habitational name from any of several places called Canales, from *canales*, plural of *canal* 'canal', 'water channel', from Latin *canalis*.
GIVEN NAMES Spanish 46%. *Jose* (81), *Juan* (23), *Manuel* (19), *Ricardo* (19), *Jorge* (18), *Miguel* (18), *Carlos* (17), *Mario* (14), *Luis* (12), *Ruben* (12), *Armando* (11), *Enrique* (11).

Canali (108) Italian: patronymic or plural form of CANALE.
GIVEN NAMES Italian 21%. *Amedeo, Angelo, Guelfo, Luigi, Paolo, Ugo*.

Canan (212) Variant of Irish CANNAN.
GIVEN NAMES Irish 6%. *Aileen, Murphy, Paddy*.

Canant (105) Origin uncertain; probably a variant of English CONANT.

Canard (166) **1.** French: from *canard* 'duck', probably a nickname for someone thought to resemble a duck in some way. **2.** Perhaps an altered spelling of Scottish **Kinnard**, an early spelling of KINNAIRD.
FOREBEARS A Canard from Tours is recorded in Quebec city by 1677.

Canary (450) **1.** Variant spelling of Irish CONNERY. **2.** Americanized form of Jewish (from Poland) **Kanarek**, a nickname meaning 'canary'.

Canas (458) Spanish (**Cañas**) and Portuguese: habitational name from a place so named from the plural of Spanish *caña*, Portuguese *canas* 'reed', from Latin *canna*.
GIVEN NAMES Spanish 50%; Portuguese 11%. *Jose* (18), *Carlos* (11), *Luis* (7), *Pedro* (6), *Juan* (5), *Ana* (4), *Enrique* (4), *Ramon* (4), *Salvador* (4), *Emilio* (3), *Jorge* (3), *Jose Luis* (3); *Ligia, Paulo*.

Canavan (1307) Irish: Anglicized form of Gaelic **Ó Ceanndubháin** 'descendant of *Ceanndubhán*', a byname meaning 'little black-headed one', from *ceann* 'head' + *dubh* 'black' + the diminutive suffix *-án*.
GIVEN NAME Irish 5%. *Brendan* (5).

Canby (236) English: probably a habitational name from Caenby in Lincolnshire, named with the Old Norse personal name *Kafni* + *býr* 'farmstead'.

Cancel (413) Spanish and French (Normandy and Picardy): topographic name for someone who lived in a house with an iron grille or iron fencing, ultimately from Latin *cancelus*. The prevalence of the name in FL suggests that it was probably brought to the U.S. chiefly from Cuba.
GIVEN NAMES Spanish 40%. *Jose* (13), *Julio* (5), *Luz* (5), *Miguel* (4), *Aida* (3), *Carlos* (3), *Jorge* (3), *Juan* (3), *Reinaldo* (3), *Ruben* (3), *Altagracia* (2), *Juanita* (2).

Cancelliere (132) Southern Italian: occupational name from *cancelliere* 'chancellor', 'clerk'.
GIVEN NAMES Italian 22%. *Angelo* (3), *Salvatore* (3), *Antonio, Domenic, Enrico*.

Cancellieri (128) Italian: patronymic or plural form of CANCELLIERE.
GIVEN NAMES Italian 24%. *Carmela* (2), *Americo* (2), *Salvatore* (2), *Antonio, Domenic, Ignazio, Libero, Roberto*.

Canchola (404) Spanish: topographic name from a derivative of *cancho* 'boulder'.
GIVEN NAMES Spanish 44%. *Jose* (15), *Juan* (6), *Raul* (6), *Manuel* (5), *Ruben* (5), *Alfonso* (4), *Jesus* (4), *Francisco* (3), *Ricardo* (3), *Salvador* (3), *Cristina* (2), *Fernando* (2).

Cancienne (214) French: probably a habitational name from Cancienes in Asturies, Spain.
GIVEN NAMES French 5%. *Alcee, Emile, Leonce, Monique*.

Cancilla (379) Southern Italian (Sicily): from a diminutive of **Canci**, from a short form of *cancelliere* 'chancellor', 'clerk'.
GIVEN NAMES Italian 10%. *Sal* (3), *Salvatore* (3), *Nunzio* (2), *Paolo*.

Cancino (251) Spanish and Asturian-Leonese: possibly a variant of **Cansino**, a habitational name from a place named Cansinos in Asturies, or from Los Cansinos in Córdoba province.
GIVEN NAMES Spanish 51%. *Jose* (5), *Carlos* (4), *Javier* (3), *Salvador* (3), *Eduardo* (2), *Francisco* (2), *Luis* (2), *Manuel* (2), *Miguel* (2), *Pablo* (2), *Pedro* (2), *Rafael* (2).

Cancio (152) Galician: probably a habitational name from a place in Lugo, Galicia called Cancio.
GIVEN NAMES Spanish 49%. *Jose* (7), *Carlos* (4), *Miguel* (4), *Humberto* (3), *Leopoldo* (3), *Catalina* (2), *Laureano* (2), *Rodolfo* (2), *Silvia* (2), *Altagracia, Arcadio, Armando*.

Cancro (167) Southern Italian (Sicily and Naples): probably a reduced form of **Càncaro**, from Sicilian Greek *kankhalos* 'hinge', but possibly a nickname meaning 'crab' (standard Italian *granchio*).
GIVEN NAMES Italian 6%. *Carmine, Ciro*.

Candee (226) **1.** Altered spelling of French **Candé**, a habitational name denoting someone from Candé in Maine-et-Loire, or from Candé-sur-Beauvron in Loire-et-Cher. **2.** Perhaps a variant spelling of CANDY.

Candela (536) Italian, Spanish, and Catalan: from *candela* 'candle' (Latin *candela*), hence a metonymic occupational name for a chandler (candlemaker) or a nickname for a tall thin person.
GIVEN NAMES Italian 18%; Spanish 9%. *Salvatore* (5), *Angelo* (4), *Americo* (3), *Antonio* (3), *Giuseppe* (3), *Giovan* (2), *Pietro* (2), *Vincenzo* (2), *Antonino, Bonaventura, Emanuele, Emilio, Ernesto, Filippo, Gerardo, Giacomo; Juan* (3), *Alejandro* (2), *Alfonso* (2), *Hilario* (2), *Ana Maria, Diego, Francisco*.

Candelaria (1244) Spanish and Portuguese: **1.** from the Marian epithet *(Maria de la) Candelaria*, referring to the Catholic feast of the Purification of the Virgin. The name derives from Latin *candela* 'candle', since on this day candles were blessed by a priest and then lit to invoke the protection of the Virgin Mary. **2.** habitational name from a place in Tenerife called Canelaria.
GIVEN NAMES Spanish 29%. *Jose* (17), *Carlos* (9), *Luis* (9), *Manuel* (8), *Juan* (7), *Rafael* (7), *Miguel* (6), *Angel* (4), *Enrique* (4), *Jesus* (4), *Pedro* (4), *Roberto* (4).

Candelario (462) Spanish: probably a habitational name from either of two places called Candelario, in Béjar and Salamanca provinces.
GIVEN NAMES Spanish 48%. *Jose* (11), *Angel* (6), *Rafael* (6), *Pedro* (5), *Carlos* (4), *Ramon* (4), *Cesar* (3), *Elena* (3), *Guillermo* (3), *Jorge* (3), *Manuel* (3), *Miguel* (3); *Antonio* (5), *Angelo, Cecilio, Ciro, Elio, Heriberto, Lucio, Marino, Romeo*.

Candella (151) Spanish and Italian: variant spelling of CANDELA.
GIVEN NAME Italian 8%. *Santo* (2).

Candia (197) **1.** Galician: habitational name from a place called Candia, in Lugo province, Galicia. **2.** Italian: see DE CANDIA.
GIVEN NAMES Spanish 38%. *Jose* (4), *Leticia* (4), *Emilio* (2), *Luz* (2), *Manuel* (2), *Mario* (2), *Roberto* (2), *Adriana, Ana, Angel, Armando, Bernardita; Lorenzo* (3), *Marcello* (2), *Antonio, Caesar, Federico*.

Candido (297) Portuguese (**Cândido**) and Italian: from Portuguese *cândido*, Italian *candito* '(shining) white' (Latin *candidus*, a derivative of *candere* 'to be white'), hence a nickname for someone with white hair. The word also came to mean 'innocent', 'simple', and the surname may often originally have had this sense.
GIVEN NAMES Spanish 16%; Italian 13%; Portuguese 7%. *Angel* (2), *Manuel* (2), *Alberto, Araceli, Arlindo, Armindo, Consuelo, Elena, Emilio, Francisco, Hilaria, Humberto; Antonio* (5), *Salvatore* (3), *Alfio, Carmelo, Cosmo, Gaetano, Giuliano, Natale, Nicola, Oronzo, Rosangela, Sal; Henrique, Joao*.

Candito (113) Italian: variant of CANDIDO.
GIVEN NAME Italian 8%. *Vito*.

Candler (897) **1.** English: variant of CHANDLER. **2.** German: variant spelling of KANDLER.

Candlish (77) Scottish and northern Irish: reduced form of MCCANDLISH, a variant of MCCANDLESS.

Candy (254) **1.** English: unexplained. **2.** There was a family of this name in Roussillon, France, descended from a partisan of James II named Kennedy, who was exiled in France in the 17th century. The family died out in France in 1868, but may have had an American branch.

Cane (700) **1.** English: nickname for a tall thin man, from Middle English, Old French *cane* 'cane', 'reed' (Latin *canna*). It may also be a topographic name for someone who lived in a damp area overgrown with reeds, or a metonymic occupational name for someone who gathered reeds, which were widely used in the Middle Ages as a floor covering, as roofing material, and for weaving small baskets. **2.** Southern Italian: either a habitational name from a place named Canè, in Bescia and Belluna, or more likely an occupational name for a basket maker or the like, from Greek *kanna* 'reed' + the occupational suffix *-(e)as*. **3.** French: Norman and Picard variant of *chane* a term denoting a particular type of elongated pitcher (ultimately from Latin *canna* 'reed'), hence possibly a metonymic occupational name for a potter who specialized in making such jugs, or a nickname for someone who resembled one. **4.** Possibly an Americanized spelling of German **Köhn** (see KUEHN).

Canedo (189) Spanish (**Cañedo**), Galician, and Portuguese: habitational name from any of various minor places called Canedo or Cañedo, from Latin *canna* 'reed' + the locative suffix *-etum*.
GIVEN NAMES Spanish 40%. *Jose* (6), *Luis* (5), *Alfonso* (4), *Jesus* (4), *Eduardo* (3), *Carlos* (2), *Claudio* (2), *Alberto*, *Alicia*, *Ana*, *Andres*, *Angel*; *Angelo*, *Antonio*, *Federico*, *Sal*.

Canedy (145) Americanized form of Irish–Scottish KENNEDY.

Canela (160) Catalan: **1.** metonymic occupational name for a candle maker, from a dialectal or obsolete variant of Catalan *candela* 'candle'. **2.** possibly also metonymic occupational name for a spicer, from a dialectal or old form of *canyella* 'cinnamon'.
GIVEN NAMES Spanish 59%. *Jose* (5), *Jesus* (4), *Manuel* (4), *Fernando* (3), *Raul* (3), *Alejandro* (2), *Angel* (2), *Ignacio* (2), *Julio* (2), *Luz* (2), *Milagros* (2), *Pedro* (2).

Canell (118) **1.** Catalan: possibly from Catalan *canell* 'wrist'. **2.** Respelling of French **Canel**, a topographic name from *canel* 'water-channel', 'pipe', or Swiss German **Känel**, also a topographic name with the same meaning.

Canepa (492) Italian: from *cànepa* 'hemp', from Latin *cannabis*, a plant cultivated for its strong fibrous stems, which were used to make rope and canvas, hence a metonymic occupational name for a grower or seller of hemp or of articles made from it, a topographic name for someone who lived in an area where the plant was grown, or a habitational name from Canèpa in Genoa province.
GIVEN NAMES Italian 9%. *Angelo* (3), *Aldo* (2), *Dante* (2), *Salvatore* (2), *Carlo*, *Domenic*, *Giacomo*, *Giovanni*, *Nicola*, *Remo*, *Sal*, *Silvio*.

Canevari (174) Italian: of uncertain derivation; it could be an occupational name either for a seller or producer of hemp, from an agent derivative of *cànepa* 'hemp' (see CANEPA), or for the keeper of an inn or wine cellar, from an agent derivative of *caneva*, *canova* 'cellar', 'pantry', 'tavern', 'wine shop'.
GIVEN NAMES Italian 8%. *Angelo*, *Carlo*, *Gino*, *Pietro*, *Silvio*, *Siro*.

Canez (161) Spanish (**Cánez**): unexplained; possibly derivative of Spanish *caña* 'reed' (from Latin *canna*).
GIVEN NAMES Spanish 38%. *Jose* (4), *Miguel* (4), *Manuel* (3), *Carlos* (2), *Facundo* (2), *Raul* (2), *Angelina*, *Araceli*, *Armando*, *Elvira*, *Ernesto*, *Fernando*.

Canfield (4384) English: **1.** habitational name from Great or Little Canfield in Essex, named with the Old English personal name *Cana* + *feld* 'open country'. **2.** in some cases the surname may be of Norman origin, a habitational name from Canville-les-Deux-Églises in Seine-Maritime, France.

Cange (101) French: occupational name for a moneychanger, from Old French *cange* 'exchange'. This is recorded as a Huguenot name.
GIVEN NAMES French 9%. *Guilene*, *Rodrigue*.

Cangelosi (547) Southern Italian: probably a variant of CANGIALOSI.
GIVEN NAMES Italian 17%. *Sal* (6), *Salvatore* (6), *Santo* (3), *Vincenzo* (3), *Antonio* (2), *Carmelo* (2), *Rocco* (2), *Vito* (2), *Carmine*, *Concetta*, *Dino*, *Gaspare*.

Cangemi (284) Southern Italian (Calabria and Sicily): occupational name from Arabic *ḥaggām* 'barber surgeon'.
GIVEN NAMES Italian 20%; Spanish 5%. *Vito* (5), *Salvatore* (4), *Mario* (2), *Agostino*, *Carmelo*, *Dante*, *Erminio*, *Gasper*, *Giacomo*, *Giuseppi*, *Rocco*; *Salvador* (2), *Barbaro*, *Gaspar*.

Cangialosi (247) Italian: of disputed origin; possibly from Arabic *ḥajar al-lawz* 'almond rock'.
GIVEN NAMES Italian 28%. *Salvatore* (5), *Sal* (3), *Angelo*, *Antonino*, *Carmelo*, *Carmine*, *Filippo*, *Giacomo*, *Gino*, *Giuseppe*, *Ignazio*, *Ottavio*.

Cangiano (168) Southern Italian: from a variant of the personal name *Canciano* or *Canziano*.

GIVEN NAMES Italian 16%; French 5%; Spanish 5%. *Antonio*, *Biaggio*, *Cosmo*, *Franco*, *Italo*, *Marco*, *Mauro*, *Michelina*; *Gaston*, *Micheline*; *Edgardo*, *Salvador*.

Canham (379) English: habitational name from a place in Suffolk called Cavenham (of which this is a reduced form), from the genitive case of an unattested Old English byname *Cāfna* (from *cāf* 'bold', 'active') + Old English *hām* 'homestead'.

Canida (159) Origin uncertain. **1.** Most probably Scottish or Irish, a respelling of KENNEDY. **2.** Alternatively, perhaps, an Americanized spelling of South German **Kaneider**, a variant of **Geineder**, a habitational name for someone from Geinöd in northern Bavaria (earlier recorded as *Kagenöd*).

Caniff (102) Irish: reduced Americanized form of Gaelic **Mac Conduibh** (see CUNNIFF).

Caniglia (298) Southern Italian: from Calabrian *caniglia* 'bran', Sicilian *canighia*, so probably a metonymic occupational name for a miller or a cereal grower.
GIVEN NAMES Italian 11%. *Umberto* (2), *Angelo*, *Antonio*, *Carmine*, *Cesare*, *Cirino*, *Domenic*, *Maurizio*, *Pasqualino*, *Renzo*, *Vincenza*, *Vito*.

Canine (120) Americanized spelling of South German **Kanein**: unexplained.

Canino (409) **1.** Spanish: nickname from *canino* 'canine'. **2.** Southern Italian: nickname from Sicilian *caninu* 'beautiful', 'dear', from Arabic *ḥanūn* 'soft', 'sweet'. **3.** Southern Italian: nickname from a diminutive of *cane* 'dog'.
GIVEN NAMES Spanish 10%; Italian 8%. *Jose* (2), *Luis* (2), *Manuel* (2), *Alberto*, *Alfredo*, *Angel*, *Arcadio*, *Feliciano*, *Hilario*, *Jesus*, *Jorge*, *Juan Raul*; *Aldo*, *Angelo*, *Constantino*, *Gino*, *Giovanni*.

Canion (133) French (Huguenot) and English: nickname from a diminutive of *caigne* 'bitch' (see CAINE).

Canipe (594) **1.** French (**Canipé**): Picard and southern occupational name for a knife-maker, from a derivative of *canif* '(small) knife'. **2.** Probably an Americanized form of German KNEIP. Compare KANIPE.

Canizales (164) Spanish (**Cañizales**): topographic name for someone who lived by a reedbed, from the plural of *cañizal* 'where there is an abundance of reeds' (from Latin *canna*).
GIVEN NAMES Spanish 49%. *Jose* (6), *Angel* (3), *Cesar* (3), *Juan* (3), *Raul* (3), *Ruben* (3), *Ricardo* (2), *Alejandro*, *Armando*, *Arnulfo*, *Auxiliadora*, *Carlos*.

Canizares (125) Spanish (**Cañizares**): variant of **Cañizales** (see CANIZALES).
GIVEN NAMES Spanish 53%. *Carlos* (4), *Juan* (4), *Mario* (3), *Rolando* (3), *Guillermo* (2), *Jesus* (2), *Luis* (2), *Miguel* (2), *Adolfo*, *Andres*, *Angel*, *Angelita*; *Antonio*, *Federico*, *Marco*.

Canlas (189) Galician: possibly a habitational name from Las Canles in Ourense province, Galicia, named from Galician *canle* 'channel' (Latin *canal*).
GIVEN NAMES Spanish 45%; French 5%. *Marcelo* (4), *Alfredo* (2), *Cesar* (2), *Domingo* (2), *Eduardo* (2), *Efren* (2), *Emiliano* (2), *Lourdes* (2), *Rolando* (2), *Abelardo*, *Aguedo*, *Amalia*; *Renald* (2), *Andre*.

Cann (1315) **1.** Reduced form of Irish Mc-CANN. **2.** English: habitational name from Cann, a place in Dorset, named from Old English *canna* 'can', used in the transferred sense of a deep valley, or a topographic name from the same word used elsewhere in southwestern England. **3.** Americanized spelling of KANN or KAHN.

Cannada (120) **1.** Italian: regional variant of CANNATA 1. **2.** Variant of CANADA.

Cannaday (511) Americanized form of Irish–Scottish KENNEDY.

Cannady (1392) Americanized form of Irish–Scottish KENNEDY.

Cannan (319) Irish: Anglicized form of Gaelic **Mac Canann** or **Ó Canann** (Ulster), or **Ó Canáin** (County Galway) (see CANNON 1).

Cannata (711) Southern Italian: occupational name for a potter or a water carrier, from *cannata* 'pitcher', 'jug' (medieval Greek *kanata*) or the medieval Greek occupational name derived from this, *kanatas* 'water carrier'.
GIVEN NAMES Italian 13%. *Sal* (4), *Rocco* (3), *Salvatore* (3), *Gaetano* (2), *Vito* (2), *Angelo*, *Antonino*, *Antonio*, *Biagio*, *Carlo*, *Carmela*, *Corrado*.

Cannavo (157) Southern Italian (**Cannovò**): **1.** nickname from Greek *kannabos* 'gray', 'hemp-colored'. **2.** habitational name from a place in Calabria called Cannavo.
GIVEN NAMES Italian 26%. *Vito* (3), *Carmine* (2), *Sal* (2), *Santo* (2), *Biagio*, *Carmelo*, *Filippo*, *Franco*, *Giuseppe*, *Nicola*.

Cannedy (255) Americanized form of Irish–Scottish KENNEDY.

Cannell (487) See CANELL.

Cannella (647) Southern Italian (Sicily and Naples): occupational name for a spice merchant, from *cannella* 'cinnamon' (from Latin *cannella*), or possibly a nickname for a tall thin man, from the same word in the sense 'thin reed'.
GIVEN NAMES Italian 14%. *Giuseppe* (3), *Sal* (3), *Salvatore* (3), *Angelo* (2), *Antonio* (2), *Luigi* (2), *Vito* (2), *Aldo*, *Carmela*, *Carmelo*, *Caterina*, *Chiara*.

Canner (181) **1.** English: occupational name for a maker or seller of cans, from an agent derivative of Old English *canne* 'can'. **2.** Respelling of KANNER.

Canney (395) Irish: variant spelling of CANNY, itself a southern variant of McCANN.

Canniff (265) Irish: variant of CUNNIFF.

Canning (1612) **1.** Irish: variant of CANNAN. **2.** English: habitational name from a place in Wiltshire called Cannings, apparently named with the Old English byname *Cana* (of uncertain origin) + *-ingas* 'people of'.

Cannistra (126) Southern Italian: metonymic occupational name for a basket maker, medieval Greek *kannistras*.
GIVEN NAMES Italian 19%. *Natale* (2), *Santo* (2), *Dante*, *Mario*, *Romana*.

Cannistraci (119) Southern Italian: metonymic occupational name for a basket maker, from Greek *kanistrakion* 'wicker basket'. Compare CANNISTRA.
GIVEN NAMES Italian 19%. *Angelo* (3), *Salvatore* (3), *Carmelo* (2), *Filomena*, *Sal*.

Cannistraro (111) Southern Italian: occupational name for a basket maker, from an agent derivative of *cannistra* 'basket' (see CANNISTRA).
GIVEN NAMES Italian 8%. *Carmelo*, *Salvatore*.

Cannizzaro (653) Southern Italian (Sicily and Calabria): **1.** occupational name, Italian *cannizzaro*, for a maker of reed matting. **2.** habitational name from a place in eastern Sicily named Cannizzaro.
GIVEN NAMES Italian 21%. *Salvatore* (6), *Sal* (4), *Rosario* (3), *Mario* (3), *Antonio* (2), *Enrico* (2), *Gaspare* (2), *Rocco* (2), *Santo* (2), *Agostino*, *Carlo*, *Carmela*, *Carmine*, *Mariano*.

Cannizzo (227) Southern Italian: metonymic occupational name for a maker of reed matting and the like, from Sicilian *cannizzu* 'reed matting', from Late Latin *cannicius* 'made of reed', or possibly a topographic name for someone who lived by a reedbed, from a collective derivative of *canna* 'reed'.
GIVEN NAMES Italian 20%. *Salvatore* (8), *Antonino*, *Filippo*, *Giovanni*, *Nunzia*, *Nunzio*, *Sal*.

Cannon (23206) **1.** Irish: Anglicized form of Gaelic **Mac Canann** or **Ó Canann** (Ulster), or **Ó Canáin** (County Galway) 'son (*Mac*) or descendant (*Ó*) of Canán', a personal name derived from *cano* 'wolf cub'. In Ulster it may also be from **Ó Canannáin** 'descendant of Canannán', a diminutive of the personal name. **2.** English: from Middle English *canun* 'canon' (Old Norman French *canonie*, *canoine*, from Late Latin *canonicus*). In medieval England this term denoted a clergyman living with others in a clergy house; the surname is mostly an occupational name for a servant in a house of canons, although it could also be a nickname or even a patronymic.

Cannone (221) Italian: from *cannone* 'cannon', applied as a metonymic occupational name for a maker of cannons, or as a nickname for a tall thin man or someone with a resounding voice.

GIVEN NAMES Italian 17%. *Salvatore* (2), *Santo* (2), *Amedeo*, *Filippo*, *Guido*, *Salavatore*, *Vito*.

Cannova (110) Italian (Sicily): variant spelling of CANOVA.
GIVEN NAMES Italian 19%. *Antonio*, *Carmela*, *Mario*, *Sal*, *Salvatore*.

Canny (328) Irish: reduced Anglicized form of Gaelic **Mac Cana** (see McCANN).
GIVEN NAME Irish 4%. *Brendan*.

Cano (3430) Spanish and Portuguese: **1.** nickname for an old man or someone with prematurely white hair, from *cano* 'white or gray haired', 'old', 'worthy' (Latin *canus*). **2.** habitational name from a place in Spain called Caño or Cano in Portugal, both named with a derivative of Latin *canna* 'reed'.
GIVEN NAMES Spanish 48%; Portuguese 10%. *Jose* (87), *Juan* (55), *Manuel* (38), *Luis* (37), *Carlos* (35), *Jesus* (32), *Miguel* (26), *Francisco* (21), *Jorge* (20), *Alberto* (18), *Raul* (18), *Javier* (17); *Adauto*, *Wenceslao*.

Canode (103) Origin uncertain. **1.** Possibly Scottish or Irish, a respelling of KENNEDY. **2.** Alternatively, perhaps, an Americanized spelling of South German **Kaneider**, a variant of **Geineder**, a habitational name for someone from Geinöd in northern Bavaria (earlier recorded as Kagenöd).

Canon (821) English: variant spelling of CANNON.

Canonico (183) Southern Italian: from *canònico* 'canon', 'church official', probably denoting the servant or even the off-spring of such a person, since canonic officials of the Greek Catholic Church were allowed to marry.
GIVEN NAMES Italian 19%. *Angelo* (3), *Carmine* (2), *Domenic* (2), *Salvatore* (2), *Rocco*, *Saverio*, *Vito*.

Canosa (108) Galician: habitational name from a place in A Coruña province, Galicia, named Canosa, from Galician *cana* 'reed' (Latin *canna*).
GIVEN NAMES Spanish 22%; Italian 7%. *Amado*, *Amador*, *Andres*, *Domingo*, *Fidel*, *Jose*, *Josefina*, *Julio*, *Manuel*, *Margarita*, *Nilda*, *Orlando*; *Antonio*, *Fabiano*, *Rocco*.

Canova (468) **1.** Southern Italian (**Cànova**): from *cànova* 'cupboard', 'cellar', 'food shop', presumably applied as a metonymic occupational name for a seller of comestibles. **2.** Northern Italian (**Canóva**): reduced form of CASANOVA.
GIVEN NAMES Italian 4%. *Antonio* (2), *Remo* (2), *Carlo*, *Enzio*, *Ettore*, *Franco*, *Sal*.

Canoy (259) **1.** Apparently of English origin, but unexplained. **2.** Filipino: unexplained.

Canright (112) Probably an American spelling of English **Kenwright**, a variant of KENDRICK or KERRICK.

Canseco (116) Spanish: habitational name from Canseco in Cármenes in León province.

GIVEN NAMES Spanish 63%. *Juan* (5), *Jose* (4), *Carlos* (3), *Alejandro* (2), *Jorge* (2), *Raimundo* (2), *Sinesio* (2), *Adelina*, *Balbina*, *Blanca*, *Cesar*, *Efren*; *Antonio*, *Bartolo*, *Donato*, *Filiberto*, *Franco*.

Cansler (632) Altered spelling of German KANZLER 'chancellor', or possibly of the English cognate CHANCELLOR.

Cant (131) **1.** Scottish: unexplained. The surname appears in Scottish records from the 15th century; in at least one case it is believed to have come from Flanders. **2.** Americanized spelling of German KANT.

Cantalupo (182) Italian: habitational name from any of various places in Italy named or named with Cantalupo, thought to be a grimly humorous name derived from Latin *cantare* 'to sing' + *lupus* 'wolf', i.e. denoting a settlement where the wolves could be heard howling in the uncleared woods around. This is a widespread place name but some scholars now dispute its derivation, believing it to have been altered by folk etymology.
GIVEN NAMES Italian 17%. *Carmine* (2), *Cesare*, *Ciro*, *Donato*, *Gennaro*, *Rocco*, *Salvatore*, *Vito*.

Cantara (209) Spanish and Portuguese (**Cántara**): from a variant of *cántaro* 'pitcher', 'jug', from Latin *cantharus*, probably applied as a metonymic occupational name for a jug maker.
GIVEN NAMES French 7%. *Alcide*, *Laurier*, *Patrice*.

Cantarella (110) Italian: of uncertain derivation, possibly **1.** aphetic form of **Alcàntara**, a topographic name for someone who lived by running water, from Arabic form *al qantarah* 'the river'. **2.** from a diminutive of *cantaro* 'night pot', presumably applied as a derogatory nickname. **3.** perhaps from a derivative of *cantare* 'to sing' (compare CANTORE).
GIVEN NAMES Italian 32%. *Canio* (2), *Carlo* (2), *Domenic* (2), *Carmine*, *Dante*, *Francesco*, *Palma*, *Paolo*, *Salvatore*.

Cantelmo (116) Southern Italian: said to be from the name of a noble family originating in Provence, taken to Italy with Carlo D'Angiò.
GIVEN NAMES Italian 13%; French 7%. *Angelo* (2), *Carmine*; *Andre* (2).

Canter (2113) **1.** English: from an agent derivative of Anglo-Norman French *cant* 'song', applied as an occupational name for a singer in a chantry or a nickname for someone who had a good voice or who sang a lot. **2.** Americanized spelling of KANTER or KANTOR.

Canterberry (143) Variant spelling of English CANTERBURY.

Canterbury (1535) English: habitational name from Canterbury in Kent, named in Old English as *Cantwaraburg* 'fortified town (*burgh*) of the people (*wara*) of Kent'.

Cantero (165) Spanish: occupational name for a stonemason, *cantero*.
GIVEN NAMES Spanish 45%. *Jose* (7), *Arnaldo* (2), *Benito* (2), *Miguel* (2), *Pedro* (2), *Alberto*, *Armando*, *Aroldo*, *Beatriz*, *Bernardina*, *Constancio*, *Consuelo*.

Cantey (386) Irish: variant of CANTY.

Cantillo (175) Spanish: topographic name for someone who lived on a street corner, *cantillo*, or, in Navarre, by irrigated land, the term being used there to denote a ridge dividing a field for the purposes of irrigation.
GIVEN NAMES Spanish 38%; Italian 7%. *Julio* (5), *Roberto* (3), *Edgardo* (2), *Jose* (2), *Lourdes* (2), *Manuel* (2), *Rafael* (2), *Abelardo*, *Alfonso*, *Alfredo*, *Alvero*, *Arcadio*; *Antonio* (4), *Ciana*, *Salvatore*.

Cantillon (100) French: metonymic occupational name for a stonemason, from a derivative of *chantille* 'canthus', 'angle'; 'thin brick' or 'stone shaped like a large brick'.

Cantin (525) French: **1.** habitational name from a place called Cantin, in Nord. **2.** spelling variant of **Quantin**, from the Old French personal name *Quentin*, *Quintin* (from Latin *Quintinus*, a derivative of *Quintus* 'fifth-born').
FOREBEARS A family called Quentin or Cantin, from Normandy, France, is documented in Quebec city in 1660. Huguenots called Cantin, Cantine, Quantin, from Saintonge, France, settled in New Rochelle, NY.
GIVEN NAMES French 17%. *Andre* (3), *Gilles* (3), *Marcel* (3), *Marielle* (2), *Pierre* (2), *Aime*, *Aldege*, *Armand*, *Edouard*, *Emile*, *Fernand*, *Herve*.

Cantley (569) English: habitational name from either of two places called Cantley, in Norfolk and South Yorkshire, named with an unattested Old English personal name *Canta* + *lēah* 'clearing'.

Cantlin (155) Irish (of Norman origin): habitational name from any of various places in Normandy and Picardy, France, named Canteloup or Canteleu, from Old Norman French *cante(r)* 'to sing' + *lou*, *leu* 'wolf'. These appear originally to have been grimly humorous names denoting settlements where the wolves could be heard howling in the uncleared woods around. Compare Italian CANTALUPO.

Cantlon (150) Probably a variant spelling of Irish CANTLIN.

Canto (289) **1.** Spanish and Portuguese: topographic for someone who lived on a corner, *canto* 'corner' (from Latin *cantus*), or a habitational name from numerous places in Spain and Portugal named with this word. **2.** Catalan (**Cantó**): habitational name from any of the minor places in Catalonia named Cantó, from Catalan *cantó* 'stone', derived from the pre-Latin form *cant-*.
GIVEN NAMES Spanish 31%. *Jose* (8), *Carlos* (6), *Manuel* (4), *Ignacio* (2), *Jorge* (2),

Juan (2), *Miguel* (2), *Pedro* (2), *Ramon* (2), *Reynaldo* (2), *Alda*, *Alejandro*; *Antonio* (2), *Silvio* (2), *Albertina*, *Angelo*, *Carlo*, *Constantino*, *Salvatore*, *Serafino*.

Canton (640) **1.** Galician (**Cantón**): habitational name from places in Lugo and Pontevedra provinces, in Galicia, named Cantón, from a derivative of *canto* 'corner' (see CANTO). **2.** Southern French: topographic name, from Occitan *canton* 'corner', 'angle', denoting someone who lived on a street corner.
GIVEN NAMES Spanish 10%. *Ana* (2), *Carlos* (2), *Cesar* (2), *Fabio* (2), *Jose* (2), *Julio* (2), *Rafael* (2), *Reinaldo* (2), *Alicia*, *Angelina*, *Beatriz*, *Berta*.

Cantone (274) Italian: **1.** habitational name from any of numerous places called Cantone, from *cantone* 'corner'. **2.** possibly from an augmentative form of the medieval personal name *Cante*, a reduced form of *Cavalcante*.
GIVEN NAMES Italian 21%. *Salvatore* (6), *Antonio* (2), *Emanuele* (2), *Alfonse*, *Clementina*, *Damiano*, *Francesca*, *Francesco*, *Giovanni*, *Pasquale*, *Pietro*, *Sebastiano*.

Cantoni (140) Italian: patronymic or plural form of CANTONE.
GIVEN NAMES Italian 7%. *Aldo*, *Attilio*, *Gianfranco*, *Marino*.

Cantor (1866) **1.** English: variant spelling of CANTER. **2.** German and Jewish (Ashkenazic): variant spelling of KANTOR. **3.** French (Picardy): learned form of *chantre* 'singer'. Compare CANTER 1.
GIVEN NAMES Jewish 5%. *Meyer* (5), *Sol* (5), *Emanuel* (3), *Miriam* (2), *Este*, *Hyman*, *Isador*, *Isadore*, *Isidor*, *Yetta*.

Cantore (137) Italian: from *cantore* 'singer' (from Latin *cantor* 'singer', 'poet'), hence an occupational name for a singer or cantor, or a nickname for someone who sang well.
GIVEN NAMES Italian 24%. *Pasquale* (2), *Amedeo*, *Claudio*, *Emilio*, *Enrico*, *Filippo*, *Rocco*, *Salvatore*.

Cantos (122) Spanish and Portuguese: variant (plural) of CANTO.
GIVEN NAMES Spanish 30%. *Cesar* (2), *Julio* (2), *Olegario* (2), *Pasqual* (2), *Adela*, *Adrina*, *Agustin*, *Alicia*, *Carlos*, *Ernesto*, *Florentina*, *Gerardo*.

Cantrall (265) English: variant of CANTRELL.

Cantrell (12163) **1.** English: habitational name from Cantrell in Devon, recorded as *Canterhulle* in 1330, from an unexplained first element + Old English *hyll* 'hill'. **2.** English: from Old French *chanterelle* 'small bell', 'treble', hence a metonymic occupational name for a bellmaker or ringer. **3.** English: diminutive of CANTER. **4.** French: nickname for someone who liked to sing.

Cantrelle (209) French: variant of CANTRELL.

GIVEN NAMES French 5%. *Emile* (2), *Armand*, *Michel*.

Cantrill (146) English: variant spelling of CANTRELL.

Cantu (6251) Mexican (**Cantú**): probably a habitational name from Cantù in Italy. This surname is extremely frequent in Mexico, but rare elsewhere.
GIVEN NAMES Spanish 48%. *Jose* (138), *Juan* (90), *Manuel* (65), *Jesus* (64), *Carlos* (63), *Ruben* (48), *Raul* (42), *Jorge* (33), *Arturo* (32), *Ricardo* (32), *Pedro* (29), *Guadalupe* (28).

Cantwell (2615) English: possibly a habitational name from Canwell in Staffordshire, named with either Old English *canne* 'can', 'cup' or the Old English personal name *Cana* + *well(a)* 'spring', 'stream'. The surname is common in Ireland as well as England.

Canty (1877) Irish (West Cork): Anglicized form of Gaelic **Ó an Cháintighe** 'descendant of the satirist', from *cáinteach* 'satirical', later shortened to **Ó Cáinte**.

Canuel (102) French: nickname from a diminutive of *canu* 'old, gray-haired man', an old or dialectal form of *chenu* (from the Latin adjective *canutus*).
GIVEN NAMES French 22%; Spanish 5%. *Adelard* (2), *Andre*, *Benoit*, *Fabien*, *Ghislain*, *Normand*; *Zosimo* (2), *Nestor*.

Canup (467) Americanized spelling of North German KNAPP or KNOPP.

Canupp (234) See CANUP.

Canzano (175) Italian (mainly southern): probably a habitational name from Canzano in Teramo province, named with the Latin personal name *Cantius* + the suffix *-anu*.
GIVEN NAMES Italian 11%. *Domenic* (3), *Carmela*, *Carmelo*, *Giovanni*, *Vittorio*.

Canzoneri (275) Southern Italian (Sicily and Naples): occupational name for a singer, Sicilian *canzonere*, Italian *canzoniere*, derivatives of *canzone* 'song'.
GIVEN NAMES Italian 25%. *Salvatore* (9), *Alfredo*, *Carmel*, *Ciro*, *Emilio*, *Mariano*, *Mario*, *Santo*, *Vito*.

Cao (1802) **1.** Chinese 曹: there are two main branches of the Cao line. One branch comes from Cao An, a great-grandson of the emperor Zhuan Xu (26th century BC). A descendant named Cao Xie was granted the state of Zhu when the Zhou dynasty came to power in 1122 BC. When Zhu was conquered by the state of Chu, many of the Zhu aristocracy adopted a modified form of the character Zhu as their surname (see CHU), but others kept the name Cao. The origin of the other branch also involves the granting of a state at the beginning of the Zhou dynasty: in 1122 BC Zhen Duo, a son of Wen Wang, was granted the state of Cao, a name subsequently adopted by his descendants. Other Romanized forms of this name include **Tso**, **Cho**, **Tsao** and **Chou**. **2.** Vietnamese: unexplained. **3.** Portuguese (**Cão**) and Galician equivalent of Spanish CANO.

GIVEN NAMES Chinese 48%; Vietnamese 38%. *Hung* (20), *Dung* (17), *Hong* (11), *Yang* (9), *Jian* (8), *Ming* (7), *Wei* (7), *Man* (4), *Ping* (4), *Qiang* (4), *Song* (4), *Yong* (4), *Feng* (3), *Jin* (3); *Thanh* (19), *Minh* (13), *Son* (13), *Lan* (11), *Nhan* (10), *Tuan* (10), *Hien* (9), *Hoa* (9), *Duc* (8), *Hai* (8); *Tam* (12), *Nam* (5), *Tuong* (5), *Chung* (4), *Min* (4), *Phong* (3), *Thai* (3), *Tinh* (3), *Chang* (2), *Manh*, *Tap*, *Thach*.

Caouette (489) North American spelling of the French topographic name CAILLOUET.
GIVEN NAMES French 13%. *Armand* (3), *Andre* (2), *Marcel* (2), *Adelard*, *Alcide*, *Alphonse*, *Emile*, *Gilberte*, *Gilles*, *Lucien*, *Ludger*, *Napoleon*.

Cap (282) **1.** Ukrainian, Jewish (from Ukraine), Polish, Serbian, and Hungarian (**Cáp**): from Ukrainian *tsap* 'billy goat', Polish *cap*, and so probably a nickname for someone thought to resemble the animal in some way or perhaps a metonymic occupational name for a goat herd. **2.** Czech (**Čáp**): nickname for a tall or long-legged man, from *čáp* 'stork'. **3.** Southern French: from Occitan *cap* 'head' (Latin *caput*); probably a nickname for a person with something distinctive about his head. The word was often used in the metaphorical sense 'chief', 'principal', and the surname may also have denoted a leader or a village elder. In some cases it may also be a topographic name from the same word used in the sense of a promontory or headland. **4.** Americanized spelling of German KAPP. **5.** English: variant spelling of CAPP.
GIVEN NAMES Polish 4%. *Bazyli*, *Wasyl*, *Witold*.

Capaccio (138) Italian: habitational name from Capàccio in Salerno province.
GIVEN NAMES Italian 22%. *Mario* (2), *Rosario* (2), *Vito* (2), *Luigi*, *Matteo*, *Salvatore*, *Vita*.

Capalbo (413) Southern Italian: nickname from Latin *caput albus* 'white head'.
GIVEN NAMES Italian 21%. *Angelo* (6), *Carlo* (3), *Carmine* (3), *Salvatore* (3), *Dante* (2), *Giuseppe* (2), *Pasquale* (2), *Antonio*, *Domenic*, *Giovanni*, *Marcello*, *Rocco*.

Capaldi (317) Italian: patronymic or plural form of CAPALDO.
GIVEN NAMES Italian 16%. *Angelo* (2), *Antonio* (2), *Domenic* (2), *Gino* (2), *Guido* (2), *Sabatino* (2), *Carlo*, *Francesco*, *Natale*, *Sandro*, *Tullio*.

Capaldo (213) Southern Italian: possibly a derivative of *capo* 'head' (Latin *caput*), perhaps equivalent to French **Capard** 'obstinate man', 'hard head'.
GIVEN NAMES Italian 15%. *Angelo* (3), *Salvatore* (3), *Aldo*, *Camillo*, *Remo*, *Sal*.

Capan (141) Perhaps from French **Capin**, a nickname for someone with a small head (see CAP).

Capano (261) Southern Italian: variant of **Capuano**, habitational name for someone from Capua in Campania.
GIVEN NAMES Italian 17%; Spanish 5%. *Carlo* (3), *Carmela* (2), *Salvatore* (2), *Alicia*, *Americo*, *Ciro*, *Dante*, *Gregorio*, *Luigi*, *Mario*, *Nicola*, *Nunzio*; *Juan*, *Juan Alberto*, *Rafael*.

Caparelli (110) Italian: variant of CAPPARELLI.
GIVEN NAMES Italian 18%. *Angelo*, *Armando*, *Camillo*, *Ernesto*, *Guido*, *Pietro*, *Ruben*.

Capasso (653) Southern Italian: possibly from an Italianized form of Spanish *capaz* 'competent', 'able'; it is the name of an old Neapolitan family.
GIVEN NAMES Italian 20%. *Salvatore* (5), *Angelo* (4), *Donato* (4), *Giuseppe* (3), *Ugo* (3), *Antonio* (2), *Pasquale* (2), *Rocco* (2), *Sal* (2), *Augustino*, *Carlo*, *Carmine*.

Capaul (103) Probably a variant spelling of French **Capoul**, a metonymic occupational name for a cook or kitchen hand, from a noun derivative of *capolar* 'to cut into small pieces'.

Cape (914) French and English: metonymic occupational name for a maker of capes and cloaks, or perhaps a nickname for someone who habitually wore a cloak or cape, from Middle English and Old Norman French *cape* 'cape', 'cloak', 'hooded cloak' (in French also 'hood' or 'hat'), from Late Latin *cappa*, *capa*, probably a derivative of *caput* 'head' (see CAPP). There is also an Old English word *cāpe* 'cape', 'cloak', from the same Late Latin word, but the normal development of this in southern England was Middle English *cope* (see COPE).

Capece (285) Southern Italian: from a reduced form of *Cacapece*, a derogatory nickname meaning 'pitch shitter'. This is the name of an old Neapolitan family.
GIVEN NAMES Italian 11%; French 4%. *Antonio* (4), *Crescenzo* (2), *Carmelo*, *Luigi*; *Alphonse*, *Henri*.

Capehart (704) Americanized form of German GEBHARDT.

Capek (255) **1.** Czech (**Čapek**): from a diminutive of *čáp* 'stork', applied as a habitational name for someone who lived at a house distinguished by the sign of a stork. In some cases the family name may have derived from a heraldic symbol. **2.** Polish: nickname from *cap* 'he-goat' (see CAP). **3.** Croatian (northwestern Croatia): nickname, perhaps from *cap* 'he-goat' or from *capa* 'paw'.

Capel (428) **1.** French (Normandy and Picardy): from a dialect variant of Old French *chape* 'hooded cloak', 'cape', 'hat' (see CAPE 2). **2.** probably a Castilianized form of Catalan CAPELL. **3.** Dutch: metonymic occupational name from Middle Dutch *capeel* 'hood', 'headgear'. **4.** English: variant of CHAPPELL 'chapel', from a Norman form with hard *c*-, applied as a topographic or occupational name, or as a habitational name for someone from any of several minor places named with this word, such as Capel in Surrey, Capel le Ferne in Kent, or Capel St. Andrew and Capel St. Mary in Suffolk.

FOREBEARS A bearer of this name from Normandy, France, with the secondary surname Desjardins, is documented in Varennes, Quebec, Canada, in 1696.

Capell (508) **1.** English: variant spelling of CAPEL. **2.** Catalan: from *capell* 'hat', 'hood', as a nickname for someone who habitually wore a hat or hood, or a metonymic occupational name for someone who made hats or hoods.

Capella (321) **1.** Spanish, Catalan, and Italian: from *capella* 'chapel', a topographic name for someone who lived by a chapel or a metonymic occupational name for someone who worked in one. **2.** Italian: habitational name from any of several places called Cappella or Capella.

GIVEN NAMES Spanish 10%; Italian 4%. *Jose* (3), *Jaime* (2), *Luis* (2), *Manuel* (2), *Angel*, *Cesar*, *Gerardo*, *Horacio*, *Javier*, *Mario*, *Miguel*, *Milagros*; *Primo* (2), *Ennio*, *Giovanni*.

Capellan (136) Spanish (**Capellán**): occupational name from *capellán* 'chaplain'.

GIVEN NAMES Spanish 48%. *Jose* (5), *Ana* (3), *Altagracia* (2), *Erasmo* (2), *Juan* (2), *Manuel* (2), *Milagros* (2), *Pedro* (2), *Reina* (2), *Romulo* (2), *Aida*, *Albania*; *Eliseo*.

Capelle (336) **1.** French (Normandy and Picardy) and Dutch: variant spelling of CAPEL. **2.** Dutch and Belgian: occupational name for someone who worked in a chapel, from Middle Dutch *kapel* 'chapel', 'church'. In some instances this may be a shortened form of **van de Capelle**, a topographic name for someone who lived by a chapel, or **van Capelle**, a habitational name for someone from any of various places named with this word, such as Kapelle-op-de-Bos or Sint-Ulriks-Kapelle, both in the Belgian province of Brabant.

Capelli (279) Italian: patronymic or plural form of CAPELLO.

GIVEN NAMES French 4%; Italian 4%. *Giampiero*, *Sal*.

Capello (342) Italian: **1.** nickname for a trickster, from *capello* 'trick' (Latin *capullum*). **2.** variant of CAPPELLO.

GIVEN NAMES Spanish 7%; Italian 6%. *Carlos* (2), *Manuel* (2), *Demetrio*, *Juan*, *Juvenal*, *Maria Angela*, *Roberto*, *Rosario*, *Santos*; *Deno* (2), *Aldo*, *Antonio*, *Dino*, *Oliviero*, *Remo*.

Capen (536) Possibly an Americanized spelling of German **Köppen**, a variant of KOPP.

Capener (163) English: habitational name from Capenor in Surrey, possibly named from an unattested Old English word *cape* 'look-out place' (genitive *capan*) + *ōra* 'hill slope', 'flat-topped hill'.

Capers (1178) **1.** English: occupational name for a cope or cape maker, from an agent derivative of Middle English *cape*. **2.** Dutch: from an agent derivative of *kap* 'hood', 'cap', hence an occupational name for a maker of such head gear, or a nickname for someone who habitually wore a hood.

Caperton (558) English: habitational name from Capton in Devon, earlier *Capieton* (1278) 'estate (Old English *tūn*) of a man called Capia'.

Capes (376) English: patronymic from CAPP.

Capetillo (212) Spanish: perhaps a habitational name from Capetillo, a place in Biscay province.

GIVEN NAMES Spanish 49%. *Pedro* (6), *Jose* (5), *Hilario* (3), *Jesus* (3), *Miguel* (3), *Alberto* (2), *Arnulfo* (2), *Carlos* (2), *Elena* (2), *Emilio* (2), *Felipe* (2), *Guadalupe* (2); *Angelo* (2), *Antonio* (2), *Cecilio*, *Marco*.

Capistran (145) Spanish (**Capistrán**): habitational name from Capistrán, named for the Franciscan preacher St. John of Capistrano (1386–1456), who was from Capistrano in Calabria, Italy.

GIVEN NAMES Spanish 30%. *Eleno* (2), *Gerardo* (2), *Jaime* (2), *Jesus* (2), *Juan* (2), *Pedro* (2), *Alfredo*, *Alonso*, *Ana*, *Armando*, *Benito*, *Bernardo*.

Capistrant (102) French: probably an altered form of Spanish CAPISTRAN.

Capitani (101) Southern Italian: patronymic or plural form of CAPITANO.

GIVEN NAMES Italian 14%. *Dino*, *Elio*, *Siro*, *Vito*.

Capitano (252) Southern Italian (Sicily and Naples): status name or nickname from *capitano*, a term denoting the master of a ship, an official of some kind, or an officer in the army.

GIVEN NAMES Italian 14%. *Salvatore* (4), *Sal* (2), *Angelo*, *Gilda*, *Orazio*, *Sarina*.

Capito (239) **1.** Italian (also **Capitò**): from a reduced form of the medieval Greek personal name *Agapitos* meaning 'dear', 'beloved'. **2.** German: Latinized form of HAUPT or KOPF 'head'.

FOREBEARS Wolfgang Capito (born 1478 or 1472) from Alsace, a Protestant reformer in Strasbourg, was originally Wolfgang Köpfel (literally, 'little head'), son of Johann Köpfel.

GIVEN NAMES Italian 4%. *Dino* (2), *Antonio*, *Gino*.

Capizzi (418) Southern Italian: habitational name from a place named Capizzi, in Messina province, Sicily.

GIVEN NAMES Italian 17%. *Salvatore* (10), *Angelo* (4), *Sal* (3), *Pasquale*, *Pietro*, *Salvatrice*, *Santo*, *Saverio*, *Savino*, *Silvio*.

Caplan (2370) **1.** Jewish (Ashkenazic): Americanized spelling of KAPLAN. **2.** Altered spelling of French and English CAPLIN, a variant of CHAPLIN.

GIVEN NAMES Jewish 5%. *Hyman* (4), *Isadore* (4), *Myer* (4), *Shlomo* (3), *Meyer* (2), *Sol* (2), *Emanuel*, *Faina*, *Miriam*, *Yetta*, *Zev*.

Caple (689) **1.** English: variant spelling of CAPEL. **2.** Americanized spelling of German KAPPEL or of **Göbel** (see GOEBEL).

Caples (641) English: variant of CAPEL, also established in Ireland.

Caplette (138) North American spelling of French **Caplet**, a diminutive of CAPEL.

GIVEN NAMES French 9%. *Andre*, *Aurore*, *Pierre*.

Capley (130) **1.** Possibly an Americanized spelling of French **Caplet** (see CAPLETTE). **2.** In some instances probably an Americanized spelling of Swiss **Käppeli**, variant of KAPPEL.

Caplin (257) **1.** English: occupational name for a chantry priest (or the servant of one), a priest endowed to sing mass daily on behalf of the souls of the dead (Late Latin *capellanus*). Compare CHAPLIN. **2.** Americanized spelling of Swiss German **Kaeppelin**, a diminutive of KAPPEL.

Caplinger (837) Americanized spelling of the German habitational name **Köpplinger** (see KEPLINGER).

Capo (511) **1.** Spanish and Italian: topographic name from *capo* 'head' (Latin *caput*), in the sense 'cape', 'headland', or habitational name from a place named with this word in this sense. **2.** Catalan (**Capó**): habitational name from any of the minor places named with Capó in Catalonia. This name is also found in the Island of Minorca. **3.** Italian: from *capo* 'head' or 'chief', applied either as a nickname for someone with something distinctive about his head (in a literal or abstract sense) or as a status name for a boss or overseer. **4.** Slovak (**Čapo**): unexplained.

GIVEN NAMES Spanish 14%; Italian 6%. *Carlos* (6), *Jose* (5), *Rafael* (4), *Juan* (3), *Aida* (2), *Dalia* (2), *Alicia*, *Cesar*, *Elba*, *Enrique*, *Ernesto*, *Eudaldo*; *Angelo* (3), *Antonio*, *Attilio*, *Carmine*, *Giovanna*, *Guglielmo*, *Lorenzo*.

Capobianco (1149) Italian: nickname for someone with white hair, from *capo* 'head' + *bianco* 'white'.

GIVEN NAMES Italian 23%. *Angelo* (13), *Rocco* (9), *Carmine* (7), *Cosmo* (6), *Fausto* (6), *Pasquale* (5), *Cono* (4), *Domenic* (4), *Vito* (4), *Carlo* (3), *Sal* (3), *Salvatore* (3).

Capoccia (123) Southern Italian: from a diminutive of *capo* 'head' (see CAPO), applied as an occupational name for a farm overseer, chief shepherd or herdsman, or occasionally perhaps for the head of a family, particularly in an immigrant community.

GIVEN NAMES Italian 28%. *Angelo* (3), *Antonio* (3), *Donato* (2), *Cesidio*, *Domenic*, *Domenico*, *Geno*, *Gino*, *Giuseppe*, *Luciano*, *Nino*, *Pasquale*.

Capodanno (116) Italian (Naples): from the personal name *Capodanno*, traditionally bestowed on male children born on the day of Capodanno, January 1st ('head of the year').

GIVEN NAMES Italian 13%. *Gaetano, Rocco, Salvatore.*

Capon (111) **1.** Spanish (**Capón**): from Spanish *capón* 'capon', applied as a derogatory nickname for a feeble man or a cuckold. **2.** French: nickname (see 1 above) from *capon* 'capon', a southern, Norman, and Picard equivalent of standard French *chapon*.

Capone (1734) Italian: **1.** from an augmentative of *capo* 'head', applied as a nickname for someone with a big head, probably in the sense 'arrogant' or 'stubborn' rather than in a strictly literal sense. **2.** from *capone* 'capon', 'castrated cock', applied as a derogatory nickname for a cuckold, or a metonymic occupational name for someone who kept poultry.

GIVEN NAMES Italian 13%. *Antonio* (10), *Carmine* (10), *Salvatore* (7), *Angelo* (5), *Gaetano* (5), *Gasper* (4), *Gennaro* (3), *Pasquale* (3), *Dino* (2), *Luigi* (2), *Rocco* (2), *Silvio* (2).

Caponera (106) Italian: nickname, literally 'black head', for someone with black hair or a black beard, or dark skin; alternatively, it could be a nickname meaning 'chief of the Blacks', perhaps designating a political group or similar.

GIVEN NAMES Italian 28%. *Sisto* (3), *Alfredo, Angelo, Claudio, Ernesto, Franca, Gianni, Mario, Renato, Savino, Umberto.*

Caponi (196) Italian: patronymic or plural form of CAPONE.

GIVEN NAMES Italian 17%. *Marco* (2), *Aldo, Damiano, Domenico, Gino, Remo, Reno, Rocco, Sabato, Saverio.*

Caponigro (194) Italian: nickname for someone with black hair, from *capo* 'head' + *nigro* 'black' (Latinized form of *nero*).

GIVEN NAMES Italian 12%. *Angelo* (2), *Rocco* (2), *Vito* (2), *Giordano, Giuseppe.*

Caporale (473) Italian and Sicilian: from *caporale* 'corporal', also, in Sicily, 'foreman of a gang of harvesters'.

GIVEN NAMES Italian 15%. *Fiore* (3), *Rocco* (3), *Domenic* (2), *Aldo, Angelo, Antonietta, Antonio, Gaetano, Giovanna, Nicola, Olindo, Pietro.*

Caporaso (209) Italian: nickname for someone with a shaven (or bald) head, from *capo* 'head' + *raso* 'shaven'.

GIVEN NAMES Italian 21%. *Rocco* (3), *Alessio* (2), *Angelo* (2), *Antonio, Carmelo, Enrico, Lorenzo, Nicola, Salvatore.*

Capote (315) Spanish and Portuguese: metonymic occupational name from *capote* 'hooded cloak', 'cape'.

GIVEN NAMES Spanish 55%; Italian 7%. *Jose* (11), *Juan* (9), *Pedro* (6), *Carlos* (5), *Evelio* (5), *Jorge* (5), *Enrique* (4), *Francisco* (4), *Armando* (3), *Gilberto* (3), *Horacio* (3), *Luis* (3); *Cira* (2), *Silvio* (2), *Antonio,*

Bartolo, Carmelo, Elio, Gino, Leonardo, Luciano.

Capotosto (99) Italian: nickname from *capo* 'head' + *tosto* 'hard'.

GIVEN NAMES Italian 21%. *Saverio* (2), *Angelo, Bruna, Carmel, Corrado, Cosmo, Domenic, Elio, Gino, Sal.*

Capozza (135) Southern Italian: variant of CAPOCCIA.

GIVEN NAMES Italian 23%. *Rocco* (4), *Angelo* (2), *Dino, Gaetano, Massimo, Pasquale, Vito.*

Capozzi (839) Italian: from a derivative of *capo* 'head'.

GIVEN NAMES Italian 18%. *Angelo* (6), *Rocco* (5), *Domenic* (4), *Pasquale* (3), *Carmine* (2), *Cosimo* (2), *Dante* (2), *Ezio* (2), *Salvatore* (2), *Tobia* (2), *Antonio, Carmelina.*

Capozzoli (348) Southern Italian: from a diminutive of CAPOZZI.

GIVEN NAMES Italian 10%. *Angelo* (2), *Pasquale* (2), *Antonio, Donato, Luciano, Rocco, Vito.*

Capp (683) **1.** English: from Middle English *cappe* 'cap', 'hat' (Old English *cæppe*), hence a metonymic occupational name for a maker of caps and hats, or a nickname for someone who wore distinctive headgear. Compare CAPPER. **2.** Americanized spelling of German KAPP.

Cappa (291) Southern Italian: from *cappa* '(hooded) cloak', 'cape' (Late Latin *cappa*), applied as a metonymic occupational name for a maker of capes, or possibly as a nickname for a habitual wearer of a distinctive cape.

GIVEN NAMES Italian 10%. *Carmine* (2), *Angelo, Antonio, Dino, Domenic, Ettore, Mauro, Quinto, Quirino, Remo, Rosaria, Salvatore.*

Cappadona (235) Southern Italian: from *cappa* 'cloak' + *dona*, from either the female personal name *Adona* or the male personal name *Donato*.

GIVEN NAMES Italian 8%. *Salvatore* (2), *Angelo, Gaetano, Nunzio, Sal.*

Capparelli (250) Italian: from a diminutive, *capparello*, of *capparo* (Latin *capparo*), an occupational name for a cloak or cape maker.

GIVEN NAMES Italian 26%. *Mario* (5), *Vincenzo* (3), *Angelo, Antonio, Carmela, Carmelo, Dino, Ezio, Franco, Gino, Marco, Nicola, Salvatore.*

Cappel (475) **1.** English (of Norman origin): variant of CHAPPELL. **2.** Variant of German KAPPEL.

Cappell (107) English (of Norman origin): variant of CHAPPELL.

GIVEN NAME French 4%. *Raoul.*

Cappella (226) Italian: **1.** habitational name from any of numerous places named with *cappella* 'chapel', or a topographic name for someone who lived by a chapel. **2.** variant of CAPPELLO.

GIVEN NAMES Italian 6%; French 5%. *Angelo, Luigi, Ugo*; *Antoine, Jacques.*

Cappelletti (277) Italian: **1.** from a diminutive of CAPPELLO. **2.** habitational name from a place called Cappelletti, for example, in Sicily.

GIVEN NAMES Italian 16%. *Vito* (3), *Cosmo* (2), *Maurizio* (2), *Aldo, Angelo, Francesca, Gaetano, Guido, Guilio, Marco, Silvio, Siro.*

Cappelli (475) Italian: patronymic or plural form of CAPPELLO.

GIVEN NAMES Italian 18%. *Angelo* (5), *Dante* (3), *Luca* (3), *Guido* (2), *Reno* (2), *Antonio, Attilio, Carmine, Cesare, Deno, Domenic, Enrico.*

Cappellini (101) Italian: patronymic or plural form of CAPPELLINO.

GIVEN NAMES Italian 7%. *Angelo, Domenic, Quinto.*

Cappellino (109) Italian: diminutive of CAPPELLO.

GIVEN NAMES Italian 15%. *Salvatore* (3), *Antonio* (2), *Carmela, Luigi.*

Cappello (918) Italian: from a diminutive of *cappa* 'cape', 'hood', 'hat', hence a metonymic occupational name for a maker or vendor of capes or hoods, or a nickname for someone who wore a distinctive cape or hat.

GIVEN NAMES Italian 15%. *Angelo* (10), *Salvatore* (5), *Vito* (3), *Giuseppe* (2), *Alessandro, Antonino, Antonio, Domenic, Domenico, Gaspare, Gasper.*

Capper (487) **1.** English: from an agent derivative of Middle English *cappe* 'cap', 'headgear', hence an occupational name for a maker of caps and hats. **2.** Dutch: variant of CAPERS.

Cappetta (218) Italian (Sicily): diminutive of CAPPA.

GIVEN NAMES Italian 15%. *Salvatore* (4), *Angelo, Aniello, Carmine, Gilda, Guido, Marco, Rocco, Saverio.*

Cappiello (590) Italian (Naples): variant of CAPPELLO.

GIVEN NAMES Italian 10%. *Donato* (2), *Salvatore* (2), *Vito* (2), *Amedeo, Concetta, Enrico, Gaetano, Luciano, Nicola, Rocco, Sal, Tonio.*

Cappo (175) Italian: unexplained.

GIVEN NAMES Italian 16%. *Rocco* (2), *Caesar, Ceasar, Domenic, Massimo, Primo, Salvatore, Secondo, Valentino.*

Cappola (133) Italian (Abruzzo): perhaps from a diminutive of CAPPA or alternatively a variant of COPPOLA.

GIVEN NAMES Italian 11%. *Antonio, Pasquale, Saverio, Vito.*

Cappon (104) French: variant of CAPON.

GIVEN NAME French 7%. *Andre* (2).

Capponi (148) Italian: **1.** augmentative of CAPPA. **2.** variant of CAPONE.

GIVEN NAMES Italian 13%. *Angelo* (2), *Silvio* (2), *Aldo, Antonio, Emidio, Giovanni.*

Capps (6623) **1.** English: variant of CAPP. **2.** Respelling of German KAPPUS, a metonymic occupational name for a cabbage grower.

Cappucci (161) Italian: patronymic or plural form of CAPPUCCIO.

GIVEN NAMES Italian 17%. *Angelo, Carlo, Carmel, Dario, Enrico, Gennaro, Rinaldo, Rocco.*

Cappuccio (309) Southern Italian (Sicily and Naples): from *cappuccio* 'hood', 'cowl', a diminutive of *cappa*, hence a metonymic occupational name for a maker of hoods, or from the same word as a pejorative form of *cappa*.

GIVEN NAMES Italian 26%. *Angelo* (6), *Gerardo* (2), *Mario* (2), *Pasquale* (2), *Aldo, Antonio, Carlo, Dante, Gelsomina, Giuseppe, Marco, Prisco, Raffaele, Rocco.*

Capra (654) Italian: from *capra* 'nanny goat' (Latin *capra*), hence a nickname for someone thought to resemble a goat in some way, a metonymic occupational name for a goatherd, or a topographic name for someone who lived in an area where goats grazed.

GIVEN NAMES Italian 9%. *Antonio* (3), *Angelo* (2), *Giulio* (2), *Guerino* (2), *Remo* (2), *Enrico, Fulvio, Gianni, Gino, Giovani, Luigi, Marco.*

Caprara (182) Southern Italian: **1.** habitational name from a place in Sicily named Caprara, from Latin *capraria* 'goat pasture', 'enclosure or shelter for goats'. **2.** from a feminine form of CAPRARO.

GIVEN NAMES Italian 14%. *Dante* (2), *Angelo, Fausto.*

Capraro (225) Southern Italian: occupational name for a goatherd, from an agent derivative of *capra* '(nanny) goat'.

GIVEN NAMES Italian 16%. *Carmine* (2), *Salvatore* (2), *Angelo, Antonio, Carmino, Giuseppina, Marco, Riccardo, Rocco, Vito.*

Capretta (115) Italian: from *capretta* 'female kid', a diminutive of *capra* 'nanny goat'.

GIVEN NAMES Italian 15%. *Antonio* (2), *Angelo, Carlo, Domenico, Nicola, Umberto.*

Capri (166) Italian: habitational name for someone from Capri, the island in the Bay of Naples.

GIVEN NAMES Italian 6%. *Natale* (2), *Angelo, Leonardo.*

Capria (100) Southern Italian: **1.** from Sicilian *capria* 'capstan', 'windlass', from Catalan or Spanish *cabria*. **2.** nickname, possibly for a shy or timid person, from Calabrian *crapia* 'female roe deer', Sicilian *crapia* 'wild goat'.

GIVEN NAMES Italian 15%. *Pasquale* (2), *Angelo, Carlo, Carmine, Pompeo.*

Capriglione (125) Italian: perhaps an augmentative form of a topographic or minor habitational name from a place named with a derivative of *caprile* 'place where goats are tendered', such as Capriglia Irpina, in Avellino province.

GIVEN NAMES Italian 21%. *Carmine* (2), *Carlo, Luca, Margherita, Pasquale, Pasqualina, Sal, Salvatore, Vito.*

Caprio (680) Southern Italian (Sicily, Naples, Cosenza): see DI CAPRIO.

GIVEN NAMES Italian 11%. *Angelo* (3), *Antonio* (3), *Aldo* (2), *Gino* (2), *Luigi* (2), *Vito* (2), *Camillo, Carlo, Cesare, Francesco, Luco, Nicola.*

Capriotti (354) Italian: from a diminutive of CAPRIO.

GIVEN NAMES Italian 12%; French 4%. *Angelo* (2), *Romeo* (2), *Amedeo, Dante, Dino, Enrico, Franco, Pasquale, Reno, Salvatore, Sante, Sylvio*; *Armand* (2), *Serge.*

Capron (739) **1.** English (of Norman origin): metonymic occupational name for a hood maker, from Old Norman French *caprun*, Old French *chaperon* 'hood or cap (worn by the nobility)'. **2.** French: from a Picard and southern form of *chaperon* (see 1, above).

Caproni (110) Italian: nickname or occupational name from a derivative of *capra* 'nanny goat' (see CAPRA).

Capshaw (358) English: unexplained. Perhaps a habitational name from Cadshaw near Blackburn, Lancashire, although the surname is not found in England.

Capstick (137) English (Lancashire and Yorkshire): variant of **Copestake**, an occupational nickname for a woodcutter, from Old French *couper* 'to cut' + Middle English *stikke* 'stick' or *stake* 'pin', 'stake'.

Captain (377) Probably an Americanized form of French **Capitaine**, from Old French *capitaine* 'head', 'chief', 'principal' (from Latin *capitaneus*), or of any of the various cognates, such as Italian **Capitani**, or German KAPITAN, all of which were used in similar way to denote a high-ranking official, a headman, or a person of military rank.

GIVEN NAMES French 4%. *Constant, Emile, Marcell.*

Capua (111) Southern Italian: habitational name from Capua in Caserta province.

GIVEN NAMES Italian 21%. *Giulio* (2), *Rosario* (2), *Angelo, Antonio, Carlo, Carmine, Guilio, Sal.*

Capuano (988) Southern Italian: habitational name for someone from Capua in Campania. The place name is Etruscan and means 'city of the marshes'.

GIVEN NAMES Italian 16%. *Rocco* (5), *Pasquale* (4), *Angelo* (3), *Carmine* (3), *Salvatore* (3), *Vito* (3), *Antonio* (2), *Elio* (2), *Umberto* (2), *Aniello, Carlo, Ciro.*

Capurro (163) Southern Italian: nickname from the southern dialect word *capurro* 'stubborn', a derivative of *capo* 'head'.

GIVEN NAMES Spanish 10%; Italian 7%. *Julio* (2), *Atilio, Carlos, Cesar, Enrique, Francisco, Gustavo, Raul*; *Dante* (2), *Giovanni, Pietro, Silvio.*

Capurso (140) Italian (Apulia): habitational name from Capurso in Bari province.

GIVEN NAMES Italian 17%. *Vito* (3), *Carlo, Filomena, Giovanni, Matteo, Nicolo.*

Caputa (115) Italian (Sicily): variant of CAPUTO.

GIVEN NAMES Italian 10%. *Carmelo* (2), *Carmello, Salvatore.*

Caputi (220) Italian: patronymic or plural form of CAPUTO.

GIVEN NAMES Italian 17%. *Vito* (3), *Saverio* (2), *Cosimo, Domenico, Marco, Nicolo, Pasquale, Salvatrice, Umberto.*

Caputo (3581) Southern Italian: nickname from *caputo* 'stubborn', 'obstinate'; also literally for someone with a large head.

GIVEN NAMES Italian 16%. *Rocco* (17), *Angelo* (16), *Vito* (15), *Pasquale* (10), *Salvatore* (10), *Antonio* (8), *Aldo* (5), *Enrico* (5), *Carmela* (3), *Giosue* (3), *Luigi* (3), *Marco* (3).

Capuzzi (113) Italian: from a diminutive of CAPO.

GIVEN NAMES Italian 15%. *Angelo* (3), *Remo, Rocco.*

Capwell (241) **1.** English (West Midlands): habitational name from a lost or unidentified place. **2.** Possibly an Americanized spelling of South German **Köpfel**, from a diminutive of KOPF 2.

Car (115) **1.** Croatian, Serbian, and eastern Slovenian: ironic nickname for an autocratic person, from *car* 'tsar'. **2.** Slovenian (**Čar**): see CHAR. **3.** Perhaps also French: metonymic occupational name for cartwright or carter, from *char* 'wagon', 'cart' (Latin *carrus*).

GIVEN NAMES French 7%; Polish 5%. *Martial* (3); *Iwan, Jaroslaw.*

Cara (129) **1.** Southern Italian: from the feminine form of *caro* 'dear' (see CARO). **2.** Spanish and Portuguese: from *cara* 'face', presumably applied as a nickname for someone with a beautiful or otherwise distinctive face.

GIVEN NAMES Italian 14%; Spanish 12%. *Rocco* (3), *Gino*; *Jose* (2), *Ana, Carlos, Demetrio, Efren, Luis.*

Carabajal (235) Spanish: variant of CARBAJAL.

GIVEN NAMES Spanish 24%. *Nestor* (8), *Jose* (2), *Manuel* (2), *Adolfo, Alfredo, Amador, Diego, Elfigo, Elvira, Felipa, Felipe, Guillermo.*

Caraballo (1081) Spanish: variant of CARBALLO.

GIVEN NAMES Spanish 46%. *Jose* (23), *Luis* (21), *Juan* (19), *Miguel* (12), *Ramon* (12), *Pedro* (9), *Angel* (7), *Rafael* (7), *Jorge* (6), *Ana* (5), *Arturo* (5), *Carlos* (5).

Carabello (167) **1.** Spanish: probably a Castilian variant of Galician *carabelo* 'basket' and hence a metonymic occupational name for a basket maker. **2.** Italian (Sicily): from a diminutive of *carabba* 'wine carrier' (from Arabic *qarābah*) or a nickname from a Sicilian bird name,

carabbeddu. **3.** Italian: from the female personal name *Carabella*, composed of the elements *cara* 'dear' + *bella* 'beautiful'.
GIVEN NAMES Spanish 11%; Italian 8%. *Jose* (2), *Alfonsina, Carlos, Guadalupe, Ivette, Luis, Luiz, Luz, Manuel, Mario; Natale* (2), *Rocco, Salvatore.*

Carabetta (135) Southern Italian (Sicily): from a diminutive of *carabba* 'wine carrier' (from Arabic *qarābah*). Compare CARABELLO.
GIVEN NAMES Italian 23%. *Salvatore* (4), *Rocco* (3), *Filippo, Pasquale, Pasqualina, Vito.*

Caracappa (137) Italian: apparently from *cara* 'dear' + *cappa* 'hood'. The application is unclear.
GIVEN NAMES Italian 20%. *Vito* (4), *Mario* (2), *Gaspare, Guido, Nichola, Sal, Salvatore.*

Caracci (195) Italian: **1.** from a derivative of CARO. **2.** possibly from a diminutive of the medieval Greek personal name *Theokharēs*, meaning 'grace of God'.
GIVEN NAMES Italian 16%. *Sal* (2), *Giovanni, Giuseppe, Rocco, Salvatore, Vito.*

Caracciolo (483) Southern Italian: diminutive of **Caraccio**, a derivative of CARO. This is the name of an old Neapolitan family.
GIVEN NAMES Italian 29%; Spanish 5%. *Giuseppe* (3), *Angelo* (2), *Aniello* (2), *Antonio* (2), *Carmine* (2), *Cosimo* (2), *Mario* (2), *Pasqualino* (2), *Rocco* (2), *Camillo, Domenica, Domenico, Donato; Cesar, Domingo, Jaime, Juan.*

Caradine (207) **1.** English: unexplained. **2.** Americanized form of German **Gardein**, itself a Germanized spelling of French JARDIN.

Caradonna (228) Italian: from a medieval female personal name *Caradonna*, or a nickname from the term of address, meaning 'dear lady', from which the personal name is derived.
GIVEN NAMES Italian 26%. *Salvatore* (3), *Carmine* (2), *Leonardo* (2), *Matteo* (2), *Alfio, Angelo, Antonio, Gaspare, Rocco, Rosaria, Sal, Salvator.*

Caraher (172) Variant spelling of Irish CARRAHER.

Caraker (159) Probably an altered spelling of Irish CARRAHER.

Caram (115) **1.** English: variant of **Carham**, a habitational name from a place so called in Northumbria, named with Old English *carrum* '(at the) rocks', dative plural of *carr* 'rock'. **2.** Spanish (and Portuguese): unexplained.
GIVEN NAMES Spanish 17%. *Carlos* (2), *Alberto, Ana Maria, Cristina, Emelinda, Guillermo, Jorge, Jose, Manuel, Pedro, Ramon, Sergio.*

Caramanica (103) Italian: habitational name from Caramanico in Pescara, which was also recorded as Caramanica in ancient documents.

GIVEN NAMES French 7%; Italian 7%. *Jean-Pierre; Luciano.*

Caranci (133) Italian: from old Italian *caranci* (from Arabic *kākanj*), denoting an invasive noxious plant (*Cardiospermum halicacabum*).
GIVEN NAMES Italian 14%. *Angelo* (2), *Emilio* (2), *Mario* (2), *Antonio, Dante, Libero, Nino.*

Carangelo (162) Italian: **1.** from a medieval personal name composed of the elements *caro* 'dear' + the personal name ANGELO. **2.** from the medieval Greek personal name *Kalangelos* 'beautiful angel'.
GIVEN NAMES Italian 11%. *Antonio, Domenic, Marco, Palma, Sal, Salvatore.*

Carano (261) Italian: habitational name from any of numerous minor places called Carano, as for example in Caserta province.
GIVEN NAMES Italian 10%. *Sergio* (2), *Aldo, Americo, Claudio, Domenic, Guerino, Remo, Salvatore, Mario, Orlando.*

Caras (279) Greek: **1.** nickname for a black-haired or gloomy individual, from *karas* 'black', 'dark' (and by extension 'moody'), from Turkish *kara* 'black'. It is also found in many compound surnames such as **Karageorgiou** 'black George' (patronymic). **2.** occupational name for a carter, Greek *karas* (from *karo* 'cart' + the occupational suffix *-as*).

Caravalho (109) Portuguese: probably a variant of CARVALHO.
GIVEN NAMES Spanish 9%. *Manuel* (3), *Estrella, Fernando.*

Caravella (292) Italian: **1.** from the female personal name *Carabella*, composed of the elements *cara* 'dear' + *bella* 'beautiful'. **2.** from *caravella* 'caravel', denoting the master or owner of a ship of this type.
GIVEN NAMES Italian 10%. *Bartolomeo, Ignazio, Leonardo, Nicola, Onofrio, Vito.*

Caravello (271) Italian: **1.** most probably a masculine variant of CARAVELLA. **2.** possibly also from Sicilian *caravellu*, denoting a variety of pear, hence a metonymic occupational name for a grower or seller of pears.
GIVEN NAMES Italian 16%. *Salvatore* (6), *Angelo* (3), *Aldo, Carina, Croce, Francesco, Santo, Saverio.*

Caraveo (209) Spanish: possibly a habitational name from Caraveu in Tenerife.
GIVEN NAMES Spanish 50%. *Manuel* (6), *Jesus* (4), *Jose* (4), *Luis* (3), *Arturo* (2), *Elvira* (2), *Enrique* (2), *Ernesto* (2), *Fernando* (2), *Guadalupe* (2), *Humberto* (2), *Juan* (2).

Carawan (303) Americanized spelling of Polish and Ukrainian **Karawan** or **Karavan**, from Polish *karawan* 'hearse'.

Caraway (2143) English: from Middle English *carewei* 'caraway' (from Old French *carvi, caroi*), probably applied as a metonymic occupational name for a spice merchant.

Carbajal (1660) Spanish: habitational name from any of numerous places called

Carabajal, from a collective noun derived from *carbajo* 'oak tree'.
GIVEN NAMES Spanish 51%. *Jose* (42), *Manuel* (18), *Carlos* (16), *Juan* (16), *Miguel* (16), *Jorge* (15), *Jesus* (14), *Raul* (13), *Enrique* (11), *Salvador* (10), *Ramiro* (9), *Ruben* (9).

Carballo (470) **1.** Spanish and Galician: from *carballo* 'oak', hence a topographic name for someone who lived by a conspicuous oak tree or in an oak wood, or a habitational name from any of several villages so named in Galicia. **2.** Castilianized form of Asturian-Leonese **Carbachu**, a habitational name from and old form of Asturian-Leonese *carbayu* 'oak', of pre-Latin origin.
GIVEN NAMES Spanish 51%. *Jose* (16), *Carlos* (10), *Jorge* (8), *Manuel* (7), *Pedro* (7), *Roberto* (5), *Enrique* (4), *Jesus* (4), *Juan* (4), *Luis* (4), *Fernando* (3), *Francisco* (3); *Antonio* (5), *Eligio, Federico, Geronimo, Giovanni, Godofredo, Heriberto, Marco.*

Carbary (154) Irish: variant spelling of CARBERRY.

Carbaugh (1092) **1.** Americanized spelling of the German habitational name **Gerbach**, from a place so named in the Palatinate. **2.** Americanized spelling of Czech **Carboch**, of unexplained etymology.

Carberry (1052) **1.** Scottish: habitational name from a place in the parish of Inveresk, Lothian, first recorded in the form *Crebarrin*, from Gaelic *craobh* 'tree' + *barran* 'hedge'. **2.** Irish: Anglicized form of Gaelic **Ó Cairbre** and **Mac Cairbre** 'descendant of *Cairbre*' and 'son of *Cairbre*', a byname probably meaning 'charioteer'.

Carbin (149) Swedish: soldier's name, from Swedish *karbin* 'carbine' (see CARBINE).

Carbine (210) French or English: nickname for someone who used a carbine, a type of short rifle or musket used by cavalry. This may also be an Americanized form of Jewish KARABIN.

Carbo (504) **1.** Catalan (**Carbó**): from *carbó* 'coal', 'jet black', probably applied as a topographic name for someone who lived by a coal outcrop, an occupational name for someone who extracted or sold coal, or a nickname for someone with exceptionally dark eyes or hair. **2.** Southern Italian (Sicily): possibly a topographic name from Sicilian *carbu* 'hollow in a tree'.
GIVEN NAMES Spanish 9%. *Jose* (5), *Jorge* (4), *Carlos* (3), *Ramon* (2), *Ricardo* (2), *Roberto* (2), *Agustin, Alfonso, Angelina, Fernando, Fidel, Jesus.*

Carbon (281) French and Spanish (**Carbón**): metonymic occupational name for a charcoal-burner, from Old French, Spanish *carbon* 'charcoal' (from Latin *carbo*, genitive *carbonis*).

Carbonara (235) Italian: habitational name from any of numerous minor places called Carbonara, from *carbonara* 'rich in coal'.

GIVEN NAMES Italian 16%. *Vito* (3), *Rocco* (2), *Antonio, Carmelo, Concetta, Domenico, Nino, Pasquale, Vincenzo.*

Carbonaro (369) Southern Italian: occupational name for a coal miner, coal merchant, or charcoal burner *carbonaro, carbonero*, an agent derivative of *carbone* '(char)coal' (see CARBONE).

GIVEN NAMES Italian 22%. *Mauro* (3), *Rocco* (3), *Fulvio* (2), *Mario* (2), *Adriano, Aldo, Alfredo, Armando, Angelo, Antonio, Bruna, Carmelo, Carmine, Gaetano, Gerardo, Gilda, Giovanni.*

Carbone (3680) Italian: from *carbone* 'coal', 'charcoal' (Latin *carbo*, genitive *carbonis*), as a metonymic occupational name for a coal miner, coal merchant, or charcoal burner or merchant; a topographic name for someone living near an outcrop of coal or in an area where charcoal was produced; or a nickname for someone with exceptionally dark skin or hair.

GIVEN NAMES Italian 14%. *Angelo* (16), *Rocco* (15), *Carmine* (14), *Salvatore* (10), *Sal* (8), *Antonio* (7), *Carmela* (5), *Ciro* (5), *Pasquale* (5), *Domenic* (4), *Silvio* (4), *Vito* (4).

Carbonell (527) **1.** English (of Norman origin): nickname for a man with dark hair or a swarthy complexion, from a diminutive of Anglo-Norman French *carbon* 'charcoal'. **2.** Catalan and southern French: from a personal name, *Carbonellus*, derived from Latin *carbo* 'coal', 'charcoal'.

GIVEN NAMES Spanish 39%. *Luis* (7), *Jorge* (6), *Jose* (6), *Juan* (6), *Eduardo* (5), *Rafael* (5), *Roberto* (5), *Carlos* (4), *Manuel* (4), *Miguel* (4), *Pablo* (4), *Rolando* (4); *Antonio* (6), *Carlo, Marino.*

Carboni (406) Italian (Sardinia): variant (plural) of CARBONE.

GIVEN NAMES Italian 22%. *Mario* (4), *Renato* (3), *Angelo* (2), *Carlo* (2), *Aldo, Ciro, Dante, Deno, Dino, Elvio, Ercole, Fausto, Francesco, Libero, Lino, Luciana, Olinto, Rafaela, Renaldo, Velia, Zelia.*

Carbonneau (450) French: variant of CARBONELL.

FOREBEARS There were Carbonneau from Provence documented in Île d'Orléans, Canada, by 1672.

GIVEN NAMES French 16%. *Adelard* (2), *Aime* (2), *Emile* (2), *Marcel* (2), *Alain, Amie, Andre, Cecile, Elphege, Gilles, Gisele, Henri.*

Carby (172) **1.** English: habitational name from Careby in Lincolnshire, which is named with the Old English personal name *Kári* + *býr* 'farmstead', 'village'. **2.** Swedish and Danish: habitational name from places in Sweden and Denmark named Karby, from *karl* '(free)man' + *býr* 'village'. **3.** Possibly an Americanized spelling of German GERBIG.

Carcamo (334) Spanish (**Cárcamo**): from *cárcavo* 'cooking pot' (from Latin *carcabus*), hence probably a metonymic occu-

pational name for a maker of such pots or for a cook.

GIVEN NAMES Spanish 52%. *Jose* (19), *Carlos* (9), *Luis* (6), *Jorge* (5), *Juan* (4), *Mario* (4), *Miguel* (4), *Pedro* (4), *Ana* (3), *Marta* (3), *Raul* (3), *Roberto* (3); *Antonio, Elio, Giovanni, Leonardo, Lorenzo, Olympia, Sal.*

Carchidi (135) Italian (of Croatian origin): variant of CARCICH.

GIVEN NAMES Italian 14%. *Saverio* (2), *Dominico, Rosaria.*

Carcich (130) Italianized form of Croatian **Karčić**, habitational name for someone from the island of Cres (Latin name *Cerso*) in the Kvarner Gulf of the Adriatic Sea.

GIVEN NAMES Italian 24%. *Aldo* (2), *Antonietta, Fabio, Gino, Giovanna, Italo, Marco, Pierina, Renato.*

Carcione (144) Southern Italian: variant of **Calcione**, which is of uncertain derivation, probably from an augmentative form of a personal name, *Calcio*, or from Latin *calceus* 'chalky'.

GIVEN NAMES Italian 9%. *Agostino, Filippo.*

Card (3567) **1.** English: metonymic occupational name for someone who carded wool (i.e. disentangled it), preparatory to spinning, from Middle English, Old French *card(e)* 'carder', an implement used for this purpose. **2.** Reduced form of Irish McCARD.

Carda (290) **1.** Spanish and Portuguese: from *carda* 'teasel', 'carder' (from Latin *carduus* 'thistle'), hence a metonymic occupational name for someone who carded (disentangled) wool, the dried heads of teasels and thistles having originally been used for this purpose. **2.** Italian (**Cardà**): probably a topographic name from Greek *kardas* 'thistle field'. **3.** Czech: nickname for a cunning, clever, or sly person, Old Czech or Moravian dialect *carda*.

Cardamone (468) Italian: of uncertain derivation, possibly from *cardamo* 'cardamom', hence a metonymic occupational name for a spicer.

GIVEN NAMES Italian 14%. *Angelo* (3), *Caesar* (2), *Aldo, Attilio, Carmela, Carmine, Dino, Enrico, Giovanni, Marco, Sal.*

Cardarelli (427) Italian: variant of CALDARELLI.

GIVEN NAMES Italian 13%. *Donato* (4), *Antonio* (3), *Carmelo* (2), *Aldo, Cesidio, Dante, Fulvio, Gino, Guilio, Marcello, Mauro, Nevio.*

Cardell (334) **1.** Probably a reduced form of Irish and Scottish McARDLE. **2.** Catalan or Asturian-Leonese: probably a topographic name from a diminutive of *card* 'thistle' (Latin *cardus*), or, less likely, a habitational name from a place so named in Asturies. **3.** Possibly an altered form of Italian CARDELLI or CARDELLO. **4.** Perhaps an Americanized spelling of German **Kardel** (see KARDELL).

Cardella (490) Southern Italian: habitational name from a place called Cardella in Sicily.

GIVEN NAMES Italian 18%. *Salvatore* (5), *Angelo* (4), *Sal* (4), *Matteo* (2), *Vito* (2), *Alfonse, Antonino, Carlo, Gaetano, Giovanni, Giulio, Guiseppe.*

Cardelli (129) Italian: patronymic or plural form of CARDELLO.

GIVEN NAMES Italian 17%. *Dino* (3), *Enzo* (2), *Aldo, Ciro, Gino, Luca, Marco.*

Cardello (262) Italian: **1.** nickname from *cardello* 'goldfinch' (see CARDILLO 1). **2.** topographic name or possibly a nickname from a diminutive of *cardo* 'thistle' (Latin *cardus*). **3.** from a diminutive of the personal name CARDO.

GIVEN NAMES Italian 15%; French 5%. *Salvatore* (4), *Angelo, Carmelo, Cosmo, Giacomo, Giovanna, Santo*; *Armand* (3), *Celine.*

Carden (3172) English: **1.** from Anglo-Norman French *cardon* 'thistle' (a diminutive of *carde*, from Latin *carduus*), probably applied as a topographic name for someone who lived on a patch of land overgrown with thistles, as an occupational name for someone involved in the carding of wool, originally carried out with thistle and teasel heads, or as a nickname for a prickly and unapproachable person. **2.** habitational name from Carden in Cheshire, which is recorded in the mid 13th century in the form *Kawrdin* and in the early 14th century as *Cawardyn*; it is probably named with Old English *carr* 'rock' + *worðign* 'enclosure'.

Cardenas (6554) Spanish (**Cárdenas**): habitational name from places in the provinces of Almería and Logroño named Cárdenas, from the feminine plural of *cárdeno* 'blue', 'bluish purple' (Late Latin *cardinus*, from *carduus* 'thistle'). Presumably the noun *tierras* 'lands' is to be understood, and the reference is to land covered with bluish plants, such as thistles or vines.

GIVEN NAMES Spanish 52%. *Jose* (200), *Juan* (99), *Jesus* (71), *Luis* (67), *Carlos* (66), *Raul* (55), *Manuel* (49), *Francisco* (48), *Jorge* (45), *Mario* (40), *Roberto* (40), *Miguel* (37).

Carder (2031) English: occupational name for a wool-carder or for a maker of carders, from an agent derivative of Middle English, Old French *card(e)* 'carder' (the implement). See also CARDA.

Cardi (157) Italian: **1.** topographic name from the plural of *cardo* 'thistle' (from Latin *cardus*). **2.** see CARDO.

GIVEN NAMES Italian 24%; French 7%. *Cesare* (4), *Gabriella* (2), *Gino* (2), *Antonio, Carlo, Erminio, Gaetano, Gioia, Guerino, Vincenzo*; *Alphonse* (6).

Cardiel (222) Spanish: habitational name from Cardiel de los Montes in Toledo province.

GIVEN NAMES Spanish 46%. *Jose* (8), *Javier* (3), *Carlos* (2), *Eloy* (2), *Felipe* (2), *Francisco* (2), *Jesus* (2), *Juan* (2), *Luis* (2), *Manuel* (2), *Marina* (2), *Mario* (2).

Cardiff (291) Welsh: habitational name from the Welsh city Cardiff in Glamorgan, named with Welsh *caer* 'fort' + the genitive singular of the river name *Taf*, from Welsh *taf* 'water', 'stream'.

Cardile (107) Italian: probably a variant of CARDILLO.

GIVEN NAMES Italian 21%. *Salvatore* (2), *Angelo*, *Concetto*, *Saverio*.

Cardillo (1116) **1.** Italian (Sicily): from *cardillu* 'goldfinch', possibly applied as a nickname for someone with a good singing voice or who wore colorful clothing. **2.** Italian: variant of CARDELLO 2.

GIVEN NAMES Italian 17%. *Rocco* (7), *Antonio* (6), *Carmine* (6), *Pasquale* (5), *Luigi* (4), *Salvatore* (4), *Oreste* (2), *Pasco* (2), *Raffaele* (2), *Serafino* (2), *Alfio*.

Cardin (1192) French: from a reduced form of the personal name *Ricardin*, a Norman and Picard pet form of RICHARD.

FOREBEARS A bearer of this name from Normandy, France, is recorded in Trois Rivières, Quebec, in 1669.

GIVEN NAMES French 6%. *Andre* (3), *Normand* (2), *Alexina*, *Armand*, *Fernand*, *Germaine*, *Gilles*, *Henri*, *Lucien*, *Lucienne*, *Napoleon*, *Patrice*.

Cardinal (1745) English, French, Spanish, and Dutch: from Middle English, Old French *cardinal* 'cardinal', the church dignitary (Latin *cardinalis*, originally an adjective meaning 'crucial'). The surname may have denoted a servant who worked in a cardinal's household, but was probably more often bestowed as a nickname on someone who habitually dressed in red or who had played the part of a cardinal in a pageant, or on one who acted in a lordly and patronizing manner, like a prince of the Church.

FOREBEARS A bearer of the name, of unknown origin, is documented in Montreal by 1666.

GIVEN NAMES French 5%. *Armand* (4), *Lucien* (2), *Adelard*, *Alberic*, *Clovis*, *Colette*, *Curley*, *Fabienne*, *Fernand*, *Francois*, *Germaine*, *Gilles*.

Cardinale (1161) Italian: from *cardinale* 'cardinal' (see CARDINAL), nickname for a haughty individual, or occupational nickname for the servant of a cardinal.

GIVEN NAMES Italian 25%. *Sal* (13), *Salvatore* (8), *Mario* (5), *Rocco* (4), *Vito* (4), *Angelo* (3), *Antonio* (3), *Cosimo* (3), *Salvador* (3), *Carlo* (2), *Cosmo* (2), *Francesca* (2), *Gasper* (2), *Gennaro* (2), *Angelina*, *Demetrio*, *Gaspar*, *Gerardo*, *Julio*, *Lucrecia*, *Romero*, *Rosario*.

Cardinali (270) Italian: variant of CARDINALE.

GIVEN NAMES Italian 15%. *Dante* (3), *Mario* (3), *Angelo* (2), *Sergio* (2), *Americo*,

Corinda, *Emilio*, *Ennio*, *Gildo*, *Ilio*, *Luigi*, *Massimo*, *Romeo*, *Serafino*, *Sisto*.

Cardo (121) **1.** Spanish and Italian: from *cardo* 'thistle', 'cardoon' (Latin *carduus*), hence a topographic name, or possibly in some cases a metonymic occupational name for a wool carder, thistles having been used for this purpose. **2.** Italian: from a short form of a personal name with this ending, such as ACCARDO, *Biancardo* (see BIANCARDI), or RICCARDO. **3.** Catalan (**Cardó**): habitational name from a place named Cardó in Catalonia.

GIVEN NAMES Spanish 17%; Italian 7%. *Carlos* (2), *Diego*, *Eladio*, *Feliciano*, *Hermina*, *Humberto*, *Jorge*, *Jose*, *Marta*, *Orlando*, *Reyes*, *Roberto*; *Vito* (3).

Cardon (444) **1.** French: from Old Norman French *cardon* 'thistle' (a diminutive of *carde*, from Latin *carduus*), hence a topographic name for someone who lived on land overgrown with thistles, an occupational name for someone who carded wool (originally a process carried out with thistles and teasels), or perhaps a nickname for a prickly and unapproachable person. **2.** French: possibly from a reduced form of the personal name *Ricardon*, a pet form of RICHARD. **3.** English: variant spelling of CARDEN, cognate with 1.

GIVEN NAMES French 4%. *Jacques*, *Marie-Claude*.

Cardona (2812) Catalan: habitational name for someone from a place in Barcelona province named Cardona. Its name dates from the pre-Roman period but the meaning is unknown.

GIVEN NAMES Spanish 47%. *Jose* (83), *Juan* (41), *Carlos* (31), *Luis* (24), *Jesus* (18), *Jorge* (18), *Angel* (17), *Ramon* (16), *Francisco* (15), *Manuel* (15), *Raul* (15), *Ana* (14).

Cardone (975) **1.** Southern Italian (Sicily and Naples): from Sicilian *carduni* 'thistle', 'teasel', 'cardoon', probably a topographic name, but, used figuratively to mean 'rough', 'uncouth' or 'stingy', 'miserly', it may also have been a nickname. **2.** Italian: from an augmentative form of the personal name CARDO.

GIVEN NAMES Italian 13%. *Antonio* (5), *Carmine* (5), *Rocco* (4), *Angelo* (3), *Aldo* (2), *Dante* (2), *Francesco* (2), *Luigi* (2), *Mauro* (2), *Nino* (2), *Pasquale* (2), *Salvatore* (2).

Cardoni (154) Italian: patronymic or plural form of CARDONE 2.

GIVEN NAMES Italian 11%. *Aldo* (2), *Angelo*, *Benvenuto*, *Dante*, *Dino*, *Primo*, *Sal*.

Cardosa (211) **1.** Galician and Portuguese: habitational name from any of various places in Portugal and Galicia named Cardosa. **2.** Southern Italian: habitational name from a place named Cardosa, probably from an adjectival derivative of *cardo* 'thistle' (Latin *cardosus* 'rich in thistles').

GIVEN NAMES Spanish 37%; Portuguese 13%. *Manuel* (6), *Jose* (4), *Adan* (2), *Carlos* (2), *Miguel* (2), *Salvador* (2), *Sergio* (2), *Adelino*, *Alejandro*, *Ana*, *Armando*, *Arnaldo*; *Joao*.

Cardosi (184) Italian: habitational name from any of numerous minor places called Cardosi or Cardoso, from Latin *cardosus* 'rich in thistles'.

GIVEN NAME French 4%. *Serge*.

Cardoso (1056) Portuguese, Galician, and Spanish: habitational name from any of numerous places with this name, denoting a place with an abundance of cardoons.

GIVEN NAMES Spanish 46%; Portuguese 18%. *Jose* (35), *Manuel* (30), *Carlos* (27), *Luis* (13), *Mario* (8), *Pedro* (8), *Angel* (7), *Francisco* (7), *Luiz* (6), *Miguel* (6), *Armando* (5), *Jesus* (5); *Joao* (7), *Joaquim* (5), *Agostinho* (2), *Duarte* (2), *Paulo* (2), *Afonso*, *Albano*, *Braz*, *Henrique*, *Marcio*, *Serafim*; *Antonio* (31), *Luciano* (2), *Albertina*, *Carmela*, *Ciriaco*, *Emidio*, *Federico*, *Filomena*, *Flavio*, *Giovanni*, *Gulio*, *Julieta*.

Cardoza (2122) Portuguese: variant of CARDOSA.

GIVEN NAMES Spanish 25%; Portuguese 7%. *Manuel* (55), *Jose* (28), *Rafael* (11), *Juan* (8), *Armando* (7), *Carlos* (7), *Mario* (7), *Jesus* (6), *Luis* (6), *Raul* (6), *Fernando* (5), *Ana* (4); *Ligia*, *Messias*.

Cardozo (386) Spanish and Portuguese: variant of CARDOSO. This name is also found in western India, where it was taken by Portuguese colonists.

GIVEN NAMES Spanish 33%; Portuguese 11%. *Carlos* (7), *Jose* (7), *Luis* (7), *Manuel* (4), *Pedro* (4), *Jaime* (3), *Mario* (3), *Alberto* (2), *Alvaro* (2), *Francisco* (2), *Juana* (2), *Orlando* (2); *Joaquim*, *Vasco*.

Carducci (343) Italian: from a diminutive of CARDO.

GIVEN NAMES Italian 15%. *Gaetano* (3), *Angelo* (2), *Romeo* (2), *Aldo*, *Antonio*, *Domenico*, *Emidio*, *Gino*, *Giovanni*, *Guido*, *Lorenzo*, *Luigi*.

Cardullo (131) Italian: diminutive of CARDO.

GIVEN NAMES Italian 17%. *Giovanni* (2), *Domenic*, *Orazio*, *Raffaela*, *Tommaso*.

Cardwell (4062) English, Scottish, and northern Irish: variant of CALDWELL.

Cardy (130) Cornish and English: habitational name from any of three places called Cardew, in the parishes of Trevalga and Warbstow, Cornwall, and in Cumbria. All are of Celtic origin, from *cair*, *ker* 'fort' + *du* 'dark', 'black'.

Care (294) **1.** English: occupational name for a locksmith, Middle English *keyere*, *kayer*, an agent derivative of *keye* 'key' (from Old English *cæg*). **2.** Probably an Americanized form of German KEHR or GEHR.

Careaga (107) Basque: topographic name for someone who lived by a limestone quarry or a lime kiln, from Basque *care* 'lime' + the locative suffix *-aga*.

GIVEN NAMES Spanish 39%. *Carlos* (2), *Jose* (2), *Orlando* (2), *Pedro* (2), *Alicia*, *Ana*, *Andres*, *Bernardo*, *Elba*, *Estrella*, *Fernando*, *Francisco*.

Carel (195) French: from Old French *quar(r)el* 'bolt (for a crossbow)' (Late Latin *quadrellum*, a diminutive of *quadrum* 'square'), hence a metonymic occupational name for a maker of crossbow bolts, or a nickname for a short, stout man.

Carella (323) Italian: diminutive of CARA.

GIVEN NAMES Italian 16%. *Angelo* (3), *Carlo*, *Carmela*, *Dino*, *Gabriele*, *Giovanni*, *Guido*, *Lorenzo*, *Rocco*, *Sandro*.

Carelli (331) Italian: patronymic or plural form of CARELLO.

GIVEN NAMES Italian 12%. *Vito* (2), *Antonio*, *Domenic*, *Luigi*, *Salvatore*, *Santina*, *Vincenzo*.

Carello (124) Italian: variant of CARILLO.

GIVEN NAMES Italian 17%; French 4%. *Rocco* (2), *Angelo*, *Concetta*, *Guiseppe*, *Saverio*, *Vito*; *Alphonse*, *Cecile*.

Carelock (153) See CARLOCK.

Caress (116) English: variant of CARRAS.

Carew (889) **1.** Welsh: habitational name from any of various minor places in Wales, in particular one near Pembroke with a major castle, named from Welsh *caer* 'fort' + *rhiw* 'hill', 'slope'. **2.** Cornish: from the cognate Cornish word *kerrow* (plural of *ker* 'fort'), which occurs seven times as a place name in Cornwall.

GIVEN NAMES Irish 5%. *Brendan* (2), *Aileen*, *James Patrick*, *Kieran*.

Carey (21038) **1.** Irish: Anglicized form of Gaelic **Ó Ciardha**, a midland family name meaning 'descendant of *Ciardha*', a personal name derived from *ciar* 'dark', 'black'. **2.** Irish: Anglicized form of Gaelic **Mac Fhiachra** 'son of *Fiachra*'. **3.** English: habitational name from Carey in Devon or Cary in Somerset, named for the rivers on which they stand; both river names probably derive from the Celtic root *car-* 'love', 'liking', perhaps with the meaning 'pleasant stream'. **4.** English (of Norman origin): habitational name from the manor of Carrey, near Lisieux, Normandy, France, of uncertain origin. **5.** Welsh and Cornish: variant of CAREW. **6.** Possibly an Americanized form of German GEHRIG or GEHRING.

Carfagna (102) Italian: unexplained. Compare CARFAGNO.

GIVEN NAMES Italian 15%. *Angelo* (2), *Benedetto*, *Dino*, *Geno*.

Carfagno (309) Italian: unexplained. In Italy the surname occurs predominantly in Campania, centered in Montella.

GIVEN NAMES Italian 10%. *Carmela* (2), *Angelo*, *Annamarie*, *Fausto*, *Gaetano*, *Gennaro*, *Sal*, *Salvatore*.

Carfora (155) Italian: perhaps a variant of **Canfora**, from *canfora* 'camphor', from Arabic *kāfūr*.

GIVEN NAMES Italian 23%. *Alfonso* (3), *Erasmo* (2), *Dino*, *Pasquale*, *Santo*.

Cargal (169) **1.** Altered spelling of Scottish CARGILL. **2.** Perhaps an Americanized spelling of German **Kargl** (see CARGLE).

Cargile (902) Possibly a variant spelling of Scottish CARGILL. A family of this name is recorded in Lincolnshire in the late 19th century.

Cargill (1576) Scottish: habitational name from Cargill, a place in eastern Perthshire.

Cargle (140) **1.** Probably a variant spelling of Scottish CARGILL. **2.** Americanized spelling of South German **Kargl**, a diminutive of KARG.

GIVEN NAMES French 4%. *Ives*, *Julienne*.

Cargo (266) **1.** Slovenian (**Čargo**): unexplained. This name comes from the westernmost part of Slovenia. **2.** It may also be an Americanized spelling of German KARGER.

Carhart (541) Americanized form of German GERHARDT.

Cariaga (133) Basque: variant of CAREAGA.

GIVEN NAMES Spanish 35%. *Carlos* (2), *Ernesto* (2), *Juan* (2), *Macedonio* (2), *Roberto* (2), *Alfonso*, *Alonzo*, *Amparo*, *Angelino*, *Armando*, *Arturo*, *Benigno*; *Angelo*, *Federico*.

Carias (169) Portuguese and Spanish (**Carías**): unexplained; probably a topographic name from the plural of a shortened form of Portuguese *alcaria* (Spanish *alquería*) 'little village' or 'shed' or denoting a kind of violet, of Arabic origin.

GIVEN NAMES Spanish 53%. *Carlos* (7), *Alfredo* (3), *Jesus* (3), *Josue* (3), *Armando* (2), *Jorge* (2), *Jose* (2), *Manuel* (2), *Miguel* (2), *Orlando* (2), *Rogelio* (2), *Alicia*.

Carico (593) Italian (Sicily): habitational name from a place called Carico, named with Arabic *kharq* 'cleft', 'slit', 'opening'.

Carideo (122) Italian: habitational name for someone from S. Pietro di Caridà, a place near Reggio Calabria. The suffix *-eo*, of Greek origin, is typical of the south.

GIVEN NAMES Italian 15%. *Angelo* (2), *Fausto*, *Pasquale*.

Caridi (217) Italian: **1.** habitational name from a place on the Messina strait called Cariddi. **2.** from Greek *karydion* 'walnut', probably applied as a metonymic occupational name for someone who gathered and sold walnuts.

GIVEN NAMES Italian 32%. *Salvatore* (6), *Angelo* (2), *Aida*, *Demetrio*, *Domenico*, *Jacobo*, *Marcello*, *Mario*, *Sergio*.

Carie (157) Scottish spelling of Irish CAREY.

Cariello (165) Italian (Naples): variant of CARILLO.

GIVEN NAMES Italian 25%. *Salvatore* (2), *Alba*, *Elvira*, *Lazaro*, *Sergio*, *Silvia*, *Vito*.

Carignan (706) French: habitational name for someone from Carignano in Piedmont, Italy.

GIVEN NAMES French 14%. *Armand* (9), *Adrien* (5), *Lucien* (3), *Andre* (2), *Aime*, *Benoit*, *Edouard*, *Emile*, *Gilles*, *Herve*, *Julien*, *Laurent*.

Cariker (185) Irish or German: see CARRIKER.

Carilli (131) Italian: patronymic or plural form of CARILLO.

GIVEN NAMES Italian 22%. *Angelo* (2), *Rocco* (2), *Santo* (2), *Giacomo*, *Sal*, *Umberto*.

Carillo (563) Spanish and southern Italian: from a diminutive of CARO.

GIVEN NAMES Spanish 43%; Italian 7%. *Jose* (8), *Manuel* (6), *Carlos* (5), *Arturo* (4), *Juan* (4), *Luis* (4), *Francisco* (3), *Guadalupe* (3), *Jesus* (3), *Ramon* (3), *Raul* (3), *Amado* (2); *Angelo* (5), *Antonio* (3), *Carmela* (2), *Albertina*, *Amadeo*, *Giovanni*, *Giuseppe*, *Leonardo*, *Mauro*, *Pasquale*, *Sal*, *Salvatore*.

Carinci (106) Italian: unexplained.

GIVEN NAMES Italian 17%. *Angelo*, *Enrico*, *Enzo*, *Gabriele*, *Geno*.

Carini (508) Italian: **1.** from a diminutive of CARO. **2.** habitational name from a place in Palermo province named Carini.

GIVEN NAMES Italian 16%. *Carlo* (2), *Francesco* (2), *Pietro* (2), *Stefano* (2), *Antonio*, *Caesar*, *Carmelo*, *Concetta*, *Cosmo*, *Domenic*, *Ercole*, *Filippa*.

Carino (654) Italian: diminutive of CARO.

GIVEN NAMES Spanish 26%; Italian 9%. *Mario* (4), *Alfredo* (3), *Angel* (3), *Manuel* (3), *Roberto* (3), *Carlos* (2), *Ernesto* (2), *Guadalupe* (2), *Jose* (2), *Julio* (2), *Lazaro* (2), *Luis* (2); *Angelo* (5), *Pasquale* (2), *Rocco* (2), *Salvatore* (2), *Biagio*, *Donato*, *Eliseo*, *Larraine*, *Leonardo*, *Rosaria*.

Caris (288) **1.** English: variant spelling of CARRAS. **2.** Dutch: from a reduced form of the Greek personal name *Makarios* (see MACARIO). **3.** Americanized spelling of German KARAS, GAREIS, or GEHRES.

Carithers (427) Altered spelling of Scottish CARRUTHERS.

Cariveau (159) French: unexplained; perhaps an occupational name for a knife maker, a Languedoc variant of **Canipeau** (see CANIPE).

Carkhuff (162) Altered spelling of German and Dutch KERKHOFF or German KIRCHHOFF or any of the numerous North German and Dutch cognates.

Carkin (100) English: unexplained.

Carl (4409) **1.** Variant spelling of Dutch, German, and Scandinavian KARL. **2.** English: from the Anglo-Scandinavian personal name *Karl(i)*, ultimately from Germanic *karl* 'man', 'freeman'. See also CHARLES. **3.** English: status name for a bondman or villein, from the vocabulary word *karl*, *carl*, which had various different meanings at various times: originally 'man', then 'ordinary man', 'peasant', and in Middle

English specialized in the senses 'free peasant', 'bondman', 'villein', and 'rough, churlish individual'.

Carlan (197) Irish: Anglicized form of Gaelic **Ó Cairealláin** (see CARLIN).

Carland (207) Irish: Anglicized form of Gaelic **Ó Cairealláin** (see CARLIN).

Carlberg (552) Swedish: habitational name from a farm named Carlberg, from *karl* 'man', 'freeman' + *berg*, a suffix often used since the 17th century in names of manorial estates.
GIVEN NAMES Scandinavian 7%. *Helmer, Lars.*

Carle (1271) **1.** English: variant of CARL. **2.** French: Norman and Picard form of CHARLES. **3.** Swiss German: variant spelling of KARLE.

Carlen (339) Probably a variant spelling of CARLIN or a respelling of KARLEN.

Carleo (117) Italian: **1.** from the medieval Greek personal name *Kaloleon* or *Kaloleos* meaning 'Leon the good'. **2.** from a variant of the personal name *Carlo* (see CHARLES). **3.** variant of **Corleo**, from Greek *kyrios* 'sir', 'lord' + the personal name *Leo*.
GIVEN NAMES Italian 22%. *Luigi* (2), *Armando, Gino, Nino, Rocco, Xavier.*

Carles (124) Catalan: from the personal name *Carles*, Catalan form of CHARLES 1.
GIVEN NAMES Spanish 14%; French 8%. *Carlos* (2), *Bienvenido, Blanca, Carlito, Cristina, Elva, Ernesto, Humberto, Juan Carlos, Mariana, Mariano; Emile* (2), *Alain, Marcel.*

Carleton (1966) English: variant spelling of CARLTON.

Carley (1972) **1.** Reduced form of Irish MCCARLEY. **2.** English: habitational name from the hamlet of Carley in Lifton, Devon, possibly named with Cornish *ker* 'fort' + Old English *lēah* 'woodland clearing'. **3.** Perhaps an Americanized form of German KEHRLI or **Kerle** (see KERLEY).

Carli (331) **1.** Italian: patronymic or plural form of CARLO. **2.** Swiss German: variant of KARLE.
GIVEN NAMES Italian 9%. *Angelo* (2), *Pio* (2), *Aldo, Alessio, Dino, Domenico, Egidio, Gino, Giovanni, Guido, Reno.*

Carlier (137) French: Norman and Picard variant of CHARLIER.
GIVEN NAMES French 13%. *Achille, Adrien, Gaston, Marcel, Philippe, Pierre.*

Carlile (1669) English: variant spelling of CARLISLE.

Carlin (4347) **1.** Irish (now also common in Scotland): Anglicized form of Gaelic **Ó Cairealláin**, an Ulster family name, also sometimes Anglicized as CARLTON, meaning 'descendant of *Caireallán*', a diminutive of the personal name *Caireall*. **2.** French: from a pet form of CHARLES. **3.** Swedish: probably a habitational name from any of various places named with *Karl-* or from the personal name + *-in*, a common suffix of Swedish family names

(originally Latin *-inus* 'descendant of'). **4.** Italian (Venice): from a pet form of the personal name *Carlo*, Italian form of CHARLES. **5.** Jewish (eastern Ashkenazic): Americanized spelling of KARLIN. **6.** German: habitational name from Carlin in Brandenburg.

Carline (243) **1.** Probably an altered spelling of CARLIN. **2.** Americanized form of German **Kärlein**, perhaps from a diminutive of Middle High German *kar* 'bowl', 'measure of grain', 'depression', 'basin', hence a metonymic occupational name for someone who made bowls or for someone who measured out grain, or a topographic name for someone who lived in a hollow.

Carling (289) **1.** Swedish: from the personal name *Karl* + the common suffix of surnames *-ing* 'belonging to'. **2.** Respelling of German **Karling**, a habitational name from Karling in Bavaria. **3.** Americanized form of German GARLING or GERLING.

Carlini (294) Italian: patronymic or plural form of CARLINO.
GIVEN NAMES Italian 16%. *Carlo* (4), *Orlando* (2), *Aldo, Alfonso, Angelo, Demetrio, Dino, Elio, Eliso, Filippo, Giuseppe, Mario, Massimo, Nicola, Pio, Vincenzo, Mauricio, Pasqual, Ricardo.*

Carlino (797) Italian: from a diminutive of the personal name *Carlo*, Italian equivalent of CHARLES. *Carlino* was also a term denoting a medieval Italian coin, and it is possible that in some cases the surname arose as a nickname, possibly for a worthless fellow, since it was a coin of low value, or as an occupational name for a moneyer.
GIVEN NAMES Italian 16%. *Angelo* (6), *Salvatore* (6), *Carlo* (4), *Mario* (3), *Antonio* (2), *Dino* (2), *Elio* (2), *Francesco* (2), *Giusto* (2), *Pasquale* (2), *Rocco* (2), *Carmelo, Ciro, Liborio* (2), *Salvadore* (2), *Carmella, Emilio, Ernesto, Isidoro.*

Carlisi (142) Italian: from a diminutive, *Carlino*, of the personal name *Carlo*, Italian equivalent of CHARLES.
GIVEN NAMES Italian 12%. *Angelo* (2), *Annamaria, Antonio, Salvatore.*

Carlisle (7225) English: habitational name from the Cumbrian city of Carlisle, in whose name Celtic *cair* 'fort' has been compounded with the Romano-British name of the settlement, *Luguvalium.*

Carll (363) English, Dutch, German, and Scandinavian: variant of CARL.

Carlo (1033) Italian: from the personal name *Carlo*, Italian equivalent of CHARLES.
GIVEN NAMES Spanish 8%; Italian 4%. *Jose* (3), *Carlos* (2), *Jorge* (2), *Juan* (2), *Julio* (2), *Luis* (2), *Orlando* (2), *Ricardo* (2), *Aida, Alicia, Andres, Angel; Angelo* (2), *Carmine* (2), *Silvio* (2), *Antonio, Carmela, Salvatore.*

Carlock (1081) **1.** Variant spelling of Scottish CARLOW. **2.** Americanized spelling of German GERLACH.

Carlon (525) Northern Italian: Venetian variant of CARLONE, Italian equivalent of CHARLES.

Carlone (286) Italian: from an augmentative form of the personal name *Carlo*, Italian equivalent of CHARLES.
GIVEN NAMES Italian 24%. *Carlo* (3), *Umberto* (3), *Angelo* (2), *Antonio* (2), *Biaggio, Corrado, Cosmo, Filippo, Gaetano, Giuseppe, Nichola, Pasquale.*

Carloni (149) Italian: patronymic or plural form of CARLONE.
GIVEN NAMES Italian 14%; German 6%. *Aldo, Domenic, Elio, Ercole, Massimo, Quinto, Reno; Hildegarde, Kurt, Otto.*

Carlos (1796) Spanish and Portuguese: from the personal name *Carlos*, Spanish equivalent of CHARLES.
GIVEN NAMES Spanish 36%; Portuguese 7%. *Jose* (27), *Juan* (19), *Manuel* (14), *Francisco* (11), *Raul* (9), *Alicia* (8), *Jesus* (8), *Luis* (8), *Armando* (7), *Jaime* (7), *Carlos* (6), *Ruben* (6); *Fernandes, Joao, Joaquim.*

Carlough (161) **1.** Variant spelling of Scottish CARLOW. **2.** Americanized spelling of German GERLACH.

Carlow (394) Scottish: according to Black, a Muiravonside (Stirlingshire) name of topographic origin.

Carlozzi (155) Italian: from the personal name *Carlozzo*, a derivative of *Carlo*, Italian equivalent of CHARLES.
GIVEN NAMES Italian 14%. *Salvatore* (2), *Carlo, Emidio, Enrico, Giuseppe.*

Carlquist (128) Swedish: ornamental name composed of the personal name CARL + *quist*, an old or ornamental spelling of *kvist* 'twig'.

Carls (402) English, Dutch, or German: patronymic from CARL.

Carlsen (1853) Danish, Norwegian, North German, and Dutch: patronymic from the personal name CARL.
GIVEN NAMES Scandinavian 8%; German 4%. *Niels* (4), *Lars* (2), *Lief* (2), *Alf, Berger, Bernt, Bjorn, Carsten, Erik, Folmer, Holger, Iver; Kurt* (11), *Bernhard, Friederike, Gerhard, Gerhardt, Hans, Helmut, Otto.*

Carlson (53787) **1.** Scandinavian: respelling of Norwegian and Danish CARLSEN or Swedish CARLSSON. **2.** Dutch and German: patronymic from CARL. See also KARLSON.
GIVEN NAMES Scandinavian 4%. *Erik* (71), *Nels* (20), *Lennart* (18), *Nils* (14), *Sven* (14), *Helmer* (13), *Iver* (9), *Berger* (8), *Erland* (8), *Lars* (8), *Anders* (7), *Evald* (7).

Carlsson (224) Swedish: patronymic from the personal name CARL.
GIVEN NAMES Scandinavian 42%; German 5%. *Bjorn* (4), *Sven* (4), *Anders* (2), *Erik* (2), *Nils* (2), *Britt, Mats, Owe, Siw; Hans* (3), *Katharina, Ulrika.*

Carlstedt (121) Swedish: ornamental name from the personal name CARL + *-stedt*, a common element of Swedish family names, originally from German *Stadt* 'city'.

GIVEN NAMES Scandinavian 8%; German 4%. *Anders, Erik; Kurt.*

Carlston (203) Altered form of Swedish CARLSSON or Danish and Norwegian CARLSEN.

Carlstrom (672) Swedish (**Carlström**): ornamental name composed of the personal name CARL + *ström* 'stream'.

GIVEN NAMES Scandinavian 4%. *Nils* (2), *Astrid, Erik, Iver, Nels.*

Carlton (7773) **1.** English: habitational name from any of various places called Carleton or Carlton, from Old Norse *karl* 'common man', 'peasant' + Old English *tūn* 'settlement' (compare CHARLTON 1). Places spelled *Carl(e)ton* (as opposed to *Charlton*) are in areas of Scandinavian settlement, mostly in northern England. **2.** Irish: Americanized and altered form of CARLIN 1.

Carlucci (941) Southern Italian: patronymic or plural form of CARLUCCIO.

GIVEN NAMES Italian 18%. *Rocco* (9), *Vito* (8), *Gino* (4), *Angelo* (3), *Antonio* (2), *Carlo* (2), *Domenic* (2), *Donato* (2), *Nicola* (2), *Salvatore* (2), *Alfonse, Attilio.*

Carluccio (111) Southern Italian: from the personal name *Carluccio*, a pet form of the personal name CARLO, Italian equivalent of CHARLES.

GIVEN NAMES Italian 19%. *Rocco* (2), *Dino, Mario, Pasquale, Sal.*

Carlyle (1166) English: variant spelling of CARLISLE.

Carlyon (204) Cornish: habitational name from any of three places in Cornwall called Carlyon, in St. Minver and Kea parishes. The first element is Celtic *ker* 'fort'; the second could represent the plural of Cornish *legh* 'slab'.

Carmack (1915) Probably a reduced and altered form of Irish MCCORMACK (see MCCORMICK), or possibly of **Carmaig**, an unexplained Scottish name, also recorded as **Carmag**.

Carman (4126) **1.** English: from an Old Norse personal name *Kar(l)maðr* (accusative *Kar(l)mann*), composed of the elements *karl* 'male', 'man' + *maðr* 'man', 'person'. **2.** English: occupational name for a carter, from Anglo-Norman French, Middle English *car(re)* 'cart' (Late Latin *carrus*) + Middle English *man* 'man'. **3.** Dutch: variant spelling of KARMAN. **4.** Altered spelling of GERMANN or KORMAN.

Carmany (158) Origin uncertain. Probably a variant of the French habitational name **Garmigny** (see GARMANY).

Carmean (591) Probably a variant of English CARMAN.

Carmel (496) **1.** Jewish: Americanized spelling of KARMEL. **2.** French: perhaps from **Carme** 'Carmelite friar'. The

Carmelites are a mendicant order, founded at Mount Carmel during the Crusades.

GIVEN NAMES Jewish 7%; French 5%. *Avi* (2), *Gerson* (2), *Nurit* (2), *Arie, Erez, Hadar, Merav, Miriam, Moshe, Ofer, Shai, Sol; Andre* (3), *Gilles, Lucien.*

Carmen (798) **1.** Spanish: from the Marian epithet *(María del) Carmen* 'Our Lady of Carmel', a reference to Mount Carmel (meaning 'garden' or 'orchard') in the Holy Land, which was populated from early Christian times by hermits. **2.** Spanish: habitational name from any of various places in Spain named El Carmen, for example in the province of Cuenca. **3.** English: variant spelling of CARMAN.

Carmer (307) Origin unidentified. The name is recorded in different parts of Germany, the Netherlands, and England in the 18th century, and was in the Hudson Valley from the 1740s on. In part at least, it may be a variant of Dutch **Kermer** 'Carmelite' (see CARMEL).

Carmical (214) Variant of Scottish CARMICHAEL.

Carmichael (7056) Scottish: habitational name from Carmichael in Lanarkshire, from British *caer* 'fort' + the personal name MICHAEL.

Carmicheal (111) Scottish: variant of CARMICHAEL.

Carmickle (142) Variant of Scottish CARMICHAEL.

GIVEN NAME French 4%. *Amie* (2).

Carmin (134) French: from *carmin* 'red' (from Arabic *qirmiz* 'cochineal' + Latin *minium* 'cinnabar'), applied perhaps as a nickname for someone with a ruddy complexion or one who habitually wore red.

GIVEN NAME French 4%. *Florent.*

Carminati (105) Italian: unexplained; probably a habitational name from a lost place called Carminate.

GIVEN NAMES Italian 12%. *Angelo, Ettore, Gaeton, Premo, Renzo.*

Carmine (261) Italian (Piedmont): from the personal name *Carmine*, a variant of *Carmelo*, from Mount Carmel in the Holy Land, which was populated from early Christian times by hermits.

Carmody (2416) Irish (Munster): Anglicized form of Gaelic **Ó Cearmada** 'descendant of *Cearmaid*', a personal name of uncertain origin.

GIVEN NAMES Irish 6%. *Brendan* (3), *Brennan, Liam, Padraic, Padraig, Padric, Patrick Joseph.*

Carmon (708) **1.** English: variant spelling of CARMAN. **2.** Altered spelling of GERMANN or KORMANN.

Carmona (2059) Spanish: habitational name from places called Carmona, in the provinces of Santander and (more famously) Seville. The place name is of pre-Roman origin and uncertain meaning.

GIVEN NAMES Spanish 49%. *Jose* (64), *Juan* (38), *Manuel* (24), *Jorge* (21), *Jesus* (18),

Carlos (15), *Miguel* (14), *Francisco* (13), *Luis* (13), *Raul* (12), *Javier* (11), *Salvador* (11).

Carmony (185) Most probably an altered spelling of the French habitational name **Garmigny** (see GARMANY).

Carmosino (126) Italian: of uncertain derivation; possibly a variant of **Carmicino**, **Carmisino**, from Sicilian *carmisinu* 'crimson', applied as a nickname for someone who habitually wore red or as a metonymic occupational name for a dyer.

GIVEN NAMES Italian 19%. *Antonio* (3), *Americo, Marco, Mario, Nicola, Nino, Vito.*

Carmouche (356) French: from a reduced form of *escarmouche* 'skirmish', a loanword from Italian *scaramuccia*. The name is found predominantly in LA.

GIVEN NAMES French 7%. *Monique* (2), *Camile, Fernest, Marcel, Numa, Pierre.*

Carn (192) **1.** Reduced form of Irish MCCARN, which is itself a reduced form of MCCARRON. **2.** Variant spelling of Cornish CARNE. **3.** Possibly a respelling of German, Dutch, and Jewish KERN.

Carnagey (121) Altered spelling of Scottish CARNEGIE.

Carnaghi (129) Italian: habitational name from Carnago in Varese province, Lombardy.

GIVEN NAMES French 5%; Italian 4%. *Aldo, Caesar.*

Carnahan (2796) Irish: Anglicized form of Gaelic **Ó Cearncháin** (see KERNAGHAN).

Carnal (148) **1.** English: variant spelling of CARNELL. **2.** French: metonymic occupational name for a maker of latches and hinges, from Old Picard *carnel*, Old French *charnel* 'hinge'.

GIVEN NAME French 5%. *Henri.*

Carnathan (210) Variant of Irish CARNAHAN (see KERNAGHAN).

Carne (251) **1.** Cornish: topographic name from Cornish *carn* 'cairn', or a habitational name from any of several places in Cornwall named Carne from this word. **2.** French: metonymic occupational name from Old Picard *carne* 'hinge' (Old French *charnel*). **3.** French (**Carné**): nickname for a thin man or alternatively for a fat one. The surname derives from the past participle of Norman, Picard, and Occitan *carner* (Old French *charner*), from *c(h)ar* 'flesh', 'meat', from Latin *caro*, genitive *carnis*. This term was used in a variety of senses, as for example 'to strip flesh from the bone' or 'to feed animals with meat', and it is from this that the ambiguity of the nickname arises.

Carneal (382) **1.** Scottish: habitational name from the lands of Carneil near Dunfermline, Fife. **2.** Possibly an altered spelling of North German **Ka(r)nehl**, an occupational name for a spicer, from *Kaneel* 'cinnamon'.

Carnegie (570) Scottish: habitational name from a place called Carnegie, near Carmyllie in Angus, probably named in Gaelic as *cathair an eige* 'fort at the gap'.

FOREBEARS The industrialist and philanthropist Andrew Carnegie (1835–1919) was born in Dunfermline, Scotland; he came with his family to Allegheny, PA, in 1848.

Carneiro (203) Portuguese: from *carneiro* 'ram' (from an unattested Latin word *carnāriu*, a derivative of *caro* 'flesh'), applied as a nickname for a good-natured person or someone's fiancé.

GIVEN NAMES Spanish 34%; Portuguese 21%. *Antonio* (11), *Jose* (10), *Manuel* (5), *Carlos* (4), *Mario* (4), *Americo* (2), *Claudio* (2), *Enrique* (2), *Aida, Aires, Alberto, Alda, Alfredo*; *Joao* (2), *Ademir, Aloisio, Heitor*.

Carnell (777) **1.** English: apparently a metonymic occupational name for a crossbowman who specialized in fighting from the battlements of castles, from Anglo-Norman French *carnel* 'battlement', 'embrasure' (a metathesized form of *crenel*, Late Latin *crenellus*, a diminutive of *crena* 'notch'). **2.** English: reduced form of CARBONELL or CARDINAL. **3.** Swedish: the second element *-ell* is a common suffix of Swedish surnames, taken from the Latin adjectival ending *-elius*. The first element is unexplained.

Carner (661) **1.** Americanized spelling of German KARNER or **Körner** (see KOERNER). **2.** Possibly also English: variant of CORNER.

Carnero (107) Spanish: nickname from *carnero* 'ram'.

GIVEN NAMES Spanish 47%. *Manuel* (5), *Jose* (3), *Fernando* (2), *Juan* (2), *Pedro* (2), *Adolfina, Alfredo, Caridad, Casimiro, Corina, Educardo, Emilio*; *Antonio, Constantino, Elio*.

Carnes (5197) **1.** Irish: variant of KEARNS. **2.** Scottish: variant of CAIRNS.

Carnett (143) Possibly an altered spelling of French **Carnet**, which may be a reduced form of **Carrenet**, a derivative of **Carré** (see CARRE), or alternatively a derivative of *carnet* 'tax register' and therefore a metonymic occupational name for a tax collector.

Carnevale (1067) Italian: from *carnevale* 'festival' (from *carnelevare* 'fast', literally 'removal of meat'; it was the normal practice to have a riotous carnival before a period of solemn fast such as Lent, and this gradually acquired a greater significance than the fast itself and usurped the meaning of the word). This was sometimes used as a personal name (Italian *Varnevale*, also *Carlevario*; Latin *Carnelevarius*), probably bestowed on someone born at the time of a carnival, or a nickname for someone with a particularly festive spirit.

GIVEN NAMES Italian 17%. *Angelo* (5), *Rocco* (4), *Antonio* (3), *Carmine* (3), *Franco* (3), *Luigi* (3), *Cosmo* (2), *Francesco* (2),

Gennaro (2), *Giulio* (2), *Guido* (2), *Oreste* (2).

Carney (12482) **1.** Irish: Anglicized form of Gaelic **Ó Catharnaigh** 'descendant of *Catharnach*', a byname meaning 'warlike'. **2.** Irish: reduced form of MCCARNEY. **3.** Irish: variant of CAIRNEY. **4.** Irish: Anglicized form of Gaelic **Ó Cearnaigh** 'descendant of *Cearnach*'. Compare KEARNEY.

GIVEN NAMES Irish 7%. *Brendan* (3), *Kieran* (3), *Aidan, Aileen, Briana, Declan, Eamon, Finbarr, Keane, Meave, Mhairi, Paddy*.

Carnicelli (107) Italian: from a diminutive of *carne* 'flesh', bestowed as a nickname for a corpulent man.

GIVEN NAMES Italian 8%. *Biago, Enrico*.

Carnicom (102) Origin unidentified.

Carnie (104) Scottish: habitational name from Carnie, near Skene, Aberdeenshire.

Carnine (169) Perhaps an Americanized spelling of South German **Karnein** (unexplained).

Carnley (561) **1.** English: habitational name, possibly from Canetley in Cumbria, named with Celtic *carn* 'cairn' + the Old Welsh personal name *Teiliau*. **2.** Americanized spelling of German **Körnle**, a diminutive of KORN.

Carns (626) Scottish: variant of CAIRNS.

Caro (1498) **1.** Spanish, Portuguese, Italian, and Jewish (Sephardic and Ashkenazic): nickname from Portuguese, Spanish, Italian *caro* 'dear', 'beloved' (Latin *carus*). In medieval Italy this was also a personal name. **2.** Italian (Sicily; **Carò**): variant of **Carrò** (see CARRO).

GIVEN NAMES Spanish 33%. *Jose* (17), *Miguel* (16), *Jesus* (13), *Carlos* (11), *Luis* (11), *Francisco* (7), *Juan* (7), *Jaime* (6), *Manuel* (6), *Ramon* (5), *Ruben* (5), *Angel* (4).

Carol (364) Irish: variant spelling of CARROLL.

Carolan (909) Irish: Anglicized form of Gaelic **Ó Cearbhalláin**, a northern and midland Irish name meaning 'descendant of *Cearbhallán*', a diminutive of the personal name *Cearbhall* (see CARROLL).

GIVEN NAMES Irish 7%. *Brendan* (2), *Connolly, Malachy*.

Carolin (103) Irish: variant of CAROLAN.

GIVEN NAME Irish 5%. *Eamon*.

Carolina (158) Spanish: from the female personal name, feminine form of CAROLUS, or a habitational name from La Carolina in Jaén province.

GIVEN NAME French 6%. *Andre*.

Caroline (111) Irish: variant of CAROLAN.

Caroll (148) Irish: variant spelling of CARROLL.

Carolla (115) Southern Italian: feminine variant of CAROLLO.

Carollo (718) Southern Italian: **1.** from a diminutive of CARO. **2.** variant of **Carolo**, from a diminutive of CARLO.

GIVEN NAMES Italian 16%. *Salvatore* (7), *Santo* (4), *Angelo* (2), *Antonio* (2), *Calogero* (2), *Damiano* (2), *Ferdinando* (2), *Sal* (2), *Vito* (2), *Aldo, Croce, Domenic*.

Carolus (242) Spanish: from the humanistic personal name *Carolus*, a Latinized form of the Germanic personal name *Karl* (see CARL and CHARLES).

Caron (5209) **1.** French: from a personal name of Gaulish origin, represented in Latin records in the form *Caraunus*. This name was borne by a 5th-century Breton saint who lived at Chartres and was murdered by robbers; his legend led to its widespread use as a personal name during the Middle Ages. **2.** English (of Norman origin) and French: habitational name for someone from Cairon in Calvados, France. **3.** English and French: metonymic occupational name for a carter, or possibly a cartwright, from a Norman and Picard form of Old French *c(h)arron* 'cart'.

FOREBEARS There was a Caron or LeCaron, a missionary priest, in Quebec in 1615. The marriage of a Caron, of unknown origin, is recorded in Quebec in 1637.

GIVEN NAMES French 14%. *Armand* (17), *Normand* (14), *Marcel* (13), *Andre* (11), *Lucien* (9), *Pierre* (7), *Fernand* (6), *Emile* (5), *Gaston* (5), *Laurent* (5), *Adrien* (4), *Alcide* (4).

Carona (105) Probably a variant of Italian **Caronna**, a habitational name from Caronna in Apulia, or possibly a respelling of CARONE.

GIVEN NAME Italian 4%. *Vito*.

Carone (416) Italian: from an augmentative of CARO.

GIVEN NAMES Italian 17%. *Vito* (4), *Carlo* (2), *Carmelo* (2), *Luigi* (2), *Saverio* (2), *Antonio, Domenic, Gaetano, Giacomo, Giancarlo, Gino, Giovanni*.

Caronia (109) Italian: habitational name from Caronìa in Messina province, Sicily.

GIVEN NAMES Italian 15%. *Vito* (2), *Angelo, Domenico, Pellegrino*.

Caronna (136) Southern Italian: habitational name from a place in Apulia named Caronna. As an American surname, it occurs chiefly in LA.

GIVEN NAMES Italian 25%. *Angelo* (2), *Salvatore* (2), *Antonino, Ettore, Gianna, Vito*.

Carosella (218) Italian: feminine variant of CAROSELLI.

GIVEN NAMES Italian 12%. *Carmine* (3), *Gino* (2), *Mario* (2), *Orlando* (2), *Santina, Silvio*.

Caroselli (201) Italian: from a diminutive of CARUSO.

GIVEN NAMES Italian 13%. *Ercole, Grazia, Remo, Vito, Vittorio*.

Carosi (100) Italian: variant (plural) of **Carosio**, a nickname from Latin *cariosus* 'withered by age'.

GIVEN NAMES Italian 19%. *Antonio, Arcangelo, Carmela, Domenic, Gasper, Guido, Italo, Pasquale, Santo*.

Carota (119) Italian: habitational name for someone from a place in Calabria called Caria, named with Greek *karyon* 'walnut'.
GIVEN NAMES Italian 12%. *Aldo, Angelo, Carlo, Dino.*

Carotenuto (144) Italian: from a compound of *caro* 'dear' + *tenuto* 'held', a term of endearment for a much loved child, also a personal name.
GIVEN NAMES Italian 18%. *Antonio, Carmela, Francesco, Pasquale.*

Carothers (1995) Scottish: variant spelling of CARRUTHERS.

Carow (156) **1.** English: variant spelling of CARROW. **2.** Respelling of German KAROW.

Carozza (291) Italian (Sicily): possibly from a derivative of the female personal name CARA.
GIVEN NAMES Italian 14%. *Dino* (2), *Salvatore* (2), *Alfonse, Antonio, Carmine, Falco, Filomena, Gaetano, Lucio, Luigi, Pietro.*

Carp (471) **1.** German, Polish, and Jewish (eastern Ashkenazic): variant spelling of KARP. **2.** English: from Middle English, Old French *carpe* 'carp', in some cases a nickname for a greedy person or for someone thought to resemble the fish in some other way; also a metonymic occupational name for a carp fisherman or a seller of the fish. **3.** English: possibly a nickname for a garrulous or complaining person, from Middle English *carp(e)* 'carping speech'.

Carpenito (175) Variant spelling of Italian **Carpeneto**, a diminutive of CARPINO.
GIVEN NAMES Italian 23%. *Angelo* (2), *Mario* (2), *Alfonso, Domenic, Guido, Salvatore.*

Carpenter (47517) **1.** English: occupational name for a worker in wood, Norman French *carpentier* (from Late Latin *carpentarius* 'cartwright'). **2.** Translation of German ZIMMERMANN, French CHARPENTIER, Italian CARPENTIERI, or cognates and equivalents in various other languages.

Carpentier (839) French: Norman, Picard, or Provençal variant of CHARPENTIER.
FOREBEARS A bearer of this name from Normandy is documented in Quebec city in 1671.
GIVEN NAMES French 13%. *Armand* (5), *Pierre* (5), *Marcel* (4), *Normand* (2), *Urgel* (2), *Aime, Alain, Andre, Cecile, Celine, Emile, Gaston.*

Carpentieri (155) Italian: from the occupational name *carpentière* 'carpenter', from Late Latin *carpentarius* 'cartwright'.
GIVEN NAMES Italian 28%. *Carmine* (4), *Angelo* (3), *Ennio* (2), *Domenic, Gaetano, Guiseppe, Nuncio, Rocco.*

Carper (2310) Origin unidentified. Perhaps an Americanized spelling of German **Körber** (see KORBER).

Carpinelli (146) Italian: habitational name from a place so named in Lucca, or from CARPINELLO.
GIVEN NAMES Italian 14%. *Angelo, Carmine, Giovanni, Pasquale, Rocco.*

Carpinello (113) Italian: habitational name from a place so named in Foril, from a diminutive of *carpino* 'hornbeam'.
GIVEN NAME Italian 7%. *Nunzio.*

Carpino (385) **1.** Southern Italian (**Càrpino**): topographic name from *carpine* 'hornbeam' (witch elm). **2.** Italian (Naples): from a diminutive of the personal name CARPIO.
GIVEN NAMES Italian 8%. *Santo* (2), *Angelo, Carmelo, Concetta, Fiore, Rocco.*

Carpio (607) **1.** Spanish: habitational name from Carpio in Valladolid province or any of various places in southern Spain named with this word (a regional term meaning 'hill'), as for example Carpio-Bernardo or El Carpio. **2.** Italian (Naples): from the personal name *Carpio*, a short form of *Eucarpio*.
GIVEN NAMES Spanish 47%. *Manuel* (12), *Jose* (11), *Luis* (9), *Francisco* (7), *Jesus* (7), *Carlos* (6), *Alfredo* (5), *Fernando* (5), *Angel* (3), *Armando* (3), *Guillermo* (3), *Juan* (3); *Antonio* (5), *Marco* (2), *Bartolina, Cecilio, Cesario, Constantino, Elio, Franco.*

Carr (41809) **1.** Northern English and Scottish: variant of KERR. **2.** Irish (Ulster): Anglicized form of Gaelic **Ó Carra** 'descendant of *Carra*', a byname meaning 'spear'. **3.** Irish: Anglicized form of Gaelic **Mac Giolla Chathair**, a Donegal name meaning 'son of the servant of *Cathair*'.

Carra (236) **1.** Italian: topographic name for someone who lived on stoney land, from *carra* 'stone', 'rock'. **2.** Spanish: topographic name from *carra* 'narrow path', 'track'.
GIVEN NAMES Italian 21%; Spanish 5%. *Salvatore* (2), *Angelo, Armando, Aurelio, Carmelo, Elio, Francesco, Gaetano, Italo, Luigi, Mario, Nicola, Primo, Roberto, Rocco, Sal; Juan* (2), *Jorge.*

Carradine (144) English: variant spelling of CARADINE.
GIVEN NAME French 4%. *Pierre.*

Carragher (209) Irish: variant spelling of CARRAHER.
GIVEN NAME Irish 7%. *Aidan.*

Carraher (323) Irish: reduced Anglicized form of Gaelic **Mac Fhearchair** 'son of *Fearchar*', a personal name derived from Celtic *fear* 'man' + *car* 'dear', 'beloved'.

Carranco (138) Spanish: habitational name from Carranco in Granada province.
GIVEN NAMES Spanish 47%. *Jose* (7), *Juan* (4), *Lupe* (4), *Manuel* (3), *Jorge* (2), *Raul* (2), *Ruben* (2), *Sergio* (2), *Agustin, Armando, Balentin, Belen.*

Carrano (490) Southern Italian: habitational name from a minor place named Carrano, in Colosimi, Cosenza province.
GIVEN NAMES Italian 14%. *Salvatore* (6), *Marco* (3), *Luigi* (2), *Romeo* (2), *Alfonse, Domenico, Gino, Rocco, Sal.*

Carranza (1910) Castilianized form of Basque **Karrantza**, a habitational name from Karrantza in Biscay province, Basque Country.
GIVEN NAMES Spanish 52%. *Jose* (70), *Carlos* (33), *Manuel* (21), *Luis* (19), *Francisco* (18), *Miguel* (17), *Jesus* (15), *Mario* (14), *Juan* (12), *Pedro* (12), *Raul* (12), *Alfredo* (11).

Carrara (420) Southern Italian: habitational name from a place named Carrara, from Latin *carraria* 'quarry'.
GIVEN NAMES Italian 13%; French 4%. *Guido* (3), *Angelo* (2), *Alessandro, Amerigo, Antonio, Arrigo, Carlo, Enzo, Gaetano, Giovanni, Guerino; Dominique, Marcel.*

Carraro (108) Italian: occupational name from a derivative of Late Latin *carrarius* 'cartwright'; 'carter'.
GIVEN NAMES Italian 8%. *Alessandro, Rinaldo.*

Carras (212) **1.** Greek: variant spelling of CARAS. **2.** English: habitational name from any of several places called Carr House or Carrhouse (examples of which are found in northern counties including Cheshire and Yorkshire), from Middle English *kerr* 'wet ground' or 'brushwood' (Old Norse with *kjarr*; see KERR) + *h(o)us* 'house' (Old English *hūs*).
GIVEN NAMES Greek 5%. *Anastasios, Costas, Spiro, Stelios.*

Carrasco (3053) Spanish: topographic name from *carrasco, carrasca* 'holm oak' (from Latin *cerrus*, from a pre-Roman Celtiberian word), or a habitational name from any of various places named with this word, as for example Carrasco in Salamanca province or Casas Carrasco in Jaén province, Spain.
GIVEN NAMES Spanish 46%. *Jose* (56), *Jesus* (43), *Manuel* (42), *Carlos* (26), *Ramon* (26), *Mario* (23), *Juan* (22), *Pedro* (17), *Luis* (16), *Miguel* (14), *Ruben* (14), *Armando* (13).

Carrasquillo (624) Spanish: possibly from a field so named, from a diminutive of CARRASCO.
GIVEN NAMES Spanish 48%. *Jose* (19), *Luis* (13), *Carlos* (11), *Juan* (11), *Pedro* (8), *Angel* (6), *Ramon* (5), *Jesus* (4), *Margarita* (4), *Santos* (4), *Ana* (3), *Francisca* (3).

Carraway (1412) English: variant spelling of CARAWAY.

Carre (198) French (**Carré**): from Old French *carré* 'square' (Latin *quadratus*), applied as a nickname for a squat, thickset man.
FOREBEARS A bearer of the name Carré from the Nivernais is documented in Montreal in 1706. Huguenots of this name, from Île de Ré, settled in Narragansett.
GIVEN NAMES French 14%. *Olivier* (2), *Antoine, Arnaud, Marcel, Marie-Noelle, Pierre, Regine.*

Carreau (137) French: variant of CARREL.
FOREBEARS A Carreau from Bordeaux, also called Lafraîcheur, is recorded in Quebec city in 1654.

GIVEN NAMES French 13%. *Armand* (2), *Donat, Marcelle, Pierre, Yves.*

Carreira (271) Portuguese and Galician: habitational name from any of various places so named in Portugal (and Galicia), from *carreira* 'road', 'thoroughfare', originally a road passable by vehicles as well as pedestrians (from Late Latin *carraria (via)*, a derivative of *carrum* 'cart').

GIVEN NAMES Spanish 18%; Portuguese 16%. *Manuel* (11), *Jose* (5), *Fernando* (4), *Jorge* (3), *Adelino* (2), *Carlos* (2), *Americo, Armando, Augusto, Dionisio, Domingo, Francisco; Ademir, Joao, Joaquim, Sebastiao.*

Carreiro (797) **1.** Galician: from *carreiro* 'passable by vehicles', hence a topographic name for someone who lived by a roadway or thoroughfare or a habitational name from a place named with this word. **2.** Portuguese and Galician: occupational name from *carreiro* 'carter'.

GIVEN NAMES Spanish 19%; Portuguese 12%. *Manuel* (27), *Jose* (19), *Carlos* (4), *Fernando* (4), *Alvaro* (3), *Francisco* (3), *Luis* (3), *Jorge* (2), *Viriato* (2), *Abilio, Agueda, Ana; Joao* (4), *Duarte* (2), *Agostinho.*

Carreker (130) Altered spelling of Irish CARRAHER.

Carrel (386) **1.** French: from Old French *quar(r)el* 'bolt (for a crossbow)', hence a metonymic occupational name for a maker of crossbow bolts or a nickname for a short, stout man. The word also meant 'paving slab', and so it could also have been a metonymic occupational name for a street layer. **2.** Probably a variant spelling of English CARRELL or Irish CARROLL.

Carrell (1760) **1.** English: from Old French *carrel*, 'pillow', 'bolster', hence a metonymic occupational name for a maker of these. **2.** In some cases perhaps an altered spelling of Irish CARROLL. In other cases perhaps an altered spelling of French CARREL.

Carrender (142) Origin unidentified.

Carreno (528) Spanish (**Carreño**): Castilianized form of Asturian-Leonese **Carreñu**, a habitational name from a place called Carreñu in Asturies.

GIVEN NAMES Spanish 52%. *Jose* (16), *Francisco* (8), *Juan* (7), *Luis* (7), *Manuel* (7), *Ricardo* (6), *Carlos* (5), *Miguel* (5), *Pedro* (5), *Ruben* (5), *Arturo* (4), *Fernando* (4); *Antonio* (12), *Dario* (3), *Leonardo* (2), *Antonino, Donato, Filiberto, Flavio, Lorenzo, Marco.*

Carreon (1163) Spanish (**Carreón**): variant of name CARRION.

GIVEN NAMES Spanish 48%. *Jose* (34), *Juan* (15), *Manuel* (13), *Arturo* (9), *Enrique* (9), *Fernando* (9), *Jesus* (9), *Alfredo* (8), *Luis* (8), *Juana* (6), *Alberto* (5), *Carlos* (5).

Carrera (1551) **1.** Spanish: topographic name for someone living by a main road, *carrera* 'thoroughfare', originally a road

passable by vehicles as well as pedestrians (Late Latin *carraria (via)*, a derivative of *carrum* 'cart'), or a habitational name from any of various places named with this word. **2.** Southern Italian: habitational name from a place named Carrera, cognate with 1.

GIVEN NAMES Spanish 44%. *Jose* (28), *Manuel* (23), *Juan* (16), *Jesus* (15), *Luis* (15), *Pedro* (11), *Carlos* (10), *Ruben* (9), *Guadalupe* (7), *Mario* (7), *Miguel* (7), *Ramon* (7); *Antonio* (6), *Salvatore* (4), *Geno* (3), *Mauro* (3), *Sal* (3), *Vito* (3), *Eliseo* (2), *Flavio* (2), *Gabino* (2), *Aldino, Aldo, Alessandro.*

Carreras (446) Spanish: topographic name for someone living by a crossroads, from the plural of *carrera* 'thoroughfare' (see CARRERA).

GIVEN NAMES Spanish 39%. *Carlos* (10), *Jose* (8), *Francisco* (6), *Juan* (5), *Luis* (5), *Angel* (4), *Eduardo* (3), *Guillermo* (3), *Jorge* (3), *Ricardo* (3), *Agustin* (2), *Alberto* (2).

Carrere (152) French (**Carrère**): variant of **Carrière** (see CARRIERE).

GIVEN NAMES French 13%. *Edouard, Elodie, Germaine, Henri, Jacques, Pierre, Raoul.*

Carrero (384) Spanish: occupational name from *carrero* 'carter', a derivative of Latin *carrum* 'cart', 'wagon'.

GIVEN NAMES Spanish 47%. *Carlos* (8), *Luis* (7), *Jose* (4), *Luz* (4), *Cesar* (3), *Enrique* (3), *Juan* (3), *Margarita* (3), *Rafael* (3), *Alejandra* (2), *Alfredo* (2), *Angel* (2).

Carretta (173) Southern Italian (Sicily and Naples): habitational name from Carretta in Sicily.

GIVEN NAMES Italian 10%. *Aldo, Carlo, Salvatore.*

Carricato (100) Italian (also **Caricato**): from *carricato*, an agent derivative of *caricare* (Sicilian *carricari*), 'to load', hence probably an occupational name for a porter, carrier, stevedore, etc.

GIVEN NAME Italian 5%. *Salvatore.*

Carrick (1501) **1.** Scottish: regional name for someone from Carrick, a steep and rocky district in Ayrshire, named in Old Welsh with *carreg* 'rock', borrowed into Gaelic as *carraig*. **2.** Irish: reduced form of McCARRICK.

Carrico (2031) Portuguese (**Carriço**): from *carrico* 'reed', hence a topographic name for someone living in a place where reeds grew, a habitational name from a place named with this word, for example in Leiria, or a nickname for a tall, thin person.

Carrie (228) **1.** French (**Carrié**): variant of CARRIER. **2.** Scottish: reduced form of **Mc-Harrie**, an Anglicized form of Gaelic **Mac Fhearadhaigh** (see McGARRY).

GIVEN NAMES French 6%. *Curley* (2), *Jacques, Pascale.*

Carrier (4736) **1.** English and southern French: from Middle English, Old French *car(r)ier* (Late Latin *carrarius*, a derivative of *carrum* 'cart', 'wagon', of Gaulish

origin); in English an occupational name for someone who transported goods, in French for a cartwright. **2.** French: occupational name for a stonemason or quarryman, *carrier.*

GIVEN NAMES French 7%. *Armand* (9), *Andre* (7), *Marcel* (7), *Emile* (5), *Lucien* (5), *Cecile* (4), *Alain* (3), *Gaetan* (3), *Gilles* (3), *Jacques* (3), *Laurent* (3), *Normand* (3).

Carriere (1006) **1.** French (**Carrière**): topographic name for someone who lived on a fairly major thoroughfare, originally a road passable by vehicles as well as pedestrians (from Late Latin *carraria (via)*, a derivative of *carrum* 'cart'). **2.** Italian: occupational name for a carter or cartwright (see CARRIERO).

FOREBEARS A bearer of the name from Guyenne is documented in Montreal in 1670.

GIVEN NAMES French 13%. *Andre* (6), *Emile* (6), *Armand* (4), *Cecile* (2), *Michel* (2), *Adrien, Antoine, Celina, Germain, Herve, Irby, Jacques.*

Carrieri (128) Italian: patronymic or plural form of CARRIERO.

GIVEN NAMES Italian 24%. *Vito* (2), *Angelo, Armando, Dario, Lino, Mario, Pasquale, Pietro, Salvatore.*

Carriero (233) Italian: occupational name for a carter or cartwright, *carraio, carraro*, from Late Latin *carrarius*, a derivative of *carrum* 'cart', 'wagon'.

GIVEN NAMES Italian 16%. *Gino* (2), *Angelo, Carlo, Carmine, Cosmo, Donato, Philomena, Remo, Vito.*

Carrig (254) Irish: **1.** reduced form of McCARRICK. **2.** Anglicization of Gaelic **de Carraig**, a topographic name referring to some particular rock, from *carraig* 'rock'.

Carrigan (2378) Irish: variant of CORRIGAN.

Carriger (328) **1.** Probably an altered spelling of Irish CARRAHER. **2.** Perhaps also an Americanized spelling of German **Kärcher** (see KARCHER) or **Kariger**, a variant of KARGER.

Carrigg (164) Variant spelling of CARRIG.

Carriker (581) **1.** Altered spelling of Irish CARRAHER. **2.** Perhaps also an Americanized spelling of German **Karricher** (see KARCHER).

Carrillo (7417) Spanish: nickname for a person with some peculiarity of the cheek or jaw, Spanish *carrillo*. The word is attested since the 13th century, but its origin is uncertain. It appears to be a diminutive of *carro* 'cart', 'wagon', and it has been suggested that the reference is to the movements of the jaw in chewing. The surname may also have denoted originally a bold or shameless person; for the semantic development compare CHEEK.

GIVEN NAMES Spanish 49%. *Jose* (164), *Juan* (115), *Carlos* (72), *Jesus* (72), *Manuel* (71), *Luis* (61), *Pedro* (51), *Francisco* (48),

Ruben (41), *Miguel* (38), *Roberto* (38), *Mario* (33).

Carringer (197) Americanized spelling of German GERINGER.

Carrington (3495) **1.** English: habitational name from a place in Greater Manchester (formerly in Cheshire) called Carrington, probably named with an unattested Old English personal name *Cāra* + *-ing-* denoting association + *tūn* 'settlement'. **2.** Scottish: habitational name from a place in Midlothian named Carrington, probably from Old English *Cēriheringa-tūn* 'settlement of Cērihere's people'.

Carrino (211) Southern Italian: **1.** from a diminutive of *carro* 'cart', 'wagon'. **2.** variant of CARLINO.
GIVEN NAMES Italian 10%. *Caesar, Fiore.*

Carrion (1111) Spanish (**Carrión**): habitational name from a place of this name in the Spanish province of Ciudad Real, or from Carrión de los Céspedes in Seville, or Carrión de los Condes in Palencia.
GIVEN NAMES Spanish 42%. *Jose* (20), *Juan* (14), *Carlos* (13), *Luis* (12), *Ramon* (12), *Angel* (6), *Manuel* (6), *Ramiro* (6), *Ricardo* (6), *Enrique* (5), *Fernando* (5), *Julio* (5).

Carris (217) **1.** English variant spelling of CARRAS. **2.** Portuguese: habitational name from any of various places, for example in Leiria, so named with the plural of *carril* 'thoroughfare' (from Latin *carrile*).

Carrithers (228) Scottish: variant spelling of CARRUTHERS.

Carriveau (328) French: topographical name from a pre-Latin term *caravu* 'rocky place'.

Carrizales (602) Spanish: from a field so named, from the plural of *carrizal* 'reedbed'.
GIVEN NAMES Spanish 52%. *Juan* (20), *Jose* (10), *Francisco* (6), *Carlos* (5), *Gustavo* (5), *Juanita* (5), *Raul* (5), *Roberto* (5), *Javier* (4), *Manuel* (4), *Ramiro* (4), *Alicia* (3).

Carro (233) **1.** Spanish and Italian (also **Del Carro**): from *carro* 'wagon', 'cart' (from Late Latin *carrum*, of Gaulish origin), hence a metonymic occupational name for a carter or cartwright. **2.** Italian (Sicily; **Carrò**): respelling of the French family name **Car(r)aud**, from Occitan *carral* 'passable by vehicles', hence a topographic name for someone who lived by such a thoroughfare. **3.** Italian: from *carro* 'cart', hence an occupational name for a carter or a cartwright. **4.** Southern Italian: topographic name from Greek *kárros*, southern Italian *carru* 'turkey oak' (*Quercus cerris*), or a habitational name from any of various places named with this word. **5.** Altered spelling of various like-sounding names, such as French CARREAU and English CARROW.
GIVEN NAMES Spanish 20%; Italian 10%. *Armando* (4), *Jose* (3), *Manuel* (2), *Mario* (2), *Adolfo, Alejandro, Angel, Aurelio,* *Concepcion, Dominga, Eduardo, Elena*; *Salvatore* (3), *Angelo, Antonio.*

Carrol (342) Irish: variant of CARROLL.

Carroll (49397) Irish: Anglicized form of Gaelic **Mac Cearbhaill** or **Ó Cearbhaill** 'son (or descendant) of *Cearbhall*', a personal name of uncertain origin, perhaps from *cearbh* 'hacking' and hence a byname for a butcher or nickname for a fierce warrior.

Carron (659) **1.** French and English: variant spelling of CARON 3. **2.** Reduced form of Irish McCARRON.

Carrothers (294) Scottish: variant spelling of CARRUTHERS.

Carrow (619) **1.** English: habitational name from either of two places: Carrow in Norfolk or Carraw in Northumberland. The first is thought to be named from Old English *carr* 'rock' (a Celtic loan word) + *hōh* 'spur of a hill', while the last may be named either from an Old British plural of *carr*, or from *carr* + Old English *rāw* 'row'. **2.** Possibly in some cases a reduced form of the Cornish surname NANCARROW.

Carroway (95) English: variant spelling of CARAWAY.

Carrozza (418) Italian: probably a topographic name from a derivative of *carra* 'stone', or a habitational name from a place named with this word.
GIVEN NAMES Italian 18%. *Carmelo* (3), *Pasquale* (3), *Falco* (2), *Giovanni* (2), *Angelo, Annunziato, Cosmo, Georgio, Gino, Giuseppe, Grazia, Ignazio.*

Carrubba (224) Southern Italian (Sicily and Naples): habitational name from any of various places in Sicily named or named with Carruba or Carrubba.
GIVEN NAMES Italian 24%. *Salvatore* (6), *Angelo* (4), *Ettore* (2), *Antonio, Camillo, Carmela, Carmelo, Corrado, Francesco, Lucio, Pietro, Rocco.*

Carruth (1445) Scottish: from the lands of Carruth in the parish of Kilmacolm in Renfrewshire.

Carruthers (1599) Scottish: habitational name from a place near Ecclefechan in Dumfries, locally pronounced 'kridders'. The name is first recorded in 1334 in the form *Carrothres*, and then more clearly in *c*.1350 as *Caer Ruther*, and derives from British *caer* 'fort' + a personal name.

Carry (227) Irish: reduced form of **McCarry** or **O'Carry** (see McCARY).

Carse (166) Scottish and northern Irish: topographic or habitational name from Scottish *kerss, carse* 'low and fertile land, generally adjacent to a river', as in Carse of Falkirk, Carse of Forth, Carse of Gowrie, etc. There are also places called Carse in Kirkcudbrightshire and Argyllshire which could have given rise to the surname.

Carsey (259) English: variant spelling of KERSEY.

Carsley (131) English: variant of KEARSLEY.

Carsner (113) Americanized spelling of German KRASNER, **Kürschner** (see KURSCHNER), or a similar name.

Carson (19978) Scottish and northern Irish: probably a variant of CURZON.
FOREBEARS The trapper and Indian agent known as Kit Carson was born Christopher Carson in 1809 in Madison Co., KY. His paternal grandfather, William, was an immigrant, probably from Scotland or northern Ireland, who in 1761 received a land grant in Iredell Co., NC.

Carstarphen (167) Altered spelling of Scottish **Corstorphine**, **Corstorphan**, a habitational name from a village in Midlothian, now a suburb of Edinburgh.

Carsten (485) North German, Dutch, and Scandinavian (chiefly Denmark): from the personal name *Carsten*, a variant of CHRISTIAN.

Carstens (1385) North German, Dutch, and Scandinavian: patronymic from CARSTEN.
GIVEN NAMES German 4%. *Kurt* (4), *Otto* (3), *Erna, Fritz, Gerhardt, Hans, Klaus, Manfred, Wilhelm, Willi.*

Carstensen (913) North German, Danish, and Norwegian: patronymic from CARSTEN.
GIVEN NAMES Scandinavian 5%; German 5%. *Carsten* (2), *Ove, Sven, Viggo; Hans* (5), *Kurt* (3), *Otto* (2), *Egon, Ingeborg, Lorenz, Siegfried.*

Carswell (1917) English and Scottish: habitational name from Carswell in south Oxfordshire (formerly Berkshire) or from any of the places mentioned at CRESWELL, all named with Old English *cærse* '(water)cress' + *well(a)* 'spring', 'stream'.

Cart (419) **1.** Scottish and northern Irish: reduced form of McCART. **2.** English: from Middle English *cart(e)* 'cart' (from Old English *cræt*, Old Norse *kartr*), hence a metonymic occupational name for a carter or cartwright. **3.** French: from Old Occitan *cart*, a variant of *quart*, a term which in the Middle Ages denoted a tax levied on wine; hence possibly a metonymic occupational name for a tax collector.

Carta (340) Italian (Sardinia and Sicily): metonymic occupational name for a notary or administrator, from *carta* 'document'.
GIVEN NAMES Italian 25%; Spanish 8%. *Salvatore* (3), *Attilio* (2), *Adolfo, Alvaro, Angelo, Antonio, Armando, Carmello, Donatella, Filomena, Francesco, Georgio, Giuseppa, Luciano, Luigi; Carlos* (2), *Julio* (2), *Salvador* (2), *Angel, Elodia, Jesus.*

Cartagena (672) Spanish: habitational name from the eastern seaport of Cartagena (earlier Carthago Nova) in Murcia province.
GIVEN NAMES Spanish 49%. *Jose* (29), *Carlos* (17), *Luis* (13), *Pedro* (10), *Angel* (8), *Manuel* (8), *Miguel* (6), *Luz* (5), *Ernesto* (4), *Francisco* (4), *Rafael* (4), *Alberto* (3).

Cartaya (109) Spanish: habitational name from Cartaya in Seville province.

GIVEN NAMES Spanish 49%. *Luis* (3), *Armando* (2), *Eduardo* (2), *Mario* (2), *Pedro* (2), *Raciel* (2), *Ramon* (2), *Sergio* (2), *Angel*, *Elba*, *Eulalia*, *Fermin*; *Dario*, *Rinaldo*.

Carte (673) **1.** English: variant spelling of CART. **2.** French: variant of CART.

Cartee (788) Possibly an altered spelling of French CARTE or Irish CARTY.

Cartelli (131) Italian: from a diminutive of CARTA.

GIVEN NAMES Italian 24%. *Salvatore* (3), *Antonino* (2), *Liliana*, *Vincenza*.

Carten (102) Northern Irish: reduced form of MCCARTAN.

Carter (116042) **1.** English: occupational name for a transporter of goods, Middle English *cartere*, from an agent derivative of Middle English *cart(e)* or from Anglo-Norman French *car(e)tier*, a derivative of Old French *caret* (see CARTIER). The Old French word coalesced with the earlier Middle English word *cart(e)* 'cart', which is from either Old Norse *kartr* or Old English *cræt*, both of which, like the Late Latin word, were probably originally derived from Celtic. **2.** Northern Irish: reduced form of MCCARTER.

Carthen (106) Probably a variant of northern Irish CARTEN.

Cartier (1061) French: variant of CHARTIER.

FOREBEARS The explorer Jacques Cartier (born in St. Malo; 1491?–1557) arrived at the site of modern Quebec in the winter of 1535–36. Hoping to get to China, he got upriver of Montreal, where he was stopped by the rapids, which he named 'Lachine' ('China').

GIVEN NAMES French 10%. *Jacques* (6), *Normand* (3), *Alphonse* (2), *Andre* (2), *Cecile* (2), *Marcel* (2), *Michel* (2), *Aristide*, *Armand*, *Colette*, *Donat*, *Francois*.

Cartin (121) Northern Irish: reduced form of MCCARTAN.

Cartledge (469) English: habitational name for someone from Cartledge in Derbyshire, named from Old Norse *kartr* 'rocky ground' + Old English *læcc* 'boggy stream' (both unattested).

Cartlidge (222) English: variant of CARTLEDGE.

Cartmell (360) English (Cumbria and Lancashire): habitational name for someone from Cartmel in Cumbria (formerly in Lancashire), the site of a famous priory, inland from Cartmel Sands. The place name is derived from Old Norse *kartr* 'rocky ground' + *melr* 'sandbank'.

Cartmill (350) English: variant of CARTMELL.

Cartner (280) **1.** English (Cumbria): unexplained. Compare CORTNER. **2.** Americanized form of German **Gärtner** (see GARTNER).

Cartolano (106) Southern Italian: variant of **Cartolaro**, an occupational name for a notary, from a derivative of Latin *cartularius*.

GIVEN NAMES Italian 21%. *Carmine* (2), *Antonio*, *Marco*, *Romeo*, *Salvatore*.

Carton (496) **1.** Irish: reduced form of MCCARTAN or MCCARTNEY. **2.** Northern French: occupational name for a carter, *charreton*, *charton*. **3.** French: from Old French *carton*, a measure of cereals; hence a metonymic occupational name for a grain merchant.

GIVEN NAMES French 5%. *Dominique*, *Jean-Paul*, *Michel*, *Pierre*.

Cartrette (297) Variant spelling of French **Cartret**, probably a derivative of Old French *cartier* 'quarter', which, among other things, denoted a measure of land equivalent to the area which could be sown with a quart of seed.

FOREBEARS A John Cartrett is recorded in Surrey, England, in 1596. Possibly this French surname was brought via England to North America, perhaps by Huguenots.

Cartright (103) Variant of English CARTWRIGHT or possibly an altered form of Dutch **Kortrijk** (see COURTRIGHT).

GIVEN NAMES French 9%; German 6%. *Fabienne*, *Fernand*; *Fritz* (2).

Cartwright (7695) English: occupational name for a maker of carts, from Middle English *cart(e)* + *wright* 'craftsman' (see WRIGHT). The surname is attested from the late 13th century, although the vocabulary word does not occur before the 15th century.

Carty (2048) Irish: Anglicized form of Gaelic **Ó Cárthaigh** 'descendant of *Cárthach*', a byname meaning 'loving'. See also MCCARTHY.

Caruana (443) Italian (Sicily): topographic name from *caruana* 'castor oil plant'.

GIVEN NAMES Italian 19%. *Angelo* (3), *Carlo* (2), *Carmel* (2), *Amante*, *Antonietta*, *Carmelo*, *Libia*, *Reno*, *Sal*, *Salvatore*, *Santo*.

Carucci (325) Southern Italian: from a diminutive of CARO.

GIVEN NAMES Italian 17%. *Donato* (3), *Pasquale* (3), *Angelo* (2), *Carmine* (2), *Marco* (2), *Biagio*, *Caesar*, *Ciro*, *Delio*, *Enrico*, *Gaetana*, *Siena*.

Carufel (134) French: unexplained.

GIVEN NAME French 6%. *Emile*.

Carulli (130) Southern Italian: patronymic or plural form of CARULLO.

GIVEN NAMES Italian 19%. *Rocco* (3), *Antonio* (2), *Americo*, *Angelo*, *Arturo*, *Carmela*, *Florindo*, *Sal*, *Salvatore*.

Carullo (136) Southern Italian: from a diminutive of CARO.

GIVEN NAMES Italian 37%. *Carmine* (2), *Emilio* (2), *Giovanni* (2), *Pasquale* (2), *Rocco* (2), *Sal* (2), *Adriano*, *Antonio*, *Gerardo*, *Lorenzo*, *Luca*, *Luigi*, *Olimpia*, *Salvatore*, *Vincenzo*.

Caruso (7587) Italian: nickname from *caruso* 'close-cropped' (Latin *cariosus* 'decayed', also 'smooth', 'bald'). This word was also used in the more general sense 'boy', 'lad', since in the Middle Ages young men of fashion sometimes wore their hair much shorter than was the prevailing style. In the Girgenti area of Sicily the term was a metonymic occupational name for a worker in the sulfur pits, since such workers were required to wear their hair short.

GIVEN NAMES Italian 15%. *Angelo* (43), *Salvatore* (36), *Enrico* (30), *Antonio* (17), *Carmine* (15), *Rocco* (12), *Sal* (12), *Vito* (11), *Giuseppe* (10), *Domenic* (8), *Saverio* (8), *Carmelo* (7).

Carusone (182) Italian: from an augmentative of CARUSO.

GIVEN NAMES Italian 31%. *Salvatore* (3), *Angelo* (2), *Geno* (2), *Giuseppe* (2), *Antonietta*, *Antonio*, *Cataldo*, *Fausto*, *Franco*, *Italia*, *Luigi*, *Matteo*.

Caruth (269) Scottish: variant of CARRUTHERS.

Caruthers (1362) Scottish: variant spelling of CARRUTHERS.

Carvajal (916) Spanish: topographic name for someone who lived near an oak grove, from a collective noun derivative of *carvallo* 'oak', or a habitational name from a place so named, for example in Málaga province. Compare CARBAJAL.

GIVEN NAMES Spanish 54%. *Jose* (22), *Juan* (22), *Carlos* (18), *Jorge* (14), *Luis* (11), *Fernando* (10), *Mario* (9), *Rafael* (9), *Jaime* (8), *Javier* (7), *Miguel* (7), *Pedro* (7).

Carvalho (2548) Portuguese: topographic name for someone who lived by a conspicuous oak tree, *carvalho*, or a habitational name from any of numerous places named with this word. This name is also found in western India, where it was taken by Portuguese colonists.

GIVEN NAMES Spanish 21%; Portuguese 16%. *Manuel* (68), *Jose* (67), *Fernando* (14), *Carlos* (10), *Luis* (9), *Francisco* (7), *Jorge* (7), *Ricardo* (7), *Luiz* (6), *Mario* (6), *Pedro* (6), *Ana* (5); *Paulo* (12), *Joao* (11), *Joaquim* (8), *Agostinho* (4), *Amadeu* (3), *Afonso* (2), *Duarte* (2), *Guilherme* (2), *Henrique* (2), *Ilidio* (2), *Marcio* (2), *Vasco* (2).

Carvell (327) **1.** English and Irish (of Norman origin): habitational name from either of two places called Carville (see CARVILLE) in Calvados and Seine-Maritime, France. **2.** Irish: variant of CARROLL.

Carvelli (142) Italian (Naples): **1.** from a reduced form of the personal name *Carobello*, *Carubello* (from Latin *carus* 'dear' + *bellus* 'beautiful'). **2.** occupational name for a baker, from medieval Greek *karbellion* denoting a type of bread.

GIVEN NAMES Italian 20%. *Carmela* (2), *Gaetano*, *Guiseppe*, *Sal*, *Salvatore*.

Carver (11359) **1.** English: occupational name for a carver of wood or a sculptor of stone, from an agent derivative of Middle English *kerve(n)* 'to cut or carve'. **2.** English: occupational name for a plowman, from Anglo-Norman French *caruier*, from Late Latin *carrucarius*, a derivative of *carruca* 'cart', 'plow'. **3.** Americanized spelling of German GARBER, GERBER, or **Körber** (see KOERBER). **4.** Irish: variant of CARVEY. **5.** Possibly also a reduced form of Irish McCARVER.

FOREBEARS John Carver (*c.* 1576–1621), one of the *Mayflower* Pilgrims, was the first governor of Plymouth Plantation. He was born in Nottinghamshire or Derbyshire, England. Emigrating to Holland in 1609, he joined the Pilgrims at Leyden.

Carvey (183) Irish: Americanized form of **Mac Cearbhaigh** 'son of *Cearbhach*', a byname from *cearbhach* 'ragged'.

Carville (215) **1.** French: habitational name from places in Calvados and Seine-Maritime named Carville, from the Scandinavian personal name *Kári* + Old French *ville* 'settlement' (see VILLA). **2.** English and Irish: variant of CARVELL.

GIVEN NAMES French 6%. *Berchman, Collette.*

Carvin (252) English: unexplained.

Carwell (160) Irish and Scottish: unexplained.

Carwile (684) Probably an Americanized spelling of German **Karweil**, a metonymic occupational name for a herbalist or herb dealer, from Middle Low German *karwe(l)* 'chervil'.

Cary (4362) Irish and English: variant spelling of CAREY.

Caryl (223) English: variant spelling of CARRELL.

Casa (418) **1.** Italian, Portuguese, and Spanish: from *casa* 'house' (Latin *casa* 'hut', 'cottage', 'cabin'), perhaps originally denoting the occupier of the most distinguished house in a village. **2.** Italian: from a short form of the personal name *Benincasa*, an omen name meaning 'welcome in (our) house'. **3.** Italian (Sicily; **Casà**): probably a metonymic occupational name for a maker of saddlecloths, from Greek *kasas* 'saddlecloth'.

GIVEN NAMES Spanish 29%; Italian 12%. *Blanca* (4), *Ernesto* (4), *Carlos* (3), *Alicia* (2), *Esperanza* (2), *Martinez* (2), *Miguel* (2), *Rafael* (2), *Adriana, Alberto, Alvarez, Benito; Antonio* (2), *Angelo, Camillo, Ciro, Dante, Domenic, Gaetano, Gennaro, Giovanna, Guido, Luigi, Onofrio.*

Casad (203) Origin uncertain; probably a reduced and altered form of Irish CASSIDY.

Casada (245) Most probably an American variant of Irish CASSIDY, altered perhaps under Hispanic influence.

Casaday (139) Variant spelling of Irish CASSIDY.

Casado (264) Spanish: status name for a married man, the head of a household, from

Spanish *casado*, past participle of *casar* 'to marry' (a derivative of *casa* 'house').

GIVEN NAMES Spanish 44%. *Jose* (6), *Luis* (6), *Ramon* (5), *Ana* (4), *Manuel* (4), *Carlos* (3), *Fernando* (3), *Gustavo* (3), *Altagracia* (2), *Arturo* (2), *Diego* (2), *Eduardo* (2).

Casados (287) Spanish: perhaps a plural form of CASADO, but more probably a topographic name from the plural of the homonym *casado* 'farmstead'.

GIVEN NAMES Spanish 19%. *Manuel* (3), *Benito* (2), *Carlos* (2), *Orlando* (2), *Abelino, Adan, Andres, Angel, Aracely, Cayetano, Cipriano, Ernesto.*

Casady (540) Variant spelling of Irish CASSIDY.

Casagranda (106) Italian (northern Italy and south Tyrol): variant of CASAGRANDE.

Casagrande (471) Italian and Spanish: habitational name from any of numerous minor places called Casagrande or Casa Grande, in Spain and Italy, from *casa* 'house' + *grande* 'big'.

GIVEN NAMES Italian 8%; French 4%. *Gino* (3), *Marco* (2), *Aldo, Angelo, Carlo, Dino, Franco, Geno, Lido, Luigi, Marino, Ottavio; Olivier, Pierre.*

Casal (245) Spanish, Catalan, and Portuguese: topographic name, from a derivative of Late Latin *casale* 'hut', 'cottage'.

GIVEN NAMES Spanish 39%; Portuguese 11%; French 4%; Italian 4%. *Jose* (11), *Carlos* (3), *Juan* (3), *Manuel* (3), *Rolando* (3), *Alina* (2), *Antonio* (2), *Javier* (2), *Jorge* (2), *Luis* (2), *Pedro* (2), *Santiago* (2), *Agustin; Pinto* (2); *Julien* (2), *Anais; Aldo, Constantino, Ettore, Romeo.*

Casale (1624) Italian: from Late Latin *casale* 'hut', 'cottage', a diminutive of *casa* 'house', hence a topographic name for someone who lived in such a dwelling or a habitational name from any of the various places named with this word, in particular a place in Piedmont.

GIVEN NAMES Italian 16%. *Angelo* (15), *Antonio* (6), *Carmine* (6), *Rocco* (4), *Salvatore* (4), *Concetta* (3), *Domenic* (3), *Pasquale* (3), *Aldo* (2), *Carlo* (2), *Domenico* (2), *Gennaro* (2).

Casaletto (100) Italian: topographic name from *casaletto*, a diminutive of Late Latin *casale* 'hut', 'cottage' (see CASALE), or a habitational name from any of various places so named.

Casali (282) Italian: habitational name from a place named Casali, from Sicilian *casali* 'hut', 'cottage', 'village'. Compare CASALE.

GIVEN NAMES Italian 25%. *Mario* (4), *Antonio* (3), *Dante* (3), *Dino* (2), *Haroldo* (2), *Otello* (2), *Rocco* (2), *Attilio, Leonardo, Marco, Marino, Paolo, Primo.*

Casalino (152) Italian: habitational name from any of various places called Casalino, for example in Sicily, Tuscany, and Liguria, from a diminutive of CASALE.

GIVEN NAMES Italian 16%; Spanish 6%. *Angelo, Gino, Orlando, Rocco, Rosaria; Alejandra, Diego.*

Casamento (168) Italian: topographic name from *casamento* 'large house', 'group of houses' (from Latin *casmentum* 'estate with house').

GIVEN NAMES Italian 19%. *Antonio, Bartolo, Carmello, Carmelo, Cira, Enzo, Lia, Sergio.*

Casano (146) Southern Italian (Sicily, Naples): possibly from the Arabic personal name *Ḥasan*, which may also have given rise to the Sicilian place names Casano and Casana.

GIVEN NAMES Italian 15%. *Rocco* (2), *Salvatore* (2), *Filippo, Giovanni.*

Casanova (1453) Catalan and Italian: topographic name from Latin *casa* 'house' + *nova* 'new', or a habitational name from any of the many places named with these words.

GIVEN NAMES Spanish 33%; Italian 4%. *Jose* (26), *Juan* (17), *Luis* (14), *Carlos* (13), *Manuel* (13), *Pedro* (9), *Francisco* (8), *Raul* (7), *Santiago* (6), *Alberto* (5), *Arturo* (5), *Eduardo* (5); *Antonio* (5), *Lorenzo* (4), *Aldo* (3), *Heriberto* (3), *Giovanni* (2), *Pasquale* (2), *Salvatore* (2), *Angelo, Carlo, Dino, Elio, Federico.*

Casarella (103) Italian: topographic name from *casarella* 'little house'.

GIVEN NAMES Italian 34%. *Vito* (3), *Sal* (2), *Aldo, Angelo, Armando, Carmine, Donato, Emidio, Gaetano, Gerardo, Mario, Serafino.*

Casares (565) Spanish and Galician: from the plural of *casar, casal* 'farm', hence a topographic name, or a habitational name from any of numerous places called Casares or named with this word, especially in Galicia.

GIVEN NAMES Spanish 48%; Portuguese 9%. *Jose* (14), *Jesus* (7), *Juan* (6), *Guadalupe* (5), *Manuel* (5), *Carlos* (4), *Eduardo* (4), *Enrique* (4), *Raul* (4), *Alfonso* (3), *Benito* (3), *Javier* (3); *Guilherme.*

Casarez (769) Probably an altered spelling of Spanish and Galician CASARES.

GIVEN NAMES Spanish 40%. *Jose* (15), *Carlos* (10), *Manuel* (10), *Juan* (8), *Guadalupe* (4), *Raul* (4), *Ricardo* (4), *Alfonso* (3), *Francisco* (3), *Jesus* (3), *Lupe* (3), *Marisol* (3).

Casas (1799) Spanish and Catalan: variant (plural) of CASA. The Catalan form is a respelling (probably Castilianization) of Catalan **Cases**.

GIVEN NAMES Spanish 53%; Portuguese 11%. *Jose* (52), *Juan* (32), *Manuel* (27), *Luis* (21), *Carlos* (20), *Francisco* (18), *Raul* (17), *Roberto* (14), *Ricardo* (12), *Ruben* (12), *Armando* (11), *Guadalupe* (11); *Joao, Ligia, Paulo.*

Casasanta (127) Italian: habitational name from a place named as 'the holy house'.

GIVEN NAMES Italian 24%. *Angelo* (3), *Antonio* (3), *Domenic, Enio, Fiore, Gaetano, Guido, Levio, Pasquale, Rinaldo, Valentino, Vincenzo.*

Casassa (197) Italian (Milan, Naples): probably from a pejorative derivative of CASA.

Casaus (241) Catalan: variant of **Casals**, from a plural of CASAL.

GIVEN NAMES Spanish 21%. *Alfonso* (2), *Carlos* (2), *Juan* (2), *Manuel* (2), *Ruben* (2), *Abenicio, Adonis, Alvino, Ana, Aurelio, Benito, Catarino.*

Casavant (514) French: topographic name from words meaning 'forward house'.

FOREBEARS A bearer of the name from Gascony, also called La Débauche, was documented in Contrecoeur, Quebec, in 1681.

GIVEN NAMES French 11%. *Marcel* (3), *Andre* (2), *Lucien* (2), *Aime, Armand, Dominique, Emile, Gedeon, Germaine, Marcelle, Normand, Oliva.*

Casazza (561) Italian: habitational name from a place named Casazza, for example in Sicily, probably from a derogatory form of CASA.

GIVEN NAMES Italian 4%. *Marco* (2), *Dino, Domenico, Enzo, Guido, Renzo, Silvio.*

Casbeer (114) Americanized spelling of German **Käsebier** (see CASEBEER).

Casbon (101) French: probably a reduced form of **Casabon**, a topographic name meaning 'house in good condition'.

GIVEN NAME French 4%. *Prosper.*

Cascella (118) Italian: feminine form of **Cascello**, a diminutive of CASCIO.

GIVEN NAMES Italian 19%. *Nicola* (2), *Carmela, Concezio.*

Casciani (112) Italian: patronymic or plural form of CASCIANO.

GIVEN NAMES Italian 22%. *Mario* (2), *Angelo, Carlo, Dino, Emidio, Franco, Geraldo, Giulio, Orlando, Paride, Renzo, Sante.*

Casciano (258) Italian: 1. habitational name from any of numerous places called Casciano. 2. habitational name for someone from Cascia in Umbria, the birthplace of St. Rita, from an adjectival form of the place name.

GIVEN NAMES Italian 14%. *Salvatore* (2), *Angelo, Carmine, Donato, Giuseppe, Nicola, Romeo.*

Casciato (224) Italian: unexplained.

GIVEN NAMES Italian 14%; French 4%. *Amelio, Antonio, Carmine, Dario, Donato, Matteo, Nicola, Romeo; Armand, Michel.*

Cascino (120) Southern Italian: 1. diminutive of CASCIO. 2. nickname from Arabic *ḥašī* 'timid', 'bashful'. 3. (**Càscino**) nickname from Arabic *ḥašin* 'coarse', 'rough', 'uncouth'.

GIVEN NAMES Italian 17%. *Salvatore* (3), *Sal* (2), *Antonio, Biagio.*

Cascio (1330) Southern Italian (Sicily, Calabria, Naples): of uncertain derivation;

possibly from a variant of *cacio* 'cheese' (Latin *caseus*).

GIVEN NAMES Italian 14%. *Salvatore* (10), *Sal* (5), *Vito* (5), *Angelo* (4), *Antonino* (3), *Carmelo* (2), *Carmine* (2), *Cosmo* (2), *Gandolfo* (2), *Santo* (2), *Antonio, Biaggio.*

Cascioli (102) Italian: from a diminutive of CASCIO.

GIVEN NAMES Italian 14%. *Aldo, Antonio, Gino, Nazzareno, Pompeo, Vito.*

Casco (152) Spanish (and Portuguese): from *casco* 'helmet', 'shell'.

GIVEN NAMES Spanish 50%. *Jose* (4), *Juan* (4), *Francisco* (3), *Salvador* (3), *Adolfo* (2), *Carlos* (2), *Jose Antonio* (2), *Manuel* (2), *Marta* (2), *Adriana, Alberto, Ana.*

Cascone (262) Italian: topographic name from an augmentative form of *casco* 'helmet', denoting a piece of land of this shape.

GIVEN NAMES Italian 18%. *Sal* (3), *Salvatore* (3), *Pasquale* (2), *Rocco* (2), *Agostino, Carmelo, Carmine, Egidio, Enrico, Giuseppe, Luigi, Remo.*

Casdorph (169) Americanized spelling of German KASDORF.

Case (15303) 1. English: from Anglo-Norman French *cas(s)e* 'case', 'container' (from Latin *capsa*), hence a metonymic occupational name for a maker of boxes or chests. 2. Americanized spelling of French CAISSE. 3. Americanized spelling of KAAS. 4. Americanized spelling of German **Käse**, a metonymic occupational name for a maker or seller of cheese. Compare KAESER.

Casebeer (322) Americanized spelling of German **Käsebier**, literally 'cheese (and) beer', a metonymic occupational name for a tavern keeper who served only cold food.

Casebier (226) Partly Americanized spelling of German **Käsebier** (see CASEBEER).

Casebolt (488) English: descriptive nickname from Middle English *casbalde* 'baldhead'.

Casella (1242) Italian: diminutive of CASA.

GIVEN NAMES Italian 12%. *Carmine* (6), *Angelo* (4), *Salvatore* (3), *Alessandra* (2), *Attilio* (2), *Carmelo* (2), *Rocco* (2), *Vito* (2), *Alfio, Antonio, Carlo, Carmello.*

Caselli (254) Italian: from *Casello*, a diminutive of the personal name CASO.

GIVEN NAMES Italian 12%. *Angelo* (2), *Cosimo* (2), *Dante* (2), *Marco* (2), *Carlo, Dario, Deno, Francesco, Orest.*

Casement (122) Manx: Anglicization of Gaelic **Mac Asmuint** 'son of *Asmundr*', an Old Norse personal name meaning 'god protector'.

Caserta (476) Italian: habitational name from Caserta, a city in Campania, named in medieval Latin as *casa irta* 'impregnable house'.

GIVEN NAMES Italian 19%. *Angelo* (6), *Salvatore* (5), *Nino* (3), *Alfio* (2), *Enzo* (2), *Santo* (2), *Annamarie, Carlo, Enio, Gaetano, Luigi, Pasquale.*

Casey (24800) Irish: reduced Anglicized form of Gaelic **Ó Cathasaigh** 'descendant of *Cathasach*', a byname meaning 'vigilant' or 'noisy'.

GIVEN NAMES Irish 7%. *Brendan* (15), *Donal* (5), *Ciaran* (2), *Dermot* (2), *John Patrick* (2), *Liam* (2), *Aileen, Cait, Caitlyn, Conor, Eamon, Joe Pat.*

Cash (10123) 1. English: variant of CASE. 2. Americanized spelling of German KIRCH or KIRSCH.

Cashatt (172) Americanized spelling of French **Cachot** or **Cachat**, a nickname for a secretive man, from *cacher* 'to hide'.

Cashdollar (227) Americanized spelling of German **Kirchthaler**, from the field name *Kirchtal* 'church valley' + the suffix *-er* denoting an inhabitant.

Cashel (121) Irish: 1. from the Norman habitational name *de Cashel*, from Cassel in northern France, and so an Irish form of the English name CASSELL. 2. (County Clare) Anglicization of Gaelic **Ó Maolchaisil** 'descendant of the chief of Cashel'.

Cashell (131) Irish: variant of CASHEL.

Cashen (450) Irish: variant spelling of CASHION.

Casher (162) Americanized spelling of German KIRCHER.

Cashin (660) Irish: variant spelling of CASHION.

Cashio (148) Perhaps an altered spelling of Italian CASCIO.

GIVEN NAMES Italian 6%. *Sal* (2), *Carlo, Vito.*

Cashion (1060) Irish: Anglicized form of Gaelic **Mac Caisin** or **Ó Caisin** 'son (or descendant) of *Caisín*', a byname based on a diminutive of *cas* 'curly'. Compare CASSIDY.

Cashman (2242) 1. English: variant of CASE. 2. Irish: Anglicized form of Gaelic **Ó Ciosáin**, which Woulfe describes as a variant of **Ó Casáin**, with the same meaning as **Ó Caisín** (see CASHION). 3. Americanized spelling of German **Kirchmann** (see KIRCHMAN).

Cashmore (155) 1. English: probably a habitational name from Cashmoor in Dorset, which is probably named with Old English *cærse* 'cress' + *mōr* 'fen', 'marsh' or *mere* 'pool'. 2. Perhaps an Americanized spelling of German KIRCHMEIER.

Cashner (109) Probably an Americanized spelling of German KIRCHNER or KIRSCHNER.

Cashon (142) Irish: variant spelling of CASHION.

Cashwell (521) 1. Probably a variant of German **Kirchwall** (see KERCHEVAL). 2. Perhaps a variant of the English habitational name CASWELL.

Casiano (454) Spanish: possibly from the personal name *Casiano*.

GIVEN NAMES Spanish 48%. *Juan* (13), *Jose* (7), *Carlos* (6), *Julio* (6), *Miguel* (6), *Angel*

(5), *Manuel* (5), *Jesus* (4), *Luis* (4), *Aurelio* (3), *Francisco* (3), *Aida* (2).

Casias (471) Spanish: possibly a topographic name related to *casa* 'house' (plural *casas*).

GIVEN NAMES Spanish 17%. *Alfonso* (3), *Alfredo* (2), *Alicia* (2), *Eloy* (2), *Jose* (2), *Juan* (2), *Pedro* (2), *Ramon* (2), *Ramona* (2), *Abran*, *Adelina*, *Alonzo*.

Casida (101) American variant spelling of Irish CASSIDY.

Casillas (2020) Spanish: from any of various places called Casillas or Las Casillas, from the plural of *casilla*, a diminutive of CASA.

GIVEN NAMES Spanish 45%. *Jose* (54), *Jesus* (23), *Juan* (21), *Carlos* (16), *Ramon* (15), *Francisco* (14), *Manuel* (14), *Jorge* (11), *Mario* (10), *Miguel* (10), *Ruben* (10), *Guadalupe* (9).

Casillo (193) Southern Italian: topographic name from medieval Latin *casellum* 'hamlet', 'farmhouse', or a habitational name from a place named Casillo in Campania.

GIVEN NAMES Italian 20%. *Angelo* (2), *Sal* (2), *Alessandro*, *Aniello*, *Cataldo*, *Gaetano*, *Nunzio*, *Pasquale*, *Salvatore*, *Santo*.

Casimir (248) French and Dutch: from the personal name *Casimir*, a name of Slavic origin meaning 'destroyer of peace'. Compare Polish KAZMIERCZAK.

GIVEN NAMES French 29%. *Jacques* (3), *Jean-Philippe* (2), *Alain*, *Andree*, *Fresnel*, *Gilberte*, *Jean Robert*, *Kettly*, *Laurent*, *Magloire*, *Marcel*, *Marthe*.

Casimiro (165) Spanish and Portuguese: from the personal name *Casimiro*, Spanish and Portuguese equivalent of CASIMIR. See also KAZMIERCZAK.

GIVEN NAMES Spanish 37%. *Jose* (10), *Francisco* (2), *Manuel* (2), *Miguel* (2), *Abilio*, *Agustin*, *Aida*, *Alberto*, *Americo*, *Apolonio*, *Avelino*, *Basilio*; *Antonio* (4), *Clemente*.

Casini (144) Italian: patronymic or plural form of CASINO.

GIVEN NAMES Italian 27%; French 5%. *Omero* (4), *Francesca* (2), *Francesco* (2), *Franco* (2), *Leno* (2), *Spartaco* (2), *Amerigo*, *Angelo*, *Carlo*, *Elio*, *Enrico*, *Fabrizio*, *Guido*, *Lino*, *Mario*, *Roberto*; *Armand*, *Lucien*.

Casino (271) Italian: **1.** habitational name from a place named Casino, from a diminutive of *casa* 'house' (see CASA). **2.** from a diminutive of the personal name *Caso*, from a diminutive of the omen name *Benincasa* (see CASA).

GIVEN NAMES Spanish 11%; Italian 7%. *Alfredo* (4), *Cesar*, *Cristina*, *Domingo*, *Efren*, *Epifania*, *Herminio*, *Margarita*, *Miguel*, *Pacita*, *Rolando*, *Romaldo*; *Salvatore* (2), *Aldo*, *Leonardo*, *Pasquale*.

Caskey (2178) Northern Irish: Anglicized form of Gaelic **Mac Ascaidh**, a patronymic from a personal name of Norse origin (see MCCASKEY).

Casler (743) **1.** Spelling variant of German KASSLER. **2.** English: perhaps a habitational name from any of several places in Cumbria called Castle Howe, from Middle English *castel* 'castle', 'earthwork' + *howe* 'mound' (Old Norse *haugr*), or alternatively a topographic or occupational name from Middle English *casteler* 'dweller or worker at a castle'.

Caslin (147) Irish: Anglicized form of Gaelic **Ó Caisealáin** 'descendant of *Caisealán*', a diminutive of *Caisile*, a variant of the byname *Caiside* (see CASSIDY).

Casner (683) American spelling of German KASSNER.

Caso (514) **1.** Castilianized form of Asturian-Leonese **Casu**, a habitational name from Campu de Casu or Sotu de Casu, both in Asturies. **2.** Southern Italian (mainly Sicily): from a masculinized form of the personal name *Casa*, a short form of the omen name *Benincasa* (see CASA).

GIVEN NAMES Spanish 15%; Italian 10%. *Luis* (5), *Carlos* (4), *Alfonso* (3), *Jose* (3), *Roberto* (3), *Diego* (2), *Eduardo* (2), *Orlando* (2), *Alfredo*, *Americo*, *Angelina*, *Evelio*; *Sal* (4), *Antonio* (3), *Angelo* (2), *Carmine* (2), *Carlo*, *Carmelo*, *Ciro*, *Damiano*, *Enrico*, *Gasper*, *Giuseppe*, *Margherita*.

Casola (147) Southern Italian (**Càsola**): diminutive of CASA.

GIVEN NAMES Italian 14%; Spanish 11%; French 5%. *Sal* (3), *Antonella*, *Carlo*, *Franco*, *Gaetano*, *Giovanna*, *Lelio*, *Salvatore*; *Adolfo*, *Carolina*, *Jaime*, *Leopoldo*, *Luis*, *Mario*, *Pura*, *Ramona*, *Rigoberto*, *Zoraida*; *Armand* (3), *Elodie*, *Germaine*.

Cason (3903) **1.** English: habitational name for someone from Cawston in Norfolk; the form of the surname reflects the local pronunciation of the place name, which is from the Old Scandinavian personal name *Kalfr* + Old English *tūn* 'settlement'. **2.** Italian (Venetia): augmentative form of CASA.

Caspar (177) German: variant spelling of KASPAR.

Caspari (112) **1.** Swiss Italian: variant spelling of Italian GASPARI. **2.** Dutch, German, Swiss, Hungarian, etc.: humanistic patronymic name from the Latin genitive form of *Caspar* (see KASPAR).

GIVEN NAMES German 10%. *Georg*, *Gottfried*, *Gunter*, *Horst*.

Caspary (128) **1.** German: patronymic from the personal name *Caspar* (see CASPER). **2.** Jewish (Ashkenazic): adoption of the German name.

Casper (4825) German and Slavic: from the personal name *Casper* or *Kaspar*, which was especially popular in central Europe up to the 18th century. Originally from Persian *kaehbaed*, *khazana-dar*, or *ganjvaer*, all meaning 'treasure bearer', it was ascribed by popular tradition in Europe to one of the three Magi. Their supposed remains were

taken to Cologne from Constantinople. in the 12th century. See also BALTAZAR and MELCHIOR.

Caspers (304) North German: patronymic from CASPER.

GIVEN NAMES German 5%. *Aloys*, *Elke*, *Erna*, *Gunter*.

Caspersen (188) Danish, Norwegian, and North German (Holstein): patronymic from the personal name CASPER.

GIVEN NAMES Scandinavian 14%. *Erik* (3), *Lars* (2), *Gunhild*, *Juel*, *Lennart*, *Thor*.

Casperson (569) Respelling of CASPERSEN or its Swedish equivalent, **Caspersson** (also **Kaspersson**).

GIVEN NAMES Scandinavian 4%. *Lars*, *Sven*.

Cass (3058) English: from the medieval female personal name *Cass*, a short form of *Cassandra*. This was the name (of uncertain, possibly non-Greek, origin) of an ill-fated Trojan prophetess of classical legend, condemned to foretell the future but never be believed; her story was well known and widely popular in medieval England.

Cassada (313) American variant of Irish CASSIDY.

Cassaday (230) Irish: variant spelling of CASSIDY.

Cassady (1729) Irish: variant spelling of CASSIDY.

Cassani (160) Italian: patronymic or plural form of CASSANO.

GIVEN NAMES Italian 8%. *Aldo*, *Angelo*, *Giulio*, *Quinto*.

Cassano (715) Italian: from the personal name *Cass(i)ano* or *Casciano* (from the Roman name *Cassianus*), which was popularized by the cults of various 1st-century saints and martyrs, including Saints Cassiano of Imola and Todi, or a habitational name from any of numerous places called (San) Cass(i)ano or (San) Casciano after these figures.

GIVEN NAMES Italian 16%. *Vito* (8), *Rocco* (7), *Angelo* (2), *Salvatore* (2), *Antonio*, *Caesar*, *Carmine*, *Domenico*, *Enrico*, *Francesco*, *Guido*, *Luigi*.

Cassar (229) Probably an altered spelling of French **Cassard**, apparently a nickname for a clumsy person, from Old French *casse(r)* 'to break', with the addition of the pejorative suffix *-ard*.

GIVEN NAMES Italian 8%; French 6%. *Salvatore* (2), *Angelo*, *Carmel*, *Luigi*, *Reno*; *Antoine*, *Francois*.

Cassara (308) Southern Italian (**Cassarà**): occupational name from medieval Greek *kassaras* 'mat maker'.

GIVEN NAMES Italian 21%. *Angelo* (4), *Vito* (4), *Salvatore* (3), *Nunzio* (2), *Sal* (2), *Agatino*, *Antonino*, *Antonio*, *Benedetto*, *Calogero*, *Carmela*, *Carmine*.

Cassarino (158) Southern Italian: diminutive of CASSARO.

GIVEN NAMES Italian 38%. *Angelo* (5), *Santo* (5), *Rosario* (2), *Sal* (2), *Aurelio*, *Gino*,

Nicola, Paolo, Salvatore, Sebastiano, Vicenzo.

Cassaro (239) Italian: **1.** (**Càssaro**) habitational name from Càssaro, a place in Sicily, named from Sicilian *càssaru* 'main street', 'street leading to the citadel', from Arabic *qaṣr* 'citadel', 'castle', which in turn is derived from Latin *castrum* 'Roman walled city'. **2.** (**Càssaro**) occupational name for a maker or seller of crates or boxes.
GIVEN NAMES Italian 13%. *Salvatore* (3), *Angelo* (2), *Vito* (2), *Giovanni, Sal.*

Cassata (236) Southern Italian: from *cassata* denoting a sweet cake made with cheese and candied fruit (from a derivative of Latin *caseus* 'cheese'), hence a metonymic occupational name for a pastry cook, or perhaps a nickname for someone with a sweet nature.
GIVEN NAMES Italian 18%. *Angelo* (2), *Luigi* (2), *Salvatore* (2), *Vito* (2), *Carlo, Carmela, Giuseppe, Vincenza.*

Cassatt (188) Origin uncertain. This is not known as a surname in Britain. It may be an Americanized form of a French name such as **Casault**.

Casseday (115) Variant spelling of Irish CASSIDY.

Cassedy (194) Irish: variant spelling of CASSIDY.

Cassel (1825) **1.** English (of Norman origin): habitational name for someone from Cassel in Nord, France. **2.** English: variant spelling of CASTLE. **3.** Americanized or older spelling of German KASSEL.

Casselberry (246) Americanized form of a German or Swiss German name (see CASTLEBERRY).

Cassell (2884) **1.** English: variant spelling of CASSEL or CASTLE. **2.** Altered spelling of German KASSEL.

Cassella (500) Italian: metonymic occupational name for a box maker, from a diminutive of *cassa* 'box', 'crate'.
GIVEN NAMES Italian 10%. *Pasquale* (3), *Angelo, Antonio, Dante, Giuseppe, Lorenzo, Rocco, Salvatore, Tiziana, Vincenzo.*

Cassells (165) Scottish variant of CASTLES.

Casselman (553) Americanized or older spelling of the German habitational name **Kasselmann**, denoting someone from Kassel (see KASSEL), or KESSELMAN.

Cassels (442) English: variant of CASTLES.

Cassens (335) Frisian: patronymic from the personal name *Cassen*, Frisian form of CHRISTIAN.

Casserly (406) Irish: Anglicization of Gaelic **Ó Caisile**, a variant of **Ó Caiside** (see CASSIDY).
GIVEN NAMES Irish 7%. *Liam, Niall.*

Cassese (325) Italian: from Arabic *qissīs* 'priest', perhaps a patronymic, but equally possibly a nickname for a learned or pious man, or alternatively denoting someone in

the service of a priest or even the offspring of one.
GIVEN NAMES Italian 14%. *Angelo* (2), *Anella, Antonio, Carmela, Carmine, Domenic, Domenico, Donato, Nunzio, Sal, Salvatore, Veto.*

Cassetta (257) Italian: metonymic occupational name for a box maker, from a diminutive of *cassa* 'crate', 'box'.
GIVEN NAMES Italian 9%. *Angelo, Bruna, Cosmo, Giacoma, Guido, Lorenzo, Nichola, Pasquale, Philomena.*

Cassetty (149) Variant of Irish CASSIDY.

Casseus (102) Probably a respelling of French **Cassius**, from the Latin personal name, which was particularly popular in France during the Renaissance.
GIVEN NAMES French 46%. *Regine* (3), *Monique* (2), *Andre, Fresnel, Jean Michel, Luce, Marie Jose, Michelin, Mirelle, Sauveur, Thierry, Yva.*

Cassiday (216) Irish: variant of CASSIDY.

Cassidy (10138) Irish (Fermanagh): reduced Anglicized form of Gaelic **Ó Caiside** 'descendant of *Caiside*', a byname from *cas* 'curly(-headed)'.
GIVEN NAMES Irish 6%. *Brendan* (13), *Conan* (2), *Liam* (2), *Murphy* (2), *Aileen, Brigid, Conal, Conley, Fergus, John Patrick, Padraic, Seamus.*

Cassie (127) Scottish: from a pet form of CASS.

Cassin (394) French: diminutive of **Casse**, a topographic name denoting someone who lived by an oak tree or in an oak wood, from Old French *casse* 'oak (tree)'.

Cassinelli (206) Italian: possibly from a diminutive of CASSINO.
GIVEN NAMES Italian 7%. *Enrico* (3), *Rino* (2), *Dante.*

Cassino (117) Italian: **1.** habitational name from any of various places called Cassino, especially the one in Frosinone province. **2.** from a diminutive of the personal name *Cassio* (Latin *Cassius*). **3.** (Sicily; **Càssino**): topographic name from Sicilian *càssinu* 'little oak'.
GIVEN NAMES Italian 12%. *Donato, Salvatore.*

Cassis (172) **1.** Portuguese: possibly from Arabic *qissīs* 'priest', 'clergyman', hence a status name, a nickname, or a metonymic occupational name for someone in the service of a priest. **2.** Possibly a habitational name from the southern French town of Cassis.
GIVEN NAMES French 6%. *Gilles, Jacques.*

Cassity (820) Variant of Irish CASSIDY.

Cassler (107) Variant spelling of German KASSLER.

Casso (234) Probably an altered spelling of Spanish CASO.
GIVEN NAMES Spanish 21%. *Alfonso* (3), *Carlos* (2), *Doroteo* (2), *Ernesto* (2), *Jesus* (2), *Manuel* (2), *Raul* (2), *Angel, Celedonio, Cesar, Elida, Esperanza;*

Antonio (2), *Angelo, Federico, Marco, Rocco.*

Casson (693) English: metronymic from CASS.

Cassone (154) Italian: possibly from an augmentative of *cassa* 'box', 'crate' or alternatively from the Arabic personal name *Ḥassūn*, commonly found in Sicilian place names.
GIVEN NAMES Italian 22%. *Rocco* (8), *Salvatore* (2), *Antonio, Palma.*

Casstevens (271) Origin unidentified; apparently of English or Scottish origin, but unexplained.

Cast (423) **1.** Americanized spelling of German KAST. **2.** English (Essex, Kent): possibly a nickname from Norman *caste* 'chaste', 'virtuous' (from Old French *chaste*). **3.** Possibly an altered spelling of French **Caste**, cognate with 2.

Castagna (712) Italian: from *castagna* 'chestnut' (the fruit, not the tree), probably a metonymic occupational name for someone who collected or sold chestnuts, or a nickname for someone with chestnut-colored hair.
GIVEN NAMES Italian 12%; French 4%. *Angelo* (3), *Antonio* (2), *Dino* (2), *Maurizio* (2), *Sal* (2), *Salvatore* (2), *Antonino, Carlo, Carmine, Ciro, Emidio, Giacomo; Armand* (5), *Andre, Aude.*

Castagno (208) Italian: topographic name for someone who lived by a chestnut tree, *castagno* (from Latin *castanea*).
GIVEN NAMES Italian 11%; French 4%. *Antonio, Battista, Dino, Francesco, Primo, Raffaele, Salvatore; Alphonse* (2), *Armand.*

Castagnola (178) Italian: diminutive of CASTAGNA.
GIVEN NAMES Italian 14%. *Angelo* (2), *Agostino, Carmela, Dante, Dario.*

Castaldi (401) Italian: patronymic or plural form of CASTALDO.
GIVEN NAMES Italian 12%; French 4%. *Salvatore* (4), *Marco* (2), *Alfonse, Carlo, Ciro, Dario, Domenic, Giacinto, Giuseppe, Vito; Andre, Armand, Ovide.*

Castaldo (638) Italian: status name or a nickname from *castaldo* (Lombard *gastald(us)*), the title of an official, originally an administrator in the service of the king, later of the estates of the dukes and counts of Lombardy or of the church.
GIVEN NAMES Italian 21%. *Carmine* (7), *Angelo* (4), *Pasquale* (4), *Vincenzo* (3), *Antonio* (2), *Gennaro* (2), *Lorenzo* (2), *Silvestro* (2), *Alessandro, Annalisa, Carlo, Carmin.*

Castaneda (5244) Spanish and Asturian-Leonese (**Castañeda**): habitational name from any of various places in Santander, Asturies, and Salamanca, named with *castañeda*, a collective of *castaña* 'chestnut'.
GIVEN NAMES Spanish 51%. *Jose* (138), *Manuel* (72), *Juan* (69), *Carlos* (55), *Luis* (48), *Jesus* (47), *Mario* (35), *Francisco*

(34), *Miguel* (34), *Raul* (31), *Salvador* (31), *Alfredo* (30).

Castano (757) **1.** Spanish and Galician (**Castaño**): from *castaño* 'chestnut (tree)' (Latin *castanea*), hence a topographic name for someone who lived by such a tree or a habitational name from any of numerous places named with this word. **2.** Southern Italian: from medieval Greek *kastanon* 'chestnut', hence a topographic name for someone who lived by a conspicuous chestnut tree, or a nickname for someone with chestnut-colored hair.

GIVEN NAMES Spanish 42%; Italian 4%. *Jose* (21), *Carlos* (16), *Luis* (13), *Manuel* (11), *Jaime* (6), *Ana* (4), *Fernando* (4), *Francisco* (4), *Juan* (4), *Cesar* (3), *Enrique* (3), *Guillermo* (3); *Antonio* (4), *Lorenzo* (2), *Caesar*, *Fausto*, *Federico*, *Heriberto*, *Leonardo*, *Marco*, *Nunzio*, *Silvio*, *Vita*.

Castanon (594) Spanish (**Castañón**): topographic name from an augmentative of *castaño* 'chestnut' or for someone who lived by a field named with this word.

GIVEN NAMES Spanish 44%. *Jose* (16), *Juan* (7), *Luis* (6), *Rafael* (6), *Jesus* (5), *Pedro* (5), *Guadalupe* (4), *Manuel* (4), *Pablo* (4), *Raul* (4), *Alicia* (3), *Armando* (3); *Antonio* (6), *Marco* (3), *Clemente*, *Domenic*, *Federico*, *Gabino*, *Gabriella*, *Heriberto*, *Lucio*, *Primo*, *Santino*.

Casteel (2903) **1.** Dutch: from Dutch *kasteel* 'castle' (from Picard *castel*, Old French *chastel*), hence a topographic name or a metonymic occupational name for someone who lived or worked in a castle. **2.** Perhaps an altered spelling of French CASTILLE.

Casteen (145) Altered spelling of Swedish **Castén**, a variant of **Kastén** (see KASTEN).

Castel (155) **1.** English: variant spelling of CASTLE. **2.** Southern French: topographic name from Occitan *castel*, a derivative of Late Latin *castellum* 'castle' (a diminutive of Latin *castrum* 'fort', 'Roman walled city'). This name is also found as a Jewish (Sephardic) name. **3.** Catalan: respelling of **Castell**.

FOREBEARS A bearer of the name from Chartres is documented in Champlain, Quebec, in 1684.

GIVEN NAMES French 14%; Spanish 6%. *Benoit* (2), *Herve*, *Jean Michel*, *Thierry*, *Yves*; *Jose* (2), *Blanco*, *Carlos*, *Rafael*.

Castelan (161) Galician (**Castelán**): generally from Galician *castelán*, an ethnic name for a Castilian (Castilian *castellano*). However, in some cases it may be a habitational name, from places in Lugo and A Coruña provinces called Castelán, or it could be an occupational name denoting a bailiff or steward.

GIVEN NAMES Spanish 52%. *Jose* (6), *Miguel* (5), *Francisco* (4), *Alejandro* (3), *Guadalupe* (3), *Concepcion* (2), *Felipe* (2), *Gerardo* (2), *Jorge* (2), *Jose Luis* (2),

Manuel (2), *Serafin* (2); *Antonio* (3), *Gabino* (2), *Leonardo* (2), *Lorenzo* (2).

Castell (338) **1.** English: variant spelling of CASTLE. **2.** Manx: from a short form of the Old Norse personal name *Ásketill*, composed of the elements *áss* 'god' + *ketill* 'kettle'. **3.** Catalan: topographic name from Catalan *castell* 'castle', a derivative of Late Latin *castellum* 'castle' (a diminutive of Latin *castrum* 'fort', 'Roman walled city'). Compare Spanish CASTILLO and Occitan (southern French) CASTEL. **4.** Probably an altered spelling of German KASTEL.

GIVEN NAMES Spanish 5%. *Roberto* (3), *Amarilys*, *Carlos*, *Eduardo*, *Estevan*, *Francisco*, *Guadalupe*, *Humberto*, *Jorge*, *Manuel*, *Mateo*, *Pablo*.

Castellana (167) Southern Italian: habitational name from a place named Castellana, notably the one in Sicily.

GIVEN NAMES Italian 24%. *Angelo* (5), *Salvatore* (2), *Vincenzo* (2), *Ambrogio*, *Carlo*, *Carmelo*, *Caterina*, *Cesare*, *Giovanni*.

Castellani (345) Italian: patronymic or plural form of CASTELLANO.

GIVEN NAMES Italian 15%. *Aldo* (3), *Angelo* (2), *Carlo* (2), *Guido* (2), *Annamarie*, *Antonio*, *Dante*, *Dino*, *Enio*, *Enrico*, *Franco*, *Gildo*.

Castellano (2527) **1.** Spanish: ethnic name for someone from Castile. **2.** Italian: status names from *castellano* (Latin *castellanus*), denoting the governor or constable of a castle, the lord of the manor, or the warder of a prison.

GIVEN NAMES Spanish 17%; Italian 12%. *Jose* (13), *Juan* (10), *Miguel* (7), *Enrique* (6), *Armando* (5), *Carlos* (5), *Roberto* (5), *Guadalupe* (4), *Jesus* (4), *Luis* (4), *Manuel* (4), *Ruben* (4); *Carmine* (13), *Rocco* (13), *Angelo* (8), *Salvatore* (7), *Vito* (7), *Antonio* (5), *Carmela* (4), *Cosmo* (3), *Battista* (2), *Carlo* (2), *Dario* (2), *Enrico* (2).

Castellanos (2316) **1.** Spanish: habitational name from any of numerous places called Castellanos, denoting a 'place founded or inhabited by Castilians'. **2.** Greek (**Kastellanos**): topographic name from an adjectival derivative of *kastello* 'castle' (from Late Latin *castellum*, a diminutive of *castrum* 'fort', 'Roman walled city').

GIVEN NAMES Spanish 54%. *Jose* (89), *Juan* (48), *Carlos* (34), *Luis* (31), *Jorge* (30), *Jesus* (21), *Manuel* (21), *Rafael* (19), *Miguel* (17), *Ricardo* (16), *Enrique* (15), *Ramon* (14).

Castellaw (193) Scottish: habitational name from any of several places in southern Scotland named as *Castle Law* 'castle hill'. The name has more or less died out in Scotland.

Castelli (1162) Italian: patronymic or plural form of CASTELLO.

GIVEN NAMES Italian 20%. *Angelo* (11), *Salvatore* (10), *Vito* (7), *Dino* (4), *Aldo* (3),

Calogero (3), *Guido* (3), *Vittorio* (3), *Antonio* (2), *Emidio* (2), *Enzo* (2), *Gino* (2).

Castellini (152) Italian: from a diminutive of CASTELLO.

GIVEN NAMES Italian 6%. *Gabriele*, *Primo*, *Renzo*.

Castello (853) **1.** Italian: from *castello* 'castle', 'fortified building' (from Late Latin *castellum*), applied as a topographic name, a habitational name from any of numerous places so named or named with this word, or a metonymic occupational name for a servant who lived and worked in such a place. **2.** Catalan (**Castelló**): habitational name from any of the places named Castelló or with that word, as for example Castelló de la Plana, one of the main towns in Valencia, or Castelló d'Empúries, a town in the Catalan district of L'Empordà.

GIVEN NAMES Spanish 7%; Italian 5%. *Jose* (5), *Manuel* (3), *Carlos* (2), *Juan* (2), *Adela*, *Arturo*, *Avelino*, *Dulce*, *Elena*, *Emilia*, *Enrique*, *Isadora*; *Angelo* (2), *Antonio* (2), *Salvatore* (2), *Vito* (2), *Aldo*, *Gaspare*, *Gaspere*, *Gino*, *Guiseppe*, *Lia*, *Luigi*, *Mino*.

Castellon (643) Spanish (**Castellón**): Castilianized form of Catalan **Castelló**, a habitational name from any of the places so named. This Castilianized form is notably applied to Castelló de la Plana, a town in Valencia, where the Castilianization process of Catalan is remarkable (see CASTELLÓ).

GIVEN NAMES Spanish 54%. *Jose* (24), *Carlos* (18), *Jesus* (9), *Juan* (9), *Ramon* (7), *Luis* (6), *Francisco* (5), *Jorge* (5), *Pedro* (5), *Sergio* (5), *Mario* (4), *Miguel* (4).

Castellow (115) Variant of Scottish CASTELLAW.

Castellucci (281) Italian: patronymic or plural form of CASTELLUCCIO.

GIVEN NAMES Italian 20%. *Angelo* (4), *Carlo* (4), *Antonio* (2), *Federico* (2), *Giovanni* (2), *Albino*, *Domenic*, *Domenica*, *Emilio*, *Filomena*, *Oreste*, *Pasquale*, *Rocco*.

Castelluccio (151) Italian: habitational name from any of numerous places named or named with Castelluccio or Castelluc-chio, from a diminutive of *castello* 'castle', 'fortified building'.

GIVEN NAMES Italian 16%. *Antonio*, *Domenic*, *Sal*, *Salvatore*.

Castelo (186) **1.** Portuguese: habitational name from any of numerous places called Castelo, from *castelo* 'castle', '(group of) fortified building(s)' (from Late Latin *castellum*). **2.** Catalan and Spanish (**Casteló**): respelling of Catalan **Castelló** (see CASTELLO).

GIVEN NAMES Spanish 46%; Portuguese 9%. *Jose* (5), *Rodolfo* (4), *Eduardo* (3), *Miguel* (3), *Ramon* (3), *Agustin* (2), *Amalia* (2), *Carlos* (2), *Juan* (2), *Narciso* (2), *Rogelio* (2), *Alberto*; *Joao*; *Antonio* (2), *Marco* (2), *Romeo*.

Casten (217) Swedish (**Castén**) and German: variant of **Kastén** (Swedish) or **Kasten** (German) (see KASTEN).

Casteneda (131) Variant of Spanish CASTANEDA.
GIVEN NAMES Spanish 54%. *Jose* (7), *Javier* (3), *Felipe* (2), *Luis* (2), *Orlando* (2), *Ruben* (2), *Alejandrina*, *Ambrosio*, *Araceli*, *Armando*, *Brijida*, *Carlos*.

Caster (1065) **1.** English: variant spelling of CASTOR. **2.** Americanized spelling of German KASTER.

Casterline (458) Origin unidentified. Perhaps an altered spelling of English **Castellain**, a status name for the governor of a castle, from Middle English, Anglo-Norman French *castelain* (see CHATELAIN).

Castetter (133) Americanized spelling of German **Kirchstetter** (see KERSTETTER).

Castiglia (365) Italian: regional name for someone from Castile in Spain (see CASTILLA).
GIVEN NAMES Italian 15%. *Salvatore* (2), *Angelo*, *Annamarie*, *Antonino*, *Benedetto*, *Carmine*, *Francesco*, *Gaetano*, *Gennaro*, *Giacomo*, *Giuseppe*, *Ignazio*.

Castiglione (730) Italian and Jewish (from Italy): habitational name from any of numerous places named with this word, from medieval Latin *castellio* (genitive *castellionis*) 'fortification', 'small castle'.
GIVEN NAMES Italian 22%. *Angelo* (15), *Salvatore* (7), *Vito* (7), *Sal* (3), *Amedeo* (2), *Carlo* (2), *Carmela* (2), *Giovanni* (2), *Luigi* (2), *Pasquale* (2), *Rocco* (2), *Aldo*.

Castiglioni (144) Italian: patronymic or plural form of CASTIGLIONE.
GIVEN NAMES Italian 17%; Spanish 7%. *Aldo*, *Armando*, *Giuseppe*, *Remo*, *Rosalinda*; *Lupe*, *Magda*, *Ramon*.

Castile (295) French: regional name for someone from Castile in Spain, a variant of French CASTILLE.

Castilla (277) Spanish: regional name for someone from Castile (Spanish *Castilla*) in Spain. An independent kingdom between the 10th and 15th centuries, it formed the largest power in the Iberian peninsula. The name derives from the many castles in the region.
GIVEN NAMES Spanish 45%. *Alfredo* (5), *Carlos* (4), *Raul* (4), *Sergio* (4), *Jesus* (3), *Jorge* (3), *Pablo* (3), *Ruben* (3), *Blanca* (2), *Elido* (2), *Francisco* (2), *Guillermo* (2); *Antonio* (2), *Aldo*, *Angelo*, *Leonardo*, *Lucio*, *Plinio*, *Primo*.

Castille (805) French: regional name for someone from Castile in central Spain (see CASTILLA).
GIVEN NAMES French 6%. *Alcee* (2), *Antoine* (2), *Armand* (2), *Maudry*, *Michel*, *Monique*, *Normand*, *Remy*, *Renella*.

Castilleja (354) Spanish: habitational name from any of various places, especially in Seville province, named with the word *castilleja* 'little castle'.

GIVEN NAMES Spanish 42%. *Jose* (5), *Manuel* (4), *Ricardo* (4), *Armando* (3), *Guadalupe* (3), *Juan* (3), *Santos* (3), *Agapito* (2), *Alberto* (2), *Alfredo* (2), *Domingo* (2), *Eusebio* (2).

Castillo (19385) Spanish: from *castillo* 'castle', 'fortified building' (Latin *castellum*), a habitational name from any of numerous places so named or named with this word.
GIVEN NAMES Spanish 48%. *Jose* (511), *Juan* (264), *Carlos* (192), *Luis* (156), *Manuel* (149), *Jesus* (146), *Francisco* (122), *Jorge* (120), *Ramon* (110), *Pedro* (105), *Roberto* (102), *Raul* (100).

Castillon (160) **1.** Aragonese and Spanish (**Castillón**): habitational name from any of the places named Castillón or with this word mainly in Aragon, as for example Castillón de Sos, from a derivative of *castillo* 'castle' (see CASTILLO). **2.** Southern French: habitational name meaning 'little castle', from any of various places so named.
GIVEN NAMES Spanish 47%. *Jesus* (5), *Carlos* (4), *Jose* (4), *Francisco* (3), *Juan* (3), *Mario* (3), *Ramon* (3), *Cristobal* (2), *Everado* (2), *Alonso*, *Angelina*, *Candelario*.

Castilow (100) See CASTELLAW.

Castine (276) Americanized spelling of German KERSTEIN, possibly also of the Jewish name.

Castle (7075) English: topographic name from Anglo-Norman French, Middle English *castel* 'castle', 'fortified building or set of buildings', especially the residence of a feudal lord (Late Latin *castellum*, a diminutive of *castrum* 'fort', 'Roman walled city'). The name would also have denoted a servant who lived and worked at such a place.

Castleberry (2812) **1.** Americanized form of Swiss German **Castelberger**, a habitational name, probably from a place in Grisons canton. **2.** Possibly also an Americanized spelling of German **Kesselberg**, a habitational name from any of the places in Bavaria, Baden, or Rhineland named Kesselberg.

Castleman (1176) Americanized spelling of German **Kasselmann** (see CASSELMAN) or **Kesselmann** (see KESSELMAN).

Castles (376) English, Scottish, and northern Irish: from a plural or genitive form of CASTLE.

Castleton (149) English: habitational name from any of various places called Castleton, for example in Derbyshire and North Yorkshire, from Old English *castel* 'castle' + *tūn* 'settlement', 'farmstead'.

Castner (843) **1.** Variant spelling of German and Jewish (Ashkenazic) KASTNER. **2.** Swedish: probably of German origin.

Casto (2619) Spanish and Italian: **1.** from the Latin personal name *Castus* 'chaste'. **2.** nickname from *casto* 'chaste', 'pure'.

Caston (920) English: habitational name from a place in Norfolk named Caston, from an unattested Old English personal name *Catt* or the Old Norse personal name *Káti* + Old English *tūn* 'farmstead', 'settlement'.

Castonguay (800) French Canadian: variant of **Gastonguay**, which is a combination of the first and last names of the first bearer of the name in Canada, Gaston Guay or Gay.
GIVEN NAMES French 17%. *Pierre* (5), *Lucien* (3), *Marcel* (3), *Normand* (3), *Alban* (2), *Andre* (2), *Armand* (2), *Camille* (2), *Adelard*, *Alcide*, *Alyre*, *Aurele*.

Castor (1652) English: habitational name from places called Caistor, in Lincolnshire and Norfolk, Caister in Norfolk, or Castor in Cambridgeshire, all named with Old English *cæster* 'Roman fort or town'.

Castorena (320) Spanish variant spelling of CASTORINA.
GIVEN NAMES Spanish 46%. *Jose* (12), *Jesus* (6), *Carlos* (4), *Juan* (4), *Pedro* (4), *Miguel* (3), *Roberto* (3), *Alberto* (2), *Alejandro* (2), *Alfonso* (2), *Emilio* (2), *Felipe* (2).

Castorina (122) Southern Italian (Sicily): from a feminine diminutive of the personal name *Castore* (Greek *Kastōr*). This is also found as a place name in Sicily, from which the surname may be a habitational name.
GIVEN NAMES Italian 29%. *Rosario* (3), *Alfio* (2), *Orlando* (2), *Carmela*, *Carmelo*, *Carmine*, *Domenic*, *Leonardo*, *Mario*, *Salvatore*.

Castoro (155) Italian: from *castoro* 'beaver' (Latin *castor*), hence a nickname for someone thought to resemble the animal in some way.
GIVEN NAMES Italian 31%. *Rocco* (4), *Saverio* (2), *Vito* (2), *Angelo*, *Carlo*, *Carmela*, *Chiara*, *Gino*, *Pasquale*, *Pietro*, *Salvatore*.

Castrejon (308) Spanish (**Castrejón**): habitational name from any of various places called Castrejón, for example in Salamanca province, or named with this word, a diminutive of *castro* 'castle', from Latin *castrum* 'fort', 'Roman walled city'.
GIVEN NAMES Spanish 60%. *Jose* (16), *Francisco* (7), *Carlos* (6), *Jaime* (5), *Pedro* (4), *Angel* (3), *Isidro* (3), *Jesus* (3), *Joaquin* (3), *Jorge* (3), *Juan* (3), *Margarito* (2); *Antonio* (5), *Lorenzo* (2), *Bartolo*, *Federico*, *Francesca*, *Lucio*, *Saturnina*.

Castricone (131) Italian: possibly from Old Italian *castrica* 'shrike', presumably a nickname for someone thought to resemble the bird in some way.
GIVEN NAMES Italian 16%. *Angelo* (2), *Camillo* (2), *Salvatore* (2), *Antonio*, *Domenica*, *Paolo*.

Castrillo (135) Spanish: habitational name from any of various places, especially in León province, named Castrillo from *castrillo* 'fort', a diminutive of CASTRO.
GIVEN NAMES Spanish 42%. *Jose* (6), *Manuel* (4), *Jorge* (3), *Angel* (2), *Carlos* (2), *Emilio*

(2), *Guillermo* (2), *Ramon* (2), *Alberto*, *Alejandro*, *Ana*, *Benito*; *Silvio* (2), *Annalisa, Antonio, Vito.*

Castrillon (110) Asturian-Leonese and Galician (**Castrillón**): habitational name from any of the three places named Castrillón, from an augmentative of *castrillo* 'fort', in Asturies, or perhaps from either of the two places so called in the provinces of Lugo and Pontevedra in Galicia.
GIVEN NAMES Spanish 56%. *Jose* (4), *Juan* (4), *Alberto* (3), *Humberto* (3), *Luis* (3), *Adriana* (2), *Guillermo* (2), *Jairo* (2), *Luis Fernando* (2), *Socorro* (2), *Ana, Edelmira.*

Castro (16365) Galician, Portuguese, Italian, and Jewish (Sephardic): topographic name from *castro* 'castle', 'fortress' (Latin *castrum* 'fort', 'Roman walled city'): in Galicia and also in northern Portugal a habitational name from any of various places named with this word; in Italy either a topographic name or a habitational name.
GIVEN NAMES Spanish 45%; Portuguese 10%. *Jose* (371), *Juan* (172), *Manuel* (169), *Carlos* (145), *Luis* (134), *Jesus* (116), *Jorge* (112), *Miguel* (91), *Francisco* (87), *Mario* (83), *Pedro* (73), *Raul* (73); *Joao* (5), *Paulo* (5), *Ligia* (2), *Vasco* (2), *Wenceslao* (2), *Armanda, Fernandes.*

Castrogiovanni (122) Southern Italian: habitational name from Castrogiovanni, the name until 1927 of Enna in central Sicily.
GIVEN NAMES Italian 19%. *Angelo* (2), *Antonio, Calogero, Giuseppe, Mario, Paolo, Pasquale, Ricardo, Silvo.*

Castronova (186) Variant of Italian CASTRONOVO.
GIVEN NAMES Italian 13%. *Fiore* (2), *Salvatore* (2), *Alfonse, Angelo, Dino.*

Castronovo (233) Southern Italian: habitational name from any of various places named Castronovo, from *castro* 'castle' (see CASTRO) + *novo* 'new'.
GIVEN NAMES Italian 22%. *Salvatore* (4), *Angelo* (2), *Santo* (2), *Cosimo, Giacomo, Graziella, Sal, Stefano.*

Castruita (145) Hispanic (Mexico): unexplained.
GIVEN NAMES Spanish 37%. *Manuel* (4), *Jesus* (3), *Jose* (2), *Natividad* (2), *Adolfo, Albino, Alfonso, Alfredo, Cruz, Esperanza, Ezequiel, Francisco.*

Caswell (3693) English: habitational name from places in Dorset, Northamptonshire, and Somerset named Caswell, from Old English *cærse* '(water)cress' + *well(a)* 'spring', 'stream'.

Catala (134) Catalan (**Català**): regional name for a Catalan, someone from Catalonia (Catalan *Catalunya*).
GIVEN NAMES Spanish 42%. *Luis* (4), *Jose* (3), *Miguel* (3), *Rafael* (3), *Ana* (2), *Antonio* (2) *Mario* (2), *Orlando* (2), *Andres, Apolo, Eduardo, Elpidio, Emilia.*

Catalan (340) Spanish (**Catalán**): regional name for someone from Catalonia (Spanish *Cataluña*).

GIVEN NAMES Spanish 48%. *Jose* (6), *Juan* (4), *Carlos* (3), *Roberto* (3), *Abelardo* (2), *Alberto* (2), *Aquiles* (2), *Armando* (2), *Francisco* (2), *Guadalupe* (2), *Julio* (2), *Lourdes* (2).

Catalani (114) Italian: patronymic or plural form of CATALANO.
GIVEN NAMES Italian 9%. *Giovanni, Guido, Renzo.*

Catalano (3467) Italian: regional name for someone from Catalonia, Italian *Catalogna* (see CATALA). The name is widespread in Italy, especially southern Italy, a reflection of the migration of Catalonians to Italy in the 11th and 13th centuries, and of the strong commercial and social links between the Catalano-Aragonese realm and the Mediterranean coast of Italy at that time.
GIVEN NAMES Italian 15%. *Angelo* (24), *Salvatore* (18), *Vito* (12), *Rocco* (7), *Carmine* (6), *Santo* (6), *Antonio* (5), *Silvio* (4), *Carlo* (3), *Giovanni* (3), *Nino* (3), *Orazio* (3).

Catalanotto (192) Italian: diminutive of CATALANO.
GIVEN NAMES Italian 18%. *Biagio, Carlo, Gasper, Gilda, Gino, Mario, Vincenza.*

Cataldi (396) Southern Italian: patronymic or plural form of CATALDO.
GIVEN NAMES Italian 28%; Spanish 6%. *Angelo* (5), *Dante* (2), *Adolfo, Alfonso, Alina, Antonio, Armando, Cosimo, Domenico, Francesco, Gino, Giulio, Mirella, Nicola, Ottavio, Paolo; Alejandro, Ines, Luis, Ramona, Victorio.*

Cataldo (1554) Southern Italian: from the personal name *Cataldo*, popularized in the Middle Ages by the cult of Saint Cataldo, an Irish monk and disciple of Saint Carthage, who on returning from a pilgrimage in the Holy Land settled in Taranto.
GIVEN NAMES Italian 16%. *Angelo* (10), *Salvatore* (9), *Vito* (5), *Carlo* (4), *Rocco* (4), *Sal* (4), *Antonio* (3), *Carmine* (3), *Giovanni* (3), *Luigi* (3), *Aldo* (2), *Domenic* (2).

Catalfamo (200) Southern Italian (Sicily): of uncertain origin; most probably a variant of **Catalfano**, a habitational name from a place called Catalfàno, named with Arabic *qal'at* 'citadel' + perhaps *ḥalfān* 'two oaths'.
GIVEN NAMES Italian 23%. *Vito* (3), *Antonio* (2), *Carmelo* (2), *Rocco* (2), *Salvatore* (2), *Carmela, Elio, Giovanna, Giuseppe, Orazio, Sal, Santo.*

Catalina (206) Spanish (Castilian): from the Castilian form of the female personal name *Catarina* (see CATHERINE).

Cataline (118) Possibly an altered spelling of Spanish CATALINA, or of the French equivalent, **Cateline**.

Catalino (107) Italian: unexplained; perhaps from a female personal name equivalent to CATHERINE.

GIVEN NAMES Italian 8%; Spanish 7%; French 5%. *Angelo, Mario, Santino; Marisol, Miguel, Tomas; Colette, Michel.*

Catallo (108) Southern Italian: possibly a variant of CATALDO, showing characteristic assimilation of *-ld-* to *-ll-*.
GIVEN NAMES Italian 11%. *Dario, Ercole, Rocco.*

Catanach (117) Scottish: variant of CATTANACH.
GIVEN NAMES French 5%; Spanish 4%. *Yolette* (2); *Alfonso, Alfredo, Crucita, Eduardo, Erlinda, Marcos.*

Catanese (579) Southern Italian: habitational name for someone from the Sicilian port of Catania, from an adjectival form of the place name.
GIVEN NAMES Italian 22%. *Santo* (5), *Salvatore* (4), *Sal* (3), *Angelo* (2), *Rocco* (2), *Vito* (2), *Antonino, Antonio, Armando, Carmella, Francesco, Gaetano, Marina, Mario, Pietro, Santi; Pedro* (2), *Ruben, Salvador.*

Catania (1132) Italian (Sicily): habitational name for someone from the city of Catania on the east coast of Sicily.
GIVEN NAMES Italian 18%; Spanish 6%. *Salvatore* (11), *Sal* (7), *Vito* (5), *Angelo* (3), *Carmelo* (3), *Nunzio* (3), *Mario* (4), *Anselmo* (2), *Biagio* (2), *Carlo* (2), *Guido* (2), *Pasquale* (2), *Rocco* (2), *Aldo* (2), *Mariana, Roberto; Manuel* (2), *Pablo* (2), *Ana, Angel, Liborio.*

Catano (177) Italian (Messina): **1.** from a variant of the personal name *Caetano* (see GAETANO). **2.** variant of **Cattano**, an occupational name for a producer or seller of cotton, from Arabic *quaṭṭān*. **3.** variant of CATTANEO. **4.** with the stress on the second *a*, it could be from Old Italian *cattano* 'captain'.
GIVEN NAMES Spanish 39%; Italian 9%. *Jose* (5), *Alfredo* (2), *Armando* (2), *Genaro* (2), *Gustavo* (2), *Jesus* (2), *Alba, Arturo, Audelia, Aurelio, Camila, Carlos; Antonio* (3), *Angelo, Carmel, Dario, Nicolo.*

Catanzano (103) Italian: variant of CATANZARO.
GIVEN NAMES Italian 20%. *Attilio, Cosmo, Dante, Gaetano, Sal, Salvatore.*

Catanzarite (194) Southern Italian: habitational name for someone from CATANZARO, with the Greek habitational suffix *-itēs*.
GIVEN NAMES Italian 23%. *Gino, Rocco, Rosario.*

Catanzaro (982) Italian (Calabria and Sicily): habitational name from Catanzaro in Calabria.
GIVEN NAMES Italian 15%. *Sal* (5), *Gasper* (4), *Salvatore* (4), *Gaspare* (3), *Giuseppe* (3), *Concetta* (2), *Cosimo* (2), *Cosmo* (2), *Ignazio* (2), *Nino* (2), *Santo* (2), *Francesco.*

Catapano (386) Southern Italian: status name from *catapano*, the title of a high-ranking official with judicial, administrative, and economic jurisdiction (a borrowing from Byzantine *catepano* 'superintendent').

GIVEN NAMES Italian 17%. *Salvatore* (4), *Carmine* (3), *Gaetano* (3), *Sal* (2), *Aniello, Carlo, Conrado, Donato, Enrico, Francesco, Pina.*

Catching (120) Probably an Americanized form of German **Göttgen**, a Rhenish surname from a pet form of the personal name GOTTFRIED, or of North German **Gätjen**, from the medieval personal name *Gado*, cognate with Middle High German *gate* 'companion' (see GADE).

Catchings (417) Probably an Americanized spelling of German **Göttgens** or **Gädjens**, patronymics from **Göttgen** and **Gädjen** respectively (see CATCHING).

Catchpole (146) English (chiefly East Anglia): from Anglo-Norman French *cachepol* (a compound of *cache(r)* 'to chase' + *pol* 'fowl'), an occupational name for a bailiff, originally one empowered to seize poultry and other livestock in case of default on debts or taxes.

Cate (2104) **1.** English: unexplained. **2.** Possibly from one of the many variants of Dutch *kat* 'cat'. See also KATH, CATT.

Catena (211) Southern Italian (Sicily and Naples): **1.** habitational name from any of several places called Catena, from Latin *catena* 'chain'. **2.** from the Marian name *(Maria della) Catena*, the patron saint of many communities in eastern Sicily.

GIVEN NAMES Italian 15%. *Pasquale* (2), *Salvatore* (2), *Silvio* (2), *Camillo, Carlo, Gino, Vittorio.*

Catenacci (112) Italian: from a derivative of *catena* 'chain'.

GIVEN NAMES Italian 18%. *Gino* (2), *Mauro* (2), *Angelo, Antonio, Dante, Dino, Giovanni, Tullio.*

Cater (1288) **1.** English: occupational name for the buyer of provisions for a large household, from a reduced form of Anglo-Norman French *acatour* (Late Latin *acceptator*, an agent derivative of *acceptare* 'to accept'). Modern English *caterer* results from the addition of a second agent suffix to the word. **2.** Slovenian (**Čater**): status name for a person who read out the Slovenian ceremonial text at the installation of the Carantanian rulers and, later, Carinthian dukes, derived from the dialect verb *čatiti* 'to read'. Carantania was the early medieval Slovenian state on the territory of present-day Carinthia and Styria, now divided between Austria and Slovenia. The people's installation of the Carantanian rulers was an exceptional example of democratic elections in medieval Europe. Thomas Jefferson knew about it and was influenced by it in his thinking about American Independence. **3.** Perhaps also an Americanized spelling of German **Köter** (see KOETTER).

Caterina (136) Italian: from the female personal name *Caterina*, a popular name in the

medieval period, which was borne by numerous early Christian saints. See also CATHERINE.

GIVEN NAMES Italian 9%. *Battista, Stefano.*

Caterino (185) Italian: masculinized variant of CATERINA.

GIVEN NAMES Italian 16%. *Sal* (4), *Cosmo* (3), *Angelo, Salvatore, Vito, Vittorio.*

Cates (6809) **1.** English: patronymic from the Old Norse byname *Káti* (from *káti* 'boy'). (*Kate* was not in use as a pet form of *Catherine* during the Middle Ages.) **2.** Probably in some instances an Americanized spelling of German GOETZ.

Cathcart (1720) Scottish: habitational name from Cathcart near Glasgow.

Cathell (216) English: unexplained.

Cather (455) **1.** Scottish: habitational name from Catter or Cather in Dumbartonshire. **2.** Altered spelling of Austrian German **Köther**, a variant of **Kötter** (see KOETTER).

Catherine (104) French and English: from the medieval female personal name *Catherine*, Latin *Caterina*. This is of uncertain origin, being first attested in Greek in the form *Aikaterinē* but later affected by folk etymological associations with Greek *katharos* 'pure'. It was borne by various early Christian saints, and was popular throughout the Middle Ages.

GIVEN NAME French 6%. *Benoit.*

Catherman (264) Probably an altered spelling of Dutch **Katherman**, a nickname for someone who was very dextrous, such as a juggler or conjuror, from Old French *quatremains* 'four hands'. Compare QUARTERMAN.

Cathers (335) Variant of the Scottish habitational name CATHER, now occurring chiefly in northern Ireland.

Catherwood (161) Scottish: variant of CALDERWOOD.

Cathey (2997) Scottish: reduced form of **MacCathay**, a Galloway surname of unexplained origin, also spelled **Cathie**.

Catino (343) **1.** Southern Italian: from a masculinized form of *Catina*, a reduced form of CATERINA. **2.** Possibly an altered spelling of French **Catineau**, from a pet form of the female personal name CATHERINE or of **Gatineau**.

GIVEN NAMES Italian 12%. *Antonio* (2), *Domenic* (2), *Ciriaco, Dante, Gaetano, Gilda, Luigi, Marcello, Nichola, Nicola, Pasquale, Tullio.*

Catizone (133) Italian (Catanzaro): unexplained.

GIVEN NAMES Italian 28%. *Antonio* (3), *Pietro* (3), *Carmine* (2), *Angelo, Domenico, Giuseppe, Luigi, Palma, Sal, Salvatore.*

Catledge (176) **1.** English: variant of CARTLEDGE. **2.** Possibly an Americanized spelling of South German **Göttlich**, from the old personal name *Godolec*, cognate with GOETZ.

Catlett (1907) English: from the medieval female personal name *Cat(e)let*, a pet form of CATLIN.

Catlin (1813) English: from the medieval female personal name *Cat(e)lin(e)*, Anglo-Norman French form of CATHERINE.

Catlow (116) English: habitational name from either of two minor places in Lancashire named Catlow.

Cato (2516) **1.** Variant of Scottish CATTO. **2.** Spanish and Catalan (**Cató**): possibly from a personal name taken with reference to the Roman republican statesman Cato. **3.** Swedish: perhaps a soldier's name, likewise bestowed with reference to Cato, the Roman statesman.

Catoe (665) Scottish and English: variant of CATTO.

Caton (2202) **1.** English: habitational name from either of two places called Caton, in Derbyshire and Lancashire. The former is probably named with the Old English personal name or byname *Cada* (see CADE) + Old English *tūn* 'enclosure', 'settlement'; the latter is from the Old Norse byname *Káti* (see CATES) + *tūn*. **2.** English and French: from a pet form of CATLIN.

Catone (204) Italian: derivative of the name of the Roman republican statesman Cato, used as a nickname.

GIVEN NAMES Italian 4%. *Angelo* (2), *Mafalda.*

Cator (109) English: variant of CATER.

Catrambone (184) Italian (Calabria): unexplained.

GIVEN NAMES Italian 18%. *Vito* (3), *Giuseppe, Rocco.*

Catrett (232) Americanized form of English CARTWRIGHT.

Catron (1942) **1.** Americanized form of English KETTERING. **2.** Possibly also French, from a pet form of the female personal name CATHERINE.

Catt (729) **1.** English: nickname from the animal, Middle English *catte* 'cat'. The word is found in similar forms in most European languages from very early times (e.g. Gaelic *cath*, Slavic *kotu*). Domestic cats were unknown in Europe in classical times, when weasels fulfilled many of their functions, for example in hunting rodents. They seem to have come from Egypt, where they were regarded as sacred animals. **2.** English: from a medieval female personal name, a short form of CATHERINE. **3.** Variant spelling of German and Dutch KATT.

Cattanach (161) Scottish: from Gaelic **Cattanaich** 'belonging to Clan Chattan', the name of a clan said to be descended from one *Gillecatain* 'servant of St. Catan'.

Cattaneo (253) Italian (Liguria): **1.** variant of CAPITANO. **2.** (**Cattanèo**) habitational name for someone from Catania.

GIVEN NAMES Italian 13%. *Giuseppe* (2), *Angelo, Antonio, Dante, Dino, Ettore,*

Fausto, Fiorenzo, Giovanna, Luca, Luciano, Marco.

Cattani (194) Southern Italian: occupational name for a cotton producer or dealer, from Arabic *qaṭṭān.* Compare CATANO 2.
GIVEN NAMES Italian 11%. *Gino* (2), *Alda, Angelina, Dante, Dino, Eduardo, Emilio, Secondo.*

Cattell (339) **1.** Welsh: variant of CADDELL. **2.** English (chiefly West Midlands): from a pet form of the female personal name CATLIN.

Catterall (167) English (Lancashire): habitational name from Catterall in Lancashire, possibly named from Old Norse *kattar-hali* 'cat's tail', referring to a long, thin piece of land.

Catterson (232) Scottish and northern Irish: reduced Anglicized form (with the redundant addition of English patronymic *-son*) of **Mac Uaitéir**, a Gaelic patronymic based on the Norman personal name WALTER. Compare McWATTERS.

Catterton (281) English: habitational name from a place in North Yorkshire named Catterton, from a Celtic hill name, *Cadeir* (from *cadeir* 'chair'), + Old English *tūn* 'settlement'. Compare CHATTERTON.

Catto (168) **1.** Scottish: development of **Cattoch**, a name of unknown origin, recorded in Aberdeenshire since the mid 15th century. **2.** Italian (Venice): of uncertain origin; possibly derived from a short form of the female personal name CATERINA.

Catton (305) English: **1.** habitational name from any of the various places called Catton, for example in Derbyshire, Norfolk, and North Yorkshire, all apparently from an Old English byname *Catta* meaning 'cat' or Old Norse *Káti* meaning 'boy' + Old English *tūn* 'enclosure', 'settlement'. **2.** from a pet form of CATHERINE.

Catts (133) **1.** English: variant of CATT. **2.** Probably an Americanized spelling of German and Jewish KATZ, Dutch KATS, or German **Götz** (see GOETZ).

Catucci (106) Italian: augmentative form of **Cati**, a variant of **Cattì**, a much-reduced pet form of the Greek personal name *Konstantinos* (see CONSTANTINE).
GIVEN NAMES Italian 24%. *Angelo* (2), *Carlo, Cosmo, Franco, Pietro, Rocco, Sal, Stefano, Vito.*

Cauble (721) Americanized form of German KABEL.

Cauchon (108) French (Normandy and Picardy): variant of **Chausson**, a metonymic occupational name for a maker or seller of slippers.
GIVEN NAMES French 8%. *Armand, Clothilde.*

Caudell (699) English, Scottish, and northern Irish: variant of CALDWELL.

Caudill (5952) English, Scottish, and northern Irish: variant of CALDWELL.

Caudillo (404) Spanish: from Spanish *caudillo* 'military leader' (from Latin *capitellum*).

GIVEN NAMES Spanish 41%. *Juan* (7), *Guadalupe* (5), *Manuel* (5), *Jose* (4), *Luis* (3), *Lupe* (3), *Ramon* (3), *Ricardo* (3), *Alfredo* (2), *Ana* (2), *Edmundo* (2), *Fernando* (2).

Caudle (2938) English, Scottish, and northern Irish: variant of CALDWELL.

Cauffman (230) Americanized spelling of German and Jewish (Ashkenazic) KAUFMAN(N).

Caufield (556) **1.** English and Irish: variant spelling of CAULFIELD. **2.** Americanized form of German **Kauffeld**, a development from **Kaufwald**, seemingly topographic names with the familiar suffixes *-feld* 'open country', *-wald* 'wood(s)', but actually derivatives or nicknames from Old High German *kouf* 'trade', 'purchase'. See KOFF.
GIVEN NAMES Irish 6%. *Aileen, Delma.*

Caughell (127) Irish: Anglicized spelling of Gaelic **Ó Cathail** (see CAHILL).

Caughey (570) Irish (pronounced 'ko-hi'): **1.** Anglicized form of Gaelic **Mac Eochadha** or **Mac Eachaidh** 'son of *Eachaidh*', a byname meaning 'horseman' (a derivative of *each* 'horse'). **2.** reduced Anglicized form of Gaelic **Ó Maolchathaigh** (see MULCAHY).

Caughlin (221) Irish: probably a reduced and altered form of McLAUGHLIN.

Caughman (424) Possibly an Americanized spelling of German and Jewish KAUFMAN(N), or German **Kochmann** (see KOCHMAN).

Caughran (130) Variant spelling of Irish and Scottish CAUGHRON.

Caughron (356) **1.** Variant of Scottish COCHRAN. **2.** Reduced variant of Irish McCAGHREN.

Caul (177) Reduced form of Irish McCAUL (see McCALL).

Caulder (695) Scottish and English: variant spelling of CALDER.

Cauldwell (133) English, Scottish, and northern Irish: variant of CALDWELL.

Cauley (1476) Irish: reduced form of McCAULEY.

Caulfield (1558) English, Scottish, and Irish: probably a habitational name from a place in England or Scotland named with Old English *cald* 'cold' + *feld* 'open country'. There is a Cauldfield near Langholm in Dumfriesshire which is a probable source of the name.
GIVEN NAMES Irish 5%. *Briana, Eamonn, Liam.*

Caulk (417) English (Norfolk): possibly a variant of CALK.

Caulkins (468) Irish: variant of CULKIN, with English patronymic *-s* added. Compare CALKINS.

Causby (362) English: perhaps a variant spelling of COSBY.

Causer (169) English (West Midlands): probably an occupational name for a maker of leggings or other apparel for the legs or

feet, from an agent derivative probably of a northern variant of Old French *chausse* 'footwear' or 'leggings' (see CHAUSSE).

Causey (3891) English (of Norman origin): topographic name for someone who lived by a causeway, Middle English *caucey* (from Old Norman French *cauciée*); the ending of the word was in time assimilated by folk etymology to Middle English *way.*

Causley (110) English: habitational name of uncertain origin, possibly from Corsley in Wiltshire, which is named with Celtic *cors* 'marsh' + Old English *lēah* 'woodland clearing'.

Cauthen (1274) Probably a variant of English CAWTHORNE.

Cauthon (169) Probably a variant of English CAWTHORNE.

Cauthorn (176) English: variant spelling of CAWTHORNE.

Cauthron (112) English: probably a variant of CAWTHORNE.

Cava (303) Italian, Catalan, Spanish, and Portuguese: from *cava* 'cave', 'cellar' (from Latin *cavea*), hence a metonymic occupational name for someone employed in the wine cellars of a great house, a topographic name for someone who lived in or near a cave, or a habitational name from any of numerous places named with this word.
GIVEN NAMES Italian 22%; Spanish 5%. *Alfonso* (2), *Alicia, Angelo* (2), *Battista, Carmine, Emilio, Eugenio, Fernando, Francisca, Fiore, Franca, Francesca, Giovanni, Pelagia; Luis, Rafael.*

Cavaco (103) Portuguese: nickname from *cavaco* 'log', but there also exist various places called Cavao or Cavacos, which could have given rise to the surname.
GIVEN NAMES Spanish 16%; Portuguese 10%. *Manuel* (4), *Belarmino, Casimiro, Fernando, Idalina; Henrique.*

Cavagnaro (374) Southern Italian: occupational name for a basketmaker, from an agent derivative of *cavagno* 'basket' (now obsolete).

Cavalcante (101) Italian: from a medieval personal name derived from *cavalcare* 'to ride', from Latin *caballicare.* The form **Cavalcanti** also became established in Spain.
GIVEN NAMES Spanish 13%; German 5%; Italian 4%. *Marcos* (3), *Claudio, Francisco, Gustavo, Lito, Orlando; Otto* (2); *Sal.*

Cavaleri (122) Southern Italian: occupational name from Sicilian *cavaleri* 'rider', 'mounted soldier', 'knight'. It was also used as a patrician title. Compare CAVALIERE.
GIVEN NAMES Italian 26%. *Rosario* (2), *Angelo, Antonio, Augustino, Francesco, Giorgio, Giuseppe, Rocco, Vito.*

Cavalier (1175) Southern French: variant of CHEVALIER (meaning 'knight', 'rider').
FOREBEARS A family Cavalier or Lecavelier, from Normandy, France, had settled in

Montreal by 1654. There are also Huguenot bearers (among whom it is also spelled **Cavalear**) who came to VA by way of London.

Cavaliere (745) Italian: from *cavaliere* 'knight', 'horseman' (from Late Latin *caballarius*), possibly a status name, but more likely a nickname or an occupational name for the servant of a knight.
GIVEN NAMES Italian 18%. *Angelo* (9), *Salvatore* (5), *Antonio* (2), *Carlo* (2), *Carmelo* (2), *Lorenzo* (2), *Pasquale* (2), *Amato*, *Amedeo*, *Biagio*, *Emanuele*, *Franca*.

Cavalieri (482) Italian: patronymic or plural form of CAVALIERE.
GIVEN NAMES Italian 15%. *Angelo* (4), *Pasquale* (3), *Rocco* (3), *Amerigo* (2), *Salvatore* (2), *Domenic*, *Ercole*, *Gennaro*, *Gianpaolo*, *Gildo*, *Giuseppe*, *Marco*.

Cavallaro (1328) Southern Italian: either a variant, under Spanish influence, of CAVALIERE, or an occupational name for a keeper or dealer in horses, Sicilian *cavaddaru*.
GIVEN NAMES Italian 17%. *Salvatore* (13), *Sal* (6), *Antonio* (5), *Alfio* (3), *Ilario* (3), *Angelo* (2), *Franco* (2), *Nunzio* (2), *Orazio* (2), *Santo* (2), *Vincenzo* (2), *Vito* (2).

Cavallero (224) Southern Italian (Sicily, Naples): either from Sicilian *cavaleri* 'rider' or an equivalent of Spanish CABALLERO 'horseman', 'knight'.
GIVEN NAMES Italian 18%; Spanish 9%. *Mario* (2), *Aldo* (2), *Angelo* (2), *Dario*, *Secondo*; *Alejandro*, *Angel*, *Felipe*, *Jose*, *Susana*, *Zulma*; *Michel* (2).

Cavalli (318) Italian: patronymic or plural form of CAVALLO.
GIVEN NAMES Italian 11%. *Aldo* (3), *Giulio* (2), *Antonio*, *Domenico*, *Fiore*, *Giorgio*, *Giovanni*, *Massimo*, *Piera*, *Pietro*.

Cavallini (133) Italian: from a diminutive of CAVALLO.
GIVEN NAMES Italian 24%; Spanish 6%. *Augusto* (2), *Manlio* (2), *Adriano*, *Alberto*, *Alessandra*, *Amilcare*, *Angelo*, *Alfredo*, *Biagio*, *Cristina*, *Lorenzo*, *Nino*, *Oreste*, *Peppino*, *Primo*, *Reno*, *Riccardo*; *Luis* (2), *Luisa*, *Delphin*.

Cavallo (1177) Italian: metonymic occupational name for a man in charge of horses, perhaps also a nickname for someone supposedly resembling a horse, from *cavallo* 'horse' (Late Latin *caballus* 'gelding').
GIVEN NAMES Italian 19%; Spanish 5%. *Angelo* (8), *Vito* (5), *Mario* (4), *Giuseppe* (3), *Guido* (3), *Rocco* (3), *Aldo* (2), *Americo* (2), *Antonio* (2), *Claudio* (2), *Gerardo* (2), *Guiseppe* (2), *Orlando* (2), *Romeo* (2), *Santo* (2), *Alessandro*, *Alberto*, *Amelio*, *Augusto*, *Fabio*, *Fernando*, *Germano*; *Luis* (2), *Alejandro*.

Cavan (221) **1.** Irish: Anglicized form of Gaelic **Ó Caomháin**, 'son of *Caomhán* (*Kevin*)', a diminutive of the personal name *Caomh* (see O'KEEFE). **2.** Irish: in some cases perhaps an alternative Anglicization

of **Caomhánach** (see KAVANAGH). **3.** Filipino or other Southeast Asian: unexplained.
GIVEN NAMES Southeast Asian 4%. *Oai*, *Onh*, *Phanh*, *Vinh*.

Cavanagh (1806) Irish: variant spelling of KAVANAGH.
GIVEN NAMES Irish 5%. *Brendan* (2), *Brennan*, *Fergus*.

Cavanah (203) Irish: variant spelling of KAVANAGH.

Cavanaugh (6930) Irish: variant spelling of KAVANAGH.
GIVEN NAMES Irish 8%. *Brendan* (3), *Brennan* (2), *Aileen*, *Dermod*, *Donal*, *Patrick Sean*.

Cavaness (261) Americanized form of the French Huguenot name CABANISS.

Cavanna (125) Italian: topographic name for someone who lived in a rough or temporary dwelling, from *capanna* 'hut', 'shelter'.
GIVEN NAMES Italian 12%; Spanish 12%; Irish 5%. *Antonio*, *Carlo*, *Dino*, *Gianni*; *Mario* (2), *Cesar*, *Eduardo*, *Eugenio*, *Maria Teresa*, *Rafael*, *Ramon*, *Vicente*.

Cavaretta (125) Southern Italian (Calabria): occupational name from Sicilian *cavaretta*, *cavarettu* 'warder', '(night) watchman' (from medieval Latin *gavarretus*).
GIVEN NAMES Italian 10%. *Carlo* (2), *Angelo*, *Salvatore*, *Vita*.

Cavataio (155) Italian: occupational name from a derivative of Latin *cavator* 'miner'.
GIVEN NAMES Italian 11%. *Salvatore* (3), *Sal*, *Vito*.

Cavazos (2267) Spanish: from Italian **Cavazzo**, a derivative of the personal name *Iacovo* (see JAMES).
GIVEN NAMES Spanish 50%. *Jose* (72), *Juan* (38), *Manuel* (33), *Jesus* (20), *Raul* (19), *Ruben* (17), *Arturo* (15), *Carlos* (14), *Guadalupe* (14), *Luis* (14), *Mario* (14), *Javier* (12).

Cave (2934) **1.** English (of Norman origin) and northern French: nickname for a bald man, from Anglo-Norman French *cauf* 'bald'. Compare CHAFFEE. **2.** English: habitational name from a place in East Yorkshire called Cave, apparently from a river name derived from Old English *cāf* 'swift'. **3.** French: metonymic occupational name for someone employed in or in charge of the wine cellars of a great house, from Old French *cave* 'cave', 'cellar' (Latin *cavea*, a derivative of *cavus* 'hollow'). **4.** French, possibly also English: topographic name for someone who lived in or near a cave, from the same word as in 3 in an older sense.

Cavell (177) English: nickname for a bald man, from a diminutive of Anglo-Norman French *cauf*.

Caven (321) Scottish and northern Irish: spelling variant of CAVAN.

Cavenaugh (269) Variant of Irish KAVANAGH.

Cavender (1554) English altered form of Irish KAVANAGH.
FOREBEARS Hugh Cavenagh (died *c.*1709) came from Bristol in England to Westmoreland County, VA, in 1658 as an indentured servant for a five-year period to a Mr. Wills. His descendants spelled their name variously **Cavenah**, **Caviner**, **Cavenner**, **Cavinder**, and **Cavender**.

Cavendish (161) English: habitational name from a place in Suffolk named Cavendish, from an Old English byname *Cāfna* (meaning 'bold', 'daring') + Old English *edisc* 'enclosed pasture'.

Cavener (109) English (London): respelling of Irish KAVANAGH. Compare CAVENDER.

Caveness (102) Americanized form of the French Huguenot name CABANISS.

Caveney (153) Irish: variant of KEAVENEY.

Caveny (132) Irish: variant of KEAVENEY.

Caver (484) French: from Gascon *caber*, *caver* 'horseman', 'knight' (from medieval Latin *caballarius*).

Caverly (458) English: reduced form of CALVERLEY.

Caves (579) English: variant of CAVE 1 or 4.

Cavett (328) Altered spelling of French **Cavet**: **1.** diminutive of CAVE 1, 3, or 4. **2.** metonymic occupational name for a laborer, from Old Occitan *cavet*, denoting a tool for clearing ground for cultivation.

Cavey (375) Irish: Anglicized form of Gaelic **Mac Dháibhidh**, and so akin to McDEVITT.

Cavicchi (137) Italian: perhaps from a derivative of Late Latin *cavicla*, a diminutive of *clavicula* 'key'.

Cavill (115) English: habitational name from Cavil, a place in the East Riding of Yorkshire, named from Old English *cā* 'jackdaw' + *feld* 'open country'.

Cavin (1219) **1.** Scottish: unexplained. **2.** French: diminutive of CAVE.

Cavinder (117) English (of Irish origin): variant of CAVENDER.

Caviness (1149) Americanized form of the French Huguenot name CABANISS.

Cavins (407) Scottish: unexplained.

Cavitt (506) Irish: reduced form of **Mc-Cavitt**, a variant of McKEVITT.

Cavnar (130) Variant of CAVENER.

Cavner (136) Variant of CAVENER.

Cavness (170) Americanized form of the French Huguenot name CABANISS.

Cawley (2108) Irish: reduced form of McCAULEY.
GIVEN NAMES Irish 6%. *William Kevin* (2), *Brendan*, *Dermot*, *Niamh*.

Cawood (434) English (Yorkshire and Lancashire): habitational name from places in North Yorkshire and Lancashire called Cawood, from Old English *cā* 'jackdaw' + *wudu* 'wood'.

Cawthon (1022) Variant of English CAWTHORNE.

Cawthorn (205) English: variant spelling of CAWTHORNE.

Cawthorne (293) English: habitational name from Cawthorn in North Yorkshire or Cawthorne in South Yorkshire; both are probably named with Old English *cald* 'cold' (i.e. 'exposed') + *þorn* 'thorn bush'.

Cawvey (111) Americanized form of an unidentified German or Slavic name, perhaps Czech KAVA.

Cay (111) **1.** Scottish: variant spelling of KAY. **2.** French: probably a variant of QUAY.

Caya (256) **1.** Southern French: of uncertain origin; perhaps a nickname from *caia* (variant of Occitan *calha*, French *caille*, Latin *quacula*) 'quail' or from regional French *caya* 'sow'. **2.** possibly also Asturian-Leonese: habitational name from the place called (La) Caya in Asturies.
GIVEN NAMES French 10%. *Adrien* (2), *Aurore, Cecile, Girard, Jacques, Normand*.

Cayce (282) Probably an altered spelling of English CASEY.

Caye (136) **1.** Americanized form of French **Caille** 'quail', a nickname or metonymic occupational name for someone who caught and sold quails. **2.** French: possibly from a variant French dialect *caye* 'sow'. Compare CAYA.

Cayea (116) Probably an Americanized form of French CAILLIER 'quail catcher'.

Cayer (500) **1.** French: probably a variant spelling of CAILLIER 'quail catcher'. **2.** Possibly an Americanized spelling of German KEHR or GEYER.
GIVEN NAMES French 16%. *Adelard* (3), *Armand* (3), *Normand* (3), *Jacques* (2), *Lucien* (2), *Andre, Benoit, Emile, Fernand, Germaine, Jean-Marc, Jean-Marie*.

Cayetano (135) Spanish (**Cajetano**): from the personal name *Caietano*, bestowed in honor of the Italian Saint Gaetano (1480–1547) (see GAETANO).
GIVEN NAMES Spanish 49%. *Francisco* (3), *Albaro, Alberto, Alfonso, Apolonia, Arsenia, Arturo, Avelino, Bernabe, Bernardino, Carlos, Carmencita*.

Caylor (1173) **1.** Variant of Scottish KEILLOR. **2.** Americanized spelling of German **Köhler** (see KOHLER).

Cayo (168) **1.** Spanish: from the personal name *Cayo*, Spanish equivalent of GAETANO. **2.** possibly also from the Castilianized form of Asturian-Leonese **Cayu**, a habitational name from either of two places in Asturies named El Cayu.
GIVEN NAMES French 9%. *Gabrielle, Michel, Pierre, Raoul*.

Cayson (183) English: unexplained.

Cayton (793) English: habitational name from either of two places in North Yorkshire called Cayton, near Scarborough and in South Stainley; both are named from the Old English personal name *Cǣga* + Old English *tūn* 'farmstead', 'settlement'.

Caywood (952) English: variant of CAWOOD.

Caza (142) Southern French: short form of any of various compound names formed with Occitan *caza*, *casa* 'house', from Latin *casa* 'hut', 'cottage', 'cabin'.
GIVEN NAMES French 10%. *Alderic, Germain, Renaud, Yvon*.

Cazares (1110) Spanish (**Cázares**): variant of CACERES.
GIVEN NAMES Spanish 55%. *Jose* (36), *Juan* (21), *Guadalupe* (15), *Jesus* (15), *Francisco* (11), *Luis* (11), *Carlos* (10), *Manuel* (10), *Javier* (9), *Rafael* (9), *Ricardo* (9), *Miguel* (8).

Cazarez (133) Spanish (**Cázarez**): variant of CAZARES.
GIVEN NAMES Spanish 56%. *Javier* (4), *Francisco* (3), *Juan* (3), *Adan* (2), *Alberto* (2), *Guadalupe* (2), *Luis* (2), *Alejandro, Amparo, Andres, Arturo, Beatriz*.

Cazes (116) French: plural derivative of Occitan *caza*, *casa* 'house' (see CAZA).
GIVEN NAME French 5%. *Emile*.

Cazier (315) French: from Old French *casier*, a term denoting an openwork basket in which cheese for tasting was displayed (from a diminutive of Latin *caseus* 'cheese'); hence by extension an occupational name for a cheesemaker.
FOREBEARS Spelled **Casier**, this is the name of a Huguenot family from Picardy, which was established early in New Amsterdam.

Cdebaca (239) Hispanic (found mainly in New Mexico): much reduced and altered form of Spanish **Cabeza de Vaca**, an unflattering nickname meaning 'cow's head'.
GIVEN NAMES Spanish 19%. *Albertano, Alicia, Amalia, Andres, Anselmo, Bernardo, Carlos, Guillermo, Jesus, Lalo, Manuel, Marcos*.

Cea (237) Spanish, Galician, and Portuguese: habitational name from any of the places called Cea, in León, in Ourense and A Coruña, Galicia, and in Portugal.
GIVEN NAMES Spanish 22%; Italian 10%. *Jose* (5), *Jorge* (4), *Miguel* (3), *Adolfo, Alberto, Almerinda, Ana, Arturo, Augusto, Berta, Blanca, Caridad*; *Rocco* (4), *Carmelo* (2), *Italia, Marco, Saverio, Vito*.

Cearley (572) Probably an Americanized spelling of German **Zierle**, a variant of ZIER, or in Swabia, a pet form of *Zyr*, a short form of the personal name *Zyriacus* (see ZILCH).

Cearlock (92) Americanized spelling of German **Gierlach**, a variant of GERLACH. Compare CARLOCK.

Ceasar (467) Americanized form of Italian CESARE or French **César** (see CAESAR).

Cease (306) Probably an Americanized spelling of German **Zies**, **Ziess**, or **Ziese**, which are of Slavic origin (see ZIESKE).

Ceaser (363) Americanized form of Italian CESARE or French **César** (see CAESAR).

Ceballos (1154) Spanish: habitational name from a place called Ceballos, a district of Santander.
GIVEN NAMES Spanish 52%. *Jose* (30), *Luis* (16), *Juan* (15), *Carlos* (14), *Manuel* (14), *Francisco* (10), *Mario* (8), *Sergio* (8), *Javier* (7), *Jesus* (7), *Miguel* (7), *Ramon* (7).

Cebula (452) Polish: from *cebula* 'onion' (Latin *cepulla*), either a nickname or a metonymic occupational name for an onion grower or seller.
GIVEN NAMES Polish 8%. *Andrzej* (2), *Kazimierz* (2), *Wieslaw* (2), *Danuta, Grzegorz, Jerzy, Marzanna, Mateusz*.

Cebulski (197) Polish: habitational name for someone from a place formerly called Cebula (now Chlebowice) in Łódź voivodeship, or possibly directly from *cebula* 'onion'. Compare CEBULA, CYBULSKI.
GIVEN NAMES Polish 4%. *Bogdan, Casimir, Jacek*.

Cecala (167) Italian: from Neapolitan *cecala* 'cicada' (standard Italian *cicala*, Latin *cicala*), probably applied as a nickname for a talkative person.
GIVEN NAMES Italian 21%. *Salvatore* (4), *Luigi, Marco, Vincenza*.

Ceccarelli (338) Italian: from the personal name *Ceccarello*, a diminutive of *Cecco*, itself a diminutive *Francesco*, from Latin *Franciscus* (FRANCIS).
GIVEN NAMES Italian 28%. *Mario* (4), *Dino* (3), *Angelo* (2), *Dante* (2), *Quinto* (2), *Sesto* (2), *Aldo, Americo, Amerigo, Arcangelo, Augusto, Aurelio, Franco, Gino, Guido, Italo, Leoncio, Renato, Roberto, Tino, Tito, Valerio*.

Cecchetti (112) Italian: from a diminutive of the personal name *Cecco*, itself a diminutive of FRANCESCO, from Latin *Franciscus* (see FRANCIS).
GIVEN NAMES Italian 14%. *Enzo* (2), *Carlo, Mauro, Sal, Spartaco*.

Cecchi (243) Italian: from the personal name *Cecco*, a diminutive of FRANCESCO, from Latin *Franciscus* (see FRANCIS).
GIVEN NAMES Italian 16%. *Giuseppe* (3), *Aldo* (2), *Luigi* (2), *Dante, Deno, Dino, Elio, Enrico, Gino, Marino, Piero, Pietro*.

Cecchini (506) Italian: from the personal name *Cecchino*, a diminutive of *Cecco*, itself a diminutive of FRANCESCO, from Latin *Franciscus* (see FRANCIS).
GIVEN NAMES Italian 12%. *Angelo* (3), *Aldo* (2), *Antonio* (2), *Dante* (2), *Nino* (2), *Battista, Dario, Elio, Evo, Geno, Gino, Graziano*.

Cecconi (157) Italian: from the personal name *Ceccone*, an augmentative of *Cecco*, a diminutive of FRANCESCO, from Latin *Franciscus* (see FRANCIS).
GIVEN NAMES Italian 8%. *Elio* (2), *Alessandro, Guido, Lucio, Muzio*.

Cece (143) **1.** Italian: from *cece*, *cecio* 'chick pea' (from Latin *cicero*), applied as a metonymic occupational name for a grower or seller of chick peas, or a nickname for a man with a growth or lump on his face. **2.** Hungarian: from the medieval ecclesiastical name *Cecilián*, from Latin *Caecilius*, or from a pet form of the female personal name *Cecília*.

GIVEN NAMES Italian 17%. *Vito* (3), *Angelo* (2), *Dino, Marco, Salvatore.*

Cecere (594) Italian: from *cecere* 'pea' (from Latin *cicer, ciceris*), hence a metonymic occupational name for a grower or seller of peas, or a nickname for a man with a growth or lump on his face.

GIVEN NAMES Italian 12%. *Ezio* (2), *Angelo, Carlo, Carmela, Carmine, Concetta, Dino, Domenic, Giulio, Guilio, Lorenzo.*

Cech (461) **1.** Czech and Slovak (**Čech**): ethnic name meaning 'Czech', used in particular to distinguish a native or inhabitant of Bohemia (Czech *Čechy*) from Slovaks, Moravians, and other ethnic groups, or a speaker of the Czech language as opposed to German. The word itself is of unknown origin. **2.** Czech and Slovak: from a short form of the personal name *Čechoslav*. **3.** Perhaps an altered spelling of German ZECH.

Ceci (213) Italian: patronymic or plural form of CECE.

GIVEN NAMES Italian 15%. *Francesco* (2), *Angelo, Cira, Filippo, Rocco, Salvatore, Valentino, Vittorio.*

Cecil (4387) Welsh (Monmouthshire): from the Old Welsh personal name *Seisyllt*, an altered form of the Latin name *Sextilius*, a derivative of *Sextus* meaning 'sixth'. The spelling has been modified as a result of folk etymological association with the Latin name *C(a)ecilius*, a derivative of *caecus* 'blind'.

FOREBEARS The great and powerful English Cecil family first came to prominence with David Cecil, a Monmouthshire gentleman who espoused the cause of Henry Tudor and came to court in London after the latter became king in 1485. His grandson William Cecil, Lord Burghley (1520–98), was Elizabeth I's chief adviser for 40 years, and his descendants have remained politically powerful and culturally influential in Britain ever since. They were originally minor Welsh gentry; their name is found in a variety of forms, including *Sitsylt, Ceyssel*, and *Sisseld*.

Cecilio (110) Spanish, Portuguese, and Italian: from the personal name *Cecilio*, from Latin name *C(a)ecilius*, a derivative of *caecus* 'blind'.

GIVEN NAMES Spanish 32%. *Manuel* (2), *Adelina, Bernabe, Catalino, Domingos, Efrain, Fernando, Jorge Luis, Jose, Joselito, Juan, Lauro; Antonio* (2), *Cecilio, Rocco.*

Cedano (107) Spanish (common in Mexico and the Dominican Republic): variant of SEDANO.

GIVEN NAMES Spanish 67%. *Ramon* (3), *Carlos* (2), *Jorge* (2), *Jose* (2), *Ofelia* (2), *Alejandro, Amado, Andres, Angel, Arturo, Berta, Blanca.*

Cedar (278) Probably an Americanized spelling of Swedish and Jewish CEDER.

Cedars (110) Origin uncertain. Possibly an Americanized form of French **Cèdre**, a topographic name for someone who lived by a cedar tree, or in a landscape characterized by cedar trees.

GIVEN NAME French 8%. *Marcelle* (3).

Cedeno (775) Spanish: from a variant of *sedeño* 'silken' or 'cloth (or rope) of tow', also 'bristle', possibly used as a nickname in the sense of Catalan *sedeny* 'very strong man'. This name is common in many parts of Latin America and in the Philippines, but rare in Spain itself.

GIVEN NAMES Spanish 48%. *Jose* (24), *Juan* (15), *Luis* (11), *Carlos* (8), *Angel* (6), *Jorge* (6), *Fernando* (5), *Jaime* (5), *Manuel* (5), *Ana* (4), *Jesus* (4), *Rafael* (4).

Ceder (134) **1.** Swedish: ornamental name from *ceder* 'cedar' (Latin *cedrus*). **2.** Jewish (from Poland): ornamental name from Yiddish *tseder* 'cedar' or German *Zeder*.

Cederberg (254) Swedish: ornamental name composed of the elements *ceder* 'cedar' + *berg* 'mountain', 'hill'.

GIVEN NAMES Scandinavian 4%. *Erik, Nils, Sven.*

Cedergren (102) Swedish: ornamental name composed of the elements *ceder* 'cedar' + *gren* 'branch'.

GIVEN NAME German 6%. *Kurt.*

Cederholm (166) Swedish: ornamental name composed of the elements *ceder* 'cedar' + *holm* 'island'.

GIVEN NAMES Scandinavian 10%; German 5%. *Lars, Sven, Vilhelm; Erwin, Kurt.*

Cederquist (160) Swedish: ornamental name composed of the elements *ceder* 'cedar' + *quist*, an old or ornamental spelling of *kvist* 'twig'.

GIVEN NAME Scandinavian 5%. *Alf.*

Cederstrom (114) Swedish (**Cederström**): ornamental name composed of the elements *ceder* 'cedar' + *ström* 'river'.

Cedillo (687) Spanish: habitational name from Cedillo in Cáceres province, Cedillo del Condado in Toledo province, or Cedillo de la Torre in Segovia province.

GIVEN NAMES Spanish 53%. *Jose* (25), *Juan* (12), *Miguel* (8), *Pedro* (8), *Ricardo* (7), *Carlos* (6), *Jesus* (6), *Luis* (6), *Manuel* (6), *Raul* (5), *Alberto* (3), *Armando* (3).

Cedillos (108) Apparently a plural form of Spanish CEDILLO, also written **Sedillos**.

GIVEN NAMES Spanish 55%. *Jose* (4), *Agustin, Alfredo, Andres, Apolonia, Carlos, Cruz, Gonzalo, Gregorio, Guillermo, Ignacio, Isidro.*

Cedotal (160) French: unexplained.

GIVEN NAMES French 6%. *Achille, Oneil.*

Cedrone (347) Italian: topographic name denoting someone who lived by a large

cedar tree, from an augmentative of *cedro* 'cedar'.

GIVEN NAMES Italian 24%. *Antonio* (6), *Donato* (5), *Franco* (3), *Angelo* (2), *Biagio* (2), *Carmelo* (2), *Carmine* (2), *Dante* (2), *Amato, Cesidio, Dino, Domenic.*

Cefalo (152) Italian (Calabria): **1.** from Greek *kephalē* 'head', applied as a nickname, probably for someone whose head was of a distinctive shape or size. The word also denotes a kind of mullet, and may have been a metonymic occupational name for a fisherman. **2.** derogatory nickname meaning 'idiot', from medieval Latin *cephalus*, of the same etymology as 1.

GIVEN NAMES Italian 8%. *Romeo* (2), *Carmine, Giancarlo, Gino, Saverio.*

Cefalu (346) Italian (Sicily; **Cefalù**): habitational name from Cefalù near Palermo, Sicily, named with Greek *kephalē* 'head'.

GIVEN NAMES Italian 10%. *Salvatore* (2), *Antonino, Antonio, Giancarlo, Marco, Sal, Vito.*

Cefaratti (138) Southern Italian: possibly altered from a diminutive of the personal name *Lucifero*.

GIVEN NAMES Italian 11%. *Amedeo, Donato, Elio, Eliseo.*

Cegelski (114) Polish: variant of CEGIELSKI.

Cegielski (207) Polish: habitational name for someone from any of the various places called Cegły, from *cegła* 'brick' or Cegielnia, from *cegielna* 'brickworks', or a topographic name for someone who lived by a brickworks.

GIVEN NAMES Polish 5%. *Ireneusz, Jozef, Tadeusz.*

Ceglia (116) Italian: habitational name from Ceglie del Campo in Bari or, more rarely, from Ceglie Messapico in Brindisi province.

GIVEN NAMES Italian 12%. *Alessandro, Carmine, Fiore, Salvatore.*

Ceja (938) Spanish: from a common field name or a habitational name from any of various minor places called Ceja Yecla in Aragon.

GIVEN NAMES Spanish 61%. *Jose* (45), *Jesus* (24), *Juan* (16), *Luis* (14), *Rafael* (13), *Francisco* (11), *Javier* (11), *Jose Luis* (10), *Manuel* (9), *Salvador* (8), *Alejandro* (7), *Enrique* (7).

Cejka (197) Czech (**Čejka**): nickname from *čejka* 'lapwing'.

Celani (166) Italian: patronymic or plural form of CELANO.

GIVEN NAMES Italian 19%. *Angelo* (3), *Domenic* (2), *Dario, Gabriele, Matteo, Natale, Salvatore, Vincenzo.*

Celano (264) Italian: habitational name from a place named Celano, in L'Aquila province.

GIVEN NAMES Italian 29%. *Salvatore* (3), *Fiore* (2), *Guido* (2), *Osvaldo* (2), *Tullio* (2), *Vito* (2), *Antonio, Bernardo, Geno,*

Giuseppe, Leonardo, Marino, Mario, Nino, Orazio.

Celaya (504) Castilianized form of Basque **Zelaia**, a habitational name from a place named Zelaia, in Biscay province, Basque Country (see ZELAYA).

GIVEN NAMES Spanish 36%. *Francisco* (8), *Jesus* (6), *Manuel* (6), *Jose* (5), *Andres* (3), *Enrique* (3), *Guillermo* (3), *Alfonzo* (2), *Camilo* (2), *Carlos* (2), *Ernesto* (2), *Juan* (2).

Celentano (577) Italian (Naples): regional name for someone from CILENTO.

GIVEN NAMES Italian 13%. *Salvatore* (4), *Gennaro* (2), *Antonio, Carmela, Enrico, Enzio, Ferdinando, Giuseppe, Maddalena, Pasquale, Rocco.*

Celenza (125) Italian: habitational name from Celenza sul Trigno in Chieti or Celenza Valfortore in Foggia.

GIVEN NAMES Italian 11%. *Domenic, Gennaro, Sisto.*

Celeste (394) French (**Céleste**), Portuguese, and Spanish: from the female personal name *Céleste, Celeste*, meaning 'celestial', 'heavenly' (Latin *caelestis*).

GIVEN NAMES Italian 10%. *Angelo* (4), *Salvatore* (4), *Antonio, Carlo, Carmine, Constantino, Rocco.*

Celestin (392) French (**Célestin**): from the personal name *Célestin*, a pet form of *Céleste* (see CELESTE).

GIVEN NAMES French 33%. *Pierre* (3), *Andre* (2), *Jacques* (2), *Remy* (2), *Serge* (2), *Clovis, Edouard, Edwige, Flore, Francois, Gratien, Henri.*

Celestine (577) Probably an altered spelling of French **Célestin** (see CELESTIN).

GIVEN NAMES French 5%. *Andre* (2), *Gabrielle, Georges, Monique.*

Celestino (286) Spanish, Portuguese, and Italian: from the personal name *Celestino*, a derivative of Latin *caelestris* 'heavenly'. It was a popular name among early Christians and was the name of several popes, including Celestino V (*c.* 1215–96), the founder of a religious order known as the Celestines.

GIVEN NAMES Spanish 27%; Italian 6%. *Carlos* (3), *Jose* (3), *Pedro* (3), *Adelina* (2), *Juan* (2), *Alejandro, Alfredo, Armando, Arturo, Ascencion, Bernabe, Candido; Salvatore* (2), *Agostino, Elio, Nevio, Pio.*

Celi (142) Southern Italian: from a short form of the personal name *Michele*, Italian equivalent of MICHAEL.

GIVEN NAMES Italian 13%; Spanish 12%. *Francesco* (2), *Carlo, Clemente, Gaetano, Giovanni, Marco; Jorge* (2), *Luis* (2), *Ana, Aurelio, Guadalupe, Hernan, Manuel, Roberto, Segundo.*

Celia (230) Italian: **1.** from the female personal name *Celia*. **2.** (southern Italian) nickname from medieval Greek *kaēlas* 'warmth', 'ardor'.

GIVEN NAMES Italian 18%. *Gino* (2), *Santo* (2), *Alfio, Angelo, Carmine, Franco, Nichola, Nicola, Salvatore, Vito.*

Celio (157) **1.** Spanish and Italian: from the personal name *Celio*, probably from Latin *Caelius*. **2.** Southern Italian: nickname from southern dialect (Sicily) *cèliu* 'inconsistent', 'changeable', or from Calabrian *céliu* 'having a squint', 'cross-eyed'.

GIVEN NAMES Spanish 18%; Italian 13%; French 4%. *Gerardo* (2), *Jesus* (2), *Alicia, Arcelia, Candelario, Carlos, Fernando, Jose, Manuel, Mario, Miguel, Orlando; Antonio* (4), *Angelo* (2), *Falco, Gennaro, Guido; Achille* (2), *Lucien.*

Celis (357) Spanish: habitational name from a place in Santander province called Celis.

GIVEN NAMES Spanish 52%. *Jose* (11), *Carlos* (6), *Jesus* (5), *Sergio* (5), *Guillermo* (4), *Miguel* (4), *Beatriz* (3), *Fernando* (3), *Francisco* (3), *Luis* (3), *Manuel* (3), *Raul* (3), *Godofredo.*

Cella (884) Italian: habitational name from any of numerous minor places called Cella or Celle (from *cella* 'cell'), because they were once the locations of hermits' cells.

GIVEN NAMES Italian 8%. *Carlo* (3), *Carmine* (2), *Geno* (2), *Amelio, Aniello, Concetta, Cosmo, Flavio, Gaetano, Gennaro, Mafalda, Raffaele.*

Celli (459) Italian: **1.** from the personal name *Cello*, a short form of *Baroncello, Marcello, Pacello, Simoncello*, or any other personal name ending in *-cello*. **2.** variant of CELI.

GIVEN NAMES Italian 8%. *Carlo* (3), *Angelo, Cosmo, Lido, Nunzio, Santina, Vittorio.*

Cellini (313) Italian: from the personal name *Cellino*, a diminutive of *Cello* (see CELLI).

GIVEN NAMES Italian 24%. *Angelo* (3), *Orlando* (3), *Rocco* (3), *Antonio* (2), *Mario* (2), *Neno* (2), *Alfonso, Benvenuto, Berta, Chiara, Cristina, Domenic, Enrico, Ermenegildo, Gino, Italia, Liliana, Marcello, Renato, Virgilio.*

Cellucci (286) Italian: from a diminutive of the personal name *Cello* (see CELLI).

GIVEN NAMES Italian 28%. *Antonio* (2), *Carlo* (2), *Donato* (2), *Luciano* (2), *Mario* (2), *Pasquale* (2), *Angelo, Biagio, Carmine, Carmino, Cesidio, Claudio, Gabriele, Massimo, Orlando.*

Cellura (102) Italian: unexplained.

GIVEN NAMES Italian 21%. *Angelo* (5), *Carlo.*

Celmer (287) Slavicized spelling of German ZELLMER.

Celona (205) Italian: **1.** from a derivative of CELI. **2.** (northern Italian) habitational name for someone from *Celona*, Italian name of Châlons-sur-Marne in France, which was named as the seat of a Gaulish tribe recorded in Latin sources as *Catalauni.* **3.** (southern Italian) nickname from Greek *khelōnē* 'turtle'.

Cena (129) **1.** Italian: of uncertain origin; possibly a topographic name from Latin *caenum* 'mud'. **2.** Polish: from *cena* 'price', presumably a nickname for a trader or dealer.

GIVEN NAMES Spanish 18%; Italian 10%. *Mario* (2), *Alberto, Alicia, Armando, Consuela, Eugenio, Imelda, Javier, Jorge, Juan, Juana, Juanito; Geno, Gino, Pasquale, Salvatore.*

Cenac (118) French: habitational name from a place called Cenac, in Gironde and Domme, or from Senac in Hautes Pyrénées, from a Romano-Gallic estate name formed with the Gallic personal name *Senos* (from *seno* 'old') + the locative suffix *-acum.*

GIVEN NAMES French 10%. *Andre, Monique, Ovide.*

Cenci (203) Italian: from the medieval personal name *Cencio*, a diminutive of *Vincenzo* (see VINCENT).

GIVEN NAMES Italian 15%. *Dante* (2), *Aldo, Angelo, Camillo, Corrado, Domenico, Enzio, Evo, Geno, Marcello.*

Cendejas (237) Spanish: habitational name from Cendejas de Enmedio or Cendejas de la Torre, both in Guadalajara province.

GIVEN NAMES Spanish 56%. *Jose* (11), *Luis* (6), *Roberto* (4), *Salvador* (4), *Jesus* (3), *Jorge* (3), *Ramon* (3), *Alfonso* (2), *Arturo* (2), *Gerardo* (2), *Guillermo* (2), *Humberto* (2); *Antonio* (2), *Federico, Heriberto, Leonardo, Salvatore.*

Ceniceros (335) Spanish: topographic name from *ceniza* 'ash(es)' (from Latin *cinis, cinesis*), or a habitational name from a place in the province of Burgos named with this word.

GIVEN NAMES Spanish 51%. *Jose* (14), *Carlos* (6), *Manuel* (5), *Juan* (4), *Ernesto* (3), *Jesus* (3), *Mario* (3), *Ramon* (3), *Raul* (3), *Alfredo* (2), *Blanca* (2), *Catalina* (2).

Cennamo (120) Italian: from Old Italian *cennamo* 'cinnamon' (from Latin *cinnamum*), probably applied as a metonymic occupational name for a spicer.

GIVEN NAMES Italian 19%. *Carmine* (2), *Angelo, Giulio, Nunzio, Salvatore, Vito.*

Centanni (337) Italian: from *cento* 'hundred' + *anno* 'year', i.e. a hundred years, a century. In Sicily this is the common name of the agave or century plant, and in some instances this may have been a topographic name for someone who lived where the plant grew.

GIVEN NAMES Italian 11%; French 4%. *Angelo* (3), *Carmine* (2), *Sal* (2), *Antonio, Concetta, Cosmo, Giuseppe; Michel* (3).

Centeno (1061) Spanish: from *centeno* 'rye' (Late Latin *centenum*, a derivative of *centum* 'hundred', so called as the plant was supposed to be capable of producing a hundred grains on each stalk). The a

surname may have arisen as a metonymic occupational name for someone who grew or sold rye, or a topographic name for someone who lived by a field given over to the cultivation of this crop.
GIVEN NAMES Spanish 47%. *Jose* (38), *Luis* (12), *Juan* (11), *Manuel* (11), *Carlos* (8), *Rafael* (7), *Raul* (7), *Roberto* (7), *Alfredo* (6), *Jesus* (6), *Mario* (6), *Francisco* (5); *Antonio* (8), *Flavio* (4), *Fausto* (2), *Lucio* (2), *Angelo*, *Carmela*, *Carmelo*, *Lelio*, *Leonardo*, *Luciano*, *Marco*, *Romeo*.

Center (1184) **1.** English: metonymic occupational name for a maker of belts and girdles, from Middle English *ceinture*, *ceintere* 'girdle'. **2.** Possibly an Americanized form of German **Zehnder**, a variant of ZEHNER.

Centers (638) Variant of CENTER.

Centner (169) Americanized spelling of German ZENTNER.

Centofanti (267) Italian: from the personal name *Centofano*, an omen name composed of the elements *cento* 'hundred' + *fante* 'child', presumably bestowed in the hope that the recipient would have a large family.
GIVEN NAMES Italian 28%. *Gino* (6), *Antonio* (2), *Domenic* (2), *Salvatore* (2), *Vito* (2), *Aldo*, *Alfredo*, *Americo*, *Armando*, *Attilio*, *Bernardo*, *Colombo*, *Dante*, *Dino*, *Edoardo*, *Egidio*, *Gennaro*, *Mario*, *Roberto*.

Centola (183) Italian: habitational name from Centola in Salerno province.
GIVEN NAMES Italian 9%. *Guido* (3), *Antonio*, *Cosmo*, *Lorenzo*, *Quido*, *Romeo*, *Sal*, *Salvatore*.

Centore (104) Italian: from *cento ore* 'hundred gold pieces', hence probably a nickname for a wealthy person.
GIVEN NAMES Italian 24%; Spanish 5%. *Antonio* (2), *Amerigo*, *Carlo*, *Domenic*, *Italo*, *Sal*, *Salvatore*.

Centrella (230) Italian (Avellino): unexplained.
GIVEN NAMES Italian 12%. *Carmine* (3), *Antonio*, *Cosimo*, *Cosmo*, *Fiore*, *Guilio*, *Lia*.

Centrone (107) Italian: from *cintrune*, in Calabrian dialect meaning 'big hammer', and probably applied as a nickname for a tall, thin person or for someone with a big head and a small body.
GIVEN NAMES Italian 25%. *Angelo* (2), *Corrado*, *Domenico*, *Francesco*, *Giacomo*, *Vito*.

Cepeda (992) Spanish: habitational name from Cepeda in Salamanca province or Cepeda la Mora in Ávila province, named from *cepeda*, a collective of *cepa* 'tree stump', 'stock' (from Latin *cippus* 'pillar').
GIVEN NAMES Spanish 53%. *Jose* (32), *Juan* (16), *Luis* (11), *Francisco* (10), *Roberto* (10), *Rafael* (9), *Jesus* (8), *Ramon* (8), *Jorge* (7), *Manuel* (7), *Pablo* (7), *Carlos* (6); *Antonio* (7), *Fausto* (3), *Marino* (2), *Clemente*, *Eligio*, *Eliseo*, *Flavio*,

Geronimo, *Giraldo*, *Leonardo*, *Lucio*, *Marco*.

Cepero (193) Spanish: topographic name from a derivative of *cepo* 'tree trunk'.
GIVEN NAMES Spanish 61%. *Juan* (7), *Ana* (4), *Enrique* (4), *Jesus* (4), *Rodolfo* (4), *Francisco* (3), *Jose* (3), *Rafael* (3), *Raul* (3), *Alfredo* (2), *Armando* (2), *Carlos* (2); *Antonio* (2), *Heriberto*.

Cephas (292) Classicized spelling of German **Zehfuss**, **Siefus**, **Ziehfuss**, literally 'toe foot', which is a folk-etymological development of the early medieval personal name *Sigifuns*, from Old High German *sigu* 'victory'.
GIVEN NAME French 4%. *Monique*.

Cephus (171) Classicized spelling of German **Zehfuss**, **Siefus**, or **Ziehfuss** (see CEPHAS).

Cera (225) Catalan: metonymic occupational name for a wax seller, from *cera* 'wax' (from Latin *cera*).
GIVEN NAMES Spanish 16%. *Jose* (2), *Raul* (2), *Alicia*, *Ana*, *Benito*, *Carlos*, *Eduardo*, *Emelita*, *Estanislao*, *Guadalupe*, *Juan*, *Manuel*.

Cerami (258) Southern Italian: from Greek *keramion* 'ceramic', 'terracotta pot' or *keramis* 'brick', 'tile', hence a metonymic occupational name for a potter, tile or brick maker, a metonymic occupational name for a tiler, or a nickname for a tough individual.
GIVEN NAMES Italian 15%; French 4%. *Rocco* (2), *Sal* (2), *Salvatore* (2), *Carmine*, *Francesco*, *Gandolfo*, *Nunzio*, *Santo*, *Valentino*, *Vito*; *Armand*, *Sylvie*.

Cerar (130) Slovenian: unexplained.

Ceraso (132) Italian: habitational name for someone from any of the numerous minor places named with the dialect word *cerasa* 'cherry tree' (Latin *cerasus*), notably Ceraso in Salerno, or possibly a topographic name for someone who lived by a cherry tree or cherry orchard.
GIVEN NAMES Italian 18%. *Angelo*, *Ettore*, *Gaetano*, *Guido*, *Matteo*, *Pasquale*, *Salvatore*.

Cerasoli (189) Italian: habitational name from any of numerous places named with *cerasa* 'cherry tree' (from Latin *cerasus*), for example Cerasuolo in Campobasso or Cerisola in Genova and Cuneo.
GIVEN NAMES Italian 12%. *Matteo* (2), *Attilio*, *Guido*, *Marco*, *Pasquale*.

Cerasuolo (130) Italian: variant of CERASOLI.
GIVEN NAMES Italian 30%. *Vito* (3), *Rocco* (2), *Angelo*, *Antonio*, *Franco*, *Giovanni*, *Giuseppi*, *Mario*, *Pasquale*, *Salvatore*, *Tobia*.

Ceravolo (167) Italian: derogatory nickname from a southern dialect word, *ceravolo* 'snake-charmer', by extension 'rogue', 'charlatan'. Compare CIRAULO.
GIVEN NAMES Italian 22%. *Rocco* (5), *Antonio*, *Domenic*, *Giuseppe*, *Pietro*, *Primo*.

Cerbone (261) Italian: **1.** probably a variant spelling of CERVONE 1. **2.** possibly from an augmentative of the personal name *Acerbo* (from Latin *Acerbus* meaning 'sour', 'tart'), with loss of the first syllable.
GIVEN NAMES Italian 17%. *Angelo* (2), *Carmine* (2), *Antonio*, *Luigia*, *Marco*, *Ottavio*, *Sal*, *Salvator*, *Silvio*, *Vincenzo*.

Cercone (358) Italian: probably from an augmentative of CIRCO.
GIVEN NAMES Italian 16%. *Antonio* (3), *Angelo* (2), *Domenic* (2), *Ettore* (2), *Gino* (2), *Carlo*, *Cesidio*, *Concezio*, *Damiano*, *Gaetano*, *Giacomo*, *Giulio*.

Cerda (1471) **1.** Spanish and Portuguese: from *cerda* 'bristle', 'hair' (Late Latin *cirra*), apparently a nickname for someone with a prominent tuft of hair. One of the sons of King Alfonso X (1221–84) was known as Fernando de la Cerda. **2.** Catalan (**Cerdà**): regional name, *cerdà*, for someone from La Cerdanya, a Catalan district in the Pyrenees which is currently situated partly in Spain and partly in France.
GIVEN NAMES Spanish 50%. *Jose* (43), *Jesus* (19), *Francisco* (16), *Manuel* (16), *Juan* (13), *Luis* (12), *Ramon* (12), *Guadalupe* (11), *Ricardo* (11), *Miguel* (10), *Pedro* (10), *Carlos* (9).

Cereghino (142) Italian (Genoa): possibly a variant of *clericus* + *-inus* (see CLERICO).
GIVEN NAMES Italian 4%. *Aldo*, *Marco*.

Ceresa (122) Italian: habitational name from a place named with Latin *ceresea* 'cherry'.
GIVEN NAMES Italian 5%. *Aldo*, *Matteo*.

Cerezo (191) Spanish: habitational name from any of numerous places, for example in Hervás and Cáceres provinces, named Cerezo, from *cerezo* 'cherry tree' (from Latin *cerasus*).
GIVEN NAMES Spanish 45%. *Luis* (5), *Francisco* (3), *Jose* (3), *Alfredo* (2), *Carlos* (2), *Filemon* (2), *Ines* (2), *Miguel* (2), *Agripina*, *Alberto*, *Amado*, *Angel*.

Cerf (155) **1.** French: from Old French *cerf* 'stag' (Latin *cervus*), applied as a nickname with reference to the presumed lustfulness of the creature, or conversely to the horns as the mark of a cuckold (see HORN 4). **2.** Jewish (Ashkenazic from France): from the personal name, French calque of the Yiddish personal name *Hirsh* (see HIRSCH).
GIVEN NAME French 4%. *Patrice*.

Cericola (138) Italian: from a compound personal name composed of *Ceri* (see CERINO) + COLA.
GIVEN NAMES Italian 6%. *Paolo*, *Vito*.

Cerini (116) Italian: patronymic or plural form of CERINO.
GIVEN NAMES Italian 7%. *Costantino*, *Dario*, *Romeo*.

Cerino (254) Italian: probably from a diminutive of the personal name *Ceri*, which has various origins: it can be a topographic name (see CERRO); a nickname for someone with curly hair, from Latin *cirrus* 'lock', 'curl'; alternatively, it can be from a diminutive of *Ricciere*, *Riccieri* (more commonly found as *Rizziero*), with loss of the first syllable; or from a short form of the Latin occupational name *cereterius* 'wax seller'.

GIVEN NAMES Italian 16%; Spanish 12%; French 4%. *Carmine, Filiberto, Geno, Nunzio, Pasquale, Sal, Vito; Jesus, Jose Luis, Juan, Maria Del Rosario, Osvaldo; Alphonse* (2), *Dominique*.

Cerio (243) Southern Italian: from a variant of the personal name *Ceri* (see CERINO).

GIVEN NAMES French 6%; Italian 4%. *Camille* (3); *Angelo, Olympia*.

Cerise (181) French: from *cerise* 'cherry' (Latin *cerasus*), applied as a metonymic occupational name for someone who grew or sold cherries.

Cermak (698) Czech and Slovak (**Čermák**): nickname meaning 'redstart', the name of a common European songbird. The Czech word was also used as a euphemism for the devil, and this no doubt affected its use as a nickname.

Cerminara (135) Southern Italian: probably from medieval Greek *kyrie Minadas* 'Mr Minada'.

GIVEN NAMES Italian 22%. *Angelo* (3), *Antonio* (2), *Carmine, Giuseppe, Lia, Santo, Serafino, Umberto*.

Cerminaro (107) Italian: variant of CERMINARA.

GIVEN NAMES Italian 26%. *Santo* (3), *Salvatore* (2), *Angelo, Cesare, Simona*.

Cerna (444) **1.** Spanish and Galician: nickname for a tough, hard-headed individual, from *cerna* 'heartwood'. **2.** Hungarian (**Cérna**): from the *cérna* 'thread', hence an metonymic occupational name for a tailor. **3.** Czech and Slovak (**Černa**): nickname from the feminine form of Czech *černý*, Slovak *čierny* 'black', 'dark'.

GIVEN NAMES Spanish 47%. *Jose* (7), *Mario* (6), *Carlos* (5), *Juan* (5), *Luis* (5), *Salvador* (5), *Fernando* (4), *Ricardo* (4), *Guadalupe* (3), *Jaime* (3), *Javier* (3), *Jesus* (3), *Gonsalo* (2).

Cernak (122) Czech (**Černák**) and Slovak (**Černak**): nickname from *čierny* 'black', 'dark'.

Cerne (128) **1.** French (**Cerné**): habitational name from any of numerous places in Calvados, Eure-et-Loire, Vienne, etc., called Cerné, named with the Roman personal name *Cernus*, a short form of *Cerenus* or *Serenus* + the locative suffix *-acum*. **2.** Slovenian (**Černe**): nickname for someone with black hair or a dark complexion, from *črn* 'black', 'dark'. **3.** Probably also Galician: variant of CERNA.

Cerney (261) **1.** Americanized form of Slovenian **Černe** (see CERNE), Czech **Černý** (see CERNY), or Slovak **Černej**. **2.** Americanized form of **Cserney**, a Hungarian habitational name for someone from a place called Cserne, formerly in Trencsény county, now in Slovakia, or Csernye in Veszprém county. **3.** Possibly also English, a habitational name from North and South Cerney or Cerney Wick, all in Gloucestershire, which are named for the Churn river, on which they stand, + Old English *ēa* 'stream'. The river name is of Celtic origin.

Cerniglia (450) Italian: perhaps from Sicilian *cirniglia, cirnigliu*, an occupational name for a grain sifter or winnower.

GIVEN NAMES Italian 15%. *Salvatore* (5), *Angelo* (3), *Sal* (2), *Santo* (2), *Amedeo, Biagio, Donato, Giusto, Ignazio, Natale, Nunzio, Vito*.

Cernik (152) Czech (**Černík**) and Slovak (**Čiernik**): from a diminutive of **Černý** 'black' (see CERNY).

GIVEN NAMES Czech and Slovak 5%. *Milan* (2), *Vlasta*.

Cernoch (108) Czech (**Černoch**): nickname for a dark-skinned, swarthy person, from *černoch* 'negro'. Compare **Černý** (see CERNY).

GIVEN NAMES German 7%. *Alois* (2), *Erwin* (2); *Zigmund*.

Cernosek (126) Czech (**Černošek**): from a derivative of *černý* 'black' (see CERNY).

Cerny (1328) **1.** Czech (**Černý**): from *černý* 'black', hence a nickname for a black-haired person, or someone with a dark complexion, sometimes used as a nickname for the devil. **2.** French: habitational name from either of two places, in Aisne and Essonne, named Cerny, from the Roman personal name *Serenus* + the suffix *-iacus*, denoting an estate.

Ceron (230) Spanish: probably a metonymic occupational name for a beekeeper, from *cerón* 'residue of wax or honeycomb'.

GIVEN NAMES Spanish 54%; French 4%. *Jose* (11), *Carlos* (6), *Juan* (4), *Julio* (4), *Sergio* (4), *Francisco* (3), *Luis* (3), *Alfonso* (2), *Andres* (2), *Enrique* (2), *Gerardo* (2), *Jaime* (2); *Antonio* (2), *Marco* (2), *Heriberto, Leonardo, Lucio; Gaston* (3), *Yves*.

Cerone (347) Southern Italian: **1.** from an augmentative form of the personal name *Ceri* (see CERINO). **2.** variant of CERRONE.

GIVEN NAMES Italian 13%. *Aldo* (2), *Carmine* (2), *Emidio* (2), *Giovanni* (2), *Angelo, Pasquale, Pietro, Vito*.

Cerqueira (133) Portuguese: habitational name from any of various places named Cerquerira, in most cases from a Latin derivative of *quercus* 'oak'. The family name also occurs in Sicily, probably of the same origin.

GIVEN NAMES Spanish 43%; Portuguese 18%; Italian 7%. *Jose* (8), *Manuel* (7), *Carlos* (5), *Ana* (2), *Fernanda* (2), *Luis* (2), *Abilio, Alvaro, Candido, Eduardo, Eloina, Ernesto; Joao; Antonio* (9), *Gasper, Luciano*.

Cerra (549) **1.** Southern Italian: habitational name from Acerra in Naples province or from any of various places called Cerra. **2.** Asturian-Leonese: possibly a habitational name from a place named Cerra or La Cerra, as for example in Asturies.

GIVEN NAMES Italian 25%; Spanish 12%. *Angelo* (5), *Emilio* (5), *Salvatore* (5), *Eduardo* (3), *Adolfo* (2), *Orlando* (2), *Alessio* (2), *Carmine* (2), *Sal* (2), *Antonino, Enzo, Ercole, Fiore, Franco, Luigina, Reno; Carlos, Estela, Maria Del Pilar, Maria Luisa*.

Cerrato (472) Spanish (also **Serrato**): regional name from Cerrato, an area of central Spain (in Valladolid, Palencia, and Burgos provinces).

GIVEN NAMES Spanish 20%; Italian 14%. *Jose* (7), *Carlos* (4), *Cesar* (3), *Miguel* (3), *Julio* (2), *Ramon* (2), *Santiago* (2), *Adalberto, Albino, Amado, Ana; Mario* (4), *Ciro* (3), *Giacomo* (2), *Domenico, Domiano, Enzo, Ferdinando, Francesca, Mauro, Raffaele, Rocco, Vita, Vito*.

Cerreta (203) Italian: topographic name for someone who lived by an oak wood or in a place with an abundance of turkey oaks, from Latin *cerretum*, plural *cerreta*.

GIVEN NAMES Italian 13%. *Angelo* (2), *Pasquale* (2), *Salvatore* (2), *Attilio, Emidio, Sal, Tullio*.

Cerri (166) Italian: topographic name from the plural of CERRO.

GIVEN NAMES Italian 14%. *Angelo* (2), *Reno* (2), *Alessio, Gianluca, Gino, Luciano, Maurizio, Salvatore, Sante, Ugo*.

Cerrillo (120) Spanish: habitational name from any of the many places called Cerrillo, a diminutive of *cerro* 'hill'.

GIVEN NAMES Spanish 51%. *Juan* (6), *Jose* (4), *Luis* (3), *Fernando* (2), *Isidro* (2), *Jesus* (2), *Manuel* (2), *Rogelio* (2), *Alfonso, Alvaro, Apolonio, Avelino*.

Cerrito (216) **1.** Italian: topographic name for someone who lived by an oak grove, Sicilian *cirritu*. Compare CERRETA. **2.** Spanish: from a common field name, from a diminutive of *cerro* 'hill'.

GIVEN NAMES Italian 16%. *Angelo* (3), *Umberto* (2), *Italia, Mario, Regino, Rigoberto, Sal*.

Cerro (148) **1.** Spanish: topographic name for someone who lived on or by a hill or ridge, Spanish *cerro*, from Latin *cirrus* 'bristle', 'hair', 'hackles', or possibly a nickname for someone with a ridge of spiky hair like an animal's hackles. Alternatively, it may be a habitational name from a place named with this word (in the sense 'ridge'), as for example El Cerro in Salamanca province. **2.** Italian: topographic name from *cerro* 'turkey oak', 'cerris' (*Quercus cerris*).

GIVEN NAMES Spanish 15%; Italian 12%. *Angel* (2), *Adolfo, Alfonso, Benito, Camilo, Guillermo, Jeronimo, Jose, Juan, Luis Miguel, Manuel, Pedro; Luigi* (2), *Antonio, Carlo, Rocco*.

Cerrone (473) Italian: augmentative form of CERRO.

Cerroni GIVEN NAMES Italian 16%. *Angelo* (3), *Elio* (3), *Carlo* (2), *Domenic* (2), *Rocco* (2), *Antonio*, *Carmela*, *Federico*, *Gino*, *Giuseppe*, *Guido*, *Luigi*.

Cerroni (102) Italian: variant of CERRONE.
GIVEN NAMES Italian 11%. *Angelo*, *Enzo*, *Luigi*.

Cerruti (205) Italian: variant spelling of CERUTTI.
GIVEN NAMES Italian 10%. *Dario* (2), *Libero* (2), *Carlo*, *Gino*, *Guido*, *Reno*, *Secondo*, *Ugo*, *Vito*.

Certa (102) Italian: variant of CERTO.
GIVEN NAMES Italian 8%; Spanish 5%. *Carlo*; *Diego*, *Xavier*.

Certain (287) **1.** French: nickname from *certain* 'certain', 'resolute', a derivative of Old French *certise* 'certitude'. **2.** English: variant spelling of SARTAIN, cognate with 1.

Certo (222) Italian: from *certo* 'certain', 'sure', from Latin *certus*, probably a nickname for a decisive, resolute, or dependable person.
GIVEN NAMES Italian 10%. *Angelo* (2), *Salvatore* (2), *Nunzio*.

Cerulli (219) Italian: patronymic or plural form of CERULLO.
GIVEN NAMES Italian 15%. *Amadeo*, *Carmine*, *Concetta*, *Enzo*, *Giro*, *Guido*, *Nicolo*, *Pasquale*, *Rocco*, *Salvatore*.

Cerullo (464) Italian: from a diminutive of *cera* 'wax', hence a metonymic occupational name for a wax seller, or of the personal name *Ceri* (see CERINO).
GIVEN NAMES Italian 15%. *Ciro* (2), *Lorenzo* (2), *Pasquale* (2), *Rocco* (2), *Vito* (2), *Amedeo*, *Angelo*, *Antonio*, *Carmel*, *Carmine*, *Dante*, *Domenic*.

Cerutti (355) Italian: from a derivative of *cero* 'curl', regional variant of *cirro* (from Latin *cirrus* 'lock', 'curl', 'ringlet'), and so a nickname for someone with curly hair, or alternatively a nickname from Late Latin *cerutus* 'hot-headed', 'strange', 'freakish'.
GIVEN NAMES Italian 5%. *Aldo* (2), *Dino*, *Francesca*, *Franco*, *Heriberto*, *Lorenzo*, *Romeo*, *Silvano*, *Silvio*.

Cervantes (5515) Galician: habitational name from a place in Lugo province named Cervantes.
GIVEN NAMES Spanish 54%; Portuguese 11%. *Jose* (200), *Juan* (82), *Jesus* (78), *Manuel* (66), *Francisco* (55), *Luis* (47), *Raul* (43), *Carlos* (41), *Miguel* (41), *Ramon* (37), *Salvador* (36), *Jorge* (32); *Wenceslao* (2), *Paulo*, *Sil*.

Cervantez (482) Latin American spelling of CERVANTES.
GIVEN NAMES Spanish 41%. *Jose* (16), *Guadalupe* (4), *Juan* (4), *Manuel* (4), *Francisco* (3), *Jesus* (3), *Jose Luis* (3), *Pablo* (3), *Ramon* (3), *Ruben* (3), *Alfonso* (2), *Andres* (2).

Cervelli (139) Italian: **1.** from *cervello* 'brain(s)', a nickname for a clever or, ironically, for a hare-brained person. **2.** from a diminutive of *cervo* 'deer', a nickname for

someone who was fleet of foot. **3.** from southern Italian *cervello*, *cevrello* '(goat) kid'. **4.** from a diminutive of the personal name *Acerbo* (Latin *Acerbus* meaning 'sour', 'tart'), with loss of the first syllable.
GIVEN NAMES Italian 11%. *Reno* (2), *Ercole*, *Orest*, *Silvio*.

Cervenka (507) Czech (**Červenka**): nickname from *červenka* 'robin', from *červený* 'red'.

Cerveny (312) Czech and Slovak (**Červený**): from *červený* 'red', 'ruddy', hence a nickname for someone with red hair or a ruddy complexion.

Cervera (314) Catalan and Spanish: habitational name from any of numerous places called Cervera, from Late Latin *cervaria* 'place of stags' (a derivative of *cervus* 'stag').
GIVEN NAMES Spanish 46%. *Jose* (7), *Juan* (7), *Carlos* (6), *Enrique* (4), *Armando* (3), *Jorge* (3), *Marta* (3), *Rafael* (3), *Ramiro* (3), *Ricardo* (3), *Alfonso* (2), *Benigno* (2); *Angelo*, *Elio*, *Leonardo*, *Salvatore*, *Silvio*.

Cervi (190) Italian: **1.** nickname from *cervo* 'stag' (Latin *cervus*), given with reference to the presumed lustiness of the creature, or conversely to the horns, supposed to be a sign of a cuckold. **2.** from the personal name *Acerbo* (see CERVELLI), with loss of the first syllable.
GIVEN NAMES Italian 22%. *Domenico* (3), *Nino* (3), *Carmine* (2), *Angelo*, *Antonio*, *Cesidio*, *Domenic*, *Fiorino*, *Gino*, *Riccardo*, *Vito*.

Cervini (181) Italian: patronymic or plural form of CERVINO.
GIVEN NAMES Italian 24%. *Orlando* (3), *Arcangelo*, *Armando*, *Carmine*, *Domenico*, *Francesco*, *Geno*, *Guilio*, *Luciano*, *Margherita*, *Pietro*, *Riccardo*, *Roberto*, *Rocco*, *Romeo*.

Cervino (132) **1.** Galician (**Cerviño**): from *cervino* denoting a species of deer (Latin *cervinus*), possibly topographic in application. **2.** Italian: perhaps a habitational name for someone from a place called Cervo, for example in Liguria.
GIVEN NAMES Spanish 13%; Italian 7%. *Jose* (4), *Angelina*, *Eduardo*, *Jacinto*, *Jorge*, *Julio*, *Lino*, *Rodolfo*; *Filomena*, *Francesca*, *Leonardo*, *Pasquale*.

Cervone (331) Italian: **1.** from an augmentative of *cervo* 'stag' (see CERVI). **2.** variant spelling of CERBONE 2.
GIVEN NAMES Italian 21%. *Angelo* (3), *Vincenzo* (2), *Alberto*, *Antonio*, *Aurelio*, *Carmela*, *Carmine*, *Gian Carlo*, *Luigi*, *Mario*, *Pasquale*, *Philomena*, *Salvatore*.

Cesa (138) Italian: habitational name from any of various places called Cesa or Cese, for example Cesa in Caserta province, Campania (Latin *Caesa*), named with a derivative of *caedere* 'to cut', denoting a place cleared of wood.
GIVEN NAMES Italian 16%. *Aldo* (2), *Gilio* (2),

Orlando (2), *Angelo*, *Carmine*, *Riccardo*, *Silvio*.

Cesar (490) **1.** French and Portuguese (**César**); from the personal name *César*, French and Portuguese equivalent of *Caesar* (see CESARE). **2.** Slovenian and Croatian (northern Croatia): from *cesar* 'emperor', nickname for a person who behaved in an imperious manner or for an administrative official in the service of the Austro-Hungarian Empire.
GIVEN NAMES Spanish 17%; French 12%; Portuguese 6%. *Julio* (10), *Jose* (8), *Carlos* (4), *Aguilar* (2), *Claudio* (2), *Luis* (2), *Alberto*, *Armando*, *Arturo*, *Constancia*, *Estela*, *Fernando*; *Jean Claude* (3), *Monique* (2), *Serge* (2), *Alies*, *Andre*, *Colette*, *Collette*, *Georges*, *Luckner*, *Marcel*, *Marie Anne*, *Pierre*; *Joao*.

Cesare (364) Italian: from the personal name *Cesare*, from the famous Roman family name *Caesar*. This was associated by folk etymology in classical times with Latin *caesaries* 'head of hair', but is probably of Etruscan origin, perhaps ultimately a cognate of CHARLES. After the spectacular success of Julius Caesar the name was adopted by his imperial successors, and eventually came to be taken as a generic title. As such it has been adopted into most European languages (see KAISER).
GIVEN NAMES Italian 14%. *Domenic* (2), *Pasquale* (2), *Sal* (2), *Antonio*, *Carmine*, *Emanuele*, *Erminio*, *Francesco*, *Giacomo*.

Cesari (128) Italian: patronymic or plural form of CESARE.
GIVEN NAMES Italian 18%. *Mario* (2), *Amato*, *Angelo*, *Cesare*, *Domenic*, *Francesco*, *Leandro*, *Luigi*, *Ricardo Romeo*.

Cesarini (117) Italian and Corsican: from a diminutive of CESARE.
GIVEN NAMES Italian 27%; French 5%. *Angelo* (3), *Armando* (3), *Dino* (2), *Francesco* (2), *Aldo*, *Annibale*, *Antonio*, *Arnaldo*, *Carlo*, *Domenico*, *Enrico*, *Giulio*, *Giuseppe*; *Antoinette*, *Pierre*.

Cesario (590) Italian: **1.** from the Late Latin personal name *Caesarius*, itself from *Caesar* (see CESARE). **2.** topographic name from the unattested Late Latin word *caesario* 'wood', 'coppice'.
GIVEN NAMES Italian 25%; Spanish 8%. *Mario* (6), *Attilio* (4), *Sal* (4), *Marco* (2), *Angelo*, *Antonio*, *Camillo*, *Carlo*, *Carmine*, *Dante*, *Donato*, *Eduardo*, *Emilia*, *Enrico*, *Eugenio*, *Orlando*; *Salvador* (2), *Alicia*, *Carlos*, *Consuelo*, *Patricio*, *Ramon*.

Cesaro (146) Italian: **1.** variant of CESARE. **2.** from Calabrian dialect *cesaru* 'water snake', presumably applied as a nickname for someone thought to resemble a snake in some way.
GIVEN NAMES Italian 9%. *Antimo*, *Edvige*, *Salvatore*.

Cesarz (148) Polish: nickname from *cesarz* 'emperor', cognate with German KAISER.
GIVEN NAME German 4%. *Hans* (2).

Cesena (183) Italian: habitational name from a place named Cesena, near Forlì in Emilia-Romagna.
GIVEN NAMES Spanish 27%. *Jose* (4), *Josefina* (2), *Manuel* (2), *Ruben* (2), *Alejandro, Amalia, Arturo, Carlos, Consuelo, Eduardo, Enrique, Estela.*

Cespedes (501) Spanish (**Céspedes**): from the plural of *cesped* 'peat', 'turf' (Latin *caespes*, genitive *caespitis*), applied as a habitational name from a place named Céspedes (for example in Burgos province) or named with this word, or a topographic name for someone who lived by an area of peat, or possibly as a metonymic occupational name for someone who cut and sold turf.
GIVEN NAMES Spanish 52%. *Carlos* (20), *Jose* (19), *Luis* (16), *Juan* (6), *Manuel* (6), *Cesar* (5), *Miguel* (5), *Pedro* (5), *Ramon* (5), *Eduardo* (4), *Alfonso* (3), *Alfredo* (3).

Cessna (807) French: unexplained; perhaps a variant of German **Kestner** (see KASTNER).

Cesta (109) Italian (Aquila): unexplained; in part at least, possibly a metonymic occupational name for someone who make or used baskets, from *cesta* 'basket'.
GIVEN NAMES Italian 11%; Spanish 5%. *Angelo, Armando, Oreste; Ramon* (2), *Lupe, Marta.*

Cestaro (214) Italian: occupational name for a basketmaker, from an agent derivative of *cesta* 'basket', from Latin *cista*.
GIVEN NAMES Italian 12%. *Giro* (3), *Alfonse, Dante, Ennio, Pasquale, Salvatore, Silvio.*

Cestone (136) Italian: from an augmentative of *cesta* 'basket'.
GIVEN NAMES Italian 11%. *Angelo, Giovanna, Michelina.*

Cetrone (118) Southern Italian (Sicily): topographic name from an augmentative of Sicilian *citru* 'citron (tree)' (Italian *cedro*).
GIVEN NAMES Italian 14%. *Domenic* (2), *Gaetana, Guido, Romeo.*

Cetta (106) Italian: **1.** from Albanian *Çetta*; *çetë* is the Albanian word for 'tribe' or 'group'. The application of this word as a surname is unclear. **2.** habitational name from a place so named in Triora in Imperia province. **3.** possibly from a feminine form of **Cetti**, from Old Tuscan *Cettus*, a pet form of a personal name ending in *-cettus*.
GIVEN NAMES Italian 20%. *Vito* (3), *Antonio, Grazio, Guglielmo, Mauro, Pasquale.*

Cevallos (319) Spanish: variant spelling of CEBALLOS.
GIVEN NAMES Spanish 52%. *Carlos* (6), *Juan* (6), *Manuel* (5), *Pedro* (5), *Fernando* (4), *Jose* (4), *Luis* (4), *Eduardo* (3), *Francisco* (3), *Jaime* (3), *Ana* (2), *Angel* (2); *Marco* (3), *Franco* (2), *Aldo, Antonio, Clemente, Fausto, Flavio, Marco Antonio, Primo.*

Cha (1268) **1.** Korean (**Ch'a**): there is only one Chinese character for the Ch'a surname, and the Yŏnan Ch'a clan is the only clan. Their founding ancestor was Ch'a Hyojŏn, son of Yu Ch'a-tal (10th century AD). Ch'a is a fairly common surname throughout the Korean peninsula, but most of the clan's members live in Kyŏngsang province, Hwanghae province, or P'yŏngan province. **2.** Chinese 查: variant of ZHA.
GIVEN NAMES Chinese/Korean 66%. *Young* (15), *Jae* (10), *Yong* (9), *Jin* (8), *Jung* (8), *Sang* (8), *Kyung* (5), *Soon* (5), *Sung* (5), *Yung* (5), *Jong* (4), *Kwang* (4); *Chong* (8), *Byung* (7), *Joo* (6), *Chang* (5), *Min* (5), *Hojoon* (3), *Jung Jin* (3), *Neng* (3), *Toua* (3), *Blia* (2), *Blong* (2), *Bok Nam* (2).

Chaban (122) Russian and Polish: nickname from *chaban* 'bad man'.
GIVEN NAMES Russian 5%; Polish 5%. *Galina, Mikhail; Irena, Michalina, Wassil.*

Chabot (1590) French: **1.** habitational name from any of several places called Chabot, from *caput* 'head', 'summit'. **2.** from *chabot* 'bull-head', a species of fish with a large head, hence a nickname for someone with a big head and a small body.
FOREBEARS A bearer of the name Chabot from Poitou is documented in Quebec city in 1661.
GIVEN NAMES French 15%. *Andre* (8), *Marcel* (5), *Pierre* (4), *Adrien* (3), *Armand* (3), *Jacques* (3), *Lucien* (3), *Emilien* (2), *Fernand* (2), *Gaetan* (2), *Laurent* (2), *Normand* (2).

Chace (844) English: variant spelling of CHASE.

Chachere (218) **1.** French (mainly LA): perhaps a variant of **Jachère**, from a word meaning 'fallow', the name of a domain. **2.** Perhaps an altered spelling of German **Tschacher**, of Polish origin (see CZACHOR).
GIVEN NAMES French 5%. *Celestine, Laure.*

Chacko (548) **1.** Indian: from a pet form of the Hebrew personal name *ya'aqobh* (see JACOB), used as a given name among Christians in Kerala (southern India) and in the U.S. as a last name among families from Kerala. **2.** Jewish: possibly an altered form of Slovak **Čačko** or Ukrainian **Chacka**, a nickname from Czech *čačka* 'toy', 'plaything', Ukrainian *tsyatska*.
GIVEN NAMES Indian 37%. *Oommen* (5), *Varughese* (5), *Eapen* (4), *Babu* (3), *Mathai* (3), *Ninan* (3), *Cheriyan* (2), *Shanti* (2), *Aleykutty, Biji, Harsha, Jaya.*

Chacon (2773) Spanish (**Chacón**): nickname from *chacón* 'gecko'.
GIVEN NAMES Spanish 43%. *Jose* (48), *Carlos* (34), *Luis* (24), *Manuel* (24), *Jorge* (22), *Juan* (22), *Raul* (20), *Mario* (18), *Jesus* (17), *Francisco* (13), *Armando* (12), *Julio* (11).

Chaconas (148) Greek: Americanized form of *Tsakonas* 'Tsakonian', an inhabitant of the eastern Peloponnese speaking an archaic variety of Greek.
GIVEN NAME Greek 5%. *Demetrios* (2).

Chad (102) **1.** English: from the personal name *Chad*, from the Old English personal name *Ceadda*, of unknown origin. St. Chad was a 7th-century archbishop of York. **2.** Indian (Gujarat): Hindu (Bhatia) name of unknown meaning.
GIVEN NAMES Indian 7%. *Jayesh, Kailash, Rao.*

Chada (124) Indian (Panjab): variant of CHADHA.
GIVEN NAMES Indian 12%. *Kiran, Prakash, Ramana, Sandeep, Srinivas, Sunil, Sushil.*

Chadbourne (575) English: variant of CHADBURN.

Chadburn (122) English: habitational name from Chatburn in Lancashire, named with the Old English personal name *Ceatta* + *burna* 'stream'.

Chadd (282) English: from the Old English personal name *Ceadd(a)*.

Chadderdon (201) Variant of English CHATTERTON.

Chadderton (104) English: variant of CHATTERTON.

Chaddick (112) English: variant of CHADWICK.

Chaddock (244) English: variant of CHADWICK.

Chadha (216) Indian (Panjab): Hindu (Khatri) and Sikh name based on the name of a clan in the Khatri community. Ramgarhia Sikhs also have a clan called Chadha.
GIVEN NAMES Indian 92%. *Deepak* (4), *Rakesh* (3), *Vijay* (3), *Arun* (2), *Ashok* (2), *Chander* (2), *Jagdish* (2), *Navin* (2), *Ramesh* (2), *Ritu* (2), *Sangeeta* (2), *Sanjay* (2).

Chadick (182) Variant spelling of English CHADWICK.
GIVEN NAME Jewish 4%. *Herschel* (2).

Chadwell (1274) English: habitational name from Chadwell St. Mary in Essex or Chadwell in Leicestershire, both named with Old English *cald* 'cold' + *well(a)* 'spring', 'stream'. Compare CALDWELL.

Chadwick (6031) English: habitational name from any of various places called Chadwick, in Merseyside (formerly in Lancashire), Warwickshire, and two in Worcestershire. One of the places in Worcestershire and the one in Warwickshire are named as 'the dairy farm (Old English *wīc*) of Ceadel'. The other in Worcestershire and the one in Merseyside are named as 'Ceadda's dairy farm'. *Ceadda* was the name of a famous Anglo-Saxon bishop, St. Chad.

Chae (483) Korean: there is only one Chinese character for the Chae surname. There are two Chae clans: the Ch'ilwŏn and the Ŭisŏng, the Ch'ilwŏn clan being the larger. Some records indicate that the Chae clans descended from another cian with the two-character surname of **Chaegal**. According to the Chaegal clan genealogy, the founding ancestor of the Korean Chaegal clan was a twentieth-generation descendant of a Chinese government official, Chae Kal-lyang, a charac-

ter who plays an important role in the epic tale of the Three Kingdoms. This descendant migrated to the Shilla kingdom sometime in the early 9th century. He and his descendants lived in the southern tip of the Korean peninsula for four centuries. Then, during the reign of Koryŏ king Kojong (1213–1259), two brothers split the Chaegal surname. One brother, Yŏng, took the surname **Kal** and the other brother, Hong, took the surname Chae. Afterward, the surnames Chaegal and Kal became all but extinct, with only a few families surviving into the 20th century. In Korea, most members of the Chae clan live in southern Kyŏngsang and Chŏlla provinces.
GIVEN NAMES Korean 63%. *Young* (8), *Sung* (6), *Jin* (5), *Hyo* (4), *Kyung* (3), *Yoon* (3), *Chin* (2), *Dong* (2), *Eunhee* (2), *Han* (2), *Hee* (2), *Joon* (2); *Chang* (4), *Byung* (3), *Chong* (3), *Kyunghee* (2), *Pyong* (2), *Seungil* (2), *Sung Do* (2), *Chong Sun*, *Dong Hun*, *Dong Jin*, *Eunmi*, *Hae*.

Chafe (150) English: variant of CHAFFEE.

Chafee (134) English: variant of CHAFFEE.

Chafetz (128) Jewish (from Belarus): variant of HEIFETZ.

Chaffee (2423) English (of Norman origin): descriptive nickname from a derivative of Old French *chauf* 'bald' (Latin *calvus*). Compare CAVE.

Chaffey (130) English (Dorset): variant spelling of CHAFFEE. In the U.K. this is the usual spelling of the surname.

Chaffin (3497) English (of Norman origin): descriptive nickname for a bald man, from Middle English *chaffin*, a diminutive of Old French *chauf* 'bald' (Latin *calvus*).
FOREBEARS All present-day English bearers of the name Chaffin are descended from John Chaffin (died 1658), a blacksmith of Bruton, Somerset. The surname is now much more common in America than in England.

Chaffins (336) English: variant of CHAFFIN.

Chafin (1345) English: variant spelling of CHAFFIN.

Chagnon (808) French: topographic name from a diminutive of *chagne* 'oak (tree)', a regional variant of *chêne* (see CHENE).
FOREBEARS A bearer of the name from Tours is documented at Contrecoeur, Quebec, in 1678, with the secondary surname Larose.
GIVEN NAMES French 12%. *Pierre* (4), *Emile* (3), *Lucien* (3), *Andre* (2), *Dominique* (2), *Fernand* (2), *Remi* (2), *Armand*, *Camille*, *Cecile*, *Herve*, *Jacques*.

Chagolla (108) Hispanic (Mexican): nickname from Mexican Spanish *chagolla* 'counterfeited or worn-down coin'.
GIVEN NAMES Spanish 47%. *Armando* (3), *Jesus* (3), *Carlos* (2), *Ignacio* (2), *Javier* (2), *Juan* (2), *Mario* (2), *Alfredo*, *Angelina*, *Bacilio*, *Estevan*, *Gerardo*; *Antonio*.

Chahal (101) Indian (Panjab): Sikh name of unknown meaning, based on the name of a Jat clan.

GIVEN NAMES Indian 85%. *Amrit*, *Bakhshish*, *Balwinder*, *Beant*, *Hardev*, *Jeet*, *Pavan*, *Raghbir*, *Sonali*, *Vinod*.

Chahine (118) Muslim (North African): probably from a variant spelling, under French influence, of the Persian personal name *Shahin* (see SHAHEEN).
GIVEN NAMES Muslim 51%; French 9%. *Mohamad* (4), *Ali* (2), *Hazem* (2), *Kamal* (2), *Salah* (2), *Talal* (2), *Youssef* (2), *Abbas*, *Abd*, *Abdallah*, *Abdulrahman*, *Akram*; *Antoine* (2), *Alain*, *Georges*, *Henri*, *Pierre*.

Chai (620) **1.** Chinese 柴: from the name of Gao Chai, a disciple of Confucius during the Spring and Autumn period (722–481 BC). His descendants adopted this character as their surname; it also means 'firewood'. **2.** Korean: variant of CHAE.
GIVEN NAMES Chinese/Korean 39%. *Soo* (4), *Jung* (3), *Kyung* (3), *Li* (3), *Liang* (3), *Sang* (3), *Han* (2), *Jin* (2), *Seung* (2), *Sung* (2), *Wai Ling* (2), *Won* (2); *Hyoun* (2), *Min* (2), *Young Kun* (2), *Chang*, *Chul*, *Chung*, *Hee Sook*, *Iksoo*, *In Sook*, *Joo*, *Junghoon*, *Kum*; *Tan* (2), *Du*, *Tek*, *Thao*, *Tok*, *Xuan*, *Yaping*.

Chaidez (390) Hispanic (Mexico): unexplained; perhaps a variant of CHAIREZ.
GIVEN NAMES Spanish 60%. *Jose* (15), *Juan* (7), *Jesus* (6), *Manuel* (6), *Ricardo* (5), *Margarita* (4), *Miguel* (4), *Amador* (3), *Angel* (3), *Francisco* (3), *Guadalupe* (3), *Librado* (3); *Antonio* (10), *Lorenzo* (3), *Lucio* (2), *Clemente*, *Heriberto*, *Marino*, *Sal*.

Chaiken (222) Americanized spelling of CHAIKIN.
GIVEN NAMES Jewish 8%. *Hyman* (2), *Miriam* (2), *Meyer*, *Yetta*.

Chaikin (277) Jewish (from Belarus): metronymic from Yiddish female personal name *Khayke*, a pet form of *Khaye*, meaning 'life'.
GIVEN NAMES Jewish 7%. *Meyer* (2), *Miriam* (2), *Sol*.

Chaille (109) French (**Chaillé**): habitational name from either of two places, in Deux-Sèvres and Vendée, which were Romano-Gallic settlements named as *Calliacum*, from the Latin personal name *Callius* + the locative suffix -*acum*.
FOREBEARS A Chaillé from Poitou is documented in Quebec city in 1665.

Chain (519) French: from Old French *chain*, a device for catching birds, possibly applied as a metonymic occupational name for a bird-catcher or a hunter. In some cases it may be an American spelling of the French topographic surname **Chêne** (see CHENE).

Chaires (206) Hispanic (Mexican): unexplained, but possibly a topographic name related to Galician *chaira* 'little valley or meadow' or *chairo* 'flat' (way, terrain).
GIVEN NAMES Spanish 23%. *Jorge* (2), *Jose* (2), *Raul* (2), *Agustin*, *Andres*, *Carlota*, *Elena*, *Ernesto*, *Faustino*, *Feliciano*, *Genaro*, *Glafiro*.

Chairez (342) Spanish (Mexico): variant (probably **Cháirez**) of CHAIRES.
GIVEN NAMES Spanish 55%. *Jose* (13), *Carlos* (5), *Juan* (5), *Luis* (5), *Francisco* (4), *Jesus* (4), *Ruben* (4), *Javier* (3), *Jose Luis* (3), *Margarita* (3), *Roberto* (3), *Alberto* (2); *Antonio* (4), *Cecilio*, *Filiberto*, *Julieta*, *Mirella*, *Sal*.

Chaisson (1104) Variant spelling of French CHIASSON, frequent in LA.
GIVEN NAMES French 6%. *Camile* (2), *Alcide*, *Alphonse*, *Amie*, *Andree*, *Angelle*, *Cecile*, *Chantel*, *Easton*, *Lucien*, *Oneil*.

Chait (406) Jewish (eastern Ashkenazic): occupational name for a tailor, Yiddish *khayet* (from Hebrew *chayat*).
GIVEN NAMES Jewish 7%; German 4%. *Arnon*, *Herschel*, *Isidor*, *Meyer*, *Nechama*, *Yossi*; *Frieda*.

Chakrabarti (101) Indian (Bengal) and Bangladeshi: Hindu (Brahman) name, *čokroborti* in Bengali, from Sanskrit *čakravartī* 'emperor'. *Čakravartī* means literally 'wheels rolling'; metaphorically, it denotes a ruler whose chariot wheels roll everywhere without obstruction (*čakra* 'wheel' + *vart*- 'to roll or turn').
GIVEN NAMES Indian 91%. *Amitabha* (3), *Alok* (2), *Sumita* (2), *Aloke*, *Anil*, *Anjan*, *Arindam*, *Arun*, *Ashok*, *Asim*, *Barin*, *Bhaskar*.

Chakraborty (166) Indian (Bengal) and Bangladeshi: variant of CHAKRABARTI.
GIVEN NAMES Indian 90%. *Amit* (3), *Asit* (3), *Dilip* (3), *Arup* (2), *Goutam* (2), *Indranil* (2), *Manju* (2), *Mita* (2), *Murali* (2), *Prabir* (2), *Soumya* (2), *Tapan* (2).

Chalcraft (122) English: habitational name from Chalcraft in Hampshire, named from Old English *cealf* 'calf' + *croft* 'enclosure', or a topographic name with the same meaning.

Chalfant (935) Variant of English **Chalfont**, habitational name from either of two places in Buckinghamshire, Chalfont St. Giles and Chalfont St. Peter, named with Old English *cealf* 'calf' + *funta* 'spring'.

Chalfin (259) Probably an American variant of English **Chalfont** (see CHALFANT).

Chalifour (136) French (Savoy): variant of **Chaufour**, from *chaux* 'lime' + *four* 'oven', 'kiln'; a topographic name for someone who lived by a lime kiln, a habitational name from any of various places named with this term, or a metonymic occupational name for a lime burner.
GIVEN NAMES French 23%. *Jacques* (2), *Alphonse*, *Andre*, *Francois*, *Henri*, *Laurent*, *Lucien*, *Marcel*, *Yvon*.

Chalifoux (323) Altered spelling of French CHALIFOUR.
FOREBEARS A bearer of the name from La Rochelle, France, is documented in Quebec city in 1648.
GIVEN NAMES French 15%. *Raoul* (5), *Armand* (2), *Gilles* (2), *Adelard*, *Adrien*, *Andre*, *Cecile*, *Luc*, *Philippe*.

Chalk (959) English: from Old English *cealc* 'chalk', applied as a topographic name for someone who lived on a patch of chalk soil, or as a habitational name from any of the various places named with this word, as for example Chalk in Kent or Chalke in Wiltshire.

Chalker (722) Southern English: **1.** topographic name for someone who lived on chalky ground; from CHALK + the suffix *-er* denoting an inhabitant. **2.** occupational name from an agent derivative of Old English *(ge)cealcian* 'to whitewash'.

Chalkley (250) English: habitational name from an unidentified place (probably in southern England, where the surname is commonest and where chalk hills abound), apparently named with Old English *cealc* 'chalk' + *lēah* 'woodland clearing'. The source may be Chalkley Farm in Hawkesbury, Gloucestershire, which is recorded from the 12th century.
FOREBEARS Quaker minister Thomas Chalkley of Southwark, England, first came to America in 1698, on a preaching journey, and in 1700 he brought his family over to MD. The next year he moved to Philadelphia, and in 1723 to a plantation he had purchased in the nearby suburb of Frankford, later a part of the city. As his family grew, he became a sea trader.

Chall (100) Probably a respelling of the French habitational name **Challe**, from any of the various places so named from Late Latin *cala* 'rock shelter'.

Challender (169) English: occupational name for a maker or seller of blankets, from an agent derivative of Middle English *chaloun* 'blanket', 'coverlet'. The articles were named from being produced in Châlons-sur-Marne, once the seat of a Gaulish tribe recorded in Latin sources as *Catalauni*.

Challenger (224) English: from an agent derivative of Middle English *chalangen* 'to challenge' (from Old French *chalonger*), possibly applied as a nickname for a quarrelsome or litigious person.

Challis (316) English (of Norman origin): habitational name from Eschalle in Pas-de-Calais, France, which is named from Old French *eschelle* 'ladder' (Latin *scala*).

Chalmers (2289) Scottish: variant of CHAMBERS. The *-l-* was originally an orthographic device to indicate the length of the vowel after assimilation of *-mb-* to *-m(m)-*.

Chaloupka (266) Czech: from a diminutive of *chalupa* 'peasant's cottage' (see CHALUPA).

Chaloux (217) Of French origin: **1.** perhaps a variant of **Jaloux**, a nickname meaning 'jealous', 'possessive'. **2.** possibly a reconstruction of **Challuz** or **Chalus**, a habitational name from places so named in Puy-de-Dôme and Haute-Vienne.
FOREBEARS A Chalou from Poitou is documented in Quebec city in 1723; a Chalut, of

unknown origin, is documented in Quebec city in 1657. A bearer of the name Chanluc or Chalut, from Poitiers, is documented in Orleans Isle, near Quebec city, in 1695.
GIVEN NAMES French 17%. *Etienne* (2), *Pierre* (2), *Aime*, *Alcide*, *Alphonse*, *Fernand*, *Marcel*, *Muguette*, *Normand*.

Chalupa (249) Czech, Slovak, and Polish (**Chałupa**): status name for a cottager, from *chalupa*, a term denoting a free peasant's cottage with very little land attached to it. Compare SEDLAK, ZAHRADNIK.

Cham (138) **1.** French: habitational name from any of various places called Chalm, often recorded as La Champ, in Ardèche, Drôme, Haute-Loire, Isère, Lozère. **2.** Arabic: ethnic name for a Syrian or habitational name for someone from Damascus, from *al shām*, Arabic name for Syria, used in Syria itself to denote the city of Damascus. **3.** Chinese 詹: variant of ZHAN. **4.** Other Southeast Asian: unexplained.
GIVEN NAMES Southeast Asian 14%; French 8%; Arabic 8%. *Chun*, *Fei*, *Heng*, *Hong*, *Kam*, *Roeun*; *Kiem* (2), *Binh*, *Pha*, *Tung*, *Tuyen*; *Francoise*, *Hancy*, *Murielle*, *Yves*; *Musa* (2), *Sheikh* (2), *Mustapha*, *Shahram*, *Suleiman*.

Chamberlain (11021) English: status name from Old French *chambrelain*, Norman French *cambrelanc*, *cambrelen(c)* 'chamberlain' (of Germanic origin, from *kamer* 'chamber', 'room', Latin *camera* (see CHAMBERS) + the diminutive suffix *-(l)ing*). This was originally the name of an official in charge of the private chambers of his master.

Chamberland (538) Americanized spelling of French CHAMBERLIN.
FOREBEARS A bearer of the name from La Rochelle is recorded at Ste-Famille, Orleans Isle, near Quebec city, in 1669. There is a Chambellan from Paris documented in Quebec city in 1617 and a Chamballon from Poitou is documented in Quebec city in 1691.
GIVEN NAMES French 15%. *Alphonse* (2), *Camille* (2), *Marcel* (2), *Normand* (2), *Adrien*, *Andre*, *Antoine*, *Armand*, *Emile*, *Fernand*, *Fernande*, *Ghislaine*.

Chamberlin (3996) **1.** French: occupational name for an official in charge of the private chambers of his master, Old French *chamberlenc*. See also CHAMBERLAIN. **2.** English: variant of CHAMBERLAIN.

Chambers (29955) English: occupational name for someone who was employed in the private living quarters of his master, rather than in the public halls of the manor. The name represents a genitive or plural form of Middle English *cha(u)mbre* 'chamber', 'room' (Latin *camera*), and is synonymous in origin with CHAMBERLAIN, but as that office rose in the social scale, this term remained reserved for more humble servants of the bedchamber.

Chamblee (1057) Possibly a respelling of the English habitational name CHAMBLEY.

Chambless (1112) English: unexplained; perhaps a variant of CHAMBERS. Compare CHAMBLISS.

Chambley (122) English: variant of CHUMBLEY (see CHUMLEY).

Chamblin (424) English: probably a reduced form of CHAMBERLIN.

Chambliss (1934) English: variant of CHAMBLESS.

Chamlee (220) American variant spelling of English CHUMLEY.

Chamness (817) English: probably a variant spelling of **Champness**, a variant of CHAMPNEY.

Chamorro (203) Spanish: nickname from *chamorro* 'shaven head', used especially to denote a boy or Portuguese man.
GIVEN NAMES Spanish 51%. *Carlos* (6), *Eduardo* (4), *Jose* (4), *Alejandro* (3), *Ernesto* (3), *Jaime* (3), *Jorge* (3), *Manuel* (3), *Alberto* (2), *Alfredo* (2), *Armando* (2), *Arturo* (2); *Antonio*, *Constantino*.

Champ (865) English and French: from Old French *champ* 'field', 'open land' (Latin *campus* 'plain', 'expanse of flat land'), a topographic name for someone who lived in or near a field or expanse of open country, or else in the countryside as opposed to a town.

Champa (250) Americanized spelling of Slovenian **Čampa**, a nickname for a left-handed person, from the dialect word *čampa* 'left hand'.

Champagne (4245) French: regional name for someone from Champagne, named in Latin as *Campania* (from *campus* 'plain', 'flat land'). This is also the name of various villages in France, and in some cases the family name may derive from one of these.
FOREBEARS In Canada this serves as a secondary surname for dozens of primary names, and is documented as a principal surname in 1703, in Quebec city. In LA some bearers of the name are descended from Jean-Baptiste Champagne of New Orleans, of unknown antecedents (he married around 1740); another branch is descended from a Canadian, Jean-Louis Champagne, who settled in LA in the early 1760s.
GIVEN NAMES French 11%. *Andre* (15), *Armand* (15), *Marcel* (12), *Lucien* (8), *Cecile* (5), *Emile* (5), *Normand* (5), *Pierre* (5), *Alain* (2), *Antoine* (2), *Evens* (2), *Fernand* (2).

Champe (109) Variant of French or English CHAMP.

Champeau (305) French: topographic name from *champeau* 'little field', or a habitational name from any of various places called Champeaux, for example in Deux-Sèvres, Manche, and Seine-et-Marne.
FOREBEARS A Champaux or Champoux, also called Jolicoeur, from Périgord was recorded in Bécancour, Quebec, in 1680.

Champigny (123) French: habitational name from any of the various places in northern and central France named Champigny, from a Romano-Gallic settlement name composed of the personal name *Campanius* + the locative suffix *-acum*.
FOREBEARS A Champigny from Paris, with the secondary surname Des Landes, was documented in Boucherville in 1688.
GIVEN NAMES French 21%. *Armand, Aurel, Calix, Jean-Pierre, Laurier, Luc, Lucien, Marcel, Mederic, Normand, Pierre*.

Champine (378) Americanized form of French CHAMPAGNE.

Champion (5798) English (of Norman origin) and French: status name for a professional champion, especially an agent employed to represent one of the parties in a trial by combat, a method of settling disputes current in the Middle Ages. The word comes from Old French *champion, campion* (Late Latin *campio*, genitive *campionis*, a derivative of *campus* 'plain', 'field of battle'). Compare CAMPION, KEMP.

Champlain (187) French: topographic name denoting someone who lived by a flat field, from *champ* 'field' (see CHAMP) + *plaine* 'level'.
FOREBEARS Samuel de Champlain, explorer, colonizer, and founder of Quebec city, was lieutenant governor of New France from 1619 to his death in 1635. He was buried in Quebec city. In 1609 he gave his name to the lake which lies between VT and NY.

Champlin (1530) English: probably a reduced form of CHAMBERLAIN.

Champney (310) English: regional name for someone from Champagne in France, from Old French *champeneis* (see CHAMPAGNE).

Champoux (286) French: **1.** habitational name from Champoux in Doubs, Burgundy. **2.** altered form of **Chamboux**, a dialect variant of **Chambon**, a habitational name from any of several places so named. There may have been some confusion with **Champeaux** (see CHAMPEAU).
GIVEN NAMES French 15%. *Andre* (6), *Amedee, Armand, Berthe, Cecile, Donat, Jacques, Luce, Pierre*.

Chan (15151) **1.** Chinese 陈: Cantonese variant of CHEN. **2.** Chinese 詹: variant transcription of ZHAN. **3.** Vietnamese (**Chân**): unexplained. **4.** Galician and Portuguese: topographic name from a field named *Chan* (Galician) or *Chã* (Portuguese), from Latin *plana* 'level', 'flat'.
GIVEN NAMES Chinese 24%; Vietnamese 8%. *Wai* (63), *Wing* (60), *Kwok* (59), *Kam* (50), *Chun* (41), *Kin* (40), *Chi* (34), *Ming* (33), *Man* (32), *Ping* (22), *Ying* (22), *Yuk* (22).

Chana (59) Indian (Panjab): Hindu (Arora) and Sikh name of unknown meaning, based on the name of a clan in the Arora community.

Chance (4670) **1.** English: from Old French *chea(u)nce* '(good) fortune' (a derivative of *cheoir* 'to fall (out)', Latin *cadere*), a nickname for an inveterate gambler, for someone considered fortunate or well favored, or perhaps for someone who had survived an accident by a remarkable piece of luck. **2.** Americanized form of German TSCHANTZ or SCHANTZ.

Chancellor (1518) English and Scottish: status name for a secretary or administrative official, from Old French *chancelier*, Late Latin *cancellarius* 'usher (in a law court)'. The King's Chancellor was one of the highest officials in the land, but the term was also used to denote the holder of a variety of offices in the medieval world, such as the secretary or record keeper in a minor manorial household. In some cases the name undoubtedly originated as a nickname or as an occupational name for someone in the service of such an official.

Chancey (1356) **1.** English (of Norman origin): habitational name from any of the various places in France named Chancé. **2.** Americanized spelling of German **Schanze**, a habitational name from Schanze, a place in the Upper Rhine, or a variant of SCHANTZ.

Chancy (240) **1.** French: habitational name, most probably from a place name derived from a Romano-Gallic estate named with the personal name *Cantius* + the locative suffix *-acum*. variant of CHANCEY. **2.** Variant spelling of CHANCEY.
GIVEN NAMES French 9%. *Altagrace, Edouard, Francois, Georges, Jacques, Marie Claude, Pierre*.

Chand (361) Indian (northern states): Hindu name found in several communities, from Sanskrit *čandra* 'pleasant', 'shining', 'moon'. It is a common final element of compound personal names, such as *Ramchand* and *Kishanchand*, and appears subsequently to have evolved into a surname. Compare CHANDRA.
GIVEN NAMES Indian 74%. *Suresh* (9), *Ramesh* (8), *Prem* (5), *Hari* (4), *Ram* (4), *Rup* (4), *Subhash* (4), *Harish* (3), *Lal* (3), *Nirmal* (3), *Prakash* (3), *Satish* (3).

Chanda (158) Indian (Bengal) and Bangladeshi: Hindu (Kayasth) name, **Čondo** in Bengali, from Sanskrit *čandra* 'pleasant', 'shining', 'moon'.
GIVEN NAMES Indian 29%. *Sanjay* (2), *Amit, Anand, Ashok, Manju, Pranab, Rajat, Rupa, Seema, Shampa, Sipra, Sreedhar*.

Chander (119) Indian (northern states): Hindu name from Sanskrit *čandra* 'pleasant', 'shining', 'moon'. This commonly occurs as the final element of a compound given name (for example, *Kishanchander*), and this final element subsequently evolved into a surname.
GIVEN NAMES Indian 93%. *Subhash* (13), *Ramesh* (8), *Harish* (6), *Satish* (4), *Subash*

(4), *Suresh* (4), *Ravi* (3), *Jagdish* (2), *Mohan* (2), *Raj* (2), *Rakesh* (2), *Renu* (2).

Chandlee (131) **1.** English: variant spelling of CHANDLEY. **2.** See CHANDLEY 2.

Chandler (27163) English: occupational name for a maker and seller of candles, from Middle English *cha(u)ndeler* (Old French *chandelier*, Late Latin *candelarius*, a derivative of *candela* 'candle'). While a medieval chandler no doubt made and sold other articles beside candles, the extended sense of modern English *chandler* does not occur until the 16th century. The name may also, more rarely, have denoted someone who was responsible for the lighting arrangements in a large house, or else one who owed rent in the form of wax or candles.

Chandley (217) **1.** English (Lancashire and Cheshire): unexplained; perhaps a habitational name from a lost or unidentified place, or an altered form of CHANDLER. **2.** Possibly an Americanized spelling of German **Schändle**, either a variant of **Schandel**, a metonymic occupational name for a candle maker, from Middle High German *schandel* (from French *chandelle* 'candle'), or a derogatory nickname for an evil-doer, from a diminutive of Middle High German *schande* 'shame', 'disgrace', 'ignominy'.

Chandonnet (180) French: from a diminutive of the habitational name **Chandon**, from places so named in Loire, Indre-et-Loire, and Savoie.
FOREBEARS A bearer of the name from the Maine region in France is documented in Quebec city in 1712, with the secondary surname L'Éveillé. There was a Chandonnet from Quebec who fought on the side of the rebelling colonists in the American Revolution and was rewarded with land in the area of Chazy, NY, at the end of the war.
GIVEN NAMES French 21%. *Emile* (2), *Andre, Cecile, Colette, Donat, Fernand, Gaetane, Hermance, Leonce, Marcel, Normand, Renaud*.

Chandra (571) Indian (Bengal) and Bangladeshi: Hindu (Kayasth) name, from Sanskrit *čandra* 'pleasant', 'shining', 'moon'. It occurs commonly as the final element of compound given names such as *Ramachandra* and *Krishnachandra*. Compare CHAND and CHANDER.
GIVEN NAMES Indian 87%. *Ramesh* (14), *Suresh* (13), *Subhash* (11), *Satish* (8), *Dinesh* (6), *Sushil* (6), *Umesh* (6), *Naveen* (5), *Amitabh* (4), *Kailash* (4), *Mahesh* (4), *Prakash* (4).

Chandran (103) Indian (Kerala, Tamil Nadu): Hindu name from Sanskrit *čandra* 'shining' (see CHANDRA) + the Tamil-Malayalam third-person masculine singular suffix *-n*. This is only a given name in India, but has come to be used as a family name in the U.S.

GIVEN NAMES Indian 91%. *Ravi* (8), *Ram* (6), *Bala* (4), *Jayanti* (2), *Mohan* (2), *Rajesh* (2), *Rama* (2), *Suresh* (2), *Anand, Biju, Chandra, Chandrika*.

Chaney (10557) **1.** English: variant of CHESNEY. **2.** French: habitational name from any of the various places called Chanet or Le Chanet, from Latin *canna* 'reed' + the suffix *-etum* denoting an inhabitant.

Chang (16309) **1.** Chinese 张: variant of ZHANG 1. **2.** Chinese 常: The emperor Huang Di (2697–2595 BC) had two advisers whose names contained this character; descendants of both of them are believed to have adopted Chang as their surname. Additionally, in the state of Wei during the Zhou dynasty (1122–221 BC) there existed a fief named Chang, the name of which was adopted by descendants of its ruling class. The Chinese character also has the meanings 'often' and 'ordinary'. **3.** Chinese 章: variant of ZHANG 2. **4.** Chinese 昌: a rare name whose Chinese character also means 'prosperous, flourishing'. This name is said to have originated 4500 years ago with Chang Yi, son of the legendary emperor Huang Di and father of emperor Zhuan Xu. **5.** Korean: there are 33 Chang clans in Korea, all but three of which use the same Chinese character for their surname. All of the Korean Chang clans had their origins in China, and, apart from the Tŏksu Chang clan and the Chŏlgang Chang clan, they all originated from a single founding ancestor, Chang Chŏn-p'il. He was born in China in 888 AD and fled to Korea with his father during a tumultuous period of Chinese history. The Tŏksu Chang clan's founding ancestor, Chang Sul-long, stayed in Korea, having escorted Koryŏ King Ch'ungyŏl's queen-to-be from China to Korea in 1275. Most of the founding ancestors of the other Chang clans arrived in Korea from Yüan China during the Koryŏ period (AD 918–1392) or during the early Chosŏn period.

GIVEN NAMES Chinese/Korean 32%. *Sung* (35), *Yong* (34), *Ming* (30), *Chi* (29), *Kyung* (24), *Hyun* (22), *Ching* (21), *Ying* (21), *Jin* (20), *Sang* (19), *Min* (11), *Pao* (11); *Young* (61), *Chung* (26), *Chong* (22), *Jae* (20), *Byung* (10), *Hak* (10), *Moon* (10), *Myong* (10), *Dae* (9), *Chul* (7), *Hae* (7), *Vang* (7).

Chanin (259) Jewish (from Belarus): metronymic from the Yiddish female personal name *Khane*, from Hebrew *Ḥannā* (see HANNA).

GIVEN NAMES Jewish 10%. *Zalman* (3), *Meyer* (2), *Miriam* (2), *Doron*.

Chanley (184) English: variant of CHANDLEY.

Channel (353) English: variant spelling of CHANNELL.

Channell (1152) English: topographic name for someone who lived near an estuary, channel, or drain, Middle English

chanel, Old French *chanel* (Latin *canalis* 'canal', 'conduit').

Channer (140) English: reduced form of CHALLENDER.

Channing (237) English: unexplained. Perhaps a variant of CHANNON.
FOREBEARS The earliest American Channing was John, who came from Dorset, England, in 1711 with his wife. Their son John became a prosperous merchant of Newport, RI, and their grandson William Ellery was born there in 1780. William Ellery Channing (1780–1842) was a Unitarian clergyman who founded the Massachusetts Peace Society, a precursor of the modern anti-war movement.

Channon (116) English (chiefly West Country): variant of CANNON 'canon', taken from the central French form *chanun*, as opposed to Norman *canun*.

Chant (272) French: from Old French *chant* 'song', applied as a metonymic occupational name for a singer in a chantry, or possibly as a nickname for a noted songster.

Chanthavong (133) Laotian: unexplained.
GIVEN NAMES Southeast Asian 62%. *Phouvanh* (2), *Amphone, Bouaphanh, Bouavanh, Khamphet, Phonesavanh, Somchith, Somnuk, Soubanh*; *Bounxou, Kham*; *Chan, Dong, Hong, Seng, Sou, Sun, Teng, Wan, Xong*; *Binh, Chanh, Douang, Phanh*.

Chantry (121) English: from Old French *chanterie*, a term which originally meant the singing or chanting of a mass, but later came to denote in turn the endowment of a priest to sing mass daily on behalf of the souls of the dead, the priest so endowed, and eventually the chapel where he officiated. The surname therefore may have arisen from a metonymic occupational name for the servant of a chantry priest, or possibly for the priest himself, or alternatively from a topographic name for someone who lived by a chantry chapel.

GIVEN NAMES French 6%. *Laurent* (2), *Colette*.

Chao (2086) **1.** Chinese 赵: variant of ZHAO. **2.** Chinese 周: variant of CHOW 1. **3.** Chinese 曹: variant of CAO. **4.** Chinese 巢: the Chinese character for this name means 'nest'. Its use as a surname has its origin in Chao Lake in modern Anwei province. The lake gave its name to the state of Chao, which dates back to the Yin dynasty (1401–1122 BC). The name of the state of Chao was in turn adopted by descendants of its ruling class. **5.** Portuguese (**Chão**) and Galician: from a common field name derived from Latin *planus* 'level', 'even', 'flat'.

GIVEN NAMES Chinese 17%; Spanish 6%. *Ming* (6), *Cheng* (5), *Ching* (5), *Wei* (5), *Chan* (4), *Chin* (4), *Kwang* (4), *Pei* (4), *Yi* (4), *Bin* (3), *Chen* (3), *Chien* (3); *Jose* (9), *Jesus* (6), *Manuel* (5), *Eduardo* (3), *Leticia*

(3), *Luis* (3), *Miguel* (3), *Raul* (3), *Roberto* (3), *Alfonso* (2), *Angel* (2), *Engracia* (2).

Chap (115) Cambodian: unexplained.
GIVEN NAMES Southeast Asian 20%. *Nhin, Phon, Saroeun, Thy*; *Ram, Sarath*.

Chapa (2048) Spanish and Portuguese: from *chapa* meaning amongst other things 'metal sheet', 'tin' and hence a metonymic occupational name for a metalworker.

GIVEN NAMES Spanish 47%. *Jose* (47), *Juan* (25), *Manuel* (18), *Carlos* (17), *Jesus* (16), *Ricardo* (16), *Mario* (15), *Ruben* (15), *Raul* (14), *Francisco* (11), *Guadalupe* (11), *Armando* (10).

Chaparro (484) Spanish and Portuguese: topographic name from *chaparro* 'oak bushes' (used as firewood), from Basque *txaparro*, or alternatively a nickname from the same word in the sense 'plump', 'chubby'.

GIVEN NAMES Spanish 46%. *Carlos* (7), *Juan* (7), *Jose* (6), *Ramon* (5), *Luis* (4), *Santos* (4), *Alfredo* (3), *Eloy* (3), *Javier* (3), *Jorge* (3), *Julio* (3), *Orlando* (3); *Carmela, Gilda, Heriberto, Marco, Marco Antonio, Riccardo*.

Chapdelaine (459) French: compound name from Old French *chape* 'hooded cloak', 'cape', 'hat' + *de laine* 'of wool', probably applied as a metonymic occupational name for a maker of such apparel, or as a nickname for someone who wore a distinctive cloak or hat.
FOREBEARS A Chapdelaine from Normandy, France, is documented at Saint-Ours, Quebec, in 1691, with the secondary surname *La Rivière*, which is thus translated *Rivers*.

GIVEN NAMES French 16%. *Andre* (4), *Adelard* (2), *Adelore* (2), *Henri* (2), *Normand* (2), *Aime, Armand, Camille, Fernand, Germain, Lisanne, Pierre*.

Chapek (179) Americanized spelling of Czech **Čapek** (see CAPEK).

Chapel (757) **1.** English: variant spelling of CHAPPELL. **2.** French: from a diminutive of Old French *chape* 'hooded cloak', 'cape', 'hood', or 'hat' (from Late Latin *cappa, capa*), hence a metonymic occupational name for a maker of cloaks or hats, or a nickname for a habitual wearer of a distinctive cloak or hat.

Chapell (167) English: variant spelling of CHAPPELL.

Chapelle (108) French: **1.** topographic name for someone living by a shrine, from French *chapelle* 'chapel', 'shrine'. **2.** variant of CHAPEL 'hat maker'.

Chapin (4420) French and Spanish: from a reduced form of French *eschapin* or Spanish *chapín*, a term for a light (woman's) shoe; perhaps a nickname for someone who habitually wore this type of footwear or possibly a metonymic occupational name for a shoemaker.

Chapla (126) Origin unidentified.

Chaplain (186) English: variant spelling of CHAPLIN 1.

Chaplin (2316) **1.** English and French: occupational name for a clergyman, or perhaps for the servant of one, from Middle English, Old French *chapelain* 'chantry priest', a priest endowed to sing mass daily on behalf of the souls of the dead (Late Latin *capellanus*). **2.** Ukrainian and Belorussian: patronymic from the nickname *Chaplya*, from the dialect word *chaplya* 'heron', 'stork' (Russian *tsaplya*), referring to a man with long, thin legs or perhaps one who was shy and easily frightened.
FOREBEARS Clement Chaplin was one of the founders of Hartford, CT, (coming from Cambridge, MA, with Thomas Hooker) in 1635.

Chapline (126) Respelling of CHAPLIN.
GIVEN NAME French 4%. *Camille*.

Chaplinski (107) **1.** Ukrainian and Belorussian: patronymic from the nickname *Chaplya* 'heron', 'stork' (see CHAPLIN 2), with the common surname suffix *-ski*. **2.** Americanized spelling of Polish CZAPLINSKI.

Chapman (45808) English: occupational name for a merchant or trader, Middle English *chapman*, Old English *cēapmann*, a compound of *cēap* 'barter', 'bargain', 'price', 'property' + *mann* 'man'.
FOREBEARS This name was brought independently to North America from England by numerous different bearers from the 17th century onward. John Chapmen (sic) was one of the free planters who assented to the 'Fundamental Agreement' of the New Haven Colony on June 4, 1639.

Chapnick (136) **1.** Americanized spelling of Polish and Jewish (eastern Ashkenazic) **Czapnik**, occupational name for a maker of caps. **2.** Americanized spelling of Polish **Chapnik** (which is pronounced 'Hapnick'), from *chapać* 'to snatch or snap at'.
GIVEN NAMES Jewish 9%. *Hyman* (2), *Meyer*.

Chapp (170) English: metonymic occupational name for a maker of ecclesiastical copes, from Old French *chape* (see CHAPEL).

Chappa (106) Probably a Spanish spelling of Italian **Ciappa**, a habitational name from a place so named in Cuneo province.
GIVEN NAMES Spanish 11%. *Jose* (2), *Alphonso, Angelita, Chino, Edelmira, Jose Luis, Tomas*.

Chappel (861) English: variant spelling of CHAPPELL.

Chappelear (304) Anglicized spelling of French **Chapel(l)ier**, an occupational name for a maker or seller of hats, from an agent derivative of *chapel* (see CHAPEL). This is a Huguenot name.

Chappell (8154) **1.** English: topographic name for someone who lived near a chapel, from Middle English *chapel(l)e* 'chapel', via Old French, from Late Latin *capella*, originally a diminutive of *capa* 'hood',

'cloak', but later transferred to the sense 'chapel', 'sanctuary', with reference to the shrine at Tours where the cloak of St. Martin was preserved as a relic. **2.** Americanized spelling of French CHAPPELLE.

Chappelle (679) French: topographic name for someone who lived by a chapel or church (see LACHAPELLE, CHAPPELL.).

Chappie (116) English: unexplained.

Chapple (1027) English (West Country): spelling variant of CHAPPELL.

Chappuis (187) French: occupational name for a carpenter or joiner, a derivative of Old French *chapuiser* 'to cut' (Late Latin *cappulare*, of uncertain origin).
GIVEN NAMES French 7%. *Laurent, Marcel, Veronique*.

Chaput (919) French: nickname for a habitual wearer of a distinctive cloak or hat, from a variant of CHAPEL.
FOREBEARS A Chaput from the Franche-Comté is recorded in Pointe-aux-Trembles, Quebec, in 1689.
GIVEN NAMES French 9%. *Armand* (4), *Andre* (2), *Fernand* (2), *Lucien* (2), *Adrien, Alcid, Alphonse, Gaetan, Germaine, Girard, Jacques, Jean Marc*.

Char (271) **1.** French: from French *char* 'cart', metonymic occupational name for a carter. **2.** Anglicized spelling of Slovenian **Čar**, a nickname from *čarati* 'to practice sorcery'. **3.** Indian (Karnataka): Hindu (Brahman) name, from Sanskrit *ācārya* 'teacher', 'spiritual guide'.
GIVEN NAMES Indian 9%. *Bharat, Gautam, Kalpana, Mohan, Padma, Rohini, Srikant, Usha, Vijay*.

Charboneau (650) Variant spelling of French CHARBONNEAU.

Charbonneau (1773) French: nickname for a man with dark hair or a swarthy complexion, from a diminutive of Old French *carbon* 'charcoal' (Latin *carbo*, genitive *carbonis*).
GIVEN NAMES French 11%. *Andre* (7), *Armand* (7), *Gaston* (3), *Marcel* (3), *Jacques* (2), *Laurent* (2), *Lucien* (2), *Normand* (2), *Pierre* (2), *Raoul* (2), *Yvon* (2), *Adrien*.

Charbonnet (217) French: variant of CHARBONNEAU.
GIVEN NAMES French 9%. *Pierre* (4), *Alphonse, Antoine, Odette*.

Chard (643) **1.** English: habitational name from Chard or South Chard in Somerset, recorded in Domesday Book as *Cerdren*, possibly from Old English *ceart* 'rough heathland' + *ærn* 'building', 'dwelling'. In some instances the surname may have arisen simply as a topographic name from *ceart*. **2.** French: from the personal name *Chard*, a short form of RICHARD; **3.** French: habitational name for someone from Chard in the department of Creuse.

Charest (923) French: variant of CHARETTE.
GIVEN NAMES French 17%. *Armand* (6), *Lucien* (4), *Jacques* (3), *Marcel* (3),

Normand (3), *Andre* (2), *Andree* (2), *Emile* (2), *Fernand* (2), *Herve* (2), *Michel* (2), *Rosaire* (2).

Charette (1357) French: from Old French *charette* 'cart', a diminutive of *char(re)*, probably acquired as a metonymic occupational name for a user or maker of carts.
FOREBEARS A Charet from Poitiers is recorded in the 1666 census of Quebec city.
GIVEN NAMES French 13%. *Lucien* (6), *Emile* (5), *Marcel* (5), *Adrien* (3), *Andre* (3), *Alban* (2), *Armand* (2), *Fernand* (2), *Gilles* (2), *Normand* (2), *Pierre* (2), *Adelard*.

Chargois (122) Of French origin; unexplained.
GIVEN NAMES French 8%. *Armand* (2), *Jacques, Monique*.

Charity (375) English: from Middle English *charite* 'charity', from Old French *charité* (Latin *caritas*), probably applied as a nickname for a benevolent, devout, or hospitable person.

Charland (744) French: perhaps from a diminutive of CHARLES.
FOREBEARS A bearer of the name Charland, from Bourges, is documented in Quebec city in 1652, with the secondary surname Francoeur.
GIVEN NAMES French 11%. *Jacques* (3), *Adelard* (2), *Emile* (2), *Aldor, Anatole, Andre, Armand, Benoit, Edouard, Euclide, Francois, Huguette*.

Charlebois (426) Of French origin: it appears in Canada first with the secondary surname **Jolibois** (literally 'joyful (or attractive) wood'), of which it may be a variant.
GIVEN NAMES French 12%. *Armand* (2), *Germaine* (2), *Monique* (2), *Remi* (2), *Aime, Eugenie, Fernand, Gaetan, Jacques, Marcel, Marcelle, Paul Emile*.

Charles (12904) **1.** French, Welsh, and English: from the French form of the Germanic personal name *Carl* 'man' (which was Latinized as *Carolus*). In France the personal name was popular from an early date, due to the fame of the Emperor Charlemagne (?742–814; Latin name *Carolus Magnus*, i.e. Charles the Great). The Old French form *Charles* was briefly introduced to England by the Normans, but was rare during the main period of surname formation. It was introduced more successfully to Scotland in the 16th century by the Stuarts, who had strong ties with France, and was brought by them to England in the 17th century. Its frequency as a Welsh surname is attributable to the late date of Welsh surname formation. Old English *Ceorl* 'peasant' is also found as a byname, but the resulting Middle English form, *Charl*, with a patronymic in *-s*, if it existed at all, would have been absorbed by the French form introduced by the Normans. Compare CARL. English variants pronounced with initial *k-* for the most part reflect the cognate Old Norse personal name

Karl, Karli. **2.** Swedish: ornamental form of a Frenchified form of the Old Norse personal name *Karl.*

FOREBEARS This name was brought independently to North America from England by numerous different bearers from the 17th century onward. John Charles was one of the free planters who assented to the 'Fundamental Agreement' of the New Haven Colony on June 4, 1639.

In Canada, a Charles, also known as **La Jeunesse**, arrived in Trois-Rivières, Quebec, from Paris in 1665.

GIVEN NAMES French 6%. *Pierre* (21), *Antoine* (9), *Andre* (8), *Francois* (7), *Patrice* (6), *Germaine* (5), *Magalie* (5), *Philippe* (5), *Yves* (5), *Alain* (4), *Jacques* (4), *Cecile* (3).

Charleson (101) **1.** English: patronymic from the personal name CHARLES. **2.** French: from the personal name *Charlesson*, a pet form of CHARLES.
GIVEN NAME French 5%. *Monique.*

Charleston (768) English: patronymic (with intrusive -*t*-) from the personal name CHARLES. The various places called Charleston are all of recent origin, so they are unlikely to be the source of the surname.

Charlesworth (675) English: habitational name from a place in Derbyshire named Charlesworth, from an Old English personal name *Ceafl* (or from the Old English word *ceafl* 'jaw', here meaning 'ravine') + *worð* 'enclosure'.

Charlet (173) French: from the personal name *Charlet*, a pet form of CHARLES.
GIVEN NAMES French 4%. *Calice, Jean-Claude.*

Charleville (106) French: habitational name from the city of Charleville in Marne.

Charley (463) **1.** English: habitational name from Charley in Leicestershire, named with Celtic *carn* 'cairn', 'pile of stones' + Old English *lēah* 'woodland clearing'. **2.** French (Burgundy): from a pet form of CHARLES.

Charlie (131) English: variant spelling of CHARLEY.

Charlier (280) French: occupational name for a cartwright, from Old French *charrelier*, a derivative of *charrel* 'cart', a diminutive of *char*, Late Latin *carrum*. Compare CARRIER.
GIVEN NAMES French 8%. *Alain, Andree, Emile, Jacques, Susette.*

Charlot (244) French: from a pet form of the personal name CHARLES.
GIVEN NAMES French 24%. *Lucien* (4), *Pierre* (3), *Jean-Baptiste* (2), *Stephane* (2), *Andre, Benoit, Constant, Dominique, Firmin, Francois, Gabrielle, Myrtha.*

Charlson (462) Americanized form of Danish and Norwegian CARLSEN or Swedish CARLSSON.

Charlton (3555) **1.** English: habitational name from any of the numerous places called Charlton, mainly in southern

England, from Old English *Ceorlatūn* 'settlement (Old English *tūn*) of the peasants'. Old English *ceorl* denoted originally a free peasant of the lowest rank, later (but probably already before the Norman conquest) a tenant in pure villeinage, a serf or bondsman. **2.** Irish: altered form of CARLIN.

Charnas (102) Jewish (eastern Ashkenazic): acronymic surname from the Hebrew phrase *Chatan Rabi Nahum Sofer* 'son-in-law of rabbi Nahum the Scribe'.
GIVEN NAMES Jewish 8%. *Chaim, Shimon.*

Charneski (118) Americanized spelling of Polish CZARNECKI.

Charney (825) **1.** French: topographic name from a derivative of *charne*, a dialect variant of Old French *charme* 'hornbeam', 'witch elm'. **2.** Americanized spelling of Jewish (eastern Ashkenazic) CZARNY.
GIVEN NAMES Jewish 4%. *Hyman* (3), *Dov* (2), *Hymie, Isack, Shulamit, Sol.*

Charnley (177) English (Lancashire): habitational name from an unidentified place, probably named with Celtic *carn* 'cairn', 'pile of stones' + Old English *lēah* 'woodland clearing'. Compare CHARLEY.

Charnock (243) **1.** English: habitational name from Charnock Richard or Heath Charnock in southern Lancashire, which are probably named with a derivative of Celtic *carn* 'cairn', 'pile of stones' (see CAIRNS). **2.** Perhaps also an Americanized spelling of Polish **Czarnoch**, a nickname for a dark-haired person, from Polish *czarny* 'black', or possibly of German **Scharnack** or **Tschernak**, nicknames from a Slavic word with the same meaning.

Charo (103) Spanish: perhaps an altered spelling of **Charro**, a nickname from *charro* 'rustic'. As a forename *Charo* is a pet form of *(María del) Rosario* (see DEL ROSARIO).
GIVEN NAMES Spanish 44%. *Ramon* (3), *Bernardino* (2), *Manuel* (2), *Ruben* (2), *Alonzo, Arturo, Carlos, Elena, Florentino, Jesus, Juan, Lupe.*

Charon (351) French: variant spelling of CHARRON.
GIVEN NAMES French 4%. *Jean-Yves* (2), *Francois, Valmore.*

Charpentier (1097) French: occupational name for a worker in wood, from Old French *charpentier* (Late Latin *carpentārius* 'cartwright').
GIVEN NAMES French 12%. *Normand* (5), *Marcel* (4), *Andre* (2), *Armand* (2), *Leodore* (2), *Adrien, Aime, Chantal, Easton, Emile, Francois, Henri.*

Charping (114) Origin unidentified. Perhaps an Americanized variant of French **Charpin**, an occupational name for a wool carder, from a derivative of *charper* 'to card', from Latin *carpere* 'to separate'
GIVEN NAME French 4%. *Irby.*

Charrette (145) French: variant spelling of CHARETTE.
GIVEN NAME French 7%. *Normand* (2).

Charrier (290) French: variant of CARRIER.
FOREBEARS A bearer of this name from the Saintonge region is recorded in Sainte-Famille, near Quebec city, in 1673, with the secondary surname Lafontaine.
GIVEN NAMES French 8%. *Benoit* (2), *Elphege* (2), *Aime, Jacques, Marcel, Rolande.*

Charron (1620) French: metonymic occupational name for a cartwright, from Old French *charron* 'cart' (Latin *carro*, genitive *carronis*, a derivative of *carrum* 'cart').
FOREBEARS A Charon of unknown origin is recorded in 1654 in Quebec city with the secondary surname La Barre, while a Charron from Champagne, secondary surname Ducharme, is recorded in Montreal in 1665 and another, from the Saintonge region, also called La Ferrière, was recorded in Quebec city in 1669.
GIVEN NAMES French 10%. *Andre* (7), *Armand* (4), *Donat* (3), *Lucien* (3), *Marcel* (3), *Alphonse* (2), *Emile* (2), *Laurent* (2), *Normand* (2), *Renald* (2), *Yves* (2), *Adrien.*

Charter (481) **1.** English: variant of CARTER. **2.** French: Breton variant of CHARTIER.

Charters (449) Scottish and English (of Norman origin): habitational name from the French city of Chartres, named for a Gaulish tribe, recorded in Latin sources as the *Carnutes*, whose seat it was.

Chartier (1815) French: reduced form of **Charretier**, an occupational name for a carter, from an agent derivative of Old French *charette* 'cart' (see CHARETTE).
FOREBEARS The Chartier-Lotbinière family, known in both its LA and Canada branches, can trace its lineage directly to the grandfather (born in Dijon in 1345) of the famous French poet and statesman Alain Chartier (c. 1385–c. 1433), author of *La belle Dame sans Mercy*. A Chartier from Paris is documented in Quebec city in 1646, and other bearers from Anjou, with the secondary surname Robert, are documented in Montreal in 1663.
GIVEN NAMES French 8%. *Andre* (6), *Armand* (4), *Normand* (4), *Jacques* (3), *Marcel* (3), *Adelard* (2), *Alcide* (2), *Emile* (2), *Gilles* (2), *Raoul* (2), *Rosaire* (2), *Alphonse.*

Charton (138) **1.** English: possibly a habitational name from either of two places named Charton, in Devon and Kent, the latter being the more likely source, to judge by the current distribution of the surname. **2.** French (Normandy and Champagne): reduced form of **Char(r)eton**, denoting a carter, from a derivative of Old French *charette* 'cart'.

Chartrand (759) French: probably a variant of **Chartrain**, a habitational name for someone from the city of Chartres.
FOREBEARS A Chartrand from Rouen, France, is documented in Montreal in 1669.
GIVEN NAMES French 10%. *Marcel* (5), *Andre* (3), *Jean Guy* (2), *Philippe* (2), *Alderic,*

Colette, Damien, Herve, Jean-Louis, Laurier, Luc, Lucien.

Charvat (346) Czech and Slovak (**Charvát**): ethnic name for a Croatian.

Charvet (118) French: diminutive of **Charve**, a regional variant of **Chauve** 'bald' (see under CHAUVIN).

GIVEN NAMES French 17%. *Andre* (2), *Emile, Josee, Julien, Marcel, Pierre.*

Chase (19875) **1.** English: metonymic occupational name for a huntsman, or rather a nickname for an exceptionally skilled huntsman, from Middle English *chase* 'hunt' (Old French *chasse*, from *chasser* 'to hunt', Latin *captare*). **2.** Southern French: topographic name for someone who lived in or by a house, probably the occupier of the most distinguished house in the village, from a southern derivative of Latin *casa* 'hut', 'cottage', 'cabin'.

FOREBEARS Thomas Chase came to MA from Chesham, Buckinghamshire, England, in the 1640s, and had many prominent descendants. Samuel Chase, born in Somerset Co., MD, in 1741, was one of the first members of the U.S. Supreme Court; Philander Chase, born in Cornish, NH, in 1741 was a prominent Episcopal clergyman, and his nephew Salmon Portland Chase (1808–73), also born in Cornish, was governor of OH, a U.S. senator, and secretary of the U.S. Treasury during the Civil War.

Chasen (231) Jewish (Ashkenazic): variant of CHAZEN.

GIVEN NAME Jewish 4%. *Hyman.*

Chasey (139) English (Somerset): unexplained.

Chasin (250) Jewish (Ashkenazic): variant of CHAZEN.

GIVEN NAMES Jewish 4%. *Hillel* (2), *Sol.*

Chason (478) Jewish (Ashkenazic): variant of CHAZEN.

Chasse (1009) French: **1.** from Old French *chasse* 'hunt', hence a metonymic occupational name for a huntsman or possibly, by ellipsis, for a gamekeeper, *garde-chasse*. **2.** (**Chassé**): habitational name from a place in Sarthe named Chassé, from the Roman personal name *Cacius* + the locative suffix *-acum*.

GIVEN NAMES French 15%. *Armand* (4), *Lucien* (4), *Andre* (3), *Emile* (3), *Adrien* (2), *Alain* (2), *Alcide* (2), *Benoit* (2), *Fernand* (2), *Marcel* (2), *Martial* (2), *Raoul* (2).

Chastain (5101) French: from Old French *castan(h)* 'chestnut tree' (Latin *castanea*), hence a topographic name for someone living near a particular chestnut tree or group of them, or possibly a nickname for someone with chestnut-colored hair.

Chastang (144) French: variant of CHASTAIN.

Chasteen (1323) Americanized spelling of French CHASTAIN.

Chasten (114) Americanized spelling of French CHASTAIN.

Chastine (106) Possibly an Americanized spelling of CHASTAIN.

Chatagnier (129) French (**Châtagnier**): topographic name for someone living near a chestnut tree. Compare CHASTAIN.

Chateau (103) French (**Château**): from Old French *chastel* 'castle', 'fortified building', a topographic name for someone who lived in or near a castle or an occupational name for someone who worked in one.

GIVEN NAMES French 18%. *Thierry* (2), *Francois, Michel.*

Chatel (118) French (**Châtel**): from Old French *chastel* 'castle', 'fortified building' (see CHATEAU).

GIVEN NAMES French 13%. *Celine, Emile, Gilles, Jacques, Lucien.*

Chatelain (572) English and French (**Châtelain**): status name for the governor or constable of a castle, or the warder of a prison, from Norman Old French *chastelain* (Latin *castellanus*, a derivative of *castellum* 'castle').

FOREBEARS A priest named Châtelain from Paris is documented in Quebec city in 1636, and a family is documented in Trois Rivières, Quebec, in 1722.

GIVEN NAMES French 10%. *Irby* (2), *Angelle, Camille, Cecile, Elzear, Fernand, Gilles, Jean Claude, Jean Robert, Jean-Luc, Marcel, Thierry.*

Chatfield (1207) English: habitational name from Chatfields in Sussex, which is named with the Old English personal name *Ceatta* (probably a variant of *Catta*) + Old English *feld* 'open country'.

Chatham (1658) English: habitational name from Chatham in Kent or possibly from Chatham Green in Essex, both named from Celtic *cēd* 'wood' (modern Welsh *coed*) + Old English *hām* 'homestead'.

Chatman (2887) **1.** English: possibly an altered spelling of CHAPMAN. **2.** Perhaps also an Americanized spelling of German **Schattmann**, a North German form of **Schatzmann** (see SCHATZMAN).

Chatmon (383) Variant of CHATMAN.

Chatt (126) English: variant of CATT.

Chatten (109) English: see CHATTIN.

Chatterjee (395) Indian (Bengal) and Bangladeshi: Hindu (Brahman) name, from *Chatta*, the name of a village, + *jhā* 'teacher' (a greatly reduced form of Sanskrit *upādhyāya*), i.e. 'teacher from the village of Chatta'. In Bengali names formed with *-jee*, the initial element is believed to indicate a village granted by Ballal Sen, an ancient king of Bengal, to an ancestor of bearers of the surname.

GIVEN NAMES Indian 86%. *Amit* (4), *Arun* (4), *Pallab* (4), *Amitabha* (3), *Anil* (3), *Arindam* (3), *Mita* (3), *Partha* (3), *Pranab* (3), *Anindya* (2), *Anjan* (2), *Aparna* (2).

Chatterton (785) English: habitational name from Chadderton in Greater Manchester (formerly in Lancashire), which is recorded in 1224 in the form

Chaterton, possibly from a Celtic hill name *Cadeir* (from *cadeir* 'chair') + Old English *tūn* 'settlement'. Compare CATTERTON.

Chattin (395) English: probably a variant spelling of **Chatton**, a habitational name from Chatton in Northumberland, named with the Old English personal name *Ceatta* + Old English *tūn* 'settlement', 'farmstead'. Compare CHATTEN.

Chatwin (170) English: habitational name from a place in Shropshire named Chetwynd, from the Old English personal name *Ceatta* + Old English *(ge)wind* 'winding ascent'.

Chau (2193) **1.** Chinese 周: Cantonese variant of CHOW 1. **2.** Chinese 邹: Cantonese variant of ZOU. **3.** Chinese 巢: Min variant of CHAO 4. **4.** Chinese 仇: variant of QIU 3. **5.** Vietnamese: unexplained.

GIVEN NAMES Vietnamese 38%; Chinese 26%. *Hung* (32), *Minh* (27), *Hoa* (19), *Thanh* (18), *Duc* (14), *Ha* (14), *Anh* (12), *Quyen* (11), *Lan* (10), *Son* (9), *Linh* (7), *Muoi* (7); *Wing* (12), *Hong* (9), *Han* (7), *Sang* (6), *Chi* (4), *Hang* (4), *Ching* (3), *Chiu* (3), *Dong* (3), *Kam* (3), *Man* (3), *Ping* (3); *Phong* (5), *Chung* (4), *Nam* (4), *Chong* (3), *Sinh* (3), *Tam* (2), *Thai* (2), *Tinh* (2), *Tuong* (2), *Yuet* (2), *Hung Kim, Manh.*

Chaudhari (112) Indian (Bengal) and Bangladeshi: variant of CHOWDHURY.

GIVEN NAMES Indian 89%. *Ajay* (2), *Arvind* (2), *Ashok* (2), *Kirit* (2), *Mohan* (2), *Prahlad* (2), *Prakash* (2), *Ram* (2), *Ramesh* (2), *Seema* (2), *Sunil* (2), *Suresh* (2).

Chaudhary (260) Indian (Bengal) and Bangladeshi: variant of CHOWDHURY.

GIVEN NAMES Muslim 50%; Indian 38%. *Mohammad* (9), *Abdul* (4), *Saleem* (4), *Khalid* (3), *Muhammad* (3), *Riaz* (3), *Ali* (2), *Imtiaz* (2), *Javed* (2), *Kamal* (2), *Mujeeb* (2), *Nazir* (2); *Bharat* (3), *Anand* (2), *Ashok* (2), *Chhaya* (2), *Kiran* (2), *Narendra* (2), *Naveen* (2), *Neeraj* (2), *Ravi* (2), *Sanjay* (2), *Shiv* (2), *Vinod* (2).

Chaudhry (642) Indian (Bengal) and Bangladeshi: variant of CHOWDHURY.

GIVEN NAMES Muslim 76%; Indian 14%. *Mohammad* (25), *Abdul* (21), *Muhammad* (17), *Khalid* (8), *Saeed* (8), *Mohammed* (7), *Aslam* (6), *Farooq* (6), *Arshad* (5), *Iqbal* (5), *Maqsood* (5), *Tahir* (5); *Vijay* (4), *Anup* (3), *Asim* (3), *Amit* (2), *Anand* (2), *Anil* (2), *Lalit* (2), *Prem* (2), *Sanjay* (2), *Subhash* (2), *Suneel* (2), *Suresh* (2).

Chaudhuri (148) Indian (Bengal) and Bangladeshi: variant of CHOWDHURY.

GIVEN NAMES Indian 84%. *Swapan* (4), *Asok* (2), *Minu* (2), *Mohan* (2), *Prabir* (2), *Santanu* (2), *Sharmila* (2), *Tarun* (2), *Ajit* (2), *Anand, Anil, Arjun.*

Chaudoin (224) Probably a variant of French **Jaudouin** (see JODOIN).

Chaudoir (119) French: from a shortened form of *échaudoir* 'scalding vat', possibly applied as a metonymic occupational name for a butcher.

GIVEN NAME French 5%. *Patrice*.

Chaudry (133) Indian (Bengal) and Bangladeshi: variant of CHOWDHURY.

GIVEN NAMES Muslim 82%; Indian 6%. *Mohammad* (7), *Javaid* (3), *Kassim* (3), *Khalid* (3), *Abdul* (3), *Irshad* (3), *Muhammad* (2), *Rafiq* (2), *Shaheen* (2), *Tariq* (2), *Abdul Hamid, Adil, Alam; Anil, Asim, Ramesh, Shanti*.

Chauhan (273) Indian (northern states): Hindu (Rajput) and Sikh name of great and ancient prestige but unknown meaning. There is a legend that the ancestor of this Rajput clan emerged from a sacrificial fire with four arms, and so it was associated with the Sanskrit word *chatur-* meaning 'four', but this is no more than folk etymology. Chauhan kings ruled in Rajasthan and in neighboring states, and conquered Delhi and its neighborhood in the 12th century. The Chauhans, along with the Solankis, the Paramaras, and the Partharas, call themselves *Agnikulas* 'Fire Tribes'. According to the Agnikula legend, after the original Kshatriyas had been exterminated by Parashurama (see ARORA), the Brahmans found themselves in need of protection from the demons that were harassing them, and so they prayed and made a special sacrifice to the god Shiva for assistance. Then, through divine intercession, there emerged from the sacrificial fire the ancestors of the four Rajput clans known as the Fire Tribes, and they vanquished the demons. Historians believe that these tribes were in reality foreign tribes that entered India and defeated the original Kshatriyas. As they became the staunch defenders of the Hindu ideals, they were admitted into the prestigious Kshatriya rank by the Brahmans. A clan of the Porwal Banias have also adopted this name and, because of the prestige associated with it, it has been adopted in many other communities as well.

GIVEN NAMES Indian 88%. *Vijay* (5), *Rajesh* (4), *Rohit* (3), *Sandip* (3), *Vinod* (3), *Amul* (2), *Arun* (2), *Bharat* (2), *Chitra* (2), *Dipak* (2), *Hemraj* (2), *Lakhbir* (2).

Chaumont (116) French: habitational name from any of numerous places called Chaumont 'bald mountain', for example in Cher, Jura, Haute-Savoie, etc.

GIVEN NAMES French 11%; Spanish 8%. *Berchman, Curley, Gilles, Raoul, Yvon; Alicia* (2), *Andres, Arturo, Beatriz, Elia, Jose, Julio, Miguel, Raul*.

Chauncey (583) English: variant of CHANCEY.

Chausse (232) French: **1.** from Old French *chausse* 'footwear' or 'leggings' (Late Latin *calcia*, for classical Latin *calceus* 'sandal', 'shoe'), hence a metonymic occupational name for a maker of shoes or leggings, or a nickname for a wearer of distinctive ones. In medieval Europe this term was used very widely, and denoted boots, shoes, leggings, leg armor, gaiters, hose, breeches, pantaloons, and so on; its modern descendants include French *chaussures* 'shoes' and *chaussettes* 'socks'. **2.** from the same root as above, the past participle *chaussé*, designating, in a rural area, a person distinctive in wearing leggings when bare legs were more common.

GIVEN NAMES French 12%. *Armand, Dominique, Henri, Lucien, Marcel, Maxime, Pierre*.

Chaussee (203) French (**Chaussée**): topographic name for someone who lived by a paved road, French *chaussée*, a relatively rare feature of the medieval countryside. The term is from Latin *(via) calciata* 'limed (way)', from *calx* 'chalk', 'limestone', genitive *calcis*. This word has also been used in naming a number of French villages, and the surname may be a habitational name from any one of these.

FOREBEARS There was a Chaussé from the Périgord region of France, also known as Lemeine, documented in L'Islet, Quebec, in 1681.

Chauvette (114) French: from a diminutive of *chauve* 'bald' (see CHAUVIN).

GIVEN NAMES French 12%. *Emile, Laurier, Normand*.

Chauvin (1495) French: diminutive of **Chauve**, a nickname for a bald man, from Old French *chauf* 'bald' (Latin *calvus*).

FOREBEARS A Chauvin from the Maine region of France is documented in Quebec city in 1647, with the secondary surname Ste. Suzanne. Another Chauvin family, from Anjou, represented by 'Grand' Pierre Chauvin, was in Montreal by 1653. Three of his sons were with Jean-Baptise Le Moyne, Sieur de Bienville, in Biloxi in 1700, and a fourth joined them in 1706. They settled in New Orleans, where their descendants achieved great prominence. Some adopted secondary surnames which in due course superseded the Chauvin name, for example **(De) Léry, (De) La Frenière**, and **(De) Beaulieu**.

GIVEN NAMES French 8%. *Armand* (4), *Andre* (3), *Marcel* (3), *Michel* (3), *Anatole* (2), *Camille* (2), *Emile* (2), *Lucien* (2), *Raoul* (2), *Amedee, Angelle, Dany*.

Chavana (103) Spanish: unexplained; perhaps related to Occitan *chabana* 'hut'.

GIVEN NAMES Spanish 45%. *Humberto* (2), *Justo* (2), *Rosalinda* (2), *Ruben* (2), *Adan, Adela, Ademar, Adolfo, Concha, Eladia, Erasmo, Ernestina*.

Chavanne (109) French: variant of **Chabane**, a topographic name from *cabane* 'hut' (from Latin *capanna*), or a habitational name from a place named with this word.

GIVEN NAMES French 8%. *Jean Pierre, Monique*.

Chavarin (160) **1.** Spanish (**Chavarín**, common in Mexico): unexplained; perhaps a derivative from *chavar* 'to bother' (Puerto Rico). The surname is not documented in Spain. **2.** French: possibly an eastern derivative of Old French *chaver* 'to dig'.

GIVEN NAMES Spanish 65%. *Jesus* (6), *Jose* (5), *Juan* (3), *Manuel* (3), *Rigoberto* (3), *Araceli* (2), *Luis* (2), *Maria Elena* (2), *Miguel* (2), *Ramon* (2), *Ramona* (2), *Ruben* (2).

Chavarria (1470) Spanish (**Chavarría**): variant of ECHEVARRIA.

GIVEN NAMES Spanish 47%. *Jose* (44), *Juan* (24), *Miguel* (13), *Carlos* (12), *Jesus* (12), *Francisco* (9), *Manuel* (9), *Raul* (9), *Alfredo* (8), *Jorge* (8), *Pedro* (8), *Ruben* (8).

Chavera (91) Spanish: from a feminine form of *chavero* 'bunch of keys', hence perhaps a metonymic occupational name for a chatelaine. Compare CLAVER.

GIVEN NAMES Spanish 56%. *Jesus* (2), *Jose* (2), *Santiago* (2), *Alejos, Amando, Anacleto, Arnoldo, Carlos, Cristina, Cruz, Efrin, Elvira*.

Chavers (840) Variant of Irish and English CHIVERS.

Chaves (1344) **1.** Portuguese: habitational name from a place in the province of Trasos-Montes named Chaves, from Latin *(aquis) Flaviis*, '(at the) waters of Flavius'. The place was the site of sulfurous springs with supposedly health-giving properties, around which a settlement was founded in the 1st century AD by the Emperor Vespasian. **2.** Portuguese and Galician: habitational name from any of numerous places called Chaves, generally from the plural of *chave* 'key', from Latin *clavis*. **3.** Variant of Irish and English CHIVERS. Compare CHAVERS.

GIVEN NAMES Spanish 32%; Portuguese 14%. *Jose* (60), *Manuel* (39), *Luis* (10), *Carlos* (9), *Juan* (6), *Roberto* (5), *Ruben* (5), *Cesar* (4), *Francisco* (4), *Jesus* (4), *Jorge* (4), *Mario* (4); *Joao* (5), *Paulo* (3), *Agostinho, Duarte, Goncalo, Ilidio, Ligia, Vasco; Antonio* (40), *Angelo* (3), *Mauro* (2), *Aldo, Caesar, Geronimo, Marco, Marino, Raimondo*.

Chavez (22835) Spanish (**Chávez**): variant spelling of CHAVES.

GIVEN NAMES Spanish 44%. *Jose* (540), *Juan* (256), *Manuel* (241), *Carlos* (183), *Jesus* (149), *Francisco* (126), *Luis* (121), *Miguel* (117), *Ramon* (98), *Rafael* (94), *Jorge* (90), *Pedro* (87).

Chavira (713) Hispanic (Mexico): unexplained.

GIVEN NAMES Spanish 50%. *Jose* (17), *Jesus* (14), *Manuel* (13), *Carlos* (8), *Francisco* (6), *Roberto* (6), *Ruben* (6), *Juan* (5), *Fernando* (4), *Ignacio* (4), *Jose Luis* (4), *Luz* (4).

Chavis (3201) **1.** Portuguese or Spanish: variant of CHAVES. **2.** Variant of Irish and English CHIVERS. **3.** The name is also associated with PeeDee Indian origin.

Chavous (242) Variant of Irish and English CHIVERS.

Chawla (386) Indian (Panjab): Hindu (Arora) and Sikh name, based on the name of a clan in the Arora community, which is apparently named with *čāwəl* 'rice'.
GIVEN NAMES Indian 89%. *Sanjay* (7), *Rajesh* (6), *Rajeev* (5), *Raj* (4), *Satish* (4), *Amar* (3), *Arvind* (3), *Ashok* (3), *Harish* (3), *Jag* (3), *Jagdish* (3), *Madhu* (3).

Chay (141) **1.** Korean: variant of CHAE. **2.** Hawaiian: unexplained. **3.** Hispanic (Guatemala and Mexico): unexplained; perhaps a variant spelling of CHE.
GIVEN NAMES Korean 14%. *Beng, Duck, Heng, Ilsoo, In, Seung, Seung Jae, Sin, Sok, Wan, Wing Kin, Won*.

Chaya (101) Origin unidentified.
GIVEN NAMES Muslim 9%; Spanish 4%. *Gazi, Ibrahim, Izzat, Karim, Nabih, Siham, Walid; Ramon* (2).

Chayer (115) French: according to Morlet, a derivative of **Chaye**, which represents Latin *cavea* 'cave', as found in the name of the church Saint-Crespin-en-Chaye at Soissons, Aisne.
GIVEN NAMES French 7%. *Phillippe* (2), *Pierre*.

Chazen (152) Jewish: status name for a cantor in a synagogue, Hebrew *chazan*.
GIVEN NAME Jewish 7%. *Aron*.

Che (268) **1.** Chinese 车: from a word meaning 'cart'. During the Han dynasty (206 BC–220 AD) there was a prime minister who became to old to walk very far unaided, so he had himself brought to and from work in a cart, and became known as 'Prime Minister Cart'. His descendants adopted the character for cart as their surname. **2.** Chinese 谢: variant of XIE 1. **3.** Vietnamese: unexplained. **4.** Korean: variant of CHAE. **5.** Spanish: from a pet form of the personal name *José*.
GIVEN NAMES Chinese/Korean 49%; Vietnamese 20%; Spanish 12%. *Wai Man* (3), *Ming* (2), *Sang* (2), *Song* (2), *Yuan* (2), *Chae, Duck, Hong, Hsiao, Hui-Wen, Jianwei, Jingbo; Hien* (2), *Hung* (2), *Khanh* (2), *Minh* (2), *Thanh* (2), *Anh, Cau, Chi Thi, Hoa Van, Liet, Linh, Mai; Chong, Chung, Manh, Mi Young, Phong, Shen, Sun Ja, Tuong; Anbrocio, Anica, Domingo, Jose, Juan, Pedro, Sevastian, Toribio, Ysidoro*.

Chea (453) Cambodian: unexplained.
GIVEN NAMES Cambodian 45%. *Seng* (5), *Hong* (4), *Eng* (3), *Khun* (3), *Kong* (3), *Han* (2), *Kheng* (2), *Leng* (2), *Sambath* (2), *Soeun* (2), *Sok* (2), *Sokhom* (2); *Yom* (2), *Chang, Hak, Hu, Kum, Savuth, Vong, Yeong; Leang* (4), *Samnang* (2), *Saroeun* (2), *Thon* (2), *Hen, Houng, Keang, Khoanh, Khon, Ky, Long, Ly; Huot* (2), *Vuthy* (2), *Chay, Chheang, Chhun, Khamma, Savoeun, Sophat, Sophath, Soun, Sovann*.

Cheadle (428) English: habitational name from places in Cheshire and Staffordshire named Cheadle, from Celtic *cēd* 'wood' + Old English *lēah* 'woodland clearing'.

Cheah (122) Chinese 谢: variant of XIE 1.
GIVEN NAMES Chinese: 34%. *Poh* (3), *Chun Wah* (2), *Siew* (2), *Chuan, Haiping, Hui, Leong, Mei, Ngan Ying, Sin, Soo, Sui Ling, Swee, Wee*.

Cheairs (135) Americanized form of **de la Chare**, a French Huguenot name of uncertain derivation. It may be a habitational name from Croix-de-la-Chaire, a district of Genis-Terrenoire.

Cheak (122) English: variant spelling of CHEEK.

Cheaney (190) English: variant of CHENEY.

Cheatham (4085) English: variant spelling of CHEETHAM.

Cheatle (114) English: variant of CHEADLE.

Cheatum (182) Altered spelling of English CHEETHAM.

Cheatwood (657) English: probably a variant of **Chetwode** (see CHITWOOD).

Checchi (108) Italian: patronymic from *Checcho*, a variant of *Cecco* (see CECCHI).
GIVEN NAMES Italian 9%; French 5%. *Gino, Giordano, Mauro; Gabrielle, Pierre*.

Check (833) **1.** Possibly an Americanized spelling of Czech and Slovak **Čech** (see CECH), or other Slavic or German ethnic names for a Czech. **2.** English: unexplained.

Checketts (171) English (Worcestershire): unexplained.

Checkley (101) English: habitational name from any of various places called Checkley, in Cheshire, Herefordshire, and Staffordshire. The first is named from an Old English personal name *Ceaddica* + *lēah* 'woodland clearing'; the other two have the same second element, combined with an Old English personal name *Ceacca* or Old English *ceacce* 'hill'.

Checo (113) Spanish: probably an ethnic name from *checo* 'Czech'.
GIVEN NAMES Spanish 59%. *Ramon* (6), *Jose* (5), *Ana* (3), *Rafael* (3), *Juan* (2), *Luis* (2), *Luisa* (2), *Mercedes* (2), *Ramona* (2), *Reina* (2), *Amarilis, Artemio*.

Chedester (128) American variant of English CHICHESTER.

Chee (603) **1.** Navajo: unexplained. **2.** Chinese: variant Romanization of QI. **3.** Korean: variant of CHI.
GIVEN NAMES Chinese/Korean 9%. *Kam* (4), *Cheng* (2), *Yong* (2), *Chan, Cheon, Chia, Chiang, Chow, Fong, Fung, Hon, Hong*.

Cheek (5891) Southern English: from Middle English *cheeke* (Old English *cē(a)ce*), used as a nickname for someone with some deformity or scar in the region of the cheek or jawbone.

Cheeks (806) Probably a variant of CHEEK, although this form does not appear in English sources.

Cheeley (135) Of German origin: see CHEELY.

Cheely (205) Americanized spelling of South German SCHIELE or Swiss German **Schieli**.

Cheema (214) Indian (Panjab): Sikh name based on the name of a Jat clan.
GIVEN NAMES Muslim 48%; Indian 38%. *Mohammad* (6), *Muhammad* (4), *Mushtaq* (4), *Zahid* (3), *Abdul* (2), *Arshad* (2), *Mohammed* (2), *Muhammed* (2), *Saeed* (2), *Saif* (2), *Yusuf* (2), *Akram; Jag* (2), *Tej* (2), *Ajit, Amritpal, Balwinder, Gurpal, Lakhbir, Mohan, Nirmal, Priya, Ravi, Vinita*.

Cheers (207) English: from a personal name or nickname from Old French *chier*, *cher* 'dear', 'precious'.

Cheeseman (807) English: occupational name for a maker or seller of cheese, from Old English *cȳse*, *cēse* 'cheese' (Latin *caseus*) + *mann* 'man'.

Cheesman (675) English: variant of CHEESEMAN.

Cheetham (341) English: habitational name from a place in Lancashire called Cheetham, apparently named with Celtic *cēd* 'wood' + Old English *hām* 'homestead'.

Cheever (872) English: from Anglo-Norman French *chivere*, *chevre* 'goat' (Latin *capra* 'nanny goat'), applied as a nickname for an unpredictable or temperamental person, or a metonymic occupational name for a goatherd.
FOREBEARS Born in London in about 1614, the son of spinner William Cheaver, Ezekiel Cheever came to Boston in June 1637. After a brief sojourn in New Haven, CT, he was master of the Boston Latin School from 1670 until his death in 1708. He had twelve children; his youngest son, also called Ezekiel, was the clerk to the court in the infamous Salem witchcraft trials of 1692.

Cheevers (157) English: patronymic from CHEEVER. This name has also been long established in Ireland.

Cheff (163) Probably a respelling of French **Chef**, from Old French *chef* 'head'. See also CAP.

Chelette (319) North American form of French **Chelet**, which is perhaps a variant of GILLETTE, or alternatively a variant of **Chalet** 'house', either a topographic name or habitational name from any of the various places called Le Chalet or Les Chalets.
GIVEN NAMES French 4%. *Emile, Honore, Marcelle*.

Chelf (296) Origin unidentified.

Chelius (144) German: humanistic name adopted in the early 16th century by Pankratius Chelius, Lutheran pastor of Oberwiddersheim, Hesse. His original German name was *Kiste*, a metonymic occupational name for a maker of chests or boxes.

Chellis (214) Of uncertain origin. **1.** Possibly Italian: from the personal name *Chello*, a short form of *Rustichello*, itself a pet form of a nickname from *rustico* 'country dweller', 'rustic'. **2.** English: unexplained.

Chelton (121) English: perhaps a variant of CHILTON.

Chen (21725) Chinese 陈: from name of the region of Chen (in present-day Henan province). After overthrowing the Shang dynasty and becoming the first king of the Zhou dynasty in 1122 BC, Wu Wang searched for a descendant of the great ancient emperors to guard their memory and offer sacrifices, to help retain the 'Mandate of Heaven', which was considered essential to remain in power. He found Gui Man, a descendant of the model emperor Shun (2257–2205 BC), and granted him the region of Chen, along with the title Marquis of Chen and one of his daughters in marriage. Gui Man was posthumously named Chen Hugong, and his descendants came to adopt the surname Chen.
GIVEN NAMES Chinese 38%. *Wei* (83), *Jian* (64), *Ming* (58), *Hong* (56), *Li* (47), *Yan* (47), *Wen* (43), *Jing* (41), *Ping* (38), *Ying* (37), *Feng* (36), *Mei* (33).

Chenard (292) French: nickname from Old French *chenes* 'white hair', from Latin *canus* 'white', 'hoary'.
FOREBEARS A bearer of the name Chenard from Limoges is recorded in Beauport, Quebec, in 1752.
GIVEN NAMES French 22%. *Marcel* (5), *Henri* (3), *Gaetan* (2), *Michel* (2), *Alcide, Berthe, Francoise, Gisele, Herve, Jeannot, Monique, Napoleon.*

Chenault (1425) French: topographic name for someone who lived near an irrigation channel, from Old French *chenal* 'channel', 'pipe' (Late Latin *canalis*, a derivative of *canna* 'reed').
FOREBEARS A Chenault from St. Malo, France is documented in Ste-Foy, Quebec, in 1731, with the variant **Chauveau**.

Chene (89) French (**Chêne**): from Old French *chesne* 'oak' (Late Latin *caxinus*), hence a topographic name denoting someone who lived near a conspicuous oak tree or in an oak wood, or perhaps occasionally a nickname for a man with a 'heart of oak'.
GIVEN NAMES French 19%. *Alain, Andre, Armand, Jean Michel, Marcel, Pierre.*

Chenery (104) English (of Norman origin): possibly a habitational name from Chenevray in Haute-Saône, France.

Chenette (188) Respelling of French **Chenet**, from a diminutive of Old French *chesne* 'oak' (see CHENE).
GIVEN NAMES French 8%. *Lucien* (2), *Armand.*

Chenevert (504) French: topographic for someone who lived 'by the green oak', from Old French *chesne* 'oak' (see CHENE) + *vert* 'green'.
GIVEN NAMES French 6%. *Theophile* (3), *Andre, Gesner, Ovide, Pierre.*

Cheney (5260) **1.** English: variant of CHESNEY. **2.** French: habitational name

from a place in Yonne, which takes its name from a Romano-Gallic estate, *Caniacum* 'estate of a man named *Canius*', from the Roman personal name + the locative suffix *-acum.*

Cheng (6220) **1.** Chinese 郑: variant of ZHENG. **2.** Chinese 程: from the name of the area of Cheng during the Shang dynasty (1766–1122 BC). A high adviser who was a descendant of the legendary emperor Zhuan Xu was granted the fiefdom of this area, and his descendants adopted its name as their surname. **3.** Chinese 成: from the name of the state of Cheng during the Zhou dynasty (1122–221 BC). The fifth son of Wen Wang was granted lordship of the state of Cheng following the fall of the Shang dynasty and the establishment of the Zhou dynasty. Subsequently, his descendants adopted the place name as their surname.
GIVEN NAMES Chinese 30%. *Ming* (15), *Kin* (14), *Wing* (14), *Ping* (13), *Wai* (11), *Chi* (10), *Wei* (10), *Yan* (10), *Hong* (8), *Kam* (8), *Ying* (8), *Chin* (7).

Chenier (358) French (**Chénier**): topographic name for someone who lived by an oak wood or in area characterized by oak trees; from a derivative of Old French *chesne* 'oak' (see CHENE).
FOREBEARS A bearer of the name Chenier from the Saintonge region was documented in Quebec city in 1651.
GIVEN NAMES French 8%. *Antoine, Fernand, Gaston, Gisele, Lucien, Normand, Osborn.*

Chennault (302) Respelling of French CHENAULT.

Chenot (119) French: from a diminutive of Old French *chesne* 'oak' (see CHENE).
GIVEN NAMES French 10%. *Armand* (2), *Albert Louis, Andre.*

Chenoweth (1908) Cornish: topographic name from the elements *chy* 'house' + *noweth* 'new'.

Chenowith (123) Cornish: variant spelling of CHENOWETH.

Cheong (360) **1.** Chinese 张: Cantonese variant of ZHANG 1. **2.** Chinese 章: Cantonese variant of ZHANG 2. **3.** Korean: variant of **Chǒng** (see CHONG).
GIVEN NAMES Chinese/Korean 42%. *Man* (2), *Yong* (2), *Young* (2), *Chan, Chang Yun, Chao, Cheok, Dong, Eui, Eunjoo, Fong, Fook; Deok* (3), *Kwang Yong* (2), *Weng* (2), *Yuet* (2), *Cho, Kok, Seok, Seungil.*

Cheramie (831) Variant spelling, frequent in LA, of French **Cheramy**, a nickname from *cher* 'dear' + *ami* 'friend', not perhaps for someone who was a 'dear friend' so much as for someone who used the expression a great deal.
FOREBEARS The LA families trace their origin to one Joseph Cheramy, or Cheramie, from Brittany, who married an Acadian refugee, and appears in the records of New Orleans in 1785.

GIVEN NAMES French 5%. *Antoine* (2), *Camille, Celestine, Dumas, Gabrielle, Ludger, Marcel, Monique, Noemie.*

Cherek (126) Americanized spelling of a Slavic name, possibly Polish **Czerek** or **Czyrek**, a nickname from *czyr* 'gnarl on a tree' or 'insect larva', or more probably from czyryk 'chirp', applied to someone with a voice thought to resemble that of a sparrow.

Cherian (244) Indian (Kerala): derivative of Hebrew-Aramaic *Zecharya* (see ZACHARIAS), and variant of ZACHARIAS among Kerala Christians. The final *-n* is the Malayalam third-person masculine singular suffix. In India it is found only as a given name, but in the U.S. it is also used as a family name among families from Kerala.
GIVEN NAMES Indian 37%. *Babu* (3), *Oommen* (2), *Shaji* (2), *Sunil* (2), *Varughese* (2), *Biju, Binny, Eapen, Jaya, Jayan, Mathai, Ninan; Yohannan* (2), *Miriam.*

Cherico (192) Italian: probably a variant spelling of **Chierico**, an occupational name for a cleric, from Latin *clericus.*
GIVEN NAMES Italian 4%. *Gennaro, Pasquale.*

Cherin (110) Anglicized spelling of Slovenian *Čerin*, proboably a topographic name derived from *čer* 'crag'.

Cherkas (104) Jewish (eastern Ashkenazic): habitational name from the city of Cherkassy in Ukraine.
GIVEN NAME Jewish 7%. *Revekka.*

Chermak (278) Americanized spelling of Czech **Čermák** (see CERMAK).
GIVEN NAMES German 4%. *Alois, Dieter, Erwin, Otto.*

Chern (195) **1.** Austrian (Styria): probably from Slovenian **Černe** (see CERNE). **2.** Chinese 陈: variant of CHEN 1.
GIVEN NAMES Chinese 10%. *Chyi* (2), *Mou* (2), *Bin, Guan, Jong, Kuo, Lih, Rong, Shyh, Sung, Swee, Yao Hui.*

Cherne (176) Americanized spelling of Slovenian **Černe** 'black', 'dark' (see CERNE) or Czech **Černý** (see CERNY), or of German **Tscherne**, a Germanized form of the Czech or Slovenian name.

Cherner (121) Jewish (eastern Ashkenazic): nickname from a derivative of Slavic *černy* 'black', 'dark'.
GIVEN NAMES Jewish 12%; Russian 5%. *Meyer, Tsilya, Yakov; Gennady, Iosif, Pinya, Yelena.*

Chernesky (125) Americanized spelling of a Slavic habitational name, perhaps of Czech or Slovak origin, from an unidentified place named with Czech *černý*, Slovak *čierny* 'black', or from the Polish habitational name **Czerniecki**, denoting someone from Czerniec in Nowy Sącz province.

Cherney (788) Americanized spelling of Czech **Černý** (see CERNY), Ukrainian **Černej**, or some other Slavic name meaning 'black', probably denoting someone with a swarthy complexion or dark hair.

Cherniak (102) Americanized spelling of a Slavic name meaning 'black'. Compare CERNIK and Polish CZARNIAK.

GIVEN NAMES Slavic 4%. *Arkadi, Vlad.*

Chernick (284) **1.** Jewish (Eastern Ashkenazic): nickname from an eastern Slavic word meaning 'black', 'dark' (see CHORNEY). The suffix *-ik* is a Slavic noun ending. **2.** Americanized form of Czech, Slovak, and Jewish **Černík**, nickname meaning 'the black one', 'the dark one'. **3.** Americanized form of Slovenian **Černic** or **Černič**, nicknames derived from *črn* 'black', 'dark'.

GIVEN NAMES Jewish 7%. *Isadore* (2), *Sarra, Shulamith.*

Chernin (209) **1.** Respelling of Czech **Černín**, from a derivative of *černý* 'black', 'sable' (see CERNA), or alternatively a habitational name for someone from Černice or some other place named with this word. **2.** Jewish (from Belarus): metronymic from the eastern Yiddish female personal name *Tsherne*, derived from Slavic *černy* 'black'.

GIVEN NAMES Jewish 12%; Russian 7%. *Aron* (2), *Sol* (2), *Isaak, Ophir, Yakov; Arkadiy, Arkady, Boris, Igor, Lev, Mikhail, Vladimir, Yevgeny.*

Chernoff (479) Russian and Jewish (from Belarus and Ukraine): alternative spelling of **Chernov**, a patronymic from the byname *Chernyj* 'black', denoting a black-haired or dark-skinned person.

GIVEN NAMES Jewish 5%. *Chaim, Isadore, Shulamith, Sol.*

Chernow (172) Variant spelling, under Polish influence, of Russian and Jewish **Chernov** (see CHERNOFF).

Cherny (166) **1.** Americanized spelling of Ukrainian **Černij**, Czech **Černý** (see CERNY), or some other Slavic name meaning 'black'. **2.** Jewish (eastern Ashkenazic): variant of CHORNEY.

GIVEN NAMES Russian 7%. *Anatoli, Galina, Grigoriy, Michail, Vladimir.*

Cherrier (142) French: variant of CHARRIER.

GIVEN NAMES French 9%. *Andre, Jean-Claude, Jean-Guy, Michel, Pascal.*

Cherrington (322) English: habitational name from any of various places called Cherington or Cherrington. Cherrington in Shropshire is probably named from the Old English personal name *Ceorra* + *-ing-* denoting association (or alternatively from Old English *cerring* 'river bend') + *tūn* 'settlement', 'estate', but others (Cherington in Gloucestershire and Cherrington in Warwickshire) are from Old English *cyrice* 'church' + *tūn*. Places called Cheriton in Devon, Hampshire, Kent, and Somerset also have this last etymology.

Cherry (11150) **1.** English: from Middle English *chirie, cherye* 'cherry', hence a metonymic occupational name for a grower or seller of cherries, or possibly a nickname for someone with rosy cheeks. **2.** Probably in some cases a translation name of German KIRSCH.

Chertok (101) Jewish (from Belarus): nickname for a wicked man, a diminutive form of eastern Slavic *chort, chert* 'devil'.

GIVEN NAMES Russian 11%; Jewish 11%. *Arcady, Boris, Lev, Raisa, Yefim, Yelena, Yury; Aron, Fira, Genya, Rakhil.*

Cherubin (104) French (**Chérubin**): nickname from Old French *chérubin* 'cherub', from ecclesiastical Latin *cherubin*.

GIVEN NAMES French 18%; Italian 5%; Polish 4%. *Sylvie* (2), *Dieudonne, Oge, Pascale; Giampaolo* (2); *Tadeusz.*

Cherubini (178) Italian: from the personal name *Cherubino*, from *cherubino* 'cherub', or a nickname from the same word.

GIVEN NAMES Italian 11%. *Guido* (2), *Angelo, Carlo, Domenic, Giorgio, Lorenzo, Marco.*

Chervenak (222) Americanized spelling of Slovak **Červenák** and Hungarian **Cservenák** (from Slovak), from a derivative of Slovak *červený* 'red', 'ruddy' (see CERVENY).

Chervenka (102) Americanized spelling of Czech **Červenka** (see CERVENKA).

Cherveny (134) Americanized spelling of Czech and Slovak **Červený** (see CERVENY).

Chery (323) French (**Chéry**): from a word meaning 'darling', perhaps used ironically. It is also the name of several places, deriving from the Latin *Cariacus* 'land belonging to Carius'.

GIVEN NAMES French 49%. *Pierre* (5), *Yves* (3), *Michel* (2), *Yolene* (2), *Altagrace, Andre, Antoine, Catheline, Claudel, Francois, Germaine, Jacques.*

Chesbro (239) Variant of English CHESBROUGH.

Chesbrough (133) English: habitational name from Cheeseburn in Northumberland, recorded in 1286 as *Cheseburgh*, possibly from Old English *cis* 'gravel' + *burh* 'stronghold'.

Chesebro (295) Variant of English CHESBROUGH.

Chesher (197) Variant spelling of English CHESHIRE.

Cheshier (395) Variant spelling of English CHESHIRE.

Cheshire (1154) English: regional name for someone from the county of Cheshire in northwestern England, the name of which is recorded in Domesday Book as *Cestrescire*, from the name of the county seat, CHESTER, + Old English *scīr* 'district', 'division'.

Chesky (144) Jewish (Ashkenazic): ethnic name for a Czech.

Chesla (107) Americanized spelling of Polish **Cieśla** (see CIESLA).

Chesler (404) Americanized spelling of Polish **Cieśla** (see CIESLA).

Chesley (1095) **1.** English: habitational name from a place in Kent named Chesley, from the Old English personal name *Cæcca* + Old English *lēah* 'woodland clearing'. **2.** Possibly an Americanized form of German **Schüssler** (see SCHUESSLER).

Cheslock (265) Americanized spelling of Polish CIESLIK or German **Tscheslog**, a surname of Slavic origin.

Chesmore (159) **1.** English: apparently a habitational name from a lost or unidentified place. **2.** Perhaps an Americanized spelling of German **Tschismar** (see CHISMAR), or of CHIZMAR.

Chesna (103) Variant of English and Irish CHESNEY.

Chesney (1576) English, northern Irish, and French: topographic name for someone who lived by or in an oak wood, from Old French *chesnai* 'oak grove'.

Chesnick (102) Jewish (eastern Ashkenazic): from an eastern Slavic word meaning 'garlic' (e.g. Russian *chesnok*, Ukrainian *chosnyk*), either a nickname or a metonymic occupational name.

Chesnut (1319) English: variant spelling of CHESTNUT.

Chesnutt (400) English: variant spelling of CHESTNUT.

Chess (658) English (Gloucestershire): unexplained.

Chesser (1999) English: variant of CHESHIRE.

Chessher (166) English: variant spelling of CHESHIRE.

Chesshir (147) English: variant spelling of CHESHIRE.

Chessman (150) English: variant of CHEESEMAN.

Chesson (575) **1.** English: unexplained. **2.** French: variant of CHIASSON.

Chessor (132) Variant of English CHESHIRE.

Chestang (158) French: variant of **Chastang**, itself a variant of CHASTAIN.

GIVEN NAMES French 5%. *Alphonse, Andre, Pierre.*

Chester (5000) English: habitational name from Chester, the county seat of Cheshire, or from any of various smaller places named with this word (as for example Little Chester in Derbyshire or Chester le Street in County Durham), which is from Old English *ceaster* 'Roman fort or walled city' (Latin *castra* 'legionary camp').

Chesterfield (135) English: habitational name from a place in Derbyshire named Chesterfield, from Old English *ceaster* 'Roman fort' + *feld* 'open country'.

Chesterman (166) English: possibly a topographic name for someone who lived by a Roman fort, Old English *ceaster*, or a habitational name for someone from any of the places mentioned at CHESTER.

Chestnut (2478) English: from early English *chesten nut* 'chestnut' (from Middle English *chesteine* 'chestnut' + *nut*), a topographic name for someone who lived by a chestnut tree, or possibly a nickname for someone with chestnut-colored hair.

Chestnutt (261) Variant spelling of English CHESTNUT.

Cheston (135) English: habitational name, perhaps from a place in Devon called Cheston, although the surname is found mainly in East Anglia rather than Devon.

Cheung (3699) **1.** Chinese 张: variant of ZHANG 1. **2.** Chinese 章: variant of ZHANG 2. **3.** Chinese 蔣: variant of JIANG.

GIVEN NAMES Chinese 35%. *Wai* (28), *Wing* (22), *Kwok* (17), *Kam* (15), *Ming* (15), *Kin* (14), *Man* (13), *Chi* (10), *Chun* (10), *Ping* (10), *Ying* (7), *Yuk* (7); *Chung* (5), *Pak* (5), *Shiu* (3), *Yiu* (3), *Nam* (2), *Sik* (2), *Yuet* (2), *Byung Chul, Chong, Choon, Dong Ho, Jaeho.*

Cheuvront (264) Possibly of French origin: unexplained.

Chevalier (2092) French: from Old French *chevalier* 'knight' (literally 'horseman', 'rider', from Late Latin *caballarius*, a derivative of *caballus* 'horse'). In the Middle Ages only men of comparative wealth were able to afford the upkeep of a riding horse. It is likely that in the majority of cases the surname was originally a nickname, or an occupational name for a knight's servant, rather than a status name, for most men of the knightly class belonged to noble families which had more specific surnames derived from their estates.

FOREBEARS A bearer of the name from Anjou is documented in 1656 in Quebec city; and another, from Rouen, is recorded in Montreal in 1670.

GIVEN NAMES French 9%. *Andre* (8), *Pierre* (4), *Patrice* (3), *Serge* (3), *Gabrielle* (2), *Jacques* (2), *Marcel* (2), *Michel* (2), *Raoul* (2), *Sylvain* (2), *Adelore, Antoine.*

Chevallier (128) French: variant of CHEVALIER.

GIVEN NAMES French 9%; Jewish 4%. *Blanchard, Christophe, Francois; Hershel.*

Cheves (234) **1.** Scottish: perhaps a variant of SHIVES or CHEVIS. **2.** Hispanic (Mexico): variant of CHAVEZ.

FOREBEARS Langdon Cheves (1776–1857), a congressman and financier, was born in Abbeville District, SC. His father was Alexander Chivas, of Buchan, Aberdeenshire, Scotland.

Chevez (141) Variant (**Chévez**) of CHAVEZ.

GIVEN NAMES Spanish 54%. *Jose* (7), *Ana* (4), *Carlos* (3), *Francisco* (3), *Alfredo* (2), *Graciela* (2), *Manuel* (2), *Miguel* (2), *Ruben* (2), *Abelino, Abimael, Alba.*

Chevis (108) English: from Middle English *cheuyn*, Old French *chevesne* 'chub', possibly applied as a nickname for someone thought to resemble the fish in some way, or as a metonymic occupational name for a fisherman or fish seller.

GIVEN NAMES French 5%. *Cecile, Monique.*

Chevrette (158) French: from a diminutive of *chèvre*, 'goat', probably applied as a nickname.

GIVEN NAMES French 14%. *Aldor, Armand, Emile, Jean-Guy, Lucien, Marcel, Normand, Pascal.*

Chevrier (174) French: occupational name for a goatherd, from an agent derivative of *chèvre* 'goat' (Latin *capra* 'nanny goat').

GIVEN NAMES French 23%. *Armand* (2), *Gilles* (2), *Aurele, Germain, Jacques, Jean-Claude, Manon, Michel, Pierre, Serge, Stephane.*

Chew (2722) **1.** English: habitational name from a place in Somerset named Chew Magna, which is named for the river on which it stands, a Celtic name, perhaps cognate with Welsh *cyw* 'young animal or bird', 'chicken'. **2.** English: habitational name from places called Chew, in West Yorkshire and in the parish of Billington, Lancashire, named with Old English *cēo* 'fish gill', used in the transferred sense of a ravine, in a similar way to Old Norse *gil*. **3.** English: derogatory nickname from Middle English *chowe* 'chough', Old English *cēo*, a bird closely related to the crow and the jackdaw, notorious for its chattering and thieving. **4.** Korean: variant of CHU. **5.** Chinese 赵: variant of ZHAO.

Chewning (978) Americanized form of German SCHOENING.

Cheyne (364) English: topographic name for someone who lived near a conspicuous oak tree, or in an oak wood, from Old French *chesne* 'oak'.

Cheyney (175) English: variant of CHESNEY.

Chez (152) French: from *chez* 'of the house of'. When a man of good lineage or repute became an outlaw this was added before his name to indicate both his status and the family of which he used to be considered a part. In some cases the *chez* was adopted as a surname in its own right and the family name was dropped.

GIVEN NAMES French 22%; Spanish 5%. *Monique* (4), *Andre* (2), *Leonie* (2), *Alain, Michel, Odette, Pascal, Patrice, Sylvain*; *Jose* (2), *Elena, Guillermo, Jorge, Julio, Marianela, Tomas.*

Chezem (148) Americanized form of Scottish CHISHOLM. Compare CHISUM.

Chhabra (172) Indian (Panjab): Hindu (Arora) and Sikh name based on the name of an Arora clan.

GIVEN NAMES Indian 95%. *Ashok* (4), *Om* (4), *Brij* (3), *Dev* (3), *Sandeep* (3), *Vinay* (3), *Ajay* (2), *Amar* (2), *Amita* (2), *Ashim* (2), *Mahesh* (2), *Manoj* (2).

Chhay (131) Cambodian: unexplained.

GIVEN NAMES Cambodian 39%; Other Southeast Asian 24%; Cambodian 12%. *Heng* (2), *Tong* (2), *Vuthy* (2), *Chhoeuth, Chhun, Choeun, Huon, Huot, Phoeun, Samoeun, Sophany, Voeun*; *Chan, Hieng, Him, Hin, Kheng, Khun, Meng, Sek, Seng,*

Siong; *Leang, Mang, Nga, Nguon, Pha, Phon, Saroeun, Son, Tha, Than, Thong.*

Chi (1240) **1.** The Romanization **Chi** represents at least thirteen different Chinese surnames and a Korean one. **2.** Chinese 池: this character means 'pond' and is found in names of lakes and areas surrounding lakes. As many Chinese surnames originated in place names (often containing the word 'pond'), so the surname Chi developed naturally from the word for 'pond'. **3.** Chinese 纪: variant of JI 1. **4.** Chinese 齐: variant of QI 1. **5.** Chinese 祁: variant of QI 2. **6.** Chinese 季: variant of JI 2. **7.** Chinese 姬: variant of JI 3. **8.** Chinese 戚: variant of QI 3. **9.** Chinese 冀: variant of JI 4. **10.** Chinese 姬: variant of JI 5. **11.** Chinese 籍: variant of JI 6. **12.** Chinese 支: variant of **Zhi**. **13.** Chinese 稽: variant of JI 7. **14.** Chinese 计: variant of JI 8. **15.** Korean: There are two Chinese characters for the Chi surname, borne by different groups. The smaller of the two groups has only one clan associated with it, the majority of whose members live in Kangwŏn and Ch'ungch'ŏn North Provinces of South Korea and North Korea's P'yŏngan North Province. The other group also has but one clan but a much larger population. Unlike many clans in Korea, the larger Chi family did not remain congregated in and around its clan seat but dispersed fairly evenly around the peninsula.

GIVEN NAMES Chinese/Korean 43%. *Young* (6), *Dong* (4), *Yun* (4), *Cheng* (3), *Jae* (3), *Yong* (3), *Cheng Chung* (2), *Chi* (2), *Chun* (2), *Duk* (2), *Fang* (2), *Feng* (2); *Chung* (6), *Chong* (3), *Jae Hong* (2), *Moon* (2), *Myong* (2), *Pong* (2), *Shen* (2), *Yoo* (2), *Byung, Chang, Chol, Chong Hun; Phi* (4), *Hung* (2), *Ly* (2), *Tu* (2), *Denh, Do Van, Duong, Hao, Kieu, Mui, Nga, Phat.*

Chia (342) **1.** Chinese 贾: see JIA. **2.** American Indian (Choctaw and other): unexplained. **3.** Spanish (**Chía**): generally a habitational name from Chía in Uesca province, but in some cases possibly a nickname from *chía*, denoting a kind of cape.

GIVEN NAMES Chinese 14%; Spanish 10%. *Li-Li* (2), *Teck* (2), *Chee, Chen, Cheng, Chin, Chu, Der, Foong, Heng, Mei Lan, Mi-Young; Luis* (3), *Jesus* (2), *Mario* (2), *Roberto* (2), *Salvador* (2), *Abelardo, Angeles, Enrique, Eulalio, Imelda, Javier, Juan.*

Chianese (237) Southern Italian: from a southern adjectival form of **Piana**, a habitational name any of numerous places named with *piana* 'plain', as for example Piana di Gioia Tauro in Calabria.

GIVEN NAMES Italian 10%. *Angelo, Domenic, Filomena, Sal.*

Chiang (1915) **1.** Chinese 纪: variant of JIANG 1. **2.** Chinese 蔣: variant of JIANG 2. **3.** Chinese 姜: variant of JIANG 3.

GIVEN NAMES Chinese 26%. *Ming* (7), *Ching* (6), *Chuan* (5), *Kuo* (5), *Wen* (4), *Yung* (4), *Chin* (3), *Fei* (3), *Feng* (3), *Hsin* (3), *Ling* (3), *Pei-Ling* (3).

Chiao (153) **1.** Chinese 焦: variant of JIAO. **2.** Chinese 乔: variant of QIAO.
GIVEN NAMES Chinese 28%. *Hsi* (2), *Meng* (2), *Cheng, Chia, Chu, Hui Ming, I-Chun, Jia, Sheng, Shu-Ying, Xin, Ya*; *Chung* (2), *Chang, Pao.*

Chiappa (147) Southern Italian: topographic name for someone who lived in rocky terrain, from Sicilian *chiappa* 'stone slab'.
GIVEN NAMES Italian 14%. *Attilio* (2), *Angelo, Gino, Giovanni, Italo, Renzo.*

Chiappetta (532) Southern Italian: **1.** diminutive of CHIAPPA. **2.** nickname from a diminutive of the southern dialect word *chiappa* 'buttock'.
GIVEN NAMES Italian 11%. *Rocco* (3), *Aldo* (2), *Domenic* (2), *Enrico* (2), *Lorenzo* (2), *Antonio, Beniamino, Gaspare, Gino, Marco, Salvatore, Vito.*

Chiappini (110) Italian: diminutive of CHIAPPA.
GIVEN NAMES Italian 9%. *Dario, Domenic, Giuseppe, Mauro, Rocco.*

Chiappone (224) Southern Italian: derogatory nickname from Sicilian *chiappuni* 'fat lazy man'.
GIVEN NAMES Italian 13%. *Santo* (3), *Angelo* (2), *Sal* (2), *Aldo, Salvatore.*

Chiara (222) Italian: from the female personal name *Chiara* or *Clara*, a name popularized in the medieval period by the cult of St. Clare of Assisi (c. 1193–1253); she was an associate of St. Francis of Assisi and founded the order of nuns known as the Poor Clares. See also CHIARO.
GIVEN NAMES Italian 10%; French 5%. *Marco* (2), *Amedeo, Angelo, Gino, Rocco*; *Andre, Flore.*

Chiaramonte (424) Italian: habitational name from any of various places called Chiaramonte or from Chiaramonte Gulfi in Ragusa, Sicily.
GIVEN NAMES Italian 17%. *Salvatore* (9), *Sal* (5), *Ceasar* (2), *Dante* (2), *Gasper* (2), *Nunzio* (2), *Angelo, Antonino, Vincenza, Vito, Vittorio.*

Chiarella (282) Italian: diminutive of CHIARA.
GIVEN NAMES Italian 17%. *Aldo, Angelo, Antonio, Costantino, Gerardo, Luigi, Pasquale, Rocco, Sal, Salvatore, Saverio.*

Chiarelli (331) Italian: patronymic or plural form of CHIARELLO.
GIVEN NAMES Italian 25%. *Salvatore* (6), *Giovanni* (3), *Angelo* (2), *Antonio, Carmelo, Eduardo, Elio, Gianfranco, Gustavo, Luciano, Orlando, Sal, Salvator, Ubaldo, Vinicio.*

Chiarello (441) Italian: from a diminutive of the personal name CHIARO.
GIVEN NAMES Italian 12%. *Angelo* (3), *Vito* (3), *Sal* (2), *Antonio, Domenico, Guido,*

Luigi, Nunzio, Reno, Rinaldo, Salvatore, Santo.

Chiarenza (111) Southern Italian: from the female personal name *Chiarenza*, from Latin *Clarentia* meaning 'shining', 'clear'.
GIVEN NAMES Italian 24%. *Angelo* (3), *Antonio, Gasper, Orazio, Roberto.*

Chiaro (203) Italian: from the personal name *Chiaro*, from Latin *Clarus* meaning 'light', 'famous'; alternatively the name may simply have arisen as a nickname from *chiaro* 'fair', 'clear', 'light'.
GIVEN NAMES Italian 13%. *Rocco* (3), *Augustino* (2), *Antonio, Carmelo, Pasquale, Salvatore, Santo.*

Chiasson (1236) French: derogatory nickname from *chiasse* 'excrement'.
FOREBEARS There was a Chiasson or Giasson from La Rochelle, France, documented in Quebec city in 1683; other sources claim a Guyon Chiasson, also known as LaValée, from La Rochelle, who settled in Acadia around 1650 and is the progenitor of the LA families.
GIVEN NAMES French 9%. *Andre* (2), *Fernand* (2), *Marcel* (2), *Rejeanne* (2), *Remy* (2), *Adelard, Aime, Alphie, Anatole, Armand, Aurelie, Camile.*

Chiaverini (120) Italian: from a diminutive of **Chiavaro**, an occupational name for a locksmith, from an agent derivative of *chiave* 'key'.
GIVEN NAMES Italian 18%. *Falco* (2), *Mauro* (2), *Carmine, Gaetano, Primo, Rino, Vito.*

Chiavetta (149) Italian: from *chiavetta*, a diminutive of *chiave* 'key'.
GIVEN NAMES Italian 16%. *Gino* (3), *Amedeo, Quintino, Sal, Santo.*

Chiba (118) Japanese: 'thousand leaves'; habitational name from Chiba-gun in Shimōsa (now part of Chiba prefecture). The Chiba were a branch of the TAIRA clan, and were powerful in Shimōsa from the 12th to 16th centuries.
GIVEN NAMES Japanese 83%. *Akira* (3), *Kazuo* (3), *Yoshi* (3), *Ichiro* (2), *Naoki* (2), *Setsuko* (2), *Takashi* (2), *Aki, Akio, Atsuko, Etsuko, Fumiko.*

Chica (128) Spanish: apparently from *chica*, feminine form of *chico* 'small', 'young' (see CHICO), but a variant of the habitational name **Checa**, from a place so named in Jaén province is also a possibility.
GIVEN NAMES Spanish 50%. *Jose* (6), *Jorge* (4), *Luis* (3), *Manuel* (3), *Orlando* (3), *Alba, Alejandro, Alfonso, Andres, Angel, Arturo, Blanca.*

Chicas (220) Spanish: variant (plural) of CHICA.
GIVEN NAMES Spanish 59%. *Jose* (22), *Carlos* (4), *Juan* (4), *Blanca* (3), *Mauricio* (3), *Atilio* (2), *Francisco* (2), *Manuel* (2), *Miguel* (2), *Miguel Angel* (2), *Pedro* (2), *Ricardo* (2).

Chichester (649) English: habitational name from the city of Chichester in Sussex, probably named with the Old English per-

sonal name *Cissa* + Old English *ceaster* 'Roman fort'. (*Cissa* is attested as the name of a historical person; it is of uncertain etymology.) Alternatively, the first element may be an Old English word *cisse* 'gravelly feature'. The name is also established in Ireland.

Chick (1688) English: **1.** from Middle English *chike* 'young fowl' (a shortened form of *chiken*), applied as a metonymic occupational name for someone who bred poultry for the table, or as a nickname from the same word used as a term of endearment. **2.** variant of CHEEK.

Chickering (437) English: unexplained. It is known that the Chickering(e)s or Chickring(e)s who were in Dedham, MA, by c.1670 were originally from Wrentham, Suffolk. However, only four Chickerings (all in Staffordshire) and one Chickring (from Devon) were recorded in the 1881 British census and the surname since seems to have died out altogether in the British Isles.

Chico (336) **1.** Spanish and Portuguese: from *chico* 'small', 'young' (of uncertain origin, perhaps from Latin *ciccum* 'trifle'), applied as a nickname for a small man, or for the younger of two bearers of the same personal name. **2.** Portuguese: from a pet form of the personal name *Francisco*, a vernacular form of *Franciscus* (see FRANCIS).
GIVEN NAMES Spanish 33%. *Jose* (4), *Manuel* (4), *Jesus* (3), *Pedro* (3), *Rafael* (3), *Bernardo* (2), *Camilo* (2), *Cirilo* (2), *Juan* (2), *Miguel* (2), *Ramona* (2), *Ruben* (2); *Antonio* (2), *Dino, Eliseo, Sal.*

Chicoine (662) Altered spelling of French **Chichoisne**, a nickname for an argumentative or quarrelsome person, from Old French *chicoisne* 'quibbler', 'carper'.
FOREBEARS A bearer of this name from Anjou is documented in Montreal in 1670. A family with the secondary surname Dozois or Dausois is documented from 1717.
GIVEN NAMES French 10%. *Armand* (3), *Normand* (3), *Laure* (2), *Andre, Donat, Gabrielle, Girard, Henri, Jacques, Michel, Ovila, Raoul.*

Chidester (978) Origin uncertain; probably an American altered form of English CHICHESTER. It is not found in English records.

Chidsey (142) **1.** English: habitational name from Chedzoy in Somerset, which is named with an Old English personal name *Cedd* + *ēg* 'island', 'dry ground in a marsh'. **2.** Americanized spelling of German **Schütze**, a variant of **Schütz** (see SCHUETZ).

Chieffo (186) Altered spelling Italian (Calabrian) **Chiefo**, which is probably from a nickname, perhaps with sinister connotations, from *ceffo* 'muzzle', 'snout', 'bestial face' (from French *chef* 'head', from Latin *caput*).

GIVEN NAMES Italian 16%. *Salvatore* (4), *Sal* (2), *Angelo, Egidio.*

Chiem (107) Vietnamese: unexplained.

GIVEN NAMES Vietnamese 52%; Chinese 12%. *Anh* (2), *Bao, Binh, Chau, Du Van, Hanh, Hen, Hia, Hoa, Hoang Thanh, Hung, Khen*; *Chi, Chu, Ho, Hong, Man, Xia.*

Chien (842) **1.** Chinese 钱: variant of QIAN. **2.** Chinese 简: variant of JIAN.

GIVEN NAMES Chinese 22%. *Ming* (3), *Shih* (3), *Yao* (3), *Kuang* (2), *Li-Jen* (2), *Mei* (2), *Pei-Ling* (2), *Shu-Jen* (2), *Wan* (2), *Ying* (2), *Chao, Chen.*

Chiera (111) Italian (Calabria): unexplained.

GIVEN NAMES Italian 22%. *Carmela, Carmelo, Salvatore.*

Chiesa (410) Italian: from *chiesa* 'church', applied a topographic name for someone living near a church, a habitational name from any of numerous places named with this word, or possibly an occupational name for someone employed in a church.

GIVEN NAMES Italian 8%. *Aldo* (2), *Reno* (2), *Attilio, Dino, Domenica, Enrico, Fabrizio, Gabriele, Luigi, Mauro, Otello, Vito.*

Chilcoat (433) Altered spelling of English CHILCOTE.

Chilcote (710) English: **1.** habitational name from places in Leicestershire and Northamptonshire named Chilcote, from Old English as *cild* 'young men' + *cot* 'cottage(s)'. **2.** variant of CHILCOTT.

Chilcott (347) English: **1.** habitational name from a place in Somerset named Childcott, from the Old English personal name *Cēola* (a short form of various compound names beginning with *cēol* 'ship') + Old English *cot* 'cottage', 'dwelling'. **2.** variant of CHILCOTE.

Chilcutt (246) Variant of English CHILCOTT.

Child (1698) English: **1.** nickname from Middle English *child* 'child', 'infant' (Old English *cild*), in various possible applications. The word is found in Old English as a byname, and in Middle English as a widely used affectionate term of address. It was also used as a term of status for a young man of noble birth, although the exact meaning is not clear; in the 13th and 14th centuries it was a technical term used of a young noble awaiting elevation to the knighthood. In other cases it may have been applied as a byname to a youth considerably younger than his brothers or to one who was a minor on the death of his father. **2.** possibly a topographic name from Old English *cielde* 'spring (water)', a rare word derived from *c(e)ald* 'cold'.

Childers (10814) English: probably a habitational name from some lost place named Childerhouse, from Old English *cildra*, genitive plural of *cild* 'child' + *hūs* 'house'. This may have referred to some form of orphanage perhaps run by a religious order,

or perhaps the first element is to be understood in its later sense as a term of status (see CHILD).

Childre (107) Probably a variant of English CHILDREY.

Childree (238) Variant of English CHILDREY.

Childres (289) English: metathesized variant of CHILDERS.

Childress (8217) English: metathesized variant of CHILDERS.

Childrey (189) English: habitational name from Childrey in Oxfordshire, which is named for Childrey Brook. This is probably 'stream (Old English *rīth*) of *Cilla* (masculine) or *Cille* (feminine)', but the first element could alternatively be Old English *cille* 'spring'. The surname has died out in England.

Childs (9316) English: patronymic from CHILD 1.

Chiles (1606) English: patronymic from CHILD 1.

Chill (167) English: variant of CHILD.

GIVEN NAME French 4%. *Michel* (2).

Chillemi (241) Southern Italian: probably a derogatory nickname from *gaèmi, gaimi* 'vile', 'base', 'cowardly', or an occupational name from *caimu* 'cheesemaker'.

GIVEN NAMES Italian 24%. *Salvatore* (4), *Luiz* (2), *Sal* (2), *Agatino, Antonino, Carmela, Carmello, Carmelo, Ennio, Giuseppe, Lorenza, Mario, Onofrio, Santo, Vito.*

Chilson (1072) English: habitational name from Chilson in Oxfordshire, named with Old English *cild* 'young man' (see CHILD) + *tūn* 'farmstead', 'settlement'.

FOREBEARS It is not known when this surname was first brought to America, but it was well established in CT in the early 18th century. Daniel Chilson of Weathersfield, CT, was born about 1720 and on 4 October 1745 married Sybil Stanclift in Middlesex County, CT.

Chilton (2444) English: habitational name from any of the various places called Chilton, for example in Berkshire, Buckinghamshire, County Durham, Hampshire, Kent, Shropshire, Somerset, Suffolk, and Wiltshire. The majority are shown by early forms to derive from Old English *cild* 'child' (see CHILD) + *tūn* 'enclosure', 'settlement'. One place of this name in Somerset possibly gets its first element from Old English *cealc* 'chalk', 'limestone', and one on the Isle of Wight from the personal name *Cēola* (compare CHILCOTT), or from Old English *ceole* 'deep valley'.

Chim (123) **1.** Cambodian: unexplained. **2.** Chinese 詹: Cantonese variant of ZHAN. **3.** Hispanic (Guatemala and Mexico): unexplained. In some cases, possibly an ethnic name, from Portuguese *chim* 'Chinese'.

GIVEN NAMES Cambodian 24%; Chinese 6%; Spanish 6%. *Than* (2), *Bopha, Chhon, Khen, Kosal, Noeun, Noy, Samnang, Sophan, Sophea; Chan, Chun, Dung, Fong, Kong, Leung, Ping, Sang, Wah; Domingo, Francisco, Jose, Juan, Pascuala.*

Chimenti (218) Southern Italian: variant of **Clementi** (see CLEMENT).

GIVEN NAMES Italian 14%; French 4%. *Vito* (4), *Angelo* (3), *Francesco* (2), *Filomena, Guido; Armand* (3), *Oliva.*

Chimento (252) Southern Italian: variant of CLEMENTE.

GIVEN NAMES Italian 14%. *Salvatore* (3), *Carmelo, Elio, Georgio, Santo.*

Chimera (127) Southern Italian: habitational name from a place in Sicily named Chimera, from *chimera* 'kid', 'young goat', from Greek *khimaira*.

GIVEN NAMES Italian 11%. *Cosimo, Domenica.*

Chimienti (114) Italian: variant of CLEMENTE (see CLEMENT).

GIVEN NAMES Italian 36%. *Angelo* (3), *Sal* (2), *Vito* (2), *Antonio, Cosimo, Fabio, Gino, Giovanni, Giuseppe, Nicola, Pietro, Saverio.*

Chin (6579) **1.** English: variant spelling of CHINN. **2.** Chinese 金: variant of JIN 1. **3.** Chinese 钱: Cantonese variant of QIAN. **4.** Chinese 秦: variant of QIN 1. **5.** Chinese 覃: variant of QIN 2. **6.** Chinese 靳: variant of JIN 2. **7.** Chinese 晋: variant of JIN 3. **8.** Korean: there are four Chinese characters for the surname Chin, representing five clans. At least three of the clans have origins in China; most of them migrated to Korea during the Koryŏ period (AD 918–1392).

GIVEN NAMES Chinese/Korean 13%. *Wing* (17), *Wai* (15), *Hong* (14), *Fook* (9), *Chun* (8), *Lun* (6), *Ying* (6), *Young* (6), *Yuk* (6), *Kin* (5), *Leung* (5), *Mee* (5).

China (202) **1.** Italian: from the feminine form of the personal name CHINO. **2.** Italian (Sicily): nickname from *chinu*, *china* 'full of water', 'bloated', 'fat'.

Chinault (121) Variant of French **Chinaud**, nickname for a grumpy person, from a derivative of *chiner* 'to snarl'.

Chinchilla (225) Spanish: habitational name from Chinchilla de Monte Aragón in Albacete province.

GIVEN NAMES Spanish 52%. *Jose* (7), *Juan* (6), *Manuel* (6), *Jorge* (5), *Luis* (5), *Roberto* (4), *Carlos* (2), *Cesar* (2), *Julio* (2), *Rogelio* (2), *Santos* (2), *Sergio* (2).

Chinen (181) Japanese: written with characters meaning 'know feelings', but the meaning could be 'one thousand years'; from the Ryūkyū Islands.

GIVEN NAMES Japanese 28%. *Harue* (2), *Kimiko* (2), *Masa* (2), *Atsuko, Hidetoshi, Hiromu, Hiroshi, Jiro, Katsuaki, Kazuhiko, Kikue, Kiyoko.*

Chinery (105) English: variant of CHENERY.

Ching (2026) **1.** English (Cornwall): unexplained. **2.** Chinese 程: Cantonese variant of CHENG 2. **3.** Chinese 景: variant of JING 1. **4.** Chinese 荆: variant of JING 2. **5.** Chinese 井: variant of JING 3. **6.** Chinese 金: variant of JING 4.

Chinn (2197) English: from Old English *cin* 'chin', as a nickname for someone with a prominent chin or else for a clean-shaven man.

Chinnici (163) Italian: probably from Sicilian *chinnici* 'fifteen', though the application as a surname is unclear.
GIVEN NAMES Italian 12%. *Salvatore* (2), *Rosario, Santo*.

Chinnock (138) English: habitational name from East or West Chinnock in Somerset, recorded in Domesday Book as *Cinioch*. The name is of uncertain origin; according to Mills, it may from a derivative of Old English *cinu* 'deep valley', or possibly from an old hill name of Celtic origin.

Chino (102) **1.** Italian: from the personal name *Chino*, a short form of *Franceschino*, a diminutive of FRANCESCO (see FRANCIS). **2.** Spanish: ethnic name for somebody from China, or possibly also nickname for somone thought to bear a resemblance to Chinese or Asian people. **3.** Japanese: in modern times this name is written with characters meaning 'field of miscanthus reeds', but there could be an ancient connection to the name *Chinu*, which is recorded in the Shinsen shōjiroku with a character meaning 'strange' or 'unusual' but actually may have denoted the reeds.
GIVEN NAMES Spanish 23%; Japanese 18%. *Jose* (2), *Avelino, Ezequiel, Fernando, Francisco, Homero, Humberto, Joaquin, Jose Hector, Manuel, Maricela, Paulino*; *Aki, Hideki, Hirohito, Hiroki, Kazumi, Kazuo, Shigeru, Taro, Yuriko, Yutaka*.

Chiodi (148) Italian: patronymic or plural form of CHIODO.
GIVEN NAMES Italian 19%. *Marcelo* (2), *Antonio, Domenic, Domenico, Francesco, Gianni, Giuseppe, Lorenzo, Mario, Pasquale, Raimondo*.

Chiodini (122) Italian: diminutive of CHIODO.
GIVEN NAME French 4%; Italian 4%. *Carlo*.

Chiodo (702) Italian: from Italian *chiodo* 'nail', applied as a metonymic occupational name for a nailmaker or as a nickname for a tall, thin man.
GIVEN NAMES Italian 9%. *Angelo* (3), *Antonio* (2), *Santo* (2), *Carmine, Concetta, Enrico, Gino, Giuseppe, Luigi, Orazio, Palma, Raffaele*.

Chiong (138) **1.** Chinese 张: Cantonese variant of ZHANG 1. **2.** Chinese 章: Cantonese variant of ZHANG 2.
GIVEN NAMES Spanish 41%. *Luis* (3), *Arturo* (2), *Carlos* (2), *Jose* (2), *Mario* (2), *Rebeca* (2), *Agustin, Aida, Alfonso, Amado, Angel, Angelina*.

Chiou (287) **1.** Chinese 邱: variant of QIU 1. **2.** Chinese 丘: variant of QIU 2. **3.** Chinese 仇: variant of QIU 3. **4.** Chinese 裘: variant of QIU 4.
GIVEN NAMES Chinese 20%. *Jin* (2), *Yueh* (2), *Chee, Chen, Chen-Yu, Chien-Chung, Chiew, Ching, Chuen, Chun Sheng, Fu, Ning*.

Chipley (220) English: habitational name from places called Chipley, in Somerset and Devon, or from Chipley Abbey in Suffolk, each having as the second element Old English *lēah* 'woodland clearing'. In the case of Chipley, Somerset, the first element was probably the Old English personal name *Cippa*, while Chipley in Devon is named with Old English *cēap* 'price', 'purchase', and the Suffolk place name derives from Old English *cipp* 'log'.

Chipman (1934) English: variant of CHAPMAN 'trader', from West Saxon *cȳpmann*.

Chipps (483) English: occupational nickname for a carpenter or woodcutter, from Middle English *chip(pe)* 'small piece of sawn or cut wood'.

Chirco (218) Italian: from a reduced form of CHIRICO.
GIVEN NAMES Italian 26%. *Salvatore* (5), *Alfonso* (3), *Antonio* (2), *Gaetano* (2), *Angelo, Carlo, Francesca, Pietro, Santo, Sergio, Tommaso, Vito*.

Chiriboga (107) Castilianized form of Basque *txiriboga* 'tavern', hence a metonymic occupational name for someone who ran a tavern, a topographic name for someone who lived by one, or a nickname for someone who frequented one.
GIVEN NAMES Spanish 53%. *Carlos* (8), *Juan* (3), *Luis* (3), *Raul* (3), *Gonzalo* (2), *Jorge* (2), *Luz* (2), *Roque* (2), *Alfonso, Alfredo, Alicia, Alonso*.

Chirichella (102) Italian: from a femininized diminutive of the personal name CHIRICO.
GIVEN NAMES Italian 17%. *Antoninette, Gennaro, Philomena*.

Chirico (471) Italian: from the personal name *Chirico*, Latin *Cyriacus* or *Quiricus*, Greek *Kyriakos* (see CYR), a personal name of the early Christian era, an adjectival form meaning 'of the Lord'. There may have been some confusion with church Latin *clericus* 'cleric' (Italian *chierico*).
GIVEN NAMES Italian 18%. *Arcangelo* (2), *Cesare* (2), *Francesco* (2), *Angelo, Biagio, Carmelo, Carmine, Domenic, Fedele, Gaetano, Gilda, Gino*.

Chirillo (114) Southern Italian: **1.** status name for the heir to an important estate, a pet form of **Chiro**, from Greek *klēros* 'inheritance', 'legacy'. **2.** nickname from Calabrian *chirillo* 'piglet', a derivative of Greek *khoiros*. **3.** altered spelling of **Cirillo**.
GIVEN NAMES Italian 8%. *Egidio, Gennaro, Gino*.

Chirino (162) Spanish: variant spelling of CIRINO.
GIVEN NAMES Spanish 56%. *Jose* (11), *Pedro* (6), *Juan* (4), *Luis* (3), *Sergio* (3), *Ana* (2), *Carlos* (2), *Concepcion* (2), *Julio* (2), *Marcial* (2), *Miguel* (2), *Modesto* (2).

Chirinos (117) Spanish: variant (plural) of CIRINO.
GIVEN NAMES Spanish 50%. *Jose* (7), *Cesar* (3), *Luis* (3), *Felipe* (2), *Jorge* (2), *Mariela* (2), *Mario* (2), *Andres, Arnaldo, Berna-dina, Carlos, Domingo*.

Chisam (159) Americanized form of Scottish CHISHOLM.

Chisenhall (142) English: habitational name from Chisnall Hall in Lancashire, which is named with Old English *cisen* 'gravelly' + *halh* 'nook or corner of land'.

Chisholm (4492) Scottish: habitational name from Chisholme near Hawick in southern Scotland, which derives its name from Old English *cȳse, cēse* 'cheese' (Latin *caseus*) + *holm* 'piece of dry land in a fen' and refers to a waterside meadow good for dairy farming and hence for producing cheeses. In the 14th century members of this family migrated to the Highlands, settling in Strathglass, where their name was Gaelicized as **Siosal**.

Chisler (142) Americanized form of German **Schüssler** (see SCHUESSLER).

Chisley (141) **1.** Americanized form of German **Schüssler** (see SCHUESSLER). **2.** English: possibly a habitational name from Chisley Vale in Norfolk, or alternatively a variant spelling of CHESLEY.

Chism (2487) Irish (Antrim): shortened form of Scottish CHISHOLM.

Chisman (134) English: variant of CHEESE-MAN.

Chismar (185) Americanized spelling of Slavic CHIZMAR or of **Tschismar**, a German form of the same name.

Chisnell (101) English: variant of CHISEN-HALL.

Chisolm (998) Scottish: variant spelling of CHISHOLM.

Chisom (179) Americanized form of Scottish CHISHOLM.

Chisum (643) Americanized form of Scottish CHISHOLM.

Chittenden (836) English: habitational name from a place in Kent named Chittenden, probably from an Old English personal name *Citta* (perhaps a byname derived from *cīð* 'shoot', 'sprout') + *-ing-* denoting association + Old English *denn* 'swine pasture'.
FOREBEARS William Chittenden came from Cranbrook, Kent, England, and settled in Guilford, CT, in 1639. His fourth-generation descendant Thomas Chittenden, born in East Guilford, CT, in 1730, received a grant of land in 1774 in VT, where he was governor, as was his son Martin. Thomas's other sons each sat in the VT assembly and held various public offices.

Chittick (333) English: nickname from a diminutive of Middle English *chitte* 'young (animal)', 'kitten', 'cub' (see CHITTY), probably used as a term of endearment.

Chittum (537) Altered spelling of English CHEETHAM.

Chitty (665) **1.** English: nickname from Middle English *chitte* 'pup', 'cub', 'young (of an animal)' (apparently related to Old English *cīð* 'shoot', 'sprout'). **2.** English: habitational name from a place named Chitty in the parish of Chislet, Kent, named from an Old English personal name *Citta* + *ēg* 'island', 'dry ground in marsh'. **3.** Possibly an Americanized form of German **Schütte** (see SCHUTTE).

Chitwood (2376) English: variant spelling of **Chetwode**, a habitational name from a place in Buckinghamshire named Chitwood, from Celtic *cēd* 'wood', with the tautological addition of Old English *wudu* when the old name was no longer understood.

Chiu (2779) **1.** Chinese 邱: variant of QIU 1. **2.** Chinese 赵: Cantonese variant of ZHAO. **3.** Chinese 丘: variant of QIU 2. **4.** Chinese 仇: variant of QIU 3. **5.** Chinese 裘: variant of QIU 4.
GIVEN NAMES Chinese 25%. *Chi* (9), *Wai* (9), *Ming* (7), *Ching* (6), *Chun* (6), *Ping* (6), *Kam* (5), *Wan* (5), *Wen* (5), *Cheng* (4), *Kwok* (4), *Man* (4).

Chiulli (123) Central Italian: from an unidentified personal name formed with the suffix *-ullo*.
GIVEN NAMES Italian 23%. *Carlo* (2), *Angelo*, *Antonio*, *Donato*, *Guido*, *Nino*, *Silvio*, *Ugo*, *Umberto*.

Chiumento (100) Italian: variant of **Clemento**.
GIVEN NAMES Italian 8%. *Alba*, *Mario*, *Salvatore*.

Chiusano (189) Italian: habitational name from a place named with *chiusa* 'lock', 'sluice', as for example Chiusano di San Domenico in Campania, or a topographic name for someone who lived by a lock.
GIVEN NAMES Italian 23%; French 4%. *Angelo* (5), *Carmine* (5), *Constantino*, *Donato*, *Pasquale*, *Salvatore*; *Armand*, *Micheline*.

Chivers (505) Irish and English (of Norman origin): derivative of Anglo-Norman French *chivere*, *chevre* 'goat' (see CHEEVER).
FOREBEARS This Norman name has been in southeast Leinster, Ireland, since the 12th century.
Thomas Chivers (*c*.1627–64) bought land in Surry County, VA, in 1659.

Chivington (112) English: habitational name from Chevington in Suffolk or from East or West Chevington in Northumberland. The first is named with an Old English personal name *Cifa* (genitive *Cifan*) + Old English *tūn* 'settlement'; the second is

from the same personal name + *-ing-*, denoting association, + *tūn*.

Chizek (252) Americanized spelling of Czech **Čížek**, Slovak **Čížik**, and Slovenian **Čižek** (see CIZEK), all nicknames meaning 'siskin' (a type of finch).

Chizmar (198) Slovak and Czech (Moravian) (**Čižmár**), and Serbian (**Čizmar**): occupational name for a cobbler or bootmaker, from Slovak *čižmar*, Serbian *čizmar* 'bootmaker'.

Chladek (108) Czech (**Chládek**): diminutive of *chlád* 'coolness', nickname for a cool, reserved man.

Chlebek (115) Polish: metonymic occupational name for a baker, from a diminutive of *chleb* 'bread'.
GIVEN NAMES Polish 8%. *Andrzej*, *Henryk*, *Wladyslaw*, *Zofia*.

Chlebowski (180) Polish and Jewish (from Poland): habitational name for someone from Chlebów or Chlebowo, both named with Polish *chleb* 'bread'.
GIVEN NAMES Polish 6%. *Casimir*, *Jozef*, *Kazimierz*.

Chludzinski (107) Polish (**Chludziński**): habitational name from a place called Chludnie in Łomża voivodeship.
GIVEN NAMES Polish 9%. *Andrzej* (2), *Miroslaw*, *Tadeusz*.

Chmela (119) Czech: from Czech *chmel* 'hops', a metonymic occupational name for a grower of hops.

Chmelik (114) Czech (**Chmelík**): occupational name for a hop grower, from a diminutive of CHMELA.

Chmiel (611) Polish and Jewish (from Poland): from Polish *chmiel* 'hops', hence a metonymic occupational name for a grower of hops. It may also be from any of various places in Poland named with this word.
GIVEN NAMES Polish 7%. *Alicja*, *Boguslaw*, *Danuta*, *Jacek*, *Janina*, *Jerzy*, *Jolanta*, *Jozef*, *Marcin*, *Mariusz*, *Piotr*, *Ryszard*.

Chmielewski (1313) Polish: habitational name for someone from one of many places called Chmielew or Chmielewo, from *chmiel* 'hops'.
GIVEN NAMES Polish 8%. *Bogdan* (2), *Janina* (2), *Jerzy* (2), *Tadeusz* (2), *Wieslaw* (2), *Witold* (2), *Zygmunt* (2), *Beata*, *Casimir*, *Darek*, *Dariusz*, *Ewa*.

Chmielinski (56) Polish (**Chmieliński**): habitational name for someone from a place called Chmieleń, in Ostrołęka voivodeship, or Chmielina, both named with *chmiel* 'hops'.
GIVEN NAMES Polish 17%. *Bronislaw*, *Krystyna*, *Piotr*, *Zygmunt*.

Chmielowiec (76) Polish: **1.** from a derivative of CHMIEL. **2.** Possibly a habitational name from a place in Piotrkow voivodeship named Chmielowiec.
GIVEN NAMES Polish 15%. *Ewa*, *Jacek*, *Thadeus*.

Chmura (612) Polish and Jewish (from Poland): nickname from *chmura* 'cloud'.
GIVEN NAMES Polish 10%. *Mieczyslaw* (2), *Zbigniew* (2), *Boguslaw*, *Darek*, *Franciszek*, *Grazyna*, *Jozef*, *Kazmir*, *Lech*, *Stanislawa*, *Tadeusz*, *Zuzanna*.

Cho (5700) **1.** Korean: there are two Chinese characters for the surname Cho. Some records indicate a total of 210 different clans which use the more common Cho character, but only fifteen can be documented with confidence. Each of these claims a different founding ancestor. Most of them trace their origins to the beginning of the Koryŏ kingdom (early 10th century). Only one clan, the Ch'angnyŏng Cho, uses the other Chinese character. The founder of this clan's name was Cho Kye-ryong. According to legend, there was a certain scholar named Yi Kwang-ok, whose daughter very much wanted to marry. A monk visited her and told her to go to Hwawang Mountain to pray at the dragon pond. The maiden did so, and upon her return found herself to be pregnant. In a dream, a young man with a crown and a jade belt appeared to her. A few months later, in the 48th year of the reign of the Shilla King Chinp'yŏng (AD 626), she gave birth to a little boy under whose arm the Chinese character for Cho appeared in red. The king, understanding the boy to be special, named him Cho Kyeryong and married him to his daughter, the princess. So began the Ch'angnyŏng Cho clan. **2.** Chinese 曹: Min variant of CAO. **3.** Chinese 卓: variant of ZHUO.
GIVEN NAMES Chinese/Korean 64%. *Young* (91), *Yong* (57), *Sung* (51), *Kyung* (31), *Jung* (28), *Sang* (27), *Kwang* (23), *Myung* (23), *Jae* (21), *Seung* (20), *Nam* (29), *Byung* (26), *Chung* (19), *Chong* (16), *Myong* (10), *Pyong* (9), *Moon* (7), *Seong* (7), *Chul* (6), *Dae* (6); *Won* (40), *Chang* (30), *Dong* (21), *Min* (6).

Choat (325) Variant spelling of English CHOATE.

Choate (4255) English: unexplained.
FOREBEARS A John Choate who emigrated from England in 1643 and settled in Ipswich, MA, was the ancestor of several prominent 19th century Choates, including Rufus Choate (1799–1859), who was one of the organizers of the Whig Party in MA, and Joseph Hodges Choate (1832–1917), U.S. ambassador to Great Britain.

Chobot (104) Polish: nickname from the dialect word *chobot* 'tail'.
GIVEN NAMES Polish 6%. *Ludwik*, *Zbigniew*.

Chock (362) **1.** Possibly a variant of English SHOCK. **2.** Alternatively, perhaps an Americanized form of German **Zschoche**, **Zschocke**, habitational names from Zschochau, Zschokau, or Zschocken in Saxony, or Tschocke in Silesia, of Slavic origin.

Chockley (110) Variant of English SHOCKLEY.

Chodosh (86) Jewish (eastern Ashkenazic): nickname from the Ashkenazic pronunciation of the Hebrew word meaning 'new'.
GIVEN NAMES Jewish 6%. *Baruch, Pinkus.*

Choe (1661) Korean (**Ch'oe**): there is only one Chinese character for the surname Ch'oe. Of the 326 Ch'oe clans listed in some sources, only 43 distinct clans can be documented. Ch'oe is the fourth most common surname in Korea. The common Romanization **Choi** represents a French transliteration of the surname, which is actually pronounced more like *Ch'wae.* The first Ch'oe, Sobŏldori, was one of the six elders of pre-Shilla Korea; he received his surname from the Shilla King Yuri Isagŭm in AD 32.
GIVEN NAMES Korean 70%. *Yong* (38), *Young* (26), *Chong* (21), *Sung* (19), *Song* (18), *Pyong* (14), *Chang* (13), *Myong* (12), *Kwang* (12), *Sang* (10), *Jong* (9), *Kyong* (9), *Man* (9), *Won* (9), *Jae* (8), *Byong* (7), *Byung* (6), *Choon* (4), *Hyong* (4), *Chol* (3), *Chong Sun* (3), *Chul* (3), *Chun Ho* (3), *Chung* (3).

Chohan (105) North Indian: variant of CHAUHAN.
GIVEN NAMES Indian 50%; Muslim 37%. *Rani* (2), *Shantilal* (2), *Amritpal, Ashok, Asim, Bawa, Kishan, Makhan, Mohan, Naina, Ramesh, Sujata; Muhammad* (4), *Abdul* (2), *Iqbal* (2), *Naseer* (2), *Shabbir* (2), *Zahid* (2), *Ahmad, Amtul, Ansar, Maqbool, Mohammad, Mukhtar.*

Choi (7827) **1.** Chinese 蔡: Cantonese variant of CAI 1. **2.** Chinese 徐: variant of XU 1. **3.** Korean: variant of CHOE.
GIVEN NAMES Chinese/Korean 66%. *Young* (153), *Yong* (77), *Sung* (73), *Sang* (51), *Jung* (50), *Jin* (49), *Jae* (44), *Jong* (43), *Kyung* (43), *Kwang* (40), *Won* (38), *Dong* (36); *Chang* (49), *Byung* (39), *Chong* (23), *Chung* (23), *Moon* (19), *Jeong* (13), *Myong* (12), *Chul* (10), *Min* (10), *Choon* (8), *Nam* (8), *Seong* (8).

Choice (455) English: probably a variant of JOYCE. There is a family tradition among bearers of the name that it means 'chosen', from Middle English, Old French *chois* (of Germanic origin). In the Middle Ages the word was used both for an 'act of choosing' and a 'thing chosen', and as an adjective with the meaning 'chosen', 'select', 'favored'. Perhaps this word gave rise to a nickname, but there is no evidence to support this speculation.

Choiniere (416) French (**Choinière**): from *choinier,* an agent derivative of *choin* 'white', hence possibly an occupational name for a baker of fancy breads. It is sometimes Americanized as SWEENEY.
GIVEN NAMES French 14%. *Armand* (5), *Alain* (2), *Alcide, Emile, Gaston, Germain, Jacques, Jean Louis, Laurent, Lucien, Marcel, Normand.*

Choinski (185) Polish (**Choiński**): habitational name for someone from a place

named Choina or Choiny, from *choina* 'fir tree'.
GIVEN NAMES Polish 11%. *Jozef, Kazimierz, Lucjan, Waclaw, Witold, Zigmund.*

Chojnacki (562) Polish: habitational name for someone from any of the many places (Choina, Chojna, Choiny, Chojna, Chojny, or Chojnata), named with *choina* 'fir tree'.
GIVEN NAMES Polish 6%. *Andrzej* (2), *Tadeusz* (2), *Zbigniew* (2), *Grzegorz, Janina, Ryszard, Zygmunt.*

Chojnowski (222) Polish: habitational name for someone from a place called Chojnowo or Chojnów, from *choina* 'fir tree', in Ciechanów, Łomża and Ostrołęka voivodeships.
GIVEN NAMES Polish 11%. *Andrzej, Kazimierz, Lech, Lucjan, Witold, Zbigniew.*

Chokshi (162) Indian (Gujarat and Bombay city): Hindu (Vania), Jain, and Parsi name, from Gujarati *čoksi* 'jeweler', 'assayer of gold and silver', from *čokəs* 'precise', 'circumspect', a compound of *čo-* 'four', 'four-way', 'all-round' (Sanskrit *čatus-* 'four') + *kəs* 'assaying' (Sanskrit *kaṣa* 'rubbing', 'touchstone').
GIVEN NAMES Indian 96%. *Dilip* (4), *Hitesh* (4), *Ramesh* (4), *Kaushik* (3), *Ketan* (3), *Pravin* (3), *Aruna* (2), *Atul* (2), *Chetan* (2), *Dinesh* (2), *Gaurang* (2), *Gautam* (2).

Cholewa (245) Polish: metonymic occupational name for a bootmaker, or a nickname for someone who habitually wore boots, from *cholewa* 'boot upper'.
GIVEN NAMES Polish 9%. *Janusz* (5), *Grazyna, Stanislawa, Wojciech.*

Cholewinski (140) Polish (**Cholewiński**): habitational name for someone from places called Cholewy in Ciechanów, Nowy Sącz, or Warszawa voivodeships, named with the personal name *Cholewa* (from *cholewa* 'boot upper').
GIVEN NAMES Polish 5%. *Jerzy, Pawel.*

Choma (271) **1.** Ukrainian and Slovak: from the personal name *Choma,* the eastern Slavic equivalent of THOMAS. **2.** Altered spelling of Hungarian **Csoma**, from the old secular personal name *Csoma.*

Chomicki (65) Polish: habitational name for someone from a place called Chomice in Warszawa voivodeship.
GIVEN NAME French 6%. *Alphonse.*

Chon (704) **1.** Korean (**Chŏn**): there are three Chinese characters for the surname Chŏn. **2.** Some sources number the clans which use the most common character as high as 178, but only seventeen have been documented. All of these descend from a common ancestor, Chŏn Sŏp. The founding king of the Koguryŏ kingdom (37 BC–AD 668) had three sons, the youngest of whom went south and established what would later become one of Koguryŏ's rival kingdoms, Paekche. This son took with him ten servants, one of whom was Chŏn Sŏp. **3.** Five clans use the second most common Chinese character for their surname. These

clans descended from different ancestors, at least two of whom migrated to Korea from China. **4.** The clan which uses the least common character, the Mun'gyŏng Chŏn, descends from an ancestor named Chŏn Yu-gŏm. Chŏn Yu-gŏm was a minister sent from China to visit the Koryŏ court in the mid 14th century. He decided to stay in Korea and married the elder sister of a famous Koryŏ general, Ch'oe Yŏng. When the Koryŏ kingdom fell to the Chosŏn kingdom in 1392, Chŏn abandoned his government post and retired to the countryside to pass the remainder of his years in peaceful obscurity.
GIVEN NAMES Korean 67%. *Young* (16), *Yong* (12), *Sang* (10), *Myong* (7), *Chang* (5), *Chong* (5), *Dong* (5), *Kyong* (5), *Myung* (5), *Kwang* (4), *Song* (4), *Sun* (4), *Tong* (4), *Chung* (3), *Hyun* (3), *Jung* (3), *Hyong* (2), *Jung Hee* (2), *Nam* (2), *Pyong* (2), *Seong* (2), *Tae Won* (2), *Bong Soo, Byung.*

Chong (3062) **1.** Korean (**Chŏng**): there are three Chinese characters used to represent the Chŏng surname. The clans that use two of these characters are quite rare and are mostly found in Chŏlla province; their origins are obscure. The more common of the three clans is the oldest and is widely distributed throughout the peninsula. Only the clans which use this more common character will be treated here. Some sources indicate that there are 215 separate Chŏng clans, but only 32 of them can be documented. The earliest and largest Chŏng clan began in 32 AD when Chibaekho, one of the six ruling elders of pre-Shilla Korea, received the surname of Chŏng from the Shilla King Yuri Isagŭm (AD 24–57). **Chŏng** is one of the most common Korean surnames. **2.** Chinese 庄: variant of ZHUANG. **3.** Chinese 臧: Cantonese form of ZANG 1. **4.** Chinese 钟: variant of ZHONG. **5.** Chinese 张: variant of ZHANG 1. **6.** Chinese 宗: variant of ZONG.
GIVEN NAMES Chinese/Korean 35%. *Yong* (20), *Sun* (15), *Young* (11), *Kyong* (10), *Sang* (9), *Hyon* (8), *Kwang* (8), *Chae* (7), *Dong* (7), *Chin* (6), *Chun* (6), *Song* (6); *Chong* (9), *Hae* (7), *Min* (6), *Chang* (5), *Byung* (4), *Chol* (4), *Myong* (4), *Chung* (3), *Pak* (3), *Pyong* (3), *Chong Su* (2), *Dae* (2).

Chonko (129) Probably Ukrainian. Compare CHUNKO.
GIVEN NAME French 5%. *Emile* (2).

Chontos (123) **1.** Greek: nickname for someone with a large nose, from Albanian *hundë* 'nose'. **2.** Americanized spelling of Hungarian **Csontos**, from *csontos* 'strong', 'heavily built', from *csont* 'bone', hence a nickname for a tough man.

Choo (416) Chinese and Korean: variant of CHU.
GIVEN NAMES Chinese/Korean 43%. *Young* (5), *Jae* (4), *Eun* (3), *Jung* (3), *Byoung* (2), *Chee* (2), *Hyo* (2), *Hyun* (2), *Joon* (2),

Kyung (2), *Meng* (2), *Yang* (2); *Byung* (4), *Young Jun* (2), *Byung Woo*, *Chang*, *Chung*, *Hyun Jae*, *Moon*, *Sangwoo*, *Siew*, *Woong*, *Yang Sook*, *Yeon*.

Chop (129) **1.** Americanized form of German TSCHOPP. **2.** Ukrainian and Slovak (**Čop**): nickname from Ukrainian *chop*, Slovak *čop* 'European pike-perch' (*Lucioperca volgensis*).

Chopin (151) **1.** French and English: nickname for a heavy drinker, from Old French *chopine*, a large liquid measure (from Middle Low German *schōpen* 'ladle'). The derived Old French verb *chopiner* has the sense 'to tipple', 'to drink to excess'. Possibly, though less likely, the surname may have been acquired as a metonymic occupational name for a maker of ladles or vessels used in the casting of metal, which were also called *chopines*. **2.** French and English: nickname for a pugnacious person, from Old French *chopin* 'violent blow' (in form a diminutive of *chop* 'blow', Latin *colpus*, from Greek *kolaphos*). **3.** Shortened and altered form, under French influence, of Polish **Szopiński** (see SZOPINSKI).
GIVEN NAMES French 10%. *Emile*, *Laurent*, *Nestor*, *Rafael*.

Choplin (192) French: diminutive of **Chopel**, a nickname for someone of unsteady gait, from *chopper* 'to knock over'.
GIVEN NAMES French 4%. *Emile*, *Pierre*.

Chopp (369) **1.** Americanized spelling of German **Tschopp** or **Zschoppe** (see TSCHOPP). **2.** Ukrainian: variant of CHOP.

Chopra (470) Indian (Panjab): Hindu (Khatri) and Sikh name of unknown meaning. The Panjabi Khatris have a clan called Chopra (see KHATRI), as also have the Ramgarhia Sikhs.
GIVEN NAMES Indian 90%. *Raj* (13), *Sanjeev* (9), *Ashok* (8), *Rakesh* (8), *Rajiv* (6), *Anil* (5), *Kewal* (5), *Sunil* (5), *Vivek* (5), *Arun* (4), *Asha* (4), *Hari* (4).

Choquette (844) Altered spelling of French **Choquet**, a Picard form of Old French *soquet*, which was the term for a tax on wines and foodstuffs, hence a metonymic occupational name for a collector of such taxes.
FOREBEARS A bearer of the name Choquet, from Picardy, is documented in Montreal in 1668, with the secondary surname Champagne.
GIVEN NAMES French 14%. *Normand* (4), *Pierre* (4), *Marcel* (3), *Armand* (2), *Donat* (2), *Francois* (2), *Gaston* (2), *Rosaire* (2), *Aime*, *Alcide*, *Berthe*, *Fernand*.

Chorba (248) **1.** Altered spelling of Hungarian **Csorba**, from *csorba* 'gaptoothed', 'mutilated', hence a nickname for a toothless, wounded, or deformed person. This name is well established in Romania. **2.** Slovak (**Čorba**): nickname from *čorba* 'soup', of Turkish derivation.

Chorley (112) English: habitational name from any of several places, notably those in Lancashire and Cheshire, named Chorley,

from Old English *ceorla*, genitive plural of *ceorl* 'peasant' + *lēah* 'woodland clearing'.

Chorney (264) Ukrainian and Jewish (Ashkenazic): nickname for someone with dark skin or dark hair, from Ukrainian *chornyj* 'black'.

Chou (2214) **1.** Chinese 周: variant of ZHOU. **2.** Chinese 仇: variant of QIU 3. **3.** Chinese 邹: Cantonese variant of ZOU. **4.** Chinese 曹: variant of CAO 1.
GIVEN NAMES Chinese 21%. *Han* (16), *Cheng* (5), *Chih* (4), *Hong* (4), *Li* (4), *Ming* (4), *Ping* (4), *Ting* (4), *Wai* (3), *Yu-Wen* (3), *Chen* (2), *Chen-Chen* (2).

Choudhary (142) Indian (Bengal) and Bangladeshi: variant of CHOWDHURY.
GIVEN NAMES Indian 48%; Muslim 44%. *Sunil* (4), *Suresh* (4), *Ashok* (2), *Kalyani* (2), *Krishna* (2), *Pramod* (2), *Subhash* (2), *Subodh* (2), *Ajay*, *Ajit*, *Alok*, *Anjani*; *Khalid* (3), *Abdul* (2), *Mohammed* (2), *Munir* (2), *Shafiq* (2), *Tahir* (2), *Zafar* (2), *Adil*, *Afzal*, *Akbar*, *Ali*, *Anjum*.

Choudhry (205) Indian (Bengal) and Bangladeshi: variant of CHOWDHURY.
GIVEN NAMES Muslim 82%; Indian 8%. *Mohammad* (11), *Tariq* (7), *Abdul* (5), *Javed* (5), *Karamat* (5), *Tahir* (4), *Arshed* (3), *Mahmood* (3), *Ahmad* (2), *Akram* (2), *Ali* (2), *Ansar* (2); *Umesh* (2), *Ashok*, *Dinesh*, *Harish*, *Sanjiv*, *Satish*, *Savita*, *Vas*, *Vasu*, *Vineet*.

Choudhury (414) Indian (Bengal) and Bangladeshi: variant of CHOWDHURY.
GIVEN NAMES Muslim 64%; Indian 23%. *Mohammed* (7), *Abdul* (6), *Gulam* (4), *Mahbub* (4), *Golam* (3), *Mahmud* (3), *Nurul* (3), *Shaukat* (3), *Abdur* (2), *Ahmed* (2), *Faria* (2), *Iftakhar* (2); *Bhaskar* (2), *Dilip* (2), *Mahbubur* (2), *Partha* (2), *Partho* (2), *Pradip* (2), *Ajit*, *Anirban*, *Apurba*, *Arindam*, *Ashish*.

Chouest (101) French (Louisiana): unexplained.
GIVEN NAMES French 4%. *Chantel*, *Germaine*, *Mechelle*.

Chouinard (1276) French: nickname from a diminutive of *cho(u)e* 'jackdaw' + the pejorative suffix -*ard*.
FOREBEARS A bearer of this name from Tours is documented in Quebec city in 1692.
GIVEN NAMES French 14%. *Andre* (5), *Armand* (4), *Adrien* (3), *Normand* (3), *Pierre* (3), *Yvon* (3), *Adelard* (2), *Camille* (2), *Emile* (2), *Fernand* (2), *Jacques* (2), *Lucien* (2).

Choung (115) **1.** Korean: variant of **Chŏng** (see CHONG). **2.** Cambodian: unexplained.
GIVEN NAMES Korean 49%. *Jin* (2), *Chan*, *Dong*, *Dongjin*, *Eun*, *Eun Suk*, *Heesun*, *Hun*, *Hyo*, *Jae Young*, *Kwang*, *Kyung*; *Moon* (2), *Byung Soo*, *Chang*, *Choon*, *Kum*, *Suk Kyu*, *Youn*.

Chovan (220) Czech and Slovak: nickname for a foster child, *chovan*, a derivative of the verb *chovat* 'to bring up'.

GIVEN NAMES Czech and Slovak 4%. *Milan* (4), *Marketa*.

Chovanec (263) Czech: from a derivative of CHOVAN.

Chow (3895) **1.** English: nickname from Middle English *chow* (Old English *cēo*) 'jackdaw or crow'. **2.** Chinese 周: variant of ZHOU. **3.** Chinese 邹: Cantonese variant of ZOU. **4.** Chinese 曹: variant of CAO 1. **5.** Chinese 巢: Cantonese variant of CHAO 4.
GIVEN NAMES Chinese 17%. *Wing* (15), *Ping* (12), *Kam* (9), *Ming* (8), *Kwok* (7), *Ying* (7), *Cheung* (6), *Hing* (6), *Wah* (6), *Wai* (6), *Wong* (6), *Chee* (5).

Chowaniec (140) Polish: from the Polish word *chowaniec* 'adopted child'.
GIVEN NAMES Polish 12%. *Danuta* (2), *Jozef* (2), *Andrzej*, *Jozefa*, *Krzysztof*, *Lucjan*.

Chowdhury (924) Indian (Bengal) and Bangladeshi: Muslim and Hindu status name for a head of a community or caste, from Sanskrit *čatus*- 'four-way', 'all-round' + *dhurīya* 'undertaking a burden (of responsibility)' (Sanskrit *dhura* 'burden'). The title was originally awarded to persons of eminence, both Muslims and Hindus, by the Mughal emperors. The Khatris have a clan called Chowdhury. In some traditions the term is said to derive from a title for a military commander controlling four different fighting forces, namely navy, cavalry, infantry, and elephant corps, but this is probably no more than folk etymology.
GIVEN NAMES Muslim 73%; Indian 14%. *Mohammed* (36), *Mohammad* (17), *Abdul* (13), *Abu* (5), *Iqbal* (5), *Shabbir* (5), *Abul* (4), *Ahmed* (4), *Akbar* (4), *Ali* (4), *Asif* (4), *Kamrul* (4), *Alam* (3); *Dipak* (3), *Shyamal* (3), *Deepak* (2), *Manik* (2), *Partha* (2), *Seema* (2), *Abhijeet*, *Ajit*, *Amit*, *Amitabha*, *Arun*.

Chown (176) English: from a Middle English personal name, *Chun(n)*.

Chowning (433) Possibly an Americanized form of German **Schöning** (see SCHOENING).

Choy (1239) **1.** Chinese 蔡: variant of CAI 1. **2.** Possibly an Americanized form of German SCHEU.
GIVEN NAMES Chinese 12%. *Kam* (5), *Young* (5), *Chan* (4), *Wai* (4), *Ming* (3), *Wing* (3), *Chee* (2), *Hon* (2), *Kwan* (2), *Kwok* (2), *Man* (2), *Sun* (2).

Choyce (160) English: variant spelling of JOYCE. See also CHOICE.

Chrest (159) Altered spelling of German CHRIST.

Chrestman (226) Probably a variant spelling of CHRISTMAN or CHRISTMANN.

Chretien (540) French (**Chrétien**): see CHRISTIAN.
FOREBEARS A bearer of the name from the Touraine area of France was documented in Quebec city in 1665.
GIVEN NAMES French 15%. *Emile* (4), *Lucien*

(3), *Marcel* (3), *Laurent* (2), *Andre, Germain, Gilles, Henri, Jacques, Normand, Prosper, Renaud.*

Chris (234) **1.** Greek: shortened form of any of various surnames formed from the personal name *Khristos* (see CHRISTOS). **2.** shortened form of CHRISTOPHER or any of its cognates or derivatives.

Chrisco (282) Origin unidentified. This name is concentrated in NC.

Chriscoe (188) Variant spelling of CHRISCO.

Chrisler (129) Americanized spelling of German and Jewish KREISLER.

Chrisley (160) **1.** English: variant of CHRISTLEY. **2.** Possibly also an Americanized form of German KREISLER.

Chrisman (2447) **1.** Respelling of German CHRISTMANN. **2.** Respelling of English CHRISTMAN. **3.** Respelling of Slovenian **Križman** (see KRIZMAN 1).

Chrismer (202) Of German origin: **1.** perhaps an altered form of **Krismer**, a nickname for a grizzled or old man, from Old High German *gris* 'gray'. **2.** alternatively, it may be a reduced form of **Griessmeyer**, from Middle High German *griez* 'sand' + *meier* 'tenant farmer' (see MEYER), a distinguishing name for a farmer whose soil was sandy.

Chrismon (186) Altered form of German CHRISTMANN, possibly also of English CHRISTMAN.

Chrisp (138) English: variant spelling of CRISP.

GIVEN NAMES French 5%. *Celestine, Damien.*

Chriss (316) English: variant of CRIST.

Christ (2694) **1.** German: from the Latin personal name *Christus* 'Christ' (see CHRISTIAN). The name *Christ* (Latin *Christus*) is from Greek *Khristos*, a derivative of *khriein* 'to anoint', a calque of Hebrew *mashiach* 'Messiah', which likewise means literally 'the anointed'. **2.** English: variant of CRIST.

GIVEN NAMES German 4%. *Otto* (4), *Fritz* (3), *Kurt* (3), *Erwin, Franz, Georg, Gerhard, Heinz, Inge, Klaus, Liselotte, Udo.*

Christain (114) Variant of CHRISTIAN.

Christakos (125) Greek: from a pet form of the personal name *Khristos* (see CHRISTOS) + the patronymic suffix *-akos*, associated mainly with the Mani peninsula in southwestern Peloponnese.

GIVEN NAMES Greek 10%. *Apostolos, Demetrios, Eleni, Vasilios.*

Christal (146) **1.** Scottish: variant spelling of CHRYSTAL. **2.** Americanized spelling of German CHRISTEL or of KRISTAL.

Christel (254) German and French (Alsace): from the personal name *Christel*, a pet form of CHRISTIAN.

Christen (1206) German and Scandinavian: from the personal name *Christen*, one of numerous vernacular forms of Latin *Christianus* (see CHRISTIAN).

GIVEN NAMES German 5%. *Hans* (4), *Ernst* (3), *Markus* (2), *Bernhard, Eldred, Fritz, Gottlieb, Otto, Rudi, Ulrich, Urs.*

Christenberry (289) English: unexplained. It is said by family historians to be a variant of **Questenbury**, but no surname or place name of that spelling is known in Britain. It may be an altered form of **Glastonbury**, a habitational name from the place of this name in Somerset.

FOREBEARS American bearers of the name Christenberry are all said to be descended from Thomas Questenbury (1600–72), who came to VA in 1624 from Bromley, Kent, England.

Christenbury (261) English: see CHRISTENBERRY.

Christensen (29669) Danish, Norwegian, and North German: patronymic from the personal name CHRISTEN.

GIVEN NAMES Scandinavian 5%. *Erik* (51), *Nels* (28), *Niels* (23), *Lars* (15), *Bent* (9), *Anders* (8), *Thor* (8), *Jorgen* (7), *Nils* (7), *Einer* (6), *Viggo* (6), *Folmer* (5).

Christenson (4491) Americanized spelling of various Scandinavian patronymics from the personal name CHRISTEN. Compare CHRISTIANSON.

Christerson (102) Swedish: patronymic from the personal name *Christer*, variant of CHRISTEN.

Christesen (116) Danish: variant of CHRISTENSEN.

Christeson (170) **1.** Scottish: variant spelling of CHRISTISON. **2.** Scandinavian: variant of CHRISTIANSON.

GIVEN NAME Scandinavian 4%. *Erik* (2).

Christian (16783) English, German, and French: from the personal name *Christian*, a vernacular form of Latin *Christianus* 'follower of Christ' (see CHRIST). This personal name was introduced into England following the Norman conquest, especially by Breton settlers. It was also used in the same form as a female name.

Christiana (338) Evidently from the female personal name *Christiana*, but the source language and status of the American surname have not been clearly identified. It is probably of German origin.

Christiano (638) Americanized spelling of Italian CRISTIANO.

GIVEN NAMES Italian 13%. *Angelo* (6), *Vito* (3), *Carmine* (2), *Donato* (2), *Salvatore* (2), *Fiore, Gilda, Mafalda, Nicolino, Philomena, Rocco, Santina.*

Christians (528) Dutch, Danish, and North German: patronymic from CHRISTIAN.

Christiansen (7869) **1.** Danish and Norwegian: variant of CHRISTENSEN. **2.** North German: patronymic from CHRISTIAN.

GIVEN NAMES Scandinavian 6%. *Erik* (9), *Niels* (7), *Nels* (5), *Holger* (4), *Bent* (3), *Carsten* (3), *Lars* (3), *Per* (3), *Sven* (3), *Ejner* (2), *Johan* (2), *Jorgen* (2).

Christianson (5017) Americanized spelling of any of the Scandinavian patronymics

from CHRISTIAN: Danish **Christiansen**, **Christensen**, Swedish **Christiansson**, etc.

GIVEN NAMES Scandinavian 4%. *Erik* (6), *Nels* (5), *Selmer* (3), *Thor* (3), *Helmer* (2), *Sven* (2), *Alf, Anders, Arlys, Hilma, Hilmar, Morten.*

Christie (6732) Scottish: from the personal name *Christie*, a pet form of CHRISTIAN.

Christin (108) English and French: variant of CHRISTIAN.

GIVEN NAMES French 7%. *Jacques, Laurent.*

Christina (287) Americanized spelling of Italian, Spanish, and Portuguese CRISTINA.

GIVEN NAMES Italian 9%; Spanish 6%. *Angelo* (2), *Carlo* (2), *Sal* (2); *Carlos* (2), *Angel, Salvador.*

Christine (434) English and French: variant of CHRISTIAN.

Christison (334) Scottish: patronymic from the personal name CHRISTIE.

Christl (116) German: variant of CHRISTEL.

GIVEN NAMES German 5%. *Kurt, Otto.*

Christle (140) Altered spelling of German CHRISTEL.

Christley (130) English: unexplained. It has the form of an English habitational name, but no place of this name has been identified in the British Isles. Compare CHRISLEY.

Christlieb (182) German: literally 'dear to Christ', a surname of Jewish and other converts to Christianity.

Christman (4531) **1.** Respelling of German CHRISTMANN. **2.** English: from Middle English *Cristeman* 'servant of Christ', *Christ* being a short form of Christian or Christopher, or possibly Christine.

Christmann (304) German: from a short form of the personal name CHRISTIAN + Middle High German *man* 'man'.

GIVEN NAMES German 6%. *Erwin, Hans, Kurt, Monika, Nikolaus.*

Christmas (1539) **1.** Southern English: nickname for someone who was born on Christmas Day or had some other particular association with that time of year, from Old English *Crīstesmæsse* 'mass (i.e. festival) of Christ'. The name was also established in County Waterford, Ireland, in 1622. **2.** Translation of French NOEL.

Christner (1053) Probably a variant spelling of German **Kristner** or of **Christiner**, both variants of CHRISTIAN.

Christo (346) **1.** Americanized spelling of Spanish, Italian, or Portuguese CRISTO. **2.** Shortened form of Greek **Christopoulos, Khristopoulos** (with the patronymic suffix *-poulos*), or any of the Greek family names derived from compound personal names formed with *Khristo* (see CHRISTOS), as for example **Khristovassilis** ('Basil, son of Christos'), **Khristogeorgis** ('George, son of Christos'), **Khristogiannis** ('John, son of Christos').

Christodoulou (162) Greek: patronymic from the genitive case of the personal name

Khristodoulos meaning 'servant of Christ'. Genitive patronymics are particularly associated with Cyprus.
GIVEN NAMES Greek 39%. *Christos* (5), *Loucas* (3), *Constantine* (2), *Costas* (2), *Athanasios, Constantinos, Dimitris, Ioannis, Kostas, Manos, Marios, Panayiotis.*

Christoferson (112) Swedish (**Christofersson**): patronymic from the personal name *Christofer* (see CHRISTOPHER).

Christoff (616) **1.** Dutch: from the personal name, a vernacular form of Latin *Christopherus*, from Greek *Khristophoros* (see CHRISTOPHER). **2.** Bulgarian: alternative spelling of **Hristov**, patronymic from the personal name *Hristo*, short form of a name such as *Hristodul* (see Greek CHRISTODOULOU) or *Hristofor* (see CHRISTOPHER).

Christoffel (197) **1.** South German: from a pet form of *Christoffer*, a German form of CHRISTOPHER. **2.** Dutch: variant of CHRISTOFF, sometimes shortened to **Stoffel**.

Christoffer (132) German and Danish: from the personal name *Christoffer* (see CHRISTOPHER).

Christoffersen (533) Danish, Norwegian, and German: patronymic from the personal name *Christoffer* (see CHRISTOPHER).
GIVEN NAMES Scandinavian 8%; German 4%. *Erik* (2), *Bendt, Ejnar, Holger, Iver, Lars, Morten; Elke, Klaus, Kurt.*

Christofferson (904) Americanized spelling of various Scandinavian patronymics from the personal name *Christoffer* (CHRISTOPHER); see for example CHRISTOFFERSEN.

Christon (190) English: habitational name from a place named Christon, possibly the one in Somerset (named with Celtic *crūg* 'hill' + Old English *tūn* 'settlement'), but more likely from Christon Bank in Northumberland, the surname now occurring predominantly in the northeastern counties of England.

Christoph (348) German: from the personal name *Christoph*, a German form of CHRISTOPHER.
GIVEN NAMES German 6%. *Fritz, Gunther, Hermann, Irmgard, Kurt, Lutz, Siegfried.*

Christophe (177) French: from the personal name *Christophe*, French form of CHRISTOPHER.
GIVEN NAMES French 10%. *Andre, Armand, Marise, Murielle, Philippe.*

Christophel (174) German: from a pet form of the personal name CHRISTOPH.

Christopher (8893) English: from a medieval personal name which ostensibly means 'bearer of Christ', Latin *Christopherus*, Greek *Khristophoros*, from *Khristos* 'Christ'. Compare CHRISTIAN + *-pher-*, *-phor-* 'carry'. This was borne by a rather obscure 3rd-century martyred saint. His name was relatively common among early Christians, who desired to bear Christ

metaphorically with them in their daily lives. Subsequently, the name was explained by a folk etymology according to which the saint carried the infant Christ across a ford and so became the patron saint of travelers. In this guise he was enormously popular in the Middle Ages, and many inns were named with the sign of St. Christopher. In some instances the surname may have derived originally from residence at or association with such an inn. As an American family name, **Christopher** has absorbed cognates from other continental European languages. (For forms, see Hanks and Hodges 1988.)

Christophersen (360) North German, Danish, and Norwegian: variant spelling of CHRISTOFFERSEN.
GIVEN NAMES German 5%; Scandinavian 4%. *Wilhelm* (2), *Gerhart, Ilse, Kurt.*

Christopherson (2406) **1.** Northern English: patronymic from the personal name CHRISTOPHER. **2.** Americanized spelling of Danish and Norwegian CHRISTOPHERSEN or Swedish **Christophersson**.

Christopoulos (180) Greek: patronymic from the Greek personal name *Khristos* (see CHRISTOS). The common Greek patronymic suffix *-poulos* is derived from Latin *pullus* 'chick', 'nestling'; it is found mainly in the Peloponnese.
GIVEN NAMES Greek 23%. *Dimitrios* (4), *Andreas* (2), *Christos* (2), *Vasilios* (2), *Charalambos, Eleni, Epaminondas, Ilias, Kostas, Nikos, Takis.*

Christos (112) Greek: from the personal name *Khristos*, a pet form of the name *Khristodoulos* 'servant of Christ' (see CHRISTODOULOU). It is probably also used as a shortened form of surnames beginning with *Christo-*, such as CHRISTOPOULOS and CHRISTAKOS.
GIVEN NAMES Greek 7%. *Constantine* (2), *Dinos, Spero.*

Christou (131) Greek: patronymic (genitive) form of the personal name CHRISTOS. Genitive patronymics are particularly associated with Cyprus.
GIVEN NAMES Greek 45%; German 4%. *Andreas* (5), *Christos* (4), *Anastase* (2), *Costas* (2), *Ioannis* (2), *Vasilios* (2), *Anastasios, Antonios, Charalambos, Christakis, Evangelos, Kosta.*

Christy (5066) Scottish and northern Irish: variant spelling of CHRISTIE.

Criswell (159) English: probably a variant spelling of **Criswell**, one of the many variants of CRESWELL.

Chrobak (171) Polish, Slovak (**Chrobák**), and Ukrainian: derogatory nickname meaning 'small worm or insect'.
GIVEN NAMES Polish 17%. *Stanislaw* (2), *Andrzey, Halina, Henryk, Jolanta, Jozef, Ludwik, Malgorzata, Slawomir, Tadeusz, Zbigniew, Zygmunt.*

Chromy (126) Polish, Ukrainian, Czech, and Slovak (**Chromý**): nickname from Slavic *chromy* 'lame'.

Chronis (157) Greek: from a short form of the personal name *Polychronis, Polychronios*, an omen name meaning '(may he be) long lived' (from *poly* 'much', 'many' + *chronos* 'time', 'year').
GIVEN NAMES Greek 7%. *Aristotle, Eleni, Kyriakos, Stavros.*

Chronister (1140) Altered spelling of South German **Kronester**, a habitational name for someone from Kronast in Bavaria.

Chrostowski (213) Polish: habitational name for someone from a place called Chrostowa, Chrostowo, or Chrostow, from Old Polish *chrost*, later *chrust* 'brushwood', 'dry twigs'.
GIVEN NAMES Polish 12%. *Tadeusz* (2), *Andrzej, Casimir, Elzbieta, Jerzy, Lech, Zbigniew.*

Chrusciel (143) Polish (**Chruściel**): nickname from *chruściel* 'corncrake', a bird with speckled plumage and reddish wings inhabiting fields and meadows. The Polish word is ultimately derived from Slavic *chrust-* 'to rustle', and so is cognate with Russian *khrushch* 'cockchafer'.
GIVEN NAMES Polish 11%. *Beata, Danuta, Ewa, Ignatius, Jadwiga, Zdzislaw.*

Chrysler (476) Americanized spelling of German and Jewish KREISLER.

Chryst (131) Variant spelling of German CHRIST.

Chrystal (239) Scottish: variant spelling of CRYSTAL (see MCCRYSTAL).

Chrzan (240) Polish: derogatory nickname for an infirm or indolent man, from Polish *chrzan* 'horseradish'.
GIVEN NAMES Polish 10%. *Tadeusz* (2), *Agnieszka, Bogdan, Casimir, Halina, Krzysztof, Lucjan.*

Chrzanowski (591) Polish: habitational name for someone from Chrzanów or Chrzanowo, villages named from CHRZAN, a derogatory nickname from *chrzan* 'horseradish'.
GIVEN NAMES Polish 9%. *Casimir* (3), *Zbigniew* (3), *Jozef* (2), *Andrzej, Jozef, Lech, Ludwik, Stanislaw, Tadeusz, Wojciech.*

Chu (5888) **1.** This form represents at least ten different Chinese family names, as well as a Korean one. **2.** Chinese 朱: variant of ZHU 1. **3.** Chinese 褚: from the name of an adminstrative position during the Spring and Autumn period (722–481 BC). At this time, many dukes of the Zhou dynasty, including the duke of the state of Song, established a high administrative position which may be roughly translated as 'Chu master'. The descendants of a Song Chu master took this title as their surname. Additionally, there was an area named Chu during the Zhou dynasty (1122–221 BC) which lent its name to the people who lived there. **4.** Chi-

nese 祝: variant of ZHU 2. **5.** Chinese 曲: variant of QU 1. **6.** Chinese 楚: from the name of the state of Chu, one of the most powerful states of the Warring States period (403–221 BC), adopted as a surname by its ruling class. **7.** Chinese 鞠: variant of JU. **8.** Chinese 瞿: variant of QU 2. **9.** Chinese 屈: variant of QU 3. **10.** Chinese 诸: variant of ZHU 3. **11.** Chinese 竺: variant of ZHU 4. **12.** Korean: there are two Chinese characters for the Chu surname in use in Korea. One character has only one clan associated with it (the Shinan Chu clan), and while some records indicate that the other has as many as 25, only four can be documented; all of these descended from a common ancestor, Chu Hwang, who was naturalized in 907. The Shinan Chu clan is descended from a man named Chu Cham, a direct descendant of the Chinese philosopher Chu-tze. Chu Cham migrated from China to Korea some time in the early 13th century. Chu is a fairly common surname and is found throughout the peninsula.
GIVEN NAMES Chinese/Korean 21%; Vietnamese 8%. *Wing* (13), *Young* (13), *Chun* (11), *Ming* (10), *Chi* (9), *Kwok* (9), *Ling* (9), *Ying* (7), *Chin* (6), *Kam* (6), *Kin* (6), *Wai* (6); *Thanh* (9), *Tien* (9), *Hai* (7), *Minh* (7), *Lan* (5), *Mai* (5), *Vinh* (5), *Chinh* (4), *Dinh* (4), *Lien* (4), *Tin* (4), *Tuan* (4).

Chua (608) **1.** Peruvian: unexplained. The etymology is not Spanish; it is probably Quechuan. **2.** Chinese 蔡: variant of CAI 1.
GIVEN NAMES Spanish 22%. *Jose* (6), *Eduardo* (4), *Jaime* (3), *Bernardo* (2), *Corazon* (2), *Elena* (2), *Ernesto* (2), *Felipe* (2), *Gregorio* (2), *Joselito* (2), *Manuel* (2), *Ramon* (2).

Chuang (722) Chinese 庄: variant of ZHUANG.
GIVEN NAMES Chinese 24%. *Ming* (6), *Mei-Yu* (4), *Cheng* (2), *Chien-Chung* (2), *Chih* (2), *Chin* (2), *Chiu* (2), *Fan* (2), *Hui* (2), *Shu-Ming* (2), *Ying* (2).

Chuba (181) **1.** Czech and Slovak (**Čuba**): derogatory nickname from *čuba* 'bitch'. **2.** Altered spelling of German **Schuba**, of Slavic origin, probably an occupational name for a furrier, from Czech and Sorbian *šuba* 'fur'.

Chubb (948) English (chiefly West Country): nickname from Middle English *chubbe* 'chub', a common freshwater fish, *Leuciscus cephalus*. The fish is notable for its short, fat shape and sluggish habits. The word is well attested in Middle English as a description of an indolent, stupid, or physically awkward person, and this is probably the origin of modern English *chubby*, although the term has lost any pejorative overtones.

Chubbuck (222) Americanized spelling of German **Schuback** or **Schubach**, from Sorbian *šuba* 'fur', hence probably an oc-cupational name for a furrier. Compare CHUBA.

Chuck (306) English: from Anglo-Norman French *chouque* 'tree stump', possibly applied as a topographic name for someone who lived near a tree stump, or alternatively as a nickname for a person of stumpy build. Compare SUCH.

Chudy (364) **1.** Czech and Slovak (**Chudý**); and Ukrainian: nickname from Czech and Slovak *chudý* 'poor', 'poverty-stricken', Ukrainian *khudyj*. **2.** Altered spelling of Swiss German **Tschudy**, **Tschudi**, a nickname for someone with thick, disheveled hair or for a silly person.
GIVEN NAMES Polish 7%. *Andrej, Bogdan, Boguslaw, Bronislaw, Halina, Jerzy, Maciej, Tadeusz, Zdzislaw.*

Chudzik (171) Polish: nickname for a thin man, from *chudy* 'thin'.
GIVEN NAMES Polish 13%; German 4%. *Janina* (2), *Aniela, Danuta, Franciszek, Kazimierz, Ludwik, Mariusz, Wieslawa; Willi.*

Chudzinski (141) Polish (**Chudziński**): habitational name for someone from a place called Chudzino (now Chudzyno), in Płock voivodeship.
GIVEN NAMES Polish 6%. *Leszek* (2), *Dariusz.*

Chugg (144) **1.** English (Devon): possibly a variant of CHUCK. **2.** Possibly an altered spelling of the Austrian (Tyrolean) surname **Tschugg**, from Romansh *tschugg* 'mountain ridge' (from Latin *iugum* 'yoke'), hence a topographic name for someone who lived near a ridge or pass.

Chui (367) **1.** Chinese 徐: Cantonese variant of XU 1. **2.** Chinese 崔: Cantonese variant of CUI.
GIVEN NAMES Chinese 33%. *Ming* (3), *Wai* (3), *Chung* (2), *Hing* (2), *Ning* (2), *Wing* (2), *Cheung, Chia, Chiming, Chun Fai, Fung, Hin, Hon, Ki Young, Pang.*

Chum (149) **1.** Cambodian: unexplained. **2.** Peruvian: unexplained. The etymology is not Spanish; it is probably Quechuan. **3.** English: unexplained.
GIVEN NAMES Cambodian 45%. *Choun* (2), *Kong* (2), *Oeun* (2), *Sophal* (2), *Chean, Chen, Cheng, Chi Sing, Chhon, Choeun, Doeun, Duong, Heng, Loeuth, Ngim, On, Ouk, Pha, Pheap, Rin, Rong, Saroeun, Soeun, Soeuth, Sok, Tho, Thoai, Thoeun, Voeuth.*

Chumbler (129) Origin unidentified. Probably English, a variant of CHUMLEY.

Chumbley (487) English: variant of CHUMLEY.

Chumley (1101) English: habitational name from Cholmondeley in Cheshire, named from the Old English personal name *Cēolmund* + *lēah* 'woodland clearing'. The spelling of the surname reflects the current pronunciation of the place name.

Chumney (304) Origin uncertain. Possibly an altered form of English CHUMLEY.

Chun (3083) **1.** Chinese 秦: Cantonese variant of QIN 1. **2.** Korean: variant of CHON. **3.** English (Wiltshire): variant spelling of CHUNN.
GIVEN NAMES Chinese/Korean 32%. *Young* (45), *Sung* (12), *Yong* (9), *Kwang* (8), *Sang* (8), *Jin* (7), *Jong* (7), *Myung* (7), *Soon* (6), *Won* (6), *Jae* (5), *Kyung* (5); *Byung* (7), *Chang* (5), *Chong* (5), *Dae* (5), *Moon* (4), *Chung* (3), *Young Chul* (3), *Choon* (2), *Chul Ho* (2), *Jeong* (2), *Joo Young* (2), *Jung Hee* (2).

Chung (8278) **1.** Chinese 钟: variant of ZHONG 1. **2.** Chinese 宗: variant of ZONG. **3.** Chinese 仲: variant of ZHONG 2. **4.** Chinese 丛: variant of CONG. **5.** Korean: variant of **Chŏng** (see CHONG).
GIVEN NAMES Chinese/Korean 46%; Vietnamese 6%. *Young* (72), *Sung* (43), *Jae* (36), *Jin* (34), *Kyung* (28), *Kwang* (24), *Yong* (24), *Sang* (21), *Soon* (20), *Won* (20), *Dong* (19), *Myung* (19); *Byung* (23), *Hae* (22), *Chang* (19), *Min* (15), *Koo* (11), *Chul* (10), *Dae* (10), *Joo* (9), *Woon* (9), *Chong* (8), *Myong* (7), *Nam* (7); *Hung* (10), *Thanh* (9), *Minh* (7), *Cuong* (6), *Hai* (5), *Sanh* (5), *Son* (5), *Vinh* (5), *Yen* (5), *Chau* (4), *Ha* (4), *Ha To* (4).

Chunko (110) Ukrainian: unexplained.

Chunn (774) **1.** English: unexplained. **2.** Possibly an altered spelling of German **Tschann**, from a short form of JOHANNES.

Chuong (137) Vietnamese: unexplained.
GIVEN NAMES Vietnamese 72%. *Minh* (3), *Mui* (3), *Chan* (2), *Duong* (2), *Hai* (2), *Hung* (2), *Kiu* (2), *Muoi* (2), *Anh, Bao, Binh, Bui, Chau, Cuong; Fong, Kwi, Mun, Pok, Sang, Ung, Yan.*

Chupka (117) Probably a respelling of eastern German **Schupke**, which is in part from a short form of the Slavic personal name *Czepan* (a vernacular form of Latin *Stephanus* (see STEVEN), and in part a nickname from Middle Low German *schupe* 'fish scale', or potentially a nickname for a tardy or indecisive person, from Middle High German *schup* 'delay', 'procrastination').

Chupp (617) Altered spelling of Swiss German TSCHOPP or **Tschupp**, variants of SCHUPPE.

Chura (185) Ukrainian: occupational name from Ukrainian *chura, dzhura* 'cossak servant'.

Church (13442) **1.** English: topographic surname for someone who lived near a church. The word comes from Old English *cyrice*, ultimately from medieval Greek *kyrikon*, for earlier *kyriakōn (dōma)* '(house) of the Lord', from *kyrios* 'lord'. **2.** Translation of German KIRCH.

Churches (111) English: probably an occupational name for someone who worked at a 'church house' (Middle English *chirche* + *h(o)us*), a building, usually adjoining the church, which served as a parish room.

Churchey (102) English: topographic name for someone who lived by a churchyard, Middle English *chircheheye* literally 'church enclosure'.

Churchill (5247) English: habitational name from any of various places named Churchill, for example in Devon, Oxfordshire, Somerset, and Worcestershire. Most were probably originally named with a Celtic element *crūg* 'hill' (which early on was reinterpreted as Old English *cyrice* 'church'), to which was added Old English *hyll* 'hill'.

Churchman (567) **1.** English: topographic name for someone who lived by a church, from Middle English *chirche* (see CHURCH) + *man*. **2.** Possibly a translation of German **Kirchmann** (see KIRCHMAN).

Churchwell (995) English: most probably a variant of CHURCHILL, or possibly a habitational name from a lost or unidentified place.

Churilla (186) Belorussian: nickname from *churila* 'untidy man'.

Churn (140) English: unexplained.

Churney (106) Americanized form of Czech **Černý** (see CERNY), Polish CZARNY, Ukrainian **Černij**, or some other Slavic name meaning 'black'.

Chustz (252) Origin unidentified. This is a LA name.
GIVEN NAMES French 5%. *Andre* (3), *Theophile*.

Chute (788) **1.** English: habitational name from any of several places in Hampshire and Wiltshire named with Chute, from Celtic *cēd* 'wood'. Compare Welsh *coed*. **2.** Americanized form of German **Schütt**, a variant of **Schütte** (see SCHUTTE).

Chvala (120) Czech: from the Old Czech personal name *Chval*, from an element meaning 'praise', a short form of *Bohuchval* 'praise God'.

Chvatal (110) Czech (**Chvátal**): nickname from the past participle of *chváatat* 'to hurry', 'rush'.

Chwalek (104) Polish (**Chwałek**): from a pet form of the personal name *Chwalimir* or *Chwalisław*, or from *chwalić* 'to prize or value' or *chwalic się* 'to boast (of something)'.
GIVEN NAMES Polish 7%; German 5%. *Czeslaw*; *Gunther*.

Chynoweth (258) Cornish: variant spelling of CHENOWETH.

Ciabattoni (119) Italian: from an augmentative of *ciabatta* 'old shoe', 'slipper', probably a nickname for someone who habitually wore old shoes or had a peculiar gait.
GIVEN NAMES Italian 28%. *Carlo, Corradino, Dino, Enrico, Ferdinando, Filippo, Franco, Guerrino, Mauro, Orlando.*

Ciaburri (109) Italian (Benevento, Campania): unexplained.
GIVEN NAMES Italian 16%. *Salvatore* (2), *Dino, Enrico, Rocco, Sal.*

Ciaccia (168) Italian: from a feminine form of CIACCIO.
GIVEN NAMES Italian 21%. *Donato* (3), *Vito* (2), *Angelo, Carlo, Giuseppe.*

Ciaccio (576) Italian: probably from a short form of a personal name ending with the suffix *-accio.*
GIVEN NAMES Italian 13%. *Salvatore* (8), *Giorgio* (2), *Rocco* (2), *Carlo, Domenica, Giovanni, Lorenzo, Sal, Vito.*

Ciak (118) Polish: of uncertain origin, possibly a nickname from *ciekać* 'to run fast'.
GIVEN NAMES Polish 10%. *Bronislawa, Janina, Jerzy, Walenty.*

Ciambrone (102) Italian (Calabria): habitational name from a minor place named Ciambrone, Ciambron, Ciambra, or Le Ciambre, from Old Italian *ciambra* 'room', probably indicating a guard post to control the territory.
GIVEN NAMES Italian 15%. *Angelo* (3), *Nichola.*

Ciampa (575) Italian: feminine form of **Ciampo** (see CIAMPI 1).
GIVEN NAMES Italian 18%. *Mario* (3), *Alfonso* (2), *Americo* (2), *Antonio* (2), *Carmine* (2), *Gerardo* (2), *Rocco* (2), *Angelo, Armando, Carmela, Carmella, Domenico, Donato, Ettore, Generoso, Gino, Ottavio, Panfilo, Pasquale, Raffaele, Rico.*

Ciampi (311) Italian: **1.** from *Ciampo*, a nickname for a bow-legged or crooked legged man, Tuscan *ciampo*. **2.** habitational name from a place named Ciampi.
GIVEN NAMES Italian 18%. *Angelo* (2), *Mario* (2), *Nunzio* (2), *Pasquale* (2), *Alfonzo, Alphonso, Amador, Antonio, Armando, Emilio, Gerardo, Giovanni, Manfredo, Sabino.*

Cianci (602) Italian: patronymic or plural form of CIANCIO.
GIVEN NAMES Italian 22%. *Angelo* (6), *Salvatore* (5), *Donato* (3), *Canio* (2), *Guilio* (2), *Sal* (2), *Amedio, Antonio, Camillo, Carmelo, Cosmo, Domenic.*

Ciancio (307) Italian: **1.** from an old Tuscan nickname *Cianci(a)*, derived from *cianciare* 'to chatter', 'to talk idly'. **2.** from an adaptation of the Spanish personal name SANCHO. **3.** topographic name for someone who lived by a boundary, from Old French *chanche* 'border'.
GIVEN NAMES Italian 25%. *Silvio* (3), *Alfonso* (2), *Emilio* (2), *Rocco* (2), *Adriana, Angelo, Antonio, Carlo, Carmelo, Elvira, Enrico, Piero, Raffaela, Salvatore, Umberto, Vincenzo.*

Cianciola (154) Italian: variant of CIANCIOLO.
GIVEN NAMES Italian 7%. *Angelo, Marco.*

Cianciolo (353) Italian: **1.** from a diminutive of CIANCIO. **2.** from the Sicilian word *cianciulu* 'night fishing lamp', probably applied as a metonymic occupational name for a night fisherman.
GIVEN NAMES Italian 9%. *Angelo, Domenic, Ercole, Guido, Salvatore, Saverio.*

Cianciulli (163) Italian: variant of CIANCIOLO.
GIVEN NAMES Italian 24%. *Angelo* (2), *Dino* (2), *Fortunato* (2), *Alfonso, Caterina, Guido, Luigi, Mario, Pasquale, Vito.*

Cianelli (105) Italian: from the personal name *Ciano*, a diminutive of *Luciano*, + the suffixe *-ello.*
GIVEN NAMES Italian 14%. *Dante* (2), *Angelo, Antonio, Egidio, Franco, Gino, Stefano.*

Cianflone (114) Italian: **1.** derogatory nickname from Spanish *chanflón* 'rough', 'crude', 'coarse'. **2.** from Calabrian *cianfruni*, the name of an old gold coin, applied possibly as a metonymic occupational name for a moneyer or as a nickname for a rich or miserly man.
GIVEN NAMES Italian 23%. *Angelo* (2), *Antonio, Concetta, Fiore, Giuseppe, Ottavio, Rocco.*

Ciani (203) Italian: patronymic or plural form of CIANO.
GIVEN NAMES Italian 10%. *Aldo, Amerigo, Annamaria, Dario, Natale, Paolo, Pasquale, Sal.*

Ciano (286) Italian: from the personal name *Ciano*, a short form of *Feliciano, Luciano, Marciano*, etc.
GIVEN NAMES Italian 13%. *Angelo* (3), *Salvatore* (2), *Cosmo, Dino, Fausto, Luigi, Pasquale, Rocco.*

Ciaramella (200) Southern Italian: from *ciaramella* 'bagpipe', applied as a metonymic occupational name for a maker of bagpipes or a piper, or possibly as a nickname for a windbag.
GIVEN NAMES Italian 14%. *Angelo* (2), *Silvio* (2), *Amedeo, Antonio, Arduino, Filomena, Pasquale.*

Ciaramitaro (302) Italian (Sicily): occupational name from *ciaramitaru* 'worker at a furnace'.
GIVEN NAMES Italian 24%. *Carlo* (5), *Salvatore* (5), *Vito* (5), *Angelo* (2), *Mercurio* (2), *Antonino, Antonio, Enza, Filippo, Gaetano, Matteo, Nino.*

Ciaravino (196) Italian: from a personal name of Germanic origin, *Giaravino, Gerevini*, reinterpreted through folk etymology as Italian *ciara* 'sniffs' + *vino* 'wine'.
GIVEN NAMES Italian 34%. *Vito* (11), *Carlo* (3), *Gaspare* (2), *Pietro* (2), *Sal* (2), *Salvatore* (2), *Angelo, Francesca, Gaetano, Ignazio, Settimo.*

Ciarcia (139) Southern Italian: **1.** occupational name for a hawker or falconer, from Greek *kyrkias*, occupational derivative of *kyrkos* 'falcon', 'hawk'. **2.** (**Ciarcià**): habitational name from a place named Giarcià.
GIVEN NAMES Italian 13%. *Salvatore* (3), *Santo* (2), *Gilda, Sal, Santina.*

Ciardi (165) Southern Italian: from the medieval personal name *Ciardo*, a short form of names such as *Acciardo, Guicciardo*, or *Ricciardo.*

GIVEN NAMES Italian 15%; Irish 5%. *Carlo* (2), *Angelo, Enzo, Guido, Italo, Libero, Mauro.*

Ciardullo (124) Italian: from a diminutive of the personal name *Ciardo* (see CIARDI).
GIVEN NAMES Italian 20%. *Biagio, Carmine, Fedele, Gino, Luigi, Rocco.*

Ciarleglio (103) Italian: unexplained.
GIVEN NAMES Italian 30%. *Pasquale* (3), *Salvatore* (2), *Angelo, Antimo, Antonietta, Antonio, Filomena, Italo, Luigi.*

Ciarlo (193) Italian: unexplained; perhaps a nickname from *ciarla* 'gossip'.
GIVEN NAMES Italian 26%. *Franco* (2), *Gino* (2), *Rocco* (2), *Angelo, Carlo, Carmelo, Dante, Dino, Domenic, Donato, Elio, Enrico.*

Ciarrocchi (159) Italian: unexplained.
GIVEN NAMES Italian 12%. *Biagio* (2), *Cosmo* (2), *Attilio, Rocco, Saturno, Serafino.*

Ciavarella (206) Southern Italian (Sicily): probably from Sicilian *ciavareddu* 'kid', 'young goat', from Old French *chevrel*, presumably applied as a nickname or as a metonymic occupational name for a goatherd.
GIVEN NAMES Italian 19%. *Angelo* (9), *Rocco* (3), *Antonio, Elio, Ginevra.*

Cibelli (122) Italian (Campania): possibly a topographic name, from Arabic *gebel* 'mountain' (compare *Mongibello*, i.e. Etna in Sicily).
GIVEN NAMES Italian 11%. *Domenic* (2), *Gennaro* (2), *Achille.*

Ciborowski (155) Polish: habitational name for someone from a place called Ciborowice, Ciborów, or Cibory, from the personal name *Czścibor*.
GIVEN NAMES Polish 11%. *Bogdan, Ewa, Henryk, Janina, Kazimierz, Pawel, Stanislaw.*

Cibula (165) Jewish (from Poland and Ukraine): nickname from Polish *cybula* 'onion', Ukrainian *tsybulya*. Compare ZWIEBEL.

Cibulka (143) Czech: from a diminutive of *cibule* 'onion', a nickname for someone with a head thought to resemble an onion or a metonymic occupational name for an onion seller.

Cicala (200) Italian: nickname for a talkative person, from Italian *cicala* 'cicada', 'grasshopper'.
GIVEN NAMES Italian 16%. *Carlo* (2), *Domenico* (2), *Pino* (2), *Alesio, Antonino, Bartolomeo, Carmela, Carmelo.*

Cicale (106) Italian: variant of CICALA.
GIVEN NAMES Italian 12%. *Sal* (3), *Elvira.*

Cicalese (201) Italian: habitational name for someone from Cicala, in Catanzaro province, or Cicalesi, an area of Nocera Inferiore in Salerno province.
GIVEN NAMES Italian 24%. *Salvatore* (3), *Sal* (2), *Aldo, Alfonse, Carmelina, Carmine, Chiara, Gennaro, Luca, Nunzio, Rocco, Sabato.*

Ciccarelli (759) Italian: patronymic or plural form of CICCARELLO.
GIVEN NAMES Italian 18%. *Angelo* (6), *Antonio* (4), *Salvatore* (4), *Carmine* (3), *Ciro* (3), *Gino* (3), *Luigi* (3), *Vito* (3), *Dino* (2), *Gennaro* (2), *Pasquale* (2), *Vita* (2).

Ciccarello (223) Italian: from a diminutive of the personal name CICCO.
GIVEN NAMES Italian 29%. *Santo* (4), *Angelo* (2), *Cosmo* (2), *Giulio* (2), *Pasqualina* (2), *Caterina, Domenico, Francesco, Gaspare, Ignazio, Nicolo, Pietro.*

Ciccarone (125) Italian: from an augmentative of the personal name CICCO.
GIVEN NAMES Italian 12%. *Aniello, Annamarie, Carlo, Enrico.*

Cicchetti (331) Italian: from a pet form of the personal name CICCO.
GIVEN NAMES Italian 18%. *Dante* (5), *Domenic* (3), *Aldo* (2), *Gino* (2), *Antonio, Carlo, Carmela, Flavio, Guido, Loredana, Orazio, Orfeo.*

Cicchini (108) Italian: patronymic or plural form of CICCHINO.
GIVEN NAMES Italian 22%. *Rinaldo* (2), *Armando, Camillo, Chiara, Claudio, Francesco, Guido, Mario, Quinta.*

Cicchino (117) Italian: from a diminutive of the personal name CICCO.
GIVEN NAMES Italian 16%. *Antonio, Carmine, Quintino.*

Cicci (137) Italian: patronymic or plural form of CICCO.
GIVEN NAMES Italian 14%. *Carmine, Dino, Domenic, Ugo, Valentino.*

Cicciarelli (104) Italian: origin uncertain. **1.** perhaps from a pet form of an otherwise unrecorded medieval personal name, *Cicciaro*, which would be from a Germanic name, *Sighari*, composed of the elements *sig* 'victory' + *hari* 'army'. **2.** alternatively, it may be a derivative of the personal name CICCO.
GIVEN NAMES Italian 14%; French 9%. *Angelo* (3), *Antonio, Remo, Romeo, Silvio*; *Ferrel* (3).

Cicco (154) Southern Italian: from a diminutive of the personal name *Francesco* (Italian equivalent of FRANCIS). In the Venetian dialect *cic(c)o* is a term of endearment meaning 'little one', 'baby', which De Felice suggests could also lie behind the surname in some instances.
GIVEN NAMES Italian 19%. *Angelo* (2), *Rocco* (2), *Antonio, Luigi, Pasquale, Sal, Santo, Vincenzo.*

Ciccolella (119) Italian: from a feminine form of **Ciccolello**, a diminutive of *Ciccolo*, which is in turn a diminutive of the personal name CICCO.
GIVEN NAMES Italian 24%. *Angelo* (2), *Edo* (2), *Cosmo, Domenic, Erasmo, Salvatore, Sergio, Vito.*

Ciccone (1426) Italian: from an augmentative form of the personal name CICCO.
GIVEN NAMES Italian 24%. *Mario* (10), *Salvatore* (7), *Rocco* (6), *Antonio* (5), *Angelo* (4), *Sal* (4), *Carlo* (3), *Dino* (3), *Luigi* (3), *Orlando* (3), *Pasquale* (3), *Armando* (2), *Carmine* (2), *Celestino* (2), *Dante* (2), *Domenico* (2), *Alberto, Alfonso, Americo, Eugenio, Fernando.*

Cicconi (148) Italian: variant of CICCONE.
GIVEN NAMES Italian 13%. *Angelo, Dino, Gino, Marino, Nino, Savino, Silvio.*

Ciccotelli (134) Italian: from the personal name *Ciccotello*, a diminutive of CICCO.
GIVEN NAMES Italian 29%. *Antonio* (3), *Enzo* (2), *Alberico, Aldo, Alessandro, Angelo, Arduino, Attilio, Gino, Lelio, Manfredo, Marco.*

Cicero (1148) Southern Italian: from *cicero* 'pea' (Latin *cicer, ciceris* 'chickpea', 'lentil'), possibly a metonymic occupational name for someone who grew or sold peas, or perhaps as a nickname for someone with a carbuncle or pimple. The Roman republican lawyer and statesman Cicero was so named because he had a growth resembling a chickpea on his face.
GIVEN NAMES Italian 12%. *Salvatore* (7), *Vito* (7), *Angelo* (5), *Giovanni* (3), *Nunzio* (3), *Carmelo* (2), *Emanuele* (2), *Giuseppe* (2), *Carmine, Concetto, Enrico, Gaetano.*

Cicerone (107) Southern Italian: augmentative of CICERO.
GIVEN NAMES Italian 13%. *Marco* (2), *Albino, Michelangelo.*

Cich (171) Polish: nickname from an Old Polish variant of *cichy* 'quiet'.

Cichocki (415) Polish: habitational name for someone from places in Nowy Sącz or Toruń voivodeships called Ciche, from *cichy* 'quiet', 'calm'.
GIVEN NAMES Polish 10%. *Zbigniew* (3), *Mieczyslaw* (2), *Stanislaw* (2), *Tadeusz* (2), *Andrzej, Ewa, Kazimierz, Krzystof, Leszek, Piotr, Slawomir.*

Cichon (596) Polish (**Cichoń**): nickname from a derivative of *cichy* 'quiet', 'calm'.
GIVEN NAMES Polish 5%. *Casimir* (2), *Andrzej, Boleslaw, Bronislawa, Iwona, Jolanta, Jozef, Krzystof, Witold, Zbigniew.*

Cichosz (101) Polish: nickname from a derivative of *cichy* 'quiet', 'calm'.
GIVEN NAMES Polish 8%. *Janusz, Mariusz, Tadeusz.*

Cichowski (193) Polish: habitational name for someone from a place called Cichowo or Cichów, from the personal name *Cichy* meaning 'quiet', 'calm'.
GIVEN NAMES Polish 6%. *Bogdan, Janusz.*

Cichy (324) Polish: nickname for a quiet person, from Polish *cichy* 'quiet', 'calm'.
GIVEN NAMES Polish 4%. *Alojzy, Krzysztof, Zigmund, Zygmunt.*

Cicio (167) Italian: **1.** from a short form of a personal name formed with the hypocoristic suffix *-cicio*. **2.** possibly a variant of *cecio, cece* 'pea' (see CICERO).
GIVEN NAMES Italian 14%. *Antonio, Carmine, Salvatore, Santo, Vito.*

Cicone (102) Italian: variant spelling of CICCONE.

GIVEN NAMES Italian 10%. *Domenico, Gaetano.*

Cicotte (100) Respelling of French SICOTTE.

Cid (304) Spanish and Portuguese: from the honorific title *Cid* (from Arabic *sayyid* 'lord'), borne by Christian overlords with Muslim vassals, most famously by Rodrigo Díaz de Vivar (1043–99), *El Cid*. This was early adopted as a personal name.

GIVEN NAMES Spanish 53%; Portuguese 14%. *Jose* (10), *Manuel* (9), *Francisco* (5), *Luis* (5), *Juan* (4), *Carlos* (3), *Jesus* (3), *Pedro* (3), *Cesar* (2), *Enrique* (2), *Fulgencio* (2), *Jaime* (2); *Joao, Manoel.*

Cielinski (103) Polish: possibly a nickname from *cielę* 'calf', with addition of the common surname suffix *-iński*, normally found with habitational names.

Cienfuegos (128) Asturian-Leonese: habitational name from Cienfuegos, a town in Asturies.

GIVEN NAMES Spanish 51%. *Juan* (4), *Armando* (2), *Francisco* (2), *Guillermo* (2), *Jose* (2), *Reynaldo* (2), *Ricardo* (2), *Adela, Alfredo, Alonzo, Angel, Apolonio.*

Cieply (117) Polish (**Ciepły**): nickname from *ciepły* 'warm'.

GIVEN NAMES Polish 7%. *Ewa, Jacek, Zigmond.*

Cieri (287) Italian: probably from a short form of a medieval personal name such as *Fulcieri*.

GIVEN NAMES Italian 24%. *Angelo* (5), *Domenic* (2), *Mauro* (2), *Salvatore* (2), *Sergio* (2), *Amerigo, Antonio, Carlo, Eligio, Federico, Filomena, Lucio, Marco, Mario, Rudolfo.*

Ciervo (144) **1.** Italian: variant of **Cervo** (see CERVI). **2.** Spanish: nickname from *ciervo* 'stag' (Latin *cervus*), probably a metonymic occupational name for a hunter.

GIVEN NAMES Italian 27%. *Alfonso* (2), *Angelo, Carlo, Francesco, Italo, Salvatore, Carmella, Mario.*

Ciesielski (551) Polish: habitational name for someone from a place called Cieśle.

GIVEN NAMES Polish 5%. *Leszek* (2), *Boleslaw, Kazimierz, Krzysztof, Pawel, Piotr, Zbigniew.*

Ciesinski (109) Polish: habitational name from Ciesina in Suwałki province.

Ciesla (437) Polish (**Cieśla**): occupational name from Polish *cieśla* 'carpenter'.

GIVEN NAMES Polish 9%. *Casimir* (5), *Zofia* (2), *Beata, Ignatius, Jadwiga, Jozef, Krzysztof, Piotr, Slawomir.*

Cieslak (621) Polish (**Cieślak**): patronymic meaning 'son of the carpenter' (see CIESLA).

GIVEN NAMES Polish 7%. *Andrzej* (2), *Miroslaw* (2), *Agnieszka, Grazyna, Ignatius, Jadwiga, Marzena, Stanislaw, Tadeusz, Tomasz, Zigmund, Zofia.*

Cieslewicz (152) Polish: patronymic meaning 'son of the carpenter' (see CIESLA).

Cieslik (193) Polish (**Cieślik**): from a diminutive of *cieśla* 'carpenter' (see CIESLA).

GIVEN NAMES Polish 16%. *Stanislaw* (2), *Wieslawa* (2), *Andrzej, Halina, Ignacy, Janina, Jerzy, Krzysztof, Mieczyslaw, Ryszard, Zbigniew.*

Cieslinski (238) Polish (**Cieśliński**): habitational name for someone from a place called Cieslin, from *cieśla* 'carpenter'.

Cieszynski (122) Polish (**Cieszyński**): habitational name for someone from a place called Cieszyn.

GIVEN NAMES Polish 8%. *Ignatius, Ruta, Zygmunt.*

Cifaldi (114) Italian: from an unidentified personal name formed with the Germanic suffix *-aldo.*

GIVEN NAMES Italian 17%. *Vito* (2), *Claudio.*

Cifarelli (131) Italian: nickname from a diminutive of the southern Italian dialect term *cifaro, cifero* 'devil', 'demon' (a reduced form of the personal name ascribed to the fallen angel, Latin *Lucifer* 'bearer of light', from *lux*, genitive *lucis*, light + *ferre* 'to bear'). The first syllable was lost because it was understood as the regional form *lu* of the definite article.

GIVEN NAMES Italian 27%. *Angelo* (2), *Carlo* (2), *Emilia, Franco, Nicolina, Pasquale.*

Cifelli (371) Italian: unexplained.

GIVEN NAMES Italian 15%. *Angelo* (3), *Antonio* (2), *Camillo* (2), *Carmine* (2), *Domenic* (2), *Alfonse, Nicola, Pasquale, Sandro, Vincenzo.*

Cifuentes (438) Spanish: habitational name probably from Cifuentes in Guadalajara, named from Spanish *cien* 'hundred' (Latin *centum*) + *fuentes* 'springs' (Latin *fontes* (see FONT), because of the abundance of natural springs in the area).

GIVEN NAMES Spanish 53%. *Carlos* (12), *Jose* (7), *Jorge* (5), *Juan* (4), *Julio* (4), *Luis* (4), *Miguel* (4), *Pedro* (4), *Alberto* (3), *Alfredo* (3), *Ana* (3), *Carolina* (3); *Antonio* (3), *Marco* (2), *Angelo, Dante.*

Ciha (105) Czech (**Číha**): occupational name for a fowler (see CIHAK).

Cihak (274) Czech (**Číhák**): **1.** occupational name for a fowler, *čihař*, from *číhat* 'to lie in wait'; **2.** metonymic occupational name for a blacksmith, from *čihák*, which denoted one of the implements used by blacksmiths.

Cihlar (177) Czech (**Cihlář**): occupational name for a brick maker, *cihlář*, a derivative of *cihla* 'brick'.

Cilento (148) Italian: regional name from Cilento in Salerno province, Campania.

GIVEN NAMES Italian 15%. *Guido* (2), *Angelo, Antonio, Enzo, Sal, Vincenzo.*

Cilia (112) **1.** Southern Italian and Maltese: nickname for a fat man, from a dialect word *cilia*, derived from Greek *koilia* 'stomach'. **2.** Spanish: unidentified; perhaps a metro-

nymic from a reduced form of the female personal name *Cecilia*.

GIVEN NAMES Italian 20%; Spanish 9%. *Angelo* (3), *Alberto, Aldo, Marino, Orest, Salvatore, Sebastiano*; *Angel, Liborio, Jorge, Maria Del Carmen, Silvana, Teodora.*

Ciliberti (159) Southern Italian: patronymic or plural form of CILIBERTO.

GIVEN NAMES Italian 18%. *Battista, Biagio, Carlo, Dante, Ercole, Vito.*

Ciliberto (201) Southern Italian: variant of GILIBERTO.

GIVEN NAMES Italian 22%. *Damiano* (2), *Angelo, Pietro, Rocco, Santo, Vito.*

Cilley (365) **1.** English: variant spelling of **Silley**, a variant of SEELEY. This is a frequent NH name. **2.** Americanized spelling of German **Zille**, perhaps a metonymic occupational name for a bargee, from Middle High German *zülle* 'barge', mainly used in Saxony and the Berlin area. **3.** Americanized form of South German **Killer**, a variant of KILIAN, or a habitational name from a place near Hechingen (Württemberg).

Cillo (216) Italian: from a reduced pet form of *Francesco* (Italian equivalent of FRANCIS).

GIVEN NAMES Italian 21%. *Americo* (2), *Aniello, Antonio, Carmine, Gianna, Giovanni, Guido, Livio, Rocco, Vito.*

Cilluffo (108) Italian: **1.** from a reduced form of the Germanic personal name *Angilulf*, composed of the ethnic name *angil* 'Angle' + *wolf, wulf* 'wolf'. **2.** possibly a nickname from Sicilian *ciluffa* 'bad mood'.

GIVEN NAMES Italian 43% *Salvatore* (3), *Vito* (2), *Angelo, Antonio, Armando, Gaetano, Guiseppe, Pietro.*

Cima (239) Italian: topographic name from *cima* 'peak', 'mountain top'.

GIVEN NAMES Italian 12%. *Giulio* (3), *Annamarie, Antonio, Edmondo, Gino, Giuseppe, Guglielmo, Rocco, Salvatore.*

Cimaglia (139) Italian: habitational name from Cimaglia in Sicily or various places named with this word (probably a derivative of *cima* 'peak', 'mountain top'), such as Cimaglia Santo Spirito in Poggio Imperiale, Foggia province.

GIVEN NAMES Italian 12%. *Angelo, Bartolo, Benedetto, Egidio, Ulisse.*

Ciminelli (117) Italian: from **Ciminello**, a diminutive of CIMINO.

GIVEN NAMES Italian 9%. *Antonio, Donato, Pasquale.*

Ciminera (102) Italian: from a dialectal variant of *ciminiera*, 'chimney', hence a metonymic occupational name for someone who someone who built chimneys or worked a furnace, oven, or kiln with a chimney or a nickname for a tall thin person.

GIVEN NAMES Italian 23%; Irish 5%; Spanish 5%. *Angelo* (4), *Carmine, Constantino, Maddalena*; *Mario* (2), *Rosario.*

Cimini (328) Italian: **1.** patronymic or plural form of CIMINO. **2.** possibly a name for someone who lived by Montecimini in Lazio.

GIVEN NAMES Italian 15%. *Domenic* (3), *Marino* (2), *Amedeo, Annamaria, Camillo, Carmel, Elvio, Emidio, Enrico, Ettore, Guido, Libero.*

Cimino (1866) Italian: metonymic occupational name for a spice dealer, from *cimino* 'cumin', Sicilian *ciminu.*

GIVEN NAMES Italian 14%. *Salvatore* (8), *Sal* (6), *Rocco* (5), *Angelo* (4), *Antonio* (4), *Cono* (4), *Domenic* (4), *Aldo* (3), *Dante* (3), *Alfonse* (2), *Carmin* (2), *Carmine* (2).

Cimmino (200) Italian: variant of CIMINO.
GIVEN NAMES Italian 24%. *Mario* (4), *Carmela* (2), *Antonio, Carmine, Franco, Pasquale, Rosario, Santa.*

Cimo (174) Italian: probably from a personal name from a regularized or masculinized form of CIMA.
GIVEN NAMES Italian 15%; French 4%. *Angelo, Antonio, Domenico, Giuseppe, Onofrio, Salvatore; Andre, Pascal.*

Cimorelli (171) Italian: unexplained.
GIVEN NAMES Italian 17%. *Sal* (3), *Angelo* (2), *Antonio, Carmine, Dante, Giuseppe, Nicandro.*

Cina (288) Southern Italian: **1.** from a feminine form of the personal name CINO. **2.** (**Cinà**) variant of **Scinà**, an occupational name from medieval Greek *skoinas* 'cord or rope seller'.
GIVEN NAMES Italian 9%. *Salvatore* (2), *Carlo, Carmelo, Paolo.*

Cinco (140) **1.** Hispanic (common in El Salvador and the Philippines): possibly from Spanish *cinco* 'five'. **2.** Italian: unexplained.
GIVEN NAMES Spanish 33%; Italian 7%; French 4%. *Gustavo* (2), *Adriana, Alejo, Alfonso, Andres, Armando, Blanca, Carlos, Corazon, Domingo, Emilia, Emilio; Antonio* (3), *Lorenzo, Salvatore, Severino; Cecile, Raoul.*

Cincotta (605) Southern Italian (Sicily): possibly from a diminutive of the medieval personal names *Cinco, Cingo,* or *Gingo.*
GIVEN NAMES Italian 13%. *Angelo* (6), *Salvatore* (3), *Gaetano* (2), *Antonio, Bartolo, Carmine, Gennaro, Rocco, Sal, Silvio, Vincenzo.*

Cindric (164) Croatian (**Cindrić**): from *cindra*, a type of old musical instrument similar to a lute, hence a metonymic occupational name for someone who played this instrument.
GIVEN NAMES South Slavic 4%. *Mile, Milivoj.*

Cindrich (149) Croatian: see CINDRIC.

Cinelli (361) Italian: from a diminutive of the personal name CINO.
GIVEN NAMES Italian 17%. *Angelo* (4), *Pasquale* (3), *Annamarie, Camillo, Carmine, Domenic, Domenico, Egidio, Gianni, Gino, Guido, Luigi.*

Cini (168) Italian: **1.** patronymic or plural form of CINO. **2.** (**Cinì**) possibly a reduced form of the habitational name **Scinia**.
GIVEN NAMES Italian 12%. *Dante* (2), *Alfio, Amedeo, Attilio, Carmela, Ezio, Pasquale, Vincenza.*

Cink (177) Altered spelling of German ZINK.

Cinnamon (318) English: in part, possibly a variant of **Cinnamond**, a Norman habitational name from Saint-Amand in Cotentin, France.

Cino (198) Italian: from the personal name *Cino*, a short form of any of the personal names ending with the hypocoristic suffix -*cino*, such as *Baroncino, Leoncino, Pacino,* and *Simoncino.*
GIVEN NAMES Italian 18%. *Salvatore* (7), *Alfonso* (2), *Fausto* (2), *Angelo, Antonio, Carmelo, Elba, Gasper, Sal.*

Cinotti (104) Italian: from a diminutive of the personal name CINO.
GIVEN NAMES Italian 12%. *Alfonse* (2), *Angelo, Antonio, Emelio.*

Cinq-Mars (105) French: literally 'March 5th'; perhaps a byname given in celebration of a date of birth or some other event.
GIVEN NAMES French 12%. *Gaston, Jean Marie, Julien, Maxime.*

Cinque (295) Italian: from *cinque* 'five', applied as a nickname for the fifth-born child of a family or for someone from a family of five, or as a nickname or occupational name for someone who served in the Florentine administrative body known as the *Magistrato dei Cinque.*
GIVEN NAMES Italian 16%. *Salvatore* (4), *Cosmo* (2), *Luigi* (2), *Amedeo, Filippa, Lorenzo, Natale, Vittorio.*

Cinquemani (156) Italian: nickname meaning 'five (*cinque*) hands (*mani*)', presumably denoting a fast worker, possibly in either a literal or figurative sense.
GIVEN NAMES Italian 34%. *Salvatore* (7), *Angelo* (3), *Sal* (3), *Luigi* (2), *Luigia* (2), *Vito* (2), *Carmelo, Dino, Francesco, Giuseppe, Pietro, Vincenzo.*

Cintron (1302) Hispanic (Puerto Rico; **Cintrón**): unexplained; perhaps a nickname from a variant of Spanish *cinturón* 'belt'.
GIVEN NAMES Spanish 40%. *Jose* (30), *Carlos* (21), *Luis* (17), *Miguel* (16), *Juan* (12), *Angel* (10), *Ana* (8), *Rafael* (8), *Julio* (7), *Manuel* (7), *Luz* (6), *Wilfredo* (6).

Ciocca (243) Italian: descriptive nickname from *ciocca* 'lock of hair', 'quiff'.
GIVEN NAMES Italian 28%. *Rocco* (4), *Angelo* (3), *Mario* (3), *Americo* (2), *Antonio* (2), *Adelmo, Alfonso, Angelina, Arturo, Emilio, Elio, Fiore, Francesco, Marco, Michelangelo, Pietro, Romano.*

Ciocco (109) Italian: variant of CIOCCA.
GIVEN NAMES Italian 10%. *Angelo, Pasquale.*

Cioffi (1124) Italian: **1.** probably a nickname from Sicilian *cioffu* 'lock of hair', Italian *ciuffo.* **2.** from a French personal name of Germanic origin, *Joff.*

GIVEN NAMES Italian 16%. *Angelo* (8), *Salvatore* (7), *Carmine* (4), *Pasquale* (3), *Alberico* (2), *Carlo* (2), *Domenico* (2), *Enrico* (2), *Gino* (2), *Luigi* (2), *Antonio, Biagio.*

Ciolek (164) Polish (**Ciołek**): nickname from Polish *ciołek* 'young bull'.
FOREBEARS There were several Polish families named Ciołek; some can be traced back to the 15th century.

Ciolino (258) Italian: **1.** probably a habitational name from Ciolino, an area of Resuttano, in Caltanisetta province, Sicily. **2.** from a diminutive of the medieval Tuscan personal name *Ciolo*, itself probably a diminutive of a personal name ending with -*cio*, with loss of the preceding syllable or syllables.
GIVEN NAMES Italian 15%. *Salvatore* (4), *Sal* (3), *Antonio* (2), *Angelo, Domenic, Girolamo, Mafalda.*

Ciolli (103) Italian: perhaps from the medieval Tuscan personal name *Ciolo* (see CIOLINO).
GIVEN NAMES Italian 9%. *Angelo, Palma.*

Cione (110) Italian: from a short form of a personal name ending with the hypocoristic suffix -*cione*, such as *Felicione, Petriccione, Simoncione, Uguccione,* or a double diminutive of names ending with -*cio.*
GIVEN NAMES Italian 14%. *Rocco* (2), *Pasquale, Sal, Salvatore.*

Cioni (127) Italian: patronymic or plural form of CIONE.
GIVEN NAMES Italian 7%. *Aldo, Battista, Dario, Pietrina.*

Cioppa (151) Italian (Campania): unexplained.
GIVEN NAMES Italian 13%. *Angelo, Antimo, Antonio, Ciro, Marco, Pasquale, Sal.*

Ciotola (119) Italian: probably a diminutive of **Ciotta**, a feminine form of **Ciotto**.
GIVEN NAMES Italian 34%. *Angelo* (3), *Gino* (3), *Pietro* (2), *Rinaldo* (2), *Carmine, Domenic, Lia, Mauro, Sabatino.*

Ciotti (502) Italian: **1.** from a nickname from Old Italian *ciotto* 'lame'. **2.** from the personal name *Ciotto*, a short form of a personal name formed with the hypocoristic suffix -*ciotto*, such as *Feliciotto, Franciotto,* or *Petrucciotto.*
GIVEN NAMES Italian 16%. *Angelo* (5), *Aldo* (2), *Giuseppe* (2), *Tullio* (2), *Antonio, Dante, Domenic, Domenico, Emidio, Ezio, Geno, Gilda.*

Cipolla (977) Italian: metonymic occupational name for a grower or seller of onions, from *cipolla* 'onion'.
GIVEN NAMES Italian 16%. *Sal* (6), *Salvatore* (6), *Angelo* (5), *Gaetano* (4), *Carmine* (3), *Pasquale* (2), *Remo* (2), *Rocco* (2), *Biagio, Caesar, Calogero, Carlo.*

Cipollone (266) **1.** Italian: nickname for someone with a big head, from an augmentative of *cipolla* 'onion'. **2.** Southern

Italian (Sicily): nickname for a large coarse individual, Sicilian *cipudduni*.

GIVEN NAMES Italian 38%. *Antonio* (9), *Domenic* (4), *Pasquale* (3), *Angelo* (2), *Domenico* (2), *Luigi* (2), *Nicola* (2), *Pietro* (2), *Rocco* (2), *Alessandra, Alfredo, Benito, Camillo, Emilio, Filomeno, Mario, Rodolfo, Silvino.*

Cipra (135) Czech: from a short form of the personal name *Cyprián* Latin *Cyprianus* (see **Cipriano**).

GIVEN NAME German 8%. *Otto* (4).

Ciprian (101) Spanish (**Ciprián**): from the personal name *Ciprián*, a vernacular form of Latin *Cyprianus* (see **Cipriano**).

GIVEN NAMES Spanish 27%. *Roque* (2), *Carlos, Estela, Fiordaliza, Herminia, Jesus, Jose, Julio, Luisa, Luz Maria, Mercedes, Pedro.*

Cipriani (635) Italian: patronymic or plural form of CIPRIANO.

GIVEN NAMES Italian 15%. *Dario* (5), *Mario* (4), *Angelo* (3), *Antonio* (3), *Gennaro* (2), *Guido* (2), *Aldo, Alfonso, Augusto, Dante, Domenic, Domenico, Elio, Emidio, Ercole, Frederico, Octavio, Renato, Roberto.*

Cipriano (1230) Italian: from the personal name *Cipriano*, from Latin *Cyprianus*, originally an ethnic name for an inhabitant of Cyprus. The name was borne by a bishop of Carthage who was martyred in 258, and by another saint, probably legendary, whose cult was suppressed by the Holy See in 1969.

GIVEN NAMES Italian 24%; Spanish 9%. *Rocco* (15), *Angelo* (9), *Salvatore* (7), *Antonio* (6), *Francisco* (6), *Carmine* (5), *Mario* (5), *Vito* (4), *Carmela* (2), *Gaetano* (2), *Giovanni* (2), *Giuseppe* (2), *Pasquale* (2), *Pietro* (2), *Jose* (4), *Luis* (4), *Diego* (3), *Guadalupe* (2), *Javier* (2), *Manuel* (2), *Pedro* (2).

Cira (200) **1.** Italian: from Sicilian *cira* 'wax', presumably a metonymic occupational name for someone who collected or sold wax. **2.** Italian: habitational name from a place named Cirà. **3.** Italian: from the personal name *Ciro*. **4.** Possibly also Albanian: topographic name from *çair* 'field', 'meadow' (from Turkish *çayir*).

GIVEN NAMES Italian 7%. *Cosimo* (3), *Salvatore.*

Ciraulo (182) Southern Italian: possibly a derogatory nickname from Calabrian *ceraulu*, Sicilian *ciraulu* 'snake charmer', by extension 'fraudster', 'charlatan'. Compare CERAVOLO.

GIVEN NAMES Italian 16%. *Domenic* (4), *Antonino, Antonio, Gandolfo, Gilda, Gioacchino, Nicoletta, Sal, Sarina.*

Circelli (117) Southern Italian (Sicily): from Sicilian *circedda, circeddu, circhetta* 'hoop earring', a desriptive epithet for someone who wore hoop earrings.

GIVEN NAMES Italian 26%. *Angelo* (3), *Carmine* (2), *Antonio, Donato, Matteo, Pasquale, Raffaele, Salvatore.*

Circle (319) Americanized spelling of German **Zirkel**, an occupational name for a watchman (one who makes the rounds), Middle High German *zirkeler*.

Circo (105) Italian (Sicily): metonymic occupational name for a falconer or nickname for someone thought to resemble a falcon or hawk, from medieval Greek *kyrkos* 'falcon', 'hawk'. Compare CIARCIA.

GIVEN NAMES Italian 9%. *Alfio* (2), *Angelo, Remo.*

Cirelli (375) Italian: from a pet form of the personal name *Ciro*, Italian equivalent of CYRUS.

GIVEN NAMES Italian 18%. *Angelo* (3), *Carlo* (2), *Gino* (2), *Aldo, Carmine, Cono, Dante, Franco, Giovanni, Giuseppe, Luigi, Pasquale.*

Ciresi (162) Italian: from a derivative of Latin *ceresa* 'cherry', probably applied as a nickname for someone with rosy cheeks or cherry lips, or as a topographic name for someone who lived in a place with an abundance of cherry trees, or as a metonymic occupational name for a grower or seller of cherries.

GIVEN NAMES Italian 17%. *Salvatore* (4), *Angelo, Gaetano, Paolo, Sal.*

Ciriello (250) Italian: probably from a diminutive of *Cirio*, a personal name derived from Greek *kyrios* 'lord'.

GIVEN NAMES Italian 19%. *Carmine* (3), *Salvatore* (3), *Dario* (2), *Agostino, Angelo, Cosmo, Domenico, Gaetano, Giulio, Luigi, Vincenzo, Vito.*

Cirigliano (253) Italian: habitational name from a place named Cirigliano, in Matera province.

GIVEN NAMES Italian 22%. *Salvatore* (3), *Rocco* (2), *Alfredo, Caesar, Carmela, Donato, Fausto, Gennaro, Luciano, Vincenzo, Vito.*

Cirilli (119) Italian: patronymic or plural form of CIRILLO.

GIVEN NAMES Italian 14%. *Angelo, Damiano, Dante, Levio.*

Cirillo (1338) Italian: from a diminutive of the personal name *Cirio*, from Greek *kyrios* 'lord'.

GIVEN NAMES Italian 16%. *Carmine* (4), *Ilario* (3), *Rocco* (3), *Sal* (3), *Salvatore* (3), *Carmin* (2), *Domenic* (2), *Gaetano* (2), *Pasquale* (2), *Vincenzo* (2), *Angelo.*

Cirilo (113) Spanish: from the personal name *Cirilo*, from Latin *Cyrillus* from Greek *Kyrillos* meaning 'of the Lord'. This name was borne by a large number of early saints, most notably the theologians Cyril of Alexandria and Cyril of Jerusalem. It was also the name of one of the Greek evangelists who took Christianity to the Slavic regions of eastern Europe.

GIVEN NAMES Spanish 40%. *Eleazar* (3), *Manuel* (3), *Roberto* (2), *Alejandro, Alfredo, Angel, Armando, Blanca, Carlos, Cruz Maria, Domingo, Efrain; Cira, Tolentino.*

Cirincione (233) Italian (Sicily): variant spelling of CIRRINCIONE.

GIVEN NAMES Italian 14%. *Salvatore* (3), *Vito* (2), *Sal, Serafino.*

Cirino (412) Italian, Spanish, and Portuguese: from the personal name *Cirino*, Greek *Kyrinos* (Latin *Quirinus*), a name borne by various early saints.

GIVEN NAMES Italian 12%; Spanish 9%. *Angelo* (2), *Antonio* (2), *Domenic* (2), *Carmin, Francesco, Franco, Natale, Rocco, Sal, Salvatore, Vincenzo; Caridad* (2), *Jose* (2), *Juan* (2), *Nestor* (2), *Heriberta, Josefina, Juanita, Julio, Justina, Lourdes.*

Cirone (331) Southern Italian: from an augmentative form of the personal name *Ciro*, from Greek *kyrios* 'lord'.

GIVEN NAMES Italian 17%. *Carmine* (2), *Cono* (2), *Domenico* (2), *Salvatore* (2), *Caterina, Marco, Nunzio, Pasquale, Romolo, Vito.*

Cirrincione (207) Italian (Sicily): from an augmentative form of a nickname from *cirrinciò* 'greenfinch'.

GIVEN NAMES Italian 21%. *Sal* (3), *Ciro* (2), *Marco* (2), *Angelo, Carlo, Carmelo, Gaetano, Pietro, Sando, Vito.*

Cirrito (105) Italian: variant of CERRITO.

GIVEN NAME Italian 6%. *Cosmo.*

Cisar (207) Czech (**Císař**): from *císař* 'emperor', probably used as a nickname for someone with an imperious manner or for someone who had played the part of an emperor in a pageant or play. See also KAISER.

Cisco (779) Southern Italian: from the personal name *Cisco*, a short form of *Francesco*, from Latin *Franciscus* (see FRANCIS).

Cisek (240) Polish: **1.** topographic name from a diminutive of *cis* 'yew tree'. **2.** nickname from *cisy* 'swarthy'.

GIVEN NAMES Polish 7%. *Andrzej, Ignatius, Jerzy, Stanislaw, Teofil.*

Cisewski (195) Variant spelling of Polish CISZEWSKI.

Ciske (109) German: of Slavic origin. Compare ZISKA.

GIVEN NAMES German 6%. *Erwin* (2), *Kurt.*

Cislo (211) Polish (**Cisło**): unflattering nickname from a derivative of *cisnąć* 'to oppress', 'bully'.

GIVEN NAMES Polish 7%. *Andrzej, Bronislawa, Danuta, Kazimierz, Krystyna.*

Cisneros (4187) Spanish: habitational name from Cisneros, a place in the province of Palencia, named with a derivative of Spanish *cisne* 'swan' (via Old French and Latin from Greek *kyknos*).

GIVEN NAMES Spanish 48%. *Jose* (120), *Juan* (54), *Jesus* (52), *Manuel* (52), *Carlos* (42), *Luis* (32), *Raul* (27), *Arturo* (26), *Francisco* (26), *Mario* (24), *Guadalupe* (22), *Pedro* (22).

Cisney (197) Americanized form of French CISSNA.

Cisse (125) **1.** French (**Cissé**): habitational name from a place called Cissé in Vienne. **2.** African: unexplained.

GIVEN NAMES African 40%; Muslim 34%. *Amadou* (4), *Aminata* (4), *Mamadou* (4), *Thierno* (2), *Aboubacar*, *Aliou*, *Alou*, *Babacar*, *Cheikh*, *Fatou*, *Keba*, *Mahamadou*; *Moussa* (4), *Ibrahima* (3), *Daouda* (2), *Mohamed* (2), *Omar* (2), *Abdoulaye*, *Abdul*, *Ali*, *Hassane*, *Ismail*, *Issa*, *Khadim*.

Cissel (133) Variant of Welsh CECIL.

Cissell (718) Variant of Welsh CECIL.

Cissna (159) French: variant of CESSNA.

Cisson (118) Probably a variant spelling of SISSON.

Ciszek (179) Polish: nickname from *cichy* 'quiet', 'calm', or *ciszyć* 'to appease', 'to calm down'.

GIVEN NAMES Polish 10%. *Ignatius* (2), *Stanislaw* (2), *Jaroslaw*, *Piotr*, *Wieslaw*.

Ciszewski (284) Polish: habitational name for someone from a place named Ciszewo, from a derivative of *cichy* 'quiet', 'calm'.

GIVEN NAMES Polish 8%. *Teofil* (2), *Andrzej*, *Janusz*, *Jaroslaw*, *Lech*, *Wojciech*, *Zbigniew*.

Citarella (151) Southern Italian (Sicily and Naples): metonymic occupational name for a guitar maker or player, from a diminutive of *citarra* 'guitar' (standard Italian *chitarra*).

GIVEN NAMES Italian 16%; Spanish 5%. *Alberto*, *Giorgio*, *Italo*, *Sal*, *Salvatore*; *Bicente*, *Vicente*.

Citizen (178) Origin uncertain. There is some evidence that it may be an altered form of an English patronymic, *Cittison*, from an unidentified personal name. Alternatively, it may be an ornamental adoption of the vocabulary word *citizen* as a surname by people with republican beliefs, in some cases representing an Americanized form of the French equivalent *citoyen*.

GIVEN NAMES French 8%. *Raoul* (2), *Lucien*, *Maudry*.

Citrano (144) Italian (Sicily): from *citru* 'cedar' (Italian *cedro*), applied as a topographic name or possibly as a habitational name from a lost or unidentified place named for its cedars.

GIVEN NAMES Italian 11%. *Salvatore* (3), *Giuseppe*.

Citrin (215) Jewish (eastern Ashkenazic): from Yiddish *tsitrin* 'lemon (tree)'. Compare CITRON.

GIVEN NAME Jewish 4%. *Sol*.

Citro (290) Southern Italian: topographic name from Sicilian *citru* 'cedar' (Italian *cedro*).

GIVEN NAMES Italian 14%. *Angelo* (3), *Antonio*, *Augustino*, *Gino*, *Michelina*, *Romolo*, *Sal*, *Santino*, *Vittorio*.

Citron (627) **1.** Jewish (eastern Ashkenazic): ornamental name from German *Zitrone* 'lemon (tree)'; in some cases it may be a metonymic occupational name as in 2 below. **2.** French: from Old French *citron* 'lemon' (from Latin *citrus* 'lemon tree'), and so a metonymic occupational name for a grower or seller of lemons, or perhaps a nickname for a sharp and disagreeable person.

GIVEN NAMES Jewish 5%. *Chaim* (2), *Dov*, *Emanuel*, *Hyman*, *Kive*, *Shira*, *Yoav*.

Cittadino (163) Italian: from *cittadino* 'townsman', probably applied as a nickname for someone who had lived in or had some association with a town or city.

GIVEN NAMES Italian 12%. *Aldo*, *Carmela*, *Elio*, *Ercole*, *Giuseppe*, *Sal*.

Ciucci (145) Italian (Naples): nickname from the dialect word *ciuccio* 'ass'.

GIVEN NAMES Italian 15%. *Alessandra*, *Alfio*, *Atilio*, *Domenico*, *Francesco*, *Luigi*.

Ciuffo (104) Italian: from *ciuffo* 'tuft', 'bunch', 'fringe', 'quiff', hence a nickname for someone with some peculiarity in the way his hair was styled.

GIVEN NAMES Italian 16%. *Angelo*, *Giuseppa*, *Salvatore*.

Ciufo (153) Italian: variant of CIUFFO.

GIVEN NAMES Italian 13%. *Alessandro*, *Angelo*, *Attilio*, *Clemente*, *Pio*, *Silvio*.

Ciulla (502) Italian: **1.** from a feminine form of CIULLO. **2.** from a diminutive of the female personal name LUCIA, with loss of the first syllable. **3.** of Albanian origin but unexplained etymology; the surname is found chiefly in Piana degli Albanesi, in Palermo province, which is one of the most ancient Albanian communities in Italy.

GIVEN NAMES Italian 14%. *Luigi* (4), *Salvatore* (4), *Santo* (3), *Giovanni* (2), *Saverio* (2), *Angelo*, *Antonio*, *Gasper*, *Pasqualino*, *Sal*.

Ciullo (225) Italian: **1.** from an old Tuscan personal name *Ciullo*, a short form of *Franciullo*, *Vincenciullo*, and other names with this suffix. **2.** derogatory nickname from *ciullo* 'ignorant', 'inept', from *fanciullo* 'little boy'.

GIVEN NAMES Italian 15%. *Angelo* (2), *Valentino* (2), *Alfonse*, *Enrico*, *Nunzio*, *Rocco*, *Salvator*, *Salvatore*.

Civello (148) Italian: possibly a habitational name from Civello near Como in Lombardy.

GIVEN NAMES Italian 8%. *Gandolfo*, *Paolo*, *Salvatore*.

Civiello (106) Italian: variant of CIVELLO.

GIVEN NAMES Italian 14%. *Rocco* (2), *Domenic*, *Guido*.

Civil (108) **1.** French, Catalan, and Spanish: nickname from *civil*, from Latin *civilis* 'civil', 'of or pertaining to a citizen', by extension 'cultivated', 'educated'. However, in Spanish the term also meant 'wicked' or 'rude' and the nickname may have come from either of these senses. **2.** Catalan: topographic name from Old French *sevil* 'fence', 'enclosure'.

Civitarese (101) Italian: habitational name for someone from a place named with Civita, most notably Civitaluparella in Chieti province, where the modern family name is frequent, also Civitaquana in Abruzzo, and Civitacampomarano in Molise.

GIVEN NAMES Italian 14%. *Antonio*, *Domenic*, *Giuseppe*.

Civitello (190) Italian: habitational name from any of numerous places named from *civitella* 'little city'.

GIVEN NAMES Italian 11%. *Carmine* (2), *Carmel*, *Domenic*, *Leonardo*, *Sal*.

Cizek (392) Czech (**Čížek**), Slovak (**Čížik**), and Slovenian (**Čižek**): nickname from *čížek* (Czech) or *čižek* (Slovenian) 'siskin' (a type of finch). In Moravia this was a nickname for someone from Bohemia.

Claar (717) Altered spelling of Dutch or German **Klaar**. The first, according to Debrabandere, is from the female personal name *Clara*. The German surname is a topographic name from a minor place near Braunschweig, or a nickname from Middle High German, Middle Low German *klar*, 'pure', 'pretty', 'sensible'.

Claassen (611) Dutch, North German, and Danish: patronymic from the personal name *Klaas*, a reduced form of *Nik(o)laas* (see NICHOLAS, CLAUS).

GIVEN NAMES German 5%. *Hans* (2), *Claus*, *Erna*, *Frieda*, *Klaas*, *Otto*, *Ulrich*.

Clabaugh (649) Probably an Americanized form of German **Kleebach** (the second element of which is German *Bach* 'stream'; the first element is unexplained) or possibly of **Klappach**, a variant of KLAPPER.

Clabby (118) Scottish: unexplained.

Clabo (211) French (**Clabaud**) and Dutch: derivative of the Germanic personal name *Hlōdbald*, composed of the elements *hlōd* 'famous', 'clear' + *bald* 'bold', 'daring'.

Claborn (440) Variant of English CLAIBORNE.

Clabough (215) Probably an Americanized form of German **Kleebach** or possibly of **Klappach** (see CLABAUGH).

Clack (1146) English: from a Middle English personal name *Clac*, which is from Old English *Clacc* or the Old Norse cognate *Klakkr*. As a personal name this is from a word meaning 'lump' and may have been used as a nickname for a large or thickset man. Reaney suggests that it could also be from *clacker* 'chatterer'.

Clady (103) Respelling of French **Cladé** or **Cladet**, an Occitan derivative of *cleda* 'hurdle', 'fence'.

Claes (125) Dutch: from a reduced form of the personal name *Nik(o)laas* (see NICHOLAS, CLAASSEN, CLAUS).

Claeys (589) Dutch: from a reduced form of the personal name *Nik(o)laas* (see NICHOLAS, CLAASSEN, CLAUS).

GIVEN NAMES French 5%. *Armand* (2), *Alphonse, Andre, Dany, Dominique, Etienne.*

Claffey (467) Irish: reduced Anglicized form of **McClaffey**, Gaelic **Mac Fhlaithimh**, a patronymic from the personal name *Flaitheamh* meaning 'prince'.
GIVEN NAME Irish 5%. *Kieran.*

Claflin (789) Irish: reduced form of Mc-LAUGHLIN. The interchange between the sounds *gh* and *f* occurs in other Americanized Irish names, for example MURPHY.

Clagett (422) Variant spelling of English CLAGGETT.

Clagg (401) **1.** English: voiced variant of CLACK. **2.** Possibly a variant spelling of Manx CLAGUE.

Claggett (448) English: probably a habitational name from Claygate in Surrey, named with Old English *clæg* 'clay' + *geat* 'gate', 'gap', or from some other similarly named place.

Claghorn (106) Scottish: variant of CLEGHORN.
FOREBEARS James Claghorn was shipped to New England in 1651 as a prisoner, having been one of the Scottish opponents of Oliver Cromwell. In 1662 he is recorded as a freeman of Barnstable, MA.

Clague (199) Manx: Anglicized form of Gaelic **Mac Liaigh** 'son of the physician', from *mac* 'son' + *liaigh* 'physician'.
GIVEN NAME Scottish 4%. *Ewan.*

Claiborne (1548) English: It has been proposed that this may be a variant of CLIBURN, but the latter is a northwestern English name whereas **Claiborne** is found mostly in Norfolk and the southeast, so it is more probably from a lost place in that part of England, perhaps named with Old English *clæg* 'clay' + *burne* 'spring', 'stream'.
FOREBEARS William Claiborne (*c*.1600–77) was a founding colonist in VA. His descendant, William Charles Claiborne (1775–1817) was the first governor of LA.

Clair (1664) French: from the personal name *Clair* (Latin *Clarus* 'illustrious'), which was borne by a 3rd-century bishop of Nantes and by the 4th-century St. Clair of Aquitaine.

Claire (406) **1.** English and Irish: variant spelling of CLARE. **2.** French: from the female personal name *Claire* (feminine form of CLAIR), which was popularized through the fame of St. Clare of Assisi (see CHIARA).

Clairmont (483) Variant of the French habitational name CLERMONT.
GIVEN NAMES French 4%. *Adelard, Aime, Antoine, Aurore, Fernand.*

Claman (134) Probably an Americanized spelling of Dutch and German **Clemen**, a patronymic from the Middle Dutch personal name *Clemin* or a variant of German CLEMENS.

Clamp (316) English: possibly from Middle English *clamp* 'clamp', 'brace', 'iron band'

(a borrowing from Middle Dutch, first recorded in the early 14th century). This may have been a metonymic occupational name for a smith who specialized in making clamps.

Clampitt (597) English: habitational name from either of two places in Devon called Clampitt or from Clampit in Cornwall, all named with Old English *clām* 'mud', 'clay' + Old English *pytt* 'pit'.

Clanahan (128) Scottish: reduced form of MCCLANAHAN.

Clancey (345) Irish: variant spelling of CLANCY.

Clancy (4949) Irish: Anglicized form of Gaelic **Mac Fhlannchaidh**, patronymic from the personal name *Flannchadh*, which is derived from *flann* 'red'.
GIVEN NAMES Irish 6%. *Brendan* (3), *John Patrick* (2), *Liam* (2), *Callahan, Clancy, Conor, Donal, Siobhan.*

Clanin (151) Probably a reduced and altered form of Scottish MCCLANAHAN.

Clanton (2616) English: probably a variant spelling of the habitational name **Clandon**, from places in Surrey and Dorset named Clandon, from Old English *clǣne* 'clean' (i.e. 'clear of weeds') + *dūn* 'hill'.

Clapham (305) English: habitational name from any of various places called Clapham, for example in Bedfordshire, Surrey, Sussex, and North Yorkshire. The first three are named with Old English *clopp(a)* 'lump', 'hillock' + *hām* 'homestead' or *hamm* 'enclosure hemmed in by water', while the Yorkshire place name is formed with an Old English word *clǣpe* 'noisy stream'.

Clapp (3813) **1.** English (chiefly Bristol): from Middle English *clop(pe)* 'lump', 'hillock' (from Old English *clopp(a)*), applied either as a topographic name or as a nickname for a large and ungainly person. **2.** Variant spelling of German KLAPP.

Clapper (1720) **1.** English: from Middle English *clapper* 'rough bridge', applied as a topographic name or as a habitational name from any of the numerous minor places named with this word. **2.** English: nickname from an agent derivative of Middle English *clappe* 'chatter'. **3.** Americanized spelling of German and Jewish KLAPPER 'chatterer'. **4.** Americanized form of German **Klopper**, a metonymic occupational name relating to several trades, from Middle Low German *klopper* 'clapper', 'bobbin', 'hammer'.

Claps (164) Origin unidentified. This name is found with Italian forenames, but is not Italian in form. It was probably imported to Italy from France, where it is a topographic name from French *Les Claps*, the name of a rock mass in Hérault.
GIVEN NAMES Italian 19%. *Vito* (4), *Rocco* (2), *Annalisa, Italia, Salvatore, Saverio.*

Clapsaddle (320) Americanized spelling of German **Klebsattel**, a nickname for a rider

(on horseback), apparently from *kleben* 'to stick' + *Sattel* 'saddle'.

Clar (133) **1.** Variant spelling of German KLAR. **2.** southern French and Catalan: from Occitan and Catalan *Clar*, equivalent to French CLAIR.
GIVEN NAMES Spanish 5%. *Alberto* (2), *Baltasar, Jorge, Juan, Luis, Ramon, Susana.*

Clara (118) **1.** Spanish, Catalan, Portuguese, and northern Italian (Piedmont): variant of CLARO. **2.** Dutch: metronymic from the female personal name *Clara* (see CLARE).
GIVEN NAMES Spanish 33%; Italian 10%. *Pedro* (2), *Raul* (2), *Amado, Benigno, Cornelio, Esteban, Genaro, Hermelinda, Joaquin, Josefa, Juan, Luis; Aldo, Antonio, Domenico, Giovanna, Remo.*

Clardy (1274) Irish or Scottish: reduced form of **McLardy**, an Anglicized form of Gaelic **Mac Fhlaithbheartaigh**, found mainly in Scotland (see MCLAFFERTY).

Clare (1624) **1.** Irish and English: habitational name from Clare in Suffolk (probably named with a Celtic river name meaning 'bright', 'gentle', or 'warm'). One of the first Normans in Ireland (1170–72) was Richard de Clare, Earl of Pembroke, better known as 'Strongbow', who took his surname from his estate in Suffolk. **2.** English: habitational name from Clare in Oxfordshire, named with Old English *clǣg* 'clay' + *ōra* 'slope'. **3.** English: from the Middle English, Old French female personal name *Cla(i)re* (Latin *Clara*, from *clarus* 'famous'), which achieved some popularity, greater on the Continent than in England, through the fame of St. Clare of Assisi. See also SINCLAIR. **4.** English: occupational name for a worker in clay, for example someone expert in building in wattle and daub, from Middle English *clayere*, an agent derivative of Old English *clǣg* 'clay'.

Clarence (104) English: Clarence was the name of a dukedom created in 1362 for Lionel, third son of Edward III, whose wife was the heiress of Clare in Suffolk. How the name came to be adopted as a surname is uncertain, but it is recorded in 1453; its use as a personal name is not attested until the late 19th century.

Clarey (382) Irish and English: variant spelling of CLARY.
GIVEN NAMES Irish 5%. *Delma* (2), *Donovan.*

Clarida (148) Origin unidentified. Compare CLARIDY.

Claridge (336) English: **1.** from the Middle English, Old French female personal name *Clarice* (Latin *Claritia* meaning 'fame', 'brightness', a derivative of *clarus* 'famous', 'bright'). **2.** habitational name from Clearhedge Wood in Sussex, which is probably named with Old English *clǣfre* 'clover' + *hrycg* 'ridge'.

Claridy (120) **1.** Probably a variant of Irish or Scottish CLARDY. **2.** Alternatively, perhaps a variant of English CLARIDGE.

Clarin (135) **1.** French: from a pet form of CLAIR. **2.** Swedish: derivative of *klar* 'clear' (possibly representing an element of a place name) + *-in* (suffix of surnames derived from Latin *-inus*, *-inius* 'descendant of').

GIVEN NAMES Spanish 15%. *Luz* (2), *Alejandro, Armida, Epifano, Florencio, Jose, Libia, Librada, Maria Luisa, Raul, Santos, Sergio.*

Clarizio (112) Italian: from a derivative of the nickname or personal name CHIARO.

GIVEN NAMES Italian 30%. *Salvatore* (2), *Arcangelo, Dino, Giacomo, Gino, Luco, Orlando, Ottavio, Rocco, Sal, Vincenzo.*

Clark (195819) English: occupational name for a scribe or secretary, originally a member of a minor religious order who undertook such duties. The word *clerc* denoted a member of a religious order, from Old English *cler(e)c* 'priest', reinforced by Old French *clerc*. Both are from Late Latin *clericus*, from Greek *klērikos*, a derivative of *klēros* 'inheritance', 'legacy', with reference to the priestly tribe of Levites (see LEVY) 'whose inheritance was the Lord'. In medieval Christian Europe, clergy in minor orders were permitted to marry and so found families; thus the surname could become established. In the Middle Ages it was virtually only members of religious orders who learned to read and write, so that the term *clerk* came to denote any literate man.

Clarke (23265) English: variant spelling of CLARK.

FOREBEARS This name was brought independently to New England by many bearers from the 17th century onward. Nicholas Clarke was one of the founders of Hartford, CT, (coming from Cambridge, MA, with Thomas Hooker) in 1635.

Clarkin (412) English: from a diminutive of CLARE or CLARK.

Clarkson (3366) English: patronymic from CLARK.

Clarkston (197) English (Nottinghamshire): variant of CLARKSON.

Clarno (127) Origin unidentified.

Claro (195) **1.** Spanish and Portuguese: nickname from *claro* 'light', 'bright', or from the personal name *Clarus*, both from Latin *clarus* 'clear', 'bright'. **2.** Italian (Piedmont): variant of CHIARO.

GIVEN NAMES Spanish 35%; Italian 10%. *Jaime* (3), *Adalberto* (2), *Emilio* (2), *Jose* (2), *Manuel* (2), *Raul* (2), *Salvador* (2), *Abilio, Adan, Agustin, Aida, Alfredo; Antonio* (2), *Elio* (2), *Rocco* (2), *Angelo, Licinio, Romeo.*

Claros (202) Spanish: possibly topographic name from the plural of Spanish *claro* 'clearing (in a forest)', or variant of CLARO.

GIVEN NAMES Spanish 47%. *Jose* (7), *Carlos* (4), *Juan* (4), *Francisco* (3), *Alberto* (2), *Mario* (2), *Mercedes* (2), *Ricardo* (2), *Valerio* (2), *Alcira, Alicia, Americo.*

Clary (4301) **1.** Irish: variant of CLEARY or a reduced form of MCCLARY. **2.** English: perhaps from Middle English *clary, clarie* 'clary' (the pot herb *Salvia sclarea*), a topographic name for someone who lived where the plant grew or a metonymic occupational name for a herb seller.

Clasby (208) Scottish, English, and Irish: apparently a habitational name from an English or Scottish place named with Old Norse *býr* 'farm', 'settlement', possibly CLEASBY or one of the three places in Lincolnshire named Claxby, named with the Old Norse personal name *Klakkr* (see CLACK).

GIVEN NAMES Irish 6%. *Brendan, Bridie.*

Clasen (639) Dutch, North German, Danish, and Norwegian: patronymic from the personal name *Claas* (see CLAASSEN).

GIVEN NAMES German 5%. *Gerhard* (2), *Erwin, Hermann, Ingeborg, Irmgard, Kurt, Otto, Ulrich.*

Clason (299) Americanized spelling of Dutch **Claasen**.

GIVEN NAMES German 4%. *Kurt* (2), *Otto.*

Class (551) **1.** English: from the medieval personal name *Classe*, a short form of NICHOLAS. See also CLAYSON. **2.** Variant of **Klaas** or **Klass**, North German forms of CLAUS.

GIVEN NAMES Spanish 7%. *Angel* (5), *Jose* (4), *Ramon* (3), *Edgardo* (2), *Manuel* (2), *Rafael* (2), *Adela, Altagracia, Ana, Beatriz, Confesora, Jorge.*

Classen (734) Dutch, North German, and Danish: patronymic from the personal name *Claas* (see CLAASSEN).

Classon (165) Swedish: patronymic from the personal name *Claes*, Swedish form of CLAUS.

GIVEN NAME Scandinavian 6%. *Hild.*

Clatterbuck (430) English (Gloucestershire): variant spelling of **Clutterbuck**, a name of unknown origin, possibly a garbled form of a Dutch name.

Claud (234) French: variant of CLAUDE.

Claude (496) French: from a medieval personal name (Latin *Claudius*, a Roman family name derived from *claudus* 'lame') which was popular as a result of having been borne by a 7th-century saint, bishop of Besançon.

GIVEN NAMES French 12%. *Medard* (2), *Pierre* (2), *Yves* (2), *Alain, Alphonse, Andre, Arnaud, Elodie, Emile, Fabienne, Fernande, Georges.*

Claudio (642) Portuguese (**Cláudio**) and Spanish: from the personal name, Portuguese *Cláudio*, Spanish *Claudio*, vernacular forms of Latin *Claudius*, a Roman family name derived from *claudus* 'lame'.

GIVEN NAMES Spanish 40%. *Jose* (16), *Angel* (7), *Carlos* (7), *Juan* (6), *Luis* (6), *Pedro*

(5), *Luz* (4), *Miguel* (4), *Rafael* (4), *Ramon* (4), *Ana* (3), *Arnaldo* (3); *Antonio* (9), *Carmello* (2), *Angelo, Carmelo, Cecilio, Cesare, Corrado, Leonardo, Lorenzo, Pio, Serverino, Silvio.*

Clauer (131) German: variant spelling of KLAUER.

GIVEN NAMES German 4%. *Egon* (2), *Monika.*

Claunch (725) Americanized form of German KLONTZ.

Claus (1409) **1.** Variant spelling of German KLAUS, which is from a popular personal name, a reduced form of *Nikolaus* (see NICHOLAS). This spelling is also found in Dutch. **2.** Occitan: topographic name for someone who lived by an enclosure of some sort, such as a courtyard or farmyard, from Late Latin *clausum* 'enclosure', 'closed', originally the past participle of *claudere* 'to close'.

GIVEN NAMES German 4%. *Hans* (3), *Bodo* (2), *Heinz* (2), *Alfons, Eberhard, Erwin, Gerhard, Gunther, Helmut, Jochen, Kurt, Otto.*

Clause (465) Dutch: variant of CLAUS.

GIVEN NAMES French 4%. *Chantel, Landry, Marcel.*

Clausell (183) Origin unidentified.

Clausen (3862) Dutch, North German, Danish, and Norwegian: patronymic from the personal name CLAUS, a reduced form of *Nikolaus* (see NICHOLAS).

GIVEN NAMES Scandinavian 4%. *Holger* (4), *Bente* (2), *Ingard* (2), *Niels* (2), *Ansgar, Astrid, Bent, Bjorn, Erik, Evald, Jorgen, Knud.*

Clauser (392) Variant spelling of German KLAUSER.

Clausing (320) Spelling variant of German KLAUSING.

GIVEN NAMES German 5%. *Kurt* (3), *Erwin* (2), *Hans.*

Clausnitzer (101) Variant spelling of German **Klausnitz**, a habitational name from a place called Klausnitz or Klaussnitz.

GIVEN NAMES German 7%. *Otto, Volker.*

Clauson (972) Variant spelling of CLAUSEN or one of its many cognates.

Clauss (779) Dutch, North German, etc.: variant of CLAUS. This spelling is also found in Alsace and Lorraine.

GIVEN NAMES German 4%. *Kurt* (3), *Helmut, Ingeborg, Otto.*

Claussen (1532) Dutch, North German, Norwegian, and Danish: patronymic from the personal name CLAUS.

Clavel (109) **1.** Spanish: from Spanish *clavel* or Catalan *clavell* 'clove', earlier also 'nail', a derivative of Latin *clavellus* 'nail', applied as a metonymic occupational name for a spice trader or a nail maker. **2.** French: metonymic occupational name for a nail maker from a derivative of Latin *clavellus*, but in some cases possibly from the same word in the sense 'smallpox', 'rash'.

GIVEN NAMES Spanish 25%; French 11%. *Jose* (2), *Alfredo, Angel, Bernardina,*

Carlos, Consuelo, Fernando, Gustavo, Jeronimo, Jorge, Luis, Margarita; Andre (2), Eugenie, Fernande, Jean-Claude, Pierre.

Claver (115) **1.** English: occupational name from Old French *clavier* 'doorkeeper' (from Latin *clavis* 'key'). **2.** Catalan: from *claver* 'keeper of the keys', 'doorkeeper', Latin *clavarius*.

Claverie (126) French: from Middle French *claverie* (a derivative of Latin *clavis* 'key'), a term denoting a receiving office for coffer keys; by extension, this was probably an occupational name for the person who administered such an office.

GIVEN NAMES French 8%. *Gaston, Monique.*

Clavette (221) French: probably a nickname or occupational name from *clavette* 'wedge'.

GIVEN NAMES French 18%. *Cecile (2), Lucien (2), Adrien, Alcide, Alphie, Armand, Aurele, Donat, Fernand, Marthe, Oneil, Yvon.*

Clavier (108) Southern French: occupational name for someone who had charge of keys, a chatelain, treasurer, or ceremonial official, from Old French *clavier* 'doorkeeper' (from Latin *clavis* 'key').

GIVEN NAMES French 11%. *Henri, Julien, Marie Ange, Monique.*

Clavijo (174) Spanish: habitational name from a place in Logroño province named Clavijo.

GIVEN NAMES Spanish 47%. *Carlos (4), Eduardo (4), Jose (3), Juan (3), Luis (3), Pedro (3), Alberto (2), Andres (2), Augusto (2), Felipe (2), Javier (2), Jorge (2); Antonio (2), Cecilio, Federico, Guido.*

Clavin (243) Irish: reduced Anglicized form of Gaelic **Mac Fhláimhín** 'son of *Flaithimhín*', a personal name from a diminutive of *flaith* 'prince', 'ruler' (see LAVIN).

GIVEN NAME Irish 4%. *Kieran.*

Clawson (4000) Americanized form of any of the Dutch, North German, or Scandinavian patronymics from short forms of the personal name *Nik(o)laus, Nikolaas*, etc. (see NICHOLAS).

Claxon (133) English: patronymic from the Middle English personal name *Clac* (see CLACK).

Claxton (1996) English: habitational name from any of various places named Claxton, for example in County Durham, Norfolk, and North Yorkshire, probably from the Old Norse personal name *Klakkr* (see CLACK) or possibly from Old English *clacc* 'hill' + Old English *tūn* 'settlement'.

Clay (14091) **1.** English: from Old English *clǣg* 'clay', applied as a topographic name for someone who lived in an area of clay soil or as a metonymic occupational name for a worker in a clay pit (see CLAYMAN). **2.** Americanized spelling of German KLEE.

FOREBEARS The relatively common English name Clay had several American forebears

in the 18th century. Henry Clay, born in Hanover, VA, in 1777, secretary of state for President John Quincy Adams, was descended from English ancestors who came to VA shortly after the founding of Jamestown. The revolutionary war officer Joseph Clay, also a member of the Continental Congress, was a native of Yorkshire, England, who emigrated to GA in 1760 and was a founder of the University of Georgia.

Claybaugh (271) Probably an Americanized form of German **Kleebach** or possibly of **Klappach** (see CLABAUGH).

Clayborn (547) English: variant of CLAIBORNE.

Clayborne (452) English: variant of CLAIBORNE.

Claybrook (398) English: habitational name from any of various minor places named Claybrook, from Old English *clǣg* 'clay' + *brōc* 'brook', for example Claybrook in Shropshire or Claybrooke Magna and Claybrooke Parva in Leicestershire.

Claybrooks (129) English: variant of CLAYBROOK.

Clayburn (240) English: variant of CLAIBORNE.

Claycamp (113) Americanized form of North German **Kleikamp**, a nickname or topographic name for a farmer on clay soil, from Low German *Klei* 'clay' + *Kamp* 'field'.

Claycomb (838) **1.** English: habitational name from some minor place named with Old English *clǣg* 'clay' + *cumb* 'combe', 'valley', for example Claycombe near Minchinhampton in Gloucestershire. **2.** Perhaps a variant of German **Kleikamp** (see CLAYCAMP).

Claydon (140) English: habitational name from any of various places named Claydon, for example in Suffolk, Buckinghamshire, and Oxfordshire, from Old English *clǣgig* 'clayey' + *dūn* 'hill'.

Clayman (472) **1.** English: occupational name for a person who worked in a clay pit or one who prepared clay for use in brick making. See CLAY. **2.** Americanized form of German and Jewish **Kleimann** (see KLEIMAN).

Claymore (105) Irish: reduced and altered form of MCLEMORE.

Claypole (104) English: variant of CLAYPOOL.

Claypool (1726) English: habitational name from Claypole in Lincolnshire, named from Old English *clǣg* 'clay' + *pōl* 'pool'.

Claypoole (401) English: variant of CLAYPOOL.

Clayson (288) English: patronymic from the personal name *Classe*, a short form of *Nicholas*. The name may have been imported to England in the Middle Ages by Flemish weavers. As an American surname it has probably absorbed some cases of Dutch CLAASSEN and its variants.

Clayton (18684) English: habitational name from any of the numerous places, in Yorkshire, Lancashire, Staffordshire, and elsewhere, named Clayton, from Old English *clǣg* 'clay' + *tūn* 'enclosure', 'settlement'.

Claytor (917) **1.** English: possibly a habitational name from Cleator in Cumbria, named from Old English *clǣte* 'burdock' + Old Norse *erg* 'hill pasture'. **2.** Possibly an Americanized spelling of North German **Klöter**, a variant of **Klüter**, a humorous nickname for a farmer, from Middle Low German *klūt(e)* 'clod'.

Claywell (258) English: habitational name from Claywell in Dorset or Claywell Farm in Oxfordshire, named from Old English *clǣg* 'clay' + *wella* 'stream', 'spring'.

Clear (742) **1.** English: probably a habitational name from *clere*, a component of several place names in north Hampshire (Highclere, Burghclere, Kingsclere). This is of uncertain origin, probably from a Celtic stream name meaning 'bright' (cognate with Latin *clarus* 'clear', 'bright'). **2.** English and Irish: variant of CLARE. **3.** Translation of German KLAR 1.

Clearman (247) **1.** Probably a translation of German **Klarmann** (see KLARMAN). **2.** Possibly English: unexplained. Just four bearers of the name are recorded in the 1881 British census; since then it appears to have died out in the British Isles.

Clearwater (373) Translation of German **Klarwasser**, a topographic name for someone who lived by a source of pure water, from Middle High German *klār* 'clear' + *wazzer* 'water'. Compare RAINWATER.

Cleary (6370) Irish: reduced Anglicized form of Gaelic **Ó Cléirigh** (or **Mac Cléirigh**) 'descendant (or son) of the scribe, clerk, or cleric (*cléireach*)', also commonly Anglicized as CLARK.

GIVEN NAMES Irish 5%. *Brendan (4), Malachy (4), Aileen (2), Brigid (2), Ronan (2), Aine, Bridie, Egan, William Kevin.*

Cleasby (110) English: habitational name from Cleasby in North Yorkshire, named from the Old Norse personal name *Kleppr* or *Kleiss* + *býr* 'farm', 'settlement'.

Cleaton (130) English: probably a variant of CLAYTON.

Cleaveland (460) Variant spelling of English CLEVELAND.

FOREBEARS A family spelling its name in this way is particularly associated with Martha's Vineyard. Moses Cleaveland (1651–1717) came to Edgartown in about 1680 from Woburn, MA; several of his descendants were captains of whaling ships.

Cleavenger (191) English: variant of CLEVENGER.

Cleaver (1728) **1.** English: from Middle English *clevere* 'one who cleaves' (a derivative of Old English *clēofan* 'to split'), hence an occupational name for someone who split wood into planks using a wedge rather than a saw, or possibly for a butcher. **2.** English: topographic name from Middle English *cleve* 'bank', 'slope' (from the dative of Old English *clif*) + the suffix *-er,* denoting an inhabitant. **3.** Americanized spelling of German KLIEWER or **Klüver** (see KLUVER).

Cleaves (695) English: habitational name from Cleaves in Devon (see CLEVE).

Cleckler (342) Americanized spelling of German **Glöckler**, an occupational name for a bellringer, sexton, or the like, from an agent derivative of GLOCK. Cleckler occurs predominantly in AL.

Cleckley (178) Americanized spelling of German **Glöckler** (see CLECKLER).

Cleckner (124) Americanized spelling of German **Klöckner** (see KLOECKNER).

Clee (101) **1.** English: habitational name from the Clee Hills in Shropshire or the nearby village of Clee St. Margaret. The hills are probably named with Old English *cleo* 'rounded', 'ball-shaped'. **2.** Possibly an altered form of Irish or Scottish McCLAY. **3.** Variant spelling of German KLEE.

GIVEN NAME French 4%. *Celestine.*

Cleek (536) **1.** English: of uncertain derivation. The first recorded instance seems to be William Cleike (Yorkshire 1176), but this may well be an error for *Clerke.* In subsequent records the name is concentrated in Devon; it seems to have been originally a habitational name connected with a piece of land in the parish of Ermington near Plymouth, first recorded in 1278 as *Clekeland(e),* and still known as Clickland; the names John de Clakelond and Robert Cleaklond occur in this parish in 1332 and 1337 respectively. The place name may be from Old English *cleaca* 'stepping stone', 'boundary stone' (of Celtic origin) + *land* 'territory'. Compare CLACK. **2.** Americanized spelling of German **Glück** (see GLUCK).

Cleere (211) English: variant spelling of CLEAR or possibly CLARE.

Cleeton (161) English: probably a variant of CLAYTON.

Clegg (2932) **1.** English (chiefly Lancashire and Yorkshire): habitational name from a place in Lancashire named Clegg, from Old Norse *kleggi* 'haystack', originally the name of a nearby hill. **2.** Manx: variant of CLAGUE.

Cleghorn (742) Scottish: habitational name from a place in Lanarkshire called Cleghorn. See also CLAGHORN.

Clein (114) Respelling of German KLEIN.

Cleland (1714) **1.** Scottish and Irish: reduced form of MCCLELLAND. **2.** Belgian: habitational name from Cleilant in East Flanders or Cleylande in West Flanders.

Clelland (414) **1.** Scottish and Irish: reduced form of MCCLELLAND. **2.** Scottish: habitational name from Clelland near

Motherwell, probably named with Old English *clæg* 'clay' + *land* 'land'.

Clem (3126) English and Dutch: from a short form of the personal name CLEMENT.

Clemans (404) **1.** Dutch: variant of CLEMENS. **2.** English: patronymic from the personal name CLEMENT. **3.** Americanized spelling of German KLEMENS.

Clemen (219) German and Dutch: variant of CLEMENS.

Clemence (397) **1.** English: patronymic from CLEMENT. **2.** French: metronymic from a feminine derivative of the personal name *Clément* (see CLEMENT).

Clemens (5395) **1.** English: patronymic from the personal name CLEMENT. **2.** German, Dutch, and Danish: from the personal name *Clemens* (see CLEMENT).

FOREBEARS Samuel Langhorne Clemens, better known by his pen name, Mark Twain, was descended from VA stock on his father's side, from a Robert Clemens, who was born in Warwickshire, England, in 1634.

Clemensen (160) Danish and Norwegian: patronymic from the personal name CLEMENS (see CLEMENT).

Clemenson (256) Americanized form of a Scandinavian patronymic from the personal name CLEMENS (see CLEMENT).

Clement (9035) English, French, and Dutch: from the Latin personal name *Clemens* meaning 'merciful' (genitive *Clementis*). This achieved popularity firstly through having been borne by an early saint who was a disciple of St. Paul, and later because it was selected as a symbolic name by a number of early popes. There has also been some confusion with the personal name *Clemence* (Latin *Clementia,* meaning 'mercy', an abstract noun derived from the adjective; in part a masculine name from Latin *Clementius,* a later derivative of *Clemens*). As an American family name, Clement has absorbed cognates in other continental European languages. (For forms, see Hanks and Hodges 1988.)

GIVEN NAMES French 4%. *Pierre* (7), *Alcide* (4), *Alphonse* (3), *Andre* (3), *Marcel* (3), *Oneil* (3), *Armand* (2), *Cecile* (2), *Christophe* (2), *Gaston* (2), *Olivier* (2), *Aime.*

Clemente (1675) Spanish, Italian, and Portuguese: from the personal name *Clemente* (see CLEMENT).

GIVEN NAMES Spanish 20%; Italian 11%; Portuguese 5%. *Jose* (22), *Carlos* (6), *Elia* (6), *Manuel* (6), *Cesar* (4), *Fernando* (4), *Luis* (4), *Rafael* (4), *Alfredo* (3), *Andres* (3), *Armando* (3), *Gerardo* (3); *Antonio* (6), *Carmine* (6), *Salvatore* (5), *Vito* (5), *Gino* (4), *Angelo* (3), *Nicola* (3), *Rocco* (3), *Enrico* (2), *Guido* (2), *Marco* (2), *Matteo* (2); *Joaquim* (2).

Clementi (417) Italian: patronymic or plural form of CLEMENTE.

GIVEN NAMES Italian 13%. *Angelo* (3), *Sandro* (3), *Amelio, Antonio, Carmela, Carmelo, Damiano, Enio, Pasquale, Primo, Riccardo, Rocco.*

Clements (14095) English: patronymic from the personal name CLEMENT. As an American family name, this form has absorbed cognates in other continental European languages. (For forms, see Hanks and Hodges 1988.)

Clementson (201) Northern English: patronymic from the personal name CLEMENT or possibly an Americanized form of a Scandinavian cognate.

Clementz (177) Altered spelling of CLEMENTS or of German **Clemenz**, a variant of CLEMENS.

Clemetson (147) Anmericanized form of a Scandinavian patronymic from the personal name *Clemet,* a variant of CLEMENS.

Clemmens (142) **1.** English: patronymic from the personal name CLEMENT. **2.** Dutch: from the personal name *Clemmin,* a medieval Dutch form of CLEMENT, or a metronymic from the personal name *Clemme,* feminine form of CLEMENT.

Clemmensen (117) Variant of Danish and Norwegian CLEMENSEN.

GIVEN NAMES Scandinavian 5%; German 4%. *Knud; Erna, Kurt.*

Clemmer (1394) Possibly an Americanized spelling of German **Klemme**, a variant of KLEMM or KLEMMER.

Clemmons (2497) Probably an altered spelling of CLEMONS, CLEMANS, CLEMENCE, or any of the other like-sounding surnames derived from the personal name CLEMENT in various European languages.

Clemo (171) English: from a Cornish form of the personal name CLEMENT.

Clemon (108) **1.** English: probably from a variant of the personal name CLEMENT. **2.** Perhaps a reduced form of Scottish and northern Irish McCLYMONT.

Clemons (7168) English: patronymic from the personal name CLEMENT.

Clemson (213) English: patronymic from a short form of the personal name CLEMENT.

Clendaniel (213) Apparently of Scottish origin, but unexplained.

Clendenen (535) Variant of Scottish GLENDENNING.

Clendenin (914) Variant of Scottish GLENDENNING.

Clendening (427) Variant of Scottish GLENDENNING.

Clendennen (117) Variant of Scottish GLENDENNING.

Clendenning (232) Variant of Scottish GLENDENNING.

Clendenon (134) Variant of Scottish GLENDENNING.

Clenney (260) Scottish or Irish: reduced form of MCCLENNEY.

Clennon (123) Reduced form of Irish **McLennon** (see LENNON) or Scottish MCLENNAN.
GIVEN NAMES Irish 5%. *Conroy, Gearoid.*

Clepper (319) Americanized spelling of German KLEPPER.

Cler (120) French: variant of CLAIR.

Clerc (145) French: occupational name for a scribe or secretary, or for a member of a minor religious order, Old French *clerc*, Latin *clericus* (see CLARK).
GIVEN NAMES French 11%. *Alain, Odette, Sebastien, Serge.*

Clerici (108) Italian: patronymic or plural form of CLERICO.
GIVEN NAME Italian 7%. *Gino* (2).

Clerico (146) Italian: occupational name for a scribe or secretary, or for a member of a minor religious order, from Latin *clericus*. See also CLARK.
GIVEN NAMES Italian 8%. *Angelo, Carlo, Dino.*

Clerk (117) English: variant spelling of CLARK. In some cases this may be an Americanized spelling of French CLERC or of the Dutch cognate **Clerck**, or of variants of these names.
GIVEN NAMES French 7%. *Pierre* (2), *Jacques.*

Clerkin (228) English: variant of CLARKIN.
GIVEN NAMES Irish 10%. *Liam* (2), *Brendan, Dympna, Seamus.*

Clermont (397) French: habitational name from any of the various places named Clermont, from Old French *clair, cler* 'bright', 'clear' + *mont* 'hill', i.e. a hill that could be seen a long way off.
GIVEN NAMES French 20%. *Jacques* (3), *Georges* (2), *Normand* (2), *Pierre* (2), *Armand, Edouard, Gaston, Ghislaine, Gilles, Henri, Herve, Jean Francois.*

Clester (133) Probably an Americanized form of Dutch KLOOSTER.

Cleve (129) **1.** English: habitational name from any of the numerous minor places, for example in Devon, Gloucestershire, and Oxfordshire, named Cleeve or Cleve '(place) at the cliff', from the dative case *clife* of Old English *clif* 'slope', 'cliff'. Compare CLIFF. **2.** Americanized spelling of KLEVE.

Cleveland (10329) **1.** English: regional name from the district around Middlesbrough named Cleveland 'the land of the cliffs', from the genitive plural (*clifa*) of Old English *clif* 'bank', 'slope' + *land* 'land'. See also CLEAVELAND. **2.** Americanized spelling of Norwegian **Kleiveland** or **Kleveland**, habitational names from any of five farmsteads in Agder and Vestlandet named with Old Norse *kleif* 'rocky ascent' or *klefi* 'closet' (an allusion to a hollow land formation) + *land* 'land'.
FOREBEARS Grover Cleveland (1837–1908), 22nd and 24th president of the U.S., was the fifth child of a country Presbyterian clergyman. His father, Richard Falley Cleveland, a graduate of Yale College and of the theological seminary at Princeton, was descended from a certain Moses Cleaveland who arrived in MA in 1635.

Cleven (227) **1.** Dutch and North German: habitational name from Kleve in North Rhine-Westphalia. **2.** Americanized spelling of Norwegian **Kleven**.

Clevenger (4452) English: variant of **Clavinger**, status name for the keeper of the keys in a great household, Latin *clavigerus*, from *clavis* 'key'.
FOREBEARS George Clevenger was born in Yonkers, NY, in 1654, the son of John Clevenger (born 1633), who probably came from Devon, England.

Clever (552) Respelling of German and Norwegian KLEVER.

Cleverley (127) English: variant of CLEVERLY.

Cleverly (166) English: habitational name, probably from Claverley in Shropshire, which is named with Old English *clǣfre* 'clover' + *lēah* 'woodland clearing'. Alternatively, it could possibly be from Cleveley in Lancashire (named with Old English *clif* 'bank', 'slope' + *lēah*), with intrusive -*r*- under the influence of *cleverly*.

Clevidence (111) Origin unidentified.

Clevinger (460) English: variant of CLEVENGER.

Clewell (301) Origin unidentified. Perhaps a variant of French CLAVEL.
FOREBEARS In at least one case, this name is a Germanized form of French CLAVEL, borne by Huguenot refugees who fled from Dauphiné to Baden in the late 17th century, when Protestants in France endured persecution following revocation of the Edict of Nantes in 1685. The name was brought to PA from Baden by Frantz Clawell in 1737.

Clewis (308) **1.** Scottish and Irish: reduced form of **McLewis** (see LEWIS 3). **2.** English: topographic name from the genitive form of Old English *clōh* 'ravine' (see CLOUGH).

Clews (125) Scottish or Irish: reduced form of **McLewis**, an Americanized form of Gaelic **Mac Lughaidh** (see LEWIS 3).
GIVEN NAME French 7%. *Noele* (3).

Cliatt (145) Americanized form of Welsh **Clwyd** (see CLUETT).

Cliburn (291) English: habitational name from Cliburn, a place in Cumbria named from Old English *clif* 'slope', 'bank' + *burna* 'stream'.

Click (2319) **1.** English: see CLEEK. **2.** Possibly an Americanized spelling of German KLICK, Jewish GLICK, or German and Jewish **Glück** (see GLUCK).

Clickner (219) Respelling of German KLECKNER.

Cliett (323) Americanized form of Welsh **Clwyd** (see CLUETT).

Cliff (884) English: habitational name from a place named with Old English *clif*

'slope', 'bank', 'cliff', or a topographic name from the same word. The Old English word was used not only in the sense of modern English *cliff* but also of much gentler slopes and frequently also of a riverbank.

Cliffe (172) English: variant spelling of CLIFF.

Clifford (8591) English: habitational name from any of various places called Clifford, for example in Devon, Gloucestershire, West Yorkshire, and in particular Herefordshire. The place name is derived from Old English *clif* 'slope' + *ford* 'ford'.
FOREBEARS A family of this name trace their descent from Walter de Clifford, who acquired the surname from Clifford Castle near Hay-on-Wye, Herefordshire, in the 12th century.

Clifft (130) Variant spelling of English CLIFT.

Clift (1701) English: **1.** topographic name for someone who lived by a crevice in rock, from Middle English *clift* 'cleft'. **2.** probably a variant of CLIFF.

Clifton (8709) English: habitational name from any of numerous places named Clifton, from Old English *clif* 'slope' (see CLIFF) + *tūn* 'enclosure', 'settlement'.

Climer (556) **1.** English (Midlands): unexplained. **2.** Perhaps also an Americanized spelling of KLIMA.

Climo (113) English: from a Cornish form of the personal name CLEMENT.

Clinard (658) French (Alsatian) or American form of German KLEINERT.

Clinch (367) English: **1.** habitational name from a place in Wiltshire named Clench, from Old English *clenc* 'lump', 'hill', which seems also to have been used of a patch of dry raised ground in fenland surroundings. In some cases the surname may be of topographic origin. **2.** metonymic occupational name for a maker or fixer of bolts and rivets, from Middle English *clinch, clench* 'door nail secured by riveting or clinching', from *clench(en)* 'to fix firmly'.

Cline (18637) **1.** Americanized spelling of German KLEIN or a Jewish (Ashkenazic) variant of this name. **2.** Variant spelling of Scottish or Irish CLYNE.

Clinebell (101) Origin unidentified. Probably an Americanized form of some German name beginning with *klein* 'small'.

Clinedinst (108) Americanized spelling of German KLEINDIENST.

Clines (334) English: habitational name from Claines in Worcestershire, named from Old English *clǣg* 'clay' + *nǣss* 'headland'.

Clinesmith (129) Americanized form of German KLEINSCHMIDT.

Clingan (699) Scottish and northern Irish: reduced form of **Mac Clingan**, an Anglicized form of Gaelic **Mac Gilla Fhinnéin**

'son of the servant of (Saint) Finnian', also Anglicized as **Mac Alingen**.

Clingenpeel (368) Americanized spelling and variant of German **Klingebeil**, a variant of KLINGBEIL.

Clinger (715) **1.** Americanized spelling of German KLINGER. **2.** Possibly a variant of **Clinker**, an English occupational name for a maker or fixer of bolts and rivets, from an agent derivative of Middle English *clinch*, *clench* 'door nail secured by riveting or clinching' (see CLINCH).

Clingerman (400) Jewish (Ashkenazic): variant spelling of KLINGERMAN.

Clingman (412) Americanized spelling of German **Klingmann** (see KLINGMAN).

Clink (292) **1.** Northern English: variant of CLINCH. **2.** Possibly an Americanized spelling of German KLING.

Clinkenbeard (443) Possibly an Americanized form of North German **Klingebiel**, a variant of KLINGBEIL.

Clinkscale (161) Scottish: variant of CLINKSCALES.

Clinkscales (645) Scottish: habitational name from a lost place in Coldingham, East Lothian.

Clint (123) English: habitational name from a place in North Yorkshire named Clint, from Old Norse *klint* 'rocky cliff', 'steep bank'.

Clinton (5167) **1.** Irish: reduced form of MCCLINTON. **2.** English: habitational name, either from Glympton in Oxfordshire, named as 'settlement (Old English *tūn*) on the Glym river', a Celtic river name meaning 'bright stream', or from Glinton in Cambridgeshire, recorded in 1060 as *Clinton* (named with an unrecorded Old English element akin to Middle Low German *glinde* 'enclosure', 'fence' + Old English *tūn*).
FOREBEARS Charles Clinton (born 1690 in Longford, Ireland) organized a group of colonists and founded the settlement of Little Britain, Ulster county, NY, in 1731. His son George Clinton (1739–1812) was governor of NY (1777–95), and they had many prominent descendants.
  An English aristocratic family called *Clinton* was founded by Geoffrey de Clinton (fl. 1130), who held lands at Glympton, Oxfordshire. He was chamberlain and treasurer to Henry I (1100–35).

Clipp (152) Probably an Americanized spelling of North German KLIPP.

Clippard (198) Americanized spelling of German KLIPPERT.

Clipper (245) Probably an altered spelling of German **Klipper**, a variant of KLIPP or KLIPPERT.

Clippinger (325) Altered form of German KLEPPINGER.

Clise (124) Americanized form of German KLEIS.

Clisham (149) Scottish and Irish (County Galway): possibly a habitational name from Clisham in the Western Isles. Woulfe, however, suggests a Gaelic form, **Mac Cliseam**, of unexplained derivation.

Clites (279) Americanized form of German **Kleitz** (unexplained; possibly a metathesized form of KLEIST).

Clive (108) English: habitational name from any of various places, for example in Shropshire and Cheshire, named Clive, from the dative case of Old English *clif* 'slope', 'bank', 'cliff' (see CLIFF), originally used after a preposition. In some cases the name may be topographical, with the same origin and meaning.
GIVEN NAME French 4%; Scottish 4%. *Celine*.

Cliver (218) Americanized spelling of German KLIEWER (or the variants **Kliver** and **Kliwer**) or KLEIBER.

Cloar (128) Perhaps of German origin: see CLOER.

Clock (366) Variant spelling of Dutch and German KLOCK.

Clodfelter (985) Americanized spelling of German **Glattfelder** (see GLADFELTER).

Cloe (213) Possibly an altered spelling of French **Clouet**: **1.** from a pet form of the Germanic personal name *Hlodald* (see CLOUD). **2.** habitational name from Les Clouets in Côtes-d'Armor.

Cloer (488) Possibly an Americanized spelling of German **Klör** or **Klor**, from a derivative of the medieval personal name *Hilarius* (see HILLARY).

Clogston (256) Scottish: variant of CLUGSTON. This seems to be a survival of an old spelling, which is no longer found in Scotland itself.

Cloherty (167) Irish (Galway): reduced Anglicized form of Gaelic **Ó Clochartaigh** 'descendant of *Clochartach*', a personal name, probably formed with *cloch* 'stone', **Stone** being an alternative Anglicization of the surname.

Clohessy (133) Irish: Anglicized form of Gaelic **Ó Clochasaigh** 'descendant of *Clochasach*', a personal name apparently derived from *cloch* 'stone'.
GIVEN NAMES Irish 16%. *Michael Patrick* (2), *Dermot, Eamon, John Patrick*.

Cloke (181) English: Devon variant of CLOUGH.

Clonch (212) Americanized form of German KLONTZ.

Cloney (131) Irish: Anglicized form of Gaelic **Ó Cluanaigh** 'descendant of *Cluanach*', a personal name derived from *cluana*, which means 'deceitful', 'flattering', or 'rogue'.

Cloninger (1036) Altered spelling of German **Kloninger**, a habitational name from a lost or unidentified place. *Kloningers Mühle* (Kloninger's Mill) near Langenlonsheim on the Nahe river attests to the surname in Germany.

Clonts (410) Variant spelling of German KLONTZ.

Clontz (883) Variant spelling of German KLONTZ.

Cloonan (391) Irish: Anglicized form of Gaelic **Ó Cluanáin** 'descendant of *Cluanan*', a personal name which Woulfe derives from a diminutive of *cluanach* 'deceitful'.

Clooney (118) Irish: Anglicized form of Gaelic **Ó Cluanaigh** 'descendant of *Cluanach*' (see CLONEY).

Cloos (127) **1.** Dutch: variant of CLAEYS. **2.** Altered spelling of North German KLOOS or the variant **Klooss**.
GIVEN NAME French 4%. *Marcel*.

Clopper (160) Dutch: from the verb *kloppen*, which has many meanings, including 'to tap', 'to knock', 'to beat', 'to sound', and could therefore have been applied in various ways as a nickname or an occupational name, for example for a bellringer.

Clopton (659) English: habitational name from any of various places, for example in Essex, Suffolk, and Warwickshire, named Clopton from Old English *clopp(a)* 'rock', 'hill' + *tūn* 'settlement'.

Cloran (110) Irish: shortened Anglicized form of a Gaelic patronymic, apparently from a diminutive of *Labhraidh* 'spokesman'. Woulfe calls it a rare Cavan surname.

Clore (636) Americanized spelling of German **Klor** (from a short form of the medieval personal name *Hilarius* (see HILLARY) or KLAR).

Clos (167) **1.** French: topographic name for someone who lived by an enclosure of some sort, Old French *clos*, from Late Latin *clausum*, past participle of *claudere* 'to close'. Compare CLOSE 1. **2.** Dutch: variant of CLAEYS. **3.** Respelling of German KLOSS.

Close (3696) **1.** English: topographic name for someone who lived by an enclosure of some sort, such as a courtyard set back from the main street or a farmyard, from Middle English *clos(e)* (Old French *clos*, from Late Latin *clausum*, past participle of *claudere* 'to close'). **2.** English: from Middle English *clos(e)* 'secret', applied as a nickname for a reserved or secretive person. **3.** Dutch: variant of CLAEYS. **4.** Altered spelling of German KLOSE.

Closs (371) **1.** English: variant of CLOSE 1. **2.** German: variant of KLOSS.

Closser (220) Probably an altered spelling of German GLASER or **Klöser**, a variant of KLOSS 1.

Closson (762) Northern French: from a reduced pet form of the Dutch personal name *Claes* (see NICHOLAS).

Clotfelter (241) Americanized spelling of German **Glattfelder** (see GLADFELTER).

Clothier (679) English: occupational name for a maker or seller of cloth and clothes, from Middle English *cloth* (Old English *clāð*) + the agent suffix *-(i)er*.

Clouatre (182) Of French origin: unexplained. This is a LA name.

GIVEN NAMES French 12%. *Andre, Armand, Arsene, Chantelle, Emile, Michel, Pierre, Serge.*

Cloud (4673) **1.** English: topographic name for someone who lived near an outcrop or hill, from Old English *clūd* 'rock' (only later used to denote vapor formations in the sky). **2.** French: from the Germanic personal name *Hlodald*, composed of the elements *hlōd* 'famous', 'clear' + *wald* 'rule', which was borne by a saint and bishop of the 6th century.

Clouden (100) Northern Irish: probably from an inflected form of English CLOUD.

Clough (3840) **1.** English: topographic name for someone who lived near a precipitous slope, Middle English *clough* (Old English *clōh* 'ravine'). **2.** Welsh: nickname from *cloff* 'lame'.

Clougherty (213) Irish: variant spelling of CLOHERTY.

GIVEN NAME Irish 8%. *Aileen.*

Clouse (2988) Probably an Americanized spelling of German KLAUS.

Clouser (1131) Americanized spelling of Swiss German KLAUSER.

Clouston (140) Scottish: habitational name from Clouston in Orkney, earlier recorded as *Cloustath*, from Norse *Klóstaðr*.

Clouthier (153) French: variant of CLOUTIER.

Cloutier (3169) French: occupational name for a nailer, someone who made and sold nails, from an agent derivative of *clou* 'nail' (Latin *clavus*).

GIVEN NAMES French 16%. *Andre* (11), *Marcel* (10), *Michel* (10), *Normand* (10), *Jacques* (9), *Lucien* (9), *Armand* (7), *Fernand* (5), *Yvon* (5), *Cecile* (4), *Donat* (4), *Emile* (4).

Clover (888) English: variant of CLEAVER.

Clovis (210) French: from the personal name *Clovis*, a derivative of the Germanic personal name *Hlodovic*, composed of the elements *hlōd* 'famous', 'clear' + *wīg* 'war'. The name is a doublet of *Louis* (see LEWIS).

Clow (1164) **1.** English: variant of CLOUGH. **2.** English: metonymic occupational name for a nailer, from Old French *clou* 'nail'. Compare CLOWER. **3.** Possibly an Americanized spelling of German **Klau**, a habitational name for someone from Klau near Aachen or Clauen in Lower Saxony, or **Glau**, a nickname for an astute person, from Old High German, Low German *glou, glau* 'circumspect'.

Cloward (363) Americanized form of German **Clauert** or **Glauert**, from a Germanic personal name composed of Old High German *glou* 'sharp witted' + *hart* 'strong'.

Clowdus (198) Probably an Americanized form of the German humanistic family name **Claudius**, **Klaudius**, or **Klaudies**, ostensibly adoptions of the noble Roman family name *Claudius* (from *claudus*

'limping'), taken as a Latinized form of the German personal name CLAUS, with which it actually has no connection.

Clowe (128) English: variant spelling CLOW.

Clower (899) **1.** English: occupational name for a nailer, from an agent derivative of Old French *clou* 'nail'. Compare CLOUTIER. **2.** Americanized spelling of German KLAUER (or the variant CLAUER) or of **Glauer**, a nickname from Middle High German *glau, glou* 'intelligent', 'circumspect'.

Clowers (715) English: patronymic from CLOWER, meaning 'son of the nailer'.

Clowes (273) **1.** English: variant spelling of CLOSE. **2.** Americanized spelling of German KLAUS.

Clowney (204) **1.** Scottish: probably a variant of **Cluny** or **Clunie**, a habitational name from a place in Perthshire called Clunie. **2.** English: possibly a habitational name of Norman origin, from Cluny in Saône-et-Loire, France.

GIVEN NAME French 4%. *Andre.*

Clowser (140) Americanized spelling of German KLAUSER.

Cloy (133) Scottish and Irish: reduced form of McCLOY.

Cloyd (1312) Welsh: variant of LLOYD.

Clubb (884) English: from Middle English *clubbe, clobbe* 'club', applied as a metonymic occupational name for a club maker or possibly as a nickname for someone who habitually carried a club. Reaney notes that 'by the Assize of Arms, every adult man had to be provided with at least a knife and a staff or club.'

Clubine (127) Origin unidentified.

Clucas (176) Irish and Scottish: reduced Americanized form of **Mac Lucais**, a patronymic from the personal name LUCAS.

Cluck (654) Probably a variant of German KLUCK or of Dutch KLOCK.

Cluckey (108) **1.** Variant spelling of Scottish **Cluckie**, a reduced form of McLUCKIE. **2.** Probably an Americanized spelling of German **Klucker** or the variant **Kluckert**, derivatives of KLUG, or an Americanized spelling of **Klucke**, a variant of KLUCK, itself a variant of GLUCK.

Cluett (111) English: regional name from Clwyd in Wales.

Cluff (975) English: variant spelling of CLOUGH.

Clugston (368) Scottish: habitational name from the barony of Clugston in Wigtownshire. Black records that the name is found several times in the records of Cupar Angus Abbey; it may alternatively be from the name of a lost place there.

Clukey (420) Variant spelling of Scottish **Cluckie**, a reduced form of McLUCKIE.

Clum (466) Americanized form of German KLUMP.

Clune (655) Irish: reduced Anglicized form of Gaelic **Mac Glúin**, a patronymic from the personal name *Glún*. This is either a byname meaning 'knee', or else a short form of various Old Irish compound personal names such as *Glúnfhionn* meaning 'fair-kneed' or *Glúiniairn* 'iron-kneed'.

GIVEN NAMES Irish 5%. *Conor, Seamus.*

Cluney (104) Irish: Anglicized form of Gaelic **Ó Cluanaigh** 'descendant of *Cluanach*' (see CLONEY).

Clunie (107) Scottish spelling of Irish CLONEY.

Clure (126) Irish: reduced form of McCLURE.

Cluster (136) Origin unidentified. **1.** Possibly a reduced form of Scottish McALLISTER. **2.** Alternatively, perhaps, an altered spelling of German KLOSTER.

Clute (811) Americanized spelling of North German KLUTH.

Clutter (1106) **1.** English: possibly from Middle English *cloutere, clutere*, an occupational name for a cobbler or patcher, from an agent derivative of *cloute, clut(e)* 'patch'. **2.** Possibly an altered form of German **Klutterer**, an occupational name for a traveling entertainer, Middle High German *kluterære*, or a shortened form of **Klüttermann** 'clodhopper', a nickname for a peasant.

Clutts (292) Probably an Americanized spelling of German **Klütz** (see KLUTZ) or KLOTZ.

Cluxton (124) Altered form of English CLAXTON.

Clyatt (203) Americanized form of Welsh **Clwyd** (see CLUETT).

Clyburn (770) English: variant spelling of CLIBURN.

Clyde (1185) Scottish and northern Irish: apparently a topographic name for someone who lived on the banks of the Clyde river (Gaelic *Cluaidh*, probably of pre-Celtic origin), which flows through Glasgow. This became established at a comparatively early date as a given name among American Blacks.

Clymer (1364) English: from a pet form of CLEMENT.

FOREBEARS George Clymer (1739–1813), a signer of the Declaration of Independence and of the Constitution, was a prosperous and well-connected Philadelphia merchant. His grandfather, Richard Clymer, came to Philadelphia in 1705 from Bristol, England.

Clyne (552) **1.** Irish (Roscommon and Longford): variant of **(Mac)Kilcline**, an Anglicization of Gaelic **Mac Giolla Chlaoin** 'son of the deceitful lad', from *claon* 'deceitful'. **2.** Scottish: habitational name from any of various places named Clyne, from Gaelic *claon* 'slope'. **3.** Americanized spelling of German and Jewish KLEIN.

GIVEN NAMES Irish 4%. *Aidan, Donal.*

Clynes (101) Irish: variant of CLYNE.

Co (222) **1.** Hispanic (Filipino): unexplained. **2.** Vietnamese: unexplained.
GIVEN NAMES Spanish 22%; Vietnamese 14%. *Cristina* (3), *Victoriano* (3), *Jose* (2), *Rogelio* (2), *Rosalinda* (2), *Alicia, Asuncion, Cayetano, Cesar, Conchita, Eduardo, Esteban*; *Hien* (2), *Dung, Ha To, Hanh, Hoa, Hue, Kiet, Lien, Linh, Long, Nhon, Quyen.*

Coach (166) Origin uncertain. **1.** Most probably a reduced form of Irish **McCoach**, which is of uncertain derivation, perhaps a variant of McCAIG. **2.** Possibly an altered spelling of French **Coache**, from the Norman and Picard term for a damson, probably applied as a metonymic occupational name for a grower or seller of plums. **3.** Possibly an altered spelling of German KOCH.
GIVEN NAME French 4%. *Celestine.*

Coachman (271) Americanized form of German **Kutschmann**, a variant of the medieval personal name *Kosmas.* The name is found mainly in GA, MD, and AL.

Coad (467) English (Devon): from Middle English *cōde* 'cobbler's wax', probably applied as an occupational nickname for a cobbler's assistant. Alternatively, it may be a topographic name from Old Cornish *cuit* 'wood'.

Coady (938) Irish: variant spelling of CODY 1.

Coaker (111) English (Devon): variant spelling of COKER.

Coakley (2151) Irish (Cork): Anglicized form of Gaelic **Mac Caochlaoich**, patronymic from *Caochlaoch*, a personal name composed of the elements *caoch* 'blind' + *laoch* 'warrior', 'hero'.

Coale (567) **1.** English: variant spelling of COLE. **2.** Possibly an Americanized spelling of German KOLL.

Coalson (389) English: patronymic form of COLE.

Coalter (132) Northern Irish: variant of COULTER.

Coan (1207) **1.** Irish: reduced form of **McCoan**, an Anglicized form of Gaelic **Mac Comhdhain** or **Mac Comhghain** 'son of *Comhdhan*', a personal name of unexplained meaning. **2.** Possibly an altered spelling of Jewish COHEN or German and Jewish KOHN.

Coar (215) **1.** Northern English: variant of CARR. **2.** Perhaps also an Americanized spelling of German KOHR.

Coard (138) **1.** English: from Old French *corde* 'string', a metonymic occupational name for a maker of cord or string, or a nickname for an habitual wearer of decorative ties and ribbons. **2.** French: variant of **Couard**, a derogatory nickname from Old French *couard* 'coward', 'poltroon', a compound of *coe* 'tail' + the pejorative suffix *-ard.*
GIVEN NAME French 4%. *Curley.*

Coash (109) Possibly an Americanized spelling of French **Coache** (see COACH) or of **Coche** 'barge', a metonymic occupational name for a bargeman.

Coast (161) Americanized spelling of German KOST, found chiefly in PA, OH, and NY.

Coate (442) **1.** English: variant of COATES, from the dative singular of *cote, cott.* **2.** Americanized spelling of German KOTH.

Coates (8145) **1.** English: status name for a cottager (see COTTER 2), or a topographic name for someone who lived in a relatively humble dwelling (from Middle English *cotes*, plural (or genitive) of *cote, cott*), or a habitational name from any of the numerous places named with this word, especially Coates in Cambridgeshire and Cotes in Leicestershire. **2.** Scottish: variant of COUTTS. **3.** Americanized spelling of German and Jewish KOTZ or German **Koths**, from a variant of the medieval personal name *Godo* (see GOTTFRIED).

Coatney (582) Altered spelling of English COURTNEY.

Coats (5377) English and Scottish: variant spelling of COATES.

Coatsworth (121) English: habitational name, probably from a lost place named Coatsworth, possibly in County Durham, where the modern surname is most frequent.

Coaxum (221) Origin unidentified.

Cobarrubias (123) Spanish: variant of **Covarrubias**, a habitational name from places named Cobarrubias, in the provinces of Burgos and Soria. The place name, according to Tibón, means 'red caves', from Latin *cava* 'cave' + *ruber* 'red'.
GIVEN NAMES Spanish 54%. *Jesus* (6), *Carlos* (3), *Francisco* (3), *Jose* (3), *Jorge* (2), *Manuel* (2), *Raul* (2), *Alberto, Alfonso, Ayala, Braulia, Enrique.*

Cobaugh (196) Probably an Americanized spelling of South German **Kuhbach** or **Kuhbauch**, or possibly North German **Kobarg**. The first, being a place name in Bavaria and Austria, indicates a habitational name; the second may be a mutated form of *Kuhbach* 'cow creek' to 'cow belly (*Bauch*)', a peasant nickname. The third is a variant of a habitational or topographic name **Kuhberg** meaning 'cow hill'.

Cobb (22792) English (mainly Dorset; also East Anglia): **1.** from the Middle English byname or personal name *Cobbe, Cobba*, or its Old Norse cognate *Kobbi*, which are probably from an element meaning 'lump', used to denote a large man. **2.** from a reduced form of JACOB.

Cobbett (154) English: from a Middle English personal name, either a reduced pet form of JACOB or the older personal name *Cutebald, Cubald*, a survival of Old English *Cūðbeald*, composed of the elements *cūð* 'famous', 'well-known' + *beald* 'bold', 'brave'.

Cobbins (162) English: perhaps a patronymic from a pet form of COBB.

Cobble (595) **1.** English: variant of COBLE. **2.** Americanized spelling of German KOBEL.

Cobbs (1539) **1.** Probably an altered spelling of German KOBS or KOPS. **2.** English: patronymic from COBB.

Coben (113) Americanized spelling of German **Koben**, a habitational name from a place named Coben, from Middle High German *kobe* 'hut', 'shelter'.

Cober (112) Variant spelling of German KOBER.

Coberley (110) Of German origin: see COBERLY.

Coberly (606) Americanized spelling of South German **Köberle**, an occupational name for a basket maker or a peddler, from Middle High German *kober* 'carrying basket' + the diminutive suffix *-le.* In some instances in eastern Germany the surname may be derived from Slavic *kovar* 'blacksmith' (see COFER).

Cobern (180) **1.** Americanized spelling of German **Kobern**, a habitational name from *Kowarren*, the German form of a place in Lithuania called Kavarskas, named in Lithuanian from *kovoti* 'to forge'. **2.** English: possibly a variant spelling of COCKBURN.

Cobert (187) **1.** Variant of French COLBERT. **2.** Variant of German KOBER.
GIVEN NAME French 5%. *Andre.*

Cobey (168) **1.** Possibly an Americanized spelling of French **Cobet**, from a reduced pet form of the personal name JACOB. **2.** English: unexplained. Compare COBY.
GIVEN NAME French 4%. *Emile.*

Cobia (159) Origin unidentified.
FOREBEARS It is probable that all American members of the Cobia family (a mainly Southern name) are descended from Daniel Cobia, who was born in SC in 1714. His ancestry is unknown.
GIVEN NAMES French 6%. *Andre* (2), *Chantal.*

Cobian (319) Spanish and Asturian-Leonese (**Cobián**), or Portuguese: possibly a habitational name from a place named Covián in Asturies.
GIVEN NAMES Spanish 50%. *Jose* (13), *Luis* (6), *Francisco* (5), *Ignacio* (4), *Sergio* (4), *Carlos* (3), *Javier* (3), *Jesus* (3), *Jorge* (3), *Manuel* (3), *Ruben* (3), *Alberto* (2).

Cobin (140) Perhaps a reduced form of Scottish McCUBBIN.

Coble (3538) **1.** English: from Middle English *cobel* 'rowboat', presumably applied as a metonymic occupational name for a maker of such or possibly as a nickname for a sailor. **2.** Americanized spelling of German KOBEL.

Cobleigh (205) English: habitational name from either of two places in Devon called Cobley, from the Old English personal name *Cobba* (see COBB 1) + Old English *lēah* 'woodland clearing'.

Coblentz (740) Jewish (Ashkenazic): habitational name from the German city of Koblenz, situated at the confluence of the Rhine and Mosel. It was founded in 9 BC as a Roman town, Latin name *Confluentes (fluvii)* 'confluent rivers', from which the modern name derives.

Cobler (331) **1.** English: occupational name for a cobbler, Middle English *cobeler*. **2.** Probably an Americanized spelling of German KOBLER.

Cobo (224) Spanish: **1.** from a variant of the medieval nickname *Calvo* 'bald' (from Latin *calvus*). **2.** habitational name from any of various minor places. They may have been named from the same word as in 1, referring to a bare and treeless appearance, or alternatively from Late Latin *cova* 'hollow'.
GIVEN NAMES Spanish 39%. *Juan* (5), *Luis* (5), *Jose* (4), *Carlos* (3), *Jorge* (3), *Ana* (2), *Armando* (2), *Florentina* (2), *Rafael* (2), *Ricardo* (2), *Alberto, Alejandra; Clemente* (2), *Angelo, Antonio, Cesario, Delio, Marino.*

Cobos (493) Spanish: habitational name from places in the provinces of Palencia and Segovia called Cobos (see COBO 2).
GIVEN NAMES Spanish 42%. *Carlos* (14), *Manuel* (6), *Armando* (5), *Arturo* (4), *Luis* (4), *Ruben* (4), *Angel* (3), *Francisco* (3), *Jesus* (3), *Jose* (3), *Lilia* (3), *Margarita* (3); *Antonio* (5), *Lorenzo* (3), *Leonardo* (2), *Eliseo, Gabino, Heriberto, Luciano, Marcello, Marco, Marco Antonio.*

Cobourn (101) Variant of northern English and Scottish COCKBURN.

Coburn (5045) **1.** Northern English and Scottish: variant of COCKBURN, reflecting the pronunciation. **2.** Altered spelling of German **Kobern**.

Coby (262) **1.** English: unexplained. Compare COBEY. **2.** Respelling, under French influence, of German KOBE 2 or of KOBER.
GIVEN NAMES French 4%. *Alain, Lucien, Michel.*

Coca (325) **1.** Spanish: habitational name from a place so named in Segovia province or from Coca de Alba in Salamanca. **2.** Italian: probably an altered spelling of COCCA, or possibly a variant of COCO.
GIVEN NAMES Spanish 30%. *Jose* (8), *Manuel* (5), *Jorge* (4), *Mario* (4), *Carlos* (3), *Luis* (3), *Domingo* (2), *Eduardo* (2), *Gilberto* (2), *Rafael* (2), *Tomas* (2), *Alberto.*

Cocanougher (136) Probably an altered spelling of Swiss German **Gochenauer** (see GOCHENOUR and compare COCHENOUR).

Cocca (229) Italian: from a feminine form of COCCO.
GIVEN NAMES Italian 11%. *Angelo* (3), *Concetta, Cosimo, Mauro, Vito.*

Coccaro (167) Southern Italian: from a diminutive of *cocchia*, a southern term for 'shell' or 'pod', also 'crust of bread'.

GIVEN NAMES Italian 11%. *Angelo* (2), *Carlo, Salvatore.*

Cocchi (158) Italian: plural or patronymic form of COCCO.
GIVEN NAMES Italian 10%. *Aldo, Amadeo, Anello, Dino, Massimo, Salvatore.*

Cocchiola (109) Italian: derivative of COCCIA.
GIVEN NAMES Italian 19%. *Amato* (2), *Carmine* (2), *Marco, Rocco, Rosaria.*

Coccia (390) Southern Italian: **1.** in Sicily and Calabria, possibly a nickname from *cuccìa*, denoting a gruel of boiled wheat mixed with oil, milk and sugar, or honey (from medieval Greek *kokkion*, ancient Greek *kokkos* 'grain', 'seed'), or alternatively, an occupational name for a cereal grower, from medieval Greek *kokkias*, from *kokkion* 'wheat' + the occupational suffix *-as*. **2.** nickname for someone with a large, hard, or otherwise remarkable head, from medieval Italian *coccia* 'head' (earlier 'shell').
GIVEN NAMES Italian 15%. *Angelo* (6), *Silvio* (3), *Tullio* (3), *Amerigo, Antonio, Emidio, Marco, Sante, Sisto.*

Cocco (501) Italian: from *Coccus*, a medieval personal name and nickname of uncertain derivation. De Felice speculates that it may be derived from a term of endearment, a regional variant of *cucco* 'cuckoo', also 'old man', or from *còcco* 'egg' (or a regional variant such as Sardinian *kòkku*). Alternatively, it may be from Greek *kokkos* 'grain', 'seed', 'pip'.
GIVEN NAMES Italian 12%. *Alberto* (3), *Americo* (2), *Luigi* (2), *Mario* (2), *Orlando* (2), *Rafael* (2), *Rocco* (2), *Aldo, Alfio, Angelo, Carmine, Erminio, Geno, Gino, Livio, Nicola, Remo.*

Cochell (116) Americanized spelling of French **Coqueral** (see COCKRELL).

Cochenour (295) Americanized spelling of Swiss German **Gochenauer** (see GOCHENOUR).

Cochran (21538) Scottish: habitational name from lands in the parish of Paisley, near Glasgow. The place name is of uncertain derivation, perhaps from Welsh *coch* 'red', although this etymology is not supported by the early spelling *Coueran*.

Cochrane (3489) Scottish: variant of COCHRAN.

Cochren (107) Scottish: variant of COCHRAN.

Cochrum (110) Probably an altered spelling of Scottish COCHRAN or English COCKERHAM.

Cockayne (127) **1.** English: nickname for an idle dreamer, from Middle English *cokayne* 'cloud-cuckooland', name of an imaginary paradise (Old French *(pays de) cocaigne*, from Middle Low German *kōkenje*, a diminutive of *kōke* 'cake', since in this land the houses were supposed to be made of cake). **2.** Americanized spelling of French **Cocagne**, from an Occitan word

meaning 'profit', 'advantage', used as a personal name from the Middle Ages.

Cockburn (334) Scottish and English (Northumberland): habitational name from a place in Berwickshire named Cockburn, from Old English *cocc* 'cock', 'rooster' (or the related byname *Cocca*) + *burna* 'stream' (see BOURNE). This surname is traditionally pronounced *Coburn*.

Cockcroft (130) English (Yorkshire and Lancashire): habitational name from a minor place of this name, for example Cockcroft in Rishworth or Cock Croft in Bingley, both in West Yorkshire. They are named with Old English *cocc* 'rooster' + *croft* 'paddock', 'smallholding'. In some cases it may be a topographic name with the same meaning.

Cocke (552) English: **1.** nickname from Middle English *cok* 'cock', 'male bird or fowl' (Old English *cocc*), given for a variety of possible reasons. Applied to a young lad who strutted proudly like a cock, it soon became a generic term for a youth and was attached with hypocoristic force to the short forms of many medieval personal names (e.g. ALCOCK, HANCOCK, *Hiscock, Mycock*). The nickname may also have referred to a natural leader, or an early riser, or a lusty or aggressive individual. The surname may also occasionally derive from a picture of a rooster used as a house sign. **2.** from the Old English personal name *Cocca*, derived from the word given in 1 above or from the homonymous *cocc* 'hillock', 'clump', 'lump', and so perhaps denoting a fat and awkward man. This name is not independently attested, but appears to lie behind a number of place names and (probably) the medieval personal name *Cock*, which was still in use in the late 13th century.

Cocker (154) **1.** English: nickname for a bellicose person, from Middle English *cock* 'to fight', 'to wrangle' (a derivative of Old English *cocc* 'cock'). **2.** English: occupational name for someone who was skilled in building haystacks, from Middle English *cock* 'heap of hay' (of Old Norse origin, or from an Old English *cocc* 'mound', 'hill'). **3.** Probably an Americanized spelling of German KOCHER.

Cockerell (170) English: variant of COCKRELL.

Cockerham (1748) English: habitational name from a place in Lancashire named Cocker, from the Cocker river (a Celtic name apparently derived from an element *kukro* 'winding') + Old English *hām* 'homestead' or *hamm* 'enclosure hemmed in by water'.

Cockerill (392) English: variant of COCKRELL.

Cockett (109) English: metonymic occupational name for a baker, from the Middle English term *cocket-bread*, denoting a high-quality leavened bread, second only to the *wastell* or finest bread. It has been suggested that this bread may have derived its name from Anglo-French *cockette* 'seal', having supposedly been marked with the seal of the King's Custom House, though there is no supporting evidence for this.

Cockey (136) English (Devon and Somerset): from a diminutive of COCKE.

Cockfield (200) English: habitational name from any of three places: the first, Cockfield in Durham, is named from an Old English personal name *Cocca* + *feld* 'open country'; the second, Cockfield in Suffolk, is named from an Old English personal name *Cohha*, with the same second element; and the third, Cuckfield in Sussex, is believed to be from an Old English personal name *Cuca* + *feld*.

Cocking (238) English: from a diminutive of Middle English *cok* 'cock' (see COCKE).

Cocklin (171) **1.** English: from a diminutive of Middle English *cok* 'cock' (see COCKE). **2.** Perhaps also an Americanized spelling of Swiss and South German **Köchlin**, **Koechlin**, or **Köchling**, all diminutives of KOCH.

Cockman (373) English: **1.** from Old English *cōc* 'cook' (Latin *coquus*) + *mann* 'man', hence an occupational name for the servant of a cook. **2.** variant of COCKER 2.

Cockram (154) Either a variant spelling of Scottish COCHRAN or a reduced form of English COCKERHAM.

Cockran (97) Variant of Scottish COCHRAN.

Cockrell (3364) English: from a diminutive of Middle English *cok* in the sense 'rooster' (see COCKE). This name has also absorbed some cases of the French cognates **Coquerille** and **Coqueral**.

Cockrill (383) English: variant spelling of COCKRELL.

Cockroft (274) English: variant of COCKCROFT.

Cockrum (844) Probably a reduced form of English COCKERHAM, or an altered spelling of Scottish COCHRAN.

Cocks (241) English: variant of COX.

Coco (1169) **1.** Italian: occupational name for a cook, a seller of cooked meats, or a keeper of an eating house, from southern Italian *coco* 'cook', Latin *cocus, coquus*. **2.** Belgian French: unexplained.
GIVEN NAMES Italian 12%; French 4%. *Salvatore* (14), *Angelo* (7), *Sal* (5), *Antonio* (4), *Alfio* (3), *Carmel* (3), *Carlo* (2), *Santo* (2), *Attilio, Carmello, Carmelo, Dante*; *Armand* (2), *Emile* (2), *Andre, Chanel, Germaine, Landry, Napoleon, Octave*.

Cocozza (208) Italian: variant of COCUZZA.
GIVEN NAMES Italian 8%; French 7%. *Angelo, Marco, Pasquale, Salvatore*; *Achille*.

Cocuzza (184) Italian: from *cocuzza* 'gourd', 'pumpkin', applied either as a metonymic occupational name for a grower or seller of gourds or a nickname for a rotund individual.
GIVEN NAMES Italian 18%. *Salvatore* (5), *Angelo* (2), *Antonio*.

Coda (196) Italian (Piedmont): topographic name for someone who lived on a long, narrow piece of land, from *coda* 'tail' (Latin *cauda*).
GIVEN NAMES Italian 4%. *Enzo, Stefano*.

Coday (253) Irish: variant spelling of CODY.

Codd (337) **1.** English: metonymic occupational name for a maker of purses and bags, from Middle English *cod* 'bag'. **2.** English: nickname for a man noted for his apparent sexual prowess, from *cod(piece)*, in Tudor times the garment worn prominently over the male genitals. **3.** English: from Middle English *cod*, the fish (of uncertain origin, perhaps a transferred use of 1), applied as a metonymic occupational name for a fisherman or seller of these fish, or possibly as a nickname for someone thought to resemble the fish in some way. **4.** Irish: variant of CODY. **5.** Irish (County Wexford): from the Anglo-Saxon personal name *Cod*.

Codding (269) **1.** Probably an Americanized spelling of North German **Kotting**. **2.** status name for a cottager or day laborer, from Middle Low German *kote* 'cottage' + the suffix *-ing*. **3.** from a personal name, *Götting* or *Kötting*, formed with Old High German *got* 'god'.

Coddington (1268) English: habitational name from any of various places, for example in Cheshire, Herefordshire, and Nottinghamshire, named Coddington, from the Old English personal name *Cot(t)a* + *-ing-* denoting association + *tūn* 'settlement'.

Code (297) English: variant spelling of COAD.

Codella (119) Italian: habitational name from a place called Coddella.
GIVEN NAMES Italian 17%. *Canio* (3), *Domenico, Nicola, Sylvio*.

Coder (757) **1.** Americanized spelling of German **Koder** or **Goder**, from a short form of any of the old personal names formed with Old High German *got* 'god', e.g. GOTTFRIED or GOTHARD. **2.** Americanized spelling of South German **Goder**, a topographic for someone living by a narrow pass or ravine, from Middle High German *goder* 'throat', 'gullet'. **3.** Americanized spelling of Slovenian KODER.

Coderre (359) French: of uncertain origin; possibly a variant of French **Godier**, from a Germanic personal name composed of the elements *god, got* 'god' + *hari, heri* 'army'.
GIVEN NAMES French 10%. *Gaetan* (2), *Marcel* (2), *Pierre* (2), *Adrien, Alcide, Armand, Donat, Fernand, Ghislaine*.

Codina (120) Catalan: topographic name from *codina* 'layer of hard, compressed earth' or a habitational name from places in Barcelona and Castelló provinces named with this word.
GIVEN NAMES Spanish 45%. *Francisco* (4), *Arturo* (3), *Cesar* (2), *Eugenio* (2), *Jose* (2),

Raul (2), *Salvador* (2), *Santiago* (2), *Alexandro, Carlos, Enrique, Epifanio*.

Codispoti (227) Southern Italian: status name or nickname from the Calabrian Greek term *kodespoti* 'head of the household', from Greek *oikos* 'house' + *despotēs* 'head', 'master'.
GIVEN NAMES Italian 23%. *Angelo* (2), *Mario* (2), *Antonio, Domenic, Emilio, Guiseppe, Leocadia, Luigi, Silvio*.

Codling (141) English (Yorkshire): **1.** from a double diminutive of CODD. **2.** from Old French *ceur de lion* 'lion heart', applied as a nickname for a brave man, or ironically for an exceptionally timorous one.

Codner (228) **1.** English: variant of CORDNER. **2.** Americanized form of Jewish **Kodner**, a habitational name for someone from Kodnya, a place in Ukraine.

Codrington (137) English: habitational name from Codrington in Gloucestershire, named from the Old English personal name *Cūþhere* + *-ing-* denoting association with + *tūn* 'settlement'.

Cody (6342) Irish: **1.** Anglicized form of Gaelic **Ó Cuidighthigh** (see CUDDIHY). **2.** Anglicized form of Gaelic **Mac Óda** 'son of *Óda*', a personal name of Germanic origin, introduced into Ireland by the Normans. This name was taken by a family in Kilkenny formerly known as Archdeacon.

Coe (6560) English (Essex and Suffolk): nickname from the jackdaw, Middle English *co*, Old English *cā* (see KAY). The jackdaw is noted for its sleek black color, raucous voice, and thievish nature, and any of these attributes could readily have given rise to the nickname.

Coelho (1386) Portuguese: from *coelho* 'rabbit' (Latin *cuniculus*), applied as a nickname for someone thought to resemble a rabbit in some way.
GIVEN NAMES Spanish 20%; Portuguese 14%. *Manuel* (39), *Jose* (24), *Carlos* (17), *Fernando* (7), *Francisco* (7), *Jorge* (5), *Ana* (4), *Armando* (4), *Luis* (4), *Julio* (3), *Luiz* (3), *Raul* (3); *Joao* (7), *Joaquim* (7), *Neuza* (2), *Albano, Altair, Conceicao, Guilherme, Henrique, Ilidio, Marcio, Paulo, Zulmira*; *Antonio* (37), *Marco* (4), *Angelo* (2), *Ceasar* (2), *Evo* (2), *Luciano* (2), *Aldo, Caesar, Carlo, Flavio, Gilda, Julieta*.

Coello (239) Galician: from *coello* 'rabbit' (Latin *cuniculus*), a nickname for someone thought to resemble a rabbit in some way.
GIVEN NAMES Spanish 51%. *Carlos* (8), *Jose* (7), *Miguel* (6), *Enrique* (4), *Jorge* (4), *Abilio* (3), *Fernando* (3), *Ignacio* (3), *Nestor* (3), *Blanca* (2), *Catalina* (2), *Cesar* (2); *Amedeo, Antonio, Bartolo, Ceasar, Ciro, Marco, Nino*.

Coen (1693) **1.** Irish: variant of COAN, or an alternative Anglicization of Gaelic **Ó Cúáin** or **Ó Cadhain** (see COYNE). **2.** Dutch and Jewish (Ashkenazic): variant spelling of KOEN.

Coenen (637) Dutch and North German: from a short form of any of the Germanic personal names formed with *kuoni* 'daring', 'experienced' (Middle Dutch *coene*, Middle Low German *kōne*).

Coers (124) Dutch: variant of KORS.
GIVEN NAME German 4%. *Erwin* (2).

Coey (225) **1.** English: nickname for a quiet or shy person, from French *coi* 'quiet', 'coy', 'shy'. **2.** Scottish: variant of COWIE.

Cofer (1684) **1.** Americanized spelling of German **Kofer**, an occupational name from Slavic *kovař* 'smith' (see KOVAR). **2.** Americanized spelling of German **Köfer**, a northern variant of **Küfer** (see KIEFFER).

Coffaro (200) Southern Italian (**Coffàro**): occupational name from Sicilian *cuffaru* 'basket-maker', an agent derivative of Latin *cophinus* 'basket'.
GIVEN NAMES Italian 10%. *Antonio, Carlo, Corrado, Giovanni, Luciano, Sal, Salvatore.*

Coffee (1975) Irish: variant of COFFEY.

Coffeen (171) Irish: possibly from a diminutive form of any of the Gaelic names mentioned at COFFEE, but just as likely a reduced form of MCCAUGHAN.
FOREBEARS The name was brought to Boston, MA, from Dublin, Ireland, in about 1721 by Michael Coffeen (1704–84), who, according to family lore, was press-ganged to serve as a sailor in a British ship and subsequently apprenticed to a Boston mercer.

Coffel (250) Probably an Americanized spelling of German **Kofel** or **Kofahl** (see KOFFEL).

Coffelt (1041) Americanized spelling of German **Kauffeld** (see CAUFIELD).

Coffer (506) **1.** English: from Old French *cof(f)re* 'chest', 'box', applied as a metonymic occupational name for a maker of coffers or chests or, by extension, for a treasurer. **2.** Probably an Americanized spelling of German **Kaufer** or **Kauffer** (see KAUFER).

Coffey (13055) Irish: **1.** Anglicized form of Gaelic **Ó Cobhthaigh** 'descendant of *Cobhthach*', a byname meaning 'victorious'. **2.** Anglicized form of Gaelic **Ó Cathbhadha** 'descendant of *Cathbhadh*' ('battle tent'), **Ó Cathbhuadhaigh** 'descendant of *Cathbhuadhach*' ('battle victorious'), or **Ó Cathmhogha** 'descendant of *Cathmhugh*', a byname meaning 'battle slave'.

Coffie (142) Variant spelling of Irish COFFEY.
GIVEN NAMES French 7%. *Jacques, Luce, Patrice.*

Coffield (671) **1.** English: altered spelling of COCKFIELD or CAULFIELD. **2.** Americanized spelling of German **Kauffeld** (see CAUFIELD).

Coffin (3514) English and French: metonymic occupational name for a basket maker, from Old French *cof(f)in* 'basket'

(Late Latin *cophinus*, Greek *kophinos*). The modern English word *coffin* is a specialized development of this term, not attested until the 16th century.
FOREBEARS Tristram Coffin came from Brixham, Devon, to Haverhill, MA, before 1647. An important line of his descendants is associated with Nantucket and Martha's Vineyard.

Coffing (219) English: variant of COFFIN.

Coffland (103) Probably a variant spelling of Irish **Coughland**, which may be an Anglicization of Gaelic **Mac Cochláin** or **Ó Cochláin** (see COUGHLIN).

Coffman (9453) Americanized spelling of German and Jewish **Kaufmann** (see KAUFMAN).

Cofield (1380) **1.** English: variant spelling of CAULFIELD. **2.** Americanized spelling of German **Kauffeld** (see CAUFIELD) or alternatively perhaps of the topographic name **Kohfeld**, a Low German variant of **Kuhfeld**, which is from Middle High German *kuo* 'cow' + *velt* 'open country'.

Cofone (120) Italian: unexplained. This is a frequent name in Calabria, especially in Catanzaro.
GIVEN NAMES Italian 18%. *Angelo* (2), *Annunziato, Benedetto, Carmine, Natale, Salvatore.*

Cofrancesco (148) Italian (Campania): of uncertain derivation; perhaps from a compound personal name composed of a reduced form of *Nicolo* (see NICHOLAS) + *Francesco* (see FRANCIS).
GIVEN NAMES Italian 12%. *Alfonse, Marino, Pasquale, Pierino, Salvatore.*

Cogan (1505) **1.** Americanized form of Jewish (from Ukraine) **Kogan**, from the Russian pronunciation of COHEN. **2.** Irish (of Welsh origin): habitational name from an area near Cardiff, which may have been named with a Welsh word meaning 'bowl', 'depression'. There is evidence of a family named *de Cogan* in the 12th century, and by the 13th century the name was also associated with Somerset, Devon, County Limerick, and County Cork. **3.** Irish (Leitrim): variant of COOGAN.

Cogar (839) **1.** English (Cornwall): unexplained. **2.** Possibly an Americanized spelling of German KOGER.

Cogbill (206) English (Warwickshire): unexplained. It could be a nickname, either from Middle English *cok* 'rooster' + *bill* 'beak' or from Middle English *cokebelle* 'small bell' (from Old French *coque* 'shell'). Compare COGDELL, COGDILL.

Cogburn (936) English: probably a variant of COCKBURN.

Cogdell (477) English: unexplained. Compare COGDILL, COGBILL.

Cogdill (812) English: unexplained. Compare COGDELL, COGBILL.

Cogen (147) Variant spelling of COGAN.
GIVEN NAMES Jewish 5%; German 4%. *Dorith; Erwin* (3).

Coger (326) Americanized spelling of German KOGER.

Coggan (127) **1.** Irish: Anglicized form of Gaelic **Mac Cogadháin** (see COOGAN). **2.** Jewish (eastern Ashkenazic): Americanized form of **Kogan**, from the Russian pronunciation of COHEN.
GIVEN NAMES Irish 4%; Jewish 4%. *Brendan, Brigid, Conal, Seamus; Hyman.*

Cogger (146) English: from an agent derivative of Middle English *cogge* 'small ship', 'cock boat', Old French *cogue*, hence an occupational name for a boat or cog builder or, more likely, for a sailor or master of a cog.

Coggeshall (318) English: habitational name from Coggeshall in Essex, named from an Old English personal name *Cogg* + *halh* 'nook'.
FOREBEARS This name was taken to America in 1632 by John Coggeshall, who became first governor of RI, and in 1635 by John Cogswell. In 1887 a descendant, Daniel Cogswell, founded Cogswell College, San Francisco.

Coggin (771) Irish: Anglicized form of Gaelic **Mac Cogadháin** (see COOGAN).

Coggins (2786) Irish: Anglicized form of Gaelic **Mac Cogadháin** (see COOGAN).

Coghill (563) **1.** English: habitational name, possibly from Cogill in Aysgarth, North Yorkshire, which is named with Old English *cot* 'cottage' + Old Norse *kelda* 'spring', or perhaps from any of the numerous places named Cowgill or Cow Gill (see COWGILL). **2.** Scottish: said to be an Americanized form of Danish **Køgel**. Compare KUGEL.

Coghlan (705) Irish: variant spelling of COUGHLIN.
GIVEN NAMES Irish 5%. *Malachy* (3), *Brendan.*

Cogle (125) Scottish (Shetland): habitational name from the lands of Cogle in Watten parish, Caithness.

Cogley (410) Irish: reduced Americanized form of Gaelic **Ó Coigligh** (see QUIGLEY).
GIVEN NAMES Irish 5%. *Conan, Delma, Liam.*

Coglianese (168) Italian: habitational name from an adjectival derivative of COGLIANO.
GIVEN NAMES Italian 10%. *Angelo* (2), *Annamarie, Carmine.*

Cogliano (178) Italian: variant of **Colliano**, a habitational name from Cogliano, a place in Salerno province, Campania.
GIVEN NAMES Italian 15%. *Salvatore* (4), *Angelo, Filomena.*

Cogswell (1379) English: **1.** habitational name from Great and Little Coxwell in Oxfordshire, named with an Old English personal name *Cocc* + Old English *wella* 'spring', 'stream'. **2.** variant of COGGESHALL.

Cohagan (109) Of Irish origin: Woulf found **McCoghegan** in Cavan, later **McCogan**, **Cogan**, from Gaelic **Mac**

Eochagáin, a patronymic from a diminutive of *Eochaidh* meaning 'horseman' (a derivative of *each* 'horse').

Cohan (1201) **1.** Variant of Irish **Cohane**, an Anglicized form of Gaelic **Ó Cadhain** (see COYNE 2). **2.** Variant spelling of Jewish (Ashkenazic) COHEN. This spelling of the Jewish name is found mainly in France.

Cohea (260) Irish: variant of COHEE.

Cohee (585) Irish: Munster variant of COFFEY.

Cohen (46018) Jewish: from Hebrew *kohen* 'priest'. Priests are traditionally regarded as members of a hereditary caste descended from Aaron, brother of Moses. See also KAPLAN.
GIVEN NAMES Jewish 8%. *Hyman* (98), *Sol* (73), *Meyer* (50), *Miriam* (45), *Isadore* (30), *Emanuel* (29), *Moshe* (28), *Shlomo* (27), *Myer* (20), *Avi* (16), *Yehuda* (16), *Chaim* (12).

Cohenour (225) Americanized spelling of German GOCHENOUR.

Cohick (249) Origin unidentified.

Cohill (191) Variant of Irish CAHILL or possibly of English COGHILL.

Cohn (5225) Jewish: variant spelling of COHEN.
GIVEN NAMES Jewish 4%. *Miriam* (5), *Dov* (3), *Emanuel* (3), *Hyman* (3), *Yaakov* (3), *Ari* (2), *Liba* (2), *Moshe* (2), *Shimon* (2), *Sol* (2), *Abbe, Aryeh.*

Cohoon (614) Irish spelling of Scottish COLQUHOUN. Compare CAHOON.

Cohran (159) Scottish: variant of COCHRAN.

Cohron (188) Variant of Scottish COCHRAN.

Cohrs (372) Americanized spelling of German KOHRS.
GIVEN NAMES German 6%. *Ewald* (2), *Otto* (2), *Dieter, Eldor.*

Coia (275) Italian (Apulia and Abruzzo): unexplained.
GIVEN NAMES Italian 11%. *Gino* (2), *Angelo, Domenic, Pasco, Pasquale, Romeo, Salvatore.*

Coil (756) **1.** Irish: variant spelling of COYLE. **2.** Possibly an altered spelling of German KEIL.

Coile (282) **1.** Irish: variant spelling of COYLE. **2.** Possibly an altered spelling of German KEIL.

Coin (241) **1.** Irish: variant spelling of COYNE. **2.** French: from French *coin* 'corner', a topographic name for someone who lived on a street corner.

Coiner (379) **1.** English: variant spelling of COYNER. **2.** Possibly an altered spelling of German KEINER.

Coiro (226) Italian: metonymic occupational name for a tanner or leatherworker, from old Italian *coiro* 'leather', Sicilian *coiru*. Compare CORIO.
GIVEN NAMES Italian 21%; French 6%. *Angelo* (2), *Ettore* (2), *Gerardo* (2), *Antonio, Arsenio, Attilio, Biagio, Filippo, Gaetano, Mario, Riccardo, Sebastiano, Silvio; Andre, Eugenie.*

Coit (466) English: from Old French *coit* 'flat stone', probably a nickname for a skilled quoits player.

Coito (116) Spanish and Portuguese: possibly a topographic name from *coito*, a variant of *couto* 'enclosed pasture' (see COUTO).
GIVEN NAMES Spanish 16%; Portuguese 9%. *Manuel* (4), *Adelino, Americo, Horacio, Joaquin, Jose, Lourdes; Conceicao.*

Coke (777) **1.** English: variant of COOK. **2.** Americanized spelling of German KOKE or KOCH.

Cokeley (163) Irish: variant spelling of COAKLEY.

Cokely (114) Irish: variant spelling of COAKLEY.
GIVEN NAMES Irish 4%. *Conroy, Fergal.*

Coker (8203) English: habitational name from a group of villages in Somerset named with Coker, from a Celtic river name meaning 'crooked'.

Cokley (213) Irish: variant spelling of COAKLEY.

Cola (297) Southern Italian: from the personal name *Cola*, a short form of *Nicola*, Italian equivalent of NICHOLAS.
GIVEN NAMES Italian 12%. *Angelo* (2), *Donato* (2), *Amelio, Dante, Domenic, Erminio, Luigi, Otello, Rino, Sal, Umberto.*

Colabella (146) Italian: nickname from the personal name COLA + *bella* 'beautiful'.
GIVEN NAMES Italian 16%. *Dante* (2), *Domenic, Nicola, Onofrio, Rocco, Sal.*

Colacino (135) Italian: from the personal name, a compound name of COLA + CINO.
GIVEN NAMES Italian 9%. *Antonio* (3), *Domenic, Franco, Mario.*

Colahan (147) Irish: possibly an Anglicized form of Gaelic **Ó Cathaláin** 'descendant of *Cathalan*', a diminutive of *Cathal* (see CAHILL). It may also be from **Mac Uallocháin** 'son of *Uallachán*', a personal name from a diminutive of *uallach* 'proud'.

Colaianni (190) Italian: from the personal name, a compound of COLA + IANNI, a reduced form of GIOVANNI, from Latin *Johannes* (see JOHN).
GIVEN NAMES Italian 17%. *Angelo* (3), *Carlo* (2), *Luigi* (2), *Cosimo, Dino, Francesco, Rocco.*

Colaizzi (168) Italian: **1.** from a personal name composed of the elements COLA + IZZO. **2.** variant of **Colarizzi**, from a personal name composed of the elements COLA + RIZZO.
GIVEN NAMES Italian 9%. *Franco* (3), *Antonio, Elio, Fausto, Quirino, Romolo, Vittorio.*

Colaluca (141) Italian: from the personal name, a compound of the personal names COLA + LUCA.

Colan (127) **1.** English and French: probably a variant of COLIN or COLLIN. **2.** Galician: unexplained.
GIVEN NAMES Spanish 6%. *Anselmo, Carlos, Juan, Luis, Marcos, Margarita, Pablo, Roberto.*

Colandrea (153) Italian: from the personal name, a compound of the personal names COLA + ANDREA.
GIVEN NAMES Italian 26%. *Antonio* (2), *Biagio* (2), *Dante* (2), *Pasquale* (2), *Rossano* (2), *Carmela, Ciro, Gino, Mario, Sal.*

Colaneri (126) Italian: from the personal name COLA + *nero* 'dark', 'black', hence a nickname meaning 'dark Nicholas', or alternatively from a compound name with the same second element as a personal name.
GIVEN NAME Italian 8%. *Tommaso.*

Colangelo (1240) Italian: from the personal name, a compound of the personal names COLA + ANGELO.
GIVEN NAMES Italian 16%. *Salvatore* (7), *Angelo* (6), *Rocco* (5), *Domenic* (4), *Sal* (4), *Dante* (3), *Amedio* (2), *Gino* (2), *Vito* (2), *Amedeo, Antonio, Attilio.*

Colantoni (104) Italian: patronymic or plural form of COLANTONIO.
GIVEN NAMES Italian 13%. *Ciro, Domenic, Marco, Mario, Renato, Rinaldo.*

Colantonio (224) Italian: from the personal name, a compound of the personal names COLA + ANTONIO.
GIVEN NAMES Italian 18%. *Giusto* (2), *Mario* (2), *Sergio* (2), *Angelo, Antonio, Domenic, Donato, Edmondo, Egidio, Emilio, Pietro, Renato, Rocco.*

Colantuoni (109) Italian: patronymic or plural form of COLANTUONO.
GIVEN NAMES Italian 12%. *Antonio, Gennaro.*

Colantuono (179) Italian: variant of COLANTONIO.
GIVEN NAMES Italian 18%. *Angelo* (2), *Carmine* (2), *Rocco* (2), *Luigi, Vito.*

Colao (176) Italian: from the personal name *Colao*, a short form of *Nicolao* (see NICHOLAS).
GIVEN NAMES Italian 22%; Spanish 10%. *Dante* (2), *Emilio* (2), *Angelo, Carmela, Fiore, Giacomo, Gino, Luigi, Saverio, Veto, Vito; Juan* (3), *Jesus* (2), *Francisco, Manuel.*

Colapietro (119) Italian: from the personal name, a compound of the personal names COLA + PIETRO.
GIVEN NAMES Italian 25%. *Sal* (2), *Vito* (2), *Angelo, Donato, Giacomo, Giulio, Luigi, Nicola.*

Colar (108) Respelling of French **Colard**, from a reduced derivative of the personal name *Nicolas* (see NICHOLAS).
GIVEN NAME French 5%. *Andre.*

Colarossi (127) Italian: patronymic or plural form of **Colarossi**, variant of COLARUSSO.

GIVEN NAMES Italian 22%. *Angelo* (2), *Antonio, Carlo, Carmine, Dino, Giuseppe, Pasquale, Pietro.*

Colarusso (451) Italian: from the personal name COLA + *russo* 'red' (southern variant of *rosso*), hence a nickname meaning 'red Nicholas', or alternatively from a compound name with the same second element as a personal name (see ROSSO).
GIVEN NAMES Italian 17%. *Angelo* (6), *Luigi* (3), *Antonio* (2), *Remo* (2), *Salvatore* (2), *Carmela, Domenic, Egidio, Enrico, Geno, Nicola, Rocco.*

Colas (171) French: from a reduced form of the personal name *Nicolas* (see NICHOLAS).
GIVEN NAMES French 20%; German 6%. *Pierre* (2), *Alain, Benoit, Christophe, Emile, Francoise, Jean Daniel, Josseline, Luc, Monique, Remy; Hermann* (2), *Fritz.*

Colasanti (195) Italian: from the personal name *Colasanto*, a compound of the personal names COLA + SANTO.
GIVEN NAMES Italian 12%. *Angelo* (2), *Biaggio, Cosimo, Rinaldo, Rocco.*

Colasuonno (125) Italian: compound name composed of the personal name *Cola* (short form of NICOLA) + *sonno* 'sleep'.
GIVEN NAMES Italian 28%. *Rocco* (2), *Angelo, Carlo, Domenico, Donato, Guiseppe, Mario, Riccardo, Sal.*

Colasurdo (225) Southern Italian: from the personal name COLA + southern Italian *surdo* 'deaf' (standard Italian *sordo*), hence a nickname meaning 'deaf Nicholas'.
GIVEN NAMES Italian 21%. *Sal* (3), *Rocco* (2), *Carmine, Giacomo, Giovanni, Giuseppe, Modesto, Nicola.*

Colavecchio (100) Southern Italian: from the personal name COLA + *vecchio* 'old', hence a nickname meaning 'old Nicholas'.

Colavita (148) Italian: possibly an altered form of **Calavitta**, a status name from medieval Greek *kalybitēs* 'dweller in a hut', from *kalybē* 'hut' + the habitational suffix *-itēs*.
GIVEN NAMES Italian 23%. *Angelo* (4), *Pasquale* (2), *Saverio* (2), *Aniello, Antonella, Donato, Leonardo, Piera, Severino.*

Colavito (258) Italian: from the personal name, a compound of the personal names COLA + VITO.
GIVEN NAMES Italian 16%. *Angelo* (2), *Vito* (2), *Carlo, Gaetano, Rocco.*

Colaw (146) Possibly an altered spelling of German **Kohlhaw**, a variant of KOHLHOFF.

Colbath (267) Northern Irish: variant of CULBREATH, itself a variant of Scottish GALBRAITH.

Colbaugh (191) Probably an Americanized spelling of German KALBACH. Compare KALBAUGH.

Colbeck (143) **1.** Northern English: habitational name from any of various minor places, such as Caldbeck in Cumbria, named with the Old Norse elements *kaldr* 'cold' + *bekkr* 'stream'. **2.** German: variant spelling of KOLBECK.

Colberg (462) Variant spelling of KOLBERG.
GIVEN NAMES Scandinavian 4%. *Erik, Thor.*

Colbert (6424) French (Normandy) and English: from a Germanic personal name composed of the elements *kol-* (akin to Old Norse *kollir* 'helmet') + *berht* 'bright', 'famous'.

Colbeth (152) Northern Irish: see COLBATH.

Colborn (414) English: variant of COLBURN.

Colbourne (108) English: variant of COLBURN.

Colburn (3909) English: habitational name from a place named with Old English *cōl* 'cool' + *burna* 'stream', as for example Colburn near Catterick in North Yorkshire.

Colby (4528) **1.** English: habitational name from places in Norfolk and Cumbria named Colby, from the Old Norse personal name *Koli* (a byname for a swarthy person, from *kol* '(char)coal') + Old Norse *býr* 'settlement'. **2.** Variant spelling of Norwegian **Kolby**, a habitational name in Akershus, with the same etymology as 1.

Colclasure (420) Americanized spelling of German **Kalklöser**, an occupational name for someone who quarried lime, from *Kalk* 'lime', 'chalk' + an agent derivative of *lösen* 'to loosen'.
FOREBEARS According to a passenger list, four persons called **Kalcklöser** arrived in Philadelphia aboard the *Allen* on September 11, 1729.

Colclough (378) English: habitational name from Cowclough in the parish of Whitworth, Lancashire, recorded in the 13th century as *Colleclogh*, probably named with the Old English byname *Cola* (see COLE 2) + Old English *clōh* 'ravine'.

Colcord (298) Probably an Americanized spelling of German **Kalkert**: **1.** occupational name for a lime burner, from an agent derivative of Middle High German *kalc* (see KALKBRENNER). **2.** habitational name for someone from Kalke in Brandenburg or Kalkar in Cleve.

Colden (179) **1.** English: habitational name from a place in West Yorkshire named Colden, from Old English *cald* 'cold' *col* 'charcoal' + *denu* 'valley'. **2.** English and Scottish: variant of COWDEN.
FOREBEARS Cadwallader Colden (1688–1778), physician, botanist, and mathematician, who for fifteen years was lieutenant-governor of New York colony, was born in Dalkeith, Scotland.
GIVEN NAMES Irish 5%. *Aileen, Conal.*

Colding (100) **1.** Danish: probably a habitational name from Kolding. This was originally the name of a river, from *kaldr* 'cold' + a derivational suffix *-ung*, hence 'the cold river'. **2.** English: perhaps a spelling variant of GOLDING.
GIVEN NAME Scandinavian 6%. *Kristoffer.*

Coldiron (711) Translation of German **Kalteis(en)**, an occupational name for a

blacksmith, from Middle High German *kalt* 'cold' + *īsen* 'iron'.

Coldren (457) Perhaps a variant of CALDERON.

Coldwell (473) English, Scottish, and northern Irish: variant of CALDWELL.

Cole (66813) **1.** English: from a Middle English pet form of NICHOLAS. **2.** English: from a Middle English personal name derived from the Old English byname *Cola* (from *col* '(char)coal', presumably denoting someone of swarthy appearance), or the Old Norse cognate *Koli*. **3.** Scottish and Irish: when not of English origin, this is a reduced and altered form of McCOOL. **4.** In some cases, particularly in New England, Cole is a translation of the French surname CHARBONNEAU. **5.** Probably an Americanized spelling of German KOHL.
FOREBEARS An Irish family by the name of Cole was established in Fermanagh by Sir William Cole (1576–1653). He was the first Provost of Enniskillen, and his descendants became earls of Enniskillen. The family is thought to have originated in Devon or Cornwall.

Colebank (191) English (Cumbria): habitational name, possibly from either of two places named Coal Bank, in Tyne and Wear and Durham.

Colee (160) Of uncertain origin; possibly an altered spelling of English COLEY.

Colegrove (905) **1.** English: probably a variant of COLGROVE. **2.** Probably an Americanized form of German **Kohlgrube**, a habitational name from any of twelve places so named, probably from Middle High German *kol* 'coal' + *gruobe* 'pit', or an altered spelling of **Kohlgraf**, an occupational name for an overseer of the coal trade.

Colella (1201) Italian: from a diminutive of the personal name COLA, a short form of *Nicola*, Italian equivalent of NICHOLAS.
GIVEN NAMES Italian 18%. *Angelo* (7), *Antonio* (6), *Vito* (6), *Benedetto* (5), *Domenic* (3), *Flavio* (3), *Rocco* (3), *Amerigo* (2), *Carlo* (2), *Carmela* (2), *Carmine* (2), *Domenico* (2).

Colello (386) Italian: variant of COLELLA.
GIVEN NAMES Italian 11%. *Angelo* (2), *Emidio* (2), *Mauro* (2), *Donato, Geno, Leonardo, Marco, Pina, Rocco.*

Coleman (63715) **1.** Irish: Anglicized form of Gaelic **Ó Colmáin** 'descendant of *Colmán*'. This was the name of an Irish missionary to Europe, generally known as St. Columban (c.540–615), who founded the monastery of Bobbio in northern Italy in 614. With his companion St. Gall, he enjoyed a considerable cult throughout central Europe, so that forms of his name were adopted as personal names in Italian (*Columbano*), French (*Colombain*), Czech (*Kollman*), and Hungarian (*Kálmán*). From all of these surnames are derived. In Irish and English, the name of this saint is identical with diminutives of the name of the 6th-century missionary known in English as St. Columba (521–97), who converted the Picts to Christianity, and who was known in Scandinavian languages as *Kalman*. **2.** Irish: Anglicized form of Gaelic **Ó Clumháin** 'descendant of *Clumhán*', a personal name from the diminutive of *clúmh* 'down', 'feathers'. **3.** English: occupational name for a burner of charcoal or a gatherer of coal, Middle English *coleman*, from Old English *col* '(char)coal' + *mann* 'man'. **4.** English: occupational name for the servant of a man named COLE. **5.** Jewish (Ashkenazic): Americanized form of KALMAN. **6.** Americanized form of German KOHLMANN or KUHLMANN.

Colen (346) Dutch: patronymic from a reduced form of the personal name *Nikolaus* (see NICHOLAS).

Coler (261) Possibly an Americanized spelling of the Swiss and South German surname KOHLER.

Coles (4093) English: patronymic from COLE.

Coleson (188) English: patronymic from COLE.

Colestock (149) Americanized spelling of the German name **Kohlstock**, from *Kohlstock* 'cabbage stalk', perhaps applied as a nickname for a stiff or formal person.

Coletta (649) Italian: from a diminutive of the personal name COLA.
GIVEN NAMES Italian 18%. *Antonio* (5), *Domenic* (3), *Flavio* (3), *Luigi* (3), *Rocco* (3), *Angelo* (2), *Carmine* (2), *Cesare* (2), *Ciro* (2), *Cosmo* (2), *Vito* (2), *Donato*.

Colette (100) North American variant spelling of French COLLET.
GIVEN NAMES French 6%. *Colette*; *Vito*.

Coletti (740) Italian: from a diminutive of COLA.
GIVEN NAMES Italian 13%. *Angelo* (6), *Aldo* (2), *Alessandro* (2), *Antonio* (2), *Carlo* (2), *Dino* (2), *Salvatore* (2), *Amelio*, *Attilio*, *Domenic*, *Elio*.

Coletto (100) Italian: patronymic or plural form of COLETTI.
GIVEN NAMES Italian 26%. *Reno* (3), *Vito* (3), *Domenico*, *Giovanni*, *Guido*, *Paride*, *Rocco*.

Coley (4436) **1.** English (West Midlands): nickname for a swarthy person, from Old English *colig* 'dark', 'black' (a derivative of *col* '(char)coal'). **2.** English: possibly a habitational name from Coaley in Gloucestershire, named in Old English as 'woodland clearing (*lēah*) with a hut or shelter (*cofa*)'. **3.** Probably an Americanized form of Swiss German KOHLI or KOHLER.

Colf (102) Americanized spelling of North German **Kalf**, a variant of KALB.

Colfer (223) Irish (County Wexford): probably an altered form of English COLFORD.

Colflesh (138) Americanized form of German KALBFLEISCH.

Colford (168) English: habitational name from either of two places called Coleford, in Somerset and Gloucestershire, which are named with Old English *col* '(char)coal' + *ford* 'ford'.

Colgan (1469) Irish and Scottish: reduced form of McCOLGAN, or an Americanized form of Irish **Ó Colgáin** 'descendant of *Colga*', a personal name based on *colg* 'thorn', 'sword'.
GIVEN NAMES Irish 5%. *Liam*, *Siobhan*.

Colgate (251) English: habitational name from Colgate in Sussex or Colgates in Kent, which are named with Old English *col* 'charcoal' + *geat* 'gate', indicating a gate leading into woodland where charcoal was burned.

Colgin (204) Irish: variant spelling of COLGAN.

Colglazier (261) Probably an Americanized spelling of German **Kalcklöser** (see COLCLASURE).

Colgrove (419) **1.** English: probably a variant of **Colgrave**, which appears to be a topographic name from Middle English *cole* 'coal' + *grave* 'pit', 'grave' (Old English *col* + *græf*), or perhaps a habitational name from a lost place so named. **2.** Probably an Americanized form of German **Kohlgrube** (see COLEGROVE).

Colicchio (145) Italian: from the personal name *Colicchio*, a pet form of COLA, or a shortened form of *Nicolicchio*, a pet form of NICOLA (see NICHOLAS).
GIVEN NAMES Italian 14%. *Angelo*, *Carlo*, *Nicola*, *Rocco*.

Colie (109) Scottish and English: probably a variant of COLEY.

Colin (897) **1.** French: from a reduced pet form of the personal name *Nicolas* (see NICHOLAS). **2.** English: variant spelling of COLLIN.
FOREBEARS A Colin from Brittany, France, is documented in St. Ours, Quebec, in 1669, with the secondary surname **LaLiberté**, which is often translated **Liberty**; Colin is often Americanized as COLLINS.
GIVEN NAMES Spanish 22%; French 5%. *Jose* (12), *Juan* (8), *Alfredo* (4), *Francisco* (4), *Jesus* (4), *Ricardo* (3), *Alberto* (2), *Angel* (2), *Arturo* (2), *Eduardo* (2), *Esteban* (2), *Faustino* (2); *Alexandre*, *Andre*, *Armand*, *Georges*, *Henri*, *Jean Claude*, *Jean-Michel*, *Laurette*, *Lucien*, *Marcel*, *Patrice*, *Pierre*.

Colina (161) Italian: from a feminine pet form of COLA.
GIVEN NAMES Spanish 45%. *Luis* (5), *Carlos* (3), *Jose* (3), *Juan* (3), *Eusebio* (2), *Javier* (2), *Orlando* (2), *Ramon* (2), *Adriana*, *Alberto*, *Alicia*, *Arturo*.

Colindres (111) Spanish: habitational name from Colindres in Santander province.
GIVEN NAMES Spanish 57%. *Jose* (8), *Luis* (3), *Alvaro* (2), *Blanca* (2), *Eladio* (2), *Jaime* (2), *Alejandro*, *Alicia*, *Carlos*, *Cesar*, *Everardo*, *Ezequiel*.

Coll (1031) **1.** English: from a reduced form of the personal name NICHOLAS. **2.** Scottish or Irish: reduced form of McCOLL. **3.** Catalan: topographic name from *coll* 'mountain pass', from Latin *collis* 'hill'. **4.** Americanized spelling of German KOLL or KOHL.
GIVEN NAMES Spanish 9%. *Carlos* (5), *Francisco* (5), *Jose* (4), *Mario* (4), *Andres* (3), *Jaime* (3), *Nestor* (3), *Pedro* (3), *Alberto* (2), *Angel* (2), *Eduardo* (2), *Fernando* (2).

Colla (198) **1.** Italian: habitational name from any of various places named with Colla, from medieval Latin *colla* 'hill', 'col' (a derivative of Latin *collis* 'hill'). **2.** Dutch: from a short form of the personal name *Nikolaas* (see NICHOLAS).
GIVEN NAMES Italian 10%. *Salvatore* (3), *Guido* (2), *Leno*, *Primo*, *Sal*.

Collado (830) Spanish: topographic name from Spanish *collado* 'hill', 'mountain pass', from Late Latin *collatum*, a derivative of Latin *collis* 'hill'.
GIVEN NAMES Spanish 50%. *Jose* (25), *Juan* (13), *Ana* (11), *Carlos* (9), *Luis* (8), *Ramon* (8), *Luz* (6), *Orlando* (6), *Pedro* (6), *Angel* (4), *Juana* (4), *Julio* (4); *Antonio* (7), *Lorenzo* (3), *Eligio* (2), *Fausto* (2), *Leonardo* (2), *Romeo* (2), *Angelo*, *Aureliano*, *Cecilio*, *Clemente*, *Dario*, *Delio*.

Collamore (155) Probably an altered form of English COLLYMORE, but see also GALLIMORE.

Collar (620) **1.** English: variant of COLLIER. **2.** Spanish: from *collar* 'collar'. **3.** Americanized spelling of German KOLLER or KOHLER.

Collard (1417) English and French: from the personal name COLL + the pejorative suffix *-ard*.
GIVEN NAMES French 5%. *Donat* (2), *Normand* (2), *Octave* (2), *Adelard*, *Aldor*, *Andre*, *Armand*, *Emile*, *Germaine*, *Marcel*.

Collazo (1396) Spanish: from *collazo* 'foster brother', 'servant'.
GIVEN NAMES Spanish 49%. *Jose* (43), *Luis* (28), *Juan* (17), *Carlos* (16), *Rafael* (13), *Miguel* (12), *Jesus* (11), *Jorge* (11), *Julio* (11), *Pedro* (10), *Angel* (7), *Francisco* (7).

Colle (155) **1.** French: from a short form of the personal name *Nicolas* (see NICHOLAS). **2.** Americanized spelling of German KOLL or the variant **Kolle**.
GIVEN NAME French 4%. *Patrice*.

Colledge (243) English: most probably a habitational name from Colwich in Staffordshire, named from Old English *col* '(char)coal' + *wīc* 'building'. Derivation from the word denoting an educational institution is less likely, but see COOLIDGE.

College (149) English: variant spelling of COLLEDGE.

Collen (201) English: variant spelling of COLLIN, a pet form of COLL 1.

Coller (471) **1.** English: variant of COL-LIER. **2.** Altered spelling of Swiss and German KOLLER or KOHLER.

Colleran (367) Irish: Anglicized form of Gaelic **Ó Callaráin** 'descendant of *Callarán*', which is probably a diminutive of the byname *Callaire* 'cryer', although Woulfe suggests it may be from the Connacht name **Mac Allmhuráin**.

Collet (346) French: from a pet form of COLLE.

FOREBEARS A Collet from Picardy, France, is documented in Montreal in 1668, with the secondary surname *Le Picard*.

GIVEN NAMES French 9%. *Patrice* (3), *Andre*, *Dominique*, *Francoise*, *Normand*, *Pierre*.

Colleton (119) **1.** Irish: variant of CULLI-TON. **2.** English: variant spelling of COLLITON.

Collett (2520) **1.** English: from a pet form of COLL 1. **2.** Respelling of French COL-LET, cognate with 1.

Colletta (249) Italian: from a feminine form of the personal name *Colletto* (see COLLETTI).

GIVEN NAMES Italian 9%. *Angelo*, *Carmine*, *Dino*, *Ignazio*, *Matteo*.

Collette (1818) French: spelling variant of COLLET or a metronymic from an reduced pet form of *Nicole*, feminine form of *Nicolas* (see NICHOLAS).

GIVEN NAMES French 5%. *Normand* (3), *Gilles* (2), *Alban*, *Alderic*, *Alyre*, *Amie*, *Fernande*, *Gaetan*, *Georges*, *Herve*, *Leandre*, *Monique*.

Colletti (968) Italian: from the personal name *Colletto*, a pet form of COLA (see NICOLAS).

GIVEN NAMES Italian 14%. *Salvatore* (5), *Ciro* (3), *Saverio* (3), *Angelo* (2), *Antonino* (2), *Biagio* (2), *Pasquale* (2), *Rocco* (2), *Sal* (2), *Carlo*, *Carmel*, *Emanuele*.

Colley (3148) **1.** English: variant spelling of COLEY. **2.** Irish: reduced form of MCCOLLEY. **3.** Americanized spelling of Swiss German KOHLI.

Colli (148) Italian: topographic name from the plural of *colle* 'hill'.

GIVEN NAMES Italian 6%. *Salvatore* (2), *Gasper*, *Giovanni*, *Guido*.

Collias (122) Greek: from *Kola*, Albanian pet form of the personal name NICHOLAS.

GIVEN NAMES Greek 6%. *Dimitris*, *Spiro*, *Stephanos*.

Collick (148) English: habitational name from a place in Nottinghamshire named Colwick, probably from Old English *col* '(char)coal' + *wīc* 'building'.

GIVEN NAME French 4%. *Albertine*.

Collicott (126) English: variant of CALLI-COTT.

Collie (1028) English: variant spelling of COLEY.

Collier (18671) English: occupational name for a burner of charcoal or a gatherer or seller of coal, from Middle English *cole* '(char)coal' + the agent suffix *-(i)er*.

FOREBEARS A Huguenot family of this name from Paris emigrated to New York. They were probably originally called **Colié**.

Colliflower (121) Altered form of French **Gorenflo**, a habitational name from a village named Gorenflos between Abbeville and Amiens, France.

FOREBEARS Georg Adam Goranflo arrived at Philadelphia on the ship *Ann* in 1749 and settled in Hagerstown, MD, the name being changed to **Colliflower** in the process. His forebear Jacques de Gorenflo was a leading Huguenot in the 17th century. Religious persecution drove the family to Germany, from where Georg Adam Goranflo emigrated to North America.

Colligan (846) Irish: variant of COLGAN; in Gaelic pronunciation a vowel is inserted between *l* and *g*.

GIVEN NAMES Irish 4%. *Brendan*, *Cathal*, *Paddy*.

Collignon (207) French: from a reduced pet form of *Nicolas* (see NICHOLAS). The concentration of the name in KY suggests that some other source may also be involved or that the surname was brought to North America via some other country.

Collin (863) **1.** English and French: from a pet form of English COLL 1, French COLLE. **2.** Probably an altered spelling of German KOLLIN. **3.** Danish: variant of COLDING. **4.** Swedish: ornamental name from an unexplained first element, probably from a place name, + the suffix *-in*, from Latin *-in(i)us* 'descendant of'.

GIVEN NAMES French 10%. *Lucien* (4), *Marcel* (4), *Leonide* (2), *Andre*, *Armand*, *Camille*, *Emile*, *Fernand*, *Firmin*, *Francois*, *Ghislaine*, *Normand*.

Colling (536) **1.** English: from the Old Norse personal name *Kollungr*, a derivative of *Koli*, or from an Old English cognate, *Colling*, a derivative of *Cola* (see COLE 2). **2.** English: from a pet form of COLL 1. **3.** Altered spelling of German **Kölling** (see KOLLING).

Collinge (214) English (Lancashire): possibly a variant of COLLING.

Collings (1178) English: patronymic from COLLING.

Collingsworth (227) English: variant of COLLINGWOOD.

Collingwood (480) English: habitational name, probably from Collingwood in Staffordshire, although the surname is now more common on Tyneside. The place name arose from a wood the ownership of which was disputed (from Middle English *calenge* 'dispute', 'challenge').

Collins (107617) **1.** Irish: Anglicized form of Gaelic **Ó Coileáin** and **Mac Coileáin** (see CULLEN 1). **2.** English: patronymic from the Middle English personal name *Col(l)in*, a pet form of COLL, itself a short form of NICHOLAS. **3.** Americanized form of French COLIN.

Collinson (459) English and Scottish: variant of COLLINS.

Collinsworth (929) English: variant spelling of **Collingsworth**, itself a variant of COLLINGWOOD.

Collis (1058) English: variant of COLLINS.

Collison (1076) English: variant of COLLINS.

Collister (303) Irish, Scottish, and Manx: reduced form of MCCOLLISTER, a variant form of MCALLISTER.

Colliton (125) **1.** Irish: variant of CULLITON. **2.** Possibly English, a habitational name from any of several places in Devon variously called Colliton, Colyton, or Collaton. Colliton and Collaton are named with the Old English personal name *Cola* (see COLE 2) + *tūn* 'settlement'; Colyton is 'settlement on the Coly river', a Celtic river name.

Colliver (257) English (Cornwall): of uncertain origin; probably a variant of CULVER. Compare CULLIFER.

Collman (240) **1.** English and Irish: variant of COLEMAN. **2.** Americanized spelling of German KOLLMANN, or of KOHLMANN.

Collom (428) Reduced form of Irish MCCOLLOM, a variant of MCCOLLUM.

Collopy (343) Irish (Limerick): Anglicized form of Gaelic **Ó Colpa**, 'son of *Colpa*', which is possibly a byname based on *colpa* 'collop'. A collop originally denoted a fully grown horse or cow, and from there came to denote an area of grazing land sufficient to support such an animal.

GIVEN NAMES Irish 5%. *Conan*, *Eamon*, *Eamonn*, *Liam*.

Colloton (100) Of uncertain origin; possibly English or Irish. It could be a habitational name from Collaton St. Mary in Devon, named with the Old English personal name *Cola* + *tūn* 'farmstead', 'settlement'. However, the modern name is recorded in Cheshire and Ireland only, suggesting a different source is probably involved.

Collum (1244) Reduced form of northern Irish MCCOLLUM.

Collums (236) Reduced form of northern Irish MCCOLLUM, with the addition of English patronymic -*s*. This name is found mainly in MS.

Collura (602) Southern Italian: metonymic occupational name for a baker, from late Greek *kolloura* denoting a type of bread. Pronounced *Collurà*, it is from medieval Greek *kollouras* 'baker'.

GIVEN NAMES Italian 17%. *Salvatore* (8), *Angelo* (6), *Sal* (4), *Santo* (4), *Rocco* (3), *Aldo*, *Carlo*, *Carmelo*, *Francesco*, *Gaspare*, *Giovanni*, *Petrina*.

Collver (214) Variant of English CULVER. Compare COLLIVER.

Collyer (432) English: variant spelling of COLLIER.

Collymore (168) English: apparently a habitational name from an unidentified place. There is a place called Colleymore Farm in Oxfordshire, but it is not clear whether this is the source of the surname. See also COLLAMORE, CULLIMORE, GALLIMORE.

Colman (1261) **1.** Irish and English: variant of COLEMAN 1–4. **2.** Americanized spelling of German KOHLMANN or KOLLMANN.

FOREBEARS William Colman migrated from London, England, to Massachusetts Bay Colony in 1671 aboard the ship *Arabella*. His sons, Benjamin and John, were active in Boston town affairs, with Benjamin as a minister of the Brattle Street Church, and John a selectman.

Colmenares (167) Spanish: habitational name from either of two places called Colmenares, in Palencia and Almería provinces, from the plural of *colmenar* 'beehive', or possibly from a field name with the same meaning.

GIVEN NAMES Spanish 56%. *Jose* (8), *Carlos* (5), *Rafael* (4), *Ruben* (4), *Jorge* (3), *Alfonso* (2), *Gustavo* (2), *Jaime* (2), *Luis* (2), *Miguel* (2), *Ramon* (2), *Adolfo*.

Colmenero (204) Spanish: **1.** occupational name for a beekeeper, *colmenero*, a derivative *colmena* 'beehive'. **2.** possibly a habitational name from a place in Badajoz province or another in Tenerife named Colmenero.

GIVEN NAMES Spanish 40%. *Jose* (5), *Jesus* (3), *Mario* (3), *Salvador* (3), *Arturo* (2), *Jaime* (2), *Juan* (2), *Manuel* (2), *Rodolfo* (2), *Alberto*, *Alfredo*, *Armando*.

Colmer (156) **1.** English: habitational name for someone from Colmore in Hampshire, recorded in Domesday Book as *Colemere*, from Old English *cōl* 'cool' + *mere* 'pool', 'pond'. **2.** Altered spelling of German **Kollmer**, an Alsatian habitational name for someone from Colmar (formerly written *Kolmar*), or of **Gollmer**, a habitational name for someone from any of various places named Golm or Golme.

Coln (129) Possibly a shortened form of **Köllner**, a habitational name for someone from the city of Cologne, German *Köln* (earlier *Cöln*), from a Roman military camp *Colonia Agrippina*.

Colo (142) Southern Italian: **1.** from the personal name *Colo*, a short form of *Nicolo* (see NICHOLAS). **2.** (**Colò**) nickname from medieval Greek *kolos* 'lame', classical Greek *kylos*.

GIVEN NAMES Italian 8%. *Angelo* (4), *Aldo*, *Guido*, *Michelina*.

Coloma (205) Catalan: from the personal name *Coloma*, a vernacular form of Latin *Columba* (see COLOMB).

GIVEN NAMES Spanish 46%. *Eduardo* (4), *Luis* (4), *Carlos* (3), *Ignacio* (3), *Jose* (2), *Manuel* (2), *Maria Isabel* (2), *Agripina*, *Alfredo*, *Arturo*, *Avelino*, *Claudio*.

Colomb (222) French: from Old French *colomb* 'pigeon' (Latin *columbus*), applied as a metonymic occupational name for a keeper of pigeons or doves.

GIVEN NAMES French 10%; Irish 5%. *Celina*, *Celine*, *Curley*, *Emile*, *Francois*, *Guillaume*, *Raoul*, *Thierry*; *Keane* (2).

Colombe (141) French: according to Morlet, possibly from a female personal name, *Colomba*, from *colombe* 'dove', borne by Saint Colombe, who was martyred at Sens in 273.

GIVEN NAMES French 7%. *Fernand*, *Lucien*.

Colombini (132) Italian: from a diminutive of COLOMBO. In Milan this was the surname regularly used for the foundlings taken into the orphanage of St. Catherine of Ruota there, which had a dove as its symbol.

GIVEN NAMES Italian 14%. *Carlo* (2), *Angelo*, *Dante*, *Dino*, *Ettore*, *Francesca*, *Marco*.

Colombo (1890) Italian: from the personal name *Colombo*, from Latin *Colombus*, *Colomba* meaning 'dove', a personal name favored by early Christians because the dove was considered to be the symbol of the Holy Spirit. In some cases the name may have arisen as a nickname for a gentle, mild-mannered person, or as a metonymic occupational name for a keeper of doves (Latin *columbus* 'dove').

GIVEN NAMES Italian 13%. *Angelo* (12), *Giovanni* (6), *Carlo* (5), *Sal* (5), *Antonio* (4), *Carmelo* (4), *Dino* (4), *Pasquale* (4), *Carmine* (3), *Gino* (3), *Salvatore* (3), *Dante* (2).

Colon (6873) Spanish (**Colón**): from the Latin *Colombus*, *Colomba* meaning 'dove', a personal name favored by early Christians because the dove was considered to be the symbol of the Holy Spirit.

GIVEN NAMES Spanish 42%. *Jose* (213), *Luis* (113), *Angel* (81), *Juan* (77), *Carlos* (72), *Jorge* (41), *Ramon* (38), *Miguel* (37), *Luz* (36), *Pedro* (36), *Ana* (34), *Rafael* (33).

Colona (147) Italian: from *colona*, feminine form of *colono* 'farmer', 'farm laborer'.

Colone (106) Italian: from an augmentative form, meaning 'big Nicolas', of the personal name COLA (see NICOLAS).

GIVEN NAMES Italian 10%. *Angelo*, *Ennio*, *Luigi*.

Colonna (890) Southern Italian: topographic name from *colonna* 'column' (from Latin *columna*).

GIVEN NAMES Italian 25%; Spanish 5%. *Vito* (6), *Mario* (4), *Orlando* (3), *Rocco* (3), *Sandro* (3), *Armando* (2), *Constantino* (2), *Enrico* (2), *Giovanni* (2), *Salvatore* (2), *Agostino*, *Alessandro*, *Berardino*, *Carmela*, *Delio*; *Ramon* (2), *Angel*, *Carlos*, *Isidoro*, *Jose*, *Julio*.

Colony (174) Probably a variant of Irish CLOONEY.

Colopy (148) Irish: variant spelling of COLLOPY.

Colorado (176) Spanish: nickname for someone with red skin or hair, from *colorado* 'reddish'.

GIVEN NAMES Spanish 53%. *Carlos* (6), *Luis* (5), *Jose* (3), *Julio* (3), *Ramon* (3), *Javier* (2), *Jorge* (2), *Juan* (2), *Manuel* (2), *Alberto*, *Alicia*, *Amador*.

Colosi (233) Italian: probably a habitational name from a short form of Nicolosi, a place in Catania, Sicily.

GIVEN NAMES Italian 18%. *Mario* (2), *Angelo*, *Antonio*, *Fausto*, *Marco*, *Neno*, *Nicola*, *Santino*, *Virgilia*.

Colosimo (559) Southern Italian: of uncertain derivation; possibly from a medieval Greek personal name *Kalosimos*, composed of the elements *kalos* 'beautiful' + *simos* meaning either 'lame' or 'snub-nosed'.

GIVEN NAMES Italian 10%. *Angelo* (4), *Filippo* (3), *Antonio* (2), *Dante* (2), *Filomena*, *Livio*, *Raffaele*, *Romeo*, *Saverio*.

Colp (103) Probably a respelling of German KOLB.

Colpitts (365) English: habitational name, probably from Colpitts Grange, Northumberland, which is named from Old English *col* '(char)coal' + *pytt* 'pit'.

Colquhoun (242) Scottish: habitational name from the barony of Colquhoun in Dumbartonshire. The name appears to derive from Gaelic *còil*, *cùil* 'nook', 'corner', or *coill(e)* 'wood' + *cumhann* 'narrow'. The usual Scottish pronunciation is *ka-hoon*.

GIVEN NAME Scottish 6%. *Alastair*.

Colquitt (770) Manx: unexplained.

Colson (3351) Northern English and Scottish: patronymic from COLE 1 or 2.

Colston (1194) English: **1.** from a Middle English personal name, *Colstan*, which is probably from Old Norse *Kolsteinn*, composed of the elements *kol* 'charcoal' + *steinn* 'stone'. **2.** habitational name from Colston Basset in Nottinghamshire, or the nearby Car Colston, both of which seem to have originally been named from the Old Norse personal name *Kolr* + Old English *tūn* 'settlement'. The first syllable of Car Colson was originally the defining prefix *kirk* 'church'. **3.** habitational name from Coulston in Wiltshire, which is named with the genitive case of an Old English personal name *Cufel* (diminutive of *Cufa*) + Old English *tūn* 'enclosure', 'settlement'.

Colt (540) English: from Middle English *colt* 'young ass', later also 'young horse', 'colt', hence a metonymic occupational name for someone who looked after asses and horses, or a nickname for an obstinate or frisky person, from the same word. In northern England *colt* was a generic term for working horses and asses.

Colten (115) English: possibly a variant spelling of COLTON.

Colter (955) **1.** English: occupational name for someone who looked after asses and horses, from an agent derivative of COLT.

Compare COULTHARD. **2.** Variant spelling of German KOLTER.

Coltharp (335) Probably an altered spelling of **Colthorpe**, an English habitational name from a lost or unidentified place possibly named with Old Norse *þorp* 'hamlet', 'settlement'.

Coltman (128) English: occupational name for someone who looked after asses and horses, from Middle English *colt* 'young ass', later also 'young horse', 'colt' + *man*.

Colton (2525) English and Scottish: habitational name from any of various places called Colton in England, perhaps also Colton House in Scotland. Examples in Norfolk, Staffordshire, and North Yorkshire are from the Old English personal name *Cola* (or the cognate Old Norse *Koli*; see COLE 2) + Old English *tūn* 'enclosure', 'settlement'. The place so named in Somerset has as its first element the Old English personal name *Cūla* (of uncertain origin). The one in Cumbria has a river name apparently derived from a Celtic word meaning 'hazel'.

Coltrain (263) Variant of northern Irish COLTRANE.

Coltrane (410) Northern Irish: Anglicized form of Gaelic **Ó Coltaráin**, a surname associated with county Down.

Coltrin (205) Variant of northern Irish COLTRANE.
GIVEN NAME French 4%. *Andre*.

Colucci (1439) Italian: patronymic or plural form of COLUCCIO.
GIVEN NAMES Italian 14%. *Rocco* (6), *Vito* (6), *Angelo* (5), *Guido* (3), *Marco* (3), *Carmine* (2), *Ceasar* (2), *Dino* (2), *Franco* (2), *Salvatore* (2), *Santo* (2).

Coluccio (230) Italian: from a diminutive of the personal name COLA.
GIVEN NAMES Italian 25%. *Rocco* (3), *Salvatore* (3), *Cosimo* (2), *Dante, Elio, Guiseppe, Luciano, Mario* (2), *Sal, Silvio*.

Columbia (290) Origin unidentified.

Columbo (265) Italian: variant spelling of COLOMBO.
GIVEN NAMES Italian 7%. *Nunzio* (2), *Angelo, Antonio, Carmine, Gino, Salvatore*.

Columbus (674) Origin unidentified.

Colunga (406) Asturian-Leonese: habitational name from a place in Asturies called Colunga.
GIVEN NAMES Spanish 44%. *Juan* (10), *Jose* (8), *Jesus* (7), *Pedro* (5), *Carlos* (4), *Lupe* (4), *Alfredo* (3), *Manuel* (3), *Mario* (3), *Ramon* (3), *Raul* (3), *Roberto* (3).

Coluzzi (110) Variant spelling of Italian **Colozzi**, from a pet form of the personal name COLA.
GIVEN NAMES Italian 12%. *Angelo* (2), *Romolo*.

Colvard (589) Variant of French and English COLVERT.

Colver (201) English (Leicestershire): variant of CULVER.

Colvert (229) English and French: **1.** Variant of **Culvert**, a nickname from Old French *culvert* 'base', 'treacherous'. **2.** variant of CALVERT. **3.** Possibly also a variant of COLBERT.
GIVEN NAMES French 4%. *Antoine, Yoland*.

Colville (557) Scottish (of Norman origin): habitational name from Colleville in Seine-Maritime, France, named with the Scandinavian personal name *Koli* (see COLE 2) + Old French *ville* 'settlement', 'village'.

Colvin (7936) Scottish and English: variant of COLVILLE, probably reflecting a local pronunciation.

Colwell (3743) English: habitational name from places in Northumberland and Devon named Colwell. The former is named with Old English *col* '(char)coal' or *cōl* 'cool' + *well(a)* 'spring', 'stream'; the latter has as the first element a Celtic river name, *Coly*, apparently meaning 'narrow'.

Colwill (120) English: variant of COLWELL.

Colyar (132) English: variant spelling of COLLIER.

Colyer (1042) English: variant spelling of COLLIER.

Coman (424) **1.** English (Norfolk): unexplained. **2.** Romanian: unexplained.
GIVEN NAMES Romanian 4%. *Vasile* (2), *Cornel, Mihaela, Nicolae, Sorin, Viorel*.

Comans (109) Variant of Irish CUMMINGS.

Comar (113) **1.** Indian (Panjab): Hindu name, probably derived from KUMAR. **2.** French: southern variant of **Commère** 'godmother', 'namer', from Latin *commater*.
GIVEN NAMES Indian 15%; French 7%. *Dipak* (3), *Anjali, Dharam, Ravi, Usha*; *Cyrille* (2), *Emile*.

Comardelle (102) Of French origin: unexplained.

Comas (282) **1.** Northern Irish: reduced form of McCOMAS. **2.** Catalan: topographic name from the plural of *coma*, from Gaulish *cumba* 'valley'.
GIVEN NAMES Spanish 25%. *Jose* (6), *Luis* (4), *Miguel* (4), *Pedro* (3), *Alberto* (2), *Arturo* (2), *Fernando* (2), *Manuel* (2), *Mario* (2), *Rafael* (2), *Raimundo* (2), *Adolfo*.

Comb (111) Irish, Scottish, and English: variant spelling of COMBE.

Combe (278) **1.** English: topographic name for someone who lived in a narrow valley, Middle English *combe* or habitational name from a place named with this word (see COOMBE). **2.** Irish: reduced form of **McCombe** (see McCOMB). **3.** French: topographic name from Gaulish *cumba* '(narrow) valley', 'combe'. Compare LACOMBE.
GIVEN NAMES French 6%. *Emile* (3), *Michel*.

Combee (182) **1.** Scottish: reduced and altered form of McCOMBIE. **2.** Perhaps a variant spelling of English CUMBY.

Comber (171) **1.** English: variant of COMER or COOMBER. **2.** Irish: reduced form of McCOMBER.

Combes (451) **1.** English: variant of COOMBS. **2.** French: habitational name from any of various places in southern France, for example in Hérault, named Combes, from Latin *cumba* 'narrow valley', 'ravine', a word of Gaulish origin.

Combest (426) Altered spelling of German **Kombst** or **Gumpost**, from Middle High German *kumpost* 'bottled fruit or vegetables', 'sauerkraut' (from Latin *compositum*); the term further denoted a particular tax and it is probably from this sense that the surname arose.

Combs (17889) **1.** Northern Irish: reduced form of McCOMBS. **2.** English: variant of COOMBS.

Comeau (2296) French: from a Gascon diminutive of COMBE. In Canada, this name is particularly associated with Acadia (see COMEAUX).
GIVEN NAMES French 8%. *Pierre* (4), *Andre* (3), *Camille* (3), *Alphie* (2), *Emile* (2), *Fernand* (2), *Herve* (2), *Jacques* (2), *Marcel* (2), *Monique* (2), *Murielle* (2), *Normand* (2).

Comeaux (2307) Variant spelling of French COMEAU. This is a frequent name in LA, where bearers are descendants of the Acadian refugees from the 18th-century expulsion by the British Canadians.
GIVEN NAMES French 6%. *Camille* (3), *Curley* (2), *Emile* (2), *Leonce* (2), *Pierre* (2), *Adrien, Alphonse, Andre, Antoine, Athanase, Berchman, Caliste*.

Comegys (279) Dutch: unexplained. In the U.S. the name occurs chiefly in MD and OH.

Comella (342) Italian: from a feminine form of **Comelli**, a diminutive of COMI.
GIVEN NAMES Italian 12%. *Angelo* (2), *Santo* (2), *Agostino, Antonino, Antonio, Carmel, Dante, Giuseppe, Saverio*.

Comer (6097) **1.** English: occupational name from Middle English *combere*, an agent derivative of Old English *camb* 'comb', referring perhaps to a maker or seller of combs, or to someone who used them to prepare wool or flax for spinning. This was an alternative process to carding, and caused the wool fibers to lie more or less parallel to one another, so that the cloth produced had a hard, smooth finish without a nap. **2.** English: variant of COOMBER. **3.** Probably an Americanized spelling of German KOMMER or KAMMER.

Comerford (1099) **1.** Irish: reduced, Anglicized, and altered form of Gaelic **Mac Cumascaigh** 'son of *Cumascach*', a byname from *cumascach* 'mixer', 'confuser'. See also COMISKEY. **2.** English: habitational name from Comberford in Staffordshire, so named with the Old English personal name *Cumbra* (originally an ethnic name for a British Celt), or from the genitive plural of the tribal name, meaning 'of the British' + Old English *ford* 'ford'.

Comes (306) French (**Comès**): from a Gascon variant of COMBE. It is likely that this was also a translation of VIENS, a particularly Canadian name.
GIVEN NAMES Italian 4%. *Giovanni* (2), *Angelo, Filippo, Nicola, Vito.*

Comey (155) Welsh: habitational name from a place called Cymau in Dyfed, near Wrexham, named with Welsh *cymau*, plural of *cwm* 'valley'.

Comfort (1375) English (Kent): probably a habitational name from a place near Birling in Kent, now called Comfortsplace Farm, earlier known as Comports Place (1559) and Comporte (1601). This was named for a family associated with it called de Cumpeworth (1255). The place from which the family took its name has not been identified.

Comi (100) Italian form of Greek **Komis** (see COMIS).
GIVEN NAMES Italian 6%. *Aldo, Salvatore.*

Comings (116) Variant spelling of Irish CUMMINGS.

Comins (286) Variant of Irish CUMMINGS.

Cominsky (176) Americanized spelling of Polish **Komiński**, a habitational name for someone from a place called Kominy.

Comis (107) Greek: from medieval Greek *komis* 'count', from Latin *comes* (see COMITO).
GIVEN NAME Greek 5%. *Spiro* (2).

Comiskey (615) Irish: reduced Americanized form of **Mac Cumascaigh** 'son of *Cumascach*', a byname from *cumascach* 'mixer', 'confuser'. Compare COMERFORD.

Comisky (138) Irish: variant spelling of COMISKEY.

Comito (329) Italian: from medieval Latin *comitus* 'count' or the medieval Greek form of this word, *komitos*, applied as a nickname for someone who gave himself airs and graces or for someone in the service of a count.
GIVEN NAMES Italian 20%. *Salvatore* (5), *Angelo* (3), *Carlo* (3), *Attilio, Carmelo, Carmine, Cosmo, Domenic, Gaspare, Larraine, Vito.*

Comley (327) English: habitational name, probably from Comley in Shropshire or Combley on the Isle of Wight; both are named with Old English *cumb* 'valley' + *lēah* 'woodland clearing'.

Comly (179) English: variant spelling of COMLEY.

Commander (449) **1.** English: from Middle English *comander, comando(u)r* 'leader', 'ruler', probably applied as a nickname, although Reaney suggests that the term, derived from Old French *comandeor*, also denoted the officer in charge of a commandery, for example of the Knights Templars, and in this sense it would have been an occupational or status name. **2.** Americanized spelling of German **Kommander**, a name of uncertain origin. Brechenmacher suggests that it may be a Classicized form of HOFFMANN.

Commer (109) **1.** German and Dutch: variant spelling of KOMMER. **2.** English: unexplained.

Commerford (247) Irish: variant spelling of COMERFORD.

Commers (109) Probably a variant of COMMER.

Commings (111) Variant spelling of Irish CUMMINGS.
GIVEN NAME German 4%. *Erhardt.*

Commins (269) Irish: variant of CUMMINS (see CUMMINGS).

Commisso (239) Southern Italian: habitational name from Comiso, in Ragusa province, Sicily.
GIVEN NAMES Italian 39%. *Rocco* (6), *Giuseppe* (5), *Cosimo* (3), *Luigi* (3), *Sal* (3), *Antonio* (2), *Cosmo* (2), *Domenico* (2), *Francesco* (2), *Salvatore* (2), *Silvia* (2), *Angelo, Dino, Orlando, Serafina.*

Commodore (198) Origin unidentified; perhaps an altered spelling of Italian **Commodari**, a derivative of *commodare* 'to furnish or supply'.

Common (195) Irish: reduced form of McCOMMON.

Commons (442) Irish: reduced form of McCOMMONS.

Como (761) **1.** Italian: from the personal name *Como*, a short form of *Giacomo*, Italian equivalent of JAMES. **2.** Italian: habitational name from Como in Lombardy. **3.** Altered spelling of French COMEAU.
GIVEN NAMES Italian 14%. *Sal* (6), *Salvatore* (5), *Giuseppe* (2), *Ignazio* (2), *Nunzio* (2), *Vito* (2), *Angelo, Antonio, Camillo, Carlo, Carmela, Caterina.*

Comolli (135) Italian: from a derivative of the personal name COMO.

Comp (327) Probably an altered spelling of Dutch or German KAMP or **Kumpf** (see KUMP).

Compagno (120) Italian: **1.** nickname from *compagno* 'companion', 'friend' (from Late Latin *companio, companionis*). **2.** from a reduced form of the Tuscan personal name *Boncompagno*.
GIVEN NAMES Italian 12%. *Antonio, Gaetano, Nicolino.*

Compagnone (113) Italian: from an augmentative form of COMPAGNO.
GIVEN NAMES Italian 43%. *Nino* (3), *Carlo* (2), *Franco* (2), *Armando, Domenic, Enrico, Francesco, Giovanna, Luigi, Mario, Pasquale, Pietro, Sal, Silvio.*

Companion (131) Origin uncertain; perhaps an Americanized form of Italian COMPAGNO or COMPAGNONE.

Comparato (101) Southern Italian: from the old personal name *Comparato*, from Latin *comparare* 'to provide or procure'.
GIVEN NAMES Italian 11%. *Calogero, Guiseppe, Vincenzo.*

Compas (110) French: habitational name from Le Compas in Creuse.

GIVEN NAMES French 15%; German 4%. *Gaston* (3), *Camille, Renel.*

Compean (190) Hispanic (Mexico): unexplained.
GIVEN NAMES Spanish 56%. *Jose* (12), *Juan* (5), *Luz* (3), *Rodolfo* (3), *Javier* (2), *Manuel* (2), *Pedro* (2), *Ricardo* (2), *Roberto* (2), *Agapito, Agustin, Aida.*

Compeau (217) Probably an altered spelling of French **Campeau**, a variant of CHAMPEAU. This is a MI name.

Compere (133) French (**Compère**): apparently from *compère* (from *compater*) in the sense 'godfather', or a respelling of the southern name **Compayre**, of the same derivation.
GIVEN NAMES French 14%. *Aliette, Franck, Francoise, Rosaire, Yves.*

Compher (191) Americanized spelling of South German **Kumpfer**, an occupational name for a maker of buckets and vats (see KUMP).

Compitello (100) Possibly an altered form of Italian **Campitello**, a topographic name meaning 'little field'.
GIVEN NAMES Italian 13%. *Rocco* (2), *Pasquale.*

Compo (189) **1.** Of Italian origin: possibly an Americanized form of CAMPO. **2.** Possibly also an Americanized spelling of French CAMPEAU (see CHAMPEAU).

Compston (177) English: see CUMPSTON.

Compton (12848) English: habitational name from any of the numerous places throughout England (but especially in the south) named Compton, from Old English *cumb* 'short, straight valley' + *tūn* 'enclosure', 'settlement'.

Comrie (181) Scottish: habitational name from any of various places called Comrie, of which there are examples in Fife and Perthshire. All are named with Gaelic *comarach*, from *comar* 'confluence', 'riverfork' + the locative suffix *-ach.*

Comstock (4062) English (Devon): probably a habitational name from an unidentified place.

Comte (125) French (**Compté**): **1.** regional name from Franche-Comté. **2.** habitational name from La Comté, Pas-de-Calais or numerous minor places named Comté.
GIVEN NAME French 5%. *Jean Jacques.*

Comtois (312) French: regional name denoting someone from Franche-Comté.
GIVEN NAMES French 25%. *Lucien* (3), *Marcel* (3), *Andre* (2), *Normand* (2), *Pierre* (2), *Camil, Fernand, Fernard, Gisele, Jean-Guy, Laurier, Michel.*

Comunale (173) Italian (Sicily): from *comunale* 'communal', hence possibly a nickname for a foundling cared for from community funds.
GIVEN NAMES Italian 18%. *Angelo* (3), *Cono* (2), *Amelio, Antonio, Pasquale, Sal, Umberto.*

Cona (179) Italian: topographic name for someone who lived by a roadside shrine, from *icona* 'icon', 'sacred image', with loss of the first syllable.

GIVEN NAMES Italian 35%. *Angelo* (6), *Gaetano* (2), *Rocco* (2), *Vito* (2), *Alessandro*, *Carmelo*, *Constantino*, *Ferdinando*, *Francesca*, *Francesco*, *Gennaro*, *Luigi*.

Conaghan (140) Irish: variant of CONAHAN.

GIVEN NAMES Irish 8%. *Cormac*, *Fergal*.

Conahan (225) Irish: reduced Anglicized form of Gaelic **Ó Connacháin** (see CUNNINGHAM).

GIVEN NAME Irish 13%. *Cormac* (4).

Conant (2099) **1.** English: from an Old Breton personal name, derived from an element meaning 'high', 'mighty', which was introduced into England by followers of William the Conqueror and subsequently into Ireland, where it still has some currency as a personal name. **2.** Scottish: habitational name from a place in Kincardineshire. The place name is of uncertain origin, possibly from an early Celtic name, *Conona* 'hound stream'.

FOREBEARS Roger Conant led a secession from Plymouth colony in about 1627 and founded the settlement that became Salem, MA. He was probably the son of Christopher Connant, who came over from England aboard the *Anne* in 1623.

Conard (1595) **1.** French: from a Germanic personal name composed of the elements *kōne*, *kuoni* 'bold' + *hard* 'brave', 'strong'. **2.** Americanized form of German **Kohnert**, a North German-Westphalian variant of KONRAD.

Conary (136) Irish: variant spelling of CONNERY.

Conatser (593) Probably an altered spelling of a variant of German KONITZER.

Conaty (322) Irish: Anglicized form of Gaelic **Ó Connachtaigh** 'descendant of *Connachtach*', a byname for someone from the province of Connacht.

Conaway (2852) Probably a spelling variant of Irish, Welsh, and Scottish CONWAY.

Conboy (859) Irish: alternative Anglicization of Gaelic **Ó Conbhuidhe** (see CONWAY).

Conca (173) Italian: topographic name for someone who lived in a hollow or depression in the land, from Latin *concha* 'shell'.

GIVEN NAMES Italian 17%. *Antonio* (3), *Saverio* (2), *Angelo*, *Gennaro*, *Luigi*, *Pietro*, *Salvatore*.

Concannon (854) Irish (County Galway): Anglicized form of Gaelic **Ó Con Cheanainn** 'descendant of *Cúcheanann*', a personal name composed of the elements *cú* 'hound' + *ceann* 'head' + *fionn* 'fair', 'white'. Bearers of this surname claim descent from a single 10th-century ancestor.

GIVEN NAMES Irish 6%. *Brendan*, *John Patrick*, *Niall*.

Conceicao (108) Portuguese (**Conceição**): from the Marian female personal name *(Nuestra Señora da) Conceição* '(Our Lady of the) Conception', alluding to the immaculate conception of the Virgin Mary.

GIVEN NAMES Spanish 34%; Portuguese 28%. *Manuel* (7), *Jose* (5), *Amandio* (2), *Agripina*, *Albino*, *Amaro*, *Candido*, *Carlos*, *Elvira*, *Ermelinda*, *Evandro*, *Francisco*; *Joao* (2), *Armanda*, *Joaquim*, *Marcio*; *Antonio* (5), *Concetta*.

Concepcion (1199) Spanish (**Concepción**): **1.** habitational name from any of numerous places named La Concepción. **2.** from the Marian female personal name (from Late Latin *conceptio*, genitive *conceptionis* 'conception'), alluding to the immaculate conception of the Virgin Mary.

GIVEN NAMES Spanish 47%. *Jose* (19), *Luis* (18), *Carlos* (13), *Juan* (11), *Miguel* (10), *Ramon* (9), *Luz* (8), *Ana* (7), *Cesar* (7), *Roberto* (7), *Angel* (6), *Orlando* (6); *Antonio* (8), *Carmelo* (2), *Angelo*, *Bartolo*, *Clemente*, *Dante*, *Fausto*, *Leonardo*, *Lorenzo*, *Pio*, *Plinio*.

Concha (263) Spanish: from *concha* 'shell' (Latin *concha*), applied as a topographic name for someone who lived in or near a hollow or depression in the land, or a habitational name from any of the places named with this word, notably the one in Guadalajara.

GIVEN NAMES Spanish 45%. *Sergio* (5), *Jose* (4), *Mario* (4), *Raul* (4), *Carlos* (3), *Fernando* (3), *Ramon* (3), *Ricardo* (3), *Roberto* (3), *Alfonso* (2), *Domingo* (2), *Felipe* (2); *Antonio* (2), *Lorenzo*, *Sal*.

Conde (1304) **1.** Spanish and Portuguese: nickname from the title of rank *conde* 'count', a derivative of Latin *comes*, *comitis* 'companion'. **2.** English: unexplained.

GIVEN NAMES Spanish 37%; Portuguese 9%. *Jose* (24), *Carlos* (19), *Manuel* (15), *Luis* (14), *Juan* (12), *Pedro* (9), *Raul* (7), *Jorge* (6), *Ruben* (6), *Angel* (5), *Cesar* (5), *Fernando* (5); *Goncalo*, *Manoel*.

Condello (143) Italian: diminutive of CONDO.

GIVEN NAMES Italian 20%. *Angelo*, *Antonio*, *Giuseppe*, *Nicola*, *Pasquale*, *Rocco*, *Sal*.

Conder (1082) **1.** Variant of Irish CONNOR. **2.** Possibly an Americanized spelling of German KANTER or GANTER.

Condict (118) Variant of Irish CONNICK, a patronymic from Gaelic **Mac Conmhaic**. The closing of palatalized *n* and *c* can sound like an excrescent *d* or *t* to non-Gaelic speakers.

GIVEN NAMES Irish 4%. *Brigid*, *Fergus*, *Liam*.

Condie (432) Scottish: topographic name for someone who lived by a water channel, Middle English, Old French *cond(u)it* (Late Latin *conductus*, a derivative of *conducere* to lead).

Condiff (108) Variant of Irish CONNIFF.

Condit (883) Southern French: from the past participle of *condir* from Latin *condi-tio* 'seasoning', 'flavoring', hence probably an occupational name or nickname for a cook.

Conditt (145) Respelling of French CONDIT.

GIVEN NAME French 4%. *Michel*.

Condo (377) Southern Italian (Calabria): nickname from medieval Greek *kontos* 'short'.

Condon (5497) Irish: Anglicized form of Gaelic **Condún**, itself a Gaelicized form of the Anglo-Norman habitational name *de Caunteton*. This seems to have been imported from Wales, but probably derives ultimately from Caunton in Nottinghamshire, which is named with the Old English personal name *Calunōð* (composed of the elements *calu* 'bald' + *nōð* 'daring') + Old English *tūn* 'enclosure', 'settlement'.

Condor (116) Probably a variant of Irish CONNOR.

Condos (216) Greek: nickname from *kontos* 'short', or a shortened form of various compound names formed with this word + a personal name, such as **Kondogiannis** ('short John'), **Kondopavlos** ('short Paul'), etc.

GIVEN NAMES Greek 11%. *Speros* (2), *Spyros* (2), *Athanasia*, *Christos*, *Despina*, *Dimo*, *Spiro*, *Spyro*.

Condra (585) Manx: variant of Irish CONROY.

Condran (104) Irish: variant of CONRAN.

Condray (174) Variant of Irish CONROY.

Condren (187) Variant of Irish CONRAN.

Condrey (473) Variant of Irish CONROY.

Condron (565) Irish: variant of CONRAN.

Condry (282) Variant of Irish CONROY.

Cone (4094) **1.** Irish: reduced form of McCONE. **2.** Americanized spelling of North German KOHN or **Köhn**, or KUHN.

Conejo (114) Spanish: from *conejo* 'rabbit' (from Latin *cuniculus*), presumably applied as a nickname with various possible connotations (big ears, timidity, etc.) or otherwise as a metonymic occupational name for a rabbit catcher or dealer.

GIVEN NAMES Spanish 54%. *Jose* (4), *Ignacio* (3), *Alberto* (2), *Javier* (2), *Juan* (2), *Miguel* (2), *Pedro* (2), *Raul* (2), *Roberto* (2), *Adela*, *Alfredo*, *Alvaro*.

Conely (179) Variant spelling of Irish CONNELLY.

GIVEN NAMES French 4%. *Musette*, *Patrice*.

Conerly (758) Americanized form of Irish CONNELLY.

Conery (184) Irish: variant of Irish CONNERY.

Cones (219) Americanized spelling of German KUNTZ, or the variants **Kunz** and KONZ.

Conetta (109) Italian (Caserta): unexplained; apparently from a diminutive of an unidentified female personal name.

GIVEN NAMES Italian 23%. *Aldo* (2), *Angelo*, *Antonio*, *Domenica*, *Enrico*, *Enzo*, *Luciano*, *Sal*.

Coney (1093) English: from Middle English *cony* 'rabbit' (a back-formation from *conies*, from Old French *conis*, plural of *conil*), a nickname for someone thought to resemble a rabbit in some way or a metonymic occupational name for a dealer in rabbits or rabbit skins.

Confair (104) Origin unidentified. Perhaps a respelling of French **Confrère**, a status name denoting a member of a fraternity, French *confrère*, from medieval Latin *confrater*, but see also CONFER.

GIVEN NAME French 4%. *Prosper*.

Confalone (113) Italian: from *gonfalone* 'standard', 'banner', from Old French *gonfalon* (of Germanic origin), a metonymic occupational name for a standard bearer, either in a military context or as the officer of a guild responsible for carrying the banner in religious processions. It was also a title borne by mayors of the Florentine republic, and by other magistrates designated more specifically as *gonfalonieri di giustizia* 'officers of justice', *gonfalonieri della chiesa* 'officers of the church', etc.

GIVEN NAMES Italian 10%. *Agostino, Antonio, Domenic, Donato, Pasquale, Romeo*.

Confer (1279) **1.** Respelling of French Swiss **Convers**, literally 'convert', a surname which Morlet believes was probably bestowed on Jewish or other converts to Christianity. The form **Confer** occurs with great frequency in central PA, its spelling reflecting the German (or Dutch) pronunciation; it may have originated in Europe (five Confers are listed in the German telephone directory) or on arrival in the U.S. **2.** Possibly an Americanized spelling of German **Kumpfer** (see COMPHER).

Conforti (811) Italian: from the personal name *Conforto*, meaning 'comfort', 'support', a name bestowed on a long-awaited child or one borne after the death of a sibling.

GIVEN NAMES Italian 12%. *Angelo* (6), *Antonio* (2), *Carmine* (2), *Saverio* (2), *Vito* (2), *Aniello, Attilio, Cosmo, Damiano, Dante, Enza, Gabriele*.

Cong (102) **1.** English: unexplained. **2.** Chinese 从: from an ancient area named Cong Yang, whose residents adopted the surname. **3.** Vietnamese: unexplained.

GIVEN NAMES Vietnamese 35%; Chinese 29%. *Hanh* (2), *Huyen* (2), *Chuong, Doan, Huong, Kieu, Lien, Minh, Pham, Phung, Qui, Quoc; Zhiyuan* (2), *Bin, Khin, Lei, Xiao Feng, Xing, Yang, Yusheng*.

Congdon (1647) **1.** Variant of Irish CONDON. **2.** English: apparently a habitational name from a lost or unidentified place, probably in Devon or Cornwall, where the modern surname is most frequent.

Conger (2621) English: unexplained.

Congleton (613) English: habitational name from a place in Cheshire named Congleton, from an Old English element *cung* 'mound' + *hyll* 'hill' + *tūn* 'settlement'.

Congo (128) Origin unidentified. It occurs in Dutch records of New Netherland as a name of African slaves: Simon and Manuel Congo.

Congrove (206) Probably an altered form of the English habitational name **Congreve** (or the variants **Congreave, Congrave**) from Congreve in Staffordshire or Congreave in Derbyshire. The first is recorded in Domesday Book as *Comegrave* 'grove (Old English *grǣfe*) in a valley (Old English *cumb*)'.

Conigliaro (281) Italian: occupational name for a dealer in rabbits, from an agent derivative of *coniglio* 'rabbit' (Latin *cuniculus*).

GIVEN NAMES Italian 34%. *Salvatore* (5), *Vito* (4), *Giovanni* (3), *Pietro* (3), *Rosario* (3), *Aurelio* (2), *Antonino* (2), *Lorenzo* (2), *Antonio, Concetta, Croce, Francesco, Giuseppe, Guiseppe*.

Coniglio (825) Italian: from *coniglio* 'rabbit' (Latin *cuniculus*), applied as a nickname for a timid person or a metonymic occupational name for a dealer in rabbits.

GIVEN NAMES Italian 15%. *Salvatore* (11), *Angelo* (5), *Carlo* (3), *Carmine* (3), *Sal* (3), *Gaetano* (2), *Santo* (2), *Aldo, Antonio, Carmelo, Dino, Eligio*.

Conine (569) Americanized spelling of Dutch **Conyn** or **Konijn**, from Middle Dutch *conijn* 'rabbit', hence a metonymic occupational name for a dealer in rabbits, or a nickname for someone thought to resemble a rabbit.

FOREBEARS The name **Conyn** is recorded in Beverwijck in New Netherland (Albany, NY) in the mid 17th century.

Conk (158) Probably an Americanized spelling of German **Kohnke**, a North German variant of KONRAD, or of **Kunke** (see KUNKA).

Conkel (182) Respelling of German and Dutch KONKEL or German KUNKEL.

Conkey (425) Scottish and Irish: reduced form of MCCONKEY.

Conkin (182) Irish: reduced form of McCONKIN, from a diminutive of MCCONAGHY.

Conkle (750) Americanized spelling of German and Dutch KONKEL or possibly German GUNKEL.

Conklin (8733) Origin unidentified. Most likely of Dutch origin (the name is found in the 18th century in the Hudson Valley), or possibly a variant of Irish COUGHLIN.

Conkling (596) See CONKLIN.

Conkright (210) Of Dutch origin: see CRONKHITE.

Conkwright (104) Of Dutch origin: see CRONKHITE.

Conlan (808) Irish: Anglicized form of Gaelic Ó Conalláin or Ó Caoindealbháin (see QUINLAN).

GIVEN NAMES Irish 6%. *Brendan* (2), *Siobhan* (2), *Dermot*.

Conlee (511) Variant spelling of Irish CONLEY.

Conley (18526) Irish: reduced form of CONNOLLY.

Conlin (1839) Irish: variant of CONLAN.

GIVEN NAMES Irish 4%. *Ronan, Seamus*.

Conlon (3193) Irish: Anglicized form of Gaelic Ó Conalláin or Ó Caoindealbháin (see QUINLAN).

GIVEN NAMES Irish 5%. *Brendan* (3), *Liam* (2), *Bridie, Dermot, Eamonn, Kieran, Patrick Michael, Sinead, Siobhan*.

Conly (304) Irish: reduced form of CONNOLLY.

Conmy (125) Irish: reduced form of MCNAMEE.

Conn (5653) Irish: from a short form of any of the personal names mentioned at MCCONNELL, CONNOLLY, CONNOR, and CONROY.

Connally (968) Irish: variant spelling of CONNOLLY.

Connard (116) **1.** English: unexplained. **2.** Probably an altered spelling of Dutch **Connart** or German **Kohnert** or KUHNERT, all of which derive from a Germanic personal name formed with *kōne kuoni* 'bold', 'daring'.

Connatser (154) Possibly an altered spelling of a variant of German KONITZER.

Connaughton (504) Irish: reduced Anglicized form of Gaelic Ó Connachtáin 'descendant of *Connachtan*' (see CONATY).

GIVEN NAMES Irish 6%. *Brendan, Ciaran, Ronan*.

Connaway (129) Irish: reduced and altered Anglicized form of any of the Gaelic names mentioned at CONWAY, or possibly of MCCONAGHY.

Connealy (129) Irish: variant of CONNOLLY.

Conneely (214) Irish: variant of CONNOLLY.

GIVEN NAMES Irish 16%. *Aine, Brendan, Cathal*.

Connel (135) Irish: variant of CONNELL.

Connell (9194) Irish and Scottish: reduced form of MCCONNELL or O'CONNELL.

Connelley (261) Irish: variant spelling of CONNOLLY.

GIVEN NAME French 4%. *Damien*.

Connelly (9208) Irish: variant of CONNOLLY.

GIVEN NAMES Irish 4%. *Kieran* (3), *Brendan* (2), *Brennan, Eamon, Maeve, Murphy, Paddy*.

Connely (252) Irish: variant spelling of CONNOLLY.

Conner (21791) **1.** Irish: variant spelling of CONNOR, now common in Scotland. **2.** English: occupational name for an inspector of weights and measures, Middle English *connere, cunnere* 'inspector', an agent derivative of *cun(nen)* 'to examine'.

Connerley (107) Irish: variant spelling of CONNOLLY.

Connerly (110) Irish: variant spelling of CONNOLLY.

Conners (1960) Irish: variant spelling of CONNORS.

Connerton (161) English and Irish: most probably a variant spelling of CONNAUGHTON.

Connery (653) Irish (Cork and Limerick): variant of CONROY.
GIVEN NAMES Irish 4%. *Cian, Seumas*.

Connett (421) English (Devon): unexplained.

Connick (339) 1. Irish (Wexford): Anglicized form of Gaelic **Mac Conmhaic** 'son of *Conmhac*', a personal name composed of the elements *cú* 'hound' (genitive *con*) + *mac* 'son'. 2. Americanized spelling of Dutch KOENNING.
GIVEN NAMES Irish 4%. *Brendan, Siobhan*.

Conniff (365) 1. Irish: variant of CUNNIFF. 2. Perhaps an Americanized spelling of German **Koneff**, from a diminutive of **Knabe** 'boy', or **Knappe** (Caneppele) 'boy', 'page'; later, 'miner' (see KONEFAL).

Connole (205) Probably a variant of Irish CONNOLLY or CONNELL.

Connolley (100) Irish: variant spelling of CONNOLLY.
GIVEN NAMES Irish 9%. *Aine, Aisling, Brendan, Ciaran, Eoin, Padraig*.

Connolly (12110) Irish: Anglicized form of Gaelic **Ó Conghaile** 'descendant of *Conghal*', a name meaning 'hound valiant' or of **Ó Conghalaigh** 'descendant of *Conghalach*', a derivative of *Conghal*; the two surnames have long been confused. Another possible origin is the West Cork name **Mac Coingheallaigh** (or **Ó Coingheallaigh**) 'son (or 'descendant') of *Coingheallach*', a personal name meaning 'faithful to pledges'.
GIVEN NAMES Irish 6%. *Brendan* (6), *Aileen* (3), *Bridie* (3), *Seamus* (3), *Aidan* (2), *Dermot* (2), *Eamon* (2), *Patrick Joseph* (2), *Colm, Cormac, Declan, Eoin*.

Connon (201) Irish: reduced form of MCCONNON, Anglicized form of Gaelic **Mac Canann** (see CANNON).
GIVEN NAME French 4%. *Berard*.

Connor (10991) Irish: reduced form of O'CONNOR, which is an Anglicization of Gaelic **Ó Conchobhair** 'descendant of *Conchobhar*'.

Connors (7949) Irish: reduced form of O'CONNOR, with the addition of English patronymic *-s*.
GIVEN NAMES Irish 4%. *Brendan* (4), *John Patrick* (2), *Aileen, Paddy*.

Conolly (212) Irish: variant spelling of CONNOLLY.
GIVEN NAMES Irish 4%. *Brendan, Donovan*.

Conoly (143) Irish: variant spelling of CONNOLLY.

Conover (3347) Americanized spelling of Dutch **Couwenhoven**, of unknown etymology, probably a habitational name. By the time the descendants of original Dutch

settlers on Long Island had reached western PA, the name had evolved into **Conover**.

Conquest (286) English: from Old French *conquest* 'conquest', probably applied as a nickname.

Conrad (16048) Americanized spelling of German KONRAD. In some cases the name may be French in origin, from the French form of the same name, or alternatively it may be an Americanized form of any of the various cognates in other languages, such as Dutch **Koenraad** or Czech **Konrád**.

Conradi (218) 1. German, Danish, and Norwegian: Latinization of a patronymic from the personal name KONRAD. 2. Italian: variant of **Corradi** (see CORRADO).
GIVEN NAMES German 5%. *Dietrich, Ewald, Hannelore*.

Conrado (107) Spanish: from the personal name *Conrado*, of Germanic origin (see KONRAD).
GIVEN NAMES Spanish 36%. *Bayardo* (2), *Carlos* (2), *Eduardo* (2), *Adriano, Alphonso, Cesar, Concepcion, Fabiola, Francisco, Jaime, Jeronimo, Jorge*.

Conradt (242) Dutch and German: variant of KONRAD.
GIVEN NAMES German 7%. *Kurt* (2), *Ernst, Hans, Heinz, Horst*.

Conrady (298) 1. Dutch: variant of KONRAD. 2. German: variant spelling of CONRADI.

Conran (229) Irish: Anglicized form of a diminutive of Gaelic **Ó Conaráin** 'descendant of *Conarán*', a personal name from a pet form of *Conaire* (see CONROY 2).
GIVEN NAMES Irish 6%. *Brendan, Siobhan*.

Conrardy (134) German or Dutch: altered form of CONRADY.

Conrath (255) Respelling of German KONRATH or a variant of the French equivalent, **Conrad** (see KONRAD).
GIVEN NAMES German 5%. *Ernst, Horst, Kurt*.

Conrey (247) Irish: variant spelling of CONROY.

Conrod (116) Respelling of CONRAD.

Conrow (307) Possibly a variant of Irish CONROY.

Conroy (6603) Irish: 1. Anglicized form of Gaelic **Ó Conraoi** 'descendant of *Cú Raoi*', a name meaning 'hound of the plain', which was stressed on the final syllable. 2. Anglicized form of Gaelic **Ó Conaire** 'descendant of *Conaire*', a byname meaning 'keeper of the hound' (an agent derivative of *cú* 'hound').
GIVEN NAMES Irish 5%. *Brendan* (7), *Tighe* (3), *Brigid* (2), *Declan* (2), *Finbarr, Fintan, Liam, Niall, Nuala, Patrick Michael*.

Conry (447) Irish: variant of CONROY.
GIVEN NAMES Irish 5%. *Brendan, Murphy*.

Consalvo (222) Southern Italian: adaptation of Spanish GONZALO.

GIVEN NAMES Italian 17%. *Angelo* (2), *Domenic* (2), *Carmine, Dante, Salvatore, Silvio, Vito*.

Consentino (150) Southern Italian: variant of COSENTINO.
GIVEN NAMES Italian 18%. *Antonio, Fabio, Mario, Sal, Salvatore, Santo*.

Conser (188) Possibly an Americanized spelling of German GANSER.

Considine (1094) 1. Irish: reduced Americanized form of **Mac Consaidín** 'son of *Consaidín*', Gaelic form of CONSTANTINE. This name is borne by a branch of the O'Briens in County Clare. 2. English: variant of CONSTANTINE.
GIVEN NAMES Irish 6%. *Brendan, John Patrick*.

Consigli (102) Italian: patronymic or plural form of CONSIGLIO.
GIVEN NAMES Italian 8%. *Aldo* (3), *Vita*.

Consiglio (510) Italian: 1. from a short form of the personal name *Buonconsiglio*, which is either an omen name (meaning 'may he give (or receive) good advice') or a Marian name from the cult of Madonna del Buon Consiglio 'Our Lady of Good Counsel'. 2. from *consiglio* 'advice', from Latin *consilium*, a nickname for a wise or thoughtful man or possibly for a fearful one (as in modern Italian), or an occupational name for a member of a council or similar body.
GIVEN NAMES Italian 25%. *Salvatore* (13), *Angelo* (4), *Vito* (4), *Santo* (3), *Dario* (2), *Fabrizio* (2), *Giovanni* (2), *Sal* (2), *Vincenzo* (2), *Aldo, Antonio, Benedetto*.

Console (135) Italian: status name (or nickname) from the title *console* 'consul'. The precise duties and powers of this office varied according to time and place, but the title generally denoted a high-ranking official.
GIVEN NAMES Italian 24%. *Aldo* (2), *Antonella, Concetta, Mario, Pasquale, Rocco, Salvatore, Saverio*.

Consoli (251) Italian: variant (plural) of CONSOLE.
GIVEN NAMES Italian 24%. *Angelo* (2), *Luigi* (2), *Vito* (2), *Antonio, Attilio, Carlo, Carmelo, Constantino, Domenico, Egidio, Franco, Innocenzo, Mario, Rosario*.

Consolo (245) Italian: variant of CONSOLE.
GIVEN NAMES Italian 16%. *Angelo* (4), *Salvatore* (2), *Alfio, Carlo, Carmelo, Rocco*.

Constable (1124) 1. English: occupational name for the law-enforcement officer of a parish, from Middle English, Old French *conestable, cunestable*, from Late Latin *comes stabuli* 'officer of the stable'. The title was also borne by various other officials during the Middle Ages, including the chief officer of the household (and army) of a medieval ruler, and this may in some cases be the source of the surname. 2. Americanized spelling of Dutch **Constapel**, an occupational name for the chief gunner aboard a ship or in the garrison of a fort.

Constance (518) English and French:
1. from the medieval female personal name *Constance*, Latin *Constantia*, originally a feminine form of *Constantius* (see CONSTANT), but later taken as the abstract noun *constantia* 'steadfastness'. **2.** habitational name from Coutances in La Manche, France, which was named *Constantia* in Latin (see above) in honor of the Roman emperor Constantius Chlorus, who was responsible for fortifying the settlement in AD 305.

Constancio (119) Portuguese and Spanish: from the personal name *Constancio*, from Latin *Constantius* (see CONSTANT).

GIVEN NAMES Spanish 38%. *Ramon* (3), *Ezequiel* (2), *Jesus* (2), *Santos* (2), *Abelino*, *Alvaro*, *Angelita*, *Ascencio*, *Carmella*, *Corina*, *Cosme*, *Edmundo*.

Constant (1175) **1.** French and English: from a medieval personal name (Latin *Constans*, genitive *Constantis*, meaning 'steadfast', 'faithful', present participle of the verb *constare* 'stand fast', 'be consistent'). This was borne by an 8th-century Irish martyr. This surname has also absorbed some cases of surnames based on *Constantius*, a derivative of *Constans*, borne by a 2nd-century martyr, bishop of Perugia. Compare CONSTANTINE. **2.** English: perhaps also a nickname from Old French *constant* 'steadfast', 'faithful'.

GIVEN NAMES French 6%. *Jacques* (2), *Anatole*, *Andre*, *Berard*, *Fernand*, *Gardy*, *Gesner*, *Jean Claude*, *Nazaire*, *Normand*, *Pierre*, *Thierry*.

Constante (115) Spanish: from the medieval personal name *Constante* meaning 'constant', 'steadfast', from Latin *Constans* (see CONSTANT), or a habitational name from a place name with the same etymology.

GIVEN NAMES Spanish 43%. *Eduardo* (2), *Ramon* (2), *Ricardo* (2), *Ruben* (2), *Ana*, *Candelario*, *Carolina*, *Cesar*, *Consuelo*, *Felipa*, *Galo*, *Guadalupe*.

Constantin (262) **1.** French and Romanian: from the medieval personal name *Constantin*, French and Romanian form of CONSTANTINE. **2.** Shortened form of Greek **Konstantinos**, from the personal name (see CONSTANTINE).

GIVEN NAMES French 13%; Romanian 12%; Spanish 5%. *Raoul* (2), *Andre*, *Antoine*, *Armand*, *Calice*, *Eusebe*, *Fernand*, *Michel*, *Micheline*, *Pierre*, *Ravis*; *Constantin* (2), *Mihaela* (2), *Petre* (2), *Cornel*, *Dragos*, *Dumitru*, *Estera*, *Floarea*, *Nicoleta*, *Sorin*, *Stelian*, *Vasile*; *Cristina* (3), *Ana* (2), *Carlos*, *Elena*, *Jesus*, *Liliana*, *Lourdes*, *Luis*.

Constantine (1939) **1.** English: from a medieval personal name, Latin *Constantinus*, a derivative of *Constans* (see CONSTANT). The name was popular in Continental Europe, and to a lesser extent in England, as having been borne by the first Christian ruler of the Roman Empire, Constantine the Great (?280–337), in whose honor Byzantium was renamed Constantinople. In some cases the name may be an Americanized form of one of the many cognates in other languages, in particular Greek **Konstantinos**. **2.** English (of Norman origin): habitational name or regional name for someone from Cotentin (Coutances) in Manche, France (see CONSTANCE 2).

Constantineau (137) French: from a pet form of the personal name CONSTANTIN.

GIVEN NAME French 10%. *Adrien* (3).

Constantini (116) Italian: patronymic or plural form of CONSTANTINO.

Constantinides (128) Greek: patronymic from the personal name *Konstantinos*, from Latin *Constantinus* (see CONSTANTINE). The *-ides* patronymic is classical, and was revived in particular by Greeks from the Black Sea during the late 19th and early 20th centuries.

GIVEN NAMES Greek 29%. *Panos* (4), *Demetrios* (2), *Theodoros* (2), *Alexandros*, *Alkis*, *Christos*, *Constantine*, *Marios*, *Spiros*.

Constantino (1258) Italian and Portuguese: from the medieval personal name *Constantino*, from Latin *Constantinus* (see CONSTANTINE).

GIVEN NAMES Spanish 13%; Italian 8%. *Jose* (6), *Francisco* (4), *Jorge* (4), *Juan* (4), *Carlos* (3), *Alicia* (2), *Angelina* (2), *Cesar* (2), *Conrado* (2), *Demetrio* (2), *Florentina* (2), *Manuel* (2); *Antonio* (7), *Angelo* (5), *Salvatore* (4), *Carlo*, *Domenic*, *Filomena*, *Geno*, *Ignazio*, *Maddalena*, *Nunzi*, *Raimondo*, *Rocco*.

Constantinou (123) Greek: patronymic from the genitive form of the personal name *Konstantinos*, from Latin *Constantinus* (see CONSTANTINE). Genitive patronymics are particularly associated with Cyprus.

GIVEN NAMES Greek 44%. *Costas* (5), *Andreas* (3), *Constantinos* (2), *Kyriacos* (2), *Marios* (2), *Angelos*, *Charalambos*, *Constantine*, *Despina*, *Kyriakos*, *Panayiotis*, *Panos*.

Consuegra (119) Spanish: habitational name from Consuegra in Toledo province.

GIVEN NAMES Spanish 45%; Italian 7%. *Jorge* (4), *Julio* (3), *Luis* (3), *Aida* (2), *Aura* (2), *Miguel* (2), *Pedro* (2), *Rodrigo* (2), *Ulises* (2), *Adan*, *Adolfo*, *Alicia*; *Antonio* (2), *Bartolo* (2), *Elio*, *Fausto*, *Pio*.

Contant (126) French: variant of CONSTANT.

GIVEN NAMES French 12%. *Andre*, *Francoise*, *Laurier*, *Michel*.

Contarino (153) Italian: from a Lombard personal name, *Guntarini*.

GIVEN NAMES Italian 19%. *Angelo* (2), *Mario* (2), *Rosario* (2), *Salvatore* (2), *Emanuele*.

Conte (3080) **1.** Italian: from the title of rank *conte* 'count' (from Latin *comes*, genitive *comitis* 'companion'). Probably in this sense (and the Late Latin sense of 'traveling companion'), it was a medieval personal name; as a title it was no doubt applied ironically as a nickname for someone with airs and graces or simply for someone who worked in the service of a count. **2.** English: variant of **Count**, cognate with 1. **3.** French: nickname for someone in the service of a count or for someone who behaved pretentiously, from Old French *conte*, *cunte* 'count' (of the same derivation as 1). **4.** French (**Conté**): variant of **Comté** (see COMTE).

GIVEN NAMES Italian 21%. *Mario* (24), *Angelo* (11), *Salvatore* (11), *Antonio* (8), *Rocco* (8), *Carmine* (7), *Pasquale* (7), *Luigi* (6), *Silvio* (6), *Silverio* (5), *Giuseppe* (4), *Sal* (4), *Alfonso* (3), *Biagio* (3), *Carlo* (3), *Emilio* (3), *Fernando* (3), *Gerardo* (3).

Contee (127) **1.** French: variant of CONTE or **Conté** (see COMTE). **2.** African: variant of CONTEH.

Conteh (122) African: unexplained.

GIVEN NAMES Muslim 26%; African 20%. *Abu* (3), *Mohamed* (3), *Abdul* (2), *Abdul Karim*, *Ahmed*, *Alusine*, *Mohammed*, *Musa*, *Mustapha*, *Zainab*; *Aminata* (3), *Isatu* (2), *Brima*, *Fatmata*, *Kadiatu*, *Kadijatu*, *Momodou*, *Sekou*, *Umaru*.

Contento (181) Italian: nickname for someone with a cheerful disposition, from *contento* 'happy', 'pleased'.

GIVEN NAMES Italian 15%. *Salvatore* (2), *Angelo*, *Dino*, *Orfeo*, *Vito*.

Conter (109) **1.** French (Alsace-Lorraine): unexplained. **2.** Dutch: variant of CANTER 'cantor'.

Contessa (120) Italian: **1.** from *contessa* 'countess', feminine form of CONTE. **2.** habitational name from Contessa Entellina in Palermo province, Sicily, which until 1875 was called simply Contessa.

GIVEN NAMES Italian 13%. *Carmela*, *Gaspare*, *Rocco*, *Santo*.

Conti (4003) Italian: patronymic or plural form of CONTE.

GIVEN NAMES Italian 13%. *Angelo* (23), *Salvatore* (21), *Antonio* (10), *Gino* (8), *Carlo* (6), *Domenic* (6), *Rocco* (6), *Sal* (6), *Aldo* (4), *Carmela* (4), *Enrico* (4), *Guido* (4).

Contini (222) Italian: patronymic or plural form of CONTINO.

GIVEN NAMES Italian 15%; French 4%. *Aniello*, *Attilio*, *Ettore*, *Gianfranco*, *Giorgio*, *Guido*, *Orest*, *Renzo*, *Rocco*, *Umberto*; *Gaston*, *Laurent*.

Contino (470) Italian: from a diminutive of *conte* 'count' (see CONTE).

GIVEN NAMES Italian 10%. *Amato* (2), *Sal* (2), *Vito* (2), *Anella*, *Carmelo*, *Carmine*, *Domiano*, *Luigi*, *Pasquale*, *Salvator*, *Salvatore*, *Vincenza*.

Conto (132) Italian: origin uncertain. In many parts of Italy the form **Contò**, suggesting a Greek origin (see CONDOS), is common.

GIVEN NAMES Spanish 5%. *Jose* (2), *Mario* (2), *Jaime, Lino, Osvaldo.*

Contois (287) French: variant of COMTOIS.

GIVEN NAMES French 8%. *Armand* (2), *Alphone, Fernand, Raoul, Raynald.*

Contos (378) **1.** Greek: variant of CONDOS. **2.** Americanized spelling of Hungarian **Csontos**, a nickname for a well-built man, from *csontos* 'strong', 'heavily built', 'bony' (from *csont* 'bone').

GIVEN NAMES Greek 4%. *Demetrios* (2), *Costas, Despina, Eleftherios, Yannis.*

Contractor (100) Indian (Gujarat and Bombay): Parsi occupational name for a supplier of goods or services, from the English word *contractor*.

GIVEN NAMES Indian 56%; Muslim 27%. *Jayshree* (2), *Lalan* (2), *Mehesh* (2), *Rashmi* (2), *Sunil* (2), *Usha* (2), *Aashish, Ashvin, Avinash, Bakul, Bhanu, Bharat; Abbas* (2), *Ali, Farokh, Gulam, Hanif, Hatim, Ibrahim, Iqbal, Kaid, Mukhtar, Munaf, Noshir.*

Contrera (107) Spanish: variant (singular) of CONTRERAS, used perhaps in a topographic sense or as a nickname in the sense 'contrary'.

GIVEN NAMES Spanish 32%; Italian 8%. *Miguel* (3), *Jose* (2), *Maria Luisa* (2), *Adolfina, Alvaro, Angelina, Aura, Bernardina, Eulojio, Felipe, Jaime, Jose Antonio; Ceasar* (2), *Marco, Salvatore.*

Contreras (9675) Spanish: habitational name from Conteraras, a place in the province of Burgos. The place name is derived from Late Latin *contraria* 'surrounding area', 'region' (from the preposition *contra* 'opposite', 'against', 'hard by').

GIVEN NAMES Spanish 49%; Portuguese 10%. *Jose* (259), *Juan* (143), *Jesus* (118), *Manuel* (90), *Carlos* (89), *Luis* (68), *Miguel* (63), *Francisco* (56), *Guadalupe* (50), *Roberto* (50), *Mario* (48), *Pedro* (47); *Duarte, Ligia, Paulo, Wenceslao.*

Contrino (108) Italian: from a diminutive of *Contro*, a short form of the omen name *Bonincontrus*, meaning 'good encounter', 'well met'.

GIVEN NAMES Italian 18%; French 7%; Spanish 6%. *Carmelo* (2), *Gasper, Luigi, Pasquale; Francois; Luis.*

Converse (1771) English: from Middle English, Old French *convers* 'convert' (Latin *conversus*, past participle of *convertere* 'to turn'), hence a nickname for a Jew converted to Christianity, or more often an occupational name for someone converted to the religious way of life, a lay member of a convent.

Convery (536) Irish: Anglicized form of Gaelic **Mac Ainmhire** 'son of *Ainmhire*', a byname meaning 'fierceness'.

Convey (178) Irish: reduced form of **McConvey**, an Anglicized form of Gaelic

Mac Conmidhe, **Mac Conmeadha** (see MCNAMEE).

Conville (179) Irish: reduced form of MCCONVILLE.

Conway (16477) **1.** Irish: Anglicized form of various Gaelic names, such as **Mac Conmidhe** (see MCNAMEE); **Ó Connmhaigh** or **Mac Connmhaigh** ('descendant (or son) of *Connmhach*', a personal name derived from *connmach* 'head-smashing'), also Anglicized as **Conoo**; and **Ó Conbhuide** ('descendant of *Cú Bhuidhe*', a personal name composed of the elements *cú* 'hound' + *buidhe* 'yellow'). **2.** Welsh: habitational name from Conwy (formerly Conway), a fortified town on the coast of North Wales, itself named for the river on which it stands. **3.** Scottish: habitational name from Conway in the parish of Beauly, recorded *c*.1215 as Coneway and in 1291 as Convathe. It probably gets its name from Gaelic *coinmheadh* 'billet', 'free quarters', being so named as the district in which the local lord's household troops were billeted.

GIVEN NAMES Irish 6%. *Brendan* (5), *Padraig* (3), *Aileen* (2), *Donal* (2), *James Patrick* (2), *Kieran* (2), *Brigid, Cliona, Colm, Conley, Declan, Delma.*

Conwell (1285) Irish: reduced variant of MCCONVILLE.

Conwill (154) Irish: reduced variant of MCCONVILLE.

Conyer (151) English: **1.** metathesized form of the occupational name COYNER. **2.** possibly an occupational name for a dealer in rabbits or rabbit skins, from an agent derivative of Middle English *cony* 'rabbit' (see CONEY).

Conyers (1802) English (of Norman origin): habitational name from either of two places in northern France: Coignières in Seine-et-Oise or Cogners in Sarthe. This surname is well established in the southern states, where it is now borne mainly by African Americans.

Conzemius (113) Luxembourgeois: unexplained.

Coody (506) Irish: variant of CODY.

Coogan (1180) Irish: Anglicized form of Gaelic **Mac Cogadháin** 'son of *Cogadhán*', a diminutive from a reduced form of the personal name *Cúchogaidh*, meaning 'hound of war'.

GIVEN NAMES Irish 5%. *Brendan, Grainne, Liam, Sinead.*

Coogle (167) Americanized spelling of German KUGEL.

Coogler (140) Americanized spelling of German KUGLER.

Cook (109743) **1.** English: occupational name for a cook, a seller of cooked meats, or a keeper of an eating house, from Old English *cōc* (Latin *coquus*). There has been some confusion with COCKE. **2.** Irish and Scottish: usually identical in origin with the English name, but in some cases a reduced

Anglicized form of Gaelic **Mac Cúg** 'son of Hugo' (see MCCOOK). **3.** In North America Cook has absorbed examples of cognate and semantically equivalent names from other languages, such as German and Jewish KOCH. **4.** Erroneous translation of French **Lécuyer** (see LECUYER).

FOREBEARS Francis Cooke (died 1663) and his eldest son John were passengers on the *Mayflower* in 1621; they were joined two years later by Francis's wife and other children. In the words of William Bradford, when he died he had 'lived to see his children's children have children'.

Cooke (12383) English, etc.: variant spelling of COOK.

Cookingham (152) This has the form of an English habitational name; however, there is no record of any such place name in the British Isles, and the surname does not appear in present-day records. It is probably an Americanized form of Jewish GUGGENHEIM.

Cookman (230) English: from a byname meaning 'servant of the cook' (see COOK).

Cooks (909) English: variant of or patronymic from COOK.

Cooksey (2512) English (chiefly West Midlands): habitational name from a place in Worcestershire named Cooksey, from the genitive case of the Old English personal name *Cucu* (perhaps a byname from Old English *cwicu* 'lively') + Old English *ēg* 'island'.

Cooksley (125) English (Somerset and Devon): habitational name from Coxley, Somerset, named from Old English *cōc* 'cook' + *lēah* 'woodland clearing'. Mills notes that the wife of a cook of the royal household is recorded in Domesday Book (1086) as holding lands near Wells in Somerset.

Cookson (1291) English (mainly Lancashire): patronymic from COOK.

Cookston (196) Scottish: habitational name from any of several places named Cookston, in Fife, Grampian, and Tayside. The surname is now rare or extinct in Scotland.

Cool (1543) **1.** Irish and Scottish: reduced form of MCCOOL. **2.** Dutch: variant spelling of KOOL. **3.** Probably an Americanized form of German **Kuhl** and **Kühl** (see KUHL).

Coolbaugh (349) Americanized spelling of German **Kühlbach**, a topographic name from Middle High German *küel* 'cool' + *bach* 'stream', 'creek', or of German **Kuhlbach**, also a topographic name, in which the first element is from Middle Low German *kule* 'pit'.

GIVEN NAMES German 4%. *Monika* (2), *Kurt, Merwin.*

Coole (169) Irish: reduced form of MCCOOL.

GIVEN NAME Scandinavian 4%. *Thor.*

Cooler (258) Americanized spelling of German **Kühler** (see KUEHLER).

Cooley (11512) **1.** Irish: Anglicized form of Gaelic **Mac Giolla Chúille** 'son of the servant of (Saint) Mochúille', a rare Clare name, or a reduced form of **McCooley**, a variant of MCCAULEY. **2.** Americanized form of German **Kuhle** or **Kühle**, variants of KUHL.

Coolidge (1261) English (Cambridgeshire): **1.** probably an occupational name for a college servant or someone with some other association with a university college, for example a tenant farmer who farmed one of the many farms in England known as College Farm, most of which are or were owned by university colleges. **2.** See COLLEDGE.

FOREBEARS John Coolidge came to Watertown, MA, in about 1631, probably from Cottenham, Cambridgeshire, England. His most notable descendant was U.S. President Calvin Coolidge (1872–1933), who was born in Plymouth Notch, VT, where his ancestors had moved in the late 18th century.

Cooling (233) English: **1.** from a medieval personal name, originally an Old English patronymic from the personal names *Cūl(a)* or *Cēola*. The former may be from a Germanic root *kūl* 'swollen'; the latter is a short form of various compound names with the first element *cēol* 'ship'. **2.** habitational name from a place in Kent named Cooling, from the Old English tribal name *Cūlingas* 'people of *Cūl(a)*'.

Coolman (204) Americanized form of KUHLMAN or KUHLMANN.

Coombe (372) English: topographic name from Middle English *combe* (Old English *cumb*, of Celtic origin) denoting a short, straight valley, or else a habitational name from a place named with this word. There are a large number of places in England, mostly spelled *Combe*, named with this word. Compare COOMBS.

Coomber (114) Southern English: variant spelling of COOMER.

Coombes (448) English: variant of COOMBS.

Coombs (3528) English: habitational name from any of various places named with a plural or possessive derivative of Old English *cumb* (see COOMBE).

Coomer (1372) **1.** English: topographic name for someone who lived in a short, straight valley, from Middle English *combe* (see COOMBE), + the suffix *-er* denoting an inhabitant. **2.** Americanized spelling of German KUMMER.

Coomes (876) English: variant of COOMBS.

Coon (6154) **1.** Irish: possibly an Anglicized form of Gaelic **Ó Cuana** (see COONEY). **2.** Americanized spelling of German KUHN. **3.** Americanized spelling of Dutch COEN or KOEN.

Coonan (275) Irish: Anglicized form of Gaelic **Ó Cuanáin** 'descendant of *Cuanán*', a diminutive of the personal name *Cuana* (see COONEY).

GIVEN NAME Irish 4%. *Liam.*

Coonce (379) Variant spelling of COONS.

Coone (204) **1.** Variant spelling of Irish COON. **2.** Possibly an Americanized spelling of German KUHNE.

Coonen (128) Irish: variant spelling of COONAN.

Cooner (262) Probably an Americanized spelling of German KUHNER.

Coones (151) See COONS.

Cooney (5136) Irish: Anglicized form of Gaelic **Ó Cuana** 'descendant of *Cuana*', a personal name either based on *cú* 'hound' or derived from *cuanna* 'elegant', 'comely'.

GIVEN NAMES Irish 5%. *Brendan* (3), *Aileen, Bridie, Brigid, Caitlin, Dermot, Eamonn, Seamus, Siobhan.*

Coonfield (107) Probably an Americanized form of German KORNFELD or a similar name.

Coonley (105) Variant spelling of Irish CONLEY.

GIVEN NAME Scottish 4%. *Matha.*

Coonradt (174) Americanized spelling of Dutch **Coenraet** or **Koenraadt** or German **Kühnrat** (see KONRAD).

Coonrod (625) Americanized spelling of Dutch **Coenraet** or **Koenraadt** or German **Kühnrat** (see KONRAD).

Coons (3227) **1.** Americanized spelling of Dutch **Couns, Cuens,** or **Cuyns**, patronymics from COEN (see KOEN). **2.** Possibly also an Americanized spelling of German KUNTZ.

Coonts (124) **1.** Americanized spelling of Dutch **Couns, Cuens,** or **Cuyns**, patronymics from COEN (see KOEN). **2.** Possibly also an Americanized spelling of German KUNTZ.

Coontz (306) Of Dutch or German origin: see COONTS.

Coop (647) **1.** English: metonymic occupational name for a cooper, from Middle English *coupe* 'tub', 'container' (see COOPER). In some cases the surname may have been derived from a pub or house sign. **2.** Dutch: from *koop* 'purchase', 'bargain', hence a nickname for a haggler or a metonymic occupational name for a merchant.

Cooper (92926) **1.** English: occupational name for a maker and repairer of wooden vessels such as barrels, tubs, buckets, casks, and vats, from Middle English *couper, cowper* (apparently from Middle Dutch *kūper*, a derivative of *kūp* 'tub', 'container', which was borrowed independently into English as *coop*). The prevalence of the surname, its cognates, and equivalents bears witness to the fact that this was one of the chief specialist trades in the Middle Ages throughout Europe. In America, the English name has absorbed some cases of like-sounding cognates and words with similar meaning in other European languages, for example Dutch KUIPER. **2.** Jewish (Ashkenazic): Americanized form of **Kupfer** and **Kupper** (see KUPER). **3.** Dutch: occupational name for a buyer or merchant, Middle Dutch *coper*.

Cooperider (149) See COOPERRIDER.

Cooperman (772) Jewish (American): Americanized spelling of KUPERMAN.

GIVEN NAMES Jewish 5%. *Sol* (6), *Emanuel, Ilysa, Isadore, Sima.*

Cooperrider (196) Americanized spelling of German **Koppenreuter** or **Kuppelreuter**, habitational names for someone from a place named in Middle Low German or Middle High German with *koppel* 'pasture' (originally denoting a fenced area of grazing land in multiple ownership) + *riute* 'cleared land'.

Coopersmith (372) Americanized form of German **Kupferschmied**, an occupational name for a smith. Although the literal meaning is 'coppersmith', according to Brechenmacher, during the Middle Ages the term was also used to denote a blacksmith.

Cooperstein (190) **1.** Partly Americanized form of Ashkenazic Jewish **Kup(f)erstein**, an ornamental name composed of German *Kupfer* 'copper', Yiddish *kuper* + German *Stein* 'stone', Yiddish *shteyn*. **2.** Respelling of German KOBERSTEIN. Compare COVERSTONE.

Coopman (172) **1.** Dutch: occupational name from *koopman* 'merchant', 'trader'. See also COPEMAN. **2.** English: variant of COPEMAN. **3.** Variant spelling of North German KOOPMANN.

Cooprider (188) See COOPERRIDER.

Coopwood (108) Origin unidentified. This has the form of an English habitational name, but neither the place name nor the surname are found in England.

Coor (152) Probably an Americanized spelling of German KUHR, an occupational name from Middle High German *kure* 'official inspector', or Middle Low German *kur(e)* 'lookout', 'watchman'.

GIVEN NAME German 4%. *Kurt* (2).

Coors (118) Dutch: variant of KORS.

Coote (207) English: from Middle English *co(o)te* 'coot', applied as a nickname for a bald or stupid man. The bird was regarded as bald because of the large white patch, an extension of the bill, on its head. It is less easy to say how it acquired the reputation for stupidity.

Cooter (205) English (Sussex): unexplained.

Coots (1097) **1.** English: patronymic from the nickname COOTE. **2.** Probably an Americanized spelling of German KUTZ.

Coover (591) Probably an Americanized form of an unidentified Dutch name or of German KOBER.

Coovert (141) Probably an Americanized form of an unidentified Dutch name.

Copas (629) **1.** Spanish: from *copa*, plural *copas* 'drinking bowl', applied possibly as a metonymic occupational name for a maker of such vessels or possibly as a topographic name for someone living in a hollow. **2.** English: unexplained. Compare COPASS, COPUS.

Copass (106) English (Surrey): unexplained. Compare COPAS, COPUS.

Cope (6782) English (common in the Midlands): from Middle English *cope* 'cloak', 'cape' (from Old English *cāp* reinforced by the Old Norse cognate *kápa*), hence a metonymic occupational name for someone who made cloaks or capes, or a nickname for someone who wore a distinctive one. Compare CAPE.

Copelan (202) **1.** Jewish (American): Americanized form of KAPLAN. **2.** Possibly also a variant of English and Scottish COPELAND.
GIVEN NAMES Jewish 4%. *Herschel, Miriam.*

Copeland (18430) Northern English and Scottish: habitational name from a place called Copeland, of which there is an example in Cumbria, or from Coupland in Northumberland, both named with Old Norse *kaupa-land* 'bought land', a feature worthy of note during the early Middle Ages, when land was rarely sold, but rather held by feudal tenure and handed down from one generation to the next.

Copelin (312) Probably a variant of English and Scottish COPELAND.

Copeman (189) **1.** English: occupational name for a merchant or trader, Middle English *copman*, from Old Norse *kaupmaðr*, cognate with Old English *cēapmann* (see CHAPMAN). *Kaupmaðr* is also found as a personal name in England, and this use may lie behind some cases of the surname. **2.** Probably an Americanized spelling of North German KOOPMANN or Dutch COOPMAN.

Copen (343) **1.** English: variant of COPPIN. **2.** Probably an Americanized spelling of German KOPPEN.

Copenhaver (1633) Probably an Americanized spelling of German **Kobenhauer**, an occupational name for a cooper (see KOPPENHAVER).

Copes (448) Probably a variant of COPE or an Americanized spelling of Dutch KOPPES or German and Dutch KOPS.

Copher (308) Probably an Americanized spelling of German KAUFER.

Coplan (313) Probably a variant of Dutch KOPEL.

Copland (268) Scottish, Dutch, etc.: variant of COPELAND.

Coplen (394) See COPLIN.

Copley (2193) English (Yorkshire): habitational name from any of various places called Copley, for example in County Durham, Staffordshire, and Yorkshire, from the Old English personal name *Coppa* (ap-

parently a byname for a tall man) or from *copp* 'hilltop' + *lēah* 'woodland clearing'.

Coplin (544) Probably a variant of Jewish KAPLAN or an Americanized spelling of German and Jewish KOPLIN.

Copp (1408) **1.** English: topographic name for someone who lived on the top of a hill, from Middle English *coppe*, Old English *copp* 'summit' (a transferred sense of *copp* 'head', 'bowl', cognate with modern English *cup*), or a habitational name from Copp in Lancashire, named with this word. **2.** English: nickname for someone with a large or deformed head, from Middle English *cop(p)* 'head' (the same word as in 1 above). **3.** Respelling of German KOPP.

Coppa (314) Southern Italian: from *coppa* 'drinking bowl', possibly applied as a metonymic occupational name or as a topographic name for someone who lived in a hollow.
GIVEN NAMES Italian 24%. *Vito* (4), *Giovanni* (2), *Mario* (2), *Attilio, Aurelio, Camillo, Carlo, Ciro, Concetta, Dino, Elio, Gaetano, Gennaro, Giosue, Gustavo.*

Coppage (805) **1.** English (West Midlands): unexplained. Compare COPPEDGE. **2.** Possibly an Americanized spelling of German **Koppitsch** or **Koppisch**, eastern German variants of JACOBUS, or of Slavic origin.

Coppedge (759) English: unexplained. Compare COPPAGE.

Coppel (104) Variant spelling of Dutch KOPEL.
GIVEN NAMES Spanish 7%. *Enrique* (2), *Alberto, Fernando, Luis, Ricardo, Ruben.*

Coppenbarger (109) Belgian: habitational name from Koppenberg in East Flanders.

Coppens (308) English: variant spelling of COPPINS.
GIVEN NAMES French 6%. *Dominique, Jean-Louis, Marcel.*

Copper (688) **1.** English: variant of COOPER, from Middle English *copere*, found from the 12th century alongside *cupere*. **2.** English: metonymic occupational name for a worker in copper, Old English *coper* (Latin *(aes) Cyprium* 'Cyprian bronze'). **3.** Respelling of German KOPPER.

Coppernoll (164) Americanized spelling of North German **Koppernagel** or otherwise of **Kupfernagel**, a metonymic occupational name for a coppersmith, from *Kupfer* 'copper' + *nagel* 'nail'.

Coppersmith (430) **1.** English: occupational name for a smith who worked in copper, Middle English *copersmith*. **2.** Translation of German **Kupferschmidt** (see KUPERSMITH) or any of the various Ashkenazic Jewish surnames with the same meaning, as for example **Kupferschmi(e)dt, Kupfershmid(t), Kupershmid(t), Kupperschmidt, Kuperschmidt, Kupershmit.**

Coppes (137) See COPPESS.

Coppess (170) Perhaps an Americanized spelling of German KAPPUS or the variant **Kappes**; both forms are concentrated in OH.
GIVEN NAME French 4%. *Pierre.*

Coppi (106) Italian: from the personal name *Coppo*, a short form of *Iacoppo* (see JACOB).
GIVEN NAMES Italian 16%. *Aldo* (2), *Dino* (2), *Gino, Renzo.*

Coppin (333) **1.** English: from a reduced pet form of the personal name JACOB. **2.** French: nickname for a good neighbor or amiable fellow worker, from Old French *compain* 'companion', 'fellow' (Late Latin *companio* 'messmate', genitive *companionis*, from *con-* 'together' + *panis* 'bread'). **3.** Possibly also Irish or Scottish: reduced form of McCOPPIN.
GIVEN NAMES French 4%. *Philippe* (2), *Camille, Christophe.*

Copping (136) English: **1.** variant of COPPIN. **2.** topographic name for someone who lived on the top of a hill, from a derivative Old English of *copp* 'summit' (see COPP 1).

Coppinger (759) **1.** English: topographic name for someone who lived on a hilltop, from COPPING 2 + the suffix *-er* denoting an inhabitant. **2.** Possibly an Americanized spelling of German **Kapfinger, Gapfinger,** or **Kopfinger,** habitational names for someone from a place named Kapfingen or Köpfingen, in southern Germany.

Coppins (123) English: patronymic from the personal name COPPIN.

Copple (893) **1.** English: habitational name from Coppull in Lancashire, recorded in the 13th century as *Cophill*, from Old English *copp* 'peak' + *hyll* 'hill'. **2.** English: nickname from Old French *curt peil* 'short hair'. **3.** Probably an Americanized spelling of German and Jewish KOPPEL or German and Dutch KAPPEL.

Coppler (117) **1.** English: unexplained. **2.** Americanized form of German **Koppler**.

Coppock (950) English (Cheshire): unexplained.

Coppola (3109) Southern Italian: from Neapolitan dialect *coppola*, denoting a type of beret characteristic of the region, hence either a nickname for a habitual wearer of such headgear, or a metonymic occupational name for a beret maker.
GIVEN NAMES Italian 18%. *Salvatore* (20), *Carmine* (15), *Angelo* (14), *Antonio* (9), *Rocco* (7), *Pasquale* (5), *Carlo* (4), *Donato* (4), *Giuseppe* (4), *Luigi* (4), *Paolo* (4), *Ciro* (3).

Coppolino (211) Italian: from a diminutive of *coppola* (see COPPOLA).
GIVEN NAMES Italian 16%. *Angelo* (3), *Domenic* (2), *Carmelo, Domenica, Salvatore.*

Copps (163) Perhaps an altered spelling of Dutch **Cops**, which is in part a patronymic from a short form of the personal name *Jacop*, Dutch form of JACOB, and in part a metonymic occupational name or a nickname from Middle Dutch *cop(pe)* 'cooking pot', 'dish', 'beaker'; 'skull'; 'crown', 'top'.

Copsey (327) English (East Anglia): apparently from a medieval personal name *Copsi* or *Cofsi*.

Copus (310) **1.** English: unexplained. Compare COPAS, COPASS. **2.** Probably a respelling of KOBUS or of German possibly **Kopes**, a variant of CASPER.

Cora (272) Galician: habitational name from places called Cora in Lugo and Pontevedra provinces.
GIVEN NAMES Spanish 27%. *Juan* (3), *Pedro* (3), *Eduardo* (2), *Jose* (2), *Luisa* (2), *Miguel* (2), *Roberto* (2), *Alberto, Ana, Candido, Diego, Edgardo.*

Corado (122) Portuguese and Galician: Portuguese or Galician equivalent of Spanish COLORADO.
GIVEN NAMES Spanish 50%. *Jose* (7), *Ana* (4), *Luis* (3), *Carlos* (2), *Cesar* (2), *Manuel* (2), *Alonzo, Alvaro, Angelita, Armando, Berardo, Blanca.*

Corallo (210) Italian: from the personal name *Corallo*, meaning 'coral'.
GIVEN NAMES Italian 18%. *Salvatore* (5), *Dante* (2), *Sal* (2), *Angelo, Francesco, Natale, Salvatora, Vincenzo.*

Coram (387) English (Devon): variant of CORUM.

Coran (150) Americanized spelling of Czech **Kořán** (see KORAN) or perhaps a variant of the Irish family name **Corran** (see CURRAN).
GIVEN NAME French 5%. *Aubert* (2).

Corazza (138) Italian: possibly a metonymic occupational name for an armorer, from *corazza* 'cuirass', or alternatively a nickname from the Calabrian dialect word *corazzu* 'generous man', probably a derivative of dialect *core* 'heart' (standard Italian *cuore*).
GIVEN NAMES Italian 14%; German 4%. *Antonio, Egidio, Francesco, Livio, Luciano, Luigi, Natale.*

Corban (223) Irish: Anglicized form of Gaelic **Ó Corbáin** 'descendant of *Corbán*' or **Ó Coirbín** 'descendant of *Coirbín*', possibly from *corb* 'chariot'. Both names are also Anglicized as CORBETT.

Corbeil (330) French: from Old French *corbeil(le)* 'basket' (Late Latin *corbicula*, a diminutive of *corbis* 'basket'), a metonymic occupational name for a maker and seller of baskets. It may also be a habitational name from any of the various places named with this word because of a depression in the ground. This surname is sometimes Americanized as KIRBY.
GIVEN NAMES French 24%. *Andre* (5), *Jacques* (4), *Fernand* (2), *Jean-Louis* (2), *Armand, Fernande, Gilles, Hugues,*

Huguette, Jean Pierre, Jean-Baptiste, Leonie.

Corbell (445) **1.** English: metonymic occupational name for a basketmaker, from Old French *corbeille* 'basket', or alternatively possibly a nickname for someone with black hair, from Old French *corbel* 'raven'. **2.** Americanized spelling of **Körbel** or KORBEL. **3.** Americanized spelling of Dutch **Corbeel**, from Old French *corbel* 'raven' (see 1 above).

Corbello (163) Italian: from a diminutive of *corbo* 'rook', 'raven' (see CORBO). This is a predominantly LA name.

Corbet (236) English: variant spelling of CORBETT.

Corbett (9843) **1.** English (Shropshire; of Norman origin): nickname meaning 'little crow', 'raven', from Anglo-Norman French, Middle English *corbet*, a diminutive of *corb*, alluding probably to someone with dark hair or a dark complexion. The name was taken from Shropshire to Scotland in the 12th century and to northern Ireland in the 17th century, and thence to North America by one group of bearers of the name. **2.** Irish: see CORBAN.

Corbi (102) Italian: patronymic or plural form of CORBO.
GIVEN NAMES Italian 11%; French 5%. *Romolo* (2), *Antonio*; *Jean-Claude* (2).

Corbin (9101) **1.** French and English: nickname meaning 'little crow', 'raven', from Old French, Middle English *corbin*, a diminutive of *corb*. Compare CORBETT. **2.** English: possibly also a Norman habitational name from places in Calvados and Orne, France, named Corbon.

Corbit (259) English: variant spelling of CORBETT.

Corbitt (1846) English: variant spelling of CORBETT.

Corbo (543) **1.** Italian: from *corbo* 'rook', 'raven', a central southern variant of *corvo* (see CORVO). **2.** Spanish: nickname from a variant of *corvo* 'crooked', 'bent' (Latin *curvus*). **3.** Spanish: possibly from a variant of Galician *corvo* 'raven' (Latin *corvus*).
GIVEN NAMES Italian 21%; Spanish 9%. *Angelo* (8), *Sal* (3), *Vito* (3), *Antonio* (2), *Roberto* (2), *Carmela* (2), *Carmine* (2), *Rocco* (2), *Salvatore* (2), *Alfonse, Attilio, Carmelo, Giovanna*; *Carlos* (2), *Eleno* (2), *Guillermo* (2), *Raimundo* (2), *Agustin, Beatriz, Blanca, Francisco.*

Corboy (127) Irish: Anglicized form of Gaelic **Mac Corrbuidhe** 'son of *Corrbuidhe*', a byname composed of the elements *corr* 'crane' + *buidhe* 'yellow'.

Corbridge (236) English (Yorkshire): habitational name from Corbridge in Northumberland, named in late Old English as *Corebricg* 'bridge near Corchester', from a shortened form of *Corstopitum*, the Celtic name of Corchester + Old English *brycg* 'bridge'.

Corby (773) **1.** English: habitational name from any of various places in northern England. Those in Lincolnshire and Northamptonshire are named with the Old Norse personal name *Kori* (see CORY) + Old Norse *býr* 'farm', 'settlement', whereas the one in Cumbria has as its first element the Old Irish personal name *Corc*. **2.** French: from a diminutive of *corb* 'crow'. **3.** Irish: variant of CORBOY.

Corchado (131) Spanish: probably a nickname meaning 'corked', from the past participle of Spanish *corchar*, a verb from *corcho* 'cork'.
GIVEN NAMES Spanish 56%. *Manuel* (4), *Jose* (3), *Juan* (3), *Angel* (2), *Juan Jose* (2), *Octaviano* (2), *Rafael* (2), *Roberto* (2), *Alfredo, Alicia, Altagracia, Antoneo.*

Corcione (101) Italian: from an augmentative of CURCIO.
GIVEN NAMES Italian 28%. *Carmine* (2), *Sabato* (2), *Luigi, Nicola, Rocco, Sal, Salvatore, Vito.*

Corcoran (7219) Irish: Anglicized form of Gaelic **Ó Corcráin** 'descendant of *Corcrán*', a diminutive of the personal name *Corcra* (see CORKERY).
GIVEN NAMES Irish 5%. *Brigid* (2), *Caitlin, Dermot, Eamon, John Patrick, Kieran, Liam, Sinead.*

Cord (376) **1.** Northern Irish: reduced form of MCCORD. **2.** Possibly an Americanized spelling of French **Corde**, from Old French *corde* 'string', 'rope' (Latin *c(h)orda*, from Greek *khordē*), a metonymic occupational name for a maker of cord or string, or a nickname for a habitual wearer of decorative ties and ribbons. **3.** Dutch: variant of KORT 'short'.

Corda (220) Italian: **1.** from *corda* 'rope', 'string' (Latin *c(h)orda*, from Greek *khordē*), hence a metonymic occupational name for a maker of cord or string, or a nickname for a habitual wearer of decorative ties and ribbons. **2.** from a short form of a medieval Tuscan personal name, *Bentaccorda*, an omen name meaning 'well granted'.
GIVEN NAMES Italian 8%. *Aldo, Ignazio, Renzo, Salvatore, Ugo.*

Cordano (147) Italian (Tuscany and Liguria): unexplained.
GIVEN NAMES Italian 6%. *Angelo, Dario, Orazio.*

Cordaro (489) Italian: occupational name from *cordaro, cordaio* 'rope maker'.
GIVEN NAMES Italian 25%. *Salvatore* (10), *Angelo* (5), *Sal* (3), *Carlo* (2), *Vincenzo* (2), *Aurelio, Carmella, Calogero, Carmelo, Francesco, Gilda, Giuseppe, Ignazio, Rocco, Rosario, Nicasio, Rito, Roberto.*

Cordasco (137) Italian: from the personal name CORDA or *Cordio* (a short form of *Accord(i)o*, literally 'agreement') + the suffix *-asco* denoting kinship.
GIVEN NAMES Italian 14%. *Carlo* (2), *Pasquale, Salvatore.*

Cordeiro (1032) Portuguese and Galician: from *cordeiro* 'young lamb' (Latin *cordarius*, a derivative of *cordus* 'young', 'new'), hence a metonymic occupational name for a shepherd, or a nickname meaning 'lamb'.
GIVEN NAMES Spanish 19%; Portuguese 11%. *Manuel* (33), *Jose* (20), *Carlos* (8), *Francisco* (5), *Luiz* (4), *Eduardo* (3), *Hermano* (3), *Luis* (3), *Abilio* (2), *Eusebio* (2), *Mariano* (2), *Mario* (2); *Joao* (5), *Paulo* (2), *Vasco* (2), *Caetano*, *Duarte*, *Guilherme*, *Serafim*.

Cordell (3098) **1.** English: occupational name for a maker of cord or string or a nickname for an habitual wearer of decorative ties and ribbons, from a diminutive of Old French *corde* 'rope' (see CORDES). **2.** Americanized spelling of German *Kardel* (see KARDELL).

Corder (2568) **1.** English: variant of CORDIER. **2.** Catalan: occupational name for a maker of cord or string, from an agent derivative of Catalan *corda* 'string', 'cord'.

Corderman (120) Dutch (**Cordeman**): occupational name for a rope maker.

Cordero (2995) Spanish: from *cordero* 'young lamb' (Latin *cordarius*, a derivative of *cordus* 'young', 'new'), hence a metonymic occupational name for a shepherd, or alternatively a nickname meaning 'lamb'.
GIVEN NAMES Spanish 43%. *Jose* (64), *Carlos* (39), *Juan* (37), *Luis* (34), *Manuel* (31), *Francisco* (17), *Jesus* (17), *Pedro* (16), *Rafael* (16), *Ana* (15), *Miguel* (14), *Ramon* (13).

Cordery (124) English: variant of CORDRAY.

Cordes (2504) **1.** English: occupational name for a maker of cord or string or a nickname for a habitual wearer of decorative ties and ribbons, from the genitive or plural form of Old French *corde* 'string' (see COARD). **2.** Variant spelling of German KORDES. **3.** French: habitational name from any of several places called Cordes.
GIVEN NAMES German 4%. *Eldor* (2), *Erwin* (2), *Heinz* (2), *Kurt* (2), *Deitrich*, *Dieter*, *Ewald*, *Franz*, *Fritz*, *Gerhard*, *Gunther*, *Heinrich*.

Cordi (128) Italian: probably from the personal name *Cordio*, a short form of *Accord(i)o* (literally 'agreement').
GIVEN NAMES Italian 23%. *Angelo* (5), *Carmine*, *Dante*, *Francesca*, *Giuseppe*.

Cordial (154) English: variant of CORDELL.

Cordier (347) French and English: occupational name for a maker of cord or string, from an agent derivative of Old French *corde* 'string'.

Cordill (158) English: spelling of CORDELL.

Cording (113) English (Somerset): unexplained.

Cordingley (119) English: most likely a habitational name from a lost or unidentified place, probably in Yorkshire, where the surname is most frequent.

Cordisco (148) Italian: variant of **Cordischi**, itself either a variant of CORDASCO, or from the Old Italian adjective *cordesco* 'of or pertaining to sheep or cows'.
GIVEN NAMES Italian 15%. *Angelo* (2), *Gino* (2), *Carlo*, *Domenic*, *Leonardo*, *Pasquale*, *Ugo*.

Cordle (1011) **1.** English: variant spelling of CORDELL. **2.** Possibly an Americanized spelling of German **Kördel**, a pet form of an old German personal name, formed with *kuoni* 'daring'. Compare CONRAD.

Cordner (305) English (now found chiefly in Ireland): **1.** occupational name from Anglo-Norman French *cordewaner* 'cordwainer', 'shoemaker'. **2.** from an agent derivative of Old French *cordon* 'ribbon', hence an occupational name for a maker or seller of cord or ribbon. **3.** occupational name for a worker in fine Spanish kid leather, from an agent derivative of Old French *cordoan* (see CORDON 2).
GIVEN NAMES French 4%. *Cecile*, *Michel*.

Cordoba (397) Spanish (**Córdoba**): habitational name from the city of Córdoba in southern Spain, of extremely ancient foundation and unknown etymology.
GIVEN NAMES Spanish 55%. *Juan* (10), *Carlos* (9), *Jose* (8), *Luis* (5), *Julio* (4), *Mario* (4), *Roberto* (4), *Arturo* (3), *Concepcion* (3), *Diego* (3), *Jorge* (3), *Miguel* (3).

Cordon (488) **1.** French, English, and Spanish (**Cordón**): from Old French *cordon* 'cord', 'ribbon', a diminutive of *corde* 'string', 'cord'; Spanish *cordón*, hence a metonymic occupational name for a maker or seller of cord or ribbon. **2.** English: metonymic occupational name for a worker in fine Spanish kid leather, from Old French *cordoan* (so named with being originally produced at Córdoba).
GIVEN NAMES Spanish 19%. *Carlos* (7), *Jorge* (4), *Julio* (3), *Ricardo* (3), *Emilio* (2), *Jose* (2), *Juan* (2), *Luis* (2), *Pablo* (2), *Rigoberto* (2), *Acevedo*, *Adan*.

Cordone (169) Italian: from *cordone* 'cord', an augmentative form of *corda* 'string' (see CORDA), hence a metonymic occupational name for a cordmaker or a nickname for a tall, thin person.
GIVEN NAMES Italian 9%. *Domenic*, *Romeo*, *Serafino*.

Cordonnier (129) French: occupational name for a worker in fine leather, Old French *cordouanier*, a derivative of *cordoan* 'kid leather' (named for Córdoba in Spain, where it was originally produced).

Cordova (5478) Spanish (**Córdova**): variant of CORDOBA.
GIVEN NAMES Spanish 31%. *Jose* (79), *Manuel* (53), *Juan* (49), *Carlos* (47), *Mario* (27), *Francisco* (26), *Miguel* (19), *Jesus* (18), *Luis* (18), *Ruben* (17), *Arturo* (15), *Jorge* (15).

Cordray (761) English: nickname for a proud man, from Old French *cuer de roi* 'king's heart'.

Cordrey (390) English: variant spelling of CORDRAY.

Cordry (173) English: variant spelling of CORDRAY.

Cords (273) **1.** English: variant spelling of CORDES. **2.** Americanized spelling of German **Kordts** (see CORDTS). **3.** Dutch: patronymic from a reduced form of the personal name *Koenraet* (see CONRAD).
GIVEN NAMES German 7%. *Arno*, *Dieter*, *Erwin*, *Frieda*, *Juergen*, *Jutta*.

Cordts (252) **1.** Dutch: variant of CORDS. **2.** Americanized spelling of North German **Kordts** or possibly of **Korz**, a variant of KURZ.
GIVEN NAMES German 9%. *Bernhard* (2), *Gerhard* (2), *Mathias* (2), *Klaus*, *Lothar*, *Manfred*.

Cordwell (130) English: habitational name from Cordwell in Derbyshire or from either of two places called Cauldwell, in Derbyshire and Bedfordshire; all are named with Old English *cauld* 'cold' + *well(a)* 'spring', 'stream'.

Cordy (262) English: unexplained.

Core (1199) **1.** English: unexplained. **2.** Southern Italian: from a short form of the personal names *Boncore*, literally 'good heart', a medieval omen name, or *Belcore*.

Corea (413) **1.** Spanish: nickname from *corea* 'chorea'. **2.** Spanish: variant of CORREA. **3.** Southern Italian: possibly a habitational name from Corea, a place in Calabria.
GIVEN NAMES Spanish 30%; Portuguese 9%. *Jose* (7), *Luis* (4), *Carlos* (3), *Cesar* (3), *Jorge* (3), *Mario* (3), *Pedro* (3), *Ana* (2), *Cristina* (2), *Guillermo* (2), *Humberto* (2), *Manuel* (2); *Paulo* (2).

Coreas (134) Spanish: **1.** variant (plural) of COREA. **2.** variant (plural) of CORREA.
GIVEN NAMES Spanish 60%. *Jose* (14), *Carlos* (5), *Ana* (3), *Francisco* (3), *Aida* (2), *Juan* (2), *Julio* (2), *Manuel* (2), *Rafael* (2), *Reyna* (2), *Ricardo* (2), *Alba*.

Corell (251) English, Irish, and German: variant of KORELL.
GIVEN NAMES German 4%. *Volker* (2), *Hans*, *Kurt*.

Corella (218) **1.** Basque: habitational name from Corella in Navarre province, Basque Country. **2.** Italian: possibly from a feminine form of CORE.
GIVEN NAMES Spanish 31%; Portuguese 10%. *Carlos* (4), *Jose* (4), *Luis* (4), *Manuel* (4), *Rafael* (3), *Angel* (2), *Francisco* (2), *Ignacio* (2), *Jesus* (2), *Julio* (2), *Agapita*, *Alba*; *Armanda*.

Corelli (112) Italian: unexplained; perhaps from a short form of a personal name ending with *-coro* + the diminutive suffix *-ello*.
GIVEN NAMES Italian 15%. *Alfio* (2), *Aldo*, *Amedeo*, *Antonio*, *Gino*.

Coren (246) Anglicized or Americanized form of Jewish, Dutch, Norwegian, or Slovenian KOREN.

GIVEN NAMES Jewish 7%. *Meyer* (2), *Gershon, Mayer, Toba.*

Corey (5978) **1.** English: from the Old Norse personal name *Kori*, which is of uncertain meaning. **2.** Northern Irish: variant of CURRY.

Corfield (125) English (Welsh Marches and West Midlands): habitational name from a place by the river Corve in Shropshire named Corfield, from the river name (which is from Old English *corf* 'cutting') + Old English *feld* 'open country'.

Corfman (130) Probably an Americanized spelling of German **Korfmann**, an occupational name for a basketmaker or seller, from Middle High German *korp* 'basket' + *man* 'man'.

Corgan (158) Possibly a variant spelling of northern Irish **Corken**, a reduced Anglicized form of Gaelic **Ó Corcáin** 'descendant of *Corcán*'.

Coria (341) Spanish: habitational name from Coria in Cáceres province (Latin *Caurium*), or from Coria del Río, a place in Seville province.

GIVEN NAMES Spanish 55%. *Jose* (16), *Juan* (5), *Luis* (5), *Jose Luis* (4), *Mario* (4), *Arturo* (3), *Carlos* (3), *Javier* (3), *Jorge* (3), *Miguel* (3), *Pablo* (3), *Alfredo* (2); *Antonio* (5), *Eliseo* (2), *Clemente, Lorenzo, Olivero, Sal, Salvatore, Severiano.*

Coriell (301) Probably of French (Huguenot) origin (see CORYELL).

Corigliano (227) Italian: habitational name from Corigliano Calabro in Cosenza province, Corigliano d'Otranto in Lecce province, or Corigliano in Sessa Aurunca in Caserta province. All are named with the Latin personal name *Corel(l)ius* or *Corilius* + the suffix *-anus*.

GIVEN NAMES Italian 24%. *Cosimo* (2), *Cosmo* (2), *Gennaro* (2), *Angelo, Carmelo, Domenic, Duilio, Francesca, Ricardo, Rosario.*

Corin (116) English (Cornwall): unexplained.

Corio (227) Southern Italian: metonymic occupational name for a tanner or leather worker, from *corio* 'leather', a dialect variant of *cuoio*. Compare COIRO.

GIVEN NAMES Italian 13%. *Salvatore* (4), *Antonio* (2), *Antonino, Francesca, Luigi, Sal.*

Cork (865) English: metonymic occupational name for a supplier of red or purple dye or for a dyer of cloth, Middle English *cork* (of Celtic origin; compare CORKERY).

Corke (123) English: variant spelling of CORK.

Corker (323) English: occupational name for a supplier of red or purple dye, from an agent derivative of Middle English *cork* (see CORK).

Corkern (331) Reduced form of Irish CORCORAN.

GIVEN NAME Irish 4%. *Murphy* (2).

Corkery (508) Irish (Munster): Anglicized form of Gaelic **Ó Corcra** 'descendant of *Corcra*', a personal name derived from *corcair* 'purple' (ultimately cognate with Latin *purpur*).

Corkill (282) Irish: reduced form of McCORKLE.

Corkins (277) Northern Irish: Anglicized form of Gaelic **Ó Corcáin** 'descendant of *Corcán*', a personal name from the diminutive of *corc* 'crimson', with the addition of redundant English genitive *-s*.

Corkran (300) Irish: reduced form of CORCORAN.

GIVEN NAMES Irish 4%. *Brendan, Connor, Donovan.*

Corkum (293) Said by family historians to be of German origin (a variant of **Gorkum**), but unexplained.

Corl (636) Possibly an Americanized form of German KARL.

Corle (342) Possibly an Americanized form of German KARL or KARLE.

Corless (368) English (chiefly Lancashire): variant of CORLISS.

Corlett (552) Manx: Anglicized form of Gaelic **Mac Thorliot**, a patronymic from a personal name of Old Norse origin, composed of the divine name *Þórr* + *ljótr* 'bright'.

Corlew (525) English: nickname for someone thought to resemble a curlew in some way, Anglo-Norman French *curleu*, Old French *corlieu*. The spelling *Corlew* is recorded in Sussex in 1327, but now appears to have died out in the British Isles, replaced by the modern form **Curlew**.

Corley (6367) **1.** Irish: variant of CURLEY. **2.** English: habitational name from Corley in Warwickshire or Coreley in Shropshire, both named with Old English *corna*, a metathesized form of *crona*, genitive plural of *cron, cran* 'crane' + *lēah* 'woodland clearing'.

Corliss (1222) English: nickname for a carefree person, from Old English *carlēas* (a compound of *caru* 'grief', 'care' + *lēas* 'free from', 'without').

Cormack (478) Scottish and Irish: reduced form of McCORMACK (see McCORMICK).

GIVEN NAMES Irish 4%. *Brendan* (2), *Dermot.*

Corman (823) **1.** Dutch: variant of KORMAN. **2.** Altered spelling of German **Kormann** (see KORMAN).

Cormany (281) Probably of French origin, a variant of CARMANY.

Cormican (195) Scottish: from a pet form of the Gaelic personal name *Cormac* (see McCORMICK).

Cormier (6088) French: topographic name for someone who lived near a sorb or service tree, Old French *cormier* (from *corme*,

the name of the fruit for which the tree was cultivated, apparently of Gaulish origin).

GIVEN NAMES French 11%. *Armand* (10), *Emile* (9), *Yvon* (9), *Aurele* (7), *Normand* (7), *Alcide* (6), *Lucien* (6), *Ulysse* (6), *Oneil* (5), *Adrien* (4), *Cecile* (4), *Curley* (4).

Corn (2684) **1.** English: nickname from Old English *corn*, a metathesized form of *cran* 'crane' (see CRANE). **2.** English: from Middle English *corn* 'grain', applied as a metonymic occupational name for a grain merchant or grower, or possibly a miller. **3.** English: metonymic occupational name for a maker or user of hand mills, Old English *cweorn*. **4.** Altered spelling of German KORN or a shortened form of any of the composite names formed with this element.

Cornacchia (176) Italian: from *cornacchia* 'crow', 'jackdaw', applied as a nickname for a talkative person or someone thought to resemble a crow or jackdaw in some other way.

GIVEN NAMES Italian 25%. *Angelo* (5), *Rocco* (4), *Antonio, Carina, Carlo, Carmine, Massimo, Paolo, Romolo, Sal, Vincenzo.*

Cornatzer (119) German: variant of **Kornatz** (see KARNATZ).

Corne (194) **1.** French: from Old French *corne* 'horn' (Late Latin *corna*), a derogatory nickname for a cuckold (see HORN 4), or a metonymic occupational name for a hornblower or worker in horn. **2.** English: variant spelling of CORN.

GIVEN NAMES French 6%. *Emile* (2), *Heloise.*

Corneau (131) French: from a diminutive of Old French *corne* 'horn' (see CORNE).

GIVEN NAMES French 10%. *Alcide, Cecile, Normand, Pierre, Yvon.*

Cornejo (1318) Spanish: topographic name for someone who lived by a dogwood tree, Spanish *cornejo* (Latin *corniculus*), or a habitational name from any of the various minor places named Cornejo, for example in the provinces of Almería, Burgos, and Ciudad Real.

GIVEN NAMES Spanish 50%. *Jose* (51), *Carlos* (23), *Juan* (18), *Manuel* (17), *Arturo* (11), *Luis* (10), *Ricardo* (10), *Francisco* (9), *Miguel* (9), *Jorge* (8), *Raul* (8), *Ruben* (8).

Cornelia (148) Italian: from the female personal name *Cornelia*, feminine form of CORNELIO.

Cornelio (252) Spanish, Italian, and Portuguese: from the personal name *Cornelio*, from Latin CORNELIUS.

GIVEN NAMES Spanish 33%; Italian 13%; Portuguese 5%. *Carlos* (5), *Jose* (3), *Guadalupe* (2), *Mario* (2), *Ramon* (2), *Adelfo, Agustin, Aniceto, Claudio, Cruz, Damaso, Eleazar; Antonio* (3), *Dante* (2), *Bartolo, Carmelo, Carmine, Cesario, Enrico, Filomena, Franco, Luciano, Nicola, Orazio; Joao.*

Cornelious (139) Respelling of CORNELIUS.

Cornelison (1334) Dutch: patronymic from *Cornelis*, vernacular form of CORNELIUS.

Cornelius (6985) Dutch, Danish, and German: from a personal name borne by a 3rd-century Christian saint and pope, Latin *Cornelius*, an old Roman family name, probably derived from *cornu* 'horn'. Compare CORNE.

Cornell (8002) **1.** Americanized form of any of the numerous Continental European surnames derived from Latin *Cornelius* (see CORNELIUS), for example French **Corneille** or German **Kornel**. **2.** Swedish: Latinized form of HORN, meaning 'horn'; probably a soldier's name. **3.** English: reduced form of CORNWELL or of **Cornhill**, a habitational name from a place in Northumberland named Cornhill, from Old English *corn*, a metathesized form of *cron*, *cran* 'crane' + *halh* 'nook', 'recess'; or from Cornhill in London, a medieval grain exchange, named with Old English *corn* 'corn', 'grain' + *hyll* 'hill', or from some other place elsewhere similarly named.
FOREBEARS Ezra Cornell (1807–74), the founder of Cornell University, was born of New England Quaker stock in Westchester Co., NY, a descendant of Thomas Cornell of Saffron Walden, Essex, England, who emigrated sometime before 1642, when he is recorded as being married in Portsmouth, Newport Co., RI.

Cornella (130) **1.** Catalan (**Cornellà**): habitational name of one the places so called in Catalonia. **2.** Italian: from the personal name *Cornella*.
GIVEN NAMES Spanish 5%. *Alonzo, Ines, Lino, Valerio.*

Cornellier (123) French: probably from a derivative of the Latin personal name *Cornelius* (see CORNELIUS, CORNELL). This name is concentrated in MA and MI.
GIVEN NAMES French 7%. *Armand, Fernand, Normand.*

Cornelsen (134) **1.** Dutch: reduced form of CORNELISON. **2.** North German: patronymic from the personal name CORNELIUS.

Cornelson (123) Respelling of Dutch and North German CORNELSEN.

Cornely (155) French (**Cornély**): from a personal name from Latin *Cornelius* (see CORNELIUS). The cathedral of St. Cornelius at Aachen was a center of pilgrimage, and the personal name was especially popular in this area in the Middle Ages.
GIVEN NAMES French 6%. *Chantal* (2), *Jean-Paul, Loubert.*

Corner (645) **1.** English: occupational name for a hornblower or worker in horn, from an agent derivative of Old French *corne* 'horn' (see CORNE). **2.** English: metonymic occupational name for a maker of hand mills, from an agent derivative of Old English *cweorn* 'hand mill' (see CORN 3). **3.** English: topographic name for someone who lived on the corner of two streets or tracks, (Middle English *corner*, from Old French *cornier* 'angle', 'corner'). **4.** Amer-

icanized spelling of German **Körner** (see KOERNER) or Swiss KORNER.

Cornet (130) French: **1.** topographic name for someone who lived on a street corner, from a derivative of *corne* 'corner'. Compare COIN. **2.** from *cornet*, denoting either a rustic horn or an object made of horn, hence a metonymic occupational name for a hornblower or for a worker in horn.
GIVEN NAMES French 24%. *Jacques* (2), *Pierre* (2), *Antoine, Jean-Claude, Jean-Luc, Marie Anne, Olivier.*

Cornett (5319) English: diminutive of CORN 1.

Cornetta (123) Italian: from a diminutive of *corno* 'horn'.
GIVEN NAMES Italian 8%. *Angelo, Gennaro, Pasquale.*

Cornette (441) French: from a diminutive of *corne* 'horn' (see CORNE).

Corney (202) English: habitational name from places in Cumbria and Hertfordshire named Corney, from Old English *corn* 'grain' or *corn*, a metathesized form of *cron*, *cran* 'crane' + *ēg* 'island'. It seems possible, from the distribution of early forms, that it may also derive from a lost place in Lancashire.

Cornfield (121) **1.** English: apparently a topographic name for someone who lived near an area of open land frequented by cranes, from Old English *corn*, a metathesized form of *cron*, *cran* 'crane' + *feld* 'open country', or a habitational name from a place name with the same origin. **2.** Translation of Jewish or German KORNFELD.

Cornforth (231) English: habitational name from Cornforth in County Durham, named with Old English *corn*, a metathesized form of *cron*, *cran* 'crane' (see CRANE) + *ford* 'ford'.

Cornia (150) Southern Italian: possibly a habitational name from a minor place named Cornia, examples of which are found in Sicily and Calabria.

Cornick (281) English (Dorset): ethnic name for a Cornishman.

Corning (635) Possibly a respelling of German **Körnig**, a nickname for a strong person, from *körnig* 'robust', 'solid', or from **Korney**, a variant of CORNELIUS.
FOREBEARS An early bearer of the name was Ensign Samuel Corning, who emigrated from England to Beverly, MA, in 1641. Erastus Corning (1794–1872) moved in 1814 from CT to Albany, NY, where he became a wealthy iron manufacturer and railroad businessman.

Cornish (2627) **1.** English: regional name for someone from the county of Cornwall, from Middle English *corneys, cornysh*. Not surprisingly, the surname is common in adjacent Devon, but it is also well established as far afield as Essex and Lancashire. **2.** Possibly also an Americanized spelling of German **Kornisch**, a nickname for a

sickly or weak person, from Sorbian *krne* 'weak', 'poor'.

Cornman (494) Americanized form of the German occupational name **Kornmann** (see KORMAN).

Cornog (104) Welsh: ethnic name for a Cornishman.

Corns (513) **1.** English: variant of CORNISH, from Old French *corneis*. **2.** Americanized form of Dutch KORNS.

Cornutt (116) **1.** Variant spelling of German **Kornutt**, which is of unexplained origin. **2.** See CURNUTT. **3.** Possibly a variant spelling of CORNETT.

Cornwall (884) English: **1.** regional name from the county of Cornwall, which is named with the Old English tribal name *Cornwealas*. This is from *Kernow* (the term that the Cornish used to refer to themselves, a word of uncertain etymology, perhaps connected with a Celtic element meaning 'horn', 'headland'), + Old English *wealas* 'strangers', 'foreigners', the term used by the Anglo-Saxons for British-speaking people. **2.** variant of CORNWELL.

Cornwell (4678) English: **1.** habitational name from Cornwell in Oxfordshire, named from Old English *corn*, a metathesized form of *cron*, *cran* 'crane' + *well(a)* 'spring', 'stream'. **2.** variant of CORNWALL.

Coro (112) Spanish: apparently from *coro* 'choir'. This name is common in Bolivia, Peru, and Ecuador.
GIVEN NAMES Spanish 27%. *Ignacio* (2), *Jesus* (2), *Abelardo, Aida, Aleida, Arturo, Carlos, Ernesto, Evaristo, Francisco, Heliodoro, Jorge.*

Corona (3295) **1.** Spanish and Italian: from Spanish, Italian *corona* 'crown' (Latin *corona* 'garland', 'chaplet', 'diadem'), perhaps applied as a habitational name for someone who lived in a house with this sign, or as a nickname for someone who had a tonsure in fulfillment of a religious vow or who had influence and power. **2.** Italian: from the female personal name *Corona*, of the same derivation as 1.
GIVEN NAMES Spanish 44%. *Jose* (100), *Juan* (43), *Jesus* (31), *Manuel* (25), *Luis* (23), *Francisco* (20), *Jorge* (19), *Rafael* (19), *Roberto* (19), *Ramon* (18), *Ricardo* (17), *Carlos* (16); *Antonio* (19), *Salvatore* (4), *Federico* (3), *Filiberto* (3), *Heriberto* (3), *Marco* (3), *Angelo* (2), *Eliseo* (2), *Fausto* (2), *Lorenzo* (2), *Lucio* (2), *Silvio* (2).

Coronado (2421) Spanish: from *coronado* 'crowned', past participle of *coronare* 'to crown', applied as a nickname for someone who behaved in an imperious manner.
GIVEN NAMES Spanish 47%. *Jose* (67), *Juan* (32), *Jesus* (23), *Mario* (22), *Francisco* (21), *Manuel* (21), *Carlos* (17), *Luis* (17), *Ramon* (16), *Pedro* (15), *Guadalupe* (14), *Rafael* (13).

Coronel (487) Spanish and Portuguese: from Italian *colonnello*, a diminutive of

colonna 'column (of troops)' (Latin *columna*), hence a metonymic occupational name for someone in command of a regiment. According to Tibón, the change of *-l-* to *-r-* may be under the influence of the word *corona* 'crown' as a symbol of power.
GIVEN NAMES Spanish 51%. *Jose* (15), *Luis* (8), *Carlos* (7), *Jorge* (6), *Armando* (5), *Manuel* (5), *Fernando* (4), *Francisco* (4), *Ramon* (4), *Cesar* (3), *Jose Luis* (3), *Juan* (3).

Corp (397) English and French: from Old French *corp* 'raven', probably applied as a nickname for someone with glossy dark hair. In some cases the English name may be derived from the cognate Old Norse *korpr*.

Corpe (119) English: variant spelling of CORP.

Corpening (325) Altered form of German **Köp(e)nick** (see KOEPNICK).

Corporon (115) Perhaps an altered form of a French habitational name **Corberon**, from a place so named in Côte-d'Or.

Corprew (140) Origin unidentified. This name is concentrated in VA and SC.

Corpus (424) Spanish: from the Latin personal name *Corpus Christi*, literally 'body of Christ', a Christian festival.
GIVEN NAMES Spanish 32%. *Jose* (4), *Gustavo* (3), *Lupe* (3), *Raul* (3), *Alfredo* (2), *Armando* (2), *Francisco* (2), *Jesus* (2), *Juan* (2), *Juanita* (2), *Rey* (2), *Rolando* (2).

Corpuz (675) Spanish (Philippines: **Córpuz**): variant spelling of CORPUS.
GIVEN NAMES Spanish 40%. *Carlito* (4), *Francisco* (4), *Juanito* (4), *Jose* (3), *Juan* (3), *Marcelo* (3), *Pacita* (3), *Adriano* (2), *Alfredo* (2), *Andres* (2), *Bernardo* (2), *Carlos* (2).

Corr (1132) Irish: Anglicized form of Gaelic **Ó Corra** 'descendant of *Corra*', a personal name from *corr* 'spear', 'pointed object'.
GIVEN NAMES Irish 5%. *Dermot* (2), *Aidan*, *Brendan*.

Corra (132) Italian (**Corrà**): from a short form of the personal name CORRADO.
GIVEN NAMES Italian 5%. *Gino* (2), *Renzo*, *Rinaldo*.

Corradetti (104) Italian: from a pet form of the personal name CORRADO.
GIVEN NAMES Italian 32%. *Adriana*, *Albino*, *Argentina*, *Carlo*, *Carmel*, *Costantino*, *Emidio*, *Mariano*, *Orlando*, *Sebastiano*, *Silvio*, *Tosca*.

Corradi (201) Italian: patronymic or plural form of CORRADO.
GIVEN NAMES Italian 23%. *Nino* (4), *Angelo* (3), *Aldo* (2), *Elio* (2), *Giulio* (2), *Dino*, *Gildo*, *Igino*, *Luciano*, *Renzo*, *Romolo*, *Stefano*.

Corradini (108) Italian: patronymic or plural form of CORRADINO.
GIVEN NAMES Italian 15%. *Angelo* (3), *Attilio*, *Corrado*, *Fabrizio*, *Stefano*.

Corradino (153) Italian: from a diminutive of the personal name CORRADO.

GIVEN NAMES Italian 17%. *Angelo*, *Carmelo*, *Gandolfo*, *Luigi*, *Sal*, *Salvatore*, *Vito*.

Corrado (1305) Italian: from the personal name *Corrado*, from Germanic *Chuonrad* (see KONRAD).
GIVEN NAMES Italian 12%. *Angelo* (6), *Luigi* (3), *Antonio* (2), *Domenic* (2), *Enrico* (2), *Pasquale* (2), *Sal* (2), *Salvatore* (2), *Alessandro*, *Attilio*, *Carlo*, *Cosmo*.

Corral (1757) Spanish: topographic name for someone who lived near an enclosure for livestock, *corral*. There are numerous places named with this word, in both the singular and plural forms, and to a large extent the surname is a habitational name from these.
GIVEN NAMES Spanish 51%. *Jose* (63), *Manuel* (31), *Jesus* (25), *Javier* (13), *Ramon* (13), *Juan* (11), *Luis* (11), *Raul* (11), *Francisco* (10), *Alfredo* (9), *Mario* (9), *Miguel* (9).

Corrales (961) Spanish: habtational name of any of the many places called (Los) Corrales, plural of CORRAL, plural of CORRAL.
GIVEN NAMES Spanish 49%. *Jose* (20), *Luis* (16), *Manuel* (13), *Carlos* (11), *Juan* (10), *Jesus* (9), *Armando* (7), *Javier* (6), *Miguel* (6), *Mario* (5), *Pedro* (5), *Sergio* (5).

Corrao (626) Italian (Sicily): reduced form of CORRADO.
GIVEN NAMES Italian 17%. *Salvatore* (11), *Sal* (4), *Giuseppe* (3), *Angelo* (2), *Antonino* (2), *Alberico*, *Biaggio*, *Biagio*, *Cesare*, *Costantino*, *Gaspare*, *Giorgio*.

Correa (3943) Spanish: possibly from *correa* 'leather strap', 'belt', 'rein', 'shoelace', plural *correas* (Latin *corrigia* 'fastening', from *corrigere* 'to straighten', 'to correct'), applied as a metonymic occupational name for a maker or seller of such articles.
GIVEN NAMES Spanish 45%. *Jose* (103), *Juan* (56), *Luis* (56), *Carlos* (46), *Manuel* (38), *Jorge* (24), *Pedro* (23), *Miguel* (21), *Jesus* (19), *Ramon* (19), *Raul* (19), *Francisco* (18).

Correale (192) Italian: from Spanish *correal* denoting a type of leather.
GIVEN NAMES Italian 14%. *Antonio* (2), *Angelo*, *Carmela*, *Carmine*, *Guiseppe*, *Pasquale*, *Rocco*, *Vincenzo*.

Correia (2574) Portuguese: from *correia* 'leather strap', 'belt', 'rein', 'shoelace' (Latin *corrigia* 'fastening', from *corrigere* 'to straighten', 'to correct'), applied as a metonymic occupational name for a maker or seller of such articles.
GIVEN NAMES Spanish 20%; Portuguese 12%. *Manuel* (82), *Jose* (54), *Carlos* (20), *Luis* (13), *Mario* (10), *Jorge* (9), *Fernando* (8), *Francisco* (8), *Alberto* (5), *Alfredo* (5), *Alvaro* (5), *Americo* (5); *Joao* (15), *Joaquim* (4), *Paulo* (4), *Albano*, *Aloisio*, *Duarte*, *Guilherme*, *Henrique*, *Vasco*.

Correira (207) Spanish: probably an altered form of CORREIA or CARREIRA.

GIVEN NAMES Spanish 11%; Portuguese 8%. *Manuel* (5), *Jose* (4), *Abilio*, *Alfredo*, *Carlos*, *Claudino*, *Dionisio*, *Germano*, *Octavio*; *Joao* (2); *Antonio* (3), *Flavio*, *Nicolina*.

Correll (2559) **1.** English: unexplained. **2.** Of Irish origin: unexplained; perhaps a variant of **Kirrell**, an Anglicized form of **Ó Coirill** (probably 'descendant of *Cairell*', an unexplained personal name). **3.** Americanized spelling of German KORELL.

Corrente (262) Italian (Milan): from *corrente* 'running', 'flowing', 'stream' (from Latin *currere* 'to run'), applied as a topographic name for someone who lived by a stream or possibly as a nickname for someone who was fleet of foot, a messenger, or someone always in a hurry.
GIVEN NAMES Italian 17%. *Pasquale* (3), *Nicola* (2), *Sal* (2), *Angelo*, *Antonio*, *Carmelo*, *Caterina*, *Cosimo*, *Damiano*, *Nichola*, *Santo*, *Umberto*.

Correnti (246) Italian: patronymic or plural form of CORRENTE.
GIVEN NAMES Italian 18%. *Angelo* (4), *Salvatore* (3), *Antonio* (2), *Domenic* (2), *Donato*, *Franca*, *Gaetano*, *Luciano*.

Corrick (230) Irish: Anglicized form of Gaelic **Mac ConChairrge** or **Mac ConChathrach** (see MCCARRICK).

Corrie (402) Scottish: **1.** habitational name from places in Arran, Dumfries, and elsewhere, named Corrie, from Gaelic *coire* 'cauldron', applied to a circular hanging valley on a mountain. **2.** Scottish spelling of northern Irish MCCORRY 'son of Godfrey'. See also CURRY, MCGORRY.

Corriea (110) Possibly an altered spelling of Portuguese CORREIA.
GIVEN NAMES Spanish 7%. *Manuel* (4), *Carlos*.

Corriere (107) Italian: occupational name from *corriere* 'messenger' (from medieval Latin *currerius*, from Latin *currere* 'to run').
GIVEN NAMES Italian 12%. *Angelo*, *Rocco*.

Corrigan (4714) Irish: Anglicized form of Gaelic **Ó Corragáin** 'descendant of *Corragán*', a double diminutive of *corr* 'pointed'.
GIVEN NAMES Irish 6%. *Malachy* (5), *Brendan* (3), *Dermot* (2), *Bridgid*, *Brigid*, *Cait*, *Niall*, *Patrick Michael*.

Corriher (252) Probably an altered spelling of Irish CARRAHER.

Corrin (165) **1.** Manx: contracted form of **Mac Oran**, Anglicized form of Gaelic **Mac Odhráin** 'son of *Odhran*', a byname from a diminutive of *odhar* 'dun'. **2.** Irish: see CURRAN.

Corrington (203) English: perhaps a variant of CARRINGTON or a habitational name from some other place now lost. See also CURRINGTON.

Corris (102) Manx: probably a reduced form of Gaelic *Mac Fheorais* 'son of *Feoras*', Gaelic form of the Anglo-Norman

French personal name *Piers* (see PIERCE). Compare BERMINGHAM.

Corriveau (1012) Altered spelling of French CARRIVEAU.

GIVEN NAMES French 17%. *Emile* (5), *Marcel* (5), *Rosaire* (5), *Fernand* (4), *Andre* (3), *Normand* (3), *Alphonse* (2), *Armand* (2), *Camille* (2), *Yves* (2), *Adrien*, *Alphee*.

Corron (179) **1.** English: Possibly a variant of CARON. **2.** Manx: variant of CORRIN.

Corrow (179) Probably an Americanized form of French **Carreau**, a variant of CARREL.

Corry (1027) Irish: **1.** Irish: reduced and altered form of MCCORRY. **2.** variant spelling of Scottish CORRIE.

Corsa (94) Italian (Apulia): from a feminine form of CORSO.

Corsaro (357) Italian (Sicily): **1.** occupational name for a scribe or copyist, from medieval Latin *cursarius*. **2.** derogatory nickname from *corsaro* 'pirate', 'corsair'.

GIVEN NAMES Italian 17%. *Angelo* (4), *Rocco* (2), *Aldo*, *Amedeo*, *Cosmo*, *Domenic*, *Franco*, *Gennaro*, *Pietro*, *Sal*, *Vito*.

Corse (255) **1.** English: habitational name from a place in Gloucestershire named Corse, from Welsh *cors* 'marsh', 'bog'. **2.** Scottish: topographic name from northern Middle English *cors*, *corse* 'cross', or a habitational name for someone from any of various places, for example in Grampian and Orkney, named with this word. **3.** Danish or Dutch: from the personal name *Corsse*, a variant of CARSTEN, which was borne by Scandinavian settlers in New Netherland in the 17th century.

Corsello (204) Italian: from a diminutive of the personal name CORSO.

GIVEN NAME Italian 7%. *Antonio* (2).

Corsentino (150) Italian (Sicily): variant of CONSENTINO.

GIVEN NAME Italian 5%. *Angelo*.

Corser (221) English: occupational name for a horse dealer, Middle English *corser*.

Corsetti (306) Italian: from a diminutive of the personal name CORSO.

GIVEN NAMES Italian 21%. *Rocco* (4), *Aldo* (2), *Gaetano* (2), *Nino* (2), *Amato*, *Amerigo*, *Angelo*, *Carlo*, *Carmelina*, *Dino*, *Domenic*, *Donato*.

Corsey (124) **1.** English: possibly a variant of DECOURCEY. **2.** Perhaps an altered spelling of French COURCY.

Corsi (713) Italian: patronymic or plural form of CORSO.

GIVEN NAMES Italian 11%. *Remo* (3), *Giampiero* (2), *Marco* (2), *Rocco* (2), *Sante* (2), *Aldo*, *Cosimo*, *Dante*, *Dario*, *Dino*, *Domenico*, *Elio*.

Corsiglia (135) Italian: habitational name from a minor place named Corsiglia, in Nerione, Genoa province.

Corsini (291) Italian: patronymic or plural form of CORSINO.

GIVEN NAMES Italian 10%. *Pasquale* (2), *Salvatore* (2), *Dante*, *Giocondo*, *Giulio*, *Giuseppe*, *Luciano*, *Riccardo*, *Vito*.

Corsino (114) Italian: from the personal name *Corsino*, a diminutive of CORSO. This name is also established in Mexico.

GIVEN NAMES Italian 24%; Spanish 11%. *Antonio* (2), *Alfonso*, *Alfredo*, *Carmela*, *Clemente*, *Nunzio*, *Salvatore*, *Tito*; *Jose* (2), *Andres*, *Belkys*, *Juan*, *Luis*, *Miguel*, *Reynaldo*.

Corso (1673) Italian: from the personal name *Corso*, a short form of *Accorso* (see ACCURSO) or BONACCORSO.

GIVEN NAMES Italian 11%. *Salvatore* (10), *Angelo* (4), *Gaetano* (3), *Sal* (3), *Agostino* (2), *Aldo* (2), *Antonio* (2), *Carlo* (2), *Domenic* (2), *Pasquale* (2), *Rocco* (2), *Annamaria*.

Corson (2220) **1.** Scottish and northern Irish: variant of CURZON. **2.** English (of Norman origin): nickname from Old French *corson*, a diminutive of *curt* 'short' (see COURT).

Cort (460) **1.** Catalan: from *cort* 'court' (Latin *cohors*, genitive *cohortis*, 'yard', 'enclosure'), an occupational name for someone who worked in a manorial court or a topographic name for someone who lived in or by one. **2.** Variant spelling of German and Jewish KORT.

Cortazzo (123) Southern Italian (Campania): possibly a topographic name from a derivative of *corte* 'court' (see CORTE).

GIVEN NAMES Italian 9%. *Carmine* (2), *Carlo*, *Leonardo*.

Corte (217) **1.** Italian, Spanish, and Portuguese: from *corte* 'court' (Latin *cohors* 'yard', 'enclosure', genitive *cohortis*), applied as an occupational name for someone who worked at a manorial court or a topographic name for someone who lived in or by one. **2.** English: variant spelling of COURT. **3.** Americanized spelling of KORTE.

GIVEN NAMES Italian 9%; Spanish 6%. *Ennio* (2), *Antonio*, *Carlo*, *Domenic*, *Gino*, *Guido*, *Silvio*; *Jose* (2), *Julio* (2), *Catalina*, *Luis*, *Manuel*, *Stelio*.

Cortelyou (132) Dutch: unexplained.

Corter (232) Origin unidentified; possibly an altered spelling of Dutch GORTER.

Cortes (3109) **1.** Spanish (**Cortés**), Catalan (**Cortès**), and Portuguese (**Cortês**): from *cortés* 'courteous', 'polite', a derivative of *corte* (see CORTE), a nickname for a refined person, sometimes no doubt given ironically. **2.** Spanish and Portuguese (**Cortes**): habitational name from any of numerous places in Spain and Portugal named with *cortes*, plural of *corte* 'court'.

GIVEN NAMES Spanish 51%. *Jose* (90), *Carlos* (49), *Juan* (41), *Luis* (33), *Jorge* (28), *Miguel* (28), *Manuel* (22), *Pedro* (21), *Jesus* (20), *Rafael* (19), *Jaime* (18), *Javier* (17).

Cortese (1489) Italian: from the personal name *Cortese*, meaning 'courteous', 'polite' and also 'dweller at a court'.

GIVEN NAMES Italian 15%. *Angelo* (9), *Salvatore* (7), *Antonio* (6), *Luigi* (5), *Vito* (5), *Rocco* (4), *Domenico* (2), *Ferdinando* (2), *Pasquale* (2), *Silvio* (2), *Vincenzo* (2), *Aldo*.

Cortesi (141) Italian: patronymic or plural form of CORTESE.

GIVEN NAMES Italian 10%; German 5%. *Gino* (2), *Angelo*, *Domenic*, *Geno*, *Reno*; *Otto* (3).

Cortez (8842) Spanish: variant of **Cortés** (see CORTES).

GIVEN NAMES Spanish 46%. *Jose* (191), *Juan* (103), *Jesus* (70), *Carlos* (69), *Manuel* (57), *Raul* (52), *Miguel* (49), *Ricardo* (47), *Francisco* (41), *Pedro* (41), *Ruben* (38), *Javier* (35).

Corthell (147) Perhaps an altered spelling of German **Körtel**, from a pet form of the personal name KONRAD.

Corti (190) Italian: from a nickname from *corto* 'short', from Latin *curtis*.

GIVEN NAMES Italian 23%. *Mario* (5), *Albino* (2), *Juana* (2), *Aldo*, *Alessio*, *Dario*, *Dino*, *Gianfranco*, *Gino*, *Livio*, *Remo*, *Vito*.

Cortina (418) **1.** Spanish, Catalan, Asturian-Leonese, Galician (**Cortiña**), and Italian: from a diminutive of CORTE. In Spain the precise meaning of the term varies from language to language: in Catalonia it denotes a farmyard, in Asturies an unfenced field, and in Galicia *cortiña* means 'vegetable garden'. In Asturies the name can also be habitational, from any of numerous minor places named with this word, as for example La Cortina. **2.** Italian: from a feminine diminutive of *corto* 'small'.

GIVEN NAMES Spanish 40%; Italian 14%. *Juan* (9), *Mario* (6), *Jose* (5), *Manuel* (5), *Pedro* (4), *Alberto* (3), *Armando* (3), *Elena* (3), *Eustaquio* (3), *Alvaro* (2), *Americo* (2), *Angel* (2); *Antonio* (6), *Angelo* (4), *Giuseppe* (2), *Pasquale* (2), *Benedetto*, *Clemente*, *Dante*, *Filippo*, *Geno*, *Geronimo*, *Gino*, *Gulio*.

Cortinas (411) Spanish, Catalan, and Asturian-Leonese: **1.** from the plural of CORTINA. The Catalan and Asturian-Leonese form are Castilianized variants of **Cortines**. **2.** Galician: habitational name from any of numerous places named Cortiñas.

GIVEN NAMES Spanish 45%. *Jose* (8), *Manuel* (8), *Ramon* (7), *Mario* (6), *Ricardo* (6), *Enrique* (5), *Jesus* (4), *Reynaldo* (4), *Carlos* (3), *Javier* (3), *Juan* (3), *Domingo* (2); *Antonio* (5), *Amadeo*, *Angelo*, *Dino*, *Filiberto*, *Marco*.

Cortis (118) Variant of English CURTIS.

Cortner (322) **1.** English (Cumbria): unexplained. Compare CARTNER. **2.** Americanized spelling of German **Kortner**, probably a habitational name from any of several places called Korten in Westphalia, the suffix *-er* denoting an inhabitant. This is also found as a Norwegian name, probably taken there from Germany.

Cortopassi (174) Italian: probably from *corto* 'short' + *passo* 'step', hence a nickname for someone who shuffled.

GIVEN NAMES Italian 12%. *Italo* (2), *Lido* (2), *Angelo, Carlo, Dario, Dino.*

Cortright (574) Americanized form of Dutch **Kortrijk** (see COURTRIGHT).

Corts (132) Americanized spelling of German KORTZ.

Corum (1179) English (Devon): habitational name from Curham near Tiverton in Devon.

Corvi (127) Italian: patronymic or plural form of CORVO.

GIVEN NAMES Italian 8%; French 5%. *Ivano, Leno, Salvatore; Armand* (3).

Corvin (341) **1.** Swedish: perhaps a habitational name from an unidentified place named with *korp* 'raven' (Latin *corvus*). **2.** English: possibly a variant of CORBIN.

Corvino (308) Italian: from a diminutive of *corvo* 'raven', 'rook' (see CORVO).

GIVEN NAMES Italian 20%. *Angelo* (5), *Pasquale* (3), *Marco* (2), *Sal* (2), *Antonio, Emidio, Enrico, Giovanni, Ottavio, Romeo, Salvatore, Serafino.*

Corvo (128) Italian: from *corvo* 'raven', 'rook' (Latin *corvus*), applied as a nickname for someone thought to resemble the bird in some way.

GIVEN NAMES Italian 13%; Spanish 11%. *Salvatore* (2), *Amerigo, Gaetano; Adela* (3), *Mario* (2), *Ana, Caridad, Humberto, Roberto, Rogelio, Rutilio.*

Corwell (111) English: possibly a habitational name from Cornwell in Oxfordshire, which in early medieval records is sometimes written without the *-n-*, for example *Corwelle* (see CORNWELL).

Corwin (2925) English: variant of CORDON.

Cory (2267) English: variant spelling of COREY.

Coryea (126) Variant of Portuguese CORREIA.

Coryell (751) Probably an altered form of French **Querelle** 'quarrel', a nickname for a quarrelsome man.

FOREBEARS The earliest record of the name in North America is of Abraham Coriell, in Piscataway, NJ, in 1702. Family tradition says that he was a Huguenot from Orleans in France, who fled to the Netherlands in 1685, when French Protestants were openly persecuted after the revocation of the Edict of Nantes, and subsequently made his way to North America.

Corzine (542) Altered form, under Dutch influence, of a French (Huguenot) name, **Corsin** or **Corsine**, of uncertain origin.

Corzo (174) Spanish (Seville and Córdoba) and Galician: from *corzo* 'roe deer', probably applied as a nickname for someone who was timid or fleet of foot, or alternatively as

a habitational name from places named with this word in A Coruña (Galicia) and Seville.

GIVEN NAMES Spanish 53%. *Juan* (5), *Jose* (4), *Mario* (4), *Miguel* (4), *Caridad* (3), *Luis* (3), *Pedro* (3), *Roberto* (3), *Carlos* (2), *Fernando* (2), *Francisco* (2), *Jorge* (2).

Cosand (108) Americanized spelling of Dutch **Kozandt**, of unexplained origin.

Cosby (3073) English: habitational name from a place in Leicestershire named Cosby, from an Old English personal name *Cossa* + Old Norse *býr* 'farm', 'settlement'.

Coscarelli (114) Southern Italian: from a diminutive of *cosca* 'rib of a leaf', or from the plural of Calabrian *coscarella* 'blackcap' (the bird).

GIVEN NAMES Spanish 6%; Italian 5%. *Alfonso, Cristina, Diego, Eraldo, Generoso; Pasquale, Spartaco.*

Coscia (619) Italian: from *coscia* 'thigh', hence a nickname for someone whose thighs were noteworthy in some way.

GIVEN NAMES Italian 13%. *Angelo* (2), *Gennaro* (2), *Rocco* (2), *Salvatore* (2), *Alessandro, Antonio, Carlo, Carmine, Emanuele, Luciano, Michelina, Raffaele.*

Cosco (132) **1.** Italian: masculinized form of **Cosca**, a topographic name from the Calabrian dialect word *c(u)oscu* 'oak', also 'wood'. **2.** Catalan (**Coscó**): topographic name for someone who lived by a dwarf holm oak, Catalan *coscó*.

GIVEN NAMES Italian 16%. *Gennaro* (2), *Domenic, Franco, Rocco, Salvatore.*

Cose (119) English: unexplained.

Cosens (150) English: variant of COUSINS.

Cosentino (1483) Southern Italian: habitational name for someone from the city of Cosenza (Latin *Consentia*), from an adjectival form of the place name.

GIVEN NAMES Italian 16%. *Salvatore* (10), *Giuseppe* (5), *Antonio* (4), *Giovanni* (4), *Luigi* (4), *Angelo* (3), *Rocco* (3), *Biagio* (2), *Enzo* (2), *Gaetano* (2), *Remo* (2), *Aldo.*

Cosenza (581) Southern Italian: habitational name from the city of Cosenza.

GIVEN NAMES Italian 20%. *Salvatore* (4), *Mario* (3), *Pasquale* (3), *Aldo* (2), *Duilio* (2), *Adamo, Angelo, Antonio, Camillo, Carmine, Cesare, Cosmo, Dante, Liborio, Ricardo.*

Cosey (318) **1.** English: variant of COSSEY. **2.** Perhaps also an Americanized spelling of French **Cossé** (see COSSE).

Cosgrave (183) English and Irish: variant of COSGROVE.

Cosgray (104) Irish: variant of Irish COSGROVE.

Cosgriff (246) Irish: variant of COSGROVE 2.

Cosgrove (3929) **1.** English: habitational name from Cosgrove in Northamptonshire, named with an Old English personal name *Cōf* + Old English *grāf* 'grove', 'thicket'. **2.** Irish: surname adopted from English by bearers of the Gaelic name **Ó Coscraigh**

'descendant of *Coscrach*', a byname meaning 'victorious', 'triumphant' (from *coscur* 'victory', 'triumph').

Cosio (275) **1.** Spanish: perhaps a habitational name from Cosio in Santander province. **2.** Italian: habitational name from any of many minor places named with this word, which is probably from the Latin personal name *Cosius.*

GIVEN NAMES Spanish 44%; Italian 6%. *Jose* (11), *Francisco* (5), *Juan* (5), *Roberto* (4), *Armando* (3), *Enrique* (3), *Jesus* (3), *Miguel* (3), *Raul* (3), *Alberto* (2), *Eduardo* (2), *Fernando* (2); *Dario* (2), *Lorenzo* (2), *Antonio, Carina, Carmela, Leonardo, Mauro.*

Coskey (113) Irish: reduced form of McCOSKEY.

Coslett (175) Welsh: variant spelling of **Corslett**, a name of unexplained etymology said to have been taken to Wales from Germany. The name, also written **Cosslett**, is currently found in north Wales and nearby Liverpool. This does not have the form of a German name; it may be an unrecognizably altered form of a German name, or it may have reached Germany from somewhere else.

Cosma (146) **1.** Romanian and Italian: from the personal name *Cosma* (from Latin *Cosmas*, Greek *Kosmas*, a derivative of *kosmos* 'order', 'arrangement', 'ordered universe'). St. Cosmas was martyred together with his brother Damian in Cilicia in the early 4th century AD. Together, they came to be widely revered as patron saints of doctors. See also DAMIAN. **2.** Possibly a shortened form of the Greek family names **Cosmaïdis** or **Cosmadopoulos**, all formed from the personal name *Kosmas.*

GIVEN NAMES Romanian 5%. *Iulian, Mihai, Nicolae.*

Cosman (313) Probably an Americanized spelling of North German and Jewish KOSMAN.

Cosme (504) Spanish, Portuguese, and French: from the personal name *Cosmé* (see COSMA).

GIVEN NAMES Spanish 46%. *Jose* (13), *Luis* (10), *Angel* (9), *Juan* (9), *Manuel* (6), *Francisco* (5), *Luz* (5), *Pedro* (5), *Carlos* (4), *Roberto* (4), *Armando* (3), *Carolina* (3); *Antonio* (2), *Angelo, Carlo, Francesca, Savino.*

Cosmo (107) Italian: from the personal name *Cosmo*, an altered form of COSMA, with the regular masculine ending *-o.*

GIVEN NAMES Italian 11%. *Vito* (2), *Donato.*

Cosmos (101) Greek: from an altered form of the personal name *Cosmas* (see COSMO).

Cosner (895) Americanized form of German KASSNER, **Köstner** or **Kostner** (see KOSTNER), or KASTNER.

Cosper (919) Altered form of CASPER.

Coss (1044) Respelling of German and Slavic KOSS.

Cossaboon (107) Probably an Americanized form of Dutch and North German **Kassebohm** 'cherry tree' (see German KASSEBAUM, KIRSCHBAUM).

Cossairt (160) **1.** Variant spelling of Dutch **Cossaert**, probably a nickname for a confidante, sweetheart, or flatterer, from an agent derivative of Middle Dutch *cosen* 'to whisper'. **2.** perhaps also a variant of the French nickname **Cossard** 'lazybones', 'idle fellow'.

Cosse (148) **1.** French (**Cossé**): habitational name from Cossé-d'Anjou in Maine-et-Loire, Cossé-en-Champagne, or Cossé-le-Vivien in Mayenne, all of which are named with the Romano-Gallic personal name *Cocceius* + the locative suffix *-acum*. **2.** French: from *cosse* 'pod', probably a nickname or perhaps a metonymic occupational name for a grower or seller of peas and similar vegetables. **3.** Greek: unexplained. Possibly the French surname, or an Americanized reduced form of COSTAS or some other surname beginning with *Cost-*.
GIVEN NAMES French 10%; Greek 7%. *Easton, Francois, Jacques, Jean-Paul, Stephane; Spiro* (4).

Cossette (558) French: from a diminutive of COSSE 2.
GIVEN NAMES French 11%. *Yves* (3), *Irby* (2), *Pierre* (2), *Florent, Gaston, Gillis, Jean-Yves, Ludger, Marcel, Marie Paule, Micheline, Normand.*

Cossey (764) **1.** English: perhaps a habitational name (reduced form) from Costessey in Norfolk, named with an Old English or Old Norse personal name *Cost* + Old English *ēg* 'island', 'dry ground in a marsh'. **2.** Americanized spelling of French **Cossé** (see COSSE).

Cossin (153) Variant of French or English COUSIN.

Cossio (168) Spanish: possibly a variant of COSIO.
GIVEN NAMES Spanish 56%. *Juan* (4), *Luis* (4), *Jose* (3), *Manuel* (3), *Alejandra* (2), *Alvaro* (2), *Antolin* (2), *Elvira* (2), *Jaime* (2), *Jesus* (2), *Jorge* (2), *Miguel* (2).

Cossman (141) Respelling of German KOSSMAN or Jewish **Kosman**.

Cosson (159) Variant of French COUSIN.
GIVEN NAME French 5%. *Andre.*

Cost (540) **1.** Variant spelling of German and Dutch KOST or German KAST. **2.** Perhaps also an altered spelling of French COSTE.

Costa (10845) Portuguese, Catalan, Italian, and southern French: **1.** topographic name for someone who lived on a slope or river bank, or on the coast (ultimately from Latin *costa* 'rib', 'side', 'flank', also used in a transferred topographical sense), or a habitational name from any of numerous places named Costa or named with this word. **2.** of Greek origin (see COSTAS).
GIVEN NAMES Spanish 13%; Portuguese 7%; Italian 7%. *Manuel* (170), *Jose* (105),

Carlos (42), *Mario* (40), *Luis* (30), *Fernando* (21), *Ana* (13), *Francisco* (13), *Julio* (13), *Eduardo* (11), *Jorge* (11), *Marcos* (11); *Joao* (27), *Joaquim* (11), *Paulo* (9), *Duarte* (5), *Vasco* (3), *Adao* (2), *Albano* (2), *Anabela* (2), *Marcio* (2), *Margarida* (2), *Serafim* (2), *Aderito*; *Antonio* (92), *Angelo* (36), *Salvatore* (25), *Rocco* (8), *Sal* (7), *Domenic* (5), *Giovanni* (5), *Giuseppe* (5), *Guido* (5), *Luciano* (5), *Pasquale* (5), *Pietro* (5).

Costabile (327) Southern Italian: **1.** occupational name from medieval Greek *kontostablēs* 'chamberlain', from medieval Latin *comes stabuli*, literally 'count of the stable' (see CONSTABLE). **2.** from the southern Italian personal name *Costabile*, from Late Latin *Constabilis* meaning 'determined', 'resolute'.
GIVEN NAMES Italian 17%. *Aldo* (3), *Antonio* (2), *Ciro* (2), *Nino* (2), *Agnese, Angelo, Duilio, Enrico, Ercole, Franco, Palma.*

Costagliola (121) Southern Italian (Sicily): topographic name from Sicilian *custigghiola* 'moderate slope', 'gentle incline', or *custigghiula* 'stony infertile ground'.
GIVEN NAMES Italian 39%. *Salvatore* (4), *Domenic* (2), *Gennaro* (2), *Sal* (2), *Angelo, Aniello, Antonio, Domenico, Francesco, Giovanni, Giro, Luigi.*

Costain (168) **1.** Scottish and Irish: Anglicized form of Gaelic **Mac Austain** 'son of Austin' (see AUSTIN). **2.** English: from a reduced form of CONSTANT or CONSTANTINE.

Costales (320) Spanish: possibly from the plural of *costal* 'bag'.
GIVEN NAMES Spanish 29%. *Manuel* (6), *Fernando* (4), *Roberto* (4), *Jorge* (3), *Alejandro* (2), *Ildo* (2), *Mariano* (2), *Teresita* (2), *Adalid, Aida, Alberto, Angel.*

Costantini (474) Southern Italian: patronymic or plural form of COSTANTINO.
GIVEN NAMES Italian 34%. *Mario* (6), *Antonio* (6), *Angelo* (3), *Dario* (3), *Luigi* (3), *Agostino* (2), *Dino* (2), *Domenic* (2), *Fedele* (2), *Ivano* (2), *Octavio* (2), *Siro* (2), *Adelmo, Arnaldo, Camillo, Carlo, Eugenio, Fabio, Gaspar, Lino.*

Costantino (1005) Southern Italian: from the personal name *Costantino* (see CONSTANTINE).
GIVEN NAMES Italian 17%. *Salvatore* (9), *Antonio* (7), *Aldo* (5), *Angelo* (5), *Gino* (4), *Rocco* (4), *Carmela* (2), *Carmine* (2), *Sal* (2), *Saverio* (2), *Silvio* (2), *Umberto* (2).

Costanza (1177) Italian: from the female personal name *Costanza*, from Latin *Constantia* (see CONSTANCE).
GIVEN NAMES Italian 15%. *Angelo* (7), *Salvatore* (7), *Sal* (5), *Vito* (5), *Rocco* (4), *Santo* (4), *Francesco* (2), *Ignazio* (2), *Luigi* (2), *Nino* (2), *Agostino, Benedetto.*

Costanzo (2210) Italian: from the personal name *Costanzo*, from Latin *Constantius* (see CONSTANT).

GIVEN NAMES Italian 18%. *Angelo* (23), *Salvatore* (11), *Sal* (6), *Carmine* (5), *Francesco* (5), *Gaetano* (5), *Rocco* (5), *Santo* (5), *Dino* (4), *Antonio* (3), *Dante* (3), *Costantino* (2).

Costas (417) **1.** Portuguese and Catalan: variant (plural) of COSTA. The Catalan form is a respelling (probably Castilianization) of Catalan **Costes**, of the same origin. **2.** Greek: from the personal name *Kostas*, a reduced form of *Konstantinos* (see CONSTANTINE).
GIVEN NAMES Spanish 14%. *Carlos* (5), *Rafael* (3), *Angel* (2), *Jose* (2), *Manuel* (2), *Marina* (2), *Ramiro* (2), *Agapito, Alfonso, Ana Maria, Andres, Antulio.*

Coste (180) French: variant of **Côte** (see COTE).
GIVEN NAMES French 14%; Spanish 5%. *Jean-Francois* (2), *Philippe* (2), *Pierre* (2), *Antoine, Aurel, Gisele, Henri; Alberto, Ana, Gonzalo, Juan, Luis, Miguelina, Rafael, Ramon, Ricardo.*

Costea (101) Romanian: unexplained.
GIVEN NAMES Romanian 9%; Russian 5%. *Vasile* (2), *Ionel; Andrei, Gavril.*

Costella (159) Italian: probably from a diminutive of COSTA.
GIVEN NAMES Italian 14%. *Armando, Aurelio, Dario, Enrico, Fernando, Reno, Rocco, Teodoro, Tino.*

Costello (12006) Irish: reduced Anglicized form of Gaelic **Mac Oisdealbhaigh** 'son of *Oisdealbhach*', a personal name composed of the elements *os* 'deer', 'fawn' + *dealbhach* 'in the form of', 'resembling'.
GIVEN NAMES Irish 4%. *Brendan* (9), *Declan* (2), *John Patrick* (2), *Seamus* (2), *Siobhan* (2), *Conley, Fergus, Liam, Mairead, Sean Patrick.*

Costen (181) English: variant spelling of COSTAIN.

Costenbader (130) Variant spelling of German KOSTENBADER.

Coster (587) **1.** English: metonymic occupational name for a grower or seller of *costards* (Anglo-Norman French, from *coste* 'rib'), a variety of large apples, so called for their prominent ribs. In some cases, it may have been a nickname (from the same word) for a person with an apple-shaped (i.e. round) head. **2.** Dutch: status name for a churchwarden, from Late Latin *custor* 'guard', 'warden'. **3.** Variant spelling of German KOSTER.
FOREBEARS This name is recorded in Beverwijck in New Netherland (Albany, NY) in the mid 17th century.

Costigan (956) Irish: Anglicized form of Gaelic **Mac Oistigín** 'son of *Oistigín*', which Woulfe says is from English *Hodgkin*, a pet form of ROGER.
GIVEN NAMES Irish 5%. *Caitlin, Donal.*

Costilla (242) Spanish: perhaps from *costilla* 'rib', but more likely from a derivative of COSTA.

GIVEN NAMES Spanish 52%. *Jesus* (5), *Jose* (5), *Manuel* (5), *Juan* (4), *Emilio* (3), *Lupe* (3), *Ana Maria* (2), *Andres* (2), *Arturo* (2), *Domingo* (2), *Javier* (2), *Marcelino* (2).

Costilow (150) Irish: probably a variant spelling of COSTELLO.

Costin (692) English: variant of COSTAIN.

Costine (139) Irish and Scottish: variant of COSTAIN.

Costley (638) Irish: variant of COSTELLO.

Costlow (418) Irish: reduced form of COSTELLO.

Costner (919) Respelling of German KOSTNER or KASTNER.

Coston (1409) French: from a diminutive of Old French *coste* 'slope', 'riverbank', 'coast' (see COTE).

Cota (1850) **1.** Galician: habitational name from any of several places in Galicia named Cota, for example in Lugo province. The place name may be from *cota* 'animal den'. **2.** Variant spelling of German COTTA.

GIVEN NAMES Spanish 19%; Portuguese 5%. *Jose* (19), *Manuel* (17), *Luis* (8), *Ruben* (7), *Carlos* (6), *Jesus* (6), *Francisco* (5), *Alvaro* (4), *Fernando* (4), *Rafael* (4), *Ramon* (4), *Alfonso* (3); *Joao, Paulo, Sebastiao*.

Cote (8719) **1.** French (**Côte**): topographic name for someone who lived on a slope or riverbank, less often on the coast, from Old French *coste* (Latin *costa* 'rib', 'side', 'flank', also used in a transferred topographical sense). There are several places in France named with this word, and the surname may also be a habitational name from any of these. **2.** English: topographic name from Middle English *cote, cott* 'shelter', 'cottage' (see COATES).

GIVEN NAMES French 14%. *Armand* (32), *Marcel* (28), *Normand* (25), *Andre* (24), *Emile* (16), *Laurent* (15), *Michel* (11), *Pierre* (11), *Jacques* (10), *Lucien* (10), *Fernand* (9), *Monique* (9).

Cotey (119) French (Burgundy): from a reduced pet form of *Nicot* or *Jacot*, pet forms of *Nicolas* (see NICHOLAS) and JACQUES.

Cotham (349) English (Merseyside): variant of COTTON.

Cotherman (101) Americanized spelling of German **Kothermann** or **Köthermann**, a habitational name for someone from a place called Köthen (earlier *Kothen*).

Cothern (711) Probably a variant of English CAWTHORNE.

Cothran (1560) **1.** Probably a variant of Scottish COCHRAN. **2.** Perhaps also a variant of English CAWTHORNE.

Cothren (579) **1.** Probably a variant of Scottish COCHRAN. **2.** Perhpas also a variant of English CAWTHORNE.

Cothron (393) **1.** Probably a variant of Scottish COCHRAN. **2.** Perhaps also a variant of English CAWTHORNE.

Cotler (155) **1.** Jewish (eastern Ashkenazic): occupational name from Yiddish *kotler* 'kettlemaker', 'boilermaker'. **2.** Americanized spelling of German **Kot(t)ler, Köttler**, or the variant **Kattler** (see KOTTLER).

GIVEN NAME Jewish 6%. *Sol*.

Cotman (231) **1.** English: status name for a cottager (see COTTER 2), or a topographic name for someone who lived in a relatively humble dwelling, from Middle English *cote, cott* + *man* (see COATES). **2.** Respelling of German KOTHMANN, **Kottmann** (see KOTTMAN), or **Kathmann** (see KATHMAN).

Cotner (979) Probably an Americanized spelling of German **Kötner** or **Köthner**, status names for a cotter, derived from Middle High German, Middle Low German *kote* 'shelter', 'cottage', specifically of a kind that was rented on a daily basis and had little or no land with it. See KOTH 1.

Cotney (250) Possibly English or Irish; perhaps a variant spelling of COURTNEY. This is an AL name.

Cotnoir (234) French: unexplained.

GIVEN NAMES French 23%. *Alain* (3), *Armand* (3), *Luc* (3), *Marcel* (3), *Yves* (2), *Adelard, Alphonse, Andre, Emile, Gilles, Pierre, Serge*.

Coto (309) Spanish and Galician: habitational name from any of various places named Coto, for example in Ciudad Real and Pontevedra provinces.

GIVEN NAMES Spanish 47%. *Jose* (13), *Manuel* (7), *Luis* (6), *Miguel* (5), *Carlos* (4), *Raul* (4), *Alberto* (3), *Armando* (3), *Juan* (3), *Marta* (3), *Rafael* (3), *Alba* (2).

Cotrell (112) English: variant spelling of COTTRELL.

Cotrone (149) Italian: habitational name for someone from Crotone, which was formerly (until 1929) called *Cotrone*.

GIVEN NAMES Italian 18%. *Luca* (2), *Vito* (2), *Angelo, Mafalda, Nunzio, Salvatore*.

Cotroneo (210) Italian: habitational name for someone from Crotone in Calabria, from an adjectival form of COTRONE.

GIVEN NAMES Italian 23%. *Rocco* (3), *Domenic* (2), *Salvatore* (2), *Angelo, Antonino, Antonio, Cosmo, Gaetano, Pasquale*.

Cott (282) **1.** English: from the Old English personal name *Cotta*. **2.** Possibly an altered spelling of French **Cotte**, a metonymic occupational name for a maker of chain mail, from Old French *cot(t)e* 'coat of mail', 'surcoat'. It may perhaps have been used as a nickname for a hard and unfeeling person, but is unlikely to have been a nickname for a wearer of a coat of mail, since only the richest classes, who already had distinguished family names of their own, could afford such protection. A later meaning of *cotte* is a long-sleeved garment, worn by both men and women. **3.** Alternatively, possibly an altered spelling of French **Cot**, from a reduced form of *Jacot* or *Nicot*, pet forms of JACQUES and *Nicolas* (see NICHOLAS). **4.** Respelling of German KOTH or the variant **Kott**.

Cotta (330) **1.** Portuguese and Spanish: possibly a nickname from *cota* 'breast armor'. **2.** Italian: from a short form of a personal name formed with the suffix *-cotta*, as for example *Ciccotta*, or a nickname from *cotta* '(ecclesiastical) habit'. **3.** French and: from medieval Latin *cotta*, Old French *cotte*, denoting a kind of long-sleeved tunic worn both by men and women, hence possibly an occupational name for someone who made such garments or a nickname for someone who habitually wore one. **4.** German: habitational name from either of two places named Cotta, near Pirna and near Dresden in Saxony.

GIVEN NAMES Spanish 5%. *Manuel* (7), *Albino, Alfonso, Margarita*.

Cottage (102) English (Cambridgeshire): unexplained; apparently from Norman French *cotage*, perhaps denoting the status of a cotter (see COTTER 2).

Cottam (367) English (chiefly Lancashire): variant of COTTON.

Cotten (2089) **1.** English: variant spelling of COTTON. **2.** Possibly an altered spelling of German **Kotten**, a habitational name from any of several places so named in Rhineland, Westphalia, Silesia, etc., or an Americanized shortened form of composite German surnames such as **Kottenhagen, Kottenhoff, Kottenkamp** (see KOTH).

Cotter (4978) **1.** Irish (co. Cork): reduced Anglicized form of Gaelic **Mac Oitir** 'son of *Oitir*', a personal name borrowed from Old Norse *Óttarr*, composed of the elements *ótti* 'fear', 'dread' + *herr* 'army'. **2.** English: status name from Middle English *cotter*, a technical term in the feudal system for a serf or bond tenant who held a cottage by service rather than rent, from Old English *cot* 'cottage', 'hut' (see COATES) + *-er* agent suffix. **3.** Probably an Americanized spelling of German KOTTER.

Cotterell (203) **1.** English: variant of COTTRELL. **2.** Possibly an altered spelling of any of the various French cognates: **Cotterel, Cotterelle, Cottereau, Cothereau**, etc.

Cotterill (194) English: variant of COTTRELL.

Cotterman (451) Probably an Americanized form of German **Kattermann**, a variant of KOTHMANN.

Cottier (175) **1.** English: variant of COTTER 2. **2.** Americanized form of French GAUTHIER.

Cottingham (1555) English: habitational name from either of two places named Cottingham ('homestead (Old English *hām*) of the people of (Old English *-inga-*) of a man named *Cott* or *Cotta*'), one in East Yorkshire and one in Northamptonshire.

Cottle (1698) English: **1.** metonymic occupational name for a maker of chain-mail, from an Anglo-Norman French diminutive of Old French *cot(t)e* 'coat of mail' (see COTT). **2.** metonymic occupational name for a cutler, from Old French *co(u)tel*, *co(u)teau* 'knife' (Late Latin *cultellus*, a diminutive of *culter* 'plowshare').

FOREBEARS Edward Cottle was in Martha's Vineyard, MA, before 1653.

Cottman (320) **1.** English: variant spelling of COTMAN. **2.** Americanized spelling of the German cognates **Kottmann** or KOTH-MANN.

Cotto (628) Spanish and Portuguese: variant spelling of COTO.

GIVEN NAMES Spanish 44%. *Jose* (17), *Angel* (13), *Rafael* (10), *Luis* (9), *Juan* (8), *Pedro* (8), *Luz* (6), *Miguel* (6), *Ramon* (6), *Jorge* (5), *Ana* (4), *Carlos* (4), *Antonio* (3), *Eliseo* (2), *Carmine*, *Eligio*.

Cottom (388) English (chiefly Lancashire): variant of COTTON.

Cotton (9587) **1.** English: habitational name from any of numerous places named from Old English *cotum* (dative plural of *cot*) 'at the cottages or huts' (or sometimes possibly from a Middle English plural, *coten*). Examples include Coton (Cambridgeshire, Northamptonshire, Staffordshire), Cottam (East Yorkshire, Lancashire, Nottinghamshire), and Cotham (Nottinghamshire). **2.** French: from a diminutive of Old French *cot(t)e* 'coat (of mail)' (see COTT).

FOREBEARS John Cotton (1584–1652) was a noted Puritan preacher, who landed at Boston, MA, from London in 1633 and became leader of the Congregationalists in America.

Cottone (650) Southern Italian (Sicily): metonymic occupational name for a dealer in cotton, from Sicilian *cuttuni* 'cotton'.

GIVEN NAMES Italian 21%. *Salvatore* (15), *Giuseppe* (3), *Sal* (3), *Vito* (3), *Damiano* (2), *Pellegrino* (2), *Antonino*, *Calogero*, *Cesare*, *Domenic*, *Filippo*, *Francesca*.

Cottongim (222) Variant of English COT-TINGHAM.

Cottrell (5652) French and English: status name for a cottager, from Old French *coterel*, a diminutive of *cotier* 'cottager' (see COTTER 2).

Cottrill (1137) English: variant spelling of COTTRELL.

Cotts (128) Scottish: variant of COUTTS.

Cotugno (235) Southern Italian (Sicily): from Sicilian *cutugnu* 'quince' (the fruit).

GIVEN NAMES Italian 16%. *Angelo* (3), *Gianluca* (2), *Amedeo*, *Gilda*, *Marino*, *Rocco*.

Coty (482) French: **1.** habitational name from a place named Coty ('old house'). **2.** (Normandy and the west): variant of **Costy**, from Old Norman French *costi* 'hill'.

Couch (9171) **1.** Cornish and Welsh: nickname for a red-haired man, from *cough*, *coch* 'red(-haired)'. Compare GOUGH.

2. English: metonymic occupational name for a maker of beds or bedding, or perhaps a nickname for a lazy man, from Middle English, Old French *couche* 'bed', a derivative of Old French *coucher* 'to lay down', Latin *collocare* 'to place'.

Couchman (465) English: occupational name for a maker of beds or bedding, from Middle English *couche* 'bed' (see COUCH) + *man*.

Couden (109) English and Scottish: variant spelling of COWDEN.

Coudriet (156) French: topographic name from a derivative of *coudrier* 'hazelnut tree'.

Couey (585) Probably an Americanized spelling of French **Coué**, from Old French *coé* 'tail'. According to Morlet during the Middle Ages this was a derogatory nickname for an Englishman, possibly by implication a coward (see note at COWARD).

Coufal (335) **1.** Czech: nickname derived from a dialect form of *couvat* 'to retreat or go backwards', probably applied to a timid or cowardly person. **2.** Variant spelling of German **Coufahl**, an occupational name from Sorbian *kowal* 'blacksmith'. Compare KUFAHL.

Coughenour (514) Probably an Americanized spelling of German **Kochenauer** (see GOCHENOUR).

Coughlan (773) Irish: variant spelling of COUGHLIN.

GIVEN NAMES Irish 7%. *Brendan* (2), *Eamonn* (2), *Dermot*, *Donal*, *Kieran*.

Coughlin (6145) Irish: Anglicized form of Gaelic **Mac Cochláin** (or **Ó Cochláin**) 'son (or descendant) of *Cochlán*', a byname derived from *cochal* 'cloak', 'hood'. The *Mac* form is found chiefly in County Offaly; the *Ó* form in County Cork.

GIVEN NAMES Irish 5%. *Brendan* (5), *Caitlin*, *Conn*, *Conor*, *Delma*, *Eamon*, *Malachy*, *Niall*, *Padraic*, *Sean Patrick*.

Coughran (272) Variant of Scottish COCH-RAN.

Cougill (119) English: variant spelling of COWGILL.

Couillard (588) French: from Old French *coille* 'testicle', hence a nickname for a man with large testicles, later (from the 16th century) for a lusty or vigorous man.

GIVEN NAMES French 7%. *Andre* (2), *Armand* (2), *Emile* (2), *Andree*, *Jean Pierre*, *Laurent*, *Monique*, *Ovide*, *Pierre*, *Remi*, *Yvon*.

Coulbourn (140) English: variant spelling of COLBURN.

Coulbourne (138) English: variant spelling of COLBURN.

Coull (180) Scottish: habitational name from Coull in Aberdeenshire. There is also another place so named, in the Highland Region, which may have given rise to the surname.

Coulombe (886) Southern French: **1.** from Old Occitan *colomb* 'dove' (Latin *colum-*

bus), hence a metonymic occupational name for a keeper of doves, or a nickname for a person of a mild and gentle disposition. **2.** from a personal name of the same origin. The name in its Latin forms *Columbus* and *Columba* was popular among early Christians because the dove was considered to be the symbol of the Holy Spirit.

GIVEN NAMES French 11%. *Lucien* (4), *Armand* (3), *Jacques* (3), *Marcel* (2), *Raoul* (2), *Adrien*, *Andre*, *Chanel*, *Donat*, *Fernand*, *Gilles*, *Henri*.

Coulon (411) French: variant of COULOMBE.

GIVEN NAMES French 9%. *Emile* (2), *Remi* (2), *Antoine*, *Dominique*, *Fernand*, *Jacques*, *Jean-Michael*, *Landry*, *Marcel*.

Coulson (1999) **1.** English: patronymic from COLE 1. **2.** Irish: from a reduced form of McCOOL, with the addition of the English patronymic suffix *-son* in place of the Gaelic prefix *mac*.

Coulston (320) English: variant spelling of COLSTON.

Coultas (371) English (Yorkshire): from early modern English *coulthus* 'stable', a compound of *co(u)lt* 'colt', 'young horse' + *hus* 'house', hence a topographic name or an occupational name for someone who lived or worked at a stables.

Coulter (7700) Scottish and northern Irish: habitational name from Coulter in Lanarkshire or Culter, Aberdeenshire.

Coulthard (267) Northern English and Scottish: occupational name for someone who looked after asses or working horses, Middle English *colthart*, *coltehird*, from Old English *colt* 'ass', 'young horse' + *hierde* 'herdsman'.

Coulton (173) English (Lancashire): habitational name from a place in North Yorkshire named Coulton, probably from Old English *col* '(char)coal' + *tūn* 'enclosure', 'settlement'.

Counce (334) Americanized spelling of German **Kauntz**, a variant of KUNTZ, or of Dutch **Coensz**, **Koensz**, a patronymic form of COEN.

Council (1837) **1.** English: nickname for a wise or thoughtful man, from Anglo-Norman French *counseil* 'consultation', 'deliberation', also 'counsel', 'advice' (Latin *consilium*, from *consulere* 'to consult'). This form was probably influenced by the similar meaning of Anglo-Norman French *councile* 'council', 'assembly' (Latin *concilium* 'assembly', from the archaic verb *concalere* 'to call together', 'to summon'), and it may also have been an occupational name for a member of a royal council or, more probably, a manorial council. **2.** Americanized spelling of German **Künzel** (see KUENZEL).

Councill (147) English: variant spelling of COUNCIL.

Councilman (214) Americanized form of German **Kunzelmann** or the variant

Konzelmann (see KUNSELMAN), or possibly a translation of RATHMANN.

Counihan (291) Irish: Anglicized form of Gaelic **Ó Cuanacháin**, from a diminutive of the personal name *Cuana* (see COONEY).

Counsell (207) English: variant spelling of COUNCIL.

Counselman (159) See COUNCILMAN.

Counter (357) English (Devon): occupational name for a treasurer or accountant, from Middle English *counter* (from Old French *conteor*).

Counterman (327) **1.** Probably an Americanized spelling of German **Kundermann**, a nickname for a devilish person, from Middle High German *kunder* 'monster' + *man* 'man', or an altered form of **Kondermann**, a habitational name for someone from Kondrau in Bavaria. **2.** The surname is found in England, though now rare, and may be an occupational name meaning 'servant of the accountant', from Middle English *countour* 'accountant' (see COUNTER) + *man* 'servant'.

Countess (129) English: from Middle English *contas(e)*, Old French *contesse* 'countess', applied as a nickname for a proud, haughty woman or for an effeminate or foppish man, or as an occupational name for a servant of a countess.

Countiss (115) English: variant spelling of COUNTESS.

Countryman (1521) Translation of German **Landmann**, **Landsmann** or Dutch **Landman**, **Landsman** (see LANDSMAN).

Counts (3463) Americanized spelling of a Dutch patronymic from COEN or of German KUNTZ. Compare COONS.

Coup (193) **1.** English: variant spelling of COUPE. **2.** Possibly an Americanized form of German KAUP.

Coupal (106) Possibly an altered spelling of French **Coupel**, from a diminutive of *coupe*, from Latin *cuppa* a measure of grain.
GIVEN NAMES French 16%. *Armand, Fernande, Germaine, Jacques, Pierre.*

Coupe (383) English (mainly Lancashire): variant spelling of COOP.

Couper (169) Scottish: **1.** habitational name from Cupar in Fife, which is probably of Pictish origin, with an unknown meaning. There are several other places similarly named, for example Couper Angus and Cupar Maculty (now Couttie), but these do not seem to have given rise to surnames. **2.** English: variant spelling of COOPER.

Coupland (244) English and Scottish: variant of COPELAND.

Courage (114) English: **1.** from Middle English *corage*, Old French *corage, curage* in the sense 'stout (of body)'. **2.** habitational name from Cowridge End in Luton, Bedfordshire, reflecting a former pronunciation of the place name. **3.** possibly a variant of KENDRICK 3, via a hypothetical variant, **Kenwright**.

Courchaine (218) Respelling of French COURCHESNE.
GIVEN NAMES French 5%. *Marcelle* (2), *Armand.*

Courchesne (181) French: probably a topographic name for someone living at a farm with an oak tree in the farmyard, from French *court* 'farmyard' + *chesne* 'oak'.
GIVEN NAMES French 20%. *Armand* (2), *Aime, Andre, Aurel, Emile, Gaston, Germain, Gilles, Jean-Claude, Marcel, Marcelle.*

Courcy (141) French: habitational name from any of the places in Calvados, Loiret, Manche, and Marne called Courcy.
GIVEN NAMES French 14%. *Alphonse, Andree, Jacques, Michel, Monique.*

Courey (127) Probably an altered spelling of French **Coury**, a habitational name from a place so named in Vienne.

Couri (104) **1.** Variant spelling of French **Courie**, a habitational name from a place called Courie, in Allier or Loiret. **2.** Finnish: unexplained.
GIVEN NAME French 4%. *Emile.*

Courier (157) French: occupational name for a messenger.

Courington (223) Probably a variant of English CURRINGTON.

Courneya (129) Variant of French CURNOYER.

Cournoyer (953) French: unexplained. **1.** Perhaps an altered spelling of **Corneyre**, a 'learned' form of **Cornier**, a topographic name for someone who lived on the corner of a street. **2.** Alternatively, it may be a French form of German KOERNER.

Coursen (273) Possibly an altered spelling of Dutch **Corsen**, attested in records of New Netherland, or perhaps an altered spelling of the French habitational names COURSON or **Coursan**, from either of two places so called, in Aude and Aube, both named for a Romano-Gallic landlord *Curtenus* (a derivative of Latin *curtus* 'short') + the locative suffix *-anum*.

Courser (186) Possibly an altered spelling of French **Coursier**, an occupational name for a messenger or runner, Old French *coursier*; alternatively it may be an Americanized spelling of German **Kurzer**, a nickname for a short man, from a noun derivative of Middle High German *kur(t)z* 'short'.

Coursey (1334) Irish (of Norman origin): habitational name from any of various places in northern France called Courcy, from the Romano-Gallic personal name *Curtius* (a derivative of *curtus* 'short') + the locative suffix *-acum*. Compare DECOURSEY.

Courson (1150) **1.** French: habitational name from either of two places named Courson, in Calvados and Essonne, from the personal name *Curtenus* (a derivative of Latin *curtus* 'short') + the locative suffix *-onem*, or from a place in Yonne named with the same personal name + Gaulish *dunum* meaning 'pride'; later, 'fortress', 'stronghold'. **2.** See COURSEN.

Court (945) **1.** English and French: topographic name from Middle English, Old French *court(e), curt* 'court' (Latin *cohors*, genitive *cohortis*, 'yard', 'enclosure'). This word was used primarily with reference to the residence of the lord of a manor, and the surname is usually an occupational name for someone employed at a manorial court. **2.** English: nickname from Old French, Middle English *curt* 'short', 'small' (Latin *curtus* 'curtailed', 'truncated', 'cut short', 'broken off'). **3.** Irish: reduced form of McCOURT.

Courtade (153) Southern French: topographic or occupational name, from an Occitan word meaning 'court', 'residence'.

Courteau (176) Altered spelling of the Huguenot name **Courtauld**, according to Dauzat, a nickname from a diminutive of French *court* 'short', 'small'.
GIVEN NAMES French 12%. *Alphonse, Girard, Ludger, Olivier, Ovila, Stephane.*

Courtemanche (663) French: apparently a nickname from *court* 'short' + *manche* 'sleeve'.
GIVEN NAMES French 9%. *Emile* (2), *Amedee, Andre, Armand, Fernand, Herve, Lucien, Marcel, Normand, Ovide, Raoul.*

Courtenay (188) English and Irish: variant spelling of COURTNEY.

Courter (998) French: probably an altered spelling of COUTURE.

Courtier (100) French: habitational name from places called Courtier (Seine-et-Marne, Aples-de-Haute-Provence), Courtié (Tarn), or Courtière (Loir-et-Cher).
GIVEN NAME French 4%. *Patrice.*

Courtland (98) Americanized form of Dutch **Kortland**: from a village called Cortlandt near Wijk bij Duurstede.
FOREBEARS Oloff Stevenszen van Cortland (1600–79), who became a prominent merchant in New Amsterdam, arrived there in 1638.

Courtney (9758) **1.** English (of Norman origin): habitational name from Courtenay near Sens in northern France, or some other place similarly named, from the name of a Romano-Gallic landlord, *Curtenus* (a derivative of Latin *curtus* 'short') + the locative suffix *-acum*. **2.** English (of Norman origin): nickname for someone with a snub nose, from Old French *c(o)urt* 'short' + *nes* 'nose' (Latin *nasus*). **3.** Irish: English surname adopted by bearers of Gaelic **Ó Curnáin** 'descendant of *Curnán*', an Old Irish personal name from a diminutive of *corn* 'horn'.

Courtois (413) French: nickname for a refined person, sometimes no doubt applied ironically, from Old French *curteis, co(u)rtois* 'refined', 'accomplished'.

GIVEN NAMES French 9%. *Jacques* (2), *Marcel* (2), *Gislaine, Luc, Pierre, Renald, Stephane.*

Courtright (1124) **1.** Americanized form of Dutch **Kortrijk**, a habitational name from a place of this name in Flanders. **2.** Perhaps also a respelling of English CARTWRIGHT.

Courts (494) **1.** English: patronymic form of COURT. **2.** Americanized spelling of German KURTZ.

Courtwright (256) **1.** See KORTRIGHT. **2.** Possibly an altered spelling of English CARTWRIGHT.

Courville (1181) French: habitational name from either of two places in Marne and Eure-et-Loir, named with Latin *curba villa*, denoting a settlement in the curve of a road.
GIVEN NAMES French 7%. *Andre* (4), *Raoul* (2), *Alberie, Alcee, Alexandre, Calice, Cecile, Chantelle, Curley, Elrick, Fernest, Flavien.*

Coury (663) **1.** Irish: reduced and altered form of MCCORRY. **2.** French: habitational name from a place in Vienne named Coury.

Cousar (276) Scottish (Ayrshire): variant spelling of COUSER.

Couse (234) English: **1.** from the medieval northern English personal name *Kouse, Kause*, corresponding to Old Norse *Kausi*, a nickname meaning 'tomcat'. **2.** Possibly an Americanized spelling of German KAUS or **Ku(h)se**, which is of unexplained origin.

Cousens (177) English: patronymic form of COUSIN.

Couser (311) Scottish and northern Irish: unexplained.

Cousin (700) English and French: nickname from Middle English, Old French *co(u)sin, cusin* (Latin *consobrinus*), which in the Middle Ages, as in Shakespearean English, had the general meaning 'relative', 'kinsman'. The surname would thus have denoted a person related in some way to a prominent figure in the neighborhood. In some cases it may also have been a nickname for someone who used the term 'cousin' frequently as a familiar term of address. The old slang word *cozen* 'cheat', perhaps derives from the medieval confidence trickster's use of the word *cousin* as a term of address to invoke a spurious familiarity. The patronymics constitute the most frequent forms of this name.
GIVEN NAMES French 5%. *Jacques* (2), *Emile, Jeanpaul, Serge.*

Cousineau (870) French: from a derivative of Old French *co(u)sin, cusin* 'cousin' (see COUSIN).
GIVEN NAMES French 10%. *Marcel* (4), *Pierre* (3), *Monique* (2), *Alain, Alcide, Anatole, Andre, Armand, Colombe, Emile, Francoise, Gilles.*

Cousino (770) Altered spelling of French COUSINEAU.

Cousins (2986) English: patronymic from the nickname COUSIN.

Coussens (119) Possibly a respelling of French COUSIN or **Coussin**, a metonymic occupational name for a cushion maker, from Old French *coissin* 'cushion'.
GIVEN NAMES French 7%. *Remi* (2), *Prudent, Remy.*

Coutant (197) French: variant of CONSTANT.
GIVEN NAMES French 6%. *Gabrielle, Serge, Sylvie.*

Coutee (227) Possibly a respelling of French **Couteau** (see COUTU).

Coutinho (195) Portuguese: diminutive of COUTO. This name is also found in western India, where it was taken by Portuguese colonists.
GIVEN NAMES Spanish 19%; Portuguese 13%. *Manuel* (4), *Jose* (3), *Adriano* (2), *Jesus* (2), *Pedro* (2), *Armando, Augusto, Decio, Eusebio, Fabiola, Fernando, Luiz; Agostinho, Joaquim, Terezinha.*

Couto (720) **1.** Portuguese: habitational name from any of numerous places so named or named with *couto* 'enclosed pasture' (Late Latin *cautum*, from the past participle of *cavere* 'to make safe'). In some cases the name may be topographic. **2.** Possibly an altered spelling of French *Couteau* (see COUTU).
GIVEN NAMES Spanish 25%; Portuguese 16%. *Jose* (22), *Manuel* (21), *Carlos* (6), *Luis* (5), *Horacio* (4), *Jorge* (4), *Mario* (4), *Ernesto* (3), *Juan* (3), *Miguel* (3), *Sergio* (3), *Armando* (2); *Joao* (4), *Agostinho* (3), *Guilherme* (2), *Joaquim* (2), *Adao, Albano, Duarte, Henrique, Margarida, Serafim, Sil, Valentim; Antonio* (22), *Guido.*

Couts (382) **1.** Scottish: variant spelling of COUTTS. **2.** Possibly an Americanized spelling of the German family names KUTZ or KAUTZ.

Coutts (635) Scottish: habitational name from Cults in Aberdeenshire, named with Gaelic *cuilt* 'nook', with the later addition of the English plural *-s*.

Coutu (657) Of French origin: probably an altered form of **Couteau**, a metonymic occupational name for a knifemaker, from *couteau* 'knife'.
GIVEN NAMES French 14%. *Andre* (3), *Armand* (3), *Marcel* (3), *Adrien* (2), *Gilles* (2), *Girard* (2), *Normand* (2), *Fernand, Florent, Laurent, Michel, Ovila.*

Couture (3366) French: **1.** metonymic occupational name for a tailor, from Old French *cousture* 'seam' (Latin *consutura*, from *(con)suere* 'to sew (together)'). **2.** metonymic occupational name for a holder of a smallholding, Old French *couture* 'small plot', 'kitchen garden' (Late Latin *cultura*, in classical Latin used in the abstract sense 'cultivation', 'agriculture', from *colere* 'to till or tend').
GIVEN NAMES French 14%. *Armand* (13), *Pierre* (13), *Jacques* (10), *Lucien* (9), *Normand* (9), *Andre* (8), *Marcel* (7), *Emile* (5), *Henri* (3), *Luc* (3), *Raoul* (3), *Adrien* (2).

Couturier (576) French: occupational name for either a tailor (from an agent derivative of Old French *cousture* 'seam') or for a smallholder, from an agent derivative of Old French *couture* 'small plot' (see COUTURE).
GIVEN NAMES French 12%. *Marcel* (5), *Adrien* (2), *Fernand* (2), *Achille, Arsene, Carolle, Firmin, Gilles, Gisele, Herve, Jacques, Michel.*

Couvillion (417) French: unexplained; compare COUVILLON, of which this may be a variant.
GIVEN NAMES French 6%. *Andre, Gaston, Jacques, Landry, Lucien, Monique, Oneil, Pierre.*

Couvillon (231) Perhaps an altered form of French **Cavillon**, a habitational name from either of two places so named in Somme and Oise.
GIVEN NAMES French 6%. *Lucien* (2), *Eugenie, Raoul.*

Couzens (183) English: patronymic form of COUSIN.

Cova (110) Catalan and Galician: topographic name from Catalan and Galician *cova* 'cave', or a habitational name from a place named with this word, in the provinces of Lugo, Ourense, Pontevedra, Catalonia and Valencia. Compare CUEVA.
GIVEN NAMES Spanish 20%; Romanian 4%. *Paola* (2), *Alfonso, Carlos, Enrique, Fidel, Guillermo, Josefina, Luis, Luz, Manuel, Mario, Oswaldo, Reno; Vasile* (2).

Coval (182) **1.** Portuguese: habitational name from any of numerous places named Coval, from *coval* 'pit', 'hollow'. **2.** Respelling of KOVAL or KOWAL.
GIVEN NAMES French 4%. *Andre, Serge.*

Covalt (201) Of Dutch origin: see COVAULT.

Covan (103) English: possibly a variant spelling of COVEN.

Covarrubias (1129) Spanish: habitational name from a place in the province of Burgos named Covarrubias. The place name, meaning 'red caves', is from the plural of *cueva* 'cave' (Latin *cova*) + *rubio* 'red' (Latin *rubeus*).
GIVEN NAMES Spanish 55%. *Jose* (36), *Carlos* (20), *Jesus* (14), *Juan* (14), *Javier* (12), *Raul* (12), *Pedro* (11), *Francisco* (9), *Guadalupe* (8), *Jorge* (8), *Luis* (8), *Manuel* (8).

Covault (230) Of Dutch origin, perhaps an Americanized form of **Koevoet.**

Cove (259) English: habitational name from a place named Cove, examples of which are found in Devon, Hampshire, and Suffolk, from Old English *cofa* 'cove', 'bay', 'inlet', also 'shelter', 'hut', or a topographic name with the same meaning.

Covel (247) English: variant spelling of COVELL.

Covell (1237) English: from Old English *cufle* 'cloak', hence a nickname for an habitual wearer of a cloak or perhaps a metonymic occupational name for a cloak maker.

Covelli (384) Italian: patronymic or plural form of COVELLO.

GIVEN NAMES Italian 13%. *Aldo* (2), *Angelo* (2), *Gabriele* (2), *Luigi* (2), *Antonio*, *Caterina*, *Cesare*, *Domenico*, *Elio*, *Guido*, *Marcello*, *Orazio*.

Covello (413) Italian: from the personal name *Covello*, a diminutive of *Iacovo*, with loss of the first syllable. Iacovo is one of many old Italian forms of JACOB, now preserved only in surnames.

GIVEN NAMES Italian 14%. *Guiseppe* (2), *Nunzio* (2), *Rocco* (2), *Angelo*, *Calogero*, *Carlo*, *Gaspare*, *Gasper*, *Geno*, *Gino*, *Gioacchino*, *Lia*.

Coven (239) English: **1.** from Old French *covine* 'fraud', 'deceit', hence a derogatory nickname for a trickster. **2.** habitational name from a place in Staffordshire named Coven '(place) at the huts or shelters (Old English *cofa*, dative plural *cofum*)'.

Coveney (321) English: habitational name from a place in Cambridgeshire named Coveney, from either the genitive case of Old English *cofa* 'shelter' (see COVE) or of a personal name *Cofa* (of uncertain origin) + Old English *ēg* 'island'. The surname is also established in Ireland.

GIVEN NAME Irish 5%. *Eamonn*.

Coventry (296) English: habitational name from the city of Coventry in the West Midlands, which is probably named with the genitive case of an Old English personal name *Cofa* (compare COVENEY) + Old English *trēow* 'tree'.

Coveny (100) English: variant spelling of COVENEY.

Cover (1357) **1.** English: occupational name for a roofer, from Old French *co(u)vreur*, an agent derivative of *co(u)vrir* 'to cover' (Latin *cooperire*). Roofing materials in the Middle Ages might be tiles (see TYLER), slates (see SLATER), or thatch (see THATCHER), depending on the regional availability of suitable materials. **2.** English (of Norman origin): occupational name for a maker of barrels and tubs, from an agent derivative of Middle English, Old French *cuve* 'vat', 'tub' (Late Latin *cupa*, of Germanic origin; compare COOPER). **3.** Americanized spelling of German KOBER.

Coverdale (492) English: habitational name from places named Coverdale in North Yorkshire and Lancashire, 'in the valley (Middle English *dale*) of the Cover river (a Celtic name)'.

Coverdell (106) Variant of English COVERDALE.

Coverstone (134) Americanized form of German KOBERSTEIN. Compare COOPERSTEIN.

Covert (3048) **1.** English: nickname for a reserved or secretive person, from Old French *covert* 'guarded', 'crafty'. **2.** Amer-

icanized spelling of an unidentified Dutch or German name, perhaps KOFOED.

Covey (3202) **1.** Irish: reduced form of **MacCovey**, an Anglicized form of Gaelic **Mac Cobhthaigh** (see COFFEY). **2.** English (Surrey and West Sussex): unexplained.

Coviello (740) Italian: variant of COVELLO.

GIVEN NAMES Italian 15%. *Sal* (5), *Domenic* (4), *Pasquale* (4), *Vito* (4), *Rocco* (3), *Salvatore* (3), *Antonio* (2), *Carmine* (2), *Martino* (2), *Ciriaco*, *Gino*, *Nino*.

Covil (109) English: variant spelling of COVELL.

Covill (222) English: variant spelling of COVELL.

Coville (303) Variant of English COVELL.

Covin (310) **1.** English: unexplained. **2.** French (Walloon): habitational name from Couvin in the Belgian province of Namur.

Covington (7977) **1.** Scottish: habitational name from Covinton in Lanarkshire, first recorded in the late 12th century in the Latin form *Villa Colbani*, and twenty years later as *Colbaynistun*. By 1422 it had been collapsed to *Cowantoun*, and at the end of the 15th century it first appears in the form *Covingtoun*. It is nevertheless clearly named with the personal name *Colban* (see COLEMAN 1) + Old English *tūn* 'enclosure'; Colban was a follower of David, Prince of Cumbria, in about 1120. **2.** English: habitational name from a place in Huntingdonshire (now Cambridgeshire) named Covington, from an Old English personal name *Cofa* + Old English *-ing* denoting association + *tūn* 'settlement'.

Covino (390) Italian: from the personal name *Covino*, a diminutive of *Iacovo*, an old Italian form of JACOB.

GIVEN NAMES Italian 17%. *Angelo* (5), *Salvatore* (5), *Carmine* (3), *Rocco* (3), *Cosmo*, *Enrico*, *Gennaro*, *Guido*, *Nino*, *Vito*.

Covitz (114) Jewish: Americanized spelling of KOWITZ (see KOVICH).

GIVEN NAME Jewish 5%. *Hyman*.

Cowan (12743) Scottish: reduced form of McCOWEN.

Cowans (315) Scottish: variant of COWAN, with redundant English patronymic *-s*.

Coward (2022) English: occupational name for a keeper of cattle, Middle English *cowherde*, Old English *cūhyrde*, from *cū* 'cow' + *hierde* 'herdsman'. (The surname has nothing to do with the modern English word *coward*, which is from Old French *cuard*, a pejorative term from *coue* 'tail' (Latin *cauda*) with reference to an animal with its tail between its legs.)

Cowardin (104) Origin unidentified.

Cowart (3985) Probably a variant of English COWARD. This name is concentrated in GA.

Cowden (1660) English and Scottish: habitational name from any of at least three

places named Cowden. One in Northumbria occurs in 1286 as *Colden* and is derived from Old English *col* '(char)coal' + *denu* 'valley'; that in East Yorkshire occurs in Domesday Book as *Coledun* and is from Old English *col* + *dūn* 'hill'; while one in Kent is recorded in 1160 as *Cudena* and is from Old English *cū* 'cow' + *denn* 'pasture'. The last does not appear to have yielded any surnames; the surname is more or less restricted to northern England, and is also found in northern Ireland, where it may be of Scottish origin, from places called Cowden near Dollar and near Dalkeith, Lothian.

Cowdery (225) English: variant spelling of COWDREY.

Cowdin (143) Variant spelling of COWDEN.

Cowdrey (452) English (of Norman origin): habitational name from Coudrai in Seine-Maritime, France, or Coudray in Eure, France, or from Cowdray or Cowdry in Sussex, England. The latter was probably named after one of the places in France. All are named with Old French *coudraie* 'hazel copse' (a collective noun from *coudre* 'hazelnut tree', Late Latin *colurus*, a metathesized form of classical Latin *corylus*, from Greek *korylos*).

Cowee (105) English: variant of COWEY.

Cowell (2452) **1.** English: habitational name from places in Lancashire and Gloucestershire called Cowhill, from Old English *cū* 'cow' + *hyll* 'hill'. **2.** possibly also an Americanized form of Polish, Jewish, and Sorbian KOWAL.

Cowen (2044) Scottish and northern English: variant spelling of COWAN.

Cowens (110) Scottish and northeastern English: variant spelling of Scottish COWANS.

Cowett (105) Origin unidentified.

Cowey (108) **1.** Southeastern English: habitational name from Cowey Green in Essex. **2.** Northern English: variant spelling of Scottish COWIE, found chiefly in County Durham.

Cowger (748) Americanized form of German GAUGER.

FOREBEARS Bearers of the name **Cowger** are descended from Johan Conrad Gauger, who came to America from Germany in 1736 and settled in Pendleton County, WV.

Cowgill (1026) English (mainly Lancashire): habitational name from any of several places named Cowgill or Cow Gill, for example in Cumbria, Yorkshire, and Lancashire; all are named with Old Norse *gil* 'narrow valley', 'ravine' with various first elements including Old English *cū* 'cow' and Old English *col* '(char)coal'.

Cowher (211) Probably a variant of German GAUGER. This name is concentrated in PA.

Cowherd (496) English: variant of COWARD, perhaps a deliberate respelling by a bearer anxious to avoid association with the unrelated modern English word *coward*.

Cowick (112) English: habitational name from any of various minor places named Cowick. Cowick in Devon and East and West Cowick in East Yorkshire are all named with Old English *cū* 'cow' + *wīc* 'outlying dairy farm'.

Cowie (674) Scottish: habitational name from any of several places, especially one near Stirling, named Cowie, probably from Gaelic *colldha*, an adjective from *coll* 'hazel'.

Cowin (471) Variant spelling of Scottish COWAN.

Cowing (274) Perhaps a variant of Scottish COWIN.

Cowles (2670) English: patronymic form of COLE.

Cowley (2209) **1.** English: habitational name from any of the various places called Cowley. One in Gloucestershire is named with Old English *cū* 'cow' + *lēah* 'woodland clearing'; two in Derbyshire have Old English *col* '(char)coal' as the first element; and one near London has it from Old English *cofa* 'shelter', 'bay' (see COVE) or the personal name *Cofa*. The largest group, however, with examples in Buckinghamshire, Devon, Oxfordshire, and Staffordshire, were apparently named as 'the wood or clearing of *Cufa*'; however, in view of the number of places named with this element, it is possible that it conceals a topographical term as well as a personal name. **2.** Irish: reduced form of **Macaulay** (see MCCAULEY).

Cowling (824) English: variant of COLLING.

Cowlishaw (106) English: habitational name from either of two minor places named Cowlishaw, in Derbyshire and Lancashire.

Cowman (410) English, Scottish, and Irish (of Norman origin): variant of CUMMING.

Cowper (236) Scottish: variant spelling of COUPER.

Cowperthwaite (183) English: habitational name from Copperthwaite in North Yorkshire, which is named with Middle English *coupere* 'maker of wooden buckets and tubs' + *thweit* 'clearing' (from Old Norse *þveit*).

Cowser (222) English: occupational name from Old French *cousere* 'tailor'.

Cowsert (352) Possibly an Americanized spelling of Dutch **Cousaert**, a nickname for a talker, from Middle Dutch *cosen* 'to talk or chatter'.

Cox (94703) **1.** English: from COCKE in any the senses described + the suffix -*s* denoting 'son of' or 'servant of'. **2.** Irish (Ulster): mistranslation of **Mac Con Coille** ('son of *Cú Choille*', a personal name meaning 'hound of the wood'), as if formed with *coileach* 'cock', 'rooster'.

Coxe (522) English: variant spelling of COX.

Coxen (176) English: variant spelling of COXON.

Coxey (118) English: from a pet form of COX.

Coxon (273) English: patronymic (*Cocke's son*) from COCKE.

Coxson (120) English: patronymic form of COCKE.

Coxwell (320) English: see COGSWELL.

Coy (4103) **1.** Irish: reduced form of MCCOY. **2.** English: nickname for a quiet and unassuming person, from Middle English, Old French *coi*, *quei* 'calm', 'quiet' (Latin *quietus*).

Coyan (108) Irish: variant of COYNE 1, 2, or 3.

Coye (179) Irish: variant spelling of COY.

Coyer (364) French: according to Morlet, from a derivative of Latin *cos*, genitive *cotis*, denoting the pouch where a reaper kept a whetstone for sharpening his sickle, hence a metonymic occupational name for a reaper or mower.

Coykendall (297) Americanized spelling of the Dutch habitational name **Kuikendaal**, from a place so named.

Coyle (7746) Irish: reduced variant of MCCOOL 1 and 2. See also HOYLE.
GIVEN NAMES Irish 6%. *Liam* (3), *Brendan* (2), *Seamus* (2), *Siobhan* (2), *Eamonn*, *Roisin*.

Coyne (4718) **1.** Irish: Anglicized form of Gaelic **Ó Cuáin** 'descendant of *Cuán*', a byname from a diminutive of *cú* 'hound', 'dog'. **2.** Irish: Anglicized form of Gaelic **Ó Cadhain** 'descendant of *Cadhan*', a byname from *cadhan* 'barnacle goose'. **3.** Irish: Anglicized form of **Ó Comhgháin** 'descendant of *Comghán*', a Connacht name usually Anglicized as COEN. **4.** Irish: variant of QUINN. **5.** English: metonymic occupational name for a minter of money, or a derogatory nickname for a miser, from Middle English *coin* 'piece of money' (earlier the die used to stamp money, from Latin *cuneus* 'wedge').
GIVEN NAMES Irish 6%. *Brendan* (13), *Colum* (2), *Colm*, *John Patrick*, *Malachy*, *Marypat*.

Coyner (424) English: occupational name for a moneyer, from an agent derivative of Middle English *coin* 'piece of money' (see COYNE).

Cozad (943) Variant of COZART.

Cozart (1412) **1.** Probably a variant spelling of Dutch **Cossaert**, a nickname for a confidante, sweetheart, or flatterer, from an agent derivative of Middle Dutch *cosen* 'to whisper'. **2.** Perhaps a variant of French **Cossard**, which is either a nickname for a lazy person or a derivative of *cosse* 'pod' (see COSSE).

Cozby (248) Altered spelling of English COSBY.

Cozens (143) English: patronymic from COUSIN.

Cozier (122) English (Oxfordshire): occupational name from Old French *cousere* 'tailor'. This name is now well established in Barbados.

Cozine (301) Variant of French or English COUSIN.

Cozort (147) Variant of COZART.

Cozza (401) Italian: **1.** nickname for someone with a large or otherwise remarkable head, from medieval Italian *coccia* 'head' (also a dialect term). **2.** from a feminine form of COZZO 1.
GIVEN NAMES Italian 14%. *Pasquale* (3), *Guido* (2), *Luigi* (2), *Angelo*, *Artilio*, *Benedetto*, *Carmine*, *Dario*, *Emilio*, *Enzo*, *Filomena*, *Francesca*, *Francesco*, *Franco*, *Mario*, *Oliverio*, *Sergio*, *Silvino*.

Cozzens (419) English: variant spelling of COZENS.

Cozzi (499) Italian: patronymic or plural form of COZZO.
GIVEN NAMES Italian 6%. *Angelo*, *Ciriaco*, *Dante*, *Dino*, *Grazia*, *Umberto*, *Vito*.

Cozzo (125) Italian: **1.** from the Germanic personal name *Gozo*. **2.** masculinized form of COZZA 1.
GIVEN NAMES Italian 22%. *Adelina*, *Aldo*, *Alfonso*, *Augustino*, *Carlo*, *Gaetano*, *Gaspere*, *Rosario*, *Ruggiero*, *Salvatore*, *Vincenzo*.

Cozzolino (354) Italian: diminutive of COZZO.
GIVEN NAMES Italian 13%. *Angelo* (3), *Antonio* (2), *Filomena* (2), *Salvatore* (2), *Ciro*, *Gennaro*, *Luigi*, *Natale*, *Pasquale*, *Rinaldo*, *Sal*, *Savino*.

Cozzone (100) Italian: augmentative form of COZZO.
GIVEN NAMES Italian 10%; French 5%. *Amerigo*, *Dino*, *Emilio*, *Marco*, *Orlando*; *Camille*, *Pierre*.

Crabb (2293) **1.** English and Scottish: from Middle English *crabbe*, Old English *crabba* 'crab' (the crustacean), a nickname for someone with a peculiar gait. **2.** English and Scottish: from Middle English *crabbe* 'crab apple (tree)' (probably of Old Norse origin), hence a topographic name for someone who lived by a crabapple tree. It may also have been a nickname for a cantankerous person, a sense which developed primarily from this word, with reference to the sourness of the fruit, but may also have been influenced by the awkward-seeming locomotion of the crustacean. **3.** Americanized spelling of German, Dutch, and Danish KRABBE.

Crabbe (587) English and Scottish: variant spelling of CRABB.

Crabbs (205) Americanized form of German and Swiss KREBS.

Crabill (568) Americanized spelling of German **Krähenbühl** (see KRAHENBUHL).

Crable (324) Americanized spelling of German **Krähenbühl** (see KRAHENBUHL).

Crabtree (9484) English: topographic name for someone who lived by a crabapple tree, Middle English *crabbetre* (see CRABB 2).

Cracchiolo (226) Italian (Sicily): probably from *cracchiola* denoting a chicory-like vegetable.

GIVEN NAMES Italian 30%. *Salvatore* (10), *Nunzio* (3), *Gaspare* (2), *Santo* (2), *Alessandro, Angelo, Antonino, Antonio, Caterina, Filippo, Giovanni, Giuseppe.*

Crace (345) English: variant of CRASS.

Crackel (149) English: habitational name from either of two places in North Yorkshire, one called Crakehall and the other Crakehill, both from Old Norse *kráka* 'crow' (or Old English *craca* 'crake') + Old English *halh* 'recess'. This form of the surname is now rare in England.

Cracraft (272) Variant of English CRAYCRAFT.

Craddick (143) English: variant of CRADDOCK.

Craddock (3001) English, from Welsh: from the Welsh personal name *Caradog* meaning 'amiable'. A British bearer of this name is recorded in the Latin form *Cara(c)tacus* and remembered for his leadership of a revolt against the Roman occupation in the 1st century AD.

Cradduck (127) English: variant of CRADDOCK.

Crader (427) Americanized spelling of German GRETHER.

Cradic (154) Probably an altered form of English CRADDOCK. This name is concentrated in TN.

Crady (307) Irish: reduced form of McCREADY.

Crafford (100) English, Scottish, and Irish: variant of CRAWFORD.

Craft (10869) **1.** English: variant of CROFT. **2.** Americanized spelling of KRAFT.

Crafton (1449) English: habitational name from Crafton in Buckinghamshire, named in Old English as 'the estate (*tūn*) where wild saffron (*croh*) grew'.

Crafts (521) English: variant of CROFT.

Crager (460) Americanized spelling of German **Kröger** (see KROGER).

Cragg (451) Scottish: variant of CRAIG, from the Middle English form *crag(g)*.

Craggs (163) Scottish: variant of CRAIG, from the Middle English form *crag(g)*.

Craghead (272) Scottish: variant of CRAIGHEAD.

Cragin (256) Probably an altered spelling of Scottish CRAIGEN.

Cragle (194) Americanized spelling of German KREGEL or **Krögel** (unexplained).

Crago (593) English (mainly Cornwall): unexplained. Compare CREGO.

Cragun (240) Probably an altered spelling of Scottish CRAIGEN. Compare CRAGIN.

Crahan (123) Irish: according to MacLysaght this is a Kerry variant of McCROHAN or a Mayo form of O'Creaghan, a variant of CREAN.

Craib (104) Scottish: variant of CRABB, found in Banff and Aberdeenshire.

Craig (33412) Scottish: topographic name for someone who lived near a steep or precipitous rock, from Gaelic *creag*, a word that has been borrowed in Middle English as *crag(g)*.

Craige (125) Variant spelling of Scottish CRAIG.

Craigen (130) Scottish: habitational name for someone from Craigie in Kyle, named with Gaelic *creag*, 'precipitous rock' (see CRAIG). Black records that in 1272 the church of Cragyn 'was confirmed to the monks of Paisley by Thomas de Cragyn, son and heir of John Hose, who had assumed his surname from his lands'.

Craiger (113) Probably an Americanized form of German and Jewish KRIEGER.

Craighead (954) Scottish: habitational name from any of various minor places named Craighead.

Craigie (182) Scottish: topographic name from the locative case of Gaelic *creagach* 'rocky place' (see CRAIGO).

Craigmile (115) Scottish: habitational name from a place called Craigmyle, in Aberdeenshire.

Craigo (235) Scottish: habitational name from Craigo in Angus, named from Gaelic *creagach* 'rocky place', from *creag* 'steep rock'.

Craik (148) Scottish: habitational name from a place in Aberdeenshire, named from Gaelic *creag* 'steep or precipitous rock' (see CRAIG).

Crail (265) Scottish: habitational name from Crail in Fife.

GIVEN NAMES German 4%. *Kurt* (2), *Dietrich, Frieda.*

Crain (6472) **1.** Irish: variant of CREHAN. **2.** English: variant spelling of CRANE.

Craine (744) Chiefly Manx form of Irish CREHAN.

Craker (236) English: variant of CROCKER 1.

Craley (149) English: unexplained.

Crall (465) Americanized spelling of German KRALL.

Cralle (114) Americanized spelling of German KRALL.

Cram (1559) **1.** Scottish: according to Black this name is from Perthshire and is a shortening of the habitational name **Crambie**, from Crombie in Fife. **2.** Americanized spelling of German KRAM.

Cramblit (152) Americanized form of German **Kramlich**, a variant of GRAMLICH.

Cramer (12050) **1.** Variant spelling of German and Dutch KRAMER or its German variant **Krämer**. It is also found in England as a Huguenot name, presumably with this origin. **2.** English: variant of CREAMER 1.

Cramm (125) **1.** German: habitational name from a place named Cramme, near Wolfenbüttel. **2.** Americanized spelling of German KRAMM (see KRAM). **3.** Dutch: metonymic occupational name for a maker of staples, clamps, clasps, and the like, from Middle Dutch *cram(me)* 'clasp', 'staple'.

Crammer (140) English, Dutch, and German: variant of CRAMER.

Cramp (186) **1.** English: variant of CRUMP. **2.** Dutch: variant spelling of KRAMP. **3.** Americanized spelling of German KRAMP.

Crampton (1125) English: variant of CRUMPTON.

Cramton (173) English: variant of CRUMPTON.

Cran (142) **1.** English: variant of CRANE. **2.** Dutch: variant of KRANE.

Crance (216) Probably an Americanized spelling of German KRANZ or KRENZ or Dutch CRANS.

Crandall (6632) Scottish: Anglicized form of Gaelic **Mac Raonuill** 'son of *Raonull*' (see RONALD).

Crandell (1314) Variant of Scottish CRANDALL, now found chiefly in Kent.

Crane (14940) **1.** English: nickname, most likely for a tall, thin man with long legs, from Middle English *cran* 'crane' (the bird), Old English *cran, cron*. The term included the heron until the introduction of a separate word for the latter in the 14th century. **2.** Dutch: variant spelling of KRANE. **3.** English translation of German KRAHN or KRANICH.

FOREBEARS The American writer Stephen Crane (1871–1900) was named for a NJ ancestor who was a delegate to the Continental Congress. He was descended from a Stephen Crane who, coming probably from England or Wales, settled at Elizabethtown, NJ, as early as 1665.

Craner (352) **1.** English (West Midlands and Staffordshire): etymology unexplained. **2.** Americanized spelling of German **Krahner**, a variant of KRAHN, or **Kröner** (see KRONER).

Craney (290) Irish: reduced Anglicized form of Gaelic **Mac Bhranaigh** (see McCRANEY).

Cranfield (262) English: habitational name from a place in Bedfordshire named Cranfield, from Old English *cran(uc)* 'crane' + *feld* 'open country'.

Cranfill (557) Perhaps an altered spelling of English CRANFIELD. It is concentrated in NC and TX.

Cranford (2803) English: habitational name from any of several places, for example in the county of Middlesex (now part of Greater London) and Northamptonshire (Cranford St. Andrew and Cranford St. John), named with Old English *cran* 'crane' + *ford* 'ford'.

Crangle (136) Scottish (now found mainly in northern Ireland): Anglicized form of

Gaelic **Mac Raonuill** 'son of *Raonull*' (see RONALD). Compare CRANDALL.

Crank (1125) **1.** English (chiefly Lancashire): from Middle English *cranke* 'lively', 'lusty', 'vigorous', hence a nickname for a cheerful, boisterous, or cocky person. **2.** English: nickname from *cranuc*, a diminutive of Middle English *cran* 'crane' (see CRANE). **3.** Possibly an Americanized spelling of German **Kranke**, from Low German *Kraneke* 'crane', applied to someone thought to resemble the bird in some way, or a nickname for a poor physical specimen, from Middle High German *kranc* 'sickly', 'ailing'.

Crankshaw (171) English: variant of CRANSHAW.

Cranmer (910) English: habitational name, probably from Cranmore in Somerset, named from Old English *cran* 'crane' + *mere* 'lake', 'pool'.

Cranmore (150) English: habitational name from any of various places named Cranmore, for example in Somerset (see CRANMER) and the Isle of Wight, which is named with Old English *cran* 'crane' + *mōr* 'moor', 'marshy ground'.

Crannell (217) Probably a variant of Scottish CRANDALL.

Cranney (173) Irish: variant spelling of CRANEY.

Cranor (364) Irish: reduced Anglicized form of Gaelic **Mac Thréinfhir** 'son of *Tréinfhear*', a byname meaning 'champion', 'strong man' (from *tréan* 'strong' + *fear* 'man'). Compare TRAINOR.

Crans (177) Dutch: from Middle Dutch *crans* 'wreath', 'garland', 'crown'; hence a nickname for someone whose hair was tonsured, or a habitational name for someone who lived at a house distinguished by the sign of a garland.

Cranshaw (177) English: habitational name from Cranshaw in Lancashire, named from Old English *cran(uc)* 'crane' + *sceaga* 'grove', 'thicket'.

Cranson (143) English: unexplained. Perhaps a variant of CRANSTON.

Cranston (1296) Scottish: habitational name from a place near Dalkeith named Cranston, from the genitive case of the Old English byname *Cran* meaning 'crane' + Old English *tūn* 'settlement'.

Cranwell (105) English: habitational name from Cranwell in Lincolnshire, named from Old English *cran* 'crane', 'heron' + *wella* 'spring', 'stream'.

Crapo (448) Americanized spelling of French **Crépaux** (see CREPEAU).

Crapps (310) **1.** Americanized spelling of German KREBS. **2.** Perhaps an altered spelling of Dutch **Craps**, which in part represents a patronymic from KRABBE and in part is derived from Middle Dutch *crappe* 'madder', a plant used to produce a red dye, and hence a metonymic occupational name for a dyer or for someone who grew madder.

Crapser (183) Americanized form of Swiss and German **Krebser**, an occupational name for a crab fisher. See also KREBS.

Crary (726) Probably Scottish or northern Irish: reduced and altered form of McCREERY.

Crase (495) Altered spelling of the English family name CRACE, a variant of CRASS.

Crask (143) English (East Anglia): nickname for a lusty man, from Middle English *craske* 'fat', 'lusty' (see CRASS).

Crass (511) **1.** English: nickname from Old French, Middle English *cras* 'big', 'fat' (Latin *crassus*). **2.** Possibly an altered spelling of German KRASS.

Crate (181) English: from Old English *cræt* 'cart', hence a metonymic occupational name for a carter or a cartwright.

Crater (620) Americanized spelling of German and Swiss German GRETHER.

Crates (107) English: variant of CRATE.

Craton (164) English (Devon): unexplained.

Cratty (303) Irish: variant of CROTTY.

Craun (408) Americanized form of German KRAHN.

Craven (5914) **1.** Irish: Anglicized form of Gaelic **Ó Crabháin** (County Galway) or **Mac Crabháin** (Louth, Monaghan) 'descendant (or 'son') of *Crabhán*'. **2.** English: regional name from the district of West Yorkshire so called, which is probably 'garlic place', from a British word, the ancestor of Welsh *craf* 'garlic'.

Cravener (122) **1.** Altered spelling of North German **Grevener**, a habitational name for someone from any of several places named Greven, probably from Middle Low German *grave* 'ditch', 'moat', referring to an early Frankish settlement with that type of fortification. **2.** Possibly also an altered spelling of North German **Grewener**, a variant of **Gräb(e)ner**, an occupational name for a miner, grave digger or the like, or for an engraver. See also GRABER.

Cravens (2333) Variant of English and Irish CRAVEN.

Craver (1491) Perhaps an Americanized spelling of the North German occupational name **Grever**, a variant of **Gräber** (see GRABER).

Cravey (555) Northern Irish: reduced form of McGREEVY. Compare McCRAVY.

Cravotta (105) Italian: from a diminutive of *crava* 'nanny goat', a dialect form of CAPRA.

GIVEN NAMES Italian 18%. *Angelo* (4), *Salvatore* (2), *Santo*.

Craw (468) **1.** Scottish and Irish: variant of CROW. **2.** Possibly an altered spelling of German GRAU or **Krahe**, a variant of KRAY 1.

Crawford (55113) **1.** Scottish, English, and northern Irish: habitational name from any of the various places, for example in

Lanarkshire (Scotland) and Dorset and Lancashire (England) called Crawford, named in Old English with *crāwe* 'crow' + *ford* 'ford'. **2.** English: variant of **Crowfoot** (see CROFOOT).

Crawley (3928) **1.** English: habitational name from any of the many places called Crawley, named with Old English *crāwe* 'crow' + *lēah* 'woodland clearing'. Compare CROWLEY. **2.** Probably also a reduced form of Irish **McCrawley**, an Anglicization of Gaelic **Mac Raghallaigh** 'son of *Raghallach*', also Anglicized as **Magreely**.

Crawmer (147) Americanized spelling of German KRAMER.

Crawshaw (313) English: habitational name from Crawshaw Booth in Lancashire, named from Old English *crāwe* 'crow' + *sceaga* 'grove', 'thicket'.

Cray (793) **1.** Irish: Anglicized form of Gaelic **Ó Craobhaigh** 'descendant of *Craobhach*', a byname meaning 'curly(-headed)' or 'prolific' (from *craobh* 'branch', 'bough'). Compare CREEVY. **2.** Respelling of German KRAY or KREY.

Craycraft (534) English (Kent): probably a habitational name from a lost or unidentified place. There is a river Cray in Kent, named with Old Welsh *crei* 'fresh'; *craft* may be Old English *cræft* 'mill'.

FOREBEARS John Craycroft came to MD in 1666 from Lincolnshire, England.

Craycroft (108) English: variant of CRAYCRAFT.

GIVEN NAME French 4%. *Sylviane* (2).

Crayne (305) Probably an altered spelling of English CRANE or possibly an Americanized spelling of German **Krain**, a habitational name from any of several places so named.

Crays (191) Americanized spelling of German KREIS.

Crayton (1325) English: habitational name, possibly a variant spelling of CREIGHTON.

Craze (186) English: variant of CRASS.

Crea (324) **1.** Italian: from the southern dialect word *crea* 'flesh' (from Greek *kreas*), presumably applied as a nickname for a fat man. **2.** Possibly a reduced form of Scottish **McCrea**, an Ayrshire variant of McCRAE (see McRAE).

GIVEN NAMES Italian 17%. *Rocco* (6), *Antonio* (2), *Salvatore* (2), *Carmela*, *Domenic*, *Giovanni*, *Nunzio*, *Pasquale*, *Romeo*, *Saverio*, *Vincenzo*.

Creach (195) **1.** Scottish: probably a variant spelling of CREECH. **2.** Perhaps an Americanized spelling of German KRIEG or **Krietsch**, from Slavic *kric* 'crier', hence an occupational name for a town crier or a nickname for a habitual shouter.

Creacy (108) English: variant spelling of CREASY.

Creagan (118) Irish: variant spelling of CREEGAN.

GIVEN NAME French 5%. *Camille*.

Creager (1180) Americanized spelling of German and Swiss KRIEGER or **Kröger** (see KRUEGER).

Creagh (237) Irish: alternative Anglicization of Gaelic **Craobhach** (see CRAY), an epithet of the O'Neills of Clare, one of whose ancestors is said to have carried a green branch into battle.

Creal (216) **1.** Possibly Irish (unexplained) or a variant spelling of Scottish CRAIL. **2.** Americanized spelling of KRIEL.

Creamer (3009) **1.** English: occupational name for a seller of dairy products, from an agent derivative of Middle English, Old French *creme* 'cream' (Late Latin *crama*, apparently of Gaulish origin). **2.** Scottish and northern Irish: occupational name for a peddler, a cognate of German **Krämer** (see KRAMER). Sir John Skene, in his *De verborum significatione* ('On the Meaning of Words', 1681), explains the term *peddler* as 'ane mechand or *cremer*, quha beris ane pack or *creame* upon his back'. **3.** Americanized spelling of **Krämer**, KRAMER, or KREMER.

Crean (534) Irish: **1.** (southern) Anglicized form of Gaelic **Ó Corraidhín** (see CURRAN). **2.** (in Ulster) Anglicized form of Gaelic **Ó Croidheáin** (see CREHAN) or **Ó Creacháin** 'descendant of *Creachán*'.
GIVEN NAMES Irish 7%. *Finbar* (2), *Bridie*.

Crear (201) Scottish: variant of the occupational name **Crerar**, from Gaelic *criathrar* 'sievewright', i.e. a maker of sieves.
GIVEN NAMES French 4%. *Celestine, Vernice.*

Creary (181) Irish: reduced form of MCCREARY.
GIVEN NAME Irish 5%. *Donovan* (2).

Creaser (127) **1.** English (Yorkshire): unexplained. **2.** Probably an Americanized spelling of German KRIESER, a variant of GRIESER, of which this could also be an Americanized spelling.

Creasey (595) **1.** English: variant spelling of CREASY. **2.** Possibly an Americanized spelling of the German names mentioned at CREASY.

Creasman (461) Probably an Americanized spelling of German **Griessmann**, a topographic name for someone who lived in a sandy place (see GRIES).

Creason (802) **1.** English: unexplained. **2.** Perhaps also an Americanized spelling of Dutch **Cruyssen** (see CRUSAN).

Creasy (1295) **1.** English: nickname from Middle English *crease* 'fine', 'elegant' (Old English *crēas*). **2.** Probably an Americanized spelling of German KRIESE, GRIESE, KRIESER, or GRIESER, or of Swiss German **Krüsi**, a variant of KRAUS.

Creath (161) Reduced form of Scottish **McCreath** (see MCCRAE).

Crecco (104) Italian: metathesized form of **Cherco**, from a reduced form of *chierico* 'cleric', 'clergyman'.

GIVEN NAMES Italian 24%. *Santino* (2), *Antonio, Attilio, Gino, Giovanni, Giulio, Italo, Umberto.*

Crecelius (428) German: humanistic Latinized form of **Kretzel, Krätzel**, shortened pet forms of the personal name PANKRATZ.

Credeur (482) French: literally 'believer', but the application as a surname is unexplained. Perhaps a nickname for a devout person. This is a LA surname.
GIVEN NAMES French 11%. *Antoine* (3), *Easton* (2), *Nolton* (2), *Alcide, Clovis, Curley, Dupre, Gilfred, Nelma, Ovide, Raoul.*

Credit (178) French (**Crédit**): unexplained.
GIVEN NAMES French 5%. *Emile, Monique.*

Credle (297) Probably an Americanized spelling of German **Kredel** or **Gredel**, variants of GRETH.

Cree (636) Scottish: reduced form of MCCREE (see MCRAE).

Creech (4961) **1.** English: possibly a topographic name from Middle English *crich(e)* 'creek', but more likely a habitational name from Creech St. Michael in Somerset or East Creech in Dorset, both named with a Celtic element *crūg* 'mound', 'hill'. **2.** Scottish: habitational name from Creich in Fife. **3.** Possibly an Americanized spelling of the German names mentioned at CREACH 2.

Creecy (301) English: variant spelling of CREASY.

Creed (1875) **1.** Southern Irish: reduced form of CREEDON. **2.** English: from the Old English personal name *Creoda*. **3.** English: habitational name from Creed Farm in Bosham, Sussex, so named with an Old English word *crēde* 'weeds', 'plants'. In part the surname may perhaps have arisen from a place called Creed in Cornwall, named for the patron saint of the church, St. Cride.

Creeden (276) Irish: variant of CREEDON.

Creedon (594) **1.** Southern Irish: Anglicized form of Gaelic **Ó Críodáin** or **Mac Críodáin** 'descendant (or 'son') of *Críodán*', an Old Irish personal name of uncertain meaning (the ending is diminutive in form). **2.** English: habitational name from Creeton in Lincolnshire, so named with an unattested Old English personal name *Crēta* + Old English *tūn*.
GIVEN NAMES Irish 5%. *Brendan, Ronan.*

Creegan (347) Irish: **1.** Anglicized form of Gaelic **Ó Croidheagáin** 'descendant of *Croidheagán*', a personal name from a diminutive of *croidhe* 'heart', used as a term of endearment. **2.** perhaps also an alternative Anglicization of **Ó Croidheáain** (see CREHAN 1).

Creeger (108) Probably an Americanized spelling of KRIEGER or *Krüger* (see KRUEGER).

Creek (1312) **1.** English: habitational name for someone from North or South Creake in

Norfolk, named from Celtic *creig* 'cliff', 'rock'. **2.** English: from Middle English *creke* 'basket' (Old French *creche*), hence a metonymic occupational name for a basket maker. **3.** Americanized spelling of German KRIEG, German and Jewish KRICK, or Dutch **Kriek**, a metonymic occupational name for a fruit grower or dealer, from Middle Dutch *krieke* 'cherry'.

Creekmore (1069) English: probably a habitational name from a place in Dorset named Creekmoor, from Middle English *crike* 'creek', 'inlet' + *more* 'moor', 'marshy ground'. However, this surname is not found in current English records.

Creekmur (153) Variant of English CREEKMORE.

Creel (3113) Possibly an Americanized spelling of German KRIEL or **Krüll**, a variant of KROLL 1.

Creelman (255) Scottish and northern Irish: probably an occupational name derived from the English word *creel*, denoting a type of large wicker basket, used for putting fish in.

Creely (173) Irish: alternative Anglicization of Gaelic **Mac Raghallaigh** (see CRAWLEY).

Creer (270) Scottish: variant spelling of CREAR.

Crees (170) English: variant of CREASY.

Creese (170) English: variant of CREASY. There is probably no connection with modern English *crease*, which is first attested in the 16th century, from earlier *crest*.

Creevy (88) Irish: reduced Anglicized form of Gaelic **Ó Craobhaigh** 'descendant of *Craobhach*', a byname meaning 'curly(-headed)' or 'prolific' (from *craobh* 'branch', 'bough').

Cregan (302) Irish: variant of CREEGAN, or possibly in some cases an Anglicized form of Gaelic **Mac Riagáin** 'son of *Riagán*' (see RYAN).
GIVEN NAMES Irish 6%. *Brendan, Liam.*

Cregar (224) Of Dutch or German origin: see CREGER.

Creger (432) **1.** Americanized spelling of German KRIEGER, or of its Dutch cognate **Krijger**. **2.** Perhaps an Americanized spelling of German **Krüger** (see KRUEGER).

Cregg (208) English: perhaps a variant of GREGG.

Cregger (367) Americanized spelling of Dutch and German **Krieger**, German KRIEGER, or German **Kröger** (see KROEGER).

Crego (489) English (Cornwall): unexplained. Compare CRAGO.

Crehan (268) Irish: **1.** (Sligo) Anglicized form of Gaelic **Ó Croidheáin** 'descendant of *Croidheán*', from a diminutive of *croidhe* 'heart'. Compare CREEGAN. **2.** (originally Mayo and Tyrone) Anglicized form of Gaelic **Ó Creacháin** or **Ó Criocháin**, from a diminutive of *creach* 'blind'.

Creighton (2891) **1.** Scottish and Irish: habitational name from Crichton, near Edinburgh, first recorded *c*.1128 in the form *Crectune*, in 1287 as *Crecton*, and in 1360 as *Creychtona*. The name is probably an early hybrid compound of Old Welsh *creic* 'rock' + Older Scots *tun* 'farm', 'settlement' (Old English *tūn*). In the British Isles, this spelling of the name is now found chiefly in northern Ireland; the more usual Scottish forms are **Crichton** and **Crighton**. **2.** Irish: sometimes used for Gaelic **Ó Creacháin** or **Ó Críocháin** (see CREHAN 2). **3.** English: habitational name from Creighton in Staffordshire or Creaton in Northamptonshire, both named with Celtic *creig* 'rock' + Old English *tūn* 'settlement'.

Creitz (119) Respelling of German KREITZ.

Crellin (209) Manx: from a metathesized form of **Crennall**, which is an Anglicized form of Gaelic **Mac Raghnaill** 'son of *Raghnall*', a personal name from Old Norse *Rǫgvaldr* meaning 'ruler of the gods'.

Cremeans (673) **1.** Probably an altered spelling of Irish CRIMMINS. **2.** Alternatively, perhaps, an altered spelling of German **Krementz**, which is probably of Slavic origin (see KREMIN).

Cremeens (239) Variant of CREMEANS.

Cremer (631) Dutch and North German: variant of KRAMER.

Cremers (137) Variant of German KREMER.

Cremin (199) **1.** Irish: variant of CRIMMINS. **2.** Jewish (Ashkenazic): see KREMIN.

Cremins (130) Irish: variant of CRIMMINS.
GIVEN NAMES Irish 6%. *Conor, Siobhan.*

Crenshaw (5474) English: variant of CRANSHAW.

Crenwelge (180) Altered spelling of South German **Krenwelge**, a metonymic occupational name for a spice dealer, from Middle High German *krēn* 'horseradish' + *welge* 'roller', 'rolling pin'.
GIVEN NAME German 5%. *Kurt.*

Crepeau (415) French (**Crépeau**): nickname for someone with curly hair, from a derivative of Latin *crispus* 'curly-haired'.
FOREBEARS A bearer of this name from the Poitou region of France was documented in Duquet, Quebec, in 1665.
GIVEN NAMES French 9%. *Marcel* (2), *Adelore, Armand, Gabrielle, Henri, Jacques, Lucien, Michel, Pierrette, Simonne.*

Creppel (117) Probably a respelling of French **Crépel**, a variant of **Crépeau** (see CREPEAU).
GIVEN NAME French 6%. *Jacques.*

Crepps (108) Variant spelling of German KREBS.

Creps (221) Variant spelling of German KREBS.

Creque (177) French: probably a southern variant of the habitational name **Créquy**, from a locality in Pas-de-Calais, so named from *Kreko*, a personal name of Germanic

origin, + the suffix *-acum*. Compare CRIQUI.
GIVEN NAMES French 5%; Spanish 4%. *Lucienne, Renold, Romain; Alejandro* (2), *Eduardo* (2), *Beatriz, Juana, Mario, Porfirio.*

Cresap (262) English: unexplained.
FOREBEARS Col. Thomas Cresap (1694–1790), Maryland surveyor, was born in 1694 in Skipton, Yorkshire, England, and came to MD in 1710.

Crescenzi (178) Italian: patronymic or plural form of CRESCENZO.
GIVEN NAMES Italian 19%. *Rocco* (3), *Francesco* (2), *Gino* (2), *Angelo, Giovani.*

Crescenzo (276) Italian: from the personal name *Crescenzo*, an omen name bestowed in the hope that the recipient will thrive and prosper.
GIVEN NAMES Italian 11%. *Angelo, Biagio, Carlo, Francesco, Giovanni, Rocco.*

Cresci (247) Italian: of uncertain origin, possibly from a short form of the medieval personal name *Crescimbene*, an omen name bestowed in the hope that the recipient will flourish (literally 'grow well'). Alternatively, it may be a variant of **Cresi**, which Caracausi links with **Clesi**, an Albanian family name.
GIVEN NAMES Italian 14%. *Dino* (4), *Aldo, Carlo, Domenic, Leno, Nino.*

Creson (220) See CREASON.

Crespi (263) **1.** Catalan (**Crespí**): from a personal name, the Catalan equivalent of CRISPIN. **2.** Northern Italian and Jewish (from Italy): either a variant of CRESPO or a habitational name from a place so called or from Crespi d'Adda in Bergamo.
GIVEN NAMES Spanish 12%; Jewish 5%. *Jaime* (2), *Juan* (2), *Mercedes* (2), *Racquel* (2), *Alberto, Alejandro, Consuelo, Eduardo, Jose, Jose Manuel, Migdalia, Pedro; Aron, Nissim.*

Crespin (417) French: variant of CRISPIN.
GIVEN NAMES Spanish 19%. *Jose* (8), *Manuel* (4), *Carlos* (2), *Raul* (2), *Vidal* (2), *Adelina, Alfonso, Amador, Andres, Aniceto, Delfino, Emilio.*

Crespo (1958) Spanish, Portuguese, and northern Italian: nickname for a man with curly hair, from Latin *crispus* 'curly-haired'.
GIVEN NAMES Spanish 45%; Portuguese 11%; Italian 6%. *Jose* (41), *Luis* (30), *Juan* (23), *Jorge* (21), *Carlos* (20), *Manuel* (19), *Francisco* (17), *Pedro* (15), *Rafael* (13), *Fernando* (12), *Miguel* (12), *Orlando* (9); *Joaquim* (2); *Antonio* (21), *Carmelo* (5), *Heriberto* (4), *Angelo* (3), *Ciro* (2), *Lorenzo* (2), *Silvio* (2), *Ceasar, Cecilio, Concetta, Elio, Fausto.*

Cress (2087) Americanized spelling of German KRESS.

Cressey (302) **1.** English: variant spelling of CRESSY or possibly of CREASY. **2.** Probably also an altered spelling of German KRESSE or KRESSER.

Cressler (178) Altered spelling of German KRESSLER.
GIVEN NAME French 4%. *Lucien.*

Cressman (741) Americanized spelling of German **Kressmann**, a variant of KRESS.

Cresswell (619) English: variant spelling of CRESWELL.

Cressy (279) **1.** French and English (of Norman origin): habitational name from places in northern France, in Saône-et-Loire, Seine-Maritime, and Somme, all named with the Gallic personal name *Crixsos* 'curly-haired man' (Latin *Crixsus*) + the Latin locative suffix *-acum*. **2.** Southern French: topographic name for someone who lived on a patch of stony ground, Occitan *cres, gres*. **3.** Possibly a variant of French **Cressé**: unexplained.
FOREBEARS A bearer of the name Cressé from Paris is documented in Quebec city in 1674.

Crest (100) English: possibly a variant of CRIST.

Cresta (154) Italian: from *cresta* 'crest' (from Latin *crista*), perhaps applied as a topographic name for someone who lived by the crest of a mountain or as a nickname with reference to the comb of a rooster.
GIVEN NAMES Italian 20%. *Gino* (3), *Angelo, Antonio, Carmela, Carmine, Fiore, Gianluca, Luca, Luigi, Marcello, Nicola, Paolo.*

Cresto (141) Italian: unexplained.
GIVEN NAMES Italian 14%. *Angelo, Marcelino, Mariana, Mercedes, Norberto, Oresto, Rodrigo.*

Creswell (1017) English: habitational name from any of the various places named Creswell, from Old English *cærse* '(water)cress' + *well(a)* 'spring', 'stream', as for example in Derbyshire, Nottinghamshire, and Staffordshire.

Crete (179) French (**Crète**, adjectival form **Crété** 'crested'): nickname for an arrogant individual, from Old French *creste* 'crest (of a hill)' (Late Latin *crista*), used with reference to the comb of a rooster. Compare Old French *crester* 'to strut'.
FOREBEARS A settler from the Perche region of France, documented as Crete and Creste, is recorded in Quebec city as early as 1654.
GIVEN NAMES French 18%. *Adrien, Alain, Camille, Fernand, Gaetan, Gilles, Gillis, Martial, Michel, Monique, Normand, Rosaire.*

Cretella (267) Italian: probably a derivative of **Creta**, a habitational name from the Greek island of Crete, which in Renaissance times was under Venetian rule.
GIVEN NAMES Italian 20%. *Salvatore* (4), *Angelo, Aniello, Carmine, Domenic, Enrico, Liberato, Matteo, Pasquale, Sal.*

Cretsinger (162) Americanized spelling of **Grötzinger** (see GRETZINGER).

Creveling (372) Northern German: probably a variant of GREVE or **Greuling**, a nickname for someone with gray hair, from

Middle Low German **grawe** 'gray' + *-ling*, a suffix denoting affiliation.

Crevier (265) French (Normandy): from Old French *creve* 'crevice', 'fissure', probably a topographic name for someone who lived on arid land.

FOREBEARS A Crevier from Normandy, France, is documented in 1639 in Trois Rivières, Quebec.

GIVEN NAMES French 11%. *Andre* (2), *Francois* (2), *Armand, Jean Pierre, Laurent, Pierre, Rejean*.

Creviston (279) Probably an Americanized form of German **Gravenstein**, a habitational name from northwestern Germany, from Middle Low German *grāve* 'governor' + *stein* 'rock', 'castle'.

Crew (1384) English: habitational name for someone from Crewe in Cheshire, named with Old Welsh *criu* 'weir'. This denoted a wickerwork fence that was stretched across a river to catch fish.

Crewdson (124) English (Lancashire): unexplained.

Crewe (199) English: variant spelling of CREW.

Crews (8109) **1.** English: variant spelling of CRUSE. **2.** Americanized spelling of German and Danish KRUSE.

Crewse (144) **1.** English: variant spelling of CRUSE. **2.** Americanized spelling of German and Danish KRUSE.

Criado (104) Portuguese and Spanish: occupational name from *criado* 'servant'.

GIVEN NAMES Spanish 35%. *Jose* (5), *Manuel* (3), *Adolfo* (2), *Agustin, Camilo, Concepcion, Elodia, Enrique, Everardo, Jose Alberto, Juan, Juanita; Antonio* (4), *Marino*.

Cribari (146) Italian: habitational name from a minor place named Cribari, in Trenta, Cosenza province.

GIVEN NAMES Italian 11%. *Angelo, Gino, Premo, Sal, Salvatore, Silvio*.

Cribb (1126) English: from Old English *crib(b)* 'manger', (later) 'ox stall', hence a metonymic occupational name for a cowherd.

Cribbs (1504) English: variant spelling of CRIBB or CRIPPS.

Crichlow (190) English: variant spelling of CRITCHLOW.

Crichton (708) **1.** Scottish spelling of CREIGHTON. **2.** Perhaps an Americanized spelling of Dutch KRUCHTEN.

FOREBEARS The Mennonite Encyclopedia lists a Wilhelm Crichton, born at Königsberg, East Prussia, in 1732.

Crick (907) **1.** English: habitational name from Crick in Northamptonshire, recorded in Domesday Book as *Crec*, from Celtic *creig* 'rock', 'cliff'. **2.** Possibly an Americanized spelling of any of the names mentioned at CREEK 3.

Crickenberger (191) Americanized spelling of German **Krückenberger**, a habitational name for someone from a place

called Krückeberg near Herford, Westphalia.

Criddle (539) English: from an Old English personal name, *Cridela*.

Crider (3731) Americanized spelling of German KREIDER.

Crifasi (107) Italian: metathesized spelling of CRISAFI.

GIVEN NAMES Italian 16%; French 7%. *Salvatore* (2), *Carlo, Dante, Dino; Jacques, Thierry*.

Criger (207) Americanized spelling of Dutch and German **Krieger**.

Crigger (661) Americanized spelling of Dutch and German **Krieger**.

Crighton (113) Scottish and Irish: variant spelling of CREIGHTON.

Crigler (420) Americanized spelling of German **Kriegler**, a nickname for a quarrelsome person, from an agent derivative of Middle High German *kriegen* 'to quarrel', 'to dispute', or an occupational name for an innkeeper or potter, a variant of **Krüger** (see KRUEGER).

Crihfield (181) Americanized form of German **Creyfelt**, a habitational name from Krefeld, Rhineland.

Crile (164) Probably an Americanized spelling of German KREIL.

Crill (199) **1.** English (Channel Islands): unexplained. **2.** Probably an Americanized spelling of German KRILL or GRILL 2.

Crilley (228) Irish: variant spelling of CRILLY.

Crilly (402) Irish: Anglicized form of Gaelic **Mac Raghailligh** 'son of *Raghailleach*'. Compare CRAWLEY.

GIVEN NAMES Irish 6%. *Brendan, Liam*.

Crim (1641) **1.** Variant of CRUM. **2.** Possibly an altered spelling of German and Jewish KRIM, or German KRIMM or GRIMM. This name is concentrated in the old South.

Crimi (323) Italian (Sicily): from an altered form of the medieval Greek personal name *Klēmēs*, from Latin *Clemens* (see CLEMENT).

GIVEN NAMES Italian 15%. *Salvatore* (3), *Angelo* (2), *Gaetano* (2), *Vita* (2), *Cosimo, Giuseppe, Luciano, Luigi, Sal, Tommaso*.

Crimm (195) Possibly an altered spelling of German KRIMM or GRIMM.

Crimmins (1046) Irish: Anglicized form of Gaelic **Ó Cruimín** 'descendant of *Cruimín*', a byname from a diminutive of *crom* 'bent', 'crooked'.

GIVEN NAMES Irish 4%. *Brendan* (2), *Siobhan*.

Criner (747) Americanized spelling of KRINER, KREINER, or GREINER.

Cripe (1345) Origin uncertain. **1.** Possibly a variant of English **Crippe**, from Middle English *crippe* 'pouch', either an occupational name for a maker of pouches or a nickname for someone who habitually wore a distinctive pouch. **2.** Americanized

spelling of German **Kreipe**, from a topographic name of uncertain origin.

Crippen (1137) English: variant of CRISPIN.

Crippin (117) English: variant of CRISPIN.

Cripps (1044) **1.** English: occupational name for a maker of pouches, from the plural of Middle English *crippes* 'pouch'. **2.** English: metathesized form of CRISP. **3.** German: variant spelling of **Krips**, a variant of KREBS.

Criqui (145) Walloon variant of French **Créquy** (see CREQUE).

Crisafi (144) Italian: metonymic occupational name for a goldsmith, from medieval Greek *khrysaphion*, a diminutive of classical Greek *khrysos* 'gold'.

GIVEN NAMES Italian 18%. *Rocco* (2), *Pasquale*.

Crisafulli (567) Southern Italian: Italianized form of the medieval Greek family names **Khrysaphoudēs** or **Khrysaphoulēs**, from medieval Greek *khrysaphēs* 'gold' + the diminutive ending *-oudi, -ouli*.

GIVEN NAMES Italian 20%. *Angelo* (7), *Carmelo* (6), *Domenic* (3), *Dante* (2), *Salvatore* (2), *Santo* (2), *Sebastiano* (2), *Vincenzo* (2), *Alessandro, Annalisa, Antonio, Attilio*.

Crisan (108) Romanian: unexplained.

GIVEN NAMES Romanian 17%; French 9%. *Cornel* (2), *Doina, Dragos, Ovidiu, Petru, Silviu, Toader; Aurel* (3), *Jean-Pierre*.

Crisanti (156) Southern Italian: from the personal name *Crisante, Grisante*, from Greek *Khrysanthos*, literally 'gold flower'.

GIVEN NAMES Italian 18%. *Salvatore* (4), *Antonino, Caesar, Dino, Ilio, Pietro, Rocco, Romeo*.

Crisci (445) Southern Italian: perhaps a variant of **Crisi**, which is from the Greek female personal name *Khrysē* 'golden'.

GIVEN NAMES Italian 17%. *Angelo* (3), *Nunzio* (2), *Salvatore* (2), *Aniello, Carmine, Cirino, Clemente, Domenico, Giuseppe, Maddalena, Nicoletta, Rocco*.

Criscione (307) Italian: augmentative of CRISCI.

GIVEN NAMES Italian 15%. *Salvatore* (6), *Angelo* (3), *Carmelo* (2), *Antonio, Carmine, Emanuele, Ignazio, Natale, Sal*.

Crisco (330) Italian: unexplained.

Criscuolo (436) Italian: derivative of CRISCO.

GIVEN NAMES Italian 18%; French 4%. *Salvatore* (9), *Guido* (2), *Marco* (2), *Aldo, Alfonse, Aniello, Antonio, Carlo, Carmine, Giulio, Luca, Luigi; Alphonse* (3).

Crise (170) Probably an Americanized spelling of KREIS or KRIES.

Crisler (731) Americanized spelling of German KREISLER or **Griessler**, a topographic name for someone who lived or farmed in an area of sand (see GRIES), or (in the south) an occupational name for a grocer, from Middle High German *griezmel* 'milled grain' (from *griez* 'sand', 'gravel').

Crislip (303) Americanized spelling of German **Christlieb**, from a fairly recent baptismal name for converts, especially from Judaism, meaning 'dear to Christ'.

Crisman (838) **1.** Respelling of German CHRISTMANN. **2.** Respelling of Slovenian **Križman** (see KRIZMAN 2). **3.** Variant of English CHRISTMAN.

Crismon (235) Variant of CRISMAN.

Crisostomo (259) Spanish (**Crisóstomo**): from the personal name, a derivative of Greek *Khrysostomos*, literally 'mouth of gold'. This was the nickname of St. John Chrysostom (4th century AD), a prominent theologian, and one of the four Fathers of the Eastern Church.
GIVEN NAMES Spanish 43%. *Jose* (6), *Alberto* (4), *Cesar* (4), *Juan* (4), *Edgardo* (3), *Manuel* (3), *Pedro* (3), *Alfredo* (2), *Ernesto* (2), *Eugenio* (2), *Honorio* (2), *Luis* (2); *Antonio*, *Domenica*, *Enrico*, *Luciano*, *Romeo*, *Salvatore*.

Crisp (4366) **1.** English: nickname for a man with curly hair, from Middle English *crisp*, Old English *crisp*, *cryps* (Latin *crispus*), reinforced in Middle English by an Old French word also from Latin *crispus*. **2.** Americanized spelling of the German cognate **Krisp**, from Middle High German *krisp*, *krispel* 'curly-haired man'. **3.** Americanized form of German **Krisp**, from a short form the medieval personal name *Krispin* (see CRISPIN).

Crispell (276) **1.** Americanized spelling of German **Krispel**, a variant of **Krisp** (see CRISP). **2.** Variant of French **Crespel** ('curly-haired'), an older form of **Crépel** (see CREPPEL).
FOREBEARS A Huguenot family from French Flanders bore this name (also in the forms **Crépel** and **Crespel**). They settled in Esopus, NY.

Crispen (148) Variant spelling of English CRISPIN or of the German cognates **Crispien** and **Krispin**.

Crispi (127) Italian: patronymic or plural form of CRISPO.
GIVEN NAME Italian 6%. *Carmine* (2).

Crispin (689) **1.** English and French: from the Middle English, Old French personal name *Crispin*, Latin *Crispinus*, a family name derived from *crispus* 'curly-haired' (see CRISP). This name was especially popular in France in the early Middle Ages, having been borne by a saint who was martyred at Soissons in AD *c.* 285 along with a companion, *Crispinianus* (whose name is a further derivative of the same word). **2.** English and French: diminutive of CRISP.
GIVEN NAMES Spanish 7%; French 4%. *Jose* (6), *Juan* (3), *Pedro* (3), *Alicia* (2), *Fernando* (2), *Manuel* (2), *Rafael* (2), *Adolfo*, *Alfredo*, *Ana*, *Areli*, *Candita*; *Adrien*, *Andre*, *Eugenie*, *Francoise*.

Crispino (273) Southern Italian: from the personal name *Crispino*, from Latin *Crispinus*, a derivative of the old Roman family name *Crispus* 'curly(-headed)' (see CRISPIN).
GIVEN NAMES Italian 17%. *Luigi* (4), *Carlo* (2), *Amato*, *Angelo*, *Antonio*, *Domenico*, *Fiore*, *Gennaro*, *Michelina*, *Rocco*, *Sal*, *Salvator*.

Crispo (154) Southern Italian: from the personal name *Crispo* meaning 'curly-haired' (from the old Roman family name *Crispus*), or a nickname from a regional variant of *crespo*, also meaning 'curly-haired'.
GIVEN NAMES Italian 12%. *Angelo* (2), *Guillermo* (2), *Adonis*, *Antonio*, *Domenica*, *Enrico*, *Italia*.

Criss (1566) Americanized spelling of German GRIES.

Crissey (287) **1.** English: unexplained. **2.** Possibly an Americanized spelling of Swiss German **Krüsi**, a variant of KRUSE, or **Kriesi**, a variant of KRIES.

Crissinger (184) Altered spelling of German GRIESINGER.

Crissman (782) Either a variant spelling of English CRISMAN or possibly a respelling of German CHRISTMANN or **Kressmann**, a variant of KRESS. Compare CRESSMAN.

Crist (4237) **1.** English: from Old English *Crīst*, probably applied as a nickname for someone who played the part of Christ in a pageant. **2.** North German: from a short form of the personal name *Kristen* or one of its variants (see CHRISTIAN). **3.** Americanized spelling of North German KRIST.

Cristaldi (115) Southern Italian: probably from Sicilian *cristaudu* 'crystal'.
GIVEN NAMES Italian 13%; Spanish 6%; French 5%. *Mario* (3), *Caterina* (2), *Salvatore* (2), *Rosario*; *Luis Carlos*, *Luisa*; *Camille*, *Lucien*.

Criste (144) German and English: variant of CRIST.

Cristello (113) Italian: from a diminutive of the personal name CRISTO.
GIVEN NAME Italian 11%. *Salvatore*.

Cristiano (328) Italian: from the personal name *Cristiano*, Latin *Christianus* 'follower of *Christ*' (see CHRISTIAN). In the Tarentine and Sicilian dialects of Italy *cristiano* is a complimentary term for a clever, judicious person.
GIVEN NAMES Italian 30%. *Antonio* (5), *Franco* (2), *Pasquale* (2), *Silvano* (2), *Vito* (2), *Antimo*, *Enrico*, *Fortunato*, *Francesco*, *Gennaro*, *Nino*, *Nunzio*, *Pietro*, *Renato*, *Rodolfo*, *Rosario*.

Cristina (154) Southern Italian: from the female personal name *Cristina*, a continuation of the Latin personal name *Christina*, derived from Latin *Christus* 'Christ'.
GIVEN NAMES Italian 16%. *Renzo* (2), *Rocco* (2), *Umberto* (2), *Giovanni*, *Vito*.

Cristo (158) Spanish, Italian (Sardinia and Lazio), and Portuguese: from the personal name *Cristo* 'Christ', Latin *Christus*, Greek *Khristos* (see CHRISTIAN).

GIVEN NAMES Spanish 12%; Italian 7%. *Adolfo*, *Carlos*, *Eduardo*, *Emilio*, *Guadalupe*, *Jorge*, *Juan*, *Juan Ramon*, *Livia*, *Manuel*, *Rebeca*, *Rey*; *Carlo*, *Dino*, *Marcello*, *Sal*.

Cristobal (267) Spanish (**Cristóbal**): from the personal name *Cristóbal*, Spanish form of CHRISTOPHER.
GIVEN NAMES Spanish 50%. *Manuel* (5), *Jesus* (3), *Jose* (3), *Aurelio* (2), *Carlos* (2), *Cielito* (2), *Luis* (2), *Mariano* (2), *Ramon* (2), *Adela*, *Adelaida*, *Alejandro*.

Cristofaro (110) Italian: variant of **Cristoforo**, from the personal name *Cristoforo*, from Latin *Christoforus* (see CHRISTOPHER).
GIVEN NAMES Italian 23%. *Angelo* (2), *Luciano* (2), *Cosmo*, *Dante*, *Franco*, *Matteo*, *Pasco*, *Tullio*.

Cristy (109) English: variant spelling of CHRISTIE.

Criswell (2907) English: variant of CRESWELL.

Critcher (245) English (Berkshire): unexplained.

Critchett (115) English: unexplained.

Critchfield (859) English: variant of CRUTCHFIELD.

Critchley (318) English (Lancashire): either a variant of CRITCHLOW or a habitational name from some other place, now lost.

Critchlow (548) English: habitational name from Critchlow in Lancashire, named from Celtic *crūg* 'hill' + Old English *hlāw* 'mound'.

Crite (98) Perhaps an Americanized spelling of South German **Kreit(h)**, a topographic name from Middle High German *geriute* 'land cleared for farming', or of North German **Kreite**, a nickname for a quarrelsome person, from Middle Low German *kreit* 'strife'.

Critelli (367) Italian: variant of CRETELLA.
GIVEN NAMES Italian 12%. *Antonio*, *Gennaro*, *Rocco*, *Salvatore*, *Vincenzo*.

Crites (2628) Americanized spelling of German KREUTZ.

Critser (197) Americanized spelling of German KRITZER or KREUTZER.

Crittenden (2264) English (Kent): habitational name from Crittenden in Kent, which is named with the Old English personal name *Gūðhere* + Old English *-ing-* denoting association with + Old English *denn* 'woodland pasture'.
FOREBEARS The statesman John Jordan Crittenden, who was born near Versailles, KY, in 1787, was of Welsh descent on his father's side. His immigrant ancestor arrived in VA before 1650. His father, a major in the American Revolution, moved from VA to KY and settled in Woodford Co.

Crittendon (428) English: variant of CRITTENDEN.

Critz (293) Variant spelling of German KRITZ.

Critzer (316) Variant spelling of German KRITZER.

Crivelli (162) Italian: patronymic or plural form of CRIVELLO.

GIVEN NAMES Italian 24%. *Geno* (3), *Franco* (2), *Angelo, Antonio, Camillo, Enzo, Nicola, Pasquale, Piero, Pietro, Sal, Salvatore.*

Crivello (445) Italian: metonymic occupational name for a maker or user of sieves, from *crivello* 'sieve', from Late Latin *cribellum*, a diminutive of classical Latin *cribrum*.

GIVEN NAMES Italian 24%; Spanish 9%. *Mario* (6), *Roberto* (4), *Antonio* (2), *Salvatore* (2), *Bartolo, Domenic, Gasper, Marco, Mariano* (2), *Neno; Manuel* (3), *Alvarino, Fernanda, Jaime, Julio, Ramona, Salvador.*

Crnkovich (223) Serbian and Croatian (**Crnković**): patronymic meaning 'son of the black-haired or dark-skinned one', from *crn* 'black'.

Croak (268) **1.** English: unexplained. **2.** Irish: variant of CROKE.

Croan (142) Irish: variant of CROGHAN.

Croasdale (132) English (Lancashire): apparently a habitational name from an unidentified place, possibly Crowsdale Wood in North Yorkshire.

Crocco (369) Italian: probably from Sicilian *croccu* 'hook', hence a metonymic occupational name for a maker of hooks, crooks, and the like, or possibly a nickname for someone who wore a hook in place of a lost hand or arm.

GIVEN NAMES Italian 17%. *Domenic* (2), *Italo* (2), *Pasquale* (2), *Salvatore* (2), *Santo* (2), *Biagio, Biago, Marino, Nicola, Oresto, Pierina, Pietro.*

Croce (1020) Italian: from *croce* 'cross' (Latin *crux*, genitive *crucis*), applied as a Christian religious personal name, a topographic name for someone who lived by a roadside cross, or a nickname for someone who carried the cross in religious processions. Compare English CROSS.

GIVEN NAMES Italian 18%. *Sal* (5), *Angelo* (4), *Carlo* (4), *Nicola* (4), *Salvatore* (4), *Vito* (3), *Antonio* (2), *Gino* (2), *Rocco* (2), *Saverio* (2), *Amadeo, Amerigo.*

Crocetti (137) Italian: from a diminutive plural form of CROCE.

GIVEN NAMES Italian 22%. *Angelo* (2), *Carlo* (2), *Emidio* (2), *Domenic, Egidio, Enrico, Ferruccio, Gino, Guerino.*

Crochet (830) French: from a diminutive of Old French *croc* 'hook', a topographic name denoting someone who lived by a bend in a river or road, or a metonymic occupational name for a maker, seller, or user of hooks.

FOREBEARS This name is frequent in LA, most families tracing their ancestry to the marriage in 1758 of Yves Crochet, from Megrit, Brittany, to Pélagie Benoist, a refugee from Acadia.

GIVEN NAMES French 7%. *Jean-Charles* (2), *Leonce* (2), *Monique* (2), *Alcide, Andree, Cecile, Emile, Kearney, Lenet, Lucien, Ovide.*

Croci (123) Italian: variant (plural) of CROCE.

GIVEN NAMES Italian 10%. *Amleto, Enrico, Filiberto, Guido, Santi.*

Crock (322) **1.** Americanized spelling of German KROCK. **2.** English: perhaps a metonymic occupational name for a potter, from Middle English *crock* 'pot'.

Crocker (7847) **1.** English (of Norman origin): habitational name from any of the various places in Normandy, France, called Crèvecoeur ('heartbreak'), from Old French *creve(r)* 'to break or destroy', 'to die' + *ceur* 'heart', a reference to the infertility and unproductiveness of the land. **2.** English: occupational name for a potter, Middle English *crockere*, an agent derivative of Middle English *crock* 'pot' (Old English *croc(ca)*). **3.** Americanized spelling of German KROCKER.

Crockett (7709) **1.** English and Scottish (Galloway): nickname for someone who affected a particular hairstyle, from Middle English *croket* 'large curl' (Old Norman French *croquet*, a diminutive of *croque* 'curl', 'hook'). **2.** Scottish: Anglicized form of Gaelic **Mac Riocaird** 'son of Richard' (see RICHARD).

Crockford (171) English: habitational name from Crockford Bridge in the parish of Chertsey, Surrey. The place name is of uncertain origin; the first element may be Old English *croc(ca)* 'pot', used of a hollow in the ground or of a place where potsherds were found; the second is Old English *ford* 'ford'.

Croes (143) Dutch: **1.** from Middle Dutch *croes(e)* 'crock', 'beaker'; hence a metonymic occupational name for a potter or seller of pottery. **2.** nickname for someone with curly hair, from Middle Dutch *croes* 'curly'. **3.** topographic name from Dutch *kruis* 'cross'.

GIVEN NAMES Spanish 6%. *Raul* (2), *Carlos, Francisca, Gilberto, Ricardo.*

Croff (311) Altered form of German GRAF or GRAFF.

Crofford (340) English: habitational name, perhaps from Croford in Somerset. However, the surname is associated more with Suffolk than Somerset, and a different source, now lost, may be involved.

Crofoot (483) **1.** Scottish: variant of CRAWFORD. **2.** English: variant of **Crowfoot**, a nickname for someone with splayed feet or some other deformity of the foot, from Old English *crāwe* 'crow' + *fōt* 'foot'. In Middle English *crou-fot* also denoted the buttercup, and it may be from this sense that the name arose, although the reason for its adoption is unclear.

Croft (4714) **1.** English: topographic name for someone who lived by an arable enclosure, normally adjoining a house, Middle English *croft*. There are several places in England named with this word (Old English *croft*), and the surname may equally be a habitational name from any of them. **2.** Possibly an Americanized spelling of KRAFT.

Crofton (390) English: habitational name from any of the various places called Crofton, for example in Cumbria, Greater London (formerly in Kent), Hampshire, Lincolnshire, Wiltshire, and West Yorkshire. Most of these are named from Old English *croft* 'paddock', 'vegetable garden' + *tūn* 'enclosure', 'settlement', but the one in Greater London probably has as its first element Old English *cropp* 'swelling', 'mound' (compare CROPPER) and that in Lincolnshire Old English *croh* 'saffron' (from Latin *crocus*).

FOREBEARS A family called Crofton was established in Ireland by John Crofton (died 1610), who held high office under Elizabeth I and acquired vast estates when he accompanied Sir Henry Sidney, Lord Deputy, into Ireland in 1565.

Crofts (451) English: variant of CROFT.

Crofut (106) Variant of Scottish and northern Irish CRAWFORD or English **Crowfoot** (see CROFOOT).

Crogan (180) Irish: variant of CROGHAN.

Croghan (518) Irish: Anglicized form of Gaelic **Mac Conchruacháin** 'son of *Cú Cruacháin*', a personal name meaning 'hound of Croghan'. Croghan in Co. Roscommon was the ancient royal site of the province of Connacht.

GIVEN NAMES Irish 6%. *Aileen, Padraic.*

Crognale (102) Italian: topographic name, indicating the presence of a cornelian cherry tree or trees (Italian *corniale*, from *corgnale*, from *corniolo*; from Latin *corneolus*).

GIVEN NAMES Italian 32%. *Caesar* (2), *Domenic* (2), *Guido* (2), *Angelo, Camillo, Carlo, Concetta, Dino, Giovanni.*

Crohn (126) Respelling of German KROHN.

GIVEN NAMES German 6%. *Sieg, Siegbert.*

Croissant (210) French: from *croissant* 'growing', present participle of *croître* 'to grow', hence a nickname for a fast-growing young man.

GIVEN NAMES French 4%; German 4%. *Olivier; Erwin* (2), *Bernd, Ingeborg.*

Croke (468) **1.** English: unexplained; possibly a nickname for someone with a rough voice. **2.** Irish: Anglicized form of Gaelic **Cróc**, from Old Norse *Krokr*.

GIVEN NAMES Irish 6%. *Aidan* (2), *Brendan, Fergus, Kieran.*

Croker (549) English: variant of CROCKER 1.

Croley (660) Irish: variant of CROWLEY.

Croll (650) **1.** Respelling of KROLL. **2.** English: variant of CURL.

Crolley (108) Variant spelling Irish **Crolly**, a variant of CRILLY in Oriel and of CROWLEY in Munster.

Crom (244) **1.** Dutch: variant of KROM. **2.** English: possibly a variant of CROOM.

Cromack (112) Metathesized variant of Scottish and Irish CORMACK (see McCORMACK).

Croman (109) Possibly of Irish or Scottish origin, but unexplained.

Cromartie (560) Scottish (now found mainly in Orkney and Aberdeen): habitational name from Cromarty in Ross and Cromarty.

GIVEN NAMES French 4%. *Celestine* (2), *Jacques*, *Pierre*.

Crombie (488) Scottish: habitational name from a place in Aberdeenshire named Crombie, from Gaelic *crom(b)* 'crooked' or possibly the British cognate of this word, ancestor of Welsh *crwm*.

Crome (104) English: variant of CROOM.

Cromer (2830) **1.** French: from a Germanic personal name, *Hrodmar*, composed of *hrōd* 'renown', 'glory' + *mār* 'famous'. **2.** English: habitational name from Cromer in Norfolk, recorded in the 13th century as *Crowemere*, from Old English *crāwe* 'crow' + *mere* 'lake'. **3.** Variant spelling of German and Jewish KROMER.

Cromie (255) Scottish and northern Irish: variant of CROMBIE.

Cromley (283) Irish: variant of CRUMLEY.

Crommett (121) English: unexplained; possibly an altered form of **Grummett**, which is from a pet form of the personal name *Grim* or of any of various Germanic personal names formed with the element *grim* 'mask' (see GRIM).

Crompton (839) English: variant of CRUMPTON.

Cromwell (2662) English: habitational name from places in Nottinghamshire and West Yorkshire named Cromwell, from Old English *crumb* 'bent', 'crooked' + *well(a)* 'spring', 'stream'.

Cron (773) **1.** Scottish: reduced form of McCRONE. **2.** Americanized spelling of German and Swedish KRON.

Cronan (777) Irish: variant spelling of CRONIN.

Cronauer (143) Americanized spelling of German **Kronauer**, a habitational name for someone from Kronau near Heidelberg or Kranau in eastern Austria (formerly *Kronau*), or of German **Gronauer**, a habitational name for someone from any of eleven places named Gronau.

Cronce (214) Americanized spelling of Dutch **Croons** (a patronymic from KROON) or of German, Dutch, or Jewish KRANTZ. Compare KRONTZ.

Crone (2073) **1.** Irish: Anglicized form of Gaelic **Ó Cróin** 'descendant of *Crón*', a name from *crón* 'swarthy'. Compare

CRONIN. **2.** Variant spelling of German KRONE.

Cronen (146) Irish: variant spelling of CRONIN.

GIVEN NAMES Irish 4%. *Conley*, *Eamon*.

Cronenwett (128) Probably an altered form of German **Kron(n)owett**, a habitational name from any of numerous places in Bavaria and Austria named Kranewitt, from Old High German *kranawitu* 'juniper tree', or possibly a topographic name for someone who lived by a juniper, Middle High German *kranewite*. See also KRONEN-WETTER.

Croner (153) Americanized spelling of German **Kroner** or **Kröner** (see KRONER).

GIVEN NAMES German 5%. *Guenther*, *Kurt*.

Croney (295) Irish: shortened Anglicized form of Gaelic **Mac Ruanaidh** (see ROONEY), or possibly of **Mac Raighne**, usually Anglicized as **Reaney** (see RAINEY).

Cronic (204) Origin uncertain. **1.** Probably a respelling of Jewish KRONICK. **2.** Possibly a variant of Serbian **Kronić**, of unexplained etymology.

Cronin (8139) Irish: Anglicized form of Gaelic **Ó Cróinín** 'descendant of *Cróinín*', a byname from a diminutive of *crón* 'swarthy'.

GIVEN NAMES Irish 5%. *Brendan* (3), *Eamon* (3), *John Patrick* (2), *Bridie*, *Caitlin*, *Colm*, *Donal*, *Paddy*, *Peadar*, *Siobhan*.

Cronister (123) German: variant of **Kronaster**, habitational name for someone from a place in Bavaria called Kronast, or from Kranest, formerly Kronest, in Upper Austria near Neumarkt. The name means 'crane's nest'.

Cronk (2062) **1.** English: variant of CRANK. **2.** Possibly an Americanized spelling of German **Kranke** (see CRANK).

Cronkhite (427) Americanized spelling of Dutch **Krankheid**, from an abstract noun meaning 'weakness', hence probably a nickname for a sickly individual.

Cronkite (115) Americanized spelling of Dutch **Krankheid** (see CRONKHITE).

FOREBEARS The ancestors of the American Cronkite family, including the broadcaster Walter Cronkite (born 1919), were Dutch merchants who settled in the 17th century in what is now New York, then the Dutch settlement of New Amsterdam.

Cronkright (143) Americanized spelling of Dutch **Krankheid** (see CRONKHITE).

Cronn (111) Variant spelling of German, Dutch, or Swedish KRON.

Cronquist (182) Swedish: ornamental name composed of the elements *kron(a)* 'crown' + *quist*, an old or ornamental spelling of *kvist* 'twig'.

Crook (5421) English: **1.** from the Old Norse byname *Krókr* meaning 'crook', 'bend', originally possibly bestowed on a cripple or hunchback or a devious schemer, but in early medieval England used as a

personal name. **2.** from Old Norse *krókr* 'hook', 'bend', borrowed into Middle English as a vocabulary word and applied as a metonymic occupational name for a maker, seller, or user of hooks or a topographic name for someone who lived by a bend in a river or road. In some instances the surname may have arisen as a habitational name from places in Cumbria and Durham named Crook from this word.

Crooke (375) English: variant spelling of CROOK.

Crooker (517) English: from a noun derivative of Old Norse *krókr* 'hook', 'bend', applied as an occupational name or a topographic or habitational name (see CROOK 2).

Crookham (140) English: habitational name from places called Crookham in Berkshire and Northumberland, or from Church Crookham in Hampshire. The one in Northumberland is named with a dative plural form of Old Scandinavian *krókr* 'crook', 'bend', while those in Berkshire and Hampshire are probably named with an Old English word *croc* 'crook', 'bend' + *hām* 'homestead'.

Crooks (3547) English: patronymic from CROOK 1.

Crookshank (136) Scottish: variant spelling of CRUICKSHANK.

Crookshanks (199) Scottish: variant of CRUICKSHANK.

Crookston (278) Scottish: habitational name, according to Black, from a place in Renfrewshire, which was named as the estate of one Robert Croc. There are other places, in the Border and Lothian regions of Scotland, with this name, from which the surname could have arisen.

Croom (1402) **1.** English: nickname for a cripple or hunchback, from Middle English *crom(p)*, Old English *crumb* 'bent', 'crooked', 'stooping'. Compare CRUMP. **2.** English: metonymic occupational name for a maker, seller, or user of hooks, from Middle English *crome*, *cromb* 'hook', 'crook' (from Old English *crumb* 'bent', reinforced by an Old French borrowing from a Germanic cognate). **3.** English: habitational name from Croom in East Yorkshire or Croome in Worcestershire. The first is named with Old English *crōhum*, dative plural (used originally after a preposition) of *crōh* 'narrow valley' (a cognate of Old Norse *krá* 'corner', 'bend', and related to the words mentioned in 1 and 2 above). The place in Worcestershire is named with an old British river name ultimately cognate with the other words mentioned here; compare Welsh *crwm* 'crooked', 'winding'. **4.** Americanized spelling of German KRUMM.

Crooms (346) English: variant of CROOM.

Croop (129) Possibly an Americanized spelling of German KRUPP.

Cropley (200) **1.** English (East Anglia): habitational name from Cropley Grove in Suffolk, which is probably named from Old English *cropp* 'swelling', 'mound' + *lēah* 'woodland clearing'. **2.** Probably an Americanized spelling of Swiss German **Kroppli**, a variant of KROPF.

Cropp (444) **1.** English: metonymic occupational name for a harvester of fruit, vegetables, or corn, from Middle English *cropp*, a noun derivative of *cropt(en)* 'to pick'. Compare CROPPER. **2.** English: topographic name for someone who lived at the top of a hill, Middle English *cropp*. **3.** Americanized spelling of German KROPP or of German and Dutch KRAPP.

Cropper (1142) English (chiefly Lancashire): occupational name for a picker of fruit or vegetables or a reaper of cereal crops, from an agent derivative of Middle English *cropt(en)* 'to pick'. The word was used also to denote the polling of cattle and the name may therefore have been given to someone who did this.

Cropsey (177) English: unexplained. Perhaps a variant of **Cripsey**, habitational name from a place of this name in Lincolnshire.

Crosbie (462) Scottish: variant spelling of CROSBY.

Crosby (13466) **1.** Scottish and English: habitational name from any of various places in southwestern Scotland and northern England that are named with Old Norse *kross* 'cross' + *býr* 'farm', 'settlement'. **2.** Irish: Scottish and English surname (see 1 above) adopted by bearers of Gaelic **Mac an Chrosáin** (see MCCROSSEN).
FOREBEARS The name of the Irish family of Crosbie is ultimately derived from providing the chief bards to the O'Mores, Chiefs of Leix (*crosán* means 'bard', 'satirist'). Pádraic Mac Crosáin or Mac An Chrosáin took the name Patrick Crosbie in about 1583.

Crose (468) **1.** Southern French: topographic name for someone who lived near a hollow in the ground. **2.** Northern Italian (Veneto): variant of CROCE.

Croshaw (149) English: variant of CRAWSHAW.

Crosier (775) English and French: variant spelling of CROZIER.

Croskey (334) Scottish and northern Irish: reduced form of **McCroskey**. Compare Irish COSGROVE.

Crosland (367) English: variant of CROSSLAND.

Crosley (664) English: variant of CROSSLEY, also established as a surname in Ireland.

Croslin (207) English: perhaps a variant of CROSSLAND.

Crosman (140) Variant of English **Crossman** or German **Crossmann** (see CROSSMAN).

Croson (248) English (North Midlands): perhaps a respelling of Irish CROSSAN.

Cross (26686) **1.** English: topographic name for someone who lived near a stone cross set up by the roadside or in a marketplace, from Old Norse *kross* (via Gaelic from Latin *crux*, genitive *crucis*), which in Middle English quickly and comprehensively displaced the Old English form *crūc* (see CROUCH). In a few cases the surname may have been given originally to someone who lived by a crossroads, but this sense of the word seems to have been a comparatively late development. In other cases, the surname (and its European cognates) may have denoted someone who carried the cross in processions of the Christian Church, but in English at least the usual word for this sense was CROZIER. **2.** Irish: reduced form of MCCROSSEN. **3.** In North America this name has absorbed examples of cognate names from other languages, such as French LACROIX.

Crossan (436) Irish: reduced form of MCCROSSEN, an Anglicized form of Gaelic **Mac an Chrosáin** 'son of the satirist'.

Crosse (146) English and Irish: variant spelling of CROSS.

Crossen (565) Irish and Scottish: reduced form of MCCROSSEN.

Crosser (381) **1.** Scottish: Black records this as an old spelling of **Crosar**, itself a variant of CROZIER. **2.** In some cases at least the name is probably a respelling of German GROSSER.

Crossett (454) Northern Irish: of uncertain derivation; perhaps from Gaelic *crosaid* 'little cross'.

Crossfield (179) English: habitational name from a place in Cambridgeshire named Crossfield, from Celtic *cors* 'marsh' + Old English *feld* 'open country'.

Crossgrove (131) Irish: possibly a variant of COSGROVE.

Crossin (185) Irish and Scottish: reduced variant of MCCROSSEN.

Crossland (1344) English (chiefly West Yorkshire): habitational name from a place in the parish of Almondbury, West Yorkshire, named Crosland, from Old English *cros* 'cross' + *land* 'newly cultivated land'.

Crossley (2045) English: habitational name from either of two places in West Yorkshire named Crossley, from Old English *cros* 'cross' + *lēah* 'woodland clearing'.

Crosslin (408) English: perhaps a variant of CROSSLAND.

Crossman (1751) **1.** English: topographic name for someone who lived by a stone cross, from Old Norse *kross* (see CROSS 1) + Middle English *man*. **2.** Altered spelling of German **Crossmann** or **Crössmann**; the first may be a habitational name from any of several places called Crossen in Saxony, Brandenburg, and East Prussia, or derived from GROSSMANN. The second is

possibly from Middle Low German *krōs*, *krüs* 'pitcher', and hence a metonymic occupational name for maker of these; alternatively it may be a metonymic occupational name for a butcher, from Middle High German *kroese* 'tripe'.

Crossno (240) Americanized form of German **Krausner**, a nickname for someone with curly hair, from a derivative of *kraus* 'curly' (see KRAUS, KRAUSER).

Crosson (1101) Reduced variant of Irish and Scottish MCCROSSEN.

Crosswell (131) English: variant of CROSWELL.

Crosswhite (628) English: either a variant of CROSTHWAITE or of **Crostwight**, a habitational name from Crostwight in Norfolk, with the same etymology.

Crosta (109) Southern Italian: nickname for a pest, from Sicilian *crusta* 'crust', 'scab'.
GIVEN NAMES Italian 4%. *Caesar, Pierina, Silvio*.

Crosthwait (149) English: variant spelling of CROSTHWAITE.

Crosthwaite (208) English: habitational name from any of several places in northwestern England named from Old Norse *kross* 'cross' + *þveit* 'clearing'.

Croston (460) English: habitational name from a place in Lancashire named Croston, from Old Norse *kross* 'cross' or Old English *cros* + Old English *tūn* 'farmstead', 'settlement'.

Croswell (372) English: habitational name from a lost or unidentified place, perhaps an altered form of CRESWELL.

Croteau (1835) French: of uncertain derivation; perhaps a diminutive of **Crotte**, a topographical name from Latin *crypta* 'grotto'. Since the name **Crotte** is spelled and pronounced the same as a word meaning 'excrement', a family might have welcomed the opportunity to vary it.
FOREBEARS A Croteau from Normandy, France, is documented in 1669 in Becquet (Cap Rouge), Quebec.
GIVEN NAMES French 12%. *Andre* (9), *Armand* (9), *Lucien* (5), *Normand* (5), *Marcel* (4), *Fernand* (3), *Aime* (2), *Gisele* (2), *Oneil* (2), *Roch* (2), *Alain, Alcide*.

Crothers (1028) Chiefly northern Irish: variant of Scottish CARRUTHERS.

Crotteau (227) French: variant of CROTEAU.

Crotts (875) Altered spelling of German KROTZ or KRATZ.

Crotty (1630) Irish: Anglicized form of Gaelic **Ó Crotaigh** 'descendant of *Crotach*', a byname for a hunchback.
GIVEN NAMES Irish 6%. *Brendan* (2), *Brigid, Dermot, Finbarr, Liam, Michael Patrick, Seamus*.

Crotwell (156) Possibly an Americanized form of South German **Grotewohl**, a late medieval nickname for a journeyman, from *es gerate wohl* 'may it (your work) turn out well'. Compare GRADWOHL, GRADWELL.

Crotzer (157) Possibly an Americanized spelling of German KRATZER.

Crouch (9266) **1.** English: from Middle English *crouch*, Old English *crūc* 'cross' (a word that was replaced in Middle English by the word *cross*, from Old Norse *kross*), applied either as a topographic name for someone who lived by a cross or possibly as a nickname for someone who had carried a cross in a pageant or procession. **2.** Dutch: from Middle Dutch *croech* 'jug', 'pitcher', hence a metonymic occupational name for a potter.

Croucher (477) English: topographic name or nickname, from a derivative of Middle English *crouch* 'cross' (see CROUCH).

Crough (172) **1.** Irish: probably a variant of CROW. **2.** Dutch: variant of CROUCH.

Crounse (193) Of Dutch origin but uncertain etymology, possibly a patronymic from KROON. This is a common name among the descendants of early Dutch settlers in the Albany area.

Crouse (5430) **1.** English: variant of CRUSE. **2.** Americanized spelling of German and Jewish KRAUS.

Crouser (152) Probably an Americanized spelling of German and Jewish KRAUSER.

Croushore (112) Americanized spelling of German and Jewish KRAUSHAAR.

Crout (353) Possibly an altered spelling of French **Croutte**, a variant of **Crotte** (see CROTEAU), or an Americanized spelling of German and Jewish KRAUT.

Crouthamel (315) Americanized spelling of German **Krauthamer**, a variant of **Krautheimer**, a habitational name for someone from any of several places named Krautheim in Baden, Bavaria, and Thuringia.

Crovo (121) Italian: metathesized spelling of CORVO.

GIVEN NAME French 4%. *Patrice.*

Crow (9725) **1.** English: from Middle English *crow*, Old English *crāwa*, applied as a nickname for someone with dark hair or a dark complexion or for someone thought to resemble the bird in some other way. **2.** Irish (Munster): Anglicized form of Gaelic **Mac Conchradha** (see MCENROE). **3.** Irish: translation of any of various Gaelic names derived from *fiach* 'raven', 'crow' (see FEE).

Crowden (162) English: habitational name from either of two places called Crowden, in Derbyshire and Devon. The first is named from Old English *crāwe* 'crow' + *denu* 'valley'; the second from Old English *crāwe* + *dūn* 'hill'.

Crowder (7718) **1.** English and Welsh: occupational name for a player on the crowd, Middle English *crouth*, *croude*, a popular medieval stringed instrument (Welsh *crwth*). **2.** Americanized spelling of German KRAUTER.

Crowe (11044) Irish (very common in northern Ireland) and English: variant spelling of CROW.

Crowell (6687) English: habitational name from a place in Oxfordshire named Crowell, from Old English *crāwe* 'crow' + *well(a)* 'spring', 'stream'.

Crowhurst (123) English: habitational name from either of two places called Crowhurst. The one in Sussex (*Croghyrste* in Old English) is named from Old English *crōh* 'nook', 'corner' + *hyrst* 'wooded hill'; the one in Surrey is from Old English *crāwe* 'crow' + *hyrst* 'wooded hill'.

Crowl (1168) **1.** English: habitational name from either of two places named Crowle. The one in Worcestershire is named with an Old English word *crōh* 'nook', 'corner' + *lēah* 'woodland clearing'; the other, in Lincolnshire, takes its name from an Old English river name meaning 'winding'. **2.** Americanized spelling of German GRAUL.

Crowley (12437) **1.** Irish: Anglicized form of Gaelic **Ó Cruadhlaoich** 'descendant of *Cruadhlaoch*', a personal name composed of the elements *cruadh* 'hardy' + *laoch* 'hero'. **2.** English: variant spelling of CRAWLEY.

GIVEN NAMES Irish 4%. *Brendan* (5), *Brennan* (2), *Kieran* (2), *Aileen*, *Assumpta*, *Bridie*, *Declan*, *Donovan*, *Kaitlin*, *Kevin Patrick*, *Maeve*, *Patrick Joseph*.

Crown (962) **1.** English (of Norman origin): habitational name from Craon in Mayenne, France. **2.** English: habitational name for someone who lived at a house distinguished by the sign of a crown, Middle English *croun*. **3.** This name has probably also assimilated examples of German or Swedish KRON 'crown', or cognates in other languages.

Crowner (198) **1.** English: status name for a coroner, Anglo-Norman French *coro(u)ner*, from Old French *coro(u)ne* 'crown', after the Latin title *custos placitorum coronæ* 'protector of the pleas of the Crown'. **2.** In some cases probably an Americanized form of German **Kroner** or **Kröner** (see KRONER).

Crowningshield (100) Origin unidentified. This name is recorded in MA from 1699 onward, but is apparently not of English origin. It is more probably an altered form of an unidentified Dutch or German original.

Crownover (929) Americanized spelling of a German name: perhaps **Kronauer**, a habitational name for someone from Kronau near Heidelberg, or **Kronhöfer**, a variant of **Grünhofer**, a habitational name for someone from a lost place called Grünhof, from Middle High German *grüene* 'green' or *kranech* 'crane' + *hof* 'farmstead'.

Crowson (1061) English: unexplained.

Crowther (1434) English (mainly Yorkshire): variant of CROWDER.

Crowthers (106) English: variant of CROWTHER.

Croxford (132) English: habitational name from an unidentified place, perhaps a variant of CROCKFORD.

Croxton (623) English: habitational name from places in Cambridgeshire, Cheshire, Lincolnshire, Leicestershire, Norfolk, and Staffordshire named Croxton, from the Old Scandinavian personal name *Krókr* (see CROOK 1) or an Old English word *crōc* 'nook' + Old English *tūn* 'farmstead', 'settlement'.

Croy (1502) **1.** Irish: reduced form of MCCROY, which is a variant of MCROY. **2.** Scottish: habitational name from any of several places named Croy, for example in Inverness-shire.

Croyle (599) English (of Norman origin): habitational name from Criel-sur-Mer, in Seine-Inférieure, France.

Crozier (1831) English and French: occupational name for one who carried a cross or a bishop's crook in ecclesiastical processions, from Middle English, Old French *croisier*.

Crubaugh (113) Probably an Americanized form of German **Grunbach** (see GRUBAUGH).

GIVEN NAMES French 4%; German 4%. *Patrice*; *Kurt*.

Cruce (750) Spanish and Galician: topographic name from *cruce* 'crossroads', or a habitational name from Cruce in Ourense province, Galicia.

Crudele (180) Italian: nickname from *crudele* 'cruel'.

GIVEN NAMES Italian 14%. *Antonio* (2), *Fernando* (2), *Giovanni* (2), *Angelo*, *Vito*, *Michael Angelo*, *Nicandro*.

Cruden (106) Scottish: habitational name from Cruden, a district of Buchan.

Crudo (139) **1.** Italian: nickname from *crudo* 'harsh', 'severe'. **2.** Romanian: from *crudo* 'raw'.

GIVEN NAMES Italian 16%. *Rocco* (2), *Angelo*, *Antonino*, *Giuseppe*.

Crudup (431) Probably an Americanized form of North German **Gratop**, a nickname for an old man, from Middle Low German *grā* 'gray' + *top* 'braid' (modern German **Zopf**).

Cruea (144) Origin uncertain; possibly an Americanized spelling of German **Krüer** (see KRUER).

Cruey (169) Probably of German origin: see CRUEA.

Cruger (176) Respelling of German and Jewish KRUGER.

FOREBEARS John Cruger, probably of German origin, came to NY from Bristol, England, in 1698 and built up a very prosperous shipping business. He was alderman for 22 years and mayor from 1739 to his death in 1744. His son of the same name was also mayor from 1756 to 1765.

Cruickshank (767) Scottish: nickname for a man with a crooked leg or legs, from older Scots *cruik* 'hook', 'bend' (Middle

English *crook*, Old Scandinavian *krókr*) + *shank* 'leg(-bone)' (Old English *sceanca*).

Cruikshank (640) Scottish: variant spelling of CRUICKSHANK.

Cruise (1075) **1.** English: variant spelling of CRUSE. **2.** Americanized spelling of German and Danish KRUSE.

Crull (578) **1.** English: variant (metathesized form) of CURL. **2.** Americanized spelling of German KRULL.

Crum (6354) **1.** Scottish and northern Irish: reduced form of MCCRUM. **2.** Scottish: reduced form of **Macilchrum**, an Americanized form of Gaelic **Mac Gille Chruim** 'son of the servant of the cripple' (see MCCRUM). **3.** Americanized spelling of German KRUMM or of Dutch and Jewish KROM.

Crumb (724) Scottish, northern Irish, and English: variant spelling of CRUM.

Crumbaker (117) Americanized spelling of Swiss German **Grumbacher** or German **Krumbacher**, habitational names for someone from Grumbach in Switzerland or from any of several places named Krumbach in southern and eastern Germany.

Crumbaugh (140) Americanized spelling of the German habitational name **Krumbach** or the Swiss habitational name **Grumbach** (see CRUMBAKER).

Crumble (108) **1.** English (Cheshire): perhaps a habitational name from Cromwell in Nottinghamshire or Cromwell Bottom in West Yorkshire, both named from Old English *crumb* 'crooked' + *wella* 'stream', 'spring'. The latter is recorded as *Crumbel* (1251) and *Crumble* (1566). **2.** Probably an altered spelling of German **Krumpel** or **Krümpel**, a nickname for someone with a deformity, from Middle High German *krum(p)* 'deformed', 'crooked'; skeletal deformities were common in the Middle Ages, often as a result of rickets.

Crumbley (669) English (Durham): probably a variant spelling of Irish CRUMLEY.

Crumbliss (113) Perhaps an Americanized spelling of German **Krumbholz** (see KRUMHOLZ).

Crumby (187) English spelling of Scottish CROMBIE.

Crume (594) Possibly an Americanized spelling of KRUM or KRUMM.

Crumley (1600) Irish: of uncertain origin. Woulfe suggests an Anglicized form of Gaelic **Ó Cromlaoich** 'descendant of *Cromlaoch*', from a byname meaning 'bent hero'. MacLysaght maintains that, in some cases at least, it is a variant of CRUMLISH.

Crumlish (127) Irish and Scottish: Anglicized form of Gaelic **Ó Cromruisc** 'descendant of *Cromrosc*', from a byname meaning 'squint-eyed'.

GIVEN NAMES Irish 7%. *Brendan, Ethna*.

Crumly (140) Irish: variant spelling of CRUMLEY.

Crumm (212) Scottish and northern Irish: variant spelling of CRUM.

Crummett (172) **1.** English (Norfolk): unexplained. **2.** Americanized form of German GRUMET.

Crummey (154) Northern Irish: variant of Scottish CROMBIE.

Crummie (110) Scottish and northern Irish: variant of CROMBIE.

Crump (6521) **1.** English (chiefly West Midlands): nickname for a cripple or hunchback, from English *cromp*, *crump* 'bent', 'crooked', 'stooping' (from Old English *crumb*). Compare CROOM. **2.** Americanized spelling of German KRUMP, the variant **Krumpp**, or German and Dutch KRAMP.

Crumpacker (218) Of German origin: see CRUMBAKER.

Crumpler (1210) English: unexplained.

Crumpley (122) Possibly a respelling of Irish CRUMLEY. Compare CRUMBLEY.

Crumpton (1581) English: habitational name from Crompton in Lancashire, named with an Old English *crumbe* 'river bend' + *tūn* 'enclosure', 'settlement'.

Crumrine (636) Americanized spelling of German **Krumreihn**, possibly from Middle High German *krum(b)* 'crooked' + *rein* 'border of a field', 'margin', and hence a topographic name for someone who lived by a field with a crooked edge, or perhaps a nickname for a farmer who plowed a crooked furrow. Alternatively, the name may be from an old personal name, *Rumerich*, from Old High German *hruom* 'fame'.

Crunk (399) Probably an Americanized spelling of German KRANK or KRONK.

Crunkleton (170) Northern English: habitational name from Cronkleton in Northumberland.

Crupi (352) Southern Italian: possibly a nickname from medieval Greek *kouroupēs* 'clipped', 'shorn'.

GIVEN NAMES Italian 19%. *Antonio* (2), *Carmelo* (2), *Pasquale* (2), *Rocco* (2), *Santo* (2), *Carlo, Cosimo, Dino, Domenic, Emanuele, Onofrio, Salvatore*.

Crupper (135) English: from Anglo-Norman French *cropere* 'crupper', the part of a horse's saddlery that passes from the tail to the back of the saddle or collar, hence a metonymic occupational name for a maker of cruppers and other harness.

Crusan (202) Probably an Americanized spelling of Dutch **Cruyssen**, habitational name for someone from any of numerous places in the Netherlands named with Dutch *cruys*, *kruis* 'cross'.

Cruse (2914) **1.** English: nickname from Middle English *cr(o)us(e)* 'bold', 'fierce'. **2.** English (of Norman origin): habitational name from a place in France, perhaps Cruys-Staëte in Nord, apparently named with a Gaulish word *crodiu* 'hard'. **3.** German: northern variant of KRAUSE.

4. Americanized spelling of German KRUSE.

Crusenberry (134) English: most probably a variant of CHRISTENBERRY.

Cruser (201) Possibly a respelling of German KRUSER.

Crush (149) Americanized spelling of German **Krusch** (see KRUSCHKE) or GROSCH.

Crusoe (144) According to Reaney and Wilson this name was taken to England by John Crusoe, a Huguenot refugee from Hownescourt in Flanders, who settled in Norwich.

GIVEN NAME French 5%. *Lucien*.

Cruson (144) Probably an Americanized spelling of Dutch **Cruyssen** (see CRUSAN).

Crust (111) English (Kent): from Middle English *crust(e)*, Old French *crouste* 'crust of bread', according to Reaney applied as a nickname for a stubborn or obstinate person.

GIVEN NAME French 5%. *Henri*.

Crutcher (1887) English: variant of CROUCHER.

Crutchfield (3046) English: habitational name probably from Cruchfield in Berkshire or Crutchfield in Surrey, both named with Celtic *crŭg* 'mound', 'hill' + Old English *feld* 'open country'.

Crutchley (185) English (West Midlands): variant of CRITCHLEY.

Crute (286) English: nickname for a dullard, from Middle English *crot*, *crote* 'lump', 'clod'.

Cruthers (109) Scottish and northern Irish: reduced form of CARRUTHERS.

Cruthirds (167) Altered form of Scottish and northern Irish CARRUTHERS. This name is found mainly in MS.

Cruthis (107) Altered form of Scottish and northern Irish CARRUTHERS. This name is found mainly in IL and NC.

Cruver (141) Possibly an Americanized form of German and Jewish GRUBER.

Cruz (25239) Spanish and Portuguese: from a common and widespread religious Christian personal name from *cruz* 'cross' (Latin *crux*), or a habitational name from any of numerous places named Cruz or La Cruz, from this word.

GIVEN NAMES Spanish 48%; Portuguese 10%. *Jose* (698), *Juan* (314), *Luis* (224), *Carlos* (217), *Manuel* (180), *Miguel* (150), *Francisco* (148), *Pedro* (146), *Jesus* (135), *Angel* (128), *Ramon* (116), *Roberto* (115); *Joao* (8), *Wenceslao* (4), *Anatolio* (2), *Godofredo* (2), *Ligia* (2), *Paulo* (2), *Sil* (2), *Albano, Joaquim, Manoel, Margarida, Omero*.

Cruzado (108) Spanish: from *cruzado* 'crusader'.

GIVEN NAMES Spanish 34%. *Jose* (3), *Manuel* (2), *Angel, Bartolome, Eloisa, Eloy, Emilio, Fernando, Genoveva, Geraldo, Isauro, Jaime; Antonio, Gabino, Santo*.

Cruzan (280) Probably an Americanized spelling of Dutch **Cruyssen** (see CRUSAN).

Cruze (408) Possibly an altered spelling of CRUSE, CRUZ, KRUS, or KRUSE.
GIVEN NAMES French 4%. *Jeanpaul* (2), *Guille*.

Cruzen (165) Probably an Americanized spelling of Dutch **Cruyssen** (see CRUSAN).

Cryan (350) Irish: reduced Anglicized form of Gaelic **Mac Ruaidhín** 'son of Ruaidhín', a byname meaning 'the little red one', from a diminutive of *ruadh* 'red'. Compare RYAN, O'RYAN.
GIVEN NAMES Irish 5%. *Brendan, Michael Patrick*.

Cryder (263) Probably an Americanized spelling of German KREIDER.

Cryderman (227) Americanized spelling of German **Kräutermann**, an occupational name of a herbalist or pharmacist, from *Kraut* 'herb' (plural *Kräuter*) + *Mann* 'man'.

Crye (250) Americanized spelling of German KREIE or the variant **Krei** (see KREY).

Cryer (1083) **1.** English: occupational name for a town crier, one whose job was to make public announcements in a loud voice, from Middle English, Old French *criere* (a derivative of Old French *crier* 'to cry aloud', Latin *quiritare*). **2.** Americanized spelling of German KREYER or the Swiss variant **Kreier**.

Crymes (224) English: possibly a variant of GRIMES.

Crysler (200) Americanized spelling of German and Jewish KREISLER. Compare CHRYSLER.

Crystal (837) Northern Irish: reduced Anglicized form of **Mac Criostal** (see MCCRYSTAL).

Crytzer (145) Respelling or Alemannic variant of German KREUTZER.
GIVEN NAME German 4%. *Kurt* (2).

Csaszar (158) Hungarian (**Császár**): from *császár* 'emperor', probably a nickname given to a self-important person or a status name for a servant of the emperor. Old Hungarian names meaning 'king', 'prince', 'noble', 'magistrate', etc. were given to serfs, not to nobles or dignitaries.
GIVEN NAMES Hungarian 9%. *Andras, Csaba, Gabor, Istvan, Jozsef*.

Cseh (131) Hungarian: ethnic name for someone of Czech ancestry.
GIVEN NAMES Hungarian 24%. *Sandor* (4), *Mihaly* (2), *Andras, Bela, Ferenc, Istvan, Jozsef, Tibor, Zoltan, Zsolt*.

Csonka (109) Hungarian: nickname from the vocabulary word *csonka* 'mutilated'.
GIVEN NAMES Hungarian 7%. *Andras, Attila, Geza*.

Cua (150) Catalan: nickname from Catalan *cua* 'tail'.
GIVEN NAMES Spanish 25%; Italian 9%. *Esperanza* (2), *Marisa* (2), *Adriana, Carlito, Carolina, Eduardo, Gonzalez Jose, Ildefonso, Jose, Juanito, Lilia, Luz; Antonio*

(3), *Annamaria, Gaetano, Leonardo, Nicola*.

Cuadra (310) Asturian-Leonese: probably a habitational name from a place in Asturies called Cuadra.
GIVEN NAMES Spanish 51%. *Jose* (10), *Carlos* (7), *Julio* (5), *Luis* (5), *Miguel* (5), *Francisco* (4), *Eduardo* (3), *Emilio* (3), *Guillermo* (3), *Gustavo* (3), *Jesus* (3), *Juan* (3).

Cuadrado (199) Spanish: nickname for a squat, thickset man, from *cuadrado* 'square' (Latin *quadratus*, past participle of *quadrare* 'to form a square').
GIVEN NAMES Spanish 47%. *Juan* (8), *Jose* (5), *Luis* (3), *Alvaro* (2), *Angel* (2), *Carlos* (2), *Efrain* (2), *Evelio* (2), *Lourdes* (2), *Margarita* (2), *Rafael* (2), *Rolando* (2).

Cuadros (133) Asturian-Leonese: habitational name from Cuadros in León province or from Los Cuadros in Asturies.
GIVEN NAMES Spanish 49%. *Jose* (6), *Carlos* (5), *Jaime* (3), *Luis* (3), *Alberto* (2), *Jorge* (2), *Socorro* (2), *Alejandro, Alicia, Ana Maria, Armando, Cristina*.

Cuaresma (101) Spanish: from *cuaresma* 'Lent', probably applied as a nickname for someone born during this period.
GIVEN NAMES Spanish 44%. *Elpidio* (2), *Josefina* (2), *Melecio* (2), *Anabel, Baldomero, Basilio, Bernardo, Celedonio, Eugenio, Felipe, Francisco, Gavino; Antonio, Federico*.

Cuba (364) **1.** Portuguese, Asturian-Leonese, Galician, and Spanish: habitational name from any of the places in Portugal (in the provinces of Alentejo and Beira Baixa) or Spain (in Aragon, Asturies, and Galicia) named Cuba, from *cuba* 'barrel' (from Latin *cupa*). **2.** Variant spelling of KUBA.
GIVEN NAMES Spanish 16%. *Juan* (3), *Carlos* (2), *Ernesto* (2), *Jose Luis* (2), *Pedro* (2), *Angel, Antero, Armando, Arnaldo, Arturo, Belen, Bernabe*.

Cubas (124) Spanish (and Portuguese): habitational name from any of the places in the provinces of Cuenca, Madrid, and Santander, or in Portugal, named Cubas, from the plural of *cuba* 'barrel'.
GIVEN NAMES Spanish 50%. *Carlos* (5), *Armando* (2), *Cesar* (2), *Francisco* (2), *Jorge* (2), *Manuel* (2), *Mario* (2), *Ramon* (2), *Raul* (2), *Roberto* (2), *Alberto, Alfonso; Lorenzo, Marco, Sisto*.

Cubbage (642) **1.** English: unexplained. Perhaps a variant of CABBAGE. **2.** Americanized spelling of German **Koppitsch** or **Koppisch** (see KOPISCHKE).

Cubberley (132) English: unexplained. Possibly a habitational name from a lost or unidentified place name.

Cubberly (108) English: variant spelling of CUBBERLEY.

Cubbison (123) Scottish: probably a reduced and altered Anglicized form of

Gaelic **Mac Giobúin** (see MCCUBBIN), with English patronymic -*son*.

Cubero (156) Spanish: occupational name for a cooper, from an agent derivative of *cuba* 'barrel', 'tub'.
GIVEN NAMES Spanish 42%. *Jose* (4), *Juan* (4), *Luis* (4), *Miguel* (3), *Ruben* (3), *Carlos* (2), *Eduardo* (2), *Ramon* (2), *Eloy, Ernesto, Francisco, Gilberto*.

Cubit (131) English: from Middle English *cubit* 'forearm' (from Latin *cubitum*), presumably applied as a nickname for someone with strong or otherwise remarkable forearms; in its extended sense, as a unit of length, it may have been a metonymic occupational name for a builder.

Cubitt (123) English: variant spelling of CUBIT.

Cuccaro (190) Italian: habitational name from any of numerous places named with this word (from Latin *cuccus* 'round prominence'), especially Cuccaro Vetere in Salerno province.
GIVEN NAMES Italian 23%. *Pasquale* (4), *Carmine* (2), *Elio* (2), *Carlo, Fiore, Lorenzo, Philomena*.

Cucchi (161) Italian: patronymic or plural form of CUCCO.
GIVEN NAMES Italian 12%. *Caesar, Cesidio, Dino, Domenic, Ercole, Fausto, Paolo*.

Cucchiara (243) Southern Italy (Sicily): from Sicilian *cucchiara* 'spoon', presumably a metonymic occupational name for a spoon maker.
GIVEN NAMES Italian 29%. *Vito* (4), *Salvatore* (3), *Orlando* (2), *Sal* (2), *Angelo, Carmelo, Giovanni, Ignazio, Margherita, Mario, Pietro*.

Cucci (235) Italian: patronymic or plural form of CUCCIO.
GIVEN NAMES Italian 14%. *Antonio* (2), *Cesare* (2), *Gennaro* (2), *Angelo, Attilio, Dino, Gilda, Salvatore*.

Cuccia (590) Italian: **1.** from a feminine form of CUCCIO. **2.** from an Albanian family name derived from *kuqi* 'red'; the surname is recorded chiefly in Piana degli Albanesi in Palermo province, the home of an ancient Albanian community.
GIVEN NAMES Italian 12%. *Carlo* (3), *Sal* (3), *Angelo* (2), *Carmelo* (2), *Salvatore* (2), *Vito* (2), *Antoninette, Antonino, Cesare, Ciro, Gaspare, Ignazio*.

Cuccio (176) Italian: from a short form of various personal names ending with the hypocoristic suffix -*cuccio*, such as *Albericuccio, Domenicuccio*, and *Enricuccio*.
GIVEN NAMES Italian 18%. *Salvatore* (3), *Rosario, Sal, Santa*.

Cucco (121) Italian: from *cucchi*, a word with several dialect meanings, including 'cuckoo', 'rounded hill', 'favorite son', any one of which could have given rise to the surname, or from the Sicilian equivalent, *cuccu*.

GIVEN NAMES Italian 24%. *Sal* (4), *Ulisse* (3), *Concetta, Enrico, Nunzio, Pasquale, Rino.*

Cucinotta (309) Italian: from a diminutive of *cugina* 'cousin' (see CUGINI).

GIVEN NAMES Italian 22%. *Salvatore* (4), *Domenic* (3), *Carmel* (2), *Santo* (2), *Vincenza* (2), *Giovanni, Marco, Nunzio, Orazio, Silvio, Tommaso.*

Cuckler (110) Americanized form of German KUGLER.

Cuda (355) **1.** Southern Italian: from Calabrian and Sicilian *cuda* 'tail', standard Italian *coda* (see CODA). **2.** Polish: nickname from *cudo, cuda* 'miracle', 'wonder'. **3.** German: probably an Americanized spelling of German **Kude** (see CUDE) or **Kuder**, a metonymic occupational name of Slavic origin for a person who prepared tow (flax or hemp broken down into fibers for spinning). **4.** Slovenian (**Čuda**): nickname for an odd fellow, from *čuden* 'strange', 'odd'.

GIVEN NAMES Italian 7%. *Angelo* (2), *Pasquale* (2), *Valentino.*

Cudahy (158) Irish: variant of CUDDIHY.

GIVEN NAMES Irish 5%. *Dermot, Murphy.*

Cudd (606) English: from the personal name *Cudd*, a short form of *Cudbert* (see CUTHBERT).

Cuddeback (250) Possibly an Americanized spelling of German **Guttenberg**, a habitational name from any of several places in Bavaria called Guttenberg.

Cuddihy (171) Irish: Anglicization of Gaelic **Ó Cuidighthigh** 'descendant of *Cuidightheach*', a personal name meaning 'helper'.

GIVEN NAMES Irish 5%. *Donal, Finbarr.*

Cuddy (957) English: from the personal name *Cuddy*, a pet form of *Cudbert* (see CUTHBERT).

Cude (565) Probably a respelling of German **Kude**, a nickname from Sorbian *khudy* 'miserable', 'poor'.

Cudmore (258) English: apparently a habitational name from a minor place, perhaps Cudmore Farm in Bampton, Devon, which is named with the Old English personal name *Cudda* + Old English *mōr* 'moor', 'marsh'.

Cudney (389) Perhaps an Americanized spelling of German **Kuttner** or the variant **Küttner** (see KUTTNER).

Cudworth (322) English: habitational name from either of two places named Cudworth, in South Yorkshire and Somerset. The first element of the Yorkshire name is the Old English personal name *Cūtha*, that of the Somerset name the Old English personal name *Cuda*; the second element of both is Old English *worð* 'enclosure'.

Cue (367) **1.** Irish: reduced form of McCUE, which is itself a variant of McCOY. **2.** Asturian-Leonese: habitational name from a place named Cue, in Asturies.

GIVEN NAMES Spanish 9%. *Jose* (3), *Alberto* (2), *Jorge* (2), *Josefina* (2), *Vicente* (2),

Alfredo, Alicia, Elena, Enrique, Fidel, Jesus, Juan.

Cuellar (2422) Spanish (**Cuéllar**): habitational name from a place called Cuéllar in Segovia province, or from minor places so named in the provinces of Soria and Salamanca.

GIVEN NAMES Spanish 47%. *Jose* (56), *Juan* (44), *Carlos* (30), *Manuel* (24), *Luis* (22), *Rafael* (19), *Jesus* (15), *Mario* (14), *Arturo* (13), *Ruben* (13), *Jorge* (12), *Raul* (12).

Cuello (171) Spanish: **1.** nickname for someone with a peculiarity of the neck, *cuello* (Latin *collum*). **2.** Castilianized form of Asturian-Leonese **Cuellu**, a habitational name from a place in Asturies called Cuellu.

GIVEN NAMES Spanish 44%. *Rafael* (5), *Armando* (4), *Julio* (4), *Jose* (3), *Francisco* (2), *Jorge* (2), *Juana* (2), *Mario* (2), *Ramon* (2), *Adela, Aida, Amado; Antonio* (2), *Francesca* (2), *Lorenzo, Silvio.*

Cuenca (305) Spanish: habitational name from Cuenca city in Castile, named from *cuenca* 'basin', 'hollow' (Latin *concha* 'shell', 'mussel').

GIVEN NAMES Spanish 53%. *Juan* (6), *Carlos* (5), *Jose* (4), *Alberto* (3), *Arturo* (3), *Benito* (3), *Blanca* (3), *Estanislao* (3), *Manuel* (3), *Miguel* (3), *Emilio* (2), *Enrique* (2); *Heriberto* (2), *Ciro, Egidio, Marco, Sal.*

Cuervo (327) Spanish: from *cuervo* 'raven', 'rook' (Latin *corvus*), applied as a nickname for a man with strikingly glossy black hair or for one with a raucous voice, or as a habitational name from a place named with this word, for example El Cuervo in Teruel province.

GIVEN NAMES Spanish 51%. *Carlos* (10), *Jose* (9), *Luis* (8), *Manuel* (7), *Gustavo* (6), *Jorge* (6), *Armando* (4), *Angel* (3), *Eduardo* (3), *Luz* (3), *Raul* (3), *Adriana* (2); *Silvio* (2), *Angelo, Antonio, Leonardo, Mauro.*

Cuesta (360) Spanish: from *cuesta* 'slope', 'bank' (Latin *costa* 'rib', 'side', 'flank', also used in a transferred topographical sense), hence a topographic name for someone who lived on a slope or riverbank, less often on the coast, or a habitational name from a place named with this word, as for example La Cuesta, in the provinces of Segovia and Soria.

GIVEN NAMES Spanish 47%. *Jose* (9), *Luis* (7), *Armando* (5), *Juan* (5), *Roberto* (5), *Angel* (4), *Carlos* (4), *Jorge* (4), *Manuel* (4), *Rafael* (4), *Ernesto* (3), *Enrique* (2); *Antonio* (6), *Anastasio* (2), *Federico, Marcello.*

Cueto (475) Galician, Asturian-Leonese, Spanish, and Basque: habitational name from any of numerous places in Galicia, Asturies, León, Santander, and Basque Country named with the topographical term *cueto* 'hill', 'fortified settlement' (from Latin *cautus* 'sheltered'. The Asturian-Leonese form is a Castilianized

variant of the Asturian-Leonese habitational name **Cuetu** (compare COTO)

GIVEN NAMES Spanish 44%. *Jose* (18), *Juan* (10), *Manuel* (8), *Pedro* (6), *Carlos* (5), *Jesus* (5), *Jorge* (4), *Alfonso* (3), *Cesar* (3), *Maximo* (3), *Angel* (2), *Bernardo* (2).

Cueva (386) Spanish: habitational name from any of the many places named with *cueva* 'cave'.

GIVEN NAMES Spanish 52%. *Jose* (17), *Luis* (9), *Juan* (6), *Mario* (5), *Genaro* (4), *Miguel* (4), *Alfredo* (3), *Blanca* (3), *Esteban* (3), *Javier* (3), *Jesus* (3), *Ricardo* (3); *Fausto* (2), *Marco* (2), *Eligio, Leonardo, Romeo.*

Cuevas (3915) Spanish: topographical name from *cueva* 'cave', plural *cuevas*, or a habitational name from any of numerous places named with this word, for example in the provinces of Burgos and Málaga.

GIVEN NAMES Spanish 46%. *Jose* (86), *Luis* (37), *Jesus* (35), *Juan* (29), *Manuel* (28), *Carlos* (27), *Raul* (25), *Pedro* (20), *Ramon* (19), *Roberto* (19), *Ruben* (18), *Fernando* (17).

Cuff (999) **1.** English: metonymic occupational name for a maker and seller of gloves or a nickname for a wearer of particularly fine gloves, from Middle English *cuffe* 'glove' (of uncertain origin; attested in this sense from the 14th century, with the modern meaning first in the 16th century). **2.** Irish: Anglicized form of Gaelic **Mac Dhuibh**, a variant of **Mac Duibh** 'son of the black one' (see DUFF). **3.** Irish: approximate translation of Gaelic **Ó Doirnín** (see DORNAN). **4.** Cornish: nickname from Cornish *cuf* 'dear', 'kind'.

Cuffe (227) English and Irish: variant spelling of CUFF.

Cuffee (304) Irish: variant of CUFF.

Cuffie (102) Irish: variant of CUFF.

Cugini (246) Italian: from the plural of *cugino* 'cousin' (Latin *consobrinus*), which in the Middle Ages had the general meaning 'relative', 'kinsman'. The surname would thus have denoted a person related in some way to a prominent figure in the neighborhood. In some cases it may have been a nickname for someone who used the word frequently as a familiar term of address.

GIVEN NAMES Italian 16%. *Cesidio* (2), *Dario* (2), *Aldo, Biagio, Carmine, Ennio, Gaetano, Lucio, Paolo, Pompeo, Rocco, Ruggiero.*

Cugno (101) Southern Italian: topographic name from Sicilian *cugnu* 'hill', 'knoll', 'barren land', or a habitational name from any of numerous minor places named with this word.

GIVEN NAMES Italian 20%. *Salvatore* (3), *Sal* (2), *Corrado, Franca, Giuseppe, Stefano.*

Cui (257) Chinese 崔: from the place name Cui, in present-day Shandong province. In the 11th century BC, the eldest son of Ding, Duke of Qi (see TING) abdicated his right of succession and moved to the area of Cui in present-day Shandong province. His descendants eventually adopted the place name Cui as their surname.

GIVEN NAMES Chinese 68%. *Hong* (5), *Yi* (5), *Yong* (4), *Yuan* (4), *Jian* (3), *Ping* (3), *Wei* (3), *Hang* (2), *Huiping* (2), *Jing* (2), *Mei Ying* (2), *Qian* (2), *Yiping*.

Culberson (1134) Probably a reduced form of CULBERTSON.

Culbert (829) English, northern Irish, and Scottish: variant of COLBERT.

Culbertson (4008) English, Scottish and northern Irish: patronymic from CULBERT.

Culbreath (608) Northern Irish: variant of GALBRAITH.

Culbreth (1082) Northern Irish: Mac-Lysaght records **Culbrath** as a Co. Monaghan variant of CULBERT, dating from the 18th century, but this name is more probably a variant of Scottish GALBRAITH.

Culhane (833) Irish: Anglicized form of Gaelic **Ó Cathláin** 'descendant of *Cathalán*', a diminutive of the personal name *Cathal* meaning 'mighty in battle'.

GIVEN NAMES Irish 6%. *Brendan* (2), *Dermot*.

Culkin (311) Irish: reduced Anglicized form of Gaelic **Mac Uilcín** 'son of *Uilcín*', a diminutive of *Ulick*, itself a diminutive of WILLIAM.

GIVEN NAMES Irish 7%. *Eamon*, *Eamonn*.

Cull (773) **1.** English: from the Old English personal name *Cula*. **2.** Americanized spelling of German and Swedish KALL or German KOLL.

Cullars (104) Reduced and altered form of Scottish MCKELLAR, with the addition of English patronymic *-s*.

Cullen (8180) **1.** Irish: Anglicized form of Gaelic **Ó Coileáin** 'descendant of *Coileán*', a byname meaning 'puppy' or 'young dog'. **2.** Irish: Anglicized form of Gaelic **Ó Cuilinn** 'descendant of *Cuileann*', a byname meaning 'holly'. **3.** Scottish: habitational name from Cullen in Banff, so named from Gaelic *cùilen*, a diminutive of *còil*, *cùil* 'nook', 'recess'. **4.** English: habitational name from the Rhineland city of Cologne (Old French form of Middle High German *Köln*, named with Latin *colonia* 'colony'). **5.** English: variant of COOLING.

GIVEN NAMES Irish 6%. *Brendan* (3), *Declan* (2), *Dermot* (2), *Donal* (2), *Fergus* (2), *Aidan*, *Brennan*, *Donovan*, *Eamon*, *Eamonn*, *Kieran*, *Liam*.

Cullens (261) Irish and Scottish: variant of CULLEN, with the addition of the English possessive *-s*.

Culler (1244) **1.** Reduced form of Scottish and Irish MCCULLER. **2.** Americanized spelling of German KOLLER, GOLLER, or GALLER.

Cullers (360) Reduced form of Scottish and Irish MCCULLER, with the addition of the English possessive *-s*.

Culleton (134) Irish: variant spelling of CULLITON.

GIVEN NAMES Irish 8%. *Nuala*, *Thomas Patrick*.

Culley (1233) Irish: variant spelling of CULLY.

Cullifer (182) English: unexplained. It may be be a variant of CULVER. Compare COLLIVER.

Culligan (505) Irish: Anglicized form of Gaelic **Ó Cuileagáin** ('descendant of *Cuileagán*'), a variant of **Ó Colgáin** (see COLGAN).

GIVEN NAMES Irish 9%. *Brendan* (2), *Caitlin*, *Ronan*, *Seamus*.

Cullimore (167) English: apparently a habitational name from an unidentified place. There is a place called Colleymore Farm in Oxfordshire, but it is not clear whether this is the source of the surname, with its many variant spellings. See also COLLAMORE, GALLIMORE, GALLIMORE.

Cullin (160) English and Irish: variant spelling of CULLEN.

Cullinan (939) Irish: Anglicized form of Gaelic **Ó Cuileannáin** 'descendant of *Cuileannán*', from a diminutive of *Cuileann* (see CULLEN 2).

GIVEN NAMES Irish 6%. *Brendan* (2), *Cormac*.

Cullinane (548) Irish: variant of CULLINAN.

GIVEN NAME Irish 4%. *Niall*.

Culling (101) English: variant of COOLING.

Cullins (743) Variant of Irish COLLINS.

Cullipher (183) English: probably a variant of CULVER.

Cullis (106) English: variant of COLLIS.

Cullison (1026) English: probably a variant of COLLISON.

Culliton (284) Irish: reduced Americanized spelling of **Mac Codlatáin** (or **Ó Codlatáin**) 'son (or 'descendant') of *Codlatán*', a byname meaning 'sleeper'.

Cullivan (141) Irish: of uncertain derivation. Woulfe traces it to **Mac Conluain**, earlier **Mac Aluain**, neither of which would account for the *v*; it could perhaps be a variant of **Ó Cuileamhain**, a Leinster name, usually Americanized as **Culloon**.

GIVEN NAME French 4%. *Curley*.

Culliver (108) English: see COLLIVER.

GIVEN NAME French 4%. *Andre*.

Cullom (341) Scottish and English: variant spelling of CULLUM.

Cullop (241) English: from Middle English *colhope*, *col(l)hop* 'fried eggs and ham or bacon', which Reaney believes to have been applied as a metonymic occupational name for the keeper of a cook house.

Cullum (1425) **1.** English: habitational name, in part probably from places in Oxfordshire and Berkshire called Culham. The first is named with an Old English personal name *Cūla* + *hamm* 'river meadow'; the Berkshire name is from Old English *cyln* 'kiln' + Old English *hām* 'homestead' or *hamm* 'river meadow'. **2.** Scottish: reduced form of MCCOLLUM.

Cully (493) Irish: Anglicized form of Gaelic **Ó Colla** 'descendant of *Colla*', originally *Conla*, an Old Irish personal name of uncertain derivation.

Culmer (152) English (Kent): variant spelling of COLMER.

Culotta (574) Southern Italian: from the personal name *Culotta*, a diminutive of COLA.

GIVEN NAMES Italian 12%. *Salvatore* (9), *Sal* (4), *Carlo*, *Carmelo*, *Cosimo*, *Gaetano*, *Giovanni*, *Marco*, *Santo*.

Culp (5055) **1.** Scottish: habitational name from Colp in Aberdeenshire. **2.** Americanized spelling of German KOLB, KOLP, or KALB.

Culpepper (3798) English: occupational name for a herbalist or spicer, from Middle English *cull(en)* 'to pick' (Old French *coillir*, from Latin *colligere* 'to collect or gather') + *peper* 'pepper'.

Cultice (102) English: variant spelling of COULTAS.

Culton (342) Scottish and English: perhaps a variant of COLTON.

Culver (6416) English: from Old English *culfre* 'dove' (Late Latin *columbula*, a diminutive of *columba*), which Reaney suggests was used as a term of endearment. It may therefore have been applied as nickname for a lovelorn youth or perhaps for someone who used the expression indiscriminately. Otherwise, it may have been a metonymic occupational name for a keeper of doves or a nickname for someone bearing some fancied resemblance to a dove, such as mildness of temper.

Culverhouse (299) English: from Old English *culfrehūs* 'dovecote', hence a topographic name for someone living near a dovecote, or possibly a metonymic occupational name for the keeper of a dovecote.

Culverson (104) English: patronymic from CULVER.

Culverwell (124) English (Somerset): habitational name from Culverwell in Somerset.

Culwell (526) English: variant spelling of COLWELL.

Cumbee (370) **1.** Variant of English CUMBY. **2.** Perhaps also Scottish: reduced and altered form of MCCOMBIE.

Cumber (176) Irish: reduced form of MCCOMBER.

Cumberbatch (309) English: habitational name for someone from Comberbach in northern Cheshire, named with the Old English personal name *Cumbra* (originally a byname meaning 'Cumbrian') or the genitive plural of *Cumbre* 'Britons' + Old English *bæce* 'stream in a valley'.

GIVEN NAMES French 4%. *Julien*, *Monique*, *Vernice*.

Cumberland (814) English: regional name for someone from Cumberland in northwestern England (now part of Cumbria).

Cumberledge (230) English: unexplained.

Cumberworth (104) English (Lincolnshire): habitational name from Cumberworth in Lincolnshire, named from an Old English personal name *Cumbre* + *worth* 'enclosure'. There is also a Lower and an Upper Cumberworth in West Yorkshire but these appear not to have contributed significantly to the modern surname, which is concentrated in Lincolnshire.

Cumbie (698) **1.** Scottish: reduced variant of McCOMBIE. **2.** Perhaps a variant spelling of English CUMBY.

Cumbo (309) Southern Italian (Sicily): nickname from medieval Greek *kombos* 'deception', 'trick', or from southern dialect *kombo* 'knot' (from medieval Greek *kombos* 'tie', 'bond').
GIVEN NAMES Italian 4%. *Salvatore* (2), *Antonio, Pasquale, Vincenza.*

Cumbow (113) **1.** Perhaps an Americanized spelling of French **Combeau**, from a diminutive of COMBE. **2.** Possibly an altered form of English CUMBY.

Cumby (327) **1.** Scottish: reduced form of McCOMBIE. **2.** English (Norfolk): unexplained. Perhaps a habitational name from a lost or unidentified place, of which the second element is Old Norse *býr* 'farm'.

Cumings (270) Scottish: see CUMMING.

Cumiskey (144) Irish: variant spelling of COMISKEY.

Cumming (1302) **1.** English, Scottish, and Irish (of Norman origin): of disputed origin. It may be from a Celtic personal name derived from the element *cam* 'bent', 'crooked' (compare CAMERON and CAMPBELL). This was relatively frequent in Norfolk, Lincolnshire, and Yorkshire in the 12th and 13th centuries, perhaps as a result of Breton immigration. According to another theory it is a habitational name from Comines near Lille, but there is no evidence for this (no early forms with *de* have been found). In southern Ireland this Anglo-Norman name has been confused with 2. **2.** Irish: Anglicized form of Gaelic **Mac Cuimín** (or **Ó Cuimín**) 'son (or 'descendant') of *Cuimín*', a personal name formed from a diminutive of *cam* 'crooked'. **3.** Americanized form of French Canadian VIEN, VIENS, based on the misconception that these derive from French *venire* 'to come'.

Cummingham (117) Scottish and Irish: variant of CUNNINGHAM.

Cummings (27316) Irish: variant of CUMMING, with the addition of English patronymic -*s*.

Cummins (7880) Irish: variant of CUMMINGS.

Cummiskey (272) Irish: variant spelling of COMISKEY.

Cumpston (317) Northern English: probably a variant of the Scottish habitational name **Cumstoun**, from Cumstoun in Kirkcudbrightshire or from Cumstone in

Dumfriesshire. There are places in Cumbria named Cumpston Hill and Cumpstone House, but both take their names from a family called Compston or Cumpston, recorded in the area in the 16th century, rather than vice versa.

Cumpton (304) English: variant of COMPTON.

Cunanan (174) Kapampangan (Philippines): unexplained.
GIVEN NAMES Spanish 46%; Italian 7%. *Angel* (2), *Ernesto* (2), *Imelda* (2), *Joaquin* (2), *Josefino* (2), *Manuel* (2), *Ramon* (2), *Renato* (2), *Roberto* (2), *Rodolfo* (2), *Alfonso, Angelina*; *Romeo* (4), *Antonio, Dino.*

Cunard (211) **1.** English: from the Old English personal name *Cyneheard*, composed of the elements *cyne* 'royal', 'kingly' + *heard* 'hardy', 'brave', 'strong'. **2.** In some instances probably an Americanized form of German KUNERT.

Cundall (165) English: habitational name from Cundall in North Yorkshire, which was probably originally named simply with Old English *cumb* 'valley' and later acquired the addition of Old Scandinavian *dalr* 'valley'.

Cundari (163) Southern Italian: nickname for a short man, from medieval Greek *kontē oura*, literally 'short tail'.
GIVEN NAMES Italian 26%. *Rocco* (2), *Angelo, Carmelo, Ellio, Natale, Rosario.*

Cundiff (2320) Irish: variant of CUNNIFF.

Cundy (293) English: variant of CONDIE.

Cuneo (907) Italian: regional name from Cuneo in Piedmont, named in Latin with *cuneus* 'wedge'.

Cunha (1364) Portuguese: habitational name from one of the numerous places called Cunha; the ancient form is *Cuinha*, probably meaning 'kitchen' (Latin *culina*).
GIVEN NAMES Spanish 20%; Portuguese 14%. *Manuel* (42), *Jose* (28), *Carlos* (14), *Mario* (6), *Luiz* (5), *Fernando* (4), *Ricardo* (4), *Domingos* (3), *Eduardo* (3), *Jorge* (3), *Alberto* (2), *Americo* (2); *Joao* (9), *Joaquim* (5), *Paulo* (4), *Agostinho, Albano, Conceicao, Henrique, Margarida, Vasco, Zulmira.*

Cunico (133) Italian (northern Veneto): of German origin. This surname was taken to northern Italy by German speakers during the 15th and 16th centuries. According to Rapelli, it may be a variant of **Cunego**, from Middle High German *künic* 'king' (see KOENIG), or alternatively from the personal name *Chunico*, a pet form of *Kuno* (see KONRAD).

Cunliffe (325) English: habitational name from a place in Lancashire, near Rishton, recorded in 1246 as *Kunteclive*, from Old English *cunte* 'cunt' + *clif* 'slope', i.e. 'slope with a slit or crack in it'.

Cunnane (202) Irish: Anglicized form of Gaelic **Ó Cuineáin** (see QUEENAN).
GIVEN NAME Irish 8%. *Liam.*

Cunneen (202) Irish: **1.** Anglicized form of Gaelic **Mac Coinín** (or **Ó Coinín**) 'son (or 'descendant') of *Coinín*', from a byname from *coinín* 'rabbit' or from *cano* 'wolf'. **2.** Connacht variant of CUNNANE (see QUEENAN).
GIVEN NAMES Irish 6%. *Brendan, Kieran.*

Cunniff (597) Irish (Connacht): reduced form of **McCunniff**, an Anglicized form of Gaelic **Mac Conduibh** 'son of *Condubh*' (earlier *Cú Dhubh*), a personal name meaning 'black hound'. This is just one of several Anglicized forms that also include McADOO and McNIFF.

Cunniffe (116) Irish: variant spelling of CUNNIFF.
GIVEN NAME Irish 10%. *Eamonn.*

Cunning (352) Northern Ireland: variant of GUNNING.

Cunningham (46903) **1.** Scottish: habitational name from a district in Ayrshire, first recorded in 1153 in the form *Cunegan*, a Celtic name of uncertain origin. The spellings in -*ham*, first recorded in 1180, and in -*ynghame*, first recorded in 1227, represent a gradual assimilation to the English place-name element -*ingham*. **2.** Irish: surname adopted from Scottish by bearers of Gaelic **Ó Cuinneagáin** 'descendant of *Cuinneagán*', a personal name from a double diminutive of the Old Irish personal name *Conn* meaning 'leader', 'chief'.

Cunnington (218) English: habitational name from either of two places in Cambridgeshire (one formerly in Huntingdonshire) called Conington, from Old Norse *kunung* 'king', 'chieftain' (probably replacing earlier Old English *cyning*) + Old English *tūn* 'enclosure', 'settlement'.

Cuny (234) **1.** English: unexplained. **2.** French (Lorraine): according to Morlet, an Alemannic variant of **Kühni** (see KUEHN). **3.** Perhaps also in some cases an Americanized form of German **Kühne** (see KUEHN).
GIVEN NAMES French 6%. *Julien* (2), *Pierre.*

Cuoco (233) Italian: occupational name for a cook, a seller of cooked meats, or a keeper of an eating house, *cuoco* (from Latin *coquus*).
GIVEN NAMES Italian 18%. *Gino* (3), *Angelo* (2), *Antonio* (2), *Carmine* (2), *Dario, Domenico, Giovanni, Guido, Lorenzo, Philomena, Salvatore.*

Cuomo (853) Italian (Campania): probably from a reduced form of *Cuosëmo*, a Neapolitan variant of the personal name *Cosimo* (see COSMA).
GIVEN NAMES Italian 15%. *Salvatore* (7), *Pasquale* (4), *Angelo* (3), *Sal* (3), *Antonio* (2), *Carmela* (2), *Giuseppe* (2), *Rocco* (2), *Amadeo, Carlo, Domenico, Franco.*

Cuozzo (366) Italian: variant of COZZO.
GIVEN NAMES Italian 14%. *Alfonse* (2), *Angelo* (2), *Rocco* (2), *Carmine, Concetta, Dante, Enza, Filippo, Francesco, Italo, Marco, Marino.*

Cupit (508) English (North Midlands): unexplained; possibly a dialect variant of CUBIT, but see also CUPPETT.

Cupo (238) Italian: nickname from *cupo* 'deep', 'dark', or, by extension, 'sullen', 'moody'.
GIVEN NAMES Italian 13%. *Aldo, Angelo, Carlo, Giovanni, Rocco.*

Cupp (2637) **1.** English: possibly a variant of COPP. **2.** Possibly an Americanized spelling of German KOPP.

Cuppett (192) Probably an altered spelling of English **Coppett**, a nickname from Middle English *copped* 'pointed', 'haughty'.

Cupples (707) Northern Irish and English: variant of COPPLE.

Cupps (377) **1.** English: perhaps a variant of COBBS. **2.** Perhaps an altered form of Dutch **Cops** (see COPPS).

Cuppy (144) Possibly an Americanized spelling of German KOPPE.
GIVEN NAME German 5%. *Otto* (2).

Cura (113) **1.** Spanish and Portuguese: from *cura* 'priest'. **2.** Italian: probably a habitational name from Cura Carpignano in Pavia province, or other places named with this word.
GIVEN NAMES Spanish 38%; Portuguese 11%; Italian 9%. *Jose* (4), *Pedro* (3), *Cayetano* (2), *Cristina* (2), *Miguel* (2), *Alfonso, Alicia, Bernardo, Enrique, Estela, Evangelina, Genaro; Joao; Aldo, Antonio, Elio, Federico, Gino, Silvio.*

Curatolo (253) Southern Italian: occupational name from Calabrian and Sicilian *curatulu* 'head herdsman or shepherd', 'foreman'.
GIVEN NAMES Italian 32%. *Rocco* (5), *Angelo* (4), *Francesco* (3), *Antonio* (2), *Carmine* (2), *Aldo, Alfonso, Amalia, Angelina, Arcangelo, Benedetto, Carlo, Carmela, Carmelo, Caterina, Marta.*

Curb (155) Probably an Americanized form of German and Jewish KORB.

Curbelo (205) Galician: nickname from Galician *curbelo* 'crow'.
GIVEN NAMES Spanish 52%. *Jose* (7), *Carlos* (5), *Luis* (5), *Juan* (4), *Pedro* (3), *Rafael* (3), *Sergio* (3), *Enrique* (2), *Guillermo* (2), *Jorge* (2), *Orlando* (2), *Roberto* (2); *Antonio* (3), *Leonardo* (3), *Lorenzo* (2), *Carmelo.*

Curbow (251) Of French (Huguenot) origin: probably an altered form of French **Corbeille** (see CORBELL) or **Corbeau**, a nickname from a derivative of Old French *corb* 'crow' (from Latin *corvus*).

Curby (171) **1.** Americanized spelling of French CORBEIL. **2.** Perhaps a variant spelling of English KIRBY or CORBY.

Curci (340) Italian: variant (plural) of CURCIO.
GIVEN NAMES Italian 11%. *Angelo* (3), *Rocco* (2), *Silvio* (2), *Caterina, Cosmo, Domenic, Franco.*

Curcio (1598) Southern Italian: nickname from southern dialect *curciu* 'short', 'small in stature' (from Latin *curtus* 'short').
GIVEN NAMES Italian 25%. *Angelo* (7), *Antonio* (6), *Carmine* (4), *Sal* (4), *Mario* (3), *Milio* (3), *Salvatore* (3), *Silverio* (3), *Benito* (2), *Domenic* (2), *Francesco* (2), *Franco* (2), *Gandolfo* (2), *Orlando* (2), *Rocco* (2), *Rosario* (2), *Aniello, Adriana, Albino, Alfonso, Armando, Basilio, Emilio, Ermando.*

Curcuru (175) Italian (Sicily; **Curcurù**): shortened form of **Curcuruto**, from a nickname from *curcurutu* 'speedy', 'fleet of foot', used particularly with reference to a horse.
GIVEN NAMES Italian 19%. *Nunzio* (3), *Antonino, Gaspare, Liborio, Ninfa, Rosario, Salvatore, Vito.*

Curd (700) English: metonymic occupational name for a seller of dairy products, from Middle English *crud(e)*, *curd(e)* 'curd (cheese)' (of uncertain, possibly Celtic, origin).

Cure (456) **1.** Scottish and Irish: reduced form of **McCure**, an Anglicized form of Gaelic **Mac Íomhair** (see MCIVER). **2.** English: possibly from Middle English *cure* 'charge', 'care', 'concern'.
GIVEN NAMES French 4%. *Gillis* (2), *Armand.*

Curenton (124) Perhaps a variant spelling of English CURRINGTON.

Curet (150) Catalan: possibly a variant of **Coret**, a nickname with various applications from *coret*, a diminutive of *cor* 'heart'.
GIVEN NAMES Spanish 22%; French 6%. *Jose* (4), *Luis* (3), *Enrique* (2), *Mario* (2), *Adalberto, Alicia, Ana, Caridad, Eduardo, Esmeraldo, Juan, Lourdes; Armand, Magalie, Matilde.*

Cureton (1160) English: habitational name probably from Curriton or Coryton in Devon; the former is named with an Old English personal name *Curra* + Old English *tūn* 'settlement'; the second is from *Curi* (a lost Celtic river name) + *tūn*.

Curfman (535) Americanized spelling of German **Korfmann**, an occupational name for a basket maker (see KORF).

Curiale (138) Southern Italian: nickname from *curiale* 'of or pertaining to a court', a derivative of *curia* '(papal) court'.
GIVEN NAMES Italian 33%. *Salvatore* (5), *Angelo* (3), *Bartolo, Carlo, Giuseppe, Mafalda, Matteo.*

Curie (104) French: from a reduced form of Old French *escuerie* 'stable', hence a metonymic occupational name for a stable hand.
GIVEN NAMES French 8%. *Celina, Philippe, Pierre.*

Curiel (866) Spanish: habitational name from a place named Curiel, in Valladolid province.
GIVEN NAMES Spanish 51%. *Jose* (26), *Juan* (13), *Francisco* (12), *Felipe* (9), *Ramon* (9), *Luis* (7), *Carlos* (6), *Jesus* (6), *Manuel* (6), *Miguel* (6), *Enrique* (5), *Pedro* (5).

Curington (285) English: variant spelling of CURRINGTON.

Curl (1939) English: nickname for a man with curly hair, from Middle English *crull(e)*, *curl(e)* 'curly (hair)'.

Curle (146) English: variant spelling of CURL.
GIVEN NAME French 4%. *Pierre.*

Curlee (981) Variant spelling of Irish or English CURLEY.

Curler (108) Dutch (**Van Curler**): probably a habitational name from a place so called.
FOREBEARS Arent van Curler (1620–67) was born at Nykerk in the Netherlands, and came to New Netherland in 1638.

Curles (116) Probably a variant of English CURL or CORLISS.

Curless (384) **1.** Americanized spelling of Dutch **Keurlis**, of unexplained origin; possibly a variant of **Cuelers**, which is ultimately a patronymic from a short form of the personal name *Nikolaas* (see NICHOLAS). **2.** English: variant of CORLISS.
FOREBEARS A Pieter Keurlis, one of the founders of Germantown, emigrated from Krefeld, Germany, in 1683.

Curlett (152) **1.** Probably a variant spelling of Manx CORLETT. **2.** Possibly a respelling of German **Gurlitt**, from a Germanic personal name, *Gaurault*, formed with a cognate of Old High German *garo* 'ready' + *waltan* 'to rule'.

Curley (3944) **1.** Irish: reduced form of MCCURLEY. **2.** English (of Norman origin): habitational name from any of several places in northern France named Corlay, for example in Côtes-du-Nord and Indre, or possibly from Corlieu, the former name of La Rue Saint Pierre in Oise. Reaney and Wilson suggest also it may have been a variant of the nickname **Curlew**, after the bird, Anglo-Norman French *curleu*.
GIVEN NAMES Irish 5%. *Kieran* (2), *Brendan, Brennan, Conan, Delma, Seamus.*

Curlin (269) **1.** English: variant of CURLING. **2.** Swedish: from an unexplained first element + the adjectival suffix *-(l)in*, derivative of Latin *-enius*. **3.** Probably also an Americanized spelling of German GERLING.

Curling (176) **1.** English: from Middle English *crulling* 'the curly one', a nickname for someone with curly hair. **2.** Possibly an Americanized spelling of German GERLING.

Curnow (422) Cornish: ethnic name for someone from Cornwall, Cornish *Kernow* 'Cornwall', the county in southwestern England where a Celtic language (Cornish) was spoken up to the 18th century.

Curnutt (374) **1.** Americanized spelling of German **Gernot(h)**, from a Germanic personal name composed of a cognate of Old High German *gēr* 'spear' + *knōt-* '(to) swing'. **2.** Alternatively, an Americanized spelling of Swiss German **Gernet**, which is either a variant of **Gernot(h)** (see 1 above) or a derivative of Middle High German *gern* 'to desire', a component of various Germanic personal names such as *Gernhard*.

Curnutte (263) Americanized spelling of German **Gernot(h)** (see CURNUTT).

Curole (138) Perhaps a respelling of French **Curiol**, which is of uncertain origin; possibly an occupational name for a man who looked after horses in a stable, from a much altered derivative of *écurie* 'stable'.
GIVEN NAME French 4%. *Alcee*.

Curran (10277) Irish: Anglicized form of Gaelic **Ó Corráin** or **Ó Corraidhín** 'descendant of *Corraidhín*', a personal name from a diminutive of *corradh* 'spear'. Compare CORR.
GIVEN NAMES Irish 5%. *Brendan* (8), *John Patrick* (2), *Siobhan* (2), *Aisling*, *Bridie*, *Caitlin*, *James Patrick*, *Keelin*, *Liam*, *Seamus*, *Shamrock*, *Tadhg*.

Curren (782) Irish: variant spelling of CURRAN.

Currence (536) Variant spelling of **Currans**, a Scottish variant of CURRAN.

Currens (264) Variant spelling of **Currans**, a Scottish variant of CURRAN.

Current (925) 1. Probably a variant spelling of English **Currant**, from Old French *courant*, present participle of *courir* 'to run', which Dauzat and Morlet suggest is an ellipse for *chien courant*, and hence a nickname for a hunter. 2. In some cases, the name may be an Americanized form of the French cognate **Courant**, for which Morlet also offers an additional source: a habitational name from any of various minor places named (Le) Courant, from *courant* 'running', in the sense of 'running water', 'water course', a derivative of *kaour* from Old Breton *cobrand*, from *cobr* 'help', 'aid'.

Curreri (318) Italian: from an occupational name for a messenger or courier, Italian *corriere*.
GIVEN NAMES Italian 19%. *Sal* (3), *Vito* (2), *Angelo*, *Carmelo*, *Gaetano*, *Ignazio*, *Pietro*, *Salvatore*, *Santo*.

Currey (1081) Variant spelling of Scottish CURRIE or Irish CURRY.

Currie (6134) Scottish: 1. habitational name from Currie in Midlothian, first recorded in this form in 1230. It is derived from Gaelic *curraigh*, dative case of *currach* 'wet plain', 'marsh'. 2. habitational name from Corrie in Dumfriesshire (see CORRIE). 3. Scottish spelling of Irish CURRY or, in Arran, an Anglicization of **Mac Mhuirich** (see MCMURRAY).

Currier (4258) English: occupational name for a person who dressed leather after it was tanned, Middle English *curreyour* (Old French *conreeur* 'currier').

Currin (1156) Irish: variant spelling of CURRAN.

Currington (258) English: of uncertain origin; possibly an altered form of CURETON or CARRINGTON. Alternatively, it may be a habitational name from a lost place, probably in the Cambridgeshire area, where the surname is most frequent.

Curro (302) 1. Southern Italian (**Currò**): from a reduced form (via *Corrào*, *Currào*) of the Germanic personal name *Corrado*, Italian equivalent of KONRAD. 2. Southern Italian: possibly a derogatory nickname from medieval Greek *korros* 'lazy'. 3. Portuguese and Galician: from any of numerous places in Portugal and Galicia so named, from *curro* 'fold', 'pen'.
GIVEN NAMES Italian 22%. *Angelo* (5), *Salvatore* (4), *Santo* (3), *Antonino*, *Carmela*, *Carmine*, *Dino*, *Filippo*, *Veto*.

Curry (23200) 1. Irish: Anglicized form of Gaelic **Ó Comhraidhe**, 'descendant of *Comhraidhe*', a personal name of uncertain meaning. 2. Irish: Anglicized form of Gaelic **Ó Corra** (see CORR). 3. Scottish and northern English: variant of CURRIE.

Curson (129) English: variant spelling of CURZON.

Curt (137) 1. English: variant of COURT. 2. Americanized spelling of German KURT. 3. Catalan: from *curt* 'short' (Latin *curtus* 'cut short', 'broken off'), hence a nickname for a short man.
GIVEN NAMES German 5%. *Dieter*, *Frieda*.

Curtain (104) 1. Irish and Scottish: variant of CURTIN. 2. Possibly an Americanized spelling of French CURTIN.
GIVEN NAME French 4%. *Cecile*.

Curti (271) Italian: patronymic or plural form of CURTO.
GIVEN NAMES Italian 11%. *Amerigo*, *Angelo*, *Cesare*, *Ciro*, *Dario*, *Evo*, *Fernando* (2), *Josafat*, *Mario*, *Olivio*, *Ruben*.

Curtice (308) 1. English: variant spelling of CURTIS. 2. Possibly an altered spelling of North German GERDES.

Curtin (3995) 1. Irish and Scottish: reduced Anglicized form of Gaelic **Mac Cruitín** 'son of *Cruitín*', a byname for a hunchback (see MCCURTAIN). 2. English: from a diminutive of COURT.
GIVEN NAMES Irish 6%. *Brendan* (2), *Conor*, *Donal*, *Donovan*, *John Patrick*, *Liam*, *Marypat*, *Senan*.

Curtis (35883) 1. English: nickname for a refined person, sometimes no doubt given ironically, from Old French, Middle English *curteis*, *co(u)rtois* 'refined', 'accomplished' (a derivative of Old French *court*, see COURT 1). 2. English: from Middle English *curt* 'short' + *hose* 'leggings', hence a nickname for a short person or one who wore short stockings. This nickname was borne by William the Conqueror's son Robert, but it is not clear whether it has given rise to any surnames. 3. Altered form of French COURTOIS.

Curtiss (2195) English: variant spelling of CURTIS.

Curtner (290) 1. Americanized spelling of Swiss German GURTNER. 2. Probably a variant spelling of CORTNER.

Curto (562) 1. Southern Italian, Spanish, and Portuguese: nickname from southern Italian *curtu*, Spanish and Portuguese *curto* 'short' (Latin *curtus* 'curtailed', 'broken off'). 2. Catalan (**Curtó**): from a diminutive of CURT.
GIVEN NAMES Italian 17%. *Angelo* (9), *Salvatore* (8), *Sal* (3), *Fausto* (2), *Giovanni* (2), *Carmelo*, *Carmine*, *Concetta*, *Dino*, *Gioacchino*, *Marcello*, *Michelangelo*.

Curtright (227) See COURTRIGHT.

Curts (363) Americanized spelling of German KURZ or KURTZ.

Curtsinger (522) Probably an Americanized spelling of German **Grötzinger** (see GRETZINGER).

Curvey (100) English: unexplained.

Curvin (246) 1. English: unexplained. Compare CORVIN. 2. Americanized spelling of German GERWIN.

Curzon (116) English (of Norman origin): habitational name from Notre-Dame-de-Courson in Calvados, France, which was named with the Romano-Gallic personal name *Curtius* (from *curtus* 'short') + the locative suffix -*o*, genitive -*onis*. There is also a place called Curzon in Vendée, but this is not the source of the English surname.

Cusack (1488) Irish (of Norman origin): habitational name from Cussac in Guienne, France, named with the Romano-Gallic personal name *Cūcius* or *Cussius* + the locative suffix -*acum*. The surname died out in England, but is common in Ireland, where it was imported at the time of the Anglo-Norman invasion in the 12th century. It has been Gaelicized as **de Cíosóg**.
GIVEN NAMES Irish 6%. *Aileen*, *Brigid*, *Eamon*, *Fergus*, *Seamus*.

Cusanelli (101) Italian: unexplained; possibly a derivative of *Cusano*, from the Latin personal name *Cusius*, which occurs as an element in place names such as Cusano Milanino (Milan province) and Cusano Mutri (Benevento).
GIVEN NAMES Italian 8%. *Angelo*, *Pierino*, *Rocco*.

Cusano (476) Italian: habitational name from Cusano Mutri in Benevento province or Cusano Milanino in Milan province.
GIVEN NAMES Italian 17%. *Angelo* (4), *Pasquale* (4), *Rocco* (3), *Domenic* (2), *Antonietta*, *Antonio*, *Carmine*, *Domenico*, *Guiseppe*, *Luigi*, *Serafino*.

Cusato (144) Italian: possibly a habitational name from any of the places named Cusato, notably in Lombardy.
GIVEN NAMES Italian 14%. *Domenic*, *Domenico*, *Salvatore*, *Vincenzo*.

Cusenza (105) Italian: variant of COSENZA.

GIVEN NAMES Italian 23%. *Antonino, Dario, Gaetano, Pasquale, Raimondo, Rocco, Salvatore, Vito.*

Cush (231) **1.** English: variant of KISS. **2.** Americanized spelling of German and Jewish KUSCH.

Cushen (112) English: variant of COUSIN.

Cushenberry (97) Americanized form of German **Kusenberg**, a habitational name from a place so named near Düsseldorf, Rhineland.

Cushing (2946) English: variant of COUSIN.

Cushion (123) English: variant of COUSIN.

Cushman (3059) Americanized spelling of Jewish KUSHMAN.

Cushner (120) Americanized spelling of Jewish KUSHNER.

GIVEN NAMES Jewish 7%. *Aviva, Meyer, Tema.*

Cusic (266) Serbian (**Ćušić**): derogatory nickname from *ćuša* 'snout', 'big mouth'.

Cusick (2064) **1.** Variant spelling of Irish CUSACK, in the British Isles now found predominantly in Scotland. **2.** Respelling of Czech **Kusik**, a nickname for a short person or someone with a physical defect, from *kusý* 'fragmentary', 'unfinished', 'truncated'.

Cusimano (661) Italian (Sicily): from a personal name which de Felice suggests may be a fusion of two saints' names: COSMA + DAMIANO, with a loss of the last syllable of one and the first of the other, but which Caracausi takes to be a regional variant of the Late Greek personal name *Kosmas* (see COSMA) or a short form of an old personal name beginning with *Kosm-*. He suggests that alternatively it could be derived from Arabic *Quzmān*.

GIVEN NAMES Italian 19%. *Sal* (8), *Angelo* (3), *Valentino* (2), *Carmela, Carmelo, Francesco, Mario, Orlando, Raffaele, Rico, Rosolino, Santo, Silvana.*

Cusmano (157) Italian: variant of CUSIMANO.

GIVEN NAMES Italian 12%. *Carmine, Corrado, Giuseppe, Salvatore.*

Cussen (140) English: variant of COUSIN.
GIVEN NAME Irish 8%. *Brendan* (2).

Cusson (453) English: variant of COUSIN.
GIVEN NAMES French 12%. *Normand* (3), *Herve* (2), *Adrien, Aime, Armand, Girard, Laurier, Lucien, Marcel, Philippe, Rejean, Thierry.*

Custard (321) English: variant of COSTER.

Custer (4097) **1.** Americanized spelling of German **Köster** or **Küster** 'sexton' (see KUSTER). **2.** English: variant of COSTER. FOREBEARS The American military officer George Custer (1839–76) was a descendant of a German officer from Hesse by the name of Küster.

Custis (473) English: unexplained. Possibly from a much altered form of the personal name AUGUSTUS. This is an old VA surname, dating from the 17th century.

Custodio (437) Spanish and Portuguese (**Custódio**): from a religious byname chosen to invoke the protection of a guardian angel, Portuguese *anjo custódio* (Late Latin *angelus custodius*, from *custos*, genitive *custodis*, 'guardian', 'keeper').

GIVEN NAMES Spanish 37%; Portuguese 9%. *Jose* (11), *Carlos* (5), *Ricardo* (4), *Enrique* (3), *Ernesto* (3), *Luis* (3), *Manuel* (3), *Pablo* (3), *Angelito* (2), *Cirilo* (2), *Fernando* (2), *Juan* (2); *Joao, Joaquim*; *Antonio* (5), *Donato, Pio, Romeo, Silvano.*

Cusumano (614) Italian (Sicily): variant of CUSIMANO.

GIVEN NAMES Italian 20%. *Salvatore* (11), *Vito* (6), *Sal* (4), *Antonio* (2), *Domenico* (2), *Filippo* (2), *Francesco* (2), *Santo* (2), *Alessandro, Alfonso, Angelina, Benedetto, Ciro, Dominico, Mario, Rosario.*

Cutaia (192) Italian: habitational name from a place named Cuttaia.

GIVEN NAMES Italian 24%. *Salvatore* (4), *Lorenzo* (2), *Angelo, Carlo, Caterina, Francesca, Guiseppe, Sebastiano, Stefano.*

Cutbirth (216) Altered form of English CUTHBERT or possibly of the variant **Cutbird.**

Cutchall (142) Possibly an Americanized form of German **Gottschall** (see GOTTSCHALK). Compare CUTSHALL.

Cutcher (253) Americanized spelling of German KUTSCHER or the variant **Gutscher**, also found in Switzerland.

Cutchin (220) Reduced and altered form of Scottish McCUTCHEON.

Cutchins (151) Reduced and altered form of Scottish McCUTCHEON, with the addition of English patronymic -*s.*

Cuthbert (945) English: from the Middle English personal name *Cudbert*, Old English *Cuðbeorht*, composed of the elements *cūð* 'famous', 'well known' + *beorht* 'bright', 'famous'. The name was borne by a 7th-century saint, bishop of Hexham and later of Lindisfarne, and remained popular because of his cult throughout the Middle Ages, especially in northern England and the lowlands of Scotland.

Cuthbertson (1109) English: patronymic from the personal name *Cudbert* (see CUTHBERT).

Cuthrell (309) Variant of English COTTRELL.

Cutillo (244) Italian (southern Latium, northern Campania): possibly a topographic name for someone who lived on stony ground, from a derivative of Sicilian *cuti* 'pebble', 'stone'.

GIVEN NAMES Italian 11%. *Carmine* (2), *Alfonse, Angelo, Antonio, Carlo, Carmela, Enrico, Giovanni, Sal.*

Cutino (102) Southern Italian: topographic name from a diminutive of Sicilian *cuti* 'pebble', 'whetstone'. This name is also well established in Mexico.

GIVEN NAMES Spanish 18%; Italian 13%. *Orlando* (2), *Pedro* (2), *Armando, Enrique,*

Ernestina, Gerardo, Juan, Lilia, Marcelino, Marta, Orestes, Renaldo; *Salvatore* (3), *Gaetano.*

Cutler (6423) **1.** English: occupational name for a maker of knives, from an agent derivative of Middle English, Old French *co(u)tel, co(u)teau* 'knife', Late Latin *cultellus*, a diminutive of *culter* 'plowshare'. Compare COTTLE. **2.** Americanized spelling of German KOTTLER or **Kattler**, which is of uncertain origin. .

Cutlip (964) **1.** English: variant of **Cudlip(p)**, a habitational name from Cudlipptown in Petertavy, Devon. **2.** Americanized form of German GOTTLIEB.

Cutone (112) Italian: possibly a variant of COTTONE.

GIVEN NAMES Italian 16%. *Mario* (2), *Antonio, Armando, Carmine, Elio, Giuseppe, Nicandro, Pasquale, Salvatore.*

Cutrell (264) Probably a variant spelling of English COTTRELL.

Cutrer (580) Altered spelling of German **Kutterer**, a nickname from an agent derivative Middle High German (and modern dialect) *kuteren* 'to laugh like a male pigeon', or of German **Gutterer**, an occupational name for glass blower who made balloon-shaped bottles, from Middle High German *kuterolf*. Compare GUTTERY.

Cutri (145) Southern Italian: **1.** nickname for someone with a big or otherwise noticeable head, from medieval Greek *koutra* 'head', or, pronounced *Cutrì*, from Greek *koutrias*, the suffix denoting a personal attribute. **2.** Alternatively, it may be a descriptive nickname from medieval Greek *koutroulas* 'maimed'.

GIVEN NAMES Italian 21%. *Rocco* (4), *Basilio, Dante, Demetrio, Guiseppe, Italia.*

Cutright (926) Altered form of Dutch **Kortrijk** (see COURTRIGHT) or of English CARTWRIGHT.

Cutrona (186) Southern Italian (Sicily): variant of CUTRONE.

GIVEN NAMES Italian 20%. *Salvatore* (6), *Sal* (2), *Carmela, Francesca, Vito.*

Cutrone (436) Southern Italian: variant of COTRONE.

GIVEN NAMES Italian 17%; French 4%. *Vito* (7), *Angelo* (4), *Domenico* (2), *Palma* (2), *Sal* (2), *Fabrizio, Francesco, Giovanni, Marco, Nicola*; *Camille* (4), *Luc.*

Cutsforth (223) English: probably a habitational name from a lost or unidentified place, possibly in the Humberside area, where the surname is most common.

Cutshall (936) Americanized form of German **Gottschall** (see GOTTSCHALK).

Cutshaw (606) Americanized form of German **Gottschall** (see GOTTSCHALK).

Cutsinger (297) Probably an altered form of **Grötzinger** (see GRETZINGER).

Cutter (1742) **1.** English: from an agent derivative of Old English *cyttan* 'to cut', possibly applied as an occupational name for a tailor or barber. **2.** Americanized form of German KOTTER.

Cutting (1237) **1.** English: patronymic from a short form of the personal name *Cudbert* (see CUTHBERT). **2.** Americanized spelling of German **Kötting** or the variant **Kotting** (see KOETTING).

Cuttino (155) Respelling of Italian CUTINO.

Cuttler (141) Variant spelling of CUTLER.

Cutts (868) **1.** English: patronymic from a short form of the personal name CUTHBERT. **2.** Probably an Americanized spelling of German KOTZ or German and Jewish KATZ.

Cuva (128) Italian: habitational name from a place called Cuva, from Old Italian *cuva* 'cupola', 'dome'.
GIVEN NAMES Italian 21%. *Angelo* (4), *Rocco* (2), *Concetta, Salvatore.*

Cuvelier (151) French: occupational name for a cooper, from an agent derivative of *cuve* 'vat', 'tun'.
FOREBEARS A Cuvelier from Arras, in Picardy, is recorded in Quebec city in 1755. In addition, there is documentation of Huguenots of this name, spelling it **Cuvilyé** and **Cuviljé.**
GIVEN NAMES French 6%. *Andre, Jean-Claude.*

Cuyler (377) Dutch: probably a variant of **Koole,** from a short form of the personal name *Nikolaas* (see NICHOLAS). This is a common Dutch name in the Albany area. A variant form of the surname in the Netherlands is **Kuilart,** suggesting perhaps that these could be occupational names for a potato grower, from *kuilen* 'to plant potatoes' (from *kuil* 'pit', 'hole').
FOREBEARS The Cuyler family were one of five prominent political families in Albany, NY, by the 1730s. Philip and Cornelius Cuyler provisioned militiamen during the French and Indian War.

Cuzick (107) Variant spelling of Irish CUSACK.

Cuzzort (136) Dutch: variant of **Cossart** (see COSSAIRT).

Cvengros (119) Origin unidentified. Some bearers of this name are recorded in Hungary, but it is not Hungarian. It may be Slavic or Romanian.

Cwalina (101) Polish: nickname from *cwalina,* a species of plant.
GIVEN NAMES Polish 23%; German 4%. *Andrzej, Izabela, Janina, Kazimierz, Krystyna, Krzysztof, Mariusz, Wieslaw, Zdzislaw.*

Cwik (236) **1.** Polish (**Ćwik**): from *ćwik* 'game bird', hence a nickname for someone thought to resemble a bird in some way, or from the same word in the sense 'experienced man'. **2.** Polish: nickname for an imbecile, from a variant of *ćwiek* 'hobnail'.
GIVEN NAMES Polish 5%. *Boleslaw, Iwona, Wieslaw, Wojciech, Zbigniew.*

Cwikla (179) Polish (**Ćwikła**): nickname for someone with a livid complexion, from *ćwikła* 'beetroot salad'.
GIVEN NAMES Polish 4%. *Boleslaw, Mikolaj.*

Cwiklinski (184) Polish (**Ćwikliński, Cwikliński**): habitational name from a place called Ćwiklin, Ćwiklinek, or Ćwikly.
GIVEN NAMES Polish 5%. *Kazimierz, Tomasz.*

Cwynar (175) Polonized form of the German surname **Zwirner,** an occupational name for a yarn or twine maker, from an agent derivative of Middle High German *zwirn* 'twine', 'yarn'
GIVEN NAMES Polish 5%. *Eugeniusz, Malgorzata.*

Cybulski (431) Polish: habitational name for someone from Cybulice or Cybulin, named with the personal name *Cybula.*
GIVEN NAMES Polish 7%. *Tomasz* (2), *Andrzej, Bogdan, Casimir, Jozef, Stanislaw, Tadeusz, Witold, Zigmund.*

Cygan (392) **1.** Polish: ethnic name or nickname from a word meaning 'gypsy', 'Romany'. **2.** Altered spelling of eastern German **Zigan,** from Hungarian *cigány* 'gypsy'.
GIVEN NAMES Polish 11%. *Stanislaw* (3), *Jerzy* (2), *Zofia* (2), *Alicja, Andrzej, Aniela, Jacek, Jolanta, Kazimierz, Krystyna, Mariusz, Michalina.*

Cypert (464) Respelling of German SEIBERT.

Cypher (499) Fanciful Americanized spelling of German SEIFER.

Cyphers (691) Fanciful Americanized spelling of German **Seifers,** a patronymic from the personal name SEIFER.

Cyphert (246) Fanciful Americanized spelling of German SEIFERT.

Cypress (205) Translation of German **Zypress,** a topographic name for someone living near a cypress tree or a habitational name for someone living at a house distinguished by the sign of a cypress, Middle High German *zipres(se)* (from Italian *cipressa,* Latin *cupressus*), or possibly of any of various Greek family names derived from *kyparissos* 'cypress', as for example **Kyparissis, Kyparissos, Kyparissiadis,** etc.
GIVEN NAME French 4%. *Damien.*

Cyprian (119) Possibly an altered spelling of French **Cyprien,** from a medieval personal name, from Latin *Cyprianus* (originally an ethnic name for an inhabitant of Cyprus), or a shortened form of Greek **Kyprianos, Kyprianis, Kyprianidis,** ethnic names for an inhabitant of Cyprus (Greek *Kypros*), or patronymics from the personal name *Kyprianos* (of the same derivation). The most prominent saint of this name was St. Cyprian of Carthage, a theologian and martyr who died in 258 AD.

Cyr (4816) French: from the Latin personal name *Quiricus* or *Cyricus,* Greek *Kyrikos* or *Kyriakos,* ultimately from Greek *kyrios*

'lord', 'master'. This name was borne by a 4th-century martyr, a small child martyred with his mother St. Julitta in 304 AD (see QUILICI). In North America it is sometimes Americanized as SEARS.
GIVEN NAMES French 12%. *Armand* (17), *Marcel* (10), *Normand* (10), *Fernand* (9), *Alban* (7), *Lucien* (7), *Adrien* (6), *Andre* (6), *Cecile* (6), *Pierre* (5), *Alphy* (4), *Emile* (4).

Cyran (200) Polish: from a derivative of *cyranka* 'teal', hence a nickname for someone thought to resemble the bird in some way.
GIVEN NAMES Polish 10%. *Zbigniew* (2), *Andrzej, Jerzy, Krystyna.*

Cyrus (1346) **1.** Polish: possibly from the personal name *Cyrus,* derived from the Greek form, *Kyros,* of the name of several kings of Persia. The origin of the name is not known, but in the early Christian period it was associated with Greek *kyrios* 'lord', and borne by various saints, including an Egyptian martyr and a bishop of Carthage. **2.** Possibly an Americanized spelling of the Greek family name **Kyros,** from the personal name (see 1 above).

Cywinski (165) Polish (**Cywiński**): habitational name, possibly for someone from Cywiny in Ciechanów province.
GIVEN NAMES Polish 7%. *Janusz* (2), *Tadeusz, Zigmund.*

Czachor (126) Polish: from a personal name like *Czabor* or *Czasław.*
GIVEN NAMES Polish 20%. *Jerzy* (2), *Zdzislaw* (2), *Andrzej, Boleslaw, Piotr, Slawomir, Zuzanna, Zygmunt.*

Czaja (439) Polish: from *czaja, czajka* 'lapwing', a nickname for someone thought to resemble the bird in some way.
GIVEN NAMES Polish 9%. *Jerzy* (2), *Krystyna* (2), *Stanislaw* (2), *Tadeusz* (2), *Janina, Ludwika, Michalina, Stanislawa, Sylwester, Thadeus.*

Czajka (426) Polish: nickname from *czajka* 'lapwing', a nickname for someone thought to resemble the bird in some way.
GIVEN NAMES Polish 6%. *Beata, Darek, Janina, Karol, Malgorzata, Stanislaw, Wasyl, Zygmunt.*

Czajkowski (913) Polish: habitational name for someone from Czajka, Czajki, Czajków, Czajkowice, or other places named with Polish *czajka* 'lapwing' (cognate with Russian *chaika* 'seagull').
GIVEN NAMES Polish 8%. *Bogdan* (2), *Franciszek* (2), *Jerzy* (2), *Tadeusz* (2), *Boleslaw, Casimir, Dorota, Eugeniusz, Janusz, Karol, Kazimierz, Mariusz.*

Czap (109) Polonized spelling of Czech **Čáp** (see CAP).

Czapiewski (109) Polish: habitational name from Czapiewice in Bydgoszcz province.
GIVEN NAMES German 4%. *Alfons, Florian.*

Czapla (312) Polish: from *czapla* 'heron', hence a nickname for a man with long, thin legs.
GIVEN NAMES Polish 6%. *Feliks, Krzysztof, Wladyslaw.*

Czaplewski (215) Polish: habitational name for someone from any of various places called Czaple, from *czapla* 'heron'.

Czaplicki (251) Polish: habitational name for someone from Czaplice, which is named with *czapla* 'heron'.
GIVEN NAMES Polish 6%. *Grazyna, Janusz, Kazimir, Zygmunt.*

Czaplinski (119) Polish (**Czapliński**): habitational name for someone from a place named Czaplin or Czaplinek, from *czapla* 'heron'.
GIVEN NAMES Polish 17%. *Jerzy (2), Bogdan, Leszek, Stanislaus, Wieslaw, Zbigniew, Zygmunt.*

Czar (113) Polish: **1.** most probably a nickname for a charming man, from *czar* 'charm'. **2.** possibly also from Polish *czar* 'tsar'.

Czarnecki (1548) Polish and Jewish (from Poland): habitational name for someone from a place called Czarnca in Kielce voivodeship, or any of the various places called Czarnocin or Czarnia, all named with Polish *czarny* 'black'.
FOREBEARS The Czarnecki and Czarniecki noble families can be traced back to the 14th century. Stefan Czarniecki (1599–1665) was a famous military man and an outstanding commander-in-chief of the Polish Army at the time of the Swedish invasion. His name is even mentioned in the Polish national anthem.
GIVEN NAMES Polish 5%. *Casimir (2), Jacek (2), Kazimierz (2), Darek, Dariusz, Grazyna, Irena, Jolanta, Leszek, Miroslaw, Piotr, Stanislaw.*

Czarniak (116) Polish: patronymic from the personal name CZARNY.
GIVEN NAMES Polish 8%. *Casimir (2), Zdzislaw.*

Czarniecki (122) Polish: variant of CZAR-NECKI.
GIVEN NAMES Polish 14%. *Zygmunt (3), Jacek, Lech, Lucjan, Mariusz.*

Czarnik (257) Polish: nickname from a diminutive of *czarny* 'black', or a patronymic from CZARNY.

GIVEN NAMES Polish 11%. *Jozef (2), Stanislaw (2), Andrzej, Casimir, Dorota, Henryka, Ryszard, Wieslaw.*

Czarnowski (117) Polish: habitational name for someone from places named Czarnowo or Czarnow, from the nickname CZARNY.
GIVEN NAMES Polish 11%. *Bogdan (2), Janina, Jerzy, Stanislaw, Zygmunt.*

Czarny (158) Polish and Jewish (eastern Ashkenazic): nickname for someone with dark hair or a dark complexion, from Polish *czarny* 'black'.
GIVEN NAMES Polish 7%. *Bronislawa, Irena, Janusz, Jozef, Tadeusz.*

Czech (855) **1.** Polish: ethnic name meaning 'Czech'. **2.** Probably also an English translation of the German cognate ZECH or Czech and Slovak **Čech** (see CECH).
GIVEN NAMES Polish 5%. *Jerzy (2), Alicja, Bogdan, Boguslaw, Bronislaw, Casimir, Elzbieta, Janusz, Leslaw, Wiktoria, Zbigniew.*

Czechowicz (111) Polish: patronymic from the ethnic name CZECH.
GIVEN NAMES Polish 9%. *Halina (2), Darek, Zygmunt.*

Czechowski (180) Polish: **1.** habitational name for someone from any of various places called Czechowice, Czechowo, or Czechów, all named with *Czech*, a short form of the personal name *Czibor* (composed of Polish *czcić* 'venerate' and Slavic *bor* 'to fight'). **2.** from a derivative of *Czech*, an ethnic name for a Czech.
GIVEN NAMES Polish 6%. *Krzysztof, Lech, Maciej, Zdzislawa.*

Czekaj (154) Polish: from *czekać* 'to wait for', possibly applied as a nickname for a patient person.
GIVEN NAMES Polish 10%. *Jozef (2), Janusz, Jaroslaw, Mariusz.*

Czelusniak (139) Polish (**Czeluśniak**): from *czelustny* 'deep', from *czeluść* 'abyss', 'gulf', also 'jaw', 'face'.
GIVEN NAMES Polish 5%. *Slawomir, Thadeus.*

Czepiel (169) Polish: from *czep* 'peg', 'stump', probably applied as a topographic name, nickname, or metonymic occupational name.
GIVEN NAMES Polish 5%. *Agnieszka, Leszek.*

Czerniak (305) Polish and Jewish (eastern Ashkenazic): nickname denoting a person

with dark hair or dark skin, from Polish *czarny* 'black'.
GIVEN NAMES Polish 4%. *Bogdan, Ryszard, Zbigniew.*

Czerniawski (104) Polish and Jewish (Ashkenazic): habitational name for someone from a place called Czerniawa, Czerniawka, or Czerniawy, all in the southern borderland of Poland.
GIVEN NAMES Polish 12%. *Benedykt, Janusz, Lech, Stanislaw.*

Czerwinski (930) Polish (**Czerwi(e)ński**): habitational name for someone from a place called Czerwin in Płock voivodeship, Czerwionka, Czerwonka, or other places in Poland named with *czerwień* 'red'.
GIVEN NAMES Polish 9%. *Jerzy (5), Casimir (2), Kazimierz (2), Aleksander, Andrzej, Beata, Bogdan, Czeslaw, Grazyna, Grzegorz, Leszek, Maciej.*

Czerwonka (247) Polish: nickname from *czerwony* 'red', presumably a nickname for someone who had red hair or a ruddy complexion, or perhaps for someone who habitually wore red.
GIVEN NAMES Polish 9%. *Iwona, Jozef, Karol, Malgorzata, Tadeusz, Thadeus, Wladyslaw, Zbigniew.*

Czuba (142) Polish: **1.** nickname from *czub* 'hair on top of the head'. **2.** nickname for a quarrelsome person, from *czubic się* 'to quarrel'.
GIVEN NAMES Polish 8%. *Jadwiga, Wieslaw, Zdislaw.*

Czupryna (101) Polish: nickname from *czupryna* 'shaggy hair'.
GIVEN NAMES Polish 14%. *Jerzy, Lech, Ludwik, Stanislaus, Tadeusz.*

Czyz (216) Polish (**Czyż**) and Ukrainian: nickname from Polish *czyżyk* 'siskin' (the bird).
GIVEN NAMES Polish 15%. *Jerzy (2), Jozef (2), Casimir, Halina, Henryk, Ignatius, Karol, Krystyna, Pawel, Stanislaw, Wieslaw, Zdzislaw.*

Czyzewski (253) Polish (**Czyżewski**): habitational name for someone from any of the many places in Poland called Czyżew or Czyżewo, from *czyż(yk)* 'siskin'.
GIVEN NAMES Polish 13%. *Piotr (2), Andrzej, Boleslaw, Casimir, Grazyna, Jacek, Jerzy, Jozef, Kazimierz, Krzysztof, Leslaw.*

D

Daane (225) Dutch: from a pet form of the personal name DANIEL.

Dabb (140) Southern English: variant of DOBB, a pet form of ROBERT.

Dabbs (1519) Southern English: patronymic from DABB.

Dabkowski (165) Polish (Dąbkowski): habitational name for someone from a place named with *dąb* 'oak', for example Dąbki or Dąbkowice.
GIVEN NAMES Polish 21%. *Slawomir* (2), *Tadeusz* (2), *Witold* (2), *Zdzislaw* (2), *Zygmund* (2), *Ferdynand, Kazimierz, Wladyslaw.*

Dabler (102) Perhaps a French (Alsatian) variant of DOBLER.
GIVEN NAME French 7%. *Amiee.*

Dabney (2039) English (of both Norman and Huguenot origin): altered form of French **d'Aubigné**, a habitational name for someone from any of the various places in northern France called Aubigny or Aubigné, named with the Romano-Gallic personal name *Albinius* (a derivative of Latin *albus* 'white'; compare ALBAN and ALBIN) + the locative suffix *-acum*.
FOREBEARS American Dabneys are probably mostly descended from Cornelius Dabney or d'Aubigné, a Huguenot who came to VA in the early 18th century, after a considerable residence in England. Some family historians trace their ancestry to an even earlier American, a Cornelius born about 1650 in King Williams Co., VA.

Dabrowski (892) Polish (Dąbrowski): habitational name from any of various places named Dąbrowa or Dąbrowka, from *dąbrowa* 'oak grove' (from *dąb* 'oak'), with the addition of *-ski*, suffix of local surnames.
GIVEN NAMES Polish 24%. *Jerzy* (6), *Andrzej* (5), *Stanislaw* (4), *Zdzislaw* (4), *Casimir* (3), *Ewa* (3), *Halina* (3), *Jozef* (3), *Miroslaw* (3), *Tadeusz* (3), *Bogdan* (2), *Dariusz* (2).

Daby (103) English: variant of DARBY.

Dacanay (123) Ilocano (Philippines): unexplained.
GIVEN NAMES Spanish 28%; Italian 9%; French 5%. *Leticia* (3), *Fernando* (2), *Joaquin* (2), *Alejandro, Camilo, Celso, Constantina, Edgardo, Filemon, Jesus; Antonio, Arnulfo, Bernardo, Eliseo, Filomena, Romeo; Armand, Julienne.*

Dace (282) English: from Old French *dars* 'dace'; a nickname for someone thought to resemble the fish of this name, or a metonymic occupational name for a fisherman or fish seller.

Dacey (684) Irish: Anglicized form of Gaelic **Déiseach**, a name for a member of the vassal community known as the *Déise*, a term of uncertain meaning and origin.
GIVEN NAME Irish 5%. *Liam.*

Dach (138) German: topographic name from Middle High German *dahe, tahe* 'mud', 'clay', for a settler on clayey soil.

Dachel (127) South German: diminutive of DACH.

D'Achille (123) Italian: patronymic from the personal name *Achille*, from Greek *Akhilleus* 'Achilles'.

Dachs (112) German and Jewish (Ashkenazic): from Middle High German *dahs*, German *Dachs* 'badger'; in German a nickname for someone thought to resemble a badger or an occupational name for a badger hunter; in Yiddish an ornamental name.
GIVEN NAMES Jewish 13%; German 4%. *Zalman* (2), *Dovid, Heshy, Shimon, Simcha; Alois.*

Dack (291) **1.** English: from an Old English personal name, *Dæcca*. **2.** Dutch: metonymic occupational name for a roofer, from *dack*, a variant of *deck* 'roof'. Compare DE DECKER.

Dacko (126) **1.** Ukrainian: from a pet form of the personal name *Danýlo*. **2.** Polish: from a pet form of an Old Polish compound personal name beginning with *Da-* (for example, *Dalebor, Dalegor, Dalemir*), or of the Biblical names DANIEL or *Dawid* (Polish form of DAVID). **3.** Bulgarian: from a pet form of *Daco*, itself a pet form of various personal names such as *Jordan, Danail,* or *David* or alternatively from a pet form of DACE.

Da Costa (1232) Portuguese, Galician, Italian, and Jewish (Sephardic): variant of the topographic name COSTA, denoting someone who lived on a slope or river bank or on the sea coast, with the addition of the preposition *da* 'from (the)', 'of (the)'.
GIVEN NAMES Spanish 24%; Portuguese 17%. *Jose* (36), *Manuel* (35), *Carlos* (13), *Francisco* (11), *Fernando* (8), *Alfredo* (4), *Jorge* (4), *Luis* (4), *Mario* (4), *Luiz* (3), *Ricardo* (3), *Alfonso* (2); *Joao* (7), *Joaquim* (4), *Marcio* (4), *Afonso, Agostinho, Albano, Conceicao, Fernandes, Henrique, Manoel, Martinho, Paulo.*

D'Acquisto (197) Italian (mainly Sicily): patronymic from a short form of the late medieval personal name *Bonacquisto*, literally 'good acquisition', 'good buy', a name bestowed on a much-wanted child.

Da Cruz (189) Portuguese: variant of CRUZ, with the addition of the preposition *da* 'of (the)', 'from (the)', probably originally an epithet with religious connotations.
GIVEN NAMES Spanish 42%; Portuguese 15%; French 4%. *Antonio* (13), *Jose* (6), *Carlos* (5), *Manuel* (3), *Domingos* (2), *Fernando* (2), *Miguel* (2), *Pedro* (2), *Abilio, Albertino, Armando, Arnaldo, Belen; Joaquim* (4), *Joao, Marcio, Paulo; Armand, Clovis, Colette, Pascal.*

Da Cunha (186) Portuguese: variant of CUNHA, with the addition of the preposition *da* 'from (the)', 'of (the)'.
GIVEN NAMES Portuguese 26%; Spanish 26%. *Joao* (3), *Joaquim* (2), *Afonso, Albano, Almir, Ilidio, Serafim; Jose* (6), *Manuel* (5), *Mario* (5), *Carlos* (4), *Alvaro* (2), *Fernando* (2), *Jorge* (2), *Rogerio* (2), *Alfonso, Alfredo, Armando, Armindo; Antonio* (5).

D'Acunto (109) Italian: patronymic from the personal name *Acunto*, from Greek *Akontes*.
GIVEN NAMES Italian 24%. *Antonio* (2), *Annalisa, Franco, Gennaro, Giuseppe, Sal, Sebastiano, Silvio.*

Dacus (773) Welsh: Anglicized form of the Welsh personal name *Deicws*, a pet form of *Dafydd*, Welsh form of DAVID.

Dacy (189) Irish: variant spelling of DACEY.

Dada (130) **1.** Muslim: from a personal name based on the Persian *dāda* 'given' (i.e. 'gift of God'). **2.** Indian (Maharashtra): Hindu and Muslim name meaning 'elder brother' in Marathi, also used as an honorific term of address.
GIVEN NAMES Muslim 52%; Indian 6%. *Abdul* (3), *Arshad* (3), *Aslam* (2), *Ghulam* (2), *Salim* (2), *Uzair* (2), *Aftab, Aleem, Aly, Aman, Ameen, Asif; Nisha* (2), *Gagan, Pradeep.*

D'Adamo (247) Italian: patronymic from the personal name *Adamo*, Italian equivalent of ADAM.
GIVEN NAMES Italian 26%. *Angelo* (2), *Pasquale* (2), *Adriano, Aldo, Amadeo, Amedeo, Antonio, Armando, Cristiano, Donato, Emilio, Erasmo, Eugenio, Gerado, Marco, Salvatore, Saverio.*

D'Addario (603) Italian: patronymic from the personal name *Addario*, a dialect vari-

401

ant of Dario, associated chiefly with Apulia.

GIVEN NAMES Italian 11%. *Carlo* (3), *Franco* (3), *Donato* (2), *Angelo, Antonio, Gaetano, Gino, Guido, Lido, Luciano, Luigino, Rinaldo.*

D'Addio (273) Italian: patronymic from the personal name *Addio, Addeo,* a short form of a compound name formed with this element, as for example *Donadeo, Donadio* 'gift of God'.

D'Addona (286) Italian: patronymic from the personal name *Addona,* which is most probably from a Germanic personal name, *Adduni.*

GIVEN NAMES Italian 20%. *Salvatore* (5), *Angelo* (3), *Nicola* (2), *Aldo, Alessandra, Amedeo, Antonietta, Antonio, Carmine, Domenic, Florindo, Nunzio.*

Dade (638) **1.** Irish: reduced form of McDade, 'son of David'. **2.** German: from the Frisian personal name *Dode,* which Bahlow explains as a form derived from baby talk. **3.** English (Norfolk): from Old English *dēd* 'deed', 'exploit', probably applied as a nickname commemorating some exploit perpetrated by the bearer or for someone noted for his derring-do. Compare Deeds.

Dadisman (168) Origin unidentified.

Dado (147) Hispanic: unexplained.

GIVEN NAMES Spanish 4%. *Amalio, Fernando, Gumersindo, Leonida, Reynaldo, Rigoberto.*

Dady (325) **1.** Irish: variant of Deady. **2.** Hungarian: habitational name for someone from a place called Dad, in Fejér and Komárom counties, or Dada, in Somogy and Szabolcs counties.

Daehn (101) North German (also **Dähn**): variant of Dehn 3.

GIVEN NAME German 5%. *Helmut.*

Daenzer (132) German (**Dänzer**): variant of Tanzer 'dancer'.

GIVEN NAMES German 6%. *Ernst, Klaus.*

Daffern (158) Probably a variant of South German **Dafferner,** an occupational name for an inn- or tavern-keeper, Middle High German *tavernære,* a borrowing from Latin *tabernarius,* or a habitational name from Tafern in Baden.

Daffin (239) English: probably a nickname for a simpleton.

Daffron (504) Possibly English: unexplained.

Dafoe (276) See Defoe.

Daft (187) English: nickname for a meek person, from Middle English *daffte* 'mild', 'gentle', 'meek' (Old English *gedæfte*). It was not until the 15th century, toward the end of the main period of surname formation in England, that the word came to mean 'stupid', 'silly'.

Dagan (159) Jewish (Israeli and Sephardic): ornamental name or metonymic occupational name from Hebrew *dagan* 'cereals'.

GIVEN NAMES Jewish 30%. *Moshe* (3), *Shlomo* (3), *Anat* (2), *Aviad* (2), *Doron* (2),

Erez (2), *Aharon, Avraham, Bezalel, Nurit, Oded, Vered.*

D'Agata (189) Italian: metronymic from the female personal name *Agata* (Latin *Agatha,* Greek *Agathē,* from Greek *agathos* 'good'). This was the name of a 3rd-century Sicilian martyr; for this reason the personal name was particularly popular in Sicily, where the surname is still concentrated today.

GIVEN NAMES Italian 14%. *Salvatore* (4), *Alfio* (3), *Angelo, Filomena, Gino, Orazio.*

Dagel (116) German (**Dägel**): **1.** Probably a Bavarian dialect variant of Diegel 'potter'. Alternatively, it may be a metonymic occupational name for a tiler or a maker of roof tiles, from Low German *tegel* 'tile'. Compare Tegeler. **2.** From a short form of a Germanic personal name based on *tac* 'day'.

Dagen (284) Variant spelling of German Degen.

Dagenais (338) French: regional name, with the preposition *d(e),* for someone from the region named for the city of Agen (see Dagen).

FOREBEARS A bearer of the name from Aunis was married in 1665 in Montreal.

GIVEN NAMES French 11%. *Andre* (2), *Alain, Armand, Dominique, Jacques, Jean Louis, Marcel, Martial, Sylvain.*

Dagenhart (315) Altered spelling of German Degenhardt.

Dager (231) **1.** English: unexplained. **2.** Possibly a variant spelling of Catalan **Daguer,** from *daguer* 'knife smith'.

GIVEN NAMES Spanish 5%. *Fernando* (2), *Alfonso, Arturo, Edilberto, Jairo, Santiago, Sergio, Viviana, Yajaira.*

Dages (173) French (**Dagès**): habitational name, with the preposition *d(e),* for someone from Agès in Landes.

Dagg (238) **1.** English: from Old French *dague* 'dagger' (of uncertain origin), hence a metonymic occupational name for a maker or seller of daggers, or a nickname for someone who carried one. Middle English **Dagger** is a later development of the same word. The surname was taken to southern Ireland in the 17th century. **2.** Scottish: on the evidence of the early spelling *Dog,* Black believed this possibly to be a form of Doig. **3.** German: from a personal name based on Old High German *tac* 'day'.

Daggett (2029) English: variant of Doggett.

FOREBEARS John Daggett came from England to Watertown, MA, in 1630, and moved to Rehoboth, MA, in 1646. He was one of the original proprietors of Martha's Vineyard in 1642 and by 1651 had settled there permanently.

Daggs (313) English: variant of Dagg.

Daggy (142) Possibly a respelling of French **Dagay,** a habitational name for someone

from Agay, a district of Saint-Raphaël in Provence.

GIVEN NAME French 4%. *Chantelle.*

Dagher (148) Arabic: variant of Daher.

GIVEN NAMES Arabic 49%; French 7%. *Ghassan* (3), *Sami* (3), *Ali* (2), *Bassel* (2), *Hassan* (2), *Marwan* (2), *Nabil* (2), *Rafik* (2), *Rifaat* (2), *Ziad* (2), *Adnan, Akram; Antoine, Emile, Marcelle, Micheline, Pierre.*

Dagle (187) Probably an altered form of German **Degel** or **Dägele,** from a short form of an old personal name formed with Old High German *tac* 'day'.

Dagley (383) **1.** English: habitational name from an unidentified place, most probably in the West Midlands, where the surname is concentrated today. **2.** Americanized spelling of German **Dägele** (see Dagle) or **Degele,** from a short form of any of several Germanic personal names formed with Old High German *diot* 'people', 'nation'.

Dagnan (100) Irish: variant of Irish Dignan.

Dagner (103) Altered spelling of German Degener.

D'Agosta (103) Italian: variant of the habitational name Agosta, with the addition of the preposition *d'.*

D'Agostino (3026) Italian: patronymic from the personal name *Agostino,* a pet form of Agosto.

GIVEN NAMES Italian 17%. *Angelo* (26), *Salvatore* (14), *Pasquale* (8), *Romeo* (8), *Carmine* (7), *Antonio* (6), *Sal* (5), *Vito* (5), *Carmelo* (4), *Domenic* (4), *Rocco* (4), *Attilio* (3).

Dague (699) French: from Old French *dague* 'dagger', applied as a nickname for someone who carried a dagger or possibly a metonymic occupational name for a maker or seller of daggers.

Dahan (239) Jewish (Sephardic): occupational name from an Arabic word meaning 'someone who coats with oil', most likely a painter or a dealer in oil.

GIVEN NAMES Jewish 31%; French 13%; Jewish Biblical 5%. *Meir* (6), *Moshe* (5), *Mazal* (3), *Chaim* (2), *Doron* (2), *Eran* (2), *Nissim* (2), *Yossi* (2), *Aharon, Ahron, Anat, Arie; Andre* (4), *Armand* (3), *Jacques* (2), *Dominique, Fernand, Gisele, Jean-Jacques, Lucienne, Marcelle.*

Daher (365) Arabic: from a personal name based on Arabic *ẓāhir* 'knowing', 'clear', 'evident'.

GIVEN NAMES Arabic 19%; French 5%. *Khalil* (3), *Mohamed* (3), *Ali* (2), *Hassan* (2), *Hussein* (2), *Sami* (2), *Shadi* (2), *Abdul, Ahmad, Aref, Badih, Bechara; Emile* (2), *Antoine, Dany, Georges, Mireille, Pierre.*

Dahill (187) Irish: reduced Anglicized form of Gaelic **Ó Dathail** 'descendant of *Dathal,*' a personal name from *daithgheal* 'fair', 'light-colored'.

Dahl (9374) Norwegian, Danish, Swedish, North German, and Jewish (Ashkenazic):

from any of the medieval and modern forms of Germanic *dala-*, Old Norse *dalr*, 'valley'. Throughout Norway and elsewhere in Scandinavia this is a common farm name. In some cases it is a habitational name from places in Germany named Dahl or Dahle, from the same word. As a Jewish family name this is a habitational name or an ornamental adoption.

GIVEN NAMES Scandinavian 5%. *Erik* (11), *Selmer* (6), *Alf* (5), *Nils* (5), *Jorgen* (3), *Per* (3), *Sven* (3), *Astrid* (2), *Helmer* (2), *Holger* (2), *Iver* (2), *Johan* (2).

Dahlberg (1485) Norwegian and Swedish: from a compound of *dal* 'valley' + *berg* 'mountain', 'hill', found as a farm name. In Sweden it is also an ornamental name.

GIVEN NAMES Scandinavian 8%. *Erik* (4), *Sven* (3), *Bjorn* (2), *Lennart* (2), *Sten* (2), *Anders*, *Kerstin*, *Sigfred*, *Tor*.

Dahlby (142) Norwegian and Danish: from a Norwegian farm name or Danish place name, both derived from Old Norse *dalr* 'valley' + *býr* 'farmstead'.

Dahle (752) 1. Norwegian: spelling variant of DALE. 2. German: habitational name from any of various places in Germany named Dahle (see DAHL).

GIVEN NAMES Scandinavian 6%; German 4%. *Erik* (2), *Bjorn*, *Thorvald*; *Rudiger* (3), *Hans* (2), *Armin*, *Erwin*, *Johannes*, *Juergen*.

Dahlem (286) 1. Norwegian: habitational name from any of several farmsteads named Dalem, from Old Norse *dalr* 'valley' + *heim* 'home'. 2. German: habitational name from any of the places in western Germany named Dahlem: near Lüneburg, Bitburg, Trier, and Berlin (now a suburb).

Dahlen (854) 1. Swedish (**Dahlén**): ornamental form of DAHL, with the suffix -*én*, from the Latin adjectival suffix -*enius* 'relating to'. 2. Norwegian: variant spelling of the farm name DALEN. 3. German: habitational name from any of various places in Germany named Dahlum, e.g. near Düsseldorf and in Eastphalia.

GIVEN NAMES Scandinavian 5%. *Arndt*, *Erik*, *Lennart*, *Ove*.

Dahler (202) 1. North German (also **Dähler**): topographic name for someone who lived in a valley (see DAHL), or habitational name for someone from a place named with this word. 2. German: from a Germanic word meaning 'proud', 'famous' (cognate with Anglo-Saxon *deal*). 3. Norwegian: from the farm name *Daler*, plural indefinite form of *dal* 'valley' (see DAL).

GIVEN NAMES German 4%. *Elke*, *Kurt*.

Dahlgren (1454) Swedish: ornamental name composed of the elements *dal* 'valley' + *gren* 'branch'.

GIVEN NAMES Scandinavian 5%. *Alf*, *Anders*, *Elof*, *Evald*, *Fredrik*, *Helmer*, *Lennart*, *Nels*, *Sven*.

Dahlheimer (196) German: habitational name for someone from a place called

Dahlheim, near Coblenz or in Lower Saxony, near Hannoversch-Münden.

Dahlin (1087) Swedish: ornamental form of DAHL, with the suffix -*in*, from the Latin adjectival ending -*inius* 'relating to'.

GIVEN NAMES Scandinavian 5%. *Erik* (2), *Torvald* (2), *Bjorn*, *Disa*, *Jarl*, *Lars*, *Nils*, *Per*, *Toralf*.

Dahling (119) 1. Norwegian: from a farm name *Daling*, composed of the elements *dal* 'valley' + *eng* 'meadow'. 2. Possibly also Swedish: ornamental form of *dal* 'valley' with the suffix -*ing*. 3. German (**Dähling**): topographic name for someone who lived in a valley (see DAHL), or habitational name for someone from a place named with this word.

Dahlinger (110) German (also **Dählinger**): topographic name for a valley dweller (see DAHLING).

GIVEN NAME German 5%. *Johann*.

Dahlke (1258) Eastern German: from a pet form of the Slavic personal names *Dalibor* or *Dalimir*, which are both derived from *dal* 'present', 'gift'.

GIVEN NAMES German 5%. *Kurt* (6), *Hans* (2), *Otto* (2), *Erwin*, *Fritz*, *Gerhardt*, *Hedwig*, *Helmuth*, *Joerg*, *Klaus*, *Reinhold*, *Willi*.

Dahlman (705) 1. Swedish: ornamental name composed of the elements *dal* 'valley' + *man* 'man'. 2. variant of German DAHLMANN.

GIVEN NAMES Scandinavian 4%. *Per* (2), *Astrid*, *Erik*, *Sven*.

Dahlmann (100) German: topographic name for someone who lived in a valley, an elaborated form of DAHL with the addition of *man* 'man'.

Dahlquist (1037) Swedish: ornamental name composed of the elements *dal* 'valley' + *quist*, an old or ornamental spelling of *kvist* 'twig'.

GIVEN NAMES Scandinavian 6%. *Nils* (2), *Sven* (2), *Erik*, *Erland*, *Nels*, *Sig*.

Dahlstrom (1166) Swedish (**Dahlström**): ornamental name composed of the elements *dal* 'valley' + *ström* 'stream'.

GIVEN NAMES Scandinavian 6%. *Bent*, *Berndt*, *Bertel*, *Erik*, *Kerstin*, *Per*, *Sven*.

Dahm (889) 1. North German, Dutch, and Danish: from a short form of the personal name ADAM. 2. German: variant of **Dahme**, a habitational name from a place so named (see DAHMER).

GIVEN NAMES German 4%. *Erna* (2), *Otto* (2), *Bodo*, *Eckhard*, *Erwin*, *Kurt*, *Reinhard*, *Uli*.

Dahman (156) Origin unidentified. Perhaps in part an altered spelling of DAHMEN, but it is also found as a Muslim name.

GIVEN NAMES Muslim 4%. *Bassam* (3), *Bachar*, *Elsayed*, *Nidal*, *Samer*.

Dahmen (336) 1. Swedish (**Dahmén**): probably an ornamental form of *Dahm* with the common suffix -*én*, from Latin -*enius* 'relating to'. 2. German: habitational name from a place in Mecklenburg called

Dahmen. 3. North German and Dutch: patronymic from the personal name DAHM.

GIVEN NAMES German 7%. *Hans* (2), *Klaus* (2), *Aloysius*, *Dieter*, *Florian*, *Kaethe*, *Kurt*, *Rinehart*, *Wilhelm*.

Dahmer (374) North German and Danish: habitational name for someone from any of various places called Dahme, in Holstein, Mecklenburg, Brandenburg, or Silesia.

Dahms (766) German and Dutch: patronymic from DAHM.

Dahn (430) German: 1. habitational name from a place in the Rhine Palatinate called Dahn. 2. (**Dähn**): ethnic name for a Dane, from Old Norse *Dan-*.

Dahnke (239) German: from a short form of the Slavic personal name *Danislaw*, from *dan-* 'gift'.

Dai (618) 1. Chinese 傣: there are two sources of this surname, both from the Spring and Autumn period (722–481 BC). At one time, there existed a state of Dai at one time (in modern Henan province). When this was defeated by the state of Cheng, residents of the defeated state adopted Dai as their surname. Additionally, a duke of the state of Song was called Dai, and his descendants adopted Dai as their surname. 2. Vietnamese: unexplained.

GIVEN NAMES Chinese 47%; Vietnamese 12%. *Wei* (5), *Cheng* (3), *Chi* (3), *Jin* (3), *Weimin* (3), *Xing* (3), *Zheng* (3), *Chung* (3), *Dong* (2), *Hong* (2), *Meng* (2), *Ning* (2), *Peihua* (2); *Hung* (3), *Quang* (3), *Thanh* (3), *Anh*, *Cuong*, *Dai*, *Khanh*, *Lam Van*, *Minh*, *Mui*, *Nghia*, *Ngoc*.

Daiber (135) German: occupational name from Middle High German *tiuber* 'dove keeper' or *töuber* 'wind player', 'musician'.

GIVEN NAMES German 8%. *Ernst*, *Hermann*, *Siegmar*.

D'Aidone (201) Southern Italian: habitational name for someone from Aidone in Enna province, Sicily.

Daigh (116) 1. Possibly of English origin: unexplained. 2. German: possibly an altered spelling of DEICH.

Daigle (5380) 1. French version of the German surname DEGLER 'potter', reinterpreted by folk etymology as *D'Aigle* 'of the eagle'. 2. Altered spelling of South German **Daigl**, a metonymic occupational name for a baker, from Middle High German *teic* 'dough' + the diminutive suffix -*el*.

GIVEN NAMES French 8%. *Lucien* (9), *Marcel* (9), *Armand* (7), *Andre* (6), *Emile* (5), *Gilles* (4), *Pierre* (4), *Rosaire* (4), *Amie* (3), *Aurele* (3), *Camille* (3), *Curley* (3).

Daigler (196) 1. South German: occupational name for a baker, from an agent derivative of Middle High German *teic* 'dough'. 2. South German: variant of **Daichler**, an occupational name for a maker or user of wooden waterpipes or ducts, from an agent derivative of Middle High German *tiuchel* 'waterpipe', 'duct'.

Daignault (325) French: from a variant of the personal name *Daniau*, a variant of DANIEL.

FOREBEARS The first Dagneau or Dagnaux in Sorel, Quebec, was from Normandy, France (1665).

GIVEN NAMES French 10%. *Andre* (2), *Marcel* (2), *Adrien, Aime, Armand, Emile*.

Daigneau (106) French: variant of DAIGNAULT, written thus under the influence of *agneau* 'lamb'.

GIVEN NAME French 4%. *Aurore*.

Daigneault (578) French: variant of DAIGNAULT.

GIVEN NAMES French 14%. *Normand* (5), *Andre* (4), *Armand* (2), *Laurent* (2), *Pierre* (2), *Aime, Anatole, Dominique, Emile, Fernande, Germain, Lucien*.

Daigre (172) French: habitational name, with the preposition *d(e)*, for someone from a place in Charente named Aigre.

FOREBEARS Jetté tells us that a Jacques Daigre was condemned to be hanged for theft in Quebec in 1665, but was spared when he agreed to become a hangman himself.

Daigrepont (200) French: of uncertain derivation; perhaps an altered spelling of **Daigremont**, a habitational name, with the preposition *d(e)*, for someone from any of several places named Aigremont, in France (Gard, Haute-Marne, Seine-et-Oise, Yonne) and the Belgian provinces of Liège and Luxembourg.

Daiker (152) Perhaps an altered spelling of English **Daker**, a habitational name from either of two places named Dacre, in Cumbria and North Yorkshire, both named from the rivers on which they stand (a Celtic river name meaning 'trickling').

Dail (1395) English: variant spelling of DALE.

Dailey (11185) Irish: variant spelling of DALY.

Daily (3885) Irish: variant spelling of DALY. In the British Isles this spelling is found mainly in Scotland.

Dain (326) **1.** English: nickname from Middle English *digne, deyne* 'worthy', 'honorable', or alternatively, as Reaney suggests, from Middle English *dain(e)* 'haughty', 'reserved' (Burgundian French *doigne*). **2.** English: variant of DEAN. **3.** English: variant of DANE. **4.** French: nickname from Old French *dain* 'agile', 'nimble'. **5.** Jewish: variant of DAYAN.

GIVEN NAMES Jewish 4%. *Khanna, Nukhim, Rakhil*.

Daines (334) English (mainly East Anglia and Essex): patronymic from DAIN.

Daino (144) **1.** Italian: from *daino* 'fallow deer', applied as a nickname, perhaps for someone who was timid or fleet of foot, or as a metonymic occupational name for a

game warden or hunter. **2.** Perhaps a respelling of French DAIGNAULT.

GIVEN NAMES Italian 6%. *Vito* (2), *Franco*.

Dains (287) English: variant spelling of DAINES.

Dainty (122) English: affectionate nickname or term of address, from Middle English *deinteth* 'pleasure', 'tidbit' (Old French *deintiet*, from Latin *dignitas* 'worth', 'value'). The word was also used as an adjective in the later form *deinte* (Old French *deint(i)é*) in the sense 'fine', 'handsome', 'pleasant'.

Dais (250) Of uncertain origin. It is found as a French Huguenot name in England. It may also be a variant of Irish DEASE.

Daise (149) Origin unidentified. Compare DAIS, DAISEY.

Daisey (258) Of uncertain origin; perhaps a variant of Irish DACEY or DEASE.

Daisley (130) **1.** English: unexplained; perhaps a habitational name from a lost or unidentified place. In England it occurs mainly in Bedfordshire, Cambridgeshire, and Norfolk. **2.** French: unexplained; possibly a habitational name for someone from a lost or unidentified place.

GIVEN NAMES French 10%. *Michel* (2), *Patrice* (2).

Daisy (207) **1.** French: habitational name, with the preposition *d(e)*, for someone from either of two places called Aisy, in Yonne and Côte-d'Or. **2.** Probably a variant of spelling Irish DACEY. **3.** English: perhaps as Reaney suggests, from a nickname from the flower, Old English *dæges-ēage*.

Daitch (131) Jewish: Americanized form of DEUTSCH.

D'Aiuto (130) Italian: patronymic from the personal name *Aiuto*, meaning 'aid', 'help', often a short form of the compound names *Bonaiuto, Diotaiuti*, or *Diolaiuti*.

Dajani (125) Muslim: unexplained.

GIVEN NAMES Muslim 71%. *Omar* (5), *Nader* (4), *Hassan* (3), *Musa* (3), *Salim* (3), *Ahmad* (2), *Jawad* (2), *Sami* (2), *Adnan, Aref, Ata, Badr*.

Dakan (151) Origin uncertain. Probably an Americanized spelling of English DEACON.

Dake (1047) Perhaps an altered spelling of German DEIKE.

Dakin (749) English (chiefly East Midlands): from a pet form of DAY 1 and 2.

Dal (31) Scandinavian, chiefly Danish and Norwegian: habitational name from a common place name, the name of several farmsteads, derived from Old Norse *dalr* 'valley'. Compare DAHL.

GIVEN NAME Scandinavian 12%. *Aase* (2).

Dalager (114) Possibly an altered spelling of Irish **Dallagher**, a reduced Anglicized form of Gaelic **Ó Dalachair**, a rare name found mainly in Co. Limerick.

Dalal (398) Indian (Panjab, Gujarat, and Bombay city): Hindu (Vania), Sikh, Jain, Parsi, and Muslim name, an occupational

name for a broker, from Arabic *dallāl* 'auctioneer'. The Jats have a tribe called *Dalal*.

GIVEN NAMES Indian 76%; Muslim 7%. *Sunil* (6), *Rajiv* (5), *Sudhir* (5), *Ajay* (4), *Dinesh* (4), *Sanjay* (4), *Apurva* (3), *Bharat* (3), *Dilip* (3), *Harsh* (3), *Jagdish* (3), *Kiran* (3); *Kamal* (3), *Samir* (3), *Hemal* (2), *Muna* (2), *Nirav* (2), *Adil, Ashraf, Bashar, Fazle, Halima, Hussein, Imtiyaz*.

Dalbec (328) Variant of French **Dalbègue**, a habitational name, with fused preposition *d'*, from Albègue (Loire).

GIVEN NAMES French 6%. *Andre, Euclide, Jean-Marc, Rosaire*.

Dalberg (146) Swedish: variant spelling of DAHLBERG.

Dalbey (390) Variant spelling of DALBY.

Dalby (659) Norwegian, Danish, and northern English: habitational name from any of various places named Dalby, named with Old Norse *dalr* 'valley' + *býr* 'farm', 'settlement'. The English surname is common in Yorkshire, where it derives mainly from Dalby in North Yorkshire, but similarly named places in Leicestershire and Lincolnshire are also possible sources. In Norway, it is common as a farm name. See also DAHLBY.

GIVEN NAMES Scandinavian 4%. *Britt, Erik, Knud, Nels, Obert*.

Dale (11095) **1.** English: from Middle English *dale* 'dale', 'valley' (Old English *dæl*, reinforced in northern England by the cognate Old Norse *dalr*), a topographic name for someone who lived in a valley, or a habitational name from any of the numerous minor places named with this word, such as Dale in Cumbria and Yorkshire. **2.** Irish: possibly in some cases of English origin, but otherwise an Anglicized form of Gaelic **Dall**, a byname meaning 'blind'. **3.** Norwegian: habitational name from a farm named from Old Norse *dali*, the dative case of *dalr* 'valley'. It is a common name in Norway, especially western Norway, and is also found in Sweden. **4.** Americanized spelling of German DAHL.

FOREBEARS With a reputation as a disciplinarian, the soldier and colonizer Sir Thomas Dale (d. 1619), was appointed marshal of VA and arrived in 1611 at Point Comfort with the *Starr, Prosperous,* and *Elizabeth,* carrying settlers, stores, and livestock. First enlisted in the service of the Netherlands, he later served Prince Henry in Scotland and was knighted as Sir Thomas Dale of Surrey.

Dalebout (105) Dutch: from the Germanic personal name *Dalbaldus*.

Daleiden (191) North German and Dutch: habitational name from a place in the Rhineland called Daleiden.

GIVEN NAME German 4%. *Meinrad* (2).

Dalen (303) **1.** Norwegian: from a very widespread farm name meaning 'the valley', the singular definite form of *dal* 'valley'. **2.** Swedish (**Dalén**): ornamental name from *dal* 'valley' + the suffix *-én*, a derivative of the Latin adjectival suffix *-enius* 'relating to'. See also DAHLEN.

GIVEN NAMES Scandinavian 6%. *Einer, Lars.*

D'Aleo (353) Italian: patronymic from the personal name ALEO.

GIVEN NAMES Italian 16%. *Carlo* (4), *Salvatore* (4), *Vito* (3), *Sal* (2), *Angelo, Camillo, Gioacchino, Pietro, Salvator.*

Dales (366) **1.** English: regional name from the area referred to as 'the Dales' in northern England. See also DALE. **2.** Jewish (eastern Ashkenazic): nickname for a needy person, from Hebrew *daluš* 'poverty'.

D'Alesandro (260) Italian: variant spelling of D'ALESSANDRO.

D'Alesio (194) Italian: variant spelling of D'ALESSIO.

D'Alessandro (2007) Italian: patronymic from the personal name *Alessandro*, from Greek *Alexandros* (see ALEXANDER).

GIVEN NAMES Italian 17%. *Angelo* (11), *Rocco* (7), *Vito* (7), *Carmine* (5), *Antonio* (4), *Domenic* (4), *Donato* (4), *Guido* (4), *Salvatore* (4), *Carlo* (3), *Elio* (3), *Attilio* (2).

D'Alessio (977) Italian: patronymic from the personal name *Alessio* (see ALEXIS).

GIVEN NAMES Italian 20%. *Angelo* (7), *Gaetano* (5), *Carmine* (4), *Domenic* (4), *Guido* (4), *Luigi* (3), *Rocco* (3), *Salvatore* (3), *Alfonse* (2), *Antonio* (2), *Carlo* (2), *Matteo* (2).

Daley (8509) Irish: variant spelling of DALY.

D'Alfonso (257) Italian: patronymic from the personal name ALFONSO; this form is typical of Abruzzo.

GIVEN NAMES Italian 18%. *Mario* (3), *Alfonso* (2), *Claudio* (2), *Ermanno* (2), *Sal* (2), *Angelo, Carmel, Delio, Domenic, Domenico, Fiore, Mauro, Nunzi, Nunzio, Pasquale.*

Dalgleish (248) Scottish: habitational name from a place near Selkirk, first recorded in 1383 in the form *Dalglas*, from Celtic *dol* 'field' + *glas* 'green' (compare GLASS 2).

D'Alia (173) **1.** Italian: patronymic from the personal name *Alia*, a variant of ELIA. **2.** Indian (Gujarat, Rajasthan): Jain name of unknown meaning, based on the name of a clan in the Godha Jain community.

GIVEN NAMES Italian 10%; Indian 6%. *Antonio, Carmine, Cira, Gaetano, Gino, Michelina, Saverio, Vincenzo; Anil, Mukund, Rachana, Raj, Satish.*

Dalin (150) **1.** Swedish: variant spelling of DAHLIN. **2.** French: patronymic from the personal name *Alin*, a short form of any of the Germanic personal names containing the element *adal* 'noble'.

Dalke (551) Variant spelling of German DAHLKE.

Dall (589) **1.** Danish: variant of DAHL. **2.** German: from a short form of a Germanic personal name, perhaps related to Anglo-Saxon *deal* 'proud', 'famous'; or alternatively from a Slavic stem *dalu* 'gift', a

nickname for a generous or gifted person perhaps.

Dallaire (352) French: probably a patronymic (**D'Allaire**) from the personal name *Allaire*, an old form of *Hilaire* (see HILLARY).

GIVEN NAMES French 25%. *Lucien* (5), *Normand* (4), *Armand* (3), *Andre* (2), *Laurent* (2), *Pierre* (2), *Amedee, Dany, Emile, Fernand, Gilles, Jacques.*

Dallal (102) Muslim: variant spelling of DALAL.

GIVEN NAMES Muslim 19%. *Amir, Farid, Fouad, Hassan, Kamal, Mahmoud, Mohammed, Naim, Said, Saleem, Yehia, Zuhair.*

Dallam (136) English: habitational name from either of two places called Dalham, one in Suffolk and one in Kent, both named from Old English *dæl* 'valley' + *hām* 'settlement', 'homestead', or from Daleham in Sussex, which is named from Old English *dæl* 'valley' + Old English *hamm* 'enclosure hemmed in by water', 'meadow'.

Dallas (2848) **1.** Scottish: habitational name from Dallas, a place near Forres, probably named from British *dol* 'meadow' (Gaelic *dail*) + *gwas* 'dwelling' (Gaelic *fas*). The surname is also established in County Derry in Ireland. **2.** English: habitational name from a place named from Old English *dæl* or Old Norse *dalr* 'valley' + *hūs* 'house', for example Dalehouse in North Yorkshire, or a topographic name with the same meaning.

Dallenbach (114) German: habitational name from a place so named, from dialect *Dalle* 'dell'.

GIVEN NAME German 4%. *Erik* (2).

D'Allesandro (109) Respelling of Italian D'ALESSANDRO.

D'Allessandro (111) Respelling of Italian D'ALESSANDRO.

D'Alleva (107) Italian: patronymic from the personal name ALLEVA.

Dalley (492) Irish: variant of DALY.

Dallin (101) English: variant of DALLING.

Dalling (109) English and Scottish: habitational name, possibly from Dalling in Norfolk, which was named in Old English as 'the place of the people (*-inga-*) of Dall(a)'.

Dallis (126) Scottish and English: variant spelling of DALLAS.

Dallman (706) Respelling of German DALLMANN.

GIVEN NAMES German 4%. *Kurt* (2), *Otto* (2), *Erwin, Florian, Gerhardt.*

Dallmann (452) German: **1.** northern habitational name for someone from Dalle near Celle. **2.** perhaps from an old personal name formed with a stem cognate with Anglo-Saxon *deal* 'proud', 'famous' + *man* 'man'. **3.** topographic name from Low German *Dalle, Delle* 'depression', 'hollow' (cognate with standard German *Tal*, English *dale*).

GIVEN NAMES German 7%. *Erwin* (3), *Armin, Dieter, Erhardt, Hans, Kurt, Leonhard, Manfred, Otto, Ulrich.*

Dallmeyer (112) German: **1.** distinguishing name for a tenant farmer (see MEYER) who lived in a valley (Middle Low German *dal*). **2.** perhaps from a Slavic personal name, *Dalemir*, composed of the elements *dale* 'further' + *mir* 'peace'.

GIVEN NAME German 5%. *Erwin.*

Dalluge (132) German (**Dallüge**): from the Slavic personal name *Daluge*.

Dally (624) **1.** Irish: variant of DALY. **2.** French: habitational name, with the preposition *d(e)*, for someone from either of two places in France called Ally, one in Cantal and one in Haute-Loire.

Dalman (314) **1.** Swedish: variant spelling of DAHLMAN. **2.** Respelling of German DALLMANN or *Dahlmann*, an elaborated form of DAHL.

D'Alo (127) Southern Italian (also **D'Alò**): patronymic from the personal name *Aloe, Aloi*, from French *Eloi, Eloy*, meaning 'chosen'.

GIVEN NAMES Italian 15%. *Donato* (2), *Salvatore* (2), *Giorgio.*

D'Aloia (245) Italian: metronymic from the personal name *Aloia*, feminine form of *Aloi* (see D'ALO).

D'Aloisio (157) Italian: patronymic from the personal name ALOISIO.

D'Alonzo (176) Italian (**D'Alonzo**): patronymic from *Alonso*, a variant of the personal name ALFONSO.

GIVEN NAMES Italian 14%. *Augustino, Domenic, Emelio, Fiore, Rocco, Romeo.*

Dalpe (169) Variant of French Canadian **Delpe** or **Delpué dit Pariseau**, which are probably forms of southern French **Delpey**, itself equivalent to northern **Dupuy**, a topographical name for someone living by a well.

FOREBEARS A bearer of this name from Rouergue was in Montreal by 1674.

GIVEN NAMES French 26%. *Andre* (2), *Marcel* (2), *Donat, Fernand, Florent, Jacques, Laurent, Luc, Lucien, Michel, Normand, Pierre.*

Dalpiaz (159) German, Italian, or Romansch name from the South Tyrol in northeast Italy: the etymology is unexplained.

GIVEN NAMES French 4%; Italian 4%. *Firmin; Angelo, Eligio.*

Dal Porto (173) Italian: topographic name from *porto* 'port', 'harbor', preceded by *dal*, fused preposition and article meaning 'from the' or 'of the'.

GIVEN NAMES Italian 7%. *Angelo, Evo, Lido, Pietro, Reno, Santino, Secondo.*

Dalrymple (2627) Scottish: habitational name from a place in Ayrshire, named with Gaelic *dail* 'field', 'meadow' + an unexplained second element.

FOREBEARS The Dalrymple family which held the earldom of Stair can be traced to William de Dalrymple, who in 1429 acquired the estate of Stair in Kyle, Ayrshire. In the muster rolls of the Scots Guards in France, the name appears as **de Romple**. John Dalrymple (1749–1821) served under Sir Henry Clinton in the American Revolution.

Dal Santo (148) Italian: patronymic from the personal name SANTO.

GIVEN NAMES Italian 10%. *Attilio, Carlo, Mauro, Santo.*

Dalsing (119) German: unexplained.

GIVEN NAME German 5%. *Kurt.*

D'Alto (193) Italian (Salerno and the south): patronymic from a nickname from *alto* 'tall', i.e. '(son) of the tall one'.

Dalton (18359) **1.** English: habitational name from any of the various places, for example in Cumbria, County Durham, Lancashire, Northumberland, and Yorkshire, named Dalton, from Old English *dæl* 'valley' (see DALE) + *tūn* 'enclosure', 'settlement'. **2.** English and Irish (of Norman origin): habitational name for someone from Autun (*d'Autun*) in Seine-et-Loire, France. The place name derives from the Latin form *Augustodunum*, a compound of the imperial name *Augustus* + the Gaulish element *dūn* 'hill', 'fort'.

Da Luz (153) Portuguese: from a religious epithet meaning 'of the light', specifically the Marian name *Nuestra Señora da Luz* 'Our Lady of the Light' (see LUX).

GIVEN NAMES Spanish 27%; Portuguese 13%; Italian 7%. *Manuel* (3), *Augusto* (2), *Bienvenido* (2), *Jose* (2), *Miguel* (2), *Sergio* (2), *Adriano, Amancio, Carlos, Felipe, Luis, Noelia; Joao, Joaquim; Antonio* (4), *Flavio.*

Daly (12883) Irish: reduced Anglicized form of Gaelic **Ó Dálaigh** 'descendant of *Dálach*', a personal name based on *dál* (modern *dáil*) 'meeting', 'assembly'.

FOREBEARS The main Irish family of this name claims descent from Dálach, tenth in descent from Niall of the Nine Hostages. From the 12th century they became famous as a poet family, and branches spread all over Ireland.

GIVEN NAMES Irish 5%. *Brendan* (14), *Kieran* (6), *Dermot* (4), *Brigid* (3), *Aileen* (2), *Declan* (2), *Finbarr* (2), *Fintan* (2), *Aidan, Brennan, Bridie, Cathal.*

Dalzell (759) Scottish: habitational name from a place in the Clyde valley, recorded in 1200 in the forms *Dalyell, Daliel* and in 1352 as *Daleel*, apparently from Gaelic *dail* 'field' + *g(h)eal* 'white'. The *z* in the spelling is not really a *z* at all; it represents Middle English *Ê'*, and the pronunciation, regardless of spelling, was normally 'Dee-ell' or 'Die-ell', sometimes 'Dalyell'. Black quotes an 'old Galloway rhyme': 'Deil (devil) and Da'yell begins with yae letter; Deil's nae gude and Da'yell's nae better'. Nowadays 'Dalzell' and 'Dalzeel' are also heard, and are standard in North America. The name was introduced in the 17th century to Ireland (Counties Louth and Down), where the normal spelling is **Dalzell**. The more common spelling Scotland is **Dalziel**.

Dalziel (277) The usual spelling in Scotland of DALZELL.

Dam (565) **1.** Vietnamese (**Đàm**): unexplained. **2.** Other Southeast Asian: unexplained. **3.** Dutch, Swedish, and Danish: topographic name for someone living by a dam or pond (*dam*). Compare Dutch VAN DAM.

GIVEN NAMES Vietnamese 36%; Other Southeast Asian 8%. *Hung* (6), *Hoa* (5), *Tuan* (5), *Ngoc* (4), *Thanh* (4), *Binh* (3), *Chanh* (3), *Duc* (3), *Hiep* (3), *Minh* (3), *Nu* (3), *Tien* (3); *Hong* (2), *Chan, Dong, Hon, Man, Oi, Ok, Phoung, Sang, Sokhom, Sun.*

Daman (237) **1.** Dutch: variant spelling of DAMMAN. **2.** Scandinavian: see DAHMAN. **3.** Belorussian: from the personal name *Daman* (see DAMIAN).

Damas (205) French: from a medieval personal name (Latin *Dalmatius*), originally an ethnic name for someone from Dalmatia (the coast of Croatia). The name may be of Illyrian origin and akin to southern Albanian *delme* 'sheep'. It was borne by a 3rd-century bishop of Pavia and a 6th-century bishop of Rodez, both of whom were popularly venerated in the Middle Ages. The surname is also established in Spain and Portugal and may be of French origin.

GIVEN NAMES Spanish 22%; Portuguese 8%; French 8%. *Manuel* (4), *Carlos* (2), *Jose* (2), *Luis* (2), *Miguel* (2), *Adan, Adela, Araceli, Arturo, Carlos Alberto, Francisco, Jorge; Joao; Jean Robert* (2), *Guylaine, Mireille, Pierre, Wilner.*

Damask (104) English: presumably an occupational name for someone who sold damask, a richly woven material of a kind originally made in Damascus. The English word also came to denote a rich pink color, and it is possible that the surname arose as a nickname with reference to someone's complexion.

Damaso (100) Portuguese and Spanish (**Dámaso**): from the personal name *Dámaso*, derived from Greek *Damasos*, meaning 'tamer', a derivative of *damazein* 'to tame'. Compare DAMIAN.

GIVEN NAMES Spanish 39%. *Manuel* (2), *Pedro* (2), *Ador, Alfredo, Alvaro, Andres, Carlos, Constancio, Eleazar, Gerardo, Lino, Luz.*

D'Amato (2379) Italian: patronymic from the personal name *Amato*, from the Latin personal name *Amatus*, meaning 'beloved'.

GIVEN NAMES Italian 15%. *Salvatore* (15), *Angelo* (13), *Antonio* (9), *Carmine* (8), *Pasquale* (6), *Luigi* (5), *Rocco* (5), *Sal* (5), *Gaetano* (4), *Vito* (4), *Francesco* (3), *Giuseppe* (3).

Dambach (187) German: habitational name from any of the numerous places called Dambach.

GIVEN NAMES German 4%. *Hans* (2), *Gottlieb.*

Damboise (129) French (**D'Amboise**): habitational name for someone 'from Amboise' in Indre-et-Loire.

GIVEN NAMES French 15%. *Cecile, Jeannot, Laurent, Marcel, Michel, Pascal.*

D'Ambra (423) Italian: metronymic from the late medieval female personal name *Ambra*, from the word for 'amber', a derivative of Arabic *'anbar*.

GIVEN NAMES Italian 19%. *Vito* (10), *Gennaro* (4), *Salvatore* (3), *Domenic* (2), *Sal* (2), *Angelo, Antonio, Carmine, Domenica, Mauro.*

Dambrose (102) **1.** French (**D'Ambrose**): patronymic from the personal name AMBROSE. **2.** Americanized version of Italian D'AMBROSIO.

D'Ambrosi (114) Italian: patronymic or plural form of D'AMBROSIO.

GIVEN NAMES Italian 24%. *Rocco* (2), *Aldo, Alfonse, Angelo, Faust, Francesca, Luigi, Mario, Rico, Valentino.*

D'Ambrosia (242) Italian: altered form of D'AMBROSIO, possibly under the influence of the vocabulary word *ambrosia*, denoting the food of the gods in classical mythology.

GIVEN NAMES Italian 10%. *Salvatore* (2), *Angelo.*

D'Ambrosio (1550) Italian: patronymic from the personal name AMBROSIO, from Latin *Ambrosius* (see AMBROSE).

GIVEN NAMES Italian 18%. *Angelo* (15), *Vito* (6), *Gaetano* (5), *Antonio* (4), *Salvatore* (4), *Carmine* (3), *Nunzio* (3), *Sal* (3), *Carmela* (2), *Corrado* (2), *Marco* (2), *Pasquale* (2).

Dame (1422) English and French: from Old French *dame* 'lady' (Latin *domina* 'mistress'), originally a nickname for a foppish man or a title of respect for a widow. It may also have been a metonymic occupational name for someone in the service of a lady.

D'Amelio (456) Italian: patronymic from the personal name AMELIO.

GIVEN NAMES Italian 18%. *Carmine* (3), *Rocco* (3), *Alesio* (2), *Amelio* (2), *Pellegrino* (2), *Angelo, Antonino, Carlo, Cosmo, Dino, Fausto, Giovanni.*

Damer (114) **1.** Dutch: variant of DAMMER. **2.** Perhaps a variant or altered spelling of German DAHMER, a variant of *Dagomar* or *Daukmar*, Germanic personal names formed with *tac, dac* 'day' or *dauk* 'thought' + *mar* 'famous'.

GIVEN NAME German 4%. *Otto.*

Dameron (1466) French: nickname for a foppish or effeminate young man, Old French *dameron*, a derivative of Latin *dominus* 'lord', 'master' plus two diminutive endings suggestive of weakness or childishness.

Damerow (107) Americanized spelling of French **Damereau**, which is a variant of DAMERON.

GIVEN NAMES German 14%. *Arno* (2), *Claus* (2), *Hans*, *Otto*.

Damery (122) French: habitational name from Damery in Somme, France, or from either of two places in present-day Belgium: Amry in the province of Liège, or Aumerie in Hainault, these last two with the fused preposition *d(e)*.

Dames (432) Variant of German DAHMS.

Damewood (364) Americanized form of German **Dammholz**, a topographic name for someone living by a wooded dike, from *Damm* 'dam', 'dike' + *Holz* 'wood'.

Damgaard (104) Danish: habitational name from a place called Damgaard.

GIVEN NAMES Scandinavian 14%; German 7%. *Erik, Nels, Niels*; *Ewald, Otto, Viktor*.

Damian (565) **1.** French, Spanish (**Damián**), Italian (Venice), Czech and Slovak (**Damián**), and Polish: from the medieval personal name *Damian*, Greek *Damianos* (from *damazein* 'to subdue'). St. Damian was an early Christian saint martyred in Cilicia in AD 303 under the emperor Domitian, together with his brother Cosmas. In some accounts the brothers are said to have been doctors, and together they were regarded as the patrons of physicians and apothecaries. A later St. Damian lived in the 7th–8th centuries and was bishop of Pavia; he may have had some influence on the popularity of the personal name in Italy. **2.** Americanized spelling of Hungarian **Damján** or **Damján** or Slovenian **Damjan, Damijan**, cognates with 1. **3.** Jewish (from Poland): either an ornamental adoption of the Polish personal name *Damian* as a surname, or a habitational name from the village of Damiany in northeastern Poland.

FOREBEARS In the form **Damien**, this name is found in Quebec in 1641, coming from Normandy, France.

GIVEN NAMES Spanish 28%. *Francisco* (8), *Juan* (6), *Jose* (4), *Pedro* (4), *Alberto* (2), *Armando* (2), *Carlos* (2), *Cesar* (2), *Elena* (2), *Felipe* (2), *Lourdes* (2), *Luis* (2).

Damiani (659) **1.** Italian: patronymic or plural form of DAMIANO. **2.** Hungarian (**Damiani**): from a Latinized form of *Damjáni*, Hungarian form of *Damianus* (see DAMIAN).

GIVEN NAMES Italian 20%; Spanish 11%; French 5%. *Antonio* (5), *Angelo* (4), *Ettore* (3), *Aldo* (2), *Luigi* (2), *Primo* (2), *Salvatore* (2), *Bruna, Camillo, Dario, Emidio, Ermanno. Luis* (3), *Carlota* (2), *Paola* (2), *Carlos, Cesar, Fernando, Juan, Liborio; Andre, Michel, Renold*.

Damiano (1087) Italian: from the personal name *Damiano* (see DAMIAN).

GIVEN NAMES Italian 14%. *Angelo* (4), *Rocco* (4), *Vincenzo* (4), *Gaetano* (3), *Salvatore* (3), *Vito* (3), *Luigi* (2), *Sal* (2), *Antonio, Camillo, Carmelo, Giuseppe*.

D'Amico (4893) Italian: patronymic from the personal name AMICO.

GIVEN NAMES Italian 14%. *Salvatore* (33), *Angelo* (21), *Sal* (17), *Antonio* (12), *Pasquale* (10), *Rocco* (9), *Carmine* (8), *Domenic* (7), *Santo* (6), *Vito* (5), *Carlo* (4), *Vincenzo* (4).

Damien (80) French: variant of DAMIAN.

Damitz (155) German: habitational name from a place in Pomerania called Damitz.

Damm (1035) **1.** German and Danish: topographic name from Middle High German *damm* 'dike'. In large parts of northern Germany (including Berlin), *damm* denoted the main, i.e. paved, road, which was generally raised in areas of swampy or sandy terrain. **2.** German: from a short form of a personal name containing the Old High German element *thank* 'thanks', 'reward'.

GIVEN NAMES German 4%. *Volker* (2), *Beate, Bernd, Frederick Fritz, Heinrich, Heinz, Ingeborg, Johann, Katharina, Klaus, Konrad, Manfred*.

Damman (266) **1.** Dutch: occupational name for someone whose responsibility was to look after a dike or dam, from *dam* 'dike' + *man* 'man'. **2.** Variant spelling of German DAMMANN.

Dammann (498) German: topographic name from Middle Low German *dam* 'dike', 'highway' + *man* 'man' (see DAMM), or a habitational name from any of the various places named Damm or Damme from this word, for example in Brandenburg, Oldenburg, and Pomerania.

Damme (128) **1.** Dutch: habitational name from any of the many places in the Netherlands named Dam or Ten Damme, from *dam* 'dam', 'dike'. **2.** German: variant of DAMM 2.

Dammen (165) **1.** Norwegian: habitational name from a farm in southeastern Norway, from the definite singular form ('the pond') of *dam* 'pond'. **2.** Dutch: patronymic from a short form of ADAM.

Dammer (156) **1.** Dutch: topographic name from *dam* 'dike' + the suffix *-er*, denoting an inhabitant. **2.** German: habitational name from any of several places in Silesia called Dammer.

GIVEN NAMES Dutch 6%; German 4%. *Sievert* (3), *Harm; Guenther*.

Dammeyer (142) North German: distinguishing name for a tenant farmer (see MEYER) whose land lay near a dike or highway, Middle Low German *damm*.

Damon (2672) **1.** English and Scottish: from the personal name *Damon*, from a classical Greek name, a derivative of *damān* 'to kill'. Compare DAMIAN. **2.** Respelling of the French surname **D'Amont**, a topographic name, with the preposition *d(e)* denoting someone who lived *à mont* 'uphill', i.e. on high ground above a village or settlement.

Damone (107) Italian: from a reduced augmentative form of the Biblical name *Adamo* (see ADAM).

GIVEN NAMES Italian 17%. *Angelo* (2), *Vito* (2), *Carlo, Ciro, Onofrio*.

D'Amore (1141) Italian: patronymic from the personal name *Amore*, meaning 'love'. *D'Amore* sometimes denoted a foundling or an illegitimate son, a 'love child'.

GIVEN NAMES Italian 16%. *Salvatore* (7), *Angelo* (5), *Vito* (5), *Pasquale* (3), *Dante* (2), *Donato* (2), *Enrico* (2), *Luigi* (2), *Natale* (2), *Nunzio* (2), *Alfonse, Antonino*.

D'Amour (290) French: patronymic from *Amour*, nickname for an amorous man or a love child.

GIVEN NAMES French 13%. *Armand* (2), *Gaston* (2), *Alain, Cecile, Donat, Jacques, Marcel, Normand, Valette, Yvon*.

Damp (108) **1.** English (Hampshire): apparently from Middle English *domp* 'vapor', 'gas' (probably a loan word from Middle Low German), applied as a topographic name. **2.** North German and Danish: habitational name from a place called Damp, for example the one near Kiel.

Dampf (121) German: from Old High German *dampf* 'steam', a Swabian dialect term for an obnoxious person.

Danuser (107) Swiss German: an Alemannic variant of **Tannhauser** or **Dannhauser**.

Dampier (660) English (of Norman origin): habitational name from any of various places in northern France named Dampierre, in honor of St. Peter. The first element, *Dam-* or *Don-*, is an Old French title of respect (from Latin *dominus* 'lord'), often prefixed to the names of saints.

Damrau (100) German: see DAMROW.

GIVEN NAME German 4%. *Theodor*.

Damron (2808) Reduced form of French DAMERON.

Damrow (218) **1.** German: habitational name from any of the 22 places so called or from any of the 37 places called Damerau. **2.** Reflex of the French family name **Damereau**, a variant of DAMERON.

GIVEN NAMES German 4%. *Dieter, Kurt, Reinhard*.

Damschroder (135) German (**Damschröder**): distinguishing name for a tailor (see SCHRODER) who lived by a dike or highway, Middle Low German *damm* (see DAMM).

Damsky (107) Jewish (eastern Ashkenazic): occupational name from Polish *damski* or eastern Slavic *damskij* 'of or relating to ladies', most likely used for a tailor of ladies' clothes.

Damuth (130) Respelling of German DEMUTH.

Dan (484) **1.** Ethnic name in various European languages (including Danish and English) meaning 'Dane'. **2.** Romanian: unexplained. **3.** Vietnamese: unexplained.

GIVEN NAMES Vietnamese 7%; Romanian 5%. *Ha To* (2), *Hieu* (2), *Lam* (2), *Chinh, Dung, Dung Anh, Long, Ly, Mai, Minh, Nga, Nguyen Van; Corneliu* (2), *Silviu* (2),

Constantin, Dumitru, Ilie, Rodica, Stelian, Vasile.

Dana (1997) **1.** Origin unidentified. There has been much speculation about the origins of this famous American family name. The most plausible theory is that it is a Huguenot name, a variant of **D'Aunay**, from any of several places in France called Aunay. However, the name acquired an Irish flavor, being associated, probably erroneously, with a Gaelic forename likewise spelled *Dana*. **2.** Hungarian: from a pet form of the personal name *Dániel* (see DANIEL). **3.** Czech and Slovak (**Daňa**); also Polish: from the personal name DANIEL, or perhaps from a short form of any of the various Old Slavic compound personal names formed with *-dan*, for example *Bogdan*.
FOREBEARS Richard Dana came from England in 1640 to Cambridge, MA, where he died in 1690. His most famous descendant was Richard Henry Dana (1815–82), author of *Two Years before the Mast*. A lawyer by profession as well as a writer and traveler, he supported the rights of fugitive slaves before and during the Civil War.

Danaher (680) Irish: Anglicized form of Gaelic **Ó Danachair** 'descendant of *Danachar*', a personal name meaning 'poetry loving', from *dán* 'craft', 'poem'.
GIVEN NAMES Irish 6%. *Brendan, Brigid.*

Danahy (371) Irish: variant of DENNEHY.

Danberry (102) Variant of English DANBURY.

Danbury (100) English: habitational name from Danbury in Essex, named in Old English as the 'stronghold (*burh*) of a man called Dene'.

Danby (161) English: habitational name from any of several places called Danby in North Yorkshire, originally named in Old Norse as *Danabýr* 'settlement of the Danes', and thus cognate with DENBY.
GIVEN NAME German 4%. *Otto* (2).

Danca (120) **1.** Portuguese (**Dança**): perhaps a nickname from *dança* 'dance'. **2.** Dutch: variant of **Dankaert** (see DANKERT). **3.** Americanized spelling of Hungarian *Dancsa*, a patronymic from *Dancs*, a pet form of *Dániel, Domonkos*, or *Damján*.
GIVEN NAMES Italian 9%. *Nicola, Salvatore.*

Dance (899) **1.** English: from Middle English, Old French *dance* 'dance', hence a nickname for a skilled or enthusiastic dancer, or a metonymic occupational name for a professional acrobat or dancer. **2.** Probably a translation or Americanized spelling of German DANZ.

Dancer (783) **1.** English: occupational name for a dancer or acrobat, from an agent derivative of Middle English, Old French *dance* 'dance' (see DANCE). **2.** Translation of German **Dänzer** or **Danser** (see DANZER).

Dancey (161) English: variant spelling of DANSIE.

Dancy (1363) English: variant spelling of DANSIE.

Dandeneau (158) Altered spelling of French **Dandonneau**, of uncertain origin; perhaps related to *se dindiner* 'to waddle'.
FOREBEARS The name Dandonneau-Lajeunesse was borne by Calvinists from La Rochelle who were in Trois-Rivières, Quebec, by 1653.
GIVEN NAMES French 16%. *Laurent* (2), *Andre, Jacques, Marcel, Pierre, Prosper, Viateur.*

Dando (314) English (Somerset; of Norman origin): habitational name for someone from Aunou in Orne, Normandy (French *d'Aunou*), which is named with Old French *aunaie* 'alder grove' (see DELANEY).

D'Andrea (2028) Italian: patronymic from the personal name *Andrea*, from Greek ANDREAS.
GIVEN NAMES Italian 18%. *Angelo* (13), *Rocco* (10), *Carmine* (5), *Domenic* (4), *Salvatore* (4), *Antonio* (3), *Fausto* (3), *Luigi* (3), *Nicola* (3), *Vito* (3), *Carmela* (2), *Gino* (2).

Dandridge (1011) English: habitational name of uncertain origin, possibly from Tandridge in Surrey, which is named from an unexplained first element + Old English *hrycg* 'ridge', 'hill'.

Dandurand (353) French: from *Dom Durand* 'Master Durand', composed of the title 'Dom', from Latin *dominus* 'lord' (see DAMPIER) + the personal name *Durand* (see DURANT).
FOREBEARS This surname was in Ile d'Orléans, Quebec, by 1696, having been brought there from Paris.
GIVEN NAMES French 8%. *Lucien* (3), *Armand, Henri, Mathieu, Normand, Serge, Yvon.*

Dandy (323) English: from the personal name, a pet form of ANDREW.

Dane (1086) **1.** English: variant of DEAN or DENCE. **2.** French (**Dané**): ethnic name for someone from Denmark. **3.** Dutch: variant spelling of DAANE. **4.** Irish: Anglicized form of Gaelic **Ó Déaghain** 'descendant of the dean', but also of English origin, a variant of DEAN. **5.** Hungarian (**Dáné**): from the personal name *Dániel*, Hungarian form of DANIEL.

Danehy (157) Variant of Irish DONAHUE.

Danek (411) **1.** Czech (**Daněk**): from a pet form of DANIEL or of any of the Slavic compound personal names formed with *dan* 'gift', as for example *Danomír, Danoslav*, and *Bohdan*. **2.** Czech (**Daněk**): nickname from *daněk* 'buck', 'fallow deer'. **3.** Polish: from a pet form of DANA. **4.** Ukrainian: from a pet form of *Danylo*, Ukrainian form of DANIEL.
GIVEN NAMES French 4%. *Gabrielle, Laurette.*

Daneker (106) North German: variant of DANNECKER.

Danella (127) Italian: of uncertain derivation; perhaps a metronymic from the personal name *Anella*, feminine form of *Anello*.
GIVEN NAMES Italian 21%. *Angelo* (4), *Rocco* (2), *Antonio, Salvatore, Saverio, Silvio.*

Danenberg (106) Jewish (Ashkenazic): possibly a habitational name from any of various places in Germany named DANNENBERG.
GIVEN NAMES Jewish 6%. *Meyer, Zvi.*

Danes (198) **1.** English: patronymic or genitive from *Dane*, variant of DEAN 2, i.e. 'son (or servant) of the dean'. **2.** Dutch: patronymic from a short form of DANIEL. **3.** Czech and Slovak (**Daneš**): variant of **Daněk** (see DANEK).

Danese (171) Italian: ethnic name for a Dane, or from the personal name *Danese*, which was introduced to and popularized in medieval Italy through French Carolingian literature, notably the epics Chanson de Roland and Ogier de Denemarche.
GIVEN NAMES Italian 14%. *Marco* (2), *Antonio, Carlo, Edo, Gino, Rocco, Vito.*

Danesi (120) Italian: patronymic or plural form of DANESE.
GIVEN NAMES Italian 23%. *Francesco* (3), *Antonio* (2), *Enzo* (2), *Gino* (2), *Aldo, Attilio, Dante, Gioia.*

Daney (146) Americanized form of French **Dané** (see DANE).

Danford (992) English: see DANFORTH.

Danforth (1818) English: probably a habitational name, perhaps from Darnford in Suffolk, Great Durnford in Wiltshire, or Dernford Farm in Sawston, Cambridgeshire, all named from Old English *dierne* 'hidden' + *ford* 'ford'.
FOREBEARS Nicholas Danforth, a man of considerable property, emigrated in about 1634 with his children to Cambridge, MA, from Framlingham, Suffolk, England, after the death of his wife Elizabeth. He was elected to various political offices in the colony. His son Thomas (1623–99) was admitted as a freeman in 1643 and was named treasurer of Harvard College in the 1650 charter granted that institution.

Dang (3476) **1.** Vietnamese (**Đặng**): unexplained. **2.** Chinese 党: The surname Dang comes from a branch of the ruling family of the Zhou dynasty (1122–221 BC) that spread to the state of Jin and the state of Lu. The character now also means 'political party'. **3.** German: from an old personal name *Tanco*, a cognate of modern German *denken* 'to think', *Gedanke* 'thoughts'.
GIVEN NAMES Vietnamese 54%; Chinese 16%. *Thanh* (47), *Minh* (44), *Hung* (36), *Dung* (32), *Tuan* (32), *Hoa* (24), *Anh* (23), *Hai* (22), *Long* (22), *Binh* (20), *Huong* (20), *Trung* (19); *Hong* (15), *Hang* (10), *Chi* (8), *Dong* (8), *Chan* (4), *Chien* (4), *Han* (4), *Ho* (4), *Hon* (4), *Sang* (4), *Song* (4), *Chu* (3); *Tam* (21), *Phong* (11), *Nam* (10), *Thai* (10), *Sinh* (6), *Thach* (4), *Tuong* (4),

Manh (3), *Tau* (3), *Chang* (2), *Cho* (2), *Byung*.

Dangel (292) Eastern German: from the personal name *Dangel*, a Slavic pet form of DANIEL.

D'Angelo (4295) Italian: patronymic from the personal name ANGELO. In Italy it is found chiefly in Naples and the south.
GIVEN NAMES Italian 18%. *Salvatore* (24), *Antonio* (22), *Angelo* (16), *Rocco* (12), *Vito* (10), *Carlo* (9), *Sal* (9), *Domenico* (7), *Nicolo* (7), *Gaetano* (6), *Giovanni* (6), *Pasquale* (6).

Danger (153) French: **1.** patronymic from the personal name ANGER. **2.** habitational name for someone from the city of Angers.
FOREBEARS A Jean Dangers was in Quebec in 1727.

Dangerfield (784) English (of Norman origin): habitational name, with fused preposition *d(e)*, for someone from any of the various places in northern France called Angerville, from the Old Norse personal name *Ásgeirr* (from *áss* 'god' + *geirr* 'spear') + Old French *ville* 'settlement', 'village'. In England the surname is now found chiefly in the West Midlands.

Dangler (461) **1.** German: variant of DENGLER. **2.** French: habitational name, with the preposition *d(e)*, denoting someone from Angleur, in the Belgian province of Liège.

Danh (143) Vietnamese: unexplained.
GIVEN NAMES Vietnamese 59%; Chinese 18%. *Dung* (3), *Hien* (2), *Hoa* (2), *Hoang* (2), *Nga* (2), *Nhan* (2), *Nhut* (2), *Son* (2), *Thao* (2), *Thuan* (2), *Tien* (2), *Ty Thi* (2), *Tinh* (2), *Vang* (2), *Manh*, *Ry*, *Tam*, *Tuoi*; *Sang* (2), *Hong*, *Man*, *On*, *Sen*, *Soon*, *Sung*, *Ung*.

Dani (119) Indian (Gujarat): Hindu (Vania) name, from the Sanskrit epithet *dānī* 'liberal in giving'.
GIVEN NAMES Indian 36%. *Narendra* (2), *Saryu* (2), *Shashi* (2), *Bachu*, *Chandu*, *Devyani*, *Dilip*, *Dinesh*, *Hasit*, *Kaushik*, *Kirit*, *Manisha*.

Daniel (25268) **1.** English, French, Spanish, Portuguese, German, Polish, Czech, Slovak, Hungarian (**Dániel**), Romanian, and Jewish: from the Hebrew personal name *Daniel* 'God is my judge', borne by a major prophet in the Bible. The major factor influencing the popularity of the personal name (and hence the frequency of the surname) was undoubtedly the dramatic story in the Book of Daniel, recounting the prophet's steadfast adherence to his religious faith in spite of pressure and persecution from the Mesopotamian kings in whose court he served: Nebuchadnezzar and Belshazzar (at whose feast Daniel interpreted the mysterious message of doom that appeared on the wall, being thrown to the lions for his pains). The name was also borne by a 2nd-century Christian martyr and by a 9th-century hermit, the legend of whose life was

popular among Christians during the Middle Ages; these had a minor additional influence on the adoption of the Christian name. Among Orthodox Christians in Eastern Europe the name was also popular as being that of a 4th-century Persian martyr, who was venerated in the Orthodox Church. **2.** Irish: reduced form of MC-DANIEL, which is actually a variant of MC-DONNELL, from the Gaelic form of Irish *Donal* (equivalent to Scottish *Donald*), erroneously associated with the Biblical personal name *Daniel*. See also O'DONNELL.
FOREBEARS Peter Daniel was one of the pioneer settlers in the 17th century in Stafford County, VA, where he was a justice of the peace. His grandson, Peter Vivian Daniel, was a U.S. Supreme Court justice from 1841 to his death in Richmond, VA, in 1860.

Daniele (532) Italian: from the personal name *Daniele*, Italian equivalent of DANIEL.
GIVEN NAMES Italian 27%. *Carlo* (6), *Mario* (5), *Antonio* (4), *Angelo* (3), *Carmine* (3), *Mauro* (3), *Aniello* (2), *Carmino* (2), *Giovanni* (2), *Rocco* (2), *Salvatore* (2), *Alberto*, *Alfredo*, *Aurelio*, *Carmel*, *Carmela*, *Ersilia*, *Fortunato*, *Luisa*, *Rico*.

Danielewicz (108) Polish: patronymic from the personal name DANIEL.
GIVEN NAMES Polish 11%. *Pawel*, *Ryszard*, *Teofil*, *Zigmund*.

Danieli (132) **1.** Italian: patronymic or plural form of DANIELE. **2.** Jewish (Israeli): Hebrew patronymic from DANIEL.
GIVEN NAMES Italian 13%; Jewish 4%. *Domenic* (2), *Aldo*, *Angelo*, *Emidio*, *Pietro*, *Rino*; *Eyal*, *Hadar*.

Danielian (109) Armenian: patronymic from the Biblical name DANIEL.
GIVEN NAMES Armenian 26%. *Anahid* (2), *Armine*, *Artour*, *Gevork*, *Hagop*, *Hakop*, *Hasmig*, *Hovsep*, *Sarkis*, *Seda*, *Tigran*.

Daniell (902) English: variant spelling of DANIEL.

D'Aniello (310) Italian: patronymic from the personal name *Aniello*, a southern variant of AGNELLO.
GIVEN NAMES Italian 16%. *Salvatore* (4), *Luigi* (2), *Carmine*, *Ciro*, *Gennaro*, *Giacomo*, *Gino*, *Giro*, *Pasquale*, *Rocco*, *Vito*.

Daniels (41682) English, North German, Dutch, and Jewish (Ashkenazic): patronymic from the personal name DANIEL.

Danielsen (555) Danish, Norwegian, and North German: patronymic from the personal name DANIEL.
GIVEN NAMES Scandinavian 9%. *Ketil* (2), *Morten* (2), *Knut*, *Oivind*, *Pehr*, *Petter*, *Thor*, *Viggo*.

Danielski (183) **1.** Polish: habitational name for someone from a place called Daniel or Daniele. **2.** Jewish (from Poland) patronymic from DANIEL.

Danielson (5482) **1.** Jewish (Ashkenazic): patronymic from DANIEL. **2.** Respelling of

Swedish **Danielsson** or Norwegian and Danish DANIELSEN.
GIVEN NAMES Scandinavian 4%. *Erik* (6), *Lars* (2), *Mauritz* (2), *Nels* (2), *Nils* (2), *Sigfrid* (2), *Alf*, *Arlys*, *Berent*, *Bjorn*, *Eskil*, *Gunner*.

Daniely (127) Jewish (Israeli): variant of DANIELI 2.
GIVEN NAMES Jewish 7%. *Ehud*, *Shlomo*, *Shmuel*.

Danis (665) **1.** French: from a short form of the personal *Jordanis*. **2.** French and English: from a pet form of DANIEL. **3.** French: habitational name, with the preposition *d(e)*, for someone from Anixhe in Fexhe-lez-Slins in the Belgian province of Liège, recorded in the 13th century as *Anis*. **4.** Hungarian: patronymic from *Dani*, a pet form of the personal name *Dániel*, Hungarian form of DANIEL. **5.** Czech and Slovak (**Daniš**): variant of **Daněk** (see DANEK). **6.** Lithuanian and Latvian: from a derivative of the personal name *Danis*, *Danielius* (see DANIEL).
FOREBEARS A Danis-Tourangeau, from Tours, was married in Montreal in 1658.
GIVEN NAMES French 10%. *Marcel* (3), *Raoul* (3), *Armand* (2), *Normand* (2), *Andre*, *Cyrille*, *Damien*, *Gaston*, *Gilles*, *Herve*, *Lucien*, *Renald*.

Danish (264) **1.** Americanized spelling of German **Danisch**, perhaps from a pet form of DANIEL or the Slavic personal names *Bogdan* or *Niedan*. **2.** Americanized spelling of Czech and Slovak **Daniš**, a derivative of DANIEL.

Danison (153) Variant of English DENNISON.

Danke (128) German: from an old personal name formed with the stem *dank* (see DANKEL).

Dankel (101) German: from an old personal name formed with the stem *dank*, cognate with modern German *denken* 'to think' and *Gedanke* 'thought'. It may be a short form of the personal name *Thanculf*. Compare DANG.

Dankenbring (127) North German: from a personal name formed with *Dank* (see DANKEL) or alternatively, as suggested by the variant **Dankenbrink**, a topographic name composed with this personal name + Low German *brink* 'grazing land', 'slope'.
GIVEN NAMES German 4%. *Kurt*, *Siegfried*.

Danker (340) German and Dutch: variant of DANKERT.
GIVEN NAMES German 6%. *Otto* (2), *Bernhard*, *Erna*, *Gerhard*, *Manfred*.

Dankers (120) German, Dutch, and Latvian: variant of DANKERT.
GIVEN NAME Latvian 4%. *Imants*.

Dankert (356) Frisian, Dutch, and North German: from an old personal name composed of Old High German, Old Saxon *thank-*, *dank* 'thought', 'intention', 'will' + *hart* 'strong'.

Danko (1138) **1.** Hungarian (**Dankó**); Czech and Slovak (**Daňko**); and Slovenian: from a pet form of the personal name DANIEL (Hungarian *Dániel*, Slovenian *Danijel*). **2.** Ukrainian: from a pet form the personal name *Danylo* (see DANIEL). **3.** Bulgarian: from a pet form of the personal name DANO.

Danks (538) English: patronymic from a pet form of DANIEL. In England the name is found chiefly in Birmingham.

Danley (1439) English: unexplained.

Dann (1249) **1.** English: topographic name for someone who lived by a woodland pasture, from Middle English *denn* 'woodland pasture, especially for swine' (Old English *denn*, *dænn*). **2.** Scottish: from a short form of the personal name DANIEL. **3.** German and French (Alsace): topographic name for someone who lived by a pine tree, from Old High German *tanna* 'pine tree'.

Danna (1382) French (also **D'Anna**): apparently a metronymic from the female personal name ANNA, although Debrabandere suggests it may be a dialect form of the surname **Dannau**, from DANIEL.
GIVEN NAMES Italian 15%. *Salvatore* (8), *Angelo* (7), *Pasquale* (6), *Vito* (6), *Biagio* (4), *Gasper* (3), *Gaetano* (2), *Alessandro*, *Antonino*, *Antonio*, *Carlo*, *Carmello*.

Dannecker (106) German: topographic or habitational name for someone from a place named Tanneck, denoting a place with pine trees.
GIVEN NAME German 5%. *Franz* (2).

Dannelley (155) Probably variant spelling of the Irish family name DONNELLY.

Dannelly (143) Probably variant spelling of the Irish family name DONNELLY.

Dannels (210) English: variant of DANIELS.

Danneman (138) German (**Dannemann**): topographic name for someone who lived by a forest, from Middle Low German *dan*, Middle High German *tan* 'pine', 'forest'.

Dannemiller (233) Part translation of German **Dann(en)müller**, distinguishing name for a miller who lived by a forest, from Middle Low German, Middle High German *tan* 'pine', 'forest' + *mūlnære* 'miller'.

Dannen (175) Probably a short form of any of the various German family names, for example **Dannenbaum**, **Dannenfeldt**, beginning with *Dannen* or *Tannen*, from Middle High German *tan* 'pine', 'forest'.

Dannenberg (438) German: habitational name from any of various places named Dannenberg or Tannenberg.
GIVEN NAMES German 6%. *Klaus* (2), *Konrad* (2), *Meinhard* (2), *Siegfried*.

Dannenfelser (109) German: habitational name for someone from a place in the Rhineland-Palatinate called Dannenfels.
GIVEN NAMES German 7%. *Horst*, *Uwe*.

Danner (3883) German: topographic name for someone who lived in or by a forest, from Middle Low German *dan*, Middle High German *tan* 'pine', 'forest' + the suffix *-er* denoting an inhabitant, or a habitational name from any of various places called Thann, named with this word, notably in Bavaria, and also in Mecklenburg and Switzerland.

D'Annunzio (246) Italian: patronymic from a reduced form of ANNUNZIATO.
GIVEN NAMES Italian 13%. *Antonio*, *Cosmo*, *Dante*, *Dario*, *Emidio*, *Fausto*, *Gaetano*, *Grazia*, *Salvatore*.

Dano (237) **1.** Hungarian (**Danó**): from a pet form of *Dániel*, Hungarian form of DANIEL. **2.** Slovak (**Daňo**): probably a derivative of the personal name DANIEL. **3.** Bulgarian: from a derivative of the personal names *Jordan* or *Danail*. **4.** Perhaps an altered spelling of French **Danot** or **Danon**, from pet forms of JOURDAN or DANIEL.
GIVEN NAMES Spanish 6%. *Anastacio*, *Efren*, *Graciela*, *Loida*, *Margarita*, *Narciso*, *Pacita*, *Pedro*, *Trinidad*.

Danoff (174) **1.** Bulgarian: alternative spelling of **Danov**, a patronymic from the personal name DANO. **2.** Jewish (American): shortened form of some eastern Ashkenazic surname, most likely from **Danowski**, a habitational name from the village of Danowo in Poland.
GIVEN NAMES Jewish 8%. *Jascha* (2), *Sol* (2), *Hyman*.

Danon (119) Spanish (**Danón**) and Jewish (Sephardic): variant of DANIEL.
GIVEN NAMES Jewish 13%; Spanish 10%. *Nissim* (2), *Arie*, *Eyal*, *Hyman*, *Isak*; *Jose* (4), *Rafael* (2), *Elia*.

Danos (580) **1.** French: habitational name, with the preposition *d(e)*, for someone from Anos in Pyrénées Atlantiques. **2.** Hungarian (**Dános**): from a pet form of the personal name *Dániel* (see DAN).
GIVEN NAMES French 6%. *Gillis* (2), *Maxime* (2), *Achille*, *Antoine*, *Emile*, *Georges*, *Leonce*, *Marcel*, *Olivier*.

Danowski (307) Polish: habitational name for someone from any of various places named Danowo or Danow.
GIVEN NAMES Polish 7%. *Bogumil*, *Ewa*, *Henryk*, *Kazimierz*, *Lucyna*, *Waclaw*.

Dansby (877) English: presumably a habitational name from a lost or unidentified place in an area of Scandinavian settlement; perhaps a variant of DANBY.

Danser (237) **1.** German: variant of DANZER. **2.** Altered spelling of English DANCER.

Dansereau (380) French: unexplained.
FOREBEARS A Pierre Dansereau from Poitou married Angélique Abirou in Varennes, Quebec, in 1708.
GIVEN NAMES French 11%. *Pierre* (3), *Aldor* (2), *Armand*, *Constant*, *Jacques*, *Jeanne Marie*, *Lucien*, *Normand*, *Raoul*.

Dansie (209) English (of Norman origin): habitational name, with fused preposition *d(e)*, for someone from Anizy in Calvados, France, recorded in 1155 in the form *Anisie*. The place name is probably derived from the Romano-Gallic personal name *Anitius* (of uncertain origin) + the locative suffix *-acum*.

Danskin (126) Scottish: habitational name for someone from DANZIG. This surname is first recorded in Scotland in this form early in the 17th century.

Dansky (170) Jewish (eastern Ashkenazic): habitational name for someone from DANZIG, the suffix *-ski* denoting association.
GIVEN NAME Jewish 6%. *Hyman*.

Danson (179) English: patronymic form a short form of ANDREW or DANIEL.

Dant (461) French: nickname for someone with large, protruding, or otherwise remarkable teeth, from Breton dialect *dant* 'tooth'.

Dante (292) Italian: from a reduced form of DURANTE.
GIVEN NAMES Italian 5%; French 4%. *Annamarie*, *Dante*, *Domenic*, *Mauro*, *Pasquale*; *Camille*, *Pierre*.

Dantes (107) Galician (or Portuguese): unexplained; probably variant spelling of **Dantas** (*d'Antas*), a habitational name from any of the many places called Antas in Portugal and Galicia, plural of *anta* 'dolmen'.
GIVEN NAMES Spanish 26%. *Adelina* (2), *Caridad*, *Cesar*, *Corazon*, *Edmundo*, *Eduardo*, *Elena*, *Graciela*, *Igmedio*, *Luisa*, *Manuel*, *Mario*.

Dantin (234) French (**D'Antin**): habitational name, with the preposition *d(e)* denoting someone from either of two places called Antin, in Hautes Pyrénées and Pas-de-Calais.
GIVEN NAMES French 4%. *Monique*, *Odile*.

Danton (163) French: habitational name, with the preposition *d(e)*, for someone from either of two places, in Isère and Haute-Savoie, called Anthon. The place name is probably from an unrecorded Gaulish personal name rather than from a version of Anthony.

D'Antona (102) Italian: metronymic from the female personal name *Antonia*, feminine form of *Antonio*. Compare D'ANTONIO.
GIVEN NAMES Italian 27%; Spanish 7%. *Aldo* (2), *Gaetano* (2), *Sal* (2), *Vito* (2), *Gabriele*, *Pasquale*, *Salvatore*; *Felipe* (2), *Rosario* (2).

D'Antoni (295) Italian: variant of D'ANTONIO.
GIVEN NAMES Italian 14%. *Aldo* (2), *Carmela*, *Federico*, *Francesca*, *Mario*, *Rosaria*, *Salvadore*, *Sergio*, *Stefano*.

D'Antonio (989) Italian: patronymic from the personal name *Antonio*, from Latin *Antonius* (see ANTHONY).
GIVEN NAMES Italian 15%. *Carlo* (5), *Domenic* (4), *Luigi* (3), *Amerigo* (2), *Dante* (2), *Domenica* (2), *Gaetano* (2), *Pasquale* (2), *Rocco* (2), *Alessandro*, *Angelo*, *Antonio*.

D'Antuono (222) Italian: southern variant of D'ANTONIO.

Dantzler (970) Altered spelling of German **Dänzler**, an occupational name for a professional acrobat or entertainer, Middle High German *tenzeler*. Compare TANZER.

Danuser (107) Swiss German: unexplained.

Danvers (100) Irish and English (of Norman origin): habitational name, with fused preposition *d(e)*, for someone from *Anvers*, the French name of the port of Antwerp in what is now Belgium.
GIVEN NAME Irish 5%. *Fitzroy*.

Danyluk (133) Ukrainian: patronymic from the personal name *Danýlo* (see DANIEL).
GIVEN NAMES Ukrainian 8%. *Bohdan* (3), *Dmytro*, *Raisa*.

Danz (592) German: **1.** from a personal name, a short form of *Tandulf*, which is of uncertain origin. **2.** possibly a nickname for someone who liked to dance, from Middle High German *tanz, danz* 'dance'.
GIVEN NAMES German 4%. *Erwin, Fritz, Gerhard, Hans*.

Danza (180) Italian: **1.** from *danza* 'dance', hence a nickname for someone who enjoyed dancing, but possibly from the same word, in Old Italian meaning 'agreement', 'pact', 'coalition'. **2.** habitational name from Danza in Salerno province.
GIVEN NAMES Italian 16%. *Angelo* (4), *Gaetano* (2), *Cosmo, Michelangelo, Salvatore*.

Danzeisen (111) German: either an occupational nickname for a blacksmith, someone who makes the 'iron (Middle High German *īsen*) dance (from Middle High German *danzen, tanzen* 'to dance')' or (from the same components) a nickname for a tireless dancer.

Danzer (209) German (**Dänzer**): occupational name for a professional acrobat or entertainer; variant of TANZER.

Danzey (104) English: variant spelling of DANSIE.

Danzi (129) Italian: of uncertain origin; possibly a variant of DANZA, or alternatively a habitational name from a minor place named Danzi, for example in Potenza province.
GIVEN NAMES Italian 11%. *Rocco* (3), *Giuseppe*.

Danzig (298) Jewish (Ashkenazic): habitational name from *Danzig*, German name of Gdańsk, the main port of Poland, on the Baltic Sea. The wide distribution of the name from an early date suggests that in many cases it may have been acquired by merchants who traded with the city, as well as those who were actually born there.
GIVEN NAMES Jewish 6%. *Josif, Mayer, Meyer, Rivka*.

Danziger (480) Jewish (Ashkenazic): habitational name for someone from DANZIG.
GIVEN NAMES Jewish 7%; German 4%. *Hillel, Mayer, Moishe, Mort, Nochum, Shai*,

Sheva, Shraga, Yaakov, Yaron; *Erwin* (2), *Hans* (2), *Gerhard, Wolfgang*.

Danzy (195) Variant of English DANSIE.

Dao (1263) Vietnamese (**Đào**): unexplained.
GIVEN NAMES Vietnamese 62%. *Hung* (23), *Minh* (16), *Dung* (15), *Hai* (13), *Hoa* (13), *Thanh* (11), *Linh* (10), *Phong* (10), *Quang* (10), *Son* (10), *Tuan* (10), *Hien* (9), *Hoang* (9), *Hong* (6), *Tam* (6), *Thai* (6), *Nam* (5), *Man* (4), *Manh* (3), *Chi* (2), *Gan* (2), *Han* (2), *Sang* (2), *Thach* (2), *Uyen* (2), *Yung* (2), *Chan, Chuan, Dong, Hang, Ho, Hung Kim, Tanh, Tinh, Vang*.

Daoud (263) Muslim: from the personal name *Dāwūd*, Arabic form of DAVID. In Islam, Dāwūd is a messenger of Allah, noted in particular as the father of the Prophet SULEIMAN.
GIVEN NAMES Muslim 57%; French 5%. *Sami* (5), *Issa* (4), *Omar* (3), *Basim* (2), *Bassam* (2), *Emad* (2), *Faris* (2), *Hassan* (2), *Mazen* (2), *Mohammed* (2), *Nabil* (2), *Abdullah*; *Georges* (4), *Alphonse, Antoine, Emile*.

Daoust (544) French: nickname, originally *d'Avout*, for someone who was born in the month of August (Old French *auoust*, from Latin *(mensis) Augustus*, from the name of the first Roman emperor), or who owed a feudal obligation to help with the harvest in that month.
FOREBEARS There was a Jacques Daoust from Normandy, France, in Montreal in 1666; and a Guillaume from Picardy, who married in Lachine in 1686.
GIVEN NAMES French 10%. *Andre* (2), *Emile* (2), *Lucien* (2), *Marcel* (2), *Pierre* (2), *Armand, Celina, Gilles, Guylaine, Jeannot, Michel, Roch*.

D'Apice (176) Southern Italian: habitational name for someone from Apice, a place in Benevento.
GIVEN NAMES Italian 15%. *Carmine* (4), *Philomena* (2), *Concetta, Dante, Lorenzo, Rocco*.

Dapkus (101) Lithuanian: of uncertain origin, probably from a Polish or Belorussian personal name *Dobka*.
GIVEN NAMES Lithuanian 6%. *Ausra, Kestutis*.

D'Apolito (185) Italian: patronymic from *Apolito*, a variant of the personal name IPPOLITO.
GIVEN NAMES Italian 12%. *Angelo* (2), *Pasquale* (2), *Antonio, Carmine, Donato*.

Da Ponte (206) Italian, Portuguese, and Galician: topographic name meaning 'from the bridge' (see PONTE).
GIVEN NAMES Spanish 22%; Portuguese 11%; Italian 9%. *Manuel* (6), *Jose* (5), *Carlos* (3), *Mario* (2), *Alvardo, Americo, Christiano, Diego, Fernando, Francisco, Hermano, Humberto*; *Joao* (2), *Albano*; *Aniello* (2), *Antonino, Antonio, Guiseppe, Lorenzo, Marino, Quido*.

Dapp (139) **1.** German: nickname for a clumsy person, from the South German dialect word *dapp, depp* 'awkward', 'clum-

sy'. See also DEPP. **2.** English (Sussex): possibly a variant of DABB.

Dapper (208) Dutch and North German: nickname from *dapper* 'brave', 'gallant'.

Da Pra (106) Italian: topographic name for someone 'from the meadow', from a northern variant, *pra*, of *prato* 'meadow'.
GIVEN NAMES Italian 4%. *Primo, Sal*.

D'Aprile (157) Italian: patronymic from the personal name APRILE.
GIVEN NAMES Italian 17%. *Vito* (3), *Rocco* (2), *Carmelo, Cesidio, Cosmo*.

D'Aquila (263) Italian: habitational name for someone from the city of L'Aquila (known locally as Aquila) in Abruzzo.

Daquin (106) French: patronymic from the personal name *Aquin*, which is either from a Germanic personal name composed of the elements *agi-* 'point (of a sword)' + *win* 'friend', or possibly a much later coinage bestowed in honor of St. Thomas Aquinas (see AQUINO).
GIVEN NAMES French 8%. *Jean-Jacques, Pascale*.

D'Aquino (143) Italian: habitational name for someone from a place called Aquino, of which there are several examples in Italy, but in particular the one in Lazio, birthplace of St. Thomas Aquinas.
GIVEN NAMES Italian 25%; Spanish 7%. *Nicola* (2), *Stefano* (2), *Gaetano, Margherita, Nunzio, Sal, Salvatore*; *Alba, Jose Alejandro, Pedro, Socorro*.

Dar (136) **1.** Muslim: from Arabic *dār* 'house (of)', 'family (of)', commonly used as a prefix in forming Arabic surnames. **2.** Indian (Kashmir): Muslim name, probably from the Persian suffix *dār* 'holder', 'possessor', 'master'. **3.** Jewish (Israeli): ornamental name from Hebrew *dar* 'mother-of-pearl'.
GIVEN NAMES Muslim 53%; Jewish 13%; Indian 7%. *Mohammad* (3), *Mohammed* (3), *Akram* (2), *Arshad* (2), *Muneer* (2), *Shahid* (2), *Tariq* (2), *Waseem* (2), *Aftab, Akbar, Amir, Anwer*; *Asaf* (4), *Reuven* (2), *Shaul* (2), *Akiva, Dalit*; *Ajay, Sanjay, Vinod*.

Dara (123) **1.** Indian (Gujarat and Bombay): Parsi name based on the Old Persian royal name *Dārayavahush* 'possessor' (see DARIUS). **2.** Indian (Panjab): Sikh name of unknown meaning.
GIVEN NAMES Indian 16%; Muslim 4%. *Anil, Ashish, Bhajan, Poornima, Ravikumar, Rupa, Vijay*; *Hasan, Mohammad, Syed, Tanvir*.

Darbonne (408) French: habitational name, with the preposition *d(e)*, denoting someone from either of two places called Arbonne, in Haute-Garonne and Seine-et-Marne.
GIVEN NAMES French 4%. *Angelle, Charlet, Jean-Paul, Yves*.

Darby (6112) **1.** English: habitational name from the city of Derby, the county seat of Derbyshire, but also from the much smaller place called West Derby in Lancashire. Both are named from Old Norse *djúr* 'deer' + *býr* 'farm', 'settlement'. The usual spelling of the surname represents the pronunciation of both the place name and the surname. **2.** Irish: adopted as an English equivalent of Gaelic **Ó Diarmada** (or **Mac Diarmada**) 'descendant (or 'son') of *Diarmaid*', a personal name meaning 'freeman'. See also DERMOTT, MACDERMOTT. Insofar as Gaelic **Ó Duibhdhiormaigh** was sometimes reinterpreted as **Ó Diarmada**, Darby could also be an Anglicization of this name too. The English surname is also established in Ireland, having been taken to County Leix in the 16th century.

Darbyshire (194) English: **1.** regional name from the hundred of West Derby in Lancashire, which was often referred to in the Middle Ages as *Derbyshire*. The surname is still chiefly common in Lancashire, rather than Derbyshire. **2.** Nevertheless, it may also be a regional name from the county of Derbyshire, centered on the city of Derby (see DARBY).

D'Arcangelo (368) Italian: patronymic from the medieval personal name *Arcangelo*, meaning 'archangel'.
GIVEN NAMES Italian 16%. *Luigi* (4), *Sante* (2), *Amedeo, Angelo, Carmine, Cosmo, Domenic, Donato, Florindo, Gaetano, Giovanni, Marco.*

Darcey (283) English: variant spelling of DARCY.

D'Arco (174) Italian: **1.** in southern Italy, a habitational name from any of various places named with this word, in particular Pomigliano d'Arco in Naples province. **2.** elsewhere, possibly a metonymic occupational name for a bowman or a maker of bows, from *arco* 'bow' (from Latin *arcus*).
GIVEN NAMES Italian 17%. *Aniello* (2), *Carlo, Gennaro, Gino, Luigi, Pino, Sal, Salvatore.*

Darcy (1883) **1.** English and Irish (of Norman origin): habitational name from Arcy in Manche, France, named from a Gaulish personal name (which, it has been suggested, may be akin to the Indo-European root *ars-* 'bear') + the locative suffix *-acum*. **2.** Irish: English surname adopted by bearers of the Gaelic surname **Ó Dorchaidhe** 'descendant of the dark one', from *dorcha* 'dark', 'gloomy'. This Connacht name has fallen together with the Norman surname, which is certainly attested in Ireland, having been introduced there by Sir William D'Arcy and Sir John D'Arcy, who was appointed Chief Justiciar of Ireland in the 14th century.
GIVEN NAMES Irish 6%; French 4%. *Eamon* (2), *Brendan, Eamonn, Maeve, Malachy, Niamh, Seamus*; *Gisele* (2), *Julien* (2), *Normand* (2), *Alain, Armand, Cecile, Clemence, Dominique, Emile, Gilles, Jean-Paul, Laure.*

Dardar (215) Possibly an altered spelling of French **Dardard**, from a Germanic personal name composed of the elements *dard*, *dart* 'lance', 'spear' + *hard* 'hardy', 'brave', 'strong'.
GIVEN NAMES French 9%. *Antoine* (2), *Armand, Etienne, Julien, Michel.*

Darden (3727) English: unexplained. Possibly a habitational name from a locality in Northumberland called Darden.

Dardenne (107) French: regional name, with the preposition *d(e)*, for someone from the Ardennes, a wooded plateau in northeastern France, southeastern Belgium, and Luxembourg, or a habitational name from a place named Ardenne, for example in Charente-Maritime and Haute-Loire.
FOREBEARS The marriage of a Dardenne or Dardains from Saintonge is recorded in 1668 in Montreal.
GIVEN NAMES French 9%. *Patrice* (2), *Jacques.*

Dardis (285) Irish (mainly Dublin): **1.** possibly a variant of French **D'Artois**, a Norman habitational name for someone from Artois, France. **2.** Woulfe, however, suggests as an origin the Ards peninsula in County Down, which was heavily settled by Normans.

Dare (1176) English: variant of DEAR.

Darensbourg (161) French: unexplained; possibly an Alsatian habitational name of German origin.
GIVEN NAMES French 11%. *Andre, Aurore, Camile, Irby, Pierre.*

D'Arezzo (120) Italian: habitational name for someone from Arezzo in central Italy.
GIVEN NAMES Italian 13%. *Guido* (4), *Antonio, Marco, Pasco, Vittorio.*

Darga (203) Polish: from a pet form of the old Pomeranian compound personal names *Dargobad, Dargorad*, and *Dargosław* (probably based on a metathesized form of Polish *drog* 'dear').

Dargan (473) Irish: reduced Anglicized form of Gaelic **Ó Deargáin** 'descendant of *Deargán*', a byname from a diminutive of *dearg* 'red'.

Dargie (153) Scottish: habitational name from a place named Dargie, in Angus (Tayside).
GIVEN NAME French 7%. *Camille* (2).

Dargis (194) **1.** Lithuanian: unflattering nickname from *dargùs* 'ugly', 'unpleasant', 'irritable'. **2.** French (**D'Argis**): probably a habitational name for someone from Argis in Ain.
GIVEN NAMES French 8%; Lithuanian 5%. *Pierre* (2), *Andre, Gaston, Yves*; *Kazys* (2), *Algimantas, Stasys.*

D'Arienzo (195) Italian: habitational name for someone from Arienzo in Caserta province.

Darilek (139) Czech (**Dařílek**): nickname for a prosperous individual, from *dařiti (se), (po)dařiti* 'to do well', 'to prosper'.

Darin (263) **1.** Serbian and Russian: metronymic from the female personal name *Dara* (Russian *Darja*). **2.** Bulgarian: from *Daro*, a pet form of the personal name *Todor* (see

THEODORE). **3.** Italian: northern variant of **Darino**, from a pet form of DARIO.
GIVEN NAMES Italian 8%. *Valentino* (2), *Angelo, Antonio, Ferruccio, Livio, Quirino, Silvio, Tullio.*

Daring (101) English: perhaps be a nickname from Middle English *daring* 'trembling', 'crouching or transfixed with fear'.

Dario (129) Spanish (**Darío**) and Italian: from the personal name *Darío* (see DARIUS).
GIVEN NAMES Italian 15%; Spanish 8%. *Mario* (4), *Enrico, Luigino, Rachele*; *Ruben* (2), *Angel, Pedro.*

Darity (139) Altered form of Irish **Dorrity**, which MacLysaght identifies as a form of DOHERTY.

Darius (110) French: from the Late Latin personal name *Darius*, Greek *Dareios*, which was borne by various kings of ancient Persia, including Darius I (522–486 BC). The ancient Persian form of the name was *Darayavahush*, meaning 'possessor', from *daraya(miy)* 'possess', 'maintain' + *vahu* 'good', 'well'. This became accepted as a Christian name in medieval Europe in honor of a saint martyred at Nicaea at an uncertain date.
GIVEN NAMES French 15%. *Gratien, Philomene, Solange.*

Dark (827) English: nickname for someone with dark hair or a dark complexion, from Middle English *darke*, Old English *deorc* 'dark'. In England, the surname is most frequent in the West Country.

Darke (157) English: variant spelling of DARK.
GIVEN NAME French 4%. *Marcelle.*

Darland (553) English: habitational name from a place in Kent named Darland, from Old English *deor* 'deer or other wild animal' + *land* 'tract of land', 'estate'.

Darley (541) English: habitational name from either of two places in Derbyshire, named Darley, from Old English *deor* 'beast', 'deer' + *leah* 'woodland clearing'. This surname was taken to Ireland in the 17th century.

Darling (6766) English and Scottish: from Middle English *derling*, Old English *deorling* 'darling', 'beloved one', a derivative of *deor* 'dear', 'beloved' (see DEAR 1). This was quite a common Old English byname, which remained current as a personal name into the 14th century. The surname probably derives at least in part from this use, probably in part also from a Middle English nickname.

Darlington (1030) English: habitational name from Darlington in County Durham, recorded in *c.*1009 as *Dearthingtun*, from Old English *Dēornōðingtūn* 'settlement (Old English *tūn*) associated with *Dēornōð*', a personal name composed of the elements *dēor* 'dear' + *nōð* 'daring'. The surname was present in Scotland from an early period.

Darmody (141) Irish: variant of DERMODY.

Darnall (758) English: habitational name from Darnall, now a district of Sheffield, Yorkshire, or Darnhall in Cheshire, both named from Old English *derne* 'hidden', 'secret' + *halh* 'nook'.

Darnell (6310) English: **1.** from Old French *darnel* 'darnel', an annual grass, *Lolium temulentum*, hence perhaps a topographic name. However, according to Reaney, the plant was believed to produce intoxication, so its adoption as a surname may have been for quite different reasons. In the British Isles the name is found chiefly in the central and east Midlands. **2.** variant spelling of DARNALL.

Darner (261) Respelling of German *Dörner* (see DOERNER) or DERNER.

Darney (112) **1.** English: possibly a habitational name from a lost or unidentified place. **2.** French: habitational name from a place so named in Vosges or from Darney-aux-Chênes in the canton of Châtenois. In some cases it may be an altered spelling of the French surname **Darné**, a habitational name, with the preposition *d(e)*, for someone from Arné in Hautes Pyrénées.

Darnley (122) English and Scottish: habitational name from Darnlee or Darnley, an estate in southwestern Glasgow.

Darnold (157) Partly Americanized form of French **Darnoud**, a patronymic from the personal name *Arnoud*, *Arnoult*.

Da Rocha (131) Portuguese and Galician: common topographic name meaning 'from the rock (*rocha*)'.
GIVEN NAMES Spanish 21%; Portuguese 16%. *Jose* (5), *Manuel* (4), *Luis* (2), *Tito* (2), *Ana*, *Ernesto*, *Fernando*, *Jorge*, *Luiz*, *Maria Emilia*; *Joaquim*, *Marcio*; *Antonio* (2), *Delio*, *Ernani*.

Daron (160) French: **1.** habitational name, with the preposition *d(e)*, denoting someone from Aron in Mayenne. **2.** from Old French *daron* 'master of the house', probably applied as a nickname, no doubt ironically in some instances.

Da Rosa (321) Portuguese: literally 'of the (*da*) rose (*rosa*)', generally a component of personal names: among women a Marian name; among men of uncertain application.
GIVEN NAMES Spanish 32%; Portuguese 21%. *Manuel* (22), *Jose* (11), *Carlos* (5), *Adelino* (4), *Fernando* (3), *Julio* (3), *Luis* (3), *Mario* (3), *Ana* (2), *Marcos* (2), *Tomas* (2), *Alfredo*; *Joao* (3), *Joaquim* (2), *Duarte*; *Antonio* (10), *Filomena* (2), *Angelo*, *Eliseo*, *Marco*, *Santina*.

D'Arpino (153) Italian: habitational name for someone from Arpino in Ciociaria, Frosinone province.
GIVEN NAMES Italian 15%. *Mario* (2), *Carlo*, *Dante*, *Elpidio*, *Enrico*, *Livio*, *Marciano*, *Marino*, *Pasquale*, *Silvio*, *Marisa*.

Darr (2490) **1.** English: perhaps a variant of DEAR. **2.** German (**Därr**): from a short form of a Germanic personal name, perhaps

related to Old High German *dart* 'spear'. **3.** Variant spelling of German DORR.

Darragh (488) Northern Irish: reduced Anglicized form of Gaelic **Ó Dhubhdarach** or **Mac Dhubhdarach** 'descendant (or son) of *Dubhdarach*', a personal name meaning 'black one of the oak tree'. For this reason it has sometimes been Anglicized as OAKES.
GIVEN NAME Irish 5%. *Murphy*.

Darrah (1353) Northern Irish: variant spelling of DARRAGH.

Darras (106) English (of Norman origin) or French: habitational name, with fused preposition *d(e)*, principally for someone from Arras in northern France, or possibly from Arras-en-Lavedan (Hautes Pyrénées) or Arras-sur-Rhône (Ardèche).

Darrell (458) English (of Norman origin): habitational name, with fused preposition *d(e)*, for someone from Airelle in Calvados, France, or Airel in La Manche, Normandy.

D'Arrigo (286) Italian: patronymic from the personal name ARRIGO.
GIVEN NAMES Italian 17%. *Carmel* (2), *Giuseppe* (2), *Antonino*, *Antonio*, *Carmelo*, *Domenic*, *Nunzio*, *Pasquale*, *Sal*, *Sebastiano*, *Stefano*.

Darrin (131) English: unexplained.

Darrington (342) English: habitational name from Darrington in West Yorkshire, recorded in Domesday Book as *Darni(n)tone* 'settlement (Old English *tūn*) associated with (a man called) *Dēornōth*'.

Darroch (169) Scottish: **1.** variant of DARROW. **2.** variant of northern Irish DARRAGH.

Darrough (262) Northern Irish: variant of DARRAGH.

Darrow (2338) Scottish: **1.** habitational name from Darroch near Falkirk, in Stirlingshire, said to be named from Gaelic *darach* 'oak tree'. **2.** Scottish variant of northern Irish DARRAGH.
FOREBEARS George Darrow (b. 1652), a paternal ancestor of legendary criminal trial lawyer Charles Seward Darrow (1857–1938), emigrated from Leigh, Lancashire, England, to New London, CT, in the mid 17th century.

Darsey (334) English: variant spelling of DARCY or possibly of Scottish **Darsie**, a habitational name from Dairsie in Fife.

Darst (737) PA-German variant of DURST.

Dart (1356) **1.** English: habitational name from a settlement on the river Dart in Devon, which is named from a British term meaning 'oak' and is thus a cognate of DARWIN 2. **2.** English: metonymic occupational name for a maker of arrows, from Middle English *dart* (from Old French *darde*).

Darter (352) English: variant of **Daughter** (see DAUGHTERS).

Dartez (394) Probably an altered spelling of French **Darthez**, a habitational name, with the preposition *d(e)*, denoting someone

from either of two places called Arthez, in Landes and Pyrénées Atlantiques.
GIVEN NAMES French 7%. *Raywood* (2), *Andre*, *Curley*, *Octa*, *Pierre*, *Vernice*.

Dartt (229) English: variant spelling of DART.

Darty (230) Origin uncertain; possibly an altered spelling of French **Dartis**, a habitational name, with the preposition *d(e)*, denoting someone from either of two places called Artix, in Ariège and Pyrénées Atlantiques. Alternatively it could be a reduced form of the Irish surname DOHERTY.

Darville (203) French: habitational name for someone from either of two places called Arville, in Loir-et-Cher and Seine-et-Marne, or from Arvillers in Somme.

Darwin (632) English: **1.** from the Old English personal name *Dēorwine*, composed of the elements *dēor* 'dear' + *wine* 'friend'. This name is attested in the 10th century, but it was not common; nevertheless it may have survived long enough to become a Middle English personal name and so given rise to the surname. **2.** habitational name from Darwen in Lancashire, named from the Darwin river (earlier *Derwent*) on which it stands. This seems to be a British name derived from a word meaning 'oak'.

Darwish (241) Muslim: status name for a Sufi holy man, from Persian and Turkish *derviş* 'dervish', a member of a Sufi Muslim religious order, from Pahlavi *driyosh* meaning 'beggar', 'one who goes from door to door'.
GIVEN NAMES Muslim 59%; Jewish 5%. *Ahmad* (4), *Ahmed* (4), *Ali* (4), *Mohamed* (4), *Mohammed* (3), *Sabet* (3), *Akram* (2), *Amal* (2), *Darwish* (2), *Kamal* (2), *Khaled* (2), *Mamdouh* (2); *Menachem* (3), *Miriam*, *Sasson*, *Shlomo*.

Dary (131) English: unexplained.

Das (1001) Indian (Bengal) and Bangladeshi: Hindu (Kayasth) name, from Bengali *daš* 'votary', 'servant', from Sanskrit *dāsa* 'slave', 'servant'. It is also commonly used as the final element of compound given names, for example *Bhagavandas* 'servant of god', *Mohandas* 'votary of Mohan (an epithet of the god Krishna)'.
GIVEN NAMES Indian 81%. *Pranab* (8), *Ajit* (7), *Pankaj* (7), *Ashok* (6), *Krishna* (6), *Anil* (5), *Dipak* (5), *Gokul* (5), *Kalyan* (5), *Mohan* (5), *Suman* (5), *Tapas* (5).

D'Asaro (143) Italian: patronymic from ASARO, a variant of the personal name *Ássoro*.
GIVEN NAMES Italian 7%. *Santo*, *Vita*.

D'Ascanio (119) Italian: patronymic from the personal name *Ascanio*, Latin *Ascanius*, from Greek *Askanios*.
GIVEN NAMES Italian 20%. *Angelo* (2), *Franco* (2), *Amedeo*, *Emidio*, *Giovanni*, *Giulio*, *Luigi*, *Pasquale*.

D'Ascenzo (193) Italian: patronymic from the personal name *Ascenzo*, a name popularly given to babies born on Ascension Day.

GIVEN NAMES Italian 10%; German 5%; Spanish 5%. *Rocco* (2), *Domenic, Franco, Gabriele, Romeo; Manfred* (3); *Anselmo, Elia, Lamberto, Ovidio.*

Dasch (217) **1.** German: variant of TASCH. **2.** German: from an old personal name formed with Old High German *tac* 'day'.

Dascher (134) South German: variant of TASCHNER 'purse maker'.

D'Ascoli (199) Italian: habitational name for someone from Ascoli Piceno or Ascoli Satriano. The name is also found among Jewish families, the Jewish community in Ascoli Piceno having been forced to disperse to the ghettoes of Rome and Ancona during the 17th and 18th centuries.

Dase (162) German: variant of DOSE.

Dasenbrock (109) Origin unidentified.

Dasgupta (180) Indian (Bengal) and Bangladeshi: Hindu (Baidya) compound name from DAS + GUPTA.

GIVEN NAMES Indian 88%. *Dipankar* (4), *Partha* (4), *Ashok* (3), *Gautam* (3), *Nivedita* (3), *Purnendu* (2), *Sandip* (2), *Soma* (2), *Tapas* (2), *Abhik, Amit, Anindita.*

Dash (1043) **1.** English: topographic name for someone who lived near an ash tree, or a habitational name from a place named with the Old English word *æsc* (see ASH). The Anglo-Norman French preposition *de* 'of', 'from' has become fused to the name. **2.** Americanized spelling of German DASCH. **3.** Indian: variant of DAS.

GIVEN NAMES Indian 5%. *Arati* (2), *Meenakshi* (2), *Raj* (2), *Binod, Kalyani, Manoj, Narayan, Padmaja, Pramod, Rajesh, Satya, Sita.*

Dasher (939) **1.** Americanized spelling of German DASCHER. **2.** Scottish: possibly a habitational name from Dasher near Kippen in Stirlingshire.

Dashiell (650) Scottish: unexplained.

Dashnaw (212) **1.** Americanized form of French Canadian DAGENAIS. **2.** Perhaps an altered spelling of German **Daschner** (see DASHNER).

Dashner (280) Americanized spelling of South German **Daschner**, variant of TASCHNER.

Da Silva (3189) Portuguese (**Da Silva**): topographic name for someone who lived by a wood, from Latin *silva* 'wood'.

GIVEN NAMES Spanish 32%; Portuguese 22%. *Jose* (127), *Manuel* (125), *Carlos* (41), *Luis* (21), *Fernando* (18), *Francisco* (18), *Luiz* (15), *Mario* (15), *Jorge* (13), *Julio* (11), *Marcelo* (10), *Roberto* (10); *Joao* (34), *Joaquim* (18), *Paulo* (18), *Duarte* (4), *Agostinho* (3), *Henrique* (3), *Marcio* (3), *Nelio* (3), *Albano* (2), *Altair* (2), *Amadeu* (2), *Catarina* (2); *Antonio* (106), *Marco* (4), *Alessandra* (3), *Marcello* (3), *Filomena* (2), *Luciano* (2), *Mauro* (2), *Romeo* (2), *Albertina, Annamaria, Antonino, Ceasar.*

Dasinger (114) German: habitational name for someone from a place near Augsburg called Dasing.

Daskal (125) Jewish (from Romania and Moldova): occupational name from Romanian *dascăl* 'teacher', 'cantor' (in a synagogue).

GIVEN NAMES Jewish 18%; Russian 4%. *Aron, Aryeh, Elimelech, Meyer, Mier, Moshe, Oded, Rivka; Anatoly.*

Daspit (153) French: LA variant of **Daspet**, a habitational name, with fused preposition *d(e)*, for someone from Aspet in Haute-Garonne.

Dass (264) Indian: variant of DAS.

GIVEN NAMES Indian 48%. *Bhagwan* (4), *Ishwar* (4), *Ram* (4), *Charan* (3), *Savitri* (3), *Bawa* (2), *Dharam* (2), *Kumar* (2), *Reena* (2), *Ajay, Anil, Anurag.*

Dassow (247) Eastern German: habitational name, of Slavic origin, from one of the places in Mecklenburg and Pomerania called Dassow.

Dastrup (133) Danish: habitational name from a place called Dastrup.

Data (122) **1.** Italy (Turin): unexplained. **2.** Polish: Polonized form of German *Dato, Date,* short forms of compound personal named formed with *Diet-* (see for example DIETRICH).

GIVEN NAMES Spanish 5%. *Domingo* (2), *Lauro, Lourdes, Virgilio.*

Date (207) **1.** Indian (Maharashtra); pronounced as two syllables: Hindu (Brahman) name found among the Konkanasth Brahmans, from Sanskrit *dātā* 'donor'. **2.** Japanese: habitational name from a place called Idate in Mutsu (now Aomori) prefecture. They were a great samurai family descended from the northern FUJIWARA clan.

GIVEN NAMES Indian 16%; Japanese 12%. *Shashank* (2), *Urmila* (2), *Ashwini, Chetan, Hari, Medha, Ravi, Santosh, Shashi, Sumit, Vandana, Vijay; Masaki* (2), *Shiro* (2), *Hiroaki, Kazuo, Nobuo, Noriko, Tomoaki, Tsutomu, Yoko, Yoshihiko.*

Datema (114) Frisian: unexplained.

Dates (340) English: unexplained.

Dato (166) Italian: from a reduced form of a personal name ending in *-ato*, for example DONATO, DIODATO.

GIVEN NAMES Spanish 15%; Italian 10%. *Sixto* (2), *Alfonso, Bartolome, Cesar, Efren, Gustavo, Juan, Orlando, Rosario, Vicente, Victorino; Carmine* (2), *Filiberto, Gaetano, Gianfranco, Giuseppe.*

D'Atri (133) Italian: habitational name for someone from Atri in Teramo province.

GIVEN NAME Greek 4%. *Arist* (3).

Datta (331) Indian (Assam, Bengal, and Panjab) and Bangladeshi: Hindu name from Sanskrit *datta* 'given', 'gift'. In ancient Sanskrit literature this name is associated with the Vaishya caste. In Assam and Bengal the Dattas belong to the Kayasth caste. In the Panjab it is a Brahman name based on the name of a clan in the Mohyal

subgroup of Saraswat Brahmans, having probably evolved from an ancestral personal name.

GIVEN NAMES Indian 83%. *Sanjay* (4), *Anuradha* (3), *Kaushik* (3), *Anil* (2), *Anindya* (2), *Arun* (2), *Asim* (2), *Babul* (2), *Biswa* (2), *Dilip* (2), *Indrani* (2), *Krishna* (2).

D'Attilio (186) Italian: patronymic from the personal name **Attilio**.

GIVEN NAMES Italian 8%. *Cosmo, Nicola.*

Dattilo (520) Southern Italian: **1.** habitational name from any of numerous minor places named Dattilo. **2.** from the personal name *Dattilo*, a pet form of a Germanic personal name, *Dado, Daddo, Datto.* **3.** patronymic from a reduced form of the personal name **Attilio**. **4.** possibly a nickname from Greek *daktylos* 'finger', which also means 'date palm' (Latin *dactylus*).

GIVEN NAMES Italian 12%. *Ignazio* (2), *Luigi* (2), *Salvatore* (2), *Angelo, Annunziato, Domenico, Franca, Gaetano, Giuseppe, Marcello, Palma, Vincenzo.*

Dattoli (112) Italian: **1.** from a pet form of *Datto*, a variant of the Germanic personal name *Dado* (see DATZ). **2.** possibly, though less likely, a topographic name from Sicilian and southern Italian *dattula* 'date palm'.

GIVEN NAME Italian 7%. *Vito.*

Datz (289) German: from a pet form of the old personal name *Dado*, cognate with Old High German *tāt* 'deed', 'action'.

Dau (433) **1.** North German and Dutch: from an Old Frisian personal name *Douwo.* **2.** South German: from *Davo*, a short form of the personal name *Tavold*, formed with Old High German *dau* 'custom', 'tradition'. **3.** Vietnamese: unexplained.

GIVEN NAMES Vietnamese 5%. *Son* (3), *Tuan* (2), *Dai, Dinh, Duong, Giao, Hoa, Huong, Khuyen, Linh, Mau, Phu.*

Daub (756) **1.** German and Jewish: variant of TAUBE. **2.** South German: byname for a deaf person, from Middle High German *toup* 'deaf'. Compare TAUB.

Daube (188) **1.** German: variant of TAUBE. **2.** German: habitational name from Dauba in eastern Germany. **3.** Jewish: variant of TAUBE 2.

GIVEN NAMES German 5%. *Fritz, Otto.*

Daubenmire (109) Americanized form of German **Daubenmeyer** 'dove farmer'. Compare DAUBENSPECK and MEYER.

Daubenspeck (352) German: habitational name from a farm near Moers, Rhineland, named from Middle Low German *dūve* 'dove' or the personal name *Dube* + Middle German *specke* 'log road'. (The humorous literal translation of the name, 'pigeon bacon', has nothing to do with its origin.)

Dauber (418) **1.** English: occupational name from Middle English *daubere*, Old French *daubier* 'whitewasher', 'plasterer'. **2.** German: variant of TAUBER or a habitational name from Dauba, near Aussig, now in Czech Republic.

GIVEN NAMES German 5%. *Dieter* (2), *Dietmar, Otto*.

Dauberman (116) German (**Daubermann**): **1.** occupational name for someone who kept doves, German *Tauben*. Compare TAUBER. **2.** alternatively, perhaps, a topographic name for someone who lived by the Tauber river.
GIVEN NAME German 6%. *Dieter*.

Daubert (635) German: **1.** variant of TAUBERT. **2.** from an old personal name formed with Old High German *dau* 'custom', 'tradition'.

Daubner (134) German: occupational name for a breeder or keeper of doves, Middle High German *daubener, tubener*. Compare TAUBE.
GIVEN NAME French 4%. *Colette*.

Daudelin (183) French: of unclear derivation; perhaps from a pet form of the personal name *Dode*, itself of obscure origin.
FOREBEARS Nicolas Daudelin, of Rouen, France, married Anne Girard in Château Richer, Quebec, in 1665.
GIVEN NAMES French 11%. *Adelard, Fernand, Gilles, Marcel, Philias, Yvon*.

Dauenhauer (295) South German: occupational name for a stave maker, from Middle High German *düge* (Latin *doga*) 'stave' + an agent derivative of *hauen* 'to cut wood', 'to carve'.

Dauer (647) German: **1.** habitational name from a place so named in Uckermark. **2.** variant of TAUER. **3.** shortened form of **Dauerer**, a variant of DAUENHAUER.

Daughdrill (234) Probably a variant of English DODRILL.
GIVEN NAMES French 4%. *Gaston, Pascal*.

Daughenbaugh (362) Americanized spelling of German **Dauchenbach**, probably from a creek so named from Middle High German *dauch* 'bog', 'moor', or **Daufenbach**, a habitational name from either of two places so named: near Neuwied on the Rhine, or near Trier.

Daugherty (12706) Irish: variant spelling of DOHERTY.

Daughety (201) Irish: variant spelling of DOHERTY.

Daughters (157) English: from Middle English, Old English *dohtor* 'daughter'. The application is unclear; perhaps it was a surname acquired by the retainers of an heiress of an important family.

Daughtery (335) English: variant of DAUGHTRY.

Daughton (153) English: probably a variant of DALTON.

Daughtrey (503) English: variant of DAUGHTRY.

Daughtridge (173) Probably an altered form of English DAUGHTRY.

Daughtry (1814) English (of Norman origin): habitational name, with fused French preposition *d(e)*, for someone from Hauterive in Orne, France, named from Old French *haute rive* 'high bank' (Latin *alta ripa*).

Daul (340) German: **1.** nickname, perhaps for a tall thin person, from Middle Low German *düle* 'reed', 'cat's tail'. **2.** variant of DAU 2.
GIVEN NAMES German 5%. *Dieter, Florian, Kurt, Liselotte, Wilhelm*.

Dault (192) French: habitational name, with the preposition *d(e)*, denoting someone from Ault in Somme.
GIVEN NAME French 4%. *Normand*.

Daulton (563) English: variant spelling of DALTON.

Daum (1333) German and Jewish (Ashkenazic): nickname for a short person, from from Middle High German *doum* 'tap', 'plug', or *düme*, German *Daumen* 'thumb'.

Daun (239) **1.** German: habitational name from Daun, a place in the Eifel region. **2.** Scottish (Aberdeenshire): variant of DON.

Daunhauer (102) German: reduced form of **Daubenhauer** or **Daugenhauer**, an occupational name for someone who made staves for barrels, from Middle High German *duge* 'dowel', + an agent noun from *houwen* 'to cut', 'hew'.
GIVEN NAME German 4%. *Kurt*.

Daunt (125) English and Irish: nickname from Middle English *daunten* 'to subdue', 'to tame', 'to intimidate'. The surname was taken to County Cork in Ireland in the 16th century.
GIVEN NAMES Irish 8%. *Brendan, Kieran*.

Dauphin (539) French: from a medieval personal name (Latin *Delphinus*, from *delphis* 'dolphin'). This name was borne by a 4th-century saint who was bishop of Bordeaux, and from the early 12th century it was in use as a hereditary personal name in the family of the counts of Albon, so that it soon came to be used as a title and led to their territory (capital Grenoble) being known as the *Dauphiné*. When it became part of the Kingdom of France in 1349, the title of *dauphin* thereafter denoted the heir-apparent to the throne, and it is possible that in some cases this is the origin of the surname, either denoting a member of the Dauphin's household or applied as a nickname in the sense of 'prince'.
GIVEN NAMES French 12%. *Andre* (2), *Armand* (2), *Emile* (2), *Antoine, Benoit, Carmelle, Fernand, Georges, Jean Claude, Laure, Luckner, Maryse*.

Dauphinais (402) French: regional name for someone from the Dauphiné region of southeastern France (see DAUPHIN).
GIVEN NAMES French 11%. *Emile* (2), *Normand* (2), *Adelard, Andre, Armand, Gilles, Henri, Lucien*.

Dauphine (120) French (**Dauphiné**): regional name for someone from the Dauphiné region of southeastern France (see DAUPHIN). This name is rare in France but fairly frequent in the New World.
GIVEN NAMES French 6%. *Armand, Aurelien*.

Dauphinee (179) Altered spelling of French **Dauphiné** (see DAUPHINE).
GIVEN NAME French 4%. *Damien*.

D'Auria (550) Italian: metronymic from the female personal name *Auria*, a derivative of Latin *aurea* 'golden'.
GIVEN NAMES Italian 13%. *Salvatore* (5), *Angelo* (3), *Lombardo* (2), *Sal* (2), *Aniello, Annamarie, Antonio, Cosmo, Gennaro, Giuseppe, Luciano, Vincenzo*.

Daus (237) **1.** German: from Middle Low German *düs* denoting the two on a die or the ace in cards, hence a nickname for an inveterate card or dice player. **2.** South German: variant of DAUSCH.

Dausch (112) South German: **1.** possibly from the dialect word *Dausch* 'breeding sow', a metonymic occupational name for a (successful) pig farmer, or a farmer in general. **2.** nickname for an inveterate dice player, from Middle High German *tūs, dūs* 'two'. Compare DEUSCHLE.

Dausman (123) German: extended form of DAUS.

Daut (129) Dutch and German: from a much reduced short form of the personal name **Diederik** (see DEDERICK) (Dutch) or DIETRICH (German).

Dautel (118) **1.** French: variant of DESAUTELS. **2.** French: topographic name, with the preposition *d(e)*, for someone who lived by a small church, from *autel* 'altar' (Latin *altare*). **3.** German: nickname from Swabian *dautel* 'indecisive or clumsy man'. **4.** Dutch and North German: from a pet form of DAUT.

Dauterive (184) French (LA): of uncertain derivation. Possibilities include *d'haute rive* 'from the high bank'; **D'Autry** 'from Autry', (places in Ardennes and Allier); or **D'Autriche** 'from Austria'.
GIVEN NAMES French 8%. *Cecile, Damien, Lucien, Raoul*.

Dauterman (132) German (**Dautermann**): probably an extended form of **Dauter**, which is derived from a short form of an old personal name formed with Old High German *diot* 'people'.
GIVEN NAMES German 4%. *Georg, Kurt*.

Dauteuil (103) French: habitational name, with the preposition *d(e)*, for someone from a place called Auteuil (Oise, Yvelines).
GIVEN NAMES French 19%. *Armand, Bibiane, Camille, Donat, Marcel, Pierre*.

Dautrich (141) French: ethnic name, with the preposition *d(e)*, for someone from Austria (French *Autriche*).

Dauzat (520) French: habitational name from Dauzat-sur-Vodable in Puy-de-Dôme.
GIVEN NAMES French 4%. *Elodie, Gaston, Landry, Michel*.

Davalos (629) Spanish (**Dávalos**): habitational name, with fused preposition *d(e)*, denoting someone from Ábalos in the province of Soria (see AVALOS).
GIVEN NAMES Spanish 49%. *Jose* (12), *Jesus* (9), *Juan* (7), *Guillermo* (6), *Pedro* (6),

Carlos (5), *Luis* (5), *Francisco* (4), *Miguel* (4), *Ramiro* (4), *Ruben* (4), *Sergio* (4); *Antonio* (9), *Lorenzo* (4), *Cecilio* (3), *Luciano* (2), *Marco* (2), *Filiberto*, *Gabino*, *Heriberto*.

D'Avanzo (423) Italian: patronymic from the personal name *Avanzo*, a popular omen name of the late Middle Ages, meaning 'advantage'.
GIVEN NAMES Italian 9%. *Carmine* (2), *Livio* (2), *Albo*, *Aldo*, *Angelo*, *Antonio*, *Giorgio*, *Giuseppe*, *Lorenzo*, *Luigi*, *Marco*, *Paolo*.

Davault (184) French: topographic name for someone who lived downstream from the main settlement, from Old French *aval* 'downstream' (Latin *ad vallem* 'towards the valley', as opposed to *ad montem* (Old French *amont*) 'towards the hill', 'upstream').

Dave (782) Indian (Gujarat); pronounced as *da-way*: Hindu (Brahman) name, from Sanskrit *dvivedī* '(one who has studied) two Vedas'.
GIVEN NAMES Indian 78%. *Rajesh* (8), *Bharat* (7), *Ashok* (6), *Kamlesh* (6), *Kiran* (6), *Amit* (5), *Dilip* (5), *Kirit* (5), *Mukesh* (5), *Prakash* (5), *Raj* (5), *Ramesh* (5).

Davee (170) Variant spelling of English DAVEY or Scottish DAVIE.

D'Avella (102) Southern Italian: habitational name for someone from Avella in Avellino province.
GIVEN NAMES Italian 28%. *Carmine* (2), *Mario* (2), *Aldo*, *Donato*, *Ernesto*, *Pompeo*, *Salvatore*, *Sebastiano*.

Davenport (18875) **1.** English: habitational name from a place in Cheshire named Davenport, from the Dane river (apparently named with a Celtic cognate of Middle Welsh *dafnu* 'to drop', 'to trickle') + Old English *port* 'market town'. **2.** Irish (County Tipperary): English surname adopted by bearers of Munster Gaelic **Ó Donndubhartaigh** 'descendant of *Donndubhartach*', a personal name composed of the elements *donn* 'brown-haired man' or 'chieftain' + *dubh* 'black' + *artach* 'nobleman'.
FOREBEARS John Davenport (died 1670) arrived in Boston, MA, in 1637. He came of an English Cheshire family associated with Capesthorne Hall, near Macclesfield.

Davern (288) **1.** Irish: reduced Anglicized form of Gaelic **Ó Dábhoireann** 'descendant of *Dábhoireann*'. The original form of this name was *Dubhdábhoireann* 'black one of the two burrens' (from *dubh* 'black' + *dá* 'two' + *boireann*), apparently denoting The Burren, a rocky area in the north of County Clare. The family was famed for its learning, and ran a literary and legal school in County Clare. **2.** In some instances, it may be an altered spelling of the French habitational name **Daverne**, originally denoting someone from either of two places called Avernes, in Orne and Val d'Oise.
GIVEN NAMES Irish 6%. *Eamon*, *Liam*, *Niall*.

D'Aversa (225) Italian: habitational name for someone from Aversa in Caserta province. The surname is widespread in southern Italy and Sicily.

Daves (1163) **1.** Probably a variant spelling of DAVIS or DAVIES. **2.** Americanized spelling of German TEWES or **Däves**, from reduced forms of the personal name *Matthäus* (see MATTHEW).

Davey (3403) English: variant spelling of DAVY.

Davi (443) **1.** Italian (Sicily): patronymic or plural form of **Davo**. **2.** English and French: variant spelling of DAVY.
GIVEN NAMES Italian 30%. *Salvatore* (16), *Antonio* (6), *Guido* (4), *Rosario* (4), *Mario* (3)*Sal* (3), *Calogero* (2), *Gino* (2), *Vincenzo* (2), *Vito* (2), *Alessandra*, *Biagio*, *Biago*, *Carmela*.

Davia (159) Italian: of uncertain derivation; possibly a topographic name from *da via* 'from the street', in some cases misdivided as **D'Avia**.
GIVEN NAMES Italian 8%. *Carmela*, *Gaetano*, *Gino*, *Marcello*, *Onorato*.

Daviau (131) French: from a derivative of *Davy*, popular form of DAVID.
GIVEN NAMES French 13%. *Armand* (2), *Aime*, *Aldor*, *Emile*, *Normand*.

David (12661) Jewish, Welsh, Scottish, English, French, Portuguese, German, Czech, Slovak (**Dávid**), and Slovenian: from the Hebrew personal name *David* 'beloved', which has been perennially popular among Jews, in honor of the Biblical king of this name, the greatest of the early kings of Israel. His prominence, and the vivid narrative of his life contained in the First Book of Samuel, led to adoption of the name in various parts of Europe, notably Britain, among Christians in the Middle Ages. The popularity of this as a personal name was increased in Britain, firstly by virtue of its being the name of the patron saint of Wales (about whom very little is known: he was probably a 6th-century monk and bishop) and secondly because it was borne by two kings of Scotland (David I, reigning 1124–53, and David II, 1329–71). Its popularity in Russia is largely due to the fact that this was the ecclesiastical name adopted by St. Gleb (died 1015), one of two sons of Prince Vladimir of Kiev who were martyred for their Christian zeal.
FOREBEARS The first French family of the name David recorded in Quebec was in Trois-Rivières around 1649; their place of origin in France is unknown. A second line, from Normandy, was in Château Richer by 1662.

Davide (112) Italian: from the Biblical name *David(e)* (see DAVID).
GIVEN NAMES Italian 16%. *Salvatore* (3), *Gandolfo*, *Marco*.

Davidge (156) English and Scottish: variant of DAVIDS.

Davidheiser (145) Respelling of German **Davidhäuser**, a habitational name for someone living or working at a house known as 'David's house', from the personal name *David* (see DAVID) + Middle High German *hūs* 'house'.

Davidian (273) Armenian: patronymic from the personal name DAVID.
GIVEN NAMES Armenian 23%. *Aram* (2), *Haig* (2), *Sark* (2), *Vartan* (2), *Armen*, *Arpine*, *Dikran*, *Diran*, *Edik*, *Garnik*, *Ghazar*, *Goharik*.

Davidoff (403) Russian, Bulgarian, and Jewish (from eastern Ukraine or eastern Belarus): alternative spelling of *Davidov* (Bulgarian, Jewish) or DAVYDOV (Russian, Jewish), a patronymic name from the personal name DAVID. In some cases it is from DAVIDOVICH, shortened in America.
GIVEN NAMES Jewish 5%. *Ari*, *Arye*, *Dov*, *Dror*.

Davidov (153) Jewish (from Russia): see DAVIDOFF.
GIVEN NAMES Jewish 20%; Russian 12%; Spanish 8%. *Yaffa* (2), *Yakov* (2), *Asher*, *Doron*, *Ilya*, *Irina*, *Izia*, *Mazal*, *Mendy*, *Nissim*, *Simcha*; *Boris* (3), *Gennadiy*, *Georgy*, *Igor*, *Michail*, *Mikhail*, *Raisa*, *Vladimir*, *Vyacheslav*; *Carlos* (3), *Rafael* (3), *Margarita* (2), *Pablo*.

Davidovich (159) Ukrainian, Belorussian; Serbian and Croatian (**Davidović**); and Jewish (eastern Ashkenazic): patronymic from the personal name DAVID.
GIVEN NAMES Jewish 13%; Russian 9%. *Rina* (2), *Avi*, *Izya*, *Mendel*, *Rifka*, *Rivka*, *Tuvia*; *Boris* (2), *Svetlana* (2), *Arkadiy*, *Ayzik*, *Fima*, *Iosif*, *Yuriy*.

Davidow (262) Jewish (eastern Ashkenzic): see DAVIDOFF.
GIVEN NAMES Jewish 5%. *Sol* (2), *Ari*, *Moshe*, *Talya*.

Davidowitz (130) Jewish: Germanized spelling of the Polish form **Dawidowicz** or the Russian form **Davidovich**, patronymics from the personal name DAVID.
GIVEN NAMES Jewish 17%. *Avi* (2), *Moshe* (2), *Chana*, *Hershel*, *Yocheved*.

Davids (864) Dutch, English, and Jewish (Ashkenazic): patronymic from the personal name DAVID.

Davidsen (149) Norwegian and Danish: patronymic from the personal name DAVID.
GIVEN NAMES Scandinavian 15%. *Petter* (2), *Bendt*, *Erik*, *Knut*, *Oluf*.

Davidson (39384) **1.** Scottish, northern English, and Jewish (Ashkenazic): patronymic from the personal name DAVID. As a Jewish name, the last element comes from German *Sohn* 'son'. **2.** Americanized spelling of Norwegian and Danish **Davidsen** or Swedish **Davidsson**, patronymics from the personal name DAVID.

Davie (1177) **1.** Scottish: from the Scottish pet form of the personal name DAVID. **2.** English: variant of WAY (see below).
FOREBEARS A family whose name is now

found as Davie originated from Wey or Way near Torrington, Devon, England. Their earliest recorded ancestor was William de Wy or de la Wey, living in the reign of Henry II (1154–89). The name later occurred as de Vye and de Vie before being assimilated to a derivative of DAVID.

Davies (13668) Welsh and English: patronymic from the personal name *Davy* (Welsh *Dafydd*, *Dewi*), a pet form of DAVID.

Davignon (434) French: habitational name, with the preposition *d(e)*, denoting someone from Avignon in Vaucluse. The place name is said to be derived from an obscure pre-Roman element, *ab-ēn*, + the Latin suffix *-ionem*.

FOREBEARS François Davignon, also called Beauregard (his place of origin unrecorded), married Madeleine Maillot at Chambly, Quebec, in 1719, and the surname was in VT by 1816. The descendants of this couple also bear the surnames names DEVINO and **Burgor**.

GIVEN NAMES French 12%. *Jacques* (3), *Armand* (2), *Lucien* (2), *Marcel* (2), *Pierre* (2), *Adlore*, *Isabele*, *Jean Guy*, *Yves*.

Davila (4534) **1.** Spanish (**D'Ávila**): habitational name for someone from Ávila (see AVILA). **2.** Galician and Portuguese (**da Vila**): topographic name for someone 'from the village (*vila*)'.

GIVEN NAMES Spanish 45%; Portuguese 9%. *Jose* (106), *Juan* (63), *Carlos* (59), *Luis* (55), *Manuel* (46), *Jesus* (42), *Mario* (25), *Raul* (22), *Angel* (21), *Javier* (21), *Jorge* (21), *Pedro* (21); *Ligia* (2), *Afonso*, *Calixtro*, *Catarina*.

Da Villa (135) Galician and Portuguese: variant of **da Vila** (see DAVILA 2).

GIVEN NAMES Spanish 34%. *Felipe* (2), *Fernando* (2), *Ivette* (2), *Manuel* (2), *Miguel* (2), *Adriana*, *Alfredo*, *Armando*, *Carlos*, *Cesar*, *Esequiel*, *Gerado*.

Davin (557) **1.** Irish (Connacht and Munster): Anglicized form of Gaelic **Ó Duibhín** or **Ó Daimhín** (see DEVINE). **2.** French: from a pet form of DAVID.

Davino (319) **1.** Italian: either a habitational name for someone from Avino in Piedmont, or from the personal name *Davino*, a pet form of DAVID, via the hypothetical form *Davidino*. This was the name of an Italian saint who died in 1051 in Lucca. **2.** Americanized spelling of French DAVIGNON.

GIVEN NAMES Italian 18%. *Angelo* (5), *Salvatore* (4), *Carmine* (2), *Carlo*, *Dino*, *Domenic*, *Gaetano*, *Giuseppe*, *Pasquale*, *Rocco*.

Davio (108) Origin uncertain. There is some evidence for it as a French and French-Belgian name, but its etymology is unexplained. Despite its *-o* ending, it is not Italian.

Davis (354880) Southern English: patronymic from DAVID.

FOREBEARS John Davis or Davys (*c.* 1550–1605) was an English navigator who searched for the Northwest Passage.

By the 18th century there were numerous persons named Davis in America, including the jurist John Davis, born in 1761 in Plymouth, MA, and Henry Davis, a clergyman and college president, who was born in 1771 in East Hampton, NY. Jefferson Davis, born in 1808 in KY, was president of the Confederate States of America from 1861 to 1865.

Davison (8410) Northern English: patronymic from DAVID.

Davisson (1159) Northern English: patronymic from DAVID.

Davitt (484) Irish: reduced form of McDAVITT.

Davlin (198) Irish: variant of DEVLIN.

Davoli (171) Italian: habitational name from Davoli, a place in Catazaro province.

GIVEN NAMES Italian 24%. *Alfonse* (2), *Enrico* (2), *Giuseppe* (2), *Alberto*, *Antonio*, *Francesco*, *Guido*, *Pietro*, *Renato*.

Davolt (155) French: hypercorrected variant of **d'Avout**, literally 'of August' (see DAOUST).

Davoren (126) Irish: variant of DAVERN.

GIVEN NAME Irish 8%. *Brendan*.

Davy (1184) **1.** English and Irish: from the personal name *Davy*, a medieval French vernacular form of the Biblical name DAVID which became common in England in the Middle Ages. **2.** Scottish: variant spelling of DAVIE 1. **3.** French: variant of DAVID.

Davydov (128) Russian and Jewish (eastern Ashkenazic): patronymic name from the personal name DAVID.

GIVEN NAMES Russian 51%; Jewish 23%. *Boris* (7), *Mikhail* (7), *Aleksandr* (4), *Vyacheslav* (4), *Grigoriy* (3), *Anatoly* (2), *Iosif* (2), *Lev* (2), *Yuriy* (2), *Alexei*, *Alexey*, *Andrei*; *Yakov* (4), *Ilya* (3), *Avrum*, *Filipp*, *Gavriel*, *Isak*, *Nuriel*.

Daw (842) **1.** English and Scottish: from a pet form of DAVID. **2.** English: nickname from the jackdaw, Middle English *dawe*, a bird noted for its sleek black color, raucous voice, and thievish nature, any of which characteristics could readily have given rise to a nickname. **3.** Irish: Anglicized form of Gaelic **Ó Deaghaidh**, 'descendant of *Deaghadh*', a personal name of uncertain origin. It may be composed of the elements *deagh-* 'good' + *ádh* 'luck', 'fate'; some such association seems to lie behind its Anglicization as GOODWIN.

Dawdy (440) Possibly Irish, an Anglicized form of Gaelic **Ó Dubhda**, which has usually been Anglicized as **O'Dowd** (see DOWD), but also as DOWDA and DUDDY, forms which preserve the final vowel.

Dawe (734) English, Scottish, and Irish: variant spelling of DAW.

Dawes (2164) **1.** English and Scottish: patronymic from DAW 1. **2.** German

(**Däwes**): either a patronymic from a personal name *Davo*, or a variant spelling of TEWES.

FOREBEARS William Dawes (1745–99) was a prominent citizen of Boston, MA, and rode with Paul Revere to warn colonists of the British invasion in 1775. He is buried in Boston's King's Chapel Burying Ground.

Dawkins (3945) English: patronymic from a pet form of DAW 1.

Dawley (929) Irish: variant of DALY.

Dawn (429) English: patronymic from DAW 1. It is suggested by Reaney and Wilson that the unusual *-n* suffix is a late survival of an Old English genitive ending, which was later superseded by the familiar *-es* suffix.

Dawood (132) Muslim: see DAOUD.

GIVEN NAMES Muslim 70%. *Mohammad* (4), *Mohamed* (3), *Mohammed* (3), *Asif* (2), *Isam* (2), *Muhammad* (2), *Saira* (2), *Samir* (2), *Sultan* (2), *Ahmed*, *Amin*, *Ashraf*.

Daws (469) English: patronymic from DAW 1.

Dawsey (337) English: unexplained.

Dawson (27672) English: patronymic from DAW 1.

Dax (136) **1.** English: patronymic from DACK. **2.** Possibly an Americanized spelling of German **Dachs**, from Middle High German *dahs* 'badger'; hence a nickname for someone who hunted badgers or was thought to resemble the animal. **3.** French: habitational name, either from Dax in Landes or (with fused preposition *d(e)*) from Ax-les-Thermes in Ariège.

Day (38582) **1.** English: from a pet form of DAVID. **2.** English: from the Middle English personal name *Day(e)* or *Dey(e)*, Old English *Dæi*, apparently from Old English *dæg* 'day', perhaps a short form of Old English personal names such as *Dægberht* and *Dægmund*. Reaney, however, points to the Middle English word *day(e)*, *dey(e)* 'dairy maid', '(female) servant' (from Old English *dæge*, cognate with Old Norse *deigja* 'female servant', ultimately from a root meaning 'to knead', and related to the word for dough), which he says came to be used for a servant of either sex. **3.** Irish: Anglicized form of Gaelic **Ó Deaghaidh** (see O'DEA). **4.** Scottish: from an Anglicized form of the Gaelic personal name *Daidh*, a colloquial form of DAVID. **5.** Welsh: from *Dai*, a pet form of the personal name *Dafydd*, Welsh form of DAVID.

FOREBEARS This name was brought independently from many parts of Britain to New England by many bearers from the 17th century onward. Robert Day was one of the founders of Hartford, CT, (coming from Cambridge, MA, with Thomas Hooker) in 1635.

Dayal (130) Indian (northern states): Hindu (Kayasth) name, from Sanskrit *dayālu* 'kind', 'compassionate'. This also commonly occurs as the final element in compound given names such as **Ramdayal** 'Rama the Compassionate', **Shankardayal** 'Shankara the Compassionate'.

GIVEN NAMES Indian 87%. *Mahesh* (3), *Akhil* (2), *Hemant* (2), *Sandeep* (2), *Satish* (2), *Seema* (2), *Vibha* (2), *Vinay* (2), *Viresh* (2), *Vivek* (2), *Aditya, Alok*.

Dayan (296) Jewish: occupational name from Hebrew *dayan* 'rabbinic judge'.

GIVEN NAMES Jewish 20%; Jewish Biblical 4%. *Moshe* (4), *Nissim* (3), *Avi* (2), *Haim* (2), *Shimshon* (2), *Shlomo* (2), *Yair* (2), *Ofer, Yacov, Yariv, Yigal, Yonah*; *Shulamit*.

Daye (875) English: variant spelling of DAY.

Dayhoff (331) Americanized spelling of German DE HOFF.

Dayhuff (127) Americanized spelling of German DE HOFF.

Daykin (134) English: from a pet form of DAY.

Dayley (223) English (of Norman origin): habitational name, with fused Norman preposition *d(e)*, for someone from any of the numerous places in northern France called Ouilly.

Daymon (114) English: variant of **Dayman**, an occupational name for a herdsman or dairyman (see DAY). It was also used as a personal name.

Days (416) Welsh: patronymic from the personal name *Dai*, a pet form of *Dafydd* (see DAVID), with the redundant addition of the English patronymic suffix *-s*.

Dayton (3411) English: probably a variant spelling of DEIGHTON.

Daywalt (169) Americanized spelling of German DEWALD.

Daza (182) **1.** Spanish: probably a topographic name from *daza* 'sorghum'. **2.** Italian: probably a habitational name from Daza in Messina province, Sicily.

GIVEN NAMES Spanish 51%. *Jose* (4), *Luis* (4), *Arturo* (3), *Carlos* (3), *Fernando* (3), *Armando* (2), *Juan* (2), *Margarita* (2), *Mauricio* (2), *Ramiro* (2), *Rolando* (2), *Alfonso*; *Antonio, Federico, Guido, Lorenzo, Marco, Raniero*.

Dazey (195) Origin uncertain: probably an Americanized spelling of English DAISY or Irish DEASY.

D'Azzo (110) Italian: patronymic from the Germanic personal name *Azzo*, from a short form of various compound names beginning with the element *Adal* 'noble'.

GIVEN NAMES Italian 19%. *Salvatore* (2), *Benito, Calogero, Carlo*.

De (160) Indian: variant of DEY.

GIVEN NAMES Indian 39%. *Dilip* (3), *Anirban* (2), *Gopal* (2), *Alok, Anindya, Arunava, Asit, Asok, Dibyendu, Goutam, Indra, Indranil*.

Dea (338) **1.** Irish: reduced form of O'DEA. **2.** Chinese 谢: possibly a variant of XIE 1.

GIVEN NAMES Chinese 4%. *Suey* (5), *Hong* (2), *Kwong* (2), *Fook, Jin, Kit Ching, Lai, Ming, Suet, Wing, Yee*.

Deacon (1288) **1.** English: occupational name for a deacon, or perhaps more probably for his servant. In Middle English two forms coalesced: *deakne*, from Old English, and *diacne*, from Old French. Both are ultimately from Late Latin *diaconus*, from Greek *diakonos* 'servant'. **2.** Irish: when not of English origin; it was taken to Ireland in the 17th century, it may be an Anglicized form of Gaelic **Ó Deocáin** 'descendant of *Deocán*', a personal name of uncertain derivation and meaning.

Deacy (127) Irish: variant spelling of DACEY.

Deaderick (106) Americanized form of Dutch **Diederik** (see DEDERICK).

Deadmond (133) Origin uncertain; probably a variant of English DEDMAN, itself a variant of DEBNAM.

Deadrick (118) Americanized form of Dutch **Diederik** (see DEDERICK).

Deadwyler (162) Americanized form of the Swiss German habitational name **Dettweiler** (see DETWILER).

Deady (375) Irish (Counties Kerry and Limerick): Anglicized form of Gaelic **Ó Déadaigh** 'descendant of *Déadach*', a personal name apparently meaning 'toothy'.

GIVEN NAME Irish 5%. *John Patrick* (2).

Deagle (109) **1.** English: variant of DIGGLE. **2.** Possibly also a respelling of German **Degel** or **Dägele** (see DAGLE).

Deahl (245) Americanized spelling of German DIEHL.

Deak (479) **1.** Hungarian (**Deák**): occupational or status name for a notary, scholar, priest teacher, or someone who could write in medieval Latin, *deák*. In old Hungarian texts the word *deák* refers to the Latin language, which was officially used in Hungary both in secular and ecclesiastical writing as late as the 18th century. The surname is also found in Austria, where it is sometimes spelled **Deack**. **2.** Possibly an Americanized spelling of German DIECK.

GIVEN NAMES Hungarian 6%. *Bela* (2), *Imre* (2), *Mihaly* (2), *Akos, Gabor, Istvan, Laszlo, Tibor*.

Deakin (419) English and Irish: variant spelling of DEACON.

Deakins (522) English: patronymic form of DEAKIN.

Deakle (106) Americanized form of German **Degel** or **Dägele** (see DAGLE).

Deakyne (100) Probably a variant spelling of English and Irish DEACON.

Deal (7314) **1.** English: variant of DALE (from the Old Kentish form *del*) or a habitational name from Deal in Kent, named with this word. **2.** Americanized spelling of German DIE(H)L.

De Alba (244) Spanish: habitational name for someone from any of numerous minor places named with the word *alba*, thought be derived either from a pre-Roman word meaning 'hill fort', 'fortified settlement' or from Latin *albus* 'white', as for example

Alba (Teruel), Alba de Tormes (Salamanca).

GIVEN NAMES Spanish 44%. *Jose* (6), *Roberto* (5), *Alfonso* (3), *Fernando* (3), *Jesus* (3), *Juan* (3), *Ramon* (3), *Felipe* (2), *Manuel* (2), *Margarita* (2), *Maria Elena* (2), *Ricardo* (2).

Deale (124) English: variant spelling of DEAL.

De Almeida (199) Spanish and Portuguese: habitational name for someone 'from (*de*) ALMEIDA'.

GIVEN NAMES Spanish 31%; Portuguese 23%. *Manuel* (6), *Jose* (4), *Ana* (3), *Carlos* (3), *Julio* (2), *Lino* (2), *Luis* (2), *Mauricio* (2), *Nilo* (2), *Sergio* (2), *Adriana, Adriano*; *Joaquim* (6), *Henrique, Joao, Serafim*; *Antonio* (4), *Leonardo, Lia*.

Dealy (287) Irish: variant spelling of DEELEY, though in County Cork it may be a variant of DALY.

Deam (217) **1.** Irish: see DEMPSTER. **2.** Americanized spelling of German DIEM, or the variant DIEHM.

Deamer (185) **1.** Irish: see DEMPSTER. **2.** Americanized spelling of German DIEMER.

De Amicis (140) Italian: patronymic from the personal name AMICO, but here probably in the broader sense 'member of the Amici family'.

GIVEN NAMES Italian 14%. *Aldo, Dante, Eliseo, Franco, Giancarlo, Giulio, Guido, Libero, Lido*.

Dean (39048) **1.** English: topographic name from Middle English *dene* 'valley' (Old English *denu*), or a habitational name from any of several places in various parts of England named Dean, Deane, or Deen from this word. In Scotland this is a habitational name from Den in Aberdeenshire or Dean in Ayrshire. **2.** English: occupational name for the servant of a dean or nickname for someone thought to resemble a dean. A dean was an ecclesiastical official who was the head of a chapter of canons in a cathedral. The Middle English word *deen* is a borrowing of Old French *d(e)ien*, from Latin *decanus* (originally a leader of ten men, from *decem* 'ten'), and thus is a cognate of DEACON. **3.** Irish: variant of DEANE. **4.** Italian: occupational name cognate with 2, from Venetian *dean* 'dean', a dialect form of *degan*, from *degano* (Italian *decano*).

De Anda (929) Spanish: habitational name for someone 'from Anda', a place in Araba province, Basque Country, named with Basque *an* 'hill' (see ANDA).

GIVEN NAMES Spanish 45%. *Jose* (24), *Raul* (18), *Juan* (11), *Jesus* (9), *Carlos* (8), *Jaime* (8), *Luis* (8), *Manuel* (8), *Eduardo* (6), *Lupe* (6), *Mario* (6), *Rodolfo* (6).

De Andrade (156) Galician and Portuguese: habitational name for someone from a place called Andrade (see ANDRADE).

GIVEN NAMES Spanish 20%; Portuguese 17%; Italian 8%; French 5%. *Jose* (5), *Manuel* (5), *Armando* (2), *Geraldo* (2), *Gustavo* (2), *Alvaro*, *Ana Paula*, *Domingos*, *Fernando*, *Jacinto*, *Luis*, *Marcelo*; *Joao* (2), *Agostinho*; *Antonio* (2), *Alfonse*, *Dino*, *Italo*, *Philomena*; *Charlet*, *Clovis*.

De Andrea (134) Italian: patronymic from the personal name *Andrea* (see ANDREAS).
GIVEN NAMES Italian 10%. *Angelo*, *Guido*, *Marco*, *Rocco*.

Deane (2450) **1.** Irish: in County Donegal this is an Anglicized form of Gaelic **Mac an Deagánaigh** 'son of the deacon' (see DEACON); in County Tipperary it can be from Gaelic **Ó Déaghain** 'descendant of the deacon'. In other cases the surname is of English origin (see DEAN 1). **2.** English: variant of DEAN 1.

Deaner (400) **1.** Southern English: topographic name for someone who lived in a valley, from Middle English *dene* 'valley' (see DEAN 1) + the suffix *-er* denoting an inhabitant. **2.** Americanized spelling of German and Jewish DIENER.

De Angelis (3017) Italian: patronymic from the personal name ANGELO, but here probably in the broader sense 'member of the Angeli family'. Alternatively, this may have been a name bestowed on a foundling in the sense 'from the angels'.
GIVEN NAMES Italian 13%. *Angelo* (13), *Domenic* (7), *Salvatore* (7), *Guido* (6), *Antonio* (4), *Pasquale* (4), *Rocco* (4), *Franco* (3), *Gaetano* (3), *Geno* (3), *Marco* (3), *Nicola* (3).

De Angelo (1560) Italian: patronymic from the personal name ANGELO.
GIVEN NAMES Italian 10%. *Salvatore* (9), *Angelo* (4), *Domenic* (3), *Mauro* (3), *Rocco* (2), *Vito* (2), *Antonio*, *Carlo*, *Carmine*, *Cesare*, *Dante*, *Elio*.

Deans (1245) Scottish: patronymic meaning 'son (or servant) of the dean' (see DEAN).

De Antonio (104) Variant of Italian D'ANTONIO.
GIVEN NAMES Italian 12%; Spanish 9%. *Antonio*, *Ciro*, *Gino*, *Pasquale*; *Angel* (2), *Alicia*, *Maria Elida*, *Ramon*.

Dear (1139) English: **1.** from the Middle English personal name *Dere*, Old English *Dēora*, in part a short form of various compound names formed with *dēore* 'dear', in part a byname meaning 'beloved', or *dēor* 'brave', 'bold'. **2.** nickname from Middle English *dere*, Old English *dēor* 'wild animal', or from the adjective of the same form, meaning 'wild', 'fierce'. By the Middle English period the adjective was falling out of use, and the noun was beginning to be restricted to the sense of modern English *deer*, so that this may be the sense behind the surname in some cases.

De Araujo (105) Portuguese and Galician: habitational name for someone from a place called Araujo (see ARAUJO).

GIVEN NAMES Spanish 36%; Portuguese 19%. *Carlos* (4), *Jose* (3), *Manuel* (3), *Luis* (2), *Marcelo* (2), *Sergio* (2), *Ailton*, *Armando*, *Augusto*, *Berenice*, *Frederico*, *Luiz*; *Henrique*, *Joaquim*.

Dearborn (1213) English: unexplained.
FOREBEARS Godfrey Dearborn (baptized September 24, 1603 in Willoughby, Lincolnshire, England) came to North America in 1639 and settled in Hampton, NH, where he died on February 4, 1686.

Dearden (475) English (Lancashire): habitational name from a place near Edenfield named Dearden, from Old English *dēor* 'beast', 'deer' + *denu* 'valley'.

Deardorff (1105) Americanized spelling of German **Dierdorf**, a habitational name from Dierdorf, a place near Koblenz.

Deardurff (123) Americanized spelling of German **Dierdorf** (see DEARDORFF).

Dearie (123) English: variant spelling of DEARY.
GIVEN NAME Scandinavian 4%. *Disa* (2).

Dearing (2098) **1.** English: patronymic from DEAR 1. **2.** Americanized spelling of German **Diering**, a variant of **Döring** (see DOERING).

Dearinger (291) Americanized spelling of German DIERINGER.

Dearman (1200) **1.** English: from a Middle English personal name, *Derman* (Old English *Dēormann*), meaning either 'beloved man' or 'spirited man' (from *dēor* 'wild creature'). See DEAR 1. **2.** Variant of Irish DEARMOND. **3.** Probably an Americanized spelling of German **Diermann** or **Thiermann**, which derive from short forms of the personal name DIETRICH or perhaps from Middle High German *tier* 'animal', 'game' + *man* 'man' and thus denote a game or venison dealer.

De Armas (386) Portuguese: from the plural of *arma* 'weapon', presumably a metonymic occupational name for someone who made or bore arms.
GIVEN NAMES Spanish 57%. *Raul* (9), *Mario* (7), *Jesus* (6), *Jorge* (6), *Alberto* (5), *Juan* (5), *Luis* (5), *Orlando* (5), *Pedro* (5), *Jose* (4), *Miguel* (4), *Rafael* (4).

Dearment (157) Variant of Irish DEARMOND.

Dearmin (97) Variant of Irish DEARMOND or English DEARMAN.

Dearmitt (119) Variant of Irish DERMOTT or DEARMOND.
GIVEN NAME French 4%. *Damien*.

Dearmon (341) Variant of Irish DEARMOND or English DEARMAN.

Dearmond (774) Irish: variant of **Dermond**, a reduced Anglicized form of Gaelic **Ó Duibhdhiorma** 'descendant of *Duibhdhiorma*' a personal name meaning 'black trooper' (see DORMER 3). There has been some confusion between the personal names *Duibhdhiorma* and *Diarmaid*, so that **Dearmond** alternates with MCDERMOTT.

Dearmore (110) Probably a variant of Irish DEARMOND.
GIVEN NAME French 4%. *Clovis*.

Dearth (921) English: nickname from Middle English *derth* 'famine' (of uncertain application) or *de(e)th* 'death', Old English *dēað*. The latter name would have been acquired by someone who had played the part of the personified figure of Death in a pageant or play, or else one who was habitually gloomy or sickly, and the insertion of the letter *-r-* may have been a deliberate attempt to dissociate the name from *death*.

Dearwester (102) Of German origin; see DEERWESTER.

Deary (268) English: **1.** nickname for a noisy or troublesome person, from Anglo-French *de(s)rei* 'noise', 'trouble', 'turbulence' (from Old French *desroi*). **2.** topographic for someone who lived by a deer enclosure, from Old English *dēor* 'deer' + *(ge)hæg* 'enclosure'.

Deas (1095) Scottish and English: from Old French *dez* 'dice', hence a metonymic occupational name for a maker or seller of dice, or a nickname for an habitual player at dice. Compare DICE.

Dease (374) Irish (Gaelic **Déise**): habitational name from Deece in County Meath.

Deason (2088) English: patronymic from DAY (1 and 2).

Deasy (503) Irish: variant of DACEY.
GIVEN NAMES Irish 5%. *Brennan*, *Oonagh*, *Siobhan*.

Deater (152) Americanized spelling of German DIETER.

Deatherage (1080) Variant spelling of English DETHERAGE.

Deatley (264) Americanized spelling of South German **Dietl**, from a pet form of DIETRICH.

Deaton (5033) English: probably a variant spelling of DEIGHTON.

Deatrick (223) Americanized spelling of German DIETRICH or Dutch **Diederik** (see DEDERICK).

Deats (334) Americanized spelling of German DIETZ.

Deaver (1712) **1.** Irish: variant of DEVER. **2.** Perhaps a respelling of German **Düwer**, **Düver**, from Middle Low German *düver* 'male pigeon', hence a nickname for someone thought to resemble the bird or a metonymic occupational name for a dove keeper.

Deavers (513) Irish: variant of DEAVER, with the addition of the English patronymic suffix *-s*.

De Avila (164) Spanish (**De Ávila**): variant of Spanish **D'Ávila** (see DAVILA 1).
GIVEN NAMES Spanish 48%; Portuguese 16%. *Jose* (6), *Jesus* (4), *Luis* (4), *Francisco* (3), *Manuel* (3), *Miguel* (3), *Alfredo* (2), *Carlos* (2), *Esperanza* (2), *Gerardo* (2), *Javier* (2), *Jorge* (2); *Joao*.

Debaca (104) Probably a short form of the Spanish family name **Cabeza de Vaca** (see CDEBACA).
GIVEN NAMES Spanish 14%. *Manuel* (2), *Benito, Elena, Isela, Leandro, Miguel, Nestor, Tomas, Tomasita.*

De Bacco (123) Italian: variant of DI BACCO.
GIVEN NAMES Italian 6%. *Deno, Sante.*

De Backer (227) Dutch: **1.** occupational name from Middle Dutch *de backere* 'the baker'. **2.** occupational name from Middle Dutch *de backer* 'the ferryman'.
GIVEN NAMES French 10%. *Achille, Florent, Francoise, Lucien, Marcel, Michel, Pierre.*

Debaere (118) **1.** Dutch: nickname from Middle Dutch *baer* 'bare', 'naked' + the definite article *de*, i.e. 'the bare (one)'. **2.** Belgian French: variant of DEBAR.

De Baker (121) Dutch: variant of DE BACKER.

Debar (104) French: habitational name for someone from a place named Bar, in Aveyron, Ardennes, and Corrèze, or possibly Bar-sur-Aube in Champagne or Bar-sur-Seine in Aube.
GIVEN NAMES French 6%. *Laurent, Pierre.*

De Bardelaben (107) Dutch: unexplained.

Debarge (123) French (Walloon): habitational name for someone from Barges in Hainault, Belgium.

De Bari (110) Italian: variant of DI BARI.
GIVEN NAMES Italian 18%. *Corrado, Nichola, Nunzia, Onofrio, Salvatore, Vito.*

Debarr (198) Probably a respelling of DEBAR.

De Barros (207) Portuguese: habitational name for someone 'from (*de*) Barros', of which there are numerous examples, all named from the plural of *barro* 'clay'.
GIVEN NAMES Spanish 19%; Portuguese 15%; French 7%. *Manuel* (7), *Marcelo* (3), *Isaura* (2), *Jose* (2), *Raul* (2), *Roberto* (2), *Dominga, Fernando, Francisco, Lauro, Mario, Natalio; Paulo* (2), *Almir, Joao, Joaquim, Manoel, Vasco; Armand, Celina, Jean Claude, Jean-Pierre, Micheline, Napoleon.*

De Bartolo (355) Italian: variant of DI BARTOLO.
GIVEN NAMES Italian 23%. *Santo* (3), *Vito* (3), *Cosmo* (2), *Luigi* (2), *Mario* (2), *Orlando* (2), *Paola* (2), *Saverio* (2), *Aldo, Angelo, Assunta, Carmella, Carmine, Enrico, Francesco, Giuseppe, Gregoria, Ignazio.*

Debates (153) Possibly an altered spelling of Walloon **Debatis**, a topographic name, with the preposition *de*, from *bati* 'common land', 'village green', or a habitational name for someone from a place named with this word, for example Batty in Nandrain or Le Baty in Xhoris, both in the Belgian province of Liège, or Les Battis in Laneffe, Namur.

Debauche (219) French: habitational name for someone from La Bauche in Savoy, named from *boscus* 'wood'.

Debaun (266) Dutch: unexplained.

Debban (110) German or Dutch: unexplained. Perhaps a variant of German DEPPEN or Dutch **de Baan**, **Debanne**, from Middle Dutch *bane* 'fives court', 'games court'.
GIVEN NAME German 4%. *Kurt.*

De Beck (133) Dutch: derogatory nickname meaning 'the (animal's) mouth'.

De Beer (151) Dutch and Jewish (from the Netherlands): nickname for someone thought to resemble a bear or a boar, from Dutch *beer* 'bear', 'boar' + the definite article *de*.
GIVEN NAMES Dutch 7%; German 4%; French 4%. *Gerrit, Harm, Thys; Hans, Otto; Jacques* (2).

Debelak (147) Slovenian: nickname from *debelak, debeljak* 'fat person', from *debel* 'fat'. It may also represent a simplified spelling of the Slovenian and Croatian surname **Debeljak**, which has the same meaning. Compare DEBEVEC.

Debell (316) English: nickname from French *debile* 'feeble' (Latin *debil, debilis*).

De Bella (187) Italian: see DI BELLA. In Italy **De Bella** is the more frequent form.
GIVEN NAMES Italian 9%. *Sal* (2), *Salvato, Salvatore, Santo.*

De Bellis (555) Italian: patronymic from the personal name BELLO, but here probably in the broader sense 'of the Belli family'.
GIVEN NAMES Italian 22%. *Mario* (6), *Vito* (4), *Domenico* (3), *Lorenzo* (3), *Americo* (2), *Angelo* (2), *Gerardo* (2), *Luca* (2), *Pasquale* (2), *Salvatore* (2), *Alfonse, Carlo, Cosmo, Catalina, Elena, Elvira, Emanuele, Gaetano, Isidoro, Julio, Salvadore.*

De Bello (181) Italian: see DI BELLO.
GIVEN NAMES Italian 12%. *Rocco* (2), *Angelo, Settimo.*

De Benedetti (150) Italian: patronymic from the personal name BENEDETTO.
GIVEN NAMES Italian 18%. *Dario* (2), *Mario* (2), *Sergio* (2), *Aldo, Arrigo.*

De Benedetto (366) Italian: patronymic from the personal name BENEDETTO.
GIVEN NAMES Italian 16%. *Rocco* (4), *Aldo* (2), *Antonio, Camillo, Corrado, Domenic, Enrico, Guido, Luigi, Marco, Mauro, Ral.*

De Benedictis (379) Italian: patronymic from a variant of the personal name BENEDETTO, in the broader sense 'of the Benedicti family'.
GIVEN NAMES Italian 19%. *Vito* (5), *Angelo* (3), *Aldo* (2), *Carlo* (2), *Carmine* (2), *Pasquale* (2), *Dante, Dario, Dino, Ezio, Lorenzo, Nicola.*

De Berardinis (145) Italian: patronymic from *Berardino*, a pet form of the personal name BERARDO, in the broader sense 'member of the Berardino family'.
GIVEN NAMES Italian 17%. *Caesar* (2), *Santino* (2), *Antonio, Attilio, Dante, Domenic, Giancarlo, Gilda, Marino, Romeo, Sante.*

De Berg (141) Dutch: from Middle Dutch *berg, barg* 'castrated pig', possibly applied as a metonymic occupational name for someone who castrated animals.

De Bernardi (198) Italian: see DI BERNARDO.
GIVEN NAMES Italian 7%. *Gilio* (2), *Attilio, Cesare, Dario, Domenic.*

De Bernardo (124) Italian: see DI BERNARDO.
GIVEN NAMES Italian 27%. *Angelo* (3), *Carlo* (2), *Gino, Luigi, Marcello, Pasquale, Reno, Vincenzo.*

Deberry (1561) Northern French: habitational name for someone from Berry-au-Bac in Aisne, France.

Debes (202) **1.** French (**Debès**): topographic name from Church Latin *bettiu* 'birch tree', 'birch wood' (from Gaulish *betu*), or a habitational name from any of the places named with this word, of which there are examples in Dordogne, Isère, and Puy-de-Dôme. **2.** German: variant of DEBUS. **3.** Hungarian: from the old secular personal name *Debes*.
GIVEN NAMES German 4%. *Otto* (2), *Inge.*

Debevec (156) Slovenian: nickname from *debelec* 'fat person', from *debel* 'fat'. Compare DEBELAK.

Debevoise (102) Possibly a reduced form of French **Debeauvois**, a habitational name for someone from a place called Beauvois, examples of which are found in Aisne, Nord, Pas-de-Calais.

De Biase (396) Italian: see DI BIASE. In Italy **De Biase** is the more frequent form.
GIVEN NAMES Italian 15%. *Angelo* (3), *Sal* (2), *Salvatore* (2), *Attilio, Cosmo, Domenic, Gaetano, Gino, Giuseppe, Guido, Marco, Rocco.*

De Blanc (168) Dutch: nickname for a pale person or one with blond hair (see BLANC).

De Blase (113) Italian: variant of DI BIASE.
GIVEN NAMES Italian 15%. *Angelo, Carmine.*

De Blasi (151) Italian: variant of DI BIASE.
GIVEN NAMES Italian 15%. *Angelo* (2), *Antonio, Duilio, Pasquale, Sal, Salvatore, Ugo.*

De Blasio (518) Italian: variant of DI BIASE.
GIVEN NAMES Italian 10%. *Vito* (3), *Aldo, Alessandra, Antonio, Carlo, Dante, Guido, Natale, Nichola, Pasquale, Philomena.*

De Blieck (135) Dutch: **1.** nickname from Middle Dutch *de bliec* 'the sprat'. **2.** patronymic from the medieval personal name *Bliec*.

De Block (185) Dutch: nickname for a man of stocky build, from Middle Dutch *de bloc* 'the block or chunk'.

Deblois (551) French: habitational name, with the preposition *de* 'from', for someone from Blois in Loir-et-Cher.
GIVEN NAMES French 11%. *Andre* (2), *Armand* (2), *Rosaire* (2), *Amelie, Damien, Emile, Fernand, Herve, Jacques, Jean Guy, Monique, Ovide.*

Debnam (316) English: habitational name for someone from Debenham in Suffolk, probably named from the genitive case of the Old English river name *Dēope* 'deep one' + Old English *hām* 'homestead'.
GIVEN NAMES French 4%. *Almira, Renella.*

Debo (267) **1.** Anglicized spelling of French **De Baux**, a habitational name for someone from Baux. This is a Huguenot name, found as such in England and the Netherlands. **2.** In North America, it is also found as a variant of DEBOSE.

De Board (532) Americanized spelling of French DEBORD.

De Bock (119) Dutch: **1.** from *de bok* 'the he-goat', applied as a nickname for a man thought to resemble a he-goat, or, alternatively, a metonymic occupational name for a goatherd. **2.** Debrabandere suggests that the name is also possibly a patronymic from a personal name that was reinterpreted as *bok* 'he-goat', 'buck'.
GIVEN NAMES French 9%. *Florent, Gabrielle, Georges.*

Deboe (200) **1.** French: variant of DUBOIS. **2.** Dutch: variant of **de Bode**, an occupational name (with definite article *de*) for a messenger.
GIVEN NAMES French 4%. *Marthe, Pierre.*

De Boer (3066) Dutch: occupational name for a farmer or landsman, from Middle Dutch *boer, boor*, with the definite article *de*. See also BAUER.
GIVEN NAMES Dutch 4%. *Dirk* (5), *Gerrit* (5), *Douwe* (4), *Hendrik* (3), *Frans* (2), *Hendrick* (2), *Klaas* (2), *Maarten* (2), *Auke, Coert, Cor, Cornelis.*

Debois (138) French: variant of DUBOIS.

Debold (251) German: variant of DIEBOLD.

Debolt (1131) German: variant of DIEBOLD.

De Bona (142) Italian: variant of DI BONA.
GIVEN NAMES Italian 11%. *Angelo* (2), *Margherita, Rocco.*

De Bonis (436) Italian: patronymic from the medieval personal name BONO, in the broader sense 'of the Boni family'.
GIVEN NAMES Italian 9%. *Flavio* (2), *Rocco* (2), *Aldo, Carmine, Domenic, Ercole, Filomena, Giacomo, Nicolina, Silvio.*

De Bono (208) Italian and Spanish: patronymic from the medieval personal name BONO.
GIVEN NAMES French 7%; Italian 6%; Spanish 4%. *Emile, Georges, Sauveur; Carmel, Carmela, Mario, Sal; Manuel* (2).

Debord (1332) French: **1.** habitational name, with the preposition *de* 'from', for someone from a place called Bord, in Creuse, or from either of two places called Bort, in Puy-de-Dôme and Corrèze. **2.** possibly a topographic name for someone who lived at the side of a road, river, or similar, from *bord* 'border', 'edge'.

Deborde (259) Variant spelling of French DEBORD.

Debose (531) Americanized form of French DUBOIS. This is well established as an African-American name, inherited from 18th-century slave owners in SC.

Debow (378) **1.** Americanized spelling of French **Debaux** (see DEBO) or DEBOSE. **2.** Americanized form of Dutch DEBOE.

Deboy (173) Americanized form of French DUBOIS.

Debree (119) **1.** Origin uncertain. Probably a respelling of French **Debré: 2.** patronymic from the personal name *Bré*, a variant of *Bref* meaning 'small'. **3.** habitational name for someone from any of various places called Bry(e), Brie, or Bré, in particular a locality in Peyreleau in Aveyron and another in Bégard, Côtes-d'Armor.

De Brito (130) Galician and Portuguese: habitational name for someone from any of various places named Brito.
GIVEN NAMES Spanish 16%; Portuguese 13%. *Fernando* (2), *Luis* (2), *Manuel* (2), *Pedro* (2), *Alvaro, Angelina, Belmira, Carlos, Jose; Margarida, Serafim; Angelo* (2), *Antonio* (2).

De Brock (115) Dutch: habitational name, with French preposition *de* 'from', for someone from a place named Broek, from Dutch *broek* 'morass', 'bog'.
GIVEN NAME French 4%. *Edouard.*

Debrosse (158) French: topographic name for someone who lived in an area of scrub, from Old French *broce* 'brushwood', 'scrub' (Late Latin *bruscia*). Occasionally it may be a metonymic occupational name for a brush maker, from the same word used in the transferred sense 'brush'.
GIVEN NAMES French 19%. *Francois* (2), *Gaston, Jacques, Leonie, Lucien, Micheline, Mireille, Pierre, Serge, Solange.*

Debroux (203) French: habitational name, with the preposition *de* 'from', denoting someone from either of two places called Broux, in Rhône and Vienne.
GIVEN NAMES French 6%. *Dominique* (2), *Alphonse, Etienne.*

Debruhl (236) Dutch: topographic name for someone living by a marshy area, from Middle Dutch *de brûl* 'the marshy area'. Compare German BRUEHL.

De Bruin (627) Dutch: nickname meaning 'the brown one', i.e. someone who had brown hair or who habitually wore brown, Middle Dutch *brune*.
GIVEN NAMES Dutch 4%. *Maarten* (3), *Gerrit* (2), *Hendrik* (2), *Annick, Cornelis, Marinus.*

Debruler (187) French: of uncertain origin. It may be an altered form of **Debruille** or **Debrulle** (see DEBRUHL).
FOREBEARS The name is believed to have been brought to North America by Jean or Georges De Bruler, who came from Orléans, France, to MD in the late 17th century.

De Bruyn (430) Dutch: variant spelling (17th century) of DE BRUIN.

GIVEN NAMES German 5%; Dutch 5%. *Hans* (5), *Otto* (3), *Erna; Dirk* (2), *Antoon, Emiel, Pieter, Wim.*

De Bruyne (187) Dutch: variant spelling (17th century) of DE BRUIN.
GIVEN NAME French 4%. *Jacques.*

Debs (189) French: from the personal name *Debus*, a variant of *Theb(u)s*, itself a short form of *Matthaeus* (see MATTHEW).
GIVEN NAMES Spanish 6%; French 4%. *Pablo* (4), *Carlos* (2), *Eduardo* (2), *Luis* (2); *Pierre* (2).

Debski (160) Polish (**Dębski**): habitational name for someone from any of various places called Dębie, Dębsk, or Dęby, named with *dąb* 'oak'. See also DEMBSKI, DEMSKI.
GIVEN NAMES Polish 25%. *Jerzy* (4), *Zygmunt* (2), *Andrzej, Dorota, Grazyna, Jozef, Miroslaw, Ryszard, Stanislaw, Tadeusz, Tomasz, Witold.*

De Buhr (205) North German: occupational name or nickname for a farmer, from the Low German definite article *de* + *buhr*, *boer* 'peasant', 'farmer' (see BAUER).
GIVEN NAME Dutch 4%. *Harm* (3).

Debus (351) **1.** German: from a personal name, a much altered variant of *Matthäus* (see MATTHEW). **2.** French: habitational name, with the preposition *de* 'from', for someone from any of various places named Bus (from a regional form of *bois* 'wood') in Eure, Pas-de-Calais, and Somme.

Debusk (727) Probably an altered spelling of the Dutch habitational name **Deboske**, itself a Frenchified form of VANDENBOSCH.

Debutts (101) **1.** Origin unidentified. Perhaps an altered form of Dutch **De But(te): 2.** from Middle Dutch *but(te), bot(te)* 'pannier', 'box', presumably a metonymic occupational name. **3.** from *but(te), bot(te)* 'flat fish', 'flounder', hence a nickname for someone thought to resemble the fish, or a metonymic occupational name for a fisherman or fish seller.

Dec (374) **1.** Czech (**Deč**): ethnic name for a German, from German *Deutsch*. **2.** Polish: from a pet form of the personal name *Dionizy*, Polish form of *Dionysius* (see DENNIS).
GIVEN NAMES Polish 9%. *Aleksander, Andrzej, Casimir, Ignacy, Jerzy, Krystyna, Krzysztof, Malgorzata, Mikolaj, Stanislaw, Tadeusz.*

Decaire (154) Origin unidentified. Possibly an American French respelling of German DECKER.

Decamp (1014) Dutch and North German: from *de camp* 'the field', hence a topographic name, or a status name denoting a small farmer.

De Candia (144) Italian: habitational name for someone from Crete or, specifically, from its capital Iraklion, formerly known as *Candia*. The name is from Arabic *qandi* 'rock sugar', transferred to Crete because

the Arabs had established a sugar refinery there; *Candia* is thus cognate with the American word *candy*. Crete was under Venetian rule at the time of surname formation.
GIVEN NAMES Italian 29%; French 4%. *Corrado* (2), *Rocco* (2), *Carmine*, *Domenic*, *Fabrizio*, *Giordano*, *Giuseppe*, *Luigi*, *Oronzo*; *Odette*, *Odile*.

De Canio (116) Italian: patronymic from the personal name *Canio* (from Latin *Canius* meaning 'white-haired'), borne by a 3rd-century martyr.
GIVEN NAMES Italian 12%. *Sal* (2), *Vito* (2), *Carmela*, *Rogelio*.

De Caprio (183) Italian: variant of DI CAPRIO.
GIVEN NAMES Italian 11%. *Angelo* (2), *Domenic*, *Edo*, *Filomena*, *Pasquale*.

De Capua (173) Italian: variant of DI CAPUA.
GIVEN NAMES Italian 13%. *Angelo* (3), *Concetta*, *Domenic*, *Libero*, *Nunzie*, *Salvatore*.

De Cardenas (108) Spanish: (**De Cárdenas**): habitational name for someone from Cárdenas, a place in Burgos province (see CARDENAS).
GIVEN NAMES Spanish 48%. *Alberto* (8), *Jorge* (5), *Juan* (3), *Raul* (3), *Silvio* (3), *Alfredo* (2), *Andres* (2), *Emilio* (2), *Jose* (2), *Mario* (2), *Mateo* (2).

De Carli (212) Italian: variant of DI CARLO.
GIVEN NAMES Italian 10%. *Angelo* (3), *Massimo* (2), *Geno*, *Maurizio*, *Silvio*.

De Carlo (2117) Italian: variant of DI CARLO.
GIVEN NAMES Italian 11%. *Vito* (14), *Angelo* (6), *Rocco* (6), *Cesare* (4), *Salvatore* (4), *Antonio* (3), *Carmine* (3), *Domenic* (2), *Francesco* (2), *Aldo*, *Caesar*, *Carlo*.

De Caro (622) Italian and Spanish (Navarre): patronymic from the medieval personal name CARO.
GIVEN NAMES Italian 21%; Spanish 5%. *Angelo* (15), *Salvatore* (5), *Antonio* (3), *Mario* (3), *Sal* (3), *Caesar* (2), *Vito* (2), *Armando*, *Arturo*, *Carmel*, *Carmelo*, *Bernardina*, *Francesco*, *Franco*, *Giuseppe*, *Matteo*; *Elvira*, *Jacinta*, *Trinidad*.

De Carolis (328) Italian: patronymic from a Latinized form of the personal name *Carlo* (see CHARLES), in the broader sense 'of or belonging to the Carli family'.
GIVEN NAMES Italian 20%. *Angelo* (4), *Antonio* (3), *Dino* (2), *Rocco* (2), *Vito* (2), *Amedeo*, *Berardino*, *Domenico*, *Enrico*, *Ercole*, *Erminio*, *Ezio*.

De Carvalho (133) Portuguese: habitational name for someone from any of numerous places called Carvalho, from *carvalho* 'oak' (compare CARVALHO), or a topographic name with the same meaning.
GIVEN NAMES Spanish 22%; Portuguese 21%; French 5%; Italian 5%. *Jose* (6), *Carlos* (3), *Manuel* (3), *Fernando* (2), *Ricardo* (2),

Ruy (2); *Albano*, *Joao*, *Marcio*; *Andre* (2), *Aide*; *Antonio* (3), *Albertina*, *Fausto*.

De Castro (1026) Galician and Portuguese: habitational name for someone from any of various places named with CASTRO 'castle', 'fortress'.
GIVEN NAMES Spanish 31%. *Jose* (18), *Carlos* (11), *Luis* (8), *Armando* (6), *Mario* (6), *Alfredo* (4), *Jorge* (4), *Julio* (4), *Manuel* (4), *Ricardo* (4), *Rolando* (4), *Alvaro* (2), *Antonio* (11), *Silvio* (2), *Adalgisa*, *Alessandro*, *Angelo*, *Donato*, *Franco*, *Gino*, *Ignazio*, *Leonardo*, *Marco*, *Romeo*.

Decato (161) Origin uncertain; perhaps a variant of DECATUR.
GIVEN NAMES French 6%. *Emile*, *Ovide*.

Decatur (333) Variant of Dutch **de Caters**, a nickname for someone thought to resemble a tomcat (see KATER).

De Cecco (160) Italian: variant of DI CICCO.
GIVEN NAMES Italian 13%. *Angelo* (2), *Carlo*, *Dante*, *Luigi*, *Secondo*.

Decell (104) Probably a respelling of French DECELLE.

Decelle (186) French: topographic name for someone who lived near a monk's hermitage, from ecclesiastic Latin *cella* 'cell', 'hermitage', or a habitational name from any of the widespread and numerous places named with this word.

Decelles (202) French: variant of DECELLE.
GIVEN NAMES French 9%. *Adrien*, *Amedee*, *Camille*, *Cecile*, *Philippe*.

De Cesare (706) Italian: variant of DI CESARE.
GIVEN NAMES Italian 12%. *Angelo* (3), *Carmine* (2), *Gaetano* (2), *Gino* (2), *Marco* (2), *Antonio*, *Carlo*, *Carmela*, *Dante*, *Dino*, *Donato*, *Edmondo*.

Dech (170) **1.** German: from an Old Slavic stem *(u)těcha* 'consolation'. **2.** Americanized spelling of Czech *Deč* (see DEC). **3.** Americanized spelling of Hungarian **Décsi**, or **Decsi**, a habitational name for someone from a place called Decs in Tolna county, or Děcs in Békés county or Nyitra county, now in Slovakia. All of these places were named from personal names derived from *Gyeü*, a Turkic name of dignity.
GIVEN NAMES German 5%. *Ernst*, *Heinrich*.

Dechaine (158) Altered spelling of French **Dechêne**, variant of **Duchêne** (see DUCHENE).
GIVEN NAME French 5%. *Micheline*.

Dechambeau (103) French: unexplained; possibly a habitational name for someone from *(de)* Champeau in Côte d'Or, or any of various places called Champeaux, for example in Manche and Seine-et-Marne.

Dechant (634) **1.** German: occupational name for the master of a guild or the supervisor of a ecclesiastical or secular administrative unit, from Middle High German *techant*, *dechent* 'one in charge of ten men' (Latin *decanus*). **2.** French (also **De Chant**): of uncertain derivation; perhaps an

altered spelling of **Deschamps** (see CHAMP).

De Chellis (197) Italian: of uncertain derivation; perhaps from the personal name *Chello*, a short form of *Rustichello*, itself a pet form of a nickname from *rustico* 'country dweller', 'rustic'.
GIVEN NAMES Italian 16%. *Antonio* (2), *Carlo* (2), *Giuseppe* (2), *Primo* (2), *Attilio*, *Fiore*, *Gino*, *Guido*, *Verino*.

Dechene (140) French (**Dechêne**): variant of **Duchêne** (see DUCHENE).
GIVEN NAMES French 15%. *Andre* (4), *Laurier*, *Lucien*, *Marcel*, *Michel*.

Dechert (260) German: from Middle High German *decher*, *techer* 'unit of ten' (from Latin *decem*). This was a measure used particularly with reference to hides, furs, and parchment; the inorganic *-t* suggests that this was an occupational name, probably for someone who handled such items.
GIVEN NAMES German 4%. *Kurt*, *Otto*.

De Chiara (120) Southern Italian: metronymic from the personal name *Chiara*, feminine form of CHIARO.
GIVEN NAMES Italian 19%. *Enzo* (2), *Amerigo*, *Armando*, *Benito*, *Carmin*, *Eduardo*, *Giuseppe*, *Orlando*, *Pasquale*, *Sergio*.

De Chiaro (100) Southern Italian: patronymic from the personal name *Chiaro*, from Latin *Clarus*, meaning 'bright', 'shining'.
GIVEN NAMES Italian 17%. *Angelo*, *Enrico*, *Vito*.

De Christopher (173) Partly Americanized form of Italian DE CRISTOFORO.
GIVEN NAMES Italian 6%. *Carmine*, *Constantino*, *Romeo*.

De Cicco (918) Italian: variant of DI CICCO.
GIVEN NAMES Italian 14%. *Angelo* (3), *Luigi* (2), *Pasquale* (2), *Remo* (2), *Rocco* (2), *Sal* (2), *Aniello*, *Antonio*, *Camillo*, *Carmela*, *Carmine*, *Cosimo*.

Deck (1998) **1.** South German: occupational name for a roofer, from Middle High German *decke* 'covering'. Compare the later form DECKER. **2.** Dutch and North German: from the personal name *Deck*, a local pet form of Dutch **Diederik** (see DEDERICK) or German DIETRICH.

Deckard (1797) Variant of German DECKERT.

Deckelman (129) German (**Deckelmann**): from either *Theodicho*, an old personal name formed with Old High German *diot* 'people', or a short form of a personal name composed with Old High German *tac* 'day' + *man* 'man'.
GIVEN NAME German 4%. *Kurt*.

Decker (21217) **1.** German: occupational name for a roofer (thatcher, tiler, slater, or shingler) or a carpenter or builder, from an agent derivative of Middle High German *decke* 'covering', a word which was normally used to refer to roofs, but sometimes also to other sorts of covering; modern German *Decke* still has the twin senses 'ceiling' and 'blanket'. **2.** Dutch: variant of DEKKER, cognate with 1. **3.** English: variant of DICKER.

Deckert (794) German: **1.** variant of DECKER 1. **2.** from an old personal name, *Tagahard*, composed of Old High German *tac* 'day' + *hart* 'strong'.

Deckman (279) German (**Deckmann**): variant of DECKER 1.

De Clark (119) Americanized form of Dutch DE CLERCQ or any of its variants.

De Cleene (153) Dutch: nickname meaning 'the little one', from Middle Dutch *cleen* 'small', preceded by the definite article *de*.

De Clerck (180) Dutch: variant spelling of DE CLERCQ.
GIVEN NAME French 4%. *Yves*.

De Clercq (251) Dutch: occupational name for a clerk or scribe, Middle Dutch *clerc*, from Latin *clericus* (see CLARK), preceded by the definite article *de*.
GIVEN NAMES French 7%. *Cyrille* (2), *Firmin*, *Remi*.

De Clerk (111) Anglicized spelling of Dutch DE CLERCQ.
GIVEN NAME German 8%. *Rainer* (3).

Declue (579) Altered spelling of French **Decloux**, a topographic or habitational name, with the preposition *de* 'from', from a regional variant of CLOS 'enclosure'.

De Cock (187) Dutch: variant of DE COOK.
GIVEN NAMES French 4%. *Gaston, Julien*.

De Cola (322) Italian: variant of DI COLA.
GIVEN NAMES Italian 8%. *Sal* (2), *Salvatore* (2), *Giacomo, Guido, Romeo, Silvio*.

De Coninck (100) Dutch: status name for the head of a craftmen's guild, or a society of archers, or minstrels, from Middle Dutch *coninc* 'king', preceded by the definite article *de*. See also KOENIG.
GIVEN NAMES French 10%. *Benoit, Lucien, Michel*.

De Cook (252) Dutch: variant of DE KOK.
GIVEN NAMES French 7%. *Andre* (2), *Armand, Firmin, Hilaire, Nicolle*.

De Cordova (106) Spanish (**De Córdova**): habitational name for someone 'from (*de*) Córdoba', the city in southern Spain.
GIVEN NAMES Spanish 6%. *Jose* (3), *Eloisa, Fernando, Jaime*.

Decorte (171) Dutch: nickname for a short person, from Middle Dutch *corte* 'short', preceded by the definite article *de*.
GIVEN NAMES French 5%. *Jacques, Serge*.

De Cosmo (110) Italian: patronymic from the personal name COSMO.
GIVEN NAMES Italian 9%. *Agostino, Benedetto, Carmelo, Vito*.

De Costa (924) Variant of Portuguese DA COSTA.

Decoste (433) French: probably a topographic name for someone who lived on the coast or at the side of a river or some other prominent feature, from *coste*, a southern variant of *côte* 'coast', 'side', with the fused preposition *de* 'from'.

GIVEN NAMES French 4%. *Antoine, Marcel, Yves*.

De Coster (467) Dutch: occupational name for a sexton, from Middle Dutch *coster(e)*, *costre*, preceded by the definite article *de*.
GIVEN NAMES French 9%. *Prosper* (3), *Alain* (2), *Lucien* (2), *Alphonse, Emile, Francois, Jacques, Marcel*.

Decoteau (495) Altered form of French **Descôteaux**, a topographic name from the plural of *côteau* 'hillside'; often translated as HILL.
GIVEN NAMES French 5%. *Raoul* (2), *Armand, Oneil, Vernice*.

De Cotis (101) Portuguese: patronymic from the personal name *Cotis*, from Latin *Cotys*.
GIVEN NAMES Italian 7%. *Antonio, Alfonso, Josefina*.

Decou (227) Variant of French DECOUX.
GIVEN NAMES French 8%. *Emile* (2), *Antoine, Eugenie, Raywood*.

Decourcey (153) English and Irish: variant spelling of DECOURSEY.

Decourcy (185) English and Irish: variant spelling of DECOURSEY.

Decoursey (373) English and Irish (of Norman origin; also written **De Coursey**): habitational name for someone from any of various places in northern France called Courcy, from the Romano-Gallic personal name *Curtius* (a derivative of Latin *curtus* 'short'; compare COURT 2) + the locative suffix *-acum*.

Decoux (164) French: habitational name, with the preposition *de* 'from', for someone from any of various places in France called Coux or Coulx.

De Crescenzo (240) Italian: patronymic from the personal name *Crescenzo*, an omen name with the implied sense 'may he grow well', from Latin *Crescens*.
GIVEN NAMES Italian 22%. *Carmine* (3), *Sabino* (2), *Sal* (2), *Amalia, Armando, Carlo, Dante, Elpidio, Rocco, Vito*.

De Cristofaro (264) Italian: variant of DI CRISTOFARO.
GIVEN NAMES Italian 13%. *Elio* (2), *Angelo, Antonio, Benedetto, Dante, Domenic, Marzio, Silvio*.

De Cristoforo (117) Italian: variant of DI CRISTOFARO.
GIVEN NAMES Italian 12%. *Antonio, Delio, Domenic, Guido*.

Decuir (488) French: **1.** possibly an occupational name for a curer of leather, from *cuir* 'leather', but *le* 'the' is normal with occupational names, not *de* 'from'. **2.** more probably, a habitational name from an unidentified place called Cuir or a variant of **De Court** (see COURT).
GIVEN NAMES French 5%. *Gaston, Marcelle, Renella*.

Dede (181) **1.** English: variant of DEEDS. **2.** Hungarian: from a pet form of *Déd*, an old secular personal name.

GIVEN NAMES French 8%. *Calixte, Damien, Dominique, Leontine, Ursule*.

Dedeaux (348) French: unexplained. This name is concentrated in MS. Probably a habitational name for someone from Deaux in Gare.
GIVEN NAMES French 4%. *Alphonse, Andre*.

De Decker (191) Dutch (**de Decker**): variant of DEKKER, with the addition of the definite article *de*.
GIVEN NAME Dutch 4%. *Willem* (2).

Dederich (133) Dutch and North German: variant of Dutch **Diederik** (see DEDERICK) or German DIETRICH.
GIVEN NAME French 5%. *Venance*.

Dederick (150) Dutch: variant of **Diederik**, from a Germanic personal name composed of the elements *theud* 'people', 'race' + *ríc* 'power(ful)', 'rich'; cognate with High German DIETRICH.

Dedic (157) Serbian and Bosnian (**Dedić**): nickname from *deda* 'grandfather'.
GIVEN NAMES South Slavic 7%; Muslim 5%. *Nenad, Ranko, Velimir; Emir, Ilyas, Ismet, Mehmed, Muhamed, Nermin, Suad*.

De Dios (170) Spanish (**De Dios**): from (*de*) *Dios* 'of God', a popular medieval addition to baptismal names.
GIVEN NAMES Spanish 56%; Italian 7%. *Angel* (7), *Jose* (6), *Francisco* (3), *Jose Luis* (3), *Carlos* (2), *Enrique* (2), *Guadalupe* (2), *Jesus* (2), *Rafael* (2), *Adan, Adelina, Alberto, Godofredo; Antonio* (2), *Dante, Heriberto, Marco, Sulpicio*.

Dedman (393) English: altered form of DEBNAM.

Dedmon (661) Probably an altered spelling of English DEDMAN.

Dedo (136) **1.** Polish: from German *Dedo*, a pet form of a compound name formed with *Diet-*, as for example DIETRICH. **2.** Americanized spelling of DEDEAUX.

De Domenico (122) Italian: variant of DI DOMENICO.
GIVEN NAMES Italian 20%. *Attilio, Carmello, Concetta, Dante, Domenic, Geno, Lorenzo*.

De Dominicis (168) Italian: patronymic from the personal name DOMENICO, in the broader sense 'member of the Domenico family'.
GIVEN NAMES Italian 20%. *Aldo* (2), *Antonio* (2), *Dante* (2), *Enzo* (2), *Ermanno* (2), *Carmine, Filomena, Luigi, Sandro*.

Dedon (114) Perhaps an altered spelling of the French habitational name **Dedun**, denoting someone from any of the various places named Dun, for example in Cher, Indre, and Meuse. According to Morlet, the habitational name is derived from Gallic *dunum* 'hill', later 'fortress'.

De Donato (116) Italian: variant of DI DONATO.
GIVEN NAMES Italian 11%. *Angelo, Carmel, Donato, Pasquale*.

Dedrick (791) Respelling of North German *Dedrich*, a variant of DIEDRICH.

Dedrickson (105) Probably a respelling of North German **Diederichsen**, a patronymic from the personal name DIEDRICH.

Dee (2396) **1.** Welsh: nickname for a swarthy person, from Welsh *du* 'dark', 'black'. **2.** Irish: variant of DAW 3. **3.** English and Scottish: habitational name from a settlement on the banks of the river Dee in Cheshire or either of the rivers so named in Scotland. The origin of both of these is a Celtic word meaning 'sacred', 'goddess'.

Deeb (571) Arabic: probably from a personal name based on Arabic *dhi'b* 'wolf'.
GIVEN NAMES Arabic 18%; French 4%. *Ziad* (4), *Ibrahim* (3), *Nabil* (3), *Samir* (3), *Fadi* (2), *Hisham* (2), *Issa* (2), *Khaled* (2), *Nidal* (2), *Abbas, Ali, Amal; Auguste, Camile, Jean-Paul, Marcell, Michel, Pierre.*

Deeble (131) **1.** English: nickname for a sickly person, from French *debile* 'frail', 'weak' (from Latin *debilis*). **2.** Americanized spelling of German DIEBEL.

Deeds (1024) English: from Old English *dǣd* 'deed', 'exploit'; probably a nickname commemorating some exploit perpetrated by the bearer or for someone noted for his derring-do.

Deeg (206) **1.** Possibly an Americanized spelling of French **Digue**, which Morlet suggests may be derived from a root *dig-* meaning 'to sting', hence 'to quarrel', and therefore a nickname for a quarrelsome, argumentative person. **2.** Americanized spelling of Hungarian **Dég**, from the old secular personal name *Dég*.
GIVEN NAMES German 10%. *Hartmut, Helmut, Horst, Kurt, Otto, Rudi.*

Deegan (1441) Irish: Anglicized form of Gaelic **Ó Duibhginn** 'descendant of *Duibhgeann*', a byname from *dubh* 'black' + *ceann* 'head', 'chief'.

Deehan (148) Irish: Anglicized form of Gaelic **Ó Díochon** 'descendant of *Díochú*', a personal name formed with *cú* 'hound'. This is a rare Ulster surname.

Deeken (122) German: from a short form of a personal name formed with the element *theudo* 'people'.
GIVEN NAME German 4%. *Gunther.*

Deeks (116) English: variant of DYKE.

Deel (1271) **1.** North German: variant of DIEHL. **2.** Probably a respelling of German DIEHL, DIEL. **3.** Variant spelling of English DEAL.

Deeley (312) Irish (Galway): Anglicized form of Gaelic **Ó Duibhghiolla** 'descendant of *Duibhghiolla*', from *dubh* 'black' + *giolla* 'lad'.

Deely (237) Irish: variant spelling of DEELEY.
GIVEN NAMES Irish 6%. *Brendan, Fergus.*

Deem (1277) **1.** English: from Old English *dēma, dōma* 'judge', hence an occupational name, or a byname for an arbiter of disputes. **2.** Altered spelling of German DIE(H)M.

Deemer (944) **1.** English: from Old English *dēmere* 'judge', an agent derivative of *dēmian* 'to judge'. Compare DEEM. **2.** Altered spelling of German DIEMER.

Deems (549) English: derivative of DEEM, meaning '(son or servant) of the judge'.

Deen (1496) **1.** English and Irish: variant of DEAN. **2.** Dutch: ethnic name for a Dane, Middle Dutch *Deen.*

Deener (156) Probably an Americanized spelling of German DIENER.

Deeney (222) Irish: Anglicized form of Gaelic **Ó Duibhne** 'descendant of *Duibhne*', a byname from *duibhne* 'disagreeable', 'ill-tempered'. Compare PEOPLES.
GIVEN NAMES Irish 7%. *Conor, Liam.*

Deep (218) **1.** Indian (northern states): Hindu name meaning 'lamp', from Sanskrit *dīpa*. It occurs commonly as the final element of compound personal names, e.g. in *Kuldeep* 'light of the family'. Subsequently, it appears to have evolved into a surname. **2.** English: presumably from the adjective *deep*, either a topographic name for someone who lived in a deep valley, or perhaps a nickname for a 'deep', thoughtful person.
GIVEN NAMES Indian 4%. *Akash, Prem, Vishal.*

Deer (930) **1.** English: variant spelling of DEAR. **2.** Scottish: habitational name from (Old and New) Deer in Aberdeenshire. **3.** Hungarian: variant of **Dér**, from the secular personal name.

Deere (580) **1.** English: variant spelling of DEAR. **2.** Irish: reduced Anglicized form of Gaelic **Ó Duibhidhir** (see DWYER).

Deering (2247) **1.** English: patronymic from DEAR 1. **2.** Americanized form of German **Thüring**, regional name for someone from Thuringia.

Deerman (214) **1.** Variant spelling of DEARMAN. **2.** German (**Deermann**): unexplained. **3.** Altered spelling of German *Diermann* (see DEARMAN 3).

Deerwester (105) Americanized form of German **Turwachter** 'door (or gate) watchman'. Compare TARWATER, WACHTER.

Deery (493) Irish: Anglicized form of Gaelic **Ó Daighre** 'descendant of *Daighre*', a byname meaning 'fiery'.
GIVEN NAMES Irish 4%. *Conn, Seamus.*

Dees (3760) **1.** English: variant spelling of DEAS. **2.** Dutch: patronymic from a short form of the personal name *Desiderius*. **3.** German: from a short form of the personal name *Matthäs*, a variant of *Matthäus* (see MATTHEW), or in some instances an Americanized spelling of **Diess** (see DIES).

Deese (2050) **1.** German: variant of DEES. **2.** Probably a variant spelling of Irish DEASE or an Americanized spelling of German **Diess** (see DIES).

Deeter (918) Either a North German form of DIETER or a respelling of the same name.

Deets (572) Variant of German DEETZ.

Deetz (337) **1.** North German: from a variant of *Deth* or some other short form of an old personal name formed with Old High German *theudō* 'people', 'nation'. **2.** Americanized spelling of German DIETZ.

De Fabio (136) Italian: variant of DI FABIO.
GIVEN NAME Italian 8%. *Rocco.*

De Falco (762) Italian: variant of DI FALCO.
GIVEN NAMES Italian 14%. *Carmine* (4), *Salvatore* (4), *Ciro* (3), *Dante* (2), *Sabato* (2), *Aniello, Carina, Domenic, Domenico, Gino, Guerino, Guido.*

De Fazio (1059) Italian: patronymic from the personal name *Fazio*, a short form of *Bonifazio* (see BONIFACE).
GIVEN NAMES Italian 13%. *Angelo* (7), *Salvatore* (5), *Dante* (2), *Domenic* (2), *Antonella, Antonio, Bruna, Carlo, Cosmo, Dino, Emelio.*

Defee (193) Origin uncertain. **1.** This name is recorded in London, England, in the 18th century, where it may be an Anglicized form of an unidentified French name. **2.** Alternatively, it may be a variant of Irish DUFFY. See also DIFFEE.

De Felice (1367) Mainly southern Italian: patronymic from the personal name *Felice*, from the Roman family name FELIX.
GIVEN NAMES Italian 12%. *Angelo* (7), *Rocco* (6), *Salvatore* (4), *Mauro* (3), *Domenic* (2), *Guido* (2), *Luciano* (2), *Pasquale* (2), *Santo* (2), *Amedeo, Amedio, Carlo.*

Defenbaugh (178) Americanized spelling of German DIEFFENBACH.

De Feo (1070) Italian: patronymic from the personal name FEO.
GIVEN NAMES Italian 15%. *Angelo* (9), *Carmine* (6), *Salvatore* (5), *Cesare* (2), *Domenic* (2), *Luigi* (2), *Pasquale* (2), *Pio* (2), *Rocco* (2), *Sal* (2), *Vito* (2), *Agostino.*

Defer (111) French: from *de fer* 'of iron'; probably a nickname for someone who was immoveable, inflexible, or remarkably tough.
GIVEN NAME French 5%. *Armand.*

Deffenbaugh (517) Americanized spelling of German DIEFFENBACH.

Deffner (116) German: dialect variant of the habitational name **Deffinger**, denoting someone from Deffingen in Swabia, earlier Tafingen.
GIVEN NAMES German 10%. *Otto* (2), *Gerhard, Hans, Helmut.*

Defibaugh (315) Americanized spelling of German DIEFFENBACH.

De Filippis (469) Italian: patronymic from the personal name FILIPPO, but here in the broader sense 'member of the Filippo family'.
GIVEN NAMES Italian 21%. *Rocco* (4), *Angelo* (2), *Marco* (2), *Aldo, Alessio, Attilio, Dino, Domenic, Donato, Enzo, Erminio, Giacomo.*

De Filippo (777) Italian: variant of DI FILIPPO.

GIVEN NAMES Italian 17%. *Salvatore* (8), *Angelo* (6), *Rocco* (5), *Marino* (4), *Antonio* (2), *Pasquale* (2), *Sal* (2), *Carmine*, *Carmino*, *Ciro*, *Cosmo*.

De Fina (214) Italian: metronymic from the female personal name FINA.
GIVEN NAMES Italian 18%. *Angelo, Angelina, Fernando, Mario, Maurizio, Mauro, Vincente.*

De Fino (275) Italian: patronymic from the personal name FINO.
GIVEN NAMES Italian 9%. *Salvatore* (2), *Antonio, Dino, Vito.*

De Fiore (232) Italian: variant of DI FIORE.
GIVEN NAMES Italian 6%. *Carmine* (2), *Giovanni, Palma.*

De Florio (145) Italian: patronymic from the personal name FLORIO.
GIVEN NAMES Italian 18%. *Angelo* (3), *Ceasar, Clementina, Domenic, Rocco, Santina, Vito.*

Defoe (577) Of uncertain origin; probably an Anglicized form of a French Huguenot name.
FOREBEARS According to family historians, the name **Defoe** or **Dafoe** was brought to North America from Switzerland in 1709 by a certain Daniel Dafoe, alias **Deffu**, **Thevou**, or **Thevoz**. A burgher family named **Thevoz** has lived in Missy, Vaud canton, Switzerland, since at least 1458.

The name is also established in England, where it was borne by the novelist, satirist, pamphleteer, and spy Daniel Defoe (1660–1731), author of *Robinson Crusoe, Moll Flanders*, and many other works. His father, a Dissenter, by trade a butcher in London, used the name **Foe**.

De Foor (441) **1.** Dutch: topographic name for someone living near a castle, fortified town, or citadel. **2.** Altered spelling of French DUFOUR.

Deford (920) Altered spelling of French **Dufort**, a patronymic from the nickname *le Fort* 'the strong'.

De Fore (242) Americanized spelling of DE FOOR.

Deforest (1019) French and Dutch: habitational name, with the preposition *de* 'from', for someone from a place named Forest, for example in Nord and Somme. The place name is derived from Old French *forest* 'forest'.
FOREBEARS The name **De Foreest** is recorded in Beverwijck in New Netherland (Albany, NY) in the mid 17th century.

Deforge (428) French: variant, with the preposition *de* 'from', of FORGE.

Deforrest (174) Variant of French DE-FOREST. This was a common form in colonial New York among Huguenots who fled first to the Netherlands and from there to New Netherland via the West India Company.

Defrain (172) **1.** French: variant, with the preposition *de* 'from', of the habitational name FRAIN. **2.** Altered spelling of French DUFRESNE.

Defrance (306) French: ethnic name for someone from France, i.e. the area of modern France which lies to the north of Paris.
GIVEN NAMES French 4%. *Emile, Henri, Jean-Paul.*

De Francesco (963) Italian: patronymic from the personal name *Francesco*, from Latin *Franciscus* (see FRANCIS).
GIVEN NAMES Italian 17%. *Carmine* (7), *Angelo* (6), *Salvatore* (6), *Vito* (4), *Carlo* (3), *Sal* (3), *Vincenzo* (3), *Aldo* (2), *Antonio* (2), *Gaetano* (2), *Nicola* (2), *Pasquale* (2).

De Francis (141) Possibly a partly Americanized form of Italian **De Francisci**, a patronymic from the personal name *Francesco*, from Latin *Franciscus* (see FRANCIS).
GIVEN NAMES Italian 6%. *Antonio, Gino.*

De Francisco (351) Italian: variant of DI FRANCESCO.
GIVEN NAMES Italian 9%. *Angelo* (3), *Caesar* (2), *Salvatore* (2), *Vito* (2), *Cosimo.*

De Franco (802) Italian: variant of DI FRANCO.
GIVEN NAMES Italian 13%. *Salvatore* (5), *Carlo* (2), *Silvio* (2), *Amelio, Angelo, Antonino, Antonio, Beniamino, Carmela, Cosmo, Dante, Domenic.*

De Frank (448) Partly Americanized form of Italian DI FRANCO, or possibly of DI FRANCESCO.
GIVEN NAMES Italian 7%. *Angelo, Emidio, Salvatore.*

Defrates (137) Variant of Portuguese DE FREITAS. This surname was also taken to India by Portuguese colonists.
GIVEN NAME Indian 4%. *Ananda* (2).

Defreece (135) Americanized spelling of Dutch DEFRIES.

Defrees (158) Americanized spelling of Dutch DEFRIES.

Defreese (242) Americanized spelling of Dutch DEFRIES.

De Freitas (643) Portuguese: variant of the habitational and topographic name FREITAS.
GIVEN NAMES Spanish 11%; Portuguese 7%. *Jose* (7), *Carlos* (6), *Luis* (3), *Juan* (2), *Luiz* (2), *Alvaro, Arlindo, Cesar, Eduardo, Ernesto, Fernando, Fidel; Joao* (4), *Adao* (2), *Goncalo.*

De Fries (333) Dutch: regional or ethnic name for a Frisian (see FRIES 1).

De Fronzo (104) Italian: patronymic from the personal name *Fronzo*, a short form of ALFONSO.
GIVEN NAMES Italian 19%. *Domenic* (2), *Rocco* (2), *Angelo, Biagio, Saverio.*

De Furia (140) Italian: apparently a patronymic from a nickname meaning 'fury'.
GIVEN NAMES Italian 9%. *Dante* (2), *Salvatore.*

De Fusco (284) Southern Italian: patronymic from the personal name *Fusco*, a southern variant of FOSCO.

GIVEN NAMES Italian 14%; French 4%. *Pasquale* (3), *Angelo* (2), *Carmine* (2), *Salvatore* (2), *Dante, Guido; Andre* (2), *Armand* (2).

De Gaetano (346) Italian: variant of DI GAETANO.
GIVEN NAMES Italian 16%. *Sal* (4), *Angelo* (2), *Alicia, Aniello, Carmella, Demetrio, Dino, Gaspar, Giuseppe, Rocco, Rosario, Sante, Santi, Santo, Tullio, Vito.*

Degan (277) **1.** Italian (Venetian) and southern French: from Venetian *degan*, Occitan *decan* 'dean', probably denoting someone in the service of a dean. See also DEAN. **2.** Irish: variant spelling of DEEGAN. **3.** Respelling of German DEGEN. **4.** French and Dutch: habitational name from the city of Ghent (Gand) in Belgium.

Degarmo (645) Americanized form of French **de Garmeaux**, said to be from a place called Garmeaux in Normandy.
FOREBEARS The name was established during the 17th century in the Dutch settlement that later became Albany, NY. Pierre Villeroy (1641–1739) had ten children, the first four of whom, born during the 1680s, were baptized as Villeroy, but later all members of the family came to be known as **Degarmeaux**.

Degeer (127) Dutch: topographic name for someone living on a triangular piece of land (Dutch *geer*). Compare English GORE.
GIVEN NAME Dutch 4%. *Dirk* (2).

De Geest (123) Dutch: nickname for someone thought to have an intellectual or spiritual aura, from the definite article *de* + *geest* 'mind', 'spirit'.

Degen (751) German and Swiss German: status name from Middle High German *degen* 'free man', 'warrior', 'vassal'. This name is also found in Slovenia.
GIVEN NAMES German 5%. *Dieter* (2), *Kurt* (2), *Bernhard, Erna, Erwin, Fritz, Gunther, Hans, Helmuth, Klaus, Otto.*

Degener (195) North German: from a Low German variant of an old personal name *Degenher* (see DEGENHARDT).

Degenhardt (568) German: from a popular personal name *Degenhar(d)t*, composed of Old High German *degan* 'young warrior', 'vassal' + *hart* 'strong'.
GIVEN NAMES German 4%. *Bodo* (2), *Winfried* (2), *Angelika, Reinhold.*

Degenhart (215) German: variant of DEGENHARDT.

De Gennaro (774) Italian: variant of DI GENNARO.
GIVEN NAMES Italian 16%. *Angelo* (3), *Luigi* (3), *Ciro* (2), *Domenic* (2), *Gennaro* (2), *Matteo* (2), *Sal* (2), *Carlo, Carmine, Corrado, Cosimo, Domenico.*

De Genova (137) Variant of Italian DI GENOVA.
GIVEN NAMES French 8%; Italian 7%. *Alphonse, Armand, Colette; Rocco, Sal.*

Degenstein (116) German: probably from a topographic name composed of DEGEN + STEIN.

Dehnel (130) German: variant of DEGEN.
GIVEN NAMES French 5%; German 4%. *Yves; Erwin, Ewald.*

De George (897) French Canadian: patronymic from GEORGE. The European French form would be **Degeorges**, but in Canada both the surname and personal name have lost the final *-s*.
GIVEN NAMES Italian 8%. *Angelo* (6), *Carmela* (2), *Sal* (2), *Antonio, Carmine, Cataldo, Giacomo, Salvatore.*

Deger (162) **1.** German: nickname for a big person, from Middle Low German *deger* 'big', 'tall'. **2.** French: habitational name, with fused preposition *d(e)* 'from', for someone from a place named Ger, of which there are examples in Manche and Pyrénées. The place name is believed to derive from a pre-Indo-European element *gar*, meaning 'rock', 'stone'.

De Geus (125) Dutch: nickname for a beggar or vagabond, *geus*, with the addition of the definite article *de*.
GIVEN NAMES Dutch 5%. *Aart, Andries.*

De Geyter (124) Dutch: occupational name for a goatherd, Middle Dutch *geyt(t)ere*, with the addition of the definite article *de*.

De Giacomo (140) Italian: variant of DI GIACOMO.
GIVEN NAMES Italian 19%. *Angelo* (3), *Gaetano, Gennaro, Luigi, Pina, Rocco, Salvatore, Vito.*

D'Egidio (195) Italian: patronymic from the personal name *Egidio*, from Latin *Aegidius* (see GILES).
GIVEN NAMES Italian 11%. *Giovanni* (2), *Nunzio* (2), *Camillo, Domenic, Pasquale.*

De Giorgio (135) Italian: variant of DI GIORGIO.
GIVEN NAMES Italian 24%. *Vito* (2), *Mario* (2), *Alessandro, Amedeo, Gino, Giovanna, Leno, Nicola, Sal, Salvatore, Saverio.*

De Girolamo (190) Italian: variant of DI GIROLAMO.
GIVEN NAMES Italian 22%. *Nicola* (4), *Mario* (2), *Salvatore* (2), *Amadeo, Domenico, Gino, Leonardo, Lorenzo, Luigi, Mauro, Norberto, Umberto.*

De Giulio (114) Variant of Italian DI GIULIO.
GIVEN NAMES Italian 14%. *Angelo, Giulio, Paride, Pasquale, Santo.*

Degler (391) German: occupational name for a potter, from an agent derivative of Low German *degel* '(earthenware) pot' (from Latin *tegula* 'tile').
GIVEN NAME German 4%. *Otto* (2).

Degn (104) **1.** Swedish and Danish: occupational name from *degn* 'deacon', from Latin *diaconus* 'servant'. **2.** German: variant of DEGEN.
GIVEN NAMES German 6%. *Hans* (2), *Otto* (2), *Erik.*

Degnan (1038) Irish: variant of DEIGNAN.

Degner (600) North German: variant of DEGENER.
GIVEN NAMES German 6%. *Otto* (3), *Hans* (2), *Kurt* (2), *Armin, Gerhard, Lorenz, Orlo, Reinholdt.*

De Golier (141) Origin uncertain; perhaps a Dutch nickname for a jester, from Dutch *de* 'the' + a word cognate with Old French *goliard* 'jester', 'buffoon' (originally 'glutton'), from Old French *gole*, Latin *gula* 'gluttony'.

Degollado (108) Spanish (Mexico): from *degollado* 'cut-throat', probably applied as a topographic name, perhaps for someone who lived near a place where a felon was caught or hanged, for example.
GIVEN NAMES Spanish 48%. *Alfredo* (2), *Francisco* (2), *Juan* (2), *Pablo* (2), *Raul* (2), *Rosalva* (2), *Ruben* (2), *Agapito, Alberto, Ana, Andres, Anselma; Lorenzo, Luciano.*

De Golyer (106) See DE GOLIER.

Degon (125) English (Devon): of uncertain origin; perhaps a variant of DEACON. The name in this spelling seems to have died out in England.

De Gonia (111) **1.** Catalan (Valencia; **(De) Goniá**): unexplained. **2.** Possibly also Spanish (from Basque): from **Goña** (Navarre), which is likewise unexplained.

De Good (152) Part translation of Dutch **de Goede**, nickname for a good man, a variant of GOEDE 2, with the addition of the definite article *de*.

De Graaf (503) Dutch: from *graaf* 'count' (see GRAF), with the addition of the definite article *de*, hence a nickname for the servant of a count or for someone supposedly resembling one.
GIVEN NAMES Dutch 5%. *Gerrit* (6), *Adriaan, Bastiaan, Cornelis, Dirk, Geert.*

De Grace (232) French (**Degrâce**): habitational name for someone from La Grâce in Marne. According to Morlet, the place takes its name from La Grâce-Notre-Dame, an abbey founded in the 13th century near Montmirail. Alternatively, it may be a habitational name, with fused preposition *de*, for someone from Grâce(-Berleur) in the Belgian province of Liège.
GIVEN NAMES French 6%. *Emile* (2), *Monique.*

De Gracia (144) Spanish or Catalan: metronymic from the female personal name *Gracia* (Spanish) or *Gràcia* (Catalan), a name with religious associations, from Latin *Gratia*, meaning 'grace' (compare GRACIA).
GIVEN NAMES Spanish 31%. *Carlos* (2), *Jose* (2), *Rolando* (2), *Rosario* (2), *Agustin, Aida, Alberto, Alfredo, Braulio, Cesar, Cristobal, Eleazar; Carmine.*

De Grado (108) Italian: **1.** patronymic from the personal name *Grado*, a variant of the omen name *Grato* ('appreciated', 'dear'), or from a short form of a personal name formed with this element, as for example *Altogrado* or *Bongrado*. **2.** habita-

tional name for someone from Grado in Gorizia province.
GIVEN NAME Italian 4%. *Salvatore.*

De Graff (762) Dutch: variant of DE GRAAF.

De Graffenreid (366) French form of Swiss German **von Graffenried**, a habitational name from an unidentified place.
FOREBEARS Christoph von Graffenried (1661–1743) was the leader of a group of immigrants from Switzerland and the Palatinate in 1710, who founded a German-speaking settlement at New Bern, NC.

De Graffenried (133) See DE GRAFFENREID.

Degrand (172) French: patronymic from the nickname *(le) grand* 'tall', 'large'. Compare GRANT.

De Grande (136) Italian: patronymic from the nickname GRANDE ('tall', 'large').
GIVEN NAME French 4%. *Romain.*

Degrange (193) French: variant, with the preposition *de* 'from', of the habitational name GRANGE.
GIVEN NAME French 4%. *Normand.*

Degrasse (234) Altered spelling of French **Degrâce** (see DEGRACE).

De Grave (303) Dutch: variant of DE GRAAF.

De Graw (788) Dutch: from Middle Dutch *gra(u)we* 'gray', with the addition of the definite article *de*, hence a nickname for someone with gray hair or a gray beard, or possibly for someone who habitually wore gray clothes.

De Gray (215) Possibly a respelling of Dutch **de Graeye**, which Debrabandere suggests could be an adaptation of French **Legraye**, a variant of **Legré**, from Old French *gré* 'Greek', with fused definite article *le*; alternatively, it could be an altered form of Dutch DE GRAVE.

De Grazia (277) Southern Italian: variant of DI GRAZIA.
GIVEN NAMES Italian 11%. *Antonio* (2), *Carlo, Carmine, Gaetano, Mafalda, Pasquale, Remo, Sal, Santo, Tullio.*

Degree (199) Altered spelling of the French habitational name **Degré**, originally denoting someone from a place in Sarthe, said to be named from Latin *gradus* 'step'.

De Gregorio (624) Italian: mainly southern variant of DI GREGORIO.
GIVEN NAMES Italian 14%. *Carmine* (3), *Pasquale* (3), *Angelo* (2), *Antonio* (2), *Guido* (2), *Matteo* (2), *Salvatore* (2), *Vincenzo* (2), *Filomena, Gennaro, Gino.*

De Gregory (184) Partly Americanized form of Italian DE GREGORIO.

De Groat (784) Americanized spelling of Dutch DE GROOT.

De Groff (579) Altered spelling of Dutch DE GRAAF. The vowel change is a common feature of New York Dutch, i.e. the lowering of long *a*, *-aa-* becoming *-aw-*.

De Groodt (101) Dutch: variant of DE GROOT.

De Groot (2069) Dutch: nickname for a big man, from Middle Dutch *grote* 'big', 'large', preceded by the definite article *de*.
GIVEN NAMES Dutch 5%. *Dirk* (5), *Gerrit* (3), *Harm* (3), *Jacobus* (3), *Cornelis* (2), *Hendrik* (2), *Pieter* (2), *Roelof* (2), *Adriaan, Annika, Cees, Cor.*

De Groote (200) Dutch: variant of DE GROOT.
GIVEN NAMES French 5%. *Jacques, Lucien.*

De Gross (118) Dutch: nickname meaning 'the big'.

De Gruy (118) French or Dutch: possibly a variant of Dutch **De Grie**, which Debrabandere describes as a part translation of French **Le Gris** 'the gray one', denoting someone who habitually wore gray, had a gray complexion or graying hair, from Old French *gris*, with the definite article *le*. This is mainly a LA name.
GIVEN NAMES French 13%. *Andre, Angelle, Pierre, Theophile.*

Deguire (241) French: unexplained. Possibly a Frenchified form of Irish MCGUIRE.
GIVEN NAMES French 6%. *Marcel* (3), *Alphonse, Armand.*

Degutis (135) Lithuanian: occupational name for someone who made or sold tar, from a derivative of *degutas* 'tar'.

De Guzman (1176) Spanish (**De Guzmán**): variant of GUZMAN.
GIVEN NAMES Spanish 41%. *Jose* (14), *Ernesto* (9), *Pedro* (9), *Manuel* (6), *Reynaldo* (6), *Ricardo* (6), *Jaime* (5), *Alberto* (4), *Alfredo* (4), *Edgardo* (4), *Francisco* (4), *Mario* (4); *Antonio* (2), *Enrico* (2), *Leonardo* (2), *Lorenzo* (2), *Romeo* (2), *Carmelo, Clemente, Concetta, Dante, Federico, Fortunata.*

De Haan (1197) Dutch: from Middle Dutch *hane* 'rooster', preceded by the definite article *de*, a nickname for someone thought to resemble a rooster, or alternatively a habitational name for someone who lived at a house distinguished by the sign of a rooster.
GIVEN NAMES Dutch 4%. *Dirk* (4), *Gerrit* (3), *Pieter* (2), *Albertus, Andries, Cornelis, Egbert, Huibert, Klaas, Marten, Nicolaas.*

De Haas (362) Dutch: from Middle Dutch *hase, haes* 'hare', preceded by the definite article *de*, a nickname for someone thought to resemble a hare, or a habitational name for someone who lived at a house distinguished by the sign of a hare.
GIVEN NAMES Dutch 4%. *Gerrit* (2), *Pieter* (2), *Bastiaan.*

De Haro (177) Spanish: habitational name for someone from a place in Logroño province named Haro; the place name is probably of Basque origin.
GIVEN NAMES Spanish 60%. *Jose* (4), *Rafael* (4), *Arturo* (3), *Jaime* (3), *Jesus* (3), *Ubaldo* (3), *Alfredo* (2), *Enrique* (2), *Felipe* (2), *Francisco* (2), *Gustavo* (2), *Juan* (2).

De Hart (3514) Dutch: 1. nickname from Middle Dutch *hart, hert* 'hard', 'strong', 'headstrong', 'unruly', preceded by the definite article *de*. 2. occupational name for a herdsman, Middle Dutch *harde, herde*, with the addition of the definite article *de*.

De Haven (1783) Possibly a Dutch variant of HAVEN, a metonymic occupational name for a potter, with the addition of the definite article *de*.

De Hay (108) French: topographic name, with the preposition *de*, for someone who lived by an enclosure, from Old French *haye* 'hedge', or a habitational name from any of the various places named with this word.

De Heer (128) Dutch (**de Heer**): from *heer* '(feudal) lord', 'master', preceded by the definite article *de*, probably applied as a nickname to someone who behaved in a lordly manner, or as a metonymic occupational name for someone in the service of a feudal lord or the like.

De Herrera (526) Spanish: habitational name for someone from any of various places in the provinces of Seville and Badajoz named Herrera, from *herrería* 'smithy', 'forge', 'ironworks' (from Latin *ferraria*).
GIVEN NAMES Spanish 12%. *Alfonso* (4), *Juan* (4), *Carlos* (2), *Frutoso* (2), *Jose* (2), *Manuel* (2), *Orlando* (2), *Alcario, Andres, Angel, Eloisa, Ernesto.*

Dehler (255) German: 1. habitational name for someone from Döhlau in Bavaria. 2. from an old personal name formed with Old High German *diot* 'people', 'nation'.

Dehlinger (174) German: habitational name for someone from any of the various places named Dehlingen.
GIVEN NAMES German 5%. *Dieter, Hans, Klaus.*

Dehm (161) 1. German: variant of DIEHM. 2. South German: occupational name or byname for someone who grazed his pigs in the woods, from the Bavarian term for this practice, *dechel*.
GIVEN NAME German 4%. *Frieda.*

Dehmer (183) 1. North German: habitational name for someone from Dehme near Minden. 2. South German: variant of DEHM.
GIVEN NAME German 4%. *Kurt, Manfred.*

Dehn (858) North German: 1. from a short form of the personal name *Degenhar(d)t* (see DEGENHARDT). 2. from the personal name DANIEL. 3. (also Danish): ethnic name for someone from Denmark, from Middle Low German, Danish *dene* 'Dane'. In the Middle Ages Denmark extended as far south as the River Eider. 4. possibly a topographic name for someone who lived in a hollow, from Middle Low German *denne* 'hollow', 'shallow valley'.

Dehne (342) North German: variant of DEHN.
GIVEN NAMES German 4%. *Ernst, Manfred, Wilfried.*

Dehnel (130) German: from a diminutive of DEHN.

GIVEN NAMES French 5%; German 4%. *Yves; Erwin, Ewald.*

Dehner (473) German: from a short form of the old personal name *Degenher*, composed of Old High German *degen* 'warrior', 'vassal' + *her* 'high', 'noble'.

Dehnert (250) German: from a reduced form of the personal name *Degenhar(d)t* (see DEGENHARDT).

Dehning (112) North German: from a derivative of *Denhard*, a variant of the personal name *Degenhar(d)t* (see DEGENHARDT).

Dehnke (121) North German: from a pet form of *Denhard*, a variant of the personal name *Degenhar(d)t* (see DEGENHARDT).

De Hoff (435) North German: from the Low German definite article *de* + *hoff*, variant of *hof* 'court', 'farmstead', 'manor farm', hence a status name for a peasant in the service of a manor or for a free land-owning farmer.

De Hoog (117) Dutch: nickname from Middle Dutch *hooch* 'high', with the addition of the definite article *de*, i.e. 'the high or exalted one', presumably applied in either a literal or figurative sense.
GIVEN NAMES Dutch 12%; French 5%. *Gerrit* (2), *Bram, Cornelis, Hendrik; Gilles* (2).

De Hoyos (536) Spanish: habitational name for someone from any of the places named Hoyos, for example in the provinces of Ávila, Cáceres, and Santander. The place name is from *hoyo* 'pit' (Latin *fovea*).
GIVEN NAMES Spanish 50%. *Jose* (18), *Juan* (17), *Carlos* (9), *Jesus* (9), *Arturo* (6), *Manuel* (6), *Mario* (6), *Luis* (5), *Ruben* (5), *Armando* (4), *Juanita* (4), *Raul* (4).

Dehring (124) German: variant of **Döhring** (see DOEHRING).
GIVEN NAME German 4%. *Alfons.*

Deibel (427) German: origin uncertain. Perhaps from a pet form of DEIBERT or a diminutive of DEIBLER.

Deibert (668) German: from a short form of a Germanic personal name *Theudobert*, composed of the elements *theud* 'people', 'race' + *berht* 'bright', 'famous'.

Deibler (457) German and Jewish (Ashkenazic): occupational name for a dove keeper, from an agent derivative of Middle High German *tûbe* 'dove' (see TAUBE), or, in the case of the Jewish surname, an ornamental adoption.

Deich (120) German: variant of TEICH, in the north a topographic name from Middle Low German *dîk* 'dike', 'dam' for someone who lived and farmed near a coastal dike.
GIVEN NAME German 4%. *Otto.*

Deichert (166) German: variant of TEICHERT.
GIVEN NAMES German 4%. *Kurt, Otto.*

Deichman (124) Jewish (Ashkenazic): variant of DEUTCH.

Deichmann (124) German: 1. variant of DIECKMANN, a partly standardized form.

2. variant spelling of the occupational or topographic surname TEICHMANN.
GIVEN NAMES German 11%. *Hans* (2), *Ewald, Helmut, Kurt, Otto.*

Deighan (173) Irish: variant of DEEGAN or DEEHAN.
GIVEN NAMES Irish 10%. *Paddy* (2), *Eamon.*

Deighton (162) English (chiefly Yorkshire): habitational name from any of several places in Yorkshire named Deighton, from Old English *dīc* 'ditch', 'dike' + *tūn* 'settlement', 'enclosure'. See also DITTON.

Deignan (348) Irish (Roscommon): reduced Anglicized form of Gaelic **Ó Duibhgeannáin** 'descendant of *Duibhgeannán*', a diminutive of *Duibhgeann* (see DEEGAN).

Deihl (302) Altered spelling of German DIEHL.

Deike (254) North German and Dutch: from an Old Frisian and Lower Saxon personal name *Deiko*, cognate with High German DIETRICH, recorded as early as the 10th century.

Deily (210) Irish: probably a variant of DALY.

Deimel (112) South German: of uncertain derivation; possibly related to DAUM.

Deimler (156) German: variant of **Däumler**, an occupational name for a torturer, from an agent derivative of Middle High German *diumeln* 'to apply the thumbscrew'.

Dein (113) German: **1.** from a short form of the personal name *Deinhart*, itself a variant of *Degenhar(d)t* (see DEGENHARDT). **2.** North German: in Westphalia, a topographic name, from field names *Deine, Dene* meaning 'moist lowland or hollow'.

Deines (771) Altered spelling of German DIENES.

Deininger (479) German: habitational name for someone from any of several places called Deining(en). This is a common place name in Bavaria.
GIVEN NAMES German 4%. *Gerhardt, Heinz, Klaus, Wolfgang.*

Deis (355) German: **1.** from a short form of the personal name *Matthias* or *Matthäus* (see MATTHEW). **2.** from an old Germanic personal name, a pet form of DIETRICH.

Deisenroth (105) Probably an altered form of German **Deiseroth**, a habitational name from a place in Thuringia named Deiseroth; the second element is *-rode* 'forest clearing'.

Deisher (271) Respelling of German **Deischer**: **1.** in southern Germany, a derogatory nickname for a peasant, from Swabian *Deisch* 'dung', Middle High German *teisch*. **2.** possibly a dialect variant of DEUTSCHER. **3.** from a short form of an old personal name, *Deisch*.

Deisler (105) Respelling of German **Deissler**, an occupational name for a maker of wagons, frames, or poles.
GIVEN NAME German 5%. *Gerhard.*

Deiss (349) **1.** German and Swiss German: from a short form of an old personal name formed with Old High German *tac* 'daily'. **2.** German: variant of DEIS.
GIVEN NAMES German 4%. *Kurt* (2), *Egon.*

Deist (208) German: habitational name from a place called Deisten, near Celle (Hannover).

Deister (131) German: regional name for someone from the Deister, a range of wooded hills between the rivers Leine and Weser.

Deitch (633) Jewish (Ashkenazic): variant of DEUTSCH.
GIVEN NAMES Jewish 5%. *Sol* (2), *Avram, Hyman, Meyer, Ronit, Yakov.*

Deitchman (129) Jewish (Ashkenazic): variant of DEUTSCH.

Deiter (426) **1.** German: from the personal names *Detert* or *Dethard*, Low German variants of *Diethard*, composed of Old High German *diot* 'people', 'nation' + *hart* 'strong'. **2.** Possibly an altered spelling of DIETER.

Deitering (149) German: variant of **Diedering**, a patronymic from a Germanic personal name formed with *diet* 'people', as for instance DIETRICH.

Deiters (177) German: patronymic form of DEITER.
GIVEN NAMES German 5%. *Kurt, Markus.*

Deitrich (380) Altered spelling of German DIETRICH.

Deitrick (523) Altered spelling of Dutch **Diederik** (see DEDERICK) or German DIETRICH.

Deitsch (287) Jewish (Ashkenazic): variant of DEUTSCH.
GIVEN NAMES Jewish 8%. *Shalom* (2), *Zalman* (2), *Aron, Avrohom, Basya, Chaya, Mendel, Mordecai, Shira.*

Deitz (1501) Variant spelling of German DIETZ.

Deja (150) Polish or Eastern German: unexplained.

De Jager (257) Dutch: occupational name meaning 'the huntsman', from Middle Dutch *jaghere* 'huntsman'.
GIVEN NAMES Dutch 5%. *Anders* (2), *Gerrit* (2), *Dirk, Durk, Huibert, Johan.*

Dejardin (108) French: variant of JARDIN, meaning 'from the garden or enclosure'.

Dejarnatt (113) French: see DEJARNETTE.

Dejarnett (222) French: see DEJARNETTE.

Dejarnette (428) French: of uncertain origin; perhaps a variant of **Dejouhanet** or **Dejouany**, patronymics from *Jou(h)anet, Jouany*, pet forms of *Jean* (the French equivalent of JOHN).

Dejaynes (127) Origin unidentified; perhaps an altered spelling of French **Degesnes**, a habitational name, with the preposition *de*, for someone from any of the places named Gesnes, of which there are examples in Meuse and Sarthe.

Dejean (536) French: patronymic from the personal name *Jean*, French equivalent of JOHN.
GIVEN NAMES French 11%. *Elrick* (2), *Fernand* (2), *Pierre* (2), *Andre, Baptiste, Colette, Guerline, Jean Charles, Jean-Robert, Manon, Marcel, Monique.*

De Jesus (3755) Spanish (**De Jesús**): patronymic from the personal name *Jesús*.
GIVEN NAMES Spanish 46%; Portuguese 10%. *Jose* (108), *Carlos* (38), *Juan* (37), *Luis* (31), *Manuel* (31), *Francisco* (27), *Miguel* (26), *Angel* (25), *Pedro* (21), *Ramon* (19), *Jorge* (18), *Rafael* (16); *Joao* (3), *Paulo* (2), *Conceicao, Vasco.*

Dejohn (600) **1.** Part translation of the Italian patronymic **De Giovanni** (see DI GIOVANNI). **2.** Possibly a part translation of some other patronymic from a personal name equivalent to JOHN, such as French DEJEAN. **3.** Perhaps an altered spelling of Dutch **Dejon**, a variant of DE JONG.
GIVEN NAMES Italian 5%. *Augustino* (2), *Domenic, Santino.*

Dejoie (106) French: metronymic from the female personal name *Joie*, meaning 'joy'.
GIVEN NAMES French 20%. *Adrien, Andre, Chantal, Constant, Leonie, Regine, Yves.*

De Jong (2412) Dutch: from the epithet *de jong* 'the young', used as a means of distinguishing between two bearers of the same personal name, usually a son from his father.
GIVEN NAMES Dutch 9%. *Dirk* (11), *Pieter* (8), *Gerrit* (7), *Gerben* (6), *Cornie* (5), *Cornelis* (4), *Hessel* (4), *Marinus* (4), *Frans* (3), *Hendrik* (3), *Kees* (3), *Maarten* (3).

De Jonge (468) Dutch: variant of DE JONG.
GIVEN NAMES Dutch 7%; German 4%. *Gerrit* (3), *Adriaan* (2), *Frans, Geert, Hendrik, Jacobus, Joop, Marinus, Marten, Maurits, Nicolaas, Pieter; Erna, Hans, Kurt.*

De Jongh (198) Dutch: variant of DE JONG.
GIVEN NAMES German 4%. *Kurt* (2), *Hans, Johannes.*

De Joseph (209) Part translation of the Italian patronymic DI GIUSEPPE.
GIVEN NAMES Italian 11%. *Tullio* (2), *Angelo, Eliseo, Salvatore, Vito.*

Dejoy (160) Possibly a part translation of the French metronymic DEJOIE.

De Julio (214) Portuguese (**De Júlio**): patronymic from the personal name JULIO.
GIVEN NAMES Italian 12%. *Angelo, Dario, Domenic, Enrico, Ettore, Fulvio, Guerino, Maurizio, Romeo, Sal.*

De Kalb (103) Dutch and North German: nickname from Middle Low German *kalb* 'calf'.

De Kam (132) Dutch: metonymic occupational name for a maker or seller of combs, from Middle Dutch *kam* 'comb', preceded by the definite article *de*.

De Kay (198) Dutch: from Middle Dutch *cade* 'piece of roast fat', hence an derogatory nickname or perhaps a metonymic occupational name for a cook.

De Keyser (305) Dutch: from Middle Dutch *keiser* 'leader' (from the Latin imperial title *Caesar*), preceded by the definite article *de*. The surname may have originated as a nickname, possibly for someone with an overbearing manner. Debrabandere suggests it may have arisen from the title of the leader of a company of marksmen, or from a house or tavern name.

Dekker (929) Dutch: occupational name for a roofer (a thatcher, slater, shingler, or tiler), Middle Dutch *deck(e)re*, an agent derivative of *decken* 'to cover'.
GIVEN NAMES Dutch 5%. *Dirk* (5), *Gerrit* (3), *Maurits* (3), *Egbert*, *Gerben*, *Hendrik*, *Henk*, *Martinus*, *Wim*.

Dekle (380) Possibly an altered spelling of German **Deckel** (see DECKELMAN).

De Kock (152) Dutch: variant of DE KOK.
GIVEN NAMES Dutch 8%; German 4%. *Pieter* (3), *Frans* (2); *Engel*, *Gerhard*.

De Kok (104) Dutch: **1.** occupational name for a cook, Middle Dutch *coc*, preceded by the definite article *de*. **2.** occupational name for an executioner or hangman, Middle Dutch *(scarp)coc*.
GIVEN NAMES Dutch 7%; French 5%. *Dirk*, *Henk*; *Andre*.

De Koning (170) Dutch: from Middle Dutch *de coninc* 'the king', a nickname for someone who gave himself royal airs, or an occupational name for someone who served in the household of a king.
GIVEN NAMES Dutch 6%; German 5%. *Gerrit* (2), *Dirk*, *Hendrikus*; *Johannes* (2), *Bernhard*, *Hans*.

De Kraker (100) Dutch: nickname meaning 'the screecher', from an agent derivative of *kraken* 'to screech'.
GIVEN NAMES Dutch 4%. *Marinus*, *Piet*.

De Lacerda (339) Portuguese (of Spanish origin): variant of LACERDA.
GIVEN NAMES Spanish 43%. *Jose* (7), *Carlos* (5), *Juan* (5), *Luis* (4), *Cornelio* (3), *Jorge* (3), *Leticia* (3), *Manuel* (3), *Vicente* (3), *Alfonso* (2), *Alicia* (2), *Fernando* (2).

Delacey (115) Irish and English: variant spelling of DELACY.

Delach (109) Origin unidentified; possibly a respelling of **Delache**, a topographic name from Walloon *lèche* 'marshland', or a habitational name from either of two places in Belgium called La Lache, in Floriffoux (Namur) or Roux (Hainault).

De la Cruz (5369) Spanish (**De la Cruz**): from the second element of a personal name formed with the religious suffix *de la cruz* 'of the cross' (Latin *crux*).
GIVEN NAMES Spanish 49%. *Jose* (140), *Juan* (83), *Luis* (49), *Francisco* (48), *Manuel* (39), *Pedro* (33), *Carlos* (29), *Jesus* (29), *Mario* (25), *Raul* (24), *Miguel* (22), *Rafael* (22).

Delacy (227) Irish and English (of Norman origin): habitational name for someone from Lassy in Calvados, France (see LACY), with the preposition *de* 'from'.
GIVEN NAME Irish 5%. *Brendan*.

De Laet (121) Dutch: status name from Middle Dutch *laet* 'retainer', with the definite article *de*.
GIVEN NAMES French 5%. *Alberic*, *Michel*.

Delafield (168) English: topographic name, apparently from Anglo-Norman French *de la* 'from the' + Middle English *feld* 'open country used for pasture or tillage'. Sometimes, however, *-field* in a Norman name represents the French word *ville* 'town', so that this name may in fact be from French **Delaville**, a topographic name for someone who lived in a town.

Delafosse (103) French: variant of the topographic name FOSSE, with the preposition and article *de la*, hence literally 'from the ditch'.
GIVEN NAMES French 12%. *Dominique*, *Francois*, *Pierre*.

De la Fuente (762) Spanish: topographic name for someone who lived by a spring, from *fuente* 'fount', 'spring' (Latin *fons*, genitive *fontis*).
GIVEN NAMES Spanish 50%. *Jose* (25), *Carlos* (18), *Juan* (14), *Manuel* (9), *Luis* (8), *Guadalupe* (6), *Ramon* (6), *Ricardo* (6), *Domingo* (5), *Javier* (5), *Jesus* (5), *Miguel* (5).

Delagardelle (114) French: habitational name for someone from Lagardelle, a place in Haute Garonne.

De la Garza (1531) Spanish: patronymic from a nickname from *garza* 'heron'.
GIVEN NAMES Spanish 46%. *Jose* (31), *Carlos* (23), *Manuel* (21), *Jesus* (15), *Luis* (15), *Rodolfo* (15), *Raul* (12), *Guadalupe* (11), *Juan* (11), *Roberto* (10), *Francisco* (9), *Mario* (9).

Delage (282) French (Burgundy, Charente, and Limousin): from the dialect word *age* 'hedge', hence a topographic name for someone who lived by or in a domain enclosed by hedges, or a habitational name for someone from any of various minor places named L'Age from this word.
GIVEN NAMES French 18%. *Armand* (3), *Andre* (2), *Marcel* (2), *Thierry* (2), *Adrien*, *Emile*, *Gilles*, *Henri*, *Laurent*, *Michel*, *Olivier*, *Phillippe*.

De la Grange (201) French: topographic and habitational name, from *de la grange* 'from the grange or farm' (see GRANGE).

Delaguila (103) Spanish (**del Águila**): probably a habitational name from any of the places called El Águila, from *águila* 'eagle'.
GIVEN NAMES Spanish 49%. *Luis* (5), *Cesar* (4), *Julio* (4), *Amparo* (3), *Carlos* (2), *Francisco* (2), *Gustavo* (2), *Miguel* (2), *Arnoldo*, *Efrain*, *Fernando*, *Jorge Luis*.

Delahanty (301) Variant spelling of Irish **Delahunty** (see DELAHUNT).

Delahoussaye (527) French: topographic name for someone who lived by a holly bush or grove, from *de la houx* 'from the holly', or habitational name for someone from a place calle Houssaye, named with *houx* 'holly'.
GIVEN NAMES French 8%. *Jean-Paul* (2), *Amedee*, *Anatole*, *Andre*, *Autrey*, *Desire*, *Ignace*, *Minos*, *Monique*, *Octa*.

Delahoz (119) Spanish (**De la Hoz**): **1.** habitational name from any of the places called La Hoz, from *hoz* 'defile'. **2.** in some cases perhaps a metonymic occupational name for a mower or a scythe maker, from *hoz* 'scythe'.
GIVEN NAMES Spanish 46%. *Manuel* (5), *Jose* (4), *Jorge* (3), *Alvaro* (2), *Carlos* (2), *Ernesto* (2), *Jairo* (2), *Juan* (2), *Luis* (2), *Miguel* (2), *Ricardo* (2), *Adela*.

Delahunt (290) Irish (Offaly and Kerry): Anglicized form of Gaelic **Ó Dulchaointigh** 'descendant of *Dulchaointeach*', a byname composed of the elements *dul* 'satirist' + *caointeach* 'plaintive'.

Delahunty (207) Irish: variant of DELAHUNT.
GIVEN NAME Irish 5%. *Malachy*.

Delain (100) Probably a respelling of French DELAINE.
GIVEN NAME French 6%. *Pascale*.

Delaine (181) French: **1.** (**Delaisne**) habitational name for someone from Aisne department. **2.** (**Delainé**): from the nickname *l'aîné* 'the oldest', denoting the firstborn son of a family.
GIVEN NAME French 4%. *Laurent*.

Delair (214) Presumably from French **Delaire**, a habitational name, with the preposition *de*, for someone from Aire-sur-l'Adour in Landes.
GIVEN NAME French 4%. *Andree*.

Delamar (163) English: **1.** (of Norman origin) habitational name from any of the places in northern France called La Mare 'the pond'. **2.** possibly a topographic name from Anglo-Norman French *de la* 'from the' + Middle English *mere* 'pond' or *more* 'marsh', 'moor'. Delamere Forest in Cheshire, 'forest of the lake (Old English *mere*)' may also account for some examples of the surname.

Delamarter (134) Evidently of French origin, from an unidentified habitational name, probably from a place named with *martre* 'martyr'. Dauzat records the name **Desmartres**, which he derives from more than one place named with *martres*. Nègre also has a place name Lamastre.

Delamater (402) Variant of French DELAMARTER.

De la Mora (139) Spanish: **1.** habitational name for someone from any of various places named Mora (from *mora* 'mulberry'), for example in the provinces of Albacete, León, Navarre, and Toledo, or a topographic name for someone who lived where mulberries grew. **2.** ethnic name meaning 'the Moorish woman's son', from *mora* '(female) Moor'.

GIVEN NAMES Spanish 55%. *Jose* (7), *Juan* (6), *Jorge* (4), *Angel* (2), *Arturo* (2), *Estela* (2), *Jesus* (2), *Leticia* (2), *Manuel* (2), *Rafael* (2), *Raul* (2), *Sergio* (2).

Delancey (808) Probably of French or English origin, a habitational name for someone from Lancey in Isère, France.

Delancy (233) See DELANCEY.

Deland (509) **1.** German: topographic name from Sorbian *delan* 'dweller in a depression'. **2.** Probably an altered spelling of French **Delande**, a regional name for someone 'from Lande' (see LANDE), or **DesLandes**, recorded as a secondary surname of CHAMPIGNY.

Delane (131) **1.** English: originally **de Laine** (see DELAINE), this is a Huguenot name, which was taken to England in the 17th century. **2.** French: possibly a habitational name for someone from Lannes in Haute-Marne.

Delaney (11805) **1.** English (of Norman origin): habitational name for someone from any of various minor places in northern France named from Old French *aunaie* 'alder grove'. **2.** Irish: Anglicized form, influenced by the Norman name, of Gaelic **Ó Dubhshláine** 'descendant of *Dubhshláine*', a personal name composed of the elements *dubh* 'black' + *slán* 'challenge', 'defiance'. MacLysaght, however, suggests that this element may be from the Sláinge river.

GIVEN NAMES Irish 4%. *Brendan* (5), *Aileen* (4), *Cormac* (3), *Clancy*, *Colm*, *Conley*, *Conor*, *Dermot*, *Donal*, *Eamon*, *Eamonn*, *Finbar*.

De Lange (448) **1.** Dutch: nickname meaning 'the tall (one)'. **2.** French: patronymic from the nickname *L'Ange* 'the angel', or a habitational name for someone who lived at a house or inn distinguished by the sign of an angel.

GIVEN NAMES Dutch 4%. *Andries*, *Cor*, *Dirk*, *Geert*, *Gerrit*, *Willem*.

Delangel (115) Spanish **Del Ángel**: from a personal name formed with *ángel* 'angel'.

GIVEN NAMES Spanish 59%. *Alfredo* (5), *Francisca* (3), *Jose* (3), *Juan* (3), *Guadalupe* (2), *Jose Luis* (2), *Margarita* (2), *Mario* (2), *Miguel* (2), *Alberto*, *Alonso*, *Ana*; *Aldo*, *Flavio*.

Delano (1963) Respelling of French **De la Noye**, habitational name, with the preposition *de*, for someone from any of various places called La Noue or La Noë, for example in Marne, Charente, Maine-et-Loire, named with Gaulish *nauda* 'moist or marshy place', 'swamp'.

FOREBEARS Franklin D. Roosevelt's mother was a Delano, descended from Philippe de la Noye (1602–81), who arrived at Plymouth in 1621 in the *Fortune*, one year after the Pilgrim Fathers.

Delanoy (190) English and French: habitational name for someone from either of two places named Lannoy, in Nord and Oise. See also DELANO.

GIVEN NAMES French 4%. *Gisele* (2), *Gabrielle*.

Delany (685) English and Irish: variant spelling of DELANEY.

Delao (607) possibly Filipino, variant of **Dalao**; unexplained.

GIVEN NAMES Spanish 44%. *Jose* (16), *Carlos* (7), *Juan* (7), *Manuel* (7), *Roberto* (7), *Luis* (6), *Jaime* (5), *Pedro* (5), *Salvador* (5), *Alfredo* (4), *Arturo* (4), *Francisco* (4).

Delap (502) Irish: **1.** alternative form of LAPPIN; **2.** in Counties Derry and Fermanagh, an alternative form of DUNLOP.

De la Paz (618) Spanish (**De la Paz**): patronymic from the second element of a personal name formed with the religious suffix *de la Paz*, from *paz* 'peace' (from Latin *pax*). Originally it was characteristically adopted by Jewish converts to Christianity, as a translation of Hebrew *shalom*.

GIVEN NAMES Spanish 51%. *Jose* (11), *Juan* (9), *Luis* (8), *Enrique* (7), *Roberto* (7), *Armando* (6), *Francisco* (4), *Javier* (4), *Jesus* (4), *Manuel* (4), *Mario* (4), *Alberto* (3); *Antonio* (6), *Marco* (2), *Angelo*, *Ciro*, *Fausto*, *Geronimo*, *Giovanni*, *Lucio*, *Romeo*.

De la Pena (554) Spanish (**De la Peña**): topographic name from *peña* 'rock', 'boulder'.

GIVEN NAMES Spanish 45%. *Jose* (11), *Carlos* (6), *Francisco* (5), *Jesus* (5), *Mario* (5), *Alfredo* (4), *Enrique* (4), *Jorge* (4), *Luis* (4), *Manuel* (4), *Miguel* (4), *Rafael* (4).

Delaplane (124) Altered spelling of French **De la Plaine**, a topographic name for someone who lived on a plain.

Delapp (459) Variant spelling of the Irish family name DELAP.

Delara (324) Variant, with the preposition *de*, of the Spanish or French habitational name LARA.

GIVEN NAMES Spanish 36%. *Carlos* (6), *Juan* (4), *Jose* (3), *Luis* (3), *Mauricio* (3), *Pedro* (3), *Alfonso* (2), *Ana* (2), *Jaime* (2), *Javier* (2), *Jorge* (2), *Merlinda* (2).

De la Riva (153) Catalan: topographic name for someone who lived by a riverbank or the shore of a lake.

GIVEN NAMES Spanish 60%. *Juan* (4), *Miguel* (4), *Rafael* (4), *Manuel* (3), *Ramiro* (3), *Andres* (2), *Enrique* (2), *Francisco* (2), *Humberto* (2), *Jesus* (2), *Jorge* (2), *Pablo* (2); *Carmelo*, *Eliseo*, *Lucio*, *Pio*, *Silvano*.

Delarm (121) Altered spelling, reflecting the North American pronunciation, of DELORME.

De la Rosa (3317) Spanish: literally 'of (*de*) the rose (*la rosa*)', generally a component of personal names: among women a Marian name; among men of uncertain application.

GIVEN NAMES Spanish 48%. *Jose* (73), *Juan* (52), *Manuel* (37), *Luis* (30), *Carlos* (26), *Jesus* (25), *Rafael* (25), *Francisco* (19), *Roberto* (17), *Ruben* (17), *Pedro* (16), *Mario* (14).

Delashmit (191) Americanized form of southern French **de la Chaumette**, a topographic name for someone who lived on a *chaumette*, a high, arid plateau with very little vegetation, derived from a diminutive of *chaume* 'bare land' (a specialized sense of Latin *calmus* 'calm', 'unruffled').

FOREBEARS Pierre de la Chaumette (born 1673) came from Rochouard, France, via England to Gloucester, NJ, in about 1698; in NJ he became known as Peter Delashmet. See DeLater he was joined by his brother Jean de la Chaumette, a wealthy colonist from Martinique and VA. Either this Jean or his nephew (Pierre's son) became known as John Shumate. See SHUMATE.

Delashmutt (194) Of French origin: see DELASHMIT.

De la Torre (2468) Spanish: topographic name 'from (*de*) the tower (*la torre*)', i.e. someone who lived by a watchtower, 'from (*de*) the tower (*la torre*)'.

GIVEN NAMES Spanish 51%. *Jose* (90), *Carlos* (33), *Juan* (33), *Manuel* (32), *Miguel* (31), *Jorge* (28), *Luis* (25), *Jesus* (20), *Francisco* (19), *Raul* (19), *Ruben* (18), *Jaime* (16).

Delatte (418) French: probably a variant of **Delattre** (see DELAUTER).

Delauder (217) Americanized form of French **Delautre** (see DELAUTER).

Delaughter (317) Americanized form of French **Delautre** (see DELAUTER).

Delaune (541) French: topographic name denoting someone who lived by an alder tree.

GIVEN NAMES French 4%. *Aubert*, *Emile*, *Octave*, *Raoul*.

De Laura (218) Italian: metronymic from the female personal name *Laura* (a derivative of Latin *laurus* 'laurel').

GIVEN NAMES Italian 6%. *Vito* (2), *Antonio*, *Dante*.

De Laurentis (322) Italian: patronymic from *Laurentius*, a Latinized form of Italian *Lorenzo* (see LAWRENCE), in the broader sense 'of or belonging to the Laurenti family'.

GIVEN NAMES Italian 20%. *Mario* (4), *Angelo* (2), *Carmella* (2), *Carlo*, *Celestino*, *Domenica*, *Ermanno*, *Marcello*, *Mariano*, *Remo*, *Rocco*, *Romeo*, *Tullio*, *Vito*.

Delaurier (115) French: singular form of **Deslauriers**, a topographic name denoting someone who lived by a laurel bush, *laurier*.

De Lauro (143) Italian: variant of DI LAURO.

GIVEN NAMES Italian 10%. *Salvatore* (2), *Carmine*.

Delauter (197) Americanized spelling of French **Delautre**. This is of uncertain etymology. It is probably a variant of **Delattre**

(a habitational name from a place called Lattre in Picardy) or possibly from **Delaitre** (a habitational name from a place in Lorraine).

Delavan (175) Origin unidentified: probably of French origin.

De la Vega (486) Spanish: topographic name from *vega* 'fertile plain or lowland', 'water meadow' (see VEGA).
GIVEN NAMES Spanish 42%. *Carlos* (9), *Mario* (8), *Enrique* (7), *Jorge* (7), *Luis* (7), *Eduardo* (6), *Jose* (6), *Jaime* (5), *Rafael* (5), *Arturo* (4), *Alberto* (3), *Armando* (3); *Ciro* (4), *Federico* (2), *Guido* (2), *Antonio*, *Julieta*, *Leonardo*, *Lorenzo*, *Marco Antonio*, *Romeo*.

Delavergne (138) French: habitational name for someone from a place called Lavergne (see LAVERGNE).
GIVEN NAMES French 12%. *Jacques* (2), *Francois*, *Hugues*.

Delaware (127) **1.** English (of Norman origin) and French: nickname for a soldier or for a belligerent person, from Old French *(de la) werre*, *(de la) guerre* '(of the) war'. Compare WARR. **2.** English: habitational name from Delaware in Brasted, Kent, named with Old English *wer* 'weir'.
GIVEN NAME French 5%. *Andre*.

Delawder (339) Americanized form of French **Delautre** (see DELAUTER).

Delay (1208) **1.** Irish: reduced Anglicized form of Gaelic **Ó Duinnshléibhe** 'descendant of *Donn Sleibhe*' (see DUNLEAVY). **2.** Altered spelling of **Delaye**, habitational name denoting someone from Lay (Loire), or from Laye (Hautes-Alpes, Eure, Loire, etc.).

Del Bene (222) Italian: patronymic from *Bene*, probably a short form of *Tornabene*, a medieval omen name meaning 'come back well', often bestowed on a child regarded as a replacement for an older child that died.
GIVEN NAMES Italian 10%. *Aldo* (2), *Carmel*, *Nino*, *Salvatore*, *Saverio*.

Del Bianco (164) Italian: literally 'of or belonging to the white one' (see BIANCO), hence a name denoting the son, apprentice, associate, or servant of a man bearing this nickname.
GIVEN NAMES Italian 31%. *Domenico* (2), *Emilio* (2), *Gino* (2), *Olympia* (2), *Aurelio*, *Aldo*, *Caesar*, *Cosmo*, *Dario*, *Domenic*, *Fortunato*, *Franco*, *Fulvio*, *Giovanni*, *Guido*, *Mario*, *Sirio*.

Delbosque (227) Altered spelling of the southern French surname **Delbosquet**, a topographic name for someone who lived by a copse or wood, from Old French *bosc* (Late Latin *boscus*).
GIVEN NAMES Spanish 47%. *Juan* (7), *Jose* (6), *Manuel* (5), *Carlos* (3), *Jesus* (3), *Armando* (2), *Fernando* (2), *Francisco* (2), *Homero* (2), *Jacinto* (2), *Mario* (2), *Rafael* (2).

Delbridge (446) **1.** English: topographic or metonymic occupational name, a variant of BRIDGE, with fused Anglo-Norman French article and preposition *del* ('of the'). **2.** Partly Americanized form of German **Delbrück**, a habitational name from any of several places named Dellbrücke, in Schleswig-Holstein, near Paderborn, and near Cologne. The place name denotes a boarded crossing through swampy terrain.

Del Buono (183) Italian: literally 'of or belonging to the good one' (see BUONO), hence a name for the son, apprentice, associate, or servant of a man known by this nickname or having *Buono* as a personal name.
GIVEN NAMES Italian 21%. *Angelo* (2), *Antonio*, *Dante*, *Domenic*, *Donato*, *Gino*, *Guido*, *Luigi*, *Mario*, *Silvio*, *Vita*.

Delcambre (424) French (Picard): from Old French *cha(u)mbre* 'chamber' (Latin *cambera*), hence an occupational name for someone who worked in the private living quarters of his master, rather than in the public halls of the manor.
GIVEN NAMES French 6%. *Patrice* (2), *Gaston*, *Jacques*, *Minos*.

Delcamp (210) Catalan and southern French: topographic name for someone who lived by a field.

Del Campo (380) Spanish: topographic name for someone 'from the (*del*) field (*campo*)', i.e. denoting someone who lived by a field.
GIVEN NAMES Spanish 39%. *Jose* (8), *Manuel* (6), *Miguel* (5), *Armando* (4), *Carlos* (4), *Raul* (4), *Enrique* (3), *Margarita* (3), *Pedro* (3), *Alberto* (2), *Alfonso* (2), *Cesar* (2); *Antonio* (2), *Clemente*, *Enrico*, *Erminio*, *Lucio*, *Silvio*.

Del Carlo (188) Italian: patronymic from *Carlo*, Italian equivalent of CHARLES.
GIVEN NAMES Italian 6%. *Evo* (2), *Gino*, *Marino*, *Rinaldo*.

Del Castillo (589) Spanish: topographic name for someone 'from the (*del*) castle or fortified building (*castillo*)' (see CASTILLO).
GIVEN NAMES Spanish 44%. *Carlos* (11), *Jose* (10), *Juan* (7), *Enrique* (5), *Gabriela* (5), *Rafael* (5), *Rosario* (5), *Eduardo* (4), *Fernando* (4), *Javier* (4), *Mario* (4), *Raul* (4).

Del Cid (321) Spanish: probably a habitational name from any of the places named El Cid; compare CID.
GIVEN NAMES Spanish 58%. *Jose* (18), *Luis* (7), *Carlos* (6), *Francisco* (5), *Blanca* (4), *Jesus* (4), *Juan* (4), *Julio* (3), *Mario* (3), *Ana* (2), *Ana Maria* (2), *Armando* (2).

Del Conte (211) Italian (chiefly Tuscany): literally 'of or belonging to the count' (see CONTE), hence a name denoting the servant or possibly the son of a count or a patronymic from the nickname.

GIVEN NAMES Italian 20%. *Dario* (2), *Rocco* (2), *Sal* (2), *Americo*, *Claudio*, *Domenic*, *Estanislao*, *Luciano*, *Mario*, *Nevio*.

Del Core (125) Italian: patronymic from the personal name *Core*, from *cuore* 'heart', probably a short form of various medieval personal names formed with this element, such as *Bonocore*, meaning 'good heart'.
GIVEN NAMES Italian 12%. *Romano* (2), *Carlo*, *Carmine*, *Francesco*, *Giovanna*, *Riccardo*.

Delcour (123) French: northern variant of **Delacourt** 'from the court' (see COURT).

Del Duca (211) Italian (Sicily and Naples): literally 'of or belonging to the duke' (see DUCA), an occupational name for a servant or retainer of a duke.
GIVEN NAMES Italian 17%. *Pasquale* (3), *Americo*, *Antonio*, *Mario*, *Matteo*, *Rocco*.

Delee (226) **1.** Irish (West Cork): see DELAY. **2.** Perhaps from French **De Lé**, itself an adaptation of English LEE, from a nobleman who followed King James II into exile.

De Leeuw (417) Dutch: nickname for a courageous or regal person, from *leeuw* 'lion' + the definite article *de*. In some cases the surname may have originated from a habitational name, from a house distinguished by the sign of a lion.
GIVEN NAMES Dutch 4%. *Gerrit* (2), *Hendrik* (2), *Jacobus*, *Roelof*.

Delehanty (393) Irish: variant of DELAHUNTY.
GIVEN NAME Irish 5%. *Brendan*.

De Lellis (224) Italian: patronymic from the personal name LELLO, but here in the broader sense 'of the Lelli family'.
GIVEN NAMES Italian 11%. *Salvatore* (2), *Angelo*, *Antonio*, *Arduino*, *Camillo*, *Fausto*, *Rocco*.

De Lello (116) Italian: patronymic from the personal name LELLO.
GIVEN NAMES Italian 7%. *Sal*, *Salvatore*.

De Lemos (104) Portuguese and Galician: habitational name for someone from LEMOS.
GIVEN NAMES Spanish 20%; Portuguese 11%; French 9%. *Jose* (4), *Mario* (3), *Altagracia*, *Arturo*, *Augusto*, *Carlos*, *Juan Carlos*, *Miguel*, *Pedro*, *Richard*, *Roberto*, *Rodolfo*; *Joaquim*; *Gaston* (4).

De Leo (1223) Southern Italian: patronymic from the personal name *Leo*, a short form of LEONE.
GIVEN NAMES Italian 13%. *Rocco* (8), *Salvatore* (6), *Angelo* (5), *Caesar* (2), *Cosimo* (2), *Nicola* (2), *Pasquale* (2), *Sante* (2), *Annamaria*, *Bonaventura*, *Carlo*.

De Leon (8841) **1.** Spanish (**De León**): habitational name, variant of *León*, with the preposition *de* (see LEON). **2.** French (**Deléon**): patronymic from *Léon* (see LYON 2).
GIVEN NAMES Spanish 45%. *Jose* (192), *Juan* (99), *Manuel* (72), *Francisco* (54), *Luis* (52), *Pedro* (52), *Carlos* (51), *Jesus* (51),

Mario (44), *Ruben* (39), *Raul* (38), *Rafael* (33).

De Leonardis (206) Italian: patronymic from the personal name LEONARDO, but in the broader sense 'of or belonging to the Leonardi family'.
GIVEN NAMES Italian 15%. *Antonio* (2), *Rocco* (2), *Vito* (2), *Alfonse, Carlo, Dante, Delio, Lorenzo, Luigi, Pietro, Sal.*

Del Favero (176) Northern Italian: literally 'of or belonging to the smith', from *favero*, a dialect form of *fabbro* (see FABBRI), hence a name for the son, apprentice, associate, or servant of a blacksmith.
GIVEN NAMES Italian 7%. *Siro* (2), *Elio, Filippo, Umberto.*

Delfin (191) Spanish (**Delfín**) and Italian (Venice): variant of DELFINO.
GIVEN NAMES Spanish 37%, Italian 5%. *Armando* (2), *Enrique* (2), *Luis Alberto* (2), *Alfonso, Andres, Angel, Benito, Carlos, Carolina, Claudio, Corina, Eduardo, Eliseo; Angelo, Antonio, Federico, Romeo.*

Delfino (567) Italian and Spanish: from the personal name *Delfino*, from Latin *Delphinus*, from *delphis* 'dolphin', regarded in medieval times as a symbol of goodness and friendliness.
GIVEN NAMES Italian 18%; Spanish 9%. *Rocco* (3), *Angelo* (2), *Carlo* (2), *Geno* (2), *Adriano, Alberto, Alfredo, Antonio, Cosmo, Domenic, Domenico, Donatella, Ezio, Filomena, Fulvio; Alejandro* (2), *Carlos* (2), *Eduardo* (2), *Adolfo, Aguilar, Enrique, Filemon.*

Delfosse (202) French: topographic name for someone who lived by a ditch or in an area where ditches were a characteristic feature, from *fosse* 'ditch' (see FOSSE).
GIVEN NAMES French 6%. *Laurent, Olivier, Pierre.*

Delfs (164) **1.** North German and Frisian: from a reduced form of **Dethlefs**, a patronymic from an old personal name formed with Old High German *diot* 'people'. **2.** Dutch: variant of **van Delft**, a habitational name for someone from Delft.
GIVEN NAMES German 5%. *Guenther, Heinz.*

Delgadillo (1140) Spanish: from a diminutive of DELGADO.
GIVEN NAMES Spanish 55%. *Jose* (39), *Juan* (16), *Luis* (13), *Manuel* (12), *Ernesto* (11), *Jesus* (11), *Francisco* (10), *Rafael* (10), *Carlos* (9), *Javier* (9), *Pedro* (9), *Enrique* (8).

Delgado (12272) Spanish and Portuguese: nickname for a thin person, from Spanish, Portuguese *delgado* 'slender' (Latin *delicatus* 'dainty', 'exquisite', a derivative of *deliciae* 'delight', 'joy').
GIVEN NAMES Spanish 48%; Portuguese 10%. *Jose* (331), *Juan* (195), *Manuel* (122), *Luis* (119), *Carlos* (109), *Francisco* (100), *Jesus* (95), *Jorge* (73), *Pedro* (73), *Raul* (71), *Julio* (55), *Roberto* (54); *Joao* (5), *Paulo* (2), *Godofredo, Guilherme, Joaquim, Ligia, Marcio, Sil.*

Del Gatto (131) Italian: literally 'of or belonging to the cat' (see GATTO), hence a name denoting the son, apprentice, associate, or servant of a man known by this nickname.
GIVEN NAMES Italian 22%. *Carlo, Gennaro, Marco, Paolo, Tullio, Vito.*

Del Gaudio (230) Italian: literally 'of or belonging to the joyful one' (see GAUDIO), hence a name denoting the son, apprentice, associate, or servant of such a man.
GIVEN NAMES Italian 14%. *Dino* (2), *Carlo, Carmela, Carmine, Enrico, Luigi, Sal, Salvatore.*

Delger (103) German: perhaps a variant of **Telger**, from *Telge*, a north German topographic name for an enclosed tree nursery.

Del Giorno (179) Italian: probably a patronymic from the personal name *Giorno*, a short form of BONGIORNO.

Del Giudice (350) Italian: literally 'of or belonging to the officer of justice' (see GIUDICE), hence a name denoting the son, apprentice, associate, or servant of such a man.
GIVEN NAMES Italian 16%. *Angelo* (5), *Sal* (2), *Amore, Antonio, Carlo, Carmine, Ercole, Fausto, Gaetano, Guiseppe, Natale.*

Del Grande (188) Italian (chiefly Venetian): literally 'of or belonging to the big one or the great one' (see GRANDE), hence a name denoting the son, apprentice, associate, or servant of such a man.
GIVEN NAMES Italian 13%. *Dino* (2), *Angelo, Domenic, Marco, Oreste, Reno.*

Del Greco (289) Italian (chiefly Tuscan): literally 'of or belonging to the Greek' (see GRECO), hence a name denoting the son, apprentice, associate, or servant of a Greek.
GIVEN NAMES Italian 24%. *Angelo* (4), *Enrico* (3), *Rocco* (3), *Antonio* (2), *Domenic* (2), *Marco* (2), *Aldo, Carmela, Carmine, Cesare, Dino, Elio.*

Del Grosso (461) Italian (chiefly Tuscan): literally 'of or belonging to the fat one' (see GROSSO), hence a name denoting the son, apprentice, associate, or servant of such a man.
GIVEN NAMES Italian 17%. *Rocco* (7), *Angelo* (2), *Antonio* (2), *Donato* (2), *Guido* (2), *Camillo, Carmelina, Dante, Dino, Enrico, Fausto, Gino.*

Del Guercio (166) Italian (chiefly Tuscan): literally 'of or belonging to the cross-eyed one' (see GUERCIO), hence a name denoting the son, apprentice, associate, or servant of such a man.
GIVEN NAMES Italian 20%. *Alfonse, Carmine, Donato, Eligio, Gino, Giuseppe, Paolo.*

Del Guidice (171) Altered spelling of Italian DEL GIUDICE.
GIVEN NAMES Italian 12%. *Angelo, Gino, Pietro, Salvator, Saverio.*

D'Elia (1634) Italian: patronymic from the personal name ELIA.
GIVEN NAMES Italian 14%. *Angelo* (8), *Cono* (7), *Salvatore* (4), *Vito* (4), *Antonio* (3), *Sal*

(3), *Battista* (2), *Carmine* (2), *Cosmo* (2), *Elio* (2), *Fedele* (2), *Nicola* (2).

Delich (233) Probably an Americanized spelling of German **Delitzsch**, a habitational name of Slavic origin from either of two places in Saxony named Delitzsch.

De Lillo (228) Italian: variant of DI LILLO.
GIVEN NAMES Italian 18%. *Cono* (3), *Alessandra, Cosmo, Florindo, Gaetano, Riccardo, Rocco, Vito.*

De Lima (292) Portuguese: habitational name for someone from any of several places in Portugal called Lima, as for example Ponte de Lima.
GIVEN NAMES Spanish 23%; Portuguese 13%. *Jose* (8), *Alfredo* (3), *Marcos* (3), *Carlos* (2), *Cesar* (2), *Francisco* (2), *Josue* (2), *Luis* (2), *Manuel* (2), *Marcelo* (2), *Agnaldo, Albertino; Joao* (4), *Paulo, Vasco.*

Delin (118) French: patronymic from the personal name *Lin*.
GIVEN NAME French 4%. *Alain.*

De Line (349) Probably an Americanized spelling of the French surname **Deligne**, a habitational name from places named Ligne in Pas-de-Calais and Roquetoire in France or in Hainault, Belgium, or from a place called Deslignes.

De Lio (265) Southern Italian: variant of DI LEO, from a local form of the personal name.
GIVEN NAMES Italian 19%. *Rocco* (5), *Carmine* (4), *Angelo* (3), *Ciro, Francesco, Pasquale, Salvatore.*

Delis (129) Greek: variant spelling of DELLIS.
GIVEN NAMES Greek 8%. *Evangelos, Spero, Spiros, Spyros.*

Delisa (200) Italian (**De Lisa** or **D'Elisa**): metronymic from the female personal names *Lisa* or *Elisa*, short forms of *Elisabetta*, Italian equivalent of ELIZABETH.
GIVEN NAMES Italian 4%. *Dino, Gino, Romeo.*

Delise (244) **1.** Italian: variant of DELISA. **2.** French: metronymic from the female personal name *Lise*, a short form of **Elisabeth**.
GIVEN NAMES Italian 15%; French 4%. *Sal* (3), *Angelo* (2), *Salvatore* (2), *Antonio, Carmel, Claudio, Elvio, Elena, Gasper, Gianni, Giovanni, Idalia, Mariano, Mario, Pasquale, Vito; Christophe, Francois.*

De Lisi (359) Italian: patronymic from a reduced form of the personal name ALOISIO.
GIVEN NAMES Italian 22%. *Salvatore* (4), *Vito* (4), *Angelo* (2), *Carmelo* (2), *Rosario* (2), *Sal* (2), *Antonino, Antonio, Bartolo, Carmella, Mario, Onofrio, Orlando, Roberto, Serafina.*

De Lisio (253) Italian: variant of DI LISIO.
GIVEN NAMES Italian 6%. *Rocco* (2), *Carmine, Natale.*

Delisle (1511) English (**De Lisle**) and French: topographic and habitational name (see LYLE).
GIVEN NAMES French 10%. *Jacques* (4), *Marcel* (4), *Armand* (3), *Fernand* (2),

Francoise (2), *Gilles* (2), *Pierre* (2), *Alain, Alcide, Alphe, Andre, Aurelie.*

Deliso (137) Italian: possibly a patronymic from a rare personal name *Lis(i)o*, a masculine form of *Elisa* (see DELISA).

GIVEN NAMES Italian 21%. *Angelo* (2), *Sebastiano* (2), *Vito* (2), *Domenico, Giovanni, Santino.*

Deliz (100) Spanish and Galician (**De Liz**): habitational name from Liz in Lugo province, Galicia.

GIVEN NAMES Spanish 25%. *Carlos* (2), *Eduardo* (2), *Roberto* (2), *Angel, Aurea, Auria, Eleuteria, Ernesto, Felipe, Fernando, Gerardo, Guadalupe.*

Delk (1674) Probably a variant of **Telke**, meaning 'proud' or 'famous' or possibly a shortened form of German DELKER or **Delkner**.

Delker (262) German: topographic name for someone from the area of swampland near Gütersloh formerly known as *Delkene*, now called Dalke.

GIVEN NAMES German 4%. *Erwin, Hannelore, Milbert, Wilfried.*

Dell (2923) **1.** English: topographic name for someone who lived in a small valley, from Middle English, Old English *dell* 'dell', 'valley', or a habitational name from any of several minor places named Dell, from this word, for example in Buckinghamshire, Essex, and Sussex. **2.** German: from Low German *delle* 'dell', 'depression' (Middle High German *telle* 'gorge').

Della Croce (148) Italian: topographic name for someone who lived by a cross (see CROCE).

GIVEN NAMES Italian 17%. *Rocco* (2), *Dino, Enrico, Geno, Giampiero, Salvatore, Ugo.*

Dell'Anno (121) Italian: unexplained.

GIVEN NAMES Italian 28%. *Cosmo* (3), *Elia* (2), *Erasmo* (2), *Sal* (2), *Salvatore* (2), *Umberto* (2), *Constantino, Domenic, Gennaro, Nicola, Pietro.*

Della Penna (242) Italian: nickname from *penna* 'feather'.

GIVEN NAMES Italian 10%. *Salvatore* (3), *Gino, Guido, Ottavio, Rocco, Vincenzo.*

Della Porta (118) Italian: topographic name for someone who lived by a gate or portal (see PORTA).

GIVEN NAMES Italian 26%. *Orlando* (2), *Pasquale* (2), *Carmine, Francesco, Gennaro, Guerino, Rosario.*

Dell'Aquila (253) Italian: regional name for someone from the region of L'Aquila in central Italy. See AQUILA.

GIVEN NAMES Italian 19%. *Nicola* (3), *Aldo, Angelo, Antonio, Carmine, Fiore, Gaetano, Nicolo, Pasquale, Stefano, Tullio, Vincenzo.*

Della Rocca (139) Italian: topographic name for someone who lived by a fortress or mountain (see ROCCA).

GIVEN NAMES Italian 15%. *Aldo, Carlo, Carmine, Cosmo, Marcello.*

Della Rocco (149) Altered form of Italian DELLA ROCCA, influenced by the male personal name *Rocco*.

GIVEN NAMES Italian 13%. *Carlo, Pasquale, Salvatore.*

Della Torre (102) Italian: topographic name for someone who lived by a tower (see TORRE).

GIVEN NAMES Spanish 5%. *Mario* (2), *Juan, Santiago.*

Della Valle (282) Italian: topographic name for someone who lived in a valley (see VALLE).

GIVEN NAMES Italian 13%. *Angelo* (3), *Aldo, Battista, Carlo, Dino, Giacomo, Nicolo, Raffaele, Remo.*

Della Vecchia (211) Italian: metronymic ('son of the old woman') from **La Vecchia**, a nickname for an old woman or for the elder of two bearers of the same personal name.

GIVEN NAMES Italian 24%. *Amato* (4), *Guido* (2), *Stefano* (2), *Angelo, Antonio, Carmin, Ernesto, Guiseppe, Liberato, Lucio, Pasquale, Raffaele, Rocco.*

Delle (101) **1.** English: unexplained. **2.** French: habitational name from Delle, a place in Territoire de Belfort. The usual French spelling of the family name is **Delles**.

Delle Donne (144) Italian: nickname, literally meaning 'of the ladies', probably denoting a servant who worked at a convent.

GIVEN NAMES Italian 19%. *Vincenzo* (2), *Antonio, Carlo, Ciro, Dante, Gaspare, Salvatore, Vittorio.*

Deller (436) **1.** English: topographic name for someone who lived in a small valley (see DELL). **2.** German: from a short form of a personal name formed with an element cognate with Old English *deal* 'proud', 'famous'.

GIVEN NAMES French 5%. *Ludger* (2), *Evens, Kettly, Michel, Pierre.*

Dellert (121) Origin unidentified; possibly French.

GIVEN NAME French 5%. *Alphonse.*

Delles (144) French: habitational name for someone from Delle in the Térritoire de Belfort (between Franche-Comté and Alsace), in eastern France.

GIVEN NAME French 5%. *Pierre.*

Delligatti (215) Italian: **1.** nickname meaning 'of the (*delli*) cats (*gatti*)'. **2.** possibly a patronymic from the nickname *Gatto*, here perhaps in the broader sense 'of or belonging to the Gatti family'.

GIVEN NAMES Italian 11%. *Amato* (2), *Angelo* (2), *Annamarie, Antonio, Carmine, Geno, Luigi, Raffaele.*

Delling (123) **1.** English: variant of DILLING. **2.** German: habitational name from Delling, a place near Starnberg (Bavaria) or another near Wipperfürth (North Rhine-Westphalia), or a topographic name from Sorbian *delenki* 'place in a valley'.

Dellinger (3053) German: habitational name for someone from any of the various places called DELLING.

Dellis (188) **1.** Greek: derogatory nickname from Turkish *deli* 'fool', 'foolish', or a shortened form of any of the surnames formed with *Deli* as a prefix, e.g. **Deligiannis** 'crazy John'. **2.** French: habitational name from Lys-les-Lannoy, Lisse in the Netherlands, or Lies in the Belgian province of Brabant.

Delli Santi (135) Italian: literally 'of the saints', probably an occupational name for a servant in a monastery or other religions house, or a keeper of holy relics. Compare DEL SANTO.

GIVEN NAMES Italian 11%. *Angelo, Nichola, Pasquale.*

Dell'Olio (159) Italian: probably an occupational name for an extractor or seller of olive oil, Italian *olio*, from Latin *oleum* 'oil'.

GIVEN NAMES Italian 25%; Jewish 4%. *Angelo* (8), *Domenic, Franco, Mauro, Nicola, Salvatore, Vito; Miriam.*

Dello Russo (172) Italian (**Dello Russo**): patronymic from the nickname RUSSO.

GIVEN NAMES Italian 9%. *Amato, Carlo, Geno, Pietro, Salvatore.*

Dell'Osso (103) Southern Italian: according to Caracausi, this is from Arabic *lawz* 'almond tree'.

GIVEN NAMES Italian 16%. *Mario* (2), *Bernardino, Gabriela, Renato, Rico.*

Dellwo (120) Origin unidentified.

Delman (348) **1.** English: variant of DELL. **2.** Jewish (Ashkenazic): unexplained.

Delmar (366) **1.** English: reduced form of DELAMAR. **2.** German: from a Germanic personal name, *Dallomirus*, composed the an element cognate with Old English *deal* 'proud', 'famous'. **3.** Catalan: topographic name for someome living beside the sea or having some other association with the sea, from the fused preposition and article *del* 'of the' + *mar* 'sea'.

GIVEN NAMES Spanish 5%; French 4%. *Francisco* (2), *Mario* (2), *Aurelio, Carlos, Carmelita, Ernesto, Estrella, Jose, Leonida, Luz, Marcelo, Marcos; Henri* (2), *Ricot.*

Delmas (146) Southern French and Catalan (**Delmàs**): topographic name for someone from a *mas*, a remote, outlying farmstead. Compare DUMAS.

GIVEN NAMES French 6%; Spanish 5%. *Armelle, Fabienne; Andres, Jose, Josue, Miguel, Ruben, Teodoro.*

Del Mastro (301) Italian: literally 'of or belonging to the scholar, teacher, or craftsman' (see MASTRO), hence a name denoting the son, apprentice, associate, or servant of such a man.

GIVEN NAMES Italian 9%. *Angelo* (2), *Umberto* (2), *Antonio, Dino, Donato, Guido, Rocco.*

Del Medico (116) Italian: literally 'of or belonging to the physician' (see MEDICO), hence a name denoting the son, apprentice, or servant of such a man.
GIVEN NAMES Italian 8%; French 5%; German 5%. *Leonardo, Veto, Vincenzo, Vito; Armand* (2), *Chantal; Otto* (2).

Del Monaco (184) Italian: literally 'of or belonging to the monk' (see MONACO), an occupational name denoting a servant of a monk.
GIVEN NAMES Italian 22%. *Angelo* (2), *Domenic* (2), *Domenico* (2), *Alfredo, Antonio, Arturo, Benito, Dino, Erminio, Giovanna, Giovanni, Guerino, Mario.*

Del Monico (361) Italian: probably a variant of DEL MONACO.
GIVEN NAMES Italian 9%. *Domenic* (2), *Antonio, Carmela, Cosmo, Donato, Gennaro, Gino, Salvatore, Vito.*

Delmont (200) Catalan: topographic name for someone 'from the mountain', Catalan *mont* (see MONT, DEL MONTE).

Del Monte (586) Italian and Spanish: topographic name for someone 'from the mountain' (see MONTE).
GIVEN NAMES Italian 19%; Spanish 5%. *Gaspar* (5), *Angelo* (3), *Rocco* (3), *Giovanni* (2), *Pompeo* (2), *Antonio, Armelio, Berta, Camillo, Carmela, Deno, Elvio, Ezio, Gilda, Giulio; Angel, Gonzalo, Guillermina, Jesus, Jose, Jose Manuel.*

Del Moral (106) Spanish: habitational name for someone from any of the many places named El Moral, from *mora(l)* 'mulberry'.
GIVEN NAMES Spanish 38%. *Jose* (3), *Juan* (3), *Antonio* (2) *Armando* (2), *Luis* (2), *Mario* (2), *Roberto* (2), *Alicia, Ana, Carlos, Engracia, Jorge, Juan Manuel.*

Delmore (272) English: probably a reduced form of **Delamore**, itself a variant of DELAMAR.

Del Negro (182) Italian: literally 'of or belonging to the black one' (see NEGRO), hence a name denoting the son, apprentice, associate, or servant of a man bearing this nickname or ethnic name.
GIVEN NAMES Italian 11%. *Angelo* (3), *Ciro* (2), *Amedeo, Luca, Marco.*

Del Nero (164) Italian: variant of DEL NEGRO, from *nero* 'black', a variant of *negro*.
GIVEN NAMES Italian 14%. *Angelo* (2), *Antonio, Carlo, Dino, Luigi, Marco, Rocco, Tillio.*

Delo (278) **1.** Croatian (southern Dalmatia): unexplained. Possibly from *delo* 'work'. **2.** Possibly an altered spelling of the French surname **De l'Eau**, a topographic name, with fused preposition and article, for someone who lived by a stretch of water, from Old French *ewe* 'water'.

Deloach (2960) Origin unidentified. Perhaps an Americanized spelling of French *Deloche* (see DELOSH).

Deloache (113) See DELOACH.

Deloatch (467) See DELOACH.

Deloera (131) Mexican: unexplained.
GIVEN NAMES Spanish 56%. *Jose* (7), *Jesus* (4), *Juan* (3), *Pedro* (3), *Ruben* (3), *Carlos* (2), *Efrain* (2), *Fernando* (2), *Ramon* (2), *Alberto, Alfredo, Alicia.*

Deloge (106) French: habitational name from any of numerous places, especially in northern France, named with Old French *loge* 'hut', 'cabin'.
GIVEN NAMES French 14%. *Rosaire* (2), *Emile, Normand, Yves.*

Delon (100) French: from a reduced form of *d'Adelon*, a patronymic from the personal name *Adelon*, a pet form of a Germanic name formed with *adel* 'noble'.
GIVEN NAMES French 6%. *Alain, Michel.*

Delone (128) Probably a respelling of French DELON.
GIVEN NAME French 4%. *Jesula.*

Deloney (413) Probably an altered spelling of French **Delaunay**, a habitational name meaning 'from Aunay'. There are numerous minor places in northern and eastern France so named, from Latin *alnus* 'alder' + the collective suffix *-etum*.

Delong (6619) French: **1.** habitational name, with the preposition *de*, denoting someone from a place named Long, of which there are examples in Cher, Dordogne, and Somme. **2.** possibly a variant of **Lelong**, a nickname from *long* 'tall', 'long'.

De Loof (110) Dutch: probably a nickname from Middle Dutch *loof, love* 'tired', 'dull'.

De Lorenzo (1370) Italian: variant of DI LORENZO.
GIVEN NAMES Italian 10%. *Sal* (4), *Rocco* (3), *Salvatore* (3), *Vito* (3), *Angelo* (2), *Aniello* (2), *Carmine* (2), *Dino* (2), *Antonio, Attilio, Caesar, Carlo.*

Delorey (319) Possibly an altered spelling of the northern French habitational name **Delory**, a variant (with the preposition *de*) of LORY.

Delorge (109) French: according to Dauzat, an occupational name for a grain merchant, from Old French *orge* 'barley'.

Deloria (148) Origin unidentified; it looks as if it could be a habitational name for someone from Lória in Treviso, Italy, but the surname is not found in Italy; in some cases it may be an altered spelling of French DESLAURIERS.

Delorme (658) French: topographic name for someone who lived by an elm tree (see ORME).
GIVEN NAMES French 11%. *Andre* (6), *Lucien* (2), *Camille, Donat, Emile, Fernand, Gaston, Henri, Ives, Jacques, Jean Claude, Laurent.*

Delos (434) **1.** Catalan (**Delós** or **Delòs**): Catalan variant of **d'Alós** or **d'Alòs**, two habitational names from any of the towns named with those words, as for example Alós d'Isil (in the district of El Pallars) or Alòs de Balaguer (in the district of La Noguera), in Catalonia. **2.** French: habita-

tional name denoting someone from either of two places named Loos, in Nord and Pas-de-Calais.
GIVEN NAMES Spanish 51%; French 6%. *Santos* (39), *Reyes* (23), *Angeles, Cristina, Efren, Jose, Orestes, Santos Jose; Achille, Jacques, Pierre.*

Delosh (181) Perhaps an Americanized spelling of French **Deloche**, a regional variant of *Deloye* (see DELOY).

De los Reyes (407) Spanish: from the religious epithet *de los Reyes* 'of the kings', a reference to the Magi.
GIVEN NAMES Spanish 50%. *Jose* (10), *Ramon* (4), *Alberto* (3), *Eduardo* (3), *Gustavo* (3), *Jorge* (3), *Juan* (3), *Mario* (3), *Reynaldo* (3), *Roberto* (3), *Adolfo* (2), *Arturo* (2).

De los Rios (102) Spanish (**De los Ríos**): habitational name for someone from any of various places called Los Ríos 'the rivers' (from *río* 'river') or a topographic name with the same meaning.
GIVEN NAMES Spanish 56%. *Jorge* (3), *Julio* (3), *Aleida* (2), *Arturo* (2), *Carlos* (2), *Luis* (2), *Roberto* (2), *Adriana, Alejandro, Alvaro, Andres, Armida; Antonio, Leonardo, Marco, Marco Antonio.*

De los Santos (1400) Spanish: literally 'of the saints', a common element of personal names, originally denoting a child born or baptized on All Saints' Day.
GIVEN NAMES Spanish 48%. *Jose* (32), *Juan* (22), *Manuel* (16), *Miguel* (14), *Francisco* (12), *Carlos* (11), *Mario* (11), *Armando* (9), *Pedro* (9), *Raul* (9), *Jesus* (8), *Roberto* (8).

Deloy (103) **1.** Possibly a variant spelling of French **Deloye**: **2.** occupational name for a keeper of geese, from French *oie* 'goose'. **3.** habitational name for someone from a place named Loy (Jura, Cher) or Loyes (Ain).

Delozier (1158) Possibly a respelling of French **Delosière**, a topographic name for someone who lived in a place where osiers grew, Old French *osier.*

Delp (1723) German: of uncertain origin. Possibly a southern nickname for a clumsy person, from Middle High German *talpe, tape* 'paw'. Alternatively it may be a northern topographic name for someone living by a ditch, Middle Low German *delf* (frequently an element in compound field names in swampy terrain). A third possibility is that it is from an old personal name, cognate with Anglo-Saxon *deal* 'proud', 'famous'.

Del Papa (104) Italian: literally 'of or belonging to the priest or pope' (see PAPA), hence a name denoting someone in the service of a priest or a patronymic from the nickname.
GIVEN NAMES Italian 13%. *Domenic, Giovanni, Rocco.*

Delph (708) English: from Middle English *delf* 'excavation', 'digging' (Old English *(ge)delf*), hence a topographic name for someone who lived by a ditch or quarry, a metonymic occupational name for a ditch-cutter or quarryman, or alternatively a habitational name from any of various places named with this word, as for example Delf in Kent and Delph in Lancashire (now Greater Manchester) and Yorkshire.

Delphia (150) Origin unidentified.

Del Pino (216) Spanish and Italian: topographic name for someone 'from the pine tree (*pino*)'.
GIVEN NAMES Spanish 42%; Italian 5%. *Jose* (4), *Francisco* (2), *Jorge* (2), *Juan* (2), *Julio* (2), *Luis* (2), *Pedro* (2), *Ramon* (2), *Vicente* (2), *Agustin, Alberto, Alfredo; Albertina, Aldo, Carlo, Fausto, Flavio, Mauro, Silvio.*

Del Pizzo (166) Southern Italian: probably a topographic name for someone 'from the (*del*) peak (*pizzo*)' or a habitational name for someone from Pizzo in Vibo Valentia province, Calabria.
GIVEN NAMES Italian 12%. *Carlo* (2), *Angelo, Pietro.*

Del Ponte (151) Italian: topographic name for someone 'from the (*del*) bridge (*ponte*)' (see PONTE).
GIVEN NAMES Italian 18%. *Aldo* (2), *Dante* (2), *Pasco* (2), *Vito* (2), *Dino, Domenic, Flavio, Giuseppe, Simeone.*

Del Pozo (129) Spanish: topographic name for someone 'from the (*del*) well (*pozo*)'.
GIVEN NAMES Spanish 33%. *Carlos* (3), *Jorge* (3), *Armando* (2), *Eduardo* (2), *Jose* (2), *Juan* (2), *Luis* (2), *Mercedes* (2), *Aida, Aleida, Alicia, Ana.*

Del Pozzo (112) Italian: topographic name for someone 'from the well', Italian *pozzo* (see POZZI).
GIVEN NAMES Italian 19%. *Angelo* (3), *Antonio, Carmine, Ettore, Salvatore.*

Del Prete (317) Italian: literally 'of or belonging to the priest' (see PRESTO), hence a name denoting someone in the service of a priest, the son of a priest, or the son of someone dubbed 'The Priest'.
GIVEN NAMES Italian 18%. *Salvatore* (4), *Carlo* (2), *Pasquale* (2), *Angelo, Donato, Filippo, Gennaro, Lucio, Marco, Piero, Raffaello, Sal.*

Del Priore (213) Italian: literally 'of or belonging to the prior' (see PRIORE), hence a name denoting someone in the service of a prior, the son of a prior, or the son of someone dubbed 'The Prior'.
GIVEN NAMES Italian 30%. *Angelo* (6), *Carmine* (6), *Rocco* (6), *Domenic, Franco, Salvatore, Vincenzo, Vito.*

Del Re (213) Italian: literally 'of or belonging to the king' (see RE), hence a name denoting someone belonging to the household or in the service of a king, or the son of someone dubbed 'The King'.
GIVEN NAMES Italian 21%. *Pietro* (4), *Vito* (4), *Angelo* (3), *Sal* (2), *Aldo, Elisabetta, Gabriele, Guido, Marino, Nicoletta.*

Del Real (331) Spanish: habitational name for someone from El Real de la Jara (Seville) or El Real de San Vicente (Toledo).
GIVEN NAMES Spanish 57%. *Manuel* (12), *Jose* (10), *Juan* (8), *Pedro* (5), *Carlos* (4), *Luis* (4), *Ramon* (4), *Graciela* (3), *Jesus* (3), *Alejandro* (2), *Anastacio* (2), *Angel* (2).

Del Rio (1117) Spanish (**Del Río**): topographic name for someone 'from the (*del*) river or stream (*río*)'.
GIVEN NAMES Spanish 49%. *Jose* (34), *Luis* (18), *Jesus* (16), *Manuel* (13), *Carlos* (10), *Miguel* (10), *Jorge* (9), *Juan* (7), *Alberto* (6), *Ana* (5), *Arturo* (5), *Enrique* (5).

Del Rosario (931) Spanish: from the second element of a personal name formed with the religious suffix *del Rosario* 'of the rosary'.
GIVEN NAMES Spanish 44%. *Ramon* (13), *Jose* (12), *Luis* (8), *Lourdes* (7), *Fernando* (6), *Roberto* (5), *Ruben* (5), *Cesar* (4), *Juan* (4), *Mariano* (4), *Mario* (4), *Rafael* (4); *Antonio* (14), *Romeo* (4), *Dante* (2), *Lorenzo* (2), *Quirino* (2), *Carlo, Carmela, Carmelo, Claudina, Constantino, Federico, Leonardo.*

Del Rossi (205) Italian: descriptive epithet for a member of a red-haired family, literally 'of the red ones'. Compare DEL ROSSO.
GIVEN NAMES Italian 10%. *Angelo, Attilio, Carmel, Giorgio, Nunzio, Rocco, Romano.*

Del Rosso (227) Italian: literally 'of or belonging to the red one' (see ROSSO), hence a name denoting the son, associate, or servant of a man bearing this nickname.
GIVEN NAMES Italian 14%. *Angelo, Antonio, Cosmo, Deno, Natale, Saverio, Vita, Vito.*

Del Santo (152) Italian: literally 'of or belonging to the holy one' (see SANTO), hence a name denoting the son, associate, or servant of a man bearing this nickname, which can have both literal or ironical connotations.
GIVEN NAMES Italian 7%. *Angelo, Antonio, Cosimo, Giovanni, Goffredo, Lorenzo.*

Del Signore (446) Italian: literally 'of or belonging to the lord (or Lord God)' (see SIGNORE), hence a name denoting the son or servant of a man bearing this title, nickname, or a devotional name.
GIVEN NAMES Italian 16%. *Santo* (3), *Angelo* (2), *Alessandra, Attilio, Bonaventura, Dino, Domenic, Domenico, Filomena, Gino, Guido, Italo.*

Del Sol (125) Southern French and Spanish: topographic name for someone 'from the communal threshing floor', Occitan and Spanish *sol* (see SOL).
GIVEN NAMES Spanish 42%; French 8%. *Carlos* (3), *Arnaldo* (2), *Diego* (2), *Jose* (2), *Juana* (2), *Julio* (2), *Rolando* (2), *Alejandro, Alicia, Alina, Argelio, Armando; Michel* (2), *Christophe, Emile, Odile.*

Delson (127) Origin unidentified.
GIVEN NAMES German 5%. *Erwin* (2), *Gerda.*

Del Sordo (114) Italian: patronymic meaning 'son of the deaf man', from *sordo* 'deaf'.

GIVEN NAMES Italian 12%. *Angelo* (2), *Amato, Antonio, Silvio.*

Del Toro (671) Spanish and Italian (**Del Toro**): literally 'of the (*del*) bull (*toro*)', hence a nickname for someone who owned a bull or possibly for a bull fighter.
GIVEN NAMES Spanish 47%. *Jose* (22), *Juan* (9), *Luis* (9), *Manuel* (6), *Raul* (6), *Guadalupe* (5), *Ramon* (5), *Salvador* (5), *Armando* (4), *Francisco* (4), *Javier* (4), *Miguel* (4).

Del Tufo (104) Italian: topographic name from *tufo* 'tuff' (a porous rock formed from volcanic ash) or 'tufa' (a porous rock formed by precipitation of calcium carbonate from water, for example near mineral springs).
GIVEN NAMES Italian 8%. *Mario, Sal.*

De Luca (5929) Italian: patronymic from the personal name *Luca*, from Latin LUCAS. See also LUKE.
GIVEN NAMES Italian 14%. *Angelo* (24), *Salvatore* (18), *Rocco* (13), *Antonio* (11), *Carmine* (10), *Domenic* (8), *Sal* (6), *Vito* (6), *Gaetano* (5), *Gino* (5), *Luigi* (5), *Carlo* (4).

De Lucca (325) Italian: **1.** patronymic from the personal name *Luca*, from Latin LUCAS (compare DE LUCA). **2.** possibly a habitational name for someone from the Italian city of Lucca. This name is also found in Uruguay and Brazil.
GIVEN NAMES Italian 7%; Spanish 9%. *Angelo, Claudio, Pio; Jorge* (3), *Ricardo* (2), *Carlos, Jose, Maria Victoria, Ruben.*

De Lucchi (248) Italian: patronymic from the personal name *Lucco*, a variant of *Luca* (see DE LUCA).
GIVEN NAMES Italian 7%. *Angelo* (2), *Domenico, Guido, Luigi.*

Deluccia (115) Respelling of Italian DE LUCIA.
GIVEN NAMES Italian 18%. *Armando* (2), *Carmine.*

De Lucia (1289) Italian: metronymic from the female personal name *Lucia*.
GIVEN NAMES Italian 16%. *Angelo* (11), *Salvatore* (8), *Antonio* (3), *Pasquale* (3), *Rocco* (3), *Vito* (3), *Aniello* (2), *Carlo* (2), *Carmine* (2), *Luigi* (2), *Rocci* (2), *Romeo* (2).

Delude (275) Possibly an altered form of French DULUDE.
GIVEN NAMES French 5%. *Normand* (2), *Lucien.*

De Luise (156) Italian: patronymic from the personal name *Luise*, an old variant of *Luigi*, from the Latinized form *Aloysius* (see ALOISIO).
GIVEN NAMES Italian 24%. *Salvatore* (4), *Piero* (2), *Constantino, Dante, Silvestro.*

Deluke (116) Possibly an Americanized spelling of French **Deluc**, a patronymic from the personal name *Luc*, French form of LUKE, or a habitational name from any of several places named Luc, from Latin *lucus* 'grove', 'wood'. Alternatively, it may be an Americanized spelling of the habitational names **Duluc** or **Dulucq**.

De Luna (960) Spanish: habitational name for someone from LUNA.
GIVEN NAMES Spanish 49%. *Jose* (29), *Jesus* (14), *Juan* (13), *Manuel* (12), *Javier* (9), *Arturo* (8), *Pedro* (7), *Ramon* (7), *Raul* (7), *Ruben* (7), *Fernande* (6), *Luis* (6).

Delva (198) French: northern equivalent of DUVAL.
GIVEN NAMES French 35%; German 4%. *Yves* (5), *Andre* (2), *Astride*, *Christophe*, *Dominique*, *Edeline*, *Evens*, *Fernande*, *Germaine*, *Guerline*, *Pascal*, *Philomene*; *Ernst*, *Fritz*, *KarlHeinz*.

Del Valle (1493) **1.** Spanish: topographic name for someone who lived in a valley, *valle*, from Latin *vallis* (see VALLE). **2.** Possibly also an altered spelling of northern French **Delvallée**, also a topographic name for someone who lived in a valley, from French *vallée* 'valley'.
GIVEN NAMES Spanish 45%. *Jose* (45), *Carlos* (24), *Manuel* (22), *Luis* (18), *Juan* (13), *Mario* (13), *Pedro* (13), *Francisco* (11), *Jorge* (11), *Angel* (10), *Miguel* (10), *Orlando* (9).

Delvaux (132) French: topographic name from a vocalized form of *vals*, plural of *val* 'valley'. Compare DUVAL.
GIVEN NAMES French 12%. *Armand, Chantal, Jacques, Jean-Pierre, Lucien, Philippe, Pierre*.

Del Vecchio (1713) Italian (**Del Vecchio**) and Jewish (from Italy): literally 'of or belonging to the old one' (see VECCHIO), hence a name denoting the son, associate, or servant of a man dubbed 'The Old Man'. According to tradition this name was taken by various Jewish families long established in Italy (allegedly since the capture of Jerusalem by the Romans in AD70) to distinguish themselves from later arrivals who migrated there on being expelled from the Iberian Peninsula after 1492.
GIVEN NAMES Italian 16%. *Pasquale* (8), *Angelo* (6), *Antonio* (5), *Domenic* (5), *Salvatore* (5), *Vito* (4), *Francesco* (3), *Attilio* (2), *Carlo* (2), *Carmela* (2), *Carmine* (2), *Cosmo* (2).

Delventhal (119) German: habitational name from a place so named near Stade in Lower Saxony.

Del Villar (172) Galician: topographic name for someone 'from the little village (*villar*)'.
GIVEN NAMES Spanish 49%. *Luis* (6), *Angel* (3), *Felipe* (3), *Alicia* (2), *Andres* (2), *Carlos* (2), *Francisco* (2), *Javier* (2), *Jorge* (2), *Jose* (2), *Manuel* (2), *Miguel* (2).

Delwiche (122) Northern French: topographic name from Picard and Walloon *wiche* 'vine tendril' (Old French *guiche*, from Latin *vitica*).

Delzell (239) Probably an altered form of Scottish DALZELL.

Delzer (397) German: habitational name originally denoting someone from Delitz or Delitzsch, both in Saxony.

De Maggio (139) Italian: variant of DI MAGGIO.
GIVEN NAMES Italian 12%. *Biagio, Santo*.

Demain (132) French: **1.** by ellipsis from '(homme) de main', from *main* 'hand'. **2.** habitational name originally denoting someone from Maing in Nord. **3.** possibly from *demain* 'tomorrow'.

Demaine (125) French: **1.** variant of DEMAIN. **2.** habitational name for someone from a place named with southern French *maine* 'residence', 'residential building', for example in Angoumois, Périgord.

De Maio (1230) Italian: patronymic from the personal name *Maio*, a southern variant of MAGGIO.
GIVEN NAMES Italian 12%. *Salvatore* (4), *Carmine* (3), *Pasquale* (3), *Angelo* (2), *Antonio* (2), *Cosmo* (2), *Dino* (2), *Enrico* (2), *Carmela, Carmelo, Carmino*.

Deman (177) **1.** French: variant of DEMAIN. **2.** English: variant of DAYMON. **3.** German: variant of DAMIAN. **4.** German: metonymic occupational name for a diamond cutter or dealer, from Middle Low German *dēmant* 'diamond'. **5.** Altered spelling of German **Dehmann**.
GIVEN NAMES French 7%; Dutch 5%; German 4%. *Marcel* (2), *Camille, Prosper*; *Heiko* (3), *Gerrit*; *Jochen* (2), *Hans*.

Demanche (103) French: from a regional variant of the personal name DOMINIQUE. Compare DEMANGE.
GIVEN NAMES French 16%. *Armand, Cecile, Marcel, Michel, Normand*.

Demand (112) German and French (Alsatian and Walloon): origin uncertain. Perhaps an altered form of **de Mandel**, a topographic name for someone who lived by an almond tree (German *Mandel*).

Demange (110) French: from a regional variant of the personal name DOMINIQUE. Compare DEMANCHE.
GIVEN NAME French 4%. *Pierre*.

Demann (124) Variant spelling of German **Dehmann**: **1.** from a short form of the personal name *Deneman* (from *Dene*, possibly a short form of DANIEL, + *man* 'man'); **2.** variant of DAMIAN; **3.** from a place named Dehme, near Minden, Westphalia.
GIVEN NAME German 5%. *Kurt* (2).

Demar (454) **1.** German: habitational name from a place called Themar (between Meiningen and Coburg). **2.** Possibly an altered spelling of the French family name DEMARS, a habitational name for someone from any of the places called Mars, for example in the Ardennes, Creuse, Gard, Loire, and Loire-Inférieure. The place name is from the personal name *Martius*, the name of the proprietor of the villa.

Demara (108) Spanish (Mexico): habitational name for someone from Mara in Zaragoza province, Spain.

GIVEN NAMES Spanish 5%. *Manuel, Rosalinda*.

Demarais (391) French: habitational name, with the preposition *de*, for someone from any of several minor places in northern France named Marais, from Old French *mareis* 'marsh'. In some cases, the name may simply have been topographical.
GIVEN NAMES French 4%. *Cecile, Liette, Prosper*.

Demaray (209) Americanized spelling of DEMARAIS.

Demarce (103) Origin unidentified. Perhaps a respelling of French DEMARS.

De Marchi (206) Italian: patronymic from the personal name *Marco*, from Latin *Marcus* (see MARK).
GIVEN NAMES Italian 13%. *Geno* (2), *Aldo, Angelo, Carlo, Carmela, Cesare, Donato, Gildo, Guido, Vita*.

De Marco (5251) Italian: variant of DI MARCO.
GIVEN NAMES Italian 13%. *Salvatore* (24), *Angelo* (23), *Carlo* (12), *Sal* (9), *Antonio* (7), *Rocco* (7), *Vito* (7), *Domenic* (6), *Carmine* (5), *Dino* (5), *Pasquale* (5), *Aldo* (4).

De Marcus (162) Evidently a Latinate patronymic from the personal name MARCUS, although the language of origin has not been satisfactorily identified.

Demare (115) **1.** Probably an altered form of Italian DI MARE. **2.** Dutch: nickname from *de mare* 'the famous (one)'.
GIVEN NAMES Italian 9%. *Angelo, Dino*.

Demaree (695) Americanized spelling of French DESMARAIS.

Demarest (1135) French: regional variant of DESMARAIS.

De Maria (1139) Italian and Spanish (**De María**): metronymic from the female personal name MARIA, or name for a devotee of the Virgin Mary.
GIVEN NAMES Italian 22%; Spanish 11%. *Mario* (7), *Angelo* (9), *Sal* (5), *Salvatore* (5), *Pasquale* (3), *Rocco* (3), *Carmine* (2), *Orlando* (2), *Vito* (2), *Antonio, Carlo, Marcelo* (2), *Alfonso, Angelina, Armando, Carlos, Carmel, Carmela, Carmelita, Elia, Ramon, Rosario*.

Demarie (121) Northern French: variant of DEMARY.

De Marinis (219) Italian: **1.** patronymic from the personal name *Marino* (from the Latin personal name *Marinus*, of Etruscan origin), but here in the broader sense 'of or belonging to the Marini family'. **2.** habitational name for someone from a place named Marino or Marini; these are common place names, particularly in central southern Italy.
GIVEN NAMES Italian 19%. *Angelo* (3), *Antonio* (2), *Vito* (2), *Nicola, Trifone, Vicenzo*.

De Marino (216) Variant of Italian DI MARINO.

GIVEN NAMES Italian 11%. *Rocco* (3), *Alfonse, Gilda, Sabatino.*

De Mario (287) Italian: variant of DI MARIO.

GIVEN NAMES Italian 9%. *Rocco* (3), *Angelo, Carina, Giuseppe, Nino, Vito.*

Demaris (293) Origin unidentified. Perhaps an altered spelling of DESMARAIS.

Demark (220) **1.** Altered spelling of the French family name **Demarcq**, a habitational name, with the preposition *de*, for someone from a place named Marcq, of which there are examples in Ardennes, Nord, and Yvelines. **2.** Northern French: habitational name, with the preposition *de*, from Marke in West Flanders, Marck in Pas de Calais, or any of the places in France and Belgium named with the Germanic element *marca* 'boundary', 'frontier'.

GIVEN NAME Italian 7%. *Angelo* (3).

Demarr (126) French: habitational name, with the preposition *de* 'from', from Marre in Meuse.

Demars (1455) French: habitational name from any of several places named Mars.

Demarse (112) Americanized form of French DEMARS.

GIVEN NAME French 5%. *Emile.*

Demarsh (163) Americanized form of French DEMARS.

Demartin (185) Partly Americanized form of Italian DE MARTINO or DE MARTINI.

De Martini (699) Italian: variant of DI MARTINO.

GIVEN NAMES Italian 4%. *Cesare* (2), *Aldo, Angelo, Delio, Elio, Luigi, Romeo, Salvatore.*

De Martinis (103) Italian: variant of DE MARTINO, in the broader sense 'of or belonging to the Martini family'.

GIVEN NAMES Italian 18%. *Antonio* (4), *Angelo, Giuseppe, Guerino, Nicola, Sal, Sandro, Tullio.*

De Martino (1019) Italian: variant of DI MARTINO.

GIVEN NAMES Italian 14%. *Salvatore* (5), *Gaetano* (4), *Angelo* (3), *Pasquale* (3), *Antonio* (2), *Gasper* (2), *Marco* (2), *Aldo, Antonino, Carmine, Dario, Domenic.*

Demary (232) Northern French: habitational name, with the preposition *de*, for someone from a place named Maury, in Pas-de-Calais.

De Marzo (171) Italian: variant of DI MARZO.

GIVEN NAMES Italian 19%. *Angelo* (2), *Antonio* (2), *Vito* (2), *Dino, Enrico, Graziano.*

Demas (584) Probably a variant of French DUMAS or DELMAS.

De Masi (589) Italian: variant of DI MASI.

GIVEN NAMES Italian 15%. *Vincenzo* (5), *Antonio* (3), *Rocco* (3), *Giuseppe* (2), *Pasquale* (2), *Sal* (2), *Amerigo, Carlo, Carmela, Carmelo, Domenic.*

De Maso (105) Variant of Italian **De Masi**, a patronymic from the personal name *Maso*,

a short form of *Tommaso*, Italian equivalent of THOMAS.

GIVEN NAMES Italian 11%. *Angelo, Mauro, Nichola.*

Demaster (112) See DEMASTERS.

Demasters (185) Origin unidentified. Possibly a part-translation of French **Demaistre**, **Demaître**, a patronymic meaning '(son) of the teacher'.

Demastus (136) See DEMASTERS.

Demato (103) Galician: variant of MATO and more particularly **Domato**, a habitational name for someone from any of the numerous places in Galicia called Mato or O Mato (formerly El Mato), from *mato* 'brushwood', or a topographic name with the same meaning.

GIVEN NAMES Italian 11%. *Americo, Giovanni, Nunzio.*

De Mattei (125) Italian: variant of DI MATTEO.

GIVEN NAMES Italian 13%. *Angelo* (3), *Gaetano* (2), *Silvio.*

De Matteis (333) Italian: patronymic from the personal name *Matteo* (see MATTHEW), in the broader sense 'of or belonging to the Mattei family'.

GIVEN NAMES Italian 13%; French 4%. *Angelo* (3), *Domenic* (2), *Agostino, Dino, Pasquale, Rocco, Salvatore, Umberto; Achille, Gaelle, Jean Marc.*

De Matteo (740) Italian: variant of DI MATTEO.

GIVEN NAMES Italian 12%. *Dante* (4), *Salvatore* (3), *Angelo* (2), *Carmine* (2), *Elio* (2), *Guido* (2), *Annamarie, Benedetto, Carlo, Emelio, Gino, Pasquale.*

De Mattia (227) Italian: variant of DI MATTIA.

GIVEN NAMES Italian 9%; French 4%. *Vito* (2), *Angelo, Antonietta, Luca, Quinto, Salvatore; Constant* (2), *Armand.*

De Mauro (308) Southern Italian: variant of DI MAURO.

GIVEN NAMES Italian 13%. *Sal* (4), *Vito* (2), *Angelo, Carlo, Enrico, Orazio, Salvatore.*

Demay (599) **1.** French: habitational name, with the preposition *de*, for someone from either of two minor places called May, in Drôme and Rhône. **2.** northern French: topographic name from *mê* 'trough', presumably denoting someone who lived in a trough-shaped hollow. **3.** Northern French: topographic name from Old French *mes*, *meis* 'house', 'dwelling' (Latin *mansus*). Compare DUMAS.

GIVEN NAMES French 4%. *Andree, Gabrielle, Henri, Jean Claude, Patrice.*

Demayo (422) Respelling of Italian DE MAIO.

GIVEN NAMES Italian 6%. *Angelo, Gaetano.*

Dembeck (173) Americanized spelling of Polish DEMBEK.

Dembek (129) **1.** Polish: variant spelling of **Dąbek**, from a pet form of the personal name *dąb*, or a nickname from *dąbek* 'small oak'. **2.** Jewish (from Poland):

ornamental adoption of Polish *dąbek* 'small oak'.

GIVEN NAMES Polish 6%. *Bogdan, Dariusz.*

Dembinski (248) Polish (**Dembiński**), Jewish (eastern Ashkenazic), Ukrainian, and Belorussian: habitational name for someone from a place named with *dąb* 'oak': in Polish *Dębin*, *Dębina*, or *Dębiny*; in Ukrainian or Belorussian *Dembino*. The usual form of the Polish surname is **Dębiński**.

GIVEN NAMES Polish 4%. *Janina, Pawel, Wlodzimierz, Zygmunt.*

Dembo (158) Jewish (from Lithuania): habitational name for someone from any of various places in Lithuania or Poland called Dęby.

GIVEN NAMES French 4%; Jewish 4%. *Michel, Patrice; Ari, Moysey.*

Dembowski (446) Polish (**Dębowski**): habitational name for someone from any of various places called Dębowa, Dębowo, or Dębów, from *dąb* 'oak'.

FOREBEARS The surnames Dembowski and Dębowski, borne by several Polish noble families, can be traced back to the 14th century.

GIVEN NAMES Polish 4%. *Casimir, Henryk, Rajmund, Zigmund, Zygmond.*

Dembski (156) Polish and Jewish (from Poland): variant spelling of **Dębski** (see DEBSKI).

GIVEN NAMES German 6%. *Kurt* (2), *Alois, Fritz.*

Demby (355) Polish: habitational name for someone from a place named Dęby.

Demchak (308) **1.** Americanized spelling of Czech and Slovak **Demčák**, or Polish **Demczak**, from a pet form of a vernacular form (Czech and Slovak *Demet(e)r*, Polish *Dymitr*) of the Greek personal name *Dēmētrios* (Latin *Demetrius*; see DEMETRIOU). **2.** Ukrainian: from a pet form of the personal name *Demjan* (see DAMIAN).

Demchuk (122) Ukrainian: patronymic from a pet form of the personal name *Demjan* (see DAMIAN) or *Dymitr* (Latin *Demetrius*; see DEMETRIOU).

GIVEN NAMES Russian 8%; Polish 7%. *Fyodor, Igor, Sergey, Vitaliy, Vladimir; Wasil* (3).

De Meester (125) Dutch: from Middle Dutch *meester* 'master' + the definite article *de*; a nickname for someone who behaved in a masterful manner, or an occupational name for someone who was a master craftsman. See also MASTER.

GIVEN NAME French 4%. *Georges.*

Demel (258) German: of uncertain origin. It may be from a pet form of the personal name THOMAS, but in most cases it is more probably an altered spelling of **Dehmel**, from an old personal name *Dagomar*, formed with Old High German *tac* 'day'.

GIVEN NAMES German 6%. *Alois, Ewald, Florian, Kurt, Reinhard, Wilhelm.*

De Mello (1040) **1.** Portuguese: variant spelling of DE MELO. The name in this spelling is also found in western India, where it was taken by Portuguese colonists. **2.** Italian: patronymic from a short form of *Giacomello*, a pet form of *Giacomo*, from Late Latin *Jac(o)mus* (see JAMES).

GIVEN NAMES Spanish 8%; Portuguese 6%. *Manuel* (17), *Jose* (11), *Fernando* (5), *Eduardo* (4), *Ana* (2), *Jaime* (2), *Mario* (2), *Sergio* (2), *Abdias, Adelino, Aires, Albino*; *Joao* (2), *Paulo* (2), *Seraphine*.

De Melo (264) Portuguese: habitational name for someone from a place named Melo (Porto), from Latin *merulus* 'blackbird'.

GIVEN NAMES Spanish 33%; Portuguese 24%; Italian 8%. *Jose* (16), *Manuel* (13), *Carlos* (6), *Luis* (4), *Armando* (3), *Mario* (3), *Alexandrina* (2), *Armindo* (2), *Francisco* (2), *Helio* (2), *Marcos* (2), *Adalberto*; *Joao* (7), *Paulo, Vasco*; *Antonio* (14), *Alberico, Emidio, Ezio, Licinio, Luciano, Marcello*.

Dement (1553) Possibly an altered spelling of German **Demant**, a metonymic occupational name for a diamond dealer or cutter, from Middle High German *dīemant* 'diamond'.

De Meo (942) Italian: variant of DI MEO.

GIVEN NAMES Italian 11%. *Angelo* (9), *Rocco* (5), *Romeo* (3), *Carmine* (2), *Salvatore* (2), *Alfonse, Amadeo, Amedeo, Antonio, Attilio, Benedetto, Caesar*.

Demerath (114) German: habitational name from a place so named in the Rhineland.

Demerchant (132) French: perhaps a Flemish occupational name for a merchant.

GIVEN NAME French 4%. *Blanchard*.

Demeritt (291) Possibly an altered form of French DESMARAIS or *Desmarest* (see DEMAREST).

GIVEN NAMES French 4%. *Andrus, Delphin*.

Demers (3804) **1.** English: patronymic from DEEMER. **2.** French: habitational name apparently associated with a specific domain; the source is unclear, because of the wide range of local variants.

GIVEN NAMES French 14%. *Mireille* (40), *Marcel* (11), *Andre* (10), *Armand* (9), *Lucien* (9), *Normand* (9), *Jacques* (6), *Alphonse* (5), *Fernand* (5), *Adrien* (4), *Alcide* (4), *Cecile* (4).

Demery (473) Probably an altered spelling of French DEMORY.

Demeter (529) **1.** German: occupational name for a weaver or cloth merchant, from an agent derivative of Middle High German *timīt, dimīt* denoting a type of cloth woven with double thread. **2.** Czech and Slovak: from the personal name *Demeter*, derived from Greek *Dēmētrios* (Latin *Demetrius*; see DEMETRIOU). **3.** Hungarian: from the ecclesiastical name *Demeter*, or *Dömötör*, from Greek *Dēmētrios* (Latin *Demetrius*; see DEMETRIOU).

GIVEN NAMES Hungarian 7%. *Attila* (3), *Bela* (3), *Laszlo* (3), *Gyula* (2), *Geza, Ildiko, Istvan, Jolan, Zsolt*.

Demetriou (217) Greek: from the genitive case of the personal name *Dēmētrios* '(follower) of Dēmēter', the classical goddess of fertility, whose name derives from an obscure element *dē*, sometimes taken as a Doric equivalent of Attic *gē* 'earth' + *mētēr* 'mother'. This name was borne by several early Christian martyrs, and its popularity in eastern Europe is largely due to the fame of a 4th-century saint executed under Diocletian. Genitive patronymics are particularly associated with Cyprus.

GIVEN NAMES Greek 27%. *Andreas* (6), *Demetrios* (4), *Christos* (2), *Demetris* (2), *Kyriacos* (2), *Marios* (2), *Savvas* (2), *Spyros* (2), *Angeliki, Angelos, Athanasios, Georgios*.

Demetro (113) Hispanic: probably a variant of Spanish **Metro**, unexplained; possibly related to *metro* 'measure; rule'.

De Meulenaere (115) Dutch: occupational name from Middle Dutch *muelnare* 'miller' + the definite article *de*.

Demeuse (134) French: habitational name for someone from a place in Haute Marne formerly called Meuse, now Montigny-le-Roi. The earlier place name derives from the river name, this, according to Morlet, being a place where various streams unite to form the Meuse river.

GIVEN NAMES Scandinavian 4%. *Hilma, Nels*.

Demey (114) French: habitational name for someone from (*de*) Mey (Moselle), which derives its name from the Romano-Gallic estate name *Maiacum*.

GIVEN NAMES French 5%; Dutch 4%. *Olivier*; *Corniel, Willem*.

De Meyer (310) Dutch: occupational name from Middle Dutch *de meyer* 'the steward', 'the bailiff' (see MEYER).

GIVEN NAMES French 6%. *Alphonse, Gaston, Marcel, Patrice*.

Demian (101) Muslim: unexplained.

GIVEN NAMES Muslim 22%; French 11%. *Ashraf* (2), *Bassem* (2), *Makram* (2), *Fawzi, Hany, Maher, Nabil, Samir, Yousef, Ziad*; *Aurel* (4), *Andre*.

Demicco (172) Variant of Italian **De Mico**, a patronymic from the personal name *Mico*, a pet form of DOMENICO.

GIVEN NAMES Italian 12%. *Angelo* (2), *Domenico, Gaetano, Quido*.

Demichael (131) Partly Americanized form of Italian DE MICHELE or any of its variants, or possibly of the French cognate **Demichel**.

GIVEN NAMES Italian 10%. *Carmine, Marino, Tullio*.

De Michele (404) Italian: variant of DI MICHELE.

GIVEN NAMES Italian 12%. *Angelo* (2), *Carlo* (2), *Antonio, Carmine, Domenic, Pasquale, Pietro, Santo, Vito*.

Demick (258) Probably an altered spelling of the German surname **Demmig** or **Demmich** (of unexplained origin), or of the Old Prussian personal name *Demeke*.

D'Emilio (206) Italian: patronymic from the personal name EMILIO.

GIVEN NAMES Italian 21%. *Rocco* (2), *Vito* (2), *Angelo, Carmine, Cesare, Domenic, Falco, Giuseppe, Guido, Luca, Luigi, Pasquale*.

Demille (434) Belgian French: habitational name, with the preposition *de*, for someone from Hamme-Mille in Belgium.

Deming (2201) English: from Old English *dēmung* 'judgement', 'act of judging', hence a metonymic occupational name for a judge or for an arbiter of minor disputes. Compare DEEMER and DEEM.

Demint (191) Origin unidentified.

Demirjian (188) Armenian: patronymic from an occupational name derived from Turkish *demirci* 'ironmonger' or 'ironsmith' a derivative of *demir* 'iron'.

GIVEN NAMES Armenian 49%. *Raffi* (3), *Yervant* (3), *Ara* (2), *Garabet* (2), *Hagop* (2), *Nerses* (2), *Vartan* (2), *Andranik, Arshalous, Avak, Avedis, Deran*.

Demko (739) **1.** Polish and Slovak: from a pet form of a personal name, Polish *Dymitr* and Slovak *Demeter*, from Greek *Dēmētrios* (Latin *Demetrius*; see DEMETRIOU). **2.** Ukrainian: from a pet form of a personal name *Demjan* (see DAMIAN).

Deml (147) German: variant of DEMEL.

GIVEN NAMES German 5%. *Bernhard, Ignaz, Wolfgang*.

Demler (296) **1.** German: from an old personal name, *Damo*, a short form of a compound name formed with Old High German *tac* 'day'. **2.** Perhaps an altered spelling of German **Demmler**, a southern nickname for a glutton, from an agent derivative of Middle High German *demmen* 'to indulge oneself', or a northern nickname from Middle Low German *damelaer*, *demeler* 'prankster', 'flirt'.

Demlow (123) Origin unidentified.

GIVEN NAME German 4%. *Armin*.

Demma (295) Italian: metronymic from the female personal name EMMA.

GIVEN NAMES Italian 13%. *Angelo* (4), *Salvatore* (2), *Carlo, Gaetano, Marco, Mattia, Petrina, Saverio*.

Demme (119) German and French: from *Thiemo*, a short form of the Germanic personal name *Theudemar*, composed of the elements *theud* 'people', 'race' + *māri*, *mēri* 'famous'.

GIVEN NAMES Scandinavian 6%; German 4%. *Nils*; *Heiner*.

Demmer (317) German: **1.** nickname for a glutton, from an agent derivative of Middle High German *demmen* 'to indulge oneself'. **2.** from the Germanic personal name *Theudemar* (see DEMME).

Demmin (133) German: habitational name from a place so named in Brandenburg.

Demming (183) **1.** German: habitational name from Demmingen in Württemberg. **2.** English: variant of DEMING.

Demmitt (110) Probably an altered spelling of German **Demit**, a metonymic occupational name for a weaver or cloth dealer, from Middle High German *dimit* 'dimity' (from Greek *dimitos*). Compare DEMETER.

Demmon (204) Altered spelling of English and Scottish DAMON.

Demmons (188) Variant of English or Scottish DEMMON.

Demmy (107) German: unexplained.

Demo (369) Greek and Southern Italian: shortened form of DEMOS.

Demonbreun (160) Possibly an altered form of the French habitational name **Monbrun**, denoting someone from Monbrun in Gers, or Montbrun in Aude, Drôme, Lot, and Lozère, presumably all named as 'brown mountain'.

Demond (283) Possibly an altered spelling of DEMONT.

Demont (253) French: topographic name, with the preposition *de*, from *mont* 'hill' (see MONT).

Demonte (333) Italian: possibly a topographic name from *monte* 'hill' (from Latin *mons*, genitive *montis*), with the preposition *de* 'from'.
GIVEN NAMES Italian 22%. *Vito* (12), *Donato* (2), *Domenico*, *Emanuele*, *Francesco*, *Giovanna*, *Nicola*, *Primo*, *Rocco*.

Demontigny (124) French: habitational name, with the preposition *de*, for someone from any of the numerous places named Montigny, from Latin *Montiniacum* (formed either from a personal name or from a derivative of *mons* 'mountain' + the locative suffix *-acum*).
GIVEN NAMES French 9%. *Aurele*, *Gilles*, *Jacques*.

Demopoulos (172) Greek: patronymic from the personal name DEMOS, pet form of *Dēmētrios* (see DEMETRIOU), + the suffix *-poulos*, derived from Latin *pullus* 'nestling', 'chick'; this ending occurs chiefly in the Peloponnese.
GIVEN NAMES Greek 14%. *Konstantinos* (2), *Angeliki*, *Anthoula*, *Athanasia*, *Christos*, *Costas*, *Kostas*, *Koula*, *Panayiotis*, *Stavros*.

Demoranville (133) French: habitational name for someone from Moranville in Meuse.

Demore (337) **1.** French: patronymic from the nickname MORE 3,4,5. **2.** Altered spelling of French D'AMOUR.

Demorest (325) Altered spelling of French DESMARAIS or **Desmarest** (see DEMAREST).

Demoret (101) Altered spelling of French DESMARAIS or **Desmarest** (see DEMAREST).

Demory (212) French: **1.** patronymic from *Mory*, a reduced form of *Amory* (see EMERY). **2.** northern French habitational name, with the preposition *de*, for someone from any of various places called Mory, in Oise, Pas-de-Calais, or Seine-et-Marne, the place name being derived from Latin *Mauriacum* (composed of a personal name *Maurius* + locative suffix *-acum*).
GIVEN NAMES French 4%. *Monique*, *Pascal*.

Demos (682) Greek: from the Greek personal name *Demos*, pet form of *Dēmētrios* (see DEMETRIOU), or from a shortened form of a Greek patronymic based on this name, for example DEMOPOULOS.
GIVEN NAMES Greek 6%. *Apostolos* (2), *Anthoula*, *Constantine*, *Costas*, *Demetrios*, *Despina*, *Eleni*, *Epaminondas*, *Kalliope*, *Kosta*, *Panagiotis*, *Spiro*.

Demoss (1904) Origin unidentified.

Demott (933) Variant spelling of French DEMOTTE.
FOREBEARS A family of this name, probably of Huguenot origin, is recorded in Pompton Plains, NJ, and Hempstead, NY, in the 18th century. The surname is now also common in MO, KS, and elsewhere.

Demotte (138) French: variant of **De la Motte**, a topographic name from *motte* 'motte' (a man-made mound forming the site of a castle), or more probably a habitational name from any of several minor places named with this word (see MOTTE).

Demoulin (153) French: topographic name, with the preposition *de*, from *moulin* 'mill', or a habitational name from any of the numerous places named with this word. See also MOULIN. In French-speaking countries DUMOULIN, or the plural, **Desmoulins**, is the more common form. All are frequently translated as MILLER.
GIVEN NAMES French 7%. *Chantel*, *Honorine*, *Yves*.

De Moura (148) Portuguese and Galician: habitational name for someone from the Portuguese town of Moura (Alentejo) or any of various similarly named places in Galicia.
GIVEN NAMES Portuguese 16%; Spanish 15%. *Joao* (3), *Joaquim* (2), *Almir*; *Jose* (3), *Renato* (2), *Adriana*, *Ezequiel*, *Joaquin*, *Julio*, *Luis*, *Luiz*, *Oswaldo*, *Rafael*, *Raymondo*; *Antonio* (5), *Giovanni*.

Dempewolf (161) North German: metonymic occupational name for a hunter, from Middle Low German *dempen* 'to choke someone (with steam)' + *wolf* 'wolf'; so literally 'strangle the wolf'.

Demps (332) Origin uncertain: possibly a variant form of DEMPSEY.

Dempsey (10114) Irish: Anglicized form of Gaelic **Ó Díomasaigh** 'descendant of *Díomasach*', a byname meaning 'proud', 'haughty', from *díomas* 'pride'. The name was occasionally Anglicized as *Proudman* (see PROUD). Compare MCGIMSEY.

Dempster (965) **1.** Scottish, Manx, and English: occupational name for a judge or arbiter of minor disputes, from Old English *dēm(e)stre*, a derivative of the verb *dēmian* 'to judge or pronounce judgement'. Although this was originally a feminine form of the masculine *dēmere*, by the Middle English period the suffix *-stre* had lost its feminine force, and the term was used of both sexes. The surname is not common in England, where the term was early replaced by Anglo-Norman French *juge* (see JUDGE), but relatively frequent in Scotland, where until 1747 every laird of a barony could have certain offenses within his territory tried by his *dempster*, and on the Isle of Man, where *deemsters* also played an important part in the administration of justice. **2.** Irish (especially County Down): as 1, but also occasionally used instead of DEMPSEY.

Demske (123) Eastern German: from a Slavic (Sorbian) word meaning 'oak', either as a topographic name or a habitational name from a place named with this word (see DEMSKI).

Demski (362) **1.** Jewish (from Poland and adjacent regions): from Polish *dąb*, *demb* 'oak', either a habitational name from a place named with this word or an ornamental name with reference to the tree and its qualities of strength and durability. **2.** Polish: variant spelling of **Dębski** (see DEBSKI).
FOREBEARS The film actor Kirk Douglas's original name was Izzi Demski; he came from a Jewish family of eastern European origin.

Demsky (150) Jewish (Ashkenazic): variant spelling of DEMSKI.

Demulling (111) Origin unidentified.

De Muro (201) **1.** Italian and Spanish: habitational name for someone from any of various places in Spain and Italy named Muro, from *muro* 'wall'. **2.** Southern Italian: topographic name for someone who lived by a mulberry tree, from the dialect word *muru*, a habitational name from a place named with this word. Compare MORA.
GIVEN NAMES French 5%; Italian 5%. *Girard*; *Alfonse*, *Filomena*.

Demus (165) German: from a short form of the personal name *Nikodemus* (see NICODEMUS).

Demuth (1174) German: byname for a modest person, from Middle High German *diemuot*, *demuot* 'humility', 'modesty', or from a female personal name of the same derivation.

Demyan (199) **1.** Ukrainian: from the personal name *Dem'jan* (see DAMIAN). **2.** Bulgarian: from the personal name, also transcribed as *Demjan*. **3.** Hungarian (**Demján**): variant of *Damján* (see DAMIAN).

Dena (118) **1.** Spanish: unexplained; it is associated with Uesca province, in Aragon. **2.** Italian: unexplained.
GIVEN NAMES Spanish 34%. *Elino* (2), *Alejandra*, *Alejandro*, *Arturo*, *Edmundo*,

Elva, Eneida, Homero, Ignacio, Isidro, Jaime, Javier.

De Napoli (203) Italian: variant of DI NAPOLI.

GIVEN NAMES Italian 9%. *Camillo* (2), *Angelo, Francesco, Philomena.*

Denard (271) French: patronymic from the personal name *Nard*, a short form of BERNARD.

De Nardis (111) Italian: patronymic from the personal name *Nardo* (see DI NARDO), in the broader sense 'of or belonging to the Nardi family'.

GIVEN NAMES Italian 10%. *Antonio, Camillo, Dante, Vito.*

De Nardo (607) Italian: variant of DI NARDO.

GIVEN NAMES Italian 14%. *Antonio* (3), *Domenic* (3), *Pasquale* (3), *Salvatore* (3), *Amedeo* (2), *Vito* (2), *Carmela, Carmine, Dino, Domenico, Remo, Sarina.*

De Naro (347) Southern Italian: habitational name for someone from Naro in Agrigento province, Sicily.

GIVEN NAMES Italian 22%. *Domenic* (2), *Sal* (2), *Salvatore* (2), *Antonio, Carmelo, Constantino, Francesco, Gasper, Giorgio, Giovanni, Mario, Marisa, Natale, Philomena, Placido, Renato.*

De Natale (156) Italian: variant of DI NATALE.

GIVEN NAMES Italian 8%. *Alfonse, Guido, Vito.*

Denault (566) French: **1.** from a northern form of DANIEL, in which the final syllable *-(i)el* has been vocalized in Picard, and the Naams and Liège dialects. **2.** northern habitational name, with the preposition *d(e)*, for someone from Hainault (French *Hainaut*, Dutch *Henegouwen*). **3.** perhaps a variant of **Denau(x)**, from a southern word meaning 'ship' (Latin *navis*). **4.** possibly a variant spelling of DAIGNAULT.

GIVEN NAMES French 7%. *Aime, Alphonse, Andre, Emile, Fernand, Jacques, Jean-Pierre, Pierre, Valmore.*

Den Bleyker (163) Old spelling of Dutch **den Bleijker**, an occupational name for someone who bleached linen.

Denbo (185) Variant of English DENBOW.

Den Boer (154) Dutch: variant of DE BOER.

GIVEN NAMES Dutch 4%. *Huibert* (2), *Willem.*

Denbow (381) English: of uncertain origin; Reaney derives it from an Old English personal name, *Denebeald*, an unrecorded compound of *Dene-*.

Denby (529) English: habitational name from places so named in Derbyshire and West Yorkshire. This place name has the same origin as DANBY, but the Old Norse first element has been replaced by the cognate Old English *Dene*.

Dence (123) English: ethnic name for someone from Denmark, from Middle English *den(s)ch* 'Danish' (Old English *denisc*). There were many Danes in England in the Middle Ages, not only the

long-established settlers in the Danelaw region, but also more recent immigrants.

GIVEN NAMES German 4%. *Erwin, Herta.*

Dencker (105) German: variant spelling of DENKER.

GIVEN NAME German 5%. *Hans* (2).

Dencklau (134) **1.** Origin unidentified; probably German. **2.** Probably a topographic or habitational name from an unexplained north German place name + *lau*, a variant of *Loh* (Middle High German *lōch*) 'brushwood' or 'a place of a former wood'.

Dendinger (196) Altered spelling of German **Dentinger**, a habitational name for someone from Dentingen near Riedlingen, Württemberg.

Dendy (839) English (Sussex): unexplained.

Deneau (232) French: **1.** habitational name for someone from Neau, a place in Mayenne. **2.** variant of DENAULT 1.

GIVEN NAME French 4%. *Huguette.*

Deneault (195) Variant spelling of DENAULT or DENEAU 1.

GIVEN NAMES French 5%. *Collette, Normand.*

Denecke (133) German: variant spelling of DENEKE.

GIVEN NAMES German 16%. *Manfred* (3), *Ernst, Gerlinde, Hans, Hermann, Juergen.*

Deneen (510) Variant of Irish DINEEN.

Denehy (137) Irish: see DENNEHY.

GIVEN NAME Irish 7%. *Brendan.*

Deneke (159) Dutch and North German: from a diminutive of *Dene* 'Dane'.

GIVEN NAMES German 5%. *Otto, Siegfried.*

Denenberg (242) Jewish (eastern Ashkenazic): ornamental name from German *Tannenberg*, Yiddish *tenenbarg* 'fir tree mountain'.

Denes (197) **1.** Hungarian (**Dénes**): from the personal name *Dénes*, from Greek *Dionysios* (see DENNIS). **2.** Jewish (from Hungary): adoption of the Hungarian surname.

GIVEN NAMES Hungarian 16%; Jewish 4%; Romanian 4%. *Bela* (3), *Laszlo* (2), *Miklos* (2), *Tibor* (2), *Aranka, Balint, Endre, Ferenc, Lajos, Zoltan; Imrich, Meyer; Doina, Matei, Radu.*

De Neui (115) Origin unidentified.

Deneve (163) **1.** Altered spelling of northern French **Denef(v)e**, a habitational name, with the preposition *de*, for someone from places called Neffe in the Belgian provinces of Namur and Luxembourg. **2.** Dutch (**de Neve**): kinship name from Middle Dutch *neve* 'grandson', '(male) cousin', 'nephew' + the definite article *de*.

GIVEN NAMES French 7%. *Egide, Marcel, Remy.*

Denfeld (104) North German: habitational name from an unidentified place named with *feld* 'open country' as the second element.

Deng (790) Chinese 邓: from the name of a state that existed during the Xia (2205–

1766 BC) and Shang (1766–1122 BC) dynasties. At a much later date, descendants of the state's rulers took the state name Deng as their surname. This was the family name of Deng Xiaoping (1904–97), effectively ruler of China from 1977 to his death twenty years later.

GIVEN NAMES Chinese 61%. *Hong* (12), *Hua* (5), *Jian* (5), *Jing* (5), *Wei* (5), *Wen* (5), *Yi* (4), *Ying* (4), *Chao* (3), *Fang* (3), *Gang* (3), *Hui* (3), *Min* (2).

Dengel (247) German: **1.** from a pet form of the medieval personal name *Anton(ius)* (see ANTHONY) or a Sorbian short form of DANIEL. **2.** Westphalian nickname for an idler, from Low German *dengel* 'sluggish'.

GIVEN NAME German 4%. *Florian.*

Denger (105) German: **1.** habitational name for someone from Tengen or Hohentengen in Baden-Württemberg, or from Tiengen or Teningen, also in Baden-Württemberg, which were earlier called Dengen and Tengen respectively. **2.** dialect variant of **Dienger**, a habitational name for someone from Oberding or Unterding in Bavaria.

Dengler (795) German: occupational name for a knife-sharpener, from an agent derivative of Middle High German *tengelen* 'to sharpen instruments' (such as large knives, sickles, and scythes), originally by carefully angled hammer blows (from Old High German *tangol* 'hammer').

GIVEN NAMES German 4%. *Claus, Dieter, Erwin, Kurt, Reinhold, Siegfried, Wolfgang.*

Denham (2857) English: habitational name from any of various places so called, for example in Buckinghamshire (near Uxbridge) and two in Suffolk, which are named from Old English *denu* 'valley' + *hām* 'homestead'.

Denhart (166) German (Bavaria and Austria): **1.** from the personal name *Degenhart* (see DEGENHART). **2.** from an old personal name *Denihart*, probably composed of the Germanic stem *dan*(compare DANE) + *hard* 'strong'.

Den Hartog (219) Dutch: from *hertog* 'duke'; a nickname for someone who adopted airs and graces, or an occupational name for someone who served in the household of a duke.

GIVEN NAMES Dutch 7%. *Gerrit* (2), *Pieter* (2), *Dirk.*

Den Herder (176) Dutch: occupational name from Middle Dutch *herde(r)*, *harde(r)* 'shepherd'.

Denholm (216) **1.** Scottish: habitational name from a place in southern Scotland near Hawick, so named from Old English *denu* 'valley' + *holm* 'piece of dry land in a fen' (see HOLME 2). **2.** English: habitational name from Denholme in West Yorkshire, so named from Old English *denu* 'valley' + Old Norse *holmr* 'water meadow'.

Deni (110) **1.** Italian: variant of **Diene**, from Greek *digenēs* 'born of two races'. **2.** French (Huguenot) and Dutch: from a variant of the personal name DENNIS.
GIVEN NAMES Italian 8%; French 4%. *Luigi, Salvatore; Camille.*

De Nicola (659) Southern Italian: patronymic from the personal name *Nicola*, from Greek *Nikolaos* (see NICHOLAS).
GIVEN NAMES Italian 18%. *Angelo* (6), *Cosmo* (3), *Fausto* (2), *Nino* (2), *Salvatore* (2), *Constantino, Dante, Dino, Donato, Franco, Gaetano, Nicola.*

De Nicolo (101) Southern Italian: patronymic from the personal name NICOLO.
GIVEN NAMES Italian 22%; French 4%. *Pietro* (2), *Donato, Remo, Rocco; Michel.*

Denier (106) **1.** French: from Old French *denier*, originally the name of a copper coin, later a term for money in general, hence probably a metonymic occupational name for a moneyer or minter. **2.** English: variant spelling of DENYER, cognate with 1.
GIVEN NAMES French 9%. *Gabrielle* (2), *Jacques, Philippe.*

Denig (132) Variant of German **Dennig**, from a short form of the personal name *Anton(ius)* (see ANTHONY).
GIVEN NAMES German 4%. *Erwin, Fritz.*

De Nigris (167) Italian: patronymic from a Latinized form of NEGRO, but here in the broader sense 'of or belonging to the Negri family'.
GIVEN NAMES Italian 15%. *Emanuele* (2), *Vito* (2), *Benedetto, Pasquale, Rocco.*

Denike (223) Altered spelling of Dutch DENEKE.

De Ninno (124) Italian: patronymic from *Ninno*, probably a nickname from a masculine form of Old Italian *ninna* 'baby', medieval Latin *ninnus*.
GIVEN NAMES Italian 21%; German 5%. *Donato* (3), *Rocco* (3), *Dante, Guido, Vito; Otto* (2).

Denio (289) Altered form of French DAIGNAULT.

Denis (1513) **1.** French, Spanish (**Denís**), and Portuguese: from the personal name *Denis* (Spanish *Denís*), variant of DENNIS. **2.** Ukrainian: from the personal name *Denys* (see DENNIS).
FOREBEARS Originally brought to Canada from Tours, France, this surname was in Quebec city by 1655.
GIVEN NAMES French 17%; Spanish 6%. *Camille* (5), *Jacques* (5), *Armand* (4), *Marcel* (4), *Andre* (3), *Pierre* (3), *Serge* (3), *Yvan* (3), *Alphonse* (2), *Edouard* (2), *Francois* (2), *Gaetane* (2); *Jose* (6), *Carlos* (3), *Jorge* (3), *Roberto* (3), *Angel* (2), *Francisco* (2), *Joaquin* (2), *Juan* (2), *Manuel* (2), *Miguel* (2), *Ramon* (2), *Rolando* (2).

Denisco (123) Italian: unexplained.
GIVEN NAMES Italian 9%. *Carmine* (2), *Aniello.*

Denise (300) French: variant of DENIS.

GIVEN NAMES French 4%. *Francois* (2), *Etienne.*

Denison (2629) **1.** English: patronymic from the personal name DENNIS. **2.** Possibly an Americanized form of cognates in other languages, for example Russian **Denisov**, from *Denis*, or Ukrainian **Denysevich**, from *Denys*.

Deniston (188) Variant spelling of Scottish DENNISTON.

Deniz (227) Spanish: possibly from a variant of the personal name *Denís* (see DENNIS).
GIVEN NAMES Spanish 34%. *Jesus* (3), *Jose* (3), *Luis* (2), *Manuel* (2), *Miguel* (2), *Pablo* (2), *Rafael* (2), *Ramon* (2), *Rosalina* (2), *Adolfo, Adonis, Aida.*

Denk (585) German: **1.** from a short form of the personal name *Dankwart*, from Old High German *thank* 'think', 'thank', 'thought' + *wart* 'guardian'. **2.** South German: nickname for a left-handed or clumsy person, from Middle High German *tenk* 'left'. **3.** variant of DENKE.
GIVEN NAMES German 4%. *Hans, Juergen, Otto, Uwe, Wilhelm, Winfried.*

Denke (127) **1.** German: from a short form of a personal name containing the Old High German element *thank* 'thank', 'think', 'thought', or a habitational name for someone from a place named Denkte, near Wolfenbüttel. **2.** Hungarian: from a pet form of any of the personal names *Dénes*, *Demeter*, or *Demjén*.
GIVEN NAMES German 15%. *Erwin* (2), *Helmuth* (2), *Elke, Erhart, Kurt.*

Denker (559) German: **1.** nickname for a left-handed person, from an agent derivative of Middle High German *tenk* 'left'. **2.** Frisian and North German variant of DANKERT.

Denkins (139) Probably an altered spelling of Dutch **Denkens**, a patronymic from a pet form of the personal name DANIEL.

Denley (293) English: apparently a habitational name from an unidentified place, probably so named from Old English *denu* 'valley' + *lēah* 'woodland clearing'. It may well be an altered form of Delly End in Oxfordshire.

Denlinger (707) Altered spelling of Swiss German **Dändlinker**, a habitational name from Dändlikon, Switzerland.

Denman (2360) English: topographic name for someone who dwelt in a valley (see DEAN 1).

Denmark (982) **1.** English: ethnic name originally denoting someone from Denmark. See also DENCE. In the British Isles the name is found chiefly in East Anglia. **2.** Americanized spelling of German **Dennemark**, ethnic name for someone from Denmark, from Middle Low German *Dennemarken.*

Denmon (334) English: variant spelling of DENMAN.

Denn (430) English: from a short form of the personal name DENNIS.

Dennard (738) Probably an altered spelling of German **Dennhardt** (see DENHART) or possibly of French DENARD.

Denne (293) English (Kent): variant spelling of DENN.

Dennee (119) Probably a variant of French DENNIS or possibly Irish DENNEHY.

Dennehy (739) Irish (Cork): Anglicized form of Gaelic **Ó Duineachdha** 'descendant of *Duineachaidh*', a personal name meaning 'humane'.
GIVEN NAMES Irish 6%. *Brendan, Donal, Paddy.*

Dennen (312) **1.** Dutch: patronymic from a short form of DANIEL, or from a short form of a Germanic personal name with the first element *Dein-* (Dutch *thegna* 'man', 'serving man', 'thane', or 'fighting man'). **2.** In some cases, probably an altered spelling of the Irish surname **Dennan**, an Americanized form of **Ó Doineannaigh** 'descendant of *Doineannaoh*', a byname from *doineannach* 'tempestuous'.

Denner (497) **1.** German: variant of DANNER, or a habitational name for someone from a place called Denn in the Rhineland. **2.** English: from an agent derivative of Middle English *denn* 'woodland pasture for swine', hence an occupational or topographic name.

Dennert (131) **1.** German: variant of DENNER. **2.** see DINEHART.
GIVEN NAMES French 5%; German 4%. *Andre* (2); *Gunther.*

Dennett (653) English: from a pet form of the personal name DENNIS.

Denney (4561) English and Scottish: variant spelling of DENNY.

Dennie (475) Scottish: variant spelling of DENNY.

Dennin (188) Origin unidentified.

Denning (2867) **1.** English: patronymic from an Old English personal name, *Dynna*. **2.** Irish: variant of DINEEN. **3.** German: habitational name from Denning in Bavaria.

Denninger (211) German: habitational name for someone from Denning in Bavaria or Danningen, near Messkirch, in Baden.
GIVEN NAME German 4%. *Gerhard.*

Dennington (253) English: habitational name from a place in Suffolk, recorded in Domesday Book as *Dingifetuna*, from the Old English female personal name *Denegifu* (composed of the elements *Dene* 'Dane' + *gifu* 'gift') + Old English *tūn* 'enclosure', 'settlement'.

Dennis (24913) **1.** English: from the medieval personal name *Den(n)is* (Latin *Dionysius*, Greek *Dionysios* '(follower) of *Dionysos*', an eastern god introduced to the classical pantheon at a relatively late date and bearing a name of probably Semitic origin). The name was borne by various early saints, including St Denis, the martyred 3rd-century bishop of Paris who became the patron of France; the popularity of the name in England from the 12th century onwards seems to have been largely due to French influence. The feminine form *Dionysia* (in the vernacular likewise *Den(n)is*) is also found, and some examples of the surname may represent a metronymic form. **2.** English: variant of **Dench**. **3.** Irish (mainly Dublin and Cork): of the same origin as 1 and 2, sometimes an alternative form to Donohue but more often to MacDonough, since the personal name *Donnchadh* was Anglicized as Donough or Denis. **4.** Irish (Ulster and Munster): Anglicized form of the rare Gaelic name Ó Donnghusa 'descendant of *Donnghus*', a personal name from *donn* 'brown-haired man' or 'chieftain' + *gus* 'vigor'.

Dennison (4829) English: patronymic from the personal name Dennis.

Denniston (823) Scottish: habitational name from Danzielstoun in Renfrewshire, named with the personal name Daniel (for the phonetic significance of the *-z-*, see Dalzell) + Middle English *toun, tone* 'settlement' (Old English *tūn*).

Dennler (122) German: topographic name denoting someone from a place with pine trees, from Middle High German *tanne*.
GIVEN NAMES French 4%; German 4%. *Jean-Jacques; Ewald.*

Denno (300) Perhaps an altered spelling of the French surname Daignault, Denault, or Deneau.
GIVEN NAME French 4%. *Antoine.*

Denny (6263) **1.** Scottish and English: from a pet form of Dennis. **2.** English: habitational name from a place in Cambridgeshire, most probably named with Old English *Dene* 'Dane' + *ēg* 'island'. **3.** Scottish: habitational name from Denny in Stirlingshire. **4.** Irish: reduced Anglicized form of Gaelic Ó Duibhne (see Deeney). **5.** Irish (Cork): less frequently, a reduced Anglicization of Gaelic Ó Duineachdha (see Dennehy).

Deno (473) Americanized spelling of French Daignault, Denault, or Deneau.

Denoble (173) Dutch: from Middle Dutch *nobel* 'noble' + the definite article *de*, applied as a nickname for someone of high birth, or ironically for someone of very humble origin.

De Noia (113) **1.** Spanish: habitational name for someone from Noia in Galicia. **2.** Italian (also **Noia, Noja, Di Noia**): habitational name from either of two places, Noicattaro in Bari province and Noepoli in Potenza province, both named Noja until the end of 19th century.
GIVEN NAMES Italian 11%. *Angelo, Nicola, Sal, Vito.*

Denomme (187) Possibly French: unexplained.

GIVEN NAMES French 7%. *Adelard, Gaston, Laurent.*

Denoncourt (132) Origin unidentified; possibly a French habitational name.
GIVEN NAMES French 12%. *Armand* (2), *Laurent* (2), *Oliva, Yvan.*

Denoon (155) Scottish: variant of **Dunoon**, a habitational name from the place on the Clyde west of Glasgow.

Denoyer (217) French: habitational name, with the preposition *de*, for someone from any of several places named Noyers, or a topographic name (see Desnoyers).
GIVEN NAME French 4%. *Monique.*

Densford (151) English: probably a variant of Dunsford.
GIVEN NAME French 4%. *Collette.*

Densley (183) English (Somerset): apparently a habitational name from an unidentified place. It is probably a variant of Denslow or possibly Denley, neither of which are of identified origin.

Denslow (340) English (Somerset and Devon): apparently a habitational name, although no place of this name is known.

Densmore (1491) English: probably a variant of Dunsmore.

Denson (3418) English: patronymic from Dean 2.

Dent (4648) **1.** English: habitational name from places in Cumbria and West Yorkshire named Dent, possibly from a British hill name cognate with Old Irish *dinn, dind* 'hill'. **2.** English and French: nickname from Old French *dent* 'tooth' (Latin *dens*, genitive *dentis*), bestowed on someone with some deficiency or peculiarity of the teeth, or of a gluttonous or avaricious nature.

Dente (343) Italian and Portuguese: from *dente* 'tooth' (Latin *dens*, genitive *dentis*), a nickname for someone with some deficiency or peculiarity of dentition, or of a gluttonous or avaricious nature.
GIVEN NAMES Italian 12%; French 4%. *Vito* (3), *Alfonse, Angelo, Carmine, Gino, Italo, Primo, Rocco, Sal; Alphonse* (2), *Colette* (2), *Octave.*

Dentel (117) German: **1.** from Middle High German *tant* 'empty prattle', as a nickname for a braggart or someone who busied himself doing nothing. **2.** from a pet form of the personal name Daniel.

Dentice (110) Italian: from *dentice* 'dentex' (a kind of sea bream); hence probably a nickname for someone thought to resemble the fish in some way or a metonymic occupational name for a fisherman.
GIVEN NAMES Italian 16%. *Santo* (3), *Gino, Sal.*

Dentinger (155) German: habitational name for someone from a place called Dentingen in Württemberg.

Dentino (159) Italian: from a diminutive of Dente.
GIVEN NAMES Italian 10%. *Vito* (3), *Carmine, Mauro.*

Dentler (244) German: nickname for a prattler, Middle High German *tendeler*.

Denton (10194) English and Scottish: habitational name from any of the numerous places so called. The vast majority, including those in Cambridgeshire, Cumbria, Dumfries, County Durham, Kent, Lancashire, Lincolnshire, Norfolk, Northumberland, Oxfordshire, Sussex, and West Yorkshire, are named from Old English *denu* 'valley' (see Dean 1) + *tūn* 'enclosure', 'settlement'. An isolated example in Northamptonshire appears in Domesday Book as *Dodintone* 'settlement associated with *Dodda*'.

Dentremont (318) French: habitational name for someone from a place called Entremont in Haute-Savoie.

Dentz (106) **1.** German: variant of Denz. **2.** Jewish (Ashkenazic): unexplained.
GIVEN NAMES Jewish 4%. *Shoshana, Sol.*

De Nucci (168) Italian: variant of Di Nucci.
GIVEN NAMES Italian 7%. *Angelo, Cosimo, Domenic, Sal.*

De Nunzio (228) Italian: variant of Di Nunzio.
GIVEN NAMES Italian 9%. *Concetta, Dino, Enzo, Silvio.*

Denver (284) English: habitational name from Denver in Norfolk, named as 'Danes' crossing', from Old English *Dene* 'Dane' (genitive *Dena*) + *fær* 'ford', 'passage', 'crossing'.

Denyer (127) **1.** English (Surrey and Sussex): nickname for a poor or insignificant man, from the name of a very small medieval coin, Middle English, Old French *denier* (Latin *denarius*, a derivative of *decem* 'ten', since the Roman coin was worth ten asses). **2.** In some cases possibly a respelling of the French cognate Denier.

Denys (122) **1.** French: variant spelling of *Denis* (see Dennis 1). **2.** Ukrainian: from the personal name *Denys* (see Dennis).
GIVEN NAMES French 6%; Polish 4%. *Luc, Lucien; Casimir, Wiktor.*

Denz (149) German: **1.** from a short form of the personal name Degen(hardt). **2.** in northeastern Germany, a habitational name denoting someone from a place called Tenze in Mecklenburg. **3.** from an old personal name formed with the stem *Dand*, which is of unknown origin.

Denzel (159) German: from a pet form of the personal name Denz.
GIVEN NAMES German 6%. *Heinz, Kurt, Otto.*

Denzer (480) German: occupational name for a professional acrobat or entertainer, a variant of Tanzer.

Denzin (151) German: habitational name, of Slavic origin, for someone from a place so named in Pomerania.
GIVEN NAMES German 8%. *Erwin* (2), *Arno, Eldred, Frieda.*

Denzler (203) German and Swiss German: **1.** occupational name for a professional acrobat or entertainer; variant of *Tänzler,* itself a variant of TANZER. **2.** from an old personal name formed with the stem *Dand* (unexplained).

Deo (271) **1.** Indian (northern states): Hindu name found in several communities, from Sanskrit *deva* 'god', 'lord'. This was a title used by ruling families in northern India. There is a Jat tribe called *Deo*. In the northeast this name is found among Kayasths, pronounced *deb*. In Maharashtra Konkanasth Brahmans have a clan called **Dev**. **2.** Italian: from a short form of the personal names *Amadeo*, *Laudadeo*, or *Sperindeo*, of which only the first now remains in use as a given name.

GIVEN NAMES Indian 38%. *Ravindra* (3), *Sohini* (2), *Vivek* (2), *Ajay*, *Alok*, *Anil*, *Annapurna*, *Daya*, *Ganga*, *Goutam*, *Harnek*, *Indra*.

Deocampo (143) Spanish (Galician): habitational name for someone from a place called Ocampo in Galicia, or a variant of the topographic name **Docampo**, from *o campo* 'the field'.

GIVEN NAMES Spanish 38%. *Roberto* (4), *Eduardo* (2), *Jose* (2), *Marina* (2), *Alberto*, *Anacleto*, *Angelita*, *Augusto*, *Bonifacio*, *Edgardo*, *Edmundo*, *Efrain*; *Antonio*, *Gabriella*, *Severino*.

Deol (102) Indian (Panjab): Sikh name based on the name of a Jat clan.

GIVEN NAMES Indian 86%. *Manjinder* (2), *Tarsem* (2), *Ajit*, *Anoop*, *Anup*, *Balwinder*, *Hardip*, *Jagroop*, *Navdeep*, *Sukhpal*.

De Oliveira (445) Portuguese: topographic name for someone who lived by an olive tree, *oliveira*.

GIVEN NAMES Spanish 33%; Portuguese 21%. *Jose* (12), *Manuel* (11), *Carlos* (5), *Francisco* (5), *Luiz* (4), *Marcos* (4), *Luis* (3), *Mario* (3), *Abilio* (2), *Adelino* (2), *Ana* (2), *Fabio* (2); *Joao* (4), *Paulo* (3), *Altair*, *Joaquim*, *Manoel*, *Sebastiao*, *Vanderlei*; *Antonio* (11), *Marco* (3), *Enio*, *Marcello*, *Mauro*, *Sebastiano*, *Severino*.

Deon (195) French (**Déon**): habitational name for someone from Eon, an ancient fief in Burgundy, which gained celebrity in 18th century through the exploits of Charles de Beaumont d'Eon.

GIVEN NAME French 4%. *Leonce*.

De Orio (133) Possibly Spanish, a habitational name for someone from (*de*) Orio, a place in Gipuzkoa, Basque Country.

GIVEN NAME Italian 6%. *Carmine*.

Depa (113) Polish: possibly an occupational name for a a weaver, from the dialect term *depaki* 'treadles in a weaver's loom'.

GIVEN NAMES Polish 9%. *Henryk*, *Jozefa*, *Krystyna*, *Ryszard*.

Depace (140) **1.** Italian (**De Pace**): variant of DI PACE. **2.** French (Walloon): habitational name from any of various places named with the French element *Pas* (from Latin *passus* 'step', 'track'), for example Pas-en-Artois. Compare DE PASS.

GIVEN NAMES Italian 14%. *Sal* (2), *Antonio*, *Nunziato*, *Tommaso*.

De Paepe (104) Dutch: from Middle Dutch *pape* 'priest'; a nickname for someone who was pious or full of religious fervor or an occupational name for someone in the service of a priest.

De Palma (1597) Italian: variant of DI PALMA.

GIVEN NAMES Italian 12%. *Angelo* (5), *Antonio* (5), *Vito* (5), *Pasquale* (4), *Carmine* (2), *Domenic* (2), *Donato* (2), *Filippo* (2), *Giuseppe* (2), *Leonardo* (2), *Marco* (2).

De Palo (280) Italian: **1.** habitational name for someone from any of various minor places named Palo, from *palo* 'pole', 'stake', 'pile'. **2.** possibly a respelling of DE PAOLO.

GIVEN NAMES Italian 22%. *Vito* (6), *Angelo* (2), *Savino* (2), *Antonio*, *Ceasar*, *Donato*, *Franco*, *Giuseppe*, *Luigi*, *Rocco*.

De Paola (467) Italian: variant of DI PAOLA.

GIVEN NAMES Italian 19%. *Cono* (5), *Gino* (4), *Salvatore* (3), *Carmine* (2), *Angelo*, *Antonietta*, *Attilio*, *Edmondo*, *Ennio*, *Francesco*, *Luigi*, *Paolo*.

De Paoli (348) Italian: variant of DE PAOLO.

GIVEN NAMES Italian 10%. *Romano* (3), *Angelo*, *Caterina*, *Dino*, *Enzo*, *Fausto*, *Marino*, *Piero*, *Silvio*, *Tullio*.

De Paolis (172) Italian: patronymic from the personal name *Paolo* (see PAUL), here in the sense 'of or belonging to the Paoli family'.

GIVEN NAMES Italian 21%. *Carlo* (2), *Lorenzo* (2), *Angelo*, *Enrico*, *Ferdinando*, *Guido*, *Igino*, *Pietro*, *Salvatore*, *Sebastiano*, *Vito*.

De Paolo (513) Italian: variant of DI PAOLO.

GIVEN NAMES Italian 12%. *Amato* (2), *Angelo* (2), *Rocco* (2), *Salvatore* (2), *Camillo*, *Carlo*, *Carmello*, *Carmine*, *Ciro*, *Cono*, *Gino*, *Nunzi*.

Depas (104) French: according to Morlet, a habitational name for someone from Pas-en-Artois, in Pas-de-Calais, so named from Latin *passus* 'pass'.

De Pascale (150) Italian: patronymic from the personal name *Pascale*, a southern variant of *Pasquale* (see PASCAL).

GIVEN NAMES Italian 32%. *Angelo* (3), *Antonio* (2), *Gennaro* (2), *Nicola* (2), *Sabino* (2), *Valentino* (2), *Luigi*, *Orlando*, *Oreste*, *Salvatore*, *Silvio*, *Vittorio*.

De Pasquale (1159) Italian: patronymic from the personal name *Pasquale* (see PASCAL).

GIVEN NAMES Italian 17%. *Salvatore* (6), *Angelo* (3), *Carmine* (3), *Rocco* (3), *Carmelo* (2), *Mauro* (2), *Sal* (2), *Antonio*, *Attilio*, *Concetta*, *Cosimo*, *Cosmo*.

De Pass (180) Probably an altered spelling of French **Depas**, a habitational name from Pas-en-Artois, named with Latin *passus* 'step', 'track'. Compare DEPACE. Alternatively, it may be an altered spelling of French **Depasse**, which is possibly a pat-

ronymic from a nickname from *passe* 'sparrow'.

Depatie (117) Origin unidentified.

GIVEN NAMES French 10%. *Marcel*, *Michel*, *Renald*.

Depaul (656) French: patronymic from the personal name PAUL.

GIVEN NAMES Italian 7%. *Rocco* (3), *Pasquale* (2), *Angelo*, *Caesar*, *Guido*, *Romeo*.

De Paula (209) **1.** Spanish: habitational name from Paola, the Italian birthplace of Saint Francis of Paola (Spanish *San Francisco de Paula*). **2.** Italian: variant of DE PAOLA.

GIVEN NAMES Spanish 23%; Portuguese 8%. *Luiz* (3), *Ignacio* (2), *Julio* (2), *Marcos* (2), *Renato* (2), *Tereza* (2), *Adriana*, *Alejandro*, *Ana*, *Ana Lucia*, *Dulce*, *Fidelia*; *Joao*, *Paulo*.

De Paulis (132) **1.** Italian: variant of DE PAOLIS. **2.** German: humanistic patronymic based on PAUL.

GIVEN NAMES Italian 12%; German 9%; Spanish 4%. *Enrico* (2), *Antonio*, *Dario*, *Giovanni*, *Paolo*, *Pietro*; *Otto* (3), *Kurt*, *Monika*; *Pablo*, *Tomas*.

De Paulo (161) Variant spelling of Italian DE PAOLO.

GIVEN NAMES Italian 11%. *Amato*, *Angelo*, *Carmine*, *Gennaro*, *Rocco*.

De Pauw (322) Dutch: from *pauw* 'peacock' + the definite article *de*, a nickname for a proud or flamboyant person, or a habitational name for someone living at a house bearing the sign of a peacock.

GIVEN NAMES French 5%. *Alphonse* (2), *Alphone*, *Amie*.

De Paz (243) Spanish and Galician: in most cases, probably a variant of DE LA PAZ, but in some possibly a habitational name for someone from (*de*) Paz in Lugo province, Galicia.

GIVEN NAMES Spanish 48%; Italian 7%. *Jose* (7), *Manuel* (4), *Pedro* (4), *Roberto* (4), *Jesus* (3), *Juan* (3), *Raul* (3), *Ana* (2), *Ana Maria* (2), *Carlos* (2), *Enrique* (2), *Margarito* (2); *Antonio* (3), *Silvio* (3), *Severino* (2), *Nino*.

De Pena (112) Galician, Asturian-Leonese (**De Peña**), and Spanish (**De Peña**): habitational name for someone from any of the numerous places in Galicia called (A) Pena, or in Asturies called (La) Peña, from Galician *pena*, Asturian-Leonese and Spanish *peña* 'rock'.

GIVEN NAMES Spanish 57%. *Francisco* (3), *Luis* (3), *Rafael* (3), *Bolivar* (2), *Manuel* (2), *Ramona* (2), *Ruben* (2), *Altagracia*, *Arturo*, *Carlos*, *Cesar*, *Ernesto*.

De Petris (143) Italian: Latinized variant of DE PIETRO.

GIVEN NAMES Italian 6%. *Giovanni*, *Nichola*, *Pasquale*.

De Petro (179) Italian: Latinized or regional variant of DE PIETRO.

GIVEN NAMES Italian 13%. *Salvatore* (6), *Gaetana, Palma, Sal, Vito.*

De Pew (1935) Altered spelling of French DUPUY or DUPUIS.

De Phillips (215) Variant of Dutch PHILLIPS, Italian DE FILIPPO, or a cognate in some other language.

GIVEN NAME Italian 4%. *Gaeton.*

De Piano (104) Italian: topographic name for someone who lived on a plain or plateau (see PIANO).

GIVEN NAMES Italian 13%. *Antonio, Carmine, Cesare, Salvatore.*

De Piero (133) Italian: variant of DI PIERO.

GIVEN NAMES Italian 10%. *Angelo, Attilio, Dante, Elio, Franco, Severino.*

De Pierro (158) Italian: variant of DI PIERRO.

GIVEN NAMES Italian 7%. *Amedio* (2), *Angelo, Sal.*

Depies (144) Origin unidentified.

De Pietro (472) Italian: variant of DI PIETRO.

GIVEN NAMES Italian 12%. *Rocco* (7), *Angelo* (2), *Silvio, Tullio, Vito.*

De Pina (302) Portuguese: habitational name for someone from Pina in Zaragoza province, Spain.

GIVEN NAMES Spanish 35%; Portuguese 20%. *Manuel* (13), *Jose* (11), *Armando* (3), *Augusto* (3), *Francisco* (3), *Carlos* (2), *Domingo* (2), *Fernando* (2), *Juan* (2), *Adelina, Alberto, Alda; Joao* (2), *Anabela, Paulo; Antonio* (11), *Gilda.*

De Pinto (316) Italian: variant of DI PINTO.

GIVEN NAMES Italian 22%. *Vito* (7), *Corrado* (2), *Cosimo, Damiano, Donato, Fedele, Luigi, Mauro, Nicola, Saverio.*

Depner (175) German: of uncertain derivation. It may be a habitational name for someone from a place called Depenau, in Schleswig-Holstein (from Middle Low German *deep* 'deep', 'low' + *owe* 'low-lying field'). Alternatively, it could be an occupational name for a potter (in west central Germany), from an agent derivative of Middle High German *düpfen, tüp(p)en* 'pot'.

GIVEN NAMES German 8%. *Kurt* (3), *Heinz, Hilde.*

Depoe (112) Origin unidentified.

De Polo (203) Italian: patronymic from the personal name *Polo*, a northern variant of *Paolo* (see PAUL).

GIVEN NAME Italian 6%. *Angelo* (2).

De Ponte (168) Italian: variant of DA PONTE.

GIVEN NAMES Italian 11%. *Angelo* (2), *Antonio, Augustino, Nicola, Nicolo.*

De Porter (134) Dutch: status name from Middle Dutch *poetere* 'burgher', with the addition of the definite article *de*.

Depoy (304) Possibly an altered spelling of French DUPUIS.

GIVEN NAME German 4%. *Kurt* (3).

Depp (304) South German: nickname for a maladroit person, from Middle High German *tāpe* 'paw'.

Deppe (711) North German: from a pet form of the personal name *Detbern*, composed of the elements *theudō* 'people', 'race' + *ber(n)* 'bear'.

Deppen (299) German: variant of DEPPE.

Depperschmidt (126) German: occupational name for a blacksmith who made metal pots (as opposed to a potter who made clay pots), from an unrounded form of Middle Low German *döpper* 'potter' + SCHMIED.

Depree (215) Altered spelling of French **Dupré** (see DUPRE).

GIVEN NAMES Dutch 4%. *Dirk* (2), *Pieter.*

Deprey (308) Altered spelling of French **Dupré** (see DUPRE), or one of its numerous variants.

GIVEN NAMES French 7%. *Aime, Alphie, Alyre, Camille, Normand, Renold, Ursule, Vernice.*

Deprez (233) Altered spelling of French **Dupré** (see DUPRE).

Depriest (1356) Origin unidentified. Possibly an altered spelling (by folk etymology) of the northern French topographic name **Deprest** denoting someone who lived by a meadow, from French *pré* 'meadow' (Latin *pratum*).

De Prima (118) Italian: variant of DI PRIMA.

GIVEN NAMES Italian 9%. *Carmine, Sal.*

De Primo (101) Variant of Italian **Di Primo**, a patronymic or habitational name from PRIMO.

GIVEN NAMES Italian 22%. *Angelo* (3), *Giro, Rocco, Sabato, Salvatore.*

De Prospero (108) Italian: patronymic from the personal name PROSPERO.

GIVEN NAMES Italian 11%; German 5%. *Aldo, Quinto; Fritz.*

De Prospo (103) Origin unidentified; perhaps a reduced form of Italian DE PROSPERO.

GIVEN NAMES Italian 16%. *Rocco* (3), *Mafalda, Nicola.*

Deptula (322) Polish (**Deptuła**): nickname from *deptać* 'to tread on something'.

GIVEN NAMES Polish 7%. *Dariusz, Jadwiga, Karol, Stanislawa, Tadeusz, Wieslaw.*

Depue (625) Perhaps a respelling of French DUPUY or DUPUIS.

Depugh (109) Origin unidentified. Perhaps a respelling of French DUPUY or DUPUIS.

Deputy (416) Origin unidentified.

Depuy (542) Probably an altered spelling of French DUPUY or DUPUIS.

GIVEN NAMES French 4%. *Jacques* (2), *Jeremie.*

De Puydt (122) Dutch: nickname from Middle Dutch *puyt, puut* 'frog', with the addition of the definite article *de*.

Der (238) Hungarian (**Dér**): from an old Hungarian secular personal name *Dér*.

GIVEN NAMES Hungarian 6%. *Zoltan* (2), *Istvan, Janos, Lajos.*

De Raad (139) Dutch: metonymic occupational name for an adviser or counselor, from Middle Dutch *raed* 'advice', 'counsel' + the definite article *de*.

Deragon (168) Altered spelling of French **D'Aragon**, ethnic name for someone from the former kingdom of Aragon, now an autonomous region of northern Spain.

GIVEN NAMES French 11%. *Normand* (2), *Monique, Pierre, Raoul, Rejean.*

Deramo (255) **1.** Italian (**D'Eramo**): patronymic from the personal name ERAMO, according to Felice a variant of **Erasmo**. **2.** (**De Ramo**): patronymic from the old personal name *Ramo*, according to Caracausi from *ramo* 'branch', an allusion to the olive branch, as Christian symbol of peace.

GIVEN NAMES Italian 19%. *Domenic* (3), *Pasquale* (3), *Angelo, Attilio, Camillo, Carmine, Giacomo, Italo, Luciano, Orest.*

Deramus (450) Origin unidentified. Probably a Latinized form of DERAMO.

Deras (208) Galician: probably a habitational name for someone from a place in A Coruña province called Ras, possibly from a plural of Galician *ra* 'frog'.

GIVEN NAMES Spanish 48%. *Jose* (9), *Carlos* (4), *Francisco* (3), *Luis* (3), *Mario* (3), *Andres* (2), *Juan* (2), *Manuel* (2), *Ricardo* (2), *Alfonso, Alfredo, Artemio; Severiano* (2), *Ennio, Lorenzo, Marco.*

Derasmo (181) Italian: patronymic from the personal name ERASMO.

GIVEN NAMES Italian 33%. *Vito* (9), *Rocco* (2), *Angelo, Domenico, Francesco, Lorenzo, Mauro, Pasquale.*

Derbes (140) German: nickname from a derivative of Middle Low German *derve* 'strong', 'tough', 'simple', or perhaps a reduced form of **Der(b)fuss**, literally 'strong foot'; presumably a nickname.

GIVEN NAME French 4%; German 4%. *Fritz.*

Derby (2302) English: variant spelling of DARBY.

Derbyshire (367) English: variant spelling of DARBYSHIRE.

Derck (125) Dutch: from a reduced form of the personal name *Die(de)rik* (see DEDERICK).

D'Ercole (210) Italian: patronymic from the personal name *Ercole*, from Latin *Hercules*, Greek *Heraklēs* (see HERCULES).

GIVEN NAMES Italian 20%. *Pasquale* (2), *Angelo, Augustino, Dante, Dino, Domenic, Ercole, Ignazio, Olindo, Remo, Salvatore, Silvio.*

Derda (117) Eastern German (under Slavic influence) and Polish: habitational name for someone from a place called Derdau.

GIVEN NAME German 4%; Polish 4%. *Czeslaw.*

Derden (191) Origin uncertain: possibly an altered spelling of English DURDEN.

Derderian (391) Armenian: patronymic from classical Armenian *derder* 'priest'.

GIVEN NAMES Armenian 21%. *Armen* (4), *Krikor* (4), *Ara* (3), *Raffi* (3), *Aris, Arra,*

Arshag, Boghos, Dicran, Dikran, Garbis, Garo.

De Rego (125) Galician: variant of **Do Rego**, a habitational name for someone from any of the numerous places in Galicia called Rego, from Galician *rego* 'rivulet'.

Deremer (400) Dutch and North German: from an old personal name *Terrimar*, which is probably from Old High German *dart* 'spear' + *mari* 'famous'.

De Remer (129) Dutch and North German (**De Remer**): occupational name for a leather worker (see REMER, German REIMER).

Deren (200) **1.** Dutch and North German: from a much reduced form of the Dutch personal name **Diederik** (see DEDERICK) or German DIETRICH. **2.** Polish: unexplained.
GIVEN NAMES Polish 7%. *Casimir, Feliks, Halina, Janusz, Jerzy.*

Derenne (116) French: habitational name for someone 'from (*de*) Renne or Rennes', examples of which are found in Aude, Doubs, Ille-et-Vilaine, and Mayenne in France, and in Liège province, Belgium.
GIVEN NAME French 4%. *Yannick.*

De Renzo (215) Italian: variant of DI RENZO.
GIVEN NAMES Italian 10%. *Pompeo* (2), *Angelo, Pasquale, Rocco, Santo.*

Derfler (107) Altered spelling of German **Dörfler** (see DOERFLER).

Derflinger (166) German (**Derfflinger**): habitational name from any of several places in Upper Austria named Derfling. Compare DOERFLINGER.

Derham (207) **1.** English: habitational name from Dearham in Cumbria or Dyrham in Gloucestershire, named from Old English *dēor* 'deer' + *hām* 'settlement', 'homestead', or *hamm* 'enclosure hemmed in by water', 'river meadow'. There are places in Norfolk called East and West Dereham, which have the same etymology. However, the present-day distribution of the surname suggests that they probably did not contribute to the surname. **2.** Irish (mainly Dublin, Drogheda, and Cork): of English origin, but MacLysaght takes this to be a variant of DURHAM.

Derhammer (163) Altered spelling of German **Dürhammer**, a habitational name from Dürrheim in Baden; -*hammer* is a common dialect form for -*heimer*.

Derian (108) Armenian: patronymic from classical Armenian *tēr* 'lord'.
GIVEN NAMES Armenian 18%. *Garo* (2), *Ara, Aram, Armen, Artine, Haig, Vahe.*

Derick (147) Dutch and North German: from a variant spelling of *Dierik*, a reduced form of the personal name *Diederik* (see DEDERICK).

Derickson (299) Dutch: patronymic from the personal name *Derick*, a reduced form of *Diederik* (see DEDERICK).

Derico (143) Italian: **1.** from the personal name *Rico*, a pet form of *Ricardo* (see

RICHARD) or *Enrico* (see HENRY). **2.** variant of D'ERRICO.
GIVEN NAMES Italian 11%; Scottish 4%. *Angelo, Giovanni, Pasquale, Rocco, Romeo, Sabatino; Evander* (2).

De Ridder (277) Dutch (**de Ridder**): from Middle Dutch *riddere, ruddere* 'knight', 'rider', 'horseman'; a status name for a mounted warrior or messenger.
GIVEN NAMES French 8%. *Andre* (2), *Constant, Laure, Marcel, Prosper.*

De Rienzo (190) Italian: variant of DI RIENZO.
GIVEN NAMES Italian 15%. *Rocco* (3), *Angelo, Antonio, Carmelina, Domenico, Gino, Pasquale.*

De Riggi (100) Italian: regional name for someone 'from (*de*) Reggio Calabria', from a dialect form of the place name.
GIVEN NAMES Italian 19%. *Angelo* (2), *Bartolomeo, Dino, Elia, Luigi, Mario, Sal.*

Dering (258) **1.** English: patronymic from DEAR 1. **2.** German: probably a variant of **Döring** (see DOERING).

Deringer (231) German: **1.** from a short form of an old personal name, a variant of *Därr* (see DARR). **2.** variant of **Döringer**, which is either from a personal name or from a regional name for someone from Thuringia (see DOERING).

Derington (131) Variant spelling of the English habitational name DERRINGTON.

Derise (150) French: habitational name originally denoting someone from Érize in Meuse. The name is sometimes Americanized as RICE as if from French *riz*.
GIVEN NAMES French 8%. *Nolton* (2), *Alphonse, Emile.*

De Riso (246) Possibly a respelling of the Italian (Sicily) family name **Di Riso**, a patronymic either from a nickname from *riso* 'laughter', but more likely from a short form of a Germanic personal name such as *Auderisius*.
GIVEN NAMES Italian 5%. *Cosmo, Salvatore.*

De Rita (114) Italian: metronymic from the personal name RITA.
GIVEN NAME Italian 7%. *Vito.*

Derk (184) North German and Dutch: variant of DIRK.

Derks (477) North German and Frisian: variant of DIRKS or DIERKS.

Derksen (342) Dutch, North German, and Danish: patronymic from the personal name DERK.
GIVEN NAMES German 4%. *Johannes, Reinhard, Ulrike.*

Derleth (185) German origin: from a Germanic personal name, perhaps composed of Old High German *dart* 'spear' + *walt* 'rule'.

Derman (211) **1.** Altered spelling of German **Dermann**, probably from an old personal name composed with Old High German *dart* 'spear' + *man* 'man'. **2.** Jewish (eastern Ashkenazic): ornamental name from German *der Mann* 'the man'.

GIVEN NAMES Jewish 5%; German 4%. *Aron* (2), *Emanuel* (2), *Miriam, Yakov; Manfred* (2).

Dermer (262) **1.** German: from an old personal name, *Terrimar*, a variant of *Därr* (see DARR). **2.** German: variant of **Dörmer** (standard German **Türmer**), an occupational name for a watchman on a tower (of a castle or town), from an agent derivative of Middle Low German *torn* or Middle High German *turn* 'tower'. **3.** Jewish: unexplained.
GIVEN NAMES Jewish 4%. *Hersh, Pinchas, Yaffa.*

Dermody (615) Irish: Anglicized form of Gaelic **Ó Diarmada** 'descendant of *Diarmaid*', the same personal name as gave rise to McDERMOTT.
GIVEN NAMES Irish 5%. *Aileen, Brigid, Donal.*

Dermott (111) Irish: reduced form of McDERMOTT.

Dern (303) German: **1.** from an old personal name based on an element cognate with Old High German *tarhnen* 'to conceal', *tarni* 'secretly'. **2.** possibly a habitational name from Derne near Dortmund or Dehrn on the Lahn river, Hesse.
GIVEN NAMES German 5%. *Klaus* (2), *Fritz.*

Dernbach (134) German: habitational name from a place so named in Hesse.
GIVEN NAME German 4%. *Helmut.*

Derner (152) German: **1.** variant of DERN, the -*er* suffix denoting an inhabitant. **2.** from an old personal name (see DERN 1). **3.** possibly from **Dürner** or **Döner**, southern and northern variants of standard German **Türmer**, an occupational name for a watchman, someone who manned a tower, German *Turm* (see DERMER).

De Robertis (198) Italian: patronymic from the personal name *Roberto*, Italian equivalent of ROBERT, in the broader sense 'of or belonging to the Roberti family'.
GIVEN NAMES Italian 22%. *Rocco* (4), *Alessandro, Donato, Gino, Giuseppe, Luigi, Nicola, Sal.*

De Rocco (163) Italian: variant of DI ROCCO.
GIVEN NAMES Italian 10%; French 5%. *Antimo* (2), *Martino, Rocco; Armand* (3).

Deroche (889) French: topographic name for someone who lived by a prominent rock, Old French *roche*, with the preposition *de* 'from'.

Derocher (359) Altered form of the French family names DUROCHER or DESROCHERS.
GIVEN NAMES French 5%. *Adrien, Emile, Etienne, Firmin.*

De Rogatis (120) Italian: patronymic from a personal name, *Rogato* (an omen name derived from Latin *rogare* 'to ask'), but here in the broader sense 'of or belonging to the Rogati family'. The surname is now very rare in Italy.
GIVEN NAMES Italian 13%. *Alfonse, Cesare, Dante, Filomena, Sal.*

De Rolf (101) Dutch: patronymic from *Rolf*, a Germanic personal name composed of the elements *hrōd* 'renown' + *wulf* 'wolf'.
GIVEN NAME Scandinavian 4%. *Kerstin.*

De Ronde (100) Dutch: from the nickname *de Ronde* 'the round one', denoting a person of ample proportions.
GIVEN NAMES Dutch 7%. *Kryn* (2), *Willem.*

De Roo (326) Dutch (**De Roo**): nickname, probably for someone with red hair, from *rood* 'red' + the definite article *de.*
GIVEN NAMES French 6%. *Alain, Colette, Jean Marie, Marcel.*

De Roos (192) Dutch (**de Roos**): from *roos* 'rose' with the addition of the definite article *de*, probably a habitational name for someone living at a house distinguished by the sign of a rose, or possibly a nickname for a man with a rosy complexion.
GIVEN NAMES Dutch 7%. *Dirk* (2), *Frans* (2), *Antoon, Derk.*

De Rosa (2904) Southern Italian: metronymic from the female personal name *Rosa*, from *rosa* 'rose'.
GIVEN NAMES Italian 13%. *Salvatore* (18), *Angelo* (9), *Pasquale* (6), *Rocco* (5), *Sal* (5), *Antonio* (3), *Ciro* (3), *Concetta* (3), *Domenic* (3), *Luigi* (3), *Santo* (3), *Amerigo* (2).

De Rose (1450) **1.** Italian: variant of DE ROSA. **2.** In some cases, possibly a partly Americanized form of Dutch DE ROOS.
GIVEN NAMES Italian 9%. *Rocco* (5), *Angelo* (4), *Antonio* (4), *Salvatore* (3), *Santo* (3), *Carmela* (2), *Dino* (2), *Francesca* (2), *Natale* (2), *Cosmo, Donato, Franca.*

Derosia (392) Possibly an altered spelling of French DE ROSIER or DESROSIERS.

De Rosier (887) French: from *rosier* 'rose (bush)', hence a topographic name for someone who lived where wild roses grew, or a habitational name from any of various minor places named with this word.
GIVEN NAMES French 6%. *Camille* (2), *Lucien* (2), *Wesner* (2), *Adelard, Alphonse, Armand, Fernand, Ferrier, Jinette, Mirielle.*

Deross (108) Origin uncertain. **1.** Variant spelling of Dutch DE ROOS. **2.** Americanized form of Italian DI RUSSO.
GIVEN NAMES Italian 5%. *Carmine, Salvatore.*

Derossett (427) Possibly Italian (**De Rossett**), a regional variant of ROSSETTI.

Derouen (893) **1.** French: habitational name for someone from Rouen. **2.** North American alteration of DEROUIN, particularly common in LA, where bearers of the name trace their descent from inhabitants of Quebec in the late 18th century.
GIVEN NAMES French 6%. *Anatole* (2), *Marcel* (2), *Minos* (2), *Ulysse* (2), *Alphonse, Autrey, Collette, Easton, Germaine, Leonie, Mechelle.*

Derouin (413) French: a hypercorrected form of DROUIN, as if the initial *D-* represented the preposition *de.*

GIVEN NAMES French 6%. *Armand* (2), *Emile* (2), *Adrien, Amiee, Jeanpaul.*

Derousse (248) Origin unidentified; possibly **1.** French: metronymic from *Rousse*, a feminine form of *Roux* meaning 'red-haired'. **2.** Frenchified spelling of Dutch DE ROOS or of **Derous**, a habitational name for someone from any of the places in Belgium called Roux, in Hainault, Liège, and Namur provinces.

Deroy (228) **1.** French: patronymic from the nickname ROY. **2.** Perhaps a variant of Dutch **de Rooi**, a nickname for a redhead.
GIVEN NAMES French 7%. *Amedee, Girard, Raoul, Yves.*

Derr (2971) Southern and eastern German: nickname for a thin person, a variant of **Dürr** (see DURR).

Derrer (117) Swiss German: occupational name for a flax or hemp worker, from Middle High German *darren, derren* 'to soak flax or hemp' (to make it pliable).

Derrick (3368) **1.** English and Dutch: from the personal name *Derrick* (now more commonly spelled *Derek* in England, earlier *Dederick*), which was introduced to England in the 15th century, from Dutch *Diederick, Dirck* (see TERRY). **2.** Irish: an English introduction of the same origin as 1, but occasionally a variant of DERRIG.

Derrickson (478) Dutch: patronymic from the personal name DERRICK.

D'Errico (756) Italian: patronymic from the personal name *Errico*, an Italian equivalent of HENRY.
GIVEN NAMES Italian 11%. *Rocco* (4), *Domenic* (2), *Salvatore* (2), *Angelo, Dante, Donato, Elio, Giampaolo, Giovanni, Marco, Matteo, Mauro.*

Derricott (116) English: habitational name, possibly a variant of **Darracott**, from Darracott in Devon. However, the present-day concentration of the form Derricott in the West Midlands and Shropshire suggests that this may be a distinct name, from a different source, now lost.

Derrig (203) Irish (Connacht): Anglicized form of Gaelic **Ó Deirg** 'descendant of *Dearg*', a byname meaning 'red'. (In Gaelic pronunciation an epenthetic vowel is inserted between *r* and *g*.)

Derringer (449) German: see DERINGER.

Derrington (235) English: habitational name from a place in Staffordshire called Derrington, recorded in Domesday Book as *Dodintone* 'settlement (*tūn*) associated with a man called *Do(d)a* or *Dud(d)a*'.

Derrow (203) Possibly an altered spelling of Scottish DARROW.

Derry (1262) **1.** English: variant of DEARY, or alternatively a nickname for a merchant or tradesman, from Anglo-French *darree* 'pennyworth', from Old French *denree*. **2.** Irish: Anglicized form of Gaelic **Ó Doiridh**, the name of an eccesiastical family from Donegal, meaning 'descendant of

Doireadh'. Derry is often confused with DEERY.

Derryberry (739) Origin unidentified.

Dersch (183) **1.** Eastern German: from the Slavic personal name *Dirslaw*. **2.** South German: nickname for a foolish person, from Middle High German *tærsch* 'foolish'.
GIVEN NAMES German 7%. *Dietrich, Eckhart, Erwin, Ilse, Jurgen.*

Derse (111) Origin unidentified.

Dersham (104) Origin unidentified. Perhaps an Americanized spelling of the French topographic name DESCHAMPS.

Dershem (201) See DERSHAM.

Derstine (333) Altered spelling of a Swiss German habitational name, from places called Dierstein in Baden and northern Bavaria.
FOREBEARS This is the name of a Swiss Mennonite family, originally from Berne canton, that was in the Palatinate in the early 18th century and subsequently came to North America.

Dertinger (111) German: habitational name for someone from Derdingen in Württemberg or Dertingen in Baden.

De Rubeis (141) Italian: patronymic from an old Latinized personal name *Rubeo*, meaning 'red' (see ROSSO), but here in the broader sense 'of or belonging to the Rubei family'.
GIVEN NAMES Italian 24%. *Cesidio* (3), *Carmine* (2), *Guido* (2), *Pompeo* (2), *Rocco* (2), *Silvio* (2), *Antonio, Deno, Enea, Francesco, Lidio, Omero, Orazio, Oresto, Orfeo.*

De Ruiter (304) Dutch: occupational name, from Middle Dutch *ruter, rutter* 'horseman'. The term also meant 'freebooter', 'tramp', 'soldier', and the surname may have arisen from any of these senses.
GIVEN NAMES Dutch 5%. *Andries, Dirk, Gerrit, Maarten, Teunis.*

Derus (136) Lithuanian: unexplained.

Derusha (287) Americanized form of French DESROCHERS.

De Russo (113) Variant of Italian DI RUSSO.
GIVEN NAMES Italian 5%. *Marco, Salvatore.*

De Ruyter (304) Dutch (**de Ruyter**): variant spelling (17th century) of DE RUITER.
GIVEN NAMES Dutch 5%. *Cornie* (3), *Dirk, Kees, Marinus.*

Dervin (152) Variant of Irish DERWIN.

Derwin (156) Irish (Connacht): Anglicized form of Gaelic **Ó Dearbháin** 'descendant of *Dearbhán*', a personal name from a diminutive of *dearbh* 'certain'.

Dery (540) **1.** French: habitational name, with the preposition *de*, for someone from a place named with Walloon *ri* 'stream', for example in Marchin, Liège, or Macquenoise, Hainault, or alternatively from the common northern French place name Rieu(x), derived from Latin *rivus* 'stream', 'river'. **2.** Probably of French origin (**Déry**), from **D'Héry**, habitational name, with the preposition *d'*, from places in Nièvre, Savoy, and Yonne. **3.** Hungarian (**Déry**): habitational name from a place called Dér in Baranya county or Dőr in Sopron county. Compare DORY.

FOREBEARS The French surname **Dery** is first found in Canada in the form **Desry-Larose**, the bearer (originally from the region of Bourges) having married in 1669 in Quebec city.

GIVEN NAMES French 17%. *Pierre* (4), *Andre* (3), *Emile* (2), *Gilles* (2), *Jacques* (2), *Normand* (2), *Alain*, *Aurel*, *Benoit*, *Camille*, *Fernand*, *Francois*.

De Rycke (104) Dutch: old spelling of **de Rijk**, a nickname meaning 'the rich'.

GIVEN NAMES French 9%; Scandinavian 6%. *Etienne*, *Henri*.

De Ryke (113) Dutch: old spelling of **de Rijk**, a nickname meaning 'the rich'.

GIVEN NAME German 4%. *Walther*.

De Sa (150) Portuguese (also **De Sá**) and Galician: habitational name for someone from any of numerous places in Portugal and Galicia called Sá or Sa. This name is also found in western India, where it was taken by Portuguese colonists.

GIVEN NAMES Spanish 25%; Portuguese 13%; French 6%; Indian 4%. *Jose* (4), *Manuel* (4), *Carlos* (2), *Fernando* (2), *Ronaldo* (2), *Abilio*, *Alejandro*, *Alfonso*, *Americo*, *Augusto*, *Cesar*, *Eduardo*; *Joao*, *Joaquim*, *Paulo*; *Hilaire*, *Valmont*; *Anil*, *Subhas*, *Thakorbhai*.

Desai (2996) Indian (Gujarat and Maharashtra): Hindu name meaning 'landlord', from Sanskrit *deša* 'country' + *svāmī* 'lord', 'master'.

GIVEN NAMES Indian 91%. *Anil* (46), *Bharat* (33), *Dilip* (29), *Mahesh* (28), *Ramesh* (24), *Vijay* (24), *Ashok* (23), *Girish* (22), *Sanjay* (22), *Harshad* (21), *Prakash* (21), *Kishor* (20).

Desalle (115) Origin unidentified; perhaps a reduced form of French **Delasalle**, a topographic name for someone 'from the (*de la*) hall (*salle*)'.

GIVEN NAMES Italian 6%. *Antonio* (3), *Marco* (2), *Reno*.

De Salvo (1109) Italian: patronymic from the personal name SALVO.

GIVEN NAMES Italian 7%. *Angelo* (4), *Salvatore* (3), *Antonino*, *Caesar*, *Carmine*, *Dino*, *Guido*, *Rocco*, *Sabato*, *Sal*, *Sylvio*.

De Sanctis (271) Italian: Latinized variant of DE SANTI, in the broader sense 'of or belonging to the Santi family'.

GIVEN NAMES Italian 21%; Spanish 6%. *Antonio* (4), *Dino* (3), *Angelo* (2), *Gildo* (2), *Julio* (2), *Nicola* (2), *Amedeo*, *Carmine*, *Eugenio*, *Francesca*, *Gaetano*, *Giovanni*, *Italo*; *Alfonsina*, *Carlos*, *Fernando*, *Graciela*, *Juan*.

De Santi (238) Italian: variant of DI SANTI.

GIVEN NAMES Italian 18%. *Pietro* (2), *Angelo*, *Aurelio*, *Carlo*, *Claudio*, *Dino*, *Guido*, *Mario*, *Vittorio*.

De Santiago (397) Spanish, Galician, and Portuguese: habitational name for someone from any of various places named SANTIAGO, named for St. James, in particular Santiago de Compostella in Galicia.

GIVEN NAMES Spanish 56%. *Jose* (13), *Jesus* (6), *Juan* (6), *Pedro* (6), *Manuel* (5), *Carlos* (4), *Miguel* (4), *Arturo* (3), *Enrique* (3), *Javier* (3), *Mario* (3), *Ricardo* (3); *Antonio* (2), *Lorenzo* (2), *Bartolo*, *Eliseo*, *Ermenegildo*, *Lucio*, *Mauro*, *Severino*.

De Santis (3670) Southern Italian: patronymic from the personal name SANTO, in the broader sense 'of or belonging to the Santi family'.

GIVEN NAMES Italian 17%. *Angelo* (17), *Vito* (14), *Antonio* (12), *Rocco* (12), *Domenic* (6), *Gino* (6), *Lorenzo* (5), *Pasquale* (5), *Sal* (5), *Salvatore* (5), *Camillo* (4), *Dante* (4).

De Santo (822) Italian: variant of DI SANTO.

GIVEN NAMES Italian 14%. *Salvatore* (5), *Angelo* (4), *Carmine* (3), *Donato* (2), *Pasquale* (2), *Rocco* (2), *Sal* (2), *Vito* (2), *Antonio*, *Caesar*, *Elio*, *Fiore*.

De Santos (162) Spanish: habitational name from a place named with Los Santos, as for example Los Santos de Maimona in Badajoz province.

GIVEN NAMES Spanish 33%. *Jose* (8), *Manuel* (4), *Albino*, *Alvaro*, *Ana*, *Armando*, *Avelardo*, *Carlos*, *Eduardo*, *Elena*, *Emilia*, *Fernando*; *Antonio*, *Enrico*, *Heriberto*, *Vincenzo*.

De Sario (139) Italian: patronymic from the personal name *Sario*, a short form of ROSARIO.

GIVEN NAMES Italian 16%. *Vito* (2), *Aldo*, *Mario*, *Orlando*, *Oronzo*, *Santo*.

De Sarno (131) Italian: habitational name for someone from Sarno in Salerno province, Campania.

GIVEN NAMES Italian 18%. *Aniello*, *Antonio*, *Fiore*, *Giovanna*, *Luigi*, *Pasquale*, *Sal*.

De Sarro (100) Italian: variant of DI SARRO.

GIVEN NAME Italian 6%. *Aldo*.

Desaulniers (263) French: topographic name denoting a property distinguished by a grove of alder trees, Old French *au(l)ne*.

GIVEN NAMES French 19%. *Andre* (3), *Francois* (2), *Marcel* (2), *Armand*, *Aurele*, *Florent*, *Germain*, *Gilles*, *Henri*, *Jacques*, *Normand*, *Serge*.

Desautel (229) French: variant of DESAUTELS.

Desautels (580) French: habitational name, with fused preposition and definite article *des*, for someone from any of several places called Les Autels, in Aisne, Calvados, Eure-et-Loire, and Seine-Maritime.

GIVEN NAMES French 17%. *Andre* (4), *Jacques* (4), *Armand* (3), *Gilles* (2), *Luc* (2), *Marcel* (2), *Napoleon* (2), *Pierre* (2), *Aldor*, *Alphonse*, *Antoine*, *Auguste*.

Desbiens (154) Canadian variant of French **Debien**, from *bien* 'property', 'possessions'.

GIVEN NAMES French 16%. *Marcel* (2), *Armand*, *Jacques*, *Jean Claude*, *Lucien*, *Yves*.

Descant (116) Perhaps an altered form of French DESCHAMPS.

GIVEN NAMES French 9%. *Jacques*, *Marcelin*, *Pierre*.

Desch (493) South German: variant of TASCH, a metonymic occupational name for maker of bags and purses, or a topographic name for someone who lived by a field with irregular angles.

GIVEN NAMES German 5%. *Dieter* (2), *Eberhardt* (2), *Armin*.

Deschaine (423) Variant of French **Duchaine** (see DUCHENE).

GIVEN NAMES French 9%. *Lucien* (2), *Rosaire* (2), *Emile*, *Gedeon*, *Monique*, *Phillippe*, *Simonne*.

Deschamp (133) Respelling of French DESCHAMPS.

Deschamps (670) French: topographic name for someone 'from the fields', French *champs* (see CHAMP).

GIVEN NAMES French 16%. *Colette* (4), *Herve* (3), *Alban* (2), *Emile* (2), *Fernand* (2), *Adrien*, *Andre*, *Auguste*, *Chantal*, *Dominique*, *Fernande*, *Francois*.

Deschene (264) Altered form of French **Duchêne** (see DUCHENE).

GIVEN NAMES French 10%. *Emile* (2), *Normand* (2), *Camille*, *Cecile*, *Ludger*.

Deschenes (755) Plural form of French **Duchêne** (see DUCHENE).

GIVEN NAMES French 16%. *Andre* (4), *Normand* (4), *Armand* (3), *Lucien* (2), *Adrien*, *Alain*, *Albertine*, *Aurele*, *Colette*, *Donat*, *Florent*, *Gaetan*.

De Schepper (149) Dutch: **1.** occupational name for a tailor, Middle Dutch *sceppre* + the definite article *de*. **2.** in some cases, perhaps a variant of **de Schipper**, an occupational name for the captain of a ship or barge.

Deschler (178) German: occupational name for a purse- or bag-maker, a variant of TESCHNER.

Deschner (144) German: variant of DESCHLER.

GIVEN NAMES German 7%. *Klaus*, *Otto*, *Reinhart*, *Rudi*.

Descoteaux (329) French: topographic name for someone living in a hilly place, from the plural of *coteau* 'small hill'. This was a secondary surname in Canada, and has often been translated as HILL.

GIVEN NAMES French 18%. *Andre* (2), *Fernand* (2), *Renald* (2), *Adelard*, *Armand*, *Cecile*, *Clovis*, *Germaine*, *Gilles*, *Gratien*, *Henri*, *Herve*.

Deselms (131) Americanized form of French DESORMEAUX 'of the elms'.

De Sena (305) Italian, Spanish, and Portuguese: habitational name for someone from the city of Siena in Italy. *Sena* is an old Italian, Spanish, and Portuguese form of the place name.

GIVEN NAMES Italian 18%; Portuguese 4%; Spanish 4%. *Carmine* (6), *Angelo* (3), *Salvatore* (3), *Aniello, Carlo, Ferdinando, Stefano; Ilidio, Margarida; Julio* (2), *Agueda, Jose.*

Desens (107) German: probably a Rhenish derivative of **Deessen**, a short and patronymic form of *Matthäus* (see MATTHEW).
GIVEN NAME German 4%. *Merwin.*

De Serio (113) Italian: patronymic from *Serio*, evidently a nickname from *serio* 'serious', 'earnest'.

GIVEN NAMES Italian 13%. *Giovanni, Leonardo, Marco, Sante, Vito.*

Desforges (133) French: habitational name originally denoting someone from a place named Forges (from *forge* 'smithy', 'workshop'), examples of which are found in Creuse and Morbihan.

GIVEN NAMES French 19%. *Andre, Emile, Gaetan, Gaston, Jacques, Octave, Pierre.*

Desfosses (131) French: **1.** habitational name from any of numerous places named Les Fosses (from Latin *fossa* 'hole', 'hollow'). This was a secondary surname in Canada, especially for **Laspron**, but also **Lacharité** and **St. Louis**. **2.** (**Des Fossés**): habitational name for someone a place called Les Fossés (from Latin *fossates* 'ditches', 'trenches').

GIVEN NAMES French 15%. *Armand, Jean-Jacques, Lucien, Marcel, Yvon.*

Desha (172) Altered form of French DESCHAMPS, meaning 'of or from the fields'.

Deshaies (296) French: topographic name, a plural variant of DE HAY.

GIVEN NAMES French 15%. *Andre* (3), *Armand* (2), *Lucien* (2), *Marcel* (2), *Cecile, Gabrielle, Germain, Leo-Paul, Telesphore.*

Deshane (219) Americanized spelling of French **Duchêne** (see DUCHENE).

Desharnais (159) Perhaps a respelling of French **Decharnais**, a habitational name for someone from for example Charnois in Ardennes, so named from a derivative of *charme* 'hornbeam'.

GIVEN NAMES French 20%. *Armand* (4), *Andre* (2), *Adrien, Emile, Fernand, Gaston, Jean-Louis, Raoul.*

Deshaw (235) **1.** Americanized spelling of the French topographic name **Duchamp**, or its plural form DESCHAMPS, meaning 'of or from the field(s)' (see CHAMP). **2.** Americanized spelling of Belgian French **Dechaux**, which comes from the common place name Chaux, or in some cases may represent **Déchaux**, a nickname from Old French *descaus* 'unshod', 'barefoot'.

Deshazer (339) Possibly French, a topographic name from a derivative of the regional term *chaze* 'house' (from Latin *casa*).

Deshazo (751) Perhaps an altered form of French **Deschazeau**, a topographic name from the Massif Central, denoting someone from a grouping of *caseaux* 'houses', i.e. a village as opposed to a farm.

Deshields (509) Possibly a part Americanized form of Dutch **de Schilder**, an occupational name for a gilder or painter (of arms), from *schilder* 'painter', a derivative of *schild* 'shield', 'scutcheon', 'coat of arms'.

Deshler (221) Americanized spelling of German DESCHLER.

Deshmukh (133) Indian (Maharashtra): Hindu name found in several communities, from Marathi *dešmukh* 'district chief', once an hereditary office (from Sanskrit *deša* 'country', 'district' + *mukha* 'face').

GIVEN NAMES Indian 90%. *Ravi* (3), *Smriti* (3), *Uday* (3), *Vinod* (3), *Ajit* (2), *Aparna* (2), *Avinash* (2), *Prakash* (2), *Sanjiv* (2), *Shankar* (2), *Shashank* (2), *Shilpa* (2).

Deshon (285) Altered form of the French topographic name DESCHAMPS (see CHAMP, DESHONG).

Deshong (596) Americanized form of the French topographic name **Duchamp** or its plural form DESCHAMPS, meaning 'of or from the field(s)' (see CHAMP). Compare DISHONG.

Deshotel (504) Altered form of French DESAUTELS.

GIVEN NAMES French 4%. *Damien, Emile, Ignace, Monique.*

Deshotels (180) Altered form of French DESAUTELS.

Deshpande (225) Indian (Karnataka and Maharashtra): Hindu (usually Brahman) name, from Marathi *dešpaṇe* 'district accountant', formerly a hereditary office (from Sanskrit *deša* 'country', 'district' + *paṇita* 'learned man').

GIVEN NAMES Indian 95%. *Ashok* (6), *Vijay* (5), *Ashish* (4), *Shantanu* (4), *Abhay* (3), *Avinash* (3), *Jayant* (3), *Milind* (3), *Sanjay* (3), *Shrikant* (2), *Achyut* (2), *Anand* (2).

Desiderio (540) Italian: from the medieval personal name *Desiderio*, from Latin *Desiderius*, a derivative of *desiderium* 'desire', 'longing', given to a longed-for son or as a devotional name, an expression of the Christian's longing for God.

GIVEN NAMES Italian 25%. *Camillo* (2), *Massimo* (2), *Mario* (3), *Alfonso, Angelo, Antonio, Braulio, Cirilo, Dante, Eladio, Elida, Elio, Falco, Gennaro, Gino, Leopoldo, Mariano, Nicolo, Nidia, Piero.*

Desilets (448) French: topographic name, with fused preposition and definite article *des* 'from the', for someone who lived by some group of small islands, from the plural of *îlet* 'islet'.

FOREBEARS In Canada this was a secondary surname associated with HUARD and COUILLARD, and first used independently there in 1748.

GIVEN NAMES French 18%. *Andre* (3), *Laurent* (3), *Lucien* (2), *Pierre* (2), *Serge* (2), *Aime, Armand, Arsene, Benoit, Camille, Cecile, Eloi.*

De Silva (1194) Respelling of Portuguese DA SILVA. This name is common in western India, where it was taken by Portuguese colonists.

GIVEN NAMES Indian 16%. *Asoka* (4), *Sumith* (4), *Lal* (3), *Nihal* (3), *Rohan* (3), *Sunil* (3), *Ananda* (2), *Anura* (2), *Chandra* (2), *Mahendra* (2), *Manjula* (2), *Nalin* (2).

De Simone (2968) Italian: patronymic from the personal name *Simone*, Italian equivalent of SIMON.

GIVEN NAMES Italian 16%. *Angelo* (22), *Salvatore* (17), *Antonio* (10), *Gino* (8), *Carmine* (7), *Rocco* (7), *Carlo* (6), *Sal* (6), *Vito* (5), *Enrico* (4), *Pasquale* (4), *Alfonse* (3).

Desio (224) Italian: patronymic from a medieval personal name, *Desio*, documented in medieval Latin as *Desigius, Desijo*, and associated with literary Italian *desio* 'desire'.

GIVEN NAMES Italian 20%. *Carmine* (3), *Achille, Camillo, Cono, Gianluca, Marco, Rocco, Vito.*

Desir (316) French (**Désir**): from the personal name *Désir*, a development of Latin *Desiderius*.

GIVEN NAMES French 43%. *Andre* (2), *Antoine* (2), *Julienne* (2), *Michel* (2), *Monique* (2), *Odette* (2), *Serge* (2), *Carolle, Chantal, Evens, Fresnel, Gisele.*

De Sisto (273) Italian: patronymic from the personal name SISTO.

GIVEN NAMES Italian 17%. *Egidio* (2), *Pasquale* (2), *Antonio, Carmine, Emelio, Fausto, Gennaro, Rocco, Salvatore, Silvio.*

Desjardin (339) Respelling of French DESJARDINS.

GIVEN NAMES French 8%. *Pierre* (3), *Armand* (2), *Emile, Lucien, Normand.*

Desjardins (1797) French: from the plural of *jardin* 'garden' (Old French *jart*), with the preposition and definite article *des* 'from the'; a topographic name or a habitational name from any of numerous minor places so named. In the U.S., this name was often translated as GARDNER.

GIVEN NAMES French 16%. *Andre* (11), *Armand* (7), *Lucien* (7), *Pierre* (7), *Jacques* (6), *Normand* (5), *Gilles* (4), *Marcel* (4), *Camille* (2), *Cecile* (2), *Clovis* (2), *Fernand* (2).

Desjarlais (382) French: unexplained. The forms **Desjarlès** and **De Gerlais** also occur; this name is associated with the secondary surname St. Amand.

GIVEN NAMES French 9%. *Andre* (2), *Gilles* (2), *Marcel* (2), *Armand, Eugenie, Germaine, Herve, Mireille, Normand.*

Deskin (291) Variant of Irish DISKIN.

Deskins (828) Most probably a variant of Irish DISKIN.

Desko (117) Origin unidentified.

Deslandes (114) French: habitational name from any of various minor places named Les Landes throughout France.
GIVEN NAMES French 15%. *Brunel, Luc, Lucien, Pierre, Rejean.*

Deslatte (161) French: habitational name from a place called Lattes, examples of which are to be found in Hérault and Jura. This surname is concentrated in LA.

Deslauriers (529) French: topographic name for someone living among laurels, a combination of the fused preposition and plural definite article *des* 'from the' + the plural of Old French *lorier* 'laurel'. It is a frequent secondary surname in Canada.
GIVEN NAMES French 13%. *Armand* (6), *Andre* (2), *Aime, Alcide, Aurore, Cecile, Edouard, Emile, Florent, Gilles, Jacques, Jean Claude.*

Desmarais (1748) French: habitational name for someone from any of various places named with Old French *mareis, maresc* 'marsh', as for example Les Marets, in Seine-et-Marne, Centre, Nord, and Picardy.
GIVEN NAMES French 15%. *Armand* (12), *Normand* (10), *Andre* (6), *Lucien* (6), *Emile* (4), *Cecile* (3), *Clovis* (3), *Gaston* (3), *Adrien* (2), *Aime* (2), *Amedee* (2), *Gilles* (2).

De Smet (482) Dutch: occupational name from *smed* 'smith' + the definite article *de*.
GIVEN NAMES French 6%. *Emile* (2), *Andre, Desire, Dominique, Gaston, Julien, Olivier.*

De Smidt (128) Dutch: variant of DE SMET.

De Smith (178) Part translation of Dutch DE SMET 'the smith'.

Desmond (2943) Irish: Anglicized form of Gaelic **Ó Deasmhumhnaigh** 'descendant of the man from southern Munster', from *deas* 'south' + *Mumhain* 'Munster', an ancient Irish kingdom named for *Mumhu*, one of its early kings. The surname Desmond has passed into common use as a personal name, not only in Ireland.
GIVEN NAMES Irish 4%. *Aidan, Aileen, Brendan, Colm, Donal, Liam, Mairead, Sean Patrick, Siobhan.*

Desnoyers (237) French: topographic name from the plural of *noyer* 'walnut tree', Old French *noier* (see NOYER).
FOREBEARS In Canada this was used as a secondary surname, appearing as early as 1640 in Quebec.
GIVEN NAMES French 16%. *Gaston* (2), *Jacques* (2), *Adelard, Armand, Cecile, Henri, Jean Pierre, Luc, Lucienne, Oliva, Rosaire, Sylvain.*

Deso (103) Origin unidentified.

De Socio (135) Italian: patronymic from a nickname from *socio* 'companion', 'friend', 'ally' or from a short form of a personal name formed with this element.

De Sorbo (108) Italian: topographic name for someone living by a sorbus tree, a rowan, or a whitebeam, Italian *sorbo* (Latin *sorbus*), or habitational name for someone from a place named with this word.
GIVEN NAMES Italian 9%. *Antonio, Carmine.*

Desormeaux (367) French: topographic name from a diminutive of Old French *orme* 'elm', or a habitational name from any of several places named Les Ormeaux from this word. See also ORME 2.
GIVEN NAMES French 10%. *Emile* (2), *Andre, Andree, Armand, Curley, Fernand, Gaston, Laurette, Leontine, Marcel, Minos, Pierre.*

Desotell (119) Americanized spelling of French DESAUTELS.

De Soto (637) Galician and Asturian-Leonese: habitational name from any of numerous minor places called Soto, notably in Galicia and Asturies, alongside the Asturian-Leonese variant **Sotu**.
GIVEN NAMES Spanish 6%; French 4%. *Hernando* (2), *Juan* (2), *Margarita* (2), *Rafael* (2), *Xavier* (2), *Aida, Aleyda, Angel, Angelina, Berta, Beto, Blanca; Ovide* (3), *Marcelle* (2), *Andre, Chantal.*

De Sousa (866) Portuguese: habitational name from any of various minor places named SOUSA.
GIVEN NAMES Spanish 30%; Portuguese 20%. *Jose* (37), *Manuel* (35), *Carlos* (12), *Mario* (9), *Fernando* (7), *Luis* (6), *Jorge* (5), *Cesar* (4), *Francisco* (4), *Geraldo* (4), *Adelino* (3), *Armando* (3); *Joao* (9), *Joaquim* (4), *Agostinho* (3), *Paulo* (3), *Vasco* (3), *Duarte, Ligia, Manoel, Valentim; Antonio* (29), *Constantino* (3), *Clemente, Filomena, Leontina, Marco.*

De Souza (1075) Portuguese: variant of DE SOUSA.
GIVEN NAMES Spanish 21%; Portuguese 12%; French 4%. *Jose* (21), *Manuel* (10), *Carlos* (9), *Geraldo* (7), *Luiz* (6), *Claudio* (4), *Mario* (4), *Eduardo* (3), *Ana* (2), *Celso* (2), *Francisco* (2), *Gustavo* (2); *Joao* (4), *Manoel* (3), *Paulo* (3), *Adauto* (2), *Marcio* (2), *Ademir, Guilherme, Joaquim, Sebastiao; Alexandre* (2), *Andre* (2), *Celine* (2), *Easton, Elcie, Marcel, Marie-France, Sylvie.*

Despain (1196) Part translation of the French family name **Despagne**, ethnic name for a Spaniard, from *d'Espagne* 'from Spain'.

Despard (122) Origin unidentified; probably French.
GIVEN NAME French 4%. *Mathieu.*

Desper (225) French: probably a nickname from Old French *despers, despert* 'rough', 'cruel', 'wild'.

De Spirito (117) Italian: variant of DI SPIRITO.
GIVEN NAMES Italian 13%. *Antonio* (2), *Attilio, Gilda, Marzio, Pasquale, Raffaele.*

D'Esposito (325) Italian: patronymic from ESPOSITO, meaning 'exposed', 'exhibited', a surname which was commonly given to foundling children.
GIVEN NAMES Italian 14%. *Sal* (3), *Angelo* (2), *Salvatore* (2), *Sergio* (2), *Carmine,*

Elvira, Filomena, Mario, Orlando, Pasquale, Rocco.

Despot (114) Serbian: nickname from *despot* 'despot', 'tyrant', a title of the 15th-century Serbian absolute rulers, from Greek *despotēs* 'master'.
GIVEN NAMES South Slavic 7%; French 6%. *Milenko* (2); *Camille* (2).

Despres (470) French (**Després**): variant (plural) of **Dupré** (see DUPRE).
FOREBEARS This name was in Quebec city by 1651.
GIVEN NAMES French 11%. *Jacques* (2), *Adelard, Aime, Alphonse, Cecile, Colette, Emile, Leonide, Marcel, Normand, Raoul.*

Desroche (102) Respelling of French DEROCHE.
GIVEN NAMES French 14%. *Armand, Emile, Etienne, Laure, Normand.*

Desrocher (146) Respelling of French DESROCHERS.
GIVEN NAMES French 9%. *Donat, Jacques, Marcel.*

Desrochers (1000) French: topographic name for someone living among boulders, from fused preposition and plural definite article *des* + the plural of *rocher* 'boulder', or a habitational name from any of several places named with this word. This name was sometimes confused with DESROSIERS, even in French language documents.
GIVEN NAMES French 18%. *Armand* (5), *Marcel* (5), *Andre* (4), *Lucien* (4), *Jacques* (3), *Pierre* (3), *Cecile* (2), *Dominique* (2), *Emile* (2), *Alphonse, Andree, Aurele.*

Desroches (633) French: topographic name for someone living among rocks, from the fused preposition and definite article *des* + the plural of French *roche* 'rock', or a habitational name from any of several places named with this word. In North America, this name has been confused with LAROCHE, and translated as ROCK.
GIVEN NAMES French 14%. *Herve* (3), *Andre* (2), *Emile* (2), *Gilles* (2), *Normand* (2), *Armand, Elphege, Elzear, Fernand, Gaspard, Gisele, Jean Marc.*

Desrosier (308) Respelling of French DESROSIERS.
GIVEN NAMES French 8%. *Armand, Herve, Manon, Philias.*

Desrosiers (1765) French: topographic name for someone living among rose bushes, from the fused preposition and definite article *des* 'from the' + the plural of Old French *rosier* 'rose bush'. This was sometimes confused with DESROCHERS, even in French language documents.
GIVEN NAMES French 20%. *Pierre* (13), *Andre* (9), *Armand* (7), *Marcel* (7), *Aime* (4), *Laurent* (4), *Lucien* (4), *Normand* (4), *Camille* (3), *Emile* (3), *Fernand* (3), *Adelard* (2).

Desruisseaux (118) French: topographic name for someone who lived in an area characterized by streams, from the fused preposition and plural definite article *des* 'from the' + *ruisseaux*, plural of *ruisseau* 'stream'.

GIVEN NAMES French 14%; German 4%. *Emile* (2), *Armand, Lucien, Pascale*; *Fritz*.

Dessauer (122) German: habitational name for someone from Dessau in Sachsen-Anhalt or Dessow in Brandenburg.

GIVEN NAMES German 8%. *Florian, Gerhard, Hans, Kurt*.

Dessel (108) Origin unidentified.

Desselle (351) French: variant spelling of DECELLE.

GIVEN NAMES French 5%. *Landry, Marcel*.

Desser (154) Jewish (Ashkenazic): habitational name from the city of Dessau in Germany.

GIVEN NAME Jewish 4%; German 4%. *Chaim*.

Dessert (238) French: topographic name, with the preposition *d(e)*, from Old French *essart* 'clearing', 'assart' (from Latin *exsartum*, a derivative of *sarire* 'to hoe'), a term denoting an area of woodland that had been cleared for cultivation or settlement, rather than a natural glade.

GIVEN NAMES French 10%. *Marcel* (3), *Alderic, Gaston, Normand*.

Desta (149) Ethiopian: unexplained.

GIVEN NAMES Ethiopian 76%. *Almaz* (3), *Abebe* (2), *Abenet* (2), *Getachew* (2), *Girma* (2), *Hirut* (2), *Saba* (2), *Tadele* (2), *Tedla* (2), *Abeba, Abiy, Alem, Alemayehu*.

De Stasio (127) Italian: variant of DI STASIO.

GIVEN NAMES Italian 13%. *Carmela, Gelsomina, Luigi, Pasquale, Sal, Salvatore*.

De Stefanis (160) Italian: patronymic from the personal name *Stefano* (see STEVEN), in the broader sense 'of or belonging to the Santi family'.

GIVEN NAMES Italian 24%. *Mario* (5), *Americo* (2), *Carmine* (2), *Alessandro, Angelo, Antonio, Dino, Domenic, Giancarlo, Nunzio, Renato, Roberto, Sergio*.

De Stefano (2548) Italian: variant of DI STEFANO.

GIVEN NAMES Italian 14%. *Carmine* (15), *Angelo* (14), *Salvatore* (11), *Rocco* (7), *Gennaro* (4), *Santo* (4), *Carlo* (3), *Pasquale* (3), *Sal* (3), *Antonio* (2), *Biagio* (2), *Cosmo* (2).

Destin (113) French: variant of DUSTIN.

GIVEN NAMES French 33%. *Pierre* (2), *Sauveur* (2), *Aurele, Frenel, Julien, Prosper, Wesner*.

Destro (106) Italian: nickname from *destro* 'dextrous', 'skilled', (literally 'right-handed').

GIVEN NAMES Italian 12%. *Carmelo, Delio, Francesco*.

De Sutter (136) Dutch: occupational name for a cobbler or tailor, from Middle Dutch *sutter* 'one who sews', (from Latin *sutor* 'shoemaker', 'cobbler').

GIVEN NAMES French 9%. *Alphonse, Antoine, Marcel, Pascal, Remy*.

Desy (112) Origin unidentified; probably French.

GIVEN NAMES French 13%. *Alain, Jacques, Pierre, Raoul*.

Detamore (256) Probably an Americanized spelling of DITTMAR.

Detar (261) **1.** Slavic variant of German DIETER. **2.** North German: variant of DETER. **3.** Hungarian (**Détári**): habitational name for someone from a place called *Déter* in Békés county.

Detemple (151) French: habitational name, with the preposition *de*, from any of several places named (Le) Temple, from Latin *templum*, denoting a settlement of the Knights Templar. The name is also found in Germany, taken there by a family which fled from France in 1789.

Deter (333) **1.** North German: from the personal name *Detert*, which is a reduced of *Dethard*, from an old personal name composed of Old Saxon *thioda* 'people', 'race' + *hard* 'strong'. This a deduced form of DIETRICH. **2.** Possibly an altered spelling of DIETER.

Deterding (252) North German: from **Detharding**, a patronymic from the Low German personal name *Dethard* (see DETER).

Detering (114) North German: patronymic from the Low German personal name *Dethard* (see DETER).

Determan (514) North German (**Determann**): elaborated form of DETER.

Deters (998) North German: **1.** patronymic from DETER. **2.** Possibly a variant of *Dieters* (see DIETER).

Detert (241) North German: variant of DETER.

GIVEN NAMES German 6%. *Gunther* (2), *Bernhard, Ewald, Ralf*.

Detherage (190) English: occupational name for someone who chopped up wood into tinder, Middle English *dethewright*, from *dethe* 'fuel', 'tinder' + *wright* 'maker'.

GIVEN NAME German 4%. *Otto* (2).

Dethlefs (154) North German and Frisian: patronymic from the personal name *Detlef*, composed of Middle Low German *theudo* 'people', 'race' + *lēf* 'life', 'offshoot'. The South German equivalent of *Detlef* is *Dietleib*.

Dethlefsen (146) Danish and North German: variant spelling of DETLEFSEN.

Dethloff (244) North German: from a personal name composed of the Germanic elements *theudō* 'people', 'race' + *wolf* 'wolf'.

Dethomas (145) French: patronymic from the personal name THOMAS.

GIVEN NAMES Italian 7%. *Natale* (2), *Dino*.

Detienne (166) French (**D'Étienne**): patronymic from the personal name *Étienne*, French form of STEVEN.

GIVEN NAMES French 4%; Scandinavian 4%. *Andre, Marcel*; *Maija*.

Detjen (178) North German, Frisian, and Danish: variant of *Dedeken*, a short form of the personal name *Dethard* (see DETER).

GIVEN NAMES French 6%; German 6%. *Emile* (2); *Dieter, Katharina, Reinhold*.

Detlefsen (249) Danish and North German: patronymic from the personal name *Ditlev, Detlef* (see DETHLEFS).

GIVEN NAMES German 4%. *Guenther, Hans, Kurt*.

Detling (101) Respelling of German DETTLING.

Detloff (218) German: variant spelling of DETHLOFF.

Detmer (419) Variant spelling of North German DETTMER.

Detmers (102) German: patronymic from the personal name *Dietmar* (see DITTMAR).

GIVEN NAME German 7%. *Fritz* (2).

De Tore (207) Southern Italian: patronymic from a short form of the personal name SALVATORE.

GIVEN NAMES French 6%; Italian 6%. *Armand* (2), *Patrice*; *Camillo* (2), *Carmine, Santo*.

De Toro (104) **1.** Italian: variant of DI TORO. **2.** Spanish: habitational name for someone from Toro, a place in Zamora province.

GIVEN NAMES Italian 14%; French 8%; Spanish 8%; Jewish 4%. *Lorenzo* (2), *Primo* (2), *Antonio*; *Armand* (4), *Laurette*; *Anamaria, Armando, Carlos, Manuel, Milagros, Pedro*; *Miriam*.

Detrich (145) Altered spelling of German DIETRICH.

GIVEN NAME German 4%. *Kurt*.

Detrick (1004) Altered spelling of German DIETRICH or Dutch **Diederik** (see DEDERICK).

Detro (136) Origin unidentified. Perhaps an altered spelling of Belgian French **Detrou**, a habitational name, with the preposition *de*, for someone from any of the various places named Trou, from Old French *trau* 'hole', 'hollow', 'well'. Compare DUTRO.

Detter (277) **1.** South German: habitational name from a place so named in Bavaria. **2.** North German: variant spelling of DETER.

GIVEN NAMES German 4%. *Helmut, Monika, Otto*.

Dettinger (172) German: habitational name for someone from any of numerous places called Dettingen.

Dettlaff (114) German: variant spelling of DETHLOFF.

GIVEN NAMES German 5%. *Alois, Erwin*.

Dettling (309) German: habitational name for someone from a place named Dettlingen in Württemberg.

Dettloff (303) German: variant spelling of DETHLOFF.

Dettman (593) Variant spelling of German DETTMANN.

Dettmann (440) German: from a derivative of the old personal name *Dettmar* (see DITTMAR).

Dettmer (570) North German: from the old personal name *Dettmar* (see DITTMAR).
GIVEN NAMES German 4%. *Erwin, Franz, Helmut, Kurt, Raimund.*

D'Ettore (182) Italian: patronymic from the personal name *Ettore*, from Greek *Hektōr* (see HECTOR 2).
GIVEN NAMES Italian 14%. *Angelo* (2), *Amedeo, Rocco, Santo.*

D'Ettorre (102) Variant spelling of Italian D'ETTORE.
GIVEN NAMES Italian 11%. *Dino, Domenic, Marco, Pasquale.*

Dettwiler (114) Swiss German: variant spelling of DETWEILER.

Detty (293) Origin unidentified.

De Turk (159) Dutch: from Middle Dutch *turc* 'Turk' + the definite article *de*, hence an ethnic name, or probably more commonly a habitational name for someone who lived at a house or tavern distinguished by the sign of the Turk.

Detweiler (1163) German: habitational name from Detweiler, a village in Zürich canton, Switzerland or from Dettwiller in the Upper Rhine region of France, near Saverne.

Detwiler (1888) Variant spelling of German DETWEILER, or a habitational name for someone from a farm named Dettwyl in Aargau canton, Switzerland.

Detzel (172) German: **1.** variant of DITZEL. **2.** possibly an altered spelling of DIETZEL.

Detzler (101) Origin unidentified.

Deubel (141) South and Swiss German: **1.** nickname from Alemannic *deubel* 'devil' (see TEUFEL). **2.** nickname, or an occupational name for a dove breeder or dealer, from a diminutive of Middle High German *tūbe* 'dove' (see TAUBE).

Deubler (145) South German and Swabian: occupational name for a dove keeper, from an agent derivative of Middle High German *tūbe* 'dove'.
GIVEN NAMES German 6%. *Horst, Klaus.*

Deubner (101) German: **1.** habitational name for someone from either of two places called Deuben (in Saxony, Saxony-Anhalt). **2.** variant of TEUBNER, an occupational name for a dove keeper.

Deuel (801) Possibly of French origin. This name is concentrated in SC and may have been brought there by Huguenots.

Deupree (240) Altered spelling of French **Du Pré** (see DUPRE).

Deur (103) Possibly an altered spelling of Scottish DEWAR.

Deus (113) Portuguese and Galician: from a variant or shortened form of *de Deus* 'from or with God', an element of various Christian personal names element (compare DIOS).

GIVEN NAMES Spanish 19%; Italian 7%; German 5%. *Manuel* (5), *Carlos* (2), *Eduardo, Guadalupe, Ladislao, Marisol, Mirta, Ramiro, Ricardo, Vincente; Antonio* (4), *Angelo, Elio, Evo; Lutz, Manfred.*

Deuschle (179) South German: from Middle High German *tiuschen, tuschen* 'to barter or trade', but also 'to deceive'; hence probably a nickname for a swindler or rogue.
GIVEN NAMES German 13%. *Kurt* (3), *Otto* (2), *Erhardt, Fritz, Manfred.*

Deuser (196) German: variant of DIETZ.
GIVEN NAMES German 4%. *Alois, Hedwig, Kurt.*

Deuster (102) German: nickname for a grim or low-spirited person, from Middle High German *dinster, duster* 'black', 'dark', 'grim'.

Deutch (247) Altered spelling of Jewish and German DEUTSCH.
GIVEN NAMES Jewish 12%. *Miriam* (3), *Chaya, Isador, Isadore, Naftali, Shlomo, Shmuel, Zvi.*

Deutchman (114) Altered spelling of German DEUTSCHMANN.

Deuter (103) German: habitational name for someone from either of two places in Hesse named Deute.
GIVEN NAME German 4%. *Ernst.*

Deutmeyer (115) German: a rounded form of **Dietmeyer**, a distinguishing name for a farmer, from DIET (see DIETRICH) + MEYER.

Deutsch (4118) **1.** German: ethnic name given in areas of mixed population to inhabitants speaking German rather than a Slavic language, from German *Deutsch* German (Middle High German *tiu(t)sch*, Old High German *diutisk*, from *diot, deot*, 'people', 'nation', from a Germanic root *theudō*). **2.** Jewish (Ashkenazic): regional name for someone who had migrated from a German-speaking area to another part of Europe.
GIVEN NAMES Jewish 6%. *Miriam* (6), *Sol* (6), *Chaim* (5), *Moshe* (4), *Meir* (3), *Mordechai* (3), *Yakov* (3), *Zalman* (3), *Baruch* (2), *Dov* (2), *Hyman* (2), *Mayer* (2).

Deutscher (345) German and Jewish (Ashkenazic): variant of DEUTSCH, with *-er*, suffix of agent nouns.
GIVEN NAMES German 5%. *Erwin, Hertha, Kurt, Siegmund.*

Deutschman (197) Respelling of German DEUTSCHMANN.

Deutschmann (154) German: ethnic name for a German-speaker, from a noun derivative of DEUTSCH.
GIVEN NAMES German 12%. *Kurt* (2), *Otto* (2), *Erhard, Hans.*

De Valk (159) Dutch: from Middle Dutch *valke* 'falcon' + the definite article *de*, hence a metonymic occupational name for a falconer, a nickname for someone thought to resemble the bird, or a habitational name

for someone who lived at a house or tavern distinguished by the sign of a falcon.

Devall (598) **1.** English: variant of DEVILLE 2. **2.** In some cases, probably an altered spelling of French **Deval** or DUVAL, topographic names from *val* 'valley'.

De Valle (105) **1.** Spanish: topographic name for someone living in a valley, or habitational name from a place named with this word (see VALLE). **2.** Possibly an Americanized spelling of French **Deval** or **Devallée**, denoting a valley dweller (see DEVALL).
GIVEN NAMES Spanish 27%. *Agustin, Alejandro, Armando, Carlos, Enrique, Fernando, Florentino, Jorge, Jose, Liliana, Martiza, Nestor.*

Devan (362) **1.** Irish: Anglicized form of Gaelic **Ó Duibhín** or **Ó Daimhín** (see DEVINE). **2.** Indian (Kerala, Tamil Nadu): Hindu name from Sanskrit *deva* 'god' + the Tamil-Malayalam third-person masculine singular suffix *-n*. This is only a given name in India, but has come to be used as a family name in the U.S.
GIVEN NAMES Indian 4%. *Santosh, Sashi, Satya, Vas, Vasu.*

Devane (802) Irish: Anglicized form of Gaelic **Ó Duibhín** or **Ó Daimhín** (see DEVINE).

Devaney (1698) Irish (eastern Ulster): **1.** Anglicized form of Gaelic **Ó Duibheannaigh** 'descendant of *Duibheannach*', a personal name of uncertain origin; the first element is *dubh* 'black', the second may be *eanach* 'marshy place'. The surname has become confused with DEVANE. **2.** Anglicized form of Gaelic **Ó Duibheamhna**, from a personal name based on *dubh* 'black' + the genitive of *Eamhain*, the Gaelic name of Navan fort, County Armagh, the legendary capital of Ulster.

Devanney (156) Irish: variant of DEVANEY.
GIVEN NAME French 5%. *Damien.*

Devantier (100) Origin unidentified.
GIVEN NAMES French 8%. *Andre, Edouard.*

Devany (166) Irish: variant of DEVANEY.

Devary (128) Probably a variant of the Irish family name **Devery**, a variant of DEVEREUX in Counties Leix and Offaly.

Devaughn (587) Altered spelling of Irish DEVINE.

Devaul (333) Americanized spelling of French DEVAULT, **Deval** (see DEVALL 2), or DUVAL 1.

Devault (1270) French: topographic name, from Old French *vau(l)x*, plural of *val* 'valley'. Compare DEVALL, DUVAL.

Devaux (234) French: variant of DEVAULT.
GIVEN NAMES French 5%. *Michel* (2), *Jean-Francois, Pierre.*

Deveau (738) Variant of French DEVAULT.
GIVEN NAMES French 6%. *Girard* (2), *Marcel* (2), *Adhemar, Alphee, Andre, Armand, Blanchard, Celine, Emile, Euclide, Henri, Lucien.*

Deveaux (322) French: variant of DEVAULT.

French 7%. *Andre* (2), *Pierre* (2), *Alain, Napoleon.*

Devendorf (200) Respelling of German DIEFENDORF.

Deveney (312) Irish: spelling variant of DEVANEY.

Devenney (292) Irish: spelling variant of DEVANEY.

Devenny (185) Irish: spelling variant of DEVANEY.

Devenport (297) Irish: variant of DAVENPORT 2; the spelling **Devonport** is found in Ireland and it may have been this form which gave rise to *Devenport.*

Devens (273) Probably a variant of Irish DEVINE. See also DEVINS.

Deveny (220) Hungarian (**Dévényi**): habitational name for someone from a place called Dévény, formerly in Hungary, now in Slovakia, or possibly from Divény in Nógrád county, or Devény (now Dövény) in Borsod county.

Dever (2015) Irish (County Mayo) and Scottish: Anglicized form of Gaelic **Ó Duibhidhir** (see DWYER).

Devera (448) Spanish: topographic name for someone 'from (*de*) an area of fertile land between a river and an upland (*vera*)'.
GIVEN NAMES Spanish 36%. *Francisco* (5), *Juanito* (4), *Alfredo* (3), *Jaime* (3), *Rodolfo* (3), *Arturo* (2), *Elvira* (2), *Jesus* (2), *Jorge* (2), *Jose* (2), *Juan* (2), *Lourdes* (2); *Antonio* (2), *Federico* (2), *Romeo* (2), *Ceasar, Cecilio, Dante, Enrico, Filomena, Leonardo, Marco.*

Deveraux (155) English and Irish: variant spelling of DEVEREUX.
GIVEN NAME Irish 4%. *Dermot.*

Devere (298) French and English: habitational name, with the French preposition *de*, from any of the numerous places named with the Gaulish element *ver(n)* 'alder', for example in Calvados and Manche.

Devereaux (1442) English and Irish (of Norman origin): variant spelling of DEVEREUX.

Deverell (168) **1.** English: habitational name from any of a group of places in Worcestershire which take their name affixes from the River Deverill (e.g. Brixton Deverill, Kingston Deverill). The river is thought to be named from Welsh *dwfr* 'river' + *iâl* 'fertile uplands'. **2.** English and Irish: variant of DEVEREUX.

Devereux (623) English and Irish (of Norman origin): habitational name, with the preposition *d(e)*, for someone from Évreux in Eure, France. See also EVEREST.
GIVEN NAMES Irish 4%. *Dermot, Sean.*

Devers (1082) Irish: variant of DEVER, with the addition of English patronymic *-s*.

Devery (170) Irish (Counties Leix and Offaly): variant of DEVEREUX.
GIVEN NAMES Irish 14%. *Kieran* (3), *Brendan* (2), *Clancy.*

Devey (205) Irish: see DEVOY.

Devi (101) Indian: honorific term used with the names of women, from Sanskrit *devī* 'goddess'. It is used as a last name by some women who do not have a surname as such.
GIVEN NAMES Indian 85%. *Shanti* (6), *Uma* (4), *Gayatri* (3), *Bimla* (2), *Chandra* (2), *Kamla* (2), *Amala, Aruna, Asha, Darshan, Durga, Indira.*

Devich (118) Serbian and Croatian (**Dević**): of uncertain origin; possibly a derivative of *deva* 'camel', denoting someone who tended camels at a place where Turkish caravans used to stop.

De Vico (110) Italian: patronymic from the personal name *Vico*, reduced form of *Lodovico* (see LEWIS 1).
GIVEN NAMES Italian 22%. *Sal* (2), *Achille, Alfonso, Assunta, Angelo, Emilio, Pasquale, Rosario.*

Devilbiss (434) Part translation of the German surname **Deubelbeiss** or the variants **Tüfelbeiss, Dübelbeiss**, which are Alemannic (Swiss) nicknames from Middle High German *düvel, tiufel* 'devil' + *beiz* 'biter'.

Deville (1231) **1.** English (of Norman origin): habitational name from Déville in Seine-Maritime, France, probably named with Latin *dei villa* 'settlement of (i.e. under the protection of) God'. This name was interpreted early on as a prepositional phrase *de ville* or *de val* and applied to dwellers in a town or valley (see VILLE and VALE). **2.** English: nickname from Middle English *devyle*, Old English *dēofol* 'devil' (Latin *diabolus*, from Greek *diabolos* 'slanderer', 'enemy'), referring to a mischievous youth or perhaps to someone who had acted the role of the Devil in a pageant or mystery play. **3.** French: variant of VILLE, with the preposition *de*.
GIVEN NAMES French 5%. *Damien* (2), *Herve* (2), *Adrien, Alexandre, Arianne, Chanel, Clovis, Delphin, Elrick, Emile, Eraste, Gilfred.*

Devillers (166) French: variant of DEVILLIER.
GIVEN NAMES French 6%. *Andre, Armand, Arnaud.*

Devillez (124) Origin unidentified.
GIVEN NAMES French 5%. *Dominique, Emile.*

Devillier (544) French: habitational name from any of the many places in France named Vill(i)er(s), from Late Latin *villare* 'outlying farm'.
GIVEN NAMES French 5%. *Andre, Cecile, Jacques, Maudry, Raoul, Silton.*

Devilliers (125) Origin unidentified.
GIVEN NAMES French 13%; Dutch 5%. *Pierre* (3), *Etienne* (2), *Andre, Raoul*; *Adriaan* (2), *Willem.*

Devin (507) **1.** Irish (County Louth): variant of DEVINE 1. **2.** English and French: variant of DEVINE 2. **3.** French: from *devin* 'sorcerer', 'fortuneteller' (related to the verb *deviner* 'to divine', 'foretell'). **4.** Russian: metronymic from *deva* 'girl',

normally a designation of an illegitimate child. Sometimes it may be a patronymic from a nickname for an effeminate man.
FOREBEARS A Breton bearer of this name was married in Quebec city in 1692.

De Vincent (199) French: patronymic from the personal name VINCENT.

De Vincentis (261) Italian: patronymic from a Latinized form of the personal name *Vincenzo*, Latin *Vincentius* (see VINCENT), but in the broader sense 'of or belonging to the Vincenzi family'.
GIVEN NAMES Italian 16%; French 4%. *Angelo* (3), *Antonio* (2), *Annibale, Attilio, Camillo, Carmine, Concetta, Cosimo, Giuseppe, Marco, Nazareno, Pasquale; Emile, Patrice, Pierre.*

De Vincenzi (203) Italian: variant of DE VINCENZO.
GIVEN NAMES Italian 9%. *Angelo* (3), *Aldo* (2), *Dario, Guido, Tullio.*

De Vincenzo (187) Italian: patronymic from the personal name *Vincenzo*, from Latin *Vincentius* (see VINCENT).
GIVEN NAMES Italian 28%. *Salvatore* (4), *Vito* (3), *Benito* (2), *Sal* (2), *Angelo, Carmine, Dante, Donato, Giorgio, Pasqualina, Rocco.*

Devine (9093) **1.** Irish: reduced Anglicized form of either of two Gaelic names, **Ó Duibhín** 'descendant of *Duibhín*', a byname meaning 'little black one', or **Ó Daimhín** 'descendant of *Daimhín*', a byname meaning 'fawn', 'little stag'. These are attenuated versions of Ó *Dubháin* and Ó *Damháin*, and are the phonetic origin of Anglicizations with an internal *v* (as opposed to *w*, as in DEWAN, or monosyllabic forms with an *o* or *u*) (see DOANE). **2.** English and French: nickname, of literal or ironic application, from Middle English, Old French *devin, divin* 'excellent', 'perfect' (Latin *divinus* 'divine').
GIVEN NAMES Irish 6%. *Brendan* (4), *Brennan* (2), *Cormac* (2), *Donal* (2), *Finbar* (2), *Seamus* (2), *Conan, John Patrick, Padraic, Patrick Michael.*

Deviney (321) Variant of Irish DEVANEY.

Devinney (473) Variant of Irish DEVANEY.

Devino (178) Probably Italian (**De Vino**): patronymic for the son, apprentice, associate, or servant of a winemaker, grower, or dealer, from a metonymic occupational name from *vino*.
GIVEN NAMES Italian 4%. *Angelo, Bruna, Carmela, Rocco.*

Devins (319) Probably a variant of Irish DEVINE.

De Visser (129) Dutch: occupational name from *de visser* 'the fisherman'.

De Vita (821) Italian: metronymic from the female personal name VITA, or from a short form of a compound personal name formed with *vita* 'life', such as the omen names *Bonavita* ('good life'), *Bellavita* ('beautiful life').

GIVEN NAMES Italian 15%. *Angelo* (4), *Carmine* (4), *Salvatore* (3), *Antonio* (2), *Carlo* (2), *Dino* (2), *Ennio* (2), *Guido* (2), *Matteo* (2), *Pasquale* (2), *Rocco* (2), *Ceasar*.

De Vitis (111) Italian: probably a patronymic from the personal name VITO, in the broader sense 'of or belonging to the Vito family'.
GIVEN NAMES Italian 12%. *Antonio, Enrico, Filippo, Nicola, Quinto*.

De Vito (2754) Italian: patronymic from the personal name VITO.
GIVEN NAMES Italian 14%. *Carmine* (12), *Angelo* (10), *Rocco* (10), *Salvatore* (8), *Vito* (7), *Antonio* (6), *Sal* (6), *Pasquale* (5), *Guido* (4), *Donato* (3), *Lorenzo* (3), *Amato* (2).

Devitt (915) Irish: reduced form of Mc-DEVITT 'son of David'.

De Vitto (113) Italian: patronymic from *Vitto*, from a short form of the various the Germanic personal names formed with the element *Wid-*.
GIVEN NAMES Italian 11%. *Carmine, Cosmo, Pasquale, Sal*.

De Vivo (403) Italian: patronymic from the nickname *Vivo* meaning 'alive' or from a shortened form of a personal name such as *Vivaldo, Vivenzio*, or *Viviano*.
GIVEN NAMES Italian 20%. *Angelo* (4), *Mario* (4), *Alfonso* (3), *Antonio* (3), *Gaetano* (2), *Salvatore* (2), *Aldo, Alphonso, Armando, Benito, Biago, Carlo, Carmine, Domenico, Emidio, Emilio, Filomena, Giovanni*.

Devlin (4960) Irish and Scottish: Anglicized form of Gaelic **Ó Dobhailéin** 'descendant of *Dobhailéan*', a personal name of uncertain origin, probably from a diminutive of *dobhail* 'unlucky', 'unfortunate'.
GIVEN NAMES Irish 6%. *Brendan* (3), *Liam* (2), *Siobhan* (2), *Brid, Caitlyn, Colum, Eamon, John Patrick, Kieran, Paddy, Seamus, Sinead*.

Devney (109) Irish: variant of DEVANEY.

Devoe (1896) Probably a variant of English DEFOE or perhaps of French DEVAUX.

Devoid (136) Dutch: variant of **De Voogd** (see VOOGD).

Devol (318) **1.** Altered form of Norwegian **Devold**, a habitational name from a farmstead in western Norway named *Devoll*, from *de* (Old Norse *digr* 'large') + *vǫllr* 'green field'. **2.** Possibly also an altered form of French **Deval** (see DEVALL 2) or DUVAL 1.

De Volder (150) Dutch: occupational name for someone employed in the cloth trade whose job was to fold sheets of cloth.
GIVEN NAMES French 7%. *Andre, Marcel*.

Devoll (277) See DEVOL.

Devon (200) **1.** English: regional name for someone from the county of Devon. In origin, this is from an ancient British tribal name, Latin *Dumnonii*, perhaps meaning 'worshipers of the god Dumnonos'. **2.** Irish (County Louth): variant of DEVINE.

Devonshire (187) English: regional name for someone from the county of DEVON.

Devor (283) Probably an altered spelling of French DEVORE.

Devore (4140) **1.** French: variant of **De Var**, a habitational name for someone from a place named Var, for example in Charente. **2.** Respelling of French **Devors**, a habitational name, with the preposition *de*, for someone from Vors in Aveyron.

Devos (830) **1.** Dutch (**De Vos**): from Middle Dutch *de vos* 'the fox'; a nickname for someone with red hair, or a crafty man. **2.** Respelling of the French topographic name DEVAULT.
GIVEN NAMES German 4%; French 4%. *Alphons* (2), *Alfons, Alois, Johannes, Wilfried; Antoine, Cecile, Fernand, Henri, Julien, Marcel, Michel, Pierre*.

Devoss (235) Dutch (**De Voss**): variant of spelling DEVOS.

Devost (112) Origin unidentified; possibly Dutch.
GIVEN NAMES French 12%. *Adrien* (2), *Armand, Camille, Monique, Rosaire*.

Devoto (193) Italian: nickname, possibly applied ironically, from *devoto* 'devout', 'pious'.
GIVEN NAMES Italian 4%. *Alberto, Andres, Angel, Horacio, Jose Antonio, Juan Antonio, Mario, Patricio*.

Devoy (253) Irish: Anglicized form of Gaelic **Ó Dubhuidhe** 'descendant of *Dubhuidhe*', a personal name probably derived from *dubh* 'dark', 'black' + *buidhe* 'sallow'.

De Vries (5295) Dutch: ethnic name for someone from Friesland (see FRIES 1).

Devroy (136) Origin unidentified.

Dew (2383) **1.** English (of Norman origin): habitational name (Old French *d'Eu*) for someone from Eu in Seine-Maritime, France (see DOE 2). **2.** Welsh: nickname for a fat person, from Welsh *tew* 'fat'.

De Waal (129) Dutch: ethnic name for a Walloon, Middle Dutch *Wale* (ultimately from a Germanic word meaning 'foreign') + the definite article *de*.
GIVEN NAMES Dutch 9%; Scandinavian 5%; German 4%. *Adriaan, Frans, Leendert; Johan; Johannes* (2).

De Waard (164) Dutch: variant of DE WEERD.
GIVEN NAMES Dutch 9%; German 5%. *Gerrit* (3), *Aart, Dirk, Frans, Gerritt, Klaas; Armin*.

De Waele (131) Dutch: variant of DE WAAL.
GIVEN NAMES French 6%. *Lucien, Marcel*.

Dewald (1372) German: from the personal name *Diebold*, from Middle High German *Dietbold*, from Old High German *diot* 'people', 'nation' + *bald* 'brave', 'strong'.

De Wall (456) Variant of Dutch DE WAAL.

Dewalt (964) Probably an altered spelling of German DEWALD.

Dewan (365) Indian and Pakistani: status name for a treasurer or court official, from Arabic *dīwān* 'royal court', 'tribunal of justice', or 'treasury'. Under the Mughal administration in India the *dewan* was usually the highest official in a state.
GIVEN NAMES Indian 37%. *Rajiv* (4), *Anil* (3), *Brij* (3), *Naresh* (3), *Rakesh* (2), *Renu* (2), *Ritu* (2), *Sanjeev* (2), *Sunil* (2), *Tarun* (2), *Vijay* (2), *Amrit*.

Dewane (171) Irish: variant of DWAN.

Dewar (1020) Scottish: **1.** occupational name for a custodian of holy relics (which was normally a hereditary office), from Gaelic *deoradh* 'pilgrim', 'stranger'. **2.** habitational name from Dewar, a place near Dalkeith, of uncertain origin.

Dewart (151) **1.** Scottish: variant of DEWAR, formerly found chiefly in Lanarkshire. **2.** Possibly an altered spelling of Dutch **de Waart**, a variant of DE WEERD. **3.** Possibly a variant spelling of German **Deward**, from an old personal name *Teudoard*, composed of Old High German *diot* 'people', 'nation' + *wart-* 'observer', 'guard'.

Dewaters (116) Americanized form of Dutch **de Wauters**, a patronymic from a Germanic personal name composed of the elements *wald* 'rule' + *hari, heri* 'army'. See also WALTER.

Dewberry (1094) **1.** English: habitational name from Dewberry Hill in Radcliffe on Trent, Nottinghamshire, which is of uncertain origin. **2.** Probably an Americanized spelling of French **Dubarry**, a topographic name from Anglo-Norman French *barri* 'rampart'; later it denoted a suburb outside the walls of a medieval city (see BARRY).

Dewbre (170) **1.** Probably an altered spelling of English or French DEWBERRY. **2.** Alternatively, an altered spelling of French **Dupré** (see DUPRE).

De Weerd (215) Dutch: occupational name for an innkeeper, from Middle Dutch *we(e)rt* 'host' + the definite article *de*.

De Weerdt (113) Dutch: variant of DE WEERD.

De Wees (924) Dutch: variant of DE WEESE.

De Weese (2263) Dutch: from Middle Dutch *weese* 'orphan' + the definite article *de*.

Dewell (297) English (West Midlands): unexplained.

DeWerff (108) Frisian: topographic name from either Middle Low German *de werve, wereft* 'the area of uncultivated land' or Middle Low German *de werf* 'the wharf'.

De Wese (111) Dutch: variant of DE WEESE.

Dewey (5015) **1.** Welsh: from the personal name *Dewi*, Welsh form of DAVID. **2.** Anglicized form of a French Huguenot name of uncertain form and origin. Traditionally it is recorded as **Douai**, from a place in northern France, but it could also be from Old Norman French *du we(z)* 'of the ford', from a variant of standard French *gué* 'ford'.

FOREBEARS Thomas Duee of Sandwich, Kent, England, emigrated to Dorchester, MA, in 1634, where his name is recorded as **Dewey**. Another line is apparently descended from a Huguenot family called **Douai**, who settled in Kent, England, in the latter half of the 16th century. The connection, if any, between the two Kentish families is not clear.

Dewhirst (316) English: variant of DEW-HURST.

Dewhurst (319) English: habitational name from a place in Lancashire, probably so named from Old English *dēawig* 'dewy' + *hyrst* 'wooded hill'.

De Wilde (322) Dutch: from Middle Dutch *wilde* 'wild', 'savage'. In the Low Countries this was used as a descriptive nickname for a man with an unruly temperament, but among the Dutch in New Netherland it was a term for native Americans, equivalent to English *savage*, French *suavage*. In many cases, therefore, it implies American Indian ancestry.
GIVEN NAMES French 6%; Dutch 4%. *Andre* (2), *Camile, Camille, Gilles*; *Cornelis, Gerrit, Henk, Klaas*.

De Windt (142) Dutch: **1.** from Middle Dutch *wint* 'wind' + the definite article *de*, hence possibly a nickname for a fast runner. **2.** ethnic name for a Wend, a member of a Slavic people.

Dewine (109) Scottish: variant of Irish DWAN.

Dewing (351) English: unexplained.

De Winter (232) Dutch: nickname for a cold or gloomy man, from Middle Dutch *winter* 'winter' + the definite article *de*.
GIVEN NAMES French 7%; German 4%. *Urbain* (2), *Marcel*; *Kurt* (2), *Johannes*.

Dewire (157) Variant spelling, under French influence, of Irish DWYER.
GIVEN NAME French 5%. *Laurent* (2).

De Wit (314) Dutch: variant spelling of DE WITT.
GIVEN NAMES Dutch 13%; French 4%. *Michiel* (3), *Gerrit* (2), *Klaas* (2), *Wim* (2), *Aart, Adriaan, Cornelis, Henk, Joost, Maarten, Pieter*; *Amiee, Marcell, Prosper*.

De Witt (9494) Dutch: nickname for someone with white or very fair hair, or an exceptionally pale complexion, from Middle Dutch *witte* 'white' + the definite article *de*.

De Witte (408) Dutch: variant spelling of DE WITT.
GIVEN NAMES French 7%. *Marcel* (3), *Adhemar* (2), *Alphonse* (2), *Cyrille, Henri, Prosper*.

Dewitz (239) German: habitational name from any of numerous places so named, for example in Altmark, Mecklenburg, and Saxony.
GIVEN NAMES German 9%. *Friederike* (2), *Kurt* (2), *Hans, Horst, Otto*.

De Wolf (864) Dutch: habitational name for someone living at a house distinguished by the sign of a wolf, from Middle Dutch *de wulf* 'the wolf', or from a nickname with the same meaning. See also WOLF.

De Wolfe (563) Variant spelling of Dutch DE WOLF.

Dewoody (236) Origin unidentified.

Dews (611) English: unexplained; perhaps variant of DEW.

De Wulf (174) Dutch: variant of DE WOLF.
GIVEN NAMES French 12%. *Lucienne* (2), *Marcel* (2), *Andre, Gaston, Laurette, Luc*.

Dexheimer (259) German: habitational name for someone from Dexheim in Hesse.
GIVEN NAMES German 5%. *Armin, Kurt, Wolfgang*.

Dexter (3783) English (East Midlands): occupational name from Middle English *dyster* 'dyer' (see DYER).

Dey (1326) **1.** English: variant of DAY 1 and 2. **2.** German: topographic name from a field name in North Rhine-Westphalia, denoting a sizeable piece of land. **3.** Welsh: from *Dai* or *Dei*, pet forms of the personal name *Dafydd*, Welsh form of DAVID. **4.** Indian (Bengal and Orissa) and Bangladeshi: Hindu (Kayasth) name, probably from Sanskrit *deya* 'suitable for a gift'.
GIVEN NAMES Indian 10%. *Ashit* (2), *Indu* (2), *Naina* (2), *Partha* (2), *Soumya* (2), *Ajit, Anjan, Anjana, Anup, Arjun, Arun, Ashim*.

Deyarmin (157) Origin unidentified.

Deyerle (101) Origin unidentified.

Deyo (1082) French (Huguenot): variant of **d'Oiau**, which is of unexplained origin.
FOREBEARS Christian Deyo, also known as Christian **d'Oiau**, was one of the founding settlers in New Palz, NY, in 1675–78.

Deyoe (295) French (Huguenot): variant of DEYO.
GIVEN NAMES French 4%. *Laurette, Pierre*.

De Young (3143) Part translation of Dutch DE JONG.

Deyton (260) Variant spelling of English DEIGHTON.

Dezarn (216) Origin unidentified.

De Zeeuw (181) Dutch: regional name for someone from Zeeland.
GIVEN NAMES Dutch 5%. *Hendrik* (2), *Gerrit, Pieter*.

Dezell (113) Variant of Scottish DALZELL.

Dezern (153) Origin unidentified. Compare DEZARN.

Deziel (192) Probably an altered form (under French influence) of Scottish **Dalziel** (see DALZELL).
GIVEN NAMES French 12%. *Alain, Benoit, Donat, Francois, Gaetan, Jacques, Pierre*.

Dhaliwal (253) Indian (Panjab): Hindu and Sikh name said to be from an ancestral place name, Daranagar. The Dhaliwals are a Jat tribe, said to be Bhatti Rajputs.
GIVEN NAMES Indian 91%. *Avtar* (4), *Darshan* (4), *Amrit* (3), *Balwinder* (2), *Ajit, Balkar, Bhajan, Charan, Gurdial, Gurmel, Hari, Jagdish*.

Dhanani (110) Hindu and Muslim name found in Gujarat, India, and among people from Sind, Pakistan, meaning 'descendant of Dhan'. *Dhan* (meaning 'wealth') is a shortened form of an ancestral name beginning with this element, for example *Dhanesh* 'lord of wealth' (from Sanskrit *dhana* 'wealth' + *īśa* 'lord') or *Dhanaraj* 'king of wealth' (from *dhana* 'wealth' + *rājā* 'king').
GIVEN NAMES Muslim 73%; Indian 15%. *Karim* (4), *Mahmood* (3), *Shiraz* (3), *Alnoor* (2), *Aly* (2), *Amir* (2), *Nasim* (2), *Nasruddin* (2), *Nizar* (2), *Noor* (2), *Shireen* (2), *Siraj* (2); *Anuja, Chandulal, Dinesh, Falguni, Harsha, Jayesh, Mukesh, Neeta, Nilam, Ramesh, Suresh, Tulsi*.

Dhar (142) **1.** Indian (Bengal) and Bangladeshi: Hindu (Kayasth) name, probably from Bengali *dhar* 'credit' (Sanskrit *uddhāra* 'deliverance'). **2.** Indian (Kashmir): Hindu (Brahman) name of unknown meaning, pronounced *dhǝr*.
GIVEN NAMES Indian 88%. *Sanjay* (8), *Ravi* (5), *Ashok* (4), *Sunil* (4), *Hari* (2), *Shashi* (2), *Veena* (2), *Abhinav, Amit, Amitava, Animesh, Anitha*.

Dhawan (123) Indian (Panjab): Hindu (Khatri) name based on the name of a clan in the Khatri community. It is popularly believed to mean 'runner', 'messenger', from Sanskrit *dhāv-* 'to run'.
GIVEN NAMES Indian 92%. *Anil* (5), *Sanjeev* (4), *Ashok* (3), *Vikram* (3), *Amit* (2), *Ashish* (2), *Madan* (2), *Manish* (2), *Prem* (2), *Raj* (2), *Rajeev* (2), *Rakesh* (2).

Dhein (168) Origin unidentified. Perhaps a variant of French **Duhain**, a topographic name, with the preposition *d(e)*, from Old French *ham* 'home', 'house', 'village'.

Dhillon (497) Indian (Panjab): Sikh name of unknown meaning. The Dhillon are one of the largest and most widely distributed Jat tribes in the Panjab. Like other Jat tribes, the Dhillon claim to be Rajputs by origin.
GIVEN NAMES Indian 84%. *Avtar* (8), *Nirmal* (5), *Balwinder* (4), *Ajay* (2), *Ajit* (2), *Ajmer* (2), *Bahadur* (2), *Balraj* (2), *Darshan* (2), *Mangal* (2), *Onkar* (2), *Param* (2).

Dhingra (117) Indian (Panjab): Hindu (Arora) and Sikh name, based on the name of a Jat clan.
GIVEN NAMES Indian 91%. *Ashok* (5), *Raj* (4), *Harish* (3), *Satish* (3), *Vijay* (3), *Ajay* (2), *Kamlesh* (2), *Pankaj* (2), *Ramesh* (2), *Sandeep* (2), *Subhash* (2), *Sunil* (2).

Dhondt (166) Dutch: from *de hond* 'the dog', a derogatory nickname for a villain or wretch. Alternatively, it may be a habitational name from a house distinguished by the sign of a dog.
GIVEN NAMES French 12%. *Marcel* (2), *Andre, Camile, Camille, Gabrielle, Jean Pierre, Valere*.

Dia (103) North African (Muslim): probably from a personal name based on of Arabic *ḍiyā'* 'light', 'glow', 'illumination'.
GIVEN NAMES African 29%; Muslim 20%. *Mamadou* (3), *Oumar* (2), *Aliou, Aminata*,

Cheikh, Djibril, Mouhamadou, Saliou, Sekou, Serigne; Abdoulaye (3), Ibrahima (2), Ahmad, Basem, Husam, Maan, Nabil, Rachid.

Diab (201) Muslim: probably from a personal name based on Arabic *dhi'b* 'wolf'.

GIVEN NAMES Muslim 51%. *Hassan (5), Khaled (3), Samer (3), Alaa (2), Chaker (2), Ibrahim (2), Khalil (2), Mahmoud (2), Mazen (2), Mohammed (2), Nasser (2), Raif (2).*

Diak (104) Respelling of Scottish **Diack, Dyack**, of uncertain derivation. According to Black, it is believed by bearers to have been taken to Scotland from Denmark or alternatively to be a local (Aberdeen) variant of DICK.

Dial (3468) **1.** English: of uncertain origin; possibly an altered form of Irish DOYLE. Compare DYAL. **2.** Name found among people of Indian origin in Guyana and Trinidad: altered spelling of DAYAL. This spelling is found in Indian names occasionally when *-dial* is the final element of a compound personal name.

Diallo (261) African: unexplained.

GIVEN NAMES African 49%; Muslim 30%; French 5%. *Mamadou (29), Amadou (7), Thierno (5), Aissatou (3), Djibril (3), Saliou (3), Fatoumata (2), Mahamadou (2), Mariama (2), Oumar (2), Ousmane (2), Seydou (2); Ibrahima (17), Souleymane (9), Mohamed (5), Ahmed (3), Abdoul (2), Abdoulaye (2), Fatima (2), Moussa (2), Moustapha (2), Abdul, Abou, Cherif; Alain, Jean-Marc, Olivier.*

Dials (262) Origin unidentified. This name is most frequent in the island of Barbados. It may be a variant of DIAL.

Diamant (240) Jewish (Ashkenazic): see DIAMOND.

GIVEN NAMES Jewish 8%. *Emanuel (2), Moshe (2), Avrohom, Moishe, Yakov.*

Diamond (8972) **1.** Jewish (Ashkenazic): Americanized form of a Jewish surname, spelled in various ways, derived from modern German *Diamant, Demant* 'diamond', or Yiddish *dime(n)t*, going back to Middle High German *dīemant* (via Latin from Greek *adamas* 'unconquerable', genitive *adamantos*, a reference to the hardness of the stone). The name is mostly ornamental, one of the many Ashkenazic surnames based on mineral names, though in some cases it may have been adopted by a jeweler. **2.** English: variant of *Dayman* (see DAY). Forms with the excrescent *d* are not found before the 17th century; they are at least in part the result of folk etymology. **3.** Irish: Anglicized form of Gaelic **Ó Diamáin** 'descendant of *Diamán*', earlier *Díomá* or *Déamán*, a diminutive of *Díoma*, itself a pet form of *Diarmaid* (see MCDERMOTT).

Diana (822) Italian: from the female personal name *Diana*, the name borne in Roman

mythology by the goddess of the moon and of hunting.

GIVEN NAMES Italian 13%. *Salvatore (8), Angelo (5), Enrico (3), Antonio (2), Gennaro (2), Giovanni (2), Nunzio (2), Pasquale (2), Ateo, Attilio, Emelio.*

Di Angelo (318) Italian: variant of D'AN-GELO.

GIVEN NAMES Italian 5%. *Gino, Reno, Vita.*

Diano (108) Italian: habitational name from Diano in Cosenza, or possibly from Teggiano in Salerno province, which was earlier called Diano.

GIVEN NAMES Italian 24%. *Angelo (2), Carlo, Domenico, Francesco, Luigi, Salvatore, Santo.*

Di Antonio (205) Italian: variant of D'AN-TONIO.

GIVEN NAMES Italian 12%. *Guido (2), Vito (2), Aniello, Donato, Rocco, Santino, Serafino.*

Dias (3087) Portuguese: patronymic from the medieval personal name *Didacus* (genitive *Didaci*). Compare DIEGO. This name is also common in the former Portuguese colony of Goa and elsewhere on the west coast of India, having been taken there by Portuguese settlers.

GIVEN NAMES Spanish 20%; Portuguese 12%. *Manuel (91), Jose (54), Carlos (24), Francisco (9), Jorge (9), Luis (9), Domingos (7), Mario (7), Pedro (7), Ana (6), Armando (6), Eduardo (6); Joao (16), Paulo (6), Joaquim (5), Manoel (3), Henrique (2), Margarida (2), Albano, Batista, Guilherme, Ligia, Mateus, Sebastiao.*

Diaz (31611) Spanish (**Díaz**): patronymic from the medieval personal name *Didacus* (see DIEGO).

GIVEN NAMES Spanish 49%. *Jose (997), Juan (401), Carlos (339), Luis (322), Manuel (318), Jesus (227), Francisco (218), Jorge (217), Rafael (200), Miguel (192), Pedro (185), Roberto (162).*

Dib (107) Muslim: variant of DEEB.

GIVEN NAMES Muslim 39%; French 8%. *Nabil (4), Eid (2), Fadi (2), Ghassan (2), Issa (2), Ahmad, Ali, Bassam, Ghazi, Hakam, Hasna, Issam; Georges (2), Antoine, Clovis.*

Di Bacco (211) Southern Italian: patronymic from the personal name BACCO.

GIVEN NAMES Italian 16%. *Attilio (2), Lorenzo (2), Rocco (2), Sal (2), Enio, Luciano, Quinto, Rachele, Salvatore, Ugo, Vittorio.*

Di Bari (180) Italian: habitational name for someone from the port of Bari in southern Italy.

GIVEN NAMES Italian 25%. *Vito (4), Angelo (3), Rocco (2), Antonio, Carmela, Cosimo, Domenic, Nicolo, Ottavio, Pasquale.*

Di Bartolo (304) Italian: patronymic from the personal name *Bartolo*, a short form of *Bartolomeo*, from Latin *Bart(h)olomaeus* (see BARTHOLOMEW).

GIVEN NAMES Italian 34%. *Salvatore (6), Carmelo (3), Giuseppe (3), Nicolo (3), Sal (3), Giovanni (2), Vito (2), Alfio, Angelo, Benedetta, Benedetto, Camillo.*

Di Bartolomeo (283) Italian: patronymic from the personal name *Bartolomeo*, Latin *Bart(h)olomaeus* (see BARTHOLOMEW).

GIVEN NAMES Italian 29%. *Mario (5), Mauro (3), Carlo (2), Mando (2), Amedeo, Angelo, Antonio, Carmine, Cesare, Claudio, Domenic, Donato, Eduardo, Gaetano, Gino, Giuseppe, Osvaldo, Renaldo, Renato.*

Di Battista (308) Italian: patronymic from the personal name BATTISTA.

GIVEN NAMES Italian 23%. *Americo (3), Carmine (3), Antonio (2), Domenic (2), Ercole (2), Angelo, Armando, Assunta, Attilio, Concetta, Corrado, Dario, Dino, Erminio, Fortunato, Franco, Mario.*

Dibb (126) English: topographic name for someone living in a hollow, Middle English *dybbe*. The surname is most common in Yorkshire, where a number of minor place names are formed from it.

Dibbern (183) German: from an Old Frisian and Low German personal name, *Dietbern* (Old High German *Thiatbarn*), a compound of *thiod* 'people' + *bero* 'bear'.

GIVEN NAMES German 5%. *Dieter, Hans, Kurt.*

Dibble (2203) English: from a variant of the medieval personal name *Tebald, Tibalt* (see THEOBALD).

Di Bella (691) Italian: metronymic from the medieval female personal name *Bella*, meaning 'beautiful'.

GIVEN NAMES Italian 25%. *Mario (6), Salvatore (6), Carmela (3), Cosimo (3), Rosario (3), Angelo (2), Alberto, Antonio (2), Agostino, Biagio, Carmelo, Carmine, Dino, Emilio, Fernando, Francesco, Leonardo, Renato, Ricardo, Roberto.*

Di Bello (387) Italian: patronymic from the personal name BELLO.

GIVEN NAMES Italian 14%. *Angelo (2), Agostino, Carmine, Ciro, Cosimo, Erminio, Gennaro, Luigi, Nicola, Onofrio, Pietro, Silvio.*

Di Benedetto (1469) Italian: patronymic from the personal name *Benedetto*, from Latin *Benedictus* (see BENEDICT).

GIVEN NAMES Italian 22%. *Salvatore (14), Angelo (13), Vito (12), Antonio (10), Gino (3), Guido (3), Nunzio (3), Pietro (3), Aldo (2), Carmine (2), Domenico (2), Emidio (2).*

Di Berardino (133) Italian: patronymic from the personal name *Berardino*, a pet form of BERARDO.

GIVEN NAMES Italian 18%. *Elio, Pietro, Salvatore, Santino.*

Di Bernardo (382) Italian: patronymic from the personal name *Bernardo*, Italian equivalent of BERNARD.

GIVEN NAMES Italian 19%. *Angelo (4), Livio (4), Luigi (3), Carmelo, Carmine,*

Concetto, Emidio, Enrico, Gasper, Gianni, Gioia, Giuseppe.

Dibert (269) North German: variant spelling of **Diebert** or an altered spelling of DEIBERT.

Di Biase (759) Italian: patronymic form of the personal name *Biase*, one of the many vernacular forms derived from Latin BLASIUS.
GIVEN NAMES Italian 20%. *Cosmo* (7), *Angelo* (4), *Antonio* (4), *Carmine* (4), *Domenic* (3), *Rocco* (3), *Salvatore* (3), *Camillo* (2), *Dante* (2), *Falco* (2), *Giro* (2), *Caterina.*

Di Biasi (114) Italian: variant of DI BIASE.
GIVEN NAMES Italian 26%. *Vito* (3), *Angelo* (2), *Nunzio* (2), *Antonio, Ettore, Giuseppe, Ottavio, Pietro.*

Di Biasio (157) Italian: variant of DI BIASE.
GIVEN NAMES Italian 25%. *Antimo* (2), *Biagio, Carmin, Carmine, Carmino, Cosmo, Gabriella, Gino, Guido, Luigi, Nicola, Pasco.*

Di Blasi (504) Italian: variant of DI BIASE.
GIVEN NAMES Italian 19%. *Angelo* (4), *Salvatore* (3), *Alberto, Alfonso, Alfonzo, Anella, Antonio, Biagio, Calogero, Domenic, Fedele, Francesco, Gino, Mariano, Mario, Natale, Pasco, Silvana, Victorio.*

Di Blasio (194) Italian: variant of DI BIASE.
GIVEN NAMES Italian 17%. *Angelo, Carmin, Dante, Dino, Ennio, Lazzaro, Marco, Remo, Rocco, Vincenzo.*

Dible (197) **1.** English: variant of DIBBLE. **2.** Altered spelling of German DEIBEL or DEUBEL.

Di Bona (472) Italian: metronymic from the medieval female personal name *Bona*, meaning 'good'.
GIVEN NAMES Italian 19%. *Angelo* (2), *Calogero* (2), *Dante* (2), *Domenic* (2), *Donato* (2), *Nunziato* (2), *Salvatore* (2), *Ateo, Dario, Egidio, Elio, Erminio.*

Dibrell (149) Americanized form of French **du Breuil**, a habitational name from Breuil in Calvados or from any of various places elsewhere in France called La Breuil. Compare English BROWELL.
FOREBEARS The name was brought to VA from Paris, France, at the beginning of the 18th century by Christoffe du Breuil (*c.*1680–1728). His son Jean Antoine du Breuil (1728–99) came to be known as Anthony Dibrell.

Di Buono (173) Italian: patronymic from the personal name *Buono* 'good'.
GIVEN NAMES Italian 14%. *Sal* (2), *Antonio, Aurelio, Italo, Pasquale, Salvatore, Vito.*

Di Camillo (300) Italian: patronymic from the personal name *Camillo*, which is derived from the old Roman family name *Camillus*, of Etruscan origin.
GIVEN NAMES Italian 19%. *Antonio* (2), *Camillo* (2), *Dante* (2), *Dino* (2), *Vito* (2), *Agostino, Domenico, Elio, Gianfranco, Italo, Lorenzo, Luigi.*

Di Caprio (219) Italian (Campania): from Latin *caprae* 'goats' or possibly from Greek *kapros* '(wild) boar', and so a metonymic occupational name for a goatherd or swineherd, or a nickname for someone thought to resemble a goat or boar.
GIVEN NAMES Italian 16%. *Angelo* (3), *Antonio* (2), *Luigi* (2), *Dante, Gino, Italo, Nicolina, Sisto, Vincenzo.*

Di Capua (133) Italian: habitational name for someone from Capua in Caserta province. The name is common in the Naples area.
GIVEN NAMES Italian 22%. *Riccardo* (2), *Salvatore* (2), *Angelo, Antonio, Federico, Mario, Nicola, Onofrio, Xavier.*

Di Carlo (1519) Italian: patronymic from the personal name *Carlo*, Italian equivalent of CHARLES.
GIVEN NAMES Italian 19%. *Salvatore* (7), *Lorenzo* (6), *Angelo* (5), *Domenic* (5), *Gino* (4), *Rocco* (4), *Antonio* (3), *Gennaro* (3), *Vito* (3), *Carlo* (2), *Dino* (2), *Dominico* (2).

Dice (1227) **1.** English: from Middle English *dyse, dyce* 'die', 'dice', 'chance', 'luck', probably applied as a nickname for an habitual dice player or gambler or as a metonymic occupational name for a maker of dice. Compare DEAS. **2.** Possibly also an Americanized spelling of German DEISS.

Di Cecco (152) Italian: variant of DI CICCO.
GIVEN NAMES Italian 12%. *Angelo, Cosmo, Luca, Rocco, Salvatore.*

Di Cello (165) Italian: patronymic from the personal name *Cello*, a short form of various pet names with this ending, such as *Baroncello, Simoncello*, etc.
GIVEN NAMES Italian 15%. *Angelo* (4), *Antonio* (3), *Domenic, Genario, Gennaro, Nicola.*

Di Censo (229) Probably a variant spelling of Italian DI CENZO.
GIVEN NAMES Italian 33%. *Angelo* (4), *Domenic* (4), *Carlo* (3), *Guido* (3), *Americo* (2), *Dante* (2), *Enrico* (2), *Orlando* (2), *Alberico, Aldo, Antonio, Arduino, Carmine, Elio, Feliciano, Fernando, Panfilo.*

Di Cenzo (298) Italian: patronymic from the personal name *Cenzo*, a short form of *Vincenzo*, from Latin *Vincentius* (see VINCENT).
GIVEN NAMES Italian 20%. *Angelo* (2), *Mario* (2), *Aldo, Antonio, Carmela, Domenic, Fiore, Guerino, Guido, Mariano, Panfilo, Pasquale, Pierino, Rinaldo, Rocco.*

Di Cerbo (114) Italian: patronymic possibly from a reduced pet form of the personal name *Acerbo* (Latin *Acerbus*) or alternatively from the nickname *Cervo* (see CERVI).
GIVEN NAMES Italian 18%. *Dino, Francesco, Gaetano, Giuseppe, Marco, Oreste, Pietro, Vito.*

Di Cesare (527) Italian: patronymic from the personal name CESARE.

GIVEN NAMES Italian 17%. *Vito* (3), *Carlo* (2), *Dino* (2), *Donato* (2), *Pasquale* (2), *Angelo, Antonio, Delio, Domenic, Domenico, Franco, Gilda.*

Dicharry (108) Probably a French habitational name, **De Char(r)ey**, for someone from (*de*) Charray in Eure et Loire, Charrey in Côte d'Or or Charey in Meurthe et Moselle.
GIVEN NAMES French 9%. *Andre, Dreux, Jean Charles, Jean-Charles.*

Di Chiara (445) Italian: metronymic from the female personal name *Chiara*, meaning 'famous', 'bright' (see CLARE).
GIVEN NAMES Italian 23%. *Rocco* (3), *Sal* (3), *Salvatore* (3), *Aldo* (2), *Alfonse, Alfredo, Angelo, Annalisa, Antonio, Armondo, Ciro, Franco, Gaetano, Generoso, Lorenzo, Mario.*

Di Chiaro (104) Italian: patronymic from the personal name *Chiaro*, meaning 'famous', 'bright', from Latin *Clarus*.
GIVEN NAMES Italian 14%. *Carmine, Domenic, Filomena, Salvatore.*

Dichter (203) **1.** South and central German: from Middle High German *diechter* 'grandchild', probably from Middle High German *dīhen* 'to thrive'. **2.** German: ostensibly an occupational name for a minstrel or poet, from an agent derivative of Middle High German *tichten* 'to write or compose' (Latin *dicere* 'to recite'). **3.** Jewish (from Germany and Poland): nickname from either German *Dichter* 'poet', or an inflected form of German *dicht* 'thick'. **4.** Jewish (from Ukraine): occupational name from a Yiddishized form of Ukrainian *dikhtyar* 'tar worker'.
GIVEN NAME German 4%. *Wilhelm.*

Di Cicco (995) Italian: patronymic from a pet form of the personal name *Francesco*, from Latin *Franciscus* (see FRANCIS).
GIVEN NAMES Italian 17%. *Angelo* (9), *Antonio* (5), *Pasquale* (4), *Carlo* (2), *Cosmo* (2), *Giovanni* (2), *Giulio* (2), *Giuseppe* (2), *Nicola* (2), *Attilio, Benedetto, Carmela.*

Di Cioccio (178) Italian: patronymic from a personal name of uncertain derivation, possibly a pet form of *Francesco* (see FRANCIS).
GIVEN NAMES Italian 32%. *Cosmo* (3), *Mario* (3), *Cesidio* (2), *Dante* (2), *Guido* (2), *Salvatore* (2), *Aldo, Americo, Benito, Biagio, Domenico, Ezio, Flavio, Nunzio, Quintino, Silverio.*

Dick (7891) **1.** Scottish and English: from a short form of RICHARD. Although found in every part of Britain, the form *Dick* is especially common in Scotland, and it was from there, in the 17th century, that the surname was taken to northern Ireland. **2.** German and Jewish (Ashkenazic): nickname from Middle High German *dic(ke)* 'thick', 'strong', 'stout', or in the case of the Jewish name from modern German *dick* 'fat' or Yiddish *dik*. **3.** German: topographic name for someone who lived by a thicket or patch of thick undergrowth, from Middle High German *dicke*, a special use of *dic(ke)* 'thick'. **4.** North German: from a short form of a Germanic personal name *Theodicho*, formed with *theud* 'people', 'race'.

Dickard (185) Variant spelling of German DICKERT, or a respelling of **Dichart**, from a personal name probably formed with Old High German *dīhan* 'to thrive'.

Dickason (299) English: variant spelling of DICKERSON.

Dicke (388) **1.** Variant spelling of DICK. **2.** German: topographic name for someone who lived by a dike, from the dative case (originally preceded by a preposition) of Middle Low German *dīk* 'dike'.

Dickel (162) German: from a pet form of the personal name *Benedikt* (see BENEDICT).

Dicken (822) English (chiefly West Midlands): from a pet form of the personal name DICK.

Dickens (5537) English (chiefly West Midlands): patronymic from the personal name DICKEN.

Dickensheets (133) Americanized spelling of German **Dickenscheid**, a habitational name from a place named Dickenschied in the Hunsrück region. The place name is from Middle High German *dicke* 'thicket', 'woods' + *-scheid* (often *schied*) 'border area' (i.e. ridge, watershed), 'settler's piece of cleared (wood)land'.

GIVEN NAME German 4%. *Hans.*

Dickenson (1552) English (Lancashire): patronymic from the personal name DICKEN.

Dicker (569) **1.** English (southwest): occupational name for a digger of ditches or a builder of dikes, or a topographic name for someone who lived by a ditch or dike, from an agent derivative of Middle English *diche*, *dike* (see DYKE). **2.** English: regional name from an area of East Sussex, near Hellingly, called 'the Dicker' (hence also the hamlets of Upper and Lower Dicker), from Middle English *dyker* unit of ten (Latin *decuria*, from *decem* 'ten'); the reason for the place being so named is not clear. It has been suggested that the reference is to a bundle of iron rods, in which sense *dicras* appears in Domesday Book. Such a bundle could have been the rent for property in this iron-working area. Surname forms such as *atte dicker* occur in the surrounding region in the 13th and 14th centuries. **3.** German and Jewish (Ashkenazic): variant of DICK 2, from an inflected form. **4.** North German: variant of Low German **Dieker**, a topographic or an occupational name for someone who lived or worked at a dike (see DIECK). **5.** Americanized spelling of French DECAIRE.

Dickerhoff (109) Dutch or North German: habitational name from a farm named Dickerhoff, from Middle Low German *dīk*

'dike' + *hof* 'farmstead', 'manor farm', 'court'.

Dickerhoof (127) Dutch: variant of DICKERHOFF.

Dickerman (542) German (**Dickermann**) and Jewish (Ashkenazic): variant of DICK 2.

Dickerson (16510) English (mainly East Anglia): patronymic from a pet form of DICK 1.

Dickert (522) **1.** Dutch and North German: shortened form of *Diekhardt*, a personal name composed of the elements *Diek*, a short form of *Diederik* (see DEDERICK) + *-hart* 'hard', 'strong'. **2.** German: from an inflected form of DICK 2, with added inorganic *-t*. **3.** German: topographic name for someone who lived near a wood or thicket, from Middle Low German *dick* + the collective suffix *-et*, enlarged to *-ert*.

Dickes (209) **1.** English: variant of DIXON. **2.** Possibly a German topographic name from a reduced form (typical of the Lower Rhine) of Middle Low German *dīk* 'dike' + *hūs* 'house'.

Dickeson (176) English: variant spelling of DICKERSON.

Dickey (9073) Northern Irish: from a pet form of the personal name DICK 1.

Dickhaus (112) North German: **1.** Habitational name from Dickhausen near Waldbröl. **2.** Perhaps a variant of DIECKHAUS.

GIVEN NAME German 4%. *Kurt.*

Dickhaut (141) German: nickname for an insensitive person, from Middle High German *dic(ke)* 'thick' + *hūt* 'skin'.

Dickherber (131) Probably of German origin: unexplained.

Dickie (905) Scottish and northern Irish: from a pet form of DICK.

Dickinson (11036) Northern English: patronymic from the personal name *Dicken*, *Dickin*, a pet form of DICK.

FOREBEARS Jonathan Dickinson, the first president of the College of New Jersey (now Princeton), was born in Hatfield, MA, in 1688. Both his parents came from pioneer Connecticut Valley stock.

Dickison (595) Northern English: variant of DICKINSON.

Dickler (102) German: probably a topographic name for someone living near a thicket, from Middle High German *dicke* 'thicket'.

Dickman (2344) **1.** English: from Middle English *diche*, *dike* 'dike', 'earthwork' + *man* 'man', hence an occupational name for a ditch digger or a topographic name for someone who lived by a ditch or dike. See also DYKE. **2.** English: occupational name meaning 'servant (Middle English *man*) of DICK'. **3.** Dutch: elaborated form of DYCK. **4.** Americanized spelling of German DICKMANN. **5.** Jewish (Ashkenazic): nickname meaning 'fat man', a noun formation from DICK 2.

Dickmann (379) **1.** German and Jewish (Ashkenazic): nickname meaning 'fat man', a noun formation from DICK 2. **2.** German: topographic name meaning either 'dweller by the thicket' (Middle High German *dicke* 'thicket') or 'dweller by the dike' (Middle Low German *dīk* 'dike'). Compare DIECKMAN.

GIVEN NAMES German 7%. *Fritz* (2), *Kurt* (2), *Ewald, Heinz, Johannes, Otto, Wilhelm.*

Dickmeyer (189) German: variant of **Die(c)kmeyer**, a topographic name for a tenant farmer whose land lay close to a dike, from Middle Low German *dīk* 'dike' + *meier* 'tenant farmer'.

Dickover (113) Probably an Americanized form of Dutch **Dijkhofer** or North German **Diekhofer**, habitational names for someone who lived at a farm by a dike.

Dicks (1401) English (West Midlands and Wales): patronymic from the personal name DICK.

Dickson (12819) Scottish and northern Irish: patronymic from the personal name DICK.

Dickstein (361) Jewish (Ashkenazic): ornamental name from German *dick* 'thick' + *Stein* 'stone'.

GIVEN NAMES Jewish 12%. *Ephraim* (2), *Velvel* (2), *Akiva, Isadore, Itzhak, Miriam, Nachum, Yehuda.*

Di Clemente (203) Italian: patronymic from the personal name CLEMENTE.

GIVEN NAMES Italian 26%. *Gino* (3), *Antonio* (2), *Emidio* (2), *Salvatore* (2), *Angelo, Dino, Domenic, Domenico, Gaetano, Giulio, Lucio, Massimo.*

Di Cocco (209) Italian: patronymic from the medieval personal name COCCO.

GIVEN NAMES Italian 31%. *Luigi* (5), *Mario* (4), *Domenic* (3), *Antonio* (2), *Duilio* (2), *Lorenzo* (2), *Aldo, Alessio, Amedeo, Celestino, Enrico, Ercole, Francesco, Milio, Ricardo, Rolando, Sergio.*

Di Cola (268) Italian: patronymic from the personal name *Cola*, a pet form of *Nicola* (see NICHOLAS).

GIVEN NAMES Italian 14%. *Salvatore* (3), *Aldo, Antimo, Antonietta, Antonio, Domenic, Gennaro, Giovanni, Marino, Nino, Oreste, Quirino.*

Di Cosola (100) Italian: probably a habitational name for someone from Cosolo in Calabria.

GIVEN NAMES Italian 30%. *Vito* (4), *Saverio* (3), *Nicola* (2), *Angelo, Gaetano.*

Di Costanzo (289) Italian: patronymic from the personal name *Costanzo*, Latin *Constans* (see CONSTANT).

GIVEN NAMES Italian 33%. *Mario* (4), *Pasquale* (3), *Gino* (2), *Giorgio* (2), *Salvatore* (2), *Angelo, Benedetto, Carmine, Cosmo, Duilio, Franco, Fulgencio, Gaetano, Giacoma.*

Di Cristofaro (111) Italian: patronymic from the personal name CRISTOFARO.

GIVEN NAMES Italian 25%. *Carlo* (4), *Santo* (2), *Antonio, Onofrio, Virna*.

Di Croce (111) Italian: topographic name for someone who lived by a cross (see CROCE).

GIVEN NAMES Italian 11%. *Guido* (2), *Antonio, Domenic, Gilda, Mafalda*.

Dicus (678) Americanized spelling of Dutch DYKHUIS.

Diddle (127) **1.** English: unexplained. Compare ADUDDELL. **2.** Perhaps an Americanized spelling of German **Dittel**, from a pet form of a personal name formed with *Diet* (Germanic *theud* 'people', 'race'), for example DIETRICH.

Didier (860) French: from the personal name (Latin *Desiderius*, a derivative of *desiderium* 'desire', 'longing', given either to a longed-for child as an expression of the Christian's spiritual longing for God). The name was borne by a 3rd-century bishop of Langres and a 6th-century bishop of Vienne in the Dauphiné, both of whom were locally venerated as saints.

FOREBEARS Brought from Champagne, this surname was in Montreal by 1703.

GIVEN NAMES French 5%. *Marcel* (2), *Michel* (2), *Alain, Andre, Camille, Jacques, Pierre, Yves*.

Di Dio (479) Italian: literally 'of God', most probably a name bestowed on a foundling, or possibly a nickname for a pious or devout person.

GIVEN NAMES Italian 13%. *Angelo* (7), *Rocco* (4), *Salvatore* (2), *Biagio, Carlo, Gino, Nazzareno, Sal, Serafino, Ugo, Vita*.

Didion (308) French: from a pet form of DIDIER.

Di Domenico (904) Italian: patronymic from the personal name DOMENICO.

GIVEN NAMES Italian 19%. *Salvatore* (5), *Aldo* (4), *Antonio* (4), *Domenic* (3), *Franco* (3), *Rocco* (3), *Angelo* (2), *Carmela* (2), *Carmine* (2), *Dino* (2), *Domenico* (2), *Elio* (2).

Di Domizio (140) Italian: patronymic from the personal name *Domizio*, from Latin *Domitius*.

GIVEN NAMES Italian 23%. *Gino* (3), *Angelo* (2), *Antonio, Carlo, Cesare, Emidio, Franco, Liberato, Marco, Nino, Pasquale, Santina*.

Di Donato (1214) Italian: patronymic from the personal name DONATO.

GIVEN NAMES Italian 16%. *Angelo* (5), *Antonio* (5), *Carmine* (5), *Pasquale* (5), *Carlo* (4), *Rocco* (4), *Carmela* (3), *Domenic* (3), *Salvatore* (3), *Santo* (3), *Enrico* (2), *Agostino*.

Di Donna (209) Italian: metronymic from DONNA.

GIVEN NAMES Italian 24%. *Vito* (6), *Ciro* (2), *Luigi* (2), *Rocco* (2), *Angelo, Aniello, Antonio, Cataldo, Giuseppe, Marino, Nicola, Nunzio*.

Didriksen (106) Danish and North German: patronymic from the Germanic personal name *Didrik* (see DIETRICH).

GIVEN NAME Scandinavian 12%. *Erik*.

Dieball (103) Probably an altered spelling of German DIEBEL or DIEBOLD.

GIVEN NAME German 5%. *Erwin*.

Diebel (346) German: from a pet form of DIEBOLD.

Diebold (761) German: from a Germanic personal name composed of the elements *theud* 'people', 'race' + *bald, bold* 'bold', 'brave' (see THEOBALD).

GIVEN NAMES French 4%. *Jean-Pierre, Marcel, Olivier*.

Diebolt (152) Variant of German DIEBOLD.

Dieck (250) North German: topographic name for someone who lived near a dike, Middle Low German *dīk*. See also DIECKMANN.

GIVEN NAMES German 6%. *Armin, Juergen, Kurt, Manfred*.

Dieckhaus (101) North German: topographic name for someone who lived at a house by a dike, from Middle Low German *dīk* 'dike' + *haus* 'house'.

Dieckhoff (123) North German: topographic name for someone who lived at a farmstead by a dike, from Middle Low German *dīk* 'dike' + *hof* 'farmstead', 'manor farm'.

GIVEN NAMES German 4%. *Frieda, Lorenz*.

Dieckman (347) Respelling of DIECKMANN.

Dieckmann (407) North German: **1.** topographic name for someone who lived by a dike, typically for someone whose job was to control pumps and water levels, a variant of DIECK, with the addition of *man* 'man'. **2.** from the personal name *Dieck*, a reduced form of the old personal name *Theodicho* (see DICK).

GIVEN NAMES German 9%. *Erwin* (2), *Otto* (2), *Erna, Ernst, Gerhard, Gunther, Hans, Kurt, Merwin, Ralf, Rudiger*.

Diede (370) North German and Dutch: from a short form of the personal name DIEDRICH.

Diederich (918) Variant of North German and Dutch DIEDRICH.

Diederichs (127) North German and Dutch: patronymic from the personal name DIEDERICH.

GIVEN NAMES German 4%. *Egon, Erwin*.

Diedrich (1461) North German and Dutch: from a regional form of the Germanic personal name DIETRICH.

Diedrick (313) Dutch: variant of DIEDRICH.

Diefenbach (414) German: habitational name from any of various places named Diefenbach, in the Rhineland and Württemberg.

GIVEN NAMES German 4%. *Kurt* (2), *Ernst, Herta*.

Diefenderfer (352) Altered spelling of German **Diefendorfer**, a derivative of DIEFENDORF.

Diefendorf (202) German: habitational name, apparently from a lost or unidentified place named Diefendorf. It is possible that the place in question is in fact Dübendorf near Zürich, Switzerland, which became to **Diebenderf** in the Palatinate (listed as a name of the Palatines), and subsequently transformed to **Diefendorf**, modified on the model of DIEFENBACH, a very frequent surname in southwestern Germany.

Dieffenbach (290) German: variant spelling of DIEFENBACH.

GIVEN NAME German 4%. *Otto* (3).

Diegel (353) German: **1.** metonymic occupational name for a potter, from Middle High German *tegel, tigel* 'pot' (from Latin *tegula* 'tile'). **2.** from a pet form of DICK 4.

GIVEN NAMES German 4%. *Heinz, Kurt, Reinhold*.

Diego (432) Spanish: from the personal name *Diego*, which is of uncertain derivation. It was early taken to be a reduced form of SANTIAGO, and is commonly taken by English speakers as being a form of JAMES, but this is no more than folk etymology. It is found in the Middle Ages in the Latin forms *Didacus* and *Didagus*, which Meyer-Lübke derived from Greek *didakhē* 'doctrine', 'teaching', but in view of the fact that it is unknown outside the Iberian Peninsula it may possibly have a pre-Roman origin.

GIVEN NAMES Spanish 44%. *Manuel* (6), *Francisco* (5), *Juan* (5), *Fernando* (4), *Jose* (4), *Miguel* (4), *Mario* (3), *Maximo* (3), *Salvador* (3), *Aida* (2), *Ana* (2), *Domingo* (2); *Federico* (2), *Angelo, Antonio, Bartolo, Eliseo, Filiberto, Romeo*.

Dieguez (205) Spanish (**Diéguez**): patronymic from the personal name DIEGO.

GIVEN NAMES Spanish 52%. *Jose* (9), *Manuel* (7), *Juan* (5), *Alberto* (4), *Luis* (4), *Miguel* (4), *Carlos* (3), *Francisco* (3), *Alejandro* (2), *Alfredo* (2), *Arturo* (2), *Enrique* (2).

Diehl (7486) German: from the personal name *Diel, Tiel*, from *Thilo*, a pet form of a personal name beginning with *Diet-*, as for example DIETRICH.

Diehm (385) North German: variant spelling of DIEM.

GIVEN NAMES German 4%. *Fritz* (2), *Inge, Siegfried, Ute*.

Diehr (109) German: variant of DIER 3.

Dieken (136) North German and Frisian: shortened form of the Frisian patronymic **Diekena**, from the Germanic personal name *Theodicho* (see DICK).

Dieker (181) German: from a noun derivative of Middle Low German *dīk* 'dike', 'ditch', applied as a topographic name or as an occupational name for someone who manned a dike or dug ditches. Compare DIECKMANN.

GIVEN NAMES German 6%. *Fritz, Hans, Kurt*.

Diekman (308) Altered spelling of German DIECKMANN.

GIVEN NAMES German 4%. *Fritz, Kurt*.

Diekmann (381) Altered or variant spelling of DIECKMANN.

GIVEN NAMES German 11%. *Kurt* (5), *Otto* (2), *Erna, Fritz, Gerhard, Horst, Joerg, Jurgen.*

Diel (500) German: variant spelling of DIEHL.

FOREBEARS A Diel Le Petit, from Rouen, was married in Montreal in 1676.

Dieleman (131) German (**Dielemann**): variant of THIELEMANN.

Dielman (102) German (**Dielmann**): southwestern variant of THIELEMANN.

GIVEN NAMES Scandinavian 4%; German 4%. *Nels*; *Helmut.*

Diem (709) German: from a reduced form of the personal name *Dietmar* (see DITTMAR).

GIVEN NAMES German 5%. *Otto* (3), *Klaus* (2), *Erna, Inge, Ingeborg, Kurt, Oskar.*

Diemer (858) North German and Frisian: from a reduced form of the personal name *Dietmar* (see DITTMAR).

Diemert (231) Variant of German DIEMER.

Diener (1191) German: **1.** occupational name for a council official, Middle High German *dienære*. In larger centers of population, the term was also used to denote a representative of the local tradespeople. **2.** from a reduced form of the Germanic personal name *Degenher*, a compound of Old High German *degan* 'warrior', 'vassal' + *hēr* 'noble', 'esteemed'.

GIVEN NAMES German 4%. *Bernhard, Erna, Erwin, Frieda, Gottlieb, Heinrich, Helmut, Kurt, Siegmund.*

Dienes (240) **1.** Hungarian: variant of **Dénes** (see DENES). **2.** German: from a vernacular pet form of the Latin personal name *Dionysius* (see DENNIS).

GIVEN NAMES Hungarian 4%. *Geza, Sandor, Zol, Zoltan.*

Dienhart (116) Probably an altered form of German **Deinhart**, from the personal name, a variant of DEGENHART.

GIVEN NAME German 7%. *Ewald* (2).

Dienst (178) German: occupational name for the servant of a lord or lady, Middle High German *dienest*. The term also meant 'service', 'tax' and in this sense may have been a status name.

GIVEN NAMES German 4%. *Juergen, Markus.*

Diep (794) Vietnamese (**Diệp**): unexplained.

GIVEN NAMES Vietnamese 60%; Chinese 14%. *Thanh* (23), *Minh* (14), *Hung* (12), *Anh* (11), *Ha* (8), *Lam* (8), *Duc* (7), *Dung* (7), *Hoa* (7), *Loi* (7), *Binh* (6), *Thai* (6), *Kien* (5), *Sinh* (2), *Tuong* (2), *Chong, Chung, Nam, Phong, Sieu, Tam, Thach, Tinh, Yang Soon*; *Hong* (5), *Chi* (4), *Man* (3), *Chu* (2), *Kiu* (2), *Sang* (2), *Cai, Chan, Choi, Dong, Han, Ming.*

Diepenbrock (140) North German: topographic name from Middle Low German *dēp* 'deep', 'channel' + *brōk* 'wooded swamp', or a habitational name denoting someone from Diepenbroich or any of several places in Westphalia and Hannover named Depenbrock.

Dier (308) **1.** English: variant of DYER. **2.** Dutch: reduced form of the French personal name DIDIER. **3.** South German: from Middle High German *dier* 'wild animal', 'game'; probably a metonymic occupational name for a hunter, or a habitational name for someone living at a house distinguished by a sign depicting a deer.

Diercks (532) Dutch and North German: patronymic from the personal name *Dierck*, a variant of DIRK.

FOREBEARS The name **Dirckse** is recorded in Beverwijck in New Netherland (Albany, NY) in the mid 17th century.

Dierickx (136) Dutch: patronymic from the personal name *Dierick*, a reduced DEDERICK.

GIVEN NAME French 7%. *Lucien* (2).

Dieringer (476) **1.** Americanized form of German **Thüringer**, regional name for someone from Thuringia, This was also used as a medieval personal name. **2.** Americanized form of German **Tieringer**, habitational name for someone from Tieringen in Württemberg.

Dierker (352) Dutch and North German: patronymic from a short form of *Diederik* (see DEDERICK).

GIVEN NAMES German 4%. *Kurt* (2), *Frieda, Otto.*

Dierkes (374) Dutch: variant of DIRKES.

GIVEN NAMES German 4%. *Kurt* (2), *Otto.*

Dierking (394) North German and Frisian: patronymic from the personal name *Dierck*, a Low German reduced form of *Diederik* (see DIETRICH).

Dierks (716) Dutch and North German: variant spelling of DIERCKS.

GIVEN NAMES German 5%. *Heinz* (2), *Detlef, Dieter, Ernst, Hans, Hermann, Jurgen, Klaus.*

Dierlam (107) German (also **Dierlamm**): variant of DIRLAM.

Dierolf (203) German: from the popular medieval personal name *Thierolf*, formed with the Old High German stem *tiuri* 'dear', 'valuable'.

GIVEN NAMES German 5%. *Ernst, Horst, Volker.*

Diers (559) North German and Dutch: patronymic from a reduced form of the personal name DIETRICH.

Diersen (123) Altered spelling of North German and Dutch **Dierssen**, a patronymic from a reduced form of the personal name DIETRICH.

GIVEN NAME German 4%. *Armin.*

Diersing (133) German: patronymic of DIERS, a patronymic of **Dierck** or DIETER.

Dies (371) **1.** Possibly an altered spelling of German **Diess**, from a short form of the Biblical name *Matthias* (see MATTHEW). **2.** German: from the Germanic personal name *Teuzo*, from *theud* 'people', 'race' (Old High German *diot*).

Diesel (193) Southern German: from a pet form of *Matthias* (see MATTHEW), or any of the Germanic compound names beginning with the element *theudō* 'people', 'race', for example DIETRICH.

Diesing (169) North German: patronymic from DIES.

Diestler (115) German: **1.** Occupational name for a maker of poles, frames, or wagons, from Middle High German *dīhsel* 'shaft'. **2.** topographic name for someone living on thistle-covered land, from Middle High German *distel*.

GIVEN NAMES German 9%. *Kurt* (2), *Armin, Otto.*

Dietel (255) German: from a pet form of DIETRICH.

GIVEN NAMES German 7%. *Arno, Fritz, Gunther, Ilse, Klaus, Lothar, Matthias.*

Dieter (1196) German: from the Germanic personal name *Theudhar*, composed of *theud* 'people', 'race' + *hari, heri* 'army'.

Dieterich (566) German: variant of DIETRICH.

GIVEN NAMES German 4%. *Otto* (3), *Erwin, Heinz, Klaus, Wolfgang.*

Dieterle (465) South German: from a pet form of the personal name DIETER.

GIVEN NAMES German 4%. *Hans* (2), *Gunther, Horst, Kurt, Ulrike.*

Dietert (130) German: variant of DIETER.

GIVEN NAMES German 10%. *Bodo, Egon, Fritz, Helmuth, Otto.*

Diethelm (100) South German: from the personal name *Diethelm*, composed of the elements *theud* 'people', 'race' + *helm* 'helmet', 'protection'.

GIVEN NAME German 5%. *Florian.*

Dietiker (111) Swiss German: habitational name for someone from Dietikon near Zürich.

GIVEN NAMES German 6%. *Fritz, Otto.*

Dietl (137) German: from a pet form of various personal names formed with *Diet* (Germanic *theud* 'people', 'race'), as for example DIETRICH.

GIVEN NAMES German 18%. *Fritz* (4), *Helmut* (2), *Elfriede, Eugen, Franz, Manfred.*

Dietlin (114) German and French (Alsatian): from a pet form of various personal names formed with *Diet* (see DIETL).

GIVEN NAME French 6%. *Camille.*

Dietrich (6755) German: from the Germanic personal name *Tederich* (*Theudoricus*), composed of the elements *theud* 'people', 'race' + *rīc* 'power(ful)', 'rich'. This surname is common throughout central and eastern Europe, particularly in the western Slavic countries. The forename occurs in a wide variety of local forms, especially in northern Germany. It is cognate with Dutch *Diederik* (see DEDERICK).

GIVEN NAMES German 4%. *Kurt* (17), *Otto* (6), *Gerhard* (4), *Dieter* (3), *Hans* (3), *Helmut* (3), *Juergen* (3), *Wolfgang* (3), *Fritz* (2), *Hans-Peter* (2), *Heinz* (2), *Jurgen* (2).

Dietrick (513) Americanized spelling of German DIETRICH.

Dietsch (510) South German: variant of DIETZ.

Dietsche (162) South German: variant of DIETZ.

Dietz (7680) German: from a short form of the personal name DIETRICH.

Dietze (269) German: variant of DIETZ.
GIVEN NAMES German 10%; Scandinavian 4%. *Arno* (2), *Claus* (2), *Friedhelm, Hans, Lothar, Manfred, Uwe; Hilmer, Holger, Sven.*

Dietzel (550) German: from the personal name *Dietzel,* a pet form of DIETZ.

Dietzen (248) German: patronymic from the personal name DIETZ.

Dietzler (185) German: patronymic from the personal name *Dietz(e)l,* a pet form of DIETZ.

Dietzman (239) German (**Dietzmann**): elaborated form of DIETZ, with the addition of *man* 'man'.

Dieu (126) Vietnamese: unexplained.
GIVEN NAMES Vietnamese 27%. *Hung* (2), *Chanh, Chau, Cuong Van, Dau, Dung, Duong, Kinh, Lam, Lan, Minh, Muoi.*

Dieudonne (112) French (**Dieudonné**): from the medieval personal name *Dieudonné* 'God-given', a vernacular form of *Deodonatus.*
GIVEN NAMES French 34%. *Carolle, Dominique, Francois, Henri, Jacinthe, Kettly, Marcel, Pierre, Regine, Viergela.*

Diez (676) **1.** Spanish (**Díez**): variant of *Díaz* (see DIAZ, DIEGO). **2.** German: variant spelling of DIETZ.
GIVEN NAMES Spanish 34%. *Jose* (10), *Carlos* (8), *Jorge* (6), *Juan* (6), *Fernando* (5), *Pedro* (5), *Rafael* (5), *Roberto* (5), *Angel* (4), *Eduardo* (4), *Mario* (4), *Ricardo* (4).

Di Fabio (290) Italian: patronymic from the personal name FABIO.
GIVEN NAMES Italian 22%. *Carmine* (3), *Mario* (3), *Rocco* (3), *Angelo* (2), *Salvatore* (2), *Anselmo, Antonio, Armando, Arturo, Carlo, Corrado, Domenico, Emilia, Emilio, Florindo, Franco, Geno, Luca, Mariano, Orlando.*

Di Falco (285) Italian: patronymic from the personal name FALCO.
GIVEN NAMES Italian 20%. *Italia* (2), *Sal* (2), *Salvatore* (2), *Vito* (2), *Angelo, Antonio, Camillo, Cosmo, Damiano, Donato, Francesco, Pasquale.*

Di Fatta (116) Italian: metronymic from the female personal name *Fatta,* a short form of *Benfatta,* literally 'well-made'.
GIVEN NAMES Italian 30%. *Salvatore* (5), *Santo* (3), *Angelo, Antonio, Benigna, Luigi, Sal, Salvato, Vincenzo.*

Di Fazio (261) Italian: variant of DE FAZIO.
GIVEN NAMES Italian 31%. *Angelo* (4), *Salvatore* (4), *Cosmo* (3), *Sal* (3), *Mauro* (2), *Pasco* (2), *Aldo, Antonio, Carmine, Egidio, Gaetano, Gennaro, Mario, Rosita, Silverio.*

Di Felice (184) Southern Italian: variant of DE FELICE.
GIVEN NAMES Italian 30%. *Mario* (4), *Antonio* (3), *Dino* (2), *Fiore* (2), *Gino* (2), *Remo* (2), *Angelo, Attilio, Camillo, Domenic, Emilio, Ennio, Firmino, Giovanni, Lino, Orlando.*

Diffee (213) Probably a variant of Irish DUFFY.
FOREBEARS William Diffee, from whom present-day American bearers of this name are descended, was born in about 1710, probably in Ireland, and died in 1790 in Randolph Co., NC.

Diffenbaugh (119) Americanized spelling of German DIEFENBACH.

Diffenderfer (362) Americanized spelling of German **Diefendörfer** (see DIEFENDERFER).

Diffey (109) **1.** English (Dorset): unexplained. **2.** See DIFFEE.

Diffin (139) Irish (Counties Tyrone and Armagh): reduced Anglicized form of Gaelic **Ó Duibhchinn**, a variant of **Ó Duibhginn** (see DEEGAN).

Diffley (212) Irish (Connacht): reduced Anglicized form of Gaelic **Ó Duibhghiolla** 'descendant of the black lad'.
GIVEN NAME Irish 8%. *Brendan.*

Di Filippo (562) Italian: patronymic from the personal name *Filippo,* Greek *Philippos* (see PHILIP).
GIVEN NAMES Italian 22%. *Donato* (3), *Gino* (3), *Nicola* (3), *Rocco* (3), *Salvatore* (3), *Angelo* (2), *Antonio* (2), *Carmine* (2), *Enrico* (2), *Luigi* (2), *Pasquale* (2), *Romeo* (2).

Di Fiore (558) Italian: patronymic or metronymic from the personal name FIORE.
GIVEN NAMES Italian 18%. *Salvatore* (8), *Antonio* (2), *Carmelo* (2), *Domenica* (2), *Giacomo* (2), *Giovanni* (2), *Giuseppe* (2), *Silvio* (2), *Angelo, Carmine, Ciro, Dante.*

Di Fonzo (212) Italian: patronymic from the personal name *Fonzo,* a short form of ALFONSO. The change of *s* to *z* is typical of southern and central Italy.
GIVEN NAMES Italian 22%. *Antonio* (3), *Angelo* (2), *Alfonso, Biagio, Carmine, Domenic, Eliseo, Eraldo, Onofrio, Panfilo, Pio, Raffaele, Renato, Salvatore, Valentino.*

Di Francesco (598) Italian: patronymic from the personal name *Francisco,* a southern variant of *Francesco,* from Latin *Franciscus* (see FRANCIS).
GIVEN NAMES Italian 18%. *Angelo* (4), *Pasquale* (3), *Domenic* (2), *Ezio* (2), *Gaetano* (2), *Guido* (2), *Mauro* (2), *Rocco* (2), *Sal* (2), *Aldo, Antonio, Carlo.*

Di Franco (609) Italian: patronymic from the personal name *Franco,* Italian equivalent of FRANK.
GIVEN NAMES Italian 32%. *Mario* (5), *Salvatore* (5), *Adelio* (4), *Adelmo* (4), *Antonio* (3), *Carmine* (3), *Dino* (3), *Remo* (3), *Rocco* (3), *Angelo* (2), *Carmelo* (2), *Dante* (2), *Flavio* (2), *Gino* (2), *Sal* (2),

Gabriela (2), *Adriana, Adriano, Alphonso, Candido, Mauricio, Tino, Valeria.*

Di Fronzo (131) Italian: patronymic from the personal name *Fronzo,* a variant of ALFONSO.
GIVEN NAMES Italian 20%. *Rocco* (3), *Vito* (2), *Angelo, Antonio, Arcangelo, Dino, Italo, Pasquale.*

Di Fulvio (104) Italian: patronymic from the personal name *Fulvio,* from Latin *Fulvius,* a personal name based on *fulvus* 'fair or reddish haired'.
GIVEN NAMES Italian 21%. *Angelo, Antonio, Camillo, Carmine, Giancarlo, Mauro, Nicola.*

Di Gaetano (155) Italian: patronymic from personal name GAETANO.
GIVEN NAMES Italian 14%. *Sal* (2), *Angelo, Dante, Pasquale, Salvatore.*

Di Gangi (302) Italian: habitational name for someone from Gangi in Palermo, Sicily.
GIVEN NAMES Italian 18%. *Angelo* (3), *Franco* (2), *Mario* (2), *Salvatore* (2), *Alberto, Antonio, Calogero, Claudio, Natale.*

Digby (545) English: habitational name from Digby in Lincolnshire, named from Old Norse *dík* 'dike', 'ditch' + *býr* 'farm', 'settlement'.

Di Gennaro (397) Italian: patronymic from the personal name GENNARO.
GIVEN NAMES Italian 27%. *Antimo* (2), *Carlo* (2), *Mario* (2), *Rocco* (2), *Agostino, Aldo, Americo, Angelo, Antonio, Bruna, Corrado, Domenic, Elena, Ernesto, Gennaro, Orlando, Rodolfo, Timoteo.*

Di Genova (138) Italian: habitational name for someone from the seaport of Genoa in Liguria, Italian GENOVA.
GIVEN NAMES Italian 36%. *Mario* (3), *Ennio* (2), *Adamo, Americo, Aniello, Antonietta, Caesar, Corrado, Enrico, Ernesto, Fiorenzo, Gennaro, Marcello, Nunzio, Remo.*

Di Geronimo (241) Italian: variant of DE GIROLAMO, from an old form of the personal name, now preserved only in the surname.
GIVEN NAMES Italian 16%. *Carmine* (2), *Angelo, Antonio, Chiara, Gino, Guido, Italo, Lorenzo, Luciano, Marcello, Mario, Sal, Salvatore.*

Digges (189) English: **1.** from Middle English *digge* 'duck', probably applied as a metonymic occupational name for someone who kept, caught, or sold ducks or as a nickname for someone thought to resemble a duck in some way. **2.** patronymic from *Digg,* a voiced variant of the personal name DICK.

Diggins (709) English and Scottish: variant of DICKENS.
GIVEN NAMES Irish 4%. *Donovan, Niall.*

Diggle (120) English: from a pet form of DICK.

Diggs (3404) English: variant spelling of DIGGES.

Dighton (129) English: variant of DEIGH-TON.

Di Giacinto (112) Italian: patronymic from the personal name GIACINTO.

GIVEN NAMES Italian 8%. *Dante, Marco.*

Di Giacomo (1402) Italian: patronymic from the personal name *Giacomo*, from Latin *Jacobus*, via Late Latin *Jacomus* (see JAMES).

GIVEN NAMES Italian 14%. *Angelo* (7), *Rocco* (5), *Salvatore* (4), *Carlo* (3), *Dino* (2) (2), *Lorenzo* (2), *Luigi* (2), *Pasquale* (2), *Sal* (2), *Agatino, Alfonse.*

Di Gilio (273) Italian: patronymic from the personal name *Gilio*, a variant of *Egidio* (see GILES).

GIVEN NAMES Italian 11%. *Rocco* (4), *Angelo.*

Di Gioia (343) Italian: patronymic from the personal name *Gioia*, or a habitational name for someone from a place called Gioia. See GIOIA.

GIVEN NAMES Italian 20%. *Vito* (3), *Angelo* (2), *Enrico* (2), *Giuseppe* (2), *Carlo, Cosmo, Domenico, Ferdinando, Gaetano, Luigi, Pietro.*

Di Giorgio (560) Italian: patronymic from the personal name *Giorgio*, from Greek *Geōrgios* (see GEORGE).

GIVEN NAMES Italian 26%. *Angelo* (5), *Mario* (4), *Rocco* (4), *Salvatore* (3), *Domenic* (2), *Domenico* (2), *Gioacchino* (2), *Giovanni* (2), *Valentino* (2), *Amedeo, Antonio, Armando, Cesare, Emilio, Erasmo, Ermano, Gerardo, Horacio, Poria.*

Di Giovanna (205) Italian: metronymic from the female personal name *Giovanna*, Italian equivalent of *Joan* (see JOHN).

GIVEN NAMES Italian 21%. *Gaspar* (3), *Alfonso, Carlo, Domenic, Gaetano, Liborio, Nunzio, Pietro, Rosario, Sal, Salvatore.*

Di Giovanni (1574) Italian: patronymic from the personal name *Giovanni*, Italian equivalent of JOHN.

GIVEN NAMES Italian 16%. *Angelo* (9), *Salvatore* (9), *Vito* (8), *Rocco* (6), *Sal* (5), *Aldo* (3), *Carlo* (3), *Gino* (3), *Giuseppe* (3), *Guido* (3), *Agostino* (2), *Carmela* (2).

Di Girolamo (724) Italian: patronymic from the personal name *Girolamo*, from Latin *Hieronymus*, Greek *Hieronymos* (see JEROME).

GIVEN NAMES Italian 19%. *Antonio* (4), *Vito* (4), *Carlo* (3), *Rocco* (3), *Dino* (2), *Domenic* (2), *Domenico* (2), *Enrico* (2), *Gasper* (2), *Gino* (2), *Livio* (2), *Angelo.*

Di Giulio (367) Italian: patronymic from the personal name *Giulio*, from Latin *Julius*, a Roman family name of uncertain origin (see JULIUS).

GIVEN NAMES Italian 20%. *Angelo* (4), *Domenic* (3), *Enrico* (2), *Nino* (2), *Pasquale* (2), *Aldo, Amedeo, Biagio, Carlo, Carmine, Cinzia, Dante.*

Di Giuseppe (175) Italian: patronymic from the personal name *Giuseppe*, Italian equivalent of JOSEPH.

GIVEN NAMES Italian 18%. *Enrico* (2), *Vito* (2), *Antonio, Carmine, Ezio, Gennaro, Marco, Mauro, Nicola, Pasquale, Rinaldo, Sal.*

Diglio (144) Italian (also **D'Iglio**): from Sicilian *jigliu*, Italian *giglio* 'lily'.

GIVEN NAMES Italian 18%. *Salvatore* (3), *Antonio, Giovanni, Giuseppe, Lorenzo, Sabatino.*

Digman (322) **1.** English: variant of DICK-MAN. **2.** Danish (**Digmann**): either a topographic name, from *dik* 'dike' + *man* 'man', or a nickname for a stout man, from *dik* 'fat' + *man*. **3.** German (**Digmann**): variant of DIECKMANN.

Dignam (160) **1.** Irish: see DIGNAN. **2.** English: of uncertain derivation. Perhaps, as Reaney suggests, a habitational name for someone from Dagenham, formerly in Essex, now in Greater London, which gets its name from an Old English personal name *Dæcca* + genitive -*n* + *hām* 'homestead'.

Dignan (428) Irish: reduced Anglicized form of Gaelic **Ó Duibhgeannáin** (see DEIGNAN).

GIVEN NAMES Irish 6%. *Aileen, Donal.*

Di Grazia (237) Italian: metronymic from the female personal name *Grazia*, a name with religious associations, from Latin *Gratia*, meaning 'grace'.

GIVEN NAMES Italian 13%. *Ugo* (2), *Annamarie, Carmine, Domenic, Domenico, Gianpaolo, Gino, Mauro, Salvatore.*

Di Gregorio (977) Italian: patronymic from the personal name *Gregorio*, Latin *Gregorius*, Greek *Grēgorios* (see GREGORY).

GIVEN NAMES Italian 19%. *Antonio* (8), *Rocco* (5), *Domenic* (4), *Adamo* (3), *Armando* (3), *Dante* (3), *Americo* (2), *Mario* (3), *Ricardo* (3), *Silvio* (3), *Angelo* (2), *Carmela* (2), *Fernando* (2), *Guido* (2), *Nino* (2), *Pasquale* (2), *Pietro* (2).

Di Guglielmo (153) Southern Italian: patronymic from the personal name *Guglielmo*, Italian equivalent of WILLIAM.

GIVEN NAMES Italian 21%. *Angelo* (3), *Pasquale* (2), *Agostino, Antonio, Nicola.*

Di Iorio (401) Italian: patronymic from the personal name *Iorio*, a southern Italian variant of GIORGIO.

GIVEN NAMES Italian 24%. *Salvatore* (4), *Antonio* (3), *Angelo* (2), *Carmine* (2), *Claudio* (2), *Cosimo* (2), *Gerardo* (2), *Gino* (2), *Amerigo, Carlo, Carmela, Dino, Francesco, Guido.*

Di Joseph (126) Partly Americanized form of Italian DI GIUSEPPE.

GIVEN NAMES Italian 12%. *Domenic, Raniero.*

Di Julio (116) Italian: variant spelling of DI GIULIO.

Dike (586) English: variant spelling of DYKE.

Dikeman (323) Probably in most cases an Americanized spelling of Dutch DYCKMAN or German TEICHMANN. However, early forms of English DIGMAN include the spelling *Dikeman*, and in some cases the name may represent a survival of this older form.

Dikes (126) English: variant of DYKE.

Di Lallo (136) Italian: patronymic from a short form of a personal name formed with the hypocoristic suffix -*lallo*.

GIVEN NAMES Italian 12%. *Angelo, Camillo, Filomena, Guido, Rocco.*

Di Laura (150) Italian: metronymic from the female personal name *Laura* (a derivative of Latin *laurus* 'laurel').

GIVEN NAMES Italian 7%. *Angelo* (2), *Antonio, Emidio, Rosaria.*

Di Lauro (219) Italian: **1.** patronymic from the personal name LAURO, of the same derivation as 2. **2.** habitational name from any of various places named Lauro, from *lauro* 'laurel', 'bay' (from Latin *laurus*).

GIVEN NAMES Italian 20%. *Amato* (3), *Antonio* (3), *Angelo* (2), *Amerigo, Camillo, Carmela, Guglielmo, Rocco, Saverio, Umberto.*

Dilbeck (705) Belgian: according to Debrabandere, possibly a habitational name from a place called Dilbeek, in the province of Brabant. It could alternatively be a variant spelling of **Delbeck**, a Frenchified form of VANDERBECK.

Dilcher (103) German: variant of DILGER 2.

Dilday (347) Origin uncertain. **1.** It is said to be a Huguenot name, probably a derivative of French **Isle d'Aix**, a habitational name from a place in Charente Maritime, or **Dildé**, which is of uncertain origin. **2.** Alternatively, perhaps, a respelling of German **Dildey**, which is likewise unexplained. The element -*dey*, which occurs in a number of German surnames (e.g. **Dauthendey, Mackeldey**), has so far received no satisfactory explanation.

Dildine (437) Origin unidentified. Perhaps a reduced form of German DINGELDEIN.

Dildy (246) Variant spelling of DILDAY.

Dile (117) **1.** Probably an Americanized form of German DIEHL. **2.** Probably also a variant of English DIAL.

Di Lella (166) Italian: metronymic from a short form of *Angiolella* or any of various other female pet names with the hypocoristic suffix -*ella* following a final consonant -*l*.

GIVEN NAMES Italian 17%. *Emidio* (2), *Angelo, Antonio, Biagio, Dante, Domenic, Gaetano.*

Di Lello (189) Italian: patronymic from the personal name LELLO, a short form of *Angiolello*, or any of various other personal names with the hypocoristic suffix -*ello*.

GIVEN NAMES Italian 32%. *Remo* (3), *Mario* (3), *Alfonso* (2), *Armando* (2), *Enrico* (2), *Angelo, Antonietta, Emilio, Franca, Giovanni, Luciano, Nicola, Nicolino, Santa.*

Di Leo (915) Southern Italian: patronymic from the personal name *Leo*, a short form of LEONE or LEONARDO.

GIVEN NAMES Italian 21%. *Angelo* (9), *Rocco* (6), *Vito* (5), *Carlo* (3), *Ignazio* (3), *Salvatore* (3), *Antonio* (2), *Carmine* (2), *Concetta* (2), *Domenic* (2), *Filippo* (2), *Romano* (2).

Di Leonardo (193) Southern Italian: patronymic from the personal name *Leonardo*, Italian equivalent of LEONARD.
GIVEN NAMES Italian 25%. *Angelo* (3), *Angelina* (2), *Mario* (2), *Carlo*, *Emidio*, *Germano*, *Gino*, *Guerino*, *Pietro*, *Salvatore*, *Santina*.

Diles (130) Origin unidentified.

Dilg (162) German: from a pet form of the medieval female personal name *Odila*, a derivative of *od* 'riches', 'fortune'. It was the name of an 8th-century saint who founded a Benedictine convent at what is now Odilienburg in Alsace; she is the patron saint of Alsace.
GIVEN NAME German 4%. *Gerhard*.

Dilger (404) German: **1.** habitational name from any of several places called Dillingen (in Bavaria, near Luxembourg, or in the Saarland) or from Tüllingen near Lörrach in Baden. **2.** metronymic from the female personal name DILG.
GIVEN NAMES German 5%. *Kurt* (2), *Benno*, *Otto*.

Di Liberti (113) Italian: see DI LIBERTO.
GIVEN NAMES Italian 22%. *Angelo* (3), *Salvatore* (2), *Enza*, *Vincenzo*, *Vito*.

Di Liberto (434) Italian (**Di Liberto**): patronymic from the personal name *Liberto*, from Latin *Libertus*, or from a short form of the Germanic personal name *Aliberto*, Italian equivalent of ALBERT.
GIVEN NAMES Italian 17%. *Salvatore* (4), *Angelo* (3), *Carlo* (2), *Guiseppe* (2), *Sal* (2), *Sante* (2), *Caesar*, *Carmine*, *Gioia*, *Giovanni*, *Innocenzo*, *Luigi*.

Di Lillo (222) Italian: patronymic from the personal name *Lillo*, a short form of various pet names formed with this suffix, such *Angelillo*, *Jacolillo*, or *Paolillo*.
GIVEN NAMES Italian 33%; Polish 8%; Spanish 6%. *Rocco* (14), *Antonio* (4), *Angelo* (2), *Carmel*, *Giro*, *Michelina*, *Salvatore*, *Vito*; *Mario*.

Di Lisio (159) Italian: either a habitational name from Lisio in Cuneo province or alternatively a patronymic from *Lisio*, a reduced form of the personal name ALOISIO.
GIVEN NAMES Italian 19%. *Angelo* (2), *Silvio* (2), *Attillo*, *Francesco*, *Guiseppe*, *Matteo*, *Pasquale*, *Piero*, *Sal*, *Salvatore*.

Dilks (525) English (chiefly East Midlands): patronymic from a pet form of the Middle English personal name *Dillo* (see DILLON).

Dill (6871) **1.** German: metonymic occupational name for a sawyer, from Middle High German *dill(e)* '(floor)board'. **2.** English: metonymic occupational name for a grower or seller of dill, an aromatic culinary and medicinal herb, Old English *dile*, *dyle*. **3.** English: nickname from Middle English *dell*, *dill*, *dull* 'dull', 'fool-

ish'. **4.** English: from an Old English personal name *Dylli* or *Dylla*. **5.** Possibly a reduced form of Scottish MCDILL.

Dilla (109) Origin unidentified.

Dillabough (109) Probably an Americanized form of a German habitational name, Dillenburg, in Hesse.

Dillahunt (173) Americanized spelling of Irish DELAHUNT.

Dillahunty (174) Altered spelling of Irish DELAHUNTY.

Dillard (9413) English: unexplained; possibly a variant of DOLLARD. The name was in VA by 1698.

Dillashaw (125) Origin unidentified. It could be an Americanized spelling of South German **Dilcher**, a variant of DILGER 2. This name is concentrated in AL and TX.

Dillavou (178) Probably an altered form of French **Delavau**, a dialect form of **Delaval**, a topographic name for someone who lived in a valley, French *val*.

Dille (733) German: **1.** from a personal name, variant of *Thiele*, which came to be used as a nickname denoting an inept or silly person. **2.** variant of DILL.

Dillehay (326) Altered spelling of French **Delahaye**, a topographic name for someone who lived on land enclosed by hedges, from *de la haye* 'from the hedge', or a habitational name from any of the various places named with this word, such as La Haye in Normandy, France.

Dillen (197) **1.** Dutch: Brabantine variant of **Gielen**, a patronymic from a vernacular form of *Ægidius* (see GILES). **2.** German: probably from a variant of *Thielen* (see THIEL). **3.** Possibly an altered spelling of DILLON.

Dillenbeck (348) Probably of German origin: perhaps an altered form DILLENBURG.

Dillenburg (209) German: habitational name from a place in Hesse now named Dillenburg, but formerly called Dillenberg. This was the ancestral home of William of Orange (*Willem van Oranje*) of the house of Nassau.

Dillender (120) Origin unidentified.

Diller (1444) **1.** German: occupational name for a sawyer, from an agent derivative of Middle High German *dille*, *dil* 'plank', '(floor)board'. **2.** German: habitational name for someone from any of various places named Dill, Dille, or Till. **3.** English: occupational name for a grower of dill, from an agent derivative of Old English *dile* (see DILL 2).

Dilley (2142) **1.** English: possibly a pet form of an unrecorded Old English personal name *Dylla*, found as the first element in the place names Dillington (in the former Huntingdonshire) and Dilton (in Wiltshire). **2.** In some cases, possibly an altered spelling of French DILLY.

Dilliard (103) Probably a variant of English DILLARD.

Dillie (156) Probably an altered spelling of DILLEY or DILLY or possibly of German **Dillier**, a variant of DILGER 2.
GIVEN NAME French 4%. *Marcel*.

Dillin (189) Variant spelling of DILLING or DILLON.

Dilling (478) **1.** English: of uncertain derivation; it may be from *Dylling* 'son of *Dylla*', or from *dylling* 'the dull one'. **2.** German: metronymic from the female personal name *Dilli*, in Westphalia a pet form of *Ottilie*. **3.** German: variant of DILLINGER.

Dillinger (916) **1.** German: habitational name for someone from Dillingen near Augsburg or Tüllingen in Baden. **2.** English: habitational name from Drellingore in Kent, which is recorded as *Dillynger* in 1264, from the Old English personal name *Dylla* + *-ing-* denoting association + Old English *ōra* 'hill slope'.

Dillingham (1846) English: habitational name, probably from Dullingham in Cambridgeshire, named in Old English as 'homestead (Old English *hām*) of the people (*-inga-*) of Dull(a)' (an unattested personal name).

Dillion (582) Irish and English: possibly a variant of DILLON.

Dillman (2159) German (**Dillmann**): variant of **Dielmann**, itself a variant of THIELEMANN.

Dillner (118) German (Saxony): metronymic from a reduced form of the medieval female personal name *Odilia* (see DILG).
GIVEN NAMES German 6%. *Gerhard*, *Helmut*.

Dillon (17784) **1.** English and French: from the Germanic personal name *Dillo* (of uncertain origin, perhaps a byname from the root *dīl* 'destroy'), introduced to Britain from France by the Normans. **2.** English: habitational name from Dilwyn near Hereford, recorded in 1138 as *Dilun*, probably from Old English *dīglum*, dative plural of *dīgle* 'recess', 'retreat', i.e. 'at the shady or secret places'. **3.** Irish (of Norman origin): altered form of **de Leon** (see LYON). **4.** Irish: reduced Anglicized form of Gaelic **Ó Duilleáin** 'descendant of *Duilleán*', a personal name, a variant of *Dallán* meaning 'little blind one'. **5.** Jewish (eastern Ashkenazic): of uncertain origin; either an ornamental name from the Biblical place name Dilon (Joshua 15:38), or an altered form of Sephardic **de León** (see LYON).

Dillow (1186) English: probably a variant of DILLON.

Dills (1254) **1.** Variant spelling of Dutch DILS. **2.** English: infrequent variant of DILL.

Dillworth (132) English: variant spelling of DILWORTH.

Dilly (235) **1.** English: variant spelling of DILLEY. **2.** French: habitational name, with the preposition *d(e)*, for someone from Illy, a place in the Ardennes. **3.** German:

from a pet form of the female personal name *Ottilie*.

Dilmore (170) Possibly a reduced form of English **Dillamore**, itself a variant of DELAMAR.

Di Lorenzo (1210) Italian: patronymic from the personal name *Lorenzo*, from Latin *Laurentius* (see LAWRENCE).

GIVEN NAMES Italian 22%. *Angelo* (9), *Mario* (8), *Sal* (7), *Rocco* (4), *Salvatore* (4), *Mauro* (3), *Pasquale* (3), *Aldo* (2), *Antimo* (2), *Antonino* (2), *Antonio* (2), *Carlo* (2), *Carmine* (2), *Emilio* (2), *Gaspar* (2), *Germano* (2), *Orlando*, *Roberto*.

Di Loreto (397) Italian: habitational name for someone from Loreto, south of Ancona. The distribution of the modern surname is coterminous with the medieval cult of the Madonna of Loreto.

GIVEN NAMES Italian 18%. *Angelo* (3), *Salvatore* (3), *Attilio* (2), *Emidio* (2), *Ettore* (2), *Guido* (2), *Nino* (2), *Antonio*, *Concetta*, *Dante*, *Domenic*, *Domenico*.

Dils (233) **1.** Dutch: Brabantine variant of **Gils**, a patronymic from the vernacular form of *Aegidius* (see GILES). **2.** Altered spelling of German **Dilz** (see DILTS).

Dilsaver (144) Probably an Americanized spelling of North German **Dellshöver**, a habitational name from someone from a minor place named with Middle Low German *delle* 'flat depression' + *hov* 'yard', 'farm'.

Dilts (907) Americanized spelling of German DILTZ.

Diltz (359) German: either from an old personal name formed with Old High German *diot* 'people', 'nation' or from *Tiltz*, a Sorbian short form of the personal name *Bartholomäus* (see BARTHOLOMEW).

Di Lullo (299) Southern Italian: patronymic from a nickname from Sicilian *lullu*, *lollu* 'stupid', 'silly'.

GIVEN NAMES Italian 20%. *Angelo* (5), *Domenic* (4), *Ugo* (2), *Amerigo*, *Carmine*, *Ciro*, *Domenico*, *Donato*, *Enrico*, *Ettore*, *Ireneo*, *Luciano*.

Di Luzio (251) Italian: patronymic from *Luzio*, an old variant of the personal name *Lucio*, from Latin *Lucius*, an ancient Roman personal name probably derived from *lux* 'light' (genitive *lucis*).

GIVEN NAMES Italian 14%. *Rocco* (2), *Attilio*, *Camillo*, *Dante*, *Gino*, *Marino*, *Nicola*, *Pasquale*.

Dilworth (1466) **1.** English: habitational name from Dilworth, a place in Lancashire named from Old English *dile* 'dill' (a medicinal and culinary herb) + *worð* 'enclosure'. **2.** Irish: English surname adopted by bearers of the Gaelic name **Ó Dubhluachra** 'descendant of *Dubhluachra*', a compound of *dubh* 'black' + *luachair* 'rushes'.

Di Maggio (1118) Italian: patronymic from the personal name or nickname MAGGIO.

GIVEN NAMES Italian 21%. *Salvatore* (13), *Rocco* (8), *Antonio* (6), *Angelo* (4), *Giovanni* (4), *Sal* (4), *Saverio* (3), *Vito* (3), *Antonino* (2), *Calogero* (2), *Cesare* (2).

Di Maio (682) Italian: variant of DI MAGGIO.

GIVEN NAMES Italian 16%. *Sal* (4), *Vito* (4), *Aldino* (2), *Carlo* (2), *Domenico* (2), *Enzo* (2), *Salvatore* (2), *Aldo*, *Carmela*, *Carmelina*, *Dante*, *Emanuele*.

Di Mambro (163) Southern Italian: of uncertain derivation. It may be a habitational name from a lost place called Mambro, or alternatively from a short form of the medieval personal names *Mambrino* or *Mambretto*.

GIVEN NAMES Italian 22%; Spanish 5%. *Antonio* (3), *Giovanni* (2), *Marino* (2), *Angelo*, *Carmine*, *Dante*, *Domenic*, *Gaetano*, *Gildo*, *Guido*, *Piero*, *Salvatore*; *Mario* (3), *Armando*, *Assunta*, *Celestino*, *Emilio*, *Germano*, *Renato*, *Roberto*.

Di Marco (1385) Italian: patronymic from the personal name *Marco*, from Latin *Marcus* (see MARK).

GIVEN NAMES Italian 21%. *Salvatore* (15), *Antonio* (8), *Angelo* (4), *Carlo* (4), *Ciro* (4), *Guido* (4), *Santo* (4), *Fiore* (3), *Giacomo* (3), *Gino* (3), *Giovanni* (3), *Luigi* (3).

Di Mare (209) Italian: most probably a patronymic from a reduced form of *Ademaro*, a personal name of Germanic origin, composed of the elements *adal* 'noble' + *māri*, *mēri* 'fame'.

GIVEN NAMES Italian 23%. *Sal* (2), *Salvatore* (2), *Ugo* (2), *Angelo*, *Antonio*, *Carmine*, *Dario*, *Domenic*, *Marcello*, *Santo*.

Di Maria (677) Italian: variant of DE MARIA.

GIVEN NAMES Italian 21%. *Salvatore* (5), *Sal* (4), *Mario* (3), *Rosario* (3), *Angelo* (2), *Antonino* (2), *Liborio* (2), *Marcello* (2), *Pasquale* (2), *Antonio*, *Calogero*, *Camillo*, *Carlo*, *Cesario*, *Domiano*.

Di Marino (200) Italian: patronymic from the personal name MARINO.

GIVEN NAMES Italian 16%. *Vito* (2), *Angelo*, *Antonio*, *Emidio*, *Modestino*, *Pasquale*, *Pietro*.

Di Mario (165) Italian: patronymic from the personal name MARIO.

GIVEN NAMES Italian 23%. *Salvatore* (5), *Angelo* (4), *Antonio*, *Carlo*, *Domenico*, *Enrico*, *Gino*.

Di Martino (1055) Italian: patronymic from the personal name *Martino*, from Latin *Martinus* (see MARTIN).

GIVEN NAMES Italian 20%. *Mario* (11), *Salvatore* (9), *Angelo* (5), *Rosario* (4), *Sal* (4), *Biagio* (3), *Domenic* (3), *Guido* (3), *Luigi* (3), *Antonio* (2), *Carlo* (2), *Emidio* (2), *Gaetano* (2), *Gino* (2), *Gustavo* (2), *Alberto*, *Alfonzo*, *Benito*, *Ernesto*, *Leopoldo*.

Di Marzio (295) Italian: patronymic from the personal name *Marzio*, which is of Latin origin, meaning 'dedicated to (the god) Mars'.

GIVEN NAMES Italian 15%. *Angelo* (3), *Antonio* (2), *Dante* (2), *Dino* (2), *Cesare*, *Domenic*, *Ermanno*, *Gino*, *Guido*, *Nunzio*, *Vittorino*.

Di Marzo (177) Italian: patronymic from the personal name MARZO.

GIVEN NAMES Italian 15%. *Domenico* (2), *Biaggio*, *Damiano*, *Filomena*, *Fiore*, *Marino*, *Onofrio*, *Pasquale*.

Dimas (642) Spanish and Portuguese: from a personal name *Dimas*, supposedly that of the repentant robber crucified alongside Christ, although no name is recorded in the Biblical account.

GIVEN NAMES Spanish 36%; Portuguese 8%. *Jose* (14), *Juan* (7), *Jesus* (5), *Guadalupe* (4), *Pedro* (4), *Carlos* (3), *Julio* (3), *Lupe* (3), *Manuel* (3), *Maria Elena* (3), *Nicasio* (3), *Roberto* (3); *Martinho*.

Di Mascio (244) Italian: name for a servant or member of the household of a master craftsman (see MASCIO).

GIVEN NAMES Italian 29%. *Orlando* (3), *Guido* (2), *Mario* (2), *Sabatino* (2), *Silvano* (2), *Aldo*, *Angelo*, *Attilio*, *Attillo*, *Biaggio*, *Camillo*, *Carmine*, *Cataldo*, *Roberto*.

Di Masi (129) Italian: patronymic from a reduced form of the personal name *Tommaso*, Italian equivalent of THOMAS.

GIVEN NAMES Italian 17%. *Angelo*, *Antonio*, *Domenic*, *Domenico*, *Giuseppe*, *Leonardo*, *Salvatore*.

Di Matteo (823) Italian: patronymic from the Biblical name *Matteo*, Italian equivalent of MATTHEW.

GIVEN NAMES Italian 22%. *Angelo* (8), *Antonio* (6), *Emilio* (5), *Pietro* (4), *Rocco* (4), *Enrico* (3), *Gaetano* (3), *Mario* (3), *Nicola* (3), *Pasquale* (3), *Attilio* (2), *Carmine* (2), *Luca* (2), *Gerardo* (2), *Orlando* (2), *Adelmo*, *Alfonso*, *Alfredo*, *Armando*, *Carmella*, *Genaro*, *Lino*.

Di Mattia (280) Italian: patronymic from the personal name MATTIA.

GIVEN NAMES Italian 17%. *Angelo* (4), *Aldo*, *Arcangelo*, *Attilio*, *Dino*, *Domenic*, *Emanuele*, *Ezio*, *Pina*, *Pio*, *Vito*, *Vittorino*.

Di Mauro (782) Southern Italian: patronymic from the personal name MAURO.

GIVEN NAMES Italian 27%. *Salvatore* (12), *Angelo* (11), *Sal* (6), *Rosario* (5), *Antonio* (4), *Domenic* (3), *Gino* (3), *Mario* (3), *Biaggio* (2), *Carmelo* (2), *Marcello* (2), *Alfonso*, *Alfredo*, *Armando*, *Arturo*, *Cesario*, *Dino*, *Emanuele*, *Emilio*, *Fortunato*, *Orlando*.

Di Meglio (475) Italian: patronymic from the personal name *Meglio*, meaning 'better'. Compare MIGLIORE.

GIVEN NAMES Italian 27%. *Angelo* (8), *Salvatore* (6), *Luigi* (4), *Pasquale* (4), *Aniello* (3), *Silvio* (3), *Antonio* (2), *Crescenzo* (2), *Domenico* (2), *Clemente*, *Concetta*, *Filomena*.

Di Menna (114) Italian: patronymic from the personal name *Menna*, from Greek *Mēnas* (see MINAS).

GIVEN NAMES Italian 15%. *Carmela, Costantino, Dante, Giuseppe, Nicola.*

Diment (121) Jewish (Ashkenazic): variant of DIAMOND.

GIVEN NAMES Russian 11%; Jewish 10%. *Lyubov* (2), *Arkady, Galya, Iosif, Konstantin, Yefim; Aron, Shlomo, Yakov.*

Di Meo (574) Italian: patronymic from a reduced form of the personal name *Bartolomeo* (see BARTHOLOMEW) or of ROMEO.

GIVEN NAMES Italian 21%; French 4%. *Salvatore* (4), *Alessandro* (3), *Angelo* (3), *Carmine* (2), *Domenic* (2), *Domenico* (2), *Adamo, Agostino, Alessio, Annunziata, Antimo, Antonio; Armand* (4), *Lucien* (2).

Di Mercurio (149) Southern Italian: patronymic from the popular medieval personal name MERCURIO.

GIVEN NAMES Italian 28%. *Salvatore* (6), *Gaetano* (3), *Sal* (2), *Antonino, Antonio, Biagio, Dino, Giuseppe, Vito.*

Dimery (99) English (Gloucestershire): unexplained.

Di Miceli (212) Southern Italian: variant of DI MICHELE.

GIVEN NAMES Italian 13%. *Biagio* (2), *Ettore* (2), *Sal* (2), *Angelo, Carmelo, Luigi, Salvatore.*

Di Michele (267) Italian: patronymic from the personal name *Michele*, Italian equivalent of MICHAEL.

GIVEN NAMES Italian 23%. *Aldo* (2), *Angelo* (2), *Antonio* (2), *Dino* (2), *Benedetto, Carlo, Dario, Enrico, Gino, Giuseppa, Giuseppe.*

Dimick (728) **1.** English: variant spelling of DIMMICK. **2.** Perhaps an Americanized form of Serbian **Dimić**, from the personal name *Dima*, a pet form of *Dimitrije*, from Greek *Dēmētrios* (Latin *Demetrius*; see DEMETRIOU). **3.** Americanized spelling of Slovenian **Dimic**: nickname for a grayhaired man, from the noun *dimec* 'graybeard', a derivative of the adjective *dimast* 'dark gray'. The form **Dimec** is also found as a Slovenian name.

Di Mino (437) Italian: patronymic from a short form of a pet name ending in *-mino*, as for example *Anselmino* (from ANSELMO), *Giacomino* (from GIACOMO), *Guglielmino* (from GUGLIELMO).

GIVEN NAMES Italian 21%. *Angelo* (4), *Salvatore* (2), *Antonio, Calogero, Carlo, Carmela, Ignazio, Luciano, Pietro, Sal, Vito.*

Dimit (109) English: variant of DIMMITT.

Dimitri (209) **1.** Southern Italian: patronymic form of the personal name *Demetrio*, from Greek *Dēmētrios* (Latin *Demetrius*; see DEMETRIOU). **2.** Bulgarian: from the personal name *Dimitri*, from Greek *Dēmētrios* (see DEMETRIOU).

GIVEN NAMES Italian 5%. *Guido* (3), *Carmine, Enrico, Marco, Salvatore.*

Dimitriou (117) Greek: variant of DEMETRIOU.

GIVEN NAMES Greek 18%. *Christos, Dimitrios, Eleni, Evangelos, Georgios, Ilias, Lambros, Spyros, Yiota.*

Dimitroff (214) Bulgarian and Macedonian: alternative spelling of DIMITROV.

Dimitrov (118) Bulgarian and Macedonian: patronymic from the personal names *Dimitr* (Bulgarian) or *Dimitar* (Macedonian), from Greek *Dēmētrios*.

GIVEN NAMES Bulgarian 46%. *Dimitar* (5), *Boris* (2), *Hristo* (2), *Mitko* (2), *Dragan, Evgeniy, Kiril, Konstantin, Lazar, Nikolai, Nikolay, Ognian, Petar, Plamen, Valeri, Veselin, Yordan; Ljubomir.*

Dimler (138) **1.** German: variant of DIEM. **2.** Variant of German **Dimmler**, a nickname or occupational name for a tumbler or a traveling entertainer, from an agent derivative of Middle High German *tumel(e)n* 'to tumble or romp'.

Dimmer (189) **1.** English: of uncertain derivation. Reaney suggests this is from Old French *dix mars* 'ten marks', presumably as a nickname for someone who owed this as a feudal due or paid it in rent. **2.** German: variant of the personal name *Dietmar* (see DITTMAR).

Dimmick (823) English: habitational name from Dymock in Gloucestershire, named perhaps from a British word akin to Welsh *tymoch* 'pigsty', but more probably from a Celtic *din* 'fort' + an adjectival suffix.

Dimmig (108) German: probably a variant of **Timmig**, from *Thiemo*, a short form of a Germanic personal name as in DIETMAR.

Dimmitt (484) English: unexplained. Perhaps an altered form of DIMMICK.

Dimmock (142) English: variant spelling of DIMMICK.

Dimock (385) English: variant spelling of DIMMICK.

Di Modica (112) Italian: metronymic from the female personal name *Modica*, from *modica*, feminine form of *modico* 'modest', 'moderate', from Latin *modicus*.

GIVEN NAMES Italian 19%. *Salvatore* (4), *Angelo, Domenic, Sal, Sebastiano.*

Dimoff (102) Bulgarian and Macedonian: unexplained.

Dimon (379) **1.** Irish: variant of DIAMOND. **2.** French: probably a southeastern variant of DEMONT.

Dimond (885) English and Irish: variant of DIAMOND.

D'Imperio (223) Italian: patronymic from the personal name *Imperio*, meaning 'empire'.

GIVEN NAMES Italian 14%. *Angelo* (3), *Francesco* (2), *Antonio, Alfonso, Alonzo, Julio, Mario, Sal.*

Dimsdale (133) English: habitational name from Dimsdale, a place in Staffordshire, possibly named from Middle English *dimple* 'dip in the ground' + *dale* 'valley'.

Di Muccio (101) Italian: patronymic from a short form of *Guglielmuccio* (from GUGLIELMO), or possibly from some other personal name ending with *-muccio*.

GIVEN NAMES Italian 12%. *Angelo, Domenic, Oreste.*

Di Muro (159) Italian: variant of DE MURO.

GIVEN NAMES Italian 20%. *Amedeo, Carmela, Concetta, Dino, Donato, Elio, Oreste, Pietro, Rocco, Salvatore, Vito.*

Di Muzio (212) Italian: patronymic from the personal name *Muzio*, from *Mucius*, of Etruscan origin.

GIVEN NAMES Italian 9%. *Pietro* (2), *Chiara, Dominico, Guido, Marco, Riccardo.*

Din (226) **1.** Muslim: shortened form of any of the many Arabic names formed with the word *dīn* 'religion', for example *Saifuddin* 'sword of religion' or *Salahuddin* 'righteousness of religion'. **2.** Indian (northern states): Hindu name derived from Sanskrit *dina* 'humble'. **3.** Scottish: unexplained. According to Black, this is an old Strathblane surname. **4.** Jewish (Ashkenazic): nickname from Yiddish *din* 'thin'.

GIVEN NAMES Muslim 51%; Indian 6%. *Munir* (3), *Riaz* (3), *Akbar* (2), *Anwar* (2), *Ashraf* (2), *Ghulam* (2), *Mohammad* (2), *Salah* (2), *Shahid* (2), *Tariq* (2), *Zahir* (2), *Abdul; Amrit, Gulab, Hemant, Jitendra, Mohi, Neena, Shingara.*

Dina (202) Italian: from the female personal name *Dina*.

GIVEN NAMES Italian 12%. *Dino* (2), *Salvatore* (2), *Carlo, Gasper, Marcellina, Nunzio.*

Di Nallo (108) Perhaps an altered form of Italian DI NELLO.

GIVEN NAMES Italian 11%. *Angelo, Dino, Giovanni.*

Dinan (562) **1.** Irish: (now mainly Counties Clare and Cork): reduced Anglicized form of Gaelic **Ó Daghnáin** 'descendant of *Daghnán*', possibly a diminutive of *dagh* 'good'. **2.** Irish: variant of DINEEN. **3.** English (of Norman origin): habitational name from Dinan, in Côtes-du-Nord, Brittany. **4.** In some cases, possibly an altered spelling of French **Dinant**, a habitational name from Dinant, a place in the Belgian province of Namur.

Di Napoli (701) Italian: habitational name for someone from the city of Naples (Italian *Napoli*).

GIVEN NAMES Italian 16%. *Rocco* (5), *Salvatore* (3), *Vito* (3), *Angelo* (2), *Antonio* (2), *Gennaro* (2), *Sal* (2), *Biagio, Canio, Cosimo, Cosmo, Domenic.*

Di Nardi (162) Italian: variant of DI NARDO.

GIVEN NAMES Italian 18%. *Antonio, Carlo, Carmel, Ciro, Gaetano, Gino, Margherita, Pietro, Rocco, Sal, Salvatore, Silvio.*

Di Nardo (1118) Italian: patronymic from the personal name *Nardo*, a short form of *Bernardo* (see BERNARD) or *Leonardo* (see LEONARD).

GIVEN NAMES Italian 18%. *Angelo* (10), *Antonio* (4), *Rocco* (4), *Amedeo* (3), *Luigi* (3), *Carmine* (2), *Enrico* (2), *Gildo* (2), *Gino* (2), *Giulio* (2), *Pasquale* (2).

Di Natale (567) Italian: patronymic from the personal name NATALE.

GIVEN NAMES Italian 27%. *Salvatore* (6), *Mario* (5), *Angelo* (3), *Antonio* (3), *Francesco* (3), *Luigi* (3), *Adolfo* (2), *Donato* (2), *Natale* (2), *Pietro* (2), *Vincenzo* (2), *Vito* (2), *Carmelo*, *Carmine*, *Americo*, *Armando*, *Sergio*.

Dinda (112) German: unexplained.

GIVEN NAMES German 9%. *Gerhard* (3), *Ernst*.

Dine (283) **1.** French: from a short form of the personal name *Claudine*, feminine form of CLAUDE. **2.** Possibly an altered spelling of DAIN.

Dineen (1254) Irish: reduced Anglicized form of Gaelic **Ó Duinnín** 'descendant of *Duinnín*', a byname from a diminutive of *donn* 'brown-haired man' or 'chieftain'.

GIVEN NAME Irish 5%. *Dermot*.

Dinehart (182) Americanized spelling of German **Deinhardt**, a variant of DEGEN-HARDT.

Di Nelli (132) Italian: variant of DI NELLO.

GIVEN NAMES Italian 13%. *Aldo*, *Antonio*, *Dante*, *Delio*, *Enrico*, *Gianfranco*, *Gino*, *Reno*, *Sal*.

Di Nello (145) Italian: patronymic from the personal name *Nello*, a short form of a pet name formed with the hypocoristic suffix *-ello* following the final consonant *-n*, as for example *Antonello* (from ANTONIO), *Brunello* (from BRUNO), *Giovanello* (from GIOVANNI).

GIVEN NAMES Italian 14%. *Pasquale* (2), *Alessandro*, *Attilio*, *Domenic*, *Donato*, *Marco*, *Vincenzo*.

Diner (137) Jewish (eastern Ashkenazic): **1.** occupational name from Yiddish *diner* 'servant'. **2.** nickname from an inflected form of Yiddish *din* 'thin'. Compare DIN.

GIVEN NAMES Russian 9%; Jewish 9%. *Boris*, *Efim*, *Igor*, *Lev*, *Mikhail*, *Semyon*, *Yev-geniy*; *Avi*, *Izrael*, *Mordecai*, *Yehuda*; *Frieda*, *Gitta*.

Dinerman (140) Jewish (eastern Ashkenazic): variant of DINER.

GIVEN NAMES Jewish 18%. *Bernhart* (2), *Tsvi* (2), *Gersh*, *Isadore*, *Miriam*, *Sima*, *Yankel*, *Yisroel*.

Dinerstein (110) Jewish (from Ukraine): ornamental name from Yiddish *diner* 'thin' + *shteyn* 'stone'.

GIVEN NAME Jewish 7%. *Shalom*.

Dines (520) English: patronymic from DAIN 1.

Ding (612) Chinese 丁: there are several sources of this surname; one of them is a certain Duke Ding who lived during the reign of Wu Wang, who established the Zhou dynasty in 1122 BC.

GIVEN NAMES Chinese 54%. *Wei* (8), *Li* (6), *Yan* (5), *Feng* (4), *Hong* (4), *Ning* (4), *Wen*
(4), *Chen* (3), *Hui* (3), *Jin* (3), *Min* (3), *Yuan* (3), *Zheng* (3), *Chong, Joo, Yeo, You*.

Dinga (101) Origin unidentified.

Dingee (243) Origin uncertain; probably English or Dutch.

FOREBEARS Robert Dingee was in Hempstead, Long Island, NY, by 1676.

Dingeldein (121) German: **1.** probably a variant of **Dingeldey**, which is unexplained. Compare DILDAY. **2.** Alternatively, it may be an occupational nickname for an armorer (literally 'sharpen the sword'), from Middle High German *dengeln* 'to sharpen', 'to hone' + *dey*, shortened form of *degen* 'sword'.

Dinger (1151) German: occupational name from Middle High German *dingære*, Middle Low German *dinger* 'judge', 'arbiter'.

Dinges (729) German: from a vernacular form of the Latin personal name *Dionysius* (see DENNIS).

Dingess (706) Altered spelling of German DINGES.

Dingfelder (104) German: topographic or habitational name from a place named Dingfeld.

GIVEN NAME German 6%. *Otto* (2).

Dingle (978) **1.** English: topographic name for someone living in a small wooded dell or hollow, Middle English *dingle* (of uncertain origin). There is a district of Liverpool called Dingle. **2.** South German: nickname or status name for a smallholder, from Middle High German *dingelīn* 'smallholding'. **3.** Americanized spelling of the old Prussian name **Dingel** or **Dyngele**, possibly from Germanic *thing* 'legal assembly'.

Dingledine (145) Americanized spelling of German DINGELDEIN.

Dingler (729) German: variant of DENGLER.

Dingley (207) English: habitational name from a place in Northamptonshire named Dingley, possibly from Middle English *dingle* 'hollow' + Old English *lēah* 'woodland clearing'.

Dingman (1805) Americanized spelling of German DINGMANN.

Dingmann (173) **1.** German: variant of DINGER. **2.** South German: habitational name for someone from Ober or Unter Ding in Bavaria.

Dings (116) Probably a respelling of German DINGES.

Dingus (720) Probably a respelling of German DINGES.

Dingwall (228) Scottish: habitational name from Dingwall, a place in Ross-shire.

Dingwell (122) Scottish: variant of DING-WALL.

Dinh (1681) Vietnamese (**Đinh**): unexplained.

GIVEN NAMES Vietnamese 61%; Chinese 18%. *Hung* (33), *Thanh* (32), *Dung* (23), *Tuan* (21), *Minh* (17), *Hoang* (16), *Hai* (15), *Tien* (15), *Long* (14), *Cuong* (13),
Hien (13), *Tam* (13), *Duc* (12), *Nam* (11), *Manh* (3), *Uyen* (3), *Phong* (2), *Sinh* (2), *Thai* (2), *Thein* (2), *Tuong* (2), *Cho, Chung, Tay*; *Hong* (7), *Chi* (3), *Dong* (3), *Lai* (3), *Tang* (3), *Chan* (2), *Hang* (2), *Ho* (2), *Man* (2), *Sang* (2), *Sen* (2), *Sung* (2).

Dini (232) Italian: patronymic or plural form of DINO.

GIVEN NAMES Italian 13%. *Angelo* (3), *Gino* (2), *Aldo, Amerigo, Carlo, Dante, Dino, Italo, Luca, Silvio*.

Di Nicola (556) Italian: patronymic, found chiefly in Naples, from the personal name *Nicola*, Italian equivalent of NICHOLAS.

GIVEN NAMES Italian 15%. *Pietro* (3), *Rocco* (3), *Antonio* (2), *Gino* (2), *Nicola* (2), *Sal* (2), *Aldo, Amerigo, Angelo, Camillo, Carlo, Carmine*.

Di Nino (161) Italian: patronymic from the personal name *Nino*, a short form of various pet names formed with the hypocoristic suffix *-ino* following the final consonant *-n*, as for example *Giovanino* (from GIOVANNI) or *Antonino* (from ANTONIO).

GIVEN NAMES Italian 24%. *Quintino* (2), *Alessandro, Biagio, Dino, Fiore, Guido, Luciano, Pierino, Salvatore, Settimio*.

Di Nitto (119) Italian: patronymic from a much reduced form of the personal name BENEDETTO.

GIVEN NAMES Italian 29%. *Cosmo* (4), *Angelo* (2), *Carmine, Domenic, Eliseo, Salvatore, Santina, Vincenzo*.

Dinius (233) Lithuanian: from the North German personal nmae *Dinies*, a reduced and altered form of *Antonius* (see ANTHONY).

Diniz (130) Portuguese: patronymic from the personal name *Dinis*, a vernacular form of *Dionysius* (see DENNIS).

GIVEN NAMES Spanish 35%; Portuguese 20%. *Jose* (4), *Manuel* (4), *Augusto* (2), *Celso* (2), *Francisco* (2), *Luis* (2), *Ricardo* (2), *Rogerio* (2), *Alvaro, Anselmo, Antero, Carlos*; *Joao, Marcio*; *Antonio* (3), *Gilda, Marco, Paolo*.

Dinkel (969) South German: metonymic occupational name for a grain farmer, from Middle High German *dinkel* 'spelt', 'wheat'.

Dinkelman (109) German (**Dinkelmann**): occupational name for a grain producer or dealer, from Middle High German *dinkel* 'spelt', 'wheat' + *man* 'man'.

GIVEN NAME German 9%. *Otto*.

Dinkin (111) **1.** Jewish (eastern Ashkenazic): metronymic from the Yiddish female name *dinke*, a pet form of biblical Dinah. **2.** Irish: shortened Anglicized form of Gaelic **Ó Duinnchinn** (see DUNCAN 2).

GIVEN NAMES Jewish 5%. *Isador, Sol*.

Dinkins (1564) Probably a variant (with English possessive *-s*) of Irish DINKIN.

Dinkle (117) Americanized spelling of German DINKEL.

Dinn (131) **1.** English: from a short form of the personal name *Dinis*, a variant of DENNIS. **2.** Vietnamese: unexplained.
GIVEN NAMES Vietnamese 6%. *Dinh, Hoa, Trang.*

Dinneen (436) Irish: variant spelling of DINEEN.

Dinner (109) English (Devon and Cornwall): perhaps a variant of DENNER.

Dinning (277) Northeastern English: variant of DENNING or Irish DINEEN.

D'Innocenzo (129) Italian: patronymic from the personal name *Innocenzo*, from Late Latin *Innocentius* (see INNOCENTI).
GIVEN NAMES Italian 11%. *Antonio, Dino, Nunzio, Pasquale.*

Dino (216) Italian (Sicily): from the personal name *Dino*, a short form of various pet names formed with the hypocoristic suffix *-ino* following the final consonant *-d*, such as *Bernardino* (from BERNARDO), *Gherardino* (from GHERARDI), *Riccardino* (from RICCARDO).
GIVEN NAMES Spanish 12%; Italian 6%. *Mario* (2), *Aida, Asuncion, Baldo, Felicitas, Leticia, Ramon, Reynaldo, Roberto, Salvadore, Valeria, Vincente*; *Dante, Romeo.*

Di Noia (106) Italian: variant of DE NOIA.
GIVEN NAMES Italian 22%. *Angelo, Cosmo, Girolamo, Pasquale, Rocco.*

Di Nolfo (112) Italian (also **Dinolfo**): patronymic from the personal name *Nolfo*, a short form of the Germanic personal names *Adinolfo* (see ADINOLFI), or *Arnolfo* (see NOLF).
GIVEN NAMES Italian 19%. *Aldo* (2), *Angelo* (2), *Sal* (2), *Baldassare, Pasquale, Salvatore.*

Di Noto (172) Italian (Sicily): habitational name for someone from Noto, a place near Syracuse.
GIVEN NAMES Italian 23%. *Salvatore* (4), *Biagio, Gabriele, Giacomo, Maurizio, Pietro, Salvator, Santo, Vincenzo.*

Di Novo (202) Italian: patronymic from a personal name from *n(u)ovo* 'new'.
GIVEN NAMES Italian 10%. *Salvatore* (3), *Carlo, Santo.*

Dinsdale (272) English: habitational name from a settlement on both sides of the Tees river, so partly in County Durham and partly in North Yorkshire. The place is named in Old English as *Dīctūneshalh* 'nook, recess (Old English *halh*) belonging to DEIGHTON'.

Dinse (175) North German: from a medieval personal name, a vernacular form of Latin *Dionysius* (see DENNIS).
GIVEN NAMES German 10%. *Egon, Erwin, Friedrich, Hans, Hartmut.*

Dinsmoor (122) Variant spelling of DINSMORE.

Dinsmore (2159) Northern Irish (mainly Counties Derry and Donegal): variant of the Scottish habitational name DUNSMORE.

D'Intino (120) Italian: unexplained.

GIVEN NAMES Italian 25%. *Carmine* (2), *Aldo, Angelo, Domenic, Donato, Fiore, Gianni, Guido, Italo, Maddalena.*

Di Nucci (130) Italian: patronymic from a reduced form of various personal names with the diminutive ending *-nucci(o)*, for example *Antonuccio, Benuccio, Stefanuccio.*
GIVEN NAMES Italian 16%. *Gino* (2), *Guido* (2), *Massimo* (2), *Donato, Ezio, Rinaldo.*

Di Nunzio (325) Italian: patronymic from the personal name *Nunzio*, a reduced masculine form of the Marian name ANNUNZIATA.
GIVEN NAMES Italian 17%. *Angelo* (3), *Gildo* (2), *Antonio, Camillo, Domenic, Donato, Gianluca, Gino, Giovanni, Guido, Matteo, Nicola.*

Di Nuzzo (117) Italian: patronymic from a short form of various pet names with the ending *-nuzzo*, such as *Antonuzzo, Giovannuzzo, Stefanuzzo.*
GIVEN NAMES Italian 24%. *Alfonso, Antonio, Domenico, Raffaele, Sabatino, Salvator, Salvatore.*

Dinwiddie (948) Scottish: habitational name for someone from Dinwoodie near Dumfries. The place name is of uncertain derivation; it is first recorded in 1296 in the form *Dinwithie, Dunwythye* (then later 1482 *Donwethy*, 1503 *Dunwedy*, 1578 *Dumwiddie*) and is probably named with British words that are ancestors of Welsh *din* 'forest' + *gwydd* 'shrubs', 'bushes'.
FOREBEARS Robert Dinwiddie, born in Glasgow in 1693, was lieutenant governor of VA from 1751 to 1758.

Dinwoodie (114) Scottish: variant of DINWIDDIE.

Diodati (155) Italian: patronymic or plural form of DIODATO.
GIVEN NAMES Italian 22%. *Angelo* (2), *Domenic* (2), *Aldo, Armando, Bernardino, Carmine, Egidio, Emidio, Flavio, Francesca, Gaetano, Giacomo, Marcello, Mario, Orlando.*

Diodato (158) Italian: from a medieval personal name *Diodato, Deodato*, meaning 'God-given', from Latin *deus* 'god' + *donatus* 'given'. This was sometimes used as a name for a foundling.
GIVEN NAMES Italian 16%. *Angelo* (2), *Vito* (2), *Dino, Salvatore.*

Dioguardi (212) Italian: from a medieval personal name *Dioguardi* or *Diotiguardi*, meaning 'God protect (you)'.
GIVEN NAMES Italian 19%. *Nunzio* (2), *Alfonse, Claudio, Guido, Pietro, Raffaele, Vincenzo.*

Dion (3168) French: habitational name from any of various places called Dion(s) and Dionne, all apparently derived from a Gaulish element *divon-* '(sacred) spring'. Compare DEE 3.
FOREBEARS The earliest Dion on record in North America, from La Rochelle, France, was married in Quebec city in 1672. The

name is sometimes rendered in English as YOUNG.
GIVEN NAMES French 12%. *Normand* (12), *Marcel* (11), *Lucien* (10), *Armand* (9), *Camille* (5), *Emile* (5), *Andre* (4), *Yvon* (4), *Aime* (3), *Pierre* (3), *Cecile* (2), *Gilles* (2).

Dionisio (339) Italian and Portuguese (**Dionísio**): from the personal name *Dionisio*, from Latin *Dionysius* (see DENNIS 1.)
GIVEN NAMES Spanish 15%; Italian 14%. *Jose* (4), *Adolfo* (2), *Carlos* (2), *Adalia, Adelino, Cesar, Efrain, Elida, Emilio, Ernesto, Faustino, Francisco*; *Antonio* (4), *Rocco* (4), *Vito* (4), *Elio, Francesca, Luco, Salvatore.*

Dionne (2586) French: variant spelling of DION.
GIVEN NAMES French 14%. *Marcel* (12), *Andre* (8), *Armand* (7), *Fernand* (6), *Lucien* (5), *Pierre* (5), *Emile* (4), *Alcide* (3), *Jacques* (3), *Michel* (3), *Normand* (3), *Adelard* (2).

Diop (166) West African: probably a variant of the Muslim name DIAB.
GIVEN NAMES African 50%; Muslim 23%; French 5%. *Mamadou* (8), *Cheikh* (6), *Serigne* (4), *Oumar* (3), *Aliou* (2), *Awa* (2), *Babacar* (2), *Idrissa* (2), *Modou* (2), *Aboubacar, Ahmadou, Amadou*; *Abdoulaye* (4), *Moustapha* (3), *Abdou* (2), *Ibrahima* (2), *Moussa* (2), *Touba* (2), *Ahmed, Daouda, Khadim, Lamine, Mohammed, Mostapha*; *Francois, Marceline, Pierre.*

Diorio (1305) Southern Italian: **1.** (**D'Iorio**): patronymic from the personal name *Iorio*, a variant of GIORGIO. **2.** (**Di Orio**): from *orio*, 'barley'; a patronymic from a metonymic occupational name for a grower or seller of barley, or a topographic name for someone who lived where barley grew.
GIVEN NAMES Italian 12%. *Carmine* (4), *Donato* (3), *Amelio* (2), *Angelo* (2), *Reno* (2), *Sal* (2), *Salvatore* (2), *Aldo, Alessio, Alfonse, Amadeo, Antonio.*

Diotte (117) Possibly a respelling of French **Diot**, which may be from an reduced form of the personal name *Didiot*, a pet form of DIDIER.
GIVEN NAMES French 7%. *Lucien, Philippe.*

Di Pace (130) Italian: patronymic from the personal name PACE.
GIVEN NAMES Italian 18%. *Ugo* (2), *Angelo, Gino, Lorenzo, Nicola, Pierina, Sal.*

Di Palma (583) Italian: **1.** habitational name for someone from any of various places in Italy and Sardinia named Palma. **2.** patronymic from the medieval personal name *Palma*, from *palma* 'palm', as a symbol of Christian faith.
GIVEN NAMES Italian 17%. *Antonio* (4), *Angelo* (3), *Salvatore* (3), *Dino* (2), *Anello, Aniello, Dante, Donato, Enzo, Federico, Fiorino, Gennaro.*

Di Palo (103) Italian: habitational name for someone from any of various places named Palo.
GIVEN NAMES Italian 14%. *Vito* (2), *Luca.*

Di Paola (644) Italian: **1.** habitational name for someone from the city of Paola in Cosenza province, Calabria. **2.** metronymic from the personal name *Paola*, feminine form of PAOLO.
GIVEN NAMES Italian 24%. *Rocco* (7), *Salvatore* (7), *Angelo* (6), *Vito* (6), *Antonio* (3), *Giuseppe* (3), *Pasquale* (3), *Giovanni* (2), *Pietro* (2), *Alfio, Amato, Carmel*.

Di Paolo (909) Italian: patronymic from the personal name *Paolo*, from Latin *Paulus* (see PAUL).
GIVEN NAMES Italian 21%. *Angelo* (5), *Antonio* (4), *Dino* (3), *Rocco* (3), *Carmine* (2), *Domenic* (2), *Gino* (2), *Luciano* (2), *Nicola* (2), *Salvatore* (2), *Umberto* (2).

Di Pasqua (104) Italian: patronymic from the personal name PASQUA.
GIVEN NAMES Italian 26%. *Aldo* (2), *Angelo, Carlo, Rino, Sylvio*.

Di Pasquale (1088) Italian: patronymic from the personal name *Pasquale* (see PASCAL).
GIVEN NAMES Italian 19%. *Angelo* (6), *Salvatore* (5), *Sal* (4), *Gaetano* (3), *Vito* (3), *Concetta* (2), *Orazio* (2), *Rocco* (2), *Antonio, Attilio, Benedetto, Biagio*.

Di Perna (217) Southern Italian: metronymic from the female personal name *Perna*, meaning 'pearl' (from Latin *perna* 'sea mussel').
GIVEN NAMES Italian 20%. *Antonio* (2), *Matteo* (2), *Angelo, Carlo, Cosmo, Dino, Enrico, Giovanni, Marcello, Nunzio, Pasquale, Rocco*.

Di Piazza (273) Italian: topographic name for someone who lived in the main square of a town, or a habitational name from a place named Piazza or Piazze, from *piazza* 'square'.
GIVEN NAMES Italian 21%. *Angelo* (4), *Giuseppe* (2), *Mario* (2), *Bernardo, Calogero, Enza, Girolamo, Guiseppe, Mariano, Rosario, Salvatore, Santo, Vito*.

Di Piero (153) Italian: patronymic from the personal name *Piero* (see PIERI).
GIVEN NAMES Italian 19%. *Domenic* (3), *Amedeo, Amerigo, Angelo, Dante, Domenico, Duilio, Livio, Nino*.

Di Pierro (262) Italian: patronymic from the personal name *Pierro*, a dialect variant of *Pietro* (see PETER). Compare French PIERRE.
GIVEN NAMES Italian 31%. *Angelo* (7), *Rocco* (5), *Cosmo* (3), *Domenic* (3), *Donato* (2), *Giovanni* (2), *Carlo, Carmine, Ciriaco, Constantino, Erminio, Gino*.

Di Pietrantonio (152) Italian: patronymic from the personal name *Pietrantonio*, a compound of PIETRO + ANTONIO.
GIVEN NAMES Italian 41%. *Antonio* (3), *Mario* (3), *Cosmo* (2), *Donato* (2), *Agostino, Aldo, Angelo, Antonello, Camillo, Constantino, Costantino, Dario, Franco, Germano, Ubaldo*.

Di Pietro (2158) Italian: patronymic from the personal name PIETRO (see PETER).

GIVEN NAMES Italian 18%. *Angelo* (15), *Salvatore* (11), *Rocco* (9), *Antonio* (7), *Vito* (6), *Gaetano* (5), *Gino* (4), *Carmine* (3), *Pina* (3), *Sal* (3), *Santo* (3), *Aldo* (2).

Di Pilato (100) Southern Italian: **1.** patronymic from the Sicilian nickname *pilatu* 'balding', 'completely bald'. **2.** habitational name from a minor place in Sicily named Pilatu, from Latin *pratum* 'meadow'.
GIVEN NAMES Italian 27%. *Angelo* (2), *Sergio* (2), *Alessandro, Domenic, Nino*.

Di Pinto (201) Italian: patronymic from the nickname *Pinto*, meaning 'painted', 'multicolored', 'speckled', 'flecked', also 'pockmarked'.
GIVEN NAMES Italian 26%. *Vito* (6), *Angelo* (2), *Domenico* (2), *Pasquale* (2), *Salvatore* (2), *Alessandro, Cosmo, Egidio, Mauro, Natale, Rosaria, Santo*.

Di Pippo (127) Italian: patronymic from a pet form of the personal name *Filippo*, from Greek *Philippos* (see PHILIP).
GIVEN NAMES Italian 22%. *Carmine* (4), *Angelo* (2), *Antonio, Carlo, Carmela, Guido*.

Di Pirro (146) Italian: patronymic from the personal name *Pirro*, from Greek *Pyrrhos*, meaning 'red (haired)', or from a local variant of the personal name *Pierro* (see PETER).
GIVEN NAMES Italian 4%. *Angelo, Dante, Romeo*.

Di Placido (116) Italian: patronymic from the personal name *Placido*, from a vocabulary word meaning 'calm', 'peaceable' (Latin *placidus*).
GIVEN NAMES Italian 30%. *Angelo* (2), *Cesidio* (2), *Nicola* (2), *Pietro* (2), *Dino, Domenic, Emidio, Fiore, Nino, Pasquale, Vito*.

Dippel (624) South German: from the personal name *Dippold*, a dialect form of *Dietbald* (see THEOBALD).

Dipple (139) **1.** Scottish: habitational name from a former parish in Morayshire. **2.** English: from the medieval personal name *Tebald, Tibalt* (see THEOBALD). **3.** possibly also an altered spelling of the South German cognate DIPPEL.
FOREBEARS John Scott (d. 1738) of Dipple emigrated to the American colonies, became minister of Overwharton parish, Stafford County, VA, and called his estate there Dipple.

Dippold (334) German: from a dialect form of the personal name *Dietbald* (see THEOBALD).

D'Ippolito (269) Southern Italian: patronymic from the personal name IPPOLITO.
GIVEN NAMES Italian 23%. *Donato* (2), *Rocco* (2), *Amerigo, Angelo, Carlo, Cesare, Costantino, Domenico, Eligio, Fiore, Gasper, Geno*.

Di Prima (336) Italian: metronymic from the female personal name *Prima*, meaning 'first'.

GIVEN NAMES Italian 13%. *Romeo* (2), *Sal* (2), *Salvatore* (2), *Biagio, Carlo, Carmine, Domenic, Francesco, Gino, Giovanna, Nino, Santo*.

Dirck (107) Dutch and North German: from the personal name *Dirck*, a reduced form of *Diederik* (see DEDERICK).

Dircks (273) Dutch and North German: variant spelling of DIERCKS.

Di Re (218) Italian: literally 'of or belonging to the king' (see RE), hence a name denoting a member of a royal entourage, or the son of someone bearing the nickname 'King'.
GIVEN NAMES Italian 18%. *Guido* (2), *Sal* (2), *Vittorio* (2), *Aldo, Alessandro, Angelo, Carmela, Carmine, Edmondo, Enzo, Gennaro, Libero*.

Director (128) Jewish (eastern Ashkenazic): occupational name from Polish *dyrektor* 'private teacher'.
GIVEN NAMES Jewish 10%. *Hyman, Isadore, Isidor, Meyer*.

Di Renzo (402) Italian: patronymic from a short form of the personal name *Lorenzo*, from Latin *Laurentius* (see LAWRENCE).
GIVEN NAMES Italian 20%. *Donato* (3), *Luigi* (3), *Antonio* (2), *Carmine* (2), *Domenic* (2), *Rocco* (2), *Bartolomeo, Corradino, Domenico, Gaetano, Marco, Mauro*.

Dirickson (187) Dutch: patronymic from the personal name DERRICK. Compare DERICKSON.

Di Rico (145) Variant of Italian *De Rico* (see DERICO).
GIVEN NAMES Italian 30%. *Rocco* (6), *Antonio* (5), *Alfonso* (2), *Camillo, Domenico, Eraldo, Filippo, Giuseppe, Luciano, Pasquale*.

Di Rienzo (503) Italian: patronymic from *Rienzo*, an old dialect variant of *Renzo*, a short form of *Lorenzo*, from Latin *Laurentius* (see LAWRENCE).
GIVEN NAMES Italian 21%. *Mario* (6), *Orlando* (4), *Angelo* (3), *Antonio* (2), *Carlo* (2), *Carmela* (2), *Domenic* (2), *Luigi* (2), *Annamarie, Berardino, Carmelina, Carmine, Giovanni, Guido, Emilio, Rolando*.

Dirk (208) Dutch and North German: from a reduced form of the personal name *Diederik* (see DEDERICK and DIETRICH).

Dirkes (232) Dutch: variant of DIRKS.

Dirks (1708) Dutch and North German: patronymic from the personal name DIRK.

Dirkse (133) Dutch and North German: variant of DIRKSEN.

Dirksen (643) Dutch and North German: patronymic from the personal name DIRK.
GIVEN NAMES German 4%. *Hans* (3), *Kurt* (2), *Erwin, Fritz, Otto, Volkmar, Willi, Wolfgang*.

Dirlam (138) German (also **Dirlamm**): habitational name from a place called Dirlammen near Lauterbach in Hesse.

Dirnberger (127) German (Austria): habitational name for someone from Dirnberg in Upper Austria.
GIVEN NAMES German 4%. *Erna, Helmut.*

Di Rocco (426) Italian: patronymic from the personal name ROCCO.
GIVEN NAMES Italian 24%. *Antonio* (4), *Mario* (4), *Orazio* (2), *Rocco* (2), *Alessandro, Alfonso, Amedeo, Angelo, Arcangelo, Cesare, Demetrio, Domenic, Domenico, Donato.*

Di Roma (105) Italian: habitational name for someone from Rome (Italian *Roma*).
GIVEN NAMES Italian 24%. *Dante* (4), *Angelo* (2), *Antonio* (2), *Agostino, Orlando.*

Di Rosa (166) Italian: variant of DE ROSA.
GIVEN NAMES Italian 26%. *Sal* (3), *Angelo* (2), *Domenic* (2), *Francesca* (2), *Antonio, Benito, Carmela, Mario, Paolo, Salvatore, Santino.*

Dirr (199) South German: variant of **Dürr** (see DURR).

Di Russo (283) Italian: patronymic from the nickname *Russo*, a southern variant of ROSSO, meaning 'red(-headed)'.
GIVEN NAMES Italian 21%. *Salvatore* (5), *Angelo* (3), *Antonio* (3), *Cosmo* (2), *Eliseo* (2), *Amedeo, Dante, Fausto, Guglielmo, Luigi, Nichola, Pasquale.*

Di Sabatino (230) Italian: patronymic from the personal name SABATINO.
GIVEN NAMES Italian 9%. *Elio, Mauro, Natale, Raffaela, Sabatino, Umberto.*

Di Sabato (154) Italian: patronymic from the nickname or personal name SABATO.
GIVEN NAMES Italian 16%. *Elvio* (2), *Aniello, Augostino, Emidio, Giuseppe, Lorenzo, Nunzio, Romeo, Silvio, Vito.*

Di Salvatore (109) Italian: patronymic from the personal name SALVATORE.
GIVEN NAMES Italian 18%. *Angelo* (3), *Carmela, Enzo, Rocco, Umberto, Valentino.*

Di Salvo (1145) Italian: patronymic from the personal name SALVO.
GIVEN NAMES Italian 17%. *Salvatore* (8), *Angelo* (7), *Mario* (7), *Sal* (5), *Antonio* (4), *Santo* (4), *Carlo* (2), *Carmine* (2), *Pasquale* (2), *Antonella, Carmel, Carmelo, Rosario.*

Di Sandro (118) Italian: patronymic from the personal name *Sandro*, a short form of ALESSANDRO or *Lissandro*, a reduced variant of the same name.
GIVEN NAMES Italian 34%. *Domenic* (5), *Antonio* (2), *Silvio* (2), *Angelo, Antonino, Cosmo, Enrico, Gabriella, Nicola, Severino.*

Di Sano (172) Italian: **1.** patronymic from the personal name *Sano* or a nickname from *sano* 'healthy'. **2.** patronymic from a short form of a habitational or ethnic name ending with *-sano*, as for example FORMISANO or PALMISANO.
GIVEN NAMES Italian 14%. *Angelo, Antonio, Carmine, Concetta, Gennaro, Mafalda, Matteo, Nicola.*

Di Santi (187) Italian: **1.** patronymic from the personal name SANTI. **2.** variant of DI SANTO.
GIVEN NAMES Italian 20%. *Angelo* (4), *Carlo, Ercole, Francesca, Gabriella, Marino, Salvatore, Vincenzo, Vito.*

Di Santis (191) Italian: variant of DE SANTIS.
GIVEN NAMES Italian 6%; French 5%. *Antonio, Italo, Valentino; Armand* (3).

Di Santo (915) Italian: patronymic from the personal name SANTO, meaning 'holy'.
GIVEN NAMES Italian 19%. *Salvatore* (7), *Angelo* (4), *Carmine* (4), *Vincenzo* (4), *Antonio* (3), *Donato* (3), *Domenic* (2), *Francesco* (2), *Geno* (2), *Luigi* (2), *Marco* (2), *Onorato* (2).

Di Sanza (105) Italian: patronymic from the Old Tuscan name *Sanza*, a short form of a compound personal name formed with this element, such as *Sanzanome*, literally 'without name', or a metronymic from *Sanza*, a personal name of Germanic origin, feminine form of SANZO.
GIVEN NAMES Italian 12%. *Salvatore* (2), *Nunzio, Vincenzo.*

Di Sarro (105) Italian: patronymic from the personal name SARRO.
GIVEN NAMES Italian 9%. *Antonio, Pietro.*

Disbennett (108) Origin unidentified.

Disbro (170) Most probably a respelling of English DISBROW.

Disbrow (718) English: variant of **Disborough**, a habitational name from places in Buckinghamshire and Northamptonshire called Desborough. The first is named from Old English *dwostle* 'pennyroyal' + *beorg* 'hill'; the second from the Old English personal name *Dēor* + *burh* 'fortress', 'stronghold'.

Di Scala (127) Variant of Italian **De Scala**, a habitational name for someone from any of numerous minor places named or named with SCALA 'steps', 'ladder', 'wharf'.
GIVEN NAMES Italian 14%. *Emidio, Luigi, Nicola, Paolo.*

Di Scenza (178) Italian: metronymic from the personal name *Scenza*, an reduced form of *Ascenza*, a devotional name referring to the Ascension.
GIVEN NAMES Italian 13%. *Biagio* (2), *Angelo, Antonio, Carmine, Gasper, Pasquale.*

Disch (508) German: from the Germanic personal name *Teuzo* (see DIETZ).

Discher (297) Northern and eastern German: occupational name for a carpenter or joiner, Middle Low German *discher*, from *disch* 'table'. Compare TISCHLER.

Dischinger (164) German: habitational name for someone from Dischingen near Neresheim or Oberdischingen near Ehingen in Württemberg.
GIVEN NAMES German 5%. *Christoph, Otto.*

Dischler (153) Northern and eastern German: variant of DISCHER.
GIVEN NAMES German 4%. *Frieda, Gerhard.*

Di Sciullo (154) Italian: patronymic from the personal name SCIULLO, variant of SULLO.
GIVEN NAMES Italian 29%. *Gino* (3), *Guido* (3), *Mario* (2), *Mariano* (2), *Camillo, Carmela, Domenic, Enrico, Francesco, Maurizio, Nicola, Oreste, Remo.*

Dise (211) Origin unidentified. **1.** Probably a variant of English DICE. **2.** It could be an Americanized spelling of German DEIS.

Disharoon (289) Americanized form of an unidentified French name, possibly **de Charente**. This name was established in MD by the end of the 17th century.

Dishaw (290) See DESHAW.

Disher (548) **1.** Americanized spelling of German DISCHER 'joiner'. **2.** English: occupational name for a maker or seller of dishes, from an agent derivative of Old English *disc* 'dish'. **3.** Possibly a respelling of any of the names mentioned at DESHAW.

Dishman (1613) Americanized form of German **Dischmann** or **Tischmann**, occupational name for a joiner, from Middle Low German *disch* 'table' + *man* 'man'.

Dishmon (149) Variant of German **Dischmann** (see DISHMAN).

Dishner (283) Americanized spelling of German **Dischner**, a variant of DISCHLER, or perhaps of the cognate **Tischner**.

Dishon (351) Respelling of French DUCHAMP or DESCHAMPS.

Dishong (358) Respelling of French DUCHAMP or DESCHAMPS.

Dishongh (109) Respelling under Dutch influence of French DUCHAMP or DESCHAMPS.

Di Silvestro (177) Italian: patronymic from the personal name SILVESTRO (see SYLVESTER).
GIVEN NAMES Italian 22%. *Sal* (3), *Santo* (2), *Angelo, Antonio, Armando, Carlo, Mario, Orlando, Pasquale, Rocco, Tino, Vittorio.*

Di Simone (145) Italian: variant of DE SIMONE.
GIVEN NAMES Italian 18%. *Carmela* (2), *Angelo, Giovanni, Lorenzo, Salvatore, Ugo, Vito.*

Disinger (108) Americanized spelling of German **Deisinger**, a habitational name for someone from Deising in Bavaria.

Diskin (459) Irish (Connacht): reduced Anglicized form of Gaelic **Ó Díscín** 'descendant of *Díscín*', which may be derived from *díosc* 'barren'. The place name Ballyeeskeen, now Ballydiscin, in County Sligo, is derived from the surname.

Disla (129) Spanish (Dominican Republic): variant of **Isla**, a habitational name for someone from a place named Isla or La Isla, from Spanish *isla* 'island', or a topographic name with the same meaning.
GIVEN NAMES Spanish 48%. *Juan* (5), *Ana* (4), *Jose* (3), *Luis* (2), *Marina* (2), *Tomas* (2), *Aida, Altagracia, Andres, Dulce, Ediberto, Epifanio, Felipe.*

Disler (129) Swiss German: probably a variant of **Distler** (see DIESTLER 2).
GIVEN NAMES German 6%. *Kurt, Otto.*

Dismang (99) Origin unidentified. Perhaps an altered form of DISHMAN, from German **Tischmann** 'joiner'.

Dismore (161) English: unexplained. It is said to be from Old French *dix marcs* 'ten marks', perhaps denoting a valuation, but this is doubtful.

Dismuke (655) Variant of DISMUKES.

Dismukes (551) Anglicized form of French **Des Meaux** (see MEAUX). At least some of the bearers are of Huguenot origin, and came to North America via England when Protestants in France were persecuted following the revocation of the Edict of Nantes in 1685. The name is also recorded in Scotland.

Disney (1319) English (of Norman origin): habitational name, with the preposition *d(e)*, for someone from Isigny in Calvados, France, named from the Romano-Gallic personal name *Isinius* (a Latinized form of Gaulish *Isina*) + the locative suffix *-acum*.

Dison (400) English: variant spelling of DYSON.

Disotell (112) Americanized spelling of French DESAUTELS.
GIVEN NAMES French 7%. *Blanchard* (2), *Antoine.*

Dispenza (261) Italian: metonymic occupational name from *dispensa* in the sense 'pantry', 'storeroom'.
GIVEN NAMES Italian 12%. *Angelo, Giuseppe, Sal, Salvatore, Santi, Veto.*

Di Spirito (136) Italian: patronymic from the personal name SPIRITO.
GIVEN NAMES Italian 21%. *Angelo* (2), *Carmine* (2), *Antimo, Antonio, Arcangelo, Constantino, Francesco, Luigi, Rocco.*

Disque (197) German (Palatinate): unexplained.

Disrud (104) Origin unidentified.
GIVEN NAME German 4%. *Otto.*

Diss (182) **1.** English: habitational name from Diss in Suffolk, which gets its name from a Norman pronunciation of Middle English *diche*, Old English *dīc* 'ditch', 'dike' (see DYKE). **2.** German: habitational name from Dissen near the Teutoburg forest.

Dissinger (288) German: possibly a derivative of *Diesing*, a variant of the personal name *Matthias* (see MATTHEW), or alternatively an altered form of **Di(e)zinger**, a habitational name for someone from Ditzingen in Württemberg.

Distad (155) Norwegian: habitational name from a farmstead named Distad, from the Old Norse female personal name *Dís* + *stad* (from Old Norse *staðr* 'farmstead', 'dwelling').

Di Stasi (148) Italian: variant of DI STASIO.
GIVEN NAMES Italian 15%. *Domenic* (2), *Angelo, Libero, Salvatore.*

Di Stasio (377) Italian: patronymic from a short form of the personal name ANASTASIO.
GIVEN NAMES Italian 18%. *Pasquale* (3), *Gennaro* (2), *Rocco* (2), *Sal* (2), *Salvatore* (2), *Antonio, Carlo, Carmelo, Dante, Donato, Giuseppe, Liberato.*

Di Stefano (2250) Italian: patronymic from the personal name *Stefano*, from Greek *Stephanos* (see STEVEN).
GIVEN NAMES Italian 17%. *Salvatore* (18), *Angelo* (13), *Sal* (8), *Domenic* (6), *Antonio* (5), *Vito* (5), *Gino* (4), *Giuseppe* (4), *Pasquale* (4), *Rocco* (4) (3), *Luigi* (3).

Distel (339) **1.** German, North German, and Dutch: topographic name for someone who lived by a patch of ground overgrown with thistles, or perhaps a nickname for a 'prickly' person, from Middle High German, Middle Low German, Middle Dutch *distel* 'thistle'. **2.** Jewish (Ashkenazic): probably in most cases an unflattering name bestowed on Jews by non-Jewish government officials in 18th- and 19th-century central Europe.

Distler (515) German: topographic name for someone who lived in a place where thistles grew, from German *Distel* 'thistle' (see DISTEL) + *-er*, suffix denoting an inhabitant.

Di Taranto (118) Italian: habitational name for someone from the city of Taranto, the provincial capital of Apulia. Compare TARANTINO.
GIVEN NAMES Italian 31%. *Rocco* (5), *Francesco* (2), *Angelo, Carmelina, Nino, Silvio.*

Ditch (376) **1.** English: variant of DYKE. **2.** Jewish (Ashkenazic): variant of DEUTSCH.

Ditman (106) Americanized spelling of German DITTMANN.

Ditmars (249) German: patronymic from DITTMAR.

Ditmer (229) Americanized spelling of DITTMAR.

Ditmore (326) Americanized spelling of German DITTMAR or one of its many variants.

Dito (121) Italian: possibly a nickname for someone with a missing, maimed, or deformed finger or fingers, from *dito* 'finger'.
GIVEN NAMES Italian 13%. *Carmine, Gino, Guido, Salvatore, Vicenzo.*

Di Tomaso (117) Italian: variant spelling of DI TOMMASO.
GIVEN NAMES Italian 18%. *Angelo, Domenic, Enzo, Pasquale, Saverio.*

Di Tomasso (143) Variant spelling of Italian DI TOMMASO.
GIVEN NAMES Italian 27%. *Amedeo, Antonio, Carlo, Dino, Elio, Emelio, Francesca, Guido, Lorenzo, Pasquale, Pietro, Remo.*

Di Tommaso (296) Italian: patronymic from the personal name *Tommaso*, Italian equivalent of THOMAS.
GIVEN NAMES Italian 28%; French 4%. *Vito* (5), *Angelo* (4), *Antonio* (4), *Salvatore* (2), *Dante, Francesco, Guerino, Lucio, Luigi, Mariano, Mario, Nino, Pietro, Roberto, Saverio; Dominique, Gabrielle, Marcel.*

Di Toro (125) Italian: patronymic from the personal name *Toro*, probably an reduced form of the personal name *Ristoro*, meaning 'recompense', a name bestowed on a son whose birth was seen as compensation for the loss of an earlier son.
GIVEN NAMES Italian 15%. *Angelo, Carlo, Domenico, Egidio, Lucio, Nicola, Salvatore.*

Ditsch (110) German: probably a variant or altered spelling of **Dietsch** or **Titsch**, variants of DIETZ.
GIVEN NAMES German 7%. *Fritz, Hans.*

Ditsworth (116) English: unexplained. It could be a habitational name from Ditsworthy in Sheepstor, Devon (which is perhaps named from a Middle English personal name *Durke* 'the dark one' + Middle English *worth(y)* 'enclosure') or from some other, unidentified place. The surname is not found in current English records.

Ditta (267) Italian: from a short form of the personal name *Benedetta*, feminine form of BENEDETTO.
GIVEN NAMES Italian 8%. *Carlo, Ciro, Elvio, Emilio, Lucrecia, Rosario, Salvatore.*

Dittberner (200) German: **1.** from the Germanic personal name *Thiatbarn*, formed with *theud, diot* 'people', 'race'. **2.** unrounded form of **Dittbörner**, a habitational name for someone from a place named Dittborn.

Dittemore (180) Perhaps an altered spelling of German **Dietmar**, a variant of DITTMAR.

Dittenber (107) Altered form of German DITTBERNER.

Ditter (327) German: variant of DIETER.

Dittman (1065) Americanized spelling of German DITTMANN.

Dittmann (300) German: variant of DITTMAR. In eastern Germany this form has been used for Dittmar since the 15th century.
GIVEN NAMES German 10%. *Manfred* (3), *Klaus* (2), *Fritz, Jurgen, Otto, Sieglinde, Ulrich.*

Dittmar (1002) North German: from a personal name composed of the elements *theud* 'people', 'race' (Old High German *diot, deot*) + *māri, mēri,* 'famous'.
GIVEN NAMES German 6%. *Hans* (4), *Kurt* (4), *Heinz* (3), *Klaus* (2), *Dieter, Ekkehard, Gerda, Gunter, Ulrich.*

Dittmer (1267) North German and Danish: variant of DITTMAR.

Ditto (887) **1.** Anglicized form of a French Huguenot name of unexplained etymology. The name was already in North America by 1700. **2.** Italian: from a short form of the personal name BENEDETTO.

Dittoe (104) Of French (Huguenot) origin: variant of DITTO 1.

Ditton (194) English: **1.** habitational name from any of the numerous places named Ditton, for example in Cheshire, Kent, Cambridgeshire, and Surrey, from Old English *dīc* 'ditch', 'dike' + *tūn* 'enclosure', 'settlement'. **2.** habitational name from Ditton Priors in Shropshire, recorded in Domesday Book as *Dodintone* 'settlement (Old English *tūn*) associated with a man called *Dod(d)a* or *Dud(d)a*'.

Dittrich (858) German: variant of DIETRICH. GIVEN NAMES German 6%. *Erwin* (2), *Florian* (2), *Hans* (2), *Otto* (2), *Alois*, *Arno*, *Bernd*, *Franz*, *Guenther*, *Helmuth*, *Horst*, *Kurt*.

Dittus (211) German: from a vernacular short form of the Latin personal name *Benedictus* (see BENNETT). GIVEN NAMES German 9%. *Gerhard* (2), *Fritz*, *Kurt*, *Otto*, *Reinhold*.

Ditty (392) Northern Irish: unexplained; perhaps from a Scottish pet form of the personal name *Dait* (a Scottish form of DAVID).

Di Tullio (453) Italian: patronymic from the personal name *Tullio*, from Latin *Tullius*, an ancient Roman personal name, borne by the orator Cicero. GIVEN NAMES Italian 19%. *Rocco* (4), *Guido* (3), *Aldo* (2), *Angelo* (2), *Donato* (2), *Ennio* (2), *Umberto* (2), *Antonio*, *Biagio*, *Cesare*, *Dante*, *Dino*.

Ditz (108) German: variant of DIETZ.

Ditzel (232) German: from a pet form of DIETZ. GIVEN NAME German 4%. *Kurt*.

Ditzler (592) Variant of German **Diezler**, a patronymic from a pet form of DIETZ.

Divan (120) **1.** Irish: variant of DEVINE. **2.** Indian and Pakistani: variant of DEWAN. GIVEN NAMES Indian 6%; German 4%. *Kishore* (2), *Deepak*; *Kurt*, *Otto*.

Divelbiss (279) One of several Americanized forms of German **Tüfelbeiss** or **Deubelbeiss** (see DEVILBISS).

Diveley (223) Variant of Irish **Divilly** (see DIVELY).

Dively (403) Variant of the Irish family name **Divilly**, a reduced Anglicized form of Gaelic **Ó Duibhghiolla**, from a personal name based on *dubh* 'black' + *giolla* 'lad'.

Diven (323) Irish: variant of DEVINE.

Divens (180) Possibly a variant of Irish DEVINE.

Diver (534) **1.** Irish (County Donegal): Anglicized form of Gaelic **Ó Duibhidhir** or sometimes of **Mac Duibhidhir** (see DWYER, also DYER). **2.** English: of uncertain derivation; possibly from *diver*, an agent derivative of Middle English *dive* 'to dip or plunge', but if so the application is obscure. It may be a nickname for someone compared to a diving bird. Compare DUCKER.

Divers (417) English: patronymic from DIVER.

Divin (125) **1.** Czech and Slovak (**Divín**): variant of **Diviš** (see DIVIS). **2.** Possibly a variant of French DEVIN.

Di Vincenzo (428) Italian: patronymic from the personal name *Vincenzo*, from Latin *Vincentius* (see VINCENT). GIVEN NAMES Italian 24%. *Mario* (5), *Angelo* (4), *Guido* (2), *Nino* (2), *Remo* (2), *Tito* (2), *Aldo*, *Alfonso*, *Alfredo*, *Antonio*, *Benito*, *Carlo*, *Carmelo*, *Carmine*, *Dante*, *Eduardo*, *Elvira*, *Gustavo*, *Olympio*, *Rodolfo*, *Sergio*.

Divine (1151) Irish, English and French: variant of DEVINE .

Diviney (178) **1.** Irish (County Mayo): reduced Anglicized form of Gaelic **Ó Duibheanaigh** (see DEVANEY). **2.** Americanized spelling of Hungarian **Divinyi**, or **Divényi** (see DEVENY). GIVEN NAME French 4%. *Michel*.

Divins (101) Scottish: probably a variant of Irish DIVEN, itself a variant of DEVINE.

Di Virgilio (264) Italian: patronymic from the personal name *Virgilio*, from Latin *Vergilius*, *Virgilius* (see VIRGIL). GIVEN NAMES Italian 30%. *Aldo* (3), *Domenic* (3), *Dante* (2), *Donato* (2), *Nicola* (2), *Salvatore* (2), *Alfio*, *Bartolomeo*, *Camillo*, *Carlo*, *Carmelina*, *Dino*.

Divis (320) Czech (**Diviš**): from the personal name *Diviš*, a vernacular form of Greek *Dionysios* (see DENNIS).

Di Vita (276) Italian: variant of DE VITA. GIVEN NAMES Italian 11%. *Angelo*, *Carlo*, *Fosco*, *Gaetano*, *Lido*, *Salvatore*, *Salvo*, *Vito*.

Di Vito (536) Italian: variant of DE VITO. GIVEN NAMES Italian 32%. *Mario* (6), *Antonio* (3), *Camillo* (2), *Domenic* (2), *Elio* (2), *Ettore* (2), *Ferdinando* (2), *Gino* (2), *Luigi* (2), *Pasqual* (2), *Salvatore* (2), *Amerigo*, *Angelo*, *Augusto*, *Aurelio*, *Emilio*, *Fernando*, *Lino*, *Magno*, *Renato*.

Di Vittorio (127) Italian: patronymic from the personal name VITTORIO. GIVEN NAMES Italian 24%. *Ciro* (3), *Giuseppe* (2), *Domenic*, *Gino*, *Rocco*, *Salvatore*, *Vito*.

Dix (3649) English: patronymic from the personal name DICK.

Dixey (135) English: variant spelling of DIXIE.

Dixie (146) English: generally from a pet form of the personal name DICK, but sometimes, according to both Reaney and Dauzat, a nickname for a chorister, from Latin *dixi* 'I have spoken', the first word of the 39th Psalm.

Dixit (135) Indian (north-central, south, and west): Hindu (Brahman) name, from Sanskrit *dīkṣita* 'priest performing initiations (*dīkṣā*)', i.e. a priest specially employed to initiate Hindu boys into the performance of their religious duties. GIVEN NAMES Indian 93%. *Krishna* (3), *Sunil* (3), *Ajit* (2), *Girish* (2), *Parmesh* (2), *Pradeep* (2), *Rahul* (2), *Sanjay* (2), *Suresh* (2), *Vaishali* (2), *Vijay* (2), *Akhilesh*.

Dixon (47409) Northern English: patronymic from the personal name DICK.

Dixson (1135) English: variant spelling of DIXON.

Dixwell (2) English: probably a habitational name from a lost or unidentified place. FOREBEARS John Dixwell (*c.* 1607–1698/9), a regicide who signed Charles I's death warrant, fled from England to Hanau, Germany. From Hanau he migrated to New England, where he was first mentioned as being in America in 1664/5. The son of William Dixwell of Coton Hall, near Rugby, Warwickshire, John settled in New Haven, CT, where he assumed the name of James Davids.

Dize (142) Origin uncertain. **1.** Perhaps a variant of English DICE. **2.** It could be an Americanized spelling of German DEIS.

Dizon (672) Filipino: variant of Spanish **Izón**, unexplained, but possibly a topographic or habitational name. GIVEN NAMES Spanish 38%. *Jose* (7), *Eduardo* (5), *Wilfredo* (5), *Edgardo* (4), *Gualberto* (4), *Manuel* (4), *Ricardo* (4), *Conrado* (3), *Domingo* (3), *Efren* (3), *Eugenio* (3), *Francisco* (3); *Romeo* (5), *Antonio* (3), *Dante* (2), *Julieta* (2), *Carina*, *Carmel*, *Dario*, *Enrico*, *Federico*, *Filomena*, *Leonardo*, *Liberato*.

Djordjevic (126) Serbian (**Djordjević**): patronymic from the personal name *Djordje*, vernacular form of the Greek personal name *Geōrgios* (see GEORGE). GIVEN NAMES South Slavic 70%. *Dragan* (5), *Bozidar* (2), *Branko* (2), *Milan* (2), *Miodrag* (2), *Momcilo* (2), *Predrag* (2), *Sinisa* (2), *Sotir* (2), *Borka*, *Djordje*, *Dragana*, *Dunja*; *Dusan*, *Mirko*, *Miroslav*, *Milutin*, *Misha*, *Vladimir*.

Dlouhy (269) Czech (**Dlouhý**): nickname for a tall person, from *dlouhý* 'long'.

Dlugos (174) Americanized spelling of Polish **Długosz** (see DLUGOSZ).

Dlugosz (181) Polish (**Długosz**): nickname for a tall person, from *długi* 'long'. GIVEN NAMES Polish 18%. *Casimir* (2), *Krystyna* (2), *Andrzej*, *Boguslaw*, *Irena*, *Jacek*, *Jerzy*, *Jozef*, *Miroslaw*, *Waclaw*, *Zofia*.

Dmitriev (31) Russian: patronymic from the personal name *Dmitri*, from Greek *Dēmētrios* (see DEMETRIOU). GIVEN NAMES Russian 64%. *Oleg* (3), *Alexei* (2), *Anatoly* (2), *Gennady*, *Leonid*, *Mikhail*, *Nikolai*, *Sergei*, *Vasili*, *Vladimir*.

Do (3200) **1.** Vietnamese (**Đỗ**): unexplained. **2.** Chinese 杜: possibly a variant of DU 1. **3.** Korean: variant of TO. GIVEN NAMES Vietnamese 58%; Chinese/Korean 21%. *Hung* (51), *Minh* (37), *Thanh* (35), *Hien* (29), *Long* (26), *Dung* (24), *Anh* (23), *Tuan* (22), *Hoang* (21), *Hai* (20), *Quang* (20), *Son* (19); *Hong* (10), *Hang* (9), *Chi* (8), *Sang* (8), *Dong* (5), *Chan* (3), *Han* (3), *Ho* (3), *Bai* (2), *Chien* (2), *Lai* (2), *Man* (2); *Phong* (14), *Tam* (14), *Nam* (11),

Thai (7), *Chung* (6), *Tinh* (5), *Sinh* (3), *Uyen* (3), *Tham* (2), *Tuoc* (2), *Tuong* (2), *Chang Yol*.

Doak (1398) **1.** Scottish and northern Irish: variant of DOIG. **2.** Irish (Ulster): reduced Anglicized form of Gaelic **Mac Dabhóc** 'son of *Dabhóc*', a pet form of DAVID.

Doan (3711) **1.** Irish: variant of DOANE. **2.** Vietnamese (**Đoàn**): unexplained.
GIVEN NAMES Vietnamese 29%. *Hung* (28), *Thanh* (21), *Duc* (17), *Minh* (14), *Trung* (14), *Vinh* (14), *Dung* (12), *Huong* (12), *Quang* (12), *Khanh* (11), *Long* (11), *Tan* (11); *Hong* (6), *Hang* (4), *Chan* (2), *Chien* (2), *Han* (2), *Man* (2), *Chi*, *Chin*, *Dong*, *Lung*, *Mija*, *Ming*.

Doane (2677) Irish: reduced Anglicized form of Gaelic **Ó Dubháin** 'descendant of *Dubhán*', meaning 'the little black one', a common name in the 16th century in southern Ireland, or **Ó Damháin** 'descendant of *Damhán*' meaning 'fawn', 'little stag', a rare Ulster name. See also DEVINE.

Doar (135) English: variant spelling of DORE.

Dobb (135) English: from the medieval personal name DOBBE.

Dobbe (159) English: from the medieval personal name *Dobbe*, one of several pet forms of ROBERT in which the initial letter was altered. Compare HOBBS.

Dobberpuhl (106) Respelling of German **Dobberpfuhl**, a habitational name from any of the places called Dobberphul, of which there are four examples in Pomerania.

Dobberstein (251) German: metonymic occupational name for a dice maker or a nickname for a dice player, from Middle High German *topel* 'die' + *stein* 'stone', 'cube'.

Dobbert (105) **1.** Eastern German: (of Slavic origin) possibly a derivative of Old Slavic *dobru* 'good'. **2.** German: from a short form of the Germanic name *Theudobert*, Old High German *Thiotprecht*, (from *diot* 'people' + *berht* 'bright', 'shining').
GIVEN NAME German 4%. *Armin*.

Dobbertin (123) German: habitational name from Dobbertin, a place in Mecklenburg.
GIVEN NAMES German 10%. *Reinhold* (2), *Kurt*.

Dobbie (173) Scottish and northern English: from a pet form of the personal name ROBERT.

Dobbin (421) English, northern Irish, and Scottish: from a pet form of ROBIN, which is itself a pet form of ROBERT.

Dobbins (5152) English: patronymic meaning 'son of Robin' (see DOBBIN).

Dobbs (6549) English: patronymic meaning 'son of Robert', common in central England (see DOBB).
FOREBEARS Arthur Dobbs (1689–1765) was born at Castle Dobbs, Co. Antrim, Ireland. In 1745 he purchased 400,000 acres of land in NC and was selected as governor in 1754. He married twice and his second wife, wed when he was age 73, was a girl in her teens from NC.

Dobbyn (125) English: variant spelling of DOBBIN.

Dobeck (110) German: from a pet form of a Slavic personal name beginning with the Old Slavic element *dob* 'courageous', 'noble', as for example *Dobeslav*.

Dobek (206) Polish and Czech: from a pet form of a traditional Slavic personal name beginning with the Old Slavic element *dob* 'courageous', 'noble', as for example *Dobeslav* (Polish *Dobiesław*), or from Czech *Tobiáš* (see TOBIAS).
GIVEN NAMES Polish 6%. *Casimir, Wojciech*.

Dober (222) German: from a byname from an agent derivative of Swabian *toben, töben* 'to rant and rage'.
GIVEN NAMES German 6%. *Alois, Erna, Erwin, Otto*.

Doberstein (208) Variant spelling of German DOBBERSTEIN.
GIVEN NAMES German 5%. *Klaus, Kurt*.

Dobert (111) Czech: from the Germanic personal name *Theudobert* (see DOBBERT).

Dobesh (204) Americanized spelling of Czech **Dobeš**, from the Czech personal name *Tobiáš*, or of German **Döbesch**, from the same Czech personal name or some other Slavic form of TOBIAS.

Dobey (157) **1.** English: variant of DOBBIE. **2.** Americanized spelling of Hungarian **Dobi** (see DOBIE).

Dobias (276) Czech and Slovak (**Dobiaš**): from the personal name *Tobiáš* (see TOBIAS).

Dobie (362) **1.** English: variant of DOBBIE. **2.** Americanized form of Hungarian **Dobi** from the personal name *Dabó* (Transylvanian form *Dobó*), from a pet form of the personal name *Dob*.

Dobies (203) Polish: dialect form of **Dobiesz**, from a pet form of any of the various Old Polish compound personal names beginning with *Dobie*, as for example *Dobiegniew, Dobiemir, Dobiesław*.

Dobin (128) Jewish (eastern Ashkenazic): metronymic from the Yiddish female name *Dobe*, a pet form of *Dobre* (see DOBRIN).
GIVEN NAMES Russian 7%; Jewish 5%; German 4%. *Boris* (2), *Mikhail, Yury*; *Ilya* (2); *Fritz, Kurt*.

Dobis (183) **1.** Czech (**Dobiš**): variant of **Dobiaš** (see DOBIAS). **2.** Lithuanian: from Lithuanian *Duoba* or Polish *Doba*, a shortened form of a traditional Slavic personal name beginning with the element *dob* 'courageous', 'noble', for example *Dobeslav* (Polish *Dobiesław*).
GIVEN NAMES German 4%. *Hedwig, Otto*.

Dobish (116) **1.** Ukrainian: perhaps an occupational name from *dovbysh* 'kettle drum player'. **2.** Americanized spelling of German **Dobisch**, from a pet form of any of various Slavic personal names, notably TOBIAS, possibly others such as *Dobeslav* and *Dobrobud*, or perhaps in some cases an altered spelling of Czech **Dobiš** (see DOBIS).

Dobkin (305) **1.** English: from a diminutive of DOBB. **2.** Jewish (from Lithuania and Belarus): metronymic from the Yiddish female personal name *Dobke*, a pet form of *Dobre* (see DOBRIN).
GIVEN NAMES Russian 6%; Jewish 5%. *Lev* (2), *Arkadiy, Arkagy, Boris, Igor, Mikhail, Svetlana*; *Ilya, Isak*.

Dobkins (155) English: patronymic from DOBKIN.

Dobkowski (124) Polish: habitational name for someone from a place called Dobkowice, Dobkowo, or Dobków.
GIVEN NAMES Polish 5%. *Casimir, Janina*.

Doble (377) **1.** English (of Norman origin): variant of DOUBLE. **2.** In some cases, probably an altered spelling of South German **Dobel** or **Döbel**, a topographic name for someone who lived in a gorge or deep valley, Middle High German southern dialect *tobel*.

Dobler (484) **1.** South German: topographic name from Middle High German (southern dialect) *tobel* 'gorge' + the suffix *-er*, denoting an inhabitant. **2.** North German (also **Döbler**): nickname for a dice player, from an agent derivative of Middle Low German *dob(e)len* 'to throw dice', 'to play (cards or board games)'.
GIVEN NAMES German 12%. *Gerhard* (2), *Hans* (2), *Katharina* (2), *Kurt* (2), *Manfred* (2), *Markus* (2), *Erwin, Franz, Gunter, Joerg, Johann, Konrad*.

Dobmeier (170) German (originally **Thumbmeyer**): distinguishing name for a tenant farmer (see MEYER) who was the tenant of land belonging to a cathedral chapter. Compare DOMEIER.

Dobner (108) German (**Döbner**): habitational name for someone from a place called Döben.

Dobos (390) **1.** Hungarian: metonymic occupational name for a drummer or for a drum maker, from *dob* 'drum'. **2.** Hungarian: from a pet form of any of various Slavic personal names such as *Dobeslav* and *Doběstoj*, or Czech *Tobiáš* or Hungarian *Tóbiás* (see TOBIAS). **3.** Czech (**Doboš**): variant of **Dobeš** (see DOBESH). **4.** Americanized spelling of Polish DOBOSZ.
GIVEN NAMES Hungarian 7%. *Gabor* (3), *Istvan* (2), *Laszlo* (2), *Balazs, Bela, Ference, Ildiko, Kalman*.

Dobosz (206) Polish: **1.** from a personal name beginning with Old Slavic *dobie* 'courageous', 'noble', for example *Dobiemir* or *Dobieslaw*. **2.** occupational name from *dobosz* 'drummer'.
GIVEN NAMES Polish 15%. *Boleslaw, Gerzy, Jacek, Jolanta, Kazimierz, Lech, Maciej, Stanislaw, Wladyslaw*.

Dobransky (199) **1.** Americanized spelling of Polish **Dobrański** or **Dobrzański**, a habitational name for someone from a place called Dobranowice, named with *Dobran*, an Old Polish pet form of a personal name formed with Old Slavic *dobr* 'good', as for example *Dobrosław*, *Dobromir*, or *Dobrogost*. **2.** Czech (**Dobřanský**): habitational name from a place called Dobřany.

Dobratz (238) German: nickname from Old Slavic *dobru* 'good'.

Dobrick (116) German: nickname from Old Slavic *dobru* 'good'.

Dobrin (182) **1.** Romanian, Bulgarian, Serbian, Croatian, and Slovenian: from the Old Slavic personal name *Dobrin*, a derivative of *dobr* 'good', 'kind'. It may also be a nickname of the same origin. **2.** Slovenian: probably a topographic name from *dob* 'oak' or from Old Slavic *dobr* 'wood', 'forest'. This name is found mainly in the foothills of the wooded mountains of Dobrča in Gorenjska region, northern central Slovenia. **3.** Jewish (eastern Ashkenazic): metronymic from the Yiddish female personal name *Dobre*, a derivative of a Slavic word meaning 'good'.
GIVEN NAMES Romanian 5%. *Mihai, Ovidiu, Stelian, Toader.*

Dobrinski (166) Americanized spelling of Polish **Dobrzyński** (see DOBRZYNSKI).
GIVEN NAME Polish 4%. *Casimir* (2).

Dobrosky (112) Variant of Polish DOBROWSKI.

Dobrovolny (116) Czech (**Dobrovolný**): nickname meaning literally 'good will' (from *dobro* 'good' + *volny* 'will'). According to Moldanová, it was bestowed on someone who voluntarily accepted serfdom.
GIVEN NAMES French 5%; German 4%. *Pierre; Otto.*

Dobrow (110) **1.** Russian: patronymic from *dobryj* 'good'. **2.** Jewish (from Ukraine): of uncertain derivation; possibly of the same origin as 1, or alternatively a habitational name from the village of Dobroe in Ukraine.
GIVEN NAMES Jewish 11%. *Hinda* (2), *Isadore, Meyer, Sol.*

Dobrowolski (424) Polish: habitational name for someone from for example Dobrowola in Lublin or Siedlce voivodeships, places named from Polish *dobry* 'good' + *volya* 'will'. According to Bystroń, it may alternatively have a nickname for a peasant who had been freed from serfdom. Compare Czech DOBROVOLNY.
GIVEN NAMES Polish 9%. *Tadeusz* (2), *Andrzej, Casimir, Czeslaw, Janusz, Krzystof, Lech, Mieczyslaw, Stanislaw.*

Dobrowski (169) Polish: **1.** habitational name for someone from a place called Dobrów, named with the personal name *Dobry* (from *dobry* 'good') + the posses-sive suffix *-ów*. **2.** variant of **Dąbrowski** (see DABROWSKI).

Dobry (264) **1.** Czech and Slovak (**Dobrý**): nickname from Czech *dobrý* 'good', 'honest', 'faithful'. **2.** French: patronymic from the personal name *Obry*, a spelling variant of AUBREY. **3.** English: altered form of the French surname **Dobrée**, which was taken to England by a Huguenot family whose ancestor had fled to Guernsey after the St. Bartholomew Massacre in 1572.

Dobrzynski (229) Polish (**Dobrzyński**): habitational name for someone from a place named Dobrzyń, from *dobry* 'good'.
GIVEN NAMES Polish 11%. *Andrzej, Bogdan, Czeslaw, Jerzy, Krystyna, Wieslaw, Witold, Zbigniew, Zdzislaw.*

Dobson (6895) English and Scottish: patronymic from the personal name DOBBE. This is also established in Ireland, notably County Leitrim.

Doby (711) **1.** English: from a pet form of the personal name DOBBE. **2.** Hungarian: habitational name for someone from a place called Dob in Sabolcs-Szatmár county, or Doba in Veszprém county.

Dobyns (519) Variant spelling of English DOBBINS.

Docherty (514) Scottish spelling of the Irish surname DOHERTY.

Dochterman (180) South German: kinship name from a dialect variant of **Tochtermann**, literally 'daughter husband', i.e. 'son-in-law'.

Dock (470) **1.** English: of uncertain derivation; possibly from Middle English *doke* 'duck' (see DUCK). **2.** Norwegian: habitational name from a farm named *Dokk*, from Old Norse *dǫkk* 'hollow', 'depression'. **3.** Possibly an altered form of German **Docke**, a metonymic occupational name for someone who worked in the cloth trade, from Middle Low German *dōk* 'fabric'.

Docken (263) **1.** German: probably a shortened form of various compound names formed with this element, for example DOCKENDORF. **2.** Altered spelling of Norwegian DOKKEN.

Dockendorf (266) German: habitational name from a place near Bitburg called Dockendorf.

Dockens (115) Irish: see DOCKINS.
GIVEN NAME Irish 6%. *Brennan.*

Dockery (3226) **1.** English: habitational name from any of several places called Dockray, of which there are four examples in Cumbria. A possible origin of the place name is Old Norse *dǫkk* 'hollow', 'valley' + *vrá* 'isolated place'; the first element is, however, more likely to be Old English *docce* 'dock' (the plant). **2.** Irish: reduced Anglicized form of Gaelic **Ó Dochraidh** 'descendant of *Dochradh*', a personal name that is a variant of *Dochartach* (see DOHERTY).

Dockett (105) English: variant of DOGGETT.

GIVEN NAMES French 6%; German 4%. *Colette; Kurt.*

Dockham (200) English: habitational name from Dockham in Donhead St. Mary, Wiltshire, named in Old English with *docce* 'dock' (the plant) + *hamm* 'enclosure', 'water meadow'. This surname has died out in England.

Dockins (623) Irish: of uncertain derivation; perhaps a variant of the English family name **Dockings**, a habitational name from Docking in Norfolk, named in Old English as 'place where docks (Old English *docce*) grow'.

Dockray (111) English and Irish: variant of DOCKERY.
GIVEN NAME French 4%. *Lucien.*

Dockrey (106) English and Irish: variant of DOCKERY.

Dockstader (358) German: topographic name for someone who lived by a landing, from Middle German *docke* 'dock' + *stade* 'embankment', 'shore', + the suffix *-er* denoting an inhabitant. In some cases, it may have been an occupational name for a docker, since *stade* also denoted a granary or warehouse.

Dockter (953) **1.** Germanized form of Latin *doctor* 'teacher', an occupational name originally denoting a university teacher (subsequently one who specialized in medicine). **2.** Scottish: old spelling of DOCTOR.

Docktor (118) See DOCKTER.

Dockum (107) **1.** Dutch habitational name from a place called Doccum in West Friesland. **2.** Alternatively, perhaps a variant of English DOCKHAM.

Dockweiler (107) German: habitational name from a place so called in the Eifel Mountains.
FOREBEARS The earliest known immigrant of this name is Rudolph Duckwell or Duckwiler, who arrived at Philadelphia from Rotterdam on the ship *Virtuous Grace* on 24 September 1737. The name is widespread in Germany, and several bearers of it brought it to North America independently of one another.

Docter (265) **1.** Scottish: variant spelling of DOCTOR. **2.** Respelling of German DOCKTER or DOKTOR.

Doctor (788) **1.** Scottish: according to Black, an hereditary occupational name for a physician, from Latin *doctor* 'teacher', but possibly in some cases it may have the same origin as DAUGHTERS. **2.** Americanized form of German, Czech, Slovak, and Hungarian DOKTOR. **3.** Indian (Gujarat and Bombay): Parsi occupational name for a physician, from the English word *doctor*.
GIVEN NAMES Indian 5%. *Ravi* (4), *Bhupendra* (2), *Umakant* (2), *Aspi, Dipak, Gopi, Jaideep, Pratibha, Saurabh, Shishir, Uday.*

Doda (107) Polish: probably a nickname from the dialect word *dodek* 'grandfather'.
GIVEN NAMES Polish 5%. *Genowefa, Michalina, Zofia.*

Dodaro (167) Italian: variant of TODARO.
GIVEN NAMES Italian 18%. *Mario* (2), *Alberto, Armando, Dino, Guido, Salvatore, Silvio, Vito.*

Dodd (11175) **1.** English and Scottish: from the Middle English personal name *Dodde, Dudde,* Old English *Dodda, Dudda,* which remained in fairly widespread and frequent use in England until the 14th century. It seems to have been originally a byname, but the meaning is not clear; it may come from a Germanic root used to describe something round and lumpish—hence a short, plump man. **2.** Irish: of English origin, taken to Sligo in the 16th century by a Shropshire family; also sometimes adopted by bearers of the Gaelic name Ó **Dubhda** (see DOWD).
FOREBEARS Daniel and Mary Dod, natives of England, emigrated to Branford, CT, in about 1645.

Doddridge (141) English: habitational name from a place in Sandford, Devon named Doddridge, from the Old English personal name *Dodda* (see DODD) + Old English *hrycg* 'ridge'.
GIVEN NAMES French 4%. *Gisele, Pierre.*

Dodds (3413) English: patronymic from DODD 1. Black suggests that the name in Scotland may sometimes be derived from a place in Berwickshire called Doddis.

Doddy (105) English: possibly a variant of DUDDY.
GIVEN NAME German 5%; Irish 5%. *Fritz.*

Dodenhoff (122) German: habitational name from a farm named Dudenhof(f) (see DUDENHOEFFER).
GIVEN NAME German 4%. *Erwin.*

Dodge (8858) English (northern England): **1.** from the Middle English personal name *Dogge,* a pet form of ROGER. **2.** possibly a nickname from Middle English *dogge* 'dog' (Old English *docga, dogga*).

Dodgen (529) English: from a pet form of *Dogge* (see DODGE).

Dodgson (164) English: patronymic form of DODGE.

Dodier (124) French: from a personal name of Germanic origin.
GIVEN NAMES French 15%. *Benoit, Hermas, Jacques, Lucien, Rosaire, Solange.*

Dodrill (483) variant of English **Dottrell**, a nickname from Middle English *dott(e)rel* '(a species of) plover', which was considered a foolish bird that was easy to catch.

Dods (127) English: patronymic form of DODD.

Dodson (13337) English: patronymic form of DODD.

Dodsworth (157) English: habitational name for someone from Dodworth in West Yorkshire (recorded as *Dodeswrde* in Domesday Book), which is named from the Old English personal name *Dodd(a)* + Old English *worð* 'enclosure'.

Dodt (127) German: variant spelling of TODT.

GIVEN NAMES French 6%; German 5%. *Cecile, Lorette; Otto, Willi.*

Doe (1302) **1.** English and Scottish: nickname for a mild and gentle man, from Middle English *do* 'doe' (Old English *dā*). **2.** English (of Norman origin): habitational name (Old French *d'Eu*) for someone from Eu in Seine-Maritime, France. The place name is either a dramatic reduction of Latin *Augusta* '(city of) Augustus', or else derives from the Germanic element *auwa* 'water meadow', 'island'.

Doebler (373) German (**Döbler**): see DOBLER 2.

Doede (115) German: **1.** (**Döde**): in the north, from a Germanic personal name *Duco* (see DIETZ). **2.** perhaps a nickname for someone with a grim or cadaverous appearance, a Low German homonym of *tot* 'dead', but probably from an old nursery word *dot* 'godfather', Middle High German *dode.*

Doeden (251) German: **1.** variant of DUDEN. **2.** variant of DOEDE 2.

Doege (312) North German (**Döge**): nickname from *döge* 'capable', 'competent'.
GIVEN NAMES German 4%. *Erwin* (3), *Gerhard.*

Doehring (220) German (**Döhring**): variant of **Döring** (see DOERING).
GIVEN NAMES German 11%. *Dietmar* (4), *Fritz, Hans, Kurt, Ralf, Volker.*

Doell (327) German (**Döll**): **1.** habitational name from Döllen near Oldenburg, Lower Saxony. **2.** from the personal name *Döl,* a Rhenish reduced form of ADOLF.
GIVEN NAMES German 7%. *Eldred, Gerhard, Hans, Heinz, Manfred, Reinhold, Wilhelmina.*

Doelling (132) German (**Dölling**): **1.** habitational name from Dolling in Bavaria, or Döllingen in Saxony. **2.** nickname from the dialect word *Dölling* 'young pike'. **3.** nickname from Middle High German *dol* 'highly or overzealous'.
GIVEN NAMES German 6%. *Erna, Hellmut, Kurt.*

Doenges (217) German (**Dönges**): variant of DONGES.
GIVEN NAME German 5%. *Gerhard.*

Doepke (203) North German (**Döpke**): **1.** from a Low German pet form of THEOBALD. **2.** metonymic occupational name for a potter, from a diminutive of Low German *doppe, duppe* 'beaker', 'jar'. See also DOPP.
GIVEN NAMES German 5%. *Guenter, Konrad, Kurt.*

Doepker (151) Variant of German **Döpke** (see DOPKE).

Doerflein (124) German (**Dörflein**): standardized form of the South German habitational name **Dörfle** (see DOERFLER).

Doerfler (602) South German (**Dörfler**): nickname from a derivative of Middle High German *dorf(l)ære* 'inhabitant of a village', or a habitational name, common in Bavaria

and Austria, from places named Dörfl or Dörfle ('little village').

Doerflinger (146) German and Swiss German (**Dörflinger**): habitational name for someone from any of several places in Bavaria named Dörfling. Compare DERFLINGER.
GIVEN NAMES German 8%. *Otto* (2), *Kurt.*

Doerge (127) German (**Dörge**): variant of **Dörries** (see DORRIES).

Doering (2022) German (**Döring**): **1.** ethnic name for someone from Thuringia (German *Thüringen*). The region is named from its former occupation by the *T(h)uringii,* a Germanic tribe. **2.** from a personal name based on cognate of *turren* 'to dare'.
GIVEN NAMES German 4%. *Otto* (4), *Hans* (2), *Heinz* (2), *Claus, Egon, Elfriede, Erna, Ernst, Gerd, Gerhard, Hellmuth, Klaus.*

Doerksen (175) North German (**Dörksen**): patronymic from a Low German form of DIETRICH.
GIVEN NAME German 4%. *Klaus.*

Doerner (376) German (**Dörner**): see DORNER.
GIVEN NAMES German 6%. *Manfred* (2), *Egon, Erwin, Otto.*

Doerr (2587) German (**Dörr**): variant of **Dürr** (see DURR).

Doerrer (121) German (**Dörrer**): from an old personal name formed with Old Saxon *diuri* 'valuable', 'dear'.

Doersam (142) North German (**Dörsam**): of uncertain derivation, but possibly a nickname from Middle Low German *dor* 'fool', 'mentally ill person' + the adjectival suffix *-sam.*
GIVEN NAMES German 8%. *Dieter* (2), *Frederich, Gerhard.*

Doescher (362) North German (**Döscher**): see DOSCHER.

Doetsch (187) South German (**Dötsch**): nickname for a lumpish person, a variant of **Detsch,** from *detsch* 'soft', 'fat (person)'.
GIVEN NAMES German 8%. *Gerhard, Gernot, Hans, Ingeborg, Volker, Wolf.*

Doffing (166) German: probably from the short form of a personal name composed with Old High German *diot* 'people' + *fridu* 'peace' + the suffix *-ing* indicating a follower or member of a clan.
GIVEN NAMES German 4%. *Mathias, Otto.*

Dogan (389) Turkish: from a first name based on Turkish *dogan* 'falcon'.
GIVEN NAMES Muslim 7%. *Kemal* (2), *Tahsin* (2), *Abdullah, Arif, Aydin, Banu, Fatih, Huseyin, Irfan, Ismail, Koray, Levent.*

Doggett (1736) English: **1.** nickname, probably with abusive connotations, from a diminutive of Middle English *dogge* 'dog' (Old English *docga*). **2.** nickname from Middle English *dogge* 'dog' + *heved* 'head' (Old English *hēafod*).

Doheny (382) Irish: reduced Anglicized form of Gaelic Ó **Dubhchonna** 'descendant of *Dubhchonna*', a personal name

based on *dubh* 'black' + *Conna*, a pet form of *Colmán* 'little dove'.
GIVEN NAME Irish 6%. *Paddy*.

Doherty (11574) Irish: reduced Anglicized form of Gaelic **Ó Dochartaigh** 'descendant of *Dochartach*', a byname from *do* + *cartach* 'not loving'. The family were chieftains in Donegal.
GIVEN NAMES Irish 5%. *Liam* (5), *Brendan* (3), *Kieran* (3), *Dermot* (2), *Niall* (2), *Aileen, Cahal, Colum, Connor, Conor, Eamon, Eoin*.

Dohm (502) German: from a pet form of the personal name THOMAS.

Dohman (155) North German (**Dohmann**): from a pet form of THOMAS.
GIVEN NAME German 5%. *Kurt* (2).

Dohmen (189) Presumably an altered spelling of German DOHMAN.
GIVEN NAMES German 4%. *Erwin* (2), *Hans, Matthias*.

Dohn (271) German (**Döhn**): from a derivative of the personal name *Ant(h)on*, German form of ANTHONY.
GIVEN NAMES German 5%. *Erwin* (2), *Armin, Kurt*.

Dohner (350) German (**Döhner**): **1.** patronymic from the personal name *Döhn* (see DOHN). **2.** habitational name for someone from Dohna near Pirna, Saxony.

Dohoney (143) Irish: probably a variant of DOHENY.

Dohr (158) North German: topographic names for someone who lived by the gates of a town or city (see THOR).

Dohrer (103) German (**Döhrer**): habitational name for someone from any of various places called Dohr, Döhra, or Döhren.

Dohrman (267) Americanized spelling of German DOHRMANN.

Dohrmann (352) North German: topographic name for someone who lived by the gates of a town or city (see THOR).

Dohrn (133) North German: topographic name for someone who lived by a 'prickly thicket', from Middle Low German *dorn* 'thorn' (the -*h*- reflects the long vowel, as in the occasional spelling **Doorn-**).
GIVEN NAMES French 5%; German 4%. *Camille; Ilse, Klaus*.

Dohse (200) German: **1.** variant of DOSE. **2.** in Friesland, a habitational name, from a place called Dohse. The place name may be identical with a North German fieldname for an island-like piece of land or a swamp.
GIVEN NAMES German 9%. *Erhard, Gerhard, Gunther, Hans, Kurt, Lothar, Rainer*.

Doi (418) Japanese: usually written with characters meaning 'earthen well'; found mainly in western Japan and the island of Shikoku. A name with the same pronunciation, but written with characters meaning 'earthen habitation', is found in eastern Japan. Both have an alternate pronunciation: **Tsuchii**.
GIVEN NAMES Japanese 46%. *Isamu* (3), *Shinobu* (3), *Daisuke* (2), *Kiyoshi* (2), *Masami*

(2), *Masaru* (2), *Norio* (2), *Toshi* (2), *Tsuneo* (2), *Yuriko* (2), *Yutaka* (2), *Akira*.

Doidge (168) English (Devon): variant of DODGE.

Doig (476) Scottish: reduced Anglicized form of Gaelic **Mac Gille Doig** 'son of the servant of *Dog*', a reduced form of the personal name *Cadog* (see CADDICK).

Doiron (1033) French: habitational name, with the preposition *d(e)* 'from', for someone from Oiron in Deux-Sèvres.
GIVEN NAMES French 8%. *Armand* (4), *Camille* (3), *Etienne* (3), *Emile* (2), *Adrien, Alcee, Alderic, Anatole, Eugenie, Germain, Lucien, Marcel*.

Doke (321) English: variant of DUCK.

Dokes (125) Variant of English DOKE.

Dokken (420) Norwegian: habitational name from any of several farms, especially in southeastern Norway, so named from Old Norse *dǫkk* 'hollow', 'depression'.
GIVEN NAMES Scandinavian 6%. *Jorgen* (2), *Arlis, Arnell, Erik, Hjalmer*.

Dokter (109) Dutch: occupational name for a schoolmaster or a doctor, from Latin *doctor*, Middle Dutch *doctoor*. In some cases it might be a status name for a scholar or learned man.
GIVEN NAMES Dutch 12%. *Marinus* (2), *Dirk, Egbert, Gerrit, Henk*.

Doktor (156) German, Czech, Slovak, Polish, and Hungarian: occupational name for a schoolmaster or a doctor. In some cases it might be a status name for a scholar or learned man.
GIVEN NAMES Russian 7%; Polish 6%. *Aleksandr, Lev, Lyudmila, Semyon, Yevgeniya; Boleslaw, Czeslaw, Zygmunt*.

Dolak (174) **1.** Czech and Slovak (**Dolák**): topographic name for someone living in the lower part of a village, a variant of **Dolejš** (see DOLES 2), or habitational name for someone from a place called Důl or Dolan. **2.** Polish: patronymic form of *Dola* meaning 'fate', 'destiny'. **3.** Polish: topographic name from a derivative of *dół* 'pit', 'hole'. **4.** Polish: possibly from a pet form of the personal name *Adolf*.

Dolan (11261) Irish: **1.** reduced Anglicized form of Gaelic **Ó Dubhshláin**, **Ó Dubhlainn**, or **Ó Dúnlaing** (see DOOLIN). **2.** Anglicized form of Gaelic **Ó Dobhailéin** (see DEVLIN).
GIVEN NAMES Irish 5%. *Brendan* (9), *James Patrick* (2), *Aisling, Brennan, Bridgid, Cormac, Donovan, Dymphna, Eamon, John Patrick, Kevin Patrick, Liam*.

Doland (263) English: variant of DOWLAND.

Dolata (167) Polish: possibly from a derivative of *dolatać* 'to reach one's destination', 'to arrive', presumably applied as a nickname, or alternatively as a topographic name from the dialect word *dolaty* 'valley', 'flat country'.
GIVEN NAMES Polish 9%. *Andrzej, Krystian, Krystyna, Lech*.

Dolbeare (109) English (Devon): unexplained. It is probably a habitational name from a lost or unidentified place. -*beare*, from Old English *bearu* 'grove', is a common place-name element in Devon.
FOREBEARS American bearers of this name are descended from Edmund Dolbeare, a pewterer who came from Ashburton, Devon, to Boston and Salem, MA, in the late 17th century.

Dolberg (100) Dutch: habitational name from Dolberg in Klimmen, Netherlands, or possibly from Dolberg in North Rhine-Westphalia in Germany.
GIVEN NAMES Russian 5%; Romanian 4%. *Boris, Yevgeniy, Zinovy; Dorel* (2).

Dolberry (108) Probably a variant of English DOLBEARE.

Dolbow (192) Probably an Americanized form of the common Swedish topographic name **Dalbo** 'valley farm'. Compare DALBY.

Dolby (544) English or Scandinavian: variant spelling of DALBY.

Dolce (778) Italian (Sicily): from the medieval personal name *Dolce*, meaning 'sweet', 'pleasant', from Latin *dulcis*.
GIVEN NAMES Italian 11%. *Giuseppe* (4), *Rocco* (4), *Salvatore* (4), *Gasper* (3), *Franco* (2), *Gaspere* (2), *Sal* (2), *Angelo, Domenica, Vita, Vito*.

Dolch (155) German: **1.** perhaps from *Dolch* 'dagger', 'knife' (of uncertain origin); presumably a metonymic occupational name for a maker of such weapons or perhaps a nickname for someone who habitually carried one. However, the vocabulary word was not recorded before 1512, and the surname may alternatively be a variant of **Dolge**, a topographic name meaning 'long', from Old Slavic *dolgy*. **2.** variant of DOLEN.
GIVEN NAMES French 4%; German 4%. *Leonie, Patrice; Bodo, Wilhelm*.

Dold (458) German: from a short form of the personal name BERTHOLD.

Dolder (181) German: **1.** variant of DOLD. **2.** South German: perhaps a topographic name denoting someone who lived in a house overshadowed by trees, from Middle High German *tolde* 'treetop'. **3.** in Swabia, a nickname for someone who was prone to stumbling.
GIVEN NAME German 4%. *Ulrich*.

Dole (1229) **1.** English: from Middle English *dole* 'portion of land' (Old English *dāl* 'share', 'portion'). The term could denote land within the common field, a boundary mark, or a unit of area; so the name may be of topographic origin or a status name. **2.** Irish: reduced and altered Anglicized form of MCDOWELL. Compare MCDOLE. **3.** French (**Dolé**): nickname for a troubled or anxious person, from Old French *dolé*, past participle of *doler* 'to regret' (Latin *dolere* 'to hurt').

Dolecki (138) Polish: habitational name for someone from a place called Doleck, in Skierniewice voivodeship, or Dołki, named from the plural of *dołek* 'depression', 'hollow'.

Doleman (143) English (Midlands): variant of DOLE or DULL. Compare DOLMAN.

Dolen (354) **1.** Irish: variant spelling of DOLAN. **2.** Perhaps a reduced form of Slovenian **Dolenc** or **Dolenec** (see DOLENCE). **3.** German: from a short form of a personal name composed with Germanic *theud* 'people', 'race'. **4.** Perhaps an Americanized spelling of Norwegian **Døhlen**, **Dæhlen**, habitational names from a number of farmsteads named from Old Norse *dalvin* (from *dalr* 'valley' + *vin* 'meadow').

Dolence (158) **1.** Altered spelling of Dutch **Dolens** (see DOLLENS). **2.** Probably an Americanized form of the Slovenian surnames **Dolenc**, variant of **Dolenjec**, a habitational name for someone from the Dolenjska region of southern Slovenia.

Doles (531) **1.** French: unexplained; perhaps a habitational name from Dole in the Jura. **2.** Variant of Czech **Dolejš** 'lower', a distinguishing epithet for one of two or more bearers of the same personal name, living in the lower part of the village. Compare **Hořejš** (see HOREJSI). **3.** Slovenian: unexplained.

Dolese (105) French: unexplained.
GIVEN NAME French 4%. *Monique.*

Dolezal (1053) Czech and Slovak (**Doležal**): nickname for a lazy man, from the past participle of *doležit* 'to lie down'. The name is also found in Croatia.

Dolfi (161) Italian: patronymic from a reduced form of a Germanic personal name ending with *-dolfo*, for example *Adolfo, Gandolfo, Rodolfo.*
GIVEN NAMES Italian 10%. *Rocco* (2), *Aldo, Cesare, Gino, Romeo, Sal.*

Dolgin (207) Jewish (from Belarus): patronymic from the Russian nickname *dolgij,* meaning 'long'.
GIVEN NAMES Jewish 12%; Russian 5%. *Giora* (2), *Avram, Etty, Osher, Sol, Yehudah; Aleksandr, Dmitriy, Semyon, Yury.*

Dolin (770) **1.** Jewish (eastern Ashkenazic): habitational name from any of several places in Ukraine and Belarus called Dolina, from Slavic *dolina* 'valley'. **2.** French: metonymic occupational name for a carpenter, from a derivative of *doler* 'to shave or plane'. **3.** Probably a variant spelling of DOLEN.

Dolinar (211) Slovenian: topographic name for someone who lived in a valley, from *dolina* 'valley'.

Dolinger (282) Altered spelling of German DOLLINGER.

Dolinski (147) Polish (**Doliński**) and Jewish (eastern Ashkenazic), Belorussian, and Ukrainian: habitational name for some-

one from any of various places in Poland, Ukraine, and Belarus named with *dolina* 'valley', for example Dolina in eastern Galicia, Poland.
GIVEN NAMES Polish 10%. *Bogdan, Janusz, Jozef, Kazimierz, Krzysztof, Zbigniew.*

Dolinsky (275) **1.** Jewish (Ashkenazic), Ukrainian, and Belorussian: variant spelling of DOLINSKI. **2.** Slovak (**Dolinský**): habitational name from a place named with *dolina* 'lowland'.
GIVEN NAMES Jewish 8%; Russian 4%. *Aron, Hyman, Inna, Mordechai, Zelig; Boris, Dmitry, Mikhail, Sergey, Yevgeny.*

Doll (3793) **1.** South German: nickname from Middle High German *tol, dol* 'foolish', 'mad'; also 'strong', 'handsome'. **2.** South German (**Döll**): variant of THIEL. **3.** South German (Bavaria): topographic name for someone living in a valley, Middle High German *tol* 'ditch'. **4.** North German: habitational name from Dolle, Dollen, or Döllen in Brandenburg. **5.** English: nickname for a foolish individual, from Middle English *dolle* 'dull', 'foolish' (Old English *dol*). The byform *dyl(le)* gave rise to Middle English *dil(le), dul(le)*, modern English *dull.* Compare DILL 3.

Dollahite (110) Irish: see DOLLARHIDE.
GIVEN NAMES Irish 4%. *Aine, Colm.*

Dollar (2328) **1.** Scottish: habitational name from Dollar in Clackmannanshire. **2.** Americanized spelling of German DAHLER, **Daler**, or **Taler**, topographic names for someone who lived in a valley, from Middle High German *tal* 'valley' + the suffix *-er* denoting an inhabitant. The American word *dollar* is from Czech *tolar*, German *Thaler*, denoting a silver coin first minted at the silver mines at *Joachimsthal* ('Joachim's valley') in Bohemia (Czech name: *Jáchymov*). **3.** Americanized spelling of Slovenian **Dolar**, topographic name for someone who lived in a valley, from *dol* 'valley', a derivative of Old High German *tal* 'valley'.

Dollard (495) **1.** English: nickname from Middle English *dull + -ard* 'dull or stupid person'. Compare DOLL 5. **2.** Irish: either an importation to Ireland of the English name or, possibly, a reduced and altered form of **de la Hyde** (see DOLLARHIDE).
GIVEN NAMES Irish 4%. *Aine, Michael Patrick.*

Dollarhide (385) Irish: of uncertain origin. It may be an altered form of **de la Hyde** (see HYDE), which was a prominent family name in Leinster from medieval times onward.
FOREBEARS Francis Dollahide, born about 1650–60 in County Dublin, Ireland, was the ancestor of Americans with the surname **Dollahide, Dollahite,** and **Dollarhide.** In 1680 he was transported to MD for some youthful misdemeanor. He appears to have been an educated man and rose to be an important landowner and politician, serving in the Lower House of the MD

legislature as an elected representative for Baltimore County from about 1705 to 1721.

Dolle (243) **1.** German: habitational name from Dolle, a place near Magdeburg. **2.** French (**Dollé**): variant of **Dolé** (see DOLE).

Dollens (151) Probably an altered spelling of Dutch **Dolens**, a patronymic from *Dolin*, a personal name of Germanic origin. Compare DOLENCE.

Dolley (260) English (of Norman origin): variant of DULEY.

Dollinger (482) German (also **Döllinger**:) habitational name for someone from a place named Dollingen, of which there are several examples in Bavaria, or from either of two places, in Saxony and Prussia, named Döllingen.
GIVEN NAMES German 4%. *Heinz, Kurt, Milbert, Reinhard.*

Dollins (424) **1.** English (Somerset): unexplained; perhaps a patronymic from a derivative of DOLL. **2.** Possibly an altered spelling of Dutch **Dolins**, a variant of **Dolens** (see DOLLENS).

Dollison (272) English: variant of **Dollinson** (see DOLLINS).
GIVEN NAME French 5%. *Monique.*

Dolliver (249) English: variant of TOLLIVER.

Dollman (130) **1.** English: variant spelling of DOLMAN, itself a variant of DOLL or DOLE. **2.** North German (**Dollmann**): habitational name for someone from Dolle, north of Magdeburg.
GIVEN NAMES German 10%. *Siegfried* (2), *Kurt, Otto.*

Dolloff (402) Probably of Dutch origin, an altered form of **Doelhoff**, a habitational name from a place named with *doel* 'target' + *hof* 'farmstead', 'manor farm', 'courtyard'. This could also have been a name for someone in charge of a firing range.
FOREBEARS The surname was brought to America before 1674 by Christian Dolloff (born *c.*1639, died 18 August 1708 in Exeter, Rockingham County, NH). His origins are a mystery. 10 October 1674 is the date of his marriage.

Dolly (412) Irish (Galway): Anglicized form of Gaelic **Ó Dathlaoich** 'descendant of *Dathlaoch*', a personal name composed of the elements *dath* 'bright', 'colored' + *laoch* 'hero', 'champion'.

Dolman (274) **1.** English: variant of DOLE or of DOLL. **2.** Dutch: nickname for a stupid person. **3.** Americanized spelling of German **Dollmann** (see DOLLMAN). **4.** Hungarian **Dolmán**: variant of **Dolmány**, metonymic occupational name or nickname from *dolmány* 'embroidered coat', named after a Szekler village in Transylvania called Dolmán. In some cases this may be an Americanized spelling of *Dolmáni*, habitational name for someone from the village itself.

Dolney (221) **1.** Possibly of French origin: a habitational name, with the preposition *d(e)*, for someone from any of several places named Aulnay, for example in Aube, Charente-Maritime, and Marne. The place name is derived from *aune* 'alder'. Compare DONAIS. **2.** Perhaps an altered spelling of Hungarian **Dolnay** or **Dolnai**, variants of **Dolinai**, a habitational name for someone from any of various places called Dolina, from Slavic *dolina* 'valley'; examples are found in Tolna and Vas counties, as well as in Trencsény, Nyitra, and other regions now in Slovakia.

Dolph (662) **1.** Scandinavian, German, and Dutch: reduced variant of ADOLF. **2.** English: variant of DELPH.

Dolphin (629) English and Irish: variant of DUFFIN. The surname was taken to Ireland at the time of the Anglo-Norman invasion in the 12th century, and the original bearers of the name settled in County Galway.

Dols (182) Dutch: nickname from Middle Dutch *dol(le)* 'mad', 'crazy'.
GIVEN NAMES German 4%. *Florian* (2), *Ewald, Kurt.*

Dolsen (95) Dutch: evidently a patronymic, presumably from **Dol**, a nickname for a madman, from Middle Dutch *dolle* 'crazy', 'mad'.

Dolson (552) English: patronymic of unexplained etymology. Perhaps an importation to England of Dutch DOLSEN.

Dolton (208) English: variant spelling of DALTON.

Dom (120) Dutch: **1.** nickname from Middle Dutch *dom(b)* 'stupid', 'dumb'. **2.** from a short form of the Biblical name ADAM. **3.** from a Germanic personal name formed with *dōm* 'judgement', 'verdict'.

Domagala (241) Polish (**Domagała**): nickname for a selfish or demanding person, from Polish *domagać się* 'to demand'.
GIVEN NAMES Polish 13%. *Karol* (2), *Andrzej, Bogdan, Bronislaus, Czeslaw, Irena, Jadwiga, Janina, Jolanta, Lucyna, Mikolaj, Walenty.*

Domagalski (190) Polish: either a habitational name from an unidentified place, or from **Domagała** (see DOMAGALA), with the addition of the surname suffix *-ski*.

Doman (801) **1.** Polish, Czech, and Slovak: from a derivative of the personal name *Tomas* (see THOMAS) or a Slavic personal name formed with *doma* 'home', 'domestic', as for example Polish *Domasław*, Czech *Domaslav* (+ *sław, slav* 'glory'), or Czech *Domorad*, Polish *Domarad* (+ *rad* 'glad'). **2.** Hungarian (**Domány**): from the personal name *Damján*. **3.** Americanized spelling of German DOMANN.

Domangue (334) Variant spelling of French DOMINGUE.
GIVEN NAMES French 5%. *Camille* (2), *Nolton.*

Domanico (151) Italian (Calabria and Piedmont): unexplained.

GIVEN NAMES Italian 5%. *Pasquale, Pietro, Valentino.*

Domann (161) **1.** Eastern German: from a Slavic personal name formed with *doma* 'home', 'domestic' (see DOMAN). **2.** North German: from a Low German pet form of THOMAS.

Domanski (437) Polish (**Domański**): habitational name for someone from Domanice or Domaniew, or various places named with DOMAN.
GIVEN NAMES Polish 11%. *Piotr* (2), *Zygmunt* (2), *Bogdan, Boguslaw, Darek, Feliks, Irena, Jaroslaw, Jerzy, Jozefa, Miroslaw, Stanislaw.*

Domas (117) Dutch: variant of THOMAS.
GIVEN NAME Dutch 5%. *Dirk* (2).

Dombeck (215) Americanized spelling of Polish and Jewish (Ashkenazic) **Dąbek** (see DOMBEK).
GIVEN NAMES German 4%. *Alois, Florian.*

Dombek (258) Americanized spelling of Polish and Jewish (from Poland) **Dąbek**, a nickname or topographic name from *dąbek* 'young oak'. As a Jewish name it is mainly ornamental.

Dombkowski (195) Polish: variant of **Dąbkowski** (see DABKOWSKI).
GIVEN NAMES Polish 9%. *Casimir* (3), *Zigmund* (2), *Zygmunt.*

Dombroski (895) Polish: variant of **Dąbrowski** (see DABROWSKI).

Dombrosky (248) Americanized spelling of Polish **Dąbrowski** (see DABROWSKI).

Dombrow (113) German: habitational name for someone from a place called Dombrowa (see DOMBROWSKI).
GIVEN NAME German 6%. *Helmut* (2).

Dombrowski (2459) Polish and Jewish (eastern Ashkenazic): habitational name for someone from any of several places named Dombrowa (Polish *Dąbrowa*). See also DABROWSKI.

Dombrowsky (138) Ukrainian, Belorussian, and Jewish (Ashkenazic): habitational name for someone from any of various places called in Russian Dombrovo, Dombrova, or Dombrovka, for example in the districts of Zhitomir, Vladimir, or Kamenets in Ukraine, or from any of various places called Dombrowa (in Polish, *Dąbrowa*) (see DABROWSKI).
GIVEN NAMES German 7%. *Dieter, Rainer, Wolf.*

Dome (256) **1.** English: occupational name from the Old English root *dōma, dēma* 'judge', 'arbiter'. Compare DEMPSTER. **2.** French: habitational name from Dome in Saône-et-Loire. **3.** Hungarian (**Döme**): from a pet form of the personal name DEMETER.

Domeier (229) German (**Dommeier**): distinguishing name for the tenant farmer (see MEYER) of land belonging to a cathedral (German *Dom*), to which he would have owed feudal tax or service obligations.

GIVEN NAMES German 4%. *Erwin, Florian, Kurt, Meinrad.*

Domek (162) Czech and Polish: from a pet form of the personal name *Dominik*, a vernacular form of Late Latin *Dominicus* (see DOMINICK), or an old personal name composed with *domo-*, from *doma* 'home', 'domestic', as for example Czech *Domorad* and *Domoslav* or Polish *Domarad* and *Domasław* (see DOMAN).

Domen (112) **1.** Dutch: patronymic from the personal name DOM. **2.** Japanese: it is unclear whether instances of this name in America are *Domen*, written with characters meaning 'surface of the earth', or *Dōmen*, written with various characters; one combination means 'surface of the road'. None of these are common in Japan.
GIVEN NAMES Japanese 6%. *Kazufumi, Minoru, Yosh.*

Domenech (252) Catalan (**Domènech**): respelling of the personal name *Domènec*, Catalan form of DOMINICK.
GIVEN NAMES Spanish 39%. *Luis* (7), *Guillermo* (5), *Jose* (4), *Armando* (3), *Angel* (2), *Carlos* (2), *Enrique* (2), *Fernando* (2), *Juan* (2), *Manuel* (2), *Orlando* (2), *Sergio* (2).

Domenici (148) Italian: patronymic or plural form of DOMENICO.
GIVEN NAMES Italian 9%. *Elvio, Evo, Fulvio, Gianna, Guido, Umberto.*

Domenick (281) From a personal name derived from Late Latin *Domenicus*, though the language of origin is uncertain: it could be a variant spelling of English or German DOMINICK or an Americanized form of French **Dominique** or Italian DOMENICO.
GIVEN NAMES Italian 7%. *Aldo, Nunzio, Rocco.*

Domenico (399) Italian: from the personal name *Domenico* (Latin *Dominicus*, meaning 'of the Lord', from *dominus* 'lord', 'master').
GIVEN NAMES Italian 7%. *Angelo* (2), *Alfonse, Concetta, Dante, Dino, Palma.*

Domer (454) German: of uncertain derivation. It may be an occupational name for a judge, Middle Low German *domer*, an agent derivative of *domen* 'to judge or pass sentence'. Alternatively it could be a nickname for a self-indulgent person, Middle Low German *domer*.

Domes (105) **1.** Czech and Slovak: from the personal name *Tomas* (see THOMAS), or a derivative of a Slavic personal name formed with *doma* 'home' (see DOMAN). **2.** Alternatively, possibly a variant of French DOME.

Domian (104) **1.** Polish: from a derivative of a personal name formed with *doma* 'home', 'domestic', for example *Domarad* or *Domasław*. **2.** Anglicized spelling of eastern Slovenian **Domjan**, a dialect form of the personal name *Damjan*, Latin *Damianus* (see DAMIAN).
GIVEN NAMES Polish 7%. *Edyta, Jerzy, Jozef.*

Domiano (162) Italian: possibly a variant of DAMIANO.
GIVEN NAMES Italian 17%. *Neno* (2), *Carlo*, *Carmelo*, *Dino*, *Gino*.

Domico (128) Origin uncertain. It may be a reduced form of Italian DOMENICO.
GIVEN NAMES Italian 4%. *Angelo*, *Pasquale*.

Domin (299) French: from Old French *domainier* 'feudal lord', hence perhaps a nickname for someone who behaved in a lordly manner.

Domina (259) Czech, Slovak, and Polish: from the personal name *Dominik*, a vernacular form of Late Latin *Dominicus* (see DOMINICK).

Domine (172) French (**Dominé**): nickname for a church cantor, from Latin *Domine* (vocative of *Dominus*, 'Lord'). In Canada, the name comports the secondary surname *Saint Sauveur* 'Holy Savior'.

Dominey (199) **1.** English (Somerset, Dorset, and Hampshire): unexplained. **2.** In some instances probably an altered spelling of French **Dominé** (see DOMINE).

Domingo (1235) Spanish: from a personal name (Latin *Dominicus* meaning 'of the Lord', from *dominus* 'lord', 'master'). This was borne by a Spanish saint (1170–1221) who founded the Dominican order of friars and whose fame added greatly to the popularity of the name, already well established because of its symbolic value.
FOREBEARS The surname Domingo is found in Quebec city by 1681, brought from Bayonne in France. Bearers of this name are also called **Carabi**, implying a connection with the former Spanish colony of Santo Domingo (now the Dominican Republic) in the Caribbean.
GIVEN NAMES Spanish 35%. *Jose* (12), *Manuel* (8), *Juan* (6), *Ernesto* (4), *Rolando* (4), *Violeta* (4), *Virgilio* (4), *Carlos* (3), *Fernando* (3), *Francisco* (3), *Jaime* (3), *Jesus* (3); *Antonio* (7), *Quirino* (4), *Dante* (3), *Federico* (3), *Jovencio* (2), *Lorenzo* (2), *Romeo* (2), *Salvatore* (2), *Carmelo*, *Ceasar*, *Enrico*, *Franco*.

Domingos (298) Portuguese: from the personal name *Domingos*, Portuguese equivalent of DOMINICK.
GIVEN NAMES Spanish 21%; Portuguese 13%. *Manuel* (16), *Jose* (10), *Carlos* (2), *Luis* (2), *Miguel* (2), *Ana*, *Arlindo*, *Cesar*, *Ernestina*, *Gilberto*, *Horacio*, *Manual*; *Agostinho*, *Joao*, *Joaquim*.

Domingue (1205) Variant of French DOMINIQUE.
GIVEN NAMES French 7%. *Andre* (2), *Alcide*, *Andree*, *Clermont*, *Clovis*, *Curley*, *Desire*, *Easton*, *Emile*, *Fernand*, *Jacques*, *Kossuth*.

Domingues (338) Portuguese: patronymic from the personal name DOMINGOS.
GIVEN NAMES Spanish 34%; Portuguese 11%. *Manuel* (9), *Carlos* (6), *Jose* (5), *Pedro* (4), *Adelino* (2), *Aires* (2), *Alejandrina* (2), *Jesus* (2), *Luis* (2), *Marcelo* (2), *Miguel* (2), *Roberto* (2); *Aderito*, *Joaquim*.

Dominguez (10114) Spanish (**Domínguez**): patronymic from the personal name DOMINGO.
GIVEN NAMES Spanish 48%. *Jose* (258), *Juan* (134), *Manuel* (101), *Carlos* (95), *Luis* (78), *Raul* (72), *Jesus* (70), *Francisco* (62), *Ramon* (54), *Ruben* (53), *Pedro* (52), *Miguel* (49).

Dominiak (198) Polish: patronymic from the personal name *Dominik*, a vernacular form of Late Latin *Dominicus* (see DOMINICK).
GIVEN NAMES Polish 9%. *Casimir*, *Krzysztof*, *Ludwik*, *Zbigniew*.

Dominic (334) **1.** English: variant spelling of DOMINICK. **2.** In some cases, probably an Americanized spelling of the French cognate DOMINIQUE.

Dominici (160) Italian: variant of DOMENICI (see DOMENICO).
GIVEN NAMES Italian 19%; Spanish 4%. *Lamberto* (2), *Angelo*, *Carlo*, *Dino*, *Enio*, *Francesca*, *Gasper*, *Guido*; *Carlos*, *Domingo*, *Elvira*.

Dominick (1550) English: from a vernacular form of the Late Latin personal name *Dominicus* 'of the Lord'. This was borne by a Spanish saint (1170–1221) who founded the Dominican order of friars. In medieval England it may have been used as a personal name for a child born on a Sunday. As an English surname it is comparatively rare, and in the U.S. it has undoubtedly absorbed cognates in other European languages; for the forms, see Hanks and Hodges 1988.

Dominik (191) Czech, Slovak, Slovenian, and Polish: from the personal name *Dominik*, Late Latin *Dominicus* (see DOMINICK).
GIVEN NAMES German 11%; Polish 4%. *Otto* (2), *Florian*, *Guenter*, *Jurgen*, *Kurt*; *Danuta*, *Janusz*, *Tadeusz*.

Dominique (564) French: from the personal name *Dominique*, a vernacular form of Late Latin *Dominicus* (see DOMINICK).
GIVEN NAMES French 12%. *Alain*, *Alcide*, *Andre*, *Angelle*, *Antoine*, *Brunel*, *Edele*, *Jean Baptiste*, *Jean Marc*, *Jean Robert*, *Jean-Claude*, *Jeanne Marie*.

Domino (630) Italian: from the personal name *Domino*, from Latin *dominus* 'lord', 'master', or a nickname with the same meaning.
GIVEN NAMES Italian 5%. *Antonio* (3), *Geronimo* (3), *Sal* (3), *Rocco* (2), *Marino*, *Salvatore*, *Tommaso*.

Dominquez (356) Hispanic (**Domínquez**): variant of Spanish DOMINGUEZ.
GIVEN NAMES Spanish 45%. *Jose* (11), *Juan* (6), *Enrique* (3), *Luis* (3), *Manuel* (3), *Mario* (3), *Alberto* (2), *Armando* (2), *Blanca* (2), *Fernando* (2), *Francisco* (2), *Jorge* (2).

Dominski (176) Polish (**Domiński**): **1.** habitational name for someone from Dominek in Słupsk voivodeship. **2.** from the personal name *Domin*, a vernacular

form of Late Latin *Dominicus* (see DOMINICK) + *-ski*, suffix of surnames.

Dominy (652) English: variant of DOMINEY.

Domitrovich (120) **1.** Ukrainian: patronymic from the personal name *Domitry*, from Greek *Dēmētrios* (Latin *Demetrius*; see DEMETRIOU). **2.** Croatian and Serbian (**Domitrović**): patronymic from the personal name *Domitar*, an old form of the personal name *Dimitrije*, from Greek *Dēmētrios* (Latin *Demetrius*; see DEMETRIOU).
GIVEN NAME Polish 5%. *Karol* (3).

Domke (486) Eastern German: from a pet form of the personal name THOMAS.

Domm (117) German: variant spelling of DUMM.

Dommer (257) German: **1.** from a Germanic personal name derived from an element cognate with Gothic *doms*, Old High German *tuom* 'judgement', 'justice', 'power'. **2.** variant of DUMMER.
GIVEN NAMES Scandinavian 4%. *Erik*, *Jarl*.

Domonkos (112) Hungarian: from the personal names *Domokos* or *Domonkos*, Hungarian equivalents of DOMINICK.
GIVEN NAMES Hungarian 4%. *Arpad*, *Istvan*.

Dompier (109) Possibly a respelling of French **Dompierre**, a habitational name from any of several places in northern France named Dompierre, from Latin *dominus Petrus*, i.e. St. Peter, or the southern variant **Dompeyre**.

Domres (154) German: habitational name for someone from a place called Dumröse, near Stolp in Pomerania.
GIVEN NAMES German 4%. *Fritz*, *Otto*.

Domzalski (222) Polish (**Domżalski**): of uncertain origin; possibly from a derivative of *domrzeć* 'to die' or from dialect *mżeć* 'to dream of something'.

Don (543) **1.** Scottish: Aberdeenshire surname, presumably a topographic name referring to the River Don, although according to Black, it may be a variant of DUNN. **2.** Italian: in northern Italy (Venetia), from the personal name *Dono*, a shortening of *dono di Dio* 'gift of God'; in the south, it is probably from the honorific title *don*, meaning 'master'. **3.** French: from the personal name *Dodo(ne)*. **4.** Spanish: unexplained; perhaps from the term of address *don* 'mister' (Latin *dominus*), in the patronymic form **De Don**, or perhaps a habitational name from a hypothetical place so called. **5.** Hungarian: from a short form of the personal name *Donát* (see DONATH). **6.** Jewish (Ashkenazic): from the personal name *Don*, a variant of *Dan*. **7.** Vietnamese (**Đôn**): unexplained.
GIVEN NAMES Spanish 7%. *Agustin* (2), *Jose* (2), *Miguel* (2), *Pablo* (2), *Ramon* (2), *Ruben* (2), *Adriana*, *Ausencio*, *Eduardo*, *Enrique*, *Erasmo*, *Francisco*.

Dona (227) **1.** Italian (**Donà**): Venetian variant of DONATO. **2.** Southern Italian: from a reduced form of *Adona*, feminine form of *Adone*. **3.** Hungarian: from a pet form of the personal name *Donát* (see DONATH). **4.** Catalan: perhaps from *dona* 'lady', 'woman'.

GIVEN NAMES Spanish 12%. *Juan* (4), *Mario* (2), *Cristobal*, *Florencio*, *Francisco*, *Lino*, *Luis*, *Luisa*, *Mariano*, *Orlando*, *Perfecto*, *Renato*.

Donabedian (111) Armenian: patronymic from classical Armenian *tōnapet* 'head of a festival'.

GIVEN NAMES Armenian 36%. *Haig* (5), *Aram* (2), *Zaven* (2), *Armen*, *Asdghig*, *Avedis*, *Berj*, *Hagop*, *Hasmig*, *Hovhannes*, *Hovig*, *Vartkes*.

Donadio (426) Southern Italian: from the medieval personal name *Donadio* meaning 'gift of God'.

GIVEN NAMES Italian 11%. *Giuseppe* (2), *Rocco* (2), *Aldo*, *Carmine*, *Emelio*, *Luigi*, *Renzo*, *Salvatore*.

Donaghey (249) Irish: variant of DONAHUE.
GIVEN NAMES Irish 4%. *Aidan*, *Fergus*.

Donaghue (238) Irish: variant of DONAHUE.
GIVEN NAMES Irish 5%. *Connor*, *Niall*.

Donaghy (707) Irish: variant of DONAHUE.
GIVEN NAMES Irish 6%. *Caitlin*, *Colm*, *Kieran*.

Donaher (118) Irish: variant of DANAHER.

Donahey (228) Irish: variant of DONAHUE.

Donaho (238) Irish: variant of DONAHUE.

Donahoe (1231) Irish: variant of DONAHUE.
GIVEN NAMES Irish 4%. *Cormac*, *Ronan*.

Donahoo (602) Variant of Irish DONAHUE.

Donahue (12455) Irish: reduced Anglicized form of Gaelic **Ó Donnchadha** 'descendant of *Donnchadh*', a personal name (sometimes Anglicized as *Duncan* in Scotland), composed of the elements *donn* 'brown-haired man' or 'chieftain' + *cath* 'battle'.

GIVEN NAMES Irish 6%. *Brendan* (6), *Aidan* (2), *Siobhan* (2), *Aileen*, *Conan*, *Fidelma*, *John Patrick*, *Kieran*, *Parnell*.

Donais (175) French: of uncertain derivation; perhaps a respelling of **Daunay**, a habitational name, with the preposition *d(e)*, for someone from a place named Aunay, for example in Calvados, Eure, and Orne. The place name is derived from *aune* 'alder'.

GIVEN NAME French 5%. *Adelard*.

Donald (3609) Scottish and Irish: reduced form of MCDONALD.

Donaldson (12604) Scottish: patronymic from DONALD, often representing a reduced Anglicized form of Gaelic **Mac Dhomhnaill** (see MCDONALD).

Donalson (358) Scottish: variant of DONALDSON.

Donarski (123) Polish: **1.** possibly a habitational name from a place called Downary, named with the personal name *Downar*, Lithuanian *Daunoras*. **2.** alternatively, perhaps, from the personal name DONAT.

Donat (440) English, French, German, Hungarian (**Donát**), Polish, and Czech

(**Donát**): from a medieval personal name (Latin *Donatus*, past participle of *donare*, frequentative of *dare* 'to give'). The name was much favored by early Christians, either because the birth of a child was seen as a gift from God, or else because the child was in turn dedicated to God. The name was borne by various early saints, among them a 6th-century hermit of Sisteron and a 7th-century bishop of Besançon, all of whom contributed to the popularity of the baptismal name in the Middle Ages, which was not checked by the heresy of a 4th-century Carthaginian bishop who also bore it. Another bearer was a 4th-century grammarian and commentator on Virgil, widely respected in the Middle Ages as a figure of great learning.

Donatelli (686) Italian: patronymic from a pet form of DONATO.

GIVEN NAMES Italian 13%. *Angelo* (4), *Dante* (4), *Dino* (2), *Silvio* (2), *Antonio*, *Biagio*, *Camillo*, *Carlo*, *Dario*, *Domenic*, *Gaetano*, *Galileo*.

Donath (422) **1.** German: variant of DONAT. **2.** Hungarian (**Donáth**): variant of **Donát** (see DONAT).

GIVEN NAMES German 6%. *Kurt* (2), *Otto* (2), *Gerhard*, *Hans*, *Horst*.

Donathan (387) Origin uncertain; perhaps an altered form of JONATHAN.

Donati (591) Italian: patronymic or plural form of DONATO.

GIVEN NAMES Italian 11%. *Dino* (5), *Enrico* (3), *Angelo* (2), *Reno* (2), *Aldo*, *Amedeo*, *Elio*, *Ettore*, *Fabrizio*, *Fausto*, *Geno*, *Gianni*.

Donato (2191) Italian: from the medieval personal name *Donato* (Latin *Donatus*, past participle of *donare*, frequentative of *dare* 'to give'). It was the name of a 4th-century Italian bishop martyred in *c.* 350 under Julian the Apostate, as well as various other early saints, and a 4th-century grammarian and commentator on Virgil, widely respected in the Middle Ages as a figure of great learning. See also DONAT.

GIVEN NAMES Italian 22%. *Antonio* (12), *Salvatore* (11), *Mario* (9), *Angelo* (6), *Domenic* (5), *Alfredo* (3), *Jose* (3), *Alberto* (2), *Armando* (2), *Cosmo* (2), *Franco* (2), *Gaetano* (2), *Gino* (2), *Rafael* (2), *Renato* (2), *Rico* (2), *Rocco* (2), *Rosario* (2), *Santo* (2).

Donavan (254) Irish: variant spelling of DONOVAN.

Donaway (162) English: unexplained. Compare DUNAWAY.

Doncaster (110) English: habitational name from Doncaster in South Yorkshire, named from the river name *Don* (a Celtic name meaning 'water', 'river') + Old English *ceaster* 'Roman fort or walled city'.

Donchez (123) Origin unidentified.

Dondero (524) Italian (Genoa): unexplained; possibly an occupational name.

Dondlinger (182) German: habitational name for someone from a place called Dondlingen in Luxembourg.

Done (235) English (Cheshire): possibly a variant spelling of DUNN.

GIVEN NAMES Spanish 9%. *Jose* (3), *Carlos* (2), *Alfredo*, *Angel*, *Berto*, *Cristobal*, *Dinora*, *Eloisa*, *Francisco*, *Generoso*, *Gustavo*, *Juan*.

Donegan (1501) Irish: reduced Anglicized form of Gaelic **Ó Donnagáin** 'descendant of *Donnagán*', a personal name from a double diminutive of *donn* 'brown-haired man' or 'chieftain'.

GIVEN NAMES Irish 4%. *Brendan* (2), *Siobhan*.

Donehoo (160) Variant spelling of Irish DONAHUE.

Donelan (415) Irish: reduced Anglicized form of Gaelic **Ó Domhnalláin** (see DONLON).

GIVEN NAME Irish 5%. *Brendan*.

Donelson (1123) Variant of Scottish DONALDSON.

Doner (571) **1.** German (**Döner**): occupational name for a musician, from an agent derivative of Middle High German *dænen* 'to sing or play'. **2.** Altered spelling of German **Döhner** (see DOHNER).

Dones (402) Catalan: possibly from the plural of Catalan *dona* 'lady', 'woman', perhaps alluding to a convent.

GIVEN NAMES Spanish 30%. *Jose* (9), *Angel* (4), *Carlos* (4), *Juan* (4), *Miguel* (4), *Fernando* (3), *Roberto* (3), *Domingo* (2), *Dulce* (2), *Luz* (2), *Pedro* (2), *Alberto*.

Doney (869) English (Devon and Cornwall): variant of DONAT.

Dong (1317) **1.** Chinese 董: from a character that also means 'to supervise' or 'to manage'. The story goes that in the 23rd century BC, an adviser to the emperor Shun was given this surname due to his ability to supervise and train dragons. Additionally, at one time during the Spring and Autumn period (722–481 BC), Dong was part of the title of official historians. The descendants of a historian of the state of Jin adopted the character for Dong from their ancestor's title and used it as a surname. **2.** Vietnamese (**Đông** and **Đồng**): unexplained.

GIVEN NAMES Chinese 38%; Vietnamese 13%. *Qing* (8), *Ming* (7), *Feng* (6), *Wei* (6), *Jian* (4), *Ying* (4), *Zheng* (4), *Fang* (3), *Gang* (3), *Hong* (3), *Mei* (3), *Wing* (3); *Hao* (3), *Lan* (3), *Minh* (3), *Nguyen* (3), *Be* (2), *Bich* (2), *Cuc* (2), *Duc* (2), *Dung* (2), *Hai* (2), *Hoa* (2), *Hue* (2).

Donges (130) North German: variant of TONJES.

Donham (508) English: variant spelling of DUNHAM.

Donica (210) Polish: **1.** from *donica* 'bowl', 'flowerpot', possibly a metonymic occupational name for a maker of such items. **2.** from the personal name *Donat* (see DONAT).

GIVEN NAMES French 6%. *Clovis, Corin, Marcel.*

Donigan (170) Irish: variant spelling of DONEGAN.

Doniger (111) German: **1.** possibly a habitational name from a place called Donningen in Luxembourg **2.** alternatively, perhaps an Americanized form of DANNECKER.

Donis (257) **1.** Catalan (**Donís**): from the personal name *Donís*, a Valencian variant of *Dionís*, a vernacular form of *Dionysius* (see DENNIS). **2.** Italian (Piedmont): possibly a variant of DONISI, cognate with 1.
GIVEN NAMES Spanish 33%. *Jose* (5), *Julio* (4), *Luis* (4), *Francisco* (3), *Juan* (2), *Agustin, Alicia, Andres, Armando, Arturo, Carlos, Carlota.*

Donisi (102) Italian: reduced form of DIONISIO.
GIVEN NAMES Italian 18%. *Paolo* (2), *Gennaro, Raffaele, Tullio.*

Donivan (126) Irish: variant spelling of DONOVAN.

Donker (138) Dutch: nickname for someone with dark hair or a dark complexion, from Middle Dutch *donker, donkel* 'dark'.

Donkin (132) Scottish: variant of DUNCAN.

Donlan (540) Irish: variant of DONLON.

Donlevy (115) Irish: variant of DUNLEAVY.

Donley (2785) Irish: probably a reduced form of DONNELLY.

Donlin (457) Irish: variant of DONLON.
GIVEN NAME Irish 4%. *Clancy.*

Donlon (946) Scottish and Irish: reduced Anglicized form of Gaelic **Ó Domhnalláin** 'descendant of *Domhnallán*', a diminutive of the personal name *Domhnall*, Anglicized in Ireland as *Donall* or *Daniel* and in Scotland as *Donald*.
GIVEN NAMES Irish 5%. *Aidan, Parnell.*

Donmoyer (206) Probably a respelling of German **Dannmeyer**, a nickname for a tenant farmer (see MEYER) whose land was sited near some pines (see DANN), or possibly of **Dommeier** (see DOMEIER).

Donn (283) **1.** English and Scottish: variant spelling of DUNN. **2.** Jewish (Ashkenazic): variant spelling of DON.
GIVEN NAMES Jewish 6%. *Chaim* (2), *Isaak, Meyer, Miriam, Zorach.*

Donna (231) Italian: metronymic from the medieval personal name *Donna*, from the appellative and title of respect meaning 'mistress' (from Latin *domina*).

Donnally (144) Irish: variant of DONNELLY.

Donnan (372) Irish (County Down): reduced Anglicized form of Gaelic **Ó Donnáin** 'descendant of *Donnán*', a diminutive of *donn* 'brown-haired man' or 'chieftain'. This surname is often confused with DOONAN.

Donnay (152) **1.** English: variant of DONAT. **2.** Possibly a respelling of French **Donné**, also a variant of DONAT.
GIVEN NAMES French 5%. *Gabrielle, Marcel.*

Donnell (2356) Irish: reduced form of MCDONNELL.

Donnellan (641) Irish and Scottish: reduced Anglicized form of Gaelic **Ó Domhnalláin** (see DONLON).
GIVEN NAMES Irish 8%. *Brendan, Brennan, Brigid, Conan, Nuala, Seamus.*

Donnelley (137) Irish: variant spelling of DONNELLY.

Donnellon (135) Irish and Scottish: reduced Anglicized form of Gaelic **Ó Domhnalláin** (see DONLON).

Donnelly (12540) Irish: reduced Anglicized form of Gaelic **Ó Donnghaile** 'descendant of *Donnghal*', a personal name composed of the elements *donn* 'brown-haired man' or 'chieftain' + *gal* 'valor'. It is claimed that most bearers of this surname in Donegal descend from Donnghal O'Neill, 17th in descent from Niall of the Nine Hostages; there were also other families of the same name in Sligo and Cork.
GIVEN NAMES Irish 5%. *Brendan* (9), *Eamon* (3), *Aileen* (2), *Kieran* (2), *Liam* (2), *Aisling, Brigid, Clodagh, Conan, Eamonn, Michael Patrick, Niall.*

Donner (1897) **1.** German: nickname for a loud or irascible man, from Middle High German *doner* 'thunder' (Old High German *thonar*). **2.** Jewish (Ashkenazic): ornamental adoption of German *Donner* 'thunder'.

D'Onofrio (2293) Southern Italian: patronymic from the personal name *Onofrio*, an adaptation of Egyptian *Onnophris* (said to mean 'always happy'), an epithet of the god Osiris. The name gained popularity in Italy through the cult of St. Onofrio, a 5th-century martyr.
GIVEN NAMES Italian 16%. *Rocco* (10), *Salvatore* (10), *Pasquale* (9), *Angelo* (8), *Carmine* (7), *Antonio* (5), *Sal* (5), *Domenic* (4), *Vito* (4), *Carlo* (3), *Agostino* (2), *Carmelo* (2).

Donoghue (1428) Irish: variant spelling of DONAHUE.
GIVEN NAMES Irish 5%. *Brendan, Bridie, Dermot, Liam, Malachy, Niall, Seamus.*

Donohew (109) Respelling of Irish DONAHUE.

Donoho (847) Irish: variant spelling of DONAHUE.

Donohoe (1422) Irish: variant spelling of DONAHUE.
GIVEN NAMES Irish 6%. *Padraic* (2), *Ronan* (2), *Donal, Liam, Meave.*

Donohoo (292) Irish: variant spelling of DONAHUE.
GIVEN NAMES Irish 8%. *Donovan* (5), *Sean Michael.*

Donohue (5896) Irish: variant spelling of DONAHUE.
GIVEN NAMES Irish 6%. *Brendan* (3), *Kieran* (2), *Declan, John Patrick, Liam, Malachy, Padraig, Parnell.*

Donoso (121) Spanish: nickname from *donoso* 'graceful'.

GIVEN NAMES Spanish 41%. *Pedro* (5), *Jose* (4), *Carlos* (3), *Alfonso* (2), *Ana* (2), *Eduardo* (2), *Jorge* (2), *Luis* (2), *Ricardo* (2), *Aida, Alberto, Alvero.*

Donovan (16544) Irish (originally of County Limerick, later of Counties Cork and Kilkenny): reduced Anglicized form of Gaelic **Ó Donndubháin** 'descendant of *Donndubhán*', a personal name composed of the elements *donn* 'brown-haired man' or 'chieftain' + *dubh* 'black' + the diminutive suffix *-án*.
GIVEN NAMES Irish 5%. *Brendan* (14), *Finbarr* (2), *Aidan, Aileen, Brigid, Declan, Delma, Siobhan.*

Donsbach (108) German: habitational name from Donsbach in Hesse.
GIVEN NAMES German 10%. *Dieter, Egon, Hermann, Siegfried.*

Donson (122) English: unexplained. Compare DUNSON, of which this may be a variant.

Donze (277) **1.** French (**Donzé**): according to Morlet, a Corsican variant of Italian **Donzelli**, from Old Italian *donzello*, denoting a young man of noble birth in the service of a king, used as a nickname for a mannered or effeminate man. **2.** Dutch: nickname from Middle Dutch *donst, donse* 'down', 'downy hair on the chin'.

Doo (124) Chinese: see TU.
GIVEN NAMES Chinese 8%. *Jin Ho* (2), *Young* (2), *Jong, Ling, Mi Sook, Quong, Yi.*

Doody (1204) Irish: variant of DOWD.

Doogan (116) Irish: variant spelling of DUGAN.
GIVEN NAME Irish 6%. *James Patrick.*

Doolan (523) Irish: variant spelling of DOOLIN.
GIVEN NAME Irish 6%. *Brendan* (2).

Doolen (224) Irish: variant spelling of DOOLIN.

Dooley (8970) Irish: reduced Anglicized form of Gaelic **Ó Dubhlaoich** 'descendant of *Dubhlaoch*', a personal name composed of the elements *dubh* 'black' (see DUFF) + *laoch* 'champion', 'hero'.

Doolin (895) Irish: reduced Anglicized form of Gaelic **1. Ó Dubhshláin** 'descendant of *Dubhshlán*', a personal name composed of the elements *dubh* 'dark', 'black' + *slán* 'challenge'. **2. Ó Dubhlainn** 'descendant of *Dubhfhlann*', a personal name composed of the elements *dubh* 'black' + *flann* 'blood-colored', 'red'. **3. Ó Dúnlaing**, a North Leinster name meaning 'descendant of *Dúnlang*'.

Dooling (508) **1.** Irish: variant of DOLAN 1. **2.** English: variant of DOWLING.

Doolittle (2696) English: nickname for a lazy man, from Middle English *do* 'do' + *little* 'little'.

Dooly (154) Irish: variant spelling of DOOLEY.

Doom (327) **1.** Dutch: from a Limburg short form of the personal name ADAM. **2.** Dutch: from *de oom* 'the uncle', proba-

bly used as an epithet to distinguish between two members of the same family with the same personal name. **3.** Americanized spelling of German DUMM or **Thum**, from a pet form of THOMAS.
GIVEN NAMES French 4%. *Collette, Gabrielle, Remi.*

Dooms (138) Dutch: patronymic from DOOM.

Doonan (558) Irish (Counties Fermanagh, Leitrim, and Roscommon): **1.** reduced Anglicized form of Gaelic **Ó Dúnáin** 'descendant of *Dúnán*', which is a pet form of a longer name beginning with *dun* 'fortress'. **2.** reduced Anglicized form of Gaelic **Ó Donnáin** (see DONNAN).

Dooner (194) **1.** German: variant of DONNER. **2.** Irish (Counties Roscommon and Leitrim): Anglicized form of Gaelic **Ó Dúnabhra, Ó Donnabhair** 'descendant of *Dúnabhra*', from *donn* 'brown' + *abhra* 'eyebrow'.
GIVEN NAME Irish 5%. *Sean Michael.*

Dooney (113) Irish: variant of DOWNEY.
GIVEN NAME Irish 10%. *Brendan.*

Door (135) **1.** Probably a variant spelling of the English topographic name DORE. **2.** Alternatively an Americanized form of the German cognate **Tür**.

Doorley (128) Irish: variant of DURLEY.

Doorn (178) Dutch: from *doorn* 'thorn', a topographic name for someone who lived by a thicket or thorn bush.
GIVEN NAMES Dutch 5%. *Harm, Klaas, Michiel.*

Doornbos (277) Dutch: topographic name from *doornbos* 'bramble bush'.
GIVEN NAMES German 4%. *Kurt, Otto.*

Doose (135) Dutch: of uncertain origin. Debrabandere proposes **D'Hoossche** as a source; possibly a reflex of **de Hoofsche**, a nickname for someone with courtly manners.

Dopke (102) German (**Döpke**): from a variant of *Depke*, a much altered pet form of the personal name *Detmar* (see DITTMAR).

Dopkins (103) English: patronymic from *Dopkin, Dobkin*, a pet form of the medieval personal name DOBBE.

Dopp (594) German: **1.** from Low German *doppe, duppe* 'beaker', 'jar', hence presumably a metonymic occupational name for a maker of such vessels. **2.** from a short form of a Germanic personal name formed with *theud, diot* 'people'. 'race'.

Doppelt (110) Jewish (Ashkenazic): from German *doppelt* 'doubled', 'twice'. The application of this term as a surname is not clear.
GIVEN NAMES Jewish 8%; German 4%. *Mandel, Moshe.*

Doppler (102) German: **1.** nickname from Middle High German *topelære* 'dice player'. **2.** habitational name for someone from either of two places called Toppel, in Saxony-Anhalt, Germany, and in Austria.
GIVEN NAME French 6%. *Etienne.*

Dopson (301) English: patronymic from the medieval personal name DOBBE.

Dora (276) **1.** Hungarian: from the female personal name *Dóra*, a short form of *Dorottya*, Hungarian form of DOROTHY. **2.** Indian (Bengal) and Bangladeshi: Hindu (Kayasth) name of unknown meaning.

Dorado (416) Spanish: from *dorado* 'golden' (from Late Latin *deaurare* 'to gild', from *aurum* 'gold'), probably applied as a nickname to someone with golden hair.
GIVEN NAMES Spanish 56%. *Juan* (12), *Jose* (11), *Manuel* (5), *Miguel* (4), *Ricardo* (4), *Agustin* (3), *Gustavo* (3), *Jesus* (3), *Jose Luis* (3), *Luis* (3), *Rafael* (3), *Raul* (3), *Antonio* (4), *Clemente* (2), *Fausto* (2), *Aureliano, Bartolo, Eliseo, Lorenzo, Sal.*

Dorais (149) French: unexplained.
GIVEN NAMES French 14%. *Laurent* (2), *Armand, Gilles, Luc, Marcel, Pierre.*

Dorame (126) Mexican: unexplained.
GIVEN NAMES Spanish 44%. *Jesus* (5), *Francisco* (4), *Jose* (3), *Ramon* (3), *Ricardo* (3), *Armida* (2), *Efren* (2), *Ana, Artemisa, Arturo, Carlos, Celso.*

Doran (6614) **1.** Irish: reduced Anglicized form of Gaelic **Ó Deoradháin** 'descendant of *Deoradhán*', a byname representing a diminutive of *deoradh* 'pilgrim', 'stranger', 'exile'. **2.** English: variant of DURANT.
GIVEN NAMES Irish 5%. *James Patrick* (2), *Kieran* (2), *Pegeen* (2), *Brendan, Caitlin, Dymphna, Dympna, Lorcan, Roisin, Siobhan.*

Dorantes (172) Spanish: apparently a variant of **Durantes, Durántez**, a patronymic from the personal name *Durant* (see DURANT, DURANTE).
GIVEN NAMES Spanish 54%. *Jose* (11), *Francisco* (4), *Miguel* (4), *Carlos* (3), *Javier* (3), *Luis* (3), *Raul* (3), *Alvaro* (2), *Joaquin* (2), *Juan* (2), *Ricardo* (2), *Roberto* (2).

Dorau (101) French: from a pet form of the personal name *Théodore* (see THEODORE) or of a Germanic personal name formed with the element *dor-*.

D'Orazio (907) Italian: patronymic from the personal name *Orazio*, from Latin *Horatius* (see HORACE).
GIVEN NAMES Italian 20%. *Angelo* (11), *Antonio* (5), *Arduino* (3), *Rocco* (3), *Carlo* (2), *Emidio* (2), *Gino* (2), *Marco* (2), *Marino* (2), *Palma* (2), *Pasquale* (2), *Pio* (2).

Dorcas (107) Irish or English: unexplained.

Dorcey (119) Irish and English: variant of DARCY.

Dorch (139) Scottish: perhaps a nickname from Gaelic *dorch* 'dark'.
GIVEN NAME French 5%. *Blanchard.*

Dorchester (104) English: habitational name either from Dorchester in Oxfordshire or Dorchester, county seat of Dorset. Both are named with a Celtic name, respec-

tively *Dorcic* and *Durnovaria*, + Old English *ceaster* 'Roman fort or walled city'.

Dore (1787) **1.** English: habitational name from either of two places, one in South Yorkshire (formerly in Derbyshire) and the other near Hereford. The former gets its name from Old English *dor* 'door', used of a pass between hills; the latter from a Celtic river name of the same origin as DOVER 1. In some cases, the name may be topographic, from Middle English *dore* 'gate'. **2.** Irish: in County Limerick a reduced Anglicized form of Gaelic **Ó Doghair** 'descendant of *Doghar*', a byname meaning 'sadness'; alternatively, according to MacLysaght, it could be from **De Hóir**, a name of Norman origin. Outside Limerick it may be from French **Doré** (see below). **3.** French (**Doré**): nickname from Old French *doré* 'golden', past participle of *dorer* 'to gild' (Late Latin *deaurare*, from *aurum* 'gold'), denoting either a goldsmith or someone with bright golden hair. **4.** Hungarian (**Dőre**): nickname from *dőre* 'stupid', 'useless' 'mad'.
GIVEN NAMES French 6%. *Andre* (3), *Sarto* (2), *Alphonse, Aymar, Chantal, Colette, Collette, Curley, Eudore, Gaetan, Gilles, Homere.*

Doremus (588) Dutch: Debrabandere suggests that this is a nickname from *Adoremus* 'We adore', from the Latin liturgy.

Doren (265) **1.** German (**Dören**): habitational name from any of the places named Döhren, in Hannover and Westphalia (several), or a shortened form of various compound names beginning with *Doren-*, for example **Dorenberg, Dorendorff**. **2.** Possibly Dutch: reflex of DOORN with epenthesis.

Dorenkamp (122) Dutch: unexplained; possibly a topographic name for someone who lived by a thorn field, from *doorn* 'bramble patch', 'thorn patch' + *kamp* 'field', 'domain' (from Latin *campus*).

Dorer (219) German: topographic name for someone who lived by the gate of a town or city, from Middle High German *tōr(e)*, Middle Low German *dore* 'gate', + the suffix *-(e)r*, denoting an inhabitant.
GIVEN NAMES German 4%. *Kurt* (2), *Oskar.*

Dorey (531) English (of Norman origin): nickname for a goldsmith or someone with golden hair, from Old French *doré* 'golden' (see DORE 3).

Dorf (496) Jewish (Ashkenazic): nickname or topographic name for someone who lived in a village, German *Dorf*.
GIVEN NAMES Jewish 6%. *Sol* (3), *Meir* (2), *Zvi* (2), *Miriam, Rebekah.*

Dorff (313) Variant spelling of DORF.

Dorfman (1478) German (**Dorfmann**) and Jewish (Ashkenazic): nickname for a villager or a countryman, literally 'village man', from Middle High German *dorf* 'village', Middle Low German *dorp*; German *Dorf*. Low German names were often standardized, i.e. adapted to High German *Dorf.*

GIVEN NAMES Jewish 8%. *Hyman* (3), *Emanuel* (2), *Inna* (2), *Isadore* (2), *Meyer* (2), *Sol* (2), *Aviva, Avram, Basya, Bentsion, Cohen, Ilya.*

Dorgan (756) Irish: **1.** reduced Anglicized form of the rare Munster name **Ó Dorcháin** 'descendant of *Dorchán*', a byname representing a diminutive of Gaelic *dorcha* 'black', 'gloomy'. **2.** variant of DARGAN.

D'Oria (638) Italian: possibly a metronymic from the female personal name *Oria* (from the Latin personal name *Area, Auria* 'golden'), or a habitational name for someone from a place named *Oria*, of which there are many examples.

Dorian (366) **1.** Irish (County Donegal): variant of DORAN 1. **2.** Variant of French DORION. **3.** Armenian: unexplained. **4.** Romanian: explained.

GIVEN NAMES French 5%; Armenian 4%. *Armand, Cecile, Celestine, Etienne, Jacques; Ara* (2), *Anahid, Ashot, Garo, Houry, Saro.*

Dorin (235) **1.** French: from a pet form of the personal name *Théodore* (see THEODORE). **2.** Jewish (eastern Ashkenazic): Slavicized form of DORN 2.

Doring (260) **1.** English: patronymic from DEAR 1. **2.** German (**Döring**): see DOERING.

GIVEN NAMES German 5%. *Heinz, Kurt, Monika, Otto.*

D'Orio (239) Italian: patronymic from the personal name *Orio*, a masculine form of *Oria* (see D'ORIA).

GIVEN NAMES Italian 17%. *Salvatore* (3), *Angelo* (2), *Carmine* (2), *Alfonse, Luigi, Sal, Vito.*

Dorion (264) French: habitational name, with the preposition *d(e)* 'from', for someone from Orion, in Picardy, believed to be named from a local tributary of the Authie river.

GIVEN NAMES French 6%. *Alphonse, Andre, Armand, Emile, Pierre.*

Doris (512) **1.** Irish (Connacht and Ulster): reduced Anglicized form of Gaelic **Ó Dubhruis** (earlier **Ó Dubhrosa**), 'descendant of *Dubhros*', a personal name composed of the elements *dubh* 'black' + *ros* 'wood'. **2.** French: habitational name, with the preposition *de* 'from', denoting someone from Oris-en-Rattier, Isère.

Dority (574) Irish: variant spelling of DORRITY.

Dorko (163) Hungarian (**Dorkó**): from a pet form of the female personal name *Dorottya*, Hungarian form of DOROTHY.

Dorland (354) French: probably a variant of **Douland**, a habitational name for someone from Doullens in the Somme, from an old form of the place name.

Dormady (113) Irish: variant of DERMODY.

Dorman (4624) **1.** English: from the Old English personal name *Dēormann*, com-

posed of Old English *dēor* (see DEAR) + *mann* 'man'. This surname became established in Ireland in the 17th century; sometimes it is found as a variant of DORNAN. **2.** German (**Dormann**): occupational name for a doorkeeper or gatekeeper or topographic name for someone who lived by the gate of a town or city. Compare DORER, DORWART. **3.** Hungarian (**Dormán**): from the old secular personal name *Dormán*. **4.** Jewish (Ashkenazic): unexplained.

Dormer (308) **1.** English (of Norman origin): nickname for a lazy man or a sleepyhead, from Old French *dormeor* 'sleeper', 'sluggard' (Latin *dormitor*, from *dormire* to sleep). **2.** English: most probably a habitational name, as medieval forms with *de* are found, but if so the place of origin has not been identified. **3.** Irish: when not of the same origin as 1 or 2, this is a reduced Anglicized form of the Donegal name **Ó Díorma**, a reduced form of **Ó Duibhdhíormaigh** 'descendant of *Duibhdhíormach*', a personal name composed of Gaelic *dubh* 'black' + *díormach* 'trooper'.

Dorminey (230) See DORMINY.

Dorminy (137) French or German: perhaps a habitational name for someone from a place called Orm(e)ignies, in Hainault, Belgium, with the preposition *d(e)* 'from'.

Dorn (4142) **1.** German: topographic name for someone who lived by a thorn bush or thorn hedge, from Middle High German *dorn* 'thorn', or a habitational name from any of numerous places named with this word. **2.** Jewish (Ashkenazic): ornamental name from German *Dorn* 'thorn'. **3.** Czech: see DORNAK.

Dornak (165) Czech (also **Dorňák**) and Slovak (**Dornák**): from the female personal name *Dorotha* or *Dorothea*, Czech equivalents of DOROTHY.

Dornan (378) Irish: reduced Anglicized form of Gaelic **Ó Dornáin** or **Ó Doirnín** 'descendant of *Doirnín*', a byname from a diminutive of *dorn* 'fist'.

Dornbusch (317) **1.** German: habitational name from any of various places named Dornbusch, or a topographic name for someone living by a briar patch or thorn bush, from Middle High German, Middle Low German *dorn* 'thorn' + Middle High German *busch, bosch* 'bush'. **2.** Jewish (eastern Ashkenazic): ornamental name from German *Dornbusch* 'thornbush', 'briar' (see 1)

GIVEN NAMES German 4%. *Rudi* (4), *Horst.*

Dornbush (218) Part translation of DORNBUSCH or a reflex of the Dutch cognate, **Doornbosch**, a topographic name for someone living by a copse of furze or thorn bushes.

Dorner (677) German (also **Dörner**): habitational name for someone from places named Dorn or Dornau in Bavaria, or either of two places named Dorna, in Saxony and Thuringia.

GIVEN NAMES German 4%. *Kurt* (2), *Erwin, Horst, Otto, Wolfgang.*

Dorney (459) **1.** English: habitational name from a place in Buckinghamshire, named from Old English *dora* 'bee' (genitive plural *dorena*) + *ēg* 'island', 'dry ground in marsh'. **2.** Irish (Counties Cork and Tipperary): reduced Anglicized form of Gaelic **Ó Doirinne** 'descendant of *Doireann*', a female personal name meaning 'sullen'. **3.** Americanized spelling of Hungarian **Dörnyei** or **Dörnyey**, habitational names for someone from a place called Dernye in former Körös county.

GIVEN NAME Irish 5%. *Conn.*

Dornfeld (306) German: topographic name for someone who lived by a field where thorn bushes grew, from Middle High German, Middle Low German *dorn* 'thorn' + *velt* 'open country'.

GIVEN NAMES German 4%. *Ernst, Heinz, Kurt.*

Dorning (160) **1.** English (mainly Lancashire and Cheshire): unexplained. **2.** Probably an altered form of German **Dornig**, which is probably a nickname for someone with a sharp tongue, from an adjectival derivative of Middle High German, Middle Low German *dorn* 'thorn'. The suffixes *-ig* and *-ing* were often interchanged in Pennsylvania German and elsewhere. The name may also refer to a sloe bush.

Dornon (131) Irish: variant spelling of DORNAN.

Doro (203) **1.** Italian: possibly from a reduced form of various personal names ending with *-doro*, such as *Eliodoro, Isidoro*, or *Teodoro*. **2.** Hungarian (**Doró**): from a pet form of the female name *Dorottya* (see DORA).

Doroff (107) Origin unidentified. Possibly a variant of Irish DARRAGH.

Doron (146) **1.** German: adaptation of the French family name **Doron** or **D'Oron**, a habitational name, with fused preposition *d(e)* 'from', for someone from Oron in Moselle. **2.** Jewish (Israeli): ornamental name from Hebrew *doron* 'gift'.

GIVEN NAMES Jewish 22%. *Yoav* (2), *Arie, Dorit, Doron, Eyal, Meir, Menashe, Merav, Meyer, Motti, Nilly, Ofer.*

Dorosh (115) Russian: unexplained.

GIVEN NAMES Russian 6%. *Anatoly, Svyatoslav, Vitali.*

Dorothy (304) **1.** adopted as an English equivalent of Gaelic **Ó Dorchiadhe** (see DARCY). **2.** Perhaps also an Americanized form of some European family name, for example French **Dorothée**, derived from a Greek female name composed of the elements *dōron* 'gift' + *theos* 'god' (the same elements as *Theodora*, but in reverse order).

Dorough (492) Variant of northern Irish DARRAGH.

Dorow (342) **1.** German (under Slavic influence): habitational name from Dorow, a place in Pomerania. **2.** Perhaps a variant of Scottish Darrow.

Dorr (2444) German (**Dörr**): variant of **Dürr** (see Durr).

Dorrance (397) English: variant of Durrance.

Dorrell (625) English (chiefly Worcestershire): variant of Darrell.

Dorrian (152) Irish: County Down variant of Doran.
given name Irish 8%. *Seamus.*

Dorries (156) German (**Dörries**): from a reduced pet form of the medieval personal name *Isidor(i)us* (Greek *Isidōros*, from *Isis*, the name of an originally Egyptian goddess + *dōron* 'gift').

Dorriety (117) Irish: variant of Dorrity.
given names Irish 4%. *Caitlin, Patrick Sean.*

Dorrington (115) English: habitational name from any of several places called Dorrington. One in Lincolnshire and one in Shropshire (near Woore) get the name from Old English *Dēoringtūn* 'settlement (*tūn*) associated with *Dēor(a)*' (see Dear); another in Shropshire (near Condover) was earlier *Dodintone* 'settlement associated with *Dodda*'.

Dorris (2307) **1.** Irish: variant spelling of Doris. **2.** Possibly in some instances a respelling of German **Dörries** (see Dorries) or French Doris.

Dorrity (107) Irish: reduced Anglicized form of Gaelic **Ó Dochartaigh** (see Doherty).

Dorroh (168) Variant spelling of **Dorrah**, an Ulster variant of Irish Darragh.

Dorrough (329) Variant spelling of **Dorrah**, an Ulster variant of Irish Darragh.

Dorsa (159) Italian: probably of Albanian origin, from **Dòrëza**, being very frequent in the Albanian settlement Piana degli Albanesi, Sicily.

Dorsch (627) **1.** North German: metonymic occupational name for a fisherman, from Middle High German *dorsch* 'cod' (a borrowing from Middle Low German *dorsch*, *dors(k)*, itself a loanword from Old Norse *þorskr* 'fish for drying', since cod was traded as dried fish). **2.** South German: from the word for a cabbage stalk or rutabaga, hence a nickname for a cabbage or turnip grower or for a tall thin man.
given names German 4%. *Hans* (2), *Erwin, Georg, Kurt, Reinhard, Rudi.*

Dorschner (141) German: variant of Dorsch 2.

Dorsett (1869) English: regional name from the county of Dorset, named from Old English *Dorn*, an early name of Dorchester (of British origin, from *durn* 'fist', probably referring to fist-sized pebbles) + *sǣte* 'dwellers'.

Dorsey (12051) English (of Norman origin): habitational name, with the preposition *d(e)*, from Orsay in Seine-et-Orne, France, recorded in the 13th century as *Orceiacum*, from the Latin personal name *Orcius* + the locative suffix *-acum*.

D'Orsi (189) Italian: variant of D'Orso.

Dorsky (106) Origin unidentified.

D'Orso (124) Italian: patronymic from the personal name Orso, meaning 'bear'.

Dorst (261) German: **1.** topographic name for someone who lived on dry, hard ground, from *dörr* 'dry', or a habitational name from places named Dorst near Cologne or Helmstedt or Dorste in the Harz Mountains. **2.** nickname from Middle Low German *dorst* 'boldness', 'cunning'. Compare Durst. **3.** metathesized variant of Droste.

Dorsten (105) German: habitational name from a place in Westphalia called Dorsten.

Dort (212) **1.** German: possibly from **Dorten**, a metronymic from the female personal name *Dorothea* (see Dorothy). **2.** Dutch: habitational name from a reduced form of Dordrecht.

Dorta (164) Portuguese and Galician: topographic name from the preposition *d(e)* 'from' + *horta* 'garden' (from Latin *hortus*), or habitational name for someone from any of numerous places named with this word in Portugal and Galicia.
given names Spanish 48%. *Jose* (8), *Gonzalo* (4), *Pedro* (4), *Roberto* (3), *Ana* (2), *Armando* (2), *Enrique* (2), *Idalia* (2), *Juan* (2), *Luis* (2), *Marcelo* (2), *Reynaldo* (2); *Antonio* (2), *Angelo, Gabino, Pio.*

Dortch (1167) Probably an altered spelling of German Dorsch.

Dorton (880) English: habitational name from a place in Buckinghamshire named Dorton, from Old English *dor* 'narrow pass' + *tūn* 'settlement'.

Dorval (297) French: habitational name, with the preposition *d(e)* 'from', from either of two places named Orval: in Cher and Manche.
given names French 13%. *Alain, Andre, Antoine, Armand, Emile, Marie-Ange, Micheline, Rosemonde, Solange, Sylvie.*

Dorward (223) **1.** Scottish: status name from Old English *duru-weard* 'doorkeeper', 'porter'. In medieval Scotland the office of king's doorward was one of considerable honor. **2.** Americanized form of German Dorwart.

Dorwart (231) **1.** German: occupational name for a doorkeeper or gatekeeper, from Middle Low German *dor*, Middle High German *tor* + *wart* 'guard'. **2.** Variant of Scottish Dorward.

Dory (291) **1.** English: variant spelling of Dorey. **2.** Hungarian (**Dőry**): habitational name for someone from a place called Dör in Sopron county or Dér in Baranya county.

Dosch (592) South German: **1.** topographic name for someone living near bushes or brush, from Middle High German *doste*, *toste* 'leafy branch', or a habitational name from a house with a sign depicting a bush. **2.** altered spelling of Dasch.

Doscher (401) **1.** North German (**Döscher**): Low German form of Drescher. **2.** Altered spelling of German Dascher (see Taschner).
given names German 5%. *Klaus* (3), *Franz.*

Dose (317) German: **1.** from the personal name *Dose*, from Germanic *Teuzo* (see Dietz). **2.** habitational name from Dose near Hannover, or Döse, a place near Hamburg.
given names German 7%. *Hans* (2), *Claus, Detlef, Erwin, Fritz, Heinz, Kurt.*

Dosen (114) Croatian and Serbian (**Došen**): unexplained.

Doser (189) German (also **Döser**): nickname for an indolent man, from an agent derivative of Middle High German *dōsen* 'to slumber or doze'.
given names German 5%. *Liesl, Lorenz, Manfred.*

Dosh (146) Americanized spelling of German Dosch.

Dosher (210) Americanized spelling of German **Döscher** (see Doscher) or an altered spelling of Dascher (see Taschner).

Doshi (507) Indian (Gujarat): Hindu name meaning 'hawker selling cloth' in Gujarati, from Persian *dush* 'shoulder' + the agent suffix *-ī* (because the cloth was carried over the hawker's shoulder).
given names Indian 93%. *Dinesh* (7), *Arvind* (6), *Bharat* (6), *Mahendra* (6), *Ramesh* (6), *Anil* (5), *Dilip* (5), *Jitendra* (5), *Kishor* (5), *Mahesh* (5), *Manish* (5), *Mukesh* (5).

Doshier (320) Origin unidentified. Possibly an American variant of French Dozier.

Dosier (172) French: variant of Dozier.

Doskocil (153) Czech (**Doskočil**): nickname for a lively or agile person, from *doskočit* 'to jump', 'spring up'.
given name French 4%. *Camille.*

Doss (6673) German: **1.** habitational name for someone from Dosse in Altmark. **2.** variant of Dose 1. **3.** in Austria (Tyrol) and Switzerland, a topographic name for someone living on a hill, from Ladin *dos* (from Latin *dorsum* 'ridge', 'hill top').

Dos Santos (700) Portuguese and Galician: from *dos Santos*, literally 'of the saints', a common element of personal names, originally denoting a child born or baptized on All Saints' Day.
given names Spanish 35%; Portuguese 21%; Italian 7%. *Jose* (24), *Manuel* (21), *Carlos* (15), *Fernando* (7), *Pedro* (7), *Ana* (4), *Francisco* (4), *Luis* (4), *Sergio* (4), *Luiz* (3), *Mario* (3), *Rafael* (3); *Joao* (7), *Paulo* (6), *Joaquim* (4), *Mateus* (2), *Aderito, Agostinho, Damiao, Henrique, Sebastiao; Antonio* (27), *Angelo* (4), *Lucio* (2), *Silvio* (2), *Alberico, Cira, Dario, Leonardo, Livio, Luciano, Marcello, Marco.*

Dosser (130) German: **1.** nickname for a loud person, from an agent derivative of Old High German *dozzen* 'to bluster or thunder'. **2.** in Austria (Tyrol) and Switzerland, topographic name for someone living on a ridge, from Ladin *dos* (Latin *dorsum* 'ridge', literally 'back'), + the suffix *-er* denoting an inhabitant.

Dossett (903) 1. English: variant of DORSETT. 2. Possibly a respelling of French **Dosset** (see DOSSEY).

Dossey (523) Possibly an altered spelling of French **Dosset**, a nickname for someone with a spinal deformity, from a diminutive of *dos* 'back'.

Dost (252) German: topographic name from Middle High German *doste, toste* 'wild thyme', also 'bunch', 'bouquet', or a habitational name from a house with a sign depicting such a plant.
GIVEN NAMES German 8%. *Erwin, Fritz, Gerhard, Helmut, Herta, Klaus, Kurt.*

Dostal (737) Czech (**Dostál**): nickname for a reliable, trustworthy person, from Czech *dostát(slovu)* 'keep, abide by (one's word)'.

Doster (1434) 1. German: from an agent derivative of Middle High German *doste, toste* 'wild thyme', 'shrub', 'bouquet' (see DOST), hence a topographic name, especially for someone whose land abutted an uncultivated piece of land, or possibly an occupational name for a dealer in herbs. 2. Belgian French: habitational name, with the preposition *d(e)*, for someone from either of two places in the province of Luxembourg named Oster.

Dostie (390) French: habitational name, with the preposition *d(e)*, denoting someone from Ostia in Italy.
GIVEN NAMES French 16%. *Normand* (3), *Andre* (2), *Armand* (2), *Jacques* (2), *Marcel* (2), *Chantal, Egide, Gaetan, Gilles, Laurier, Lucienne, Ludger.*

Doswell (214) English: probably a habitational name from Dowdeswell in Gloucestershire, named from an Old English personal name *Dogod* + Old English *wella* 'spring', 'stream'.

Doten (294) English: 1. said to be a variant of DOTY. 2. Perhaps an altered spelling of English **Dotten**, a habitational name from Dotton Farm in Colaton Raleigh, Devon, named in Old English as 'settlement (Old English *tūn*) associated with *Dudda*', or from Dutton in Lancashire, 'Dudda's settlement'.

Doto (172) Italian: unexplained.
GIVEN NAMES Italian 10%. *Rocco* (2), *Francesco, Sal, Salvatore.*

Dotseth (121) Norwegian: unexplained.

Dotson (9817) English: patronymic from the personal name *Dodde* (see DODD).

Dott (137) 1. English: of uncertain derivation. Reaney suggests it could be from bynames associated with Old Norse *dottr* 'lazy', or Old English *dott* 'head of a boil'. 2. South German: from a term meaning 'godfather'. 3. North German: from a short form of the personal name *Dietrich* or a related name.

D'Ottavio (175) Italian: patronymic from the personal name Ottavio, from Latin *Octavius* (from *octavus* 'eighth'). This was a Roman imperial family name, the *gens* name of the Roman Emperor Augustus.
GIVEN NAMES Italian 15%. *Angelo, Antonio, Domenica, Gianni, Guido, Nino, Salvatore, Stefano.*

Dotter (346) German (**Dötter**): from a Germanic personal name formed with *theud* 'people', 'race' + *hard* 'hardy', 'strong' or *hari, heri* 'army'.

Dotterer (316) German: 1. (**Dötterer**): variant of **Dötter** (see DOTTER). 2. possibly a nickname for a person with a tottering gait, from a dialect agent noun based on *dottern* 'to totter'.

Dotterweich (158) German: habitational name from a place in Württemberg named Todtenweis, literally 'meadow of the dead', altered by folk etymology to *Dotterweich*, literally 'yolk soft'.

Dotts (437) Possibly an Americanized spelling of **Dötz** or **Dotz**, a Swabian and Swiss German nickname for a small, soft-hearted man; or a Sorbian short form of a Germanic personal name, cognate with DIETZ.

Doty (7096) English: probably an early variant of DOUGHTY.
FOREBEARS Edward Doty (*c.*1600–55) was one of the passengers on the Mayflower, a servant of Stephen Hopkins. He became comparatively wealthy and moved to Duxbury MA, where he left nine children.

Dotzler (177) German: habitational name from a place called Dotzlar, near Wittgenstein, Hesse.

Doub (403) Altered spelling of German and Jewish DAUB.

Doubek (327) Czech: nickname for a strong man from *doubek* 'small oak' (also 'nice oak'), a diminutive of DUB.

Douberly (104) English: variant of DUBBERLY.

Doubet (204) Possibly a respelling of French **Dubet**, a Gascon variant of DUBEAU.
GIVEN NAMES French 4%. *Jean Baptiste, Monique.*

Double (325) English (of Norman origin): nickname from Old French *doubel* 'twin' (literally 'double', from Late Latin *duplus*, classical Latin *duplex*, from *du(o)* 'two' + *plek*, a root meaning 'fold').

Doubleday (442) English: possibly from the nickname or byname *Do(u)bel* 'the twin' or the personal name *Dobbel* (a pet form of ROBERT) + Middle English *day(e)* 'servant' (see DAY).

Doublin (118) Possibly French: unexplained.

Doubrava (177) Czech: topographic name from *doubrava* 'oak forest'.

Doucet (1989) French: nickname for a gentle-natured person, from Old French *dolz, dous* 'sweet', 'pleasant' (from Latin *dulcis*).

GIVEN NAMES French 9%. *Albon* (2), *Alexandre* (2), *Benoit* (2), *Clovis* (2), *Fernand* (2), *Leonce* (2), *Lucien* (2), *Michel* (2), *Odile* (2), *Pierre* (2), *Serge* (2), *Adelard.*

Doucett (113) Respelling of French DOUCET.

Doucette (3197) Respelling of French DOUCET.
GIVEN NAMES French 5%. *Armand* (7), *Alyre* (2), *Emile* (2), *Marcel* (2), *Alphie, Alphy, Alvine, Arianne, Aurele, Calixte, Damien, Donat.*

Doud (1118) 1. Irish: variant of DOWD 1. 2. Muslim: variant of DAOUD.

Doudna (175) Variant spelling of English **Dowdney**, from a vernacular form of the Latin personal name *Deodonatus* 'God-given'.

Douds (211) Northern Irish: variant of DOWD 1, with the addition of English patronymic *-s*.

Dougal (215) Scottish: variant spelling of DOUGALL.

Dougall (222) Scottish: reduced Anglicized form of Gaelic **Mac Dubhghaill** (see McDOUGALL).

Dougan (1260) Scottish and Irish: variant spelling of DUGAN.

Douget (118) French: Breton nickname for a man of respect.

Dougharty (113) Irish: variant of DOHERTY.

Dougher (295) 1. Irish: reduced Anglicized form of Gaelic **Ó Dubhchair** 'descendant of *Dubhchar*', a personal name composed of the elements *dubh* 'black' + *car* 'dear'. 2. Possibly an Americanized spelling of South German **Daucher**, a topographic name for someone living near a marsh, Swabian dialect *Dauch*.

Dougherty (15019) Irish: variant spelling of DOHERTY.
GIVEN NAMES Irish 4%. *Brendan* (4), *Conan* (2), *Daley, Donal, Paddy.*

Doughman (264) Possibly an altered spelling of the English surname **Dowman**, 'servant of *Dow*' (see DAVID) or an occupational name for a baker from Middle English *dogh* 'dough' (Old English *dāh*) + *man*.

Doughten (197) Altered spelling of English DOUGHTON.

Doughtie (260) English and Scottish: variant spelling of DOUGHTY.

Doughton (145) English: habitational name from either of two places, in Gloucestershire and Norfolk, named Doughton, from Old English *dūce* 'duck' + *tūn* 'farmstead'.

Doughty (4343) English and Scottish (also established in Ireland, especially Dublin): nickname for a powerful or brave man, especially a champion jouster, from Middle English *doughty*, Old English *dohtig, dyhtig* 'valiant', 'strong'.

Douglas (31010) Scottish: habitational name from any of the various places called Douglas from their situation on a river named with Gaelic *dubh* 'dark', 'black' +

glas 'stream' (a derivative of *glas* 'blue'). There are several localities in Scotland and Ireland so named, but the one from which the surname is derived in most if not all cases is 20 miles south of Glasgow, the original stronghold of the influential Douglas family and their retainers.

Douglass (6004) Scottish: variant spelling of DOUGLAS.

FOREBEARS William Douglass, a physician recognized for his identification and description of an epidemic of scarlet fever, was born in about 1691 in Gifford, Haddington County, Scotland, and settled in Boston in 1718. The abolitionist, orator, and journalist Frederick Douglass assumed the name after escaping from slavery in 1838 and traveling to Massachusetts. Son of a white father and a slave with some Indian blood, he was born Frederick Augustus Washington Bailey about 1817 in Tuckahoe, MD.

Doukas (249) Greek: from medieval Greek *doukas* 'duke', 'lord', from Latin *dux*. This was the name of a family of imperial rank in medieval Byzantium.
GIVEN NAMES Greek 12%. *Spyros* (2), *Anastasios*, *Aphrodite*, *Apostolos*, *Athanasios*, *Constantine*, *Costas*, *Dimitrios*, *Kalliopi*, *Kimon*, *Panagiotis*.

Douma (388) Frisian: patronymic from the Old Frisian personal name *Douw(o)*.

Doup (129) German: variant of TAUB.

Doupe (103) Irish name of German origin (a variant of TAUBE), brought to Ireland by immigrants from the Palatinate in the 17th or 18th century.

Douse (176) **1.** Dutch (**Douwse(n)**): patronymic from the Old Frisian personal name *Douw(o)*. **2.** Americanized spelling of German DAUS.

Douthat (235) English: variant spelling of DOUTHIT.

Douthett (141) English: variant spelling of DOUTHIT.

Douthit (965) English: variant of **Douthwaite**, a habitational name from Dowthwaite in Cumbria or Dowthwaite Hall in North Yorkshire. The first is from the Old Norse personal name *Dúfa* + Old Norse *þveit* 'clearing'; the second is from the Old Irish personal name *Dubhan* + Old Norse *þveit*. The elliptic form of the surname probably reflects the local pronunciation of the place names.

Douthitt (484) English: variant spelling of DOUTHIT.

Doutt (245) Origin uncertain. It is probably an Americanized form of Dutch and German DAUT.

FOREBEARS Doutt is a PA name. Bearers claim descent from a certain John Daut/ Doutt, born in 1778.

Douty (223) English: variant spelling of DOUGHTY.

Douville (358) French: **1.** habitational name from either of two places named Douville, in Calvados and Eure. **2.** habitational name, with the preposition *d(e)* 'from', for someone from a place named Ouville, examples of which are found in Calvados, Manche, and Seine-Maritime, or from Houville, in Eure and Eure-et-Loire .
GIVEN NAMES French 8%. *Aime*, *Armand*, *Bonard*, *Jean-Paul*, *Josee*, *Lucien*, *Mireille*, *Normand*.

Dove (4961) **1.** English: from Middle English *dove*, Old English *dūfe* 'dove' (or perhaps occasionally from the Old Norse cognate *dúfa*), applied as a nickname for a mild and gentle person or as a metonymic occupational name for a keeper of doves. The Old English word was used as a personal name for either sex in the early Middle English period, and the surname at least in part derives from this use. **2.** Scottish: translation of **Mac Calmáin** (see COLEMAN 1). **3.** Scottish: variant of DUFF. **4.** North German: nickname for a deaf or dull man, Middle Low German *dōf*.

FOREBEARS David James Dove was born about 1696 in Portsmouth, England, where his father was a tailor. He arrived with his wife in Philadelphia in 1750 and in 1751 opened an academy for young ladies. He was the first person in PA who attempted to supply higher education for women.

Dovel (330) **1.** English: variant spelling of DOVELL. **2.** Respelling of Swedish DOVELL.

Dovell (109) **1.** English (Devon): probably a variant of DUVALL. **2.** Swedish: ornamental name composed of an unexplained first element + -*ell*, a common ornamental suffix derived from the Latin adjectival ending -*elius*.

Dover (3157) **1.** English: habitational name from the port of Dover in Kent, named from the river on which it stands, a Celtic name meaning 'the waters' (from the word which became modern Welsh *dwfr* 'water'). **2.** North German: habitational name from Doveren in the Rhineland, of uncertain etymology; the origin is possibly Celtic and so related ultimately to 1, or a variant of DOVE 4.

Doverspike (271) Americanized spelling of German DAUBENSPECK.

Dovey (166) **1.** Irish and Scottish: variant of DUFFY. **2.** Perhaps an Americanized spelling of Norwegian **Dåvøy**, a habitational name from a farm so named in western Norway, from *dove* 'shaking bog' + *øy* 'island'.

D'Ovidio (155) Italian: patronymic from the personal name *Ovidio*.

Dow (6158) **1.** Scottish (also found in Ireland): reduced form of McDOW. This surname is borne by a sept of the Buchanans. **2.** English: variant of DAW. **3.** Americanized spelling of Dutch **Douw**, an Old Frisian personal name. **4.** Americanized spelling of German DAU.

FOREBEARS Henry Dow (1634–1707), NH soldier and statesman, was born at Ormsby in Norfolkshire, England. His father migrated with his family to Watertown in the colony of Massachusetts Bay in 1637 and moved to Hampton in the province of NH in 1644. Henry became an influential and prosperous figure in Hampton. He married twice and had four sons.

The Dutch name **Douw** is recorded in Beverwijck in New Netherland (Albany, NY) in the mid 17th century.

Dowd (5456) **1.** Irish: reduced Anglicized form of Gaelic **Ó Dubhda** 'descendant of *Dubhda*', a byname derived from *dubh* 'dark', 'black'. The family were chieftains in Sligo and Mayo. **2.** English: from the personal name *Dowd*, a variant of DAVID.
GIVEN NAMES Irish 5%. *Brendan* (4), *Aileen*, *Cathal*, *Dermot*, *Liam*, *Seamus*, *Siobhan*.

Dowda (159) Irish: variant of DOWD.

Dowdall (272) **1.** Irish (of English origin): habitational name from Dovedale in Derbyshire, 'valley (Middle English *dale*) of the river Dove' (see DOVE 1). **2.** Irish: English surname adopted by bearers of Gaelic **Ó Dubhdáleithe** (see DUDLEY 2). **3.** English: habitational name from a lost place Ovedale or Uvedale, which gave rise to the 14th-century surname *de Uvedale* alias *de Ovedale*, connected with the manor of D'Oversdale in Litlington, Cambridgeshire; this is first recorded as 'manor of Overdale otherwise *Dowdale*' in 1408.
GIVEN NAMES Irish 5%. *John Patrick*, *Niall*.

Dowdell (1246) Irish and English: variant of DOWDALL.

Dowden (1352) English: patronymic from an Old English personal name, *Dogod* (probably a derivative of *dugan* 'to avail', 'to be of use'). In England the surname is chiefly found in Gloucestershire and Somerset.

Dowdey (129) **1.** English: unexplained. **2.** Variant spelling of Scottish **Dowdie**, which is probably a variant of Irish DUDDY.

Dowding (363) English: variant of DOWDEN.

Dowdle (858) **1.** English: variant spelling of DOWDELL. **2.** Possibly an altered spelling of German **Daudel**, **Dautel**, variants of DIETZ.

Dowds (177) Northern Irish: variant of DOWD 1, with the addition of English patronymic -*s*.

Dowdy (4664) Northern Irish: variant of DOWD.

Dowe (476) English and Scottish: variant spelling of DOW.

Dowell (5080) Irish: reduced Anglicized form of Gaelic **Mac Dubhghaill** (see McDOWELL).

Dowen (184) English (chiefly Midlands): unexplained.

Dower (520) **1.** English: occupational name for a baker, *doghere*, from an agent derivative of Middle English *dogh* 'dough'.

2. Probably an Americanized spelling of German DAUER.

Dowers (311) English: variant of DOWER.

Dowey (101) English and Irish: variant of DUFFY.

Dowie (139) **1.** Scottish and northern Irish: variant of DUFFY. **2.** Scottish: probably a reduced form of **MacIldowie**, an Anglicized form of Gaelic **Mac Gille Dhuibh** 'son of the black lad'.

Dowis (293) Probably a Scottish variant of DAWES.

Dowland (158) **1.** English: habitational name from Dowland in Devon, named from Old English *dūfe* 'dove' + *feld* 'open country' + *land* 'estate'. **2.** Irish: of uncertain derivation, possibly a variant of DOWLIN or DOLAN. **3.** Altered spelling of Norwegian **Dovland**, a habitational name from a farm on the south coast of Norway, so named from *dove* 'shaking bog' + *land* 'land'.

Dowlen (292) English: perhaps a variant of DOWLAND.

Dowler (974) English: occupational name for a maker of dowels and similar objects, from an agent derivative of Middle English *dowle* 'dowel', 'headless peg', 'bolt'.

Dowless (227) English: unexplained.

Dowley (100) Irish: variant of DOOLEY.

Dowlin (133) Irish: variant of DOLAN.

Dowling (6430) **1.** English: nickname for a stupid person, Middle English *dolling*, a derivative of Old English *dol* 'dull', 'stupid' (see DOLL). **2.** Irish: variant of DOLAN 1.

Down (496) **1.** English: topographic name for a downland dweller, from Old English *dūn* 'down', 'low hill'. See also DOWNER. **2.** English: variant of DUNN 2. **3.** Scottish: possibly a habitational name from Doune in Perthshire.

Downard (647) English (Sussex and Kent): probably a variant of DOWNER.

Downen (481) English: habitational name from a place such as Downend in Gloucestershire, which is named from Old English *dūn* 'down', 'low hill' + *ende* 'end', or a topographic name with the same meaning.

Downer (1721) **1.** Southern English: topographic name for someone who lived in an area of downland (the rolling chalk hills of Sussex, Surrey, and Kent), from Old English *dūn* 'down', 'low hill' (of Celtic origin) + the suffix *-er*, denoting an inhabitant. *Dun* is a common element of English place names. **2.** Irish: variant of DOONER 2.

Downes (2317) **1.** English: variant (plural) of DOWN. **2.** Irish (Counties Clare and Limerick): reduced Anglicized form of Irish Gaelic **Ó Dubháin** (see DOANE).

Downey (10160) **1.** Irish: reduced Anglicized form of Gaelic **Ó Dúnadhaigh** 'descendant of *Dúnadhach*', a personal name meaning 'fortress-holder' (from *dún* 'fortress', 'fortified hill'). **2.** Irish: reduced

Anglicized form of Gaelic **Ó Maol Dhomhnaigh**, or of **Mac Giolla Dhomhnaigh** (see MALONEY). **3.** Scottish: habitational name from the Scottish barony of Downie or Duny in the parish of Monikie in Angus (on Tayside), named from Gaelic *dùn* 'hill' + the locative suffix *-ach*.

Downham (197) English: **1.** habitational name from any of various places called Downham, in Cambridgeshire, Essex, Norfolk, Suffolk, Lancashire, and Northumberland. The last two are named from Old English *dūn*, dative plural *dūnum* '(at) the hills', while the others are named from Old English *dūn* 'hill' + *hām* 'homestead'. **2.** Variant spelling of DUNHAM.

Downhour (128) Americanized spelling of German DAUNHAUER.

Downie (1033) Scottish and Irish: variant spelling of DOWNEY.

Downin (136) Variant spelling of Irish DOWNING.

GIVEN NAME French 4%. *Andre*.

Downing (10831) **1.** Irish: sometimes of English origin, but in County Kerry it is usually an Anglicized form of Gaelic **Ó Duinnín** (see DINEEN). **2.** English: patronymic from a variant of DUNN 2.

FOREBEARS Sir George Downing (1623–84), baronet, member of Parliament, and ambassador to the Netherlands in the time of both Cromwell and King Charles II, was the second graduate of the first class (1642) at Harvard College. He was born in Dublin, Ireland, the son of Emmanuel Downing of the Inner Temple and his second wife, Lucy Winthrop, sister of John Winthrop. The family emigrated to New England in 1638 and settled at Salem, MA.

Downs (12254) English: **1.** patronymic from a variant of DUNN 2. **2.** variant (plural) of DOWN.

Downton (116) English: variant of DUNTON; there are place names spelled thus in Herefordshire, Shropshire, and Wiltshire.

Downum (227) Altered spelling of DOWNHAM.

Dowse (252) English: variant spelling of DUCE. In this spelling, the name has also been found in Ireland since the 14th century.

Dowsett (144) **1.** English: from a diminutive of DUCE. **2.** Americanized spelling of French DOUCET.

Dowson (135) English: **1.** patronymic from *Dow*, a variant of DAW. **2.** metronymic from a medieval female personal name (see DUCE).

Dowtin (101) Origin unidentified. Possibly an Anglicized form of French **Dautin**, a patronymic from the personal name AUTIN.

GIVEN NAME French 4%. *Andre*.

Dowty (380) English: variant spelling of DOUGHTY.

Doxey (497) English: habitational name from Doxey in Staffordshire, named in

Domesday Book as *Dochesig*, 'island, or piece of dry ground in a marsh, (*ēg*) of a man called Docc'.

Doxsee (138) Variant spelling of English DOXEY.

Doxtater (147) Respelling of German DOCKSTADER.

Doxtator (115) Respelling of German DOCKSTADER.

Doyal (504) Irish: variant spelling of DOYLE.

Doyel (277) Irish: variant spelling of DOYLE.

Doyen (332) French: from *doyen* 'dean', hence probably a nickname for someone thought to resemble a dean, or an occupational name for someone in the service of a dean.

Doyle (29099) Irish: reduced Anglicized form of Gaelic **Ó Dubhghaill** 'descendant of *Dubhghall*', a personal name composed of the elements *dubh* 'black' + *gall* 'stranger'. This was used as a byname for Scandinavians, in particular to distinguish the darker-haired Danes from fair-haired Norwegians. Compare McDOUGALL, McDOWELL.

GIVEN NAMES Irish 6%. *Brendan* (17), *Sean* (9), *Kieran* (5), *Seamus* (4), *Aileen* (3), *Dermot* (3), *Liam* (3), *Niall* (3), *Brennan* (2), *Brigid* (2), *Conal* (2), *Conan* (2), *Donal* (2).

Doyne (118) Irish: reduced Anglicized form of Gaelic **Ó Duinn**, **Ó Doinn** (see DUNNE); this is an earlier Anglicization.

Doyon (870) French: habitational name from Doyon in the province of Namur in present-day Belgium.

GIVEN NAMES French 22%. *Marcel* (7), *Lucien* (4), *Andre* (3), *Armand* (3), *Laurent* (3), *Normand* (3), *Yvan* (3), *Adrien* (2), *Donat* (2), *Fernand* (2), *Henri* (2), *Laurier* (2).

Dozer (135) Americanized spelling of German DOSER.

Dozier (4577) French (Huguenot): from Old French *osier* 'osier', 'willow', with the preposition *d(e)* 'from', applied as a topographic name for someone who lived near a plantation of willows, or perhaps as a metonymic occupational name for a basket maker.

Dozois (110) French: probably a variant of DOZIER.

GIVEN NAMES French 18%. *Chantal*, *Emilien*, *Fernand*, *Jean-Paul*, *Normand*, *Pierre*.

Drab (153) **1.** Czech and Slovak (**Dráb**): occupational name from Czech *dráb*, which originally meant a foot soldier, but also came to denote a servant or retainer, especially an overseer of workers on an estate. **2.** Polish: nickname from *drab* 'mercenary'; later 'tall, strapping fellow', and finally 'ruffian'. Etymologically, this is the same word as in 1, but the sense development has been very different. **3.** Slovenian: unexplained.

Drabant (104) German: occupational name from Middle High German *drabant* 'foot soldier'.

Drabek (374) **1.** Czech (**Drábek**): from a diminutive of *Dráb* 'retainer', 'steward' (see DRAB 1). **2.** Polish: from a diminutive of DRAB 2.

Drabick (101) Americanized spelling of Slavic DRABIK.

Drabik (264) Polish, Czech (**Drabík**), and Slovak (**Drábik**): from a diminutive of DRAB.

GIVEN NAMES Polish 10%. *Leszek* (2), *Aniela, Basia, Casimir, Grazyna, Henryk, Jaroslaw, Leslaw, Urszula.*

Drabkin (101) Jewish (from Belarus): metronymic from Yiddish *drabke* 'loose woman'.

GIVEN NAMES Russian 18%; Jewish 10%. *Vladimir* (3), *Aleksandr, Maksim, Mikhail, Yelena, Yevgeny, Yuriy; Inna, Sol.*

Drace (146) Possibly an Americanized spelling of German DREES.

Drach (242) **1.** German: from Middle High German *trache, drache* 'dragon', hence probably a habitational name for someone who lived at a house distinguished by the sign of a dragon, or a nickname for someone with a fierce or fiery temperament. **2.** Jewish (Ashkenazic): ornamental adoption of 1. **3.** Polish: possibly of German origin (see 1).

GIVEN NAMES Jewish 4%. *Hersz, Naum, Sol.*

Drachenberg (147) German: habitational name, probably adapted from Dutch Drakenburg or from Drakenburg in Lower Saxony.

GIVEN NAMES German 11%. *Otto* (3), *Gunter, Sieg.*

Drachman (121) Jewish (Ashkenazic): variant of DRACH.

GIVEN NAMES Jewish 6%. *Miriam* (2), *Pincus.*

Draeger (943) **1.** North German (also **Dräger**) and Dutch: occupational name, from Middle Low German *dreger, drager*, Middle Dutch *drager* 'porter', 'carrier'; sometimes 'guarantor', 'negotiator'. **2.** North German, occupational name for a wood turner, Middle Low German *dreyer, dreger.*

GIVEN NAMES German 4%. *Erwin* (2), *Bernhard, Eldred, Hartmut, Horst, Joerg, Klaus, Otto, Reinhard.*

Draffen (137) **1.** Scottish: habitational name from Draffan in Lanarkshire. **2.** Probably an altered spelling of German **Draffehn**, an ethnic name for a Slavic speaker from Lüneburg Heath, from Polabic (a West Slavic language) *Dråwën*. This was the westernmost region where a Slavic language was spoken. In some cases the name was habitational, from a place called Drawehn, near Köslin in Pomerania.

Drafts (103) Origin unidentified.

Drag (131) **1.** Polish (**Drąg**): from *drąg* 'pole', 'rod', presumably a nickname for a tall thin person. **2.** Norwegian: habitational name from any of several farms named Drag. The place name is related to Old Norse *draga* 'to pull' and originally denoted a place where boats were pulled along a river or across an isthmus.

GIVEN NAMES Polish 13%. *Andrze, Casimir, Genowefa, Irena, Iwona, Jerzy, Kinga.*

Dragan (320) **1.** Serbian and Croatian: from the personal name *Dragan*, from the adjective *drag* 'dear', 'beloved'. This is also found as a Romanian name. **2.** Polish and Ukrainian: nickname from *dragan* 'dragon' (later also *dragon*). Compare DRAGON. **3.** German: from a Germanic personal name *Trago*, cognate with Anglo-Saxon *dragan* 'to roam or wander', or a habitational name from a place named Drage, near Hamburg or Schleswig-Holstein.

GIVEN NAMES Romanian 5%; Polish 4%. *Alexandru, Florin, Mihaela, Radu, Sorin, Stelian; Ewa, Halina, Janusz, Zosia.*

Drage (175) **1.** English: variant of DREDGE. **2.** German: from a Germanic personal name *Trago*, or a habitational name from a place named Drage, near Hamburg or in Schleswig-Holstein. **3.** Norwegian: variant of DRAG, from the dative case.

Drager (598) Dutch and German (**Dräger**): see DRAEGER.

Draghi (129) Italian: patronymic or plural form of DRAGO.

GIVEN NAMES Italian 5%. *Aldo, Angelo, Camillo.*

Dragich (141) Serbian and Croatian (**Dragić**): patronymic from the personal name *Dragan*, from *drag* 'dear', 'beloved'.

GIVEN NAMES South Slavic 7%. *Slavko* (2), *Branko, Zorica.*

Drago (1050) **1.** Italian: from *drago* 'dragon', hence a nickname, or in some cases from a personal name, a continuation of Latin *Draco, Draconis*, from *draco* 'dragon'. **2.** French: variant of DRAGOO.

GIVEN NAMES Italian 11%. *Salvatore* (7), *Angelo* (5), *Sal* (3), *Carlo* (2), *Domenic* (2), *Gaspare* (2), *Gasper* (2), *Leonardo* (2), *Antonino, Antonio, Domenico, Francesco.*

Dragon (778) **1.** French: from the Germanic personal name *Drago*, a short form of *Dragwald*, composed of the elements *drag-* 'to carry' + *wald* 'power', 'rule'. **2.** French and English (of Norman origin): nickname or occupational name for someone who carried a standard in battle or else in a pageant or procession, from Middle English, Old French *dragon* 'snake', 'monster' (Latin *draco*, genitive *draconis*, from Greek *drakōn*, ultimately from *derkesthai* 'to flash'). This word was applied in Late Latin to military standards in the form of windsocks, so resembling snakes. **3.** Polish and Ukrainian: from *dragon* 'dragoon'. **4.** Polish, Jewish (from Poland), and Ukrainian: from Polish *dragon* 'dragoon'. As a Jewish name it is of ornamental origin. **5.** New England form of French **D'Aragon** (see DERAGON).

FOREBEARS Francois D'Aragon 'dit La France' married Marie Guillemet in 1697. They are the ancestors of all the Dragons in VT.

GIVEN NAMES French 5%. *Armand* (2), *Emile* (2), *Adelard, Alphonse, Andre, Antoine, Jean Robert, Marcel, Michel.*

Dragone (264) Italian: probably a variant of DRAGO (from the genitive *draconis*).

GIVEN NAMES Italian 24%. *Amato* (3), *Angelo* (3), *Silvio* (2), *Vito* (2), *Antonio, Corrado, Donato, Gaeton, Olindo, Rocco, Salvatore, Santo.*

Dragonetti (141) Italian: patronymic from a diminutive of DRAGO or DRAGONE.

GIVEN NAMES Italian 12%. *Aldo, Pasquale, Raffaele, Rocco.*

Dragoo (666) Americanized form of French (Huguenot) **Dragaud**, from the Germanic personal name *Dragwald* (see DRAGON).

FOREBEARS The Dragaud ancestors were Huguenots who came to England in the 1680s. On November 12, 1699 Pierre Dragaud married Elizabeth Tavaud in Bristol and shortly afterwards they came to America. They are probably the ancestors of all American bearers of this surname.

Dragos (160) **1.** Romanian (**Dragoş**), and Serbian, Croatian (central Dalmatia), and Slovenian (**Dragoš**): from a derivative of the South Slavic personal name *Dragoslav*, based on the adjective *drag* 'dear', 'beloved'. **2.** Americanized spelling of Hungarian **Drágosi**, a habitational name for someone from a place called Drágos(falva) in Transylvania. In some cases, perhaps a Magyarized form of Slavic **Dragoš** (see 1).

GIVEN NAMES Romanian 9%. *Gheorghe* (3), *Octavian* (2), *Savu.*

Dragotta (121) Italian: from a feminine diminutive of DRAGO.

GIVEN NAMES Italian 28%. *Salvatore* (3), *Carmine* (2), *Angelo, Giovanni, Sal.*

Dragovich (214) Serbian and Croatian (**Dragović**): patronymic from the personal name *Drago*, from *drag* 'dear', 'beloved'.

Draheim (440) German: habitational name from a place called Draheim, near Stettin in Pomerania or in East Prussia.

Drahos (272) Czech (**Drahoš**): from a pet form of the personal names *Drahoslav* or *Drahomir.*

Drain (1190) **1.** Irish: reduced Anglicized form of Gaelic **Ó Dreain** 'descendant of *Drean*', a byname possibly from *dreán* 'wren'. The name is also found in Scotland. **2.** Irish (Cork): reduced Anglicized form of Gaelic **Ó Druacháin** (see DROHAN). **3.** English: from Middle English *dreine* 'drain', 'ditch', hence a metonymic occupational name for a ditch digger or a topographic name. **4.** English: variant spelling of DRANE. **5.** French: reduced form of **Derain**, from Old French *dererain* 'last', hence a nickname for the youngest son of a family. **6.** French: habitational name from a place in Maine-et-Loire called Drain.

Draine (227) English: variant spelling of DRAIN.

Drake (22035) **1.** English: from the Old English byname *Draca*, meaning 'snake' or 'dragon', Middle English *Drake*, or sometimes from the Old Norse cognate *Draki*. Both are common bynames and, less frequently, personal names. Both the Old English and the Old Norse forms are from Latin *draco* 'snake', 'monster' (see DRAGON). **2.** English and Dutch: from Middle English *drake*, Middle Dutch *drāke* 'male duck' (from Middle Low German *andrake*), hence a nickname for someone with some fancied resemblance to a drake, or perhaps a habitational name for someone who lived at a house distinguished by the sign of a drake. **3.** North German: nickname from Low German *drake* 'dragon' (see DRACH 1).

Drakeford (365) English (West Midlands): probably a habitational name from a lost or unidentified place.
GIVEN NAMES French 4%. *Andre, Antoine.*

Drakes (195) **1.** English: variant of DRAKE. **2.** In some cases, perhaps an Americanized form of a like-sounding cognate in some other language.

Drakos (134) Greek: from the personal name *Drakos*, from *drakos* 'dragon', 'ogre' (classical Greek *drakōn*, ultimately from *derkesthai* 'to flash'), an omen name expressing the wish that the boy so named will grow up to be as strong as an ogre. Compare DRAGON.
GIVEN NAMES Greek 11%. *Antonios, Christos, Diamantis, Fotios, Konstantinos, Kostas.*

Drakulich (106) Croatian and Serbian (**Drakulić**): patronymic from the Romanian personal name *Drakul*, a derivative of Latin *draco* 'dragon'.
GIVEN NAME Southern Slavic 4%. *Milan* (2).

Dralle (242) North German: nickname from *drall, drell* 'stout', 'earthy'.
GIVEN NAMES German 4%. *Monika, Rainer.*

Drane (808) **1.** English: nickname for a lazy man, from Middle English *drone* 'drone', 'male honey bee', long taken as a symbol of idleness (Old English *drān*). **2.** English: variant spelling of DRAIN.

Draney (243) Variant spelling of Scottish **Drainie**, a habitational name from Drainie, a place in Moray.

Dransfield (130) English (mainly Yorkshire): habitational name, perhaps from Dransfield Hill in Mirfield, West Yorkshire, which contains the Old English genitive of *drān* 'drone' + *feld* 'open country'. *Drān* may be a byname in this instance.

Drape (102) English: metonymic occupational name for a maker and seller of woolen cloth, from Old French *drap* 'cloth'.
GIVEN NAMES German 5%. *Erwin, Hans, Otto.*

Drapeau (484) French: metonymic occupational name for a maker and seller of woolen cloth, from a derivative of Old French *drap* 'cloth'.
FOREBEARS A family of this name from Poitou had settled in Île d'Orléans, Quebec, by 1669.
GIVEN NAMES French 16%. *Armand* (3), *Marcel* (3), *Normand* (3), *Andre* (2), *Julien* (2), *Lucien* (2), *Philippe* (2), *Camille, Emile, Francois, Gilles, Jacques.*

Draper (8480) English and Irish: occupational name for a maker and seller of woolen cloth, Anglo-Norman French *draper* (Old French *drapier*, an agent derivative of *drap* 'cloth'). The surname was introduced to Ulster in the 17th century. Draperstown in County Londonderry was named for the London Company of Drapers, which was allocated the land in the early 17th century.

Drapkin (164) Jewish (from Belarus): variant of DRABKIN.
GIVEN NAMES Russian 8%; Jewish 8%. *Leonid* (2), *Aleksandr, Arkady, Igor, Semion; Emanuel, Faina, Meyer, Sol.*

Drass (133) German: of uncertain derivation. It could be a variant of **Drasch**, from the Slavic stem *dragi* 'dear', as in the personal name *Dragomir*. Alternatively, it may be a variant of **Drasse**, perhaps from a Germanic personal name formed with *thras* (an element of uncertain etymology).

Drath (149) German: metonymic occupational name for a wire maker, from Middle High German *drāt*.
GIVEN NAME German 10%. *Kurt* (4).

Draudt (128) German: originally from the female personal name DRUDE, which later became associated by folk etymology with Middle Low German, Middle High German *drūt, trūt* 'dear', 'related' and applied as a nickname, presumably for someone who frequently used this term of endearment or was referred to by it.
GIVEN NAME German 4%. *Gunther.*

Draughn (633) Variant of Irish DROHAN.

Draughon (545) Variant of Irish DROHAN.

Draus (180) Polish: of uncertain derivation; perhaps taken from German *draussen* 'outside', thus meaning 'outsider', 'someone who came from outside'.
GIVEN NAMES Polish 7%. *Maciej, Ryszard, Wladyslaw.*

Draves (664) **1.** Variant spelling of German DREWES. **2.** English: topographic name, from Old English *drāf* 'drove', 'cattle track'.

Dravis (158) **1.** English: variant of TRAVIS. **2.** English: variant of DRAVES. **3.** Perhaps an Americanized form of German DREWES.

Drawbaugh (192) Of German origin: probably an Americanized spelling of **Trarbach**, a habitational name from a place so named on the Mosel river (now part of the twin towns of Traben-Trarbach).

Drawdy (687) Altered spelling of Irish **Droody** or **Drudy**, Anglicized forms of Gaelic **Ó Draoda**, an old and rare Connacht name.

Draxler (163) South German (Bavaria and Austria): variant of DRESSLER.

Dray (608) English: from Middle English *dregh*, probably as a nickname from any of its several senses: 'lasting', 'patient', 'slow', 'tedious', 'doughty'. Alternatively, in some cases, the name may derive from Old English *drȳge* 'dry', 'withered', also applied as a nickname.

Drayer (517) Dutch: occupational name for a wood or bone turner, Middle Dutch *drayere*, an agent derivative of *draaien* 'to turn'.

Drayton (1576) English: habitational name from any of the very numerous places in England named Drayton, from Old English *dræg* 'drag', 'portage', 'slipway', or 'sledge' (a place where boats were dragged across land or where loads had to be dragged uphill or on sledges across wet ground, from *dragan* 'to draw or drag') + *tūn* 'enclosure', 'settlement'.

Drazek (103) Polish (**Drążek**): from a diminutive of **Drąg** (see DRĄG).
GIVEN NAMES Polish 19%. *Jerzy, Jozef, Krysztof, Leszek, Mieczyslaw, Piotr, Teofil.*

Drazkowski (116) Polish (**Drążkowski**): habitational name from a place named with **Drążek** (see DRAZEK).

Drea (101) Irish: reduced Americanized form of **Ó Draoi** (see DREW).

Drechsel (263) German: occupational name from Old High German *drāsil* 'turner'. See also DRESSLER.
GIVEN NAMES German 7%. *Gerhardt, Hans, Heinz, Kurt, Siegfried.*

Drechsler (400) German and Jewish (Ashkenazic): variant of DRESSLER. *Drechsler* became the standard German term for the occupation of wood turner.
GIVEN NAMES German 10%. *Kurt* (3), *Gerhard* (2), *Erwin, Ewald, Guenther, Gunther, Jochen.*

Dreckman (102) North German (**Dreckmann**): topographic name for someone who lived in a muddy place, from Middle Low German *dreck* 'mire', 'morass' + *man* 'man', or a habitational name for someone from any of the places in Rhineland and Hannover called Dreck, Drecke, or Dreeke.

Dredge (195) English: from Old French *dragie, dragé* 'mixture of grains sown together', hence probably an metonymic occupational name for a farmer or a grain merchant.

Drees (794) **1.** North German and Dutch: from the personal name *Drees*, a short form of the Biblical name *Andreas* (see ANDREW). **2.** German: habitational name from a place named Drees in the Rhineland.

Dreese (197) Altered spelling of German DREES.

Dreesen (170) North German: patronymic from the personal name DREES.

Dreessen (142) North German and Danish: variant of DREESEN.

Dreger (457) North German: variant of DREYER.

GIVEN NAMES German 6%. *Kurt* (5), *Erwin* (3), *Fritz, Hans.*

Dreher (2191) South German and Swiss German: occupational name for a turner, from an agent derivative of Middle High German *dræhen, dræjen* 'to turn'. See also DRESSLER.

Dreibelbis (366) Variant of Swiss and South German **Deubelbeiss** or **Tüfelbeiss** (see DEVILBISS).

Dreier (913) North German, Scandinavian, and Jewish (Ashkenazic): variant spelling of DREYER.

GIVEN NAMES German 4%. *Armin, Ernst, Franz, Fritz, Heinz, Kurt, Udo, Uwe.*

Dreiling (832) German: **1.** from Middle High German *drīling* 'third (part)', possibly denoting a service or tax obligation, and hence a status name, or a triplet. **2.** habitational name from Drelingen near Uelzen, Lower Saxony.

Dreis (160) **1.** Dutch and North German: variant of DREES. **2.** German: habitational name from a place named Dreis, for example in the Eifel region.

GIVEN NAMES French 4%. *Chantal, Monique.*

Dreisbach (457) German: habitational name from any of several places in Hesse called Dreisbach.

Dreith (109) German: unexplained.

Drell (104) Jewish (eastern Ashkenazic): metonymic occupational name from eastern Slavic *drel* 'borer', 'gimlet'.

GIVEN NAMES Jewish 7%. *Hyman, Isadore.*

Drendel (127) German and French (Alsace–Lorraine): unexplained.

Drennan (1626) Irish and Scottish (mainly Galloway): Anglicized form of Gaelic **Ó Draighneáin** 'descendant of *Draighneán*', a byname from *draighneán* 'blackthorn'.

Drennen (781) Irish: variant spelling of DRENNAN.

Drenner (123) Variant of German TRENNER.

Drenning (203) Anglicized form of Irish and Scottish DRENNAN.

Drennon (354) Irish: variant spelling of DRENNAN.

Drenth (273) Dutch: habitational name from a place in the Netherlands called Drente.

GIVEN NAMES Dutch 4%. *Derk* (2), *Henk, Maarten.*

Drerup (119) North German: topographic or habitational name probably from Schleswig, where the suffix *-rup* is comon.

Dresbach (167) German: habitational name from any of three places near Cologne called Dresbach.

Dresch (220) German: **1.** variant of DREES 1. **2.** old form of DRESCHER.

GIVEN NAMES German 4%. *Franz, Heinz.*

Drescher (1172) German and Jewish (Ashkenazic): occupational name for a thresher, German *Drescher*, Yiddish *dresher*, agent derivatives of Middle High German *dreschen*, Yiddish *dresh(e)n* 'to thresh'.

GIVEN NAMES German 5%. *Otto* (3), *Eldred* (2), *Christl, Erhard, Erwin, Fritz, Gerhard, Goetz, Hans, Kurt, Uwe, Wolfgang.*

Dresden (156) German, Scandinavian, and Jewish (Ashkenazic): habitational name denoting someone from Dresden in Saxony.

GIVEN NAME Scandinavian 4%. *Knute.*

Dresel (133) German: **1.** occupational name for a turner, Middle High German *drēhsel*. **2.** habitational name from a place in Westphalia called Dresel. **3.** from a reduced pet form of the personal name ANDREAS.

Dresen (256) **1.** German: habitational name from a reduced form of DRESDEN. **2.** Probably a variant spelling of German DREESEN.

Dresher (219) Americanized spelling of German DRESCHER, also found as a Jewish name.

Dresner (256) German and Jewish (Ashkenazic): habitational name for someone from the city of Dresden.

GIVEN NAMES Jewish 4%. *Avram, Miriam, Sol.*

Dress (238) German: of uncertain derivation; possibly from a short form of the Germanic personal name *Thrasolt*, composed with a stem meaning 'to fight', or alternatively from the personal name ANDREAS.

Dressel (1082) German: **1.** from a pet form of the personal name ANDREAS. **2.** variant of DRESS and of DRESEL 3. **3.** occupational name for a turner, from Middle High German *drehsel*.

GIVEN NAMES German 4%. *Erwin* (3), *Kurt* (3), *Adelheid, Alois, Armin, Johann, Lorenz, Markus, Otto.*

Dressen (294) Probably an altered spelling of German DRESEN or DREESSEN.

Dresser (1047) **1.** German: eastern variant of DRESCHER. **2.** English: from an agent derivative of Middle English *dressen* 'to arrange' (in certain specific senses), possibly an occupational name for someone who dressed or finished cloth. Compare FULLER.

Dressler (1812) German and Jewish (Ashkenazic): occupational name for a turner, from Middle High German *dreseler* or *dræselære* (formed by the addition of a superfluous agent suffix to Old High German *drāsil* 'turner', a primary derivative of *drāen* 'turn', 'spin'). A turner would make small objects not just from wood, but also from bone, ivory, and amber, all of which were widely used in the Middle Ages for their decorative value.

Dressman (168) **1.** Americanized spelling of Dutch **Dreszmann**, a patronymic from the personal name DREES. **2.** German: probably of the same origin as 1.

Dreves (117) German: variant of DREWES.

Drew (8731) **1.** English: from a short form of ANDREW. **2.** English (Norman): from the Germanic personal name *Drogo*, which is of uncertain origin; it is possibly akin to Old Saxon *(gi)drog* 'ghost', 'phantom', or with a stem meaning 'to bear', 'to carry' (Old High German *tragan*). Whatever its origin, the name was borne by one of the sons of Charlemagne, and was subsequently popular throughout France in the forms *Dreus, Drues* (oblique case *Dreu, Dr(i)u*), whence it was introduced to England by the Normans. Drogo de Monte Acuto (as his name appears in its Latinized form) was a companion of William the Conqueror and founder of the **Montagu** family, among whom the personal name *Drogo* was revived in the 19th century. **3.** English (of Norman origin): nickname from Middle English *dreue, dru*, Old French *dru* 'favorite', 'lover' (originally an adjective, apparently from a Gaulish word meaning 'strong', 'vigorous', 'lively', but influenced by the sense of the Old High German element *trūt, drūt* 'dear', 'beloved'). **4.** English (of Norman origin): habitational name from any of various places in France called Dreux, from the Gaulish tribal name *Durocasses*. **5.** English (of Norman origin): habitational name, with the preposition *de*, from any of the numerous places in France named from Old French *rieux* 'streams'. **6.** Irish: when not an adoption of the English surname, a reduced Anglicized form of Gaelic **Mac an Druaidh** or **Ó Druaidh** or **Ó Draoi** 'son' and 'descendant of the druid', from *draoi* 'druid', genitive *druadh* or *draoi*.

Drewek (130) Polish: from a diminutive of *drewo*, dialect form of *drewno* 'wood', probably a metonymic occupational name for a woodcutter.

Drewery (357) English and Irish: variant spelling of DRURY.

Drewes (635) **1.** English and Scottish: patronymic from the personal name DREW. **2.** Danish, Dutch, and German: from a vernacular form of the personal name ANDREAS.

GIVEN NAMES German 4%. *Claus, Erna, Frieda, Guenter, Horst, Klaus, Wolfram.*

Drewett (171) English: from a diminutive of DREW 2 or 3.

Drewniak (150) Polish: status name for someone who lived in a wooden hut, *drewniak*, a derivative of *drewno* 'timber', 'wood'.

GIVEN NAMES Polish 14%. *Krzysztof* (2), *Andrzej, Malgorzata, Tomasz, Zbigniew.*

Drewry (853) English and Irish: variant spelling of DRURY.

Drews (1616) **1.** English and Scottish: patronymic from the personal name DREW, a short form of ANDREW. **2.** Danish, Dutch, and German: from a vernacular form of the personal name ANDREAS.
GIVEN NAMES German 5%. *Erwin* (3), *Gerhard* (2), *Gunter* (2), *Hans* (2), *Heinz* (2), *Helmut* (2), *Otto* (2), *Reinhold* (2), *Bernd, Detlef, Egon, Erna.*

Drexel (367) German: variant spelling of DRECHSEL.

Drexler (1397) German and Jewish (Ashkenazic): variant spelling of DRECHSLER (see DRESSLER).

Drey (259) **1.** German: habitational name from Dreyen, a place near Herford, or Dreye, a place near Bremen. **2.** English: variant spelling of DRAY.

Dreyer (2831) **1.** German and Jewish (Ashkenazic): nickname derived from German *drei* 'three', Middle High German *drī(e)*, with the addition of the suffix *-er*. This was the name of a medieval coin worth three hellers (see HELLER), and it is possible that the German surname may have been derived from this word. More probably, the nickname is derived from some other connection with the number three, too anecdotal to be even guessed at now. **2.** North German and Scandinavian: occupational name for a turner of wood or bone, from an agent derivative of Middle Low German *dreien, dregen* 'to turn'. See also DRESSLER. **3.** Jewish (Ashkenazic): occupational name from Yiddish *dreyer* 'turner', or a nickname from a homonym meaning 'swindler, cheat'. **4.** English: variant spelling of DRYER.
GIVEN NAMES German 4%. *Hans* (4), *Erwin* (2), *Fritz* (2), *Johannes* (2), *Kurt* (2), *Baerbel, Bernhard, Christoph, Claus, Dieter, Ernst, Hedwig.*

Dreyfus (443) Jewish (western Ashkenazic): habitational name from *Trevis*, an old name of the city of Trier on the Mosel, known in French as *Trèves*; both the French and German names come from Latin *Augusta Treverorum* 'city of Augustus among the *Treveri*', a Celtic tribal name of uncertain origin. The form of the surname has been altered from *Trevis* by folk etymological association with modern German *Dreifuss* 'tripod'. Compare TRIER.
GIVEN NAMES French 9%. *Philippe* (2), *Pierre* (2), *Andre, Benoit, Camille, Dominique, Emile, Georges, Julien, Marcel, Sylvie.*

Dreyfuss (363) Jewish (western Ashkenazic): variant spelling of DREYFUS.
GIVEN NAMES French 5%; German 5%. *Jacques* (2), *Andre*; *Hans* (2), *Kurt* (2), *Hedwig.*

Drier (322) Probably an Americanized spelling of DREYER.

Dries (469) Dutch and North German: variant spelling of DREES.

Driesbach (115) Probably a respelling of German DREISBACH.
GIVEN NAME German 4%. *Kurt.*

Driesen (109) Probably a respelling of Dutch and North German DRIESSEN.
GIVEN NAMES German 5%. *Armin, Hans.*

Driessen (285) Dutch and North German: patronymic from the personal name *Dries* (see DREES).

Driggers (2464) Origin unidentified. Possibly an Americanized form of German DRAEGER.

Driggs (701) Possibly a variant of English TRIGGS.

Drill (191) Possibly a variant of German **Trill**, a topographic name for someone who lived by the turnstile at the entrance to a village, or an Americanized spelling of German **Trüll** (see TRULL).
GIVEN NAMES German 4%. *Fritz, Wolfgang.*

Drilling (247) German: nickname for one of triplets, from Middle High German *dri* 'three' + *-ling* suffix denoting affiliation.

Drinan (127) Irish (County Cork): variant of DRENNAN.

Dring (189) English: from Old Norse *drengr* 'young man', but with more than one possible interpretation. It may reflect the personal name (originally a byname) of this form, which had some currency in the most Scandinavian-influenced areas of medieval England. Alternatively it may reflect the Middle English borrowing of the vocabulary word in the sense 'servant', later a technical term of the feudal system of Northumbria for a free tenant who held land by military and agricultural service, sometimes paying rent as well or in commutation.

Drinkard (757) Perhaps an altered spelling of German **Trinkart** or **Trinkert**, nicknames for a drinker, or Dutch **Drinckwaard**, which Debrabandere suggests could be an occupational name for a publican or innkeeper, though he thinks it is more likely to be a reinterpreted form of DRINKWATER.

Drinkwater (855) English: nickname from Middle English *drink* + *water*. In the Middle Ages weak ale was the universal beverage among the poorer classes, and so cheap as to be drunk like water, whereas water itself was only doubtfully potable. The surname was perhaps a joking nickname given to a pauper or miser allegedly unable or unwilling to afford beer, or may have been given in irony to an innkeeper or a noted tippler. Compare French BOILEAU, German **Trinkwasser**.

Drinkwine (285) Translation of the French family name BOIVIN.

Drinnen (124) Irish: variant of DRENNAN.

Drinnon (368) Variant of Irish DRENNAN.

Dripps (187) Scottish: habitational name from a place in Lanarkshire called Dripps.

Driscoll (9699) Irish: reduced Anglicized form of Gaelic **Ó hEidirsceóil** 'descendant of the messenger', from *eidirsceól* 'go-between', 'intermediary', 'news bearer' (a compound of *eidir* 'between' + *scéal* 'story', 'news'). Bearers of this Irish surname claim descent from a single 10th-century ancestor.
GIVEN NAMES Irish 5%. *Donovan* (2), *Brendan, John Patrick.*

Drish (132) Probably a variant of North German **Driesch**, a topographic name for someone who lived by an uncultivated piece of land used for pasture, or a habitational name from any of several places in Rhineland called Driesch.

Driskel (102) Irish: variant spelling of DRISCOLL.
GIVEN NAME Irish 5%. *Paddy.*

Driskell (1498) Irish: variant spelling of DRISCOLL.

Driskill (1285) Irish: variant spelling of DRISCOLL.

Drisko (125) Irish: variant spelling of DRISCOLL.

Drivas (117) Greek: **1.** most probably a variant of GRIVAS. **2.** possibly from a derivative of Slavic *drvo* 'tree'.
GIVEN NAMES Greek 8%. *Chrisoula, Constantine, Spyros, Theodoros.*

Driver (5255) English: occupational name for a driver of horses or oxen attached to a cart or plow, or of loose cattle, from a Middle English agent derivative of Old English *drīfan* 'to drive'.

Drobnick (113) **1.** Americanized spelling of Czech and Polish **Drobnik**, a derivative of DROBNY. **2.** Americanized or Germanized spelling of Slovenian **Drobnič**, a nickname derived from *droben* 'tiny', 'small'.

Drobny (215) Czech and Slovak (**Drobný**); Polish: nickname from Czech *drobný*, Polish *drobny* 'small'.
GIVEN NAMES Polish 4%. *Wladyslaw* (2), *Jozef.*

Droddy (172) Possibly a variant of the Irish family name **Draddy**, a reduced Anglicized form of Gaelic **Ó Dreada**.

Droege (441) North German (**Dröge**): from Middle Low German *droge* 'dry', probably applied as a topographic name for someone who lived in an area of dry ground.
GIVEN NAMES German 4%. *Wolfgang* (2), *Heinz, Helmut, Kurt.*

Droessler (201) German (**Drössler**): variant, found mainly in East Franconia and Thuringia, of DRESSLER.

Droge (197) **1.** German (**Dröge**): see DROEGE. **2.** German: from a byname of uncertain derivation, cognate with German *Trug-* 'deception', 'illusion' or Old Norse *drog* 'load'. **3.** Dutch: nickname from Middle Dutch *droog* 'dry', 'boring', 'unfriendly'.

Drohan (346) Irish: reduced Anglicized form of Gaelic **Ó Druacháin** 'descendant of *Druachán*', a byname representing a diminutive of *druach* 'wise man'.

Droke (265) Respelling of DROGE.

Drolet (437) French: probably a nickname, from a diminutive of *drôle* 'lively', 'cheeky'.

FOREBEARS A Parisian family by this name had settled in Quebec city by 1654.

GIVEN NAMES French 15%. *Adrien* (2), *Andre* (2), *Pierre* (2), *Aime*, *Benoit*, *Cecile*, *Francois*, *Gilles*, *Jean-Jacques*, *Jean-Paul*, *Lucien*, *Normand*.

Droll (266) German: **1.** nickname for a chubby funny man, from Middle Low German *dral* 'round', 'whirly'. **2.** variant of the nickname TROLL 'demon'.

Drollinger (319) German: ethnic or regional name for someone from Tyrol.

Dromgoole (171) Irish: habitational name from the Gaelic place name *Dromgabhail* in County Lough, source of the modern name Drumgoolestown. MacLysaght says this was a family of prominent Jacobites.

Drone (345) **1.** Probably an altered spelling of North German **Drohne**, a habitational name from a place in Westphalia called Drohne, or from a fieldname, from Middle Low German *drōn(e)*, a unit of land. **2.** Possibly a variant of English DRANE, Irish DROHAN, or Scottish **Dron**, a habitational name from a place so called in Perthshire.

Dronen (138) Variant spelling of Scottish **Dronan**, a habitational name from a place named The Dronnan in Kirkcudbrightshire.

Dronet (176) Possibly an altered spelling of French **Dronnet**, a pet form of *Dron*, a derivative of the Germanic personal name *Drogo* (see DREW 2).

GIVEN NAMES French 9%; Irish 5%. *Alcee*, *Desire*, *Olympe*; *Daley*, *Murphy*.

Droney (163) Irish (especially eastern County Clare): reduced Anglicized form of Gaelic **Ó Dróna** 'descendant of *Dróna*', an unexplained personal name.

GIVEN NAMES Irish 10%. *Kieran*, *Seamus*.

Drop (122) Dutch: nickname from Middle Dutch *drope* 'dropsy', 'gout'.

Dropkin (136) Jewish (from Belarus): nickname from Belorussian *drobka* 'crumb'+ the eastern Slavic patronymic suffix *-in*.

Dropp (105) Probably a variant of German TROPP.

Dross (180) **1.** German: variant of DROSTE. This name is also found in Germany as a Huguenot name, from French DROZ. **2.** German: variant of TROSS. **3.** Perhaps an altered spelling of **Dros**, a Dutch variant of DROST.

Drost (986) **1.** Dutch: occupational name for a steward or head servant, Middle Dutch *drost*, *drossaert*. Like the German cognate DROSTE, the term was also used as a title for various officials. **2.** Danish and Polish: from German DROSTE.

Droste (447) North German: occupational name for a steward or head servant, Middle Low German *drotsete* (a cognate of Middle High German *truhsæze*). The term derives

from Old High German *truht* 'body of vassals' (later servants) + *sizzen* 'to sit' (i.e. preside). The term was also used as a title in various different contexts.

Drotar (226) Slovak (**Drotár**): occupational name for a tinker.

Drott (132) Dutch: variant of the German family name **Trott(e)**, an ironical nickname for a slow awkward person, from Middle High German *trotten* 'to trot' (see TROTT).

Drought (142) Irish: **1.** (Leinster) reduced Anglicized form of Gaelic **Ó Drochtaigh**, which according to Woulfe is a derivative of *drocht* 'millwheel', i.e. a byname for a miller. **2.** (Counties Limerick and Clare) reduced Anglicized form of Gaelic **Ó Droichid**, from *droichead* 'bridge', more usually Anglicized as BRIDGEMAN.

Drouhard (105) French: from a derivative of *Droue*, an unattested variant of *Dreue*, from the Germanic personal name *Drogo* (see DREW 2).

Drouillard (440) French: **1.** probably a derogatory nickname, from a derivative of the regional term *drouiller* 'to defecate', which also has various figurative senses. **2.** re-formation of the habitational name **Drouillac**, from a place so named in Corrèze.

FOREBEARS The name was present in Canada as early as 1689; the marriage of a man of this name from Saintonge is recorded in Quebec city in 1698.

GIVEN NAMES French 4%. *Amede*, *Collette*, *Girard*, *Gisele*, *Huguette*, *Ovila*.

Drouin (988) French: from a pet form of *Droue*, an unattested variant of the personal name *Dreue*. This is from the Germanic personal name *Drogo* (see DREW 2).

FOREBEARS A family of this name from Perche was established in Quebec city by 1637.

GIVEN NAMES French 17%. *Marcel* (8), *Armand* (5), *Benoit* (3), *Jacques* (3), *Andre* (2), *Clermont* (2), *Emile* (2), *Gaston* (2), *Gilles* (2), *Ovide* (2), *Pierre* (2), *Serge* (2).

Drover (107) English: occupational name for someone who drove herds of cattle across the country to a market, from an agent derivative of Old English *drāf* 'drove', 'herd'.

Drown (1007) **1.** English (Cornwall and Devon): unexplained. **2.** Possibly a reflex of French DROUIN.

Drowne (122) Variant spelling of DROWN.

Droz (307) Swiss and Alsatian French: from the Germanic personal name *Drogo* (see DREW 2).

GIVEN NAMES Spanish 6%. *Aida*, *Cruz Maria*, *Diego*, *Jose*, *Miguel*, *Milagros*, *Nydia*, *Osvaldo*, *Rodriguez*, *Vidal*.

Drozd (632) Polish, Czech, Slovak, and Jewish (eastern Ashkenazic): nickname for someone thought to resemble a thrush, from Polish and Czech *drozd* 'thrush'. As a Jewish name it is mainly ornamental.

GIVEN NAMES Polish 8%. *Krystyna* (3), *Zbigniew* (3), *Boleslaw*, *Danuta*, *Dariusz*, *Janina*, *Katarzyna*, *Leszek*, *Malgorzata*, *Piotr*, *Stanislawa*, *Wieslaw*.

Drozda (166) Polish: variant of DROZD, with the addition of the genitive suffix *-a*.

Drozdowski (309) Polish: habitational name for someone from any of various places called Drozdowo or Drozdów, for example.

GIVEN NAMES Polish 13%. *Zygmunt* (2), *Alicja*, *Casimir*, *Danuta*, *Jerzy*, *Krzystof*, *Tadeusz*, *Witold*, *Wladyslawa*, *Wlodzimierz*, *Zigmund*.

Druce (162) **1.** English: variant spelling of DREWES. **2.** Possibly an altered spelling of Dutch and German DREWES.

Druck (240) Jewish (Ashkenazic): from German *Druck* 'print', 'printing'; hence a metonymic occupational name for a printer. Compare DRUCKER.

Druckenmiller (258) Partly Americanized form of German **Druckenmüller**, a distinguishing name for a miller (see MUELLER) whose mill was situated in a dry place.

Drucker (1337) Jewish (Ashkenazic): occupational name for a printer, from German *Drucker* or Yiddish *druker* 'printer', agent derivatives of German *drucken*, Yiddish *drukn* 'to print', derived from a southern dialect variant of *drücken* 'to press'. Printing was first developed in Mainz in the 15th century.

GIVEN NAMES Jewish 4%. *Meyer* (2), *Golda*, *Isadore*, *Jakob*, *Meirav*, *Mort*, *Myer*, *Reuven*, *Rina*, *Shalom*, *Sol*, *Yifat*.

Druckman (150) Jewish (Ashkenazic): occupational name for a printer (see DRUCKER).

GIVEN NAMES Jewish 9%. *Meyer* (2), *Elihu*.

Drude (103) North German: from a short form of the female personal name *Gertrud* (see TRUDE).

GIVEN NAME German 6%. *Heinz*.

Drudge (157) English: variant of DREDGE.

Druffel (132) German: habitational name from Druffel near Minden, in North Rhine-Westphalia.

Drugan (159) Irish: reduced Anglicized form of Gaelic **Ó Druagáin** 'descendant of *Druagán*', an unexplained personal name.

Druker (144) Jewish: variant spelling of DRUCKER.

GIVEN NAMES Jewish 10%; Russian 5%; Jewish Biblical 4%. *Galit* (3), *Ari*, *Naum*, *Polina*, *Rahil*, *Yoel*; *Igor*, *Pyotr*.

Druley (106) Americanized spelling of French DROLET.

Drum (1730) **1.** Irish: reduced Anglicized form of Gaelic **Ó Droma** 'descendant of *Droma*', a personal name, which may be from *druim* 'back', 'ridge' and have been given originally to someone with a deformed back. **2.** Scottish: habitational name from a place and castle in Aberdeenshire named from Gaelic *druim* 'ridge'. **3.** German: nickname from Middle Low

German *drum*, Middle High German *trum* 'woodblock', 'uncouth person'.

Drumgoole (123) Irish: variant of DROM-GOOLE.

Drumheller (750) Americanized spelling of German **Trum(pf)heller**, an occupational name for a drummer, from an enlarged form of Middle High German *trumbeler* 'drummer' (from *trumbe* 'drum' + the agent suffix *-er*).

Drumm (1604) **1.** Irish: variant spelling of DRUM 1. **2.** German: from Middle Low German *drum* 'lump of wood' (Middle High German *trum*), used as a nickname for an uncouth man.

Drummer (525) German: variant of TRUMMER.

Drummey (204) Variant of the Irish family name DRUM.

Drummond (5954) Scottish: habitational name from any of the various places, as for example Drymen near Stirling and Drummond (Castle) in Perthshire, that are named from Gaelic *drumainn*, a derivative of *druim* 'ridge'.

Drummonds (221) Variant of Scottish DRUMMOND.

Drumright (157) Variant of DRUMWRIGHT.

Drumwright (169) Origin unidentified. The name has 18th-century associations with Louisa county, VA.

Drury (4224) **1.** English (Norman) and French: nickname from Old French *druerie* 'love', 'friendship', a derivative of *dru* 'lover', 'friend' (see DREW 3). In Middle English the word also had the concrete meanings 'love affair', 'love token', 'sweetheart'. **2.** English (Norman) and French: from a Germanic personal name composed of Old High German *triuwa* 'truth', 'trust' + *rīc* 'power(ful)'. **3.** Irish (County Roscommon): English name adopted by bearers of Gaelic **Mac an Druaidh** 'son of the druid'. Compare DREW 6.

Druschel (132) German: from a pet form of any of the various personal names beginning with Old High German *trūt, drūt* 'dear', 'beloved' (see DRAUDT).

Druse (116) North German: nickname from Low German *drus* 'sullen'.

Drust (113) English (Lincolnshire): unexplained. Black identified this as a Scottish name of Pictish origin. However, the modern distribution of the surname, almost exclusively in Lincolnshire and adjoining counties, suggests a more localized eastern English origin.

Dry (849) English: variant of DRAY.

Dryburgh (120) Scottish: habitational name for someone from either of two places in the Borders named Dryburgh.

Dryden (2052) English: habitational name from a lost or unidentified place, probably in Cumbria or Northumberland, where the name is still common, and perhaps named

from Old English *drȳge* 'dry' + *denu* 'valley'.

Drye (683) English: variant of DRAY.

Dryer (1097) **1.** English: from an agent derivative of Old English *drȳgean* 'to dry'; possibly an occupational name for a drier of cloth. In the Middle Ages, after cloth had been dyed and fulled, it was stretched out in tenterfields to dry. **2.** Altered spelling of German DREIER or DREYER.

Dryman (111) Scottish: habitational name from the village of Drymen in Stirlingshire.

Drymon (100) Variant of Scottish DRYMAN.

Drysdale (728) Scottish: habitational name from Dryfesdale near Dumfries, named from the river *Dryfe* + Old English *dæl* 'valley'.

Drzal (102) Polish (**Drzał**): nickname from *drzeć* 'to tear'.

GIVEN NAMES Polish 8%. *Jolanta, Stanislaw, Tadeusz.*

Drzewiecki (316) Polish: habitational name from any of the many places called Drzewce or Drzewiec, from *drzewa* 'trees', or possibly a topographic name from the same word.

D'Souza (586) Portuguese: habitational name for someone from any of the various places named SOUSA. The surname is also common in Goa and elsewhere on the west coast of India, having been taken there by Portuguese colonists.

GIVEN NAMES Indian 6%. *Sanjeev (2), Anil, Arvind, Asha, Naveen, Pradeep, Prafulla, Praveen, Rattan, Rohit, Sandeep, Shalini.*

Du (868) **1.** Chinese 杜: from the name of a state that existed during the Zhou dynasty (in present-day Shaanxi province). When the second king of the Zhou dynasty, Cheng Wang (1115–1079 BC), defeated the state of Tang in present-day Shaanxi province, he changed its name to Du and granted it to a descendant of the model emperor Yao. Descendants of the new ruler subsequently adopted the place name as their surname. **2.** Chinese 都: from the names of two princes of ancient territories, one from the state of Qi, and the other from the state of Zhen. **3.** Vietnamese (**Dư**): unexplained.

GIVEN NAMES Chinese 40%; Vietnamese 27%. *Wei (10), Hong (6), Jian (3), Jing (3), Li (3), Ping (3), Yan (3), Yang (3), Yong (3), Bin (2), Chan (2), Cheng (2); Thanh (8), Quang (6), Cuong (5), Dung (5), Hung (5), Binh (4), Minh (4), Duong (3), Hao (3), Hien (3), Liem (3), Lien (3).*

Dua (121) Indian (Panjab): Hindu (Arora) and Sikh name based on the name of a clan in the Arora community. The Arabic word *du'ā* 'invocation', 'good wish' is familiar to Panjabi speakers, but it is not clear whether it is connected with this name.

GIVEN NAMES Indian 76%. *Anil (4), Prem (3), Shyam (3), Anuj (2), Naresh (2), Raj (2), Ramesh (2), Satish (2), Usha (2), Aashish, Anit, Aparna.*

Duan (177) Chinese 段: from the name of the youngest son of Duke Wu Gong of the state of Zheng during the Spring and Autumn period (722–481 BC). He was brought up by a doting mother and became an arrogant and domineering man. Upon being granted a fief, he raised an army with the goal of overthrowing his elder brother, Duke Zhuang Gong. Hearing of this, the latter remarked, 'excessive unrighteous behavior must die of itself', and as he expected, his younger brother failed. Nevertheless some of his descendants adopted **Duan** as their surname. Another source of the name is from Duan-gan Mu of the state of Wei during the Warring States period (403–221 BC). His descendants simplified *Duan-gan* to *Duan* and adopted that as their surname.

GIVEN NAMES Chinese 51%. *Lian (2), Ling (2), Xiaofeng (2), Zheng (2), Chang Min, Dongsheng, Guohong, Hongwei, Hongyi, Hongyu, Hui, Jian Ping Hai Long (4), Cao, Hao, Long.*

Duane (816) Irish: reduced Anglicized form of Gaelic **Ó Dubháin** or **Ó Damháin** (see DOANE).

Duarte (4562) Portuguese: from the personal name *Duarte*, Portuguese equivalent of EDWARD.

GIVEN NAMES Spanish 40%; Portuguese 10%. *Jose (108), Manuel (69), Carlos (42), Jesus (40), Juan (33), Jorge (28), Luis (24), Ruben (22), Francisco (19), Miguel (19), Raul (19), Pedro (15), Joao (5), Joaquim (3), Agostinho (2), Henrique (2), Paulo (2), Albano, Almir, Anabela, Ilidio, Ligia, Marcio, Margarida.*

Dub (129) Jewish (eastern Ashkenazic), Czech, and Slovak: nickname for someone of great strength, from eastern Slavic, Czech and Slovak *dub* 'oak', or a habitational name from a place named with this word.

GIVEN NAMES Russian 7%; Jewish 5%; Polish 4%. *Leonid (2), Galina, Lev, Semion, Vladimir; Zigmund.*

Duba (268) **1.** Hungarian: from the old secular Hungarian personal names *Duba*, or *Doba*, pet forms of *Dub* or *Dob*. **2.** Possibly French, a variant of French DUBEAU.

Dubach (194) Possibly an altered form of German **Tubach**, which may be from Swiss **Tübach**, a habitational name from a place so named near Rorschach.

GIVEN NAME French 4%. *Marcel (2).*

Dubard (116) Probably a variant of French **Dubart**, a patronymic from the Germanic personal name *Bardo*, a short form of a compound name formed with *bard*, from Old High German *barta* 'battle axe'.

Dubas (249) French: topographic name for someone who lived in the lower part of a village, from *bas* 'low'.

GIVEN NAMES French 4%. *Andre, Colette.*

Dubay (1095) **1.** Hungarian: habitational name for someone from a place called

Duba in Zala county. **2.** Possibly also an Americanized spelling of French **Dubé** (see DUBE).

Dubberly (292) English: unexplained. It is probably a habitational name from a lost or unidentified place in west central England, where the modern surname is most frequent.

Dubbert (138) Frisian (also **Dübbert**): variant of **Dibbert**, itself a variant of DIBBERN.

Dubbs (622) English: probably a variant of DOBBS.

Dube (3457) **1.** French (**Dubé**): of uncertain origin. It may be a habitational name for someone from any of various places called Le Bec, which are named either from Gaulish *becco* 'high ground' or from Germanic *bec* 'stream' (see BECK). **2.** Breton: nickname meaning 'pigeon'. **3.** Eastern German, Sorbian, or other Slavic: from Sorbian or Slavic *dub* 'oak', hence a nickname for a strong or solid man, a topographic name for someone who lived by a prominent oak or in an area where oak trees were abundant, or a habitational name for someone from a place named with this word, for example Dubá or Doubé, both frequent Czech place names. **4.** North German: variant of DUWE. **5.** Indian (northern states); pronounced as two syllables: Hindu (Brahman) name meaning 'one who knows (or has studied) two Vedas', from Sanskrit *dvivedī* 'one who knows two Vedas', from *dvi* 'two' + *veda* 'Veda', 'knowledge'. This name is a cognate of Gujarati DAVE.
FOREBEARS A Poitevin family of this name had settled in Île d'Orléans before 1670.
GIVEN NAMES French 16%. *Lucien* (20), *Normand* (19), *Armand* (12), *Pierre* (8), *Emile* (7), *Fernand* (7), *Marcel* (7), *Andre* (6), *Laurent* (6), *Gilles* (5), *Herve* (4), *Jacques* (4).

Dubeau (230) French: patronymic from LEBEAU.
GIVEN NAMES French 6%. *Cecile, Lucien, Marcel, Normand.*

Dubel (137) **1.** French: variant of DUBEAU 1. **2.** North German (**Dübel**): Low German form of TEUFEL.

Dubell (129) Americanized spelling of DUBEL.

Duberstein (122) German: variant of DOBBERSTEIN.

Dubey (454) Indian: variant of DUBE.
GIVEN NAMES Indian 23%. *Neeraj* (3), *Aditi* (2), *Ashutosh* (2), *Atul* (2), *Devendra* (2), *Pradeep* (2), *Rajeev* (2), *Sanjay* (2), *Abha, Anasuya, Bal, Dilip.*

Dubicki (127) Polish: habitational name for someone from a place called Dubica or Dubicze.
GIVEN NAMES Polish 16%. *Boguslaw, Henryk, Janina, Piotr, Ryszard, Stanislaw, Waclaw, Zbignew.*

Dubie (189) French (**Dubié**): topographic name for someone who lived by a mill race, with the fused preposition and definite article *du* 'from the' + *bié* 'mill race'.

Dubiel (597) Polish: nickname from *dubiel* 'stupid person'.
GIVEN NAMES Polish 7%. *Tadeusz* (3), *Irena* (2), *Alicja, Andrzej, Jacek, Jozef, Leszek, Ryszard, Wladyslaw, Zdzislaw, Zygmunt.*

Dubin (1438) **1.** Jewish (from Belarus and Lithuania): habitational name from Dubno in Ukraine or various places in Belarus and elsewhere called Dubin, Dubno, Dubina, Dubiny, and Duby, named with Slavic *dub* 'oak'. **2.** Czech (**Dubín**): habitational name from a place called Dubiny. **3.** French: from a pet form of the personal name ROBERT.
GIVEN NAMES Jewish 7%. *Miriam* (4), *Sol* (3), *Hyman* (2), *Yakov* (2), *Yetta* (2), *Abbe, Avrohom, Chaim, Emanuel, Gershon, Hinda, Ilya.*

Dubinski (134) **1.** Polish (**Dubiński**) and Jewish (from Poland): habitational name for someone from any of the places called Dubin, from *dub, dąb* 'oak'. **2.** Jewish (from Belarus, Lithuania, and Ukraine): habitational name, a variant of DUBIN + the locative suffix *-ski.*

Dubinsky (510) **1.** Slovak (**Dubinský**): topographic name for somone who lived by an oak tree, from Slavic *dub* 'oak', 'oak forest'. **2.** Altered spelling of Polish **Dubiński** (see DUBINSKI), also found as a Jewish name.
GIVEN NAMES Russian 10%; Jewish 10%. *Boris* (10), *Leonid* (3), *Vladimir* (3), *Dmitry, Galina, Iosif, Konstantin, Lev, Mikhail, Misha, Savva, Semyon; Aron, Faina, Inna, Marat, Meir, Mendel, Ophir.*

Dubis (159) Variant of Polish **Dubisz**, a derivative of *dub, dąb* 'oak' (see DUB).
GIVEN NAMES Polish 6%. *Ludwik, Stanislaw, Tadeusz.*

Duble (111) Altered spelling of German **Döble** (see DOBLE) or of English DOBLE.

Dubler (132) Probably an Americanized spelling of German **Döbler** (see DOBLER).

Dublin (550) Apparently a habitational name referring to Dublin, the capital of Ireland, but if so it would have been adopted outside Ireland, since place names were not normally used as surnames in Ireland.

Dubner (132) **1.** German (**Dübner**): habitational name for someone from either of two places named Düben, in Saxony and Thuringia. **2.** Jewish (eastern Ashkenazic): habitational name for someone from a place called Dubno, in Ukraine.
GIVEN NAMES Russian 4%. *Arkadiy, Yevgeniy.*

Duboff (137) **1.** Russian and Jewish (from Belarus and Ukraine): alternative spelling of **Dubov**, a patronymic from a nickname or topographic name from a derivative of *dub* 'oak' (cognate with Czech *dub*, Polish *dąb*). In some cases the Jewish name may be a habitational name from Dubova, a village in Ukraine, or from Dubovoe in Belarus. **2.** Americanized form of French **Duboeuf**, a patronymic from LEBOEUF.

Dubois (8805) French and English (Norman and Huguenot): topographic name for someone who lived in a wood, from the fused preposition and definite article *du* 'from the' + French *bois* 'wood' (see BOIS). In both England and America the name has been translated as WOOD.
GIVEN NAMES French 9%. *Andre* (24), *Armand* (18), *Normand* (13), *Jacques* (11), *Pierre* (11), *Fernand* (10), *Marcel* (10), *Emile* (9), *Lucien* (9), *Michel* (5), *Alain* (4), *Luc* (4).

Duboise (209) North American spelling of DUBOIS.

Dubon (193) French: patronymic from the epithet **Le Bon** 'the good' (see BON).
GIVEN NAMES Spanish 43%. *Jose* (5), *Armando* (2), *Luis* (2), *Mario* (2), *Pedro* (2), *Adelmo, Aida, Alberto, Alicia, Alvaro, Anabella, Argentina.*

Dubord (311) French: of uncertain derivation; **1.** possibly a patronymic from *bord* 'bastard'. **2.** alternatively, a topographic name from *bord* 'edge', 'margin'.
GIVEN NAMES French 10%. *Andre, Camille, Fleurette, Marcel, Marie-Claude, Matilde, Normand, Raoul, Rosaire, Serge.*

Dubose (4006) Probably an altered spelling of French DUBOIS.

Dubow (241) **1.** Russian and Jewish (eastern Ashkenazic): alternative form of DUBOFF. **2.** Possibly also an Americanized spelling of French DUBEAU.
GIVEN NAMES Jewish 5%. *Avrum* (2), *Emanuel, Ori.*

Dubray (224) French: **1.** habitational name, with the preposition and definite article *du*, for someone from any of various minor places named in Old French with *brai* 'mud', 'mire' (Late Latin *bracium*, a word of Gaulish origin). **2.** Perhaps also an altered form of DUBREUIL.
GIVEN NAME French 4%. *Napoleon.*

Dubree (206) Probably an altered spelling of DUBRAY.

Dubreuil (380) French: topographic name from Old French *breuil* 'marshy woodland' (Late Latin *brogilum*, of Gaulish origin). In French the term later came to mean 'enclosed woodland' and then 'cleared woodland', and both these senses may also be reflected in the surname.
GIVEN NAMES French 16%. *Andre* (2), *Edouard* (2), *Adelard, Adrien, Alain, Aldea, Betrand, Camille, Chantal, Emile, Girard, Jean-Pierre.*

Dubroc (199) French: patronymic from **Broc**: **1.** nickname, probably for a person with a prickly temperament, from Old French *broc* 'point', 'spur' (of Gaulish origin). The word has many other meanings—'pointed weapon for stabbing', 'deer's antler', 'needle', 'spit', 'jug with a pointed handle', 'spiny vegetation', etc.—and any of these senses may also have contributed to the surname, which may equally well have been a topographic name. **2.** nickname from Breton *broc'h* 'badger' (see BROCK 2).

GIVEN NAMES French 11%. *Andre* (4), *Camile, Florien, Gaston, Pierre.*

Dubrow (345) **1.** Eastern German: habitational name from any of several places in Brandenburg called Dubrow. **2.** Jewish (eastern Ashkenazic): habitational name for someone from any of various villages called Dubrova, Dubrovo, or Dubrovy in Belarus and Ukraine. **3.** Possibly also Bulgarian: Germanized spelling of **Dubrov** (unexplained).

GIVEN NAMES Jewish 6%. *Meyer* (2), *Hyman, Miriam, Sol.*

Dubs (328) German: from a Germanic personal name formed with *theud, diot* 'people', 'race'.

Dubsky (116) **1.** Czech (**Dubský**): habitational name for someone from any of various places called Dub, Dubá, Dubí, Dubsko, or Duby, named with *dub* 'oak'. **2.** Belorussian and Jewish (Ashkenazic): habitational name from any of various places called Duby in Belarus and elsewhere. See also DUB.

Dubuc (478) French (Normandy and Picardy): habitational name, with fused preposition and definite article *du*, for someone from any of the numerous minor places named with *buc*, a dialect form of *bois* 'wood'.

GIVEN NAMES French 16%. *Auguste* (2), *Fernand* (2), *Gaston* (2), *Armand, Donat, Emile, Florent, Gilles, Jean Claude, Lucien, Ludger, Marcel.*

Dubuisson (277) French: topographic name for someone who lived in an area of scrub land or by a prominent clump of bushes, from Old French *buisson* 'bush', 'scrub'.

GIVEN NAMES French 14%. *Alphonse, Arsene, Chantal, Gesner, Jacques, Jean Claude, Jean-Robert, Luc, Pierre, Serge, Wilner.*

Dubuque (536) French: variant spelling of DUBUC.

GIVEN NAMES French 5%. *Andre, Calice, Normand.*

Duby (507) French: **1.** habitational name, with fused preposition and definite article *du*, for someone from a place in Doubs called Le By. **2.** variant of **Dubié** (see DUBIE).

Duca (461) **1.** Italian: from the title of rank *duca* 'duke' (Latin *dux*, genitive *ducis* 'leader'), an occupational name for someone who lived or worked in the household of a duke or a nickname for someone who gave himself airs and graces like a duke. **2.** Hungarian: of uncertain derivation, probably a nickname for a fat person.

GIVEN NAMES Italian 6%. *Antonio* (2), *Gino, Maurizio, Philomena.*

Ducas (134) French (southern): habitational name, with fused French preposition and definite article *du*, from any of various minor places named with French or

Occitan *cas* 'house' (Latin *capsum* 'house', 'building').

GIVEN NAMES French 10%. *Leonide, Marcel, Normand.*

Ducasse (119) French: topographic name for someone who lived by an oak tree, from Old French *casse* 'oak (tree)' (Late Latin *cassanos*, a word of Celtic origin), with the fused preposition and article *du* 'from the'. This is found in England as a Huguenot name.

GIVEN NAMES French 11%; Spanish 8%. *Jean Baptiste, Jean Daniel, Veronique; Carlos Alberto, Herminia, Jose, Juan, Luis, Rafael.*

Ducat (236) **1.** English: occupational name for a moneylender or minter or a nickname for a rich man, from Old French *ducat* (Italian *ducato*), name of a gold coin. This was spelled *duket* in Middle English; *Ducat* is a 'restored' form. It has been confused with DUCKETT. **2.** Scottish: probably a variant of DUGUID. **3.** French: patronymic from the nickname **Cat**, from a dialect variant of *chat* 'cat'. **4.** Variant spelling of German and Jewish **Dukat**, cognate with 1.

Duce (197) **1.** English: nickname from Middle English *douce, dowce* 'sweet', 'pleasant' (Old French *dolz, dous*, from Latin *dulcis*). This was also in occasional use as a female personal name in the Middle Ages, and some examples may derive from it. **2.** Italian: from *duce* 'leader', 'chief', probably applied as a nickname.

Ducey (564) Irish: reduced Anglicized form of Gaelic **Ó Dubhghusa** 'descendant of *Dubhghusa*', a personal name composed of the elements *dubh* 'black' + *gus* meaning 'choice' or 'vigor'.

Duch (293) **1.** Polish and Ukrainian: nickname from *duch* 'spirit', 'breath'. **2.** Czech: from a short form of the Old Czech personal name *Duchoslav*, composed of the elements *duch* 'spirit' + *slav* 'glory'. **3.** Catalan: respelling of **Duc**, nickname or status name from *duc* 'duke' (see DUKE). **4.** Dutch: variant of DUYCK. **5.** East Asian: unexplained.

GIVEN NAMES East Asian 4%; German 4%. *Nga, Phal, Phan, Sophan, Tha, Thang, Yen; Kurt* (2), *Klaus.*

Duchaine (204) French: variant of **Duchêne** (see DUCHENE).

GIVEN NAMES French 9%. *Alain, Jacques, Julien, Marcel, Normand.*

Duchamp (70) French: topographic name meaning 'from the field'.

Ducharme (2349) French: topographic name for someone who lived by a hornbeam, from Old French *charme* 'hornbeam' (Latin *carpinus*), with fused preposition and article *du* 'from the'.

GIVEN NAMES French 8%. *Andre* (5), *Marcel* (4), *Michel* (4), *Armand* (3), *Lucien* (3), *Normand* (3), *Pierre* (3), *Fernand* (2), *Adelard, Adrien, Alphee, Aurelie.*

Duchateau (157) French (**Duchâteau**): topographic name for someone who lived or worked in a castle, French *du château* 'from the castle'.

GIVEN NAMES French 7%. *Andre, Andree, Armand, Philippe.*

Duchemin (168) French: topographic name for someone who lived beside a path (rather than in a town), with fused preposition and article *du* 'from the' + French *chemin* 'path', 'way' (from Late Latin *caminus*, a word of Celtic origin).

GIVEN NAMES French 10%. *Emile* (2), *Dominique, Mathieu, Olivier.*

Duchene (468) French (**Duchêne**): variant of DUCHESNE.

GIVEN NAMES French 4%. *Alain, Jean-Charles, Philippe.*

Duchesne (389) French (**Duchesne**): topographic name from Old French *chesne* 'oak', with fused preposition and definite article *du* 'from the'.

GIVEN NAMES French 14%. *Camille* (2), *Jacques* (2), *Marcel* (2), *Normand* (2), *Aime, Aldege, Andre, Cecile, Laurier, Lucien, Michel, Rosaire.*

Duchesneau (275) French: from a diminutive of DUCHESNE.

FOREBEARS A family of this name, from Tours, was settled in Quebec city by 1667.

GIVEN NAMES French 14%. *Francois* (2), *Adelard, Alphie, Andre, Collette, Fernand, Luce, Lucien, Marcel, Pierre, Raoul.*

Duchin (108) Jewish (eastern Ashkenazic): from Hebrew *dukhan* 'pulpit (for a preacher)'.

GIVEN NAMES Jewish 6%. *Meyer, Mordechai.*

Duchon (144) French: **1.** from a diminutive of **Duc** 'duke', hence a nickname for someone who gave himself airs and graces or an occupational nickname for someone who worked in the household of a duke. **2.** Americanized (NH) spelling of French DUCHAMP.

Duchow (175) Eastern German: nickname from Sorbian *duch* 'spirit', 'breath'.

GIVEN NAMES German 7%. *Reinhardt* (2), *Willi.*

Duck (1506) **1.** English: from Middle English *doke*, hence a nickname for someone with some fancied resemblance to a duck or a metonymic occupational name for someone who kept ducks or for a wild fowler. **2.** Irish: English name adopted as an equivalent of **Lohan** (an Anglicized form of Gaelic **Ó Leocháin** 'descendant of *Leochán*') by mistranslation, as if from *lacha* 'duck'. **3.** Dutch: variant of DUYCK. In a German-speaking environment, this is also a variant of (VAN) DYCK. **4.** North German (also **Dück**): probably a nickname for a coward, from Low German *duken* 'to duck or dive'. **5.** German (**Dück(e)**): from a pet form of an old Germanic personal name formed with *theud, diot* 'people', 'race'.

Ducker (479) **1.** English (East Anglia): nickname meaning 'diver', from an agent derivative of Middle English *douke(n)* 'to dive' (a word that is probably related to *duck* (the bird)). **2.** Jewish (Ashkenazic): unexplained. **3.** North German (**Dücker**) and Dutch: from the term for a duck or diving bird (from *du(c)ken* 'to dive or duck'), probably applied as a nickname for someone thought to resemble the duck, but perhaps in some cases a metonymic occupational name for fowler or for a furrier who used the pelts of diving birds in his trade.

Duckett (2436) English: **1.** nickname from a diminutive of Middle English *douke*, *duk(ke)* 'duck' (Old English *dūce*). **2.** nickname from Middle English *douke*, *duk(ke)* 'duck' + *heved* 'head'. **3.** nickname from Old French *ducquet* 'owl', a diminutive of *duc* 'guide', 'leader' (see DUKE 1). **4.** from a Middle English diminutive of the Old English personal name or byname *Ducca*. **5.** from a Middle English pet form of the personal name DUKE.

Ducksworth (213) English: habitational name from a place in Cambridgeshire called Duxford, recorded *c.* 960 as *Dukeswrthe* 'enclosure (Old English *worð*) of a man called *Duc(c)*'.

Duckwall (170) Americanized form of German DOCKWEILER.

Duckwitz (102) German: habitational name from a place so named near Rostock.

Duckworth (4387) English (chiefly Lancashire): habitational name from Duckworth Fold, in the borough of Bury, Lancashire, which is named from Old English *fūce* 'duck' + *worð* 'enclosure'.

Duclos (797) French: topographic name, with fused preposition and definite article *du* 'from the', from Old French *clos* 'enclosure' (from Late Latin *clausum*, past participle of *claudere* 'to close').
GIVEN NAMES French 10%. *Armand* (6), *Emile* (3), *Rejean* (2), *Aime*, *Alain*, *Colette*, *Fernand*, *Franck*, *Marcel*, *Normand*, *Pascale*, *Pierre*.

Ducommun (156) French: **1.** nickname for someone who held or guarded a common good. **2.** habitational name from any of the places called Le Commun, for example in Hainault, Belgium.
GIVEN NAME French 4%. *Marcel*.

Ducote (1230) French: probably a topographic name, with fused preposition and definite article *du* 'from the' + *côté* 'side'.
GIVEN NAMES French 4%. *Andre* (2), *Irby* (2), *Emile*, *Jacques*, *Maudry*, *Remy*.

Ducre (139) French (**Ducré**): habitational name, with fused preposition and definite article *du* 'from the', from any of numerous minor places called Le Cret, named with Old French *cret*, *creste* 'crest', 'ridge'.
GIVEN NAMES French 8%. *Marcel* (2), *Alvine*, *Renald*.

Duda (2326) **1.** Polish, Ukrainian, Czech, and Slovak: nickname for a player of the bagpipes, from Slavic *duda* 'bagpipe'. **2.** Czech: nickname for someone thought to resemble a hoopoe (*dudek*). **3.** Hungarian: from the old secular personal name *Duda*, or in some cases possibly a shortened form of **Dudás** (see DUDAS).
GIVEN NAMES Polish 5%. *Tadeusz* (4), *Casimir* (3), *Janusz* (3), *Danuta* (2), *Jacek* (2), *Piotr* (2), *Andrzej*, *Beata*, *Boguslaw*, *Dariusz*, *Eugeniusz*, *Genowefa*.

Dudak (122) Czech (**Dudák**): occupational name for a bagpipe player, a derivative of DUDA.

Dudas (657) Hungarian (**Dudás**), Serbian (**Dudáš**), and Ukrainian: occupational name for a piper, from Slavic *dude* 'bagpipes'.

Dudash (539) Americanized spelling of Hungarian **Dudás** or Serbian **Dudáš** (see DUDAS).

Dudding (308) English: patronymic from the Old English personal name *Dudda*.

Duddleston (118) English: habitational name from Dudleston in Shropshire, so named from an Old English personal name, *Dud(d)el* or *Dod(d)el*, + Old English *tūn* 'settlement'.

Duddy (432) **1.** English: habitational name from a lost place in Sussex named Dudehay '*Dudda*'s enclosure (Old English *hæg*). **2.** Irish: reduced Anglicized form of Gaelic **Ó Dubhda** (see DOWD).
GIVEN NAMES Irish 5%. *Brendan*, *Dympna*.

Dudeck (365) Americanized spelling of DUDEK.

Dudek (2136) Polish, Ukrainian, Czech, and Slovak: nickname from *dudek* 'hoopoe', with reference to some attribute of the bird such as its repetitive call or its bright plumage. In Polish the word also means 'simpleton' and this no doubt contributed to the Polish surname.
GIVEN NAMES Polish 7%. *Zbigniew* (5), *Andrzej* (3), *Kazimierz* (3), *Wladyslaw* (3), *Jozef* (2), *Tadeusz* (2), *Thadeus* (2), *Arkadiusz*, *Beata*, *Casimir*, *Danuta*, *Dorota*.

Duden (241) North German: **1.** patronymic from the Germanic personal name *Dudo* (see DUE). **2.** habitational name from Duden, a place near (former) Gumbinnen in East Prussia.

Dudenhoeffer (202) German (**Dudenhöffer**): habitational name from a farm named Dudenhof(f), from the personal name *Dudo* (see DUE) + Middle High German *hof* 'farmstead', 'manor farm', 'courtyard'.
GIVEN NAMES German 4%. *Alfons*, *Aloysius*, *Kurt*.

Duderstadt (135) German (also **Duderstädt**): habitational name from Duderstadt, a place near Göttingen, Lower Saxony.
GIVEN NAMES German 5%. *Franz*, *Frieda*.

Dudgeon (673) English and Scottish: of uncertain derivation, but possibly a metonymic occupational name for a turner or cutler; the word *dudgeon* denoted the wood (probably boxwood) used in the handles of knives and daggers in the Middle Ages. Alternatively, it could be a diminutive form of DODGE. The name was taken to northern Ireland in the 17th century.

Dudick (140) **1.** Americanized or Germanized spelling of Serbian **Dudić** (from a pet form of *Dušan*), Ukrainian DUDIK or DUDEK, or Polish DUDZIK. **2.** German: from a Czech loanword meaning 'blood sausage', presumably applied as an occupational nickname for a butcher.

Dudik (129) **1.** Czech and Slovak (**Dudík**) and Polish (**Dudzik**): from a diminutive of DUDA. **2.** Ukrainian: either a nickname from Ukrainian *dudyk* 'small stone found in clay', or an occupational name for a player on a reed pipe, from *dudyty* 'to play the reed pipe'.

Dudley (12179) **1.** English and Irish: habitational name from Dudley in the West Midlands, named from the Old English personal name *Dudda* (see DODD) + Old English *lēah* 'woodland clearing'. **2.** Irish (County Cork): English name adopted by bearers of Gaelic **Ó Dubhdáleithe** 'descendant of *Dubhdáleithe*', a personal name composed of the elements *dubh* 'black' + *dá* 'two' + *léithe* 'sides'.
FOREBEARS Thomas Dudley (1576–1653), born at Northampton, England, sailed on the *Arbella* to Salem, MA, in 1630 with the chief men of the Massachusetts Bay Company. They first settled at Newtown. Dudley subsequently moved to Ipswich but then permanently settled at Roxbury. He was elected four times as governor of the Massachusetts Bay Colony and as one of the two commissioners for the colony when the New England Confederation was formed in 1643. He was one of the first overseers of Harvard University, and in 1650, as governor, signed the charter for that institution. Dudley's seventh and most noted child, Joseph (1647–1720) was also governor of MA (1702–15).

Dudman (108) English: from the Old English personal name *Dudemann*.

Dudney (243) English: apparently a habitational name from a lost or unidentified place, possibly in southeastern England, where the modern surname is most frequent.

Dudziak (182) Polish: from a patronymic form of DUDA.
GIVEN NAMES Polish 6%. *Halina*, *Iwona*, *Miroslawa*, *Piotr*.

Dudzik (343) Polish: from a diminutive of DUDA.
GIVEN NAMES Polish 4%. *Bronislawa*, *Czeslaw*, *Ignatius*, *Karol*, *Marcin*.

Dudzinski (363) Polish (**Dudziński**): **1.** habitational name for someone from a place called Duda or Dudy. **2.** derivative of DUDA, with the addition of the surname suffix *-iński*.

GIVEN NAMES Polish 10%. *Andrzej* (2), *Feliks* (2), *Tomasz* (2), *Andrze*, *Janusz*, *Jerzy*, *Tadeusz*, *Zygmund*.

Due (488) **1.** North German (**Düe**): from the Germanic personal name *Dudo*, which is of uncertain derivation. In some cases it is said to be a pet form of the compound name *Liudolf* (composed of Old Saxon *liud* 'people', 'tribe' + *wolf* 'wolf'); in other cases it may be a derivative of Germanic *theud* 'people', 'race'. **2.** Danish: from *due* 'pigeon', 'dove', applied as a metonymic occupational name for a dove keeper or as a nickname. **3.** In some cases, perhaps an altered form of French LEDOUX. **4.** Possibly a variant of Welsh DEWEY.

Dueck (146) German (**Dück**): nickname for a shirker or a sneak.

GIVEN NAMES German 12%. *Gerhard* (2), *Horst* (2), *Johannes*, *Klaus*, *Reinhard*.

Duecker (189) German (**Dücker**): see DUCKER.

GIVEN NAMES German 10%. *Fritz* (2), *Kurt* (2), *Otto* (2).

Duehring (116) German (**Dühring**): regional name for someone from Thuringia (see DURING).

GIVEN NAME German 5%. *Manfred*.

Dueitt (168) Perhaps an altered spelling of Dutch DE WITT.

Dueker (163) North German (**Düker**): **1.** variant of **Dücker** (see DUCKER). **2.** nickname from a Westphalian euphemism for the devil (see TEUFEL).

Duel (110) Altered spelling of German **Düll** (see DUELL).

Duell (919) **1.** South German (**Düll**): nickname for a stubborn man. **2.** German (**Düll**): variant of DILL 5. **3.** English: unexplained.

Duellman (165) German (**Düllmann**): habitational name for someone from Dülmen in Westphalia.

Duenas (1066) Spanish (**Dueñas**): habitational name from Dueñas, a place in Palencia, named from the plural of *dueña* 'nun' (Latin *domina*).

GIVEN NAMES Spanish 50%. *Jose* (32), *Luis* (12), *Manuel* (12), *Jesus* (11), *Jorge* (11), *Juan* (10), *Francisco* (9), *Carlos* (7), *Rafael* (7), *Alberto* (6), *Alfonso* (6), *Joaquin* (6), *Antonio* (9), *Lorenzo* (3), *Marco* (3), *Carmelo*, *Ciro*, *Clemente*, *Eligio*, *Gabino*, *Marco Antonio*, *Marco Tulio*, *Silvano*.

Duenes (122) Hispanic: possibly a respelling of Spanish **Dueñas** (see DUENAS).

GIVEN NAMES Spanish 38%. *Jose* (6), *Gerardo* (2), *Jorge* (2), *Juan* (2), *Manuel* (2), *Adela*, *Alfredo*, *Alicia*, *Ana*, *Aristeo*, *Cruz*, *Edmundo*.

Duenez (111) Hispanic (**Dueñez**): altered or regional spelling of Spanish **Dueñas** (see DUENAS).

GIVEN NAMES Spanish 47%. *Juan* (4), *Manuel* (3), *Francisco* (2), *Gerardo* (2), *Jesus* (2), *Marcos* (2), *Ana*, *Angel*, *Braulio*, *Cesar*, *Domingo*, *Doroteo*; *Antonio*, *Eliseo*.

Duenow (155) Eastern German (**Dünow**): habitational name for someone from a place near Stettin in Pomerania called Dünow.

Duensing (353) North German (**Dünsing**): habitational name from a reduced form of Dudensing, recorded in the 17th century as *Du(d)ensiek*, from *siek* 'swamp'.

Duer (542) **1.** German (**Dür**): variant of **Dürr** (see DURR). **2.** German: either a variant of **Dühr** or a short form of any of various compound names, such as **Dürholdt** or **Dürkop**, all formed with Old High German *tiuri* 'dear' or Middle Low German *dür* 'dear', 'expensive'. **3.** Danish: habitational name, from a short form of a place called Duerlund.

Duerksen (377) North German: variant of DIRKSEN.

GIVEN NAMES German 4%. *Erwin* (2), *Ewald*, *Kurt*.

Duerr (1121) German: alternative spelling of **Dürr** (see DURR).

GIVEN NAMES German 5%. *Hans* (3), *Gerhart* (2), *Frieda*, *Friedrich*, *Gerhard*, *Heinz*, *Hermann*, *Lorenz*, *Ralf*, *Wolf*.

Duerson (166) Probably a variant spelling of North German **Dührssen** or **Dyrssen**, a patronymic from an old personal name, from Old High German *tiuri* 'dear', 'valuable'.

Duerst (224) German: variant of DURST 1.

Dues (243) Dutch and North German (**Düs**): variant of DUIS.

Duesing (183) German (**Düsing**): variant of DUSING.

GIVEN NAMES German 4%. *Ernst* (2), *Willi*.

Duesler (163) German (**Düsler**): from an old personal name of uncertain derivation (probably related to Sanskrit *tavas* 'strength').

Duet (459) French: **1.** topographic name from Old French *du wez* 'from the ford'. **2.** reduced form of the patronymic (*fils*) *d'Huet*, '(son) of Huet'.

GIVEN NAMES French 6%. *Alcide*, *Alphonse*, *Andre*, *Antoine*, *Armand*, *Leonce*, *Simonne*, *Sylvian*.

Duett (112) Respelling of French DUET.

Duey (277) **1.** Altered spelling of Welsh DEWEY. **2.** Possibly an Americanized spelling of French DUET.

Dufault (782) French: altered spelling of **Dufau**, a topographic name for someone who lived near a prominent beech tree or in a beech wood, from Occitan *fau* 'beech' (from Latin *fagus*), with fused preposition and definite article *du* 'from the'.

GIVEN NAMES French 10%. *Aime* (2), *Armand* (2), *Jean-Guy* (2), *Raoul* (2), *Aldea*, *Aldor*, *Andre*, *Emile*, *Gilles*, *Marcel*, *Michel*, *Napoleon*.

Dufek (345) Czech: from a noun derivative of *dufat* 'to hope'.

Duff (6329) Scottish and Irish: reduced Anglicized form of Gaelic **Ó Duibh** ('descendant of *Dubh*'), **Mac Giolla Duibh** ('son of the servant of *Dubh*'), or a short

form of DUFFIN 2 (County Wexford), **MacElduff** (County Tyrone; see KILDUFF), **Mac Duibh**, and DUFFY, all of which are formed from personal names containing the element *dubh* 'dark', 'black' (widely used as a nickname or byname for a dark-haired man or man of dark temperament and as an element of personal names).

Duffany (122) Americanized form of English TIFFANY.

Duffee (332) Anglicized form of Gaelic **Mac Duibhshíthe** (see McDUFFIE).

Duffek (176) Variant spelling of Czech DUFEK.

GIVEN NAME German 4%. *Alfons* (2).

Duffel (157) English: variant of DUFFIELD.

Duffell (137) English: variant of DUFFIELD.

GIVEN NAME German 4%. *Irmgard*.

Duffer (423) Origin uncertain. **1.** In at least some cases it seems to be a variant of Irish DUFFY. **2.** Perhaps a variant of South German **Tüffer**, a habitational name for someone from Tüffen in Switzerland or Tiefen (earlier *Tüeffen*) near Freiburg, place names based on Old High German *tiufi* 'gorge' or *tuf*, *taf* 'bog', 'swamp'. Compare DUFFNER. **3.** Possibly an altered spelling of French **Dufer**, a nickname from *du fer* '(man) of iron'.

Duffett (190) **1.** Altered spelling of French **Duffet**, variant of *Dufay* (see DUFFEE). **2.** English: nickname from Middle English *d(o)uve*, *dofe* 'dove' + *hed* 'head' or *fote* 'foot'.

Duffey (2201) Scottish and Irish: variant spelling of DUFFY.

Duffie (585) Scottish and Irish: variant spelling of DUFFY.

Duffield (1538) English: habitational name from places in Derbyshire and East Yorkshire, so named from Old English *dūfe* 'dove' + *feld* 'open country'.

Duffin (894) **1.** English: from the Old Norse personal name *Dólgfinnr*, composed of the elements *dólgr* 'wound', 'scar' + *Finnr* 'Finn'. **2.** Irish: reduced Anglicized form of Gaelic **Ó Duibhchinn** (see DIFFIN), **Ó Duibhghinn** (see DEEGAN), or perhaps **Ó Daimhín** (see DEVINE).

Duffner (205) German: probably a variant of South German **Tüffer** (see DUFFER).

Duffney (147) Possibly of Irish origin, a reduced Anglicized form of Gaelic **Ó Duibheannaigh** or **Ó Duibheamhna** (see DEVANEY).

Dufford (219) See DUFORD.

Duffus (208) **1.** English: from Middle English *dufhus* 'dovecote', applied as a topographic name or as a metonymic occupational name for a dove keeper. **2.** Scottish: habitational name from a place in Moray called Duffus.

Duffy (15487) **1.** Irish: reduced Anglicized form of Gaelic **Ó Dubhthaigh** 'descendant of *Dubhthach*', a byname derived from *dubh* 'black' (see DUFF). This name was

borne by a 6th-century saint who was arch-bishop of Armagh. **2.** Scottish and Irish: reduced Anglicized form of Gaelic **Mac Dhuibhshíthe** 'son of *Duibhshíth*', a personal name composed of the elements *dubh* 'black' (see DUFF) + *síth* 'peace'.
GIVEN NAMES Irish 6%. *Brendan* (21), *Seamus* (3), *Siobhan* (3), *Aidan* (2), *Brigid* (2), *Eamon* (2), *Kieran* (2), *Malachy* (2), *Aileen, Briana, Bridie, Caitlin.*

Dufner (209) German: variant of DUFFNER.

Duford (224) **1.** Variant of French DUFORT. **2.** English: apparently a habitational name, perhaps from Dulford in Broadhembury, Devon, which is named from an unattested Old English word *dylfet* 'pit', 'quarry'.
GIVEN NAMES French 5%. *Lucien, Marcelle, Veronique.*

Dufort (225) French: patronymic meaning 'son of the strong one' or 'son of someone called *Fort*', from *fort* 'strong' (see FORT).
GIVEN NAMES French 9%. *Cecile, Marcel, Marie Jose.*

Dufour (1838) French: occupational nickname for a baker, from *du four* '(the man) from the oven'.
GIVEN NAMES French 12%. *Emile* (4), *Jacques* (4), *Normand* (4), *Andre* (3), *Armand* (3), *Gaston* (3), *Pierre* (3), *Yvon* (3), *Donat* (2), *Fernand* (2), *Julien* (2), *Marcel* (2).

Dufrane (221) Americanized spelling of French DUFRESNE.

Dufrene (1074) French (**Dufrêne**): variant spelling of DUFRESNE.
GIVEN NAMES French 6%. *Fernand* (4), *Landry* (3), *Emile* (2), *Monique* (2), *Antoine, Desire, Eves, Francoise, Gaston, Gillis, Jacques, Jean-Paul.*

Dufresne (1743) French: topographic name for someone who lived near a prominent ash tree, from Old French *fresne* 'ash' (from Latin *fraxinus*), with fused preposition and definite article *du* 'from the'.
GIVEN NAMES French 11%. *Armand* (6), *Normand* (5), *Andre* (4), *Edouard* (3), *Gabrielle* (2), *Gaston* (2), *Jacques* (2), *Lucien* (2), *Olivier* (2), *Pierre* (2), *Ulysse* (2), *Aime.*

Dufur (159) Altered spelling of French DUFOUR.

Duga (100) Southern French: southern variant of **Duguet**, an occupational name for a watchman, literally '(the man) of the watch (*guet*)'.
GIVEN NAME French 4%. *Adelore.*

Dugal (268) **1.** Scottish: either an Anglicized form of the Gaelic personal name *Dùghall* (see DOYLE) or a reduced form of McDOUGALL. **2.** Possibly of French origin but unexplained. **3.** Indian (Panjab): Hindu (Khatri) and Sikh name based on the name of a Khatri clan. In India the name is more commonly spelled **Duggal**.
GIVEN NAMES French 5%; Indian 4%. *Andree, Gilles, Maurille; Bani, Kavita, Rajeev.*

Dugan (8101) Irish: **1.** reduced Anglicized form of Gaelic **Ó Dubhagáin** 'descendant of *Dubhagán*', a byname representing a double diminutive of *dubh* 'black', 'dark' (see DUFF). **2.** reduced Anglicized form of **Ó Duibhginn** (see DEEGAN).
GIVEN NAMES Irish 8%. *Brendan* (3), *Caitlin* (2), *Aileen, Kieran, Sean Patrick, Siobhan.*

Dugar (162) **1.** Indian (Panjab): Sikh name of unknown meaning. **2.** Indian (Rajasthan): Jain name of unknown meaning. **3.** Perhaps also an altered spelling of French DUGARD.
GIVEN NAMES Indian 21%. *Rajesh* (4), *Amit* (2), *Amitabh, Kirti, Mala, Meera, Sanjeev, Santosh, Sumer, Sundeep.*

Dugard (100) French: topographic name for someone who lived by a garden, from *du gard* 'from the garden', or, by extension an occupational name for a gardener (see GARD).

Dugas (2637) French: topographic name for someone who lived by a patch of waste land, Old French *gast*. Compare GAST.
FOREBEARS This name is frequent in LA, where it is sometimes spelled **Dugat**. Most if not all bearers of it trace their origins to the Acadian exile of the 18th century.
GIVEN NAMES French 7%. *Andre* (5), *Armand* (3), *Clovis* (3), *Emile* (3), *Amedee* (2), *Dumas* (2), *Normand* (2), *Ovide* (2), *Pierre* (2), *Theogene* (2), *Alcee, Alcide.*

Dugay (124) **1.** French: patronymic, meaning 'son of the cheerful one', from the nickname GAY 'cheerful'. **2.** Filipino: probably a variant of Spanish **Ducay**, unexplained.
GIVEN NAMES Spanish 11%; Italian 4%. *Pedro* (2), *Alejandro, Bernarda, Bonifacio, Catalina, Celestina, Conrado, Erlinda, Marcelina; Giovanni* (2), *Rizalino, Romeo.*

Dugdale (399) English (Lancashire): habitational name from a place called Dugdale, probably the hamlet near Uttoxeter, Staffordshire, now known as Dagdale, from the Old English personal name or byname *Ducca* + Old English *dæl* or Old Norse *dalr* 'valley'.

Duggan (5207) **1.** Scottish and Irish: variant spelling of DUGAN. **2.** English (Herefordshire): from a reduced and altered form of the Welsh personal name *Cadwgan* (see CADOGAN).
GIVEN NAMES Irish 5%. *Brigid* (3), *Eamonn* (2), *Liam* (2), *Aileen, Brid, Dermot, Donovan, John Patrick, Seamus.*

Duggar (295) Origin unidentified. Possibly a respelling of French **Dugard** (see DUGAR).

Dugger (3131) Origin unidentified. **1.** It may be an altered spelling of French **Dugard** (see DUGAR). **2.** Alternatively it could be a variant of German **Duggert**, from an old personal name from Old High German *tugan* 'to be capable, competent, or useful', 'to be strong'.

Duggin (149) Irish: variant of DUGAN.

Duggins (1082) Irish: variant of DUGGIN, with English patronymic *-s*.

Dugo (154) **1.** Italian and French (also **D'Ugo**): patronymic from the Germanic personal name *Ugo* or *Hugo* (see HUGH). **2.** French: in the south, a habitational name derived from any of the many minor places named Le Got 'the Goth', an echo, Morlet suggests, of the Visigoth occupation of Gaul below the Loire.
GIVEN NAMES Italian 14%. *Angelo* (3), *Carmela, Orfeo, Raimondo, Salvatore.*

Duguay (568) French: **1.** habitational name for someone from a place named Dugay, for example in Charente, Dordogne, and Rhône. **2.** Spelling variant of **Du Gué**, a topographic name for someone who lived by a ford, *gué*.
FOREBEARS A family from Autun named Du Gué was established in Trois-Rivières, Quebec, by 1672; and another, from Saintonge, was in Ange-Gardien by 1694.
GIVEN NAMES French 9%. *Emile* (2), *Gilles* (2), *Andre, Camille, Donat, Fernande, Laurent, Marcel, Normand, Yves, Yvon.*

Duguid (243) Scottish (mainly northeastern Scotland): perhaps from northern Middle English *du* 'do' + *gu(i)d* 'good', a nickname for a well-intentioned person or do-gooder.

Duh (119) Slovenian: nickname from *duh* 'spirit', 'soul', 'ghost'.

Duhaime (447) French: possibly a re-formation of **Du Hain**, meaning 'from the village'. Compare DUHAMEL.
GIVEN NAMES French 12%. *Andre* (4), *Marcel* (3), *Armand* (2), *Ovila* (2), *Alphee, Alphonse, Donat, Jean-Paul, Michel, Raoul, Rejean.*

Duhamel (653) French: topographic name for someone who lived in a hamlet, from Old French *hamel*, a diminutive of *ham* 'homestead', with fused preposition and definite article *du*.
GIVEN NAMES French 14%. *Laurent* (3), *Marcel* (3), *Andre* (2), *Gaston* (2), *Jean-Michael* (2), *Philippe* (2), *Adrien, Armand, Euclide, Fernand, Gaetan, Jacques.*

Duhart (287) French: habitational name, with fused preposition *d(e)*, for someone from a place called Uhart in the Pyrenees.

Duhe (443) French (**Duhé**): **1.** possibly a variant of DUET 2. **2.** alternatively a respelling of Walloon **Duhez**, **Duhait**, a habitational name for someone from any of various minor places in the Belgian province of Liège called Hez, from Walloon *hé* 'heath'.
GIVEN NAMES French 8%. *Gaston* (2), *Marcel* (2), *Aime, Antoine, Leonce.*

Duhl (124) German: variant of DUELL 2.

Duhon (2140) **1.** French: Gascon variant of **Dufond**, a topographic name, from *du fond* 'from the hollow or bottom'. **2.** Czech and Slovak (**Duhoň**): from *duha* 'rainbow'.
GIVEN NAMES French 6%. *Clovis* (4), *Andrus* (3), *Eulice* (2), *Leonce* (2), *Minos* (2),

Alcee, Alcide, Andree, Angelle, Antoine, Autrey, Celestine.

Duhr (125) North German (**Dühr**): nickname from Low German *dühr* 'costly', 'dear'.
GIVEN NAMES German 6%. *Jurgen, Karl Heinz.*

Duignan (258) Irish: reduced Anglicized form of Gaelic **Ó Duibhgeannáin** (see DEIGNAN).
GIVEN NAME Irish 5%. *Conor.*

Duin (100) **1.** Dutch and North German: patronymic from the Germanic personal name *Duno*. **2.** Dutch: shortened form of **Van Duin**, a variant of VAN DUYNE. **3.** Dutch and North German: Dutch spelling of a topographic name for someone who settled near or in dunes, from Middle Dutch *dune, duun*. The German word *Düne* came as a loan word from Dutch in the 17th century, which explains the Dutch spelling of the German name.

Duis (130) **1.** North German and Dutch: from a Germanic personal name *Theudo*, meaning 'people', 'tribe'. **2.** North German: topographic name from Westphalian dialect *düs* 'pile', 'decay'.

Duitsman (175) Dutch: ethnic name for a German.
GIVEN NAMES German 5%. *Kurt, Monika.*

Dujardin (117) French: topographic or occupational name meaning 'from the garden', from Old French *jardin* 'garden', 'enclosure' (see JARDIN), with fused preposition and definite article *du*.
GIVEN NAMES French 16%. *Pascal* (2), *Christophe, Julien, Pierre, Yves.*

Dukart (240) German: variant spelling of **Duckart**, from a medieval personal name based on Old High German *tugan* 'to be capable, useful, or strong'.

Dukas (115) Greek: variant of DOUKAS.

Duke (12758) **1.** English and Irish: from Middle English *duk(e)* 'duke' (from Old French *duc*, from Latin *dux*, genitive *ducis* 'leader'), applied as an occupational name for someone who worked in the household of a duke, or as a nickname for someone who gave himself airs and graces. **2.** English and Irish: possibly also from the personal name *Duke*, a short form of *Marmaduke*, a personal name said to be from Irish *mael Maedoc* 'devotee (*mael, maol* 'bald', 'tonsured one') of *Maedoc*', a personal name (*M'Aodhóg*) meaning 'my little *Aodh*', borne by various early Irish saints, in particular a 6th-century abbot of Clonmore and a 7th-century bishop of Ferns. **3.** Scottish: compare the old Danish personal name *Duk* (Old Norse *Dūkr*). **4.** In some cases, possibly an Americanized form of French LEDUC or Spanish DUQUE. **5.** Possibly an Americanized spelling of Polish **Duk**, a nickname from *dukac* 'to stammer or falter'.

Dukelow (125) Origin unidentified. It may be an Anglicized form of a French Huguenot name such as DUCLOS. It is established in Ireland as well as England.

Dukeman (162) Origin unidentified.

Duker (153) **1.** Dutch: from Middle Dutch *duker* 'diver', 'diving bird' (see DUCKER). **2.** North German (**Düker**): see DUEKER.

Dukes (5797) English: patronymic from DUKE 1 or 2.

Dukette (138) Americanized spelling of French DUQUETTE.

Dul (115) **1.** Polish: nickname for an empty chatterer, from *duldać* 'to make a loud tinkling noise'. **2.** Dutch: nickname from Middle Dutch *dul, dol* 'foolish', 'feeble-minded'. **3.** Hungarian: from the old secular personal name *Dúl*.
GIVEN NAMES Polish 17%. *Andrzey, Bronislaw, Jerzy, Jolanta, Stanislaw, Wieslaw, Wladyslaw.*

Dula (656) **1.** Polish: nickname from *gdula, dula* 'pear' or 'quince'. **2.** Polish: derivative of DUL. **3.** Slovak: unexplained.

Dulac (398) French: topographic name, with fused preposition and definite article *du* 'from the', for someone who lived by a lake, French *lac*.
GIVEN NAMES French 15%. *Marcel* (3), *Michel* (2), *Andre, Clermont, Emile, Fernand, Gilles, Henri, Jacques, Jean-Louis, Jean-Paul, Laurent.*

Dulak (181) **1.** Altered spelling of DULAC. **2.** Polish: from a derivative of DUL or DULA. **3.** Slovak (**Dulák**): possibly a topographic name for someone who lived by a quince tree, from Slovak *dula* 'quince'.

Dulaney (1967) Variant of Irish DELANEY.

Dulany (253) Variant of Irish DELANEY.
FOREBEARS Born in Queen's County, Ireland, Daniel Dulany (1685–1753) emigrated with two brothers, William and Joseph, to Port Tobacco, MD, in about 1703. In 1721 Daniel moved permanently to Annapolis, MD, where he served as attorney general, member of the MD assembly for 20 years, and held several high provincial offices.

Dulay (222) **1.** Filipino: unexplained. **2.** Hungarian: habitational name for someone from a place called Duló in Trencsény county.
GIVEN NAMES Spanish 34%. *Adolfo* (6), *Anacleto, Angeles, Angelita, Anicia, Artemio, Arturo, Carlos, Carmelita, Carolina, Catalina, Cipriano; Cecilio, Leonardo.*

Dulberg (136) German: variant of **Dolberg, Dölberg**, with a first element *Dölle* 'ditch' in the south or *Dul* 'bog' in the north. These appear in various place names, for instance Dollbergen near Hannover.

Duley (830) English: **1.** (of Norman origin): habitational name from any of several places in Calvados, France, called Ouilly, named with the Gallo-Roman personal name *Ollius* + the locative suffix *-acum*. **2.** Possibly also an altered spelling of DOOLEY.

Dulik (111) Slavic: unexplained.

Dulin (1390) **1.** French: from *du lin* 'from or of the flax', hence a topographic name for someone who lived in a place where flax was grown, or, by extension, an occupational name for someone who grew flax or made linen or canvas. **2.** Serbian: from the personal name *Dula*, a pet form of *Dušan*. **3.** Perhaps also a respelling of Irish DOOLIN.

Duling (407) **1.** English (Kent): unexplained. **2.** Possibly an altered spelling of the German surname **Dulling**, which is likewise unexplained.

Dulka (101) Slavic: unexplained.

Dull (1893) **1.** South German (**Düll**): nickname for a stubborn man ('thick head'), probably from a south German dialect word *tull* 'stout', "corpulent". **2.** German: variant of THIEL. **3.** Scottish: habitational name from Dull in Perthshire.

Dulle (228) Dutch: variant of DUL.

Dullea (211) Irish (west Cork): possibly one of the many Anglicized forms of Gaelic **Ó Duinnshléibhe** 'descendant of *Donn Sleibhe*' (see DUNLEAVY).

Dullinger (108) Possibly a respelling of German DOLLINGER.
GIVEN NAMES German 7%. *Alois* (2), *Aloysius, Gitta, Kurt.*

Dullum (157) Norwegian: habitational name from a farm in central Norway named Dullum, from Old Norse *dalum*, dative plural of *dalr* 'valley'.

Dulmage (154) Americanized spelling of German **Dolmetsch**, an occupational name for an interpreter, late Middle High German *tolmetsche*, from Turkish *tilmaç*, via Hungarian *tolmács*. It is recorded as a surname in 1350 in Swabia.

Dulong (274) French: patronymic from the nickname LONG.

Dulski (209) Polish: **1.** habitational name for someone from a place called Dulsk. **2.** derivative of DUL or DULA, with the addition of the surname suffix *-ski*.

Dulude (268) French: habitational name, with fused preposition and definite article *du*, for someone from a place called Le Lude in Sarthe.
GIVEN NAMES French 9%. *Marcel* (3), *Damien, Gilles, Normand, Octave.*

Dulworth (192) Probably an altered form of the English habitational name DILWORTH.

Duma (165) Polish: nickname from *duma* 'pride', 'self-respect', or *dumać* 'to ponder or reflect'.
GIVEN NAMES Polish 6%. *Iwan, Jozef, Stanislawa, Zbigniew.*

Dumaine (154) French: regional name for someone from the province of Maine in northwestern France, or a topographic name from Old French *demeure* 'dwelling', 'residence', a derivative of the verb *manoir* (from Latin *manere* 'stay', 'remain'), or a habitational name from any of numerous minor places named with this word.

FOREBEARS A Dumaine is recorded in Quebec city in 1671.

GIVEN NAMES French 15%. *Adelard, Andre, Francois, Herve, Jean Louis, Jean-Pierre, Pierre.*

Dumais (691) French: in its earliest Canadian manifestations this name is found as **Dumay**, with spelling variants **Dumé**, **Dumetz**, etc., indicating that it is probably a variant of DUMAS. However, there has been confusion with various other names, including DEMERS, **Demerce**, and **Massé** (see MASSE).

FOREBEARS A bearer of the name **Dumay** was in Quebec in 1666, and the marriage of another bearer of this name is recorded in Quebec in 1685.

GIVEN NAMES French 14%. *Adrien* (3), *Normand* (3), *Aldor* (2), *Marcel* (2), *Alain, Alcid, Armand, Camille, Cecile, Cyrille, Emile, Gaetan.*

Duman (240) French: habitational name, with fused preposition and definite article *du*, for someone from Mant in Savoy, or a variant spelling of **Dumans**, also a habitational name, for someone from Le Mans in Sarthe.

Dumars (148) Altered form of French DEMERS or perhaps DUMAS.

Dumas (5210) Southern French: topographic name, with fused preposition and definite article *du*, for someone who lived in an isolated dwelling in the country rather than in a village, from Occitan *mas* 'farmstead', from Late Latin *mansum, mansus*.

FOREBEARS A family of this name from Charente is recorded in Île d'Orléans, Quebec, in 1667, and one from Tours in Quebec city in 1671.

GIVEN NAMES French 6%. *Andre* (8), *Armand* (5), *Normand* (5), *Michel* (4), *Pierre* (3), *Antoine* (2), *Camille* (2), *Emile* (2), *Jacques* (2), *Marcel* (2), *Philippe* (2), *Raoul* (2).

Dumbauld (108) Origin unidentified. Possibly a Frenchified spelling of German **Dambold(t)**, from an old personal name composed of an earlier form of Old High German *tac* 'day' + *bald* 'bold'.

Dumbleton (121) English: habitational name from a place in Gloucestershire named Dumbleton, probably from Old English *dumbel* 'shady hollow' + *tūn* 'farmstead'.

GIVEN NAMES Irish 4%. *Donovan, Siobhan.*

Dumesnil (152) French: from Old French *du mesnil* 'from the house' (from Late Latin *mansionile*, a diminutive of *mansio* 'house', 'dwelling'), hence a topographic name denoting someone who lived in an isolated dwelling, or a habitational name for someone from one of the minor places named Le Ménil or Le Mesnil.

FOREBEARS A family of this name from Normandy, France, is recorded in Quebec city in 1668.

GIVEN NAMES French 8%. *Armand, Emile, Pascal, Romain, Ulysse.*

Dumford (152) English: probably a variant of DUNFORD.

Dumire (176) Origin unidentified; possibly an Americanized spelling of German DOMEIER.

Dumitru (106) Romanian: from the personal name *Dumitru*, equivalent to Greek *Dēmētrios* (Latin *Demetrius*; see DEMETRIOU).

GIVEN NAMES Romanian 30%. *Alexandru, Constantin, Dimitrie, Florea, Gelu, Niculae, Rodica, Valeriu*; *Avram.*

Dumke (470) German: variant of DOMKE.

GIVEN NAMES German 6%. *Albrecht, Erwin, Gunter, Hans, Hubertus, Kurt, Otto, Rainer.*

Dumlao (201) Filipino: unexplained.

GIVEN NAMES Spanish 34%. *Manuel* (3), *Eugenio* (2), *Justo* (2), *Miguel* (2), *Ruben* (2), *Vicente* (2), *Conrado, Corazon, Crecencio, Crescencio, Cristina, Encarnacion*; *Donato, Eliseo, Federico, Lorenzo.*

Dumler (354) German: probably an altered form of **Dümmler** or **Thümmler**, a nickname for a noisy, unruly person or an occupational name for a traveling entertainer, from Middle High German *tumelen* 'to move quickly or irregularly'.

Dumm (335) German: nickname for a gullible person, from Middle High German *tump* 'simple', 'naïve' (from Old High German *tumb* 'dumb').

Dummer (535) German: **1.** nickname meaning 'the foolish one', from a noun derivative of Middle High German *tump* 'simple' (see DUMM). **2.** (**Dümmer**) from the name of a lake near Oldenburg, in Mecklenburg.

FOREBEARS Richard Dummer, father of master colonial silversmith and magistrate Jeremiah Dummer (1645–1718), is said to have been a native of Bishopstoke, England, who settled at Newbury, MA, and later at Boston, and in 1635–36 was one of the governor's assistants.

Dummitt (175) English (of Norman origin): habitational name from Dumart-en-Ponthieu in Somme, France.

Dumond (951) French: altered form of DUMONT.

GIVEN NAMES French 4%. *Donat, Leonide, Onezime, Rosaire.*

Dumont (2556) French: topographic name, from Old French *du mont* 'from the mount'.

GIVEN NAMES French 14%. *Armand* (7), *Normand* (7), *Andre* (6), *Emile* (5), *Donat* (4), *Julien* (4), *Lucien* (4), *Marcel* (4), *Michel* (4), *Pierre* (4), *Gilles* (3), *Laurent* (3).

Dumouchel (134) French: patronymic from a diminutive of **Mouche**, meaning 'fly', a nickname for an importunate man.

GIVEN NAMES French 20%. *Monique* (2), *Alain, Andre, Hermas, Lucien, Normand, Philippe, Treffle, Yves.*

Dumoulin (227) French: from *du moulin* 'from the mill', applied as a topographic name for someone who lived at a mill, or, by extension, as an occupational name for a miller. In North America this name is particularly associated with **Fonteneau** (see FONTENOT). See also DEMOULIN.

GIVEN NAMES French 19%. *Jacques* (4), *Serge* (2), *Armand, Aurel, Fernand, Francoise, Marcel, Michel, Normand, Philippe, Thierry.*

Dun (162) **1.** Variant spelling of DUNN. **2.** Dutch: nickname from Middle Dutch *dun* 'thin'.

Dunagan (1284) Variant spelling of the Irish surname DONEGAN, possibly from Gaelic variant **Ó Duinneagáin**.

Dunagin (117) Irish: variant of DONEGAN, possibly from the Gaelic variant **Ó Duinneagáin**.

Dunahoo (196) Variant of Irish DONAHUE.

Dunaj (128) **1.** Polish: topographic name from *dunaj* 'distant or unfamiliar river', also 'abyss'. **2.** Jewish (from Poland): habitational name from either the village Dunaj in central Poland, or ornamental name from *Dunaj*, the Polish name for the Danube river.

GIVEN NAME Polish 4%. *Krzysztof.*

Dunavan (180) Irish: variant of DONOVAN.

Dunavant (449) Probably a variant of Irish DONOVAN.

Dunavin (115) Irish: variant of DONOVAN.

Dunaway (3957) English (Hampshire and Sussex): unexplained.

Dunay (210) **1.** Hungarian: habitational name for someone who lived in a settlement on the Danube river (Hungarian *Duna*). In some cases the name may simply be ornamental. **2.** Ukrainian: see DUNAJ 1. **3.** Jewish (Ashkenazic): variant of DUNAJ 2. **4.** Possibly an Americanized spelling of the unexplained French surname **Duné** or **Dunet**, a habitational name from a place in Indre so named, from Gallic *dunum* 'hill', later 'fortress', 'stronghold'.

Dunbar (8619) Scottish: habitational name from Dunbar, a place on the North Sea coast near Edinburgh, named with Gaelic *dùn* 'fort' + *barr* 'top', 'summit'.

Duncan (46466) **1.** Scottish and Irish (of Scottish origin): from the Gaelic personal name *Donnchadh*, composed of the elements *donn* 'brown-haired man' or 'chieftain' + a derivative of *cath* 'battle', Anglicized in Ireland as *Donagh* or *Donaghue*. Compare DONAHUE. **2.** Irish (Sligo): used as an Anglicized equivalent of Gaelic **Ó Duinnchinn** 'descendant of *Donncheann*', a byname composed of the elements *donn* 'brown-haired man' or 'chieftain' + *ceann* 'head'.

Duncanson (461) Scottish: patronymic from DUNCAN 1.

Duncil (101) Origin unidentified.

Dunckel (167) Variant of German DUNKEL.

Duncombe (169) English: **1.** habitational name from any of various minor places named Duncombe, probably from Old English *dūn* 'hill' + Old English *cumb* 'valley'. **2.** probably a variant of DUNCAN.

Dundas (549) Scottish and northern Irish (Counties Leitrim and Fermanagh): habitational name from Dundas, a place near Edinburgh, Scotland, which is named from Gaelic *dùn* 'hill' (compare DOWN 1) + *deas* 'south'.

Dundee (130) Mainly northern Irish: habitational name from the city of Dundee in Scotland.

Dundon (562) **1.** English: habitational name for someone from Dundon, a place in Somerset, named from Old English *dūn* 'hill' + *denu* 'valley'. **2.** Irish (of Norman origin): habitational name, *de Aunou* (from a place in Orne, France) or *de Auney*, from any of various places named Aunay, for example in Calvados and Seine-et-Oise, France.

GIVEN NAMES Irish 5%. *Caitlin, Dermot, Liam.*

Dundore (171) Perhaps an altered spelling of Scottish **Dundower**, which is most probably a habitational name from a lost or unidentified place.

Dunegan (208) Irish: variant spelling of DONEGAN.

Dunevant (147) Probably a variant of Irish DONOVAN.

Dunfee (774) Variant of Irish DUNPHY.

Dunfield (100) English (of Norman origin): habitational name for someone from Donville in Calvados, France.

Dunford (1266) English: habitational name from Dunford Bridge, a hamlet near Penistone, West Yorkshire, so called from the river *Don* (a British name, possibly meaning 'river') + Old English *ford* 'ford', or from Dunford House in Methley, West Yorkshire, which is named in Old English as 'Dunn's ford' (see DUNN 2). Reaney suggests that the name may also have arisen from places called Durnford in Somerset and Wiltshire. (Great) Durnford in Wiltshire was named in Old English as 'hidden ford' (*dierne* + *ford*).

Dung (135) **1.** Vietnamese (**Dũng**): unexplained. **2.** Chinese 董: variant of DONG 1. **3.** North German: topographic name for someone who lived on a piece of raised dry land in marshy surroundings, Middle Low German *dung, dunk* 'hummock', or a habitational name from any of the various places named with this word.

GIVEN NAMES Vietnamese 36%; Chinese 21%. *Nguyen* (4), *Duc* (2), *Pham* (2), *Tran* (2), *Truong* (2), *Binh, Doan, Doi Van, Duong, Ha, Hoa, Kien; Chi, Hin, Ho, Liang, Tong, Wan, Yan Li, Yu Jen.*

Dungan (1513) Irish: reduced Anglicized form of Gaelic **Mac Donnagáin** 'descendant of *Donnagán*' (see DONEGAN).

Dungee (148) Variant of DUNGEY.

Dungey (303) **1.** English (Kent): possibly a habitational name for someone from Denge or Dungeness in Kent. **2.** Perhaps also an altered spelling of French DANGER.

Dungy (99) Variant of DUNGEY.

Dunham (8863) English (chiefly Norfolk): habitational name from any of several places called Dunham, of which one is in Norfolk. Most are named from Old English *dūn* 'hill' + *hām* 'homestead'. A place in Lincolnshire now known as Dunholme appears in Domesday Book as *Duneham* and this too may be a source of the surname; here the first element is probably the Old English personal name *Dunna*.

FOREBEARS John Dunham (1590–1668) was a Puritan linen weaver who came to Plymouth, MA, via Leiden, Netherlands, in 1633. He had many prominent descendants.

Dunigan (1007) Irish: variant of DONEGAN.

Dunivan (324) Irish: variant of DONOVAN.

Dunivant (113) Possibly an altered form of DONOVAN.

Dunk (376) German: variant of DUNKER.

Dunkel (779) German: nickname from Middle Low German *dunkel*, a byform of *dunker* 'dark', 'conceited', 'unclear', also applied as a byname for a blind person.

Dunkelberger (526) **1.** Jewish (Ashkenazic): ornamental name, literally meaning 'man from the dark mountain', from German *dunkel* 'dark' + *Berg* 'mountain', 'hill' + *-er*, suffix denoting an inhabitant. **2.** topographic name for someone living on a dark hillside, from *Dunk* (see DUNKER) + *Berg* 'mountain', 'hill'.

Dunker (695) **1.** North German: nickname from Middle Low German *dunker* 'dark', 'conceited', or 'unclear'. **2.** Dutch: variant of DONKER.

Dunkerley (230) English: variant of DUNKLEY.

Dunkerson (133) Scottish, Irish, and northern English: variant of **Dunkinson**, a patronymic from DUNKIN.

Dunkin (1226) **1.** Scottish and Irish: variant of DUNCAN. **2.** Irish: Anglicized form of Gaelic **Ó Duinnchinn** (see DINKINS).

Dunkle (1229) Respelling of German DUNKEL.

Dunkleberger (173) Respelling of DUNKELBERGER.

Dunklee (152) Respelling of DUNKLEY.

Dunkley (664) English: of uncertain derivation, possibly a habitational name from Dinckley in Lancashire, recorded in 1246 as *Dunkythele* and *Dinkedelay*, and probably named with an old British name, composed of elements meaning 'fort' + 'wood', with the addition of Old English *lēah* 'woodland clearing'. In the British Isles

the surname is now most common in Northamptonshire.

Dunklin (294) English: unexplained. Perhaps a variant of DUNKLEY.

Dunkum (109) English: variant spelling of DUNCOMBE.

Dunlap (14133) Scottish and English: variant of DUNLOP.

Dunlavey (256) Irish: variant of DUNLEAVY.

GIVEN NAME Irish 6%. *Brigid.*

Dunlavy (304) Irish: variant of DUNLEAVY.

GIVEN NAMES Irish 5%. *Donal, Kieran.*

Dunlay (168) Scottish: perhaps an altered spelling of Irish DUNLEA, itself a variant of DELAY.

Dunlea (124) Irish: variant of DELAY.

Dunleavy (1032) Irish: reduced Anglicized form of Gaelic **Mac Duinnshléibhe** 'son of *Donn Sléibhe*', a personal name composed of the elements *donn* 'brown-haired man' or 'chieftain' + *sléibhe* 'of the mountain'.

GIVEN NAMES Irish 8%. *Brendan* (3), *Aidan, Connor, John Patrick, Siobhan.*

Dunlevy (443) Irish: variant spelling of DUNLEAVY.

Dunlop (1767) **1.** Scottish: habitational name a place near Kilmarnock named Dunlop, from Gaelic *dùn* 'fort' + possibly *lápach* 'muddy'. The traditional pronunciation places the stress on the second syllable, although nowadays it is usually placed on the first. **2.** Irish: variant of DUNLEAVY. **3.** Irish: Scottish surname adopted by bearers of Gaelic **Ó Lapáin** 'descendant of *Lapán*', a byname or from *lápán* 'mire', 'dirt' (used figuratively of a poor man) or 'little paw'.

Dunlow (159) English: unexplained.

Dunman (181) Southern English: variant of **Downman**, a topographic name for a downland dweller. Compare DOWNER.

Dunmire (748) **1.** Perhaps a variant of Scottish **Dunmore**, a variant of DUNMORE. **2.** Alternatively, a respelling of German **Dannmeyer** or **Dannmeier**, a distinguishing name for a farmer (see MEYER) whose farm was by a pine forest (Middle Low German *dan*, Middle High German *tan* 'pine tree', 'pine forest').

Dunmore (296) English and Scottish: habitational name from Dunmore Farm in Oxfordshire or from any of many places in Scotland named in Gaelic as *Dún Mór* 'great hill'. The surname is most common in the Midland counties of England.

Dunmyer (151) See DUNMIRE.

Dunn (51549) **1.** Irish: reduced Anglicized form of Gaelic **Ó Duinn, Ó Doinn** 'descendant of *Donn*', a byname meaning 'brown-haired' or 'chieftain'. **2.** English: nickname for a man with dark hair or a swarthy complexion, from Middle English *dunn* 'dark-colored'. **3.** Scottish: habitational name from Dun in Angus, named with

Gaelic *dùn* 'fort'. **4.** Scottish: nickname from Gaelic *donn* 'brown'. Compare 1.

Dunnagan (269) Variant spelling of Irish DONEGAN.

Dunnam (634) Variant of English DUNHAM.

Dunnavant (388) Probably a variant of Irish DONOVAN. Compare DUNAVANT.

Dunnaway (168) English: variant spelling of DUNAWAY.

Dunne (3583) **1.** Variant spelling of DUNN; this is the usual spelling of the Irish name. **2.** German (**Dünne**): nickname for a slender, skinny person, from Middle High German *dünne* 'thin'. **3.** German (**Dünne**): habitational name, for example from Dünne near Herford, Westphalia.
GIVEN NAMES Irish 6%. *Dermot* (2), *Kieran* (2), *Liam* (2), *Cahal, Eamonn, Grainne.*

Dunnell (174) English: variant of DUNWELL 1.
GIVEN NAME French 4%. *Gaston.*

Dunner (112) German: **1.** habitational name for someone from a lost place near Ditzingen (near Leonberg) called Dunn. **2.** (**Dünner**) habitational name from Dünne near Herford.
GIVEN NAMES German 6%. *Hans, Ulrich.*

Dunnett (165) **1.** English: from a diminutive of DUNN. **2.** English: habitational name from Downhead in Somerset or Donhead in Wiltshire, both named from Old English *dūn* 'hill', 'down' + Old English *hēafod* 'head', 'end'. **3.** Scottish: habitational name from a place in Caithness.

Dunnigan (833) Irish: variant of DONEGAN.
GIVEN NAMES Irish 4%. *Brendan* (2), *Michael Patrick.*

Dunning (4012) **1.** Scottish: habitational name from a place in Perthshire, recorded in 1200 as *Dunine* and later as *Dunyn*, from Gaelic *dùnan*, a diminutive of *dùn* 'fort'. **2.** English: patronymic from DUNN. **3.** Irish: variant of DOWNING.

Dunnington (485) English: habitational name for someone from Dunnington in East Yorkshire, named from the Old English personal name *Dunna* + *-ing-* denoting association + *tūn* 'settlement'.

Dunnuck (115) English: variant spelling of **Dunnock**, a nickname from Old English *dunnoc* 'hedge sparrow'.

Dunphy (1543) Irish: reduced Anglicized form of Gaelic **Mac Donnchaidh** 'son of *Donnchadh*' or **Ó Donnchaidh** 'descendant of *Donnchadh*' (see DONAHUE).
GIVEN NAMES Irish 5%. *Donal* (4), *Dermot* (2), *Brendan, Colm, Eamonn, Kieran.*

Dunsford (141) English: habitational name from Dunsford in Devon or Dunsforth in West Yorkshire, both named from the genitive case of the Old English personal name *Dunn* (see DUNN) + Old English *ford* 'ford'.

Dunshee (211) Altered spelling of the Irish family name **Dunshea**, according to MacLysaght, a name found in Counties Tyrone and Antrim since the 17th century.

Dunsmoor (232) Variant spelling of Scottish and English DUNSMORE.

Dunsmore (761) **1.** Scottish: habitational name from a now forgotten place called Dundemore in Fife. **2.** English: habitational name from Dunsmoor in Devon or from an old district of Warwickshire called Dunsmore (preserved in Ryton-on-Dunsmore and Stretton-on-Dunsmore); both are named from the Old English personal name *Dunn(a)* 'dark' + *mōr* 'moor'.
FOREBEARS A Scottish family of this name was established in County Antrim, northern Ireland, in the early 17th century. From there they emigrated in 1723 to Londonderry, NH (now called Windham).

Dunson (1083) English and Scottish: probably a patronymic from DUNN 2 or 4. Compare DONSON.

Dunst (170) German: from Middle High German *dunst* 'steam', 'haze'; figuratively, 'need', 'care'; probably a nickname for someone beset with cares and worries.

Dunstan (575) **1.** English: from a Middle English personal name *Dunstan*, composed of Old English *dunn* 'dark', 'brown' + *stān* 'stone'. This name was borne by a 10th-century archbishop of Canterbury who was later canonized. **2.** English: habitational name from Dunstone in Devon, named from Old English *Dunstānestūn* 'settlement of *Dunstan*' (as in 1). The surname is still chiefly common in Devon, but there are places in other parts of the country with similar names but different etymologies (e.g. Dunstan in Northumbria, Dunston in Lincolnshire, Norfolk, Staffordshire, and Derbyshire), which may possibly have contributed to the surname. **3.** Scottish: partly perhaps the same as 1, but there is a place named Dunstane in Roxburghshire, which may also be a source of the surname.

Dunster (150) English: habitational name for someone from Dunster in Somerset, recorded in 1138 as *Dunestore* 'craggy pinnacle (Old English *torr*) of a man named *Dun(n)*'.
FOREBEARS Henry Dunster emigrated to MA in 1640 from Bury, Lancashire, England, and was made the first president of Harvard College (1640–54) almost immediately upon arrival in MA.

Dunston (851) English: variant spelling of DUNSTAN.

Dunsworth (275) English: probably a habitational name from a lost or unidentified place.

Dunton (1220) English: habitational name from any of various places called Dunton. Most (for example those in Bedfordshire, Essex, Leicestershire, Norfolk, and Warwickshire) are named from Old English *dūn* 'hill' (see DOWN 1) + *tūn* 'enclosure', 'settlement'. One in Buckinghamshire probably has as its first element the Old English personal name *Dudda* (see DODD).

Duntz (103) French (Alsatian): probably a variant of an unexplained German name.

Dunwell (116) English (Yorkshire): **1.** topographic name from Middle English *dun* 'dark' + *wella* 'stream', 'spring'. **2.** from the Old English personal name *Dunweald.*

Dunwoodie (101) Scottish: variant of DINWIDDIE.

Dunwoody (479) Scottish: variant of DINWIDDIE.

Dunworth (201) Of uncertain origin. Dunworth is found both in England and Ireland, but it is not clear which was the original source. Most likely, it is an English habitational name, from a lost or unidentified place, which was then adopted in Ireland by bearers of Gaelic **Ó Donndubhartaigh** (see DAVENPORT 2).
GIVEN NAMES Irish 4%. *Eamon, Niall.*

Duong (2751) Vietnamese (**Dương**): unexplained.
GIVEN NAMES Vietnamese 80%. *Thanh* (40), *Hung* (38), *Minh* (35), *Quang* (30), *Dung* (26), *Hoa* (26), *Duc* (21), *Vinh* (21), *Long* (20), *Son* (19), *Hai* (18), *Khanh* (18), *Nam* (16), *Hong* (14), *Tam* (14), *Phong* (12), *Dong* (9), *Chi* (8), *Sinh* (6), *Chan* (5), *Chien* (5), *Ho* (5), *Hang* (4), *Tong* (4), *Thai* (4), *Tinh* (4), *Tuong* (3).

Dupay (107) Altered spelling of French DUPUY, or of **Dupé**, a regional variant occurring chiefly in Anjou and Vendée.

Dupee (346) Altered spelling of French **Dupé** (see DUPAY) or DUPUY.

Dupell (105) Respelling of French **Dupel**, a topographic name, with fused preposition and definite article *du* 'from the', from Old French *pel* 'stake', 'pale' (Latin *palus*).

Dupere (115) French: possibly representing **Du Père**, 'of the father,' meaning one who exercises the functions of protection, or teaching, like a father; alternatively a form of **Du Peyre**, patronymic from a regional variant of the personal name *Pierre*.
FOREBEARS In Charlesbourg, Quebec, in 1686 there was a family named Dupéré (also called LARIVIERE), originally from Tours.
GIVEN NAMES French 27%. *Fernand* (4), *Normand* (2), *Armand, Jean Guy, Lucien, Ludger, Yves.*

Dupes (130) Probably an altered spelling of German **Dups**, a southern nickname for a clumsy person.

Dupin (176) French: from Old French *du pin* 'from the pine' (from Latin *pinus*), hence a topographic name for someone who lived near a prominent pine tree, or a habitational name from any of the numerous minor places named Le Pin ('the pine').
GIVEN NAMES French 9%. *Henri, Laurent, Serge.*

Duplantier (115) French: topographic name for someone who lived by a plantation of trees, Old French *plantier*, with fused preposition and definite article *du* 'from the', or a habitational name for someone from a place called Le Plantier in Dordogne.

GIVEN NAME French 11%. *Andre* (4).

Duplantis (739) French: topographic name for someone who lived by vineyard or plantation, Old French *plantis*, with fused preposition and definite article *du* 'from the', or a habitational name for someone from Le Plantis in Orne.

GIVEN NAMES French 5%. *Camille* (3), *Camile*, *Easton*, *Jacques*, *Luc*, *Minos*, *Monique*.

Duplechain (300) Of French origin: unexplained. Possibly an Americanized form of French **Du Plachon**, a topographic name from *plachon*, a northern French diminutive of *place* 'village square'.

Duplechin (257) French: unexplained. See DUPLECHAIN.

Dupler (434) Respelling of German **Duppler**, a nickname for a dice player or an occupational name for a dice maker, from an agent derivative of from Middle High German *topel* 'die'.

Duplessis (678) French: topographic name for someone who lived by a quickset fence, Old French *pleis* (from Latin *plexum* past participle of *plectere* 'plait', 'weave'), with fused preposition and definite article *du* 'from the'. This is a Huguenot name, well established in South Africa and elsewhere.

GIVEN NAMES French 14%. *Antoine* (4), *Jacques* (3), *Alphonse* (2), *Francois* (2), *Valere* (2), *Andre*, *Armand*, *Camille*, *Colombe*, *Emile*, *Eugenie*, *Jean Louis*.

Duplisea (111) Americanized form of French DUPLESSIS.

Duplissey (103) Americanized form of French DUPLESSIS.

Dupont (3855) French: topographic name for someone 'from the bridge', French *pont* (see PONT), with fused preposition and definite article *du* 'from the'.

GIVEN NAMES French 9%. *Andre* (10), *Armand* (6), *Emile* (6), *Jacques* (6), *Laurent* (5), *Pierre* (5), *Adrien* (3), *Cecile* (3), *Emilien* (3), *Gaston* (3), *Henri* (3), *Alain* (2).

Dupper (102) German: **1.** nickname from Middle High German *dupper* 'idiot'. **2.** (**Düpper**): variant of the occupational name **Tüpper** 'potter' (see TUPPER).

GIVEN NAMES German 7%; Scandinavian 5%. *Ernst*, *Manfred*; *Hilmer*.

Dupras (268) Altered spelling of French **Duprat**, a southern form of **Dupré** (see DUPRE).

GIVEN NAMES French 6%. *Andre* (2), *Adelard*, *Normand*, *Pierre*.

Dupre (2906) French (**Dupré**): topographic name for someone 'from the (*du*) meadow *pré*' (Old French *pred*).

GIVEN NAMES French 8%. *Marcel* (7), *Antoine* (4), *Jacques* (3), *Alcee* (2), *Andre*

(2), *Armand* (2), *Camille* (2), *Lucien* (2), *Pierre* (2), *Adrien*, *Albertine*, *Alcide*.

Dupree (4714) Respelling of **Dupré** (see DUPRE).

Duprey (1103) French: variant spelling of **Dupré** (see DUPRE).

Dupriest (265) Probably an altered spelling of French **Dupriez**, a habitational name for someone from (*du*) a place called Priez, for example in Aisne, Nièvre, or Somme. Alternatively, this may be a variant of any of the following versions of **Dupré** (see DUPRE): **Dupret**, **Dupretz**, **Duprey**, **Duprez**.

Dupuis (3422) French: **1.** topographic name for someone 'from the well' (Old French *puis*). **2.** variant spelling of DUPUY 1.

GIVEN NAMES French 12%. *Andre* (12), *Jacques* (11), *Pierre* (8), *Armand* (6), *Cecile* (5), *Normand* (5), *Emile* (4), *Lucien* (4), *Marcel* (3), *Rosaire* (3), *Alphonse* (2), *Henri* (2).

Dupuy (1395) Southern French: **1.** topographic name for someone who lived on or near a hill with a rounded summit, Occitan *puy* (from Latin *podium*), with fused preposition and definite article *du* 'from the', or from any of various places called Le Puy. **2.** variant spelling of DUPUIS 1.

GIVEN NAMES French 6%. *Pierre* (5), *Andre* (2), *Armand* (2), *Antoine*, *Emile*, *Gaston*, *Jacques*, *Jean-Francois*, *Lucien*, *Macaire*, *Michel*, *Octave*.

Duquaine (134) Northern French: variant of DUCHESNE.

Duque (821) **1.** Spanish and Portuguese: from *duque* 'duke' (from Latin *dux*, genitive *ducis* 'leader'), an occupational name for someone who worked in the household of a duke, or as a nickname for someone who gave himself airs and graces. **2.** French (also **Duqué**): nickname from *duquet*, a diminutive of French *duc* 'duke' (see DUCHON).

GIVEN NAMES Spanish 47%. *Jose* (21), *Carlos* (17), *Juan* (15), *Jorge* (11), *Mario* (9), *Fernando* (8), *Luis* (8), *Francisco* (7), *Manuel* (7), *Miguel* (6), *Diego* (5), *Javier* (5).

Duquette (1751) French: altered spelling of **Duquet**, a topographic name for someone who lived by a quayside, or alternatively of **Duguet** (see DUGA).

FOREBEARS This surname, in the spelling **Duquet**, is attested in Quebec city in 1638.

GIVEN NAMES French 10%. *Lucien* (6), *Armand* (4), *Camille* (3), *Adrien* (2), *Arsene* (2), *Fernand* (2), *Jacques* (2), *Marcel* (2), *Normand* (2), *Raoul* (2), *Achille*, *Amie*.

Dura (200) **1.** Italian (Campania): from the feminine form of DURO. **2.** Polish: topographic name from Old Polish *dura* 'hollow', 'cavity', 'hole'. **3.** Czech and Slovak: from a pet form of the female name *Dorota* (see DOROTHY). **4.** Bulgarian: from the female personal name *Dura* (see

DOROTHY). **5.** Altered spelling of French **Duras**, a habitational name from Duras, a place in Lot-et-Garonne.

Durall (259) English: probably a variant of DURRELL.

Duran (9689) **1.** Spanish (**Durán**) and Catalan: from the personal name *Durand* (see DURANT, DURANTE). **2.** English: variant of DURANT. **3.** Polish: from a derivative of DURA. **4.** Czech: from a derivative of DURA.

GIVEN NAMES Spanish 38%. *Jose* (174), *Juan* (107), *Manuel* (76), *Carlos* (59), *Jesus* (55), *Luis* (47), *Francisco* (45), *Mario* (38), *Miguel* (34), *Ramon* (32), *Raul* (30), *Ruben* (30).

Duranceau (109) French: from a derivative of the personal name *Duran*, a variant of the personal name DURANT.

Durand (2921) **1.** English and French: variant of DURANT. **2.** Americanized form of Hungarian **Durándi**, a habitational name for someone from a place called Duránd, in former Szepes county.

FOREBEARS There was a Parisian family of this name in Quebec city in 1661. In 1662 a Durand from Saintonge married Catherine Anenontha, daughter of Nicolas Arendanki and Jeanne Otrihouandit, Hurons. A family called Durand from Angoumois was in Quebec by 1665; and two from Chartres were in Quebec by 1669 and 1673.

GIVEN NAMES French 9%. *Lucien* (5), *Pierre* (5), *Jacques* (4), *Jean Claude* (4), *Michel* (4), *Andre* (3), *Marcel* (3), *Adrien* (2), *Benoit* (2), *Dominique* (2), *Gaston* (2), *Gilles* (2).

Durando (132) **1.** Italian: Ligurian and Piedmontese variant of DURANTE, from the French cognate, DURAND. **2.** Americanized spelling of French **Durandeau**, from a diminutive of the personal name DURANT.

GIVEN NAMES German 4%. *Erna*, *Frieda*.

Durant (3510) French and English (Norman): from the Latin omen name *Durandus*, meaning 'enduring', which was in common use especially in the Jewish communities of southern France and from there spread out across France, into England, Italy, and the Iberian peninsula.

Durante (1106) Italian: from the medieval personal name *Durante*, ultimately from the Latin verb *durare* 'to last or endure'; like the French and English cognate DURANT, the name may also originally have had the sense 'stubborn', 'obstinate'.

GIVEN NAMES Italian 13%. *Salvatore* (9), *Angelo* (8), *Antonio* (3), *Carlo* (3), *Domenic* (3), *Carmine* (2), *Gennaro* (2), *Sal* (2), *Amedeo*, *Ciro*, *Concetta*, *Egidio*.

Duray (199) French: **1.** habitational name, with fused preposition and definite article *du* 'from the', for someone from any of various minor places named Ray, in Inre, Mayenne, Nièvre, and Tarn. **2.** Americanized spelling of **Duret** (see DURETTE).

3. Hungarian: habitational name for someone from a place called Dura.

Durazo (250) Spanish: probably a nickname from *durazo*, a modified form of *duro* 'hard'.

GIVEN NAMES Spanish 44%. *Jose* (7), *Armando* (5), *Manuel* (5), *Alfonso* (3), *Carlos* (3), *Ernesto* (3), *Ignacio* (3), *Mario* (3), *Raul* (3), *Agustin* (2), *Alejandro* (2), *Angel* (2); *Antonio* (2), *Lorenzo* (2), *Francesca, Marco*.

Durban (150) **1.** French: southern variant of DURBIN. **2.** French: habitational name from any of various places called Durban, in Ariège, Aude, and Gers. **3.** In some cases, possibly German, from the personal name URBAN, the initial *d-* having been acquired by a misdivision of *Sankt Urban* 'St. Urban'.

GIVEN NAME French 4%. *Fernande*.

D'Urbano (109) Italian: patronymic from the personal name *Urbano* (see URBAN).

GIVEN NAMES Italian 14%. *Berardino* (2), *Carmela, Edmondo, Franco, Rinaldo, Rocco*.

Durben (190) Variant spelling of French DURBAN.

Durbin (5040) French: patronymic from the personal name *Urbain*, a vernacular form of *Urbanus* (see URBAN).

Durborow (134) English: variant of **Durborough**, a Somerset name of unexplained orgin.

Durden (2161) English: **1.** variant of DEARDEN. **2.** nickname from Old French *dur* 'hard' + *dent* 'tooth'.

Durdin (151) English: variant spelling of DURDEN.

Duree (198) Altered spelling of either of two French family names: **Duré**, a nickname from *dur* 'hard', 'obdurate', or DURY.

Durel (116) **1.** French: nickname from a diminutive of Old French *dur* 'hard(y)'. **2.** Variant spelling of English DURRELL, cognate with 1.

Durell (199) Variant spelling of English DURRELL, or an altered spelling of the French cognate DUREL.

Duren (1340) German (**Düren**): habitational name from any of numerous places named Düren in northern Germany, in particular the one near Cologne.

Durette (196) French: either a respelling of **Duret**, a nickname from a diminutive of *dur* 'hard', 'obstinate', or a feminine form of the same name.

GIVEN NAMES French 13%. *Emile* (2), *Philippe* (2), *Aime, Luc, Marcel*.

Durfee (1423) Americanized spelling of French (Huguenot) **D'Urfé**, a habitational name, with the preposition *d(e)* 'from', for someone from the castle of Urfé, Loire.

FOREBEARS The name was brought to England by Huguenot refugees in the early 17th century. Thomas Durfee, the ancestor of the Durfee family in America, was born

in 1643 and came to Providence, RI, in 1660.

Durfey (404) Variant of French DURFEE.

Durflinger (197) Altered spelling of German **Dörflinger** (see DOERFLINGER).

Durgan (281) Irish: probably a variant of DURKIN.

Durgin (953) Irish: variant of DURKIN.

Durham (14539) English: habitational name from Durham, a city in northeastern England, named from Old English *dūn* 'hill' (see DOWN 1) + Old Norse *holmr* 'island'.

Durheim (125) Respelling of German **Dürrheim**, a habitational name from Bad Dürrheim in Baden Württemberg.

Durian (100) German and Swiss German: unexplained.

Durica (104) Czech and Slovak: patronymic from the personal name *Juraj*, a vernacular form of Greek *Geōrgios* (see GEORGE).

Durick (172) **1.** Probably an Americanized spelling of eastern German (Saxony, Silesia, Bohemia) **Dürich**, a regional name from Thuringia (see DOERING), or the Swiss German cognate **Dürig**. **2.** Perhaps an altered spelling of Irish **Durack**, an Anglicized form of Gaelic **Ó Dubhraic**, thought to be from **Ó Dubhratha** 'descendant of *Dubhratha*', a personal name meaning 'black one of prosperity'.

Durie (141) **1.** Scottish: habitational name from Durie, a place in Fife, named from Gaelic *dobhar* 'stream' + the locative suffix *-ach*. **2.** French (Walloon): variant of DURY, from Walloon *ri* 'stream'.

Durig (145) Swiss German (**Dü(h)rig**): regional name from Thuringia cognate with **Dürich** (see DURICK).

During (104) German (**Düring**): variant of **Dürich** (see DURICK).

GIVEN NAME French 4%. *Remi*.

Durio (238) French: regional variant of **Durieu**, a topographic name meaning 'from the stream' (French *rieu*). Compare DURY.

GIVEN NAMES French 5%. *Clotile, Clovis, Eugenie*.

Duris (188) **1.** French: variant of DURY 2. **2.** Irish: reduced Anglicized form of Gaelic **Ó Dubhruis** (see DORIS 1). **3.** Scottish (Kincardineshire): possibly a habitational name from Dores in Perthshire, or from Durris in Kincardineshire, now in Aberdeenshire. **4.** Czech (Moravian) (**Duriš**) and Slovak (**Ďuriš**): patronymic from a Moravian and Slovak form of the personal name *Jiři*, vernacular form of Greek *Geōrgios* (see GEORGE).

GIVEN NAMES Czech and Slovak 5%. *Milan* (3), *Zdenek* (2).

Durivage (133) French: topographic name for someone who lived by the seashore or the shore of a lake, Old French *rivage*.

GIVEN NAMES French 7%. *Alain, Gilles, Michel*.

Durk (99) **1.** English: variant of DARK. **2.** German (**Dürk**): variant of **Türk** 'Turk',

a nickname for a wild or unruly person, or sometimes for a prisoner of war (from the Turkish Wars). **3.** German: possibly a variant of DIRK.

Durkan (144) Irish: variant spelling of DURKIN.

GIVEN NAMES Irish 13%. *Kieran, Liam, Niall*.

Durkee (1702) Irish: of uncertain origin; perhaps a variant of DURKIN.

FOREBEARS The name was brought to the Massachusetts Bay Colony by William Durgy, who was born in Ireland in about 1632. He arrived from Barbados on November 9, 1663, as the indentured servant of Thomas Bishop.

Durkin (3082) **1.** Irish: reduced Anglicized form of Gaelic **Mac Duarcáin** 'son of *Duarcán*', a byname representing a diminutive of *duairc* 'surly'. **2.** Polish: from Russian **Durkin**, from *durak* 'fool', 'idiot'.

GIVEN NAMES Irish 6%. *Brendan* (2), *Brigid, Kieran*.

Durland (367) Origin unidentified; perhaps a Dutch respelling of French DORLAND.

Durley (171) **1.** Irish: reduced Anglicized form of Gaelic **Ó Dubhurthuille** 'descendant of *Dubhurthuille*', a personal name of unexplained origin. **2.** English: habitational name from Durley in Hampshire or Durleigh in Somerset, both named from Old English *dēor* 'deer' + *lēah* 'woodland clearing', or from Durley in Wiltshire, so named from Old English *dierne* 'hidden' + *lēah*.

Durling (467) English: variant of DARLING.

Durm (102) Variant of German **Turm**, a topographic name for someone who lived by a tower, Middle High German *turm*.

Durman (107) German (**Durmann**): occupational name for a doorkeeper.

Durnal (101) English: variant spelling of DURNELL.

Durnan (143) Irish: variant of DURNIN.

GIVEN NAME Irish 5%. *Liam*.

Durnell (341) English (Avon): perhaps a variant of DARNELL.

Durner (115) German (**Dürner**): **1.** habitational name for someone from Dürn, a place in Bavaria, or Dürnau in Württemberg. **2.** variant of TURNER.

Durney (256) Irish: variant of DORNEY.

Durnil (156) English: variant spelling of DURNELL.

Durnin (318) Irish (County Louth and eastern Ulster): shortened Anglicized form of Gaelic **Ó Duirnín** 'descendant of *Duirnín*' (see DORNAN).

GIVEN NAMES Irish 4%. *Conan* (2), *Siobhan* (2), *Padraic*.

Durning (371) Scottish: of uncertain origin. It is found primarily in Glasgow, and it may be a respelling of DURNIN. MacLysaght, however, suggests that this name is of English origin.

Duro (114) Italian: nickname for a tough or unyielding man, from *duro* 'hard', 'tough' (Latin *durus*). The word had both the approving sense 'steadfast', 'enduring' and the less favorable sense 'stubborn', 'obstinate', 'cruel'.
GIVEN NAMES Spanish 6%. *Alfonso, Dominador, Francisco, Roberto, Virgilio.*

Durocher (964) **1.** French: topographic name denoting someone who lived in a rocky place, literally 'from the (*du*) crag (*rocher*)'. In North America the surname has often become confused with DESROCHERS and DESROSIERS. **2.** Variant of German **Duracher**, a habitational name for someone from Durach near Kempten in Bavaria.
GIVEN NAMES French 8%. *Andre* (2), *Fernand* (2), *Gilles* (2), *Marcel* (2), *Normand* (2), *Alain, Antoine, Armand, Bibiane, Emile, Emilien, Gaetan.*

Duron (616) **1.** Spanish (**Durón**): habitational name from Durón, a town in Guadalajara province. **2.** French: possibly a nickname from a derivative of *dur* 'hard'. **3.** Czech (**Duroň**): variant of DURAN.
GIVEN NAMES Spanish 38%. *Jose* (16), *Manuel* (13), *Juan* (10), *Ruben* (10), *Ramon* (6), *Mario* (5), *Ignacio* (4), *Jesus* (4), *Alfredo* (3), *Armando* (3), *Enrique* (3), *Francisco* (3), *Adauto* (2).

Duross (182) Irish: reduced Anglicized form of Gaelic **Ó Dubhruis** (see DORIS).

Durow (117) English (Midlands): unexplained.

Durr (2103) German (**Dürr**): nickname from Middle High German *dürre* 'thin', 'gaunt', 'dry'.

Durrah (150) Variant of Irish DARRAH (see DARRAGH).

Durrance (532) English: variant of **Durants**, a patronymic from DURANT.

Durrani (132) Pathan: from an Afghan tribal name based on Pathan *durrān* 'pearl'.
GIVEN NAMES Muslim 89%. *Zahid* (5), *Mohammed* (4), *Abdul* (3), *Amir* (2), *Badruddin* (2), *Mohammad* (2), *Nadir* (2), *Rahima* (2), *Serdar* (2), *Shahid* (2), *Tariq* (2), *Aamir.*

Durrant (738) English and French: variant of DURANT.

Durre (121) German (**Dürre**): variant of **Dürr** (see DURR).
GIVEN NAME German 4%. *Inge* (2).

Durrell (319) English (Norman): nickname from a diminutive of Old French *dur* 'hard(y)'.

Durrenberger (104) German and Swiss German (**Dürrenberger**): habitational name from any of the numerous places in Bavaria, Thuringia, Saxony, and Silesia named Dür(r)nberg or Dürrenberg.

Durrence (288) Altered spelling of English DURRANCE.

Durrer (147) German (also **Dürrer**): nickname for a thin man, from a noun derivative of *Dürr* (see DURR).

Durrett (1275) Irish: altered form of Scottish **Durrat**, itself an altered form of DORWARD.

Durrette (127) Respelling, under French influence, of Irish DURRETT.

D'Urso (1114) Southern Italian (**D'Urso**): patronymic from the personal name *Urso*, a southern (or Latinized) variant of ORSO.
GIVEN NAMES Italian 15%. *Angelo* (8), *Salvatore* (6), *Sal* (4), *Camillo* (2), *Carmelo* (2), *Dino* (2), *Donato* (2), *Mauro* (2), *Vito* (2), *Antonietta, Antonino, Antonio.*

Durst (2366) German: **1.** (also **Dürst**): nickname from Middle High German *turst* 'boldness'. **2.** from Middle High German *durst* 'thirst', applied as nickname, probably for a heavy drinker; or a habitational name from a farmstead in the Tyrol named with the same word, probably indicating a dry location.

Durston (118) English (Somerset): habitational name from Durston in Somerset, named with the Old English personal name *Dēor* + *tūn* 'settlement', 'farmstead'.

Durtschi (131) Swiss German: unexplained.

Dury (139) **1.** French: habitational name from any of several places named Dury, in Aisne, Pas-de-Calais, and Somme. **2.** French and Swiss German: topographic name for someone who lived by a stream, *du ry* 'from the stream'. Because *ry* has fallen out of use, the name has been translated as RICE, the French word for 'rice', *riz*, being a homophone. **3.** English: either a habitational name from Dury in Lydford, Devon, or of French origin (see 1), the surname having been taken to England by the Huguenots.

Duryea (764) Possibly an Americanized spelling of French **Durieu** (see DURIO).

Duryee (223) Possibly an Americanized spelling of French **Durieu** (see DURIO).
GIVEN NAMES French 4%. *Amie, Celine.*

Dusablon (127) French: topographic name for someone who lived by a beach or on sandy soil, literally 'from the (*du*) (fine) sand (*sablon*)'.
GIVEN NAMES French 13%. *Armand* (2), *Andre, Gilles, Michel, Normand.*

Dusch (191) **1.** German: from a short form of the personal name *Theodosius*. **2.** German: habitational name from Dusch, a place in Grison canton, Switzerland. **3.** German: (**Düsch**): unexplained. **4.** German: topographic name from Bavarian dialect *Dosch, Dusch* 'bush', 'thick bunch'. **5.** French (Alsace and Lorraine): ethnic name for a German, from Middle High German *diusch*, variant of *diutsch*.

Dusek (852) Czech (**Dušek**): from a pet form of the Old Czech personal name *Duchoslav*, composed of the elements *duch* 'spirit' + *slav* 'glory'.

Dusel (126) German: from a southern word for a ghost that walks at night or for a mentally confused person or perhaps a variant of **Düsler** (see DUESLER).

Dusenberry (447) Americanized form of Dutch **(van) Doesburg**, a habitational name from Doesburg in Gelderland or possibly Duisburg in Germany.
FOREBEARS Johannes Hendricksen van Doesburg (b. 1666 in Manhattan) had children called John and Mary Dosenborrow, Dusenbury, or Dusenberry.

Dusenbery (234) Variant spelling of DUSENBERRY.

Dusenbury (287) Variant spelling of DUSENBERRY.

Dush (147) **1.** Americanized spelling of DUSCH. **2.** Americanized spelling of Hungarian **Dús**, a nickname for a rich person.

Dushane (283) Americanized spelling of French **Duchêne** (see DUCHENE).

Dusing (198) German (also **Düsing**): **1.** from Middle High German *duz ing*, Middle Low German *dūsinc*, the term for a particular type of belt, often ornate and richly decorated with bells, worn both by men and women, although often locally prohibited by the Church. **2.** probably a patronymic from one of the numerous old personal names related to DIETZ.

Duskey (145) **1.** Americanized spelling of Polish **Duski**, a habitational name from a place called Dusze, in Łomża voivodeship. **2.** Reduced form of Polish **Sandowski** (see SANDUSKY). **3.** Possibly also Scottish, a variant spelling of **Duskie**, which may be a habitational name; Black mentions Deskie in Banff.

Duskin (235) **1.** Russian: unexplained. **2.** Bulgarian: derivative of *Duska*, the feminine form of the male personal name *Dusan*; alternatively from a pet form of *Radus*.

Duso (150) Filipino: unexplained.

Dusold (110) Origin unidentified; perhaps a variant of French DUSSAULT.

Dussault (595) French: **1.** topographic name, with fused preposition and definite article *du* 'from the', from Old French *sauz*, the old subjective case of *salix* 'willow'. **2.** topographic name, with fused preposition and definite article *du* 'from the', from Old French *saut* 'grove', 'copse' (from Latin *saltus*), or a habitational name from any of the places named Le Sault, for example in Ain and Vaucluse.
FOREBEARS There was a family of this name from La Rochelle in Quebec city in 1663; one from Paris in Sillery in 1676.
GIVEN NAMES French 14%. *Andre* (3), *Henri* (2), *Lucien* (2), *Marcel* (2), *Pierre* (2), *Aime, Armand, Cecile, Jacques, Luc, Michel, Monique.*

Dusseau (301) French: habitational name, with the preposition *d(e)*, denoting someone from either of two places named Usseau, in Deux-Sèvres and Vienne.
GIVEN NAME French 4%. *Alphonse.*

Dusseault (179) French: variant spelling of DUSSAULT.

GIVEN NAMES French 23%. *Adelard* (2), *Andre* (2), *Alphee, Armand, Camille, Herve, Jean-Paul, Marcel, Marielle, Pierre, Rejean, Yvan.*

Dust (364) **1.** English: from Old English *dūst* 'dust', applied as a nickname, possibly for someone with a dusty complexion or hair (as, for example, a miller), or for a worthless person. **2.** North German: possibly a Westphalian habitational name from a farm named with *dost* 'bush', 'brush'. However, the word also means 'fine dust', 'flour' and may have been applied as an occupational nickname for a miller. Compare 1.

Dustin (881) **1.** English: possibly from a medieval personal name *Tustin*, derived via Old French *Toustin* from Old Norse *Þorsteinn* 'Thor's stone'. Compare THURSTON. **2.** Altered form of French **D'Estaing**, a topographic name, with the preposition *d(e)* 'from', for someone who lived by a pond, Old French *esta(i)ng*, or a habitational name for someone from a place named with this word, for example Estaing in Aveyron and Hautes Pyrénées. **3.** French: habitational name, with preposition *de*, for someone from Stain in the Belgian province of Namur.

Dustman (242) North German (**Dustmann**): possibly a habitational name for someone from the village of Dusnem or Dussem near Wolfenbüttel, now lost.

Duston (195) English: habitational name for someone from a place in Northamptonshire, named from Old English *dus* 'mound' or *dūst* 'dust' + *tūn* 'settlement', 'farmstead'.

Dusza (176) **1.** Polish: from *dusza* 'soul', probably a nickname in the sense 'bighearted'. **2.** Hungarian: see DUCA.

GIVEN NAMES Polish 5%. *Tadeusz* (2), *Jozef, Urszula.*

Duszynski (228) Polish (**Duszyński**): habitational name for someone from a place called Dusin or Dusina (earlier *Duszyn, Duszyna*).

GIVEN NAMES Polish 6%. *Andrzej, Casimir, Jacek, Janusz, Leszek.*

Dutch (310) **1.** Americanized spelling of German DEUTSCH. **2.** English: ethnic name for a Dutchman, especially an immigrant Dutch weaver.

Dutcher (2002) Americanized spelling of German **Deutscher** or Swiss German **Tütscher**, ethnic names for a German (see DEUTSCH).

Duthie (291) **1.** Scottish: reduced Anglicized form of Gaelic **Mac Gille Dubhthaigh**, a patronymic from the personal name *Gille Dubhthaigh* 'servant of (Saint) *Dubhthach*' (see DUFFY 1). **2.** Belgian French (**Duthie, Duthié**): variant of DUTIL, or alternatively a habitational name for someone from Thy in the province of Namur.

GIVEN NAME Scottish 4%. *Iain* (2).

Dutil (205) French: topographic name, from Old French *du til* 'from the lime(tree)' (from Latin *tilia*), or a habitational name, with fused preposition and definite article *du* 'from', for someone from a place named with this word, in particular Le Thil in Pas-de-Calais or Thil in Meurthe-et-Moselle.

GIVEN NAMES French 21%. *Marcel* (4), *Aime* (2), *Alain, Amedee, Amie, Armand, Cecile, Emile, Gilles, Jean Noel, Manon, Placide.*

Dutka (287) **1.** Polish and Ukrainian: nickname from a variant of *dudka* 'small bagpipe'. **2.** Hungarian: nickname for a poor person, from *dutka* 'small change'.

Dutkiewicz (303) Polish: patronymic from DUTKA or DUTKO.

GIVEN NAMES Polish 4%. *Halina, Jacek, Jerzy.*

Dutko (275) Polish and Ukrainian: variant of DUTKA.

Dutoit (148) French: **1.** from Old French *teit* 'roof' (from Latin *tectum*), also 'hut', 'cottage'; the name therefore may have denoted someone who lived in a small cottage or it may have been an occupational name for a roofer. **2.** habitational name from Duthoit, a hamlet in Nord.

GIVEN NAMES French 5%. *Francois, Monique.*

Dutra (1125) Portuguese: habitational name for someone from Utra, a place in Flanders or Utrecht.

GIVEN NAMES Spanish 10%; Portuguese 7%. *Manuel* (31), *Jose* (8), *Carlos* (7), *Joaquin* (2), *Luis* (2), *Mario* (2), *Rogerio* (2), *Alberto, Amalia, Americo, Ana, Angelina; Ilidio, Joao, Zulmira.*

Dutro (272) Origin unidentified. **1.** There is some evidence that it may be an American variant of German DOTTERER. **2.** Alternatively, perhaps, it may be a Walloon habitational name (equivalent of French **Dutraux, Dutroux**), from a place named with Walloon *trô* 'hole' (standard French *trou*).

Dutrow (171) Origin unidentified. Compare DUTRO.

Dutson (284) English: probably a variant of DOTSON.

Dutt (459) **1.** English: nickname from Middle English *dut* 'joy', 'delight'. **2.** Indian: variant of DATTA. **3.** German: from the Germanic personal name *Dudo* (see DUE).

GIVEN NAMES Indian 35%. *Anil* (3), *Prem* (3), *Raj* (3), *Deepak* (2), *Deo* (2), *Indar* (2), *Jitendra* (2), *Kushal* (2), *Ragini* (2), *Rajesh* (2), *Satish* (2), *Som* (2).

Dutta (282) Indian: variant of DATTA.

GIVEN NAMES Indian 88%. *Partha* (5), *Ajit* (3), *Amitava* (3), *Sandeep* (3), *Sanjay* (3), *Subhash* (3), *Sudhir* (3), *Aloke* (2), *Anindya* (2), *Arup* (2), *Bani* (2), *Bhaskar* (2).

Dutter (174) Probably a respelling of German DOTTER.

Dutterer (107) Variant spelling of German DOTTERER.

GIVEN NAME French 4%. *Michel.*

Dutton (6318) English: habitational name from any of the places called Dutton, especially those in Cheshire and Lancashire. The first of these is named from Old English *dūn* 'hill' + *tūn* 'enclosure', 'settlement'; the second is from Old English personal name *Dudd(a)* (see DODD 1) + Old English *tūn*.

Duttry (128) Origin unidentified; perhaps an Americanized form of French DAUTRICH.

Duty (1438) **1.** English: unexplained. **2.** Possibly a Americanized spelling of French **Duthie** or **Dutey**, both variants of DUTIL, or a translation of French **Dudevoir**, which is probably a dit-name in origin, from one of the regiments that served in New France, perhaps a nickname for someone obsessed with duty.

FOREBEARS A family named Dudevoir, from the Auvergne, settled in Montreal in 1690.

Duus (113) Danish and North German: from Middle Low German *dūs* denoting the two on a die or the ace in cards, hence a nickname for a card or dice player. Compare DAUS.

GIVEN NAMES Scandinavian 20%; German 5%. *Erik* (2), *Dagny, Oluf, Per, Viggo; Hans* (2), *Frieda.*

D'Uva (347) Italian: literally 'of the grapes', hence a metonymic occupational name for someone who grew, processed, or sold grapes.

GIVEN NAMES Italian 18%. *Angelo* (5), *Carmine* (4), *Sal* (2), *Dino, Gaetano, Giacomo, Luciano, Luigi, Onofrio, Riccardo, Rocco, Sebastiano.*

Duval (3203) **1.** French: topographic name from Old French *du val* 'from the valley' (from Latin *vallis*). **2.** English: variant of DUVALL 1.

GIVEN NAMES French 9%. *Andre* (12), *Armand* (8), *Pierre* (6), *Lucien* (4), *Marcel* (4), *Fernand* (3), *Edouard* (2), *Jacques* (2), *Normand* (2), *Rosaire* (2), *Alcide, Arsene.*

Duvall (7227) **1.** English: in most cases of French origin (see DUVAL 1), taken to England by a Huguenot refugee from Rouen. It may also be from a pet form of an Old English female personal name, *Dūfe*, meaning 'dove'. **2.** According to Black, this is also found as a Swedish variant of Scottish McDOUGALL.

Duve (158) German: variant of DUWE.

GIVEN NAMES German 11%. *Otto* (3), *Helmut* (2), *Rainer, Wolfgang.*

Duvernay (171) French: topographic name, with fused preposition and definite article *du*, for someone who lived near a copse of alders, French *vernay*, a derivative of *verne* 'alder' + the Latin collective suffix *-etum*.

GIVEN NAMES French 10%. *Armand* (2), *Emile, Michel, Orelia, Patrice.*

Duwe (285) **1.** North German: from Middle Low German *dūve* 'dove', hence a metonymic occupational name for someone who bred or sold doves, or perhaps a nickname for a gentle person. **2.** Eastern German, Sorbian: variant of DUBE.

GIVEN NAMES German 5%. *Kurt* (3), *Horst*.

Dux (199) German: **1.** topographic name denoting someone from Dux in Bohemia. **2.** Latinized form of German *Herzog* 'duke', hence probably a metonymic occupational name for someone in the employ of a duke or a nickname for the illegitimate son of a duke. **3.** (**Düx**): from a reduced form of the medieval personal name *Benedictus* (see BENEDICT).

GIVEN NAMES German 8%. *Erwin* (2), *Arno*, *Dieter*, *Fritz*, *Kurt*.

Duxbury (376) English: habitational name from a place in Lancashire, recorded in the early 13th century as *D(e)ukesbiri*, from the genitive case of the Old English personal name *Deowuc* or *Duc(c)* (both of uncertain origin) + Old English *burh* 'fort' (see BURKE).

Duyck (163) Dutch: nickname from Middle Dutch *duuc* 'duck'; in some cases the name may be a derivative of Middle Dutch *duken* 'to dive' and cognate with DUCKER 3. Compare also DUCK 4.

Duzan (259) Probably an Americanized form of Slovenian **Dolžan** or **Dovžan**, habitational names for someone from places named Dovje, Dovže, or Dolž.

Dvoracek (164) Czech (**Dvořáček**): from a diminutive of **Dvořák** (see DVORAK).

Dvorak (3197) Czech (**Dvořák**): status name for a rich farmer, one who owned a manor house, from Czech *dvůr* 'manor', 'estate', or in some cases an occupational name for someone who worked at a manor house rather than on the land. Compare SEDLAK. In Moravia the term denoted a freeholder subject only to the king. This is the fourth most common surname in the Czech lands.

Dvorkin (149) Jewish (eastern Ashkenazic): variant of DWORKIN.

GIVEN NAMES Russian 23%; Jewish 16%. *Mikhail* (4), *Igor* (3), *Vladimir* (3), *Arkady* (2), *Iosif* (2), *Anatoly*, *Arkadiy*, *Efim*, *Garri*, *Grigoriy*, *Grigory*, *Michail*; *Marat*, *Moisey*, *Shira*, *Yakov*.

Dvorsky (197) Czech and Slovak (**Dvorský**): habitational name for someone from a place called Dvůr or Dvory, from Old Czech *dvůr* 'manor', 'estate'.

Dwan (215) Irish: Anglicized form of Gaelic **Ó Dubháin** or **Ó Damháin** (see DOANE).

Dweck (288) Jewish: unexplained.

GIVEN NAMES Jewish 15%. *Haim* (2), *Haskel* (2), *Moshe* (2), *Hillel*, *Shlomo*.

Dwelle (161) Part translation of French DUPUIS.

Dwelley (156) English: nickname from Middle English *dwele* 'foolish', 'erring', 'heretical', from an Old English *dweollīc*, from *dwelian*, *dweolian*, *dwolian* 'to err'.

Dwenger (138) North German: from an agent derivative of Middle Low German *dwengen* 'to press or oppress', probably a nickname for a violent person or a torturer.

Dwiggins (387) **1.** Irish: Anglicized form (with English genitive -*s*) of Gaelic **Ó Dubhagáin** (see DUGAN) or, more likely, of **Ó Duibhginn** (see DEEGAN). **2.** Possibly a variant (by misdivision) of English WIGGINS.

Dwight (775) English: from *Diot*, a pet form of the female personal name DYE. Reaney also suggests that this may also be an altered form of **Thwaite** (see THWAITES).

FOREBEARS Timothy Dwight (1752–1817), Congregational divine, author, and president of Yale College (1795–1817), was the dominant figure in the established order of CT. He was born in Northampton, MA, a descendant of John Dwight who came from Dedham, England, in 1635 and settled in Dedham, MA, and the grandson of Jonathan Edwards, the great theologian of American Puritanism.

Dwinell (305) English: unexplained.

Dwire (282) Variant spelling of Irish DWYER.

Dworaczyk (114) Polish: from a diminutive or patronymic form of DWORAK.

GIVEN NAME Polish 4%. *Jerzy*.

Dworak (414) Polish: status name for someone who worked at a manor house rather than on the land, from Polish *dwór* 'manor', 'court'. Compare Czech DVORAK.

Dworkin (649) Jewish (eastern Ashkenazic): metronymic from a pet form of the Yiddish female personal name *Dvoyre* (from the Hebrew name *Devorah*, literally 'bee', whence English *Deborah*). The name *Devorah* was borne in the Bible by Rebecca's nurse (Genesis 35:8) and by a prophetess and judge (Judges 4:4). The popularity of the Yiddish name is due largely to the latter.

GIVEN NAMES Jewish 6%. *Chaim* (2), *Sol* (2), *Amram*, *Miriam*, *Moshe*.

Dworshak (110) **1.** Altered spelling of Czech **Dvořák** (see DVORAK). **2.** Altered spelling of Slovenian **Dvoršak**, derivative of *dvor* 'farmyard', 'manor house'. Compare German HOFFMANN.

Dworsky (189) Jewish (eastern Ashkenazic): **1.** habitational name from places called Dvortsy, or (Novy) Dvor, in Belarus and Ukraine. **2.** topographic name from Polish *dworski* 'manorial'. Compare DWORAK.

GIVEN NAMES Jewish 7%. *Meyer* (3), *Baila*.

Dwyer (11340) Irish: reduced Anglicized form of Gaelic **Ó Dubhuidhir**, a variant of **Ó Duibhidhir** (see DIVER) 'descendant of *Duibhuidhir*', a personal name composed of the elements *dubh* 'dark', 'black' + *odhar* 'sallow', 'tawny'.

GIVEN NAMES Irish 5%. *Brendan* (4), *Parnell* (3), *Liam* (2), *Brigid*, *Cormac*, *Oonagh*, *Patrick Michael*.

Dy (258) Filipino: unexplained.

GIVEN NAMES Spanish 25%. *Jose* (6), *Elpidio* (2), *Octavio* (2), *Alberto*, *Andres*, *Angelito*, *Benito*, *Erlinda*, *Ernesto*, *Estela*, *Felicisimo*, *Felipe*.

Dyal (715) **1.** English: of uncertain origin; possibly an altered form of Irish DOYLE. Compare DIAL. **2.** Indian: variant spelling of DAYAL.

Dyar (698) Probably an altered spelling of English and Irish DYER.

Dyas (347) English (Shropshire): of uncertain derivation. Reaney suggests it may be topographic for someone who lived at the 'dye-house', from Old English *dēag* + *hūs*.

Dybala (93) Polish (**Dybała**): nickname from *dybać* 'to lurk', 'to watch for somebody'.

GIVEN NAMES Polish 6%. *Pawel*, *Tomasz*.

Dybas (208) Polish (**Dybaś**): nickname from *dybać* 'to lurk', 'to watch for somebody'.

GIVEN NAMES Polish 5%. *Janina*, *Miroslaw*, *Zbigniew*.

Dybdahl (145) Norwegian: habitational name from a widespread farm name composed of *dyb* 'deep' + *dal* 'valley'.

GIVEN NAMES Scandinavian 9%. *Bjorn*, *Johan*.

Dyce (143) English: variant spelling of DICE.

Dyche (370) Jewish (eastern Ashkenazic): Americanized spelling of Yiddish *Daykhe*, a female personal name of uncertain origin.

Dyches (406) Jewish (eastern Ashkenazic): Americanized spelling of Yiddish *Daykhes*, metronymic from the female personal name Daykhe, of uncertain origin.

Dyck (652) Dutch: topographic name for someone who lived by a dike, Dutch *dijk*. Compare DYKE.

Dyckman (203) Dutch: occupational name for someone who tended a dike, Dutch *dijk* + *man* 'man'.

Dycus (745) Americanized spelling of Dutch DYKHUIS.

Dye (9790) English: from a pet form of the personal name DENNIS. In Britain the surname is most common in Norfolk, but frequent also in Yorkshire.

Dyer (17694) **1.** English: occupational name for a dyer of cloth, Middle English *dyer* (from Old English *dēag* 'dye'; the verb is a back-formation from the agent noun). This surname also occurs in Scotland, but LISTER is a more common equivalent there. **2.** Irish (Counties Sligo and Roscommon): usually a short form of **MacDyer**, an Anglicized form of Gaelic **Mac Duibhir** 'son of *Duibhir*', a short form of a personal name composed of the elements *dubh* 'dark', 'black' + *odhar* 'sallow', 'tawny'.

Dyes (115) **1.** Americanized spelling of German DEIS. **2.** English: probably a variant of DICE or DYE.

GIVEN NAME German 7%. *Uwe* (3).

Dyess (1153) **1.** Americanized spelling of German DEIS. **2.** English: unexplained. Possibly a variant of DICE or DYE.

Dygert (476) Probably an altered spelling of German **Deikert** or **Teikert**, both from old compound personal names formed with Old High German *dīhan* 'to thrive' or *diot* 'people' as a first element.

Dyk (216) **1.** Dutch: variant spelling of DYCK. **2.** Czech: from a short form of the personal name *Benedikt* (see BENEDICT).

Dykas (152) Polish: possibly a nickname from a dialect term *dykas* 'fat', 'pot-bellied'.

Dyke (1998) **1.** English: from Middle English *diche*, *dike*, Old English *dīc* 'dike', 'earthwork', hence a metonymic occupational name for a ditcher or a topographic name for someone who lived by a ditch or dike. The medieval dike was larger and more prominent than the modern ditch, and was usually constructed for purposes of defense rather than drainage. **2.** Americanized spelling of Dutch **Dijk** (see DYCK).

Dykema (641) Frisian: derivative of DYK.

Dykeman (525) Probably a translation of Dutch DYCKMAN.

Dykes (4891) English and Scottish: variant of DYKE. The Scottish name may also derive in part from any of several places named Dykes, although Black singles out one in the barony of Avondale or Strathaven in Lanarkshire.

Dykhouse (199) Partly Americanized form of Dutch **Dijkhuis** (see DYKHUIS).

Dykhuis (106) Variant spelling of Dutch **Dijkhuis**, a topographic name for someone who lived in a house by a dike, from *dijk* 'dike', 'ditch' + *huis* 'house'.

Dykhuizen (128) Variant (plural) of Dutch **Dijkhuis** (see DYKHOUSE), or a habitational name from Dijkhuizen in Gelderland.

GIVEN NAMES Dutch 4%. *Marinus, Willem.*

Dykman (328) Dutch: variant spelling of DYCKMAN; a variant of DYCK.

GIVEN NAMES German 4%. *Claus, Viktor.*

Dykstra (2971) Frisian: topographic name for someone who lived in the vicinity of a dike, from a locative agent noun based on Old Frisian *dīk* 'dike'.

Dylewski (162) Polish: habitational name for someone from any of various places called Dylew or Dylewo.

Dylla (139) German: probably a Westphalian variant of THIELE.

Dym (109) Jewish (eastern Ashkenazic): ornamental name from Polish *dym* 'smoke'.

GIVEN NAMES Jewish 14%. *Chaim* (2), *Emanuel, Hyman, Meyer, Miriam.*

Dymek (220) Polish and Czech (**Dýmek**): nickname from a diminutive of Polish *dym*, Czech *dým* 'smoke'.

GIVEN NAMES Polish 14%. *Jerzy* (3), *Waclaw* (2), *Bogumil, Boleslaw, Bronislaw, Kazimierz, Zofia.*

Dyment (219) English: variant of DIAMOND 2.

Dymond (644) English and Irish: variant of DIAMOND 2 and 3.

Dynan (122) Irish: variant spelling of DINAN.

Dynes (324) Irish (of English origin): patronymic from DAIN.

Dyrdahl (104) Norwegian: habitational name from a farm so named, from *dyr* 'deer', 'elk', 'moose' + Old Norse *dalr* 'valley'.

GIVEN NAME Scandinavian 7%. *Nels* (2).

Dysart (761) Scottish: habitational name from any of various places, for example those in Fife and Angus, named from Gaelic *dìseart* 'hermit's cell', 'church' (from Latin *desertum* 'desert', 'waste', 'solitary spot').

Dysert (187) Scottish: variant spelling of DYSART.

Dysinger (228) Americanized spelling of German **Deisinger**, a habitational name for someone from Deising in Bavaria.

Dyson (3811) **1.** English (chiefly Yorkshire): metronymic from DYE. **2.** Possibly an Americanized spelling of Danish, German, and Norwegian THEISEN or German THEISSEN.

Dziadosz (124) Polish: **1.** from a pet form of an Old Polish personal name such as *Dziadumił* or *Biezdziad*. **2.** from a derivative of *dziad* 'grandfather', 'old man'.

GIVEN NAME Polish 6%. *Ryszard* (2).

Dziak (246) **1.** Polish: Polonized form of *diak*, originally denoting a clerk in the chancellery of the dukes of Ruthenia; later a singer in the Orthodox Church. **2.** Slovak: unexplained.

Dzialo (180) Polish (**Działo**): nickname from *działać* 'to do or act', or alternatively a metonymic occupational name from *działo* 'gun', 'cannon'.

GIVEN NAME Polish 4%. *Casimir.*

Dziedzic (770) Polish: status name from Polish *dziedzic* 'landowner', 'squire'.

GIVEN NAMES Polish 11%. *Jerzy* (3), *Ryszard* (3), *Alicja* (2), *Zbigniew* (2), *Augustyn, Bogdan, Boleslaw, Casimir, Halina, Ignatius, Irena, Janina.*

Dziekan (182) Polish: occupational name from *dziekan* 'dean', 'deacon'.

GIVEN NAMES Polish 8%. *Grzegorz, Jacek, Jolanta, Kazimierz, Wladyslaw.*

Dzik (181) **1.** Polish: nickname from *dzik* 'wild boar'. **2.** Ukrainian: unexplained.

GIVEN NAMES Polish 6%. *Ewa, Tadeusz, Waclaw.*

Dzikowski (158) Polish and Jewish (Ashkenazic): habitational name for someone from any of the many places called Dzikowo or Dzików, from Polish *dzik* 'wild boar' + the possessive suffix *-ów*, often used in forming place names.

GIVEN NAMES Polish 9%; Slavic 4%; German 4%. *Casimir, Danuta, Jaroslaw, Ryszard, Zofia; Kazmer* (2); *Juergen.*

Dziuba (231) **1.** Polish: from a derivative of *dziub* 'nose', 'peak', also sometimes applied as a nickname for someone with a pock-marked complexion. **2.** Ukrainian and Jewish (from Ukraine): nickname from Ukrainian *dzyuba* 'pock-marked person'.

GIVEN NAMES Polish 10%. *Czeslaw, Janusz, Jerzy, Ryszard, Stanislaw, Urzula, Zofia, Zosia.*

Dziuk (216) Polish and Ukrainian: from the dialect word *dziuk* 'palmer'.

GIVEN NAMES German 4%. *Aloys, Florian, Fritz.*

Dziura (117) Polish: nickname from *dziura* 'hole', also applied to a place that was a 'hole' and for someone who never stopped talking.

GIVEN NAMES Polish 28%. *Casimir* (2), *Zofia* (2), *Dorota, Eugeniusz, Janusz, Kazimierz, Leszek, Pawel, Tadeusz, Wieslaw, Wladyslaw.*

E

Eachus (229) English (Cheshire): habitational name from any of various minor places named with Old English *ēcels* 'additional part of an estate', from *ēcan* 'to increase'. Compare ETCHELLS.
FOREBEARS The earliest record of this surname is in Church Minshull, Cheshire, England, in 1566, when John, son of Thomas Eachus, was baptized. Peter Eachus married Margaret Pownall in Church Minshull on 21 April 1594.

Eacker (132) Altered spelling of German ECKER.

Eacret (133) Origin unidentified.
GIVEN NAME Jewish 4%. *Hershel* (2).

Eaddy (769) English: from a pet form of EADE.

Eade (278) **1.** English and Scottish: from a Middle English short form of *Adam*, found mainly in Scotland and northern England. **2.** English: from *Eda*, a Middle English short form of the female personal name *Edith* (Old English *Ēadgȳð* 'prosperity battle'). **3.** Americanized spelling of Norwegian EIDE.

Eader (138) Respelling of German EDER.

Eades (1834) English: patronymic or metronymic from EADE.

Eadie (511) Scottish spelling of *Eady*, a pet form of EADE.

Eads (3078) English: patronymic or metronymic from EADE.

Eady (1067) English: from a pet form of EADE.

Eagan (2302) Irish: variant spelling of EGAN.

Eagar (207) English: variant of EDGAR.

Eagen (414) Irish: variant spelling of EGAN.
GIVEN NAMES Irish 4%. *Conal, Keane.*

Eager (868) English: variant of EDGAR.

Eagerton (112) English: variant of EDGERTON.

Eagle (2877) **1.** English (mainly East Anglia): nickname for a lordly, impressive, or sharp-eyed man, from Middle English *egle* 'eagle' (from Old French *aigle*, from Latin *aquila*). **2.** English (of Norman origin): habitational name from Laigle in Orne, France, the name of which ostensibly means 'the eagle', although it is possible that the recorded forms result from the operation of early folk etymology on some unknown original. Matilda de Aquila is recorded in 1129 as the widow of Robert Mowbray, Earl of Northumberland. **3.** Jewish: translation into English of ADLER.

Eagleburger (107) Americanized form of German **Adelberger**, a habitational name for someone from a place called Adelberg near Stuttgart.

Eagles (421) English: **1.** patronymic from EAGLE. **2.** Americanized form of French **Eglise**, a topographic name for someone who lived near a church (Old French *eclise*, from Latin *ecclesia*; compare ECCLES).

Eagleson (468) Scottish and northern Irish: altered form of **Eaglesham**, a habitational name from an old barony so named in Renfrewshire.

Eagleston (114) English: variant of EGGLESTON.

Eagleton (382) English: variant of EGGLETON.

Eaglin (386) English: possibly a variant of EAGLE.

Eagon (191) Variant of Irish EAGAN or German **Egon**.

Eaken (138) Variant spelling of Irish or English EAKIN.

Eaker (895) **1.** English: variant of EDGAR. **2.** Perhaps also a respelling of German ECKER or EGGER.

Eakes (598) Origin unidentified. This surname is concentrated in NC. **1.** Family tradition has it that this name is from northern Ireland, perhaps an Anglicized form of Scottish MCEACHIN. This is consistent with the Anglicized form of other names of Gaelic origin. **2.** Alternatively, it may be an Americanized spelling of German ECKES.

Eakin (1544) **1.** Irish: variant of EGAN. **2.** English and Irish: from a pet form of any of the personal names mentioned at EADE.

Eakins (1170) English: patronymic or metronymic from EAKIN.

Eakle (357) Americanized spelling of German ECKEL.

Eakman (120) Americanized spelling of Dutch **Eeckman**, **Eekman**, an occupational name for someone who gauged the contents of barrels.

Eales (174) English: patronymic from a medieval personal name of uncertain origin, probably a short form of any of several Old English personal names beginning with the elements *Ægel-*, *Æðel-*, or *Ealh-*.

Ealey (514) English: variant spelling of ELY.

Ealy (1090) English: variant spelling of ELY.

Eames (1147) English: **1.** probably from the possessive case of the Middle English word *eam* 'uncle', denoting a retainer in the household of the uncle of some important local person. **2.** possibly also a variant of AMES.

Eanes (1002) **1.** Perhaps a variant of English EAMES. In the U.S., this name is found predominantly in VA. **2.** Portuguese: variant of ANES.

Eardley (353) English (Staffordshire): habitational name, probably from a place called Ardley in Oxfordshire, named in Old English as 'the clearing (*lēeah*) of Eardwulf'.

Eargle (335) See ERGLE. This surname is concentrated in SC.

Earhart (1380) Americanized spelling of German EHRHARDT.

Earl (5158) English: originally, like most of the English names derived from the ranks of nobility, either a nickname or an occupational name for a servant employed in a noble household. The vocabulary word is a native one, from Old English *eorl* 'nobleman', and in the Middle Ages was often used as an equivalent of Norman *count*.

Earle (3240) English: variant spelling of EARL.

Earles (909) English: patronymic from EARL.

Earley (3588) **1.** Irish and English: variant spelling of EARLY. **2.** Americanized spelling of German EHRLE.

Earll (235) English: variant spelling of EARL.

Earls (1894) English: from EARL with genitive *-s*, probably referring to a servant or retainer of a particular earl.

Early (5148) **1.** Irish: translation of Gaelic **Ó Mocháin** (see MOHAN; Gaelic *moch* means 'early' or 'timely'), or of some other similar surname, for example **Ó Mochóir**, a shortened form of **Ó Mochéirghe**, **Ó Maoil-Mhochéirghe**, from a personal name meaning 'early rising'. **2.** English: habitational name from any of various places, such as Earley in Berkshire and Arley in Cheshire, Lancashire, Warwickshire, and Worcestershire, which derive their names from Old English *earn* 'eagle' + *lēah* 'woodland clearing'. **3.** English: nickname from Old English *eorllīc* 'manly', 'noble', a derivative of *eorl* (see EARL). **4.** Americanized spelling of German EHRLE.

Earlywine (324) Americanized spelling of German **Erlewein** (see ERLEWINE).

Earman (118) Probably an Americanized spelling of German EHRMANN.

Earnest (2943) **1.** Americanized form of German ERNST. **2.** English: variant spelling of ERNEST.

Earney (247) English and northern Irish: shortened form of *McInerny*, which sometimes also appears as **Nerney**.

Earnhardt (648) Americanized spelling of German **Ehrenhardt**, a variant of EHRHARDT.

Earnhart (472) Americanized spelling of German **Ehrenhardt**, a variant of EHRHARDT.

Earnheart (211) Americanized spelling of German **Ehrenhardt**, a variant of EHRHARDT.

Earnshaw (389) English: habitational name from a place in Lancashire, named in Old English as 'eagle's nook' or 'Earn's nook', from Old English *halh* 'nook' (see HALE). *Earn* is the Old English word meaning 'eagle'; it is also found as a personal name.

Earnst (100) Americanized spelling of German and Jewish ERNST.

Earp (1445) **1.** English (Midlands): nickname for a dark-complexioned man, from Old English *earp* 'swarthy'. **2.** Americanized spelling of German ERP.

Earthman (118) Americanized form of German ERDMANN.

Earwood (565) English: perhaps an altered spelling of YARWOOD.

Eary (200) English (Essex): perhaps a variant of AIREY.

Eash (557) Americanized form of Swiss German ISCH. This name is concentrated in IN and PA.

Easler (464) Americanized spelling of German and Swiss German ISLER or ESLER, found predominantly in SC.

Easley (5226) **1.** Americanized form of German EISELE. Compare ISLEY. **2.** English: unexplained. This name is quite widespread in Britain.

Easlick (126) English (Devon and Cornwall): variant of ESLICK.

Easom (255) English: variant of EASON.

Eason (5344) **1.** English: patronymic from EADE. **2.** Scottish and Irish: alternate Anglicization of Gaelic **Mac Aoidh** (see McKAY).

East (4451) English: topographic name for someone who lived in the eastern part of a town or settlement, or outside it to the east, or a regional name for someone who had migrated from the east of a place. As an American family name, this surname has absorbed various other European names with similar meaning.

Eastburn (611) English: habitational name from either of two places, one in Humberside and one in West Yorkshire, so named from Old English *ēast, ēasten* 'east' + *burna* 'stream'.

Eastep (481) Altered spelling of English **Eastop**, a habitational name from a place in Shropshire called Easthope, named with Old English *ēst* 'east', 'eastern' + *hop* 'enclosed valley'.

Easter (3805) **1.** English: topographic name for someone living to the east of a main settlement, from Middle English *easter* 'eastern', Old English *ēasterra*, in form a comparative of *ēast* 'east' (see EAST). **2.** English: habitational name from a group of villages in Essex, named from Old English *eowestre* 'sheepfold'. **3.** English: nickname for someone who had some connection with the festival of Easter, such as being born or baptized at that time (Old English *ēastre*, perhaps from the name of a pagan festival connected with the dawn). **4.** Translation of the German family name OSTER.

Easterbrook (262) English: topographic name for someone who lived by a brook to the east of a main settlement, from Middle English *easter* 'eastern' (see EASTER 1) + *brook* 'stream'.

Easterday (1025) Translation of the German family name OSTERTAG.

Easterlin (147) Americanized form of German **Österlin**: **1.** from the personal name *Österlin*, composed of the elements *oster* 'Easter' + the hypocoristic suffix *-lin*, thus denoting a child born on Easter Day. **2.** nickname for someone living to the east of a settlement or coming from a place in the east, from late Middle High German *ost* 'east'.

Easterling (2624) **1.** Americanized form of German OESTERLING. **2.** English: derivative of EASTER 1, with the addition of the Germanic suffix *-ling*.

Easterly (907) Americanized form of German OESTERLE or a variant of the English topographic name **Eastley**, from Old English *ēast* 'east' + *lēah* 'woodland clearing'.

Easterwood (668) Translation of German **Osterholz**, a habitational name from any of several places in northern Germany or Württemberg.

Eastes (237) English: variant of EAST. Compare ESTES.

Eastham (880) English: habitational name, now chiefly found in Lancashire, from any of various places so named from Old English *ēast* 'east' + *hām* 'homestead' or *hamm* 'river meadow'. There are places so named in Cheshire, Somerset, and Worcestershire, the first of which seems to have contributed most to the surname.

Eastin (711) Probably a variant spelling of Scottish or English EASTON.

Eastlack (103) Probably a variant of English **Eastlake** (see ESLICK).

Eastland (455) English: habitational name from any of various minor places named in Old English as *ēast land* 'the eastern estate'.

Eastlick (188) English (Devon and Cornwall): variant of ESLICK.

Eastling (130) English: unexplained; possibly a topographic name for someone who lived in the eastern part of a settlement.

Eastlund (149) Americanized form of Swedish **Östlund** (see OSTLUND).

GIVEN NAMES Scandinavian 4%. *Erik, Nels*.

Eastman (6531) English: **1.** topographic name, a variant of EAST. **2.** variant of EASTMOND.

Eastmond (114) English: from the Old English personal name *Ēastmund*, composed of the elements *ēast* 'grace' (or *ēast* 'east') + *mund* 'protection'. The name survived the Norman Conquest, although it was never very frequent, and is attested in the 13th and 14th centuries in the forms *Estmund* and *Es(t)mond*.

Easton (3856) Scottish and English: habitational name from any of the numerous places so called. Most are from Old English *ēast* 'east' + *tūn* 'enclosure', 'settlement'; examples in Devon and the Isle of Wight get their names from the Old English phrase *beēastan tūne* '(place) to the east of the settlement'. Another in Devon gets its first element from the genitive case of the Old English personal name *Ælfrīc* (composed of the elements *ælf* 'elf' + *rīc* 'power') or *Aðelrīc* (composed of the elements *aðel* 'noble' + *rīc* 'power'). One in Essex is from Old English *ēg* 'island' + *stān(as)* 'stone(s)'. Finally Easton Neston in Northamptonshire gets its name from Old English *Ēadstānestūn* 'settlement of *Ēadstān*', a personal name composed of the elements *ēad* 'prosperity', 'riches' + *stān* 'stone'.

FOREBEARS Nicholas Easton (1593–1675) was a tanner by trade who emigrated from Wales to MA in 1634, bringing his two sons with him on the *Mary and John*. He first settled at Ipswich, and in 1638 settled at Pocasset (Portsmouth) in RI, where he was governor in 1672–74. He had nine children.

Eastridge (710) Origin uncertain. **1.** Possibly English, a habitational name from any of various minor places named Eastridge, for example in Wiltshire and West Sussex. However, the surname is not known in the British Isles. **2.** It may alternatively be of German origin, an Americanized form of **Estrich**, a topographic name for someone who lived by a paved road (Middle High German *esterich*, from Late Latin *astricus*), or an Americanized form of OESTERREICH.

Eastwood (2011) English: habitational name from any of various places called Eastwood. Most, such as the one in Essex, get the name from Old English *ēast* 'east' + *wudu* 'wood', but an example in Nottinghamshire originally had as its final element Old Norse *þveit* 'meadow' (see THWAITES).

Eatherly (189) Probably an altered spelling of English ATHERLEY. This name is found chiefly in TN.

Eatherton (210) English: probably a variant spelling of ATHERTON.

Eatman (296) See EATMON.

Eatmon (596) Probably a variant of English EDMAN.

Eaton (17798) English: habitational name from any of the numerous places so named from Old English *ēa* 'river' or *ēg* 'island', 'low-lying land' + *tūn* 'enclosure', 'settlement'.

FOREBEARS Nathaneal Eaton, born in Coventry, England, in about 1609, came to MA in 1637 and was the first head of Harvard College, in 1638–39.

Eavenson (264) Altered spelling of Welsh EVANSON.

Eaves (2876) English: metronymic from the medieval female personal name EVE.

Eavey (134) Origin uncertain. **1.** Possibly an altered spelling of English AVEY. However, this name is not known in the British Isles. **2.** It is also said to be an altered form of German **Ebby**, of unexplained origin; perhaps a variant of EBBEN or EWIG.

Ebach (100) German: habitational name from a place named Ebach in Franconia.
GIVEN NAME French 4%. *Collette.*

Ebanks (415) English (Midlands): probably a variant of EUBANKS.

Ebarb (363) Said to be an Americanized form of the Hispanic name YBARBO. This name is found predominantly in LA, where there is also a place so called.

Ebaugh (369) Americanized form of German IBACH.

Ebben (322) North German: patronymic from a short form of EBBERT.

Ebbers (202) North German: patronymic from EBBERT.
GIVEN NAMES German 5%. *Erwin, Gerhard, Kurt.*

Ebbert (569) Dutch and North German: from a Germanic personal name composed of the elements *agi(l)* 'edge', 'point (of a weapon)' + *berht* 'bright', 'famous'. This was one of the most popular names among the peoples living in the Low Countries in the Middle Ages. The English cognate *Egbert* is not found as a surname, despite the fame of King Egbert of Wessex.

Ebberts (121) Dutch: patronymic from the personal name EBBERT.

Ebbing (138) North German: patronymic from a short form of EBBERT.

Ebbs (256) **1.** English: metronymic or patronymic from *Ebbe*, a pet form of ISABEL or HERBERT. **2.** North German: patronymic from a short form of EBBERT.

Ebel (1476) North German and Dutch: from a pet form EBBERT.

Ebeling (1026) North German: patronymic from EBEL.
GIVEN NAMES German 5%. *Otto* (3), *Gerd* (2), *Klaus* (2), *Kurt* (2), *Dieter, Erhardt, Erwin, Gerhard, Theodor.*

Ebell (104) Dutch and German: from a pet form of the personal name EBBERT.
GIVEN NAMES Spanish 8%. *Fernando* (2), *Alfonso, Alicia, Andres, Hilario, Horacio.*

Eben (169) German (also common in the Czech lands): habitational name for someone from a place of this name in Bavaria.
GIVEN NAMES German 7%. *Hermann* (2), *Gunther, Kurt.*

Eber (442) **1.** South German: from a short form of any of the various Germanic compound personal names formed with *eber* 'boar'. **2.** South German: from Middle High German *eber* 'boar', applied as nickname for a man of strength or as a habitational name for someone who lived at a house distinguished by the sign of boar. **3.** Jewish (Ashkenazic): from German *Eber* 'boar' (see 1), most likely a name assigned by Christian government officials.
GIVEN NAMES Jewish 5%. *Dov, Eliahu, Miriam, Sheva, Yehuda.*

Eberhard (907) German: variant spelling of EBERHARDT.
GIVEN NAMES German 4%. *Dieter, Erhard, Heinz, Helmuth, Kurt.*

Eberhardt (2527) German: from a Germanic personal name composed of the elements *eber* 'wild boar' (Old High German, Old Saxon *ebur*) + *hard* 'brave', 'hardy', 'strong'.

Eberhardy (114) Americanized form of German EBERHARDT.
GIVEN NAME German 4%. *Mathias.*

Eberhart (1766) German: variant of EBERHARDT.

Eberl (176) German (Bavarian): from a pet form of EBERHARDT.
GIVEN NAMES German 8%. *Hans* (3), *Dieter, Kurt, Wolfgang.*

Eberle (2520) German (Swabian) and Swiss German: from a pet form of EBERHARDT.
GIVEN NAMES German 4%. *Erwin* (2), *Gerhard* (2), *Horst* (2), *Kurt* (2), *Otto* (2), *Alois, Christoph, Erhard, Ernst, Georg, Gernot, Guenther.*

Eberlein (363) German (Swabian) and Swiss German: variant of EBERLE.
GIVEN NAMES German 5%. *Erwin* (2), *Arno, Dietmar, Irmgard, Ralf.*

Eberlin (173) German (Alemannic): variant of EBERLE.

Eberline (118) Americanized spelling of EBERLEIN, especially in French-speaking areas.
GIVEN NAME French 5%. *Patrice.*

Eberling (252) Altered form of German EBERLEIN.
GIVEN NAMES German 4%. *Kurt* (2), *Georg.*

Eberly (1747) Swiss German: variant of EBERLE.

Ebers (197) North German: patronymic from *Ebert*, a Low German form of EBERHARDT.

Ebersold (197) Swiss German: see EBERSOLE.

Ebersole (1587) Altered spelling of the Swiss habitational names **Ebersol, Ebersold, Äbersold, Aebersold**, from any of several places so named, from Middle High

German *eber* 'wild boar' + *sol, sul* 'wallow'.

Eberspacher (143) German: habitational name from any of several southern German places named Ebersbach (from Middle High German *eber* 'wild boar' + *bach* 'creek', 'stream') + -*er* suffix denoting origin.
GIVEN NAMES German 6%. *Kurt, Otto.*

Ebert (5322) North German: from a Germanic personal name composed of the elements *eber* 'wild boar' + *hard* 'brave', 'hardy', 'strong'.

Eberts (385) German (Rhineland): patronymic from EBERT.

Eberwein (277) German: from a Germanic personal name composed of the elements *eber* 'wild boar' + *win* 'friend'.

Ebey (178) Swiss German: see EBY.

Ebinger (330) **1.** German: habitational name from any of various places in Bavaria named Ebing or from Ebingen in Württemberg, the -*er* suffix denoting origin. **2.** Americanized form of **Aebinger** (see AVINGER).

Eble (364) **1.** German: variant of EBLEN. **2.** Americanized spelling of EBEL.

Eblen (417) German (Württemberg): from a pet form of EBERHARDT.

Eblin (180) Swiss German: variant of EBLEN.

Ebling (555) North German: variant of EBELING.

Ebner (1469) South German: topographic name for someone who lived on a piece of flat ground or a plateau, from Middle High German *ebene* 'plateau' + -*er*, suffix denoting an inhabitant.
GIVEN NAMES German 4%. *Kurt* (3), *Fritz* (2), *Aloysius, Arno, Christoph, Erhard, Frieda, Hans, Markus, Reinhard, Wolfgang.*

Ebnet (144) German: topographic name for someone who lived on a plain near mountains, from Middle High German *eben* 'flat', or a habitational name from a place so called, in particular one near Freiburg.
GIVEN NAMES German 4%. *Klaus, Reinhard.*

Ebrahim (146) Muslim: from the personal name *Ibrāhīm*, Arabic form of ABRAHAM.
GIVEN NAMES Muslim 77%; German 4%. *Ahmed* (5), *Mohamed* (5), *Azmy* (3), *Maher* (2), *Mehboob* (2), *Sadruddin* (2), *Salah* (2), *Sami* (2), *Yasser* (2), *Abbas, Abdul, Adil; Kurt* (3).

Ebrahimi (181) Muslim: from an adjectival derivative of EBRAHIM.
GIVEN NAMES Muslim 65%; Armenian 4%. *Ali* (5), *Mohammad* (4), *Ahmad* (3), *Mehdi* (3), *Ebrahim* (2), *Hadi* (2), *Hassan* (2), *Mohsen* (2), *Abbas, Ali Reza, Alireza, Arshia; Anahid, Anoush, Arshak, Roobik, Rouben.*

Ebright (535) Americanized form of German **Ebrecht**, a variant of EGGEBRECHT.

Ebron (292) Probably a variant of HEBRON. This name is found chiefly in NC.

Ebsen (137) North German: patronymic from a pet form of the personal name EGGEBRECHT.

Eby (2590) Americanized spelling of Swiss German **Ăbi**, **Ăby**, **Aby**, **Aebi**, or **Ebi**, from a pet form of EBERHARDT.

Eccher (150) Variant of German ECKER, from South Tyrol, a German-speaking region in northern Italy.
GIVEN NAMES Italian 4%. *Aldo*, *Domenica*, *Silvio*, *Vittorio*.

Eccles (1110) English and Scottish: habitational name from places near Manchester, in Berwickshire Dumfriesshire, and elsewhere, all named from the British word that lies behind Welsh *eglwys* 'church' (from Latin *ecclesia*, Greek *ekklēsia* 'gathering', 'assembly'). Such places would have been the sites of notable pre-Anglo-Saxon churches or Christian communities.

Eccleston (663) English: habitational name from any of several places so named in Cheshire and Lancashire, which get their names from an ancient British word meaning 'church' (see ECCLES) + Old English *tūn* 'enclosure', 'settlement'.

Echard (327) Swiss French spelling of German ECKHARDT.

Echavarria (269) Spanish (**Echavarría**): variant of **Echevarría**, a Castilianized form of Basque **Etxeberria** (see ECHEVARRIA).
GIVEN NAMES Spanish 47%. *Jose* (9), *Angel* (3), *Jesus* (3), *Juan* (3), *Mario* (3), *Adriana* (2), *Alejandro* (2), *Carlos* (2), *Fernando* (2), *Guillermo* (2), *Julio* (2), *Luz* (2).

Echelbarger (127) Americanized spelling of German EICHELBERGER.

Echelberger (139) Americanized spelling of German EICHELBERGER.

Echerd (120) Probably an altered spelling of German **Eckerdt** (see ECKERT).

Echevarria (1016) Spanish form (**Echevarría**) of Basque **Etxeberria**: topographic or habitational name from the Basque elements *etxe* 'house' + *berri* 'new' + the definite article *-a*. This is the origin of the name of a village near Pamplona, now called Xabier, the birthplace of St. Francis Xavier (1506–52), missionary to East Asia.
GIVEN NAMES Spanish 46%. *Jose* (25), *Pedro* (11), *Carlos* (10), *Juan* (10), *Luis* (10), *Angel* (8), *Manuel* (8), *Miguel* (8), *Ramon* (8), *Roberto* (7), *Alberto* (6), *Jorge* (6).

Echeverri (177) Castilianized variant of Basque **Etxeverri**, a town in Navarre province, Basque Country, from a topographic name from the Basque elements *etxe* 'house' + *berri* 'new'.
GIVEN NAMES Spanish 53%. *Jose* (6), *Luis* (6), *Carlos* (5), *Diego* (4), *Francisco* (4), *Arturo* (3), *Fernando* (3), *Alberto* (2), *Alfonso* (2), *Andres* (2), *Cesar* (2), *Mario* (2).

Echeverria (810) Spanish form (**Echeverría**) of Basque **Etxeberria** (see ECHEVARRIA).

GIVEN NAMES Spanish 50%. *Carlos* (18), *Jose* (16), *Luis* (14), *Juan* (13), *Raul* (12), *Jorge* (9), *Manuel* (9), *Julio* (7), *Eduardo* (6), *Rafael* (6), *Alberto* (5), *Alfonso* (5).

Echeverry (132) Variant of Basque **Etxeberri** (see ECHEVERRI).
GIVEN NAMES Spanish 56%. *Jose* (4), *Carlos* (3), *Julio* (3), *Cesar* (2), *Fernando* (2), *Jaime* (2), *Javier* (2), *Jorge* (2), *Mauricio* (2), *Rodrigo* (2), *Rosalba* (2), *Alejandro*.

Echols (4201) Respelling of German ECKELS.

Echternach (104) German: habitational name from a place so named in Luxembourg.

Eck (2981) **1.** German, Dutch, and Jewish (Ashkenazic): topographic name from Middle High German *ecke*, *egge* 'corner', German *Eck(e)* (Yiddish *ek*). This could have been the corner of two streets or, in the case of the German name, the corner of a field or area of land or a rocky outcrop. **2.** German: short form of any of the various Germanic compound personal names with a first element *agi(n)*, *agil* 'edge', 'point of a sword', akin to the word in 1 above. **3.** Swedish: topographic or ornamental name, from *ek* 'oak'.

Eckard (1107) German: variant of ECKERT.

Eckardt (448) German: variant of ECKERT.
GIVEN NAMES German 7%. *Kurt* (3), *Hans* (2), *Arno*, *Gunther*, *Heinz*, *Lothar*, *Otto*.

Eckart (688) German: variant of ECKERT.

Eckberg (309) Probably an altered spelling of Scandinavian EKBERG or a similar Norwegian compound.
GIVEN NAMES Scandinavian 5%; German 4%. *Gunner*, *Lars*; *Kurt* (2).

Eckdahl (100) Swedish: variant spelling EKDAHL.

Ecke (138) Dutch and German: variant of ECK.
GIVEN NAME German 6%; Scandinavian 4%. *Achim*.

Eckel (1062) South German: from a pet form of the personal name *Eckehard* (see ECKERT).

Eckelberry (167) Respelling of German **Eckelberg**, a northern variant of EICHELBERG.

Eckelkamp (147) North German: probably from Middle Low German *ekel* 'acorn' + *kamp* 'field', 'domain'; a topographic name for someone who lived by a field with oak trees, or for someone who owned such a piece of land.

Eckelman (136) German (**Eckelmann**): from an elaborated form of the personal name ECKEL.
GIVEN NAMES German 6%. *Hans*, *Kurt*, *Otto*.

Eckels (565) German: patronymic from ECKEL.

Eckenrod (229) Variant of North German ECKENRODE.

Eckenrode (893) North German: from Middle Low German *eke* 'oak' (plural *eken*) + *rot* 'cleared land'; a topographic name for someone who lived by a piece of land which had been cleared of oaks, or perhaps a nickname for some who owned a piece of such land.

Eckenroth (192) Variant of North German ECKENRODE.

Ecker (2055) **1.** Dutch and German: from a medieval personal name, probably a short form of *Eckhard* (see ECKERT). **2.** German: topographic name for someone who lived in a corner house or kept a corner shop, from Middle High German *ecke* 'corner' + the suffix *-er*, denoting an inhabitant. **3.** Jewish (Ashkenazic): variant of ECK 1. **4.** Jewish (eastern Ashkenazic): occupational name from a Yiddish dialect *eker* '(wood)cutter', 'chopper'. **5.** Jewish (eastern Ashkenazic): ornamental name from German *Ecker* 'beechnut'.

Eckerd (139) Variant spelling of German ECKERT.

Eckerle (320) South German: from a pet form or patronymic of ECKERT.

Eckerman (326) **1.** Americanized spelling of German ECKERMANN. **2.** Jewish: variant of ECK and ECKER 4.

Eckermann (115) German: topographic name for someone lived by the Ecker, a small river in the Harz Mountains.

Eckersley (209) English (Lancashire): habitational name from a lost place in the parish of Leigh, near Wigan, probably so named from the genitive case of the Old English personal name *Ecgheard* (see ECKERT) or *Ecghere* + Old English *lēah* 'woodland clearing'.

Eckerson (299) Patronymic from the Dutch personal name ECKER (see ECKERT).
FOREBEARS Jan Thomszen Eckerson came to America in 1669; his son Thomas Eckerson was born the same year. The family settled in Tappan, NY.

Eckert (7140) German: from a Germanic personal name composed of the elements *agi* 'edge', 'point' + *hard* 'hardy', 'brave', 'strong'.

Eckes (410) North German: patronymic from a short form of **Eckhardt** (see ECKERT).

Eckford (126) English and Scottish: habitational name from a place in Roxburghshire named Eckford.
FOREBEARS The surname Eckford appears in North America in the 18th and 19th centuries, most notably with a shipbuilder from Irvine, Scotland, named Henry Eckford (1775–1832). At age 16 he emigrated to Quebec, then to New York City (1796), where he ran shipyards and built steamboats, including the *Robert Fulton*.

Eckhardt (2010) Variant of German ECKERT.

Eckhart (1061) Variant of German ECKERT.

Eckhaus (106) Jewish (Ashkenazic): topographic or ornamental name from German *Eckhaus* 'corner house'.

GIVEN NAMES Jewish 21%. *Chaya* (2), *Baila*, *Irit*, *Isidor*, *Mordechai*, *Sol*.

Eckhoff (965) North German (Westphalia): topographic name for someone who lived on a farm surrounded by oaks or by an oak wood, from Middle Low German *eke* 'oak' + *hof* 'farmstead', 'manor farm'.

Eckholm (157) Respelling of Swedish EKHOLM.

GIVEN NAME Scandinavian 8%. *Erik*.

Eckl (180) South German: variant of ECKEL.

GIVEN NAME German 4%. *Otto*.

Eckland (188) Probably a respelling either of a Norwegian habitational name from several farmsteads named with *eik* 'oak' + *land* 'land', or of a Swedish ornamental compound with the same elements.

Eckler (494) South German: patronymic from ECKEL.

Eckles (898) Altered spelling of English ECCLES.

Eckley (705) **1.** English: variant of ACKLEY, found mainly in the Welsh marches. **2.** Americanized form of Swiss German EGLI.

Ecklund (935) Respelling of Swedish EKLUND.

GIVEN NAMES Scandinavian 4%. *Anders* (2), *Lars* (2), *Astrid*, *Gunvor*.

Eckman (1913) German (**Eckmann**) and Jewish: see ECKMANN.

Eckmann (289) German and Jewish: topographic name for someone who lived on a corner (see ECK).

GIVEN NAMES German 4%. *Claus*, *Gerhard*.

Eckols (105) Respelling of German ECKELS.

Eckrich (206) German: from a Germanic personal name composed of the elements *agi* 'edge (of a sword)' + *ric* 'power(ful)'.

GIVEN NAMES German 6%. *Kurt* (2), *Franz*, *Gunter*.

Eckrote (146) Variant of North German ECKENRODE.

Eckroth (311) Variant of North German ECKENRODE.

Eckstein (1996) **1.** German: from Middle High German *ecke* 'corner' + *stein* 'stone', hence a metonymic occupational name for a stonemason or bricklayer, or a topographic name for someone who lived by a rocky outcrop. **2.** Jewish (Ashkenazic): ornamental name from German *Eckstein* 'cornerstone' (see 1).

GIVEN NAMES Jewish 4%. *Meyer* (3), *Zvi* (3), *Isadore* (2), *Moshe* (2), *Yehuda* (2), *Abbe*, *Aharon*, *Aron*, *Ayal*, *Chana*, *Emanuel*, *Eran*.

Eckstine (119) Americanized spelling of German and Jewish ECKSTEIN.

Eckstrom (492) Altered spelling of Swedish **Ekström** (see EKSTROM).

Economides (128) Greek: patronymic meaning 'son of the steward', from ECONOMOS. The *-ides* patronymic is classical, and was revived in particular by Greeks

from the Black Sea during the late 19th and early 20th centuries.

GIVEN NAMES Greek 13%. *Constantine* (2), *Achilleas*, *Andreas*, *Demetre*, *Dimitrios*, *Lambros*, *Spyros*; *Mino* (2).

Economos (240) Greek: status name for a steward, someone who managed a property, particularly church-owned land, from ancient Greek *oikos* 'household' + *nomos* 'law', 'rule'.

GIVEN NAMES Greek 6%. *Andreas* (2), *Constantine* (2), *Soterios*, *Spiro*, *Themis*.

Economou (370) Greek: patronymic from the genitive form of ECONOMOS. Genitive patronymics are particularly associated with Cyprus.

GIVEN NAMES Greek 14%. *Ioannis* (2), *Christos*, *Costas*, *Demetrios*, *Demetris*, *Efthimios*, *Fotios*, *Fotis*, *Kaliopi*, *Kosta*, *Kostas*, *Lefteris*.

Economy (180) Americanized form of Greek ECONOMOS 'steward', or of the patronymic form ECONOMOU.

Ecton (219) English: habitational name from places in Northamptonshire and Staffordshire, so named from the Old English personal name *Ecca* + *tun* 'settlement', 'enclosure'.

Ector (234) Spanish and Portuguese: from a vernacular form of HECTOR.

Edberg (327) Swedish: ornamental name composed of the elements *ed* 'isthmus' + *berg* 'mountain'.

Edde (121) English: probably a variant of EADE. This name is also found in Normandy, France.

GIVEN NAMES French 6%. *Georges*, *Pierre*.

Eddie (340) English and Scottish: variant spelling of EDDY.

Eddinger (362) Variant spelling of German EDINGER.

Eddings (1227) English: patronymic from the Old English personal name *Eadda*.

Eddington (957) Scottish and English: variant spelling of EDINGTON.

Eddins (1427) English: variant of EDDINGS. This is a common name in TX, NC, and FL.

Eddleman (816) Americanized form of German EDELMANN.

Eddlemon (231) Americanized form of German EDELMANN.

Edds (311) English: perhaps, as Reaney suggests, a patronymic from a personal name, a short form of EDWIN or EDWARD, or for EADE 1.

Eddy (7618) English (Devon): from the Middle English personal name *Edwy*, Old English *Eadwig*, composed of the elements *ead* 'prosperity', 'fortune' + *wig* 'war'.

Ede (298) **1.** Southern English: variant spelling of EADE. **2.** North German: from the Germanic personal name *Edo*.

Edel (441) **1.** German: from a short form of the Germanic personal name *Edilo*, formed with Old High German *adal* 'tribe', 'family', 'nobility'. **2.** German: status name

from Middle High German *edel* 'noble'. See also EDELMANN. **3.** Jewish (Ashkenazic): from the Yiddish female personal name *Eydl*, meaning 'noble'. **4.** Jewish (Ashkenazic): ornamental name from modern German *edel* 'noble', 'splendid', 'fine'. See also ADEL 3.

GIVEN NAMES German 4%. *Erwin* (2), *Rudi* (2), *Alois*, *Bernhard*, *Ernst*.

Edelberg (114) Swedish and Jewish (Ashkenazic): ornamental name composed of German *edel* 'noble' + BERG 'hill'.

Edelbrock (135) **1.** Northwestern German: topographic name from *edel*, *adel* 'dirty water' (or possibly the personal name EDEL) + Low German *brök* 'swamp'. **2.** Variant of German **Edelbruch**, a habitational name from Edelbruch in Upper Austria.

GIVEN NAME German 4%. *Kurt*.

Edelen (845) Americanized spelling of French **Edeline**.

FOREBEARS Bearers of this name originally from Brittany were in Boucherville, Quebec, by 1675.

Edell (197) Altered spelling of German EDEL.

Edelman (2624) **1.** Respelling of German EDELMANN. **2.** Jewish (Ashkenazic): ornamental name from *edel* 'noble', 'splendid', 'fine' + *man* 'man'.

GIVEN NAMES Jewish 5%. *Meyer* (4), *Asher* (3), *Hyman* (3), *Miriam* (3), *Sol* (3), *Abbe*, *Beril*, *Golda*, *Irit*, *Isadore*, *Mayer*, *Rimma*.

Edelmann (290) **1.** German (**Edelmann**): status name, from Middle High German *edel* 'noble' + *man* 'man'. In the Middle Ages, the *Edelmann* ranked below the *Graf* and the *Ritter* and above the free citizens and the masses of the servile population. **2.** Jewish (Ashkenazic): variant spelling of EDELMAN.

GIVEN NAMES German 12%. *Kurt* (3), *Frieda*, *Gunther*, *Heinz*, *Helmuth*, *Manfred*, *Udo*, *Ute*, *Winfried*.

Edelson (626) Jewish (Ashkenazic): metronymic from EDEL 2.

GIVEN NAMES Jewish 5%. *Sol* (2), *Ari*, *Elihu*, *Yacov*.

Edelstein (1709) Jewish (Ashkenazic): ornamental name, from German *Edelstein* 'gem', 'precious stone'.

GIVEN NAMES Jewish 6%. *Sol* (7), *Emanuel* (2), *Hyman* (2), *Shmuel* (2), *Chaim*, *Chanie*, *Gitty*, *Hershel*, *Isadore*, *Liba*, *Meyer*, *Miriam*.

Eden (2622) **1.** English: from the Middle English personal name *Edun*, Old English *Eadhun*, composed of the elements *ead* 'prosperity', 'wealth' + *hun* 'bear-cub'. **2.** English: habitational name from Castle Eden or Eden Burn in County Durham, both of which derive from a British river name perhaps meaning 'water', recorded by the Greek geographer Ptolemy in the 2nd century AD in the form *Ituna*. **3.** German: habitational name any of several places, mainly in Bavaria and Austria, so named from Middle High German *œde* 'wasteland' + the dative suffix *-n*. **4.** Frisian: patronymic from the personal name *Ede*.

FOREBEARS Charles Eden (1673–1722), colonial governor of NC under the lords proprietors from 1714 onward, used the armorial bearings of the family of Eden of the county palatine of Durham in the north of England. Of the same connection was Sir Robert Eden, last royal governor of MD.

Edenfield (1054) Probably English: habitational name from a place in Greater Manchester (formerly in Lancashire), so named from Old English *ēg* 'well-watered land' + *tūn* 'farmstead', 'settlement' + *feld* 'open country'. However, there are no records of this as a surname in the British Isles today, and it may have been adopted by settlers on arrival in the U.S. This name is concentrated in the GA and FL.

Edens (2334) English: patronymic from EDEN 1.

Eder (1568) South German (also common in the Czech lands): topographic name for someone who lived on a patch of bare, uncultivated land, from Middle High German *(o)ed(e)* 'wasteland'. It may also be a habitational name from any of the numerous places named with this element.
GIVEN NAMES German 5%. *Otto* (3), *Alois* (2), *Fritz* (2), *Bernd*, *Erwin*, *Florian*, *Friedrich*, *Georg*, *Gerda*, *Hans*, *Heinz*, *Irmgard*.

Ederer (259) South German: variant of EDER.
GIVEN NAMES German 4%. *Kurt*, *Lothar*.

Edes (150) **1.** English: patronymic or metronymic from EADE. **2.** Hungarian (**Édes**): nickname from *édes* 'sweet' 'charming'.

Edgar (4603) Scottish and English: from the Old English personal name *Ēadgār*, composed of the elements *ēad* 'prosperity', 'fortune' + *gār* 'spear'. The name is found in Middle English in various forms, e.g. *Edgar*, *Adger*, *Agar*.

Edgcomb (101) English: variant spelling of EDGECOMBE.

Edge (3987) English: topographic name, especially in Lancashire and the West Midlands, for someone who lived on or by a hillside or ridge, from Old English *ecg* 'edge'. Compare ECK.

Edgecomb (504) English: variant spelling of EDGECOMBE.

Edgecombe (217) English: habitational name from Edgcumbe in Devon.

Edgell (732) English: probably from the Old English personal name *Ecgwulf*, meaning 'sword wolf'.

Edgeman (108) See EDGEMON.

Edgemon (308) Origin uncertain. **1.** Perhaps an altered spelling of English **Hedgeman**, a variant of HEDGE. **2.** Alternatively, it may be an Americanized form of German **Etschmann**, a topographic name from

Middle High German *ezzisch* 'open field', 'unenclosed cultivated land'.

Edger (154) English: variant spelling of EDGAR.

Edgerly (590) English: habitational name from any of numerous minor places named Edgerley, Edgerely, or Hedgerley.

Edgerton (1844) English: habitational name from either of two places, in Kent and Cheshire, called Egerton. The former is so called from Old English *Ecgheardingtūn* 'settlement (Old English *tūn*) associated with *Ecgheard*' (see ECKERT); the second, which is the main source of the surname, is more likely to have been named as the 'settlement of *Ecghere*' (in which the second element is Old English *here* 'army').

Edgett (299) English: from the Old English personal name *Ecggēat*, or in some cases perhaps from *Ecgheard* (see ECKERT).

Edgeworth (408) English: habitational name from places in Gloucestershire and Lancashire, so named from Old English *ecg* 'hillside', 'ridge' + *worð* 'enclosure'.

Edghill (114) English: variant of **Edgell**, from the Old English personal name *Ecgwulf* 'sword wolf'.

Edgin (350) English: unexplained.

Edgington (1086) English (West Midlands): probably a habitational name, of uncertain origin. It may be from a lost place, so named as the 'settlement (Old English *tūn*) associated with *Ecgi*', a short form of the various compound names with the first element *ecg* 'edge', 'point' (of a weapon). Alternatively, it may be a variant of **Erdington** (see EDRINGTON).

Edginton (103) English: variant spelling of EDGINGTON.

Edgley (161) English: habitational name from places in Cheshire and Shropshire named Edgeley, from Old English *edisc* 'enclosed pasture' + *lēah* 'woodland clearing'.

Edgmon (351) See EDGEMON.

Edgren (212) Swedish: ornamental name composed of the elements *ed* 'isthmus' + *gren* 'branch'.
GIVEN NAME Scandinavian 5%. *Lars*.

Edholm (114) Swedish: ornamental name composed of the elements *ed* 'isthmus' + *holm* 'small island'.
GIVEN NAME Scandinavian 10%. *Nels* (2).

Edick (490) Probably a variant of German **Addic** or **Eddix**, from short forms of a Germanic personal name formed with the Germanic element *adal* 'noble'.

Edie (547) English: probably from a pet form of EADE or a variant of EDDY.

Ediger (527) German: habitational name from Ediger, a place in the Mosel, or from Edigheim in the Palatinate.

Edin (193) French: from a pet form of the Germanic personal name *Edhard*.
GIVEN NAMES Scandinavian 4%. *Algot*, *Erik*, *Nils*.

Eding (103) German: probably a shortened form of EDINGER, or an altered spelling of **Edding**, a patronymic of the Low German and Frisian personal name *Addo*.

Edinger (1221) German: habitational name from any of several places called Edingen, including one northwest of Heidelberg.

Edington (1131) Northern English and Scottish: habitational name from any of various places so named, especially one in Northumbria originally named in Old English as *Idingtūn* 'settlement (Old English *tūn*) associated with *Ida*' (see IDE).

Edison (1130) English: patronymic or metronymic from EADE.

FOREBEARS The inventor Thomas Alva Edison, born in 1847 in Milan, OH, came from a Canadian family first established in North America by John Edison, a loyalist during the American Revolution, who served under the British General Richard Howe and went into exile in Nova Scotia after the Revolutionary War.

Edkins (123) English: patronymic or metronymic from a pet form of EADE.

Edleman (130) Americanized spelling of German and Jewish EDELMANN.

Edler (870) German: status name meaning 'nobleman' (see EDEL).
GIVEN NAMES German 4%. *Klaus* (2), *Eldred*, *Fritz*, *Hilde*, *Horst*, *Kurt*.

Edlin (498) English: from a personal name.

Edling (228) **1.** English: variant of EDLIN. **2.** German and Swedish: status name from Middle High German *edel* 'noble' (see EDELMAN) + *-ing* suffix denoting affiliation.
GIVEN NAMES Scandinavian 5%; German 4%. *Lars*, *Nils*; *Otto*.

Edlund (745) Swedish: ornamental name composed of the elements *ed* 'isthmus' + *lund* 'grove'.
GIVEN NAMES Scandinavian 5%. *Elof*, *Erik*, *Nels*, *Ragner*.

Edman (602) **1.** English: from the Old English personal name *Ēadmann* (unattested), meaning 'prosperity man'. Compare EDMOND. **2.** Scandinavian: Swedish: ornamental name composed of the elements *ed* 'isthmus' + *man* 'man'.
GIVEN NAMES Scandinavian 4%. *Erik*, *Swen*, *Thor*.

Edmands (135) English: variant of EDMAN.

Edminster (202) Probably a variant of Scottish EDMISTON.

Edmison (163) Scottish: variant of EDMISTON.

Edmisten (374) Variant of Scottish EDMISTON.

Edmister (156) Variant of Scottish EDMISTON.

Edmiston (1763) Scottish: habitational name from Edmonstone, near Edinburgh, so named from the Old English personal name *Ēadmund* (see EDMOND) + *tūn* 'settlement'.

Edmon (116) French variant of EDMOND.

Edmond (1748) Scottish, English, and French: from the Middle English personal name *Edmund* (Old English *Ēadmund*), composed of the elements *ēad* 'prosperity', 'fortune' + *mund* 'protection'. In medieval England and France the name was often bestowed in honor of the East Anglian King St. Edmund the Martyr (died 869), who was killed by pagan Danish invaders, and about whom many legends grew up.
GIVEN NAMES French 5%. *Curley* (2), *Monique* (2), *Amie*, *Andre*, *Cecile*, *Desire*, *Dumas*, *Jacques*, *Lucienne*, *Luckner*, *Napoleon*, *Patrice*.

Edmonds (7867) English: patronymic from EDMOND.

Edmondson (4917) Northern English: patronymic from EDMOND.

Edmonson (1428) English: variant of EDMONDSON.

Edmonston (310) Scottish: see EDMISTON.

Edmund (323) English and Scottish: variant spelling of EDMOND.
GIVEN NAMES French 4%. *Andre*, *Jean Pierre*.

Edmunds (2450) English (also common in South Wales): patronymic from the personal name *Edmund* (see EDMOND).

Edmundson (1236) Northern English and Scottish: patronymic from *Edmund* (see EDMOND).

Edney (618) English: from a medieval personal name (of which the Latin form was *Idonea*, feminine *Idonia*) of unknown origin.

Ednie (103) Scottish: variant of English EDNEY.

Edouard (198) French: from the personal name *Edouard*, French equivalent of EDWARD.
GIVEN NAMES French 49%. *Pierre* (4), *Andre* (2), *Alain*, *Alphonse*, *Auguste*, *Carolle*, *Chantel*, *Damien*, *Edouard*, *Ermite*, *Eunide*, *Gabrielle*.

Edquist (150) Swedish: ornamental name composed of the elements *ed* 'isthmus' + *quist*, an old or ornamental spelling of *kvist* 'twig'.
GIVEN NAMES German 8%; Scandinavian 7%. *Erhart*, *Erna*, *Reinhold*; *Nels*.

Edrington (414) English: habitational name from an unidentified place. It may be a metathesized spelling of *Erdington* in the West Midlands, which derives its name from the Old English personal name *Ēanrēd* + Old English *tūn* 'enclosure', 'settlement'.
FOREBEARS Christopher Edrington is recorded in Rappahannock co., VA, in 1666–71.

Edris (188) **1.** Welsh: from the Welsh personal name *Edris* or *Idris*, a compound of *iud* 'lord' + *rīs* 'ardent', 'impulsive'. **2.** Muslim: see IDRIS.

Edsall (630) **1.** English: habitational name from a place called High Edser in Ewhurst, Surrey. **2.** It is possible that in some cases

the name may be an Americanized form of the German family name ETZEL.

Edsell (145) English: variant spelling of EDSALL.

Edson (1731) English: patronymic or metronymic from EADE.

Edstrom (599) Swedish (**Edström**): ornamental name composed of the elements *ed* 'isthmus' + *ström* 'stream', 'current'.
GIVEN NAMES Scandinavian 5%. *Jarl*, *Joakim*, *Johan*, *Lennart*, *Nils*.

Edward (1221) English: from the Middle English personal name *Edward*, Old English *Ēadward*, composed of the elements *ēad* 'prosperity', 'fortune' + *w(e)ard* 'guard'. The English personal name also became popular on the Continent as a result of the fame of the two canonized kings of England, Edward the Martyr (962–79) and Edward the Confessor (1004–66). They certainly contributed largely to its great popularity in England.

Edwards (105393) English (also common in Wales): patronymic from EDWARD.
FOREBEARS One of the earliest American bearers of this very common English surname was William Edwards, the son of Rev. Richard Edwards, a London clergyman in the age of Elizabeth I, who came to New England about 1640. His descendant Jonathan (1703–58), of East Windsor, CT, was a prominent Congregational clergyman whose New England theology led to the first Great Awakening, a great religious revival.

Edwardsen (130) Americanized spelling of Danish and Norwegian **Edvardsen**, a patronymic from the personal name *Edvard*, Scandinavian form of EDWARD.
GIVEN NAMES Scandinavian 8%; German 5%. *Egil*; *Fritz*, *Hans*.

Edwardson (360) Northern English: patronymic from EDWARD; also an Americanized form of Scandinavian cognates (Danish and Norwegian *Edvardsen*, Swedish *Edvardsson*).
GIVEN NAMES Scandinavian 4%. *Hokan*, *Nels*.

Edwin (222) **1.** English: from the Middle English personal name *Edwine*, Old English *Ēadwine*, composed of the elements *ēad* 'prosperity', 'fortune' + *wine* 'friend'. **2.** Indian (southern states): name in the Christian community. It is only found as a given name in India (from the English personal name), but has come to be used as a family name among South Indian Christians in the U.S.
GIVEN NAMES Indian 7%. *Arul*, *Chandra*, *Chitra*, *Kumar*.

Eells (570) English: variant of EALES.

Eernisse (135) Dutch: probably from a medieval variant of ERNEST (see ERNST).
GIVEN NAME French 4%. *Monique*.

Efaw (270) Origin unidentified. This name is concentrated in WV, and is said to be of

German origin, though the etymology remains a mystery.

Efferson (146) Origin unidentified. Probably a reduced form of JEFFERSON.

Effertz (258) German (Rhineland): variant spelling of EVERTS.

Effinger (593) German and Swiss German: habitational name from a place near Zurich named Effingen or a place in Swabia, near Stuttgart, now called Öffingen.

Effler (289) German: variant of EIFLER.

Effron (218) Altered spelling of EFRON.
GIVEN NAME Jewish 4%. *Abbe*.

Efird (754) **1.** Variant spelling of English **Efford**, a habitational name from any of various places in Devon called Efford. **2.** Perhaps an Americanized spelling of German **Effert** or EVERT. This is a common name in NC.

Efron (208) Jewish (eastern Ashkenazic): ornamental name, taken from the Biblical place name *Efron*, a mountain mentioned in Joshua 15:9 and a Benjaminite city mentioned in 2 Chronicles 13:19, or from the identical Biblical personal name, mentioned in Genesis 25:9.
GIVEN NAMES Jewish 15%. *Gershon* (2), *Hyman*, *Menashe*, *Meyer*, *Mordecai*, *Morry*, *Sima*, *Uzi*, *Yael*.

Eftink (123) Dutch: unexplained.

Efurd (149) English or German: variant of EFIRD.

Egan (9385) Irish: reduced Anglicized form of Gaelic **Ó hAodhagáin** (see HAGAN).
GIVEN NAMES Irish 5%. *Brendan* (6), *Seamus* (4), *Kieran* (2), *Parnell* (2), *Siobhan* (2), *Aileen*, *Aine*, *Aisling*, *Dermot*, *Donal*, *Fergus*, *Finola*.

Egbers (113) Dutch or North German: patronymic from EGBERT.

Egbert (1870) Dutch or North German: variant EGGEBRECHT, assimilated to the form of an English personal name. See also EBBERT.

Ege (349) **1.** German: variant of ECK 2. **2.** Norwegian: variant of **Eike**, a habitational name from any of several farms in southwestern Norway, so named from Old Norse *eiki* 'oak grove'. **3.** Danish: topographic name for someone living near an oak tree, from *ek* 'oak', or a nickname for someone considered to share some of the oak tree's characteristics, such as reliability and strength.
GIVEN NAMES German 5%; Scandinavian 4%. *Hans* (2), *Ernst*, *Konrad*, *Raimund*, *Wolfgang*; *Bendt*, *Selmer*.

Egeberg (111) Danish and Norwegian: habitational name from a place named with *ege* 'oak' + *berg* 'mountain', 'hill'.

Egeland (429) Norwegian: habitational name from any of various farms in southwestern Norway named Eikeland, from *eiki* 'oak', 'oak grove' + *land* 'land'.
GIVEN NAMES Scandinavian 9%. *Lars* (2), *Erik*, *Iver*, *Karsten*, *Morten*, *Sig*, *Thor*.

Egeler (142) German: variant of EGLER.

Egelhoff (158) German: from the Germanic personal name *Egilolf* (see EGLOFF).

Egelston (188) Spelling variant of EGGLESTON.

Eger (693) **1.** English: variant of EDGAR. **2.** Hungarian: habitational name for someone from any of various places called Eger, in Fehér, Heves, and Zala counties, or former Nyitra county, now in Slovakia. In some cases the name may derive from *éger* 'alder'. **3.** German: habitational name from Eger in western Bohemia (Czech name Cheb).

Egerer (151) South German: variant of EGER.
GIVEN NAMES German 8%; Japanese 4%. *Egmont* (2), *Kurt*, *Manfred*; *Aki* (2), *Sawako*.

Egert (230) **1.** German (Bavaria and Austria): from Middle High German *egerte* 'fallow (land)'; a topographic name for someone who lived near land taken out of production, or a status name for someone who owned such a plot of land. **2.** German: from the old German personal name *Eckhart* (see ECKERT). **3.** Jewish (Ashkenazic): unexplained; perhaps an adoption of 2.
GIVEN NAMES Jewish 5%. *Zev* (2), *Emanuel*, *Meir*, *Shimon*.

Egerton (349) English: variant spelling of EDGERTON.

Egge (539) **1.** Norwegian: habitational name from any of several farmsteads so named, from Old Norse *egg* 'ridge', 'edge'. **2.** German: variant of ECK.
GIVEN NAMES Scandinavian 6%. *Karsten* (2), *Iver*, *Nels*, *Ordell*.

Eggebraaten (114) Norwegian: habitational name from a farm so named, from *egge* (Old Norse *egg* 'ridge', 'edge') + *braaten* (Old Norse *broti* 'land cleared for cultivation by burning').

Eggebrecht (242) German: from a Germanic personal name composed of the elements *agi(l)* 'edge', 'point' (of a weapon) + *berht* 'bright', 'famous'. See also EBBERT.
GIVEN NAMES German 5%. *Kurt* (3), *Otto*.

Eggeman (104) German: variant of ECKMANN.

Eggemeyer (268) German: distinguishing name for a tenant farmer (see MEYER) who lived on a corner or by a rocky outcrop (see ECK).
GIVEN NAMES German 4%. *Fritz* (2), *Gerhardt*.

Eggen (707) **1.** North German: patronymic from EGGE. **2.** Swiss German: possibly of the same origin as 1, but otherwise a topographic name, a derivative of ECK 1. **3.** Norwegian: habitational name from any of about 20 farms, notably in Trøndelag, so named with the definite singular form of *egg* (see EGGE).
GIVEN NAMES Scandinavian 5%. *Anders*, *Erik*, *Nels*.

Eggenberger (236) Swiss German: probably a habitational name for someone from a place called Eggenberg near Ravensburg.

Egger (1411) **1.** South German: topographic name for someone who lived on a corner (either a street corner, or the corner of a valley running around a mountain), from an altered form of ECK + the suffix *-er*, denoting an inhabitant. **2.** Dutch and German: from a Germanic personal name composed of the elements *agi* 'point (of a sword)' + *heri* 'army'. **3.** South German (Swabia): occupational name for a farmer, from an agent derivative of *eggen* 'to harrow'. **4.** English: variant of EDGAR 1.
GIVEN NAMES German 4%. *Fritz* (3), *Hans* (3), *Kurt* (2), *Oskar* (2), *Erwin*, *Franz*, *Helmut*, *Johannes*, *Mathias*, *Otto*, *Siegfried*, *Wolfgang*.

Eggers (3274) **1.** North German: patronymic from the personal name *Eggert* (see ECKERT). **2.** Dutch: patronymic from the personal name EGGER 2. **3.** English: variant of EDGAR.

Eggert (2194) North German: variant of ECKERT.
GIVEN NAMES German 4%. *Kurt* (7), *Erwin* (3), *Lutz* (3), *Hans* (2), *Manfred* (2), *Eldor*, *Ernst*, *Gunther*, *Hartmut*, *Horst*, *Karl Heinz*, *Matthias*.

Eggett (127) English (East Anglia): possibly a variant of **Edgett**, from the Old English personal name *Ecggēat*, or occasionally possibly from *Ecgheard*.

Eggler (127) South German: topographic name for someone living near the corner of a street or mountain, or by a promontory, from Middle High German *egge* 'corner' + diminutive *-l* + *-er* suffix denoting an inhabitant. Compare ECK, EGGER.

Eggleston (3635) English: habitational name from a place in County Durham so called, or from Egglestone in North Yorkshire, both named in Old English as *Egleston*, probably from the Old English personal name *Ecgel* (unattested) + *tūn* 'settlement', 'farmstead'.

Eggleton (335) English: habitational name from Eggleton in Herefordshire or Egleton in Rutland, both named in Old English as 'settlement associated with Ecgwulf or Ecgel'.

Eggum (122) Norwegian: habitational name from a farm so named from the dative case of Old Norse *egg* 'ridge'. In the U.S. this name is concentrated in Minneapolis.

Egland (206) **1.** Norwegian: variant of EGELAND. **2.** In some instances possibly an Americanized spelling of Swedish EKLUND.

Egle (210) **1.** English: variant of EAGLE. **2.** German and Swiss German: see EGLI.
GIVEN NAMES Scandinavian 4%. *Astrid*, *Erik*.

Egler (263) Probably a variant of the German family name EGGLER.
GIVEN NAMES German 5%. *Dieter* (2), *Bodo*.

Egleston (266) English: variant spelling of EGGLESTON.

Egley (176) Americanized spelling of German EGLI.

Egli (562) **1.** Swiss German: from a pet form of the personal name *Egenolf* or *Egilolf* (see EGLOFF). **2.** Possibly also Norwegian, a habitational name from a farm named Eik(e)li, from *eik* 'oak' + *li* 'hillside', 'slope'.
GIVEN NAMES German 4%. *Konrad* (2), *Kurt* (2), *Otto* (2).

Eglin (188) **1.** English: from a Norman form of a female personal name, *Agilina*, of Germanic origin. **2.** Swiss German: variant of EGLI.
GIVEN NAME German 4%. *Erhard* (2).

Egloff (322) German and Swiss German: from the Germanic personal name *Egilolf*, composed of the elements *agi(l)* 'edge', 'point' (of a sword) + *wolf* 'wolf', cognate with Old English *Ecgwulf*. This was the name of several Lombard kings (ancestors of the Bavarian ducal line of the Agilolfinger), who introduced the name to Italy.
GIVEN NAMES German 5%. *Georg*, *Hans*, *Hedwig*, *Heiner*.

Egly (194) Swiss German: variant spelling of EGLI.

Egner (679) **1.** South German: from a Germanic personal name formed with the element *agi* 'point (of a sword)'. **2.** Norwegian: habitational name from a farmstead so named, of unexplained origin.
GIVEN NAMES German 4%. *Ernst*, *Francis Fritz*, *Fritz*, *Karl-Heinz*, *Reinhard*, *Wilhelmina*.

Egnew (138) Probably an altered spelling of AGNEW.

Egnor (222) Altered spelling of German or Norwegian EGNER.

Egolf (467) German: variant of EGLOFF.

Eguchi (149) Japanese: 'mouth of the river'; the name is found mostly on the island of Kyūshū.
GIVEN NAMES Japanese 73%. *Ikushi* (23), *Hiroshi* (3), *Junko* (3), *Koji* (2), *Noboru* (2), *Takehisa* (2), *Yoko* (2), *Fujio*, *Hidenori*, *Hiromi*, *Hitoshi*, *Katsuki*.

Eguia (129) Castilianized form (**Eguía**) from Basque **Egia**, a habitational name from either of two places named Egia in Biscay province, Basque Country.
GIVEN NAMES Spanish 55%. *Juan* (4), *Luis* (4), *Jesus* (3), *Eduardo* (2), *Juventino* (2), *Mario* (2), *Pedro* (2), *Raul* (2), *Teodoro* (2), *Alfredo*, *Alicia*, *Araceli*; *Antonio* (2), *Gabriella*, *Lorenzo*, *Marino*.

Ehart (100) German: variant of **Ehard(t)**, from the personal name *Ehard*, composed of the Old High German elements *ē* 'law', 'order' + *hart(i)* 'hard', 'firm'. Compare AHART.

Ehinger (299) German: habitational name for someone from any of various places named Ehingen.

Ehl (101) Shortened form of North German EHLE or EHLEN.

Ehle (489) North German: from a short form of the personal name *Ehlebrecht*, from Germanic *agil* 'edge', 'point' (of a sword) + *berht* 'bright', 'shining'.

Ehlen (385) German: habitational name from any of various places so named.
GIVEN NAMES German 4%. *Ernst, Wilhelm.*

Ehler (658) North German: variant of EHLERT.

Ehlers (3279) North German: patronymic from EHLERT.

Ehlert (1143) North German: from a Germanic personal name composed of the elements *agil* 'edge', 'point' (of a sword) + *hard* 'brave', 'hardy', 'strong' or *ward* 'guard'.
GIVEN NAMES German 5%. *Kurt* (5), *Alois, Benno, Dieter, Eldred, Ernst, Gerhard, Heinz, Ilse, Joerg, Juergen.*

Ehli (157) Swiss German: variant of EHLE.

Ehling (157) North German: patronymic from EHLE.
GIVEN NAMES German 9%. *Kurt* (2), *Helmut.*

Ehlinger (378) German: habitational name for someone from Ehlingen in the Palatinate.

Ehlke (190) North German: from a pet form of EHLE.
GIVEN NAME German 4%. *Ewald* (2).

Ehly (229) Swiss German: variant of EHLE.

Ehm (101) Variant of German OHM.
GIVEN NAME German 4%. *Otto.*

Ehman (353) Americanized spelling of German EHMANN.

Ehmann (403) **1.** South German: byname for someone under feudal obligations of some particular kind, from Middle High German *ē* 'law', 'contract' + *man* 'man'. **2.** Jewish: (Ashkenazic): nickname from modern German *Ehemann* 'husband' (the word *Ehe* having progressively become restricted to the marriage contract and then to the state of matrimony itself). At one time in the Austrian Empire, only one son in a Jewish family was officially permitted to marry and start a family of his own: this may have been a surname adopted by such a person.

Ehmen (128) North German: patronymic from a short form of EHMER.
GIVEN NAMES German 6%. *Eldred, Erwin, Otto.*

Ehmer (142) North German: from a Germanic personal name composed of the elements *agi* 'point' (of a sword) + *mar* 'fame'.
GIVEN NAMES German 14%. *Heinz* (5), *Kurt, Lorenz, Manfred.*

Ehmke (374) North German: from the personal name, a pet form of EHMER.
GIVEN NAMES German 4%. *Fritz, Gerhard, Siegfried.*

Ehn (112) Swedish: ornamental name from *ehn*, ornamental spelling of *en* 'juniper'.

GIVEN NAMES Scandinavian 9%. *Lennart, Sven.*

Ehnert (108) German: from a Germanic personal name *Eginhard*, formed with *agi* 'point (of a sword)' + *hard* 'hardy', 'strong'.

Ehnes (133) German: from a short form of a Germanic personal name formed with *agi* 'point (of a sword)'.

Ehr (150) German: habitational name from Ehr, a place south of Boppard on the Rhine.
GIVEN NAMES French 7%. *Esme* (2), *Raoul* (2).

Ehren (103) German: from a short form of a Germanic personal name composed with *ēra* 'honor'.
GIVEN NAMES German 4%. *Alois, Fritz.*

Ehrenberg (562) **1.** German: habitational name from any of several places so named. **2.** Jewish (Ashkenazic): ornamental compound of German *Ehre* 'honor' + *Berg* 'mountain', 'hill'.
GIVEN NAMES German 4%. *Otto* (2), *Gottfried, Kurt, Theodor.*

Ehrenfeld (194) **1.** German: habitational name from a place so named, perhaps the one near Cologne. **2.** Jewish (Ashkenazic): ornamental compound name composed of German *Ehre* 'honor' + *Feld* 'field'.
GIVEN NAMES Jewish 16%. *Itzhak* (3), *Moshe* (2), *Aron, Chaim, Cheskel, Dov, Faigy, Hersh, Rivky, Shulem.*

Ehrenreich (236) **1.** German: from a medieval personal name composed of Middle High German *ēre* 'honor' + the plural suffix *-n* + *reich* 'rich'. **2.** Jewish (Ashkenazic): ornamental compound name composed of German *Ehre* 'honor' + *reich* 'rich'.
GIVEN NAMES German 5%; Jewish 5%. *Kurt*; *Naftoli* (2), *Faigie, Naftali.*

Ehresman (313) Respelling of German EHRESMANN.

Ehresmann (124) German: from the Germanic personal name *Erizo*, based on Old High German *ēra* 'honor' + *man* 'man'.
GIVEN NAMES German 8%. *Ewald, Reinhold.*

Ehret (790) German: reduced form of EHRHARDT.

Ehrgott (153) German: apparently a pious nickname meaning 'honor God', but more probably an altered form of Swiss German **Ehrengut** 'possessions'.
GIVEN NAME German 4%. *Kurt.*

Ehrhard (190) German: variant spelling of EHRHARDT.

Ehrhardt (1322) German: from a Germanic personal name composed of Old High German *ēra* 'honor' (compare EHRLICH) + *hard* 'brave', 'hardy', 'strong'. The name was popularized by the cult of an 8th century bishop of Regensburg of this name; hence the present high frequency of the family name in Bavaria. The form *Erhard* has also been adopted by Ashkenazic Jews.
GIVEN NAMES German 5%. *Fritz* (2), *Helmut* (2), *Kurt* (2), *Achim, Armin, Arno, Bernd, Erwin, Franz, Hanns, Heinz, Joerg.*

Ehrhart (867) German: variant spelling of EHRHARDT.

Ehrich (360) North German: from a Germanized form of the Old Norse personal name *Eiríkr* (see ERICKSON). The spelling of the first syllable has been influenced by German names beginning with *Ehr-* such as EHRHARDT.
GIVEN NAMES German 4%. *Manfred* (2), *Gunter.*

Ehrig (211) Variant of German EHRICH.
GIVEN NAMES German 6%. *Helmuth, Kurt, Otto, Ulrich.*

Ehrke (220) North German: from a pet form of a Germanic personal name formed with Old High German *ēra* 'honor'.
GIVEN NAMES German 5%. *Erwin, Frieda, Gerhard, Jutta.*

Ehrle (109) German: from a pet form of a Germanic personal name formed with *ēra* 'honor'.
GIVEN NAMES German 8%. *Ernst, Hannelore, Kurt.*

Ehrler (240) German: variant spelling of ERLER.
GIVEN NAMES German 5%. *Alfons, Kurt, Theodor.*

Ehrlich (3240) **1.** German: from a byname from Middle High German *ērlich* 'respected', 'honorable'. **2.** Jewish (Ashkenazic): nickname or ornamental name from German *ehrlich* 'honorable', 'honest', or Yiddish *erlekh* 'honest', 'virtuous'.
GIVEN NAMES German 4%; Jewish 4%. *Kurt* (4), *Otto* (4), *Egon, Erwin, Fritz, Gerd, Gottfried, Guenter, Gunter, Hanns, Hedwig, Heiner*; *Emanuel* (5), *Hyman* (5), *Sol* (3), *Chaim* (2), *Myer* (2), *Avrohom, Avron, Batya, Genya, Irit, Jakob, Kieve.*

Ehrman (694) **1.** Jewish (Ashkenazic): variant of EHRMANN. **2.** Americanized spelling of German EHRMANN 1.

Ehrmann (368) **1.** German: from a byname from Middle High German *ēre* 'honor', 'esteem' + *man* 'man'. **2.** German: habitational name for someone from any of the several places named Ehren or Ehr. **3.** Jewish (Ashkenazic): ornamental name from German *Ehre* 'honor' + *Mann* 'man'.
GIVEN NAMES German 6%. *Erna, Erwin, Gerhardt, Hans, Kurt, Oskar, Siegfried.*

Ehrmantraut (142) Americanized spelling of German **Ehrmanntraut**, metronymic from a Germanic female personal name composed of the elements *irmin* 'world', 'all-encompassing' + *trud* 'strength'.
GIVEN NAME German 4%. *Kurt.*

Ehrsam (241) German: from a byname from Middle High German *ērsam* 'having honor and esteem'.
GIVEN NAMES German 6%. *Erwin, Fritz, Kurt, Lorenz, Otto.*

Eib (149) German (Bavarian): habitational name from any of several places called Eib or Eyb.

Eiben (275) **1.** North German: patronymic from the personal name *Eibe*. **2.** South

German: from a Germanic personal name based on Old High German *īwa* 'yew tree', or a topographic name for someone living by a yew tree, from Middle High German *eibe* 'yew'.

GIVEN NAMES German 4%. *Bernhard, Kurt, Otto*.

Eich (845) German: from Middle High German *eich(e)* 'oak', hence a topographic name for someone who lived near an oak tree. In some cases, it may be a habitational name for someone from any of several places named with this word, for example Eiche or Eichen, or for someone who lived at a house distinguished by the sign of an oak.

Eichacker (103) German: from a topographic name meaning 'oak field', from Middle High German *eich(e)* 'oak' + *acker* 'field'.

Eichberger (113) German: habitational name from any of several places called Eichberg 'oak hill', from Middle High German *eich(e)*, Middle Low German *ēk(e)* 'oak' + *berg* 'hill', 'mountain' + *-er* denoting an inhabitant.

Eiche (144) Variant of German EICH.

Eichel (319) **1.** German: topographic name of uncertain origin, possibly related to modern German *Eichel* 'acorn'. **2.** German: habitational name for someone who lived at a house distinguished by the sign of an acorn. **3.** Jewish (Ashkenazic): ornamental adoption of 1.

GIVEN NAMES German 4%. *Gerd, Otto*.

Eichelberg (115) **1.** German: habitational name from any of various places, notably one southeast of Heidelberg, named from Middle High German *eichel* 'acorn' + *berc* 'mountain', 'hill', or topographic name for someone who lived on an oak-covered hill. **2.** Jewish (Ashkenazic): ornamental compound of German *Eichel* 'acorn' + *Berg* 'mountain', 'hill'.

GIVEN NAMES German 9%. *Kurt* (2), *Erwin, Fritz*.

Eichelberger (1798) German: habitational name for someone from any of the various places called EICHELBERG.

Eichen (150) **1.** German: habitational name from any of various places named Eichen, for example near Siegen or Hanau in Hesse. **2.** Jewish (Ashkenazic): ornamental name from German *eichen* '(of) oak', or alternatively a shortened form of any of various compound names beginning with this element (see for example EICHENBAUM).

GIVEN NAME Jewish 4%. *Yetta*.

Eichenauer (117) German: habitational name for someone from Eichenau, a village in Hesse.

GIVEN NAME German 7%. *Hasso*.

Eichenbaum (174) **1.** German: topographic name for someone who lived near an oak tree, from Middle High German *eiche* 'oak' + *boum* 'tree'. **2.** Jewish (Ashkenazic): ornamental adoption of 1.

GIVEN NAMES Jewish 10%. *Baruch* (2), *Mort* (2), *Imrich, Isadore, Zehava*.

Eichenberg (220) German: from Middle High German *eichen* 'oaks' + *berc* 'mountain', 'hill'; a topographic name for someone who lived on an oak-covered hillside, or a habitational name from a place so named near Kassel in Hesse.

Eichenberger (431) German: habitational name for someone from EICHENBERG.

Eichenlaub (435) **1.** German: from **Eichenlau**, a topographic name from Middle High German *eichen* 'oaks' + *lōch*, *lō* 'brush', 'undergrowth', reinterpreted through folk etymology as *Eichenlaub* 'oak leaf'. **2.** Jewish (Ashkenazic): ornamental name from German *Eichenlaub* 'oak leaf'.

Eicher (1432) **1.** German: topographic name for someone living by an oak tree, or habitational name for someone from a place called Eiche or Eichen. See EICH. **2.** South German: occupational name for a person who checked weights and measures against official specifications, from Middle High German *īcher*.

Eichert (132) German: topographic name for someone who lived near an oak wood, from Middle High German *eich(e)* 'oak' + *-ert* suffix denoting profusion.

GIVEN NAMES German 6%. *Deiter, Hans, Irmgard*.

Eichholz (309) **1.** German: from Middle High German *eich(e)* 'oak' + *holz* 'wood', 'forest'; a topographic name for someone who lived near an oak wood or a habitational name from any of several places so named. **2.** Jewish (Ashkenazic): ornamental adoption of 1.

GIVEN NAMES German 9%. *Friedrich, Fritz, Gerhard, Gunther, Horst, Jurgen, Klaus, Kurt, Manfred*.

Eichhorn (1164) **1.** German: topographic name for someone who lived on or near an oak-covered promontory, from Middle High German *eich(e)* 'oak' + *horn* 'horn', 'promontory'. **2.** German: from Middle High German *eichhorn* 'squirrel' (from Old High German *eihhurno*, a compound of *eih* 'oak' + *urno*, from the ancient Germanic and Indo-European name of the animal, which was later wrongly associated with *hurno* 'horn'); probably a nickname for someone thought to resemble the animal, or alternatively a habitational name for someone who lived at a house distinguished by the sign of a squirrel. **3.** Jewish (Ashkenazic): ornamental adoption of 2.

GIVEN NAMES German 5%. *Hans* (3), *Erwin* (2), *Hermann* (2), *Kurt* (2), *Dieter, Fritz, Guenther, Gunther, Heinrich, Heinz, Klaus, Lotti*.

Eichhorst (241) North German: from German *Eiche* 'oak' (probably standardized from Middle Low German *eke*) + Middle Low German *horst* 'brushy area'; a topographic name for someone who lived in an area of oak scrubland, or a habitational name from any of several northeastern Ger-

man places so named, for example in Mecklenburg and Pomerania.

GIVEN NAMES German 5%. *Eldor, Reinhold, Siegbert, Siegfried*.

Eichinger (397) German: habitational name for someone from any of several southern German places named Eiching or Aiching.

GIVEN NAMES German 6%. *Erwin, Hermann, Kurt, Manfred, Mathias*.

Eichler (1311) South German: variant of EICH, the *-ler* suffix denoting association.

GIVEN NAMES German 4%. *Fritz* (2), *Gunther* (2), *Hans* (2), *Helmut* (2), *Ernst, Gottfried, Heinrich, Helmuth, Otto, Rudi, Wenzel*.

Eichman (701) Americanized spelling of German EICHMANN.

Eichmann (286) German: variant of EICH, the suffix *-mann* denoting association.

GIVEN NAMES German 6%. *Erwin, Gerhardt, Kurt, Otto, Wilhelm*.

Eichner (707) German: variant of EICH, the *-ner* suffix denoting association.

GIVEN NAMES German 4%. *Hermann* (2), *Manfred* (2), *Hans, Horst, Rudie*.

Eicholtz (183) Altered spelling of German EICHHOLZ.

Eichorn (437) Altered spelling of German EICHHORN.

Eichorst (140) Altered spelling of German EICHHORST.

Eichstadt (169) Americanized spelling of German **Eichstädt** (see EICHSTAEDT).

GIVEN NAME German 4%. *Otto*.

Eichstaedt (142) German (**Eichstädt**): habitational name from Eichstädt in Brandenburg.

GIVEN NAMES German 4%. *Erwin, Ullrich*.

Eichten (158) German: unexplained. The name is mainly from the Eifel area, near Luxembourg and Belgium.

Eick (547) North German: topographic name for someone who lived by an oak tree or in an oak wood, from Middle Low German *eke* 'oak'. The South German cognate EICH is sometimes Americanized as *Eick*.

Eicke (107) German: from a short form (*Agico*) of a Germanic personal name formed with *agi* 'point (of a sword)'.

GIVEN NAMES German 10%. *Claus, Dieter, Hermann*.

Eickhoff (775) North German (Westphalia): topographic name for someone who lived at or owned a farm or estate that was marked by oaks, from Middle Low German *eke* + *hof* 'farmstead', 'manor farm'.

Eickholt (210) North German: topographic name for someone who lived near or owned an oak wood, from Middle Low German *eke* 'oak' + *holt* 'wood', 'forest'.

Eickman (138) Americanized spelling of North German **Eickmann** or the cognate EICHMANN.

Eickmeyer (126) North German: compound of Middle Low German *eke* 'oak' + MEYER, hence a distinguishing name for a tenant farmer who lived by an oak wood.

GIVEN NAMES German 11%. *Otto* (3), *Kurt*.

Eid (442) **1.** Muslim: from a personal name based on Arabic *'eid* 'festivity'. The two principal religious festivals observed by Muslims are 'Eidul Fitr and 'Eidul Aḍḥā. 'Eidul Fitr is observed after completion of fasting in Ramadan, 'Eidul Aḍḥā is observed as a day of sacrifice commemorating the example of the Prophet Ibrahim, or after completion of the Hajj. *Eid* is sometimes used as part of the name of a child born on one of these two feast days. **2.** Norwegian: habitational name from any of several farmsteads so named, from Old Norse *eið* 'isthmus' (see EIDE). **3.** Perhaps an Americanized spelling of German EIDT.
GIVEN NAMES Muslim 36%; French 5%. *Ahmed* (4), *Eid* (3), *Hassan* (3), *Mohammed* (3), *Amin* (2), *Diab* (2), *Fouad* (2), *Ghassan* (2), *Mohamed* (2), *Mounir* (2), *Omar* (2), *Riad* (2); *Michel* (2), *Alain, Andre, Antoine, Emile, Francois, Georges, Jean Michel, Lucien, Pierre*.

Eidam (125) German: variant of EIDEM.

Eide (1534) **1.** North German: variant of EDE. **2.** Norwegian: habitational name from any of various farmsteads, especially in western Norway, so named, from Old Norse *eiði*, dative case of *eið* 'isthmus'.
GIVEN NAMES Scandinavian 9%. *Erik* (5), *Iver* (3), *Lars* (3), *Alf* (2), *Bjorn* (2), *Ansgar, Britt, Hjalmer, Jarle, Jorgen, Kjersti, Nels*.

Eidelman (122) Jewish (eastern Ashkenazic): ornamental name from Yiddish *eydl* 'noble' (also a female personal name) + Yiddish *man* 'man' (or 'husband'). Compare EDELMAN.
GIVEN NAMES Jewish 31%; Russian 4%. *Isak* (2), *Shloma* (2), *Yisrael* (2), *Yitzchok* (2), *Dvorah, Meir, Mendel, Naum, Shmuel, Tsilya, Yosef, Efim, Leonid, Vladimir*.

Eidem (259) **1.** German: from Middle High German *eidem* 'son-in-law'. See EIDEN. **2.** Norwegian: habitational name from any of various farmsteads in central Norway so named, from Old Norse *Eiðheimr* (*eið* 'isthmus' + *heimr* 'farm').

Eidemiller (132) Americanized form of German **Heidemüller**, topographic name for a miller who kept a mill on a heath, from *Heide* 'heath' (see HEID).

Eiden (525) German: from Middle High German *eiden* 'son-in-law', probably signifying the son-in-law of a person of some importance or fame.

Eidenschink (103) German: unexplained. Probably a topographic name.

Eidman (129) German: from the short form (*Aido*) of a Germanic personal name composed with *eid* 'oath' or *eit* 'fire'.

Eidsness (120) Norwegian: habitational name from a farmstead so named in western Norway, from Old Norse *eid* 'isthmus' + *nes* 'headland', 'promontory'.
GIVEN NAME Scandinavian 9%. *Lars*.

Eidson (1773) English or Scottish: patronymic, perhaps a variant of ADDISON, from a pet form of ADAM. Compare EDSON, EADE.
FOREBEARS Edward Eidson is recorded in VA in 1706.

Eidt (133) German: of uncertain origin. Perhaps a metronymic from a short form of the personal name *Agatha* (from Greek, meaning 'good') or from a short form of a Germanic personal name based on *eid* 'oath'.

Eiermann (137) German: occupational name for an egg collector or dealer in eggs, from Middle High German *ei* 'egg' + *man* 'man'.
GIVEN NAMES German 9%. *Erwin, Heinz, Hilde, Joerg, Kurt*.

Eifert (514) North German: from the personal name *Agafrid*, composed of the Germanic elements *agi* 'point (of a sword)' + *frid* 'peace'.

Eiffert (130) Variant of North German EIFERT.

Eifler (212) German and French: regional name for someone originally from the district bounded by the mid-Rhine, Mosel, and Ardennes known as the *Eifel*. The first record of the place name occurs AD *c*.800 in the Latin form *in pago Aflense* or *E(i)flense*.
GIVEN NAMES German 6%. *Kurt* (3), *Franz*.

Eigen (141) German and Jewish (Ashkenazic): from Middle High German *aigen* 'own', denoting an independent smallholder (see EIGNER).
GIVEN NAMES Jewish 6%; German 4%. *Tikva, Zev; Inge*.

Eighmey (159) Probably an Americanized form of German EICKMEYER.

Eighmy (163) Probably of German origin: see EIGHMEY.

Eigner (192) **1.** German: from an agent derivative of Middle High German *aigen* 'own', a status name originally denoting a smallholder who held his land outright, rather than by rent or feudal obligation. In the Middle Ages this was sufficiently rare to be worthy of remark and was normally a special privilege granted in recognition of some exceptional service. **2.** Jewish (Ashkenazic): from German *Eigner* 'owner', presumably adopted as an indication of property-owning status.
GIVEN NAMES Jewish 5%; German 4%. *Gershon, Mordechai, Raizy; Kurt* (2), *Hans*.

Eigsti (110) South German or Swiss German: unexplained.

Eike (199) **1.** Norwegian: habitational name from various farms in southwestern Norway so named, from Old Norse *eiki* 'oak', 'oak grove' (see EGE). **2.** German: from a short form of a Germanic personal name formed with *Egi-, Agi-*, from Old High German *ecka* 'point (of a sword or lance)'.
GIVEN NAME Scandinavian 4%. *Erik*.

Eiken (130) Norwegian: habitational name from any of various farms so named from the definite singular form of *eik* 'oak'.

GIVEN NAMES Scandinavian 9%. *Arndt, Holger, Thoralf*.

Eikenberry (346) Americanized form of German EICHENBERG.

Eiker (127) **1.** German: from a Germanic personal name formed with *egi* 'point (of a sword or lance)' (Old High German *ecka*). **2.** Perhaps a respelling of German EICHER. **3.** Norwegian: variant (plural) of EIKE.

Eikleberry (108) Probably an altered form of EIKENBERRY (see EICHENBERG).

Eiland (970) North German: topographic name for someone who lived on or owned property surrounded by water, from Middle High German *eilant* 'island'.

Eiler (832) **1.** North German: variant of EHLERT. **2.** German: variant of EULER.

Eilerman (223) Americanized spelling of the German family name **Eilermann**, a variant of EHLERT + Middle Low German *man* 'man'.

Eilers (1569) North German: patronymic from EHLERT.

Eilert (289) Danish and North German: from a Germanic personal name composed of the elements *agil* 'edge', 'point' (of a sword) + *hard* 'brave', 'hardy', 'strong' or *ward* 'guard'.

Eilertsen (102) Danish and Norwegian: patronymic from the personal name EILERT.
GIVEN NAMES Scandinavian 24%; German 7%. *Thor* (2), *Bente, Per; Hans, Kurt*.

Eilertson (128) Respelling of Norwegian and Danish **Eilertsen**, or Swedish **Eilertsson**, patronymics from the personal name EILERT.

Eilts (214) German and French (Alsace): patronymic from a reduced form of the personal name EILERT.
GIVEN NAMES French 4%. *Manon, Patrice*.

Eimer (290) North German: from a Germanic personal name composed of the elements *agi(n)* 'edge', 'point' (of sword) + *mar* 'fame'.
GIVEN NAMES German 8%. *Kurt* (2), *Willi* (2), *Erhard, Guenther, Manfred*.

Eimers (209) North German: patronymic from EIMER.

Einbinder (158) Jewish (Ashkenazic): occupational name from Yiddish *aynbinder* 'book binder'. Compare BINDER.
GIVEN NAMES Jewish 14%. *Kalmen* (3), *Meyer* (2), *Devorah, Itamar*.

Einck (146) German: from a short form of a Germanic personal name formed with Old High German *ecka* 'point (of a sword)', 'corner'.

Einerson (110) Americanized spelling of Swedish **Einarsson**, a patronymic from *Einar*, from the Old Norse personal name *Einarr*, composed of the elements *ein* 'alone', 'only' + *arr* 'warrior'.

Einhorn (973) **1.** German: habitational name for someone who lived at a house distinguished by the sign of a unicorn, Middle

High German *einhorn*. **2.** Jewish (Ashkenazic): ornamental adoption of 1.

GIVEN NAMES Jewish 10%. *Chaim* (4), *Isadore* (3), *Moshe* (3), *Meyer* (2), *Miriam* (2), *Mordechai* (2), *Sol* (2), *Avinoam*, *Avrum*, *Hersh*, *Leib*, *Shaul*.

Einspahr (262) German: from *ein* 'one' + Middle Low German *spare* 'spur', a nickname for a farmer or mercenary with only one horse.

Einstein (373) **1.** German and Jewish (Ashkenazic): habitational name from any of various places named with a Middle High German derivative of *einsteinen* 'to enclose or surround with stone'. In the unsettled social climate of the Middle Ages even relatively minor settlements were commonly surrounded with stone walls as a defense against attack. **2.** Jewish (Ashkenazic): ornamental name composed of German *ein* 'one' + *Stein* 'stone'.

Eirich (169) German: from the Germanic personal name *Agarich*, composed of the elements *agi* 'point (of a sword)' + *rīh* 'powerful'.

Eiring (115) German: variant spelling of EYRING.

Eis (228) German: **1.** from the Germanic personal name *Iso*. **2.** habitational name for someone from Eisa, the name of a former town in Hesse.

Eisaman (179) Americanized spelling of German **Eisermann** (see EISERMAN).

Eisch (128) German: **1.** nickname from Middle High German *eisch* 'ugly'. **2.** Possibly a topographic name from *Eisch*, the name of a river in Luxembourg or from *Eysche*, *Eisch*, 14th-century forms of *Aisch*, the name of a river in Bavaria.

Eischeid (193) German: unexplained.

Eischen (367) German: habitational name from Eischen in Luxembourg, named for the EISCH river on which it stands.

Eischens (241) German: variant of EISCHEN.

Eisel (392) Probably a shortened form of German EISELE.

GIVEN NAMES German 4%. *Ewald* (2), *Aloysius*, *Helmut*.

Eisele (1466) South German: **1.** from a short pet form of the personal name *Isenhart*, from Old High German *īsan* 'iron' + *hart* 'hardy', 'strong'. **2.** from *Isenlin*, a compound of Middle High German *īsen* 'iron' + the hypocoristic suffix *-līn*, hence a nickname for a blacksmith, ironworker, or dealer in iron.

GIVEN NAMES German 4%. *Hans* (3), *Kurt* (2), *Alfons*, *Ewald*, *Gebhard*, *Gerda*, *Helmut*, *Heribert*, *Hermann*, *Ingeborg*, *Juergen*, *Jurgen*.

Eiseman (516) Americanized spelling of German **Eisemann** (see EISENMANN).

Eisemann (240) German and Jewish: variant of EISENMANN.

GIVEN NAMES German 7%; Jewish 5%. *Erwin*, *Friedrich*, *Kurt*, *Otto*; *Naftoli* (2), *Meier*, *Moshe*, *Yael*.

Eisen (1291) German and Jewish (Ashkenazic): metonymic occupational name for an ironworker or smith, or an ironmonger, from Middle High German *īsen* 'iron', German *Eisen*. It may also have been used as a nickname, with reference to the strength and hardness of iron or to its color, while as a Jewish name it was also adopted as an ornamental name from modern German *Eisen* 'iron' or the Yiddish cognate *ayzn*.

GIVEN NAMES Jewish 5%; German 4%. *Chaim* (4), *Gavriel* (2), *Avram*, *Hyman*, *Moshe*, *Naftali*, *Noam*, *Ori*, *Shai*, *Shloime*, *Yoel*; *Erwin* (2), *Kurt* (2), *Benno*, *Eldor*, *Helmut*, *Horst*, *Ilse*, *Karlheinz*, *Reiner*, *Wolfgang*.

Eisenach (107) German: habitational name from a place so named near Trier.

GIVEN NAME German 4%. *Kurt*.

Eisenbach (169) South German and Jewish (Ashkenazic): habitational name from any of the several places so named, from Middle High German *īsen* 'iron' + *bach* 'stream'. As a Jewish name it is sometimes ornamental.

GIVEN NAMES Jewish 17%. *Meyer* (2), *Aron*, *Moishe*, *Mordechai*, *Moshe*, *Pinchas*, *Rivki*, *Ronit*, *Shalom*, *Yaakov*.

Eisenbarth (321) South German: from a Germanic personal name composed of Old High German *īsan-* 'iron' + *berht* 'bright', 'shining'. By folk etymology, the second element has been confused with *Bart* 'beard' (formerly spelled *Barth*).

Eisenbeis (235) German (**Eisenbeiss**): nickname for a show-off or boastful person, from Middle High German *īsenbīss* (literally 'iron biter') 'braggart'.

Eisenberg (3589) **1.** German: habitational name from any of the several places so named, from Middle High German *īsen* 'iron' + *berg* 'hill', 'mountain'. **2.** Jewish (Ashkenazic): ornamental adoption of 1.

GIVEN NAMES Jewish 6%. *Sol* (9), *Hyman* (7), *Miriam* (6), *Meyer* (4), *Moshe* (4), *Isadore* (3), *Akiva* (2), *Aron* (2), *Avner* (2), *Chaim* (2), *Emanuel* (2), *Isidor* (2).

Eisenberger (290) German and Jewish (Ashkenazic): habitational name for someone from any of the several places called EISENBERG. As a Jewish name it is also an ornamental name.

GIVEN NAMES German 7%; Jewish 6%. *Erwin* (2), *Otto*, *Siegfried*; *Asher*, *Dov*, *Ephraim*, *Mayer*, *Mordche*, *Yakov*.

Eisenbraun (300) **1.** German: probably from the Middle High German personal name *Isenbrun*, or a nickname for someone with a swarthy complexion, from Middle High German *īsen* 'iron' + *brūn* 'brown'. **2.** Jewish (Ashkenazic): ornamental compound of German *Eisen* 'iron' + *braun* 'brown'.

GIVEN NAMES German 10%. *Erwin* (3), *Helmuth* (2), *Reinhold* (2), *Erhard*, *Georg*, *Otto*, *Wilhelm*.

Eisenhard (144) Variant of German EISENHARDT.

Eisenhardt (349) **1.** German: from the Middle High German personal name *Isenhard*, composed of the elements *īsen* 'iron' + *hard* 'hardy', 'brave', 'strong'. **2.** Jewish (Ashkenazic): ornamental name from modern German *eisenhart* 'as strong as iron'.

GIVEN NAMES German 5%. *Gunter*, *Kurt*, *Otto*, *Ulrike*.

Eisenhart (680) Variant of German EISENHARDT.

Eisenhauer (1229) German: occupational name for a worker in iron, from Middle High German *īsen* 'iron' (see EISEN) + *houwære*, a derivative of *houwen* 'to cut, chop, or hew'. As a vocabulary word, this is found in west central (Palatine) Germany only; elsewhere the standard term is SCHMIDT. In the United States, the Eisenhauers (and bearers of the various Americanized forms of the name) are found mainly in PA.

Eisenhour (269) Americanized spelling of German EISENHAUER.

Eisenhower (390) Americanized spelling of German EISENHAUER.

FOREBEARS Hans Nikolaus Eisenhauer, the ancestor of Dwight D. Eisenhower, the 34th president of the U.S., was born about 1691 in Eiterbach in southern Odenwald, a part of the former Electorate of the Palatinate, in what is now Hesse. In 1741, at the age of 50, he sailed with his wife and children from Rotterdam to America and settled in Lebanon County, PA.

Eisenhut (218) German: metonymic occupational name for a helmet maker, from Middle High German *īsenhūt* 'iron helmet'.

GIVEN NAME German 4%. *Wolfgang* (2).

Eisenhuth (172) Variant of German EISENHUT.

Eisenlohr (129) German (Swabian): habitational name for someone from a place named Eisenloh, that is a place where iron nuggets for smelting were found.

GIVEN NAMES German 4%. *Kurt*, *Otto*.

Eisenman (737) Americanized or Jewish spelling of German EISENMANN.

Eisenmann (411) German: variant of EISEN, with the addition of the suffix *-mann* 'man'.

GIVEN NAMES German 8%. *Kurt* (4), *Erwin*, *Friedrich*, *Guenther*, *Hermann*, *Reinhard*, *Ulrich*.

Eisenmenger (268) German: occupational name for an iron dealer, from Middle High German *īsen* 'iron' + *mengære* 'dealer'.

Eisenreich (116) German: from the Germanic personal name *Isanrich*, composed of *īsan* 'iron' + *rīch* 'powerful', 'rich'.

Eisenstadt (239) Jewish (Ashkenazic): habitational name from a place, formerly in Hungary, now in Austria, known in Yiddish as *Ayznshtot* 'Iron City'. See also ASH 3.
GIVEN NAMES Jewish 8%; German 5%. *Zolman* (2), *Herzl, Hyman, Mendel, Sol*; *Eugen, Frieda, Kurt*.

Eisenstat (110) Variant spelling of Jewish EISENSTADT.
GIVEN NAME Jewish 6%. *Meyer*.

Eisenstein (581) **1.** German: topographic name for someone who lived by a place where iron ore was extracted, or perhaps a habitational name from a place named for its iron workings. **2.** Jewish (Ashkenazic): ornamental compound of German *Eisen* 'iron' + *Stein* 'stone'.
GIVEN NAMES Jewish 9%. *Hyman* (3), *Miriam* (2), *Aron, Avi, Channa, Hinda, Nachum, Rivki, Yaacov*.

Eisenzimmer (128) German: from *Eisen* 'iron' + *Zimmer* 'room', 'building', also 'carpenter', hence probably an occupational name for one who made things in iron, for instance, support structures in a mine.

Eiser (136) German: occupational name for an ironworker (see EISEN).
GIVEN NAME German 5%. *Matthias*.

Eiserman (132) German (**Eisermann**): variant of EISENMANN.

Eisert (279) North German: probably from an unattested Germanic personal name *Ishard*, composed of the elements *īsan* 'iron' + *hard* 'hardy', 'brave', 'strong'.
GIVEN NAMES German 6%. *Lothar* (2), *Dieter, Erwin*.

Eisiminger (104) German: altered form of **Eisenmenger**, from Middle High German *īsenmenger* 'iron dealer', an occupational name.
GIVEN NAME German 4%. *Franz*.

Eisinger (368) South German: habitational name from any of various places named Eisingen.
GIVEN NAMES German 6%. *Orlo* (2), *Armin, Claus, Ernst, Kurt*.

Eisler (477) South German: variant of EISNER.

Eisley (123) Americanized form of Swiss German EISELE.

Eisman (445) German (**Eismann**): variant of EISEN.

Eismann (104) Variant of German EISEN.
GIVEN NAMES German 18%. *Detlef, Franz, Frederich, Irmgard, Kurt*.

Eisnaugle (86) Altered form of German **Eisnagel**, a metonymic occupational name for a dealer in ironware, from Middle High German *īsen* 'iron' + *nagel* 'nail'.

Eisner (1383) German and Jewish (Ashkenazic): occupational name for an ironworker, smith, or ironmonger, from an agent derivative of Middle High German *īsen* and German *Eisen* 'iron' (see EISEN).
GIVEN NAMES Jewish 5%. *Chaskel* (2), *Emanuel* (2), *Gadi* (2), *Shlomit* (2), *Yaffa*

(2), *Arie, Batya, Chaya, Dov, Heshy, Hyman, Mayer*.

Eison (204) Altered spelling of the German family name EISEN. This name occurs chiefly in SC.

Eiss (111) German: variant of EIS.

Eissler (180) German: variant spelling of EISLER.

Eister (130) German: variant of EYSTER.

Eiswerth (106) German: from a house name for an innkeeper or a tavern owner or for a farmer, from Middle High German *īsen* 'iron', also 'horse shoe' + *wirt* (Low German *wērt*) 'inn keeper', 'landlord', 'farmer'; *Isen, Eisen* are also found as the first part of numerous personal names.

Eitel (671) German: **1.** from a short form of a Germanic personal name formed with *agi* 'point (of a sword)', 'corner' (Old High German *ecka*). **2.** nickname from Middle High German *ītel* 'bare', 'only'. In the days before surnames had begun to make their mark, bearers of common personal names would often have a second personal name as a distinguishing feature; someone who did not have a second such name could be distinguished by this fact in itself, as for example *ītel Hans* as against *Hans Joachim*. The meaning 'vain', 'conceited' is comparatively late and has probably not contributed to the family name.
GIVEN NAMES German 4%. *Gerhard* (2), *Otto* (2), *Bernd, Franz, Ute*.

Eiting (140) German: unexplained.

Eitner (104) German: metronymic from the female personal name *Eite*, a vernacular form of *Agatha*.
GIVEN NAMES German 12%. *Lorenz* (2), *Hermann, Manfred*.

Eitniear (102) Probably an altered spelling of German EITNER.

Eitzen (172) German: **1.** habitational name from any of several places in Hannover province named Eitzen or Eitzum. **2.** from a short form of a Germanic personal name formed with *agi* 'point (of a sword)', 'corner' (Old High German *ecka*).

Ek (531) Swedish: ornamental name from *ek* 'oak'.
GIVEN NAMES Scandinavian 6%; German 4%. *Anders* (2), *Erik* (2), *Knut*; *Kurt* (2), *Bernhard, Ewald, Otto*.

Ekberg (486) Swedish: ornamental name composed of the elements *ek* 'oak' + *berg* 'hill'.
GIVEN NAMES Scandinavian 9%. *Nils* (4), *Erland* (2), *Sten* (2), *Erik, Nels*.

Ekblad (192) Swedish: ornamental name composed of the elements *ek* 'oak' + *blad* 'leaf'.

Ekdahl (300) Swedish: ornamental name composed of the elements *ek* 'oak' + *dahl*, an ornamental spelling of *dal* 'valley'.

Eke (104) **1.** Dutch and North German: variant of ECK. **2.** English: unexplained.

Ekelund (109) Variant spelling of Swedish EKLUND.
GIVEN NAMES Scandinavian 10%; German 6%. *Borge, Lars*; *Kurt*.

Ekern (223) Norwegian: habitational name from a farm in eastern Norway so named, from Old Norse *ekra* 'meadow', 'field'.

Ekey (115) Probably a variant of Dutch or German EKE.

Ekholm (288) Swedish: ornamental name composed of the elements *ek* 'oak' + *holm* 'island'.
GIVEN NAME Scandinavian 8%. *Erik* (3).

Ekins (171) English: patronymic or metronymic from EADE.

Ekis (102) Latvian (**Eķis, Ēķis**): from the German personal name *Eckehard* (see ECKERT).
GIVEN NAMES Latvian 5%. *Ervins, Imants*.

Ekker (133) Dutch: variant spelling of ECKER.

Ekleberry (115) Americanized form of German **Eckelberg**. Compare ECKELBERRY.

Eklof (146) Swedish (**Eklöf**): ornamental name composed of the elements *ek* 'oak' + *löv* 'leaf'.
GIVEN NAMES Scandinavian 18%. *Estrid* (2), *Sven* (2), *Anders, Erik, Klas, Nels*.

Eklund (1821) Swedish: ornamental name composed of the elements *ek* 'oak' + *lund* 'grove'.
GIVEN NAMES Scandinavian 7%. *Erik* (5), *Lennart* (3), *Nils* (2), *Thor* (2), *Bertel, Hilmer, Lars, Per, Sven*.

Ekman (433) Swedish: ornamental name composed of the elements *ek* 'oak' + *man* 'man'.
GIVEN NAMES Scandinavian 10%; German 4%. *Erik* (4), *Sven* (3), *Bjorn, Gudrun, Lennart, Mats*; *Ernst, Erwin, Hans, Ulrika*.

Ekstein (108) German and Jewish: variant of ECKSTEIN.
GIVEN NAMES Jewish 25%; German 6%. *Mendel* (2), *Shalom* (2), *Asher, Meir, Menachem, Moshe, Shloma, Shlomo*; *Otto, Rudi*.

Ekstrand (314) Swedish: ornamental name composed of the elements *ek* 'oak' + *strand* 'shore'.
GIVEN NAMES Scandinavian 10%. *Anders, Bertel, Erik, Lars, Matts*.

Ekstrom (1221) Swedish (**Ekström**): ornamental name composed of the elements *ek* 'oak' + *ström* 'river', 'current'.
GIVEN NAMES Scandinavian 7%. *Erik* (5), *Algot, Helmer, Hilma, Johan, Nels, Nils, Per*.

Ekwall (104) Swedish: ornamental name composed of the elements *ek* 'oak' + *wall*.
GIVEN NAME Scandinavian 5%. *Erik*.

Ela (147) Origin unidentified.

Elam (4660) English: habitational name for someone from a place called Elham, in Kent, or a lost place of this name in Crayford, Kent. The first is derived from Old English *æl* 'eel' + *hām* 'homestead' or *hamm* 'enclosure hemmed in by water'. There is also an Elam Grange in Bingley, West Yorkshire, but the current distribution of the name in the British Isles suggests that it did not contribute significantly to the surname.

Elamin (234) Muslim: from an Arabic epithet meaning 'the trustworthy'. Compare AMIN.
GIVEN NAMES Muslim 54%. *Abdul* (3), *Bilal* (3), *Hassan* (2), *Rashid* (2), *Saleem* (2), *Aisha, Ameenah, Aneesah, Ayesha, Bashir, Bayyinah, Dawud.*

Eland (252) **1.** English: habitational name for someone from Little Eland in Northumberland, or Elland in West Yorkshire, or Ealand in Lincolnshire, all of which derived their names from Old English *ēaland* 'cultivated land by water or a river'. **2.** Dutch: from a Germanic personal name composed of the elements *adel* 'noble' + *land* 'land'.

Elander (137) Swedish: ornamental name composed of an unexplained first element + *-ander*, suffix adapted from Greek *anēr, andros* 'man', a common element of Swedish surnames.
GIVEN NAMES Scandinavian 4%. *Bjorn, Nils.*

Elardo (134) Italian: possibly from a variant of the Germanic personal name *Ilardo* (see ILARDI).
GIVEN NAMES Italian 4%. *Sal, Santo.*

Elbaum (244) Jewish (Ashkenazic): ornamental name from German *(O:)lbaum* 'olive tree'.
GIVEN NAMES Jewish 18%. *Aron* (2), *Chaim* (2), *Isaak* (2), *Avron, Batya, Irina, Izak, Jechiel, Shlomo, Shmuel, Sol, Yaakov.*

Elbaz (104) Muslim and Jewish (Sephardic): from Persian and Arabic *baz* 'falcon', with the addition of *el* (*al*) 'the'. Compare BAZ.
GIVEN NAMES Jewish 30%; Arabic 15%. *Avi* (2), *Shimon* (2), *Arie, Chaim, Eran, Gilad, Itzik, Malky, Mordechai, Nissim, Ori, Shlomi; Abdel, Ayman, Farouk, Hazim, Khalil, Mohamad, Mohamed, Nabil, Samir, Youssef.*

Elbe (162) German: **1.** habitational name from any of various places named Elbe or from the river name. **2.** from a short form of a Germanic personal name beginning *Alf-*, from an element cognate with Middle Low German *alf* 'ghost', Middle High German *alp* (plural *elbe*).
GIVEN NAME German 4%. *Otto.*

Elbel (101) German: from a pet form of the personal name mentioned at ELBE 2.

Elberg (101) Jewish (Ashkenazic): ornamental name from German *Ölberg* 'olive mountain'.
GIVEN NAMES Jewish 7%; Russian 4%. *Sol, Symcha, Zinaida; Grigory, Mikhail.*

Elbers (128) Dutch and North German: patronymic from the personal name ELBERT.
GIVEN NAMES German 4%. *Johan* (2); *Kurt.*

Elberson (129) Dutch and North German: patronymic from the personal name ELBERT.

Elbert (1164) North German: from a Germanic personal name composed of the elements *agil* 'edge', 'tip' (of a sword) + *berht* 'bright', 'famous'.

Elbon (116) English: unexplained. This name occurs chiefly in WV.

Elbrecht (103) German: from a Germanic personal name composed of the elements *agil* 'edge', 'tip' (of a sword) + *berht* 'bright', 'famous'. Compare ELBERT.
GIVEN NAMES German 6%. *Erwin, Hermann.*

Elchert (122) Dutch or North German: from a Germanic personal name composed of the elements *agil* 'edge', 'tip' (of a sword) + *hard* 'hardy', 'bold'. This name is found chiefly in OH.

Elcock (208) English: from a pet form of ELLIS.

Eld (107) **1.** English: distinguishing name for the older of two bearers of the same personal name, from Middle English *eld* 'old' (from Old English *eald*). **2.** Swedish: ornamental name from Old Norse *eldr* 'flame', 'fire'.

Elden (213) **1.** Norwegian: habitational name from a farm so named, from a river name derived from Old Norse *eldr* 'flame', 'fire', possibly with ironic reference to the icy coldness of the water. **2.** Altered spelling of ELDON.

Elder (11017) **1.** Scottish and English: distinguishing nickname bestowed on the elder (Old English *ealdra*) of two bearers of the same personal name. It may also denote an elder of a Church, in the sense of a senior and respected member of a congregation. **2.** Americanized form of German ELTER, which has the same meaning as 1.

Elderkin (301) English: from a pet form of ELDER.

Elders (552) English: variant of ELDER.

Eldon (149) **1.** English: habitational name for someone from Eldon in County Durham or Elveden in Suffolk. The first is named from the Old English personal name *Ella* + *dūn* 'hill'; the second from Old English *elfitu* 'swan' or *elf* 'elf', 'fairy' + *denu* 'valley'. **2.** English: nickname from Middle English *eld* 'old' + *hine* 'servant'.

Eldred (1815) English: variant of ALDRED.

Eldredge (1821) English: variant of ALDRIDGE (see ALDRICH).

Eldreth (248) Variant of English ELDRIDGE.

Eldridge (8491) English: from a Middle English personal name, *Eldric*, a variant of ALDRICH.

Eleazer (248) German and Jewish: from the Biblical personal name *Eleazar* 'God is my salvation'.

Eleby (108) Probably an altered spelling of the English family name ELLERBY. This name is found chiefly in TX.

Eledge (141) See ELLEDGE.

Elefante (168) Southern Italian: from *elefante* 'elephant' (Latin *elephas*, genitive

elephantis), presumably applied as a nickname.
GIVEN NAMES Italian 13%; Spanish 5%. *Vito* (3), *Antonio* (2), *Dino, Salvatore; Brigido, Rey, Silvestre.*

Elek (191) Hungarian: from the personal name *Elek*, from Latin *Alexius* (see ALEXIS).
GIVEN NAMES Hungarian 11%. *Zoltan* (3), *Bela, Dezso, Gabor, Imre, Kalman.*

Elenbaas (261) Dutch: reinterpretation of **Elenbos** or **Elebaers**, from a Germanic personal name composed of the elements *alja* 'other' or *agil* 'point or edge (of a sword)' + *berht* 'bright'.

Elert (104) Variant of German EHLERT.
GIVEN NAME German 5%. *Gunter.*

Eley (1490) **1.** English: variant spelling of ELY. **2.** German: from a short form of the personal name *Eligius* (see LOY).

Elfenbein (144) Jewish (eastern Ashkenazic): ornamental name from German *Elfenbein* 'ivory'.
GIVEN NAMES Jewish 8%. *Emanuel* (3), *Isadore, Sol.*

Elfering (176) Dutch and German: patronymic from the personal name *Elfer* (see ELFERS).

Elfers (243) Dutch and German: patronymic from *Elfer*, a medieval short form of the Germanic personal name *Alberich*, a compound of *alf, alp* 'ghost', 'sprite' + *rīhhi* 'powerful', 'ruler'.
GIVEN NAMES German 8%. *Wilhelm* (3), *Gerhardt, Kurt, Otto.*

Elfman (170) **1.** German (**Elfmann**): habitational name for someone from a place called Elvede or Elbe. **2.** German (**Elfmann**): from a short form of a Germanic personal name composed of the elements *alf* 'ghost' + *man* 'man'. **3.** Jewish (eastern Ashkenazic):
GIVEN NAME Jewish 4%. *Isadore.*

Elford (188) English: habitational name from a place so named, from the Old English personal name *Ella* (see ELLINGTON) + *ford* 'ford', or from Old English *alor, elre* 'alder tree' + *ford*. There is a place of this name in Staffordshire and another in Northumbria, but the surname now occurs chiefly in Devon.

Elfrink (193) Probably a North German variant of **Elfering**, from a Germanic personal name formed with *alf, alp* 'ghost', 'sprite'.

Elfstrom (157) Probably of Swedish origin, an ornamental name composed of the elements *elf*, an ornamental (old) spelling of *älv* 'river' + *ström* 'stream', 'current'.
GIVEN NAMES Scandinavian 6%. *Anders* (2), *Sven.*

Elg (153) Swedish: ornamental name from *elg*, an ornamental (old) spelling of *älg* 'moose'.
GIVEN NAMES Scandinavian 7%. *Evald, Fredrik, Iver.*

Elgart (181) **1.** Jewish (Ashkenazic): ornamental name from German *Ölgarten* 'olive garden'. **2.** German: habitational name for someone from Elgert in the Rhineland.
GIVEN NAMES Jewish 5%. *Bracha, Myer, Uri.*

Elgersma (155) Frisian: patronymic from the Germanic personal name *Ellger*, *Agilger*, composed of the elements *agil* 'point (of a sword)' + *gēr* 'spear'.

Elgin (1128) Scottish: habitational name from Elgin, a place in Moray.

Elhard (138) German (**Elhar(d)t**): from a Germanic personal name composed of *adal* 'noble' + *hard* 'hard', 'strong'.

Eli (449) Jewish: from a short form of *Elia*.

Elia (951) **1.** Southern Italian: from the personal name *Elia*, Italian equivalent of ELIAS. **2.** Basque: habitational name from Elia, a town in Navarre, Basque Country.
GIVEN NAMES Italian 16%; Spanish 11%. *Angelo* (3), *Sal* (3), *Claudio* (2), *Rocco* (2), *Rosario* (2), *Salvatore* (2), *Amleto*, *Calogero, Concetta, Enrico, Filippo, Giovanni, Nicola, Rocci; Jose* (3), *Carlos* (2), *Ana Lucia, Blanca, Gonzalez, Gutierrez, Jaime.*

Eliades (143) Greek: patronymic from the Biblical name ELIAS. The *-ides* patronymic is classical, and was revived in particular by Greeks from the Black Sea during the late 19th and early 20th centuries.
GIVEN NAMES Greek 18%. *Eleni* (2), *Constantine, Costas, Demetris, Kyriaki, Panayotis, Pavlos, Prodromos, Savvas, Tasos.*

Elias (4874) Greek, Spanish (**Elías**), Catalan, Portuguese, English, Welsh, French (**Élias**), German, Dutch, Hungarian (**Éliás**), Czech (**Eliáš**), and Jewish: from a medieval personal name, the New Testament Greek form of Hebrew *Eliyahu* 'Jehovah is God' (Anglicized as ELIJAH in the Old Testament of the King James Bible). This name was borne by a Biblical prophet, but its popularity among Christians in the Middle Ages was a result of its adoption by various early saints, including a 7th-century bishop of Syracuse and a 9th-century Spanish martyr.
GIVEN NAMES Spanish 12%. *Jose* (27), *Miguel* (16), *Carlos* (15), *Manuel* (15), *Juan* (12), *Luis* (12), *Mario* (10), *Jorge* (9), *Ramon* (9), *Francisco* (7), *Fernando* (6), *Jesus* (6).

Eliasen (172) Danish, Norwegian, and North German: variant of ELIASSEN.
GIVEN NAMES Scandinavian 13%. *Erik* (2), *Lars, Per.*

Eliason (1457) Swedish (**Eliasson**): patronymic from the personal name ELIAS.
GIVEN NAMES Scandinavian 4%. *Iver* (2), *Nels* (2), *Sven* (2), *Anders, Erik, Lennart, Maren.*

Eliassen (173) Danish, Norwegian, and North German: patronymic from the personal name ELIAS.

GIVEN NAMES Scandinavian 18%. *Erik* (2), *Nels* (2), *Knut, Lars, Svein, Thor.*

Eliasson (123) Swedish form or Americanization of various other Scandinavian patronymics from the personal name ELIAS.
GIVEN NAMES Scandinavian 25%. *Anders* (2), *Pehr* (2), *Sven* (2), *Fredrik, Lennart.*

Elich (129) Variant of the North German family name **Ehlich**, from a byname from Middle Low German *edelik* 'noble'.
GIVEN NAME German 5%. *Fritz* (2).

Elick (193) Americanized spelling of German ELICH or ILLIG.

Elicker (191) Probably a respelling of Swiss German **Elliker**, a habitational name from either of two places in Switzerland called Ellikon.

Elie (540) French: variant of ELIAS.
FOREBEARS Immigrants bearing this name from Brittany were in Quebec by 1669, notably in the Ile d'Orléans.
GIVEN NAMES French 18%. *Luc* (3), *Emile* (2), *Jacques* (2), *Lucien* (2), *Monique* (2), *Odette* (2), *Pierre* (2), *Regine* (2), *Achille, Andre, Gilles, Jean Claude.*

Elijah (216) Welsh, Jewish, and American: from the personal name *Elijah*, the usual English transliteration in the King James Bible (Old Testament) of the Hebrew name *Eliyahu* 'Jehovah is God', name of one of the Biblical prophets (see ELIAS). As a Welsh surname, this is a comparatively late adoption of the personal name, adopted after Old Testament given names became popular among Nonconformists.

Elin (102) **1.** English: variant of HILLIAN. **2.** Russian: variant of ELLEN.
GIVEN NAMES Russian 5%. *Grigory, Matvey.*

Eline (143) **1.** English: variant of HILLIAN. **2.** Russian: variant of ELLEN.

Eliopoulos (181) Greek: patronymic from the personal name ELIAS, formed with the patronymic suffix *-poulos*, derived from Latin *pullus* 'nestling', 'chick'; this ending occurs chiefly in the Peloponnese.
GIVEN NAMES Greek 8%. *Christos* (2), *Dimitrios, Pericles, Sotirios.*

Eliot (321) English and Scottish: variant spelling of ELLIOTT.
FOREBEARS Andrew Eliot, a shoemaker of East Coker, Somerset, England, who emigrated to Boston MA in 1670, was the founder of a distinguished American family which included the poet T. S. Eliot (1888–1965), who was born in St. Louis, MO.
The earliest Eliot recorded in North America was John Eliot (1604–90), a Puritan missionary known as the 'Indian Apostle', who was born in Hertfordshire and sailed to Boston in 1631. He later settled in Roxbury MA.

Elison (204) **1.** English: patronymic from ELLIS. **2.** Scandinavian: Americanized form of ELIASSEN or ELIASSON.

Elizabeth (163) Americanized spelling of the Dutch family name **Elisabeth**, from the

female personal name derived from the Biblical name meaning 'God is my oath'. The name was particularly popular in the Middle Ages, notably after the canonization of Elisabeth, Duchess of Thuringia around 1230.
GIVEN NAME French 5%. *Dominique.*

Elizalde (452) Basque: habitational name from Elizalde, a town in Gipuzkoa, Basque Country, or topographic name for someone who lived by a church, from *eleiza* 'church' + the suffix *-alde* 'by'.
GIVEN NAMES Spanish 53%. *Raul* (12), *Jose* (10), *Juan* (8), *Luis* (5), *Jaime* (4), *Javier* (4), *Jorge* (4), *Alberto* (3), *Alfredo* (3), *Arturo* (3), *Enrique* (3), *Francisco* (3).

Elizondo (1893) Basque: habitational name from Elizondo, a town in Navarre, or topographic name for someone who lived near a church, from *eleiza* 'church' + the suffix *-ondo* 'near', 'beside'.
GIVEN NAMES Spanish 48%. *Jose* (35), *Juan* (29), *Carlos* (27), *Jesus* (20), *Manuel* (15), *Roberto* (14), *Ruben* (14), *Luis* (13), *Guadalupe* (12), *Javier* (12), *Armando* (11), *Enrique* (10).

Elk (171) Perhaps a shortened form of the Dutch family name **van Elk**, a habitational name from someone from Othée (Dutch: *Elch*) in the province of Liège.

Elkin (1525) **1.** English: from a pet form of *Elis* (see ELLIS). **2.** Jewish (eastern Ashkenazic): metronymic from the Yiddish female personal name *Elke* + the Slavic suffix *-in*. **3.** Jewish (eastern Ashkenazic): patronymic from the Yiddish male personal name *Elke*, a pet form of ELIJAH + the Slavic suffix *-in*.
GIVEN NAMES Jewish 5%. *Ilya* (3), *Hyman* (2), *Miriam* (2), *Sol* (2), *Yakov* (2), *Aron, Hymen, Itta, Meyer, Pinchas, Rakhil, Rimma.*

Elkind (262) Jewish (eastern Ashkenazic): variant of ELKIN 2 and 3.
GIVEN NAMES Jewish 9%; Russian 9%. *Faina, Ilya, Mort, Yakov; Anatoly, Arkadiy, Dmitriy, Grigoriy, Liliya, Lyubov, Mikhail, Semyon, Sofiya, Valeriy, Vladimir.*

Elkington (197) English: habitational name from North or South Elkington in Lincolnshire, so named from an Old English personal name (possibly *Ēa(n)lāc*) + Old English *tūn* 'enclosure', 'settlement'. Elkington in Northamptonshire is not the source of the family name: it did not acquire the name until 1617, before which it was *Eltington* or *Elteton*.

Elkins (8912) English: patronymic from ELKIN 1.

Elko (410) Origin unidentified.

Elks (309) English: reduced form of ELKINS.

Ell (509) **1.** German and Dutch: metonymic occupational name for a dealer in cloth or a tailor, from Middle High German, Middle Low German *el(l)e* 'yardstick', 'length of the lower arm'. **2.** German: from a short form, *Edilo*, from any of various Germanic personal names composed with *adal* 'noble family'. **3.** English: from the female personal name *Ela*, a reduced form of *Elena* and possibly also of *Eleanor*.

Ellard (622) English: variant of ALLARD.

Ellebracht (124) German: variant of EL-BERT.

Elledge (1541) Of English origin: unexplained. Possibly a much altered form of ALDRICH, which was established from an early date in North America, with a number of variant spellings.

FOREBEARS The name Elledge is first recorded in the early 18th century in MD and VA. An important ancestor is Francis Elledge, born in 1750 in Yadkin District, NC.

Ellefsen (136) Norwegian: patronymic from *Ellef*, from the Old Norse personal name *Eilífr*, a compound of *ei* 'alone', 'sole' or 'always' + *lífr* 'living', 'alive'.
GIVEN NAMES Scandinavian 11%; German 5%. *Astrid*; *Hans*, *Kurt*.

Ellefson (969) Americanized spelling of Norwegian ELLEFSEN.

Ellegood (167) Americanized spelling of German **Ellguth**, a habitational name from any of several places in Silesia, which were dubbed *lgota* 'relief from (taxes)' in Slavic; these were German settlements which were exempt from taxation.

Elleman (141) **1.** German (**Ellemann**): habitational name for someone from a place named Ell, probably the one near Aachen. **2.** Perhaps in some cases an altered spelling of ELLERMAN (see ELLER 1–3).

Ellen (444) **1.** English: from the usual medieval vernacular form of the female personal name *Helen* (Greek *Helenē*). This was the name of the mother of Constantine the Great, a devout Christian who was credited with finding the True Cross. It was a popular name in Britain, due to the legend (which has no historical basis) that she was born in Britain. **2.** English: variant of HILLIAN. **3.** Dutch: from a short form of any of several Germanic personal names beginning with the element *Ellen-*, as, for example, *Ellenborg*.

Ellena (170) Italian: from the female personal name *Ellena*, or possibly an ethnic name from the Greek word *Hellēnas* 'Greek'. From late classical times onward this word meant only 'pagan', until it was revived in the 19th century as an ethnic term used by Greeks to refer to themselves.

Ellenbecker (292) Americanized spelling of German **Ellenbecher**, a habitational name for someone from any of various places named Ellenbach or Ehlenbach.

Ellenberg (322) **1.** German, Swiss German, and Jewish (Ashkenazic): habitational name from any of various places called Ellenberg, for example near Ellwangen and Salzwedel. **2.** Jewish (Ashkenazic): ornamental name from German *Ölenberg*, literally 'olive mountain'.

GIVEN NAMES German 4%; Jewish 4%. *Eldred*, *Gerhard*, *Klaus*; *Gilad* (2), *Sholom*, *Shoshana*, *Sol*.

Ellenberger (853) German and Swiss German: habitational name for someone from any of the various places called ELLEN-BERG.
GIVEN NAMES German 4%. *Kurt* (4), *Johann*, *Konrad*, *Manfred*.

Ellenbogen (238) **1.** German: topographic name for someone who lived by a bend in a river, from Middle High German *el(l)enboge* 'elbow', or habitational name from any of several places named Ellenbogen or Ehlenbogen from this word. **2.** Jewish (Ashkenazic): ornamental name from German *Ellenbogen* 'elbow' (see 1).
GIVEN NAMES Jewish 10%; German 7%. *Miriam* (4), *Hyman* (2), *Hershel*, *Sol*, *Zipora*; *Kurt* (3), *Maximilian* (2).

Ellenburg (778) German: habitational name for someone from Nellenburg (formerly Ellenburg), near Lake Constance.

Ellender (359) **1.** English: variant of ALLENDER. **2.** Respelling of German **Elender**, a nickname for a stranger or newcomer, from Middle High German *ellende* 'strange', 'foreign', or a habitational name for someone from any of twenty places named Elend, denoting a remote settlement, as for example in the Harz Mountains or in Carinthia, Austria.

Ellens (144) **1.** English: metronymic from ELLEN. **2.** Dutch: patronymic from ELLEN.

Ellenson (176) Respelling of Swedish **Ellensson**, probably a patronymic from the personal name *Erland* (from Old Norse *erlendr* 'foreign'), or alternatively, though less likely, a metronymic from the female personal name *Ellen*.

Ellenwood (326) English: habitational name from an unidentified place.
FOREBEARS Ralph Ellenwood (born 1607) came to Salem, MA, in September 1635 in the Truelove, and later settled in Beverly.

Eller (5106) **1.** North German: topographic name for someone who lived by an alder tree, from Middle Low German *elre*, *alre* 'alder'. **2.** German: habitational name from places in the North Rhine and Mosel areas, so called from an old stream name *Elera*, *Alira*, of Celtic origin. **3.** Jewish (eastern Ashkenazic): variant of HELLER, reflecting varieties of Yiddish in which there is no *h*.

Ellerbe (585) Variant of English ELLERBY.

Ellerbeck (102) German: habitational name from any of various minor places named as the 'stream where the alder trees grow'.
FOREBEARS Heinrich Ellerbeck was born in 1818 in Holzfelde in Prussia. In 1845 he came to America, joining his uncle August Broemmelsieck on the Brommelsieck farm in Franklin County, MO.

Ellerbee (437) Variant of English ELLERBY.

Ellerbrock (353) North German: topographic name for someone who lived by a

low-lying swamp overgrown with alders, from Middle Low German *elre* 'alder' + *brock* 'swamp'.

Ellerbusch (101) German: topographic name for someone living by an alder bush.
GIVEN NAME German 4%. *Otto*.

Ellerby (131) English: habitational name from a place in North Yorkshire so named, from the Old English personal name *Ælfweard* + Old Scandinavian *býr* 'farmstead', 'village'.

Ellerd (102) English: origin uncertain, perhaps a variant of ALLARD.

Ellerman (518) **1.** English: variant of ELMAN 3. **2.** Americanized spelling of German **Ellermann**, a variant of ELLER 1.

Ellers (196) **1.** Respelling of German EHLERS. **2.** English: habitational name from High and Low Ellers in West Yorkshire, named from Old English *alras*, plural of *alor* 'alder'.
GIVEN NAMES German 4%. *Fritz*, *Manfred*.

Ellerson (152) English: variant of ELLISON.

Ellert (172) **1.** English: variant of ALLARD. **2.** Perhaps a shortened form of Swedish **Ellertsson** (see ELLERTSON).
GIVEN NAMES German 4%. *Merwin* (2), *Traude*.

Ellertson (182) Americanized form of Scandinavian EILERTSON.

Ellery (278) English: variant of HILLARY.
FOREBEARS William Ellery, a signer of the Declaration of Independence, was born in Newport, RI, in 1727.

Elles (108) Probably a variant spelling of English and Welsh ELLIS.

Ellestad (183) Norwegian: habitational name from a farm so named, from the Old Norse personal name *Eilífr* (see ELLEFSEN) + *stad* (from Old Norse *staðr* 'farmstead', 'dwelling').
GIVEN NAME Scandinavian 4%. *Erik*.

Elletson (101) English: metronymic from the female personal name *Ellet*, *Ellot* (see ELLETT).

Ellett (787) English: from a pet form of the female personal name ELLEN.

Elley (159) Welsh and English: probably from a pet form of ELLIS.

Ellick (113) **1.** Americanized form of German ILLIG. One family bearing this name and known to have made this change in form came to OH from Alsace in the 19th century. **2.** English: habitational name from either of two places called Elwick, in North Yorkshire and Northumberland, named with the Old English personal name *Ella* (or in the case of the first, possibly an unattested *Ægla*) + Old English *wīc* 'outlying (dairy) farm'.

Ellickson (147) English or German: patronymic from ELLICK.

Ellicott (184) English: **1.** habitational name from an unidentified place, probably in Devon, where there is a place called Ellicombe and where the surname is most frequent today. **2.** Possibly also a variant of ELLIOTT.

GIVEN NAME French 4%. *Eugenie*.

Elliff (201) English: **1.** from the Middle English female personal name *Ayleve*, *Aylgive*, Old English *Æðelgifu*, composed of the elements *æðel* 'noble' + *gifu* 'gift', which was borne by a daughter of King Alfred the Great, who became abbess of Shaftesbury. **2.** from the Old Norse byname *Eilífr*, which is composed of the elements *ei* 'always' + *lífr* 'life'.

Ellifritz (101) German: probably a variant of ILGENFRITZ.

Ellig (109) German: unexplained.

Ellin (145) **1.** English: variant spelling of ELLEN. **2.** Jewish (eastern Ashkenazic): habitational name from the village Elna in Belarus.

GIVEN NAMES Spanish 6%; Jewish 5%. *Efrain* (2), *Eduvigis*, *Enrique*, *Jose*, *Juan*, *Omayra*; *Baruch*.

Elling (499) North German: habitational name for someone from any of several places in northern Germany named Ellingen or Eldingen.

GIVEN NAMES German 5%. *Monika* (2), *Eldor*, *Frieda*, *Kurt*, *Lorenz*, *Otto*.

Ellingboe (154) Scandinavian: from a compound of *Elling* (either a personal name from Old Norse *Erlingr*, probably meaning 'son of an earl', or a Danish patronymic from the Frisian personal name *Elle*) + *boe* 'dwelling', 'abode'.

Ellinger (928) German: habitational name for someone from any of various places named Ellingen, or from Öllingen near Ulm.

Ellingham (109) English: habitational name from places so named in Hampshire, Northumbria, and Norfolk. The first of these is named from Old English *Ēdlingahām* 'homestead (Old English *hām*) of the people of *Ēdla*', a personal name derived from a short form of the various compound names with a first element *ēad* 'prosperity', 'fortune'; the others may have the same origin or incorporate the personal name *Ella* (see ELLINGTON).

Ellingsen (324) **1.** Norwegian: patronymic from *Elling*, from the Old Norse personal name *Erlingr*, meaning 'son of an earl'. **2.** North German: habitational name for someone from a place called Ellinghausen, Ellingesen, or similar.

GIVEN NAMES Scandinavian 10%. *Per* (2), *Egil*, *Nils*, *Selmer*, *Svein*, *Sven*.

Ellingson (2450) American spelling of Norwegian ELLINGSEN.

Ellingsworth (431) English: habitational name from an unidentified place.

Ellington (3596) English: habitational name from places in Cambridgeshire, Kent, Northumbria, and North Yorkshire; most are so named from Old English *Ellingtūn* 'settlement (Old English *tūn*) associated with *Ella*', a short form of the various com-

pound names with a first element *ælf* 'elf', but the one in Kent has its first element from the Old English byname *Ealda* meaning 'old'.

Ellingwood (404) Variant of English ELLENWOOD.

Ellinwood (262) Variant of English ELLENWOOD.

Elliot (2734) Scottish and English: variant spelling of ELLIOTT. This spelling is mainly Scottish. Compare ELIOT.

Elliott (51038) **1.** English: from a Middle English personal name, *Elyat*, *Elyt*. This represents at least two Old English personal names which have fallen together: the male name *Aðelgēat* (composed of the elements *aðel* 'noble' + *Gēat*, a tribal name; see JOCELYN), and the female personal name *Aðelgȳð* (composed of the elements *aðel* 'noble' + *gȳð* 'battle'). The Middle English name seems also to have absorbed various other personal names of Old English or Continental Germanic origin, as for example Old English *Ælfweald* (see ELLWOOD). **2.** English: from a pet form of ELLIS. **3.** Scottish: Anglicized form of the originally distinct Gaelic surname **Elloch**, **Eloth**, a topographic name from Gaelic *eileach* 'dam', 'mound', 'bank'. Compare ELIOT.

Ellis (64053) English and Welsh: from the medieval personal name *Elis*, a vernacular form of *Elijah* (see ELIAS). In Wales this surname absorbed forms derived from the Welsh personal name *Elisedd*, a derivative of *elus* 'kindly', 'benevolent'.

Ellison (14050) English: patronymic from ELLIS.

Ellisor (391) Of German origin: altered form of ELEAZER.

Elliston (430) **1.** English: patronymic from ELLIS. **2.** Scottish: habitational name from the lands of Elliston, near Bowden, in Roxburghshire.

Ellithorpe (202) English: habitational name from an unidentified place, probably in Lincolnshire. The surname has died out in the British Isles but thrives in the U.S.

FOREBEARS This name is recorded in Ipswich, MA, in 1678, and the marriage of Mary Elithorp is recorded in Boston, MA, in 1727.

Ellman (631) **1.** English: variant spelling of ELMAN. **2.** Variant spelling of Jewish ELMAN.

Ellmore (120) English: variant spelling of ELMORE.

Ellner (234) **1.** German: habitational name for someone from a place named Ellen, in particular one near Düren. **2.** Jewish (from Belarus): habitational name for someone from the village of Elnya in Belarus.

GIVEN NAMES Jewish 4%. *Miriam* (2), *Hyman*.

Ells (573) English (Kent): probably a variant of ELLIS.

Ellson (156) English: **1.** reduced form of ELLISON. **2.** variant spelling of ELSON.

Ellstrom (152) Swedish (**Ellström**): ornamental name composed of an uncertain first element (perhaps from *eld* 'fire') + *ström* 'stream', 'current'.

GIVEN NAMES Scandinavian 13%. *Tor* (2), *Kerstin*, *Sven*.

Ellsworth (5018) English: habitational name from a place in Cambridgeshire named Elsworth, from the genitive case of the Old English personal name *Elli* (see ELLINGTON) + Old English *worð* 'enclosure' (see WORTH).

Ellwanger (363) German: habitational name for someone from any of the several places named Ellwangen, the largest of which is in Swabia, on the Jagst river.

Ellwein (173) German: from a Germanic personal name composed of the elements *adal* 'noble' + *wini* 'friend'.

GIVEN NAMES German 9%. *Armin*, *Erhardt*, *Erna*, *Erwin*, *Gerhard*, *Milbert*.

Ellwood (662) English: variant spelling of ELWOOD.

Ellyson (279) Probably an altered spelling of ELLISON.

GIVEN NAME French 4%. *Yvon*.

Ellzey (677) Perhaps an altered spelling of ELSEY.

Elm (359) **1.** English: topographic name for someone who lived near an elm tree or in an elm grove, from Middle English *elm* 'elm'. **2.** German: habitational name from any of the various places so named. **3.** Swedish: ornamental name from *älm(e)* 'elm grove'.

Elman (472) **1.** Jewish (eastern Ashkenazic): variant of **Hellmann** (see HELLER), reflecting varieties of Yiddish in which there is no *h*. **2.** German (**Elmann**): from a short form of the Germanic personal name *Adelman*, composed of the elements *adal* 'noble (family)' + *man* 'man'. **3.** English: occupational name for a seller of oil, from Middle English *ele* 'oil' + *man* 'man'.

GIVEN NAMES Jewish 8%; Russian 4%. *Meyer* (2), *Yaakov* (2), *Hyman*, *Mandel*, *Polina*, *Shmul*, *Yitzhak*; *Boris* (2), *Igor*, *Leya*, *Misha*, *Semyon*, *Sofiya*, *Vladimir*, *Yefim*, *Yevgeny*.

Elmendorf (412) North German: habitational name from a village so named in the province of Oldenburg.

Elmer (2208) **1.** English: from the Middle English personal name *Ailmar*, Old English *Æðelmǣr*, composed of the elements *æðel* 'noble' + *mǣr* 'famous', which was reinforced after the Conquest by the introduction of Old French *Ailmer*, from a Continental cognate. **2.** North German: from a Germanic personal name composed of the elements *agi(l)* 'edge or tip (of a sword)' + *man* 'man'. **3.** South German: topographic name for someone who lived by an elm tree, Middle High German *elm(e)*. **4.** Swiss German: habitational name from a village so named in Glarus canton.

FOREBEARS Edward Elmer was one of the founders of Hartford, CT, (coming from Cambridge, MA, with Thomas Hooker) in 1635.

Elmes (182) English: variant of ELM.
GIVEN NAME French 4%. *Patrice*.

Elmo (146) Italian: **1.** from the personal name *Elmo*, probably a Germanic name derived from *helm* 'helmet', 'protection'. **2.** from a vernacular altered form of the personal name *Erasmus* (see ERAMO).
GIVEN NAMES Italian 13%. *Angelo* (3), *Loredana* (2), *Sal* (2), *Salvatore*.

Elmore (8727) English: habitational name from Elmore in Gloucestershire, named from Old English *elm* 'elm' + *ōfer* 'river bank' or *ofer* 'ridge'.

Elmquist (377) Swedish: ornamental name composed of the elements *älm(e)* 'elm grove' + *quist*, an old or ornamental spelling of *kvist* 'twig'.

Elms (911) English: variant of ELM.

Elo (136) **1.** Finnish: ornamental name from *elo* 'life', 'harvest'; 'grain'. It was adopted by many Finns during the name conversion movement in the 19th and early 20th centuries, especially in southern and western parts of the country. **2.** Hungarian (**Élő**): from a pet form of **Éliás** (see ELIAS).
GIVEN NAMES Finnish 8%; Scandinavian 5%; Hungarian 4%. *Arto, Kauko, Reino, Seppo*; *Jarl*; *Arpad, Atle, Csaba*.

Elofson (143) Swedish (**Elofsson**): patronymic from the personal name *Elof* (from Old Norse name *Eileifr*) (see ELLEFSON).
GIVEN NAMES Scandinavian 8%; German 4%. *Lars*; *Otto*.

Elpers (275) Dutch: probably, Debrabandere suggests, a variant of **Elbers**, a patronymic from a Germanic personal name composed of the elements *ali* 'other', 'foreign' + *berht* 'bright', 'shining'.

Elrick (178) **1.** English: variant of ALDRICH. **2.** Scottish: habitational name from Elrick in Aberdeenshire.

Elrod (4056) Altered spelling of North German **Ellrott**, **Ellrodt**, perhaps a habitational name from Ellierode near Northeim, Lower Saxony, either of two places in Hesse named Ellingerode, or two lost places so named. In the U.S. this name is very frequent in GA, TN, and TX.

Els (118) Dutch and North German: from a vernacular form of the Biblical name *Elijah* (see ELIAS).
GIVEN NAMES German 9%. *Ewald, Wilhelm*.

Elsaesser (138) German (**Elsässer**) and Jewish (western Ashkenazic): see ELSASSER.
GIVEN NAMES German 5%. *Armin, Kurt*.

Elsass (229) German and Jewish (western Ashkenazic): regional name for someone from Alsace, German *Elsass* (see ELSASSER).

Elsasser (570) German and Jewish (western Ashkenazic): regional name for someone from Alsace (German *Elsass*, Yiddish *Elzes*), with the suffix *-er* indicating a native or inhabitant of a place. The name of the region (first attested in Latin documents in the form *Alisatia*) has traditionally been derived from Old High German *ali* 'other', 'foreign' + *saz* 'seat', 'possession', but Bahlow traces the first element back to a river name *Ill* or *Ell*.
GIVEN NAMES German 4%. *Arno* (2), *Alois, Caspar, Fritz, Volker*.

El-Sayed (211) Muslim: see SAYED.

Elsbernd (142) German: metronymic name meaning 'Bernd, son of Els' or 'Bernd, husband of Els'.

Elsberry (607) Variant of English ELSBURY. This name occurs chiefly in IA and GA.

Elsbree (139) American variant spelling of English ALSBURY.

Elsbury (227) English: variant of ALSBURY.

Else (413) **1.** English: variant of ELL. **2.** North German: topographic name for someone who lived by an alder or alders, Middle Low German *else*.

Elsea (522) Probably an altered spelling of English ELSEY or German ELSE. This name occurs chiefly in TN, OH, and VA.

Elsen (472) Dutch: **1.** metronymic from a short form of the female personal name *Elisabeth* (see ELIZABETH). **2.** probably also a shortened form of **van Elsen**, a habitational name for someone from any of various places named Elzen, for example in North Brabant, or in the Belgian provinces of Brabant and Liège. Alternatively, it may be from **van den Elsen**, a topographic name from the plural of *els* 'alder'.

Elsenpeter (108) German: variant of **Elspeter**, a metronymic from *Elisabeth* or a habitational name from Elsbethen near Salzburg, Austria.

Elser (548) South German: metronymic from ELSE.

Elsesser (244) Variant spelling of German **Elsässer** (see ELSASSER).
GIVEN NAMES German 4%. *Bernd, Kurt, Mathias*.

Elsey (573) English: from the Middle English personal name *El(f)si*, Old English *Ælfsige*, composed of the elements *ælf* 'elf' + *sige* 'victory'.

Elsing (149) German: from a variant of the old personal name **Elsung**.

Elsinger (134) Swiss German: probably a derivative of ELSING.
GIVEN NAMES German 5%. *Helmut, Rainer*.

Elsmore (116) English (Staffordshire): habitational name from Ellesmere in Shropshire, named from the Old English personal name *Elli* + Old English *mere* 'lake', 'pool'.

Elsner (1028) German: in Silesia, a topographic name from Slavic *olesna* 'alder'. In northern Germany it has the same meaning,

but is derived from Middle Low German *else* 'alder'. It may also be a habitational name from a place named with this word.
GIVEN NAMES German 4%. *Wolfgang* (2), *Alfons, Dieter, Egon, Ernst, Erwin, Eward, Hans, Heinz, Lutz, Manfred*.

Elson (1259) **1.** English: habitational name from places in Hampshire and Shropshire named Elson. The former is named from the Old English personal name *Æðelswīð* (composed of the elements *æðel* 'noble' + *swīð* 'strong') + Old English *tūn* 'enclosure', 'settlement'; the latter from the genitive case of the Old English personal name *Elli* (see ELLINGTON) + Old English *tūn* 'settlement' or *dūn* 'hill'. **2.** English: variant spelling of ELLSON. **3.** Jewish (Ashkenazic): patronymic from the Yiddish male personal name *Elye*, from Hebrew *Eliyahu* 'Elijah' (see ELIAS).

Elstad (220) Norwegian: habitational name from any of several farmsteads so named, from an Old Norse personal name (*Eldfríðr* (female), *Eilífr* (male), or *Elfr* (female)) + *stad* (from Old Norse *staðr* 'farmstead', 'dwelling').
GIVEN NAMES Scandinavian 4%. *Erik* (2), *Helmer*.

Elster (304) German: habitational name from any of several places so named. This is also the name of a river in Saxony, which in some cases may have given rise to the family name.
GIVEN NAMES German 5%. *Kurt, Reinhardt*.

Elston (1933) English: habitational name from any of various places so named. One in Lancashire is named from the Old English female personal name *Æðelsige* (composed of the elements *aðel* 'noble' + *sige* 'victory') + Old English *tūn* 'enclosure', 'settlement'; one in Nottinghamshire originally had as its first element the genitive case of the Old Norse byname *Eilífr* meaning 'everlasting'; one in Wiltshire was so named from ELIAS Giffard, holder of the manor in the 12th century.

Elswick (1123) English: habitational name from a place in Lancashire, so named from the Old English personal name *Æðelsige* (see ELSTON) + *wīc* 'dairy farm'.

Elsworth (157) English: variant spelling of ELLSWORTH.

Elter (116) German: distinguishing nickname bestowed on the elder (Middle High German *elter*) of two bearers of the same personal name. In North America, this surname has frequently been assimilated to English and Scottish ELDER.
GIVEN NAME German 6%. *Reinhold* (2).

Elting (245) German: habitational name from a place in Württemberg called Eltingen. It is frequent in New Netherland, in mid Hudson valley.

Elton (848) English: habitational name from any of the various places so called. For the most part they derive from the Old English personal name *Ella* or *Elli* (see ELLING-

TON) + Old English *tūn* 'enclosure', 'settlement'. One in Berkshire, however, gets its first element from the Old English female personal name *Æðelflæd* (composed of the elements *æðel* 'noble' + *flǣd* 'beauty'). One in Cambridgeshire has its first element from the personal name *Æðelhēah* (composed of the elements *æðel* 'noble' + *hēah* 'high'). The place of this name in County Durham probably gets its first element from Old English *ǣl* 'eel'.

Eltringham (175) English: habitational name from a village in Northumbria, named from Old English *Ælfheringahām* 'homestead (Old English *hām*) of the people of *Ælfhere*'; the *t* was inserted for the sake of euphony after the name had been collapsed in pronunciation. The surname is still largely restricted to the Newcastle area.

Eltz (116) German: habitational name (originally a river name) from Elz near Limburg (Hesse) or from Eltz on the Mosel river or the Neckar river.
GIVEN NAMES German 8%. *Franz, Kurt.*

Eltzroth (191) North German: unexplained. It is probably a habitational name from a lost place or a topographic name for someone who lived in a clearing (Middle Low German *rot* 'cleared land') by a stream called *El(t)ze*, of which there are several examples. It may also be an altered form of **Elsenroth**, a habitational name from a place so called near Waldbröl in the Westerwald Mountains.

Elvidge (137) English: from the Middle English personal name *Elfegh, Alfeg*, Old English *Ælfhēah*, composed of the elements *ælf* 'elf' + *hēah* 'high'. The name was sometimes bestowed in honor of St. Alphege (954–1012), archbishop of Canterbury, who was stoned to death by the Danes, and came to be revered as a martyr.

Elvin (297) English (chiefly Norfolk): variant of ALWINE.

Elvington (165) English: habitational name from a place in North Yorkshire, named in Old English 'farmstead (Old English *tūn*) of a man called Ælfwine or a woman called Ælfwynn'. This is now a very rare name in England.

Elward (148) English: variant of AYLWARD. In the British Isles the name is found chiefly in Wales, particularly Cardiff.

Elwell (2198) English: habitational name, most probably from a place in Dorset, named from Old English *hǣl* 'omen' + *well(a)* 'spring', 'stream'; the reference is presumably to pagan river worship. Two minor places with this name in Devon are probably named as 'elder-tree spring', from Old English *ellern* 'elder tree' + *well(a)*. The surname is now found chiefly in the West Midlands. Compare HALLIWELL.

Elwood (1938) English: **1.** habitational name from a place in Gloucestershire, which is probably named from Old English *ellern* 'elder tree' + *wudu* 'wood'. **2.** from the Old English personal name *Ælfweald*, composed of the elements *ælf* 'elf' + *weald* 'rule'. In the British Isles this spelling is now found predominantly in northern Ireland.

Ely (5083) **1.** English: habitational name from the cathedral city on an island in the fens north of Cambridge. It is so named from Old English *ǣl* 'eel' + *gē* 'district'. **2.** Probably also an Americanized form of German ELEY.
FOREBEARS Nathaniel Ely was one of the founders of Hartford, CT, (coming from Cambridge, MA, with Thomas Hooker) in 1635.

Elyea (101) Americanized form of a French Canadian name, probably **Allier** or **Hélier** (see ALYEA).

Elza (194) From a short form of the personal name *Elisabeth* (see ELIZABETH), though the language of origin is unidentified.

Elzer (104) German: habitational name for someone from Elze, a place on the Leine River.
GIVEN NAME German 5%. *Otto.*

Elzey (458) English: altered spelling of ELSEY.

Elzie (121) **1.** Altered spelling of English ELSEY. **2.** Americanized spelling of German **Eltze**, probably a habitational name for someone from either of two places named Eltz, on the Mosel and the Neckar.
GIVEN NAME French 4%. *Pierre.*

Elzinga (312) Dutch: see ELSINGER.
GIVEN NAMES Dutch 4%. *Gerrit* (3), *Martinus, Pieter, Roelof.*

Elzy (278) Altered spelling of English ELSEY.

Emami (127) Muslim: from an adjectival derivative of IMAM.
GIVEN NAMES Muslim 80%. *Ali* (7), *Abbas* (3), *Ahmad* (3), *Hamid* (3), *Ehsan* (2), *Hossein* (2), *Masoud* (2), *Nasser* (2), *Alireza, Baha, Bahereh, Firooz.*

Emans (108) English: of uncertain origin; from documentary evidence, there appears to be from a medieval English female personal name, *Ismaine* or *Ismenia*.
GIVEN NAME German 4%. *Kurt.*

Emanuel (2032) From the Hebrew personal name *Imanuel* 'God is with us', found as a personal name in many European languages.

Emanuele (375) Italian: from the medieval personal name *Emanuele*, Italian form of EMANUEL.
GIVEN NAMES Italian 23%. *Salvatore* (6), *Vincenzo* (3), *Rocco* (2), *Santo* (2), *Angelo, Antonio, Carmelo, Cono, Enrico, Ezio, Filiberto.*

Emanuelson (245) Scandinavian: patronymic from EMANUEL.
GIVEN NAMES Scandinavian 5%. *Erik, Eskil, Thor.*

Emard (184) French (**Émard**): from a Germanic personal name (modern *Emhardt*), composed of Old High German *irmin* 'world' + *hard* 'strong', 'hardy'.
FOREBEARS Bearers of this name from Rheims were in Quebec city from 1698; others, from Poitiers, were in Quebec by 1702.
GIVEN NAMES French 12%. *Marcel* (2), *Normand* (2), *Emilienne, Jean Guy, Laurier.*

Emberson (201) English: patronymic from **Amery**.

Emberton (481) English: habitational name from a place in Buckinghamshire, so named from the Old English personal name *Ēanbeorht* + *tūn* 'enclosure', 'settlement'.

Embler (212) German (also common in the Czech lands): patronymic from EMEL.

Embleton (161) Northern English: habitational name from any of various places so called. One in Northumbria is probably from the Old English personal name *Æmele* + *dūn* 'hill'; one in County Durham was earlier *Elmedene*, from Old English *elm* 'elm' + *denu* 'valley'. Embleton in Cumbria is probably from the personal name *Ēanbald* + Old English *tūn* 'enclosure', 'settlement'.

Embree (995) Variant of English EMBURY or EMERY.

Embrey (1325) English: variant of EMBURY or EMERY.

Embry (2777) English: variant of EMBURY or EMERY.

Embury (194) English: habitational name from Emborough in Somerset, named from Old English *emn* 'flat topped' + *beorg* 'hill', 'mound', or possibly from Hembury in Devon.

Emch (413) Swiss German: variant of German **Emich**, a reduced form of EMMERICH.

Emde (266) **1.** North German: habitational name for someone from Emden in northwest Germany. **2.** South German: from Middle High German *āmad* 'second (grass) cut', dialect *emd*, hence a nickname for the owner of a field or meadow suitable for a second harvest.
GIVEN NAMES German 8%. *Ewald, Hannelore, Helmut, Otto, Ralf.*

Emeigh (117) Americanized form of German EMICH.

Emel (198) German: from a short form of any of various Germanic personal names beginning with the element *amal* 'strength', 'vigor'.

Emenheiser (104) Americanized spelling of German **Immenhauser**, a habitational name from any of several places called Immenhausen.

Emenhiser (106) Of German origin: see EMENHEISER.

Emens (186) English: probably a variant of EMMONS.

Emer (103) Jewish (eastern Ashkenazic): metonymic occupational name from Yiddish *emer* 'pail', 'bucket'.
GIVEN NAME Jewish 4%. *Pinkas.*

Emerich (410) Variant spelling of German EMMERICH.

Emerick (2216) Americanized spelling of German EMMERICH.

Emerine (168) Probably an Americanized spelling of German AMRHEIN.

Emerling (152) Altered spelling of German EMMERLING.

Emerson (11763) English: patronymic from the personal name EMERY.

FOREBEARS The poet and essayist Ralph Waldo Emerson (1803–82) was born in Boston of a line on his father's side that can be traced back through preachers to the first colonial generation. The name Emerson was brought over from England independently by various other people, including a Thomas Emerson who settled at Ipswich, MA, in about 1636.

Emert (695) Variant spelling of German EMMERT.

Emerton (166) English: of uncertain origin; probably a habitational name from a place that has not been identified, perhaps a reduced form of EMBERTON.

Emery (10003) English and French: from a Germanic personal name, *Emaurri*, composed of the elements *amja* 'busy', 'industrious' + *rīc* 'power'. The name was introduced into England from France by the Normans. There has been some confusion with AMORY.

FOREBEARS This name is recorded in Quebec in 1674, having been taken there from Dordogne, France.

Emfinger (309) Variant of German **Empfinger**, a habitational name for someone from Empfingen in Württemberg or Empfing in Bavaria.

Emge (359) German: probably a variant of **Emke** (see EHMKE).

Emhoff (129) North German (Westphalia): variant of IMHOFF.

Emich (102) German: reduced form of EMMERICH.

GIVEN NAMES German 6%. *Armin, Otto.*

Emick (183) German: variant of EMIG.

Emig (838) German: reduced form of EMMERICH.

Emigh (468) Variant spelling of German EMIG.

Emile (120) French (**Émile**) and Dutch: from the personal name (French *Émile*, Dutch *Emile*), from Latin *Aemilius* (see EMILIO).

GIVEN NAMES French 26%; Dutch 4%. *Arianne, Francois, Georges, Germaine, Jacques, Pierre, Yanick, Yvon.*

Emilio (105) Italian: from the personal name *Emilio* (Roman *Aemilius*, probably of Etruscan origin).

GIVEN NAMES Italian 16%. *Beniamino, Carlo, Carmelo, Domenic, Ferdinando, Francesco, Romeo, Sal.*

Emily (251) **1.** Respelling of German and Swiss German **Emele**, a variant of EMEL. **2.** English: variant of EMLEY.

Eminger (105) German: probably a habitational name from a place called Emmingen in Württemberg.

Emison (180) **1.** Variant spelling of **Emmison**, a metronymic from EMMETT. This name is found chiefly in TN. **2.** Jewish (American): Americanized form of some like-sounding Ashkenazic surname.

GIVEN NAMES Jewish 4%. *Herschell, Hershel.*

Emler (237) German (common in Switzerland, also in the Czech lands): **1.** from the Germanic personal name *Amalhari*, composed of the elements *amal* 'strength', 'vigor' + *hari, heri* 'army'. **2.** possibly a variant spelling of **Emmler**, a habitational name for someone from Emmeln in northwestern Germany.

Emley (296) **1.** English: habitational name from a place in West Yorkshire, so named from the Old English male personal name *Em(m)a* (which has nothing to do with the modern girl's name) + *lēah* 'woodland clearing'. **2.** Altered spelling of German EMLER or *Emele* (see EMEL).

Emling (213) **1.** Variant of German **Emeling**, a patronymic from a short form of any of the Germanic personal names beginning with Old High German *amal* 'strength', 'vigor'. **2.** Alternatively, it may be an altered spelling of the English family name **Emlyn**, a variant of EMMETT.

Emm (115) English: from the female personal name *Emm*; this was the English form of *Emma*, which was a popular Norman name of Germanic origin, originally a short form of compound names formed with *erm(en), irm(en)* 'entire'.

Emma (386) Italian (Sicily): apparently from the female personal name *Emma* (see EMM).

GIVEN NAMES Italian 10%. *Rocco* (4), *Francesco* (2), *Salvatore* (2), *Pasquale, Sal, Vito.*

Emmanuel (396) Variant spelling (mainly French and South Indian) of EMANUEL, which was used in the Middle Ages by Christians as an alternative name for Christ. The name was also borne by a 3rd-century martyr. Among Christians in India it is used as a given name, and in the U.S. it has come to be used as a last name among families from southern India.

GIVEN NAMES French 14%. *Pierre* (3), *Andre* (2), *Serge* (2), *Francois, Jacques, Jean Pierre, Kettly, Marcellin, Michel, Micheline, Sylvain.*

Emme (179) North German and Frisian: from the personal name *Emme*, of uncertain origin.

GIVEN NAMES German 9%. *Fritz* (2), *Otto* (2), *Siegfried.*

Emmel (437) South German and Rhineland: variant spelling of EMEL.

Emmendorfer (134) Altered spelling of North German **Emmendörffer**, a habitational name for someone from Emmendorf in Lower Saxony.

Emmer (474) German (Bavaria): from Middle High German *emmer* 'grain', a topographic name for someone who lived by land where grain was grown, a status name for someone who owned such land, or a metonymic occupational name for someone who grew or dealt in grain.

Emmerich (710) German and Dutch: **1.** from a Germanic personal name composed of Old High German *heim* 'home', 'house' or *amal* 'strength' + *rīhhi* 'powerful', 'rich'. **2.** habitational name from any of the places on the Lower Rhine named Emmerich.

GIVEN NAMES German 4%. *Kurt* (5), *Fritz, Gerhard, Klaus.*

Emmerling (298) German (Bavaria) and Austria: from the dialect word *Emmerling* 'yellowhammer', a bird with bright plumage, hence a nickname for a pretentious person.

GIVEN NAMES German 4%. *Kurt* (2), *Fritz.*

Emmerson (372) English: variant spelling of EMERSON.

Emmert (1574) German: **1.** variant of EMMER. **2.** from the Germanic personal name *Ehmhard*, composed of the elements *irmin* 'all encompassing' + *hard* 'strong'.

Emmet (157) English: variant spelling of EMMETT.

Emmett (1312) English: from a Middle English pet form of the female personal name *Emma*, introduced into England from France by the Normans, among whom it was extremely popular. The name is of Germanic origin, probably originating as a hypocoristic form of women's names with a first element *ermin* 'entire'.

Emmi (157) Italian: probably from the personal name EMMA.

GIVEN NAMES Italian 21%. *Angelo* (3), *Carmello, Francesca, Gino, Giuseppina, Natale, Palma, Paolo.*

Emmick (214) Altered spelling of German EMICH.

Emminger (165) German and Swiss German: habitational name for someone from either of two places in Württemberg named Emmingen.

Emmitt (216) English: variant spelling of EMMETT.

Emmons (5224) English: from the medieval female personal name *Ismaine*, *Ismenia* (found as *Emonie, Emeny* until the end of the 18th century), which is of uncertain origin.

Emmott (116) English: variant spelling of EMMETT.

Emmrich (103) German: variant of EMMERICH.

GIVEN NAMES German 6%. *Kurt, Manfred.*

Emond (912) **1.** Scottish (Selkirk): unexplained. **2.** French (**Émond**): variant of HAYMOND.
FOREBEARS The name has been found in Quebec since 1663, taken there from La Rochelle, France.
GIVEN NAMES French 13%. *Andre* (6), *Normand* (5), *Armand* (4), *Marcel* (4), *Pierre* (3), *Yves* (2), *Adelard*, *Benoit*, *Camille*, *Cecile*, *Cyr*, *Fernand*.

Emory (1984) English: variant spelling of EMERY.

Empey (465) Altered spelling of the English habitational name **Impey**, from any of various minor places named with Old English *imp* 'young tree', 'sapling' + *(ge)hæg* or *haga* 'enclosure'.

Empie (175) Altered spelling of the English habitational name **Impey**, from any of various minor places named with Old English *imp* 'young tree', 'sapling' + *(ge)hæg* or *haga* 'enclosure'.

Empson (291) English: metronymic from EMMETT.

Emrich (863) German: reduced form of EMMERICH.
GIVEN NAMES German 4%. *Konrad* (2), *Otto* (2), *Arno*, *Florian*, *Franz*, *Gehard*, *Hans*, *Manfred*, *Siegfried*.

Emrick (1035) Americanized spelling of German EMRICH.

Emry (339) Probably a variant spelling of EMERY.

Ems (136) German: habitational name from any of several places so named.

Emshoff (124) North German (Westphalia): habitational name from a place named 'farm or manor (Middle Low German *hof*) on the Ems river'.
GIVEN NAMES German 6%. *Erna*, *Erwin*, *Fritz*.

Emslie (183) Scottish (Aberdeen): evidently a habitational name, probably from an unidentified place named with the Old English elements *elm* 'elm' + *lēah* 'woodland clearing', with an intrusive -*s*-. There are places called Elmley in Kent and Worcestershire.

Emswiler (242) Probably a respelling of German **Emmersweiler**, a habitational name from Emmersweiler, a place near St. Wedel on the French-German border, so named from a short form of a Germanic personal name formed with *amal* 'strength', 'vigor' + Middle High German *wīler* 'small village', 'single building' (from medieval Latin *villare*, Latin *villa* 'house').

Emter (105) German: variant of **Empter**, an occupational name for a farmer who took a second cut of hay from a field in a single season, from German *Öhmt*, *Empte*, 'second cut of hay'.
GIVEN NAME French 4%; German 4%. *Math*.

Enberg (170) **1.** Swedish: probably an ornamental name composed of the elements *en* 'juniper' + *berg* 'mountain', 'hill'.

2. Norwegian: habitational name from a farmstead so named, from Old Norse *einir* 'juniper' + *berg* 'mountain', 'hill'.
GIVEN NAMES Scandinavian 8%. *Erik* (2), *Johan*, *Nels*.

Encarnacion (560) Spanish (**Encarnación**): from a short form of the Marian name *María de la Encarnación* 'Mary of the Incarnation' (from Latin *incarnatio*, from *incarnare* 'to make flesh', a derivative of *caro*, genitive *carnis*, flesh).
GIVEN NAMES Spanish 44%. *Jose* (16), *Rafael* (9), *Juan* (7), *Pedro* (5), *Ana* (4), *Alfonso* (3), *Fernando* (3), *Francisco* (3), *Jesus* (3), *Lourdes* (3), *Luisa* (3), *Manuel* (3); *Fausto* (3), *Antonio* (2), *Santo* (2), *Ciriaco*, *Dino*, *Eliseo*, *Emelio*, *Gabino*, *Heriberto*, *Leonardo*, *Marco Antonio*, *Romeo*.

Ence (126) English: variant spelling of INCE.

Encinas (461) **1.** Spanish: habitational name from any of various places, for example in the provinces of Salamanca, Valladolid, and Segovia, so named *encina* 'holm oak' (Old Spanish *lecina*, Late Latin *ilicina*, a derivative of classical Latin *ilex*, genitive *ilicis*). **2.** Galician (**Enciñas**): topographic name from the plural from of *enciña*, a Galician variant of *encina*.
GIVEN NAMES Spanish 38%. *Carlos* (9), *Jose* (7), *Jesus* (6), *Juan* (5), *Manuel* (4), *Mario* (4), *Francisco* (3), *Ramona* (3), *Ruben* (3), *Catalina* (2), *Ernesto* (2), *Fernando* (2).

Encinias (257) Respelling of Galician **Enciñas** (see ENCINAS 2).
GIVEN NAMES Spanish 22%. *Manuel* (3), *Benito* (2), *Cipriano* (2), *Orlando* (2), *Ruben* (2), *Santos* (2), *Segundo* (2), *Abelina*, *Adan*, *Alfredo*, *Ancelmo*, *Ascencion*.

Enciso (375) Spanish: habitational name from a place named Enciso, examples of which are found in Logroño and Rioja.
GIVEN NAMES Spanish 49%. *Jose* (11), *Manuel* (7), *Miguel* (6), *Carlos* (4), *Jorge* (4), *Julio* (4), *Raul* (4), *Alvaro* (3), *Fernando* (3), *Jesus* (3), *Mario* (3), *Vicente* (3); *Antonio* (4), *Angelo* (2), *Aldo*, *Benoni*, *Carlo*, *Cecilio*, *Donato*, *Giovanna*, *Guido*, *Marco*, *Marco Antonio*.

Enck (413) North German: from a pet form of the Low German and Frisian personal name *Enno*.

End (135) English: topographic name for someone who lived at the end of a village or settlement, from Middle English *end* (Old English *ende*).

Ende (236) German: topographic name for someone living at the end of a settlement or street, from Middle High German *ende* 'end'.

Ender (381) South German: from a short form of the personal name *Anders*, a vernacular form of ANDREAS.
GIVEN NAMES German 5%. *Dieter*, *Elke*, *Ingo*, *Otto*, *Siegfried*.

Enderby (172) English: habitational name from places in Leicestershire and Lincolnshire, so named from the Old Norse personal name *Eindriði* (see ENDERSON) + Old Norse *bŷr* 'farm', 'settlement'.

Enderle (797) South German: from a pet form of ENDER.
GIVEN NAMES German 4%. *Erwin* (2), *Hans* (2), *Arno*, *Heinz*, *Markus*, *Mathias*, *Otto*.

Enderlin (183) South German: from a pet form of ENDER.
GIVEN NAME German 6%. *Hans* (3).

Enders (1446) German: from a variant of the personal name *Anders*, vernacular form of ANDREAS.

Enderson (273) **1.** Altered spelling of Danish **Endersen**, a patronymic from the personal name *Endricht*, probably of Low German or Frisian origin. **2.** Altered spelling of Norwegian **Endresen**, a common patronymic from *Endre*, from the Old Norse personal name *Eindriði*, composed of the elements *ein* 'one', 'sole' + *riði* 'rider'. **3.** English: variant of ANDERSON, a patronymic from the personal name ANDERS.

Endicott (1713) English (Devon): topographic name for someone who lived 'at the end of the cottages', from Middle English, Old English *ende* 'end' + *cot* 'cottage'. One locality so named is Endicott in Cadbury, Devon; another is now called Youngcott, in Milton Abbot.
FOREBEARS John Endecott (1588–1665) was a prominent figure in the early history of MA, being one of the founding fathers of Salem, MA, in 1638. He served as governor of Massachusetts Bay Colony (1629–30), and worked harmoniously with his successor, John Winthrop, despite differences on points of religious doctrine. He served as governor again in 1644–45, 1649–50, 1651–54, and 1655–64, and as deputy governor in many of the intervening years. He is buried in the King's Chapel Burying Ground in Boston.

Endler (223) German: **1.** patronymic from *Endel*, a pet form of ENDERS. **2.** habitational name for someone from any of various places called Endel or Endeln.
GIVEN NAMES German 6%. *Gerhard* (2), *Alfons*, *Hellmuth*.

Endlich (170) German: byname from Middle High German *endelīch* 'eager', 'competent', 'efficient'.

Endo (512) Japanese (**Endō**): 'far wisteria'; designating Fujiwara of Tōtōmi. *En* 'far' is a Sino-Japanese pronunciation of the *tō* element in the place name *Tō-tsu-umi* 'farther lake' (now part of Shizuoka prefecture). The name refers to Lake Hamana and was shortened by usage to Tōtōmi. The name is found mainly in eastern Japan, where it is borne by several families descended from the TAIRA and southern FUJIWARA clans.
GIVEN NAMES Japanese 61%. *Akira* (4), *Koichi* (4), *Minoru* (4), *Yoshio* (4), *Akiko*

(3), *Hideo* (3), *Hiroyuki* (3), *Junko* (3), *Keiko* (3), *Masahiro* (3), *Takashi* (3), *Tsuguo* (3).

Endorf (103) German: habitational name from any of three places so named: in Bavaria, North Rhine-Westphalia, and Saxony-Anhalt.
GIVEN NAME German 5%. *Otto.*

Endres (2071) German: variant of ENDERS.

Endresen (135) Norwegian: see ENDERSON 2.
GIVEN NAMES Scandinavian 13%; German 4%. *Alf, Borge, Erik; Otto.*

Endress (404) Variant of German ENDRES.
GIVEN NAMES German 5%. *Erwin, Gerhard, Horst, Kurt, Lorenz.*

Endries (112) Variant of German ENDRES.

Endris (158) **1.** Hungarian: from a pet form of the personal name *Endre.* **2.** German: variant of ENDRES.
GIVEN NAME German 4%. *Kurt.*

Endriss (105) Variant of German ENDRES.
GIVEN NAME German 7%. *Kurt.*

Endrizzi (150) Italian: from a pet form of *Endrigo,* a variant of *Enrico,* Italian form of HENRY.
GIVEN NAMES Italian 4%. *Angelo, Bruna, Ezio, Marino.*

Endsley (1106) English: habitational name from Endsleigh in Devon.

Endy (223) Perhaps a variant of ANDY.

Enea (219) Italian: from the personal name *Enea,* Italian form of *Aeneas,* the Latin name of the Trojan hero credited in classical legend with founding the Roman state.
GIVEN NAMES Italian 21%. *Salvatore* (6), *Ascanio* (2), *Gaetano* (2), *Sal* (2), *Antonio, Francesca, Francesco, Gennaro, Girolamo, Giuseppe, Neno, Orazio, Rocco, Teobaldo.*

Enerson (248) Americanized spelling of Norwegian **Enersen,** a patronymic from *Ener,* from the Old Norse personal name *Einarr,* composed of the elements *ein* 'alone', 'only' + *arr* 'warrior'.

Enes (112) **1.** Portuguese (Azores): variant of ANES. **2.** Dutch and North German: habitational name from a place called Henis in Limburg, eastern Belgium.
GIVEN NAMES Spanish 13%; Portuguese 11%. *Manuel* (3), *Albino, Arlindo, Armando, Gaspar, Jeremias, Marta, Ramon; Ilidio, Joao; Antonio, Luciano.*

Enevoldsen (140) Norwegian and Danish: patronymic from the personal name *Enevold, Einvald,* a compound of *ein* 'one', 'sole', 'unique' + *vald* 'ruler'.
GIVEN NAMES Scandinavian 9%. *Kjeld* (2), *Erik, Niels.*

Enfield (561) English: habitational name from a place in Middlesex named with the Old English personal name *Ēana* or Old English *ēan* 'lamb' + *feld* 'open field'.

Enfinger (504) German: **1.** variant of EMFINGER. **2.** variant of INFINGER.

Eng (2902) **1.** Norwegian: common habitational name from any of various farmsteads

so named, from Old Norse *eng* 'meadow'. **2.** Swedish: ornamental name from *äng* 'meadow', in some cases perhaps chosen as a topographic name by someone who lived beside a meadow. This is one of the many Swedish surnames that were coined in the 19th century from words denoting aspects of the countryside, and which were also used more or less arbitrarily to form compound surnames. **3.** German: variant of ENGE. **4.** Chinese 吴: variant of WU 1. **5.** Chinese 伍: variant of WU 4.
GIVEN NAMES Chinese 9%. *Wai* (12), *Kwok* (6), *Wah* (5), *Wing* (5), *Chun* (4), *Gim* (4), *Hon* (4), *Fong* (3), *Hong* (3), *Lai* (3), *Ping* (3), *Shee* (3).

Engard (107) Americanized form of Dutch or German ENGERT.

Engberg (556) Swedish: ornamental name composed of the elements *äng* 'meadow' + *berg* 'mountain', 'hill'.
GIVEN NAMES Scandinavian 6%. *Holger* (2), *Lars* (2), *Bjorn, Erik, Jarl.*

Engblom (158) Swedish: ornamental name composed of the elements *äng* 'meadow' + *blom* 'flower'.
GIVEN NAMES Scandinavian 11%. *Nels* (2), *Kerstin, Thor.*

Engbrecht (151) German: variant of ENGELBERT.

Engdahl (572) Swedish: ornamental name composed of the elements *äng* 'meadow' + *dahl,* an ornamental (old) spelling of *dal* 'valley'.
GIVEN NAMES Scandinavian 5%. *Erik* (2), *Anders, Niels.*

Enge (316) **1.** German: topographic name for someone who lived in a narrow place, such as a valley, from *eng* 'narrow'. **2.** Norwegian: variant of ENG.
GIVEN NAMES Scandinavian 6%; German 5%. *Holger, Per, Tor; Erna, Gerhard, Guenther, Hans, Kurt.*

Engebretsen (197) Norwegian: patronymic from *Engelbrekt,* from German ENGELBRECHT.
GIVEN NAMES Scandinavian 16%. *Lars* (3), *Espen, Jorgen, Nels.*

Engebretson (961) Americanized spelling of Norwegian ENGEBRETSEN.
GIVEN NAMES Scandinavian 4%. *Iver* (2), *Arnt, Egil, Juel, Obert, Selmer, Thor.*

Engel (9588) **1.** German and Dutch: from a short form of various Germanic personal names (see, for example, ENGELBERT and ENGELHARD). A number of different elements have fallen together in *Engel-,* mainly *Ingal,* extended form of *Ing,* the name of a Germanic god or folk hero, and *Angel* 'Angle'. The Angles were a Germanic tribe living on the Jutland peninsula; in the 5th–6th centuries they invaded eastern and northern Britain and gave their name to England (Old English *Englaland* 'land of the Angles'). **2.** German and Dutch: in some cases a habitational name for someone living at a house bearing the sign of an

angel, Middle High German *engel.* **3.** Jewish (Ashkenazic): ornamental name from German *Engel* 'angel' (see 2).
GIVEN NAMES German 4%. *Kurt* (15), *Hans* (7), *Fritz* (6), *Heinz* (6), *Rainer* (5), *Otto* (4), *Albrecht* (2), *Alois* (2), *Benno* (2), *Dieter* (2), *Elfriede* (2), *Erwin* (2).

Engelbart (125) Probably an altered spelling of ENGELBERT.
GIVEN NAMES German 6%. *Fritz, Gerda, Kurt.*

Engelberg (211) Jewish (Ashkenazic): ornamental name, a compound of German ENGEL 'angel' + BERG 'mountain', 'hill'.
GIVEN NAMES Jewish 10%. *Moshe* (2), *Ari, Dov, Pincus.*

Engelbert (297) German, English, and French: from a Germanic personal name composed of *engel* (see ENGEL) + *berht* 'bright', 'famous'. The widespread popularity of the name in France during the Middle Ages was largely a result of the fact that it had been borne by a son-in-law of Charlemagne; in the Rhineland it was more often given in memory of a bishop of Cologne (1216–25) of this name, who was martyred.
GIVEN NAMES German 6%. *Kurt* (2), *Erwin, Guenter, Johann.*

Engelbrecht (904) German: variant of ENGELBERT.
GIVEN NAMES German 8%. *Otto* (4), *Heinz* (3), *Klaus* (2), *Kurt* (2), *Ralf* (2), *Claus, Eldor, Ernst, Horst, Irmgard, Monika, Rudi.*

Engelby (103) English: habitational name from any of various places in North Yorkshire, Derbyshire, and Lincolnshire named Ingleby, from Old Norse *Englar* 'Englishmen' + *bý* 'farmstead', 'settlement'.

Engeldinger (129) German: of uncertain origin; it could be a patronymic or alternatively a habitational name from an unidentified place called Engeldingen or similar.

Engelhard (333) German: variant of ENGELHARDT.
GIVEN NAMES German 5%. *Dieter, Kurt.*

Engelhardt (2080) German: from a Germanic personal name composed of the elements *engel* (see ENGEL) + *hard* 'brave', 'hardy', 'strong'.
GIVEN NAMES German 5%. *Kurt* (4), *Almut* (2), *Armin* (2), *Gerhard* (2), *Otto* (2), *Claus, Dieter, Erwin, Gunther, Hans, Heinrich, Heinz.*

Engelhart (624) Dutch and German: variant of ENGELHARDT.
GIVEN NAMES German 4%. *Kurt* (2), *Erwin, Ewald, Otto.*

Engelhaupt (124) German: from a house name, literally 'angel's head', taken from a sign depicting an angel's head.

Engelke (690) North German: from a pet form of ENGEL.
GIVEN NAMES German 4%. *Hans* (2), *Otto* (2), *Erwin, Ewald, Hartmut.*

Engelken (226) North German: from a pet form of ENGEL.

Engelkes (162) North German: patronymic from ENGELKE.

Engelking (435) North German: patronymic from a pet form of ENGEL.
GIVEN NAMES German 5%. *Dietrich, Fritz, Kurt, Otto, Wilhelm.*

Engell (100) North German and Danish: variant of ENGEL.
GIVEN NAME Scandinavian 4%. *Jorgen.*

Engelland (102) North German and Danish: ethnic name for someone from England, or nickname for someone with some other connection with England.

Engelman (1013) **1.** Jewish (Ashkenazic): ornamental name composed of German ENGEL 'angel' + *man(n)* 'man', 'husband'. **2.** Respelling of German ENGELMANN.

Engelmann (710) **1.** German: variant of ENGEL 1, with the addition of the personal suffix *-mann* 'man', sometimes denoting a pet form. **2.** Jewish (Ashkenazic): variant spelling of ENGELMAN.
GIVEN NAMES German 13%. *Kurt* (6), *Franz* (2), *Fritz* (2), *Lothar* (2), *Manfred* (2), *Otto* (2), *Ralf* (2), *Armin, Bernd, Dieter, Ernst, Erwin.*

Engelmeyer (122) South German: variant of ANGERMEIER.

Engels (1224) German and Dutch: patronymic from ENGEL 1.

Engelsman (143) **1.** German (**Engelsmann**): ethnic name from Middle Low German *Engelsman* 'person from England'. **2.** German: nickname for a gentle person, from Middle High German *engelsch* 'angelic' + the personal suffix *-man* 'man'. **3.** Jewish (Ashkenazic): variant of ENGELMAN.

Engelson (233) **1.** Swedish: patronymic from a short form of the Germanic personal name ENGELBERT. **2.** Partly Americanized form of German **Engelsohn**, a patronymic from ENGEL 1. **3.** Jewish (Ashkenazic): ornamental name from German *Engelsohn* 'son of an angel'.
GIVEN NAMES German 4%; Jewish 4%. *Engel* (2); *Avrohom, Shmuel, Yerachmiel.*

Engelstad (264) Norwegian: habitational name from any of five farmsteads in eastern Norway, so named from *Engel*, from the Old Norse personal name *Ingjaldr*, + *stad* (from Old Norse *staðr* 'farmstead', 'dwelling').
GIVEN NAMES Scandinavian 4%. *Erik, Selmer, Sigfred.*

Engeman (178) **1.** Swedish: either a variant of ENGMAN or of German origin. **2.** Americanized spelling of German ENGEMANN.

Engemann (165) German: variant of ENGE, with the addition of the personal suffix *-mann* 'man'.
GIVEN NAME German 5%. *Kurt.*

Engen (983) **1.** Norwegian: habitational name from the widespread farm name

Engen, from the singular definite form of Old Norse *eng* 'meadow'. **2.** Dutch: from a pet form of the Germanic personal name *Ingo* (borne by the hero of the *Ingweones* tribe). **3.** Dutch: reduced form of VAN ENGEN.
GIVEN NAMES Scandinavian 7%. *Erik* (2), *Lars* (2), *Thorkild* (2), *Alf, Anders, Bjorn, Tor.*

Enger (976) **1.** Norwegian: habitational name from various farmsteads, notably in eastern Norway, so named from the plural indefinite form of Old Norse *eng* 'meadow'. **2.** South German: habitational name for someone from any of various places named Enge or Engen.
GIVEN NAMES Scandinavian 5%. *Lars* (2), *Alf, Bjorn, Erik, Iver, Juel, Kristoffer, Selmer.*

Engert (258) Dutch and German: from a personal name, a reduced form of *Ingohart* or ENGELHARDT.
GIVEN NAMES German 8%. *Erwin* (6), *Armin, Bernd, Hans, Theodor.*

Engesser (137) South German: topographic name for someone who lived in a narrow street, from Middle High German *enge* 'narrow' + *gazze* 'street', 'lane'.

Engfer (124) North German: from the Germanic personal name *Ingofrid*, a compound of the personal name *Ing* + *frid* 'peace'.

Engh (422) Swedish or Norwegian: variant of ENG 1, 2.
GIVEN NAMES Scandinavian 4%. *Erland, Helmer, Svein.*

Engholm (175) Swedish: ornamental name composed of the elements *äng* 'meadow' + *holm* 'small island'.

England (10384) **1.** English: ethnic name (see ENGLISH 1). **2.** Norwegian: habitational name from any of various farmsteads, so named from Old Norse *eng* 'meadow' + *land* 'land'. **3.** Swedish: ornamental name with the same meaning as 2.

Englander (518) **1.** Jewish (Ashkenazic) and German (**Engländer**): ethnic name from German *Engländer* 'Englishman'. See also ENGLISH. In some cases the Jewish name may be an ornamental adoption. **2.** Swedish: ornamental name either from *äng* 'meadow' + *land* 'land' + the suffix *-er* denoting origin, or from *äng(e)l* 'angel' + *-ander*, suffix derived from Greek *anēr, andros* 'man'.
GIVEN NAMES Jewish 6%. *Chaim* (3), *Baruch, Mendel, Meyer, Moshe, Shaya, Sol.*

Engle (7575) Americanized spelling of German ENGEL.

Englebert (334) Americanized spelling of German ENGELBERT.

Englebrecht (124) Variant spelling of German ENGELBRECHT.
GIVEN NAME German 4%. *Horst.*

Englebright (115) Americanized form of German ENGELBRECHT.

Engledow (121) English: nickname from Latin *angelus dei*, Old French *angele* 'angel' + *Dieu* 'God'.

Englehardt (328) Partly Americanized spelling of German ENGELHARDT.

Englehart (974) Americanized spelling of German ENGELHARDT.

Engleman (836) Variant spelling of ENGELMAN(N).

Engler (2530) South German: patronymic from ENGEL.

Englert (1809) German: variant of ENGELHARDT.

Englerth (158) German: variant of ENGELHARDT.

Engles (463) Altered spelling of ENGELS.
GIVEN NAMES French 4%. *Michel, Remi.*

English (16065) **1.** English: from Old English *Englisc*. The word had originally distinguished Angles (see ENGEL) from Saxons and other Germanic peoples in the British Isles, but by the time surnames were being acquired it no longer had this meaning. Its frequency as an English surname is somewhat surprising. It may have been commonly used in the early Middle Ages as a distinguishing epithet for an Anglo-Saxon in areas where the culture was not predominantly English—for example the Danelaw area, Scotland, and parts of Wales—or as a distinguishing name after 1066 for a non-Norman in the regions of most intensive Norman settlement. However, explicit evidence for these assumptions is lacking, and at the present day the surname is fairly evenly distributed throughout the country. **2.** Irish: see GOLIGHTLY.

Englund (1309) Swedish: ornamental name composed of the elements *äng* 'meadow' + *lund* 'grove'.
GIVEN NAMES Scandinavian 6%. *Sven* (3), *Erik* (2), *Jarl* (2), *Nils* (2), *Alf, Bjorn, Lars, Per.*

Engman (489) **1.** Swedish: ornamental name composed of the elements *äng* 'meadow' + *man* 'man'. **2.** German (**Engmann**): variant of ENGEMANN.
GIVEN NAMES Scandinavian 6%. *Erik, Iver, Lars.*

Engquist (246) Swedish: ornamental name composed of the elements *äng* 'meadow' + *quist*, an old or ornamental spelling of *kvist* 'twig'.
GIVEN NAMES Scandinavian 5%. *Erik* (2), *Arnell, Bjorn.*

Engram (420) English: variant spelling of INGRAM. This form, recorded in the 13th century, now appears to have died out in the British Isles.

Engstrand (157) Swedish: ornamental name composed of the elements *äng* 'meadow' + *strand* 'shore'.
GIVEN NAMES Scandinavian 6%. *Alvar, Helmer.*

Engstrom (2753) Swedish (**Engström**): ornamental name composed of the elements *äng* 'meadow' + *ström* 'river'.
GIVEN NAMES Scandinavian 6%. *Erik* (7), *Arnell* (2), *Erland* (2), *Johan* (2), *Lars* (2),

Mats (2), *Per* (2), *Thor* (2), *Alrik, Astrid, Britt, Helmer.*

Engwall (154) Swedish: ornamental name composed of the elements *äng* 'meadow' + *vall* 'field'.

Enis (241) **1.** Irish: variant spelling of ENNIS. **2.** German and Latvian: variant of **Ehnis**, from a short form of a Germanic personal name composed with *agi(n)* 'point (of a sword)' (Old High German *ecka*).

Enix (256) English: unexplained. Perhaps a patronymic from ENOCH or a variant of Irish ENNIS.

Enke (295) South German: occupational name from Middle High German *enke* 'servant', 'worker'.
GIVEN NAMES German 4%. *Horst, Kurt, Uwe.*

Enloe (1134) English: probably a variant of ENSLOW.

Enlow (1048) English: probably a variant of ENSLOW.

Enman (241) Altered spelling of English INMAN.

Enneking (207) North German: patronymic from *Encke* (see ENCK).

Ennen (254) North German and Frisian: patronymic from the personal name *Enno.*

Ennenga (103) Frisian: patronymic from the personal name *Enno.*
GIVEN NAMES German 6%. *Fritz, Heinz.*

Ennes (152) Portuguese: variant of ANES.

Ennis (5969) Irish: **1.** Anglicized form of Gaelic **Ó hAonghuis** 'descendant of Angus', a variant of **Ó hAonghusa** (see HENNESSY). **2.** variant of Scottish and Manx INNES.

Enns (484) German: from a reduced form of the Germanic personal name ANSELM.

Eno (660) **1.** English: unexplained. **2.** Possibly in some cases a respelling of French **Énos** (see ENOS).
GIVEN NAMES French 4%. *Adrien, Camille, Pierre.*

Enoch (987) Mainly Welsh (not recorded before the 18th century): from the Biblical personal name *Enoch* (Hebrew *Chanoch* 'experienced' or 'dedicated'). This was the name borne in the Bible by the eldest son of Cain (Genesis 4:17) and by the father of Methuselah who was said to have 'walked with God' (Genesis 5:22). The surname is relatively common in Wales, but much rarer in England, where it is concentrated on the Warwickshire/Oxfordshire border, usually in the form **Enock**.

Enochs (732) Patronymic from ENOCH, concentrated in IN, TX, MO, and OH.

Enomoto (177) Japanese: from a common place name meaning '(one who lives) beneath the hackberry tree'. It is found as a surname in the Kyōto–Ōsaka area and the Ryūkyū Islands, and is listed in the Shinsen shōjiroku.
GIVEN NAMES Japanese 55%. *Mitsuo* (3), *Shigeki* (2), *Yoshio* (2), *Yuko* (2), *Akiko,*

Daisuke, Etsuko, Fusako, Haru, Haruko, Hideo, Hiro.

Enos (2686) **1.** Of multiple origin and uncertain etymology. Possible origins include: **2.** French and Portuguese: from the Biblical name *Enos* (see ENOCH). **3.** Possibly in some cases an altered form of French **Hénault** (see HENAULT). **4.** Perhaps also an altered form of Scottish INNES.

Enquist (222) Swedish: ornamental name composed of the elements *en* 'juniper' + *quist*, an old or ornamental spelling of *kvist* 'twig'.
GIVEN NAMES Scandinavian 8%. *Erik* (2), *Eskil, Nels.*

Enrico (195) Italian: from the personal name *Enrico*, Italian form of HENRY 1.
GIVEN NAMES Spanish 8%; Italian 7%. *Carlos, Domingo, Leoncio, Luis, Manuel, Melquiades, Nestor*; *Alberto, Aldo, Domenic, Gino, Livio, Pio.*

Enright (2685) Irish: Anglicized form of the Gaelic byname **Mac Ionnrachtaigh** 'son of *Ionnrachtach*', a name meaning 'attacker'. Compare HANRATTY.
GIVEN NAMES Irish 5%. *Brendan, Brigid, Caitlin, Oonagh, Seamus.*

Enrique (158) Spanish: from the personal name *Enrique*, Spanish form of HENRY.
GIVEN NAMES Spanish 51%. *Jose* (4), *Luis* (4), *Santiago* (3), *Julio* (2), *Nelida* (2), *Raul* (2), *Alberto, Alejandro, Alejo, Alicia, Amalia, Andres.*

Enriques (106) Spanish: variant of ENRIQUEZ.
GIVEN NAMES Spanish 42%. *Jose* (3), *Andres* (2), *Agustin, Alberto, Alejandro, Alfredo, Anselmo, Arturo, Blanca, Carlos, Edgardo, Efren*; *Antonio* (2), *Fausto, Luca, Marco Antonio.*

Enriquez (3483) Spanish (**Enríquez**): patronymic from ENRIQUE.
GIVEN NAMES Spanish 50%. *Jose* (94), *Juan* (46), *Jesus* (42), *Carlos* (39), *Manuel* (36), *Luis* (32), *Raul* (28), *Miguel* (19), *Jaime* (17), *Jorge* (16), *Pedro* (16), *Roberto* (16).

Ens (113) German: variant of ENNS.
GIVEN NAME French 4%. *Leontine.*

Enser (107) German: habitational named for someone from any of several places called Ense.
GIVEN NAME German 4%. *Heribert* (2).

Ensey (293) Probably an altered form of German ENSER.

Ensign (1016) English: of uncertain etymology. From the 16th to the 19th century, the English vocabulary word *ensign* denoted a junior rank of infantry officer, which may be the source of the surname.
FOREBEARS James Ensign (known as 'the Puritan') was born in Chilham, Kent, England, in 1606 and came to Hartford, CT, before 1644.

Ensing (150) German: habitational name from any of various places named Ensingen.

Ensinger (181) German: habitational name for someone from any of various places named Ensingen.

Enslen (149) Probably a respelling of German ENSLIN.

Ensley (1419) Americanized spelling of German **Ensli** or **Ensle**, pet forms of ANSELM.

Enslin (172) South German: from a pet form of the personal name *Ens* (see ENNS).
GIVEN NAMES German 4%. *Helmut, Johann.*

Enslow (240) English: habitational name from a place so named near Woodstock in Oxfordshire.

Ensminger (1034) German: of uncertain origin; probably a habitational name from a lost or unidentified place.

Ensor (948) English: habitational name for someone from Edensor in Derbyshire, which derives its name from the genitive case of the Old English personal name *Ēadhūn* (see EDEN 1) + Old English *ofer* 'ridge'.

Enstad (158) Norwegian: habitational name from a farm so named, from the Old Norse personal name *Eindriði* (see ENDERSON) + *stad* (from Old Norse *staðr* 'farmstead', 'dwelling').
GIVEN NAMES Scandinavian 6%. *Knute, Obert.*

Enstrom (234) Swedish (**Enström**): ornamental name composed of the elements *en* 'juniper' + *ström* 'river'.
GIVEN NAMES Scandinavian 7%. *Bjorn, Erik, Sven.*

Ensz (274) German: from a short form of the Germanic personal name ANSELM.

Ent (181) Dutch: variant of **Ente(n)**, a patronymic from a derivative of the Germanic personal name *Ando.*

Enter (104) German: occupational name for a poultry dealer, from an agent noun based on *Ente* 'duck'.
GIVEN NAME German 4%. *Gerhardt.*

Enterkin (110) Scottish: habitational name from a place of this name in Dumfriesshire.

Enterline (364) Americanized spelling of the South German family name **Enterlein**, from a pet form of *Ender*, a Bavarian form of ANDREAS.

Entin (194) Jewish (from Belarus): metronymic from Yiddish female name *Yente*, of Romance origin, + the Slavic suffix *-in.*
GIVEN NAMES Jewish 11%; Russian 5%. *Hyman* (2), *Jacov, Yakov*; *Leonid* (3), *Gennady, Yefim.*

Entler (191) **1.** German: variant of ENDLER. **2.** Jewish (Ashkenazic): unexplained.
GIVEN NAMES Jewish 4%. *Aron, Ronit.*

Entrekin (674) Scottish: habitational name from a place called Enterkin in the parish of Durrisdeer, Dumfriesshire.

Entrikin (135) Scottish: variant spelling of ENTREKIN.

Entringer (165) German: habitational name for someone from Entringen, near Tübingen in Swabia.

Entsminger (222) Altered spelling of German ENSMINGER.

GIVEN NAME German 7%. *Kurt* (4).

Entwisle (176) English: variant of EN-TWISTLE.

Entwistle (642) English: habitational name from the village of Entwisle in Lancashire, named from Old English *henna* '(water) hen' or *ened* 'duck' + *twisla* 'tongue of land in a river fork'.

Entz (272) German: variant of ENZ.

Entzminger (187) Respelling of German ENSMINGER.

Enwright (147) Variant of Irish ENRIGHT.

GIVEN NAMES Irish 4%. *Brendan, Sean*.

Enyart (580) Of Dutch origin, but unexplained etymology.

Enyeart (467) See ENYART.

Enz (343) South German: from a short form of the personal name ANSELM. Compare ENNS.

GIVEN NAMES German 8%. *Kurt* (3), *Ilse* (2), *Erwin, Hans, Helmuth, Hermann, Rainer*.

Enzor (248) English: variant spelling of ENSOR.

Enzweiler (137) German: habitational name from a place so named.

Eoff (587) Probably an altered spelling of German **Ehoff**, a status name for the tenant of an unfree feudal holding, from Middle High German *ē* 'law' + *hof* 'farmstead', 'manor farm'.

Epes (113) English and Dutch: Variant of EPPS.

Ephraim (269) Mainly Jewish: from the Biblical name, which is probably from a Hebrew word meaning 'fruitful'. In Genesis 41:52, Ephraim is one of the sons of Joseph and the founder of one of the twelve tribes of Israel.

GIVEN NAMES Jewish 5%. *Isidor, Miriam, Yariv, Yoel*.

Epifano (102) Italian: from a personal name bestowed in honor of the feast of the Epiphany, from Greek *epiphaneia* 'showing', 'manifestation'. This was given in particular to children born on the feast of the Epiphany (January 6th), commemorating the manifestation of the infant Christ to the three Magi.

GIVEN NAMES Italian 14%. *Silvio* (3), *Angelo, Antonio*.

Episcopo (145) Italian: from *episcopo* 'bishop' (Latin *episcopus* (see BISHOP), probably a nickname for someone who had a pious manner or perhaps a metonymic occupational name for someone in the service of a bishop).

GIVEN NAMES Italian 13%. *Angelo, Orazio, Pasquale, Rocco*.

Epler (530) Altered spelling of German EPPLER.

Epley (1314) **1.** Altered spelling of German EPPLE. **2.** English: altered spelling of the habitational name APLEY.

Eplin (153) German: variant of German **Epplin**, a variant of EPPLE.

Epling (656) German: variant of EPLIN (see EPPLE).

Epp (907) South German: from a short form of EBERHARDT.

GIVEN NAMES German 4%. *Otto* (2), *Frieda, Fritz, Gerhard, Helmut, Kurt*.

Eppard (408) Variant of German EPPERT.

Eppel (111) Jewish (eastern Ashkenazic): ornamental name or metonymic occupational name from Yiddish *epl* 'apple'.

GIVEN NAMES Jewish 7%; German 6%; Russian 4%. *Mendel, Moysey, Yakov; Dieter, Heinz, Ilse; Aleksandr, Yelena*.

Epperley (129) See EPPERLY.

Epperly (873) **1.** Perhaps Americanized spelling of German **Epperle**, from a pet form of EBERHARDT. **2.** Altered spelling of English **Apperl(e)y**, a habitational name from places named Apperley in Gloucestershire, Northumbria, and Somerset or from Apperley Bridge in West Yorkshire.

Eppers (190) North German: patronymic from a short form of EBERHARDT.

Epperson (4467) Probably German, a patronymic from a short form of EBERHARDT.

Eppert (126) North German: from the personal name EBERHARDT or EGBERT.

Eppes (297) Perhaps of English origin: unexplained.

Eppich (236) German (Austria): from Middle High German *eppich* 'ivy', presumably a topographic name.

GIVEN NAMES German 8%. *Alois* (2), *Alfons, Erna, Hedwig, Helmut*.

Eppinette (130) French: nickname or topographic name from *épinette* 'thorn', 'prickle'.

Epping (263) German: **1.** patronymic from EPPERT. **2.** habitational name for someone from Epping in Alsace or Eppingen in Baden.

GIVEN NAMES German 4%. *Otto* (2), *Dieter, Hans*.

Eppinger (417) German: habitational name for someone from Epping or Eppingen (see EPPING).

Epple (445) South German (Swabian) and Swiss German: from a pet form of EBERHARDT or ALBRECHT.

GIVEN NAMES German 4%. *Helmut* (2), *Erwin*.

Eppler (697) South German: occupational name for a fruit grower or dealer, from Middle High German *epfeler* 'grower of or dealer in apples'.

GIVEN NAMES German 6%. *Kurt* (4), *Heinz* (3), *Klaus* (2), *Otto* (2).

Eppley (690) **1.** Respelling of German EPPLE. **2.** Variant of English APLEY.

Eppolito (194) Italian: variant of Italian IPPOLITO.

GIVEN NAMES Italian 11%. *Antonio* (2), *Salvatore* (2), *Santo*.

Epps (5009) **1.** English: variant of APPS or EBBS. **2.** English: from the Old English personal name *Eoppa* or Old Danish *Øpi*. **3.** Dutch: patronymic from *Epp(e)*, a pet form of the Germanic personal name EBERHARDT. **4.** Dutch: habitational name for someone from a place called Epse (see VAN EPPS).

Epright (103) Americanized form of German **Ebrecht**, a variant of EGGEBRECHT.

Epshteyn (115) Jewish (eastern Ashkenazic): variant of EPSTEIN.

GIVEN NAMES Russian 40%; Jewish 33%. *Boris* (4), *Iosif* (4), *Leonid* (4), *Mikhail* (4), *Vladimir* (3), *Grigory* (2), *Igor* (2), *Mayya* (2), *Yefim* (2), *Aleksandr, Anatoliy, Arkady; Semen* (3), *Isaak* (2), *Rimma* (2), *Aron, Berka, Bronya, Esfir, Ilya, Meyer, Miriam, Naum, Ruvin*.

Epstein (7647) German and Jewish (Ashkenazic): habitational name for someone from any of the places named Eppstein, for example in the Palatinate and Hesse, from Old High German *ebur* 'wild boar' + *stein* 'stone'.

GIVEN NAMES Jewish 6%. *Hyman* (11), *Emanuel* (8), *Isadore* (7), *Sol* (7), *Miriam* (4), *Moshe* (4), *Aron* (3), *Chaim* (3), *Meyer* (3), *Shlomo* (3), *Yoav* (3), *Ari* (2).

Epting (506) German: habitational name for someone from any of various places named Eptingen, for example in Baden and Switzerland.

Eramo (180) Italian: from the personal name *Erasmo* (from Greek *Erasmos*, a derivative of *erān* 'to love'). St. Erasmos (died 303) was a bishop of Formia in Campania, who was martyred under Diocletian. Compare ELMO.

GIVEN NAMES Italian 17%. *Umberto* (2), *Ennio, Guido, Rocco, Salvatore, Santino, Vito*.

Erath (163) German: variant of EHRHARDT.

Erazo (335) Variant spelling of Basque **Eraso**, a habitational name from any of the places in Navarre, Basque Country, so named, from Basque *ira*, *era* 'fern', 'bracken' + the suffix *-so* indicating abundance.

GIVEN NAMES Spanish 52%. *Jose* (16), *Jorge* (6), *Juan* (6), *Luis* (6), *Carlos* (5), *Francisco* (5), *Mario* (5), *Cesar* (3), *Javier* (3), *Marcos* (3), *Miguel* (3), *Pedro* (3).

Erb (3510) German and Swiss German: from the medieval personal name *Erbe*, meaning 'descendant', 'heir', which was popular in the Upper Rhineland.

Erbach (119) German: habitational name for someone from any of several places named Erbach, for example in Hesse, Rhineland, and Württemberg.

Erbacher (149) German: habitational name for someone from any of the places called ERBACH.

GIVEN NAMES German 8%. *Otto* (2), *Kurt*.

Erbaugh (139) Americanized spelling of German ERBACH.

Erbe (634) German: variant of ERB.

Erben (128) German: patronymic from ERB or ERBE. This name was common in Bohemia in the 19th century.
GIVEN NAMES German 7%. *Kurt, Magdalena.*

Erber (206) **1.** German: of uncertain derivation; several etymologies have been suggested: **2.** habitational name for someone from any of the places called Erb or Erp. **3.** from the personal name *Erb* (Germanic *Erpo*). **4.** status name for the owner of an inherited farm, *Erbhof.* **5.** from a byname from Middle High German *ērbære* 'honorable', 'noble'.
GIVEN NAMES German 8%. *Gerhart* (2), *Franz, Hans, Heinz, Jutta.*

Erbes (318) German: from Middle High German *erweiz* 'pea', a metonymic occupational name for a grower of peas, or perhaps a nickname for someone who was small and round.

Erbland (102) French (Alsace): habitational name for someone who lived on inherited land, German *Erbland.*

Erby (300) English: variant of IRBY.

Ercanbrack (139) Americanized form of German **Erkenbrecht**, a Germanic personal name composed of the elements *erkan* 'pure', 'perfect' + *berht* 'bright', 'famous'.

Erceg (173) Croatian (Dalmatia) and Serbian: nickname from a colloquial form of *herceg* 'duke', derived via Hungarian from German *Herzog.* Compare HERCEG, HERZOG.
GIVEN NAMES South Slavic 9%. *Dragan, Miodrag, Pero, Ratko, Slavko, Vinko.*

Erck (219) **1.** Dutch and German: from a Germanic personal name formed with *erkan* 'pure', 'perfect'. **2.** English: reduced form of HERRICK.

Ercolani (129) Italian: patronymic or plural form of ERCOLANO.
GIVEN NAMES Italian 14%. *Rinaldo* (2), *Domenic, Primo, Santi.*

Ercolano (129) Southern Italian: **1.** habitational name from Ercolano in Naples province, Campania. **2.** from the personal name *Ercolano*, originally an adjectival derivative (meaning 'Herculean') of *Hercules* (see ERCOLE).
GIVEN NAMES Italian 27%. *Sal* (2), *Assunta, Carmine, Emilio, Enrico, Franco, Julio, Romolo, Salvatore.*

Ercole (155) Italian: from the personal name *Ercole*, a Renaissance revival of the Latin name *Hercules* (Greek *Hēraklēs*), famous in classical mythology as the name of a hero of immense strength and courage.
GIVEN NAMES Italian 13%. *Angelo, Caesar, Erminio, Guido, Remo, Vincenzo, Vito.*

Erdahl (367) Norwegian: habitational name from a farmstead named Erdal, from Old Norse *elri* 'alder' + *dal* 'valley'.

Erdely (116) Variant of Hungarian ERDELYI.

GIVEN NAMES Hungarian 8%. *Laszlo* (3), *Antal.*

Erdelyi (102) Hungarian (**Erdélyi**): habitational name for someone from Transylvania (now in Romania), Hungarian *Erdély.*
GIVEN NAMES Hungarian 24%; German 4%. *Csaba* (2), *Sandor* (2), *Tibor* (2), *Andras, Antal, Gabor, Jozsef, Lajos, Zoltan; Brunhilde, Katharina.*

Erdle (112) Probably an Americanized spelling of Hungarian ERDELYI.

Erdley (128) **1.** Americanized spelling of Hungarian ERDELYI. **2.** Variant of English EARDLEY.

Erdman (2849) Variant spelling of ERDMANN.

Erdmann (1729) German: probably from the personal name *Ertmar*, from Germanic *ert-, erde* 'earth' + *māri, mēri* 'famous'.
GIVEN NAMES German 5%. *Kurt* (3), *Otto* (3), *Rudiger* (3), *Erwin* (2), *Hans* (2), *Armin, Eldor, Ernst, Frederich, Gerhardt, Guenter, Gunther.*

Erdos (208) Hungarian (**Erdős**): **1.** from the old secular name *Erdő.* **2.** from *erdő* 'forest', probably a shortened form of various occupational names such as *erdőőr* or *erdőőrző* 'forest guard', 'forest ranger'.
GIVEN NAMES Hungarian 11%. *Geza* (2), *Lajos* (2), *Zoltan* (2), *Arpad, Imre, Jeno.*

Erekson (171) Altered spelling of any of the Scandinavian patronymics derived from the Old Norse personal name *Eiríkr* (see ERICKSON).
GIVEN NAMES Scandinavian 4%; French 4%. *Erik, Thor; Marielle, Normand.*

Ereth (121) English: habitational name from Erith in Greater London, named from Old English *ēar* 'muddy', 'gravelly' + *hȳth* 'landing place'.

Ergas (114) Jewish (Sephardic, from North Africa): from Berber *argas* 'man'.
GIVEN NAMES Jewish 5%; Spanish 5%. *Shimon; Jose* (2), *Carlos, Eduardo.*

Ergle (280) Variant of German **Ergele**, from a pet form of *Erko*, a short form of a Germanic personal name composed of the elements *erkan* 'pure', 'perfect' + *berht* 'bright', 'famous'.

Erhard (407) German: variant spelling of EHRHARDT.
GIVEN NAMES German 4%. *Helmut* (2), *Angelika, Kurt.*

Erhardt (920) German: variant spelling of EHRHARDT.
GIVEN NAMES German 4%. *Eberhard, Erwin, Heinrich, Helmut, Ingo, Johannes, Mathias, Otto, Sigi.*

Erhart (621) German: variant spelling of EHRHARDT.

Eric (113) French: from the personal name *Erich*, of Old Norse origin (see ERICKSON).
GIVEN NAME French 5%. *Lucien.*

Erich (221) North German: from the personal name *Erich*, of Old Norse origin (see ERICKSON).

Erichsen (320) Danish, Norwegian, and North German: patronymic from the personal name *Eirik* or *Erich* (see ERICKSON).
GIVEN NAMES German 12%; Scandinavian 6%. *Fritz* (2), *Kurt* (2), *Ernst, Ewald, Hans, Horst, Karl Heinz, Otto; Erik, Knut, Maren, Sven.*

Erick (174) Americanized spelling of North German ERICH or Scandinavian *Eirik* (see ERICKSON).

Ericksen (1353) Danish, Norwegian, and North German: patronymic from *Erick*, from the Old Norse personal name *Eirīkr* (see ERICKSON).
GIVEN NAMES Scandinavian 8%. *Alf* (2), *Eyvind* (2), *Astrid, Bent, Lars, Lief, Nels, Nils, Sig.*

Erickson (36236) Respelling of a Scandinavian and North German patronymic derived from the Old Norse personal name *Eiríkr*, which is composed of *ei* 'ever', 'always' (or a reduced form of *ein* 'one', 'only') + *rík* 'power'. The main forms are ERICHSEN, ERIKSEN, ERICSSON, and ERIKSSON.
GIVEN NAMES Scandinavian 4%. *Erik* (16), *Nels* (13), *Thor* (13), *Nils* (12), *Lars* (11), *Sven* (11), *Lief* (9), *Anders* (8), *Lennart* (7), *Iver* (6), *Elof* (5), *Erland* (5).

Ericson (2628) Scandinavian and North German: see ERICKSON.
GIVEN NAMES Scandinavian 7%. *Nils* (12), *Lars* (3), *Lennart* (3), *Erik* (2), *Anders, Erland, Eskil, Lief, Mats, Nelle, Nels, Sven.*

Ericsson (399) Swedish: variant spelling of ERIKSSON.
GIVEN NAMES Scandinavian 17%; German 5%. *Lars* (3), *Sven* (2), *Anders, Britt, Gunvor, Johan, Kerstin, Tor; Hans* (2), *Kurt* (2).

Erie (297) Origin uncertain. It may be derived from the place name *Erie*, the name of one of the Great Lakes and various counties and townships on its southern shores. The etymology is from the name of an American Indian people who lived there before the arrival of Europeans, and indeed the surname may denote a member of this people. Their name is said to mean 'cat' or 'cat people'.

Eriksen (1273) Norwegian and Danish: patronymic from the personal name *Erik*, Old Norse *Eiríkr* (see ERICKSON).
GIVEN NAMES Scandinavian 19%. *Erik* (25), *Niels* (4), *Morten* (3), *Alf* (2), *Johan* (2), *Aase, Bjorn, Einer, Fredrik, Helle, Iver, Knud.*

Erikson (1136) See ERICKSON.
GIVEN NAMES Scandinavian 13%; German 4%. *Erik* (21), *Anders* (3), *Nils* (3), *Astrid* (2), *Berndt* (2), *Iver, Karsten, Lars, Lennart, Lief, Thor; Gerhart* (3), *Ernst.*

Eriksson (469) Swedish: patronymic from the personal name *Erik*, Old Norse *Eiríkr* (see ERICKSON).
GIVEN NAMES Scandinavian 36%; German 5%. *Erik* (10), *Lars* (6), *Anders* (3), *Nils*

(3), *Per* (2), *Alf, Algot, Alvar, Bjorn, Elof, Knut, Mats; Hans* (2), *Kurt* (2), *Konrad.*

Erion (233) German: variant of IRION.

Erisman (332) Swiss German (**Erismann**): variant of EHRESMANN.

Erk (143) German: from a short form of *Erkenbrecht*, a Germanic personal name composed of the elements *erkan* 'pure', 'perfect' + *berht* 'bright', 'famous'.
GIVEN NAMES German 4%. *Bernhardt, Georg.*

Erker (234) German: byname for someone who lived in a house with a conspicuous oriel, Middle High German *ärkēr, erker.*
GIVEN NAMES German 7%. *Alois, Erna, Erwin, Frieda, Gottfried, Siegfried.*

Erkkila (197) Finnish (**Erkkilä**): habitational name from a farm so named, from the personal name *Erkki* (Finnish form of ERIC (see ERICKSON) + the local suffix *-la*).
GIVEN NAMES Finnish 13%; Scandinavian 9%. *Reino* (7), *Armas* (2), *Eino* (2), *Kristiina; Mauritz.*

Erland (125) **1.** Norwegian: habitational name from a farm in southwestern Norway so named, from Old Norse *elri* 'alder' + *land* 'land', 'farm'. **2.** Swedish: probably an ornamental name or possibly a shortened form of the patronymic **Erlandsson** (see ERLANDSON).
GIVEN NAME Scandinavian 7%. *Obert.*

Erlandson (915) Americanized spelling of Swedish **Erlandsson** or Norwegian and Danish **Erlandsen**, patronymics from *Erland*, from the Old Norse byname **Erlandr, Erlendr**, meaning 'foreign', 'from a foreign country'.
GIVEN NAMES Scandinavian 7%. *Erland* (3), *Erik* (2), *Lars* (2), *Mats* (2), *Alf, Alvar, Bjorn, Helmer, Iver, Nils, Sven.*

Erlanger (127) German and Jewish (Ashkenazic): habitational name for someone from Erlangen in Bavaria.
GIVEN NAMES Jewish 7%; German 5%. *Esti, Hillel, Jechiel, Meyer, Yechezkel; Hans, Wilhelmine.*

Erle (112) German: topographic name for someone who lived near a prominent alder tree or trees, from Middle High German *erle* 'alder'.

Erler (376) German: topographic name for someone who lived among alder trees, from Middle High German *erle* 'alder' + *-er*, suffix denoting an inhabitant.
GIVEN NAMES German 4%. *Gebhard, Kurt, Otto, Rudi.*

Erlewine (137) Americanized spelling of German **Erlewein**, from the personal name *Erlwin*, composed of the elements *erl* 'free man', 'noble fighter' + *win* 'friend'.

Erlich (376) Jewish (Ashkenazic): variant of EHRLICH.
GIVEN NAMES Jewish 12%. *Berish* (2), *Moshe* (2), *Myer* (2), *Avi, Hymie, Isadore, Ori, Shai, Shlomo, Yechiel, Yetta, Zvi.*

Erlichman (136) Jewish (Ashkenazic): variant of EHRLICH.

GIVEN NAMES Jewish 8%. *Hyman, Yehuda, Yisrael.*

Erling (153) **1.** Scandinavian and North German: from a Germanic personal name. **2.** German: habitational name from any of several places in Bavaria named Erling or Erlingen.
GIVEN NAMES Scandinavian 11%; German 6%. *Aksel, Astrid, Erik; Bernhard, Erwin, Gerd.*

Erlinger (123) German: habitational name for someone from a place called named Erling or Erlingen (see ERLING).

Erman (265) Americanized spelling of German EHRMANN.
GIVEN NAMES German 5%. *Kurt* (3), *Hans, Otto.*

Ermel (133) German: from Middle High German *ermel* 'sleeve', a metonymic occupational name for a sleeve maker. Alternatively, it may have been a nickname for someone who wore clothing with conspicuous sleeves; in medieval times the size of sleeves was regulated by luxury laws.
GIVEN NAMES German 11%. *Heinz, Jurgen, Markus, Matthias.*

Ermer (195) German: from a Germanic personal name of uncertain etymology.

Ermis (201) Czech: **1.** most probably from a reduced form of the personal name *Jeremiáš*, from Greek *Hierōnymos* (see HIERONYMUS, JEROME). **2.** alternatively, possibly from the German personal name EMMERICH.

Erne (192) German (Alemannic): from a short form of ARNOLD.

Ernest (1836) **1.** English and Dutch: from the Germanic byname mentioned at ERNST. However, Reaney cites medieval evidence for Norman spellings such as *Ernais*, and derives it from a Germanic personal name *Arn(e)gis*, possibly composed of the elements *arn* 'eagle' + *gīsil* 'pledge', 'hostage', 'noble youth' (see GIESEL). The name may have been altered by folk etymology to coincide with the word meaning 'combat'. Compare HARNESS. **2.** Dutch: variant of ERNST.

Ernesti (101) German or Dutch: humanistic name, from the genitive of *Ernestus*, Latinized form of ERNST.

Erney (209) Altered spelling of German ERNE. It is heavily concentrated in PA.

Erno (168) **1.** Americanized form of French ARNAUD. **2.** German (Alemannic): variant of ERNE.

Ernsberger (287) Probably an altered spelling of German **Ernstberger**, a habitational name for someone from a place called Ernstberg in East Prussia, or from any of several places called Arnsberg.

Ernst (7944) **1.** German and Dutch: from the personal name *Ernst*, which is most probably a byname from Middle High German and Middle Dutch *ern(e)st* 'combat', 'serious business'. However, see ERNEST. **2.** Jewish (Ashkenazic): nickname or orna-

mental from German *ernst* 'earnest', 'serious'.
GIVEN NAMES German 4%. *Otto* (10), *Erwin* (8), *Kurt* (5), *Heinz* (4), *Helmut* (3), *Manfred* (3), *Reinhold* (3), *Ulrich* (3), *Fritz* (2), *Gunter* (2), *Hans* (2), *Heinrich* (2).

Ernster (237) Jewish (Ashkenazic): variant of ERNST, from an inflected form of the German adjective.

Ernsting (109) German: patronymic from the personal name ERNST.

Erny (246) **1.** Altered form of German ERNE. **2.** French: habitational name from a place in the Pas-de-Calais, so named from the Germanic personal name *Erno* + the Latin suffix *-iacum*.
GIVEN NAMES German 5%. *Aloysius, Frieda, Horst, Otto.*

Ernzen (106) Luxembourgeois: probably a patronymic from the personal name ERNST.

Eroh (203) Origin unidentified. This name is found chiefly in PA. It may be a reduced form of French HEROUX or, under French influence, of German HEROLD.

Eros (100) Hungarian (**Erős**): unexplained.

Erp (155) North German: variant of ARP.

Erpelding (353) German: patronymic from any of the various personal names beginning with the element *Erp-, Erb-*.

Erpenbach (119) German: Probably an altered form of **Erpenbeck** (the Low German form), a habitational name from an unidentified place.

Erps (141) Jewish (Ashkenazic): variant of HERBST.
GIVEN NAMES Jewish 9%. *Baruch, Chaim, Fishel, Shaya, Yisroel, Yosef.*

Errante (119) Italian: from *errante* 'wandering', probably applied as a nickname for a wandering minstrel, an eccentric person, or a philanderer.
GIVEN NAMES Italian 15%. *Salvatore* (3), *Giuseppe, Vincenzo.*

Errett (234) English: from the Old English personal name *Ēadrǣd*, meaning 'prosperity-council'.

Errickson (251) Probably an altered spelling of ERIKSEN, ERIKSON, etc.
GIVEN NAME German 4%. *Kurt.*

Errico (568) Italian: variant of ENRICO.
GIVEN NAMES Italian 16%. *Vito* (6), *Carmine* (4), *Rocco* (3), *Antonio* (2), *Erminio* (2), *Angelo, Canio, Carlo, Ciro, Cosimo, Enzo, Federico.*

Errigo (133) Italian: variant of ENRICO.
GIVEN NAMES Italian 10%. *Pasquale* (2), *Antonio, Fausto, Nunzio.*

Errington (298) English (Northumberland): habitational name from a place in Northumbria, so called from a British river name akin to Welsh *arian* 'silvery', 'bright' + Old English *tūn* 'enclosure', 'settlement'.

Erskin (155) Scottish: variant spelling of ERSKINE.

Erskine (1965) Scottish: habitational name from a place on the south bank of the Clyde outside Glasgow, first recorded in 1225 in the form **Erskin**. Other early spellings vary (1227 **Yrskin**; 1262 **Ireskin**; 1300 **Harskin**, **Irschen**).

Ersland (112) Norwegian: habitational name from a farmstead in western Norway, so named from the personal name *Eirik* (see ERICKSON) + *land* 'land', 'farm'.

Erspamer (155) South German and Austrian: topographic name from Middle High German *esban*, *espan* 'pasture' (Bavarian and Swabian *Espan*).
GIVEN NAMES German 4%. *Florian, Kurt*.

Erstad (175) Norwegian: habitational name from any of ten farmsteads so named, from the Old Norse personal name *Eiríkr* or *Erpr* + *stad* (from Old Norse *staðr* 'farmstead', 'dwelling').
GIVEN NAME Scandinavian 6%. *Nels* (2).

Ertel (894) South German: from a pet form of a personal name beginning with *Ort-*, from Old High German *ort* 'point (of a sword or lance)'.

Ertl (516) South German: variant of ERTEL. The name in this spelling is also found in Slovenia.
GIVEN NAMES German 7%. *Lorenz* (2), *Wolfgang* (2), *Benno, Dieter, Heinrich, Hermann, Rainer, Xaver*.

Ertle (291) Americanized spelling of German ERTEL.

Ertman (183) Variant of ERDMANN.

Ertz (256) German: variant of **Ersch**, from a pet form of *Aro* or *Arez*.

Erven (146) Scottish, English, and Irish: altered spelling of ERVIN or ERWIN.

Ervin (7423) **1.** Scottish, English, and Irish: variant spelling of IRVIN. **2.** Americanized spelling of German ERWIN.

Ervine (148) Scottish, English, and Irish: variant of IRVIN.

Erving (296) Scottish, English, and Irish: variant of IRVIN.

Erway (279) Origin unidentified.

Erwin (8778) **1.** Scottish, English, and Irish: variant of IRVIN. **2.** German: from the personal name *Erwin*, from *Herwin*, a compound of Old High German *heri* 'army' + *wini* 'friend'.

Erwine (103) English (Cumbria): variant of IRVIN.

Erwood (66) Welsh: habitational name from Erwood in Breconshire.

Erxleben (176) German: habitational name from either of two places so named in the Magdeburg-Helmstedt area.
GIVEN NAMES German 4%. *Kurt, Lorenz*.

Esarey (144) English: variant of ESSARY or USSERY, both of unexplained origin.

Esau (401) Welsh: from the Biblical personal name *Esau*, meaning 'hairy' in Hebrew (Genesis 25:25).

Esbenshade (194) Altered spelling of German ESPENSCHIED.

Escajeda (110) Spanish: from a field name from a collective form of *escajo* 'fallow land' (a variant of *escalio*).
GIVEN NAMES Spanish 45%. *Jose* (6), *Guadalupe* (2), *Jesus* (2), *Juanita* (2), *Adela, Alfredo, Andres, Armida, Cruz, Enrique, Francisco, Gorgonio*.

Escalante (1591) Spanish: habitational name from a place in Santoña in Santander province, whose name derives from *escala* 'ladder' (Latin *scala*), referring to a terraced slope.
GIVEN NAMES Spanish 46%. *Jose* (31), *Juan* (23), *Manuel* (19), *Jorge* (14), *Jesus* (11), *Carlos* (10), *Francisco* (10), *Pedro* (10), *Roberto* (10), *Lupe* (9), *Ernesto* (8), *Fernando* (8).

Escalera (484) Spanish and Galician: habitational name from any of several places called Escalera, for example in Lugo, Guadalajara, and Málaga, from *escalera* 'stairs', 'ladder', probably denoting in some cases a terraced slope.
GIVEN NAMES Spanish 48%. *Jose* (17), *Jesus* (9), *Juan* (9), *Carlos* (5), *Manuel* (5), *Ana* (4), *Javier* (4), *Ruben* (4), *Miguel* (3), *Pedro* (3), *Rafael* (3), *Roberto* (3).

Escalona (285) Spanish: habitational name probably from Escalona in Toledo province; otherwise from Escalona del Prado in Soria.
GIVEN NAMES Spanish 46%. *Manuel* (6), *Luis* (5), *Alfredo* (4), *Jorge* (3), *Jose* (3), *Miguel* (3), *Rafael* (3), *Reynaldo* (3), *Arturo* (2), *Cesar* (2), *Fernando* (2), *Justo* (2); *Antonio, Marco, Maximinio, Paolino, Reno, Romeo*.

Escamilla (1787) Spanish: habitational name from Escamilla, a place in Guadalajara province.
GIVEN NAMES Spanish 47%. *Jose* (43), *Juan* (29), *Manuel* (22), *Carlos* (20), *Jesus* (14), *Luis* (13), *Raul* (13), *Ruben* (13), *Jorge* (12), *Mario* (12), *Pedro* (10), *Alfredo* (9).

Escandon (192) Spanish (**Escandón**): possibly from a field name derived from *escanda*, denoting a type of wheat.
GIVEN NAMES Spanish 44%. *Juan* (5), *Manuel* (4), *Jaime* (3), *Jose* (3), *Ricardo* (3), *Armando* (2), *Mario* (2), *Pedro* (2), *Ramiro* (2), *Ruben* (2), *Adriana, Alberto*.

Escarcega (206) Spanish (**Escárcega**): probably a Castilianized form of Basque **Eskarzaga**, a place in Biscay, Basque Country, named from Basque *(h)azkar* 'maple'.
GIVEN NAMES Spanish 45%. *Jesus* (8), *Carlos* (3), *Manuel* (3), *Jaime* (2), *Jose* (2), *Jose Antonio* (2), *Juan* (2), *Mario* (2), *Raul* (2), *Adela, Alfonso, Alicia*.

Escareno (216) Mexican: unexplained.
GIVEN NAMES Spanish 55%. *Jesus* (6), *Jose* (6), *Manuel* (5), *Juan* (4), *Mario* (3), *Adan* (2), *Alicia* (2), *Efren* (2), *Ernesto* (2), *Gerardo* (2), *Guadalupe* (2), *Isidro* (2).

Esch (1193) German: **1.** habitational name from any of several places named Esch, from Old High German *asc* 'ash', or a

topographic name for someone who lived near a prominent ash tree. **2.** from Middle High German *ezzisch* 'seeded field', hence a topographic name for someone who lived by an area where grain was grown or perhaps a status name for someone who owned such land.

Eschbach (369) German: habitational name from any of numerous places so named, from Old High German *asc* 'ash' + *bah* 'stream'.
GIVEN NAMES German 6%. *Kurt* (4), *Johann, Reiner*.

Esche (162) German: variant of ESCH or habitational name from Esche in northwest Germany.
GIVEN NAMES German 8%; Scandinavian 4%. *Kurt* (4), *Gerd*; *Sven*.

Eschen (128) German: probably a habitational name from Eschen near Bayreuth, of which the original form was Middle High German *ze den eschen* 'at the ash trees' (from the dative plural of *esch* 'ash').
GIVEN NAME German 4%. *Otto*.

Eschenbach (144) German: habitational name from any of several places so named.
GIVEN NAME French 4%. *Jeanmarie* (2).

Eschenbacher (104) German: habitational name for someone from any of the various places called ESCHENBACH.
GIVEN NAME German 6%. *Kurt*.

Eschenbrenner (109) German: occupational name for someone who prepared ash from wood fires for use in glassworks and soapworks, a variant of ASCHENBRENNER.
GIVEN NAME French 4%; German 4%. *Gunther*.

Eschenburg (158) German: habitational name from a place so called.

Escher (357) German: habitational name for someone from any of the various places called ESCH, ESCHE, or ESCHEN.

Eschete (221) French: habitational name from Eschette in the Grand Duchy of Luxembourg.

Eschler (104) German: **1.** topographic name for someone who lived by an ash tree or an ash wood (see ESCH 1). **2.** topographic name for someone who lived by an area where grain was grown or perhaps a status name for someone who owned such land (see ESCH 2).
GIVEN NAMES German 6%. *Erwin, Kurt*.

Eschliman (103) Variant of Swiss German **Äschlimann** (see ESHLEMAN).

Eschman (115) Variant of German and Swiss ESCHMANN.
GIVEN NAME German 7%. *Kurt* (3).

Eschmann (229) German and Swiss German: topographic name for someone who lived by an area of land where grain was grown, or perhaps a status name for someone who owned such land, from ESCH + *Mann* 'man'.
GIVEN NAMES German 5%. *Jurgen, Kurt*.

Eschrich (142) German: from a Germanic personal name composed of the elements *ask* 'ash', 'spear' + *rik* 'mighty', 'rich'.

Esco (214) **1.** English: probably an altered spelling of Askew. This is a southern U.S. name, concentrated in AL and GA. Compare Escoe, Escue, and Eskew. **2.** American spelling of Finnish or Estonian **Esko**, from a personal name derived from Swedish *Eskil* (see Eskildsen).

Escobar (5079) Spanish: topographic name for someone who lived in a place overgrown with broom, from a collective form of *escoba* 'broom' (Late Latin *scopa*), or a habitational name from any of the various places named with this word: for example, Escobar de Campos (León), Escobar de Polendos (Segovia), and three minor places in Murcia.

GIVEN NAMES Spanish 51%. *Jose* (167), *Carlos* (82), *Manuel* (65), *Juan* (60), *Luis* (56), *Jorge* (41), *Miguel* (41), *Francisco* (33), *Mario* (33), *Ana* (28), *Jesus* (27), *Raul* (26).

Escobedo (2317) Spanish: topographic name from a collective form of *escoba* 'broom' (Late Latin *scopa*), or a habitational name from either of two minor places in Santander province called Escobedo.

GIVEN NAMES Spanish 52%. *Jose* (74), *Juan* (50), *Carlos* (20), *Francisco* (20), *Jesus* (19), *Manuel* (19), *Javier* (18), *Ruben* (18), *Luis* (17), *Fernando* (16), *Mario* (15), *Pedro* (15).

Escoe (147) Altered form of English Askew. This name occurs chiefly in GA. Compare Esco, Escue, and Eskew.

Escoto (414) Spanish: ethnic name from *escoto*, originally denoting a Gaelic speaker from Ireland or Scotland; later, a Scot, someone from Scotland. See Scott.

GIVEN NAMES Spanish 46%. *Jose* (10), *Manuel* (7), *Jesus* (5), *Rafael* (5), *Ramon* (4), *Ana* (3), *Armando* (3), *Carlos* (3), *Cesar* (3), *Felipe* (3), *Luis* (3), *Miguel* (3).

Escott (362) **1.** English: habitational name from any of various places called Eastcott (Wiltshire), Eastcotts (Bedfordshire), Eastcote (Greater London), or Eastcourt (Wiltshire), all named from Old English *ēast* 'eastern' + *cot* 'cottage(s)'. **2.** In some cases the name may be an altered spelling of the French ethnic name **Escot**, a cognate of Scott.

Escovedo (103) Spanish or Portuguese: variant of Escobedo.

GIVEN NAMES Spanish 46%. *Jose* (4), *Juan* (2), *Manuel* (2), *Mario* (2), *Ruben* (2), *Alfredo*, *Armando*, *Bacilio*, *Esperanza*, *Guadalupe*, *Jaime*, *Javier*; *Angelo*, *Federico*, *Mauro*.

Escudero (427) Spanish: occupational name for a squire, a young man of good birth attendant on a knight, or shield bearer, *escudero* (medieval Latin *scutarius*, a derivative of Latin *scutum* 'shield').

GIVEN NAMES Spanish 47%. *Jose* (16), *Juan* (8), *Carlos* (7), *Francisco* (6), *Manuel* (6), *Margarita* (6), *Raul* (5), *Mario* (4), *Miguel* (4), *Eduardo* (3), *Ernesto* (3), *Luis* (3).

Escue (420) Probably an altered spelling of English Askew. Compare Eskew. This name is concentrated in TN.

Escutia (106) Catalan: possibly from a derivative of Catalan *escutiar* 'to burl', denoting a textile worker.

GIVEN NAMES Spanish 61%. *Jose* (7), *Jesus* (3), *Juan* (3), *Rafael* (3), *Mario* (2), *Sergio* (2), *Adalberto*, *Adan*, *Agustin*, *Alberto*, *Arturo*, *Chico*; *Antonio*, *Bartolo*.

Esguerra (211) Probably a variant of Basque **Ezkerra**, a nickname from Basque *ezker* 'left-handed'.

GIVEN NAMES Spanish 41%. *Jorge* (3), *Angel* (2), *Aurelio* (2), *Carlos* (2), *Fernando* (2), *Juan* (2), *Mario* (2), *Raul* (2), *Alberto*, *Alfredo*, *Amando*, *Angelita*; *Antonio*, *Cecilio*, *Dante*, *Dario*, *Enrico*, *Federico*, *Romeo*.

Esh (222) Americanized spelling of German Esch.

Esham (210) English: variant of Isham. The surname is no longer found in the U.K. In the U.S. it occurs chiefly in MD.
FOREBEARS The name is first recorded in Northamton Co., VA, when Daniel Esham came over as an indentured servant in 1651.

Eshbach (175) Americanized spelling of Eschbach.

Eshbaugh (215) Americanized spelling of Eschbach.

Eshelman (1158) Americanized spelling of Swiss German **Äschlimann** (see Eshleman).

Eshleman (1012) Americanized spelling of Swiss German **Äschlimann**, **Aeschlimann**, of disputed origin; some authorities believe it to be a topographic name for someone living by a prominent ash tree, from Old High German *asc* 'ash'; others derive it from *Öschli*, a pet form of the personal name *Oswald*.

Eshom (108) Variant of English Esham (see Isham).

Eskelson (150) Scandinavian: variant of Eskildsen.

Eskenazi (224) Jewish: variant of Ashkenazi (reflecting a Sephardic pronunciation).

GIVEN NAMES Jewish 10%. *Sol* (3), *Moises* (2), *Ari*, *Eyal*, *Nissim*, *Shabtay*.

Esker (282) German (Westphalia): unexplained.

Eskew (1429) English: variant of Askew. This is a common name in GA, MO, and SC.

Eskildsen (153) Scandinavian: patronymic from the personal name *Eskil(d)*, Old Norse *Áskell*, *Ásketill*, a compound of elements meaning 'god' + 'kettle' or 'helmet'.

GIVEN NAMES Scandinavian 12%. *Erik* (2), *Lars* (2), *Ludvig*.

Eskin (244) Jewish (from Belarus): metronymic from Yiddish personal name *Eske*, a pet form of *Ester* (see Esther).

GIVEN NAMES Jewish 8%; Russian 4%. *Avram*, *Ilya*, *Jakov*, *Marat*, *Semen*; *Boris*, *Mikhail*, *Semyon*.

Eskins (121) English: unexplained.

Eskola (121) Finnish: habitational name from a farmstead so named, from the personal name *Esko* (Finnish form of Scandinavian *Eskil* (see Eskildsen) + the local suffix *-la*). In some cases the surname is a later ornamental adoption; it occurs chiefly in western Finland.

GIVEN NAMES Finnish 6%; Scandinavian 4%. *Esko*, *Reino*, *Sulo*, *Toivo*; *Nels*.

Eskra (134) Variant of Polish or Slovenian Iskra.

Eskridge (1310) English: habitational name, probably from Eskrigg in Cumbria or Eskrigge in Lancashire.

Esler (432) German: byname or occupational name for someone who drove donkeys, from Middle High German *esel* 'donkey' + the agent suffix *-er*.

Eslick (559) English (Devon and Cornwall): altered form of **Eastlake**, habitational name from Eastlake in Devon, named in Old English as *ēast lacu* 'the eastern stream'.

Eslinger (1014) Altered spelling of German Esslinger.

Esmay (103) English: variant of **Ismay**, from a medieval female personal name of uncertain origin.

Esmond (275) English: from an Old English personal name composed of the elements *ēast* 'grace', 'beauty' + *mund* 'protection'. This name was also used by the Norman, among whom it represents a continental Germanic cognate of the Old English name.

Espada (240) Spanish and Portuguese: metonymic occupational name for an armorer or a swordsman, from *espada* 'sword' (Latin *spata*, from Greek *spathē*, originally denoting a broad, two-edged sword without a point). In some cases the surname may be a Catalan cognate, from Old Catalan *espada* (now *espasa*).

GIVEN NAMES Spanish 40%; Portuguese 13%. *Carlos* (6), *Jose* (6), *Pedro* (4), *Jorge* (3), *Francisco* (2), *Luis* (2), *Miguel* (2), *Rigoberto* (2), *Roberto* (2), *Alfredo*, *Angel*, *Aurelio*; *Joao*.

Espaillat (123) perhaps Catalan and southern French (Occitan): occupational name from Catalan *espallat*, in an old spelling, or directly from Occitan *espaiat*, *espalhat*, past participle of *espallar* 'to winnow', 'to separate the wheat from the chaff'.

GIVEN NAMES Spanish 56%. *Jose* (5), *Rafael* (5), *Francisco* (4), *Juana* (3), *Ana* (2), *Julio* (2), *Leopoldo* (2), *Yaniris* (2), *Adriano*, *Aida*, *Antonieta*, *Aura*; *Antonio*, *Eliseo*, *Federico*, *Francesca*, *Marco*.

Espana (265) Spanish (**España**): ethnic name for someone from Spain, *España*, from Latin *Hispania*.

GIVEN NAMES Spanish 51%. *Jose* (7), *Carlos* (6), *Jorge* (4), *Juan* (3), *Luis* (3), *Pedro* (3), *Ramon* (3), *Ricardo* (3), *Salvador* (3), *Angel* (2), *Argemiro* (2), *Estela* (2); *Angelo*, *Ceasar*, *Heriberto*, *Marco*.

Esparza (3662) Castilianized form of Basque **Espartza**, a habitational name from Espartza, a village in Navarre province.

GIVEN NAMES Spanish 48%. *Jose* (82), *Juan* (49), *Jesus* (46), *Manuel* (44), *Raul* (30), *Francisco* (25), *Ruben* (25), *Carlos* (23), *Miguel* (23), *Luis* (21), *Ramon* (20), *Guadalupe* (19).

Espe (324) **1.** German: habitational name from a place called Espe or Espa, or a topographic name from Middle Low German *espe* 'aspen', Middle High German *aspe*. **2.** Norwegian: habitational name from any of several farmsteads so named, from Old Norse *espi* 'aspen'.

GIVEN NAMES German 6%. *Claus* (3), *Kurt* (2), *Erwin*.

Espejo (284) Spanish: habitational name, probably from Espejo in Córdoba province, or otherwise from one of the minor places so named in Málaga and Araba provinces; the place name is evidently connected with *espejo* 'mirror' (Latin *speculum*).

GIVEN NAMES Spanish 45%. *Jose* (9), *Luis* (5), *Juan* (4), *Eusebio* (3), *Pancho* (3), *Alberto* (2), *Alfredo* (2), *Cesar* (2), *Javier* (2), *Manuel* (2), *Pablo* (2), *Pedro* (2); *Antonio* (4), *Dante*, *Leonardo*, *Lorenzo*, *Lucio*, *Pio*, *Sarina*.

Espeland (212) Norwegian: habitational name from any of several farms, notably in southwestern Norway, so named from Old Norse *espi* 'aspen' + *land* 'land'.

GIVEN NAMES Scandinavian 12%. *Berger*, *Jorgen*, *Lars*, *Obert*.

Espenschied (148) German: variant of the German topographic name **Espenscheidt** 'pasture at the crossroads', from Middle High German *espan* 'open space', 'unenclosed pasture' + *scheit* 'crossroads' (see SCHEIDT).

GIVEN NAME German 5%. *Otto*.

Espenshade (201) Americanized spelling of German ESPENSCHIED.

Esper (434) **1.** German: most likely a topographic name for a personal who lived by or owned an area of pasture, from Middle High German *esban*, *espan* 'pasture' (Bavarian and Swabian *Espan*). **2.** North German and Danish: variant of **Jesper**, Low German and Danish form of KASPAR.

GIVEN NAME French 4%. *Andre*.

Esperanza (120) Spanish: metronymic from the female personal name *Esperanza*, from *esperanza* 'hope', or a habitational name from a place named Esperanza of La Esperanza for its church dedicated to a 2nd-century saint bearing this name.

GIVEN NAMES Spanish 45%. *Jose* (3), *Abelardo*, *Armando*, *Blanco*, *Carlos*, *Concepcion*, *Coronado*, *Domingo*, *Ernestina*, *Esteban*, *Francisco*, *Joaquin*; *Caesar* (2), *Dante*, *Marco*.

Espersen (119) Danish: patronymic from the personal name *Esper*, from Old Norse *Ásbjórn*, a compound of *áss* 'god' + *bjǫrn* 'bear'.

Espeseth (170) Norwegian: habitational name from any of several farmsteads so named, from *espe* 'aspen' + *set* 'dwelling', 'farmstead'.

GIVEN NAMES Scandinavian 6%; German 4%. *Nels*; *Otto* (2).

Espey (463) **1.** Scottish: variant of ESPY. **2.** German: topographic name for someone who lived by a stretch of water or marsh edged by aspen trees, from Middle High German, Middle Low German *espe* 'aspen' + *-ey*, a suffix denoting the presence of water.

Espin (105) Spanish (**Espín**): variant of ESPINO.

Espina (161) Asturian-Leonese, Spanish, and Catalan: habitational name from any of several minor places named Espina (notably in Asturies), from *espina* 'thorn', 'prickle', probably applied in the sense 'thorn bush'.

GIVEN NAMES Spanish 41%. *Pedro* (3), *Cesar* (2), *Filemon* (2), *Jose* (2), *Juan* (2), *Lourdes* (2), *Manuel* (2), *Adelaida*, *Aida*, *Arturo*, *Carlos*, *Cayetano*.

Espinal (1023) Spanish: from any of numerous fields named Espinal or Espinar, from a collective of *espina* 'thorn'.

GIVEN NAMES Spanish 57%. *Jose* (40), *Juan* (23), *Ana* (16), *Rafael* (15), *Ramon* (14), *Juana* (9), *Luis* (9), *Francisco* (8), *Andres* (7), *Miguel* (7), *Ramona* (7), *Carlos* (6); *Antonio* (7), *Leonardo* (3), *Eligio* (2), *Adalgisa*, *Carmela*, *Carmelo*, *Ceasar*, *Cecilio*, *Elio*, *Filomena*, *Flavio*, *Lia*.

Espindola (168) Portuguese (**Espíndola**): of uncertain origin, but possibly a topographic name. It was taken to Portugal by an immigrant family from Genoa, Italy.

GIVEN NAMES Spanish 45%. *Jesus* (4), *Francisco* (3), *Jose* (3), *Manuel* (3), *Raul* (3), *Gerardo* (2), *Juana* (2), *Luz* (2), *Miguel* (2), *Ruben* (2), *Alejandrino*, *Alida*; *Antonio* (3), *Ciro*, *Eliseo*.

Espino (1114) Spanish: topographic name for someone living by a hawthorn or in an area characterized by hawthorns, *espino*.

GIVEN NAMES Spanish 52%. *Jose* (37), *Juan* (21), *Jesus* (12), *Manuel* (12), *Francisco* (9), *Felipe* (8), *Jorge* (8), *Luis* (8), *Miguel* (7), *Ramon* (7), *Mario* (6), *Rafael* (6).

Espinola (330) Portuguese (**Espínola**): variant of ESPINDOLA.

GIVEN NAMES Spanish 29%; Portuguese 12%. *Manuel* (11), *Jose* (4), *Julio* (4), *Arturo* (3), *Francisco* (3), *Alberto* (2), *Albino* (2), *Arlindo* (2), *Mario* (2), *Tomas* (2), *Adolfo*, *Aida*; *Duarte*, *Joao*, *Messias*, *Serafim*, *Valentim*.

Espinosa (4713) Spanish: habitational name from any of the numerous places named Espinosa, from a collective form of *espina* 'thorn'.

GIVEN NAMES Spanish 44%. *Jose* (127), *Juan* (64), *Carlos* (56), *Luis* (50), *Manuel* (45), *Jesus* (35), *Miguel* (29), *Jorge* (28), *Pedro* (25), *Francisco* (23), *Raul* (20), *Roberto* (20).

Espinoza (8007) South American spelling of Spanish ESPINOSA; the spelling with *-z-* represents a voiced pronunciation heard in some Latin-American countries, whereas in Castilian Spanish it now has an unvoiced *-s-*.

GIVEN NAMES Spanish 48%. *Jose* (185), *Juan* (105), *Jesus* (89), *Manuel* (83), *Carlos* (79), *Luis* (70), *Miguel* (52), *Pedro* (51), *Raul* (51), *Jorge* (46), *Francisco* (45), *Roberto* (43).

Espiritu (505) Spanish (**Espíritu**): from a short form of a religious compound name formed with a personal name + 'del Espíritu Santo' (Latin *Spiritus Sanctus*), often bestowed on children born on Easter Sunday.

GIVEN NAMES Spanish 40%. *Jose* (5), *Pedro* (4), *Ernesto* (3), *Esteban* (3), *Marcelo* (3), *Teofilo* (3), *Alfonso* (2), *Angel* (2), *Arsenio* (2), *Carmelita* (2), *Cesar* (2), *Crisanto* (2).

Espitia (281) Aragonese: from Fraga, in Uesca province, Aragon; unexplained.

GIVEN NAMES Spanish 51%. *Jose* (13), *Jesus* (5), *Alfonso* (4), *Juan* (4), *Pedro* (4), *Guadalupe* (3), *Manuel* (3), *Raul* (3), *Ruben* (3), *Angel* (2), *Bacilio* (2), *Carlos* (2); *Antonio* (2), *Carmel*, *Clemente*, *Federico*, *Geronimo*, *Salustia*, *Silvano*.

Esplin (265) Scottish: variant of ASPLIN.

Esposito (8120) Italian: surname commonly denoting a foundling, meaning literally 'exposed' (Latin *expositus*, past participle of *exponere* 'to place outside'). At the present day this is the commonest surname in Naples and fourth in Italy as a whole.

GIVEN NAMES Italian 16%. *Salvatore* (68), *Angelo* (34), *Sal* (27), *Antonio* (23), *Carmine* (19), *Rocco* (18), *Pasquale* (15), *Ciro* (7), *Domenic* (6), *Gennaro* (6), *Marco* (6), *Lorenzo* (5).

Espy (736) **1.** Scottish: shortened form of GILLESPIE. **2.** French: southeastern topographic name for someone living near a prominent thorn bush or in an area characterized by such vegetation, from Old French *espine* (Latin *spina*). Occasionally the name may derive from the same word used in a transferred sense of the crest or ridge of a hill. **3.** Variant spelling of German ESPEY.

Esqueda (498) Spanish or Aragonese: of uncertain origin; perhaps connected with the place name Esquedas, found in Uesca, Aragon.

GIVEN NAMES Spanish 49%. *Jose* (16), *Jesus* (10), *Ruben* (8), *Juan* (7), *Armando* (6), *Alfonso* (5), *Carlos* (4), *Jorge* (4), *Manuel*

(4), Arturo (3), Ignacio (3), Jaime (3);
Antonio (8), Carlo, Elio, Fausto, Leonardo,
Lorenzo.

Esquer (164) Castilianized form of Basque
Ezker, a nickname for a left-handed person, from _ezker_ 'left (hand)'.
GIVEN NAMES Spanish 39%; Italian 8%.
Francisco (4), Manuel (4), Mario (4),
Macario (3), Margarita (2), Adriana,
Alicia, Ana, Bernarda, Carlos, Concepcion, Cristina; Antonio (5), Antonino,
Heriberto.

Esquibel (839) Castilianized form of
Basque **Ezkibel**, a habitational name in
Araba province, Basque Country, possibly
from a topographic name from Basque
(h)aizkibel 'behind the cliffs'.
GIVEN NAMES Spanish 24%. _Jose (12),_
Manuel (9), Juan (7), Jesus (4), Eloy (3),
Emilio (3), Adolfo (2), Alfonso (2), Cosme
(2), Felicita (2), Gerardo (2), Isidro (2).

Esquilin (143) Spanish (**Esquilín**): nickname from Spanish _esquilín_ 'small bell'.
GIVEN NAMES Spanish 41%. _Jose (4), Angel_
(3), Ines (2), Jorge (2), Juan (2), Margarita
(2), Santos (2), Adelina, Adriana, Ana,
Angel Luis, Arnaldo; Antonio (2), Carmelo,
Cecilio, Fausto.

Esquivel (2871) Spanish: variant of ES-
QUIBEL.
GIVEN NAMES Spanish 50%. _Jose (72), Juan_
(53), Manuel (37), Carlos (26), Jesus (26),
Luis (25), Raul (22), Jorge (18), Mario
(18), Ramon (18), Pedro (17), Gerardo
_(15)._

Ess (225) **1.** North German: topographic
name for someone living on or owning land
that was waterlogged or partly surrounded
by water, from Middle Low German _es_
'swamp', 'water'. **2.** Swiss German: unexplained.

Essa (121) Arabic: variant of ISSA.
GIVEN NAMES Arabic 48%. _Abdul (3),_
Mohamed (3), Hasan (2), Ahmad, Ahmed,
Ehab, Emran, Essa, Faisal, Farooq, Hanif,
Hodan.

Essary (988) English: of uncertain origin.
Many hypotheses have been put forward as
to its origin. The most plausible is that a
habitational name from Essworthy (pronounced _Essery_ locally), near Hatherleigh,
Devon. Compare USSERY and ESWORTHY.

Esse (141) **1.** Norwegian: habitational
name from a farmstead named with Old
Norse _æsin_ 'hill' + _vin_ 'meadow'. **2.** German: unexplained. **3.** English: unexplained.
GIVEN NAME Scandinavian 4%. _Erik._

Esselman (261) German (**Esselmann**):
habitational name for someone from a
place called Essel near Bremen, meaning
'swampy lowland'.

Essen (197) German: habitational name
from any of several places called Essen, for
example in the Ruhr.

Essenburg (159) Of Dutch or German origin, a habitational name from an unidenti-

fied place, perhaps Dutch **Essenbroek**,
named as 'the marsh (Dutch _broek_) where
the ash trees grow'. In the U.S. this name is
found chiefly in MI.

Essenmacher (135) North German: variant of **Assenmacher**, an occupational
name for a cartwright, from Middle Low
German _asse_ 'axle' (hence meronymically
'cart' or 'wagon') + _Macher_ 'maker'.

Esser (1745) **1.** German: occupational
name for a wheelwright or cartmaker, from
Middle Low German _asse_ 'axle' + the
agent suffix _-er_. **2.** German: variant of
ESSNER. **3.** English: perhaps a variant of
Asser, itself a variant of ASHER.
GIVEN NAMES German 4%. _Kurt (3), Ernst_
(2), Eberhard, Elke, Gunter, Hans, Karlheinz, Klaus, Lieselotte, Lothar, Reiner,
Rudi.

Essert (110) German: variant of ESSER 1.

Esses (184) Jewish (eastern Ashkenazic):
metronymic from Yiddish personal name
Ese, a pet form of _Ester_ (see ESTHER).
GIVEN NAMES Jewish 11%. _Hyman (2),_
Moshe.

Essex (1302) English: regional name for
someone from the county of Essex, which
is named from Old English _ēast_ 'east' +
Seaxe 'Saxons'. In England the surname is
now particularly common in Birmingham.

Essick (456) Americanized spelling of German ESSIG.

Essig (908) German: metonymic occupational name for a maker or seller of wine
vinegar, from Middle High German _ezzich_
'vinegar'.

Essinger (102) German: habitational name
for someone from Essing in Bavaria.

Essington (117) English: habitational
name from Essington in Staffordshire,
named in Old English as the farmstead (_tū_
_n_) of the people (_-inga-_) of a man called
Esne.

Essler (133) German: from a short form of
a Germanic personal name composed with
adel 'noble'. Compare ADOLF.
GIVEN NAME German 4%. _Horst._

Esslinger (661) German: habitational name
from any of several places named
Esslingen, for example in Bavaria,
Rhineland, and Württemberg.

Essman (459) German (**Essmann**): habitational name, a variant of ESSEN, with the
suffix _man_ 'man'.

Essner (213) German: probably a reduced
form of **Essener**, a habitational name for
someone from a place named Essen, of
which there are several in northern Germany.

Esson (173) **1.** Scottish: patronymic or
metronymic from the personal name
EADE. **2.** Americanized spelling of German ESSEN.
GIVEN NAMES German 4%. _Kurt (2), Hans._

Esswein (126) German: **1.** perhaps a variant of **Ösenwein**, a nickname for a heavy
drinker of wine, from Middle High German

ösen 'to guzzle' + _wīn_ 'wine'.
2. Alternatively, it may be from a personal
name _Össwin_, a variant of _Oswin_, composed of the Germanic elements _ans_
'demigod' + _win_ 'friend'.
GIVEN NAMES German 7%. _Gunther, Lieselotte._

Estabrook (1016) English: variant of
EASTERBROOK.

Estabrooks (194) English: variant of ESTA-
BROOK.

Estacio (138) Portuguese, Galician and
Spanish: variant of **Eustacio** (see EUS-
TACE).
GIVEN NAMES Spanish 38%. _Carlos (3), Jose_
(3), Manuel (2), Adolfo, Aida, Benigno,
Carolina, Celedonio, Cosme, Edgardo,
Emilio, Enrique.

Estay (118) Spanish: unexplained; probably
topographic.
GIVEN NAMES Spanish 17%. _Pedro (3), Juan_
(2), Angel, Aquiles, Hernan, Horacio,
Juanita, Luis, Luz, Marcelo, Ricardo,
Rodrigo.

Esteban (389) Spanish (**Esteban**): from
the personal name _Esteban_, Spanish vernacular form of Latin _Stephanus_ (see
STEVEN).
GIVEN NAMES Spanish 46%. _Jose (8), Manuel_
(6), Alfredo (4), Juan (4), Luis (4), Ricardo
(4), Roberto (4), Eduardo (3), Julio (3),
Miguel (3), Pedro (3), Ana (2); Antonio (3),
Leonardo (2), Angelo, Cecilio, Donato.

Estel (146) French: variant spelling of
ESTELLE.

Estell (612) French: variant spelling of
ESTELLE.

Estelle (542) French: metronymic from the
female personal name _Estelle_, from Latin
stella 'star'; the name was popularized by a
3rd century martyr.

Esten (110) English: probably a variant of
EASTON.
FOREBEARS The Esten family has been associated with Scituate, MA, and Providence,
RI, since the 17th century.

Estenson (191) Scandinavian: patronymic
from the Old Norse personal name
Eysteinn, a compound of _ey_ 'luck', 'happiness', 'gift' + _steinn_ 'stone'.

Estep (4504) Variant of English **Eastop**
(see EASTEP). This name is common in OH,
WV, and VA.
FOREBEARS Thomas Estep, son of Richard
Eastop, came to MD in 1647. His son
Shadrach established a family in Kanawha
Co., WV.

Estepp (334) Variant of English **Eastop**
(see EASTEP).

Ester (480) **1.** German: topographic name
for someone who lived by a gate leading to
cultivated land, from Middle High German
ezzisch 'seed field' + _tor_ 'gate'. **2.** Jewish:
variant of ESTHER.

Esterbrook (107) English: variant of
EASTERBROOK.

Esterle (102) Variant of German **Österle**, variant of **Österlein** (see ESTERLINE).
GIVEN NAME German 4%. *Otto* (2).

Esterline (425) Americanized spelling of **Esterlein**, variant of **Österlein**, a topographic name for someone whose home was to the east of a settlement, from Middle High German *ōster-* 'easterly' + the hypocoristic suffix *līn*, or a nickname for someone born at Easter, from Middle High German *ōster-* 'Easter'.

Esterly (324) Americanized spelling of German ESTERLE.

Esterman (131) Jewish (eastern Ashkenazic): variant of ESTHER, the element *man* meaning 'husband' in Yiddish.
GIVEN NAMES Russian 8%; Jewish 6%. *Efim, Igor, Leonid, Mikhail, Raisa*; *Filipp, Sarra*.

Esters (340) Dutch: patronymic from a Germanic personal name composed of the elements *ast* 'branch' + *heri, hari* 'army'.

Estes (13648) English: variant of EASTES, still pronounced today as two syllables, as it was in medieval times.
FOREBEARS This name was brought to New England by Matthew (1645–1723) and Richard (born 1647) Estes, sons of Robert and Dorothy Estes of Dover, England. Probably unconnected is the founder of the VA and TN family of this name, Benjamin Estes (born 1736 in VA; died 1811 in TN).

Estess (158) English: variant of EASTES.

Esteve (129) **1.** Catalan and southern French (**Estève**): from the personal name *Esteve*, Catalan and Occitan vernacular form of Latin *Stephanus* (see STEVEN). **2.** In some cases, possibly Portuguese, an old variant of **Estévão**, cognate with 1.
GIVEN NAMES Spanish 21%; French 6%. *Eduardo* (3), *Ernesto* (2), *Humberto* (2), *Jorge* (2), *Elenita, Ignacio, Javier, Juan, Marcos, Milagros, Pablo, Pepe*; *Andre, Francoise, Laurent*.

Esteves (592) Portuguese: patronymic from *Estévão*, Portuguese vernacular form of Latin *Stephanus* (see STEVEN).
GIVEN NAMES Spanish 34%; Portuguese 16%. *Manuel* (21), *Jose* (13), *Carlos* (5), *Sergio* (4), *Eduardo* (3), *Francisco* (3), *Jorge* (3), *Luis* (3), *Mario* (3), *Angel* (2), *Cesar* (2), *Fernando* (2); *Joao* (5), *Joaquim* (4), *Ilidio, Ligia, Marcio, Paulo*; *Antonio* (13), *Fausto* (2), *Romeo* (2), *Marco, Nonato*.

Estevez (1043) Variant of Portuguese ESTEVES.
GIVEN NAMES Spanish 53%. *Jose* (42), *Ramon* (23), *Carlos* (20), *Rafael* (15), *Juan* (12), *Miguel* (10), *Manuel* (9), *Francisco* (8), *Enrique* (7), *Luis* (7), *Alberto* (6), *Mario* (6).

Estey (760) English: of uncertain origin; perhaps a variant of EASTES.

Esther (142) **1.** French and Jewish: metronymic from the female name *Esther*, from Hebrew *Ester*, the name borne in the Bible by a Jewish captive of the Persian King Ahasuerus. According to the Biblical story,

she became his favorite concubine and by her wise persuasion managed to save the Jews of Persia from the machinations of the royal counselor Haman. Her name is probably a derivative of Persian *esther* 'star'. **2.** German: habitational name from any of various places in Bavaria named Ester.
GIVEN NAMES French 9%. *Andre, Odette, Prosper, Yves*.

Estill (518) English (Yorkshire): variant of **Eastall**, topographic name for someone who lived and worked 'at the east hall'.

Estis (203) **1.** English: variant of ESTES. **2.** Jewish (from Ukraine): metronymic from the Yiddish personal name *Este*, a pet form of *Ester* (see ESTHER).

Estle (166) Probably an altered spelling of South German **Esterl**, a variant of ESTER.

Estock (246) Americanized spelling of ESTOK.

Estok (223) Hungarian (**Estók**): variant of *Istók*, a pet form of the personal name *István*, Hungarian vernacular form of Latin *Stephanus* (see STEVEN).

Estopinal (117) Spanish: probably a derivative of Spanish *estopa* 'tow', the coarse part of flax, or 'burlap', a material made from it (from Latin *stuppa*). Compare ESTUPINAN.
GIVEN NAMES French 7%. *Marcel* (2), *Angelle*.

Estrada (10301) Spanish and Catalan: habitational name from any of the numerous places in Spain and Portugal named Estrada, from *estrada* 'road', Latin *stata (via)* (from *sternere* 'to strew or cover'), a term denoting a paved way.
GIVEN NAMES Spanish 49%. *Jose* (259), *Juan* (123), *Jesus* (111), *Carlos* (107), *Manuel* (93), *Francisco* (79), *Luis* (79), *Ramon* (58), *Ruben* (58), *Jorge* (55), *Raul* (48), *Miguel* (46).

Estrella (1276) Spanish: from *estrella* 'star' (Latin *stella*). Although in some cases it may derive from the medieval female personal name *Estrella*, also a Marian name (*María de la Estrella*) or from a nickname, in most instances it was probably a habitational name from any of the numerous places named Estrella or from La Estrella in Toledo; other possibilities are a topographic name for someone who lived at a place from which roads radiated out in a star shape or a habitational name for someone who lived at a house distinguished by the sign of a star.
GIVEN NAMES Spanish 40%. *Jose* (41), *Manuel* (17), *Juan* (13), *Luis* (11), *Miguel* (10), *Carlos* (9), *Rafael* (9), *Angel* (7), *Jesus* (7), *Javier* (6), *Ana* (5), *Julio* (5).

Estrem (149) Norwegian: variant of OSTREM.

Estremera (117) Spanish: habitational name from a place in Madrid province called Estremera.
GIVEN NAMES Spanish 43%. *Jose* (6), *Francisco* (4), *Alberto, Alejandro, Arcadio,*

Carlos, Gustavo, Jorge, Juan, Lourdes, Luis, Magda.

Estridge (531) English: from Old French *estreis* 'eastern'; probably a regional name for someone who had migrated from the east. The term was applied in particular to Germans in 13th-century London.

Estrin (309) Jewish (eastern Ashkenazic): metronymic from the Yiddish personal name *Estra*, a variant of *Ester* (see ESTHER).
GIVEN NAMES Jewish 6%; Russian 4%. *Aron, Hyman, Moisey, Semen*; *Igor* (2), *Anisim, Arkady, Grigory, Lev, Yevgeniy*.

Estupinan (119) Aragonese and Spanish (**Estupiñán**, also **Estopiñán, Estopañán**): habitational name from Estopiñán d'o Castiello, in Uesca province, Aragon.
FOREBEARS In the late 15th century the family migrated from Aragon in northeastern Spain to Jerez de la Frontera in the south, and from there to the Canary Islands. During the 1600s one descendant went to Guatemala, and his son Antonio moved to Mexico in about 1636. Lorenzo Estopinan was living in Lima, Peru, as early as 1565.
GIVEN NAMES Spanish 58%. *Juan* (4), *Francisco* (3), *Jose* (3), *Miguel* (3), *Adan* (2), *Alfonso* (2), *Carlos* (2), *Eduardo* (2), *Jesus* (2), *Mario* (2), *Pablo* (2), *Alfredo*.

Estus (150) English: variant of ESTES.

Esty (305) English: variant of ESTES.

Esworthy (184) English: habitational name from Essworthy, a small place near Hatherleigh, Devon. Compare ESSARY, USSERY.

Etchells (130) English (Lancashire): habitational name from any of various minor places in northern and central England named with the Old English term *ēcels* 'piece of land added to an estate' (a derivative of *ēcan* 'to increase').

Etcheverry (212) Americanized spelling of Basque **Etxeberri** (see ECHEVERRI).
GIVEN NAMES French 17%; Spanish 7%. *Andre* (2), *Marcel* (2), *Pierre* (2), *Alain, Chantelle, Dominique, Etienne, Jean Louis, Michel, Monique*; *Elena* (2), *Pedro* (2), *Alicia, Felisa, Horacio, Jorge, Juan Martin, Justo, Leandro, Paz, Tomas.*

Etchison (588) Variant of Scottish ATCHISON.

Ethen (104) Origin unidentified; probably of German origin.

Etheredge (990) English: variant spelling of ETHERIDGE.

Etheridge (3776) English: altered form of **Edrich**, from the Middle English personal name *Edrich, Ederick*, Old English *Ēadrīc*, composed of the elements *ēad* 'prosperity', 'fortune' + *rīc* 'power'. Current since the beginning of the 17th century, it developed from the late 16th-century forms *Et(t)riche, Et(t)ridge.*

Etherington (452) English: variant of HETHERINGTON.

Etherton (632) English: variant of ATHERTON.

Ethier (790) French: perhaps from Old French *estier*, 'canal', designating someone living near a canal; or perhaps a variant of **Astier** or **Hatier**. This name is sometimes Americanized as **Achy**.
FOREBEARS A family so named from Limoges settled in Montreal before 1670.
GIVEN NAMES French 14%. *Andre* (4), *Armand* (3), *Marcel* (3), *Emile* (2), *Jacques* (2), *Laurent* (2), *Roch* (2), *Sylvie* (2), *Yvon* (2), *Adelard*, *Aime*, *Alain*.

Ethington (531) Possibly an English habitational name. However, no appropriate place name has been identified and the surname is not found in the U.K.

Ethridge (2760) English: variant of ETHERIDGE.

Etie (115) French: unexplained.

Etienne (1049) French: from the personal name *Étienne*, French vernacular form of Latin *Stephanus* (see STEVEN).
FOREBEARS Bearers of this name from Saintes in western France are found in the records of Trois Rivières (Quebec) since 1635; also families from Toulouse and Lorraine occur in Quebec City as early as 1640; and bearers from Rouen are found in Montreal from 1657.
GIVEN NAMES French 25%. *Jacques* (7), *Pierre* (7), *Andre* (4), *Luc* (3), *Yves* (3), *Dieudonne* (2), *Fernand* (2), *Francois* (2), *Jean Claude* (2), *Mathieu* (2), *Philomene* (2), *Renald* (2).

Etkin (152) **1.** Jewish (eastern Ashkenazic): metronymic from Yiddish personal name *Etke*, a pet form of *Ester* (see ESTHER). **2.** Variant spelling of English ATKIN.
GIVEN NAME Jewish 5%. *Asher*.

Etling (303) **1.** Either a French form (Alsace and Lorraine) or a respelling of German **Ettling**: **2.** patronymic from a short form of any of the Germanic personal names formed with *adal* 'noble' as the first element. **3.** (among German bearers) a habitational name from any of several places named Ettling or Ettlingen, all in southern Germany.

Eto (104) Japanese (**Etō**): 'river wisteria'. It is found mainly in western Japan. Despite the element *-tō* (*fuji*) in the name, bearers are descended from the TAIRA clan rather than from the Fujiwara.
GIVEN NAMES Japanese 41%. *Hiroaki* (2), *Miho* (2), *Hirohiko*, *Hirokazu*, *Junichi*, *Kazuo*, *Keiji*, *Kenta*, *Masaji*, *Masazumi*, *Nami*, *Seiji*.

Etris (116) Variant of ETTERS.

Ettel (111) South German: from the personal name *Ettel*, a pet form of OTTO.

Etten (162) **1.** Shortened form of the Dutch habitational name **van Etten**, denoting someone from a place in North Brabant called Etten. **2.** North German and Frisian: variant of EDEN 4.

Etter (2040) **1.** South German and Swiss German: topographic name for someone who lived near the boundary fence of a village, from Middle High German *eter* 'woven boundary fence'. **2.** German and Dutch: from Middle High and Low German *etter* 'uncle' or 'cousin'.

Etters (246) Variant of German ETTER 2. The name is associated mainly with NC and SC, from the 18th century onward.

Ettinger (1145) German: habitational name for someone from any of several places in southern Germany, northern Alsace, or Switzerland named Etting, Ettingen, or Öttingen.

Ettlinger (145) German: habitational name from any of several places named Ettling or Ettlingen.
GIVEN NAMES German 6%. *Hans* (2), *Erna*.

Etue (132) Origin unidentified.

Etzel (810) South German: **1.** from *Atzilo*, a short form of any of the Germanic personal names beginning with *adal* 'noble'. **2.** from a reflex of *Attila* 'little father'.

Etzkorn (211) German: unexplained.

Etzler (367) German: habitational name from Etzel, a place in northwestern Germany.
GIVEN NAMES German 4%. *Erwin*, *Gunther*, *Otto*, *Reinhard*, *Wilhelm*.

Eubank (2278) English: see EUBANKS.

Eubanks (6680) English: topographic name for someone who lived by a bank of yew trees, Old English *īw*, + *bank*.

Eucker (123) German: unexplained.

Eudy (1154) **1.** Cornish: unexplained. **2.** Possibly also an altered form of an unidentified German name.

Euell (110) English: variant spelling of EWELL.
GIVEN NAME French 6%. *Patrice*.

Eugene (563) French (**Eugène**): from the personal name *Eugène* (Latin *Eugenius*, from Greek *Eugenios* meaning 'well-born', 'noble'). This was borne by a 3rd-century bishop and martyr, who gave the personal name some currency during the Middle Ages. In some cases it may also represent an Americanized form of a Greek patronymic family name of this origin, for example **Eugeniadis** or **Eugenidis**.
GIVEN NAMES French 19%. *Jacques* (3), *Gesner* (2), *Lucienne* (2), *Yanick* (2), *Alphonse*, *Amie*, *Andre*, *Dany*, *Edwige*, *Jean Marc*, *Jean-Robert*, *Lafontant*.

Eugenio (259) Spanish and Italian: from the personal name *Eugenio*, cognate of *Eugène* (see EUGENE).
GIVEN NAMES Spanish 34%; Italian 6%. *Estanislao* (2), *Jaime* (2), *Jose* (2), *Manuel* (2), *Pedro* (2), *Alda*, *Ana Maria*, *Andres*, *Armando*, *Artemio*, *Aurea*, *Berta*; *Marco* (2), *Antonio*, *Cesario*, *Dante*, *Emiliana*, *Federico*, *Lorenzo*, *Romeo*.

Eul (100) Probably an Americanized spelling of German JUHL.
GIVEN NAMES German 6%. *Otto*, *Reiner*.

Eulberg (149) German: of uncertain origin. Possibly a habitational name from Eilenburg (near Leipzig) or from Eulenburg in northern Germany.

Euler (682) German and Jewish (Ashkenazic): occupational name for a potter, most common in the Rhineland and Hesse, from Middle High German *ūl(n)ære* (an agent derivative of the dialect word *ūl*, *aul* 'pot', from Latin *olla*), German *Euler*.
GIVEN NAMES German 6%. *Franz* (2), *Fritz* (2), *Ursel* (2), *Bernhard*, *Frieda*, *Klaus*, *Konrad*, *Kurt*, *Ute*, *Wilfried*, *Wilhelm*.

Euliss (111) Of uncertain origin; perhaps an altered spelling of English **Youles** (see YULE).

Eull (122) **1.** Variant of English EWELL. **2.** Possibly also a respelling of German JUHL.
GIVEN NAMES French 5%. *Collette*, *Jacques*.

Eunice (185) Americanized form of Spanish **Núñez** (see NUNEZ) in a family of Portuguese Jewish origin. This family name occurs chiefly in GA. The etymology of the female given name *Eunice* is from Greek *eu* 'good' + *nikē* 'victory', but no historical connection has been established between the given name and the surname.
FOREBEARS At the time of the Civil War, Cole Nunez, a descendant of Samuel Nunez of Savannah, GA, changed his surname to **Eunice**.

Eure (674) Origin uncertain. **1.** Probably of English origin, a topographic name from Middle English *evre* 'edge of an escarpment', 'brow of a hill', Old English (unattested) *yfer*. **2.** Alternatively, perhaps a variant of Scottish URE.

Eurich (364) Possibly a respelling of Swiss German *Urech*, a variant of ULRICH.
GIVEN NAMES German 5%. *Detlef*, *Gottfried*, *Reinold*, *Sigi*.

Eury (319) French: variant spelling of **Oury**, a French form of ULRICH.

Eusebio (195) Spanish and Portuguese (**Eusébio**): from the personal name *Eusebio* (Greek *Eusebios* meaning 'revered', from *eu-* 'good', 'well' + a derivative of *sebesthai* 'to honor', 'respect'). This was borne by a large number of early saints, including a 5th-century friend of Jerome popularly credited with the foundation of the monastery of Guadalupe. A 4th-century bishop of Samosata in Syria who bore this name is one of many bearers of this name venerated in the Orthodox Church.
GIVEN NAMES Spanish 35%; Portuguese 11%. *Eduardo* (5), *Ernesto* (4), *Julio* (3), *Alberto* (2), *Raul* (2), *Ricardo* (2), *Abran*, *Adolfo*, *Ana*, *Belarminio*, *Bienvenido*, *Carlos*; *Joao*.

Eustace (501) English: from the personal name *Eustace* (Latin *Eustacius*, from Greek *Eustakhyos*, meaning 'fruitful', blended with the originally distinct name

Eustathios 'orderly'). The name was borne by various minor saints, but little is known of the most famous St. Eustace, patron saint of hunters, said to have been converted by the vision of a crucifix between the antlers of a hunted stag. In some cases this may be an Americanized form of a Greek family name based on *Eusthathios*, such as **Eustathiadis** or **Eustathidis**.

Eustice (458) English: variant spelling of EUSTACE.

Eustis (332) English: variant spelling of EUSTACE.

Eutsey (187) Origin uncertain. **1.** It is most probably a metathesized form of Scottish or English **Eustie**, a pet form of EUSTACE. **2.** Alternatively, it may be a respelling of Swiss German **Uetze**, a variant of UTZ.

Eutsler (307) Americanized spelling of German and Swiss UTSLER.

Eva (193) Spanish and Portuguese: from the female personal name *Eva* (see EVE).

Evan (478) **1.** Welsh: from the personal name *Iefan*, a Welsh form of JOHN. (The modern form of the personal name is *Ieuan*.) **2.** Scottish: variant of EWAN.

Evancho (265) Possibly Ukrainian: variant of EVANKO.

Evangelist (182) Shortened form of Italian EVANGELISTA or EVANGELISTI.

GIVEN NAMES Italian 5%. *Angelo, Mario*.

Evangelista (1420) Italian: from *Evangelista* 'evangelist' (a derivative of Greek *euangelos* 'bringer of good news', from *eu* 'well', 'good' + *angelos* 'messenger'). This is the term used to denote any of the four gospel writers of the New Testament (Matthew, Mark, Luke, and John), in particular St. John the Evangelist.

GIVEN NAMES Spanish 22%; Italian 11%. *Mario* (9), *Carlos* (8), *Jose* (7), *Armando* (6), *Jesus* (6), *Pablo* (4), *Alfredo* (3), *Andres* (3), *Enrique* (3), *Juan* (3), *Manuel* (3), *Pedro* (3); *Angelo* (7), *Antonio* (7), *Gino* (3), *Luigi* (3), *Amato* (2), *Italo* (2), *Pietro* (2), *Salvatore* (2), *Umberto* (2), *Aldo, Alessio, Antimo, Enea, Paulo*.

Evangelisti (133) Italian: variant of EVANGELISTA.

GIVEN NAMES Italian 16%. *Carlo, Domenic, Eligio, Giancarlo, Lorenzo, Luciano, Marco, Marino, Pasquale, Santino*.

Evanko (256) Ukrainian: from a pet form of the personal name IVAN.

Evanoff (608) Russian, Belorussian, and Bulgarian: alternative spelling of IVANOV.

Evans (117387) Welsh: patronymic from the personal name *Iefan* (see EVAN), with redundant English patronymic -*s*.

Evanson (575) Welsh: patronymic from the personal name *Iefan* (see EVAN), with English patronymic -*son*. This form of the surname is found chiefly in the English counties bordering on Wales, particularly Shropshire and Cheshire.

Evard (100) Swiss French: reduced form of EVRARD.

GIVEN NAMES French 10%. *Henri, Jean-Claude, Remy*.

Evarts (464) Variant spelling of North German and Dutch EVERTS.

Evatt (433) English: variant spelling of **Ivatt**, from a pet form of the Old French female personal name *Iva*, feminine of *Ivo* (see IWEN).

Evavold (135) Origin unidentified.

Eve (367) English and Dutch: from the rare medieval female personal name *Eve, Eva* (from Hebrew *Chava*, of uncertain origin). This was, according to the Book of Genesis, the name of the first woman, and in some cases the name may have been acquired by someone (invariably a man) who had played the part in a drama dealing with the Creation.

Eveland (984) Origin uncertain; most probably a respelling of German IFFLAND.

Eveleigh (134) English (Devon): habitational name from Eveleigh in Broad Clyst, Devon.

Eveler (117) Americanized spelling of German **Uebler** (see UEBEL).

Eveleth (212) American variant of English EVELEIGH.

Evelyn (284) English: from the Middle English, Old French female personal name *Aveline*, a double diminutive of the Germanic personal name *Avo*, from the element *avi*, perhaps meaning 'desired', 'wished for'.

Even (703) **1.** Breton: cognate of EVAN 1. **2.** In some cases perhaps an altered spelling of EVAN or IVAN. **3.** Shortened form of the Dutch topographic name **van Even**, from Middle Dutch *even(e)* 'black oats'.

Evenhouse (101) Americanized form of Norwegian **Evenhus**, a habitational name from a farmstead so named from the Old Norse personal name *Eyvindr* (see EVENSEN) + *hus* 'dwelling', 'farmstead'.

GIVEN NAME Scandinavian 5%. *Thor*.

Evens (650) English and Welsh: variant spelling of Welsh EVANS.

Evensen (465) Norwegian: patronymic from the Old Norse personal name *Eyvindr*, composed of the elements *ey* 'luck', 'happiness', 'gift' + *vindr* 'winner'.

GIVEN NAMES Scandinavian 11%. *Erik* (2), *Lars, Per*.

Evenson (2535) Variant spelling of EVENSEN or EVANSON.

GIVEN NAMES Scandinavian 4%. *Erik* (3), *Helmer* (3), *Thor* (2), *Juel, Obert, Selmer, Swen, Thorval, Tor*.

Evenstad (112) Norwegian: habitational name from any of five farmsteads so named, from a personal name (Old Norse personal name *Eyvindr*; see EVENSEN) + *stad* (from Old Norse *staðr* 'farmstead', 'dwelling').

Everage (349) English: variant spelling of EVERIDGE.

Everard (257) English: variant of EVERETT.

Everding (212) North German: patronymic from EVERT.

Everest (356) English (of Norman origin): habitational name from Evreux in Eure, France, probably named from its association with the *Eburovices*, a Gaulish tribe.

Everett (13756) English: from a Germanic personal name composed of the elements *eber* 'wild boar' + *hard* 'brave', 'hardy', 'strong'. The surname was at first found mainly in East Anglia (still one of the principal locations of the variant *Everett*), which was an area of heavy Norman and Breton settlement after the Conquest. This suggests that the personal name may be of Continental (Norman) origin, but it is also possible that it swallowed up an unattested Old English cognate, *Eoforheard*.

Everette (1016) Altered spelling, under French influence, of English EVERETT.

Everetts (238) English: variant of EVERETT.

Everhard (101) North German: variant of EBERHARDT.

Everhardt (163) North German: variant of EBERHARDT.

Everhart (3729) North German: variant of EBERHARDT.

Everidge (332) English: from an unattested Old English personal name *Eoforīc*, composed of the elements *eofor* 'wild boar' + *rīc* 'rich'.

Everingham (285) English: habitational name from a place in Humberside named in Old English *Yferingaham* 'homestead' (*hām*) of the people (-*inga*-) of *Eofor*'.

Everist (155) English: variant spelling of EVEREST.

Everitt (1363) English: variant spelling of EVERETT.

Everley (105) English: habitational name from Everleigh in Wiltshire, named from Old English *eofor* 'wild boar' + *lēah* 'woodland clearing'. There is an Everley in North Yorkshire (of the same derivation), which may be the source of the surname in some instances.

Everling (191) North German (Westphalia): patronymic from EVERT.

Everly (1176) English: variant spelling of EVERLEY.

Everman (649) North German (**Evermann**): patronymic from or pet form of EVERT.

Everroad (112) Probably an Americanized form of North German EVERHART (see EBERHARDT).

Evers (3692) **1.** English: topographic name for someone who lived on the edge of an escarpment, from Middle English *evere* 'edge', a word that is probably of Old English origin, though unattested. **2.** English: patronymic from the Middle English personal name *Ever*, from Old English *Eofor* 'boar'. **3.** North German and Dutch: patronymic from EVERT.

Eversley (107) English: habitational name from places in Essex and Hampshire named Eversley. The second is named from Old English *eofor* 'boar' or the personal name *Eofor* + *lēah* 'woodland clearing'. The surname is now more frequent in the midlands than the south of England, and it may be that another, lost or unidentified source is involved.

Eversman (189) German: unexplained. Possibly a derivative of EVERT.

Eversole (1587) Of Swiss German origin: see EBERSOLE.

Eversoll (109) Of Swiss German origin: see EBERSOLE.

Everson (2782) English: patronymic from the personal name *Ever* (see EVERS 2).

Evert (972) North German and Dutch: reduced form of the personal name EBERHARDT.

Everton (337) English: habitational name from any of various places, in Bedfordshire, Merseyside, and Nottinghamshire, so named from Old English *eofor* 'wild boar' + *tūn* 'settlement'.

FOREBEARS Described as being from Kent, England, Walter **Everendon** (d. 1725) was a colonial gunpowder manufacturer who ran a mill in Neponset in the township of Milton, across the river from Dorchester, MA. The first person to make gunpowder in America, Everendon eventually took majority interest in the mill and sold out to his son. The family, which also spelled their name Everden and Everton, continued to manufacture powder until after the Revolution.

Everts (842) North German and Dutch: patronymic from EVERT.

Evertsen (113) North German and Dutch: patronymic from EVERT.

Evertz (107) North German and Dutch: patronymic from EVERT.

GIVEN NAMES German 9%. *Dieter, Wilhelm.*

Every (488) Americanized spelling of English AVERY.

Eves (516) English: metronymic from EVE.

Eveslage (109) German: probably a habitational name from a minor place in the Oldenburg-Osnabrück area, probably named with an unidentified personal name + *-lage*, denoting a deforested area.

Evett (357) English: from a pet form of the female personal name EVE.

Evetts (234) English: metronymic from EVETT.

Evey (135) See EAVEY.

Evick (136) Americanized spelling of German EWIG.

FOREBEARS Johan Rufus Ewig (otherwise Evick) came from Heidelberg, Germany, to Philadelphia in 1737.

Evilsizer (143) Americanized form of German **Ebelshäuser, Ebelsheuser, Ebel-**

sheiser, a habitational name from a lost or unidentified place.

Evilsizor (126) Americanized form of German **Ebelshäuser** (see EVILSIZER).

Evinger (173) German: **1.** habitational name for someone from Eving, a place near Dortmund. **2.** Variant of AVINGER.

Evink (104) Respelling of Dutch **Evinck**, from a short form of a Germanic personal name formed with *ebur* 'wild boar'.

Evins (423) Variant spelling of Welsh EVANS.

Evitt (164) English: variant spelling of EVETT.

Evitts (311) English: metronymic from EVETT.

Evjen (183) Norwegian: habitational name from a common farm name from Old Norse *efja* 'eddy', 'backwater'.

GIVEN NAMES Scandinavian 5%. *Obert, Thor.*

Evola (276) Italian: perhaps a topographic name from *ebbio* 'danewort' (*Sambucus ebulus*), from Latin *ebullus*, or possibly a habitational name from a minor place named with this word.

GIVEN NAMES Italian 23%. *Giuseppe* (4), *Salvatore* (4), *Damiano* (3), *Nunzio* (2), *Vito* (2), *Concetta, Domenica, Francesco, Gaspare, Leonardo, Marcello, Matteo.*

Evon (264) Probably a variant spelling of Welsh EVAN.

Evora (117) Portuguese (**Évora**): habitational name from Évora in Alentejo.

GIVEN NAMES Spanish 38%; Portuguese 9%. *Jose* (2), *Orlando* (2), *Viriato* (2), *Almerinda, Angelito, Armando, Carlos, Elisio, Gabriela, Gilberto, Jose Antonio, Jose Miguel; Joao.*

Evoy (139) Irish: shortened form of McEVOY.

Evrard (235) English and French: from the Germanic personal name *Eberhard* (see EVERETT).

GIVEN NAMES French 9%. *Alain, Emile, Herard, Jean Claude, Jean-Marc, Jean-marie, Marcel.*

Ewald (1885) North German: from a Germanic personal name composed of the elements *ēo* 'law', 'custom', 'right' (a rare element in personal names, found mostly in Old Saxon) + *wald* 'rule'. This name was borne in the 7th century by two brothers (distinguished as 'Ewald the White' and 'Ewald the Black') who were missionaries in North Germany. They became the patron saints of Cologne and Westphalia, and so contributed to the popularity of the personal name (and hence the eventual frequency of the surname) in these areas.

GIVEN NAMES German 4%. *Hans* (3), *Kurt* (3), *Bernhard* (2), *Helmut* (2), *Otto* (2), *Alois, Armin, Arno, Erwin, Franziska, Fritz, Gerhard.*

Ewalt (477) Variant of North German EWALD.

Ewan (409) Scottish: variant spelling of EWEN.

Ewart (854) Scottish and northern English: **1.** from the personal name *Ewart*, an Anglo-Norman French form of EDWARD. **2.** occupational name for a shepherd, from Middle English *ewehirde*, from Old English *eowu* 'ewe' + *hierde* 'herdsman'. **3.** habitational name from a place in Northumbria named Ewart, from Old English *ēa* 'river' + *worð* 'enclosure'; it is enclosed on three sides by the rivers Glen and Till.

Ewbank (303) English: variant spelling of EUBANK.

Ewell (1534) English: habitational name from Ewell in Surrey or from Ewell Minnis or Temple Ewell in Kent, all named with Old English *æwell* 'river source'.

Ewen (784) **1.** Scottish: reduced Anglicized form of Gaelic **Mac Eòghainn** 'son of *Eòghann*' (see McEWEN). **2.** Jewish (Israeli): from Hebrew *even* 'stone', a translation of the surname STEIN or any of its compounds.

Ewens (156) Scottish: variant of EWEN, formed with the addition of English patronymic *-s*.

Ewer (378) English: occupational name for a transporter or server of water, Middle English *ewer* (Old Northern French *evier*, Old French *aiguier*, from Latin *aquarius*, a derivative of *aqua* 'water'). There has been considerable confusion with URE.

Ewers (999) English: variant of EWER.

Ewert (1185) North German: variant of EBERHARDT.

GIVEN NAMES German 4%. *Gerd* (2), *Claus, Dieter, Frieda, Fritz, Gerhard, Gunter, Horst, Jurgen, Klaus, Kurt, Otto.*

Ewig (160) German: habitational name from a place named Ewich near Attendorn, Westphalia.

GIVEN NAMES German 4%; French 4%. *Otto; Monique, Patrice.*

Ewin (131) Scottish: variant of EWING.

Ewing (12421) Scottish: altered form of EWEN (itself a shortened Anglicized form of Gaelic **Mac Eòghainn** 'son of *Eòghann*'), formed as if it were an English patronymic ending in *-ing*. See also McEWEN.

Ewings (202) Scottish: variant of EWING, formed with the addition of English patronymic *-s*.

Ewoldt (332) North German: variant of EWALD.

GIVEN NAMES German 5%. *Kurt* (2), *Arno, Hans, Otto.*

Ewton (193) Possibly an English habitational name; however, no appropriate place name has been identified and the surname is not recorded in the U.K.

Ewy (245) Polish: origin uncertain; perhaps a metronymic from the female personal name *Ewa*, Polish form of EVE.

Excell (101) English (Kent): habitational name from either of two places in Warwickshire named Exhall.

Exler (142) Americanized spelling of German **Öchsler**, from Middle High German *ochse* 'ox' + diminutive suffix *-l* + *-er* suffix denoting human agency; an occupational name for someone who tended cattle or for a cattle dealer, or a nickname for a farmer who used oxen for plowing.

Exley (611) **1.** English: habitational name from a place in West Yorkshire, near Halifax, so named from a British *ecclēsia* name meaning 'church' (see ECCLES) + Old English *lēah* 'woodland clearing'. The surname is common in West Yorkshire. **2.** Americanized spelling of the German family name **Öchsle**, a diminutive of OCHS.

Exline (522) Altered spelling of German **Exlein**, a variant of **Öchslein**, from Middle High German *ochse* 'ox' + the diminutive suffix *-lin*; an occupational name for someone who tended the cattle or for a cattle dealer. Alternatively, it may have been a nickname for a farmer who had only oxen for plowing, or perhaps for someone thought to resemble an ox.

Exner (435) German: variant of OXNER.
GIVEN NAMES German 5%. *Otto* (2), *Wolfgang* (2), *Jurgen*.

Exposito (173) Spanish (**Expósito**): from *expósito* 'exposed' (Latin *expositus* past participle of *exponere* 'to place outside'), a surname commonly bestowed on a foundling.
GIVEN NAMES Spanish 46%. *Jose* (4), *Andres* (3), *Jorge* (3), *Rafael* (3), *Agustin* (2), *Carlos* (2), *Eladio* (2), *Jesus* (2), *Pedro* (2), *Rosendo* (2), *Santiago* (2), *Adelfa*.

Exton (164) English: habitational name from places so called in Devon, Hampshire, Leicestershire, and Somerset. The first and last derive their name from the Celtic river name *Exe*, while the place in Hampshire, recorded in 940 as *East Seaxnatune*, is named from Old English *Ēastseaxe* 'East Saxon', and the Leicestershire place name is from Old English *oxa* 'of the oxen'. In each case the final element is from Old English *tūn* 'settlement'.

Exum (880) English: probably a variant of AXSOM. This name is concentrated in NC.

Ey (150) Origin uncertain. Possibilities include: **1.** German and Dutch: variant of AYE. **2.** variant of English: a variant spelling of EYE.
GIVEN NAME German 4%. *Wolfgang* (2).

Eye (589) English: habitational name from places in Cambridge, Hereford, and Suffolk named from Old English *ēg*, a term denoting low-lying land, an island or promontory, or an area of dry land in a marsh.

Eyer (721) **1.** English: variant of AYER. **2.** German: variant of EGGER 2.

Eyerly (223) Possibly an altered spelling of German **Eyerle**, from a Germanic personal name formed with *ecke* 'sword', 'blade'.

Eyerman (204) **1.** German (**Eyermann**): variant spelling of EIERMANN. **2.** Possibly a variant of the Dutch family name **Heyermans**, a topographic name for someone who lived on a heath or a variant of HERMAN.

Eyestone (188) **1.** Americanized form of German AUGENSTEIN. **2.** Possibly an altered spelling of English **Eyston**, a variant of EASTON.

Eyler (1095) **1.** Americanized spelling of German EILER or EULER. **2.** Also, perhaps an altered spelling of the English family name AYLER.

Eyles (138) English: variant spelling of ILES.

Eyman (368) **1.** Dutch: variant of the topographic name for a dweller on heathland VANDERHEIDEN. **2.** Dutch: variant of HEINEMAN. **3.** German (**Eymann**): from a Germanic personal name composed of the elements *agi* 'point (of a sword or lance)' + *man* 'man', 'retainer'.

Eymann (124) Dutch: occupational name for an egg merchant.
GIVEN NAMES German 4%. *Fritz, Hans*.

Eymard (123) French: from *Haimrad*, a personal name of Germanic origin composed of *haim* 'home' + *hard* 'hardy', 'strong'.
GIVEN NAME French 6%. *Emile*.

Eynon (326) Welsh: from the personal name *Einion*, which used to be extremely common in Wales. It is probably ultimately derived from the Latin personal name *Anmianus*, but no doubt enjoyed its wide popularity as a result of folk etymological associations with Welsh *einion* 'anvil' and/or *uniawn* 'upright', 'just'.

Eyre (844) English: variant spelling of AYER.

Eyres (121) English: variant spelling of AYERS.

Eyrich (249) German: variant spelling of EIRICH.
GIVEN NAMES German 4%. *Gunter, Hans, Kurt*.

Eyring (188) German: from a Germanic personal name *Iring*, of uncertain etymology. Compare IHRIG.

Eyster (539) German: probably a habitational name from Eisten in Emsland district.

Eytcheson (126) Variant spelling of Scottish AITCHISON.

Ezekiel (294) From the Hebrew Biblical personal name *Yechezkel* 'God will strengthen'. This is found, not only as a Jewish family name, but also as a comparatively late surname in the British Isles among Nonconformists, especially in Wales.

Ezell (3713) **1.** English: of unknown origin. The name was well established in the Carolinas by the mid 18th century. In one branch of the family the name was changed to ISRAEL; this is a derivative, not the origin. **2.** Americanized form (under French influence) of German **Esel**, a nickname from Middle High German *esel* 'donkey'.

Ezelle (229) Variant spelling (under French influence) of EZELL.

Ezernack (151) Americanized spelling of German **Eisenach**, a habitational name from either of two places named Eisenach, one near Trier, the other in Thuringia.

Ezra (177) Jewish: from the Hebrew personal name *Ezra*, meaning 'help'. Ezra was a Biblical prophet of the 5th century BC who played an important role in the rebuilding of Jerusalem after the Babylonian exile.
GIVEN NAMES Jewish 15%. *Moshe* (3), *Ehud, Haskel, Shalom, Shoshanna, Yoram*.

Ezzell (895) Variant of EZELL.

Ezzo (327) Italian: variant of IZZO.
GIVEN NAMES Italian 8%. *Angelo* (2), *Antonio, Gennaro, Gino, Salvatore*.

F

Faaborg (105) Danish: habitational name from a place so called.

GIVEN NAMES Scandinavian 11%; German 5%. *Niels* (2), *Britt, Erik, Folmer*; *Otto* (2).

Faas (433) **1.** Dutch: from a short form of the medieval personal name *Bonefaas*, Dutch form of BONIFACE. **2.** South German (especially Baden-Württemberg): from a short form of the personal name *Gervasius*, the name of the patron saint of Breisach on the Rhine. **3.** North German (especially Lower Rhine): from a short form of the personal name *Servaes*, dialect form of *Servatius*, the name of the patron saint of Maastricht, one of the three so-called 'Ice Saints', or of the personal name *Bonifatius* (see BONIFACE), also borne by a saint.

GIVEN NAMES German 4%. *Gunther* (2), *Jochen, Theresia.*

Faatz (115) German: from a short form of the Late Latin personal name *Bonifatius* (see BONIFACE). In the Rhineland area it may also be from the dialect personal name *Servaes* (see FAAS).

Fabacher (115) German: probably a habitational name from an unidentified place. This name is common in LA.

GIVEN NAMES French 5%. *Andre, Emile.*

Fabbri (395) Italian: occupational name for a smith (see FABBRO).

GIVEN NAMES Italian 29%. *Gino* (3), *Mario* (3), *Angelo* (2), *Antonio* (2), *Dante* (2), *Eduardo* (2), *Fabio* (2), *Fabrizio* (2), *Julio* (2), *Nino* (2), *Orfeo* (2), *Aldo, Alfio, Amelio, Attilio, Benito, Bruna, Fernando, Francisco, Lucindo, Marisa, Octavio.*

Fabbro (119) Italian: occupational name for an ironworker, from *fabbro* 'smith' (Latin *faber* 'craftsman').

GIVEN NAMES Italian 14%. *Fausto* (2), *Aldo, Angelo, Dante, Dario, Giovanni, Santo, Silvio.*

Fabel (217) South German: from the personal name, a pet form of FABIAN.

GIVEN NAMES French 5%. *Jacques, Patrice.*

Fabela (320) Spanish: variant of FAVELA.

GIVEN NAMES Spanish 46%. *Jose* (6), *Carlos* (3), *Guillermo* (3), *Juan* (3), *Manuel* (3), *Alejandro* (2), *Domingo* (2), *Edmundo* (2), *Enrique* (2), *Fidel* (2), *Francisco* (2), *Julio* (2).

Faber (4175) **1.** Occupational name for a smith or ironworker, from Latin *faber* 'craftsman'. This was in use as a surname in England, Scotland, and elsewhere in the Middle Ages and is also found as a personal name. At the time of the Reformation, it was much used as a humanistic name, a translation into Latin of vernacular surnames such as German *Schmidt* and Dutch *Smit.* **2.** Secondary surname in French Canada for LEFEBVRE. The name *Fabert* appears in Kaskaskia, IL, in 1725.

Fabian (2941) **1.** English, French, German, Italian (Venetian), Polish, Czech and Slovak (**Fabián**), and Hungarian (**Fábián**): from a personal name, Latin *Fabianus*, a derivative of the Roman family name *Fabius*. The personal name achieved considerable popularity in Europe in the Middle Ages, having been borne by a 3rd-century pope and saint. **2.** Americanized or Italianized spelling of Slovenian **Fabjan** or **Fabijan** (see 1). **3.** Jewish: adoption of the non-Jewish surname under the influence of the Yiddish personal name *Fayvish.*

GIVEN NAMES Spanish 6%. *Juan* (11), *Jose* (7), *Francisco* (5), *Pedro* (5), *Ana* (4), *Lourdes* (4), *Gerardo* (3), *Luis* (3), *Manuel* (3), *Mario* (3), *Ricardo* (3), *Aurelio* (2).

Fabiani (187) **1.** Italian and Corsican: patronymic or plural form of FABIANO. **2.** Hungarian (**Fábiáni**): patronymic from the personal name *Fábián* (see FABIAN).

GIVEN NAMES Italian 18%; French 4%. *Mario* (3), *Dante, Emanuele, Geno, Germano, Gino, Marco, Natale, Silvio*; *Andre, Benoit.*

Fabiano (688) Italian: from the personal name *Fabiano*, a continuation of the Roman family name *Fabianus*, a derivative of *Fabius* (see FABIAN).

GIVEN NAMES Italian 21%. *Angelo* (3), *Orlando* (3), *Alberto* (2), *Carlo* (2), *Carmine* (2), *Fedele* (2), *Leonardo* (2), *Luigi* (2), *Mario* (2), *Matteo* (2), *Rocco* (2), *Antonio, Carmelo, Cosmo, Fabio, Franco, Gaspar, Gerardo, Lupercio, Maurilio, Rosario.*

Fabin (100) Polish: variant of FABIAN.

GIVEN NAME Polish 4%. *Zbigniew.*

Fabio (172) Italian: from the personal name *Fabio*, from Latin *Fabius*, a Roman family name.

GIVEN NAMES Italian 14%. *Rocco* (2), *Adolfo, Alfredo, Camillo, Carmine, Fausto, Franco, Salvatore.*

Fabish (116) **1.** Americanized spelling of German **Fabisch**, Czech and Slovak **Fabiš**, Polish **Fabiś**, or other derivatives of the personal name FABIAN. **2.** Jewish (Ashkenazic): from a male personal name derived from Latin *Vivus.*

Fabozzi (116) Italian: from a diminutive of **Fabbo**, which is probably a variant of FALBO.

GIVEN NAMES Italian 12%. *Aniello, Nicola, Saverio.*

Fabre (577) Southern French and Catalan: occupational name for a smith (see FABER).

GIVEN NAMES French 7%; Spanish 6%. *Emile* (2), *Oneil* (2), *Alain, Amede, Cecile, Colette, Gilles, Michel, Rodolphe*; *Luis* (4), *Alvaro* (2), *Ernesto* (2), *Jose* (2), *Angel, Brunilda, Carols, Digna, Elina, Fernando, Ines, Jorge.*

Fabregas (107) Catalan (**Fàbregas**): respelling of **Fàbregues**, a habitational name from any of the places in Barcelona province named Fàbregues, from the plural of *fàbrega* 'forge'.

GIVEN NAMES Spanish 39%. *Jose* (9), *Adalberto, Adolpho, Alfredo, Ana, Carlos, Fernando, Fransico, Juan Carlos, Lazaro, Luis, Maria Luisa.*

Fabri (126) Italian (mainly Venetian): variant spelling of FABBRI.

GIVEN NAMES Italian 6%; French 4%. *Oresto* (2), *Lucio, Umberto*; *Armand, Chantale.*

Fabricant (160) Jewish (Ashkenazic): variant spelling of FABRIKANT.

GIVEN NAMES Jewish 6%. *Aviva, Hyman.*

Fabricius (141) Humanistic name (mainly Dutch, Danish, and German): from a medieval personal name adopted from Latin *Fabricius* (see FABRIZIO). This was sometimes taken as a Latinized equivalent of SCHMIDT 'smith'.

GIVEN NAMES Scandinavian 7%; German 5%. *Erik*; *Dietrich, Hans.*

Fabrikant (118) Jewish (Ashkenazic): occupational name for a factory owner or manufacturer of any type of goods, from Russian *fabrikant* 'manufacturer', Polish *fabrykant* 'manufacturer', German *Fabrikant*, from Latin *fabricans, fabricantis*, present participle of *fabricare* 'to make', a derivative of *faber.*

GIVEN NAMES Russian 11%; Jewish 7%. *Boris* (2), *Anatoly, Gennadiy, Leonid, Natalya, Oleg, Yevsey*; *Ilya, Rakhil.*

Fabris (184) Italian (also **De Fabris**): patronymic from FABBRO, i.e. 'son of the smith'.

GIVEN NAMES Italian 12%. *Antonio* (3), *Aldo, Dante, Dino, Domenic, Fiorenzo, Humberto, Luigia, Marino, Mario, Sergio, Valentino, Manuel.*

Fabrizi (191) Italian: patronymic or plural form of FABRIZIO.

GIVEN NAMES Italian 19%. *Angelo* (3), *Rinaldo* (2), *Benedetto, Ezio, Giovanni, Guerino, Rocco, Sandro, Silvio.*

Fabrizio (1112) Italian: **1.** from the medieval personal name *Fabrizio,* Latin *Fabricius,* a Roman family name of unknown, possibly Etruscan, origin. Already in the Roman period the name was associated by folk etymology with *faber,* and Latin forms of the name were extensively used in the late Middle Ages as equivalents of vernacular terms denoting a smith or other craftsman. **2.** habitational name from Fabrizio, a locality of Corigliano Calabro in Cosenza province.
GIVEN NAMES Italian 13%. *Angelo* (5), *Antonio* (4), *Dino* (4), *Rocco* (4), *Carmine* (3), *Vito* (3), *Aldo, Carmelo, Ciriaco, Dante, Deno, Domenic.*

Fabrizius (121) German (humanistic name): variant of FABRICIUS.

Fabro (110) Italian: **1.** variant spelling of FABBRO. **2.** habitational name from Fabro, a place in Perugia.
GIVEN NAMES Spanish 18%. *Mauricio* (2), *Reynaldo* (2), *Apolonia, Cristino, Dominador, Guillermo, Josefina, Mario, Pelagio, Violeta.*

Fabry (546) **1.** Slovak and Hungarian (**Fábry**): occupational name for a blacksmith or ironworker, from a derivative of Latin *faber* 'craftsman'. **2.** Southern French: variant of FABRE.

Facchini (173) Southern Italian: occupational name from *facchino* 'porter', 'carrier of goods', formerly meaning 'scribe', 'clerk', from Arabic *faqīh* 'expert in the law'.
GIVEN NAMES Italian 28%; Spanish 10%. *Antonio* (3), *Angelo* (2), *Mauro* (2), *Primo* (2), *Dino, Enio, Ermanno, Erminio, Evo, Geno, Livio, Luca; Sergio* (3), *Fabio* (2), *Mario* (2), *Elena, Emilio, Eugenio, Marisa, Ramona, Sabino.*

Facciolo (110) Italian (Sicilian): unflattering nickname from Sicilian *facciolu* 'false man'.
GIVEN NAMES Italian 14%. *Guiseppe, Palma, Rocco.*

Face (166) **1.** English: from a short form of the personal name BONIFACE. **2.** Perhaps an Americanized spelling of German **Fese**, a variant of FEESE.

Facemire (197) Americanized spelling of German **Fehsmeier**, an occupational name for a spelt farmer, from Middle High German, Middle Low German *vese* 'chaff', 'husk', 'spelt' + Middle High German *meier* '(tenant) farmer', 'bailiff'.

Facer (314) **1.** English (chiefly Northamptonshire): probably from the obsolete slang term *facer,* denoting a braggart or bully. The earliest citation for this term in OED is *c.* 1515. **2.** Americanized spelling of German FEESER.

Facey (357) **1.** English (southwestern, also found in South Wales): variant of VEAZEY.

2. Americanized spelling of German **Fehse, Vehse,** variants of FEESE.
3. Americanized spelling of Swiss German **Fäsi,** from a pet form of the personal name *Gervasius* (see GERVAIS).
GIVEN NAMES French 4%. *Alette, Charlot, Monique, Patrice.*

Faciane (170) French: unexplained. Perhaps a variant, under French influence, of Italian FASCIANO.
GIVEN NAME French 5%. *Emile* (2).

Facio (136) American variant of Italian FAZIO.
GIVEN NAMES Spanish 40%. *Fernando* (2), *Jose* (2), *Juan* (2), *Margarita* (2), *Rafael* (2), *Ruben* (2), *Alfredo, Amparo, Araceli, Bino, Blanca, Estela.*

Fackelman (124) German (**Fackelmann**): occupational name for someone whose job was to make torches or to light or carry a torch, from Middle High German *vackel* 'torch' + *man* 'man'.

Facklam (104) German: habitational name from a Sorbian place name probably in Mecklenburg-West Pomerania.
GIVEN NAMES German 5%. *Gerhard, Rainer.*

Fackler (864) German: **1.** occupational name for a torchmaker or for someone whose job was to light or carry a torch, from Middle High German *vackel* 'torch' + agent suffix *-er.* **2.** Eastern German: from a short form of the Slavic personal name *Wenceslaw* or other Slavic names beginning with *Vech-* or *Vach-.* **3.** Americanized spelling of **Fachler,** an occupational name for a surveyor of fish pens (see FECHER).

Fackrell (280) English (Somerset): unexplained.
FOREBEARS James Fackrell (1787–1867) came to NY and VT from North Petherton, Somerset, England, in or before 1812, and subsequently moved to MI and thence to East Bountiful, UT.

Facteau (147) French Canadian: variant of FECTEAU.

Factor (581) **1.** German and Dutch: humanistic name, a translation into Latin of any of various names meaning 'steward' or 'agent', for example HOFFMANN or MEYER. **2.** Scottish and English: from Latin *factor* 'agent', literally 'doer', from *facere* 'to do'. In 15th-century English, this word developed the specialist sense of a merchant's agent in another town; it also came to denote a steward in charge of an estate, the usual meaning in Scotland.

Facundo (116) Spanish and Portuguese: from the personal name *Facundo* (from Latin *facundus* 'talkative', 'eloquent'). This was the name of a 4th-century martyr of Leon, who is commemorated in the place name San Facundo.
GIVEN NAMES Spanish 50%. *Jose* (7), *Jose Antonio* (2), *Mario* (2), *Romualdo* (2), *Sergio* (2), *Agapito, Alicia, Auturo, Carlos, Cesar, Chavez, Claudio; Antonio* (2), *Carmelo.*

Fadden (608) Reduced form of Scottish McFADDEN.

Faddis (336) Variant of Scottish or Irish FIDDES.

Fadel (260) Muslim: from a personal name based on Arabic *fāḍil* 'virtuous', 'generous', 'excellent'.
GIVEN NAMES Muslim 28%. *Deeb* (2), *Hossam* (2), *Mahmoud* (2), *Tarek* (2), *Ziad* (2), *Abbas, Abdallah, Abdul, Ahmad, Akram, Ali, Amin.*

Fadeley (175) Variant spelling of English FADLEY.

Fadely (238) Variant spelling of English FADLEY.

Faden (159) German and Jewish (Ashkenazic): metonymic occupational name for a tailor, from respectively Middle High German *vadem* and modern German *Faden,* both meaning 'thread'.
GIVEN NAMES Jewish 4%; German 4%. *Gerson* (2), *Ilya, Isadore; Otto* (2).

Fader (658) **1.** German; of uncertain derivation; possibly a nickname from Old High German (or modern Low German) *fader* 'father', or alternatively an occupational name for a carpenter who fashioned roof beams, from *pfate* 'beam', 'timber'. **2.** Respelling of German FEDER.

Fadler (134) **1.** South German: probably a nickname for a spinner or tailor, from the verb *fädeln* 'to work with thread'. See also FADEN. **2.** Respelling of **Fed(d)eler,** North German form of FIEDLER, or **Pfadler,** a variant of **Pfader** (see FADER).

Fadley (100) English: habitational name from Faddiley, a place in Cheshire, named from an Old English personal name *Fad(d)a* + Old English *lēah* 'woodland clearing'.

Fadness (216) Norwegian: habitational name from a farm so named in Hordaland county; the first element is probably a river name derived from *ferja* 'to ferry'; the second element is *nes* 'headland', 'promontory'.

Faenza (106) Italian: habitational name from Faenza in Ravenna.
GIVEN NAMES Italian 15%. *Angelo* (2), *Corrado, Giuseppe, Salvatore.*

Faerber (326) German (**Färber**): see FARBER.
GIVEN NAMES German 7%. *Fritz* (3), *Otto* (2), *Arno, Erwin, Irmgard.*

Faeth (213) German (**Fäth**): Franconian variant of VOGT. Compare FAUTH.

Fafard (161) French: from a diminutive of any of various words of diverse meaning containing the onomatopoeic element *faf.*
GIVEN NAMES French 17%. *Herve* (2), *Camille, Donat, Emile, Gilles, Luc, Marcel.*

Faga (141) **1.** Southern Italian (**Fagà**): nickname for a big eater, from Greek *phagas* 'glutton'. **2.** Variant of French **Fagaie.**
GIVEN NAMES Italian 17%; French 4%. *Aldo* (2), *Angelo* (2), *Vito* (2), *Agostino, Antonio, Enzo, Rocco, Salvatore; Jeremie* (2).

Fagan (6754) Irish: **1.** Gaelicized version of a surname of Norman origin, from the personal name *Pagan* meaning 'rustic'. **2.** in some cases it is a reduced Anglicized form of Gaelic **Ó Fágáin** or **Ó Faodhagáin**, which are probably dialect forms of **Ó hÓgáin** (see HOGAN, HAGAN) and **Ó hAodhagáin** (see HAGAN). Irish lenited *f* (spelled *fh*) is soundless, and a number of words beginning with vowels have gained an initial *f* in some dialects; such seems to be the case here. **3.** occasionally an Anglicized form of **Mac Phaidín** (see MCFADDEN) or **Ó Fiacháin** (see FEEHAN).

Fagen (431) Irish: variant spelling of FAGAN.

Fager (679) **1.** Swedish: ornamental name or from a byname meaning 'handsome', 'beautiful'. **2.** German: nickname for a handsome person, from the Old High German *fagar* 'fair', 'pretty'.

Fagerberg (137) Scandinavian: ornamental name composed of the elements *fager* 'beautiful' + *berg* 'mountain', 'hill', or topographic name from a place so called.
GIVEN NAME Scandinavian 7%; German 5%. *Egon*.

Fagerland (121) Norwegian: habitational name from a farmstead so named, from *fager* 'beautiful', 'fair' + *land* 'land', 'farmstead'.
GIVEN NAME Scandinavian 4%. *Ansgar*.

Fagerstrom (265) Swedish (**Fagerström**): ornamental name composed of the elements *fager* 'beautiful' + *ström* 'river'.
GIVEN NAME Scandinavian 7%. *Erik*.

Fagg (655) English (Kent): of uncertain origin. Reaney suggests that it may be a metonymic occupational name for a fish seller or a baker, from Middle English *fagge*, Old English *facg*, which denoted a kind of flatfish, and perhaps also a flat loaf. Another Middle English word *fagge* apparently denoted a fault in the weave of a piece of cloth.

Faggart (177) Dutch: from a personal name composed with the Germanic element *Fag*, which may related to any of various roots meaning 'to be glad', 'fitting', or 'fence', 'wall'.

Fagin (480) Jewish (eastern Ashkenazic): variant spelling of FEIGIN.

Fagley (166) **1.** English: probably a habitational name from Fagley in West Yorkshire, so named from a dialect word *feg* 'coarse grass' + *leye* 'pasture'. **2.** Altered spelling of South German **Vögele**, **Vögeli** (see VOEGELE) or of **Vög(e)ler** (see VOGELER).

Faglie (102) Variant of English FAGLEY.

Fagnani (102) Southern Italian: probably a habitational name from Fagnano in Cosenza or from any of several other places called Fagnani.
GIVEN NAMES Italian 16%. *Attilio, Carlo, Dario, Domenico, Enrico*.

Fagnant (134) French: nickname from *fainéant* 'do-nothing'.

GIVEN NAMES French 12%. *Alcide, Armand, Elzear, Fernand, Normand*.

Fago (121) Southern Italian (Sicilian): from southern Italian and Sicilian *fagu* 'beech', from Latin *fagus*, hence a topographic name for someone who lived by a beech wood or beech tree.

Fagot (83) French: from Old French *fagot* 'bundle of firewood'; probably a metonymic occupational name for a gatherer or seller of firewood.
FOREBEARS A Fagot from Poitou settled in Quebec by 1669.

Fagundes (425) Portuguese: patronymic from the personal name *Fagundo* (see FACUNDO).
GIVEN NAMES Spanish 15%; Portuguese 10%. *Manuel* (11), *Jose* (8), *Francisco* (4), *Carlos* (2), *Adriano, Alvarino, Americo, Augusto, Avelina, Berta, Domingos, Edmundo*; *Fernandes, Joaquim, Marcio, Terezinha*.

Faherty (617) Irish (Galway): reduced Anglicized form of Gaelic **Ó Fathartaigh** 'descendant of *Fathartach*', a personal name (also spelled *Faghartach*) meaning 'noisy', from a derivative of *foghar* 'noise'.
GIVEN NAMES Irish 7%. *Brendan, Colm, Conor, Declan, Eoin*.

Fahey (3796) Irish: reduced Anglicized form of Gaelic **Ó Fathaidh** or **Ó Fathaigh** 'descendant of *Fathadh*', a personal name derived from *fothadh* 'base', 'foundation'. This name is sometimes Anglicized as *Green(e)* as a result of erroneous association with *faithche* 'lawn'.
GIVEN NAMES Irish 6%. *Brendan* (3), *Donal* (2), *Eamon* (2), *Conor, Kieran, Liam, Padraic, Siobhan*.

Fahl (268) German: nickname for someone with a pale complexion or with very fair hair, from Middle High German *val* 'pale', 'wan'. In some cases it may be a shortened form of any of various Germanic compound names with *Fahl* as the first element.
GIVEN NAMES German 4%. *Gunther, Wolfgang*.

Fahle (111) German: variant of FAHL.

Fahlgren (119) Swedish: ornamental-habitational name formed with the place-name element *fal-* 'plain', 'flat land' + *gren* 'branch'.

Fahlstrom (101) Swedish (**Fahlström**): ornamental-habitational name formed with the place-name element *fal-* 'plain', 'flat land' + *ström* 'river'.
GIVEN NAMES Scandinavian 10%; German 5%. *Erland, Mats, Per*; *Viktor*.

Fahmy (182) Muslim: from a personal name based on Arabic *fahmi* 'intelligent', 'quick-witted'.
GIVEN NAMES Muslim 72%. *Nabil* (9), *Mohamed* (5), *Hany* (4), *Amr* (3), *Mohammed* (3), *Mounir* (3), *Samir* (3), *Abdel* (2), *Baha* (2), *Faten* (2), *Haytham* (2), *Hazem* (2).

Fahn (109) **1.** North German: topographic name for someone who lived by a bog, from a Westphalian field name *van* 'marsh', or a habitational name from a place named with this word. **2.** German: a short form of the personal name **Stephan** (see STEVEN).
GIVEN NAME German 5%. *Heinrich* (2).

Fahner (105) German, mainly Swiss German.

Fahnestock (592) German: apparently from *Fahnestock*, literally 'flag pole', but according to family history an altered form of **Fahrenstuck** (**Fahrenstück**), which is a topographic name either from Middle Low German *vor(n)* 'swamp', 'bog', or from the fused preposition and definite article *vorn* 'before the', 'in front of the' + Middle High German *stück* 'piece (of land)', 'field'.
FOREBEARS Johann Diedrich Fahrenstuck arrived in 1726 in New York from Hagen, Germany. From the second generation onward, the name has been conventionally spelled as **Fahnestock**, after a variety of spellings of the name in early colonial records.

Fahr (235) German and Swiss German: topographic name for someone who lived near a crossing point on a river, from Middle High German *vare* 'ferry'.

Fahrbach (124) German: topographic name, in northwestern Germany, from an old creek name, composed of Middle Low German *vor(n)* 'bog, swamp' + Middle High German *bach* 'stream'; in southern Germany (Baden) the first element is from Middle High German *varch* 'pig(let)'.

Fahrenholz (120) German: habitational and topographic name from any of various places, in particular in Westphalia, named with Middle Low German *vor(n)* 'bog' + *holz* 'wood', 'forest', or elsewhere from Middle Low German *vär* 'in front of' or Middle High German *varn* 'fern', *vāre* 'furrow', 'lane', 'border'.

Fahrenkrug (151) German: habitational name from any of several places in northern Germany, including one in Holstein, so named from Middle Low German *krōch* 'inn', 'tavern' + Middle Low German *vor(n)* 'bog', 'swamp'.
GIVEN NAME German 4%. *Alois*.

Fahrer (174) German: topographic name for someone living by a ferry or an occupational name for a ferryman, from Middle High German *vare* 'ferry' + the *-er* suffix of agent nouns.
GIVEN NAME French 4%. *Armand* (3).

Fahringer (310) German: habitational name for someone from a place called Fahring, in Bavaria.

Fahrner (282) German and Swiss German: variant of FARNER.

Fahrney (203) Americanized form of Swiss German FAHRNI.

Fahrni (110) Swiss German: perhaps a variant of **Farni**, a topographic name for someone who lived in an area with ferns, from Middle High German *varn*.

Fahs (276) **1.** Variant spelling of German FAAS. **2.** Muslim: from a personal name based on Arabic *fahṣ* 'investigation', 'inquiry'.
GIVEN NAMES Muslim 7%. *Hussein* (3), *Abeer, Adnan, Ahmad, Ali, Hani, Hassan, Ibrahim, Mohamed, Mouna, Mounir, Rafic.*

Fahy (995) Irish: variant of FAHEY.
GIVEN NAMES Irish 7%. *Declan* (2), *Brendan, Bridie, Cathal, Eamonn, Eoin, Liam, Ronan.*

Faia (129) Southern Italian: probably from Greek **Phagas**, a nickname meaning 'heavy eater' or 'glutton'.
GIVEN NAMES Italian 14%. *Salvatore* (4), *Angelo, Carmel, Franco, Santo.*

Faidley (191) Americanized form of South German FEDERLE or the Swiss German form of this name, **Federli**.

Faiella (262) Italian: unexplained.
GIVEN NAMES Italian 19%. *Pasquale* (3), *Angelo* (2), *Francesco* (2), *Salvatore* (2), *Benedetto, Carlo, Carmela, Domenico, Fabiano, Gennaro, Luigi, Sal.*

Faigle (111) German: Swabian variant of FEIGE 1.
GIVEN NAMES German 7%. *Ernst, Gotthilf.*

Fail (420) **1.** Scottish: reduced form of MCPHAIL. Black suggests that it may also be a habitational name from Fail in Ayrshire. **2.** Northern English (Scottish Borders): Reaney has it as a nickname from Old French *faille* 'erring' or 'failure', but a more probable source is the southern Scots dialect adjective *fail*, meaning 'frail' or 'weak'. **3.** Altered spelling of French FAILE. **4.** Altered spelling of German **Föhl, Fehl**, variants of FEIL 2.

Faile (439) **1.** Possibly a variant spelling of English or Scottish FAIL. **2.** French: of uncertain origin. It may be from *Fail*, a domain name mentioned by Dauzat. Alternatively, it may be a variant of FAILLE.

Failing (343) Americanized spelling of German FEHLING.

Failla (573) Italian: from Latin *favilla* 'spark', a nickname for a lively individual.
GIVEN NAMES Italian 22%. *Salvatore* (4), *Mario* (3), *Natale* (3), *Sal* (3), *Emanuele* (2), *Francesca* (2), *Vito* (2), *Angelo, Antonino, Carmelo, Domenica, Domenico, Elia, Lino, Orlando, Sofio.*

Faillace (151) Italian: probably a nickname meaning 'sparky', from a diminutive of FAILLA 'spark' (influenced by the medieval Greek form *phabrillakēs*).
GIVEN NAMES Italian 16%. *Attilio, Osualdo, Ricardo* (2), *Emilio, Ernesto, Rogerio, Sal, Salvatore.*

Faille (114) French: **1.** metonymic occupational name for a torchbearer, from Old French *faille* 'torch' (Late Latin *facilla*). **2.** metonymic occupational name for a maker or seller of a kind of silk material known in Old French as *faille* (Middle

High German *pfelle*, from Latin *palliolum*, a type of light garment). **3.** nickname for an inept or luckless individual, from Old French *faille* 'fault', 'failing', 'mistake'. **4.** variant spelling of FAILE.
GIVEN NAMES French 9%. *Agathe, Andre.*

Failor (289) Americanized spelling of German **Failer** or **Fehler**, variants of FEILER.

Fails (456) Scottish or Irish: reduced form of MCPHAIL, with the addition of English patronymic *-s*.

Faiman (114) Jewish (Ashkenazic): variant of FEINMAN.
GIVEN NAME Jewish 5%. *Aharon.*

Fain (2916) **1.** French: habitational name from any of various places in France, deriving their names mostly from Old French *fain* 'swamp', but Latin *fanum* 'temple' is also a source in some cases. **2.** English: variant spelling of FAYNE.

Faine (142) English: variant spelling of FAYNE.

Faiola (210) Italian: probably a topographic name from a diminutive of Sicilian *faju* 'beech' (Latin *fageus*), or possibly a habitational name from *Faiolo*, a locality in Montegabbione in Umbria.
GIVEN NAMES Italian 16%. *Angelo, Carmine, Dino, Emelio, Giacinto, Giulio, Guido, Marco, Pietro, Vittorio.*

Fair (6030) **1.** English: nickname meaning 'handsome', 'beautiful', 'fair', Middle English *fair, fayr*, Old English *fæger*. The word was also occasionally used as a personal name in Middle English, applied to both men and women. **2.** Irish: translation of Gaelic *fionn* 'fair', which Woulfe describes as 'a descriptive epithet that supplanted the real surname', or a reduced Anglicized form of Gaelic *Mac F(h)inn*, a variant of *Mag Fhinn* (see MCGINN).

Fairall (226) English: of uncertain origin; perhaps a variant of the Sussex personal name **Fairhall**, which Reaney has as a habitational name from an unidentified place named in Old English as *fæger healh* 'fair nook' or 'fair hollow'.

Fairbairn (546) Scottish: probably a nickname from Older Scottish *fair bairn* 'fair child'. Black, however, suggests that it is perhaps a metathesized variant of **Frebern** (see FREEBORN).

Fairbank (452) English: topographic name for someone who lived 'by the fair bank' or habitational name from a minor place so named, of which there are examples in Cheshire and Cumbria.

Fairbanks (3347) English: habitational name from Fair Banks in Derbyshire or any of various other minor places so called.

Fairbrother (505) English (Lancashire): probably 'brother of someone called Fair' or else a descriptive name for the better-looking of a pair of brothers.

Fairburn (295) Northern English: habitational name from Fairburn in North York-

shire, so named from Old English *fearn* 'fern' + *burna* 'stream'.

Fairchild (5228) Southern English: nickname from Middle English *fair child* 'handsome child' or 'handsome youth of noble birth' (see CHILD).

Faircloth (3181) English (Essex and southeastern counties): variant of the Lancashire name FAIRCLOUGH, altered by folk etymology.

Fairclough (288) English (Lancashire): habitational name from Fairclough Farm near Clitheroe in Lancashire, named in Middle English as *fair clough* 'beautiful ravine' (see CLOUGH).

Faires (413) English: variant of FAIR.

Fairey (226) English: **1.** nickname from Middle English *fair eie* 'fair eye', Old English *fæger ēage*. **2.** habitational name from Fairy Farm in Wethersfield, Essex, or from Fairyhall in Felsted, Essex, both probably so named from Old English *fearh* 'pig', 'hog' + *(ge)hæg* 'enclosure'.

Fairfax (476) English: nickname for someone with beautiful long hair, from Middle English *fair feax* 'beautiful tresses'. This was a common descriptive phrase in Middle English; the alliterative poem *Sir Gawain and the Green Knight* refers to 'fair fanning fax' encircling the shoulders of the doughty warrior.
FOREBEARS Thomas Fairfax (1693–1781), an army officer from Leeds Castle, Kent, England, first came to VA in 1735 and settled on maternal estates there as a proprietor in 1747.

Fairfield (1037) English: habitational name from any of various places, for example Fairfield in Derbyshire or Kent, both named from Old English as *fæger* 'beautiful' + *feld* 'open country', or Fairfield in Worcestershire, which is named with Old English *fō* 'hog' + *feld*.
FOREBEARS John Fairfield was an immigrant to Charlestown, MA, in 1635.

Fairhurst (314) English (Lancashire): habitational name from a hamlet near Parbold, not far from Wigan, so named from Old English *fæger* 'beautiful' + *hyrst* 'wooded hill'.

Fairleigh (108) English: possibly a variant of Scottish FAIRLEY.

Fairless (278) English (Northumberland): said to be a variant of Scottish FAIRLIE.

Fairley (1546) Scottish: habitational name from one of several places named from Old English *fæger* 'beautiful' or *fearn* 'fern' + *lēah* 'woodland clearing'. Black associates the name in this spelling particularly with the barony of Fairley or Fairlie near Largs in Ayrshire.

Fairlie (151) **1.** Scottish: habitational name from any of several places in Scotland so called (see FAIRLEY). **2.** Possibly also an Americanized spelling of South German **Fährle, Värli**, a metonymic occupational name for a hog farmer, from a diminutive of Middle High German *varch* 'pig', 'piglet'.

Fairman (846) **1.** English: occupational name for the servant of someone named *Fair*, or a nickname meaning 'handsome man'. **2.** Jewish (Ashkenazic): Americanized form of one or more like-sounding Jewish surnames, notably **Feuerman** (see FEUER). **3.** Probably an Americanized spelling of German **Fährmann**, a variant of FEHRMANN.

Fairweather (640) English and Scottish: nickname for a person with a sunny temperament. Compare MERRYWEATHER. There is a legend that a Scottish family of Highland origin assumed this name in punning allusion to Job 37:22, 'Fair weather cometh out of the north'. At the present time the surname is most frequent in East Anglia.

Faison (1991) Probably an Americanized form of English, Dutch, or French **Faisant** 'pheasant', either a metonymic occupational name for a breeder of pheasants or a nickname for someone who was thought to resemble the bird. **Faisant** is found as a surname of Old French origin in Middle English, but is not found in present-day Britain.

Faist (173) German: variant of FEIST.

Fait (287) **1.** Czech and Polish: from German **Feit** (see VEIT). **2.** German: variant spelling of VEIT. **3.** German: occupational name for a steward or bailiff, Middle High German *voit*. Compare FAUTH, VOGT. **4.** Perhaps from an obsolete English personal name derived from Anglo-Norman French *afaitie* 'accomplished', 'skillful'.

Faith (1317) English (most frequent in northern Ireland): from Middle English *fe(i)th* 'belief (especially Christian belief)', 'faithfulness', 'loyalty'. This may have been a nickname for a trustworthy person, but was more probably bestowed on one who used 'Faith!' frequently as a mild oath or exclamation.

Faivre (209) French (Lorraine, Franche-Comté): variant of **Fèvre**, an occupational name for a smith (see LEFEVRE).
GIVEN NAMES French 10%. *Marcel* (2), *Henri, Jean Francois, Nadege.*

Faix (128) **1.** French: metonymic occupational name for a gatherer or seller of firewood, from Old French *fais* 'bundle of firewood'. See also FAGOT. **2.** Czech and Slovak: from the personal name *Veits*, from the Latin personal name *Vitus*. **3.** German: variant spelling of **Feix** (see VEIT).

Fajardo (1371) Galician: topographic name for someone who lived by a beech tree or in a beech wood, from Late Latin *fagea (arbor)* 'beech (tree)', a derivative of classical Latin *fagus* 'beech'.
GIVEN NAMES Spanish 46%. *Jose* (29), *Juan* (25), *Manuel* (20), *Carlos* (12), *Luis* (12), *Miguel* (12), *Rafael* (11), *Jorge* (10), *Alfonso* (9), *Alfredo* (9), *Fernando* (9), *Mario* (9); *Antonio* (6), *Leonardo* (3),

Marco (3), *Angelo* (2), *Aldo, Ciriaco, Dino, Fausto, Federico, Julieta, Lorenzo, Mirella.*

Fake (335) **1.** English (mainly Norfolk and Suffolk): variant of FAULKS. **2.** Dutch: from the Germanic personal name *Facco*, a variant of *Falco*, itself probably a short form of a personal name formed with *fal*, a tribal name (as in West*phal*ia) or alternatively a byname meaning 'falcon'.

Fakes (106) English (Suffolk): variant of FAULKS.

Fakhoury (131) Arabic: from a personal name based on either *fakhūrī* or *fakhrī*, both meaning 'proud', 'associated with a noble cause'.
GIVEN NAMES Muslim 63%. *Amin* (2), *Awni* (2), *Hani* (2), *Ibrahim* (2), *Karem* (2), *Mahmoud* (2), *Nabil* (2), *Akram, Atef, Bassem, Chakib, Daoud.*

Fakler (101) German: variant of FACKLER.
GIVEN NAME German 4%. *Helmut.*

Falanga (218) Southern Italian: from Sicilian *falanca, falanga* 'plank', 'gangplank', 'temporary bridge'; also 'ravine', 'gorge'.
GIVEN NAMES Italian 17%. *Angelo* (2), *Antonio* (2), *Fiore, Gennaro, Natale, Nunzio, Pasquale, Salvatore, Vincenza.*

Falardeau (206) Variant of French Canadian **Follardeau**, a derivative of Spanish FERNANDO.
FOREBEARS A bearer of the name from Saintonge is recorded in Beauport as **Foulardeau** by 1694.
GIVEN NAMES French 15%. *Andree* (2), *Andre, Aurele, Cecile, Emile, Fernand, Laurent, Marcel, Marie-Noelle.*

Falasca (122) Southern Italian: topographic name for someone who lived where fescue grew, from Italian *falasca* 'fescue', or a habitational name from a place so named.
GIVEN NAMES Italian 15%. *Angelo, Italo, Lirio, Nino, Pio.*

Falasco (152) Italian: topographic name from *falasco* 'bog grass'.
GIVEN NAMES Italian 10%. *Antonio, Emidio, Santo.*

Falb (155) German: nickname for someone with a pale complexion or fair hair, from Middle High German *valwe, val* 'pale'. The word *Falb(e)* is used today only to denote the color of a horse.

Falbo (543) Italian: nickname, probably for someone with fair hair or a blond beard, from *falbo* 'pale yellow', usually applied to the color of an animal's coat, from medieval Latin *falvus* 'tawny', usually applied to the color of an animal's coat. Compare Sicilian *farbu* 'blond', 'reddish'.
GIVEN NAMES Italian 9%. *Salvatore* (4), *Santo* (2), *Angelo, Carmelo, Francesco, Giacomo, Peppino, Vincenzo.*

Falcione (160) Italian: from a derivative of *falce* 'sickle' (from Latin *falx*).
GIVEN NAMES Italian 18%. *Domenic* (2), *Geno* (2), *Orest* (2), *Amedeo, Angelo, Giuseppe, Pasquale, Romeo.*

Falck (434) German and Scandinavian: variant spelling of FALK.
GIVEN NAMES German 4%. *Hans* (2), *Kurt, Otto, Wolfgang.*

Falco (1446) Italian and Catalan (**Falcó**): from *falco* 'falcon'. This was generally a metonymic occupational name for a falconer or a nickname for someone thought to resemble a hawk, but it is also a Germanic personal name.
GIVEN NAMES Italian 15%. *Salvatore* (6), *Carmine* (5), *Pasquale* (5), *Angelo* (4), *Carlo* (4), *Vincenzo* (3), *Vito* (3), *Corrado* (2), *Domenico* (2), *Enzo* (2), *Santo* (2), *Antonio.*

Falcon (2365) **1.** English: from Middle English, Old French *faucon, falcun* 'falcon', either a metonymic occupational name for a falconer, or a nickname for someone thought to resemble the falcon, which was regarded as a symbol of speed and courage in the Middle Ages. In a few cases, it may also have been a metonymic occupational name for a man who operated the piece of artillery named after the bird of prey. Compare FAULKNER. **2.** In Louisiana, the name **Falcón** is borne by the descendants of Canary Islanders brought in to settle in 1779.
GIVEN NAMES Spanish 29%. *Jose* (32), *Juan* (21), *Manuel* (14), *Luis* (13), *Pedro* (9), *Alberto* (8), *Miguel* (8), *Pablo* (8), *Ramon* (8), *Angel* (7), *Jesus* (7), *Julio* (7).

Falcone (2582) Italian: from *falcone* 'falcon', either a personal name, or a nickname, or a metonymic occupational name for a falconer. See also FALCON.
GIVEN NAMES Italian 15%. *Angelo* (14), *Salvatore* (10), *Carmine* (6), *Vito* (6), *Domenic* (5), *Sal* (5), *Antonio* (4), *Lorenzo* (4), *Carmelo* (3), *Gaetano* (3), *Giovanni* (3), *Rocco* (3).

Falconer (1265) Scottish: occupational name for someone who kept and trained falcons (see FAULKNER).

Falconi (181) Italian: from *falcone* 'falcon', a personal name, a nickname, or a metonymic occupational name for a falconer. See also FALCON, FALCONE.
GIVEN NAMES Spanish 18%; Italian 10%. *Cesar* (2), *Jorge* (2), *Alicia, Carlos, Enrique, Jose, Josue, Juan, Magdalena*; *Salvatore* (2), *Alberto, Edvige, Fausto, Fulvio, Guillermo.*

Falen (123) German and Swedish: ethnic name for someone from East or Westphalia, from *fal*, presumably referring to a plain.

Faler (308) **1.** Altered spelling of German **Pfahler, Pfähler** from Middle High German *pfāl* 'stake', 'post', an early loan word from Latin *palus*. It was a topographic name for someone who lived near a post marking the village boundary, or just outside a city wall; or alternatively an occupational name for a postmaker. **2.** Perhaps an Americanized spelling of German FEHLER.

Fales (953) Czech (**Fáles**): from a pet form of the personal name VALENTIN.

Faletti (147) Italian: of uncertain origin. **1.** Perhaps from a pet form of an unidentified personal name ending in -*falo*. **2.** Alternatively, it may be from *Falletti*, an outlying district of Sagliano Micca in Piedmont.

Faley (191) English: probably a variant of FAWLEY.

Falgoust (238) Variant of French **Falgoux**, a habitational name from a place named Le Falgoux in Cantal.

Falgout (673) French: variant of FALGOUST. FOREBEARS This name is borne by a LA family descended from Louis-Marseille Falgoust, from Beaumont, north of Tours, living in about 1737.

GIVEN NAMES French 4%. *Amie* (2), *Alcee*, *Armand*, *Collette*, *Ferrel*, *Pierre*.

Falin (223) **1.** Irish: variant spelling of FALLON. **2.** Russian and Jewish (from Belarus): patronymic from the personal name *Fal*, a derivative of Greek *Thallos*, from *thallos* 'branch', 'shoot'. This was the name of a martyr venerated in the Eastern Church.

Falk (5380) **1.** German: from Middle High German *valke* 'falcon', hence a nickname or a metonymic occupational name for a falconer. **2.** Scandinavian: ornamental name from *falk* 'falcon'. **3.** Jewish (Ashkenazic): ornamental name from German *Falke* 'falcon', or, in Bohemia, from Czech *vlk* 'wolf'. **4.** Jewish (Ashkenazic): ornamental name from Yiddish *falk* 'falcon' or from the personal name *Falk* with the same meaning.

Falke (332) German: variant of FALK.

GIVEN NAMES German 4%. *Erwin*, *Heinz*, *Rainer*, *Wolfgang*.

Falkenberg (466) **1.** German: habitational name from any of several places, especially in eastern Germany and Bavaria, named from Old High German *falk* 'falcon' + *berg* 'mountain', 'hill'; such place names are often associated with the presence of a castle, as falconry was a privilege of the nobility. **2.** Scandinavian: habitational name or ornamental name from *falk* 'falcon' + *berg* 'mountain', 'hill'. **3.** Jewish (Ashkenazic): ornamental name composed of the German elements *Falke(n)* 'falcon' + *Berg* 'mountain', 'hill'.

GIVEN NAMES German 7%; Scandinavian 4%. *Hans* (4), *Kurt* (4), *Erhardt*, *Erwin*, *Fritz*, *Otto*, *Ulrika*; *Carsten* (2), *Erik* (2), *Tryg*.

Falkenhagen (117) German: habitational name from any of several places named from Old High German *falke* 'falcon' + *hag* 'hedge', 'fencing'. A place so named is documented west of Berlin in the 14th century.

GIVEN NAME German 4%. *Erwin*.

Falkenstein (506) **1.** German: habitational name from any of several places named Falkenstein, from Old High German *falke*

'falcon' + *stein* 'stone', 'rock', here indicating a medieval castle. This has been a common surname in Germany since the late 14th century. **2.** Jewish (Ashkenazic): habitational name as in 1 or an ornamental name composed of German *Falke* 'falcon' + *Stein* 'stone'.

FOREBEARS George Ness Falkenstein (1859–1949), educator, minister, and historian, wrote a history of the German Baptist Brethren (1900), became a pastor at the Germantown, PA, German Baptist Brethren congregation in 1893, and was ordained in 1899.

GIVEN NAMES German 6%. *Kurt* (4), *Alois* (3), *Hans* (2), *Alfons*, *Fritz*, *Otto*.

Falkner (1081) **1.** German: occupational name for a falconer, Middle High German *vakenoere*. In medieval times falconry was a sport practised only by the nobility; it was the task of the falconer to look after the birds and train young ones. **2.** English: variant spelling of FAULKNER.

FOREBEARS Daniel Falckner (1666–*c*.1745), German Lutheran pastor and agent for the Frankfurt Land Company, founded the first German Lutheran congregation in America.

Falkowitz (84) Jewish (eastern Ashkenazic): patronymic from the personal name FALK 'falcon'.

GIVEN NAMES Jewish 24%. *Moshe* (3), *Alter* (2), *Hersch*, *Isadore*, *Mechel*, *Mordche*.

Falkowski (655) Polish and Jewish (eastern Ashkenazic): habitational name for someone from a place called Falkow (now Fałków) for example, probably named from *Fałek*, a pet form of *Chwał*, a short form of the personal name *Chwalisław*. In some instances the Jewish name is a patronymic from the Yiddish personal name FALK.

GIVEN NAMES Polish 6%. *Bogdan*, *Casimir*, *Dariusz*, *Feliks*, *Henryk*, *Jadwiga*, *Jozef*, *Justyna*, *Miroslaw*, *Tadusz*, *Zigmund*.

Fall (1375) **1.** Scottish or Irish: reduced form of MCFALL. **2.** English: topographic name for someone who lived by a waterfall, declivity, or forest clearing, Middle English *fall* (from Old English (*ge*)*fall* 'a felling of trees', Old Norse *fall* 'forest clearing'). **3.** German: topographic name from Middle High German *val* 'fall (of trees)'; in some cases 'waterfall' or 'landslide', or a habitational name from a minor place named with this word, or in Tyrol from Ladine *val* 'valley'. **4.** African: unexplained.

GIVEN NAMES African 4%. *Cheikh* (6), *Amadou* (3), *Serigne* (3), *Mamadou* (2), *Modou* (2), *Aboubacar*, *Awa*, *Fatou*, *Idrissa*, *Matar*, *Moctar*, *Oumou*.

Falla (166) **1.** Spanish and Catalan (**(de) Falla**): probably a nickname from Catalan *falla* 'torch' or 'bonfire' (in particular, one which was lit in the streets of a city on public festivals), or an occupational name for one who lit such a bonfire. **2.** Spanish: perhaps a nickname from *falla* 'flaw', 'error',

'doubt' (Latin *falla*). **3.** Scottish: habitational name from any of various places named Falla, Fala, or Fallaw, especially Fala in Midlothian. The second element is probably *law* 'hill'. **4.** Norwegian: habitational name from a farm so named in southeastern Norway, so named from *fall* 'fall', probably with reference to the site of a landslide or to tree felling.

GIVEN NAMES Spanish 27%. *Luis* (4), *Jose* (3), *Juan* (3), *Carlos* (2), *Enrique* (2), *Lourdes* (2), *Ana*, *Arturo*, *Cristina*, *Ernesto*, *Guillermo*, *Hernan*.

Fallas (146) **1.** English (Yorkshire): variant spelling of FALLIS. **2.** Spanish: probably nickname from the plural of FALLA. **3.** Jewish (Sephardic): borrowing of the Spanish surname.

GIVEN NAMES Spanish 13%; Jewish 6%. *Jose* (4), *Luis* (2), *Carlos*, *Geovanny*, *Humberto*, *Juan Carlos*, *Mario*, *Rodrigo*; *Isadore*, *Meyer*, *Sol*.

Fallat (146) Polish (also **Fałat**) and Ukrainian: nickname from Polish dialect *fałat* 'piece', 'chunk', 'wisp', or 'bunch', from Hungarian.

Fallaw (180) Scottish: variant of FALLA 2.

Fallen (358) Scottish and northern Irish: variant spelling of Irish FALLON.

Faller (999) South German: **1.** habitational name for someone from Ober- or Unter-Fall near Triberg in the Black Forest. **2.** topographical name for someone living by a waterfall or the site of a landslide, from Middle High German *val* 'fall', 'waterfall', 'landslide'. **3.** in some cases it may derive from FALTER, through assimilation of the consonants. **4.** Scandinavian: unexplained.

Fallert (213) South German: probably from FALLER, with the addition of an inorganic -*t*.

Falletta (198) Southern Italian: of uncertain origin. Compare FALETTI.

GIVEN NAMES Italian 21%. *Salvatore* (10), *Angelo*, *Dino*, *Enrico*, *Gaetano*, *Luciano*.

Fallick (103) English (Hampshire): unexplained.

Fallin (739) **1.** Irish: variant spelling of FALLON. **2.** German: from *Fällin*, a south German pet form of the personal name *Valentin* (see VALENTINE).

Fallis (716) **1.** English and Scottish (of Norman origin): habitational name from Falaise in Calvados, France, the birthplace of William the Conqueror. The place is so named from Old French *falaise* 'cliff' (a word of Germanic origin). **2.** Scottish and northern Irish: reduced form of MCFALLS.

Fallo (145) Italian: from *fallo* 'error', 'mistake', also 'sin', presumably applied as a nickname.

GIVEN NAMES French 8%; Italian 7%. *Emile* (3), *Achille*; *Gaetana*, *Santo*.

Fallon (4669) Irish: reduced Anglicized form of Gaelic **Ó Fallamhain** 'descendant of *Fallamhan*', a byname meaning 'leader' (from *follamhnas* 'supremacy').

GIVEN NAMES Irish 5%. *Malachy* (6), *Kieran* (5), *Eamon* (2), *Aidan*, *Declan*, *Fergus*, *John Patrick*, *Kilian*.

Fallone (113) Italian: from an augmentative of FALLO, probably in the sense 'error', also 'blame', 'sin', or possibly related to Fallo, the name of a hamlet in the province of Chieti, which derives from *faldo* 'layer', 'slope'.
GIVEN NAMES Italian 32%. *Mario* (w), *Carmine* (2), *Franco* (2), *Rocco* (2), *Silvano* (2), *Antonio*, *Enrico*, *Giovanni*, *Guido*, *Oreste*, *Pasquale*, *Tommaso*.

Fallows (155) **1.** English: topographic name for someone who lived by a patch of fallow land, Middle English *falwe* (Old English *f(e)alg*). This word was used to denote both land left uncultivated for a time to recover its fertility and land recently brought into cultivation. **2.** The name is also borne by Ashkenazic Jews, as an Americanized form of one or more like-sounding Jewish surnames.

Falls (2578) **1.** Northern Irish: variant of FALLIS. **2.** Americanized spelling of German VOLZ.

Faloon (148) Northern Irish: variant of FALLON.

Falor (171) Probably altered spelling of German **Fehler** or **Failer** (see FEILER).

Falotico (155) Southern Italian: from southern Italian *falotico* 'eccentric', 'strange', Greek *kephalōtikos*, a derivative of Greek *kephalē* 'head'.
GIVEN NAMES Italian 16%. *Rocco* (4), *Salvatore*.

Falsetta (109) Italian: feminine form of FALSETTI.
GIVEN NAMES Italian 10%. *Angelo* (2), *Fausto* (2).

Falsetti (122) Italian: from a diminutive of a nickname from *falso* 'false', 'untrue', or alternatively a nickname from *falsetto* denoting a man using a singing voice above the normal register.
GIVEN NAMES Italian 14%. *Aldo*, *Dino*, *Ettore*, *Santo*.

Falso (129) Italian: nickname for a deceiver, from *falso* 'false', 'fake'.
GIVEN NAMES Italian 19%. *Ercole* (2), *Antonio*, *Ennio*, *Enzo*, *Giovanna*, *Mattia*.

Falsone (137) Italian: from an augmentative of FALSO.
GIVEN NAMES Italian 21%. *Marco* (2), *Salvatore* (2), *Alfonse*, *Angelo*, *Giovanni*, *Giuseppe*, *Sebastiano*.

Falstad (115) Norwegian: habitational name from either of two farmsteads in Trøndelag so named, from an uncertain first element + *stad* (from Old Norse *staðir*, plural of *staðr* 'farmstead', 'dwelling').

Falter (545) South German: topographic name from Middle High German *valletor*, *valter*, the term for a self-closing gate, placed between a village and the adjacent fields.

Falvey (768) Irish (Kerry): reduced Anglicized form of Gaelic **Ó Fáilbhe** 'descendant of *Fáilbhe*', a byname meaning 'lively'.
GIVEN NAME Irish 6%. *Brendan* (2).

Falvo (371) **1.** Italian: variant of FALBO. **2.** Southern French: from Occitan *falvo* 'tawny', a nickname probably referring to hair or skin color, cognate with 1.
GIVEN NAMES Italian 13%. *Salvatore* (2), *Angelo*, *Antonio*, *Carmino*, *Gennaro*, *Giuseppe*, *Italo*, *Remo*, *Sal*, *Sante*, *Vito*.

Falwell (195) Possibly an Americanized form of German FULWILER.

Falzarano (234) Italian: unexplained; possibly a habitational name from a lost or unidentified place.
GIVEN NAMES Italian 15%. *Carmine* (2), *Lorenzo* (2), *Agostino*, *Angelo*, *Antonella*, *Giorgio*, *Nunzio*, *Sabatino*, *Sal*, *Santino*.

Falzon (177) Italian: variant of FALZONE.
GIVEN NAMES Italian 10%. *Carmel* (3), *Grazio*, *Reno*.

Falzone (760) Italian: **1.** variant of FALSONE. **2.** possibly from a northern equivalent of *falcione* denoting a type of weapon derived from the agricultural sickle.
GIVEN NAMES Italian 17%; French 4%. *Salvatore* (16), *Angelo* (5), *Carlo* (3), *Sal* (3), *Luciano* (2), *Amadeo*, *Attilio*, *Carmine*, *Cataldo*, *Cosimo*, *Dino*, *Gasper*; *Alphonse*, *Armand*, *Gabrielle*, *Michel*, *Monique*.

Fama (370) **1.** Southern Italian (**Famà**): from Greek *phamē* 'speech', hence a nickname for a garrulous person. **2.** Italian, Spanish, and Portuguese: nickname from *fama* 'rumor' or 'renown'.
GIVEN NAMES Italian 26%. *Salvatore* (5), *Angelo* (4), *Rocco* (4), *Santo* (3), *Sal* (2), *Silvio* (2), *Antonio*, *Massimo*, *Romualdo*, *Salavatore*, *Santi*, *Ugo*.

Fambro (255) Variant of English FAMBROUGH.

Fambrough (296) Perhaps an altered form of the English habitational name **Farmborough**, from a place near Bath, so named from Old English *fearn* 'fern' + *beorg* 'hill', 'mound'.

Famiglietti (387) Italian: occupational name from *famiglia*, from old Italian *famiglio* 'familiar', 'servant', 'domestic'.
GIVEN NAMES Italian 18%. *Rocco* (7), *Carmine* (5), *Antonio* (4), *Angelo* (2), *Marco* (2), *Amato*, *Donato*, *Ezio*, *Gaetano*, *Sabatino*, *Vito*.

Famularo (271) Italian: occupational name for a servant, retainer, or courtier, from Latin *famulus* + the suffix of agent nouns -*arius*.
GIVEN NAMES Italian 13%. *Sal* (2), *Angelo*, *Carmela*, *Giacomo*, *Leonardo*.

Fan (1233) **1.** Chinese 范: from the name of a place called Fan, which existed during the Zhou dynasty. The Western Zhou dynasty's penultimate king, Xuan Wang (827–781 BC), executed a direct descendant of the model emperor Yao. The latter's son

fled to the state of Jin, where he became a distinguished general and was granted the area called Fan. His descendants adopted the place name as their surname. **2.** Chinese 樊: from a different place of the same period, also written in English as **Fan**. Zhong Shanfu, a senior adviser to Xuan Wang (827–781 BC), the penultimate king of the Western Zhou dynasty, is considered to have been a major factor in the exceptional success of this king during a period of generally declining authority for the Zhou kings. He was successful in conquering and pacifying tribes to the north, south, and west, and for this service he was granted the area of Fan. His descendants took the place name Fan as their surname.
GIVEN NAMES Chinese 45%. *Li* (7), *Ming* (5), *Yi* (5), *Chen* (4), *Chung* (4), *Lei* (4), *Liang* (4), *Wei* (4), *Cheng* (3), *Chi* (3), *Chin* (3), *Hong* (3), *Jian* (3), *Chang*, *Sook*, *Yiping*.

Fanara (200) Southern Italian (Sicily): occupational name from medieval Greek *phanaras* 'lamp maker' or 'beacon keeper', from *phanos* 'torch', 'beacon', 'lamp'.
GIVEN NAMES Italian 15%. *Angelo* (3), *Carlo*, *Natale*, *Sal*, *Salvatore*, *Santo*, *Vito*.

Fancher (2315) **1.** Probably a variant spelling of French FANGER. **2.** It could alternatively be an altered form of English **Fanshaw**, which Reaney believes to be a habitational name from Fanshaw Gate, near Holmesfield, Derbyshire. However, the earliest records of the place name, *le Faunchalle-gate* (1456, 1472, etc.), indicate that the place takes its name from the Faunchall or Fanshaw family and not the other way about. Further, the early form of the surname suggests a French origin.

Fancy (133) English (Dorset): unexplained. This name is frequent in Nova Scotia.

Fandel (308) South German: **1.** from a diminutive of FENDT. **2.** metonymic occupational name for a maker of copper or iron pans, from *Pfand(e)l*.

Fandrey (125) German: variant of FANDRICH.
GIVEN NAMES German 6%. *Ewald* (2), *Erna*.

Fandrich (259) German: **1.** variant of FENRICH. **2.** from a Sorbian vernacular form of the personal name ANDREAS.
GIVEN NAMES German 6%. *Helmut* (2), *Erwin*, *Gerhart*, *Otto*.

Fane (206) English: variant spelling of FAYNE.

Fanella (112) Italian: variant of FANELLI.
GIVEN NAMES Italian 5%. *Ermanno*, *Silvio*.

Fanelli (1298) Italian: patronymic or plural form of *Fanello*, a reduced pet form of the personal name *Stefano*.
GIVEN NAMES Italian 15%. *Salvatore* (9), *Rocco* (6), *Angelo* (5), *Carlo* (3), *Antonio* (2), *Carmine* (2), *Donato* (2), *Filomena* (2), *Mauro* (2), *Alfonse*, *Arcangelo*, *Caesar*.

Fang (1294) **1.** Chinese 方: from the name of Ji Fang Shu, a senior adviser to the penultimate king of the Western Zhou

dynasty, Xuan Wang (827–781 BC). He is known for the expeditions he undertook to calm southern tribes. His descendants adopted part of his name, Fang, as their surname. **2.** Chinese 房: from the name of the ancient state of Fang (in present-day Henan province). The model emperor Yao (2357–2257 BC) was admired by Confucius for his virtuous leadership and his selection of his successor, Shun, on grounds of merit rather than heredity. (Yao passed over his own son, Dan Zhu, who did not display governing ability, and chose Shun.) When Shun ascended the throne, he granted the state of Fang to Dan Zhu's son. His descendants eventually adopted the name of the state Fang as their surname. **3.** German: from Middle High German *vanc* 'catch', 'enclosure', hence a topographic name for someone who lived by an enclosed plot of land, a hunting ground, a place where traps were set (for game or fish), or a pit; or a byname, meaning 'the catch', for a foreigner who had been forced into bondage.
GIVEN NAMES Chinese 48%. *Ming* (9), *Wei* (9), *Rong* (8), *Yi* (7), *Fang* (6), *Hong* (6), *Ping* (6), *Min* (5), *Peng* (5), *Chien* (4), *Hua* (4), *Jing* (4), *Qing* (4), *Chung* (2), *Jang* (2), *Xou* (2), *Choua, Neng, Pai, Tian, Yeong, Youa.*

Fanger (190) **1.** German (**Fänger**) and Swiss German (**Fanger**): occupational name for a trapper, from an agent derivative of *fangen* 'to catch'. **2.** Possibly French: habitational name from Le Fanget in Haute Loire, named from Old French *fange* 'mud', 'mire' (Old Occitan *fanga*).

Fangman (447) Jewish (Ashkenazic): occupational name for a trapper (see FANGER). In some cases it is an ornamental name.

Fangmeier (101) North German: topographic name for a (tenant) farmer (see MEYER) who owned an enclosed piece of land on which animals were kept (Middle Low German *vanc*).
GIVEN NAMES German 7%. *Frederick Fritz, Kurt.*

Fanguy (227) French: topographic name from *fange* 'mud', 'mire'.
GIVEN NAMES French 6%. *Camille, Celestin, Emile, Ulysse.*

Faniel (91) French: topographic name for someone who lived on or near marshy ground, from a diminutive of *fagne* 'quagmire'. This, rhyming with *Daniel*, is how the name **Faneuil** is pronounced.
FOREBEARS The wealthy merchant who donated Boston's Faneuil Hall marketplace, Peter Faneuil (1700–43), was the son of one of three Huguenot brothers from La Rochelle who came to America by way of Holland after the revocation of the Edict of Nantes in 1685. Admitted members of the MA colony in 1691, they were among the small number of French Huguenot refugees who were able to bring considerable property with them to North America.

GIVEN NAMES Spanish 6%. *Juanita* (2), *Felipe.*

Fanjoy (121) Variant of French FANGUY.

Fank (108) German: **1.** nickname for quick and lively person, from Middle High German *vank(e)* 'spark'. **2.** shortened form of FANKHAUSER.
GIVEN NAME French 4%. *Monique.*

Fankhauser (594) South German and Swiss German: topographic name for someone living by a *Fanghaus*, literally 'capture house', a building or enclosure in which live animals captured by hunting were kept.
GIVEN NAMES German 4%. *Fritz* (2), *Christoph, Erwin, Hanspeter, Kurt.*

Fann (1073) **1.** English: variant of FENN. **2.** Reduced form of Irish McFANN.
FOREBEARS The first recorded bearer of this name in North America is John Fann, who was born in Richmond Co., VA, in 1688.

Fannin (2335) Irish: reduced Anglicized form of Gaelic **O Fionnáin** 'descendant of *Fionnán*', a diminutive of FINN.

Fanning (4290) English: variant of FENNING.

Fannon (708) Irish: variant of FANNIN.

Fano (133) **1.** Danish: unexplained. **2.** Asturian-Leonese: habitational name (alongside its variant **Fanu**) from any of the places in Asturies named Fano or Fanu.
GIVEN NAMES Spanish 11%; Danish 5%; Italian 4%. *Arturo* (2), *Manuel* (2), *Cesar, Elena, Mario, Valeriano, Viviana; Erwin, Wilhelm; Antonio, Ugo.*

Fansler (750) German: habitational name for someone from Vanselow, a place in Pomerania.

Fant (1345) **1.** English: from Old French *enfant* 'child', hence a nickname for someone of a childish (or childlike) disposition. This name arose when, in medieval England, Anglo-Norman French *l'enfant* was wrongly understood as *le fant*. **2.** Italian: Venetian variant of INFANTE.

Fanta (205) **1.** Spanish and Italian: unexplained. **2.** Ethiopian: unexplained.
GIVEN NAMES Ethiopian 4%. *Alemayehu, Legesse, Tesfaye, Yosief.*

Fantasia (280) Southern Italian: from the personal name *Fantasia*, feminine form of *Fantasio*, or possibly a nickname for someone with a vivid imagination, from *fantasia* 'imagination'.
GIVEN NAMES Italian 11%. *Angelo, Carmine, Cosmo, Elio, Romolo, Serafino.*

Fantauzzi (110) Southern Italian: of uncertain origin. It may be a patronymic from the personal name FANTE.
GIVEN NAMES Spanish 25%; Italian 7%. *Jose* (2), *Agustina, Andres, Assunta, Blanca, Claudio, Ernesto, Francisco, Ines, Juan, Luz, Maribel; Dino, Pasquale.*

Fante (102) Northern Italian: from the medieval personal name *Fante*, from *fante* 'child', 'youth', or from a short form of the omen names *Bonfante* 'good child' or

Belfante 'beautiful child', formed with this word.
GIVEN NAMES Italian 4%. *Antonio, Guglielmo.*

Fanti (114) Northern Italian: patronymic or plural form of FANTE.
GIVEN NAMES Italian 17%. *Paolo* (3), *Egisto* (2), *Aldo, Angelo, Caesar, Dino, Edo, Luigi, Marco, Mario, Orlando.*

Fantin (106) Italian: from a northern variant of *fantino* 'baby', 'boy', 'young (unmarried) man'.
GIVEN NAMES Italian 13%. *Aldo* (2), *Angelo, Antonietta, Antonio, Attilio, Giuseppe, Luciano.*

Fantini (245) Italian: from a pet form of **Fante** (see FANTI).
GIVEN NAMES Italian 20%; Spanish 5%. *Mario* (3), *Mauro* (2), *Aldo, Amedeo, Antonio, Carlo, Ceasar, Gaspare, Giovanni, Guido, Luciano, Raffaele, Remo, Renato, Ricardo; Alvino, Leonida, Nestor, Olimpia, Oralia.*

Fanto (116) Italian: possibly a habitational name from Fanto in Calabria.
GIVEN NAME Italian 8%. *Salvatore.*

Fanton (186) Italian: from an augmentative of **Fante** (see FANTI).

Fantozzi (263) Italian: from a derivative of **Fante** (see FANTI).
GIVEN NAMES Italian 22%. *Angelo* (5), *Domenico* (2), *Gino* (2), *Umberto* (2), *Antonio, Carlo, Dante, Luigi, Nichola, Otello, Reno, Ugo.*

Fantroy (121) Possibly a respelling of eastern German **Fandrey**, from Slavic *Wandrey*, a pet form of the personal name ANDREAS.
GIVEN NAME French 5%. *Patrice.*

Fanucchi (197) Italian: from a reduced form of the personal name *Stefanucchio*, a pet form of *Stefano* (see STEVEN).
GIVEN NAMES Italian 18%. *Angelo* (4), *Gino* (3), *Geno* (2), *Attilio, Dante, Elio, Gulio, Lorenzo, Marino, Oreste.*

Fanucci (110) Italian: from a reduced form of the personal name *Stefanuccio*, a pet form of *Stefano* (see STEVEN).
GIVEN NAMES Italian 10%. *Angelo, Santino, Secondo.*

Fara (115) **1.** Southern Italian: from a short form of a female personal name formed with a Germanic element, *fara*, as in (for example) *Burgundofara*. **2.** Czech (also **Fára**) and Slovak: from the personal name *Farnacius*; or alternatively a topographic name from *fara* 'priest's house'.
GIVEN NAMES Spanish 5%. *Eduardo* (2), *Carlos, Mario.*

Farabaugh (451) Americanized spelling of German **Fa(h)renbach**, a habitational name from any of numerous places so named in Hesse, Baden, and Bavaria, or of FEHRENBACH.

Farabee (366) English: variant of FEREBEE.

Farace (299) Italian: apparently from a medieval personal name, perhaps, as Caracausi suggests, Arabic FARAJ.

GIVEN NAMES Italian 13%. *Cesare* (2), *Nuncio* (2), *Salvatore* (2), *Biagio*, *Cosimo*, *Luigi*.

Faraci (378) Italian: patronymic or plural form of FARACE.

GIVEN NAMES Italian 23%. *Salvatore* (10), *Angelo* (5), *Rocco* (3), *Ciro* (2), *Luciano* (2), *Antonino*, *Biagio*, *Caesar*, *Carmelo*, *Carmine*, *Caterina*, *Cesare*.

Farag (227) Muslim: Egyptian form of FARAJ.

GIVEN NAMES Muslim 69%. *Nabil* (5), *Samir* (5), *Emad* (4), *Farag* (4), *Hany* (4), *Safwat* (4), *Ahmed* (3), *Aziz* (3), *Fouad* (3), *Ashraf* (2), *Badie* (2), *Hassan* (2).

Faragher (161) Irish: reduced Anglicized form of **Ó Fearchair** 'descendant of *Fearchar*', a Gaelic personal name meaning 'philanthropist', 'man-loving', or of the personal name itself. Compare Scottish FARQUHAR.

Farago (220) Hungarian (**Faragó**): from *faragó* 'cutter' (from *faragni* 'to cut'), hence an occupational name for a woodcutter (*fafaragó*) or a stonecutter (*kőfaragó*).

GIVEN NAMES Italian 6%; Hungarian 5%. *Dante*, *Gianna*, *Nicolina*, *Salvatore*; *Laszlo* (3), *Sandor*.

Farah (881) Muslim: from a personal name based on Arabic *faraḥ* 'joy', 'happiness', 'delight'.

GIVEN NAMES Muslim 31%. *Abdi* (5), *Abdulkadir* (5), *Ahmed* (3), *Aziz* (3), *Charbel* (3), *Ibrahim* (3), *Mohamed* (3), *Omar* (3), *Samir* (3), *Yacoub* (3), *Zahra* (3), *Abdirashid* (2).

Faraj (120) Muslim: from a personal name based on Arabic *faraj* 'remedy (for troubles or grief)', 'comfort'.

GIVEN NAMES Muslim 74%; French 4%. *Hassan* (4), *Hani* (2), *Mahmoud* (2), *Ramzi* (2), *Sami* (2), *Talal* (2), *Walid* (2), *Abdul*, *Aimen*, *Ali*, *Amin*, *Atallah*; *Alexandre*, *Almira*, *Pierre*.

Faranda (151) Italian: possibly from *Faranda(s)*, a personal name of Greek origin.

Faraone (318) Italian: probably a nickname from *faraone* 'pharaoh', although various other sources have been proposed.

GIVEN NAMES Italian 17%. *Angelo* (3), *Gaeton* (2), *Camillo*, *Dante*, *Emidio*, *Ercole*, *Gaetano*, *Giuseppa*, *Rocco*, *Rosolino*, *Sebastiano*, *Umberto*.

Farb (177) Jewish (Ashkenazic): metonymic occupational name for a dyer, from German *Farbe* 'color'. Compare FARBER.

GIVEN NAME French 5%. *Esme* (2).

Farber (3326) German (**Färber**) and Jewish (Ashkenazic): occupational name for a dyer, from Middle High German *varwer* (an agent derivative of *varwe* 'color') or from Yiddish *farber*.

GIVEN NAMES Jewish 5%. *Sol* (5), *Miriam* (4), *Emanuel* (3), *Hyman* (3), *Doron* (2), *Ilya* (2), *Aron*, *Esfir*, *Faina*, *Hinda*, *Hymie*, *Isadore*.

Farbman (199) Jewish (eastern Ashkenazic): occupational name for a dyer, from Yiddish *farb* 'dye' + *man* 'man'. Compare FARBER.

GIVEN NAMES Jewish 9%; Russian 4%. *Sol* (3), *Izak*; *Leonid*, *Lev*, *Motya*, *Vladimir*.

Fare (154) **1.** Italian (**Faré**): Lombard variant of FERRARI. **2.** English: topographic name for a dweller by the roadside, Middle English *fare* (Old English *fær*). **3.** English: variant spelling of FAIR.

Farella (143) Italian: from a pet form of the female personal name FARA.

GIVEN NAMES Italian 15%. *Angelo*, *Damiano*, *Rosaria*, *Vito*.

Fares (241) **1.** Muslim: from a personal name based on Arabic *fāris* 'horseman', 'knight'. **2.** English: variant spelling of FAIRES.

GIVEN NAMES Muslim 40%. *Nabil* (6), *Mohamad* (2), *Nafez* (2), *Nagib* (2), *Onsi* (2), *Ramzi* (2), *Sameer* (2), *Samir* (2), *Abdelkader*, *Abdulaziz*, *Ali*, *Amer*.

Farese (260) Italian: topographic or habitational name from an adjectival form of FARO.

GIVEN NAMES Italian 26%. *Carmine* (5), *Sabino* (4), *Biagio* (2), *Domenic* (2), *Agostino*, *Alberto*, *Antonio*, *Elio*, *Francesca*, *Genaro*, *Marco*, *Romeo*, *Vito*.

Farewell (159) English: **1.** variant of FARWELL. **2.** according to Reaney the name 'appears frequently in Suffolk from 1275 to 1417, always without a preposition, and is, no doubt, a phrase name, *Fare well!*'.

Farfan (299) Spanish: **1.** probably from *farfán*, a term denoting one of a group of Spaniards who went to Morocco in the 8th century; there they retained their Christian faith and in 1390 their descendants returned to Spain. **2.** in some cases, a habitational name from Farfán in Granada.

GIVEN NAMES Spanish 49%. *Jose* (7), *Carlos* (6), *Jorge* (5), *Francisco* (4), *Raul* (4), *Eduardo* (3), *Luis* (3), *Mauricio* (3), *Miguel* (3), *Alfredo* (2), *Armando* (2), *Cesar* (2); *Fausto* (3), *Marco* (2), *Dino*, *Romeo*.

Fargason (121) Variant of Scottish FERGUSON.

Fargnoli (192) Italian: probably a topographic name from old Italian *fargna* a species of oak (from Latin *farnus* 'ash').

GIVEN NAMES Italian 21%. *Angelo* (2), *Enrico* (2), *Gaetano* (2), *Alessandro*, *Antonio*, *Dante*, *Domenico*, *Italo*, *Salvatore*, *Silvio*, *Sylvio*, *Tommaso*.

Fargo (809) See VARGO.

FOREBEARS This name is said to have been brought from Wales to America in about 1670 and established in CT. At this time, however, surnames were not generally in use in Wales. William Fargo (1818–81), who, with Henry Wells, founded the Wells Fargo express company in 1844, was a member of this family, born in New York.

Farha (210) Muslim: from a personal name based on Arabic *farḥa* 'joy', 'glad tidings'. Compare FARAH.

GIVEN NAMES Muslim 16%. *Ayham* (3), *Maen* (2), *Samer* (2), *Abdel*, *Abdul*, *Aisha*, *Amjad*, *Fayez*, *Hassan*, *Ihsan*, *Issa*, *Jamal*.

Farhat (379) Muslim: from a personal name based on Arabic *farḥāt* 'joys', plural of Arabic *faraḥ* 'happiness', 'joy' (see FARAH), or from Persian *faerhaet* 'grandeur', 'splendor', 'status'. In Persian literature, Farhād is the name of a stonemason who rivals King Khusrau for the love of the Armenian princess Shīrīn.

GIVEN NAMES Muslim 46%; French 4%. *Ali* (7), *Jamal* (4), *Mohamad* (4), *Ahmad* (3), *Hassan* (3), *Issam* (3), *Jamil* (3), *Mohamed* (3), *Said* (3), *Samir* (3), *Bassam* (2), *Fadi* (2); *Camille* (2), *Michel* (2), *Andre*, *Antoine*.

Faria (1464) **1.** Portuguese: habitational name from either of two places called Faria, in Braga and Aveiro. **2.** Southern Italian (Sicily): topographic name from Greek *pharias*, a derivative of *pharos* 'beacon', 'lighthouse'.

GIVEN NAMES Spanish 20%; Portuguese 12%. *Manuel* (63), *Jose* (32), *Carlos* (9), *Luis* (9), *Alberto* (5), *Mario* (5), *Fernando* (4), *Fernanda* (3), *Jaime* (3), *Juan* (3), *Celestino* (2), *Dulce* (2); *Joao* (4), *Joaquim* (2), *Vasco* (2), *Agostinho*, *Almir*, *Henrique*, *Ligia*, *Lourenco*, *Paulo*, *Sebastiao*, *Serafim*.

Farias (1665) **1.** Portuguese (and Spanish): apparently a plural form of FARIA. **2.** Southern Italian: topographic name from Greek *pharias*, a derivative of *pharos* 'beacon', 'lighthouse'.

GIVEN NAMES Spanish 45%; Portuguese 9%. *Jose* (31), *Manuel* (26), *Juan* (22), *Jesus* (19), *Carlos* (12), *Pedro* (11), *Francisco* (9), *Jorge* (9), *Roberto* (9), *Jose Luis* (8), *Luis* (8), *Raul* (8); *Joao* (4), *Messias* (2), *Joaquim*, *Paulo*, *Serafim*.

Farid (135) Muslim: from a personal name based on Arabic *farīd* 'unique', 'matchless'.

GIVEN NAMES Muslim 78%. *Farid* (5), *Mohammad* (4), *Hisham* (3), *Ali* (2), *Hani* (2), *Mohamad* (2), *Samir* (2), *Abbas*, *Abdullah*, *Abid*, *Ahmad*, *Ahmed*.

Fariello (174) Italian: probably from a reduced form of the personal name *Cristofariello*, a pet form of CRISTOFARO.

GIVEN NAMES Italian 11%. *Angelo*, *Gabriele*, *Guido*, *Rocco*.

Faries (433) English: probably an altered form of Irish or Scottish FERRIS, or of English FARRAR.

Farin (110) **1.** Swedish (common in Finland): ornamental name formed with the common surname suffix *-in* and an unexplained first element. **2.** German:

unexplained. **3.** English: unexplained. **4.** Spanish (**Farín**): unexplained.

GIVEN NAMES Spanish 14%; Italian 6%; German 4%. *Alberto, Alfonso, Dominador, Florendo, Jose, Mercedes, Nestor, Rey, Romulo, Vicente*; *Antonio* (2), *Federico*; *Ingo.*

Farina (1933) **1.** Italian: from *farina* 'wheat flour' (Latin *farina*), a metonymic occupational name for a miller or flour merchant. In some cases it may also have been a nickname for someone with a pale complexion. **2.** Galician and Asturian-Leonese (**Fariña**): from Galician and Asturian-Leonese *fariña* 'wheat flour' (Latin *farina*; compare 1). **3.** possibly also Catalan: from *farina* 'flour' (from Latin *farina*; compare 1).

Farinacci (216) Italian: from a derivative of FARINA.

GIVEN NAMES Italian 16%. *Domenic* (3), *Angelo* (2), *Salvatore* (2), *Dino, Gino, Reno, Rosaria.*

Farinas (237) From the plural of FARINA, probably applied as a metonymic occupational name for a flour dealer.

GIVEN NAMES Spanish 49%; Italian 7%. *Manuel* (5), *Jesus* (4), *Jose* (4), *Luis* (4), *Alberto* (3), *Benito* (3), *Guillermo* (3), *Juan* (3), *Orlando* (3), *Pedro* (3), *Segundo* (3), *Vicente* (3), *Enrico* (3), *Antonella, Antonio, Cecilio, Federico, Lucio, Saturnina.*

Farinella (307) Italian: from a diminutive of FARINA.

GIVEN NAMES Italian 14%. *Alfonso* (2), *Carmelo* (2), *Elia* (2), *Salvatore* (2), *Adriano, Antonino, Luigina, Mario.*

Farinelli (168) Italian: patronymic or plural form of FARINELLA.

GIVEN NAMES Italian 8%. *Angelo* (2), *Giancarlo, Gino, Mauro, Reno.*

Farinha (104) Portuguese: from *farinha* 'wheat flour' (see FARINA).

GIVEN NAMES Spanish 18%. *Jose* (3), *Manuel* (2), *Pedro* (2), *Carlos, Fernando, Joaquin, Lourdes, Luis, Mario.*

Farino (283) Italian: probably from a reduced pet form of the personal name CRISTOFARO, or alternatively a topographic name from a diminutive of *faro* 'beacon', 'lighthouse'.

GIVEN NAMES Italian 10%. *Angelo, Carmine, Fiore, Salvatore, Vito.*

Faris (1963) **1.** Variant of Irish and Scottish FERRIS. **2.** Muslim: from a personal name based on Arabic *fāris* 'horseman', 'knight'. Compare FARES.

Farish (499) Variant of Irish or Scottish FARRISH.

Fariss (375) Variant of Irish and Scottish FERRIS.

Farkas (2637) **1.** Hungarian: from the old secular personal name (later also ecclesiastical name) *Farkas.* **2.** Hungarian: nickname from *farkas* 'wolf'. **3.** Slovenian, Czech, and Slovak (**Farkaš**): nickname from Old Slavic *farkaš* 'wolf', a word of Hungarian origin. **4.** Jewish (from Hun-

gary): translation of the Yiddish personal name *Volf* meaning 'wolf', or else an ornamental adoption of the Hungarian word.

GIVEN NAMES Hungarian 7%; Jewish 5%. *Laszlo* (10), *Tibor* (8), *Attila* (6), *Sandor* (6), *Zoltan* (6), *Gabor* (4), *Geza* (4), *Janos* (4), *Istvan* (3), *Miklos* (3), *Bela* (2), *Csaba* (2); *Arie* (16), *Chaim* (5), *Moshe* (4), *Liat* (2), *Mayer* (2), *Zev* (2), *Ari, Asher, Eliezer, Faigy, Fishel, Mendel.*

Farland (349) Scottish and northern Irish: reduced form of MCFARLAND.

GIVEN NAMES French 6%. *Armand* (2), *Julien* (2), *Alphee, Monique, Normand.*

Farlee (133) Variant spelling of English or Irish FARLEY.

Farleigh (108) English: habitational name from any of various places named Farleigh, of which there are examples in Hampshire, Kent, Somerset, Surrey, and Wiltshire, from Old English as *fearn* 'fern' + *lēah* 'woodland clearing'. See also FARLEY, FAIRLEY, FAIRLIE.

Farler (192) Americanized form of German PFAHLER.

Farless (253) English (formerly common in Kent): unexplained. This name seems to have died out in Britain.

Farley (13511) **1.** English: habitational name from any of various places named Farley, of which there are examples in Berkshire, Derbyshire, Hampshire, Kent, Somerset, and Staffordshire, from Old English as *fearn* 'fern' + *lēah* 'woodland clearing'. See also FARLEIGH, FAIRLEY, FAIRLIE. **2.** Irish: reduced Anglicized form of Gaelic *Ó Fearghaile* (see FARRELLY).

Farling (152) Perhaps a variant of Scottish and northern Irish FARLAND.

Farlow (1135) English: habitational name from a place in Shropshire, so named from Old English *fearn* 'fern' + *hlāw* 'hill', 'tumulus'.

Farm (200) Scottish and English: possibly a metonymic occupational name for a tax farmer, from Middle English *ferme* 'fixed yearly amount payable as tax, rent, or the like' (see FARMER). The English word *farm* did not come to mean 'farmhouse' or 'cultivated land' until the 16th century. Compare FARMER.

Farman (203) **1.** English and French: from an Old Norse personal name, *Farmaðr*, denoting a seafarer or traveling merchant. **2.** English: occupational name for a peddler or itinerant merchant, Middle English *far(e)man*, from an Old Norse word meaning 'traveling man' (see 1). **3.** Muslim: from the Arabic personal name based on *faraman* 'command', 'order', 'decree'. It is also found in compound names such as *Faraman-ullah* 'order of Allah'.

Farmer (23822) **1.** English: occupational name from Middle English, Old French *ferm(i)er* (Late Latin *firmarius*). The term denoted in the first instance a tax farmer, one who undertook the collection of taxes,

revenues, and imposts, paying a fixed (Latin *firmus*) sum for the proceeds, and only secondarily someone who rented land for the purpose of cultivation; it was not applied to an owner of cultivated land before the 17th century. **2.** Irish: Anglicized (part translated) form of Gaelic **Mac an Scolóige** 'son of the husbandman', a rare surname of northern and western Ireland.

Farnam (365) English: variant spelling of FARNHAM.

Farnan (389) Irish: shortened Anglicization of Gaelic **Ó Farannáin** 'descendant of *Forannán*', a personal name possibly based on *forrán* 'attack'. The family bearing this name was connected with the church of Ardstraw in Ulster.

Farnell (419) English: habitational name from any of the many places, such as Farnell (Kent, Wiltshire), Farnhill (West Yorkshire), and Fernhill (Cheshire), named from Old English *fearn* 'fern' + *hyll* 'hill'. In a few cases it may also derive from Farnell in Angus, Scotland, although the surname is not now common in Scotland.

Farnen (107) Irish: variant spelling of FARNAN.

Farner (700) German and Swiss German: habitational name for someone from a place called Farn near Oberkirch, or Fahrnau in Baden. Compare FAHRNER.

Farnes (207) **1.** English: variant of FERN 1. **2.** Norwegian: habitational name from a farm so named, from *far* 'road', 'track' + *nes* 'headland', 'promontory'.

Farney (599) **1.** English and Scottish: of uncertain origin; perhaps a topographic name from Middle English *fern* 'fern' + *heye* 'enclosure', or possibly a habitational name from a minor place so named. Compare FORNEY, FURNEY. **2.** Variant of German FARNER.

Farnham (2009) English: habitational name from any of various places so called. Most, including those in Buckinghamshire, Dorset, Essex, Suffolk, Surrey, and West Yorkshire, are named from Old English *fearn* 'fern' + *hām* 'homestead' or *hamm* 'enclosure hemmed in by water'.

Farnsley (126) English: of uncertain origin. It is probably a habitational name; there is a Farnsley Farm in Derbyshire, or it could perhaps be from any of three places in Yorkshire named Farnley, named in Old English with *fearn* 'fern' + *lēah* 'woodland clearing'. The surname seems to have died out in England.

Farnsworth (4430) English: variant of FARNWORTH.

Farnum (847) English: variant spelling of FARNHAM.

Farnworth (256) English: habitational name from either of two places, one formerly in Lancashire, now in Greater Manchester; the other in Cheshire, both so named from Old English as *fearn* 'fern' + *worð* 'enclosure'.

Faro (414) **1.** Italian (Sicily and Calabria) and Portuguese: topographic name from *faro* 'beacon', 'lighthouse' (Greek *pharos*), or a habitational name from any of several places named with this word. Compare ALFARO and HARO. **2.** English: variant of FARROW.
GIVEN NAMES Italian 12%. *Alfio* (5), *Angelo* (3), *Annamarie* (2), *Domenic* (2), *Salvatore* (2), *Santo* (2), *Amedeo, Concetta, Gaetano, Marco*.

Faron (234) French: from an inflected form of *Faro*, a personal name of Germanic origin.
GIVEN NAMES French 4%. *Andre, Colette*.

Farone (229) Italian: probably a derivative of FARO.
GIVEN NAMES Italian 8%. *Angelo, Gino*.

Farooq (173) Muslim: from a personal name based on Arabic *fārūq* 'distinguisher', i.e. 'one who distinguishes truth from falsehood'. *Al-Fārūq* was a byname of 'Umar ibn al-Khaṭṭāb, the second 'rightly guided' khalif (ruled 634–644), renowned for his stern and uncompromising execution of justice.
GIVEN NAMES Muslim 86%. *Mohammad* (17), *Mohammed* (9), *Muhammad* (5), *Tariq* (5), *Arshad* (4), *Khalid* (4), *Omar* (4), *Ghulam* (3), *Sheikh* (3), *Umar* (3), *Zafar* (3), *Abid* (2).

Farooqui (105) Muslim: Arabic family name (**Fārūqī**), denoting someone descended from or associated with someone called FAROOQ, in particular a descendant of the khalif 'Umar.
GIVEN NAMES Muslim 92%. *Mohammed* (7), *Mohammad* (5), *Abdul* (4), *Javed* (3), *Anwar* (2), *Muhammed* (2), *Noman* (2), *Tariq* (2), *Zafar* (2), *Zaheer* (2), *Ali, Arif*.

Farquhar (1184) Scottish (Aberdeenshire): reduced Anglicized form of Gaelic **Mac Fhearchair** 'son of *Fearchar*', a personal name composed of the elements *fear* 'man' + *car* 'loving', 'beloved'.

Farquharson (506) Scottish: patronymic from FARQUHAR.
GIVEN NAME Scottish 4%. *Iain*.

Farr (7217) **1.** English: from Middle English *farre* 'bull', applied as a nickname for a fierce or lusty man or a metonymic occupational name for someone who kept a bull. **2.** German: nickname from Middle High German *varne, var*, with the same meaning as 1.

Farra (276) **1.** English: variant of FARRAR. **2.** Muslim: variant of FARAH.
GIVEN NAMES Muslim 5%; French 4%. *Ammar* (2), *Bassel, Fadi, Fadia, Farid, Hazem, Nabil, Nadim, Salem, Samir, Waseem, Yasser; Henri, Marcel*.

Farragher (144) Manx and Irish: variant of Scottish FARQUHAR.
GIVEN NAME Irish 8%. *Liam*.

Farrah (279) **1.** English: variant of FARRAR. **2.** Muslim: variant of FARAH.

Farrall (130) Irish: variant spelling of FARRELL.

Farran (255) **1.** Catalan: variant of FERRAN. **2.** Irish: variant of FARREN. **3.** English: variant of FARRAND. **4.** Muslim: variant of **Farhan**, from a personal name based on Arabic *farḥān* 'glad', 'happy', an adjectival derivative of *faraḥ* 'joy' (see FARAH).
GIVEN NAMES Muslim 6%. *Ahmed, Bilal, Fatme, Ghada, Haisam, Jamal, Khalil, Mohamad, Mustapha, Ramzi, Randa, Samir*.

Farrand (688) English: **1.** nickname for a person with gray hair or for someone who used to dress in gray, from Old French *ferrant* 'iron-gray' (a derivative of *fer* 'iron'). **2.** from the medieval personal name *Fer(r)ant*, an Old French form of FERDINAND, which came to be associated with the color.

Farrant (132) English: variant of FARRAND.

Farrar (5807) Northern English: occupational name for a smith or worker in iron, from Middle English and Old French *farrour, ferour*, from medieval Latin *ferrator*, an agent derivative of *ferrare* 'to shoe horses', from *ferrum* 'iron', in medieval Latin 'horseshoe'. Compare FERRIER and FARROW.

Farrel (137) Irish: variant spelling of FARRELL.

Farrell (20639) Irish: reduced Anglicized form of Gaelic **Ó Fearghail** 'descendant of *Fearghal*', a personal name composed of the elements *fear* 'man' + *gal* 'valor'.
GIVEN NAMES Irish 5%. *Brendan* (5), *Aileen* (2), *Eamon* (2), *Kieran* (2), *Brigid, Kaitlin, Liam, Niall, Oona, Paddy, Padraic, Patrick Michael*.

Farrelly (583) Irish: reduced Anglicized form of Gaelic **Ó Fearghaile**, from the personal name *Fearghal* ('man of valor'), of which *Fearghaile* is an older genitive form (see FARRELL).
GIVEN NAMES Irish 7%. *Brendan, Clodagh, Fintan, Kieran*.

Farren (1124) **1.** Irish: reduced Anglicized form of Gaelic **Ó Farracháin** 'descendant of *Farachán*', a personal name perhaps derived from *Ánrothán* (see HANRAHAN) with the addition of an initial *F-*. **2.** Irish: shortened Anglicized form of Gaelic **Ó Fearáin**, from a diminutive of *fear* 'man' or of the personal name *Fearadhach* (see FERRY). **3.** Possibly also English: according to Reaney, a nickname composed of Old English *fæger* 'fair' + *hine* 'servant' or an occupational name from Old English *fearr* 'bull' + *hine*, i.e. 'bull keeper'. **4.** Possibly also German: from Middle High German *var(r)e* '(young) bull', 'steer'.

Farrenkopf (153) German: nickname for a reckless or clumsy man, from Middle High German, Middle Low German *var(r)e* 'steer', 'bullock' + *kopf* 'head'.
GIVEN NAMES German 5%. *Kurt, Markus*.

Farrens (195) Irish: variant of FARREN, with English patronymic *-s*.

Farrer (663) **1.** English: variant spelling of FARRAR. **2.** German: variant of FORER or FAHRER.

Farrey (180) Irish: variant spelling of FARRY.

Farrier (536) English: occupational name for a blacksmith (see FERRIER).

Farrin (159) English and Irish: variant spelling FARREN.

Farringer (105) Americanized form of FAHRINGER.

Farrington (3497) English: habitational name from a place called Farrington. There is one in Somerset, but the surname is associated mainly with Farington, Lancashire. Both are named from Old English *fearn* 'fern' + *tūn* 'settlement'. The surname probably reached America also via Ireland, where it is recorded as early as the 14th century.

Farrior (443) Altered spelling of English FARRIER.

Farris (10373) **1.** Scottish: variant of FERGUS, in which the Gaelic *gh* sound has been dropped rather than being altered to *g*. Compare FARRISH, FERRIS. **2.** Probably also a variant of English FARRAR; the name is quite common in southeast England.

Farrish (317) Scottish and Irish: reduced Anglicized form of Gaelic **Ó Fearghuis** 'descendant of *Fearghus*' (see FERGUS).

Farro (204) **1.** English: variant of FARROW. **2.** Italian: from *farro*, the common name of two varieties of wheat (from Latin *far, farris*), probably applied as a topographic name or a metonymic occupational name for a farmer. **3.** Catalan (**Farró**): probably an occupational name from *ferró* 'smith'.
GIVEN NAMES Italian 12%; Spanish 7%. *Enrico* (2), *Agostino, Angelo, Aurelio, Onorato; Antero, Jesus, Reynaldo, Ruben*.

Farron (107) English and Irish: variant spelling of FARREN.

Farrow (3567) Northern English: hypercorrected form of FARRAR, occupational name for a smith or worker in iron. The original *-ar* or *-er* ending of this name came to be regarded as an error, and was changed to *-ow*.

Farruggia (182) Italian: **1.** nickname from Arabic *farrūj* 'chicken', *farrūja* 'hen'. **2.** (Calabria) nickname from the dialect word *ferruggia* 'staff', 'rod', 'bishop's crosier'.
GIVEN NAMES Italian 22%. *Salvatore* (6), *Sal* (3), *Alfonso, Angelo, Gaetano, Giovanna, Pasquale, Rosario, Salvator, Vittorio*.

Farruggio (105) Italian: variant of FARRUGGIA.
GIVEN NAMES Italian 21%. *Angelo* (2), *Giovanni, Remo, Salvatore, Sarina, Vincenzo*.

Farrugia (240) Italian: variant spelling of FARRUGGIA.
GIVEN NAMES Italian 15%; Spanish 5%. *Salvatore* (4), *Carmel* (3), *Angelo* (2), *Carmelo; Jaime, Luis, Manuel*.

Farry (261) Northern Irish: variant of FERRY.

GIVEN NAMES Irish 4%. *Donal, Liam.*

Farson (257) Northern English: nickname from Middle English *fair* 'fair' + *son* 'son'.

Farstad (106) Swedish: habitational name from a place so named.

GIVEN NAMES Scandinavian 14%. *Lars* (2), *Erik, Johan, Knut, Monrad, Nils.*

Farthing (1206) English: **1.** habitational name from a place named in Old English with *fēorðing* 'fourth (part)', 'quarter', being the fourth part of a larger administrative area. There are fifteen or more minor places with this name in southern England. As a surname, it may also denote someone who paid a farthing in rent, from the same word in the sense 'farthing', 'quarter of a penny'. **2.** from the Old Norse personal name *Farþegn*, composed of the elements *fara* 'to go' + *þegn* 'warrior', 'hero'.

Farve (156) Possibly of French origin, but unexplained; perhaps a metathesized form of FAVRE.

GIVEN NAME French 5%. *Cecile.*

Farver (546) **1.** Danish: occupational name for a dyer, from *farve* 'color'. **2.** Variant of German **Farwer**, a variant of FARBER.

Farwell (1226) English: habitational name from a place in Staffordshire, so named from Old English *fæger* 'pleasant' + *wella* 'spring', 'stream'.

Farwick (100) German: habitational name for someone from a place so named in Oldenburg province.

Fary (122) Variant of Irish FARRY, FERRY.

Fasanella (126) Italian: probably a habitational name from a place so called, or a diminutive of **Fasana**, a habitational name from any of various places in southern Italy with this name. A female personal name *Fasana* is recorded in 957, and it is possible that the surname could have arisen from a diminutive form of this.

GIVEN NAMES Italian 15%. *Domenica, Giacomo, Rocco, Salvatore, Vito.*

Fasano (1065) Italian: **1.** habitational name from Fasano in Brindisi province. **2.** from the personal name *Fasanus*. **3.** possibly from *fasano* 'pheasant', perhaps a nickname for someone thought to resemble the bird.

GIVEN NAMES Italian 16%. *Angelo* (8), *Rocco* (5), *Carmine* (4), *Domenic* (4), *Gennaro* (4), *Pasquale* (4), *Salvatore* (4), *Antonio* (2), *Attilio* (2), *Dante* (2), *Luciano* (2), *Vincenzo* (2).

Fasbender (179) Americanized spelling of German FASSBENDER.

Fasching (265) South German and Austrian: from Middle High German *vaschanc* 'Shrovetide carnival', possibly a nickname for an exuberant, high-spirited person or for someone born between the end of Christmas and the start of Lent.

Fasciano (168) Italian: from a dialect variant of *fagiano* 'pheasant', possibly applied as a nickname for someone thought to resemble the bird.

GIVEN NAMES Italian 11%. *Salvatore* (4), *Angelo, Cosmo.*

Fasel (121) German and Swiss German: **1.** from Middle High German, Middle low German *vasel* 'young male breeding animal' or 'brood', 'offspring', probably applied as a nickname for a man with a large family or a derisive nickname for a worthless person. **2.** from a form of the personal name *Gervasius* (see GERVAIS).

Fash (119) Respelling of German **Fasch**: **1.** in Westphalia, a nickname for a lively person, from Low German *fasch, fersk*. **2.** in southern Germany, possibly a metonymic occupational name, from Middle High German *fasch(e)* 'band', 'bandage', or a nickname for a soft, weak person.

Fasick (197) Altered spelling of German **Fäseke** or **Feseke**, a metonymic occupational name for a grain farmer or miller, or a nickname for a small and delicate person or for a person of no account from Middle Low German *väseke(n)* 'grain husk', 'chaff', 'fiber', 'little thing' or central German *fasig* 'small and delicate'.

Fasig (165) Variant of German **Fäseke** or **Feseke** (see FASICK).

Faske (108) **1.** Variant of German **Fäseke** (see FASICK). **2.** spelling variant of **Vaske**, a short form of the medieval personal name *Servatius*.

Fasnacht (434) South German and Swiss German: from *Fastnacht* 'Shrovetide carnival', 'Shrove Tuesday' (literally 'fast eve'); probably, like FASCHING, it was a nickname for a lively, exuberant person or someone born between Christmas and Lent, in particular on Shrove Tuesday.

Faso (233) Southern Italian: **1.** nickname from a Sicilian modification of *falso* 'false', 'untrue', 'erroneous', also 'untruth', 'falsehood'. **2.** from a short form of the personal name *Bonifasio* (see BONIFACIO).

GIVEN NAMES Italian 13%. *Salvatore* (3), *Angelo* (2), *Calogero, Filippo, Giovanni.*

Fasold (130) German: from a popular medieval personal name *Fasolt, Fasold*, presumably derived from *Wasu* (the name of a Germanic deity) + the name suffix *-olt*.

GIVEN NAMES German 9%. *Ewald, Franz, Jurgen, Ulrich.*

Fasolino (108) Southern Italian: from a diminutive of FASOLO.

GIVEN NAMES Italian 17%. *Angelo* (2), *Achille, Alfonse, Mario, Silvio.*

Fasolo (100) Italian: from a diminutive of FASO.

GIVEN NAMES Italian 15%. *Aurelio, Carlo, Guido, Luciano, Nicola.*

Fason (188) English: variant of FAISON.

Fasone (149) Italian: possibly an augmentative form of FASO.

GIVEN NAMES Italian 18%. *Rosario* (2), *Santa* (2), *Giuseppe, Natale, Pasquale, Sal.*

Fass (524) **1.** German and Jewish (Ashkenazic): from Middle High German *faz*, German *Fass* 'cask', 'keg', hence a metonymic occupational name for a maker or seller of casks and kegs, or a nickname for someone as rotund as a barrel. **2.** German: variant of FASSE, FAAS.

GIVEN NAMES Jewish 6%. *Shimon* (2), *Aron, Hyman, Malca, Meyer, Shira, Sol, Yehudis.*

Fassbender (315) German: occupational name for a cooper, (standard German *Fassbinder*) from Middle High German *faz* 'cask', 'barrel' + *binder* 'joiner'. This is a term used in northern Germany; terms used in other German-speaking regions are *Böttcher, Büttner, Küfer*, and *Schäffler*.

GIVEN NAMES German 8%. *Franz* (3), *Helmut* (2), *Achim, Friedrich, Guenther, Hans, Kurt, Monika.*

Fasse (138) German: from the personal name *Fass* or *Vass*, a vernacular short form of the Late Latin personal name *Gervasius* (see GERVAIS).

GIVEN NAMES German 10%. *Arno* (2), *Bodo, Fritz, Ingeborg, Kurt.*

Fassel (110) South German: from a dialect diminutive of *Fass* 'cask', 'barrel'; probably a nickname for a short, rotund person, or a habitational name for someone living at a house or tavern distinguished by the sign of a barrel. In some cases it may be an Americanized spelling of **Fässle** or **Fassl**, of like meaning and application.

Fassett (771) English: variant of FAWCETT.

Fassio (125) Italian: variant of FAZIO.

GIVEN NAMES Italian 14%. *Mario* (2), *Silvio* (2), *Angelo, Armando, Dario, Pierino, Tino.*

Fassler (378) German (also **Fässler**): occupational name for a cooper, from Middle High German *vaz, vezzel* 'keg' (a diminutive of *vaz* 'barrel') + the agent suffix *-er*.

Fassnacht (238) Swiss and South German: variant spelling of FASNACHT.

GIVEN NAMES German 5%. *Gerhard, Hans, Kurt.*

Fast (1956) North German: nickname for a reliable steadfast person, or from a short form of any of the various personal names beginning with the element *fast* 'steadfast', 'firm', for example *Fastert*.

Fasullo (116) Italian: diminutive of FASO.

GIVEN NAMES Italian 12%. *Gaetano, Guiseppe, Sal.*

Fasulo (380) Southern Italian: nickname or occupational name from a dialect variant of *fagiolo* 'bean'.

GIVEN NAMES Italian 17%. *Salvatore* (3), *Angelo* (2), *Pasquale* (2), *Rocco* (2), *Benedetto, Carlo, Enzo, Gasper, Gino, Lorenzo, Margherita, Palma.*

Fata (268) **1.** Southern Italian: possibly a variant of *Fato*, a short form of *Bonifato* (see BONIFACIO), but more likely a nickname from *fata*, meaning 'fairy' in standard Italian or 'praying mantis' in Calabrian dialect. **2.** Hungarian (**Fáta**): from the old pagan personal name *Fáta*.

GIVEN NAMES Italian 16%. *Angelo* (5), *Luigi* (3), *Antonio, Domenico, Gino, Giovanni, Lorenzo, Oreste, Salvatore*.

Fate (352) Scottish: reduced form of MCFATE.

Fath (520) South German: **1.** variant of VOGT. **2.** topographic name for someone living near a grass- or moss-covered spot or an enclosure, Middle High German *vate, vade*. **3.** metonymic occupational name for a carpenter who made roof trusses, from *phate* 'roof beam', a derivative of medieval Latin *patena*. **4.** from a cognate of Gothic *faths* 'man', a byname also contained in *Vetter* 'paternal uncle', 'cousin'.

Fatheree (229) Possibly of Irish origin, a shortened Americanized form of **Ó Fiachra**, which is found as **Feigh(e)ry** in Ireland.

Fatica (177) Italian: perhaps a nickname from *fatica* 'hard work'.

GIVEN NAMES Italian 14%. *Domenic* (2), *Antonio, Attilio, Gianni, Liberato, Rinaldo*.

Fatta (123) Italian: from a reduced form of the medieval personal name *Benfatta*.

GIVEN NAMES Italian 20%. *Angelo* (3), *Gasper* (2), *Nicola* (2), *Biagio, Salvatore*.

Fattore (118) Italian: status name from *fattore* 'factor', 'administrator', 'steward'.

GIVEN NAMES Italian 22%. *Alfonse, Carmine, Dino, Elio, Giulio, Guerino, Italo, Renzo, Santo*.

Fatula (168) Origin unidentified.

Fatzinger (224) South German: variant of **Fatzer**, a nickname for a joker, from Middle High German *fatzen* 'to tease', 'make fun of'.

Faubel (155) German: **1.** variant of VAUPEL. **2.** from a pet form of the personal name FABIAN.

Fauber (330) Variant of French FAUBERT.

Faubert (222) French: from a personal name composed of the Germanic elements *falc-* 'falcon' + *berht* 'bright', 'famous'.

FOREBEARS A bearer of the name from Charente is recorded in Lachine, Canada, in 1704.

GIVEN NAMES French 14%. *Alcide, Armand, Emile, Gilles, Henri, Jean-Louis, Laurent, Marcel, Pierre*.

Faubion (473) **1.** French in form, but not found in Tanguay or any other French source. **2.** Possibly an altered spelling of German FABIAN.

Fauble (211) Variant of German FAUBEL.

Faucett (774) English: variant spelling of FAWCETT.

Faucette (615) Possibly a French name, but more probably a Frenchified spelling of English FAWCETT.

Faucheaux (125) Variant spelling of French FAUCHEUX.

GIVEN NAMES French 7%. *Lucien, Prudent*.

Faucher (931) French Canadian form of FAUCHEUX 'mower'.

FOREBEARS A Faucher from Limoges is found in Quebec by 1669.

GIVEN NAMES French 18%. *Andre* (6), *Marcel* (6), *Armand* (3), *Jacques* (3), *Antoine* (2), *Camille* (2), *Evariste* (2), *Fernand* (2), *Germain* (2), *Lucien* (2), *Monique* (2), *Pierre* (2).

Faucheux (197) French: variant of **Faucheur**, an occupational name for a mower, from an agent derivative of Old French *faucher* 'to mow'.

GIVEN NAMES French 11%; Irish 6%. *Emile* (2), *Lucien* (2), *Felicien; Clancy* (2), *James Patrick*.

Fauci (205) Southern Italian: metonymic occupational name for a sickle maker or someone who used a sickle, from Sicilian *fauci* 'sickle'.

GIVEN NAMES Italian 15%. *Salvatore* (3), *Angelo* (2), *Benigna, Carmel, Carmine*.

Faudree (123) French: unexplained.

Fauerbach (116) German: habitational name from any of several places in Hesse, earlier named *Vurbach* 'mud stream'.

GIVEN NAMES German 7%. *Kurt* (2), *Erwin*.

Faughn (277) Welsh: variant of VAUGHAN.

Faughnan (250) Irish: reduced Anglicized form of Gaelic **Ó Fachtnáin** 'descendant of *Fachtnán*', a personal name representing a diminutive of *Fachtna*, an ancient name meaning 'hostile'.

Faught (1197) Americanized spelling of German VOGT.

Faul (893) **1.** Irish or Scottish: reduced form of MCFAUL. **2.** English: variant of FALL 2. **3.** South German: from a byname for a weakling, from Middle High German *vūl, voul* 'frail', 'decayed', 'foul', 'weak'. Later the term took on the meaning 'lazy' and in some cases the surname may have arisen from this sense.

Faulcon (168) Variant spelling of English FALCON.

Faulconer (541) **1.** English: variant spelling of FAULKNER. **2.** Americanized form of the French cognate **Fauconnier** 'falconer'.

Faulds (317) **1.** English: variant of FOLDS. **2.** Scottish: habitational name from any of various places called Faulds, as for example in Ayrshire, Lanarkshire, and Perth.

Faulhaber (590) South German: from Middle High German *vûl, voul* 'weak', 'rotten' + *haber* 'oats', presumably a nickname for a farmer who sold rotten grain or whose crops were infested with an oats fungus.

GIVEN NAMES German 4%. *Fritz* (4), *Hans, Kurt*.

Faulk (3688) Probably an Americanized spelling of FALK.

Faulkenberry (683) Americanized spelling of German FALKENBERG.

Faulkingham (151) English (Yorkshire): evidently a habitational name from an unidentified place, perhaps Falkenham in Suffolk, which is named from an Old English personal name, *Falta* (+ genitive *-n*) + Old English *hām* .

Faulkner (13091) English: occupational name for someone who kept and trained falcons (a common feudal service). Falconry was a tremendously popular sport among the aristocracy in medieval Europe, and most great houses had their falconers. The surname could also have arisen as metonymic occupational name for someone who operated the siege gun known as a *falcon*.

Faulks (332) English: from the Anglo-Norman French personal name *Fau(l)ques* (oblique case *Fau(l)que*), originally a Germanic byname meaning 'falcon'.

Faull (182) **1.** English: variant of FALL. **2.** Variant spelling of German FAUL.

Fauls (104) Scottish: variant of FAULDS.

Faulstich (261) German: nickname for a bad or lazy tailor or shoemaker, from Middle High German *vūl, voul* 'weak', 'lazy' + *stich* 'stitch'.

GIVEN NAMES German 7%. *Elfriede, Gerd, Gerhard, Johann*.

Faunce (586) **1.** English: nickname for a lively person, from Middle English *faun, foun* 'fawn' 'cub', Old French *faon*, or from the same word used as a personal name. **2.** Possibly an Americanized spelling of French **Fonce**, a topographic name for someone living in a hollow.

Fauntleroy (368) English: from Old French *enfant* 'child' + *roi* 'king', denoting a royal prince and, as a surname, a member of a royal prince's household.

Faupel (158) German: variant of FAUBEL.

Fauquier (33) French: probably a variant of northern French **Fauqueur** 'mower' (standard French **Faucheur**; see FAUCHEUX).

FOREBEARS The Fauquier name was introduced to VA by Francis Fauquier (1720–68), an Englishman of Huguenot ancestry, who was appointed lieutenant governor of VA in 1758 and assumed the duties of the governorship when the colony was in the midst of the French and Indian War.

Faure (227) Southern French: occupational name for an ironworker or smith, Old French *fevre* (Latin *faber* 'craftsman'). This surname is associated with Huguenot emigration.

GIVEN NAMES French 16%. *Andre* (3), *Marcel* (2), *Pierre* (2), *Adrien, Eugenie, Jean-Claude, Laurent, Michel, Olivier*.

Faurot (198) French: from a diminutive FAURE.

Faurote (102) Probably a variant of French FAUROT.

Faus (184) German (also **Pfaus**): variant of PFAUTZ, a nickname for a self-important person.

Fauser (225) South German: nickname for a self-important person, from an agent derivative of Middle High German *phūsen* 'to snort or puff (oneself up)'.

GIVEN NAMES German 9%. *Kurt* (3), *Uli* (2), *Fritz, Otto*.

Fausett (423) English: variant spelling of FAWCETT.

Fausey (162) **1.** Possibly an Americanized spelling of Swiss German **Fasi**, from a pet form of *Gervasius* (see GERVAIS). **2.** Altered spelling of Swiss German **Fausi**, a nickname for a prankster.

Fausnaugh (147) Americanized spelling of German FASNACHT.

Fauss (179) Americanized spelling of German *Pfaus*, a variant of PFAUTZ, a nickname for a self-important person, or possibly an altered spelling of FASS.

Faust (6102) **1.** German, Jewish (Ashkenazic), and French (Alsace-Lorraine): from Middle High German *fūst* 'fist', presumably a nickname for a strong or pugnacious person or for someone with a club hand or other deformity of the hand. **2.** German and French (Alsace-Lorraine): from a personal name (Latin *Faustus*, meaning 'fortunate', 'lucky', a derivative of *favere* 'to favor'). This was borne by at least one Christian martyr.

Faustin (127) French: from *Faustin*, a pet form of the personal name FAUST.

GIVEN NAMES French 28%. *Andre* (2), *Pierre* (2), *Felicite, Fresnel, Gaston, Ghislaine, Jean Michel, Joseph Jean, Marcelle, Myrtha, Pierrette, Prosper*.

Faustini (106) Italian: patronymic or plural form of FAUSTINO.

GIVEN NAMES Italian 19%. *Fernando* (2), *Sante* (2), *Sebastiano* (2), *Americo, Armando, Giuseppe, Lino, Livio, Mario, Nicola, Renato*.

Faustino (210) Italian: from a pet form of the personal name FAUSTO.

GIVEN NAMES Italian 16%; Spanish 14%; Portuguese 13%. *Adriano* (3), *Antonio* (3), *Luciano* (2), *Albino, Arnulfo, Benedicto, Benigno, Bernardino, Nicola; Jose* (4), *Abilio* (2), *Francisco* (2), *Luis* (2), *Nicanor* (2), *Carlito; Joaquim* (3), *Joao* (2).

Fausto (141) Italian: from the personal name *Fausto*, Latin *Faustus* 'fortunate', 'lucky', a derivative of *favere* 'favor'. See also FAUST. *Fausto* is quite common today as an Italian personal name, but was not so used until the Renaissance.

GIVEN NAMES Spanish 41%; Italian 9%. *Jose* (4), *Jesus* (3), *Cesar* (2), *Fernando* (2), *Francisca* (2), *Lilia* (2), *Ricardo* (2), *Alfonso, Angelina, Armando, Edmundo, Esteban; Gino* (3), *Oreste, Rocco, Vito*.

Fauteux (194) French: variant of **Faudeux**, dit Bonsecours.

FOREBEARS A bearer of the name from Normandy, France, is documented in Neuville, Quebec, from 1679.

GIVEN NAMES French 35%. *Emile* (2), *Jacques* (2), *Laurier* (2), *Pierre* (2), *Remi*

(2), *Alain, Andre, Armand, Dominique, Edmour, Fernand, Francois*.

Fauth (492) German: occupational name for a steward or bailiff, from a South German dialect form of VOGT.

GIVEN NAMES German 4%. *Otto* (2), *Helmut, Jurgen, Milbert*.

Fauver (519) Americanized spelling of French FAVRE.

Faux (415) **1.** English: variant of FAULKS. **2.** French: probably a metonymic occupational name for a reaper or scythe maker, from *faux* 'scythe'.

Fava (500) Italian, Catalan, and Portuguese: from *fava* 'broad bean', applied as a metonymic occupational name for a grower or seller of broad beans, a nickname for a bean eater, or a topographic name for someone living in an area characterized by the cultivation of this plant.

GIVEN NAMES Italian 16%; Spanish 8%. *Sal* (5), *Rocco* (4), *Carmine* (3), *Mario* (3), *Carlo* (2), *Giovanni* (2), *Amerigo, Angelo, Dante, Dino, Ferdinando, Gino, Italo; Adela, Aura, Esteban, Juan, Juanita, Luis, Mercedes, Otila, Pablo, Rosario*.

Favale (152) Italian: topographic name for someone who lived by a bean field, from Latin *fabalis* 'bean field'.

GIVEN NAMES Italian 25%. *Mario* (3), *Aldo, Alfonso, Alicia, Americo, Cosmo, Dino, Egidio, Fabrizio, Gabriele, Gaetano, Raffaele, Rocco*.

Favaloro (179) Southern Italian: occupational name from Sicilian *favaloru* 'grower or seller of beans', a term also denoting a scrounger.

GIVEN NAMES Italian 15%. *Salvatore* (4), *Cosimo* (2), *Vito* (2), *Caesar, Ercole*.

Favara (118) Southern Italian (Sicily): from Arabic *fawwarah* 'fount', 'spring' (whence Sicilian *favara*), hence a topographic or habitational name from any of numerous places in Sicily named with this word, notably Favara in Agrigento province.

GIVEN NAMES Italian 13%. *Angelo* (2), *Sal, Salvatore, Vito*.

Favaro (130) Italian: **1.** variant of FABBRO, peculiar to the Venice area. **2.** from a derivative of FAVA, denoting a bean grower or seller. **3.** perhaps a nickname for someone who wore brightly colored clothes. Compare Calabrian *favaru* 'multicolored'.

GIVEN NAMES Italian 9%. *Angelo* (2), *Camillo, Ennio*.

Favata (290) Southern Italian: topographic name from Sicilian *favara* 'bean field'.

GIVEN NAMES Italian 14%. *Angelo* (3), *Ricardo* (2), *Rocco* (3), *Alfonso, Antonino, Clemente, Eduardo, Giuseppe, Salvatore, Vito*.

Favazza (193) Southern Italian: from a derogatory derivative of FAVA 'bean'.

GIVEN NAMES Italian 18%. *Salvatore* (4), *Carlo* (3), *Vito* (2), *Francesco, Gaetana, Sarina*.

Favela (500) **1.** Spanish: of uncertain origin; possibly from a Visigothic personal name *Fafila*, or alternatively from a derivative of *faba*, a regional form of *haba* 'broad bean'. Possibly in some instances, it could be based on Portuguese and Galician *fabela* 'small plot'. **2.** Southern Portuguese (also Brazilian): topographic name from *favela* 'slum'.

GIVEN NAMES Spanish 57%. *Juan* (16), *Jose* (14), *Jaime* (8), *Jesus* (7), *Manuel* (7), *Roberto* (5), *Francisco* (4), *Luis* (4), *Alvaro* (3), *Cruz* (3), *Enrique* (3), *Fernando* (3), *Adauto, Catarina*.

Faver (248) Variant of French LEFEVRE.

Favero (331) **1.** Italian: Venetian variant of FABBRO. **2.** Possibly a respelling of French FAVREAU.

GIVEN NAMES Italian 11%. *Domenic* (5), *Franco* (2), *Giovanni* (2), *Nino* (2), *Aldo, Carlo, Gino, Luigi, Romeo, Valentino*.

Favia (168) Italian: possibly, as Caracausi proposes, from the personal name *Fabia*, feminine form of FABIO.

GIVEN NAMES Italian 20%. *Vito* (3), *Giacomo* (2), *Angelo, Donato, Lorenzo, Nicola, Rocco, Salvatore, Saverio*.

Favier (112) French: variant of **Favre**.

GIVEN NAMES French 8%. *Etienne, Jean Jacques, Philippe, Yves*.

Favinger (170) Origin unidentified.

Favor (349) Americanized form of French FAVRE.

Favorite (453) Americanized form of Italian FAVORITO.

Favorito (134) Italian: probably from a personal name, an omen name from *favorito* 'favorite'.

GIVEN NAMES Italian 19%; Spanish 14%. *Angelo, Antonio, Enrico, Francesca, Onofrio; Alfredo* (2), *Delfin* (2), *Manuel* (2), *Alfonso, Mariano, Mario, Sabino*.

Favors (833) Americanized form of French FAVRE.

Favre (478) Southern French and Swiss French: occupational name for a smith or ironworker, Occitan *fevre* (Latin *faber* 'craftsman'). Compare FABER.

GIVEN NAMES French 6%. *Alphonse, Cecile, Chantal, Francoise, Jacques, Julien, Laurent*.

Favreau (716) Southern French: from a diminutive of FAVRE.

FOREBEARS This surname is documented in Contrecoeur, Quebec, in 1668.

GIVEN NAMES French 10%. *Armand* (4), *Andre* (2), *Fernand* (2), *Alain, Arsene, Emile, Gabrielle, Gaetan, Gaston, Jacques, Jean Marie, Jean-Philippe*.

Favret (139) French: diminutive of FAVRE.

GIVEN NAMES French 12%. *Jacques* (3), *Andre, Chantel, Raoul*.

Favro (172) **1.** Italian: Venetian variant of FABBRO. **2.** French: variant of FAVREAU.

GIVEN NAMES Italian 5%. *Aldo, Carlo, Remo, Silvio*.

Faw (530) Americanized spelling of South German PFAU or the variant **Pfoh**, a nickname for someone thought to resemble a peacock in some way, or a habitational name for someone who lived at a house or tavern distinguished by the sign of a peacock.

Fawaz (102) Muslim: from a personal name based on Arabic *fawāz* 'winner of victories'.

GIVEN NAMES Muslim 71%. *Hassan* (6), *Ali* (5), *Hussein* (5), *Ayman* (2), *Fawzi* (2), *Rania* (2), *Ahmad, Ahmed, Bassam, Darwish, Hasan, Hicham.*

Fawbush (247) North American variant of the Scottish name FORBES, which is pronounced as two syllables in Aberdeenshire. Compare FORBUSH.

Fawcett (2584) Northern English: habitational name from Fawcett in Cumbria or Facit in Lancashire, both named from Old English *fāh* '(brightly) colored' + *sīde* 'slope', 'hillside'. A further possible source, Forcett in North Yorkshire, is named from Old English *ford* 'ford' + *set* 'animal fold'.

Fawkes (121) English: variant of FAULKS.

Fawley (483) English: habitational name from any of various places named Fawley, in Berkshire, Buckinghamshire, and Hampshire. The first is probably so named from Old English as *fealu* 'fallow' (probably used in the sense 'fallow deer') + *lēah* 'woodland clearing', while the last two are from either Old English *fealu* 'fallow-colored' or *fealg* 'plowed land' + *lēah*.

Fawver (281) North American variant of French **Fèvre** (see LEFEVRE).

Fax (158) English: in part probably an Americanized spelling of German **Fachse**.

Faxon (331) English: unexplained.

Fay (6145) **1.** English: nickname for a person believed to have supernatural qualities, from Middle English, Old French *faie* 'fairy' (Late Latin *fata* 'fate', 'destiny'). **2.** English: nickname for a trustworthy person, from Middle English, Old French *fei* 'loyalty', 'trust'. **3.** English (of Norman origin) and French: habitational name from any of various places in France named with Old French *faie* 'beech', or a topographic name from someone living by a beech wood. Compare LAFAYETTE. **4.** Irish: variant of FAHEY. **5.** Irish: variant of FEE.

GIVEN NAMES Irish 4%. *Brendan* (9), *John Patrick* (3), *Donovan, Fergus, Kieran, Liam, Nuala.*

Fayad (136) Muslim: from a personal name based on Arabic *fayāḍ* 'generous'.

GIVEN NAMES Muslim 42%; French 4%. *Farid* (3), *Abdalla* (2), *Hassan* (2), *Mohamed* (2), *Salim* (2), *Sami* (2), *Samir* (2), *Walid* (2), *Ahmad, Akram, Amgad, Amira; Michel, Pierre.*

Fayard (372) Southern French: topographic name for someone living by a beech wood, from a derivative of FAY 3.

GIVEN NAMES French 5%. *Emile* (2), *Camille, Cecile, Gaston.*

Faye (480) **1.** English: variant spelling of FAY. **2.** Southern French: variant of FAY 3.

Fayer (146) **1.** Jewish (eastern Ashkenazic): ornamental name from Yiddish *fayer* 'fire' or Yiddishized form of FEUER. **2.** English: variant of FAIR.

GIVEN NAMES Russian 15%; Jewish 6%. *Gennady* (2), *Mikhail* (2), *Alik, Dmitry, Efim, Ganna, Grigoriy, Igor, Savely, Vladimir; Emanuel, Rakhil, Rivka.*

Fayette (221) Southern French: from a diminutive of FAYE.

GIVEN NAME French 4%. *Andre.*

Fayle (105) Manx: variant of MCPHAIL.

Faylor (126) Variant of German FEILER.

Fayne (225) English: nickname from Middle English *fein, fayn, fane* 'glad', 'well disposed' (Old English *fægen*). The word seems also to have been occasionally used as a personal name in the Middle Ages, from which the surname may derive in some instances.

Faz (204) Hispanic (Mexico): unexplained.

GIVEN NAMES Spanish 48%. *Jose* (6), *Jesus*(3), *Juan* (3), *Ramiro* (3), *Roberto* (3), *Adelita* (2), *Alfredo* (2), *Armando* (2), *Carlos* (2), *Domingo* (2), *Ignacio* (2), *Mario* (2); *Antonio* (3), *Eliseo* (2).

Fazekas (595) Hungarian: occupational name for a potter, *fazekas*, from *fazék* 'pot'.

GIVEN NAMES Hungarian 8%. *Laszlo* (3), *Attila* (2), *Imre* (2), *Sandor* (2), *Balazs, Bela, Ferenc, Geza, Istvan, Karoly, Lajos, Tamas.*

Fazel (107) Iranian: from a personal name based on *fazl*, Persian form of Arabic *faḍl* 'favor', 'grace', 'kindness', 'gift'. This name is also found in the Indian subcontinent.

GIVEN NAMES Muslim 46%; Indian 4%. *Ali* (3), *Abbas* (2), *Hassan* (2), *Ahmad, Bahram, Ebrahim, Fahima, Fazel, Foad, Hafizullah, Karim, Magid; Bahadur, Navin.*

Fazenbaker (318) Americanized spelling of South German **Fesenbecker**, an occupational nickname for a baker who used mainly spelt or who sold bread full of husks, Middle High German, Middle Low German *vese* 'chaff', 'husk', 'spelt' + *becker* 'baker'.

Fazio (2708) Italian: from the personal name *Fazio*, a short form of *Bonifazio* (see BONIFACIO).

GIVEN NAMES Italian 16%. *Salvatore* (21), *Angelo* (14), *Antonio* (8), *Carlo* (7), *Domenic* (6), *Nunzio* (6), *Rocco* (5), *Natale* (4), *Pasquale* (4), *Sal* (4), *Filippo* (3), *Ignazio* (3).

Fazzari (124) Italian: according to Caracausi, from an Arabic name, *al-Fazārī*.

GIVEN NAMES Italian 22%. *Antonio* (2), *Franco* (2), *Mario* (2), *Angelo, Pasquale, Rocco, Salvatore, Saverio.*

Fazzi (105) Italian: variant of FAZIO.

GIVEN NAMES Italian 6%. *Aldo, Alessandro.*

Fazzina (100) Italian: variant (feminine form) of FAZZINO.

GIVEN NAMES Italian 23%. *Carmelo* (3), *Antonio, Gaetana, Massimo, Nino, Sebastiano.*

Fazzini (137) Italian: patronymic or plural form of FAZZINO.

GIVEN NAMES Italian 7%. *Amilcare, Enrico, Siro.*

Fazzino (312) Italian: from a pet form of the personal name FAZIO.

GIVEN NAMES Italian 29%. *Salvatore* (10), *Sal* (3), *Angelo* (2), *Antonio, Benito, Carlo, Carmelo, Gaetano, Giovanni, Matteo, Salvator, Sebastiano, Umberto.*

Fazzio (280) Italian: variant of FAZIO.

GIVEN NAMES Italian 10%. *Carlo* (2), *Carmel, Massimo, Nunzio, Silvio.*

Fazzolari (107) Italian: from Old Italian *fazzulo* 'kerchief', from Late Latin *faciolum*, probably a nickname for someone who habitually wore a kerchief, or an occupational name for someone who made kerchiefs.

GIVEN NAMES Italian 44%. *Salvatore* (5), *Rocco* (2), *Carina, Carlo, Carmela, Carmine, Domenico, Giovanni, Giuseppe, Pasquale, Sandro, Saverio.*

Fazzone (137) Italian: from an augmentative of the personal name FAZIO.

GIVEN NAME Italian 8%. *Salvatore.*

Feagan (278) Irish: variant spelling of FAGAN.

Feagans (248) Irish: variant of FAGAN, with English patronymic -*s*.

Feagin (752) Irish: variant spelling of FAGAN.

Feagins (269) Irish: variant of FAGAN, with English patronymic -*s*.

Feagle (152) Americanized spelling of German FIEGEL.

Feagley (115) Americanized form of German **Fiegele** (see FIEGEL) or, more likely, of **Vögele, Vögeli** (see [VOGEL]).

Fealy (117) Irish: variant spelling of FEELEY.

GIVEN NAME Irish 8%. *Eamon.*

Feamster (110) English and Scottish: variant spelling of FEEMSTER.

Fear (678) English: **1.** nickname for a sociable person, from Middle English *fe(a)re* 'comrade', 'companion' (Old English *(ge)fēra*). **2.** nickname for a proud or haughty person, from Middle English *fere* 'proud' (Old French *fier*).

Fearing (441) **1.** English: habitational name from Feering, a village in Essex, named from the Old English personal name *Fēra* + -*ingas* 'people of', i.e. '(settlement of) Fēra's people'. **2.** Americanized spelling of German **Viering**, a topographic name for someone from a swampy area, from a derivative of Germanic *vir* 'bog', 'swamp', or a variant of FEHRING 2.

Fearn (429) English: variant spelling of FERN 1.

Fearnley (110) English (Yorkshire): variant of FARLEY.

Fearnow (201) Americanized spelling of German FERNAU or of **Virnau** (also **Viernow**), habitational name from Viernau in Thuringia.

Fearon (596) English (of Norman origin): occupational name for a blacksmith or worker in iron, from Old French *ferron* 'blacksmith', Latin *ferro*, genitive *ferrōnis*, a derivative of *ferrum* 'iron'. Compare FERRO.
GIVEN NAMES Irish 4%. *Brendan, Eamon.*

Fearrington (141) Perhaps an altered spelling of FARRINGTON.

Fears (1401) English: patronymic from FEAR.

Feasel (382) Americanized spelling of South German **Fiesel**, a nickname for a womanizer, from Middle High German *visel* 'penis'.

Feaster (1327) Americanized spelling of German PFISTER, occupational name for a baker. Compare FISTER.

Feather (998) **1.** English: from Middle English *fether* 'feather', applied as a metonymic occupational name for a trader in feathers and down, a maker of quilts, or possibly a maker of pens. Feathermongers are recorded from the 13th century onwards. In some cases the surname may have arisen from a nickname denoting a very light person or perhaps a person of no account. **2.** Americanized form of German FEDER.

Featherly (145) Americanized form of German FEDERLE.

Featherman (103) Americanized form of German **Federmann** (see FEDERMAN).
GIVEN NAME German 4%. *Dieter.*

Feathers (940) **1.** English: variant of FEATHER. **2.** Americanized form of German FEDER.

Featherston (1109) English: variant of FEATHERSTONE.

Featherstone (1014) Northern English: habitational name from places in Staffordshire, West Yorkshire, and Northumberland, which are so called from Old English *feðerstān* 'tetralith', a prehistoric structure consisting of three upright stones capped with a headstone (from Old English *fe(o)ðer-* 'four' + *stān* 'stone').

Feazel (188) German: variant spelling of FEASEL.
GIVEN NAME German 4%. *Kurt* (2).

Feazell (378) German: variant spelling of FEASEL.

Febles (185) Spanish: possibly a nickname from *feble* 'feeble', 'weak', though the reason for the plural form is not clear.
GIVEN NAMES Spanish 49%. *Carlos* (4), *Roberto* (4), *Jose* (3), *Juan* (3), *Mercedes* (3), *Abundio* (2), *Alberto* (2), *Eduardo* (2), *Gregorio* (2), *Juana* (2), *Luis* (2), *Manuel* (2).

Febo (110) **1.** Spanish: habitational name from Febo in the autonomous region of Valencia. **2.** Italian: from the personal name *Febo*, from Latin *Phoebus*, Greek *Phoibos*, name of the sun god.
GIVEN NAMES Spanish 25%; Italian 21%. *Jose* (3), *Ramon* (2), *Raul* (2), *Wilfredo* (2), *Alicia, Angel, Beatriz, Edgardo, Jose Angel; Aida, Angelo, Aurelio, Cosmo, Ernesto, Gabriele, Giuseppe, Guido, Salvatore.*

Febus (161) Spanish: unexplained.
GIVEN NAMES Spanish 21%. *Jose* (4), *Ana* (2), *Felipe* (2), *Marta* (2), *Amalia, Carlos, Crucita, Ernesto, Fernando, Gilberto, Juan, Juana.*

Fecher (210) German: occupational name for a surveyor of fish pens, from a noun derivative of Middle High German *vach* 'compartment', 'division', in fishing, an area of water penned off with logs.

Fechner (339) German: **1.** patronymic from a dialect variant of WENZEL. **2.** occupational name for a furrier, from Middle High German *vēch* 'colorful (fur)'.
GIVEN NAMES German 9%; Scandinavian 4%. *Manfred* (2), *Egon, Erhard, Erwin, Gehard, Jurgen, Klaus, Ulrich, Wolfram; Knud* (2), *Erik, Jarl.*

Fecht (279) German: topographic name from various river and moorland names in North Germany and the Netherlands containing the element *fecht*.

Fechter (438) South German: occupational name for a professional fencer or duelist, from Middle High German *vehten* 'to fence'. This may have denoted someone who fought for public entertainment at fairgrounds and markets.
GIVEN NAMES German 4%. *Alois* (3), *Kurt* (2), *Gunter, Hildegarde.*

Feck (164) North German: from a short form of the Frisian personal name *Feddeke*, a pet form of *Fre(de)rik* (see FRIEDERICH). Compare FICK.

Fecko (117) **1.** Slovak (also **Fečko**): from a pet form of the personal name FEDOR. **2.** Altered spelling of Polish **Feczko**, **Fiecko**, or **Fiećko**, cognates of 1.

Fecteau (697) French Canadian: altered spelling of **Filteau** or **Feuilleteau**, diminutives of **Feuillet**, which is itself a diminutive of **Feuille**, meaning 'leaf,' with a wide variety of applications that make the semantic identification doubtful.
GIVEN NAMES French 15%. *Armand* (4), *Andre* (3), *Gilles* (3), *Lucien* (3), *Emile* (2), *Viateur* (2), *Anatole, Armande, Aurel, Cecile, Clovis, Gaston.*

Fedak (409) **1.** Polish: from a derivative of the personal name FEDOR. **2.** Ukrainian and Slovak (**Fedák**): from a pet form of the personal name FEDOR.

Fedde (116) German (Frisian): from a short form of *Feddercke*, Frisian form of the personal name FRIEDRICH.
GIVEN NAMES German 8%. *Hans, Otto, Uwe.*

Fedder (300) **1.** English: variant of FEATHER. **2.** North German, Dutch, and Danish: from the Frisian personal name *Vetter*, meaning 'relative'. Relationship terms were commonly used as personal names in Friesland.

Fedders (140) North German and Danish: variant of FEDDERSEN.
GIVEN NAMES Dutch 4%. *Gerrit* (2), *Marinus.*

Feddersen (414) North German, Dutch, and Danish: Frisian patronymic from FEDDER 2.
GIVEN NAMES German 5%. *Kurt* (2), *Hans, Lauritz, Reinhard, Uwe.*

Fede (132) Italian: **1.** from the female personal name *Fede*, from Latin *fides* 'faith'. **2.** reduced form of the personal name FEDERICO. **3.** short form of the medieval personal name *Bonafede*, an omen name meaning 'good faith'.
GIVEN NAMES Italian 20%; French 7%. *Bartolo, Croce, Dante, Domenico, Giorgio, Luigi, Pietro, Salvatore, Vincenzo, Vito; Guerline, Jean Marie.*

Fedele (687) Italian: from the personal name *Fedele*, a continuation of the Latin personal name *Fidelis*, meaning 'of the faith' (from *fides* 'faith'), which was adopted in Christian circles.
GIVEN NAMES Italian 18%. *Salvatore* (9), *Cosmo* (5), *Angelo* (3), *Antonino* (2), *Gennaro* (2), *Nicolina* (2), *Sal* (2), *Biagio, Carmela, Franco, Nunzio.*

Fedeli (158) Italian: patronymic or plural form of FEDELE.
GIVEN NAMES Italian 25%. *Umberto* (4), *Gino* (2), *Aldo, Amedeo, Amerigo, Dante, Guido, Nunzio, Paolo, Settimio.*

Feder (1403) German and Jewish (Ashkenazic): metonymic occupational name for a trader in feathers (see FEATHER) or in quill pens, from Middle High German *veder(e)*, German *Feder* 'feather', 'quill', 'pen'.
GIVEN NAMES Jewish 9%. *Sol* (5), *Hyman* (4), *Moshe* (4), *Baruch* (3), *Aron* (2), *Chaim* (2), *Meyer* (2), *Miriam* (2), *Zev* (2), *Arie, Aryeh, Avi.*

Federer (329) German, Swiss, and Jewish (Ashkenazic): occupational name for a trader in feathers or quill pens, or an upholsterer, from FEDER + agent suffix *-er*.

Federici (437) Italian: patronymic or plural form of FEDERICO.
GIVEN NAMES Italian 28%. *Mario* (4), *Gino* (3), *Ovidio* (3), *Benigno* (2), *Italo* (2), *Vito* (2), *Aldo, Americo, Angelo, Dario, Domenico, Francesco, Gaetano, Herculano, Luigi, Nicola, Ricci, Silvia, Valerio.*

Federico (1585) Italian: from the personal name *Federico*, Italian equivalent of FRIEDERICH.
GIVEN NAMES Italian 22%; Spanish 9%. *Domenic* (8), *Antonio* (6), *Guerino* (6), *Armando* (5), *Salvatore* (5), *Domenico* (4), *Gino* (4), *Mario* (4), *Nino* (4), *Sal* (4), *Carmine* (3), *Guido* (3), *Alfredo* (2), *Angelo* (2), *Benito* (2), *Carmela* (2); *Jose*

(5), *Ruben* (4), *Carlos* (3), *Jesus* (3), *Rosario* (3), *Enrique* (2), *Francisco* (2), *Juan* (2).

Federle (165) South German: from a diminutive of FEDER.
GIVEN NAMES German 5%. *Helmut, Ingo*.

Federline (115) Americanized form of German **Federlein**, from a diminutive of FEDER.

Federman (463) German (**Federmann**) and Jewish (Ashkenazic): occupational name for a trader in feathers or quill pens, or an upholsterer, from FEDER + -*man* 'man'.
GIVEN NAMES Jewish 5%. *Hyman* (2), *Isak, Zahava*.

Federoff (124) **1.** Russian: alternative spelling of **Fedorov**, a patronymic from the personal name *Fedor* (see THEODORE). **2.** Alternatively, it could be an Americanized form of Jewish (from Ukraine) *Fedorovsky*, a habitational name from any of the villages in Ukraine named Fedorovka.

Federowicz (111) Altered spelling of Polish **Fedorowicz** or **Fiederowicz**, patronymics from FEDOR.

Federspiel (292) South German and Swiss German: metonymic occupational name for a falconer, from Middle High German *vederspil* 'bird of prey (trained for hunting)'.

Fedewa (308) Origin unidentified.

Fedie (166) Probably a respelling of French **Fedit**, **Fedi**, or **Fedy**, variants of **Faidit**, from the past participle of *faidir* 'to outlaw', 'to treat as an enemy', hence a nickname for an exile or outcast.

Fedler (170) North German: variant of FIEDLER.

Fedor (1064) Slovak, Ukrainian, and Polish: from the personal name *Fedor*, Greek *Theodōros* 'gift of God' (see THEODORE).

Fedora (200) Ukrainian: from the female personal name *Fedora*, Ukrainian form of *Theodora*. See also THEODORE.

Fedorchak (251) Ukrainian and Slovak (**Fedorčak**): from a pet form of the personal name FEDOR.

Fedorka (147) Ukrainian: from a pet form of the personal name *Fedor* (see THEODORE).

Fedorko (260) Ukrainian and Slovak: from a pet form of the personal name *Fedor* (see THEODORE).

Fedorowicz (106) Polish: patronymic from the personal name *Fedor* (see THEODORE).
GIVEN NAMES Polish 7%. *Genowefa, Wasyl, Zofia*.

Fedrick (245) Irish: variant of PATRICK, from Gaelic **Mac Phádraig**, *Ph*- being the lenited form of *P*- used after *mac* 'son of'.

Fee (2431) Irish: reduced form of **O'Fee**, Anglicized form of Gaelic **Ó Fiaich** 'descendant of *Fiach*', a byname meaning 'raven'. This name has sometimes been mistranslated as *Hunt* as a result of confu-

sion with *fiach*, the modern spelling of *fiadhach* 'hunt'.

Feeback (194) Americanized form of Silesian **Fieback**, a variant of FIEBIG, or North German **Viebeck**, which may be a topographic name from Middle Low German *vi(he)* 'swamp', 'moor' + *be(c)k* 'stream', or a habitational name from Viehbach in the south.

Feehan (686) Irish: reduced Anglicized form of Gaelic **Ó Fiacháin** or **Ó Feichín**, a name meaning 'little raven', from a diminutive of *fiach*.
GIVEN NAMES Irish 6%. *Brendan, Colm, Declan*.

Feeler (173) Possibly an Americanized spelling of German VIELE.

Feeley (1699) Irish: **1.** reduced Anglicized form of Gaelic **Ó Fithcheallaigh** 'descendant of *Fithcheallach*', a byname meaning 'chess player'. See also MCFEELEY. **2.** reduced Anglicized form of Gaelic **Ó Fáilbhe** (see FALVEY).
GIVEN NAMES Irish 6%. *Brendan* (6), *Eamon, Siobhan*.

Feely (585) Irish: variant spelling of FEELEY. See also MCFEELEY.
GIVEN NAME Irish 6%. *Brendan* (2).

Feeman (137) Americanized form of German **Viehmann**, an occupational name for a cattle dealer, from Middle High German *vihe* 'animal', 'cattle' + *man* 'man'.

Feemster (369) English and Scottish: occupational name for a senior herdsman, from Middle English *fee* 'cattle' + *master* 'master' (see MASTER).

Feener (114) Origin unidentified.

Feeney (3957) Irish: **1.** reduced Anglicized form of Gaelic **Ó Fiannaidhe** 'descendant of *Fiannaidhe*', a byname meaning 'warrior', 'champion' (from *fian* 'army'). **2.** shortened Anglicized form of Gaelic **Ó Fidhne** 'descendant of *Fidhne*', a personal name probably derived from *fiodh* 'wood'.
GIVEN NAMES Irish 6%. *Brendan* (7), *Patrick James* (2), *Aileen, Colm, Fergal, Kiera, Ronan, Siobhan*.

Feenstra (389) Frisian: topographic name for someone who lived in a boggy area, a variant of VEENSTRA.
GIVEN NAMES Dutch 4%. *Hendrik* (2), *Cornie, Dirk, Gerrit, Wouter*.

Feeny (189) Irish: variant spelling of FEENEY.

Feerick (150) Irish: reduced Anglicized form of Gaelic **Mac Phiaraic** 'son of Piers or Peter'. Compare FERRICK.

Fees (332) Variant of German FEESE.

Feese (296) German: from Middle High German, Middle Low German *vese* 'spelt', 'chaff', 'husk'; a nickname for a small person or an indirect occupational name for a cereal farmer or miller.

Feeser (362) German: metonymic occupational name for a cereal farmer or a miller, an agent derivative of FEESE.

Feest (143) Eastern German: variant of FEIST.

Feezor (181) Americanized spelling of German FEESER.

Feffer (142) Silesian and Bohemian variant spelling of German PFEFFER.

Fegan (523) Irish: reduced Anglicized form of Gaelic **Ó Fiacháin** or **Ó Feichín** (see FEEHAN).
GIVEN NAME Irish 5%. *Aileen*.

Fegely (108) Perhaps an Americanized spelling of German **Vögele**, a metonymic occupational name for a bird catcher or a nickname for someone with birdlike features, a diminutive of VOGEL (compare FEGLEY), or alternatively of Swiss German **Fügle** or **Fügli**, a nickname for a skillful person, from Middle High German *vuoc*, *vüege* 'skill'.

Feger (269) South German: occupational name for an armorer or weapon maker, from an agent derivative of Middle High German *fegen* 'to clean or sweep' or 'to polish a sword'.

Fegley (681) Americanized spelling of German **Vögli**, metonymic occupational name for a bird catcher or nickname for someone with birdlike features, from a diminutive of VOGEL.

Feher (593) **1.** Hungarian and Jewish (from Hungary) (**Fehér**): nickname for someone with a pale complexion or fair or white hair, from Hungarian *fehér* 'white'. This name is also found in eastern Slovenia. **2.** Variant of German FEHR.
GIVEN NAMES Hungarian 11%. *Bela* (5), *Sandor* (4), *Antal* (3), *Andras* (2), *Istvan* (2), *Akos, Arpad, Denes, Ferenc, Geza, Imre, Janos*.

Fehl (331) German: **1.** in northwestern Germany, a topographic name from *vel* 'marsh', 'bog'. **2.** in parts of central and southern Germany this surname and its Alemannic variant **Föhl** are related to FEILER 'file maker'.

Fehlberg (106) **1.** North German: probably a topographic name for someone living near a marshy area of high ground (see FEHL). **2.** South German: habitational name from Fehlberg, a place in Bavaria.
GIVEN NAMES German 13%. *Kurt* (2), *Otto* (2), *Erwin*.

Fehler (122) German: **1.** variant of FEILER 'file maker', altered by folk etymology to the form of the German word *Fehler* 'mistake'. **2.** topographic name for someone living near a marsh, a derivative of FEHL 1.
GIVEN NAME German 4%. *Otto*.

Fehling (185) North German: habitational name for an inhabitant of Eastphalia or Westphalia (German *Ostfalen, Westfalen*), the suffix -*ling* denoting affiliation and habitation.

Fehlman (183) German (**Fehlmann**): topographic name for someone who lived in open country, a variant of FELDMANN, especially in the Rhine and Mosel area.

Fehn (236) **1.** North German: topographic name for someone who lived by a bog or marsh, from Frisian *fehn* 'bog', related to Dutch *veen*. **2.** Norwegian: habitational name from any of three farms in southeastern Norway named *Fen*, probably from Old Norse *Fávin*, of which the second element is *vin* 'meadow'; the first element is unexplained.

Fehnel (181) South German: nickname for the standard bearer of a town guild or occupational name for an ensign, from a dialect diminutive of *Fahne* 'flag', 'banner' (Middle High German *van(e)*).

Fehr (1460) South German and Swiss German: metonymic occupational name for a ferryman, from Middle High German *ver(e)*. The name is common in Zurich, where, according to Bahlow, a journeyman of the boatmen's guild named Feer is recorded in 1468.

Fehrenbach (415) German: habitational name from any of several places so named (earlier *Vöhrenbach*) in Württemberg and Thuringia.

GIVEN NAMES German 5%. *Kurt* (2), *Erwin*, *Gerhard, Helmut, Otto, Rainer, Reiner*.

Fehrenbacher (237) German: habitational name for someone from any of the numerous places called FEHRENBACH.

Fehring (223) **1.** German (Holstein, Hamburg): patronymic from the Old Frisian personal name *Fero*. **2.** North German: nickname or status name alluding to a tax obligation, from Middle Low German *verdinc*, a term denoting a quarter of a weight or coin ('farthing'). This is the equivalent of South German **Vierdinc**, from Middle High German *vierdinc*.

Fehringer (190) South German: habitational name from any of several places named Fehringen (earlier *Vehringen*).

Fehrman (332) Americanized spelling of FEHRMANN.

Fehrmann (146) South and Swiss German: occupational name for a ferryman, from Middle High German *ver(e)* 'ferry' + *man* 'man'.

Fei (137) Chinese 费: this surname has three main sources. Two of them are from the state of Lu during the Spring and Autumn period (722–481 BC), part of present-day Shandong province. A senior official of the state of Lu was granted a city named Fei, while the son of a certain duke was granted a county named Fei. Both of these place names were adopted by descendants as surnames. A third source of the name is Fei Zhong, a high minister of the Yin dynasty (1401–1122 BC).

GIVEN NAMES Chinese 40%. *Wei* (4), *Jia* (3), *Yanjun* (2), *Bin, Chen, Chen-Yu, Chiang, Guoping, Hong, Hua, Li Ping, Ling-Ling*.

Feicht (118) South German and Austrian: variant of FEUCHT.

Feichter (100) German: variant of FEUCHT or FICHTER.

Feick (379) German: possibly a derivative of the Frisian personal name *Feiko*, a pet form of *Fre(de)rik* (see FREDERICK).

Feickert (172) German: of uncertain origin; a relatively recent surname which is not recorded as an older personal name.

GIVEN NAMES German 4%. *Hans, Otto*.

Feider (128) German: probably a nickname for a quarrelsome person, from Middle High German *feid* 'hate', 'strife', a short form of *vēede*.

Feidt (142) German: variant spelling of FEIT.

Feierabend (113) German and Swiss German: nickname for an idler, from late Middle High German *vīrābent*, originally 'eve (*ābent*) of a (religious) festival (*vīre*)' (modern German *Feierabend* now denotes 'evening', 'free time after work').

GIVEN NAMES German 20%. *Ewald, Hans, Helmut, Kurt, Otto, Ute*.

Feierstein (111) Jewish: variant of FEUERSTEIN.

GIVEN NAMES Jewish 16%. *Hyman* (3), *Chaim, Mayer, Sol*.

Feiertag (136) German: variant of FEIERABEND (literally 'holiday', from Middle High German *vīre* 'festival', 'feast' + *tag, tac* 'day').

Feig (382) **1.** South German: nickname for a coward, from the Middle High German *veic* 'fated to die', which then took on the meaning 'intimidated', 'fearful', 'cowardly'. **2.** German: variant of FEIGE 2. **3.** German: in some cases the Slavic word *voj* 'man', 'warrior' (variants *vojko, vojka*) may have been adapted, since, according to Brechenmacher, several 16th-century documents from eastern Germany report the name. **4.** Jewish (Ashkenazic): ornamental name from German *Feige* 'fig'.

GIVEN NAMES Jewish 6%; German 4%. *Chaim* (2), *Ephraim, Eran, Irina, Menachem, Miriam, Nachman, Yehuda; Hans, Irmgard*.

Feige (215) **1.** German: variant of FEIG. **2.** German: topographic name for someone who lived by a fig tree, or metonymic occupational name for a grower or seller of figs, from Middle High German *vīge* (Old High German *fīga*, from Latin *ficus*). **3.** Jewish (Ashkenazic): from the Yiddish female personal name *Feyge*, a back-formation from *Feygl* (see FEIGEL), as if this contained the diminutive suffix -*l*.

GIVEN NAMES German 6%. *Frankl, Gerhard, Hans, Manfred*.

Feigel (173) **1.** South German: variant of FEIGE 2. **2.** German: nickname from Middle High German *vīol* 'violet'. **3.** Jewish (Ashkenazic): from the Yiddish female personal name *Feygl*, which is from Yiddish *foygl* 'bird' (compare VOGEL), a translation of the Hebrew name *Tsipora* (*Zipporah*) 'bird', borne by the wife of Moses.

GIVEN NAMES French 5%; German 5%. *Jeanmarie; Waltraud*.

Feigen (104) German: variant of FEIGEL.

Feigenbaum (557) Jewish (Ashkenazic): ornamental name from German *Feigenbaum* 'fig tree'.

GIVEN NAMES Jewish 9%. *Aron, Aryeh, Avraham, Chana, Chaya, Eran, Haim, Hyman, Miriam, Sender, Shimon, Tzvi*.

Feighner (184) South German: **1.** probably an altered spelling of **Feigner**, a variant of FIEGER. **2.** possibly a variant of **Fichtner** (see FICHTER).

Feight (269) Respelling of German FEUCHT.

Feightner (126) Respelling of German **Fi(e)chtner, Feichtner**, or **Feuchtner** (see FICHTER).

Feigen (104) German: metronymic from a reduced form of the personal name *Sophia*.

Feik (132) Czech: see FEIG.

Feikema (106) Frisian: patronymic from the personal name *Feike*, a diminutive of *Feie*, a derivative of a Germanic personal name formed with *frid(u)* 'peace'.

GIVEN NAME Dutch 6%. *Dirk* (2).

Feil (837) German: **1.** from Middle High German *vīol* 'violet', presumably applied as a nickname; this surname occurs mostly in southern Germany. **2.** metonymic occupational name for a filemaker, from Middle High German *vīle* 'file'. **3.** metonymic occupational name for an arrowsmith, a variant of PFEIL, with the initial consonant cluster reduced to 'f' as is common in northern pronunciation *Pfeil*.

GIVEN NAMES German 5%. *Guenther* (2), *Kurt* (2), *Otto* (2), *Reinhardt* (2), *Bernhard, Helmut, Walburga, Wilhelm*.

Feild (234) English: variant of FIELD.

Feiler (497) German: occupational name for a filemaker, from FEIL + the agent suffix -*er*.

GIVEN NAMES German 7%. *Otto* (4), *Erwin* (2), *Gerhard* (2), *Ewald, Klaus, Kurt, Taube*.

Feimster (215) English and Scottish: variant of FEEMSTER.

Fein (1324) **1.** German: nickname from Middle High German *fīn* 'fine', 'splendid' (a cognate of FINE). **2.** Jewish (Ashkenazic): ornamental name from German *fein*, Yiddish *fayn* 'fine', 'excellent'.

GIVEN NAMES Jewish 4%. *Hyman* (5), *Elihu, Emanuel, Maier, Malca, Shifra, Sol*.

Feinauer (151) German: of uncertain origin. Perhaps from a topographic or habitational name composed with Middle High German *ouwe* 'water meadow' and a personal name *Fin, Vin*. (The Middle High German adjective *fīn*, a loan word from French, did not enter German before the middle of the 13th century, and the place names predate that time.)

Feinberg (2669) Jewish (Ashkenazic): ornamental name composed of German *fein* 'fine' + *Berg* 'mountain', 'hill'.

GIVEN NAMES Jewish 5%. *Meyer* (4), *Emanuel* (3), *Miriam* (3), *Sol* (3), *Avi* (2),

Hyman (2), *Isadore* (2), *Aron*, *Avrom*, *Batya*, *Chaim*, *Eliahu*.

Feind (117) German: nickname meaning 'enemy', from Middle High German *viant*, mostly in compounds, for instance **Bauernfeind**.

Feiner (560) **1.** German and Jewish (Ashkenazic): variant of FEIN. **2.** German: occupational name for a refiner and polisher of gold and other metals, from Middle High German *vīnen* 'to refine, polish, or gild' (a derivative of *vīn* 'pure', 'pretty').

GIVEN NAMES Jewish 4%. *Azriel*, *Cyla*, *Eitan*, *Hyman*, *Miriam*, *Moishe*, *Yetta*, *Yigal*.

Feingold (896) Jewish (Ashkenazic): ornamental name composed of German *fein* 'fine' + *Gold* 'gold'.

GIVEN NAMES Jewish 5%. *Sol* (4), *Anat*, *Emanuel*, *Inna*, *Myer*, *Nili*, *Oded*, *Yaron*.

Feinman (509) Jewish (Ashkenazic) and German (**Feinmann**): variant of FEIN.

GIVEN NAMES Jewish 4%. *Mayer*, *Miriam*, *Sol*.

Feinstein (1797) Jewish (Ashkenazic): ornamental name composed of German *fein* 'fine' + *Stein* 'stone'.

GIVEN NAMES Jewish 5%. *Hyman* (4), *Sol* (3), *Ari* (2), *Meyer* (2), *Mordecai* (2), *Reuven* (2), *Yetta* (2), *Avi*, *Baila*, *Dov*, *Eyal*, *Isadore*.

Feintuch (102) Jewish (eastern Ashkenazic): ornamental name composed of German *fein* 'fine' and *Tuch* 'cloth'.

GIVEN NAMES Jewish 16%; German 4%. *Elihu* (2), *Moshe* (2), *Zev*.

Feiock (128) Altered spelling of German FEICK. Compare FYOCK.

GIVEN NAMES German 4%. *Erwin*, *Theresia*.

Feist (1449) German and Jewish (Ashkenazic): nickname for a stout person, from, respectively, Middle High German *veiz(e)t* and modern German *feist* 'well covered', 'well fed'.

Feister (138) South German: nickname for a stout man, from a noun derivative of Middle High German *veiz(e)t* 'well covered', 'well fed'.

Feit (702) South German and Jewish (Ashkenazic): **1.** variant of VEIT. **2.** nickname from Middle High German *feit* 'adorned', 'pretty' (the same word as French *fait*, Latin *factus*).

GIVEN NAMES Jewish 6%. *Akiva* (2), *Sol* (2), *Aron*, *Chanie*, *Devorah*, *Gadi*, *Hyman*, *Peretz*, *Yosi*, *Zeev*.

Feith (167) German: variant of VEIT.

Fejes (158) Hungarian: from *fej* 'head', probably a nickname for someone with a big head. In modern Hungarian *fejes* means 'stubborn', but as this meaning dates back to the mid-18th century, it probably did not contributed to the origin of the surname.

Fekete (678) Hungarian and Jewish (from Hungary): nickname for a dark-haired or swarthy person, from Hungarian *fekete* 'black'.

GIVEN NAMES Hungarian 10%; Jewish 7%. *Laszlo* (5), *Istvan* (4), *Miklos* (4), *Karoly* (2), *Tibor* (2), *Zoltan* (2), *Akos*, *Balazs*, *Ferenc*, *Gyula*, *Imre*, *Janos*; *Hershel* (2), *Hershy* (2), *Aron*, *Avraham*, *Baruch*, *Boruch*, *Chaim*, *Chana*, *Chaya*, *Ezriel*, *Izidor*, *Nechama*.

Felan (281) **1.** Variant spelling of Irish PHELAN. **2.** Mexican: unexplained.

GIVEN NAMES Spanish 28%. *Guadalupe* (3), *Ignacio* (2), *Jose* (2), *Marcos* (2), *Ruben* (2), *Agustin*, *Alfredo*, *Alvino*, *Amalio*, *Ana*, *Apolonio*, *Carlos*.

Feland (147) Americanized form of German **Fehlandt**, **Fa(h)land**, a nickname for a wild or devilish person, from Middle High German *vālant* 'devil'.

Felber (661) **1.** German and Swiss German: topographic name for someone who lived by a conspicuous willow tree or a group of such trees, from Middle High German *velwe* 'willow' (presumably from an unrecorded Old High German cognate of Old English *welig*). As a vocabulary word this has now been entirely supplanted by WEIDE. Both words ultimately derive from a root meaning 'bent', 'twisted', and refer to the useful suppleness of willow twigs. Some examples of the surname may derive from places called Felben, from the dative plural of the word (originally used after a preposition). **2.** Jewish (Ashkenazic): ornamental name, from the tree (see 1).

GIVEN NAMES German 4%. *Hans* (2), *Dietrich*, *Frederich*, *Helmut*, *Johann*, *Kurt*, *Siegfried*, *Wenzel*.

Felch (412) Americanized spelling of German **Felsch**: **1.** nickname from Middle High German *vals* 'false'. **2.** in eastern Germany, from the Slavic personal name *Velislav* (from *velij* 'big'), which became *Velisch*, *Felsch*. **3.** variant of North German **Fölsch**, **Völsch**, based on the Frisian-Low German personal name *Fölske*, *Völske* (from the common name component *volc* 'people', 'tribe'); unrounding of *-ö-* to *-e-* changes *Fölsch* to *Felsch*.

Feld (1259) **1.** German: topographic name for someone who lived on ground which had been cleared of forest, but not brought into cultivation, from Middle High German *velt* 'area of open country'. **2.** Jewish (Ashkenazic): ornamental from German *Feld* (see 1). In some cases it could be a shortened form of any of the various compound names beginning with German *Feld*.

GIVEN NAMES Jewish 5%. *Sol* (3), *Chaim* (2), *Hyman* (2), *Baruch*, *Charna*, *Erez*, *Haya*, *Isadore*, *Itzchak*, *Lipman*, *Semen*, *Sheva*.

Feldbauer (108) German: topographic name for a peasant living and working on an area of open country (see FELD, BAUER).

Feldberg (174) **1.** German: habitational name from any of several places named Feldberg, for example in Hesse or the Black Forest. **2.** Jewish (Ashkenazic): or-

namental name composed of German *Feld* 'field' + *Berg* 'mountain', 'hill'.

GIVEN NAMES Jewish 11%. *Meyer* (2), *Chaim*, *Hyman*, *Shloma*.

Felde (224) German (**von dem Felde**): topographic name for someone living by an area of open country (see FELD).

GIVEN NAMES German 6%. *Kurt* (2), *Fritz*, *Johann*.

Felder (3049) German: variant of the topographic name FELD, or habitational name for someone from a place named with this word.

Felderman (178) Jewish (Ashkenazic): ornamental extension of FELD.

Feldhaus (398) German: habitational name from a place named Feldhaus, after a house (Middle High German *hūs*) standing in open country (Middle High German *velt*).

GIVEN NAMES German 4%. *Bernhard*, *Ewald*, *Hermann*.

Feldhausen (106) German: from the (old) dative plural of FELDHAUS.

Feldkamp (539) North German: topographic name for someone living by a field in open country, from Middle Low German *feld* 'open country' + *kamp* (from Latin *campus*) 'grazing place', 'small tree nursery', apparently for someone who owned or farmed land in an unprotected area, away from a settlement.

Feldman (12053) **1.** Jewish (Ashkenazic): ornamental extension of FELD. **2.** Americanized spelling of German FELDMANN.

GIVEN NAMES Jewish 7%. *Sol* (24), *Hyman* (14), *Miriam* (12), *Meyer* (11), *Yakov* (10), *Emanuel* (7), *Mendel* (6), *Myer* (6), *Naum* (6), *Isadore* (5), *Moshe* (4), *Aron* (3).

Feldmann (1087) German: topographic name for someone who lived in open country; a variant of FELD, with the addition of Middle High German *man* 'man'.

GIVEN NAMES German 6%. *Hans* (3), *Helmut* (3), *Frieda* (2), *Kurt* (2), *Oskar* (2), *Alois*, *Claus*, *Ernst*, *Erwin*, *Fritz*, *Gerda*, *Hermann*.

Feldmeier (209) German: distinguishing name for a tenant farmer (see MEYER) whose farm was in open country (see FELD).

Feldner (307) **1.** German: from Middle High German *veldener* (a derivative of Old High German *feld* 'open country'), a feudal term denoting a vassal or bondsman who was granted the land (but not the dwelling and barn) for his services. **2.** South German: habitational name for someone from any of various places named Felden or Velden. **3.** Jewish (Ashkenazic): ornamental extension of FELD.

GIVEN NAMES German 4%. *Fritz*, *Klaus*, *Kurt*, *Markus*.

Feldpausch (295) German: probably from a term meaning literally 'field bundle', hence 'scarecrow', applied as an occupational nickname for a farmer, a nickname for an unkempt individual, or a topographic name for someone who lived by a piece of cultivated land with a scarecrow.

Feldstein (672) Jewish (Ashkenazic): ornamental name composed of German *Feld* 'field' + *Stein* 'stone'.

GIVEN NAMES Jewish 5%. *Chaim, Elihu, Gerson, Sima, Sol, Yaakov, Yetta.*

Feldt (625) North German: variant of FELD.

Felgar (133) Altered spelling of German FELGER.

Felgenhauer (151) German: occupational name for a wheelwright, from Middle High German *velgenhouwer* 'maker of wooden rims for wheels'.

GIVEN NAMES German 11%. *Gerhard* (2), *Erwin, Otto, Reinhold, Wolfgang.*

Felger (338) German: **1.** occupational name for a wheelwright, from an agent derivative of Middle High German *velge* 'wooden rim of a wheel'. Compare FELGENHAUER. **2.** in some cases possibly an occupational name for a plowman, from an agent derivative of Middle High German *valgen, velgen* 'to plow'.

Felice (1101) **1.** Italian: from the personal name *Felice*, from the Roman family name *Felix* (Latin *felix*, genitive *felicis* 'lucky', 'fortunate'). **2.** English: variant of FELIX.

GIVEN NAMES Italian 8%. *Angelo* (3), *Salvatore* (3), *Antonio* (2), *Sal* (2), *Concetta, Dante, Dario, Domenic, Filippo, Fulvio, Gabriella, Gino.*

Felicetti (156) Italian: from a pet form of the personal name FELICE.

GIVEN NAMES Italian 12%; French 7%. *Fausto, Natale, Salvatore; Armand* (2), *Dominique, Monique.*

Felici (121) Italian: patronymic or plural form of FELICE.

GIVEN NAMES Italian 31%. *Angelo* (4), *Aldo* (2), *Roberto* (2), *Alberto, Americo, Fernando, Franco, Giulio, Lilia, Liliana, Luciano, Massimo, Romolo, Vincenzo.*

Feliciano (2109) Italian, Spanish, and Portuguese: from a medieval personal name (Latin *Felicianus*, a derivative of FELIX). The name was borne by a number of early saints, most notably a 3rd-century bishop of Foligno and apostle of Umbria.

GIVEN NAMES Spanish 42%; Portuguese 9%. *Jose* (70), *Luis* (27), *Angel* (20), *Carlos* (19), *Juan* (14), *Pedro* (13), *Wilfredo* (11), *Ana* (9), *Manuel* (9), *Margarita* (9), *Francisco* (8), *Ruben* (8); *Almir.*

Felipe (498) Spanish: from the personal name *Felipe*, Spanish form of PHILIP.

GIVEN NAMES Spanish 48%. *Jose* (11), *Juan* (6), *Manuel* (5), *Francisco* (4), *Juana* (4), *Miguel* (4), *Orlando* (4), *Pedro* (4), *Angel* (3), *Carlos* (3), *Emilio* (3), *Jesus* (3); *Antonio* (4), *Marco* (2), *Mauro* (2), *Fausto, Gaetano, Lorenzo, Nicoletta, Sylvio.*

Feliu (109) Catalan: from the Catalan form of the personal name *Felix*, borne by several saints, or perhaps a nickname from *feliu* 'happy', 'fortunate'.

GIVEN NAMES Spanish 37%. *Jose* (3), *Rafael* (3), *Ignacia* (2), *Jorge* (2), *Juan* (2), *Alejandro, Carlos, Fernando, Heberto, Jaime, Javier, Josue.*

Felix (5089) Spanish (**Félix**), Portuguese, English, German, and Jewish (Ashkenazic): from a medieval personal name (Latin *Felix*, genitive *Felicis*, meaning 'lucky', 'fortunate'). This was a relatively common Roman family name, said to have been first adopted as a nickname by Sulla. It was very popular among early Christians and was borne by a large number of early saints.

GIVEN NAMES Spanish 23%. *Jose* (53), *Manuel* (33), *Juan* (29), *Jesus* (24), *Francisco* (21), *Luis* (19), *Ramon* (17), *Raul* (16), *Carlos* (14), *Pedro* (14), *Rafael* (14), *Mario* (13).

Feliz (402) Spanish and Portuguese: from the byname *Feliz*, from *feliz* 'fortunate', 'happy'.

GIVEN NAMES Spanish 40%. *Jose* (9), *Luis* (8), *Carlos* (4), *Manuel* (4), *Miguel* (4), *Altagracia* (3), *Francisco* (3), *Luz* (3), *Angel* (2), *Cesar* (2), *Guillermo* (2), *Josefa* (2).

Felkel (167) German: from a pet form of the personal name VOLKMAR.

Felker (1648) German: **1.** from a variant of the Germanic personal name *Volker*, composed of the elements *folk* 'people', 'tribe' + *heri* 'army'. **2.** probably a variant of **Fälker**, itself a variant of FALKNER.

Felkins (307) Variant of English FILKINS.

Felkner (201) German: variant of FALKNER.

Fell (2174) **1.** English (chiefly northern): topographic name for someone who lived by an area of high ground or by a prominent crag, from northern Middle English *fell* 'high ground', 'rock', 'crag' (Old Norse *fjall, fell*). **2.** English, German, and Jewish (Ashkenazic): metonymic occupational name for a furrier, from Middle English *fell*, Middle High German *vel*, or German *Fell* or Yiddish *fel*, all of which mean 'skin', 'hide', or 'pelt'. Yiddish *fel* refers to untanned hide, in contrast to *pelts* 'tanned hide' (see PILCHER).

Fella (128) English: variant of FELL.

GIVEN NAME French 6%. *Laurent.*

Felland (148) Norwegian: habitational name from a farmstead in Telemark, so named from Old Norse *fall* 'fall', probably with reference to the site of a landslide + *land* 'land', 'farmstead'.

Fellbaum (109) German: variant of FELLENBAUM.

Fellenbaum (112) German: occupational nickname for a woodman, literally 'fell the tree', or possibly a topographic name for someone who lived by a fallen tree.

Fellenz (250) German: perhaps a habitational name from Veldenz on the Mosel.

Feller (2630) **1.** English, German, and Jewish (Ashkenazic): occupational name for a furrier, from an agent derivative of Middle English *fell*, Middle Low German,

Middle High German *vel*, or German *Fell* or Yiddish *fel* 'hide', 'pelt'. See also FELL. **2.** German: variant of FELDER. **3.** German: habitational name for someone from a place called Feld(e) or Feld(a) in Hesse.

Fellers (948) English: variant of FELLER.

Fellhauer (109) South German: occupational name for a metal finisher, from Middle High German *vīle* 'metal file' + an agent derivative of *houwen* 'to chop or beat'.

GIVEN NAMES German 8%. *Hans, Horst, Reiner.*

Fellin (297) **1.** Italian: Venetian variant of **Fellino, Fellini**, from a pet form of *Fel(l)o*, a short form of the personal name *Raffaello* (see RAPHAEL). **2.** Swedish: ornamental name, probably from a place-name element cognate with English FELL + the Swedish adjectival suffix *-in*, based on Latin *-inius*.

Felling (228) **1.** habitational name from Felling in Bavaria. **2.** Americanized spelling of German FEHLING.

Fellinger (167) German: habitational name for someone from Felling in Bavaria.

GIVEN NAMES German 7%. *Franz, Kurt, Nikolaus.*

Fellman (572) German and Swiss German (**Fellmann**), Jewish (Ashkenazic): occupational name for a furrier (see FELL 2).

Fellner (383) German: variant of FELDNER or FELLMAN.

GIVEN NAMES German 5%. *Franz* (2), *Alois, Dieter, Fritz, Hans, Rudi.*

Fellows (3033) English: patronymic from **Fellow**, from Middle English *felagh, felaw* late Old English *fēolaga* 'partner', 'shareholder' (Old Norse *félagi*, from *fé* 'fee', 'money' + *legja* to lay down). In Middle English the term was used in the general sense of a companion or comrade, and the surname thus probably denoted a (fellow) member of a trade guild. Compare FEAR 1.

Fells (425) **1.** English: variant of FELL. **2.** Jewish (Ashkenazic): variant of FELS.

Fellure (113) Origin unidentified.

Felman (135) **1.** Jewish (Ashkenazic): variant spelling of FELLMAN. **2.** Respelling of German **Fehlmann**, a variant of FELDMANN, or of **Fellmann** (see FELLMAN).

GIVEN NAMES Jewish 6%. *Meir, Moises, Rina, Sol.*

Felmlee (181) Possibly an altered spelling of South German **Völmle**, from a pet form of the personal name VOLKMAR.

Felps (192) Variant spelling of PHELPS.

Fels (384) **1.** German: topographic name for someone who lived near high ground or by a prominent crag, from Middle High German *vels* 'rock', 'cliff'. **2.** Jewish (Ashkenazic): ornamental name from German *Fels* 'rock'.

GIVEN NAMES German 4%. *Klaus, Kurt, Sieglinde, Wolfgang.*

Felsen (125) German: **1.** variant of FELS. **2.** habitational name for someone from any of several places named Felsen, Velsen, or Velzen in northwestern Germany.

Felsenthal (111) Jewish (Ashkenazic): ornamental name composed of German *Felsen* 'rock' and *Tal* 'valley'.
GIVEN NAME Jewish 4%. *Chani* (2).

Felser (100) German: topographic name for someone who lived in a rocky place or by a cliff (*Fels*).

Felsher (138) Origin unidentified. Perhaps a variant of FELSER.

Felsing (109) **1.** German: of Slavic origin; a nickname for a tall person, from Slavic *velij* 'big', 'tall'. **2.** Danish: habitational name from a place so called.

Felske (216) German: from a pet form of the Slavic personal names *Velislav*, or *Velimir*, both composed with *velij* 'big'.

Felt (1195) **1.** English: metonymic occupational name for a felt maker, from Old English *felt* 'felt'. **2.** Said to be an Americanized or Germanized spelling of a Hungarian name, of uncertain identity.

Felten (502) German: from the medieval personal name *Velten*, a vernacular form of Latin *Valentinus* (see VALENTINE).

Feltenberger (139) German: probably from a habitational name, which may be composed with *Felten*, a variant of *Velten*, a short form of the medieval personal name VALENTIN, + *berg* 'hill'.

Felter (662) German: **1.** habitational name for someone from any of several places named Felten or Velten. **2.** shortened form of any of various habitational names or topographic names formed with *-feld* 'open country' (see FELD), as for example KLEINFELDER. **3.** variant of FALTER.

Feltes (352) Dutch and North German: patronymic from a pet form of the personal name VALENTINE. Compare VELTEN.

Feltham (133) English: habitational name from either of two places so named: one southwest of London and the other in Somerset. The former is named from Old English *feld* 'open country' or *felte* 'mullein' (or a similar plant) + *hām* 'homestead' or *hamm* 'enclosure hemmed in by water'; the latter from Old English *fileðe* 'hay' + *hām* or *hamm*.

Feltis (111) Dutch and North German: variant of FELTES.

Feltman (874) Respelling of FELDMAN or FELDMANN.

Feltmann (106) Respelling of German FELDMANN.

Feltner (971) German: variant of FELDNER.

Felton (4814) English: habitational name from any of various places so called. Most of them, including those in Herefordshire, Shropshire, and Somerset (Winford), are named from Old English *feld* 'pasture', 'open country' + *tūn* 'enclosure', 'settlement'. Another place of the same name in Somerset, also known as Whitchurch, has as its first element Old English *fileðe* 'hay'.

Felton Hill in Northumberland is named with the Old English personal name *Fygla* (a derivative of *fugol* 'bird'; compare FOWLE).

Felts (2504) Dutch and German: variant of FELTZ.

Feltus (168) Dutch: patronymic from a pet form of the personal name VALENTINE. Compare FELTES, VELTEN.

Felty (1149) Americanized spelling of South German **Velte**, from a short form of the personal name *Valentin* (see VALENTINE).

Feltz (690) Alsatian and German: **1.** variant of **Völtz**, from a pet form of the personal name *Vol(k)mar* (see VOLKMAR). **2.** patronymic from a pet form of the personal name VALENTINE.

Felver (129) Variant of German FELBER.

Femia (216) Italian: from the southern Italian female personal name *Femìa*, from Greek *Phēmia*, short form of *Euphēmia*, a Greek Christian name composed of the elements *eu* 'well', 'good' + *phēmē* 'speech'.
GIVEN NAMES Italian 30%. *Rocco* (10), *Luigi* (2), *Nicola* (2), *Angelo*, *Antonio*, *Attilio*, *Cosmo*, *Fiore*, *Natale*, *Raffaele*, *Salvatore*.

Femino (132) Southern Italian (Sicily): from a reduced form of the personal name *Eufemiano*, from Greek *Euphēmianos* 'speaking well' or 'well spoken of' (see FEMIA).
GIVEN NAMES Italian 12%. *Angelo* (2), *Antonio*, *Domenic*, *Salvatore*.

Femrite (158) Norwegian: habitational name from a farm in Sogn, named with *fim* 'early growth in spring' + *reit* 'small field'.
GIVEN NAMES Scandinavian 11%. *Nels* (2), *Sig* (2), *Ingman*.

Fenchel (113) German: metonymic occupational name for a dealer in herbs or spices, from Middle High German *vönichel* (from Latin *faeniculum* 'fennel').
GIVEN NAMES German 6%. *Gerd*, *Kurt*.

Fencl (274) Polish or Czech: from German *Ventzl*, *Fentzl*, variants of WENZEL.
GIVEN NAMES Czech and Slovak 4%. *Jaroslav*, *Miroslav*, *Zdenek*.

Fendel (78) Altered spelling of English **Fendall**, a habitational name from Fenhale in Norfolk, recorded in medieval records as *Fendhale*.
FOREBEARS Josias Fendall (*c.* 1620–*c.* 1687) was granted 2,000 acres of land and appointed colonial governor of MD in 1656. He later established an estate in Charles Co. with his family, including a brother. In 1681 he was found guilty of attempting to raise a mutiny against a subsequent administration; banished from the province, he relocated to VA.

Fender (2182) **1.** English: nickname from *fend*, a shortened form of *defend*, thus 'defender'. **2.** South German: from Alemannic *Venner* 'flag bearer', 'ensign' or *Fähndrich*, which has the same meaning (see

FENRICH). **3.** South German: variant of FENDLER.

Fenderson (461) Scottish: ostensibly a variant of HENDERSON, but according to family historians an altered form of FINLAYSON.

Fendler (138) German: of uncertain origin; perhaps an occupational name for a flag-bearer, from an agent derivative of Middle Low German *vendel* (compare FENDER) or a nickname for a pilgrim, wanderer, or wayward person, from Middle High German *wandeler*, *wendeler* 'wanderer', 'pilgrim'.
GIVEN NAMES German 6%; French 4%. *Ernst*, *Hilde*, *Kurt*; *Emile*, *Regine*.

Fendley (674) Americanized spelling of German FENDLER.

Fendrich (140) German: variant of FENRICH 'standard bearer'.

Fendrick (243) Americanized form of German FENDRICH.

Fendt (166) German: nickname for a lad or a young man or farmer, from Middle High German *vende*, *vent*, *vendel(in)*, Middle Low German *vent* 'lad', 'page', 'little boy'. (In Old High German it denoted a foot soldier.)
GIVEN NAMES German 9%. *Berthold* (2), *Erwin*, *Ilse*, *Kurt*, *Ulrich*.

Fenech (189) Respelling of German **Fen(n)ich**, a metonymic occupational name for a millet farmer, from Middle High German *venich* 'millet'.
GIVEN NAMES Italian 8%. *Carmel* (4), *Angelo*, *Salvo*.

Fenelon (248) **1.** French (**Fénelon**): habitational name from Fénelon in the Dordogne, which is of uncertain origin. **2.** Irish: variant spelling of FENLON 1.
GIVEN NAMES French 16%. *Luckner* (2), *Edouard*, *Evens*, *Huguette*, *Jean Claude*, *Jean-Claude*, *Raoul*, *Ricot*, *Serge*, *Yvrose*.

Fenerty (125) Irish: variant of **O'Fenaghty**, an Anglicized form of Gaelic **Ó Fionnachta** (see FINNERTY).

Feng (1231) **1.** Chinese 冯: from the name of the city of Feng in the state of Wei during the Zhou dynasty (1122–221 BC). The fifteenth son of the virtuous duke Wen Wang, Bi Gonggao, was granted the state of Wei soon after the founding of the Zhou dynasty in 1122 BC. A descendant of Bi Gonggao, Bi Wan, was granted Feng city, and his descendants took the city name as their surname. **2.** Chinese 封: from the name of a territory in what is now Henan province. A descendant of the second legendary emperor, Shen Nong (2734–2697 BC), was a tutor of the third legendary emperor, Huang Di (2697–2595 BC). In honor of this service he was granted an area called Feng, and his descendants adopted the place name as their surname. **3.** Chinese 丰: from the name of a personage who lived during the Spring and Autumn period (722–481 BC). At this time, Duke Mu of the

state of Zheng had a son whose name contained this character for Feng, and his descendants adopted it as their surname. **4.** Chinese 鄷: from the name of an area called Feng (location unknown). The seventeenth son of the virtuous duke Wen Wang, who lived in the twelfth century BC, was granted an area called Feng, along with the title Marquis of Feng. His descendants adopted the name of the place as their surname.
GIVEN NAMES Chinese 55%. *Li* (9), *Wei* (9), *Yi* (8), *Jian* (7), *Ming* (6), *Yan* (6), *Chen* (5), *Ping* (5), *Fang* (4), *Hui* (4), *Cheng* (3), *Feng* (3); *Tian* (5), *Chung* (2), *Min* (2), *Chang, Pao, Shen, Yiming, Yiping*.

Fenger (176) **1.** German: variant of FANGER. **2.** Possibly an Americanized form of Polish **Węgier**, an ethnic name for someone from Hungary.
GIVEN NAMES German 6%; Scandinavian 5%. *Irmgard* (2), *Ewald, Manfred*.

Fengler (102) German: Silesian variant of WENGLER.
GIVEN NAMES German 13%; Scandinavian 4%. *Gerda*(2), *Frieda, Kurt, Wolfgang, Wolfram*; *Alf*.

Fenicle (102) Origin unidentified.

Fenimore (710) English: nickname from Old French *fin* 'fine', 'splendid' + *amour* 'love' (Latin *amor*).

Fenlason (119) Variant spelling of Scottish FINLAYSON.

Fenley (511) **1.** English: perhaps a variant spelling of Scottish FINLEY. **2.** Possibly a respelling of South German **Fähnle**, an occupational name for an ensign bearer, from a diminutive of Middle High German *van(e)* 'flag', 'banner' (from Old High German *fano* 'cloth').

Fenlon (408) **1.** Irish: reduced Anglicized form of Gaelic **Ó Fionnaláin** 'descendant of *Fionnalán*', a personal name from a diminutive of *fionn* 'fair', 'white' (see FINN 1). **2.** English (Huguenot): altered form of French **Fénelon** (see FENELON).

Fenn (1841) **1.** English: topographic name for someone who lived in a low-lying marshy area, from Middle English *fenn* 'marsh', 'bog'. **2.** South German: topographic name from Old High German *fenni*, Middle Low German and Old Frisian *fenne* 'bog'. Compare FEHN.

Fennel (295) English and Irish: variant spelling of FENNELL.

Fennell (3855) **1.** English: metonymic occupational name for a grower or seller of fennel (Old English *finugle, fenol*, from Late Latin *fenuculum*). Fennel was widely used in the Middle Ages as a herb for seasoning. The surname may also have been a topographic name for someone who lived near a place where the herb grew or was grown. **2.** English: Reaney also identifies this as a derivative of **Fitz Neal** 'son of Neal', citing as an example Fennells Wood, a place name recorded in 1391 as *Fenel-*

grove and named for a Robert FitzNeel (1283). **3.** Irish: reduced Anglicized form of Gaelic **Ó Fionnghail** 'descendant of *Fionnghal*', a personal name composed of the elements *fionn* 'fair', 'white' + *gal* 'valor'.

Fennelly (466) Irish: variant of FENNELL 3, from the earlier Gaelic form of the genitive **Ó Fionnghaile** or **Ó Fionnghalaigh**.
GIVEN NAME Irish 6%. *Kieran* (2).

Fennema (210) Frisian: variant of VENEMA.

Fenner (2577) **1.** English: topographic name for someone who lived in a low-lying marshy area (see FENN). **2.** South German: occupational name for an ensign or standard bearer, from Middle High German *vener*, an agent derivative of Middle High German *vane* 'flag'. See also FENRICH.

Fennern (102) Origin unidentified.

Fennessey (275) Irish: variant spelling of FENNESSY.

Fennessy (368) Irish: reduced Anglicized form of Gaelic **Ó Fionnghusa** 'descendant of *Fionnghus*', a personal name composed of the elements *fionn* 'fair', 'white' + *gus* 'vigor', 'force'.
GIVEN NAMES Irish 11%. *Conor* (5), *Eamon, Niall, Siobhan*.

Fennewald (179) Variant spelling of German **Vennewald**, a topographic name from Middle Low German *fenne* 'bog' + *wald* 'wood', 'forest'.
GIVEN NAMES German 4%. *Kurt, Theresia*.

Fenney (127) English: origin uncertain; most probably a variant of FINNEY.

Fennig (150) Variant spelling of German **Pfennig** (see PFENNING).

Fennimore (292) English: variant spelling of FENIMORE.

Fenning (154) English: topographic name for a fen dweller, from a derivative of Old English *fenn* (see FENN).

Fenno (234) English: unexplained.

Fenoglio (212) Italian (Piedmont): variant of FINOCCHIO.

Fenrich (144) German: from a byname for the standard bearer of a town guild, from early New High German *fenrich*. The term was formed and came into use around 1500, replacing Middle High German *vener*, from which the older surnames FENNER and the Alemannic form VENNER were derived, and giving rise to **Fähn-(d)rich**, the standard German spelling.
GIVEN NAME German 4%. *Kurt*.

Fenske (1458) German form of a Slavic personal name equivalent to VINCENT (e.g. Polish *Winzenz*) or *Vaclav* (Polish *Wacław*; Czech *Vęceslav, Václav*; see VACEK).

Fenstemaker (100) Partial Americanized form of German FENSTERMACHER.

Fenster (612) German and Jewish (Ashkenazic): **1.** metonymic occupational name for a window maker, from Middle High German *venster*, German *Fenster* 'window'. Medieval windows were often just

holes in the wall; indeed, the English word *window* derives from Old Norse *vindauga* 'wind eye'. Later they were filled with a frame containing thin layers of translucent horn, and eventually glass, normally only in small pieces leaded together. **2.** possibly a habitational name from any of various minor places so named from being in a gap in a range of hills or a clearing in a wood; it may also have been a topographic name for someone who lived in a house remarkable for its windows.
GIVEN NAMES French 4%; Jewish 4%. *Remy* (2), *Aristide, Colette, Norvin, Pierre; Yaacov* (2), *Chaim, Chana, Dov, Hyman*.

Fenstermacher (676) German and Jewish (Ashkenazic): occupational name for a window maker, from Middle High German *venster* (from Latin *fenestra*), German *Fenster* 'window' + Middle High German *macher*, German *Macher* 'maker'. See also FENSTER.

Fenstermaker (769) Partly Americanized form of German FENSTERMACHER or Americanized spelling of the Dutch cognate **Venstermaker**.

Fent (196) German: variant of FENDT.

Fenter (266) German: from a vernacular reduced form of the personal name *Bonaventura*, which became popular as a personal name around 1500.

Fenters (119) Patronymic derivative of German FENTER.

Fenton (6076) **1.** English: habitational name from any of various places, in Lincolnshire, Northumberland, Staffordshire, and South Yorkshire, so called from Old English *fenn* 'marsh', 'fen' + *tūn* 'enclosure', 'settlement' **2.** Irish: English surname adopted by bearers of Gaelic *Ó Fionnachta* (see FINNERTY) or **Ó Fiachna** 'descendant of *Fiachna*', an old personal name Anglicized as **Feighney** and sometimes mistranslated as HUNT (see FEE). **3.** Jewish (Ashkenazic): Americanized form of various like-sounding names, for example **Finkelstein** (see FUNKE).

Fentress (793) English and Scottish: variant of VENTRESS, itself a variant of VENTERS, a nickname for a daring person, from Middle English *aventurous* 'bold', 'venturesome'.

Fenty (129) Northern English and Scottish: unexplained.

Fenwick (1591) Northern English and Scottish: habitational name from either of two places in Northumberland or from one in West Yorkshire, all of which are so named from Old English *fenn* 'marsh', 'fen' + *wīc* 'outlying dairy farm'. There is also a place in Ayrshire, Scotland, which has the same name and origin. This last is the source of at least some early examples of the surname: Nicholaus Fynwyk was provost of Ayr in 1313, and Reginald de Fynwyk or Fynvyk appears as bailie and alderman of the same burgh in 1387 and

1401. The name is usually pronounced 'Fennick'.

FOREBEARS The name was brought over from England by several forebears, including George Fenwick (1603–56/7), a colonist from Brinkburn, Northumberland. He was one of the group of lords and gentlemen to whom the earl of Warwick, president of the Council for New England, granted forty leagues of territory west of the Narragansett River. George took up residence with his family at Saybrook, CT, in 1639.

John Fenwick of Bynfield, Berkshire, England, established himself at Salem, NJ, in June 1675, the first Quaker settlement on the Delaware.

Fenzel (124) German (Sudetenland): variant of WENZEL.

Feo (111) **1.** Southern Italian: from the personal name *Feo*, a short form of *Maffeo*; an Italian form of MATTHEW. **2.** Spanish: from the byname *Feo*, from *feo* 'ugly'.

GIVEN NAMES Italian 17%; Spanish 14%. *Antonio* (4), *Giovanni, Nunzio, Rocco, Saverio, Stefano*; *Ricardo* (2), *Alphonso, Amalia, Armando, Augusto, Jose, Paulina, Raul, Sixto*.

Feola (511) Italian: from a derivative of FEO.

GIVEN NAMES Italian 17%. *Angelo* (4), *Luigi* (3), *Salvatore* (3), *Marco* (2), *Rocco* (2), *Sal* (2), *Agostino, Amato, Amedeo, Aniello, Augostino, Carmine*.

Feole (140) Italian: from a derivative of FEO.

GIVEN NAMES Italian 13%. *Carmino* (2), *Angelo, Antonio, Dante, Luigi, Pasquale, Rino*.

Fera (369) Italian: from Latin *fera* 'wild animal' (Italian *fiera*) or Calabrian *fera* 'dolphin'.

GIVEN NAMES Italian 9%. *Angelo, Carmine, Carmino, Domenic, Domenico, Nicola, Rocco, Veto*.

Feraco (120) Italian (Calabria): from an old personal name, recorded in the 11th century in the Latinized form *Faracus*. This is of uncertain origin; it may be an Italianized version of Arabic FAROOQ.

GIVEN NAMES Italian 19%. *Angelo* (2), *Luigi* (2), *Carmine, Gino, Santo*.

Ferber (1112) German and Jewish (Ashkenazic): variant of **Färber** (see FARBER).

GIVEN NAMES German 5%. *Erwin* (4), *Kurt* (4), *Bernd, Fritz, Helmut, Herta, Ignaz, Konrad, Matthias, Otto*.

Ferch (292) **1.** German: variant of FERG. **2.** Americanized form of German **Förtsch** (see FOERTSCH). **3.** Americanized form of German **Förch**, a habitational name from a place so named, from Old High German word *for(a)ha* 'fir tree'. There are several such places in southern Germany.

Ferderer (203) German: unexplained.

GIVEN NAME German 4%. *Kurt* (2).

Ferdig (203) Variant of German FERTIG.

Ferdinand (657) German and French: from a Spanish (Visigothic) personal name composed of the elements *farð* 'journey', 'expedition' (or a metathesized form of *frið* 'peace') + *nanð* 'daring', 'brave'. The surname is of comparatively recent origin in German-speaking countries and in France, for the personal name was not introduced from Spain until the late 15th century. It was brought to Austria by the Habsburg dynasty, among whom it was a hereditary name, and from Austria it spread to France. The Iberian cognates are of more ancient origin and more frequently found today, since the name was much favored in the royal house of Castile. It owes its popularity in large part to King Ferdinand III of Castile and León (1198–1252), who recaptured large areas of Spain from the Moors and was later canonized.

GIVEN NAMES French 8%. *Andre* (3), *Michel* (2), *Alain, Cecile, Dieudonne, Jean Robert, Ludger, Magalie, Micheline*.

Ferdman (123) Jewish (eastern Ashkenazic): occupational name for a coachman, from Yiddish *ferd* 'horse' + *man* 'man'.

GIVEN NAMES Russian 19%; Jewish 18%. *Mikhail* (4), *Boris* (2), *Vladimir* (2), *Lev, Svetlana, Vlagimir, Yefim*; *Aron, Ilya, Irina, Khana, Naum, Semen*.

Ferdon (233) Possibly French: from a metathesized short form of a Germanic personal name containing *frid* 'peace'.

Ferebee (570) English: habitational name from North Ferriby in East Yorkshire or South Ferriby in Lincolnshire, both named from Old Norse *ferja* 'ferry' + *býr* 'farmstead'.

Fereday (116) **1.** Irish (Galway): reduced Anglicized form of Gaelic **Ó Fearadhaigh** (see FERRY). **2.** English: from the Old English personal name *Fæger* 'fair' + *dæge* 'servant', hence 'servant of (a man called) Fair'.

GIVEN NAME French 5%. *Andre*.

Ferenc (214) Hungarian (also found in Poland): from the personal name *Ferenc*, a vernacular form of Latin *Franciscus* (see FRANCIS).

GIVEN NAMES Polish 7%. *Andrzej, Casimir, Iwan, Zbigniew*.

Ference (593) **1.** Hungarian: patronymic form of FERENC. **2.** Americanized spelling of Hungarian *Ferencei, Ferenci*, or some other derivative of FERENC. **3.** Probably also English: patronymic from FARRANT.

Ferencz (218) Hungarian: from an old spelling of the personal name, now spelled FERENC.

GIVEN NAMES Hungarian 5%. *Arpad* (2), *Denes, Jolan, Sandor*.

Ferenz (151) **1.** Polish: from the Hungarian personal name FERENC. **2.** Germanized spelling of Hungarian FERENC.

GIVEN NAMES French 5%; German 4%. *Jean-Marie* (2); *Helmuth, Wilhelm*.

Feret (137) French: from a pet form of a compound personal name such as *Férart* or *Féraud*.

GIVEN NAME French 4%. *Philippe*.

Ferg (176) German: occupational name for a ferryman, Middle High German *verje, verge*.

Fergason (168) Altered spelling of Scottish and Irish FERGUSON.

Ferge (107) German: variant of FERG.

Fergen (130) German: probably from a shortened form of a compound name with FERG, as for example **Fergenheinz** 'Henry (son) of the ferryman'.

Ferger (182) German: hypercorrected form of FERG 'ferryman', the *-er* occupational suffix having been added to what was already an occupational name. Compare BECK and BECKER, where the same process has taken place.

Fergerson (370) Scottish: variant of FERGUSON.

Fergeson (124) Scottish: variant of FERGUSON.

Fergus (698) **1.** Irish: reduced Anglicized form of Gaelic **Ó Fearghuis** or **Ó Fearghasa** 'descendant of *Fearghus*', a personal name composed of the elements *fear* 'man' + *gus* 'vigor', 'force', or possibly 'choice'. This was the name of an early Irish mythological figure, a valiant warrior, also of the grandfather of St. Columba. **2.** Scottish: from the Gaelic personal name *Fearghus* (see 1 above).

Ferguson (51167) Scottish: patronymic from the personal name FERGUS.

Fergusson (296) Scottish: variant spelling of FERGUSON.

Feria (187) Spanish and Portuguese (**Féria**): possibly from *feria* 'fair', 'market' (Latin *feria* 'holiday', 'feast day').

GIVEN NAMES Spanish 45%. *Carlos* (4), *Eduardo* (3), *Fernando* (3), *Jose* (3), *Ana* (2), *Arturo* (2), *Juan* (2), *Luis* (2), *Manuel* (2), *Mario* (2), *Miguel* (2), *Rafael* (2).

Ferko (272) Hungarian (**Ferkó**), Polish, and Slovenian: from a pet form of the Hungarian personal name FERENC.

Ferland (800) Of French origin: possibly an Americanized spelling of **Ferlin**, from a term denoting a small weight, perhaps applied as a nickname for a slight person or a metonymic occupational name for someone whose work involved the making or use of weights.

FOREBEARS A Ferlin from Poitou is recorded in Orleans Isle, Quebec, in 1708.

GIVEN NAMES French 17%. *Armand* (9), *Marcel* (4), *Andre* (2), *Cecile* (2), *Emile* (2), *Gilles* (2), *Jacques* (2), *Normand* (2), *Origene* (2), *Pierre* (2), *Adrien, Aime*.

Ferlazzo (136) Italian: augmentative form of **Ferla**, from Latin *ferula* 'giant fennel', hence a topographic name for someone who lived where fennel grew or an occupational name for a herb seller or a herbalist.

GIVEN NAMES Italian 18%. *Gaetano* (2), *Sal* (2), *Angelo, Gasper, Natale, Salvatore.*

Ferlita (130) Italian: from a diminutive of Latin *ferula* 'fennel', hence a topographic name for someone who lived in an area where fennel grew or was cultivated; or alternatively an occupational name for a grower or seller of the herb.
GIVEN NAMES Italian 13%. *Salvatore* (2), *Carlo, Francesco.*

Ferlito (105) Southern Italian (Sicily): topographic name from Latin *feruletum* 'giant fennel patch'.
GIVEN NAMES Italian 11%; Spanish 4%. *Angelo, Domenic, Salvatore; Catalina, Jose, Juan.*

Ferm (210) Swedish: soldier's name from Swedish *färm* 'prompt', 'ready'.
GIVEN NAMES Scandinavian 7%. *Dagny, Lennart.*

Ferman (391) Altered spelling of German and Swiss FEHRMANN.
GIVEN NAMES Spanish 12%. *Jose* (4), *Santos* (3), *Ana* (2), *Marta* (2), *Rafael* (2), *Alejandro, Amada, Angel, Antolin, Apolinario, Berta, Carlos.*

Fermin (365) **1.** Spanish (**Fermín**): from the medieval personal name *Fermín*, Spanish form of Latin *Firminus* (see FIRMIN). **2.** French: variant of FIRMIN.
GIVEN NAMES Spanish 51%. *Jose* (11), *Luis* (8), *Ana* (6), *Rafael* (6), *Juan* (5), *Ramon* (4), *Carlos* (3), *Mercedes* (3), *Miguel* (3), *Santiago* (3), *Alejandro* (2), *Cristina* (2).

Fern (911) English: topographic name for someone who lived in a place where there was an abundance of ferns, from Old English *fearn* 'fern' (sometimes used as a collective noun).

Fernald (916) Origin uncertain; perhaps an altered form of English **Furnell**, a topographic name from Old French *fournel* 'furnace'. This name is common in ME.

Fernandes (3643) Portuguese: patronymic from the personal name FERNANDO. This is one of the most common surnames in Portugal. This surname is also common in Goa and elsewhere on the west coast of India, having been taken there by Portuguese colonists.
GIVEN NAMES Spanish 21%; Portuguese 14%. *Manuel* (92), *Jose* (72), *Carlos* (24), *Luis* (11), *Fernando* (10), *Jorge* (10), *Mario* (10), *Francisco* (9), *Orlando* (8), *Ana* (7), *Abilio* (6), *Americo* (6); *Joao* (17), *Joaquim* (8), *Henrique* (6), *Ilidio* (4), *Paulo* (4), *Agostinho* (3), *Amadeu* (3), *Manoel* (3), *Aderito* (2), *Lourenco* (2), *Marcio* (2), *Serafim* (2).

Fernandez (23665) Spanish (**Fernández**): patronymic from the personal name FERNANDO. The surname (and to a lesser extent the variant HERNANDEZ) has also been established in southern Italy, mainly in Naples and Palermo, since the period of Spanish dominance there, and as a result of the expulsion of the Jews from Spain and Portugal at the end of the 15th century, many of whom moved to Italy.
GIVEN NAMES Spanish 45%; Portuguese 11%. *Jose* (761), *Manuel* (343), *Juan* (267), *Carlos* (243), *Luis* (215), *Jorge* (167), *Miguel* (145), *Fernando* (143), *Mario* (141), *Jesus* (132), *Pedro* (132), *Francisco* (131); *Ligia* (5), *Joao* (2), *Armanda, Godofredo, Wenceslao.*

Fernando (681) Spanish and Portuguese: from a Germanic personal name composed of a metathesized form of *frið* 'peace' (or *farð* 'journey', 'expedition') + *nanð* 'daring', 'boldness'. See also FERDINAND. This family name is also found in western India, where it was taken by Portuguese colonists.
GIVEN NAMES Spanish 23%; Indian 12%. *Jose* (4), *Manuel* (4), *Luis* (3), *Orlando* (3), *Aida* (2), *Carlos* (2), *Jesusa* (2), *Rodolfo* (2), *Ruben* (2), *Adela, Alfredo, Alicia; Rohan* (6), *Lalith* (3), *Nimal* (2), *Rajiv* (2), *Sanjeeva* (2), *Shanthi* (2), *Anil, Anusha, Dushan, Kapila, Lakshman, Mallika.*

Fernau (184) German: habitational name from a place called Fernau or Fernow.

Fernbach (128) German: habitational name, probably a reduced form of FEHRENBACH.

Ferneau (107) Origin uncertain; perhaps a variant of English **Furneaux**, a Norman habitational name from places called Fourneaux in Manche and Calvados, France.

Fernelius (105) Swedish: unexplained.

Ferner (194) German: habitational name for someone from any of various places named Ferna, Fernau, or Fernow.

Fernholz (210) German: habitational name from a large farm and manor in Westphalia called *Fernhott*, of which *Fernholz* is a standardized form.

Fernicola (151) Italian: probably from a compound of a personal name derived from the Latin name *Fernus* + *Cola*, a short form of NICOLA.
GIVEN NAMES Italian 24%. *Giacomo* (2), *Attilio, Emilio, Gerardo, Nicola, Pasquale, Silvio.*

Fernow (104) German: habitational name from a place called Fernau or Fernow.

Ferns (228) English: variant of FERN 1.

Fernsler (104) Altered spelling of German **Förnsler** or **Firnsler**, presumably an occupational name for a varnish maker, from an agent derivative of Middle High German *firnīs* 'varnish', a loanword from Old French *vernī*.

Fernstrom (139) Swedish (**Fernström**): ornamental name composed of the elements *Fern* (probably German *fern* 'far', 'distant') + *ström* 'stream', 'river'.

Fero (292) **1.** Hungarian (**Feró**): probably from a pet form of the personal name *Ferenc*, Hungarian form of FRANCIS. **2.** Possibly an altered spelling of Italian FERRO. **3.** Possibly an Americanized spelling of French **Ferraud**, a diminutive of FERRON.

Ferone (103) Italian: possibly from an augmentative form of FERA or alternatively from a short form of *Cristofarone*, an augmentative of *Cristofaro, Cristoforo.*
GIVEN NAMES Italian 22%. *Carmine* (3), *Salvatore* (2), *Fiore, Gaetano, Santi.*

Ferra (195) **1.** Catalan (**Ferrà**): variant of FERRAN. **2.** Southern Italian: habitational name from Ferla. **3.** Portuguese: probably from a derivative of *ferrar* 'to shoe' (animals).
GIVEN NAMES Spanish 14%. *Manuel* (4), *Francisco* (3), *Adan, Ernesto, Gustavo, Jorge Luis, Jose, Juan, Ovidio, Ruben, Salvador; Annalisa, Nicola, Rocco.*

Ferragamo (127) Italian (Avellino province): unexplained.
GIVEN NAMES Italian 13%. *Antonio, Concetta, Domenico, Enzo, Massimo, Sal, Salvatore.*

Ferraioli (145) Italian: patronymic or plural form of FERRAIOLO.
GIVEN NAMES Italian 27%. *Salvatore* (3), *Antonio* (2), *Luigi* (2), *Sal* (2), *Agostino, Alfredo, Alphonso, Ciro, Enrico, Gennaro, Mario, Renato.*

Ferraiolo (177) Italian: occupational name for a smith or worker in iron, *ferraiolo.*
GIVEN NAMES Italian 13%. *Antonio, Carlo, Gaetano, Pasquale, Pietro.*

Ferraiuolo (160) Italian: variant of FERRAIOLO.
GIVEN NAMES Italian 11%. *Alessandro, Domenic, Pasquale, Salvatore.*

Ferrall (220) Irish: variant of FARRELL.

Ferran (272) **1.** Catalan: from the medieval personal name *Ferran*, Catalan form of FERDINAND. **2.** Irish: variant of FARREN. **3.** English: variant of FARRAND.
GIVEN NAMES Spanish 18%. *Carlos* (3), *Alberto* (2), *Francisco* (2), *Jose* (2), *Rosendo* (2), *Xavier* (2), *Ana, Angel, Arturo, Ernesto, Estela, Horacio.*

Ferrand (262) **1.** French: nickname for someone with gray hair, from Old French *ferrand* 'iron gray'. **2.** Catalan: from a regional variant of the personal name FERNANDO. **3.** English: variant of FARRAND.
GIVEN NAMES French 10%; Spanish 8%. *Olivier* (2), *Armand, Cecile, Francois, Monique, Paulet, Pierre, Stephane; Jose* (3), *Jesus* (2), *Luis* (2), *Valeria* (2), *Atilio, Carlos, Javier, Liliana, Nestor.*

Ferrandino (148) Italian: from a diminutive of FERRANDO.
GIVEN NAMES Italian 20%. *Angelo* (2), *Salvatore* (2), *Ciro, Egidio, Giovanni.*

Ferrando (303) Italian: **1.** nickname for someone with gray hair or for a person who dressed in gray, from an Italianized form of Old French *ferrand* 'iron gray'. **2.** from a Late Latin personal name *Ferrandus*, which was either a variant of FERDINAND or a byname meaning 'gray'.
GIVEN NAMES Italian 15%; Spanish 9%. *Mario* (3), *Carlo* (2), *Dante, Giovanni,*

Paolo, Reno, Salvatore; Javier (2), *Luis* (2), *Jesus, Jose, Marcelo, Marta, Miguel, Pilar.*

Ferrante (2273) Italian: **1.** Italianized form of French FERRAND. Compare FERRANDO 1. **2.** habitational name from Ferrante, a locality of Acri in Cosenza province.
GIVEN NAMES Italian 20%. *Salvatore* (16), *Angelo* (14), *Domenic* (9), *Rocco* (8), *Vito* (6), *Antonio* (5), *Enrico* (4), *Francesco* (4), *Luigi* (4), *Pasquale* (4), *Santino* (4), *Carmine* (3).

Ferranti (545) Italian: variant of FERRANDO 1.
GIVEN NAMES Italian 15%. *Rocco* (4), *Giuseppe* (3), *Aldo* (2), *Angelo* (2), *Albo, Amerigo, Caesar, Carlo, Francesca, Gildo, Gino, Giovanna.*

Ferrantino (104) Italian: diminutive of FERRANTE.
GIVEN NAMES Italian 22%. *Mario* (2), *Angelina, Emilio, Matteo.*

Ferrar (145) English: variant of **Farrar**.

Ferrara (5004) Southern Italian: topographic name for someone who lived by a forge or iron workings, from *ferrara*, Latin *ferraria*, a derivative of *ferrum* 'iron', or a habitational name from the provincial capital of Ferrara, in Emilia-Romagna.
GIVEN NAMES Italian 15%. *Salvatore* (38), *Angelo* (33), *Sal* (13), *Pasquale* (11), *Rocco* (8), *Vito* (8), *Carmine* (7), *Antonio* (4), *Carlo* (4), *Domenico* (4), *Giovanni* (4), *Giuseppe* (4).

Ferrare (108) Variant of Italian **Ferrari** (see FERRARO).
GIVEN NAMES Italian 24%. *Angelo, Dino, Erenio, Gino, Giovanna, Justo, Rocco, Severino.*

Ferrari (3009) Italian: patronymic or plural form of FERRARO.
GIVEN NAMES Italian 16%. *Mario* (18), *Angelo* (14), *Dino* (9), *Aldo* (8), *Antonio* (5), *Alberto* (4), *Alfredo* (4), *Carlo* (4), *Geno* (4), *Lino* (4), *Roberto* (4), *Cesare* (3), *Enzo* (3), *Giuseppe* (3), *Guido* (3), *Marino* (3), *Paolo* (3), *Adolfo* (2), *Albino* (2), *Armando* (2), *Emilio* (2).

Ferrarini (113) Italian: from a diminutive of FERRARI.
GIVEN NAMES Italian 14%. *Aldo, Angelo, Dante, Italo, Marco, Mauro, Sante, Silvio, Sylvio.*

Ferrario (200) Italian: variant of FERRARO.
GIVEN NAMES Italian 7%. *Angelo* (3), *Antonio, Gino, Reno, Renzo.*

Ferraris (201) Italian and Swiss Italian (**De Ferraris**): patronymic from FERRARO, in the broader sense 'of the Ferrari family'.
GIVEN NAMES Italian 8%; Spanish 5%; German 4%. *Aldo, Angelo, Dino, Enzo, Gerardo, Rinaldo, Roberto; Jose* (2), *Carlos, Concepcion, Francisca, Julio, Mercedes; Franz* (2).

Ferraro (4564) Italian: occupational name for a smith or iron worker, from *ferro* 'iron' (Latin *ferrum*).

GIVEN NAMES Italian 14%. *Angelo* (24), *Salvatore* (20), *Antonio* (13), *Carmine* (12), *Sal* (12), *Rocco* (10), *Domenic* (6), *Pasquale* (5), *Carlo* (4), *Cosimo* (4), *Francesco* (4), *Natale* (4).

Ferraz (107) Spanish and Portuguese: evidently based on Latin *ferrum* 'iron', probably an unattested derivative, *ferraceus* 'iron', 'inflexible'. It is not clear if it is a nickname or a medieval personal name. The cradle of this name (variant **Ferràs**, Spanish **Herraz**) is Catalonia.
GIVEN NAMES Spanish 34%; Portuguese 23%. *Jose* (7), *Eduardo* (2), *Francisco* (2), *Virginio* (2), *Adriano, Aleida, Arlindo, Claudio, Esteban, Fabio, Gilberto, Joaquin; Paulo* (4), *Joao* (2); *Antonio* (3), *Leonardo.*

Ferre (270) **1.** Possibly a variant of French **Ferré** (see FERREE). **2.** Catalan (**Ferré**): respelling of Catalan **Ferrer**, from *ferrer* 'smith', reflecting the pronunciation.
GIVEN NAMES French 6%; Spanish 6%. *Alain, Andre, Francois, Laurette, Olivier; Francisco* (3), *Fernando* (2), *Mario* (2), *Abelardo, Carlos, Eduardo, Humberto, Jose, Juan, Mariana, Mirta.*

Ferrebee (213) English: variant spelling of FEREBEE.

Ferree (1171) **1.** Probably an altered spelling of Irish FERRY 1. **2.** Americanized form of French **Ferré**, a nickname meaning 'of iron', i.e. 'armed'.

Ferreira (5588) Galician and Portuguese: common topographic name for someone who lived by a forge or iron workings, from Latin *ferraria* 'forge', 'iron working'.
GIVEN NAMES Spanish 24%; Portuguese 13%. *Manuel* (145), *Jose* (124), *Carlos* (41), *Luis* (28), *Fernando* (26), *Mario* (23), *Francisco* (20), *Armando* (15), *Ana* (14), *Jorge* (14), *Miguel* (11), *Sergio* (10); *Joao* (26), *Paulo* (15), *Joaquim* (13), *Henrique* (4), *Agostinho* (3), *Albano* (2), *Amadeu* (2), *Duarte* (2), *Ligia* (2), *Marcio* (2), *Vasco* (2), *Adao; Antonio* (116), *Angelo* (4), *Luciano* (4), *Marco* (4), *Elio* (3), *Flavio* (3), *Alessandra* (2), *Caesar* (2), *Carlo* (2), *Dario* (2), *Alfonse, Annalisa.*

Ferreiro (149) Galician and Portuguese: occupational name for a smith or worker in iron.
GIVEN NAMES Spanish 56%. *Jose* (11), *Carlos* (6), *Juan* (6), *Julio* (5), *Luis* (4), *Alberto* (3), *Jorge* (3), *Manuel* (3), *Amalia* (2), *Enrique* (2), *Raul* (2), *Vicente* (2).

Ferrel (620) Irish: variant of FARRELL.
GIVEN NAMES Spanish 6%. *Manuel* (4), *Carlos* (2), *Jesus* (2), *Jose* (2), *Luis* (2), *Pedro* (2), *Trinidad* (2), *Angel, Cipriano, Enrique, Francisco, Gabriela.*

Ferrell (11277) Irish: variant of FARRELL.

Ferrelli (189) Italian: patronymic or plural form, probably from a diminutive of *ferro* 'iron'.

GIVEN NAMES Italian 11%. *Antonio* (2), *Domenic, Ercole, Ferdinando, Remo, Rocci.*

Ferren (394) Perhaps a variant spelling of English *Ferran*, itself a variant of FARRAND, or a variant of Irish FARREN, or a shortened form of Irish McFERRAN.

Ferrence (119) Americanized spelling of Hungarian FERENCZ.

Ferrentino (189) Italian: variant of **Ferrantino**, a diminutive of FERRANTE.
GIVEN NAMES Italian 16%. *Alfonso* (4), *Mario* (2), *Francesco.*

Ferrer (2217) **1.** Catalan: occupational name for a blacksmith or a worker in iron, from Latin *ferrarius*. This is the commonest Catalan surname. **2.** English: variant of FARRAR.
GIVEN NAMES Spanish 44%. *Jose* (58), *Luis* (33), *Francisco* (26), *Miguel* (24), *Juan* (22), *Jorge* (18), *Carlos* (17), *Angel* (16), *Pedro* (16), *Roberto* (15), *Manuel* (14), *Ramon* (13).

Ferrera (655) **1.** Italian (northwest and Liguria): variant of FERRARA. **2.** Italian: habitational name from various places named with this word: Ferrera Cenisio (now Moncenisio) in Piemonte; and Ferrera di Varese and Ferrera Erbognone, both in Lombardy. **3.** Spanish and Catalan: topographic name for someone who lived near a forge or ironworks, from Latin *ferraria*.
GIVEN NAMES Spanish 17%; Italian 10%. *Carlos* (3), *Manuel* (3), *Rafael* (3), *Augusto* (2), *Francisco* (2), *Jorge* (2), *Jose* (2), *Luis* (2), *Miguel* (2), *Pedro* (2), *Ramona* (2), *Ricardo* (2); *Salvatore* (6), *Antonio* (5), *Biagio* (2), *Domenic* (2), *Sal* (2), *Aldo, Angelo, Attilio, Carmelo, Elio, Enrico.*

Ferreri (478) Southern Italian: variant of FERRARI.
GIVEN NAMES Italian 10%. *Salvatore* (5), *Sal* (4), *Antonio, Carlo, Dario, Ignazio, Nunzio, Paolo.*

Ferrero (736) **1.** Italian (Piedmont and Liguria): variant of FERRARO. **2.** Catalan (**Ferreró**): from a diminutive of FERRER.
GIVEN NAMES Italian 7%. *Reno* (3), *Angelo* (2), *Attilio* (2), *Luca* (2), *Marco* (2), *Alessandro, Domenic, Elisabetta, Franco, Giorgio, Giovanni, Giuseppe.*

Ferrett (129) English (southern counties): nickname from Middle English *ferette, fyrette* 'ferret', literally 'little thief' (Old French *fuiret, furet*).

Ferretti (982) Italian: from a diminutive of FERRO.
GIVEN NAMES Italian 12%. *Aldo* (4), *Antonio* (2), *Carlo* (2), *Dante* (2), *Domenic* (2), *Quinto* (2), *Alessandro, Attilio, Carmello, Ceasar, Cosimo, Cosmo.*

Ferreyra (110) Galician and Portuguese: variant of FERREIRA.
GIVEN NAMES Spanish 50%. *Jose* (5), *Jorge* (3), *Natividad* (3), *Juan* (2), *Luis* (2), *Adalberto, Alfredo, Arcelia, Armando, Arturo, Augusto, Carlos.*

Ferri (1148) Italian: patronymic or plural form of FERRO.

GIVEN NAMES Italian 16%. *Domenic* (6), *Antonio* (5), *Enrico* (4), *Pasquale* (4), *Rocco* (4), *Vito* (4), *Angelo* (3), *Aldo* (2), *Carlo* (2), *Carmine* (2), *Dino* (2), *Geno* (2).

Ferrick (372) Irish (County Mayo): shortened Americanized form of *Mac Phiaraic* 'son of Piers or Peter'. The Piers in question is probably the 12th-century Norman baron Piers de Bermingham, founder of the **McCorish** family, of which this is a branch.

Ferrie (336) Scottish spelling of Irish FERRY.

Ferriell (120) Origin unidentified.

Ferrier (1178) **1.** Scottish: occupational name for a smith, one who shoed horses, Middle English and Old French *ferrier*, from medieval Latin *ferrarius*, from *ferrus* 'horseshoe', from Latin *ferrum* 'iron'. Compare FARRAR. **2.** Scottish: possibly an occupational name for a ferryman. Black reports that lands called Ferrylands in Dumbarton, by a ferry across the Clyde, belonged to Robert Ferrier in 1512. **3.** Possibly southern French: occupational name for a smith, a variant of **Ferrié** (see FERRIE).

Ferriera (178) **1.** Southern Italian: variant of FERRERA, itself a variant of FERRARA. **2.** Variant of Spanish FERREIRA.

GIVEN NAMES Spanish 12%; Italian 5%. *Jose* (2), *Americo, Armando, Augusto, Carlos, Ferando, Jacinto, Jaime, Luiz, Manuel, Marta, Pedro*; *Antonio* (3), *Antonietta, Marcello, Silvio*.

Ferries (111) Scottish: according to Black, either a shortened form of **MacFerries**, an Anglicized form of Gaelic **Mac Fearghuis** 'son of FERGUS', or an altered form of FERGUS itself. Compare FERRIS.

Ferrigno (575) Southern Italian: from the adjective *ferrigno* 'made of or resembling iron' (a derivative of Latin *ferrum* 'iron'), applied as a nickname to someone who was very strong or thought to resemble the metal in some other way.

GIVEN NAMES Italian 26%. *Angelo* (7), *Carmelo* (4), *Carmine* (3), *Massimo* (3), *Pasquale* (3), *Salvatore* (3), *Emanuele* (2), *Vito* (2), *Alfonse, Alfonso, Bartolomeo, Benito, Bernardo, Cesar, Dante, Mario, Rafael*.

Ferrill (542) Irish: variant of FARRELL.

Ferrin (855) **1.** Irish: variant of FARREN or a shortened form of MCFERRIN. **2.** Spanish (**Ferrín**): from a derivative of *ferro* 'iron'. **3.** Italian: dialect variant of *Ferrino*, a diminutive of FERRO 1.

Ferring (129) English: habitational name from a place in West Sussex, so named from the Old English personal name *Fēra* + *-ingas* 'people of', 'family of', or 'followers of'.

Ferringer (144) Probably a respelling of German FEHRINGER.

Ferrington (174) English (Shropshire): variant of FARRINGTON.

Ferrini (179) Italian: patronymic or plural form of *Ferrino*, a diminutive of FERRO.

GIVEN NAMES Italian 16%. *Mario* (2), *Aldo, Carlo, Carmela, Dino, Gilda, Gino, Raul, Renato*.

Ferriola (114) Variant of Italian **Ferriolo**, which is either an occupational name for a blacksmith or iron worker, from *ferraiolo*, or alternatively from a homonym (Sicilian *firriolu, furriolu*) denoting a type of cloak, typically of silk, worn by clerics and high-ranking officials.

GIVEN NAMES Italian 9%; French 5%. *Constantino*; *Patrice* (2).

Ferris (8268) **1.** Irish and Scottish: reduced Anglicized form of Irish **Ó Fearghuis** or **Ó Fearghasa** 'descendant of *Fearghus*', or from the Scottish-Gaelic form of this personal name, *Fearghus* (see FERGUS). **2.** English: variant of FARRAR.

Ferriss (174) Irish, Scottish, or English: variant of FERRIS.

Ferriter (225) Possibly an Americanized spelling of German **Vorreiter**, an occupational name for someone who rides ahead, Middle High German, Middle Low German *vorrīter*, from *vor* 'before', 'ahead' + *rīter* 'rider'.

Ferritto (110) Italian: variant of FERLITO.

GIVEN NAMES Italian 18%. *Angelo, Domenic, Florindo, Geno, Pasquale*.

Ferro (2228) **1.** Italian, Spanish, Portuguese, and Jewish (Sephardic): metonymic occupational name for someone who produced or worked iron (Latin *ferrum*). **2.** Italian: from a medieval personal name, preserved in the modern pet form *Ferrucio*.

GIVEN NAMES Italian 10%; Spanish 10%. *Salvatore* (12), *Antonio* (7), *Angelo* (6), *Mario* (5), *Pasquale* (4), *Alberto* (3), *Antonino* (3), *Bernardo* (3), *Guido* (3), *Carmine* (2), *Concetta* (2), *Dino* (2), *Ottavio* (2), *Pietro* (2), *Rocco* (2); *Manuel* (12), *Jose* (10), *Luis* (6), *Carlos* (4), *Ramon* (4), *Eduardo* (3), *Fermin* (3), *Sixto* (3), *Angel* (2).

Ferron (556) **1.** French: occupational name for a blacksmith or worker in iron, from Old French *ferron* 'blacksmith' (Latin *ferro*, genitive *ferronis*, a derivative of *ferrum* 'iron'). **2.** Italian: from an augmentative of FERRO. **3.** Possibly also a reduced form of northern Irish MCFERRON.

GIVEN NAMES French 6%. *Armand* (2), *Aime, Fernand, Luce, Marthe, Remy*.

Ferrone (396) Italian: from an augmentative of FERRO.

GIVEN NAMES Italian 6%. *Rocco* (2), *Cosmo, Marco, Vito*.

Ferroni (120) Italian: patronymic or plural form of FERRONE.

GIVEN NAMES Italian 23%. *Alberto, Alessandro, Amedeo, Elvio, Enrico, Germano, Grazia, Lorenzo, Mario, Serafino, Stefano*.

Ferrucci (425) Italian: patronymic or plural form of a diminutive from FERRO.

GIVEN NAMES Italian 15%. *Nunzio* (3), *Aldo, Alessandro, Angelo, Dario, Egidio, Enzo, Fiore, Franco, Giovanna, Luigi, Nicola*.

Ferry (3718) **1.** Irish: reduced Anglicized form of Gaelic **Ó Fearadhaigh** 'descendant of *Fearadhach*', a personal name of uncertain origin, probably an adjective derivative of *fear* 'man'. **2.** English: metonymic occupational name for a ferryman, or a topographic name for someone who lived by a ferry crossing on a river. Middle English *feri* 'ferry' is from Old Norse *ferja* 'ferry', ultimately cognate with the Old English verb *ferian* 'to carry'.

Ferryman (169) English: occupational name for a ferryman (see FERRY).

Fersch (119) German: **1.** nickname for someone with a deformed heel, from Middle High German *verse(n)* 'heel'. **2.** nickname for a handsome, young person, from Middle Low German *versch* 'fresh', 'new'.

GIVEN NAME German 5%. *Wendelin*.

Ferson (113) Probably a shortened form of MCPHERSON.

GIVEN NAME French 5%. *Minot* (2).

Ferst (110) German: unrounded form of **Först**, a variant of FORST 1.

Ferster (127) German: variant of FORSTER 1.

GIVEN NAMES German 6%. *Eldred, Erwin, Kurt*.

Fertal (116) Jewish (eastern Ashkenazic): variant of FERTEL.

Fertel (122) Jewish (eastern Ashkenazic): nickname from Yiddish *fertl* 'a quarter'; perhaps applied to a very small person.

GIVEN NAMES Jewish 8%. *Cohen, Hyman, Isadore*.

Fertig (772) German and Jewish (Ashkenazic): nickname from Middle High German *vertec* 'skillful', 'ready', 'prepared' (German *fertig*), Old High German *fertīg*, a derivative of *vart* 'journey', 'expedition', and so meaning originally 'ready for an expedition'.

Fertitta (346) Sicilian: said to be from a personal name based on an Arabic word meaning 'butterfly'.

GIVEN NAMES Italian 11%. *Salvatore* (7), *Angelo, Domenic*.

Ferullo (254) Italian: from a diminutive of FERA.

GIVEN NAMES Italian 11%; French 4%. *Pasquale* (2), *Antonio, Domenic, Domenica, Rocco, Salvator, Vincenzo*; *Alphonse, Andre, Michel*.

Ferwerda (168) German: of uncertain origin; possibly from East Frisian **Ferweerda**, composed of the elements *Fer-*, *Ver-* 'woman' (German *Frau*) + *Weerda*, from a short form of a personal name related to Old High German *wer* 'worthy' or Old Saxon *werd* 'innkeeper', 'householder'.

Feser (180) German: variant of FEESE.

Fesko (145) possibly an Americanized spelling of Slovak **Fečko** (see FECKO).

Fesler (601) Variant of German and Jewish FESSLER.

Fesmire (342) Americanized spelling of German **Fes(en)meyer** or **Fess(en)maier**, from Middle High German, Middle Low German *vesen* 'husk', 'chaff', 'spelt' + *meier* 'steward', '(tenant) farmer', hence an occupational name for an overseer or tax official in the grain trade or for a spelt grower.

Fesperman (311) German: **1.** in northern Germany, a topographic name for someone living by a field named as *Fesper*. **2.** in the south of Germany, probably an occupational name for someone who rang the bell for vespers.

Fess (231) German: variant of FEESE.

Fessel (195) South German: **1.** variant spelling of FASSEL. **2.** perhaps occupational name for a maker of leather straps, from Middle High German *vezzel* 'shackle', 'strap'.

Fessenden (733) English (Kent): unexplained; probably from a lost or unidentified place in Kent, named with an unexplained first element + Old English *denu* 'valley'. The variant **Fishenden** is also found.

Fessler (1330) **1.** German and Jewish (Ashkenazic): occupational name for a cooper, Middle High German *vezzeler*, an agent derivative of *faz* 'barrel', 'keg'. **2.** Swiss German: nickname for a complainer, probably from Middle High German *vassen* 'to enquire', 'to investigate'.

Fest (190) German: nickname for a strong, steadfast person, from Middle High German *veste* 'strong', 'firm'.

Festa (894) **1.** Southern Italian: possibly from *festa* 'festival', 'holiday', but more likely from a short form of the medieval omen names *Carafesta* or *Cattafesta*. **2.** Portuguese: from *festa* 'festival', 'holiday'.
GIVEN NAMES Italian 12%. *Carmine* (6), *Salvatore* (3), *Antonio* (2), *Enrico* (2), *Luigino* (2), *Angelo, Carlo, Cosmo, Domenic, Giuseppi, Italia, Libero.*

Fester (223) **1.** German: from a short form of the personal name SILVESTER. **2.** Jewish (Ashkenazic): nickname from inflected form of Yiddish *fest* 'firm'.
GIVEN NAMES German 4%; Jewish 4%. *Gottlieb, Guenther, Hans; Arieh* (2), *Mordechai.*

Fetch (216) Americanized spelling of Swiss German FETSCH.

Fetchko (109) Americanized spelling of Slovak **Fečko** (see FECKO).

Fetcho (119) Origin unidentified. Possibly an altered form of Slovak FECKO.

Feth (107) German: spelling variant of **Veth**, a variant of FATH.
GIVEN NAMES German 10%. *Aloysius, Siegbert.*

Fetherolf (216) Of German origin, but unexplained. Compare FETTEROLF, FETTERHOFF. This name is found predominantly in OH.

Fetherston (227) English: variant spelling of FEATHERSTONE.

Fetner (283) Altered spelling of German **Fettner, Pfet(t)ner**, an occupational name for a timber worker, from an agent derivative of Middle High German *phate* 'beam', 'roof timber' (see FATH).

Fetrow (315) Origin unidentified.

Fetsch (230) **1.** German (Swabia): topographic name for someone who lived in an area of marsh or moorland, from Swabian *Fätsche* 'marsh'. **2.** Swiss German: occupational nickname for a mountain farmer, from Alemannic *fätsche* 'mountain hay'.

Fetsko (190) Variant spelling of Slovak **Fečko** (see FECKO).

Fett (609) **1.** North German: nickname for a fat man, from Middle Low German *vett* 'fat'. **2.** English: nickname from Old French *fait*, Middle English *fet* 'suitable', 'comely'. **3.** Norwegian: habitational name from any of several farms named with Old Norse *fit* 'meadow'.

Fette (292) Variant of German FETT or FATH 4.

Fetter (1493) **1.** German: variant spelling of VETTER. **2.** Jewish (Ashkenazic): nickname for a fat man, from modern German *fett*, Yiddish *fet* 'fat'.

Fetterhoff (294) Of German origin, but unexplained. Compare FETHEROLF, FETTEROLF. This name is found chiefly in PA.

Fetterly (266) Americanized spelling of German **Vetterle** or **Vätterli**, from a pet form of Middle High German *vetter* 'secondary male relative', i.e. uncle or cousin, but not father or son.

Fetterman (931) Jewish (Ashkenazic): variant of FETTER.

Fetterolf (444) Of German origin, but unexplained. Compare FETHEROLF, FETTERHOFF. This name is found chiefly in PA.

Fetters (1504) English: nickname for a cheat, from Middle English, Anglo-French *faitour* 'imposter', 'cheat', a specialized sense of Old French *faitor* 'doer', 'maker'.

Fettes (147) **1.** Scottish: variant of FETT 'comely'. **2.** German: unexplained; probably a Rhenish dialect form.

Fettig (812) German: **1.** in the north, a patronymic from FETT. **2.** in the south, from Middle High German *vetich* 'wing (of a bird)'. **3.** variant of FATH 4.
GIVEN NAMES German 4%. *Mathias* (4), *Benno, Helmut, Kurt, Wendelin.*

Fetting (213) North German: **1.** patronymic from FETT. **2.** variant of FETTIG 2. **3.** variant of FATH 4.
GIVEN NAMES German 7%. *Erwin, Fritz, Hans, Johann, Siegfried.*

Fettinger (110) German: variant of FATH 1 and 4.

Fetty (611) German: variant of FATH 4.

Fetz (169) South German: **1.** nickname for a sloppy, disorderly person, from Middle High German *vetze* 'scrap', 'rag'. **2.** probably a variant of FATH 2.
GIVEN NAMES German 5%. *Hannelore, Kurt, Manfred.*

Fetzer (1470) German: **1.** occupational name for a ragman, from an agent derivative of Middle High German *vetze* 'scrap', 'rag' or *vetzen* 'to tear or shred'. **2.** topographic name for someone who lived in a marshy area, from Swabian *Fätsche* 'marsh'. **3.** altered spelling of **Pfetzer**, a nickname from Middle High German *phetzen* 'to pinch'.

Fetzner (131) South German: variant of FETZER.
GIVEN NAME German 4%. *Kurt.*

Feucht (453) German: topographic name for someone who lived by a conspicuous pine tree or by a pine forest, from Middle High German *viehte* 'pine'. The vowel of the first syllable underwent a variety of changes in different dialects.
GIVEN NAMES German 4%. *Frieda, Gottlieb, Guenter.*

Feuer (786) **1.** German: metonymic occupational name for a stoker in a smithy or public baths, or nickname for someone with red hair or a fiery temper, from Middle High German *viur* 'fire'. **2.** Jewish (Ashkenazic): ornamental name from modern German *Feuer* 'fire'.
GIVEN NAMES Jewish 7%; German 4%. *Hyman* (2), *Moshe* (2), *Sol* (2), *Avi, Avrohom, Rochel, Shimon, Shula, Simcha, Tema, Yetta, Zehava; Frieda* (3), *Georg, Kurt, Otto.*

Feuerbach (131) German: habitational name for someone from any of several places so named. According to Bahlow, Feuerbach near Stuttgart was named from a prehistoric term for a marsh + Old High German *bah* 'stream' (see BACH 1).

Feuerbacher (139) German: habitational name for someone from any of the places called FEUERBACH.
GIVEN NAMES German 5%. *Fritz, Reinhard.*

Feuerborn (221) German: **1.** probably a topographic name for someone living near a spring or a well used for fighting fires, from Middle High German *viur* 'fire' + *born* 'spring'. **2.** alternatively, perhaps, a respelling of **Feuerbaum**, which is either a Rhenish nickname for a tall man or a topographic name for someone who lived by a juniper, Middle High German *viurboum*.

Feuerhelm (162) German: nickname from a compound of *Feuer* 'fire' + *Helm* 'helmet', probably an occupational nickname for a stoker or smelter.

Feuerman (125) Jewish (Ashkenazic): ornamental name from a compound of German *Feuer* 'fire' + *Mann* 'man'.
GIVEN NAMES Jewish 7%; German 5%. *Chaim* (2), *Simcha, Zipora; Frieda, Kurt.*

Feuerstein (654) **1.** German: metonymic occupational name for a seller of flints, or topographic name for someone who lived near an outcrop of flint, from Middle High German *viur* 'fire' + *stein* 'stone'. **2.** Jewish (Ashkenazic): ornamental name composed of German FEUER 'fire' + *Stein* 'stone', or an ornamental name from the German *Feuerstein* 'flint'.
GIVEN NAMES Jewish 4%. *Hyman* (3), *Giora*, *Miriam*, *Shira*, *Zvi*.

Feuling (121) German: unexplained.

Feulner (216) German: **1.** Franconian (dialect) form of **Feilner** (see FEILER). **2.** habitational name from Feuln near Kulmbach, Bavaria.
GIVEN NAMES German 4%. *Bernhardt*, *Willi*.

Feurer (112) German: occupational name for a stoker in a smithy, salt works, or public baths, from an agent derivative of Middle High German *viur* 'fire'.

Feury (166) Irish: variant of FUREY.
GIVEN NAMES Irish 6%. *Caitlin*, *Gearold*.

Feustel (151) South German: from a pet form of FAUST.

Feutz (183) **1.** Possibly a variant of German **Feuth**, itself a variant of **Voit** or **Foit**, common variants of VOGT. The final *-z* suggests a Rhineland origin. **2.** variant spelling of Swiss German **Feuz**, of unexplained origin.

Fevold (110) Norwegian: unexplained.

Few (795) English (Wiltshire and Cambridgeshire): unexplained.

Fewell (755) English: unexplained.

Fewkes (142) **1.** English: chiefly East Midlands variant of FOULKES. **2.** Americanized spelling of German FUCHS.

Fey (1439) **1.** English: variant of FAY. **2.** Southern French: topographic name for someone who lived by a beech tree or beech wood. **3.** German: nickname for a vagrant, from Middle High German *vēhe* 'enmity', 'strife'. **4.** German: from a popular medieval pet form of the female personal name *Sophie*, honored as a martyr and saint. **5.** Danish: unexplained.

Feyen (168) German: metronymic from FEY, with the genitive suffix *-en*.

Feyereisen (127) Variant of German and French (Alsace) **Feuereisen**, literally 'fire iron', an occupational nickname for a smith or steelmaker, from Middle High German *viurīsen*.

Fiacco (217) Italian: nickname from *fiacco* 'tired', 'weak', 'listless'.
GIVEN NAMES Italian 11%. *Angelo*, *Dario*, *Egidio*, *Ezio*, *Gino*, *Giovanna*, *Guido*, *Sal*, *Valentino*.

Fiala (1118) Czech and Slovak: from *fial(k)a* 'violet' (the flower). This may have given rise to a surname in various possible ways: as a nickname for a shy, delicate person; as a topographic name for someone who lived where violets grew or a habitational name for someone who lived at a house distinguished with the sign of a bunch of violets.

Fialkowski (182) Polish (**Fiałkowski**): **1.** variant of **Fijałkowski** (see FIJALKOWSKI). **2.** from the personal name *Fija–ek* (from *fiołek* 'violet') + *-owski*, a suffix of surnames.

Fiallo (150) Galician: from a byname derived from Galician *fiallo* 'little thread'.
GIVEN NAMES Spanish 54%. *Jose* (6), *Carlos* (5), *Jesus* (4), *Galo* (3), *Guillermo* (3), *Jorge* (3), *Rafael* (3), *Alfredo* (2), *Ernesto* (2), *Luis* (2), *Osvaldo* (2), *Pedro* (2); *Antonio*, *Clemente*, *Federico*, *Lorenzo*, *Marco*, *Mirella*.

Fiandaca (109) Southern Italian: hypercorrected form of **Fianndaca**, from Sicilian *cannacca*, *çiannaca*, Calabrian *cannacca*, *fannacca* denoting a necklace of gold, coral, or gems, from Arabic *hannāqah*, *hinnāqah* 'pearl or gold necklace', presumably applied as a metonymic occupational name for a jeweler or possibly as a nickname for someone noted for their fine jewelry.
GIVEN NAMES Italian 18%. *Massimo* (3), *Salvatore* (2), *Angelo*, *Gilda*, *Pasquale*.

Fiano (106) Italian: habitational name from Fiano or Fiano Romano, in the provinces of Turin and Rome respectively.
GIVEN NAMES Italian 20%; French 11%. *Domenic* (2), *Rocco* (2), *Angelo*, *Antonio*, *Enrico*, *Sabato*, *Salvatore*; *Andre* (4), *Marcel*.

Fiaschetti (100) Italian: from a diminutive of **Fiasco**, a metonymic occupational name for a maker of goatskin flasks, or a nickname for someone who habitually used a flask or who was thought to look like one, from *fiasco* 'flask', 'bottle'.
GIVEN NAMES Italian 16%. *Americo* (2), *Margarita* (2), *Ezio*.

Fiato (128) Italian: unexplained; perhaps related to modern Italian *fiato* 'breath'.
GIVEN NAMES Italian 11%. *Rocco* (2), *Marco*, *Salvatore*.

Ficara (101) Southern Italian: topographic name from Sicilian *ficara* 'fig tree' or 'plantation of fig trees'.
GIVEN NAMES Italian 33%. *Cosmo* (2), *Rocco* (2), *Salvatore* (2), *Santo* (2), *Angelo*, *Nazzareno*, *Paolo*.

Ficarra (295) Southern Italian (Sicily): habitational name from Ficarra in Messina province, Sicily, so named from *ficara* 'fig tree', 'fig plantation'.
GIVEN NAMES Italian 11%. *Angelo* (2), *Salvatore* (2), *Carmelo*, *Rocco*, *Sal*.

Ficca (150) Italian: probably from a short form of a name composed of a verb + a name, in particular of *Ficcadenti* meaning roughly 'meddler', 'busybody'; otherwise, possibly from a feminine form of FICCO.
GIVEN NAMES Italian 11%. *Antonio* (2), *Remo* (2), *Gianni*, *Mauro*, *Nicola*.

Ficco (148) Italian: unexplained; perhaps a variant of FICO.

GIVEN NAMES Italian 10%. *Angelo*, *Cosmo*, *Guido*, *Luigi*, *Vito*.

Ficek (256) Polish and Czech: from a pet form of the personal name *Wicenty* (Polish), *Vincenc* (Czech), vernacular forms of Latin *Vincentius* (see VINCENT).

Fichera (359) Southern Italian: topographic name from Sicilian and Calabrian *fichera* 'fig tree', 'fig plantation' or habitational name from Fichera in Sicily, named with this word.
GIVEN NAMES Italian 23%. *Salvatore* (10), *Alfio* (4), *Angelo* (4), *Pasquale* (2), *Santo* (2), *Alessandro*, *Camillo*, *Carmelina*, *Concetto*, *Filippo*, *Gaspere*, *Nunzio*.

Fichtel (140) South German: topographic name for someone who lived near pine trees (see FICHTER).

Fichter (737) German: **1.** topographic name for someone who lived near pine trees (originally *bei den Fichten*, *Feichten*, or *Feuchten*), from Old High German *fiohta*. The vowel of the first syllable underwent a variety of changes in different dialects. **2.** habitational name deriving from places named with this word in Württemberg, Bavaria, Saxony, or Austria.

Fichtner (458) German: variant of FICHTER.
GIVEN NAMES German 5%. *Fritz* (2), *Erwin*, *Horst*, *Kurt*.

Fick (2094) **1.** English: variant of FITCH. **2.** North German: from a pet form of the personal name FRIEDRICH.

Fickbohm (103) North German: probably a habitational name from a minor place so called from *Fick*, a reduced form of the personal name FRIEDRICH, + *bohm*, variant of *Baum* 'tree'.

Ficke (301) **1.** North German: variant of FICK. **2.** English: variant of FITCH.

Fickel (363) German: **1.** in northern and central Germany, from a pet form of FRIEDRICH. **2.** in northern Germany, a nickname for a dirty person, from Low German *fickel* 'piglet', 'sow'. **3.** in southern Germany, from a pet form of *Vigil(ius)*.

Ficken (553) **1.** English: diminutive of FITCH. **2.** German: variant of FICK 2.

Ficker (285) German: **1.** nickname for a restless person, from an agent derivative of Middle High German *vicken* 'to rub or fidget'. **2.** from a short form of a Germanic personal name composed with Old High German *fridu* 'peace' or *frik* 'battle happy'.
GIVEN NAMES German 7%. *Hermann* (2), *Kurt* (2), *Eckhard*.

Fickert (121) German: variant of FICKER.
GIVEN NAME German 4%. *Kurt*.

Fickes (477) German: **1.** possibly a Rhenish variant of FICK. **2.** variant spelling of *Ficus*, *Fi(c)kus*, humanistic form (translation) of the surname FEIGENBAUM.

Fickett (398) **1.** English: diminutive of FITCH. **2.** Possibly an Americanized spelling of German FICKERT.

Fickey (101) Americanized form of German **Füge** (see FUGE) or FICKE.

Fickle (291) Americanized spelling of German FICKEL.

Ficklin (530) Americanized spelling of German **Wicklein**, probably from Middle High German *wickelīn* 'sweet pea', hence an indirect occupational name for a flower seller.

Fickling (291) English (Norfolk): probably a variant of HICKLING.

Fico (258) Italian: from *fico* 'fig', applied as a metonymic occupational name for someone who grew or sold figs, a topographic name for someone who lived in an area where figs grew, or a habitational name from a place named with this word, such as the district so named in Valderice, Trapani province, Sicily.

GIVEN NAMES Italian 16%. *Gennaro* (2), *Pasquale* (2), *Sal* (2), *Aldo*, *Angelo*, *Aniello*, *Salvatore*.

Fidalgo (143) Portuguese: from *fidalgo* 'nobleman' (see Spanish HIDALGO).

GIVEN NAMES Spanish 33%; Portuguese 13%. *Carlos* (6), *Jose* (4), *Manuel* (4), *Jorge* (2), *Orlando* (2), *Americo*, *Casimira*, *Elida*, *Enrique*, *Jacinto*, *Jose Manuel*, *Juan*; *Joao* (2), *Joaquim*; *Antonio* (2), *Angelo*, *Federico*, *Lorenzo*, *Luciano*, *Ludovina*.

Fidanza (115) Italian: from Old Tuscan *fidanza* 'trust', probably applied as a nickname for an honest reliable person.

GIVEN NAMES Italian 18%. *Salvatore* (2), *Agostino*, *Antonio*, *Carmine*, *Franco*, *Gianni*, *Nino*.

Fiddes (118) **1.** Irish: Anglicized form of the Norman surname *de Sancto Fide* 'of the Holy Faith'. **2.** Scottish: habitational name from a barony in former Kincardineshire called Fiddes (earlier *Futhos* or *Fothes*).

Fiddler (450) **1.** English: occupational name for a fiddle player or a nickname for a skilled or enthusiastic amateur, from Old English *fiðelere* 'fiddler'. **2.** German: variant of FIEDLER.

Fidel (203) **1.** Italian, Catalan, Galician, and Spanish: from the personal name *Fidel*, from Latin *fidelis* 'of the faith'. **2.** Jewish (Ashkenazic): metonymic occupational name for a fiddler, from Yiddish *fidl* 'fiddle'.

GIVEN NAMES Spanish 6%; Jewish 4%. *Angel*, *Carlos*, *Jorge*, *Jose*, *Mario*, *Marta*, *Pascual*, *Reyes*, *Sanchez*, *Ventura*; *Tsilya*.

Fidler (1988) **1.** English: variant spelling of FIDDLER. **2.** Probably an Americanized spelling of German FIEDLER.

Fiebelkorn (243) German: nickname for a farmer who sold substandard grain, from Middle High German *wibel* 'grain beetle', 'weevil' + *korn* 'grain'.

Fieber (213) German: from a short form of a personal name composed with Old High German *fridu* 'peace'.

Fiebig (284) German: topographic name for someone who lived by a drovers' road, Middle High German *vihewec*, from *vehe*, *vihe*, *vich* 'cattle' + *wec* 'way', 'path'. The surname originated chiefly in Saxony, Silesia, and Bohemia.

GIVEN NAMES German 10%. *Angelika*, *Bernd*, *Detlef*, *Dieter*, *Erna*, *Erwin*, *Hans*, *Heinz*, *Horst*, *Kurt*.

Fiebiger (173) German: topographic name for someone who lived by a drovers' road (see FIEBIG).

GIVEN NAMES German 5%. *Dieter*, *Joerg*, *Kurt*.

Fiechter (136) German: variant spelling of FICHTER.

GIVEN NAMES French 5%; German 4%. *Jacques*, *Michel*.

Fiechtner (141) German: variant spelling of FICHTNER.

Fiedler (3099) German and Jewish (Ashkenazic): occupational name for a professional fiddle player, or a nickname for a skilled amateur, from Middle High German *videlære*, German *Fiedler* (Yiddish *fidler*). The instrument (Old High German *fidula*) is named from Late Latin *vitula*.

GIVEN NAMES German 5%. *Hans* (6), *Kurt* (6), *Otto* (6), *Armin* (4), *Erwin* (3), *Fritz* (3), *Gerhardt* (2), *Alfons*, *Ernst*, *Gerhard*, *Gottfried*, *Hannelore*.

Fiedor (126) Polish: variant of FEDOR.

GIVEN NAMES Polish 10%. *Andrzej*, *Jozef*, *Krzysztof*, *Stanislaw*, *Zdzislaw*.

Fiege (103) Variant of German **Füge** (see FUGE).

Fiegel (311) South German: **1.** metonymic occupational name for a fiddler, from the dialect word *figele* 'fiddle', 'violin' (from Late Latin *figella*). **2.** diminutive of **Fiege**, a variant of **Füge**, from Middle High German *vüege* 'skillful', 'adroit'. **3.** nickname from a dialect form of Middle High German *vīol* 'violet'. Compare FEIGEL.

GIVEN NAMES French 4%; German 4%. *Remy*; *Kurt* (3), *Ernst*.

Fieger (112) German: **1.** occupational name for a steward or overseer, from an agent derivative of Middle High German *vüegen* 'to arrange or dispose' (Old High German *fuogen*, a derivative of *fuog* 'neat', 'smart'). **2.** variant of FICKER 2.

Fiegl (116) German: variant of FIEGEL.

Fiel (181) Portuguese and Spanish: from a byname derived from *fiel* 'faithful', 'true'.

GIVEN NAME Jewish 4%. *Miriam* (3).

Field (10758) **1.** English: topographic name for someone who lived on land which had been cleared of forest, but not brought into cultivation, from Old English *feld* 'pasture', 'open country', as opposed on the one hand to *æcer* 'cultivated soil', 'enclosed land' (see ACKER) and on the other to *weald* 'wooded land', 'forest' (see WALD). **2.** Possibly also Scottish or Irish: reduced form of **McField** (see MCPHAIL). **3.** Jewish (American): Americanized and shortened form of any of the many Jewish surnames containing *Feld*.

Fielden (529) English: variant of FIELD, from the dative plural of Old English *feld* 'open country'.

Fielder (2607) Southern English: from Middle English *felder* 'dweller by the open country'.

Fieldhouse (187) English (chiefly West Midlands and northern England): topographic name for someone who lived in a house (Middle English *hous*) in open pasture land (see FIELD). Reaney draws attention to the form *de Felhouse* (Staffordshire 1332), and suggests that this may have become FELLOWS.

Fielding (2247) English: topographic name from an Old English *felding* 'dweller in open country'.

Fieldman (154) Americanized form of the Jewish ornamental name FELDMAN.

Fields (31799) English: topographic name from Middle English *feldes*, plural or possessive of *feld* 'open country'. This name is also found as a translation of equivalent names in other languages, in particular French DESCHAMPS, DUCHAMP.

Fien (140) Variant of German FIENE 1.

Fiene (358) North German: **1.** nickname for an elegant person, from Middle Low German *fīn* 'fine'. **2.** habitational name from several fields and places named with *Fiene*.

Fier (233) **1.** Americanized form of German FEUER. **2.** French: nickname for someone who considered himself superior to others, from Old French *fier* 'terrible'.

GIVEN NAMES German 5%. *Kurt* (2), *Erwin*, *Frieda*.

Fierce (127) Probably a respelling of Swiss German **Fierz**, of unexplained origin.

Fierke (104) North German: nickname of uncertain origin, a byname for the Devil in Pomerania, Holstein, Hamburg, and Bremen.

Fierman (157) English: variant of FAIRMAN.

Fiero (267) Variant of Italian FIERRO.

Fierro (1938) **1.** Asturian-Leonese and Spanish: from *fierro* 'iron' (Latin *ferrum*) in Asturian-Leonese (alongside the variant *fierru*) and in a regional variant of Castilian. **2.** Italian: Campanese variant of FERRO.

GIVEN NAMES Spanish 34%; Italian 6%. *Jose* (32), *Carlos* (16), *Luis* (14), *Manuel* (14), *Mario* (14), *Jesus* (12), *Raul* (11), *Ruben* (11), *Juan* (10), *Arturo* (8), *Ramon* (7), *Alfredo* (6); *Antonio* (10), *Salvatore* (4), *Angelo* (3), *Ettore* (3), *Aldo* (2), *Eligio* (2), *Federico* (2), *Guido* (2), *Lorenzo* (2), *Marco* (2), *Nicola* (2), *Pasquale* (2).

Fierros (219) Asturian-Leonese: habitational name from a place called Los Fierros (from the plural of FIERRO) in Léon.

GIVEN NAMES Spanish 48%. *Jose* (9), *Jesus* (4), *Carlos* (3), *Ramon* (3), *Renaldo* (3), *Ruben* (3), *Fernando* (2), *Juan* (2), *Manuel* (2), *Mario* (2), *Pedro* (2), *Agustin*.

Fiers (121) See FIERCE.

GIVEN NAME French 4%. *Philippe*.

Fierst (192) Probably an Americanized spelling of **Fürst** (see FURST).

Fierstein (153) Jewish (American): Americanized spelling of FEUERSTEIN.
GIVEN NAME Jewish 7%. *Miriam* (2).

Fies (113) German: nickname for an unpleasant, bullying, or repulsive person, from Middle Low German *vies* 'disgusting', Middle High German *viez* 'violent'.

Fieseler (109) German: nickname for a womanizer, from an agent derivative of Middle High German *visel* 'penis'.

Fieser (152) German: **1.** nickname for an unpleasant or repulsive person, from an agent noun based on Middle Low German *vies* 'disgusting', Middle High German *viez* 'violent', 'devil of a man'. **2.** habitational name for someone from Viesen, near Jerichow, Brandenburg.

Fiest (142) Possibly an altered spelling of German WIEST.

Fiester (139) Perhaps an altered spelling of German FEISTER.

Fietz (115) German (under Slavic influence): **1.** from a Silesian short form of the personal name *Viezenz* (see VINCENT). **2.** possibly from a short form of the medieval personal name *Vitus* (see VITO).

Fife (2367) Scottish: regional name from the former kingdom of Fife in East Scotland, a name of obscure etymology. Tradition has it that the name is derived from an eponymous *Fib*, one of the seven sons of Cruithne, legendary founding father of the Picts.

Fifer (1069) **1.** Americanized spelling of German PFEIFFER. **2.** Slovenian spelling of German PFEIFFER, associated in particular with Maribor in eastern Slovenia.

Fifield (1048) English: habitational name from any of various places called Fifield or Fyfield, of which there are instances in Berkshire, Essex, Oxfordshire, and Wiltshire, all so named from Old English *fif* 'five' + *hīd* 'hide'. (A hide was a measurement of land area.)

Figard (108) French: from a derivative of *figue* 'fig', apparently applied as an offensive nickname.

Figaro (193) Of uncertain origin and derivation; the name is recorded in France, Italy, and Catalonia (**Figaró**, alongside its variant **Figueró**), and is possibly related to French *figuier*, Italian *fico*, or Catalan *figuera* 'fig tree'.
GIVEN NAMES French 18%; Italian 4%. *Rodolphe* (2), *Ghislaine, Jacques, Jean Claude, Nadege, Nicolle, Patrice, Pierre, Yves; Luigi, Sando*.

Figel (177) Variant of German FIEGEL or FEIGEL.

Figg (499) English: of uncertain origin. **1.** Perhaps a topographic name for someone who lived near a fig tree, or a metonymic occupational name for someone who sold figs, from Old French *figue* (Latin *ficus*). **2.** Reaney has it as a variant of

FITCH. **3.** It may also be from an unidentified personal name.

Figge (256) **1.** English: variant spelling of FIGG. **2.** German: from a short form of a personal name composed with *Fried-*, as for example FRIEDRICH. **3.** In southwestern Germany, a nickname for a tease, from Middle High German *vicken* 'to rub or fidget'.
GIVEN NAMES German 6%. *Erwin, Gerhard, Klaus, Kurt, Ulrich*.

Figgins (628) English: origin uncertain; apparently a pet form of FIGG.

Figgs (268) English: variant of FIGG.

Fightmaster (127) Americanized form of German **Feichtmeister** 'pine master', i.e. a master joiner.

Figiel (164) Polish: nickname for a prankster, from *figiel* 'trick', 'joke'.
GIVEN NAMES Polish 20%. *Ewa* (2), *Bogdan, Boguslaw, Dariusz, Dorota, Genowefa, Irena, Jadwiga, Janusz, Jerzy, Kazimierz, Thadeus*.

Figler (209) Americanized spelling of German FIEGLER.

Figley (284) Altered form of German **Figle** or **Fiegle**, variants of FIEGEL.

Figliola (115) Italian: diminutive of **Figlia**, from 'daughter', 'girl', Latin *filia*, perhaps used to distinguish a mother and daughter bearing the same given name, or from a female short form of a compound name formed with the element *-figlio* ('son', 'boy'), such as BONFIGLIO.
GIVEN NAMES Italian 15%. *Flavio, Rocco, Veto, Vito*.

Figone (160) Italian: from an augmentative of the personal name *Figo*, which may be a pet form of *Federico*. The surname occurs in northern Italy and Tuscany, where Germanic names are commonly Italianized with the suffix *-igo* (for example *Arrigo, Alberigo*).
GIVEN NAMES Italian 8%. *Angelo* (3), *Giovanni* (2), *Aldo*.

Figueira (191) Portuguese and Galician: topographic name for someone who lived near a fig tree from *figueira* 'fig tree' (from Latin *ficaria*), or a habitational name from a place named with this word.
GIVEN NAMES Spanish 18%; Portuguese 10%. *Avelino* (2), *Jacinto* (2), *Jose* (2), *Manuel* (2), *Adelino, Aires, Alberto, Alvero, Ana Lucia, Carlos, Fabio, Fernando; Vasco*.

Figueiredo (597) Portuguese and Galician: habitational name from any of numerous places named Figueiredo, from the collective noun *figueiredo* 'grove of fig trees'.
GIVEN NAMES Spanish 29%; Portuguese 17%; Italian 7%. *Jose* (27), *Manuel* (9), *Carlos* (5), *Francisco* (3), *Luis* (3), *Mario* (3), *Aurelio* (2), *Cesar* (2), *Fernando* (2), *Horacio* (2), *Jacinto* (2), *Luiz* (2); *Joao* (5), *Afonso* (2), *Joaquim* (2), *Paulo* (2), *Henrique, Ilidio, Marcio, Margarida, Vasco; Antonio* (27), *Marco* (2), *Angelo, Ceasar, Fabiano, Guido, Sandro*.

Figueras (178) Catalan: respelling of **Figueres**, a habitational name from a town called Figueres in the district of L'Empordà, Catalonia.
GIVEN NAMES Spanish 41%. *Jose* (8), *Juan* (5), *Carlos* (4), *Wilfredo* (3), *Ana* (2), *Fernando* (2), *Jorge* (2), *Josefa* (2), *Mario* (2), *Sabino* (2), *Alba, Alfredo; Antonio* (2).

Figueredo (338) Galician: variant of FIGUEIREDO.
GIVEN NAMES Spanish 50%. *Jorge* (8), *Jose* (8), *Luis* (8), *Fernando* (6), *Jesus* (5), *Roberto* (5), *Carlos* (4), *Manuel* (4), *Rafael* (4), *Ana* (3), *Francisco* (3), *Juan* (3).

Figueroa (8428) Galician: habitational name from any of the places in Galicia named Figueroa, from a derivative of *figueira* 'fig tree'.
GIVEN NAMES Spanish 49%; Portuguese 10%. *Jose* (242), *Luis* (121), *Juan* (107), *Carlos* (104), *Angel* (73), *Rafael* (66), *Miguel* (62), *Jorge* (56), *Jesus* (55), *Manuel* (53), *Francisco* (45), *Ramon* (45); *Ligia* (3), *Godofredo*.

Figura (326) **1.** Polish, Slovak, Ukrainian, and Hungarian: nickname for someone with a comic appearance, from *figura* 'figure', 'character', 'strange fellow' (from Latin *figura* 'form', 'shape'). **2.** Southern Italian: possibly from a short form of a personal name formed with *figura* 'form', 'shape' (Latin *figura*; possibly with the same meaning as in 1).
GIVEN NAMES Polish 5%. *Jozef* (2), *Casimir, Jerzy, Krzysztof, Waclaw*.

Figures (126) English: unexplained.
FOREBEARS Bartholomew Figures came from England to Surry County, VA, before 1677.

Figurski (174) Polish: variant of FIGURA, with the addition of the surname suffix *-ski*.
GIVEN NAMES Polish 6%. *Tadeusz* (2), *Mieczyslaw*.

Fijalkowski (77) Polish (**Fijałkowski**): habitational name for someone from any of various places called Fijałkowo, for example in Ostrołęka and Włocławek voivodeships, named with the nickname *Fijałek* or *Fijałka*, from Polish *fijałek* 'violet'.
GIVEN NAMES Polish 10%. *Jozef, Zygmunt*.

Fike (2428) Americanized spelling of German FEICK.

Fikes (763) Americanized spelling of *Faix* or *Feix*, variants of German VEIT.

Fila (199) **1.** Czech and Polish: from a pet form of *Filip* (see PHILIP). **2.** Polish: from a pet form of *Teofil* (from the Greek personal name *Theophilos*, derived from Greek *theos* 'god' + *philos* 'friend'). **3.** Polish: nickname from *chwila* 'moment'.
GIVEN NAMES Polish 5%. *Casimir, Leslaw, Stanislaw*.

Filak (115) Polish: from a derivative of FILA.
GIVEN NAMES Polish 7%. *Mikolaj* (2), *Jolanta*.

Filan (128) Polish: from a derivative of FILA.

Filar (133) Polish: nickname for a dependable, reliable man, from Polish *filar* 'pillar', 'support'.
GIVEN NAME Polish 5%. *Andrzej*.

Filardi (131) Italian: patronymic or plural form of FILARDO.
GIVEN NAMES Italian 18%. *Angelo, Ciro, Demetrio, Raul, Rocco, Salvatore*.

Filardo (132) Southern Italian: derogatory nickname from a dialect word akin to French *fillard* 'thief'.
GIVEN NAMES Italian 14%. *Domenic, Filippa, Salvatore, Silvio*.

Filas (123) **1.** Czech and Polish: derivative of the personal name *Filip* (see PHILIP). **2.** Ukrainian: unexplained.

Filbeck (113) English: habitational name from an unidentified place, possibly Fell Beck in North Yorkshire. The name has died out in England.

Filbert (418) **1.** English and German: from the medieval personal name, composed of the Germanic elements *fila* 'much' + *berht* 'bright', 'famous'. **2.** In some cases the name may be of French origin, a variant of **Filibert**, cognate with 1.

Filbin (122) English and Irish: variant spelling of PHILBIN.

Filby (191) English: habitational name from a place in Norfolk, so called from the Old Norse personal name *Fili* or *Fila* (of uncertain origin) + Old Norse *býr* 'farm', 'settlement'.

Fildes (130) English and Scottish (Aberdeen): regional name from a district in Lancashire called The Fylde, from Old English *(ge)filde* 'plain'.

File (617) **1.** Americanized spelling of German FEIL or PFEIL. **2.** Hungarian: variant of *Füle*, pet form of the personal name *Fülöp*, Hungarian form of PHILIP. **3.** Translation of French LALIME.

Fileccia (107) Southern Italian: from Sicilian *fieccia* 'arrow', applied as a metonymic occupational name for a fletcher or a nickname.
GIVEN NAMES Italian 22%. *Antonio, Camillo, Giovanni, Nicola, Salvatore, Stefano, Vincenzo*.

Filene (25) Jewish (from the Poznan area, now in western Poland): variant spelling of *Filehne*, habitational name for someone from the town called Wielen in Polish (*Filehne* in German), near Poznan.
FOREBEARS The patriarch of the family who established the prominent Boston retail department store Filene's, William Filene (1830–99), was a native of Poznan, Poland, the son of a well-to-do Jewish dealer in ribbons. He left Europe in 1848, at the age of 18, and opened a retail store in Salem, MA, in 1856. His sons Edward Filene (1860–1937) and Lincoln Filene (1865–1957) were not only successful businessmen but also influential thinkers and innovators from a liberal political and economic standpoint.

Filer (816) English: **1.** occupational name for a maker or user of files, from an agent derivative of Middle English *file* 'file'. **2.** occupational name for a spinner, from an agent derivative of Middle English, Old French *fil* 'thread' (Latin *filum*). **3.** Americanized spelling of German FEILER, cognate of 1.

Files (1271) **1.** Hungarian: variant of *Füles*, pet form of the personal name *Fülöp* (see PHILIP). **2.** Hungarian: nickname for someone with prominent ears, from *fül* 'ear'.

Filiatrault (103) French (southwestern France): from a diminutive of Occitan *filiatre*, an epithet meaning 'son-in-law'.
GIVEN NAMES French 15%. *Jacques, Jean Guy, Lucien, Pierre*.

Filiault (102) Southern French: variant of Occitan *filiol*, an epithet meaning 'godson'.
GIVEN NAMES French 11%. *Alain, Armand, Donat, Normand, Origene*.

Filice (258) Italian: **1.** (with the stress on the first syllable): variant of FELICE. **2.** (with the stress on the second syllable): topographic name from Sicilian *filici* 'fern'.
GIVEN NAMES Italian 16%. *Carmine* (3), *Angelo* (2), *Carlo* (2), *Antonio, Egidio, Franca, Francesco, Gennaro, Pasquale, Santo, Serafino, Vittorio*.

Filion (302) Variant spelling of French FILLION.
GIVEN NAMES French 17%. *Marcel* (3), *Andre, Denys, Gaetan, Germain, Gilles, Herve, Jacques, Jean-Louis, Joffre, Laurette, Laurier*.

Filip (497) Romanian, Polish, Czech, Slovak, and other European: from the personal name *Filip*, a vernacular form of the Greek personal name *Philippos* (see PHILIP).
GIVEN NAMES Romanian 7%; Polish 5%. *Mircea* (2), *Nicolae* (2), *Constantin, Doina, Dorel, Ilie, Ionel, Liviu, Petre, Radu, Stelian, Viorel; Bogdan, Henryka, Ireneusz, Janina, Stanislaw, Tadeusz, Wojciech, Zbigniew*.

Filipek (336) Czech (**Filípek**) and Polish: from a pet form of the personal name *Filip*, a vernacular form of Greek *Philippos* (see PHILIP).
GIVEN NAMES Polish 8%. *Jozef* (2), *Krystyna* (2), *Wladyslaw* (2), *Arkadiusz, Czeslaw, Ludwik*.

Filipi (142) Italian: variant of FILIPPI.

Filipiak (462) Polish: patronymic from the personal name *Filip*, a vernacular form of Greek *Philippos* (see PHILIP).
GIVEN NAMES Polish 5%. *Ewa, Henryk, Irek, Izabela, Marzena, Tadeusz, Tomasz*.

Filipkowski (168) Polish: habitational name for someone from any of various places named Filipki, from the personal name *Filip*, a vernacular form of Greek *Philippos* (see PHILIP), with the addition of the common suffix of surnames *-ski*.

GIVEN NAMES Polish 14%. *Franciszek, Genowesa, Jozef, Kazimerz, Krzysztof, Piotr, Slawomir, Zdzislaw, Zigmont, Zigmund*.

Filipovich (108) Serbian and Croatian (**Filipović**); also Ukrainian: patronymic from the personal name *Filip*, a vernacular form of Greek *Philippos* (see PHILIP).
GIVEN NAMES South Slavic 6%. *Dragan, Dusko*.

Filipowicz (273) Polish: patronymic from the personal name *Filip*, a vernacular form of Greek *Philippos* (see PHILIP).
GIVEN NAMES Polish 14%. *Casimir* (2), *Alojzy, Danuta, Ewa, Halina, Irena, Jadwiga, Jerzy, Ryszard, Stanislaw, Tadeusz, Zbigniew*.

Filipowski (124) Polish: habitational name for someone of any of various places called Filipowice or Filipów, from the personal name *Filip* (see PHILIP).
GIVEN NAMES Polish 7%. *Piotr, Tadeusz, Zbigniew*.

Filippelli (258) Italian: patronymic from a pet form of the personal name FILIPPO.
GIVEN NAMES Italian 26%. *Luigi* (3), *Mario* (3), *Carlo* (2), *Giovanni* (2), *Aldo, Carmela, Carmine, Cataldo, Dante, Domenico, Enrico, Franco, Eugenio, Isolina, Orlando, Pasquale, Roberto*.

Filippi (483) Italian: patronymic from the personal name FILIPPO.
GIVEN NAMES Italian 15%; French 4%. *Angelo* (2), *Carlo* (2), *Elio* (2), *Leno* (2), *Marcello* (2), *Primo* (2), *Reno* (2), *Amelio, Baldassare, Carmine, Elvio, Enzo; Andre, Jean Pierre, Veronique*.

Filippini (264) Italian: patronymic from the personal name *Filippino*, a pet form FILIPPO.
GIVEN NAMES Italian 14%. *Emidio* (2), *Luciano* (2), *Aldo, Amato, Antonio, Deno, Dino, Ezio, Federico, Guiseppe, Luigi, Marco*.

Filippo (144) Italian: from the personal name *Filippo*, from Greek *Philippos* (see PHILIP).
GIVEN NAMES Italian 10%. *Carlo, Elio, Libero, Marco, Rocco*.

Filippone (475) Italian: from an augmentative of the personal name FILIPPO.
GIVEN NAMES Italian 15%. *Salvatore* (5), *Antonio* (2), *Carmine* (2), *Angelo, Antonino, Dante, Ennio, Italia, Luciano, Mauro, Nicoletta, Pasquale*.

Filipski (183) Polish: **1.** habitational name for someone from a place called Filipy. **2.** from the personal name *Filip*, a vernacular form of Greek *Philippos* (see PHILIP) + the surname suffix *-ski*.

Filkins (611) English: **1.** patronymic from the medieval personal name *Filkin*, a diminutive from a short form of PHILIP. **2.** habitational name from a place so called in Oxfordshire, whose name is probably a tribal derivative (with Old English *-ingas* 'people of') of the Old English personal name *Filica* (of uncertain origin). Surname forms such as *de Filking(es)* are found in the surrounding area from the 12th and 13th centuries.

Fill (226) English: from a short form of the personal name PHILIP.

Filla (278) Czech: see FILA.

Fillebrown (104) Origin unidentified.

Filler (751) **1.** South German: occupational name for a flayer or skinner, from Middle High German *viller* 'knacker', from *villen* 'to skin'. **2.** Possibly a respelling of German **Füller**, an occupational name for a person whose work involved filling, such as a dauber, or a nickname for a gourmand or glutton.

Fillers (235) German: variant of FILLER 1.

Filley (283) English: from Middle English *filli* 'filly' (young female horse), perhaps a nickname for a temperamental or skittish person.

Fillingame (158) Variant of English FILLINGHAM. Compare FILLINGIM.

Fillinger (341) German: habitational name for someone from Villingen in the Black Forest, a market town since at least the 10th century, and a thriving trade center in the 12th century. The name derives from a 9th-century personal name, *Filo*, + the suffix *-ingen*, denoting 'people or followers of'.
GIVEN NAME German 4%. *Eldred.*

Fillingham (127) English: habitational name from a place in Lincolnshire, so named from the Old English personal name *Fygla* (from *fugol* 'bird') + *-inga-* 'of the people of' + *hām* 'homestead'.

Fillingim (367) Variant spelling of English FILLINGHAM.

Fillion (487) French: from a diminutive of Old French *fils* 'son' (Latin *filius*), used to denote the youngest son of a family.
FOREBEARS A bearer of the name from Paris is recorded in Quebec city in 1661.
GIVEN NAMES French 16%. *Andre* (3), *Armand* (3), *Gaston* (3), *Emile* (2), *Lucien* (2), *Marcel* (2), *Aime, Cecile, Donat, Fernand, Gisele, Jean Luc.*

Fillman (484) German (**Fillmann**): variant of FILLER 1.

Fillmore (1521) English: from a Norman personal name, *Filimor*, composed of the Germanic elements *filu* 'very' + *māri, mēri* 'famous'.
FOREBEARS The home of the main English branch of the Fillmore family in Tudor times was East Sutton, Kent, but the immigrant John Fillmore (1678–*c.*1710) was a mariner who came from Manchester, England, to Ipswich, MA, in about 1700. His son, also called John Fillmore (1702–77), had seven sons and three daughters. One of these sons, Nathaniel, was the father of President Millard Fillmore (1800–74).

Fillyaw (123) Americanized spelling of French FILIAULT.

Filmer (119) English: variant spelling of FILLMORE.

Filmore (215) English: variant spelling of FILLMORE.

Filo (173) Slovak (also **Fillo**): from a pet form of the personal name *Filip* (see PHILIP).

Filosa (235) Southern Italian: probably an occupational nickname for a fisherman, from Sicilian *filuòsa* 'fishing net'.
GIVEN NAMES Italian 9%; French 5%. *Sal* (3), *Antonio* (2), *Salvatore* (2), *Gennaro, Gilda, Pasquale*; *Lucien* (2), *Andre.*

Fils (102) French: from *fils* 'son', used to identify the younger of two bearers of the same personal name in a family.
GIVEN NAMES French 26%. *Guillaume* (2), *Antoine, Dieudonne, Etienne, Jean Claude, Jinette, Pierre.*

Fils-Aime (127) French (**Fils-Aimé**): nickname for a favorite son, from *fils* 'son' + *aimé* 'loved', 'beloved'.
GIVEN NAMES French 46%. *Pierre* (3), *Antoine* (2), *Andre, Argentine, Edeline, Fernande, Gessy, Gisele, Jean Claude, Lamartine, Leonne, Lucien.*

Filsinger (223) German: habitational name for someone from Filzingen in Württemberg.
GIVEN NAMES German 13%. *Manfred* (3), *Otto* (3), *Armin, Erna, Erwin, Kurt, Siegfried.*

Filson (497) English: patronymic from FILL.

Filteau (91) French: see FACTEAU.
FOREBEARS The surname Filteau first appears in Quebec in 1666.
GIVEN NAMES French 13%. *Alphonse, Emile, Gilles.*

Filter (295) North German: from Low German *vilt* 'felt' (from Old Saxon *filt*), an occupational name for someone who made felt or a metonymic occupational name for a hatter.
GIVEN NAMES German 6%. *Otto* (2), *Erna, Ewald, Guenther, Kurt.*

Filtz (135) German: **1.** occupational name for a maker or seller of felt. **2.** unflattering nickname for a stingy person.

Filyaw (182) Americanized spelling of French FILIAULT; probably a Huguenot name. The spelling **Philyaw** is also found.

Filzen (100) German: habitational name from any of several places so named in the Rhineland, Bavaria, and the Saar region.
GIVEN NAMES German 5%. *Armin, Erwin.*

Fimbres (234) Hispanic: unexplained.
GIVEN NAMES Spanish 35%. *Manuel* (7), *Francisco* (5), *Jose* (3), *Armando* (2), *Carlos* (2), *Fernando* (2), *Javier* (2), *Miguel* (2), *Abelardo, Adan, Angel, Arely.*

Fimple (106) Origin uncertain; possibly an Americanization of German **Fimmel**, occupational name for a hemp farmer or a dealer in hemp, from *Fimmel* 'hemp'.

Fina (246) Italian: from the female personal name *Fina* or a short form of any of various female personal names ending *-fina*, for example *Serafina*. Compare FINO.

GIVEN NAMES Italian 10%. *Silvio* (2), *Carmine, Gaetano, Gino, Oreste, Pasquale, Piera, Vincenzo.*

Finamore (334) **1.** English: variant of FENIMORE. Usually spelled *Finnamore*, this name is also found in Ireland, recorded in Leinster as early as the 13th century. **2.** Italian: from the medieval personal name *Finamore.*
GIVEN NAMES Italian 10%. *Angelo* (2), *Lorenzo* (2), *Antonio, Carmela, Emidio, Filippo, Gabriele, Giuseppe, Renzo.*

Finan (782) Irish (County Mayo): reduced Anglicized form of Gaelic **Ó Fionnáin** 'descendant of *Fionnán*', from the diminutive of *fionn* 'fair'.
GIVEN NAMES Irish 5%. *Aileen, Declan.*

Finau (101) Hawaiian: unexplained.
GIVEN NAMES Hawaiian 19%; Slavic 4%. *Tevita* (3), *Sione* (2), *Siaosi, Viliami*; *Milika.*

Finazzo (232) Southern Italian: from a pet form of FINO.
GIVEN NAMES Italian 30%. *Vito* (7), *Salvatore* (6), *Carlo* (3), *Sal* (2), *Antonio, Benedetto, Camillo, Mariano, Nicolo, Pina, Rosario, Stefano.*

Finberg (213) **1.** Jewish (Ashkenazic): variant of FEINBERG. **2.** Swedish: probably an ornamental name from *fin* 'fine' or *finn* 'Finnish' + *berg* 'mountain', 'hill'.
GIVEN NAMES Jewish 6%. *Meyer* (2), *Aron, Polina.*

Fincannon (217) Probably an American altered form of Irish CONCANNON. This name occurs predominantly in NC. Compare VONCANNON, VUNCANNON.

Finch (10965) English: nickname from Middle English *finch* 'finch' (Old English *finc*). In the Middle Ages this bird had a reputation for stupidity. It may perhaps also in part represent a metonymic occupational name for someone who caught finches and sold them as songsters or for the cooking pot. The surname is found in all parts of Britain but is most common in Lancashire. See also FINK.

Fincham (567) English: habitational name from a place in Norfolk, so called from Old English *finc* 'finch' + *hām* 'homestead' or *hamm* 'enclosure hemmed in by water', 'river meadow'.

Fincher (3033) English: unexplained.

Finchum (521) English: spelling of FINCHAM.

Finck (905) German: variant spelling of FINK.

Fincke (180) German: variant of FINK.
GIVEN NAME French 4%. *Jacques.*

Findeisen (140) German: occupational nickname for an apprentice blacksmith or journeyman, from Middle High German *vind-* (from *vinden* 'to find') + *īsen* 'iron', 'metal', literally 'find iron'. Apprentice names were often humorous; they were traditionally bestowed at high-spirited initiation ceremonies.

GIVEN NAMES German 19%. *Kurt* (4), *Hans* (2), *Erwin, Fritz, Heinz, Horst, Johannes, Otto*.

Finder (309) German: from Middle High German *vinder* 'inventor', possibly a nickname for a teller of tall stories or a person of great ingenuity.
GIVEN NAME French 4%. *Marcel* (2).

Findlay (1711) Scottish: variant spelling of FINLEY.

Findley (3421) Scottish: variant spelling of FINLEY.

Findling (202) German and Jewish (Ashkenazic): nickname for a foundling, from Middle High German *vindelīn*, German *Findling*.

Fine (5502) **1.** English: nickname for a clever or elegant man, from Old French *fin* 'fine', 'delicate', 'skilled', 'cunning' (originally a noun from Latin *finis* 'end', 'extremity', 'boundary', later used also as an adjective in the sense 'ultimate', 'excellent'). **2.** Jewish (American): Americanized spelling of FEIN.

Fineberg (332) Jewish (American): partly Americanized form of the ornamental compound name FEINBERG.
GIVEN NAMES Jewish 5%. *Hyman* (2), *Emanuel*.

Finefrock (152) Variant of German FINFROCK.
GIVEN NAME French 4%. *Camille*.

Finegan (729) Irish: variant spelling of FINNEGAN.
GIVEN NAME Irish 5%. *Liam*.

Finegold (200) Jewish (American): English translation of the ornamental compound name FEINGOLD.
GIVEN NAMES Jewish 8%. *Hyman* (2), *Chaya, Shoshanah*.

Finelli (514) Italian: patronymic from a pet form of FINO.
GIVEN NAMES Italian 17%. *Angelo* (5), *Domenic* (4), *Fiore* (2), *Rocco* (2), *Sal* (2), *Salvatore* (2), *Aniello, Antimo, Antonio, Biagio, Carmine, Domenico*.

Fineman (413) Americanized form or English translation of Jewish FEINMAN.
GIVEN NAMES Jewish 4%. *Gerson, Hyman, Isadore, Sol*.

Fineout (109) Probably an Americanized altered form of Dutch VAN HOUT.

Finer (354) **1.** English: occupational name for a refiner of gold and other metals, from Middle English *fine(n)* 'to refine or purify' (a derivative of *fine* 'fine', 'pure'). **2.** Probably a translated form of German FEINER.

Fineran (188) Irish: variant spelling of FINNERAN.

Finerty (209) Irish: variant spelling of FINNERTY.
GIVEN NAME Irish 7%. *James Patrick*.

Fines (229) English: variant of FINE.

Finestone (123) Americanized form of Jewish FEINSTEIN.
GIVEN NAME Jewish 4%. *Yaakov*.

Finfrock (351) German: nickname for a rich man (literally, the owner of five coats), from Middle High German *finf* 'five' + *roc* 'coat', 'jacket'.

Fingar (150) Variant (in Slavic regions) of German FINGER.

Finger (2172) English, German, and Jewish (Ashkenazic): from Middle English, Middle High German, Yiddish *finger* (modern German *Finger*), probably applied as a nickname for a man who had some peculiarity of the fingers, such as possessing a supernumerary one or having lost one or more of them through injury, or for someone who was small in stature or considered insignificant. As a Jewish name, it can also be an ornamental name.

Fingerhut (293) German and Jewish (Ashkenazic): metonymic occupational name for a tailor, from Middle High German *vingerhuot*, Yiddish *fingerhut* 'thimble' (literally 'finger hat'). The word also means 'foxglove', but this sense is unlikely to be relevant to the surname.
GIVEN NAMES Jewish 4%. *Sol* (2), *Iren, Shimon, Sima*.

Fingerman (138) Jewish (Ashkenazic): from Yiddish *finger*, 'finger', of uncertain application.
GIVEN NAME Jewish 6%. *Avrum*.

Fini (203) Italian: patronymic or patronymic from FINO.
GIVEN NAMES Italian 31%. *Mario* (3), *Aldo* (2), *Angelo* (2), *Delfo* (2), *Rosalina* (2), *Salvatore* (2), *Vincenzo* (2), *Alda, Anselmo, Armando, Benito, Carlo, Elvio, Francesco, Giovanni, Guido, Guilio, Luciano, Maurizio*.

Finigan (271) Irish: variant spelling of FINNEGAN.

Finizio (153) Italian: from the personal name *Finizio*.
GIVEN NAMES Italian 15%. *Vito* (2), *Amando, Americo, Cira, Gennaro, Giosue, Vincenzo*.

Fink (12178) German, Slovenian, English, and Jewish (Ashkenazic): nickname for a lively and cheerful person, or, in the case of the Jewish name, an ornamental name, from a Germanic word meaning 'finch' (see FINCH). As a Slovenian surname, it may also be a translation into German of the Slovenian surname **Šinkovec** (from an old spelling of *ščinkovec* or *ščinkavec* 'finch').

Finkbeiner (733) German: altered form of **Finkbunter**, a habitational name from any of various farmsteads named Finkbunt, from Middle High German *vinke* 'finch' (or perhaps *viehten* 'pine trees') + *biunte* 'enclosed plot'.
GIVEN NAMES German 6%. *Kurt* (4), *Otto* (3), *Albrecht, Armin, Erwin, Hans*.

Finkbiner (201) Respelling of German FINKBEINER.

Finke (1533) German: variant of FINK.

GIVEN NAMES German 4%. *Kurt* (3), *Dieter* (2), *Gerhard* (2), *Bernhard, Detmar, Erwin, Frieda, Fritz, Helmut, Rainer*.

Finkel (1396) **1.** German: from a diminutive of FINK. **2.** German: indirect occupational name for a blacksmith, from a derivative of *finken* 'to make sparks'. **3.** Jewish (eastern Ashkenazic): ornamental name from Yiddish *finkl* 'sparkle'. **4.** English: variant spelling of FINKLE.
GIVEN NAMES Jewish 7%. *Asher* (4), *Sol* (4), *Myer* (2), *Avram, Avrohom, Basya, Berko, Bronia, Einat, Fira, Golda, Irina*.

Finkelman (248) Jewish (eastern Ashkenazic): ornamental compound of Yiddish *finkl* 'sparkle' + *man* 'man'.
GIVEN NAMES Jewish 13%; Russian 4%. *Sol* (3), *Mordechai* (2), *Ofer* (2), *Eliezer, Hagit, Moshe, Shimon, Simcha*; *Arkady, Iosif, Leonid, Raisa, Valeriy, Yefim*.

Finkelstein (2710) Jewish (eastern Ashkenazic): ornamental compound name, literally 'sparkle stone', from Yiddish *finkl* 'sparkle' + *stein* 'stone'.
GIVEN NAMES Jewish 8%. *Sol* (6), *Meyer* (5), *Miriam* (4), *Hyman* (3), *Nachum* (3), *Aron* (2), *Chaim* (2), *Emanuel* (2), *Mayer* (2), *Alter, Avram, Bluma*.

Finken (311) German: variant of FINK or perhaps a short form of any of the various German compound names beginning with *Finken*.
GIVEN NAMES German 4%. *Guenther, Gunther, Karl-Heinz, Meinrad*.

Finkenbinder (181) Partly Americanized spelling of German **Finkenbeinder**, a variant of FINKBEINER, commonly found in Baden and Württemberg.

Finkle (824) **1.** English: habitational name (reflecting the pronunciation of the place name) for someone from Finchale in Durham, named from Old English *finc* 'finch' + *halh* 'nook or corner of land'. **2.** English: possibly a metonymic occupational name or topographic name from Middle English *fenkel* 'fennel'. Compare FENNELL. **3.** Respelling of German FINKEL.

Finklea (466) Altered spelling of English FINKLEY.
GIVEN NAMES French 4%. *Andre, Celestine, Chanel, Lucien*.

Finkler (257) Jewish (Ashkenazic): variant of FINKEL.
GIVEN NAMES Jewish 4%. *Bronia, Isadore*.

Finkley (137) English: habitational name from a place in Hampshire named Finkley, from Old English *finc* 'finch' + *lēah* 'woodland clearing'.

Finks (319) Probably a variant of German FINK.

Finlan (122) Irish (midlands): reduced Anglicized form of Gaelic **Ó Fionnaláin** (see FENLON).

Finlay (1206) Scottish: variant spelling of FINLEY.

Finlayson (1003) Scottish: patronymic from FINLAY.

Finley (12842) Scottish: from the Gaelic personal name *Fionnlagh* (Old Irish *Findlaech*), composed of the elements *fionn* 'white', 'fair' (see FINN) + *laoch* 'warrior', 'hero', which seems to have been reinforced by an Old Norse personal name composed of the elements *finn* 'Finn' + *leikr* 'fight', 'battle', 'hero'.

Finlinson (137) Variant of Scottish FINLAYSON.

Finn (8459) **1.** Irish: reduced Anglicized form of Gaelic **Ó Finn** 'descendant of *Fionn*', a byname meaning 'white' or 'fair-haired'. This name is borne by several families in the west of Ireland. **2.** English: from the Old Norse personal name *Finnr* 'Finn', used both as a byname and as a short form of various compound names with this first element. **3.** German: ethnic name for someone from Finland.
GIVEN NAMES Irish 6%. *Brendan* (7), *Liam* (2), *Aidan, Bridie, Brigid, Declan, Dierdra, Eoin, Keelin, Maeve, Niall, Seamus.*

Finnan (183) Irish: variant spelling of FINAN.

Finne (179) **1.** Variant spelling of FINN 1, 2, and 4. **2.** Norwegian: habitational name from any of several farms so named, from *finn* 'matgrass (Nardus stricta)' or *finn* 'Lapp' + *vin* 'meadow'. **3.** Danish: habitational name from various fields or places so named in Germany. **4.** North German: nickname for a sponger or freeloader or for an ugly old woman, from Middle Low German *vinne* 'pimple', 'blackhead'.
GIVEN NAMES Scandinavian 10%; French 4%. *Fredrik, Hilmer, Nils; Arnaud, Marie Ange.*

Finnegan (4182) Irish: shortened Americanized form of Irish **Ó Fionnagáin** 'descendant of *Fionnagán*', a double diminutive of *Fionn* (see FINN).
GIVEN NAMES Irish 6%. *Brendan* (8), *Clancy, Donal, Eamonn, Liam, Mairead, Padraic.*

Finnell (1109) English: variant of FENNELL.

Finneman (133) German (**Finnemann**): variant of FINN 3.

Finnemore (150) English: variant of FENIMORE.

Finnen (135) Irish: variant spelling of FINAN.
GIVEN NAME Irish 5%. *Malachy.*

Finner (104) **1.** German: ethnic name for a Finn (see FINN 3) or a topographic name, from an agent derivative of Old High German *fenni*, Middle Low German and Old Frisian *fenne* 'bog' (see FENN). **2.** English: possibly a variant of FENNER.
GIVEN NAME German 6%; Scottish 4%. *Kurt* (2).

Finneran (630) Irish: reduced Anglicized form of Gaelic **Ó Finnthighearn** 'descendant of *Finnthighearn*', from *fionn tighearna* 'fair lord'.

Finnerty (1570) Irish: reduced Anglicized form of Gaelic **Ó Fionnachta** (often now written **Ó Fiannachta**) 'descendant of *Fionnachta*', a personal name composed of the elements *fionn* 'fair', 'white' + *sneachta* 'snow'.
GIVEN NAMES Irish 5%. *Aidan, Cormac.*

Finney (5959) English: habitational name from any of several places in Cheshire called Finney or from Fenay in West Yorkshire, probably named from Old English *finig* 'heap' (especially one of wood), or from Old English and Old Norse *finn* 'coarse grass' + *(ge)hæg* 'enclosure'.

Finnicum (158) Altered form of Irish FINEGAN.

Finnie (536) Scottish or English: variant spelling of FINNEY.

Finnigan (788) Irish: variant spelling of FINNEGAN.
GIVEN NAME Irish 6%. *Brendan.*

Finnin (117) Irish: variant spelling of FINAN.

Fino (306) Italian: from a short form of any of various personal names with the ending *-fino* (for example, *Adolfino, Rodolfino, Serafino*). This name is also well established in Mexico.
GIVEN NAMES Italian 11%; Spanish 10%. *Anselmo, Apolonio, Armando, Domenic, Franco, Giulio, Pasquale; Fernando* (2), *Jose* (2), *Manuel* (2), *Elvira, Enriqueta, Juanita, Marcelo, Marcos.*

Finocchiaro (323) Southern Italian: occupational name for a grower or seller of fennel, from an agent derivative of *finnocchio* 'fennel', or in some cases possibly a habitational name from Finochiaro in Sicily.
GIVEN NAMES Italian 22%; Jewish 4%. *Salvatore* (12), *Angelo* (3), *Sal* (3), *Alfio* (2), *Biagio, Gaetano, Guido, Lucio, Orazio, Santo, Sebastiano; Isadore* (3).

Finocchio (215) Italian: metonymic occupational name for a grower or seller of fennel, *finocchio* (from Late Latin *fenuculum*).
GIVEN NAMES Italian 14%. *Domenic* (2), *Carlo.*

Finseth (164) Norwegian: habitational name from any of several farms so named, especially in the north, from *finnr* 'Finn', 'Lapp' or the personal name *Finnr* (of the same etymology) + *set* 'farmstead'.
GIVEN NAME Scandinavian 5%; German 4%. *Ralf.*

Finstad (391) Norwegian: habitational name from any of several farms so named, especially in southeastern Norway, from the personal name *Finnr*, meaning 'Finn', 'Lapp' + *stad* (from Old Norse *staðr* 'farmstead', 'dwelling').
GIVEN NAME Scandinavian 5%. *Birgit.*

Finster (283) German and Jewish (Ashkenazic): nickname from German *finster* 'dark', 'gloomy', or Yiddish *fintster* (Middle High German *vinster*). The name may have referred to a person's habitual character, or it may have been acquired as a result of some now irrecoverable anecdote.
GIVEN NAMES German 4%. *Kurt* (2), *Arno, Gerhard.*

Fintel (134) German: habitational name from a place so named in northern Germany. The place name probably referred to boggy or low-lying terrain.
GIVEN NAMES German 4%. *Erwin, Otto.*

Finton (227) English and Irish: variant of FENTON.

Finucan (152) Irish: variant of FINUCANE.

Finucane (359) Irish (Munster): reduced Anglicized form of Gaelic **Ó Fionnmhacáin** 'descendant of *Fionnmhacán*', from *fionn* 'fair' + the diminutive of *mac* 'son'.
GIVEN NAMES Irish 10%. *Brendan* (6), *Niamh.*

Finzel (170) German: from a pet form of the personal name *Vinzenz*, German form of VINCENT.
GIVEN NAME German 5%. *Hans* (2).

Fiocca (115) Italian: **1.** from a feminine form of *fiocco* 'tuft of wool' or 'ribbon', 'tape', also recorded as a personal name. **2.** from southern Italian *fiocca* '(broody) hen', also used in the figurative sense 'mother hen'.
GIVEN NAMES Italian 13%. *Deno* (2), *Angelo, Dante, Enrico, Salvatore.*

Fiocchi (123) Italian: from *fiocchi* (plural) 'tufts of wool' or 'ribbons', either a descriptive nickname or possibly from the singular form, *fiocco*, used as a personal name.
GIVEN NAMES Italian 12%. *Dino* (2), *Aldo, Caesar, Edo, Elio.*

Fiola (156) Italian (Naples): of uncertain origin; possibly a variant of FEOLA.
GIVEN NAMES French 6%; Italian 4%. *Armand, Monique; Sal* (2), *Tommaso.*

Fioravanti (250) Italian: from the personal name *Fiorvante*, which was popularized by the hero of the 14th-century romance *I reali di Francia*, by Andrea da Barberino.
GIVEN NAMES Italian 23%. *Aldo* (3), *Gino* (3), *Angelo* (2), *Dino* (2), *Luca* (2), *Amedio, Carlo, Domenic, Emidio, Ercole, Giulio.*

Fiore (3511) Italian: from the medieval male and female personal name *Fiore*, in part a continuation of the Late Latin personal name *Flos* (from *flos* 'flower', genitive *floris*), in part a term of endearment.
GIVEN NAMES Italian 13%. *Angelo* (20), *Vito* (13), *Rocco* (10), *Salvatore* (10), *Sal* (7), *Antonio* (5), *Pasquale* (5), *Gino* (4), *Luigi* (4), *Giuseppe* (3), *Marco* (3), *Carlo* (3).

Fiorella (364) Italian: from the personal name *Fiorella*, female form of FIORELLO.
GIVEN NAMES Italian 13%. *Salvatore* (5), *Angelo* (2), *Pietro* (2), *Carlo, Carmine, Sal, Valentino.*

Fiorelli (335) Italian: patronymic or plural form of FIORELLO.
GIVEN NAMES Italian 14%. *Luigi* (2), *Alfonso, Angelo, Antonio, Enzo, Mario, Rocco, Romolo, Sal, Vittorio.*

Fiorello (430) Italian: from a pet form of FIORE.
GIVEN NAMES Italian 22%. *Angelo* (3), *Antonio* (2), *Carmela* (2), *Dino* (2), *Marco* (2), *Saverio* (2), *Vito* (2), *Emilio, Franco, Gaspare, Graziano, Luciano, Nicola.*

Fiorentino (988) Italian: **1.** from the personal name *Fiorentino* (Latin *Florentinus*). **2.** from *fiorentino* 'Florentine', a habitational name for someone from the city of Florence, Italian *Firenze* (Latin *Florentia*), or from a personal name of the same origin.
GIVEN NAMES Italian 19%. *Angelo* (10), *Sal* (5), *Salvatore* (4), *Antonio* (3), *Domenic* (3), *Gennaro* (3), *Aniello* (2), *Carlo* (2), *Carmela* (2), *Carmine* (2), *Francesco* (2), *Luigi* (2).

Fiorenza (431) Italian: from the personal name *Fiorenza* (Latin *Florentia*), feminine form of *Fiorenzo*.
GIVEN NAMES Italian 23%. *Pasquale* (4), *Antonio* (3), *Angelo* (2), *Orlando* (2), *Rocco* (2), *Vito* (2), *Aurelio*, *Cataldo*, *Caterina*, *Clemente*, *Enrico*, *Enzo*, *Giacomo*, *Gilda*, *Pasqual*, *Ruben*.

Fioretti (261) Italian: patronymic from a pet form of FIORE.
GIVEN NAMES Italian 14%. *Carlo* (3), *Ettore*, *Fabrizio*, *Gaetano*, *Giulio*, *Luigi*, *Oreste*, *Pasquale*, *Renzo*, *Salvatore*, *Santo*.

Fiori (542) Italian: patronymic from FIORE.
GIVEN NAMES Italian 10%. *Angelo* (2), *Dino* (2), *Marco* (2), *Domenico*, *Filiberto*, *Franco*, *Gino*, *Maurizio*, *Mauro*, *Remo*, *Rinaldo*, *Rocco*.

Fiorilli (111) Italian: variant (plural or patronymic) of *Fiorillo*, itself a variant of FIORELLO.
GIVEN NAMES Italian 15%. *Carlo*, *Carmine*, *Cosmo*, *Romualdo*.

Fiorillo (540) Southern Italian: from a pet form of the personal name FIORE.
GIVEN NAMES Italian 16%. *Nunzio* (4), *Salvatore* (3), *Antonio* (2), *Carmine* (2), *Maddalena* (2), *Rocco* (2), *Angelo*, *Antimo*, *Carlo*, *Cosimo*, *Domenic*, *Lorenzo*.

Fiorini (479) Italian: patronymic from FIORINO.
GIVEN NAMES Italian 12%. *Dante* (3), *Geno* (3), *Aldo* (2), *Alfonse* (2), *Gaetano* (2), *Romeo* (2), *Angelo*, *Antonio*, *Constantino*, *Domenico*, *Egidio*, *Guido*.

Fiorino (347) Italian: from a pet form of FIORE.
GIVEN NAMES Italian 21%. *Angelo* (2), *Gasper* (2), *Luigi* (2), *Santo* (2), *Saverio* (2), *Biagio*, *Carmelo*, *Concetta*, *Cosimo*, *Dante*, *Giovanna*, *Giuseppe*.

Fiorita (102) Southern Italian: from the female personal name *Fiorita*, a derivative of FIORE.
GIVEN NAMES Italian 16%. *Mario* (2), *Antonio*, *Pietro*, *Rocco*.

Fiorito (464) Italian: nickname from *fiorito* 'strong', 'vigorous', 'blooming'.
GIVEN NAMES Italian 10%. *Angelo* (2), *Antonio* (2), *Ciro* (2), *Salvatore* (2), *Carmine*, *Giuseppe*, *Luciano*, *Marco*, *Matteo*, *Paolo*, *Sal*.

Fiorucci (106) Italian: from a diminutive of FIORE.
GIVEN NAMES Italian 12%. *Amato*, *Ciro*, *Giorgio*, *Silvio*.

Fipps (287) Altered spelling of PHIPPS, a patronymic from PHILIP.

Fire (134) English translation of German and Jewish FEUER.

Firebaugh (375) Americanized spelling of German FEUERBACH.

Fireman (168) **1.** Jewish (American): English translation of **Feuerman** (see FEUER). **2.** English: variant of FAIRMAN.
GIVEN NAMES Jewish 14%. *Hyman* (3), *Orah* (3), *Ahron*, *Ari*.

Firestine (229) Americanized form of German and Jewish FEUERSTEIN.

Firestone (1802) English translation of German and Jewish FEUERSTEIN.
FOREBEARS The rubber manufacturer Harvey Samuel Firestone, who established the Firestone Tire and Rubber Company in 1900 in Akron, OH, came from an Alsatian family on his father's side; Nicholas Firestone was an immigrant in PA in 1752.

Firkins (279) English (West Midlands): patronymic from **Firkin**, a metonymic occupational name for a maker of casks and barrels, or a nickname for a stout man or a heavy drinker, from Middle English *fer(de)kyn* 'small cask' (probably from a Middle Dutch diminutive of *vierde* 'fourth (part)'; as a measure of capacity a firkin was reckoned as a quarter of a barrel).

Firkus (243) Variant spelling of Lithuanian **Virkus** (see WIRKUS).

Firman (455) **1.** English: variant of FIRMIN. **2.** Muslim: variant of FARMAN.

Firment (109) Probably an altered form of English or French FIRMIN.

Firmin (416) English and French: from the medieval personal name *Firmin* (Latin *Firminus*, a derivative of *firmus* 'firm', 'resolute'). This name was borne by several early saints, including two bishops of Amiens of the 2nd and 3rd centuries.
GIVEN NAMES French 5%. *Emile*, *Fernand*, *Francois*, *Ghislaine*, *Irby*, *Marceau*.

Firpo (168) Southern Italian: from the personal name *Firpo*, a dialect variant of *Filippo* (see PHILIP) associated with Liguria.
GIVEN NAMES Spanish 12%; Italian 8%. *Sergio* (2), *Carlos*, *Eduardo*, *Gonzalo*, *Juan*, *Juana*, *Magda*, *Maxima*, *Ricardo*, *Rodolfo*, *Socorro*; *Angelo* (2), *Guido*, *Leonardo*, *Romeo*.

First (642) **1.** Jewish (eastern Ashkenazic): ornamental name from Yiddish *first* 'prince'. **2.** Americanized form of German **Fürst** (see FURST).

Firth (1295) **1.** English and Scottish: topographic name from Old English *(ge)fyrhþe* 'woodland' or 'scrubland on the edge of a forest'. **2.** Scottish: habitational name from Firth in Orkney. **3.** Welsh: topographic name from Welsh *ffrith*, *ffridd* 'barren land', 'mountain pasture' (a borrowing of the Old English word mentioned in 1).

Fiscella (138) Southern Italian: **1.** from a feminine pet form of *Fisco*, itself a reduced form of *Frisco*, a medieval pet form of the personal name *Francesco* (from the Latin form *Franciscus*). **2.** from Sicilian *fiscella* 'small wicker basket for conserving cheese', presumably a metonymic occupational name for a cheesemaker or basket maker.
GIVEN NAMES Italian 9%. *Angelo*, *Primo*, *Santo*.

Fisch (1027) German and Jewish (Ashkenazic): metonymic occupational name for a fisherman or fish seller, or a nickname for someone thought to resemble a fish, from Middle High German *visch* 'fish'. As a Jewish name it is also an ornamental name.
GIVEN NAMES Jewish 5%. *Isadore* (3), *Hyman* (2), *Aba*, *Dov*, *Ichak*, *Lazer*, *Liba*, *Malky*, *Meyer*, *Tzvi*, *Zahava*, *Zelig*.

Fischbach (788) **1.** German: habitational name from a place named Fischbach, or a topographic name for someone living by a stream (Middle High German *bach*) noted for its fish (Middle High German *visch*). **2.** Jewish (Ashkenazic): ornamental name from German *Fisch* 'fish' + *Bach* 'stream'.

Fischbeck (134) North German form of FISCHBACH.
GIVEN NAMES German 8%. *Heinz*, *Helmut*, *Manfred*.

Fischbein (188) Jewish (Ashkenazic): ornamental name, from German *Fischbein* 'whalebone'.
GIVEN NAMES Jewish 4%. *Ari*, *Nuchem*, *Yehuda*.

Fischel (221) **1.** South German: from a diminutive of FISCH. **2.** Jewish (Ashkenazic): from the Yiddish personal name **Fishl** (see FISHEL).
GIVEN NAMES German 6%. *Gunther*, *Hans*, *Heinz*, *Kurt*.

Fischer (31257) German, Danish, and Jewish (Ashkenazic): occupational name for a fisherman, from FISCH + the agent suffix *-er*. This name is widespread throughout central and eastern Europe.
GIVEN NAMES German 5%. *Kurt* (52), *Hans* (32), *Otto* (32), *Erwin* (30), *Gerhard* (15), *Helmut* (12), *Fritz* (11), *Klaus* (11), *Horst* (10), *Dieter* (9), *Franz* (9), *Ernst* (8).

Fischetti (563) Italian: **1.** possibly from a pet form of the personal name *Fisco*, an altered form of *Frisco*, itself a reduced form of the personal name *Francesco*, Latin *Franciscus*. **2.** from *fischetto* 'whistle'.
GIVEN NAMES Italian 21%. *Carmine* (8), *Rocco* (5), *Sal* (4), *Donato* (3), *Gaetano* (3), *Salvatore* (3), *Alessandro* (2), *Angelo* (2), *Carmela* (2), *Enrico* (2), *Aldo*, *Alessandra*.

Fischl (236) South German and Jewish (Ashkenazic): variant spelling of FISCHEL.
GIVEN NAMES German 4%. *Hans*, *Kurt*, *Otto*.

Fischler (313) South German and Jewish (Ashkenazic): variant of FISCHER.
GIVEN NAMES German 7%; Jewish 5%. *Mathias* (2), *Arnd*, *Ernst*, *Erwin*, *Inge*, *Kurt*, *Reinhardt*; *Sol* (4), *Emanuel*, *Nurit*.

Fischman (473) German (**Fischmann**) and Jewish (Ashkenazic): occupational name for a fish seller, from Middle High German *visch* 'fish' (modern German *Fisch*, Yiddish *fish*) + Middle High German and Yiddish *man* 'man' (modern German *Mann*).
GIVEN NAMES Jewish 11%; German 4%. *Chaim* (2), *Mendel* (2), *Aharon*, *Dov*, *Moshe*, *Raizy*, *Sabi*, *Shalom*, *Shlomie*, *Shlomo*, *Simcha*, *Sol*; *Kurt* (3), *Wolf*.

Fisco (121) Italian: reduced form of FRISCO.
GIVEN NAMES Italian 11%. *Pasquale* (2), *Antonio*, *Concetta*, *Domenic*, *Nino*, *Pino*.

Fiscus (1211) German: from Latin *fiscus* 'basket', a humanistic Latinization of the German name KORB. This is a metonymic occupational name for a basketmaker or a peddler, or a habitational name for someone who lived at a house distinguished by the sign of a basket.

Fiser (349) Czech, Slovak, and Slovenian (**Fišer**): occupational name for a fisherman, from German FISCHER.

Fisette (244) French Canadian spelling of **Fiset**, which may be related to **Fuset**, a metonymic occupational name for a weaver or seamstress, from Old French *fuset* 'small spindle'.
FOREBEARS A bearer of the name from Normandy, France, is recorded in Trois Rivières, Quebec, in 1667.
GIVEN NAMES French 9%. *Normand* (3), *Armand*, *Benoit*, *Philippe*.

Fish (10070) **1.** English: from Middle English *fische*, *fish* 'fish', a metonymic occupational name for a fisherman or fish seller, or a nickname for someone thought to resemble a fish. **2.** Americanized spelling of German and Jewish FISCH.

Fishback (733) Americanized spelling of German and Jewish FISCHBACH.

Fishbaugh (213) Americanized spelling of German FISCHBACH.

Fishbeck (169) Americanized spelling of German FISCHBACH.

Fishbein (601) Jewish (Ashkenazic): variant of FISCHBEIN.
GIVEN NAMES Jewish 6%. *Meyer* (3), *Hyman* (2), *Tema* (2), *Emanuel*, *Hirsch*.

Fishburn (741) **1.** English: habitational name from Fishbourne in Sussex and the Isle of Wight or Fishburn in Durham, all named from Old English *fisc* 'fish' + *burna* 'stream'. **2.** In some cases, possibly a translation of FISCHBACH.

Fishburne (211) English: variant spelling of FISHBURN.

Fishel (1168) Jewish (Ashkenazic): from the Yiddish personal name *Fishl*, literally 'little fish', used as a vernacular equivalent for the Biblical *Efraym* (Ephraim). Ephraim became associated with the fish because he was blessed by his father Jacob (Genesis 48:16) with the words *veyidgu larov* 'Let them grow into a multitude', the verb *yidgu*, containing the root letters of Hebrew *dag* 'fish'.

Fishell (170) Respelling of Jewish FISHEL or German and Jewish FISCHEL.

Fisher (78653) **1.** English: occupational name for a fisherman, Middle English *fischer*. The name has also been used in Ireland as a loose equivalent of BRADEN. As an American family name, this has absorbed cognates and names of similar meaning from many other European languages, including German **Fischer**, Dutch **Visser**, Hungarian **Halász**, Italian **Pescatore**, Polish **Rybarz**, etc. **2.** In a few cases, the English name may in fact be a topographic name for someone who lived near a fish weir on a river, from the Old English term *fisc-gear* 'fish weir'. **3.** Jewish (Ashkenazic): occupational name for a fisherman, Yiddish *fisher*, German *Fischer*. **4.** Irish: translation of Gaelic **Ó Bradáin** 'descendant of *Bradán*', a personal name meaning 'salmon'. See BRADEN. **5.** Mistranslation of French POISSANT, meaning 'powerful', but understood as *poisson* 'fish' (see POISSON), and assimilated to the more frequent English name.

Fishkin (348) Jewish (from Belarus): patronymic from the personal name *Fishke*, a pet form of *Fishl* (see FISHEL).
GIVEN NAMES Jewish 8%; Russian 4%. *Gitty* (2), *Semen* (2), *Emanuel*, *Inna*, *Yakov*; *Boris* (3), *Igor* (3), *Mikhail*, *Semyon*, *Vladimir*.

Fishler (194) Jewish (Ashkenazic): variant spelling of FISCHLER.

Fishman (3705) Jewish (Ashkenazic): variant of FISCHMAN.
GIVEN NAMES Jewish 10%; Russian 4%. *Miriam* (8), *Sol* (7), *Emanuel* (4), *Hyman* (4), *Isadore* (4), *Meyer* (4), *Mordechai* (4), *Yitzchok* (4), *Nachum* (3), *Yakov* (3), *Anshel* (2), *Yaffa* (2); *Mikhail* (8), *Vladimir* (8), *Arkady* (5), *Leonid* (5), *Oleg* (5), *Aleksandr* (4), *Lev* (4), *Boris* (2), *Igor* (2), *Jirina* (2), *Raisa* (2), *Semyon* (2).

Fishwick (135) English (Lancashire): habitational name from a place in Lancashire, so named from Old English *fisc* 'fish' + *wīc* 'trading place'.

Fisk (3912) English (East Anglia): metonymic occupational name for a fisherman or fish seller, or a nickname for someone supposedly resembling a fish in some way, from Old Norse *fiskr* 'fish' (cognate with Old English *fisc*).

Fiske (1661) **1.** Norwegian: habitational name from a farm in western Norway, named from Old Norse *fiskr* 'fish' + *vin* 'meadow'. **2.** Danish: metonymic occupational name for a fisherman or fish seller, from Old Norse *fiskr* 'fish'. **3.** English: variant of FISK.

Fisler (197) South German: variant of FIESELER.

Fiss (125) Dutch and North German: from a Frisian and Dutch variant of *vis* 'fish' (see FISCH, VIS).

Fissel (254) German: nickname for a womanizer or a slut, from Middle High German *visel* 'penis'.

Fister (573) **1.** South German: respelling of PFISTER, an occupational name for a baker. **2.** Slovenian (**Fišter**): occupational name for a baker, from German PFISTER.

Fistler (101) German: variant of FIESELER, or a nickname for a person prone to boils, from Middle High German *fistel* 'boil', 'carbuncle' (from Latin *fistula*).
GIVEN NAME German 4%. *Otto*.

Fitch (7085) English: of disputed origin. Reaney rejects the traditional explanation that it is a nickname derived from early modern English *fitch* 'polecat', as this word is not recorded in this form until the 16th century, whereas the byname or surname *Fitchet* is found as early as the 12th century. He proposes instead that the name may be from Old French *fiche* 'stake' (used as a boundary marker), but with the sense 'iron point', and so a metonymic occupational name for a workman who used an iron-pointed implement.
FOREBEARS The Fitches of CT, a wealthy and prominent family, were established in Norwalk, CT, before 1657 by Thomas Fitch (1612–1704). His great-grandson Thomas Fitch (c. 1700–74) was a lawyer and colonial governor of CT.

Fitchett (598) English: see FITCH.

Fite (2095) Americanized spelling of German VEIT.

Fithen (105) English and Welsh: **1.** probably a variant of FITHIAN. **2.** Alternatively, it may be an altered form of Welsh GETHIN.

Fithian (384) English: from a medieval variant of VIVIAN.

Fitschen (119) North German: Frisian patronymic from FRIEDRICH.
GIVEN NAMES German 6%; Scandinavian 4%. *Grete*, *Hermann*; *Iver*.

Fitt (164) English (chiefly Norfolk): nickname for a polite and amiable person, from Middle English *fit* 'proper', 'suited' (of uncertain origin).

Fitterer (345) Americanized spelling of German **Fütterer**, an occupational name for a feed merchant, Middle High German *fuoterer*.

Fitting (390) German: from a pet form of the personal name FRIEDRICH.

Fittipaldi (129) Italian: from *Fi' Tipaldo*, a reduced form of *Figlio di Tipaldo* 'son of Tipaldo', a personal name of unknown etymology.
GIVEN NAMES Italian 16%. *Silvio* (3), *Adelina*, *Mario*.

Fitton (411) English (chiefly Lancashire): **1.** nickname from Middle English *fitten* 'lying', 'deceit' (of unknown origin). **2.** possibly a habitational name from Fitton Hall in Cambridgeshire, named in Anglo-Scandinavian as 'settlement (Old English *tūn*) on the *fit* (Old Norse *fit*)', a term denoting grassland on the bank of a river.

Fittro (192) Origin unidentified. Compare FETROW, likewise unidentified.

Fitts (2149) English: most probably a patronymic from FITT, or perhaps a variant spelling of FITZ.

Fitz (1363) **1.** English: generally said to be from Anglo-Norman French *fi(t)z* 'son', used originally to distinguish a son from a father bearing the same personal name. **2.** It could also be a habitational name from a place in Shropshire called Fitz, recorded in 1194 as *Fittesho*, from an Old English personal name, *Fitt*, + *hōh* 'hill spur'. **3.** In one family at least, it is an altered form of English FITCH. **4.** German: unexplained. Possibly from a vernacular pet form of the personal name VINCENT.

FOREBEARS Johann Peter Fitz, an immigrant from Germany, arrived in Philadelphia in 1750. Bearers of the name from Britain were already established in North America before that date.

Fitzer (314) South German: **1.** occupational name for a weaver (of ornate patterns), from an agent derivative of Middle High German *vitzen*. **2.** Americanized spelling of PFITZER.

Fitzgerald (29318) Irish: Anglo-Norman French patronymic from the personal name *Gerald* (see GARRETT). The name was formed by the addition of the Anglo-Norman French prefix *fi(t)z* 'son of' (Latin *filius*) to the personal name. The Gaelicized form **Mac Gearailt** is common in the Gaelic-speaking areas of West Kerry.

GIVEN NAMES Irish 6%. *Brendan* (16), *Eamon* (3), *Liam* (3), *Aidan* (2), *Bridgid* (2), *Caitlin* (2), *Donal* (2), *Fitz* (2), *Fitzgerald* (2), *Ciaran*, *Colum*, *Dermot*.

Fitzgibbon (941) Irish: Anglo-Norman French patronymic (see FITZGERALD) from the medieval personal name GIBBON.

Fitzgibbons (944) Irish: variant of FITZGIBBON with the addition of the English patronymic suffix *-s*.

Fitzharris (169) Irish: Anglo-Norman French patronymic (see FITZGERALD) from HARRIS. MacLysaght describes this as the name of a distinguished Co. Wexford family, also known as FITZHENRY.

GIVEN NAME Irish 5%. *Aileen*.

Fitzhenry (283) Irish: Anglo-Norman French patronymic (see FITZGERALD) from the personal name HENRY.

Fitzherbert (102) Irish: Anglo-Norman French patronymic (see FITZGERALD) from the personal name HERBERT.

Fitzhugh (1233) English (Northamptonshire): Anglo-Norman French patronymic (see FITZGERALD) from the personal name HUGH.

FOREBEARS William Fitzhugh (1651–1701), from Bedford, England, emigrated to VA about 1670 and established himself on the Potomac River in what was then Stafford Co., VA, as a planter and exporter. He also practiced law, was a member of the Virginia House of Burgesses, and served in 1687 as lieutenant colonel of the county militia.

Fitzke (117) German: probably a Germanized form of Czech **Vítek** (see VITEK), or a cognate in a related Slavic language.

Fitzmaurice (971) Irish: Anglo-Norman French patronymic (see FITZGERALD) from the personal name *Maurice* (see MORRIS 1).

GIVEN NAMES Irish 5%. *Aidan*, *Ciaran*, *Colm*.

Fitzmorris (291) Irish: variant spelling of FITZMAURICE.

Fitzner (238) German (Silesian): **1.** from Middle High German *pfütze* 'puddle' (Latin *puteus* 'well'), hence a topographic name for someone who lived by a pond. See also PFITZER. **2.** German: from the southern form of the personal name *Vincenz* (see VINCENT).

GIVEN NAMES German 7%. *Kurt*, *Otto*, *Reinhart*, *Wolfgang*.

Fitzpatrick (15131) Irish: occasionally this may be a genuine Anglo-Norman French patronymic (see FITZGERALD) from the personal name PATRICK, but more often it has been adopted as an Anglicized form of Gaelic **Mac Giolla Pádraig** (see KILPATRICK).

GIVEN NAMES Irish 5%. *Brendan* (11), *Kieran* (4), *Declan* (3), *Ronan* (3), *Liam* (2), *Seamus* (2), *Sinead* (2), *Siobhan* (2), *Aileen*, *Bridie*, *Brigid*, *Conan*.

Fitzroy (100) Irish: Anglo-Norman French patronymic from *fi(t)z* 'son' + ROY in one or other of its senses. It is usually taken to imply that the original bearer was a bastard son of the king, though 'son of *Ruadh*' (a Gaelic nickname meaning 'red') is also a possible interpretation.

Fitzsimmons (3886) Irish: Anglo-Norman French patronymic (see FITZGERALD) from the personal name SIMON. The name is also found in the Gaelicized form **Mac Síomóin**.

Fitzsimons (788) Irish: variant of FITZSIMMONS.

GIVEN NAMES Irish 6%. *Brendan*, *Caitlin*, *Niamh*.

Fitzwater (1416) Irish: altered spelling of the Anglo-Norman French patronymic **Fitzwalter** 'son of Walter' (see WALTER). Compare FITZGERALD.

Fiumara (227) Southern Italian: habitational name from Fiumara in Reggio Calabria or from the locality so named in San Piero Patti, in Messina province. In some cases the surname may be topographic from *fiumara* 'torrent'.

GIVEN NAMES Italian 20%. *Salvatore* (4), *Angelo* (2), *Antonio*, *Carmin*, *Dino*, *Pasquale*, *Pietro*, *Reno*, *Santo*, *Vito*.

Fiveash (342) English: probably a topographic name for someone who lived by a group of five ash trees (Middle English *ashe*) or a habitational name from a place so named, for example Five Ashes in East Sussex.

Fivecoat (170) Translation of German FINFROCK.

Fix (2192) German: patronymic from a medieval personal name *Veit* (Latin *Vitus*) (see VITO).

Fixler (181) Jewish (Ashkenazic): ornamental name from Yiddish *fuks*, German *Fuchs* 'fox' + the agent noun suffix *-ler*.

GIVEN NAMES Jewish 11%. *Isidor* (2), *Aron*, *Bernat*, *Bezalel*, *Shaul*, *Zev*.

Fizer (546) German: variant spelling of FITZER or PFITZER.

Fjeld (266) Norwegian: habitational name from any of the many farms named with *fjell* 'mountain', 'rock'.

GIVEN NAMES Scandinavian 9%. *Obert* (2), *Erik*.

Fjelstad (216) Norwegian: habitational name from any of several farms so named, from *fjell* 'mountain', 'rock' + *stad* (from Old Norse *staðr* 'farmstead', 'dwelling').

GIVEN NAME Scandinavian 6%. *Per* (2).

Fjerstad (124) Norwegian: habitational name from a farmstead in Trøndelag so named, from an uncertain first element + *stad* (from Old Norse *staðir*, plural of *staðr* 'farmstead', 'dwelling').

Flaa (152) Norwegian: habitational name from a farm named *Flå*, either from Old Norse *flá* 'terrace', 'plain' or *flói* 'bog', 'swamp'.

Flach (582) German: **1.** nickname (especially in the Silesian-Bohemian area) from Czech *Vlach* 'foreigner', denoting specifically someone who spoke a Romance language, in particular an Italian. **2.** topographic name for someone living in flat terrain, from Middle Low German *vlak* 'flat', or a nickname for a superficial or silly person, from the same word in the sense 'shallow'. **3.** metonymic occupational name for a blacksmith, from Middle High German *vlach* 'smooth', 'straight'. It is recorded as a surname in Bavaria around 1500.

GIVEN NAMES German 4%. *Ernst* (2), *Kurt*, *Mathias*, *Otto*.

Flack (2316) **1.** English: probably from Middle English *flack*, *flak* 'turf', 'sod' (as found in the place name Flatmoor, in Cambridgeshire), and hence perhaps a metonymic occupational name for a turf cutter. **2.** North German: topographic name probably derived from a lost word denoting stagnant water.

Flad (150) German: **1.** from Middle High German *vlade* 'thin (sheet) cake'; probably a metonymic occupational name for a baker. **2.** in southern Germany, a topographic name from *Flad(e)* 'reed', 'sedge'. **3.** variant of FLATH 2.

GIVEN NAMES German 8%. *Egon* (2), *Christoph*, *Erwin*, *Friedrich*.

Fladung (117) German: habitational name from a place called Fladungen in Lower Franconia.

GIVEN NAMES German 6%. *Hans* (3), *Winfried*.

Flagel (126) **1.** French: metonymic occupational name for a flute or whistle player, from Old French *flegeole*, Latin *flageolum* 'flute'. **2.** German (**Flägel**): variant of FLEGEL.

Flager (103) Americanized spelling of German PFLEGER.

Flagg (2323) English: habitational name from places such as Flagg in Derbyshire and Flags in Nottinghamshire, named from Old English *flage* or Old Norse *flaga* 'slab', or from Old Norse *flag* 'turf', 'sod'.

Flagler (366) German: occupational name for a maker or user of threshing flails, from an agent derivative of Middle High German *vlegel* 'flail'.

Flaharty (224) Irish: variant spelling of FLAHERTY.

Flaherty (7632) Irish (Connacht): reduced Anglicized form of Gaelic **Ó Flaithbheartaigh** 'descendant of *Flaithbheartach*', a byname meaning 'generous', 'hospitable' (from *flaith(eamh)* 'prince', 'ruler' + *beartach* 'acting', 'behaving').
GIVEN NAMES Irish 6%. *Brendan* (8), *John Patrick* (2), *Brigid, Ciaran, Colm, Colum, Kieran, Liam, Paddy*.

Flahive (311) Irish: shortened Anglicized form of Gaelic **Ó Flaithimh** (see LAFFEY).
GIVEN NAME Irish 5%. *Connor*.

Flaig (543) German: from a Swabian-Alemannic word cognate with the word for 'fly' (standard German *Fliege*), a nickname for an agile, physically, and mentally flexible person.
GIVEN NAMES German 5%. *Kurt* (3), *Gottlob* (2), *Gunther* (2), *Otto, Rudie*.

Flaim (280) Italian: unexplained. The surname occurs mainly in South Tyrol; it may be from an unidentified place name of Germanic etymology.
GIVEN NAMES Italian 16%. *Guido* (3), *Angelo* (2), *Silvano* (2), *Claudio, Fabio, Gino, Isidoro, Lino, Luigi, Mariano, Maurizio, Silvio, Tino, Umberto*.

Flair (119) English: unexplained.

Flak (167) **1.** Polish: nickname from *flak* 'bowel', 'gut', also 'rag'. **2.** German and Danish: according to Søndergaard, a topographic or field name, from Low German *flak* 'swampy grassland', 'shallow water'. **3.** German: topographic name for someone who lived in flat terrain, from Middle High German *vlak* 'flat', or, according to Bahlow, a variant of FLAKE.
GIVEN NAMES Polish 8%. *Henryk* (2), *Boguslaw, Halina*.

Flake (1284) German: topographic name mostly in northwestern Germany for someone who lived near a swamp.

Flaker (117) Probably a variant of English **Flacker**, an occupational name for a turf cutter, from an agent derivative of Middle English *flak* 'turf'.

Flakes (265) Probably an Americanized spelling of German **Flachs** (see FLAX).

Flam (209) **1.** Jewish (eastern Ashkenazic): ornamental name from Yiddish *flam* 'flame'. **2.** German: ethnic name for someone from Flanders.
GIVEN NAMES Jewish 14%. *Dovid, Gerson, Hersh, Isadore, Meyer, Moshe, Shira, Shmuel, Sol*.

Flamand (139) French: ethnic name for a Fleming, someone from Flanders, from Old French *flamenc*.
GIVEN NAMES French 11%. *Armand, Colette, Julien, Ludger*.

Flamer (162) German: ethnic name for a Fleming (someone from Flanders).

Flaming (396) **1.** German: ethnic name for someone from Flanders, from Middle High German *vlaeminc*. See also FLEMMING. **2.** Variant spelling of Dutch **Vlaming**, ethnic name for someone from Flanders, cognate with 1.

Flaminio (105) Italian: from the personal name *Flaminio* (Latin *Flaminius*).
GIVEN NAMES Italian 6%. *Alesio, Fernando, Rocco*.

Flamm (497) **1.** South German and Jewish (Ashkenazic): metonymic occupational name for a blacksmith, from Middle High German *vlamme* 'flame'. As a Jewish name, it is mainly an ornamental name. **2.** Possibly also an Americanized form of French LAFLAMME.
GIVEN NAMES Jewish 4%. *Ari* (3), *Miriam* (2), *Chani, Ephraim, Yossi*.

Flammang (174) French (Alsace and Lorraine): local form of FLAMAND.

Flammer (157) German: **1.** (also **Flämmer**) metonymic occupational name for a blacksmith, from an agent derivative Middle High German *vlamme* 'flame'. **2.** variant spelling of FLAMER.
GIVEN NAMES German 6%. *Kurt* (2), *Bernhard*.

Flammia (195) Southern Italian: nickname from Latin *flammula* 'little flame', or alternatively from Latin *flammeus* 'flaming', also 'flame red', 'ardent'.
GIVEN NAMES Italian 14%. *Carmine* (2), *Angelo, Dino, Domenic, Giovanni, Rocco, Vito*.

Flanagan (11884) Irish: reduced Anglicized form of Gaelic **Ó Flannagáin** 'descendant of *Flannagán*', a personal name derived from a double diminutive of *flann* 'scarlet', 'ruddy'.
GIVEN NAMES Irish 5%. *Brendan* (9), *Brigid* (3), *Aine* (2), *Fintan* (2), *Aileen, Brian Patrick, Cormac, Fergus, Fidelma, Padraig, Ronan, Seamus*.

Flanagin (244) Irish: variant spelling of FLANAGAN.

Flanary (774) Irish: variant spelling of FLANNERY.

Flanders (3299) English: ethnic name for someone from Flanders. Compare FLEMING.

Flanery (565) Irish: variant spelling of FLANNERY.

Flanigan (2779) Irish: variant spelling of FLANAGAN.
GIVEN NAME Irish 4%. *Brigid* (3).

Flannagan (495) Irish: variant spelling of FLANAGAN.

Flannery (3875) Irish: reduced Anglicized form of Gaelic **Ó Flannabhra** 'descendant of *Flannabhra*' meaning 'red eyebrows', or (with *r* for the second *l*) a possible Anglicized form of **Ó Flannghaile** 'descendant of *Flannghal*', a personal name composed of the elements *flann* 'red', 'ruddy' + *gal* 'valor'. Both are Connacht names.
GIVEN NAMES Irish 5%. *Brendan, Brian Patrick, Declan, Donal, Kiernan, Paddy, Seamus, Senan*.

Flannigan (790) Irish: variant spelling of FLANAGAN.

Flansburg (368) German: habitational name for someone from Flensburg in Schleswig Holstein.

Flasch (188) German and Jewish (Ashkenazic): metonymic occupational name for a maker of flasks and bottles, from Middle High German *vlasche*, Yiddish *flash* 'bottle', 'flask'. For the ordinary households of the Middle Ages, bottles were made more often from leather than glass, but also sometimes from wood and metal.

Flash (169) **1.** English: topographic name from Middle English *flasshe* 'pool', 'marsh'. This is thought to be from Old Danish *flask* 'swamp', 'swampy grassland', 'shallow water'. **2.** Jewish (Ashkenazic): variant spelling of FLASCH. **3.** Possibly an Americanized spelling of German FLASCH.

Flasher (137) **1.** English: topographic name for someone living by a pool or marsh (see FLASH). **2.** Possibly also an Americanized form of German **Flaschner**, an occupational name for a bottle maker, from an agent derivative of Middle High German *vlashe* 'bottle'.

Flaster (118) Jewish (Ashkenazic): occupational name from Yiddish *flaster* 'plaster'.
GIVEN NAME Jewish 10%. *Mendel* (2).

Flatau (148) German: variant of FLATOW.

Flaten (480) Norwegian: habitational name from any of several farms so named, from Old Norse *flati, flǫtr* 'plain', 'meadow'.
GIVEN NAMES Scandinavian 4%. *Hilmar, Nord, Nordahl*.

Flater (220) South German: topographic name for someone who lived by a reedbed, a derivative of FLAD.

Flath (372) **1.** North German: habitational name from a place or field named from Middle Low German *flad* 'flowing water in a bog'. **2.** German: nickname from Middle High German *vlāt* 'cleanliness', 'neatness', 'beauty', or from a personal name derived from this word.

Flathers (187) English: variant of or patronymic from **Flather**, a metonymic occupational name for a maker of flathes or flawns, a type of pancake or custard, Middle English *flather, flathir*.

Flatley (592) Irish: reduced Anglicized form of Gaelic **Ó Flaithfhileadh**, an earlier form of **Ó Flaitile** 'descendant of the prince poet'.
GIVEN NAMES Irish 6%. *Brigid, Liam*.

Flatow (147) German and Jewish (Ashkenazic): habitational name for someone from either of two places called Flatow, in Brandenburg and Mecklenburg.
GIVEN NAME Jewish 5%. *Meyer*.

Flatt (1708) **1.** English (chiefly East Anglia): topographic name for someone who lived on a flat, a patch of level or low-lying ground (Old Norse *flat, flǫt*). **2.** South German: variant of FLATH 2.

Flatten (148) Norwegian: variant of FLATEN.

Flatter (131) English (Berkshire): topographic name for someone who lived on a flat, a patch of level or low-lying ground (see FLATT).

Flattery (280) Irish: reduced Anglicized form of Gaelic **Ó Flaitire**, a variant of **Ó Flaitile** (see FLATLEY).
GIVEN NAMES Irish 7%. *Brendan, Brigid, Declan*.

Flattum (104) Norwegian: unexplained.

Flaugh (157) Americanized spelling of German FLACH.

Flaugher (383) Americanized spelling of German **Flacher**, a variant of FLACH, or of **Flaucher** (standard German **Flucher**), a nickname, from an agent derivative of Middle High German *vluochen* 'to swear'.

Flaum (238) **1.** German and Jewish (Ashkenazic): metonymic occupational name for a feather dealer, from Middle Low German *vlūm* 'down', 'feather'. **2.** Jewish (eastern Ashkenazic): ornamental name from German *Pflaume* 'plum'.
GIVEN NAMES Jewish 10%. *Akiva, Hyman, Iser, Tzvi*.

Flautt (102) Origin unidentified.

Flavell (187) English (Midlands): Normanized form of **Flyford**, a habitational name from Flyford, Worcestershire, named from Old English *(ge)fyrðe* 'woodland', with an obscure first element.

Flavin (808) Irish: reduced Anglicized form of Gaelic **Ó Flaithimhín** and **Ó Flaitheamháin** 'descendant of *Flaithimhín* and *Flaitheamhán*'. Both personal names are from diminutives of *flaith(eamh)* 'prince', 'ruler'.
GIVEN NAMES Irish 5%. *Aileen, Mhairi*.

Flaws (104) Scottish (Orkney and Shetland): possibly a habitational name from Flawis in South Ronaldsay.

Flax (672) English (East Anglia) and Jewish (Ashkenazic): metonymic occupational name for someone who grew, sold, or treated flax for weaving into linen cloth, from (respectively) Middle English *flax*, German *Flachs*.

GIVEN NAMES Jewish 4%. *Hyman* (2), *Elihu, Emanuel, Herschel, Herzl, Miriam, Shira, Sol*.

Flaxman (198) **1.** English and Jewish (Ashkenazic): occupational name for a flax grower or dealer or for someone who processed it for weaving (see FLAX). **2.** Probably a respelling of German **Flachsmann**, of the same meaning as 1, from Middle High German *vlahs* 'flax' + *man* 'man'.
GIVEN NAMES Jewish 4%. *Hyman, Sol*.

Fleagle (280) Americanized spelling of German **Flügel** (see FLUEGEL).

Fleak (102) **1.** English: unexplained. **2.** Probably an Americanized form of German FLICK. Compare FLEEK.

Flechsig (100) German: probably a nickname from Middle High German *vlehsīn* 'flaxen', 'of flax', applied to someone with flaxen hair.
GIVEN NAMES German 12%. *Kurt* (4), *Otto*.

Fleck (3513) German and Jewish (Ashkenazic): from Middle High German *vlec(ke)*, German *Fleck* 'patch', 'spot' or Yiddish *flek*, of varied application. Bahlow suggests that this may be a metonymic occupational name for a user of patches in repairing shoes, clothes, or utensils, or a habitational name from a place named with this word. In some parts of Germany this was the term for a type of round, flat loaf; the surname could therefore have arisen as a metonymic occupational name for a baker. In some cases the Jewish name was probably ornamental.

Fleckenstein (692) **1.** German: habitational name from a lost place called Fleckenstein, in the Vosges mountains (Alsace). **2.** Jewish (Ashkenazic): ornamental name, from German *Flecken* 'stain', 'spot' (Yiddish *flekn*) + STEIN 'stone'.

Flecker (106) German: **1.** topographic name from Middle High German *vleck(e)* 'place', 'spot', frequent in place and farm names, often referring to a settlement on open land surrounded by woods. **2.** occupational name from agent derivative of Middle High German *vlec(ke)* 'patch', 'spot' (see FLECK).

Fledderman (112) North German: habitational name for someone from Fledder in the Lübbecke district in Westphalia.

Fleece (172) Americanized spelling of German **Fliess**, a topographic name for someone living near flowing water, from Middle High German *vliezen* 'to flow', or of **Fleiss**, a variant of FLEISCH.

Fleege (133) North German: nickname for a restless person or someone of little importance, from Middle Low German *fleege* 'fly'.

Fleeger (301) Americanized spelling of German PFLUEGER.

Fleegle (147) Americanized spelling of German FLUEGEL.

Fleek (200) **1.** English: unexplained. **2.** Probably an Americanized form of German FLICK. Compare FLEAK.

Fleeman (597) English: variant of FLEMING.

Fleener (729) Americanized spelling of German **Fleiner**, a habitational name for someone from Flein near Heilbronn.

Fleenor (1394) Americanized spelling of German **Fleiner**, a habitational name for someone from Flein near Heilbronn.

Fleer (273) Altered spelling of German **Flieher**, a nickname for a refugee, from an agent derivative of Middle High German *vliehen* 'to flee'.

Flees (149) Americanized spelling of Dutch **(van der) Vlies**, a topographic name from *vlies* 'water place'.

Fleet (895) English: **1.** habitational name from one of the places called Fleet, in Dorset, Hampshire, Kent, and Lincolnshire, or from Holt Fleet on the Severn river in Worcestershire, all named with Old English *flēot* 'stream' or 'estuary'. It may also be a topographic name from the same word used independently. **2.** nickname for a swift runner, from Middle English *flete* 'fleet', 'rapid' (probably from Old English *flēotan* 'to float or glide rapidly', and so ultimately akin to 1).

Fleetwood (1315) English: probably a habitational name from a lost or unidentified place named with Old English *flēot* 'stream', 'estuary' + *wudu* 'wood'. The place of this name in Lancashire got its name in the 19th century from its founder, Sir Peter Hesketh Fleetwood, and is not the source of the surname.

Flegal (221) Altered spelling of German FLEGEL or FLUEGEL.

Flegel (301) German: metonymic occupational name for a farmhand, originally a thresher, from Middle High German *vlegel* 'flail'.
GIVEN NAMES German 4%. *Gerhard* (2), *Kurt, Wilhelm*.

Fleharty (167) Variant spelling of the Irish family name FLAHERTY.

Fleig (377) German: nickname for a restless or insignificant person from Middle Low German *vleige* 'fly'.
GIVEN NAMES German 5%. *Otto* (3), *Kuno*.

Fleisch (151) German: metonymic occupational name for a butcher, from Middle High German *fleisch, vleisch* 'flesh', 'meat'.
GIVEN NAMES German 5%. *Helmut, Johann, Wolf*.

Fleischauer (174) Variant of German FLEISCHHAUER.

Fleischer (1870) German and Jewish (Ashkenazic): occupational name for a butcher, from FLEISCH 'flesh', 'meat' + the agent suffix *-er*.
GIVEN NAMES German 6%. *Kurt* (4), *Otto* (4), *Manfred* (3), *Erhard* (2), *Dieter, Egon,*

Erna, Erwin, Fritz, Georg, Gerhard, Guenter.

Fleischhacker (185) German and Jewish (Ashkenazic): occupational name for a butcher, from German FLEISCH 'flesh', 'meat' + an agent derivative of *hacken* 'to chop or cut'.
GIVEN NAME German 5%. *Friedrich.*

Fleischhauer (106) German: occupational name for a butcher, from Middle High German *fleisch, vleisch* 'flesh', 'meat' + an agent derivative of Middle High German *houwen* 'to cut'.
GIVEN NAMES German 17%; Scottish 4%. *Wolfgang* (3), *Dieter, Hans, Klaus, Otto, Udo.*

Fleischman (1580) Altered spelling of German and Jewish FLEISCHMANN.
GIVEN NAMES Jewish 4%. *Tovia* (3), *Sol* (2), *Aron, Benyamin, Chanie, Dov, Leib, Lipot, Meyer, Pincus, Shraga, Yitzchak.*

Fleischmann (988) German and Jewish (Ashkenazic): occupational name for a butcher, literally 'meatman', from Middle High German *fleisch* 'flesh', 'meat' + *man* 'man'.
GIVEN NAMES German 6%. *Alois* (2), *Heinz* (2), *Kurt* (2), *Annice, Berthold, Erwin, Franz, Fritz, Hans, Jurgen, Otto, Siegfried.*

Fleisher (1038) Americanized spelling of German and Jewish FLEISCHER, or Czech and Slovak **Fleišer**, which is from German FLEISCHER.
GIVEN NAMES Jewish 4%. *Miriam* (2), *Chaim, Isadore, Leib, Mendel, Meyer, Pnina, Rebekah, Simcha, Sol.*

Fleishman (725) Americanized spelling of German and Jewish FLEISCHMANN.
GIVEN NAMES Jewish 5%. *Meyer* (2), *Ari, Avrom, Dovid, Ilya, Isadore, Yankel.*

Fleissner (195) German: variant of FLEISCHER (*-ner* is a frequent variant of the agent suffix *-er*).
GIVEN NAMES German 6%; Scandinavian 4%. *Erwin, Gerhard, Hans, Kurt; Gudrun.*

Fleitas (143) Spanish: variant of Portuguese FREITAS.
GIVEN NAMES Spanish 51%. *Juan* (4), *Jorge* (3), *Jose* (3), *Luis* (3), *Orlando* (3), *Alberto* (2), *Angel* (2), *Carlos* (2), *Jesus* (2), *Mirta* (2), *Sergio* (2), *Adalberto; Antonio* (3).

Fleites (136) Spanish: probably a variant of Portuguese FREITAS.
GIVEN NAMES Spanish 55%. *Jose* (5), *Juan* (4), *Conrado* (3), *Humberto* (3), *Manuel* (3), *Ovidio* (3), *Pedro* (3), *Rafael* (3), *Agustin* (2), *Alfredo* (2), *Armando* (2), *Eulogio* (2); *Aldo, Antonio, Elio, Mirella.*

Fleitman (103) North German: topographic name, the Low German equivalent of FLEITZ, from Middle Low German *vlēt* 'running water', 'river', 'channel', used occasionally as a field name, + *man* 'man'.

Fleitz (108) German: probably a variant of **Flaitz, Flaiss,** Swabian variants of **Floss,** a topographic name for someone near running water or a channel, or a metonymic occupational name for a raftsman, from

Middle High German *vlōz* 'current', 'stream'. Compare FLOSS.

Fleming (32093) **1.** English: ethnic name for someone from Flanders. In the Middle Ages there was considerable commercial intercourse between England and the Netherlands, particularly in the wool trade, and many Flemish weavers and dyers settled in England. The word reflects a Norman French form of Old French *flamenc,* from the stem *flam-* + the Germanic suffix *-ing.* The surname is also common in south and east Scotland and in Ireland, where it is sometimes found in the Gaelicized form **Pléimeann. 2.** German: variant of FLEMMING, cognate with 1.

Flemings (281) **1.** English: patronymic or plural variant of FLEMING. **2.** Anglicized form of Dutch **Vlemincks,** a patronymic from **Vleminck,** an ethnic name for someone from Flanders, Middle Dutch *vleminc.*

Flemister (265) Anglicized form of Dutch *Vlaamster* 'person from Flanders', 'Fleming'.

Flemmer (251) German: variant of FLAMMER.
GIVEN NAMES German 4%. *Bernhardt, Erwin.*

Flemming (1828) **1.** German: ethnic name for someone from Flanders, Middle High German *vlaeminc.* People from Flanders spread throughout Germany, as well as England, in the Middle Ages as clothmakers and dyers. **2.** English: variant spelling of FLEMING.

Flemmings (107) English: variant of FLEMMINGS.

Flemons (156) English: variant of FLEMINGS.

Flener (336) Variant spelling of German FLENNER.

Flenner (223) German: nickname for a whiner, from Middle High German *flenner* 'someone who cries'.

Flenniken (306) Probably of Dutch origin, a diminutive of **Vlaming** or **Flanderinck,** both ethnic names for someone from Flanders.

Flentge (118) Variant of the unexplained Frisian name **Flentje.**
GIVEN NAMES German 5%. *Hans, Otto.*

Flesch (610) **1.** German: metonymic occupational name for a maker of flasks and bottles, from Middle High German *vlashe* 'bottle' (Old High German *flasca*). **2.** North German: variant of FLEISCH.

Flesher (1211) English: occupational name for a butcher. In part it is from Middle English *flescher,* an agent derivative of Old English *flæsc* 'flesh', 'meat'; in part a reduced form of Middle English *fleschewere,* Old English *flǣschēawere,* in which the second element is an agent noun from *hēawan* 'to hew or cut'.

Fleshman (932) Americanized form of German FLEISCHMANN.

Flesner (316) German: variant spelling of FLESSNER.

Flessner (236) North German: variant of FLEISSNER, or of **Flechsner,** an occupational name for a flax grower or seller, from an agent derivative of Middle High German *vlahs* 'flax'.

Fleszar (129) Polish: Polonized form of German FLEISCHER ('butcher').
GIVEN NAMES Polish 9%. *Casimir, Ignatius, Tadeusz.*

Fletchall (242) English: unexplained.

Fletcher (28518) English: occupational name for an arrowsmith, Middle English, Old French *flech(i)er* (from Old French *fleche* 'arrow').

Fletes (126) Spanish: possibly a metonymic occupational name for a carrier, from the plural of *flete* 'freight'.
GIVEN NAMES Spanish 55%. *Jose* (5), *Rafael* (3), *Raul* (3), *Adan* (2), *Concepcion* (2), *Jesus* (2), *Agustin, Alberto, Alejandro, Alfonso, Ana, Angel.*

Flett (346) Scottish: probably a habitational name originating in the Orkneys, from a place in the parish of Delting, Shetland, named with an Old Norse term denoting a strip of arable land or pasture. On the other hand it may be from the Old Norse byname *Fljótr* 'swift', 'speedy'. Compare FLEET 2. The surname is now most common around Aberdeen and in Orkney.

Fleury (1654) French and English (of Norman origin): **1.** from the medieval personal name *Fleuri* (Latin *Florius,* a derivative of the Roman family name *Florus,* from *flos* 'flower', genitive *floris*). This name was borne by a 3rd-century saint martyred in Nicomedia under the emperor Decius. There seems to have been some confusion with a Germanic personal name composed of the elements *hlōd* 'fame' + *rīc* 'power'. **2.** habitational name from any of the various places in northern France which get their names from the Gallo-Roman personal name *Florus* (see above) + the locative suffix *-acum.* **3.** nickname from Old French *fluri* 'flowered', 'variegated' (a derivative of *flur* FLOWER). This could have denoted someone who dressed in an extravagant mixture of colors or perhaps one who had a blotchy complexion.
FOREBEARS A bearer of the name from Ardennes was in Quebec in 1642. The surname was also brought to the U.S. from Germany, having been taken there by Huguenot refugees (see FLORY).
GIVEN NAMES French 9%. *Armand* (8), *Lucien* (3), *Yvon* (3), *Andre* (2), *Gilles* (2), *Herve* (2), *Jacques* (2), *Michel* (2), *Adrien, Benoit, Camille, Evariste.*

Flewellen (197) Anglicized form of Welsh LLEWELLYN.

Flewelling (548) Anglicized form of Welsh LLEWELLYN.

Flexer (151) English: variant of FLAX.
GIVEN NAME French 5%. *Alain.*

Flicek (164) Czech (**Flíček**): from a diminutive of *flek* 'patch', 'stain', 'spot', possibly applied as a nickname for someone with patchy skin or as a metonymic occupational name for someone who patched or mended shoes, clothes, or utensils. Compare German FLECK.

Flick (3112) German: **1.** nickname for a quick and lively person from Middle High German *vlücke* 'awake', 'bright', 'energetic'. **2.** variant of FLECK.

Flicker (310) German: occupational name for a mender or repairer, from an agent derivative of Middle High German *vlicken* 'to patch or repair'.

Flickinger (1637) German: variant of FLICKER.

Flickner (143) German: variant of FLICKER.

Fliegel (175) German: see FLUEGEL.
GIVEN NAMES German 8%. *Wolfram* (2), *Alfons, Fritz, Hans, Ulrich.*

Fliegelman (103) Jewish (Ashkenazic): ornamental name from Yiddish *fligl* 'wing' + *man* 'man', or nickname from the same phrase, used to denote a very quick person.
GIVEN NAME German 6%; Jewish 4%. *Emanuel* (2).

Flieger (106) German: variant of *Pflieger*, itself a variant of *Pflüger*, a metonymic occupational name for a farmer or metonymic occupational name for a plow maker (see PFLUEGER).
GIVEN NAME German 5%. *Otto* (2).

Flier (146) German: variant of **Flieher** (see FLEER).
GIVEN NAME German 5%. *Kurt.*

Flight (172) English: unexplained.

Flikkema (102) Frisian: unexplained.

Flinchbaugh (287) Americanized spelling of German **Flinschbach**, a habitational name from any of several places named Flinsbach, Flinzbach, or Flintsbach, from Old High German *flins* 'pebble', 'flint' + *bah* 'creek'.

Flinchum (581) Origin unidentified.

Flinders (228) **1.** English: variant of FLANDERS. **2.** Anglicized form of Dutch **Vlinder**, a nickname from *vlinder* 'butterfly'.

Fling (391) English or Irish: perhaps a hypercorrected spelling of FLYNN.

Flink (527) Swedish and Jewish (Ashkenazic): nickname from Swedish, German, or Yiddish *flink* 'quick', 'agile', 'nimble'. As a Swedish name it is one of the group of 'soldiers' names', monothematic names adopted by peasants serving in the army and later transmitted to their descendants.
GIVEN NAMES Scandinavian 5%; German 4%. *Lars* (2), *Anders; Hans* (3), *Stephanus.*

Flinn (2147) Irish: variant spelling of FLYNN.

Flinner (144) German: probably a variant of FLENNER.

Flint (5607) **1.** English and German: topographic name for someone who lived near a significant outcrop of flint, Old English, Low German *flint*, or a nickname for a

hard-hearted or physically tough individual. **2.** Welsh: habitational name from Flint in Clwyd, which gave its name to the old county of Flintshire. **3.** Jewish (Ashkenazic): ornamental name from German *Flinte* 'shotgun'.

Flippen (615) Dutch: patronymic from a variant of the personal name PHILIP.

Flippin (908) Altered spelling of FLIPPEN.

Flippo (758) Reduced form of Italian FILIPPO.

Flipse (117) Dutch: reduced and altered form of **Phillipsen** (see PHILLIPS).

Flis (258) **1.** Polish and Jewish (from Poland): occupational name from *flis* 'raftsman'. **2.** eastern Slovenian: common but unexplained.
GIVEN NAMES Polish 16%. *Pawel* (2), *Tadeusz* (2), *Kazimierz, Lech, Leslaw, Lucja, Maciej, Mariusz, Mieczyslaw, Slawomir, Zigmund.*

Fliss (236) Jewish (eastern Ashkenazic): variant of FLIS.

Flitcraft (131) Altered spelling of English **Flitcroft**, a Lancashire surname, which is probably a habitational name from a lost or unidentified place named with Old English *croft* 'paddock'.

Flitter (129) English: nickname for an argumentative person, from Old English *flitere* 'disputer', an agent derivative of *flitan* 'to wrangle'.
GIVEN NAME German 4%. *Math.*

Flitton (133) English: habitational name from a place in Bedfordshire called Flitton. The meaning of the place name, recorded in Domesday Book (1086) as *Flictham*, is unexplained.

Floberg (125) Swedish: unexplained.

Flocco (129) Italian: from *fiocco* 'staple of wool', from Latin *floccus* 'lock', possibly a nickname for someone with hair thought to resemble wool or a metonymic occupational name for a wool dealer.
GIVEN NAMES Italian 21%. *Angelo* (3), *Antonio, Biagio, Gennaro, Giuseppe, Luigi, Nunzio, Umberto.*

Floch (141) German: variant of FLACH.
GIVEN NAMES French 5%; German 4%. *Pierre; Klaus, Wolfgang.*

Flock (756) **1.** English: of uncertain origin; possibly a nickname for someone with thick curly hair, from Old French *floc* 'stable of wool'. Alternatively, it may be a metonymic occupational name for a shepherd, from Old English *flocc* 'herd', 'company'. **2.** German: unexplained. **3.** German (**Flöck**): variant of **Flück** (see FLUCK), or from a pet form of a personal name formed with Old Saxon *flod* 'flood'.

Flockhart (164) Scottish: of uncertain origin; probably a metathesized form of **Folkard**.

Floden (100) **1.** Norwegian: habitational name from a farmstead named with *floe* 'tarn', 'pool in a bog'. **2.** Swedish: orna-

mental name composed with the suffix *-én*, from Latin *-in(i)us* 'descendant of'.
GIVEN NAMES Scandinavian 13%. *Bjorn, Erik, Tor.*

Flodin (198) Swedish: ornamental name from *flod* 'river', 'stream' + the ornamental suffix *-in*, derived from Latin *-in(i)us* 'relating to'.
GIVEN NAMES Scandinavian 9%. *Erik, Nils, Ove.*

Floerchinger (107) German: habitational name for someone from Flörchingen in the Saar region.

Floerke (126) German (**Flörke**): from a pet form of the personal names FLORIAN or *Florentinus*, from Latin *Florus* (from *florere* 'to bloom').

Flohr (713) **1.** German: from a short form of the medieval personal name *Florentius* (see FLORENCE), the name of a saint who died in 693, or of FLORIAN (see also FLORY). **2.** Jewish (Ashkenazic): ornamental name from German *Flor* 'array of flowers' or metonymic occupational name from German *Flor* 'gauze'.
GIVEN NAMES Jewish 5%. *Chaim* (2), *Mort* (2), *Aron, Aviva, Avrohom, Chaya, Eliyahu, Emanuel, Shimon, Sholom, Yehuda, Yosef.*

Flom (653) **1.** Jewish (Ashkenazic): ornamental name from Yiddish *floym* 'plum'. **2.** Norwegian: habitational name from any of several farmsteads named *Flom* or *Flåm*, from Old Norse *flá* 'terrace', 'shelf', referring to a feature of a hillside.
GIVEN NAMES Scandinavian 6%. *Erik* (4), *Birgit, Jalmer, Nels, Selmer, Sig.*

Flood (6295) **1.** English: topographic name for someone who lived by a small stream or an intermittent spring (Old English *flod(e)*, from *flowan* 'to flow'). **2.** Anglicized form of the Welsh personal name *Llwyd* (see LLOYD). **3.** Irish: translation of various names correctly or erroneously associated with Gaelic *tuile* 'flood' (see TOOLE).

Flook (380) **1.** English: from the Old Norse personal name *Flóki*, originally a byname meaning 'outspoken', 'enterprising'. **2.** Altered spelling of German FLUCK.

Floor (199) **1.** English: habitational name from a place in Northamptonshire named Flore, from Old English *flor(e)* 'floor', probably with reference to a lost tessellated pavement. **2.** Danish: from a short form of the personal name *Florentz* or the Frisian *Flores* (see FLORENCE).

Flor (418) **1.** Portuguese, Spanish, and Catalan: from the female personal name *Flor* (from Latin *Flos, Floris*), or, more likely, a byname from *flor* 'flower' (from Latin *flos, floris*). **2.** Czech: from a short form of the personal name *Florián* (see FLORIAN). **3.** German: variant of FLOHR.
GIVEN NAMES Spanish 17%; Portuguese 6%. *Jose* (6), *Carlos* (4), *Edmundo* (2), *Fernando* (2), *Francisco* (2), *Jaime* (2), *Juan* (2), *Adelaida, Alfredo, Alvaro, Angel, Armando; Paulo* (2), *Joao.*

Flora (2814) **1.** Spanish, Portuguese, and Italian: from the female personal name *Flora*. **2.** Czech, Austrian, and Polish: from a vernacular form of the Latin personal name *Florianus* (see FLORIAN). **3.** Hungarian (**Flóra**): from the female personal name *Flóra* (see FLORENCE).

Florance (240) French: variant of FLORENCE.

Florczak (122) Polish: patronymic from *Florek*, a pet form of the personal name FLORIAN.
GIVEN NAMES Polish 10%; German 4%. *Casimir, Janusz, Lech, Wojciech; Kurt.*

Flore (132) **1.** Dutch and North German: from a vernacular short form of the Latin personal name *Florentius* (see FLORENCE), the name of a saint who died in 693, or of FLORIAN (see also FLORY). **2.** Italian or Portuguese: perhaps from the personal name FLORA. *Flore* is also found as a Romanian family name.
GIVEN NAMES Italian 7%. *Alessandro, Angelo, Ornella.*

Florea (368) Romanian: from the medieval personal name *Florea*, probably a derivative of *floare* (from Latin *flos, floris*), with the diminutive suffix *-ea*.
GIVEN NAMES Romanian 5%. *Gheorghe (2), Floare, Mircea, Razvan, Vacile, Vasile, Viorel.*

Florek (582) Polish and Slovak: from a pet form of the medieval personal name FLORIAN.
GIVEN NAMES Polish 5%. *Bronislaw, Danuta, Maciej, Mieczyslaw, Stanislawa, Tadeusz, Wladyslaw, Wojciech.*

Floren (213) Swedish (**Florén**): ornamental name from Latin *flor* 'flower' + the frequent suffix of surnames *-én*, derived from Latin *-enius*.
GIVEN NAMES Scandinavian 5%. *Erik, Lennart.*

Florence (2903) English and French: **1.** from the personal name *Florence*, used by both sexes (Latin *Florentius* (masculine) and *Florentia* (feminine), ultimately from *flos*, genitive *floris* 'flower'). Both names were borne by several early Christian martyrs, but in the Middle Ages the masculine name was far more common. **2.** local name for someone from Florence in Italy, originally named in Latin as *Florentia*.

Florendo (136) Hispanic (mainly Filipino): unexlained, perhaps a variant of the Spanish personal and family name **Florindo**, a literary name, based on the element *flor-*, 'flower'.
GIVEN NAMES Spanish 24%; Italian 14%. *Jose (2), Luis (2), Adela, Adelina, Alfredo, Andres, Angelita, Ernesto, Herminia, Jaime, Joselito, Josue; Romeo (2), Antonio, Clemente, Federico, Leonardo, Lorenzo.*

Florentine (182) Americanized form of FIORENTINO.

Florentino (239) Spanish: **1.** from the personal name *Florentino* (Latin *Florentinus*).

2. in some cases possibly from *florentino* 'Florentine', a habitational name for someone from the city of Florence in Tuscany.
GIVEN NAMES Spanish 33%. *Jose (2), Maximo (2), Ramon (2), Rodolfo (2), Adolfo, Alfonso, Amarilis, Andres, Angel, Basilisa, Corazon, Cristobal; Romeo, Sal.*

Florer (184) German: variant of FLOHR 1.

Flores (35258) Spanish: from the plural of *flor* 'flower'.
GIVEN NAMES Spanish 49%. *Jose (935), Juan (485), Carlos (317), Jesus (306), Manuel (306), Luis (281), Francisco (208), Miguel (196), Pedro (191), Raul (178), Ruben (176), Roberto (161).*

Florey (393) **1.** English: variant of FLEURY. **2.** German variant of the Huguenot name **Fleury** (see FLORY).

Florez (1042) Spanish (**Flórez**): probably a patronymic from the Visigothic personal name *Froila*, a derivative of *fro* 'lord', 'master'. The name is also borne by Sephardic Jews.
GIVEN NAMES Spanish 40%. *Jose (16), Luis (14), Manuel (12), Juan (11), Raul (11), Carlos (10), Francisco (8), Jesus (6), Jorge (6), Ramon (6), Blanca (5), Miguel (5).*

Flori (162) Italian: patronymic or plural form of FLORIO.
GIVEN NAMES Italian 18%. *Geno (3), Dino (2), Angelo, Armando, Attilio, Luigi, Romeo, Silvio.*

Floria (130) Spanish and Italian: from the personal name *Floria*, feminine form of *Florius*, from a derivative of *flor* 'flower'.
GIVEN NAMES Italian 7%. *Pasquale (2), Angelo, Salvatore.*

Florian (791) Italian, French, Spanish (**Florián**), Polish, Czech and Slovak (**Florián**), Slovenian (**Florjan, Florijan**), German (Austrian), Hungarian (**Flórián**), and Romanian: from a medieval personal name (Latin *Florianus*, a further derivative of *Florius*); (see FLEURY) borne by a 3rd-century saint who was drowned in Noricum during the persecutions of Christians under Diocletian and became the patron of Upper Austria, widely invoked as a protector from the danger of fires.
GIVEN NAMES Spanish 5%; German 4%. *Jose (4), Luis (3), Carlos (2), Juan (2), Mario (2), Adolfo, Alfonso, Ana, Beatriz, Cesar, Cristobal, Esteban; Kurt (5), Alois, Manfred, Manfried, Monika, Rudi, Theodor, Ute.*

Florida (416) **1.** Spanish and southern Italian: from the female personal name *Florida*. **2.** Spanish: habitational name from any of the numerous places called Florida or La Florida, from Spanish *florido* 'blooming', 'full of blossom'.

Florin (292) **1.** Swedish: ornamental name, a variant of FLOREN. **2.** Spanish (**Florín**): possibly from *florín* 'florin' (the coin).
GIVEN NAMES German 4%; French 4%. *Hans, Heinz, Hermann; Francoise, Laurette.*

Florio (1422) Italian and Portuguese: from the medieval personal name *Florio* (Latin *Florius*), which was popularized by the medieval French romance *Floire et Blanchefleur*.
GIVEN NAMES Italian 15%. *Vito (10), Rocco (9), Antonio (8), Pasquale (6), Angelo (4), Domenic (3), Salvatore (3), Domenico (2), Guido (2), Mauro (2), Carlo, Carmela.*

Florkowski (110) Polish: habitational name for someone from Florków in Częstochowa voivodeship, or Florki from Przemyśl voivodeship, both so named from *Florek*, a pet form of the personal name *Florian*.
GIVEN NAME Polish 4%. *Wojciech.*

Florman (108) **1.** German (**Flormann**): derivative of the personal name *Flor* (see FLOHR). **2.** German (**Flohrmann**): occupational name for a watchman over fields, from Middle High German *vluor* (modern German *Flur*) 'cultivated field' + *man* 'man'. **3.** Swedish: ornamental name from Latin *flor* 'flower' + *man* 'man'.
GIVEN NAMES Scandinavian 5%; German 4%. *Nils(2); Kurt.*

Floro (222) Spanish and Italian: from the personal name *Floro*, from Latin *Florus* 'flower'.
GIVEN NAMES Italian 18%; Spanish 14%. *Mariano (3), Domenic (2), Antonio, Bonifacio, Emilio, Fiore, Franca, Gino, Ignazio, Tommaso; Ramon (3), Teresita (3), Angel, Juan, Juanita, Lourdes, Pedro.*

Floros (117) Greek: from the personal name *Phlōros* 'green' (from classical Greek *khlōros*), or a nickname from the same word in the sense 'greenfinch'. In some cases it may also be a shortened form of a derivative of this name, such as **Phloropoulos**.
GIVEN NAMES Greek 22%. *Nikolaos (2), Andreas, Constantine, Constantinos, Costas, Fotios, Ourania, Spiro, Spyridon.*

Flory (2122) **1.** English: variant of FLEURY. **2.** German form of a French Huguenot name, taken to the Palatinate by a family presumed to have fled from Fleury, France (but see FLEURY). **3.** South German (mainly Austrian; also **Flöry**): from a short form of the medieval personal name FLORIAN.
FOREBEARS Joseph J. (1683–1741) and Mary Fleure and six children (including four sons) arrived in Philadelphia from the Palatinate in 1733 and settled in Lancaster Co. Two sons are the progenitors of the PA and MD Florys. One son moved to VA; descendants Latinized their name as **Flora**.

Floss (118) German: topographic name for someone who lived by a river, Middle High German *vlōz*, modern German *Fluss*.
GIVEN NAME German 7%. *Heinz (2).*

Floto (213) German: habitational name from a place on the Weser called Vlotho (earlier *Vlotuwe*, from a cognate of FLOOD), or another in Mecklenburg, near Penzlin, called Flotow, which is of Slavic origin.

Flott (157) North German: **1.** probably a short form of, for example, **Flottmann** or **Flottweder**, topographic names for someone who lived at a shallow crossing or ford, from Middle Low German *vlōt* 'shallow'. **2.** from an Old Saxon personal name formed with *flōd* 'flood'.

Flournoy (1664) French: probably a topographic name for someone who lived in a place where flowers grew. This name is associated with Huguenots who settled in VA.

Flow (162) English: unexplained; possibly a variant of **Flew**, a metonymic occupational name for a fisherman, from Middle English *flue*, denoting a kind of fishing net.

Flowe (262) English: see FLOW.

Flower (1424) **1.** English: nickname from Middle English *flo(u)r* 'flower', 'blossom' (Old French *flur*, from Latin *flos*, genitive *floris*). This was a conventional term of endearment in medieval romantic poetry, and as early as the 13th century it is also regularly found as a female personal name. **2.** English: metonymic occupational name for a miller or flour merchant, or perhaps a nickname for a pasty-faced person, from Middle English *flo(u)r* 'flour'. This is in origin the same word as in 1, with the transferred sense 'flower, pick of the meal'. Although the two words are now felt to be accidental homophones, they were not distinguished in spelling before the 18th century. **3.** English: occupational name for an arrowsmith, from an agent derivative of Middle English *flō* 'arrow' (Old English *flā*). **4.** Welsh: Anglicized form of the Welsh personal name *Llywarch*, of unexplained origin. **5.** Translation of French LAFLEUR.

Flowers (15853) English: patronymic from FLOWER 1.

Floyd (21077) Welsh: variant of LLOYD.

Fluck (369) **1.** English: variant spelling of FLOOK. **2.** South German and Swiss German (also **Flück**): nickname for a bright and lively person, from Middle High German *vlücke* 'fully fledged'.

GIVEN NAMES German 4%. *Reinhold, Udo.*

Fluckiger (144) German and Swiss German (**Flückiger**): habitational name for someone from a place in Bern, Switzerland, called Flückingen.

GIVEN NAMES German 4%. *Hans, Rudi.*

Flud (171) Variant of English and Welsh FLOOD.

Fludd (217) Variant of English and Welsh FLOOD.

Fluegel (299) German (also **Flügel**): **1.** Americanized spelling of south German **Pflügl, Pfliegl**, metonymic occupational names for a plow maker or, by extension, for a farmer, from a diminutive of Middle High German *pfluoc* 'plow'. **2.** topographic name from the field name *Flügel*, literally 'wing', denoting a jutting piece of land extending beyond the boundaries of a farmer's land.

Fluegge (172) North German (**Flügge**): variant of FLUCK 2.

GIVEN NAMES German 10%. *Otto* (3), *Erwin, Heinz, Helmut, Kurt.*

Fluellen (325) Anglicized form of Welsh LLEWELLYN.

Fluet (180) French: nickname for a weak or languid individual, from Old French *flo, flou* 'feeble', 'lethargic'.

GIVEN NAMES French 15%. *Cecile, Donat, Emile, Germaine, Gillis, Normand, Renald.*

Flug (158) German: variant of German PFLUG.

Fluharty (812) Possibly a variant of Irish FLAHERTY.

Fluhr (223) German: probably an occupational name, from *Flu(h)rer* (rarely Swabian *Pflurer*) 'field guard', an agent derivative of Middle High German *vluor* 'field'.

Fluitt (212) **1.** Dutch: metonymic occupational name for a pipe or flute player, from Middle Dutch *fluut* 'pipe', 'flute'. **2.** Possibly an altered spelling of French FLUET.

Fluke (528) **1.** English: variant spelling of FLOOK. **2.** Americanized spell of German FLUCK or PFLUG.

Fluker (564) Americanized spelling of German PFLUEGER.

Flum (108) **1.** Americanized spelling of German PFLAUM. **2.** nickname for someone with a downy beard, from Middle High German *vlume* 'feathers', 'down'.

Flurry (318) Variant spelling of FLEURY or **Flöry** (see FLORY).

Flury (404) **1.** English: variant of FLEURY. **2.** Swiss German: variant of FLORY 2.

GIVEN NAMES German 4%. *Claus, Darrold, Fritz, Markus, Mathias.*

Flusche (141) German: variant of FLASCH.

GIVEN NAME German 6%. *Otto.*

Fluty (238) Origin unidentified.

Fly (821) **1.** English: unexplained. **2.** Danish: unexplained. **3.** Perhaps an altered spelling of Dutch **Vlij**, a topographic name from *vallei* 'lowland', 'marsh'; in New Netherland this became a common term for a swamp.

Flye (209) English: variant spelling of FLY.

Flygare (165) Swedish: ornamental adoption of the occupational term *flygare* 'flier', 'aviator'.

GIVEN NAMES German 5%. *Hans* (2), *Kurt* (2).

Flynn (25237) Irish: reduced Anglicized form of Gaelic **Ó Floinn** 'descendant of *Flann*', a byname meaning 'red(dish)', 'ruddy'. There were families of this name in various parts of Ireland.

GIVEN NAMES Irish 5%. *Brendan* (15), *Connor* (3), *Declan* (3), *Kieran* (3), *Aidan* (2), *Brigid* (2), *Cathal* (2), *Dermot* (2), *Donal* (2), *Eamon* (2), *John Patrick* (2), *Kiernan* (2).

Flynt (1038) English: variant spelling of FLINT.

Flyte (110) North German: apparently a respelling of **Fleith** (see FLYTHE).

Flythe (308) Americanization of an unexplained German family name, **Fleith**.

FOREBEARS Johannes Fleith and his wife Margaretha arrived in Philadelphia in 1752 from Freudenstadt, Württemberg, Germany.

Foard (408) English: variant spelling of FORD.

Foat (121) English: nickname from Middle English *fōde* 'child', literally 'that which is fed', from Old English *fōda* 'food'.

Fobbs (240) Variant of Scottish FORBES.

Fobes (326) Variant of Scottish FORBES.

Fochs (149) North German: nickname for someone thought to resemble a fox in some way; North German form of FUCHS.

Focht (838) **1.** Possibly an altered spelling of Dutch **(de) Vocht**, an occupational name for a custodian, commander, or leader, Middle Dutch *vo(e)cht*. **2.** German: variant of VOGT.

Fochtman (188) German (**Fochtmann**): variant of **Vogtmann**.

Focke (123) North German, Dutch, and Frisian: from a short form of any of the many personal names formed with *Volk*.

Fockler (298) German (**Föckler**): **1.** variant of FOCKE. **2.** variant of **Feckler**, presumably an occupational name for a tailor or mender.

Fode (145) Origin unidentified. In part, at least, it is a Moldovian name of unexplained etymology.

Foden (109) English and Scottish: origin uncertain; perhaps a nickname for a foster parent, from Middle English *foden* 'to nurse or nourish'.

GIVEN NAME Scottish 4%. *Athol.*

Fodera (153) Sicilian (**Foderà**): nickname from medieval Greek *phōtēros* 'bright', 'radiant', or perhaps from the same word used as a personal name. It may alternatively be a topographic name, from the dialect word *foderò* 'hard', in the sense 'hard to cultivate', 'rocky'.

GIVEN NAMES Italian 31%. *Vito* (5), *Salvatore* (3), *Biagio* (2), *Angelo, Antonio, Benedetto, Camillo, Ciro, Domenico, Gaetano, Giuseppe, Vincenzo.*

Fodge (131) Possibly an Americanized form of German FOERTSCH.

Fodness (152) Norwegian: habitational name from either of two farmsteads so named, from Old Norse *Fornesjar* 'protruding mountain' from *for* 'front', 'foremost' + *nesjar*, plural of *nes* 'headland'.

Fodor (778) Hungarian: nickname for a person with curly hair, from *fodor* 'curl'.

GIVEN NAMES Hungarian 8%. *Laszlo* (4), *Sandor* (3), *Tibor* (3), *Zoltan* (3), *Zsolt* (3), *Gabor* (2), *Jozsef* (2), *Kalman* (2), *Antal, Balazs, Bela, Denes.*

Foe (119) Possibly an altered spelling of FAUX.

Foell (273) German (**Föll**): **1.** from a short form of the personal name *Volker*. **2.** variant of FELD.

Foeller (168) German (**Föller**): variant of FELDER.
GIVEN NAME German 4%. *Dieter*.

Foerst (148) German: shortened form of **Foerster** or **Förstner** (see FORSTER 1).
GIVEN NAMES German 8%. *Kurt* (2), *Dieter*, *Klaus*.

Foerster (1191) German (**Förster**): see FORSTER 1.
GIVEN NAMES German 9%. *Gerda* (3), *Hans* (3), *Kurt* (3), *Otto* (3), *Claus* (2), *Erwin* (2), *Alois*, *Bernd*, *Christoph*, *Detlef*, *Erna*, *Gerd*.

Foertsch (272) German (**Förtsch**): **1.** in Bavaria, a variant of **Pfoertsch**, probably a derisive nickname from Middle High German *verz*, *vorz* 'fart'. **2.** habitational name for someone from a place named Förtschach or Förtschendorf.
GIVEN NAMES German 4%. *Erwin*, *Hanns*, *Manfred*.

Fofana (116) West African: unexplained.
GIVEN NAMES Muslim 42%; African 28%. *Mohamed* (5), *Lamine* (2), *Sheriff* (2), *Souleymane* (2), *Abdoulaye*, *Abdul*, *Abdulai*, *Abdur*, *Abou*, *Aly*, *Habib*, *Ibrahima*; *Mamadou* (3), *Amadou* (2), *Foday* (2), *Lassana* (2), *Mariama* (2), *Alieu*, *Fatou*, *Mahamadou*, *Modou*, *Sekou*.

Fogal (270) Variant spelling (in Slavic regions) of German VOGEL.

Fogarty (3299) Irish: reduced Anglicized form of Gaelic **Ó Fógartaigh** 'son of *Fógartach*', a personal name from *fógartha* 'proclaimed', 'banished', 'outlawed'. It is sometimes Anglicized as HOWARD.
GIVEN NAMES Irish 5%. *Brendan* (2), *James Patrick*, *Kieran*, *Seamus*, *Siobhan*.

Fogel (2071) Jewish (Ashkenazic): variant spelling of VOGEL.
GIVEN NAMES Jewish 8%. *Chaim* (6), *Meyer* (4), *Asher* (3), *Avi* (3), *Mayer* (3), *Moshe* (3), *Efi* (2), *Isadore* (2), *Ori* (2), *Akiva*, *Alter*, *Ber*.

Fogelberg (160) Swedish: ornamental compound name composed of the elements *fogel*, an ornamental (old) spelling of *fågel* 'bird' + *berg* 'hill'.
GIVEN NAMES Scandinavian 8%; German 7%. *Erik*, *Erland*, *Johan*; *Kurt* (3).

Fogelman (346) Jewish (Ashkenazic): variant of VOGELMAN.
GIVEN NAMES Jewish 8%. *Avron* (3), *Chaim* (2), *Hershel* (2), *Nuchem*, *Shmuel*.

Fogelson (232) Jewish (Ashkenazic): Germanized form of **Feigelso(h)n**, a metronymic from FEIGEL.
GIVEN NAMES Jewish 4%. *Hershel*, *Irina*.

Fogerson (111) Probably an altered form, under French influence, of Scottish FERGUSON.
GIVEN NAME French 4%. *Patrice*.

Fogerty (336) Irish: variant spelling of FOGARTY.

Fogg (2262) Northern English: from Middle English *fogge* 'aftermath', i.e. grass left to grow after the hay has been cut, also applied to long grass in a water meadow. The surname arose from either a topographic name or a metonymic occupational name for someone who grazed cattle on such grass in the winter. The vocabulary word, which is probably of Old Norse origin, is still in use as a dialect term in Craven, Yorkshire, and in eastern Lancashire. Modern English *fog* 'thick mist' is first attested in the 16th century and is unlikely to be the source for a surname.

Fogle (3469) Americanized spelling of FOGEL or VOGEL.

Fogleman (1042) Americanized spelling of VOGELMAN.

Fogler (275) From VOGLER, an occupational name for a bird-catcher; this may be a variant spelling of the Jewish surname or an Americanized spelling of the German surname.

Foglesong (413) Americanized form of German and Jewish **Vogelsang** 'bird song'.

Foglia (388) Italian: **1.** habitational name from Foglia, the name of a locality in Magliano Sabina. **2.** possibly from the feminine form of the Latin personal name *Folius*.
GIVEN NAMES Italian 16%. *Angelo* (3), *Vito* (3), *Donato* (2), *Carmela*, *Carmine*, *Dario*, *Domenico*, *Enrico*, *Filomena*, *Franco*, *Guido*, *Matteo*.

Foglio (158) Italian: probably from the Latin personal name *Folius* (which is embodied in the common place name Fogliano).
GIVEN NAMES Italian 13%. *Carmine*, *Dino*, *Flavio*, *Julieta*, *Sal*, *Salvatore*.

Fogo (143) Portuguese: from Portuguese *fogo* 'fire', possibly from a place name.

Fogt (303) **1.** Danish: occupational name from Danish *foged* 'bailiff'. **2.** Americanized spelling of German VOGT.
GIVEN NAMES Scandinavian 4%. *Anders*, *Arlis*, *Arlys*, *Niels*.

Fogus (101) Probably an altered form, under French influence, of Scottish FERGUS.

Fohey (105) Irish: variant spelling of FAHEY.

Fohl (179) German: **1.** nickname for someone who behaved in a skittish or unpredictable manner, from Middle High German, Middle Low German *vole* 'foal'. **2.** (**Föhl**): variant of FEIL 2. **3.** from Swabian *Föhl* 'spark', 'embers', possibly applied as a metonymic occupational name for a blacksmith or smelter, or as a nickname for a hot-tempered person.
GIVEN NAMES German 4%. *Aloys*, *Kurt*, *Otto*.

Fohn (108) German and Swiss German (also **Föhn**): unexplained.
GIVEN NAME German 5%. *Kurt*.

Fohrman (109) North German: topographic name for someone living by a ford, Low German *Fohr*.

Foil (241) Variant spelling of English or Scottish FOYLE.

Foiles (247) Probably English or Scottish, a topographic name for someone living by two or more pits (see FOYLE).

Foist (122) Perhaps an Americanized form of German **Fürst** (see FURST) or of FEIST.

Foister (167) English: variant of FORSTER 3.

Foisy (358) French Canadian variant of French **Foissy**, a habitational name from a place so named in Yonne. In French Canada Foisy is also a secondary surname for **Frenière** or **La Frenière** (see LAFRENIERE), and Americanized as FREEMAN.
FOREBEARS A bearer of the name from Champagne is documented in Trois Rivières, Quebec, in 1667.
GIVEN NAMES French 11%. *Armand* (2), *Emile* (2), *Aime*, *Alphonse*, *Aurore*, *Fernand*, *Florent*, *Gilles*, *Manon*, *Michel*.

Foit (131) Americanized spelling of German **Voit**, a variant of VOGT.
GIVEN NAMES German 12%. *Beate*, *Dieter*, *Frieda*, *Guenter*, *Heinz*, *Lothar*.

Fojtik (201) Czech (**Fojtík**): occupational name for a bailiff, farm manager, or local administrative official, from German VOGT + the Slavic diminutive suffix *-ik*.

Fok (170) **1.** Dutch: variant of FOCKE. **2.** Chinese 霍: variant of HUO.
GIVEN NAMES Chinese 22%. *Cheong*, *Chi*, *Chi Ming*, *Chichung*, *Kai Hong*, *Kin*, *Kin Ming*, *Ping*, *Siu Ping*, *Wai*, *Wai Ching*; *Kam* (5).

Fokken (109) German: spelling variant of **Focken**, patronymic from FOCKE.
GIVEN NAMES German 9%. *Bernhard*, *Hartmut*, *Markus*.

Folan (398) Irish: reduced Anglicized form of Gaelic **Ó Faoláin** 'descendant of *Faolán*' (see WHELAN).
GIVEN NAMES Irish 8%. *Brendan*, *Liam*.

Foland (675) German: variant of VOLLAND.

Folck (157) German: variant spelling of VOLK.

Folden (519) Norwegian: habitational name from either of two farmsteads in central Norway, originally taking their names from a fjord named 'the wide (fjord)'.

Folds (518) English: topographic name for someone who lived near a pen for animals, or an occupational name for someone who worked in one, from Middle English *fold* 'pen', 'enclosure' (Old English *falod*, *fald*).

Foley (20828) Irish: **1.** (southern) reduced Anglicized form of Gaelic **Ó Foghladha** 'descendant of *Foghlaidh*', a byname meaning 'pirate', 'marauder'. **2.** (northern) Anglicized form of Gaelic *Mac Searraigh* (see McSHARRY), chosen because of its phonetic approximation to English *foal*.
GIVEN NAMES Irish 6%. *Brendan* (16), *Donal* (3), *Siobhan* (3), *Aidan* (2), *Aileen* (2),

Delma (2), *Eamonn* (2), *John Patrick* (2), *Brennan, Brian Patrick, Briana, Brigid.*

Folger (938) **1.** English: variant of FULCHER. **2.** German: nickname from Middle High German, Middle Low German *volger* 'companion', 'supporter'.
FOREBEARS John Folger came from Norwich, England, to Dedham, MA, in 1635. By 1652 he was on Martha's Vineyard. His son Peter had ten children.

Folino (340) Italian: from a short form of **Cristofolino**, a pet form of *Cristofolo*, Italian form of CHRISTOPHER.
GIVEN NAMES Italian 19%. *Domenic* (2), *Dømenico* (2), *Giuseppe* (2), *Antonio, Attilio, Carmelo, Dominico, Guido, Luigi, Mario, Pasquale, Rodolfo, Sal, Santino.*

Folio (109) Origin uncertain. There is evidence for it as an Italian, French, and English name.

Folk (2045) Variant of German VOLK or the English cognate FOULKS.

Folker (242) Variant of English FULCHER or Americanized form of the German cognate VOLKER.

Folkers (423) German: variant of FOLKERTS.
GIVEN NAMES German 5%. *Eldred, Erwin, Gerhard, Kurt, Otto.*

Folkert (159) German: Frisian form of VOLKERT.

Folkerts (516) German: Frisian patronymic from the personal name *Volkert.*
GIVEN NAMES German 4%. *Hildegarde, Jurgen, Otto, Wessel.*

Folkes (320) English: variant of FOULKS.

Folkestad (124) Norwegian: habitational name from any of five farmsteads named with the personal name *Folke* + *stad* (from Old Norse *staðr* 'farmstead', 'dwelling').
GIVEN NAME Scandinavian 5%. *Nels.*

Folkins (114) Probably a variant of English FILKINS.

Folkman (316) Variant spelling of Jewish (Ashkenazic) or Americanized spelling of German VOLKMANN.

Folkner (129) German: variant of FALKNER.
GIVEN NAME French 5%. *Henri.*

Folks (693) English: variant of FOULKS.

Folland (158) **1.** Norwegian: habitational name from a farmstead in Nordmøre, named from Old Norse *forland* 'coastal plain below high mountains'. **2.** German: variant spelling VOLLAND.
GIVEN NAMES German 5%; Scandinavian 5%. *Erwin, Fritz, Johann.*

Follansbee (345) Probably an altered form of an English habitational name, from an unidentified place.
GIVEN NAMES French 4%. *Aurore, Cecile, Celina, Marcel.*

Follen (106) English and Irish: apparently a variant spelling of FOLLIN.

Follett (1172) English: nickname for a foolish or eccentric person, from a diminutive of *Foll*, from Old French *fol* 'mad', 'stupid'

(Late Latin *follis*, originally a noun denoting any of various objects filled with air, but later transferred to vain and empty-headed notions).

Follette (223) French Canadian spelling of French **Follet**, a nickname from Old French *fol* 'mad', 'stupid'. Compare LAFOLLETTE.

Folley (185) English **1.** habitational name from any of the minor places in Wiltshire, Warwickshire, and other counties called (The) Folly, usually from Middle English *folie* in the sense 'folly', 'foolish enterprise', but otherwise from Old French *feuillie* 'leafy bower or shelter', later 'clump of trees'. In some cases, the name may be topographic. **2.** nickname for an eccentric or foolish person, from Old French *folie* 'foolishness'.

Follin (211) **1.** English: nickname from a diminutive of Old French *folet* 'fool'. **2.** Irish: unexplained; possibly a variant of PHELAN, itself a variant of WHELAN. **3.** Swedish and Danish: from a short form of **Follinius**, a humanistic name of unexplained origin.

Follis (731) Northern Irish: variant of FALLIS.

Follman (182) **1.** Americanized spelling of German **Vollmann**, from the personal name VOLKMANN. **2.** Jewish (Ashkenazic): of uncertain origin.
GIVEN NAMES Jewish 12%. *Chaim* (2), *Hyman* (2), *Yochanan* (2), *Ahron, Eluzer, Sol, Tzvi, Yehuda, Yitzchock.*

Follmer (539) German (also **Föllmer**): variant spelling of **Vollmer.**

Followell (247) English (Midlands): probably an anecdotal nickname meaning 'fall in the well'.

Follweiler (121) German: variant of FULWILER.

Folmar (632) Americanized spelling of German VOLLMAR.

Folmer (262) Americanized spelling of German VOLLMER.

Folmsbee (106) Origin unidentified. Compare FOLLANSBEE.

Folse (731) **1.** Americanized spelling of German VOLZ. **2.** Perhaps an altered spelling of English **False**, a nickname for a deceiver, from Old French *fals, faus* 'false'.
GIVEN NAMES French 5%. *Emile* (3), *Amie, Antoine, Celestine, Fernand, Leandre.*

Folsom (2986) English: variant of **Foulsham**, a habitational name from Foulsham in Norfolk, so named from the Old English personal name *Fugol* + *hām* 'homestead'.

Folson (127) English: variant of FOLSOM.

Folstad (116) Norwegian: habitational name from a farmstead in Trøndelag, so named from the river name *Folla* 'the wide' + *stad* 'farmstead', 'dwelling'.
GIVEN NAMES Scandinavian 10%. *Arnt, Thor.*

Folta (210) Czech and Polish: from the German personal name *Valentin*, a vernacular form of Latin *Valentinus* (see VALENTINE).
GIVEN NAMES Polish 6%; German 5%. *Janina, Jerzy, Karol, Krystyna, Witold; Dieter, Erna.*

Folts (353) Americanized spelling of German VOLZ.

Foltyn (110) Polish: from the personal name *Foltyn*, Polish form of German FELTEN, a vernacular form of Latin *Valentinus* (see VALENTINE).
GIVEN NAMES Polish 5%; German 5%. *Janina, Malgorzata; Mathias.*

Foltz (3551) Americanized spelling of German VOLZ.

Folwell (185) English (Midlands): variant of FOLLOWELL.

Folz (516) Americanized spelling of German VOLZ.

Fomby (285) Probably an altered form, under French influence, of English FORMBY.
GIVEN NAMES French 4%. *Andre, Gaston.*

Fonda (489) **1.** Dutch: topographic name from *fonda* 'mine' (from Latin *fundus, funda*). **2.** Catalan: possibly a topographic name from *fonda* 'inn', from Arabic *funduq*, or perhaps a nickname from *fonda* 'slingshot'. **3.** The name may also be Italian, a habitational name from a place named with the adjective *fondo, fonda* 'deep', for example *Cavafonda* 'deep cave' or *Vallefonda.*
FOREBEARS Jelles Fonda, son of Douw Fonda, came to North America from the Netherlands in 1642. His family was of Spanish or Catalan origin, having arrived in the Netherlands about a hundred years earlier via Genoa, according to some accounts fleeing from the Inquisition. Fonda, NY (county seat of Montgomery County), is named for Jelles Fonda; the actor Henry Fonda donated the Dutch family Bible to the library there.

Fonder (215) French and Belgian (Ardennes): occupational name for a metal caster, from French *fondeur.*

Fondren (855) Americanized spelling of German **Vondran**, variant of **Vorndran**, a nickname meaning 'ahead of all'.

Fones (334) **1.** English (West Midlands): unexplained; perhaps from Middle English *fon(ne)* 'stupid person', 'fool' (origin unknown) or Middle English *foun* 'fawn', 'young deer' (from Old French *feon, foun, faon*). **2.** Possibly an Americanized spelling of German **Fanz**, a nickname for a roguish or mischievous person, from Middle High German *vanz* 'joker', 'rogue'.

Fong (4276) **1.** Chinese 方: variant of FANG 1. **2.** Chinese 冯: variant of FENG 1. **3.** Chinese 房: variant of FANG 2.
GIVEN NAMES Chinese 12%. *Wing* (13), *Ming* (8), *Yee* (7), *Ching* (6), *Ping* (6), *Chun* (5), *Kam* (5), *Kin* (5), *Kwok* (5), *Lai* (5), *Wai* (5), *Hing* (4).

Fonger (153) **1.** German: variant of **Fanger**, a habitational name for someone from any of various places called Fang. A large family by this name comes from Unterwalden, Switzerland. **2.** Possibly a respelling of German **Vongehr**.

Fonk (113) Dutch and North German: variant spelling of FUNK.

Fonner (387) **1.** Possibly an altered spelling of English **Fanner**: **2.** occupational name for a winnower, from a derivative of Old English *fannian* 'to winnow', or alternatively for a maker of winnowing baskets, from Old English *fann* 'fan', 'winnowing basket'. **3.** topographic name for a fen or marsh dweller, from a derivative of Middle English *fann* 'fen'.

Fons (247) Catalan and southern French: respelling of **Fonts**, topographic name from the plural of *font* 'spring' (see FONT).

Fonseca (2917) Spanish and Portuguese: habitational name from any of several places named for a spring that dried up during the summer months, from *fonte seca* 'dry well'.
GIVEN NAMES Spanish 40%; Portuguese 12%. *Jose* (93), *Manuel* (42), *Juan* (32), *Carlos* (31), *Luis* (21), *Francisco* (20), *Pedro* (18), *Jesus* (14), *Jorge* (14), *Rafael* (14), *Raul* (12), *Fernando* (11); *Joao* (7), *Joaquim* (4), *Agostinho* (2), *Amadeu*, *Henrique*, *Ilidio*, *Ligia*, *Manoel*, *Margarida*, *Paulo*, *Sebastiao*.

Font (442) Southern French and Catalan: topographic name for someone living near a spring or well, Occitan and Catalan *font* (Latin *fons*, genitive *fontis*).
GIVEN NAMES Spanish 34%. *Jose* (18), *Carlos* (5), *Juan* (5), *Luis* (5), *Miguel* (5), *Rafael* (5), *Eduardo* (4), *Raul* (4), *Eugenio* (3), *Pedro* (3), *Roberto* (3), *Aida* (2).

Fontaine (4433) Northern and central French: topographic name for someone who lived near a spring or well, Old French *fontane*, Late Latin *fontana*, a derivative of classical Latin *fons* (see FONT).
FOREBEARS A Fontaine from Normandy, France, is documented in Quebec in 1656; another, from Poitou, arrived after 1683. There has been some alternation with ROBERT.
GIVEN NAMES French 13%. *Armand* (14), *Andre* (13), *Normand* (12), *Pierre* (9), *Emile* (6), *Fernand* (6), *Lucien* (5), *Marcel* (5), *Adelard* (4), *Henri* (4), *Jacques* (4), *Laurent* (4).

Fontan (152) Spanish and Galician (**Fontán**; also **Fontao**): habitational name from any of the many places named Fontán, from *fontán* 'spring'.
GIVEN NAMES Spanish 26%. *Angel* (4), *Benigno* (3), *Carlos* (2), *Jose* (2), *Juana* (2), *Manuel* (2), *Pedro* (2), *Adolfo*, *Aida*, *Alfredo*, *Candido*, *Emilia*.

Fontana (2756) Italian, Spanish, and Catalan: topographic name for someone who lived near a spring, from Romance de-

scendants of Late Latin *fontana*, a derivative of classical Latin *fons*, or in Italy possibly a habitational name from any of the numerous minor places named with this word. The surname is also established in Portugal, imported form Italy.
GIVEN NAMES Italian 15%. *Salvatore* (13), *Antonio* (8), *Sal* (8), *Aldo* (6), *Vito* (6), *Dante* (5), *Elio* (4), *Angelo* (3), *Caesar* (3), *Camillo* (3), *Carlo* (3), *Gaetano* (3).

Fontanella (262) Italian: from diminutive of FONTANA.
GIVEN NAMES Italian 20%. *Mario* (4), *Aldo*, *Angelo*, *Ateo*, *Atilio*, *Cristina*, *Enzo*, *Guido*, *Orazio*, *Primo*, *Tulio*.

Fontanez (360) Spanish (**Fontánez**): variant spelling of Galician **Fontanes**, a habitational name from either of the two places in Pontevedra province named Fontanes, from the plural of *fontán* 'spring'.
GIVEN NAMES Spanish 43%. *Jose* (11), *Angel* (9), *Francisco* (5), *Luis* (4), *Ruben* (4), *Carlos* (3), *Juan* (3), *Luz* (3), *Pedro* (3), *Rafael* (3), *Ramon* (3), *Roberto* (3); *Antonio* (3), *Angelo* (2), *Annamaria*, *Carmelo*, *Marcello*.

Fontanilla (190) Spanish: diminutive of FONTANA.
GIVEN NAMES Spanish 42%. *Manuel* (3), *Rogelio* (3), *Ernesto* (2), *Eugenio* (2), *Francisco* (2), *Mariano* (2), *Maximo* (2), *Ricardo* (2), *Adelina*, *Alberto*, *Alfredo*, *Alicia*; *Clemente* (2), *Romeo* (2), *Geronimo*.

Fonte (518) Portuguese and Italian: topographic name for someone who lived near a spring or well, from Latin *fons*, genitive *fontis*, 'spring', 'well', or a habitational name from a place named with this word.
GIVEN NAMES Spanish 15%; Italian 10%; Portuguese 4%. *Jose* (5), *Armando* (2), *Carlos* (2), *Gilberto* (2), *Manuel* (2), *Roberto* (2), *Salvador* (2), *Agusto*, *Alfredo*, *Ana*, *Andres*, *Benito*; *Angelo* (4), *Salvatore* (2), *Carmello*, *Francesca*, *Vincenza*, *Vincenzo*, *Vito*; *Joaquim*, *Serafim*.

Fontecchio (119) Italian: habitational name from Fontecchio in Aquila province or a topographic name from a diminutive of *fonte* 'spring'.
GIVEN NAMES Spanish 7%; Italian 6%. *Osvaldo* (2), *Isidoro*, *Julio*, *Lino*; *Giovanni*, *Remo*, *Silvio*.

Fontenette (184) French: diminutive of FONTAINE.

Fontenot (6517) French: from a diminutive of *fontane* 'spring', 'fountain'. Written **Fonteneau**, **Fonteneault** in French Canada, this is a secondary surname of **Desmoulins**, DUMOULIN, frequently found in English as MILLER. Fontenot is common in LA.
FOREBEARS There are Fonteneaus, also called Saint Jean, from Anjou, recorded in Lachenaie, Quebec, in 1681.
GIVEN NAMES French 4%. *Emile* (5), *Ulysse* (5), *Andrus* (3), *Curley* (3), *Nolton* (3),

Alcide (2), *Andre* (2), *Edouard* (2), *Lucien* (2), *Marise* (2), *Monique* (2), *Remy* (2).

Fontes (923) Portuguese and Galician: habitational name from any of the numerous places named Fontes, from the plural of *fonte* 'fount', 'source', 'spring'.
GIVEN NAMES Spanish 23%; Portuguese 10%. *Manuel* (28), *Carlos* (11), *Jose* (9), *Alfredo* (4), *Miguel* (4), *Alda* (3), *Francisco* (3), *Jesus* (3), *Mario* (3), *Octavio* (3), *Alicia* (2), *Gustavo* (2); *Joao* (3), *Catarina*, *Henrique*, *Paulo*.

Fonti (120) Italian: variant (plural) of FONTE.
GIVEN NAME Italian 13%. *Salvatore* (3).

Fonville (456) French: habitational name from a place named Fonville or Fontvieille.

Fonzi (109) Italian: from *Fonzo*, a short form of the personal name ALFONSO (see DI FONZO).
GIVEN NAMES Italian 13%. *Angelo*, *Carmine*, *Giovanni*, *Rinaldo*, *Santina*.

Foo (310) Chinese: see FU.
GIVEN NAMES Chinese 16%. *Fook* (2), *Hong* (2), *Kam* (2), *Chee*, *Chen*, *Chi Hung*, *Chiang*, *Chin*, *Chow*, *Chuan*, *Chun*, *Hon*.

Foody (171) Irish: reduced Anglicized form of Gaelic **Ó Fuada**, 'descendant of *Fuada*', a personal name from *fuad* 'haste'. Compare RUSH, SPEED, and SWIFT.
GIVEN NAME Irish 4%. *Siobhan*.

Fooks (269) **1.** English: variant of FOULKS. **2.** Americanized spelling of German FUCHS.

Foor (1079) Americanized spelling of German FUHR.

Foos (903) Americanized spelling of German FUSS.

Foose (513) Americanized spelling of German FUSS.

Fooshee (171) Probably an Americanized spelling of French **Fouché** (see FOUCHE), or alternatively a respelling of French names FAUCHEUX or FORTIER.

Foot (176) English: variant spelling of FOOTE.
GIVEN NAMES French 4%. *Dominique*, *Raymonde*.

Foote (6155) English (Somerset): **1.** nickname for someone with a peculiarity or deformity of the foot, from Middle English *fot* (Old English *fōt*), or in some cases from the cognate Old Norse byname *Fótr*. **2.** topographic name for someone who lived at the foot of a hill.

Footer (102) English (Norfolk and Suffolk): topographic name for someone who lived at the foot of a hill.

Footman (209) English: from Middle English *fotman*, applied in various senses, but most probably an occupational name for a foot soldier, or possibly for an attendant or servant (a meaning first recorded in late Middle English).

Foots (101) English: probably a variant of FOOT.
GIVEN NAME French 4%. *Landry*.

Foppe (129) Dutch, Frisian, and North German: from a pet form of the Germanic personal name *Volkbrecht*, *Volkbrand*, or a similar name, composed with *folk* 'people', 'warriors' as the first element.

Foppiano (162) Italian: habitational name from any of several places named Foppiano.
GIVEN NAMES French 4%; Italian 4%. *Sal* (2), *Angelo*, *Dino*.

Foraker (591) **1.** Americanized form of German **Vieregger** or **Vierecker** (see VIERECK). **2.** Alternatively, it could be an old or altered spelling of English **Fouracre**, a topographic or status name for someone occupying or owning a holding of four acres.

Foral (111) Origin unidentified.

Foran (1233) **1.** Irish: reduced Anglicized form of Gaelic **Ó Fuartháin** 'descendant of *Fuarthán*', a personal name derived from *fuar* 'cold'. (The word *fuarán* also means 'spring' or 'pool'.) The form *Fuarthán* was understood as *fuarathán* 'cold little ford', and the name has thus sometimes been translated as FORD. **2.** See FORAND.

Forand (262) French-Canadian: unexplained.
FOREBEARS A bearer of the name from La Rochelle is documented in La Prairie, Quebec, in 1684.
GIVEN NAMES French 13%. *Jacques* (2), *Normand* (2), *Adrien*, *Andre*, *Armand*, *Germain*.

Forbeck (119) Respelling of German **Vorbeck**, a habitational name from Vorbeck near Güstrow in Mecklenburg-West Pomerania.

Forberg (126) **1.** Scandinavian: unexplained. **2.** German: topographic and habitational name from either of two places called Vorberg or from Vorberg-Heide in Mecklenburg-West Pomerania. According to one opinion the original form is *Vorwerk* and denotes the operating farm (barns and stables) in front (*'vor'*) of a manor house in a parklike setting.

Forbes (11880) **1.** Scottish: habitational name from a place near Aberdeen, so named from Gaelic *forba* 'field', 'district' + the locative suffix *-ais*. The place name is pronounced in two syllables, with the stress on the second, and the surname until recently reflected this. Today, however, it is generally a monosyllable. **2.** Irish: reduced Anglicized form of Gaelic **Mac Firbhisigh** 'son of *Fearbhisigh*', a personal name composed of Celtic elements meaning 'man' + 'prosperity'. A family of this name in Connacht was famous for its traditional historians, compilers of the Book of Lecan.

Forbess (163) Variant spelling of Scottish FORBES, reflecting the traditional pronunciation as two syllables.

Forbis (837) Variant spelling of Scottish FORBES, reflecting the traditional pronunciation as two syllables.

Forbus (520) Altered spelling of Scottish FORBES, reflecting the traditional pronunciation as two syllables.

Forbush (470) **1.** Scottish: altered form of the Scottish name FORBES, which was traditionally pronounced as two syllables. **2.** Respelling of German **Vorbusch**, a topographic name for someone living on the edge of a wood, from *vor* 'in front of' + North German *Busch* 'wood', 'bush'.

Force (1495) **1.** English: variant of FOSSE. There has been some confusion with northwestern English *force* in the sense of 'waterfall'; it is possible that the surname may also have arisen as a topographic name for someone living by a waterfall. **2.** French: topographic name for someone who lived by a fortress or stronghold, Old French *force*, Late Latin *fortia*, a derivative of *fortis* 'strong' (see FORT). There are several places named with this word (for example in Aude, and baronial lands in the Dordogne), and it may also be a habitational name from any of these.

Forcey (140) French: habitational name from a place so named in Haute-Marne.

Forcht (103) German: topographic name for someone who lived by a pine forest, from Middle High German *vohre* 'pine' (Old High German *foraha*).

Forcier (843) French: variant of FORTIER.
FOREBEARS A bearer of this name from Brittany is recorded in Sorel, Quebec, in 1674.
GIVEN NAMES French 11%. *Normand* (5), *Andre* (2), *Edouard* (2), *Emile* (2), *Herve* (2), *Lucien* (2), *Monique* (2), *Armand*, *Camille*, *Cecile*, *Fernand*, *Germaine*.

Forcina (102) Italian: of uncertain derivation; it may be a diminutive of **Forca**, a habitational name, or **Folco**, probably a variant of FULCO; or alternatively it could be from Salentino dialect *furcina* 'fork'.
GIVEN NAMES Italian 26%. *Carmine* (2), *Giovanni* (2), *Mario*, *Orlando*, *Rodolfo*, *Renzo*, *Salvatore*.

Forck (119) Variant spelling of Scottish and Irish FORK.

Forcucci (123) Italian: from a derivative of *forca* 'pitchfork', hence perhaps a nickname for a peasant.
GIVEN NAMES Italian 16%. *Antonio*, *Domenic*, *Guiseppe*, *Mario*, *Tito*.

Forcum (210) See FORKUM.

Ford (59533) **1.** English: topographic name for someone who lived near a ford, Middle English, Old English *ford*, or a habitational name from one of the many places named with this word, such as Ford in Northumberland, Shropshire, and West Sussex, or Forde in Dorset. **2.** Irish: Anglicized form (quasi-translation) of various Gaelic names, for example **Mac Giolla na Naomh** 'son of *Gilla na Naomh*' (a personal name meaning 'servant of the saints'), **Mac Conshámha** 'son of *Conshnámha*' (a personal name composed of the elements *con* 'dog' + *snámh* 'to swim'), in all of which the final syllable was wrongly thought to be *áth* 'ford', and **Ó Fuar(th)áin** (see FORAN). **3.** Jewish: Americanized form of one or more like-sounding Jewish surnames. **4.** Translation of German *Fürth* (see FURTH).

Forde (1448) **1.** English and Irish: variant spelling of FORD 1 and 2. This is a very common spelling in Ireland. **2.** Norwegian: habitational name from any of numerous farmsteads named Førde (there are eleven on the west coast), from Old Norse *fyrði*, dative of *fjórðr* 'fjord'.
GIVEN NAMES Irish 5%. *Declan* (2), *Dermot* (2), *Aine*, *Fionnuala*, *Liam*, *Nuala*.

Fordham (1598) English: habitational name from any of the places in Cambridgeshire, Essex, and Norfolk named Fordham, from Old English *ford* 'ford' + *hām* 'homestead' or *hamm* 'enclosure hemmed in by water'.

Fordice (119) Scottish: variant spelling of FORDYCE.

Fordyce (1089) Scottish: habitational name from Fordyce, a place near Banff.

Fore (2156) Americanized spelling of German FAHR.

Foree (316) Possibly an Americanized spelling of French **Fauré** (see FAURE).

Forehand (1347) Possibly an altered spelling of French Canadian FORAND.

Foreman (9190) **1.** English: variant spelling of FORMAN 1 and 2. **2.** Respelling of North German **Formann**, a variant of FUHRMANN.

Foren (102) Irish: variant spelling of FORAN.

Forer (142) **1.** German: topographic name for someone living by a prominent fir tree, from Middle High German *vorhe* 'fir'. **2.** Altered spelling of German FAHRER.

Forero (254) Spanish: from *forero* 'someone obliged to pay tribute', 'tribute collector'.
GIVEN NAMES Spanish 47%. *Luis* (10), *Jorge* (9), *Jose* (7), *Alvaro* (5), *Hernando* (5), *Gustavo* (3), *Jaime* (3), *Juan* (3), *Manuel* (3), *Mauricio* (3), *Ricardo* (3), *Alberto* (2).

Foresman (406) Possibly an altered spelling of German FORSMAN.

Forest (1700) **1.** English: variant spelling of FORREST. It is also found in both French and Catalan as a surname in this spelling, with the same origin and meaning. **2.** Translation of French **Laforêt** (see LAFOREST).
GIVEN NAMES French 4%. *Andre* (4), *Pascal* (2), *Amie*, *Armand*, *Bertice*, *Etienne*, *Fernand*, *Germaine*, *Jacques*, *Normand*, *Sylvain*.

Foresta (157) Italian: presumably a topographic name for someone living by a forest, *foresta*.
GIVEN NAME Italian 9%. *Nino*.

Forester (1775) English: variant of FORREST.

Forestier (125) French: topographic name for someone who lived in a royal forest or an occupational name for a forester or keeper, from an agent derivative of Old French *forest* 'forest' (see FORET).

GIVEN NAMES French 6%. *Alcide, Jean Claude.*

Foret (899) French (**Forêt**): from Old French *forest* 'forest', a topographic name for someone who lived in or near a royal forest, or an occupational name for a keeper or worker in one. See also FORREST. This surname is frequent in LA.

GIVEN NAMES French 7%. *Alain* (2), *Alcide* (2), *Antoine* (2), *Camille* (2), *Emile* (2), *Oneil* (2), *Anatole, Armand, Chantal, Clemile, Clovis, Gillis.*

Forgacs (112) Hungarian (**Forgács**) and Jewish (from Hungary): from the vocabulary word *forgács* 'splinter'.

GIVEN NAMES Hungarian 6%; Jewish 4%. *Ferenc, Gabor, Sandor; Arie* (2), *Miriam.*

Forgash (112) Americanized spelling of Hungarian FORGACS.

Forge (200) English and French: topographic name for someone who lived near a forge or smithy, Middle English, Old French *forge* (from Latin *fabrica* 'workshop', a derivative of *faber* 'smith', 'workman'; compare LEFEVRE). The surname is thus in most cases a metonymic occupational name for a smith or someone employed by a smith.

GIVEN NAMES German 5%. *Kurt* (2), *Franz.*

Forget (366) French: from a diminutive of FORGE, designating a blacksmith.

FOREBEARS One family from Saintonge, France, had arrived in Varennes, Quebec, by 1681; another, from Poitiers, was in Boucherville by 1671; and a third, from Normandy, was in Quebec city by 1653.

GIVEN NAMES French 25%. *Pierre* (4), *Armand* (3), *Julien* (3), *Marcel* (3), *Cecile* (2), *Michel* (2), *Yvon* (2), *Adrien, Aime, Alphonse, Andre, Camille.*

Forgette (259) French Canadian spelling of FORGET, reflecting the Canadian pronunciation of the final *-t.*

GIVEN NAMES French 4%. *Adrien, Jeanmarie, Marcel.*

Forgey (543) Perhaps an Americanized spelling of French FORGET or an altered spelling of Scottish FORGIE.

Forgie (164) Scottish: of uncertain origin. Black suggests it could be a habitational name from a place so named near Montrose or alternatively from an altered form of the personal name *Fergie*, a pet form of FERGUS.

Forgione (630) Italian: occupational name for a blacksmith, from Old Italian *forgione.*

GIVEN NAMES Italian 17%. *Vito* (5), *Angelo* (4), *Salvatore* (4), *Carmine* (3), *Antonio* (2), *Rocco* (2), *Agostino, Alfonse, Carlo, Dino, Domenic, Gaetano.*

Forgue (220) Southern French: variant of FORGE.

FOREBEARS A bearer of the name Forgue from Haute Garonne is recorded in Quebec city in 1668.

GIVEN NAMES French 6%. *Armand, Lucien, Wilner, Zoel.*

Forgues (129) Southern French: variant of FORGUE.

GIVEN NAMES French 22%. *Gaston* (2), *Patrice* (2), *Camille, Fernand, Marie Anne, Normand, Raoul.*

Forgy (268) See FORGEY.

Forhan (141) Origin uncertain. Perhaps: **1.** an altered spelling of Irish **Foran**, **Forahan**, or **Forhane**, reduced Anglicized forms of Gaelic **Ó Fuartháin**, a name based on the adjective *fuar* 'cold'. **2.** an Americanized spelling of French Canadian FORAND.

GIVEN NAMES German 5%. *Markus, Monika, Rudi.*

Forinash (168) Origin unidentified.

Foringer (120) Americanized form of German FAHRINGER.

Forino (110) Italian: **1.** from a short form of the personal name *Cristoforino*, a pet form of *Cristoforo* (see CRISTOFARO). **2.** perhaps a nickname for a rogue or thief, from Latin *fur, furis* (Italian *furino* 'cunning', 'wily'). This sense is believed to lie behind the place name Forino, in Avellino province.

GIVEN NAMES Italian 15%. *Aldo, Carmine, Domenic, Gaetana, Luigi.*

Forish (117) Variant of Scottish and Irish FARRISH.

Forister (164) English: variant spelling of FORESTER.

Fork (127) Scottish and Irish: possibly an Anglicized form of Irish Gaelic **Ó Gabhlaigh** 'descendant of *Gabhalach*', from *gabhlach* 'forked'.

Forker (380) **1.** Scottish: variant of FARQUHAR. **2.** German: variant of VOLKER.

Forkey (202) New England respelling of French FORTIER.

Forkin (129) **1.** Irish: Anglicized form (quasi-translation) of Gaelic **Ó Gabhláin**, a name from the diminutive of *gabhal* 'fork'. **2.** North German: possibly a nickname for a hog farmer or an unkempt person, from Middle Low German *verken* 'piglet'.

Forkner (363) Probably an altered spelling of FAULKNER.

Forkum (117) Origin uncertain; perhaps an altered form of Irish FORKIN. This name is found chiefly in TN; there is also a large family in Paragould, AR.

Forland (102) English: apparently a habitational name from North or South Foreland in Kent, both named in Old English as 'promontory' (*fore + land*).

Forlano (122) Italian: variant of FURLAN.

GIVEN NAMES Italian 22%. *Domenic* (2), *Roberto* (2), *Vito* (2), *Armando, Enrico, Mario, Rico.*

Forlenza (264) Italian: metathesized form of **Florenza**, from a variant of FIORENZA.

GIVEN NAMES Italian 14%. *Vito* (3), *Nunzi* (2), *Orazio* (2), *Salvatore* (2), *Angelo, Carmine, Donato, Sal.*

Forlines (102) Origin unidentified.

Forlini (110) Italian: unexplained.

GIVEN NAMES Italian 19%. *Aldo, Dino, Emidio, Nazzareno, Pasquale, Quinto.*

Forman (5052) **1.** English: occupational name for a keeper of swine, Middle English *foreman*, from Old English *fōr* 'hog', 'pig' + *mann* 'man'. **2.** English: status name for a leader or spokesman for a group, from Old English *fore* 'before', 'in front' + *mann* 'man'. The word is attested in this sense from the 15th century, but is not used specifically for the leader of a gang of workers before the late 16th century. **3.** Czech and Jewish (from Bohemia, Moravia): occupational name for a carter, Czech *forman*, a loanword from German.

Formanek (291) Czech (**Formánek**): from a diminutive of FORMAN.

GIVEN NAME French 4%. *Camille.*

Formato (147) Italian: probably a nickname from *formato* 'mature', 'fully grown', but possibly from a reduced form of a compound name, *Benformato* 'well made', 'well built'.

GIVEN NAMES Italian 16%. *Giuseppe* (2), *Angelo, Rinaldo, Rocco.*

Formby (379) English: habitational name from the place on Merseyside, so named from Old Norse *forn* 'old' (or perhaps a by-name *Forni* with this meaning) + *býr* 'farm', 'settlement'.

Formella (112) Polish: derivative of the German personal name *Formel*, metathesized form of *Frommel* (see FROMMELT).

GIVEN NAMES Polish 5%. *Krzysztof, Tadeusz.*

Formica (495) Southern Italian: nickname for an active, assiduous person, from Latin *formica* 'ant'.

GIVEN NAMES Italian 23%. *Salvatore* (8), *Santo* (3), *Ennio* (2), *Rocco* (2), *Vito* (2), *Angelo, Ferdinando, Francesco, Franco, Gaetano, Giuseppe, Larraine.*

Formisano (152) Italian: habitational name from Formia, a city in Latina province.

GIVEN NAMES Italian 25%. *Ciro* (3), *Alfonso* (2), *Mario* (2), *Carmine, Gianna, Giuseppe, Paolo.*

Formo (106) Norwegian: unexplained.

Formosa (150) Portuguese, Galician, and Catalan: possibly a habitational name from a place called Formosa, from *formoso* 'beautiful'.

GIVEN NAMES Italian 11%; Spanish 4%. *Angelo* (2), *Carmelo, Sal, Saverio, Ugo; Carmella, Jose, Joselito.*

Formoso (140) Portuguese and Galician: nickname for a handsome man, from *formoso* 'handsome' (Spanish *hermoso*, Latin *formosus*), or in some cases possibly from a place name with the same etymology.

GIVEN NAMES Spanish 46%; Italian 9%. *Jose* (8), *Juan* (8), *Manuel* (5), *Eusebio* (3), *Carlos* (2), *Enrique* (2), *Leopoldo* (2),

Adela, Adelino, Alina, Anastacio, Artemio; Gino (2), *Vita* (2), *Aldo, Amadeo, Antonio, Ignazio.*

Fornal (173) Polish: occupational name from *fornal* 'stable boy'.

GIVEN NAMES Polish 5%; German 4%. *Casimir; Aloysius, Hedwig.*

Fornaro (153) Italian: occupational name for a baker, from Late Latin *furnarius*, a derivative of *furnus* 'oven'.

GIVEN NAMES Italian 13%. *Antonio, Carmine, Luigi, Marco, Natale, Sal.*

Fornash (101) Origin unidentified. Compare FORINASH.

Forner (256) **1.** Italian (Venetian): variant of FORNARO. **2.** Catalan: occupational name for a baker, Catalan *forner* (from Late Latin *furnarius*, a derivative of *furnus* 'oven'), cognate with 1 above.

Fornes (223) **1.** Norwegian: habitational name from any of the twelve farmsteads so named, from either Old Norse *fura* 'pine' or *for* 'foremost', 'front' + *nes* 'headland', 'promontory' (the latter etymology suggests a headland jutting out farther than others near it). **2.** Catalan (**Fornés**): respelling of **Forners**, either an occupational or a topographic name from the plural of FORNER 2.

GIVEN NAMES Spanish 9%. *Pedro* (2), *Rafael* (2), *Caridad, Jesus, Jose, Juan, Juan Jose, Mercedes, Raul, Ricardo, Salvador.*

Forness (243) Probably an altered spelling of FORNES or FURNESS.

Forney (2347) **1.** Of German origin (also found in Alsace and French Switzerland): perhaps a variant of FARNER. Compare FAHRNI. **2.** The surname is also found in England and could be a habitational name from a lost or unidentified place. Compare FARNEY, FURNEY.

Forni (259) Italian: from *forno* 'oven', Late Latin *furnus*, hence an occupational name for a baker, a topographic name for someone who lived near a bread oven, or a habitational name from any of numerous minor places named with this word.

GIVEN NAMES Italian 11%. *Alfonso* (2), *Mario* (2), *Aldo, Alfredo, Aurelio, Carlo, Dante, Delfo, Giancarlo, Orlando, Richardo.*

Fornoff (169) Variant of the German topographic name **Vornhof** 'in front of the farm'.

GIVEN NAMES German 5%. *Heinz, Kurt.*

Fornshell (115) Origin unidentified.

Fornwalt (189) German: topographic name for someone living 'in front of a wood'.

Foronda (134) Basque: habitational name from Foronda in Araba province, Basque Country.

GIVEN NAMES Spanish 46%. *Celedonio* (2), *Paquito* (2), *Pedro* (2), *Renato* (2), *Amancio, Armando, Augusto, Aurelio, Bartolome, Constante, Dionicio, Eduardo; Federico, Quirino.*

Forquer (263) French: variant of FORTIER.

Forren (142) Norwegian: habitational name from a farmstead in Trøndelag, so named from a river name derived from a word meaning 'hollow', 'gorge'.

Forrer (334) Swiss German: variant of FURRER.

Forrest (8123) English: topographic name for someone who lived in or near a royal forest, or a metonymic occupational name for a keeper or worker in one. Middle English *forest* was not, as today, a near-synonym of *wood*, but referred specifically to a large area of woodland reserved by law for the purposes of hunting by the king and his nobles. The same applied to the European cognates, both Germanic and Romance. The English word is from Old French *forest*, Late Latin *forestis (silva)*. This is generally taken to be a derivative of *foris* 'outside'; the reference was probably to woods lying outside a habitation. On the other hand, Middle High German *for(e)st* has been held to be a derivative of Old High German *foraha* 'fir' (see FORSTER), with the addition of a collective suffix.

Forrestal (142) Irish: according to MacLysaght, from a dialect word meaning 'paddock'. It was the name of a prominent Anglo-Norman family.

Forrester (4855) English: occupational or topographic name, from a derivative of FORREST.

Forrey (239) English: unexplained; perhaps a respelling of the southern French name FAURE, which was taken to England as early as the 13th century.

Forristall (132) Variant spelling of Irish FORRESTAL.

Forrister (152) English: variant spelling of FORRESTER, a variant of FORREST.

Forry (524) Possibly an Americanized or Anglicized form of French **Forêt** (see FORET).

Fors (381) Swedish: ornamental name from Swedish *fors* 'waterfall', or a habitational name from any of various places named with this element as first or second element.

GIVEN NAMES Scandinavian 6%. *Birgit, Gunner, Johan, Nels.*

Forsberg (1847) Swedish: ornamental name composed of the elements *fors* 'waterfall' + *berg* 'mountain', 'hill'.

GIVEN NAMES Scandinavian 7%. *Erik* (4), *Johan* (3), *Lars* (3), *Alf* (2), *Nels* (2), *Nils* (2), *Bjoern, Bjorn, Elof, Evald, Klas, Nanna.*

Forsch (112) South German (also **Försch**): topographic name for someone near a forest or in charge of a tree nursery, from Middle High German *forst* 'forest'.

Forse (176) **1.** English (Somerset and Avon): variant of FOSSE. **2.** Americanized form of French FORTIER.

GIVEN NAME French 4%. *Camille.*

Forsee (185) **1.** Americanized form of French FORTIER. **2.** See FORSHEE.

Forsell (262) Swedish: ornamental name from *fors* 'waterfall' + *-ell*, a common suffix of Swedish surnames taken from the Latin adjectival ending *-elius*.

GIVEN NAMES Scandinavian 6%. *Erik, Sven.*

Forseth (439) Norwegian: habitational name from any of seven farmsteads, notably in Trøndelag, so named either from Old Norse *fors* 'waterfall' or *fura* 'pine' + *set* 'farmstead'.

GIVEN NAMES Scandinavian 5%. *Nils, Thor.*

Forsey (143) **1.** English (Somerset and Avon): topographic name for someone living in or by a furze-covered enclosure, from Old English *fyrs* 'furze' + *hæg* 'enclosure'. **2.** Americanized spelling of French FORTIER.

Forsgren (337) Swedish: ornamental name composed of the elements *fors* 'waterfall' + *gren* 'branch'.

GIVEN NAMES Scandinavian 5%. *Erik* (4), *Lars, Tor.*

Forsha (133) Origin unidentified. Perhaps a respelling of English FORSHAW.

Forshaw (129) English (Lancashire): habitational name from a place so called, perhaps Forshaw Heath in Solihull, Warwickshire, although the modern distribution is much further north.

Forshay (128) **1.** Americanized spelling of French FORTIER. **2.** Possibly also a variant of English FORSEY.

Forshee (745) Americanized spelling of French FORTIER.

Forshey (395) Americanized spelling of French FORTIER.

Forslund (421) Swedish: ornamental name composed of the elements *fors* 'waterfall' + *lund* 'grove'.

GIVEN NAMES Scandinavian 5%. *Helmer, Hilmer, Nils, Sven, Walfrid.*

Forsman (865) **1.** Swedish: ornamental name composed of the elements *fors* 'waterfall' + *man* 'man'. **2.** German (**Forsmann**): variant of **Forstmann**, itself a variant of **Förster** (see FORSTER).

GIVEN NAMES Scandinavian 6%. *Knute* (2), *Nels* (2), *Nils* (2), *Gunner, Jarl, Johan, Lars.*

Forson (146) **1.** Scottish: unexplained. Perhaps a variant of FARSON. **2.** Possibly a respelling of Swedish **Forsén** or **Forssén**, an ornamental name from *fors* 'waterfall' + the adjectival suffix *-én*, a derivative of Latin *-enius*.

Forss (130) Swedish: variant of FORS.

GIVEN NAMES Scandinavian 7%. *Halvar, Lennart, Obert.*

Forst (941) **1.** German: topographic name for someone who lived in or near a royal forest or an occupational name for someone who worked in one, from Middle High German *forst* 'forest'. **2.** Czech (**Foršt**): from German (see 1).

Forster (3770) **1.** English: occupational and topographic name for someone who lived or worked in a forest (see FORREST).

2. English: Norman French nickname or occupational name from Old French *forcetier* 'cutter', an agent noun from *forcettes* 'scissors'. **3.** English: occupational name, by metathesis, from Old French *fust(r)ier* 'blockmaker' (a derivative of *fustre* 'block of wood'). **4.** German (**Förster**): occupational and topographic name for someone who lived and worked in a forest (see FORST). **5.** Jewish (Ashkenazic): ornamental name from German *Forst* 'forest'.

Forstner (210) German: variant of FORSTER.
GIVEN NAMES German 10%. *Alois* (2), *Gerhard* (2), *Erna, Heinz, Ignaz, Ilse, Monika.*

Forston (118) Possibly an English habitational name from Forston, a place in Dorset, recorded in 1236 as *Fosardeston* 'estate (*tūn*) of the Forsard family'; a family which was there from the early 13th century.

Forstrom (199) Swedish (**Forsström**): ornamental name composed of the elements *fors* 'waterfall' + *ström* 'river'.
GIVEN NAME German 5%. *Fritz.*

Forsyth (3403) Scottish: variant spelling of FORSYTHE.
FOREBEARS The statesman John Forsyth (1780–1841) was born at Fredericksburg, VA, a descendant of James Forsyth, who came to VA from Scotland in 1680. John was in public service for 30 years as representative, U.S. senator, governor of Georgia, minister to Spain, and secretary of state.

Forsythe (4324) Scottish: from an Anglicized form of the Gaelic personal name *Fearsithe*, composed of the elements *fear* 'man' + *sith* 'peace'. Some early forms with prepositions, as for example William *de Fersith* (Edinburgh 1365), seem to point to an alternative origin as a habitational name, but no place name of suitable form is known. The spelling *Forsythe* is associated chiefly with northern Ireland.

Fort (2739) **1.** English, French, and Catalan: nickname from Old French, Middle English, Catalan *fort*, 'strong', 'brave' (Latin *fortis*). In some cases it may be from the Latin personal name derived from this word; this was borne by an obscure saint whose cult was popular during the Middle Ages in southern and southwestern France. **2.** English and French: topographic name for someone who lived near a fortress or stronghold, or an occupational name for someone employed in one. Compare FORTIER 1. **3.** Czech (**Fořt**): variant of FORST.

Forte (3667) **1.** Italian: from the personal name *Forte*, from Late Latin *fortis* 'strong' (see FORT) or from a short form of a medieval personal name formed with this element, as for example *Fortebraccio* ('strong arm'). **2.** Slovenian: shortened form of the

personal name *Fortunat*, Latin *Fortunatus*.
3. English: variant of FORT.
GIVEN NAMES Italian 9%. *Angelo* (11), *Antonio* (6), *Carmine* (6), *Rocco* (6), *Guido* (5), *Salvatore* (5), *Aldo* (4), *Gaetano* (4), *Pasquale* (4), *Carlo* (3), *Matteo* (3), *Annamaria* (2).

Fortenberry (2378) Probably an altered spelling of German **Fortenbach**, a habitational name from a minor place in Bavaria named Furtenbach.

Fortes (274) Portuguese: from the old personal name *Fortes* (Latin *Fortis*, from *fortis* 'strong').
GIVEN NAMES Spanish 27%; Portuguese 13%. *Jose* (7), *Manuel* (5), *Alfredo* (2), *Alberto, Ana, Armando, Arminda, Aurelio, Avelino, Cecelio, Cesar, Diosdado; Joao* (2), *Vasco.*

Fortgang (111) Jewish (Ashkenazic): ornamental from German abstract word *Fortgang* 'continuation', 'departure'.
GIVEN NAMES Jewish 10%. *Chaim* (2), *Meyer, Pinkas.*

Forth (583) **1.** English: variant of FORD 1. **2.** German: topographic name for someone who lived by a ford, Middle High German *vurt* 'ford', or a habitational name from a place in Franconia named Forth.

Forthman (123) Americanized spelling of German FORTMANN.

Forti (293) Italian: patronymic from the personal name *Forte*, a continuation of Late Latin *Fortis* (*fortis* 'brave', 'strong'), a name chosen by early Christians as a symbol of moral strength and steadfastness.
GIVEN NAMES Italian 12%. *Angelo, Antonio, Dante, Edvige, Geno, Giancarlo, Giovanni, Pasquale, Romeo, Salvatore, Santo.*

Fortier (3118) French: **1.** occupational name for someone employed at a fortress or castle, from a derivative of Old French *fort* 'stronghold' (from the adjective *fort* 'strong'). **2.** possibly a variant of FORESTIER.
FOREBEARS A Fortier from Calvados, Normandy, France, settled in Quebec city, in 1664.
GIVEN NAMES French 11%. *Andre* (9), *Lucien* (7), *Armand* (6), *Jacques* (5), *Marcel* (5), *Normand* (5), *Emile* (3), *Michel* (3), *Ovide* (3), *Rosaire* (3), *Adrien* (2), *Aime* (2).

Fortin (3369) French: diminutive of FORT.
FOREBEARS A family from Maine, France, is recorded in Quebec city in 1652; others, from Normandy and Brittany, arrived in Montreal in 1672 and 1674.
GIVEN NAMES French 16%. *Marcel* (17), *Andre* (15), *Armand* (14), *Lucien* (8), *Fernand* (7), *Laurent* (7), *Pierre* (7), *Jacques* (6), *Normand* (6), *Yvon* (5), *Adrien* (4), *Alain* (3).

Fortini (241) Italian: patronymic or plural form of FORTINO.
GIVEN NAMES Italian 7%. *Angelo, Carlo, Dante, Luciano, Luigi, Marco, Saverio.*

Fortino (490) Italian: from a pet form of the personal name *Forte* (see FORTI).

GIVEN NAMES Italian 9%. *Domenic* (2), *Santo* (2), *Gino, Ignazio, Luigi, Pasquale, Rocco, Salvatore, Silvio.*

Fortman (502) Americanized spelling of German FORTMANN.

Fortmann (123) German: topographic name for someone who lived by a ford, Middle High German *vurt* 'ford'.
GIVEN NAME German 5%. *Guenther.*

Fortna (146) Of German origin: Americanized form of **Pförtner** (see FORTNER).

Fortner (4002) German: variant (also **Förtner**) or Americanized form of **Pförtner**, occupational name for the gatekeeper of a walled town or city, or the doorkeeper in a great house, castle, or monastery, Middle High German *portenaere* (from Latin *porta* 'door', 'gate'). Compare English PORTER.

Fortney (1824) **1.** Americanized form of German **Pförtner** (see FORTNER). **2.** Americanized form of the Norwegian habitational name FORTUN.

Forton (271) **1.** English: habitational name from places in Hampshire, Lancashire, Shropshire, and Staffordshire named Forton, from Old English *ford* 'ford' + *tūn* 'settlement', 'enclosure'. **2.** French: variant of FORTIN.

Fortson (1234) Possibly of English origin; unexplained.

Fortun (130) **1.** Norwegian: habitational name from either of two farmsteads on the west coast of Norway, named with Old Norse *for* 'front', 'foremost' + *tún* 'enclosure', indicating the frontmost of two farmsteads. **2.** Spanish: reduced form of the omen name *Fortunato*, Late Latin *Fortunatus*, from the Latin adjective *fortunatus* 'prosperous', 'happy'. **3.** Castilianized form (**Fortuñ**) of Catalan **Fortuny**, habitational name from any of several places in Catalonia (Latin *Fortunius*). **4.** Slovenian: shortened form of the personal name *Fortunat*, Latin *Fortunatus* (see FORTUNATO).
GIVEN NAMES Spanish 13%; Scandinavian 9%. *Orlando* (3), *Alberto, Alicia, Enrique, Eugenio, Juan, Luis, Mariluz, Marta, Pedro, Roberto; Tryg* (4).

Fortuna (968) **1.** Italian, Spanish, Catalan, and Portuguese: from *fortuna* 'chance', 'luck', possibly applied as a nickname for a gambler or lucky person or in some cases as a continuation of the Late Latin personal name. **2.** Slovenian: nickname from Latin *fortuna* 'fate', 'luck', probably denoting a lucky person (see 1). **3.** Slovenian: shortened form of the personal name *Fortunat*, Latin *Fortunatus* (see FORTUNATO).
GIVEN NAMES Italian 18%; Spanish 8%. *Angelo* (3), *Emilio* (2), *Salvatore* (2), *Albino, Aldo, Alfredo, Alonzo, Antonio, Benedetto, Carmelo, Donato, Filippo, Francesco, Gaetano, Guido, Lorenzo; Jose* (4), *Francisco* (3), *Ramona* (3), *Manuel* (2), *Andres, Carlos, Concepcion.*

Fortunato (1323) Italian: from the omen name *Fortunato*, a continuation of the Late Latin personal name *Fortunatus*, from the Latin adjective *fortunatus* 'prosperous', 'happy'.
GIVEN NAMES Italian 28%; Spanish 5%. *Mario* (8), *Rocco* (6), *Angelo* (4), *Vito* (4), *Gino* (3), *Salvatore* (3), *Alfonse* (2), *Antonio* (2), *Biagio* (2), *Carmine* (2), *Guido* (2), *Lorenzo* (2), *Alfredo*, *Armando*, *Bienvenido*, *Claudio*, *Dionicio*, *Eduardo*; *Julio* (3), *Jose* (2), *Agustin*.

Fortune (3547) **1.** English and French: nickname for a gambler or for someone considered fortunate or well favored, from Middle English, Old French *fortune* 'chance', 'luck'. In some cases it may derive from the rare medieval personal name *Fortune* (Latin *Fortunius*). **2.** French (**Fortuné**): from the personal name *Fortuné*, a vernacular form of the Late Latin personal name *Fortunatus* meaning 'prosperous', 'happy'. **3.** Scottish: habitational name from a place in Lothian, probably so named from Old English *fōr* 'hog', 'pig' + *tūn* 'settlement', 'enclosure'; John de Fortun was servant to the abbot of Kelso *c.* 1200.
GIVEN NAMES French 4%. *Andre* (4), *Camille* (2), *Dominique* (2), *Monique* (2), *Arianne*, *Elodie*, *Germaine*, *Gisele*, *Homere*, *Jean-Pierre*, *Lucien*, *Lucienne*.

Forward (570) English: occupational name for a keeper of swine, from Old English *fōr* 'hog', 'pig' (compare FORMAN 1) + *weard* 'guardian' (see WARD 1).

Forwood (153) English: variant of FORWARD.

Forys (169) Polish (**Foryś**): occupational name from *foryś* 'carter's assistant', 'coachman'.
GIVEN NAMES Polish 8%. *Andrzej*, *Bronislaw*, *Jerzy*, *Wladyslaw*.

Fosberg (185) **1.** Swedish: unexplained. **2.** Norwegian: habitational name from a farm named Fossberg, from Old Norse *fors* 'waterfall' + *berg* 'mountain'.

Fosburg (116) Swedish: unexplained.

Fosco (182) **1.** Italian: variant of FUSCO, from standard Italian *fosco*. **2.** Portuguese and Spanish: nickname from *fosco* 'dull', 'opaque' (Latin *fuscus* 'dark', 'swarthy').
GIVEN NAMES Italian 19%. *Antonio* (5), *Rocco* (3), *Domenico* (2), *Giuseppe*, *Marco*, *Rinaldo*.

Fosdick (539) English: habitational name from a place in Lincolnshire, so called from the genitive case of the Old English byname *Fōt*, meaning 'foot' (or the Old Norse cognate *Fótr*), + Old English *dīc* 'ditch', 'dike' (see DITCH).

Foshay (160) Americanized form of French FAUCHEUX.

Foshee (1185) Americanized form of French FAUCHEUX.

Foskett (269) English: habitational name from any of various places, such as Foscott (Buckinghamshire, Oxfordshire), Foscote (Northamptonshire, Wiltshire), Foxcott (Hampshire), Foxcote (Gloucestershire, Warwickshire), so named from Old English *fox* 'fox' + *cot* 'shelter', 'burrow'.

Foskey (591) English: unexplained. Perhaps a variant of FOSKETT.

Fosler (182) Altered spelling of German FOSSLER.

Fosmire (125) Americanized form of German **Fossmeyer**, **Vossmeyer**, a distinguishing name from Middle Low German *vos* 'fox' (see FUCHS) + MEYER.

Fosnaugh (248) Americanized spelling of German FASNACHT.

Fosnight (117) Americanized form of German FASNACHT.

Fosnot (101) Americanized form of German FASNACHT.

Foss (5948) **1.** English: variant spelling of FOSSE. **2.** Danish: from *fos*, *vos* 'fox'; a nickname for a sly or cunning person or a habitational name for someone living at a house distinguished by the sign of a fox. **3.** Norwegian: habitational name from a farmstead so named from Old Norse *fors* 'waterfall', examples of which are found throughout Norway. **4.** Altered spelling of German VOSS or the Dutch cognate VOS.

Fosse (355) **1.** English and French: habitational name from any of the various minor places named with Old English *foss* 'ditch' (Latin *fossa*). The Old English word did not survive into the period when surnames were acquired, so it is unlikely to be a topographic name, unless it is from the Old French cognate *fosse*. The reference may be to the Roman road Fosse Way, itself named in the Old English period from the ditch that ran alongside it, or to the river Foss in Yorkshire. **2.** Norwegian: habitational name from any of the fifteen west-coast farmsteads so named, from the dative form of *foss* 'waterfall' (from Old Norse *fors*).
GIVEN NAMES Scandinavian 6%. *Alf*, *Bernt*, *Egil*, *Gudrun*.

Fosselman (136) German: variant of FUSSELMAN.

Fossen (313) **1.** Norwegian: habitational name from any of the numerous farmsteads throughout Norway named Fossen, from the definite form of *foss* 'waterfall' (from Old Norse *fors*). **2.** German: variant of **Fassen**, a short form of *Servatius* (see FAAS 3).
GIVEN NAMES Scandinavian 5%. *Hilmer*, *Peer*.

Fossett (571) **1.** English: variant spelling of FAWCETT. **2.** French: diminutive of FOSSE.

Fossey (126) English (Bedfordshire): habitational name from a lost place in Bedfordshire, recorded in 969 as *Foteseige*, from Old English *foss* 'ditch', 'dike' + *ēg* 'island', 'dry land in marsh', 'promontory', or a topographic name for someone who lived on low lying land by a ditch or dike.

Fossler (118) South German: derogatory nickname or term of abuse, from an agent noun based on Middle High German *votze(l)* 'vulva'.

Fossum (846) Norwegian: habitational name from a farmstead so named, especially in eastern Norway. The farm name, *Forsheimr* in Old Norse, is composed of the elements *fors* 'waterfall' + *heimr* 'homestead'.
GIVEN NAMES Scandinavian 7%. *Arnt* (2), *Erik* (2), *Fritjof*, *Jarl*, *Nels*, *Ove*, *Sig*, *Thor*.

Foster (76761) **1.** English: reduced form of FORSTER. **2.** English: nickname from Middle English *foster* 'foster parent' (Old English *fōstre*, a derivative of *fōstrian* 'to nourish or rear'). **3.** Jewish: probably an Americanized form of one or more like-sounding Jewish surnames, such as FORSTER.
FOREBEARS This name was brought to North America by many different bearers from the 17th century onward. Thomas Foster (1640–79) is buried in the old burial ground in Cambridge, MA. John Foster, born 1648 in Dorchester, MA, was the earliest wood engraver in America.

Foston (81) English: habitational name from any of various places in Derbyshire, Lincolnshire, and East and North Yorkshire, all named Foston, from the Old Norse personal name *Fótr* + Old English *tūn*.

Foth (450) **1.** North German and Dutch: from Middle Low German *vōt* 'foot'; probably a nickname for someone with some peculiarity or deformity of the foot. **2.** North German: variant of VOGT.
GIVEN NAMES German 4%. *Kurt* (2), *Armin*, *Frieda*, *Heino*, *Ullrich*.

Fothergill (339) English: habitational name from Fothergill in Cumbria or some other place similarly named (for example in West Yorkshire), from Old Norse *fóðr* 'fodder', 'forage' + *gil* 'steep valley', 'ravine'.

Fotheringham (223) Scottish: habitational name from Fotheringham near Forfar, which seems to have been named after Fotheringhay in Northamptonshire, which was held in the 12th century by the royal family of Scotland as part of the honor of Huntingdon. The Northamptonshire place appears in Domesday Book as *Fodringeia*, probably from Old English *fōdring* 'grazing' (a derivative of *fōdor* 'fodder') + *ēg* 'island', 'low-lying land'. In the case of the Scottish place, the final element has early been replaced by *-hām* 'homestead'.

Foti (1009) **1.** Southern Italian: from the Greek personal name *Photios*, a derivative of Greek *phōs* 'light' (genitive *phōtos*). **2.** Hungarian (**Fóti**): habitational name for someone from a village called Fót in Pest county.
GIVEN NAMES Italian 14%. *Salvatore* (5), *Domenic* (4), *Angelo* (3), *Carmelo* (3),

Franco (3), *Gaetano* (3), *Santo* (3), *Antonio* (2), *Alessandro*, *Biagio*, *Carlo*, *Carmela*.

Foto (127) Italian: patronymic or plural form of FOTI.
GIVEN NAMES Italian 6%; French 4%. *Francesco*, *Giuseppe*; *Monique*, *Pascal*.

Fotopoulos (169) Greek: patronymic from the personal name *Fotis* (formally *Phōtios*) + the patronymic ending *-poulos*. This ending occurs chiefly in the Peloponnese. It is derived from Latin *pullus* 'nestling', 'chick'.
GIVEN NAMES Greek 28%. *Dimitrios* (3), *Panagiotis* (2), *Spiro* (2), *Theofilos* (2), *Anastasios*, *Christos*, *Constantine*, *Demos*, *Eleni*, *Evangelos*, *Fotios*, *Panos*.

Fotos (104) Greek: from the personal name *Fotos*, a pet form of *Fotis* (formally *Phōtios*), a derivative of Greek *phōs* 'light'. It may also be shortened form of patronymic surnames based on *Fotis*, such as FOTOPOULOS,
GIVEN NAMES Greek 5%. *Demetre*, *Demetrios*.

Foucault (149) French: from an ancient Germanic personal name composed of the elements *folk* 'people' + *wald* 'rule'.
FOREBEARS A bearer of the name Foucault from Perigord was in Quebec city in 1671; another, from Tours, is documented in Montreal in 1691; and a third, from Gascony, in 1718.
GIVEN NAMES French 14%. *Andre* (3), *Achille*, *Germain*, *Lucien*, *Pascal*, *Pierre*.

Fouch (442) **1.** French: variant of FOUCHE. **2.** Americanized spelling of German **Pfautz** (see FOUTCH).

Fouche (377) French (**Fouché**): from a Germanic personal name composed of the elements *folk* 'people' + *hari*, *heri* 'army'.
FOREBEARS A Fouché from Angoulême was in Quebec city by 1659; another, from Poitou, is documented in Quebec in 1668.
GIVEN NAMES French 8%. *Alphonse* (2), *Chantal*, *Dominique*, *Francois*, *Herve*, *Michel*, *Rodolphe*, *Serge*.

Foucher (166) Variant of French FAUCHEUX.
GIVEN NAMES French 12%. *Andre*, *Etienne*, *Henri*, *Lydie*, *Marcel*, *Rosaire*.

Fougere (210) French (**Fougère**): topographic name for someone who lived in a place densely grown with ferns, from Old French *foug(i)ere* 'fern', 'bracken' (from Late Latin *filicaria*).
FOREBEARS A bearer of the name from Saintonge is documented in Ile d'Orléans in 1703.
GIVEN NAMES French 10%. *Alain*, *Alcide*, *Armand*, *Emile*, *Fleurette*, *Thierry*.

Fought (543) Americanized form of German VOGT.

Fouke (107) **1.** English: variant of FOULKS. **2.** Possibly also an Anglicized form of French FOUQUET.
GIVEN NAME French 5%. *Lucien* (2).

Foulds (295) English: variant spelling of FOLDS.

Foulger (161) English: variant of FULCHER.

Foulk (861) English (Derbyshire): variant of FOULKS.

Foulke (538) English (Derbyshire): variant of FOULKS.

Foulkes (388) English: variant spelling of FOULKS.

Foulkrod (142) Origin unidentified.

Foulks (518) English: from a Norman personal name, a short form of various Germanic names formed with *folk* 'people'. See also VOLK.

Founds (135) English: unexplained.

Fountain (6264) English: topographic name for someone who lived near a spring or well, from Old French *fontane*, Middle English *fontayne* 'fountain'; in some cases the name may have arisen from French habitational names (FONTAINE, *Fonteyne*, *Lafontaine*) of the same derivation.

Fountaine (461) English: variant spelling of FOUNTAIN.

Fouquet (108) French: from a pet form of any of various Germanic personal names formed with *folk* 'people' (see for example German VOLKER), a cognate of English FOULKS.
GIVEN NAMES French 13%. *Alain* (2), *Jean-Michel*, *Marcel*, *Raoul*.

Fouraker (115) See FORAKER.

Fourman (258) English: variant spelling of FORMAN 1 and 2.

Fournet (194) French: metonymic occupational name for a baker, from a diminutive of *four* 'oven'.
GIVEN NAMES French 11%. *Marcel* (2), *Emile*, *Fernand*, *Henri*, *Jacques*, *Monique*.

Fournier (5786) French: occupational name for a baker, Old French *fournier* (Latin *furnarius*), originally the man responsible for cooking the dough in the *fourneau* 'oven' (see BAKER). This surname is frequently Americanized as FULLER.
FOREBEARS There are many points of origin for the name Fournier in North America; bearers of this name arrived from all over France: from Limoges, Normandy (to Quebec city, 1651), Paris (to Trois Rivières, Quebec, 1657), La Rochelle (to Quebec city, 1670), Picardy (to Boucherville, 1688), and Orléans (to Quebec, 1670).
GIVEN NAMES French 12%. *Andre* (18), *Armand* (16), *Normand* (15), *Pierre* (10), *Lucien* (9), *Emile* (8), *Fernand* (7), *Marcel* (7), *Aime* (6), *Donat* (5), *Jacques* (5), *Yves* (5).

Fouse (450) **1.** Altered spelling of French **Fousse**, a southern variant of FOSSE. **2.** Americanized spelling of German *Pfaus*, a variant of PFAUTZ, a nickname for a self-important person.

Fousek (162) Czech: nickname from *fousek*, *vousek* 'moustache'.

Foushee (535) Altered spelling of French **Fouché** (see FOUCHE).

Foust (4427) Probably an altered spelling of FAUST.

Fout (601) Altered spelling of German FAUTH.

Foutch (735) Of German origin: see FOUTS.
FOREBEARS The Brethren Encyclopedia lists a James Fouch (Pfautz) (1769–1850) as an early immigrant.

Fouts (2202) Americanized spelling of German PFAUTZ, a nickname for a self-important person.

Fouty (208) Swiss German: of uncertain origin; possibly a variant of VOGT.

Foutz (727) Americanized spelling of German PFAUTZ, a nickname for a self-important person.

Fowble (210) Americanized spelling of German FAUBEL.

Fowers (180) English: status name from Old French *fouuer*, Latin *focarius* 'hearth-keeper'.

Fowkes (303) English: variant spelling of FOULKS.

Fowle (398) **1.** English: nickname for someone who resembled a bird, in part representing a Middle English continuation of the Old English personal name *Fugol*, meaning 'bird', originally a byname, or possibly a metonymic occupational name for a fowler. **2.** Americanized spelling of German FAUL.

Fowler (37927) English: occupational name for a bird-catcher (a common medieval occupation), Middle English *fogelere*, *foulere* (Old English *fugelere*, a derivative of *fugol* 'bird').

Fowles (534) English: patronymic from FOWLE.

Fowlie (145) Scottish (Aberdeen): habitational name from a place named Foulzie in Aberdeenshire.

Fowlkes (1478) English: variant spelling of FOULKS.

Fox (58103) **1.** English: nickname from the animal, Middle English, Old English *fox*. It may have denoted a cunning individual or been given to someone with red hair or for some other anecdotal reason. This relatively common and readily understood surname seems to have absorbed some early examples of less transparent surnames derived from the Germanic personal names mentioned at FAULKS and FOULKS. **2.** Irish: part translation of Gaelic **Mac an tSionnaigh** 'son of the fox' (see TINNEY). **3.** Jewish (American): translation of the Ashkenazic Jewish surname FUCHS. **4.** Americanized spelling of **Focks**, a North German patronymic from the personal name *Fock* (see VOLK). **5.** Americanized spelling of **Fochs**, a North German variant of FUCHS, or in some cases no doubt a translation of FUCHS itself.

Foxall (137) English (West Midlands): habitational name from some minor locality, probably the lost Foxhale near Claverley, Shropshire, the name of which is derived from Old English *fox* 'fox' + *halh* 'hollow', 'recess'. It is less likely that the surname is derived from Foxhall in Suffolk (earlier *Foxhole*), which is named from Old English *fox* + *hol(h)* 'hollow', 'depression': the surname is not established in East Anglia.

Foxen (143) English: patronymic from FOULKS.

Foxhoven (138) Perhaps a part-translation of Dutch **Voshoven**.
GIVEN NAME French 4%. *Damien*.

Foxman (143) Jewish (American): variant of FOX.
GIVEN NAMES Jewish 7%. *Charna, Isadore, Shmuel*.

Foxwell (349) English (Somerset): probably a habitational name from a lost or unidentified place, possibly named from Old English *fox* 'fox' + *well(a)* 'spring', 'stream'.

Foxworth (989) Variant of English FOX-WORTHY. In the U.S. this name is found predominantly in SC.

Foxworthy (381) English (Devon): habitational name from a place in Devon named Foxworthy, probably from an Old English personal name *Færoc* + Old English *worðig* 'enclosure'.

Foxx (801) Variant spelling of FOX.

Foy (4195) **1.** Irish: variant of FAHEY. **2.** Irish: variant of FEE. **3.** French: nickname, from Old French *foi* 'faith' (Latin *fides*), either for a pious person or for someone who frequently used this term in oaths. **4.** French: from the medieval female personal name *Foy*, which is from *foi* 'faith', as above.

Foye (711) French: **1.** habitational name for someone from La Foye-Monthjault (Deux-Sèvres), so named from Latin *fagea* 'beech wood'. **2.** variant spelling of FOY.

Foyle (154) English and Scottish: topographic name for someone who lived near a pit or man-made hollow, from Old French *fouille* 'pit'. The pit in question could have been a lime pit, a clay pit, or an excavation designed to receive refuse. There are several minor places in England named with this word, as for example Foyle Farm in Oxted, Surrey, and in some instances the surname may be a habitational name derived from one of these rather than directly from the physical feature.
GIVEN NAME Scottish 9%. *Colum* (2).

Foyt (141) Respelling of German **Foyth**, a variant of VOGT.

Fraas (152) German: derogatory nickname for a glutton, from Middle Low German *vrās*, Middle High German *vrāz* 'muck'.
GIVEN NAMES German 4%. *Erwin, Otto*.

Frable (241) **1.** Variant spelling of German **Fräbel**, from a field name or nickname from Middle Low German *vrevel* 'brave', 'bold', later 'impudent', 'heinous'. **2.** Re-

spelling of German **Fröbel**, a topographic name for someone living near a willow tree, from Slavic *vrba* 'willow tree'.

Frabotta (154) Italian: from a metathesized form of **Fabrotta**, from a feminine derivative of *fabbro* 'smith'.
GIVEN NAMES Italian 19%. *Alberto* (3), *Alfredo* (2), *Remo* (2), *Americo, Fortunato Antonio, Dante, Elisabetta, Americo, Fortunato, Gabriella, Guido, Luciano, Santina, Silvio*.

Fracassi (118) Italian: plural or patronymic variant of FRACASSO.
GIVEN NAMES Italian 9%. *Guido, Primo*.

Fracasso (128) Italian: from *fracasso* 'din', 'row', 'uproar', 'ruin', probably applied as a nickname for a rowdy person. However, the word is also used to refer to derelict buildings; it may be a topographic name from this sense.
GIVEN NAMES Italian 13%. *Angelo* (2), *Antonio* (2), *Dario, Dino, Emidio, Enzo, Nicola*.

Frace (148) Americanized form of German FREIS or FROESE.

Frachiseur (119) French: probably an occupational name (**Frachisseur**) for someone who made or used tipcarts, from an agent derivative of Occitan *frachisso*.

Frack (150) German: probably a nickname for a greedy, stingy person, from Middle Low German *vrak* 'greedy', 'stingy', or for an invalid, from Middle Low German *vrak* 'damaged', 'useless'; also used as a derogatory nickname.

Fradella (101) Italian: **1.** diminutive of **Frada**, an altered form of **Fruda**, a nickname probably derived from Greek *phrydas* 'having thick eyebrows'. **2.** metathesized form of **Fardella**, a variant of **Fardello**, which may be a diminutive of **Faldo**, a short form of a pet name ending in *-faldo* such as *Ruffaldo*. **3.** alternatively, from Sicilian *faldella*, a diminutive of *falda* 'skirt'.
GIVEN NAMES Italian 16%. *Salvatore* (3), *Sal*.

Fradette (186) French: variant of FRE-DETTE 1.
FOREBEARS A bearer of the name Fradet from Bordeaux was in Ile d'Orléans by 1692.
GIVEN NAMES French 17%; Irish 5%. *Henri* (2), *Lucien* (2), *Aime, Alain, Armand, Arsene, Marcel, Michel, Pierre, Priscille*; *Kiernan* (3).

Fradin (140) Jewish (eastern Ashkenazic): metronymic from the Yiddish female personal name *Frade*, a variant of *Freyde*, meaning 'joy'.
GIVEN NAMES Jewish 9%; Russian 6%. *Ilya, Isadore*; *Boris* (3), *Mikhail, Yevgeny*.

Fradkin (235) Jewish (from eastern Belarus): metronymic from the Yiddish female personal name *Fradke*, a pet form of *Freyde*, meaning 'joy'.
GIVEN NAMES Russian 10%; Jewish 9%. *Dmitrii* (2), *Grigory* (2), *Leonid* (2), *Mikhail* (2), *Boris, Efim, Gennadiy,*

Grigoriy; *Bronya, Hillel, Morry, Naum, Yakov, Yonah*.

Frady (1006) German: Americanized form of WREDE and FREDE.

Fraedrich (103) German: variant of FRIED-RICH.
GIVEN NAME German 5%. *Gerhard*.

Fraenkel (107) German and Jewish (Ashkenazic): variant of FRANKL.
GIVEN NAMES Spanish 6%; German 4%. *Pablo* (3), *Ines*; *Kurt*.

Fraga (741) Spanish and Portuguese: habitational name from any of numerous places in Galicia in Spain and northern Portugal named Fraga, or, less likely, from the place so named in Uesca province, Aragon; all are named from *fraga* 'steep cliff'.
GIVEN NAMES Spanish 38%. *Jose* (21), *Manuel* (14), *Carlos* (7), *Juan* (6), *Pedro* (5), *Andres* (4), *Armando* (4), *Jesus* (4), *Luis* (4), *Raul* (4), *Ana* (3).

Fragale (402) Italian: probably a topographic name for someone who lived by strawberry fields, from medieval Italian *fragara* 'strawberry', modern Italian *fragola*.
GIVEN NAMES Italian 14%. *Antonio* (3), *Angelo, Carmelo, Ezio, Filippo, Giovanni, Giuseppe, Guiseppe, Leonardo, Marco, Michelangelo, Philomena*.

Frager (223) **1.** German (also **Fräger**): occupational name for a councilman whose duty it was carry out a poll required to make a council decision, Middle High German *vrägaere*, an agent derivative of Middle High German *vrägaere* 'to ask'. **2.** Jewish (Ashkenazic): ornamental name from an agent derivative of modern German *fragen* 'to ask' (see 1).
GIVEN NAMES Jewish 6%. *Yehuda* (2), *Arnon, Sholom*.

Fragola (139) Italian: apparently from *fragola* 'strawberry', probably applied as a topographic name for someone who lived by a patch of wild strawberries, a metonymic occupational name for a grower or seller of soft fruits, or a nickname for someone with a conspicuous strawberry mark.
GIVEN NAMES Italian 28%. *Vito* (5), *Rocco* (3), *Giuseppe* (2), *Carmelo, Domenic, Federico, Giacomo, Livio, Nunzie, Salvatore*.

Fragoso (363) Galician and Portuguese: habitational name from any of the places named Fragoso, from *fragoso* 'rocky', 'uneven', an adjectival form of *fraga* 'steep cliff'.
GIVEN NAMES Spanish 47%; Portuguese 12%. *Jose* (7), *Manuel* (7), *Francisco* (6), *Jesus* (5), *Rodolfo* (5), *Carlos* (4), *Genaro* (4), *Juan* (4), *Pedro* (4), *Pablo* (3), *Ruben* (3), *Alfonso* (2); *Joao, Joaquim*; *Antonio* (4), *Marco* (2), *Agostino, Albertina, Lorenzo, Luciano*.

Fraher (301) Irish (Munster): shortened Anglicization of Gaelic **Ó Fearchair**, from *fearchar* 'dear man', 'beloved', or 'loving'. Compare FARAGHER.

GIVEN NAMES Irish 6%. *Brendan* (2), *Mairead*.

Frahm (1154) North German: nickname for an honorable man, from Middle High German *vrum*, *vrom* 'noble', 'honorable', 'trustworthy' (see FROMM).

Fraijo (110) Galician: habitational name from either of two places, in Lugo and A Coruña, Galicia, named Fraijo, probably from a Castilianized spelling of Galician *freixo* 'ash'.

GIVEN NAMES Spanish 27%. *Manuel* (3), *Guadalupe* (2), *Alberto, Anamaria, Arquimedes, Blanca, Carlos, Fidel, Maria Luisa, Paz, Raul, Reynaldo*.

Frail (117) English: variant of FREEL.

Frailey (599) Americanized spelling of German FROHLICH.

Fraim (189) Altered spelling of FRAME.

Frain (571) **1.** English (of Norman origin): topographic name for someone who lived near an ash tree or ash wood, from Old French *fraisne, fresne* 'ash' (Latin *fraxinus*). **2.** French: habitational name from a place in Vosges named Frain.

Fraioli (220) Italian: unexplained; in Italy it occurs chiefly in Ciociaria (Lazio) and Abruzzo.

GIVEN NAMES Italian 23%. *Carmine* (5), *Pasquale* (2), *Rocco* (2), *Angelo, Antonio, Carlo, Domenic, Elio, Francesco, Guerino, Marco, Stefano*.

Fraire (278) Spanish: from a derivative of Latin *frater* 'brother', a status name for a member of a religious order, especially a mendicant order, and possibly also a nickname for a pious person or someone who worked in a monastery.

GIVEN NAMES Spanish 58%. *Jesus* (7), *Jose* (7), *Carlos* (5), *Juan* (5), *Armando* (4), *Miguel* (4), *Alberto* (3), *Gerardo* (3), *Manuel* (3), *Roberto* (3), *Amador* (2), *Esperanza* (2); *Antonio* (3), *Aureliano, Dario, Gabino, Lorenzo*.

Fraise (108) Probably a respelling of French **Fraisse**, a topographic name for someone who lived by a prominent ash tree or by an ash wood, from a southern variant of Old French *fresne*.

GIVEN NAMES French 8%. *Pierre* (2), *Henri*.

Fraiser (166) Altered spelling of Scottish FRASER.

Fraize (100) Probably a variant spelling of French FRAISE.

Fraizer (311) Altered spelling of Scottish FRASER.

Frake (103) English: unexplained.

Fraker (712) Jewish (eastern Ashkenazic): occupational name for a tailor who made dress coats, from Yiddish *frak* 'dress coat' + the agent suffix *-er*.

Frakes (1301) English (Midlands): unexplained. Compare FRAKE.

Fraleigh (213) Americanized form of German FROHLICH.

Fraley (4057) Americanized form of German FROHLICH.

Fralick (599) Americanized form of German FROHLICH.

Fralin (233) **1.** French: nickname for a frail timorous person, from a derivative of Old French *fraile* 'frail', from Latin *fragilis* 'frail', 'brittle'. **2.** Altered spelling of German **Freiling**, a status name from Middle High German *vrīlinc* 'freed man'.

Fralix (181) Americanized form of German FROHLICH.

Fram (200) Scottish: see FRAME.

Frame (3369) **1.** Scottish: unexplained. Black notes that 'several persons of this name are recorded in the Commissariot Records of Campsie and of Lanark'. It is now very common in Scotland, especially around Glasgow. **2.** Jewish (of Sephardic origin): probably an Anglicized form of EPHRAIM.

Frampton (1092) English: habitational name from any of various places so called, of which there are several in Gloucestershire and one in Dorset. Most take the name from the Frome river (which is probably from a British word meaning 'fair', 'brisk') + Old English *tūn* 'enclosure', 'settlement'. One near Tewkesbury was originally named in Old English as *Frēolingtūn* 'settlement associated with *Frēola*', a short form of any of the various compound names with the first element *frēo* 'free'. Frampton in Lincolnshire probably gets its name from an Old English byname *Frameca* (a derivative of *fram* 'valiant') + *tūn*.

Frana (183) Czech (**Fráňa**) and Slovak (**Fraňa, Fraňo**): short form of the personal name *František* (see FRANCIS).

Franc (216) **1.** French: from a Germanic personal name derived from the ethnic name for a FRANK. **2.** French: nickname or status name from *franc* 'free' (usually denoting a freed slave). **3.** Slovenian and Croatian (northwestern Croatia): from the personal name *Franc*, Slavic form of German *Franz*, all from Latin *Franciscus* (see FRANCIS). **4.** Polish, Czech, and Slovak: from the German personal name FRANZ.

Franca (127) **1.** Portuguese, Spanish, and Catalan: of uncertain derivation. The name is frequent in Catalonia, with the variants **de Franca** and **de la Franca**, and seems to refer to a place, perhaps to be interpreted as *França*, i.e. France. In this case we must also include the Portuguese family name **França**. On the other hand, **Franca** could be from the female personal name *Franca*. **2.** Italian: variant (feminine form) of FRANCO.

GIVEN NAMES Spanish 28%; Italian 12%. *Carlos* (3), *Jose* (3), *Alicia* (2), *Fernando* (2), *Mario* (2), *Ailton, Alfonso, Blanca, Eduardo, Elcio, Fabio, Jeremias*; *Antonio, Carina, Leonardo, Sandro*.

Francavilla (161) Southern Italian: habitational name from any of various places named with this word (from *franc* 'free (of taxes)' + *villa* 'place', 'settlement'), for example Francavilla Marittima (Cosenza), Francavilla Angitola (Vibo Valentia), Francavilla al Mare (Chieti), Francavilla d'Ete (Ascoli), Francavilla in Sinni (Potenza), Francavilla di Sicilia (Messina, Sicily). Cognates of the place name occur widely across Europe, for example *Villefranche, Vilafranca*.

GIVEN NAMES Italian 16%. *Gino* (3), *Carlo* (2), *Antonio, Filippo, Geno*.

France (4024) **1.** French: ethnic name for an inhabitant of France (i.e., of what is now the northern part of the country, where langue d'oïl was spoken). See also LAFRANCE. **2.** Czech (**Franče**): see FRANC 4. **3.** Slovenian: from the personal name *France*, a vernacular form of *Frančišek*, Latin *Franciscus* (see FRANCIS). **4.** Possibly also an Americanized spelling of German FRANZ.

Frances (679) **1.** English: variant spelling of FRANCIS. **2.** Spanish (**Francés**), Portuguese (**Francês**), and southern French and Catalan (**Francès**): from an ethnic name meaning 'Frenchman' (see FRANCIS).

GIVEN NAMES Spanish 8%; French 5%. *Francisco* (3), *Carlos* (2), *Cruz* (2), *Gustavo* (2), *Amador, Anastacia, Colon, Gaspar, Hiran, Ignacio, Joaquin, Juan*; *Dominique, Jacques, Jean-Marie, Remy, Yves*.

Franceschi (318) Italian: patronymic from a variant of FRANCESCO.

GIVEN NAMES Spanish 15%; Italian 10%. *Gonzalo* (3), *Juan* (3), *Amalia* (2), *Carlos* (2), *Francisco* (2), *Mario* (2), *Adriano, Armando, Egisto, Elena, Elvira, Enrique*; *Aldo* (2), *Dino* (2), *Antonio, Dario, Franco, Geronimo, Gino, Giuseppe, Marco, Paolo, Remo, Reno*.

Franceschini (317) Italian: patronymic or plural form of *Francheschino*, a pet form of FRANCESCO.

GIVEN NAMES Italian 14%; Spanish 8%. *Lido* (2), *Mario* (2), *Pasquale* (2), *Aldo, Angelo, Caesar, Dino, Elba, Fabio, Francesco, Fulvio, Giosue, Giulio, Luigi, Mauro, Orlando*; *Ana, Angel, Jose, Juan, Rafael, Ramon*.

Francesco (150) Italian: from the personal name *Francesco* (Latin *Franciscus*), Italian form of FRANCIS.

GIVEN NAMES Italian 19%; Spanish 6%. *Angelo, Gabriele, Giovanni, Pasquale, Rocco, Salvatore*; *Carlota* (2), *Garcia, Romana*.

Francesconi (257) Italian: patronymic from an augmentative of FRANCESCO.

GIVEN NAMES Italian 10%. *Gino* (4), *Salvino* (2), *Angelo, Antonio, Franco, Giancarlo, Giulio*.

Francese (232) Italian: ethnic name for a Frenchman.

GIVEN NAMES Italian 21%. *Carmine* (3), *Angelo* (2), *Enrico* (2), *Vito* (2), *Attilio*, *Carmela*, *Domenico*, *Donato*, *Gaetano*.

Franchetti (148) Italian: patronymic from a diminutive of FRANCO.

GIVEN NAMES Italian 8%. *Cosmo*, *Dario*, *Livio*.

Franchi (436) Italian: patronymic or plural form of FRANCO.

GIVEN NAMES Italian 25%; Spanish 7%. *Reno* (3), *Alessandro* (2), *Angelo* (2), *Antonio* (2), *Dante* (2), *Dino* (2), *Franco* (2), *Giulio* (2), *Mariano* (2), *Mario* (2), *Rafael* (2), *Rocco* (2), *Adriana*, *Augusto*, *Bruna*, *Carmine*, *Dario*, *Eugenio*, *Sergio*; *Jorge* (2), *Eduardo*, *Jose Carlos*, *Miguel*.

Franchina (112) Italian: variant (feminine in form) of FRANCHINO.

GIVEN NAMES Italian 29%. *Antonio*, *Gaetano*, *Nino*, *Rosaria*, *Sal*.

Franchini (230) Italian: patronymic from FRANCHINO.

GIVEN NAMES Italian 21%; Spanish 5%. *Marino* (3), *Franco* (2), *Roberto* (2), *Cosimo*, *Edmundo*, *Elisabetta*, *Gerardo*, *Gino*, *Guiseppe*, *Marcello*, *Marco*, *Mario*, *Paride*, *Primo*, *Remo*, *Rino*; *Carlos*, *Felipe*, *Luisa*, *Ruben*.

Franchino (162) Italian: from a pet form of FRANCO.

GIVEN NAMES Italian 9%. *Dino* (2), *Salvatore*.

Francia (230) **1.** Italian and Spanish: literally 'France', hence an ethnic name denoting a Frenchman. However, *Francia* is also found in Renaissance Italy as a personal name (both male and female), and in some instances the surname may be from this use. **2.** Hungarian: ethnic name for a Frenchman, from *francia* 'French'.

GIVEN NAMES Spanish 22%; Italian 7%. *Jose* (5), *Alejandro* (2), *Alberto*, *Angelico*, *Candelario*, *Fidencio*, *Jesus*, *Juan*, *Manuel*, *Margarito*, *Maximo*, *Nilo*; *Federico*, *Marco*, *Rocco*, *Romeo*, *Salvatore*.

Francies (126) English: variant spelling of FRANCIS.

Francione (106) Italian: from an augmentative form of FRANCIA.

GIVEN NAMES Italian 15%. *Adelmo*, *Gino*, *Mario*, *Orlando*, *Salvatore*.

Franciosa (107) Italian: variant (feminine in form) of **Francioso**, a form of the French personal name **François** (see FRANCOIS) found in Salento, or a variant of *francioso* 'Frenchman', a loan word from French *françois*.

GIVEN NAMES Italian 21%. *Emilio* (2), *Enrico* (2), *Gerardo* (2), *Salvatore* (2), *Americo*, *Giacomo*, *Mario*, *Mauro*, *Sal*, *Vito*.

Francis (23447) **1.** English: from the personal name *Francis* (Old French form *Franceis*, Latin *Franciscus*, Italian *Francisco*). This was originally an ethnic name meaning 'Frank' and hence 'Frenchman'. The personal name owed much of its popularity during the Middle Ages to the fame of St. Francis of Assisi (1181–1226),

whose baptismal name was actually *Giovanni* but who was nicknamed *Francisco* because his father was absent in France at the time of his birth. As an American family name this has absorbed cognates from several other European languages (for forms, see Hanks and Hodges 1988). **2.** Jewish (American): an Americanization of one or more like-sounding Jewish surnames, or an adoption of the non-Jewish surname.

Francisco (3803) Spanish and Portuguese: from the personal name *Francisco* (see FRANCIS).

GIVEN NAMES Spanish 15%; Portuguese 5%. *Jose* (35), *Manuel* (20), *Juan* (13), *Luis* (9), *Ana* (8), *Pedro* (8), *Rolando* (6), *Alfredo* (5), *Carlos* (5), *Gregorio* (5), *Arturo* (4), *Ramon* (4); *Joaquim* (4), *Duarte* (2), *Amadeu*, *Catarina*, *Joao*.

Franciscus (118) German and Scandinavian: humanistic name from the Latin personal name *Franciscus* (see FRANCIS).

Franck (1386) Dutch, Danish, and German: variant spelling of FRANK.

GIVEN NAMES French 4%. *Armand*, *Camille*, *Edouard*, *Francois*, *Oneil*, *Pierre*, *Yanick*.

Francke (270) Dutch, Danish, and German: variant spelling of FRANK.

GIVEN NAMES German 7%. *Lothar* (2), *Bernhard*, *Hans*, *Markus*, *Mathias*.

Franckowiak (229) Polish: patronymic from the personal name *Francek*, a Silesian pet form of *Franciszek* (see FRANCIS).

Franco (8262) **1.** Spanish and Italian: from a personal name, in origin an ethnic name for a Frank, a member of the Germanic people who inhabited the lands around the river Rhine in Roman times. See also FRANK. The personal name was popularized by the cult of San Franco di Assergi. **2.** Italian and Spanish: nickname or status name from *franco* 'free' (usually denoting a freed slave). **3.** Jewish (Sephardic): adoption of the Spanish surname.

GIVEN NAMES Spanish 35%; Portuguese 8%; Italian 7%. *Jose* (190), *Manuel* (72), *Carlos* (54), *Juan* (51), *Luis* (45), *Jesus* (44), *Francisco* (40), *Ruben* (37), *Alfredo* (29), *Miguel* (28), *Ricardo* (28), *Jorge* (27); *Paulo* (6), *Joao* (3), *Godofredo*, *Nelio*; *Antonio* (39), *Salvatore* (15), *Marco* (11), *Angelo* (10), *Carmine* (8), *Lorenzo* (7), *Carlo* (6), *Elio* (4), *Enrico* (4), *Mauro* (4), *Rocco* (4), *Dante* (3).

Francoeur (602) French: from *franc* 'open', 'generous' + *coeur* 'heart'; a nickname for a warm generous person or a habitational name from places so named in Côtes d'Armor and Yonne. This surname is often Americanized as HART.

GIVEN NAMES French 14%. *Armand* (5), *Jacques* (4), *Aime* (2), *Marcel* (2), *Normand* (2), *Alcide*, *Amie*, *Anselme*, *Cecile*, *Clemence*, *Dominique*, *Georges*.

Francois (2097) French (**François**): from the personal name *François*, originally an

ethnic name meaning 'Frenchman', (see FRANCIS).

FOREBEARS Bearers of the name from Picardy and La Rochelle arrived in Quebec city by 1670.

GIVEN NAMES French 23%. *Pierre* (11), *Andre* (7), *Jacques* (6), *Jean Claude* (5), *Serge* (5), *Franck* (4), *Luc* (4), *Yves* (4), *Dieudonne* (3), *Evens* (3), *Herve* (3), *Mimose* (3).

Francom (203) English (chiefly Bristol): status name from the Anglo-Norman French feudal term *franchomme* 'free man' (see FREE), composed of the elements *franc* 'free' (see FRANK 2) + *homme* 'man' (Latin *homo*). The spelling has been altered as the result of folk etymological association with the common English place name endings *-combe* and *-ham*.

Francone (92) Italian: augmentative of FRANCO.

GIVEN NAMES Italian 21%. *Luigi*, *Nunzio*, *Rocco*, *Vito*.

Francy (116) English and Scottish: variant of FRANCIS.

Franczak (145) Polish: from the personal name *Franciszek*, a vernacular form of Latin *Franciscus* (see FRANCIS).

Franczyk (123) Polish: from a pet form of the personal name *Franciszek*, a vernacular form of Latin *Franciscus* (see FRANCIS).

GIVEN NAMES Polish 5%. *Ireneusz*, *Piotr*.

Frandsen (974) Norwegian and Danish: patronymic from the German personal name *Franz*, Latin *Franciscus* (see FRANCIS).

GIVEN NAMES Scandinavian 5%. *Erik* (3), *Lars* (2), *Niels* (2), *Anders*, *Bent*, *Ejner*, *Jorgen*, *Thor*.

Frane (167) English: variant spelling of FRAIN.

Franek (277) Czech (**Franěk**): from a reduced form of the personal name *František*, a vernacular form of Latin *Franciscus* (see FRANCIS).

Franey (478) **1.** English: topographic name for someone who lived by an ash grove, from a collective form of FRAIN. **2.** Possibly an Americanized spelling of French **Frênay**, **Fresnay**, cognate with 1.

GIVEN NAMES French 4%. *Pierre* (2), *Gabrielle*, *Jacques*, *Marceline*.

Frangella (122) Italian: from a feminine form of **Frangello**, a diminutive of the personal or ethnic name FRANCO. The feminine form is probably due to the influence of the Italian word *famiglia* 'family'.

GIVEN NAMES Italian 20%; Spanish 5%. *Angelo* (2), *Carmine*, *Gilda*, *Nicola*, *Ottavio*, *Silvestro*; *Alfonso*, *Jaime*, *Luis*.

Frangione (134) Southern Italian: from an augmentative of southern Italian *Frangi*, a short form of a personal name formed with *frangi-*.

GIVEN NAMES Italian 15%. *Alfredo*, *Angelo*, *Gaetano*, *Mario*, *Pietro*.

Frangipane (100) Italian: nickname, of uncertain application, from a phrase meaning 'break bread'.

GIVEN NAMES Italian 12%. *Salvatore* (2), *Angelo*.

Frangos (254) Greek: from *Frankos*, literally 'French' or 'Frankish' (see FRANK), but applied by extension to all Western Europeans and all Catholics (including ethnic Greek Catholics). In some cases, **Frangos** is a short form of Greek patronymic surnames such as **Frangopoulos** 'son of (the) Frank', **Frangoglou**, and compounds such as **Frangogiannis** 'Frank John' (i.e. 'John the Westerner' or 'John the Catholic'), **Frangodimitris** 'Dimitri, son of Frank', and **Frangomikhalis** 'Michael, son of Frank'.

GIVEN NAMES Greek 17%. *Costas* (2), *Koula* (2), *Christos, Demetrios, Despina, Dimitrios, Ilias, Pantelis, Speros, Spiros, Spyridon, Stamatios.*

Franich (125) Croatian (**Franić, Franjić**): patronymic from the personal name *Frano* or *Franjo*, Croatian forms of FRANCIS.

Frank (26921) **1.** German, Dutch, Scandinavian, Slovenian, Czech, Hungarian, and Jewish (Ashkenazic): ethnic or regional name for someone from Franconia (German *Franken*), a region of southwestern Germany so called from its early settlement by the Franks, a Germanic people who inhabited the lands around the river Rhine in Roman times. In the 6th–9th centuries, under leaders such as Clovis I (*c.* 466–511) and Charlemagne (742–814), the Franks established a substantial empire in western Europe, from which the country of France takes its name. The term *Frank* in eastern Mediterranean countries was used, in various vernacular forms, to denote the Crusaders and their descendants, and the American surname may also be an Americanized form of such a form. **2.** English, Dutch, German, etc.: from the personal name *Frank*, in origin an ethnic name for a Frank. This also came be used as an adjective meaning 'free', 'open-hearted', 'generous', deriving from the fact that in Frankish Gaul only people of Frankish race enjoyed the status of fully free men. It was also used as a Jewish personal name.

Frankart (141) German: probably a habitational name from a place named with FRANK + Middle High German *hard* 'woods for grazing'.

Franke (3308) German, Dutch, and Czech: variant of FRANK 3.

GIVEN NAMES German 6%. *Kurt* (13), *Hans* (8), *Fritz* (6), *Erwin* (5), *Otto* (4), *Armin* (3), *Wolfgang* (3), *Ernst* (2), *Guenter* (2), *Horst* (2), *Klaus* (2), *Siegfried* (2).

Frankel (3614) German (also **Fränkel**) and Jewish (Ashkenazic): diminutive of FRANK.

GIVEN NAMES Jewish 8%. *Sol* (10), *Moshe* (5), *Benzion* (3), *Hyman* (3), *Leibish* (3),

Mayer (3), *Meyer* (3), *Nachum* (3), *Yitzchok* (3), *Ari* (2), *Chaim* (2), *Dov* (2).

Franken (534) **1.** Dutch: patronymic from FRANK. **2.** Jewish (Ashkenazic) variant of FRANK. In some cases it may be a shortened form of the various Jewish ornamental compound names beginning with German *Franken* 'Franconian'.

GIVEN NAMES German 4%. *Ernst, Erwin, Gerhard, Klaus.*

Frankenberg (304) **1.** German: habitational name from a place in northern Hesse named as 'fort (Old High German *burg*) of the Franks'. Situated on the border with the Saxons, Frankenberg was founded *c.* 1230. **2.** Jewish (Ashkenazic): habitational name from this place or an ornamental name from German *Franken* + *Berg* 'mountain', 'hill', 'mountain'.

GIVEN NAMES German 4%. *Diether, Ernst, Kurt.*

Frankenberger (258) German or Jewish (Ashkenazic): habitational name for someone from FRANKENBERG.

GIVEN NAMES German 5%. *Florian, Gerd, Joerg.*

Frankenberry (114) Possibly a respelling of German or Jewish FRANKENBERGER or FRANKENBERG.

Frankenfield (547) Americanized form of **Frankenfeld**, a German habitational name from any of several places named Frankenfeld in central Germany and Bavaria, literally, 'Franconian open country', or from the same term as a Jewish (Ashkenazic) ornamental name.

Frankenstein (125) German and Jewish (Ashkenazic): habitational name from any of several places named Frankenstein, in Saxony, Hesse, the Palatinate, and Silesia.

GIVEN NAMES German 5%. *Guenther, Hans.*

Frankford (126) Jewish (Ashkenazic): variant of FRANKFORT.

Frankfort (144) Jewish (Ashkenazic): habitational name from either of the German cities of Frankfurt an der Oder or Frankfurt am Main.

Frankhauser (94) German: habitational name for someone from any of several places named Frankenhausen, in Thuringia (recorded as *Franchenhausen* 12th century), Hesse, and Saxony.

Frankhouser (257) Americanized spelling of FRANKHAUSER.

Frankie (153) **1.** Americanized spelling of German FRANKE. **2.** Perhaps an American shortened form of Polish FRANKIEWICZ.

Frankiewicz (155) Polish: patronymic from the personal name *Franek*, a pet form of *Franciszek*, a vernacular form of Latin *Franciscus* (see FRANCIS).

GIVEN NAMES Polish 6%. *Henryk, Janusz.*

Frankl (231) German (**Fränkl**) and Jewish (Ashkenazic): from a diminutive of FRANK.

GIVEN NAMES German 7%; Jewish 4%. *Armin* (2), *Erwin, Gerda, Gitta, Gunther, Rainer; Chaim, Chaskel, Meyer, Miriam.*

Frankland (271) English: status name for someone who lived on a piece of land held without obligations of rent or service, from Anglo-Norman French *frank* 'free' (see FRANK 2) + Middle English *land* 'land'. Compare FREELAND.

Frankle (150) Americanized form of German **Fränkel** (see FRANKEL).

Franklin (35741) **1.** English: status name from Middle English *frankelin* 'franklin', a technical term of the feudal system, from Anglo-Norman French *franc* 'free' (see FRANK 2) + the Germanic suffix *-ling*. The status of the franklin varied somewhat according to time and place in medieval England; in general, he was a free man and a holder of fairly extensive areas of land, a gentleman ranked above the main body of minor freeholders but below a knight or a member of the nobility. **2.** The surname is also borne by Jews, in which case it represents an Americanized form of one or more like-sounding Jewish surnames. **3.** In modern times, this has been used to Americanize *François*, the French form of FRANCIS.

FOREBEARS The American statesman and scientist Benjamin Franklin (1706–90) was the son of Josiah Franklin, a chandler (dealer in soap and candles), who had emigrated in about 1682 from Ecton, Northamptonshire, to Boston, MA, where his son was born.

Franklyn (171) English: variant spelling of FRANKLIN.

Franko (745) **1.** Ukrainian: from the personal name *Franko*, a vernacular form of Latin *Franciscus* (see FRANCIS). **2.** Polish, Czech and Slovak, and Slovenian: from a pet form of the Polish personal name *Franciszek*, or Czech and Slovak *František*, or Slovenian *Frančišek*, vernacular forms of Latin *Franciscus* (see FRANCIS). **3.** As a Slovenian surname it may also be a derivative of the personal name *Frank* (see FRANK 2), formed with the diminutive suffix *-ko*. **4.** Jewish (eastern Ashkenazic): from a Slavicized form of the personal name FRANK.

Frankovich (303) Croatian (**Franković**) and Slovenian (southern Slovenia; **Frankovič**): patronymic from the personal name FRANKO.

Frankowski (317) Polish: habitational name for someone from places called Franki (in Łomża and Płock voivodeships), Frankowo, or Frankowa, so named from the personal names *Franek* or *Franko*, derivatives of the personal name *Franciszek*, a vernacular form of Latin *Franciscus* (see FRANCIS).

GIVEN NAMES Polish 8%. *Janusz* (2), *Wieslaw* (2), *Halina, Stanislaw, Witold.*

Franks (10512) English and German: patronymic from FRANK.

Frankson (145) English: patronymic from FRANK.

Frankum (278) English: variant spelling of FRANCOM.

Frano (103) **1.** Slovak (**Fraňo**): from the personal name *Fraňo*, a variant of *František*, a vernacular form of Latin *Franciscus* (see FRANCIS). **2.** Polish: from a pet form of the personal name *Franciszek*, a vernacular form of Latin *Franciscus* (see FRANCIS).

Franqui (141) Spanish: from a pet form of the personal name FRANCO.
GIVEN NAMES Spanish 36%. *Jose* (3), *Ana* (2), *Angel* (2), *Eugenio* (2), *Juan* (2), *Manuel* (2), *Mario* (2), *Wilfredo* (2), *Aida, Alberto, Benito, Eduardo; Antonio* (2).

Frans (268) Dutch: from the personal name *Frans*, Dutch form of FRANCIS.

Fransen (737) Dutch and Danish: patronymic from the personal name *Frans* (see FRANCIS).
GIVEN NAMES Scandinavian 6%. *Erik, Knute, Nels, Sig.*

Franson (675) Respelling of FRANSEN or the Swedish cognate **Fransson**.
GIVEN NAMES Scandinavian 7%. *Anders, Thorval.*

Franssen (186) Dutch: patronymic from *Frans*, Dutch form of FRANCIS.
GIVEN NAMES French 4%. *Monique* (2), *Alphonse.*

Franta (295) Czech: from a pet form of the personal name *František*, Czech form of FRANCIS.

Frantom (135) English: unexplained; perhaps a variant of FRANCOM.

Frantz (4832) German: older spelling of FRANZ.
FOREBEARS Between 1721 and 1780 over 30 families named Frantz came to America. The first three immigrants were born at St. Jacob near Basel, Switzerland.

Frantzen (270) North German, Norwegian, and Danish: patronymic from the personal name *Fran(t)z* (see FRANCIS).
GIVEN NAMES Scandinavian 6%. *Erik, Gunn, Thor.*

Franz (4861) German: from the personal name *Franz*, a vernacular form of Latin *Franciscus* (see FRANCIS).
GIVEN NAMES German 5%. *Helmut* (6), *Hans* (4), *Kurt* (4), *Wilhelm* (4), *Dieter* (3), *Fritz* (3), *Johannes* (3), *Manfred* (3), *Otto* (3), *Erwin* (2), *Ewald* (2), *Gerhard* (2).

Franza (109) **1.** Italian: variant of FRANCIA. **2.** Slovenian and Croatian: derivative of the Italian personal name *Francisco* (see FRANCIS).
GIVEN NAMES Italian 14%. *Alfredo, Eliodoro, Emilio, Giorgio, Lorenzo, Lucio, Orfeo, Rocco.*

Franzblau (110) Jewish (Ashkenazic): of uncertain origin. Compare BLAU.

Franze (191) **1.** Italian (**Franzè**): from a shortened and altered form of *francese* 'French'. **2.** Variant of Dutch **Franzen** or **Frans(s)en**, patronymics from the personal name *Frans* (see FRANCIS); the final -*n* is often dropped in Dutch, especially in the Amsterdam dialect.
GIVEN NAMES Italian 11%; German 4%. *Carmine, Cosimo, Rocco, Salvatore; Fritz, Gerhard.*

Franzel (204) German (**Fränzel**): from a pet form of FRANZ.

Franzen (2328) **1.** Dutch, Norwegian, and Danish: patronymic from the personal name FRANZ. **2.** Swedish (Franzén): from the personal name *Franz* + -*én*, from Latin -*enius* 'descendant of'.
GIVEN NAMES Scandinavian 4%. *Lennart* (3), *Erik* (2), *Sven* (2), *Anders, Bjorn, Helmer, Hjalmer, Iver, Nels, Paal.*

Franzese (411) Variant of Italian FRANCESE.
GIVEN NAMES Italian 20%. *Antonio* (4), *Carmine* (3), *Pasquale* (3), *Angelo* (2), *Giovanni* (2), *Salvatore* (2), *Vito* (2), *Amelio, Carlo, Cesare, Fiore, Gaetano.*

Franzke (122) North German: from a pet form of the personal name FRANZ.
GIVEN NAMES German 10%. *Alois* (2), *Horst, Klaus, Wilhelm.*

Franzman (98) **1.** German (**Franzmann**) and Jewish (Ashkenazic): from the personal name FRANZ + *man*, which later (after 1678, and hence outside the period of surname formation) came to mean 'Frenchman'. As a Jewish name it can be either an ornamental name or an ethnic name for someone from France. **2.** Possibly an altered spelling of Dutch **Fransman**, an ethnic name for a Frenchman, Middle Dutch *fransman*.

Franzone (189) Italian: from an augmentative form of the personal name FRANZA.
GIVEN NAMES Italian 15%. *Angelo* (2), *Mario* (2), *Salvatore* (2), *Amedeo, Amparo, Francesco, Vita.*

Franzoni (170) Italian: patronymic or plural form of FRANZONE.
GIVEN NAMES Italian 9%. *Carlo, Enzo, Italo, Orfeo, Salvatore.*

Frappier (423) French: possibly an occupational name from Old French *fripier, frappier* 'second-hand dealer'.
FOREBEARS Bearers of the name, originally from La Rochelle and Poitou, arrived before 1668 in Quebec city.
GIVEN NAMES French 11%. *Armand* (2), *Emile, Fernand, Germain, Lorette, Luc, Marcel, Michel, Normand, Pierre, Sebastien.*

Frary (451) English: variant of the Germanic personal name FRIEDERICH.

Frasca (556) Southern Italian: habitational name for someone from Frasca in Sicily, or a topographic name from *frasca* 'branch', which in Sicily also denotes a type of tree resembling the ash. Alternatively, it may be a nickname linked with the practice of collecting twigs to support vegetable crops.
GIVEN NAMES Italian 17%. *Angelo* (4), *Antonio* (3), *Salvatore* (3), *Enrico* (2), *Nicola* (2), *Rocco* (2), *Sandro* (2), *Agostino, Carlo, Carmela, Carmelo, Carmine.*

Frascella (165) Southern Italian: origin uncertain; perhaps from a diminutive of *frascio*, from Greek *phraxos* 'ash (tree)', 'barricade'.
GIVEN NAMES Italian 11%. *Gaetano, Lorenzo, Luigi.*

Frasch (229) **1.** South German: nickname for a courageous, steadfast person, from Middle High German *vrast* 'courage'. **2.** variant spelling of **Fraasch** (see FRAAS).
GIVEN NAMES German 4%. *Erhard, Helmut.*

Frasco (261) Portuguese and Spanish: nickname from Latin *frasco* 'flask', 'bottle'.
GIVEN NAMES Italian 6%. *Carlo, Gilda, Graciliano, Sal.*

Frascone (101) Italian: variant of **Frascona**, from Greek *phlaskonas*, an occupational name from medieval Greek *phlaskon*, a loan word from Late Latin *flasco, flasconis*, with the addition of the occupational suffix -*as*.
GIVEN NAMES Italian 14%. *Dante, Mario, Pierina.*

Frase (510) German: variant of FRAAS.

Fraser (10281) Scottish: of uncertain origin. The earliest recorded forms of this family name, dating from the mid-12th century, are *de Fresel, de Friselle*, and *de Freseliere*. These appear to be Norman, but there is no place in France with a name answering to them. It is possible, therefore, that they represent a Gaelic name corrupted beyond recognition by an Anglo-Norman scribe. The modern Gaelic form is **Friseal**, sometimes Anglicized as **FRIZZELL**. The surname *Fraser* is also borne by Jews, in which case it represents an Americanized form of one or more like-sounding Jewish surnames.

Frasher (509) **1.** Scottish and northern Irish: variant of FRASER. **2.** Altered form of German **Fratzscher** (see FRUTCHEY).

Frashier (101) Scottish and northern Irish: variant of FRASER.

Frasier (2251) Scottish and northern Irish: variant of FRASER.

Frasure (523) Altered form of Scottish FRASER.

Fratangelo (149) Italian: from a compound name meaning 'Brother Angelo' (*frate* 'bother' + the personal name ANGELO).
GIVEN NAMES Italian 14%. *Antonio, Guido, Nunzio, Pierino, Velio.*

Frate (188) Italian: from an appellative derived from *frate* 'brother', 'friar' (Latin *frater* 'brother').
GIVEN NAMES Italian 20%. *Remo* (3), *Angelo* (2), *Antonio* (2), *Gino* (2), *Valentino* (2), *Domenico, Donato, Ermanno, Matteo, Nunzio, Reno.*

Fratello (123) Italian: relationship name from *fratello* 'brother' (Latin *fratellus*), presumably denoting the brother of someone of note or notoriety.

GIVEN NAMES Italian 11%. *Carmelo, Cosmo, Gaspare, Santino, Vito.*

Frater (237) French and Hungarian (**Fráter**): status name for a member a religious order, especially a mendicant order; alternatively, possibly a nickname for a pious person or for someone employed in a monastery, from a Latinized form of Old French *fratre* 'brother', Hungarian *fráter* (from Latin *frater*).
GIVEN NAMES French 4%. *Julienne, Vernice.*

Frates (418) Origin unidentified.

Fraticelli (153) Italian: from a diminutive of FRATE, literally 'little friar'. This name is well established in Puerto Rico.
GIVEN NAMES Spanish 26%; Italian 6%. *Carlos* (6), *Jose* (5), *Luis* (2), *Milagros* (2), *Alicia, Domingo, Elba, Felicita, Felipe, Gilberto, Jorge, Juan; Angelo, Dario, Lorenzo, Pasquale, Umberto.*

Frattaroli (126) Italian: topographic name from a derivative of *fratta* 'shrub', 'bramble', also 'deforested place', a common element of place names such as Frattaminore and Frattamaggiore in Naples province.
GIVEN NAMES Italian 38%. *Mario* (4), *Claudio* (3), *Elio* (3), *Costantino* (2), *Aldo, Antonio, Dino, Guerino, Nino, Rocco.*

Frattini (131) Southern Italian: probably a topographic name from Calabrian dialect *frattina* 'scrubland', Sicilian *frattina* 'rugged place' (from *fratta* 'shrub', 'bramble', also 'deforested place'). Alternatively, it may be a habitational name from a place named with this word, for example one in Sicily.
GIVEN NAMES Italian 8%. *Dante, Filippo, Marco, Sante, Silvio.*

Fratto (282) Southern Italian: variant of **Fratta**, a habitational name from a place named with Sicilian *fratta* 'thicket', 'scrub', 'undergrowth', or a topographic name from this word.
GIVEN NAMES Italian 12%; French 4%. *Salvatore* (2), *Carmine, Caterina, Dante, Domenico, Luigi, Ugo; Andre, Marcel.*

Fratus (343) Origin uncertain. Perhaps an altered form of Portuguese FREITAS. The name has been common in New England since the early 19th century.

Fratzke (203) German: possibly of Slavic origin or, in northern Germany, a nickname for a glutton, from a diminutive of Middle Low German *vrātz, vrās* 'glutton'.
GIVEN NAMES German 5%. *Alois, Erwin, Sigismund.*

Frausto (642) Portuguese (**Fraústo**) or Spanish (very common in Mexico): unexplained, but apparently from a personal name, probably a variant of FAUSTO.
GIVEN NAMES Spanish 53%. *Jose* (30), *Juan* (13), *Jesus* (9), *Manuel* (8), *Ruben* (7), *Ramon* (6), *Francisco* (5), *Guadalupe* (5), *Armando* (4), *Arturo* (4), *Carlos* (4), *Luis* (4).

Fravel (462) Probably a respelling of German **Frevel**, a nickname for an evil doer,

from Middle High German *vrevel, vrävel* 'bold', 'intrepid', later 'impudent'.

Frawley (1207) Irish: reduced Anglicized form of Gaelic **Ó Freaghaile**, a metathesized form of **Ó Fearghaile** (see FARRELLY).
GIVEN NAMES Irish 5%. *Brendan* (4), *Liam* (2), *Eamonn.*

Fray (505) **1.** French (Alsace): Frenchified form of German FREY. **2.** French and English: from an Old French personal name *Fray*, of unknown origin.

Frayer (349) Variant of English FREER or Americanized form of French FRERE.

Frayne (174) English: variant spelling of FRAIN.

Frayser (127) Probably a North American spelling of FRASER.

Fraze (314) Americanized spelling of German FREESE or **Fröse** (see FROESE).

Frazee (1963) Origin uncertain: an Americanized spelling of a Dutch or German name, possibly FREESE.

Frazell (123) Variant of English FRIZZELL.

Frazer (2841) Variant spelling of FRASER, associated chiefly with northern Ireland.

Frazier (27795) Variant of Scottish and northern Irish FRASER.

Frazzini (156) Italian: of uncertain origin; possibly from a variant of Sicilian *vrazza* 'bracelet', 'armlet'.
GIVEN NAMES Italian 9%. *Caesar, Emidio, Lorenzo, Marco, Oreste.*

Fread (184) Jewish (American) or German: Americanized spelling of FRIED.

Frear (293) English: variant spelling of FREER.

Freas (546) Respelling of German FRIES, FRIESS, or FRIESE.

Frease (139) Americanized spelling of German FRIES, FRIESS, or FRIESE.

Freberg (158) **1.** Swedish: habitational name from a farm or village named Freberg(a), of which there are at least three examples in Sweden, possibly with the same etymology as 2. **2.** Norwegian: habitational name from any of three farmsteads named Freberg, from *Freyja* (the Old Norse goddess of love) + *berg* 'mountain'.

Frech (485) German and Swiss German: nickname from Middle High German *vrech* 'eager', 'bold', 'brave'.

Frechette (1425) French Canadian spelling of French **Fréchet**, a habitational name from places in Haute Garonne and Hautes Pyrénées, so named from Gascon dialect *frèche, herèche* 'ash tree' + the diminutive ending *-et*.
FOREBEARS Bearers of this name from Poitou arrived in Beaupré, Quebec, before 1671.
GIVEN NAMES French 13%. *Andre* (7), *Fernand* (3), *Lucien* (3), *Marcel* (3), *Aldee* (2), *Armand* (2), *Cecile* (2), *Emile* (2), *Napoleon* (2), *Normand* (2), *Renald* (2), *Adrien.*

Freck (190) North German form of FRECH.

Freckleton (102) English: habitational name from a place in Lancashire named Freckleton, from an Old English personal name *Frecia* + *tūn* 'farmstead', 'settlement'.

Fred (710) Swedish: ornamental name from *fred* 'peace'.

Freda (774) Italian: from a short form of the personal name *Gioffreda*, feminine form of *Goffredo*, composed of the Germanic elements *god, got* 'god' + *fred, frid* 'peace'.
GIVEN NAMES Italian 12%. *Angelo* (5), *Carmine* (3), *Giovanni* (3), *Aldo* (2), *Dino* (2), *Pasquale* (2), *Carmello, Carmelo, Domenic, Enrico, Fiore, Giacomo.*

Frede (166) North German: from a short form of any of the various personal names beginning with the Old High German element *frid, fred* 'peace'.
GIVEN NAMES German 4%. *Helmut, Klaus.*

Fredell (191) **1.** Swedish: ornamental name from *fred* 'peace' + the suffix *-ell*, taken from the Latin adjectival ending *-elius*. **2.** Altered spelling of German FRIEDEL.

Fredenberg (121) Swedish: ornamental name from *fred* 'peace' + *berg* 'mountain'. The infix *-en*, ultimately of German origin, is a relatively common feature of Swedish surnames.

Fredenburg (427) German: possibly a habitational name from either of two places called Fredeburg, in Westphalia and southeast of Hamburg.

Frederic (297) French (**Frédéric**): from the personal name, French form of FRIEDERICH.
GIVEN NAMES French 10%. *Alphonse* (2), *Antoine* (2), *Andre, Armand, Eugenie, Leonne, Loubert.*

Frederick (14816) English: from a Germanic personal name composed of the elements *frid, fred* 'peace' + *ric* 'power', introduced into England from France by the Normans. See also FRIEDRICH.

Fredericks (2948) English: patronymic from FREDERICK.

Fredericksen (653) Altered spelling of Danish and Norwegian FREDERIKSEN or North German **Frederichsen**, a patronymic from FRIEDRICH.
GIVEN NAMES Scandinavian 5%. *Thor* (2), *Bodil, Erik, Nels.*

Frederickson (1548) Probably a respelling of Danish and Norwegian FREDERIKSEN or Swedish **Frederiksson**, also a patronymic from *Frederik* (see FRIEDRICH).

Frederico (161) Italian and Portuguese: from the personal name *Frederico*, Italian and Portuguese equivalent of FRIEDRICH.
GIVEN NAMES Italian 13%. *Domenic, Nino, Santo.*

Frederiksen (683) Danish and Norwegian: patronymic from *Frederik*, Danish form of FRIEDRICH.

GIVEN NAMES Scandinavian 15%. *Erik* (6), *Jorgen* (2), *Borge, Folmer, Gunner, Knut, Lars, Mauritz, Niels, Nils, Viggo.*

Frederking (150) German: patronymic from *Frederik* (see FRIEDRICH) + patronymic suffix *-ing.*

GIVEN NAMES German 5%. *Eldor, Erwin, Traugott.*

Fredette (1070) French: from the personal name *Fredet*, a pet form of *Frédéric* (see FRIEDRICH), or of the Germanic personal names *Fredaud, Frébaud*, or *Frébert*. The *-ette* ending is standard in Canadian French family names, indicating that the final *-t* is pronounced.

GIVEN NAMES French 9%. *Emile* (6), *Armand* (5), *Andre* (4), *Alcide, Alphonse, Camille, Herve, Marcel, Normand, Patrice, Pierre, Roch.*

Frediani (185) Italian: from the personal name *Frediano*, which gained popularity through the cult of San Frediano, a 6th century bishop of Lucca. The personal name is of Germanic origin, a compound of *frithu* 'peace', 'amity' + the Latin suffix *-ianus*, in the sense 'lover of peace'.

GIVEN NAMES Italian 10%; French 6%. *Cesare, Dino, Enrico, Federico, Fulvio, Leno, Livio, Paolo, Silvio; Camille* (2), *Monique.*

Fredieu (115) Possibly French: unexplained; perhaps related to a Germanic personal name formed with *frid(u)* 'peace'.

GIVEN NAME French 4%. *Andre.*

Fredin (182) Swedish: ornamental name from *fred* 'peace' + the suffix *-in*, from the Latin genitive suffix *-in(i)us.*

GIVEN NAMES Scandinavian 6%; German 5%. *Lars; Kurt, Otto.*

Fredlund (278) Swedish: ornamental name composed of the elements *fred* 'peace' + *lund* 'grove'.

Fredman (233) **1.** Swedish: ornamental name composed of the elements *fred* 'peace' + *man* 'man'. **2.** Jewish (Ashkenazic): variant of FRIEDMANN.

GIVEN NAMES Jewish 6%. *Izak, Rina, Shlomo, Yonah, Zev.*

Fredo (117) Italian: from a reduced form of the Germanic personal name *Goffredo* (see FREDA).

GIVEN NAMES Italian 11%. *Rocco* (2), *Geno.*

Fredrich (211) North German form of FRIEDRICH.

Fredrick (2102) **1.** Dutch: from a Germanic personal name composed of the elements *frid, fred* 'peace' + *rīc* 'power' (see FRIEDRICH). **2.** In some cases possibly an altered spelling of FREDERICK or likesounding cognates in other languages.

Fredricks (929) **1.** English: variant of FREDERICKS. **2.** Variant of Dutch **Fredriks**, a patronymic from the personal name FREDRICK.

Fredricksen (306) Variant spelling of FREDRIKSEN or FREDERIKSEN.

GIVEN NAMES Scandinavian 9%. *Erik* (3), *Knute, Thor.*

Fredrickson (3715) Americanized spelling of any of the various Scandinavian patronymics derived from the Germanic personal name *Fred(e)rik* (see FREDERICK), such as Swedish **Fredriksson**, Norwegian FREDRIKSEN, etc.

GIVEN NAMES Scandinavian 4%. *Erik* (7), *Lars* (3), *Eskil* (2), *Nels* (2), *Sven* (2), *Einer, Knute, Selmer.*

Fredriksen (203) Norwegian: patronymic from the personal name *Fredrik* (see FRIEDRICH).

GIVEN NAMES Scandinavian 23%. *Astrid, Audun, Bodil, Erik, Lars, Ove, Per, Thor.*

Fredrikson (136) Scandinavian: see FREDRIKSEN, FREDRICKSON.

GIVEN NAMES Scandinavian 10%. *Erik, Johan, Lars.*

Free (3651) **1.** English (chiefly East Anglia): nickname or status name from Old English *frēo* 'free(-born)', i.e. not a serf. **2.** North German: topographic or habitational name from a place named Frede or Frede(n). **3.** North German: nickname from a variant of Middle Low German *wrēd* 'crooked'.

Freebairn (104) Scottish and English: status name from Old English *frēo* 'free' + *bearn* 'child'.

Freeberg (484) Partly Americanized form of German FREIBERG or **Freiburg** (see FREIBURGER).

Freebern (107) English: variant of FREEBORN.

Freeborn (550) English: term of status for someone who was born a free man (from Old English *frēo* 'free' + *boren* 'born'), rather than a serf emancipated in late life. Compare FREEDMAN.

Freeburg (489) Partly Americanized form of German **Freiburg** or FREIBERG.

Freeburn (178) English: variant of FREEBORN.

Freeby (123) English: possibly a variant spelling of **Friby**, a habitational name from either of two places in Yorkshire: Firby in Westow or Firby in Bedale .

Freed (4154) Jewish and German: Americanized spelling of FRIED.

Freedberg (120) Americanized spelling of Jewish FRIEDBERG.

GIVEN NAME Jewish 6%. *Sol.*

Freedland (165) Americanized form of Jewish and German FRIEDLAND.

GIVEN NAMES Jewish 10%. *Hyman, Hymen, Meyer, Yosef.*

Freedle (177) Americanized spelling of German FRIEDEL.

GIVEN NAME French 4%. *Lucien* (2).

Freedman (5182) **1.** English (Yorkshire): status name in the feudal system for a serf who had been freed. **2.** Jewish (American): Americanized form of **Friedmann** (see FRIED).

GIVEN NAMES Jewish 4%. *Sol* (11), *Isadore* (7), *Miriam* (6), *Hyman* (5), *Moshe* (3), *Rina* (3), *Emanuel* (2), *Hersh* (2), *Tzvi* (2), *Aron, Avi, Avraham.*

Freeh (126) German: perhaps a variant of FREE 2.

Freehill (154) American translation into English of the German habitational name FREIBERG.

Freehling (207) Variant spelling of North German **Frie(h)ling**, a nickname for a serf who had been freed, Middle Low German *vrilink*, or a habitational name from a place called Frielingen. Alternatively it could be a respelling of South German **Frühling** meaning 'spring', the season (from *früh* 'early' + the suffix *-ling* denoting affiliation).

Freel (733) **1.** English: nickname from Middle English *freil, frel(i)e* 'frail', 'weak'. **2.** Possibly an Americanized spelling of German FRIEL 2.

Freeland (3310) English: status name for someone who lived on a piece of land held without obligations of rent or service, from Old English *frēo* 'free' + *land* 'land'. Compare FRANKLAND.

Freeling (121) Respelling of German or Jewish FRIELING.

Freelove (131) English: from the Old English personal name *Friðulāf* 'peace-survivor'.

Freels (720) North German: from a Frisian reduced form of the personal name *Fredlefs*, or a patronymic from *Fridulf*.

Freeman (55281) **1.** English: variant of FREE. **2.** Irish: Anglicized ('translated') form of Gaelic **Ó Saoraidhe** (see SEERY). **3.** In New England, an English equivalent of French **Foissy** (see FOISY). **4.** Translation of German **Freimann** (see FREIMAN).

Freemon (205) Variant spelling of FREEMAN.

Freemyer (179) Americanized form of South German **Freimeier**, a status name for a free steward, i.e. one who was exempt from feudal service.

Freeney (188) English: variant of FRANEY.

Freeny (200) English: variant of FRANEY.

Freer (1376) **1.** English: from Old French and Middle English *frere* 'friar' (Latin *frater*, literally 'brother'). This was a status name for a member a religious order, especially a mendicant order, and may also have been a nickname for a pious person or for someone employed at a monastery. **2.** Americanized spelling of French **Frère** (see FRERE). **3.** North German and Dutch: cognate of FRIEDRICH.

Freerksen (110) Frisian and North German: patronymic from a Frisian and Low German form of the personal name FREDERICK.

Frees (391) Variant of Dutch FRESE or German FRIES, ethnic names for someone from Friesland.

Freese (2589) **1.** North German form of FRIES 1. **2.** Dutch: variant of FRESE. **3.** English: metonymic occupational name for a weaver of frieze, a coarse woolen cloth with a thick nap, Old French *frise*.

Freestone (401) English (chiefly East Anglia and East Midlands): from the Old English personal name *Frēostān*, composed of the elements *frēo* 'free', 'noble', 'generous' + *stān* 'stone'.

Freet (247) Americanized form of German FRIED.

Freeze (1460) Altered spelling of FREES(E) or FRIES(E) 1.

Fregeau (230) French (**Frégeau**): unexplained.
GIVEN NAMES French 12%. *Marcel* (2), *Armand, Camille, Eloi, Fernand, Lucien, Michel, Normand.*

Fregia (210) Origin unidentified. This name is concentrated in TX.

Fregoso (338) Spanish: probably a variant of FRAGOSO.
GIVEN NAMES Spanish 57%. *Jose* (18), *Francisco* (6), *Carlos* (4), *Fernando* (4), *Javier* (4), *Luis* (4), *Roberto* (4), *Salvador* (4), *Armando* (3), *Felipe* (3), *Jesus* (3), *Ricardo* (3).

Frehner (118) South German and Swiss: metronymic from the female personal name *Frene* or an occupational name meaning 'bondsman of a woman called Frene'. The name is testified in old documents as the name of St. Verena of Zurzach in Aargau, Switzerland.

Frei (923) German: status name for a free man in the feudal system, a variant of FREY.
GIVEN NAMES German 8%. *Hans* (8), *Otto* (4), *Franz* (3), *Alois* (2), *Erwin* (2), *Dieter, Ernst, Ewald, Hedwig, Heinz, Hermann, Juerg.*

Freiberg (789) German: habitational name from any of several places named Freiberg, from Middle High German *vrī* 'free', 'independent' + *berg* 'mountain', 'hill' (possibly an altered form of *burg* 'castle', 'fortified town').

Freiberger (294) German: habitational name for someone from any of the places named FREIBERG.
GIVEN NAMES German 5%. *Kurt* (2), *Gerhard, Inge, Rudi.*

Freiburger (431) German: habitational name for someone from any of several places named Freiburg, named with Middle High German *vrī* 'free', 'independent' + *burg* 'castle', 'fortified town'.

Freid (279) Altered spelling of German FRIED or FREUD.

Freidel (164) Altered spelling of German FRIEDEL.

Freidhof (103) Jewish (American): altered spelling of FRIEDHOFF.

Freidman (221) **1.** Jewish (eastern Ashkenazic): metronymic from the Yiddish female personal name *Freyde* 'joy'. **2.** Jewish (eastern Ashkenazic): ornamental name from Yiddish *freyd* 'joy' + *man* 'man'. **3.** Altered spelling of German **Friedmann** (see FRIEDMAN).
GIVEN NAMES Jewish 9%. *Naum* (2), *Avi, Moshe, Shulim, Yehudit, Yocheved.*

Freier (508) German: **1.** status name of the feudal system denoting a free man, as opposed to a bondsman, from an inflected form of Middle High German *vrī* 'free'. **2.** archaic occupational name, from Middle High German, Middle Low German *vrier, vriger*, denoting a man who had the ceremonial duty of asking guests to a wedding.
GIVEN NAMES German 4%. *Otto* (3), *Fritz, Hartmut.*

Freiermuth (177) German: variant of FREIMUTH.

Freifeld (135) Jewish (Ashkenazic): ornamental compound name from German *frei* 'free' + *Feld* 'field'.
GIVEN NAMES Jewish 8%; German 4%. *Ezriel, Mendel; Armin.*

Freiheit (191) German: **1.** either a nickname or an occupational name, from Middle High German *vrīheit* 'tramp', 'vagrant'; 'court usher'. **2.** habitational name from any of various places in northern Germany named Freiheit (literally 'freedom'), originally a topographic name for an area which had been granted immunity, as for example a cathedral, castle, or diocese.
GIVEN NAMES German 5%. *Erwin, Theodor.*

Freihofer (100) German (also **Freihöfer**): status name for an owner of a farm that was free of feudal obligations, from Middle High German *frī* 'free' + *hof* 'farm', farmyard'.
GIVEN NAME German 5%. *Otto.*

Freije (139) Asturian-Leonese: habitational name from places called Freije, in Asturies.

Freilich (391) German and Jewish (Ashkenazic): nickname for a person with a cheerful disposition, from Middle High German *vrīlīch* 'open', Yiddish *freylekh* 'happy', 'cheerful'. In modern German, the word *freilich* has become specialized as an adverb meaning 'certainly', but the surname is most probably from the older adjectival sense. As a Jewish surname it can also be ornamental. In America there has been some confusion with FROEHLICH.
GIVEN NAMES Jewish 11%. *Isak* (2), *Yosef* (2), *Akiva, Este, Mendel, Schlomo, Shlomo, Sima, Sura, Yaakov, Zelig.*

Freiling (103) German: status name from Middle High German *vrīlinc* 'freedman'.

Freiman (356) **1.** Jewish (Ashkenazic): ornamental name from German *frei* 'free' + *Mann* 'man'. **2.** German (**Freimann**): status name in the feudal system for a free man as opposed to a bondman or serf (see FREIER).
GIVEN NAMES Jewish 8%. *Shlomo* (2), *Shmuel* (2), *Bluma, Efroim, Emanuel, Meyer, Tziporah, Yetta.*

Freimark (183) German: topographic name from a field name denoting land that was free of tax obligation, composed of the elements *frei* 'free' + *mark* 'unit of land', 'border land'.

Freimuth (369) German: from a personal name denoting someone of a free and courageous disposition, from Middle High German *vrī* + *muot* 'mind', 'spirit'.
GIVEN NAMES German 7%. *Franz, Gerhard, Lisel, Lothar, Reinhold, Siegfried, Wilhelmina.*

Frein (179) German: from a short form of the personal name *Severin*. This was the name of two saints in particular: the first was an early bishop of Cologne (died *c.* 400); the second was a missionary in the Roman province of Noricum (Austria), who died in 482.

Freire (385) Portuguese and Galician: occupational name for a friar, or a nickname for a pious person or someone employed at a monastery, from Latin *frater* 'brother'.
GIVEN NAMES Spanish 41%; Portuguese 17%. *Jose* (13), *Jorge* (6), *Luis* (6), *Manuel* (6), *Fernando* (5), *Francisco* (4), *Joaquin* (4), *Mario* (4), *Carlos* (3), *Jesus* (3), *Maribel* (3), *Miguel* (3); *Paulo* (3), *Joao* (2), *Sebastiao, Vasco; Antonio* (6), *Federico.*

Freis (144) South German: nickname for a violent man or someone with a menacing appearance, from Middle High German *vreise* 'cruel', 'terrible'.
GIVEN NAME German 4%. *Otto.*

Freise (188) Low German variant of FRIES.

Freisinger (104) German: habitationa name from any of several places (especially in Bavaria) called Freising.
GIVEN NAMES German 5%. *Eugen, Ilse.*

Freitag (1954) German and Jewish (Ashkenazic): nickname from (respectively) Middle High German *vrītac* and German *Freitag* 'Friday' (Old High German *frīatag, frījetag*, a translation of Late Latin *Veneris dies*: Freya was the Germanic goddess of love, sometimes considered as equivalent to the Roman Venus). The German name may have denoted someone born on a Friday or who performed some feudal service then. However, Friday was considered unlucky throughout Christendom in the Middle Ages (because it was the day on which Christ was crucified), and it seems more likely that the name was given to a person considered ill-omened. It is found as a byname in this sense in Old High German. This is by far the commonest of the surnames drawn from the days of the week, followed by SONNTAG 'Sunday', traditionally a day of good omen. Among Jews, it seems to have been one of the names that were distributed at random by government officials.
GIVEN NAMES German 6%. *Otto* (5), *Kurt* (4), *Gunther* (2), *Arno, Bernhard, Bodo, Elfriede, Ernst, Erwin, Gerd, Gerhard, Gunter.*

Freitas (3102) Portuguese and Galician: habitational name from any of the numerous places named Freitas, or a topographic name for someone who lived on a patch of stony ground, from Portuguese *(pedras) freitas* 'broken stones', Late Latin *(petrae) fractae*. Compare FRAGOSO.
GIVEN NAMES Spanish 10%; Portuguese 7%. *Manuel* (55), *Jose* (31), *Fernando* (9), *Carlos* (6), *Mario* (5), *Luis* (4), *Sergio* (4), *Armando* (3), *Augusto* (3), *Jorge* (3), *Juanita* (3), *Ana* (2); *Joao* (8), *Joaquim* (3), *Marcio* (2), *Mateus* (2), *Paulo* (2), *Afonso*, *Agostinho*, *Caetano*, *Duarte*, *Guilherme*, *Henrique*, *Margarida*.

Freiwald (170) Eastern German: habitational name from places named Freiwalde, Freienwalde, or Freiwaldau.
GIVEN NAMES German 7%. *Frieda*, *Fritz*, *Reinhard*.

Freking (176) North German: patronymic from a short form of the personal name *Fredeke* (see FRIEDRICH) + patronymic suffix *-ing*.

Frelich (130) Respelling of German and Jewish FROEHLICH.
GIVEN NAMES Polish 4%. *Casimir*, *Wencil*.

Freligh (105) Americanized spelling of German and Jewish FROEHLICH.

Frelinghuysen (35) Dutch: habitational name from a place called Frelinghuizen.
FOREBEARS Theodorus Jacobus Frelinghuysen (1691–c. 1748) was a Dutch Reformed clergyman born at Lingen on the Ems, Germany, near the Dutch border. He accepted a call to the Dutch congregations of the Raritan Valley in NJ (founded 1699) and was influential in the 'Great Awakening' in the Middle Colonies.

Frels (116) German: variant of FREELS.

Fremin (234) French (**Frémin**): variant of FIRMIN.
GIVEN NAMES French 5%. *Camille*, *Curley*, *Monique*.

Fremont (304) French (**Frémont**): from a Germanic personal name composed of the elements *frid*, *fred* 'peace' (or *frija* 'free', 'noble', 'generous') + *mund* 'protection'.
FOREBEARS John Charles Frémont (1813–90), explorer of the American West, was born in Savannah, GA, of French ancestry.
GIVEN NAMES French 5%. *Marcel* (2), *Macaire*.

French (24588) English and Scottish: **1.** ethnic name for someone from France, Middle English *frensche*, or in some cases perhaps a nickname for someone who adopted French airs. **2.** variant of Anglo-Norman French FRAIN.

Frenette (471) North American form of French **Frenet**, a topographic name for someone who lived on a property of which ash trees were a characteristic feature, from a diminutive of Old French *fresne* (French *frêne*) 'ash tree'.
FOREBEARS A bearer of the name from Nor-

mandy, France, was in Neuville, Quebec, by 1684.
GIVEN NAMES French 16%. *Andre* (2), *Emile* (2), *Fernand* (2), *Benoit*, *Colette*, *Donat*, *Francois*, *Jean Marc*, *Jean-Robert*, *Julien*, *Laurier*, *Luc*.

Freni (132) Southern Italian: patronymic or plural form of **Freno**, a nickname from Calabrian *freno* 'hay' (Italian *fieno*, from Latin *fenum*).
GIVEN NAMES Italian 32%. *Salvatore* (3), *Rocco* (2), *Santo* (2), *Carmelo*, *Costantino*, *Domenic*, *Franco*, *Giovanna*, *Giuseppe*, *Orazio*, *Pina*, *Sante*.

Frenier (115) French: topographic name for someone who lived where there was an abundance of ash trees, from a derivative of French *frêne* 'ash tree' (Old French *fresne*).
GIVEN NAMES French 7%. *Andre*, *Antoine*.

Frenkel (495) Jewish (Ashkenazic) and German: variant of FRANKEL.
GIVEN NAMES Jewish 17%; Russian 12%; German 4%. *Chaim* (4), *Gerson* (4), *Yakov* (4), *Aron* (2), *Moisey* (2), *Volf* (2), *Feyga*, *Filipp*, *Irina*, *Irit*, *Isidor*, *Izak*; *Boris* (9), *Leonid* (4), *Arkadiy* (3), *Lev* (3), *Mikhail* (3), *Anatoly* (2), *Galina* (2), *Vladimir* (2), *Aleksandr*, *Grigoriy*, *Igor*, *Konstantin*; *Armin* (2), *Dieter*, *Frieda*, *Hans*, *Lothar*, *Viktor*, *Wolf*.

Frens (127) Dutch: variant of FRANS.

Frensley (113) Americanized spelling of German **Frenzle**, **Fränzle**, a South German pet form of the personal name FRANZ.

Frentz (193) German: variant spelling of FRENZ.
GIVEN NAMES German 5%. *Dieter*, *Gerlinde*, *Gunter*, *Konrad*.

Frentzel (139) German: variant spelling of FRENZEL.

Frenz (234) **1.** South German: variant of FRANZ. **2.** North German: from a short form of the personal name *Lafrens*, a variant of *Laurens* (see LAWRENCE).
GIVEN NAMES German 7%. *Armin*, *Gerhard*, *Gerhart*, *Horst*, *Konrad*, *Mathias*.

Frenzel (623) South German: from a pet form of FRANZ.
GIVEN NAMES German 9%. *Otto* (5), *Kurt* (4), *Alois*, *Florian*, *Gerhard*, *Guenter*, *Heinz*, *Helmut*, *Reinhard*, *Rudi*, *Uwe*, *Wilhelm*.

Frere (153) **1.** English: variant of FREER 1. **2.** French (**Frère**): from *frère* 'brother', used as a byname for the younger of two brothers.
GIVEN NAMES French 13%. *Emile*, *Henri*, *Jacques*, *Marcel*, *Michel*.

Freres (100) Luxembourgeois: presumably a variant of French FRERE.
GIVEN NAMES German 6%. *Heinz*, *Manfred*.

Frerich (168) North German: from a Low German form of FRIEDRICH.

Frerichs (1046) North German: patronymic from FRERICH.
GIVEN NAMES German 4%. *Erwin* (2), *Arno*, *Franz*, *Fritz*, *Gerhard*, *Kurt*, *Reinhard*.

Frericks (287) North German: patronymic from a Frisian form of FRIEDRICH.

Frerking (225) North German: variant of FREDERKING.
GIVEN NAMES German 4%. *Armin*, *Otto*.

Fresch (118) Probably an Americanized form of German FRISCH 2.

Fresco (146) Italian: from a reduced form of the personal name *Francisco* (see FRANCIS).
GIVEN NAMES Italian 11%; Spanish 10%; French 7%. *Angelo*, *Antonio*, *Cira*, *Dante*, *Franco*, *Nicola*, *Rocco*; *Alfredo*, *Arcadio*, *Jose*, *Luis*, *Manuel*, *Ramon*, *Rogelio*, *Sergio*; *Alain*, *Jacques*, *Raoul*.

Frese (704) North German: variant of FRIES.
GIVEN NAMES German 5%. *Wolfgang* (2), *Dieter*, *Egon*, *Ernst*, *Erwin*, *Hermann*, *Markus*.

Fresh (279) Possibly an Americanized form of German and Jewish FRISCH or a translation of French LEDOUX.

Freshley (117) Probably an Americanized spelling of German **Fröschli** or **Fröschle**, diminutives of FROSCH.

Freshman (144) Americanized form of German and Jewish **Frischmann** (see FRISCHMAN).
GIVEN NAMES Jewish 4%. *Hyman*, *Myer*.

Freshour (673) Americanized spelling of German **Froschauer** (or **Fröschauer**), a habitational name from any of several places named Froschau, from Old High German *frosc* 'frog' + *ouwa* 'wet land'.

Freshwater (422) English: topographic name for someone who lived by a source of clear drinking water, from Middle English *fresch* 'fresh', 'not salty' (Old French *freis*, of Germanic origin). There is a place of this name on the Isle of Wight (named from Old English *fersc* 'fresh' + *wæter* 'water'), which may also be a source of the surname.

Freson (101) French (common in Belgium; also **Fréson**): from a pet form of *frère* 'brother'.

Fresquez (407) Hispanic (**Frésquez**): unexplained.
GIVEN NAMES Spanish 18%. *Manuel* (5), *Juan* (3), *Anselmo* (2), *Ramon* (2), *Adela*, *Alvino*, *Araceli*, *Arturo*, *Bernardo*, *Delfino*, *Demetrio*, *Emilio*.

Fretheim (125) **1.** Norwegian: habitational name from either of two farmsteads so named in Sogn, probably from a river name + *heim* 'homestead', 'farmstead'. **2.** German: unexplained.
GIVEN NAMES Scandinavian 12%; German 8%. *Erik*; *Gerhard* (2), *Inge*.

Frett (230) English: from Middle English *frette*, Old French *frete* 'interlaced work (in metal and precious stones)' such as was used for hair ornaments and the like, hence a metonymic occupational name for a maker of such pieces.
GIVEN NAMES French 4%. *Camille*, *Monique*.

Fretwell (733) English: habitational name from a minor place in West Yorkshire, where the surname is commonest, probably so called from Old English *freht* 'augury' + *well(a)* 'spring', 'stream'. Fritwell in Oxfordshire is of the same derivation, but appears not to have contributed to the surname.

Fretz (706) German: variant of FRITZ.

Freud (101) **1.** German and Jewish (Ashkenazic): nickname for a person of a cheerful disposition, from Middle High German *vröude, vreude* 'joy', German *Freud(e)*. As a Jewish name it can also be an ornamental name. **2.** Jewish (Ashkenazic): metronymic from the Yiddish personal name *Freyde* meaning 'joy'.

Freudenberg (307) **1.** Jewish (Ashkenazic): ornamental name composed of German *Freude* 'joy' + *Berg* 'mountain', 'hill'. **2.** German and Jewish (Ashkenazic): habitational name from any of several places named Freudenberg, from Middle High German *vreude* 'joy' + *berc* 'hill'.
GIVEN NAMES German 7%. *Erwin* (2), *Albrecht, Kurt, Otto, Wolf.*

Freudenberger (148) **1.** German: habitational name from any of the places called FREUDENBERG. **2.** Jewish (Ashkenazic): ornamental name, an extension of FREUDENBERG 1.

Freudenthal (186) Eastern German and Jewish (Ashkenazic): habitational name for someone from any of several places named Freudenthal, from Middle High German *vreude* 'joy' + *tal* 'valley'. In some cases the Jewish surname may be ornamental.
GIVEN NAMES German 7%. *Kurt* (2), *Theodor.*

Freund (3223) **1.** German: nickname for a companionable person, from Middle High German *vriunt* 'friend'. **2.** Jewish (Ashkenazic): ornamental name from German *Freund* 'friend'.
GIVEN NAMES German 5%; Jewish 4%. *Kurt* (7), *Otto* (5), *Erwin* (2), *Gerhard* (2), *Hans* (2), *Angelika, Benno, Egon, Erna, Eugen, Friedrich, Fritz; Chaim* (5), *Moshe* (3), *Emanuel* (2), *Itzhak* (2), *Leibish* (2), *Miriam* (2), *Pincus* (2), *Shaya* (2), *Aryeh, Avi, Avner, Avrohom.*

Freundlich (239) German and Jewish (Ashkenazic): nickname meaning 'friendly', a derivative of FREUND. Among Jews this is mainly an ornamental name.
GIVEN NAMES German 6%; Jewish 5%. *Herta, Kurt; Miriam, Yehudah, Zev.*

Frevert (235) North German: presumably from the personal name *Fredebert*. This surname is documented in Westphalia in the 17th century.
GIVEN NAMES German 6%. *Otto* (2), *Heinz, Kurt.*

Frew (779) Scottish: habitational name from the Fords of Frew, a fortified site on the Forth river, probably so called from a British element *frwd* 'current', 'stream'. This place was the lowest crossing point on the river Forth, and so an important strategic location in the Middle Ages.

Frey (13851) German: status name for a free man, as opposed to a bondsman or serf, in the feudal system, from Middle High German *vrī* 'free', 'independent'.

Freye (112) German: variant of FREY.
GIVEN NAME German 5%. *Kurt* (2).

Freyer (482) German: variant spelling of FREIER.
GIVEN NAMES German 5%. *Kurt* (2), *Hans, Heinz, Klaus, Rainer, Uwe, Wolfang.*

Freyermuth (156) German: variant of FREIMUTH.
GIVEN NAME German 4%. *Lorenz.*

Freyman (173) **1.** Jewish (Ashkenazic): variant of FREIMAN 1. **2.** German (**Freymann**): status name for a free man in the feudal system (see FREY, FREIER).
GIVEN NAMES Russian 7%; Jewish 7%. *Lev* (2), *Boris, Igor, Semyon, Yevgenia; Bronya, Ilya, Irina, Meyer, Zinaida.*

Freymiller (108) German: status name for a miller who was a free man, not a bondsman, in the feudal system.

Freyre (148) Probably a variant spelling of Portuguese and Galician FREIRE.
GIVEN NAMES Spanish 43%. *Jose* (6), *Armando* (3), *Arturo* (3), *Carlos* (2), *Fernando* (2), *Jorge* (2), *Julio* (2), *Mario* (2), *Ruben* (2), *Sulma* (2), *Alba, Alvaro.*

Freytag (453) German and Jewish (Ashkenazic): variant spelling of FREITAG.
GIVEN NAMES German 8%. *Friedhelm* (2), *Kurt* (2), *Baerbel, Bernd, Dietrich, Erwin, Hans, Otto, Rainer.*

Frezza (211) Southern Italian: metonymic occupational name for an arrow maker, from *frezza* 'arrow', a variant of Italian *freccia*.
GIVEN NAMES Italian 16%. *Dante* (2), *Agostino, Alessio, Carlo, Carmine, Domenic, Elio, Francesco, Luigi, Nicola, Reno, Salvatore.*

Friant (185) French: nickname for a glutton (culinary or amorous), from Old French *friand* 'gourmand'. This occurs as a secondary surname for **Claudet**.
GIVEN NAMES French 5%. *Patrice* (2), *Andre.*

Friar (592) English: variant of FREER.

Frias (1476) Spanish (**Frías**) and Portuguese: habitational name from any of various places, for example in the provinces of Burgos and Teruel, so called from the feminine plural form of the adjective *frío* 'cold' (Latin *frigidus*); a noun such as *aguas* 'waters' or *fuentes* 'springs' has been lost.
GIVEN NAMES Spanish 50%; Portuguese 10%. *Jose* (39), *Juan* (33), *Luis* (18), *Carlos* (15), *Rafael* (15), *Manuel* (13), *Ramon* (13), *Francisco* (11), *Pedro* (10), *Jesus* (8), *Mario* (8), *Ana* (7); *Duarte, Wenceslao.*

Friberg (603) **1.** Scandinavian: either an ornamental name composed of *fri* 'free' + *berg* 'hill', 'mountain' or a habitational name from a place so named. **2.** German and Jewish (Ashkenazic): variant spelling of FREIBERG.

GIVEN NAMES Scandinavian 9%. *Birgit, Elof, Lars, Nils, Per, Viljo.*

Fricano (258) Italian: ethnic name for someone from Africa, from a reduced form of *africano* 'African'.
GIVEN NAMES Italian 24%. *Salvatore* (5), *Antonio* (4), *Onofrio* (2), *Sal* (2), *Carlo, Cosimo, Maddalena, Nicolo, Rosario.*

Frick (4044) German and Swiss German: **1.** from a short form of any of the Low German forms of FRIEDRICH. **2.** habitational name from a place so named in the Swiss canton of Aargau.

Fricke (2203) German and Swiss German: variant of FRICK.
GIVEN NAMES German 4%. *Otto* (3), *Gerd* (2), *Hans* (2), *Klaus* (2), *Armin, Ernst, Gerhard, Gotthilf, Hartmut, Juergen, Kurt, Manfred.*

Frickel (128) German: from a pet form of FRIEDRICH.

Fricker (501) **1.** English: nickname from an agent derivative of Middle English *frik(i)en* 'to move briskly or nimbly' (from Old English *frician* 'to dance'). **2.** Swiss and German: variant of FRICK 2. **3.** German and Swiss German: habitational name for someone from the Frick valley in Baden.
GIVEN NAMES German 5%. *Helmut* (2), *Georg, Manfred, Markus, Otto.*

Frickey (260) **1.** English: unexplained. **2.** Perhaps an Americanized spelling of German **Fricke**, a variant of FRICK.

Fricks (546) Altered form of German FRITZ.

Frid (167) **1.** Jewish (eastern Ashkenazic): variant of FRIED. **2.** Swedish: ornamental name from *frid* 'peace'.
GIVEN NAMES Russian 18%; Jewish 13%; Scandinavian 7%. *Leonid* (4), *Arkady* (2), *Boris* (2), *Vladimir* (2), *Aleksandr, Genady, Gennady, Igor, Lev, Mikhail, Semyon, Svetlana; Gershon, Ilya, Mariya, Nurit, Polina, Simcha; Lars* (2), *Nels* (2).

Friday (2285) Americanized form of German or Jewish FREITAG; in some cases the surname may be the much rarer English cognate, from Old English *friggandæg* 'Friday', which Reaney suggests may also have been used to denote a person with a gloomy disposition.

Friddell (112) Probably a variant spelling of FRIDELL.

Friddle (452) Probably an Americanized spelling of FRIDELL.

Fridell (137) **1.** Swedish: ornamental name from *frid* 'peace' + *-ell*, a common suffix of Swedish surnames, taken from the Latin adjectival ending *-elius*. **2.** Altered spelling of German FRIEDEL.

Fridge (113) Scottish and English: apparently a variant spelling of **Frigge**, which Reaney believes may be a nickname for a timid person, derived from Middle English *friggen* 'to quiver'.

Fridley (852) Americanized spelling of German FRIEDLI.

Fridman (470) Jewish (eastern Ashkenazic): variant of FRIEDMANN.

GIVEN NAMES Russian 33%; Jewish 27%. *Boris* (22), *Mikhail* (10), *Vladimir* (10), *Leonid* (8), *Lev* (6), *Yefim* (6), *Iosif* (4), *Galina* (3), *Grigoriy* (3), *Semyon* (3), *Svetlana* (3), *Yelena* (3); *Ilya* (4), *Moisey* (4), *Semen* (3), *Yakov* (3), *Aron* (2), *Isaak* (2), *Leyb* (2), *Miriam* (2), *Naum* (2), *Zelik* (2), *Ayelet*, *Basya*.

Fridrich (163) Czech: from the personal name *Fridrich*, Czech form of FRIEDRICH.

GIVEN NAME German 5%. *Heinz* (3).

Frie (246) German: variant of FREY.

GIVEN NAMES German 5%. *Friedrich*, *Ulrike*, *Wolfgang*.

Friebel (178) German: from a pet form of any of various Germanic personal names formed with *frid* 'peace', as for example *Fredebert* or *Fredbern*.

GIVEN NAMES German 5%. *Otto*, *Winfried*.

Frieberg (102) Danish, Swedish, and North German: variant of German FREIBERG.

GIVEN NAMES Scandinavian 6%. *Erik*, *Lars*.

Fried (3318) **1.** Jewish (Ashkenazic): from Yiddish *frid* 'peace'. Compare modern German *Friede*, which was sometimes chosen as a translation of the Hebrew personal name *Shlomo*, whose root letters are the same as those of *shalom* 'peace' (see SOLOMON), although in most cases it is simply an ornamental name. **2.** German: from a short form of the personal name FRIEDRICH.

GIVEN NAMES Jewish 7%; German 4%. *Sol* (5), *Asher* (4), *Chaim* (4), *Hyman* (4), *Meyer* (4), *Chani* (3), *Dov* (3), *Miriam* (3), *Yetta* (3), *Aron* (2), *Doron* (2), *Esti* (2); *Erwin* (6), *Wolf* (3), *Armin* (2), *Arno* (2), *Gottlieb* (2), *Kurt* (2), *Otto* (2), *Bernhard*, *Berthold*, *Erhard*, *Eugen*, *Gottlob*.

Friedberg (789) German and Jewish (Ashkenazic): habitational name from any of several places so named, from Middle High German *vride* 'peace', 'security', 'protection' + *berg* 'mountain', 'hill'. In some cases the Jewish name may be ornamental, from German *Friede* 'peace' + *berg* 'hill', 'mountain'.

GIVEN NAMES Jewish 4%. *Ahron* (2), *Miriam* (2), *Abbe*, *Dov*, *Gilah*, *Mort*, *Myer*.

Friede (244) German: from a short form of FRIEDRICH.

GIVEN NAMES German 9%. *Dieter* (2), *Heinz* (2), *Alois*, *Gerhard*, *Hasso*, *Kurt*, *Wolf*.

Friedel (978) German: from a pet form of FRIEDRICH.

Friedemann (136) German and Jewish (Ashkenazic): variant of FRIEDMANN.

GIVEN NAMES German 8%. *Konrad* (2), *Frieda*, *Heinrich*, *Jutta*.

Frieden (431) Jewish (Ashkenazic): variant of FRIED or a short form of any of the various compound names beginning *Frieden-* of the same derivation.

GIVEN NAMES German 4%. *Fritz*, *Hans*, *Kurt*.

Friedenberg (257) Jewish (Ashkenazic): variant of FRIEDBERG.

GIVEN NAMES Jewish 8%; German 6%. *Isadore*, *Isidor*, *Pinhas*; *Erwin*, *Frieda*, *Otto*.

Frieder (190) **1.** German and Hungarian: from a short form of the personal name FRIEDRICH. **2.** Jewish (Ashkenazic): ornamental extension of FRIED, with the agent suffix *-er*.

GIVEN NAMES Jewish 7%; Hungarian 4%. *Ophir* (2), *Sol* (2), *Miriam*; *Jeno* (3).

Friederich (392) German: variant of FRIEDRICH.

GIVEN NAMES German 7%. *Kurt* (4), *Armin*, *Fritz*, *Gernot*, *Reinhard*.

Friederichs (168) German: patronymic from FRIEDERICH.

GIVEN NAMES German 5%. *Arno*, *Hans*, *Kurt*.

Frieders (144) North German: patronymic from FRIEDER.

GIVEN NAME German 4%. *Kurt* (2).

Friedhoff (182) Jewish (Ashkenazic): ornamental name composed of the German elements *Friede* 'peace' + *hof* 'courtyard'. Alternatively, it may be a topographic name from the German *Friedhof* 'graveyard', 'cemetery' (from Middle Low German, Middle High German *vrīthof* 'enclosed farmstead or courtyard', later 'cemetery').

GIVEN NAMES German 4%. *Fritz*, *Wolf*.

Friedl (501) South German: from a pet form of the personal name FRIEDRICH.

GIVEN NAMES German 7%. *Hans* (3), *Kurt* (2), *Bernhard*, *Friedrich*, *Guenther*, *Gunther*, *Horst*, *Oskar*.

Friedland (1235) German and Jewish (Ashkenazic): habitational name from any of various places bearing this name, for example in the former German territories of Prussia, Upper Silesia, and Bohemia. As a Jewish name, it is in many cases an ornamental name from the German elements *Friede* 'peace' and *Land* 'land'.

GIVEN NAMES Jewish 5%. *Sol* (3), *Miriam* (2), *Shaul* (2), *Avrom*, *Avron*, *Emanuel*, *Hyman*, *Meyer*, *Shai*, *Shulamith*, *Yitzchok*.

Friedlander (1574) German (also **Friedländer**) and Jewish (Ashkenazic): habitational name for someone from a place called FRIEDLAND, or a Jewish ornamental name from the elements *Friede* 'peace' and *Land* 'land'.

GIVEN NAMES Jewish 6%. *Miriam* (5), *Itzhak* (2), *Moshe* (2), *Sholom* (2), *Chaim*, *Emanuel*, *Golda*, *Hyman*, *Ilan*, *Leib*, *Liba*, *Menachem*.

Friedlein (124) German: from a pet form of the personal name FRIED.

Friedler (119) Jewish (Ashkenazic): ornamental name, an extension of *Fried*, with the agent suffix *-ler*.

GIVEN NAMES Jewish 13%; German 4%. *Aharon*, *Chana*, *Miriam*, *Moshe*, *Naftoli*, *Sol*, *Yossi*; *Otto*.

Friedley (192) Americanized spelling of Swiss German FRIEDLI.

Friedli (219) Swiss German: from a pet form of the personal name FRIEDRICH.

GIVEN NAMES German 8%. *Armin* (3), *Hans* (2), *Otto* (2).

Friedline (255) Americanized spelling of **Friedlein**, from a South German pet form of the personal name FRIEDRICH.

Friedly (211) Variant spelling of Swiss German FRIEDLI.

Friedman (19782) **1.** Respelling of South German and Swiss FRIEDMANN. **2.** Jewish (Ashkenazic): elaborated form of FRIED.

GIVEN NAMES Jewish 8%. *Sol* (37), *Hyman* (28), *Chaim* (21), *Emanuel* (20), *Moshe* (20), *Meyer* (19), *Miriam* (19), *Isadore* (17), *Zvi* (14), *Aron* (12), *Ari* (8), *Mendel* (8).

Friedmann (574) **1.** German and Swiss German: from a derivative of FRIEDRICH. **2.** Jewish (Ashkenazic): variant of FRIEDMAN.

GIVEN NAMES German 6%. *Kurt* (4), *Hans* (3), *Alois*, *Bernhard*, *Ingeborg*, *Reiner*, *Siegfried*.

Friedrich (2650) German: from a personal name composed of the Germanic elements *frid*, *fred* 'peace' + *rīc* 'power'. The name was borne by a canonized 9th-century bishop of Utrecht, and was a hereditary name among the Hohenstaufen ruling family; hence its popularity in central Europe.

GIVEN NAMES German 8%. *Kurt* (7), *Otto* (6), *Hans* (4), *Ernst* (3), *Ewald* (3), *Franz* (3), *Gerhard* (3), *Heiner* (3), *Heinz* (3), *Helmuth* (3), *Klaus* (3), *Reinhard* (3).

Friedrichs (620) German: patronymic from FRIEDRICH.

GIVEN NAMES German 5%. *Hans* (5), *Manfred* (3), *Alois*, *Erwin*, *Gunther*, *Heinz*, *Joerg*.

Friedrichsen (355) North German and Danish: patronymic from FRIEDRICH.

GIVEN NAMES German 9%; Scandinavian 4%. *Hans* (6), *Kurt* (2), *Darrold*, *Detlef*, *Dieter*, *Hermann*, *Inge*, *Nicolaus*, *Otto*.

Friedt (214) Variant of German FRIED.

Friel (1788) **1.** Irish (common in Donegal, and now also in Glasgow): from Gaelic **Ó Frighil**, which is probably a metathesized variant of **Ó Fearghail** (see FARRELL). **2.** German: from a pet form of FRIEDRICH.

GIVEN NAMES Irish 5%. *Aileen*, *Brendan*, *Brigid*, *Colm*, *Colum*, *Kieran*.

Frieling (171) **1.** Jewish (Ashkenazic): ornamental name from Yiddish *friling* 'spring', or a Yiddishized form of FRUHLING. **2.** German: from a status name meaning 'free man' (as opposed to bondsman in the feudal system), Middle High German *vrīling* 'free man'. **3.** German: habitational name from any of several places named Frieling. **4.** German: variant of **Frühling** (see FRUHLING).

GIVEN NAME German 5%. *Gerhardt*.

Frieman (173) **1.** Jewish (American): Americanized spelling of FREIMAN. **2.** North German form (**Friemann**) of FREI.

GIVEN NAMES Jewish 9%. *Herschel, Iren, Shlomo, Varda.*

Friemel (118) German: variant of FROMMELT.

Friend (6371) **1.** English: nickname for a companionable person, from Middle English *frend* 'friend' (Old English *frēond*). In the Middle Ages the term was also used to denote a relative or kinsman, and the surname may also have been acquired by someone who belonged to the family of someone who was a more important figure in the community. **2.** American translation of Jewish and German FREUND.

Friendly (117) American translated form of German and Jewish FREUNDLICH.

Friends (127) English: variant of FRIEND.

Frier (512) **1.** English: variant of FREER 1. **2.** North German: from a reduced form of FRIEDER. **3.** Danish: of uncertain origin; possibly the same as 2.

Frierson (1374) English: patronymic from **Frier** (see FREER 1).

Fries (3354) German, Dutch, Jewish (from the Netherlands), Danish, and Swedish: **1.** ethnic name for someone from Friesland. The name of this region is ancient and of uncertain origin; the most plausible speculation derives it from an Indo-European root *prei-* 'to cut', with reference to the dikes necessary for the cultivation of low-lying land. There is archaeological evidence of the construction of ditches and dams along the southern shores of the North Sea from at least the time of Christ. **2.** occupational name for a builder of dams and dikes. The word was used in this sense in various parts of Germany during the Middle Ages, and is probably a transferred use of the ethnic term, dike building being a characteristic occupation of Frieslanders. **3.** diminutive of FRIEDRICH.

Friese (775) German, Dutch, Danish, and Swedish: variant of FRIES.

GIVEN NAMES German 5%. *Otto* (3), *Kurt* (2), *Ulrich* (2), *Egon, Gerhard, Guenther, Hans, Horst, Juergen, Rudi, Wolf.*

Friesen (2581) German and Dutch: patronymic from FRIES.

Friesenhahn (247) German: presumably a reduced form of **Friesenhagen**, a habitational name from Friesenhagen near Siegen.

GIVEN NAMES German 6%. *Erhardt, Gottlieb, Liesl, Ottmar.*

Friesner (300) German: **1.** possibly a habitational name from a place in eastern Germany named Friesen. **2.** occupational name for a builder of dikes (see FRIES 2).

Frieson (189) Altered spelling of German FRIESEN.

Friess (484) German: variant of FRIES.

GIVEN NAMES German 5%. *Kurt* (3), *Florian, Otto, Wolfgang.*

Friesz (293) **1.** German: from a short form of FRIEDRICH. **2.** Dutch: patronymic from FRIES, **Vries**, ethnic name for a Frisian.

GIVEN NAME French 4%. *Damien.*

Friez (112) Possibly a respelling of northern French **Fries**, a variant of **Friche**, a topographic name for someone who lived by fallow land, *friche* (from Old French *fresche*).

GIVEN NAMES French 7%. *Julien, Nicolle.*

Frieze (355) Probably an altered spelling of FREESE or FRIES(E).

Frigo (279) **1.** Italian: from a short form of *Federigo*, an Italian form of FRIEDERICH. **2.** Americanized spelling of French **Frigault**, from the personal name *Frigowald, Frigald*, composed of the Germanic elements *fric* 'hard', 'harsh' + *waldan* 'to govern'.

GIVEN NAMES Italian 11%; French 5%. *Gino* (2), *Amedeo, Antonio, Dario, Dino, Enio, Erminio, Reno, Renzo, Rinaldo, Ulisse, Vitina; Andre, Dominique.*

Frigon (246) French: possibly from a byname from Old French *frigon* 'thread', 'strand'.

GIVEN NAMES French 12%. *Armand* (3), *Normand* (2), *Alphe, Celine, Emile.*

Friis (230) Scandinavian: ethnic name for someone from Friesland (see FRIES).

GIVEN NAMES Scandinavian 12%; German 6%. *Erik* (4), *Bente, Carsten, Johan, Niels, Nils; Fritz, Hans, Otto.*

Friley (161) Americanized spelling of German FREILICH.

Frilot (118) Variant of French FRILOUX.

GIVEN NAMES French 7%. *Alphonse, Andrus, Antoine.*

Friloux (104) French: according to Morlet, a nickname for someone who fears the cold, from a derivative of *friller* 'to shiver'.

GIVEN NAME French 6%. *Henri.*

Fringer (141) **1.** German: habitational name for someone from Efringen, Baden. **2.** possibly a partly Americanized variant of German **Wringer**, an occupational name for the operator of a cider or oil press or a nickname for an oppressor, from an agent derivative of Middle Low German *wringen* 'to twist or turn', 'to torture'.

Frings (102) North German: patronymic from a pet form of the personal name SEVERIN (see FRINK).

GIVEN NAMES German 16%. *Otto* (2), *Johannes, Kurt, Manfred, Wilhelm.*

Frink (1469) North German: reduced and altered pet form of the personal name SEVERIN. This surname is common in the Lower Rhine area. Compare FREIN.

Fripp (123) English: of uncertain derivation; possibly a metonymic occupational name for a dealer in old clothes, from a derivative of Old French *frepe* 'rag', from *frip(i)er* 'to tear to rags'.

Frisbee (649) English: variant spelling of FRISBY.

Frisbey (148) English: variant spelling of FRISBY.

Frisbie (1545) English: variant spelling of FRISBY.

Frisby (1139) English: habitational name from Frisby on the Wreake or Frisby by Gaulby, or another lost Frisby in Leicestershire, all named with Old Norse *Frísir* 'Frisians' (see FRIES 1) + *býr* 'farm', 'settlement'.

Frisch (2050) **1.** German and Scandinavian: from a medieval personal name, a pet form of FRIEDRICH. See also FRITZ. **2.** German: nickname for someone who was handsome, cheerful, or energetic, Middle High German *vrisch*. **3.** Jewish (Ashkenazic): ornamental name or nickname from modern German *frisch*, Yiddish *frish* 'fresh'.

GIVEN NAMES German 4%. *Kurt* (5), *Hans* (3), *Markus* (2), *Otto* (2), *Walther* (2), *Franz, Gottlieb, Ignatz, Klaus, Konrad, Manfred, Mathias.*

Frischkorn (139) **1.** Jewish (Ashkenazic): ornamental name composed of German *frisch* 'fresh' + *Korn* 'grain'. **2.** German: occupational nickname for a farmer, with the same meaning as 1.

Frischman (136) **1.** Respelling of German FRISCHMANN. **2.** Jewish (Ashkenazic): elaborated form of FRISCH.

GIVEN NAMES Jewish 12%; German 6%. *Meir* (3), *Sol* (2), *Hillel, Moshe, Ruchie; Eldor, Ewald, Kurt.*

Frischmann (110) **1.** German: from FRISCH with the addition of Middle High German *man* 'man' (modern German *Mann*). **2.** Jewish (Ashkenazic): see FRISCHMAN.

GIVEN NAMES German 10%. *Kurt* (2), *Erwin, Lieselotte.*

Friscia (300) Southern Italian (Sicily): if not of Albanian origin, possibly from an ethnic name from a female palatalized form of *frisius* 'Frisian'.

GIVEN NAMES Italian 22%. *Salvatore* (4), *Agostino, Antonio, Giuseppe, Palma, Pasquale, Pellegrino, Sal, Vito.*

Frisco (334) Spanish and Italian: from a reduced form of the personal name FRANCISCO (Spanish) or FRANCESCO (Italian); but here from the Latin form *Franciscus*.

Frisella (158) Italian: possibly from a diminutive of *Fresia* and hence an ethnic name for someone from Friesland, also applied as a personal name.

GIVEN NAMES Italian 9%. *Angelo, Salvatore, Vincenza.*

Frishman (248) **1.** Jewish (Ashkenazic): variant of FRISCHMAN(N). **2.** Americanized spelling of German FRISCHMANN.

GIVEN NAMES Jewish 7%. *Basya, Boruch, Hillel, Khana.*

Frisina (276) Italian: **1.** from a diminutive of *Fresia* and hence an ethnic name for someone from Friesland, also applied as a personal name. **2.** possibly a variant of **Frosina**, from a reduced form of the Greek personal name *Euphrosynē* 'joy', 'happiness'.

GIVEN NAMES Italian 23%. *Salvatore* (5), *Antonio* (3), *Angelo, Antonietta, Antonino, Carmine, Egidio, Giacomo, Giovanni, Luigi, Natale, Palma*.

Frisinger (199) South German: habitational name for someone from any of several places called Fri(e)sing or Freising. The place names probably derive from an Old High German personal name *Frīgis* + the patronymic suffix *-ing*.

Frisk (615) Danish and Swedish: from *Frisk*, a byname meaning 'healthy'.
GIVEN NAMES Scandinavian 4%. *Anders, Erik, Mats*.

Friske (343) German: presumably a derivative of FRIES, perhaps related to **Friesecke**.

Frison (389) French: ethnic name from *frison* 'Frisian'.

Frisone (134) Italian: ethnic name for a Frisian, Italian *frisone*.
GIVEN NAMES Italian 26%. *Antonio* (2), *Giovanni* (2), *Marco* (2), *Domenic, Francesco, Gino, Giulio, Giuseppe, Orazio, Pasquale*.

Frisque (138) French: nickname for a robust, healthy person, from Old French *frisque* 'lively', 'vigorous'.

Frissell (116) Variant spelling of English FRIZZELL.

Fristoe (236) Apparently of English or Welsh origin, but unexplained. The family was established in the Rappahannock valley in the 1660s.

Fritch (752) Americanized spelling of FRITSCH.

Fritcher (182) Americanized spelling of German FRITSCHE.

Fritchey (130) English (east midlands): habitational name from Fritchley in Derbyshire.

Fritchie (127) Americanized spelling of German **Fritsche** or the Alemannic (Swiss) form **Fritschi** (see FRITSCH).

Fritchman (237) Americanized spelling of German **Fritschmann**, a variant of FRITSCH.

Frith (1212) English and Scottish: variant of FIRTH.

Fritsch (1752) German: from a reduced form of FRIEDRICH.
GIVEN NAMES German 5%. *Kurt* (5), *Arno* (2), *Beate* (2), *Erwin* (2), *Gerhard* (2), *Dieter, Guenther, Hans, Helmut, Jutta, Klaus, Rudi*.

Fritsche (777) German: variant of FRITSCH.
GIVEN NAMES German 6%. *Erwin* (4), *Johann* (3), *Otto* (2), *Eldor, Erhard, Manfred, Reinhard, Siegfried, Ulrich*.

Fritter (171) English: variant of **Fretter**, an occupational name for a maker of ornaments (especially for the hair) consisting of jewels set in a lattice network, from an agent derivative of Middle English *frette*, Old French *frete* 'interlaced work'.

Fritts (2248) Americanized spelling of FRITZ.

Fritz (13225) German: from a pet form of FRIEDRICH. It is also found as a surname in Denmark, Sweden, and elsewhere.

Fritze (347) Variant of German FRITZ.
GIVEN NAMES German 6%. *Erwin* (2), *Erna, Gunther, Hans, Kurt, Otto*.

Fritzen (142) German and Danish: patronymic or pet form of FRITZ (see FRIEDRICH).
GIVEN NAME German 5%. *Claus* (2).

Fritzinger (310) German: patronymic from FRITZ.

Fritzler (390) German: patronymic from a pet form of FRITZ.
GIVEN NAMES German 6%. *Kurt* (3), *Ulrich* (2), *Gerhart*.

Fritzsche (319) German: variant of FRITSCHE.
GIVEN NAMES German 11%. *Kurt* (3), *Gerhard* (2), *Dieter, Eldred, Hellmut, Otto, Ulrich, Wolfgang*.

Frix (235) Altered form of German FRITZ. Compare FRICKS.

Frizell (224) English: variant spelling of FRIZZELL.

Frizzell (2182) Irish and English (of Norman origin): **1.** nickname for someone who affected an ornate style of dress, from Old French *frisel, fresel* 'decoration', 'ribbon', 'tassel', 'fringe' (a diminutive of *frese*, of Germanic origin). **2.** Anglicized form of **Friseal**, Scottish Gaelic form of FRASER.

Frizzle (119) English: variant spelling of FRIZZELL.

Froberg (247) **1.** North German: habitational name for someone from Frohburg, Saxony (also recorded as *Froberg*, in the 16th century). **2.** North German: possibly from the female personal name *Froburg* (recorded in the 13th century in Hamburg). **3.** Danish (**Frøberg**): habitational name from a place called Frøbjerg. **4.** Anglicized form of Swedish **Fröberga**, habitational name from any of several places in Sweden of this name (either from *frö* 'fertile', 'rich', or from the name of the goddess *Fröja*), or possibly an ornamental name from the same elements.
GIVEN NAMES German 4%; Scandinavian 4%. *Eward, Kurt; Nils, Sven*.

Frock (424) English: **1.** metonymic occupational name for a maker or seller of men's outer garments, Old French *froc*. **2.** possibly a variant of FROGGE.

Frodge (104) English or Scottish: probably an altered form of the nickname **Frog** (see FROGGE).

Froebel (101) German: **1.** from a pet form of a personal name formed with the first element Old High German *frō* 'swift', 'happy'. **2.** in some cases, possibly a nickname from Sorbian *wrobel* 'sparrow'.
GIVEN NAMES German 11%; Scandinavian 6%. *Kurt* (2), *Helmuth; Gunner*.

Froedge (111) Altered form of German **(P)Frötzschner**, a variant of **Fretschner**, an occupational name from Middle High German *pfretzner* 'small trader', 'huckster'. The *-ö-* variant was common in the Upper Palatinate and Saxony.

Froehle (174) German and Swiss German (**Fröhle**): from a pet form of the Germanic name element *Frod-*, represented in the Old and Middle High German adjective *fruot* 'wise', 'sensible'.

Froehlich (1899) German (**Fröhlich**) and Jewish (Ashkenazic): nickname for a person with a cheerful temperament, from German *fröhlich* 'happy', 'cheerful' (a derivative of *froh* 'happy', Middle High German *frō*).
GIVEN NAMES German 7%. *Erwin* (9), *Kurt* (9), *Hans* (5), *Ulrich* (3), *Gerhard* (2), *Otto* (2), *Reinhardt* (2), *Claus, Dieter, Dietrich, Franz, Fritz*.

Froehling (120) Variant of German **Frühling** (see FRUHLING).

Froelich (1204) German (**Frölich**): variant of FROEHLICH.
GIVEN NAMES German 4%. *Kurt* (6), *Otto* (2), *Herta, Horst, Rudi*.

Froemming (346) North German (**Frömming**): patronymic from FROMM.

Froese (306) Eastern German (**Fröse**): probably a habitational name of Slavic origin from either of two places: Frohse or Frose.
GIVEN NAMES German 9%. *Dieter* (2), *Arno, Detlef, Helmut, Kurt, Otto, Willi*.

Froggatt (121) English: habitational name from Froggatt in Derbyshire.

Frogge (195) English: derogatory nickname for someone thought to resemble a frog in some way, from Old English *frogga* 'frog'.

Froh (166) German: perhaps a shortened form of any of a number of compound names formed with Froh-, from Middle High German *vrô* 'cheerful, happy'.
GIVEN NAMES German 4%. *Erwin, Wolfgang*.

Frohlich (515) German (**Frölich**) and Jewish (Ashkenazic): see FROEHLICH.
GIVEN NAMES German 9%. *Gerhard* (3), *Hans* (3), *Heinz* (3), *Franz, Gunter, Horst, Johann, Kurt, Otto, Reinhard, Willi, Wolfgang*.

Frohling (166) South German: variant of **Frühling** (see FRUHLING).
GIVEN NAME French 4%. *Lucien* (2).

Frohman (245) German (**Frohmann**): variant of *Frommann*, itself a variant of FROMM 1, or alternatively an assimilated form of **Fronmann**, a status name for someone in the service or retinue of a feudal lord, from Old High German *frôn* 'lord', 'master' + *man* 'man', 'follower'.

Frohn (148) German: occupational name from Middle High German *vrône* 'court messenger', 'bailiff'.
GIVEN NAMES German 5%. *Helmut, Otto*.

Frohock (156) English (Cambridgeshire): unexplained.

Froiland (105) Norwegian: habitational name from a farmstead named Froyland, from *Frey(a)*, the name of an Old Norse deity, + *land* 'farmstead'.
GIVEN NAME Scandinavian 11%. *Erik*.

Froio (221) Italian (Sicily): unexplained.
GIVEN NAMES Italian 17%. *Salvatore* (3), *Angelo, Antonio, Domenic, Rocco, Saverio*.

Frolich (103) German (**Frölich**) and Jewish (Ashkenazic): variant of FROEHLICH.
GIVEN NAMES German 7%. *Fritz, Helmut*.

From (230) **1.** Jewish (Ashkenazic): variant spelling of FROMM. **2.** Swedish: soldier's name based on Swedish *from* 'quiet', 'pious'. **3.** Danish: adoption of German FROMM 1. **4.** Altered spelling of German FROHMAN.

Froman (691) **1.** Respelling of Jewish (Ashkenazic) **Fromman(n)**, from FROMM, with the addition of Yiddish *man* or German *Mann* 'man'. **2.** Respelling of German **Frommann**, a variant of FROMM 1, with the addition of Middle High German *man* 'man', or of **Frohmann** (see FROHMAN).

Frome (200) English: habitational name from any of various places so called from the rivers on which they stand, or simply a name for someone living beside a river of this name, which is probably cognate with Welsh *ffraw* 'fair', 'fine', 'brisk'. Compare FRAMPTON.

Fromer (204) **1.** German: nickname from Middle Low German *vromer* 'hero', 'outstanding man'. **2.** Jewish (Ashkenazic): nickname for a pious man, from a noun derivative or inflected form of FROMM.
GIVEN NAMES Jewish 6%. *Miriam, Sol*.

Fromm (1319) **1.** German: nickname for an honorable man, from Middle High German *vrum, vrom* 'capable', 'honorable', 'trustworthy'. **2.** Jewish (Ashkenazic): nickname for a pious man, from German *fromm* 'devout', 'pious' (a later sense of the same word as in 1).
GIVEN NAMES German 4%. *Erwin* (3), *Egon* (2), *Fritz* (2), *Hilde* (2), *Kurt* (2), *Bernhard, Heinz*.

Fromme (376) German: variant of FROMM.
GIVEN NAMES German 5%. *Klaus* (2), *Kurt* (2), *Hermann*.

Frommelt (232) German: from the medieval personal name (once favored by the nobility) *Frumold, Fromolt*, from Middle High German *vrum, vrom* 'valiant', 'steadfast' + *-old* from Germanic *walt* 'leader'.

Frommer (301) German: from the nominalized form of the adjective *frommer*, an inflected form of *fromm*, originally meaning 'outstanding man'.
GIVEN NAMES German 6%. *Manfred* (2), *Wolf* (2), *Hans, Otto*.

Fron (122) French: from a reduced form of the medieval personal name *Frodon*, citation form of *Frodo*, based on Germanic *frod* 'wise', 'sensible'.
GIVEN NAME French 5%. *Camille*.

Fronczak (329) Polish: variant of FRANCZAK.
GIVEN NAMES Polish 4%. *Henryka, Lucjan, Miroslaw, Zygmond*.

Fronczek (129) Polish: variant of **Franczek**, from a pet form of the personal name *Franciszek*, a vernacular form of Latin *Franciscus* (see FRANCIS).

Froneberger (115) German: habitational name for someone from any of several places called Fronberg or Frohneberg. *Fron* is a common initial element of compound place names; from Middle High German *vrôn* 'lord', 'domain', it indicates a feudal estate.

Fronek (182) Czech (**Froněk**): from a pet form of the personal name *František*, a vernacular form of Latin *Franciscus* (see FRANCIS).

Frongillo (122) Italian: unexplained.
GIVEN NAMES Italian 5%. *Carmine, Filiberto, Guido*.

Fronheiser (141) Variant of German **Fronhäuser**, a habitational name for someone from any of several places called Fro(h)nhausen.

Froning (177) German (also **Fröning**): patronymic from *Fron*, a common element of names, from Old High German *frôno* 'belonging to a lord', 'master', hence a status name for someone in the service of a feudal lord.

Fronk (517) Variant of German FRANK.

Frontera (208) Spanish: topographic name for someone who lived on the boundary of an estate or some other geographical divide, from *frontera* 'frontier', 'boundary' (Latin *frons*, genitive *frontis* 'front'), or a habitational name from La Frontera in the province of Cuenca.
GIVEN NAMES Spanish 8%; Italian 5%. *Carlos* (2), *Miguel* (2), *Guillermo, Jaime, Luis, Raul, Roberto*; *Antonio* (3), *Vincenzo*.

Frontiero (102) Italian: probably a variant of **Frontiera**, from *frontiera* 'ornament worn on the forehead by women'.
GIVEN NAMES Italian 13%. *Salvatore* (2), *Gaetano, Gasper, Sal*.

Frontino (156) Italian: descriptive nickname from *frontino* 'forehead'.
GIVEN NAMES Italian 12%. *Vincenzo* (2), *Carmelo, Domenico*.

Frontz (173) Altered form of German FRANTZ.

Froom (121) **1.** English: variant spelling of FROME. **2.** German: from a short form of a personal name composed with Middle High German *vrom, vrum* 'valiant', 'steadfast' (see FROMMELT).

Frosch (371) German: from Middle High German *vrosch* 'frog', applied as a nickname for someone thought to resemble a frog, perhaps because he had bulging eyes (a common symptom of a disorder of the thyroid gland), but also attested as a house name, from which the surname may have arisen in some instances.

Froseth (116) Norwegian: unexplained.

Fross (199) Variant of German FRAAS.

Frost (15682) English, German, Danish, and Swedish: nickname for someone of an icy and unbending disposition or who had white hair or a white beard, from Old English, Old High German, Old Norse *frost* 'frost', or in the case of the Swedish name from a byname with the same meaning.

Frostad (109) Norwegian: habitational name from a farmstead in western Norway, so named from the personal name *Frode* + *stad* (from Old Norse *staðr* 'farmstead', 'dwelling').
GIVEN NAMES Scandinavian 17%; German 6%. *Lars* (3), *Berger, Hjalmer, Knut, Theodor*.

Frothingham (173) English: habitational name from Frodingham in Lincolnshire or North Frodingham in East Yorkshire, both named as 'homestead (Old English *hām*) of Frôd(a)'s people'. Medieval forms in *Froth-* are common, possibly as a result of Scandinavian influence. The surname is not found in current English records.

Frownfelter (145) Americanized spelling of German **Frauenfelder**, a habitational name for someone from any of several places called Frauenfeld. The place name is a compound probably of Middle High German *vrôn* 'lord', 'ruler', 'feudal domain' + *velt* 'open country', (later) 'field'.

Fruchey (179) Of German origin: see FRUTCHEY.

Fruchter (229) Jewish (Ashkenazic): metonymic occupational name for a grower or seller of fruit, from an agent derivative of German *Frucht* 'fruit', Yiddish *frukht*.
GIVEN NAMES Jewish 21%. *Yaakov* (2), *Akiva, Chaim, Chana, Dov, Emanuel, Hadassah, Haim, Hersh, Mayer, Menachem, Merav*.

Fruchtman (187) Jewish: variant of FRUCHTER.

Frueh (441) German and Swiss German (**Früh**): from Middle High German *vruo* 'early', applied as a nickname for an early riser or, more likely, used ironically for a sloth, and sometimes for a child born before or very early in the marriage.
GIVEN NAMES German 6%. *Franz* (2), *Mathias* (2), *Dieter, Erwin, Otto*.

Fruehauf (134) German (**Frühauf**): nickname for an early riser or an industrious person, from the phrase *früh auf* 'up early'.
GIVEN NAMES German 7%. *Alois, Heiner*.

Fruehling (122) German (**Frühling**) and Jewish (Ashkenazic): see FRUHLING.
GIVEN NAMES German 5%. *Eldor, Erwin*.

Fruge (1027) French (**Frugé**): probably an altered form of **Frugier, Fruger**, a habitational name from Frugière-le-Pin in Haute Loire.
FOREBEARS This name is very frequent in LA, where almost all bearers are descended from Pierre François Frugé, who arrived around 1754.

GIVEN NAMES French 5%. *Andre* (2), *Andrus* (2), *Romain* (2), *Antoine, Auguste, Curley, Octave, Pascal, Pierre.*

Fruhling (136) **1.** German (**Frühling**): nickname from Middle High German *vrüelinc* 'spring', in some cases for an early-born child. **2.** Jewish (Ashkenazic): from German *Frühling* 'spring'. It may be an ornamental name, or it may be one of the surnames that were distributed at random by government officials.

Fruhwirth (103) South German (**Frühwirth**): nickname for an innkeeper who was an early riser. The German word *fruh* 'early' is found in several such combinations.

GIVEN NAME German 4%. *Mathias.*

Fruin (258) English: from the Middle English personal name *Frewine*, Old English *Frēowine*, composed of the elements *frēo* 'free', 'noble', 'generous' (or the rarer *frēa* 'lord', 'master') + *wine* 'friend'.

Fruit (328) **1.** Translation of German **Frucht**, a nickname from Middle High German *vrucht* 'fruit', 'child', 'offspring', or possibly a Jewish ornamental name or a metonymic occupational name for a fruit grower, from German *Frucht* 'fruit'. **2.** Americanized spelling of German FRUTH. **3.** French: metonymic occupational name for a grower or seller of fruit, from *fruit* 'fruit' (Latin *fructus*).

Fruits (206) Apparently a variant of FRUIT or a folk translation of German **Früchte**, which, however, derives not from Middle High German *vrucht* 'fruit' (see FRUIT), but from Middle High German *vruchte* 'fear'.

Frum (253) **1.** Jewish (Ashkenazic): Yiddish form of FROMM. **2.** German: variant of FROMM.

Frumkin (240) Jewish (from Belarus): metronymic from the Yiddish female personal name *Frumke*, a pet form of *Frumet* (borrowed from German Christians) + the Slavic suffix *-in*.

GIVEN NAMES Russian 7%; Jewish 6%. *Arkady, Dmitri, Emanuil, Iosif, Lev, Tsilia, Veniamin, Vladimr, Zhanna; Ilya, Isak.*

Frush (167) Americanized spelling of German FROSCH.

Frushour (150) Americanized spelling of German **Froschauer** (see FRESHOUR).

Frutchey (151) Americanized form of Swiss German **Frutschi** or **Frautschi**, a pet form of the personal name FRIEDRICH.

Fruth (457) German: nickname from Middle High German *vruot* 'clever', 'astute'.

Frutiger (164) Swiss German: habitational name from a place called Fruttigen.

Frutos (114) **1.** Spanish: occupational or topographic name from the plural of Spanish *fruto* 'fruit'. **2.** Catalan (**Frutós**): variant of the Catalan personal names *Fructuós* or *Fruitós* (from Latin *Fructuosus*), or variant of the habitational name

from Sant Fruitós del Bages, a town in the district of El Bages, in Catalonia.

GIVEN NAMES Spanish 53%. *Andres* (2), *Cesar* (2), *Leticia* (2), *Manuel* (2), *Ruben* (2), *Salvador* (2), *Agustin, Ana, Angelina, Armando, Arturo, Benito; Antonio* (3).

Fry (14632) **1.** English (chiefly south and southwestern England): variant of FREE, from the Old English byform *frīg*. **2.** English: nickname for a small person, from Middle English *fry* 'small person', 'child', 'offspring' (Old Norse *frjó* 'seed'). **3.** Americanized spelling of German FREI, FREY.

Fryar (952) English: variant of FRIAR.

Frybarger (101) Variant spelling of German FREIBERGER.

Fryberger (235) Variant spelling of German FREIBERGER.

Frydenlund (159) Scandinavian (especially Norwegian): either an ornamental name or a more recent habitational name from a place in southeast Norway from *fryd* 'delight', 'joy' + *lund* 'grove'.

Frydman (166) Polish spelling of German and Jewish FRIEDMAN(N).

GIVEN NAMES Jewish 17%; Polish 6%. *Avraham* (2), *Barak, Efroim, Gershon, Gerson, Miriam, Uziel; Zygmunt* (3), *Bogdan.*

Frydrych (111) Polish form of German FRIEDRICH.

GIVEN NAMES Polish 13%; German 4%. *Henryk, Krystyna, Wojciech, Zbignew; Aloysius.*

Frye (13110) **1.** English: variant spelling of FRY. **2.** North German: variant of FREY.

FOREBEARS Joseph Frye (1711/12–94) was a military officer from Andover, MA, where the family had long been of local prominence. In 1762, he was granted a township in ME, later named Fryeburg after him, and moved his family there. His great-great-grandson William Pierce Frye was born in Lewiston, ME, and served in Congress, first as a member of the House of Representatives and then the Senate from 1871 until his death in 1911.

Fryer (2763) **1.** English: variant of FREER. **2.** German: variant spelling of FREIER.

Frykman (113) Swedish: ornamental name formed from the place-name element *Fryk-* (of unknown origin and meaning) + the common second element *man* 'man'.

Fryling (193) **1.** Polish spelling of Jewish FRUHLING. **2.** German: variant spelling of **Freiling** (see FRIELING) or of **Frühling** (see FRUHLING).

Fryman (1086) Variant spelling of German **Freimann** (see FREIMAN).

Frymire (308) Americanized spelling of German **Freimeier** (see FREEMYER).

Frymoyer (136) Americanized spelling of German **Freimeier** (see FREEMYER).

Frymyer (106) Americanized spelling of German **Freimeier** (see FREEMYER).

Fryrear (143) Almost certainly of French origin, but unexplained. Perhaps a variant of **Frère** (see FRERE).

FOREBEARS The brothers John, Francis, and Jeremiah Fryrear are recorded in VA in the late 18th century.

Frysinger (171) Variant spelling of German FRISINGER.

Fu (1290) **1.** Chinese 傅: according to ancient texts, this name originated in the time of the Shang dynasty king Wu Ding (1324–1266 BC). Wu Ding dreamed about a man looking like a prisoner, and was told by a god that this was the wise man that he had been seeking. Wu Ding immediately commissioned a portrait of the mysterious man and searched everywhere for him. Finally, a man who looked exactly like the man in the dream was found performing hard labor building walls in Fu Cliffs (in present-day Shanxi province, by the Great Wall). Wu Ding rescued the man, whose name was Yue, and gave him the name Fu Yue. Fu Yue was made prime minister and, as expected, went on to become a great administrator. His descendants adopted Fu as their surname. **2.** Chinese 符: from a character meaning 'symbol', 'tally', or 'magic figure'. This was one of the characters in a title meaning 'keeper of the royal seals'. During the Spring and Autumn period (722–481 BC), a grandson of a duke of the state of Lu held a post as the keeper of royal seals. His descendants adopted a character from the job title as their surname. **3.** Chinese 富: name borne by descendants of Fu Chen, a senior minister during the Zhou dynasty (1122–221 BC), and of Fu Fu, a member of the royal family of the state of Lu dring the Spring and Autumn period (722–481 BC).

GIVEN NAMES Chinese 39%. *Chi* (6), *Qiang* (6), *Hong* (5), *Lei* (5), *Min* (5), *Li* (4), *Ning* (4), *Tao* (4), *Bin* (3), *Chee* (3), *Chun* (3), *Dong* (3), *Gang* (3), *Chang* (2), *Chung* (2), *Yiping* (2), *Chong, Jang, Yeh.*

Fucci (512) Italian: from the plural of *Fuccio*, a short form of any of various personal names with a root ending in *-f* (as for example *Rodolfo, Gandolfo*) to which has been attached the hypocoristic suffix *-uccio*, or alternatively from a reduced form of a personal name such as *Fantuccio, Feduccio*.

GIVEN NAMES Italian 12%. *Domenic* (3), *Carmine* (2), *Salvatore* (2), *Amerigo, Angelo, Antonio, Caesar, Dante, Donato, Francesca, Giovanni.*

Fuccillo (106) Italian: possibly from a pet form of the Old Tuscan personal name *Fuccius*, a short form of a personal name ending with *-fuccius*, such as *Grifuccius, Ridolfuccius.*

GIVEN NAMES Italian 17%. *Carmine, Cosimo, Domenic, Nicola, Pasquale, Veto.*

Fuchs (5387) German and Jewish (Ashkenazic): from Middle High German *vuhs*, German *Fuchs* 'fox', nickname for a sly or cunning person, or for someone with red hair. This name is widespread throughout central Europe. As a Jewish name, it is mainly an ornamental name.

GIVEN NAMES German 6%. *Otto* (13), *Hans* (12), *Kurt* (9), *Gerhard* (6), *Fritz* (4), *Mathias* (4), *Matthias* (4), *Armin* (3), *Eldred* (3), *Ulrich* (3), *Erwin* (2), *Helmut* (2).

Fucile (133) Southern Italian: habitational name from Fucile, so named from Sicilian *fucile* 'flint', or a topographic name with the same meaning.

GIVEN NAMES Italian 22%. *Salvatore* (5), *Carmine, Sal, Vincenzo.*

Fuda (124) Italian: habitational name from Fuda, in Careri, Reggio Calabria.

GIVEN NAMES Italian 19%. *Rocco* (2), *Cosimo, Cosmo, Giovanni, Guiseppe, Pasquale, Vincenzo.*

Fudala (203) Polish: nickname from Romanian *fudul* 'conceited', 'proud'.

GIVEN NAMES Polish 7%; German 4%. *Andrzej, Janina, Krzysztof, Stanistaw.*

Fudge (1300) English (chiefly Somerset): from a pet form of FULCHER.

Fuehrer (331) German (**Führer**): see FUHRER.

GIVEN NAMES German 6%. *Hans* (2), *Kurt* (2), *Armin, Helmuth, Jochen.*

Fuelling (272) Possibly an Americanized spelling of German **Fühling**, a habitational name from a place near Cologne named Fühlingen, from Middle Low German *vūl* 'rotten', 'low lying'.

Fuemmeler (119) German: probably a variant of **Fimmler**, an occupational name for a grower or dealer of hemp. Compare FIMPLE.

Fuente (122) Spanish: habitational name from any of the numerous places in Spain named with *fuente* 'spring', 'well' (Latin *fons*, genitive *fontis*), as for example Fuente Álamo (in Albacete, Jaén, Córdoba, and Murcia provinces), Fuente del Maestre (Badajoz), or Fuente Palmera (Córdoba). This is one of the most common Spanish place name elements.

GIVEN NAMES Spanish 32%. *Jose* (6), *Pedro* (2), *Alfredo, Ana, Carlos, Consuelo, Cristino, Digna, Domingo, Felipe, Jorge, Julio.*

Fuentes (6619) Spanish: habitational name from any of numerous places named with *fuentes*, plural of *fuente* 'spring', 'well' (see FUENTE), as for example Fuentes (Cuenca, Albacete, and Segovia provinces), Fuentes Calientes (Teruel), Fuentes de León (Badajoz), Fuentes de Valdepero (Palencia).

GIVEN NAMES Spanish 50%. *Jose* (205), *Juan* (99), *Carlos* (79), *Francisco* (55), *Luis* (52), *Manuel* (52), *Jesus* (48), *Miguel* (42), *Pedro* (41), *Ruben* (36), *Jorge* (35), *Julio* (34).

Fuentez (199) Variant of Spanish FUENTES.

GIVEN NAMES Spanish 35%. *Ruben* (3), *Guadalupe* (2), *Lorenza* (2), *Ramon* (2), *Salvador* (2), *Adon, Alfredo, Andres, Armando, Arturo, Bernardo, Cesar; Antonio* (3), *Silvano* (2), *Angelo, Cecilio, Lucio.*

Fuerst (926) German (**Fürst**): see FURST.

GIVEN NAMES German 5%. *Otto* (3), *Lorenz* (2), *Erwin, Fritz, Gerhard, Hedwig, Juergen, Klaus, Kurt, Reinhold.*

Fuerstenau (111) German (**Fürstenau**): habitational name from any of various places named Fürstenau, for example in Brandenburg, North Rhine-Westphalia, Saxony, and Lower Saxony.

GIVEN NAMES German 8%. *Florian, Kurt, Lothar, Reinhold.*

Fuerstenberg (192) German (**Fürstenberg**): see FURSTENBERG.

GIVEN NAMES German 4%. *Erwin, Helmut, Otto.*

Fuerte (141) Spanish: nickname from *fuerte* 'strong', 'brave' (Latin *fortis*).

GIVEN NAMES Spanish 54%. *Jose* (7), *Gustavo* (3), *Luis* (3), *Pedro* (3), *Alberto* (2), *Elvira* (2), *Mario* (2), *Adolfo, Alfonso, Alfredo, Alicia, Alvaro; Antonio, Leonzo, Lorenzo.*

Fuertes (156) Spanish: from an old personal name from Latin *Fortis*, from *fortis* 'strong'. Compare Portuguese FORTES.

GIVEN NAMES Spanish 41%. *Jose* (10), *Luis* (3), *Mario* (3), *Angel* (2), *Basilio* (2), *Carlos* (2), *Francisco* (2), *Guillermo* (2), *Jorge* (2), *Raul* (2), *Alberto, Amparo.*

Fuess (149) German: Alemannic variant of FUSS.

Fugate (3279) English: unexplained; most probably a variant of FUGETT.

Fugatt (146) Variant spelling of English FUGETT.

Fugazzi (105) Italian: perhaps a variant of **Fogazza**, itself a variant of **Focaccia**, from *focaccia* 'flat bread', hence a metonymic occupational name for a baker of such bread.

GIVEN NAMES Italian 5%. *Carlo, Gino.*

Fuge (172) **1.** English: from a pet form of FULCHER. **2.** German (also **Füge**): nickname for a skillful, adroit person, from Middle High German *vüege* 'skillful', 'fitting' (see FIEGEL).

Fugere (373) French (**Fugère**): regional (Massif central) variant of **Fougère** (see FOUGERE).

GIVEN NAMES French 9%. *Aime, Celine, Emile, Gilles, Lucien, Normand, Philippe, Pierre, Sylvian.*

Fugett (326) English (Hampshire): unexplained; perhaps of French origin, an adaptation of **Fuget**, a topographic name from *fuge*, a regional term for *fougère* 'fern'.

Fugit (111) English: variant spelling of FUGETT.

Fugitt (521) Variant spelling of English FUGETT.

Fugleberg (115) **1.** Norwegian: habitational name from any of several farmsteads so named, for example in Ringerike, from *fugl* 'bird' + *berg* 'mountain'. **2.** Danish: from any of several places called Fuglebjerg, composed of the same elements as the Norwegian name.

Fugler (130) **1.** German: variant of VOGLER. **2.** English: variant of FOWLER.

Fuglestad (121) Norwegian: habitational name from a farm in Rogaland, named with *fugl* 'bird' + *stad* 'farmstead', 'dwelling' (from Old Norse *staðr* 'farmstead', 'dwelling').

GIVEN NAMES Scandinavian 15%; German 4%. *Erik* (2), *Jorgen; Gerhard, Oskar.*

Fuhr (661) German: topographic name for someone who lived near a ferry or ford, from Middle High German *vuore* 'load', 'place where one drives' (related to English *fare*), or a habitational name from one of the many places named with this word.

GIVEN NAMES German 4%. *Kurt* (3), *Achim, Gerhard, Wolf.*

Fuhrer (535) South German and Swiss German: **1.** (**Führer**): occupational name for a carrier or carter, a driver of horse-drawn vehicles, Middle High German *vüerer* (from the Middle High German verb *vüeren* 'to lead', 'transport'). See also FUHRMANN. **2.** topographic name for someone who lived near a ferry or ford, a derivative of FUHR + the suffix *-er* denoting an inhabitant.

Fuhriman (171) Swiss German: variant of FUHRMANN.

Fuhrman (2092) Respelling of German FUHRMANN.

Fuhrmann (877) German: from Middle High German *vuorman* 'carter', 'driver'.

GIVEN NAMES German 6%. *Kurt* (3), *Eugen* (2), *Aloys, Erwin, Ewald, Gerhard, Hans, Helmuth, Juergen, Klaus, Konrad, Manfred.*

Fuhrmeister (132) German: occupational name for an overseer or manager of a haulage business, composed of Middle High German *vuore* 'load', 'transport' + *meister* 'master'.

GIVEN NAMES German 6%. *Kurt, Lorenz.*

Fuhs (361) German: nickname from Old High German *funs* 'quick', 'active'.

Fujii (810) Japanese: 'wisteria well'; mostly found in west central Japan and the Ryūkyū Islands. Some bearing this name descend from the FUJIWARA clan. Listed in the Shinsen shōjiroku.

GIVEN NAMES Japanese 50%. *Hiroshi* (4), *Masao* (4), *Takao* (4), *Kenji* (3), *Minoru* (3), *Satoshi* (3), *Takeo* (3), *Tetsuya* (3), *Toshio* (3), *Yoshiko* (3), *Yoshio* (3), *Aki* (2).

Fujikawa (210) Japanese: 'wisteria river'; most common in western Japan. Bearers of this name are descended from the southern FUJIWARA through the Kudō family.

GIVEN NAMES Japanese 47%. *Masao* (4), *Hiroshi* (3), *Eiji* (2), *Kenji* (2), *Takeo* (2),

Taro (2), *Tetsuo* (2), *Atsushi, Daisuke, Fumiko, Haruki, Hideo.*

Fujimori (102) Japanese: 'wisteria forest'; the name is found mostly in central Japan.
GIVEN NAMES Japanese 64%. *Taro* (3), *Hideharu* (2), *Yoshio* (2), *Akiko, Akira, Hideaki, Hiroshi, Hiroyuki, Ichiro, Iwao, Kenzo, Manami.*

Fujimoto (868) Japanese: '(one who lives) under the wisteria'; found mostly in western Japan and the Ryūkyū Islands, descended from the FUJIWARA clan.
GIVEN NAMES Japanese 43%. *Akira* (5), *Yoshio* (4), *Hiroshi* (3), *Junichi* (3), *Masami* (3), *Masao* (3), *Midori* (3), *Minoru* (3), *Sakae* (3), *Tetsuo* (3), *Toshio* (3), *Tsugio* (3).

Fujimura (102) Japanese: 'wisteria village'; the name is found mostly in western Honshū and the Ryūkyū Islands.
GIVEN NAMES Japanese 51%. *Jitsuo* (2), *Kaoru* (2), *Kaz, Keiji, Kikuo, Koya, Kunio, Micho, Morio, Noboru, Nobuki, Osamu.*

Fujino (104) Japanese: 'wisteria field'; this version of the name is found mostly in eastern Japan, while the pronunciation *Tōno* comes from western Japan.
GIVEN NAMES Japanese 49%. *Koji* (3), *Mikio* (2), *Takashi* (2), *Akira, Fujio, Haruhiko, Harumi, Haruno, Hiroshi, Itsuo, Kaori, Katsuhiro.*

Fujioka (276) Japanese: 'wisteria hill'; habitational name from a village in Shinano (now Nagano prefecture), and found mostly in western Japan and the Ryūkyū Islands. The family is descended from a branch of the FUJIWARA clan which took the name **Ashikaga**, but is not directly related to the more famous Ashikaga family, which is of Minamoto descent.
GIVEN NAMES Japanese 46%. *Taira* (3), *Akira* (2), *Hiroyuki* (2), *Isamu* (2), *Makoto* (2), *Satoshi* (2), *Tsutomu* (2), *Yoshiko* (2), *Atsushi, Futoshi, Hajime, Haruko.*

Fujita (584) Japanese: 'wisteria rice paddy'; common place name and surname in western Japan and the Ryūkyū Islands. Some bearers descend from the TAIRA clan, others from the northern FUJIWARA.
GIVEN NAMES Japanese 58%. *Tetsuya* (5), *Ichiro* (4), *Satoshi* (4), *Atsushi* (3), *Masato* (3), *Mayumi* (3), *Takeshi* (3), *Teruo* (3), *Yasuo* (3), *Akira* (2), *Hideaki* (2), *Hideo* (2).

Fujiwara (353) Japanese: 'wisteria plain'; the greatest noble clan of classical Japan. They descend from the statesman Nakatomi no Kamatari (614–669), who was awarded the Fujiwara surname by Emperor Tenji for his part in crushing the powerful Soga family and placing Tenji on the throne. *Fujiwara* is a common place name in Japan. Kamatari's birthplace was Fujiwara in Yamato (in present-day Kashiharashi, Nara prefecture). The surname is listed in the Shinsen shōjiroku, as is the ancestral name, Nakatomi. The family claims

descent from Ame no Koyane, a son of the deity Takamimusubi and a companion of the mythical hero Ninigi.
FOREBEARS Two major branches of the clan are the 'northern' and 'southern' Fujiwara, named for the relative locations of the mansions of their founders, two grandsons of Fujiwara Kamatari: Muchimaro (680–737; northern) and Fusasaki (682–737; southern). The family rose to greatness during the 10th and 11th centuries by marrying daughters to emperors and other important court figures. The name is no longer common in its original form, but local variants such as Satō, Itō, Saitō, and Katō make the Fujiwara the largest clan in Japan. Many variants of the name were created by taking the first syllable of the name of a family head's residence, or of his official title, and adding to it the suffix *-tō*, which is the Sino-Japanese reading of the word *fuji* ('wisteria'). Thus, for example, the Fujiwara of Sano (*Sano no Fujiwara*) are called *Satō*. The name Fujiwara appears in Hawaiian records in the late 18th century.
GIVEN NAMES Japanese 57%. *Makoto* (3), *Masataka* (3), *Akihiko* (2), *Akio* (2), *Hideo* (2), *Junko* (2), *Kazuhiro* (2), *Kiyoto* (2), *Koji* (2), *Miho* (2), *Minoru* (2), *Toru* (2).

Fuks (121) Jewish (Ashkenazic): variant of FUCHS.
GIVEN NAMES Jewish 27%; Russian 22%; Polish 6%; Jewish Biblical 5%. *Faina* (3), *Joachim* (2), *Anchel, Avram, Fridrikh, Froim, Gersh, Irina, Izy, Meyer, Mikhel, Perlya*; *Boris* (4), *Mikhail* (3), *Oleg* (3), *Arkady* (2), *Igor* (2), *Yuriy* (2), *Aleksandr, Aleksandra, Gennadiy, Kuzma, Leonid, Lyudmila*; *Andrzej, Bogumil, Henryk, Jozef.*

Fukuda (545) Japanese: 'blessed rice paddy'; variously written; common place name and surname throughout Japan and the Ryūkyū Islands. Branches of the FUJIWARA, TAIRA, and other important families have taken the name.
GIVEN NAMES Japanese 63%. *Koichi* (8), *Akira* (6), *Hiroyuki* (5), *Kenji* (4), *Minoru* (4), *Toshio* (4), *Hiroshi* (3), *Isao* (3), *Masao* (3), *Takashi* (3), *Haruto* (2), *Hiroko* (2).

Fukuhara (137) Japanese: 'blessed plain'; common place name and surname throughout Japan. Branches of the FUJIWARA, MINAMOTO, and other important clans have taken this name. It is pronounced **Fukibaru** in the Ryūkyū Islands.
GIVEN NAMES Japanese 35%. *Katsuya* (2), *Akira, Hidenori, Hiromichi, Hitoshi, Kame, Kenichi, Kenji, Kiyoshi, Masami, Mitsugi, Miyoko.*

Fukui (175) Japanese: 'blessed well'; found mostly in western Japan and the Ryūkyū Islands. There are several unrelated bearers of the name, the noble ones descending from Izumo no Ōmi, an ancient chief of present-day Shimane prefecture. Some others descend from the southern FUJIWARA,

and another group from a branch of the MINAMOTO.
GIVEN NAMES Japanese 69%. *Masamichi* (4), *Kenji* (2), *Mayumi* (2), *Mitsuo* (2), *Tsuyoshi* (2), *Yuji* (2), *Akihide, Akito, Chieko, Chikashi, Chiyono, Haruo.*

Fukumoto (270) Japanese: 'blessed origin'; found in western Japan and the Ryūkyū Islands.
GIVEN NAMES Japanese 42%. *Akira* (2), *Kazuo* (2), *Kiyoshi* (2), *Masahiko* (2), *Masashi* (2), *Masato* (2), *Takashi* (2), *Asao, Eiji, Hidefumi, Hideo, Hiroshi.*

Fukunaga (194) Japanese: 'blessed longevity'; most common in western Japan and the Ryūkyū Islands. There are several unrelated bearers of the name, from such widely separated places as Awa (now Tokushima prefecture), Hyūga (now Miyazaki prefecture), and a family descended from the Sasaki of Ōmi (now Shiga prefecture).
GIVEN NAMES Japanese 48%. *Kaoru* (2), *Shiro* (2), *Takayuki* (2), *Eiichiro, Etsuo, Fumie, Hajime, Hideyuki, Ikuo, Jiro, Kazuma, Koichi.*

Fukushima (306) Japanese: 'blessed island'; common place name and surname throughout Japan and the Ryūkyū Islands.
GIVEN NAMES Japanese 61%. *Hiroshi* (3), *Eiichi* (2), *Miho* (2), *Shigeo* (2), *Shigeru* (2), *Tadashi* (2), *Takashi* (2), *Takshi* (2), *Tsutomu* (2), *Yasuo* (2), *Yutaka* (2), *Akiko.*

Fulbright (1156) Americanized form of VOLLBRECHT.

Fulcher (2482) English (chiefly East Anglia): from a Germanic personal name composed of the elements *folk* 'people' + *hari, heri* 'army', which was introduced into England from France by the Normans; isolated examples may derive from the cognate Old English *Folchere* or Old Norse *Folkar*, but these names were far less common.

Fulco (232) Italian: from a short form of a Germanic personal name formed with *folk* 'people'.
GIVEN NAMES Italian 11%; Spanish 10%, French 5%. *Salvatore* (3), *Guido, Mario, Mauricio, Osvaldo*; *Jose* (3), *Ana, Angel, Jorge*; *Armand* (2), *Camille.*

Fuld (150) German and Jewish (western Ashkenazic): habitational name from the city or river named Fulda in northern Germany.
GIVEN NAMES German 7%; Jewish 4%. *Kurt* (2), *Ulrike*; *Chaya, Moshe.*

Fulenwider (183) German; habitational name of uncertain origin. The second element is probably a derivative of German *Weide* 'pasture', 'meadow'. This is most probably a field name; the first element may be **Fohlen-** or **Füllen-**, both meaning 'foal', or perhaps a dialect form of Low German *voghel* 'bird'. On the other hand, the second element may be was *-weiler* (as in **Fulweiler**), indicating a habitational name, perhaps meaning 'foal hamlet'. A third possibility is that the original form may have been Low German **Fulentwiete**, meaning 'low-lying, wet pasture', which then became altered through a process of folk etymology.

Fulfer (292) Perhaps an altered spelling of German **Pfülwer** or **Fülfe**, an occupational name for an upholsterer or a nickname for a soft person, from Middle High German *phülwe* 'feather cushion'.

Fulford (1560) English: habitational name from places in Devon, Oxfordshire, Somerset, Staffordshire, and East Yorkshire, all so named from Old English *fūl* 'dirty', 'muddy' + *ford* 'ford'.

Fulgencio (100) Spanish: from a personal name (Latin *Fulgentius*, from *fulgens* 'shining', 'brilliant'), borne by a saint who lived in the 5th–6th centuries.
GIVEN NAMES Spanish 49%. *Jose* (4), *Juan* (2), *Alfonso*, *Aquilino*, *Armando*, *Bernabe*, *Bernardino*, *Cristobal*, *Enrique*, *Estevan*, *Fabiola*, *Gerardo*; *Carina*, *Dino*.

Fulgenzi (122) Italian: patronymic or plural form of the personal name *Fulgenzio* (from Latin *Fulgentius*, from *fulgens* 'shining', 'brilliant'), borne by a saint who lived in the 5th–6th centuries.
GIVEN NAMES Italian 5%. *Antonio*, *Gilda*, *Guido*, *Lelio*.

Fulgham (868) Variant of English **Foulsham** (see FOLSOM). This form is found chiefly in MS.

Fulghum (780) Variant of English **Foulsham** (see FOLSOM). This form is found chiefly in NC, GA, and TN.

Fulginiti (238) Italian: habitational name from Forciniti (Fulginiti is a variant), San Sostene, Catanzaro.
GIVEN NAMES Italian 11%. *Luciano* (2), *Domenic*, *Salvatore*, *Saverio*.

Fulk (1719) **1.** English: variant of FOULKS. **2.** Respelling of German VOLK.

Fulkerson (2377) Americanized spelling of German *Volkertsen*, a north German patronymic from VOLKERT.

Fulks (1204) English: variant of FOULKS.

Full (265) **1.** English: unexplained. **2.** Possibly a shortened form of any of several German compound surnames formed with *Full-* or *Füll-*.

Fullam (358) English: variant spelling of **Fulham**, a habitational name from Fulham, now part of Greater London, recorded in Domesday Book as *Fuleham*, from an Old English personal name *Fulla* + *hamm* 'land in a river bend'. Both forms of the name have been recorded in Ireland, in County Dublin, since the 13th century.

Fullard (228) **1.** English: unexplained; possibly from the Germanic personal name mentioned at 2. **2.** In some cases, possibly an altered spelling of German **Vollert**, **Fullert**, or **Füllert**, from the personal name *Vol(l)hard(t)*, from *Volkhart*, a compound

of Old High German *volc* 'tribe', 'people', *hart* 'bold'.

Fullbright (334) Americanized form of German VOLLBRECHT.

Fullem (113) Respelling of English **Fulham** (see FULLAM).

Fullen (681) English: occupational name for a fuller (see FULLER), from Old French *fulun*, *foul(l)on*.

Fullenkamp (280) Altered spelling of the German topographic names **Fuhlenkamp** (from Middle Low German *vūl* 'rotten', 'stinking' + *kamp* 'field', 'domain') or **Fohlenkamp** (from Middle Low German *vol* (*volle*) 'foal' + *kamp* 'field', 'domain').

Fullenwider (161) Of German origin: see FULENWIDER.

Fuller (38130) **1.** English: occupational name for a dresser of cloth, Old English *fullere* (from Latin *fullo*, with the addition of the English agent suffix). The Middle English successor of this word had also been reinforced by Old French *fouleor*, *foleur*, of similar origin. The work of the fuller was to scour and thicken the raw cloth by beating and trampling it in water. This surname is found mostly in southeast England and East Anglia. See also TUCKER and WALKER. **2.** In a few cases the name may be of German origin with the same form and meaning as 1 (from Latin *fullare*). **3.** Americanized version of French FOURNIER.
FOREBEARS Samuel Fuller (1589–1633), born in Redenhall, Norfolk, England, was among the Pilgrim Fathers who sailed on the *Mayflower* in 1620. He was a deacon of the church and until his death functioned as Plymouth Colony's physician.

Fullerton (3392) Scottish and northern Irish: habitational name from a place so called from Old English *fuglere* 'bird-catcher' (see FOWLER) + *tūn* 'enclosure', 'settlement'. There is a place with this spelling in Hampshire, but the surname derives chiefly if not exclusively from Fullarton in Ayrshire, Scotland.

Fullilove (229) English: nickname for an amorous person, from a translation of French *pleyn d'amour*.
GIVEN NAME Scottish 4%. *Morag* (2).

Fullingim (109) Most probably a variant of English FILLINGHAM.

Fullington (508) English: habitational name from an unidentified place, or possibly an altered form of FULLERTON.

Fullman (153) North German (**Fullmann**): variant of **Vollmann** (see VOLLMAN).
GIVEN NAME Scandinavian 4%. *Nels*.

Fullmer (1563) **1.** Altered spelling of English FULMER. **2.** German (**Füllmer**): variant of VOLKMAR.

Fullwood (552) English (Midlands): habitational name from places in Nottinghamshire and Lancashire called Fulwood, from Old English *fūl* 'dirty', 'muddy' + *wudu* 'wood'.

Fulmer (3655) **1.** English: habitational name from Fulmer in Buckinghamshire or Fowlmere in Cambridgeshire, so named from Old English *fugol* 'bird' + *mere* 'lake'. **2.** German: variant of VOLKMAR.

Fulmore (274) Possibly an altered spelling of FULMER.

Fulop (262) **1.** Hungarian (**Fülöp**): from the personal name *Fülöp*, Hungarian form of PHILIP. **2.** Jewish (from Hungary): adoption of the Hungarian surname.
GIVEN NAMES Hungarian 22%; Jewish 4%. *Laszlo* (7), *Jozsef* (4), *Karoly* (3), *Csaba* (2), *Imre* (2), *Zoltan* (2), *Gabor*, *Lajos*, *Miklos*, *Sandor*, *Tamas*, *Tibor*; *Menashe*, *Shimon*, *Sol*, *Surie*.

Fulp (632) **1.** Perhaps an Americanized spelling of German FALB or of **Pfülb**, a metonymic occupational name for an upholsterer or cushion maker, or a nickname for a soft person. Compare FULFER. **2.** Alternatively, possibly a variant of Dutch or English PHILLIP.

Fulps (102) Variant, apparently under French influence, of Dutch or English PHILLIPS.
GIVEN NAME French 4%. *Charolet*.

Fuls (103) Probably an Americanized form of German VOLZ.
GIVEN NAME German 5%. *Otto*.

Fulton (11529) Scottish and northern Irish: **1.** probably a reduced form of FULLERTON. **2.** habitational name from a place in Roxburghshire, Scotland, so named from Old English *fugol* 'bird' + *tūn* 'enclosure', 'settlement'.

Fults (898) Americanized spelling of German VOLZ.

Fultz (3625) Americanized spelling of German VOLZ.

Fulwider (252) Of German origin: see FULENWIDER.

Fulwiler (205) Of German origin: see FULENWIDER.

Fulwood (232) English: variant spelling of FULLWOOD.

Fumo (104) Italian (mainly Veneto and Lombardy): from the medieval personal name *Fumeus*, a pet form of *Bartholomeus* or *Thomasus*.
GIVEN NAMES Italian 14%. *Osvaldo* (2), *Lorenzo*, *Luigi*, *Roberto*, *Vincenzo*.

Funai (106) Japanese: written with the characters for 'boat' and 'well', the name is more common in western Japan. It may possibly derive from the city of Funai, formerly the capital of Bungo (now Ōita prefecture), but the city's name is written with characters meaning 'seat of government'.
GIVEN NAMES Japanese 13%. *Masaru* (2), *Kazuo*, *Masami*, *Satoru*, *Satsuki*.

Funari (238) Italian (Sicilian): habitational name from Funari, a district of Messina.
GIVEN NAMES Italian 13%. *Angelo* (2), *Dino*, *Franco*, *Geno*, *Gilio*, *Gino*, *Naldo*, *Primo*, *Quinto*, *Reno*, *Santino*.

Funaro (338) Italian: variant (singular in form) of FUNARI.

GIVEN NAMES Italian 13%; French 4%. *Angelo* (2), *Concetta, Gino, Giuseppe, Palma, Pasquale, Santo, Silvio; Alphonse* (3), *Achille*.

Funches (293) Americanized spelling of German **Funccius**, a Latinized form of FUNKE, recorded since the 16th century.

Funchess (273) Americanized spelling of German **Funccius** (see FUNCHES).

Funck (258) German and Swedish: variant spelling of FUNK.

Fund (129) Jewish (Ashkenazic): from German *Pfund* 'pound', either a nickname or one of the names chosen at random from vocabulary words in the 18th and 19th centuries by government officials at the time when surnames became compulsory.

GIVEN NAME Jewish 6%. *Myer* (2).

Funderburg (690) Americanized spelling of German **von der Burg** 'from the castle', occupational or topographic name for someone who lived and worked at a castle.

FOREBEARS Walter von der Burg fled Western Germany under political persecution and arrived in Philadelphia in 1738.

Funderburk (2103) Of German origin: see FUNDERBURG.

Funderburke (223) Of German origin: see FUNDERBURG.

Fundora (182) Hispanic: unexplained.

GIVEN NAMES Spanish 53%; Italian 7%. *Luis* (5), *Ramon* (5), *Alberto* (4), *Julio* (4), *Adolfo* (3), *Fernando* (3), *Jose* (3), *Rosendo* (3), *Carlos* (2), *Jesus* (2), *Jorge* (2), *Juan* (2); *Lorenzo* (2), *Aldo, Antonio, Marco*.

Funes (410) Basque: habitational name from Funes, a place in Navarre province, Basque Country.

GIVEN NAMES Spanish 49%. *Jose* (19), *Carlos* (9), *Luis* (6), *Ana* (4), *Eduardo* (4), *Juan* (4), *Cesar* (3), *Jose Luis* (3), *Roberto* (3), *Alberto* (2), *Armando* (2), *Blanca* (2).

Fung (1836) **1.** Chinese 冯: variant of FENG 1. **2.** Chinese 封: variant of FENG 2. **3.** Chinese 丰: variant of FENG 3. **4.** Chinese 鄷: variant of FENG 4.

GIVEN NAMES Chinese 21%. *Wing* (12), *Ming* (6), *Wai* (6), *Kam* (5), *Kwan* (5), *Kwok* (5), *Kwong* (5), *Kin* (4), *Chi* (3), *Chow* (3), *Yee* (3), *Bor* (2).

Funk (9693) German: nickname for a blacksmith, or for a small and lively or irritable individual, from Middle High German *vunke* 'spark'.

FOREBEARS Between 1709 and 1772 nine families bearing this name emigrated to America. Most noted was Heinrich Funck from the Palatinate, who came to PA in 1719. In the 18th century there were Funks in Ephrata, PA.

Funke (1073) German: variant of FUNK.

GIVEN NAMES German 6%. *Kurt* (3), *Klaus* (2), *Otto* (2), *Armin, Detlef, Dietrich,*

Erwin, Georg, Gerhard, Hans, Lothar, Lutz.

Funkhouser (1600) Respelling of German FRANKHAUSER.

Funnell (210) English: variant of FENNELL 1, found predominantly in East Sussex.

Funston (362) Northern Irish: unexplained.

Funt (118) Altered spelling of German **Pfund(t)**, meaning 'pound', an metonymic occupational name for a city sealer of weights or for a wholesale merchant

Fuoco (313) Italian: from *fuoco* 'fire' or alternatively from Latin *focus* 'hearth', 'fireplace', possibly applied as a metonymic occupational name for someone employed to light and maintain a fire or someone who had the task of counting domestic hearths.

GIVEN NAMES Italian 20%. *Antonio* (2), *Cosmo* (2), *Luigi* (2), *Pasquale* (2), *Vito* (2), *Angelo, Carmine, Dino, Domenic, Donato, Egidio, Ettore.*

Fuoss (134) Variant of German FUSS.

Fuqua (3096) Probably an Americanized spelling of French FOUQUET. This name is concentrated in TN and TX.

Fuquay (341) Probably an Americanized spelling of French FOUQUET.

Furbee (303) Altered spelling of English FURBY.

Furber (245) English: from the Old French verb *fourbir* 'to burnish', 'to furbish' (a word of Germanic origin), an occupational name for a polisher of metal, in particular someone employed by an armorer to put the finishing touches to his work.

Furbish (125) See FURBUSH.

Furbush (358) Probably an altered form of the Scottish name FORBES, which is traditionally pronounced as two syllables.

Furby (178) English: habitational name from either of two places in North and East Yorkshire named Firby, from the Old Danish personal name *Frithi* + Old Norse *býr* 'farm', 'settlement'.

Furches (192) Origin unidentified.

Fure (123) Norwegian: habitational name from a farmstead in western Norway named from *fure* 'fir', 'pine'.

GIVEN NAME Scandinavian 5%. *Bjorn.*

Furer (147) **1.** Jewish (eastern Ashkenazic): occupational name from Yiddish *furer* 'coachman', 'driver'. **2.** Respelling of German **Führer** (see FUHRER).

GIVEN NAMES Jewish 7%; Russian 5%; German 4%. *Josif, Menashe, Semen; Anatoly, Fanya, Iosif, Mikhail, Savely; Hanspeter* (2).

Furey (1172) Irish: reduced Anglicized form of Gaelic **Ó Fiúra**, earlier *Ó Fiodhabhra* 'bushy eyebrows', from *fiodh* 'wood' + *(f)abhra* 'eyebrow'.

GIVEN NAMES Irish 4%. *Brigid, Conall.*

Furfaro (157) Italian: nickname for a speedy or restless person, from Sicilian *furfareddu* 'fretful child', 'speedy worker', or

alternatively a nickname related to Sicilian *forfaru* 'matchstick'.

GIVEN NAMES Italian 22%. *Angelo* (4), *Antonio* (2), *Domenic, Filippo, Giuseppe, Salvatore, Vincenzo.*

Furgason (319) Altered spelling of Scottish FERGUSON.

Furgerson (312) Altered spelling of Scottish FERGUSON.

Furgeson (184) Altered spelling of Scottish FERGUSON.

Furia (238) Italian: nickname for an irascible man, from *furia* 'fury', 'rage'.

GIVEN NAMES Italian 13%. *Salvatore* (2), *Aldo, Domenic, Enrico, Geno, Luigi, Quinto, Rocco, Sal, Silvio.*

Furino (152) Italian: from a pet form of the personal name FURIO.

GIVEN NAMES Italian 22%. *Carmine* (3), *Antonio* (2), *Salvatore* (2), *Domenic, Francesco, Marco, Pasquale.*

Furio (130) Southern Italian: from the personal name *Furio* (from Latin *Furius*, probably of Etruscan origin), which was particularly popular during the Renaissance.

GIVEN NAMES Italian 28%. *Romeo* (2), *Vito* (2), *Angelo, Carmine, Domenic, Giovanni, Girolamo, Oronzo, Rocco, Vincenza.*

Furlan (266) Slovenian and Italian (Venetia): ethnic name for someone from Friuli (Slovenian name *Furlanija*), or for a person of Friulian origin, from the medieval Latin adjective *furlanus*.

GIVEN NAMES Italian 16%; Spanish 6%. *Marco* (3), *Giorgio* (2), *Mario* (2), *Amerigo, Antonio, Dino, Leopoldo, Lino, Massimo, Roberto, Rogerio, Sal, Umberto; Alicia, Enriqueta, Jorge, Jose Antonio.*

Furlong (2711) **1.** English and Irish: apparently a topographic name from Middle English *furlong* 'length of a field' (from Old English *furh* 'furrow' + *lang* 'long'), the technical term for the block of strips owned by several different persons which formed the unit of cultivation in the medieval open-field system of farming, or a habitational name from a minor place named with this word, such as Furlong in Devon or Shropshire. The surname is now chiefly common in Ireland, where a family of this name settled at the end of the 13th century. **2.** Possibly an Americanized form of French FERLAND.

GIVEN NAMES Irish 4%. *Brendan* (3), *Donovan* (2), *Aidan, Eamon, Padric, Seamus.*

Furlough (253) Probably an altered spelling of English FARLOW.

Furlow (964) English: probably a variant of FARLOW.

Furman (3583) **1.** Polish, Czech, Slovak, Jewish (eastern Ashkenazic), and Slovenian: occupational name for a carter or drayman, the driver of a horse-drawn delivery vehicle, from Polish, Yiddish, and Slovenian *furman*, a loanword from German (see FUHRMANN). See also FORMAN.

2. English: variant of FIRMIN. **3.** Americanized spelling of German FUHRMANN.
GIVEN NAMES Jewish 4%. *Yakov* (5), *Irina* (3), *Mayer* (3), *Semen* (3), *Sol* (3), *Faina* (2), *Ilya* (2), *Isaak* (2), *Naum* (2), *Anchel*, *Aron*, *Bronia*.

Furmanek (130) Polish, Czech (**Furmanék**), and Slovak (also **Furmánek**): from a pet form of FURMAN or FORMAN.
GIVEN NAMES Polish 6%. *Witold*, *Wladyslaw*.

Furmanski (147) Polish and Jewish (eastern Ashkenazic): occupational name for a driver of a horse-drawn delivery vehicle, *furman* (see FURMAN).
GIVEN NAMES Polish 7%. *Andrze*, *Jaroslaw*, *Wojtek*.

Furnace (111) English (Cumbria and Durham): variant spelling of FURNESS.
GIVEN NAME French 5%. *Andre*.

Furnari (359) Southern Italian: **1.** habitational name from Furnari in Messina province, Sicily. **2.** occupational name for a baker, from Late Latin *furnarius*, a derivative of *furnus* 'oven'.
GIVEN NAMES Italian 16%. *Angelo* (3), *Salvatore* (3), *Mario* (2), *Vito* (2), *Carmelo*, *Domenic*, *Filippo*, *Gilda*, *Ignazio*, *Luigi*, *Mariano*, *Rosario*.

Furnas (275) Variant spelling of FURNESS.

Furner (209) English: occupational name for a baker, from Old French *fo(u)rnier* (Late Latin *furnarius*, a derivative of *furnus* 'oven').

Furness (577) **1.** English: regional name from the district on the south coast of Cumbria (formerly in Lancashire), earlier *Fuðarnes*, so named from the genitive case (*Fuðar*) of Old Norse *Fuð*, meaning 'rump', the name of the peninsula, formerly of an island opposite the southern part of this district + Old Norse *nes* 'headland', 'nose'. **2.** Norwegian: habitational name from any of various farms, particularly in Møre og Romsdal, named Furnes, from Old Norse *fura* 'pine' + *nes* 'headland'.

Furney (338) English: of unknown origin; perhaps a habitational name from an unidentified place. Compare FARNEY, FORNEY.

Furnish (531) English: variant spelling of FURNESS.

Furniss (567) English: variant spelling of FURNESS.

Furno (169) Italian: occupational nickname for a baker or smith, from *furno* 'oven' (Latin *furnus*).
GIVEN NAMES Italian 16%. *Angelo* (3), *Salvatore* (2), *Aldo*, *Dino*, *Gaetano*, *Luigi*, *Sal*.

Furr (3093) English: from Middle English *furre* 'coat or garment made of or trimmed with fur', applied as a metonymic occupational name for a maker or seller of such garments, or a nickname for someone who habitually wore one.

Furrer (471) Swiss German: topographic name from the regional term *furre* 'cleft in the ground'.

GIVEN NAMES German 5%. *Armin* (2), *Hans* (2), *Urs* (2).

Furrey (101) Variant spelling of Irish FUREY.

Furrh (173) Perhaps an altered spelling of FURR or FARR.

Furrow (746) Probably an altered spelling of English **Farrow** (see FARRAR).

Furry (646) Irish: variant spelling of FUREY or possibly of **Farry**, a variant of FERRY.

Furse (193) English (chiefly Devon): topographic name for someone who lived on a piece of land that was thickly grown with gorse, from Old English *fyrse* 'gorse', or a habitational name from a place named with this word, as for example Furze in Devon and Cornwall.

Furst (1158) **1.** German (**Fürst**): nickname from Old High German *furisto* 'the first', 'most noble one', a cognate of Old English *fyrest* 'first', 'foremost'. **2.** Jewish (Ashkenazic): ornamental name from German *Fürst* 'prince'.
GIVEN NAMES German 4%. *Erwin* (2), *Eugen* (2), *Kurt* (2), *Gunter*, *Hans*, *Herta*, *Maximilian*, *Ulrich*.

Furstenberg (152) German and Jewish (Ashkenazic) (**Fürstenberg**): habitational name from a place in Swabia, so named from the genitive case of Old High German *furisto* 'prince', modern German *Fürst* (see FURST) + *berg* 'mountain', 'hill'. As a Jewish surname, it is mainly ornamental.
GIVEN NAME German 4%. *Arno*.

Furtado (1509) Portuguese: from *furtado* 'illegitimate'. Compare Spanish *hurtado*. This name is also found in western India, where it was taken by Portuguese colonists.
GIVEN NAMES Spanish 14%; Portuguese 10%. *Manuel* (51), *Jose* (25), *Mario* (8), *Carlos* (6), *Jorge* (4), *Humberto* (3), *Alberto* (2), *Pedro* (2), *Roberto* (2), *Tiberio* (2), *Adelino*, *Adolfo*; *Joao* (7), *Vasco* (2), *Caetano*, *Duarte*, *Guilherme*, *Joaquim*, *Serafim*, *Zulmira*.

Furtak (138) Polish: unflattering nickname from Polish *furtak* 'trifler', 'frivolous person'.
GIVEN NAMES Polish 9%. *Grzegorz*, *Jerzy*, *Stanislaw*.

Furtaw (123) Americanized form of French **Fertault**, a reduced form of an unexplained name, **Ferretault**.

Furth (260) **1.** German (also **Fürth**): topographic name for someone living at a ford, Middle High German *vurt* 'ford', 'path', or a habitational name from any of several places called Fürth, for example near Nuremberg. **2.** Jewish (western Ashkenazic): habitational name of the same origin as 1. **3.** Possibly also a variant spelling of FIRTH.
GIVEN NAMES German 6%. *Helmut* (2), *Otto*.

Furtick (198) Americanized spelling of German FERTIG.

Furtney (110) Probably an Americanized form of southeastern French **Fortineu(x)**,

from a derivative of **Fortin**, a pet form of the personal name *Fort* 'strong', 'courageous' (Latin *Fortis*).
GIVEN NAME French 4%. *Camille*.

Furukawa (376) Japanese: 'old river'; found throughout Japan. Descended from the MINAMOTO, NITTA, and northern FUJIWARA families. A common alternate reading is **Kogawa**; both are later variants of the ancient name KOGA.
GIVEN NAMES Japanese 50%. *Hiroshi* (3), *Kenji* (3), *Masaaki* (3), *Hideo* (2), *Hiroko* (2), *Hiroyuki* (2), *Kazuo* (2), *Shigeru* (2), *Takashi* (2), *Yasushi* (2), *Aiko*, *Akio*.

Furuta (154) Japanese: 'old rice paddy'; one family descends from a great family of Shinano (now Nagano prefecture). Others descend from families in Ise (now Mie prefecture), or from the MINAMOTO through the NITTA family.
GIVEN NAMES Japanese 50%. *Akinori*, *Chiaki*, *Eiichi*, *Harumi*, *Haruto*, *Hideto*, *Hiroshi*, *Hiroto*, *Ichiro*, *Isami*, *Isamu*, *Itsuko*.

Furutani (54) Japanese: alternate reading of FURUYA.
GIVEN NAMES Japanese 45%. *Fumio* (2), *Akihide*, *Akio*, *Asao*, *Hisao*, *Isamu*, *Norio*, *Ryoichi*, *Sadao*, *Takeshi*.

Furuya (154) Japanese: 'old valley'; more correctly written with characters meaning 'old room'. Some bearers are descended from the TAIRA clan, others from the MINAMOTO through the Satake and TAKEDA. The name is most common in the Tōkyō area. It is pronounced *Furutani* or *Kotani* in western Japan.
GIVEN NAMES Japanese 67%. *Junko* (2), *Mikiko* (2), *Reiko* (2), *Yasuko* (2), *Akira*, *Chiho*, *Daisuke*, *Eiichiro*, *Eiko*, *Hidemi*, *Hiroaki*, *Hiroki*.

Fury (400) Irish: variant spelling of FUREY.

Furze (119) Southern English: variant of FURSE.

Fusaro (544) Italian: occupational name for a spindle or axel maker, from *fusaro*, a dialect variant of standard Italian *fusaio*.
GIVEN NAMES Italian 15%; Spanish 6%. *Angelo* (6), *Rafael* (3), *Abramo*, *Aldo*, *Antonio*, *Armando*, *Carmine*, *Dino*, *Ettore*, *Fabrizio*, *Guiseppe*, *Mario*, *Pasquale*, *Sal*, *Santo*; *Ramon* (2), *Concha*, *Domingo*, *Jose*, *Juanita*.

Fuscaldo (111) Italian (Campania): from the medieval personal name *Foscolo*, a derivative of the Latin name *Fuscus*, which is from *fuscus* 'dark', i.e. having dark hair or dark skin.
GIVEN NAMES Italian 21%. *Pasquale* (2), *Angelo*, *Carmella*, *Francisco*, *Noemi*.

Fusco (3270) Italian: nickname for someone with dark hair or a swarthy complexion, from Italian *fusco* 'dark' (Latin *fuscus*); in some cases it may be from a medieval personal name derived from the Roman family name *Fuscus*, originally of the same meaning.

GIVEN NAMES Italian 14%. *Salvatore* (18), *Angelo* (17), *Rocco* (10), *Sal* (8), *Carmine* (7), *Domenic* (6), *Luigi* (5), *Pasquale* (5), *Caesar* (4), *Carlo* (4), *Saverio* (3).

Fuse (115) **1.** Japanese: 'alms'; a noble family of Yamato (now Nara prefecture), descended from Prince Ōyamamori (5th century), a son of Emperor Ōjin, who died rebelling against his brother, Emperor Nintoku, after their father's death. Others of the same name descend from the MINAMOTO, TAIRA, and other prominent clans. Listed in the Shinsen shōjiroku. The name is most common in eastern Japan. **2.** German: topographic name for someone living by the Fuse river near Celle (Hannover) or habitational name from a place called Fuse in eastern Germany.

GIVEN NAMES Japanese 19%; German 5%. *Ayuko, Eiji, Hiroshi, Hitomi, Koji, Masaru, Tomoki, Tsuneko, Yoshiharu, Yoshio*; *Dieter* (2), *Irmgard* (2).

Fuselier (875) French: metonymic occupational name for a spindle-maker or for a spinner, from Old French *fusel* 'spindle', 'bobbin' (Late Latin *fusellus*, a diminutive of classical Latin *fusus*).

FOREBEARS Centered chiefly in LA, the Fuselier family is most probably descended from Gabriel Fusilier de la Claire, a merchant from Lyon.

GIVEN NAMES French 6%; Irish 4%. *Marcel* (2), *Monique* (2), *Silton* (2), *Andre, Catheline, Eraste, Jacques*; *Murphy* (2), *Conley*.

Fusilier (251) French: according to Morlet, an occupational name for someone who made or sold small pieces of steel used to strike flints in order to make sparks to start a fire.

GIVEN NAMES French 4%. *Olivier, Vernice*.

Fusillo (108) Italian: from a pet form of *Fuso*, a short form of the personal name *Anfuso*, one of the many regional variants of ALFONSO.

GIVEN NAMES Italian 9%. *Nunzio, Vito*.

Fuson (994) English: unexplained. A less common alternative spelling is **Fewson**. This name is found mainly in KY, OH, TN, and IN.

Fuss (833) German: from Middle High German *fus* 'foot', hence most probably a nickname for someone with some peculiarity or deformity of the foot, but perhaps also a topographic name for someone who lived at the foot of a hill.

GIVEN NAMES German 4%. *Dieter* (2), *Erwin, Gunter, Kurt, Reinhard, Wolfgang*.

Fussell (1839) **1.** English (Bristol): of uncertain derivation; perhaps a Norman metonymic occupational name for a spinner or a maker of spindles, from Old French *fusel* 'spindle' (Late Latin *fusellus*, a diminutive of classical Latin *fusus*). **2.** Americanized spelling of German **Füssel**, a diminutive of FUSS.

Fusselman (225) German (**Füsselmann**): perhaps from a diminutive of Middle High German *vuoz* 'foot' + *man* 'man', for someone with very small feet or a dancing gait.

Fussner (157) German: from a pet form of a personal name or nickname based on Old High German *funs* 'quick', 'active'.

Fust (177) North German form of FAUST 1.

Fuster (119) Catalan: occupational name from *fuster* 'carpenter'.

GIVEN NAMES Spanish 39%. *Jose* (4), *Luis* (4), *Armando* (3), *Blanca* (3), *Ricardo* (3), *Carlos* (2), *Pedro* (2), *Vicente* (2), *Alfredo, Ana, Angelina, Barbaro*; *Angelo* (2), *Marco*.

Fuston (212) Perhaps a variant of the English habitational name FORSTON, which

was often written *Furston* in the 16th century. In the U.S., it occurs predominantly in TN and TX.

Futch (1605) Perhaps an altered form of English FUDGE. In the U.S., it is heavily concentrated in FL and GA and to a lesser extent in LA and TX.

Futral (278) Perhaps a variant spelling of English FUTRELL.

Futrell (1964) English: of uncertain derivation, perhaps a derogatory nickname from a diminutive of Old French *foutre* 'sexual intercourse'.

Futter (109) **1.** German: derivative of any of several compound names formed with Middle High German *vuoter* 'feed', 'fodder'. **2.** Jewish (Ashkenazic): metonymic occupational name for a furrier, from Yiddish 'fur', 'fur coat'.

GIVEN NAMES Jewish 4%. *Dror, Menachem*.

Futterman (261) Jewish (eastern Ashkenazic): occupational name for a furrier, from Yiddish *futer* 'fur', 'fur coat' + Yiddish *man* 'man'.

GIVEN NAMES Jewish 7%. *Miriam* (2), *Mort, Nachman, Sol*.

Fye (868) **1.** Irish: Anglicized form of Gaelic **Ó Fiaich** (see FEE). **2.** Americanized spelling of German FEY.

Fyfe (724) Scottish: variant spelling of FIFE.

Fyffe (760) Scottish: variant spelling of FIFE.

Fyke (231) Americanized spelling of German FEICK.

Fyler (128) Americanized spelling of German FEILER.

Fyock (344) Altered form of the German surname FEICK. This form is common in PA.